Fourth Edition

O*NET
Dictionary of
Occupational Titles

Based on information obtained from the U.S. Department of Labor,
the U.S. Census Bureau, and other reliable sources

*Developed under the direction of Michael Farr
and Laurence Shatkin, Ph.D.*

jist ®
Works
America's Career Publisher

O*NET Dictionary of Occupational Titles, Fourth Edition

© 2007 by JIST Publishing, Inc.

Published by JIST Works, an imprint of JIST Publishing, Inc.
8902 Otis Avenue
Indianapolis, IN 46216-1033

Phone: 1-800-648-JIST   Fax: 1-800-JIST-FAX
E-mail: info@jist.com   Web site: www.jist.com

About career materials published by JIST: Our materials encourage people to be self-directed and to take control of their destinies. We work hard to provide excellent content, solid advice, and techniques that get results. If you have questions about this book or other JIST products, call 1-800-648-JIST or visit www.jist.com.

Quantity discounts are available for JIST products. Have future editions of JIST books automatically delivered to you on publication through our convenient standing order program. Please call 1-800-648-JIST or visit www.jist.com for a free catalog and more information.

Visit www.jist.com for information on JIST, free job search information, book excerpts, and ordering information on our many products.

Acquisitions Editor: Susan Pines
Development Editor: Stephanie Koutek
Cover Designer: Honeymoon Image & Design, Inc.
Interior Design and Layout: Aleata Howard
Proofreaders: Paula Lowell, Jeanne Clark

Printed in Canada

12 11 10 09 08 07   9 8 7 6 5 4 3 2 1

Library of Congress Cataloging-in-Publication Data

O*NET : dictionary of occupational titles. -- 4th ed.
    p. cm.
  "Based on information obtained from the U.S. Department of Labor, the U.S. Census Bureau, and other reliable sources."
  "Developed under the direction of Michael Farr with database work by Laurence Shatkin."
  Includes index.
  ISBN 978-1-59357-415-4 (hardcover : alk. paper) -- ISBN 978-1-59357-416-1 (softcover : alk. paper)
1. Occupations--United States--Dictionaries. 2. Occupations--United States--Classification. I. Farr, J. Michael. II. Shatkin, Laurence. III. United States. Dept. of Labor. IV. JIST Works, Inc. V. Title: ONET dictionary of occupational titles.
  HB2595.O16 2007
  331.7003--dc22

2007000652

We have been careful to provide accurate information in this book, but it is possible that errors and omissions have been introduced. Please consider this in making any career plans or other important decisions. Trust your own judgment above all else and in all things.

Trademarks: All brand names and product names used in this book are trade names, service marks, trademarks, or registered trademarks of their respective owners. O*NET™ is a trademark of the U.S. Department of Labor, Employment and Training Administration.

ISBN 978-1-59357-415-4 Hardcover
ISBN 978-1-59357-416-1 Softcover

This Book Is Easier to Use Than It Looks

Please don't be intimidated by the formal look and large size of this book, as it is very helpful and easy to use. This reference puts the nearly 950 job descriptions from the nation's main occupational information database into practical print form, which makes it useful to job seekers, students, educators, career counselors, businesses, and others. In addition to the job descriptions, this book features facts that do not appear in the database (called the Occupational Information Network, or O*NET for short), including information on earnings, education and training required, and growth.

Part I provides six easy methods to find job descriptions that interest you. You can (1) browse the jobs by O*NET number; (2) review lists of jobs organized by interest; (3) find jobs according to the education or training required; (4) use the lists of jobs with highest earnings, fastest growth, and most openings; (5) find civilian jobs related to military jobs; or (6) look for jobs alphabetically by their job title. When you find a job title that interests you, look it up in Part II. Simple. You can also use the appendix to locate jobs according to their personality type.

The Best and Most Up-to-Date Source of Career Information

The information database used to create this book was developed by the U.S. Department of Labor (DOL) and replaces an older information system used in the *Dictionary of Occupational Titles*. This database represents a major change from the past. Many governmental, business, educational, and other organizations now rely on the O*NET system as the standard occupational classification and information system.

The O*NET is clearly an important information source. But the government maintains the O*NET in electronic form only and releases the database to developers so they can adapt the data into print and software formats that reach a wide audience.

This book uses the most recent O*NET 11.0 database and includes the following new features:

- A revised selection of job titles eliminates some redundant jobs and adds some new high-technology jobs

- New and revised job descriptions present a better picture of tasks that are core to the occupation

- Easier than ever to use with several ways to quickly find the job information you need

- Most current information on wages, growth, and openings

- Related job titles from the *Occupational Outlook Handbook* and the Standard Occupational Classification System

- A new chart that links 5,700 military job titles to civilian occupations

- A new appendix that matches personality types to O*NET jobs

- Updated career interest areas in each job description that correspond to the 16 U.S. Department of Education career clusters

Credits

Although two people have their names on the cover, this book represents many years of work by hundreds of dedicated individuals. The O*NET database that serves as this book's basis was created by researchers and developers under the direction of the U.S. Department of Labor. They, in turn, were assisted by thousands of employers who provided details on the nature of work in many thousands of job samplings used in the database's development. Although the O*NET database was first released several years ago, it is based on the substantial work done on an earlier database used to develop the *Dictionary of Occupational Titles (DOT)*. That *DOT* database was first used in the 1939 *DOT* edition and had its final update in 1991. The *DOT* formed the basis for much of the occupational information used by employers, job seekers, career counselors, educational and training institutions, researchers, policy makers, and others. Because of their large numbers, most who worked on the occupational material used in this book are not credited. Even so, we appreciate their efforts and present this book in their honor and in the honor of the good people at the U.S. Department of Labor who made the O*NET database and earlier sources of career information possible. Thanks.

Other Career Information Sources to Consider

Here are other career information resources that may interest you. Many are available at your library or bookstore, or go to www.jist.com for details.

Occupational Outlook Handbook

Enhanced Occupational Outlook Handbook

New Guide for Occupational Exploration

Best Jobs for the 21st Century

300 Best Jobs Without a Four-Year Degree

200 Best Jobs for College Graduates

40 Best Fields for Your Career

Important Notice on the Limitations of Use of This Book

Occupational information in this book reflects jobs as they have been found to occur, but they may not coincide in every respect with jobs as performed in particular establishments or at certain localities. Readers demanding specific job information should supplement it with local data. Note that the U.S. Department of Labor and JIST Publishing have no responsibility for establishing wage levels or settling jurisdictional matters for occupations. In preparing vocational definitions, no data were collected concerning these and related matters. Therefore, the occupational information in this book cannot be regarded as determining standards for any aspect of the employer-employee relationship. Data contained in this publication should not be considered a judicial or legislative standard for wages, hours, or other contractual or bargaining elements.

Table of Contents

Quick Summary of Major Sections

Introduction. Provides a brief overview of the O*NET system and this book. Includes a sample O*NET job description and reviews its many elements, such as job duties, education required, earnings, skills, abilities, personality type, working conditions, and more. Offers tips to help students, job seekers, career changers, employers, career counselors, and others use this reference. *The introduction starts on page 1.*

Part I: Six Easy Ways to Find O*NET Jobs of Interest.

Presents a variety of ways to find jobs to explore:

Part II: O*NET Job Descriptions. This large section provides information-packed descriptions for the nearly 950 jobs in the O*NET database. Descriptions are arranged by their O*NET number and within logical groupings of related jobs. The major job groups, subgroups, and jobs are listed starting in the column to the right, with the major groups listed below. *The job descriptions start on page 65.*

Management Occupations 11-0000
Business and Financial Operations Occupations 13-0000
Computer and Mathematical Occupations 15-0000
Architecture and Engineering Occupations 17-0000
Life, Physical, and Social Science Occupations 19-0000
Community and Social Services Occupations 21-0000
Legal Occupations 23-0000
Education, Training, and Library Occupations 25-0000
Arts, Design, Entertainment, Sports, and Media Occupations 27-0000
Healthcare Practitioners and Technical Occupations 29-0000
Healthcare Support Occupations 31-0000
Protective Service Occupations 33-0000
Food Preparation and Serving Related Occupations 35-0000
Building and Grounds Cleaning and Maintenance Occupations 37-0000
Personal Care and Service Occupations 39-0000
Sales and Related Occupations 41-0000
Office and Administrative Support Occupations 43-0000
Farming, Fishing, and Forestry Occupations 45-0000
Construction and Extraction Occupations 47-0000
Installation, Maintenance, and Repair Occupations 49-0000
Production Occupations 51-0000
Transportation and Material Moving Occupations 53-0000
Military Specific Occupations 55-0000

Appendix: O*NET Jobs by Personality Type. The appendix lists the jobs according to their primary and secondary Holland personality types. *The appendix starts on page 651.*

Index of O*NET Job Titles. All job titles in the O*NET database (and, therefore, in this book) appear here in alphabetical order. *The index starts on page 663.*

Introduction

We know that many people skip the introduction and dive directly into the book. Our objective was to make this introduction easy to read and nontechnical. We admit that some information here is, well, dull. But we tried to format it so you can quickly browse the headings and disregard or read material as desired. For example, this introduction presents a sample job description with its elements pointed out and explained, which is very helpful in understanding the book's second part.

Also, please note that although there may be technical differences between the terms *occupation* and *job*, we use them interchangeably in this book.

What Is the O*NET?

The O*NET is not a book—it is a computerized database of information on occupations. Developed by the U.S. Department of Labor, O*NET is short for "The Occupational Information Network," the database's formal name.

In its current form (Release 11.0, the one we used in this book), the O*NET database provides information on about 950 occupations. In the years to come, occupations will be added and deleted, and the information on all occupations will be updated regularly. For example, this book's fourth edition includes several computer-related jobs that have been added since the first edition was released in 1998.

The Department of Labor has stated that its role is to create and maintain the O*NET as a database, and it has no plans to release it in print. The *O*NET Dictionary of Occupational Titles* was the first book to provide the O*NET in a useful printed form. This new edition presents the newest O*NET updates, including new and revised descriptions that present a better picture of core occupational tasks.

The O*NET Replaces an Older Occupational Information System

The O*NET was designed to replace an earlier occupational information system, also developed by the Department of Labor. This older system was used as the basis for a book titled the *Dictionary of Occupational Titles*, or *DOT*, published for the final time in 1991.

The old *DOT* gave details on 12,741 occupational titles—far more than the approximately 950 jobs in the O*NET database. To create the O*NET, the Department of Labor collapsed most of the *DOT* jobs into more broadly defined job titles and eliminated a few *DOT* jobs that were highly specialized or employed few people. The result is a list of O*NET occupations that is smaller and far more useful for many purposes.

The new O*NET and the old *DOT* system have similarities because the new O*NET is built on the solid foundation provided by the older *DOT* system. If you are familiar with the *Dictionary of Occupational Titles*, you will probably feel quite comfortable with the O*NET descriptions in this book. Because this book bridges the new O*NET and the *DOT*, we refer to both systems in the title—*O*NET Dictionary of Occupational Titles*.

The O*NET Has Too Much Information to Be Useful for Many Purposes

Remember that the O*NET is not a book—it is a database with many details about each occupation. The O*NET database includes a narrative description of each job, plus details on about 500 data element descriptors. If you were to print the complete O*NET information for one occupation, you would have a very long, boring, and confusing description.

Consider this: If you were asked to describe your best friend, you would most likely omit many details. For example, you probably would not mention your friend's blood type, cholesterol level, or mom's name; if he or she were good at reading maps; and what he or she had for breakfast, lunch, and dinner. Instead, you would select details that you felt best described this person. More specific details could be very important to someone at some time, but not in many situations.

In a similar way, if you looked at all the information available for each occupation in the O*NET database, you would quickly understand why printing it all in book form would not make sense. For example, the following figure is the summary information on just one of the approximately 500 O*NET data elements available for one occupation.

The ability called control precision is very important for a job such as Airline Pilot, but it means little to most office workers, for example. So including control precision information on each occupation would not be helpful—and giving details on the approximately 500 data elements for every job would create many pages of little interest to most people.

In addition, a book with all this information would be thousands of pages long and require many volumes. Who would buy or read it? For this reason, we used a variety of techniques to reduce the information provided for each occupation and increase the usefulness of each description for most readers. For example, if control precision is an ability that the job requires at a high level, we include it among the abilities for the job. If not, we do not mention it.

Sample of One O*NET Data Element

Element:	Rate Control			
Description:	The ability to quickly and repeatedly adjust the controls of a machine or a vehicle to exact positions.			
Content Model Key:	1.A.2.b.1			
	I. Worker Characteristics			
	A. Abilities			
	2. Psychomotor Abilities			
	b. Control Movement Abilities			
	1. Control Precision			
Scale Used for Ratings:				
Scale ID	Scale Name		Minimum	Maximum
LV	Level		0	7
Anchors Used for Ratings:				
Anchor Value	Anchor Description			
2	Adjust a room light with a dimmer switch			
4	Adjust farm tractor controls			
6	Drill a tooth			

How This Book Is Organized

This book is organized in two parts. Part I shows you six ways to find job descriptions that interest you. You can browse the jobs by O*NET number; by interest area; by amount of education and training required; by ranking on earnings, growth, and openings lists; by related military job; and by title. You can read more about these criteria later in the following section and in Part I. Part II presents the job descriptions in order by O*NET number.

A Sample O*NET Description—and What It Includes

It would take more than 10 pages to print all the data on one job in the O*NET database, and much of that data would be in coded form that is not easy to understand without study. That's simply too much information for most people, and it would result in a book of more than 10,000 pages. So our challenge was to create a description of each O*NET occupation that would be useful to most people and would also be practical in book form.

We stayed up late many nights considering how to do this. The result is the carefully thought-out job descriptions you find in this book. Because a picture is worth a thousand words, we provide a sample O*NET job description next. To help you understand all that it includes, we point out its many elements and then explain each one.

Details on Each Information Element in the Job Descriptions

While short, each description is packed with useful information that will be quite helpful for most readers. Most content is easy enough to understand, although some details will interest only those who require them. Other elements require some explanation. Following are details on each information element included in the job descriptions. Some of this information may be more detailed than you need, so skim the content to find what you want to know.

We tried to keep our explanation nontechnical. However, some of the O*NET is technical, and some readers have inquiring minds that want to know such details. For this reason, we felt compelled to add more information than some of you might want. Too much, too little—it's a balancing act we hope gives most of you what you need.

O*NET Number

Each O*NET occupation is assigned a unique number. These are not random numbers because they are based on the Standard Occupational Classification (SOC) system established by the federal government. The SOC is a structure for organizing jobs based on the work performed, and it has been adopted by all federal agencies that collect and distribute occupation-related data. Because the O*NET numbering system puts job titles into groupings of related jobs, it's pretty logical to use. You can see how this system works by looking at the list of O*NET occupations in the Table of Contents. Occupations in this book are presented in numerical order, using their assigned O*NET number. Although some numbers appear to be missing, these absent numbers allow for future expansion of the numbering system or represent places where jobs have been deleted.

Quick tip on how to use this information: The O*NET number allows you to quickly cross-reference other O*NET information sources, including the government's Web site that provides more details on the O*NET jobs.

O*NET Occupational Title

This title, which appears in bold, is assigned to the job by the Department of Labor. We include the newest O*NET titles, which are based on those used in the SOC system.

Education/Training Required

This line lists the education or training typically required for entry into a job. Please note, however, that some (or many) who work in the job may have higher or lower

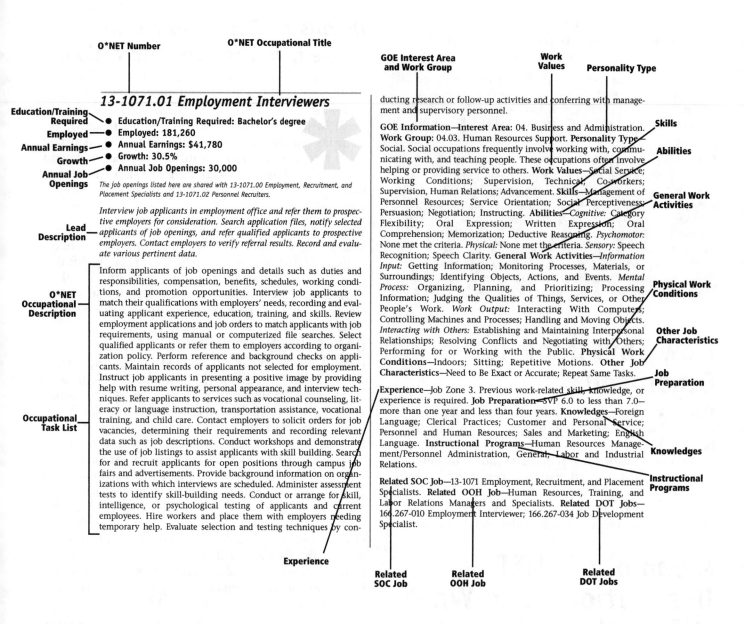

O*NET Number

O*NET Occupational Title

GOE Interest Area and Work Group

Work Values

Personality Type

13-1071.01 Employment Interviewers

Education/Training Required — ● Education/Training Required: Bachelor's degree

Employed — ● Employed: 181,260

Annual Earnings — ● Annual Earnings: $41,780

Growth — ● Growth: 30.5%

Annual Job Openings — ● Annual Job Openings: 30,000

The job openings listed here are shared with 13-1071.00 Employment, Recruitment, and Placement Specialists and 13-1071.02 Personnel Recruiters.

Lead Description — *Interview job applicants in employment office and refer them to prospective employers for consideration. Search application files, notify selected applicants of job openings, and refer qualified applicants to prospective employers. Contact employers to verify referral results. Record and evaluate various pertinent data.*

O*NET Occupational Description

Occupational Task List — Inform applicants of job openings and details such as duties and responsibilities, compensation, benefits, schedules, working conditions, and promotion opportunities. Interview job applicants to match their qualifications with employers' needs, recording and evaluating applicant experience, education, training, and skills. Review employment applications and job orders to match applicants with job requirements, using manual or computerized file searches. Select qualified applicants or refer them to employers according to organization policy. Perform reference and background checks on applicants. Maintain records of applicants not selected for employment. Instruct job applicants in presenting a positive image by providing help with resume writing, personal appearance, and interview techniques. Refer applicants to services such as vocational counseling, literacy or language instruction, transportation assistance, vocational training, and child care. Contact employers to solicit orders for job vacancies, determining their requirements and recording relevant data such as job descriptions. Conduct workshops and demonstrate the use of job listings to assist applicants with skill building. Search for and recruit applicants for open positions through campus job fairs and advertisements. Provide background information on organizations with which interviews are scheduled. Administer assessment tests to identify skill-building needs. Conduct or arrange for skill, intelligence, or psychological testing of applicants and current employees. Hire workers and place them with employers needing temporary help. Evaluate selection and testing techniques by con-

Experience

ducting research or follow-up activities and conferring with management and supervisory personnel.

GOE Information—Interest Area: 04. Business and Administration. **Work Group:** 04.03. Human Resources Support. **Personality Type**—Social. Social occupations frequently involve working with, communicating with, and teaching people. These occupations often involve helping or providing service to others. **Work Values**—Social Service; Working Conditions; Supervision, Technical; Co-workers; Supervision, Human Relations; Advancement. **Skills**—Management of Personnel Resources; Service Orientation; Social Perceptiveness; Persuasion; Negotiation; Instructing. **Abilities**—*Cognitive:* Category Flexibility; Oral Expression; Written Expression; Oral Comprehension; Memorization; Deductive Reasoning. *Psychomotor:* None met the criteria. *Physical:* None met the criteria. *Sensory:* Speech Recognition; Speech Clarity. **General Work Activities**—*Information Input:* Getting Information; Monitoring Processes, Materials, or Surroundings; Identifying Objects, Actions, and Events. *Mental Process:* Organizing, Planning, and Prioritizing; Processing Information; Judging the Qualities of Things, Services, or Other People's Work. *Work Output:* Interacting With Computers; Controlling Machines and Processes; Handling and Moving Objects. *Interacting with Others:* Establishing and Maintaining Interpersonal Relationships; Resolving Conflicts and Negotiating with Others; Performing for or Working with the Public. **Physical Work Conditions**—Indoors; Sitting; Repetitive Motions. **Other Job Characteristics**—Need to Be Exact or Accurate; Repeat Same Tasks.

Experience—Job Zone 3. Previous work-related skill, knowledge, or experience is required. **Job Preparation**—SVP 6.0 to less than 7.0—more than one year and less than four years. **Knowledges**—Foreign Language; Clerical Practices; Customer and Personal Service; Personnel and Human Resources; Sales and Marketing; English Language. **Instructional Programs**—Human Resources Management/Personnel Administration, General; Labor and Industrial Relations.

Related SOC Job—13-1071 Employment, Recruitment, and Placement Specialists. **Related OOH Job**—Human Resources, Training, and Labor Relations Managers and Specialists. **Related DOT Jobs**—166.267-010 Employment Interviewer; 166.267-034 Job Development Specialist.

Skills

Abilities

General Work Activities

Physical Work Conditions

Other Job Characteristics

Job Preparation

Knowledges

Instructional Programs

Related SOC Job

Related OOH Job

Related DOT Jobs

levels of education than indicated. Certification or licensing may be required for some jobs, but accurate information on such requirements is not available yet from the O*NET database. You need to determine such requirements from other sources, such as the *Occupational Outlook Handbook*.

The Department of Labor uses 11 levels of education or training to classify the education, training, and experience needs of a job. One of these levels is assigned to each job in this book.

The 11 Education and Training Levels

Short-term on-the-job training. It is possible to work in these occupations and achieve an average level of performance within a few days or weeks through on-the-job training.

Moderate-term on-the-job training. Occupations that require this type of training can be performed adequately after a 1- to 12-month period of combined on-the-job and informal training. Typically, untrained workers observe experienced workers performing tasks and are gradually moved into progressively more difficult assignments.

Long-term on-the-job training. This training requires more than 12 months of on-the-job training or combined work experience and formal classroom instruction. This includes occupations that use formal apprenticeships for training workers that may take up to 4 years. It also includes intensive occupation-specific, employer-sponsored training like police academies. Furthermore, it includes occupations that require natural talent that must be developed over many years.

Work experience in a related occupation. This type of job requires experience in a related occupation. For example, police detectives are selected based on their experience as police patrol officers.

Postsecondary vocational training. This requirement can vary from training that involves a few months to usually less than 1 year. In a few instances, there may be as many as 4 years of training.

Associate degree. This degree usually requires 2 years of full-time academic work beyond high school.

Bachelor's degree. This degree requires approximately 4 to 5 years of full-time academic work beyond high school.

Work experience plus degree. Jobs in this category are often management-related and require some experience in a related nonmanagerial position.

Master's degree. Completion of a master's degree usually requires 1 to 2 years of full-time study beyond the bachelor's degree.

Doctoral degree. This degree normally requires 2 or more years of full-time academic work beyond the bachelor's degree.

First professional degree. This type of degree normally requires a minimum of 2 years of education beyond the bachelor's degree and frequently requires 3 years.

Quick tip on how to use this information: We put this information at the top of the description to give you a quick idea of the job's education or training requirements.

Employed

The number of people employed in the occupation can be used to estimate job availability. This information, released in 2005 and representing 2004, comes from the Department of Labor's Bureau of Labor Statistics (BLS) and is the most current available. Note that self-employed workers are not included in this number, and in some occupations they can be a significant segment of the workforce. In entry-level jobs, the figure for employment may be low in comparison to annual job openings because of the large amount of job turnover.

Quick tip on how to use this information: Occupations employing a large number of people often have more openings than those employing smaller numbers. This is one useful measure of job opportunity.

Annual Earnings

This figure represents the median earnings for all people in the job nationwide. The median means that half the people earn more and half earn less. This annual amount, released in May 2006 and representing May 2005, comes from the Occupational Employment Statistics (OES) division of the BLS and is the most current available. The BLS reports earnings information by SOC codes, and an SOC job sometimes cross-references to more than one O*NET job. For example, the O*NET has separate information for Accountants and for Auditors, but the OES reports earnings for a single SOC occupation called Accountants and Auditors. Therefore, you may notice that the salary we report for Accountants ($52,210) is identical to the salary we report for Auditors. In reality there probably is a difference, but this is the best information that is available.

The median figure represents straight-time gross pay exclusive of premium pay. More specifically, the OES earnings include the job's base rate; cost-of-living allowances; guaranteed pay; hazardous-duty pay; incentive pay, including commissions and production bonuses; on-call pay; and tips but do not include back pay, jury duty pay, overtime pay, severance pay, shift differentials, non-production bonuses, or tuition reimbursements. The earnings of self-employed workers are not included in the estimates, and when data on earnings for an occupation is highly unreliable (for example, the income of Actors), OES does not report a figure.

Quick tips on how to use this information: Earnings figures can be misleading for several reasons. For example, new or recent entrants to the occupation often earn substantially less because they usually have much less experience than the average person working in the job. Pay rates also often vary considerably in different regions of the country. In addition, smaller employers often pay less. So consider the earnings information as a guideline that may not apply to your situation. You can often obtain local earnings information from your state employment service or other sources; ask your librarian for help. You also can ask people employed in an occupation what workers in your geographic area earn at differing experience levels.

Growth

This part of the description lists the percent of projected new jobs for the 10-year period ending in 2014. The figure comes from the Office of Occupational Statistics and Employment Projections in BLS and is the most up-to-date available. Like the earnings figures, the figures on projected growth and job openings are reported according to the SOC classification, so again you will find that some of the SOC jobs crosswalk to more than one O*NET job. To continue the example we used earlier, SOC reports growth of 22.4 percent for one occupation called Accountants and Auditors, but in this book we also report these figures separately for the occupation Accountants and for the occupation Auditors. When you see Accountants with 22.4 percent projected growth and Auditors with the same figure, you should realize that the 22.4 percent rate of projected growth represents the *average* of these two occupations—one may actually experience higher growth than the other.

Quick tip on how to use this information: Jobs with high projected growth frequently provide many opportunities. Low and negative growth numbers may reflect stagnant or declining areas.

Annual Job Openings

The number of openings available each year for the job appears next. It is based on the new jobs created plus openings due to resignations, terminations, retirement, and death. This data, representing the 10-year period ending in 2014, comes from the Office of Occupational Statistics and Employment Projections in BLS and is the most current available. Once again, BLS reports the information in terms of SOC jobs and sometimes we must crosswalk these to more than one O*NET job. When this happens—for example, when we report 157,000 job openings for the occupation Accountants and the same figure for the occupation Auditors—you should realize that these two occupations *share* the 157,000 job openings. To prevent confusion, wherever this sharing occurs we include a note such as the following: "The job openings listed here are shared with 13-2011.00 Accountants and Auditors and 13-2011.02 Auditors."

Quick tip on how to use this information: Occupations with many annual openings often offer opportunity and may be easier to obtain. Note that even if an occupation has negative *growth*, it still may have many job openings due to retirements, resignations, and so forth.

O*NET Occupational Description

This section gives you a brief but useable description for each job. The first part is the lead description, which is printed in italics. This text is sometimes followed by statements (also in italics) such as "Include wholesale or retail trade merchandising managers" or "Exclude procurement managers" that provide related titles that may be described in other O*NET occupations. This section is then followed, in regular type, by an occupational task list that describes occupational tasks specific to the job. For some jobs, the list of tasks in the O*NET database was extremely long and we needed to delete some tasks. When we did this, we deleted only the least important tasks.

Quick tips on how to use this information: The brief lead information gives you a quick way to understand the job. If it interests you, the more detailed task statement gives you a good review of the work that someone in the job does.

GOE Interest Area and Work Group

The Guide for Occupational Exploration is a system for organizing jobs based on interests. Originally developed by the U.S. Department of Labor, the GOE was designed as an intuitive way to help counselors, students, job seekers, career changers, and others identify occupations for further exploration. In 2005 JIST created a revised GOE based on the 16 career clusters that were developed by the U.S. Department of Education's Office of Vocational and Adult Education around 1999. Since this 16-cluster system is being used by many states to organize their career-oriented programs and career information, we provide GOE information in the descriptions so you can cross-reference other systems that use this classification scheme.

The GOE organizes all jobs into 16 major interest areas and then into more specific subgroups (called *work groups*) of related jobs. Note that we use the latest GOE interest area and work group names and numbers throughout this book. This new GOE information comes from a major revision of the GOE system released in a book titled *New Guide for Occupational Exploration: Linking Interests, Learning, and Careers* (JIST Works). The many changes and improvements make the old GOE system obsolete.

We include the four-digit GOE work group number for each job. (A handful of jobs do not fit into any one work group and do not have GOE information.) The first two digits of the work group number represent the major interest area where the job is assigned. The last two digits indicate the GOE work group where the job is found.

Here is a list of the GOE's 16 major interest areas.

The 16 GOE Interest Areas

01	Agriculture and Natural Resources
02	Architecture and Construction
03	Arts and Communication
04	Business and Administration
05	Education and Training
06	Finance and Insurance
07	Government and Public Administration
08	Health Science
09	Hospitality, Tourism, and Recreation
10	Human Service
11	Information Technology
12	Law and Public Safety
13	Manufacturing
14	Retail and Wholesale Sales and Service
15	Scientific Research, Engineering, and Mathematics
16	Transportation, Distribution, and Logistics

Quick tips on how to use this information: The GOE information is a very helpful way to find jobs that you might otherwise overlook. GOE codes in the job descriptions allow you to cross-reference any career information system using the new 16-cluster structure developed by the U.S. Department of Education. Also, Part I lists all the O*NET jobs that fall into each interest area. If you take an interest assessment that gives you a GOE code or U.S. Department of Education cluster, Part I allows you to cross-reference it to related O*NET jobs.

Personality Type

This information is useful for those who use a career interest inventory called the *Self-Directed Search* or related career information systems based on these personality types. The *SDS* author, John L. Holland, developed a popular theory that suggests a person can be classified into one of six personality types based on work-related preferences. Many people also identify with a secondary personality type. Each personality type relates to jobs that fit the descriptions listed next.

The 6 Personality Types

Artistic. These occupations frequently involve working with forms, designs, and patterns. They often require self-expression, and the work can be done without following a clear set of rules.

Conventional. These occupations frequently involve following set procedures and routines. These occupations can include working with data and details more than with ideas. Usually there is a clear line of authority to follow.

Enterprising. These occupations frequently involve starting up and carrying out projects. These occupations can involve leading people and making many decisions. They sometimes require risk taking and often deal with business.

Investigative. These occupations frequently involve working with ideas and require an extensive amount of thinking. These occupations can involve searching for facts and figuring out problems mentally.

Realistic. These occupations frequently involve work activities that include practical, hands-on problems and solutions. They often deal with plants; animals; and real-world materials like wood, tools, and machinery. Many of the occupations require working outside and do not involve a lot of paperwork or working closely with others.

Social. These occupations frequently involve working with, communicating with, and teaching people. These occupations often involve helping or providing service to others.

Quick tips on how to use this information: The *SDS* and other career interest inventories, like the *Strong Campbell Interest Inventory* and the *Armed Services Vocational Aptitude Battery,* use the *SDS* personality types. If you have used one of these popular tests, you might recall your personality type and use it to identify jobs that match it. You can also use the personality type information even if you haven't taken one of the assessments. Simply read the personality type definitions and determine the one or two that most closely describe jobs that interest you. Then compare jobs you have held or are considering to see if they are close matches. The appendix lists the O*NET jobs by their primary and secondary personality types.

Work Values

The O*NET database includes information on 21 work values for each job. The work values information helps you identify jobs that match your personal values, such as wanting security or independence in the work you do. For most jobs, relatively few work values receive high ratings, so giving numeric data for all 21 values is not useful. Instead, we selected the work values for each job that exceeded an "average" rating by the greatest amount. In most cases, we include the top 6 work values.

The 21 work values are arranged into 6 major groupings.

The 21 Work Values

Achievement. Occupations that satisfy these work values are results-oriented and allow employees to use their strongest abilities, giving them a feeling of accomplishment.

Ability Utilization. Workers on this job make use of their individual abilities.

Achievement. Workers on this job get a feeling of accomplishment.

Altruism. Occupations that satisfy these work values allow employees to provide service to others and work with co-workers in a friendly, noncompetitive environment.

Moral Values. Workers on this job are never pressured to do things that go against their sense of right and wrong.

Co-workers. Workers on this job have co-workers who are easy to get along with.

Social Service. Workers on this job have work where they do things for other people.

Autonomy. Occupations that satisfy this work value allow employees to work on their own and make decisions.

Autonomy. Workers on this job plan their work with little supervision.

Creativity. Workers on this job try out their own ideas.

Responsibility. Workers on this job make decisions on their own.

Comfort. Occupations that satisfy these work values offer job security and good working conditions.

Activity. Workers on this job are busy all the time.

Compensation. Workers on this job are paid well in comparison with other workers.

Working Conditions. Workers on this job have good working conditions.

Independence. Workers on this job do their work alone.

Security. Workers on this job have steady employment.

Variety. Workers on this job have something different to do every day.

Safety. Occupations that satisfy these work values offer supportive management that stands behind employees and provides a predictable and stable work environment.

Company Policies and Practices. Workers on this job are treated fairly by the company.

Supervision, Human Relations. Workers on this job have supervisors who back up their workers with management.

Supervision, Technical. Workers on this job have supervisors who train their workers well.

Status. Occupations that satisfy these work values offer advancement and potential for leadership and are often considered prestigious.

Advancement. Workers on this job have opportunities for advancement.

Authority. Workers on this job give directions and instructions to others.

Recognition. Workers on this job receive recognition for the work they do.

Social Status. Workers on this job are looked up to by others in their company and their community.

Quick tips on how to use this information: Though often overlooked by job seekers, work values are a very important part of what makes a job enjoyable or miserable. So think about which work values are particularly important to include in your career and write down those that are most important to you. Later, as you review the job descriptions, look for ones that meet your criteria.

Skills

This section lists skills needed to perform in each job. Depending on the occupation, some of these skills are quite complex, while others are relatively basic. All of us possess thousands of skills, although we take most of them for granted. For example, have you ever considered the complexity of physical skills needed to drive a car? This task is so complex that the most sophisticated machines cannot do it nearly as well as most 16-year-olds. While all of the many skills we possess are not listed in the O*NET database, it does include many skills that are important across a range of jobs. To avoid overwhelming you with details, only those skills with higher numerical ratings in the database are listed for each job.

The O*NET database provides measures for 35 skills for each job. Each skill is rated on two scales. One rates the skill on its importance to the job, and the other rates the skill on the level of performance required for the job. To create useful skills information for the job descriptions, we primarily used the level-of-performance measure, since that is, we believe, the more useful measure.

For each job, we included skills whose level-of-performance scores exceeded the average for all jobs by the greatest amount and whose ratings on the importance scale were not very low. We included as many as 6 such skills for each job, and we ranked them by the extent to which their rating exceeds the average.

Some jobs have fewer than 6 and sometimes no skills with numeric measures higher than the average measure for all jobs for each skill. For example, no skill is rated higher than average for Singers. For this job, skills with the highest ratings include Active Listening, Coordination, Speaking, and Reading Comprehension. However, the respective ratings for these 4 skills are 3.0 (compared to the average rating of 3.9 for *all* occupations), 2.8 (compared to 3.7), 2.7 (compared to 3.7), and 2.5 (compared to 4.1). Because none of these skills has a rating that exceeds the average rating for all occupations, listing these skills would not be an accurate representation of skills needed to perform this job. So, in situations such as this, we include the phrase "None met the criteria." Now, you may object that Singers must be highly skilled to perform professionally—but the particular musical skills that are required for this job are not included in the O*NET database or are classified as *abilities* (such as Hearing Sensitivity), so we are unable to list any here.

Following are the 35 skills used in the job descriptions, along with brief explanations for each one. These skills are classified as either Basic Skills or Cross-Functional Skills.

The 35 Skills

Basic Skills. These capacities facilitate the acquisition of new knowledge and skills.

Active Learning. Working with new material or information to grasp its implications.

Active Listening. Listening to what other people are saying and asking questions as appropriate.

Critical Thinking. Using logic and analysis to identify the strengths and weaknesses of different approaches.

Learning Strategies. Using multiple approaches when learning or teaching new things.

Mathematics. Using mathematics to solve problems.

Monitoring. Assessing how well one is doing when learning or doing something.

Reading Comprehension. Understanding written sentences and paragraphs in work-related documents.

Science. Using scientific methods to solve problems.

Speaking. Talking to others to effectively convey information.

Writing. Communicating effectively with others in writing as indicated by the needs of the audience.

Cross-Functional Skills. These skills facilitate performance in a variety of job settings.

Complex Problem Solving. Identifying complex problems, reviewing the options, and implementing solutions.

Coordination. Adjusting actions in relation to others' actions.

Equipment Maintenance. Performing routine maintenance and determining when and what kind of maintenance is needed.

Equipment Selection. Determining the kind of tools and equipment needed to do a job.

Installation. Installing equipment, machines, wiring, or programs to meet specifications.

Instructing. Teaching others how to do something.

Judgment and Decision Making. Weighing the relative costs and benefits of a potential action.

Management of Financial Resources. Determining how money will be spent to get the work done and accounting for these expenditures.

Management of Material Resources. Obtaining and seeing to the appropriate use of equipment, facilities, and materials needed to do certain work.

Management of Personnel Resources. Motivating, developing, and directing people as they work; identifying the best people for the job.

Negotiation. Bringing others together and trying to reconcile differences.

Operation and Control. Controlling operations of equipment or systems.

Operation Monitoring. Watching gauges, dials, or other indicators to make sure a machine is working properly.

Operations Analysis. Analyzing needs and product requirements to create a design.

Persuasion. Persuading others to approach things differently.

Programming. Writing computer programs for various purposes.

Quality Control Analysis. Evaluating the quality or performance of products, services, or processes.

Repairing. Repairing machines or systems using the needed tools.

Service Orientation. Actively looking for ways to help people.

Social Perceptiveness. Being aware of others' reactions and understanding why they react the way they do.

Systems Analysis. Determining how a system should work and how changes will affect outcomes.

(continued)

(continued)

Systems Evaluation. Looking at many indicators of system performance and taking into account their accuracy.

Technology Design. Generating or adapting equipment and technology to serve user needs.

Time Management. Managing one's own time and the time of others.

Troubleshooting. Determining what is causing an operating error and deciding what to do about it.

Quick tips on how to use this information: A big part of successful career decision making depends on your knowing what skills you enjoy and are good at. So look over the list of skills and write down those that you would most like to use in your next job. These are the ones to include in your career planning as much as possible. If you are looking for a job, the skills in the job descriptions are those you should emphasize in the interview because they are the ones likely to be valued by employers.

Abilities

This section contains "enduring attributes" that influence the job performance of workers. These attributes don't change over long periods of time. Abilities affect how quickly a person can learn new skills and the level of skill that can be achieved. Sometimes people refer to this as aptitude or even talent. Usually an ability increases your interest in learning and practicing a skill. For example, you may find that math is easy for you. So when you are taught a concept like calculating the mean and standard deviation (to help control product quality, for example), you are able to quickly learn how to use this in your job.

The O*NET database provides measures on 52 abilities for each job. (I trust that you are now beginning to understand our wisdom in including only the more important measures in each job description.) The abilities are organized into four subgroups: Cognitive (with 21 abilities), Psychomotor (10 abilities), Physical (9 abilities), and Sensory (12 abilities).

We used the O*NET's level-of-ability rating to select the top abilities (as many as 6) in each subgroup. We set a requirement that an ability must have a measure on the level-of-ability scale higher than the average of that ability for all jobs, and it must also have a rating on the importance scale higher than a very low level. We then ranked the abilities by the extent to which their rating on level exceeds the average. For example, the highest-ranked physical abilities for Employment Interviewers (by level)

include Trunk Strength and Static Strength—but the numeric ratings for these abilities are only 0.5 (compared to the average rating of 2.0 for *all* occupations) and 0.4 (compared to 1.7). Obviously, these are not important abilities for an Employment Interviewer, and that is why we set the average as a minimum. When no ability has a rating higher than the average for all jobs, we write "None met the criteria."

Here are the 52 abilities that are included in the job descriptions, along with brief explanations for each.

The 52 Abilities

Cognitive Abilities. These are mental processes that influence the acquisition and application of knowledge in problem solving.

Category Flexibility. The ability to produce many rules so that each rule tells how to group or combine a set of things in a different way.

Deductive Reasoning. The ability to apply general rules to specific problems to come up with logical answers. It involves deciding whether an answer makes sense or provides a logical explanation for why a series of seemingly unrelated events occur together.

Flexibility of Closure. The ability to identify or detect a known pattern (a figure, object, word, or sound) that is hidden in other distracting material.

Fluency of Ideas. The ability to come up with a number of ideas about a given topic. It concerns the number of ideas produced and not the quality, correctness, or creativity of the ideas.

Inductive Reasoning. The ability to combine separate pieces of information, or specific answers to problems, to form general rules or conclusions. It includes coming up with a logical explanation for why a series of seemingly unrelated events occur together.

Information Ordering. The ability to correctly follow a given rule or set of rules in order to arrange things or actions in a certain order. The things or actions can include numbers, letters, words, pictures, procedures, sentences, and mathematical or logical operations.

Mathematical Reasoning. The ability to understand and organize a problem and then to select a mathematical method or formula to solve the problem.

Memorization. The ability to remember information such as words, numbers, pictures, and procedures.

Number Facility. The ability to add, subtract, multiply, or divide quickly and correctly.

Oral Comprehension. The ability to listen to and understand information and ideas presented through spoken words and sentences.

Oral Expression. The ability to communicate information and ideas in speaking so others will understand.

Originality. The ability to come up with unusual or clever ideas about a given topic or situation or to develop creative ways to solve a problem.

Perceptual Speed. The ability to quickly and accurately compare letters, numbers, objects, pictures, or patterns. The things to be compared may be presented at the same time or one after the other. This ability also includes comparing a presented object with a remembered object.

Problem Sensitivity. The ability to tell when something is wrong or is likely to go wrong. It does not involve solving the problem, only recognizing that there is a problem.

Selective Attention. The ability to concentrate and not be distracted while performing a task over a period of time.

Spatial Orientation. The ability to know one's location in relation to the environment or to know where other objects are in relation to one's self.

Speed of Closure. The ability to quickly make sense of information that seems to be without meaning or organization. It involves quickly combining and organizing different pieces of information into a meaningful pattern.

Time Sharing. The ability to efficiently shift back and forth between two or more activities or sources of information (such as speech, sounds, touch, or other sources).

Visualization. The ability to imagine how something will look after it is moved around or when its parts are moved or rearranged.

Written Comprehension. The ability to read and understand information and ideas presented in writing.

Written Expression. The ability to communicate information and ideas in writing so others will understand.

Psychomotor Abilities. These abilities influence the capacity to manipulate and control objects primarily using fine motor skills.

Arm-Hand Steadiness. The ability to keep the hand and arm steady while making an arm movement or while holding the arm and hand in one position.

Control Precision. The ability to quickly and repeatedly make precise adjustments in moving the controls of a machine or vehicle to exact positions.

Finger Dexterity. The ability to make precisely coordinated movements of the fingers of one or both hands to grasp, manipulate, or assemble very small objects.

Manual Dexterity. The ability to quickly make coordinated movements of one hand, a hand together with its arm, or two hands to grasp, manipulate, or assemble objects.

Multilimb Coordination. The ability to coordinate movements of two or more limbs together (for example, two arms, two legs, or one leg and one arm) while sitting, standing, or lying down. It does not involve performing the activities while the body is in motion.

Rate Control. The ability to time the adjustments of a movement or equipment control in anticipation of changes in the speed and/or direction of a continuously moving object or scene.

Reaction Time. The ability to quickly respond (with the hand, finger, or foot) to one signal (sound, light, picture, and so on) when it appears.

Response Orientation. The ability to choose quickly and correctly between two or more movements in response to two or more signals (lights, sounds, pictures, and so on). It includes the speed with which the correct response is started with the hand, foot, or other body parts.

Speed of Limb Movement. The ability to quickly move the arms or legs.

Wrist-Finger Speed. The ability to make fast, simple, repeated movements of the fingers, hands, and wrists.

Physical Strength Abilities. These abilities influence strength, endurance, flexibility, balance, and coordination.

Dynamic Flexibility. The ability to quickly and repeatedly bend, stretch, twist, or reach out with the body, arms, and/or legs.

Dynamic Strength. The ability to exert muscle force repeatedly or continuously over time. This involves muscular endurance and resistance to muscle fatigue.

Explosive Strength. The ability to use short bursts of muscle force to propel oneself (as in jumping or sprinting) or to throw an object.

Extent Flexibility. The ability to bend, stretch, twist, or reach out with the body, arms, and/or legs.

Gross Body Coordination. The ability to coordinate the movement of the arms, legs, and torso together in activities where the whole body is in motion.

Gross Body Equilibrium. The ability to keep or regain one's body balance or stay upright when in an unstable position.

Stamina. The ability to exert one's self physically over long periods of time without getting winded or out of breath.

Static Strength. The ability to exert maximum muscle force to lift, push, pull, or carry objects.

(continued)

(continued)

Trunk Strength. The ability to use one's abdominal and lower back muscles to support part of the body repeatedly or continuously over time without giving out or fatiguing.

***Sensory Abilities.* These abilities influence visual, auditory, and speech perception.**

Auditory Attention. The ability to focus on a single source of auditory (hearing) information in the presence of other distracting sounds.

Depth Perception. The ability to judge which of several objects is closer or farther away from the observer or to judge the distance between an object and the observer.

Far Vision. The ability to see details at a distance.

Glare Sensitivity. The ability to see objects in the presence of glare or bright lighting.

Hearing Sensitivity. The ability to detect or tell the difference between sounds that vary over broad ranges of pitch and loudness.

Near Vision. The ability to see details of objects at a close range (within a few feet of the observer).

Night Vision. The ability to see under low light conditions.

Peripheral Vision. The ability to see objects or movement of objects to one's side when the eyes are focused forward.

Sound Localization. The ability to tell the direction from which a sound originated.

Speech Clarity. The ability to speak clearly so that it is understandable to a listener.

Speech Recognition. The ability to identify and understand the speech of another person.

Visual Color Discrimination. The ability to match or detect differences between colors, including shades of color and brightness.

Quick tips on how to use this information: Many of the abilities are similar to the skills. This overlap should not concern you, because skills and abilities are alike in some important ways. As with skills, you can select abilities that are important to you and look for career options that include them.

Abilities and Disabilities

We encourage you to use the data on abilities with care. The O*NET information does not take into account how a person with a disability might perform a job. Many jobs can be redesigned to accommodate disabilities. For this reason, the O*NET data should not be used to exclude people from jobs.

This is but one example of how even carefully collected data can lead to inaccurate conclusions. Data has its limitations, and you need to use common sense in interpreting the contents of this book and other references.

General Work Activities

This section lists the general types of activities involved in performing the job described. As with the skills section, some jobs list very complex activities as well as more basic ones. There are four subgroups within general work activities: Information Input (5 activities), Mental Process (10 activities), Work Output (9 activities), and Interacting with Others (17 activities). For each job, we included work activities whose rating on level exceeded the average for all jobs by the greatest amount and that were not rated very low on importance. We then ranked them by the extent to which their rating exceeds the average. For each subgroup of activities, we listed as many as 3.

Here are brief descriptions for the 41 general work activities in the O*NET database. (In some cases we simplified the names of the activities for easier reading.)

The 41 General Work Activities

***Information Input.* Activities that gain the information and data gained needed to perform the job.**

Estimating the Needed Characteristics of Products, Events, or Information. Estimating sizes, distances, and quantities or determining time, costs, resources, or materials needed to perform a work activity.

Getting Information. Observing, receiving, and otherwise obtaining information from all relevant sources.

Identifying Objects, Actions, and Events. Identifying information received by making estimates or categorizations, recognizing differences or similarities, or sensing.

Inspecting Equipment, Structures, or Materials. Inspecting or diagnosing equipment, structures, or materials to identify the causes of errors or other problems or defects.

Monitoring Processes, Materials, or Surroundings. Monitoring and reviewing information from materials, events, or the environment, often to detect problems or to find out when things are finished.

***Mental Process:* Processing, planning, problem-solving, decision-making, and innovating activities performed with job-relevant information.**

Analyzing Data or Information. Identifying underlying principles, reasons, or facts by breaking down information or data into separate parts.

Developing Objectives and Strategies. Establishing long-range objectives and specifying the strategies and actions to achieve these objectives.

Evaluating Information Against Standards. Evaluating information against a set of standards and verifying that it is correct.

Judging Qualities of Things, Services, or Other People's Work. Making judgments about or assessing the value, importance, or quality of things or people's work.

Making Decisions and Solving Problems. Combining, evaluating, and reasoning with information and data to make decisions and solve problems. These processes involve making decisions about the relative importance of information and choosing the best solution.

Organizing, Planning, and Prioritizing. Developing plans to accomplish work and prioritizing and organizing one's work.

Processing Information. Compiling, coding, categorizing, calculating, tabulating, auditing, verifying, or processing information or data.

Scheduling Work and Activities. Scheduling events, programs, and activities, as well as the work of others.

Thinking Creatively. Originating, inventing, designing, or creating new applications, ideas, relationships, systems, or products, including artistic contributions.

Updating and Using Relevant Knowledge. Keeping up-to-date technically and knowing the functions of one's job and related jobs.

Work Output: Physical activities, operation or control of equipment or vehicles, and complex/technical activities accomplished as job outputs.

Controlling Machines and Processes. Using either control mechanisms or direct physical activity to operate machines or processes (not including computers or vehicles).

Documenting or Recording Information. Entering, transcribing, recording, storing, or maintaining information either in written form or by electronic/magnetic recording.

Drafting and Specifying Technical Devices. Providing documentation, detailed instructions, drawings, or specifications to inform others about how devices, parts, equipment, or structures are to be fabricated, constructed, assembled, modified, maintained, or used.

Handling and Moving Objects. Using one's hands and arms in handling, installing, forming, positioning, and moving materials or in manipulating things. Includes the use of keyboards.

Interacting with Computers. Controlling computer functions by using programs, setting up functions, writing software, or otherwise communicating with computer systems.

Operating Vehicles or Equipment. Running, maneuvering, navigating, or driving vehicles or mechanized equipment, such as forklifts, passenger vehicles, aircraft, or watercraft.

Performing General Physical Activities. Performing physical activities that require moving one's whole body, such as in climbing, lifting, balancing, walking, and stooping, where the activities often also require considerable use of the arms and legs, such as in the physical handling of materials.

Repairing and Maintaining Electronic Equipment. Fixing, servicing, adjusting, regulating, calibrating, fine-tuning, or testing machines, devices, and equipment that operate primarily on the basis of electrical or electronic (not mechanical) principles.

Repairing and Maintaining Mechanical Equipment. Fixing, servicing, aligning, setting up, adjusting, and testing machines, devices, moving parts, and equipment that operate primarily on the basis of mechanical (not electronic) principles.

Interacting with Others: **Interactions with other persons or supervisory activities that occur while performing the job.**

Assisting and Caring for Others. Providing assistance or personal care to others.

Coaching and Developing Others. Identifying developmental needs of others and coaching or otherwise helping others to improve their knowledge or skills.

Communicating with Other Workers. Providing information to supervisors, fellow workers, and subordinates. This information can be exchanged face-to-face, in writing, or via telephone/electronic transfer.

Communicating with Persons Outside Organization. Communicating with persons outside the organization and representing the organization to customers, the public, government, and other external sources. Information can be exchanged face-to-face, in writing, or via telephone/electronic transfer.

Coordinating Work and Activities of Others. Coordinating members of a work group to accomplish tasks.

Developing and Building Teams. Encouraging and building mutual trust, respect, and cooperation among team members.

Establishing and Maintaining Relationships. Developing constructive and cooperative working relationships with others.

Guiding, Directing, and Motivating Subordinates. Providing guidance and direction to subordinates, including setting performance standards and monitoring subordinates.

Influencing Others or Selling. Convincing others to buy merchandise/goods or otherwise changing their minds or actions.

Interpreting Meaning of Information to Others. Translating or explaining what information means and how it can be understood or used to support responses or feedback to others.

Monitoring and Controlling Resources. Monitoring and controlling resources and overseeing the spending of money.

Performing Administrative Activities. Approving requests, handling paperwork, and performing day-to-day administrative tasks.

Performing for or Working with the Public. Performing for people or dealing directly with the public, including serving persons in restaurants and stores and receiving clients or guests.

(continued)

(continued)

Providing Consultation and Advice to Others. Providing consultation and expert advice to management or other groups on technical, systems-related, or process-related topics.

Resolving Conflict and Negotiating with Others. Handling complaints, arbitrating disputes, resolving grievances, or otherwise negotiating with others.

Staffing Organizational Units. Recruiting, interviewing, selecting, hiring, and promoting persons for the organization.

Teaching Others. Identifying educational needs, developing formal training programs or classes, and teaching or instructing others.

Quick tip on how to use this information: This information gives you a good idea of the types of activities that require higher-than-average skills for the job. So, for example, if a job requires higher-than-average skills in "staffing organizational units," you need to decide whether you have or want to develop these skills to perform well on this job.

Physical Work Conditions

The O*NET provides 55 measures on a variety of work environments and working conditions, including work setting, environmental conditions, job hazards, body positioning, and work attire. Of these, 27 may be considered physical work conditions, of which 23 have ratings for all fully described jobs in the O*NET database. From this set of 23 physical work conditions we include any whose rating exceeds the midpoint of the rating scale. The ordering of the work conditions does not reflect importance; instead, we try to keep logically related conditions together. In some cases we simplify the names of the work conditions for easier reading, and sometimes we use wording that combines two work conditions into a single phrase. For example, if both Sitting and Standing are significant for the job, with Sitting rated higher, we use the phrase "More Often Sitting Than Standing." Keep in mind that when hazards are present (for example, contaminants), protective equipment and procedures are provided to keep you safe. Brief descriptions for each measure follow, except in cases where the definition is obvious.

The 23 Physical Work Conditions

Bending or Twisting the Body.

Climbing Ladders, Scaffolds, or Poles.

Contaminants. Contaminants present, such as pollutants, gases, dust, odors, and so on.

Cramped Work Space, Awkward Positions. Working in cramped work spaces that require getting into awkward positions.

Diseases or Infections. Potential diseases/infections (for example, patient care, some laboratory work, and sanitation control).

Noisy. Sounds and noise levels that are distracting and uncomfortable.

Very Bright or Dim Lighting. Extremely bright or inadequate lighting conditions.

Hazardous Conditions. For example, high-voltage electricity, combustibles, explosives, chemicals; does not include hazardous equipment or situations.

Hazardous Equipment. For example, saws and machinery/mechanical parts. Includes exposure to vehicular traffic but not driving a vehicle.

High Places. For example, heights above 8 feet on ladders, poles, scaffolding, and catwalks.

Indoors. Working indoors in an environmentally controlled setting.

Keeping or Regaining Balance.

Kneeling, Crouching, Stooping, or Crawling.

Repetitive Motions.

Minor Burns, Cuts, Bites, or Stings. Amount job involves likelihood of cuts, bites, stings, or minor burns.

Outdoors. Working outdoors exposed to weather.

Radiation. Potential exposure to radiation.

Sitting.

Standing.

Using Hands on Objects, Tools, or Controls. Using hands to handle, control, or feel objects, tools, or controls.

Very Hot or Cold. Very hot (above 90°F) or very cold (under 32°F) temperatures.

Walking and Running. Job requires walking and running.

Whole-Body Vibration. For example, operating a jackhammer or earthmoving equipment.

Quick tips on how to use this information: For people with physical limitations or reactions to chemicals, for example, the importance of these measures is obvious. You can use this information to avoid jobs that are likely to cause you problems or provide tasks you cannot handle. All of us have limitations of some kind, and all of us have preferences for our working conditions. All jobs require some compromise, and the information here helps you clearly understand what a job may require of you.

Other Job Characteristics

This section of the job description provides other information you may find helpful. The O*NET includes 13 job characteristics under the category "Structural Job Characteristics." All fully described occupations are rated on 5 of these, which are defined below. For each job, we include any characteristics from this set whose score exceeds the midpoint of the rating scale, and we rank them in descending order of importance. In some cases we also simplify the names of the characteristics for easier reading. Here are brief definitions for these characteristics.

The 5 Other Job Characteristics

Errors Have Important Consequences. A mistake would cause a serious problem that was not readily correctable.

Automation. An above-average level of automation.

Need to Be Exact or Accurate. An above-average importance of being very exact or highly accurate in performing this job.

Repeat Same Tasks. Above-average importance of repeating the same physical activities (for example, key entry) or mental activities (for example, checking entries in a ledger) over and over without stopping.

Pace Determined by Speed of Equipment. Pace of work tends to be determined by the speed of equipment or machinery. (This does not refer to keeping busy at all times on this job.)

Quick tip on how to use this information: You may find that some of these items overlap with other data collected in the O*NET database (for example, work task statements). Still, we think you will find this information useful in helping you consider one job over another.

Experience

This section of the job description presents information the O*NET refers to as "job zones." The information presented in the O*NET job zones is a bit technical and hard to interpret, so we extracted one easily understood element from the job zones that gives the level of experience needed for each job. The O*NET assigns 1 of 5 levels of experience to each job, and we included this information in our job descriptions. Please note that sometimes discrepancies occur between the education data listed at a job description's beginning and the job zone data because the information comes from different agencies within the Department of Labor.

Here are the 5 levels the O*NET provides to help define the experience needed for entry into various jobs.

The 5 Levels of Experience

Job Zone 1. Little or no preparation needed. No previous work-related skill, knowledge, or experience is needed for these occupations. For example, a person can become a general office clerk even if the person has never worked in an office before.

Job Zone 2. Some preparation needed. Some previous work-related skill, knowledge, or experience may be helpful in these occupations but usually is not needed. For example, a drywall installer might benefit from experience installing drywall, but an inexperienced person could still learn to be an installer with little difficulty.

Job Zone 3. Medium preparation needed. Previous work-related skill, knowledge, or experience is required for these occupations. For example, an electrician must have completed 3 or 4 years of apprenticeship or several years of vocational training and often must have passed a licensing exam to perform the job.

Job Zone 4. Considerable preparation needed. A minimum of 2 to 4 years of work-related skill, knowledge, or experience is needed for these occupations. For example, an accountant must complete 4 years of college and work for several years in accounting to be considered qualified.

Job Zone 5. Extensive preparation needed. Extensive skill, knowledge, and experience are needed for these occupations. Many require more than 5 years of experience. For example, surgeons must complete 4 years of college and an additional 5 to 7 years of specialized medical training to be able to do the job.

Quick tip on how to use this information: This helps you understand the amount of training or education needed to qualify for entry into a job.

Job Preparation

The Department of Labor uses a system called the Standard Vocational Preparation (SVP) to assign 1 of 5 levels of training or education to a job. This SVP system has been used by the department for many years in standard reference systems such as the *Dictionary of Occupational Titles,* and SVP information has been included in the O*NET database. Please note that sometimes discrepancies occur between the education data listed at a job description's beginning and the job preparation data because the information comes from different agencies within the Department of Labor.

The 5 Standard Vocational Preparation (SVP) Codes

SVP below 4.0—Less than six months.

SVP 4.0 to less than 6.0—Six months to less than two years.

SVP 6.0 to less than 7.0—More than one year and less than four years.

SVP 7.0 to less than 8.0—Two years to less than 10 years.

SVP 8.0 and above—Four years to more than 10 years.

Quick tip on how to use this information: This measure is very similar to the one used for experience and can be used in a similar way to consider jobs that interest you.

Knowledges

Our job descriptions include information from the O*NET on the knowledge required to successfully perform in the occupation described. The knowledge may be obtained from formal or informal sources, including high school or college courses or majors, training programs, self-employment, military, paid or volunteer work experience, and other life experiences. There are 33 O*NET knowledge descriptors. We select the 5 whose ratings exceed the average rating on that knowledge for all jobs, and we rank them by the amount by which their rating exceeds the average.

Here are brief descriptions of the 33 knowledge items used in the O*NET and included in our job descriptions. They are arranged within the useful clusters shown here.

The 33 Knowledge Descriptors

Arts and Humanities. **Knowledge of facts and principles related to the branches of learning concerned with human thought, language, and the arts.**

English Language. Knowledge of the structure and content of the English language, including the meaning and spelling of words, rules of composition, and grammar.

Fine Arts. Knowledge of theory and techniques required to produce, compose, and perform works of music, dance, visual arts, drama, and sculpture.

Foreign Language. Knowledge of the structure and content of a foreign (non-English) language, including the meaning and spelling of words, rules of composition and grammar, and pronunciation.

History and Archeology. Knowledge of past historical events and their causes, indicators, and impact on particular civilizations and cultures.

Philosophy and Theology. Knowledge of different philosophical systems and religions, including their basic principles, values, ethics, ways of thinking, customs, and practices and their impact on human culture.

Business and Management. **Knowledge of principles and facts related to business administration and accounting, human and material resource management in organizations, sales and marketing, economics, and office information and organizing systems.**

Administration and Management. Knowledge of principles and processes involved in business and organizational planning, coordination, and execution. This includes strategic planning, resource allocation, manpower modeling, leadership techniques, and production methods.

Clerical Studies. Knowledge of administrative and clerical procedures and systems such as word-processing systems, filing and records management systems, stenography and transcription, forms, design principles, and other office procedures and terminology.

Customer and Personal Service. Knowledge of principles and processes for providing customer and personal services, including needs assessment techniques, quality service standards, alternative delivery systems, and customer satisfaction evaluation techniques.

Economics and Accounting. Knowledge of economic and accounting principles and practices, the financial markets, banking, and the analysis and reporting of financial data.

Personnel and Human Resources. Knowledge of policies and practices involved in personnel/human resource functions. This includes recruitment, selection, training, and promotion regulations and procedures; compensation and benefits packages; labor relations and negotiation strategies; and personnel information systems.

Sales and Marketing. Knowledge of principles and methods involved in showing, promoting, and selling products or services. This includes marketing strategies and tactics, product demonstration and sales techniques, and sales control systems.

Communications. **Knowledge of the science and art of delivering information.**

Communications and Media. Knowledge of media production, communication, and dissemination techniques and methods, including alternative ways to inform and entertain via written, oral, and visual media.

Telecommunications. Knowledge of transmission, broadcasting, switching, control, and operation of telecommunications systems.

Education and Training

Education and Training. Knowledge of instructional methods and training techniques, including curriculum design principles, learning theory, group and individual teaching techniques, design of individual development plans, and test design principles.

Health Services. Knowledge of principles and facts regarding diagnosing, curing, and preventing disease and improving and preserving physical and mental health and well-being.

Medicine and Dentistry. Knowledge of the information and techniques needed to diagnose and treat injuries, diseases, and deformities. This includes symptoms, treatment alternatives, drug properties and interactions, and preventive health-care measures.

Therapy and Counseling. Knowledge of information and techniques needed to rehabilitate physical and mental ailments and to provide career guidance, including alternative treatments, rehabilitation equipment and its proper use, and methods to evaluate treatment effects.

Law and Public Safety. Knowledge of regulations and methods for maintaining people and property free from danger, injury, or damage; the rules of public conduct established and enforced by legislation; and the political process establishing such rules.

Law and Government. Knowledge of laws, legal codes, court procedures, precedents, government regulations, executive orders, agency rules, and the democratic political process.

Public Safety and Security. Knowledge of weaponry; public safety; security operations, rules, regulations, precautions, and prevention; and the protection of people, data, and property.

Manufacturing and Production. Knowledge of principles and facts related to the production, processing, storage, and distribution of manufactured and agricultural goods.

Building and Construction. Knowledge of materials, methods, and the appropriate tools to construct objects, structures, and buildings.

Computers and Electronics. Knowledge of electric circuit boards, processors, chips, and computer hardware and software, including applications and programming.

Design. Knowledge of design techniques, principles, tools, and instruments involved in the production and use of precision technical plans, blueprints, drawings, and models.

Engineering and Technology. Knowledge of equipment, tools, and mechanical devices and their uses to produce motion, light, power, technology, and other applications.

Food Production. Knowledge of techniques and equipment for planting, growing, and harvesting of food for consumption, including crop rotation methods, animal husbandry, and food storage/handling techniques.

Mechanical Devices. Knowledge of machines and tools, including their designs, uses, benefits, repair, and maintenance.

Production and Processing. Knowledge of inputs, outputs, raw materials, waste, quality control, costs, and techniques for maximizing the manufacture and distribution of goods.

Mathematics and Science. Knowledge of the history, theories, methods, and applications of the physical, biological, social, mathematical, and geography.

Biology. Knowledge of plant and animal living tissue, cells, organisms, and entities, including their functions, interdependencies, and interactions with each other and the environment.

Chemistry. Knowledge of the composition, structure, and properties of substances and of the chemical processes and transformations that they undergo. This includes uses of chemicals and their interactions, danger signs, production techniques, and disposal methods.

Geography. Knowledge of various methods for describing the location and distribution of land, sea, and air masses, including their physical locations, relationships, and characteristics.

Mathematics. Knowledge of numbers and their operations and interrelationships, including arithmetic, algebra, geometry, calculus, and statistics and their applications.

Physics. Knowledge and prediction of physical principles, laws, and applications, including air, water, material dynamics, light, atomic principles, heat, electric theory, earth formations, and meteorological and related natural phenomena.

Psychology. Knowledge of human behavior and performance, mental processes, psychological research methods, and the assessment and treatment of behavioral and affective disorders.

Sociology and Anthropology. Knowledge of group behavior and dynamics; societal trends and influences; and cultures and their history, migrations, ethnicity, and origins.

Transportation

Transportation. Knowledge of principles and methods for moving people or goods by air, rail, sea, or road, including their relative costs, advantages, and limitations.

Quick tips on how to use this information: If you are considering additional education or training, this section gives you some idea of the courses or programs that would be helpful for each job. It helps you to decide whether you have some or all of the knowledge needed for a new job and what you need to improve on through additional training. In also gives an additional indication of whether the job is a good match for your interests.

Instructional Programs

The Classification of Instructional Programs (CIP) is a system of naming and categorizing training and educational programs and courses. Developed by the U.S. Department of Education, the CIP is widely used in occupational, education, and training reference systems. We list the latest CIP program or course names related to each occupation.

Quick tip on how to use this information: The CIP information helps you identify the names of training or educational programs that prepare you for a job. The U.S. Department of Education has a reference guide describing all of the CIP programs. Titled the *Classification of Instructional Programs*, it is available through state libraries and directly from the Department of Education at www.ed.gov. Keep in mind that educational institutions may use titles that differ from CIP. For example, a program called Biological Systems Engineering at a particular college may be essentially the same as the program called Agricultural/Biological Engineering and Bioengineering in CIP.

Related SOC Job

The taxonomy of jobs used in O*NET is based on the Standard Occupational Classification (SOC), which the federal government uses for reporting all job-related information (for example, in Census results). Each SOC occupation is coded by a six-digit number—for example, 11-3031 Financial Managers. O*NET uses a similar code but adds two digits to allow for specializations within the SOC occupation. To continue the preceding example, O*NET contains not only 11-3031.00 Financial Managers, but also 11-3031.01 Treasurers and Controllers and 11-3031.02 Financial Managers, Branch or Department. To make it easy for you to see the connection between O*NET and SOC, we present the code and name of the related SOC job.

Quick tips on how to use this information: If you need to explore an O*NET job using a source based on SOC, this topic will guide you to the correct code and title.

Related *OOH* Job

The *Occupational Outlook Handbook (OOH)* is a vital resource for people exploring career goals. In some ways its information is more detailed than O*NET's. For example, it very thoroughly describes alternatives for education and training, plus requirements for certification and licensing where relevant. It also identifies the economic forces expected to affect job opportunities. On the other hand, it breaks down the workforce into only 269 major jobs. (It describes 129 additional jobs without details.) For example, it uses a single article called "Broadcast and Sound Engineering Technicians and Radio Operators" to describe four O*NET jobs: Audio and Video Equipment Technicians, Broadcast Technicians, Radio Operators, and Sound Engineering Technicians.

Quick tips on how to use this information: Because the *OOH* often uses somewhat different job titles from O*NET, the reference here will help you locate the relevant article easily.

Related *DOT* Jobs

The last topic in each description is one or more *DOT* codes and job titles related to the O*NET job title. We obtained these by cross-referencing the O*NET title to the older occupational classification system titled the *Dictionary of Occupational Titles*. Although the O*NET has replaced the *DOT*, some career information systems still use the *DOT* system, so we included the related *DOT* number(s) here to allow you to make cross-references easily.

Quick tips on how to use this information: Even if you never use the *DOT*, the alternative titles help you identify the wide range of specialized jobs that are available. The *DOT* has more than 12,000 job titles, and most of them are now merged into the more general job titles used in the O*NET. This makes the O*NET much easier to use when identifying jobs that interest you, and the *DOT* job titles can give you ideas on more specialized jobs that may interest you even more. If you want, you can then learn more about the more specialized *DOT* jobs by reading their descriptions in the *Dictionary of Occupational Titles*. One of these specialized jobs may be just what you want to do with your career.

An Explanation of Some Curious Things in the Job Descriptions

As you read the job descriptions in this book, you may notice some odd things. For example, some job descriptions do not include information found in most other descriptions. And other details here and there may not seem right to you. We explain some of these points here, although you may notice others.

The basic reason for apparent errors is that the job descriptions are based on data we assemble from and cross-reference to several enormous databases of information. These databases are not perfect. They may have missing data, may not provide precise cross-references to other systems, and may have other limitations. We did our best to create a useful resource but had to base it on the limitations of our information sources. So here are explanations of a few things you may notice as you read the job descriptions.

Information in the Descriptions May Overlap

As you read the job descriptions, you may note that information in one section of a description is similar to information in another. This is not an error, as the O*NET data sometimes overlaps. For example, the general work activities statements are often similar to the occupational task list section. The skills statements may be similar to content provided elsewhere in the description.

The reason lies in how the information was developed. The occupational task lists were written specifically for each job, based on information collected from employer surveys and other sources. Work values, knowledge, abilities, skills, general work activities, and physical work conditions were created quite differently. For these, a list of characteristics was developed that applies to many or all jobs. Each occupation was given a numerical rating for each characteristic, with higher numbers referring to higher levels of competence. Because there are so many measures, listing all for each job would be impractical and, we think, confusing. Instead, we developed a method for listing the more important characteristics for each job—the ones that are most important to have or develop.

"None Met the Criteria"

The criteria we used to select data for inclusion in the job descriptions differ from one part to another. These criteria were explained earlier in this introduction.

When you see the statement "None met the criteria" in the abilities or other parts of a job description, this doesn't mean abilities are not important in these jobs. Rather, the job had no measure in the O*NET high enough to meet our criteria for inclusion. We adjusted our criteria to keep this situation from occurring too often, but you see this statement in some descriptions.

Information That Seems Incorrect

You may notice that some information in a job description seems contradictory, inaccurate, or incorrect. This is

simply a reflection of the data that was available from the database. So, as you review the descriptions, keep in mind that data has its limitations.

For example, you may notice that several jobs in a row share the same education, openings, growth, and salary data. The O*NET system is used for most information in this book, but the information sources for the education requirements, employment data, projected growth, and earnings for each occupation are coded by the Standard Occupational Classification (SOC) system. Sometimes one SOC job is linked to multiple O*NET jobs, so the O*NET jobs "share" information. The preceding discussions of these topics explain how to interpret duplicate information.

It is also possible that a work task listed for a job is not actually permitted in your state. In some jobs the workers are limited by law to performing certain tasks and not others, but the laws often vary from state to state. O*NET identifies the tasks that are most common and important, but they are not necessarily allowed in every state and jurisdiction.

"No Data Available"

When you see this statement in a job description, it means just what it says. This tends to happen for recent O*NET job entries, where the data has not yet been collected or processed for one or more of that job's measures. Sometimes the information is not available because it is very hard to collect. For example, several jobs in the performing arts have no earnings data available because annual earnings are so uneven in these jobs that no meaningful average figure can be determined.

"Others"

You see this statement at the end of some entries for the Instructional Programs and Related *DOT* Jobs sections. We did this only when there is a very long list of similar or related instructional programs or *DOT* jobs. When this is so, we cut off the *DOT* job titles at 500 characters and the program names at 2,000 characters. This section's purpose is to introduce you to the many specialized programs and jobs related to each O*NET title, so we think that listing these amounts of information gives you a good idea of the many related occupations and programs. For some O*NET job titles, there are hundreds of related *DOT* titles. Many of these jobs are similar to each other, like "Manager, Bakery" and "Manager, Cemetery," and going on and on with similar job titles isn't helpful.

Some Job Descriptions Are Shorter Than Others

Some job descriptions are substantially shorter than others. When this occurs, you see the statement "The Department of Labor has not collected some data for this job, so it has fewer details than the other descriptions."

You will see this statement under job titles that end with "All Other" and that have a code number ending in "99"—for example, 11-3049.99 Human Resources Managers, All Other. You will also see it under job titles that encapsulate other detailed jobs as part of the numbering structure. To get full information, you need to review the detailed jobs' descriptions. For example, Accountants and Auditors is listed as one job (with a shorter description), but it is then followed by longer, separate descriptions for Accountants and for Auditors.

Tips for Using This Book

The O*NET is now the major and most authoritative source of occupational information for employers, job seekers, students, career changers, and many others. Most occupational information sources now rely on or cross-reference the O*NET as the standard for detailed, reliable data on jobs.

As a major revision, the *O*NET Dictionary of Occupational Titles,* Fourth Edition, is intended for use by a variety of audiences. Following are brief tips for the major users of this book. Note that these tips are in addition to the quick tips we provide throughout our explanation of the various data elements included in the job descriptions.

Tips for Employers and Human Resource Development Professionals

The O*NET descriptions in this book provide a variety of valuable information for use in business. Some of these uses include the following.

- **Write job descriptions.** Each O*NET description has been carefully constructed to accurately reflect the tasks, skills, abilities, and other attributes required. These details provide an excellent source of objective information to use in writing job descriptions. As an example, look back at the sample description for Employment Interviewers presented earlier in the introduction. You find the key skills needed in the position, the responsibility level required, the education and training required, and the knowledge needed to succeed in the job—most of the content for a solid job description. Of course, you will need to customize the information for your organization, and you need to be careful with what you say about required physical abilities, but the O*NET descriptions provide an excellent starting point.

- **Structure employment interviews and hiring decisions.** You can use the O*NET descriptions to identify key skills and experiences to look for when screening applicants during interviews. This can be done informally, or a formal list of required competencies could be developed and then used by interviewers to more objectively rate each applicant. Of course, employer-specific requirements should be added as needed to the basic requirements for job performance provided by the O*NET descriptions.

- **Set pay levels.** We have noted the limitations for using pay information, and those same cautions apply when used by employers setting pay levels. The salary information does, however, provide some guidance on the pay rate for an experienced worker. Entry-level workers are often paid less (sometimes much less), and local conditions often determine the going rate to attract the employee skills needed. There are no hard guidelines, so use your judgment.

- **Identify training requirements.** You can use the descriptions to identify training needed for current or prospective employees to gain proficiency in various jobs. You may also identify skills deficiencies or other weaknesses in a potential employee that can be corrected through brief training and therefore increase the applicant pool for certain positions. The O*NET information is also helpful for existing employees seeking upward mobility to a more challenging or different job with the same employer. It can help them identify skills, training, knowledge, and other factors that they need to develop for success.

For more information about using the O*NET in human resources settings, download the *O*NET Toolkit for Business* at http://www.onetcenter.org/toolkit.html.

Tips for People Exploring Career Alternatives

Virtually all workers in North America work in one of the occupations described in this book. While the descriptions are quite brief, they provide substantial information that can be used as a preliminary source for identifying one or more career options to explore more thoroughly.

If you are using this book to explore career options, the best way to begin is by identifying jobs or clusters of jobs that interest you most. Part I presents six ways to find jobs in the O*NET: by SOC number, by interest area, by education and training requirements, by placement in three best jobs lists, by related military job, and alphabetically by job title. Read the O*NET descriptions for those jobs that most interest you and, for those you want to know even more about, use one of the resources that follow:

- **Read the *Occupational Outlook Handbook*.** Each O*NET description relates to one or more job titles found in a separate book titled the *Occupational Outlook Handbook*. We like the *OOH* and recommend it highly. Its descriptions are longer and provide details that are useful to anyone considering the occupation. The *OOH* is available in most libraries and through many bookstores. The *OOH* descriptions are also provided in a book titled *Top 300 Careers* (JIST Works). One of these books should be available in most libraries and bookstores.

- **Read the *Dictionary of Occupational Titles* and the *New Guide for Occupational Exploration*.** The *DOT* and *GOE* are widely used reference books with organizational systems cross-referenced by many other books, interest inventories, and other materials. The O*NET descriptions in this book include related *DOT* and *GOE* numbers and job titles or interest groups, allowing you to cross-reference these important systems. The *DOT* was published by the U.S. Department of Labor and provides brief descriptions for more than 12,000 job titles. The last edition of the *DOT* was released in 1991. Because the O*NET database replaces the older *DOT* database of occupational information, there are no plans to update the *DOT* in the future. Even so, it will remain a rich source of information on many specific job titles that are simply not described elsewhere. The *New Guide for Occupational Exploration: Linking Interests, Learning,*

and Careers (JIST Works) organizes jobs into groupings based on interests and provides useful information on these groupings and the jobs within the groups.

- **Get additional information from the library or the Internet.** Ask a librarian to direct you to books, periodicals, and other sources of information on an occupation that interests you. Professional journals are often available for a wide variety of occupations and industries. You can also often obtain substantial information from professional associations and sources on the Internet. JIST's Web site provides links to other career-related sites. Visit the company at www.jist.com.

- **Talk to people who work in the jobs that interest you.** The best source of information is often overlooked—the people who work in jobs that interest you. They are often willing to answer your questions and to direct you to sources of additional information.

Tips for Those Considering Education or Training Options

People with more training or education tend to earn more than those with less. While most training and education programs benefit you in some way, many people do not spend enough time investigating such an important decision. Before you spend substantial time and money on courses or training programs, spend some time investigating what you hope to gain.

Each O*NET description provides several sources of education and training information. The education section of each job description is the most obvious one, but additional information is found in the knowledge and instructional programs sections. Following are some details on how each of these sections can be used to better understand the training or education needed for a given job.

- **The education section.** This includes information on the training or education level typically required for entry into the listed occupation.

- **The knowledge section.** This section gives you some idea of the courses or programs that would be helpful for each job.

- **The instructional program section.** Each occupational description includes one or more CIP titles. This refers to the Classification of Instructional

Programs, a widely used system for organizing training and education programs. The CIP title tells you the type of training or educational programs typically available for preparing for that occupation. Program names used in various schools and training programs may differ from those listed in the CIP, but the CIP information gives you some idea of the programs available.

While the O*NET descriptions provide some information on the level of training, education, and experience required for various occupations, you obviously need more detail. As with occupational data, a wide variety of training and education information is available. Bookstores and libraries have many books on the topic, much is available on the Internet, and local schools and training programs provide orientation and admission information. All these resources should be used before making an important decision on education or training.

Tips for Job Seekers

The O*NET job descriptions in this book can help you in two important ways:

- **Identify new job targets.** Many job seekers miss employment opportunities by overlooking jobs they can do but that are unfamiliar. For this reason, you should carefully review all the O*NET job titles, with particular emphasis on those in clusters you are already considering. A listing of O*NET jobs within clusters appears in the table of contents. Review it if you are looking for a job. As you identify possible new job targets, look up their O*NET descriptions to determine whether you might qualify. If you do, consider pursuing these jobs. In the interview, point out the qualities that you have and state that you can quickly learn any needed skills.

- **Prepare for interviews.** The O*NET descriptions offer very useful information that can help you prepare for interviews. For example, once you have set up an interview for a position, carefully review the O*NET description for that job. Doing so helps you identify skills and experience you should emphasize. We also encourage you to carefully review the O*NET descriptions of jobs you have held in the past. Doing so identifies skills and other characteristics that you can present in your interview for a new position.

- Even past jobs that seem unrelated to your current interests often provide skills and experience that you can use to convince an employer that you can

handle the position you seek. Careful interview preparation can make the difference between getting a job offer and not getting one. We have often found that better-prepared job seekers get jobs over those with superior credentials. The difference is in how well they present themselves in interviews. Those who read and understand the skills they have for doing the job they seek—and communicate this to an employer—have a distinct advantage.

Tips for Teachers and Educators

O*NET descriptions provide excellent information on the skills and knowledge needed to succeed in a given job. If you are responsible for developing or teaching a course or curriculum for a school or training program, the descriptions provide exact points that need to be learned. An outcome-oriented program could be developed to teach specific, measurable knowledge or competencies. Remember that the O*NET database provides specific measures for many elements included in this book, and these measures can be obtained by accessing the database itself.

Tips for Those Researching Technical and Legal Issues— "Caveat Datum"

You have probably heard of "caveat emptor," which is Latin for "let the buyer beware." We think "caveat datum," which (loosely translated) means "beware of the data," is particularly appropriate as our advice regarding the O*NET data as the basis for settling legal and other important issues.

The O*NET database—and the O*NET descriptions in this book—provide substantial technical information on jobs and their many characteristics and requirements. The U.S. government provides this information, and great care has been taken to make it both accurate and reliable. Even so, the information does have limitations. For example, for the single O*NET job title Sales Managers you could find enormous differences in conditions from one employer to another regarding such matters as responsibility, stress, travel requirements, computer literacy requirements, product knowledge, and physical lifting of samples. These differences simply cannot be included in one description, and many job-to-job differences exist. That is why the U.S. Department of Labor has never approved or encouraged the use of its occupational information to support formal litigation or as the final, authoritative basis for legal and other formal matters.

In a similar way, we urge you to understand that the validity of the underlying information has limitations. For example, an occupation that lists a bachelor's degree as a typical training requirement for entry often has some or even many people successfully working in the job with less education—or much more.

One information source simply cannot cover all variations of a given job. Too many differences exist in the requirements for the same job title among different employers. That is why we recommend that you use your own judgment in understanding the information. While it has been carefully collected and reviewed, it has limitations and should not be used as the final authoritative source for legal or technical issues.

Other Major Career Information Resources

The information in this book will be very useful, but you may want or need additional information. Here are additional resources to consider.

The *Occupational Outlook Handbook* (or the *OOH*): Updated every two years by the U.S. Department of Labor, this book provides descriptions for almost 270 major jobs covering more than 85 percent of the workforce.

The *Enhanced Occupational Outlook Handbook:* Includes all descriptions in the *OOH* plus descriptions of more than 6,300 more-specialized jobs that are related to them.

The *O*NET Career Interests Inventory:* Allows users to identify their job interests by responding to 180 work activity statements. It then guides them to match those interests to potential careers organized by interest area and preparation required. In-depth suggestions for further research and a Job Information/Action Plan worksheet help them pursue their goals. The inventory is self-scoring and self-interpreting and takes less than thirty minutes to complete.

The *O*NET Career Values Inventory:* Helps individuals explore more than 900 O*NET job titles based on their work values and motivators. It then guides them to match their results to potential careers organized by values and preparation required. In-depth suggestions for further research and a Job Information/Action Plan worksheet help them pursue their goals. The inventory is self-scoring and self-interpreting and takes less than thirty minutes to complete.

The *New Guide for Occupational Exploration:* An important career reference that allows you to explore all major O*NET jobs based on your interests.

Best Jobs for the 21st Century: Includes descriptions for the 500 jobs (out of more than 1,100) with the best combination of earnings, growth, and number of openings. Useful lists make jobs easy to explore (examples: highest-paying jobs by level of education or training; best jobs overall; and best jobs for different ages, personality types, interests, and many more).

Exploring Careers—A Young Person's Guide to 1,000 Jobs: For youth exploring career and education opportunities, this book covers 1,000 job options in an interesting and useful format.

Your Suggestions Are Welcome

While it was impractical to include details on all data elements for each occupation found in the O*NET database, the O*NET descriptions in this book include substantial details in a useful format. In addition to the narrative description, we include higher-than-average requirements for many data elements for each occupation—plus the crosswalk information for the GOE, CIP, SOC, *OOH*, and *DOT* (all explained earlier). While some compromises were involved in constructing helpful descriptions, we think the information is valuable for many uses. We hope you agree.

Because we intend to revise this book as updated O*NET data becomes available, please let us know what you would like us to include in future editions. Please send your comments and suggestions to Editor, *O*NET Dictionary of Occupational Titles,* JIST Works, 8902 Otis Ave., Indianapolis, IN 46216-1033. You can also send an e-mail to info@jist.com. Thanks!

Six Easy Ways to Find O*NET Jobs of Interest

This book provides nearly 950 job descriptions, so how do you pinpoint those that are most relevant to you? This part provides six easy ways for you to find job descriptions. The lists included in this part can help you narrow the selection and consider jobs that you qualify for or are interested in. Several kinds of lists sort the jobs in helpful ways:

- Interest area lists sort jobs according to 16 career interest areas.
- Education and training level lists sort jobs according to their education and training requirements.
- Best-paying, fastest-growing, and most openings lists present the top 50 jobs in each of those three categories.

You can also browse the job titles by related military job, alphabetically, or by O*NET number.

Method 1: Browse the Jobs by O*NET Number

The jobs are listed in the table of contents by their O*NET numbers, which are based on the Standard Occupational Classification (SOC) system. The SOC is a structure established by the federal government that organizes the jobs according to the work performed.

If you know the O*NET number for a job, look it up in the table of contents and then turn to the corresponding page for the complete job description. The table of contents starts on page v.

When to Use This Method: You may have obtained the O*NET number for a job in several ways, including in the *Occupational Outlook Handbook,* another resource by the U.S. Department of Labor. The *OOH* lists the O*NET numbers for more than 250 jobs held by about 90 percent of the labor force. Use the O*NET number to locate the job description in Part II of this book. You can also browse other descriptions in the same section, as they are likely to have similar tasks and responsibilities.

Method 2: Browse the Jobs Based on Your Interests

You can use the following lists to find jobs that fall into each of the 16 career interest areas used in the *New Guide for Occupational Exploration (GOE)* as adapted from the U.S. Department of Education career clusters. This system is explained in more detail in the introduction. The jobs within each interest area are listed alphabetically, and each job is listed with its O*NET number to help you locate it in Part II.

When to Use This Method: If certain types of careers interest you, the following lists help you narrow your search. Simply find the career areas that interest you most, review the list of related jobs, and then look up their descriptions in Part II using the O*NET number.

01: Agriculture and Natural Resources

O*NET Number	Job Title
19-4011.00	Agricultural and Food Science Technicians
17-2021.00	Agricultural Engineers
45-2091.00	Agricultural Equipment Operators
19-4011.01	Agricultural Technicians
19-1011.00	Animal Scientists
11-9011.03	Aquacultural Managers
19-1031.00	Conservation Scientists
47-5041.00	Continuous Mining Machine Operators
11-9011.02	Crop and Livestock Managers
47-5011.00	Derrick Operators, Oil and Gas
47-5021.00	Earth Drillers, Except Oil and Gas
17-2081.00	Environmental Engineers
19-4091.00	Environmental Science and Protection Technicians, Including Health
53-7032.00	Excavating and Loading Machine and Dragline Operators

O*NET Number	Job Title
47-5031.00	Explosives Workers, Ordnance Handling Experts, and Blasters
45-4021.00	Fallers
45-1012.00	Farm Labor Contractors
11-9011.00	Farm, Ranch, and Other Agricultural Managers
11-9012.00	Farmers and Ranchers
45-2092.02	Farmworkers and Laborers, Crop
45-2092.00	Farmworkers and Laborers, Crop, Nursery, and Greenhouse
45-2093.00	Farmworkers, Farm and Ranch Animals
45-1011.07	First-Line Supervisors/Managers of Agricultural Crop and Horticultural Workers
45-1011.08	First-Line Supervisors/Managers of Animal Husbandry and Animal Care Workers
45-1011.06	First-Line Supervisors/Managers of Aquacultural Workers
47-1011.00	First-Line Supervisors/Managers of Construction Trades and Extraction Workers
45-1011.00	First-Line Supervisors/Managers of Farming, Fishing, and Forestry Workers
37-1012.00	First-Line Supervisors/Managers of Landscaping, Lawn Service, and Groundskeeping Workers
45-1011.05	First-Line Supervisors/Managers of Logging Workers
45-3011.00	Fishers and Related Fishing Workers
19-4011.02	Food Science Technicians
19-1012.00	Food Scientists and Technologists
19-4093.00	Forest and Conservation Technicians
45-4011.00	Forest and Conservation Workers
19-1032.00	Foresters
19-4041.00	Geological and Petroleum Technicians
19-4041.02	Geological Sample Test Technicians
19-4041.01	Geophysical Data Technicians
47-5081.00	Helpers—Extraction Workers
45-3021.00	Hunters and Trappers
37-3011.00	Landscaping and Groundskeeping Workers
53-7033.00	Loading Machine Operators, Underground Mining
45-4023.00	Log Graders and Scalers
45-4022.00	Logging Equipment Operators
47-5042.00	Mine Cutting and Channeling Machine Operators
17-2151.00	Mining and Geological Engineers, Including Mining Safety Engineers
11-9011.01	Nursery and Greenhouse Managers
45-2092.01	Nursery Workers
19-1031.03	Park Naturalists
37-2021.00	Pest Control Workers
37-3012.00	Pesticide Handlers, Sprayers, and Applicators, Vegetation
17-2171.00	Petroleum Engineers
13-1021.00	Purchasing Agents and Buyers, Farm Products
19-1031.02	Range Managers

47-5051.00	Rock Splitters, Quarry
47-5061.00	Roof Bolters, Mining
47-5012.00	Rotary Drill Operators, Oil and Gas
47-5071.00	Roustabouts, Oil and Gas
47-5013.00	Service Unit Operators, Oil, Gas, and Mining
53-7111.00	Shuttle Car Operators
19-1013.00	Soil and Plant Scientists
19-1031.01	Soil and Water Conservationists
37-3013.00	Tree Trimmers and Pruners
53-7073.00	Wellhead Pumpers
19-1023.00	Zoologists and Wildlife Biologists

02: Architecture and Construction

O*NET Number	Job Title
17-1011.00	Architects, Except Landscape and Naval
17-3011.00	Architectural and Civil Drafters
17-3011.01	Architectural Drafters
47-2011.00	Boilermakers
47-2021.00	Brickmasons and Blockmasons
47-2041.00	Carpet Installers
47-2051.00	Cement Masons and Concrete Finishers
17-3011.02	Civil Drafters
49-9092.00	Commercial Divers
47-2031.01	Construction Carpenters
47-2061.00	Construction Laborers
11-9021.00	Construction Managers
53-7021.00	Crane and Tower Operators
47-2081.00	Drywall and Ceiling Tile Installers
49-2095.00	Electrical and Electronics Repairers, Powerhouse, Substation, and Relay
49-9051.00	Electrical Power-Line Installers and Repairers
47-2111.00	Electricians
47-4021.00	Elevator Installers and Repairers
47-4031.00	Fence Erectors
47-2042.00	Floor Layers, Except Carpet, Wood, and Hard Tiles
47-2043.00	Floor Sanders and Finishers
47-2121.00	Glaziers
47-4041.00	Hazardous Materials Removal Workers
49-9021.01	Heating and Air Conditioning Mechanics and Installers
47-3011.00	Helpers—Brickmasons, Blockmasons, Stonemasons, and Tile and Marble Setters
47-3012.00	Helpers—Carpenters
47-3013.00	Helpers—Electricians
49-9098.00	Helpers—Installation, Maintenance, and Repair Workers
47-3014.00	Helpers—Painters, Paperhangers, Plasterers, and Stucco Masons
47-3015.00	Helpers—Pipelayers, Plumbers, Pipefitters, and Steamfitters
47-3016.00	Helpers—Roofers
47-4051.00	Highway Maintenance Workers
47-2131.00	Insulation Workers, Floor, Ceiling, and Wall
47-2132.00	Insulation Workers, Mechanical
17-1012.00	Landscape Architects
49-9042.00	Maintenance and Repair Workers, General
49-9095.00	Manufactured Building and Mobile Home Installers
47-2073.00	Operating Engineers and Other Construction Equipment Operators
47-2141.00	Painters, Construction and Maintenance
47-2142.00	Paperhangers
47-2071.00	Paving, Surfacing, and Tamping Equipment Operators
47-2072.00	Pile-Driver Operators
47-2152.01	Pipe Fitters and Steamfitters
47-2151.00	Pipelayers
47-2161.00	Plasterers and Stucco Masons
47-2152.02	Plumbers
47-2152.00	Plumbers, Pipefitters, and Steamfitters
47-4061.00	Rail-Track Laying and Maintenance Equipment Operators
49-9045.00	Refractory Materials Repairers, Except Brickmasons
49-9021.02	Refrigeration Mechanics and Installers
47-2171.00	Reinforcing Iron and Rebar Workers
49-9096.00	Riggers
47-2181.00	Roofers
47-2031.02	Rough Carpenters
49-2098.00	Security and Fire Alarm Systems Installers
47-4091.00	Segmental Pavers
47-4071.00	Septic Tank Servicers and Sewer Pipe Cleaners
47-2211.00	Sheet Metal Workers
51-9195.03	Stone Cutters and Carvers, Manufacturing
47-2022.00	Stonemasons
47-2221.00	Structural Iron and Steel Workers
17-1022.00	Surveyors
47-2082.00	Tapers
49-2022.00	Telecommunications Equipment Installers and Repairers, Except Line Installers
49-9052.00	Telecommunications Line Installers and Repairers
47-2053.00	Terrazzo Workers and Finishers
47-2044.00	Tile and Marble Setters

03: Arts and Communication

O*NET Number	Job Title
27-2011.00	Actors
13-1011.00	Agents and Business Managers of Artists, Performers, and Athletes
53-2021.00	Air Traffic Controllers

(continued)

(continued)

03: Arts and Communication

O*NET Number	Job Title
53-2022.00	Airfield Operations Specialists
27-1011.00	Art Directors
27-4011.00	Audio and Video Equipment Technicians
27-3021.00	Broadcast News Analysts
27-4012.00	Broadcast Technicians
27-4031.00	Camera Operators, Television, Video, and Motion Picture
27-2032.00	Choreographers
27-1021.00	Commercial and Industrial Designers
27-3043.04	Copy Writers
39-3092.00	Costume Attendants
27-1012.00	Craft Artists
27-2031.00	Dancers
27-2012.02	Directors—Stage, Motion Pictures, Television, and Radio
43-5032.00	Dispatchers, Except Police, Fire, and Ambulance
27-3041.00	Editors
27-1022.00	Fashion Designers
27-4032.00	Film and Video Editors
27-1013.00	Fine Artists, Including Painters, Sculptors, and Illustrators
27-1023.00	Floral Designers
27-1024.00	Graphic Designers
27-1025.00	Interior Designers
27-3091.00	Interpreters and Translators
39-5091.00	Makeup Artists, Theatrical and Performance
27-1026.00	Merchandise Displayers and Window Trimmers
27-1014.00	Multi-Media Artists and Animators
27-2041.04	Music Composers and Arrangers
27-2041.01	Music Directors
27-2041.00	Music Directors and Composers
49-9063.00	Musical Instrument Repairers and Tuners
27-2042.00	Musicians and Singers
27-2042.02	Musicians, Instrumental
27-4021.00	Photographers
27-3043.05	Poets, Lyricists, and Creative Writers
43-5031.00	Police, Fire, and Ambulance Dispatchers
51-9195.05	Potters, Manufacturing
27-2012.01	Producers
27-2012.00	Producers and Directors
27-2012.03	Program Directors
27-3012.00	Public Address System and Other Announcers
11-2031.00	Public Relations Managers
27-3031.00	Public Relations Specialists
27-3011.00	Radio and Television Announcers
27-4013.00	Radio Operators
27-3022.00	Reporters and Correspondents
27-1027.00	Set and Exhibit Designers
27-2042.01	Singers
27-4014.00	Sound Engineering Technicians
27-2012.04	Talent Directors
27-2012.05	Technical Directors/Managers
27-3042.00	Technical Writers
43-2021.00	Telephone Operators
27-3043.00	Writers and Authors

04: Business and Administration

O*NET Number	Job Title
13-2011.01	Accountants
13-2011.00	Accountants and Auditors
11-3011.00	Administrative Services Managers
13-2011.02	Auditors
43-3021.00	Billing and Posting Clerks and Machine Operators
43-3021.02	Billing, Cost, and Rate Clerks
43-3021.03	Billing, Posting, and Calculating Machine Operators
43-3031.00	Bookkeeping, Accounting, and Auditing Clerks
43-4011.00	Brokerage Clerks
13-2031.00	Budget Analysts
11-1011.00	Chief Executives
11-3041.00	Compensation and Benefits Managers
13-1072.00	Compensation, Benefits, and Job Analysis Specialists
43-4021.00	Correspondence Clerks
43-9021.00	Data Entry Keyers
13-1071.01	Employment Interviewers
13-1071.00	Employment, Recruitment, and Placement Specialists
43-6011.00	Executive Secretaries and Administrative Assistants
43-4071.00	File Clerks
37-1011.00	First-Line Supervisors/Managers of Housekeeping and Janitorial Workers
43-1011.00	First-Line Supervisors/Managers of Office and Administrative Support Workers
11-1021.00	General and Operations Managers
43-4161.00	Human Resources Assistants, Except Payroll and Timekeeping
11-3040.00	Human Resources Managers
17-3026.00	Industrial Engineering Technicians
43-6012.00	Legal Secretaries
13-1081.00	Logisticians
43-9051.00	Mail Clerks and Mail Machine Operators, Except Postal Service
13-1111.00	Management Analysts
43-5081.02	Marking Clerks
43-6013.00	Medical Secretaries
13-1121.00	Meeting and Convention Planners
43-5041.00	Meter Readers, Utilities

43-9061.00	Office Clerks, General
43-9071.00	Office Machine Operators, Except Computer
15-2031.00	Operations Research Analysts
43-5081.04	Order Fillers, Wholesale and Retail Sales
43-3051.00	Payroll and Timekeeping Clerks
13-1071.02	Personnel Recruiters
43-5051.00	Postal Service Clerks
43-5053.00	Postal Service Mail Sorters, Processors, and Processing Machine Operators
43-3061.00	Procurement Clerks
43-5061.00	Production, Planning, and Expediting Clerks
43-6014.00	Secretaries, Except Legal, Medical, and Executive
43-5071.00	Shipping, Receiving, and Traffic Clerks
43-3021.01	Statement Clerks
43-5081.00	Stock Clerks and Order Fillers
43-5081.01	Stock Clerks, Sales Floor
43-5081.03	Stock Clerks—Stockroom, Warehouse, or Storage Yard
43-2011.00	Switchboard Operators, Including Answering Service
13-2082.00	Tax Preparers
11-3042.00	Training and Development Managers
13-1073.00	Training and Development Specialists
43-5111.00	Weighers, Measurers, Checkers, and Samplers, Recordkeeping
43-9022.00	Word Processors and Typists

05: Education and Training

O*NET Number	Job Title
25-3011.00	Adult Literacy, Remedial Education, and GED Teachers and Instructors
25-1041.00	Agricultural Sciences Teachers, Postsecondary
25-1061.00	Anthropology and Archeology Teachers, Postsecondary
25-1031.00	Architecture Teachers, Postsecondary
25-4011.00	Archivists
25-1062.00	Area, Ethnic, and Cultural Studies Teachers, Postsecondary
25-1121.00	Art, Drama, and Music Teachers, Postsecondary
25-1051.00	Atmospheric, Earth, Marine, and Space Sciences Teachers, Postsecondary
25-9011.00	Audio-Visual Collections Specialists
25-1042.00	Biological Science Teachers, Postsecondary
25-1011.00	Business Teachers, Postsecondary
25-1052.00	Chemistry Teachers, Postsecondary
25-1122.00	Communications Teachers, Postsecondary
25-1021.00	Computer Science Teachers, Postsecondary
25-1111.00	Criminal Justice and Law Enforcement Teachers, Postsecondary
25-4012.00	Curators
25-1063.00	Economics Teachers, Postsecondary

11-9032.00	Education Administrators, Elementary and Secondary School
11-9033.00	Education Administrators, Postsecondary
11-9031.00	Education Administrators, Preschool and Child Care Center/Program
25-1081.00	Education Teachers, Postsecondary
21-1012.00	Educational, Vocational, and School Counselors
25-2021.00	Elementary School Teachers, Except Special Education
25-1032.00	Engineering Teachers, Postsecondary
25-1123.00	English Language and Literature Teachers, Postsecondary
25-1053.00	Environmental Science Teachers, Postsecondary
25-9021.00	Farm and Home Management Advisors
39-9031.00	Fitness Trainers and Aerobics Instructors
25-1124.00	Foreign Language and Literature Teachers, Postsecondary
25-1043.00	Forestry and Conservation Science Teachers, Postsecondary
25-1064.00	Geography Teachers, Postsecondary
25-1191.00	Graduate Teaching Assistants
21-1091.00	Health Educators
25-1071.00	Health Specialties Teachers, Postsecondary
25-1125.00	History Teachers, Postsecondary
25-1192.00	Home Economics Teachers, Postsecondary
25-9031.00	Instructional Coordinators
25-2012.00	Kindergarten Teachers, Except Special Education
25-1112.00	Law Teachers, Postsecondary
25-4021.00	Librarians
43-4121.00	Library Assistants, Clerical
25-1082.00	Library Science Teachers, Postsecondary
25-4031.00	Library Technicians
25-1022.00	Mathematical Science Teachers, Postsecondary
25-2022.00	Middle School Teachers, Except Special and Vocational Education
25-4013.00	Museum Technicians and Conservators
25-1072.00	Nursing Instructors and Teachers, Postsecondary
25-1126.00	Philosophy and Religion Teachers, Postsecondary
25-1054.00	Physics Teachers, Postsecondary
25-1065.00	Political Science Teachers, Postsecondary
25-2011.00	Preschool Teachers, Except Special Education
25-1066.00	Psychology Teachers, Postsecondary
25-1193.00	Recreation and Fitness Studies Teachers, Postsecondary
25-2031.00	Secondary School Teachers, Except Special and Vocational Education
25-3021.00	Self-Enrichment Education Teachers
25-1113.00	Social Work Teachers, Postsecondary
25-1067.00	Sociology Teachers, Postsecondary
25-2042.00	Special Education Teachers, Middle School
25-2041.00	Special Education Teachers, Preschool, Kindergarten, and Elementary School
25-2043.00	Special Education Teachers, Secondary School

(continued)

(continued)

05: Education and Training

O*NET Number	Job Title
25-9041.00	Teacher Assistants
25-2023.00	Vocational Education Teachers, Middle School
25-1194.00	Vocational Education Teachers, Postsecondary
25-2032.00	Vocational Education Teachers, Secondary School

06: Finance and Insurance

O*NET Number	Job Title
13-2021.00	Appraisers and Assessors of Real Estate
13-2021.02	Appraisers, Real Estate
13-2021.01	Assessors
43-3011.00	Bill and Account Collectors
13-1031.00	Claims Adjusters, Examiners, and Investigators
13-1031.01	Claims Examiners, Property and Casualty Insurance
13-1051.00	Cost Estimators
13-2041.00	Credit Analysts
43-4041.01	Credit Authorizers
43-4041.00	Credit Authorizers, Checkers, and Clerks
43-4041.02	Credit Checkers
13-2051.00	Financial Analysts
11-3031.00	Financial Managers
11-3031.02	Financial Managers, Branch or Department
13-1031.02	Insurance Adjusters, Examiners, and Investigators
13-1032.00	Insurance Appraisers, Auto Damage
43-9041.00	Insurance Claims and Policy Processing Clerks
43-9041.01	Insurance Claims Clerks
43-9041.02	Insurance Policy Processing Clerks
41-3021.00	Insurance Sales Agents
13-2053.00	Insurance Underwriters
13-2071.00	Loan Counselors
43-4131.00	Loan Interviewers and Clerks
13-2072.00	Loan Officers
19-3021.00	Market Research Analysts
43-4141.00	New Accounts Clerks
13-2052.00	Personal Financial Advisors
43-9081.00	Proofreaders and Copy Markers
41-3031.02	Sales Agents, Financial Services
41-3031.01	Sales Agents, Securities and Commodities
41-3031.00	Securities, Commodities, and Financial Services Sales Agents
19-3022.00	Survey Researchers
43-3071.00	Tellers
11-3031.01	Treasurers and Controllers

07: Government and Public Administration

O*NET Number	Job Title
45-2011.00	Agricultural Inspectors
53-6051.01	Aviation Inspectors
19-4061.01	City and Regional Planning Aides
13-1041.00	Compliance Officers, Except Agriculture, Construction, Health and Safety, and Transportation
47-4011.00	Construction and Building Inspectors
43-4031.01	Court Clerks
23-2091.00	Court Reporters
43-4031.00	Court, Municipal, and License Clerks
13-1041.01	Environmental Compliance Inspectors
13-1041.03	Equal Opportunity Representatives and Officers
13-2061.00	Financial Examiners
33-2021.01	Fire Inspectors
33-3031.00	Fish and Game Wardens
33-2022.00	Forest Fire Inspectors and Prevention Specialists
53-6051.08	Freight and Cargo Inspectors
13-1041.04	Government Property Inspectors and Investigators
33-3021.05	Immigration and Customs Inspectors
43-4031.03	License Clerks
13-1041.02	Licensing Examiners and Inspectors
43-4031.02	Municipal Clerks
19-4051.02	Nuclear Monitoring Technicians
29-9011.00	Occupational Health and Safety Specialists
29-9012.00	Occupational Health and Safety Technicians
11-9151.00	Social and Community Service Managers
13-2081.00	Tax Examiners, Collectors, and Revenue Agents
53-6051.07	Transportation Vehicle, Equipment and Systems Inspectors, Except Aviation
19-3051.00	Urban and Regional Planners

08: Health Science

O*NET Number	Job Title
29-1061.00	Anesthesiologists
45-2021.00	Animal Breeders
39-2011.00	Animal Trainers
29-9091.00	Athletic Trainers
29-1121.00	Audiologists
19-4021.00	Biological Technicians
29-2031.00	Cardiovascular Technologists and Technicians
29-1011.00	Chiropractors
13-1041.06	Coroners
31-9091.00	Dental Assistants
29-2021.00	Dental Hygienists
29-1021.00	Dentists, General

29-2032.00	Diagnostic Medical Sonographers
29-2051.00	Dietetic Technicians
29-1031.00	Dietitians and Nutritionists
39-4011.00	Embalmers
29-1062.00	Family and General Practitioners
31-1011.00	Home Health Aides
29-1063.00	Internists, General
29-2061.00	Licensed Practical and Licensed Vocational Nurses
31-9011.00	Massage Therapists
29-2012.00	Medical and Clinical Laboratory Technicians
29-2011.00	Medical and Clinical Laboratory Technologists
11-9111.00	Medical and Health Services Managers
31-9092.00	Medical Assistants
31-9093.00	Medical Equipment Preparers
29-2071.00	Medical Records and Health Information Technicians
31-9094.00	Medical Transcriptionists
39-2021.00	Nonfarm Animal Caretakers
29-2033.00	Nuclear Medicine Technologists
31-1012.00	Nursing Aides, Orderlies, and Attendants
29-1064.00	Obstetricians and Gynecologists
31-2012.00	Occupational Therapist Aides
31-2011.00	Occupational Therapist Assistants
29-1122.00	Occupational Therapists
29-2081.00	Opticians, Dispensing
29-1041.00	Optometrists
29-1022.00	Oral and Maxillofacial Surgeons
29-1023.00	Orthodontists
29-2091.00	Orthotists and Prosthetists
29-1065.00	Pediatricians, General
29-1051.00	Pharmacists
31-9095.00	Pharmacy Aides
29-2052.00	Pharmacy Technicians
31-2022.00	Physical Therapist Aides
31-2021.00	Physical Therapist Assistants
29-1123.00	Physical Therapists
29-1071.00	Physician Assistants
29-1081.00	Podiatrists
29-1024.00	Prosthodontists
31-1013.00	Psychiatric Aides
29-2053.00	Psychiatric Technicians
29-1066.00	Psychiatrists
29-1124.00	Radiation Therapists
29-2034.02	Radiologic Technicians
29-2034.01	Radiologic Technologists
29-2034.00	Radiologic Technologists and Technicians
29-1125.00	Recreational Therapists
29-1111.00	Registered Nurses
29-1126.00	Respiratory Therapists
29-2054.00	Respiratory Therapy Technicians
29-1127.00	Speech-Language Pathologists
29-1067.00	Surgeons

29-2055.00	Surgical Technologists
29-1131.00	Veterinarians
31-9096.00	Veterinary Assistants and Laboratory Animal Caretakers
29-2056.00	Veterinary Technologists and Technicians

09: Hospitality, Tourism, and Recreation

O*NET Number	Job Title
39-3091.00	Amusement and Recreation Attendants
27-2021.00	Athletes and Sports Competitors
39-6011.00	Baggage Porters and Bellhops
39-5011.00	Barbers
35-3011.00	Bartenders
51-3021.00	Butchers and Meat Cutters
35-1011.00	Chefs and Head Cooks
27-2022.00	Coaches and Scouts
35-3021.00	Combined Food Preparation and Serving Workers, Including Fast Food
39-6012.00	Concierges
35-2011.00	Cooks, Fast Food
35-2012.00	Cooks, Institution and Cafeteria
35-2013.00	Cooks, Private Household
35-2014.00	Cooks, Restaurant
35-2015.00	Cooks, Short Order
35-3022.00	Counter Attendants, Cafeteria, Food Concession, and Coffee Shop
35-9011.00	Dining Room and Cafeteria Attendants and Bartender Helpers
35-9021.00	Dishwashers
35-1012.00	First-Line Supervisors/Managers of Food Preparation and Serving Workers
39-1021.00	First-Line Supervisors/Managers of Personal Service Workers
39-6031.00	Flight Attendants
35-2021.00	Food Preparation Workers
35-3041.00	Food Servers, Nonrestaurant
11-9051.00	Food Service Managers
39-3012.00	Gaming and Sports Book Writers and Runners
39-3011.00	Gaming Dealers
11-9071.00	Gaming Managers
39-1011.00	Gaming Supervisors
39-5012.00	Hairdressers, Hairstylists, and Cosmetologists
35-9031.00	Hosts and Hostesses, Restaurant, Lounge, and Coffee Shop
43-4081.00	Hotel, Motel, and Resort Desk Clerks
37-2011.00	Janitors and Cleaners, Except Maids and Housekeeping Cleaners
39-3093.00	Locker Room, Coatroom, and Dressing Room Attendants
11-9081.00	Lodging Managers
37-2012.00	Maids and Housekeeping Cleaners

(continued)

(continued)

09: Hospitality, Tourism, and Recreation

O*NET Number	Job Title
39-5092.00	Manicurists and Pedicurists
39-3021.00	Motion Picture Projectionists
39-9032.00	Recreation Workers
43-4181.00	Reservation and Transportation Ticket Agents and Travel Clerks
39-5093.00	Shampooers
39-5094.00	Skin Care Specialists
39-1012.00	Slot Key Persons
39-6021.00	Tour Guides and Escorts
39-6032.00	Transportation Attendants, Except Flight Attendants and Baggage Porters
41-3041.00	Travel Agents
39-6022.00	Travel Guides
27-2023.00	Umpires, Referees, and Other Sports Officials
39-3031.00	Ushers, Lobby Attendants, and Ticket Takers
35-3031.00	Waiters and Waitresses

10: Human Service

O*NET Number	Job Title
39-9011.00	Child Care Workers
21-1021.00	Child, Family, and School Social Workers
21-2011.00	Clergy
19-3031.02	Clinical Psychologists
19-3031.00	Clinical, Counseling, and School Psychologists
19-3031.03	Counseling Psychologists
21-2021.00	Directors, Religious Activities and Education
43-4061.00	Eligibility Interviewers, Government Programs
39-4021.00	Funeral Attendants
43-4111.00	Interviewers, Except Eligibility and Loan
21-1013.00	Marriage and Family Therapists
21-1022.00	Medical and Public Health Social Workers
21-1023.00	Mental Health and Substance Abuse Social Workers
21-1014.00	Mental Health Counselors
39-9011.01	Nannies
39-9021.00	Personal and Home Care Aides
21-1092.00	Probation Officers and Correctional Treatment Specialists
21-1015.00	Rehabilitation Counselors
39-9041.00	Residential Advisors
21-1093.00	Social and Human Service Assistants
21-1011.00	Substance Abuse and Behavioral Disorder Counselors

11: Information Technology

O*NET Number	Job Title
49-9091.00	Coin, Vending, and Amusement Machine Servicers and Repairers
15-1011.00	Computer and Information Scientists, Research
11-3021.00	Computer and Information Systems Managers
43-9011.00	Computer Operators
15-1021.00	Computer Programmers
15-1071.01	Computer Security Specialists
15-1031.00	Computer Software Engineers, Applications
15-1032.00	Computer Software Engineers, Systems Software
15-1041.00	Computer Support Specialists
15-1051.00	Computer Systems Analysts
15-1099.02	Computer Systems Engineers/Architects
49-2011.00	Computer, Automated Teller, and Office Machine Repairers
15-1061.00	Database Administrators
15-1071.00	Network and Computer Systems Administrators
15-1099.03	Network Designers
15-1081.00	Network Systems and Data Communications Analysts
15-1099.01	Software Quality Assurance Engineers and Testers
15-1099.05	Web Administrators
15-1099.04	Web Developers

12: Law and Public Safety

O*NET Number	Job Title
23-1021.00	Administrative Law Judges, Adjudicators, and Hearing Officers
55-3011.00	Air Crew Members
55-1011.00	Air Crew Officers
55-1012.00	Aircraft Launch and Recovery Officers
55-3012.00	Aircraft Launch and Recovery Specialists
33-9011.00	Animal Control Workers
23-1022.00	Arbitrators, Mediators, and Conciliators
55-3013.00	Armored Assault Vehicle Crew Members
55-1013.00	Armored Assault Vehicle Officers
55-3014.00	Artillery and Missile Crew Members
55-1014.00	Artillery and Missile Officers
33-3011.00	Bailiffs
55-1015.00	Command and Control Center Officers
55-3015.00	Command and Control Center Specialists
33-3012.00	Correctional Officers and Jailers
33-3021.03	Criminal Investigators and Special Agents
33-9091.00	Crossing Guards
33-3021.00	Detectives and Criminal Investigators
13-1061.00	Emergency Management Specialists

29-2041.00	Emergency Medical Technicians and Paramedics
33-2011.00	Fire Fighters
33-2021.02	Fire Investigators
55-2011.00	First-Line Supervisors/Managers of Air Crew Members
55-2013.00	First-Line Supervisors/Managers of All Other Tactical Operations Specialists
33-1011.00	First-Line Supervisors/Managers of Correctional Officers
33-1021.00	First-Line Supervisors/Managers of Fire Fighting and Prevention Workers
33-1012.00	First-Line Supervisors/Managers of Police and Detectives
55-2012.00	First-Line Supervisors/Managers of Weapons Specialists/Crew Members
19-4092.00	Forensic Science Technicians
33-2011.02	Forest Fire Fighters
33-1021.02	Forest Fire Fighting and Prevention Supervisors
33-9031.00	Gaming Surveillance Officers and Gaming Investigators
55-3016.00	Infantry
55-1016.00	Infantry Officers
23-1023.00	Judges, Magistrate Judges, and Magistrates
23-2092.00	Law Clerks
23-1011.00	Lawyers
33-9092.00	Lifeguards, Ski Patrol, and Other Recreational Protective Service Workers
33-2011.01	Municipal Fire Fighters
33-1021.01	Municipal Fire Fighting and Prevention Supervisors
23-2011.00	Paralegals and Legal Assistants
33-3041.00	Parking Enforcement Workers
33-3051.00	Police and Sheriff's Patrol Officers
33-3021.01	Police Detectives
33-3021.02	Police Identification and Records Officers
33-3051.01	Police Patrol Officers
33-9021.00	Private Detectives and Investigators
55-3017.00	Radar and Sonar Technicians
33-9032.00	Security Guards
33-3051.03	Sheriffs and Deputy Sheriffs
55-3018.00	Special Forces
55-1017.00	Special Forces Officers
23-2093.00	Title Examiners, Abstractors, and Searchers
33-3052.00	Transit and Railroad Police
33-9099.01	Transportation Security Screeners

13: Manufacturing

O*NET Number	Job Title
49-3011.00	Aircraft Mechanics and Service Technicians
51-2011.00	Aircraft Structure, Surfaces, Rigging, and Systems Assemblers

49-3021.00	Automotive Body and Related Repairers
49-3022.00	Automotive Glass Installers and Repairers
49-3023.01	Automotive Master Mechanics
49-3023.00	Automotive Service Technicians and Mechanics
49-3023.02	Automotive Specialty Technicians
49-2091.00	Avionics Technicians
51-3011.00	Bakers
49-3091.00	Bicycle Repairers
51-5011.00	Bindery Workers
51-5012.00	Bookbinders
49-3031.00	Bus and Truck Mechanics and Diesel Engine Specialists
51-7011.00	Cabinetmakers and Bench Carpenters
49-9061.00	Camera and Photographic Equipment Repairers
51-9191.00	Cementing and Gluing Machine Operators and Tenders
51-9011.00	Chemical Equipment Operators and Tenders
51-8091.00	Chemical Plant and System Operators
51-9192.00	Cleaning, Washing, and Metal Pickling Equipment Operators and Tenders
51-9121.00	Coating, Painting, and Spraying Machine Setters, Operators, and Tenders
51-2021.00	Coil Winders, Tapers, and Finishers
51-4011.00	Computer-Controlled Machine Tool Operators, Metal and Plastic
49-9012.00	Control and Valve Installers and Repairers, Except Mechanical Door
53-7011.00	Conveyor Operators and Tenders
51-9193.00	Cooling and Freezing Equipment Operators and Tenders
51-9021.00	Crushing, Grinding, and Polishing Machine Setters, Operators, and Tenders
51-9031.00	Cutters and Trimmers, Hand
51-9032.00	Cutting and Slicing Machine Setters, Operators, and Tenders
51-4031.00	Cutting, Punching, and Press Machine Setters, Operators, and Tenders, Metal and Plastic
51-9081.00	Dental Laboratory Technicians
43-9031.00	Desktop Publishers
51-4032.00	Drilling and Boring Machine Tool Setters, Operators, and Tenders, Metal and Plastic
49-2092.00	Electric Motor, Power Tool, and Related Repairers
51-2022.00	Electrical and Electronic Equipment Assemblers
49-2093.00	Electrical and Electronics Installers and Repairers, Transportation Equipment
49-2094.00	Electrical and Electronics Repairers, Commercial and Industrial Equipment
51-2023.00	Electromechanical Equipment Assemblers
49-2096.00	Electronic Equipment Installers and Repairers, Motor Vehicles
49-2097.00	Electronic Home Entertainment Equipment Installers and Repairers
51-2031.00	Engine and Other Machine Assemblers

(continued)

(continued)

13: Manufacturing

O*NET Number	Job Title
51-9194.00	Etchers and Engravers
51-4021.00	Extruding and Drawing Machine Setters, Operators, and Tenders, Metal and Plastic
51-6091.00	Extruding and Forming Machine Setters, Operators, and Tenders, Synthetic and Glass Fibers
51-9041.00	Extruding, Forming, Pressing, and Compacting Machine Setters, Operators, and Tenders
51-6092.00	Fabric and Apparel Patternmakers
49-9093.00	Fabric Menders, Except Garment
49-3041.00	Farm Equipment Mechanics
51-2091.00	Fiberglass Laminators and Fabricators
53-1021.00	First-Line Supervisors/Managers of Helpers, Laborers, and Material Movers, Hand
49-1011.00	First-Line Supervisors/Managers of Mechanics, Installers, and Repairers
51-1011.00	First-Line Supervisors/Managers of Production and Operating Workers
51-3091.00	Food and Tobacco Roasting, Baking, and Drying Machine Operators and Tenders
51-3092.00	Food Batchmakers
51-3093.00	Food Cooking Machine Operators and Tenders
51-4022.00	Forging Machine Setters, Operators, and Tenders, Metal and Plastic
51-4071.00	Foundry Mold and Coremakers
51-9051.00	Furnace, Kiln, Oven, Drier, and Kettle Operators and Tenders
51-7021.00	Furniture Finishers
53-7071.00	Gas Compressor and Gas Pumping Station Operators
51-8092.00	Gas Plant Operators
51-9071.06	Gem and Diamond Workers
51-9195.04	Glass Blowers, Molders, Benders, and Finishers
45-2041.00	Graders and Sorters, Agricultural Products
51-9022.00	Grinding and Polishing Workers, Hand
51-4033.00	Grinding, Lapping, Polishing, and Buffing Machine Tool Setters, Operators, and Tenders, Metal and Plastic
51-4191.00	Heat Treating Equipment Setters, Operators, and Tenders, Metal and Plastic
51-9198.00	Helpers—Production Workers
53-7041.00	Hoist and Winch Operators
49-9031.00	Home Appliance Repairers
49-9041.00	Industrial Machinery Mechanics
11-3051.00	Industrial Production Managers
53-7051.00	Industrial Truck and Tractor Operators
51-9061.00	Inspectors, Testers, Sorters, Samplers, and Weighers
51-9071.01	Jewelers
51-9071.00	Jewelers and Precious Stone and Metal Workers
51-5021.00	Job Printers
51-4034.00	Lathe and Turning Machine Tool Setters, Operators, and Tenders, Metal and Plastic
51-6011.00	Laundry and Dry-Cleaning Workers
51-4192.00	Lay-Out Workers, Metal and Plastic
49-9094.00	Locksmiths and Safe Repairers
53-7063.00	Machine Feeders and Offbearers
51-4041.00	Machinists
49-9043.00	Maintenance Workers, Machinery
51-3022.00	Meat, Poultry, and Fish Cutters and Trimmers
49-9011.00	Mechanical Door Repairers
51-9082.00	Medical Appliance Technicians
49-9062.00	Medical Equipment Repairers
51-4051.00	Metal-Refining Furnace Operators and Tenders
51-4035.00	Milling and Planing Machine Setters, Operators, and Tenders, Metal and Plastic
49-9044.00	Millwrights
51-9023.00	Mixing and Blending Machine Setters, Operators, and Tenders
49-3042.00	Mobile Heavy Equipment Mechanics, Except Engines
51-4061.00	Model Makers, Metal and Plastic
51-7031.00	Model Makers, Wood
51-9195.07	Molding and Casting Workers
51-4072.00	Molding, Coremaking, and Casting Machine Setters, Operators, and Tenders, Metal and Plastic
49-3051.00	Motorboat Mechanics
49-3052.00	Motorcycle Mechanics
51-4081.00	Multiple Machine Tool Setters, Operators, and Tenders, Metal and Plastic
51-8011.00	Nuclear Power Reactor Operators
51-4012.00	Numerical Tool and Process Control Programmers
51-9083.00	Ophthalmic Laboratory Technicians
49-3053.00	Outdoor Power Equipment and Other Small Engine Mechanics
51-9111.00	Packaging and Filling Machine Operators and Tenders
53-7064.00	Packers and Packagers, Hand
51-9122.00	Painters, Transportation Equipment
51-9123.00	Painting, Coating, and Decorating Workers
51-9196.00	Paper Goods Machine Setters, Operators, and Tenders
51-4062.00	Patternmakers, Metal and Plastic
51-7032.00	Patternmakers, Wood
51-8093.00	Petroleum Pump System Operators, Refinery Operators, and Gaugers
51-9131.00	Photographic Process Workers
51-9132.00	Photographic Processing Machine Operators
51-4193.00	Plating and Coating Machine Setters, Operators, and Tenders, Metal and Plastic
51-4052.00	Pourers and Casters, Metal
51-8012.00	Power Distributors and Dispatchers

51-8013.00	Power Plant Operators
51-9071.07	Precious Metal Workers
51-5022.00	Prepress Technicians and Workers
51-6021.00	Pressers, Textile, Garment, and Related Materials
51-5023.00	Printing Machine Operators
53-7072.00	Pump Operators, Except Wellhead Pumpers
49-2021.00	Radio Mechanics
49-3043.00	Rail Car Repairers
49-3092.00	Recreational Vehicle Service Technicians
53-7081.00	Refuse and Recyclable Material Collectors
51-4023.00	Rolling Machine Setters, Operators, and Tenders, Metal and Plastic
51-7041.00	Sawing Machine Setters, Operators, and Tenders, Wood
51-9141.00	Semiconductor Processors
51-9012.00	Separating, Filtering, Clarifying, Precipitating, and Still Machine Setters, Operators, and Tenders
51-6051.00	Sewers, Hand
51-6031.00	Sewing Machine Operators
53-5031.00	Ship Engineers
51-6041.00	Shoe and Leather Workers and Repairers
51-6042.00	Shoe Machine Operators and Tenders
49-9097.00	Signal and Track Switch Repairers
51-3023.00	Slaughterers and Meat Packers
51-4121.07	Solderers and Brazers
51-8021.00	Stationary Engineers and Boiler Operators
51-2041.00	Structural Metal Fabricators and Fitters
51-6052.00	Tailors, Dressmakers, and Custom Sewers
53-7121.00	Tank Car, Truck, and Ship Loaders
51-2092.00	Team Assemblers
51-6061.00	Textile Bleaching and Dyeing Machine Operators and Tenders
51-6062.00	Textile Cutting Machine Setters, Operators, and Tenders
51-6063.00	Textile Knitting and Weaving Machine Setters, Operators, and Tenders
51-6064.00	Textile Winding, Twisting, and Drawing Out Machine Setters, Operators, and Tenders
51-2093.00	Timing Device Assemblers, Adjusters, and Calibrators
51-9197.00	Tire Builders
49-3093.00	Tire Repairers and Changers
51-4111.00	Tool and Die Makers
51-4194.00	Tool Grinders, Filers, and Sharpeners
51-6093.00	Upholsterers
49-9064.00	Watch Repairers
51-8031.00	Water and Liquid Waste Treatment Plant and System Operators
51-4121.06	Welders, Cutters, and Welder Fitters
51-4121.00	Welders, Cutters, Solderers, and Brazers
51-4122.00	Welding, Soldering, and Brazing Machine Setters, Operators, and Tenders
51-7042.00	Woodworking Machine Setters, Operators, and Tenders, Except Sawing

14: Retail and Wholesale Sales and Service

O*NET Number	Job Title
11-2011.00	Advertising and Promotions Managers
41-3011.00	Advertising Sales Agents
41-2011.00	Cashiers
41-2021.00	Counter and Rental Clerks
43-4051.00	Customer Service Representatives
41-9011.00	Demonstrators and Product Promoters
41-9091.00	Door-To-Door Sales Workers, News and Street Vendors, and Related Workers
41-1012.00	First-Line Supervisors/Managers of Non-Retail Sales Workers
41-1011.00	First-Line Supervisors/Managers of Retail Sales Workers
11-9061.00	Funeral Directors
43-3041.00	Gaming Cage Workers
41-2012.00	Gaming Change Persons and Booth Cashiers
11-2021.00	Marketing Managers
41-9012.00	Models
43-4151.00	Order Clerks
41-2022.00	Parts Salespersons
11-9141.00	Property, Real Estate, and Community Association Managers
13-1023.00	Purchasing Agents, Except Wholesale, Retail, and Farm Products
11-3061.00	Purchasing Managers
41-9021.00	Real Estate Brokers
41-9022.00	Real Estate Sales Agents
43-4171.00	Receptionists and Information Clerks
41-2031.00	Retail Salespersons
41-9031.00	Sales Engineers
11-2022.00	Sales Managers
41-4012.00	Sales Representatives, Wholesale and Manufacturing, Except Technical and Scientific Products
41-4011.00	Sales Representatives, Wholesale and Manufacturing, Technical and Scientific Products
53-6031.00	Service Station Attendants
41-9041.00	Telemarketers
13-1022.00	Wholesale and Retail Buyers, Except Farm Products

15: Scientific Research, Engineering, and Mathematics

O*NET Number	Job Title
15-2011.00	Actuaries
17-3021.00	Aerospace Engineering and Operations Technicians

(continued)

(continued)

15: Scientific Research, Engineering, and Mathematics

O*NET Number	Job Title
17-2011.00	Aerospace Engineers
19-3091.01	Anthropologists
19-3091.00	Anthropologists and Archeologists
19-3091.02	Archeologists
19-2011.00	Astronomers
19-2021.00	Atmospheric and Space Scientists
19-1021.00	Biochemists and Biophysicists
19-1020.01	Biologists
17-2031.00	Biomedical Engineers
17-1021.00	Cartographers and Photogrammetrists
17-2041.00	Chemical Engineers
19-4031.00	Chemical Technicians
19-2031.00	Chemists
17-3022.00	Civil Engineering Technicians
17-2051.00	Civil Engineers
17-2061.00	Computer Hardware Engineers
19-3011.00	Economists
17-3023.00	Electrical and Electronic Engineering Technicians
17-3012.00	Electrical and Electronics Drafters
17-3012.02	Electrical Drafters
17-3023.03	Electrical Engineering Technicians
17-2071.00	Electrical Engineers
17-3024.00	Electro-Mechanical Technicians
17-3012.01	Electronic Drafters
17-3023.01	Electronics Engineering Technicians
17-2072.00	Electronics Engineers, Except Computer
11-9041.00	Engineering Managers
17-3025.00	Environmental Engineering Technicians
19-2041.00	Environmental Scientists and Specialists, Including Health
19-1041.00	Epidemiologists
17-2111.02	Fire-Prevention and Protection Engineers
19-3092.00	Geographers
19-2042.00	Geoscientists, Except Hydrologists and Geographers
17-2111.00	Health and Safety Engineers, Except Mining Safety Engineers and Inspectors
19-3093.00	Historians
19-2043.00	Hydrologists
17-2112.00	Industrial Engineers
17-2111.01	Industrial Safety and Health Engineers
19-3032.00	Industrial-Organizational Psychologists
17-3031.02	Mapping Technicians
17-2121.02	Marine Architects
17-2121.01	Marine Engineers
17-2121.00	Marine Engineers and Naval Architects
17-2131.00	Materials Engineers
19-2032.00	Materials Scientists
15-2091.00	Mathematical Technicians
15-2021.00	Mathematicians
17-3013.00	Mechanical Drafters
17-3027.00	Mechanical Engineering Technicians
17-2141.00	Mechanical Engineers
19-1042.00	Medical Scientists, Except Epidemiologists
19-1022.00	Microbiologists
11-9121.00	Natural Sciences Managers
17-2161.00	Nuclear Engineers
19-4051.01	Nuclear Equipment Operation Technicians
19-4051.00	Nuclear Technicians
19-2012.00	Physicists
19-3094.00	Political Scientists
17-2111.03	Product Safety Engineers
19-3031.01	School Psychologists
19-4061.00	Social Science Research Assistants
19-3041.00	Sociologists
43-9111.00	Statistical Assistants
15-2041.00	Statisticians
17-3031.00	Surveying and Mapping Technicians
17-3031.01	Surveying Technicians

16: Transportation, Distribution, and Logistics

O*NET Number	Job Title
53-1011.00	Aircraft Cargo Handling Supervisors
53-2011.00	Airline Pilots, Copilots, and Flight Engineers
53-3011.00	Ambulance Drivers and Attendants, Except Emergency Medical Technicians
53-6011.00	Bridge and Lock Tenders
53-3022.00	Bus Drivers, School
53-3021.00	Bus Drivers, Transit and Intercity
53-5021.00	Captains, Mates, and Pilots of Water Vessels
43-5011.00	Cargo and Freight Agents
53-7061.00	Cleaners of Vehicles and Equipment
53-2012.00	Commercial Pilots
43-5021.00	Couriers and Messengers
53-7031.00	Dredge Operators
53-3031.00	Driver/Sales Workers
53-1031.00	First-Line Supervisors/Managers of Transportation and Material-Moving Machine and Vehicle Operators
53-7062.00	Laborers and Freight, Stock, and Material Movers, Hand
53-4011.00	Locomotive Engineers
53-4012.00	Locomotive Firers
53-5021.02	Mates—Ship, Boat, and Barge
53-5022.00	Motorboat Operators
53-6021.00	Parking Lot Attendants
53-5021.03	Pilots, Ship
43-5052.00	Postal Service Mail Carriers

11-9131.00	Postmasters and Mail Superintendents
53-4013.00	Rail Yard Engineers, Dinkey Operators, and Hostlers
53-4021.00	Railroad Brake, Signal, and Switch Operators
53-4031.00	Railroad Conductors and Yardmasters
53-5011.00	Sailors and Marine Oilers
53-5021.01	Ship and Boat Captains
11-3071.02	Storage and Distribution Managers
53-4041.00	Subway and Streetcar Operators
53-3041.00	Taxi Drivers and Chauffeurs
53-6041.00	Traffic Technicians
11-3071.01	Transportation Managers
11-3071.00	Transportation, Storage, and Distribution Managers
53-3032.00	Truck Drivers, Heavy and Tractor-Trailer
53-3033.00	Truck Drivers, Light or Delivery Services

Method 3: Browse the Jobs by Education and Training Requirements

The following lists sort the jobs according to the amount of education and training that they require. You can find descriptions of the various education and training levels in the introduction, and O*NET numbers are included for the jobs so that you can find the descriptions in Part II easily. The jobs are listed alphabetically in each level, and jobs without education or training information have not been included in the lists.

When to Use This Method: If you have achieved, are working toward, or are considering a certain level of education and training, these lists help you find the jobs that meet your qualifications. Simply find your education or training level here, review the list of related jobs, and then look up their descriptions in Part II using the O*NET number.

Jobs Requiring Short-Term On-the-Job Training

O*NET Number	Job Title
39-3091.00	Amusement and Recreation Attendants
39-6011.00	Baggage Porters and Bellhops
35-3011.00	Bartenders
43-3011.00	Bill and Account Collectors
51-5011.00	Bindery Workers
53-6011.00	Bridge and Lock Tenders
53-3022.00	Bus Drivers, School
41-2011.00	Cashiers
39-9011.00	Child Care Workers
53-7061.00	Cleaners of Vehicles and Equipment
51-2021.00	Coil Winders, Tapers, and Finishers
35-3021.00	Combined Food Preparation and Serving Workers, Including Fast Food

43-2099.99	Communications Equipment Operators, All Other
53-7011.00	Conveyor Operators and Tenders
35-2011.00	Cooks, Fast Food
35-2015.00	Cooks, Short Order
43-4021.00	Correspondence Clerks
39-3092.00	Costume Attendants
41-2021.00	Counter and Rental Clerks
35-3022.00	Counter Attendants, Cafeteria, Food Concession, and Coffee Shop
43-5021.00	Couriers and Messengers
43-4031.01	Court Clerks
43-4031.00	Court, Municipal, and License Clerks
43-4041.01	Credit Authorizers
43-4041.00	Credit Authorizers, Checkers, and Clerks
43-4041.02	Credit Checkers
33-9091.00	Crossing Guards
51-9031.00	Cutters and Trimmers, Hand
35-9011.00	Dining Room and Cafeteria Attendants and Bartender Helpers
35-9021.00	Dishwashers
41-9091.00	Door-To-Door Sales Workers, News and Street Vendors, and Related Workers
53-3031.00	Driver/Sales Workers
51-2022.00	Electrical and Electronic Equipment Assemblers
51-2023.00	Electromechanical Equipment Assemblers
51-2031.00	Engine and Other Machine Assemblers
45-2092.02	Farmworkers and Laborers, Crop
45-2092.00	Farmworkers and Laborers, Crop, Nursery, and Greenhouse
45-2093.00	Farmworkers, Farm and Ranch Animals
43-4071.00	File Clerks
51-3091.00	Food and Tobacco Roasting, Baking, and Drying Machine Operators and Tenders
51-3092.00	Food Batchmakers
51-3093.00	Food Cooking Machine Operators and Tenders
35-2021.00	Food Preparation Workers
35-3041.00	Food Servers, Nonrestaurant
39-4021.00	Funeral Attendants
43-3041.00	Gaming Cage Workers
41-2012.00	Gaming Change Persons and Booth Cashiers
31-9099.99	Healthcare Support Workers, All Other
47-3019.99	Helpers, Construction Trades, All Other
47-3011.00	Helpers—Brickmasons, Blockmasons, Stonemasons, and Tile and Marble Setters
47-3012.00	Helpers—Carpenters
47-3013.00	Helpers—Electricians
47-5081.00	Helpers—Extraction Workers
49-9098.00	Helpers—Installation, Maintenance, and Repair Workers
47-3014.00	Helpers—Painters, Paperhangers, Plasterers, and Stucco Masons
47-3015.00	Helpers—Pipelayers, Plumbers, Pipefitters, and Steamfitters

(continued)

(continued)

Jobs Requiring Short-Term On-the-Job Training

O*NET Number	Job Title
51-9198.00	Helpers—Production Workers
47-3016.00	Helpers—Roofers
31-1011.00	Home Health Aides
35-9031.00	Hosts and Hostesses, Restaurant, Lounge, and Coffee Shop
43-4081.00	Hotel, Motel, and Resort Desk Clerks
43-4161.00	Human Resources Assistants, Except Payroll and Timekeeping
53-7051.00	Industrial Truck and Tractor Operators
43-4199.99	Information and Record Clerks, All Other
43-4111.00	Interviewers, Except Eligibility and Loan
37-2011.00	Janitors and Cleaners, Except Maids and Housekeeping Cleaners
53-7062.00	Laborers and Freight, Stock, and Material Movers, Hand
37-3011.00	Landscaping and Groundskeeping Workers
43-4121.00	Library Assistants, Clerical
25-4031.00	Library Technicians
43-4031.03	License Clerks
33-9092.00	Lifeguards, Ski Patrol, and Other Recreational Protective Service Workers
43-4131.00	Loan Interviewers and Clerks
39-3093.00	Locker Room, Coatroom, and Dressing Room Attendants
53-7063.00	Machine Feeders and Offbearers
37-2012.00	Maids and Housekeeping Cleaners
43-9051.00	Mail Clerks and Mail Machine Operators, Except Postal Service
49-9043.00	Maintenance Workers, Machinery
43-5081.02	Marking Clerks
51-3022.00	Meat, Poultry, and Fish Cutters and Trimmers
31-9093.00	Medical Equipment Preparers
43-5041.00	Meter Readers, Utilities
39-3021.00	Motion Picture Projectionists
53-3099.99	Motor Vehicle Operators, All Other
43-4031.02	Municipal Clerks
39-9011.01	Nannies
39-2021.00	Nonfarm Animal Caretakers
45-2092.01	Nursery Workers
31-1012.00	Nursing Aides, Orderlies, and Attendants
31-2012.00	Occupational Therapist Aides
43-9061.00	Office Clerks, General
43-9071.00	Office Machine Operators, Except Computer
43-4151.00	Order Clerks
43-5081.04	Order Fillers, Wholesale and Retail Sales
51-9111.00	Packaging and Filling Machine Operators and Tenders
53-7064.00	Packers and Packagers, Hand
51-9123.00	Painting, Coating, and Decorating Workers
33-3041.00	Parking Enforcement Workers
53-6021.00	Parking Lot Attendants
39-9021.00	Personal and Home Care Aides
39-9099.99	Personal Care and Service Workers, All Other
31-9095.00	Pharmacy Aides
51-9132.00	Photographic Processing Machine Operators
31-2022.00	Physical Therapist Aides
43-5051.00	Postal Service Clerks
43-5052.00	Postal Service Mail Carriers
43-5053.00	Postal Service Mail Sorters, Processors, and Processing Machine Operators
51-6021.00	Pressers, Textile, Garment, and Related Materials
43-3061.00	Procurement Clerks
43-5061.00	Production, Planning, and Expediting Clerks
43-9081.00	Proofreaders and Copy Markers
31-1013.00	Psychiatric Aides
43-4171.00	Receptionists and Information Clerks
53-7081.00	Refuse and Recyclable Material Collectors
43-4181.00	Reservation and Transportation Ticket Agents and Travel Clerks
41-2031.00	Retail Salespersons
49-9096.00	Riggers
53-5011.00	Sailors and Marine Oilers
33-9032.00	Security Guards
53-6031.00	Service Station Attendants
51-6051.00	Sewers, Hand
39-5093.00	Shampooers
43-5071.00	Shipping, Receiving, and Traffic Clerks
53-7111.00	Shuttle Car Operators
43-5081.00	Stock Clerks and Order Fillers
43-5081.03	Stock Clerks—Stockroom, Warehouse, or Storage Yard
43-5081.01	Stock Clerks, Sales Floor
43-2011.00	Switchboard Operators, Including Answering Service
53-3041.00	Taxi Drivers and Chauffeurs
25-9041.00	Teacher Assistants
41-9041.00	Telemarketers
43-2021.00	Telephone Operators
43-3071.00	Tellers
51-6099.99	Textile, Apparel, and Furnishings Workers, All Other
49-3093.00	Tire Repairers and Changers
53-6041.00	Traffic Technicians
39-6032.00	Transportation Attendants, Except Flight Attendants and Baggage Porters
53-6099.99	Transportation Workers, All Other
37-3013.00	Tree Trimmers and Pruners
53-3033.00	Truck Drivers, Light or Delivery Services
39-3031.00	Ushers, Lobby Attendants, and Ticket Takers
31-9096.00	Veterinary Assistants and Laboratory Animal Caretakers

35-3031.00	Waiters and Waitresses
43-5111.00	Weighers, Measurers, Checkers, and Samplers, Recordkeeping

Jobs Requiring Moderate-Term On-the-Job Training

O*NET Number	Job Title
41-3011.00	Advertising Sales Agents
45-2091.00	Agricultural Equipment Operators
55-3011.00	Air Crew Members
55-3012.00	Aircraft Launch and Recovery Specialists
53-3011.00	Ambulance Drivers and Attendants, Except Emergency Medical Technicians
45-2021.00	Animal Breeders
33-9011.00	Animal Control Workers
39-2011.00	Animal Trainers
55-3013.00	Armored Assault Vehicle Crew Members
55-3014.00	Artillery and Missile Crew Members
51-2099.99	Assemblers and Fabricators, All Other
25-9011.00	Audio-Visual Collections Specialists
33-3011.00	Bailiffs
49-3091.00	Bicycle Repairers
43-3021.00	Billing and Posting Clerks and Machine Operators
43-3021.02	Billing, Cost, and Rate Clerks
43-3021.03	Billing, Posting, and Calculating Machine Operators
51-5012.00	Bookbinders
43-3031.00	Bookkeeping, Accounting, and Auditing Clerks
43-4011.00	Brokerage Clerks
53-3021.00	Bus Drivers, Transit and Intercity
49-9061.00	Camera and Photographic Equipment Repairers
27-4031.00	Camera Operators, Television, Video, and Motion Picture
43-5011.00	Cargo and Freight Agents
47-2041.00	Carpet Installers
47-2051.00	Cement Masons and Concrete Finishers
51-9191.00	Cementing and Gluing Machine Operators and Tenders
51-9011.00	Chemical Equipment Operators and Tenders
51-9192.00	Cleaning, Washing, and Metal Pickling Equipment Operators and Tenders
51-9121.00	Coating, Painting, and Spraying Machine Setters, Operators, and Tenders
49-9091.00	Coin, Vending, and Amusement Machine Servicers and Repairers
55-3015.00	Command and Control Center Specialists
49-9092.00	Commercial Divers
43-9011.00	Computer Operators
51-4011.00	Computer-Controlled Machine Tool Operators, Metal and Plastic

39-6012.00	Concierges
47-4099.99	Construction and Related Workers, All Other
47-2061.00	Construction Laborers
47-5041.00	Continuous Mining Machine Operators
49-9012.00	Control and Valve Installers and Repairers, Except Mechanical Door
35-2012.00	Cooks, Institution and Cafeteria
51-9193.00	Cooling and Freezing Equipment Operators and Tenders
33-3012.00	Correctional Officers and Jailers
53-7021.00	Crane and Tower Operators
51-9021.00	Crushing, Grinding, and Polishing Machine Setters, Operators, and Tenders
43-4051.00	Customer Service Representatives
51-9032.00	Cutting and Slicing Machine Setters, Operators, and Tenders
51-4031.00	Cutting, Punching, and Press Machine Setters, Operators, and Tenders, Metal and Plastic
43-9021.00	Data Entry Keyers
41-9011.00	Demonstrators and Product Promoters
31-9091.00	Dental Assistants
47-5011.00	Derrick Operators, Oil and Gas
29-2051.00	Dietetic Technicians
43-5032.00	Dispatchers, Except Police, Fire, and Ambulance
53-7031.00	Dredge Operators
51-4032.00	Drilling and Boring Machine Tool Setters, Operators, and Tenders, Metal and Plastic
47-2081.00	Drywall and Ceiling Tile Installers
47-5021.00	Earth Drillers, Except Oil and Gas
43-4061.00	Eligibility Interviewers, Government Programs
53-7032.00	Excavating and Loading Machine and Dragline Operators
43-6011.00	Executive Secretaries and Administrative Assistants
47-5031.00	Explosives Workers, Ordnance Handling Experts, and Blasters
47-5099.99	Extraction Workers, All Other
51-4021.00	Extruding and Drawing Machine Setters, Operators, and Tenders, Metal and Plastic
51-6091.00	Extruding and Forming Machine Setters, Operators, and Tenders, Synthetic and Glass Fibers
51-9041.00	Extruding, Forming, Pressing, and Compacting Machine Setters, Operators, and Tenders
49-9093.00	Fabric Menders, Except Garment
45-4021.00	Fallers
47-4031.00	Fence Erectors
51-2091.00	Fiberglass Laminators and Fabricators
33-2021.01	Fire Inspectors
33-2021.00	Fire Inspectors and Investigators
45-3011.00	Fishers and Related Fishing Workers
47-2042.00	Floor Layers, Except Carpet, Wood, and Hard Tiles
47-2043.00	Floor Sanders and Finishers

(continued)

(continued)

Jobs Requiring Moderate-Term On-the-Job Training

O*NET Number	Job Title
27-1023.00	Floral Designers
45-4011.00	Forest and Conservation Workers
33-2022.00	Forest Fire Inspectors and Prevention Specialists
51-4022.00	Forging Machine Setters, Operators, and Tenders, Metal and Plastic
51-4071.00	Foundry Mold and Coremakers
51-9051.00	Furnace, Kiln, Oven, Drier, and Kettle Operators and Tenders
33-9031.00	Gaming Surveillance Officers and Gaming Investigators
53-7071.00	Gas Compressor and Gas Pumping Station Operators
51-9195.04	Glass Blowers, Molders, Benders, and Finishers
51-9022.00	Grinding and Polishing Workers, Hand
51-4033.00	Grinding, Lapping, Polishing, and Buffing Machine Tool Setters, Operators, and Tenders, Metal and Plastic
47-4041.00	Hazardous Materials Removal Workers
51-4191.00	Heat Treating Equipment Setters, Operators, and Tenders, Metal and Plastic
47-4051.00	Highway Maintenance Workers
53-7041.00	Hoist and Winch Operators
45-3021.00	Hunters and Trappers
55-3016.00	Infantry
51-9061.00	Inspectors, Testers, Sorters, Samplers, and Weighers
49-9099.99	Installation, Maintenance, and Repair Workers, All Other
47-2131.00	Insulation Workers, Floor, Ceiling, and Wall
47-2132.00	Insulation Workers, Mechanical
43-9041.00	Insurance Claims and Policy Processing Clerks
43-9041.01	Insurance Claims Clerks
43-9041.02	Insurance Policy Processing Clerks
51-4034.00	Lathe and Turning Machine Tool Setters, Operators, and Tenders, Metal and Plastic
51-6011.00	Laundry and Dry-Cleaning Workers
51-4192.00	Lay-Out Workers, Metal and Plastic
53-7033.00	Loading Machine Operators, Underground Mining
49-9094.00	Locksmiths and Safe Repairers
45-4023.00	Log Graders and Scalers
45-4022.00	Logging Equipment Operators
45-4029.99	Logging Workers, All Other
49-9042.00	Maintenance and Repair Workers, General
49-9095.00	Manufactured Building and Mobile Home Installers
17-3031.02	Mapping Technicians
53-7199.99	Material Moving Workers, All Other
49-9011.00	Mechanical Door Repairers
27-4099.99	Media and Communication Equipment Workers, All Other
31-9092.00	Medical Assistants
27-1026.00	Merchandise Displayers and Window Trimmers
51-4199.99	Metal Workers and Plastic Workers, All Other
51-4051.00	Metal-Refining Furnace Operators and Tenders
51-4035.00	Milling and Planing Machine Setters, Operators, and Tenders, Metal and Plastic
47-5042.00	Mine Cutting and Channeling Machine Operators
47-5049.99	Mining Machine Operators, All Other
51-9023.00	Mixing and Blending Machine Setters, Operators, and Tenders
51-4061.00	Model Makers, Metal and Plastic
41-9012.00	Models
51-9195.00	Molders, Shapers, and Casters, Except Metal and Plastic
51-9195.07	Molding and Casting Workers
51-4072.00	Molding, Coremaking, and Casting Machine Setters, Operators, and Tenders, Metal and Plastic
53-5022.00	Motorboat Operators
51-4081.00	Multiple Machine Tool Setters, Operators, and Tenders, Metal and Plastic
47-2073.00	Operating Engineers and Other Construction Equipment Operators
51-9083.00	Ophthalmic Laboratory Technicians
49-3053.00	Outdoor Power Equipment and Other Small Engine Mechanics
47-2141.00	Painters, Construction and Maintenance
51-9122.00	Painters, Transportation Equipment
51-9196.00	Paper Goods Machine Setters, Operators, and Tenders
47-2142.00	Paperhangers
41-2022.00	Parts Salespersons
51-4062.00	Patternmakers, Metal and Plastic
47-2071.00	Paving, Surfacing, and Tamping Equipment Operators
43-3051.00	Payroll and Timekeeping Clerks
37-2021.00	Pest Control Workers
37-3012.00	Pesticide Handlers, Sprayers, and Applicators, Vegetation
29-2052.00	Pharmacy Technicians
51-9131.00	Photographic Process Workers
47-2072.00	Pile-Driver Operators
47-2151.00	Pipelayers
51-4193.00	Plating and Coating Machine Setters, Operators, and Tenders, Metal and Plastic
43-5031.00	Police, Fire, and Ambulance Dispatchers
51-9195.05	Potters, Manufacturing
51-4052.00	Pourers and Casters, Metal
51-5023.00	Printing Machine Operators
51-9199.99	Production Workers, All Other
29-2053.00	Psychiatric Technicians

53-7072.00	Pump Operators, Except Wellhead Pumpers
55-3017.00	Radar and Sonar Technicians
27-3011.00	Radio and Television Announcers
27-4013.00	Radio Operators
47-4061.00	Rail-Track Laying and Maintenance Equipment Operators
49-9045.00	Refractory Materials Repairers, Except Brickmasons
39-9041.00	Residential Advisors
47-5051.00	Rock Splitters, Quarry
51-4023.00	Rolling Machine Setters, Operators, and Tenders, Metal and Plastic
47-5061.00	Roof Bolters, Mining
47-2181.00	Roofers
47-5012.00	Rotary Drill Operators, Oil and Gas
47-5071.00	Roustabouts, Oil and Gas
41-4012.00	Sales Representatives, Wholesale and Manufacturing, Except Technical and Scientific Products
51-7041.00	Sawing Machine Setters, Operators, and Tenders, Wood
43-6014.00	Secretaries, Except Legal, Medical, and Executive
47-4091.00	Segmental Pavers
51-9012.00	Separating, Filtering, Clarifying, Precipitating, and Still Machine Setters, Operators, and Tenders
47-4071.00	Septic Tank Servicers and Sewer Pipe Cleaners
47-5013.00	Service Unit Operators, Oil, Gas, and Mining
51-6031.00	Sewing Machine Operators
47-2211.00	Sheet Metal Workers
51-6042.00	Shoe Machine Operators and Tenders
49-9097.00	Signal and Track Switch Repairers
51-3023.00	Slaughterers and Meat Packers
21-1093.00	Social and Human Service Assistants
43-3021.01	Statement Clerks
43-9111.00	Statistical Assistants
51-9195.03	Stone Cutters and Carvers, Manufacturing
51-2041.00	Structural Metal Fabricators and Fitters
53-4041.00	Subway and Streetcar Operators
17-3031.00	Surveying and Mapping Technicians
17-3031.01	Surveying Technicians
53-7121.00	Tank Car, Truck, and Ship Loaders
47-2082.00	Tapers
13-2082.00	Tax Preparers
51-2092.00	Team Assemblers
51-6061.00	Textile Bleaching and Dyeing Machine Operators and Tenders
51-6062.00	Textile Cutting Machine Setters, Operators, and Tenders
51-6064.00	Textile Winding, Twisting, and Drawing Out Machine Setters, Operators, and Tenders
51-2093.00	Timing Device Assemblers, Adjusters, and Calibrators
51-9197.00	Tire Builders
23-2093.00	Title Examiners, Abstractors, and Searchers
51-4194.00	Tool Grinders, Filers, and Sharpeners
39-6021.00	Tour Guides and Escorts
39-6022.00	Travel Guides
53-3032.00	Truck Drivers, Heavy and Tractor-Trailer
51-4122.00	Welding, Soldering, and Brazing Machine Setters, Operators, and Tenders
53-7073.00	Wellhead Pumpers
51-7099.99	Woodworkers, All Other
51-7042.00	Woodworking Machine Setters, Operators, and Tenders, Except Sawing
43-9022.00	Word Processors and Typists

Jobs Requiring Long-Term On-the-Job Training

O*NET Number	Job Title
27-2011.00	Actors
55-1011.00	Air Crew Officers
53-2021.00	Air Traffic Controllers
55-1012.00	Aircraft Launch and Recovery Officers
51-2011.00	Aircraft Structure, Surfaces, Rigging, and Systems Assemblers
53-2022.00	Airfield Operations Specialists
55-1013.00	Armored Assault Vehicle Officers
55-1014.00	Artillery and Missile Officers
27-1019.99	Artists and Related Workers, All Other
27-2021.00	Athletes and Sports Competitors
27-4011.00	Audio and Video Equipment Technicians
49-3021.00	Automotive Body and Related Repairers
49-3022.00	Automotive Glass Installers and Repairers
51-3011.00	Bakers
47-2011.00	Boilermakers
47-2021.00	Brickmasons and Blockmasons
51-3021.00	Butchers and Meat Cutters
51-7011.00	Cabinetmakers and Bench Carpenters
47-2031.00	Carpenters
51-8091.00	Chemical Plant and System Operators
13-1031.00	Claims Adjusters, Examiners, and Investigators
13-1031.01	Claims Examiners, Property and Casualty Insurance
27-2022.00	Coaches and Scouts
55-1015.00	Command and Control Center Officers
13-1041.00	Compliance Officers, Except Agriculture, Construction, Health and Safety, and Transportation
47-2031.01	Construction Carpenters
35-2013.00	Cooks, Private Household
35-2014.00	Cooks, Restaurant
27-2031.00	Dancers
51-9081.00	Dental Laboratory Technicians
49-9051.00	Electrical Power-Line Installers and Repairers
47-2111.00	Electricians

(continued)

(continued)

Jobs Requiring Long-Term On-the-Job Training

O*NET Number	Job Title
47-4021.00	Elevator Installers and Repairers
27-2099.99	Entertainers and Performers, Sports and Related Workers, All Other
13-1041.01	Environmental Compliance Inspectors
13-1041.03	Equal Opportunity Representatives and Officers
51-9194.00	Etchers and Engravers
51-6092.00	Fabric and Apparel Patternmakers
11-9012.00	Farmers and Ranchers
27-1013.00	Fine Artists, Including Painters, Sculptors, and Illustrators
33-2011.00	Fire Fighters
33-3031.00	Fish and Game Wardens
39-6031.00	Flight Attendants
33-2011.02	Forest Fire Fighters
51-7021.00	Furniture Finishers
51-8092.00	Gas Plant Operators
47-2121.00	Glaziers
13-1041.04	Government Property Inspectors and Investigators
49-9021.01	Heating and Air Conditioning Mechanics and Installers
49-9021.00	Heating, Air Conditioning, and Refrigeration Mechanics and Installers
49-9031.00	Home Appliance Repairers
49-9041.00	Industrial Machinery Mechanics
55-1016.00	Infantry Officers
13-1031.02	Insurance Adjusters, Examiners, and Investigators
13-1032.00	Insurance Appraisers, Auto Damage
27-3091.00	Interpreters and Translators
51-5021.00	Job Printers
13-1041.02	Licensing Examiners and Inspectors
51-4041.00	Machinists
27-3099.99	Media and Communication Workers, All Other
51-9082.00	Medical Appliance Technicians
55-1019.99	Military Officer Special and Tactical Operations Leaders/Managers, All Other
49-9044.00	Millwrights
51-7031.00	Model Makers, Wood
49-3051.00	Motorboat Mechanics
49-3052.00	Motorcycle Mechanics
33-2011.01	Municipal Fire Fighters
49-9063.00	Musical Instrument Repairers and Tuners
27-2042.00	Musicians and Singers
27-2042.02	Musicians, Instrumental
51-8011.00	Nuclear Power Reactor Operators
51-4012.00	Numerical Tool and Process Control Programmers
29-2081.00	Opticians, Dispensing
51-7032.00	Patternmakers, Wood
51-8093.00	Petroleum Pump System Operators, Refinery Operators, and Gaugers
27-4021.00	Photographers
47-2152.01	Pipe Fitters and Steamfitters
51-8099.99	Plant and System Operators, All Other
47-2161.00	Plasterers and Stucco Masons
47-2152.02	Plumbers
47-2152.00	Plumbers, Pipefitters, and Steamfitters
33-3051.00	Police and Sheriff's Patrol Officers
33-3051.01	Police Patrol Officers
51-8012.00	Power Distributors and Dispatchers
51-8013.00	Power Plant Operators
49-9069.99	Precision Instrument and Equipment Repairers, All Other
51-5022.00	Prepress Technicians and Workers
49-3043.00	Rail Car Repairers
49-3092.00	Recreational Vehicle Service Technicians
49-9021.02	Refrigeration Mechanics and Installers
47-2171.00	Reinforcing Iron and Rebar Workers
47-2031.02	Rough Carpenters
33-3051.03	Sheriffs and Deputy Sheriffs
51-6041.00	Shoe and Leather Workers and Repairers
27-2042.01	Singers
51-4121.07	Solderers and Brazers
55-3018.00	Special Forces
55-1017.00	Special Forces Officers
51-8021.00	Stationary Engineers and Boiler Operators
47-2022.00	Stonemasons
47-2221.00	Structural Iron and Steel Workers
51-6052.00	Tailors, Dressmakers, and Custom Sewers
27-2012.04	Talent Directors
27-2012.05	Technical Directors/Managers
49-2022.00	Telecommunications Equipment Installers and Repairers, Except Line Installers
49-9052.00	Telecommunications Line Installers and Repairers
47-2053.00	Terrazzo Workers and Finishers
51-6063.00	Textile Knitting and Weaving Machine Setters, Operators, and Tenders
47-2044.00	Tile and Marble Setters
51-4111.00	Tool and Die Makers
33-3052.00	Transit and Railroad Police
27-2023.00	Umpires, Referees, and Other Sports Officials
51-6093.00	Upholsterers
49-9064.00	Watch Repairers
51-8031.00	Water and Liquid Waste Treatment Plant and System Operators
51-4121.06	Welders, Cutters, and Welder Fitters
51-4121.00	Welders, Cutters, Solderers, and Brazers

Jobs Requiring Work Experience in a Related Occupation

O*NET Number	Job Title
45-2011.00	Agricultural Inspectors
53-1011.00	Aircraft Cargo Handling Supervisors
53-6051.01	Aviation Inspectors
53-5021.00	Captains, Mates, and Pilots of Water Vessels
35-1011.00	Chefs and Head Cooks
27-2032.00	Choreographers
47-4011.00	Construction and Building Inspectors
13-1041.06	Coroners
13-1051.00	Cost Estimators
33-3021.03	Criminal Investigators and Special Agents
33-3021.00	Detectives and Criminal Investigators
13-1061.00	Emergency Management Specialists
45-1012.00	Farm Labor Contractors
55-2011.00	First-Line Supervisors/Managers of Air Crew Members
55-2013.00	First-Line Supervisors/Managers of All Other Tactical Operations Specialists
47-1011.00	First-Line Supervisors/Managers of Construction Trades and Extraction Workers
33-1011.00	First-Line Supervisors/Managers of Correctional Officers
45-1011.00	First-Line Supervisors/Managers of Farming, Fishing, and Forestry Workers
33-1021.00	First-Line Supervisors/Managers of Fire Fighting and Prevention Workers
35-1012.00	First-Line Supervisors/Managers of Food Preparation and Serving Workers
53-1021.00	First-Line Supervisors/Managers of Helpers, Laborers, and Material Movers, Hand
37-1011.00	First-Line Supervisors/Managers of Housekeeping and Janitorial Workers
37-1012.00	First-Line Supervisors/Managers of Landscaping, Lawn Service, and Groundskeeping Workers
49-1011.00	First-Line Supervisors/Managers of Mechanics, Installers, and Repairers
41-1012.00	First-Line Supervisors/Managers of Non-Retail Sales Workers
43-1011.00	First-Line Supervisors/Managers of Office and Administrative Support Workers
39-1021.00	First-Line Supervisors/Managers of Personal Service Workers
33-1012.00	First-Line Supervisors/Managers of Police and Detectives
51-1011.00	First-Line Supervisors/Managers of Production and Operating Workers
41-1011.00	First-Line Supervisors/Managers of Retail Sales Workers
53-1031.00	First-Line Supervisors/Managers of Transportation and Material-Moving Machine and Vehicle Operators
55-2012.00	First-Line Supervisors/Managers of Weapons Specialists/Crew Members
33-1099.99	First-Line Supervisors/Managers, Protective Service Workers, All Other
11-9051.00	Food Service Managers
33-1021.02	Forest Fire Fighting and Prevention Supervisors
53-6051.08	Freight and Cargo Inspectors
11-9071.00	Gaming Managers
39-1011.00	Gaming Supervisors
45-2041.00	Graders and Sorters, Agricultural Products
33-3021.05	Immigration and Customs Inspectors
11-3051.00	Industrial Production Managers
53-4011.00	Locomotive Engineers
11-9081.00	Lodging Managers
11-9199.99	Managers, All Other
53-5021.02	Mates—Ship, Boat, and Barge
33-1021.01	Municipal Fire Fighting and Prevention Supervisors
43-4141.00	New Accounts Clerks
53-5021.03	Pilots, Ship
33-3021.01	Police Detectives
33-3021.02	Police Identification and Records Officers
11-9131.00	Postmasters and Mail Superintendents
33-9021.00	Private Detectives and Investigators
13-1021.00	Purchasing Agents and Buyers, Farm Products
13-1023.00	Purchasing Agents, Except Wholesale, Retail, and Farm Products
53-4013.00	Rail Yard Engineers, Dinkey Operators, and Hostlers
53-4021.00	Railroad Brake, Signal, and Switch Operators
53-4031.00	Railroad Conductors and Yardmasters
41-9021.00	Real Estate Brokers
25-3021.00	Self-Enrichment Education Teachers
53-5021.01	Ship and Boat Captains
11-3071.02	Storage and Distribution Managers
53-6051.00	Transportation Inspectors
11-3071.01	Transportation Managers
33-9099.01	Transportation Security Screeners
53-6051.07	Transportation Vehicle, Equipment and Systems Inspectors, Except Aviation
11-3071.00	Transportation, Storage, and Distribution Managers
25-1194.00	Vocational Education Teachers, Postsecondary
13-1022.00	Wholesale and Retail Buyers, Except Farm Products

Jobs Requiring Postsecondary Vocational Training

O*NET Number	Job Title
49-3011.00	Aircraft Mechanics and Service Technicians
13-2021.00	Appraisers and Assessors of Real Estate
13-2021.02	Appraisers, Real Estate

(continued)

(continued)

Jobs Requiring Postsecondary Vocational Training

O*NET Number	Job Title
17-3011.00	Architectural and Civil Drafters
17-3011.01	Architectural Drafters
13-2021.01	Assessors
49-3023.01	Automotive Master Mechanics
49-3023.00	Automotive Service Technicians and Mechanics
49-3023.02	Automotive Specialty Technicians
49-2091.00	Avionics Technicians
39-5011.00	Barbers
49-3031.00	Bus and Truck Mechanics and Diesel Engine Specialists
17-3011.02	Civil Drafters
53-2012.00	Commercial Pilots
49-2011.00	Computer, Automated Teller, and Office Machine Repairers
23-2091.00	Court Reporters
43-9031.00	Desktop Publishers
17-3019.99	Drafters, All Other
49-2092.00	Electric Motor, Power Tool, and Related Repairers
17-3012.00	Electrical and Electronics Drafters
49-2093.00	Electrical and Electronics Installers and Repairers, Transportation Equipment
49-2094.00	Electrical and Electronics Repairers, Commercial and Industrial Equipment
49-2095.00	Electrical and Electronics Repairers, Powerhouse, Substation, and Relay
17-3012.02	Electrical Drafters
17-3012.01	Electronic Drafters
49-2096.00	Electronic Equipment Installers and Repairers, Motor Vehicles
49-2097.00	Electronic Home Entertainment Equipment Installers and Repairers
39-4011.00	Embalmers
29-2041.00	Emergency Medical Technicians and Paramedics
49-3041.00	Farm Equipment Mechanics
39-9031.00	Fitness Trainers and Aerobics Instructors
39-3012.00	Gaming and Sports Book Writers and Runners
39-3011.00	Gaming Dealers
51-9071.06	Gem and Diamond Workers
39-5012.00	Hairdressers, Hairstylists, and Cosmetologists
51-9071.01	Jewelers
51-9071.00	Jewelers and Precious Stone and Metal Workers
43-6012.00	Legal Secretaries
29-2061.00	Licensed Practical and Licensed Vocational Nurses
53-4012.00	Locomotive Firers
39-5091.00	Makeup Artists, Theatrical and Performance
39-5092.00	Manicurists and Pedicurists
31-9011.00	Massage Therapists
17-3013.00	Mechanical Drafters
43-6013.00	Medical Secretaries
31-9094.00	Medical Transcriptionists
49-3042.00	Mobile Heavy Equipment Mechanics, Except Engines
51-9071.07	Precious Metal Workers
25-2011.00	Preschool Teachers, Except Special Education
49-2021.00	Radio Mechanics
41-9022.00	Real Estate Sales Agents
29-2054.00	Respiratory Therapy Technicians
49-2098.00	Security and Fire Alarm Systems Installers
53-5031.00	Ship Engineers
39-5094.00	Skin Care Specialists
39-1012.00	Slot Key Persons
27-4014.00	Sound Engineering Technicians
29-2055.00	Surgical Technologists
41-3041.00	Travel Agents

Jobs Requiring an Associate Degree

O*NET Number	Job Title
17-3021.00	Aerospace Engineering and Operations Technicians
19-4011.00	Agricultural and Food Science Technicians
19-4011.01	Agricultural Technicians
19-4021.00	Biological Technicians
27-4012.00	Broadcast Technicians
29-2031.00	Cardiovascular Technologists and Technicians
19-4031.00	Chemical Technicians
19-4061.01	City and Regional Planning Aides
17-3022.00	Civil Engineering Technicians
15-1099.99	Computer Specialists, All Other
15-1041.00	Computer Support Specialists
27-1012.00	Craft Artists
29-2021.00	Dental Hygienists
29-2032.00	Diagnostic Medical Sonographers
17-3023.00	Electrical and Electronic Engineering Technicians
17-3023.03	Electrical Engineering Technicians
17-3024.00	Electro-Mechanical Technicians
17-3023.01	Electronics Engineering Technicians
17-3029.99	Engineering Technicians, Except Drafters, All Other
17-3025.00	Environmental Engineering Technicians
19-4091.00	Environmental Science and Protection Technicians, Including Health
45-1011.07	First-Line Supervisors/Managers of Agricultural Crop and Horticultural Workers
45-1011.08	First-Line Supervisors/Managers of Animal Husbandry and Animal Care Workers
45-1011.06	First-Line Supervisors/Managers of Aquacultural Workers

19-4011.02	Food Science Technicians
19-4092.00	Forensic Science Technicians
19-4093.00	Forest and Conservation Technicians
11-9061.00	Funeral Directors
19-4041.00	Geological and Petroleum Technicians
19-4041.02	Geological Sample Test Technicians
19-4041.01	Geophysical Data Technicians
17-3026.00	Industrial Engineering Technicians
19-4099.99	Life, Physical, and Social Science Technicians, All Other
17-3027.00	Mechanical Engineering Technicians
29-2012.00	Medical and Clinical Laboratory Technicians
49-9062.00	Medical Equipment Repairers
29-2071.00	Medical Records and Health Information Technicians
19-4051.01	Nuclear Equipment Operation Technicians
29-2033.00	Nuclear Medicine Technologists
19-4051.02	Nuclear Monitoring Technicians
19-4051.00	Nuclear Technicians
29-9012.00	Occupational Health and Safety Technicians
31-2011.00	Occupational Therapist Assistants
23-2011.00	Paralegals and Legal Assistants
31-2021.00	Physical Therapist Assistants
27-3012.00	Public Address System and Other Announcers
29-1124.00	Radiation Therapists
29-2034.02	Radiologic Technicians
29-2034.01	Radiologic Technologists
29-2034.00	Radiologic Technologists and Technicians
29-1111.00	Registered Nurses
29-1126.00	Respiratory Therapists
41-4011.00	Sales Representatives, Wholesale and Manufacturing, Technical and Scientific Products
51-9141.00	Semiconductor Processors
19-4061.00	Social Science Research Assistants
29-2056.00	Veterinary Technologists and Technicians

Jobs Requiring a Bachelor's Degree

O*NET Number	Job Title
13-2011.01	Accountants
13-2011.00	Accountants and Auditors
25-3011.00	Adult Literacy, Remedial Education, and GED Teachers and Instructors
17-2011.00	Aerospace Engineers
17-2021.00	Agricultural Engineers
53-2011.00	Airline Pilots, Copilots, and Flight Engineers
19-1011.00	Animal Scientists
17-1011.00	Architects, Except Landscape and Naval
29-9091.00	Athletic Trainers
19-2021.00	Atmospheric and Space Scientists

13-2011.02	Auditors
17-2031.00	Biomedical Engineers
27-3021.00	Broadcast News Analysts
13-2031.00	Budget Analysts
13-1199.99	Business Operations Specialists, All Other
17-1021.00	Cartographers and Photogrammetrists
17-2041.00	Chemical Engineers
19-2031.00	Chemists
21-1021.00	Child, Family, and School Social Workers
17-2051.00	Civil Engineers
27-1021.00	Commercial and Industrial Designers
13-1072.00	Compensation, Benefits, and Job Analysis Specialists
17-2061.00	Computer Hardware Engineers
15-1021.00	Computer Programmers
15-1071.01	Computer Security Specialists
15-1031.00	Computer Software Engineers, Applications
15-1032.00	Computer Software Engineers, Systems Software
15-1051.00	Computer Systems Analysts
19-1031.00	Conservation Scientists
11-9021.00	Construction Managers
27-3043.04	Copy Writers
21-1019.99	Counselors, All Other
13-2041.00	Credit Analysts
15-1061.00	Database Administrators
29-1031.00	Dietitians and Nutritionists
21-2021.00	Directors, Religious Activities and Education
27-3041.00	Editors
17-2071.00	Electrical Engineers
17-2072.00	Electronics Engineers, Except Computer
25-2021.00	Elementary School Teachers, Except Special Education
13-1071.01	Employment Interviewers
13-1071.00	Employment, Recruitment, and Placement Specialists
17-2199.99	Engineers, All Other
17-2081.00	Environmental Engineers
25-9021.00	Farm and Home Management Advisors
27-1022.00	Fashion Designers
27-4032.00	Film and Video Editors
13-2051.00	Financial Analysts
13-2061.00	Financial Examiners
13-2099.99	Financial Specialists, All Other
33-2021.02	Fire Investigators
17-2111.02	Fire-Prevention and Protection Engineers
45-1011.05	First-Line Supervisors/Managers of Logging Workers
19-1012.00	Food Scientists and Technologists
19-1032.00	Foresters
27-1024.00	Graphic Designers
17-2111.00	Health and Safety Engineers, Except Mining Safety Engineers and Inspectors

(continued)

(continued)

Jobs Requiring a Bachelor's Degree

O*NET Number	Job Title
13-1079.99	Human Resources, Training, and Labor Relations Specialists, All Other
17-2112.00	Industrial Engineers
17-2111.01	Industrial Safety and Health Engineers
41-3021.00	Insurance Sales Agents
13-2053.00	Insurance Underwriters
27-1025.00	Interior Designers
25-2012.00	Kindergarten Teachers, Except Special Education
17-1012.00	Landscape Architects
23-2092.00	Law Clerks
23-2099.99	Legal Support Workers, All Other
19-1099.99	Life Scientists, All Other
13-2071.00	Loan Counselors
13-2072.00	Loan Officers
13-1081.00	Logisticians
17-2121.02	Marine Architects
17-2121.01	Marine Engineers
17-2121.00	Marine Engineers and Naval Architects
17-2131.00	Materials Engineers
19-2032.00	Materials Scientists
17-2141.00	Mechanical Engineers
29-2011.00	Medical and Clinical Laboratory Technologists
21-1022.00	Medical and Public Health Social Workers
13-1121.00	Meeting and Convention Planners
25-2022.00	Middle School Teachers, Except Special and Vocational Education
17-2151.00	Mining and Geological Engineers, Including Mining Safety Engineers
27-1014.00	Multi-Media Artists and Animators
25-4013.00	Museum Technicians and Conservators
15-1071.00	Network and Computer Systems Administrators
15-1081.00	Network Systems and Data Communications Analysts
17-2161.00	Nuclear Engineers
29-2091.00	Orthotists and Prosthetists
19-1031.03	Park Naturalists
13-2052.00	Personal Financial Advisors
13-1071.02	Personnel Recruiters
17-2171.00	Petroleum Engineers
19-2099.99	Physical Scientists, All Other
29-1071.00	Physician Assistants
27-3043.05	Poets, Lyricists, and Creative Writers
21-1092.00	Probation Officers and Correctional Treatment Specialists
17-2111.03	Product Safety Engineers
11-9141.00	Property, Real Estate, and Community Association Managers
27-3031.00	Public Relations Specialists
19-1031.02	Range Managers
39-9032.00	Recreation Workers
29-1125.00	Recreational Therapists
21-2099.99	Religious Workers, All Other
27-3022.00	Reporters and Correspondents
41-3031.02	Sales Agents, Financial Services
41-3031.01	Sales Agents, Securities and Commodities
41-9031.00	Sales Engineers
25-2031.00	Secondary School Teachers, Except Special and Vocational Education
41-3031.00	Securities, Commodities, and Financial Services Sales Agents
27-1027.00	Set and Exhibit Designers
11-9151.00	Social and Community Service Managers
21-1029.99	Social Workers, All Other
19-1013.00	Soil and Plant Scientists
19-1031.01	Soil and Water Conservationists
25-2042.00	Special Education Teachers, Middle School
25-2041.00	Special Education Teachers, Preschool, Kindergarten, and Elementary School
25-2043.00	Special Education Teachers, Secondary School
17-1022.00	Surveyors
13-2081.00	Tax Examiners, Collectors, and Revenue Agents
25-3099.99	Teachers and Instructors, All Other
27-3042.00	Technical Writers
13-1073.00	Training and Development Specialists
27-3043.00	Writers and Authors

Jobs Requiring Work Experience Plus Degree

O*NET Number	Job Title
15-2011.00	Actuaries
23-1021.00	Administrative Law Judges, Adjudicators, and Hearing Officers
11-3011.00	Administrative Services Managers
11-2011.00	Advertising and Promotions Managers
13-1011.00	Agents and Business Managers of Artists, Performers, and Athletes
11-9011.03	Aquacultural Managers
23-1022.00	Arbitrators, Mediators, and Conciliators
27-1011.00	Art Directors
11-1011.00	Chief Executives
11-3041.00	Compensation and Benefits Managers
11-3021.00	Computer and Information Systems Managers
11-9011.02	Crop and Livestock Managers
27-2012.02	Directors—Stage, Motion Pictures, Television, and Radio
11-9039.99	Education Administrators, All Other
11-9032.00	Education Administrators, Elementary and Secondary School
11-9033.00	Education Administrators, Postsecondary

11-9031.00	Education Administrators, Preschool and Child Care Center/Program
11-9041.00	Engineering Managers
11-9011.00	Farm, Ranch, and Other Agricultural Managers
11-3031.00	Financial Managers
11-3031.02	Financial Managers, Branch or Department
11-1021.00	General and Operations Managers
11-3040.00	Human Resources Managers
11-3049.99	Human Resources Managers, All Other
23-1023.00	Judges, Magistrate Judges, and Magistrates
11-1031.00	Legislators
13-1111.00	Management Analysts
11-2021.00	Marketing Managers
11-9111.00	Medical and Health Services Managers
27-2041.04	Music Composers and Arrangers
11-9121.00	Natural Sciences Managers
11-9011.01	Nursery and Greenhouse Managers
27-2012.01	Producers
27-2012.00	Producers and Directors
27-2012.03	Program Directors
11-2031.00	Public Relations Managers
11-3061.00	Purchasing Managers
11-2022.00	Sales Managers
11-3042.00	Training and Development Managers
11-3031.01	Treasurers and Controllers
25-2023.00	Vocational Education Teachers, Middle School
25-2032.00	Vocational Education Teachers, Secondary School

Jobs Requiring a Master's Degree

O*NET Number	Job Title
25-1041.00	Agricultural Sciences Teachers, Postsecondary
19-3091.01	Anthropologists
19-3091.00	Anthropologists and Archeologists
25-1061.00	Anthropology and Archeology Teachers, Postsecondary
19-3091.02	Archeologists
25-1031.00	Architecture Teachers, Postsecondary
25-4011.00	Archivists
25-1062.00	Area, Ethnic, and Cultural Studies Teachers, Postsecondary
25-1121.00	Art, Drama, and Music Teachers, Postsecondary
25-1051.00	Atmospheric, Earth, Marine, and Space Sciences Teachers, Postsecondary
29-1121.00	Audiologists
25-1042.00	Biological Science Teachers, Postsecondary
25-1011.00	Business Teachers, Postsecondary
25-1052.00	Chemistry Teachers, Postsecondary
21-2011.00	Clergy
25-1122.00	Communications Teachers, Postsecondary
25-1021.00	Computer Science Teachers, Postsecondary

25-1111.00	Criminal Justice and Law Enforcement Teachers, Postsecondary
25-4012.00	Curators
25-1063.00	Economics Teachers, Postsecondary
19-3011.00	Economists
25-1081.00	Education Teachers, Postsecondary
21-1012.00	Educational, Vocational, and School Counselors
25-1032.00	Engineering Teachers, Postsecondary
25-1123.00	English Language and Literature Teachers, Postsecondary
25-1053.00	Environmental Science Teachers, Postsecondary
19-2041.00	Environmental Scientists and Specialists, Including Health
19-1041.00	Epidemiologists
25-1124.00	Foreign Language and Literature Teachers, Postsecondary
25-1043.00	Forestry and Conservation Science Teachers, Postsecondary
19-3092.00	Geographers
25-1064.00	Geography Teachers, Postsecondary
19-2042.00	Geoscientists, Except Hydrologists and Geographers
25-1191.00	Graduate Teaching Assistants
21-1091.00	Health Educators
25-1071.00	Health Specialties Teachers, Postsecondary
19-3093.00	Historians
25-1125.00	History Teachers, Postsecondary
25-1192.00	Home Economics Teachers, Postsecondary
19-2043.00	Hydrologists
19-3032.00	Industrial-Organizational Psychologists
25-9031.00	Instructional Coordinators
25-4021.00	Librarians
25-1082.00	Library Science Teachers, Postsecondary
19-3021.00	Market Research Analysts
21-1013.00	Marriage and Family Therapists
15-2099.99	Mathematical Science Occupations, All Other
25-1022.00	Mathematical Science Teachers, Postsecondary
15-2091.00	Mathematical Technicians
15-2021.00	Mathematicians
21-1023.00	Mental Health and Substance Abuse Social Workers
21-1014.00	Mental Health Counselors
27-2041.01	Music Directors
27-2041.00	Music Directors and Composers
25-1072.00	Nursing Instructors and Teachers, Postsecondary
29-9011.00	Occupational Health and Safety Specialists
29-1122.00	Occupational Therapists
15-2031.00	Operations Research Analysts
25-1126.00	Philosophy and Religion Teachers, Postsecondary
29-1123.00	Physical Therapists
25-1054.00	Physics Teachers, Postsecondary
25-1065.00	Political Science Teachers, Postsecondary
19-3094.00	Political Scientists

(continued)

(continued)

Jobs Requiring a Master's Degree

O*NET Number	Job Title
25-1199.99	Postsecondary Teachers, All Other
19-3039.99	Psychologists, All Other
25-1066.00	Psychology Teachers, Postsecondary
25-1193.00	Recreation and Fitness Studies Teachers, Postsecondary
21-1015.00	Rehabilitation Counselors
25-1069.99	Social Sciences Teachers, Postsecondary, All Other
19-3099.99	Social Scientists and Related Workers, All Other
25-1113.00	Social Work Teachers, Postsecondary
19-3041.00	Sociologists
25-1067.00	Sociology Teachers, Postsecondary
29-1127.00	Speech-Language Pathologists
15-2041.00	Statisticians
21-1011.00	Substance Abuse and Behavioral Disorder Counselors
19-3022.00	Survey Researchers
19-3051.00	Urban and Regional Planners

Jobs Requiring a Doctoral Degree

O*NET Number	Job Title
19-2011.00	Astronomers
19-1021.00	Biochemists and Biophysicists
19-1029.99	Biological Scientists, All Other
19-1020.01	Biologists
19-3031.02	Clinical Psychologists
19-3031.00	Clinical, Counseling, and School Psychologists
15-1011.00	Computer and Information Scientists, Research
19-3031.03	Counseling Psychologists
19-1042.00	Medical Scientists, Except Epidemiologists
19-1022.00	Microbiologists
19-2012.00	Physicists
19-3031.01	School Psychologists
19-1023.00	Zoologists and Wildlife Biologists

Jobs Requiring a First Professional Degree

O*NET Number	Job Title
29-1061.00	Anesthesiologists
29-1011.00	Chiropractors
29-1029.99	Dentists, All Other Specialists
29-1021.00	Dentists, General
29-1062.00	Family and General Practitioners
29-1063.00	Internists, General
25-1112.00	Law Teachers, Postsecondary
23-1011.00	Lawyers
29-1064.00	Obstetricians and Gynecologists
29-1041.00	Optometrists
29-1022.00	Oral and Maxillofacial Surgeons
29-1023.00	Orthodontists
29-1065.00	Pediatricians, General
29-1051.00	Pharmacists
29-1069.99	Physicians and Surgeons, All Other
29-1081.00	Podiatrists
29-1024.00	Prosthodontists
29-1066.00	Psychiatrists
29-1067.00	Surgeons
29-1131.00	Veterinarians

Method 4: Browse the Best Jobs in Three Categories

If you are interested in jobs with high pay, a high percentage of growth, or a high number of annual openings, you can find the 50 highest-rated jobs in each of these three categories in the lists in this section. Occupations with a high rate of growth can be desirable because growth provides opportunities for advancement and occupations with many openings can provide more opportunities for new workers to enter the field and can make it easier for workers to move from one position to another.

When to Use This Method: If you are looking for jobs that provide good growth potential, many opportunities, or good wages, the following lists help you narrow your search. Simply find the category that is important to you, review the list of related jobs, and then look up their descriptions in Part II using the O*NET number.

For more lists of "best jobs," consult *Best Jobs for the 21st Century*, also from JIST Publishing. Also available are *300 Best Jobs Without a Four-Year Degree*, *200 Best Jobs for College Graduates*, and several other books in this series.

The 50 Best-Paying Jobs

Rank	O*NET Number	Job Title	Annual Earnings
1.	29-1061.00	Anesthesiologists	more than $145,600
2.	29-1063.00	Internists, General	more than $145,600
3.	29-1064.00	Obstetricians and Gynecologists	more than $145,600
4.	29-1022.00	Oral and Maxillofacial Surgeons	more than $145,600
5.	29-1023.00	Orthodontists	more than $145,600
6.	29-1024.00	Prosthodontists	more than $145,600
7.	29-1066.00	Psychiatrists	more than $145,600
8.	29-1067.00	Surgeons	more than $145,600
9.	29-1069.99	Physicians and Surgeons, All Other	$143,480

10.	11-1011.00	Chief Executives	$142,440
11.	29-1062.00	Family and General Practitioners	$140,400
12.	53-2011.00	Airline Pilots, Copilots, and Flight Engineers	$138,170
13.	29-1065.00	Pediatricians, General	$136,600
14.	29-1021.00	Dentists, General	$125,300
15.	53-2021.00	Air Traffic Controllers	$107,590
16.	19-2011.00	Astronomers	$104,670
17.	11-9041.00	Engineering Managers	$100,760
18.	29-1081.00	Podiatrists	$100,550
19.	23-1011.00	Lawyers	$98,930
20.	23-1023.00	Judges, Magistrate Judges, and Magistrates	$97,570
21.	11-3021.00	Computer and Information Systems Managers	$96,520
22.	29-1029.99	Dentists, All Other Specialists	$94,600
23.	11-9121.00	Natural Sciences Managers	$93,090
24.	17-2171.00	Petroleum Engineers	$93,000
25.	11-2021.00	Marketing Managers	$92,680
26.	15-1011.00	Computer and Information Scientists, Research	$91,230
27.	29-1051.00	Pharmacists	$89,820
28.	19-2012.00	Physicists	$89,810
29.	25-1112.00	Law Teachers, Postsecondary	$89,790
30.	17-2161.00	Nuclear Engineers	$88,290
31.	29-1041.00	Optometrists	$88,040
32.	11-2022.00	Sales Managers	$87,580
33.	11-3031.00	Financial Managers	$86,280
34.	11-3031.02	Financial Managers, Branch or Department	$86,280
35.	11-3031.01	Treasurers and Controllers	$86,280
36.	19-3032.00	Industrial-Organizational Psychologists	$84,690
37.	17-2061.00	Computer Hardware Engineers	$84,420
38.	11-3049.99	Human Resources Managers, All Other	$84,190
39.	19-3094.00	Political Scientists	$84,100
40.	17-2011.00	Aerospace Engineers	$84,090
41.	19-2099.99	Physical Scientists, All Other	$83,300
42.	15-1032.00	Computer Software Engineers, Systems Software	$82,120
43.	15-2011.00	Actuaries	$81,640
44.	11-1021.00	General and Operations Managers	$81,480
45.	15-2021.00	Mathematicians	$80,920
46.	11-9199.99	Managers, All Other	$79,170
47.	17-2072.00	Electronics Engineers, Except Computer	$78,030
48.	17-2199.99	Engineers, All Other	$77,150
49.	17-2041.00	Chemical Engineers	$77,140
50.	15-1031.00	Computer Software Engineers, Applications	$77,090

The 50 Fastest-Growing Jobs

Rank	O*NET Number	Job Title	Percent Growth Through 2014
1.	31-1011.00	Home Health Aides	56.0%
2.	15-1081.00	Network Systems and Data Communications Analysts	54.6%
3.	31-9092.00	Medical Assistants	52.1%
4.	29-1071.00	Physician Assistants	49.6%
5.	15-1031.00	Computer Software Engineers, Applications	48.4%
6.	31-2021.00	Physical Therapist Assistants	44.2%
7.	29-2021.00	Dental Hygienists	43.3%
8.	15-1032.00	Computer Software Engineers, Systems Software	43.0%
9.	31-9091.00	Dental Assistants	42.7%
10.	39-9021.00	Personal and Home Care Aides	41.0%
11.	15-1071.01	Computer Security Specialists	38.4%
12.	15-1071.00	Network and Computer Systems Administrators	38.4%
13.	15-1061.00	Database Administrators	38.2%
14.	29-1123.00	Physical Therapists	36.7%
15.	19-4092.00	Forensic Science Technicians	36.4%
16.	29-2056.00	Veterinary Technologists and Technicians	35.3%
17.	29-2032.00	Diagnostic Medical Sonographers	34.8%
18.	31-2022.00	Physical Therapist Aides	34.4%
19.	31-2011.00	Occupational Therapist Assistants	34.1%
20.	19-1042.00	Medical Scientists, Except Epidemiologists	34.1%
21.	29-1122.00	Occupational Therapists	33.6%
22.	25-2011.00	Preschool Teachers, Except Special Education	33.1%
23.	29-2031.00	Cardiovascular Technologists and Technicians	32.6%
24.	25-1000.00	Teachers, Postsecondary	32.2%
25.	21-1099.99	Community and Social Service Specialists, All Other	31.9%
26.	19-2043.00	Hydrologists	31.6%
27.	15-1051.00	Computer Systems Analysts	31.4%
28.	47-4041.00	Hazardous Materials Removal Workers	31.2%
29.	17-2031.00	Biomedical Engineers	30.7%
30.	13-1071.02	Personnel Recruiters	30.5%
31.	13-1071.00	Employment, Recruitment, and Placement Specialists	30.5%
32.	13-1071.01	Employment Interviewers	30.5%
33.	17-2081.00	Environmental Engineers	30.0%
34.	23-2011.00	Paralegals and Legal Assistants	29.7%
35.	21-1093.00	Social and Human Service Assistants	29.7%

(continued)

(continued)

The 50 Fastest-Growing Jobs

Rank	O*NET Number	Job Title	Percent Growth Through 2014
36.	29-2055.00	Surgical Technologists	29.5%
37.	29-1111.00	Registered Nurses	29.4%
38.	29-9091.00	Athletic Trainers	29.3%
39.	29-2071.00	Medical Records and Health Information Technicians	28.9%
40.	39-9041.00	Residential Advisors	28.9%
41.	21-1011.00	Substance Abuse and Behavioral Disorder Counselors	28.7%
42.	29-2052.00	Pharmacy Technicians	28.6%
43.	29-1126.00	Respiratory Therapists	28.4%
44.	39-3091.00	Amusement and Recreation Attendants	28.0%
45.	53-3011.00	Ambulance Drivers and Attendants, Except Emergency Medical Technicians	28.0%
46.	39-3011.00	Gaming Dealers	28.0%
47.	11-9031.00	Education Administrators, Preschool and Child Care Center/Program	27.9%
48.	25-9031.00	Instructional Coordinators	27.5%
49.	47-4099.99	Construction and Related Workers, All Other	27.5%
50.	29-2041.00	Emergency Medical Technicians and Paramedics	27.3%

*Job 24 is not a single O*NET job; it combines 38 postsecondary teaching jobs in the O*NET, numbered 25-1011.00 through 25-1199.99.*

The 50 Jobs with the Most Openings

Rank	O*NET Number	Job Title	Annual Openings
1.	41-2031.00	Retail Salespersons	1,350,000
2.	41-2011.00	Cashiers	1,211,000
3.	35-3031.00	Waiters and Waitresses	800,000
4.	35-3021.00	Combined Food Preparation and Serving Workers, Including Fast Food	751,000
5.	43-9061.00	Office Clerks, General	695,000
6.	53-7062.00	Laborers and Freight, Stock, and Material Movers, Hand	671,000
7.	37-2011.00	Janitors and Cleaners, Except Maids and Housekeeping Cleaners	528,000
8.	43-4051.00	Customer Service Representatives	510,000
9.	39-9011.00	Child Care Workers	439,000
10.	39-9011.01	Nannies	439,000
11.	43-5081.02	Marking Clerks	351,000
12.	43-5081.04	Order Fillers, Wholesale and Retail Sales	351,000
13.	43-5081.00	Stock Clerks and Order Fillers	351,000
14.	43-5081.01	Stock Clerks, Sales Floor	351,000
15.	43-5081.03	Stock Clerks—Stockroom, Warehouse, or Storage Yard	351,000
16.	25-1000.00	Teachers, Postsecondary	329,000
17.	37-2012.00	Maids and Housekeeping Cleaners	314,000
18.	31-1012.00	Nursing Aides, Orderlies, and Attendants	307,000
19.	43-4171.00	Receptionists and Information Clerks	299,000
20.	35-2021.00	Food Preparation Workers	294,000
21.	43-3031.00	Bookkeeping, Accounting, and Auditing Clerks	291,000
22.	53-3032.00	Truck Drivers, Heavy and Tractor-Trailer	274,000
23.	51-2092.00	Team Assemblers	262,000
24.	25-9041.00	Teacher Assistants	252,000
25.	47-2061.00	Construction Laborers	245,000
26.	37-3011.00	Landscaping and Groundskeeping Workers	243,000
27.	43-6014.00	Secretaries, Except Legal, Medical, and Executive	231,000
28.	39-9021.00	Personal and Home Care Aides	230,000
29.	33-9032.00	Security Guards	230,000
30.	41-1011.00	First-Line Supervisors/Managers of Retail Sales Workers	229,000
31.	29-1111.00	Registered Nurses	229,000
32.	43-6011.00	Executive Secretaries and Administrative Assistants	218,000
33.	47-2031.00	Carpenters	210,000
34.	47-2031.01	Construction Carpenters	210,000
35.	47-2031.02	Rough Carpenters	210,000
36.	11-1021.00	General and Operations Managers	208,000
37.	35-2014.00	Cooks, Restaurant	207,000
38.	25-2021.00	Elementary School Teachers, Except Special Education	203,000
39.	35-3022.00	Counter Attendants, Cafeteria, Food Concession, and Coffee Shop	199,000
40.	53-7064.00	Packers and Packagers, Hand	194,000
41.	13-1199.99	Business Operations Specialists, All Other	193,000
42.	35-1012.00	First-Line Supervisors/Managers of Food Preparation and Serving Workers	187,000
43.	35-2011.00	Cooks, Fast Food	174,000
44.	35-9011.00	Dining Room and Cafeteria Attendants and Bartender Helpers	174,000
45.	31-1011.00	Home Health Aides	170,000

46.	41-4012.00	Sales Representatives, Wholesale and Manufacturing, Except Technical and Scientific Products	169,000
47.	25-3099.99	Teachers and Instructors, All Other	169,000
48.	53-3033.00	Truck Drivers, Light or Delivery Services	169,000
49.	43-1011.00	First-Line Supervisors/Managers of Office and Administrative Support Workers	167,000
50.	35-9021.00	Dishwashers	164,000

Jobs 9 and 10 share 439,000 job openings. Jobs 11, 12, 13, 14, and 15 share 351,000 job openings. Job 16 is not a single O*NET job; it combines 38 postsecondary teaching jobs in the O*NET, numbered 25-1011.00 through 25-1199.99. Jobs 33, 34, and 35 share 210,000 job openings.

Method 5: Related Military Job

Many military jobs are similar to civilian jobs—similar work tasks, similar skill requirements, similar work context, and so forth. In fact, many people leaving the military find work in civilian jobs for which they qualify because of their military training and work experience. The following list links military jobs to similar O*NET jobs. The military jobs are organized into major occupational categories (for example, Administrative Occupations) and are listed alphabetically within those categories. The military occupational titles are based on the MOTD (Military Occupational Title Database) classification, and each title actually represents several, perhaps dozens, of specific military jobs. For example, the title Administrative Support Specialists represents the Army job called Administrative Specialist, the Marines job called Administrative Clerk, the Coast Guard job called Petty Officer, the Air Force job called Information Management Journeyman, and the Navy job called Flag Officer Writer—among many others.

When to Use This Method: If you have served or are considering serving in the armed forces, you may want to find the equivalent of your (former or planned) military job in the list and then make a note of the O*NET job or jobs that are considered similar. Use the code number of the O*NET job to find the complete job description.

Administrative Occupations

O*NET Number	Job Title

Administrative Support Specialists
13-1023.00	Purchasing Agents, Except Wholesale, Retail, and Farm Products
13-1079.99	Human Resources, Training, and Labor Relations Specialists, All Other
13-1199.99	Business Operations Specialists, All Other
15-1051.00	Computer Systems Analysts
19-3093.00	Historians
37-1011.00	First-Line Supervisors/Managers of Housekeeping and Janitorial Workers
43-1011.00	First-Line Supervisors/Managers of Office and Administrative Support Workers

43-3061.00	Procurement Clerks
43-4199.99	Information and Record Clerks, All Other
43-5021.00	Couriers and Messengers
43-5051.00	Postal Service Clerks
43-6011.00	Executive Secretaries and Administrative Assistants
43-6014.00	Secretaries, Except Legal, Medical, and Executive
43-9011.00	Computer Operators
43-9022.00	Word Processors and Typists
43-9031.00	Desktop Publishers
43-9061.00	Office Clerks, General
43-9199.99	Office and Administrative Support Workers, All Other

Finance and Accounting Specialists
13-1023.00	Purchasing Agents, Except Wholesale, Retail, and Farm Products
43-1011.00	First-Line Supervisors/Managers of Office and Administrative Support Workers
43-3031.00	Bookkeeping, Accounting, and Auditing Clerks
43-3051.00	Payroll and Timekeeping Clerks
43-3061.00	Procurement Clerks
43-3071.00	Tellers
43-4199.99	Information and Record Clerks, All Other

Flight Operations Specialists
13-1199.99	Business Operations Specialists, All Other
53-1011.00	Aircraft Cargo Handling Supervisors
53-2022.00	Airfield Operations Specialists

Legal Specialists and Court Reporters
23-2011.00	Paralegals and Legal Assistants
23-2091.00	Court Reporters
23-2092.00	Law Clerks
43-6012.00	Legal Secretaries

Preventive Maintenance Analysts
13-1081.00	Logisticians
43-1011.00	First-Line Supervisors/Managers of Office and Administrative Support Workers
43-4199.99	Information and Record Clerks, All Other
43-5061.00	Production, Planning, and Expediting Clerks
49-9042.00	Maintenance and Repair Workers, General

Sales and Stock Specialists
41-1011.00	First-Line Supervisors/Managers of Retail Sales Workers
41-2031.00	Retail Salespersons
43-5071.00	Shipping, Receiving, and Traffic Clerks
43-5081.01	Stock Clerks, Sales Floor
43-5081.03	Stock Clerks—Stockroom, Warehouse, or Storage Yard
43-5081.04	Order Fillers, Wholesale and Retail Sales

Combat Specialty Occupations

O*NET Number	Job Title

Artillery and Missile Crew Members

49-9099.99	Installation, Maintenance, and Repair Workers, All Other

Artillery and Missile Officers

11-9041.00	Engineering Managers
49-1011.00	First-Line Supervisors/Managers of Mechanics, Installers, and Repairers

Infantry Officers

11-1021.00	General and Operations Managers

Construction Occupations

O*NET Number	Job Title

Building Electricians

47-1011.00	First-Line Supervisors/Managers of Construction Trades and Extraction Workers
47-2111.00	Electricians
49-1011.00	First-Line Supervisors/Managers of Mechanics, Installers, and Repairers

Construction Equipment Operators

47-1011.00	First-Line Supervisors/Managers of Construction Trades and Extraction Workers
47-2071.00	Paving, Surfacing, and Tamping Equipment Operators
47-2073.00	Operating Engineers and Other Construction Equipment Operators
47-4051.00	Highway Maintenance Workers
47-5021.00	Earth Drillers, Except Oil and Gas
47-5031.00	Explosives Workers, Ordnance Handling Experts, and Blasters
47-5051.00	Rock Splitters, Quarry
53-7021.00	Crane and Tower Operators

Construction Specialists

13-1041.00	Compliance Officers, Except Agriculture, Construction, Health and Safety, and Transportation
17-3011.01	Architectural Drafters
17-3011.02	Civil Drafters
17-3022.00	Civil Engineering Technicians
17-3031.01	Surveying Technicians
17-3031.02	Mapping Technicians
47-1011.00	First-Line Supervisors/Managers of Construction Trades and Extraction Workers
47-2021.00	Brickmasons and Blockmasons

47-2022.00	Stonemasons
47-2031.00	Carpenters
47-2031.01	Construction Carpenters
47-2031.02	Rough Carpenters
47-2051.00	Cement Masons and Concrete Finishers
47-2081.00	Drywall and Ceiling Tile Installers
47-2181.00	Roofers
47-2221.00	Structural Iron and Steel Workers
47-4011.00	Construction and Building Inspectors
47-4021.00	Elevator Installers and Repairers
47-4061.00	Rail-Track Laying and Maintenance Equipment Operators
47-4099.99	Construction and Related Workers, All Other
47-5031.00	Explosives Workers, Ordnance Handling Experts, and Blasters
51-7011.00	Cabinetmakers and Bench Carpenters

Plumbers and Pipe Fitters

47-2011.00	Boilermakers
47-2151.00	Pipelayers
47-2152.00	Plumbers, Pipefitters, and Steamfitters
47-2152.01	Pipe Fitters and Steamfitters
47-2152.02	Plumbers

Electronic/Electrical Equipment Repair Occupations

O*NET Number	Job Title

Avionics Technicians

49-1011.00	First-Line Supervisors/Managers of Mechanics, Installers, and Repairers
49-2011.00	Computer, Automated Teller, and Office Machine Repairers
49-2021.00	Radio Mechanics
49-2091.00	Avionics Technicians
49-2094.00	Electrical and Electronics Repairers, Commercial and Industrial Equipment
49-3011.00	Aircraft Mechanics and Service Technicians
51-2011.00	Aircraft Structure, Surfaces, Rigging, and Systems Assemblers

Electrical Products Repairers

49-1011.00	First-Line Supervisors/Managers of Mechanics, Installers, and Repairers
49-2021.00	Radio Mechanics
49-2092.00	Electric Motor, Power Tool, and Related Repairers
49-2094.00	Electrical and Electronics Repairers, Commercial and Industrial Equipment
49-2096.00	Electronic Equipment Installers and Repairers, Motor Vehicles
49-2097.00	Electronic Home Entertainment Equipment Installers and Repairers

49-2098.00	Security and Fire Alarm Systems Installers
49-9031.00	Home Appliance Repairers
49-9062.00	Medical Equipment Repairers
49-9069.99	Precision Instrument and Equipment Repairers, All Other
51-4194.00	Tool Grinders, Filers, and Sharpeners

Electronic Instrument and Equipment Repairers

15-1071.00	Network and Computer Systems Administrators
15-1071.01	Computer Security Specialists
27-4013.00	Radio Operators
43-1011.00	First-Line Supervisors/Managers of Office and Administrative Support Workers
43-2099.99	Communications Equipment Operators, All Other
43-9011.00	Computer Operators
49-1011.00	First-Line Supervisors/Managers of Mechanics, Installers, and Repairers
49-2011.00	Computer, Automated Teller, and Office Machine Repairers
49-2021.00	Radio Mechanics
49-2022.00	Telecommunications Equipment Installers and Repairers, Except Line Installers
49-2091.00	Avionics Technicians
49-2093.00	Electrical and Electronics Installers and Repairers, Transportation Equipment
49-2094.00	Electrical and Electronics Repairers, Commercial and Industrial Equipment
49-2096.00	Electronic Equipment Installers and Repairers, Motor Vehicles
49-2097.00	Electronic Home Entertainment Equipment Installers and Repairers
49-3011.00	Aircraft Mechanics and Service Technicians
49-9052.00	Telecommunications Line Installers and Repairers
49-9069.99	Precision Instrument and Equipment Repairers, All Other

Power Plant Electricians

47-2111.00	Electricians
49-2093.00	Electrical and Electronics Installers and Repairers, Transportation Equipment
49-2094.00	Electrical and Electronics Repairers, Commercial and Industrial Equipment
49-2095.00	Electrical and Electronics Repairers, Powerhouse, Substation, and Relay
49-9012.00	Control and Valve Installers and Repairers, Except Mechanical Door
49-9041.00	Industrial Machinery Mechanics
49-9051.00	Electrical Power-Line Installers and Repairers
51-8021.00	Stationary Engineers and Boiler Operators

Precision Instrument and Equipment Repairers

| 49-1011.00 | First-Line Supervisors/Managers of Mechanics, Installers, and Repairers |

49-2011.00	Computer, Automated Teller, and Office Machine Repairers
49-2094.00	Electrical and Electronics Repairers, Commercial and Industrial Equipment
49-9041.00	Industrial Machinery Mechanics
49-9061.00	Camera and Photographic Equipment Repairers
49-9062.00	Medical Equipment Repairers
49-9063.00	Musical Instrument Repairers and Tuners
49-9064.00	Watch Repairers
49-9069.99	Precision Instrument and Equipment Repairers, All Other
49-9094.00	Locksmiths and Safe Repairers
51-1011.00	First-Line Supervisors/Managers of Production and Operating Workers
51-9061.00	Inspectors, Testers, Sorters, Samplers, and Weighers

Ship Electricians

47-2111.00	Electricians
47-4021.00	Elevator Installers and Repairers
49-2022.00	Telecommunications Equipment Installers and Repairers, Except Line Installers
49-2092.00	Electric Motor, Power Tool, and Related Repairers
49-2093.00	Electrical and Electronics Installers and Repairers, Transportation Equipment
49-2094.00	Electrical and Electronics Repairers, Commercial and Industrial Equipment
49-2095.00	Electrical and Electronics Repairers, Powerhouse, Substation, and Relay
49-2098.00	Security and Fire Alarm Systems Installers
49-9031.00	Home Appliance Repairers
49-9052.00	Telecommunications Line Installers and Repairers
49-9069.99	Precision Instrument and Equipment Repairers, All Other

Weapons Maintenance Technicians

37-1011.00	First-Line Supervisors/Managers of Housekeeping and Janitorial Workers
47-5031.00	Explosives Workers, Ordnance Handling Experts, and Blasters
49-1011.00	First-Line Supervisors/Managers of Mechanics, Installers, and Repairers
49-2011.00	Computer, Automated Teller, and Office Machine Repairers
49-2021.00	Radio Mechanics
49-2091.00	Avionics Technicians
49-2094.00	Electrical and Electronics Repairers, Commercial and Industrial Equipment
49-3011.00	Aircraft Mechanics and Service Technicians
49-3031.00	Bus and Truck Mechanics and Diesel Engine Specialists
49-9042.00	Maintenance and Repair Workers, General

(continued)

(continued)

Electronic/Electrical Equipment Repair Occupations

O*NET Number	Job Title
49-9069.99	Precision Instrument and Equipment Repairers, All Other
49-9099.99	Installation, Maintenance, and Repair Workers, All Other
51-2011.00	Aircraft Structure, Surfaces, Rigging, and Systems Assemblers

Engineering, Science, and Technical Occupations

O*NET Number	Job Title

Aerospace Engineers

11-9041.00	Engineering Managers
11-9121.00	Natural Sciences Managers
17-2011.00	Aerospace Engineers
17-2071.00	Electrical Engineers
17-2072.00	Electronics Engineers, Except Computer
17-2141.00	Mechanical Engineers

Civil Engineers

11-3011.00	Administrative Services Managers
11-9021.00	Construction Managers
11-9041.00	Engineering Managers
17-1011.00	Architects, Except Landscape and Naval
17-1021.00	Cartographers and Photogrammetrists
17-2051.00	Civil Engineers
17-2141.00	Mechanical Engineers
17-2199.99	Engineers, All Other

Communications Equipment Operators

27-4012.00	Broadcast Technicians
27-4013.00	Radio Operators
27-4031.00	Camera Operators, Television, Video, and Motion Picture
43-2099.99	Communications Equipment Operators, All Other
49-1011.00	First-Line Supervisors/Managers of Mechanics, Installers, and Repairers
49-2021.00	Radio Mechanics
49-2022.00	Telecommunications Equipment Installers and Repairers, Except Line Installers
49-2094.00	Electrical and Electronics Repairers, Commercial and Industrial Equipment
49-9052.00	Telecommunications Line Installers and Repairers

Communications Managers

11-3021.00	Computer and Information Systems Managers
11-9199.99	Managers, All Other
13-1111.00	Management Analysts
15-1081.00	Network Systems and Data Communications Analysts
17-2199.99	Engineers, All Other
49-1011.00	First-Line Supervisors/Managers of Mechanics, Installers, and Repairers

Computer Systems Officers

11-3021.00	Computer and Information Systems Managers
11-9199.99	Managers, All Other
13-1111.00	Management Analysts
15-1021.00	Computer Programmers
15-1031.00	Computer Software Engineers, Applications
15-1032.00	Computer Software Engineers, Systems Software
15-1051.00	Computer Systems Analysts
15-1061.00	Database Administrators
15-1071.01	Computer Security Specialists
15-1081.00	Network Systems and Data Communications Analysts
17-2061.00	Computer Hardware Engineers
17-2071.00	Electrical Engineers
49-1011.00	First-Line Supervisors/Managers of Mechanics, Installers, and Repairers

Computer Systems Specialists

15-1021.00	Computer Programmers
15-1041.00	Computer Support Specialists
15-1051.00	Computer Systems Analysts
15-1061.00	Database Administrators
15-1071.00	Network and Computer Systems Administrators
15-1071.01	Computer Security Specialists
15-1081.00	Network Systems and Data Communications Analysts
19-4099.99	Life, Physical, and Social Science Technicians, All Other
43-1011.00	First-Line Supervisors/Managers of Office and Administrative Support Workers
43-2099.99	Communications Equipment Operators, All Other
43-9011.00	Computer Operators
49-2011.00	Computer, Automated Teller, and Office Machine Repairers
49-2094.00	Electrical and Electronics Repairers, Commercial and Industrial Equipment

Divers

49-9092.00	Commercial Divers

Electrical and Electronics Engineers

11-9041.00	Engineering Managers
17-2011.00	Aerospace Engineers
17-2061.00	Computer Hardware Engineers
17-2071.00	Electrical Engineers

17-2072.00   Electronics Engineers, Except Computer
49-1011.00   First-Line Supervisors/Managers of Mechanics, Installers, and Repairers

Environmental Health and Safety Officers
11-9111.00   Medical and Health Services Managers
17-2031.00   Biomedical Engineers
17-2041.00   Chemical Engineers
17-2051.00   Civil Engineers
17-2081.00   Environmental Engineers
17-2111.01   Industrial Safety and Health Engineers
19-2031.00   Chemists
19-2041.00   Environmental Scientists and Specialists, Including Health
29-1069.99   Physicians and Surgeons, All Other
29-9011.00   Occupational Health and Safety Specialists

Environmental Health and Safety Specialists
29-2056.00   Veterinary Technologists and Technicians
29-9011.00   Occupational Health and Safety Specialists
29-9012.00   Occupational Health and Safety Technicians
31-9096.00   Veterinary Assistants and Laboratory Animal Caretakers
37-2021.00   Pest Control Workers
45-2011.00   Agricultural Inspectors
47-4041.00   Hazardous Materials Removal Workers

Industrial Engineers
11-3042.00   Training and Development Managers
11-3051.00   Industrial Production Managers
11-9021.00   Construction Managers
11-9041.00   Engineering Managers
15-2021.00   Mathematicians
15-2031.00   Operations Research Analysts
15-2041.00   Statisticians
17-2072.00   Electronics Engineers, Except Computer
17-2112.00   Industrial Engineers
17-2199.99   Engineers, All Other

Intelligence Officers
11-1021.00   General and Operations Managers
15-2021.00   Mathematicians
17-1021.00   Cartographers and Photogrammetrists
17-3031.02   Mapping Technicians
19-3099.99   Social Scientists and Related Workers, All Other
25-3099.99   Teachers and Instructors, All Other
27-3091.00   Interpreters and Translators
33-1012.00   First-Line Supervisors/Managers of Police and Detectives
49-1011.00   First-Line Supervisors/Managers of Mechanics, Installers, and Repairers

Intelligence Specialists
13-1111.00   Management Analysts
15-1071.00   Network and Computer Systems Administrators
15-1071.01   Computer Security Specialists
15-2021.00   Mathematicians
17-1021.00   Cartographers and Photogrammetrists
17-1022.00   Surveyors
17-3031.02   Mapping Technicians
19-3099.99   Social Scientists and Related Workers, All Other
27-3091.00   Interpreters and Translators
43-2099.99   Communications Equipment Operators, All Other

Lawyers and Judges
23-1011.00   Lawyers
23-1023.00   Judges, Magistrate Judges, and Magistrates

Life Scientists
11-9111.00   Medical and Health Services Managers
11-9121.00   Natural Sciences Managers
19-1012.00   Food Scientists and Technologists
19-1021.00   Biochemists and Biophysicists
19-1022.00   Microbiologists
19-1029.99   Biological Scientists, All Other
19-1042.00   Medical Scientists, Except Epidemiologists
19-1099.99   Life Scientists, All Other
19-2041.00   Environmental Scientists and Specialists, Including Health
29-1011.00   Chiropractors
29-1124.00   Radiation Therapists
29-1131.00   Veterinarians
29-2011.00   Medical and Clinical Laboratory Technologists

Marine Engineers
11-1021.00   General and Operations Managers
11-9041.00   Engineering Managers
11-9121.00   Natural Sciences Managers
11-9199.99   Managers, All Other
17-2121.01   Marine Engineers
17-2121.02   Marine Architects
19-2042.00   Geoscientists, Except Hydrologists and Geographers
19-2043.00   Hydrologists
53-5031.00   Ship Engineers

Meteorological Specialists
19-2021.00   Atmospheric and Space Scientists
19-4099.99   Life, Physical, and Social Science Technicians, All Other

Non-Destructive Testers
17-3021.00   Aerospace Engineering and Operations Technicians

(continued)

(continued)

Engineering, Science, and Technical Occupations

O*NET Number	Job Title
17-3027.00	Mechanical Engineering Technicians
17-3029.99	Engineering Technicians, Except Drafters, All Other
19-4031.00	Chemical Technicians
19-4051.01	Nuclear Equipment Operation Technicians
49-2094.00	Electrical and Electronics Repairers, Commercial and Industrial Equipment
49-3011.00	Aircraft Mechanics and Service Technicians
49-9069.99	Precision Instrument and Equipment Repairers, All Other
51-8093.00	Petroleum Pump System Operators, Refinery Operators, and Gaugers
51-9061.00	Inspectors, Testers, Sorters, Samplers, and Weighers

Nuclear Engineers

11-9041.00	Engineering Managers
17-2161.00	Nuclear Engineers
19-2099.99	Physical Scientists, All Other

Ordnance Officers

11-3051.00	Industrial Production Managers
11-3071.01	Transportation Managers
11-3071.02	Storage and Distribution Managers
11-9041.00	Engineering Managers
13-1061.00	Emergency Management Specialists
17-2072.00	Electronics Engineers, Except Computer
17-2111.01	Industrial Safety and Health Engineers
17-2112.00	Industrial Engineers
17-2131.00	Materials Engineers
17-2161.00	Nuclear Engineers
17-2199.99	Engineers, All Other
49-1011.00	First-Line Supervisors/Managers of Mechanics, Installers, and Repairers
51-1011.00	First-Line Supervisors/Managers of Production and Operating Workers

Ordnance Specialists

13-1061.00	Emergency Management Specialists
47-5021.00	Earth Drillers, Except Oil and Gas
47-5031.00	Explosives Workers, Ordnance Handling Experts, and Blasters
47-5051.00	Rock Splitters, Quarry
49-1011.00	First-Line Supervisors/Managers of Mechanics, Installers, and Repairers
49-2094.00	Electrical and Electronics Repairers, Commercial and Industrial Equipment
49-9042.00	Maintenance and Repair Workers, General
49-9092.00	Commercial Divers
49-9099.99	Installation, Maintenance, and Repair Workers, All Other

Physical Scientists

17-2041.00	Chemical Engineers
17-2171.00	Petroleum Engineers
17-2199.99	Engineers, All Other
19-2011.00	Astronomers
19-2012.00	Physicists
19-2021.00	Atmospheric and Space Scientists
19-2031.00	Chemists
19-2041.00	Environmental Scientists and Specialists, Including Health
19-2042.00	Geoscientists, Except Hydrologists and Geographers
19-2043.00	Hydrologists
19-2099.99	Physical Scientists, All Other
49-1011.00	First-Line Supervisors/Managers of Mechanics, Installers, and Repairers

Radar and Sonar Operators

43-9011.00	Computer Operators
49-2094.00	Electrical and Electronics Repairers, Commercial and Industrial Equipment

Space Operations Officers

13-1111.00	Management Analysts
19-1029.99	Biological Scientists, All Other
19-2021.00	Atmospheric and Space Scientists
53-2011.00	Airline Pilots, Copilots, and Flight Engineers

Space Operations Specialists

43-2099.99	Communications Equipment Operators, All Other

Surveying, Mapping, and Drafting Technicians

17-1021.00	Cartographers and Photogrammetrists
17-1022.00	Surveyors
17-3011.01	Architectural Drafters
17-3011.02	Civil Drafters
17-3022.00	Civil Engineering Technicians
17-3029.99	Engineering Technicians, Except Drafters, All Other
17-3031.00	Surveying and Mapping Technicians
17-3031.01	Surveying Technicians
17-3031.02	Mapping Technicians

Executive/Administrative/Managerial Occupations

O*NET Number	Job Title

Administrative Officers

11-1021.00	General and Operations Managers
11-3011.00	Administrative Services Managers
11-9081.00	Lodging Managers
11-9131.00	Postmasters and Mail Superintendents

11-9141.00	Property, Real Estate, and Community Association Managers
11-9199.99	Managers, All Other
13-1041.04	Government Property Inspectors and Investigators
13-1199.99	Business Operations Specialists, All Other
43-1011.00	First-Line Supervisors/Managers of Office and Administrative Support Workers
53-1011.00	Aircraft Cargo Handling Supervisors
53-1031.00	First-Line Supervisors/Managers of Transportation and Material-Moving Machine and Vehicle Operators

Finance and Accounting Managers

11-3031.01	Treasurers and Controllers
11-3031.02	Financial Managers, Branch or Department
13-2011.01	Accountants
13-2011.02	Auditors
13-2031.00	Budget Analysts

Health Services Administrators

| 11-9111.00 | Medical and Health Services Managers |
| 11-9199.99 | Managers, All Other |

International Relations Officers

11-1021.00	General and Operations Managers
13-1199.99	Business Operations Specialists, All Other
19-3094.00	Political Scientists
27-3031.00	Public Relations Specialists

Logisticians

11-3071.00	Transportation, Storage, and Distribution Managers
11-3071.01	Transportation Managers
13-1081.00	Logisticians
13-1111.00	Management Analysts

Management Analysts and Planners

11-1021.00	General and Operations Managers
11-9199.99	Managers, All Other
13-1041.04	Government Property Inspectors and Investigators
13-1111.00	Management Analysts
15-2031.00	Operations Research Analysts

Purchasing and Contracting Managers

11-1021.00	General and Operations Managers
11-3051.00	Industrial Production Managers
11-3061.00	Purchasing Managers
11-9041.00	Engineering Managers
11-9199.99	Managers, All Other
13-1023.00	Purchasing Agents, Except Wholesale, Retail, and Farm Products
13-1081.00	Logisticians

Store Managers

11-1021.00	General and Operations Managers
11-3071.02	Storage and Distribution Managers
41-1011.00	First-Line Supervisors/Managers of Retail Sales Workers

Supply and Warehousing Managers

11-3061.00	Purchasing Managers
11-3071.01	Transportation Managers
11-3071.02	Storage and Distribution Managers
11-9199.99	Managers, All Other

Health Care Occupations

O*NET Number	Job Title

Cardiopulmonary and EEG Technicians

29-2031.00	Cardiovascular Technologists and Technicians
29-2054.00	Respiratory Therapy Technicians
29-2099.99	Health Technologists and Technicians, All Other
31-9092.00	Medical Assistants

Dental and Optical Laboratory Technicians

| 51-9081.00 | Dental Laboratory Technicians |
| 51-9083.00 | Ophthalmic Laboratory Technicians |

Dental Specialists

29-2021.00	Dental Hygienists
29-2055.00	Surgical Technologists
29-9099.99	Healthcare Practitioners and Technical Workers, All Other
31-9091.00	Dental Assistants

Dentists

11-9111.00	Medical and Health Services Managers
29-1021.00	Dentists, General
29-1022.00	Oral and Maxillofacial Surgeons
29-1023.00	Orthodontists
29-1024.00	Prosthodontists
29-1029.99	Dentists, All Other Specialists

Medical Care Technicians

29-2032.00	Diagnostic Medical Sonographers
29-2033.00	Nuclear Medicine Technologists
29-2053.00	Psychiatric Technicians
29-2054.00	Respiratory Therapy Technicians
29-2055.00	Surgical Technologists
29-2061.00	Licensed Practical and Licensed Vocational Nurses
29-2071.00	Medical Records and Health Information Technicians
29-2091.00	Orthotists and Prosthetists

(continued)

(continued)

Health Care Occupations

O*NET Number	Job Title
29-2099.99	Health Technologists and Technicians, All Other
31-1012.00	Nursing Aides, Orderlies, and Attendants
31-9092.00	Medical Assistants
31-9093.00	Medical Equipment Preparers
49-9062.00	Medical Equipment Repairers
51-9082.00	Medical Appliance Technicians

Medical Laboratory Technicians
19-4021.00	Biological Technicians
19-4031.00	Chemical Technicians
29-2011.00	Medical and Clinical Laboratory Technologists
29-2012.00	Medical and Clinical Laboratory Technicians

Medical Record Technicians
29-1071.00	Physician Assistants
29-2071.00	Medical Records and Health Information Technicians
43-1011.00	First-Line Supervisors/Managers of Office and Administrative Support Workers

Medical Service Technicians
11-9111.00	Medical and Health Services Managers
13-1079.99	Human Resources, Training, and Labor Relations Specialists, All Other
29-2041.00	Emergency Medical Technicians and Paramedics
29-9011.00	Occupational Health and Safety Specialists
29-9099.99	Healthcare Practitioners and Technical Workers, All Other
31-2011.00	Occupational Therapist Assistants
31-9092.00	Medical Assistants
31-9093.00	Medical Equipment Preparers

Optometric Technicians
29-2081.00	Opticians, Dispensing
31-9092.00	Medical Assistants
31-9093.00	Medical Equipment Preparers
51-9083.00	Ophthalmic Laboratory Technicians

Optometrists
29-1041.00	Optometrists

Pharmacists
29-1051.00	Pharmacists

Pharmacy Technicians
29-2052.00	Pharmacy Technicians

Physical and Occupational Therapists
29-1122.00	Occupational Therapists
29-1123.00	Physical Therapists

Physical and Occupational Therapy Specialists
29-2091.00	Orthotists and Prosthetists
31-2011.00	Occupational Therapist Assistants
31-2021.00	Physical Therapist Assistants

Physician Assistants
29-1071.00	Physician Assistants

Physicians and Surgeons
11-9111.00	Medical and Health Services Managers
19-1042.00	Medical Scientists, Except Epidemiologists
29-1061.00	Anesthesiologists
29-1062.00	Family and General Practitioners
29-1063.00	Internists, General
29-1064.00	Obstetricians and Gynecologists
29-1065.00	Pediatricians, General
29-1066.00	Psychiatrists
29-1067.00	Surgeons
29-1069.99	Physicians and Surgeons, All Other
29-1081.00	Podiatrists
29-9011.00	Occupational Health and Safety Specialists

Psychologists
19-3031.00	Clinical, Counseling, and School Psychologists
19-3031.02	Clinical Psychologists
19-3031.03	Counseling Psychologists
19-3032.00	Industrial-Organizational Psychologists
19-3039.99	Psychologists, All Other
19-3099.99	Social Scientists and Related Workers, All Other

Registered Nurses
29-1111.00	Registered Nurses

Speech Therapists
29-1121.00	Audiologists
29-1127.00	Speech-Language Pathologists

Human Resource Development

O*NET Number	Job Title

Personnel Managers
11-1021.00	General and Operations Managers
11-3041.00	Compensation and Benefits Managers
11-3042.00	Training and Development Managers
11-3049.99	Human Resources Managers, All Other
13-1079.99	Human Resources, Training, and Labor Relations Specialists, All Other

Personnel Specialists
13-1071.00	Employment, Recruitment, and Placement Specialists
13-1071.02	Personnel Recruiters

13-1072.00   Compensation, Benefits, and Job Analysis Specialists

13-1073.00   Training and Development Specialists

13-1079.99   Human Resources, Training, and Labor Relations Specialists, All Other

13-1111.00   Management Analysts

43-1011.00   First-Line Supervisors/Managers of Office and Administrative Support Workers

43-4161.00   Human Resources Assistants, Except Payroll and Timekeeping

43-9011.00   Computer Operators

43-9061.00   Office Clerks, General

Recruiting Managers

11-3049.99   Human Resources Managers, All Other

13-1071.00   Employment, Recruitment, and Placement Specialists

13-1071.02   Personnel Recruiters

Recruiting Specialists

13-1071.02   Personnel Recruiters

13-1072.00   Compensation, Benefits, and Job Analysis Specialists

43-4161.00   Human Resources Assistants, Except Payroll and Timekeeping

Teachers and Instructors

13-1073.00   Training and Development Specialists

23-1011.00   Lawyers

25-1011.00   Business Teachers, Postsecondary

25-1021.00   Computer Science Teachers, Postsecondary

25-1022.00   Mathematical Science Teachers, Postsecondary

25-1031.00   Architecture Teachers, Postsecondary

25-1032.00   Engineering Teachers, Postsecondary

25-1041.00   Agricultural Sciences Teachers, Postsecondary

25-1042.00   Biological Science Teachers, Postsecondary

25-1043.00   Forestry and Conservation Science Teachers, Postsecondary

25-1051.00   Atmospheric, Earth, Marine, and Space Sciences Teachers, Postsecondary

25-1052.00   Chemistry Teachers, Postsecondary

25-1053.00   Environmental Science Teachers, Postsecondary

25-1054.00   Physics Teachers, Postsecondary

25-1061.00   Anthropology and Archeology Teachers, Postsecondary

25-1062.00   Area, Ethnic, and Cultural Studies Teachers, Postsecondary

25-1063.00   Economics Teachers, Postsecondary

25-1064.00   Geography Teachers, Postsecondary

25-1065.00   Political Science Teachers, Postsecondary

25-1066.00   Psychology Teachers, Postsecondary

25-1067.00   Sociology Teachers, Postsecondary

25-1069.99   Social Sciences Teachers, Postsecondary, All Other

25-1071.00   Health Specialties Teachers, Postsecondary

25-1072.00   Nursing Instructors and Teachers, Postsecondary

25-1081.00   Education Teachers, Postsecondary

25-1082.00   Library Science Teachers, Postsecondary

25-1111.00   Criminal Justice and Law Enforcement Teachers, Postsecondary

25-1112.00   Law Teachers, Postsecondary

25-1113.00   Social Work Teachers, Postsecondary

25-1121.00   Art, Drama, and Music Teachers, Postsecondary

25-1122.00   Communications Teachers, Postsecondary

25-1123.00   English Language and Literature Teachers, Postsecondary

25-1124.00   Foreign Language and Literature Teachers, Postsecondary

25-1125.00   History Teachers, Postsecondary

25-1126.00   Philosophy and Religion Teachers, Postsecondary

25-1191.00   Graduate Teaching Assistants

25-1192.00   Home Economics Teachers, Postsecondary

25-1193.00   Recreation and Fitness Studies Teachers, Postsecondary

25-1194.00   Vocational Education Teachers, Postsecondary

25-1199.99   Postsecondary Teachers, All Other

25-3011.00   Adult Literacy, Remedial Education, and GED Teachers and Instructors

25-3099.99   Teachers and Instructors, All Other

Training and Education Directors

11-3042.00   Training and Development Managers

11-3049.99   Human Resources Managers, All Other

11-9033.00   Education Administrators, Postsecondary

11-9039.99   Education Administrators, All Other

25-3099.99   Teachers and Instructors, All Other

25-9031.00   Instructional Coordinators

27-3041.00   Editors

Training Specialists and Instructors

13-1073.00   Training and Development Specialists

25-3099.99   Teachers and Instructors, All Other

39-9032.00   Recreation Workers

Machine Operator/Production Occupations

O*NET Number	Job Title

Machinists

49-9041.00   Industrial Machinery Mechanics

51-2041.00   Structural Metal Fabricators and Fitters

51-4011.00   Computer-Controlled Machine Tool Operators, Metal and Plastic

51-4012.00   Numerical Tool and Process Control Programmers

51-4041.00   Machinists

(continued)

(continued)

Machine Operator/Production Occupations

O*NET Number | **Job Title**

Power Plant Operators

19-4051.01	Nuclear Equipment Operation Technicians
49-1011.00	First-Line Supervisors/Managers of Mechanics, Installers, and Repairers
49-2095.00	Electrical and Electronics Repairers, Powerhouse, Substation, and Relay
49-9041.00	Industrial Machinery Mechanics
51-1011.00	First-Line Supervisors/Managers of Production and Operating Workers
51-8011.00	Nuclear Power Reactor Operators
51-8013.00	Power Plant Operators
51-8021.00	Stationary Engineers and Boiler Operators
51-8092.00	Gas Plant Operators
51-8099.99	Plant and System Operators, All Other

Printing Specialists

51-5011.00	Bindery Workers
51-5021.00	Job Printers
51-5022.00	Prepress Technicians and Workers
51-5023.00	Printing Machine Operators

Survival Equipment Specialists

49-1011.00	First-Line Supervisors/Managers of Mechanics, Installers, and Repairers
49-3011.00	Aircraft Mechanics and Service Technicians
49-9041.00	Industrial Machinery Mechanics
49-9042.00	Maintenance and Repair Workers, General
49-9043.00	Maintenance Workers, Machinery
49-9093.00	Fabric Menders, Except Garment
49-9096.00	Riggers
49-9099.99	Installation, Maintenance, and Repair Workers, All Other
51-9061.00	Inspectors, Testers, Sorters, Samplers, and Weighers

Water and Sewage Treatment Plant Operators

47-2151.00	Pipelayers
49-1011.00	First-Line Supervisors/Managers of Mechanics, Installers, and Repairers
49-9041.00	Industrial Machinery Mechanics
51-1011.00	First-Line Supervisors/Managers of Production and Operating Workers
51-8031.00	Water and Liquid Waste Treatment Plant and System Operators

Welders and Metal Workers

47-2152.01	Pipe Fitters and Steamfitters
47-2152.02	Plumbers
47-2211.00	Sheet Metal Workers
47-2221.00	Structural Iron and Steel Workers
49-1011.00	First-Line Supervisors/Managers of Mechanics, Installers, and Repairers
49-3011.00	Aircraft Mechanics and Service Technicians
51-1011.00	First-Line Supervisors/Managers of Production and Operating Workers
51-2041.00	Structural Metal Fabricators and Fitters
51-4011.00	Computer-Controlled Machine Tool Operators, Metal and Plastic
51-4041.00	Machinists
51-4121.00	Welders, Cutters, Solderers, and Brazers
51-4121.06	Welders, Cutters, and Welder Fitters
51-4121.07	Solderers and Brazers
51-4191.00	Heat Treating Equipment Setters, Operators, and Tenders, Metal and Plastic
51-4192.00	Lay-Out Workers, Metal and Plastic

Media and Public Affairs Occupations

O*NET Number | **Job Title**

Audiovisual and Broadcast Directors

11-1021.00	General and Operations Managers
11-2031.00	Public Relations Managers
11-3042.00	Training and Development Managers
23-2091.00	Court Reporters
27-1011.00	Art Directors
27-1013.00	Fine Artists, Including Painters, Sculptors, and Illustrators
27-2012.02	Directors—Stage, Motion Pictures, Television, and Radio
27-2012.03	Program Directors
27-2012.04	Talent Directors
27-2012.05	Technical Directors/Managers
27-3031.00	Public Relations Specialists
27-3041.00	Editors
27-4021.00	Photographers

Audiovisual and Broadcast Technicians

27-2012.02	Directors—Stage, Motion Pictures, Television, and Radio
27-2012.03	Program Directors
27-2012.05	Technical Directors/Managers
27-3011.00	Radio and Television Announcers
27-3021.00	Broadcast News Analysts
27-3022.00	Reporters and Correspondents
27-3043.04	Copy Writers
27-3099.99	Media and Communication Workers, All Other
27-4011.00	Audio and Video Equipment Technicians
27-4012.00	Broadcast Technicians
27-4031.00	Camera Operators, Television, Video, and Motion Picture
27-4032.00	Film and Video Editors
27-4099.99	Media and Communication Equipment Workers, All Other

49-2097.00 Electronic Home Entertainment Equipment
Installers and Repairers

Broadcast Journalists and Newswriters
23-2091.00 Court Reporters
27-3011.00 Radio and Television Announcers
27-3021.00 Broadcast News Analysts
27-3022.00 Reporters and Correspondents
27-3031.00 Public Relations Specialists
27-3041.00 Editors
27-3043.04 Copy Writers
27-3043.05 Poets, Lyricists and Creative Writers
27-4021.00 Photographers

Graphic Designers and Illustrators
27-1011.00 Art Directors
27-1012.00 Craft Artists
27-1013.00 Fine Artists, Including Painters, Sculptors, and
Illustrators
27-1014.00 Multi-Media Artists and Animators
27-1024.00 Graphic Designers
27-4099.99 Media and Communication Equipment Workers,
All Other
43-9031.00 Desktop Publishers

Interpreters and Translators
27-3091.00 Interpreters and Translators
43-9061.00 Office Clerks, General

Music Directors
27-2041.01 Music Directors
27-2041.04 Music Composers and Arrangers

Musicians
27-2041.01 Music Directors
27-2041.04 Music Composers and Arrangers
27-2042.00 Musicians and Singers
27-2042.01 Singers
27-2042.02 Musicians, Instrumental

Photographic Specialists
27-4021.00 Photographers
27-4031.00 Camera Operators, Television, Video, and
Motion Picture
51-9131.00 Photographic Process Workers
51-9132.00 Photographic Processing Machine Operators

Public Information Officers
11-2031.00 Public Relations Managers
27-3031.00 Public Relations Specialists
27-3041.00 Editors

Protective Service Occupations

O*NET Number	Job Title

Emergency Management Officers
11-1021.00 General and Operations Managers
13-1061.00 Emergency Management Specialists

Emergency Management Specialists
13-1061.00 Emergency Management Specialists
19-4099.99 Life, Physical, and Social Science Technicians,
All Other
49-9099.99 Installation, Maintenance, and Repair Workers,
All Other

Firefighters
13-1061.00 Emergency Management Specialists
33-1021.01 Municipal Fire Fighting and Prevention
Supervisors
33-2011.01 Municipal Fire Fighters

Law Enforcement and Security Officers
11-1021.00 General and Operations Managers
11-9199.99 Managers, All Other
33-1011.00 First-Line Supervisors/Managers of Correctional
Officers
33-1012.00 First-Line Supervisors/Managers of Police and
Detectives
33-1099.99 First-Line Supervisors/Managers, Protective
Service Workers, All Other
33-3021.03 Criminal Investigators and Special Agents

Law Enforcement and Security Specialists
33-1012.00 First-Line Supervisors/Managers of Police and
Detectives
33-3012.00 Correctional Officers and Jailers
33-3021.01 Police Detectives
33-3021.03 Criminal Investigators and Special Agents
33-3051.00 Police and Sheriff's Patrol Officers
33-3051.01 Police Patrol Officers
33-3051.03 Sheriffs and Deputy Sheriffs
33-3052.00 Transit and Railroad Police
33-9032.00 Security Guards
33-9092.00 Lifeguards, Ski Patrol, and Other Recreational
Protective Service Workers

Support Service Occupations

O*NET Number	Job Title

Caseworkers and Counselors
21-1023.00	Mental Health and Substance Abuse Social Workers
21-1029.99	Social Workers, All Other
21-1092.00	Probation Officers and Correctional Treatment Specialists
21-1093.00	Social and Human Service Assistants
29-2053.00	Psychiatric Technicians

Chaplains
21-2011.00	Clergy
21-2021.00	Directors, Religious Activities and Education

Food Service Managers
11-9051.00	Food Service Managers
35-1012.00	First-Line Supervisors/Managers of Food Preparation and Serving Workers

Food Service Specialists
35-1011.00	Chefs and Head Cooks
35-1012.00	First-Line Supervisors/Managers of Food Preparation and Serving Workers
35-2012.00	Cooks, Institution and Cafeteria
35-2014.00	Cooks, Restaurant
35-2015.00	Cooks, Short Order
35-2021.00	Food Preparation Workers
35-3021.00	Combined Food Preparation and Serving Workers, Including Fast Food

Religious Program Specialists
21-2021.00	Directors, Religious Activities and Education
21-2099.99	Religious Workers, All Other
43-9061.00	Office Clerks, General

Social Workers
21-1021.00	Child, Family, and School Social Workers
21-1022.00	Medical and Public Health Social Workers
21-1023.00	Mental Health and Substance Abuse Social Workers
21-1029.99	Social Workers, All Other

Transportation Management Occupations

O*NET Number	Job Title

Air Traffic Control Managers
11-3071.01	Transportation Managers
53-2021.00	Air Traffic Controllers

Airplane Navigators
53-2011.00	Airline Pilots, Copilots, and Flight Engineers
53-2012.00	Commercial Pilots

Airplane Pilots
53-2011.00	Airline Pilots, Copilots, and Flight Engineers
53-2012.00	Commercial Pilots

Helicopter Pilots
53-2011.00	Airline Pilots, Copilots, and Flight Engineers
53-2012.00	Commercial Pilots

Ship and Submarine Officers
11-1021.00	General and Operations Managers
11-9199.99	Managers, All Other
49-1011.00	First-Line Supervisors/Managers of Mechanics, Installers, and Repairers
49-9092.00	Commercial Divers
53-5021.01	Ship and Boat Captains
53-5021.03	Pilots, Ship

Ship Engineers
17-2131.00	Materials Engineers
17-2141.00	Mechanical Engineers
17-2199.99	Engineers, All Other
49-1011.00	First-Line Supervisors/Managers of Mechanics, Installers, and Repairers
53-1031.00	First-Line Supervisors/Managers of Transportation and Material-Moving Machine and Vehicle Operators
53-5031.00	Ship Engineers

Transportation Maintenance Managers
11-3051.00	Industrial Production Managers
11-3071.01	Transportation Managers
17-2011.00	Aerospace Engineers
17-2112.00	Industrial Engineers
49-1011.00	First-Line Supervisors/Managers of Mechanics, Installers, and Repairers
51-1011.00	First-Line Supervisors/Managers of Production and Operating Workers

Transportation Managers
11-1021.00	General and Operations Managers
11-3071.00	Transportation, Storage, and Distribution Managers
11-3071.01	Transportation Managers
11-3071.02	Storage and Distribution Managers
13-1081.00	Logisticians
53-2022.00	Airfield Operations Specialists

Transportation/Material Handling Occupations

O*NET Number	Job Title

Air Traffic Controllers
53-2021.00	Air Traffic Controllers

Aircraft Launch and Recovery Specialists
33-2011.01	Municipal Fire Fighters

Cargo Specialists
11-3071.02	Storage and Distribution Managers
43-5011.00	Cargo and Freight Agents
43-5051.00	Postal Service Clerks
43-5071.00	Shipping, Receiving, and Traffic Clerks
43-5081.04	Order Fillers, Wholesale and Retail Sales
53-1011.00	Aircraft Cargo Handling Supervisors
53-5011.00	Sailors and Marine Oilers
53-7064.00	Packers and Packagers, Hand
53-7199.99	Material Moving Workers, All Other

Flight Engineers
53-2011.00	Airline Pilots, Copilots, and Flight Engineers
53-2012.00	Commercial Pilots

Petroleum Supply Specialists
11-3071.02	Storage and Distribution Managers
19-4031.00	Chemical Technicians
49-9099.99	Installation, Maintenance, and Repair Workers, All Other
51-1011.00	First-Line Supervisors/Managers of Production and Operating Workers
51-8093.00	Petroleum Pump System Operators, Refinery Operators, and Gaugers
51-9061.00	Inspectors, Testers, Sorters, Samplers, and Weighers
53-6031.00	Service Station Attendants
53-7072.00	Pump Operators, Except Wellhead Pumpers

Quartermasters and Boat Operators
53-5011.00	Sailors and Marine Oilers
53-5021.01	Ship and Boat Captains
53-5021.02	Mates—Ship, Boat, and Barge
53-5021.03	Pilots, Ship
53-5022.00	Motorboat Operators

Seamen
53-5011.00	Sailors and Marine Oilers
53-5021.02	Mates—Ship, Boat, and Barge

Transportation Specialists
13-1081.00	Logisticians
39-1021.00	First-Line Supervisors/Managers of Personal Service Workers
39-6031.00	Flight Attendants
41-3041.00	Travel Agents
43-1011.00	First-Line Supervisors/Managers of Office and Administrative Support Workers
43-4181.00	Reservation and Transportation Ticket Agents and Travel Clerks
43-5011.00	Cargo and Freight Agents
43-5061.00	Production, Planning, and Expediting Clerks
43-5071.00	Shipping, Receiving, and Traffic Clerks
53-1011.00	Aircraft Cargo Handling Supervisors
53-1031.00	First-Line Supervisors/Managers of Transportation and Material-Moving Machine and Vehicle Operators
53-4021.00	Railroad Brake, Signal, and Switch Operators
53-7051.00	Industrial Truck and Tractor Operators

Vehicle Drivers
47-2073.00	Operating Engineers and Other Construction Equipment Operators
53-1031.00	First-Line Supervisors/Managers of Transportation and Material-Moving Machine and Vehicle Operators
53-3021.00	Bus Drivers, Transit and Intercity
53-3032.00	Truck Drivers, Heavy and Tractor-Trailer
53-3033.00	Truck Drivers, Light or Delivery Services
53-3041.00	Taxi Drivers and Chauffeurs
53-3099.99	Motor Vehicle Operators, All Other

Warehousing and Distribution Specialists
13-1081.00	Logisticians
15-1061.00	Database Administrators
43-1011.00	First-Line Supervisors/Managers of Office and Administrative Support Workers
43-3031.00	Bookkeeping, Accounting, and Auditing Clerks
43-3061.00	Procurement Clerks
43-5051.00	Postal Service Clerks
43-5061.00	Production, Planning, and Expediting Clerks
43-5071.00	Shipping, Receiving, and Traffic Clerks
43-5081.03	Stock Clerks—Stockroom, Warehouse, or Storage Yard
43-5081.04	Order Fillers, Wholesale and Retail Sales
43-9011.00	Computer Operators
53-7062.00	Laborers and Freight, Stock, and Material Movers, Hand

Vehicle and Machinery Mechanic Occupations

O*NET Number	Job Title

Aircraft Mechanics
43-5061.00	Production, Planning, and Expediting Clerks
49-1011.00	First-Line Supervisors/Managers of Mechanics, Installers, and Repairers
49-2091.00	Avionics Technicians

(continued)

(continued)

Vehicle and Machinery Mechanic Occupations

O*NET Number	Job Title
49-2094.00	Electrical and Electronics Repairers, Commercial and Industrial Equipment
49-3011.00	Aircraft Mechanics and Service Technicians
51-2011.00	Aircraft Structure, Surfaces, Rigging, and Systems Assemblers
51-9122.00	Painters, Transportation Equipment

Automotive and Heavy Equipment Mechanics

47-1011.00	First-Line Supervisors/Managers of Construction Trades and Extraction Workers
47-4021.00	Elevator Installers and Repairers
49-1011.00	First-Line Supervisors/Managers of Mechanics, Installers, and Repairers
49-2093.00	Electrical and Electronics Installers and Repairers, Transportation Equipment
49-2094.00	Electrical and Electronics Repairers, Commercial and Industrial Equipment
49-2096.00	Electronic Equipment Installers and Repairers, Motor Vehicles
49-3021.00	Automotive Body and Related Repairers
49-3023.01	Automotive Master Mechanics
49-3023.02	Automotive Specialty Technicians
49-3031.00	Bus and Truck Mechanics and Diesel Engine Specialists
49-3042.00	Mobile Heavy Equipment Mechanics, Except Engines
49-3043.00	Rail Car Repairers
49-9041.00	Industrial Machinery Mechanics
49-9042.00	Maintenance and Repair Workers, General

Heating and Cooling Mechanics

47-2151.00	Pipelayers
47-2152.02	Plumbers
49-1011.00	First-Line Supervisors/Managers of Mechanics, Installers, and Repairers
49-9021.01	Heating and Air Conditioning Mechanics and Installers
49-9021.02	Refrigeration Mechanics and Installers
49-9041.00	Industrial Machinery Mechanics

Marine Engine Mechanics

47-4021.00	Elevator Installers and Repairers
49-2094.00	Electrical and Electronics Repairers, Commercial and Industrial Equipment
49-3031.00	Bus and Truck Mechanics and Diesel Engine Specialists
49-3042.00	Mobile Heavy Equipment Mechanics, Except Engines
49-3051.00	Motorboat Mechanics
49-9041.00	Industrial Machinery Mechanics
49-9042.00	Maintenance and Repair Workers, General
51-8013.00	Power Plant Operators
53-5031.00	Ship Engineers

Powerhouse Mechanics

49-1011.00	First-Line Supervisors/Managers of Mechanics, Installers, and Repairers
49-2095.00	Electrical and Electronics Repairers, Powerhouse, Substation, and Relay
49-3042.00	Mobile Heavy Equipment Mechanics, Except Engines
49-3053.00	Outdoor Power Equipment and Other Small Engine Mechanics
49-9012.00	Control and Valve Installers and Repairers, Except Mechanical Door
49-9041.00	Industrial Machinery Mechanics
49-9042.00	Maintenance and Repair Workers, General
51-8013.00	Power Plant Operators
51-8021.00	Stationary Engineers and Boiler Operators

Method 6: Browse an Alphabetical Listing of Job Titles

Another way you can use the book is to find jobs by their titles. The index, which starts on page 663, contains an alphabetical listing of all job titles.

When to Use This Method: If you are interested in more information about certain jobs, use the index to find the job title. Then turn to the page listed to find the complete job description.

PART II

O*NET Job Descriptions

This is the book's main section, and it provides information-packed descriptions for the nearly 950 jobs in the O*NET database. Descriptions are arranged by their O*NET number and in logical groupings of related jobs.

See the introduction for more details on how this section is organized. In addition, a sample job description there points out the important features of each entry. The introduction also offers helpful information on how to use and interpret the descriptions.

If you are looking for a list of the job descriptions included here, see the table of contents. Also, all job titles appear alphabetically in the index.

11-0000
Management Occupations

11-1000 Top Executives

11-1011.00 Chief Executives

- **Education/Training Required: Work experience plus degree**
- **Employed: 321,300**
- **Annual Earnings: $142,440**
- **Growth: 14.9%**
- **Annual Job Openings: 38,000**

Determine and formulate policies and provide the overall direction of companies or private and public sector organizations within the guidelines set up by a board of directors or similar governing body. Plan, direct, or coordinate operational activities at the highest level of management with the help of subordinate executives and staff managers.

Direct and coordinate an organization's financial and budget activities in order to fund operations, maximize investments, and increase efficiency. Confer with board members, organization officials, and staff members to discuss issues, coordinate activities, and resolve problems. Analyze operations to evaluate performance of a company and its staff in meeting objectives and to determine areas of potential cost reduction, program improvement, or policy change. Direct, plan, and implement policies, objectives, and activities of organizations or businesses in order to ensure continuing operations, to maximize returns on investments, and to increase productivity. Prepare budgets for approval, including those for funding and implementation of programs. Direct and coordinate activities of businesses or departments concerned with production, pricing, sales, and/or distribution of products. Negotiate or approve contracts and agreements with suppliers, distributors, federal and state agencies, and other organizational entities. Review reports submitted by staff members in order to recommend approval or to suggest changes. Appoint department heads or managers and assign or delegate responsibilities to them. Direct human resources activities, including the approval of human resource plans and activities, the selection of directors and other high-level staff, and establishment and organization of major departments. Preside over or serve on boards of directors, management committees, or other governing boards. Prepare and present reports concerning activities, expenses, budgets, government statutes and rulings, and other items affecting businesses or program services. Establish departmental responsibilities and coordinate functions among departments and sites. Implement corrective action plans to solve organizational or departmental problems. Coordinate the development and implementation of budgetary control systems, record-keeping systems, and other administrative control processes. Direct non-merchandising departments such as advertising, purchasing, credit, and accounting. Deliver speeches, write articles, and present information at meetings or conventions in order to promote services, exchange ideas, and accomplish objectives.

GOE Information—**Interest Area:** 04. Business and Administration. **Work Group:** 04.01. Managerial Work in General Business. **Personality Type**—Enterprising. Enterprising occupations frequently involve starting up and carrying out projects. These occupations can involve leading people and making many decisions. They sometimes require risk taking and often deal with business. **Work Values**—Authority; Social Status; Working Conditions; Creativity; Autonomy; Responsibility. **Skills**—Management of Financial Resources; Management of Material Resources; Negotiation; Judgment and Decision Making; Management of Personnel Resources; Systems Evaluation. **Abilities**—*Cognitive:* Number Facility; Written Expression; Mathematical Reasoning; Memorization; Fluency of Ideas; Written Comprehension. *Psychomotor:* None met the criteria. *Physical:* None met the criteria. *Sensory:* Speech Clarity; Speech Recognition; Near Vision; Auditory Attention. **General Work Activities**—*Information Input:* Getting Information; Identifying Objects, Actions, and Events; Monitoring Processes, Materials, or Surroundings. *Mental Process:* Making Decisions and Solving Problems; Developing Objectives and Strategies; Organizing, Planning, and Prioritizing. *Work Output:* Interacting With Computers. *Interacting with Others:* Communicating with Persons Outside Organization; Establishing and Maintaining Interpersonal Relationships; Communicating with Other Workers. **Physical Work Conditions**—Indoors; Sitting. **Other Job Characteristics**—Need to Be Exact or Accurate; Errors Have Important Consequences; Repeat Same Tasks.

Experience—Job Zone 5. Extensive skill, knowledge, and experience are needed. **Job Preparation**—SVP 8.0 and above—four years to more than 10 years. **Knowledges**—Administration and Management; Economics and Accounting; Sales and Marketing; Personnel and Human Resources; Law and Government; Customer and Personal Service. **Instructional Programs**—Business Administration/Management; Business/Commerce, General; Entrepreneurship/Entrepreneurial Studies; International Business/Trade/Commerce; International Relations and Affairs; Public Administration; Public Administration and Services, Other; Public Policy Analysis; Transportation/Transportation Management.

Related SOC Job—11-1011 Chief Executives. **Related OOH Job**—Top Executives. **Related DOT Jobs**—050.117-010 Director, Employment Research and Planning; 079.167-010 Community-Services-and-Health-Education Officer; 090.117-034 President, Educational Institution; 099.117-022 Superintendent, Schools; 137.137-010 Director, Translation; 168.167-090 Manager, Regulated Program; 169.117-010 Executive Secretary, State Board of Nursing; 185.117-010 Manager, Department Store; 185.167-062 Supervisor, Liquor Stores and Agencies; 186.117-022 Deputy Insurance Commissioner; others.

11-1021.00 General and Operations Managers

- **Education/Training Required: Work experience plus degree**
- **Employed: 1,663,810**
- **Annual Earnings: $81,480**
- **Growth: 17.0%**
- **Annual Job Openings: 208,000**

Plan, direct, or coordinate the operations of companies or public and private sector organizations. Duties and responsibilities include formulating policies, managing daily operations, and planning the use of materials and human resources, but are too diverse and general in nature to be classified in any one functional area of management or administration, such as personnel, purchasing, or administrative services. Includes owners and managers who head small business establishments whose duties are primarily managerial.

Direct and coordinate activities of businesses or departments concerned with the production, pricing, sales, or distribution of products. Manage staff, preparing work schedules and assigning specific duties. Review financial statements, sales and activity reports, and other performance data to measure productivity and goal achievement and to determine areas needing cost reduction and program improvement. Establish and implement departmental policies, goals, objectives, and procedures, conferring with board members, organization officials, and staff members as necessary. Determine staffing requirements and interview, hire, and train new employees or oversee those personnel processes. Monitor businesses and agencies to ensure that they efficiently and effectively provide needed services while staying within budgetary limits. Oversee activities directly related to making products or providing services. Direct and coordinate organization's financial and budget activities to fund operations, maximize investments, and increase efficiency. Determine goods and services to be sold and set prices and credit terms based on forecasts of customer demand. Manage the movement of goods into and out of production facilities. Locate, select, and procure merchandise for resale, representing management in purchase negotiations. Perform sales floor work such as greeting and assisting customers, stocking shelves, and taking inventory. Develop and implement product marketing strategies including advertising campaigns and sales promotions. Plan and direct activities such as sales promotions, coordinating with other department heads as required. Direct non-merchandising departments of businesses, such as advertising and purchasing. Recommend locations for new facilities or oversee the remodeling of current facilities. Plan store layouts and design displays.

GOE Information—Interest Area: 04. Business and Administration. **Work Group:** 04.01. Managerial Work in General Business. **Personality Type**—No data available. **Work Values**—No data available. **Skills**—Management of Financial Resources; Management of Personnel Resources; Management of Material Resources; Monitoring; Negotiation; Persuasion. **Abilities**—*Cognitive:* Mathematical Reason-ing; Number Facility; Originality; Fluency of Ideas; Deductive Reasoning; Inductive Reasoning. *Psychomotor:* None met the criteria. *Physical:* Trunk Strength. *Sensory:* Speech Recognition; Speech Clarity; Depth Perception; Far Vision; Near Vision; Auditory Attention. **General Work Activities**—*Information Input:* Getting Information; Identifying Objects, Actions, and Events; Monitoring Processes, Materials, or Surroundings. *Mental Process:* Scheduling Work and Activities; Making Decisions and Solving Problems; Evaluating Information Against Standards. *Work Output:* Documenting or Recording Information; Interacting With Computers. *Interacting with Others:* Establishing and Maintaining Interpersonal Relationships; Communicating with Other Workers; Resolving Conflicts and Negotiating with Others. **Physical Work Conditions**—Indoors; Standing; Noisy; Walking and Running. **Other Job Characteristics**—Need to Be Exact or Accurate; Repeat Same Tasks; Errors Have Important Consequences.

Experience—Job Zone 4. A minimum of two to four years of work-related skill, knowledge, or experience is needed. **Job Preparation**—SVP 7.0 to less than 8.0—two years to less than 10 years. **Knowledges**—Sales and Marketing; Administration and Management; Personnel and Human Resources; Economics and Accounting; Customer and Personal Service; Law and Government. **Instructional Programs**—Business Administration/Management; Entrepreneurship/Entrepreneurial Studies; International Business/Trade/Commerce; Public Administration.

Related SOC Job—11-1021 General and Operations Managers. **Related OOH Job**—Top Executives. **Related DOT Jobs**—185.117-010 Manager, Department Store; 189.117-022 Manager, Industrial Organization.

11-1031.00 Legislators

- **Education/Training Required:** Work experience plus degree
- **Employed:** 61,060
- **Annual Earnings:** $15,740
- **Growth:** 2.0%
- **Annual Job Openings:** 3,000

Develop laws and statutes at the federal, state, or local level.

Attend receptions, dinners, and conferences to meet people, exchange views and information, and develop working relationships. Analyze and understand the local and national implications of proposed legislation. Represent their government at local, national, and international meetings and conferences. Promote the industries and products of their electoral districts. Oversee expense allowances, ensuring that accounts are balanced at the end of each fiscal year. Organize and maintain campaign organizations and fundraisers in order to raise money for election or re-election. Evaluate the structure, efficiency, activities, and performance of government agencies. Establish personal offices in local districts or states and manage office staff. Encourage and support party candidates for political office. Conduct "head counts" to help predict the outcome of upcoming votes. Speak to students to encourage and support the development of future political leaders. Alert constituents of government actions and programs by way of newsletters, personal appearances at town meetings, phone calls, and individual meetings. Write, prepare, and deliver statements for the Congressional Record. Vote on motions, amendments, and decisions on whether or not to report a bill out from committee to the assembly floor. Serve on commissions, investigative panels, study groups, and committees in order to examine specialized areas and recommend action. Develop expertise in subject matters related to committee assignments. Appoint nominees to leadership posts or approve such appointments. Determine campaign strategies for media advertising, positions on issues, and public appearances. Debate the merits of proposals and bill amendments during floor sessions, following the appropriate rules of procedure. Seek federal funding for local projects and programs. Hear testimony from constituents, representatives of interest groups, board and commission members, and others with an interest in bills or issues under consideration. Keep abreast of the issues affecting constituents by making personal visits and phone calls, reading local newspapers, and viewing or listening to local broadcasts.

Note: The Department of Labor has not collected some data for this job, so it has fewer details than the other descriptions.

Instructional Programs—Public Administration; Public Administration and Services, Other; Public Policy Analysis.

Related SOC Job—11-1031 Legislators. **Related OOH Job**—Legislators. **Related DOT Job**—No data available.

11-2000 Advertising, Marketing, Promotions, Public Relations, and Sales Managers

11-2011.00 Advertising and Promotions Managers

- **Education/Training Required:** Work experience plus degree
- **Employed:** 41,710
- **Annual Earnings:** $68,860
- **Growth:** 20.3%
- **Annual Job Openings:** 9,000

Plan and direct advertising policies and programs or produce collateral materials, such as posters, contests, coupons, or giveaways, to create extra interest in the purchase of a product or service for a department, for an entire organization, or on an account basis.

Prepare budgets and submit estimates for program costs as part of campaign plan development. Plan and prepare advertising and promotional material to increase sales of products or services, working with customers, company officials, sales departments, and advertising agencies. Assist with annual budget development. Inspect layouts and advertising copy and edit scripts, audiotapes and videotapes, and other promotional material for adherence to specifications. Coordinate activities of departments, such as sales, graphic arts, media, finance, and research. Prepare and negotiate advertising and sales contracts. Identify and develop contacts for promotional campaigns and industry programs that meet identified buyer targets, such as dealers, distributors, or consumers. Gather and organize information to plan advertising campaigns. Confer with department heads or staff to discuss topics such as contracts, selection of advertising media, or product to be advertised. Confer with clients to provide marketing or technical advice. Monitor and analyze sales promotion results to determine cost-effectiveness of promotion campaigns. Read trade journals and professional literature to stay informed on trends, innovations, and changes that affect media planning. Formulate plans to extend business with established accounts and to transact business as agent for advertising accounts. Provide presentation and product demonstration support during the introduction of new products and services to field staff and customers. Direct, motivate, and monitor the mobilization of a campaign team to advance campaign goals. Plan and execute advertising policies and strategies for organizations. Track program budgets and expenses and campaign response rates to evaluate each campaign based on program objectives and industry norms. Assemble and communicate with a strong, diverse coalition of organizations or public figures, securing their cooperation, support, and action to further campaign goals. Train and direct workers engaged in developing and producing advertisements. Coordinate with the media to disseminate advertising.

GOE Information—Interest Area: 14. Retail and Wholesale Sales and Service. **Work Group:** 14.01. Managerial Work in Retail/Wholesale Sales and Service. **Personality Type—**Artistic. Artistic occupations frequently involve working with forms, designs, and patterns. They often require self-expression, and the work can be done without following a clear set of rules. **Work Values—**Creativity; Authority; Working Conditions; Compensation; Ability Utilization; Achievement. **Skills—**Management of Financial Resources; Service Orientation; Persuasion; Negotiation; Time Management; Coordination. **Abilities—***Cognitive:* Fluency of Ideas; Originality; Number Facility; Written Expression; Mathematical Reasoning; Speed of Closure. *Psychomotor:* None met the criteria. *Physical:* None met the criteria. *Sensory:* Speech Clarity; Speech Recognition; Visual Color Discrimination; Near Vision. **General Work Activities—***Information Input:* Getting Information; Identifying Objects, Actions, and Events; Estimating the Needed Characteristics of Products, Events, or Information. *Mental Process:* Organizing, Planning, and Prioritizing; Making Decisions and Solving Problems; Scheduling Work and Activities. *Work Output:* Interacting With Computers; Documenting or Recording Information. *Interacting with Others:* Communicating with Other Workers; Resolving Conflicts and Negotiating with Others; Establishing and Maintaining Interpersonal Relationships. **Physical Work Conditions—**Sitting; Repetitive Motions. **Other Job Characteristics—**Need to Be Exact or Accurate; Repeat Same Tasks.

Experience—Job Zone 4. A minimum of two to four years of work-related skill, knowledge, or experience is needed. **Job Preparation—**SVP 7.0 to less than 8.0—two years to less than 10 years. **Knowledges—**Sales and Marketing; Fine Arts; Design; Production and Processing; Communications and Media; Clerical Practices. **Instructional Programs—**Advertising; Marketing/Marketing Management, General; Public Relations/Image Management.

Related SOC Job—11-2011 Advertising and Promotions Managers. **Related OOH Job—**Advertising, Marketing, Promotions, Public Relations, and Sales Managers. **Related DOT Jobs—**159.167-022 Executive Producer, Promos; 163.117-018 Manager, Promotion; 164.117-010 Manager, Advertising; 164.117-014 Manager, Advertising Agency; 164.117-018 Media Director; 164.167-010 Account Executive.

11-2021.00 Marketing Managers

- **Education/Training Required: Work experience plus degree**
- **Employed: 166,470**
- **Annual Earnings: $92,680**
- **Growth: 20.8%**
- **Annual Job Openings: 23,000**

Determine the demand for products and services offered by a firm and its competitors and identify potential customers. Develop pricing strategies with the goal of maximizing the firm's profits or share of the market while ensuring that the firm's customers are satisfied. Oversee product development or monitor trends that indicate the need for new products and services.

Develop pricing strategies, balancing firm objectives and customer satisfaction. Identify, develop, and evaluate marketing strategy, based on knowledge of establishment objectives, market characteristics, and cost and markup factors. Evaluate the financial aspects of product development, such as budgets, expenditures, research and development appropriations, and return-on-investment and profit-loss projections. Formulate, direct, and coordinate marketing activities and policies to promote products and services, working with advertising and promotion managers. Direct the hiring, training, and performance evaluations of marketing and sales staff and oversee their daily activities. Negotiate contracts with vendors and distributors to manage product distribution, establishing distribution networks and developing distribution strategies. Consult with product development personnel on product specifications such as design, color, and packaging. Compile lists describing product or service offerings. Use sales forecasting and strategic planning to ensure the sale and profitability of products, lines, or services, analyzing business developments and monitoring market trends. Select products and accessories to be displayed at trade or special production shows. Confer with legal staff to resolve problems such as copyright infringement and royalty sharing with outside producers and distributors. Coordinate and participate in promotional activities and trade shows, working with developers, advertisers, and production managers to market products and services. Advise business and other groups on local, national, and international factors affecting the buying and selling of products and services. Initiate market research studies and analyze their findings. Consult with buying personnel to gain advice regarding the types of products or services expected to be in demand. Conduct economic and commercial surveys to identify potential markets for products and services.

GOE Information—Interest Area: 14. Retail and Wholesale Sales and Service. **Work Group:** 14.01. Managerial Work in Retail/Wholesale Sales and Service. **Personality Type—**Enterprising. Enterprising occupations frequently involve starting up and carrying out projects. These occupations can involve leading people and making many decisions. They sometimes require risk taking and often deal with business. **Work Values—**Creativity; Working Conditions; Authority; Recognition; Ability Utilization; Autonomy. **Skills—**Management of

Financial Resources; Management of Personnel Resources; Operations Analysis; Negotiation; Persuasion; Coordination. **Abilities**—*Cognitive:* Fluency of Ideas; Mathematical Reasoning; Originality; Deductive Reasoning; Written Expression; Inductive Reasoning. *Psychomotor:* None met the criteria. *Physical:* None met the criteria. *Sensory:* Speech Recognition; Near Vision; Speech Clarity. **General Work Activities**—*Information Input:* Getting Information; Identifying Objects, Actions, and Events; Monitoring Processes, Materials, or Surroundings. *Mental Process:* Making Decisions and Solving Problems; Organizing, Planning, and Prioritizing; Updating and Using Relevant Knowledge. *Work Output:* Interacting With Computers; Documenting or Recording Information. *Interacting with Others:* Communicating with Persons Outside Organization; Establishing and Maintaining Interpersonal Relationships; Resolving Conflicts and Negotiating with Others. **Physical Work Conditions**—Indoors; Sitting. **Other Job Characteristics**—Need to Be Exact or Accurate.

Experience—Job Zone 4. A minimum of two to four years of work-related skill, knowledge, or experience is needed. **Job Preparation**—SVP 7.0 to less than 8.0—two years to less than 10 years. **Knowledges**—Sales and Marketing; Customer and Personal Service; Administration and Management; Personnel and Human Resources; Communications and Media; Psychology. **Instructional Programs**—Apparel and Textile Marketing Management; Consumer Merchandising or Retailing Management; International Marketing; Marketing Research; Marketing, Other; Marketing/Marketing Management, General.

Related SOC Job—11-2021 Marketing Managers. **Related OOH Job**—Advertising, Marketing, Promotions, Public Relations, and Sales Managers. **Related DOT Jobs**—162.117-034 Media Buyer; 163.117-022 Director, Media Marketing; 164.117-022 Media Planner; 185.157-010 Fashion Coordinator; 185.157-014 Supervisor of Sales; 187.167-170 Manager, World Trade and Maritime Division.

11-2022.00 Sales Managers

- **Education/Training Required: Work experience plus degree**
- **Employed: 317,970**
- **Annual Earnings: $87,580**
- **Growth: 19.7%**
- **Annual Job Openings: 40,000**

Direct the actual distribution or movement of a product or service to the customer. Coordinate sales distribution by establishing sales territories, quotas, and goals and establish training programs for sales representatives. Analyze sales statistics gathered by staff to determine sales potential and inventory requirements and monitor the preferences of customers.

Resolve customer complaints regarding sales and service. Monitor customer preferences to determine focus of sales efforts. Direct and coordinate activities involving sales of manufactured products, services, commodities, real estate, or other subjects of sale. Determine price schedules and discount rates. Review operational records and reports to project sales and determine profitability. Direct, coordinate, and review activities in sales and service accounting and record-keeping and in receiving and shipping operations. Confer or consult with department heads to plan advertising services and to secure information on equipment and customer specifications. Advise dealers and distributors on policies and operating procedures to ensure functional effectiveness of business. Prepare budgets and approve budget expenditures. Represent company at trade association meetings to promote products. Plan and direct staffing, training, and performance evaluations to develop and control sales and service

programs. Visit franchised dealers to stimulate interest in establishment or expansion of leasing programs. Confer with potential customers regarding equipment needs and advise customers on types of equipment to purchase. Oversee regional and local sales managers and their staffs. Direct clerical staff to keep records of export correspondence, bid requests, and credit collections and to maintain current information on tariffs, licenses, and restrictions. Direct foreign sales and service outlets of an organization. Assess marketing potential of new and existing store locations, considering statistics and expenditures.

GOE Information—**Interest Area:** 14. Retail and Wholesale Sales and Service. **Work Group:** 14.01. Managerial Work in Retail/Wholesale Sales and Service. **Personality Type**—Enterprising. Enterprising occupations frequently involve starting up and carrying out projects. These occupations can involve leading people and making many decisions. They sometimes require risk taking and often deal with business. **Work Values**—Authority; Compensation; Creativity; Advancement; Autonomy; Working Conditions. **Skills**—Management of Personnel Resources; Negotiation; Persuasion; Service Orientation; Time Management; Operations Analysis. **Abilities**—*Cognitive:* Mathematical Reasoning; Number Facility; Originality; Fluency of Ideas; Speed of Closure; Memorization. *Psychomotor:* Multilimb Coordination. *Physical:* None met the criteria. *Sensory:* Speech Recognition; Speech Clarity; Depth Perception; Near Vision. **General Work Activities**—*Information Input:* Getting Information; Identifying Objects, Actions, and Events; Monitoring Processes, Materials, or Surroundings. *Mental Process:* Organizing, Planning, and Prioritizing; Making Decisions and Solving Problems; Thinking Creatively. *Work Output:* Interacting With Computers; Handling and Moving Objects; Documenting or Recording Information. *Interacting with Others:* Communicating with Persons Outside Organization; Establishing and Maintaining Interpersonal Relationships; Communicating with Other Workers. **Physical Work Conditions**—Indoors; Sitting. **Other Job Characteristics**—Need to Be Exact or Accurate; Repeat Same Tasks.

Experience—Job Zone 4. A minimum of two to four years of work-related skill, knowledge, or experience is needed. **Job Preparation**—SVP 7.0 to less than 8.0—two years to less than 10 years. **Knowledges**—Sales and Marketing; Computers and Electronics; Mathematics; Law and Government; Administration and Management; Customer and Personal Service. **Instructional Programs**—Business Administration/Management; Business/Commerce, General; Consumer Merchandising or Retailing Management; Marketing, Other; Marketing/Marketing Management, General.

Related SOC Job—11-2022 Sales Managers. **Related OOH Job**—Advertising, Marketing, Promotions, Public Relations, and Sales Managers. **Related DOT Jobs**—163.117-014 Manager, Export; 163.167-010 Manager, Advertising; 163.167-018 Manager, Sales; 163.167-022 Manager, Utility Sales and Service; 163.267-010 Field Representative; 185.117-014 Area Supervisor, Retail Chain Store; 185.167-042 Manager, Professional Equipment Sales-and-Service; 187.167-162 Manager, Vehicle Leasing and Rental; 189.117-018 Manager, Customer Technical Services.

11-2031.00 Public Relations Managers

- **Education/Training Required: Work experience plus degree**
- **Employed: 43,770**
- **Annual Earnings: $76,450**
- **Growth: 21.7%**
- **Annual Job Openings: 5,000**

Plan and direct public relations programs designed to create and maintain a favorable public image for employer or client or, if engaged in fundraising, plan and direct activities to solicit and maintain funds for special projects and nonprofit organizations.

Identify main client groups and audiences and determine the best way to communicate publicity information to them. Write interesting and effective press releases, prepare information for media kits, and develop and maintain company Internet or intranet Web pages. Develop and maintain the company's corporate image and identity, which includes the use of logos and signage. Manage communications budgets. Manage special events such as sponsorship of races, parties introducing new products, or other activities the firm supports to gain public attention through the media without advertising directly. Draft speeches for company executives and arrange interviews and other forms of contact for them. Assign, supervise, and review the activities of public relations staff. Evaluate advertising and promotion programs for compatibility with public relations efforts. Establish and maintain effective working relationships with local and municipal government officials and media representatives. Confer with labor relations managers to develop internal communications that keep employees informed of company activities. Direct activities of external agencies, establishments, and departments that develop and implement communication strategies and information programs. Formulate policies and procedures related to public information programs, working with public relations executives. Respond to requests for information about employers' activities or status. Establish goals for soliciting funds, develop policies for collection and safeguarding of contributions, and coordinate disbursement of funds. Facilitate consumer relations or the relationship between parts of the company such as the managers and employees or different branch offices. Maintain company archives. Manage in-house communication courses. Produce films and other video products, regulate their distribution, and operate film library. Observe and report on social, economic, and political trends that might affect employers.

GOE Information—Interest Area: 03. Arts and Communication. **Work Group:** 03.01. Managerial Work in Arts and Communication. **Personality Type—**No data available. **Work Values—**No data available. **Skills—**Management of Financial Resources; Social Perceptiveness; Monitoring; Service Orientation; Writing; Persuasion. **Abilities—***Cognitive:* Written Expression; Fluency of Ideas; Originality; Number Facility; Written Comprehension; Oral Expression. *Psychomotor:* None met the criteria. *Physical:* None met the criteria. *Sensory:* Speech Recognition; Speech Clarity; Far Vision; Near Vision; Visual Color Discrimination. **General Work Activities—***Information Input:* Getting Information; Monitoring Processes, Materials, or Surroundings; Identifying Objects, Actions, and Events. *Mental Process:* Organizing, Planning, and Prioritizing; Updating and Using Relevant Knowledge; Making Decisions and Solving Problems. *Work Output:* Interacting With Computers; Documenting or Recording Information. *Interacting with Others:* Establishing and Maintaining Interpersonal Relationships; Communicating with Persons Outside Organization; Communicating with Other Workers. **Physical Work Conditions—**Indoors; Sitting. **Other Job Characteristics—**Need to Be Exact or Accurate.

Experience—Job Zone 4. A minimum of two to four years of work-related skill, knowledge, or experience is needed. **Job Preparation—**SVP 7.0 to less than 8.0—two years to less than 10 years. **Knowledges—**Sales and Marketing; Economics and Accounting; Foreign Language; Education and Training; Law and Government; English Language. **Instructional Program—**Public Relations/Image Management.

Related SOC Job—11-2031 Public Relations Managers. **Related OOH Job—**Advertising, Marketing, Promotions, Public Relations, and Sales Managers. **Related DOT Jobs—**163.117-026 Director, Underwriter Solicitation; 165.117-010 Director, Fundraising; 165.117-014 Director, Funds Development; 165.167-014 Public-Relations Representative; 293.157-010 Fund Raiser I.

11-3000 Operations Specialties Managers

11-3011.00 Administrative Services Managers

- **Education/Training Required: Work experience plus degree**
- **Employed: 239,410**
- **Annual Earnings: $64,020**
- **Growth: 16.9%**
- **Annual Job Openings: 25,000**

Plan, direct, or coordinate supportive services of an organization, such as recordkeeping, mail distribution, telephone operator/receptionist, and other office support services. May oversee facilities planning and maintenance and custodial operations.

Monitor the facility to ensure that it remains safe, secure, and well-maintained. Direct or coordinate the supportive services department of a business, agency, or organization. Set goals and deadlines for the department. Prepare and review operational reports and schedules to ensure accuracy and efficiency. Analyze internal processes and recommend and implement procedural or policy changes to improve operations such as supply changes or the disposal of records. Acquire, distribute, and store supplies. Plan, administer, and control budgets for contracts, equipment, and supplies. Oversee construction and renovation projects to improve efficiency and to ensure that facilities meet environmental, health, and security standards and comply with government regulations. Hire and terminate clerical and administrative personnel. Oversee the maintenance and repair of machinery, equipment, and electrical and mechanical systems. Manage leasing of facility space. Participate in architectural and engineering planning and design, including space and installation management. Conduct classes to teach procedures to staff. Dispose of, or oversee the disposal of, surplus or unclaimed property.

GOE Information—Interest Area: 04. Business and Administration. **Work Group:** 04.02. Managerial Work in Business Detail. **Personality Type—**Enterprising. Enterprising occupations frequently involve starting up and carrying out projects. These occupations can involve leading people and making many decisions. They sometimes require risk taking and often deal with business. **Work Values—**Authority; Working Conditions; Responsibility; Advancement; Autonomy; Creativity. **Skills—**Management of Financial Resources; Management of Personnel Resources; Programming; Service Orientation; Coordination; Monitoring. **Abilities—***Cognitive:* Written Expression; Memorization; Number Facility; Originality; Oral Expression; Fluency of Ideas. *Psychomotor:* None met the criteria. *Physical:* Trunk Strength. *Sensory:* Near Vision; Speech Recognition; Far Vision; Speech Clarity. **General Work Activities—***Information Input:* Identifying Objects, Actions, and Events; Getting Information; Monitoring Processes, Materials, or Surroundings. *Mental Process:* Organizing, Planning, and Prioritizing; Making Decisions and Solving Problems; Updating and Using Relevant Knowledge. *Work Output:* Documenting or Recording Information; Interacting With

Computers. *Interacting with Others:* Establishing and Maintaining Interpersonal Relationships; Communicating with Other Workers; Resolving Conflicts and Negotiating with Others. **Physical Work Conditions**—Indoors; More Often Sitting Than Standing. **Other Job Characteristics**—Need to Be Exact or Accurate; Repeat Same Tasks; Errors Have Important Consequences; Automation.

Experience—Job Zone 4. A minimum of two to four years of work-related skill, knowledge, or experience is needed. **Job Preparation**—SVP 7.0 to less than 8.0—two years to less than 10 years. **Knowledges**—Personnel and Human Resources; Clerical Practices; Economics and Accounting; Customer and Personal Service; Administration and Management; Law and Government. **Instructional Programs**—Business Administration/Management; Business/Commerce, General; Medical Staff Services Technology/Technician; Medical/Health Management and Clinical Assistant/Specialist; Public Administration; Purchasing, Procurement/Acquisitions, and Contracts Management; Transportation/Transportation Management.

Related SOC Job—11-3011 Administrative Services Managers. **Related OOH Job**—Administrative Services Managers. **Related DOT Jobs**—163.167-026 Property-Disposal Officer; 169.167-034 Manager, Office; 187.117-062 Radiology Administrator; 188.117-130 Court Administrator; 188.167-106 Unclaimed Property Officer; 189.167-014 Director, Service.

11-3021.00 Computer and Information Systems Managers

- **Education/Training Required: Work experience plus degree**
- **Employed: 259,330**
- **Annual Earnings: $96,520**
- **Growth: 25.9%**
- **Annual Job Openings: 25,000**

Plan, direct, or coordinate activities in such fields as electronic data processing, information systems, systems analysis, and computer programming.

Manage backup, security, and user help systems. Consult with users, management, vendors, and technicians to assess computing needs and system requirements. Direct daily operations of department, analyzing workflow, establishing priorities, developing standards, and setting deadlines. Assign and review the work of systems analysts, programmers, and other computer-related workers. Stay abreast of advances in technology. Develop computer information resources, providing for data security and control, strategic computing, and disaster recovery. Review and approve all systems charts and programs prior to their implementation. Evaluate the organization's technology use and needs and recommend improvements, such as hardware and software upgrades. Control operational budget and expenditures. Meet with department heads, managers, supervisors, vendors, and others to solicit cooperation and resolve problems. Develop and interpret organizational goals, policies, and procedures. Recruit, hire, train, and supervise staff or participate in staffing decisions. Review project plans to plan and coordinate project activity. Evaluate data-processing proposals to assess project feasibility and requirements. Prepare and review operational reports or project progress reports. Purchase necessary equipment.

GOE Information—**Interest Area:** 11. Information Technology. **Work Group:** 11.01. Managerial Work in Information Technology. **Personality Type**—Enterprising. Enterprising occupations frequently involve starting up and carrying out projects. These occupations can involve leading people and making many decisions. They sometimes require risk taking and often deal with business. **Work Values**—Authority; Working Conditions; Creativity; Responsibility; Compensation; Advancement. **Skills**—Programming; Management of Financial Resources; Systems Analysis; Operations Analysis; Systems Evaluation; Management of Material Resources. **Abilities**—*Cognitive:* Deductive Reasoning; Originality; Written Comprehension; Oral Comprehension; Inductive Reasoning; Oral Expression. *Psychomotor:* None met the criteria. *Physical:* None met the criteria. *Sensory:* Near Vision; Speech Recognition. **General Work Activities**—*Information Input:* Identifying Objects, Actions, and Events; Getting Information; Monitoring Processes, Materials, or Surroundings. *Mental Process:* Making Decisions and Solving Problems; Updating and Using Relevant Knowledge; Processing Information. *Work Output:* Interacting With Computers; Documenting or Recording Information; Performing General Physical Activities. *Interacting with Others:* Communicating with Other Workers; Resolving Conflicts and Negotiating with Others; Teaching Others. **Physical Work Conditions**—Indoors; Noisy; Sitting; Using Hands on Objects, Tools, or Controls; Repetitive Motions. **Other Job Characteristics**—Need to Be Exact or Accurate.

Experience—Job Zone 5. Extensive skill, knowledge, and experience are needed. **Job Preparation**—SVP 8.0 and above—four years to more than 10 years. **Knowledges**—Clerical Practices; Computers and Electronics; Economics and Accounting; Engineering and Technology; Design; Telecommunications. **Instructional Programs**—Computer and Information Sciences, General; Computer Science; Information Resources Management/CIO Training; Information Science/Studies; Knowledge Management; Management Information Systems, General; Operations Management and Supervision; System Administration/Administrator.

Related SOC Job—11-3021 Computer and Information Systems Managers. **Related OOH Job**—Computer and Information Systems Managers. **Related DOT Jobs**—169.167-030 Manager, Data Processing; 169.167-082 Manager, Computer Operations.

11-3031.00 Financial Managers

- **Education/Training Required: Work experience plus degree**
- **Employed: 471,950**
- **Annual Earnings: $86,280**
- **Growth: 14.8%**
- **Annual Job Openings: 63,000**

The job openings listed here are shared with 11-3031.01 Treasurers and Controllers and 11-3031.02 Financial Managers, Branch or Department.

Plan, direct, and coordinate accounting, investing, banking, insurance, securities, and other financial activities of a branch, office, or department of an establishment.

No task data available.

GOE Information—**Interest Area:** 06. Finance and Insurance. **Work Group:** 06.01. Managerial Work in Finance and Insurance. **Note:** The Department of Labor has not collected some data for this job, so it has fewer details than the other descriptions.

Instructional Programs—Accounting and Business/Management; Accounting and Finance; Credit Management; Finance and Financial Management Services, Other; Finance, General; International Finance; Public Finance.

Related SOC Job—11-3031 Financial Managers. **Related OOH Job**—Financial Managers. **Related DOT Job**—No data available.

11-3031.01 Treasurers and Controllers

- **Education/Training Required: Work experience plus degree**
- **Employed: 471,950**
- **Annual Earnings: $86,280**
- **Growth: 14.8%**
- **Annual Job Openings: 63,000**

The job openings listed here are shared with 11-3031.00 Financial Managers and 11-3031.02 Financial Managers, Branch or Department.

Direct financial activities, such as planning, procurement, and investments, for all or part of an organization.

Prepare and file annual tax returns or prepare financial information so that outside accountants can complete tax returns. Prepare or direct preparation of financial statements, business activity reports, financial position forecasts, annual budgets, and/or reports required by regulatory agencies. Supervise employees performing financial reporting, accounting, billing, collections, payroll, and budgeting duties. Delegate authority for the receipt, disbursement, banking, protection, and custody of funds, securities, and financial instruments. Maintain current knowledge of organizational policies and procedures, federal and state policies and directives, and current accounting standards. Conduct or coordinate audits of company accounts and financial transactions to ensure compliance with state and federal requirements and statutes. Receive and record requests for disbursements; authorize disbursements in accordance with policies and procedures. Monitor financial activities and details such as reserve levels to ensure that all legal and regulatory requirements are met. Monitor and evaluate the performance of accounting and other financial staff; recommend and implement personnel actions such as promotions and dismissals. Develop and maintain relationships with banking, insurance, and non-organizational accounting personnel in order to facilitate financial activities. Coordinate and direct the financial planning, budgeting, procurement, or investment activities of all or part of an organization. Develop internal control policies, guidelines, and procedures for activities such as budget administration, cash and credit management, and accounting. Analyze the financial details of past, present, and expected operations in order to identify development opportunities and areas where improvement is needed. Advise management on short-term and long-term financial objectives, policies, and actions. Provide direction and assistance to other organizational units regarding accounting and budgeting policies and procedures and efficient control and utilization of financial resources. Evaluate needs for procurement of funds and investment of surpluses and make appropriate recommendations.

GOE Information—Interest Area: 06. Finance and Insurance. **Work Group:** 06.01. Managerial Work in Finance and Insurance. **Personality Type**—Enterprising. Enterprising occupations frequently involve starting up and carrying out projects. These occupations can involve leading people and making many decisions. They sometimes require risk taking and often deal with business. **Work Values**—Authority; Working Conditions; Advancement; Ability Utilization; Activity; Creativity. **Skills**—Management of Financial Resources; Management of Material Resources; Management of Personnel Resources; Judgment and Decision Making; Negotiation; Time Management. **Abilities**—*Cognitive:* Number Facility; Mathematical Reasoning; Problem Sensitivity; Written Expression; Deductive Reasoning; Written Comprehension. *Psychomotor:* None met the criteria. *Physical:* None met the criteria. *Sensory:* Speech Recognition; Speech Clarity; Far Vision; Near Vision. **General Work Activities**—*Information Input:* Getting Information; Identifying Objects, Actions, and Events; Estimating the Needed Characteristics of Products, Events, or Information. *Mental Process:* Updating and Using Relevant Knowledge; Organizing, Planning, and Prioritizing; Processing Information. *Work Output:* Interacting With Computers; Documenting or Recording Information. *Interacting with Others:* Establishing and Maintaining Interpersonal Relationships; Monitoring and Controlling Resources; Communicating with Other Workers. **Physical Work Conditions**—Indoors; Sitting. **Other Job Characteristics**—Need to Be Exact or Accurate; Repeat Same Tasks; Errors Have Important Consequences; Automation.

Experience—Job Zone 5. Extensive skill, knowledge, and experience are needed. **Job Preparation**—SVP 8.0 and above—four years to more than 10 years. **Knowledges**—Economics and Accounting; Administration and Management; Personnel and Human Resources; Law and Government; Mathematics; English Language. **Instructional Programs**—Accounting and Business/Management; Accounting and Finance; Credit Management; Finance and Financial Management Services, Other; Finance, General; International Finance; Public Finance.

Related SOC Job—11-3031 Financial Managers. **Related OOH Job**—Financial Managers. **Related DOT Jobs**—160.167-058 Controller; 161.117-018 Treasurer; 186.117-070 Treasurer, Financial Institution; 186.117-078 Vice President, Financial Institution; 186.167-054 Reserve Officer.

11-3031.02 Financial Managers, Branch or Department

- **Education/Training Required: Work experience plus degree**
- **Employed: 471,950**
- **Annual Earnings: $86,280**
- **Growth: 14.8%**
- **Annual Job Openings: 63,000**

The job openings listed here are shared with 11-3031.00 Financial Managers and 11-3031.01 Treasurers and Controllers.

Direct and coordinate financial activities of workers in a branch, office, or department of an establishment, such as branch bank, brokerage firm, risk and insurance department, or credit department.

Establish and maintain relationships with individual and business customers and provide assistance with problems these customers may encounter. Examine, evaluate, and process loan applications. Plan, direct, and coordinate the activities of workers in branches, offices, or departments of such establishments as branch banks, brokerage firms, risk and insurance departments, or credit departments. Oversee the flow of cash and financial instruments. Recruit staff members and oversee training programs. Network within communities to find and attract new business. Approve or reject, or coordinate the approval and rejection of, lines of credit and commercial, real estate, and personal loans. Prepare financial and regulatory reports required by laws, regulations, and boards of directors. Establish procedures for custody and control of assets, records, loan collateral, and securities in order to ensure safekeeping. Review collection reports to determine the status of collections and the amounts of outstanding balances. Prepare operational and risk reports for management analysis. Evaluate financial reporting systems, accounting and collection procedures, and investment activities and make recommendations for changes to procedures, operating systems, budgets, and other financial control functions. Plan, direct, and coordinate risk and insurance programs of establishments to control risks and losses. Submit delinquent accounts to attorneys or outside agencies for collection. Communicate with stockholders and other investors to provide information and to raise capital. Evaluate data pertaining to costs in order to plan budgets. Analyze and classify risks and investments to determine their potential impacts on companies. Review reports of securities transactions and price lists in order to analyze market conditions. Develop and analyze information to assess the current and future financial status of firms. Direct insurance negotiations, select insurance brokers and carriers, and place insurance.

GOE Information—Interest Area: 06. Finance and Insurance. **Work Group:** 06.01. Managerial Work in Finance and Insurance. **Personality Type—**Enterprising. Enterprising occupations frequently involve starting up and carrying out projects. These occupations can involve leading people and making many decisions. They sometimes require risk taking and often deal with business. **Work Values—**Authority; Working Conditions; Recognition; Ability Utilization; Responsibility; Autonomy. **Skills—**Management of Personnel Resources; Management of Financial Resources; Service Orientation; Instructing; Persuasion; Time Management. **Abilities—***Cognitive:* Number Facility; Mathematical Reasoning; Written Expression; Originality; Fluency of Ideas; Deductive Reasoning. *Psychomotor:* None met the criteria. *Physical:* None met the criteria. *Sensory:* Speech Recognition; Speech Clarity; Near Vision. **General Work Activities—***Information Input:* Monitoring Processes, Materials, or Surroundings; Getting Information; Identifying Objects, Actions, and Events. *Mental Process:* Processing Information; Making Decisions and Solving Problems; Updating and Using Relevant Knowledge. *Work Output:* Documenting or Recording Information; Interacting With Computers. *Interacting with Others:* Influencing Others or Selling; Performing for or Working with the Public; Guiding, Directing, and Motivating Subordinates. **Physical Work Conditions—**Indoors; Sitting. **Other Job Characteristics—**Need to Be Exact or Accurate; Automation; Repeat Same Tasks; Errors Have Important Consequences.

Experience—Job Zone 4. A minimum of two to four years of work-related skill, knowledge, or experience is needed. **Job Preparation—**SVP 7.0 to less than 8.0—two years to less than 10 years. **Knowledges—**Economics and Accounting; Sales and Marketing; Personnel and Human Resources; Customer and Personal Service; Clerical Practices; Administration and Management. **Instructional Programs—**Accounting and Finance; Credit Management; Finance and Financial Management Services, Other; Finance, General; International Finance; Public Finance.

Related SOC Job—11-3031 Financial Managers. **Related OOH Job—**Financial Managers. **Related DOT Jobs—**169.167-086 Manager, Credit and Collection; 186.117-066 Risk and Insurance Manager; 186.117-074 Trust Officer; 186.117-082 Foreign-Exchange Dealer; 186.117-086 Manager, Exchange Floor; 186.137-014 Operations Officer; 186.167-070 Assistant Branch Manager, Financial Institution; 186.167-082 Factor; 186.167-086 Manager, Financial Institution.

11-3040.00 Human Resources Managers

- **Education/Training Required: Work experience plus degree**
- **Employed: 156,748**
- **Annual Earnings: No data available**
- **Growth: 20.3%**
- **Annual Job Openings: 4,000**

Plan, direct, and coordinate human resource management activities of an organization to maximize the strategic use of human resources and maintain functions such as employee compensation, recruitment, personnel policies, and regulatory compliance.

Administer compensation, benefits, and performance management systems and safety and recreation programs. Identify staff vacancies and recruit, interview, and select applicants. Allocate human resources, ensuring appropriate matches between personnel. Provide current and prospective employees with information about policies, job duties, working conditions, wages, opportunities for promotion, and employee benefits. Perform difficult staffing duties, including dealing with understaffing, refereeing disputes, firing employees, and administering disciplinary procedures. Advise managers on organizational policy matters such as equal employment opportunity and sexual harassment and recommend needed changes. Analyze and modify compensation and benefits policies to establish competitive programs and ensure compliance with legal requirements. Plan and conduct new employee orientation to foster positive attitude toward organizational objectives. Serve as a link between management and employees by handling questions, interpreting and administering contracts, and helping resolve work-related problems. Plan, direct, supervise, and coordinate work activities of subordinates and staff relating to employment, compensation, labor relations, and employee relations. Analyze training needs to design employee development, language training, and health and safety programs. Maintain records and compile statistical reports concerning personnel-related data such as hires, transfers, performance appraisals, and absenteeism rates. Analyze statistical data and reports to identify and determine causes of personnel problems and develop recommendations for improvement of organization's personnel policies and practices. Plan, organize, direct, control, or coordinate the personnel, training, or labor relations activities of an organization. Conduct exit interviews to identify reasons for employee termination. Investigate and report on industrial accidents for insurance carriers. Represent organization at personnel-related hearings and investigations. Negotiate bargaining agreements and help interpret labor contracts.

GOE Information—Interest Area: 04. Business and Administration. **Work Group:** 04.01. Managerial Work in General Business. **Personality Type—**Enterprising. Enterprising occupations frequently involve starting up and carrying out projects. These occupations can involve leading people and making many decisions. They sometimes require risk taking and often deal with business. **Work Values—**Authority; Social Service; Working Conditions; Ability Utilization; Autonomy; Responsibility. **Skills—**Management of Personnel Resources; Negotiation; Persuasion; Management of Financial Resources; Social Perceptiveness; Active Listening. **Abilities—***Cognitive:* Mathematical Reasoning; Number Facility; Speed of Closure; Memorization; Written Expression; Fluency of Ideas. *Psychomotor:* None met the criteria. *Physical:* None met the criteria. *Sensory:* Speech Clarity; Speech Recognition; Near Vision; Far Vision; Auditory Attention. **General Work Activities—***Information Input:* Getting Information; Identifying Objects, Actions, and Events; Monitoring Processes, Materials, or Surroundings. *Mental Process:* Making Decisions and Solving Problems; Updating and Using Relevant Knowledge; Organizing, Planning, and Prioritizing. *Work Output:* Documenting or Recording Information; Interacting With Computers. *Interacting with Others:* Establishing and Maintaining Interpersonal Relationships; Resolving Conflicts and Negotiating with Others; Staffing Organizational Units. **Physical Work Conditions—**Indoors; Sitting. **Other Job Characteristics—**Need to Be Exact or Accurate; Automation; Repeat Same Tasks.

Experience—Job Zone 4. A minimum of two to four years of work-related skill, knowledge, or experience is needed. **Job Preparation—**SVP 7.0 to less than 8.0—two years to less than 10 years. **Knowledges—**Personnel and Human Resources; Clerical Practices;

Law and Government; Economics and Accounting; Therapy and Counseling; Education and Training. **Instructional Program**—No related CIP programs.

Related SOC Job—11-3040 Human Resources Managers. **Related OOH Job**—Human Resources, Training, and Labor Relations Managers and Specialists. **Related DOT Jobs**—166.117-010 Director, Industrial Relations; 166.117-018 Manager, Personnel; 166.167-030 Manager, Employment; 166.167-034 Manager, Labor Relations; 188.117-086 Director, Merit System; 188.217-010 Commissioner Of Conciliation.

11-3041.00 Compensation and Benefits Managers

- **Education/Training Required: Work experience plus degree**
- **Employed: 51,470**
- **Annual Earnings: $69,130**
- **Growth: 21.5%**
- **Annual Job Openings: 4,000**

Plan, direct, or coordinate compensation and benefits activities and staff of an organization.

Advise management on such matters as equal employment opportunity, sexual harassment, and discrimination. Direct preparation and distribution of written and verbal information to inform employees of benefits, compensation, and personnel policies. Administer, direct, and review employee benefit programs, including the integration of benefit programs following mergers and acquisitions. Plan and conduct new employee orientations to foster positive attitude toward organizational objectives. Plan, direct, supervise, and coordinate work activities of subordinates and staff relating to employment, compensation, labor relations, and employee relations. Identify and implement benefits to increase the quality of life for employees by working with brokers and researching benefits issues. Design, evaluate, and modify benefits policies to ensure that programs are current, competitive, and in compliance with legal requirements. Analyze compensation policies, government regulations, and prevailing wage rates to develop competitive compensation plan. Formulate policies, procedures, and programs for recruitment, testing, placement, classification, orientation, benefits and compensation, and labor and industrial relations. Mediate between benefits providers and employees, such as by assisting in handling employees' benefits-related questions or taking suggestions. Fulfill all reporting requirements of all relevant government rules and regulations, including the Employee Retirement Income Security Act (ERISA). Maintain records and compile statistical reports concerning personnel-related data such as hires, transfers, performance appraisals, and absenteeism rates. Analyze statistical data and reports to identify and determine causes of personnel problems and develop recommendations for improvement of organization's personnel policies and practices. Develop methods to improve employment policies, processes, and practices and recommend changes to management. Negotiate bargaining agreements. Investigate and report on industrial accidents for insurance carriers. Represent organization at personnel-related hearings and investigations.

GOE Information—Interest Area: 04. Business and Administration. **Work Group**: 04.01. Managerial Work in General Business. **Personality Type**—Enterprising. Enterprising occupations frequently involve starting up and carrying out projects. These occupations can involve leading people and making many decisions. They sometimes require risk taking and often deal with business. **Work Values**—

Authority; Social Service; Working Conditions; Ability Utilization; Autonomy; Responsibility. **Skills**—Management of Personnel Resources; Management of Financial Resources; Management of Material Resources; Monitoring; Social Perceptiveness; Time Management. **Abilities**—*Cognitive:* Mathematical Reasoning; Number Facility; Written Expression; Deductive Reasoning; Originality; Category Flexibility. *Psychomotor:* None met the criteria. *Physical:* None met the criteria. *Sensory:* Speech Clarity; Speech Recognition; Near Vision; Auditory Attention; Far Vision. **General Work Activities**—*Information Input:* Getting Information; Identifying Objects, Actions, and Events; Monitoring Processes, Materials, or Surroundings. *Mental Process:* Organizing, Planning, and Prioritizing; Making Decisions and Solving Problems; Processing Information. *Work Output:* Interacting With Computers; Documenting or Recording Information; Updating and Using Relevant Knowledge. *Interacting with Others:* Communicating with Other Workers; Establishing and Maintaining Interpersonal Relationships; Communicating with Persons Outside Organization. **Physical Work Conditions**—Indoors; Sitting. **Other Job Characteristics**—Need to Be Exact or Accurate; Repeat Same Tasks.

Experience—Job Zone 3. Previous work-related skill, knowledge, or experience is required. **Job Preparation**—SVP 6.0 to less than 7.0—more than one year and less than four years. **Knowledges**—Personnel and Human Resources; Economics and Accounting; Clerical Practices; Administration and Management; Law and Government; Education and Training. **Instructional Programs**—Human Resources Management/Personnel Administration, General; Labor and Industrial Relations.

Related SOC Job—11-3041 Compensation and Benefits Managers. **Related OOH Job**—Human Resources, Training, and Labor Relations Managers and Specialists. **Related DOT Jobs**—166.167-018 Manager, Benefits; 166.167-022 Manager, Compensation.

11-3042.00 Training and Development Managers

- **Education/Training Required: Work experience plus degree**
- **Employed: 28,720**
- **Annual Earnings: $74,180**
- **Growth: 25.9%**
- **Annual Job Openings: 3,000**

Plan, direct, or coordinate the training and development activities and staff of an organization.

Conduct orientation sessions and arrange on-the-job training for new hires. Evaluate instructor performance and the effectiveness of training programs, providing recommendations for improvement. Develop testing and evaluation procedures. Conduct or arrange for ongoing technical training and personal development classes for staff members. Confer with management and conduct surveys to identify training needs based on projected production processes, changes, and other factors. Develop and organize training manuals, multimedia visual aids, and other educational materials. Plan, develop, and provide training and staff development programs, using knowledge of the effectiveness of methods such as classroom training, demonstrations, on-the-job training, meetings, conferences, and workshops. Analyze training needs to develop new training programs or modify and improve existing programs. Review and evaluate training and apprenticeship programs for compliance with government standards. Train instructors and supervisors in techniques and skills for training and dealing with employees. Coordinate established courses with technical and professional courses provided by community schools and designate training procedures. Prepare training budget for department or organization.

GOE Information—Interest Area: 04. Business and Administration. **Work Group:** 04.01. Managerial Work in General Business. **Personality Type—**Enterprising. Enterprising occupations frequently involve starting up and carrying out projects. These occupations can involve leading people and making many decisions. They sometimes require risk taking and often deal with business. **Work Values—**Authority; Social Service; Working Conditions; Co-workers; Creativity; Achievement. **Skills—**Management of Personnel Resources; Management of Financial Resources; Learning Strategies; Negotiation; Service Orientation; Social Perceptiveness. **Abilities—***Cognitive:* Fluency of Ideas; Memorization; Written Expression; Originality; Inductive Reasoning; Oral Expression. *Psychomotor:* Control Precision; Arm-Hand Steadiness; Finger Dexterity. *Physical:* Trunk Strength. *Sensory:* Speech Clarity; Speech Recognition; Far Vision; Near Vision; Auditory Attention; Visual Color Discrimination. **General Work Activities—***Information Input:* Monitoring Processes, Materials, or Surroundings; Identifying Objects, Actions, and Events; Getting Information. *Mental Process:* Organizing, Planning, and Prioritizing; Updating and Using Relevant Knowledge; Making Decisions and Solving Problems. *Work Output:* Interacting With Computers; Documenting or Recording Information. *Interacting with Others:* Establishing and Maintaining Interpersonal Relationships; Communicating with Other Workers; Teaching Others. **Physical Work Conditions—**Indoors; Sitting; Using Hands on Objects, Tools, or Controls. **Other Job Characteristics—**Errors Have Important Consequences; Need to Be Exact or Accurate.

Experience—Job Zone 4. A minimum of two to four years of work-related skill, knowledge, or experience is needed. **Job Preparation—**SVP 7.0 to less than 8.0—two years to less than 10 years. **Knowledges—**Personnel and Human Resources; Clerical Practices; Administration and Management; Psychology; Education and Training; Computers and Electronics. **Instructional Programs—**Human Resources Development; Human Resources Management/ Personnel Administration, General.

Related SOC Job—11-3042 Training and Development Managers. **Related OOH Job—**Human Resources, Training, and Labor Relations Managers and Specialists. **Related DOT Jobs—**166.167-026 Manager, Education and Training; 188.117-010 Apprenticeship Consultant; 375.167-054 Police Academy Program Coordinator.

11-3049.99 Human Resources Managers, All Other

- **Education/Training Required: Work experience plus degree**
- **Employed: 57,830**
- **Annual Earnings: $84,190**
- **Growth: 15.9%**
- **Annual Job Openings: 4,000**

All Human Resources Managers not listed separately.

No task data available.

Note: The Department of Labor has not collected some data for this job, so it has fewer details than the other descriptions.

Related SOC Job—11-3049 Human Resources Managers, All Other. **Related OOH Job—**Human Resources, Training, and Labor Relations Managers and Specialists. **Related DOT Jobs—**166.117-014 Manager, Employee Welfare; 166.167-014 Director Of Placement.

11-3051.00 Industrial Production Managers

- **Education/Training Required: Work experience in a related occupation**
- **Employed: 153,950**
- **Annual Earnings: $75,580**
- **Growth: 0.8%**
- **Annual Job Openings: 13,000**

Plan, direct, or coordinate the work activities and resources necessary for manufacturing products in accordance with cost, quality, and quantity specifications.

Direct and coordinate production, processing, distribution, and marketing activities of industrial organization. Develop budgets and approve expenditures for supplies, materials, and human resources, ensuring that materials, labor, and equipment are used efficiently to meet production targets. Review processing schedules and production orders to make decisions concerning inventory requirements, staffing requirements, work procedures, and duty assignments, considering budgetary limitations and time constraints. Review operations and confer with technical or administrative staff to resolve production or processing problems. Hire, train, evaluate, and discharge staff and resolve personnel grievances. Initiate and coordinate inventory and cost control programs. Prepare and maintain production reports and personnel records. Set and monitor product standards, examining samples of raw products or directing testing during processing to ensure finished products are of prescribed quality. Develop and implement production tracking and quality control systems, analyzing production, quality control, maintenance, and other operational reports to detect production problems. Review plans and confer with research and support staff to develop new products and processes. Institute employee suggestion or involvement programs. Coordinate and recommend procedures for facility and equipment maintenance or modification, including the replacement of machines. Maintain current knowledge of the quality control field, relying on current literature pertaining to materials use, technological advances, and statistical studies. Negotiate materials prices with suppliers.

GOE Information—Interest Area: 13. Manufacturing. **Work Group:** 13.01. Managerial Work in Manufacturing. **Personality Type—**Enterprising. Enterprising occupations frequently involve starting up and carrying out projects. These occupations can involve leading people and making many decisions. They sometimes require risk taking and often deal with business. **Work Values—**Authority; Autonomy; Creativity; Responsibility; Compensation; Variety. **Skills—**Management of Material Resources; Systems Evaluation; Management of Personnel Resources; Systems Analysis; Operations Analysis; Quality Control Analysis. **Abilities—***Cognitive:* Mathematical Reasoning; Speed of Closure; Visualization; Originality; Deductive Reasoning; Perceptual Speed. *Psychomotor:* None met the criteria. *Physical:* Trunk Strength. *Sensory:* Depth Perception; Auditory Attention; Speech Recognition; Far Vision; Hearing Sensitivity; Near Vision. **General Work Activities—***Information Input:* Monitoring Processes, Materials, or Surroundings; Identifying Objects, Actions, and Events; Getting Information. *Mental Process:* Organizing, Planning, and Prioritizing; Making Decisions and Solving Problems; Scheduling Work and Activities. *Work Output:* Documenting or Recording Information; Controlling Machines and Processes; Performing General Physical Activities. *Interacting with Others:* Guiding, Directing, and Motivating Subordinates; Coordinating the Work and Activities of Others;

Developing and Building Teams. **Physical Work Conditions—** Indoors; Sitting. **Other Job Characteristics—**Need to Be Exact or Accurate; Repeat Same Tasks.

Experience—Job Zone 4. A minimum of two to four years of work-related skill, knowledge, or experience is needed. **Job Preparation—** SVP 7.0 to less than 8.0—two years to less than 10 years. **Knowledges—**Production and Processing; Personnel and Human Resources; Mechanical Devices; Education and Training; Engineering and Technology; Design. **Instructional Programs—**Business Administration/Management; Business/Commerce, General; Operations Management and Supervision.

Related SOC Job—11-3051 Industrial Production Managers. **Related OOH Job—**Industrial Production Managers. **Related DOT Jobs—** 180.167-054 Superintendent; 182.167-022 Superintendent, Concrete-Mixing Plant; 183.117-010 Manager, Branch; 183.117-014 Production Superintendent; 183.161-014 Wine Maker; 183.167-010 Brewing Director; 183.167-014 General Superintendent, Milling; 183.167-018 General Supervisor; 183.167-022 General Supervisor; 183.167-026 Manager, Food Processing Plant; 183.167-034 Superintendent, Car Construction; 187.167-090 Manager, Dental Laboratory; others.

11-3061.00 Purchasing Managers

- **Education/Training Required: Work experience plus degree**
- **Employed: 69,300**
- **Annual Earnings: $76,270**
- **Growth: 7.0%**
- **Annual Job Openings: 8,000**

Plan, direct, or coordinate the activities of buyers, purchasing officers, and related workers involved in purchasing materials, products, and services.

Maintain records of goods ordered and received. Locate vendors of materials, equipment, or supplies and interview them to determine product availability and terms of sales. Prepare and process requisitions and purchase orders for supplies and equipment. Control purchasing department budgets. Interview and hire staff and oversee staff training. Review purchase order claims and contracts for conformance to company policy. Analyze market and delivery systems to assess present and future material availability. Develop and implement purchasing and contract management instructions, policies, and procedures. Participate in the development of specifications for equipment, products, or substitute materials. Resolve vendor or contractor grievances and claims against suppliers. Represent companies in negotiating contracts and formulating policies with suppliers. Review, evaluate, and approve specifications for issuing and awarding bids. Direct and coordinate activities of personnel engaged in buying, selling, and distributing materials, equipment, machinery, and supplies. Prepare bid awards requiring board approval. Prepare reports regarding market conditions and merchandise costs. Administer online purchasing systems. Arrange for disposal of surplus materials.

GOE Information—Interest Area: 14. Retail and Wholesale Sales and Service. **Work Group:** 14.01. Managerial Work in Retail/Wholesale Sales and Service. **Personality Type—**Enterprising. Enterprising occupations frequently involve starting up and carrying out projects. These occupations can involve leading people and making many decisions. They sometimes require risk taking and often deal with business. **Work Values—**Authority; Working Conditions; Activity; Advancement; Co-workers; Company Policies and Practices. **Skills—** Management of Material Resources; Management of Financial Resources; Negotiation; Operations Analysis; Systems Evaluation; Mathematics. **Abilities—***Cognitive:* Number Facility; Mathematical

Reasoning; Memorization; Speed of Closure; Flexibility of Closure; Written Expression. *Psychomotor:* Multilimb Coordination; Arm-Hand Steadiness; Finger Dexterity; Manual Dexterity. *Physical:* Trunk Strength; Static Strength. *Sensory:* Speech Recognition; Near Vision; Hearing Sensitivity; Speech Clarity; Depth Perception; Visual Color Discrimination. **General Work Activities—***Information Input:* Getting Information; Identifying Objects, Actions, and Events; Monitoring Processes, Materials, or Surroundings. *Mental Process:* Organizing, Planning, and Prioritizing; Making Decisions and Solving Problems; Judging the Qualities of Things, Services, or Other People's Work. *Work Output:* Documenting or Recording Information; Handling and Moving Objects; Interacting With Computers. *Interacting with Others:* Communicating with Other Workers; Providing Consultation and Advice to Others; Establishing and Maintaining Interpersonal Relationships. **Physical Work Conditions—**Indoors; Noisy; Sitting. **Other Job Characteristics—** Need to Be Exact or Accurate; Repeat Same Tasks.

Experience—Job Zone 4. A minimum of two to four years of work-related skill, knowledge, or experience is needed. **Job Preparation—** SVP 7.0 to less than 8.0—two years to less than 10 years. **Knowledges—**Economics and Accounting; Personnel and Human Resources; Production and Processing; Administration and Management; Mathematics; Transportation. **Instructional Program—**Purchasing, Procurement/Acquisitions, and Contracts Management.

Related SOC Job—11-3061 Purchasing Managers. **Related OOH Job—** Purchasing Managers, Buyers, and Purchasing Agents. **Related DOT Jobs—**162.117-014 Contract Administrator; 162.167-014 Buyer, Tobacco, Head; 162.167-022 Manager, Procurement Services; 184.117-078 Superintendent, Commissary; 185.167-034 Manager, Merchandise.

11-3071.00 Transportation, Storage, and Distribution Managers

- **Education/Training Required: Work experience in a related occupation**
- **Employed: 84,870**
- **Annual Earnings: $69,120**
- **Growth: 12.7%**
- **Annual Job Openings: 15,000**

The job openings listed here are shared with 11-3071.01 Transportation Managers and 11-3071.02 Storage and Distribution Managers.

Plan, direct, or coordinate transportation, storage, or distribution activities in accordance with governmental policies and regulations.

No task data available.

GOE Information—Interest Area: 16. Transportation, Distribution, and Logistics. **Work Group:** 16.01. Managerial Work in Transportation. **Note:** The Department of Labor has not collected some data for this job, so it has fewer details than the other descriptions.

Instructional Programs—Aeronautics/Aviation/Aerospace Science and Technology, General; Aviation/Airway Management and Operations; Business Administration/Management; Business/ Commerce, General; Logistics and Materials Management; Public Administration; Transportation/Transportation Management.

Related SOC Job—11-3071 Transportation, Storage, and Distribution Managers. **Related OOH Job—**Transportation, Storage, and Distribution Managers. **Related DOT Job—**No data available.

11-3071.01 Transportation Managers

- **Education/Training Required: Work experience in a related occupation**
- **Employed:** 84,870
- **Annual Earnings:** $69,120
- **Growth:** 12.7%
- **Annual Job Openings:** 15,000

The job openings listed here are shared with 11-3071.00 Transportation, Storage, and Distribution Managers and 11-3071.02 Storage and Distribution Managers.

Plan, direct, and coordinate the transportation operations within an organization or the activities of organizations that provide transportation services.

Direct activities related to dispatching, routing, and tracking transportation vehicles such as aircraft and railroad cars. Plan, organize, and manage the work of subordinate staff to ensure that the work is accomplished in a manner consistent with organizational requirements. Direct investigations to verify and resolve customer or shipper complaints. Serve as contact persons for all workers within assigned territories. Implement schedule and policy changes. Collaborate with other managers and staff members to formulate and implement policies, procedures, goals, and objectives. Monitor operations to ensure that staff members comply with administrative policies and procedures, safety rules, union contracts, and government regulations. Promote safe work activities by conducting safety audits, attending company safety meetings, and meeting with individual staff members. Develop criteria, application instructions, procedural manuals, and contracts for federal and state public transportation programs. Monitor spending to ensure that expenses are consistent with approved budgets. Direct and coordinate, through subordinates, activities of operations department to obtain use of equipment, facilities, and human resources. Direct activities of staff performing repairs and maintenance to equipment, vehicles, and facilities. Conduct investigations in cooperation with government agencies to determine causes of transportation accidents and to improve safety procedures. Analyze expenditures and other financial information to develop plans, policies, and budgets for increasing profits and improving services. Negotiate and authorize contracts with equipment and materials suppliers and monitor contract fulfillment. Supervise workers assigning tariff classifications and preparing billing. Set operations policies and standards, including determination of safety procedures for the handling of dangerous goods. Recommend or authorize capital expenditures for acquisition of new equipment or property to increase efficiency and services of operations department. Prepare management recommendations, such as proposed fee and tariff increases or schedule changes.

GOE Information—Interest Area: 16. Transportation, Distribution, and Logistics. **Work Group:** 16.01. Managerial Work in Transportation. **Personality Type**—Enterprising. Enterprising occupations frequently involve starting up and carrying out projects. These occupations can involve leading people and making many decisions. They sometimes require risk taking and often deal with business. **Work Values**—Authority; Autonomy; Ability Utilization; Variety; Creativity; Responsibility. **Skills**—Negotiation; Time Management; Coordination; Management of Financial Resources; Monitoring; Management of Material Resources. **Abilities**—*Cognitive:* Mathematical Reasoning; Number Facility; Memorization; Problem Sensitivity; Originality; Selective Attention. *Psychomotor:* None met the criteria. *Physical:* None met the criteria. *Sensory:* Auditory Attention; Speech Recognition; Speech Clarity; Hearing Sensitivity; Far Vision; Near Vision. **General Work Activities**—*Information Input:* Getting Information; Monitoring Processes, Materials, or Surroundings; Identifying Objects, Actions, and Events. *Mental Process:* Making Decisions and Solving Problems; Judging the Qualities of Things, Services, or Other People's Work; Updating and Using Relevant Knowledge. *Work Output:* Documenting or Recording Information; Interacting With Computers. *Interacting with Others:* Communicating with Persons Outside Organization; Providing Consultation and Advice to Others; Resolving Conflicts and Negotiating with Others. **Physical Work Conditions**—Indoors; Noisy; Sitting. **Other Job Characteristics**—Need to Be Exact or Accurate; Repeat Same Tasks; Errors Have Important Consequences.

Experience—Job Zone 3. Previous work-related skill, knowledge, or experience is required. **Job Preparation**—SVP 6.0 to less than 7.0—more than one year and less than four years. **Knowledges**—Transportation; Clerical Practices; Customer and Personal Service; Sales and Marketing; Production and Processing; Administration and Management. **Instructional Programs**—Aeronautics/Aviation/Aerospace Science and Technology, General; Aviation/Airway Management and Operations; Business Administration/Management; Logistics and Materials Management; Public Administration; Transportation/Transportation Management.

Related SOC Job—11-3071 Transportation, Storage, and Distribution Managers. **Related OOH Job**—Transportation, Storage, and Distribution Managers. **Related DOT Jobs**—180.167-062 Manager, Aerial Planting and Cultivation; 184.117-014 Director, Transportation; 184.117-018 District Supervisor; 184.117-026 Manager, Airport; 184.117-034 Manager, Automotive Services; 184.117-038 Manager, Flight Operations; 184.117-042 Manager, Harbor Department; 184.117-050 Manager, Operations; 184.117-054 Manager, Regional; 184.117-058 Manager, Schedule Planning; 184.117-066 Manager, Traffic; 184.117-086 Manager, Car Inspection and Repair; others.

11-3071.02 Storage and Distribution Managers

- **Education/Training Required: Work experience in a related occupation**
- **Employed:** 84,870
- **Annual Earnings:** $69,120
- **Growth:** 12.7%
- **Annual Job Openings:** 15,000

The job openings listed here are shared with 11-3071.00 Transportation, Storage, and Distribution Managers and 11-3071.01 Transportation Managers.

Plan, direct, and coordinate the storage and distribution operations within an organization or the activities of organizations that are engaged in storing and distributing materials and products.

Supervise the activities of workers engaged in receiving, storing, testing, and shipping products or materials. Plan, develop, and implement warehouse safety and security programs and activities. Review invoices, work orders, consumption reports, and demand forecasts to estimate peak delivery periods and to issue work assignments. Schedule and monitor air or surface pickup, delivery, or distribution of products or materials. Interview, select, and train warehouse and supervisory personnel. Confer with department heads to coordinate warehouse activities, such as production, sales, records control, and purchasing. Respond to customers' or shippers' questions and complaints regarding storage and distribution services. Inspect physical conditions of warehouses, vehicle fleets, and equipment and order testing, maintenance, repair, or replacement as necessary. Develop and document standard and emergency operating procedures for receiving, handling, storing, shipping, or salvaging products or materials. Examine products or materials to estimate quantities or weight and type of container required for storage or transport. Negotiate with carriers, warehouse operators, and insurance company representatives for services and preferential rates. Issue shipping instructions and provide routing information to ensure that delivery times and locations are coordinated. Examine invoices and shipping manifests for conformity to tariff and customs regulations. Prepare and manage departmental budgets. Prepare or direct preparation of correspondence; reports; and operations, maintenance, and safety manuals. Arrange for necessary shipping documentation and contact customs officials to effect release of shipments. Advise sales and billing departments of transportation charges for customers' accounts. Evaluate freight costs and the inventory costs associated with transit times to ensure that costs are appropriate. Participate in setting transportation and service rates. Track and trace goods while they are en route to their destinations, expediting orders when necessary. Arrange for storage facilities when required.

GOE Information—Interest Area: 16. Transportation, Distribution, and Logistics. **Work Group:** 16.01. Managerial Work in Transportation. **Personality Type—**Enterprising. Enterprising occupations frequently involve starting up and carrying out projects. These occupations can involve leading people and making many decisions. They sometimes require risk taking and often deal with business. **Work Values—**Authority; Creativity; Autonomy; Responsibility; Company Policies and Practices; Security. **Skills—**Management of Personnel Resources; Operations Analysis; Monitoring; Management of Material Resources; Systems Analysis; Systems Evaluation. **Abilities—***Cognitive:* Number Facility; Mathematical Reasoning; Category Flexibility; Fluency of Ideas; Perceptual Speed; Written Expression. *Psychomotor:* None met the criteria. *Physical:* None met the criteria. *Sensory:* Speech Recognition; Speech Clarity; Far Vision; Auditory Attention; Hearing Sensitivity; Near Vision. **General Work Activities—***Information Input:* Getting Information; Identifying Objects, Actions, and Events; Monitoring Processes, Materials, or Surroundings. *Mental Process:* Organizing, Planning, and Prioritizing; Making Decisions and Solving Problems; Updating and Using Relevant Knowledge. *Work Output:* Handling and Moving Objects; Interacting With Computers; Documenting or Recording Information. *Interacting with Others:* Communicating with Other Workers; Monitoring and Controlling Resources; Resolving Conflicts and Negotiating with Others. **Physical Work Conditions—**Indoors; Noisy; Contaminants; More Often Sitting Than Standing. **Other Job Characteristics—**Need to Be Exact or Accurate; Repeat Same Tasks.

Experience—Job Zone 3. Previous work-related skill, knowledge, or experience is required. **Job Preparation—**SVP 6.0 to less than 7.0—more than one year and less than four years. **Knowledges—**Sales and Marketing; Administration and Management; Personnel and Human Resources; Customer and Personal Service; Production and Processing; Education and Training. **Instructional Programs—**Aeronautics/Aviation/Aerospace Science and Technology, General; Aviation/Airway Management and Operations; Business Administration/Management; Logistics and Materials Management; Public Administration; Transportation/Transportation Management.

Related SOC Job—11-3071 Transportation, Storage, and Distribution Managers. **Related OOH Job—**Transportation, Storage, and Distribution Managers. **Related DOT Jobs—**181.117-010 Manager, Bulk Plant; 184.117-022 Import-Export Agent; 184.161-014

Superintendent, Water-And-Sewer Systems; 184.167-038 Dispatcher, Chief I; 184.167-086 Manager, Telegraph Office; 184.167-114 Manager, Warehouse; 184.167-118 Operations Manager; 184.167-146 Superintendent, Compressor Stations; 184.167-154 Superintendent, Distribution II; 184.167-190 Superintendent, Measurement; 184.167-198 Superintendent, Pipelines; 184.167-238 Supervisor, Sewer System; others.

11-9000 Other Management Occupations

11-9011.00 Farm, Ranch, and Other Agricultural Managers

- **Education/Training Required:** Work experience plus degree
- **Employed:** 4,070
- **Annual Earnings:** $51,160
- **Growth:** 4.0%
- **Annual Job Openings:** 20,000

The job openings listed here are shared with 11-9011.01 Nursery and Greenhouse Managers, 11-9011.02 Crop and Livestock Managers, and 11-9011.03 Aquacultural Managers.

On a paid basis, manage farms, ranches, aquacultural operations, greenhouses, nurseries, timber tracts, cotton gins, packing houses, or other agricultural establishments for employers. Carry out production, financial, and marketing decisions relating to the managed operations, following guidelines from the owner. May contract tenant farmers or producers to carry out the day-to-day activities of the managed operation. May supervise planting, cultivating, harvesting, and marketing activities. May prepare cost, production, and other records. May perform physical work and operate machinery.

No task data available.

GOE Information—Interest Area: 01. Agriculture and Natural Resources. **Work Group:** 01.01. Managerial Work in Agriculture and Natural Resources. **Note:** The Department of Labor has not collected some data for this job, so it has fewer details than the other descriptions.

Instructional Programs—Agribusiness/Agricultural Business Operations; Agricultural Animal Breeding; Agricultural Business and Management, General; Agricultural Business and Management, Other; Agricultural Production Operations, General; Agricultural Production Operations, Other; Agronomy and Crop Science; Animal Nutrition; Animal Sciences, General; Animal/Livestock Husbandry and Production; Crop Production; Dairy Husbandry and Production; Dairy Science; Farm/Farm and Ranch Management; Greenhouse Operations and Management; Horse Husbandry/Equine Science and Management; Horticultural Science; Livestock Management; Ornamental Horticulture; Plant Nursery Operations and Management; Plant Protection and Integrated Pest Management; Plant Sciences, General; Poultry Science; Range Science and Management.

Related SOC Job—11-9011 Farm, Ranch, and Other Agricultural Managers. **Related OOH Job—**Farmers, Ranchers, and Agricultural Managers. **Related DOT Job—**No data available.

11-9011.01 Nursery and Greenhouse Managers

- **Education/Training Required: Work experience plus degree**
- **Employed: 4,070**
- **Annual Earnings: $51,160**
- **Growth: 4.0%**
- **Annual Job Openings: 20,000**

The job openings listed here are shared with 11-9011.00 Farm, Ranch, and Other Agricultural Managers, 11-9011.02 Crop and Livestock Managers, and 11-9011.03 Aquacultural Managers.

Plan, organize, direct, control, and coordinate activities of workers engaged in propagating, cultivating, and harvesting horticultural specialties, such as trees, shrubs, flowers, mushrooms, and other plants.

Construct structures and accessories such as greenhouses and benches. Prepare soil for planting and plant or transplant seeds, bulbs, and cuttings. Position and regulate plant irrigation systems and program environmental and irrigation control computers. Negotiate contracts such as those for land leases or tree purchases. Inspect facilities and equipment for signs of disrepair and perform necessary maintenance work. Graft plants. Coordinate clerical, recordkeeping, inventory, requisitioning, and marketing activities. Confer with horticultural personnel in order to plan facility renovations or additions. Provide information to customers on the care of trees, shrubs, flowers, plants, and lawns. Cut and prune trees, shrubs, flowers, and plants. Determine types and quantities of horticultural plants to be grown, based on budgets, projected sales volumes, and/or executive directives. Determine plant growing conditions, such as greenhouses, hydroponics, or natural settings, and set planting and care schedules. Assign work schedules and duties to nursery or greenhouse staff and supervise their work. Explain and enforce safety regulations and policies. Hire employees and train them in gardening techniques. Identify plants as well as problems such as diseases, weeds, and insect pests. Manage nurseries that grow horticultural plants for sale to trade or retail customers, for display or exhibition, or for research. Select and purchase seeds, plant nutrients, disease control chemicals, and garden and lawn care equipment. Tour work areas to observe work being done, to inspect crops, and to evaluate plant and soil conditions. Apply pesticides and fertilizers to plants.

GOE Information—Interest Area: 01. Agriculture and Natural Resources. **Work Group:** 01.01. Managerial Work in Agriculture and Natural Resources. **Personality Type—**Enterprising. Enterprising occupations frequently involve starting up and carrying out projects. These occupations can involve leading people and making many decisions. They sometimes require risk taking and often deal with business. **Work Values—**Authority; Creativity; Autonomy; Ability Utilization; Responsibility; Variety. **Skills—**Management of Personnel Resources; Management of Financial Resources; Management of Material Resources; Negotiation; Systems Analysis; Systems Evaluation. **Abilities—***Cognitive:* Number Facility; Mathematical Reasoning; Written Expression; Originality; Written Comprehension; Oral Expression. *Psychomotor:* None met the criteria. *Physical:* None met the criteria. *Sensory:* None met the criteria. **General Work Activities—***Information Input:* Getting Information; Identifying Objects, Actions, and Events; Monitoring Processes, Materials, or Surroundings. *Mental Process:* Making Decisions and Solving Problems; Scheduling Work and Activities; Thinking Creatively. *Work Output:* Handling and Moving Objects; Performing General Physical Activities. *Interacting with Others:* Monitoring and Controlling Resources; Communicating with Persons Outside Organization;

Resolving Conflicts and Negotiating with Others. **Physical Work Conditions—**More Often Indoors Than Outdoors; Standing; Kneeling, Crouching, Stooping, or Crawling. **Other Job Characteristics—**None met the criteria.

Experience—Job Zone 4. A minimum of two to four years of work-related skill, knowledge, or experience is needed. **Job Preparation—**SVP 7.0 to less than 8.0—two years to less than 10 years. **Knowledges—**Biology; Food Production; Chemistry; Personnel and Human Resources; Administration and Management; Production and Processing. **Instructional Programs—**Agribusiness/Agricultural Business Operations; Agricultural Business and Management, General; Greenhouse Operations and Management; Horticultural Science; Ornamental Horticulture; Plant Nursery Operations and Management; Plant Protection and Integrated Pest Management.

Related SOC Job—11-9011 Farm, Ranch, and Other Agricultural Managers. **Related OOH Job—**Farmers, Ranchers, and Agricultural Managers. **Related DOT Jobs—**180.117-010 Manager, Christmas-Tree Farm; 180.161-014 Superintendent, Horticulture; 180.167-042 Manager, Nursery.

11-9011.02 Crop and Livestock Managers

- **Education/Training Required: Work experience plus degree**
- **Employed: 4,070**
- **Annual Earnings: $51,160**
- **Growth: 4.0%**
- **Annual Job Openings: 20,000**

The job openings listed here are shared with 11-9011.00 Farm, Ranch, and Other Agricultural Managers, 11-9011.01 Nursery and Greenhouse Managers, and 11-9011.03 Aquacultural Managers.

Direct and coordinate, through subordinate supervisory personnel, activities of workers engaged in agricultural crop production for corporations, cooperatives, or other owners.

Record information such as production figures, farm management practices, and parent stock data and prepare financial and operational reports. Confer with buyers to arrange for the sale of crops. Contract with farmers or independent owners for raising of crops or for management of crop production. Evaluate financial statements and make budget proposals. Analyze soil to determine types and quantities of fertilizer required for maximum production. Purchase machinery, equipment, and supplies, such as tractors, seed, fertilizer, and chemicals. Analyze market conditions to determine acreage allocations. Direct and coordinate worker activities such as planting, irrigation, chemical application, harvesting, and grading. Inspect orchards and fields to determine maturity dates of crops or to estimate potential crop damage from weather. Hire, discharge, transfer, and promote workers. Enforce applicable safety regulations. Negotiate with bank officials to obtain credit. Plan and direct development and production of hybrid plant varieties with high yields or with disease or insect resistance. Inspect equipment to ensure proper functioning. Determine procedural changes in drying, grading, storage, and shipment processes in order to provide greater efficiency and accuracy. Coordinate growing activities with activities of related departments such as engineering, equipment maintenance, and packing.

GOE Information—Interest Area: 01. Agriculture and Natural Resources. **Work Group:** 01.01. Managerial Work in Agriculture and Natural Resources. **Personality Type—**Enterprising. Enterprising occupations frequently involve starting up and carrying out projects. These occupations can involve leading people and making many decisions. They sometimes require risk taking and often deal with business. **Work Values**—Authority; Creativity; Autonomy; Responsibility; Variety; Social Status. **Skills**—Management of Financial Resources; Negotiation; Management of Material Resources; Persuasion; Management of Personnel Resources; Judgment and Decision Making. **Abilities**—*Cognitive:* Number Facility; Mathematical Reasoning; Written Expression; Originality; Fluency of Ideas; Speed of Closure. *Psychomotor:* None met the criteria. *Physical:* None met the criteria. *Sensory:* Far Vision; Near Vision; Speech Recognition. **General Work Activities**—*Information Input:* Getting Information; Identifying Objects, Actions, and Events; Monitoring Processes, Materials, or Surroundings. *Mental Process:* Organizing, Planning, and Prioritizing; Making Decisions and Solving Problems; Updating and Using Relevant Knowledge. *Work Output:* Documenting or Recording Information; Interacting With Computers; Operating Vehicles or Equipment. *Interacting with Others:* Resolving Conflicts and Negotiating with Others; Monitoring and Controlling Resources; Establishing and Maintaining Interpersonal Relationships. **Physical Work Conditions**—More Often Indoors Than Outdoors; Sitting. **Other Job Characteristics**—Need to Be Exact or Accurate.

Experience—Job Zone 4. A minimum of two to four years of work-related skill, knowledge, or experience is needed. **Job Preparation**—SVP 7.0 to less than 8.0—two years to less than 10 years. **Knowledges**—Food Production; Economics and Accounting; Biology; Sales and Marketing; Geography; Chemistry. **Instructional Programs**—Agribusiness/Agricultural Business Operations; Agricultural Animal Breeding; Agricultural Business and Management, General; Agricultural Business and Management, Other; Agricultural Production Operations, General; Agricultural Production Operations, Other; Agronomy and Crop Science; Animal Nutrition; Animal Sciences, General; Animal/Livestock Husbandry and Production; Crop Production; Dairy Husbandry and Production; Dairy Science; Farm/Farm and Ranch Management; Horse Husbandry/Equine Science and Management; Horticultural Science; Livestock Management; Plant Protection and Integrated Pest Management; Plant Sciences, General; Poultry Science; Range Science and Management.

Related SOC Job—11-9011 Farm, Ranch, and Other Agricultural Managers. **Related OOH Job**—Farmers, Ranchers, and Agricultural Managers. **Related DOT Jobs**—180.161-010 Manager, Production, Seed Corn; 180.167-018 General Manager, Farm; 180.167-058 Superintendent, Production; 180.167-066 Manager, Orchard.

11-9011.03 Aquacultural Managers

- **Education/Training Required: Work experience plus degree**
- **Employed: 4,070**
- **Annual Earnings: $51,160**
- **Growth: 4.0%**
- **Annual Job Openings: 20,000**

The job openings listed here are shared with 11-9011.00 Farm, Ranch, and Other Agricultural Managers, 11-9011.01 Nursery and Greenhouse Managers, and 11-9011.02 Crop and Livestock Managers.

Direct and coordinate, through subordinate supervisory personnel, activities of workers engaged in fish hatchery production for corporations, cooperatives, or other owners.

Grow fish and shellfish as cash crops or for release into fresh water or salt water. Supervise and train aquaculture and fish hatchery support workers. Collect and record growth, production, and environmental data. Conduct and supervise stock examinations to identify diseases or parasites. Account for and disburse funds. Devise and participate in activities to improve fish hatching and growth rates and to prevent disease in hatcheries. Monitor environments to ensure maintenance of optimum conditions for aquatic life. Direct and monitor trapping and spawning of fish, egg incubation, and fry rearing, applying knowledge of management and fish culturing techniques. Coordinate the selection and maintenance of brood stock. Direct and monitor the transfer of mature fish to lakes, ponds, streams, or commercial tanks. Determine, administer, and execute policies relating to operations administration and standards and facility maintenance. Determine how to allocate resources and how to respond to unanticipated problems such as insect infestation, drought, and fire. Collect information regarding techniques for fish collection and fertilization, spawn incubation, and treatment of spawn and fry. Operate and maintain cultivating and harvesting equipment. Confer with biologists, fish pathologists, and other fishery personnel to obtain data concerning fish habits, diseases, food, and environmental requirements. Prepare reports required by state and federal laws. Identify environmental requirements of a particular species and select and oversee the preparation of sites for species cultivation. Scuba dive to inspect sea farm operations. Design and construct pens, floating stations, and collector strings or fences for sea farms.

GOE Information—**Interest Area:** 01. Agriculture and Natural Resources. **Work Group:** 01.01. Managerial Work in Agriculture and Natural Resources. **Personality Type**—Enterprising. Enterprising occupations frequently involve starting up and carrying out projects. These occupations can involve leading people and making many decisions. They sometimes require risk taking and often deal with business. **Work Values**—Authority; Creativity; Autonomy; Responsibility; Variety; Compensation. **Skills**—Management of Financial Resources; Management of Material Resources; Technology Design; Science; Systems Evaluation; Management of Personnel Resources. **Abilities**—*Cognitive:* Number Facility; Mathematical Reasoning; Written Expression; Originality; Fluency of Ideas; Category Flexibility. *Psychomotor:* Control Precision; Multilimb Coordination; Arm-Hand Steadiness; Manual Dexterity; Finger Dexterity. *Physical:* None met the criteria. *Sensory:* Visual Color Discrimination; Depth Perception; Auditory Attention; Hearing Sensitivity; Far Vision; Speech Recognition. **General Work Activities**—*Information Input:* Monitoring Processes, Materials, or Surroundings; Identifying Objects, Actions, and Events; Getting Information. *Mental Process:* Making Decisions and Solving Problems; Updating and Using Relevant Knowledge; Organizing, Planning, and Prioritizing. *Work Output:* Handling and Moving Objects; Performing General Physical Activities; Repairing and Maintaining Mechanical Equipment. *Interacting with Others:* Coordinating the Work and Activities of Others; Establishing and Maintaining Interpersonal Relationships; Monitoring and Controlling Resources; Communicating with Other Workers. **Physical Work Conditions**—More Often Outdoors than Indoors; Noisy; Very Hot or Cold; Standing; Using Hands on Objects, Tools, or Controls. **Other Job Characteristics**—Need to Be Exact or Accurate; Errors Have Important Consequences.

Experience—Job Zone 4. A minimum of two to four years of work-related skill, knowledge, or experience is needed. **Job Preparation**—SVP 7.0 to less than 8.0—two years to less than 10 years. **Knowledges**—Food Production; Biology; Engineering and Technology; Building and Construction; Chemistry; Design. **Instructional Programs**—Agribusiness/Agricultural Business Operations; Agricultural Business and Management, General; Agricultural Business and Management, Other; Agricultural Production Operations, General; Agricultural Production

Operations, Other; Animal/Livestock Husbandry and Production; Crop Production; Farm/Farm and Ranch Management.

Related SOC Job—11-9011 Farm, Ranch, and Other Agricultural Managers. **Related OOH Job**—Farmers, Ranchers, and Agricultural Managers. **Related DOT Job**—180.167-030 Manager, Fish Hatchery.

11-9012.00 Farmers and Ranchers

- **Education/Training Required: Long-term on-the-job training**
- **Employed: 350**
- **Annual Earnings: $34,140**
- **Growth: –14.5%**
- **Annual Job Openings: 96,000**

On an ownership or rental basis, operate farms, ranches, greenhouses, nurseries, timber tracts, or other agricultural production establishments that produce crops, horticultural specialties, livestock, poultry, finfish, shellfish, or animal specialties. May plant, cultivate, harvest, perform post-harvest activities on, and market crops and livestock; may hire, train, and supervise farm workers or supervise a farm labor contractor; may prepare cost, production, and other records. May maintain and operate machinery and perform physical work.

Monitor crops as they grow in order to ensure that they are growing properly and are free from diseases and contaminants. Select animals for market and provide transportation of livestock to market. Select and purchase supplies and equipment such as seed, fertilizers, and farm machinery. Remove lower-quality or older animals from herds and purchase other livestock to replace culled animals. Purchase and store livestock feed. Plan crop activities based on factors such as crop maturity and weather conditions. Negotiate and arrange with buyers for the sale, storage, and shipment of crops. Determine types and quantities of crops or livestock to be raised according to factors such as market conditions, federal program availability, and soil conditions. Milk cows, using milking machinery. Maintain pastures or grazing lands to ensure that animals have enough feed, employing pasture-conservation measures such as arranging rotational grazing. Install and shift irrigation systems to irrigate fields evenly or according to crop need. Harvest crops and collect specialty products such as royal jelly, wax, pollen, and honey from bee colonies. Evaluate product marketing alternatives and then promote and market farm products, acting as the sales agent for livestock and crops. Assist in animal births and care for newborn livestock. Breed and raise stock such as cattle, poultry, and honeybees, using recognized breeding practices to ensure continued improvement in stock. Clean and disinfect buildings and yards and remove manure. Clean and sanitize milking equipment, storage tanks, collection cups, and cows' udders or ensure that procedures are followed to maintain sanitary conditions for handling of milk. Clean, grade, and package crops for marketing. Control the spread of disease and parasites in herds by using vaccination and medication and by separating sick animals. Destroy diseased or superfluous crops. Perform crop production duties such as planning, tilling, planting, fertilizing, cultivating, spraying, and harvesting. Set up and operate farm machinery to cultivate, harvest, and haul crops.

GOE Information—**Interest Area:** 01. Agriculture and Natural Resources. **Work Group:** 01.01. Managerial Work in Agriculture and Natural Resources. **Personality Type**—Realistic. Realistic occupations frequently involve work activities that include practical, hands-on problems and solutions. They often deal with plants; animals; and real-world materials like wood, tools, and machinery. Many of the occupations require working outside and do not involve a lot of paperwork or working closely with others. **Work Values**—Autonomy; Creativity; Responsibility; Authority; Variety; Achievement. **Skills**—

Management of Financial Resources; Operation and Control; Installation; Management of Material Resources; Equipment Selection; Management of Personnel Resources. **Abilities**—*Cognitive:* Number Facility; Visualization; Information Ordering; Deductive Reasoning; Mathematical Reasoning; Oral Expression. *Psychomotor:* Wrist-Finger Speed; Control Precision; Manual Dexterity; Multilimb Coordination. *Physical:* Static Strength; Dynamic Strength; Stamina; Trunk Strength; Extent Flexibility. *Sensory:* None met the criteria. **General Work Activities**—*Information Input:* Getting Information; Identifying Objects, Actions, and Events; Monitoring Processes, Materials, or Surroundings. *Mental Process:* Organizing, Planning, and Prioritizing; Updating and Using Relevant Knowledge; Scheduling Work and Activities. *Work Output:* Performing General Physical Activities; Handling and Moving Objects; Controlling Machines and Processes. *Interacting with Others:* Monitoring and Controlling Resources; Coordinating the Work and Activities of Others; Communicating with Persons Outside Organization. **Physical Work Conditions**—Outdoors; Contaminants; Hazardous Equipment; Minor Burns, Cuts, Bites, or Stings; Standing; Using Hands on Objects, Tools, or Controls. **Other Job Characteristics**—Errors Have Important Consequences.

Experience—Job Zone 3. Previous work-related skill, knowledge, or experience is required. **Job Preparation**—SVP 6.0 to less than 7.0—more than one year and less than four years. **Knowledges**—Food Production; Economics and Accounting; Personnel and Human Resources; Production and Processing; Biology; Sales and Marketing. **Instructional Programs**—Agribusiness/Agricultural Business Operations; Agricultural Animal Breeding; Agricultural Business and Management, General; Agricultural Production Operations, General; Agricultural Production Operations, Other; Agronomy and Crop Science; Animal Nutrition; Animal Sciences, General; Animal/Livestock Husbandry and Production; Aquaculture; Crop Production; Dairy Husbandry and Production; Dairy Science; Farm/Farm and Ranch Management; Greenhouse Operations and Management; Horticultural Science; Livestock Management; Ornamental Horticulture; Plant Nursery Operations and Management; Plant Protection and Integrated Pest Management; Plant Sciences, General; Poultry Science; Range Science and Management.

Related SOC Job—11-9012 Farmers and Ranchers. **Related OOH Job**—Farmers, Ranchers, and Agricultural Managers. **Related DOT Jobs**—169.171-010 Gamekeeper; 180.167-026 Manager, Dairy Farm; 180.167-034 Manager, Game Breeding Farm; 180.167-046 Manager, Poultry Hatchery; 401.161-010 Farmer, Cash Grain; 402.161-010 Farmer, Vegetable; 403.161-010 Farmer, Tree-Fruit-and-Nut Crops; 403.161-014 Farmer, Fruit Crops, Bush and Vine; 404.161-010 Farmer, Field Crop; 405.161-010 Bonsai Culturist; 405.161-014 Horticultural-Specialty Grower, Field; 405.161-018 Horticultural-Specialty Grower, Inside; 405.361-010 Plant Propagator; others.

11-9021.00 Construction Managers

- **Education/Training Required: Bachelor's degree**
- **Employed: 192,610**
- **Annual Earnings: $72,260**
- **Growth: 10.4%**
- **Annual Job Openings: 28,000**

Plan, direct, coordinate, or budget, usually through subordinate supervisory personnel, activities concerned with the construction and maintenance of structures, facilities, and systems. Participate in the conceptual development of a construction project and oversee its organization, scheduling, and implementation.

Confer with supervisory personnel, owners, contractors, and design professionals to discuss and resolve matters such as work procedures, complaints, and construction problems. Plan, organize, and direct activities concerned with the construction and maintenance of structures, facilities, and systems. Schedule the project in logical steps and budget time required to meet deadlines. Determine labor requirements and dispatch workers to construction sites. Inspect and review projects to monitor compliance with building and safety codes and other regulations. Prepare contracts and negotiate revisions, changes, and additions to contractual agreements with architects, consultants, clients, suppliers, and subcontractors. Interpret and explain plans and contract terms to administrative staff, workers, and clients, representing the owner or developer. Obtain all necessary permits and licenses. Direct and supervise workers. Study job specifications to determine appropriate construction methods. Select, contract, and oversee workers who complete specific pieces of the project, such as painting or plumbing. Requisition supplies and materials to complete construction projects. Prepare and submit budget estimates and progress and cost tracking reports. Take actions to deal with the results of delays, bad weather, or emergencies at construction site. Develop and implement quality control programs. Investigate damage, accidents, or delays at construction sites to ensure that proper procedures are being carried out. Evaluate construction methods and determine cost-effectiveness of plans, using computers. Direct acquisition of land for construction projects.

GOE Information—Interest Area: 02. Architecture and Construction. **Work Group:** 02.01. Managerial Work in Architecture and Construction. **Personality Type**—Enterprising. Enterprising occupations frequently involve starting up and carrying out projects. These occupations can involve leading people and making many decisions. They sometimes require risk taking and often deal with business. **Work Values**—Authority; Autonomy; Variety; Responsibility; Compensation; Creativity. **Skills**—Repairing; Installation; Troubleshooting; Management of Material Resources; Coordination; Management of Financial Resources. **Abilities**—*Cognitive:* Visualization; Originality; Fluency of Ideas; Mathematical Reasoning; Information Ordering; Written Expression. *Psychomotor:* None met the criteria. *Physical:* None met the criteria. *Sensory:* Near Vision; Speech Clarity; Far Vision; Speech Recognition. **General Work Activities**—*Information Input:* Monitoring Processes, Materials, or Surroundings; Inspecting Equipment, Structures, or Materials; Getting Information. *Mental Process:* Organizing, Planning, and Prioritizing; Scheduling Work and Activities; Updating and Using Relevant Knowledge. *Work Output:* Handling and Moving Objects; Documenting or Recording Information; Performing General Physical Activities. *Interacting with Others:* Coordinating the Work and Activities of Others; Resolving Conflicts and Negotiating with Others; Establishing and Maintaining Interpersonal Relationships. **Physical Work Conditions**—Indoors; Noisy; Sitting. **Other Job Characteristics**—Need to Be Exact or Accurate; Errors Have Important Consequences.

Experience—Job Zone 3. Previous work-related skill, knowledge, or experience is required. **Job Preparation**—SVP 6.0 to less than 7.0—more than one year and less than four years. **Knowledges**—Building and Construction; Design; Mechanical Devices; Administration and Management; Public Safety and Security; Sales and Marketing. **Instructional Programs**—Business Administration/Management; Business/Commerce, General; Construction Engineering Technology/Technician; Operations Management and Supervision.

Related SOC Job—11-9021 Construction Managers. **Related OOH Job**—Construction Managers. **Related DOT Jobs**—181.117-014 Mine Superintendent; 181.167-014 Superintendent, Drilling And Production; 181.167-018 Supervisor, Mine; 182.167-010 Contractor; 182.167-014 Landscape Contractor; 182.167-018 Railroad-Construction Director; 182.167-026 Superintendent, Construction; 182.167-030 Superintendent, Maintenance of Way; 182.167-034 Supervisor, Bridges and Buildings.

11-9031.00 Education Administrators, Preschool and Child Care Center/Program

- **Education/Training Required: Work experience plus degree**
- **Employed: 47,670**
- **Annual Earnings: $37,010**
- **Growth: 27.9%**
- **Annual Job Openings: 9,000**

Plan, direct, or coordinate the academic and nonacademic activities of preschool and child care centers or programs.

Confer with parents and staff to discuss educational activities and policies and students' behavioral or learning problems. Prepare and maintain attendance, activity, planning, accounting, or personnel reports and records for officials and agencies or direct preparation and maintenance activities. Set educational standards and goals and help establish policies, procedures, and programs to carry them out. Monitor students' progress and provide students and teachers with assistance in resolving any problems. Determine allocations of funds for staff, supplies, materials, and equipment and authorize purchases. Recruit, hire, train, and evaluate primary and supplemental staff and recommend personnel actions for programs and services. Direct and coordinate activities of teachers or administrators at daycare centers, schools, public agencies, or institutions. Plan, direct, and monitor instructional methods and content of educational, vocational, or student activity programs. Review and interpret government codes and develop procedures to meet codes and to ensure facility safety, security, and maintenance. Determine the scope of educational program offerings and prepare drafts of program schedules and descriptions to estimate staffing and facility requirements. Review and evaluate new and current programs to determine their efficiency; effectiveness; and compliance with state, local, and federal regulations, and recommend any necessary modifications. Teach classes or courses or provide direct care to children. Prepare and submit budget requests or grant proposals to solicit program funding. Write articles, manuals, and other publications and assist in the distribution of promotional literature about programs and facilities. Collect and analyze survey data, regulatory information, and demographic and employment trends to forecast enrollment patterns and the need for curriculum changes. Inform businesses, community groups, and governmental agencies about educational needs, available programs, and program policies. Organize and direct committees of specialists, volunteers, and staff to provide technical and advisory assistance for programs.

GOE Information—Interest Area: 05. Education and Training. **Work Group:** 05.01. Managerial Work in Education. **Personality Type**—Social. Social occupations frequently involve working with, communicating with, and teaching people. These occupations often involve helping or providing service to others. **Work Values**—Authority; Ability Utilization; Creativity; Social Status; Recognition; Social Service. **Skills**—Management of Financial Resources; Management of Personnel Resources; Learning Strategies; Management of Material Resources; Social Perceptiveness; Monitoring. **Abilities**—*Cognitive:* Originality; Written Expression; Number Facility; Problem Sensitivity; Fluency of Ideas; Oral Expression. *Psychomotor:* None met the criteria. *Physical:* None met the criteria. *Sensory:* Speech Recognition; Hearing Sensitivity; Speech Clarity; Visual Color Discrimination; Far Vision; Auditory Attention. **General Work**

Activities—*Information Input:* Monitoring Processes, Materials, or Surroundings; Getting Information; Identifying Objects, Actions, and Events. *Mental Process:* Making Decisions and Solving Problems; Organizing, Planning, and Prioritizing; Scheduling Work and Activities. *Work Output:* Documenting or Recording Information; Handling and Moving Objects; Interacting With Computers. *Interacting with Others:* Coordinating the Work and Activities of Others; Resolving Conflicts and Negotiating with Others; Guiding, Directing, and Motivating Subordinates. **Physical Work Conditions**—Indoors; Standing. **Other Job Characteristics**—Need to Be Exact or Accurate.

Experience—Job Zone 4. A minimum of two to four years of work-related skill, knowledge, or experience is needed. **Job Preparation**—SVP 7.0 to less than 8.0—two years to less than 10 years. **Knowledges**—Personnel and Human Resources; Education and Training; Clerical Practices; Philosophy and Theology; Therapy and Counseling; Sociology and Anthropology. **Instructional Programs**—Educational Administration and Supervision, Other; Educational Leadership and Administration, General; Educational, Instructional, and Curriculum Supervision; Elementary and Middle School Administration/Principalship.

Related SOC Job—11-9031 Education Administrators, Preschool and Child Care Center/Program. **Related OOH Job**—Education Administrators. **Related DOT Jobs**—092.167-010 Director, Day Care Center; 094.167-014 Director, Special Education; 097.167-010 Director, Vocational Training; 099.117-010 Director, Educational Program; 099.117-018 Principal.

11-9032.00 Education Administrators, Elementary and Secondary School

- **Education/Training Required:** Work experience plus degree
- **Employed:** 213,250
- **Annual Earnings:** $75,400
- **Growth:** 10.4%
- **Annual Job Openings:** 27,000

Plan, direct, or coordinate the academic, clerical, or auxiliary activities of public or private elementary or secondary-level schools.

Review and approve new programs or recommend modifications to existing programs, submitting program proposals for school board approval as necessary. Prepare, maintain, or oversee the preparation and maintenance of attendance, activity, planning, or personnel reports and records. Confer with parents and staff to discuss educational activities, policies, and student behavioral or learning problems. Prepare and submit budget requests and recommendations or grant proposals to solicit program funding. Direct and coordinate school maintenance services and the use of school facilities. Counsel and provide guidance to students regarding personal, academic, vocational, or behavioral issues. Organize and direct committees of specialists, volunteers, and staff to provide technical and advisory assistance for programs. Teach classes or courses to students. Advocate for new schools to be built or for existing facilities to be repaired or remodeled. Plan and develop instructional methods and content for educational, vocational, or student activity programs. Develop partnerships with businesses, communities, and other organizations to help meet identified educational needs and to provide school-to-work programs. Direct and coordinate activities of teachers, administrators, and support staff at schools, public agencies, and institutions. Evaluate curricula, teaching methods, and programs to determine their effectiveness, efficiency, and utilization and to ensure that school activities comply with federal, state, and local reg-

ulations. Set educational standards and goals and help establish policies and procedures to carry them out. Recruit, hire, train, and evaluate primary and supplemental staff. Enforce discipline and attendance rules. Observe teaching methods and examine learning materials to evaluate and standardize curricula and teaching techniques and to determine areas where improvement is needed. Establish, coordinate, and oversee particular programs across school districts, such as programs to evaluate student academic achievement. Review and interpret government codes and develop programs to ensure adherence to codes and facility safety, security, and maintenance.

GOE Information—**Interest Area:** 05. Education and Training. **Work Group:** 05.01. Managerial Work in Education. **Personality Type**—Social. Social occupations frequently involve working with, communicating with, and teaching people. These occupations often involve helping or providing service to others. **Work Values**—Authority; Ability Utilization; Creativity; Social Status; Recognition; Social Service. **Skills**—Management of Personnel Resources; Management of Financial Resources; Negotiation; Learning Strategies; Social Perceptiveness; Monitoring. **Abilities**—*Cognitive:* Originality; Written Expression; Fluency of Ideas; Deductive Reasoning; Written Comprehension; Inductive Reasoning. *Psychomotor:* None met the criteria. *Physical:* None met the criteria. *Sensory:* Speech Clarity; Speech Recognition; Near Vision. **General Work Activities**—*Information Input:* Getting Information; Monitoring Processes, Materials, or Surroundings; Identifying Objects, Actions, and Events. *Mental Process:* Organizing, Planning, and Prioritizing; Making Decisions and Solving Problems; Updating and Using Relevant Knowledge. *Work Output:* Documenting or Recording Information; Interacting With Computers; Performing General Physical Activities. *Interacting with Others:* Establishing and Maintaining Interpersonal Relationships; Resolving Conflicts and Negotiating with Others; Communicating with Other Workers. **Physical Work Conditions**—Indoors; Standing. **Other Job Characteristics**—Need to Be Exact or Accurate.

Experience—Job Zone 5. Extensive skill, knowledge, and experience are needed. **Job Preparation**—SVP 8.0 and above—four years to more than 10 years. **Knowledges**—Education and Training; Therapy and Counseling; Personnel and Human Resources; Psychology; Sociology and Anthropology; History and Archeology. **Instructional Programs**—Educational Administration and Supervision, Other; Educational Leadership and Administration, General; Educational, Instructional, and Curriculum Supervision; Elementary and Middle School Administration/Principalship; Secondary School Administration/Principalship.

Related SOC Job—11-9032 Education Administrators, Elementary and Secondary School. **Related OOH Job**—Education Administrators. **Related DOT Jobs**—091.107-010 Assistant Principal; 094.117-010 Director, Commission for the Blind; 094.167-014 Director, Special Education; 097.167-010 Director, Vocational Training; 099.117-010 Director, Educational Program; 099.117-018 Principal; 099.167-034 Director Of Pupil Personnel Program.

11-9033.00 Education Administrators, Postsecondary

- **Education/Training Required:** Work experience plus degree
- **Employed:** 105,360
- **Annual Earnings:** $70,350
- **Growth:** 21.3%
- **Annual Job Openings:** 18,000

Plan, direct, or coordinate research, instructional, student administration and services, and other educational activities at postsecondary institutions, including universities, colleges, and junior and community colleges.

Recruit, hire, train, and terminate departmental personnel. Plan, administer, and control budgets; maintain financial records; and produce financial reports. Represent institutions at community and campus events, in meetings with other institution personnel, and during accreditation processes. Participate in faculty and college committee activities. Provide assistance to faculty and staff in duties such as teaching classes, conducting orientation programs, issuing transcripts, and scheduling events. Establish operational policies and procedures and make any necessary modifications, based on analysis of operations, demographics, and other research information. Confer with other academic staff to explain and formulate admission requirements and course credit policies. Appoint individuals to faculty positions and evaluate their performance. Direct activities of administrative departments such as admissions, registration, and career services. Develop curricula and recommend curricula revisions and additions. Determine course schedules and coordinate teaching assignments and room assignments to ensure optimum use of buildings and equipment. Consult with government regulatory and licensing agencies to ensure the institution's conformance with applicable standards. Direct, coordinate, and evaluate the activities of personnel engaged in administering academic institutions, departments, and/or alumni organizations. Teach courses within their department. Participate in student recruitment, selection, and admission, making admissions recommendations when required to do so. Review student misconduct reports requiring disciplinary action and counsel students regarding such reports. Supervise coaches. Assess and collect tuition and fees. Direct scholarship, fellowship, and loan programs, performing activities such as selecting recipients and distributing aid. Coordinate the production and dissemination of university publications such as course catalogs and class schedules. Review registration statistics and consult with faculty officials to develop registration policies. Audit the financial status of student organizations and facility accounts.

GOE Information—Interest Area: 05. Education and Training. **Work Group:** 05.01. Managerial Work in Education. **Personality Type—**Enterprising. Enterprising occupations frequently involve starting up and carrying out projects. These occupations can involve leading people and making many decisions. They sometimes require risk taking and often deal with business. **Work Values—**Authority; Social Status; Working Conditions; Recognition; Creativity; Ability Utilization. **Skills—**Management of Financial Resources; Management of Personnel Resources; Systems Evaluation; Persuasion; Monitoring; Judgment and Decision Making. **Abilities—***Cognitive:* Written Expression; Fluency of Ideas; Oral Expression; Number Facility; Mathematical Reasoning; Originality. *Psychomotor:* None met the criteria. *Physical:* None met the criteria. *Sensory:* Speech Recognition; Speech Clarity; Hearing Sensitivity; Far Vision; Auditory Attention. **General Work Activities—***Information Input:* Getting Information; Identifying Objects, Actions, and Events; Monitoring Processes, Materials, or Surroundings. *Mental Process:* Organizing, Planning, and Prioritizing; Updating and Using Relevant Knowledge; Making Decisions and Solving Problems. *Work Output:* Documenting or Recording Information; Interacting With Computers. *Interacting with Others:* Establishing and Maintaining Interpersonal Relationships; Communicating with Other Workers; Guiding, Directing, and Motivating Subordinates. **Physical Work Conditions—**Indoors; Sitting. **Other Job Characteristics—**Need to Be Exact or Accurate.

Experience—Job Zone 5. Extensive skill, knowledge, and experience are needed. **Job Preparation—**SVP 8.0 and above—four years to more than 10 years. **Knowledges—**Education and Training; Personnel and Human Resources; Sociology and Anthropology; Administration and Management; Sales and Marketing; English Language. **Instructional Programs—**Community College Education; Educational Administration and Supervision, Other; Educational Leadership and Administration, General; Educational, Instructional, and Curriculum Supervision; Higher Education/Higher Education Administration.

Related SOC Job—11-9033 Education Administrators, Postsecondary. **Related OOH Job—**Education Administrators. **Related DOT Jobs—**075.117-030 Director, School Of Nursing; 090.117-010 Academic Dean; 090.117-014 Alumni Secretary; 090.117-018 Dean of Students; 090.117-022 Director, Athletic; 090.117-026 Director, Extension Work; 090.117-030 Financial-Aid Officer; 090.167-010 Department Head, College or University; 090.167-014 Director of Admissions; 090.167-018 Director of Institutional Research; 090.167-022 Director of Student Affairs; 090.167-026 Director, Summer Sessions; 090.167-030 Registrar, College or University; others.

11-9039.99 Education Administrators, All Other

- **Education/Training Required: Work experience plus degree**
- **Employed: 24,710**
- **Annual Earnings: $64,180**
- **Growth: 20.3%**
- **Annual Job Openings: 4,000**

All education administrators not listed separately.

No task data available.

Note: The Department of Labor has not collected some data for this job, so it has fewer details than the other descriptions.

Related SOC Job—11-9039 Education Administrators, All Other. **Related OOH Job—**Education Administrators. **Related DOT Jobs—**075.117-018 Director, Educational, Community-Health Nursing; 099.117-014 Education Supervisor, Correctional Institution; 099.117-030 Director, Education.

11-9041.00 Engineering Managers

- **Education/Training Required: Work experience plus degree**
- **Employed: 187,410**
- **Annual Earnings: $100,760**
- **Growth: 13.0%**
- **Annual Job Openings: 15,000**

Plan, direct, or coordinate activities in such fields as architecture and engineering or research and development in these fields.

Confer with management, production, and marketing staff to discuss project specifications and procedures. Coordinate and direct projects, making detailed plans to accomplish goals and directing the integration of technical activities. Analyze technology, resource needs, and market demand to plan and assess the feasibility of projects. Plan and direct the installation, testing, operation, maintenance, and repair of facilities and equipment. Direct, review, and approve product design and changes. Recruit employees; assign, direct, and evaluate their work; and oversee the development and maintenance of staff competence. Prepare budgets, bids, and contracts and direct the negotiation of research contracts. Develop and implement policies, standards, and procedures for the engineering and technical work performed in the department, service, laboratory, or firm. Review and recommend or approve contracts and cost estimates. Perform administrative functions such as reviewing and writing reports, approving expenditures, enforcing rules, and making decisions about the purchase of materials or services. Present and explain proposals, reports, and findings to clients. Consult or negotiate with clients to prepare project specifications. Set scientific and technical goals within broad outlines provided by top management. Administer highway planning, construction, and maintenance. Direct the engineering of water control, treatment, and distribution projects. Plan, direct, and coordinate survey work with other staff activities, certifying survey work and writing land legal descriptions. Confer with and report to officials and the public to provide information and solicit support for projects.

GOE Information—Interest Area: 15. Scientific Research, Engineering, and Mathematics. **Work Group:** 15.01. Managerial Work in Scientific Research, Engineering, and Mathematics. **Personality Type—**Enterprising. Enterprising occupations frequently involve starting up and carrying out projects. These occupations can involve leading people and making many decisions. They sometimes require risk taking and often deal with business. **Work Values—**Authority; Compensation; Autonomy; Creativity; Working Conditions; Ability Utilization. **Skills—**Technology Design; Science; Operations Analysis; Installation; Management of Financial Resources; Quality Control Analysis. **Abilities—***Cognitive:* Mathematical Reasoning; Fluency of Ideas; Visualization; Written Comprehension; Originality; Oral Comprehension. *Psychomotor:* None met the criteria. *Physical:* None met the criteria. *Sensory:* Far Vision; Near Vision; Speech Recognition; Visual Color Discrimination; Speech Clarity; Depth Perception. **General Work Activities—***Information Input:* Getting Information; Identifying Objects, Actions, and Events; Monitoring Processes, Materials, or Surroundings. *Mental Process:* Making Decisions and Solving Problems; Updating and Using Relevant Knowledge; Organizing, Planning, and Prioritizing. *Work Output:* Drafting and Specifying Technical Devices; Documenting or Recording Information; Interacting With Computers. *Interacting with Others:* Communicating with Other Workers; Establishing and Maintaining Interpersonal Relationships; Resolving Conflicts and Negotiating with Others. **Physical Work Conditions—**Indoors; Noisy; Sitting. **Other Job Characteristics—**Need to Be Exact or Accurate.

Experience—Job Zone 5. Extensive skill, knowledge, and experience are needed. **Job Preparation—**SVP 8.0 and above—four years to more than 10 years. **Knowledges—**Engineering and Technology; Design; Physics; Building and Construction; Personnel and Human Resources; Mathematics. **Instructional Programs—**Aerospace, Aeronautical, and Astronautical Engineering; Agricultural/Biological Engineering and Bioengineering; Architectural Engineering; Architecture (BArch, BA/BS, MArch, MA/MS, PhD); Biomedical/Medical Engineering; Ceramic Sciences and Engineering; Chemical Engineering; City/Urban, Community, and Regional Planning; Civil Engineering, General; Civil Engineering, Other; Computer Engineering, General; Computer Engineering, Other; Computer Hardware Engineering; Computer Software Engineering; Construction Engineering; Electrical, Electronics, and Communications Engineering; Engineering Mechanics; Engineering Physics; Engineering Science; Engineering, General; Engineering, Other; Environmental Design/Architecture; Environmental/Environmental Health Engineering; Forest Engineering; Geological/Geophysical Engineering; Geotechnical Engineering; Industrial Engineering; Interior Architecture; Landscape Architecture (BS, BSLA, BLA, MSLA, MLA, PhD); Manufacturing Engineering; Materials Engineering; Materials Science; Mechanical Engineering; Metallurgical Engineering; Mining and Mineral Engineering; Naval Architecture and Marine Engineering; Nuclear Engineering; Ocean Engineering; Petroleum Engineering; Polymer/Plastics Engineering; Structural Engineering; Surveying Engineering; Systems Engineering; Textile Sciences and Engineering; Transportation and Highway Engineering; Water Resources Engineering.

Related SOC Job—11-9041 Engineering Managers. **Related OOH Job—**Engineering and Natural Sciences Managers. **Related DOT Jobs—**003.167-034 Engineer-in-Charge, Transmitter; 003.167-070 Engineering Manager, Electronics; 005.167-010 Chief Engineer, Waterworks; 005.167-022 Highway-Administrative Engineer; 007.167-014 Plant Engineer; 010.161-014 Chief Petroleum Engineer; 010.167-018 Superintendent, Oil-Well Services; 018.167-022 Manager, Land Surveying; 019.167-014 Project Engineer; 162.117-030 Research-Contracts Supervisor.

11-9051.00 Food Service Managers

- **Education/Training Required: Work experience in a related occupation**
- **Employed: 191,420**
- **Annual Earnings: $41,340**
- **Growth: 11.5%**
- **Annual Job Openings: 61,000**

Plan, direct, or coordinate activities of an organization or department that serves food and beverages.

Test cooked food by tasting and smelling it to ensure palatability and flavor conformity. Investigate and resolve complaints regarding food quality, service, or accommodations. Schedule and receive food and beverage deliveries, checking delivery contents to verify product quality and quantity. Monitor food preparation methods, portion sizes, and garnishing and presentation of food to ensure that food is prepared and presented in an acceptable manner. Monitor budgets and payroll records and review financial transactions to ensure that expenditures are authorized and budgeted. Monitor compliance with health and fire regulations regarding food preparation and serving and building maintenance in lodging and dining facilities. Schedule staff hours and assign duties. Coordinate assignments of cooking personnel to ensure economical use of food and timely preparation. Keep records required by government agencies regarding sanitation and food subsidies when appropriate. Establish standards for personnel performance and customer service. Estimate food, liquor, wine, and other beverage consumption to anticipate amounts to be purchased or requisitioned. Review work procedures and operational problems to determine ways to improve service, performance, or safety. Perform some food preparation or service tasks such as cooking, clearing tables, and serving food and drinks when necessary. Maintain food and equipment inventories and keep inventory records. Organize and direct worker training programs, resolve personnel problems, hire new staff, and evaluate employee performance in dining and lodging facilities. Order and purchase equipment and supplies. Review menus and analyze recipes to determine labor and overhead costs and assign prices to menu items. Record the number, type, and cost of items sold to determine which items may be unpopular or less profitable. Assess staffing needs and recruit staff, using methods such as newspaper advertisements or attendance at job fairs. Arrange for equipment maintenance and repairs and coordinate a variety of services such as waste removal and pest control.

GOE Information—Interest Area: 09. Hospitality, Tourism, and Recreation. Work Group: 09.01. Managerial Work in Hospitality and Tourism. Personality Type—Enterprising. Enterprising occupations frequently involve starting up and carrying out projects. These occupations can involve leading people and making many decisions. They sometimes require risk taking and often deal with business. Work Values—Authority; Creativity; Autonomy; Responsibility; Security; Recognition. Skills—Management of Personnel Resources; Management of Financial Resources; Management of Material Resources; Systems Evaluation; Monitoring; Time Management; Speaking. Abilities—Cognitive: Mathematical Reasoning; Memorization; Perceptual Speed; Number Facility; Originality; Fluency of Ideas. Psychomotor: Speed of Limb Movement; Manual Dexterity; Arm-Hand Steadiness; Multilimb Coordination; Control Precision; Finger Dexterity. Physical: Extent Flexibility; Stamina; Trunk Strength; Gross Body Coordination; Static Strength. Sensory: Visual Color Discrimination; Auditory Attention; Speech Recognition; Hearing Sensitivity; Far Vision; Near Vision. General Work Activities—Information Input: Identifying Objects, Actions, and Events; Getting Information; Monitoring Processes, Materials, or Surroundings. Mental Process: Organizing, Planning, and Prioritizing; Scheduling Work and Activities; Making Decisions and Solving Problems. Work Output: Performing General Physical Activities; Handling and Moving Objects; Controlling Machines and Processes. Interacting with Others: Establishing and Maintaining Interpersonal Relationships; Resolving Conflicts and Negotiating with Others; Communicating with Other Workers. Physical Work Conditions—Indoors; Very Hot or Cold; Standing; Walking and Running; Using Hands on Objects, Tools, or Controls; Repetitive Motions. Other Job Characteristics—Need to Be Exact or Accurate; Repeat Same Tasks.

Experience—Job Zone 3. Previous work-related skill, knowledge, or experience is required. Job Preparation—SVP 6.0 to less than 7.0—more than one year and less than four years. Knowledges—Food Production; Sales and Marketing; Production and Processing; Customer and Personal Service; Administration and Management; Personnel and Human Resources. Instructional Programs—Hospitality Administration/Management, General; Hotel/Motel Administration/Management; Restaurant, Culinary, and Catering Management/Manager; Restaurant/Food Services Management.

Related SOC Job—11-9051 Food Service Managers. Related OOH Job—Food Service Managers. Related DOT Jobs—185.137-010 Manager, Fast Food Services; 187.161-010 Executive Chef; 187.167-026 Director, Food Services; 187.167-050 Manager, Agricultural-Labor Camp; 187.167-066 Manager, Camp; 187.167-106 Manager, Food Service; 187.167-126 Manager, Liquor Establishment; 187.167-206 Dietary Manager; 187.167-210 Director, Food and Beverage; 319.137-014 Manager, Flight Kitchen; 319.137-018 Manager, Industrial Cafeteria; 320.137-010 Manager, Boarding House.

11-9061.00 Funeral Directors

- Education/Training Required: Associate degree
- Employed: 21,960
- Annual Earnings: $47,630
- Growth: 6.7%
- Annual Job Openings: 3,000

Perform various tasks to arrange and direct funeral services, such as coordinating transportation of body to mortuary for embalming, interviewing family or other authorized person to arrange details, selecting pallbearers, procuring official for religious rites, and providing transportation for mourners.

Consult with families or friends of the deceased to arrange funeral details such as obituary notice wording, casket selection, and plans for services. Plan, schedule, and coordinate funerals, burials, and cremations, arranging such details as the time and place of services. Obtain information needed to complete legal documents such as death certificates and burial permits. Oversee the preparation and care of the remains of people who have died. Contact cemeteries to schedule the opening and closing of graves. Provide information on funeral service options, products, and merchandise and maintain a casket display area. Manage funeral home operations, including hiring and supervising embalmers, funeral attendants, and other staff. Offer counsel and comfort to bereaved families and friends. Close caskets and lead funeral corteges to churches or burial sites. Arrange for clergy members to perform needed services. Provide or arrange transportation between sites for the remains, mourners, pallbearers, clergy, and flowers. Perform embalming duties as necessary. Direct preparations and shipment of bodies for out-of-state burial. Discuss and negotiate prearranged funerals with clients. Inform survivors of benefits for which they may be eligible. Maintain financial records, order merchandise, and prepare accounts. Plan placement of caskets at funeral sites and place and adjust lights, fixtures, and floral displays. Arrange for pallbearers and inform pallbearers and honorary groups of their duties. Receive people and usher them to their seats for services.

GOE Information—Interest Area: 14. Retail and Wholesale Sales and Service. Work Group: 14.01. Managerial Work in Retail/Wholesale Sales and Service. Personality Type—Enterprising. Enterprising occupations frequently involve starting up and carrying out projects. These occupations can involve leading people and making many decisions. They sometimes require risk taking and often deal with business. Work Values—Social Service; Autonomy; Authority; Security; Compensation; Responsibility. Skills—Service Orientation; Management of Financial Resources; Social Perceptiveness; Management of Personnel Resources; Management of Material Resources; Coordination. Abilities—Cognitive: Number Facility; Memorization; Written Expression; Oral Expression; Mathematical Reasoning; Written Comprehension. Psychomotor: None met the criteria. Physical: None met the criteria. Sensory: Speech Recognition; Speech Clarity; Near Vision; Depth Perception; Visual Color Discrimination. General Work Activities—Information Input: Getting Information; Identifying Objects, Actions, and Events; Monitoring Processes, Materials, or Surroundings. Mental Process: Making Decisions and Solving Problems; Updating and Using Relevant Knowledge; Processing Information. Work Output: Handling and Moving Objects; Documenting or Recording Information; Performing General Physical Activities. Interacting with Others: Performing for or Working with the Public; Assisting and Caring for Others; Establishing and Maintaining Interpersonal Relationships. Physical Work Conditions—More Often Indoors Than Outdoors; Contaminants; Disease or Infections; Standing. Other Job Characteristics—Need to Be Exact or Accurate; Repeat Same Tasks.

Experience—Job Zone 3. Previous work-related skill, knowledge, or experience is required. Job Preparation—SVP 6.0 to less than 7.0—more than one year and less than four years. Knowledges—Therapy and Counseling; Philosophy and Theology; Customer and Personal Service; Sales and Marketing; Clerical Practices; Psychology. Instructional Programs—Funeral Direction/Service; Funeral Service and Mortuary Science, General.

Related SOC Job—11-9061 Funeral Directors. Related OOH Job—Funeral Directors. Related DOT Job—187.167-030 Director, Funeral.

11-9071.00 Gaming Managers

- Education/Training Required: Work experience in a related occupation
- Employed: 3,310
- Annual Earnings: $59,940
- Growth: 22.6%
- Annual Job Openings: 1,000

Plan, organize, direct, control, or coordinate gaming operations in a casino. Formulate gaming policies for their area of responsibility.

Resolve customer complaints regarding problems such as payout errors. Remove suspected cheaters, such as card counters and other players who may have systems that shift the odds of winning to their favor. Maintain familiarity with all games used at a facility, as well as strategies and tricks employed in those games. Train new workers and evaluate their performance. Circulate among gaming tables to ensure that operations are conducted properly, that dealers follow house rules, and that players are not cheating. Explain and interpret house rules, such as game rules and betting limits. Monitor staffing levels to ensure that games and tables are adequately staffed for each shift, arranging for staff rotations and breaks and locating substitute employees as necessary. Interview and hire workers. Prepare work schedules and station assignments and keep attendance records. Direct the distribution of complimentary hotel rooms, meals, and other discounts or free items given to players based on their length of play and betting totals. Establish policies on issues such as the type of gambling offered and the odds, the extension of credit, and the serving of food and beverages. Track supplies of money to tables and perform any required paperwork. Set and maintain a bank and table limit for each game. Monitor credit extended to players. Review operational expenses, budget estimates, betting accounts, and collection reports for accuracy. Record, collect, and pay off bets, issuing receipts as necessary. Direct workers compiling summary sheets that show wager amounts and payoffs for races and events. Notify board attendants of table vacancies so that waiting patrons can play.

GOE Information—Interest Area: 09. Hospitality, Tourism, and Recreation. **Work Group:** 09.01. Managerial Work in Hospitality and Tourism. **Personality Type—**Enterprising. Enterprising occupations frequently involve starting up and carrying out projects. These occupations can involve leading people and making many decisions. They sometimes require risk taking and often deal with business. **Work Values—**Authority; Responsibility; Social Service; Creativity; Autonomy; Working Conditions. **Skills—**Management of Personnel Resources; Management of Financial Resources; Systems Evaluation; Service Orientation; Negotiation; Social Perceptiveness. **Abilities—** *Cognitive:* Number Facility; Mathematical Reasoning; Problem Sensitivity; Selective Attention; Flexibility of Closure; Inductive Reasoning. *Psychomotor:* None met the criteria. *Physical:* Trunk Strength. *Sensory:* Far Vision; Speech Clarity; Speech Recognition; Visual Color Discrimination; Auditory Attention. **General Work Activities—***Information Input:* Getting Information; Monitoring Processes, Materials, or Surroundings; Identifying Objects, Actions, and Events. *Mental Process:* Organizing, Planning, and Prioritizing; Evaluating Information Against Standards; Updating and Using Relevant Knowledge. *Work Output:* Documenting or Recording Information; Handling and Moving Objects; Interacting With Computers. *Interacting with Others:* Establishing and Maintaining Interpersonal Relationships; Resolving Conflicts and Negotiating with Others; Communicating with Other Workers. **Physical Work Conditions—**Indoors; Noisy; Contaminants; Standing; Walking and Running. **Other Job Characteristics—**Need to Be Exact or Accurate; Repeat Same Tasks; Errors Have Important Consequences.

Experience—Job Zone 3. Previous work-related skill, knowledge, or experience is required. **Job Preparation—**SVP 6.0 to less than 7.0—more than one year and less than four years. **Knowledges—**Sales and Marketing; Customer and Personal Service; Personnel and Human Resources; Administration and Management; Economics and Accounting; Mathematics. **Instructional Program—**Personal and Culinary Services, Other.

Related SOC Job—11-9071 Gaming Managers. **Related OOH Job—**Gaming Managers. **Related DOT Jobs—**187.167-014 Bookmaker; 187.167-070 Manager, Casino; 187.167-134 Manager, Mutuel Department; 343.137-010 Manager, Cardroom.

11-9081.00 Lodging Managers

- Education/Training Required: Work experience in a related occupation
- Employed: 31,040
- Annual Earnings: $40,610
- Growth: 16.6%
- Annual Job Openings: 10,000

Plan, direct, or coordinate activities of an organization or department that provides lodging and other accommodations.

Greet and register guests. Answer inquiries pertaining to hotel policies and services and resolve occupants' complaints. Assign duties to workers and schedule shifts. Coordinate front-office activities of hotels or motels and resolve problems. Participate in financial activities such as the setting of room rates, the establishment of budgets, and the allocation of funds to departments. Confer and cooperate with other managers to ensure coordination of hotel activities. Collect payments and record data pertaining to funds and expenditures. Manage and maintain temporary or permanent lodging facilities. Observe and monitor staff performance to ensure efficient operations and adherence to facility's policies and procedures. Train staff members. Show, rent, or assign accommodations. Develop and implement policies and procedures for the operation of a department or establishment. Inspect guest rooms, public areas, and grounds for cleanliness and appearance. Prepare required paperwork pertaining to departmental functions. Interview and hire applicants. Purchase supplies and arrange for outside services such as deliveries, laundry, maintenance and repair, and trash collection. Arrange telephone answering services, deliver mail and packages, or answer questions regarding locations for eating and entertainment. Organize and coordinate the work of staff and convention personnel for meetings to be held at a particular facility. Perform marketing and public relations activities. Receive and process advance registration payments, mail letters of confirmation, or return checks when registrations cannot be accepted. Meet with clients to schedule and plan details of conventions, banquets, receptions, and other functions. Provide assistance to staff members by inspecting rooms, setting tables, or doing laundry. Book tickets for guests for local tours and attractions.

GOE Information—Interest Area: 09. Hospitality, Tourism, and Recreation. **Work Group:** 09.01. Managerial Work in Hospitality and Tourism. **Personality Type—**Enterprising. Enterprising occupations frequently involve starting up and carrying out projects. These occupations can involve leading people and making many decisions. They sometimes require risk taking and often deal with business. **Work Values—**Authority; Autonomy; Social Service; Responsibility; Working Conditions; Creativity. **Skills—**Management of Financial Resources; Management of Material Resources; Negotiation; Social Perceptiveness; Management of Personnel Resources; Monitoring. **Abilities—***Cognitive:* Memorization; Mathematical Reasoning;

Written Expression; Time Sharing; Problem Sensitivity; Deductive Reasoning. *Psychomotor:* None met the criteria. *Physical:* None met the criteria. *Sensory:* Speech Recognition. **General Work Activities—** *Information Input:* Getting Information; Identifying Objects, Actions, and Events; Monitoring Processes, Materials, or Surroundings. *Mental Process:* Organizing, Planning, and Prioritizing; Making Decisions and Solving Problems; Processing Information. *Work Output:* Documenting or Recording Information; Interacting With Computers. *Interacting with Others:* Establishing and Maintaining Interpersonal Relationships; Resolving Conflicts and Negotiating with Others; Performing for or Working with the Public. **Physical Work Conditions—**Indoors; Sitting. **Other Job Characteristics—**Repeat Same Tasks; Need to Be Exact or Accurate.

Experience—Job Zone 3. Previous work-related skill, knowledge, or experience is required. **Job Preparation—**SVP 6.0 to less than 7.0—more than one year and less than four years. **Knowledges—**Sales and Marketing; Clerical Practices; Personnel and Human Resources; Economics and Accounting; Customer and Personal Service; Psychology. **Instructional Programs—**Hospitality Administration/Management, General; Hospitality and Recreation Marketing Operations; Hotel/Motel Administration/Management; Resort Management; Selling Skills and Sales Operations.

Related SOC Job—11-9081 Lodging Managers. **Related OOH Job—**Lodging Managers. **Related DOT Jobs—**187.117-038 Manager, Hotel or Motel; 187.137-018 Manager, Front Office; 320.137-014 Manager, Lodging Facilities.

11-9111.00 Medical and Health Services Managers

- **Education/Training Required: Work experience plus degree**
- **Employed: 230,130**
- **Annual Earnings: $69,700**
- **Growth: 22.8%**
- **Annual Job Openings: 33,000**

Plan, direct, or coordinate medicine and health services in hospitals, clinics, managed care organizations, public health agencies, or similar organizations.

Direct, supervise, and evaluate work activities of medical, nursing, technical, clerical, service, maintenance, and other personnel. Establish objectives and evaluative or operational criteria for units they manage. Direct or conduct recruitment, hiring, and training of personnel. Develop and maintain computerized record management systems to store and process data such as personnel activities and information and to produce reports. Develop and implement organizational policies and procedures for the facility or medical unit. Conduct and administer fiscal operations, including accounting, planning budgets, authorizing expenditures, establishing rates for services, and coordinating financial reporting. Establish work schedules and assignments for staff according to workload, space, and equipment availability. Maintain communication between governing boards, medical staff, and department heads by attending board meetings and coordinating interdepartmental functioning. Monitor the use of diagnostic services, inpatient beds, facilities, and staff to ensure effective use of resources and assess the need for additional staff, equipment, and services. Maintain awareness of advances in medicine, computerized diagnostic and treatment equipment, data processing technology, government regulations, health insurance changes, and financing options. Manage change in integrated health care delivery systems, such as work restructuring, technological innovations, and shifts in the focus of care. Prepare activity reports to inform management of the status and implementation plans of programs, services, and quality initiatives. Plan, implement, and administer programs and services in a health care or medical facility, including personnel administration, training, and coordination of medical, nursing, and physical plant staff. Consult with medical, business, and community groups to discuss service problems, respond to community needs, enhance public relations, coordinate activities and plans, and promote health programs. Inspect facilities and recommend building or equipment modifications to ensure emergency readiness and compliance to access, safety, and sanitation regulations.

GOE Information—Interest Area: 08. Health Science. **Work Group:** 08.01. Managerial Work in Medical and Health Services. **Personality Type—**Enterprising. Enterprising occupations frequently involve starting up and carrying out projects. These occupations can involve leading people and making many decisions. They sometimes require risk taking and often deal with business. **Work Values—**Authority; Social Service; Creativity; Working Conditions; Social Status; Responsibility. **Skills—**Management of Material Resources; Management of Personnel Resources; Management of Financial Resources; Systems Evaluation; Persuasion; Service Orientation. **Abilities—***Cognitive:* Mathematical Reasoning; Number Facility; Originality; Deductive Reasoning; Written Expression; Oral Comprehension. *Psychomotor:* None met the criteria. *Physical:* Trunk Strength. *Sensory:* Speech Clarity; Speech Recognition; Far Vision; Near Vision. **General Work Activities—***Information Input:* Monitoring Processes, Materials, or Surroundings; Getting Information; Identifying Objects, Actions, and Events. *Mental Process:* Organizing, Planning, and Prioritizing; Updating and Using Relevant Knowledge; Making Decisions and Solving Problems. *Work Output:* Interacting With Computers; Documenting or Recording Information; Performing General Physical Activities. *Interacting with Others:* Establishing and Maintaining Interpersonal Relationships; Resolving Conflicts and Negotiating with Others; Guiding, Directing, and Motivating Subordinates. **Physical Work Conditions—**Indoors; Noisy; Disease or Infections; Sitting. **Other Job Characteristics—**Need to Be Exact or Accurate.

Experience—Job Zone 5. Extensive skill, knowledge, and experience are needed. **Job Preparation—**SVP 8.0 and above—four years to more than 10 years. **Knowledges—**Therapy and Counseling; Medicine and Dentistry; Philosophy and Theology; Personnel and Human Resources; Sociology and Anthropology; Biology. **Instructional Programs—**Community Health and Preventive Medicine; Health and Medical Administrative Services, Other; Health Information/Medical Records Administration/Administrator; Health Services Administration; Health Unit Manager/Ward Supervisor; Health/Health Care Administration/Management; Hospital and Health Care Facilities Administration/Management; Nursing Administration (MSN, MS, PhD); Public Health, General (MPH, DPH).

Related SOC Job—11-9111 Medical and Health Services Managers. **Related OOH Job—**Medical and Health Services Managers. **Related DOT Jobs—**075.117-014 Director, Community-Health Nursing; 075.117-022 Director, Nursing Service; 075.117-026 Director, Occupational Health Nursing; 076.117-010 Coordinator of Rehabilitation Services; 079.117-010 Emergency Medical Services Coordinator; 079.167-014 Medical-Record Administrator; 169.167-090 Quality Assurance Coordinator; 187.117-010 Administrator, Health Care Facility; 187.117-058 Director, Outpatient Services.

11-9121.00 Natural Sciences Managers

- Education/Training Required: **Work experience plus degree**
- Employed: **40,400**
- Annual Earnings: **$93,090**
- Growth: **13.6%**
- Annual Job Openings: **5,000**

Plan, direct, or coordinate activities in such fields as life sciences, physical sciences, mathematics, and statistics and research and development in these fields.

Confer with scientists, engineers, regulators, and others to plan and review projects and to provide technical assistance. Develop client relationships and communicate with clients to explain proposals, present research findings, establish specifications, or discuss project status. Plan and direct research, development, and production activities. Prepare project proposals. Design and coordinate successive phases of problem analysis, solution proposals, and testing. Review project activities and prepare and review research, testing, and operational reports. Hire, supervise, and evaluate engineers, technicians, researchers, and other staff. Determine scientific and technical goals within broad outlines provided by top management and make detailed plans to accomplish these goals. Develop and implement policies, standards, and procedures for the architectural, scientific, and technical work performed to ensure regulatory compliance and operations enhancement. Develop innovative technology and train staff for its implementation. Provide for stewardship of plant and animal resources and habitats, studying land use; monitoring animal populations; and providing shelter, resources, and medical treatment for animals. Conduct own research in field of expertise. Recruit personnel and oversee the development and maintenance of staff competence. Advise and assist in obtaining patents or meeting other legal requirements. Prepare and administer budget, approve and review expenditures, and prepare financial reports. Make presentations at professional meetings to further knowledge in the field.

GOE Information—Interest Area: 15. Scientific Research, Engineering, and Mathematics. **Work Group:** 15.01. Managerial Work in Scientific Research, Engineering, and Mathematics. **Personality Type—**Investigative. Investigative occupations frequently involve working with ideas and require an extensive amount of thinking. These occupations can involve searching for facts and figuring out problems mentally. **Work Values—**Authority; Creativity; Working Conditions; Responsibility; Autonomy; Co-workers. **Skills—**Science; Mathematics; Active Learning; Management of Personnel Resources; Reading Comprehension; Writing. **Abilities—***Cognitive:* Number Facility; Mathematical Reasoning; Oral Comprehension; Deductive Reasoning; Written Expression; Originality. *Psychomotor:* None met the criteria. *Physical:* None met the criteria. *Sensory:* Speech Clarity; Speech Recognition; Near Vision. **General Work Activities—***Information Input:* Getting Information; Identifying Objects, Actions, and Events; Monitoring Processes, Materials, or Surroundings. *Mental Process:* Updating and Using Relevant Knowledge; Organizing, Planning, and Prioritizing; Processing Information. *Work Output:* Documenting or Recording Information; Interacting With Computers. *Interacting with Others:* Communicating with Other Workers; Establishing and Maintaining Interpersonal Relationships; Coordinating the Work and Activities of Others. **Physical Work Conditions—**Indoors; Noisy; Sitting. **Other Job Characteristics—**Need to Be Exact or Accurate.

Experience—Job Zone 5. Extensive skill, knowledge, and experience are needed. **Job Preparation—**SVP 8.0 and above—four years to more than 10 years. **Knowledges—**Biology; Chemistry; Engineering and Technology; Law and Government; Administration and Management; Production and Processing. **Instructional Programs—**Acoustics; Algebra and Number Theory; Analysis and Functional Analysis; Analytical Chemistry; Anatomy; Animal Genetics; Animal Physiology; Applied Mathematics; Applied Mathematics, Other; Astronomy; Astrophysics; Atmospheric Chemistry and Climatology; Atmospheric Physics and Dynamics; Atmospheric Sciences and Meteorology, General; Atmospheric Sciences and Meteorology, Other; Atomic/Molecular Physics; Biochemistry; Biological and Biomedical Sciences, Other; Biological and Physical Sciences; Biology/Biological Sciences, General; Biometry/Biometrics; Biophysics; Biopsychology; Biostatistics; Biotechnology; Botany/Plant Biology; Botany/Plant Biology, Other; Cell/Cellular Biology and Anatomical Sciences, Other; Cell/Cellular Biology and Histology; Chemical Physics; Chemistry, General; Chemistry, Other; Computational Mathematics; Ecology; Ecology, Evolution, and Systematics, Other; Elementary Particle Physics; Entomology; Evolutionary Biology; Geochemistry; Geochemistry and Petrology; Geological and Earth Sciences/Geosciences, Other; Geology/Earth Science, General; Geometry/Geometric Analysis; Geophysics and Seismology; Hydrology and Water Resources Science; Immunology; Inorganic Chemistry; Logic; Marine Biology and Biological Oceanography; Mathematics and Computer Science; Mathematics and Statistics, Other; Mathematics, General; Medical Microbiology and Bacteriology; Meteorology; Microbiology, General; Molecular Biology; Natural Sciences; Neuroscience; Nuclear Physics; Nutrition Sciences; Oceanography, Chemical and Physical; Operations Research; Optics/Optical Sciences; Organic Chemistry; Paleontology; Parasitology; Pathology/Experimental Pathology; Pharmacology; Physical and Theoretical Chemistry; Physical Sciences; Physical Sciences, Other; Physics, General; Physics, Other; Planetary Astronomy and Science; Plant Genetics; Plant Pathology/Phytopathology; Plant Physiology; Plasma and High-Temperature Physics; Polymer Chemistry; Radiation Biology/Radiobiology; others.

Related SOC Job—11-9121 Natural Sciences Managers. **Related OOH Job—**Engineering and Natural Sciences Managers. **Related DOT Jobs—**008.167-010 Technical Director, Chemical Plant; 022.161-010 Chemical Laboratory Chief; 029.167-014 Project Manager, Environmental Research.

11-9131.00 Postmasters and Mail Superintendents

- Education/Training Required: **Work experience in a related occupation**
- Employed: **26,120**
- Annual Earnings: **$52,710**
- Growth: **0.0%**
- Annual Job Openings: **2,000**

Direct and coordinate operational, administrative, management, and supportive services of a U.S. post office or coordinate activities of workers engaged in postal and related work in assigned post office.

Organize and supervise activities such as the processing of incoming and outgoing mail. Direct and coordinate operational, management, and supportive services of one or a number of postal facilities. Resolve customer complaints. Hire and train employees and evaluate their performance. Prepare employee work schedules. Negotiate labor disputes. Prepare and submit detailed and summary reports of post office activities to designated supervisors. Collect rents for post office boxes. Issue and cash money orders. Inform the public of available services and of postal laws and regulations. Select and train postmasters and managers of associate postal units. Confer with suppliers to obtain bids for proposed purchases and to requisition supplies; disburse funds according to federal regulations.

GOE Information—Interest Area: 16. Transportation, Distribution, and Logistics. **Work Group:** 16.01. Managerial Work in Transportation. **Personality Type**—Enterprising. Enterprising occupations frequently involve starting up and carrying out projects. These occupations can involve leading people and making many decisions. They sometimes require risk taking and often deal with business. **Work Values**—Authority; Security; Company Policies and Practices; Working Conditions; Compensation; Variety. **Skills**—Negotiation; Persuasion; Monitoring; Management of Personnel Resources; Service Orientation; Management of Financial Resources. **Abilities**—*Cognitive:* Number Facility; Written Expression; Mathematical Reasoning; Originality; Category Flexibility; Written Comprehension. *Psychomotor:* None met the criteria. *Physical:* None met the criteria. *Sensory:* Speech Recognition; Visual Color Discrimination. **General Work Activities**—*Information Input:* Getting Information; Monitoring Processes, Materials, or Surroundings; Identifying Objects, Actions, and Events. *Mental Process:* Organizing, Planning, and Prioritizing; Processing Information; Scheduling Work and Activities. *Work Output:* Documenting or Recording Information; Interacting With Computers. *Interacting with Others:* Communicating with Other Workers; Guiding, Directing, and Motivating Subordinates; Coaching and Developing Others. **Physical Work Conditions**—Indoors; Contaminants; Standing. **Other Job Characteristics**—Need to Be Exact or Accurate; Repeat Same Tasks.

Experience—Job Zone 3. Previous work-related skill, knowledge, or experience is required. **Job Preparation**—SVP 6.0 to less than 7.0—more than one year and less than four years. **Knowledges**—Production and Processing; Personnel and Human Resources; Public Safety and Security; Clerical Practices; Economics and Accounting; Education and Training. **Instructional Program**—Public Administration.

Related SOC Job—11-9131 Postmasters and Mail Superintendents. **Related OOH Job**—Postmasters and Mail Superintendents. **Related DOT Jobs**—188.167-066 Postmaster; 188.167-086 Sectional Center Manager, Postal Service.

11-9141.00 Property, Real Estate, and Community Association Managers

- **Education/Training Required:** Bachelor's degree
- **Employed:** 154,230
- **Annual Earnings:** $41,900
- **Growth:** 15.3%
- **Annual Job Openings:** 58,000

Plan, direct, or coordinate selling, buying, leasing, or governance activities of commercial, industrial, or residential real estate properties.

Meet with prospective tenants to show properties, explain terms of occupancy, and provide information about local areas. Direct collection of monthly assessments; rental fees; and deposits and payment of insurance premiums, mortgage, taxes, and incurred operating expenses. Inspect grounds, facilities, and equipment routinely to determine necessity of repairs or maintenance. Investigate complaints, disturbances, and violations and resolve problems, following management rules and regulations. Manage and oversee operations, maintenance, administration, and improvement of commercial, industrial, or residential properties. Plan, schedule, and coordinate

general maintenance, major repairs, and remodeling or construction projects for commercial or residential properties. Negotiate the sale, lease, or development of property and complete or review appropriate documents and forms. Maintain records of sales, rental or usage activity, special permits issued, maintenance and operating costs, or property availability. Determine and certify the eligibility of prospective tenants, following government regulations. Prepare detailed budgets and financial reports for properties. Direct and coordinate the activities of staff and contract personnel and evaluate their performance. Maintain contact with insurance carriers, fire and police departments, and other agencies to ensure protection and compliance with codes and regulations. Market vacant space to prospective tenants through leasing agents, advertising, or other methods. Solicit and analyze bids from contractors for repairs, renovations, and maintenance. Review rents to ensure that they are in line with rental markets. Prepare and administer contracts for provision of property services such as cleaning, maintenance, and security services. Purchase building and maintenance supplies, equipment, or furniture. Act as liaisons between on-site managers or tenants and owners. Confer regularly with community association members to ensure their needs are being met. Meet with boards of directors and committees to discuss and resolve legal and environmental issues or disputes between neighbors.

GOE Information—Interest Area: 14. Retail and Wholesale Sales and Service. **Work Group:** 14.01. Managerial Work in Retail/Wholesale Sales and Service. **Personality Type**—Enterprising. Enterprising occupations frequently involve starting up and carrying out projects. These occupations can involve leading people and making many decisions. They sometimes require risk taking and often deal with business. **Work Values**—Authority; Autonomy; Responsibility; Variety; Activity; Working Conditions. **Skills**—Management of Financial Resources; Management of Personnel Resources; Management of Material Resources; Time Management; Repairing; Judgment and Decision Making. **Abilities**—*Cognitive:* Written Comprehension; Written Expression; Number Facility; Oral Expression; Fluency of Ideas; Problem Sensitivity. *Psychomotor:* None met the criteria. *Physical:* None met the criteria. *Sensory:* Near Vision; Speech Recognition; Speech Clarity. **General Work Activities**—*Information Input:* Getting Information; Monitoring Processes, Materials, or Surroundings; Inspecting Equipment, Structures, or Materials. *Mental Process:* Organizing, Planning, and Prioritizing; Judging the Qualities of Things, Services, or Other People's Work; Processing Information. *Work Output:* Documenting or Recording Information. *Interacting with Others:* Establishing and Maintaining Interpersonal Relationships; Communicating with Persons Outside Organization; Resolving Conflicts and Negotiating with Others. **Physical Work Conditions**—More Often Indoors Than Outdoors; Sitting. **Other Job Characteristics**—Need to Be Exact or Accurate; Repeat Same Tasks.

Experience—Job Zone 3. Previous work-related skill, knowledge, or experience is required. **Job Preparation**—SVP 6.0 to less than 7.0—more than one year and less than four years. **Knowledges**—Sales and Marketing; Clerical Practices; Economics and Accounting; Customer and Personal Service; Administration and Management; Personnel and Human Resources. **Instructional Program**—Real Estate.

Related SOC Job—11-9141 Property, Real Estate, and Community Association Managers. **Related OOH Job**—Property, Real Estate, and Community Association Managers. **Related DOT Jobs**—186.117-042 Manager, Land Development; 186.117-046 Manager, Leasing; 186.117-058 Real-Estate Agent; 186.117-062 Rental Manager, Public Events Facilities; 186.167-018 Manager, Apartment House; 186.167-030 Manager, Housing Project; 186.167-038 Manager, Land

Leases-And-Rentals; 186.167-042 Manager, Market; 186.167-046 Manager, Property; 186.167-062 Condominium Manager; 186.167-066 Manager, Real-Estate Firm; 187.167-190 Superintendent, Building; 191.117-050 Right-Of-Way Supervisor.

11-9151.00 Social and Community Service Managers

- **Education/Training Required: Bachelor's degree**
- **Employed: 112,910**
- **Annual Earnings: $49,500**
- **Growth: 25.5%**
- **Annual Job Openings: 17,000**

Plan, organize, or coordinate the activities of a social service program or community outreach organization. Oversee the program or organization's budget and policies regarding participant involvement, program requirements, and benefits. Work may involve directing social workers, counselors, or probation officers.

Establish and maintain relationships with other agencies and organizations in community to meet community needs and to ensure that services are not duplicated. Prepare and maintain records and reports, such as budgets, personnel records, or training manuals. Direct activities of professional and technical staff members and volunteers. Evaluate the work of staff and volunteers to ensure that programs are of appropriate quality and that resources are used effectively. Establish and oversee administrative procedures to meet objectives set by boards of directors or senior management. Participate in the determination of organizational policies regarding such issues as participant eligibility, program requirements, and program benefits. Research and analyze member or community needs to determine program directions and goals. Speak to community groups to explain and interpret agency purposes, programs, and policies. Recruit, interview, and hire or sign up volunteers and staff. Represent organizations in relations with governmental and media institutions. Plan and administer budgets for programs, equipment, and support services. Analyze proposed legislation, regulations, or rule changes to determine how agency services could be impacted. Act as consultants to agency staff and other community programs regarding the interpretation of program-related federal, state, and county regulations and policies. Implement and evaluate staff training programs. Direct fundraising activities and the preparation of public relations materials.

GOE Information—Interest Area: 07. Government and Public Administration. **Work Group:** 07.01. Managerial Work in Government and Public Administration. **Personality Type—**Social. Social occupations frequently involve working with, communicating with, and teaching people. These occupations often involve helping or providing service to others. **Work Values—**Social Service; Authority; Security; Autonomy; Creativity; Activity. **Skills—**Management of Personnel Resources; Social Perceptiveness; Negotiation; Service Orientation; Systems Evaluation; Persuasion. **Abilities—***Cognitive:* Mathematical Reasoning; Memorization; Originality; Fluency of Ideas; Written Expression; Visualization. *Psychomotor:* None met the criteria. *Physical:* None met the criteria. *Sensory:* Speech Clarity; Speech Recognition; Near Vision; Far Vision. **General Work Activities—***Information Input:* Getting Information; Identifying Objects, Actions, and Events; Monitoring Processes, Materials, or Surroundings. *Mental Process:* Making Decisions and Solving Problems; Thinking Creatively; Organizing, Planning, and Prioritizing. *Work Output:* Documenting or Recording Information; Interacting With Computers. *Interacting with Others:* Establishing

and Maintaining Interpersonal Relationships; Communicating with Persons Outside Organization; Coordinating the Work and Activities of Others. **Physical Work Conditions—**Indoors; Noisy; Sitting. **Other Job Characteristics—**Need to Be Exact or Accurate.

Experience—Job Zone 4. A minimum of two to four years of work-related skill, knowledge, or experience is needed. **Job Preparation—**SVP 7.0 to less than 8.0–two years to less than 10 years. **Knowledges—**Sociology and Anthropology; Therapy and Counseling; Psychology; Education and Training; Philosophy and Theology; Clerical Practices. **Instructional Programs—**Business Administration/Management; Business, Management, Marketing, and Related Support Services; Business/Commerce, General; Community Organization and Advocacy; Entrepreneurship/Entrepreneurial Studies; Human Services, General; Non-Profit/Public/Organizational Management; Public Administration.

Related SOC Job—11-9151 Social and Community Service Managers. **Related OOH Job—**Social and Community Service Managers. **Related DOT Jobs—**187.117-022 District Adviser; 187.117-026 Executive Director, Sheltered Workshop; 187.117-046 Program Director, Group Work; 187.117-066 Executive Director, Red Cross; 187.134-010 Supervisor, Contract-Sheltered Workshop; 187.137-014 Supervisor, Volunteer Services; 187.167-022 Coordinator, Volunteer Services; 187.167-038 Director, Volunteer Services; 187.167-214 Director, Service; 187.167-234 Director, Community Organization; 195.117-010 Administrator, Social Welfare; 195.167-022 Director, Field; others.

11-9199.99 Managers, All Other

- **Education/Training Required: Work experience in a related occupation**
- **Employed: 340,720**
- **Annual Earnings: $79,170**
- **Growth: 7.8%**
- **Annual Job Openings: 105,000**

All managers not listed separately.

No task data available.

Note: The Department of Labor has not collected some data for this job, so it has fewer details than the other descriptions.

Related SOC Job—11-9199 Managers, All Other. **Related OOH Job—**None. **Related DOT Jobs—**072.117-010 Director, Dental Services; 075.117-010 Consultant, Educational, State Board Of Nursing; 075.117-034 Executive Director, Nurses' Association; 090.164-010 Laboratory Manager; 090.167-034 Director, Field Services; 096.161-010 Home-Service Director; 096.167-010 District Extension Service Agent; 096.167-014 Specialist-In-Charge, Extension Service; 153.137-010 Manager, Pool; 168.167-066 Quality-Control Coordinator; 169.267-022 Secretary, Board-Of-Education; others.

13-0000

Business and Financial Operations Occupations

13-1000 Business Operations Specialists

13-1011.00 Agents and Business Managers of Artists, Performers, and Athletes

- **Education/Training Required: Work experience plus degree**
- **Employed: 10,640**
- **Annual Earnings: $53,800**
- **Growth: 11.8%**
- **Annual Job Openings: 2,000**

Represent and promote artists, performers, and athletes to prospective employers. May handle contract negotiation and other business matters for clients.

Schedule promotional or performance engagements for clients. Advise clients on financial and legal matters such as investments and taxes. Hire trainers or coaches to advise clients on performance matters such as training techniques or performance presentations. Prepare periodic accounting statements for clients. Manage business and financial affairs for clients, such as arranging travel and lodging, selling tickets, and directing marketing and advertising activities. Collect fees, commissions, or other payments according to contract terms. Obtain information about and inspect performance facilities, equipment, and accommodations to ensure that they meet specifications. Conduct auditions or interviews in order to evaluate potential clients. Negotiate with managers, promoters, union officials, and other persons regarding clients' contractual rights and obligations. Confer with clients to develop strategies for their careers and to explain actions taken on their behalf. Develop contacts with individuals and organizations and apply effective strategies and techniques to ensure their clients' success. Keep informed of industry trends and deals. Arrange meetings concerning issues involving their clients.

GOE Information—Interest Area: 03. Arts and Communication. **Work Group:** 03.01. Managerial Work in Arts and Communication. **Personality Type—**Enterprising. Enterprising occupations frequently involve starting up and carrying out projects. These occupations can involve leading people and making many decisions. They sometimes require risk taking and often deal with business. **Work Values—**Social Service; Autonomy; Working Conditions; Authority; Compensation; Variety. **Skills—**Management of Financial Resources; Negotiation; Management of Personnel Resources; Systems Evaluation; Systems Analysis; Speaking. **Abilities—***Cognitive:* Mathematical Reasoning; Number Facility; Oral Expression; Memorization; Fluency of Ideas; Originality. *Psychomotor:* None met the criteria. *Physical:* None met the criteria. *Sensory:* Speech Clarity. **General Work Activities—***Information Input:* Getting Information; Identifying Objects, Actions, and Events; Monitoring Processes, Materials, or Surroundings. *Mental Process:* Organizing, Planning, and Prioritizing; Scheduling Work and Activities; Making Decisions and Solving Problems. *Work Output:* Documenting or Recording Information. *Interacting with Others:* Resolving Conflicts and Negotiating with Others; Monitoring and Controlling Resources; Communicating with Persons Outside Organization. **Physical Work Conditions—**Indoors; Sitting. **Other Job Characteristics—**Errors Have Important Consequences.

Experience—Job Zone 3. Previous work-related skill, knowledge, or experience is required. **Job Preparation—**SVP 6.0 to less than 7.0—more than one year and less than four years. **Knowledges—**Economics and Accounting; Sales and Marketing; Personnel and

Human Resources; Fine Arts; Administration and Management; Law and Government. **Instructional Programs—**Arts Management; Purchasing, Procurement/Acquisitions, and Contracts Management.

Related SOC Job—13-1011 Agents and Business Managers of Artists, Performers, and Athletes. **Related OOH Job—**Agents and Business Managers of Artists, Performers, and Athletes. **Related DOT Jobs—**153.117-014 Manager, Athlete; 191.117-010 Artist's Manager; 191.117-014 Booking Manager; 191.117-018 Business Manager; 191.117-022 Circus Agent; 191.117-026 Jockey Agent; 191.117-034 Literary Agent; 191.117-038 Manager, Touring Production; 191.167-010 Advance Agent.

13-1021.00 Purchasing Agents and Buyers, Farm Products

- **Education/Training Required: Work experience in a related occupation**
- **Employed: 12,970**
- **Annual Earnings: $46,680**
- **Growth: 7.0%**
- **Annual Job Openings: 2,000**

Purchase farm products for further processing or resale.

Advise farm groups and growers on land preparation and livestock care techniques that will maximize the quantity and quality of production. Arrange for processing or resale of purchased products. Arrange for transportation and/or storage of purchased products. Examine and test crops and products to estimate their value, determine their grade, and locate any evidence of disease or insect damage. Maintain records of business transactions and product inventories, reporting data to companies or government agencies as necessary. Negotiate contracts with farmers for the production or purchase of farm products. Review orders to determine product types and quantities required to meet demand. Estimate land production possibilities, surveying property and studying factors such as crop rotation history, soil fertility, and irrigation facilities. Sell supplies such as seed, feed, fertilizers, and insecticides, arranging for loans or financing as necessary. Coordinate and direct activities of workers engaged in cutting, transporting, storing, or milling products and in maintaining records. Purchase for further processing or for resale farm products such as milk, grains, and Christmas trees. Calculate applicable government grain quotas.

GOE Information—Interest Area: 01. Agriculture and Natural Resources. **Work Group:** 01.01. Managerial Work in Agriculture and Natural Resources. **Personality Type—**Enterprising. Enterprising occupations frequently involve starting up and carrying out projects. These occupations can involve leading people and making many decisions. They sometimes require risk taking and often deal with business. **Work Values—**Co-workers; Responsibility; Authority; Autonomy; Advancement; Creativity. **Skills—**Negotiation; Management of Financial Resources; Writing; Mathematics; Management of Material Resources; Speaking. **Abilities—***Cognitive:* Number Facility; Mathematical Reasoning; Written Expression; Memorization; Oral Expression; Written Comprehension. *Psychomotor:* Wrist-Finger Speed. *Physical:* None met the criteria. *Sensory:* Speech Clarity. **General Work Activities—***Information Input:* Identifying Objects, Actions, and Events; Getting Information; Inspecting Equipment, Structures, or Materials. *Mental Process:* Making Decisions and Solving Problems; Organizing, Planning, and Prioritizing; Judging the Qualities of Things, Services, or Other People's Work. *Work Output:* Documenting or Recording Information. *Interacting with*

Others: Resolving Conflicts and Negotiating with Others; Communicating with Persons Outside Organization; Providing Consultation and Advice to Others. **Physical Work Conditions—**Indoors; More Often Standing Than Sitting; Walking and Running; Using Hands on Objects, Tools, or Controls. **Other Job Characteristics—**Need to Be Exact or Accurate.

Experience—Job Zone 4. A minimum of two to four years of work-related skill, knowledge, or experience is needed. **Job Preparation—**SVP 7.0 to less than 8.0—two years to less than 10 years. **Knowledges—**Food Production; Production and Processing; Biology; Communications and Media; Economics and Accounting; Sales and Marketing. **Instructional Program—**Agricultural/Farm Supplies Retailing and Wholesaling.

Related SOC Job—13-1021 Purchasing Agents and Buyers, Farm Products. **Related OOH Job—**Purchasing Managers, Buyers, and Purchasing Agents. **Related DOT Jobs—**162.117-010 Christmas-Tree Contractor; 162.117-022 Field Contractor; 162.117-026 Field-Contact Technician; 162.167-010 Buyer, Grain; 162.167-018 Clean-Rice Broker.

13-1022.00 Wholesale and Retail Buyers, Except Farm Products

- **Education/Training Required: Work experience in a related occupation**
- **Employed: 132,900**
- **Annual Earnings: $42,870**
- **Growth: 8.4%**
- **Annual Job Openings: 20,000**

Buy merchandise or commodities, other than farm products, for resale to consumers at the wholesale or retail level, including both durable and nondurable goods. Analyze past buying trends, sales records, price, and quality of merchandise to determine value and yield. Select, order, and authorize payment for merchandise according to contractual agreements. May conduct meetings with sales personnel and introduce new products.

Examine, select, order, and purchase at the most favorable price merchandise consistent with quality, quantity, specification requirements, and other factors. Negotiate prices, discount terms, and transportation arrangements for merchandise. Analyze and monitor sales records, trends, and economic conditions to anticipate consumer buying patterns and determine what the company will sell and how much inventory is needed. Interview and work closely with vendors to obtain and develop desired products. Authorize payment of invoices or return of merchandise. Inspect merchandise or products to determine value or yield. Set or recommend markup rates, markdown rates, and selling prices for merchandise. Confer with sales and purchasing personnel to obtain information about customer needs and preferences. Consult with store or merchandise managers about budget and goods to be purchased. Conduct staff meetings with sales personnel to introduce new merchandise. Manage the department for which they buy. Use computers to organize and locate inventory and operate spreadsheet and word processing software. Provide clerks with information to print on price tags, such as price, markups or markdowns, manufacturer number, season code, and style number. Train and supervise sales and clerical staff. Determine which products should be featured in advertising, the advertising medium to be used, and when the ads should be run. Monitor competitors' sales activities by following their advertisements in newspapers and other media.

GOE Information—Interest Area: 14. Retail and Wholesale Sales and Service. **Work Group:** 14.05. Purchasing. **Personality Type—**Enterprising. Enterprising occupations frequently involve starting up and carrying out projects. These occupations can involve leading people and making many decisions. They sometimes require risk taking and often deal with business. **Work Values—**Advancement; Working Conditions; Creativity; Variety; Responsibility; Co-workers. **Skills—**Management of Financial Resources; Management of Material Resources; Negotiation; Operations Analysis; Quality Control Analysis; Service Orientation. **Abilities—***Cognitive:* Mathematical Reasoning; Deductive Reasoning; Speed of Closure; Inductive Reasoning; Number Facility; Originality. *Psychomotor:* None met the criteria. *Physical:* None met the criteria. *Sensory:* Speech Recognition; Speech Clarity; Near Vision. **General Work Activities—***Information Input:* Estimating the Needed Characteristics of Products, Events, or Information; Monitoring Processes, Materials, or Surroundings; Inspecting Equipment, Structures, or Materials. *Mental Process:* Organizing, Planning, and Prioritizing; Updating and Using Relevant Knowledge; Thinking Creatively. *Work Output:* Performing General Physical Activities; Interacting With Computers; Handling and Moving Objects. *Interacting with Others:* Establishing and Maintaining Interpersonal Relationships; Performing for or Working with the Public; Influencing Others or Selling. **Physical Work Conditions—**Indoors; Sitting; Repetitive Motions. **Other Job Characteristics—**Need to Be Exact or Accurate; Repeat Same Tasks.

Experience—Job Zone 3. Previous work-related skill, knowledge, or experience is required. **Job Preparation—**SVP 6.0 to less than 7.0—more than one year and less than four years. **Knowledges—**Sales and Marketing; Economics and Accounting; Clerical Practices; Customer and Personal Service; Administration and Management; Transportation. **Instructional Programs—**Apparel and Accessories Marketing Operations; Apparel and Textile Marketing Management; Fashion Merchandising; Merchandising and Buying Operations; Sales, Distribution, and Marketing Operations, General.

Related SOC Job—13-1022 Wholesale and Retail Buyers, Except Farm Products. **Related OOH Job—**Purchasing Managers, Buyers, and Purchasing Agents. **Related DOT Jobs—**162.157-018 Buyer; 162.157-022 Buyer, Assistant.

13-1023.00 Purchasing Agents, Except Wholesale, Retail, and Farm Products

- **Education/Training Required: Work experience in a related occupation**
- **Employed: 267,410**
- **Annual Earnings: $49,030**
- **Growth: 8.1%**
- **Annual Job Openings: 19,000**

Purchase machinery, equipment, tools, parts, supplies, or services necessary for the operation of an establishment. Purchase raw or semi-finished materials for manufacturing.

Purchase the highest-quality merchandise at the lowest possible price and in correct amounts. Prepare purchase orders, solicit bid proposals, and review requisitions for goods and services. Research and evaluate suppliers based on price, quality, selection, service, support, availability, reliability, production and distribution capabilities, and the supplier's reputation and history. Analyze price proposals, financial reports, and other data and information to determine reasonable prices. Monitor and follow applicable laws and regulations. Negotiate, or renegotiate, and administer contracts with suppliers, vendors, and other representatives. Monitor shipments to ensure that goods come in on time and trace shipments and follow up undelivered goods in the event of problems. Confer with staff, users, and vendors to discuss defective or unacceptable goods or services and determine corrective action. Evaluate and monitor contract performance to ensure compliance with contractual obligations and to determine need for changes. Maintain and review computerized or manual records of items purchased, costs, delivery, product performance, and inventories. Review catalogs, industry periodicals, directories, trade journals, and Internet sites and consult with other department personnel to locate necessary goods and services. Study sales records and inventory levels of current stock to develop strategic purchasing programs that facilitate employee access to supplies. Interview vendors and visit suppliers' plants and distribution centers to examine and learn about products, services, and prices. Arrange the payment of duty and freight charges. Hire, train, and/or supervise purchasing clerks, buyers, and expediters. Write and review product specifications, maintaining a working technical knowledge of the goods or services to be purchased. Monitor changes affecting supply and demand, tracking market conditions, price trends, or futures markets. Formulate policies and procedures for bid proposals and procurement of goods and services. Attend meetings, trade shows, conferences, conventions, and seminars to network with people in other purchasing departments.

GOE Information—Interest Area: 14. Retail and Wholesale Sales and Service. **Work Group:** 14.05. Purchasing. **Personality Type—** Enterprising. Enterprising occupations frequently involve starting up and carrying out projects. These occupations can involve leading people and making many decisions. They sometimes require risk taking and often deal with business. **Work Values—**Authority; Advancement; Variety; Compensation; Autonomy; Working Conditions. **Skills—**Management of Financial Resources; Operations Analysis; Management of Personnel Resources; Management of Material Resources; Speaking; Writing. **Abilities—***Cognitive:* Deductive Reasoning; Written Expression; Category Flexibility; Mathematical Reasoning; Oral Expression; Inductive Reasoning. *Psychomotor:* None met the criteria. *Physical:* None met the criteria. *Sensory:* Near Vision; Speech Recognition. **General Work Activities—** *Information Input:* Monitoring Processes, Materials, or Surroundings; Getting Information; Identifying Objects, Actions, and Events. *Mental Process:* Organizing, Planning, and Prioritizing; Making Decisions and Solving Problems; Processing Information. *Work Output:* Interacting With Computers; Documenting or Recording Information; Drafting and Specifying Technical Devices. *Interacting with Others:* Establishing and Maintaining Interpersonal Relationships; Communicating with Other Workers; Communicating with Persons Outside Organization. **Physical Work Conditions—**Indoors; Sitting; Using Hands on Objects, Tools, or Controls; Repetitive Motions. **Other Job Characteristics—**Need to Be Exact or Accurate; Repeat Same Tasks; Automation.

Experience—Job Zone 3. Previous work-related skill, knowledge, or experience is required. **Job Preparation—**SVP 6.0 to less than 7.0— more than one year and less than four years. **Knowledges—**Clerical Practices; Economics and Accounting; Production and Processing; Administration and Management; Computers and Electronics; Communications and Media. **Instructional Programs—**Merchandising and Buying Operations; Sales, Distribution, and Marketing Operations, General.

Related SOC Job—13-1023 Purchasing Agents, Except Wholesale, Retail, and Farm Products. **Related OOH Job—**Purchasing Managers, Buyers, and Purchasing Agents. **Related DOT Jobs—**162.117-018 Contract Specialist; 162.157-030 Outside Property Agent; 162.157-034 Procurement Engineer; 162.157-038 Purchasing Agent; 163.117-010 Manager, Contracts.

13-1031.00 Claims Adjusters, Examiners, and Investigators

- **Education/Training Required: Long-term on-the-job training**
- **Employed: 234,030**
- **Annual Earnings: $46,190**
- **Growth: 15.1%**
- **Annual Job Openings: 28,000**

The job openings listed here are shared with 13-1031.01 Claims Examiners, Property and Casualty Insurance and 13-1031.02 Insurance Adjusters, Examiners, and Investigators.

Review settled claims to determine that payments and settlements have been made in accordance with company practices and procedures, ensuring that proper methods have been followed. Report overpayments, underpayments, and other irregularities. Confer with legal counsel on claims requiring litigation.

No task data available.

GOE Information—Interest Area: 06. Finance and Insurance. **Work Group:** 06.02. Finance/Insurance Investigation and Analysis. **Note:** The Department of Labor has not collected some data for this job, so it has fewer details than the other descriptions.

Instructional Programs—Health/Medical Claims Examiner; Insurance.

Related SOC Job—13-1031 Claims Adjusters, Examiners, and Investigators. **Related OOH Job—**Claims Adjusters, Appraisers, Examiners, and Investigators. **Related DOT Job—**No data available.

13-1031.01 Claims Examiners, Property and Casualty Insurance

- **Education/Training Required: Long-term on-the-job training**
- **Employed: 234,030**
- **Annual Earnings: $46,190**
- **Growth: 15.1%**
- **Annual Job Openings: 28,000**

The job openings listed here are shared with 13-1031.00 Claims Adjusters, Examiners, and Investigators 13-1031.02 Insurance Adjusters, Examiners, and Investigators.

Review settled insurance claims to determine that payments and settlements have been made in accordance with company practices and procedures. Report overpayments, underpayments, and other irregularities. Confer with legal counsel on claims requiring litigation.

Investigate, evaluate, and settle claims, applying technical knowledge and human relations skills to effect fair and prompt disposal of cases and to contribute to a reduced loss ratio. Pay and process claims within designated authority level. Adjust reserves or provide reserve recommendations to ensure that reserve activities are consistent with corporate policies. Enter claim payments, reserves, and new claims on computer system, inputting concise yet sufficient file documentation. Resolve complex severe exposure claims, using high-service-oriented file handling. Maintain claim files such as records of settled claims and an inventory of claims requiring detailed analysis. Verify and analyze data used in settling claims to ensure that claims are valid and that settlements are made according to company practices and procedures. Examine claims investigated by insurance adjusters, further investigating questionable claims to determine whether to authorize payments. Present cases and participate in their discussion at claim committee meetings. Contact or interview claimants, doctors, medical specialists, or employers to get additional information.

Confer with legal counsel on claims requiring litigation. Report overpayments, underpayments, and other irregularities. Communicate with reinsurance brokers to obtain information necessary for processing claims. Supervise claims adjusters to ensure that adjusters have followed proper methods. Conduct detailed bill reviews to implement sound litigation management and expense control. Prepare reports to be submitted to company's data-processing department.

GOE Information—Interest Area: 06. Finance and Insurance. **Work Group:** 06.02. Finance/Insurance Investigation and Analysis. **Personality Type**—Conventional. Conventional occupations frequently involve following set procedures and routines. These occupations can include working with data and details more than with ideas. Usually there is a clear line of authority to follow. **Work Values**—Advancement; Supervision, Human Relations; Company Policies and Practices; Working Conditions; Responsibility; Security. **Skills**—Judgment and Decision Making; Persuasion; Writing; Negotiation; Reading Comprehension; Instructing. **Abilities**—*Cognitive:* Number Facility; Mathematical Reasoning; Deductive Reasoning; Written Expression; Fluency of Ideas; Written Comprehension. *Psychomotor:* None met the criteria. *Physical:* None met the criteria. *Sensory:* Speech Recognition; Speech Clarity; Auditory Attention; Near Vision. **General Work Activities**—*Information Input:* Getting Information; Identifying Objects, Actions, and Events; Monitoring Processes, Materials, or Surroundings. *Mental Process:* Making Decisions and Solving Problems; Organizing, Planning, and Prioritizing; Processing Information. *Work Output:* Documenting or Recording Information; Interacting With Computers. *Interacting with Others:* Establishing and Maintaining Interpersonal Relationships; Communicating with Persons Outside Organization; Communicating with Other Workers. **Physical Work Conditions**—Indoors; Sitting; Using Hands on Objects, Tools, or Controls; Repetitive Motions. **Other Job Characteristics**—Need to Be Exact or Accurate; Repeat Same Tasks.

Experience—Job Zone 3. Previous work-related skill, knowledge, or experience is required. **Job Preparation**—SVP 6.0 to less than 7.0—more than one year and less than four years. **Knowledges**—Customer and Personal Service; Clerical Practices; Medicine and Dentistry; Law and Government; Computers and Electronics; English Language. **Instructional Program**—Health/Medical Claims Examiner.

Related SOC Job—13-1031 Claims Adjusters, Examiners, and Investigators. **Related OOH Job**—Claims Adjusters, Appraisers, Examiners, and Investigators. **Related DOT Job**—168.267-014 Claim Examiner.

13-1031.02 Insurance Adjusters, Examiners, and Investigators

- **Education/Training Required: Long-term on-the-job training**
- **Employed: 234,030**
- **Annual Earnings: $46,190**
- **Growth: 15.1%**
- **Annual Job Openings: 28,000**

The job openings listed here are shared with 13-1031.00 Claims Adjusters, Examiners, and Investigators and 13-1031.01 Claims Examiners, Property and Casualty Insurance.

Investigate, analyze, and determine the extent of insurance company's liability concerning personal, casualty, or property loss or damages and attempt to effect settlement with claimants. Correspond with or interview medical specialists, agents, witnesses, or claimants to compile information. Calculate benefit payments and approve payment of claims within a certain monetary limit.

Interview or correspond with claimant and witnesses, consult police and hospital records, and inspect property damage to determine extent of liability. Investigate and assess damage to property. Examine claims forms and other records to determine insurance coverage. Analyze information gathered by investigation and report findings and recommendations. Negotiate claim settlements and recommend litigation when settlement cannot be negotiated. Collect evidence to support contested claims in court. Prepare report of findings of investigation. Interview or correspond with agents and claimants to correct errors or omissions and to investigate questionable claims. Refer questionable claims to investigator or claims adjuster for investigation or settlement. Examine titles to property to determine validity and act as company agent in transactions with property owners. Obtain credit information from banks and other credit services. Communicate with former associates to verify employment record and to obtain background information regarding persons or businesses applying for credit.

GOE Information—Interest Area: 06. Finance and Insurance. **Work Group:** 06.02. Finance/Insurance Investigation and Analysis. **Personality Type**—Enterprising. Enterprising occupations frequently involve starting up and carrying out projects. These occupations can involve leading people and making many decisions. They sometimes require risk taking and often deal with business. **Work Values**—Advancement; Company Policies and Practices; Supervision, Human Relations; Ability Utilization; Responsibility; Supervision, Technical. **Skills**—Negotiation; Persuasion; Time Management; Judgment and Decision Making; Management of Financial Resources; Reading Comprehension. **Abilities**—*Cognitive:* Written Expression; Flexibility of Closure; Inductive Reasoning; Oral Expression; Deductive Reasoning; Written Comprehension. *Psychomotor:* None met the criteria. *Physical:* None met the criteria. *Sensory:* Far Vision; Near Vision; Speech Recognition; Speech Clarity. **General Work Activities**—*Information Input:* Identifying Objects, Actions, and Events; Getting Information; Monitoring Processes, Materials, or Surroundings. *Mental Process:* Organizing, Planning, and Prioritizing; Judging the Qualities of Things, Services, or Other People's Work; Updating and Using Relevant Knowledge. *Work Output:* Documenting or Recording Information; Interacting With Computers. *Interacting with Others:* Establishing and Maintaining Interpersonal Relationships; Communicating with Persons Outside Organization; Communicating with Other Workers. **Physical Work Conditions**—Indoors; Noisy; Sitting; Using Hands on Objects, Tools, or Controls; Repetitive Motions. **Other Job Characteristics**—Need to Be Exact or Accurate; Repeat Same Tasks; Errors Have Important Consequences; Automation.

Experience—Job Zone 3. Previous work-related skill, knowledge, or experience is required. **Job Preparation**—SVP 6.0 to less than 7.0—more than one year and less than four years. **Knowledges**—Customer and Personal Service; Clerical Practices; Computers and Electronics; Law and Government; Medicine and Dentistry; Therapy and Counseling. **Instructional Program**—Insurance.

Related SOC Job—13-1031 Claims Adjusters, Examiners, and Investigators. **Related OOH Job**—Claims Adjusters, Appraisers, Examiners, and Investigators. **Related DOT Jobs**—191.167-014 Claim Agent; 241.217-010 Claim Adjuster; 241.267-018 Claim Examiner.

13-1032.00 Insurance Appraisers, Auto Damage

- **Education/Training Required:** Long-term on-the-job training
- **Employed:** 12,900
- **Annual Earnings:** $48,090
- **Growth:** 16.6%
- **Annual Job Openings:** 2,000

Appraise automobile or other vehicle damage to determine cost of repair for insurance claim settlement and seek agreement with automotive repair shop on cost of repair. Prepare insurance forms to indicate repair cost or cost estimates and recommendations.

Estimate parts and labor to repair damage, using standard automotive labor and parts-cost manuals and knowledge of automotive repair. Review repair-cost estimates with automobile-repair shop to secure agreement on cost of repairs. Examine damaged vehicle to determine extent of structural, body, mechanical, electrical, or interior damage. Evaluate practicality of repair as opposed to payment of market value of vehicle before accident. Determine salvage value on total-loss vehicle. Prepare insurance forms to indicate repair-cost estimates and recommendations. Arrange to have damage appraised by another appraiser to resolve disagreement with shop on repair cost.

GOE Information—Interest Area: 06. Finance and Insurance. **Work Group:** 06.02. Finance/Insurance Investigation and Analysis. **Personality Type—**Conventional. Conventional occupations frequently involve following set procedures and routines. These occupations can include working with data and details more than with ideas. Usually there is a clear line of authority to follow. **Work Values—**Advancement; Company Policies and Practices; Supervision, Human Relations; Responsibility; Supervision, Technical; Social Service. **Skills—**Negotiation; Service Orientation; Persuasion; Judgment and Decision Making; Time Management; Active Listening. **Abilities—***Cognitive:* Written Expression; Written Comprehension; Oral Expression; Deductive Reasoning; Oral Comprehension; Mathematical Reasoning. *Psychomotor:* None met the criteria. *Physical:* None met the criteria. *Sensory:* Speech Clarity; Near Vision; Speech Recognition. **General Work Activities—***Information Input:* Identifying Objects, Actions, and Events; Getting Information; Inspecting Equipment, Structures, or Materials. *Mental Process:* Processing Information; Organizing, Planning, and Prioritizing; Judging the Qualities of Things, Services, or Other People's Work. *Work Output:* Documenting or Recording Information; Interacting With Computers. *Interacting with Others:* Communicating with Persons Outside Organization; Resolving Conflicts and Negotiating with Others; Communicating with Other Workers. **Physical Work Conditions—**More Often Indoors Than Outdoors; Noisy; Very Hot or Cold; Contaminants; Sitting. **Other Job Characteristics—**Need to Be Exact or Accurate; Repeat Same Tasks; Automation.

Experience—Job Zone 3. Previous work-related skill, knowledge, or experience is required. **Job Preparation—**SVP 6.0 to less than 7.0—more than one year and less than four years. **Knowledges—**Customer and Personal Service; Law and Government; Computers and Electronics; Medicine and Dentistry; Transportation; Telecommunications. **Instructional Program—**Insurance.

Related SOC Job—13-1032 Insurance Appraisers, Auto Damage. **Related OOH Job—**Claims Adjusters, Appraisers, Examiners, and Investigators. **Related DOT Job—**241.267-014 Appraiser, Automobile Damage.

13-1041.00 Compliance Officers, Except Agriculture, Construction, Health and Safety, and Transportation

- **Education/Training Required:** Long-term on-the-job training
- **Employed:** 161,810
- **Annual Earnings:** $49,360
- **Growth:** 11.6%
- **Annual Job Openings:** 17,000

The job openings listed here are shared with 13-1041.01 Environmental Compliance Inspectors, 13-1041.02 Licensing Examiners and Inspectors, 13-1041.03 Equal Opportunity Representatives and Officers, 13-1041.04 Government Property Inspectors and Investigators, and 13-1041.06 Coroners.

Examine, evaluate, and investigate eligibility for or conformity with laws and regulations governing contract compliance of licenses and permits and other compliance and enforcement inspection activities not classified elsewhere.

No task data available.

GOE Information—Interest Area: 07. Government and Public Administration. **Work Group:** 07.03. Regulations Enforcement. **Note:** The Department of Labor has not collected some data for this job, so it has fewer details than the other descriptions.

Instructional Program—No related CIP programs.

Related SOC Job—13-1041 Compliance Officers, Except Agriculture, Construction, Health and Safety, and Transportation. **Related OOH Job—**Compliance Officers, Except Agriculture, Construction, Health and Safety, and Transportation. **Related DOT Job—**No data available.

13-1041.01 Environmental Compliance Inspectors

- **Education/Training Required:** Long-term on-the-job training
- **Employed:** 161,810
- **Annual Earnings:** $49,360
- **Growth:** 11.6%
- **Annual Job Openings:** 17,000

The job openings listed here are shared with 13-1041.00 Compliance Officers, Except Agriculture, Construction, Health and Safety, and Transportation, 13-1041.02 Licensing Examiners and Inspectors, 13-1041.03 Equal Opportunity Representatives and Officers, 13-1041.04 Government Property Inspectors and Investigators, and 13-1041.06 Coroners.

Inspect and investigate sources of pollution to protect the public and environment and ensure conformance with federal, state, and local regulations and ordinances.

Determine the nature of code violations and actions to be taken and issue written notices of violation; participate in enforcement hearings as necessary. Examine permits, licenses, applications, and records to ensure compliance with licensing requirements. Prepare, organize, and maintain inspection records. Interview individuals to determine the nature of suspected violations and to obtain evidence of violations. Prepare written, oral, tabular, and graphic reports summarizing requirements and regulations, including enforcement and chain of custody documentation. Monitor follow-up actions in cases where violations were found and review compliance monitoring reports. Investigate complaints and suspected violations regarding illegal dumping, pollution, pesticides, product quality, or labeling laws. Inspect waste pretreatment, treatment, and disposal facilities and systems for conformance to federal, state, or local regulations. Inform individuals and groups of pollution control regulations and inspection findings and explain how problems can be corrected. Determine sampling locations and methods and collect water or wastewater samples for analysis, preserving samples with appropriate containers and preservation methods. Verify that hazardous chemicals are handled, stored, and disposed of in accordance with regulations. Research and keep informed of pertinent information and developments in areas such as EPA laws and regulations. Determine which sites and violation reports to investigate and coordinate compliance and enforcement activities with other government agencies. Observe and record field conditions, gathering, interpreting, and reporting data such as flow meter readings and chemical levels. Learn and observe proper safety precautions, rules, regulations, and practices so that unsafe conditions can be recognized and proper safety protocols implemented. Evaluate label information for accuracy and conformance to regulatory requirements. Inform health professionals, property owners, and the public about harmful properties and related problems of water pollution and contaminated wastewater.

GOE Information—Interest Area: 07. Government and Public Administration. **Work Group:** 07.03. Regulations Enforcement. **Personality Type—**Investigative. Investigative occupations frequently involve working with ideas and require an extensive amount of thinking. These occupations can involve searching for facts and figuring out problems mentally. **Work Values—**Supervision, Human Relations; Advancement; Achievement; Authority; Autonomy; Co-workers. **Skills—**Science; Negotiation; Writing; Reading Comprehension; Persuasion; Active Listening. **Abilities—***Cognitive:* Written Expression; Spatial Orientation; Problem Sensitivity; Inductive Reasoning; Mathematical Reasoning; Flexibility of Closure. *Psychomotor:* Multilimb Coordination; Control Precision; Finger Dexterity; Arm-Hand Steadiness. *Physical:* None met the criteria. *Sensory:* Visual Color Discrimination; Auditory Attention; Far Vision; Speech Recognition; Depth Perception; Speech Clarity. **General Work Activities—***Information Input:* Getting Information; Identifying Objects, Actions, and Events; Monitoring Processes, Materials, or Surroundings. *Mental Process:* Evaluating Information Against Standards; Processing Information; Updating and Using Relevant Knowledge. *Work Output:* Documenting or Recording Information; Performing General Physical Activities; Interacting With Computers. *Interacting with Others:* Establishing and Maintaining Interpersonal Relationships; Communicating with Other Workers; Communicating with Persons Outside Organization; Communicating with Other Workers. **Physical Work Conditions—**More Often Indoors than Outdoors; Contaminants; Sitting. **Other Job Characteristics—**Need to Be Exact or Accurate.

Experience—Job Zone 4. A minimum of two to four years of work-related skill, knowledge, or experience is needed. **Job Preparation—**SVP 7.0 to less than 8.0—two years to less than 10 years. **Knowledges—**Biology; Chemistry; Law and Government; Geography; Physics; Engineering and Technology. **Instructional Program—**No related CIP programs.

Related SOC Job—13-1041 Compliance Officers, Except Agriculture, Construction, Health and Safety, and Transportation. **Related OOH Job—**Compliance Officers, Except Agriculture, Construction, Health and Safety, and Transportation. **Related DOT Jobs—**168.267-054 Inspector, Industrial Waste; 168.267-082 Agricultural-Chemicals Inspector; 168.267-086 Hazardous-Waste Management Specialist; 168.267-090 Inspector, Water-Pollution Control; 168.267-098 Pesticide-Control Inspector; 168.267-106 Registration Specialist, Agricultural Chemicals; 168.267-110 Sanitation Inspector.

13-1041.02 Licensing Examiners and Inspectors

- **Education/Training Required: Long-term on-the-job training**
- **Employed: 161,810**
- **Annual Earnings: $49,360**
- **Growth: 11.6%**
- **Annual Job Openings: 17,000**

The job openings listed here are shared with 13-1041.00 Compliance Officers, Except Agriculture, Construction, Health and Safety, and Transportation, 13-1041.01 Environmental Compliance Inspectors, 13-1041.03 Equal Opportunity Representatives and Officers, 13-1041.04 Government Property Inspectors and Investigators, and 13-1041.06 Coroners.

Examine, evaluate, and investigate eligibility for, conformity with, or liability under licenses or permits.

Issue licenses to individuals meeting standards. Evaluate applications, records, and documents to gather information about eligibility or liability issues. Administer oral, written, road, or flight tests to license applicants. Score tests and observe equipment operation and control to rate ability of applicants. Advise licensees and other individuals or groups concerning licensing, permit, or passport regulations. Warn violators of infractions or penalties. Prepare reports of activities, evaluations, recommendations, and decisions. Prepare correspondence to inform concerned parties of licensing decisions and of appeals processes. Confer with and interview officials, technical or professional specialists, and applicants to obtain information or to clarify facts relevant to licensing decisions. Report law or regulation violations to appropriate boards and agencies. Visit establishments to verify that valid licenses and permits are displayed and that licensing standards are being upheld.

GOE Information—Interest Area: 07. Government and Public Administration. **Work Group:** 07.03. Regulations Enforcement. **Personality Type—**Conventional. Conventional occupations frequently involve following set procedures and routines. These occupations can include working with data and details more than with ideas. Usually there is a clear line of authority to follow. **Work Values—**Social Service; Supervision, Human Relations; Company Policies and Practices; Supervision, Technical; Authority; Security. **Skills—**Speaking; Service Orientation; Judgment and Decision Making; Active Listening; Social Perceptiveness; Reading Comprehension. **Abilities—***Cognitive:* Perceptual Speed; Time Sharing; Oral Expression; Written Expression; Speed of Closure; Written Comprehension. *Psychomotor:* Response Orientation; Reaction Time; Control Precision; Multilimb Coordination; Finger Dexterity; Manual Dexterity. *Physical:* None met the criteria. *Sensory:* Glare Sensitivity; Depth Perception; Far Vision; Speech Recognition; Auditory Attention; Hearing Sensitivity. **General Work Activities—***Information Input:* Monitoring Processes, Materials, or Surroundings; Getting Information; Identifying Objects, Actions, and Events. *Mental Process:* Updating and Using Relevant Knowledge; Evaluating Information Against Standards; Processing Information. *Work Output:* Documenting or Recording Information; Interacting With Computers; Handling and Moving Objects. *Interacting with Others:* Performing for or Working with the Public; Establishing and Maintaining Interpersonal Relationships; Communicating with Persons Outside Organization. **Physical Work Conditions—**More Often Indoors than Outdoors; Contaminants; Sitting; Using Hands on Objects, Tools, or Controls; Repetitive Motions. **Other Job Characteristics—**Need to Be Exact or Accurate; Repeat Same Tasks; Errors Have Important Consequences; Automation.

Experience—Job Zone 2. Some previous work-related skill, knowledge, or experience may be helpful in these occupations, but usually is not needed. **Job Preparation**—SVP 4.0 to less than 6.0—six months to less than two years. **Knowledges**—Customer and Personal Service; Clerical Practices; Law and Government; Psychology; Foreign Language; Public Safety and Security. **Instructional Program**—No related CIP programs.

Related SOC Job—13-1041 Compliance Officers, Except Agriculture, Construction, Health and Safety, and Transportation. **Related OOH Job**—Compliance Officers, Except Agriculture, Construction, Health and Safety, and Transportation. **Related DOT Jobs**—168.167-074 Reviewing Officer, Driver's License; 168.267-034 Driver's License Examiner; 168.267-066 License Inspector; 169.267-014 Examiner; 169.267-030 Passport-Application Examiner; 196.163-010 Flight-Operations Inspector.

13-1041.03 Equal Opportunity Representatives and Officers

- **Education/Training Required: Long-term on-the-job training**
- **Employed: 161,810**
- **Annual Earnings: $49,360**
- **Growth: 11.6%**
- **Annual Job Openings: 17,000**

The job openings listed here are shared with 13-1041.00 Compliance Officers, Except Agriculture, Construction, Health and Safety, and Transportation, 13-1041.01 Environmental Compliance Inspectors, 13-1041.02 Licensing Examiners and Inspectors, 13-1041.04 Government Property Inspectors and Investigators, and 13-1041.06 Coroners.

Monitor and evaluate compliance with equal opportunity laws, guidelines, and policies to ensure that employment practices and contracting arrangements give equal opportunity without regard to race, religion, color, national origin, sex, age, or disability.

Investigate employment practices and alleged violations of laws to document and correct discriminatory factors. Interpret civil rights laws and equal opportunity regulations for individuals and employers. Study equal opportunity complaints to clarify issues. Meet with persons involved in equal opportunity complaints to verify case information and to arbitrate and settle disputes. Coordinate, monitor, and revise complaint procedures to ensure timely processing and review of complaints. Prepare reports of selection, survey, and other statistics and recommendations for corrective action. Conduct surveys and evaluate findings to determine if systematic discrimination exists. Develop guidelines for non-discriminatory employment practices and monitor their implementation and impact. Review company contracts to determine actions required to meet governmental equal opportunity provisions. Counsel newly hired members of minority and disadvantaged groups, informing them about details of civil rights laws. Provide information, technical assistance, and training to supervisors, managers, and employees on topics such as employee supervision, hiring, grievance procedures, and staff development. Verify that all job descriptions are submitted for review and approval and that descriptions meet regulatory standards. Act as liaisons between minority placement agencies and employers or between job search committees and other equal opportunity administrators. Consult with community representatives to develop technical assistance agreements in accordance with governmental regulations. Meet with job search committees or coordinators to explain the role of the equal opportunity coordinator, to provide resources for advertising, and to explain expectations for future contacts. Participate in the recruitment of employees through job fairs, career days, and advertising plans.

GOE Information—Interest Area: 07. Government and Public Administration. **Work Group**: 07.03. Regulations Enforcement. **Personality Type**—Social. Social occupations frequently involve working with, communicating with, and teaching people. These occupations often involve helping or providing service to others. **Work Values**—Working Conditions; Social Service; Responsibility; Social Status; Supervision, Human Relations; Company Policies and Practices. **Skills**—Negotiation; Persuasion; Social Perceptiveness; Service Orientation; Complex Problem Solving; Active Listening. **Abilities**—*Cognitive:* Written Expression; Fluency of Ideas; Number Facility; Deductive Reasoning; Originality; Mathematical Reasoning. *Psychomotor:* Finger Dexterity. *Physical:* None met the criteria. *Sensory:* Speech Recognition; Speech Clarity; Far Vision; Near Vision; Auditory Attention. **General Work Activities**—*Information Input:* Getting Information; Identifying Objects, Actions, and Events; Monitoring Processes, Materials, or Surroundings. *Mental Process:* Organizing, Planning, and Prioritizing; Evaluating Information Against Standards; Making Decisions and Solving Problems. *Work Output:* Documenting or Recording Information; Interacting With Computers. *Interacting with Others:* Resolving Conflicts and Negotiating with Others; Communicating with Other Workers; Communicating with Persons Outside Organization; Establishing and Maintaining Interpersonal Relationships. **Physical Work Conditions**—Indoors; Sitting; Repetitive Motions. **Other Job Characteristics**—Need to Be Exact or Accurate; Repeat Same Tasks.

Experience—Job Zone 4. A minimum of two to four years of work-related skill, knowledge, or experience is needed. **Job Preparation**—SVP 7.0 to less than 8.0—two years to less than 10 years. **Knowledges**—Law and Government; Personnel and Human Resources; Clerical Practices; English Language; Customer and Personal Service; Administration and Management. **Instructional Program**—No related CIP programs.

Related SOC Job—13-1041 Compliance Officers, Except Agriculture, Construction, Health and Safety, and Transportation. **Related OOH Job**—Compliance Officers, Except Agriculture, Construction, Health and Safety, and Transportation. **Related DOT Jobs**—168.167-014 Equal-Opportunity Representative; 168.267-114 Equal Opportunity Officer.

13-1041.04 Government Property Inspectors and Investigators

- **Education/Training Required: Long-term on-the-job training**
- **Employed: 161,810**
- **Annual Earnings: $49,360**
- **Growth: 11.6%**
- **Annual Job Openings: 17,000**

The job openings listed here are shared with 13-1041.00 Compliance Officers, Except Agriculture, Construction, Health and Safety, and Transportation, 13-1041.01 Environmental Compliance Inspectors, 13-1041.02 Licensing Examiners and Inspectors, 13-1041.03 Equal Opportunity Representatives and Officers, and 13-1041.06 Coroners.

Investigate or inspect government property to ensure compliance with contract agreements and government regulations.

Examine records, reports, and documents in order to establish facts and detect discrepancies. Submit samples of products to government laboratories for testing as required. Testify in court or at administrative proceedings concerning investigation findings. Monitor investigations of suspected offenders to ensure that they are conducted in accordance with constitutional requirements. Investigate applications for special licenses or permits, as well as alleged license or permit violations. Coordinate with and assist law enforcement agencies in matters of mutual concern. Prepare correspondence, reports of inspections or investigations, and recommendations for action. Locate and interview plaintiffs, witnesses, or representatives of business or government to gather facts relevant to inspections or alleged violations. Inspect government-owned equipment and materials in the possession of private contractors in order to ensure compliance with contracts and regulations and to prevent misuse. Collect, identify, evaluate, and preserve case evidence. Recommend legal or administrative action to protect government property. Inspect manufactured or processed products to ensure compliance with contract specifications and legal requirements.

GOE Information—Interest Area: 07. Government and Public Administration. **Work Group:** 07.03. Regulations Enforcement. **Personality Type**—Enterprising. Enterprising occupations frequently involve starting up and carrying out projects. These occupations can involve leading people and making many decisions. They sometimes require risk taking and often deal with business. **Work Values**—Advancement; Supervision, Human Relations; Company Policies and Practices; Variety; Security; Social Status. **Skills**—Systems Analysis; Speaking; Judgment and Decision Making; Systems Evaluation; Negotiation; Writing. **Abilities**—*Cognitive:* Memorization; Written Comprehension; Written Expression; Oral Expression; Problem Sensitivity; Speed of Closure. *Psychomotor:* Wrist-Finger Speed. *Physical:* None met the criteria. *Sensory:* Speech Clarity. **General Work Activities**—*Information Input:* Getting Information; Identifying Objects, Actions, and Events; Inspecting Equipment, Structures, or Materials. *Mental Process:* Evaluating Information Against Standards; Judging the Qualities of Things, Services, or Other People's Work; Analyzing Data or Information. *Work Output:* Documenting or Recording Information; Handling and Moving Objects. *Interacting with Others:* Communicating with Other Workers; Communicating with Persons Outside Organization; Interpreting the Meaning of Information for Others. **Physical Work Conditions**—Indoors; More Often Sitting Than Standing; Walking and Running; Using Hands on Objects, Tools, or Controls. **Other Job Characteristics**—Need to Be Exact or Accurate; Errors Have Important Consequences.

Experience—Job Zone 3. Previous work-related skill, knowledge, or experience is required. **Job Preparation**—SVP 6.0 to less than 7.0—more than one year and less than four years. **Knowledges**—Law and Government; Personnel and Human Resources; Public Safety and Security; Communications and Media; English Language; Mathematics. **Instructional Program**—No related CIP programs.

Related SOC Job—13-1041 Compliance Officers, Except Agriculture, Construction, Health and Safety, and Transportation. **Related OOH Job**—Compliance Officers, Except Agriculture, Construction, Health and Safety, and Transportation. **Related DOT Jobs**—168.267-050 Inspector, Government Property; 168.267-062 Investigator; 168.287-014 Inspector, Quality Assurance.

13-1041.06 Coroners

- **Education/Training Required: Work experience in a related occupation**
- **Employed: 161,810**
- **Annual Earnings: $49,360**
- **Growth: 11.6%**
- **Annual Job Openings: 17,000**

The job openings listed here are shared with 13-1041.00 Compliance Officers, Except Agriculture, Construction, Health and Safety, and Transportation, 13-1041.01 Environmental Compliance Inspectors, 13-1041.02 Licensing Examiners and Inspectors, 13-1041.03 Equal Opportunity Representatives and Officers, and 13-1041.04 Government Property Inspectors and Investigators.

Direct activities such as autopsies, pathological and toxicological analyses, and inquests relating to the investigation of deaths occurring within a legal jurisdiction to determine cause of death or to fix responsibility for accidental, violent, or unexplained deaths.

Perform medico-legal examinations and autopsies, conducting preliminary examinations of the body in order to identify victims, to locate signs of trauma, and to identify factors that would indicate time of death. Inquire into the cause, manner, and circumstances of human deaths and establish the identities of deceased persons. Direct activities of workers who conduct autopsies, perform pathological and toxicological analyses, and prepare documents for permanent records. Complete death certificates, including the assignment of a cause and manner of death. Observe and record the positions and conditions of bodies and of related evidence. Collect and document any pertinent medical history information. Observe, record, and preserve any objects or personal property related to deaths, including objects such as medication containers and suicide notes. Complete reports and forms required to finalize cases. Remove or supervise removal of bodies from death scenes, using the proper equipment and supplies, and arrange for transportation to morgues. Testify at inquests, hearings, and court trials. Interview persons present at death scenes to obtain information useful in determining the manner of death. Provide information concerning the circumstances of death to relatives of the deceased. Locate and document information regarding the next of kin, including their relationship to the deceased and the status of notification attempts. Confer with officials of public health and law enforcement agencies in order to coordinate interdepartmental activities. Inventory personal effects, such as jewelry or wallets, that are recovered from bodies. Coordinate the release of personal effects to authorized persons and facilitate the disposition of unclaimed corpses and personal effects. Arrange for the next of kin to be notified of deaths. Record the disposition of minor children, as well as details of arrangements made for their care. Collect wills, burial instructions, and other documentation needed for investigations and for handling of the remains. Witness and certify deaths that are the result of a judicial order.

GOE Information—Interest Area: 08. Health Science. **Work Group:** 08.01. Managerial Work in Medical and Health Services. **Personality Type**—Investigative. Investigative occupations frequently involve working with ideas and require an extensive amount of thinking. These occupations can involve searching for facts and figuring out problems mentally. **Work Values**—Authority; Autonomy; Responsibility; Security; Ability Utilization; Social Service. **Skills**—Science; Management of Financial Resources; Management of Personnel Resources; Reading Comprehension; Critical Thinking; Speaking. **Abilities**—*Cognitive:* Inductive Reasoning; Flexibility of Closure; Written Expression; Information Ordering; Speed of Closure; Fluency of Ideas. *Psychomotor:* Arm-Hand Steadiness; Manual Dexterity; Multilimb Coordination; Finger Dexterity; Control Precision. *Physical:* Static Strength; Trunk Strength. *Sensory:* Visual Color Discrimination; Far Vision; Speech Recognition; Speech Clarity; Depth Perception; Near Vision. **General Work Activities**—*Information Input:* Identifying Objects, Actions, and Events; Getting Information; Monitoring Processes, Materials, or Surroundings. *Mental Process:* Updating and Using Relevant Knowledge; Making Decisions and Solving Problems; Analyzing Data or Information.

Work Output: Documenting or Recording Information; Handling and Moving Objects; Performing General Physical Activities. *Interacting with Others:* Communicating with Persons Outside Organization; Performing for or Working with the Public; Teaching Others. **Physical Work Conditions**—More Often Indoors Than Outdoors; Contaminants; Disease or Infections; Hazardous Equipment; Using Hands on Objects, Tools, or Controls. **Other Job Characteristics**—Need to Be Exact or Accurate; Errors Have Important Consequences.

Experience—Job Zone 5. Extensive skill, knowledge, and experience are needed. **Job Preparation**—SVP 8.0 and above—four years to more than 10 years. **Knowledges**—Medicine and Dentistry; Biology; Psychology; Therapy and Counseling; Chemistry; Law and Government. **Instructional Program**—No related CIP programs.

Related SOC Job—13-1041 Compliance Officers, Except Agriculture, Construction, Health and Safety, and Transportation. **Related OOH Job**—Compliance Officers, Except Agriculture, Construction, Health and Safety, and Transportation. **Related DOT Job**—168.161-010 Coroner.

13-1051.00 Cost Estimators

- **Education/Training Required: Work experience in a related occupation**
- **Employed: 204,330**
- **Annual Earnings: $52,020**
- **Growth: 18.2%**
- **Annual Job Openings: 15,000**

Prepare cost estimates for product manufacturing, construction projects, or services to aid management in bidding on or determining price of product or service. May specialize according to particular service performed or type of product manufactured.

Analyze blueprints and other documentation to prepare time, cost, materials, and labor estimates. Assess cost-effectiveness of products, projects, or services, tracking actual costs relative to bids as the project develops. Consult with clients, vendors, personnel in other departments, or construction foremen to discuss and formulate estimates and resolve issues. Confer with engineers, architects, owners, contractors, and subcontractors on changes and adjustments to cost estimates. Prepare estimates used by management for purposes such as planning, organizing, and scheduling work. Prepare estimates for use in selecting vendors or subcontractors. Review material and labor requirements to decide whether it is more cost-effective to produce or purchase components. Prepare cost and expenditure statements and other necessary documentation at regular intervals for the duration of the project. Prepare and maintain a directory of suppliers, contractors, and subcontractors. Set up cost-monitoring and -reporting systems and procedures. Establish and maintain tendering process and conduct negotiations. Conduct special studies to develop and establish standard hour and related cost data or to effect cost reduction. Visit site and record information about access, drainage and topography, and availability of services such as water and electricity.

GOE Information—Interest Area: 06. Finance and Insurance. **Work Group:** 06.02. Finance/Insurance Investigation and Analysis. **Personality Type**—Conventional. Conventional occupations frequently involve following set procedures and routines. These occupations can include working with data and details more than with ideas. Usually there is a clear line of authority to follow. **Work Values**—Working Conditions; Independence; Advancement; Responsibility; Autonomy; Supervision, Human Relations. **Skills**—

Management of Financial Resources; Mathematics; Management of Personnel Resources; Negotiation; Operations Analysis; Equipment Selection. **Abilities**—*Cognitive:* Number Facility; Mathematical Reasoning; Speed of Closure; Memorization; Oral Expression; Originality. *Psychomotor:* None met the criteria. *Physical:* None met the criteria. *Sensory:* Near Vision; Depth Perception; Speech Recognition; Speech Clarity. **General Work Activities**—*Information Input:* Monitoring Processes, Materials, or Surroundings; Identifying Objects, Actions, and Events; Estimating the Needed Characteristics of Products, Events, or Information. *Mental Process:* Scheduling Work and Activities; Organizing, Planning, and Prioritizing; Making Decisions and Solving Problems. *Work Output:* Drafting and Specifying Technical Devices; Interacting With Computers; Documenting or Recording Information. *Interacting with Others:* Resolving Conflicts and Negotiating with Others; Coordinating the Work and Activities of Others; Communicating with Other Workers. **Physical Work Conditions**—Indoors; Contaminants; Sitting. **Other Job Characteristics**—Need to Be Exact or Accurate; Errors Have Important Consequences; Repeat Same Tasks.

Experience—Job Zone 4. A minimum of two to four years of work-related skill, knowledge, or experience is needed. **Job Preparation**—SVP 7.0 to less than 8.0—two years to less than 10 years. **Knowledges**—Economics and Accounting; Production and Processing; Administration and Management; Sales and Marketing; Clerical Practices; Personnel and Human Resources. **Instructional Programs**—Business Administration/Management; Business/Commerce, General; Construction Engineering; Construction Engineering Technology/Technician; Manufacturing Engineering; Materials Engineering; Mechanical Engineering.

Related SOC Job—13-1051 Cost Estimators. **Related OOH Job**—Cost Estimators. **Related DOT Job**—169.267-038 Estimator.

13-1061.00 Emergency Management Specialists

- **Education/Training Required: Work experience in a related occupation**
- **Employed: 11,240**
- **Annual Earnings: $45,980**
- **Growth: 22.8%**
- **Annual Job Openings: 2,000**

Coordinate disaster response or crisis management activities, provide disaster-preparedness training, and prepare emergency plans and procedures for natural (e.g., hurricanes, floods, earthquakes), wartime, or technological (e.g., nuclear power plant emergencies, hazardous materials spills) disasters or hostage situations.

Keep informed of activities or changes that could affect the likelihood of an emergency, as well as those that could affect response efforts and details of plan implementation. Prepare plans that outline operating procedures to be used in response to disasters or emergencies such as hurricanes, nuclear accidents, and terrorist attacks and in recovery from these events. Propose alteration of emergency response procedures based on regulatory changes, technological changes, or knowledge gained from outcomes of previous emergency situations. Maintain and update all resource materials associated with emergency-preparedness plans. Coordinate disaster response or crisis management activities such as ordering evacuations, opening public shelters, and implementing special needs plans and programs. Develop and maintain liaisons with municipalities, county departments, and similar entities in order to facilitate plan development, response effort coordination, and exchanges of personnel and equipment. Keep informed of federal, state, and local regulations affecting emergency plans and ensure that plans adhere to these regulations. Design and administer emergency and disaster-preparedness training courses that teach people how to effectively respond to major emergencies and disasters. Prepare emergency situation status reports that describe response and recovery efforts, needs, and preliminary damage assessments. Inspect facilities and equipment such as emergency management centers and communications equipment to determine their operational and functional capabilities in emergency situations. Consult with officials of local and area governments, schools, hospitals, and other institutions in order to determine their needs and capabilities in the event of a natural disaster or other emergency. Develop and perform tests and evaluations of emergency management plans in accordance with state and federal regulations. Attend meetings, conferences, and workshops related to emergency management to learn new information and to develop working relationships with other emergency management specialists.

GOE Information—Interest Area: 12. Law and Public Safety. **Work Group:** 12.01. Managerial Work in Law and Public Safety. **Personality Type—**No data available. **Work Values—**No data available. **Skills—**Management of Material Resources; Service Orientation; Complex Problem Solving; Judgment and Decision Making; Coordination; Management of Financial Resources. **Abilities—***Cognitive:* Fluency of Ideas; Originality; Written Expression; Problem Sensitivity; Visualization; Deductive Reasoning. *Psychomotor:* None met the criteria. *Physical:* None met the criteria. *Sensory:* Speech Clarity; Far Vision; Speech Recognition; Near Vision; Visual Color Discrimination. **General Work Activities—***Information Input:* Monitoring Processes, Materials, or Surroundings; Getting Information; Identifying Objects, Actions, and Events. *Mental Process:* Updating and Using Relevant Knowledge; Organizing, Planning, and Prioritizing; Making Decisions and Solving Problems. *Work Output:* Documenting or Recording Information; Interacting With Computers; Performing General Physical Activities. *Interacting with Others:* Establishing and Maintaining Interpersonal Relationships; Communicating with Persons Outside Organization; Communicating with Other Workers. **Physical Work Conditions—**Indoors; Sitting. **Other Job Characteristics—**Need to Be Exact or Accurate; Errors Have Important Consequences.

Experience—Job Zone 4. A minimum of two to four years of work-related skill, knowledge, or experience is needed. **Job Preparation—**SVP 7.0 to less than 8.0—two years to less than 10 years. **Knowledges—**Public Safety and Security; Customer and Personal Service; Education and Training; Law and Government; Physics; Telecommunications. **Instructional Programs—**Community Organization and Advocacy; Public Administration.

Related SOC Job—13-1061 Emergency Management Specialists. **Related OOH Job—**Emergency Management Specialists. **Related DOT Job—**188.117-022 Civil Preparedness Officer.

13-1071.00 Employment, Recruitment, and Placement Specialists

- **Education/Training Required:** Bachelor's degree
- **Employed:** 181,260
- **Annual Earnings:** $41,780
- **Growth:** 30.5%
- **Annual Job Openings:** 30,000

The job openings listed here are shared with 13-1071.01 Employment Interviewers and 13-1071.02 Personnel Recruiters.

Recruit and place workers.

No task data available.

GOE Information—Interest Area: 04. Business and Administration. **Work Group:** 04.03. Human Resources Support. **Note:** The Department of Labor has not collected some data for this job, so it has fewer details than the other descriptions.

Instructional Programs—Human Resources Management/Personnel Administration, General; Labor and Industrial Relations.

Related SOC Job—13-1071 Employment, Recruitment, and Placement Specialists. **Related OOH Job—**Human Resources, Training, and Labor Relations Managers and Specialists. **Related DOT Job—**No data available.

13-1071.01 Employment Interviewers

- **Education/Training Required:** Bachelor's degree
- **Employed:** 181,260
- **Annual Earnings:** $41,780
- **Growth:** 30.5%
- **Annual Job Openings:** 30,000

The job openings listed here are shared with 13-1071.00 Employment, Recruitment, and Placement Specialists and 13-1071.02 Personnel Recruiters.

Interview job applicants in employment office and refer them to prospective employers for consideration. Search application files, notify selected applicants of job openings, and refer qualified applicants to prospective employers. Contact employers to verify referral results. Record and evaluate various pertinent data.

Inform applicants of job openings and details such as duties and responsibilities, compensation, benefits, schedules, working conditions, and promotion opportunities. Interview job applicants to match their qualifications with employers' needs, recording and evaluating applicant experience, education, training, and skills. Review employment applications and job orders to match applicants with job requirements, using manual or computerized file searches. Select qualified applicants or refer them to employers according to organization policy. Perform reference and background checks on applicants. Maintain records of applicants not selected for employment. Instruct job applicants in presenting a positive image by providing help with resume writing, personal appearance, and interview techniques. Refer applicants to services such as vocational counseling, literacy or language instruction, transportation assistance, vocational training, and child care. Contact employers to solicit orders for job vacancies, determining their requirements and recording relevant data such as job descriptions. Conduct workshops and demonstrate the use of job listings to assist applicants with skill building. Search for and recruit applicants for open positions through campus job fairs and advertisements. Provide background information on organizations with which interviews are scheduled. Administer assessment tests to identify skill-building needs. Conduct or arrange for skill, intelligence, or psychological testing of applicants and current employees. Hire workers and place them with employers needing temporary help. Evaluate selection and testing techniques by conducting research or follow-up activities and conferring with management and supervisory personnel.

GOE Information—Interest Area: 04. Business and Administration. **Work Group:** 04.03. Human Resources Support. **Personality Type—** Social. Social occupations frequently involve working with, communicating with, and teaching people. These occupations often involve helping or providing service to others. **Work Values—**Social Service; Working Conditions; Supervision, Technical; Co-workers; Supervision, Human Relations; Advancement. **Skills—**Management of Personnel Resources; Service Orientation; Social Perceptiveness; Persuasion; Negotiation; Instructing. **Abilities—***Cognitive:* Category Flexibility; Oral Expression; Written Expression; Oral Comprehension; Memorization; Deductive Reasoning. *Psychomotor:* None met the criteria. *Physical:* None met the criteria. *Sensory:* Speech Recognition; Speech Clarity. **General Work Activities—***Information Input:* Getting Information; Monitoring Processes, Materials, or Surroundings; Identifying Objects, Actions, and Events. *Mental Process:* Organizing, Planning, and Prioritizing; Processing Information; Judging the Qualities of Things, Services, or Other People's Work. *Work Output:* Interacting With Computers; Controlling Machines and Processes; Handling and Moving Objects. *Interacting with Others:* Establishing and Maintaining Interpersonal Relationships; Resolving Conflicts and Negotiating with Others; Performing for or Working with the Public. **Physical Work Conditions—**Indoors; Sitting; Repetitive Motions. **Other Job Characteristics—**Need to Be Exact or Accurate; Repeat Same Tasks.

Experience—Job Zone 3. Previous work-related skill, knowledge, or experience is required. **Job Preparation—**SVP 6.0 to less than 7.0—more than one year and less than four years. **Knowledges—**Foreign Language; Clerical Practices; Customer and Personal Service; Personnel and Human Resources; Sales and Marketing; English Language. **Instructional Programs—**Human Resources Management/Personnel Administration, General; Labor and Industrial Relations.

Related SOC Job—13-1071 Employment, Recruitment, and Placement Specialists. **Related OOH Job—**Human Resources, Training, and Labor Relations Managers and Specialists. **Related DOT Jobs—**166.267-010 Employment Interviewer; 166.267-034 Job Development Specialist.

13-1071.02 Personnel Recruiters

- **Education/Training Required: Bachelor's degree**
- **Employed: 181,260**
- **Annual Earnings: $41,780**
- **Growth: 30.5%**
- **Annual Job Openings: 30,000**

The job openings listed here are shared with 13-1071.00 Employment, Recruitment, and Placement Specialists and 13-1071.01 Employment Interviewers.

Seek out, interview, and screen applicants to fill existing and future job openings and promote career opportunities within an organization.

Establish and maintain relationships with hiring managers to stay abreast of current and future hiring and business needs. Interview applicants to obtain information on work history, training, education, and job skills. Maintain current knowledge of Equal Employment Opportunity (EEO) and affirmative action guidelines and laws, such as the Americans with Disabilities Act (ADA). Perform searches for qualified candidates according to relevant job criteria, using computer databases, networking, Internet recruiting resources, cold calls, media, recruiting firms, and employee referrals. Prepare and maintain employment records. Contact applicants to inform them of employment possibilities, consideration, and selection.

Inform potential applicants about facilities, operations, benefits, and job or career opportunities in organizations. Screen and refer applicants to hiring personnel in the organization, making hiring recommendations when appropriate. Arrange for interviews and provide travel arrangements as necessary. Advise managers and employees on staffing policies and procedures. Review and evaluate applicant qualifications or eligibility for specified licensing according to established guidelines and designated licensing codes. Hire applicants and authorize paperwork assigning them to positions. Conduct reference and background checks on applicants. Evaluate recruitment and selection criteria to ensure conformance to professional, statistical, and testing standards, recommending revision as needed. Recruit applicants for open positions, arranging job fairs with college campus representatives. Advise management on organizing, preparing, and implementing recruiting and retention programs. Supervise personnel clerks performing filing, typing, and recordkeeping duties. Project yearly recruitment expenditures for budgetary consideration and control. Serve on selection and examination boards to evaluate applicants according to test scores, contacting promising candidates for interviews. Address civic and social groups and attend conferences to disseminate information concerning possible job openings and career opportunities.

GOE Information—Interest Area: 04. Business and Administration. **Work Group:** 04.03. Human Resources Support. **Personality Type—** Enterprising. Enterprising occupations frequently involve starting up and carrying out projects. These occupations can involve leading people and making many decisions. They sometimes require risk taking and often deal with business. **Work Values—**Working Conditions; Social Service; Supervision, Human Relations; Company Policies and Practices; Advancement; Responsibility. **Skills—** Management of Personnel Resources; Negotiation; Persuasion; Management of Financial Resources; Service Orientation; Judgment and Decision Making. **Abilities—***Cognitive:* Memorization; Speed of Closure; Mathematical Reasoning; Category Flexibility; Flexibility of Closure; Inductive Reasoning. *Psychomotor:* None met the criteria. *Physical:* None met the criteria. *Sensory:* Speech Recognition; Speech Clarity; Near Vision; Auditory Attention; Far Vision. **General Work Activities—***Information Input:* Getting Information; Identifying Objects, Actions, and Events; Monitoring Processes, Materials, or Surroundings. *Mental Process:* Organizing, Planning, and Prioritizing; Judging the Qualities of Things, Services, or Other People's Work; Making Decisions and Solving Problems. *Work Output:* Documenting or Recording Information; Interacting With Computers. *Interacting with Others:* Establishing and Maintaining Interpersonal Relationships; Communicating with Other Workers; Resolving Conflicts and Negotiating with Others. **Physical Work Conditions—**Indoors; Sitting. **Other Job Characteristics—**Need to Be Exact or Accurate; Repeat Same Tasks.

Experience—Job Zone 4. A minimum of two to four years of work-related skill, knowledge, or experience is needed. **Job Preparation—** SVP 7.0 to less than 8.0—two years to less than 10 years. **Knowledges—**Personnel and Human Resources; Clerical Practices; Sales and Marketing; Education and Training; Administration and Management; Computers and Electronics. **Instructional Programs—** Human Resources Management/Personnel Administration, General; Labor and Industrial Relations.

Related SOC Job—13-1071 Employment, Recruitment, and Placement Specialists. **Related OOH Job—**Human Resources, Training, and Labor Relations Managers and Specialists. **Related DOT Jobs—** 099.167-010 Certification and Selection Specialist; 166.267-026 Recruiter; 166.267-038 Personnel Recruiter; 205.367-050 Supervisor, Contingents.

13-1072.00 Compensation, Benefits, and Job Analysis Specialists

- **Education/Training Required:** Bachelor's degree
- **Employed:** 97,740
- **Annual Earnings:** $48,870
- **Growth:** 20.4%
- **Annual Job Openings:** 15,000

Conduct programs of compensation and benefits and job analysis for employer. May specialize in specific areas, such as position classification and pension programs.

Evaluate job positions, determining classification, exempt or non-exempt status, and salary. Ensure company compliance with federal and state laws, including reporting requirements. Advise managers and employees on state and federal employment regulations, collective agreements, benefit and compensation policies, personnel procedures, and classification programs. Plan, develop, evaluate, improve, and communicate methods and techniques for selecting, promoting, compensating, evaluating, and training workers. Provide advice on the resolution of classification and salary complaints. Prepare occupational classifications, job descriptions, and salary scales. Assist in preparing and maintaining personnel records and handbooks. Prepare reports such as organization and flow charts and career path reports to summarize job analysis and evaluation and compensation analysis information. Administer employee insurance, pension, and savings plans, working with insurance brokers and plan carriers. Negotiate collective agreements on behalf of employers or workers and mediate labor disputes and grievances. Develop, implement, administer, and evaluate personnel and labor relations programs, including performance appraisal, affirmative action, and employment equity programs. Perform multifactor data and cost analyses that may be used in areas such as support of collective bargaining agreements. Research employee benefit and health and safety practices and recommend changes or modifications to existing policies. Analyze organizational, occupational, and industrial data to facilitate organizational functions and provide technical information to business, industry, and government. Advise staff of individuals' qualifications. Assess need for and develop job analysis instruments and materials. Review occupational data on Alien Employment Certification Applications to determine the appropriate occupational title and code; provide local offices with information about immigration and occupations. Research job and worker requirements, structural and functional relationships among jobs and occupations, and occupational trends.

GOE Information—Interest Area: 04. Business and Administration. **Work Group:** 04.03. Human Resources Support. **Personality Type—**Investigative. Investigative occupations frequently involve working with ideas and require an extensive amount of thinking. These occupations can involve searching for facts and figuring out problems mentally. **Work Values—**Working Conditions; Responsibility; Co-workers; Authority; Ability Utilization; Autonomy. **Skills—**Service Orientation; Persuasion; Management of Financial Resources; Judgment and Decision Making; Negotiation; Coordination. **Abilities—***Cognitive:* Number Facility; Mathematical Reasoning; Written Expression; Deductive Reasoning; Fluency of Ideas; Category Flexibility. *Psychomotor:* None met the criteria. *Physical:* None met the criteria. *Sensory:* Speech Clarity; Speech Recognition; Near Vision; Far Vision. **General Work Activities—***Information Input:* Getting Information; Identifying Objects, Actions, and Events; Monitoring Processes, Materials, or Surroundings. *Mental Process:* Organizing, Planning, and Prioritizing; Processing Information; Updating and Using Relevant Knowledge. *Work Output:* Documenting or Recording Information; Interacting With Computers. *Interacting with Others:* Establishing and Maintaining Interpersonal Relationships; Communicating with Other Workers; Performing Administrative Activities. **Physical Work Conditions—**Indoors; Noisy; Sitting; Using Hands on Objects, Tools, or Controls; Repetitive Motions. **Other Job Characteristics—**Need to Be Exact or Accurate; Repeat Same Tasks.

Experience—Job Zone 4. A minimum of two to four years of work-related skill, knowledge, or experience is needed. **Job Preparation—**SVP 7.0 to less than 8.0—two years to less than 10 years. **Knowledges—**Personnel and Human Resources; Clerical Practices; Customer and Personal Service; Administration and Management; English Language; Education and Training. **Instructional Programs—**Human Resources Management/Personnel Administration, General; Labor and Industrial Relations.

Related SOC Job—13-1072 Compensation, Benefits, and Job Analysis Specialists. **Related OOH Job—**Human Resources, Training, and Labor Relations Managers and Specialists. **Related DOT Jobs—**166.067-010 Occupational Analyst; 166.267-018 Job Analyst.

13-1073.00 Training and Development Specialists

- **Education/Training Required:** Bachelor's degree
- **Employed:** 206,860
- **Annual Earnings:** $45,870
- **Growth:** 20.8%
- **Annual Job Openings:** 32,000

Conduct training and development programs for employees.

Keep up with developments in area of expertise by reading current journals, books, and magazine articles. Present information, using a variety of instructional techniques and formats such as role playing, simulations, team exercises, group discussions, videos, and lectures. Schedule classes based on availability of classrooms, equipment, and instructors. Organize and develop, or obtain, training procedure manuals and guides and course materials such as handouts and visual materials. Offer specific training programs to help workers maintain or improve job skills. Monitor, evaluate, and record training activities and program effectiveness. Attend meetings and seminars to obtain information for use in training programs or to inform management of training program status. Coordinate recruitment and placement of training program participants. Evaluate training materials prepared by instructors, such as outlines, text, and handouts. Develop alternative training methods if expected improvements are not seen. Assess training needs through surveys; interviews with employees; focus groups; or consultation with managers, instructors, or customer representatives. Screen, hire, and assign workers to positions based on qualifications. Select and assign instructors to conduct training. Devise programs to develop executive potential among employees in lower-level positions. Design, plan, organize, and direct orientation and training for employees or customers of industrial or commercial establishment. Negotiate contracts with clients, including desired training outcomes, fees, and expenses. Supervise instructors, evaluate instructor performance, and refer instructors to classes for skill development. Monitor training costs to ensure budget is not exceeded and prepare budget reports to justify expenditures. Refer trainees to employer relations representatives, to locations offering job placement assistance, or to appropriate social services agencies if warranted.

GOE Information—Interest Area: 04. Business and Administration. Work Group: 04.03. Human Resources Support. Personality Type—Social. Social occupations frequently involve working with, communicating with, and teaching people. These occupations often involve helping or providing service to others. Work Values—Authority; Social Service; Creativity; Co-workers; Working Conditions; Responsibility. Skills—Writing; Service Orientation; Speaking; Social Perceptiveness; Persuasion; Active Learning. Abilities—*Cognitive:* Fluency of Ideas; Oral Expression; Written Expression; Originality; Written Comprehension; Memorization. *Psychomotor:* None met the criteria. *Physical:* Trunk Strength. *Sensory:* Speech Clarity; Speech Recognition; Auditory Attention; Far Vision; Near Vision. General Work Activities—*Information Input:* Getting Information; Identifying Objects, Actions, and Events; Monitoring Processes, Materials, or Surroundings. *Mental Process:* Organizing, Planning, and Prioritizing; Updating and Using Relevant Knowledge; Thinking Creatively. *Work Output:* Interacting With Computers; Documenting or Recording Information. *Interacting with Others:* Communicating with Other Workers; Teaching Others; Establishing and Maintaining Interpersonal Relationships. Physical Work Conditions—Indoors; Noisy; Standing; Repetitive Motions. Other Job Characteristics—Need to Be Exact or Accurate; Automation.

Experience—Job Zone 4. A minimum of two to four years of work-related skill, knowledge, or experience is needed. Job Preparation—SVP 7.0 to less than 8.0—two years to less than 10 years. Knowledges—Sociology and Anthropology; Psychology; Personnel and Human Resources; Therapy and Counseling; Customer and Personal Service; Public Safety and Security. Instructional Programs—Human Resources Management/Personnel Administration, General; Organizational Behavior Studies.

Related SOC Job—13-1073 Training and Development Specialists. Related OOH Job—Human Resources, Training, and Labor Relations Managers and Specialists. Related DOT Jobs—079.127-010 Inservice Coordinator, Auxiliary Personnel; 166.167-038 Port Purser; 166.167-054 Technical Training Coordinator; 169.167-062 Coordinator, Skill-Training Program; 239.137-010 Commercial-Instructor Supervisor.

13-1079.99 Human Resources, Training, and Labor Relations Specialists, All Other

- Education/Training Required: Bachelor's degree
- Employed: 171,880
- Annual Earnings: $48,440
- Growth: 24.1%
- Annual Job Openings: 26,000

All human resources, training, and labor relations specialists not listed separately.

No task data available.

Note: The Department of Labor has not collected some data for this job, so it has fewer details than the other descriptions.

Related SOC Job—13-1079 Human Resources, Training, and Labor Relations Specialists, All Other. Related OOH Job—Human Resources, Training, and Labor Relations Managers and Specialists. Related DOT Jobs—166.167-042 Senior Enlisted Advisor; 166.167-050 Program Specialist, Employee-Health Maintenance; 166.257-010 Employer Relations Representative; 166.267-030 Retirement Officer; 166.267-042 Employee Relations Specialist; 166.267-046 Human Resource Advisor; 169.107-010 Arbitrator; 169.207-010 Conciliator.

13-1081.00 Logisticians

- Education/Training Required: Bachelor's degree
- Employed: 52,220
- Annual Earnings: $60,110
- Growth: 13.2%
- Annual Job Openings: 7,000

Analyze and coordinate the logistical functions of a firm or organization. Responsible for the entire life cycle of a product, including acquisition, distribution, internal allocation, delivery, and final disposal of resources.

Maintain and develop positive business relationships with a customer's key personnel involved in or directly relevant to a logistics activity. Develop an understanding of customers' needs and take actions to ensure that such needs are met. Direct availability and allocation of materials, supplies, and finished products. Collaborate with other departments as necessary to meet customer requirements, to take advantage of sales opportunities, or, in the case of shortages, to minimize negative impacts on a business. Protect and control proprietary materials. Review logistics performance with customers against targets, benchmarks, and service agreements. Develop and implement technical project management tools such as plans, schedules, and responsibility and compliance matrices. Direct team activities, establishing task priorities, scheduling and tracking work assignments, providing guidance, and ensuring the availability of resources. Report project plans, progress, and results. Direct and support the compilation and analysis of technical source data necessary for product development. Explain proposed solutions to customers, management, or other interested parties through written proposals and oral presentations. Provide project management services, including the provision and analysis of technical data. Develop proposals that include documentation for estimates. Plan, organize, and execute logistics support activities such as maintenance planning, repair analysis, and test equipment recommendations. Participate in the assessment and review of design alternatives and design change proposal impacts. Support the development of training materials and technical manuals. Stay informed of logistics technology advances and apply appropriate technology in order to improve logistics processes. Redesign the movement of goods in order to maximize value and minimize costs. Manage subcontractor activities, reviewing proposals, developing performance specifications, and serving as liaisons between subcontractors and organizations. Manage the logistical aspects of product life cycles, including coordination or provisioning of samples and the minimization of obsolescence.

GOE Information—Interest Area: 04. Business and Administration. Work Group: 04.05. Accounting, Auditing, and Analytical Support. Personality Type—No data available. Work Values—No data available. Skills—Management of Financial Resources; Systems Analysis; Management of Material Resources; Management of Personnel Resources; Operations Analysis; Persuasion. Abilities—*Cognitive:* Originality; Mathematical Reasoning; Deductive Reasoning; Fluency of Ideas; Number Facility; Inductive Reasoning. *Psychomotor:* Finger Dexterity. *Physical:* None met the criteria. *Sensory:* Far Vision; Speech Recognition; Speech Clarity; Near Vision. General Work Activities—*Information Input:* Monitoring Processes, Materials, or Surroundings; Getting Information; Identifying Objects, Actions, and Events. *Mental Process:* Scheduling Work and Activities; Evaluating Information Against Standards; Organizing, Planning, and Prioritizing. *Work Output:* Interacting With Computers; Documenting or Recording Information. *Interacting with Others:* Communicating with Other Workers; Establishing and Maintaining Interpersonal Relationships; Communicating with Persons Outside

Organization. **Physical Work Conditions**—Indoors; Sitting. **Other Job Characteristics**—Need to Be Exact or Accurate.

Experience—Job Zone 4. A minimum of two to four years of work-related skill, knowledge, or experience is needed. **Job Preparation**—SVP 7.0 to less than 8.0—two years to less than 10 years. **Knowledges**—Telecommunications; Computers and Electronics; Administration and Management; Geography; Economics and Accounting; Public Safety and Security. **Instructional Programs**—Logistics and Materials Management; Operations Management and Supervision; Transportation/Transportation Management.

Related SOC Job—13-1081 Logisticians. **Related OOH Job**—Logisticians. **Related DOT Job**—019.167-010 Logistics Engineer.

13-1111.00 Management Analysts

- **Education/Training Required: Work experience plus degree**
- **Employed: 441,000**
- **Annual Earnings: $66,380**
- **Growth: 20.1%**
- **Annual Job Openings: 82,000**

Conduct organizational studies and evaluations, design systems and procedures, conduct work simplifications and measurement studies, and prepare operations and procedures manuals to assist management in operating more efficiently and effectively. Includes program analysts and management consultants.

Gather and organize information on problems or procedures. Analyze data gathered and develop solutions or alternative methods of proceeding. Confer with personnel concerned to ensure successful functioning of newly implemented systems or procedures. Develop and implement records management program for filing, protection, and retrieval of records and assure compliance with program. Review forms and reports and confer with management and users about format, distribution, and purpose and to identify problems and improvements. Document findings of study and prepare recommendations for implementation of new systems, procedures, or organizational changes. Interview personnel and conduct on-site observation to ascertain unit functions; work performed; and methods, equipment, and personnel used. Prepare manuals and train workers in use of new forms, reports, procedures, or equipment according to organizational policy. Design, evaluate, recommend, and approve changes of forms and reports. Plan study of work problems and procedures, such as organizational change, communications, information flow, integrated production methods, inventory control, or cost analysis. Recommend purchase of storage equipment and design area layout to locate equipment in space available.

GOE Information—**Interest Area:** 04. Business and Administration. **Work Group:** 04.05. Accounting, Auditing, and Analytical Support. **Personality Type**—Enterprising. Enterprising occupations frequently involve starting up and carrying out projects. These occupations can involve leading people and making many decisions. They sometimes require risk taking and often deal with business. **Work Values**—Creativity; Working Conditions; Authority; Achievement; Social Status; Compensation. **Skills**—Systems Evaluation; Installation; Management of Financial Resources; Operations Analysis; Quality Control Analysis; Systems Analysis. **Abilities**—*Cognitive:* Written Expression; Inductive Reasoning; Deductive Reasoning; Fluency of Ideas; Written Comprehension; Mathematical Reasoning. *Psychomotor:* None met the criteria. *Physical:* None met the criteria. *Sensory:* Near Vision; Speech Recognition; Speech Clarity. **General Work Activities**—*Information Input:* Getting Information;

Monitoring Processes, Materials, or Surroundings; Identifying Objects, Actions, and Events. *Mental Process:* Organizing, Planning, and Prioritizing; Processing Information; Updating and Using Relevant Knowledge. *Work Output:* Documenting or Recording Information; Interacting With Computers; Performing General Physical Activities. *Interacting with Others:* Establishing and Maintaining Interpersonal Relationships; Communicating with Other Workers; Resolving Conflicts and Negotiating with Others. **Physical Work Conditions**—Indoors; Sitting. **Other Job Characteristics**—Need to Be Exact or Accurate; Errors Have Important Consequences.

Experience—Job Zone 4. A minimum of two to four years of work-related skill, knowledge, or experience is needed. **Job Preparation**—SVP 7.0 to less than 8.0—two years to less than 10 years. **Knowledges**—Personnel and Human Resources; Clerical Practices; Sales and Marketing; Customer and Personal Service; Economics and Accounting; Administration and Management. **Instructional Programs**—Business Administration/Management; Business/Commerce, General.

Related SOC Job—13-1111 Management Analysts. **Related OOH Job**—Management Analysts. **Related DOT Jobs**—161.117-014 Director, Records Management; 161.167-010 Management Analyst; 161.167-014 Manager, Forms Analysis; 161.167-018 Manager, Records Analysis; 161.167-022 Manager, Reports Analysis; 161.267-010 Clerical-Methods Analyst; 161.267-018 Forms Analyst; 161.267-022 Records-Management Analyst; 161.267-026 Reports Analyst.

13-1121.00 Meeting and Convention Planners

- **Education/Training Required: Bachelor's degree**
- **Employed: 40,040**
- **Annual Earnings: $41,280**
- **Growth: 22.2%**
- **Annual Job Openings: 4,000**

Coordinate activities of staff and convention personnel to make arrangements for group meetings and conventions.

Consult with customers to determine objectives and requirements for events such as meetings, conferences, and conventions. Monitor event activities to ensure compliance with applicable regulations and laws, satisfaction of participants, and resolution of any problems that arise. Confer with staff at a chosen event site to coordinate details. Plan and develop programs, agendas, budgets, and services according to customer requirements. Review event bills for accuracy and approve payment. Coordinate services for events, such as accommodation and transportation for participants, facilities, catering, signage, displays, special needs requirements, printing, and event security. Arrange the availability of audio-visual equipment, transportation, displays, and other event needs. Inspect event facilities to ensure that they conform to customer requirements. Maintain records of event aspects, including financial details. Conduct post-event evaluations to determine how future events could be improved. Negotiate contracts with such service providers and suppliers as hotels, convention centers, and speakers. Meet with sponsors and organizing committees to plan scope and format of events, to establish and monitor budgets, or to review administrative procedures and event progress. Direct administrative details such as financial operations, dissemination of promotional materials, and responses to inquiries. Evaluate and select providers of services according to customer requirements. Read trade publications, attend seminars, and consult with other meeting professionals to keep abreast of meeting management standards and trends. Organize registration of event participants. Design and implement efforts to publicize events and promote sponsorships. Hire, train, and supervise volunteers and support staff required for events. Obtain permits from fire and health departments to erect displays and exhibits and serve food at events. Promote conference, convention, and trades show services by performing tasks such as meeting with professional and trade associations and producing brochures and other publications.

GOE Information—Interest Area: 04. Business and Administration. **Work Group:** 04.02. Managerial Work in Business Detail. **Personality Type—**Enterprising. Enterprising occupations frequently involve starting up and carrying out projects. These occupations can involve leading people and making many decisions. They sometimes require risk taking and often deal with business. **Work Values—**Authority; Working Conditions; Creativity; Social Service; Recognition; Variety. **Skills—**Service Orientation; Operations Analysis; Management of Financial Resources; Negotiation; Coordination; Time Management. **Abilities—**_Cognitive:_ Visualization; Memorization; Number Facility; Fluency of Ideas; Mathematical Reasoning; Time Sharing. _Psychomotor:_ Finger Dexterity. _Physical:_ None met the criteria. _Sensory:_ Speech Recognition; Far Vision; Speech Clarity; Visual Color Discrimination; Near Vision; Auditory Attention. **General Work Activities—**_Information Input:_ Getting Information; Identifying Objects, Actions, and Events; Estimating the Needed Characteristics of Products, Events, or Information. _Mental Process:_ Organizing, Planning, and Prioritizing; Scheduling Work and Activities; Processing Information. _Work Output:_ Interacting With Computers; Documenting or Recording Information. _Interacting with Others:_ Establishing and Maintaining Interpersonal Relationships; Communicating with Other Workers; Communicating with Persons Outside Organization. **Physical Work Conditions—**Indoors; Sitting. **Other Job Characteristics—**Need to Be Exact or Accurate; Repeat Same Tasks.

Experience—Job Zone 4. A minimum of two to four years of work-related skill, knowledge, or experience is needed. **Job Preparation—**SVP 7.0 to less than 8.0—two years to less than 10 years. **Knowledges—**Sales and Marketing; Customer and Personal Service; Personnel and Human Resources; Economics and Accounting; Administration and Management; Communications and Media. **Instructional Program—**Selling Skills and Sales Operations.

Related SOC Job—13-1121 Meeting and Convention Planners. **Related OOH Job—**Meeting and Convention Planners. **Related DOT Jobs—**169.117-022 Meeting Planner; 187.167-078 Manager, Convention.

13-1199.99 Business Operations Specialists, All Other

- Education/Training Required: Bachelor's degree
- Employed: 916,290
- Annual Earnings: $54,550
- Growth: 27.0%
- Annual Job Openings: 193,000

All business operations specialists not listed separately.

No task data available.

Note: The Department of Labor has not collected some data for this job, so it has fewer details than the other descriptions.

Related SOC Job—13-1199 Business Operations Specialists, All Other. **Related OOH Job—**None. **Related DOT Jobs—**100.117-014 Library Consultant; 110.167-010 Bar Examiner; 152.067-018 Cue Selector; 162.167-030 Purchase-Price Analyst; 166.267-014 Hospital-Insurance Representative; 168.267-026 Dealer-Compliance Representative; 168.367-010 Attendance Officer; 168.367-014 Rater, Travel Accommodations; 169.117-014 Grant Coordinator; 169.117-018 Provider Relations Representative; 169.167-022 Fire Assistant; 169.167-026 Laboratory Assistant, Liaison Inspection; 169.167-066 Legislative Assistant; others.

13-2000 Financial Specialists

13-2011.00 Accountants and Auditors

- Education/Training Required: Bachelor's degree
- Employed: 1,051,220
- Annual Earnings: $52,210
- Growth: 22.4%
- Annual Job Openings: 157,000

The job openings listed here are shared with 13-2011.01 Accountants and 13-2011.02 Auditors.

Examine, analyze, and interpret accounting records for the purpose of giving advice or preparing statements. Install or advise on systems of recording costs or other financial and budgetary data.

No task data available.

GOE Information—Interest Area: 04. Business and Administration. **Work Group:** 04.05. Accounting, Auditing, and Analytical Support. **Note:** The Department of Labor has not collected some data for this job, so it has fewer details than the other descriptions.

Instructional Programs—Accounting; Accounting and Business/Management; Accounting and Computer Science; Accounting and Finance; Auditing; Taxation.

Related SOC Job—13-2011 Accountants and Auditors. **Related OOH Job—**Accountants and Auditors. **Related DOT Job—**No data available.

13-2011.01 Accountants

- Education/Training Required: Bachelor's degree
- Employed: 1,051,220
- Annual Earnings: $52,210
- Growth: 22.4%
- Annual Job Openings: 157,000

The job openings listed here are shared with 13-2011.00 Accountants and Auditors and 13-2011.02 Auditors.

Analyze financial information and prepare financial reports to determine or maintain record of assets, liabilities, profit and loss, tax liability, or other financial activities within an organization.

Prepare, examine, or analyze accounting records, financial statements, or other financial reports to assess accuracy, completeness, and conformance to reporting and procedural standards. Compute taxes owed and prepare tax returns, ensuring compliance with payment, reporting, or other tax requirements. Analyze business operations, trends, costs, revenues, financial commitments, and obligations to project future revenues and expenses or to provide advice. Report to management regarding the finances of establishment. Establish tables of accounts and assign entries to proper accounts. Develop, maintain, and analyze budgets, preparing periodic reports that compare budgeted costs to actual costs. Develop, implement, modify, and document recordkeeping and accounting systems, making use of current computer technology. Prepare forms and manuals for accounting and bookkeeping personnel and direct their work activities. Survey operations to ascertain accounting needs and to recommend, develop, or maintain solutions to business and financial problems. Work as Internal Revenue Service (IRS) agents. Advise management about issues such as resource utilization, tax strategies, and the assumptions underlying budget forecasts. Provide internal and external auditing services for businesses or individuals. Advise clients in areas such as compensation, employee health care benefits, the design of accounting or data processing systems, or long-range tax or estate plans. Investigate bankruptcies and other complex financial transactions and prepare reports summarizing the findings. Represent clients before taxing authorities and provide support during litigation involving financial issues. Appraise, evaluate, and inventory real property and equipment, recording information such as the description, value, and location of property. Maintain or examine the records of government agencies. Serve as bankruptcy trustees or business valuators.

GOE Information—Interest Area: 04. Business and Administration. **Work Group:** 04.05. Accounting, Auditing, and Analytical Support. **Personality Type—**Conventional. Conventional occupations frequently involve following set procedures and routines. These occupations can include working with data and details more than with ideas. Usually there is a clear line of authority to follow. **Work Values—**Working Conditions; Compensation; Social Status; Security; Ability Utilization; Responsibility. **Skills—**Management of Financial Resources; Systems Analysis; Systems Evaluation; Operations Analysis; Judgment and Decision Making; Programming. **Abilities—**Cognitive: Number Facility; Mathematical Reasoning; Deductive Reasoning; Flexibility of Closure; Written Expression; Speed of Closure. Psychomotor: None met the criteria. Physical: None met the criteria. Sensory: Near Vision; Speech Recognition; Speech Clarity. **General Work Activities—**Information Input: Getting Information; Identifying Objects, Actions, and Events; Estimating the Needed Characteristics of Products, Events, or Information. Mental Process: Processing Information; Organizing, Planning, and Prioritizing; Analyzing Data or Information. Work Output: Interacting With Computers; Documenting or Recording Information. Interacting with Others: Communicating with Other Workers; Establishing and Maintaining Interpersonal Relationships; Providing Consultation and Advice to Others. **Physical Work Conditions—**Indoors; Sitting. **Other Job Characteristics—**Need to Be Exact or Accurate; Automation; Repeat Same Tasks.

Experience—Job Zone 4. A minimum of two to four years of work-related skill, knowledge, or experience is needed. **Job Preparation—**SVP 7.0 to less than 8.0—two years to less than 10 years. **Knowledges—**Economics and Accounting; Clerical Practices; Mathematics; Law and Government; Computers and Electronics; Personnel and Human Resources. **Instructional Programs—**Accounting; Accounting and Business/Management; Accounting and Computer Science; Accounting and Finance.

Related SOC Job—13-2011 Accountants and Auditors. **Related OOH Job—**Accountants and Auditors. **Related DOT Jobs—**160.162-010 Accountant, Tax; 160.162-018 Accountant; 160.162-022 Accountant, Budget; 160.162-026 Accountant, Cost; 160.167-022 Accountant, Property; 160.167-026 Accountant, Systems; 160.167-042 Bursar.

13-2011.02 Auditors

- **Education/Training Required: Bachelor's degree**
- **Employed: 1,051,220**
- **Annual Earnings: $52,210**
- **Growth: 22.4%**
- **Annual Job Openings: 157,000**

The job openings listed here are shared with 13-2011.00 Accountants and Auditors and 13-2011.01 Accountants.

Examine and analyze accounting records to determine financial status of establishment and prepare financial reports concerning operating procedures.

Collect and analyze data to detect deficient controls; duplicated effort; extravagance; fraud; or non-compliance with laws, regulations, and management policies. Report to management about asset utilization and audit results and recommend changes in operations and financial activities. Prepare detailed reports on audit findings. Review data about material assets, net worth, liabilities, capital stock, surplus, income, and expenditures. Inspect account books and accounting systems for efficiency, effectiveness, and use of accepted accounting procedures to record transactions. Examine and evaluate financial and information systems, recommending controls to ensure system reliability and data integrity. Supervise auditing of establishments and determine scope of investigation required. Prepare, analyze, and verify annual reports, financial statements, and other records, using accepted accounting and statistical procedures to assess financial condition and facilitate financial planning. Confer with company officials about financial and regulatory matters. Inspect cash on hand, notes receivable and payable, negotiable securities, and canceled checks to confirm that records are accurate. Examine inventory to verify journal and ledger entries. Examine whether the organization's objectives are reflected in its management activities and whether employees understand the objectives. Examine records and interview workers to ensure recording of transactions and compliance with laws and regulations. Direct activities of personnel engaged in filing, recording, compiling, and transmitting financial records. Produce up-to-the-minute information, using internal computer systems, to allow management to base decisions on actual, not historical, data. Conduct pre-implementation audits to determine if systems and programs under development will work as planned. Review taxpayer accounts and conduct audits on site, by correspondence, or by summoning taxpayer to office. Evaluate taxpayer finances to determine tax liability, using knowledge of interest and discount rates, annuities, valuation of stocks and bonds, and amortization valuation of depletable assets.

GOE Information—Interest Area: 04. Business and Administration. **Work Group:** 04.05. Accounting, Auditing, and Analytical Support. **Personality Type—**Conventional. Conventional occupations frequently involve following set procedures and routines. These occupations can include working with data and details more than with ideas. Usually there is a clear line of authority to follow. **Work Values—**Authority; Advancement; Working Conditions; Compensation; Co-workers; Company Policies and Practices. **Skills—**Management of Financial Resources; Writing; Mathematics; Time Management; Negotiation; Service Orientation. **Abilities—**Cognitive: Number Facility; Mathematical Reasoning; Flexibility of Closure; Inductive Reasoning; Problem Sensitivity; Deductive Reasoning. Psychomotor: Finger Dexterity. Physical: None met the criteria. Sensory: Near Vision; Speech Recognition; Speech Clarity; Far Vision; Auditory Attention. **General Work Activities—**Information Input: Getting Information; Monitoring Processes, Materials, or

Surroundings; Identifying Objects, Actions, and Events. _Mental Process:_ Organizing, Planning, and Prioritizing; Analyzing Data or Information; Evaluating Information Against Standards. _Work Output:_ Interacting With Computers; Documenting or Recording Information. _Interacting with Others:_ Establishing and Maintaining Interpersonal Relationships; Communicating with Other Workers; Providing Consultation and Advice to Others. **Physical Work Conditions**—Indoors; Noisy; Sitting; Using Hands on Objects, Tools, or Controls; Repetitive Motions. **Other Job Characteristics**—Need to Be Exact or Accurate; Repeat Same Tasks; Errors Have Important Consequences; Automation.

Experience—Job Zone 4. A minimum of two to four years of work-related skill, knowledge, or experience is needed. **Job Preparation**—SVP 7.0 to less than 8.0—two years to less than 10 years. **Knowledges**—Economics and Accounting; Sales and Marketing; Mathematics; Law and Government; Computers and Electronics; Customer and Personal Service. **Instructional Programs**—Accounting; Accounting and Business/Management; Accounting and Computer Science; Accounting and Finance; Auditing.

Related SOC Job—13-2011 Accountants and Auditors. **Related OOH Job**—Accountants and Auditors. **Related DOT Jobs**—160.162-030 Auditor, Data Processing; 160.167-030 Auditor, County or City; 160.167-034 Auditor, Internal; 160.167-038 Auditor, Tax; 160.167-054 Auditor; 160.267-014 Director, Utility Accounts.

13-2021.00 Appraisers and Assessors of Real Estate

- **Education/Training Required: Postsecondary vocational training**
- **Employed: 63,800**
- **Annual Earnings: $43,440**
- **Growth: 22.8%**
- **Annual Job Openings: 9,000**

The job openings listed here are shared with 13-2021.01 Assessors and 13-2021.02 Appraisers, Real Estate.

Appraise real property to determine its fair value. May assess taxes in accordance with prescribed schedules.

No task data available.

GOE Information—Interest Area: 06. Finance and Insurance. **Work Group:** 06.02. Finance/Insurance Investigation and Analysis. **Note:** The Department of Labor has not collected some data for this job, so it has fewer details than the other descriptions.

Instructional Program—Real Estate.

Related SOC Job—13-2021 Appraisers and Assessors of Real Estate. **Related OOH Job**—Appraisers and Assessors of Real Estate. **Related DOT Job**—No data available.

13-2021.01 Assessors

- **Education/Training Required: Postsecondary vocational training**
- **Employed: 63,800**
- **Annual Earnings: $43,440**
- **Growth: 22.8%**
- **Annual Job Openings: 9,000**

The job openings listed here are shared with 13-2021.00 Appraisers and Assessors of Real Estate and 13-2021.02 Appraisers, Real Estate..

Appraise real and personal property to determine its fair value. May assess taxes in accordance with prescribed schedules.

Determine taxability and value of properties, using methods such as field inspection, structural measurement, calculation, sales analysis, market trend studies, and income and expense analysis. Inspect new construction and major improvements to existing structures to determine values. Explain assessed values to property owners and defend appealed assessments at public hearings. Inspect properties, considering factors such as market value, location, and building or replacement costs to determine appraisal value. Prepare and maintain current data on each parcel assessed, including maps of boundaries, inventories of land and structures, property characteristics, and any applicable exemptions. Identify the ownership of each piece of taxable property. Conduct regular reviews of property within jurisdictions to determine changes in property due to construction or demolition. Complete and maintain assessment rolls that show the assessed values and status of all property in a municipality. Issue notices of assessments and taxes. Review information about transfers of property to ensure its accuracy, checking basic information on buyers, sellers, and sales prices and making corrections as necessary. Maintain familiarity with aspects of local real estate markets. Analyze trends in sales prices, construction costs, and rents to assess property values or determine the accuracy of assessments. Approve applications for property tax exemptions or deductions. Establish uniform and equitable systems for assessing all classes and kinds of property. Write and submit appraisal and tax reports for public record. Serve on assessment review boards. Hire staff members. Provide sales analyses to be used for equalization of school aid. Calculate tax bills for properties by multiplying assessed values by jurisdiction tax rates.

GOE Information—Interest Area: 06. Finance and Insurance. **Work Group:** 06.02. Finance/Insurance Investigation and Analysis. **Personality Type**—Conventional. Conventional occupations frequently involve following set procedures and routines. These occupations can include working with data and details more than with ideas. Usually there is a clear line of authority to follow. **Work Values**—Independence; Responsibility; Autonomy; Compensation; Security; Working Conditions. **Skills**—Mathematics; Systems Analysis; Negotiation; Speaking; Persuasion; Systems Evaluation. **Abilities**—_Cognitive:_ Number Facility; Mathematical Reasoning; Category Flexibility; Deductive Reasoning; Written Comprehension; Fluency of Ideas. _Psychomotor:_ None met the criteria. _Physical:_ None met the criteria. _Sensory:_ Near Vision; Speech Recognition; Far Vision; Speech Clarity; Depth Perception. **General Work Activities**—_Information Input:_ Getting Information; Identifying Objects, Actions, and Events; Monitoring Processes, Materials, or Surroundings. _Mental Process:_ Updating and Using Relevant Knowledge; Organizing, Planning, and Prioritizing; Processing Information. _Work Output:_ Documenting or Recording Information; Interacting With Computers; Performing General Physical Activities. _Interacting with Others:_ Performing for or Working with the Public; Resolving Conflicts and Negotiating with Others; Communicating with Persons Outside Organization. **Physical Work Conditions**—More Often Indoors Than Outdoors; Sitting; Using Hands on Objects, Tools, or Controls; Repetitive Motions. **Other Job Characteristics**—Need to Be Exact or Accurate; Repeat Same Tasks; Automation.

Experience—Job Zone 3. Previous work-related skill, knowledge, or experience is required. **Job Preparation**—SVP 6.0 to less than 7.0—more than one year and less than four years. **Knowledges**—Building and Construction; Clerical Practices; Law and Government; Mathematics; Computers and Electronics; Economics and Accounting. **Instructional Program**—Real Estate.

Related SOC Job—13-2021 Appraisers and Assessors of Real Estate. **Related OOH Job**—Appraisers and Assessors of Real Estate. **Related DOT Job**—188.167-010 Appraiser.

13-2021.02 Appraisers, Real Estate

- **Education/Training Required: Postsecondary vocational training**
- **Employed: 63,800**
- **Annual Earnings: $43,440**
- **Growth: 22.8%**
- **Annual Job Openings: 9,000**

The job openings listed here are shared with 13-2021.00 Appraisers and Assessors of Real Estate and 13-2021.01 Appraisers.

Appraise real property to determine its value for purchase, sales, investment, mortgage, or loan purposes.

Prepare written reports that estimate property values, outline methods by which the estimations were made, and meet appraisal standards. Compute final estimation of property values, taking into account such factors as depreciation, replacement costs, value comparisons of similar properties, and income potential. Search public records for transactions such as sales, leases, and assessments. Inspect properties to evaluate construction, condition, special features, and functional design and to take property measurements. Photograph interiors and exteriors of properties in order to assist in estimating property value, substantiate findings, and complete appraisal reports. Evaluate land and neighborhoods where properties are situated, considering locations and trends or impending changes that could influence future values. Obtain county land values and sales information about nearby properties in order to aid in establishment of property values. Verify legal descriptions of properties by comparing them to county records. Check building codes and zoning bylaws in order to determine any effects on the properties being appraised. Estimate building replacement costs, using building valuation manuals and professional cost estimators. Examine income records and operating costs of income properties. Interview persons familiar with properties and immediate surroundings, such as contractors, homeowners, and realtors, in order to obtain pertinent information. Examine the type and location of nearby services such as shopping centers, schools, parks, and other neighborhood features in order to evaluate their impact on property values. Draw land diagrams that will be used in appraisal reports to support findings. Testify in court as to the value of a piece of real estate property.

GOE Information—**Interest Area:** 06. Finance and Insurance. **Work Group:** 06.02. Finance/Insurance Investigation and Analysis. **Personality Type**—Enterprising. Enterprising occupations frequently involve starting up and carrying out projects. These occupations can involve leading people and making many decisions. They sometimes require risk taking and often deal with business. **Work Values**—Responsibility; Independence; Autonomy; Social Status; Working Conditions; Ability Utilization. **Skills**—Mathematics; Writing; Critical Thinking; Management of Financial Resources; Complex Problem Solving; Speaking. **Abilities**—*Cognitive:* Mathematical Reasoning; Number Facility; Written Expression; Category Flexibility; Inductive Reasoning; Visualization. *Psychomotor:* None met the criteria. *Physical:* None met the criteria. *Sensory:* Far Vision; Near Vision; Speech Recognition. **General Work Activities**—

Information Input: Getting Information; Identifying Objects, Actions, and Events; Monitoring Processes, Materials, or Surroundings. *Mental Process:* Processing Information; Updating and Using Relevant Knowledge; Analyzing Data or Information. *Work Output:* Interacting With Computers; Documenting or Recording Information; Performing General Physical Activities. *Interacting with Others:* Communicating with Persons Outside Organization; Establishing and Maintaining Interpersonal Relationships; Performing Administrative Activities. **Physical Work Conditions**—More Often Outdoors Than Indoors; Sitting. **Other Job Characteristics**—Need to Be Exact or Accurate; Repeat Same Tasks.

Experience—Job Zone 4. A minimum of two to four years of work-related skill, knowledge, or experience is needed. **Job Preparation**—SVP 7.0 to less than 8.0—two years to less than 10 years. **Knowledges**—Building and Construction; Economics and Accounting; Geography; Clerical Practices; Law and Government; Customer and Personal Service. **Instructional Program**—Real Estate.

Related SOC Job—13-2021 Appraisers and Assessors of Real Estate. **Related OOH Job**—Appraisers and Assessors of Real Estate. **Related DOT Job**—191.267-010 Appraiser, Real Estate.

13-2031.00 Budget Analysts

- **Education/Training Required: Bachelor's degree**
- **Employed: 53,510**
- **Annual Earnings: $58,910**
- **Growth: 13.5%**
- **Annual Job Openings: 6,000**

Examine budget estimates for completeness, accuracy, and conformance with procedures and regulations. Analyze budgeting and accounting reports for the purpose of maintaining expenditure controls.

Direct the preparation of regular and special budget reports. Consult with managers to ensure that budget adjustments are made in accordance with program changes. Match appropriations for specific programs with appropriations for broader programs, including items for emergency funds. Provide advice and technical assistance with cost analysis, fiscal allocation, and budget preparation. Summarize budgets and submit recommendations for the approval or disapproval of funds requests. Seek new ways to improve efficiency and increase profits. Review operating budgets to analyze trends affecting budget needs. Perform cost-benefit analyses to compare operating programs, review financial requests, or explore alternative financing methods. Interpret budget directives and establish policies for carrying out directives. Compile and analyze accounting records and other data to determine the financial resources required to implement a program. Testify before examining and fund-granting authorities, clarifying and promoting the proposed budgets.

GOE Information—**Interest Area:** 04. Business and Administration. **Work Group:** 04.05. Accounting, Auditing, and Analytical Support. **Personality Type**—Conventional. Conventional occupations frequently involve following set procedures and routines. These occupations can include working with data and details more than with ideas. Usually there is a clear line of authority to follow. **Work Values**—Advancement; Working Conditions; Supervision, Human Relations; Authority; Compensation; Ability Utilization. **Skills**—Management of Financial Resources; Mathematics; Operations Analysis; Quality Control Analysis; Complex Problem Solving; Monitoring. **Abilities**—*Cognitive:* Number Facility; Mathematical Reasoning; Deductive Reasoning; Speed of Closure; Written Comprehension; Category Flexibility. *Psychomotor:* None met the criteria. *Physical:* None met the criteria. *Sensory:* Near Vision; Speech Recognition; Speech Clarity. **General Work Activities**—*Information Input:* Getting Information; Monitoring Processes, Materials, or Surroundings; Identifying Objects, Actions, and Events. *Mental Process:* Organizing, Planning, and Prioritizing; Analyzing Data or Information; Processing Information. *Work Output:* Interacting With Computers; Documenting or Recording Information. *Interacting with Others:* Monitoring and Controlling Resources; Establishing and Maintaining Interpersonal Relationships; Coordinating the Work and Activities of Others. **Physical Work Conditions**—Indoors; Sitting. **Other Job Characteristics**—Need to Be Exact or Accurate; Repeat Same Tasks; Automation.

Experience—Job Zone 4. A minimum of two to four years of work-related skill, knowledge, or experience is needed. **Job Preparation**—SVP 7.0 to less than 8.0—two years to less than 10 years. **Knowledges**—Economics and Accounting; Administration and Management; Clerical Practices; Computers and Electronics; Mathematics; Personnel and Human Resources. **Instructional Programs**—Accounting; Finance, General.

Related SOC Job—13-2031 Budget Analysts. **Related OOH Job**—Budget Analysts. **Related DOT Jobs**—161.117-010 Budget Officer; 161.267-030 Budget Analyst.

13-2041.00 Credit Analysts

- **Education/Training Required: Bachelor's degree**
- **Employed: 61,500**
- **Annual Earnings: $50,370**
- **Growth: 3.6%**
- **Annual Job Openings: 3,000**

Analyze current credit data and financial statements of individuals or firms to determine the degree of risk involved in extending credit or lending money. Prepare reports with this credit information for use in decision-making.

Evaluate customer records and recommend payment plans based on earnings, savings data, payment history, and purchase activity. Confer with credit association and other business representatives to exchange credit information. Complete loan applications, including credit analyses and summaries of loan requests, and submit to loan committees for approval. Generate financial ratios, using computer programs, to evaluate customers' financial status. Review individual or commercial customer files to identify and select delinquent accounts for collection. Compare liquidity, profitability, and credit histories of establishments being evaluated with those of similar establishments in the same industries and geographic locations. Consult with customers to resolve complaints and verify financial and credit transactions. Analyze financial data such as income growth, quality of management, and market share to determine expected profitability of loans.

GOE Information—Interest Area: 06. Finance and Insurance. **Work Group:** 06.02. Finance/Insurance Investigation and Analysis. **Personality Type**—Conventional. Conventional occupations frequently involve following set procedures and routines. These occupations can include working with data and details more than with ideas. Usually there is a clear line of authority to follow. **Work Values**—Advancement; Working Conditions; Supervision, Human Relations; Company Policies and Practices; Activity; Responsibility. **Skills**—Speaking; Writing; Operations Analysis; Negotiation; Active Listening; Systems Evaluation. **Abilities**—*Cognitive:* Number Facility; Mathematical Reasoning; Flexibility of Closure; Deductive

Reasoning; Written Expression; Inductive Reasoning. *Psychomotor:* Finger Dexterity. *Physical:* None met the criteria. *Sensory:* Near Vision; Speech Recognition. **General Work Activities**—*Information Input:* Getting Information; Identifying Objects, Actions, and Events. *Mental Process:* Processing Information; Evaluating Information Against Standards; Updating and Using Relevant Knowledge. *Work Output:* Documenting or Recording Information; Interacting With Computers. *Interacting with Others:* Establishing and Maintaining Interpersonal Relationships; Communicating with Other Workers. **Physical Work Conditions**—Indoors; Sitting; Repetitive Motions. **Other Job Characteristics**—Need to Be Exact or Accurate; Repeat Same Tasks.

Experience—Job Zone 4. A minimum of two to four years of work-related skill, knowledge, or experience is needed. **Job Preparation**—SVP 7.0 to less than 8.0—two years to less than 10 years. **Knowledges**—Economics and Accounting; Clerical Practices; Mathematics; Law and Government; Administration and Management; Customer and Personal Service. **Instructional Programs**—Accounting; Credit Management; Finance, General.

Related SOC Job—13-2041 Credit Analysts. **Related OOH Job**—Credit Analysts. **Related DOT Jobs**—160.267-022 Credit Analyst; 186.267-022 Loan Review Analyst; 241.267-022 Credit Analyst.

13-2051.00 Financial Analysts

- **Education/Training Required: Bachelor's degree**
- **Employed: 180,910**
- **Annual Earnings: $63,860**
- **Growth: 17.3%**
- **Annual Job Openings: 28,000**

Conduct quantitative analyses of information affecting investment programs of public or private institutions.

Assemble spreadsheets and draw charts and graphs used to illustrate technical reports, using computer. Analyze financial information to produce forecasts of business, industry, and economic conditions for use in making investment decisions. Maintain knowledge and stay abreast of developments in the fields of industrial technology, business, finance, and economic theory. Interpret data affecting investment programs, such as price, yield, stability, future trends in investment risks, and economic influences. Monitor fundamental economic, industrial, and corporate developments through the analysis of information obtained from financial publications and services, investment banking firms, government agencies, trade publications, company sources, and personal interviews. Recommend investments and investment timing to companies, investment firm staff, or the investing public. Determine the prices at which securities should be syndicated and offered to the public. Prepare plans of action for investment based on financial analyses. Evaluate and compare the relative quality of various securities in a given industry. Present oral and written reports on general economic trends, individual corporations, and entire industries. Contact brokers and purchase investments for companies according to company policy. Collaborate with investment bankers to attract new corporate clients to securities firms.

GOE Information—Interest Area: 06. Finance and Insurance. **Work Group:** 06.02. Finance/Insurance Investigation and Analysis. **Personality Type**—Investigative. Investigative occupations frequently involve working with ideas and require an extensive amount of thinking. These occupations can involve searching for facts and figuring out problems mentally. **Work Values**—Autonomy;

Compensation; Creativity; Recognition; Social Status; Working Conditions. **Skills**—Management of Financial Resources; Judgment and Decision Making; Systems Evaluation; Programming; Complex Problem Solving; Mathematics. **Abilities**—*Cognitive:* Number Facility; Mathematical Reasoning; Deductive Reasoning; Written Expression; Written Comprehension; Flexibility of Closure. *Psychomotor:* None met the criteria. *Physical:* None met the criteria. *Sensory:* Near Vision; Speech Recognition; Speech Clarity. **General Work Activities**—*Information Input:* Getting Information; Monitoring Processes, Materials, or Surroundings; Identifying Objects, Actions, and Events. *Mental Process:* Processing Information; Analyzing Data or Information; Making Decisions and Solving Problems. *Work Output:* Documenting or Recording Information; Interacting With Computers. *Interacting with Others:* Communicating with Other Workers; Establishing and Maintaining Interpersonal Relationships; Interpreting the Meaning of Information for Others. **Physical Work Conditions**—Indoors; Sitting. **Other Job Characteristics**—Need to Be Exact or Accurate; Repeat Same Tasks; Automation.

Experience—Job Zone 4. A minimum of two to four years of work-related skill, knowledge, or experience is needed. **Job Preparation**—SVP 7.0 to less than 8.0—two years to less than 10 years. **Knowledges**—Economics and Accounting; Mathematics; Law and Government; Administration and Management; Clerical Practices; English Language. **Instructional Programs**—Accounting and Business/Management; Accounting and Finance; Finance, General.

Related SOC Job—13-2051 Financial Analysts. **Related OOH Job**—Financial Analysts and Personal Financial Advisors. **Related DOT Job**—160.267-026 Investment Analyst.

13-2052.00 Personal Financial Advisors

- **Education/Training Required: Bachelor's degree**
- **Employed: 108,640**
- **Annual Earnings: $63,500**
- **Growth: 25.9%**
- **Annual Job Openings: 17,000**

Advise clients on financial plans, utilizing knowledge of tax and investment strategies, securities, insurance, pension plans, and real estate. Duties include assessing clients' assets, liabilities, cash flow, insurance coverage, tax status, and financial objectives to establish investment strategies.

Open accounts for clients and disburse funds from account to creditors as agents for clients. Research and investigate available investment opportunities to determine whether they fit into financial plans. Recommend strategies clients can use to achieve their financial goals and objectives, including specific recommendations in such areas as cash management, insurance coverage, and investment planning. Sell financial products such as stocks, bonds, mutual funds, and insurance if licensed to do so. Collect information from students to determine their eligibility for specific financial aid programs. Conduct seminars and workshops on financial planning topics such as retirement planning, estate planning, and the evaluation of severance packages. Contact clients' creditors to arrange for payment adjustments so that payments are feasible for clients and agreeable to creditors. Meet with clients' other advisors, including attorneys, accountants, trust officers, and investment bankers, to fully understand clients' financial goals and circumstances. Authorize release of financial aid funds to students. Participate in the selection of candidates for specific financial aid awards. Determine amounts of aid to be granted to students, considering such factors as funds available,

extent of demand, and financial needs. Build and maintain client bases, keeping current client plans up to date and recruiting new clients on an ongoing basis. Review clients' accounts and plans regularly to determine whether life changes, economic changes, or financial performance indicate a need for plan reassessment. Prepare and interpret information for clients such as investment performance reports, financial document summaries, and income projections. Answer clients' questions about the purposes and details of financial plans and strategies. Contact clients periodically to determine if there have been changes in their financial status. Devise debt liquidation plans that include payoff priorities and timelines. Explain and document for clients the types of services that are to be provided and the responsibilities to be taken by the personal financial advisor.

GOE Information—**Interest Area:** 06. Finance and Insurance. **Work Group:** 06.05. Finance/Insurance Sales and Support. **Personality Type**—Social. Social occupations frequently involve working with, communicating with, and teaching people. These occupations often involve helping or providing service to others. **Work Values**—Social Service; Working Conditions; Social Status; Authority; Co-workers; Responsibility. **Skills**—Management of Financial Resources; Speaking; Service Orientation; Mathematics; Active Listening; Judgment and Decision Making. **Abilities**—*Cognitive:* Number Facility; Mathematical Reasoning; Written Expression; Problem Sensitivity. *Psychomotor:* None met the criteria. *Physical:* None met the criteria. *Sensory:* Speech Clarity. **General Work Activities**—*Information Input:* Getting Information; Identifying Objects, Actions, and Events; Estimating the Needed Characteristics of Products, Events, or Information. *Mental Process:* Analyzing Data or Information; Processing Information; Developing Objectives and Strategies. *Work Output:* Documenting or Recording Information. *Interacting with Others:* Communicating with Persons Outside Organization; Providing Consultation and Advice to Others; Assisting and Caring for Others. **Physical Work Conditions**—Indoors; Sitting. **Other Job Characteristics**—Need to Be Exact or Accurate; Errors Have Important Consequences.

Experience—Job Zone 3. Previous work-related skill, knowledge, or experience is required. **Job Preparation**—SVP 6.0 to less than 7.0—more than one year and less than four years. **Knowledges**—Economics and Accounting; Mathematics. **Instructional Programs**—Finance, General; Financial Planning and Services.

Related SOC Job—13-2052 Personal Financial Advisors. **Related OOH Job**—Financial Analysts and Personal Financial Advisors. **Related DOT Job**—160.207-010 Credit Counselor.

13-2053.00 Insurance Underwriters

- **Education/Training Required: Bachelor's degree**
- **Employed: 98,970**
- **Annual Earnings: $51,270**
- **Growth: 8.0%**
- **Annual Job Openings: 13,000**

Review individual applications for insurance to evaluate degree of risk involved and determine acceptance of applications.

Examine documents to determine degree of risk from such factors as applicant financial standing and value and condition of property. Decline excessive risks. Write to field representatives, medical personnel, and others to obtain further information, quote rates, or explain company underwriting policies. Evaluate possibility of losses due to catastrophe or excessive insurance. Decrease value of policy when risk is substandard and specify applicable endorsements or apply rating to ensure safe profitable distribution of risks, using reference materials. Review company records to determine amount of insurance in force on single risk or group of closely related risks. Authorize reinsurance of policy when risk is high.

GOE Information—Interest Area: 06. Finance and Insurance. **Work Group:** 06.02. Finance/Insurance Investigation and Analysis. **Personality Type**—Conventional. Conventional occupations frequently involve following set procedures and routines. These occupations can include working with data and details more than with ideas. Usually there is a clear line of authority to follow. **Work Values**—Advancement; Supervision, Human Relations; Responsibility; Working Conditions; Company Policies and Practices; Supervision, Technical. **Skills**—Writing; Service Orientation; Speaking; Active Learning; Learning Strategies; Active Listening. **Abilities**—*Cognitive:* Flexibility of Closure; Mathematical Reasoning; Number Facility; Deductive Reasoning; Category Flexibility; Inductive Reasoning. *Psychomotor:* None met the criteria. *Physical:* None met the criteria. *Sensory:* Near Vision; Speech Recognition. **General Work Activities**—*Information Input:* Getting Information; Identifying Objects, Actions, and Events; Monitoring Processes, Materials, or Surroundings. *Mental Process:* Organizing, Planning, and Prioritizing; Processing Information; Making Decisions and Solving Problems. *Work Output:* Interacting With Computers; Documenting or Recording Information. *Interacting with Others:* Establishing and Maintaining Interpersonal Relationships; Communicating with Other Workers; Communicating with Persons Outside Organization. **Physical Work Conditions**—Indoors; Sitting; Using Hands on Objects, Tools, or Controls; Repetitive Motions. **Other Job Characteristics**—Need to Be Exact or Accurate; Repeat Same Tasks.

Experience—Job Zone 3. Previous work-related skill, knowledge, or experience is required. **Job Preparation**—SVP 6.0 to less than 7.0—more than one year and less than four years. **Knowledges**—Customer and Personal Service; Clerical Practices; Sales and Marketing; Economics and Accounting; Computers and Electronics; Law and Government. **Instructional Program**—Insurance.

Related SOC Job—13-2053 Insurance Underwriters. **Related OOH Job**—Insurance Underwriters. **Related DOT Job**—169.267-046 Underwriter.

13-2061.00 Financial Examiners

- **Education/Training Required: Bachelor's degree**
- **Employed: 22,160**
- **Annual Earnings: $63,090**
- **Growth: 9.5%**
- **Annual Job Openings: 3,000**

Enforce or ensure compliance with laws and regulations governing financial and securities institutions and financial and real estate transactions. May examine, verify correctness of, or establish authenticity of records.

Investigate activities of institutions in order to enforce laws and regulations and to ensure legality of transactions and operations or financial solvency. Review and analyze new, proposed, or revised laws, regulations, policies, and procedures in order to interpret their meaning and determine their impact. Plan, supervise, and review work of assigned subordinates. Recommend actions to ensure compliance with laws and regulations or to protect solvency of institutions. Examine the minutes of meetings of directors, stockholders, and committees in order to investigate the specific authority extended at various levels of management. Prepare reports, exhibits, and other supporting schedules that detail an institution's safety and soundness, compliance with laws and regulations, and recommended solutions to questionable financial conditions. Review balance sheets, operating income and expense accounts, and loan documentation in order to confirm institution assets and liabilities. Review audit reports of internal and external auditors in order to monitor adequacy of scope of reports or to discover specific weaknesses in internal routines. Train other examiners in the financial examination process. Establish guidelines for procedures and policies that comply with new and revised regulations and direct their implementation. Direct and participate in formal and informal meetings with bank directors, trustees, senior management, counsels, outside accountants, and consultants in order to gather information and discuss findings. Verify and inspect cash reserves, assigned collateral, and bank-owned securities in order to check internal control procedures. Review applications for mergers, acquisitions, establishment of new institutions, acceptance in Federal Reserve System, or registration of securities sales in order to determine their public interest value and conformance to regulations and recommend acceptance or rejection. Resolve problems concerning the overall financial integrity of banking institutions, including loan investment portfolios, capital, earnings, and specific or large troubled accounts.

GOE Information—Interest Area: 07. Government and Public Administration. **Work Group:** 07.03. Regulations Enforcement. **Personality Type**—Enterprising. Enterprising occupations frequently involve starting up and carrying out projects. These occupations can involve leading people and making many decisions. They sometimes require risk taking and often deal with business. **Work Values**—Working Conditions; Authority; Advancement; Social Status; Compensation; Responsibility. **Skills**—Monitoring; Management of Financial Resources; Quality Control Analysis; Systems Analysis; Systems Evaluation; Operations Analysis. **Abilities**—*Cognitive:* Number Facility; Mathematical Reasoning; Deductive Reasoning; Fluency of Ideas; Inductive Reasoning; Problem Sensitivity. *Psychomotor:* None met the criteria. *Physical:* None met the criteria. *Sensory:* Near Vision; Speech Recognition; Far Vision; Speech Clarity. **General Work Activities**—*Information Input:* Getting Information; Identifying Objects, Actions, and Events; Monitoring Processes, Materials, or Surroundings. *Mental Process:* Evaluating Information Against Standards; Organizing, Planning, and Prioritizing; Analyzing Data or Information. *Work Output:* Interacting With Computers; Documenting or Recording Information. *Interacting with Others:* Establishing and Maintaining Interpersonal Relationships; Interpreting the Meaning of Information for Others; Guiding, Directing, and Motivating Subordinates. **Physical Work Conditions**—Indoors; Sitting. **Other Job Characteristics**—Need to Be Exact or Accurate; Repeat Same Tasks.

Experience—Job Zone 4. A minimum of two to four years of work-related skill, knowledge, or experience is needed. **Job Preparation**—SVP 7.0 to less than 8.0—two years to less than 10 years. **Knowledges**—Economics and Accounting; Law and Government; Clerical Practices; Mathematics; English Language; Administration and Management. **Instructional Programs**—Accounting; Taxation.

Related SOC Job—13-2061 Financial Examiners. **Related OOH Job**—Financial Examiners. **Related DOT Jobs**—160.167-046 Chief Bank Examiner; 186.117-090 Compliance Officer; 188.167-038 Director, Securities and Real Estate.

13-2071.00 Loan Counselors

- **Education/Training Required: Bachelor's degree**
- **Employed: 28,030**
- **Annual Earnings: $35,680**
- **Growth: 17.7%**
- **Annual Job Openings: 5,000**

Provide guidance to prospective loan applicants who have problems qualifying for traditional loans. Guidance may include determining the best type of loan and explaining loan requirements or restrictions.

Check loan agreements to ensure that they are complete and accurate according to policies. Refer loans to loan committees for approval. Approve loans within specified limits. Submit applications to credit analysts for verification and recommendation. Analyze applicants' financial status, credit, and property evaluations to determine feasibility of granting loans. Interview applicants and request specified information for loan applications. Establish payment priorities according to credit terms and interest rates in order to reduce clients' overall costs. Contact applicants or creditors to resolve questions about applications or to assist with completion of paperwork. Maintain current knowledge of credit regulations. Calculate amount of debt and funds available in order to plan methods of payoff and to estimate time for debt liquidation. Analyze potential loan markets to find opportunities to promote loans and financial services. Review billing for accuracy. Supervise loan personnel. Maintain and review account records, updating and recategorizing them according to status changes. Assist in selection of financial award candidates, using electronic databases to certify loan eligibility. Confer with underwriters to resolve mortgage application problems. Inform individuals and groups about the financial assistance available to college or university students. Match students' needs and eligibility with available financial aid programs in order to provide informed recommendations. Contact creditors to explain clients' financial situations and to arrange for payment adjustments so that payments are feasible for clients and agreeable to creditors. Petition courts to transfer titles and deeds of collateral to banks. Contact borrowers with delinquent accounts to obtain payment in full or to negotiate repayment plans. Compare data on student aid applications with eligibility requirements of assistance programs. Counsel clients on personal and family financial problems, such as excessive spending and borrowing of funds. Review accounts to determine write-offs for collection agencies. Locate debtors, using post office directories, utility services account listings, and mailing lists.

GOE Information—Interest Area: 06. Finance and Insurance. **Work Group:** 06.02. Finance/Insurance Investigation and Analysis. **Personality Type**—Enterprising. Enterprising occupations frequently involve starting up and carrying out projects. These occupations can involve leading people and making many decisions. They sometimes require risk taking and often deal with business. **Work Values**—Advancement; Working Conditions; Co-workers; Social Service; Responsibility; Autonomy. **Skills**—Service Orientation; Active Listening; Speaking; Persuasion; Instructing; Coordination. **Abilities**—*Cognitive:* Number Facility; Mathematical Reasoning; Fluency of Ideas; Originality; Perceptual Speed; Deductive Reasoning. *Psychomotor:* None met the criteria. *Physical:* None met the criteria. *Sensory:* Speech Recognition; Speech Clarity; Near Vision; Auditory Attention. **General Work Activities**—*Information Input:* Getting Information; Identifying Objects, Actions, and Events; Monitoring Processes, Materials, or Surroundings. *Mental Process:* Organizing, Planning, and Prioritizing; Thinking Creatively;

Updating and Using Relevant Knowledge. *Work Output:* Documenting or Recording Information; Interacting With Computers. *Interacting with Others:* Establishing and Maintaining Interpersonal Relationships; Communicating with Persons Outside Organization; Providing Consultation and Advice to Others. **Physical Work Conditions**—More Often Indoors Than Outdoors; Noisy; Sitting. **Other Job Characteristics**—Need to Be Exact or Accurate; Errors Have Important Consequences; Repeat Same Tasks.

Experience—Job Zone 4. A minimum of two to four years of work-related skill, knowledge, or experience is needed. **Job Preparation**—SVP 7.0 to less than 8.0—two years to less than 10 years. **Knowledges**—Economics and Accounting; Law and Government; Clerical Practices; Customer and Personal Service; Administration and Management; Fine Arts. **Instructional Programs**—Banking and Financial Support Services; Finance and Financial Management Services, Other.

Related SOC Job—13-2071 Loan Counselors. **Related OOH Job**—Loan Counselors. **Related DOT Jobs**—160.207-010 Credit Counselor; 169.267-018 Financial-Aid Counselor.

13-2072.00 Loan Officers

- **Education/Training Required: Bachelor's degree**
- **Employed: 332,690**
- **Annual Earnings: $49,440**
- **Growth: 8.3%**
- **Annual Job Openings: 38,000**

Evaluate, authorize, or recommend approval of commercial, real estate, or credit loans. Advise borrowers on financial status and methods of payments. Includes mortgage loan officers and agents, collection analysts, loan servicing officers, and loan underwriters.

Meet with applicants to obtain information for loan applications and to answer questions about the process. Approve loans within specified limits and refer loan applications outside those limits to management for approval. Analyze applicants' financial status, credit, and property evaluations to determine feasibility of granting loans. Explain to customers the different types of loans and credit options that are available, as well as the terms of those services. Obtain and compile copies of loan applicants' credit histories, corporate financial statements, and other financial information. Review and update credit and loan files. Review loan agreements to ensure that they are complete and accurate according to policy. Compute payment schedules. Stay abreast of new types of loans and other financial services and products to better meet customers' needs. Submit applications to credit analysts for verification and recommendation. Handle customer complaints and take appropriate action to resolve them. Work with clients to identify their financial goals and to find ways of reaching those goals. Confer with underwriters to aid in resolving mortgage application problems. Negotiate payment arrangements with customers who have delinquent loans. Market bank products to individuals and firms, promoting bank services that may meet customers' needs. Supervise loan personnel. Set credit policies, credit lines, procedures, and standards in conjunction with senior managers. Provide special services such as investment banking for clients with more specialized needs. Analyze potential loan markets and develop referral networks to locate prospects for loans. Prepare reports to send to customers whose accounts are delinquent and forward irreconcilable accounts for collector action. Arrange for maintenance and liquidation of delinquent properties. Interview, hire, and train new employees. Petition courts to transfer titles and deeds of collateral to banks.

GOE Information—Interest Area: 06. Finance and Insurance. Work Group: 06.02. Finance/Insurance Investigation and Analysis. Personality Type—Enterprising. Enterprising occupations frequently involve starting up and carrying out projects. These occupations can involve leading people and making many decisions. They sometimes require risk taking and often deal with business. Work Values—Advancement; Working Conditions; Co-workers; Social Service; Responsibility; Autonomy. Skills—Persuasion; Social Perceptiveness; Service Orientation; Complex Problem Solving; Negotiation; Instructing. Abilities—Cognitive: Mathematical Reasoning; Number Facility; Oral Expression; Deductive Reasoning; Written Comprehension; Written Expression. Psychomotor: None met the criteria. Physical: None met the criteria. Sensory: Near Vision; Speech Recognition; Speech Clarity. General Work Activities—Information Input: Getting Information; Monitoring Processes, Materials, or Surroundings; Identifying Objects, Actions, and Events. Mental Process: Processing Information; Analyzing Data or Information; Making Decisions and Solving Problems. Work Output: Documenting or Recording Information; Interacting With Computers. Interacting with Others: Performing for or Working with the Public; Communicating with Persons Outside Organization; Establishing and Maintaining Interpersonal Relationships. Physical Work Conditions—Indoors; Sitting; Repetitive Motions. Other Job Characteristics—Need to Be Exact or Accurate; Repeat Same Tasks; Automation.

Experience—Job Zone 3. Previous work-related skill, knowledge, or experience is required. Job Preparation—SVP 6.0 to less than 7.0—more than one year and less than four years. Knowledges—Economics and Accounting; Sales and Marketing; Law and Government; English Language; Customer and Personal Service; Mathematics. Instructional Programs—Credit Management; Finance, General.

Related SOC Job—13-2072 Loan Officers. Related OOH Job—Loan Officers. Related DOT Jobs—186.167-078 Commercial Loan Collection Officer; 186.267-018 Loan Officer; 186.267-026 Underwriter, Mortgage Loan.

13-2081.00 Tax Examiners, Collectors, and Revenue Agents

- Education/Training Required: Bachelor's degree
- Employed: 72,290
- Annual Earnings: $44,210
- Growth: 5.1%
- Annual Job Openings: 4,000

Determine tax liability or collect taxes from individuals or business firms according to prescribed laws and regulations.

Collect taxes from individuals or businesses according to prescribed laws and regulations. Maintain knowledge of tax code changes and of accounting procedures and theory to properly evaluate financial information. Maintain records for each case, including contacts, telephone numbers, and actions taken. Confer with taxpayers or their representatives to discuss the issues, laws, and regulations involved in returns and to resolve problems with returns. Contact taxpayers by mail or telephone to address discrepancies and to request supporting documentation. Send notices to taxpayers when accounts are delinquent. Notify taxpayers of any overpayment or underpayment and either issue a refund or request further payment. Conduct

independent field audits and investigations of income tax returns to verify information or to amend tax liabilities. Review filed tax returns to determine whether claimed tax credits and deductions are allowed by law. Review selected tax returns to determine the nature and extent of audits to be performed on them. Enter tax return information into computers for processing. Examine accounting systems and records to determine whether accounting methods used were appropriate and in compliance with statutory provisions. Process individual and corporate income tax returns and sales and excise tax returns. Impose payment deadlines on delinquent taxpayers and monitor payments to ensure that deadlines are met. Check tax forms to verify that names and taxpayer identification numbers are correct, that computations have been performed correctly, or that amounts match those on supporting documentation. Examine and analyze tax assets and liabilities to determine resolution of delinquent tax problems. Recommend criminal prosecutions or civil penalties. Determine appropriate methods of debt settlement, such as offers of compromise, wage garnishment, or seizure and sale of property. Secure a taxpayer's agreement to discharge a tax assessment or submit contested determinations to other administrative or judicial conferees for appeals hearings. Prepare briefs and assist in searching and seizing records to prepare charges and documentation for court cases.

GOE Information—Interest Area: 07. Government and Public Administration. Work Group: 07.03. Regulations Enforcement. Personality Type—Conventional. Conventional occupations frequently involve following set procedures and routines. These occupations can include working with data and details more than with ideas. Usually there is a clear line of authority to follow. Work Values—Working Conditions; Supervision, Human Relations; Security; Company Policies and Practices; Authority; Advancement. Skills—Service Orientation; Mathematics; Active Learning; Speaking; Complex Problem Solving; Instructing. Abilities—Cognitive: Number Facility; Mathematical Reasoning; Written Comprehension; Speed of Closure; Oral Comprehension; Inductive Reasoning. Psychomotor: None met the criteria. Physical: None met the criteria. Sensory: Speech Recognition; Near Vision. General Work Activities—Information Input: Getting Information; Identifying Objects, Actions, and Events; Monitoring Processes, Materials, or Surroundings. Mental Process: Updating and Using Relevant Knowledge; Organizing, Planning, and Prioritizing; Evaluating Information Against Standards. Work Output: Documenting or Recording Information; Interacting With Computers. Interacting with Others: Communicating with Other Workers; Communicating with Persons Outside Organization; Establishing and Maintaining Interpersonal Relationships. Physical Work Conditions—Indoors; Sitting; Repetitive Motions. Other Job Characteristics—Need to Be Exact or Accurate; Repeat Same Tasks.

Experience—Job Zone 3. Previous work-related skill, knowledge, or experience is required. Job Preparation—SVP 6.0 to less than 7.0—more than one year and less than four years. Knowledges—Law and Government; Customer and Personal Service; Computers and Electronics; Economics and Accounting; Clerical Practices; Psychology. Instructional Programs—Accounting; Taxation.

Related SOC Job—13-2081 Tax Examiners, Collectors, and Revenue Agents. Related OOH Job—Tax Examiners, Collectors, and Revenue Agents. Related DOT Jobs—160.167-050 Revenue Agent; 188.167-074 Revenue Officer.

13-2082.00 Tax Preparers

- **Education/Training Required: Moderate-term on-the-job training**
- **Employed: 58,850**
- **Annual Earnings: $25,700**
- **Growth: 10.6%**
- **Annual Job Openings: 11,000**

Prepare tax returns for individuals or small businesses, but do not have the background or responsibilities of an accredited or certified public accountant.

Compute taxes owed or overpaid, using adding machines or personal computers, and complete entries on forms, following tax form instructions and tax tables. Prepare or assist in preparing simple to complex tax returns for individuals or small businesses. Use all appropriate adjustments, deductions, and credits to keep clients' taxes to a minimum. Interview clients to obtain additional information on taxable income and deductible expenses and allowances. Review financial records such as income statements and documentation of expenditures in order to determine forms needed to prepare tax returns. Furnish taxpayers with sufficient information and advice in order to ensure correct tax form completion. Consult tax law handbooks or bulletins in order to determine procedures for preparation of atypical returns. Calculate form preparation fees according to return complexity and processing time required. Check data input or verify totals on forms prepared by others to detect errors in arithmetic, data entry, or procedures.

GOE Information—Interest Area: 04. Business and Administration. **Work Group:** 04.06. Mathematical Clerical Support. **Personality Type**—Conventional. Conventional occupations frequently involve following set procedures and routines. These occupations can include working with data and details more than with ideas. Usually there is a clear line of authority to follow. **Work Values**—Working Conditions; Social Service; Independence; Co-workers; Supervision; Human Relations; Compensation. **Skills**—Service Orientation; Mathematics; Complex Problem Solving; Active Learning; Learning Strategies; Management of Financial Resources. **Abilities**—*Cognitive:* Number Facility; Mathematical Reasoning; Written Comprehension; Deductive Reasoning; Category Flexibility; Oral Expression. *Psychomotor:* None met the criteria. *Physical:* None met the criteria.

Sensory: Near Vision; Speech Recognition. **General Work Activities—** *Information Input:* Getting Information; Identifying Objects, Actions, and Events; Monitoring Processes, Materials, or Surroundings. *Mental Process:* Processing Information; Updating and Using Relevant Knowledge; Evaluating Information Against Standards. *Work Output:* Interacting With Computers; Documenting or Recording Information. *Interacting with Others:* Establishing and Maintaining Interpersonal Relationships; Performing for or Working with the Public; Performing Administrative Activities. **Physical Work Conditions**—Indoors; Sitting. **Other Job Characteristics**—Need to Be Exact or Accurate; Repeat Same Tasks; Errors Have Important Consequences.

Experience—Job Zone 3. Previous work-related skill, knowledge, or experience is required. **Job Preparation**—SVP 6.0 to less than 7.0— more than one year and less than four years. **Knowledges**— Economics and Accounting; Clerical Practices; Mathematics; Computers and Electronics; Customer and Personal Service; Law and Government. **Instructional Programs**—Accounting Technology/ Technician and Bookkeeping; Taxation.

Related SOC Job—13-2082 Tax Preparers. **Related OOH Job**—Tax Preparers. **Related DOT Job**—219.362-070 Tax Preparer.

13-2099.99 Financial Specialists, All Other

- **Education/Training Required: Bachelor's degree**
- **Employed: 122,320**
- **Annual Earnings: $51,260**
- **Growth: 14.4%**
- **Annual Job Openings: 14,000**

All financial specialists not listed separately.

No task data available.

Note: The Department of Labor has not collected some data for this job, so it has fewer details than the other descriptions.

Related SOC Job—13-2099 Financial Specialists, All Other. **Related OOH Job**—None. **Related DOT Job**—169.267-042 Letter-Of-Credit Document Examiner.

15-0000

Computer and Mathematical Occupations

15-1000 Computer Specialists

15-1011.00 Computer and Information Scientists, Research

- **Education/Training Required: Doctoral degree**
- **Employed: 25,890**
- **Annual Earnings: $91,230**
- **Growth: 25.6%**
- **Annual Job Openings: 2,000**

Conduct research into fundamental computer and information science as theorists, designers, or inventors. Solve or develop solutions to problems in the field of computer hardware and software.

Evaluate project plans and proposals to assess feasibility issues. Direct daily operations of departments, coordinating project activities with other departments. Consult with users, management, vendors, and technicians to determine computing needs and system requirements. Participate in staffing decisions and direct training of subordinates. Participate in multidisciplinary projects in areas such as virtual reality, human-computer interaction, or robotics. Meet with managers, vendors, and others to solicit cooperation and resolve problems. Maintain network hardware and software, direct network security measures, and monitor networks to ensure availability to system users. Develop performance standards and evaluate work in light of established standards. Develop and interpret organizational goals, policies, and procedures. Approve, prepare, monitor, and adjust operational budgets. Design computers and the software that runs them. Analyze problems to develop solutions involving computer hardware and software. Apply theoretical expertise and innovation to create or apply new technology, such as adapting principles for applying computers to new uses. Conduct logical analyses of business, scientific, engineering, and other technical problems, formulating mathematical models of problems for solution by computers. Assign or schedule tasks in order to meet work priorities and goals.

GOE Information—Interest Area: 11. Information Technology. **Work Group:** 11.02. Information Technology Specialties. **Note:** The Department of Labor has not collected some data for this job, so it has fewer details than the other descriptions.

Instructional Programs—Artificial Intelligence and Robotics; Computer and Information Sciences and Support Services, Other; Computer and Information Sciences, General; Computer Science; Computer Systems Analysis/Analyst; Information Science/Studies; Medical Informatics.

Related SOC Job—15-1011 Computer and Information Scientists, Research. **Related OOH Job—**Computer Scientists and Database Administrators. **Related DOT Job—**030.062-010 Software Engineer.

15-1021.00 Computer Programmers

- **Education/Training Required: Bachelor's degree**
- **Employed: 389,090**
- **Annual Earnings: $63,420**
- **Growth: 2.0%**
- **Annual Job Openings: 28,000**

Convert project specifications and statements of problems and procedures to detailed logical flow charts for coding into computer language. Develop and write computer programs to store, locate, and retrieve specific documents, data, and information. May program Web sites.

Correct errors by making appropriate changes and rechecking the program to ensure that the desired results are produced. Conduct trial runs of programs and software applications to be sure that they will produce the desired information and that the instructions are correct. Compile and write documentation of program development and subsequent revisions, inserting comments in the coded instructions so others can understand the program. Write, update, and maintain computer programs or software packages to handle specific jobs such as tracking inventory, storing or retrieving data, or controlling other equipment. Consult with managerial, engineering, and technical personnel to clarify program intent, identify problems, and suggest changes. Perform or direct revision, repair, or expansion of existing programs to increase operating efficiency or adapt to new requirements. Write, analyze, review, and rewrite programs, using workflow chart and diagram and applying knowledge of computer capabilities, subject matter, and symbolic logic. Write or contribute to instructions or manuals to guide end users. Investigate whether networks, workstations, the central processing unit of the system, or peripheral equipment are responding to a program's instructions. Prepare detailed workflow charts and diagrams that describe input, output, and logical operation and convert them into a series of instructions coded in a computer language. Perform systems analysis and programming tasks to maintain and control the use of computer systems software as a systems programmer. Consult with and assist computer operators or system analysts to define and resolve problems in running computer programs. Assign, coordinate, and review work and activities of programming personnel. Collaborate with computer manufacturers and other users to develop new programming methods. Train subordinates in programming and program coding.

GOE Information—Interest Area: 11. Information Technology. **Work Group:** 11.02. Information Technology Specialties. **Personality Type—**Investigative. Investigative occupations frequently involve working with ideas and require an extensive amount of thinking. These occupations can involve searching for facts and figuring out problems mentally. **Work Values—**Creativity; Advancement; Ability Utilization; Autonomy; Compensation; Security. **Skills—**Programming; Operations Analysis; Technology Design; Systems Analysis; Troubleshooting; Installation. **Abilities—***Cognitive:* Written Expression; Information Ordering; Originality; Written Comprehension; Oral Comprehension; Flexibility of Closure. *Psychomotor:* None met the criteria. *Physical:* None met the criteria. *Sensory:* Near Vision. **General Work Activities—***Information Input:* Getting Information; Monitoring Processes, Materials, or Surroundings; Identifying Objects, Actions, and Events. *Mental Process:* Making Decisions and Solving Problems; Organizing, Planning, and Prioritizing; Updating and Using Relevant Knowledge. *Work Output:* Interacting With Computers; Documenting or Recording Information. *Interacting with Others:* Communicating with Other Workers; Establishing and Maintaining Interpersonal Relationships; Providing Consultation and Advice to Others. **Physical Work Conditions—**Indoors; Sitting; Using Hands on Objects, Tools, or Controls; Repetitive Motions. **Other Job Characteristics—**Need to Be Exact or Accurate; Errors Have Important Consequences; Automation.

Experience—Job Zone 4. A minimum of two to four years of work-related skill, knowledge, or experience is needed. **Job Preparation—**SVP 7.0 to less than 8.0—two years to less than 10 years. **Knowledges—**Computers and Electronics; Design; Mathematics; Telecommunications; Economics and Accounting; Engineering and Technology. **Instructional Programs—**Artificial Intelligence and Robotics; Bioinformatics; Computer Graphics; Computer

Programming, Specific Applications; Computer Programming, Vendor/Product Certification; Computer Programming/Programmer, General; E-Commerce/Electronic Commerce; Management Information Systems, General; Medical Informatics; Medical Office Computer Specialist/Assistant; Web Page, Digital/Multimedia, and Information Resources Design; Web/Multimedia Management and Webmaster.

Related SOC Job—15-1021 Computer Programmers. **Related OOH Job**—Computer Programmers. **Related DOT Jobs**—030.162-010 Computer Programmer; 030.162-018 Programmer, Engineering and Scientific; 030.167-010 Chief, Computer Programmer.

15-1031.00 Computer Software Engineers, Applications

- **Education/Training Required: Bachelor's degree**
- **Employed: 455,980**
- **Annual Earnings: $77,090**
- **Growth: 48.4%**
- **Annual Job Openings: 54,000**

Develop, create, and modify general computer applications software or specialized utility programs. Analyze user needs and develop software solutions. Design software or customize software for client use with the aim of optimizing operational efficiency. May analyze and design databases within an application area, working individually or coordinating database development as part of a team.

Confer with systems analysts, engineers, programmers, and others to design system and to obtain information on project limitations and capabilities, performance requirements, and interfaces. Modify existing software to correct errors, allow it to adapt to new hardware, or improve its performance. Analyze user needs and software requirements to determine feasibility of design within time and cost constraints. Consult with customers about software system design and maintenance. Coordinate software system installation and monitor equipment functioning to ensure specifications are met. Design, develop, and modify software systems, using scientific analysis and mathematical models to predict and measure outcome and consequences of design. Develop and direct software system testing and validation procedures, programming, and documentation. Analyze information to determine, recommend, and plan computer specifications and layouts and peripheral equipment modifications. Supervise the work of programmers, technologists, and technicians and other engineering and scientific personnel. Obtain and evaluate information on factors such as reporting formats required, costs, and security needs to determine hardware configuration. Determine system performance standards. Train users to use new or modified equipment. Store, retrieve, and manipulate data for analysis of system capabilities and requirements. Specify power supply requirements and configuration. Recommend purchase of equipment to control dust, temperature, and humidity in area of system installation.

GOE Information—Interest Area: 11. Information Technology. **Work Group:** 11.02. Information Technology Specialties. **Personality Type**—Investigative. Investigative occupations frequently involve working with ideas and require an extensive amount of thinking. These occupations can involve searching for facts and figuring out problems mentally. **Work Values**—Creativity; Ability Utilization; Working Conditions; Responsibility; Social Status; Authority. **Skills**—Programming; Troubleshooting; Technology Design; Systems Analysis; Quality Control Analysis; Operations

Analysis. **Abilities**—*Cognitive:* Mathematical Reasoning; Originality; Written Comprehension; Deductive Reasoning; Number Facility; Information Ordering. *Psychomotor:* Finger Dexterity. *Physical:* None met the criteria. *Sensory:* Speech Clarity; Speech Recognition; Near Vision. **General Work Activities**—*Information Input:* Identifying Objects, Actions, and Events; Getting Information; Monitoring Processes, Materials, or Surroundings. *Mental Process:* Updating and Using Relevant Knowledge; Making Decisions and Solving Problems; Thinking Creatively. *Work Output:* Interacting With Computers; Documenting or Recording Information. *Interacting with Others:* Communicating with Other Workers; Interpreting the Meaning of Information for Others; Establishing and Maintaining Interpersonal Relationships. **Physical Work Conditions**—Indoors; Sitting; Using Hands on Objects, Tools, or Controls; Repetitive Motions. **Other Job Characteristics**—Need to Be Exact or Accurate; Errors Have Important Consequences; Repeat Same Tasks.

Experience—Job Zone 4. A minimum of two to four years of work-related skill, knowledge, or experience is needed. **Job Preparation**—SVP 7.0 to less than 8.0—two years to less than 10 years. **Knowledges**—Computers and Electronics; Telecommunications; Engineering and Technology; Design; Mathematics; Physics. **Instructional Programs**—Artificial Intelligence and Robotics; Bioinformatics; Computer Engineering Technologies/Technicians, Other; Computer Engineering, General; Computer Science; Computer Software Engineering; Information Technology; Medical Illustration and Informatics, Other; Medical Informatics.

Related SOC Job—15-1031 Computer Software Engineers, Applications. **Related OOH Job**—Computer Software Engineers. **Related DOT Job**—030.062-010 Software Engineer.

15-1032.00 Computer Software Engineers, Systems Software

- **Education/Training Required: Bachelor's degree**
- **Employed: 320,720**
- **Annual Earnings: $82,120**
- **Growth: 43.0%**
- **Annual Job Openings: 37,000**

Research, design, develop, and test operating systems-level software, compilers, and network distribution software for medical, industrial, military, communications, aerospace, business, scientific, and general computing applications. Set operational specifications and formulate and analyze software requirements. Apply principles and techniques of computer science, engineering, and mathematical analysis.

Modify existing software to correct errors, to adapt it to new hardware, or to upgrade interfaces and improve performance. Design and develop software systems, using scientific analysis and mathematical models to predict and measure outcome and consequences of design. Consult with engineering staff to evaluate interface between hardware and software, develop specifications and performance requirements, and resolve customer problems. Analyze information to determine, recommend, and plan installation of a new system or modification of an existing system. Develop and direct software system testing and validation procedures. Direct software programming and development of documentation. Consult with customers or other departments on project status, proposals, and technical issues such as software system design and maintenance. Advise customer about, or perform, maintenance of software system. Coordinate installation of software system. Monitor functioning of equipment to ensure system operates in conformance with specifications. Store, retrieve, and manipulate data for analysis of system capabilities and requirements. Confer with data processing and project managers to obtain information on limitations and capabilities for data-processing projects. Prepare reports and correspondence concerning project specifications, activities, and status. Evaluate factors such as reporting formats required, cost constraints, and need for security restrictions to determine hardware configuration. Supervise and assign work to programmers, designers, technologists and technicians, and other engineering and scientific personnel. Train users to use new or modified equipment. Utilize microcontrollers to develop control signals; implement control algorithms; and measure process variables such as temperatures, pressures, and positions. Recommend purchase of equipment to control dust, temperature, and humidity in area of system installation. Specify power supply requirements and configuration.

GOE Information—Interest Area: 11. Information Technology. **Work Group:** 11.02. Information Technology Specialties. **Personality Type**—Investigative. Investigative occupations frequently involve working with ideas and require an extensive amount of thinking. These occupations can involve searching for facts and figuring out problems mentally. **Work Values**—Creativity; Ability Utilization; Working Conditions; Responsibility; Social Status; Authority. **Skills**—Programming; Technology Design; Systems Analysis; Troubleshooting; Operations Analysis; Complex Problem Solving. **Abilities**—*Cognitive:* Mathematical Reasoning; Number Facility; Deductive Reasoning; Written Comprehension; Oral Expression; Written Expression. *Psychomotor:* None met the criteria. *Physical:* None met the criteria. *Sensory:* Near Vision; Speech Clarity; Speech Recognition. **General Work Activities**—*Information Input:* Identifying Objects, Actions, and Events; Monitoring Processes, Materials, or Surroundings; Getting Information. *Mental Process:* Updating and Using Relevant Knowledge; Processing Information; Thinking Creatively. *Work Output:* Interacting With Computers; Documenting or Recording Information; Drafting and Specifying Technical Devices. *Interacting with Others:* Establishing and Maintaining Interpersonal Relationships; Providing Consultation and Advice to Others; Communicating with Other Workers. **Physical Work Conditions**—Indoors; Sitting; Using Hands on Objects, Tools, or Controls; Repetitive Motions. **Other Job Characteristics**—Need to Be Exact or Accurate; Repeat Same Tasks; Errors Have Important Consequences.

Experience—Job Zone 4. A minimum of two to four years of work-related skill, knowledge, or experience is needed. **Job Preparation**—SVP 7.0 to less than 8.0—two years to less than 10 years. **Knowledges**—Computers and Electronics; Design; Engineering and Technology; Telecommunications; Mathematics; Education and Training. **Instructional Programs**—Artificial Intelligence and Robotics; Computer Engineering Technologies/Technicians, Other; Computer Engineering, General; Computer Science; Information Science/Studies; Information Technology.

Related SOC Job—15-1032 Computer Software Engineers, Systems Software. **Related OOH Job**—Computer Software Engineers. **Related DOT Job**—030.062-010 Software Engineer.

15-1041.00 Computer Support Specialists
- **Education/Training Required: Associate degree**
- **Employed: 499,860**
- **Annual Earnings: $40,610**
- **Growth: 23.0%**
- **Annual Job Openings: 87,000**

Provide technical assistance to computer system users. Answer questions or resolve computer problems for clients in person, via telephone, or from remote location. May provide assistance concerning the use of computer hardware and software, including printing, installation, word processing, electronic mail, and operating systems.

Answer user inquiries regarding computer software or hardware operation to resolve problems. Enter commands and observe system functioning to verify correct operations and detect errors. Install and perform minor repairs to hardware, software, or peripheral equipment, following design or installation specifications. Oversee the daily performance of computer systems. Set up equipment for employee use, performing or ensuring proper installation of cables, operating systems, or appropriate software. Maintain records of daily data communication transactions, problems and remedial actions taken, or installation activities. Read technical manuals, confer with users, or conduct computer diagnostics to investigate and resolve problems or to provide technical assistance and support. Confer with staff, users, and management to establish requirements for new systems or modifications. Develop training materials and procedures or train users in the proper use of hardware or software. Refer major hardware or software problems or defective products to vendors or technicians for service. Prepare evaluations of software or hardware and recommend improvements or upgrades. Read trade magazines and technical manuals or attend conferences and seminars to maintain knowledge of hardware and software. Supervise and coordinate workers engaged in problem-solving, monitoring, and installing data communication equipment and software. Inspect equipment and read order sheets to prepare for delivery to users. Modify and customize commercial programs for internal needs. Conduct office automation feasibility studies, including workflow analysis, space design, or cost comparison analysis.

GOE Information—Interest Area: 11. Information Technology. **Work Group:** 11.02. Information Technology Specialties. **Personality Type**—Investigative. Investigative occupations frequently involve working with ideas and require an extensive amount of thinking. These occupations can involve searching for facts and figuring out problems mentally. **Work Values**—Creativity; Advancement; Variety; Autonomy; Social Service; Working Conditions. **Skills**—Repairing; Troubleshooting; Installation; Equipment Maintenance; Writing; Persuasion. **Abilities**—*Cognitive:* Written Comprehension; Inductive Reasoning; Deductive Reasoning; Visualization; Written Expression; Fluency of Ideas. *Psychomotor:* Finger Dexterity; Arm-Hand Steadiness. *Physical:* None met the criteria. *Sensory:* Near Vision; Speech Recognition; Speech Clarity. **General Work Activities**—*Information Input:* Identifying Objects, Actions, and Events; Getting Information; Inspecting Equipment, Structures, or Materials. *Mental Process:* Updating and Using Relevant Knowledge; Making Decisions and Solving Problems. *Work Output:* Interacting With Computers; Documenting or Recording Information; Repairing and Maintaining Electronic Equipment. *Interacting with Others:* Establishing and Maintaining Interpersonal Relationships; Communicating with Other Workers; Developing and Building Teams. **Physical Work Conditions**—Indoors; Noisy; Sitting; Repetitive Motions. **Other Job Characteristics**—Repeat Same Tasks; Need to Be Exact or Accurate.

Experience—Job Zone 3. Previous work-related skill, knowledge, or experience is required. **Job Preparation**—SVP 6.0 to less than 7.0—more than one year and less than four years. **Knowledges**—Computers and Electronics; Telecommunications; Engineering and Technology; Production and Processing; Design; Customer and Personal Service. **Instructional Programs**—Accounting and Computer Science; Agricultural Business Technology; Computer

Hardware Technology/Technician; Computer Software Technology/ Technician; Data Processing and Data Processing Technology/ Technician; Medical Office Computer Specialist/Assistant.

Related SOC Job—15-1041 Computer Support Specialists. Related OOH Job—Computer Support Specialists and Systems Administrators. Related DOT Jobs—031.132-010 Supervisor, Network Control Operators; 031.262-014 Network Control Operator; 032.132-010 User Support Analyst Supervisor; 032.262-010 User Support Analyst; 032.262-900 Office Automation Technician; 033.162-018 Technical Support Specialist; 039.264-010 Microcomputer Support Specialist.

15-1051.00 Computer Systems Analysts

- **Education/Training Required: Bachelor's degree**
- **Employed: 492,120**
- **Annual Earnings: $68,300**
- **Growth: 31.4%**
- **Annual Job Openings: 56,000**

Analyze science, engineering, business, and all other data-processing problems for application to electronic data processing systems. Analyze user requirements, procedures, and problems to automate or improve existing systems and review computer system capabilities, workflow, and scheduling limitations. May analyze or recommend commercially available software. May supervise computer programmers.

Provide staff and users with assistance solving computer-related problems, such as malfunctions and program problems. Test, maintain, and monitor computer programs and systems, including coordinating the installation of computer programs and systems. Use object-oriented programming languages as well as client and server applications development processes and multimedia and Internet technology. Confer with clients regarding the nature of the information processing or computation needs a computer program is to address. Coordinate and link the computer systems within an organization to increase compatibility and so information can be shared. Consult with management to ensure agreement on system principles. Expand or modify system to serve new purposes or improve workflow. Interview or survey workers, observe job performance, or perform the job to determine what information is processed and how it is processed. Determine computer software or hardware needed to set up or alter system. Train staff and users to work with computer systems and programs. Analyze information processing or computation needs and plan and design computer systems, using techniques such as structured analysis, data modeling, and information engineering. Assess the usefulness of pre-developed application packages and adapt them to a user environment. Define the goals of the system and devise flow charts and diagrams describing logical operational steps of programs. Develop, document, and revise system design procedures, test procedures, and quality standards. Review and analyze computer printouts and performance indicators to locate code problems; correct errors by correcting codes. Recommend new equipment or software packages. Read manuals, periodicals, and technical reports to learn how to develop programs that meet staff and user requirements. Supervise computer programmers or other systems analysts or serve as project leaders for particular systems projects. Utilize the computer in the analysis and solution of business problems such as development of integrated production and inventory control and cost analysis systems.

GOE Information—Interest Area: 11. Information Technology. Work Group: 11.02. Information Technology Specialties. Personality Type—Investigative. Investigative occupations fre-

quently involve working with ideas and require an extensive amount of thinking. These occupations can involve searching for facts and figuring out problems mentally. Work Values—Creativity; Compensation; Company Policies and Practices; Ability Utilization; Responsibility; Autonomy. Skills—Installation; Quality Control Analysis; Systems Analysis; Programming; Technology Design; Troubleshooting. Abilities—*Cognitive:* Mathematical Reasoning; Number Facility; Originality; Deductive Reasoning; Written Expression; Fluency of Ideas. *Psychomotor:* None met the criteria. *Physical:* None met the criteria. *Sensory:* Visual Color Discrimination; Near Vision; Speech Recognition; Far Vision. General Work Activities—*Information Input:* Identifying Objects, Actions, and Events; Getting Information; Monitoring Processes, Materials, or Surroundings. *Mental Process:* Thinking Creatively; Processing Information; Updating and Using Relevant Knowledge. *Work Output:* Interacting With Computers; Documenting or Recording Information. *Interacting with Others:* Interpreting the Meaning of Information for Others; Establishing and Maintaining Interpersonal Relationships; Communicating with Other Workers. Physical Work Conditions—Indoors; Sitting. Other Job Characteristics—Need to Be Exact or Accurate; Repeat Same Tasks; Errors Have Important Consequences.

Experience—Job Zone 4. A minimum of two to four years of work-related skill, knowledge, or experience is needed. Job Preparation—SVP 7.0 to less than 8.0—two years to less than 10 years. Knowledges—Computers and Electronics; Telecommunications; Design; Customer and Personal Service; Law and Government; Education and Training. Instructional Programs—Computer and Information Sciences, General; Computer Systems Analysis/Analyst; Information Technology; Web/Multimedia Management and Webmaster.

Related SOC Job—15-1051 Computer Systems Analysts. Related OOH Job—Computer Systems Analysts. Related DOT Jobs—030.162-014 Programmer-Analyst; 030.162-022 Systems Programmer; 030.167-014 Systems Analyst; 033.262-010 Quality Assurance Analyst.

15-1061.00 Database Administrators

- **Education/Training Required: Bachelor's degree**
- **Employed: 99,380**
- **Annual Earnings: $63,250**
- **Growth: 38.2%**
- **Annual Job Openings: 9,000**

Coordinate changes to computer databases; test and implement the database, applying knowledge of database management systems. May plan, coordinate, and implement security measures to safeguard computer databases.

Develop standards and guidelines to guide the use and acquisition of software and to protect vulnerable information. Modify existing databases and database management systems or direct programmers and analysts to make changes. Test programs or databases, correct errors, and make necessary modifications. Plan, coordinate, and implement security measures to safeguard information in computer files against accidental or unauthorized damage, modification, or disclosure. Approve, schedule, plan, and supervise the installation and testing of new products and improvements to computer systems, such as the installation of new databases. Train users and answer questions. Establish and calculate optimum values for database parameters, using manuals and calculator. Specify users and user access levels for each segment of database. Develop data model describing data elements and how they are used, following procedures and using pen, template, or computer software. Develop methods for integrating different products so they work properly together, such as customizing commercial databases to fit specific needs. Review project requests describing database user needs to estimate time and cost required to accomplish project. Review procedures in database management system manuals for making changes to database. Work as part of a project team to coordinate database development and determine project scope and limitations. Select and enter codes to monitor database performance and to create production database. Identify and evaluate industry trends in database systems to serve as a source of information and advice for upper management. Write and code logical and physical database descriptions and specify identifiers of database to management system or direct others in coding descriptions. Review workflow charts developed by programmer analyst to understand tasks computer will perform, such as updating records. Revise company definition of data as defined in data dictionary.

GOE Information—Interest Area: 11. Information Technology. **Work Group:** 11.02. Information Technology Specialties. **Personality Type**—Investigative. Investigative occupations frequently involve working with ideas and require an extensive amount of thinking. These occupations can involve searching for facts and figuring out problems mentally. **Work Values**—Creativity; Compensation; Security; Company Policies and Practices; Responsibility; Working Conditions. **Skills**—Troubleshooting; Systems Evaluation; Operations Analysis; Persuasion; Systems Analysis; Programming. **Abilities**—*Cognitive:* Originality; Fluency of Ideas; Written Comprehension; Visualization; Mathematical Reasoning; Flexibility of Closure. *Psychomotor:* Finger Dexterity. *Physical:* None met the criteria. *Sensory:* Visual Color Discrimination; Far Vision; Near Vision; Speech Recognition; Speech Clarity; Auditory Attention. **General Work Activities**—*Information Input:* Identifying Objects, Actions, and Events; Getting Information; Monitoring Processes, Materials, or Surroundings. *Mental Process:* Thinking Creatively; Processing Information; Analyzing Data or Information. *Work Output:* Interacting With Computers; Documenting or Recording Information; Handling and Moving Objects. *Interacting with Others:* Establishing and Maintaining Interpersonal Relationships; Communicating with Other Workers; Teaching Others. **Physical Work Conditions**—Indoors; Noisy; Sitting; Using Hands on Objects, Tools, or Controls; Repetitive Motions. **Other Job Characteristics**—Need to Be Exact or Accurate; Repeat Same Tasks; Errors Have Important Consequences.

Experience—Job Zone 4. A minimum of two to four years of work-related skill, knowledge, or experience is needed. **Job Preparation**—SVP 7.0 to less than 8.0—two years to less than 10 years. **Knowledges**—Computers and Electronics; Economics and Accounting; Clerical Practices; Administration and Management; Mathematics; Customer and Personal Service. **Instructional Programs**—Computer and Information Sciences, General; Computer and Information Systems Security; Computer Systems Analysis/Analyst; Data Modeling/Warehousing and Database Administration; Management Information Systems, General.

Related SOC Job—15-1061 Database Administrators. **Related OOH Job**—Computer Scientists and Database Administrators. **Related DOT Jobs**—039.162-010 Data Base Administrator; 039.162-014 Data Base Design Analyst; 109.067-010 Information Scientist.

15-1071.00 Network and Computer Systems Administrators

- **Education/Training Required: Bachelor's degree**
- **Employed: 270,330**
- **Annual Earnings: $59,930**
- **Growth: 38.4%**
- **Annual Job Openings: 34,000**

The job openings listed here are shared with 15-1071.01 Computer Security Specialists.

Install, configure, and support an organization's local area network (LAN), wide area network (WAN), and Internet system or a segment of a network system. Maintain network hardware and software. Monitor network to ensure network availability to all system users and perform necessary maintenance to support network availability. May supervise other network support and client server specialists and plan, coordinate, and implement network security measures.

Diagnose hardware and software problems and replace defective components. Perform data backups and disaster recovery operations. Maintain and administer computer networks and related computing environments, including computer hardware, systems software, applications software, and all configurations. Plan, coordinate, and implement network security measures to protect data, software, and hardware. Operate master consoles to monitor the performance of computer systems and networks and to coordinate computer network access and use. Perform routine network startup and shutdown procedures and maintain control records. Design, configure, and test computer hardware, networking software, and operating system software. Recommend changes to improve systems and network configurations and determine hardware or software requirements related to such changes. Confer with network users about how to solve existing system problems. Monitor network performance to determine whether adjustments need to be made and to determine where changes will need to be made in the future. Train people in computer system use. Load computer tapes and disks and install software and printer paper or forms. Gather data pertaining to customer needs and use the information to identify, predict, interpret, and evaluate system and network requirements. Analyze equipment performance records to determine the need for repair or replacement. Maintain logs related to network functions as well as maintenance and repair records. Research new technology and implement it or recommend its implementation. Maintain an inventory of parts for emergency repairs. Coordinate with vendors and with company personnel to facilitate purchases.

GOE Information—Interest Area: 11. Information Technology. **Work Group:** 11.01. Managerial Work in Information Technology. **Personality Type**—No data available. **Work Values**—No data available. **Skills**—Troubleshooting; Installation; Programming; Repairing; Systems Evaluation; Systems Analysis. **Abilities**—*Cognitive:* Speed of Closure; Inductive Reasoning; Memorization; Visualization; Flexibility of Closure; Deductive Reasoning. *Psychomotor:* Finger Dexterity; Arm-Hand Steadiness; Manual Dexterity; Control Precision. *Physical:* Static Strength. *Sensory:* Visual Color Discrimination; Far Vision; Near Vision; Speech Recognition; Auditory Attention; Depth Perception. **General Work Activities**—*Information Input:* Monitoring Processes, Materials, or Surroundings; Getting Information; Identifying Objects, Actions, and Events. *Mental Process:* Updating and Using Relevant Knowledge; Organizing, Planning, and Prioritizing; Thinking Creatively. *Work Output:* Interacting With Computers; Repairing and Maintaining Electronic Equipment; Handling and Moving Objects. *Interacting with Others:*

Communicating with Other Workers; Establishing and Maintaining Interpersonal Relationships; Providing Consultation and Advice to Others. **Physical Work Conditions**—Indoors; Sitting; Using Hands on Objects, Tools, or Controls; Repetitive Motions. **Other Job Characteristics**—Need to Be Exact or Accurate; Errors Have Important Consequences; Repeat Same Tasks.

Experience—Job Zone 4. A minimum of two to four years of work-related skill, knowledge, or experience is needed. **Job Preparation**—SVP 7.0 to less than 8.0—two years to less than 10 years. **Knowledges**—Computers and Electronics; Telecommunications; Engineering and Technology; Customer and Personal Service; Education and Training; Design. **Instructional Programs**—Computer and Information Sciences and Support Services, Other; Computer and Information Sciences, General; Computer and Information Systems Security; Computer Systems Analysis/Analyst; Computer Systems Networking and Telecommunications; Information Science/Studies; System Administration/Administrator; System, Networking, and LAN/WAN Management/Manager.

Related SOC Job—15-1071 Network and Computer Systems Administrators. **Related OOH Job**—Computer Support Specialists and Systems Administrators. **Related DOT Job**—No data available.

15-1071.01 Computer Security Specialists

- **Education/Training Required: Bachelor's degree**
- **Employed: 270,330**
- **Annual Earnings: $59,930**
- **Growth: 38.4%**
- **Annual Job Openings: 34,000**

The job openings listed here are shared with 15-1071.00 Network and Computer Systems Administrators.

Plan, coordinate, and implement security measures for information systems to regulate access to computer data files and prevent unauthorized modification, destruction, or disclosure of information.

Train users and promote security awareness to ensure system security and to improve server and network efficiency. Develop plans to safeguard computer files against accidental or unauthorized modification, destruction, or disclosure and to meet emergency data processing needs. Confer with users to discuss issues such as computer data access needs, security violations, and programming changes. Monitor current reports of computer viruses to determine when to update virus protection systems. Modify computer security files to incorporate new software, correct errors, or change individual access status. Coordinate implementation of computer system plan with establishment personnel and outside vendors. Monitor use of data files and regulate access to safeguard information in computer files. Perform risk assessments and execute tests of data-processing system to ensure functioning of data-processing activities and security measures. Encrypt data transmissions and erect firewalls to conceal confidential information as it is being transmitted and to keep out tainted digital transfers. Document computer security and emergency measures policies, procedures, and tests. Review violations of computer security procedures and discuss procedures with violators to ensure violations are not repeated. Maintain permanent fleet cryptologic and carry-on direct support systems required in special land, sea surface, and subsurface operations.

GOE Information—**Interest Area:** 11. Information Technology. **Work Group:** 11.02. Information Technology Specialties. **Personality Type**—Investigative. Investigative occupations frequently involve working with ideas and require an extensive amount

of thinking. These occupations can involve searching for facts and figuring out problems mentally. **Work Values**—Working Conditions; Compensation; Creativity; Responsibility; Autonomy; Social Status. **Skills**—Systems Evaluation; Systems Analysis; Programming; Installation; Management of Material Resources; Operations Analysis. **Abilities**—*Cognitive:* Originality; Written Comprehension; Category Flexibility; Flexibility of Closure; Deductive Reasoning; Speed of Closure. *Psychomotor:* Arm-Hand Steadiness. *Physical:* None met the criteria. *Sensory:* Hearing Sensitivity; Visual Color Discrimination; Speech Recognition. **General Work Activities**—*Information Input:* Getting Information; Monitoring Processes, Materials, or Surroundings; Identifying Objects, Actions, and Events. *Mental Process:* Updating and Using Relevant Knowledge; Processing Information; Thinking Creatively. *Work Output:* Interacting With Computers; Repairing and Maintaining Electronic Equipment; Documenting or Recording Information. *Interacting with Others:* Communicating with Other Workers; Communicating with Persons Outside Organization; Providing Consultation and Advice to Others. **Physical Work Conditions**—Indoors; Sitting. **Other Job Characteristics**—Need to Be Exact or Accurate; Errors Have Important Consequences; Repeat Same Tasks.

Experience—Job Zone 4. A minimum of two to four years of work-related skill, knowledge, or experience is needed. **Job Preparation**—SVP 7.0 to less than 8.0—two years to less than 10 years. **Knowledges**—Computers and Electronics; Telecommunications; Design; Engineering and Technology; Education and Training; Therapy and Counseling. **Instructional Program**—Computer and Information Systems Security.

Related SOC Job—15-1071 Network and Computer Systems Administrators. **Related OOH Job**—Computer Support Specialists and Systems Administrators. **Related DOT Jobs**—033.162-010 Computer Security Coordinator; 033.162-014 Data Recovery Planner; 033.362-010 Computer Security Specialist.

15-1081.00 Network Systems and Data Communications Analysts

- **Education/Training Required: Bachelor's degree**
- **Employed: 185,190**
- **Annual Earnings: $61,750**
- **Growth: 54.6%**
- **Annual Job Openings: 43,000**

Analyze, design, test, and evaluate network systems, such as local area networks (LAN); wide area networks (WAN); and Internet, intranet, and other data communications systems. Perform network modeling, analysis, and planning. Research and recommend network and data communications hardware and software. Includes telecommunications specialists who deal with the interfacing of computer and communications equipment. May supervise computer programmers.

Maintain needed files by adding and deleting files on the network server and backing up files to guarantee their safety in the event of problems with the network. Monitor system performance and provide security measures, troubleshooting, and maintenance as needed. Assist users to diagnose and solve data communication problems. Set up user accounts, regulating and monitoring file access to ensure confidentiality and proper use. Design and implement systems, network configurations, and network architecture, including hardware and software technology, site locations, and integration of technologies. Maintain the peripherals, such as printers, that are connected to the network. Identify areas of operation that need upgraded equipment such as modems, fiber-optic cables, and telephone wires. Train users in use of equipment. Develop and write procedures for installation, use, and troubleshooting of communications hardware and software. Adapt and modify existing software to meet specific needs. Work with other engineers, systems analysts, programmers, technicians, scientists, and top-level managers in the design, testing, and evaluation of systems. Test and evaluate hardware and software to determine efficiency, reliability, and compatibility with existing system and make purchase recommendations. Read technical manuals and brochures to determine which equipment meets establishment requirements. Consult customers, visit workplaces, or conduct surveys to determine present and future user needs. Visit vendors, attend conferences or training, and study technical journals to keep up with changes in technology.

GOE Information—Interest Area: 11. Information Technology. **Work Group:** 11.02. Information Technology Specialties. **Personality Type**—Investigative. Investigative occupations frequently involve working with ideas and require an extensive amount of thinking. These occupations can involve searching for facts and figuring out problems mentally. **Work Values**—Compensation; Creativity; Advancement; Ability Utilization; Autonomy; Working Conditions. **Skills**—Installation; Systems Analysis; Technology Design; Troubleshooting; Programming; Systems Evaluation. **Abilities**—*Cognitive:* Number Facility; Originality; Fluency of Ideas; Mathematical Reasoning; Written Comprehension; Inductive Reasoning. *Psychomotor:* Finger Dexterity; Arm-Hand Steadiness; Manual Dexterity. *Physical:* None met the criteria. *Sensory:* Visual Color Discrimination; Hearing Sensitivity; Near Vision; Far Vision; Speech Recognition; Auditory Attention. **General Work Activities**—*Information Input:* Identifying Objects, Actions, and Events; Monitoring Processes, Materials, or Surroundings; Getting Information. *Mental Process:* Thinking Creatively; Organizing, Planning, and Prioritizing; Updating and Using Relevant Knowledge. *Work Output:* Interacting With Computers; Repairing and Maintaining Electronic Equipment; Documenting or Recording Information. *Interacting with Others:* Establishing and Maintaining Interpersonal Relationships; Communicating with Other Workers; Communicating with Persons Outside Organization. **Physical Work Conditions**—Indoors; Sitting. **Other Job Characteristics**—Need to Be Exact or Accurate; Repeat Same Tasks; Errors Have Important Consequences.

Experience—Job Zone 3. Previous work-related skill, knowledge, or experience is required. **Job Preparation**—SVP 6.0 to less than 7.0— more than one year and less than four years. **Knowledges**— Telecommunications; Computers and Electronics; Customer and Personal Service; Engineering and Technology; Education and Training; Design. **Instructional Programs**—Computer and Information Sciences, General; Computer and Information Systems Security; Computer Systems Analysis/Analyst; Computer Systems Networking and Telecommunications; Information Technology.

Related SOC Job—15-1081 Network Systems and Data Communications Analysts. **Related OOH Job**—Computer Support Specialists and Systems Administrators. **Related DOT Jobs**—031.262-010 Data Communications Analyst; 823.261-900 Internetworking Technician.

15-1099.01 Software Quality Assurance Engineers and Testers

- **Education/Training Required: No data available**
- **Employed: 116,760**
- **Annual Earnings: $59,420**
- **Growth: 19.0%**
- **Annual Job Openings: 15,000**

The job openings listed here are shared with 15-1099.02 Computer Systems Engineers/Architects, 15-1099.03 Network Designers, 15-1099.04 Web Developers, 15-1099.05 Web Administrators, and 15-1099.99 Computer Specialists, All Other.

Develop and execute software test plans in order to identify software problems and their causes.

Develop or specify standards, methods, or procedures to determine product quality or release readiness. Update automated test scripts to ensure currency. Conduct software compatibility tests with programs, hardware, operating systems, or network environments. Create or maintain databases of known test defects. Design test plans, scenarios, scripts, or procedures. Design or develop automated testing tools. Perform initial debugging procedures by reviewing configuration files, logs, or code pieces to determine breakdown source. Visit beta testing sites to evaluate software performance. Monitor bug resolution efforts and track successes. Document test procedures to ensure replicability and compliance with standards. Evaluate or recommend software for testing or bug tracking. Identify program deviance from standards and suggest modifications to ensure compliance. Identify, analyze, and document problems with program function, output, online screen, or content. Install and configure recreations of software production environments to allow testing of software performance. Install, maintain, or use software testing programs. Investigate customer problems referred by technical support. Review software documentation to ensure technical accuracy, compliance, or completeness or to mitigate risks. Participate in product design reviews to provide input on functional requirements, product designs, schedules, or potential problems. Develop testing programs that address areas such as database impacts, software scenarios, regression testing, negative testing, error or bug retests, or usability. Plan test schedules or strategies in accordance with project scope or delivery dates. Provide feedback and recommendations to developers on software usability and functionality. Test system modifications to prepare for implementation. Collaborate with field staff or customers to evaluate or diagnose problems and recommend possible solutions. Provide technical support during software installation or configuration. Conduct historical analyses of test results. Coordinate user or third-party testing. Document software defects, using a bug tracking system, and report defects to software developers.

GOE Information—Interest Area: 11. Information Technology. **Work Group:** 11.02. Information Technology Specialties. **Note:** The Department of Labor has not collected some data for this job, so it has fewer details than the other descriptions.

Instructional Programs—Computer and Information Sciences and Support Services, Other; Computer and Information Sciences, General; Computer Engineering Technologies/Technicians, Other; Computer Engineering, General; Computer Science; Computer Software Engineering; Information Science/Studies; Information Technology.

Related SOC Job—15-1099 Computer Specialists, All Other. **Related OOH Job**—Computer Scientists and Database Administrators. **Related DOT Job**—No data available.

15-1099.02 Computer Systems Engineers/Architects

- **Education/Training Required: No data available**
- **Employed: 116,760**
- **Annual Earnings: $59,420**
- **Growth: 19.0%**
- **Annual Job Openings: 15,000**

The job openings listed here are shared with 15-1099.01 Software Quality Assurance Engineers and Testers, 15-1099.03 Network Designers, 15-1099.04 Web Developers, 15-1099.05 Web Administrators, and 15-1099.99 Computer Specialists, All Other.

Design and develop solutions to complex applications problems, system administration issues, or network concerns. Perform systems management and integration functions.

Perform security analyses of developed or packaged software components. Perform ongoing hardware and software maintenance operations, including installing or upgrading hardware or software. Complete models and simulations, using manual or automated tools, to analyze or predict system performance under different operating conditions. Define and analyze objectives, scope, issues, or organizational impact of information systems. Develop efficient and effective system controllers. Develop application-specific software. Configure servers to meet functional specifications. Verify stability, interoperability, portability, security, or scalability of system architecture. Train system users in system operation or maintenance. Provide guidelines for implementing secure systems to customers or installation teams. Provide technical guidance or support for the development or troubleshooting of systems. Monitor system operation to detect potential problems. Communicate project information through presentations, technical reports, or white papers. Communicate with staff or clients to understand specific system requirements. Investigate system component suitability for specified purposes and make recommendations regarding component use. Identify system data, hardware, or software components required to meet user needs. Evaluate existing systems to determine effectiveness and suggest changes to meet organizational requirements. Evaluate current or emerging technologies to consider factors such as cost, portability, compatibility, or usability. Establish functional or system standards to ensure operational requirements, quality requirements, and design constraints are addressed. Document design specifications, installation instructions, and other system-related information. Direct the analysis, development, and operation of complete computer systems. Direct the installation of operating systems, network or application software, or computer or network hardware. Develop system engineering, software engineering, system integration, or distributed system architectures. Design and conduct hardware or software tests.

GOE Information—Interest Area: 11. Information Technology. **Work Group:** 11.02. Information Technology Specialties. **Note:** The Department of Labor has not collected some data for this job, so it has fewer details than the other descriptions.

Instructional Programs—Computer and Information Sciences and Support Services, Other; Computer and Information Sciences, General; Computer Engineering Technologies/Technicians, Other; Computer Engineering, General; Computer Science; Computer Software Engineering; Information Science/Studies; Information Technology.

Related SOC Job—15-1099 Computer Specialists, All Other. **Related OOH Job**—Computer Scientists and Database Administrators. **Related DOT Job**—No data available.

15-1099.03 Network Designers

- **Education/Training Required: No data available**
- **Employed: 116,760**
- **Annual Earnings: $59,420**
- **Growth: 19.0%**
- **Annual Job Openings: 15,000**

The job openings listed here are shared with 15-1099.01 Software Quality Assurance Engineers and Testers, 15-1099.02 Computer Systems Engineers/Architects, 15-1099.04 Web Developers, 15-1099.05 Web Administrators, and 15-1099.99 Computer Specialists, All Other.

Determine user requirements and design specifications for computer networks. Plan and implement network upgrades.

Develop network-related documentation. Design, build, or operate equipment configuration prototypes, including network hardware, software, servers, or server operation systems. Coordinate network operations, maintenance, repairs, or upgrades. Adjust network sizes to meet volume or capacity demands. Communicate with vendors to gather information about products, to alert them to future needs, to resolve problems, or to address system maintenance issues. Coordinate installation of new equipment. Coordinate network or design activities with designers of associated networks. Design, organize, and deliver product awareness, skills transfer, and product education sessions for staff and suppliers. Determine specific network hardware or software requirements, such as platforms, interfaces, bandwidths, or routine schemas. Develop disaster recovery plans. Communicate with customers, sales staff, or marketing staff to determine customer needs. Explain design specifications to integration or test engineers. Develop plans or budgets for network equipment replacement. Prepare design presentations and proposals for staff or customers. Supervise engineers and other staff in the design or implementation of network solutions. Use network computer-aided design (CAD) software packages to optimize network designs. Develop or maintain project reporting systems. Participate in network technology upgrade or expansion projects, including installation of hardware and software and integration testing. Research and test new or modified hardware or software products to determine performance and interoperability. Develop and implement solutions for network problems. Prepare or monitor project schedules, budgets, or cost control systems. Monitor and analyze network performance and data input/output reports to detect problems, identify inefficient use of computer resources, or perform capacity planning. Evaluate network designs to determine whether customer requirements are met efficiently and effectively. Estimate time and materials needed to complete projects. Develop or recommend network security measures, such as firewalls, network security audits, or automated security probes.

GOE Information—Interest Area: 11. Information Technology. **Work Group:** 11.02. Information Technology Specialties. **Note:** The Department of Labor has not collected some data for this job, so it has fewer details than the other descriptions.

Instructional Programs—Computer and Information Sciences and Support Services, Other; Computer and Information Sciences, General; Computer Engineering Technologies/Technicians, Other; Computer Engineering, General; Computer Science; Computer Software Engineering; Computer Systems Networking and Telecommunications; Information Science/Studies; Information Technology; System, Networking, and LAN/WAN Management/Manager.

Related SOC Job—15-1099 Computer Specialists, All Other. **Related OOH Job**—Computer Scientists and Database Administrators. **Related DOT Job**—No data available.

15-1099.04 Web Developers

- **Education/Training Required:** No data available
- **Employed:** 116,760
- **Annual Earnings:** $59,420
- **Growth:** 19.0%
- **Annual Job Openings:** 15,000

The job openings listed here are shared with 15-1099.01 Software Quality Assurance Engineers and Testers, 15-1099.02 Computer Systems Engineers/Architects, 15-1099.03 Network Designers, 15-1099.05 Web Administrators, and 15-1099.99 Computer Specialists, All Other.

Develop and design Web applications and Web sites. Create and specify architectural and technical parameters. Direct Web site content creation, enhancement, and maintenance.

Recommend and implement performance improvements. Perform or direct Web site updates. Develop and document style guidelines for Web site content. Renew domain name registrations. Design and implement Web site security measures such as firewalls or message encryption. Establish appropriate server directory trees. Identify or maintain links to and from other Web sites and check links to ensure proper functioning. Create searchable indices for Web page content. Back up files from Web sites to local directories for instant recovery in case of problems. Write supporting code for Web applications or Web sites. Register Web sites with search engines to increase Web site traffic. Respond to user e-mail inquiries or set up automated systems to send responses. Collaborate with management or users to develop e-commerce strategies and to integrate these strategies with Web sites. Communicate with network personnel or Web site hosting agencies to address hardware or software issues affecting Web sites. Evaluate or recommend server hardware or software. Develop or implement procedures for ongoing Web site revision. Perform Web site tests according to planned schedules or after any Web site or product revisions. Create Web models or prototypes that include physical, interface, logical, or data models. Maintain understanding of current Web technologies or programming practices through continuing education; reading; or participation in professional conferences, workshops, or groups. Identify problems uncovered by testing or customer feedback and correct problems or refer problems to appropriate personnel for correction. Research, document, rate, or select alternatives for Web architecture or technologies. Write, design, or edit Web page content or direct others producing content. Document technical factors such as server load, bandwidth, database performance, and browser and device types. Design, build, or maintain Web sites, using authoring or scripting languages, content creation tools, management tools, and digital media. Confer with management or development teams to prioritize needs, resolve conflicts, develop content criteria, or choose solutions.

GOE Information—Interest Area: 11. Information Technology. **Work Group:** 11.02. Information Technology Specialties. **Note:** The Department of Labor has not collected some data for this job, so it has fewer details than the other descriptions.

Instructional Programs—Computer and Information Sciences and Support Services, Other; Computer and Information Sciences, General; Computer Engineering Technologies/Technicians, Other; Computer Engineering, General; Computer Science; Computer Software Engineering; E-Commerce/Electronic Commerce; Information Science/Studies; Information Technology; Web Page, Digital/Multimedia and Information Resources Design; Web/Multimedia Management and Webmaster.

Related SOC Job—15-1099 Computer Specialists, All Other. **Related OOH Job—**Computer Scientists and Database Administrators. **Related DOT Job—**No data available.

15-1099.05 Web Administrators

- **Education/Training Required:** No data available
- **Employed:** 116,760
- **Annual Earnings:** $59,420
- **Growth:** 19.0%
- **Annual Job Openings:** 15,000

The job openings listed here are shared with 15-1099.01 Software Quality Assurance Engineers and Testers, 15-1099.02 Computer Systems Engineers/Architects, 15-1099.03 Network Designers, 15-1099.04 Web Developers, and 15-1099.99 Computer Specialists, All Other.

Manage Web environment design, deployment, development, and maintenance activities. Perform testing and quality assurance of Web sites and Web applications.

Gather, analyze, or document user feedback to locate or resolve sources of problems. Perform user testing or usage analyses to determine Web sites' effectiveness or usability. Set up or maintain monitoring tools on Web servers or Web sites. Check and analyze operating system or application logfiles regularly to verify proper system performance. Develop testing routines and procedures. Evaluate testing routines or procedures for adequacy, sufficiency, and effectiveness. Test issues such as system integration, performance, and system security on a regular schedule or after any major program modifications. Determine sources of Web page or server problems and take action to correct such problems. Track, compile, and analyze Web site usage data. Recommend Web site improvements and develop budgets to support recommendations. Identify or address interoperability requirements. Evaluate or recommend server hardware or software. Develop or implement procedures for ongoing Web site revision. Implement updates, upgrades, and patches in a timely manner to limit loss of service. Identify, standardize, and communicate levels of access and security. Implement Web site security measures, such as firewalls or message encryption. Collaborate with Web developers to create and operate internal and external Web sites or to manage projects such as e-marketing campaigns. Develop Web site performance metrics. Correct testing-identified problems or recommend actions for their resolution. Provide training or technical assistance in Web site implementation or use. Back up or modify applications and related data to provide for disaster recovery. Test backup or recovery plans regularly and resolve any problems. Document application and Web site changes or change procedures. Document installation or configuration procedures to allow maintenance and repetition. Test new software packages for use in Web operations or other applications. Inform Web site users of problems, problem resolutions, or application changes and updates. Monitor Web developments through continuing education; reading; or participation in professional conferences, workshops, or groups.

GOE Information—Interest Area: 11. Information Technology. **Work Group:** 11.02. Information Technology Specialties. **Note:** The Department of Labor has not collected some data for this job, so it has fewer details than the other descriptions.

Instructional Programs—Computer and Information Sciences and Support Services, Other; Computer and Information Sciences, General; Computer Engineering Technologies/Technicians, Other; Computer Engineering, General; Computer Science; Computer Software Engineering; E-Commerce/Electronic Commerce; Information Science/Studies; Information Technology; Web/Multimedia Management and Webmaster.

Related SOC Job—15-1099 Computer Specialists, All Other. **Related OOH Job—**Computer Scientists and Database Administrators. **Related DOT Job—**No data available.

15-1099.99 Computer Specialists, All Other

- **Education/Training Required: Associate degree**
- **Employed: 116,760**
- **Annual Earnings: $59,420**
- **Growth: 19.0%**
- **Annual Job Openings: 15,000**

The job openings listed here are shared with 15-1099.01 Software Quality Assurance Engineers and Testers, 15-1099.02 Computer Systems Engineers/Architects, 15-1099.03 Network Designers, 15-1099.04 Web Developers, and 15-1099.05 Web Administrators.

All computer specialists not listed separately.

No task data available.

Note: The Department of Labor has not collected some data for this job, so it has fewer details than the other descriptions.

Related SOC Job—15-1099 Computer Specialists, All Other. **Related OOH Job**—Computer Scientists and Database Administrators. **Related DOT Jobs**—019.062-010 Geographic Information System Specialist; 033.167-010 Computer Systems Hardware Analyst.

15-2000 Mathematical Science Occupations

15-2011.00 Actuaries

- **Education/Training Required: Work experience plus degree**
- **Employed: 15,770**
- **Annual Earnings: $81,640**
- **Growth: 23.2%**
- **Annual Job Openings: 3,000**

Analyze statistical data, such as mortality, accident, sickness, disability, and retirement rates, and construct probability tables to forecast risk and liability for payment of future benefits. May ascertain premium rates required and cash reserves necessary to ensure payment of future benefits.

Ascertain premium rates required and cash reserves and liabilities necessary to ensure payment of future benefits. Analyze statistical information to estimate mortality, accident, sickness, disability, and retirement rates. Design, review, and help administer insurance, annuity, and pension plans, determining financial soundness and calculating premiums. Collaborate with programmers, underwriters, accounts, claims experts, and senior management to help companies develop plans for new lines of business or improving existing business. Determine or help determine company policy and explain complex technical matters to company executives, government officials, shareholders, policyholders, or the public. Testify before public agencies on proposed legislation affecting businesses. Provide advice to clients on a contract basis, working as a consultant. Testify in court as expert witness or to provide legal evidence on matters such as the value of potential lifetime earnings of a person who is disabled or killed in an accident. Construct probability tables for events such as fires, natural disasters, and unemployment, based on analysis of statistical data and other pertinent information. Determine policy contract provisions for each type of insurance. Manage credit and help price corporate security offerings. Provide expertise to help financial institutions manage risks and maximize returns associated

with investment products or credit offerings. Determine equitable basis for distributing surplus earnings under participating insurance and annuity contracts in mutual companies. Explain changes in contract provisions to customers.

GOE Information—Interest Area: 15. Scientific Research, Engineering, and Mathematics. **Work Group:** 15.06. Mathematics and Data Analysis. **Personality Type—**Conventional. Conventional occupations frequently involve following set procedures and routines. These occupations can include working with data and details more than with ideas. Usually there is a clear line of authority to follow. **Work Values—**Autonomy; Working Conditions; Advancement; Independence; Supervision, Human Relations; Recognition. **Skills—**Programming; Mathematics; Active Learning; Complex Problem Solving; Operations Analysis; Quality Control Analysis. **Abilities—***Cognitive:* Mathematical Reasoning; Number Facility; Inductive Reasoning; Written Expression; Fluency of Ideas; Deductive Reasoning. *Psychomotor:* None met the criteria. *Physical:* None met the criteria. *Sensory:* Speech Recognition; Near Vision; Speech Clarity. **General Work Activities—***Information Input:* Getting Information; Identifying Objects, Actions, and Events; Estimating the Needed Characteristics of Products, Events, or Information. *Mental Process:* Processing Information; Analyzing Data or Information; Updating and Using Relevant Knowledge. *Work Output:* Interacting With Computers; Documenting or Recording Information. *Interacting with Others:* Communicating with Other Workers; Establishing and Maintaining Interpersonal Relationships; Providing Consultation and Advice to Others. **Physical Work Conditions—**Indoors; Sitting; Using Hands on Objects, Tools, or Controls; Repetitive Motions. **Other Job Characteristics—**Need to Be Exact or Accurate; Repeat Same Tasks.

Experience—Job Zone 5. Extensive skill, knowledge, and experience are needed. **Job Preparation—**SVP 8.0 and above—four years to more than 10 years. **Knowledges—**Mathematics; Economics and Accounting; Sales and Marketing; Computers and Electronics; Personnel and Human Resources; English Language. **Instructional Program—**Actuarial Science.

Related SOC Job—15-2011 Actuaries. **Related OOH Job—**Actuaries. **Related DOT Job—**020.167-010 Actuary.

15-2021.00 Mathematicians

- **Education/Training Required: Master's degree**
- **Employed: 2,930**
- **Annual Earnings: $80,920**
- **Growth: −1.3%**
- **Annual Job Openings: Fewer than 500**

Conduct research in fundamental mathematics or in application of mathematical techniques to science, management, and other fields. Solve or direct solutions to problems in various fields by mathematical methods.

Apply mathematical theories and techniques to the solution of practical problems in business, engineering, the sciences, or other fields. Develop computational methods for solving problems that occur in areas of science and engineering or that come from applications in business or industry. Maintain knowledge in the field by reading professional journals, talking with other mathematicians, and attending professional conferences. Perform computations and apply methods of numerical analysis to data. Develop mathematical or statistical models of phenomena to be used for analysis or for computational simulation. Assemble sets of assumptions and explore the consequences of each set. Address the relationships of quantities, magnitudes, and forms through the use of numbers and symbols. Develop new principles and new relationships between existing mathematical principles to advance mathematical science. Design, analyze, and decipher encryption systems designed to transmit military, political, financial, or law-enforcement-related information in code. Conduct research to extend mathematical knowledge in traditional areas, such as algebra, geometry, probability, and logic.

GOE Information—Interest Area: 15. Scientific Research, Engineering, and Mathematics. **Work Group:** 15.06. Mathematics and Data Analysis. **Personality Type—**Investigative. Investigative occupations frequently involve working with ideas and require an extensive amount of thinking. These occupations can involve searching for facts and figuring out problems mentally. **Work Values—**Autonomy; Ability Utilization; Creativity; Independence; Working Conditions; Responsibility. **Skills—**Programming; Mathematics; Science; Complex Problem Solving; Critical Thinking; Active Learning. **Abilities—***Cognitive:* Mathematical Reasoning; Number Facility; Originality; Fluency of Ideas; Speed of Closure; Written Comprehension. *Psychomotor:* None met the criteria. *Physical:* None met the criteria. *Sensory:* Speech Clarity; Near Vision. **General Work Activities—***Information Input:* Getting Information; Identifying Objects, Actions, and Events; Estimating the Needed Characteristics of Products, Events, or Information. *Mental Process:* Thinking Creatively; Updating and Using Relevant Knowledge; Analyzing Data or Information. *Work Output:* Interacting With Computers; Documenting or Recording Information. *Interacting with Others:* Interpreting the Meaning of Information for Others; Providing Consultation and Advice to Others; Communicating with Other Workers. **Physical Work Conditions—**Indoors; Sitting. **Other Job Characteristics—**Need to Be Exact or Accurate.

Experience—Job Zone 5. Extensive skill, knowledge, and experience are needed. **Job Preparation—**SVP 8.0 and above—four years to more than 10 years. **Knowledges—**Mathematics; Physics; Computers and Electronics; Engineering and Technology; English Language. **Instructional Programs—**Algebra and Number Theory; Analysis and Functional Analysis; Applied Mathematics; Applied Mathematics, Other; Computational Mathematics; Geometry/Geometric Analysis; Logic; Mathematical Statistics and Probability; Mathematics and Statistics, Other; Mathematics, General; Mathematics, Other; Topology and Foundations.

Related SOC Job—15-2021 Mathematicians. **Related OOH Job—**Mathematicians. **Related DOT Job—**020.067-014 Mathematician.

15-2031.00 Operations Research Analysts

- **Education/Training Required: Master's degree**
- **Employed: 52,530**
- **Annual Earnings: $62,180**
- **Growth: 8.4%**
- **Annual Job Openings: 7,000**

Formulate and apply mathematical modeling and other optimizing methods, using a computer to develop and interpret information that assists management with decision making, policy formulation, or other managerial functions. May develop related software, service, or products. Frequently concentrates on collecting and analyzing data and developing decision support software. May develop and supply optimal time, cost, or logistics networks for program evaluation, review, or implementation.

Formulate mathematical or simulation models of problems, relating constants and variables, restrictions, alternatives, and conflicting objectives and their numerical parameters. Collaborate with others in the organization to ensure successful implementation of chosen problem solutions. Analyze information obtained from management in order to conceptualize and define operational problems. Perform validation and testing of models to ensure adequacy; reformulate models as necessary. Collaborate with senior managers and decision-makers to identify and solve a variety of problems and to clarify management objectives. Define data requirements; then gather and validate information, applying judgment and statistical tests. Study and analyze information about alternative courses of action in order to determine which plan will offer the best outcomes. Prepare management reports defining and evaluating problems and recommending solutions. Break systems into their component parts, assign numerical values to each component, and examine the mathematical relationships between them. Specify manipulative or computational methods to be applied to models. Observe the current system in operation and gather and analyze information about each of the parts of component problems, using a variety of sources. Design, conduct, and evaluate experimental operational models in cases where models cannot be developed from existing data. Develop and apply time and cost networks in order to plan, control, and review large projects. Develop business methods and procedures, including accounting systems, file systems, office systems, logistics systems, and production schedules.

GOE Information—Interest Area: 04. Business and Administration. **Work Group:** 04.05. Accounting, Auditing, and Analytical Support. **Personality Type—**Investigative. Investigative occupations frequently involve working with ideas and require an extensive amount of thinking. These occupations can involve searching for facts and figuring out problems mentally. **Work Values—**Creativity; Autonomy; Ability Utilization; Responsibility; Working Conditions; Recognition. **Skills—**Programming; Systems Analysis; Operations Analysis; Mathematics; Systems Evaluation; Science. **Abilities—***Cognitive:* Mathematical Reasoning; Number Facility; Fluency of Ideas; Originality; Written Expression; Category Flexibility. *Psychomotor:* None met the criteria. *Physical:* None met the criteria. *Sensory:* Speech Clarity; Near Vision; Speech Recognition. **General Work Activities—***Information Input:* Getting Information; Identifying Objects, Actions, and Events; Estimating the Needed Characteristics of Products, Events, or Information. *Mental Process:* Analyzing Data or Information; Processing Information; Thinking Creatively. *Work Output:* Interacting With Computers; Documenting or Recording Information. *Interacting with Others:* Providing Consultation and Advice to Others; Interpreting the Meaning of Information for Others; Communicating with Other Workers. **Physical Work Conditions—**Indoors; Sitting. **Other Job Characteristics—**Need to Be Exact or Accurate.

Experience—Job Zone 5. Extensive skill, knowledge, and experience are needed. **Job Preparation—**SVP 8.0 and above—four years to more than 10 years. **Knowledges—**Mathematics; Engineering and Technology; Computers and Electronics; Production and Processing; Economics and Accounting; Administration and Management. **Instructional Programs—**Management Science, General; Management Sciences and Quantitative Methods, Other; Operations Research.

Related SOC Job—15-2031 Operations Research Analysts. **Related OOH Job—**Operations Research Analysts. **Related DOT Job—**020.067-018 Operations-Research Analyst.

15-2041.00 Statisticians

- **Education/Training Required: Master's degree**
- **Employed: 17,480**
- **Annual Earnings: $62,450**
- **Growth: 4.6%**
- **Annual Job Openings: 2,000**

Engage in the development of mathematical theory or apply statistical theory and methods to collect, organize, interpret, and summarize numerical data to provide usable information. May specialize in fields such as bio-statistics, agricultural statistics, business statistics, economic statistics, or other fields.

Report results of statistical analyses, including information in the form of graphs, charts, and tables. Process large amounts of data for statistical modeling and graphic analysis, using computers. Identify relationships and trends in data, as well as any factors that could affect the results of research. Analyze and interpret statistical data in order to identify significant differences in relationships among sources of information. Prepare data for processing by organizing information, checking for any inaccuracies, and adjusting and weighting the raw data. Evaluate the statistical methods and procedures used to obtain data in order to ensure validity, applicability, efficiency, and accuracy. Evaluate sources of information in order to determine any limitations in terms of reliability or usability. Plan data collection methods for specific projects and determine the types and sizes of sample groups to be used. Design research projects that apply valid scientific techniques and utilize information obtained from baselines or historical data in order to structure uncompromised and efficient analyses. Develop an understanding of fields to which statistical methods are to be applied in order to determine whether methods and results are appropriate. Supervise and provide instructions for workers collecting and tabulating data. Apply sampling techniques or utilize complete enumeration bases in order to determine and define groups to be surveyed. Adapt statistical methods in order to solve specific problems in many fields, such as economics, biology, and engineering. Develop and test experimental designs, sampling techniques, and analytical methods. Examine theories, such as those of probability and inference, in order to discover mathematical bases for new or improved methods of obtaining and evaluating numerical data.

GOE Information—Interest Area: 15. Scientific Research, Engineering, and Mathematics. **Work Group:** 15.06. Mathematics and Data Analysis. **Personality Type—**Investigative. Investigative occupations frequently involve working with ideas and require an extensive amount of thinking. These occupations can involve searching for facts and figuring out problems mentally. **Work Values—** Autonomy; Ability Utilization; Independence; Creativity; Working Conditions; Responsibility. **Skills—**Programming; Science; Mathematics; Active Learning; Writing; Negotiation. **Abilities—** *Cognitive:* Mathematical Reasoning; Number Facility; Written Expression; Written Comprehension; Inductive Reasoning; Deductive Reasoning. *Psychomotor:* None met the criteria. *Physical:* None met the criteria. *Sensory:* Far Vision; Near Vision; Speech Clarity; Speech Recognition. **General Work Activities—***Information Input:* Getting Information; Monitoring Processes, Materials, or Surroundings; Identifying Objects, Actions, and Events. *Mental Process:* Organizing, Planning, and Prioritizing; Analyzing Data or Information; Updating and Using Relevant Knowledge. *Work Output:* Interacting With Computers; Documenting or Recording Information. *Interacting with Others:* Communicating with Other Workers; Communicating with Persons Outside Organization;

Establishing and Maintaining Interpersonal Relationships. **Physical Work Conditions—**Indoors; Sitting; Using Hands on Objects, Tools, or Controls; Repetitive Motions. **Other Job Characteristics—**Need to Be Exact or Accurate; Repeat Same Tasks.

Experience—Job Zone 5. Extensive skill, knowledge, and experience are needed. **Job Preparation—**SVP 8.0 and above—four years to more than 10 years. **Knowledges—**Mathematics; Computers and Electronics; English Language; Education and Training; Law and Government; Administration and Management. **Instructional Programs—**Applied Mathematics; Biostatistics; Business Statistics; Mathematical Statistics and Probability; Mathematics, General; Statistics, General; Statistics, Other.

Related SOC Job—15-2041 Statisticians. **Related OOH Job—** Statisticians. **Related DOT Jobs—**020.067-022 Statistician, Mathematical; 020.167-026 Statistician, Applied.

15-2091.00 Mathematical Technicians

- **Education/Training Required: Master's degree**
- **Employed: 1,430**
- **Annual Earnings: $36,470**
- **Growth: 3.4%**
- **Annual Job Openings: Fewer than 500**

Apply standardized mathematical formulas, principles, and methodology to technological problems in engineering and physical sciences in relation to specific industrial and research objectives, processes, equipment, and products.

Process data for analysis, using computers. Reduce raw data to meaningful terms, using the most practical and accurate combination and sequence of computational methods. Confer with scientific or engineering personnel to plan projects. Modify standard formulas so that they conform to project needs and data-processing methods. Apply standardized mathematical formulas, principles, and methodology to the solution of technological problems involving engineering or physical science. Translate data into numbers, equations, flow charts, graphs, or other forms.

GOE Information—Interest Area: 15. Scientific Research, Engineering, and Mathematics. **Work Group:** 15.06. Mathematics and Data Analysis. **Personality Type—**Investigative. Investigative occupations frequently involve working with ideas and require an extensive amount of thinking. These occupations can involve searching for facts and figuring out problems mentally. **Work Values—** Advancement; Working Conditions; Ability Utilization; Supervision, Human Relations; Independence; Creativity. **Skills—**Programming; Mathematics; Science; Operations Analysis; Critical Thinking; Active Learning. **Abilities—***Cognitive:* Mathematical Reasoning; Number Facility; Deductive Reasoning; Oral Comprehension; Fluency of Ideas; Speed of Closure. *Psychomotor:* None met the criteria. *Physical:* None met the criteria. *Sensory:* None met the criteria. **General Work Activities—***Information Input:* Getting Information; Identifying Objects, Actions, and Events; Estimating the Needed Characteristics of Products, Events, or Information. *Mental Process:* Processing Information; Analyzing Data or Information; Updating and Using Relevant Knowledge. *Work Output:* Interacting With Computers; Documenting or Recording Information; Handling and Moving Objects. *Interacting with Others:* Communicating with Other Workers; Interpreting the Meaning of Information for Others; Providing Consultation and Advice to Others. **Physical Work Conditions—**Indoors; Sitting; Using Hands on Objects, Tools, or Controls. **Other Job Characteristics—**Need to Be Exact or Accurate.

Experience—Job Zone 4. A minimum of two to four years of work-related skill, knowledge, or experience is needed. **Job Preparation**—SVP 7.0 to less than 8.0—two years to less than 10 years. **Knowledges**—Mathematics; Computers and Electronics; Engineering and Technology; English Language; Clerical Practices. **Instructional Program**—No related CIP programs.

Related SOC Job—15-2091 Mathematical Technicians. **Related OOH Job**—Mathematical Technicians. **Related DOT Jobs**—020.162-010 Mathematical Technician; 020.167-030 Weight Analyst.

15-2099.99 Mathematical Science Occupations, All Other

- **Education/Training Required: Master's degree**
- **Employed: 7,320**
- **Annual Earnings: $61,860**
- **Growth: 6.2%**
- **Annual Job Openings: 1,000**

All mathematical scientists not listed separately.

No task data available.

Note: The Department of Labor has not collected some data for this job, so it has fewer details than the other descriptions.

Related SOC Job—15-2099 Mathematical Scientists, All Other. **Related OOH Job**—None. **Related DOT Job**—199.267-014 Cryptanalyst.

17-0000

Architecture and Engineering Occupations

17-1000 Architects, Surveyors, and Cartographers

17-1011.00 Architects, Except Landscape and Naval

- **Education/Training Required: Bachelor's degree**
- **Employed: 96,740**
- **Annual Earnings: $62,850**
- **Growth: 17.3%**
- **Annual Job Openings: 7,000**

Plan and design structures, such as private residences, office buildings, theaters, factories, and other structural property.

Prepare information regarding design, structure specifications, materials, color, equipment, estimated costs, or construction time. Consult with client to determine functional and spatial requirements of structure. Direct activities of workers engaged in preparing drawings and specification documents. Plan layout of project. Prepare contract documents for building contractors. Prepare scale drawings. Integrate engineering element into unified design. Conduct periodic on-site observation of work during construction to monitor compliance with plans. Administer construction contracts. Represent client in obtaining bids and awarding construction contracts. Prepare operating and maintenance manuals, studies, and reports.

GOE Information—Interest Area: 02. Architecture and Construction. **Work Group:** 02.02. Architectural Design. **Personality Type—**Artistic. Artistic occupations frequently involve working with forms, designs, and patterns. They often require self-expression, and the work can be done without following a clear set of rules. **Work Values—**Creativity; Recognition; Ability Utilization; Social Status; Achievement; Compensation. **Skills—**Operations Analysis; Management of Financial Resources; Complex Problem Solving; Management of Personnel Resources; Coordination; Negotiation. **Abilities—***Cognitive:* Visualization; Originality; Fluency of Ideas; Deductive Reasoning; Category Flexibility; Mathematical Reasoning. *Psychomotor:* Finger Dexterity; Arm-Hand Steadiness; Control Precision. *Physical:* None met the criteria. *Sensory:* Near Vision; Far Vision; Visual Color Discrimination; Speech Recognition; Depth Perception; Speech Clarity. **General Work Activities—***Information Input:* Getting Information; Inspecting Equipment, Structures, or Materials; Identifying Objects, Actions, and Events. *Mental Process:* Thinking Creatively; Organizing, Planning, and Prioritizing; Making Decisions and Solving Problems. *Work Output:* Drafting and Specifying Technical Devices; Interacting With Computers; Documenting or Recording Information. *Interacting with Others:* Coordinating the Work and Activities of Others; Establishing and Maintaining Interpersonal Relationships; Communicating with Persons Outside Organization. **Physical Work Conditions—**Indoors; Sitting. **Other Job Characteristics—**Need to Be Exact or Accurate; Repeat Same Tasks; Errors Have Important Consequences.

Experience—Job Zone 5. Extensive skill, knowledge, and experience are needed. **Job Preparation—**SVP 8.0 and above—four years to more than 10 years. **Knowledges—**Building and Construction; Design; Engineering and Technology; Fine Arts; Law and Government; Physics. **Instructional Programs—**Architectural History and Criticism; Architecture (BArch, BA/BS, MArch, MA/MS, PhD); Architecture and Related Programs, Other; Environmental Design/Architecture.

Related SOC Job—17-1011 Architects, Except Landscape and Naval. **Related OOH Job—**Architects, Except Landscape and Naval. **Related DOT Jobs—**001.061-010 Architect; 001.167-010 School-Plant Consultant.

17-1012.00 Landscape Architects

- **Education/Training Required: Bachelor's degree**
- **Employed: 20,220**
- **Annual Earnings: $54,220**
- **Growth: 19.4%**
- **Annual Job Openings: 1,000**

Plan and design land areas for such projects as parks and other recreational facilities; airports; highways; hospitals; schools; land subdivisions; and commercial, industrial, and residential sites.

Prepare site plans, specifications, and cost estimates for land development, coordinating arrangement of existing and proposed land features and structures. Confer with clients, engineering personnel, and architects on overall program. Compile and analyze data on conditions such as location, drainage, and location of structures for environmental reports and landscaping plans. Inspect landscape work to ensure compliance with specifications, approve quality of materials and work, and advise client and construction personnel.

GOE Information—Interest Area: 02. Architecture and Construction. **Work Group:** 02.02. Architectural Design. **Personality Type—**Artistic. Artistic occupations frequently involve working with forms, designs, and patterns. They often require self-expression, and the work can be done without following a clear set of rules. **Work Values—**Creativity; Ability Utilization; Social Status; Recognition; Achievement; Autonomy. **Skills—**Operations Analysis; Management of Financial Resources; Coordination; Mathematics; Social Perceptiveness; Persuasion. **Abilities—***Cognitive:* Visualization; Originality; Fluency of Ideas; Mathematical Reasoning; Written Expression; Speed of Closure. *Psychomotor:* None met the criteria. *Physical:* None met the criteria. *Sensory:* Far Vision; Near Vision; Depth Perception; Visual Color Discrimination; Speech Recognition. **General Work Activities—***Information Input:* Getting Information; Monitoring Processes, Materials, or Surroundings; Identifying Objects, Actions, and Events. *Mental Process:* Thinking Creatively; Making Decisions and Solving Problems; Organizing, Planning, and Prioritizing. *Work Output:* Drafting and Specifying Technical Devices; Documenting or Recording Information; Interacting With Computers. *Interacting with Others:* Coordinating the Work and Activities of Others; Communicating with Persons Outside Organization; Communicating with Other Workers. **Physical Work Conditions—**More Often Indoors Than Outdoors; Very Hot or Cold; Hazardous Equipment; Minor Burns, Cuts, Bites, or Stings; Sitting. **Other Job Characteristics—**Need to Be Exact or Accurate; Errors Have Important Consequences.

Experience—Job Zone 4. A minimum of two to four years of work-related skill, knowledge, or experience is needed. **Job Preparation—**SVP 7.0 to less than 8.0—two years to less than 10 years. **Knowledges—**Design; Building and Construction; Geography; Engineering and Technology; Biology; Fine Arts. **Instructional Programs—**Environmental Design/Architecture; Landscape Architecture (BS, BSLA, BLA, MSLA, MLA, PhD).

Related SOC Job—17-1012 Landscape Architects. **Related OOH Job—**Landscape Architects. **Related DOT Job—**001.061-018 Landscape Architect.

17-1021.00 Cartographers and Photogrammetrists

- **Education/Training Required: Bachelor's degree**
- **Employed: 11,260**
- **Annual Earnings: $48,250**
- **Growth: 15.3%**
- **Annual Job Openings: 1,000**

Collect, analyze, and interpret geographic information provided by geodetic surveys, aerial photographs, and satellite data. Research, study, and prepare maps and other spatial data in digital or graphic form for legal, social, political, educational, and design purposes. May work with Geographic Information Systems (GIS). May design and evaluate algorithms, data structures, and user interfaces for GIS and mapping systems.

Identify, scale, and orient geodetic points, elevations, and other planimetric or topographic features, applying standard mathematical formulas. Collect information about specific features of the Earth, using aerial photography and other digital remote sensing techniques. Revise existing maps and charts, making all necessary corrections and adjustments. Compile data required for map preparation, including aerial photographs, survey notes, records, reports, and original maps. Inspect final compositions to ensure completeness and accuracy. Determine map content and layout, as well as production specifications such as scale, size, projection, and colors, and direct production to ensure that specifications are followed. Examine and analyze data from ground surveys, reports, aerial photographs, and satellite images to prepare topographic maps, aerial-photograph mosaics, and related charts. Select aerial photographic and remote sensing techniques and plotting equipment needed to meet required standards of accuracy. Delineate aerial photographic detail such as control points, hydrography, topography, and cultural features, using precision stereoplotting apparatus or drafting instruments. Build and update digital databases. Prepare and alter trace maps, charts, tables, detailed drawings, and three-dimensional optical models of terrain, using stereoscopic plotting and computer graphics equipment. Determine guidelines that specify which source material is acceptable for use. Study legal records to establish boundaries of local, national, and international properties. Travel over photographed areas to observe, identify, record, and verify all relevant features.

GOE Information—Interest Area: 15. Scientific Research, Engineering, and Mathematics. **Work Group:** 15.09. Engineering Technology. **Personality Type**—Conventional. Conventional occupations frequently involve following set procedures and routines. These occupations can include working with data and details more than with ideas. Usually there is a clear line of authority to follow. **Work Values**—Autonomy; Responsibility; Ability Utilization; Working Conditions; Independence; Creativity. **Skills**—Science; Technology Design; Mathematics; Active Learning; Troubleshooting; Reading Comprehension. **Abilities**—*Cognitive:* Number Facility; Mathematical Reasoning; Flexibility of Closure; Written Comprehension; Written Expression; Visualization. *Psychomotor:* Arm-Hand Steadiness; Finger Dexterity. *Physical:* None met the criteria. *Sensory:* Visual Color Discrimination; Near Vision; Far Vision. **General Work Activities**—*Information Input:* Identifying Objects, Actions, and Events; Getting Information; Estimating the Needed Characteristics of Products, Events, or Information. *Mental Process:* Updating and Using Relevant Knowledge; Processing Information; Analyzing Data or Information. *Work Output:* Interacting With Computers; Documenting or Recording Information; Drafting and

Specifying Technical Devices. *Interacting with Others:* Establishing and Maintaining Interpersonal Relationships; Communicating with Other Workers; Interpreting the Meaning of Information for Others. **Physical Work Conditions**—Indoors; Sitting; Using Hands on Objects, Tools, or Controls; Repetitive Motions. **Other Job Characteristics**—Need to Be Exact or Accurate; Repeat Same Tasks; Automation.

Experience—Job Zone 3. Previous work-related skill, knowledge, or experience is required. **Job Preparation**—SVP 6.0 to less than 7.0— more than one year and less than four years. **Knowledges**— Geography; Design; Engineering and Technology; Computers and Electronics; Production and Processing; Mathematics. **Instructional Programs**—Cartography; Surveying Technology/Surveying.

Related SOC Job—17-1021 Cartographers and Photogrammetrists. **Related OOH Job**—Surveyors, Cartographers, Photogrammetrists, and Surveying Technicians. **Related DOT Jobs**—018.131-010 Supervisor, Cartography; 018.261-010 Drafter, Cartographic; 018.261-026 Photogrammetrist; 018.262-010 Field-Map Editor.

17-1022.00 Surveyors

- **Education/Training Required: Bachelor's degree**
- **Employed: 54,220**
- **Annual Earnings: $45,860**
- **Growth: 15.9%**
- **Annual Job Openings: 4,000**

Make exact measurements and determine property boundaries. Provide data relevant to the shape, contour, gravitation, location, elevation, or dimension of land or land features on or near the earth's surface for engineering, mapmaking, mining, land evaluation, construction, and other purposes.

Prepare and maintain sketches, maps, reports, and legal descriptions of surveys to describe, certify, and assume liability for work performed. Verify the accuracy of survey data, including measurements and calculations conducted at survey sites. Direct or conduct surveys to establish legal boundaries for properties based on legal deeds and titles. Record the results of surveys, including the shape, contour, location, elevation, and dimensions of land or land features. Calculate heights, depths, relative positions, property lines, and other characteristics of terrain. Prepare or supervise preparation of all data, charts, plots, maps, records, and documents related to surveys. Write descriptions of property boundary surveys for use in deeds, leases, or other legal documents. Plan and conduct ground surveys designed to establish baselines, elevations, and other geodetic measurements. Search legal records, survey records, and land titles to obtain information about property boundaries in areas to be surveyed. Coordinate findings with the work of engineering and architectural personnel, clients, and others concerned with projects. Adjust surveying instruments to maintain their accuracy. Establish fixed points for use in making maps, using geodetic and engineering instruments. Determine longitudes and latitudes of important features and boundaries in survey areas, using theodolites, transits, levels, and satellite-based global positioning systems (GPS). Train assistants and helpers and direct their work in such activities as performing surveys or drafting maps. Analyze survey objectives and specifications to prepare survey proposals or to direct others in survey proposal preparation. Compute geodetic measurements and interpret survey data to determine positions, shapes, and elevations of geomorphic and topographic features. Develop criteria for survey methods and procedures. Develop criteria for the design and modification of survey instruments. Conduct research in surveying and mapping methods, using knowledge of techniques of photogrammetric map compilation and electronic data processing.

GOE Information—Interest Area: 02. Architecture and Construction. **Work Group:** 02.03. Architecture/Construction Engineering Technologies. **Personality Type—**Investigative. Investigative occupations frequently involve working with ideas and require an extensive amount of thinking. These occupations can involve searching for facts and figuring out problems mentally. **Work Values—**Achievement; Autonomy; Social Status; Authority; Variety; Responsibility. **Skills—**Mathematics; Management of Personnel Resources; Science; Coordination; Equipment Selection; Critical Thinking. **Abilities—***Cognitive:* Spatial Orientation; Number Facility; Mathematical Reasoning; Speed of Closure; Information Ordering; Written Expression. *Psychomotor:* Arm-Hand Steadiness; Finger Dexterity; Control Precision; Manual Dexterity; Multilimb Coordination. *Physical:* Gross Body Coordination. *Sensory:* Far Vision; Depth Perception; Near Vision; Visual Color Discrimination; Auditory Attention. **General Work Activities—***Information Input:* Getting Information; Identifying Objects, Actions, and Events; Monitoring Processes, Materials, or Surroundings. *Mental Process:* Making Decisions and Solving Problems; Processing Information; Analyzing Data or Information. *Work Output:* Documenting or Recording Information; Drafting and Specifying Technical Devices; Handling and Moving Objects. *Interacting with Others:* Guiding, Directing, and Motivating Subordinates; Monitoring and Controlling Resources; Resolving Conflicts and Negotiating with Others. **Physical Work Conditions—**More Often Outdoors Than Indoors; Very Hot or Cold; Hazardous Equipment; Minor Burns, Cuts, Bites, or Stings; Standing. **Other Job Characteristics—**Need to Be Exact or Accurate; Repeat Same Tasks.

Experience—Job Zone 3. Previous work-related skill, knowledge, or experience is required. **Job Preparation—**SVP 6.0 to less than 7.0—more than one year and less than four years. **Knowledges—**Building and Construction; Geography; Design; Engineering and Technology; Mathematics; Computers and Electronics. **Instructional Program—**Surveying Technology/Surveying.

Related SOC Job—17-1022 Surveyors. **Related OOH Job—**Surveyors, Cartographers, Photogrammetrists, and Surveying Technicians. **Related DOT Jobs—**018.161-010 Surveyor, Mine; 018.167-018 Land Surveyor; 018.167-026 Photogrammetric Engineer; 018.167-038 Surveyor, Geodetic; 018.167-042 Surveyor, Geophysical Prospecting; 018.167-046 Surveyor, Marine; 024.061-014 Geodesist; 184.167-026 Director, Photogrammetry Flight Operations.

17-2000 Engineers

17-2011.00 Aerospace Engineers

- **Education/Training Required:** Bachelor's degree
- **Employed:** 81,100
- **Annual Earnings:** $84,090
- **Growth:** 8.3%
- **Annual Job Openings:** 6,000

Perform a variety of engineering work in designing, constructing, and testing aircraft, missiles, and spacecraft. May conduct basic and applied research to evaluate adaptability of materials and equipment to aircraft design and manufacture. May recommend improvements in testing equipment and techniques.

Formulate conceptual design of aeronautical or aerospace products or systems to meet customer requirements. Direct and coordinate activities of engineering or technical personnel designing, fabricating, modifying, or testing aircraft or aerospace products. Develop design criteria for aeronautical or aerospace products or systems, including testing methods, production costs, quality standards, and completion dates. Plan and conduct experimental, environmental, operational, and stress tests on models and prototypes of aircraft and aerospace systems and equipment. Evaluate product data and design from inspections and reports for conformance to engineering principles, customer requirements, and quality standards. Formulate mathematical models or other methods of computer analysis to develop, evaluate, or modify design according to customer engineering requirements. Write technical reports and other documentation, such as handbooks and bulletins, for use by engineering staff, management, and customers. Analyze project requests and proposals and engineering data to determine feasibility, productibility, cost, and production time of aerospace or aeronautical product. Review performance reports and documentation from customers and field engineers and inspect malfunctioning or damaged products to determine problem. Direct research and development programs. Evaluate and approve selection of vendors by study of past performance and new advertisements. Plan and coordinate activities concerned with investigating and resolving customers' reports of technical problems with aircraft or aerospace vehicles. Maintain records of performance reports for future reference.

GOE Information—Interest Area: 15. Scientific Research, Engineering, and Mathematics. **Work Group:** 15.07. Research and Design Engineering. **Personality Type—**Investigative. Investigative occupations frequently involve working with ideas and require an extensive amount of thinking. These occupations can involve searching for facts and figuring out problems mentally. **Work Values—**Creativity; Ability Utilization; Social Status; Authority; Responsibility; Autonomy. **Skills—**Systems Evaluation; Systems Analysis; Science; Judgment and Decision Making; Persuasion; Technology Design. **Abilities—***Cognitive:* Mathematical Reasoning; Deductive Reasoning; Information Ordering; Inductive Reasoning; Written Expression; Problem Sensitivity. *Psychomotor:* None met the criteria. *Physical:* None met the criteria. *Sensory:* Near Vision; Speech Recognition. **General Work Activities—***Information Input:* Monitoring Processes, Materials, or Surroundings; Getting Information; Estimating the Needed Characteristics of Products, Events, or Information. *Mental Process:* Making Decisions and Solving Problems; Updating and Using Relevant Knowledge; Processing Information. *Work Output:* Interacting With Computers; Drafting and Specifying Technical Devices; Documenting or Recording Information. *Interacting with Others:* Establishing and Maintaining Interpersonal Relationships; Communicating with Other Workers; Coordinating the Work and Activities of Others. **Physical Work Conditions—**Indoors; Sitting; Repetitive Motions. **Other Job Characteristics—**Need to Be Exact or Accurate; Errors Have Important Consequences; Repeat Same Tasks.

Experience—Job Zone 5. Extensive skill, knowledge, and experience are needed. **Job Preparation—**SVP 8.0 and above—four years to more than 10 years. **Knowledges—**Engineering and Technology; Physics; Design; Mechanical Devices; Production and Processing; Mathematics. **Instructional Program—**Aerospace, Aeronautical, and Astronautical Engineering.

Related SOC Job—17-2011 Aerospace Engineers. **Related OOH Job—**Engineers. **Related DOT Jobs—**002.061-010 Aerodynamicist; 002.061-014 Aeronautical Engineer; 002.061-018 Aeronautical Test Engineer; 002.061-022 Aeronautical-Design Engineer; 002.061-026

Aeronautical-Research Engineer; 002.061-030 Stress Analyst; 002.167-010 Value Engineer; 002.167-014 Field-Service Engineer; 002.167-018 Aeronautical Project Engineer.

17-2021.00 *Agricultural Engineers*

- **Education/Training Required: Bachelor's degree**
- **Employed: 3,170**
- **Annual Earnings: $64,890**
- **Growth: 12.0%**
- **Annual Job Openings: Fewer than 500**

Apply knowledge of engineering technology and biological science to agricultural problems concerned with power and machinery, electrification, structures, soil and water conservation, and processing of agricultural products.

Visit sites to observe environmental problems, to consult with contractors, or to monitor construction activities. Design agricultural machinery components and equipment, using computer-aided design (CAD) technology. Test agricultural machinery and equipment to ensure adequate performance. Design structures for crop storage, animal shelter and loading, and animal and crop processing and supervise their construction. Provide advice on water quality and issues related to pollution management, river control, and ground and surface water resources. Conduct educational programs that provide farmers or farm cooperative members with information that can help them improve agricultural productivity. Discuss plans with clients, contractors, consultants, and other engineers so that they can be evaluated and necessary changes made. Supervise food processing or manufacturing plant operations. Design and supervise environmental and land reclamation projects in agriculture and related industries. Design food processing plants and related mechanical systems. Plan and direct construction of rural electric-power distribution systems and irrigation, drainage, and flood control systems for soil and water conservation. Prepare reports, sketches, working drawings, specifications, proposals, and budgets for proposed sites or systems. Meet with clients, such as district or regional councils, farmers, and developers, to discuss their needs. Design sensing, measuring, and recording devices and other instrumentation used to study plant or animal life.

GOE Information—Interest Area: 01. Agriculture and Natural Resources. **Work Group:** 01.02. Resource Science/Engineering for Plants, Animals, and the Environment. **Personality Type—** Investigative. Investigative occupations frequently involve working with ideas and require an extensive amount of thinking. These occupations can involve searching for facts and figuring out problems mentally. **Work Values—**Creativity; Ability Utilization; Responsibility; Autonomy; Social Status; Authority. **Skills—**Science; Programming; Technology Design; Operations Analysis; Management of Material Resources; Management of Financial Resources. **Abilities—***Cognitive:* Originality; Mathematical Reasoning; Deductive Reasoning; Number Facility; Fluency of Ideas; Visualization. *Psychomotor:* Control Precision; Reaction Time; Finger Dexterity; Multilimb Coordination; Arm-Hand Steadiness. *Physical:* None met the criteria. *Sensory:* Depth Perception; Hearing Sensitivity; Far Vision; Visual Color Discrimination; Auditory Attention; Speech Recognition. **General Work Activities—** *Information Input:* Identifying Objects, Actions, and Events; Getting Information; Inspecting Equipment, Structures, or Materials. *Mental Process:* Thinking Creatively; Updating and Using Relevant Knowledge; Processing Information. *Work Output:* Drafting and Specifying Technical Devices; Documenting or Recording

Information; Interacting With Computers. *Interacting with Others:* Coordinating the Work and Activities of Others; Providing Consultation and Advice to Others; Communicating with Other Workers. **Physical Work Conditions—**More Often Indoors Than Outdoors; Noisy; Sitting. **Other Job Characteristics—**Need to Be Exact or Accurate; Errors Have Important Consequences.

Experience—Job Zone 4. A minimum of two to four years of work-related skill, knowledge, or experience is needed. **Job Preparation—** SVP 7.0 to less than 8.0–two years to less than 10 years. **Knowledges—**Food Production; Engineering and Technology; Physics; Design; Biology; Building and Construction. **Instructional Program—**Agricultural/Biological Engineering and Bioengineering.

Related SOC Job—17-2021 Agricultural Engineers. **Related OOH Job—**Engineers. **Related DOT Jobs—**013.061-010 Agricultural Engineer; 013.061-014 Agricultural-Research Engineer; 013.061-018 Design-Engineer, Agricultural Equipment; 013.061-022 Test Engineer, Agricultural Equipment.

17-2031.00 *Biomedical Engineers*

- **Education/Training Required: Bachelor's degree**
- **Employed: 11,660**
- **Annual Earnings: $71,840**
- **Growth: 30.7%**
- **Annual Job Openings: 1,000**

Apply knowledge of engineering, biology, and biomechanical principles to the design, development, and evaluation of biological and health systems and products, such as artificial organs, prostheses, instrumentation, medical information systems, and health management and care delivery systems.

Evaluate the safety, efficiency, and effectiveness of biomedical equipment. Install, adjust, maintain, and/or repair biomedical equipment. Advise hospital administrators on the planning, acquisition, and use of medical equipment. Advise and assist in the application of instrumentation in clinical environments. Develop models or computer simulations of human bio-behavioral systems in order to obtain data for measuring or controlling life processes. Research new materials to be used for products such as implanted artificial organs. Design and develop medical diagnostic and clinical instrumentation, equipment, and procedures, utilizing the principles of engineering and bio-behavioral sciences. Conduct research, along with life scientists, chemists, and medical scientists, on the engineering aspects of the biological systems of humans and animals. Teach biomedical engineering or disseminate knowledge about field through writing or consulting. Design and deliver technology to assist people with disabilities. Diagnose and interpret bioelectric data, using signal-processing techniques. Adapt or design computer hardware or software for medical science uses. Analyze new medical procedures in order to forecast likely outcomes. Develop new applications for energy sources, such as using nuclear power for biomedical implants.

GOE Information—Interest Area: 15. Scientific Research, Engineering, and Mathematics. **Work Group:** 15.07. Research and Design Engineering. **Personality Type—**No data available. **Work Values—**No data available. **Skills—**Technology Design; Science; Installation; Operations Analysis; Quality Control Analysis; Systems Evaluation. **Abilities—***Cognitive:* Originality; Mathematical Reasoning; Deductive Reasoning; Visualization; Inductive Reasoning; Number Facility. *Psychomotor:* Control Precision; Finger Dexterity; Arm-Hand Steadiness; Manual Dexterity; Reaction Time; Multilimb Coordination. *Physical:* Gross Body Coordination; Static Strength;

Trunk Strength. *Sensory:* Hearing Sensitivity; Visual Color Discrimination; Depth Perception; Far Vision; Auditory Attention; Speech Clarity. **General Work Activities**—*Information Input:* Monitoring Processes, Materials, or Surroundings; Inspecting Equipment, Structures, or Materials; Getting Information. *Mental Process:* Updating and Using Relevant Knowledge; Thinking Creatively; Organizing, Planning, and Prioritizing. *Work Output:* Interacting With Computers; Documenting or Recording Information; Repairing and Maintaining Electronic Equipment. *Interacting with Others:* Communicating with Other Workers; Establishing and Maintaining Interpersonal Relationships; Monitoring and Controlling Resources. **Physical Work Conditions**—Indoors; Contaminants; Disease or Infections; Hazardous Conditions; Sitting; Using Hands on Objects, Tools, or Controls. **Other Job Characteristics**—Need to Be Exact or Accurate; Errors Have Important Consequences; Repeat Same Tasks.

Experience—Job Zone 4. A minimum of two to four years of work-related skill, knowledge, or experience is needed. **Job Preparation**—SVP 7.0 to less than 8.0—two years to less than 10 years. **Knowledges**—Engineering and Technology; Computers and Electronics; Physics; Design; Mechanical Devices; Chemistry. **Instructional Program**—Biomedical/Medical Engineering.

Related SOC Job—17-2031 Biomedical Engineers. **Related OOH Job**—Engineers. **Related DOT Job**—019.061-010 Biomedical Engineer.

17-2041.00 Chemical Engineers

- **Education/Training Required: Bachelor's degree**
- **Employed: 27,550**
- **Annual Earnings: $77,140**
- **Growth: 10.6%**
- **Annual Job Openings: 3,000**

Design chemical plant equipment and devise processes for manufacturing chemicals and products, such as gasoline, synthetic rubber, plastics, detergents, cement, paper, and pulp, by applying principles and technology of chemistry, physics, and engineering.

Perform tests throughout stages of production to determine degree of control over variables, including temperature, density, specific gravity, and pressure. Develop safety procedures to be employed by workers operating equipment or working in close proximity to ongoing chemical reactions. Determine most effective arrangement of operations such as mixing, crushing, heat transfer, distillation, and drying. Prepare estimate of production costs and production progress reports for management. Direct activities of workers who operate or who are engaged in constructing and improving absorption, evaporation, or electromagnetic equipment. Perform laboratory studies of steps in manufacture of new product and test proposed process in small-scale operation such as a pilot plant. Develop processes to separate components of liquids or gases or generate electrical currents by using controlled chemical processes. Conduct research to develop new and improved chemical manufacturing processes. Design measurement and control systems for chemical plants based on data collected in laboratory experiments and in pilot plant operations. Design and plan layout of equipment.

GOE Information—**Interest Area:** 15. Scientific Research, Engineering, and Mathematics. **Work Group:** 15.07. Research and Design Engineering. **Personality Type**—Investigative. Investigative occupations frequently involve working with ideas and require an extensive amount of thinking. These occupations can involve searching for facts and figuring out problems mentally. **Work Values**—Creativity; Ability Utilization; Social Status; Authority; Responsibility; Autonomy. **Skills**—Science; Technology Design; Troubleshooting; Programming; Systems Analysis; Systems Evaluation. **Abilities**—*Cognitive:* Originality; Mathematical Reasoning; Category Flexibility; Deductive Reasoning; Number Facility; Fluency of Ideas. *Psychomotor:* Arm-Hand Steadiness; Finger Dexterity. *Physical:* None met the criteria. *Sensory:* Auditory Attention; Visual Color Discrimination; Near Vision; Speech Clarity; Hearing Sensitivity; Speech Recognition. **General Work Activities**—*Information Input:* Identifying Objects, Actions, and Events; Monitoring Processes, Materials, or Surroundings; Getting Information. *Mental Process:* Processing Information; Organizing, Planning, and Prioritizing; Updating and Using Relevant Knowledge. *Work Output:* Interacting With Computers; Documenting or Recording Information; Controlling Machines and Processes. *Interacting with Others:* Communicating with Other Workers; Providing Consultation and Advice to Others; Establishing and Maintaining Interpersonal Relationships. **Physical Work Conditions**—Indoors; Noisy; Hazardous Conditions; Sitting. **Other Job Characteristics**—Need to Be Exact or Accurate; Errors Have Important Consequences; Repeat Same Tasks.

Experience—Job Zone 4. A minimum of two to four years of work-related skill, knowledge, or experience is needed. **Job Preparation**—SVP 7.0 to less than 8.0—two years to less than 10 years. **Knowledges**—Engineering and Technology; Chemistry; Physics; Design; Production and Processing; Mathematics. **Instructional Program**—Chemical Engineering.

Related SOC Job—17-2041 Chemical Engineers. **Related OOH Job**—Engineers. **Related DOT Jobs**—008.061-010 Absorption-and-Adsorption Engineer; 008.061-014 Chemical Design Engineer, Processes; 008.061-018 Chemical Engineer; 008.061-022 Chemical Research Engineer; 008.061-026 Chemical-Test Engineer.

17-2051.00 Civil Engineers

- **Education/Training Required: Bachelor's degree**
- **Employed: 229,700**
- **Annual Earnings: $66,190**
- **Growth: 16.5%**
- **Annual Job Openings: 19,000**

Perform engineering duties in planning, designing, and overseeing construction and maintenance of building structures and facilities, such as roads, railroads, airports, bridges, harbors, channels, dams, irrigation projects, pipelines, power plants, water and sewage systems, and waste disposal units. Includes architectural, structural, traffic, ocean, and geotechnical engineers.

Analyze survey reports, maps, drawings, blueprints, aerial photography, and other topographical or geologic data to plan projects. Plan and design transportation or hydraulic systems and structures, following construction and government standards and using design software and drawing tools. Compute load and grade requirements, water flow rates, and material stress factors to determine design specifications. Inspect project sites to monitor progress and ensure conformance to design specifications and safety or sanitation standards. Direct construction, operations, and maintenance activities at project site. Direct or participate in surveying to lay out installations and establish reference points, grades, and elevations to guide construction. Estimate quantities and cost of materials, equipment, or labor to determine project feasibility. Prepare or present public reports on topics such as bid proposals, deeds, environmental impact statements, or property and right-of-way descriptions. Test soils and materials to determine the adequacy and strength of foundations, concrete, asphalt, or steel. Provide technical advice regarding design, construction, or program modifications and structural repairs to industrial and managerial personnel. Conduct studies of traffic patterns or environmental conditions to identify engineering problems and assess the potential impact of projects.

GOE Information—Interest Area: 15. Scientific Research, Engineering, and Mathematics. **Work Group:** 15.07. Research and Design Engineering. **Personality Type—**Realistic. Realistic occupations frequently involve work activities that include practical, hands-on problems and solutions. They often deal with plants; animals; and real-world materials like wood, tools, and machinery. Many of the occupations require working outside and do not involve a lot of paperwork or working closely with others. **Work Values—**Creativity; Ability Utilization; Autonomy; Social Status; Authority; Variety. **Skills—**Science; Mathematics; Operations Analysis; Coordination; Negotiation; Persuasion. **Abilities—**_Cognitive:_ Visualization; Mathematical Reasoning; Speed of Closure; Deductive Reasoning; Number Facility; Originality. _Psychomotor:_ Control Precision; Finger Dexterity; Arm-Hand Steadiness; Multilimb Coordination. _Physical:_ None met the criteria. _Sensory:_ Far Vision; Near Vision; Depth Perception; Visual Color Discrimination; Speech Clarity; Speech Recognition. **General Work Activities—**_Information Input:_ Getting Information; Monitoring Processes, Materials, or Surroundings; Estimating the Needed Characteristics of Products, Events, or Information. _Mental Process:_ Making Decisions and Solving Problems; Organizing, Planning, and Prioritizing; Updating and Using Relevant Knowledge. _Work Output:_ Interacting With Computers; Drafting and Specifying Technical Devices; Documenting or Recording Information. _Interacting with Others:_ Resolving Conflicts and Negotiating with Others; Communicating with Other Workers; Coordinating the Work and Activities of Others. **Physical Work Conditions—**More Often Outdoors Than Indoors; Very Hot or Cold; Contaminants; Hazardous Equipment; Sitting. **Other Job Characteristics—**Need to Be Exact or Accurate; Errors Have Important Consequences.

Experience—Job Zone 4. A minimum of two to four years of work-related skill, knowledge, or experience is needed. **Job Preparation—**SVP 7.0 to less than 8.0—two years to less than 10 years. **Knowledges—**Engineering and Technology; Design; Building and Construction; Physics; Mathematics; Transportation. **Instructional Programs—**Civil Engineering, General; Civil Engineering, Other; Transportation and Highway Engineering; Water Resources Engineering.

Related SOC Job—17-2051 Civil Engineers. **Related OOH Job—**Engineers. **Related DOT Jobs—**005.061-010 Airport Engineer; 005.061-014 Civil Engineer; 005.061-018 Hydraulic Engineer; 005.061-022 Irrigation Engineer; 005.061-026 Railroad Engineer; 005.061-030 Sanitary Engineer; 005.061-034 Structural Engineer; 005.061-038 Transportation Engineer; 005.167-014 Drainage-Design Coordinator; 005.167-018 Forest Engineer; 005.167-026 Production Engineer, Track; 019.167-018 Resource-Recovery Engineer.

17-2061.00 Computer Hardware Engineers

- **Education/Training Required: Bachelor's degree**
- **Employed: 78,580**
- **Annual Earnings: $84,420**
- **Growth: 10.1%**
- **Annual Job Openings: 5,000**

Research, design, develop, and test computer or computer-related equipment for commercial, industrial, military, or scientific use. May supervise the manufacturing and installation of computer or computer-related equipment and components.

Update knowledge and skills to keep up with rapid advancements in computer technology. Provide technical support to designers, marketing and sales departments, suppliers, engineers, and other team members throughout the product development and implementation process. Test and verify hardware and support peripherals to ensure that they meet specifications and requirements, analyzing and recording test data. Monitor functioning of equipment and make necessary modifications to ensure system operates in conformance with specifications. Analyze information to determine, recommend, and plan layout, including type of computers and peripheral equipment modifications. Build, test, and modify product prototypes, using working models or theoretical models constructed using computer simulation. Analyze user needs and recommend appropriate hardware. Direct technicians, engineering designers, or other technical support personnel as needed. Confer with engineering staff and consult specifications to evaluate interface between hardware and software and operational and performance requirements of overall system. Select hardware and material, assuring compliance with specifications and product requirements. Store, retrieve, and manipulate data for analysis of system capabilities and requirements. Write detailed functional specifications that document the hardware development process and support hardware introduction. Specify power supply requirements and configuration, drawing on system performance expectations and design specifications. Provide training and support to system designers and users. Assemble and modify existing pieces of equipment to meet special needs. Evaluate factors such as reporting formats required, cost constraints, and need for security restrictions to determine hardware configuration. Design and develop computer hardware and support peripherals, including central processing units (CPUs), support logic, microprocessors, custom integrated circuits, and printers and disk drives. Recommend purchase of equipment to control dust, temperature, and humidity in area of system installation.

GOE Information—Interest Area: 15. Scientific Research, Engineering, and Mathematics. **Work Group:** 15.07. Research and Design Engineering. **Personality Type—**Investigative. Investigative occupations frequently involve working with ideas and require an extensive amount of thinking. These occupations can involve searching for facts and figuring out problems mentally. **Work Values—**Creativity; Ability Utilization; Working Conditions; Responsibility; Social Status; Authority. **Skills—**Programming; Systems Analysis; Systems Evaluation; Troubleshooting; Operations Analysis; Technology Design. **Abilities—**_Cognitive:_ Deductive Reasoning; Fluency of Ideas; Written Expression; Originality; Visualization; Mathematical Reasoning. _Psychomotor:_ Finger Dexterity. _Physical:_ None met the criteria. _Sensory:_ Visual Color Discrimination; Speech Recognition. **General Work Activities—**_Information Input:_ Monitoring Processes, Materials, or Surroundings; Identifying Objects, Actions, and Events; Getting Information. _Mental Process:_ Updating and Using Relevant Knowledge; Thinking Creatively; Processing Information. _Work Output:_ Interacting With Computers; Repairing and Maintaining Electronic Equipment; Documenting or Recording Information. _Interacting with Others:_ Providing Consultation and Advice to Others; Establishing and Maintaining Interpersonal Relationships; Communicating with Other Workers. **Physical Work Conditions—**Indoors; Sitting. **Other Job Characteristics—**Need to Be Exact or Accurate.

Experience—Job Zone 4. A minimum of two to four years of work-related skill, knowledge, or experience is needed. **Job Preparation**—SVP 7.0 to less than 8.0—two years to less than 10 years. **Knowledges**—Computers and Electronics; Engineering and Technology; Telecommunications; Design; Physics; Education and Training. **Instructional Programs**—Computer Engineering, General; Computer Hardware Engineering.

Related SOC Job—17-2061 Computer Hardware Engineers. **Related OOH Job**—Engineers. **Related DOT Job**—003.061-030 Electronics Engineer.

17-2071.00 Electrical Engineers

- Education/Training Required: Bachelor's degree
- Employed: 144,920
- Annual Earnings: $73,510
- Growth: 11.8%
- Annual Job Openings: 12,000

Design, develop, test, or supervise the manufacturing and installation of electrical equipment, components, or systems for commercial, industrial, military, or scientific use.

Confer with engineers, customers, and others to discuss existing or potential engineering projects and products. Design, implement, maintain, and improve electrical instruments, equipment, facilities, components, products, and systems for commercial, industrial, and domestic purposes. Operate computer-assisted engineering and design software and equipment to perform engineering tasks. Direct and coordinate manufacturing, construction, installation, maintenance, support, documentation, and testing activities to ensure compliance with specifications, codes, and customer requirements. Perform detailed calculations to compute and establish manufacturing, construction, and installation standards and specifications. Inspect completed installations and observe operations to ensure conformance to design and equipment specifications and compliance with operational and safety standards. Plan and implement research methodology and procedures to apply principles of electrical theory to engineering projects. Prepare specifications for purchase of materials and equipment. Supervise and train project team members as necessary. Investigate and test vendors' and competitors' products. Oversee project production efforts to assure projects are completed satisfactorily, on time, and within budget. Prepare and study technical drawings, specifications of electrical systems, and topographical maps to ensure that installation and operations conform to standards and customer requirements. Investigate customer or public complaints, determine nature and extent of problem, and recommend remedial measures. Plan layout of electric-power-generating plants and distribution lines and stations. Assist in developing capital project programs for new equipment and major repairs. Develop budgets, estimating labor, material, and construction costs. Compile data and write reports regarding existing and potential engineering studies and projects. Collect data relating to commercial and residential development, population, and power system interconnection to determine operating efficiency of electrical systems. Conduct field surveys and study maps, graphs, diagrams, and other data to identify and correct power system problems.

GOE Information—Interest Area: 15. Scientific Research, Engineering, and Mathematics. **Work Group:** 15.07. Research and Design Engineering. **Personality Type**—Investigative. Investigative occupations frequently involve working with ideas and require an extensive amount of thinking. These occupations can involve searching for facts and figuring out problems mentally. **Work Values**—

Creativity; Ability Utilization; Social Status; Responsibility; Autonomy; Working Conditions. **Skills**—Technology Design; Systems Analysis; Troubleshooting; Science; Systems Evaluation; Equipment Selection. **Abilities**—*Cognitive:* Mathematical Reasoning; Visualization; Oral Comprehension; Deductive Reasoning; Written Expression; Originality. *Psychomotor:* None met the criteria. *Physical:* None met the criteria. *Sensory:* Near Vision; Far Vision; Speech Recognition. **General Work Activities**—*Information Input:* Getting Information; Identifying Objects, Actions, and Events; Estimating the Needed Characteristics of Products, Events, or Information. *Mental Process:* Updating and Using Relevant Knowledge; Organizing, Planning, and Prioritizing; Thinking Creatively. *Work Output:* Interacting With Computers; Documenting or Recording Information; Drafting and Specifying Technical Devices. *Interacting with Others:* Communicating with Other Workers; Establishing and Maintaining Interpersonal Relationships; Interpreting the Meaning of Information for Others. **Physical Work Conditions**—Indoors; Sitting. **Other Job Characteristics**—Need to Be Exact or Accurate.

Experience—Job Zone 4. A minimum of two to four years of work-related skill, knowledge, or experience is needed. **Job Preparation**—SVP 7.0 to less than 8.0—two years to less than 10 years. **Knowledges**—Engineering and Technology; Design; Physics; Telecommunications; Computers and Electronics; Mathematics. **Instructional Program**—Electrical, Electronics, and Communications Engineering.

Related SOC Job—17-2071 Electrical Engineers. **Related OOH Job**—Engineers. **Related DOT Jobs**—003.061-010 Electrical Engineer; 003.061-014 Electrical Test Engineer; 003.061-018 Electrical-Design Engineer; 003.061-022 Electrical-Prospecting Engineer; 003.061-026 Electrical-Research Engineer; 003.061-046 Illuminating Engineer; 003.167-014 Distribution-Field Engineer; 003.167-018 Electrical Engineer, Power System; 003.167-022 Electrolysis-and-Corrosion-Control Engineer; 003.167-026 Engineer of System Development; 003.167-038 Induction-Coordination Power Engineer; others.

17-2072.00 Electronics Engineers, Except Computer

- Education/Training Required: Bachelor's degree
- Employed: 130,050
- Annual Earnings: $78,030
- Growth: 9.7%
- Annual Job Openings: 11,000

Research, design, develop, and test electronic components and systems for commercial, industrial, military, or scientific use, utilizing knowledge of electronic theory and materials properties. Design electronic circuits and components for use in fields such as telecommunications, aerospace guidance and propulsion control, acoustics, or instruments and controls.

Design electronic components, software, products, or systems for commercial, industrial, medical, military, or scientific applications. Provide technical support and instruction to staff or customers regarding equipment standards, assisting with specific, difficult in-service engineering. Operate computer-assisted engineering and design software and equipment to perform engineering tasks. Analyze system requirements, capacity, cost, and customer needs to determine feasibility of project and develop system plan. Confer with engineers, customers, vendors, or others to discuss existing and potential engineering projects or products. Review and evaluate work of others inside and outside the organization to ensure effectiveness, technical adequacy, and compatibility in the resolution of complex engineering problems. Determine material and equipment needs and order supplies. Inspect electronic equipment, instruments, products, and systems to ensure conformance to specifications, safety standards, and applicable codes and regulations. Evaluate operational systems, prototypes, and proposals and recommend repair or design modifications based on factors such as environment, service, cost, and system capabilities. Prepare documentation containing information such as confidential descriptions and specifications of proprietary hardware and software, product development and introduction schedules, product costs, and information about product performance weaknesses. Direct and coordinate activities concerned with manufacture, construction, installation, maintenance, operation, and modification of electronic equipment, products, and systems. Develop and perform operational, maintenance, and testing procedures for electronic products, components, equipment, and systems. Plan and develop applications and modifications for electronic properties used in components, products, and systems to improve technical performance. Plan and implement research, methodology, and procedures to apply principles of electronic theory to engineering projects. Prepare engineering sketches and specifications for construction, relocation, and installation of equipment, facilities, products, and systems.

GOE Information—Interest Area: 15. Scientific Research, Engineering, and Mathematics. **Work Group:** 15.07. Research and Design Engineering. **Personality Type—**Investigative. Investigative occupations frequently involve working with ideas and require an extensive amount of thinking. These occupations can involve searching for facts and figuring out problems mentally. **Work Values—**Creativity; Ability Utilization; Responsibility; Social Status; Autonomy; Working Conditions. **Skills—**Troubleshooting; Installation; Technology Design; Operations Analysis; Science; Systems Evaluation. **Abilities—**_Cognitive:_ Mathematical Reasoning; Visualization; Deductive Reasoning; Number Facility; Written Comprehension; Perceptual Speed. _Psychomotor:_ Finger Dexterity; Arm-Hand Steadiness; Manual Dexterity. _Physical:_ None met the criteria. _Sensory:_ Visual Color Discrimination; Hearing Sensitivity; Depth Perception; Far Vision; Speech Clarity; Auditory Attention. **General Work Activities—**_Information Input:_ Identifying Objects, Actions, and Events; Inspecting Equipment, Structures, or Materials; Monitoring Processes, Materials, or Surroundings. _Mental Process:_ Updating and Using Relevant Knowledge; Thinking Creatively; Processing Information. _Work Output:_ Repairing and Maintaining Electronic Equipment; Documenting or Recording Information; Interacting With Computers. _Interacting with Others:_ Communicating with Other Workers; Providing Consultation and Advice to Others; Coaching and Developing Others. **Physical Work Conditions—**Indoors; Noisy; Sitting. **Other Job Characteristics—**Need to Be Exact or Accurate; Errors Have Important Consequences.

Experience—Job Zone 4. A minimum of two to four years of work-related skill, knowledge, or experience is needed. **Job Preparation—**SVP 7.0 to less than 8.0—two years to less than 10 years. **Knowledges—**Engineering and Technology; Design; Computers and Electronics; Physics; Telecommunications; Production and Processing. **Instructional Program—**Electrical, Electronics, and Communications Engineering.

Related SOC Job—17-2072 Electronics Engineers, Except Computer. **Related OOH Job—**Engineers. **Related DOT Jobs—**003.061-030 Electronics Engineer; 003.061-034 Electronics-Design Engineer; 003.061-038 Electronics-Research Engineer; 003.061-042 Electronics-Test Engineer; 003.061-050 Planning Engineer, Central Office Facilities; 003.167-010 Cable Engineer, Outside Plant; 003.167-030 Engineer-in-Charge, Studio Operations; 003.167-042 Outside-Plant Engineer; 003.167-058 Supervisor, Microwave; 003.167-066 Transmission-and-Protection Engineer; 003.187-010 Central-Office Equipment Engineer; others.

17-2081.00 Environmental Engineers

- **Education/Training Required: Bachelor's degree**
- **Employed: 50,140**
- **Annual Earnings: $68,090**
- **Growth: 30.0%**
- **Annual Job Openings: 5,000**

Design, plan, or perform engineering duties in the prevention, control, and remediation of environmental health hazards, utilizing various engineering disciplines. Work may include waste treatment, site remediation, or pollution control technology.

Prepare, review, and update environmental investigation and recommendation reports. Collaborate with environmental scientists, planners, hazardous waste technicians, engineers, and other specialists and experts in law and business to address environmental problems. Obtain, update, and maintain plans, permits, and standard operating procedures. Provide technical-level support for environmental remediation and litigation projects, including remediation system design and determination of regulatory applicability. Monitor progress of environmental improvement programs. Inspect industrial and municipal facilities and programs to evaluate operational effectiveness and ensure compliance with environmental regulations. Provide administrative support for projects by collecting data, providing project documentation, training staff, and performing other general administrative duties. Develop proposed project objectives and targets and report to management on progress in attaining them. Advise corporations and government agencies of procedures to follow in cleaning up contaminated sites to protect people and the environment. Advise industries and government agencies about environmental policies and standards. Inform company employees and other interested parties of environmental issues. Assess the existing or potential environmental impact of land use projects on air, water, and land. Assist in budget implementation, forecasts, and administration. Develop site-specific health and safety protocols, such as spill contingency plans and methods for loading and transporting waste. Coordinate and manage environmental protection programs and projects, assigning and evaluating work. Serve as liaison with federal, state, and local agencies and officials on issues pertaining to solid and hazardous waste program requirements. Design systems, processes, and equipment for control, management, and remediation of water, air, and soil quality. Prepare hazardous waste manifests and land disposal restriction notifications. Serve on teams conducting multimedia inspections at complex facilities, providing assistance with planning, quality assurance, safety inspection protocols, and sampling.

GOE Information—Interest Area: 01. Agriculture and Natural Resources. **Work Group:** 01.02. Resource Science/Engineering for Plants, Animals, and the Environment. **Personality Type—**No data available. **Work Values—**No data available. **Skills—**Science; Management of Financial Resources; Mathematics; Writing; Systems Analysis; Technology Design. **Abilities—**_Cognitive:_ Written Expression; Oral Expression; Deductive Reasoning; Originality; Oral Comprehension; Problem Sensitivity. _Psychomotor:_ None met the criteria. _Physical:_ None met the criteria. _Sensory:_ Near Vision; Speech Recognition. **General Work Activities—**_Information Input:_ Getting Information; Monitoring Processes, Materials, or Surroundings; Identifying Objects, Actions, and Events. _Mental Process:_ Evaluating

Information Against Standards; Updating and Using Relevant Knowledge; Organizing, Planning, and Prioritizing. *Work Output:* Documenting or Recording Information; Interacting With Computers; Performing General Physical Activities. *Interacting with Others:* Communicating with Other Workers; Communicating with Persons Outside Organization; Establishing and Maintaining Interpersonal Relationships. **Physical Work Conditions**—Indoors; Sitting. **Other Job Characteristics**—Need to Be Exact or Accurate; Repeat Same Tasks.

Experience—Job Zone 5. Extensive skill, knowledge, and experience are needed. **Job Preparation**—SVP 8.0 and above—four years to more than 10 years. **Knowledges**—Chemistry; Biology; Education and Training; Law and Government; Engineering and Technology; Design. **Instructional Program**—Environmental/Environmental Health Engineering.

Related SOC Job—17-2081 Environmental Engineers. **Related OOH Job**—Engineers. **Related DOT Jobs**—019.081-018 Pollution-Control Engineer; 029.081-010 Environmental Analyst.

17-2111.00 Health and Safety Engineers, Except Mining Safety Engineers and Inspectors

- **Education/Training Required: Bachelor's degree**
- **Employed: 25,330**
- **Annual Earnings: $65,210**
- **Growth: 13.4%**
- **Annual Job Openings: 2,000**

The job openings listed here are shared with 17-2111.01 Industrial Safety and Health Engineers, 17-2111.02 Fire-Prevention and Protection Engineers, and 17-2111.03 Product Safety Engineers.

Promote worksite or product safety by applying knowledge of industrial processes, mechanics, chemistry, psychology, and industrial health and safety laws.

No task data available.

GOE Information—**Interest Area:** 15. Scientific Research, Engineering, and Mathematics. **Work Group:** 15.08. Industrial and Safety Engineering. **Note:** The Department of Labor has not collected some data for this job, so it has fewer details than the other descriptions.

Instructional Program—Environmental/Environmental Health Engineering.

Related SOC Job—17-2111 Health and Safety Engineers, Except Mining Safety Engineers and Inspectors. **Related OOH Job**—Engineers. **Related DOT Job**—No data available.

17-2111.01 Industrial Safety and Health Engineers

- **Education/Training Required: Bachelor's degree**
- **Employed: 25,330**
- **Annual Earnings: $65,210**
- **Growth: 13.4%**
- **Annual Job Openings: 2,000**

The job openings listed here are shared with 17-2111.00 Health and Safety Engineers, Except Mining Safety Engineers and Inspectors, 17-2111.02 Fire-Prevention and Protection Engineers, and 17-2111.03 Product Safety Engineers.

Plan, implement, and coordinate safety programs requiring application of engineering principles and technology to prevent or correct unsafe environmental working conditions.

Investigate industrial accidents, injuries, or occupational diseases to determine causes and preventive measures. Report or review findings from accident investigations, facilities inspections, or environmental testing. Maintain and apply knowledge of current policies, regulations, and industrial processes. Inspect facilities, machinery, and safety equipment to identify and correct potential hazards and to ensure safety regulation compliance. Conduct or coordinate worker training in areas such as safety laws and regulations, hazardous condition monitoring, and use of safety equipment. Review employee safety programs to determine their adequacy. Interview employers and employees to obtain information about work environments and workplace incidents. Review plans and specifications for construction of new machinery or equipment to determine whether all safety requirements have been met. Compile, analyze, and interpret statistical data related to occupational illnesses and accidents. Interpret safety regulations for others interested in industrial safety, such as safety engineers, labor representatives, and safety inspectors. Recommend process and product safety features that will reduce employees' exposure to chemical, physical, and biological work hazards. Conduct or direct testing of air quality, noise, temperature, or radiation levels to verify compliance with health and safety regulations. Provide technical advice and guidance to organizations on how to handle health-related problems and make needed changes. Confer with medical professionals to assess health risks and to develop ways to manage health issues and concerns. Install safety devices on machinery or direct device installation. Maintain liaisons with outside organizations such as fire departments, mutual aid societies, and rescue teams so that emergency responses can be facilitated. Evaluate adequacy of actions taken to correct health inspection violations. Write and revise safety regulations and codes. Check floors of plants to ensure that they are strong enough to support heavy machinery. Plan and conduct industrial hygiene research.

GOE Information—**Interest Area:** 15. Scientific Research, Engineering, and Mathematics. **Work Group:** 15.08. Industrial and Safety Engineering. **Personality Type**—Investigative. Investigative occupations frequently involve working with ideas and require an extensive amount of thinking. These occupations can involve searching for facts and figuring out problems mentally. **Work Values**—Creativity; Authority; Social Status; Responsibility; Autonomy; Ability Utilization. **Skills**—Management of Financial Resources; Science; Systems Analysis; Persuasion; Systems Evaluation; Management of Personnel Resources. **Abilities**—*Cognitive:* Number Facility; Originality; Written Expression; Inductive Reasoning; Problem Sensitivity; Fluency of Ideas. *Psychomotor:* None met the criteria. *Physical:* None met the criteria. *Sensory:* Hearing Sensitivity; Visual Color Discrimination; Speech Recognition; Depth Perception; Far Vision; Auditory Attention. **General Work Activities**—*Information Input:* Getting Information; Monitoring Processes, Materials, or Surroundings; Inspecting Equipment, Structures, or Materials. *Mental Process:* Organizing, Planning, and Prioritizing; Updating and Using Relevant Knowledge; Making Decisions and Solving Problems. *Work Output:* Documenting or Recording Information; Interacting With Computers; Drafting and Specifying Technical Devices. *Interacting with Others:* Establishing and Maintaining Interpersonal Relationships; Providing Consultation and Advice to Others; Communicating with Other Workers. **Physical Work Conditions**—More Often Indoors Than Outdoors; Noisy; Sitting. **Other Job Characteristics**—Need to Be Exact or Accurate; Errors Have Important Consequences.

Experience—Job Zone 4. A minimum of two to four years of work-related skill, knowledge, or experience is needed. **Job Preparation**—SVP 7.0 to less than 8.0—two years to less than 10 years. **Knowledges**—Building and Construction; Education and Training; Chemistry; Physics; Engineering and Technology; Biology. **Instructional Program**—Environmental/Environmental Health Engineering.

Related SOC Job—17-2111 Health and Safety Engineers, Except Mining Safety Engineers and Inspectors. **Related OOH Job**—Engineers. **Related DOT Jobs**—012.061-014 Safety Engineer; 012.167-034 Industrial-Health Engineer; 012.167-058 Safety Manager.

17-2111.02 Fire-Prevention and Protection Engineers

- **Education/Training Required: Bachelor's degree**
- **Employed: 25,330**
- **Annual Earnings: $65,210**
- **Growth: 13.4%**
- **Annual Job Openings: 2,000**

The job openings listed here are shared with 17-2111.00 Health and Safety Engineers, Except Mining Safety Engineers and Inspectors, 17-2111.01 Industrial Safety and Health Engineers, and 17-2111.03 Product Safety Engineers.

Research causes of fires, determine fire protection methods, and design or recommend materials or equipment such as structural components or fire-detection equipment to assist organizations in safeguarding life and property against fire, explosion, and related hazards.

Design fire detection equipment, alarm systems, and fire extinguishing devices and systems. Inspect buildings or building designs to determine fire protection system requirements and potential problems in areas such as water supplies, exit locations, and construction materials. Advise architects, builders, and other construction personnel on fire prevention equipment and techniques and on fire code and standard interpretation and compliance. Prepare and write reports detailing specific fire prevention and protection issues, such as work performed and proposed review schedules. Determine causes of fires and ways in which they could have been prevented. Direct the purchase, modification, installation, maintenance, and operation of fire protection systems. Consult with authorities to discuss safety regulations and to recommend changes as necessary. Develop plans for the prevention of destruction by fire, wind, and water. Study the relationships between ignition sources and materials to determine how fires start. Attend workshops, seminars, or conferences to present or obtain information regarding fire prevention and protection. Develop training materials and conduct training sessions on fire protection. Evaluate fire department performance and the laws and regulations affecting fire prevention or fire safety. Conduct research on fire retardants and the fire safety of materials and devices.

GOE Information—Interest Area: 15. Scientific Research, Engineering, and Mathematics. **Work Group:** 15.08. Industrial and Safety Engineering. **Personality Type**—Investigative. Investigative occupations frequently involve working with ideas and require an extensive amount of thinking. These occupations can involve searching for facts and figuring out problems mentally. **Work Values**—Creativity; Social Status; Authority; Responsibility; Autonomy; Ability Utilization. **Skills**—Science; Management of Financial Resources; Operations Analysis; Mathematics; Systems Analysis; Negotiation. **Abilities**—*Cognitive:* Originality; Fluency of Ideas; Deductive Reasoning; Written Expression; Visualization; Flexibility

of Closure. *Psychomotor:* None met the criteria. *Physical:* None met the criteria. *Sensory:* Far Vision; Visual Color Discrimination; Speech Clarity; Speech Recognition; Depth Perception; Hearing Sensitivity. **General Work Activities**—*Information Input:* Getting Information; Inspecting Equipment, Structures, or Materials; Identifying Objects, Actions, and Events. *Mental Process:* Updating and Using Relevant Knowledge; Evaluating Information Against Standards; Organizing, Planning, and Prioritizing. *Work Output:* Drafting and Specifying Technical Devices; Documenting or Recording Information; Interacting With Computers. *Interacting with Others:* Communicating with Persons Outside Organization; Establishing and Maintaining Interpersonal Relationships; Communicating with Other Workers. **Physical Work Conditions**—Indoors; Sitting. **Other Job Characteristics**—Need to Be Exact or Accurate.

Experience—Job Zone 4. A minimum of two to four years of work-related skill, knowledge, or experience is needed. **Job Preparation**—SVP 7.0 to less than 8.0—two years to less than 10 years. **Knowledges**—Design; Engineering and Technology; Building and Construction; Physics; Chemistry; Public Safety and Security. **Instructional Program**—Environmental/Environmental Health Engineering.

Related SOC Job—17-2111 Health and Safety Engineers, Except Mining Safety Engineers and Inspectors. **Related OOH Job**—Engineers. **Related DOT Jobs**—012.167-022 Fire-Prevention Research Engineer; 012.167-026 Fire-Protection Engineer.

17-2111.03 Product Safety Engineers

- **Education/Training Required: Bachelor's degree**
- **Employed: 25,330**
- **Annual Earnings: $65,210**
- **Growth: 13.4%**
- **Annual Job Openings: 2,000**

The job openings listed here are shared with 17-2111.00 Health and Safety Engineers, Except Mining Safety Engineers and Inspectors, 17-2111.01 Industrial Safety and Health Engineers, and 17-2111.02 Fire-Prevention and Protection Engineers.

Develop and conduct tests to evaluate product safety levels and recommend measures to reduce or eliminate hazards.

Report accident investigation findings. Conduct research to evaluate safety levels for products. Evaluate potential health hazards or damage that could occur from product misuse. Investigate causes of accidents, injuries, or illnesses related to product usage in order to develop solutions to minimize or prevent recurrence. Participate in preparation of product usage and precautionary label instructions. Recommend procedures for detection, prevention, and elimination of physical, chemical, or other product hazards.

GOE Information—Interest Area: 15. Scientific Research, Engineering, and Mathematics. **Work Group:** 15.08. Industrial and Safety Engineering. **Personality Type**—Investigative. Investigative occupations frequently involve working with ideas and require an extensive amount of thinking. These occupations can involve searching for facts and figuring out problems mentally. **Work Values**—Creativity; Ability Utilization; Achievement; Autonomy; Responsibility; Social Status. **Skills**—Quality Control Analysis; Science; Operations Analysis; Mathematics; Technology Design; Systems Evaluation. **Abilities**—*Cognitive:* Written Expression; Deductive Reasoning; Fluency of Ideas; Number Facility; Problem Sensitivity; Written Comprehension. *Psychomotor:* None met the criteria. *Physical:* None met the criteria. *Sensory:* None met the criteria. **General Work Activities**—*Information Input:* Getting Information;

Identifying Objects, Actions, and Events; Monitoring Processes, Materials, or Surroundings. *Mental Process:* Processing Information; Analyzing Data or Information; Making Decisions and Solving Problems. *Work Output:* Documenting or Recording Information; Interacting With Computers; Handling and Moving Objects. *Interacting with Others:* Interpreting the Meaning of Information for Others; Providing Consultation and Advice to Others; Communicating with Other Workers. **Physical Work Conditions—**Indoors; Sitting; Using Hands on Objects, Tools, or Controls. **Other Job Characteristics—**Need to Be Exact or Accurate; Errors Have Important Consequences.

Experience—Job Zone 5. Extensive skill, knowledge, and experience are needed. **Job Preparation—**SVP 8.0 and above—four years to more than 10 years. **Knowledges—**Chemistry; Engineering and Technology; Physics; Biology; Public Safety and Security; Production and Processing. **Instructional Program—**Environmental/Environmental Health Engineering.

Related SOC Job—17-2111 Health and Safety Engineers, Except Mining Safety Engineers and Inspectors. **Related OOH Job—**Engineers. **Related DOT Job—**012.061-010 Product-Safety Engineer.

17-2112.00 Industrial Engineers

- **Education/Training Required: Bachelor's degree**
- **Employed: 191,640**
- **Annual Earnings: $66,670**
- **Growth: 16.0%**
- **Annual Job Openings: 13,000**

Design, develop, test, and evaluate integrated systems for managing industrial production processes, including human work factors, quality control, inventory control, logistics and material flow, cost analysis, and production coordination.

Analyze statistical data and product specifications to determine standards and establish quality and reliability objectives of finished product. Develop manufacturing methods, labor utilization standards, and cost analysis systems to promote efficient staff and facility utilization. Recommend methods for improving utilization of personnel, material, and utilities. Plan and establish sequence of operations to fabricate and assemble parts or products and to promote efficient utilization. Apply statistical methods and perform mathematical calculations to determine manufacturing processes, staff requirements, and production standards. Coordinate quality control objectives and activities to resolve production problems, maximize product reliability, and minimize cost. Confer with vendors, staff, and management personnel regarding purchases, procedures, product specifications, manufacturing capabilities, and project status. Draft and design layout of equipment, materials, and workspace to illustrate maximum efficiency, using drafting tools and computer. Review production schedules, engineering specifications, orders, and related information to obtain knowledge of manufacturing methods, procedures, and activities. Communicate with management and user personnel to develop production and design standards. Estimate production cost and effect of product design changes for management review, action, and control. Formulate sampling procedures and designs and develop forms and instructions for recording, evaluating, and reporting quality and reliability data. Record or oversee recording of information to ensure currency of engineering drawings and documentation of production problems. Study operations sequence, material flow, functional statements, organization charts, and project information to determine worker functions and responsibilities. Direct workers engaged in product

measurement, inspection, and testing activities to ensure quality control and reliability. Implement methods and procedures for disposition of discrepant material and defective or damaged parts and assess cost and responsibility.

GOE Information—Interest Area: 15. Scientific Research, Engineering, and Mathematics. **Work Group:** 15.08. Industrial and Safety Engineering. **Personality Type—**Enterprising. Enterprising occupations frequently involve starting up and carrying out projects. These occupations can involve leading people and making many decisions. They sometimes require risk taking and often deal with business. **Work Values—**Creativity; Authority; Ability Utilization; Autonomy; Social Status; Responsibility. **Skills—**Equipment Selection; Technology Design; Systems Analysis; Troubleshooting; Installation; Judgment and Decision Making. **Abilities—***Cognitive:* Mathematical Reasoning; Visualization; Deductive Reasoning; Fluency of Ideas; Information Ordering; Written Expression. *Psychomotor:* None met the criteria. *Physical:* None met the criteria. *Sensory:* Auditory Attention; Near Vision. **General Work Activities—***Information Input:* Getting Information; Monitoring Processes, Materials, or Surroundings; Identifying Objects, Actions, and Events. *Mental Process:* Organizing, Planning, and Prioritizing; Processing Information; Making Decisions and Solving Problems. *Work Output:* Interacting With Computers; Drafting and Specifying Technical Devices; Documenting or Recording Information. *Interacting with Others:* Communicating with Other Workers; Establishing and Maintaining Interpersonal Relationships; Resolving Conflicts and Negotiating with Others. **Physical Work Conditions—**Indoors; Noisy; Contaminants; Hazardous Equipment; More Often Standing Than Sitting. **Other Job Characteristics—**Need to Be Exact or Accurate; Repeat Same Tasks.

Experience—Job Zone 4. A minimum of two to four years of work-related skill, knowledge, or experience is needed. **Job Preparation—**SVP 7.0 to less than 8.0—two years to less than 10 years. **Knowledges—**Engineering and Technology; Design; Production and Processing; Mechanical Devices; Physics; Mathematics. **Instructional Program—**Industrial Engineering.

Related SOC Job—17-2112 Industrial Engineers. **Related OOH Job—**Engineers. **Related DOT Jobs—**011.161-010 Supervisor, Metallurgical-and-Quality-Control-Testing; 012.061-018 Standards Engineer; 012.067-010 Metrologist; 012.167-010 Configuration Management Analyst; 012.167-014 Manager, Quality Control; 012.167-018 Factory Lay-Out Engineer; 012.167-030 Industrial Engineer; 012.167-038 Liaison Engineer; 012.167-042 Manufacturing Engineer; 012.167-046 Production Engineer; 012.167-050 Production Planner; 012.167-054 Quality Control Engineer; 012.167-062 Supervisor, Vendor Quality; others.

17-2121.00 Marine Engineers and Naval Architects

- **Education/Training Required: Bachelor's degree**
- **Employed: 6,550**
- **Annual Earnings: $72,920**
- **Growth: 8.5%**
- **Annual Job Openings: Fewer than 500**

The job openings listed here are shared with 17-2121.01 Marine Engineers and 17-2121.02 Marine Architects.

Design, develop, and evaluate the operation of marine vessels; ship machinery; and related equipment, such as power supply and propulsion systems.

No task data available.

GOE Information—Interest Area: 15. Scientific Research, Engineering, and Mathematics. Work Group: 15.07. Research and Design Engineering. Note: The Department of Labor has not collected some data for this job, so it has fewer details than the other descriptions.

Instructional Program—Naval Architecture and Marine Engineering.

Related SOC Job—17-2121 Marine Engineers and Naval Architects. Related OOH Job—Engineers. Related DOT Job—No data available.

17-2121.01 Marine Engineers

- **Education/Training Required:** Bachelor's degree
- **Employed:** 6,550
- **Annual Earnings:** $72,920
- **Growth:** 8.5%
- **Annual Job Openings:** Fewer than 500

The job openings listed here are shared with 17-2121.00 Marine Engineers and Naval Architects and 17-2121.02 Marine Architects.

Design, develop, and take responsibility for the installation of ship machinery and related equipment, including propulsion machines and power supply systems.

Prepare, or direct the preparation of, product or system layouts and detailed drawings and schematics. Inspect marine equipment and machinery in order to draw up work requests and job specifications. Conduct analytical, environmental, operational, or performance studies in order to develop designs for products such as marine engines, equipment, and structures. Design and oversee testing, installation, and repair of marine apparatus and equipment. Prepare plans, estimates, design and construction schedules, and contract specifications, including any special provisions. Investigate and observe tests on machinery and equipment for compliance with standards. Coordinate activities with regulatory bodies in order to ensure repairs and alterations are at minimum cost consistent with safety. Prepare technical reports for use by engineering, management, or sales personnel. Conduct environmental, operational, or performance tests on marine machinery and equipment. Maintain contact with, and formulate reports for, contractors and clients to ensure completion of work at minimum cost. Evaluate operation of marine equipment during acceptance testing and shakedown cruises. Analyze data in order to determine feasibility of product proposals. Determine conditions under which tests are to be conducted, as well as sequences and phases of test operations. Procure materials needed to repair marine equipment and machinery. Confer with research personnel to clarify or resolve problems and to develop or modify designs. Review work requests and compare them with previous work completed on ships to ensure that costs are economically sound. Act as liaisons between ships' captains and shore personnel to ensure that schedules and budgets are maintained and that ships are operated safely and efficiently. Perform monitoring activities to ensure that ships comply with international regulations and standards for lifesaving equipment and pollution preventatives. Check, test, and maintain automatic controls and alarm systems. Supervise other engineers and crewmembers and train them for routine and emergency duties.

GOE Information—Interest Area: 15. Scientific Research, Engineering, and Mathematics. Work Group: 15.07. Research and Design Engineering. Personality Type—Realistic. Realistic occupa-

tions frequently involve work activities that include practical, hands-on problems and solutions. They often deal with plants; animals; and real-world materials like wood, tools, and machinery. Many of the occupations require working outside and do not involve a lot of paperwork or working closely with others. Work Values—Creativity; Ability Utilization; Authority; Autonomy; Social Status; Responsibility. Skills—Science; Technology Design; Installation; Mathematics; Operations Analysis; Systems Analysis. Abilities—*Cognitive:* Mathematical Reasoning; Number Facility; Deductive Reasoning; Written Expression; Visualization; Written Comprehension. *Psychomotor:* Reaction Time; Multilimb Coordination; Control Precision; Finger Dexterity; Arm-Hand Steadiness. *Physical:* Static Strength; Trunk Strength. *Sensory:* Visual Color Discrimination; Hearing Sensitivity; Far Vision; Depth Perception; Auditory Attention; Speech Recognition. General Work Activities—*Information Input:* Monitoring Processes, Materials, or Surroundings; Inspecting Equipment, Structures, or Materials; Getting Information. *Mental Process:* Thinking Creatively; Organizing, Planning, and Prioritizing; Updating and Using Relevant Knowledge. *Work Output:* Documenting or Recording Information; Drafting and Specifying Technical Devices; Interacting With Computers. *Interacting with Others:* Coordinating the Work and Activities of Others; Providing Consultation and Advice to Others; Communicating with Persons Outside Organization. Physical Work Conditions—Outdoors; Noisy; Sitting. Other Job Characteristics—Need to Be Exact or Accurate; Repeat Same Tasks; Errors Have Important Consequences.

Experience—Job Zone 4. A minimum of two to four years of work-related skill, knowledge, or experience is needed. Job Preparation—SVP 7.0 to less than 8.0—two years to less than 10 years. Knowledges—Design; Engineering and Technology; Mechanical Devices; Physics; Building and Construction; Computers and Electronics. Instructional Program—Naval Architecture and Marine Engineering.

Related SOC Job—17-2121 Marine Engineers and Naval Architects. Related OOH Job—Engineers. Related DOT Jobs—014.061-010 Design Engineer, Marine Equipment; 014.061-014 Marine Engineer; 014.061-018 Research Engineer, Marine Equipment; 014.061-022 Test Engineer, Marine Equipment; 014.167-010 Marine Surveyor; 014.167-014 Port Engineer.

17-2121.02 Marine Architects

- **Education/Training Required:** Bachelor's degree
- **Employed:** 6,550
- **Annual Earnings:** $72,920
- **Growth:** 8.5%
- **Annual Job Openings:** Fewer than 500

The job openings listed here are shared with 17-2121.00 Marine Engineers and Naval Architects and 17-2121.01 Marine Engineers.

Design and oversee construction and repair of marine craft and floating structures such as ships, barges, tugs, dredges, submarines, torpedoes, floats, and buoys. May confer with marine engineers.

Design complete hull and superstructure according to specifications and test data and in conformity with standards of safety, efficiency, and economy. Design layout of craft interior, including cargo space, passenger compartments, ladder wells, and elevators. Study design proposals and specifications to establish basic characteristics of craft, such as size, weight, speed, propulsion, displacement, and draft. Confer with marine engineering personnel to establish arrangement of boiler room equipment and propulsion machinery, heating and ventilating systems, refrigeration equipment, piping, and other functional equipment. Evaluate performance of craft during dock and sea trials to determine design changes and conformance with national and international standards. Oversee construction and testing of prototype in model basin and develop sectional and waterline curves of hull to establish center of gravity, ideal hull form, and buoyancy and stability data.

GOE Information—Interest Area: 15. Scientific Research, Engineering, and Mathematics. **Work Group:** 15.07. Research and Design Engineering. **Personality Type—**Realistic. Realistic occupations frequently involve work activities that include practical, hands-on problems and solutions. They often deal with plants; animals; and real-world materials like wood, tools, and machinery. Many of the occupations require working outside and do not involve a lot of paperwork or working closely with others. **Work Values—**Creativity; Ability Utilization; Social Status; Achievement; Recognition; Autonomy. **Skills—**Science; Mathematics; Operations Analysis; Technology Design; Complex Problem Solving; Systems Analysis. **Abilities—***Cognitive:* Mathematical Reasoning; Visualization; Number Facility; Fluency of Ideas; Written Comprehension; Deductive Reasoning. *Psychomotor:* None met the criteria. *Physical:* None met the criteria. *Sensory:* Far Vision; Visual Color Discrimination; Depth Perception; Speech Recognition; Near Vision; Hearing Sensitivity. **General Work Activities—***Information Input:* Getting Information; Identifying Objects, Actions, and Events; Monitoring Processes, Materials, or Surroundings. *Mental Process:* Updating and Using Relevant Knowledge; Thinking Creatively; Organizing, Planning, and Prioritizing. *Work Output:* Drafting and Specifying Technical Devices; Documenting or Recording Information; Interacting With Computers. *Interacting with Others:* Communicating with Persons Outside Organization; Providing Consultation and Advice to Others; Establishing and Maintaining Interpersonal Relationships. **Physical Work Conditions—**Indoors; Sitting. **Other Job Characteristics—**Need to Be Exact or Accurate; Errors Have Important Consequences.

Experience—Job Zone 4. A minimum of two to four years of work-related skill, knowledge, or experience is needed. **Job Preparation—**SVP 7.0 to less than 8.0—two years to less than 10 years. **Knowledges—**Engineering and Technology; Design; Physics; Building and Construction; Mechanical Devices; Production and Processing. **Instructional Program—**Naval Architecture and Marine Engineering.

Related SOC Job—17-2121 Marine Engineers and Naval Architects. **Related OOH Job—**Engineers. **Related DOT Job—**001.061-014 Architect, Marine.

17-2131.00 Materials Engineers

- **Education/Training Required: Bachelor's degree**
- **Employed: 20,950**
- **Annual Earnings: $69,660**
- **Growth: 12.2%**
- **Annual Job Openings: 2,000**

Evaluate materials and develop machinery and processes to manufacture materials for use in products that must meet specialized design and performance specifications. Develop new uses for known materials. Includes those working with composite materials or specializing in one type of material, such as graphite, metal and metal alloys, ceramics and glass, plastics and polymers, and naturally occurring materials.

Analyze product failure data and laboratory test results in order to determine causes of problems and develop solutions. Monitor material performance and evaluate material deterioration. Supervise the work of technologists, technicians, and other engineers and scientists. Design and direct the testing and/or control of processing procedures. Evaluate technical specifications and economic factors relating to process or product design objectives. Conduct or supervise tests on raw materials or finished products in order to ensure their quality. Perform managerial functions such as preparing proposals and budgets, analyzing labor costs, and writing reports. Solve problems in a number of engineering fields, such as mechanical, chemical, electrical, civil, nuclear, and aerospace. Plan and evaluate new projects, consulting with other engineers and corporate executives as necessary. Review new product plans and make recommendations for material selection based on design objectives, such as strength, weight, heat resistance, electrical conductivity, and cost. Design processing plants and equipment. Modify properties of metal alloys, using thermal and mechanical treatments. Guide technical staff engaged in developing materials for specific uses in projected products or devices. Plan and implement laboratory operations for the purpose of developing material and fabrication procedures that meet cost, product specification, and performance standards. Determine appropriate methods for fabricating and joining materials. Conduct training sessions on new material products, applications, or manufacturing methods for customers and their employees. Supervise production and testing processes in industrial settings such as metal refining facilities, smelting or foundry operations, or non-metallic materials production operations. Write for technical magazines, journals, and trade association publications. Replicate the characteristics of materials and their components with computers. Teach in colleges and universities.

GOE Information—Interest Area: 15. Scientific Research, Engineering, and Mathematics. **Work Group:** 15.07. Research and Design Engineering. **Personality Type—**Investigative. Investigative occupations frequently involve working with ideas and require an extensive amount of thinking. These occupations can involve searching for facts and figuring out problems mentally. **Work Values—**Creativity; Ability Utilization; Responsibility; Autonomy; Social Status; Working Conditions. **Skills—**Science; Mathematics; Quality Control Analysis; Reading Comprehension; Troubleshooting; Technology Design. **Abilities—***Cognitive:* Mathematical Reasoning; Number Facility; Written Expression; Originality; Category Flexibility; Visualization. *Psychomotor:* None met the criteria. *Physical:* None met the criteria. *Sensory:* Visual Color Discrimination; Near Vision; Speech Clarity; Far Vision; Auditory Attention. **General Work Activities—***Information Input:* Monitoring Processes, Materials, or Surroundings; Getting Information; Identifying Objects, Actions, and Events. *Mental Process:* Processing Information; Thinking Creatively; Analyzing Data or Information. *Work Output:* Documenting or Recording Information; Drafting and Specifying Technical Devices; Interacting With Computers. *Interacting with Others:* Communicating with Other Workers; Establishing and Maintaining Interpersonal Relationships; Providing Consultation and Advice to Others. **Physical Work Conditions—**Indoors; Noisy; Contaminants; Sitting. **Other Job Characteristics—**Need to Be Exact or Accurate; Errors Have Important Consequences.

Experience—Job Zone 4. A minimum of two to four years of work-related skill, knowledge, or experience is needed. **Job Preparation—**SVP 7.0 to less than 8.0—two years to less than 10 years. **Knowledges—**Engineering and Technology; Chemistry; Physics; Design; Mathematics; Mechanical Devices. **Instructional Programs—**Ceramic Sciences and Engineering; Materials Engineering; Metallurgical Engineering.

Related SOC Job—17-2131 Materials Engineers. **Related OOH Job**—Engineers. **Related DOT Jobs**—006.061-010 Ceramic Design Engineer; 006.061-014 Ceramic Engineer; 006.061-018 Ceramic Research Engineer; 006.061-022 Ceramics Test Engineer; 011.061-010 Foundry Metallurgist; 011.061-014 Metallographer; 011.061-018 Metallurgist, Extractive; 011.061-022 Metallurgist, Physical; 011.061-026 Welding Engineer; 019.061-014 Materials Engineer.

17-2141.00 Mechanical Engineers

- **Education/Training Required: Bachelor's degree**
- **Employed: 220,750**
- **Annual Earnings: $67,590**
- **Growth: 11.1%**
- **Annual Job Openings: 11,000**

Perform engineering duties in planning and designing tools, engines, machines, and other mechanically functioning equipment. Oversee installation, operation, maintenance, and repair of such equipment as centralized heat, gas, water, and steam systems.

Read and interpret blueprints, technical drawings, schematics, and computer-generated reports. Confer with engineers and other personnel to implement operating procedures, resolve system malfunctions, and provide technical information. Research and analyze customer design proposals, specifications, manuals, and other data to evaluate the feasibility, cost, and maintenance requirements of designs or applications. Specify system components or direct modification of products to ensure conformance with engineering design and performance specifications. Research, design, evaluate, install, operate, and maintain mechanical products, equipment, systems, and processes to meet requirements, applying knowledge of engineering principles. Investigate equipment failures and difficulties to diagnose faulty operation and to make recommendations to maintenance crew. Assist drafters in developing the structural design of products, using drafting tools or computer-assisted design (CAD) or drafting equipment and software. Provide feedback to design engineers on customer problems and needs. Oversee installation, operation, maintenance, and repair to ensure that machines and equipment are installed and functioning according to specifications. Conduct research that tests and analyzes the feasibility, design, operation, and performance of equipment, components, and systems. Recommend design modifications to eliminate machine or system malfunctions. Develop and test models of alternate designs and processing methods to assess feasibility, operating condition effects, possible new applications, and necessity of modification. Develop, coordinate, and monitor all aspects of production, including selection of manufacturing methods, fabrication, and operation of product designs. Estimate costs and submit bids for engineering, construction, or extraction projects and prepare contract documents. Perform personnel functions such as supervision of production workers, technicians, technologists, and other engineers or design of evaluation programs. Solicit new business and provide technical customer service. Establish and coordinate the maintenance and safety procedures, service schedule, and supply of materials required to maintain machines and equipment in the prescribed condition.

GOE Information—Interest Area: 15. Scientific Research, Engineering, and Mathematics. **Work Group:** 15.07. Research and Design Engineering. **Personality Type**—Realistic. Realistic occupations frequently involve work activities that include practical, hands-on problems and solutions. They often deal with plants; animals; and real-world materials like wood, tools, and machinery. Many of the occupations require working outside and do not involve a lot of

paperwork or working closely with others. **Work Values**—Creativity; Autonomy; Social Status; Authority; Ability Utilization; Responsibility. **Skills**—Science; Operations Analysis; Installation; Complex Problem Solving; Mathematics; Systems Analysis. **Abilities**—*Cognitive:* Number Facility; Mathematical Reasoning; Originality; Visualization; Written Comprehension; Oral Comprehension. *Psychomotor:* Finger Dexterity. *Physical:* Trunk Strength. *Sensory:* Visual Color Discrimination; Hearing Sensitivity; Near Vision; Auditory Attention; Far Vision; Depth Perception. **General Work Activities**—*Information Input:* Identifying Objects, Actions, and Events; Getting Information; Monitoring Processes, Materials, or Surroundings. *Mental Process:* Making Decisions and Solving Problems; Organizing, Planning, and Prioritizing; Processing Information. *Work Output:* Interacting With Computers; Drafting and Specifying Technical Devices; Documenting or Recording Information. *Interacting with Others:* Communicating with Other Workers; Establishing and Maintaining Interpersonal Relationships; Communicating with Persons Outside Organization. **Physical Work Conditions**—Indoors; Sitting. **Other Job Characteristics**—Need to Be Exact or Accurate; Errors Have Important Consequences.

Experience—Job Zone 4. A minimum of two to four years of work-related skill, knowledge, or experience is needed. **Job Preparation**—SVP 7.0 to less than 8.0—two years to less than 10 years. **Knowledges**—Design; Engineering and Technology; Mechanical Devices; Production and Processing; Physics; Administration and Management. **Instructional Program**—Mechanical Engineering.

Related SOC Job—17-2141 Mechanical Engineers. **Related OOH Job**—Engineers. **Related DOT Jobs**—007.061-010 Automotive Engineer; 007.061-014 Mechanical Engineer; 007.061-018 Mechanical-Design Engineer, Facilities; 007.061-022 Mechanical-Design Engineer, Products; 007.061-026 Tool Designer; 007.061-030 Tool-Designer Apprentice; 007.061-034 Utilization Engineer; 007.061-038 Applications Engineer, Manufacturing; 007.061-042 Stress Analyst; 007.161-022 Mechanical Research Engineer; 007.161-034 Test Engineer, Mechanical Equipment; 007.161-038 Solar-Energy-Systems Designer.

17-2151.00 Mining and Geological Engineers, Including Mining Safety Engineers

- **Education/Training Required: Bachelor's degree**
- **Employed: 5,680**
- **Annual Earnings: $70,070**
- **Growth: −1.5%**
- **Annual Job Openings: Fewer than 500**

Determine the location and plan the extraction of coal, metallic ores, nonmetallic minerals, and building materials such as stone and gravel. Work involves conducting preliminary surveys of deposits or undeveloped mines and planning their development; examining deposits or mines to determine whether they can be worked at a profit; making geological and topographical surveys; evolving methods of mining best suited to character, type, and size of deposits; and supervising mining operations.

Inspect mining areas for unsafe structures, equipment, and working conditions. Select locations and plan underground or surface mining operations, specifying processes, labor usage, and equipment that will result in safe, economical, and environmentally sound extraction of minerals and ores. Examine maps, deposits, drilling locations, or mines to determine the location, size, accessibility, contents, value, and potential profitability of mineral, oil, and gas deposits. Supervise and coordinate the work of technicians, technologists, survey personnel, engineers, scientists, and other mine personnel. Prepare schedules, reports, and estimates of the costs involved in developing and operating mines. Monitor mine production rates to assess operational effectiveness. Design, implement, and monitor the development of mines, facilities, systems, or equipment. Select or develop mineral location, extraction, and production methods based on factors such as safety, cost, and deposit characteristics. Prepare technical reports for use by mining, engineering, and management personnel. Implement and coordinate mine safety programs, including the design and maintenance of protective and rescue equipment and safety devices. Test air to detect toxic gases and recommend measures to remove them, such as installation of ventilation shafts. Design, develop, and implement computer applications for use in mining operations such as mine design, modeling, or mapping or for monitoring mine conditions. Select or devise materials-handling methods and equipment to transport ore, waste materials, and mineral products efficiently and economically. Devise solutions to problems of land reclamation and water and air pollution, such as methods of storing excavated soil and returning exhausted mine sites to natural states. Lay out, direct, and supervise mine construction operations, such as the construction of shafts and tunnels. Evaluate data to develop new mining products, equipment, or processes. Conduct or direct mining experiments to test or prove research findings. Design mining and mineral treatment equipment and machinery in collaboration with other engineering specialists.

GOE Information—Interest Area: 01. Agriculture and Natural Resources. **Work Group:** 01.02. Resource Science/Engineering for Plants, Animals, and the Environment. **Personality Type—** Investigative. Investigative occupations frequently involve working with ideas and require an extensive amount of thinking. These occupations can involve searching for facts and figuring out problems mentally. **Work Values—**Authority; Responsibility; Creativity; Autonomy; Social Status; Ability Utilization. **Skills—**Operations Analysis; Programming; Management of Financial Resources; Science; Mathematics; Management of Material Resources. **Abilities—** *Cognitive:* Number Facility; Mathematical Reasoning; Written Expression; Inductive Reasoning; Category Flexibility; Originality. *Psychomotor:* Reaction Time; Control Precision. *Physical:* None met the criteria. *Sensory:* Far Vision; Auditory Attention; Hearing Sensitivity; Speech Recognition; Visual Color Discrimination; Depth Perception. **General Work Activities—***Information Input:* Getting Information; Monitoring Processes, Materials, or Surroundings; Estimating the Needed Characteristics of Products, Events, or Information. *Mental Process:* Organizing, Planning, and Prioritizing; Making Decisions and Solving Problems; Analyzing Data or Information. *Work Output:* Documenting or Recording Information; Interacting With Computers; Drafting and Specifying Technical Devices. *Interacting with Others:* Communicating with Other Workers; Establishing and Maintaining Interpersonal Relationships; Coordinating the Work and Activities of Others. **Physical Work Conditions—**More Often Indoors Than Outdoors; Very Hot or Cold; Contaminants; Hazardous Equipment; Sitting. **Other Job Characteristics—**Need to Be Exact or Accurate; Errors Have Important Consequences; Repeat Same Tasks.

Experience—Job Zone 4. A minimum of two to four years of work-related skill, knowledge, or experience is needed. **Job Preparation—** SVP 7.0 to less than 8.0—two years to less than 10 years. **Knowledges—**Engineering and Technology; Design; Chemistry; Production and Processing; Physics; Geography. **Instructional Program—**Mining and Mineral Engineering.

Related SOC Job—17-2151 Mining and Geological Engineers, Including Mining Safety Engineers. **Related OOH Job—**Engineers. **Related DOT Jobs—**010.061-010 Design Engineer, Mining-and-Oil-Field Equipment; 010.061-014 Mining Engineer; 010.061-022 Research Engineer, Mining-and-Oil-Well Equipment; 010.061-026 Safety Engineer, Mines; 010.061-030 Test Engineer, Mining-and-Oil-Field Equipment; 168.267-074 Mine Inspector.

17-2161.00 Nuclear Engineers

- **Education/Training Required: Bachelor's degree**
- **Employed: 14,290**
- **Annual Earnings: $88,290**
- **Growth: 7.3%**
- **Annual Job Openings: 1,000**

Conduct research on nuclear engineering problems or apply principles and theory of nuclear science to problems concerned with release, control, and utilization of nuclear energy and nuclear waste disposal.

Examine accidents to obtain data that can be used to design preventive measures. Monitor nuclear facility operations to identify any design, construction, or operation practices that violate safety regulations and laws or that could jeopardize the safety of operations. Keep abreast of developments and changes in the nuclear field by reading technical journals and by independent study and research. Perform experiments that will provide information about acceptable methods of nuclear material usage, nuclear fuel reclamation, and waste disposal. Design and oversee construction and operation of nuclear reactors and power plants and nuclear fuels reprocessing and reclamation systems. Design and develop nuclear equipment such as reactor cores, radiation shielding, and associated instrumentation and control mechanisms. Initiate corrective actions or order plant shutdowns in emergency situations. Recommend preventive measures to be taken in the handling of nuclear technology, based on data obtained from operations monitoring or from evaluation of test results. Write operational instructions to be used in nuclear plant operation and nuclear fuel and waste handling and disposal. Conduct tests of nuclear fuel behavior and cycles and performance of nuclear machinery and equipment to optimize performance of existing plants. Direct operating and maintenance activities of operational nuclear power plants to ensure efficiency and conformity to safety standards. Synthesize analyses of test results and use the results to prepare technical reports of findings and recommendations. Prepare construction project proposals that include cost estimates and discuss proposals with interested parties such as vendors, contractors, and nuclear facility review boards. Analyze available data and consult with other scientists to determine parameters of experimentation and suitability of analytical models. Design and direct nuclear research projects to discover facts, to test or modify theoretical models, or to develop new theoretical models or new uses for current models.

GOE Information—Interest Area: 15. Scientific Research, Engineering, and Mathematics. **Work Group:** 15.07. Research and Design Engineering. **Personality Type—**Investigative. Investigative occupations frequently involve working with ideas and require an extensive amount of thinking. These occupations can involve searching for facts and figuring out problems mentally. **Work Values—** Creativity; Ability Utilization; Social Status; Responsibility; Authority; Autonomy. **Skills—**Operation Monitoring; Technology Design; Systems Analysis; Systems Evaluation; Quality Control Analysis; Mathematics. **Abilities—***Cognitive:* Mathematical Reasoning; Number Facility; Written Expression; Written Comprehension;

Originality; Oral Comprehension. *Psychomotor:* Finger Dexterity. *Physical:* None met the criteria. *Sensory:* Visual Color Discrimination; Hearing Sensitivity; Speech Recognition; Far Vision; Auditory Attention; Depth Perception. **General Work Activities—***Information Input:* Identifying Objects, Actions, and Events; Monitoring Processes, Materials, or Surroundings; Getting Information. *Mental Process:* Processing Information; Analyzing Data or Information; Evaluating Information Against Standards. *Work Output:* Documenting or Recording Information; Interacting With Computers; Drafting and Specifying Technical Devices. *Interacting with Others:* Communicating with Other Workers; Establishing and Maintaining Interpersonal Relationships; Interpreting the Meaning of Information for Others. **Physical Work Conditions—**Indoors; Noisy; Radiation; Sitting. **Other Job Characteristics—**Need to Be Exact or Accurate; Errors Have Important Consequences; Repeat Same Tasks.

Experience—Job Zone 4. A minimum of two to four years of work-related skill, knowledge, or experience is needed. **Job Preparation—**SVP 7.0 to less than 8.0—two years to less than 10 years. **Knowledges—**Engineering and Technology; Physics; Design; Chemistry; Mechanical Devices; Building and Construction. **Instructional Program—**Nuclear Engineering.

Related SOC Job—17-2161 Nuclear Engineers. **Related OOH Job—**Engineers. **Related DOT Jobs—**005.061-042 Waste-Management Engineer, Radioactive Materials; 015.061-010 Design Engineer, Nuclear Equipment; 015.061-014 Nuclear Engineer; 015.061-018 Research Engineer, Nuclear Equipment; 015.061-022 Test Engineer, Nuclear Equipment; 015.061-026 Nuclear-Fuels Reclamation Engineer; 015.061-030 Nuclear-Fuels Research Engineer; 015.067-010 Nuclear-Criticality Safety Engineer; 015.137-010 Radiation-Protection Engineer; 015.167-010 Nuclear-Plant Technical Advisor; others.

17-2171.00 Petroleum Engineers

- **Education/Training Required: Bachelor's degree**
- **Employed: 14,860**
- **Annual Earnings: $93,000**
- **Growth: –0.1%**
- **Annual Job Openings: 1,000**

Devise methods to improve oil and gas well production and determine the need for new or modified tool designs. Oversee drilling and offer technical advice to achieve economical and satisfactory progress.

Assess costs and estimate the production capabilities and economic value of oil and gas wells to evaluate the economic viability of potential drilling sites. Monitor production rates and plan rework processes to improve production. Analyze data to recommend placement of wells and supplementary processes to enhance production. Specify and supervise well modification and stimulation programs to maximize oil and gas recovery. Direct and monitor the completion and evaluation of wells, well testing, or well surveys. Assist engineering and other personnel to solve operating problems. Develop plans for oil and gas field drilling and for product recovery and treatment. Maintain records of drilling and production operations. Confer with scientific, engineering, and technical personnel to resolve design, research, and testing problems. Write technical reports for engineering and management personnel. Evaluate findings to develop, design, or test equipment or processes. Assign work to staff to obtain maximum utilization of personnel. Interpret drilling and testing information for personnel. Design and implement environmental controls on oil and gas operations. Coordinate the installation, maintenance, and operation of mining and oilfield equipment. Supervise the removal of drilling equipment, the removal of any waste, and the safe return of land to structural stability when wells or pockets are exhausted. Inspect oil and gas wells to determine that installations are completed. Simulate reservoir performance for different recovery techniques, using computer models. Take samples to assess the amount and quality of oil, the depth at which resources lie, and the equipment needed to properly extract them. Coordinate activities of workers engaged in research, planning, and development. Design or modify mining and oilfield machinery and tools, applying engineering principles. Test machinery and equipment to ensure that it is safe and conforms to performance specifications. Conduct engineering research experiments to improve or modify mining and oil machinery and operations.

GOE Information—Interest Area: 01. Agriculture and Natural Resources. **Work Group:** 01.02. Resource Science/Engineering for Plants, Animals, and the Environment. **Personality Type—**Realistic. Realistic occupations frequently involve work activities that include practical, hands-on problems and solutions. They often deal with plants; animals; and real-world materials like wood, tools, and machinery. Many of the occupations require working outside and do not involve a lot of paperwork or working closely with others. **Work Values—**Creativity; Social Status; Authority; Ability Utilization; Autonomy; Variety. **Skills—**Management of Financial Resources; Science; Troubleshooting; Operations Analysis; Mathematics; Technology Design. **Abilities—***Cognitive:* Number Facility; Mathematical Reasoning; Written Expression; Originality; Written Comprehension; Inductive Reasoning. *Psychomotor:* None met the criteria. *Physical:* None met the criteria. *Sensory:* Far Vision; Hearing Sensitivity; Visual Color Discrimination; Auditory Attention; Depth Perception; Speech Recognition. **General Work Activities—***Information Input:* Getting Information; Identifying Objects, Actions, and Events; Estimating the Needed Characteristics of Products, Events, or Information. *Mental Process:* Making Decisions and Solving Problems; Organizing, Planning, and Prioritizing; Analyzing Data or Information. *Work Output:* Documenting or Recording Information; Drafting and Specifying Technical Devices; Interacting With Computers. *Interacting with Others:* Communicating with Other Workers; Providing Consultation and Advice to Others; Monitoring and Controlling Resources. **Physical Work Conditions—**Indoors; Sitting. **Other Job Characteristics—**Need to Be Exact or Accurate.

Experience—Job Zone 4. A minimum of two to four years of work-related skill, knowledge, or experience is needed. **Job Preparation—**SVP 7.0 to less than 8.0—two years to less than 10 years. **Knowledges—**Engineering and Technology; Physics; Geography; Chemistry; Design; Economics and Accounting. **Instructional Program—**Petroleum Engineering.

Related SOC Job—17-2171 Petroleum Engineers. **Related OOH Job—**Engineers. **Related DOT Jobs—**010.061-010 Design Engineer, Mining-and-Oil-Field Equipment; 010.061-018 Petroleum Engineer; 010.061-022 Research Engineer, Mining-and-Oil-Well Equipment; 010.061-030 Test Engineer, Mining-and-Oil-Field Equipment; 010.161-010 Chief Engineer, Research; 010.167-010 Chief Engineer; 010.167-014 District Supervisor, Mud-Analysis Well Logging.

17-2199.99 Engineers, All Other

- **Education/Training Required: Bachelor's degree**
- **Employed: 152,940**
- **Annual Earnings: $77,150**
- **Growth: 15.4%**
- **Annual Job Openings: 19,000**

All engineers not listed separately.

No task data available.

Note: The Department of Labor has not collected some data for this job, so it has fewer details than the other descriptions.

Related SOC Job—17-2199 Engineers, All Other. **Related OOH Job**—Engineers. **Related DOT Jobs**—019.061-010 Biomedical Engineer; 019.061-018 Optical Engineer; 019.061-022 Ordnance Engineer; 019.061-026 Reliability Engineer; 019.081-010 Maintainability Engineer; 019.081-014 Photographic Engineer; 019.187-010 Packaging Engineer.

17-3000 Drafters, Engineering, and Mapping Technicians

17-3011.00 Architectural and Civil Drafters

- **Education/Training Required: Postsecondary vocational training**
- **Employed: 101,040**
- **Annual Earnings: $40,390**
- **Growth: 4.6%**
- **Annual Job Openings: 9,000**

The job openings listed here are shared with 17-3011.01 Architectural Drafters and 17-3011.02 Civil Drafters.

Prepare detailed drawings of architectural and structural features of buildings or drawings and topographical relief maps used in civil engineering projects, such as highways, bridges, and public works. Utilize knowledge of building materials, engineering practices, and mathematics to complete drawings.

No task data available.

GOE Information—Interest Area: 02. Architecture and Construction. **Work Group:** 02.03. Architecture/Construction Engineering Technologies. **Note:** The Department of Labor has not collected some data for this job, so it has fewer details than the other descriptions.

Instructional Programs—Architectural Drafting and Architectural CAD/CADD; Architectural Technology/Technician; CAD/CADD Drafting and/or Design Technology/Technician; Civil Drafting and Civil Engineering CAD/CADD; Drafting and Design Technology/Technician, General.

Related SOC Job—17-3011 Architectural and Civil Drafters. **Related OOH Job**—Drafters. **Related DOT Job**—No data available.

17-3011.01 Architectural Drafters

- **Education/Training Required: Postsecondary vocational training**
- **Employed: 101,040**
- **Annual Earnings: $40,390**
- **Growth: 4.6%**
- **Annual Job Openings: 9,000**

The job openings listed here are shared with 17-3011.00 Architectural and Civil Drafters and 17-3011.02 Civil Drafters.

Prepare detailed drawings of architectural designs and plans for buildings and structures according to specifications provided by architect.

Analyze building codes, by-laws, space and site requirements, and other technical documents and reports to determine their effect on architectural designs. Operate computer-aided drafting (CAD) equipment or conventional drafting station to produce designs, working drawings, charts, forms, and records. Coordinate structural, electrical, and mechanical designs and determine a method of presentation to graphically represent building plans. Obtain and assemble data to complete architectural designs, visiting job sites to compile measurements as necessary. Lay out and plan interior room arrangements for commercial buildings, using computer-assisted drafting (CAD) equipment and software. Draw rough and detailed scale plans for foundations, buildings, and structures based on preliminary concepts, sketches, engineering calculations, specification sheets, and other data. Supervise, coordinate, and inspect the work of draftspersons, technicians, and technologists on construction projects. Represent architect on construction site, ensuring builder compliance with design specifications and advising on design corrections under architect's supervision. Check dimensions of materials to be used and assign numbers to lists of materials. Determine procedures and instructions to be followed according to design specifications and quantity of required materials. Analyze technical implications of architect's design concept, calculating weights, volumes, and stress factors. Create freehand drawings and lettering to accompany drawings. Prepare colored drawings of landscape and interior designs for presentation to client. Reproduce drawings on copy machines or trace copies of plans and drawings, using transparent paper or cloth, ink, pencil, and standard drafting instruments. Prepare cost estimates, contracts, bidding documents, and technical reports for specific projects under an architect's supervision. Calculate heat loss and gain of buildings and structures to determine required equipment specifications, following standard procedures. Build landscape, architectural, and display models.

GOE Information—Interest Area: 02. Architecture and Construction. **Work Group:** 02.03. Architecture/Construction Engineering Technologies. **Personality Type**—Realistic. Realistic occupations frequently involve work activities that include practical, hands-on problems and solutions. They often deal with plants; animals; and real-world materials like wood, tools, and machinery. Many of the occupations require working outside and do not involve a lot of paperwork or working closely with others. **Work Values**—Working Conditions; Independence; Ability Utilization; Social Status; Compensation; Moral Values. **Skills**—Operations Analysis; Coordination; Active Learning; Technology Design; Mathematics; Complex Problem Solving. **Abilities**—*Cognitive:* Visualization; Mathematical Reasoning; Deductive Reasoning; Originality; Information Ordering; Fluency of Ideas. *Psychomotor:* Arm-Hand Steadiness; Finger Dexterity; Manual Dexterity; Control Precision. *Physical:* None met the criteria. *Sensory:* Visual Color Discrimination; Near Vision; Far Vision; Depth Perception; Speech Recognition; Speech Clarity. **General Work Activities**—*Information Input:* Monitoring Processes, Materials, or Surroundings; Getting Information; Identifying Objects, Actions, and Events. *Mental Process:* Thinking Creatively; Organizing, Planning, and Prioritizing; Evaluating Information Against Standards. *Work Output:* Drafting and Specifying Technical Devices; Interacting With Computers; Documenting or Recording Information. *Interacting with Others:* Communicating with Persons Outside Organization; Establishing and Maintaining Interpersonal Relationships; Communicating with Other Workers. **Physical Work Conditions**—Indoors; Noisy; Sitting; Using Hands on Objects, Tools, or Controls; Repetitive Motions.

Other Job Characteristics—Need to Be Exact or Accurate; Repeat Same Tasks.

Experience—Job Zone 3. Previous work-related skill, knowledge, or experience is required. **Job Preparation**—SVP 6.0 to less than 7.0—more than one year and less than four years. **Knowledges**—Design; Building and Construction; Engineering and Technology; Computers and Electronics; Mathematics; Public Safety and Security. **Instructional Programs**—Architectural Drafting and Architectural CAD/CADD; Architectural Technology/Technician; CAD/CADD Drafting and/or Design Technology/Technician; Civil Drafting and Civil Engineering CAD/CADD; Drafting and Design Technology/Technician, General.

Related SOC Job—17-3011 Architectural and Civil Drafters. **Related OOH Job**—Drafters. **Related DOT Jobs**—001.261-010 Drafter, Architectural; 001.261-014 Drafter, Landscape; 005.281-014 Drafter, Structural; 014.281-010 Drafter, Marine; 017.261-026 Drafter, Commercial; 017.261-034 Drafter, Heating and Ventilating; 017.261-038 Drafter, Plumbing; 017.281-018 Drafter, Assistant; 017.281-030 Drafter, Oil and Gas.

17-3011.02 Civil Drafters

- **Education/Training Required: Postsecondary vocational training**
- **Employed: 101,040**
- **Annual Earnings: $40,390**
- **Growth: 4.6%**
- **Annual Job Openings: 9,000**

The job openings listed here are shared with 17-3011.00 Architectural and Civil Drafters and 17-3011.01 Architectural Drafters.

Prepare drawings and topographical and relief maps used in civil engineering projects, such as highways, bridges, pipelines, flood control projects, and water and sewerage control systems.

Produce drawings, using computer-assisted drafting systems (CAD) or drafting machines or by hand, using compasses, dividers, protractors, triangles, and other drafting devices. Draft plans and detailed drawings for structures, installations, and construction projects such as highways, sewage disposal systems, and dikes, working from sketches or notes. Draw maps, diagrams, and profiles, using cross-sections and surveys, to represent elevations, topographical contours, subsurface formations, and structures. Correlate, interpret, and modify data obtained from topographical surveys, well logs, and geophysical prospecting reports. Finish and duplicate drawings and documentation packages according to required mediums and specifications for reproduction, using blueprinting, photography, or other duplicating methods. Review rough sketches, drawings, specifications, and other engineering data received from civil engineers to ensure that they conform to design concepts. Supervise and train other technologists, technicians, and drafters. Supervise or conduct field surveys, inspections, or technical investigations to obtain data required to revise construction drawings. Determine the order of work and method of presentation, such as orthographic or isometric drawing. Calculate excavation tonnage and prepare graphs and fill-hauling diagrams for use in earth-moving operations. Explain drawings to production or construction teams and provide adjustments as necessary. Locate and identify symbols located on topographical surveys to denote geological and geophysical formations or oilfield installations. Calculate weights, volumes, and stress factors and their implications for technical aspects of designs. Determine quality, cost, strength, and quantity of required materials and enter figures on materials lists. Plot characteristics of boreholes for oil and gas wells from photographic subsurface survey recordings and other data, representing depth, degree, and direction of inclination.

GOE Information—**Interest Area:** 02. Architecture and Construction. **Work Group:** 02.03. Architecture/Construction Engineering Technologies. **Personality Type**—Realistic. Realistic occupations frequently involve work activities that include practical, hands-on problems and solutions. They often deal with plants; animals; and real-world materials like wood, tools, and machinery. Many of the occupations require working outside and do not involve a lot of paperwork or working closely with others. **Work Values**—Working Conditions; Ability Utilization; Moral Values; Independence; Advancement; Activity. **Skills**—Mathematics; Operations Analysis; Technology Design; Coordination; Active Learning; Instructing. **Abilities**—*Cognitive:* Visualization; Mathematical Reasoning; Number Facility; Flexibility of Closure; Originality; Written Comprehension. *Psychomotor:* Arm-Hand Steadiness; Finger Dexterity. *Physical:* None met the criteria. *Sensory:* Far Vision; Near Vision; Visual Color Discrimination; Depth Perception; Speech Recognition; Speech Clarity. **General Work Activities**—*Information Input:* Getting Information; Identifying Objects, Actions, and Events; Monitoring Processes, Materials, or Surroundings. *Mental Process:* Updating and Using Relevant Knowledge; Organizing, Planning, and Prioritizing; Evaluating Information Against Standards. *Work Output:* Drafting and Specifying Technical Devices; Interacting With Computers; Documenting or Recording Information. *Interacting with Others:* Communicating with Other Workers; Establishing and Maintaining Interpersonal Relationships; Communicating with Persons Outside Organization. **Physical Work Conditions**—Indoors; Sitting; Repetitive Motions. **Other Job Characteristics**—Need to Be Exact or Accurate; Repeat Same Tasks; Automation.

Experience—Job Zone 3. Previous work-related skill, knowledge, or experience is required. **Job Preparation**—SVP 6.0 to less than 7.0—more than one year and less than four years. **Knowledges**—Design; Engineering and Technology; Geography; Computers and Electronics; Mathematics; Law and Government. **Instructional Programs**—Architectural Drafting and Architectural CAD/CADD; Architectural Technology/Technician; CAD/CADD Drafting and/or Design Technology/Technician; Civil Drafting and Civil Engineering CAD/CADD; Drafting and Design Technology/Technician, General.

Related SOC Job—17-3011 Architectural and Civil Drafters. **Related OOH Job**—Drafters. **Related DOT Jobs**—005.281-010 Drafter, Civil; 010.281-010 Drafter, Directional Survey; 010.281-014 Drafter, Geological; 010.281-018 Drafter, Geophysical.

17-3012.00 Electrical and Electronics Drafters

- **Education/Training Required: Postsecondary vocational training**
- **Employed: 30,270**
- **Annual Earnings: $45,550**
- **Growth: 1.2%**
- **Annual Job Openings: 3,000**

The job openings listed here are shared with 17-3012.01 Electrical Drafters and 17-3012.02 Electronics Drafters.

Prepare wiring diagrams, circuit board assembly diagrams, and layout drawings used for manufacture, installation, and repair of electrical equipment in factories, power plants, and buildings.

No task data available.

GOE Information—Interest Area: 15. Scientific Research, Engineering, and Mathematics. **Work Group:** 15.09. Engineering Technology. **Note:** The Department of Labor has not collected some data for this job, so it has fewer details than the other descriptions.

Instructional Program—Electrical/Electronics Drafting and Electrical/Electronics CAD/CADD.

Related SOC Job—17-3012 Electrical and Electronics Drafters. **Related OOH Job**—Drafters. **Related DOT Job**—No data available.

17-3012.01 Electronic Drafters

- **Education/Training Required:** Postsecondary vocational training
- **Employed:** 30,270
- **Annual Earnings:** $45,550
- **Growth:** 1.2%
- **Annual Job Openings:** 3,000

The job openings listed here are shared with 17-3012.00 Electrical and Electronics Drafters and 17-3012.02 Electronics Drafters.

Draw wiring diagrams, circuit board assembly diagrams, schematics, and layout drawings used for manufacture, installation, and repair of electronic equipment.

Draft detail and assembly drawings of design components, circuitry, and printed circuit boards, using computer-assisted equipment or standard drafting techniques and devices. Consult with engineers to discuss and interpret design concepts and determine requirements of detailed working drawings. Locate files relating to specified design project in database library, load program into computer, and record completed job data. Examine electronic schematics and supporting documents to develop, compute, and verify specifications for drafting data, such as configuration of parts, dimensions, and tolerances. Supervise and coordinate work activities of workers engaged in drafting, designing layouts, assembling, and testing printed circuit boards. Compare logic element configuration on display screen with engineering schematics and calculate figures to convert, redesign, and modify element. Review work orders and procedural manuals and confer with vendors and design staff to resolve problems and modify design. Review blueprints to determine customer requirements and consult with assembler regarding schematics, wiring procedures, and conductor paths. Train students to use drafting machines and to prepare schematic diagrams, block diagrams, control drawings, logic diagrams, integrated circuit drawings, and interconnection diagrams. Generate computer tapes of final layout design to produce layered photo masks and photo plotting design onto film. Select drill size to drill test head, according to test design and specifications, and submit guide layout to designated department. Key and program specified commands and engineering specifications into computer system to change functions and test final layout. Copy drawings of printed circuit board fabrication, using print machine or blueprinting procedure. Plot electrical test points on layout sheets and draw schematics for wiring test fixture heads to frames.

GOE Information—Interest Area: 15. Scientific Research, Engineering, and Mathematics. **Work Group:** 15.09. Engineering Technology. **Personality Type**—Realistic. Realistic occupations frequently involve work activities that include practical, hands-on problems and solutions. They often deal with plants; animals; and real-world materials like wood, tools, and machinery. Many of the occupations require working outside and do not involve a lot of paperwork or working closely with others. **Work Values**—Working Conditions; Ability Utilization; Social Status; Compensation; Authority; Advancement. **Skills**—Technology Design; Operations Analysis; Installation; Mathematics; Equipment Selection; Negotiation. **Abilities**—*Cognitive:* Visualization; Mathematical Reasoning; Written Comprehension; Oral Comprehension; Oral Expression; Written Expression. *Psychomotor:* Finger Dexterity; Arm-Hand Steadiness. *Physical:* None met the criteria. *Sensory:* Visual Color Discrimination; Near Vision. **General Work Activities**—*Information Input:* Getting Information; Identifying Objects, Actions, and Events; Monitoring Processes, Materials, or Surroundings. *Mental Process:* Updating and Using Relevant Knowledge; Thinking Creatively; Processing Information. *Work Output:* Drafting and Specifying Technical Devices; Interacting With Computers; Documenting or Recording Information. *Interacting with Others:* Communicating with Other Workers; Establishing and Maintaining Interpersonal Relationships; Communicating with Persons Outside Organization. **Physical Work Conditions**—Indoors; Noisy; Sitting; Using Hands on Objects, Tools, or Controls; Repetitive Motions. **Other Job Characteristics**—Need to Be Exact or Accurate; Repeat Same Tasks; Automation.

Experience—Job Zone 3. Previous work-related skill, knowledge, or experience is required. **Job Preparation**—SVP 6.0 to less than 7.0—more than one year and less than four years. **Knowledges**—Design; Engineering and Technology; Mechanical Devices; Physics; Telecommunications; Mathematics. **Instructional Program**—Electrical/Electronics Drafting and Electrical/Electronics CAD/CADD.

Related SOC Job—17-3012 Electrical and Electronics Drafters. **Related OOH Job**—Drafters. **Related DOT Jobs**—003.131-010 Supervisor, Drafting and Printed Circuit Design; 003.261-018 Integrated Circuit Layout Designer; 003.261-022 Printed Circuit Designer; 003.281-014 Drafter, Electronic; 003.362-010 Design Technician, Computer-Aided; 017.261-014 Design Drafter, Electromechanisms; 726.364-014 Test Fixture Designer.

17-3012.02 Electrical Drafters

- **Education/Training Required:** Postsecondary vocational training
- **Employed:** 30,270
- **Annual Earnings:** $45,550
- **Growth:** 1.2%
- **Annual Job Openings:** 3,000

The job openings listed here are shared with 17-3012.00 Electrical and Electronics Drafters and 17-3012.01 Electrical Drafters.

Develop specifications and instructions for installation of voltage transformers, overhead or underground cables, and related electrical equipment used to conduct electrical energy from transmission lines or high-voltage distribution lines to consumers.

Use computer-aided drafting equipment and/or conventional drafting stations; technical handbooks; tables; calculators; and traditional drafting tools such as boards, pencils, protractors, and T-squares. Draft working drawings, wiring diagrams, wiring connection specifications, or cross-sections of underground cables as required for instructions to installation crew. Confer with engineering staff and other personnel to resolve problems. Draw master sketches to scale, showing relation of proposed installations to existing facilities and exact specifications and dimensions. Measure factors that affect installation and arrangement of equipment, such as distances to be spanned by wire and cable. Assemble documentation packages and produce drawing sets, which are then checked by an engineer or an architect. Review completed construction drawings and cost estimates for accuracy and conformity to standards and regulations. Prepare and interpret specifications, calculating weights, volumes, and stress factors. Explain drawings to production or construction teams and provide adjustments as necessary. Supervise and train other technologists, technicians, and drafters. Study work order requests to determine type of service, such as lighting or power, demanded by installation. Visit proposed installation sites and draw rough sketches of location. Determine the order of work and the method of presentation, such as orthographic or isometric drawing. Reproduce working drawings on copy machines or trace drawings in ink. Write technical reports and draw charts that display statistics and data.

GOE Information—Interest Area: 15. Scientific Research, Engineering, and Mathematics. **Work Group:** 15.09. Engineering Technology. **Personality Type—**Conventional. Conventional occupations frequently involve following set procedures and routines. These occupations can include working with data and details more than with ideas. Usually there is a clear line of authority to follow. **Work Values—**Authority; Ability Utilization; Autonomy; Creativity; Advancement; Achievement. **Skills—**Mathematics; Active Learning; Installation; Critical Thinking; Management of Personnel Resources; Quality Control Analysis. **Abilities—***Cognitive:* Written Expression; Visualization; Mathematical Reasoning; Written Comprehension; Information Ordering; Number Facility. *Psychomotor:* None met the criteria. *Physical:* None met the criteria. *Sensory:* Far Vision; Near Vision. **General Work Activities—***Information Input:* Monitoring Processes, Materials, or Surroundings; Identifying Objects, Actions, and Events; Getting Information. *Mental Process:* Updating and Using Relevant Knowledge; Processing Information; Thinking Creatively. *Work Output:* Drafting and Specifying Technical Devices; Interacting With Computers; Documenting or Recording Information. *Interacting with Others:* Establishing and Maintaining Interpersonal Relationships; Communicating with Other Workers; Communicating with Persons Outside Organization. **Physical Work Conditions—**Indoors; Sitting. **Other Job Characteristics—**Need to Be Exact or Accurate; Repeat Same Tasks.

Experience—Job Zone 3. Previous work-related skill, knowledge, or experience is required. **Job Preparation—**SVP 6.0 to less than 7.0—more than one year and less than four years. **Knowledges—**Design; Engineering and Technology; Building and Construction; Computers and Electronics; Telecommunications; Clerical Practices. **Instructional Program—**Electrical/Electronics Drafting and Electrical/Electronics CAD/CADD.

Related SOC Job—17-3012 Electrical and Electronics Drafters. **Related OOH Job—**Drafters. **Related DOT Jobs—**003.281-010 Drafter, Electrical; 019.161-010 Supervisor, Estimator, and Drafter; 019.261-014 Estimator and Drafter.

17-3013.00 Mechanical Drafters

- **Education/Training Required: Postsecondary vocational training**
- **Employed: 74,650**
- **Annual Earnings: $43,350**
- **Growth: 5.5%**
- **Annual Job Openings: 7,000**

Prepare detailed working diagrams of machinery and mechanical devices, including dimensions, fastening methods, and other engineering information.

Develop detailed design drawings and specifications for mechanical equipment, dies, tools, and controls, using computer-assisted drafting (CAD) equipment. Coordinate with and consult other workers to design, lay out, or detail components and systems and to resolve design or other problems. Review and analyze specifications, sketches, drawings, ideas, and related data to assess factors affecting component designs and the procedures and instructions to be followed. Position instructions and comments onto drawings. Compute mathematical formulas to develop and design detailed specifications for components or machinery, using computer-assisted equipment. Modify and revise designs to correct operating deficiencies or to reduce production problems. Design scale or full-size blueprints of specialty items such as furniture and automobile body or chassis components. Check dimensions of materials to be used and assign numbers to the materials. Lay out and draw schematic, orthographic, or angle views to depict functional relationships of components, assemblies, systems, and machines. Confer with customer representatives to review schematics and answer questions pertaining to installation of systems. Draw freehand sketches of designs, trace finished drawings onto designated paper for the reproduction of blueprints, and reproduce working drawings on copy machines. Supervise and train other drafters, technologists, and technicians. Lay out, draw, and reproduce illustrations for reference manuals and technical publications to describe operation and maintenance of mechanical systems. Shade or color drawings to clarify and emphasize details and dimensions or eliminate background, using ink, crayon, airbrush, and overlays.

GOE Information—Interest Area: 15. Scientific Research, Engineering, and Mathematics. **Work Group:** 15.09. Engineering Technology. **Personality Type—**Realistic. Realistic occupations frequently involve work activities that include practical, hands-on problems and solutions. They often deal with plants; animals; and real-world materials like wood, tools, and machinery. Many of the occupations require working outside and do not involve a lot of paperwork or working closely with others. **Work Values—**Working Conditions; Authority; Ability Utilization; Moral Values; Creativity; Activity. **Skills—**Technology Design; Installation; Quality Control Analysis; Equipment Selection; Operations Analysis; Mathematics. **Abilities—***Cognitive:* Mathematical Reasoning; Visualization; Number Facility; Written Expression; Originality; Fluency of Ideas. *Psychomotor:* Arm-Hand Steadiness; Manual Dexterity; Finger Dexterity. *Physical:* None met the criteria. *Sensory:* Visual Color Discrimination; Near Vision; Far Vision; Speech Recognition. **General Work Activities—***Information Input:* Getting Information; Identifying Objects, Actions, and Events; Monitoring Processes, Materials, or Surroundings. *Mental Process:* Processing Information; Updating and Using Relevant Knowledge; Analyzing Data or Information. *Work Output:* Drafting and Specifying Technical Devices; Documenting or Recording Information; Interacting With Computers. *Interacting with Others:* Establishing and Maintaining Interpersonal Relationships; Communicating with Other Workers; Communicating with Persons Outside Organization. **Physical Work Conditions—**Indoors; Noisy; Sitting; Using Hands on Objects, Tools, or Controls; Repetitive Motions. **Other Job Characteristics—**Need to Be Exact or Accurate; Repeat Same Tasks; Errors Have Important Consequences.

Experience—Job Zone 3. Previous work-related skill, knowledge, or experience is required. **Job Preparation—**SVP 6.0 to less than 7.0—more than one year and less than four years. **Knowledges—**Design; Engineering and Technology; Building and Construction; Physics; Mathematics; English Language. **Instructional Program—**Mechanical Drafting and Mechanical Drafting CAD/CADD.

Related SOC Job—17-3013 Mechanical Drafters. Related OOH Job—Drafters. Related DOT Jobs—002.261-010 Drafter, Aeronautical; 003.261-014 Controls Designer; 007.161-010 Die Designer; 007.161-014 Die-Designer Apprentice; 007.161-018 Engineering Assistant, Mechanical Equipment; 007.261-014 Drafter, Castings; 007.261-018 Drafter, Patent; 007.261-022 Drafter, Tool Design; 007.261-560 Mold Designer; 007.281-010 Drafter, Mechanical; 017.261-018 Detailer; 017.261-022 Detailer, Furniture; 017.261-030 Drafter, Detail; 017.261-042 Drafter, Automotive Design; 017.281-010 Auto-Design Detailer; others.

17-3019.99 Drafters, All Other

- **Education/Training Required: Postsecondary vocational training**
- **Employed: 20,870**
- **Annual Earnings: $42,310**
- **Growth: 14.0%**
- **Annual Job Openings: 2,000**

All drafters not listed separately.

No task data available.

Note: The Department of Labor has not collected some data for this job, so it has fewer details than the other descriptions.

Related SOC Job—17-3019 Drafters, All Other. Related OOH Job—Drafters. Related DOT Jobs—007.261-010 Chief Drafter; 017.161-010 Drafter, Chief, Design.

17-3021.00 Aerospace Engineering and Operations Technicians

- **Education/Training Required: Associate degree**
- **Employed: 9,950**
- **Annual Earnings: $52,450**
- **Growth: 8.5%**
- **Annual Job Openings: 1,000**

Operate, install, calibrate, and maintain integrated computer/communications systems consoles; simulators; and other data acquisition, test, and measurement instruments and equipment to launch, track, position, and evaluate air and space vehicles. May record and interpret test data.

Inspect, diagnose, maintain, and operate test setups and equipment to detect malfunctions. Record and interpret test data on parts, assemblies, and mechanisms. Confer with engineering personnel regarding details and implications of test procedures and results. Adjust, repair, or replace faulty components of test setups and equipment. Identify required data, data acquisition plans, and test parameters, setting up equipment to conform to these specifications. Construct and maintain test facilities for aircraft parts and systems according to specifications. Operate and calibrate computer systems and devices to comply with test requirements and to perform data acquisition and analysis. Test aircraft systems under simulated operational conditions, performing systems readiness tests and pre- and post-operational checkouts, to establish design or fabrication parameters. Fabricate and install parts and systems to be tested in test equipment, using hand tools, power tools, and test instruments. Finish vehicle instrumentation and deinstrumentation. Exchange cooling system components in various vehicles.

GOE Information—Interest Area: 15. Scientific Research, Engineering, and Mathematics. **Work Group:** 15.09. Engineering Technology. **Personality Type**—Investigative. Investigative occupations frequently involve working with ideas and require an extensive amount of thinking. These occupations can involve searching for facts and figuring out problems mentally. **Work Values**—Activity; Working Conditions; Compensation; Advancement; Achievement; Social Status. **Skills**—Installation; Technology Design; Operation Monitoring; Troubleshooting; Repairing; Science. **Abilities**—*Cognitive:* Visualization; Mathematical Reasoning; Perceptual Speed; Number Facility; Fluency of Ideas; Oral Comprehension. *Psychomotor:* Finger Dexterity; Manual Dexterity; Arm-Hand Steadiness; Control Precision; Multilimb Coordination. *Physical:* None met the criteria. *Sensory:* Visual Color Discrimination; Hearing Sensitivity; Auditory Attention; Depth Perception; Far Vision. **General Work Activities**—*Information Input:* Monitoring Processes, Materials, or Surroundings; Inspecting Equipment, Structures, or Materials; Identifying Objects, Actions, and Events. *Mental Process:* Updating and Using Relevant Knowledge; Organizing, Planning, and Prioritizing; Processing Information. *Work Output:* Documenting or Recording Information; Drafting and Specifying Technical Devices; Repairing and Maintaining Electronic Equipment. *Interacting with Others:* Communicating with Other Workers; Establishing and Maintaining Interpersonal Relationships; Resolving Conflicts and Negotiating with Others; Communicating with Other Workers. **Physical Work Conditions**—Indoors; Noisy; Sitting; Using Hands on Objects, Tools, or Controls; Repetitive Motions. **Other Job Characteristics**—Need to Be Exact or Accurate; Repeat Same Tasks; Errors Have Important Consequences.

Experience—Job Zone 4. A minimum of two to four years of work-related skill, knowledge, or experience is needed. **Job Preparation**—SVP 7.0 to less than 8.0—two years to less than 10 years. **Knowledges**—Engineering and Technology; Mechanical Devices; Computers and Electronics; Production and Processing; Public Safety and Security; Design. **Instructional Program**—Aeronautical/Aerospace Engineering Technology/Technician.

Related SOC Job—17-3021 Aerospace Engineering and Operations Technicians. Related OOH Job—Engineering Technicians. Related DOT Jobs—002.261-014 Research Mechanic; 002.262-010 Flight-Test Data Acquisition Technician; 710.361-014 Test Equipment Mechanic; 869.261-026 Wind Tunnel Mechanic.

17-3022.00 Civil Engineering Technicians

- **Education/Training Required: Associate degree**
- **Employed: 90,390**
- **Annual Earnings: $39,210**
- **Growth: 14.1%**
- **Annual Job Openings: 10,000**

Apply theory and principles of civil engineering in planning, designing, and overseeing construction and maintenance of structures and facilities under the direction of engineering staff or physical scientists.

Calculate dimensions, square footage, profile and component specifications, and material quantities, using calculator or computer. Draft detailed dimensional drawings and design layouts for projects and to ensure conformance to specifications. Analyze proposed site factors and design maps, graphs, tracings, and diagrams to illustrate findings. Read and review project blueprints and structural specifications to determine dimensions of structure or system and material requirements. Prepare reports and document project activities and data. Confer with supervisor to determine project details such as plan preparation, acceptance testing, and evaluation of field conditions. Inspect project site and evaluate contractor work to detect design malfunctions and ensure conformance to design specifications and applicable codes. Plan and conduct field surveys to locate new sites and analyze details of project sites. Develop plans and estimate costs for installation of systems, utilization of facilities, or construction of structures. Report maintenance problems occurring at project site to supervisor and negotiate changes to resolve system conflicts. Conduct materials test and analysis, using tools and equipment and applying engineering knowledge. Respond to public suggestions and complaints. Evaluate facility to determine suitability for occupancy and square footage availability.

GOE Information—Interest Area: 15. Scientific Research, Engineering, and Mathematics. **Work Group:** 15.09. Engineering Technology. **Personality Type—**Realistic. Realistic occupations frequently involve work activities that include practical, hands-on problems and solutions. They often deal with plants; animals; and real-world materials like wood, tools, and machinery. Many of the occupations require working outside and do not involve a lot of paperwork or working closely with others. **Work Values—**Advancement; Working Conditions; Supervision, Human Relations; Ability Utilization; Activity; Supervision, Technical. **Skills—**Mathematics; Science; Operations Analysis; Complex Problem Solving; Writing; Active Learning. **Abilities—***Cognitive:* Mathematical Reasoning; Number Facility; Visualization; Deductive Reasoning; Written Expression; Written Comprehension. *Psychomotor:* Arm-Hand Steadiness. *Physical:* Trunk Strength. *Sensory:* Far Vision; Near Vision; Speech Recognition; Depth Perception; Visual Color Discrimination; Auditory Attention. **General Work Activities—***Information Input:* Monitoring Processes, Materials, or Surroundings; Estimating the Needed Characteristics of Products, Events, or Information; Identifying Objects, Actions, and Events. *Mental Process:* Updating and Using Relevant Knowledge; Processing Information; Thinking Creatively. *Work Output:* Drafting and Specifying Technical Devices; Documenting or Recording Information; Interacting With Computers. *Interacting with Others:* Communicating with Other Workers; Establishing and Maintaining Interpersonal Relationships; Interpreting the Meaning of Information for Others. **Physical Work Conditions—**More Often Indoors Than Outdoors; Sitting. **Other Job Characteristics—**Need to Be Exact or Accurate; Errors Have Important Consequences; Repeat Same Tasks.

Experience—Job Zone 3. Previous work-related skill, knowledge, or experience is required. **Job Preparation—**SVP 6.0 to less than 7.0—more than one year and less than four years. **Knowledges—**Design; Building and Construction; Engineering and Technology; Mathematics; Computers and Electronics; Transportation. **Instructional Programs—**Civil Engineering Technology/Technician; Construction Engineering Technology/Technician.

Related SOC Job—17-3022 Civil Engineering Technicians. **Related OOH Job—**Engineering Technicians. **Related DOT Jobs—**005.261-014 Civil Engineering Technician; 019.261-018 Facility Planner; 019.261-026 Fire-Protection Engineering Technician; 199.261-014 Parking Analyst.

17-3023.00 Electrical and Electronic Engineering Technicians

- **Education/Training Required: Associate degree**
- **Employed: 165,850**
- **Annual Earnings: $48,040**
- **Growth: 9.8%**
- **Annual Job Openings: 18,000**

The job openings listed here are shared with 17-3023.01 Electronics Engineering Technicians and 17-3023.03 Electrical Engineering Technicians.

Apply electrical and electronic theory and related knowledge, usually under the direction of engineering staff, to design, build, repair, calibrate, and modify electrical components, circuitry, controls, and machinery for subsequent evaluation and use by engineering staff in making engineering design decisions.

No task data available.

GOE Information—Interest Area: 15. Scientific Research, Engineering, and Mathematics. **Work Group:** 15.09. Engineering Technology. **Note:** The Department of Labor has not collected some data for this job, so it has fewer details than the other descriptions.

Instructional Programs—Computer Engineering Technology/Technician; Electrical and Electronic Engineering Technologies/Technicians, Other; Electrical, Electronic and Communications Engineering Technology/Technician; Telecommunications Technology/Technician.

Related SOC Job—17-3023 Electrical and Electronic Engineering Technicians. **Related OOH Job—**Engineering Technicians. **Related DOT Job—**No data available.

17-3023.01 Electronics Engineering Technicians

- **Education/Training Required: Associate degree**
- **Employed: 165,850**
- **Annual Earnings: $48,040**
- **Growth: 9.8%**
- **Annual Job Openings: 18,000**

The job openings listed here are shared with 17-3023.00 Electrical and Electronic Engineering Technicians and 17-3023.03 Electrical Engineering Technicians.

Lay out, build, test, troubleshoot, repair, and modify developmental and production electronic components, parts, equipment, and systems, such as computer equipment, missile control instrumentation, electron tubes, test equipment, and machine tool numerical controls, applying principles and theories of electronics, electrical circuitry, engineering mathematics, electronic and electrical testing, and physics. Usually work under direction of engineering staff.

Test electronics units, using standard test equipment, and analyze results to evaluate performance and determine need for adjustment. Perform preventative maintenance and calibration of equipment and systems. Read blueprints, wiring diagrams, schematic drawings, and engineering instructions for assembling electronics units, applying knowledge of electronic theory and components. Identify and resolve equipment malfunctions, working with manufacturers and field representatives as necessary to procure replacement parts. Maintain system logs and manuals to document testing and operation of equipment. Assemble, test, and maintain circuitry or electronic components according to engineering instructions, technical manuals, and knowledge of electronics, using hand and power tools. Adjust and replace defective or improperly functioning circuitry and electronics components, using hand tools and soldering iron. Procure parts and maintain inventory and related documentation. Maintain working knowledge of state-of-the-art tools or software by reading or attending conferences, workshops, or other training. Provide user applications and engineering support and recommendations for new and existing equipment with regard to installation, upgrades, and enhancement. Write reports and record data on testing techniques, laboratory equipment, and specifications to assist engineers. Provide customer support and education, working with users to identify needs, determine sources of problems, and provide information on product use. Design basic circuitry and draft sketches for clarification of details and design documentation under engineers' direction, using drafting instruments and computer-aided design (CAD) equipment. Build prototypes from rough sketches or plans. Develop and upgrade preventative maintenance procedures for components, equipment, parts, and systems. Fabricate parts, such as coils, terminal boards, and chassis, using bench lathes, drills, or other machine tools. Research equipment and component needs, sources, competitive prices, delivery times, and ongoing operational costs. Write computer or microprocessor software programs.

GOE Information—Interest Area: 15. Scientific Research, Engineering, and Mathematics. **Work Group:** 15.09. Engineering Technology. **Personality Type—**Realistic. Realistic occupations frequently involve work activities that include practical, hands-on problems and solutions. They often deal with plants; animals; and real-world materials like wood, tools, and machinery. Many of the occupations require working outside and do not involve a lot of paperwork or working closely with others. **Work Values—**Advancement; Working Conditions; Ability Utilization; Activity; Achievement; Supervision, Human Relations. **Skills—**Repairing; Installation; Equipment Maintenance; Troubleshooting; Operation Monitoring; Technology Design. **Abilities—***Cognitive:* Visualization; Written Comprehension; Deductive Reasoning; Written Expression; Oral Comprehension; Information Ordering. *Psychomotor:* Manual Dexterity; Finger Dexterity; Control Precision; Reaction Time; Arm-Hand Steadiness. *Physical:* None met the criteria. *Sensory:* Visual Color Discrimination; Near Vision. **General Work Activities—***Information Input:* Getting Information; Identifying Objects, Actions, and Events; Monitoring Processes, Materials, or Surroundings. *Mental Process:* Making Decisions and Solving Problems; Analyzing Data or Information; Updating and Using Relevant Knowledge. *Work Output:* Repairing and Maintaining Electronic Equipment; Interacting With Computers; Repairing and Maintaining Mechanical Equipment. *Interacting with Others:* Communicating with Other Workers; Establishing and Maintaining Interpersonal Relationships; Providing Consultation and Advice to Others. **Physical Work Conditions—**Indoors; Contaminants; Hazardous Conditions; Hazardous Equipment; Sitting; Using Hands on Objects, Tools, or Controls. **Other Job Characteristics—**Need to Be Exact or Accurate; Repeat Same Tasks.

Experience—Job Zone 3. Previous work-related skill, knowledge, or experience is required. **Job Preparation—**SVP 6.0 to less than 7.0—more than one year and less than four years. **Knowledges—**Engineering and Technology; Computers and Electronics; Mechanical Devices; Design; Telecommunications; Mathematics. **Instructional Programs—**Computer Engineering Technology/Technician; Electrical and Electronic Engineering Technologies/Technicians, Other; Electrical, Electronic, and Communications Engineering Technology/Technician; Telecommunications Technology/Technician.

Related SOC Job—17-3023 Electrical and Electronic Engineering Technicians. **Related OOH Job—**Engineering Technicians. **Related DOT Jobs—**003.161-014 Electronics Technician; 003.161-018 Technician, Semiconductor Development; 003.261-010 Instrumentation Technician; 019.281-010 Calibration Laboratory Technician; 710.261-010 Instrument Repairer; 710.281-026 Instrument Mechanic; 710.281-030 Instrument Technician; 710.281-042 Instrument-Technician Apprentice; 711.281-014 Instrument Mechanic, Weapons System; 725.381-010 Tube Rebuilder; 726.261-010 Electronics Assembler, Developmental; 729.281-026 Electrical-Instrument Repairer; others.

17-3023.03 Electrical Engineering Technicians

- **Education/Training Required: Associate degree**
- **Employed: 165,850**
- **Annual Earnings: $48,040**
- **Growth: 9.8%**
- **Annual Job Openings: 18,000**

The job openings listed here are shared with 17-3023.00 Electrical and Electronic Engineering Technicians and 17-3023.01 Electronics Engineering Technicians.

Apply electrical theory and related knowledge to test and modify developmental or operational electrical machinery and electrical control equipment and circuitry in industrial or commercial plants and laboratories. Usually work under direction of engineering staff.

Assemble electrical and electronic systems and prototypes according to engineering data and knowledge of electrical principles, using hand tools and measuring instruments. Provide technical assistance and resolution when electrical or engineering problems are encountered before, during, and after construction. Install and maintain electrical control systems and solid state equipment. Modify electrical prototypes, parts, assemblies, and systems to correct functional deviations. Set up and operate test equipment to evaluate performance of developmental parts, assemblies, or systems under simulated operating conditions and record results. Collaborate with electrical engineers and other personnel to identify, define, and solve developmental problems. Build, calibrate, maintain, troubleshoot, and repair electrical instruments or testing equipment. Analyze and interpret test information to resolve design-related problems. Write commissioning procedures for electrical installations. Prepare project cost and work-time estimates. Evaluate engineering proposals, shop drawings, and design comments for sound electrical engineering practice and conformance with established safety and design criteria and recommend approval or disapproval. Draw or modify diagrams and write engineering specifications to clarify design details and functional criteria of experimental electronics units. Conduct inspections for quality control and assurance programs, reporting findings and recommendations. Prepare contracts and initiate, review, and coordinate modifications to contract specifications and plans throughout the construction process. Plan, schedule, and monitor work of support personnel to assist supervisor. Review existing electrical engineering criteria to identify necessary revisions, deletions, or amendments to outdated material. Perform supervisory duties such as recommending work assignments, approving leaves, and completing performance evaluations. Plan method and sequence of operations for developing and testing experimental electronic and electrical equipment. Visit construction sites to observe conditions impacting design and to identify solutions to technical design problems involving electrical systems equipment that arise during construction.

GOE Information—Interest Area: 15. Scientific Research, Engineering, and Mathematics. Work Group: 15.09. Engineering Technology. Personality Type—Realistic. Realistic occupations frequently involve work activities that include practical, hands-on problems and solutions. They often deal with plants; animals; and real-world materials like wood, tools, and machinery. Many of the occupations require working outside and do not involve a lot of paperwork or working closely with others. Work Values—Advancement; Working Conditions; Ability Utilization; Activity; Achievement; Moral Values. Skills—Repairing; Installation; Troubleshooting; Science; Mathematics; Equipment Maintenance. Abilities—Cognitive: Written Expression; Visualization; Deductive Reasoning; Written Comprehension; Information Ordering; Oral Expression. Psychomotor: Manual Dexterity; Arm-Hand Steadiness; Finger Dexterity. Physical: None met the criteria. Sensory: Visual Color Discrimination; Near Vision. General Work Activities—Information Input: Identifying Objects, Actions, and Events; Monitoring Processes, Materials, or Surroundings; Inspecting Equipment, Structures, or Materials. Mental Process: Updating and Using Relevant Knowledge; Processing Information; Evaluating Information Against Standards. Work Output: Handling and Moving Objects; Repairing and Maintaining Electronic Equipment; Documenting or Recording Information. Interacting with Others: Communicating with Other Workers; Establishing and Maintaining Interpersonal Relationships; Providing Consultation and Advice to Others. Physical Work Conditions—Indoors; Noisy; Sitting; Using Hands on Objects, Tools, or Controls. Other Job Characteristics—Need to Be Exact or Accurate; Repeat Same Tasks; Errors Have Important Consequences.

Experience—Job Zone 3. Previous work-related skill, knowledge, or experience is required. Job Preparation—SVP 6.0 to less than 7.0—more than one year and less than four years. Knowledges—Engineering and Technology; Design; Computers and Electronics; Physics; Mechanical Devices; Telecommunications. Instructional Programs—Computer Engineering Technology/Technician; Computer Technology/Computer Systems Technology; Electrical and Electronic Engineering Technologies/Technicians, Other; Electrical, Electronic, and Communications Engineering Technology/Technician; Telecommunications Technology/Technician.

Related SOC Job—17-3023 Electrical and Electronic Engineering Technicians. Related OOH Job—Engineering Technicians. Related DOT Jobs—003.161-010 Electrical Technician; 726.261-014 Electrician, Research.

17-3024.00 Electro-Mechanical Technicians

- Education/Training Required: Associate degree
- Employed: 15,130
- Annual Earnings: $43,880
- Growth: 9.7%
- Annual Job Openings: 2,000

Operate, test, and maintain unmanned, automated, servo-mechanical, or electromechanical equipment. May operate unmanned submarines, aircraft, or other equipment at worksites, such as oil rigs, deep ocean exploration, or hazardous waste removal. May assist engineers in testing and designing robotics equipment.

Test performance of electromechanical assemblies, using test instruments such as oscilloscopes, electronic voltmeters, and bridges. Read blueprints, schematics, diagrams, and technical orders to determine methods and sequences of assembly. Install electrical and electronic parts and hardware in housings or assemblies, using soldering equipment and hand tools. Align, fit, and assemble component parts, using hand tools, power tools, fixtures, templates, and microscopes. Inspect parts for surface defects. Analyze and record test results and prepare written testing documentation. Verify dimensions and clearances of parts to ensure conformance to specifications, using precision measuring instruments. Operate metalworking machines to fabricate housings, jigs, fittings, and fixtures. Repair, rework, and calibrate hydraulic and pneumatic assemblies and systems to meet operational specifications and tolerances. Train others to install, use, and maintain robots. Develop, test, and program new robots.

GOE Information—Interest Area: 15. Scientific Research, Engineering, and Mathematics. Work Group: 15.09. Engineering Technology. Personality Type—Realistic. Realistic occupations frequently involve work activities that include practical, hands-on problems and solutions. They often deal with plants; animals; and real-world materials like wood, tools, and machinery. Many of the occupations require working outside and do not involve a lot of paperwork or working closely with others. Work Values—Independence; Moral Values; Supervision, Technical; Supervision, Human Relations; Company Policies and Practices; Advancement. Skills—Equipment Maintenance; Operation Monitoring; Installation; Quality Control Analysis; Operation and Control; Troubleshooting. Abilities—Cognitive: Visualization; Perceptual Speed; Number Facility; Selective Attention; Flexibility of Closure; Memorization. Psychomotor: Reaction Time; Control Precision; Finger Dexterity; Manual Dexterity; Rate Control; Arm-Hand Steadiness. Physical: Static Strength; Trunk Strength. Sensory: Auditory Attention; Depth Perception; Visual Color Discrimination; Hearing Sensitivity; Far Vision; Near Vision. General Work Activities—Information Input: Monitoring Processes, Materials, or Surroundings; Inspecting Equipment, Structures, or Materials; Identifying Objects, Actions, and Events. Mental Process: Updating and Using Relevant Knowledge; Organizing, Planning, and Prioritizing; Analyzing Data or Information. Work Output: Repairing and Maintaining Electronic Equipment; Handling and Moving Objects; Controlling Machines and Processes. Interacting with Others: Communicating with Other Workers; Establishing and Maintaining Interpersonal Relationships. Physical Work Conditions—Indoors; Noisy; Contaminants; Hazardous Equipment; Standing; Using Hands on Objects, Tools, or Controls; Repetitive Motions. Other Job Characteristics—Need to Be Exact or Accurate; Repeat Same Tasks; Errors Have Important Consequences; Pace Determined by Speed of Equipment; Automation.

Experience—Job Zone 3. Previous work-related skill, knowledge, or experience is required. Job Preparation—SVP 6.0 to less than 7.0—more than one year and less than four years. Knowledges—Mechanical Devices; Engineering and Technology; Computers and Electronics; Mathematics; Design; Physics. Instructional Program—Engineering Related Technologies/Technicians, Other.

Related SOC Job—17-3024 Electro-Mechanical Technicians. Related OOH Job—Engineering Technicians. Related DOT Jobs—710.281-018 Electromechanical Technician; 828.381-018 Assembler, Electromechanical.

17-3025.00 Environmental Engineering Technicians

- **Education/Training Required: Associate degree**
- **Employed: 19,900**
- **Annual Earnings: $39,810**
- **Growth: 24.4%**
- **Annual Job Openings: 2,000**

Apply theory and principles of environmental engineering to modify, test, and operate equipment and devices used in the prevention, control, and remediation of environmental pollution, including waste treatment and site remediation. May assist in the development of environmental pollution remediation devices under direction of engineer.

Receive, set up, test, and decontaminate equipment. Maintain project logbook records and computer program files. Perform environmental quality work in field and office settings. Conduct pollution surveys, collecting and analyzing samples such as air and groundwater. Review technical documents to ensure completeness and conformance to requirements. Perform laboratory work such as logging numerical and visual observations, preparing and packaging samples, recording test results, and performing photo documentation. Review work plans to schedule activities. Obtain product information, identify vendors and suppliers, and order materials and equipment to maintain inventory. Arrange for the disposal of lead, asbestos, and other hazardous materials. Inspect facilities to monitor compliance with regulations governing substances such as asbestos, lead, and wastewater. Provide technical engineering support in the planning of projects such as wastewater treatment plants to ensure compliance with environmental regulations and policies. Improve chemical processes to reduce toxic emissions. Oversee support staff. Assist in the cleanup of hazardous material spills. Produce environmental assessment reports, tabulating data and preparing charts, graphs, and sketches. Maintain process parameters and evaluate process anomalies. Work with customers to assess the environmental impact of proposed construction and to develop pollution prevention programs. Perform statistical analysis and correction of air or water pollution data submitted by industry and other agencies. Develop work plans, including writing specifications and establishing material, manpower, and facilities needs.

GOE Information—Interest Area: 15. Scientific Research, Engineering, and Mathematics. **Work Group:** 15.09. Engineering Technology. **Personality Type—**No data available. **Work Values—**No data available. **Skills—**Science; Repairing; Troubleshooting; Equipment Maintenance; Operation Monitoring; Mathematics. **Abilities—***Cognitive:* Mathematical Reasoning; Number Facility; Written Comprehension; Category Flexibility; Problem Sensitivity; Inductive Reasoning. *Psychomotor:* Reaction Time; Control Precision; Manual Dexterity; Arm-Hand Steadiness; Multilimb Coordination. *Physical:* Static Strength; Trunk Strength; Extent Flexibility. *Sensory:* Visual Color Discrimination; Near Vision; Far Vision; Speech Recognition; Auditory Attention. **General Work Activities—***Information Input:* Monitoring Processes, Materials, or Surroundings; Identifying Objects, Actions, and Events; Inspecting Equipment, Structures, or Materials. *Mental Process:* Updating and Using Relevant Knowledge; Evaluating Information Against Standards; Processing Information. *Work Output:* Performing General Physical Activities; Handling and Moving Objects; Documenting or Recording Information. *Interacting with Others:* Communicating with Other Workers; Establishing and Maintaining Interpersonal Relationships; Communicating with Persons Outside Organization. **Physical Work Conditions—**More Often Indoors Than Outdoors; Contaminants; Hazardous Conditions; Hazardous Equipment; Standing. **Other Job Characteristics—**Need to Be Exact or Accurate; Errors Have Important Consequences.

Experience—Job Zone 3. Previous work-related skill, knowledge, or experience is required. **Job Preparation—**SVP 6.0 to less than 7.0—more than one year and less than four years. **Knowledges—**Engineering and Technology; Building and Construction; Design; Physics; Biology; Chemistry. **Instructional Programs—**Environmental Engineering Technology/Environmental Technology; Hazardous Materials Information Systems Technology/Technician.

Related SOC Job—17-3025 Environmental Engineering Technicians. **Related OOH Job—**Engineering Technicians. **Related DOT Jobs—**012.261-010 Air Analyst; 029.261-014 Pollution-Control Technician.

17-3026.00 Industrial Engineering Technicians

- **Education/Training Required: Associate degree**
- **Employed: 73,310**
- **Annual Earnings: $45,280**
- **Growth: 10.5%**
- **Annual Job Openings: 7,000**

Apply engineering theory and principles to problems of industrial layout or manufacturing production, usually under the direction of engineering staff. May study and record time, motion, method, and speed involved in performance of production, maintenance, clerical, and other worker operations for such purposes as establishing standard production rates or improving efficiency.

Recommend revision to methods of operation, material handling, equipment layout, or other changes to increase production or improve standards. Study time, motion, methods, and speed involved in maintenance, production, and other operations to establish standard production rate and improve efficiency. Interpret engineering drawings, schematic diagrams, or formulas and confer with management or engineering staff to determine quality and reliability standards. Recommend modifications to existing quality or production standards to achieve optimum quality within limits of equipment capability. Aid in planning work assignments in accordance with worker performance, machine capacity, production schedules, and anticipated delays. Observe workers using equipment to verify that equipment is being operated and maintained according to quality assurance standards. Observe workers operating equipment or performing tasks to determine time involved and fatigue rate, using timing devices. Prepare charts, graphs, and diagrams to illustrate workflow, routing, floor layouts, material handling, and machine utilization. Evaluate data and write reports to validate or indicate deviations from existing standards. Read worker logs, product processing sheets, and specification sheets to verify that records adhere to quality assurance specifications. Prepare graphs or charts of data or enter data into computer for analysis. Record test data, applying statistical quality control procedures. Select products for tests at specified stages in production process and test products for performance characteristics and adherence to specifications. Compile and evaluate statistical data to determine and maintain quality and reliability of products.

GOE Information—Interest Area: 04. Business and Administration. **Work Group:** 04.05. Accounting, Auditing, and Analytical Support. **Personality Type—**Investigative. Investigative occupations frequently involve working with ideas and require an extensive amount of thinking. These occupations can involve searching for facts and figuring out problems mentally. **Work Values**—Advancement; Supervision, Human Relations; Supervision, Technical; Ability Utilization; Achievement; Company Policies and Practices. **Skills**—Operations Analysis; Technology Design; Troubleshooting; Repairing; Systems Evaluation; Systems Analysis. **Abilities**—*Cognitive:* Number Facility; Mathematical Reasoning; Fluency of Ideas; Perceptual Speed; Originality; Visualization. *Psychomotor:* None met the criteria. *Physical:* None met the criteria. *Sensory:* Near Vision; Far Vision; Speech Clarity; Auditory Attention; Hearing Sensitivity; Speech Recognition. **General Work Activities**—*Information Input:* Monitoring Processes, Materials, or Surroundings; Getting Information; Identifying Objects, Actions, and Events. *Mental Process:* Organizing, Planning, and Prioritizing; Making Decisions and Solving Problems; Updating and Using Relevant Knowledge. *Work Output:* Documenting or Recording Information; Drafting and Specifying Technical Devices; Interacting With Computers. *Interacting with Others:* Establishing and Maintaining Interpersonal Relationships; Communicating with Other Workers; Coordinating the Work and Activities of Others. **Physical Work Conditions**—Indoors; Noisy; Contaminants; Hazardous Equipment; Standing; Walking and Running. **Other Job Characteristics**—Need to Be Exact or Accurate; Repeat Same Tasks.

Experience—Job Zone 3. Previous work-related skill, knowledge, or experience is required. **Job Preparation**—SVP 6.0 to less than 7.0— more than one year and less than four years. **Knowledges**—Production and Processing; Engineering and Technology; Design; Clerical Practices; Mathematics; Mechanical Devices. **Instructional Programs**—Industrial Management; Industrial Production Technologies/Technicians, Other; Industrial Technology/Technicians; Manufacturing Technology/Technician.

Related SOC Job—17-3026 Industrial Engineering Technicians. **Related OOH Job**—Engineering Technicians. **Related DOT Jobs**—012.261-014 Quality Control Technician; 012.267-010 Industrial Engineering Technician; 168.367-022 Personnel Quality Assurance Auditor.

17-3027.00 Mechanical Engineering Technicians

- **Education/Training Required: Associate degree**
- **Employed: 46,580**
- **Annual Earnings: $44,830**
- **Growth: 12.3%**
- **Annual Job Openings: 5,000**

Apply theory and principles of mechanical engineering to modify, develop, and test machinery and equipment under direction of engineering staff or physical scientists.

Prepare parts sketches and write work orders and purchase requests to be furnished by outside contractors. Draft detail drawing or sketch for drafting room completion or to request parts fabrication by machine, sheet, or wood shops. Review project instructions and blueprints to ascertain test specifications, procedures, and objectives and testing requirements created by technical problems such as redesign. Review project instructions and specifications to identify, modify, and plan requirements for fabrication, assembly, and testing. Devise, fabricate, and assemble new or modified mechanical components for products such as industrial machinery or equipment and measuring instruments. Discuss changes in design, method of manufacture and assembly, and drafting techniques and procedures with staff and coordinate corrections. Set up and conduct tests of complete units and components under operational conditions to investigate proposals for improving equipment performance. Inspect lines and figures for clarity and return erroneous drawings to designer for correction. Analyze test results in relation to design or rated specifications and test objectives and modify or adjust equipment to meet specifications. Evaluate tool drawing designs by measuring drawing dimensions and comparing with original specifications for form and function, using engineering skills. Confer with technicians and submit reports of test results to engineering department and recommend design or material changes. Calculate required capacities for equipment of proposed system to obtain specified performance and submit data to engineering personnel for approval. Record test procedures and results, numerical and graphical data, and recommendations for changes in product or test methods. Read dials and meters to determine amperage, voltage, and electrical output and input at specific operating temperature to analyze parts performance. Estimate cost factors, including labor and material, for purchased and fabricated parts and costs for assembly, testing, or installing. Set up prototype and test apparatus and operate test-controlling equipment to observe and record prototype test results.

GOE Information—**Interest Area:** 15. Scientific Research, Engineering, and Mathematics. **Work Group:** 15.09. Engineering Technology. **Personality Type**—Realistic. Realistic occupations frequently involve work activities that include practical, hands-on problems and solutions. They often deal with plants; animals; and real-world materials like wood, tools, and machinery. Many of the occupations require working outside and do not involve a lot of paperwork or working closely with others. **Work Values**—Advancement; Achievement; Supervision, Human Relations; Supervision, Technical; Variety; Activity. **Skills**—Installation; Troubleshooting; Technology Design; Operations Analysis; Equipment Selection; Systems Evaluation. **Abilities**—*Cognitive:* Mathematical Reasoning; Visualization; Deductive Reasoning; Written Comprehension; Information Ordering; Inductive Reasoning. *Psychomotor:* Control Precision; Multilimb Coordination; Reaction Time; Finger Dexterity; Manual Dexterity; Arm-Hand Steadiness. *Physical:* Static Strength; Trunk Strength. *Sensory:* Visual Color Discrimination; Depth Perception; Hearing Sensitivity; Near Vision; Far Vision; Auditory Attention. **General Work Activities**—*Information Input:* Monitoring Processes, Materials, or Surroundings; Identifying Objects, Actions, and Events; Getting Information. *Mental Process:* Updating and Using Relevant Knowledge; Thinking Creatively; Evaluating Information Against Standards. *Work Output:* Handling and Moving Objects; Controlling Machines and Processes; Repairing and Maintaining Mechanical Equipment. *Interacting with Others:* Communicating with Other Workers; Establishing and Maintaining Interpersonal Relationships; Interpreting the Meaning of Information for Others. **Physical Work Conditions**—Indoors; Noisy; Contaminants; Hazardous Equipment; Sitting. **Other Job Characteristics**—Errors Have Important Consequences; Need to Be Exact or Accurate.

Experience—Job Zone 3. Previous work-related skill, knowledge, or experience is required. **Job Preparation**—SVP 6.0 to less than 7.0— more than one year and less than four years. **Knowledges**—Engineering and Technology; Design; Mechanical Devices; Physics; Production and Processing; Chemistry. **Instructional Programs**—Mechanical Engineering Related Technology/Technician, Other; Mechanical Engineering/Mechanical Technology/Technician.

Related SOC Job—17-3027 Mechanical Engineering Technicians. **Related OOH Job**—Engineering Technicians. **Related DOT Jobs**—007.161-026 Mechanical-Engineering Technician; 007.161-030 Optomechanical Technician; 007.167-010 Die-Drawing Checker;

007.181-010 Heat-Transfer Technician; 007.267-010 Drawings Checker, Engineering; 007.267-014 Tool Design Checker; 017.261-010 Auto-Design Checker.

17-3029.99 Engineering Technicians, Except Drafters, All Other

- Education/Training Required: Associate degree
- Employed: 78,300
- Annual Earnings: $52,530
- Growth: 12.3%
- Annual Job Openings: 10,000

All engineering technicians, except drafters, not listed separately.

No task data available.

Note: The Department of Labor has not collected some data for this job, so it has fewer details than the other descriptions.

Related SOC Job—17-3029 Engineering Technicians, Except Drafters, All Other. **Related OOH Job**—Engineering Technicians. **Related DOT Jobs**—011.261-010 Metallurgical Technician; 011.261-014 Welding Technician; 011.261-018 Nondestructive Tester; 011.261-022 Laboratory Assistant, Metallurgical; 011.281-014 Spectroscopist; 011.361-010 Tester; 013.161-010 Agricultural-Engineering Technician; 019.261-022 Test Technician; 196.263-026 Controller, Remotely-Piloted Vehicle; 196.263-042 Test Pilot.

17-3031.00 Surveying and Mapping Technicians

- Education/Training Required: Moderate-term on-the-job training
- Employed: 63,910
- Annual Earnings: $31,290
- Growth: 9.6%
- Annual Job Openings: 9,000

The job openings listed here are shared with 17-3031.01 Surveying Technicians and 17-3031.02 Mapping Technicians.

Perform surveying and mapping duties, usually under the direction of a surveyor, cartographer, or photogrammetrist, to obtain data used for construction, mapmaking, boundary location, mining, or other purposes. May calculate mapmaking information and create maps from source data such as surveying notes, aerial photography, satellite data, or other maps to show topographical features, political boundaries, and other features. May verify accuracy and completeness of topographical maps.

No task data available.

GOE Information—Interest Area: 15. Scientific Research, Engineering, and Mathematics. **Work Group:** 15.09. Engineering Technology. **Note:** The Department of Labor has not collected some data for this job, so it has fewer details than the other descriptions.

Instructional Programs—Cartography; Surveying Technology/Surveying.

Related SOC Job—17-3031 Surveying and Mapping Technicians. **Related OOH Job**—Surveyors, Cartographers, Photogrammetrists, and Surveying Technicians. **Related DOT Job**—No data available.

17-3031.01 Surveying Technicians

- Education/Training Required: Moderate-term on-the-job training
- Employed: 63,910
- Annual Earnings: $31,290
- Growth: 9.6%
- Annual Job Openings: 9,000

The job openings listed here are shared with 17-3031.00 Surveying and Mapping Technicians and 17-3031.02 Mapping Technicians.

Adjust and operate surveying instruments, such as theodolite and electronic distance-measuring equipment, and compile notes, make sketches, and enter data into computers.

Adjust and operate surveying instruments such as prisms, theodolites, and electronic distance-measuring equipment. Compile information necessary to stake projects for construction, using engineering plans. Run rods for benches and cross-section elevations. Position and hold the vertical rods, or targets, that theodolite operators use for sighting to measure angles, distances, and elevations. Record survey measurements and descriptive data, using notes, drawings, sketches, and inked tracings. Perform calculations to determine earth curvature corrections, atmospheric impacts on measurements, traverse closures and adjustments, azimuths, level runs, and placement of markers. Conduct surveys to ascertain the locations of natural features and man-made structures on the Earth's surface, underground, and underwater, using electronic distance-measuring equipment and other surveying instruments. Search for section corners, property irons, and survey points. Operate and manage land-information computer systems, performing tasks such as storing data, making inquiries, and producing plots and reports. Direct and supervise work of subordinate members of surveying parties. Set out and recover stakes, marks, and other monumentation. Lay out grids and determine horizontal and vertical controls. Compare survey computations with applicable standards to determine adequacy of data. Collect information needed to carry out new surveys, using source maps, previous survey data, photographs, computer records, and other relevant information. Prepare topographic and contour maps of land surveyed, including site features and other relevant information such as charts, drawings, and survey notes. Maintain equipment and vehicles used by surveying crews. Place and hold measuring tapes when electronic distance-measuring equipment is not used. Provide assistance in the development of methods and procedures for conducting field surveys. Perform manual labor, such as cutting brush for lines; carrying stakes, rebar, and other heavy items; and stacking rods.

GOE Information—Interest Area: 15. Scientific Research, Engineering, and Mathematics. **Work Group:** 15.09. Engineering Technology. **Personality Type**—Realistic. Realistic occupations frequently involve work activities that include practical, hands-on problems and solutions. They often deal with plants; animals; and real-world materials like wood, tools, and machinery. Many of the occupations require working outside and do not involve a lot of paperwork or working closely with others. **Work Values**—Authority; Moral Values; Advancement; Supervision, Technical; Company Policies and Practices. **Skills**—Mathematics; Troubleshooting; Equipment Maintenance; Coordination; Equipment Selection; Technology Design. **Abilities**—*Cognitive:* Spatial Orientation; Number Facility; Mathematical Reasoning; Flexibility of Closure; Perceptual Speed; Time Sharing. *Psychomotor:* Arm-Hand Steadiness;

Response Orientation; Reaction Time; Control Precision; Finger Dexterity; Manual Dexterity. *Physical:* Static Strength; Gross Body Coordination; Stamina; Extent Flexibility; Trunk Strength. *Sensory:* Glare Sensitivity; Depth Perception; Far Vision; Hearing Sensitivity; Visual Color Discrimination. **General Work Activities**—*Information Input:* Identifying Objects, Actions, and Events; Getting Information; Monitoring Processes, Materials, or Surroundings. *Mental Process:* Updating and Using Relevant Knowledge; Organizing, Planning, and Prioritizing; Processing Information. *Work Output:* Handling and Moving Objects; Performing General Physical Activities; Controlling Machines and Processes. *Interacting with Others:* Establishing and Maintaining Interpersonal Relationships; Communicating with Other Workers; Coordinating the Work and Activities of Others. **Physical Work Conditions**—Outdoors; Very Hot or Cold; Very Bright or Dim Lighting; Hazardous Equipment; Minor Burns, Cuts, Bites, or Stings; Using Hands on Objects, Tools, or Controls. **Other Job Characteristics**—Need to Be Exact or Accurate; Repeat Same Tasks; Errors Have Important Consequences.

Experience—Job Zone 3. Previous work-related skill, knowledge, or experience is required. **Job Preparation**—SVP 6.0 to less than 7.0—more than one year and less than four years. **Knowledges**—Building and Construction; Design; Geography; Engineering and Technology; Mathematics; Computers and Electronics. **Instructional Programs**—Cartography; Surveying Technology/Surveying.

Related SOC Job—17-3031 Surveying and Mapping Technicians. **Related OOH Job**—Surveyors, Cartographers, Photogrammetrists, and Surveying Technicians. **Related DOT Jobs**—018.167-010 Chief of Party; 018.167-034 Surveyor Assistant, Instruments.

17-3031.02 Mapping Technicians

- **Education/Training Required: Moderate-term on-the-job training**
- **Employed: 63,910**
- **Annual Earnings: $31,290**
- **Growth: 9.6%**
- **Annual Job Openings: 9,000**

The job openings listed here are shared with 17-3031.00 Surveying and Mapping Technicians and 17-3031.01 Surveying Technicians.

Calculate mapmaking information from field notes and draw and verify accuracy of topographical maps.

Check all layers of maps to ensure accuracy, identifying and marking errors and making corrections. Determine scales, line sizes, and colors to be used for hard copies of computerized maps, using plotters. Monitor mapping work and the updating of maps to ensure accuracy, the inclusion of new and/or changed information, and compliance with rules and regulations. Identify and compile database information to create maps in response to requests. Produce and update overlay maps to show information boundaries, water locations, and topographic features on various base maps and at different scales. Trace contours and topographic details to generate maps that denote specific land and property locations and geographic attributes. Lay out and match aerial photographs in sequences in which they were taken and identify any areas missing from photographs. Compare topographical features and contour lines with images from aerial photographs, old maps, and other reference materials to verify the accuracy of their identification. Compute and measure scaled distances between reference points to establish relative positions of adjoining prints and enable the creation of photographic mosaics. Research resources such as survey maps and legal descriptions to verify property lines and to obtain information needed for mapping. Form three-dimensional images of aerial photographs taken from different locations, using mathematical techniques and plotting instruments. Enter GPS data, legal deeds, field notes, and land survey reports into GIS workstations so that information can be transformed into graphic land descriptions such as maps and drawings. Analyze aerial photographs to detect and interpret significant military, industrial, resource, or topographical data. Redraw and correct maps, such as revising parcel maps to reflect tax code area changes, using information from official records and surveys. Train staff members in duties such as tax mapping, the use of computerized mapping equipment, and the interpretation of source documents.

GOE Information—**Interest Area:** 15. Scientific Research, Engineering, and Mathematics. **Work Group:** 15.09. Engineering Technology. **Personality Type**—Conventional. Conventional occupations frequently involve following set procedures and routines. These occupations can include working with data and details more than with ideas. Usually there is a clear line of authority to follow. **Work Values**—Authority; Moral Values; Autonomy; Independence; Supervision, Technical; Activity. **Skills**—Programming; Technology Design; Quality Control Analysis; Operations Analysis; Troubleshooting; Mathematics. **Abilities**—*Cognitive:* Mathematical Reasoning; Number Facility; Flexibility of Closure; Visualization; Information Ordering; Speed of Closure. *Psychomotor:* Finger Dexterity; Arm-Hand Steadiness; Control Precision. *Physical:* None met the criteria. *Sensory:* Visual Color Discrimination; Far Vision; Depth Perception; Near Vision; Hearing Sensitivity; Speech Recognition. **General Work Activities**—*Information Input:* Identifying Objects, Actions, and Events; Monitoring Processes, Materials, or Surroundings; Getting Information. *Mental Process:* Processing Information; Updating and Using Relevant Knowledge; Analyzing Data or Information. *Work Output:* Documenting or Recording Information; Interacting With Computers; Drafting and Specifying Technical Devices. *Interacting with Others:* Communicating with Other Workers; Establishing and Maintaining Interpersonal Relationships; Providing Consultation and Advice to Others. **Physical Work Conditions**—Indoors; Sitting; Using Hands on Objects, Tools, or Controls; Repetitive Motions. **Other Job Characteristics**—Need to Be Exact or Accurate; Repeat Same Tasks.

Experience—Job Zone 3. Previous work-related skill, knowledge, or experience is required. **Job Preparation**—SVP 6.0 to less than 7.0—more than one year and less than four years. **Knowledges**—Geography; Design; Computers and Electronics; Engineering and Technology; Mathematics; Sales and Marketing. **Instructional Programs**—Cartography; Surveying Technology/Surveying.

Related SOC Job—17-3031 Surveying and Mapping Technicians. **Related OOH Job**—Surveyors, Cartographers, Photogrammetrists, and Surveying Technicians. **Related DOT Jobs**—018.167-014 Geodetic Computator; 018.167-030 Supervisor, Mapping; 018.260-580 Photogrammetric Technician; 018.261-018 Editor, Map; 018.261-022 Mosaicist; 018.281-010 Stereo-Plotter Operator; 029.167-010 Aerial-Photograph Interpreter.

19-0000

Life, Physical, and Social Science Occupations

19-1000 Life Scientists

19-1011.00 Animal Scientists

- **Education/Training Required:** Bachelor's degree
- **Employed:** 3,000
- **Annual Earnings:** $43,170
- **Growth:** 12.9%
- **Annual Job Openings:** Fewer than 500

Conduct research in the genetics, nutrition, reproduction, growth, and development of domestic farm animals.

Conduct research concerning animal nutrition, breeding, or management to improve products or processes. Advise producers about improved products and techniques that could enhance their animal production efforts. Study nutritional requirements of animals and nutritive values of animal feed materials. Study effects of management practices, processing methods, feed, or environmental conditions on quality and quantity of animal products, such as eggs and milk. Develop improved practices in feeding, housing, sanitation, or parasite and disease control of animals. Research and control animal selection and breeding practices to increase production efficiency and improve animal quality. Determine genetic composition of animal populations and heritability of traits, utilizing principles of genetics. Crossbreed animals with existing strains or cross strains to obtain new combinations of desirable characteristics.

GOE Information—Interest Area: 01. Agriculture and Natural Resources. **Work Group:** 01.02. Resource Science/Engineering for Plants, Animals, and the Environment. **Personality Type—** Investigative. Investigative occupations frequently involve working with ideas and require an extensive amount of thinking. These occupations can involve searching for facts and figuring out problems mentally. **Work Values—**Autonomy; Creativity; Independence; Responsibility; Ability Utilization; Achievement. **Skills—**Science; Management of Financial Resources; Systems Analysis; Writing; Complex Problem Solving; Reading Comprehension. **Abilities—** *Cognitive:* Deductive Reasoning; Written Comprehension; Inductive Reasoning; Problem Sensitivity; Originality; Fluency of Ideas. *Psychomotor:* None met the criteria. *Physical:* None met the criteria. *Sensory:* Speech Recognition; Near Vision; Speech Clarity. **General Work Activities—***Information Input:* Getting Information; Identifying Objects, Actions, and Events; Monitoring Processes, Materials, or Surroundings. *Mental Process:* Updating and Using Relevant Knowledge; Processing Information; Analyzing Data or Information. *Work Output:* Documenting or Recording Information; Interacting With Computers. *Interacting with Others:* Communicating with Persons Outside Organization; Interpreting the Meaning of Information for Others; Teaching Others. **Physical Work Conditions—**More Often Indoors Than Outdoors; Sitting. **Other Job Characteristics—**Need to Be Exact or Accurate.

Experience—Job Zone 5. Extensive skill, knowledge, and experience are needed. **Job Preparation—**SVP 8.0 and above—four years to more than 10 years. **Knowledges—**Food Production; Biology; Chemistry; Education and Training; Mathematics; Physics. **Instructional Programs—**Agricultural Animal Breeding; Agriculture, General; Animal Health; Animal Nutrition; Animal Sciences, General; Animal Sciences, Other; Dairy Science; Poultry Science; Range Science and Management.

Related SOC Job—19-1011 Animal Scientists. **Related OOH Job—** Agricultural and Food Scientists. **Related DOT Jobs—**040.061-014 Animal Scientist; 040.061-018 Dairy Scientist; 040.061-042 Poultry Scientist; 041.061-014 Animal Breeder.

19-1012.00 Food Scientists and Technologists

- **Education/Training Required:** Bachelor's degree
- **Employed:** 7,570
- **Annual Earnings:** $51,440
- **Growth:** 10.9%
- **Annual Job Openings:** 1,000

Use chemistry, microbiology, engineering, and other sciences to study the principles underlying the processing and deterioration of foods; analyze food content to determine levels of vitamins, fat, sugar, and protein; discover new food sources; research ways to make processed foods safe, palatable, and healthful; and apply food science knowledge to determine the best ways to process, package, preserve, store, and distribute food.

Test new products for flavor, texture, color, nutritional content, and adherence to government and industry standards. Check raw ingredients for maturity or stability for processing and finished products for safety, quality, and nutritional value. Confer with process engineers, plant operators, flavor experts, and packaging and marketing specialists in order to resolve problems in product development. Evaluate food processing and storage operations and assist in the development of quality assurance programs for such operations. Study methods to improve aspects of foods such as chemical composition, flavor, color, texture, nutritional value, and convenience. Study the structure and composition of food or the changes foods undergo in storage and processing. Develop new or improved ways of preserving, processing, packaging, storing, and delivering foods, using knowledge of chemistry, microbiology, and other sciences. Develop food standards and production specifications, safety and sanitary regulations, and waste management and water supply specifications. Demonstrate products to clients. Inspect food processing areas in order to ensure compliance with government regulations and standards for sanitation, safety, quality, and waste management standards. Search for substitutes for harmful or undesirable additives, such as nitrites.

GOE Information—Interest Area: 01. Agriculture and Natural Resources. **Work Group:** 01.03. Resource Technologies for Plants, Animals, and the Environment. **Personality Type—**Investigative. Investigative occupations frequently involve working with ideas and require an extensive amount of thinking. These occupations can involve searching for facts and figuring out problems mentally. **Work Values—**Creativity; Autonomy; Responsibility; Security; Independence; Ability Utilization. **Skills—**Quality Control Analysis; Science; Troubleshooting; Operation Monitoring; Monitoring; Reading Comprehension. **Abilities—***Cognitive:* Originality; Mathematical Reasoning; Fluency of Ideas; Deductive Reasoning; Number Facility; Category Flexibility. *Psychomotor:* Arm-Hand Steadiness; Finger Dexterity. *Physical:* None met the criteria. *Sensory:* Far Vision; Visual Color Discrimination; Depth Perception; Speech Clarity; Speech Recognition; Near Vision. **General Work Activities—** *Information Input:* Getting Information; Identifying Objects, Actions, and Events; Monitoring Processes, Materials, or Surroundings. *Mental Process:* Processing Information; Organizing, Planning, and Prioritizing; Updating and Using Relevant Knowledge. *Work Output:* Documenting or Recording Information; Interacting With Computers; Performing General Physical Activities. *Interacting with Others:* Communicating with Other Workers; Establishing and Maintaining Interpersonal Relationships; Interpreting the Meaning of Information for Others. **Physical Work Conditions—**Indoors; Noisy; Hazardous Conditions; Sitting. **Other Job Characteristics—** Need to Be Exact or Accurate; Repeat Same Tasks.

Experience—Job Zone 5. Extensive skill, knowledge, and experience are needed. **Job Preparation**—SVP 8.0 and above—four years to more than 10 years. **Knowledges**—Food Production; Chemistry; Production and Processing; Biology; Physics; Mathematics. **Instructional Programs**—Agriculture, General; Food Science; Food Technology and Processing; International Agriculture.

Related SOC Job—19-1012 Food Scientists and Technologists. **Related OOH Job**—Agricultural and Food Scientists. **Related DOT Job**—041.081-010 Food Technologist.

19-1013.00 Soil and Plant Scientists

- Education/Training Required: Bachelor's degree
- Employed: 10,100
- Annual Earnings: $54,530
- Growth: 13.9%
- Annual Job Openings: 1,000

Conduct research in breeding, physiology, production, yield, and management of crops and agricultural plants, their growth in soils, and control of pests or study the chemical, physical, biological, and mineralogical composition of soils as they relate to plant or crop growth. May classify and map soils and investigate effects of alternative practices on soil and crop productivity.

Communicate research and project results to other professionals and the public or teach related courses, seminars or workshops. Provide information and recommendations to farmers and other landowners regarding ways in which they can best use land, promote plant growth, and avoid or correct problems such as erosion. Investigate responses of soils to specific management practices to determine the use capabilities of soils and the effects of alternative practices on soil productivity. Develop methods of conserving and managing soil that can be applied by farmers and forestry companies. Conduct experiments to develop new or improved varieties of field crops, focusing on characteristics such as yield, quality, disease resistance, nutritional value, or adaptation to specific soils or climates. Investigate soil problems and poor water quality to determine sources and effects. Study soil characteristics to classify soils on the basis of factors such as geographic location, landscape position, and soil properties. Develop improved measurement techniques, soil conservation methods, soil sampling devices, and related technology. Conduct experiments investigating how soil forms and changes and how it interacts with land-based ecosystems and living organisms. Identify degraded or contaminated soils and develop plans to improve their chemical, biological, and physical characteristics. Survey undisturbed and disturbed lands for classification, inventory, mapping, environmental impact assessments, environmental protection planning, and conservation and reclamation planning. Plan and supervise land conservation and reclamation programs for industrial development projects and waste management programs for composting and farming. Perform chemical analyses of the microorganism content of soils to determine microbial reactions and chemical mineralogical relationships to plant growth. Provide advice regarding the development of regulatory standards for land reclamation and soil conservation. Develop new or improved methods and products for controlling and eliminating weeds, crop diseases, and insect pests.

GOE Information—**Interest Area:** 01. Agriculture and Natural Resources. **Work Group:** 01.02. Resource Science/Engineering for Plants, Animals, and the Environment. **Personality Type**—Investigative. Investigative occupations frequently involve working with ideas and require an extensive amount of thinking. These occupations can involve searching for facts and figuring out problems

mentally. **Work Values**—Creativity; Autonomy; Independence; Responsibility; Ability Utilization; Recognition. **Skills**—Science; Writing; Management of Personnel Resources; Management of Material Resources; Reading Comprehension. **Abilities**—*Cognitive:* Mathematical Reasoning; Number Facility; Written Comprehension; Inductive Reasoning; Deductive Reasoning; Category Flexibility. *Psychomotor:* None met the criteria. *Physical:* None met the criteria. *Sensory:* None met the criteria. **General Work Activities**—*Information Input:* Getting Information; Identifying Objects, Actions, and Events; Monitoring Processes, Materials, or Surroundings. *Mental Process:* Updating and Using Relevant Knowledge; Processing Information; Organizing, Planning, and Prioritizing. *Work Output:* Documenting or Recording Information; Interacting With Computers; Handling and Moving Objects. *Interacting with Others:* Communicating with Persons Outside Organization; Communicating with Other Workers; Establishing and Maintaining Interpersonal Relationships. **Physical Work Conditions**—More Often Indoors Than Outdoors; Sitting. **Other Job Characteristics**—Need to Be Exact or Accurate.

Experience—Job Zone 5. Extensive skill, knowledge, and experience are needed. **Job Preparation**—SVP 8.0 and above—four years to more than 10 years. **Knowledges**—Biology; Food Production; Geography; Chemistry; Physics; Education and Training. **Instructional Programs**—Agricultural and Horticultural Plant Breeding; Agriculture, General; Agronomy and Crop Science; Horticultural Science; Plant Protection and Integrated Pest Management; Plant Sciences, General; Plant Sciences, Other; Range Science and Management; Soil Chemistry and Physics; Soil Microbiology; Soil Science and Agronomy, General.

Related SOC Job—19-1013 Soil and Plant Scientists. **Related OOH Job**—Agricultural and Food Scientists. **Related DOT Jobs**—040.061-010 Agronomist; 040.061-038 Horticulturist; 040.061-058 Soil Scientist; 041.061-018 Apiculturist; 041.061-038 Botanist; 041.061-046 Entomologist; 041.061-082 Plant Breeder; 041.061-086 Plant Pathologist.

19-1020.01 Biologists

- Education/Training Required: Doctoral degree
- Employed: 77,099
- Annual Earnings: No data available
- Growth: 17.0%
- Annual Job Openings: No data available.

Research or study basic principles of plant and animal life, such as origin, relationship, development, anatomy, and functions.

Develop and maintain liaisons and effective working relations with groups and individuals, agencies, and the public to encourage cooperative management strategies or to develop information and interpret findings. Program and use computers to store, process, and analyze data. Study aquatic plants and animals and environmental conditions affecting them, such as radioactivity or pollution. Collect and analyze biological data about relationships among and between organisms and their environment. Communicate test results to state and federal representatives and general public. Identify, classify, and study structure, behavior, ecology, physiology, nutrition, culture, and distribution of plant and animal species. Prepare environmental impact reports for industry, government, or publication. Represent employer in a technical capacity at conferences. Plan and administer biological research programs for government, research firms, medical industries, or manufacturing firms. Research environmental effects of present and potential uses of land and water areas, determining methods of improving environmental conditions or such outputs as crop yields. Review reports such as those relating to land use classifications and recreational development for accuracy and adequacy. Measure salinity, acidity, light, oxygen content, and other physical conditions of water to determine their relationship to aquatic life. Teach, supervise students, and perform research at universities and colleges. Supervise biological technicians and technologists and other scientists. Study basic principles of plant and animal life such as origin, relationship, development, anatomy, and function. Study and manage wild animal populations. Prepare requests for proposals or statements of work. Cultivate, breed, and grow aquatic life such as lobsters, clams, or fish. Prepare plans for management of renewable resources. Develop methods and apparatus for securing representative plant, animal, aquatic, or soil samples. Study reactions of plants, animals, and marine species to parasites. Develop pest management and control measures and conduct risk assessments related to pest exclusion, using scientific methods.

GOE Information—Interest Area: 15. Scientific Research, Engineering, and Mathematics. **Work Group:** 15.03. Life Sciences. **Personality Type**—Investigative. Investigative occupations frequently involve working with ideas and require an extensive amount of thinking. These occupations can involve searching for facts and figuring out problems mentally. **Work Values**—Creativity; Autonomy; Ability Utilization; Independence; Recognition; Responsibility. **Skills**—Science; Management of Financial Resources; Judgment and Decision Making; Negotiation; Persuasion; Management of Material Resources. **Abilities**—*Cognitive:* Inductive Reasoning; Category Flexibility; Oral Expression; Written Expression; Written Comprehension; Flexibility of Closure. *Psychomotor:* None met the criteria. *Physical:* None met the criteria. *Sensory:* Speech Clarity; Speech Recognition; Visual Color Discrimination; Near Vision; Auditory Attention. **General Work Activities**—*Information Input:* Identifying Objects, Actions, and Events; Monitoring Processes, Materials, or Surroundings; Getting Information. *Mental Process:* Processing Information; Updating and Using Relevant Knowledge; Organizing, Planning, and Prioritizing. *Work Output:* Documenting or Recording Information; Interacting With Computers. *Interacting with Others:* Establishing and Maintaining Interpersonal Relationships; Communicating with Other Workers; Communicating with Persons Outside Organization. **Physical Work Conditions**—Indoors; Noisy; Sitting. **Other Job Characteristics**—Need to Be Exact or Accurate.

Experience—Job Zone 5. Extensive skill, knowledge, and experience are needed. **Job Preparation**—SVP 8.0 and above—four years to more than 10 years. **Knowledges**—Biology; Chemistry; Law and Government; Geography; Physics; Computers and Electronics. **Instructional Program**—No related CIP programs.

Related SOC Job—19-1020 Biological Scientists. **Related OOH Job**—Biological Scientists. **Related DOT Jobs**—041.061-022 Aquatic Biologist; 041.061-030 Biologist; 041.061-042 Cytologist; 041.061-050 Geneticist; 041.061-062 Mycologist; 041.061-066 Nematologist; 041.061-078 Physiologist.

19-1021.00 Biochemists and Biophysicists

- Education/Training Required: Doctoral degree
- Employed: 17,690
- Annual Earnings: $71,000
- Growth: 21.0%
- Annual Job Openings: 1,000

Study the chemical composition and physical principles of living cells and organisms and their electrical and mechanical energy and related phenomena. May conduct research to further understanding of the complex chemical combinations and reactions involved in metabolism, reproduction, growth, and heredity. May determine the effects of foods, drugs, serums, hormones, and other substances on tissues and vital processes of living organisms.

Investigate damage to cells and tissues caused by X rays and nuclear particles. Research how characteristics of plants and animals are carried through successive generations. Research the chemical effects of substances such as drugs, serums, hormones, and food on tissues and vital processes. Share research findings by writing scientific articles and by making presentations at scientific conferences. Study physical principles of living cells and organisms and their electrical and mechanical energy, applying methods and knowledge of mathematics, physics, chemistry, and biology. Study the chemistry of living processes, such as cell development, breathing, and digestion, and living energy changes such as growth, aging, and death. Study the mutations in organisms that lead to cancer and other diseases. Design and build laboratory equipment needed for special research projects. Prepare reports and recommendations based upon research outcomes. Develop and execute tests to detect diseases, genetic disorders, or other abnormalities. Develop methods to process, store, and use foods, drugs, and chemical compounds. Investigate the transmission of electrical impulses along nerves and muscles. Manage laboratory teams and monitor the quality of a team's work. Research cancer treatment, using radiation and nuclear particles. Research transformations of substances in cells, using atomic isotopes. Study how light is absorbed in processes such as photosynthesis or vision. Study spatial configurations of submicroscopic molecules such as proteins, using X rays and electron microscopes. Determine the three-dimensional structure of biological macromolecules. Investigate the nature, composition, and expression of genes and research how genetic engineering can impact these processes. Develop new methods to study the mechanisms of biological processes. Develop and test new drugs and medications intended for commercial distribution. Design and perform experiments with equipment such as lasers, accelerators, and mass spectrometers. Analyze brain functions such as learning, thinking, and memory and the dynamics of seeing and hearing.

GOE Information—Interest Area: 15. Scientific Research, Engineering, and Mathematics. **Work Group:** 15.03. Life Sciences. **Personality Type**—Investigative. Investigative occupations frequently involve working with ideas and require an extensive amount of thinking. These occupations can involve searching for facts and figuring out problems mentally. **Work Values**—Autonomy; Creativity; Ability Utilization; Responsibility; Independence; Social Status. **Skills**—Science; Programming; Mathematics; Reading Comprehension; Writing; Active Learning. **Abilities**—*Cognitive:* Written Expression; Inductive Reasoning; Written Comprehension; Memorization; Category Flexibility; Deductive Reasoning. *Psychomotor:* Arm-Hand Steadiness. *Physical:* None met the criteria. *Sensory:* Near Vision. **General Work Activities**—*Information Input:* Identifying Objects, Actions, and Events; Getting Information; Monitoring Processes, Materials, or Surroundings. *Mental Process:* Analyzing Data or Information; Processing Information; Updating and Using Relevant Knowledge. *Work Output:* Documenting or Recording Information; Interacting With Computers; Controlling Machines and Processes. *Interacting with Others:* Interpreting the Meaning of Information for Others; Providing Consultation and Advice to Others; Communicating with Other Workers. **Physical Work Conditions**—Indoors; Sitting; Using Hands on Objects, Tools, or Controls. **Other Job Characteristics**—Need to Be Exact or Accurate; Errors Have Important Consequences.

Experience—Job Zone 5. Extensive skill, knowledge, and experience are needed. **Job Preparation**—SVP 8.0 and above—four years to more than 10 years. **Knowledges**—Biology; Chemistry; Physics; Mathematics. **Instructional Programs**—Biochemistry; Biochemistry/ Biophysics, and Molecular Biology; Biophysics; Cell/Cellular Biology and Anatomical Sciences, Other; Molecular Biochemistry; Molecular Biophysics; Soil Chemistry and Physics; Soil Microbiology.

Related SOC Job—19-1021 Biochemists and Biophysicists. **Related OOH Job**—Biological Scientists. **Related DOT Jobs**—022.081-010 Toxicologist; 041.061-026 Biochemist; 041.061-034 Biophysicist; 041.061-094 Staff Toxicologist.

19-1022.00 Microbiologists

- **Education/Training Required: Doctoral degree**
- **Employed: 15,250**
- **Annual Earnings: $56,870**
- **Growth: 17.2%**
- **Annual Job Openings: 1,000**

Investigate the growth, structure, development, and other characteristics of microscopic organisms, such as bacteria, algae, or fungi. Includes medical microbiologists who study the relationship between organisms and disease or the effects of antibiotics on microorganisms.

Isolate and make cultures of bacteria or other microorganisms in prescribed media, controlling moisture, aeration, temperature, and nutrition. Perform tests on water, food, and the environment to detect harmful microorganisms and to obtain information about sources of pollution and contamination. Examine physiological, morphological, and cultural characteristics, using microscope, to identify and classify microorganisms in human, water, and food specimens. Provide laboratory services for health departments, for community environmental health programs, and for physicians needing information for diagnosis and treatment. Observe action of microorganisms upon living tissues of plants, higher animals, and other microorganisms and on dead organic matter. Investigate the relationship between organisms and disease, including the control of epidemics and the effects of antibiotics on microorganisms. Supervise biological technologists and technicians and other scientists. Study growth, structure, development, and general characteristics of bacteria and other microorganisms to understand their relationship to human, plant, and animal health. Prepare technical reports and recommendations based upon research outcomes. Study the structure and function of human, animal, and plant tissues, cells, pathogens, and toxins. Use a variety of specialized equipment such as electron microscopes, gas chromatographs and high-pressure liquid chromatographs, electrophoresis units, thermocyclers, fluorescence-activated cell sorters, and phosphoimagers. Conduct chemical analyses of substances such as acids, alcohols, and enzymes. Research use of bacteria and microorganisms to develop vitamins, antibiotics, amino acids, grain alcohol, sugars, and polymers.

GOE Information—**Interest Area:** 15. Scientific Research, Engineering, and Mathematics. **Work Group:** 15.03. Life Sciences. **Personality Type**—Investigative. Investigative occupations frequently involve working with ideas and require an extensive amount of thinking. These occupations can involve searching for facts and figuring out problems mentally. **Work Values**—Creativity; Autonomy; Independence; Ability Utilization; Social Status; Responsibility. **Skills**—Science; Operation Monitoring; Repairing; Equipment Maintenance; Quality Control Analysis; Technology Design. **Abilities**—*Cognitive:* Inductive Reasoning; Category Flexibility; Written Expression; Problem Sensitivity; Mathematical

Reasoning; Deductive Reasoning. *Psychomotor:* Arm-Hand Steadiness; Manual Dexterity; Finger Dexterity; Control Precision; Multilimb Coordination. *Physical:* None met the criteria. *Sensory:* Near Vision; Visual Color Discrimination; Depth Perception; Speech Clarity. **General Work Activities**—*Information Input:* Identifying Objects, Actions, and Events; Monitoring Processes, Materials, or Surroundings; Getting Information. *Mental Process:* Updating and Using Relevant Knowledge; Processing Information; Evaluating Information Against Standards. *Work Output:* Documenting or Recording Information; Controlling Machines and Processes; Handling and Moving Objects. *Interacting with Others:* Interpreting the Meaning of Information for Others; Communicating with Other Workers; Teaching Others. **Physical Work Conditions**—Indoors; Contaminants; Disease or Infections; Hazardous Conditions; Using Hands on Objects, Tools, or Controls; Repetitive Motions. **Other Job Characteristics**—Need to Be Exact or Accurate; Errors Have Important Consequences; Repeat Same Tasks.

Experience—Job Zone 4. A minimum of two to four years of work-related skill, knowledge, or experience is needed. **Job Preparation**—SVP 7.0 to less than 8.0—two years to less than 10 years. **Knowledges**—Biology; Chemistry; Clerical Practices; English Language; Computers and Electronics; Administration and Management. **Instructional Programs**—Biochemistry/Biophysics and Molecular Biology; Cell/Cellular Biology and Anatomical Sciences, Other; Microbiology, General; Neuroanatomy; Soil Microbiology; Structural Biology.

Related SOC Job—19-1022 Microbiologists. **Related OOH Job**—Biological Scientists. **Related DOT Job**—041.061-058 Microbiologist.

19-1023.00 Zoologists and Wildlife Biologists

- **Education/Training Required: Doctoral degree**
- **Employed: 16,440**
- **Annual Earnings: $52,050**
- **Growth: 13.0%**
- **Annual Job Openings: 1,000**

Study the origins, behavior, diseases, genetics, and life processes of animals and wildlife. May specialize in wildlife research and management, including the collection and analysis of biological data to determine the environmental effects of present and potential use of land and water areas.

Study animals in their natural habitats, assessing effects of environment and industry on animals, interpreting findings, and recommending alternative operating conditions for industry. Inventory or estimate plant and wildlife populations. Analyze characteristics of animals to identify and classify them. Make recommendations on management systems and planning for wildlife populations and habitat, consulting with stakeholders and the public at large to explore options. Disseminate information by writing reports and scientific papers or journal articles and by making presentations and giving talks for schools, clubs, interest groups, and park interpretive programs. Study characteristics of animals such as origin, interrelationships, classification, life histories and diseases, development, genetics, and distribution. Perform administrative duties such as fundraising, public relations, budgeting, and supervision of zoo staff. Organize and conduct experimental studies with live animals in controlled or natural surroundings. Oversee the care and distribution of zoo animals, working with curators and zoo directors to determine the best way to contain animals, maintain their habitats, and manage facilities. Coordinate preventive programs to control the outbreak of wildlife diseases. Prepare collections of preserved specimens or microscopic slides for species identification and study of development or disease. Raise specimens for study and observation or for use in experiments. Collect and dissect animal specimens and examine specimens under microscope.

GOE Information—Interest Area: 01. Agriculture and Natural Resources. **Work Group:** 01.02. Resource Science/Engineering for Plants, Animals, and the Environment. **Personality Type—** Investigative. Investigative occupations frequently involve working with ideas and require an extensive amount of thinking. These occupations can involve searching for facts and figuring out problems mentally. **Work Values—**Creativity; Autonomy; Achievement; Ability Utilization; Responsibility; Recognition. **Skills—**Science; Management of Financial Resources; Writing; Coordination; Persuasion; Management of Personnel Resources. **Abilities—***Cognitive:* Written Expression; Inductive Reasoning; Category Flexibility; Problem Sensitivity; Oral Expression; Oral Comprehension. *Psychomotor:* Arm-Hand Steadiness; Multilimb Coordination. *Physical:* None met the criteria. *Sensory:* Far Vision; Near Vision; Speech Clarity; Visual Color Discrimination. **General Work Activities—***Information Input:* Monitoring Processes, Materials, or Surroundings; Getting Information; Identifying Objects, Actions, and Events. *Mental Process:* Processing Information; Organizing, Planning, and Prioritizing; Updating and Using Relevant Knowledge. *Work Output:* Performing General Physical Activities; Handling and Moving Objects; Documenting or Recording Information. *Interacting with Others:* Communicating with Persons Outside Organization; Establishing and Maintaining Interpersonal Relationships; Communicating with Other Workers. **Physical Work Conditions—**More Often Indoors Than Outdoors; Sitting. **Other Job Characteristics—**Need to Be Exact or Accurate.

Experience—Job Zone 5. Extensive skill, knowledge, and experience are needed. **Job Preparation—**SVP 8.0 and above—four years to more than 10 years. **Knowledges—**Biology; Geography; English Language; Law and Government; Administration and Management; Computers and Electronics. **Instructional Programs—**Animal Behavior and Ethology; Animal Physiology; Cell/Cellular Biology and Anatomical Sciences, Other; Ecology; Entomology; Wildlife and Wildlands Science and Management; Wildlife Biology; Zoology/Animal Biology; Zoology/Animal Biology, Other.

Related SOC Job—19-1023 Zoologists and Wildlife Biologists. **Related OOH Job—**Biological Scientists. **Related DOT Job—**041.061-090 Zoologist.

19-1029.99 Biological Scientists, All Other

- **Education/Training Required: Doctoral degree**
- **Employed: 26,200**
- **Annual Earnings: $60,190**
- **Growth: 17.0%**
- **Annual Job Openings: 3,000**

All biological scientists not listed separately.

No task data available.

Note: The Department of Labor has not collected some data for this job, so it has fewer details than the other descriptions.

Related SOC Job—19-1029 Biological Scientists, All Other. **Related OOH Job—**Biological Scientists. **Related DOT Job—**No data available.

19-1031.00 Conservation Scientists

- **Education/Training Required: Bachelor's degree**
- **Employed: 15,540**
- **Annual Earnings: $53,350**
- **Growth: 6.3%**
- **Annual Job Openings: 2,000**

The job openings listed here are shared with 19-1031.01 Soil and Water Conservationists, 19-1031.02 Range Managers, and 19-1031.03 Park Naturalists.

Manage, improve, and protect natural resources to maximize their use without damaging the environment. May conduct soil surveys and develop plans to eliminate soil erosion or to protect rangelands from fire and rodent damage. May instruct farmers, agricultural production managers, or ranchers in best ways to use crop rotation, contour plowing, or terracing to conserve soil and water; in the number and kind of livestock and forage plants best suited to particular ranges; and in range and farm improvements, such as fencing and reservoirs for stock watering.

No task data available.

GOE Information—Interest Area: 01. Agriculture and Natural Resources. **Work Group:** 01.02. Resource Science/Engineering for Plants, Animals, and the Environment. **Note:** The Department of Labor has not collected some data for this job, so it has fewer details than the other descriptions.

Instructional Programs—Forest Management/ Forest Resources Management; Forest Sciences; Forestry, General; Forestry, Other; Land Use Planning and Management/Development; Natural Resources and Conservation, Other; Natural Resources Management and Policy, General; Natural Resources Management and Policy, Other; Water, Wetlands, and Marine Resources Management; Wildlife and Wildlands Science and Management.

Related SOC Job—19-1031 Conservation Scientists. **Related OOH Job—**Conservation Scientists and Foresters. **Related DOT Job—**No data available.

19-1031.01 Soil and Water Conservationists

- **Education/Training Required: Bachelor's degree**
- **Employed: 15,540**
- **Annual Earnings: $53,350**
- **Growth: 6.3%**
- **Annual Job Openings: 2,000**

The job openings listed here are shared with 19-1031.00 Conservation Scientists, 19-1031.02 Range Managers, and 19-1031.03 Park Naturalists.

Plan and develop coordinated practices for soil erosion control, soil and water conservation, and sound land use.

Develop and maintain working relationships with local government staff and board members. Advise land users such as farmers and ranchers on conservation plans, problems, and alternative solutions and provide technical and planning assistance. Apply principles of specialized fields of science, such as agronomy, soil science, forestry, or agriculture, to achieve conservation objectives. Plan soil management and conservation practices, such as crop rotation, reforestation, permanent vegetation, contour plowing, or terracing, to maintain soil and conserve water. Visit areas affected by erosion problems to seek sources and solutions. Monitor projects during and after construction to ensure projects conform to design specifications.

Compute design specifications for implementation of conservation practices, using survey and field information technical guides, engineering manuals, and calculator. Revisit land users to view implemented land use practices and plans. Coordinate and implement technical, financial, and administrative assistance programs for local government units to ensure efficient program implementation and timely responses to requests for assistance. Analyze results of investigations to determine measures needed to maintain or restore proper soil management. Participate on work teams to plan, develop, and implement water and land management programs and policies. Develop, conduct, and/or participate in surveys, studies, and investigations of various land uses, gathering information for use in developing corrective action plans. Survey property to mark locations and measurements, using surveying instruments. Compute cost estimates of different conservation practices based on needs of land users, maintenance requirements, and life expectancy of practices. Provide information, knowledge, expertise, and training to government agencies at all levels to solve water and soil management problems and to assure coordination of resource protection activities. Respond to complaints and questions on wetland jurisdiction, providing information and clarification. Initiate, schedule, and conduct annual audits and compliance checks of program implementation by local government.

GOE Information—Interest Area: 01. Agriculture and Natural Resources. Work Group: 01.02. Resource Science/Engineering for Plants, Animals, and the Environment. Personality Type—Investigative. Investigative occupations frequently involve working with ideas and require an extensive amount of thinking. These occupations can involve searching for facts and figuring out problems mentally. Work Values—Autonomy; Creativity; Responsibility; Ability Utilization; Independence; Variety. Skills—Persuasion; Operations Analysis; Science; Quality Control Analysis; Judgment and Decision Making; Installation. Abilities—*Cognitive:* Number Facility; Mathematical Reasoning; Inductive Reasoning; Originality; Flexibility of Closure; Written Expression. *Psychomotor:* Control Precision; Multilimb Coordination; Arm-Hand Steadiness. *Physical:* Gross Body Coordination; Extent Flexibility; Static Strength; Trunk Strength. *Sensory:* Far Vision; Speech Recognition; Visual Color Discrimination; Depth Perception; Speech Clarity; Hearing Sensitivity. General Work Activities—*Information Input:* Monitoring Processes, Materials, or Surroundings; Identifying Objects, Actions, and Events; Getting Information. *Mental Process:* Organizing, Planning, and Prioritizing; Making Decisions and Solving Problems; Updating and Using Relevant Knowledge. *Work Output:* Handling and Moving Objects; Performing General Physical Activities; Drafting and Specifying Technical Devices. *Interacting with Others:* Communicating with Persons Outside Organization; Establishing and Maintaining Interpersonal Relationships; Providing Consultation and Advice to Others. Physical Work Conditions—More Often Outdoors Than Indoors; Contaminants; Sitting. Other Job Characteristics—Need to Be Exact or Accurate; Errors Have Important Consequences.

Experience—Job Zone 4. A minimum of two to four years of work-related skill, knowledge, or experience is needed. Job Preparation—SVP 7.0 to less than 8.0—two years to less than 10 years. Knowledges—Geography; Biology; Engineering and Technology; Design; History and Archeology; Physics. Instructional Programs—Forest Management/ Forest Resources Management; Forest Sciences; Forestry, General; Forestry, Other; Land Use Planning and Management/Development; Natural Resources and Conservation, Other; Natural Resources Management and Policy, General; Natural Resources Management and Policy, Other; Natural Resources/

Conservation, General; Water, Wetlands, and Marine Resources Management; Wildlife and Wildlands Science and Management.

Related SOC Job—19-1031 Conservation Scientists. Related OOH Job—Conservation Scientists and Foresters. Related DOT Job—040.061-054 Soil Conservationist.

19-1031.02 Range Managers

- **Education/Training Required: Bachelor's degree**
- **Employed: 15,540**
- **Annual Earnings: $53,350**
- **Growth: 6.3%**
- **Annual Job Openings: 2,000**

The job openings listed here are shared with 19-1031.00 Conservation Scientists, 19-1031.01 Soil and Water Conservationists, and 19-1031.03 Park Naturalists.

Research or study range land management practices to provide sustained production of forage, livestock, and wildlife.

Regulate grazing and help ranchers plan and organize grazing systems to manage, improve, and protect rangelands and maximize their use. Measure and assess vegetation resources for biological assessment companies, environmental impact statements, and rangeland monitoring programs. Maintain soil stability and vegetation for nongrazing uses, such as wildlife habitats and outdoor recreation. Mediate agreements among rangeland users and preservationists as to appropriate land use and management. Study rangeland management practices and research range problems to provide sustained production of forage, livestock, and wildlife. Manage forage resources through fire, herbicide use, or revegetation to maintain a sustainable yield from the land. Offer advice to rangeland users on water management, forage production methods, and control of brush. Plan and direct construction and maintenance of range improvements such as fencing, corrals, stock-watering reservoirs, and soil-erosion control structures. Tailor conservation plans to landowners' goals, such as livestock support, wildlife, or recreation. Develop technical standards and specifications used to manage, protect, and improve the natural resources of rangelands and related grazing lands. Study grazing patterns to determine number and kind of livestock that can be most profitably grazed and to determine the best grazing seasons. Plan and implement revegetation of disturbed sites. Study forage plants and their growth requirements to determine varieties best suited to particular range. Develop methods for protecting range from fire and rodent damage and for controlling poisonous plants. Manage private livestock operations. Develop new and improved instruments and techniques for activities such as range reseeding.

GOE Information—Interest Area: 01. Agriculture and Natural Resources. Work Group: 01.02. Resource Science/Engineering for Plants, Animals, and the Environment. Personality Type—Investigative. Investigative occupations frequently involve working with ideas and require an extensive amount of thinking. These occupations can involve searching for facts and figuring out problems mentally. Work Values—Autonomy; Creativity; Independence; Responsibility; Ability Utilization; Recognition. Skills—Negotiation; Science; Management of Financial Resources; Persuasion; Coordination; Systems Evaluation. Abilities—*Cognitive:* Written Expression; Originality; Fluency of Ideas; Spatial Orientation; Problem Sensitivity; Number Facility. *Psychomotor:* Multilimb Coordination; Control Precision. *Physical:* Trunk Strength. *Sensory:* Depth Perception; Far Vision; Visual Color Discrimination; Hearing Sensitivity; Speech Recognition; Speech Clarity. General Work Activities—*Information Input:* Monitoring Processes, Materials, or

Surroundings; Getting Information; Identifying Objects, Actions, and Events. *Mental Process:* Organizing, Planning, and Prioritizing; Making Decisions and Solving Problems; Updating and Using Relevant Knowledge. *Work Output:* Handling and Moving Objects; Performing General Physical Activities; Documenting or Recording Information. *Interacting with Others:* Establishing and Maintaining Interpersonal Relationships; Communicating with Other Workers; Resolving Conflicts and Negotiating with Others. **Physical Work Conditions**—More Often Outdoors Than Indoors; Noisy; Very Hot or Cold; Minor Burns, Cuts, Bites, or Stings; Sitting. **Other Job Characteristics**—Need to Be Exact or Accurate; Repeat Same Tasks.

Experience—Job Zone 4. A minimum of two to four years of work-related skill, knowledge, or experience is needed. **Job Preparation**—SVP 7.0 to less than 8.0—two years to less than 10 years. **Knowledges**—Biology; Geography; Food Production; History and Archeology; Law and Government; Engineering and Technology. **Instructional Programs**—Forest Management/ Forest Resources Management; Forest Sciences; Forestry, General; Forestry, Other; Land Use Planning and Management/Development; Natural Resources and Conservation, Other; Natural Resources Management and Policy, General; Natural Resources Management and Policy, Other; Natural Resources/Conservation, General; Water, Wetlands, and Marine Resources Management; Wildlife and Wildlands Science and Management.

Related SOC Job—19-1031 Conservation Scientists. **Related OOH Job**—Conservation Scientists and Foresters. **Related DOT Job**—040.061-046 Range Manager.

19-1031.03 Park Naturalists

- **Education/Training Required: Bachelor's degree**
- **Employed: 15,540**
- **Annual Earnings: $53,350**
- **Growth: 6.3%**
- **Annual Job Openings: 2,000**

The job openings listed here are shared with 19-1031.00 Conservation Scientists, 19-1031.01 Soil and Water Conservationists, and 19-1031.02 Range Managers.

Plan, develop, and conduct programs to inform public of historical, natural, and scientific features of national, state, or local park.

Provide visitor services by explaining regulations; answering visitor requests, needs, and complaints; and providing information about the park and surrounding areas. Conduct field trips to point out scientific, historic, and natural features of parks, forests, historic sites, or other attractions. Prepare and present illustrated lectures and interpretive talks about park features. Perform emergency duties to protect human life, government property, and natural features of park. Confer with park staff to determine subjects and schedules for park programs. Assist with operations of general facilities, such as visitor centers. Plan, organize, and direct activities of seasonal staff members. Perform routine maintenance on park structures. Prepare brochures and write newspaper articles. Construct historical, scientific, and nature visitor-center displays. Research stories regarding the area's natural history or environment. Interview specialists in desired fields to obtain and develop data for park information programs. Compile and maintain official park photographic and information files. Take photographs and motion pictures for use in lectures and publications and to develop displays. Survey park to determine forest conditions and distribution and abundance of fauna and flora. Plan and develop audiovisual devices for public programs.

GOE Information—Interest Area: 01. Agriculture and Natural Resources. **Work Group:** 01.01. Managerial Work in Agriculture and Natural Resources. **Personality Type**—Social. Social occupations frequently involve working with, communicating with, and teaching people. These occupations often involve helping or providing service to others. **Work Values**—Autonomy; Creativity; Responsibility; Recognition; Variety; Achievement. **Skills**—Management of Personnel Resources; Management of Financial Resources; Service Orientation; Writing; Science; Management of Material Resources. **Abilities**—*Cognitive:* Originality; Oral Expression; Written Expression; Fluency of Ideas; Flexibility of Closure; Memorization. *Psychomotor:* Multilimb Coordination; Arm-Hand Steadiness; Manual Dexterity. *Physical:* Static Strength; Trunk Strength. *Sensory:* Speech Clarity; Speech Recognition; Far Vision; Hearing Sensitivity; Visual Color Discrimination; Depth Perception. **General Work Activities**—*Information Input:* Getting Information; Monitoring Processes, Materials, or Surroundings; Identifying Objects, Actions, and Events. *Mental Process:* Organizing, Planning, and Prioritizing; Updating and Using Relevant Knowledge; Thinking Creatively. *Work Output:* Handling and Moving Objects; Performing General Physical Activities; Documenting or Recording Information. *Interacting with Others:* Communicating with Persons Outside Organization; Performing for or Working with the Public; Establishing and Maintaining Interpersonal Relationships. **Physical Work Conditions**—More Often Indoors Than Outdoors; Very Hot or Cold; Minor Burns, Cuts, Bites, or Stings; Sitting; Using Hands on Objects, Tools, or Controls. **Other Job Characteristics**—Need to Be Exact or Accurate; Repeat Same Tasks.

Experience—Job Zone 4. A minimum of two to four years of work-related skill, knowledge, or experience is needed. **Job Preparation**—SVP 7.0 to less than 8.0—two years to less than 10 years. **Knowledges**—Biology; History and Archeology; Geography; Customer and Personal Service; Sociology and Anthropology; Communications and Media. **Instructional Programs**—Forest Management/Forest Resources Management; Forest Sciences; Forestry, General; Forestry, Other; Land Use Planning and Management/Development; Natural Resources and Conservation, Other; Natural Resources Management and Policy, Other; Natural Resources/Conservation, General; Water, Wetlands, and Marine Resources Management; Wildlife and Wildlands Science and Management.

Related SOC Job—19-1031 Conservation Scientists. **Related OOH Job**—Conservation Scientists and Foresters. **Related DOT Job**—049.127-010 Park Naturalist.

19-1032.00 Foresters

- **Education/Training Required: Bachelor's degree**
- **Employed: 10,750**
- **Annual Earnings: $48,670**
- **Growth: 6.7%**
- **Annual Job Openings: 1,000**

Manage forested lands for economic, recreational, and conservation purposes. May inventory the type, amount, and location of standing timber; appraise the timber's worth; negotiate the purchase; and draw up contracts for procurement. May determine how to conserve wildlife habitats, creek beds, water quality, and soil stability and how best to comply with environmental regulations. May devise plans for planting and growing new trees, monitor trees for healthy growth, and determine the best time for harvesting. Develop forest management plans for public and privately-owned forested lands.

Monitor contract compliance and results of forestry activities to assure adherence to government regulations. Establish short- and long-term plans for management of forest lands and forest resources. Supervise activities of other forestry workers. Choose and prepare sites for new trees, using controlled burning, bulldozers, or herbicides to clear weeds, brush, and logging debris. Plan and supervise forestry projects, such as determining the type, number, and placement of trees to be planted; managing tree nurseries; thinning forest; and monitoring growth of new seedlings. Negotiate terms and conditions of agreements and contracts for forest harvesting, forest management, and leasing of forest lands. Direct and participate in forest-fire suppression. Determine methods of cutting and removing timber with minimum waste and environmental damage. Analyze effect of forest conditions on tree growth rates and tree species prevalence and the yield, duration, seed production, growth viability, and germination of different species. Monitor forest-cleared lands to ensure that they are reclaimed to their most suitable end use. Plan and implement projects for conservation of wildlife habitats and soil and water quality. Plan and direct forest surveys and related studies and prepare reports and recommendations. Perform inspections of forests or forest nurseries. Map forest area soils and vegetation to estimate the amount of standing timber and future value and growth. Conduct public educational programs on forest care and conservation. Procure timber from private landowners. Subcontract with loggers or pulpwood cutters for tree removal and to aid in road layout. Plan cutting programs and manage timber sales from harvested areas, helping companies to achieve production goals. Monitor wildlife populations and assess the impacts of forest operations on population and habitats. Plan and direct construction and maintenance of recreation facilities, fire towers, trails, roads, and bridges, ensuring that they comply with guidelines and regulations set for forested public lands. Contact local forest owners and gain permission to take inventory of the type, amount, and location of all standing timber on the property.

GOE Information—Interest Area: 01. Agriculture and Natural Resources. **Work Group:** 01.02. Resource Science/Engineering for Plants, Animals, and the Environment. **Personality Type—**Realistic. Realistic occupations frequently involve work activities that include practical, hands-on problems and solutions. They often deal with plants; animals; and real-world materials like wood, tools, and machinery. Many of the occupations require working outside and do not involve a lot of paperwork or working closely with others. **Work Values—**Autonomy; Responsibility; Creativity; Authority; Ability Utilization; Achievement. **Skills—**Management of Financial Resources; Science; Programming; Quality Control Analysis; Mathematics; Operations Analysis. **Abilities—***Cognitive:* Spatial Orientation; Originality; Fluency of Ideas; Category Flexibility; Flexibility of Closure; Problem Sensitivity. *Psychomotor:* Control Precision; Multilimb Coordination; Reaction Time; Arm-Hand Steadiness. *Physical:* Static Strength; Dynamic Strength; Trunk Strength; Stamina. *Sensory:* Auditory Attention; Depth Perception; Far Vision; Near Vision. **General Work Activities—***Information Input:* Monitoring Processes, Materials, or Surroundings; Identifying Objects, Actions, and Events; Getting Information. *Mental Process:* Organizing, Planning, and Prioritizing; Processing Information; Making Decisions and Solving Problems. *Work Output:* Performing General Physical Activities; Documenting or Recording Information; Handling and Moving Objects. *Interacting with Others:* Communicating with Other Workers; Performing for or Working with the Public; Resolving Conflicts and Negotiating with Others. **Physical Work Conditions—**More Often Indoors Than Outdoors; Noisy; Sitting. **Other Job Characteristics—**Errors Have Important Consequences; Need to Be Exact or Accurate.

Experience—Job Zone 4. A minimum of two to four years of work-related skill, knowledge, or experience is needed. **Job Preparation—**SVP 7.0 to less than 8.0—two years to less than 10 years. **Knowledges—**Biology; Geography; Mathematics; Law and Government; Computers and Electronics; English Language. **Instructional Programs—**Forest Management/Forest Resources Management; Forest Resources Production and Management; Forest Sciences; Forestry, General; Forestry, Other; Natural Resources and Conservation, Other; Natural Resources Management and Policy, General; Natural Resources Management and Policy, Other; Natural Resources/Conservation, General; Urban Forestry; Wood Science and Wood Products/Pulp and Paper Technology.

Related SOC Job—19-1032 Foresters. **Related OOH Job—**Conservation Scientists and Foresters. **Related DOT Jobs—**040.061-030 Forest Ecologist; 040.061-050 Silviculturist; 040.167-010 Forester.

19-1041.00 Epidemiologists

- **Education/Training Required: Master's degree**
- **Employed: 3,630**
- **Annual Earnings: $52,170**
- **Growth: 26.2%**
- **Annual Job Openings: 1,000**

Investigate and describe the determinants and distribution of disease, disability, and other health outcomes and develop the means for prevention and control.

Oversee public health programs, including statistical analysis, health care planning, surveillance systems, and public health improvement. Investigate diseases or parasites to determine cause and risk factors, progress, life cycle, or mode of transmission. Plan and direct studies to investigate human or animal disease, preventive methods, and treatments for disease. Plan, administer, and evaluate health safety standards and programs to improve public health, conferring with health department, industry personnel, physicians, and others. Provide expertise in the design, management, and evaluation of study protocols and health status questionnaires, sample selection, and analysis. Conduct research to develop methodologies, instrumentation, and procedures for medical application, analyzing data and presenting findings. Consult with and advise physicians, educators, researchers, government health officials, and others regarding medical applications of sciences such as physics, biology, and chemistry. Supervise professional, technical, and clerical personnel. Identify and analyze public health issues related to foodborne parasitic diseases and their impact on public policies or scientific studies or surveys. Teach principles of medicine and medical and laboratory procedures to physicians, residents, students, and technicians. Standardize drug dosages, methods of immunization, and procedures for manufacture of drugs and medicinal compounds. Prepare and analyze samples to study effects of drugs, gases, pesticides, or microorganisms on cell structure and tissue.

GOE Information—Interest Area: 15. Scientific Research, Engineering, and Mathematics. **Work Group:** 15.03. Life Sciences. **Personality Type—**Investigative. Investigative occupations frequently involve working with ideas and require an extensive amount of thinking. These occupations can involve searching for facts and figuring out problems mentally. **Work Values—**Social Status; Creativity; Achievement; Recognition; Compensation; Ability Utilization. **Skills—**Science; Programming; Reading Comprehension; Mathematics; Writing; Complex Problem Solving. **Abilities—***Cognitive:* Inductive Reasoning; Problem Sensitivity; Written Comprehension; Oral Expression; Written Expression; Oral

Comprehension. *Psychomotor:* None met the criteria. *Physical:* None met the criteria. *Sensory:* Speech Clarity; Near Vision; Speech Recognition. **General Work Activities**—*Information Input:* Identifying Objects, Actions, and Events; Monitoring Processes, Materials, or Surroundings; Getting Information. *Mental Process:* Processing Information; Updating and Using Relevant Knowledge; Analyzing Data or Information. *Work Output:* Documenting or Recording Information; Interacting With Computers. *Interacting with Others:* Communicating with Other Workers; Communicating with Persons Outside Organization; Establishing and Maintaining Interpersonal Relationships. **Physical Work Conditions**—Indoors; Noisy; Sitting; Repetitive Motions. **Other Job Characteristics**—Need to Be Exact or Accurate; Repeat Same Tasks.

Experience—Job Zone 5. Extensive skill, knowledge, and experience are needed. **Job Preparation**—SVP 8.0 and above—four years to more than 10 years. **Knowledges**—Biology; Sociology and Anthropology; Medicine and Dentistry; English Language; Mathematics; Computers and Electronics. **Instructional Programs**—Cell/Cellular Biology and Histology; Epidemiology; Medical Scientist (MS, PhD).

Related SOC Job—19-1041 Epidemiologists. **Related OOH Job**—Medical Scientists. **Related DOT Jobs**—041.061-054 Histopathologist; 041.167-010 Environmental Epidemiologist.

19-1042.00 Medical Scientists, Except Epidemiologists

- Education/Training Required: Doctoral degree
- Employed: 73,670
- Annual Earnings: $61,730
- Growth: 34.1%
- Annual Job Openings: 15,000

Conduct research dealing with the understanding of human diseases and the improvement of human health. Engage in clinical investigation or other research, production, technical writing, or related activities.

Conduct research to develop methodologies, instrumentation, and procedures for medical application, analyzing data and presenting findings. Plan and direct studies to investigate human or animal disease, preventive methods, and treatments for disease. Follow strict safety procedures when handling toxic materials to avoid contamination. Evaluate effects of drugs, gases, pesticides, parasites, and microorganisms at various levels. Teach principles of medicine and medical and laboratory procedures to physicians, residents, students, and technicians. Prepare and analyze organ, tissue, and cell samples to identify toxicity, bacteria, or microorganisms or to study cell structure. Standardize drug dosages, methods of immunization, and procedures for manufacture of drugs and medicinal compounds. Investigate cause, progress, life cycle, or mode of transmission of diseases or parasites. Confer with health department, industry personnel, physicians, and others to develop health safety standards and public health improvement programs. Study animal and human health and physiological processes. Consult with and advise physicians, educators, researchers, and others regarding medical applications of physics, biology, and chemistry. Use equipment such as atomic absorption spectrometers, electron microscopes, flow cytometers, and chromatography systems.

GOE Information—**Interest Area:** 15. Scientific Research, Engineering, and Mathematics. **Work Group:** 15.03. Life Sciences. **Personality Type**—Investigative. Investigative occupations frequently involve working with ideas and require an extensive amount of thinking. These occupations can involve searching for facts and figuring out problems mentally. **Work Values**—Social Status; Creativity; Achievement; Recognition; Compensation; Ability Utilization. **Skills**—Science; Management of Financial Resources; Judgment and Decision Making; Reading Comprehension; Writing; Time Management. **Abilities**—*Cognitive:* Inductive Reasoning; Written Comprehension; Problem Sensitivity; Oral Comprehension; Oral Expression; Deductive Reasoning. *Psychomotor:* Finger Dexterity. *Physical:* None met the criteria. *Sensory:* Speech Clarity; Near Vision; Visual Color Discrimination; Speech Recognition; Far Vision. **General Work Activities**—*Information Input:* Getting Information; Monitoring Processes, Materials, or Surroundings; Identifying Objects, Actions, and Events. *Mental Process:* Processing Information; Updating and Using Relevant Knowledge; Making Decisions and Solving Problems. *Work Output:* Documenting or Recording Information; Interacting With Computers. *Interacting with Others:* Communicating with Other Workers; Communicating with Persons Outside Organization; Interpreting the Meaning of Information for Others. **Physical Work Conditions**—Indoors; Sitting; Using Hands on Objects, Tools, or Controls. **Other Job Characteristics**—Need to Be Exact or Accurate.

Experience—Job Zone 5. Extensive skill, knowledge, and experience are needed. **Job Preparation**—SVP 8.0 and above—four years to more than 10 years. **Knowledges**—Biology; Medicine and Dentistry; Chemistry; Communications and Media; Personnel and Human Resources; Mathematics. **Instructional Programs**—Anatomy; Biochemistry; Biomedical Sciences, General; Biophysics; Biostatistics; Cardiovascular Science; Cell Physiology; Cell/Cellular Biology and Histology; Endocrinology; Environmental Toxicology; Epidemiology; Exercise Physiology; Human/Medical Genetics; Immunology; Medical Microbiology and Bacteriology; Medical Scientist (MS, PhD); Molecular Biology; Molecular Pharmacology; Molecular Physiology; Molecular Toxicology; Neurobiology and Neurophysiology; Neuropharmacology; Oncology and Cancer Biology; Pathology/Experimental Pathology; Pharmacology; Pharmacology and Toxicology; Pharmacology and Toxicology, Other; Physiology, General; Physiology, Pathology, and Related Sciences, Other; Reproductive Biology; Toxicology; Vision Science/Physiological Optics.

Related SOC Job—19-1042 Medical Scientists, Except Epidemiologists. **Related OOH Job**—Medical Scientists. **Related DOT Jobs**—041.061-010 Anatomist; 041.061-070 Parasitologist; 041.061-074 Pharmacologist; 041.067-010 Medical Coordinator, Pesticide Use; 079.021-014 Medical Physicist.

19-1099.99 Life Scientists, All Other

- Education/Training Required: Bachelor's degree
- Employed: 12,790
- Annual Earnings: $56,370
- Growth: 20.6%
- Annual Job Openings: 3,000

All life scientists not listed separately.

No task data available.

Note: The Department of Labor has not collected some data for this job, so it has fewer details than the other descriptions.

Related SOC Job—19-1099 Life Scientists, All Other. **Related OOH Job**—None. **Related DOT Job**—041.261-010 Public-Health Microbiologist.

19-2000 Physical Scientists

19-2011.00 Astronomers

- **Education/Training Required: Doctoral degree**
- **Employed: 970**
- **Annual Earnings: $104,670**
- **Growth: 10.4%**
- **Annual Job Openings: Fewer than 500**

Observe, research, and interpret celestial and astronomical phenomena to increase basic knowledge and apply such information to practical problems.

Study celestial phenomena, using a variety of ground-based and space-borne telescopes and scientific instruments. Analyze research data to determine its significance, using computers. Present research findings at scientific conferences and in papers written for scientific journals. Measure radio, infrared, gamma, and X-ray emissions from extraterrestrial sources. Develop theories based on personal observations or on observations and theories of other astronomers. Raise funds for scientific research. Collaborate with other astronomers to carry out research projects. Develop instrumentation and software for astronomical observation and analysis. Teach astronomy or astrophysics. Develop and modify astronomy-related programs for public presentation. Calculate orbits and determine sizes, shapes, brightness, and motions of different celestial bodies. Direct the operations of a planetarium.

GOE Information—Interest Area: 15. Scientific Research, Engineering, and Mathematics. **Work Group:** 15.02. Physical Sciences. **Personality Type—**Investigative. Investigative occupations frequently involve working with ideas and require an extensive amount of thinking. These occupations can involve searching for facts and figuring out problems mentally. **Work Values—**Independence; Autonomy; Creativity; Ability Utilization; Responsibility; Achievement. **Skills—**Science; Programming; Mathematics; Complex Problem Solving; Active Learning; Critical Thinking. **Abilities—***Cognitive:* Mathematical Reasoning; Flexibility of Closure; Number Facility; Written Expression; Written Comprehension; Category Flexibility. *Psychomotor:* None met the criteria. *Physical:* None met the criteria. *Sensory:* Far Vision; Speech Clarity; Visual Color Discrimination; Speech Recognition; Near Vision. **General Work Activities—***Information Input:* Getting Information; Identifying Objects, Actions, and Events; Estimating the Needed Characteristics of Products, Events, or Information. *Mental Process:* Analyzing Data or Information; Thinking Creatively; Processing Information. *Work Output:* Interacting With Computers; Documenting or Recording Information. *Interacting with Others:* Interpreting the Meaning of Information for Others; Teaching Others; Communicating with Other Workers. **Physical Work Conditions—**Indoors; Sitting. **Other Job Characteristics—**Need to Be Exact or Accurate.

Experience—Job Zone 5. Extensive skill, knowledge, and experience are needed. **Job Preparation—**SVP 8.0 and above—four years to more than 10 years. **Knowledges—**Physics; Mathematics; Engineering and Technology; Chemistry; Computers and Electronics; Education and Training. **Instructional Programs—**Astronomy; Astronomy and Astrophysics, Other; Astrophysics; Planetary Astronomy and Science.

Related SOC Job—19-2011 Astronomers. **Related OOH Job—**Physicists and Astronomers. **Related DOT Job—**021.067-010 Astronomer.

19-2012.00 Physicists

- **Education/Training Required: Doctoral degree**
- **Employed: 15,160**
- **Annual Earnings: $89,810**
- **Growth: 7.0%**
- **Annual Job Openings: 1,000**

Conduct research into the phases of physical phenomena, develop theories and laws on the basis of observation and experiments, and devise methods to apply laws and theories to industry and other fields.

Perform complex calculations as part of the analysis and evaluation of data, using computers. Describe and express observations and conclusions in mathematical terms. Analyze data from research conducted to detect and measure physical phenomena. Report experimental results by writing papers for scientific journals or by presenting information at scientific conferences. Design computer simulations to model physical data so that it can be better understood. Collaborate with other scientists in the design, development, and testing of experimental, industrial, or medical equipment, instrumentation, and procedures. Direct testing and monitoring of contamination of radioactive equipment and recording of personnel and plant area radiation exposure data. Observe the structure and properties of matter and the transformation and propagation of energy, using equipment such as masers, lasers, and telescopes, to explore and identify the basic principles governing these phenomena. Develop theories and laws on the basis of observation and experiments and apply these theories and laws to problems in areas such as nuclear energy, optics, and aerospace technology. Teach physics to students. Develop manufacturing, assembly, and fabrication processes of lasers, masers, and infrared and other light-emitting and light-sensitive devices. Conduct application evaluations and analyze results to determine commercial, industrial, scientific, medical, military, or other uses for electro-optical devices. Develop standards of permissible concentrations of radioisotopes in liquids and gases. Conduct research pertaining to potential environmental impacts of atomic energy–related industrial development to determine licensing qualifications. Advise authorities of procedures to be followed in radiation incidents or hazards and assist in civil defense planning.

GOE Information—Interest Area: 15. Scientific Research, Engineering, and Mathematics. **Work Group:** 15.02. Physical Sciences. **Personality Type—**Investigative. Investigative occupations frequently involve working with ideas and require an extensive amount of thinking. These occupations can involve searching for facts and figuring out problems mentally. **Work Values—**Creativity; Autonomy; Recognition; Ability Utilization; Social Status; Achievement. **Skills—**Programming; Science; Mathematics; Complex Problem Solving; Management of Financial Resources; Systems Analysis. **Abilities—***Cognitive:* Mathematical Reasoning; Number Facility; Originality; Fluency of Ideas; Written Expression; Written Comprehension. *Psychomotor:* None met the criteria. *Physical:* None met the criteria. *Sensory:* Speech Clarity; Far Vision; Speech Recognition; Visual Color Discrimination; Depth Perception; Hearing Sensitivity. **General Work Activities—***Information Input:* Getting Information; Identifying Objects, Actions, and Events; Estimating Needed Characteristics of Products, Events, or Information. *Mental Process:* Thinking Creatively; Processing Information; Making Decisions and Solving Problems. *Work Output:* Interacting With Computers; Documenting or Recording Information. *Interacting with Others:* Interpreting the Meaning of Information for Others; Providing Consultation and Advice to Others; Communicating with Persons Outside Organization.

Physical Work Conditions—Indoors; Sitting. **Other Job Characteristics**—Need to Be Exact or Accurate.

Experience—Job Zone 5. Extensive skill, knowledge, and experience are needed. **Job Preparation**—SVP 8.0 and above—four years to more than 10 years. **Knowledges**—Physics; Mathematics; Engineering and Technology; Computers and Electronics; English Language; Telecommunications. **Instructional Programs**—Acoustics; Astrophysics; Atomic/Molecular Physics; Elementary Particle Physics; Health/Medical Physics; Nuclear Physics; Optics/Optical Sciences; Physics, General; Physics, Other; Plasma and High-Temperature Physics; Solid State and Low-Temperature Physics; Theoretical and Mathematical Physics.

Related SOC Job—19-2012 Physicists. **Related OOH Job**—Physicists and Astronomers. **Related DOT Jobs**—015.021-010 Health Physicist; 023.061-010 Electro-Optical Engineer; 023.061-014 Physicist; 023.067-010 Physicist, Theoretical.

19-2021.00 Atmospheric and Space Scientists

- Education/Training Required: Bachelor's degree
- Employed: 7,050
- Annual Earnings: $73,940
- Growth: 16.5%
- Annual Job Openings: 1,000

Investigate atmospheric phenomena and interpret meteorological data gathered by surface and air stations, satellites, and radar to prepare reports and forecasts for public and other uses.

Study and interpret data, reports, maps, photographs, and charts to predict long- and short-range weather conditions, using computer models and knowledge of climate theory, physics, and mathematics. Broadcast weather conditions, forecasts, and severe weather warnings to the public via television, radio, and the Internet or provide this information to the news media. Gather data from sources such as surface and upper air stations, satellites, weather bureaus, and radar for use in meteorological reports and forecasts. Prepare forecasts and briefings to meet the needs of industry, business, government, and other groups. Apply meteorological knowledge to problems in areas including agriculture, pollution control, and water management and to issues such as global warming or ozone depletion. Conduct basic or applied meteorological research into the processes and determinants of atmospheric phenomena, weather, and climate. Operate computer graphic equipment to produce weather reports and maps for analysis, distribution, or use in weather broadcasts. Measure wind, temperature, and humidity in the upper atmosphere, using weather balloons. Develop and use weather forecasting tools such as mathematical and computer models. Direct forecasting services at weather stations or at radio or television broadcasting facilities. Research and analyze the impact of industrial projects and pollution on climate, air quality, and weather phenomena. Collect air samples from planes and ships over land and sea to study atmospheric composition. Conduct numerical simulations of climate conditions to understand and predict global and regional weather patterns. Collect and analyze historical climate information such as precipitation and temperature records help predict future weather and climate trends. Consult with agencies, professionals, or researchers regarding the use and interpretation of climatological information. Design and develop new equipment and methods for meteorological data collection, remote sensing, or related applications. Make scientific presentations and publish reports, articles, or texts.

GOE Information—**Interest Area:** 15. Scientific Research, Engineering, and Mathematics. **Work Group:** 15.02. Physical Sciences. **Personality Type**—Investigative. Investigative occupations frequently involve working with ideas and require an extensive amount of thinking. These occupations can involve searching for facts and figuring out problems mentally. **Work Values**—Social Status; Recognition; Responsibility; Autonomy; Ability Utilization; Security. **Skills**—Science; Programming; Judgment and Decision Making; Operation Monitoring; Technology Design; Operations Analysis. **Abilities**—*Cognitive:* Mathematical Reasoning; Oral Expression; Written Expression; Number Facility; Written Comprehension; Oral Comprehension. *Psychomotor:* None met the criteria. *Physical:* None met the criteria. *Sensory:* Speech Clarity; Far Vision; Visual Color Discrimination; Near Vision. **General Work Activities**—*Information Input:* Getting Information; Monitoring Processes, Materials, or Surroundings; Identifying Objects, Actions, and Events. *Mental Process:* Processing Information; Updating and Using Relevant Knowledge; Analyzing Data or Information. *Work Output:* Interacting With Computers; Documenting or Recording Information. *Interacting with Others:* Performing for or Working with the Public; Establishing and Maintaining Interpersonal Relationships; Communicating with Persons Outside Organization. **Physical Work Conditions**—Indoors; Noisy; Sitting; Repetitive Motions. **Other Job Characteristics**—Need to Be Exact or Accurate; Repeat Same Tasks; Automation.

Experience—Job Zone 4. A minimum of two to four years of work-related skill, knowledge, or experience is needed. **Job Preparation**—SVP 7.0 to less than 8.0—two years to less than 10 years. **Knowledges**—Geography; Physics; Computers and Electronics; Mathematics; Communications and Media; Customer and Personal Service. **Instructional Programs**—Atmospheric Chemistry and Climatology; Atmospheric Physics and Dynamics; Atmospheric Sciences and Meteorology, General; Atmospheric Sciences and Meteorology, Other; Meteorology.

Related SOC Job—19-2021 Atmospheric and Space Scientists. **Related OOH Job**—Atmospheric Scientists. **Related DOT Job**—025.062-010 Meteorologist.

19-2031.00 Chemists

- Education/Training Required: Bachelor's degree
- Employed: 76,540
- Annual Earnings: $57,890
- Growth: 7.3%
- Annual Job Openings: 5,000

Conduct qualitative and quantitative chemical analyses or chemical experiments in laboratories for quality or process control or to develop new products or knowledge.

Analyze organic and inorganic compounds to determine chemical and physical properties, composition, structure, relationships, and reactions, utilizing chromatography, spectroscopy, and spectrophotometry techniques. Develop, improve, and customize products, equipment, formulas, processes, and analytical methods. Compile and analyze test information to determine process or equipment operating efficiency and to diagnose malfunctions. Confer with scientists and engineers to conduct analyses of research projects, interpret test results, or develop nonstandard tests. Direct, coordinate, and advise personnel in test procedures for analyzing components and physical properties of materials. Induce changes in composition of substances by introducing heat, light, energy, and chemical catalysts for quantitative and qualitative analysis. Write technical papers and reports and prepare standards and specifications for processes, facilities, products, or tests. Study effects of various methods of processing, preserving, and packaging on composition and properties of foods. Prepare test solutions, compounds, and reagents for laboratory personnel to conduct test.

GOE Information—Interest Area: 15. Scientific Research, Engineering, and Mathematics. **Work Group:** 15.02. Physical Sciences. **Personality Type—**Investigative. Investigative occupations frequently involve working with ideas and require an extensive amount of thinking. These occupations can involve searching for facts and figuring out problems mentally. **Work Values—**Creativity; Ability Utilization; Responsibility; Autonomy; Achievement; Independence. **Skills—**Science; Quality Control Analysis; Technology Design; Operation Monitoring; Management of Financial Resources; Management of Material Resources. **Abilities—***Cognitive:* Written Expression; Oral Comprehension; Mathematical Reasoning; Inductive Reasoning; Deductive Reasoning; Written Comprehension. *Psychomotor:* Arm-Hand Steadiness; Control Precision. *Physical:* None met the criteria. *Sensory:* Near Vision; Visual Color Discrimination. **General Work Activities—***Information Input:* Getting Information; Monitoring Processes, Materials, or Surroundings; Identifying Objects, Actions, and Events. *Mental Process:* Processing Information; Updating and Using Relevant Knowledge; Organizing, Planning, and Prioritizing. *Work Output:* Handling and Moving Objects; Repairing and Maintaining Electronic Equipment; Documenting or Recording Information. *Interacting with Others:* Establishing and Maintaining Interpersonal Relationships; Communicating with Other Workers; Providing Consultation and Advice to Others. **Physical Work Conditions—**Indoors; Contaminants; Hazardous Conditions; Standing. **Other Job Characteristics—**Need to Be Exact or Accurate; Errors Have Important Consequences.

Experience—Job Zone 4. A minimum of two to four years of work-related skill, knowledge, or experience is needed. **Job Preparation—**SVP 7.0 to less than 8.0—two years to less than 10 years. **Knowledges—**Chemistry; Mathematics; Engineering and Technology; Production and Processing; Computers and Electronics; Law and Government. **Instructional Programs—**Analytical Chemistry; Chemical Physics; Chemistry, General; Chemistry, Other; Inorganic Chemistry; Organic Chemistry; Physical and Theoretical Chemistry; Polymer Chemistry.

Related SOC Job—19-2031 Chemists. **Related OOH Job—**Chemists and Materials Scientists. **Related DOT Jobs—**022.061-010 Chemist; 022.061-014 Chemist, Food; 022.137-010 Laboratory Supervisor.

19-2032.00 Materials Scientists

- **Education/Training Required:** Bachelor's degree
- **Employed:** 7,880
- **Annual Earnings:** $71,450
- **Growth:** 8.0%
- **Annual Job Openings:** Fewer than 500

Research and study the structures and chemical properties of various natural and manmade materials, including metals, alloys, rubber, ceramics, semiconductors, polymers, and glass. Determine ways to strengthen or combine materials or develop new materials with new or specific properties for use in a variety of products and applications.

Plan laboratory experiments to confirm feasibility of processes and techniques used in the production of materials having special characteristics. Confer with customers in order to determine how materials can be tailored to suit their needs. Conduct research into the structures and properties of materials such as metals, alloys, polymers, and ceramics to obtain information that could be used to develop new products or enhance existing ones. Prepare reports of materials study findings for the use of other scientists and requestors. Devise testing methods to evaluate the effects of various conditions on particular materials. Determine ways to strengthen or combine materials or develop new materials with new or specific properties for use in a variety of products and applications. Recommend materials for reliable performance in various environments. Test individual parts and products to ensure that manufacturer and governmental quality and safety standards are met. Visit suppliers of materials or users of products to gather specific information. Research methods of processing, forming, and firing materials to develop such products as ceramic fillings for teeth, unbreakable dinner plates, and telescope lenses. Study the nature, structure, and physical properties of metals and their alloys and their responses to applied forces. Monitor production processes to ensure that equipment is used efficiently and that projects are completed within appropriate time frames and budgets. Test material samples for tolerance under tension, compression, and shear to determine the cause of metal failures. Test metals to determine whether they meet specifications of mechanical strength; strength-weight ratio; ductility; magnetic and electrical properties; and resistance to abrasion, corrosion, heat, and cold. Teach in colleges and universities.

GOE Information—Interest Area: 15. Scientific Research, Engineering, and Mathematics. **Work Group:** 15.02. Physical Sciences. **Personality Type—**Investigative. Investigative occupations frequently involve working with ideas and require an extensive amount of thinking. These occupations can involve searching for facts and figuring out problems mentally. **Work Values—**Creativity; Autonomy; Ability Utilization; Responsibility; Social Status; Working Conditions. **Skills—**Science; Programming; Technology Design; Quality Control Analysis; Mathematics; Installation. **Abilities—***Cognitive:* Originality; Mathematical Reasoning; Written Expression; Inductive Reasoning; Flexibility of Closure; Category Flexibility. *Psychomotor:* None met the criteria. *Physical:* None met the criteria. *Sensory:* Visual Color Discrimination; Hearing Sensitivity; Auditory Attention; Far Vision; Near Vision; Speech Recognition. **General Work Activities—***Information Input:* Identifying Objects, Actions, and Events; Getting Information; Monitoring Processes, Materials, or Surroundings. *Mental Process:* Processing Information; Updating and Using Relevant Knowledge; Analyzing Data or Information. *Work Output:* Documenting or Recording Information; Controlling Machines and Processes; Interacting With Computers. *Interacting with Others:* Communicating with Other Workers; Interpreting the Meaning of Information for Others; Establishing and Maintaining Interpersonal Relationships. **Physical Work Conditions—**Indoors; Noisy; Hazardous Conditions; Sitting. **Other Job Characteristics—**Need to Be Exact or Accurate; Errors Have Important Consequences.

Experience—Job Zone 5. Extensive skill, knowledge, and experience are needed. **Job Preparation—**SVP 8.0 and above—four years to more than 10 years. **Knowledges—**Chemistry; Engineering and Technology; Physics; Mathematics; Production and Processing; Administration and Management. **Instructional Program—**Materials Science.

Related SOC Job—19-2032 Materials Scientists. **Related OOH Job—**Chemists and Materials Scientists. **Related DOT Job—**029.081-014 Materials Scientist.

19-2041.00 Environmental Scientists and Specialists, Including Health

- **Education/Training Required:** Master's degree
- **Employed:** 72,000
- **Annual Earnings:** $52,630
- **Growth:** 17.1%
- **Annual Job Openings:** 8,000

Conduct research or perform investigation for the purpose of identifying, abating, or eliminating sources of pollutants or hazards that affect either the environment or the health of the population. Utilizing knowledge of various scientific disciplines, may collect, synthesize, study, report, and take action based on data derived from measurements or observations of air, food, soil, water, and other sources.

Conduct environmental audits and inspections and investigations of violations. Evaluate violations or problems discovered during inspections to determine appropriate regulatory actions or to provide advice on the development and prosecution of regulatory cases. Communicate scientific and technical information through oral briefings, written documents, workshops, conferences, and public hearings. Review and implement environmental technical standards, guidelines, policies, and formal regulations that meet all appropriate requirements. Provide technical guidance, support, and oversight to environmental programs, industry, and the public. Provide advice on proper standards and regulations or the development of policies, strategies, and codes of practice for environmental management. Analyze data to determine validity, quality, and scientific significance and to interpret correlations between human activities and environmental effects. Collect, synthesize, and analyze data derived from pollution emission measurements, atmospheric monitoring, meteorological and mineralogical information, and soil or water samples. Determine data collection methods to be employed in research projects and surveys. Prepare charts or graphs from data samples, providing summary information on the environmental relevance of the data. Develop the technical portions of legal documents, administrative orders, or consent decrees. Investigate and report on accidents affecting the environment. Monitor environmental impacts of development activities. Supervise environmental technologists and technicians. Develop programs designed to obtain the most productive, non-damaging use of land. Research sources of pollution to determine their effects on the environment and to develop theories or methods of pollution abatement or control. Monitor effects of pollution and land degradation and recommend means of prevention or control. Design and direct studies to obtain technical environmental information about planned projects. Conduct applied research on topics such as waste control and treatment and pollution control methods.

GOE Information—Interest Area: 15. Scientific Research, Engineering, and Mathematics. **Work Group:** 15.03. Life Sciences. **Personality Type—**Investigative. Investigative occupations frequently involve working with ideas and require an extensive amount of thinking. These occupations can involve searching for facts and figuring out problems mentally. **Work Values—**Autonomy; Creativity; Ability Utilization; Achievement; Recognition; Independence. **Skills—**Science; Service Orientation; Negotiation; Coordination; Reading Comprehension; Complex Problem Solving. **Abilities—***Cognitive:* Mathematical Reasoning; Inductive Reasoning; Problem Sensitivity; Number Facility; Written Expression; Speed of Closure. *Psychomotor:* None met the criteria. *Physical:* Trunk Strength. *Sensory:* Speech Clarity; Far Vision; Visual Color Discrimination; Near Vision; Hearing Sensitivity; Auditory Attention. **General Work**

Activities—*Information Input:* Monitoring Processes, Materials, or Surroundings; Getting Information; Identifying Objects, Actions, and Events. *Mental Process:* Processing Information; Updating and Using Relevant Knowledge; Organizing, Planning, and Prioritizing. *Work Output:* Documenting or Recording Information; Interacting With Computers; Performing General Physical Activities. *Interacting with Others:* Establishing and Maintaining Interpersonal Relationships; Communicating with Other Workers; Communicating with Persons Outside Organization. **Physical Work Conditions—**More Often Indoors Than Outdoors; Noisy; Sitting. **Other Job Characteristics—**Need to Be Exact or Accurate; Repeat Same Tasks.

Experience—Job Zone 5. Extensive skill, knowledge, and experience are needed. **Job Preparation—**SVP 8.0 and above—four years to more than 10 years. **Knowledges—**Biology; Geography; Chemistry; Law and Government; Engineering and Technology; Physics. **Instructional Programs—**Environmental Science; Environmental Studies.

Related SOC Job—19-2041 Environmental Scientists and Specialists, Including Health. **Related OOH Jobs—**Geoscientists; Environmental Scientists and Hydrologists. **Related DOT Job—**029.081-010 Environmental Analyst.

19-2042.00 Geoscientists, Except Hydrologists and Geographers

- **Education/Training Required:** Master's degree
- **Employed:** 27,430
- **Annual Earnings:** $71,640
- **Growth:** 8.3%
- **Annual Job Openings:** 2,000

Study the composition, structure, and other physical aspects of the earth. May use geological, physics, and mathematics knowledge in exploration for oil, gas, minerals, or underground water or in waste disposal, land reclamation, or other environmental problems. May study the earth's internal composition, atmospheres, and oceans and its magnetic, electrical, and gravitational forces. Includes mineralogists, crystallographers, paleontologists, stratigraphers, geodesists, and seismologists.

Analyze and interpret geological, geochemical, and geophysical information from sources such as survey data, well logs, bore holes, and aerial photos. Plan and conduct geological, geochemical, and geophysical field studies and surveys, sample collection, or drilling and testing programs used to collect data for research or application. Investigate the composition, structure, and history of the Earth's crust through the collection, examination, measurement, and classification of soils, minerals, rocks, or fossil remains. Prepare geological maps, cross-sectional diagrams, charts, and reports concerning mineral extraction, land use, and resource management, using results of fieldwork and laboratory research. Locate and estimate probable natural gas, oil, and mineral ore deposits and underground water resources, using aerial photographs, charts, or research and survey results. Assess ground and surface water movement to provide advice regarding issues such as waste management, route and site selection, and the restoration of contaminated sites. Identify risks for natural disasters such as mud slides, earthquakes, and volcanic eruptions, providing advice on mitigation of potential damage. Conduct geological and geophysical studies to provide information for use in regional development, site selection, and development of public works projects. Inspect construction projects to analyze engineering problems, applying geological knowledge and using test equipment and drilling machinery. Advise construction firms and government agencies on dam and road construction, foundation design, or land use and resource management. Communicate geological findings by writing research papers, participating in conferences, or teaching geological science at universities. Measure characteristics of the Earth, such as gravity and magnetic fields, using equipment such as seismographs, gravimeters, torsion balances, and magnetometers. Test industrial diamonds and abrasives, soil, or rocks to determine their geological characteristics, using optical, X-ray, heat, acid, and precision instruments. Identify deposits of construction materials and assess the materials' characteristics and suitability for use as concrete aggregates, as road fill, or in other applications.

GOE Information—Interest Area: 15. Scientific Research, Engineering, and Mathematics. **Work Group:** 15.02. Physical Sciences. **Personality Type**—Investigative. Investigative occupations frequently involve working with ideas and require an extensive amount of thinking. These occupations can involve searching for facts and figuring out problems mentally. **Work Values**—Responsibility; Ability Utilization; Autonomy; Creativity; Achievement; Independence. **Skills**—Science; Management of Financial Resources; Active Learning; Time Management; Coordination; Equipment Selection. **Abilities**—*Cognitive:* Category Flexibility; Inductive Reasoning; Mathematical Reasoning; Flexibility of Closure; Written Expression; Oral Comprehension. *Psychomotor:* None met the criteria. *Physical:* None met the criteria. *Sensory:* Near Vision; Speech Clarity; Far Vision. **General Work Activities**—*Information Input:* Identifying Objects, Actions, and Events; Getting Information; Estimating the Needed Characteristics of Products, Events, or Information. *Mental Process:* Processing Information; Analyzing Data or Information; Thinking Creatively. *Work Output:* Documenting or Recording Information; Interacting With Computers; Performing General Physical Activities. *Interacting with Others:* Interpreting the Meaning of Information for Others; Communicating with Other Workers; Establishing and Maintaining Interpersonal Relationships. **Physical Work Conditions**—More Often Indoors Than Outdoors; Sitting. **Other Job Characteristics**—Need to Be Exact or Accurate; Errors Have Important Consequences; Repeat Same Tasks.

Experience—Job Zone 5. Extensive skill, knowledge, and experience are needed. **Job Preparation**—SVP 8.0 and above—four years to more than 10 years. **Knowledges**—Geography; Physics; Chemistry; Biology; Engineering and Technology; Mathematics. **Instructional Programs**—Geochemistry; Geochemistry and Petrology; Geological and Earth Sciences/Geosciences, Other; Geology/Earth Science, General; Geophysics and Seismology; Oceanography; Oceanography, Chemical and Physical; Paleontology.

Related SOC Job—19-2042 Geoscientists, Except Hydrologists and Geographers. **Related OOH Job**—Geoscientists. **Related DOT Jobs**—024.061-010 Crystallographer; 024.061-018 Geologist; 024.061-022 Geologist, Petroleum; 024.061-026 Geophysical Prospector; 024.061-038 Mineralogist; 024.061-042 Paleontologist; 024.061-046 Petrologist; 024.061-054 Stratigrapher; 024.161-010 Engineer, Soils; 024.284-010 Prospector.

19-2043.00 Hydrologists

- **Education/Training Required: Master's degree**
- **Employed: 8,360**
- **Annual Earnings: $63,820**
- **Growth: 31.6%**
- **Annual Job Openings: 1,000**

Research the distribution, circulation, and physical properties of underground and surface waters; study the form and intensity of precipitation, its rate of infiltration into the soil, its movement through the earth, and its return to the ocean and atmosphere.

Study and document quantities, distribution, disposition, and development of underground and surface waters. Draft final reports describing research results, including illustrations, appendices, maps, and other attachments. Coordinate and supervise the work of professional and technical staff, including research assistants, technologists, and technicians. Prepare hydrogeologic evaluations of known or suspected hazardous waste sites and land treatment and feedlot facilities. Design and conduct scientific hydrogeological investigations to ensure that accurate and appropriate information is available for use in water resource management decisions. Study public water supply issues, including flood and drought risks, water quality, wastewater, and impacts on wetland habitats. Collect and analyze water samples as part of field investigations and/or to validate data from automatic monitors. Apply research findings to help minimize the environmental impacts of pollution, water-borne diseases, erosion, and sedimentation. Measure and graph phenomena such as lake levels, stream flows, and changes in water volumes. Investigate complaints or conflicts related to the alteration of public waters, gathering information, recommending alternatives, informing participants of progress, and preparing draft orders. Develop or modify methods of conducting hydrologic studies. Answer questions and provide technical assistance and information to contractors and/or the public regarding issues such as well drilling, code requirements, hydrology, and geology. Install, maintain, and calibrate instruments such as those that monitor water levels, rainfall, and sediments. Evaluate data and provide recommendations regarding the feasibility of municipal projects such as hydroelectric power plants, irrigation systems, flood warning systems, and waste treatment facilities. Conduct short-term and long-term climate assessments and study storm occurrences. Study and analyze the physical aspects of the Earth in terms of the hydrological components, including atmosphere, hydrosphere, and interior structure. Conduct research and communicate information to promote the conservation and preservation of water resources.

GOE Information—Interest Area: 15. Scientific Research, Engineering, and Mathematics. **Work Group:** 15.02. Physical Sciences. **Personality Type**—Investigative. Investigative occupations frequently involve working with ideas and require an extensive amount of thinking. These occupations can involve searching for facts and figuring out problems mentally. **Work Values**—Autonomy; Creativity; Ability Utilization; Responsibility; Independence; Achievement. **Skills**—Science; Programming; Management of Financial Resources; Mathematics; Management of Personnel Resources; Complex Problem Solving. **Abilities**—*Cognitive:* Mathematical Reasoning; Written Expression; Number Facility; Flexibility of Closure; Written Comprehension; Oral Comprehension. *Psychomotor:* None met the criteria. *Physical:* None met the criteria. *Sensory:* Visual Color Discrimination; Far Vision; Speech Clarity; Speech Recognition; Near Vision. **General Work Activities**—*Information Input:* Getting Information; Identifying Objects, Actions, and Events; Monitoring Processes, Materials, or Surroundings. *Mental Process:* Analyzing Data or Information; Processing Information; Updating and Using Relevant Knowledge. *Work Output:* Documenting or Recording Information; Interacting With Computers; Performing General Physical Activities. *Interacting with Others:* Communicating with Other Workers; Communicating with Persons Outside Organization; Providing Consultation and Advice to Others. **Physical Work Conditions**—More Often Indoors

Than Outdoors; Sitting. **Other Job Characteristics**—Need to Be Exact or Accurate.

Experience—Job Zone 5. Extensive skill, knowledge, and experience are needed. **Job Preparation**—SVP 8.0 and above—four years to more than 10 years. **Knowledges**—Geography; Physics; Engineering and Technology; Chemistry; Biology; Mathematics. **Instructional Programs**—Geology/Earth Science, General; Hydrology and Water Resources Science; Oceanography, Chemical and Physical.

Related SOC Job—19-2043 Hydrologists. **Related OOH Jobs**—Geoscientists; Environmental Scientists and Hydrologists. **Related DOT Jobs**—024.061-030 Geophysicist; 024.061-034 Hydrologist; 024.061-050 Seismologist; 024.167-010 Geophysical-Laboratory Chief.

19-2099.99 Physical Scientists, All Other

- **Education/Training Required: Bachelor's degree**
- **Employed: 23,800**
- **Annual Earnings: $83,300**
- **Growth: 14.6%**
- **Annual Job Openings: 2,000**

All physical scientists not listed separately.

No task data available.

Note: The Department of Labor has not collected some data for this job, so it has fewer details than the other descriptions.

Related SOC Job—19-2099 Physical Scientists, All Other. **Related OOH Job**—None. **Related DOT Job**—040.061-062 Wood Technologist.

19-3000 Social Scientists and Related Workers

19-3011.00 Economists

- **Education/Training Required: Master's degree**
- **Employed: 12,470**
- **Annual Earnings: $73,690**
- **Growth: 5.6%**
- **Annual Job Openings: 1,000**

Conduct research, prepare reports, or formulate plans to aid in solution of economic problems arising from production and distribution of goods and services. May collect and process economic and statistical data, using econometric and sampling techniques.

Study economic and statistical data in area of specialization, such as finance, labor, or agriculture. Provide advice and consultation on economic relationships to businesses, public and private agencies, and other employers. Compile, analyze, and report data to explain economic phenomena and forecast market trends, applying mathematical models and statistical techniques. Formulate recommendations, policies, or plans to solve economic problems or to interpret markets. Develop economic guidelines and standards and prepare points of view used in forecasting trends and formulating economic policy. Testify at regulatory or legislative hearings concerning the estimated effects of changes in legislation or public policy and present recommendations based on cost-benefit analyses. Supervise research projects and students' study projects. Forecast production

and consumption of renewable resources and supply, consumption, and depletion of non-renewable resources. Teach theories, principles, and methods of economics.

GOE Information—**Interest Area:** 15. Scientific Research, Engineering, and Mathematics. **Work Group:** 15.04. Social Sciences. **Personality Type**—Investigative. Investigative occupations frequently involve working with ideas and require an extensive amount of thinking. These occupations can involve searching for facts and figuring out problems mentally. **Work Values**—Autonomy; Creativity; Authority; Ability Utilization; Working Conditions; Responsibility. **Skills**—Mathematics; Programming; Persuasion; Judgment and Decision Making; Complex Problem Solving; Writing. **Abilities**—*Cognitive:* Number Facility; Written Expression; Mathematical Reasoning; Oral Expression; Fluency of Ideas; Written Comprehension. *Psychomotor:* None met the criteria. *Physical:* None met the criteria. *Sensory:* Speech Clarity; Speech Recognition. **General Work Activities**—*Information Input:* Getting Information; Estimating the Needed Characteristics of Products, Events, or Information; Identifying Objects, Actions, and Events. *Mental Process:* Analyzing Data or Information; Processing Information; Updating and Using Relevant Knowledge. *Work Output:* Interacting With Computers; Documenting or Recording Information. *Interacting with Others:* Communicating with Other Workers; Communicating with Persons Outside Organization; Interpreting the Meaning of Information for Others. **Physical Work Conditions**—Indoors; Sitting. **Other Job Characteristics**—Need to Be Exact or Accurate.

Experience—Job Zone 5. Extensive skill, knowledge, and experience are needed. **Job Preparation**—SVP 8.0 and above—four years to more than 10 years. **Knowledges**—Economics and Accounting; Mathematics; Sales and Marketing; Geography; Computers and Electronics; English Language. **Instructional Programs**—Agricultural Economics; Applied Economics; Business/Managerial Economics; Development Economics and International Development; Econometrics and Quantitative Economics; Economics, General; Economics, Other; International Economics.

Related SOC Job—19-3011 Economists. **Related OOH Job**—Economists. **Related DOT Job**—050.067-010 Economist.

19-3021.00 Market Research Analysts

- **Education/Training Required: Master's degree**
- **Employed: 195,710**
- **Annual Earnings: $57,300**
- **Growth: 19.6%**
- **Annual Job Openings: 20,000**

Research market conditions in local, regional, or national areas to determine potential sales of a product or service. May gather information on competitors, prices, sales, and methods of marketing and distribution. May use survey results to create a marketing campaign based on regional preferences and buying habits.

Collect and analyze data on customer demographics, preferences, needs, and buying habits to identify potential markets and factors affecting product demand. Prepare reports of findings, illustrating data graphically and translating complex findings into written text. Measure and assess customer and employee satisfaction. Forecast and track marketing and sales trends, analyzing collected data. Seek and provide information to help companies determine their position in the marketplace. Measure the effectiveness of marketing, advertising, and communications programs and strategies. Conduct research on consumer opinions and marketing strategies, collaborating with marketing professionals, statisticians, pollsters, and other professionals. Attend staff conferences to provide management with information and proposals concerning the promotion, distribution, design, and pricing of company products or services. Gather data on competitors and analyze their prices, sales, and method of marketing and distribution. Monitor industry statistics and follow trends in trade literature. Devise and evaluate methods and procedures for collecting data, such as surveys, opinion polls, or questionnaires, or arrange to obtain existing data. Develop and implement procedures for identifying advertising needs. Direct trained survey interviewers.

GOE Information—Interest Area: 06. Finance and Insurance. **Work Group:** 06.02. Finance/Insurance Investigation and Analysis. **Personality Type**—Investigative. Investigative occupations frequently involve working with ideas and require an extensive amount of thinking. These occupations can involve searching for facts and figuring out problems mentally. **Work Values**—Autonomy; Working Conditions; Recognition; Advancement; Creativity; Variety. **Skills**—Negotiation; Persuasion; Writing; Judgment and Decision Making; Reading Comprehension; Coordination. **Abilities**—*Cognitive:* Mathematical Reasoning; Written Expression; Inductive Reasoning; Deductive Reasoning; Originality; Oral Expression. *Psychomotor:* None met the criteria. *Physical:* None met the criteria. *Sensory:* Speech Clarity; Speech Recognition. **General Work Activities**—*Information Input:* Getting Information; Estimating the Needed Characteristics of Products, Events, or Information; Identifying Objects, Actions, and Events. *Mental Process:* Analyzing Data or Information; Updating and Using Relevant Knowledge; Processing Information. *Work Output:* Documenting or Recording Information; Interacting With Computers. *Interacting with Others:* Communicating with Other Workers; Communicating with Persons Outside Organization; Establishing and Maintaining Interpersonal Relationships. **Physical Work Conditions**—Indoors; Sitting. **Other Job Characteristics**—Need to Be Exact or Accurate; Repeat Same Tasks.

Experience—Job Zone 4. A minimum of two to four years of work-related skill, knowledge, or experience is needed. **Job Preparation**—SVP 7.0 to less than 8.0–two years to less than 10 years. **Knowledges**—Sales and Marketing; Administration and Management; Communications and Media; Economics and Accounting; Clerical Practices; Computers and Electronics. **Instructional Programs**—Applied Economics; Business/Managerial Economics; Econometrics and Quantitative Economics; Economics, General; International Economics; Marketing Research.

Related SOC Job—19-3021 Market Research Analysts. **Related OOH Job**—Market and Survey Researchers. **Related DOT Jobs**—050.067-014 Market-Research Analyst I; 169.267-034 Research Analyst.

19-3022.00 Survey Researchers

- **Education/Training Required: Master's degree**
- **Employed: 21,650**
- **Annual Earnings: $31,140**
- **Growth: 25.9%**
- **Annual Job Openings: 3,000**

Design or conduct surveys. May supervise interviewers who conduct the survey in person or over the telephone. May present survey results to client.

Prepare and present summaries and analyses of survey data, including tables, graphs, and fact sheets that describe survey techniques and results. Consult with clients in order to identify survey needs and any specific requirements, such as special samples. Analyze data from

surveys, old records, and/or case studies, using statistical software programs. Review, classify, and record survey data in preparation for computer analysis. Conduct research in order to gather information about survey topics. Conduct surveys and collect data, using methods such as interviews, questionnaires, focus groups, market analysis surveys, public opinion polls, literature reviews, and file reviews. Collaborate with other researchers in the planning, implementation, and evaluation of surveys. Direct and review the work of staff members, including survey support staff and interviewers who gather survey data. Monitor and evaluate survey progress and performance, using sample disposition reports and response rate calculations. Produce documentation of the questionnaire development process, data collection methods, sampling designs, and decisions related to sample statistical weighting. Determine and specify details of survey projects, including sources of information, procedures to be used, and the design of survey instruments and materials. Support, plan, and coordinate operations for single or multiple surveys. Direct updates and changes in survey implementation and methods. Hire and train recruiters and data collectors. Write training manuals to be used by survey interviewers.

GOE Information—Interest Area: 06. Finance and Insurance. **Work Group:** 06.02. Finance/Insurance Investigation and Analysis. **Personality Type**—No data available. **Work Values**—No data available. **Skills**—Management of Financial Resources; Management of Personnel Resources; Time Management; Persuasion; Writing; Active Learning. **Abilities**—*Cognitive:* Number Facility; Mathematical Reasoning; Written Expression; Originality; Fluency of Ideas; Written Comprehension. *Psychomotor:* None met the criteria. *Physical:* None met the criteria. *Sensory:* Speech Clarity; Speech Recognition; Near Vision. **General Work Activities**—*Information Input:* Identifying Objects, Actions, and Events; Monitoring Processes, Materials, or Surroundings; Getting Information. *Mental Process:* Processing Information; Analyzing Data or Information; Organizing, Planning, and Prioritizing. *Work Output:* Documenting or Recording Information; Interacting With Computers. *Interacting with Others:* Communicating with Persons Outside Organization; Interpreting the Meaning of Information for Others; Communicating with Other Workers. **Physical Work Conditions**—Indoors; Noisy; Sitting. **Other Job Characteristics**—Need to Be Exact or Accurate.

Experience—Job Zone 4. A minimum of two to four years of work-related skill, knowledge, or experience is needed. **Job Preparation**—SVP 7.0 to less than 8.0–two years to less than 10 years. **Knowledges**—Administration and Management; Mathematics; Sociology and Anthropology; Economics and Accounting; Personnel and Human Resources; Clerical Practices. **Instructional Programs**—Applied Economics; Business/Managerial Economics; Economics, General; Marketing Research.

Related SOC Job—19-3022 Survey Researchers. **Related OOH Job**—Market and Survey Researchers. **Related DOT Job**—No data available.

19-3031.00 Clinical, Counseling, and School Psychologists

- **Education/Training Required: Doctoral degree**
- **Employed: 98,820**
- **Annual Earnings: $57,170**
- **Growth: 19.1%**
- **Annual Job Openings: 10,000**

The job openings listed here are shared with 19-3031.01 School Psychologists, 19-3031.02 Clinical Psychologists, and 19-3031.03 Counseling Psychologists.

Diagnose and treat mental disorders; learning disabilities; and cognitive, behavioral, and emotional problems, using individual, child, family, and group therapies. May design and implement behavior modification programs.

No task data available.

GOE Information—Interest Area: 10. Human Service. **Work Group:** 10.01. Counseling and Social Work. **Note:** The Department of Labor has not collected some data for this job, so it has fewer details than the other descriptions.

Instructional Programs—Clinical Child Psychology; Clinical Psychology; Counseling Psychology; Developmental and Child Psychology; Psychoanalysis and Psychotherapy; Psychology, General; School Psychology.

Related SOC Job—19-3031 Clinical, Counseling, and School Psychologists. **Related OOH Job**—Psychologists. **Related DOT Job**—No data available.

19-3031.01 School Psychologists

- **Education/Training Required: Doctoral degree**
- **Employed: 98,820**
- **Annual Earnings: $57,170**
- **Growth: 19.1%**
- **Annual Job Openings: 10,000**

The job openings listed here are shared with 19-3031.00 Clinical, Counseling, and School Psychologists, 19-3031.02 Clinical Psychologists, and 19-3031.03 Counseling Psychologists.

Investigate processes of learning and teaching and develop psychological principles and techniques applicable to educational problems.

Compile and interpret students' test results, along with information from teachers and parents, to diagnose conditions and to help assess eligibility for special services. Report any pertinent information to the proper authorities in cases of child endangerment, neglect, or abuse. Assess an individual child's needs, limitations, and potential, using observation, review of school records, and consultation with parents and school personnel. Select, administer, and score psychological tests. Provide consultation to parents, teachers, administrators, and others on topics such as learning styles and behavior modification techniques. Promote an understanding of child development and its relationship to learning and behavior. Collaborate with other educational professionals to develop teaching strategies and school programs. Counsel children and families to help solve conflicts and problems in learning and adjustment. Develop individualized educational plans in collaboration with teachers and other staff members. Maintain student records, including special education reports, confidential records, records of services provided, and behavioral data. Serve as a resource to help families and schools deal with crises, such as separation and loss. Attend workshops, seminars, or professional meetings to remain informed of new developments in school psychology. Design classes and programs to meet the needs of special students. Refer students and their families to appropriate community agencies for medical, vocational, or social services. Initiate and direct efforts to foster tolerance, understanding, and appreciation of diversity in school communities. Collect and analyze data to evaluate the effectiveness of academic programs and other services, such as behavioral management systems. Provide educational programs on topics such as classroom management, teaching strategies, or parenting skills. Conduct research to generate new knowledge that can be used to address learning and behavior issues.

GOE Information—Interest Area: 15. Scientific Research, Engineering, and Mathematics. **Work Group:** 15.04. Social Sciences. **Personality Type**—Investigative. Investigative occupations frequently involve working with ideas and require an extensive amount of thinking. These occupations can involve searching for facts and figuring out problems mentally. **Work Values**—Social Service; Creativity; Autonomy; Ability Utilization; Achievement; Responsibility. **Skills**—Social Perceptiveness; Negotiation; Learning Strategies; Persuasion; Writing; Active Listening. **Abilities**—*Cognitive:* Inductive Reasoning; Problem Sensitivity; Written Expression; Originality; Oral Expression; Written Comprehension. *Psychomotor:* None met the criteria. *Physical:* None met the criteria. *Sensory:* Speech Clarity; Speech Recognition; Near Vision. **General Work Activities**—*Information Input:* Getting Information; Identifying Objects, Actions, and Events; Monitoring Processes, Materials, or Surroundings. *Mental Process:* Making Decisions and Solving Problems; Analyzing Data or Information; Updating and Using Relevant Knowledge. *Work Output:* Documenting or Recording Information; Interacting With Computers. *Interacting with Others:* Establishing and Maintaining Interpersonal Relationships; Interpreting the Meaning of Information for Others; Communicating with Other Workers. **Physical Work Conditions**—Indoors; Sitting. **Other Job Characteristics**—Need to Be Exact or Accurate; Repeat Same Tasks; Errors Have Important Consequences.

Experience—Job Zone 5. Extensive skill, knowledge, and experience are needed. **Job Preparation**—SVP 8.0 and above—four years to more than 10 years. **Knowledges**—Therapy and Counseling; Psychology; Sociology and Anthropology; Philosophy and Theology; Education and Training; Customer and Personal Service. **Instructional Programs**—Clinical Psychology; Counseling Psychology; Developmental and Child Psychology; Psychoanalysis and Psychotherapy; Psychology, General; School Psychology.

Related SOC Job—19-3031 Clinical, Counseling, and School Psychologists. **Related OOH Job**—Psychologists. **Related DOT Jobs**—045.067-010 Psychologist, Educational; 045.067-018 Psychometrist; 045.107-034 Psychologist, School.

19-3031.02 Clinical Psychologists

- **Education/Training Required: Doctoral degree**
- **Employed: 98,820**
- **Annual Earnings: $57,170**
- **Growth: 19.1%**
- **Annual Job Openings: 10,000**

The job openings listed here are shared with 19-3031.00 Clinical, Counseling, and School Psychologists, 19-3031.01 School Psychologists, and 19-3031.03 Counseling Psychologists.

Diagnose or evaluate mental and emotional disorders of individuals through observation, interview, and psychological tests and formulate and administer programs of treatment.

Identify psychological, emotional, or behavioral issues and diagnose disorders, using information obtained from interviews, tests, records, and reference materials. Develop and implement individual treatment plans, specifying type, frequency, intensity, and duration of therapy. Interact with clients to assist them in gaining insight, defining goals, and planning action to achieve effective personal, social, educational, and vocational development and adjustment. Discuss the treatment of problems with clients. Utilize a variety of treatment methods such as psychotherapy, hypnosis, behavior modification, stress reduction therapy, psychodrama, and play therapy. Counsel individuals and groups regarding problems such as stress, substance abuse, and family situations to modify behavior or to improve personal, social, and vocational adjustment. Write reports on clients and maintain required paperwork. Evaluate the effectiveness of counseling or treatments and the accuracy and completeness of diagnoses; then modify plans and diagnoses as necessary. Obtain and study medical, psychological, social, and family histories by interviewing individuals, couples, or families and by reviewing records. Consult reference material such as textbooks, manuals, and journals to identify symptoms, make diagnoses, and develop approaches to treatment. Maintain current knowledge of relevant research. Observe individuals at play, in group interactions, or in other contexts to detect indications of mental deficiency, abnormal behavior, or maladjustment. Select, administer, score, and interpret psychological tests to obtain information on individuals' intelligence, achievements, interests, and personalities. Refer clients to other specialists, institutions, or support services as necessary. Develop, direct, and participate in training programs for staff and students. Provide psychological or administrative services and advice to private firms and community agencies regarding mental health programs or individual cases. Provide occupational, educational, and other information to individuals so that they can make educational and vocational plans.

GOE Information—Interest Area: 10. Human Service. **Work Group:** 10.01. Counseling and Social Work. **Personality Type**—Investigative. Investigative occupations frequently involve working with ideas and require an extensive amount of thinking. These occupations can involve searching for facts and figuring out problems mentally. **Work Values**—Social Service; Creativity; Autonomy; Responsibility; Ability Utilization; Working Conditions. **Skills**—Social Perceptiveness; Service Orientation; Complex Problem Solving; Learning Strategies; Negotiation; Active Listening. **Abilities**—*Cognitive:* Problem Sensitivity; Inductive Reasoning; Written Expression; Deductive Reasoning; Oral Expression; Written Comprehension. *Psychomotor:* None met the criteria. *Physical:* None met the criteria. *Sensory:* Speech Recognition; Speech Clarity. **General Work Activities**—*Information Input:* Identifying Objects, Actions, and Events; Getting Information; Monitoring Processes, Materials, or Surroundings. *Mental Process:* Updating and Using Relevant Knowledge; Judging the Qualities of Things, Services, or Other People's Work; Making Decisions and Solving Problems. *Work Output:* Documenting or Recording Information; Interacting With Computers. *Interacting with Others:* Assisting and Caring for Others; Establishing and Maintaining Interpersonal Relationships; Resolving Conflicts and Negotiating with Others. **Physical Work Conditions**—Indoors; Sitting. **Other Job Characteristics**—Need to Be Exact or Accurate.

Experience—Job Zone 5. Extensive skill, knowledge, and experience are needed. **Job Preparation**—SVP 8.0 and above—four years to more than 10 years. **Knowledges**—Therapy and Counseling; Psychology; Sociology and Anthropology; Philosophy and Theology; Customer and Personal Service; Medicine and Dentistry. **Instructional Programs**—Clinical Child Psychology; Clinical Psychology; Counseling Psychology; Developmental and Child Psychology; Psychoanalysis and Psychotherapy; Psychology, General; School Psychology.

Related SOC Job—19-3031 Clinical, Counseling, and School Psychologists. **Related OOH Job**—Psychologists. **Related DOT Jobs**—045.061-010 Psychologist, Developmental; 045.061-018 Psychologist, Experimental; 045.107-022 Clinical Psychologist; 045.107-046 Psychologist, Chief; 045.107-050 Clinical Therapist.

19-3031.03 Counseling Psychologists

- **Education/Training Required: Doctoral degree**
- **Employed: 98,820**
- **Annual Earnings: $57,170**
- **Growth: 19.1%**
- **Annual Job Openings: 10,000**

The job openings listed here are shared with 19-3031.00 Clinical, Counseling, and School Psychologists 19-3031.01 School Psychologists, and 19-3031.02 Clinical Psychologists.

Assess and evaluate individuals' problems through the use of case history, interview, and observation and provide individual or group counseling services to assist individuals in achieving more effective personal, social, educational, and vocational development and adjustment.

Collect information about individuals or clients, using interviews, case histories, observational techniques, and other assessment methods. Counsel individuals, groups, or families to help them understand problems, define goals, and develop realistic action plans. Develop therapeutic and treatment plans based on clients' interests, abilities, and needs. Consult with other professionals to discuss therapies, treatments, counseling resources, or techniques and to share occupational information. Analyze data such as interview notes, test results, and reference manuals in order to identify symptoms and to diagnose the nature of clients' problems. Advise clients on how they could be helped by counseling. Evaluate the results of counseling methods to determine the reliability and validity of treatments. Provide consulting services to schools, social service agencies, and businesses. Refer clients to specialists or to other institutions for non-counseling treatment of problems. Select, administer, and interpret psychological tests to assess intelligence, aptitudes, abilities, or interests. Conduct research to develop or improve diagnostic or therapeutic counseling techniques.

GOE Information—Interest Area: 10. Human Service. **Work Group:** 10.01. Counseling and Social Work. **Personality Type**—Social. Social occupations frequently involve working with, communicating with, and teaching people. These occupations often involve helping or providing service to others. **Work Values**—Social Service; Creativity; Autonomy; Achievement; Working Conditions; Ability Utilization. **Skills**—Social Perceptiveness; Active Listening; Persuasion; Service Orientation; Negotiation; Coordination. **Abilities**—*Cognitive:* Inductive Reasoning; Problem Sensitivity; Fluency of Ideas; Deductive Reasoning; Written Expression; Originality. *Psychomotor:* None met the criteria. *Physical:* None met the criteria. *Sensory:* Speech Recognition; Speech Clarity; Near Vision. **General Work Activities**—*Information Input:* Identifying Objects, Actions, and Events; Monitoring Processes, Materials, or Surroundings; Getting Information. *Mental Process:* Updating and Using Relevant Knowledge; Making Decisions and Solving Problems; Analyzing Data or Information. *Work Output:* Documenting or Recording Information; Interacting With Computers. *Interacting with Others:* Performing for or Working with the Public; Assisting and Caring for Others; Establishing and Maintaining Interpersonal Relationships. **Physical Work Conditions**—Indoors; Sitting. **Other Job Characteristics**—Need to Be Exact or Accurate.

Experience—Job Zone 5. Extensive skill, knowledge, and experience are needed. **Job Preparation**—SVP 8.0 and above—four years to more than 10 years. **Knowledges**—Therapy and Counseling; Philosophy and Theology; Sociology and Anthropology; Psychology; English Language; Customer and Personal Service. **Instructional Programs**—Clinical Child Psychology; Clinical Psychology; Counseling Psychology; Developmental and Child Psychology; Psychoanalysis and Psychotherapy; Psychology, General; School Psychology.

Related SOC Job—19-3031 Clinical, Counseling, and School Psychologists. **Related OOH Job**—Psychologists. **Related DOT Job**—045.107-026 Psychologist, Counseling.

19-3032.00 Industrial-Organizational Psychologists

- **Education/Training Required: Master's degree**
- **Employed: 1,070**
- **Annual Earnings: $84,690**
- **Growth: 20.4%**
- **Annual Job Openings: Fewer than 500**

Apply principles of psychology to personnel, administration, management, sales, and marketing problems. Activities may include policy planning; employee screening, training, and development; and organizational development and analysis. May work with management to reorganize the work setting to improve worker productivity.

Develop and implement employee selection and placement programs. Analyze job requirements and content in order to establish criteria for classification, selection, training, and other related personnel functions. Observe and interview workers in order to obtain information about the physical, mental, and educational requirements of jobs as well as information about aspects such as job satisfaction. Write reports on research findings and implications in order to contribute to general knowledge and to suggest potential changes in organizational functioning. Advise management concerning personnel, managerial, and marketing policies and practices and their potential effects on organizational effectiveness and efficiency. Identify training and development needs. Conduct research studies of physical work environments, organizational structures, communication systems, group interactions, morale, and motivation in order to assess organizational functioning. Formulate and implement training programs, applying principles of learning and individual differences. Develop interview techniques, rating scales, and psychological tests used to assess skills, abilities, and interests for the purpose of employee selection, placement, and promotion. Assess employee performance. Study organizational effectiveness, productivity, and efficiency, including the nature of workplace supervision and leadership. Facilitate organizational development and change. Analyze data, using statistical methods and applications, to evaluate the outcomes and effectiveness of workplace programs. Counsel workers about job and career-related issues. Study consumers' reactions to new products and package designs and to advertising efforts, using surveys and tests. Participate in mediation and dispute resolution.

GOE Information—**Interest Area:** 15. Scientific Research, Engineering, and Mathematics. **Work Group:** 15.04. Social Sciences. **Personality Type**—Investigative. Investigative occupations frequently involve working with ideas and require an extensive amount of thinking. These occupations can involve searching for facts and figuring out problems mentally. **Work Values**—Creativity; Autonomy; Working Conditions; Compensation; Recognition; Authority. **Skills**—Science; Management of Personnel Resources; Systems Evaluation; Judgment and Decision Making; Complex Problem Solving; Writing. **Abilities**—*Cognitive:* Written Expression; Originality; Fluency of Ideas; Mathematical Reasoning; Written Comprehension; Oral Comprehension. *Psychomotor:* None met the criteria. *Physical:* None met the criteria. *Sensory:* Speech Clarity; Speech Recognition. **General Work Activities**—*Information Input:* Getting Information; Identifying Objects, Actions, and Events;

Monitoring Processes, Materials, or Surroundings. *Mental Process:* Judging the Qualities of Things, Services, or Other People's Work; Making Decisions and Solving Problems; Processing Information. *Work Output:* Documenting or Recording Information; Interacting With Computers. *Interacting with Others:* Providing Consultation and Advice to Others; Interpreting the Meaning of Information for Others; Establishing and Maintaining Interpersonal Relationships. **Physical Work Conditions**—Indoors; Sitting. **Other Job Characteristics**—Need to Be Exact or Accurate; Errors Have Important Consequences.

Experience—Job Zone 5. Extensive skill, knowledge, and experience are needed. **Job Preparation**—SVP 8.0 and above—four years to more than 10 years. **Knowledges**—Personnel and Human Resources; Psychology; Education and Training; Sales and Marketing; Sociology and Anthropology; Therapy and Counseling. **Instructional Programs**—Industrial and Organizational Psychology; Psychology, General.

Related SOC Job—19-3032 Industrial-Organizational Psychologists. **Related OOH Job**—Psychologists. **Related DOT Jobs**—045.061-014 Psychologist, Engineering; 045.107-030 Psychologist, Industrial-Organizational.

19-3039.99 Psychologists, All Other

- **Education/Training Required: Master's degree**
- **Employed: 6,750**
- **Annual Earnings: $74,260**
- **Growth: 9.9%**
- **Annual Job Openings: 1,000**

All psychologists not listed separately.

No task data available.

Note: The Department of Labor has not collected some data for this job, so it has fewer details than the other descriptions.

Related SOC Job—19-3039 Psychologists, All Other. **Related OOH Job**—Psychologists. **Related DOT Job**—045.067-014 Psychologist, Social.

19-3041.00 Sociologists

- **Education/Training Required: Master's degree**
- **Employed: 3,500**
- **Annual Earnings: $52,760**
- **Growth: 4.7%**
- **Annual Job Openings: Fewer than 500**

Study human society and social behavior by examining the groups and social institutions that people form, as well as various social, religious, political, and business organizations. May study the behavior and interaction of groups, trace their origin and growth, and analyze the influence of group activities on individual members.

Analyze and interpret data in order to increase the understanding of human social behavior. Prepare publications and reports containing research findings. Plan and conduct research to develop and test theories about societal issues such as crime, group relations, poverty, and aging. Collect data about the attitudes, values, and behaviors of people in groups, using observation, interviews, and review of documents. Develop, implement, and evaluate methods of data collection, such as questionnaires or interviews. Teach sociology. Direct work of statistical clerks, statisticians, and others who compile and evaluate research data. Consult with and advise individuals such as administrators, social workers, and legislators regarding social issues and policies, as well as the implications of research findings. Collaborate with research workers in other disciplines. Develop approaches to the solution of groups' problems based on research findings in sociology and related disciplines. Observe group interactions and role affiliations to collect data, identify problems, evaluate progress, and determine the need for additional change. Develop problem intervention procedures, utilizing techniques such as interviews, consultations, role-playing, and participant observation of group interactions.

GOE Information—Interest Area: 15. Scientific Research, Engineering, and Mathematics. **Work Group:** 15.04. Social Sciences. **Personality Type—**Investigative. Investigative occupations frequently involve working with ideas and require an extensive amount of thinking. These occupations can involve searching for facts and figuring out problems mentally. **Work Values—**Creativity; Autonomy; Responsibility; Working Conditions; Ability Utilization; Achievement. **Skills—**Science; Writing; Management of Financial Resources; Reading Comprehension; Critical Thinking; Complex Problem Solving. **Abilities—***Cognitive:* Written Expression; Mathematical Reasoning; Oral Expression; Originality; Deductive Reasoning; Inductive Reasoning. *Psychomotor:* None met the criteria. *Physical:* None met the criteria. *Sensory:* Speech Clarity; Speech Recognition; Near Vision. **General Work Activities—***Information Input:* Getting Information; Identifying Objects, Actions, and Events; Estimating the Needed Characteristics of Products, Events, or Information. *Mental Process:* Analyzing Data or Information; Processing Information; Thinking Creatively. *Work Output:* Documenting or Recording Information; Interacting With Computers. *Interacting with Others:* Interpreting the Meaning of Information for Others; Teaching Others; Communicating with Persons Outside Organization. **Physical Work Conditions—**Indoors; Sitting. **Other Job Characteristics—**Need to Be Exact or Accurate.

Experience—Job Zone 5. Extensive skill, knowledge, and experience are needed. **Job Preparation—**SVP 8.0 and above—four years to more than 10 years. **Knowledges—**Sociology and Anthropology; Philosophy and Theology; History and Archeology; Psychology; English Language; Mathematics. **Instructional Programs—**Criminology; Demography and Population Studies; Sociology; Urban Studies/Affairs.

Related SOC Job—19-3041 Sociologists. **Related OOH Job—**Social Scientists, Other. **Related DOT Jobs—**054.067-010 Research Worker, Social Welfare; 054.067-014 Sociologist; 054.107-010 Clinical Sociologist.

19-3051.00 Urban and Regional Planners

- **Education/Training Required: Master's degree**
- **Employed: 31,650**
- **Annual Earnings: $55,170**
- **Growth: 15.2%**
- **Annual Job Openings: 3,000**

Develop comprehensive plans and programs for use of land and physical facilities of local jurisdictions such as towns, cities, counties, and metropolitan areas.

Design, promote, and administer government plans and policies affecting land use, zoning, public utilities, community facilities, housing, and transportation. Hold public meetings and confer with government, social scientists, lawyers, developers, the public, and special interest groups to formulate and develop land use or community plans. Recommend approval, denial, or conditional approval of proposals. Determine the effects of regulatory limitations on projects. Assess the feasibility of proposals and identify necessary changes. Create, prepare, or requisition graphic and narrative reports on land use data, including land area maps overlaid with geographic variables such as population density. Conduct field investigations, surveys, impact studies, or other research to compile and analyze data on economic, social, regulatory, and physical factors affecting land use. Advise planning officials on project feasibility, cost-effectiveness, regulatory conformance, and possible alternatives. Discuss with planning officials the purpose of land use projects such as transportation, conservation, residential, commercial, industrial, and community use. Keep informed about economic and legal issues involved in zoning codes, building codes, and environmental regulations. Mediate community disputes and assist in developing alternative plans and recommendations for programs or projects. Coordinate work with economic consultants and architects during the formulation of plans and the design of large pieces of infrastructure. Review and evaluate environmental impact reports pertaining to private and public planning projects and programs. Supervise and coordinate the work of urban planning technicians and technologists. Investigate property availability.

GOE Information—Interest Area: 07. Government and Public Administration. **Work Group:** 07.02. Public Planning. **Personality Type—**Investigative. Investigative occupations frequently involve working with ideas and require an extensive amount of thinking. These occupations can involve searching for facts and figuring out problems mentally. **Work Values—**Creativity; Autonomy; Ability Utilization; Achievement; Social Status; Recognition. **Skills—**Complex Problem Solving; Persuasion; Coordination; Writing; Service Orientation; Speaking. **Abilities—***Cognitive:* Visualization; Written Expression; Originality; Written Comprehension; Deductive Reasoning; Fluency of Ideas. *Psychomotor:* None met the criteria. *Physical:* None met the criteria. *Sensory:* Far Vision; Near Vision; Depth Perception; Speech Recognition; Speech Clarity. **General Work Activities—***Information Input:* Identifying Objects, Actions, and Events; Getting Information; Monitoring Processes, Materials, or Surroundings. *Mental Process:* Making Decisions and Solving Problems; Organizing, Planning, and Prioritizing; Updating and Using Relevant Knowledge. *Work Output:* Documenting or Recording Information; Interacting With Computers. *Interacting with Others:* Establishing and Maintaining Interpersonal Relationships; Communicating with Persons Outside Organization; Performing for or Working with the Public. **Physical Work Conditions—**Indoors; Noisy; Very Bright or Dim Lighting; Sitting; Using Hands on Objects, Tools, or Controls; Repetitive Motions. **Other Job Characteristics—**Need to Be Exact or Accurate.

Experience—Job Zone 4. A minimum of two to four years of work-related skill, knowledge, or experience is needed. **Job Preparation—**SVP 7.0 to less than 8.0—two years to less than 10 years. **Knowledges—**Design; Building and Construction; Geography; Customer and Personal Service; History and Archeology; Law and Government. **Instructional Program—**City/Urban, Community and Regional Planning.

Related SOC Job—19-3051 Urban and Regional Planners. **Related OOH Job—**Urban and Regional Planners. **Related DOT Jobs—**188.167-110 Planner, Program Services; 199.167-014 Urban Planner.

19-3091.00 Anthropologists and Archeologists

- **Education/Training Required: Master's degree**
- **Employed: 4,790**
- **Annual Earnings: $45,910**
- **Growth: 17.0%**
- **Annual Job Openings: Fewer than 500**

The job openings listed here are shared with 19-3091.01 Anthropologists and 19-3091.02 Archeologists.

Study the origin, development, and behavior of humans. May study the way of life, language, or physical characteristics of existing people in various parts of the world. May engage in systematic recovery and examination of material evidence, such as tools or pottery remaining from past human cultures, to determine the history, customs, and living habits of earlier civilizations.

No task data available.

GOE Information—Interest Area: 15. Scientific Research, Engineering, and Mathematics. **Work Group:** 15.04. Social Sciences. **Note:** The Department of Labor has not collected some data for this job, so it has fewer details than the other descriptions.

Instructional Programs—Anthropology; Archeology; Physical Anthropology.

Related SOC Job—19-3091 Anthropologists and Archeologists. **Related OOH Job—**Social Scientists, Other. **Related DOT Job—**No data available.

19-3091.01 Anthropologists

- **Education/Training Required: Master's degree**
- **Employed: 4,790**
- **Annual Earnings: $45,910**
- **Growth: 17.0%**
- **Annual Job Openings: Fewer than 500**

The job openings listed here are shared with 19-3091.00 Anthropologists and Archeologists and 19-3091.02 Archeologists.

Research, evaluate, and establish public policy concerning the origins of humans; their physical, social, linguistic, and cultural development; and their behavior, as well as the cultures, organizations, and institutions they have created.

Collect information and make judgments through observation, interviews, and the review of documents. Plan and direct research to characterize and compare the economic, demographic, health care, social, political, linguistic, and religious institutions of distinct cultural groups, communities, and organizations. Write about and present research findings for a variety of specialized and general audiences. Advise government agencies, private organizations, and communities regarding proposed programs, plans, and policies and their potential impacts on cultural institutions, organizations, and communities. Identify culturally-specific beliefs and practices affecting health status and access to services for distinct populations and communities in collaboration with medical and public health officials. Build and use text-based database management systems to support the analysis of detailed first-hand observational records, or "field notes." Develop intervention procedures, utilizing techniques such as individual and focus group interviews, consultations, and participant observation of social interaction. Construct and test data collection methods. Explain the origins and physical, social, or cultural development of humans, including physical attributes, cultural traditions, beliefs, languages, resource management practices, and settlement patterns. Conduct participatory action research in communities and organizations to assess how work is done and to design work systems, technologies, and environments. Train others in the application of ethnographic research methods to solve problems in organizational effectiveness, communications, technology development, policy-making, and program planning. Formulate general rules that describe and predict the development and behavior of cultures and social institutions. Collaborate with economic development planners to decide on the implementation of proposed development policies, plans, and programs based on culturally institutionalized barriers and facilitating circumstances. Create data records for use in describing and analyzing social patterns and processes, using photography, videography, and audio recordings.

GOE Information—Interest Area: 15. Scientific Research, Engineering, and Mathematics. **Work Group:** 15.04. Social Sciences. **Personality Type—**Investigative. Investigative occupations frequently involve working with ideas and require an extensive amount of thinking. These occupations can involve searching for facts and figuring out problems mentally. **Work Values—**Creativity; Autonomy; Ability Utilization; Responsibility; Variety; Achievement. **Skills—**Writing; Social Perceptiveness; Complex Problem Solving; Science; Systems Evaluation; Reading Comprehension. **Abilities—***Cognitive:* Written Expression; Speed of Closure; Written Comprehension; Category Flexibility; Inductive Reasoning; Originality. *Psychomotor:* None met the criteria. *Physical:* None met the criteria. *Sensory:* Speech Clarity; Far Vision; Near Vision; Speech Recognition. **General Work Activities—***Information Input:* Getting Information; Identifying Objects, Actions, and Events; Monitoring Processes, Materials, or Surroundings. *Mental Process:* Processing Information; Analyzing Data or Information; Thinking Creatively. *Work Output:* Documenting or Recording Information; Interacting With Computers. *Interacting with Others:* Establishing and Maintaining Interpersonal Relationships; Communicating with Persons Outside Organization; Teaching Others. **Physical Work Conditions—**Indoors; Sitting. **Other Job Characteristics—**Need to Be Exact or Accurate.

Experience—Job Zone 5. Extensive skill, knowledge, and experience are needed. **Job Preparation—**SVP 8.0 and above—four years to more than 10 years. **Knowledges—**Sociology and Anthropology; History and Archeology; Foreign Language; Philosophy and Theology; Geography; Biology. **Instructional Programs—**Anthropology; Physical Anthropology.

Related SOC Job—19-3091 Anthropologists and Archeologists. **Related OOH Job—**Social Scientists, Other. **Related DOT Jobs—**055.067-010 Anthropologist; 055.067-014 Anthropologist, Physical; 055.067-022 Ethnologist.

19-3091.02 Archeologists

- **Education/Training Required: Master's degree**
- **Employed: 4,790**
- **Annual Earnings: $45,910**
- **Growth: 17.0%**
- **Annual Job Openings: Fewer than 500**

The job openings listed here are shared with 19-3091.00 Anthropologists and Archeologists and 19-3091.01 Anthropologists.

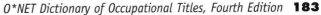

Conduct research to reconstruct record of past human life and culture from human remains, artifacts, architectural features, and structures recovered through excavation, underwater recovery, or other means of discovery.

Write, present, and publish reports that record site history, methodology, and artifact analysis results, along with recommendations for conserving and interpreting findings. Compare findings from one site with archeological data from other sites to find similarities or differences. Research, survey, or assess sites of past societies and cultures in search of answers to specific research questions. Study objects and structures recovered by excavation to identify, date, and authenticate them and to interpret their significance. Develop and test theories concerning the origin and development of past cultures. Consult site reports, existing artifacts, and topographic maps to identify archeological sites. Create a grid of each site and draw and update maps of unit profiles, stratum surfaces, features, and findings. Record the exact locations and conditions of artifacts uncovered in diggings or surveys, using drawings and photographs as necessary. Assess archeological sites for resource management, development, or conservation purposes and recommend methods for site protection. Describe artifacts' physical properties or attributes, such as the materials from which artifacts are made and their size, shape, function, and decoration. Teach archeology at colleges and universities. Collect artifacts made of stone, bone, metal, and other materials, placing them in bags and marking them to show where they were found. Create artifact typologies to organize and make sense of past material cultures. Lead field training sites and train field staff, students, and volunteers in excavation methods. Clean, restore, and preserve artifacts.

GOE Information—Interest Area: 15. Scientific Research, Engineering, and Mathematics. **Work Group:** 15.04. Social Sciences. **Personality Type**—Investigative. Investigative occupations frequently involve working with ideas and require an extensive amount of thinking. These occupations can involve searching for facts and figuring out problems mentally. **Work Values**—Autonomy; Creativity; Responsibility; Achievement; Recognition; Ability Utilization. **Skills**—Management of Financial Resources; Science; Writing; Management of Personnel Resources; Active Learning; Reading Comprehension. **Abilities**—*Cognitive:* Flexibility of Closure; Written Expression; Speed of Closure; Inductive Reasoning; Category Flexibility; Fluency of Ideas. *Psychomotor:* Arm-Hand Steadiness; Finger Dexterity; Manual Dexterity; Multilimb Coordination; Control Precision. *Physical:* Extent Flexibility; Trunk Strength; Dynamic Strength; Static Strength; Gross Body Coordination; Stamina. *Sensory:* Far Vision; Speech Clarity; Depth Perception; Near Vision; Visual Color Discrimination; Speech Recognition. **General Work Activities**—*Information Input:* Getting Information; Identifying Objects, Actions, and Events; Monitoring Processes, Materials, or Surroundings. *Mental Process:* Processing Information; Organizing, Planning, and Prioritizing; Analyzing Data or Information. *Work Output:* Documenting or Recording Information; Handling and Moving Objects; Performing General Physical Activities. *Interacting with Others:* Establishing and Maintaining Interpersonal Relationships; Communicating with Persons Outside Organization; Interpreting the Meaning of Information for Others. **Physical Work Conditions**—More Often Indoors Than Outdoors; Sitting; Using Hands on Objects, Tools, or Controls. **Other Job Characteristics**—Need to Be Exact or Accurate; Repeat Same Tasks.

Experience—Job Zone 5. Extensive skill, knowledge, and experience are needed. **Job Preparation**—SVP 8.0 and above—four years to more than 10 years. **Knowledges**—History and Archeology; Sociology and

Anthropology; Geography; Philosophy and Theology; Foreign Language; English Language. **Instructional Program**—Archeology.

Related SOC Job—19-3091 Anthropologists and Archeologists. **Related OOH Job**—Social Scientists, Other. **Related DOT Job**—055.067-018 Archeologist.

19-3092.00 Geographers

- ● **Education/Training Required: Master's degree**
- ● **Employed: 810**
- ● **Annual Earnings: $63,550**
- ● **Growth: 6.8%**
- ● **Annual Job Openings: Fewer than 500**

Study nature and use of areas of earth's surface, relating and interpreting interactions of physical and cultural phenomena. Conduct research on physical aspects of a region, including land forms, climates, soils, plants, and animals, and conduct research on the spatial implications of human activities within a given area, including social characteristics, economic activities, and political organization, as well as researching interdependence between regions at scales ranging from local to global.

Create and modify maps, graphs, or diagrams, using geographical information software and related equipment and principles of cartography such as coordinate systems, longitude, latitude, elevation, topography, and map scales. Write and present reports of research findings. Develop, operate, and maintain geographical information (GIS) computer systems, including hardware, software, plotters, digitizers, printers, and video cameras. Locate and obtain existing geographic information databases. Analyze geographic distributions of physical and cultural phenomena on local, regional, continental, or global scales. Teach geography. Gather and compile geographic data from sources including censuses, field observations, satellite imagery, aerial photographs, and existing maps. Conduct fieldwork at outdoor sites. Study the economic, political, and cultural characteristics of a specific region's population. Provide consulting services in fields including resource development and management, business location and market area analysis, environmental hazards, regional cultural history, and urban social planning. Collect data on physical characteristics of specified areas, such as geological formations, climates, and vegetation, using surveying or meteorological equipment. Provide geographical information systems support to the private and public sectors.

GOE Information—Interest Area: 15. Scientific Research, Engineering, and Mathematics. **Work Group:** 15.02. Physical Sciences. **Personality Type**—Investigative. Investigative occupations frequently involve working with ideas and require an extensive amount of thinking. These occupations can involve searching for facts and figuring out problems mentally. **Work Values**—Autonomy; Creativity; Ability Utilization; Responsibility; Social Status; Independence. **Skills**—Programming; Science; Complex Problem Solving; Writing; Management of Financial Resources; Reading Comprehension. **Abilities**—*Cognitive:* Written Expression; Written Comprehension; Oral Expression; Inductive Reasoning; Originality; Deductive Reasoning. *Psychomotor:* None met the criteria. *Physical:* None met the criteria. *Sensory:* Speech Clarity; Far Vision; Near Vision; Speech Recognition. **General Work Activities**—*Information Input:* Getting Information; Identifying Objects, Actions, and Events; Estimating the Needed Characteristics of Products, Events, or Information. *Mental Process:* Analyzing Data or Information; Updating and Using Relevant Knowledge; Processing Information. *Work Output:* Documenting or Recording Information; Interacting

With Computers. *Interacting with Others:* Communicating with Other Workers; Teaching Others; Communicating with Persons Outside Organization. **Physical Work Conditions**—Indoors; Sitting. **Other Job Characteristics**—Need to Be Exact or Accurate.

Experience—Job Zone 5. Extensive skill, knowledge, and experience are needed. **Job Preparation**—SVP 8.0 and above—four years to more than 10 years. **Knowledges**—Geography; Sociology and Anthropology; History and Archeology; Biology; Education and Training; Philosophy and Theology. **Instructional Program**—Geography.

Related SOC Job—19-3092 Geographers. **Related OOH Job**—Social Scientists, Other. **Related DOT Jobs**—029.067-010 Geographer; 029.067-014 Geographer, Physical.

19-3093.00 Historians

- Education/Training Required: Master's degree
- Employed: 2,850
- Annual Earnings: $44,400
- Growth: 4.3%
- Annual Job Openings: Fewer than 500

Research, analyze, record, and interpret the past as recorded in sources such as government and institutional records; newspapers and other periodicals; photographs; interviews; films; and unpublished manuscripts, such as personal diaries and letters.

Gather historical data from sources such as archives, court records, diaries, news files, and photographs, as well as collect data sources such as books, pamphlets, and periodicals. Organize data and analyze and interpret its authenticity and relative significance. Trace historical development in a particular field, such as social, cultural, political, or diplomatic history. Conduct historical research as a basis for the identification, conservation, and reconstruction of historic places and materials. Teach and conduct research in colleges, universities, museums, and other research agencies and schools. Conduct historical research and publish or present findings and theories. Speak to various groups, organizations, and clubs to promote the aims and activities of historical societies. Prepare publications and exhibits or review those prepared by others in order to ensure their historical accuracy. Research the history of a particular country or region or of a specific time period. Determine which topics to research or pursue research topics specified by clients or employers. Present historical accounts in terms of individuals or social, ethnic, political, economic, or geographic groupings. Organize information for publication and for other means of dissemination, such as use in CD-ROMs or Internet sites. Research and prepare manuscripts in support of public programming and the development of exhibits at historic sites, museums, libraries, and archives. Advise or consult with individuals and institutions regarding issues such as the historical authenticity of materials or the customs of a specific historical period. Translate or request translation of reference materials. Collect detailed information on individuals for use in biographies. Interview people in order to gather information about historical events and to record oral histories. Recommend actions related to historical art, such as which items to add to a collection or which items to display in an exhibit. Coordinate activities of workers engaged in cataloging and filing materials. Edit historical society publications.

GOE Information—**Interest Area:** 15. Scientific Research, Engineering, and Mathematics. **Work Group:** 15.04. Social Sciences. **Personality Type**—Investigative. Investigative occupations frequently involve working with ideas and require an extensive amount

of thinking. These occupations can involve searching for facts and figuring out problems mentally. **Work Values**—Autonomy; Working Conditions; Creativity; Responsibility; Achievement; Recognition. **Skills**—Reading Comprehension; Management of Financial Resources; Writing; Management of Personnel Resources; Speaking; Social Perceptiveness. **Abilities**—*Cognitive:* Written Expression; Oral Expression; Written Comprehension; Oral Comprehension; Inductive Reasoning; Fluency of Ideas. *Psychomotor:* None met the criteria. *Physical:* None met the criteria. *Sensory:* Speech Clarity; Near Vision; Speech Recognition. **General Work Activities**—*Information Input:* Getting Information; Identifying Objects, Actions, and Events; Inspecting Equipment, Structures, or Materials. *Mental Process:* Processing Information; Analyzing Data or Information; Updating and Using Relevant Knowledge. *Work Output:* Documenting or Recording Information; Interacting With Computers. *Interacting with Others:* Communicating with Persons Outside Organization; Providing Consultation and Advice to Others; Establishing and Maintaining Interpersonal Relationships. **Physical Work Conditions**—Indoors; Noisy; Very Bright or Dim Lighting; Contaminants; Cramped Work Space, Awkward Positions; Using Hands on Objects, Tools, or Controls. **Other Job Characteristics**—Need to Be Exact or Accurate; Repeat Same Tasks; Errors Have Important Consequences.

Experience—Job Zone 5. Extensive skill, knowledge, and experience are needed. **Job Preparation**—SVP 8.0 and above—four years to more than 10 years. **Knowledges**—History and Archeology; Computers and Electronics; English Language; Geography; Communications and Media; Clerical Practices. **Instructional Programs**—American History (United States); Ancient Studies/Civilization; Architectural History and Criticism; Asian History; Canadian History; Classical, Mediterranean, and Near Eastern/Oriental Studies and Archaeology; Cultural Resource Management and Policy Analysis; European History; Historic Preservation and Conservation; Historic Preservation and Conservation, Other; History and Philosophy of Science and Technology; History, General; History, Other; Holocaust and Related Studies; Medieval and Renaissance Studies.

Related SOC Job—19-3093 Historians. **Related OOH Job**—Social Scientists, Other. **Related DOT Jobs**—052.067-014 Director, State-Historical Society; 052.067-018 Genealogist; 052.067-022 Historian; 052.067-026 Historian, Dramatic Arts; 052.167-010 Director, Research.

19-3094.00 Political Scientists

- Education/Training Required: Master's degree
- Employed: 5,010
- Annual Earnings: $84,100
- Growth: 7.3%
- Annual Job Openings: Fewer than 500

Study the origin, development, and operation of political systems. Research a wide range of subjects, such as relations between the United States and foreign countries, the beliefs and institutions of foreign nations, or the politics of small towns or a major metropolis. May study topics such as public opinion, political decision making, and ideology. May analyze the structure and operation of governments, as well as various political entities. May conduct public opinion surveys, analyze election results, or analyze public documents.

Teach political science. Disseminate research results through academic publications, written reports, or public presentations. Identify issues for research and analysis. Develop and test theories, using information from interviews, newspapers, periodicals, case law, historical papers, polls, and/or statistical sources. Maintain current knowledge of government policy decisions. Collect, analyze, and interpret data such as election results and public opinion surveys; report on findings, recommendations, and conclusions. Interpret and analyze policies; public issues; legislation; and the operations of governments, businesses, and organizations. Evaluate programs and policies and make related recommendations to institutions and organizations. Write drafts of legislative proposals and prepare speeches, correspondence, and policy papers for governmental use. Forecast political, economic, and social trends. Consult with and advise government officials, civic bodies, research agencies, the media, political parties, and others concerned with political issues. Provide media commentary and/or criticism related to public policy and political issues and events.

GOE Information—Interest Area: 15. Scientific Research, Engineering, and Mathematics. **Work Group:** 15.04. Social Sciences. **Personality Type**—Investigative. Investigative occupations frequently involve working with ideas and require an extensive amount of thinking. These occupations can involve searching for facts and figuring out problems mentally. **Work Values**—Autonomy; Creativity; Working Conditions; Responsibility; Ability Utilization; Recognition. **Skills**—Writing; Reading Comprehension; Critical Thinking; Speaking; Active Learning; Instructing. **Abilities**—*Cognitive:* Written Expression; Written Comprehension; Originality; Inductive Reasoning; Oral Expression; Deductive Reasoning. *Psychomotor:* None met the criteria. *Physical:* None met the criteria. *Sensory:* Speech Clarity; Speech Recognition; Near Vision. **General Work Activities**—*Information Input:* Getting Information; Identifying Objects, Actions, and Events; Estimating the Needed Characteristics of Products, Events, or Information. *Mental Process:* Thinking Creatively; Analyzing Data or Information; Processing Information. *Work Output:* Documenting or Recording Information; Interacting With Computers. *Interacting with Others:* Teaching Others; Interpreting the Meaning of Information for Others; Communicating with Persons Outside Organization. **Physical Work Conditions**—Indoors; Sitting. **Other Job Characteristics**—Need to Be Exact or Accurate.

Experience—Job Zone 5. Extensive skill, knowledge, and experience are needed. **Job Preparation**—SVP 8.0 and above—four years to more than 10 years. **Knowledges**—History and Archeology; Law and Government; Philosophy and Theology; Sociology and Anthropology; Foreign Language; Geography. **Instructional Programs**—American Government and Politics (United States); Canadian Government and Politics; International Relations and Affairs; International/Global Studies; Political Science and Government, General; Political Science and Government, Other.

Related SOC Job—19-3094 Political Scientists. **Related OOH Job**—Social Scientists, Other. **Related DOT Job**—051.067-010 Political Scientist.

19-3099.99 Social Scientists and Related Workers, All Other

- **Education/Training Required:** Master's degree
- **Employed:** 31,900
- **Annual Earnings:** $62,650
- **Growth:** 12.3%
- **Annual Job Openings:** 3,000

All social scientists and related workers not listed separately.

No task data available.

Note: The Department of Labor has not collected some data for this job, so it has fewer details than the other descriptions.

Related SOC Job—19-3099 Social Scientists and Related Workers, All Other. **Related OOH Job**—Social Scientists, Other. **Related DOT Jobs**—059.067-010 Philologist; 059.067-014 Scientific Linguist; 059.167-010 Intelligence Research Specialist; 059.267-010 Intelligence Specialist; 059.267-014 Intelligence Specialist.

19-4000 Life, Physical, and Social Science Technicians

19-4011.00 Agricultural and Food Science Technicians

- **Education/Training Required:** Associate degree
- **Employed:** 19,340
- **Annual Earnings:** $31,360
- **Growth:** 13.4%
- **Annual Job Openings:** 1,000

The job openings listed here are shared with 19-4011.01 Agricultural Technicians and 19-4011.02 Food Science Technicians.

Work with agricultural scientists in food, fiber, and animal research, production, and processing; assist with animal breeding and nutrition work; under supervision, conduct tests and experiments to improve yield and quality of crops or to increase the resistance of plants and animals to disease or insects. Includes technicians who assist food scientists or food technologists in the research, development, production technology, quality control, packaging, processing, and use of foods.

No task data available.

GOE Information—Interest Area: 01. Agriculture and Natural Resources. **Work Group:** 01.03. Resource Technologies for Plants, Animals, and the Environment. **Note:** The Department of Labor has not collected some data for this job, so it has fewer details than the other descriptions.

Instructional Programs—Agricultural Animal Breeding; Agronomy and Crop Science; Animal Nutrition; Animal Sciences, General; Animal/Livestock Husbandry and Production; Crop Production; Dairy Science; Food Science.

Related SOC Job—19-4011 Agricultural and Food Science Technicians. **Related OOH Job**—Science Technicians. **Related DOT Job**—No data available.

19-4011.01 Agricultural Technicians

- **Education/Training Required:** Associate degree
- **Employed:** 19,340
- **Annual Earnings:** $31,360
- **Growth:** 13.4%
- **Annual Job Openings:** 1,000

The job openings listed here are shared with 19-4011.00 Agricultural and Food Science Technicians and 19-4011.02 Food Science Technicians.

Set up and maintain laboratory equipment and collect samples from crops or animals. Prepare specimens and record data to assist scientist in biology or related science experiments.

Receive and prepare laboratory samples for analysis, following proper protocols to ensure that they will be stored, prepared, and disposed of efficiently and effectively. Record data pertaining to experimentation, research, and animal care. Collect samples from crops or animals so testing can be performed. Prepare data summaries, reports, and analyses that include results, charts, and graphs to document research findings and results. Adjust testing equipment and prepare culture media, following standard procedures. Operate laboratory equipment such as spectrometers, nitrogen determination apparatus, air samplers, centrifuges, and potential hydrogen (pH) meters to perform tests. Measure or weigh ingredients used in testing or for purposes such as animal feed. Provide food and water to livestock and laboratory animals and record details of their food consumption. Plant seeds in specified areas and count the resulting plants to determine the percentage of seeds that germinated. Supervise pest or weed control operations, including locating and identifying pests or weeds, selecting chemicals and application methods, scheduling application, and training operators. Measure and mark plot areas and plow, disc, level, and otherwise prepare land for cultivated crops, orchards, and vineyards. Conduct insect and plant disease surveys. Examine animals and specimens to determine the presence of diseases or other problems. Perform general nursery duties such as propagating standard varieties of plant materials, collecting and germinating seeds, maintaining cuttings of plants, and controlling environmental conditions. Operate farm machinery, including tractors, plows, mowers, combines, balers, sprayers, earthmoving equipment, and trucks. Perform crop production duties such as tilling, hoeing, pruning, weeding, and harvesting crops. Devise cultural methods and environmental controls for plants for which guidelines are sketchy or nonexistent. Maintain and repair agricultural facilities, equipment, and tools to ensure operational readiness, safety, and cleanliness. Provide routine animal care such as taking and recording body measurements, applying identification, and assisting in the birthing process.

GOE Information—Interest Area: 01. Agriculture and Natural Resources. Work Group: 01.03. Resource Technologies for Plants, Animals, and the Environment. Personality Type—Realistic. Realistic occupations frequently involve work activities that include practical, hands-on problems and solutions. They often deal with plants; animals; and real-world materials like wood, tools, and machinery. Many of the occupations require working outside and do not involve a lot of paperwork or working closely with others. Work Values—Supervision, Technical; Variety. Skills—Science; Equipment Maintenance; Troubleshooting; Operation Monitoring; Mathematics; Operation and Control. Abilities—*Cognitive:* Written Expression; Flexibility of Closure; Inductive Reasoning; Written Comprehension; Oral Comprehension; Visualization. *Psychomotor:* Arm-Hand Steadiness; Manual Dexterity; Control Precision; Finger Dexterity. *Physical:* None met the criteria. *Sensory:* Depth Perception; Far Vision; Near Vision; Auditory Attention. General Work Activities—*Information Input:* Monitoring Processes, Materials, or Surroundings; Identifying Objects, Actions, and Events; Getting Information. *Mental Process:* Updating and Using Relevant Knowledge; Processing Information; Organizing, Planning, and Prioritizing. *Work Output:* Handling and Moving Objects; Documenting or Recording Information; Controlling Machines and Processes. *Interacting with Others:* Communicating with Other Workers; Establishing and Maintaining Interpersonal Relationships; Coordinating the Work and Activities of Others. Physical Work Conditions—Indoors; Contaminants; Hazardous Conditions; Standing; Using Hands on Objects, Tools, or Controls. Other Job Characteristics—Need to Be Exact or Accurate; Repeat Same Tasks; Errors Have Important Consequences; Pace Determined by Speed of Equipment.

Experience—Job Zone 3. Previous work-related skill, knowledge, or experience is required. Job Preparation—SVP 6.0 to less than 7.0—more than one year and less than four years. Knowledges—Biology; Food Production; Chemistry; Mechanical Devices; Engineering and Technology; Production and Processing. Instructional Programs—Agricultural Animal Breeding; Animal Nutrition; Animal Sciences, General; Animal/Livestock Husbandry and Production; Crop Production; Dairy Science; Food Science.

Related SOC Job—19-4011 Agricultural and Food Science Technicians. Related OOH Job—Science Technicians. Related DOT Jobs—040.361-014 Seed Analyst; 049.364-010 Feed-Research Aide; 049.364-018 Biological Aide; 411.364-010 Blood Tester, Fowl; 559.384-010 Laboratory Assistant, Culture Media.

19-4011.02 Food Science Technicians

- **Education/Training Required: Associate degree**
- **Employed: 19,340**
- **Annual Earnings: $31,360**
- **Growth: 13.4%**
- **Annual Job Openings: 1,000**

The job openings listed here are shared with 19-4011.00 Agricultural and Food Science Technicians and 19-4011.01 Agricultural Technicians.

Perform standardized qualitative and quantitative tests to determine physical or chemical properties of food or beverage products.

Conduct standardized tests on food, beverages, additives, and preservatives in order to ensure compliance with standards and regulations regarding factors such as color, texture, and nutrients. Provide assistance to food scientists and technologists in research and development, production technology, and quality control. Compute moisture or salt content, percentages of ingredients, formulas, or other product factors, using mathematical and chemical procedures. Record and compile test results and prepare graphs, charts, and reports. Clean and sterilize laboratory equipment. Analyze test results to classify products or compare results with standard tables. Taste or smell foods or beverages in order to ensure that flavors meet specifications or to select samples with specific characteristics. Examine chemical and biological samples in order to identify cell structures and to locate bacteria or extraneous material, using microscope. Mix, blend, or cultivate ingredients in order to make reagents or to manufacture food or beverage products. Measure, test, and weigh bottles, cans, and other containers in order to ensure hardness, strength, and dimensions that meet specifications. Prepare slides and incubate slides with cell cultures. Order supplies needed to maintain inventories in laboratories or in storage facilities of food or beverage processing plants.

GOE Information—Interest Area: 01. Agriculture and Natural Resources. Work Group: 01.03. Resource Technologies for Plants, Animals, and the Environment. Personality Type—Realistic. Realistic occupations frequently involve work activities that include practical, hands-on problems and solutions. They often deal with plants; animals; and real-world materials like wood, tools, and machinery. Many of the occupations require working outside and do not involve a lot of paperwork or working closely with others. Work Values—Security; Working Conditions; Supervision, Human Relations; Advancement; Variety; Supervision, Technical. Skills—Science; Quality Control Analysis; Operation Monitoring; Technology Design; Equipment Maintenance; Troubleshooting. Abilities—*Cognitive:* Written Expression; Mathematical Reasoning; Number Facility; Flexibility of Closure; Perceptual Speed; Oral Expression. *Psychomotor:* Finger Dexterity; Manual Dexterity. *Physical:* None met the criteria. *Sensory:*

Visual Color Discrimination; Auditory Attention. **General Work Activities**—*Information Input:* Monitoring Processes, Materials, or Surroundings; Identifying Objects, Actions, and Events; Getting Information. *Mental Process:* Updating and Using Relevant Knowledge; Processing Information; Evaluating Information Against Standards. *Work Output:* Documenting or Recording Information; Handling and Moving Objects; Interacting With Computers. *Interacting with Others:* Communicating with Other Workers; Establishing and Maintaining Interpersonal Relationships; Teaching Others. **Physical Work Conditions**—Indoors; Noisy; Contaminants; Hazardous Conditions; Standing; Using Hands on Objects, Tools, or Controls. **Other Job Characteristics**—Need to Be Exact or Accurate; Repeat Same Tasks; Errors Have Important Consequences.

Experience—Job Zone 3. Previous work-related skill, knowledge, or experience is required. **Job Preparation**—SVP 6.0 to less than 7.0—more than one year and less than four years. **Knowledges**—Food Production; Chemistry; Biology; Production and Processing; Mathematics; English Language. **Instructional Programs**—Agricultural Animal Breeding; Animal Nutrition; Animal Sciences, General; Animal/Livestock Husbandry and Production; Crop Production; Dairy Science; Food Science.

Related SOC Job—19-4011 Agricultural and Food Science Technicians. **Related OOH Job**—Science Technicians. **Related DOT Jobs**—022.261-014 Malt-Specifications-Control Assistant; 022.381-010 Yeast-Culture Developer; 029.361-010 Bottle-House Quality-Control Technician; 029.361-014 Food Tester; 199.251-010 Tester, Food Products; 526.381-018 Baker, Test.

19-4021.00 Biological Technicians

- **Education/Training Required: Associate degree**
- **Employed: 67,080**
- **Annual Earnings: $34,270**
- **Growth: 17.2%**
- **Annual Job Openings: 8,000**

Assist biological and medical scientists in laboratories. Set up, operate, and maintain laboratory instruments and equipment; monitor experiments; make observations; and calculate and record results. May analyze organic substances, such as blood, food, and drugs.

Keep detailed logs of all work-related activities. Monitor laboratory work to ensure compliance with set standards. Isolate, identify, and prepare specimens for examination. Use computers, computer-interfaced equipment, robotics, or high-technology industrial applications to perform work duties. Conduct research or assist in the conduct of research, including the collection of information and samples such as blood, water, soil, plants, and animals. Set up, adjust, calibrate, clean, maintain, and troubleshoot laboratory and field equipment. Provide technical support and services for scientists and engineers working in fields such as agriculture, environmental science, resource management, biology, and health sciences. Clean, maintain, and prepare supplies and work areas. Participate in the research, development, or manufacturing of medicinal and pharmaceutical preparations. Conduct standardized biological, microbiological, or biochemical tests and laboratory analyses to evaluate the quantity or quality of physical or chemical substances in food or other products. Analyze experimental data and interpret results to write reports and summaries of findings. Measure or weigh compounds and solutions for use in testing or animal feed. Monitor and observe experiments, recording production and test data for evaluation by research personnel. Examine animals and specimens to detect the presence of disease or other problems. Conduct or

supervise operational programs such as fish hatcheries, greenhouses, and livestock production programs. Feed livestock or laboratory animals.

GOE Information—Interest Area: 08. Health Science. **Work Group:** 08.06. Medical Technology. **Personality Type**—Realistic. Realistic occupations frequently involve work activities that include practical, hands-on problems and solutions. They often deal with plants; animals; and real-world materials like wood, tools, and machinery. Many of the occupations require working outside and do not involve a lot of paperwork or working closely with others. **Work Values**—Supervision, Technical; Variety. **Skills**—Science; Equipment Maintenance; Active Learning; Quality Control Analysis; Troubleshooting; Mathematics. **Abilities**—*Cognitive:* Number Facility; Mathematical Reasoning; Written Comprehension; Problem Sensitivity; Category Flexibility; Written Expression. *Psychomotor:* Control Precision; Arm-Hand Steadiness; Manual Dexterity; Finger Dexterity; Multilimb Coordination. *Physical:* None met the criteria. *Sensory:* Near Vision; Visual Color Discrimination; Far Vision; Depth Perception; Hearing Sensitivity; Auditory Attention. **General Work Activities**—*Information Input:* Identifying Objects, Actions, and Events; Monitoring Processes, Materials, or Surroundings; Inspecting Equipment, Structures, or Materials. *Mental Process:* Processing Information; Updating and Using Relevant Knowledge; Organizing, Planning, and Prioritizing. *Work Output:* Documenting or Recording Information; Handling and Moving Objects; Repairing and Maintaining Electronic Equipment. *Interacting with Others:* Communicating with Other Workers; Establishing and Maintaining Interpersonal Relationships; Coaching and Developing Others. **Physical Work Conditions**—Indoors; Standing; Using Hands on Objects, Tools, or Controls; Repetitive Motions. **Other Job Characteristics**—Need to Be Exact or Accurate; Repeat Same Tasks; Errors Have Important Consequences.

Experience—Job Zone 4. A minimum of two to four years of work-related skill, knowledge, or experience is needed. **Job Preparation**—SVP 7.0 to less than 8.0—two years to less than 10 years. **Knowledges**—Chemistry; Biology; Mathematics. **Instructional Program**—Biology Technician/Biotechnology Laboratory Technician.

Related SOC Job—19-4021 Biological Technicians. **Related OOH Job**—Science Technicians. **Related DOT Jobs**—040.061-022 Dairy Technologist; 040.061-026 Fiber Technologist; 040.361-010 Laboratory Technician, Artificial Breeding; 040.361-014 Seed Analyst; 041.381-010 Biology Specimen Technician; 041.384-010 Herbarium Worker; 049.364-010 Feed-Research Aide; 049.364-018 Biological Aide; 411.364-010 Blood Tester, Fowl; 411.384-010 Poultry Inseminator; 418.384-010 Artificial Inseminator; 418.384-014 Artificial-Breeding Technician; 559.384-010 Laboratory Assistant, Culture Media.

19-4031.00 Chemical Technicians

- **Education/Training Required: Associate degree**
- **Employed: 59,790**
- **Annual Earnings: $38,500**
- **Growth: 4.4%**
- **Annual Job Openings: 7,000**

Conduct chemical and physical laboratory tests to assist scientists in making qualitative and quantitative analyses of solids, liquids, and gaseous materials for purposes such as research and development of new products or processes; quality control; maintenance of environmental standards; and other work involving experimental, theoretical, or practical application of chemistry and related sciences.

Monitor product quality to ensure compliance to standards and specifications. Set up and conduct chemical experiments, tests, and analyses using techniques such as chromatography, spectroscopy, physical and chemical separation techniques, and microscopy. Conduct chemical and physical laboratory tests to assist scientists in making qualitative and quantitative analyses of solids, liquids, and gaseous materials. Compile and interpret results of tests and analyses. Provide technical support and assistance to chemists and engineers. Prepare chemical solutions for products and processes following standardized formulas or create experimental formulas. Maintain, clean, and sterilize laboratory instruments and equipment. Write technical reports or prepare graphs and charts to document experimental results. Order and inventory materials to maintain supplies. Develop and conduct programs of sampling and analysis to maintain quality standards of raw materials, chemical intermediates, and products. Direct or monitor other workers producing chemical products. Operate experimental pilot plants, assisting with experimental design. Develop new chemical engineering processes or production techniques. Design and fabricate experimental apparatus to develop new products and processes.

GOE Information—Interest Area: 15. Scientific Research, Engineering, and Mathematics. **Work Group:** 15.05. Physical Science Laboratory Technology. **Personality Type—**Realistic. Realistic occupations frequently involve work activities that include practical, hands-on problems and solutions. They often deal with plants; animals; and real-world materials like wood, tools, and machinery. Many of the occupations require working outside and do not involve a lot of paperwork or working closely with others. **Work Values—**Supervision, Technical; Advancement; Supervision, Human Relations; Variety; Co-workers; Working Conditions. **Skills—**Operation Monitoring; Science; Quality Control Analysis; Equipment Maintenance; Operation and Control; Repairing. **Abilities—***Cognitive:* Category Flexibility; Flexibility of Closure; Inductive Reasoning; Oral Comprehension; Mathematical Reasoning; Information Ordering. *Psychomotor:* Arm-Hand Steadiness; Control Precision; Finger Dexterity; Multilimb Coordination. *Physical:* Trunk Strength. *Sensory:* Near Vision; Visual Color Discrimination. **General Work Activities—***Information Input:* Identifying Objects, Actions, and Events; Monitoring Processes, Materials, or Surroundings; Inspecting Equipment, Structures, or Materials. *Mental Process:* Processing Information; Updating and Using Relevant Knowledge; Organizing, Planning, and Prioritizing. *Work Output:* Documenting or Recording Information; Controlling Machines and Processes; Handling and Moving Objects. *Interacting with Others:* Communicating with Other Workers; Establishing and Maintaining Interpersonal Relationships; Teaching Others. **Physical Work Conditions—**Indoors; Noisy; Contaminants; Hazardous Conditions; Standing. **Other Job Characteristics—**Need to Be Exact or Accurate; Repeat Same Tasks.

Experience—Job Zone 3. Previous work-related skill, knowledge, or experience is required. **Job Preparation—**SVP 6.0 to less than 7.0—more than one year and less than four years. **Knowledges—**Chemistry; Mechanical Devices; Computers and Electronics; Mathematics; Engineering and Technology. **Instructional Programs—**Chemical Technology/Technician; Food Science.

Related SOC Job—19-4031 Chemical Technicians. **Related OOH Job—**Science Technicians. **Related DOT Jobs—**008.261-010 Chemical-Engineering Technician; 019.261-030 Laboratory Technician; 022.161-018 Perfumer; 022.261-010 Chemical Laboratory Technician; 022.281-010 Assayer; 022.281-018 Laboratory Tester; 029.261-010 Laboratory Tester; 029.381-010 Cloth Tester; 029.381-014 Laboratory Assistant; 582.384-010 Dye-Lab Technician.

19-4041.00 Geological and Petroleum Technicians

- **Education/Training Required: Associate degree**
- **Employed: 11,130**
- **Annual Earnings: $43,750**
- **Growth: 6.5%**
- **Annual Job Openings: 1,000**

The job openings listed here are shared with 19-4041.01 Geophysical Data Technicians and 19-4041.02 Geological Sample Test Technicians.

Assist scientists in the use of electrical, sonic, or nuclear measuring instruments in both laboratory and production activities to obtain data indicating potential sources of metallic ore, gas, or petroleum. Analyze mud and drill cuttings. Chart pressure, temperature, and other characteristics of wells or bore holes. Investigate and collect information leading to the possible discovery of new oil fields.

No task data available.

GOE Information—Interest Area: 01. Agriculture and Natural Resources. **Work Group:** 01.03. Resource Technologies for Plants, Animals, and the Environment. **Note:** The Department of Labor has not collected some data for this job, so it has fewer details than the other descriptions.

Instructional Program—Petroleum Technology/Technician.

Related SOC Job—19-4041 Geological and Petroleum Technicians. **Related OOH Job—**Science Technicians. **Related DOT Job—**No data available.

19-4041.01 Geophysical Data Technicians

- **Education/Training Required: Associate degree**
- **Employed: 11,130**
- **Annual Earnings: $43,750**
- **Growth: 6.5%**
- **Annual Job Openings: 1,000**

The job openings listed here are shared with 19-4041.00 Geological and Petroleum Technicians and 19-4041.02 Geological Sample Test Technicians.

Measure, record, and evaluate geological data, using sonic, electronic, electrical, seismic, or gravity-measuring instruments to prospect for oil or gas. May collect and evaluate core samples and cuttings.

Prepare notes, sketches, geological maps, and cross-sections. Read and study reports to compile information and data for geological and geophysical prospecting. Interview individuals and research public databases to obtain information. Assemble, maintain, and distribute information for library or record systems. Operate and adjust equipment and apparatus used to obtain geological data. Plan and direct activities of workers who operate equipment to collect data. Set up or direct setup of instruments used to collect geological data. Record readings to compile data used in prospecting for oil or gas. Supervise oil, water, and gas well drilling activities. Collect samples and cuttings, using equipment and hand tools. Develop and print photographic recordings of information, using equipment. Measure geological characteristics used in prospecting for oil or gas, using measuring instruments. Evaluate and interpret core samples and cuttings and other geological data used in prospecting for oil or gas. Diagnose and repair malfunctioning instruments and equipment, using manufacturers' manuals and hand tools. Prepare and attach packing instructions to shipping containers. Develop and design packing materials and handling procedures for shipping of objects.

GOE Information—Interest Area: 01. Agriculture and Natural Resources. Work Group: 01.03. Resource Technologies for Plants, Animals, and the Environment. Personality Type—Realistic. Realistic occupations frequently involve work activities that include practical, hands-on problems and solutions. They often deal with plants; animals; and real-world materials like wood, tools, and machinery. Many of the occupations require working outside and do not involve a lot of paperwork or working closely with others. Work Values—Variety; Compensation; Creativity; Supervision, Technical; Authority; Company Policies and Practices. Skills—Science; Technology Design; Mathematics; Operations Analysis; Operation Monitoring; Persuasion. Abilities—Cognitive: Written Comprehension; Mathematical Reasoning; Oral Expression; Number Facility; Written Expression; Oral Comprehension. Psychomotor: Finger Dexterity; Multilimb Coordination; Arm-Hand Steadiness. Physical: None met the criteria. Sensory: Hearing Sensitivity; Depth Perception; Auditory Attention; Far Vision; Visual Color Discrimination. General Work Activities—Information Input: Identifying Objects, Actions, and Events; Monitoring Processes, Materials, or Surroundings; Getting Information. Mental Process: Updating and Using Relevant Knowledge; Processing Information; Analyzing Data or Information. Work Output: Documenting or Recording Information; Controlling Machines and Processes; Handling and Moving Objects. Interacting with Others: Establishing and Maintaining Interpersonal Relationships; Communicating with Other Workers; Coaching and Developing Others. Physical Work Conditions—Indoors; Sitting. Other Job Characteristics—Need to Be Exact or Accurate; Repeat Same Tasks.

Experience—Job Zone 4. A minimum of two to four years of work-related skill, knowledge, or experience is needed. Job Preparation—SVP 7.0 to less than 8.0—two years to less than 10 years. Knowledges—Geography; Engineering and Technology; Physics; Computers and Electronics; Mathematics; Design. Instructional Program—Petroleum Technology/Technician.

Related SOC Job—19-4041 Geological and Petroleum Technicians. Related OOH Job—Science Technicians. Related DOT Jobs—010.161-018 Observer, Seismic Prospecting; 010.261-014 Observer, Electrical Prospecting; 010.261-018 Observer, Gravity Prospecting; 010.261-022 Surveyor, Oil-Well Directional; 010.267-010 Scout; 024.267-010 Geological Aide; 194.382-010 Section-Plotter Operator; 930.167-010 Technical Operator.

19-4041.02 Geological Sample Test Technicians

- Education/Training Required: Associate degree
- Employed: 11,130
- Annual Earnings: $43,750
- Growth: 6.5%
- Annual Job Openings: 1,000

The job openings listed here are shared with 19-4041.00 Geological and Petroleum Technicians and 19-4041.01 Geophysical Data Technicians.

Test and analyze geological samples, crude oil, or petroleum products to detect presence of petroleum, gas, or mineral deposits indicating potential for exploration and production or to determine physical and chemical properties to ensure that products meet quality standards.

Test and analyze samples in order to determine their content and characteristics, using laboratory apparatus and testing equipment. Collect and prepare solid and fluid samples for analysis. Assemble, operate, and maintain field and laboratory testing, measuring, and mechanical equipment, working as part of a crew when required. Compile and record testing and operational data for review and further analysis. Adjust and repair testing, electrical, and mechanical equipment and devices. Supervise well exploration and drilling activities and well completions. Inspect engines for wear and defective parts, using equipment and measuring devices. Prepare notes, sketches, geological maps, and cross sections. Participate in geological, geophysical, geochemical, hydrographic, or oceanographic surveys; prospecting field trips; exploratory drilling; well logging; or underground mine survey programs. Plot information from aerial photographs, well logs, section descriptions, and other databases. Assess the environmental impacts of development projects on subsurface materials. Collaborate with hydrogeologists in order to evaluate groundwater and well circulation. Prepare, transcribe, and/or analyze seismic, gravimetric, well log, or other geophysical and survey data. Participate in the evaluation of possible mining locations.

GOE Information—Interest Area: 01. Agriculture and Natural Resources. Work Group: 01.03. Resource Technologies for Plants, Animals, and the Environment. Personality Type—Realistic. Realistic occupations frequently involve work activities that include practical, hands-on problems and solutions. They often deal with plants; animals; and real-world materials like wood, tools, and machinery. Many of the occupations require working outside and do not involve a lot of paperwork or working closely with others. Work Values—Advancement; Supervision, Technical; Compensation; Company Policies and Practices; Authority; Moral Values. Skills—Science; Equipment Maintenance; Operation Monitoring; Quality Control Analysis; Mathematics; Installation. Abilities—Cognitive: Number Facility; Mathematical Reasoning; Flexibility of Closure; Perceptual Speed; Category Flexibility; Visualization. Psychomotor: Rate Control; Reaction Time; Speed of Limb Movement; Response Orientation; Control Precision; Arm-Hand Steadiness. Physical: Static Strength; Trunk Strength. Sensory: Visual Color Discrimination; Far Vision; Depth Perception; Auditory Attention; Hearing Sensitivity; Near Vision. General Work Activities—Information Input: Monitoring Processes, Materials, or Surroundings; Identifying Objects, Actions, and Events; Getting Information. Mental Process: Processing Information; Analyzing Data or Information; Updating and Using Relevant Knowledge. Work Output: Handling and Moving Objects; Documenting or Recording Information; Repairing and Maintaining Electronic Equipment. Interacting with Others: Communicating with Other Workers; Establishing and Maintaining Interpersonal Relationships; Providing Consultation and Advice to Others. Physical Work Conditions—Indoors; Noisy; Contaminants; More Often Sitting Than Standing; Using Hands on Objects, Tools, or Controls. Other Job Characteristics—Need to Be Exact or Accurate; Errors Have Important Consequences; Repeat Same Tasks.

Experience—Job Zone 3. Previous work-related skill, knowledge, or experience is required. Job Preparation—SVP 6.0 to less than 7.0—more than one year and less than four years. Knowledges—Chemistry; Geography; Physics; Mechanical Devices; Mathematics; Computers and Electronics. Instructional Program—Petroleum Technology/Technician.

Related SOC Job—19-4041 Geological and Petroleum Technicians. Related OOH Job—Science Technicians. Related DOT Jobs—010.131-010 Well-Logging Captain, Mud Analysis; 010.261-010 Field Engineer, Specialist; 010.261-026 Test-Engine Evaluator; 010.281-022 Well-Logging Operator, Mud Analysis; 024.381-010 Laboratory Assistant; 029.261-018 Test-Engine Operator; 029.261-022 Tester.

19-4051.00 Nuclear Technicians

- Education/Training Required: Associate degree
- Employed: 6,050
- Annual Earnings: $61,120
- Growth: 13.7%
- Annual Job Openings: 1,000

The job openings listed here are shared with 19-4051.01 Nuclear Equipment Operation Technicians and 19-4051.02 Nuclear Monitoring Technicians.

Assist scientists in both laboratory and production activities by performing technical tasks involving nuclear physics, primarily in operation, maintenance, production, and quality control support activities.

No task data available.

GOE Information—Interest Area: 15. Scientific Research, Engineering, and Mathematics. Work Group: 15.05. Physical Science Laboratory Technology. Note: The Department of Labor has not collected some data for this job, so it has fewer details than the other descriptions.

Instructional Programs—Industrial Radiologic Technology/Technician; Nuclear and Industrial Radiologic Technologies/Technicians, Other; Nuclear Engineering Technology/Technician; Nuclear/Nuclear Power Technology/Technician; Radiation Protection/Health Physics Technician.

Related SOC Job—19-4051 Nuclear Technicians. Related OOH Job—Science Technicians. Related DOT Job—No data available.

19-4051.01 Nuclear Equipment Operation Technicians

- Education/Training Required: Associate degree
- Employed: 6,050
- Annual Earnings: $61,120
- Growth: 13.7%
- Annual Job Openings: 1,000

The job openings listed here are shared with 19-4051.00 Nuclear Technicians and 19-4051.02 Nuclear Monitoring Technicians.

Operate equipment used for the release, control, and utilization of nuclear energy to assist scientists in laboratory and production activities.

Follow policies and procedures for radiation workers to ensure personnel safety. Modify, devise, and maintain equipment used in operations. Set control panel switches, according to standard procedures, to route electric power from sources and direct particle beams through injector units. Submit computations to supervisors for review. Calculate equipment operating factors, such as radiation times, dosages, temperatures, gamma intensities, and pressures, using standard formulas and conversion tables. Perform testing, maintenance, repair, and upgrading of accelerator systems. Warn maintenance workers of radiation hazards and direct workers to vacate hazardous areas. Monitor instruments, gauges, and recording devices in control rooms during operation of equipment under direction of nuclear experimenters. Write summaries of activities and record experimental data, such as accelerator performance, systems status, particle beam specification, and beam conditions obtained.

GOE Information—Interest Area: 15. Scientific Research, Engineering, and Mathematics. Work Group: 15.05. Physical Science Laboratory Technology. Personality Type—Realistic. Realistic occupations frequently involve work activities that include practical,

hands-on problems and solutions. They often deal with plants; animals; and real-world materials like wood, tools, and machinery. Many of the occupations require working outside and do not involve a lot of paperwork or working closely with others. Work Values—Compensation; Supervision, Technical; Supervision, Human Relations; Independence; Company Policies and Practices; Advancement. Skills—Operation Monitoring; Operation and Control; Science; Mathematics; Equipment Maintenance; Quality Control Analysis. Abilities—*Cognitive:* Mathematical Reasoning; Perceptual Speed; Number Facility; Selective Attention; Problem Sensitivity; Speed of Closure. *Psychomotor:* Reaction Time; Control Precision; Response Orientation; Multilimb Coordination; Wrist-Finger Speed; Arm-Hand Steadiness. *Physical:* Gross Body Equilibrium; Extent Flexibility; Gross Body Coordination; Static Strength; Trunk Strength. *Sensory:* Hearing Sensitivity; Auditory Attention; Depth Perception; Visual Color Discrimination; Far Vision. General Work Activities—*Information Input:* Inspecting Equipment, Structures, or Materials; Identifying Objects, Actions, and Events; Monitoring Processes, Materials, or Surroundings. *Mental Process:* Updating and Using Relevant Knowledge; Processing Information; Evaluating Information Against Standards. *Work Output:* Handling and Moving Objects; Controlling Machines and Processes; Performing General Physical Activities. *Interacting with Others:* Communicating with Other Workers; Coaching and Developing Others; Establishing and Maintaining Interpersonal Relationships. Physical Work Conditions—Indoors; Noisy; Very Hot or Cold; Radiation; Hazardous Conditions; Hazardous Equipment. Other Job Characteristics—Need to Be Exact or Accurate; Errors Have Important Consequences; Repeat Same Tasks.

Experience—Job Zone 3. Previous work-related skill, knowledge, or experience is required. Job Preparation—SVP 6.0 to less than 7.0—more than one year and less than four years. Knowledges—Physics; Chemistry; Engineering and Technology; Public Safety and Security; Mechanical Devices; Telecommunications. Instructional Programs—Industrial Radiologic Technology/Technician; Nuclear and Industrial Radiologic Technologies/Technicians, Other; Nuclear Engineering Technology/Technician; Nuclear/Nuclear Power Technology/Technician; Radiation Protection/Health Physics Technician.

Related SOC Job—19-4051 Nuclear Technicians. Related OOH Job—Science Technicians. Related DOT Jobs—015.362-010 Accelerator Operator; 015.362-014 Gamma-Facilities Operator; 015.362-018 Hot-Cell Technician; 015.362-022 Radioisotope-Production Operator; 015.362-026 Reactor Operator, Test-and-Research.

19-4051.02 Nuclear Monitoring Technicians

- Education/Training Required: Associate degree
- Employed: 6,050
- Annual Earnings: $61,120
- Growth: 13.7%
- Annual Job Openings: 1,000

The job openings listed here are shared with 19-4051.00 Nuclear Technicians and 19-4051.01 Nuclear Equipment Operation Technicians.

Collect and test samples to monitor results of nuclear experiments and contamination of humans, facilities, and environment.

Calculate safe radiation exposure times for personnel, using plant contamination readings and prescribed safe levels of radiation. Provide initial response to abnormal events and to alarms from radiation monitoring equipment. Monitor personnel in order to determine the amounts and intensities of radiation exposure. Inform supervisors when individual exposures or area radiation levels approach maximum permissible limits. Instruct personnel in radiation safety procedures and demonstrate use of protective clothing and equipment. Determine intensities and types of radiation in work areas, equipment, and materials, using radiation detectors and other instruments. Collect samples of air, water, gases, and solids to determine radioactivity levels of contamination. Set up equipment that automatically detects area radiation deviations and test detection equipment to ensure its accuracy. Determine or recommend radioactive decontamination procedures according to the size and nature of equipment and the degree of contamination. Decontaminate objects by cleaning with soap or solvents or by abrading with wire brushes, buffing wheels, or sandblasting machines. Place radioactive waste, such as sweepings and broken sample bottles, into containers for disposal. Calibrate and maintain chemical instrumentation sensing elements and sampling system equipment, using calibration instruments and hand tools. Place irradiated nuclear fuel materials in environmental chambers for testing and observe reactions through cell windows. Enter data into computers in order to record characteristics of nuclear events and locating coordinates of particles. Operate manipulators from outside cells to move specimens into and out of shielded containers, to remove specimens from cells, or to place specimens on benches or equipment workstations. Prepare reports describing contamination tests, material and equipment decontaminated, and methods used in decontamination processes. Confer with scientists directing projects to determine significant events to monitor during tests. Immerse samples in chemical compounds to prepare them for testing.

GOE Information—Interest Area: 07. Government and Public Administration. **Work Group:** 07.03. Regulations Enforcement. **Personality Type—**Realistic. Realistic occupations frequently involve work activities that include practical, hands-on problems and solutions. They often deal with plants; animals; and real-world materials like wood, tools, and machinery. Many of the occupations require working outside and do not involve a lot of paperwork or working closely with others. **Work Values—**Compensation; Supervision, Technical; Company Policies and Practices; Social Status; Supervision, Human Relations; Recognition. **Skills—**Science; Operation Monitoring; Equipment Maintenance; Mathematics; Systems Analysis; Operation and Control. **Abilities—***Cognitive:* Mathematical Reasoning; Number Facility; Perceptual Speed; Selective Attention; Problem Sensitivity; Speed of Closure. *Psychomotor:* Reaction Time; Finger Dexterity; Arm-Hand Steadiness; Manual Dexterity; Control Precision; Multilimb Coordination. *Physical:* Gross Body Equilibrium; Extent Flexibility. *Sensory:* Far Vision; Auditory Attention; Visual Color Discrimination; Hearing Sensitivity; Speech Clarity. **General Work Activities—***Information Input:* Monitoring Processes, Materials, or Surroundings; Inspecting Equipment, Structures, or Materials; Identifying Objects, Actions, and Events. *Mental Process:* Updating and Using Relevant Knowledge; Evaluating Information Against Standards; Processing Information. *Work Output:* Documenting or Recording Information; Repairing and Maintaining Electronic Equipment; Interacting With Computers. *Interacting with Others:* Communicating with Other Workers; Establishing and Maintaining Interpersonal Relationships; Interpreting the Meaning of Information for Others. **Physical Work Conditions—**Indoors; Noisy; Very Hot or Cold; Contaminants; Radiation; Hazardous Conditions. **Other Job Characteristics—**Need to Be Exact or Accurate; Errors Have Important Consequences; Repeat Same Tasks.

Experience—Job Zone 3. Previous work-related skill, knowledge, or experience is required. **Job Preparation—**SVP 6.0 to less than 7.0—more than one year and less than four years. **Knowledges—**Physics; Chemistry; Public Safety and Security; Engineering and Technology; Design; Biology. **Instructional Programs—**Industrial Radiologic Technology/Technician; Nuclear and Industrial Radiologic Technologies/Technicians, Other; Nuclear Engineering Technology/Technician; Nuclear/Nuclear Power Technology/Technician; Radiation Protection/Health Physics Technician.

Related SOC Job—19-4051 Nuclear Technicians. **Related OOH Job—**Science Technicians. **Related DOT Jobs—**015.261-010 Chemical-Radiation Technician; 015.384-010 Scanner; 199.167-010 Radiation Monitor; 199.384-010 Decontaminator.

19-4061.00 Social Science Research Assistants

- **Education/Training Required: Associate degree**
- **Employed: 16,320**
- **Annual Earnings: $33,950**
- **Growth: 17.4%**
- **Annual Job Openings: 4,000**

The job openings listed here are shared with 19-4061.01 City and Regional Planning Aides.

Assist social scientists in laboratory, survey, and other social research. May perform publication activities, laboratory analysis, quality control, or data management. Normally these individuals work under the direct supervision of a social scientist and assist in those activities which are more routine.

Develop and implement research quality control procedures. Verify the accuracy and validity of data entered in databases; correct any errors. Conduct Internet-based and library research. Provide assistance with the preparation of project-related reports, manuscripts, and presentations. Collect specimens such as blood samples as required by research projects. Supervise the work of survey interviewers. Present research findings to groups of people. Perform needs assessments and/or consult with clients to determine the types of research and information that are required. Perform data entry and other clerical work as required for project completion. Screen potential subjects to determine their suitability as study participants. Allocate and manage laboratory space and resources. Edit and submit protocols and other required research documentation. Track research participants and perform any necessary follow-up tasks. Code data in preparation for computer entry. Provide assistance in the design of survey instruments such as questionnaires. Prepare, manipulate, and manage extensive databases. Prepare tables, graphs, fact sheets, and written reports summarizing research results. Obtain informed consent of research subjects and their guardians. Design and create special programs for tasks such as statistical analysis and data entry and cleaning. Administer standardized tests to research subjects or interview them to collect research data. Recruit and schedule research participants. Perform descriptive and multivariate statistical analyses of data, using computer software. Track laboratory supplies and expenses such as participant reimbursement.

GOE Information—Interest Area: 15. Scientific Research, Engineering, and Mathematics. **Work Group:** 15.06. Mathematics and Data Analysis. **Note:** The Department of Labor has not collected some data for this job, so it has fewer details than the other descriptions.

Instructional Program—Social Sciences, General.

Related SOC Job—19-4061 Social Science Research Assistants. **Related OOH Job**—Social Science Research Assistants. **Related DOT Job**—No data available.

19-4061.01 City and Regional Planning Aides

- **Education/Training Required:** Associate degree
- **Employed:** 16,320
- **Annual Earnings:** $33,950
- **Growth:** 17.4%
- **Annual Job Openings:** 4,000

The job openings listed here are shared with 19-4061.00 Social Science Research Assistants.

Compile data from various sources, such as maps, reports, and field and file investigations, for use by city planner in making planning studies.

Prepare, maintain, and update files and records, including land use data and statistics. Respond to public inquiries and complaints. Research, compile, analyze, and organize information from maps, reports, investigations, and books for use in reports and special projects. Prepare, develop, and maintain maps and databases. Serve as liaison between planning department and other departments and agencies. Prepare reports, using statistics, charts, and graphs, to illustrate planning studies in areas such as population, land use, or zoning. Participate in and support team planning efforts. Provide and process zoning and project permits and applications. Perform clerical duties such as composing, typing, and proofreading documents; scheduling appointments and meetings; handling mail; and posting public notices. Conduct interviews, surveys, and site inspections concerning factors that affect land usage, such as zoning, traffic flow, and housing. Perform code enforcement tasks. Inspect sites and review plans for minor development permit applications.

GOE Information—**Interest Area:** 07. Government and Public Administration. **Work Group:** 07.02. Public Planning. **Personality Type**—Conventional. Conventional occupations frequently involve following set procedures and routines. These occupations can include working with data and details more than with ideas. Usually there is a clear line of authority to follow. **Work Values**—Working Conditions; Advancement; Supervision, Human Relations; Company Policies and Practices; Variety; Supervision, Technical. **Skills**—Service Orientation; Coordination; Writing; Social Perceptiveness; Persuasion; Complex Problem Solving. **Abilities**—*Cognitive:* Number Facility; Written Expression; Fluency of Ideas; Mathematical Reasoning; Oral Expression; Time Sharing. *Psychomotor:* None met the criteria. *Physical:* None met the criteria. *Sensory:* Visual Color Discrimination; Far Vision; Speech Recognition; Hearing Sensitivity; Near Vision. **General Work Activities**—*Information Input:* Getting Information; Monitoring Processes, Materials, or Surroundings; Identifying Objects, Actions, and Events. *Mental Process:* Organizing, Planning, and Prioritizing; Updating and Using Relevant Knowledge; Analyzing Data or Information. *Work Output:* Interacting With Computers; Documenting or Recording Information; Drafting and Specifying Technical Devices. *Interacting with Others:* Establishing and Maintaining Interpersonal Relationships; Communicating with Persons Outside Organization; Communicating with Other Workers. **Physical Work Conditions**—Indoors; Noisy; Sitting. **Other Job Characteristics**—Need to Be Exact or Accurate; Errors Have Important Consequences.

Experience—Job Zone 3. Previous work-related skill, knowledge, or experience is required. **Job Preparation**—SVP 6.0 to less than 7.0—more than one year and less than four years. **Knowledges**—Geography; Design; Law and Government; Clerical Practices; English Language; Building and Construction. **Instructional Program**—Social Sciences, General.

Related SOC Job—19-4061 Social Science Research Assistants. **Related OOH Job**—Social Science Research Assistants. **Related DOT Job**—199.364-010 City Planning Aide.

19-4091.00 Environmental Science and Protection Technicians, Including Health

- **Education/Training Required:** Associate degree
- **Employed:** 32,460
- **Annual Earnings:** $36,260
- **Growth:** 16.3%
- **Annual Job Openings:** 6,000

Perform laboratory and field tests to monitor the environment and investigate sources of pollution, including those that affect health. Under direction of an environmental scientist or specialist, may collect samples of gases, soil, water, and other materials for testing and take corrective actions as assigned.

Record test data and prepare reports, summaries, and charts that interpret test results. Collect samples of gases, soils, water, industrial wastewater, and asbestos products to conduct tests on pollutant levels and identify sources of pollution. Respond to and investigate hazardous conditions or spills or outbreaks of disease or food poisoning, collecting samples for analysis. Provide information and technical and program assistance to government representatives, employers, and the general public on the issues of public health, environmental protection, or workplace safety. Calibrate microscopes and test instruments. Make recommendations to control or eliminate unsafe conditions at workplaces or public facilities. Inspect sanitary conditions at public facilities. Prepare samples or photomicrographs for testing and analysis. Calculate amount of pollutant in samples or compute air pollution or gas flow in industrial processes, using chemical and mathematical formulas. Initiate procedures to close down or fine establishments violating environmental or health regulations. Determine amounts and kinds of chemicals to use in destroying harmful organisms and removing impurities from purification systems. Discuss test results and analyses with customers. Maintain files such as hazardous waste databases, chemical usage data, personnel exposure information, and diagrams showing equipment locations. Perform statistical analysis of environmental data. Set up equipment or stations to monitor and collect pollutants from sites such as smokestacks, manufacturing plants, or mechanical equipment. Distribute permits, closure plans, and cleanup plans. Inspect workplaces to ensure the absence of health and safety hazards such as high noise levels, radiation, or potential lighting hazards. Weigh, analyze, and measure collected sample particles, such as lead, coal dust, or rock, to determine concentration of pollutants. Examine and analyze material for presence and concentration of contaminants such as asbestos, using variety of microscopes. Develop testing procedures or direct activities of workers in laboratory.

GOE Information—**Interest Area:** 01. Agriculture and Natural Resources. **Work Group:** 01.03. Resource Technologies for Plants, Animals, and the Environment. **Personality Type**—Investigative. Investigative occupations frequently involve working with ideas and require an extensive amount of thinking. These occupations can involve searching for facts and figuring out problems mentally. **Work Values**—Recognition; Independence; Creativity; Security; Variety; Advancement. **Skills**—Science; Persuasion; Active Learning; Mathematics; Reading Comprehension; Quality Control Analysis. **Abilities**—*Cognitive:* Inductive Reasoning; Mathematical Reasoning; Written Expression; Flexibility of Closure; Problem Sensitivity; Oral Expression. *Psychomotor:* Arm-Hand Steadiness; Control Precision; Multilimb Coordination. *Physical:* None met the criteria. *Sensory:* Near Vision; Far Vision; Speech Recognition; Depth Perception; Speech Clarity. **General Work Activities**—*Information Input:* Identifying Objects, Actions, and Events; Getting Information; Monitoring Processes, Materials, or Surroundings. *Mental Process:* Organizing, Planning, and Prioritizing; Updating and Using Relevant Knowledge; Processing Information. *Work Output:* Documenting or Recording Information; Performing General Physical Activities; Handling and Moving Objects. *Interacting with Others:* Establishing and Maintaining Interpersonal Relationships; Communicating with Other Workers; Resolving Conflicts and Negotiating with Others. **Physical Work Conditions**—More Often Indoors Than Outdoors; Noisy; Very Hot or Cold; Contaminants; Sitting. **Other Job Characteristics**—Need to Be Exact or Accurate; Errors Have Important Consequences.

Experience—Job Zone 4. A minimum of two to four years of work-related skill, knowledge, or experience is needed. **Job Preparation**—SVP 7.0 to less than 8.0—two years to less than 10 years. **Knowledges**—Biology; Engineering and Technology; Chemistry; Physics; Building and Construction; Design. **Instructional Programs**—Environmental Science; Environmental Studies; Physical Science Technologies/Technicians, Other; Science Technologies/ Technicians, Other.

Related SOC Job—19-4091 Environmental Science and Protection Technicians, Including Health. **Related OOH Job**—Science Technicians. **Related DOT Jobs**—012.261-010 Air Analyst; 012.281-010 Smoke Tester; 022.261-018 Chemist, Instrumentation; 022.261-022 Chemist, Wastewater-Treatment Plant; 022.281-014 Chemist, Water Purification; 029.261-014 Pollution-Control Technician; 029.261-030 Microscopist, Asbestos; 029.361-018 Laboratory Assistant.

19-4092.00 Forensic Science Technicians

- **Education/Training Required: Associate degree**
- **Employed: 11,030**
- **Annual Earnings: $44,590**
- **Growth: 36.4%**
- **Annual Job Openings: 2,000**

Collect, identify, classify, and analyze physical evidence related to criminal investigations. Perform tests on weapons or substances such as fiber, hair, and tissue to determine significance to investigation. May testify as expert witnesses on evidence or crime laboratory techniques. May serve as specialists in area of expertise, such as ballistics, fingerprinting, handwriting, or biochemistry.

Testify in court about investigative and analytical methods and findings. Keep records and prepare reports detailing findings, investigative methods, and laboratory techniques. Interpret laboratory findings and test results to identify and classify substances, materials, and other evidence collected at crime scenes. Operate and maintain laboratory equipment and apparatus. Prepare solutions, reagents, and sample formulations needed for laboratory work. Analyze and classify biological fluids, using DNA typing or serolog-

ical techniques. Collect evidence from crime scenes, storing it in conditions that preserve its integrity. Identify and quantify drugs and poisons found in biological fluids and tissues, in foods, and at crime scenes. Analyze handwritten and machine-produced textual evidence to decipher altered or obliterated text or to determine authorship, age, or source. Reconstruct crime scenes to determine relationships among pieces of evidence. Examine DNA samples to determine if they match other samples. Collect impressions of dust from surfaces to obtain and identify fingerprints. Analyze gunshot residue and bullet paths to determine how shootings occurred. Visit morgues, examine scenes of crimes, or contact other sources to obtain evidence or information to be used in investigations. Examine physical evidence such as hair, fiber, wood, or soil residues to obtain information about its source and composition. Determine types of bullets used in shooting and whether they were fired from a specific weapon. Examine firearms to determine mechanical condition and legal status, performing restoration work on damaged firearms to obtain information such as serial numbers. Confer with ballistics, fingerprinting, handwriting, document, electronics, medical, chemical, or metallurgical experts concerning evidence and its interpretation. Interpret the pharmacological effects of a drug or a combination of drugs on an individual. Compare objects such as tools with impression marks to determine whether a specific object is responsible for a specific mark.

GOE Information—**Interest Area:** 12. Law and Public Safety. **Work Group:** 12.04. Law Enforcement and Public Safety. **Personality Type**—Investigative. Investigative occupations frequently involve working with ideas and require an extensive amount of thinking. These occupations can involve searching for facts and figuring out problems mentally. **Work Values**—Autonomy; Recognition; Creativity; Variety; Achievement; Ability Utilization. **Skills**—Science; Quality Control Analysis; Troubleshooting; Speaking; Active Learning; Reading Comprehension. **Abilities**—*Cognitive:* Flexibility of Closure; Inductive Reasoning; Category Flexibility; Visualization; Oral Expression; Deductive Reasoning. *Psychomotor:* Arm-Hand Steadiness; Control Precision; Multilimb Coordination; Finger Dexterity. *Physical:* None met the criteria. *Sensory:* Near Vision; Depth Perception; Visual Color Discrimination; Far Vision; Speech Recognition; Speech Clarity. **General Work Activities**—*Information Input:* Identifying Objects, Actions, and Events; Getting Information; Monitoring Processes, Materials, or Surroundings. *Mental Process:* Updating and Using Relevant Knowledge; Processing Information; Making Decisions and Solving Problems. *Work Output:* Documenting or Recording Information; Handling and Moving Objects; Interacting With Computers. *Interacting with Others:* Communicating with Persons Outside Organization; Interpreting the Meaning of Information for Others; Communicating with Other Workers. **Physical Work Conditions**—Indoors; Contaminants; Disease or Infections; Hazardous Conditions; Sitting. **Other Job Characteristics**—Need to Be Exact or Accurate; Errors Have Important Consequences.

Experience—Job Zone 4. A minimum of two to four years of work-related skill, knowledge, or experience is needed. **Job Preparation**—SVP 7.0 to less than 8.0—two years to less than 10 years. **Knowledges**—Chemistry; Law and Government; Biology; Public Safety and Security; English Language; Clerical Practices. **Instructional Program**—Forensic Science and Technology.

Related SOC Job—19-4092 Forensic Science Technicians. **Related OOH Job**—Science Technicians. **Related DOT Jobs**—029.261-026 Criminalist; 199.267-010 Ballistics Expert, Forensic.

19-4093.00 Forest and Conservation Technicians

- Education/Training Required: Associate degree
- Employed: 29,940
- Annual Earnings: $28,540
- Growth: 6.6%
- Annual Job Openings: 6,000

Compile data pertaining to size, content, condition, and other characteristics of forest tracts under direction of foresters; train and lead forest workers in forest propagation and fire prevention and suppression. May assist conservation scientists in managing, improving, and protecting rangelands and wildlife habitats and help provide technical assistance regarding the conservation of soil, water, and related natural resources.

Train and lead forest and conservation workers in seasonal activities such as planting tree seedlings, putting out forest fires, and maintaining recreational facilities. Monitor activities of logging companies and contractors. Select and mark trees for thinning or logging, drawing detailed plans that include access roads. Thin and space trees and control weeds and undergrowth, using manual tools and chemicals, or supervise workers performing these tasks. Manage forest protection activities, including fire control, fire crew training, and coordination of fire detection and public education programs. Survey, measure, and map access roads and forest areas such as burns, cut-over areas, experimental plots, and timber sales sections. Patrol park or forest areas to protect resources and prevent damage. Provide information about, and enforce, regulations such as those concerning environmental protection, resource utilization, fire safety, and accident prevention. Keep records of the amount and condition of logs taken to mills. Supervise forest nursery operations, timber harvesting, land use activities such as livestock grazing, and disease or insect control programs. Issue fire permits, timber permits, and other forest use licenses. Develop and maintain computer databases. Measure distances, clean site lines, and record data to help survey crews. Plan and supervise construction of access routes and forest roads. Provide forestry education and general information, advice, and recommendations to woodlot owners, community organizations, and the general public. Perform reforestation, or forest renewal, including nursery and silviculture operations, site preparation, seeding and tree planting programs, cone collection, and tree improvement. Conduct laboratory or field experiments with plants, animals, insects, diseases, and soils. Provide technical support to forestry research programs in areas such as tree improvement, seed orchard operations, insect and disease surveys, or experimental forestry and forest engineering research. Inspect trees and collect samples of plants, seeds, foliage, bark, and roots to locate insect and disease damage.

GOE Information—Interest Area: 01. Agriculture and Natural Resources. **Work Group:** 01.06. Forestry and Logging. **Personality Type—**No data available. **Work Values—**No data available. **Skills—**Management of Financial Resources; Science; Operations Analysis; Equipment Selection; Management of Personnel Resources; Mathematics. **Abilities—***Cognitive:* Spatial Orientation; Flexibility of Closure; Written Expression; Inductive Reasoning; Oral Expression; Visualization. *Psychomotor:* Multilimb Coordination; Manual Dexterity; Control Precision; Arm-Hand Steadiness. *Physical:* Dynamic Strength; Static Strength; Stamina; Extent Flexibility. *Sensory:* Depth Perception; Far Vision. **General Work Activities—***Information Input:* Getting Information; Identifying Objects, Actions, and Events; Monitoring Processes, Materials, or Surroundings. *Mental Process:* Organizing, Planning, and Prioritizing; Making Decisions and Solving Problems; Updating and Using Relevant Knowledge. *Work Output:* Performing General Physical Activities; Handling and Moving Objects; Operating Vehicles or Equipment. *Interacting with Others:* Communicating with Other Workers; Establishing and Maintaining Interpersonal Relationships; Performing for or Working with the Public. **Physical Work Conditions—**Outdoors; Very Hot or Cold; Contaminants; Hazardous Equipment; Minor Burns, Cuts, Bites, or Stings; Walking and Running. **Other Job Characteristics—**Need to Be Exact or Accurate; Errors Have Important Consequences.

Experience—Job Zone 3. Previous work-related skill, knowledge, or experience is required. **Job Preparation—**SVP 6.0 to less than 7.0—more than one year and less than four years. **Knowledges—**Biology; Geography; Mechanical Devices; Law and Government; Transportation; Building and Construction. **Instructional Programs—**Forest Management/Forest Resources Management; Forest Resources Production and Management; Forest Sciences; Forest Technology/Technician; Forestry, General; Forestry, Other; Land Use Planning and Management/Development; Natural Resources and Conservation, Other; Natural Resources Management and Policy, Other; Natural Resources/Conservation, General; Urban Forestry; Water, Wetlands, and Marine Resources Management.

Related SOC Job—19-4093 Forest and Conservation Technicians. **Related OOH Job—**Science Technicians. **Related DOT Jobs—**040.261-010 Soil-Conservation Technician; 452.364-010 Forester Aide.

19-4099.99 Life, Physical, and Social Science Technicians, All Other

- Education/Training Required: Associate degree
- Employed: 63,810
- Annual Earnings: $40,030
- Growth: 20.0%
- Annual Job Openings: 18,000

All life, physical, and social science technicians not listed separately.

No task data available.

Note: The Department of Labor has not collected some data for this job, so it has fewer details than the other descriptions.

Related SOC Job—19-4099 Life, Physical, and Social Science Technicians, All Other. **Related OOH Job—**None. **Related DOT Jobs—**019.261-034 Laser Technician; 022.161-014 Colorist; 024.364-010 Paleontological Helper; 025.264-010 Hydrographer; 025.267-010 Oceanographer, Assistant; 025.267-014 Weather Observer; 029.383-010 Pilot, Submersible; 049.364-014 Vector Control Assistant; 199.364-014 Scientific Helper; 850.684-010 Excavator.

21-0000

Community and Social Services Occupations

21-1000 Counselors, Social Workers, and Other Community and Social Service Specialists

21-1011.00 Substance Abuse and Behavioral Disorder Counselors

- Education/Training Required: Master's degree
- Employed: 72,210
- Annual Earnings: $32,580
- Growth: 28.7%
- Annual Job Openings: 11,000

Counsel and advise individuals with alcohol; tobacco; drug; or other problems, such as gambling and eating disorders. May counsel individuals, families, or groups or engage in prevention programs.

Counsel clients and patients individually and in group sessions to assist in overcoming dependencies, adjusting to life, and making changes. Complete and maintain accurate records and reports regarding the patients' histories and progress, services provided, and other required information. Develop client treatment plans based on research, clinical experience, and client histories. Review and evaluate clients' progress in relation to measurable goals described in treatment and care plans. Interview clients, review records, and confer with other professionals to evaluate individuals' mental and physical condition and to determine their suitability for participation in a specific program. Intervene as advocate for clients or patients to resolve emergency problems in crisis situations. Provide clients or family members with information about addiction issues and about available services and programs, making appropriate referrals when necessary. Modify treatment plans to comply with changes in client status. Coordinate counseling efforts with mental health professionals and other health professionals such as doctors, nurses, and social workers. Attend training sessions to increase knowledge and skills. Plan and implement follow-up and aftercare programs for clients to be discharged from treatment programs. Conduct chemical dependency program orientation sessions. Counsel family members to assist them in understanding, dealing with, and supporting clients or patients. Participate in case conferences and staff meetings. Act as liaisons between clients and medical staff. Coordinate activities with courts, probation officers, community services, and other post-treatment agencies. Confer with family members or others close to clients to keep them informed of treatment planning and progress. Instruct others in program methods, procedures, and functions. Follow progress of discharged patients to determine effectiveness of treatments. Develop, implement, and evaluate public education, prevention, and health promotion programs, working in collaboration with organizations, institutions, and communities.

GOE Information—Interest Area: 10. Human Service. **Work Group:** 10.01. Counseling and Social Work. **Personality Type**—Social. Social occupations frequently involve working with, communicating with, and teaching people. These occupations often involve helping or providing service to others. **Work Values**—Social Service; Creativity; Autonomy; Responsibility; Achievement; Authority. **Skills**—Social Perceptiveness; Persuasion; Service Orientation; Negotiation; Learning Strategies; Active Listening. **Abilities**—*Cognitive:* Problem Sensitivity; Oral Expression; Written Expression; Inductive Reasoning; Originality; Oral Comprehension. *Psychomotor:* None met the criteria. *Physical:* None met the criteria. *Sensory:* Speech Recognition; Speech Clarity; Near Vision. **General Work Activities**—

Information Input: Getting Information; Monitoring Processes, Materials, or Surroundings; Identifying Objects, Actions, and Events. *Mental Process:* Organizing, Planning, and Prioritizing; Making Decisions and Solving Problems; Updating and Using Relevant Knowledge. *Work Output:* Documenting or Recording Information; Interacting With Computers. *Interacting with Others:* Establishing and Maintaining Interpersonal Relationships; Assisting and Caring for Others; Resolving Conflicts and Negotiating with Others. **Physical Work Conditions**—Indoors; Disease or Infections; Sitting. **Other Job Characteristics**—Need to Be Exact or Accurate; Repeat Same Tasks.

Experience—Job Zone 5. Extensive skill, knowledge, and experience are needed. **Job Preparation**—SVP 8.0 and above—four years to more than 10 years. **Knowledges**—Therapy and Counseling; Psychology; Sociology and Anthropology; Philosophy and Theology; Customer and Personal Service; Education and Training. **Instructional Programs**—Clinical/Medical Social Work; Mental and Social Health Services and Allied Professions, Other; Substance Abuse/Addiction Counseling.

Related SOC Job—21-1011 Substance Abuse and Behavioral Disorder Counselors. **Related OOH Job**—Counselors. **Related DOT Job**—045.107-058 Substance Abuse Counselor.

21-1012.00 Educational, Vocational, and School Counselors

- Education/Training Required: Master's degree
- Employed: 214,160
- Annual Earnings: $46,440
- Growth: 14.8%
- Annual Job Openings: 32,000

Counsel individuals and provide group educational and vocational guidance services.

Counsel students regarding educational issues such as course and program selection, class scheduling, school adjustment, truancy, study habits, and career planning. Counsel individuals to help them understand and overcome personal, social, or behavioral problems affecting their educational or vocational situations. Maintain accurate and complete student records as required by laws, district policies, and administrative regulations. Confer with parents or guardians, teachers, other counselors, and administrators to resolve students' behavioral, academic, and other problems. Provide crisis intervention to students when difficult situations occur at schools. Identify cases involving domestic abuse or other family problems affecting students' development. Meet with parents and guardians to discuss their children's progress and to determine their priorities for their children and their resource needs. Prepare students for later educational experiences by encouraging them to explore learning opportunities and to persevere with challenging tasks. Encourage students and/or parents to seek additional assistance from mental health professionals when necessary. Observe and evaluate students' performance, behavior, social development, and physical health. Enforce all administration policies and rules governing students. Meet with other professionals to discuss individual students' needs and progress. Provide students with information on such topics as college degree programs and admission requirements, financial aid opportunities, trade and technical schools, and apprenticeship programs. Evaluate individuals' abilities, interests, and personality characteristics, using tests, records, interviews, and professional sources. Collaborate with teachers and administrators in the development, evaluation, and revision of school programs. Establish and enforce behavioral rules and procedures to maintain order among students.

Teach classes and present self-help or information sessions on subjects related to education and career planning. Attend professional meetings, educational conferences, and teacher training workshops to maintain and improve professional competence.

GOE Information—Interest Area: 05. Education and Training. **Work Group:** 05.06. Counseling, Health, and Fitness Education. **Personality Type—**Social. Social occupations frequently involve working with, communicating with, and teaching people. These occupations often involve helping or providing service to others. **Work Values—**Social Service; Authority; Achievement; Creativity; Working Conditions; Responsibility. **Skills—**Social Perceptiveness; Service Orientation; Negotiation; Persuasion; Active Listening; Learning Strategies. **Abilities—***Cognitive:* Written Expression; Inductive Reasoning; Written Comprehension; Oral Expression; Problem Sensitivity; Oral Comprehension. *Psychomotor:* None met the criteria. *Physical:* None met the criteria. *Sensory:* Speech Recognition; Speech Clarity. **General Work Activities—***Information Input:* Getting Information; Identifying Objects, Actions, and Events; Monitoring Processes, Materials, or Surroundings. *Mental Process:* Organizing, Planning, and Prioritizing; Making Decisions and Solving Problems; Updating and Using Relevant Knowledge. *Work Output:* Documenting or Recording Information; Interacting With Computers. *Interacting with Others:* Establishing and Maintaining Interpersonal Relationships; Communicating with Other Workers; Resolving Conflicts and Negotiating with Others. **Physical Work Conditions—**Indoors; Sitting. **Other Job Characteristics—**Need to Be Exact or Accurate.

Experience—Job Zone 5. Extensive skill, knowledge, and experience are needed. **Job Preparation—**SVP 8.0 and above—four years to more than 10 years. **Knowledges—**Therapy and Counseling; Psychology; Sociology and Anthropology; Education and Training; Philosophy and Theology; Clerical Practices. **Instructional Programs—**College Student Counseling and Personnel Services; Counselor Education/School Counseling and Guidance Services.

Related SOC Job—21-1012 Educational, Vocational, and School Counselors. **Related OOH Job—**Counselors. **Related DOT Jobs—**045.107-010 Counselor; 045.107-014 Counselor, Nurses' Association; 045.107-018 Director of Counseling; 045.107-038 Residence Counselor; 045.117-010 Director of Guidance in Public Schools; 090.107-010 Foreign-Student Adviser; 094.224-022 Employment Training Specialist; 169.267-026 Supervisor, Special Services; 187.167-198 Veterans Contact Representative.

21-1013.00 Marriage and Family Therapists

- **Education/Training Required: Master's degree**
- **Employed: 18,500**
- **Annual Earnings: $42,300**
- **Growth: 25.4%**
- **Annual Job Openings: 3,000**

Diagnose and treat mental and emotional disorders, whether cognitive, affective, or behavioral, within the context of marriage and family systems. Apply psychotherapeutic and family systems theories and techniques in the delivery of professional services to individuals, couples, and families for the purpose of treating such diagnosed nervous and mental disorders.

Ask questions that will help clients identify their feelings and behaviors. Counsel clients on concerns such as unsatisfactory relationships, divorce and separation, child rearing, home management, and financial difficulties. Encourage individuals and family members to develop and use skills and strategies for confronting their problems in a constructive manner. Maintain case files that include activities, progress notes, evaluations, and recommendations. Collect information about clients, using techniques such as testing, interviewing, discussion, and observation. Develop and implement individualized treatment plans addressing family relationship problems. Determine whether clients should be counseled or referred to other specialists in such fields as medicine, psychiatry, and legal aid. Confer with clients in order to develop plans for post-treatment activities. Confer with other counselors to analyze individual cases and to coordinate counseling services. Follow up on results of counseling programs and clients' adjustments to determine effectiveness of programs. Provide instructions to clients on how to obtain help with legal, financial, and other personal issues. Contact doctors, schools, social workers, juvenile counselors, law enforcement personnel, and others to gather information in order to make recommendations to courts for the resolution of child custody or visitation disputes. Provide public education and consultation to other professionals or groups regarding counseling services, issues, and methods. Supervise other counselors, social service staff, and assistants. Provide family counseling and treatment services to inmates participating in substance abuse programs. Write evaluations of parents and children for use by courts deciding divorce and custody cases, testifying in court if necessary.

GOE Information—Interest Area: 10. Human Service. **Work Group:** 10.01. Counseling and Social Work. **Personality Type—**No data available. **Work Values—**No data available. **Skills—**Social Perceptiveness; Negotiation; Active Listening; Persuasion; Service Orientation; Monitoring. **Abilities—***Cognitive:* Speed of Closure; Inductive Reasoning; Problem Sensitivity; Oral Expression; Written Expression; Fluency of Ideas. *Psychomotor:* None met the criteria. *Physical:* None met the criteria. *Sensory:* Speech Recognition; Far Vision; Speech Clarity; Auditory Attention. **General Work Activities—***Information Input:* Monitoring Processes, Materials, or Surroundings; Identifying Objects, Actions, and Events; Getting Information. *Mental Process:* Making Decisions and Solving Problems; Updating and Using Relevant Knowledge; Judging the Qualities of Things, Services, or Other People's Work. *Work Output:* Documenting or Recording Information; Interacting With Computers. *Interacting with Others:* Assisting and Caring for Others; Establishing and Maintaining Interpersonal Relationships; Resolving Conflicts and Negotiating with Others. **Physical Work Conditions—**Indoors; Sitting. **Other Job Characteristics—**Errors Have Important Consequences; Need to Be Exact or Accurate.

Experience—Job Zone 5. Extensive skill, knowledge, and experience are needed. **Job Preparation—**SVP 8.0 and above—four years to more than 10 years. **Knowledges—**Therapy and Counseling; Psychology; Philosophy and Theology; Sociology and Anthropology; Medicine and Dentistry; Customer and Personal Service. **Instructional Programs—**Clinical Pastoral Counseling/Patient Counseling; Marriage and Family Therapy/Counseling; Social Work.

Related SOC Job—21-1013 Marriage and Family Therapists. **Related OOH Job—**Counselors. **Related DOT Job—**045.107-054 Counselor, Marriage and Family.

21-1014.00 Mental Health Counselors

- **Education/Training Required: Master's degree**
- **Employed: 87,220**
- **Annual Earnings: $34,010**
- **Growth: 27.2%**
- **Annual Job Openings: 14,000**

Counsel with emphasis on prevention. Work with individuals and groups to promote optimum mental health. May help individuals deal with addictions and substance abuse; family, parenting, and marital problems; suicide; stress management; problems with self-esteem; and issues associated with aging and mental and emotional health.

Maintain confidentiality of records relating to clients' treatment. Guide clients in the development of skills and strategies for dealing with their problems. Encourage clients to express their feelings and discuss what is happening in their lives and help them to develop insight into themselves and their relationships. Prepare and maintain all required treatment records and reports. Counsel clients and patients, individually and in group sessions, to assist in overcoming dependencies, adjusting to life, and making changes. Collect information about clients through interviews, observation, and tests. Act as client advocates to coordinate required services or to resolve emergency problems in crisis situations. Develop and implement treatment plans based on clinical experience and knowledge. Collaborate with other staff members to perform clinical assessments and develop treatment plans. Evaluate clients' physical or mental condition based on review of client information. Meet with families, probation officers, police, and other interested parties to exchange necessary information during the treatment process. Refer patients, clients, or family members to community resources or to specialists as necessary. Evaluate the effectiveness of counseling programs and clients' progress in resolving identified problems and moving towards defined objectives. Counsel family members to assist them in understanding, dealing with, and supporting clients or patients. Plan, organize, and lead structured programs of counseling, work, study, recreation, and social activities for clients. Modify treatment activities and approaches as needed to comply with changes in clients' status. Learn about new developments in their field by reading professional literature, attending courses and seminars, and establishing and maintaining contact with other social service agencies. Discuss with individual patients their plans for life after leaving therapy. Gather information about community mental health needs and resources that could be used in conjunction with therapy. Monitor clients' use of medications. Supervise other counselors, social service staff, and assistants.

GOE Information—Interest Area: 10. Human Service. **Work Group:** 10.01. Counseling and Social Work. **Personality Type**—Social. Social occupations frequently involve working with, communicating with, and teaching people. These occupations often involve helping or providing service to others. **Work Values**—Social Service; Creativity; Autonomy; Responsibility; Achievement; Authority. **Skills**—Social Perceptiveness; Service Orientation; Negotiation; Persuasion; Learning Strategies; Active Listening. **Abilities**—*Cognitive:* Inductive Reasoning; Problem Sensitivity; Written Comprehension; Deductive Reasoning; Oral Expression; Written Expression. *Psychomotor:* None met the criteria. *Physical:* None met the criteria. *Sensory:* Speech Recognition; Speech Clarity. **General Work Activities**—*Information Input:* Identifying Objects, Actions, and Events; Monitoring Processes, Materials, or Surroundings; Getting Information. *Mental Process:* Organizing, Planning, and Prioritizing; Thinking Creatively; Updating and Using Relevant Knowledge. *Work Output:* Documenting or Recording Information; Interacting With Computers. *Interacting with Others:* Establishing and Maintaining Interpersonal Relationships; Resolving Conflicts and Negotiating with Others; Communicating with Other Workers. **Physical Work Conditions**—Indoors; Noisy; Sitting. **Other Job Characteristics**—None met the criteria.

Experience—Job Zone 5. Extensive skill, knowledge, and experience are needed. **Job Preparation**—SVP 8.0 and above—four years to more than 10 years. **Knowledges**—Therapy and Counseling; Psychology; Sociology and Anthropology; Philosophy and Theology; Medicine and Dentistry; Education and Training. **Instructional Programs**—Clinical/Medical Social Work; Mental and Social Health Services and Allied Professions, Other; Mental Health Counseling/Counselor; Substance Abuse/Addiction Counseling.

Related SOC Job—21-1014 Mental Health Counselors. **Related OOH Job**—Counselors. **Related DOT Job**—195.107-050 Bereavement Counselor.

21-1015.00 Rehabilitation Counselors

- **Education/Training Required: Master's degree**
- **Employed: 117,230**
- **Annual Earnings: $28,330**
- **Growth: 23.9%**
- **Annual Job Openings: 19,000**

Counsel individuals to maximize the independence and employability of persons coping with personal, social, and vocational difficulties that result from birth defects, illness, disease, accidents, or the stress of daily life. Coordinate activities for residents of care and treatment facilities. Assess client needs and design and implement rehabilitation programs that may include personal and vocational counseling, training, and job placement.

Monitor and record clients' progress in order to ensure that goals and objectives are met. Confer with clients to discuss their options and goals so that rehabilitation programs and plans for accessing needed services can be developed. Prepare and maintain records and case files, including documentation such as clients' personal and eligibility information, services provided, narratives of client contacts, and relevant correspondence. Arrange for physical, mental, academic, vocational, and other evaluations to obtain information for assessing clients' needs and developing rehabilitation plans. Analyze information from interviews, educational and medical records, consultation with other professionals, and diagnostic evaluations to assess clients' abilities, needs, and eligibility for services. Develop rehabilitation plans that fit clients' aptitudes, education levels, physical abilities, and career goals. Maintain close contact with clients during job training and placements to resolve problems and evaluate placement adequacy. Locate barriers to client employment, such as inaccessible work sites, inflexible schedules, and transportation problems, and work with clients to develop strategies for overcoming these barriers. Develop and maintain relationships with community referral sources such as schools and community groups. Arrange for on-site job coaching or assistive devices such as specially equipped wheelchairs in order to help clients adapt to work or school environments. Confer with physicians, psychologists, occupational therapists, and other professionals to develop and implement client rehabilitation programs. Develop diagnostic procedures for determining clients' needs. Participate in job development and placement programs, contacting prospective employers, placing clients in jobs, and evaluating the success of placements. Collaborate with clients' families to implement rehabilitation plans that include behavioral, residential, social, and/or employment goals. Collaborate with community agencies to establish facilities and programs to assist persons with disabilities.

GOE Information—Interest Area: 10. Human Service. **Work Group:** 10.01. Counseling and Social Work. **Personality Type**—No data available. **Work Values**—No data available. **Skills**—Management of Financial Resources; Social Perceptiveness; Writing; Service Orientation; Monitoring; Coordination. **Abilities**—*Cognitive:* Originality; Inductive Reasoning; Fluency of Ideas; Oral Comprehension; Oral Expression; Problem Sensitivity. *Psychomotor:* Finger Dexterity. *Physical:* None met the criteria. *Sensory:* Speech Recognition; Speech Clarity; Far Vision; Near Vision. **General Work Activities**—*Information Input:* Identifying Objects, Actions, and Events; Getting Information; Monitoring Processes, Materials, or Surroundings. *Mental Process:* Organizing, Planning, and Prioritizing; Updating and Using Relevant Knowledge; Scheduling Work and Activities. *Work Output:* Documenting or Recording Information; Performing General Physical Activities. *Interacting with Others:* Communicating with Other Workers; Assisting and Caring for Others; Coaching and Developing Others. **Physical Work Conditions**—More Often Indoors Than Outdoors; Sitting; Walking and Running. **Other Job Characteristics**—Need to Be Exact or Accurate; Repeat Same Tasks.

Experience—Job Zone 4. A minimum of two to four years of work-related skill, knowledge, or experience is needed. **Job Preparation**—SVP 7.0 to less than 8.0—two years to less than 10 years. **Knowledges**—Psychology; Therapy and Counseling; Philosophy and Theology; Education and Training; Personnel and Human Resources; Sales and Marketing. **Instructional Programs**—Assistive/Augmentative Technology and Rehabiliation Engineering; Rehabilitation Counseling/Counselor.

Related SOC Job—21-1015 Rehabilitation Counselors. **Related OOH Job**—Counselors. **Related DOT Jobs**—045.107-042 Vocational Rehabilitation Counselor; 076.117-010 Coordinator of Rehabilitation Services; 094.117-018 Vocational Rehabilitation Consultant.

21-1019.99 Counselors, All Other

- **Education/Training Required: Bachelor's degree**
- **Employed: 21,390**
- **Annual Earnings: $37,250**
- **Growth: 23.1%**
- **Annual Job Openings: 4,000**

All counselors not listed separately.

No task data available.

Note: The Department of Labor has not collected some data for this job, so it has fewer details than the other descriptions.

Related SOC Job—21-1019 Counselors, All Other. **Related OOH Job**—Counselors. **Related DOT Job**—No data available.

21-1021.00 Child, Family, and School Social Workers

- **Education/Training Required: Bachelor's degree**
- **Employed: 256,430**
- **Annual Earnings: $35,350**
- **Growth: 19.0%**
- **Annual Job Openings: 31,000**

Provide social services and assistance to improve the social and psychological functioning of children and their families and to maximize the family well-being and the academic functioning of children. May assist single parents, arrange adoptions, and find foster homes for abandoned or abused children. In schools, they address such problems as teenage pregnancy, misbehavior, and truancy. May also advise teachers on how to deal with problem children.

Interview clients individually, in families, or in groups, assessing their situations, capabilities, and problems, to determine what services are required to meet their needs. Counsel individuals, groups, families, or communities regarding issues including mental health, poverty, unemployment, substance abuse, physical abuse, rehabilitation, social adjustment, child care, or medical care. Maintain case history records and prepare reports. Counsel students whose behavior, school progress, or mental or physical impairment indicate a need for assistance, diagnosing students' problems and arranging for needed services. Consult with parents, teachers, and other school personnel to determine causes of problems such as truancy and misbehavior and to implement solutions. Counsel parents with child rearing problems, interviewing the child and family to determine whether further action is required. Develop and review service plans in consultation with clients and perform follow-ups assessing the quantity and quality of services provided. Collect supplementary information needed to assist clients, such as employment records, medical records, or school reports. Address legal issues, such as child abuse and discipline, assisting with hearings and providing testimony to inform custody arrangements. Provide, find, or arrange for support services, such as child care, homemaker service, prenatal care, substance abuse treatment, job training, counseling, or parenting classes, to prevent more serious problems from developing. Refer clients to community resources for services such as job placement, debt counseling, legal aid, housing, medical treatment, or financial assistance and provide concrete information, such as where to go and how to apply. Arrange for medical, psychiatric, and other tests that may disclose causes of difficulties and indicate remedial measures. Work in child and adolescent residential institutions. Administer welfare programs. Evaluate personal characteristics and home conditions of foster home or adoption applicants. Serve as liaisons between students, homes, schools, family services, child guidance clinics, courts, protective services, doctors, and other contacts to help children who face problems such as disabilities, abuse, or poverty.

GOE Information—Interest Area: 10. Human Service. **Work Group:** 10.01. Counseling and Social Work. **Personality Type**—Social. Social occupations frequently involve working with, communicating with, and teaching people. These occupations often involve helping or providing service to others. **Work Values**—Social Service; Autonomy; Activity; Authority; Variety; Achievement. **Skills**—Social Perceptiveness; Service Orientation; Speaking; Monitoring; Negotiation; Learning Strategies. **Abilities**—*Cognitive:* Problem Sensitivity; Written Expression; Originality; Fluency of Ideas; Inductive Reasoning; Oral Expression. *Psychomotor:* None met the criteria. *Physical:* None met the criteria. *Sensory:* Speech Recognition; Speech Clarity; Near Vision. **General Work Activities**—*Information Input:* Identifying Objects, Actions, and Events; Getting Information; Monitoring Processes, Materials, or Surroundings. *Mental Process:* Organizing, Planning, and Prioritizing; Making Decisions and Solving Problems; Evaluating Information Against Standards. *Work Output:* Documenting or Recording Information; Interacting With Computers. *Interacting with Others:* Establishing and Maintaining Interpersonal Relationships; Communicating with Other Workers; Resolving Conflicts and Negotiating with Others. **Physical Work Conditions**—Indoors; Sitting. **Other Job Characteristics**—Need to Be Exact or Accurate.

Experience—Job Zone 5. Extensive skill, knowledge, and experience are needed. **Job Preparation**—SVP 8.0 and above—four years to more than 10 years. **Knowledges**—Therapy and Counseling; Psychology;

Sociology and Anthropology; Customer and Personal Service; Philosophy and Theology; Law and Government. **Instructional Programs**—Juvenile Corrections; Social Work; Youth Services/Administration.

Related SOC Job—21-1021 Child, Family, and School Social Workers. **Related OOH Job**—Social Workers. **Related DOT Jobs**—189.267-010 Field Representative; 195.107-010 Caseworker; 195.107-014 Caseworker, Child Welfare; 195.107-018 Caseworker, Family; 195.107-022 Social Group Worker; 195.107-026 Social Worker, Delinquency Prevention; 195.107-038 Social Worker, School; 195.137-010 Casework Supervisor; 195.164-010 Group Worker; 195.167-010 Community Organization Worker; 195.167-014 Community-Relations-And-Services Advisor, Public Housing; 195.367-018 Community Worker.

21-1022.00 Medical and Public Health Social Workers

- **Education/Training Required: Bachelor's degree**
- **Employed: 112,220**
- **Annual Earnings: $41,120**
- **Growth: 25.9%**
- **Annual Job Openings: 14,000**

Provide persons, families, or vulnerable populations with the psychosocial support needed to cope with chronic, acute, or terminal illnesses, such as Alzheimer's, cancer, or AIDS. Services include advising family caregivers, providing patient education and counseling, and making necessary referrals for other social services.

Collaborate with other professionals to evaluate patients' medical or physical condition and to assess client needs. Investigate child abuse or neglect cases and take authorized protective action when necessary. Refer patient, client, or family to community resources to assist in recovery from mental or physical illness and to provide access to services such as financial assistance, legal aid, housing, job placement, or education. Counsel clients and patients in individual and group sessions to help them overcome dependencies, recover from illness, and adjust to life. Organize support groups or counsel family members to assist them in understanding, dealing with, and supporting the client or patient. Advocate for clients or patients to resolve crises. Identify environmental impediments to client or patient progress through interviews and review of patient records. Utilize consultation data and social work experience to plan and coordinate client or patient care and rehabilitation, following through to ensure service efficacy. Modify treatment plans to comply with changes in clients' status. Monitor, evaluate, and record client progress according to measurable goals described in treatment and care plan. Supervise and direct other workers providing services to clients or patients. Develop or advise on social policy and assist in community development. Oversee Medicaid- and Medicare-related paperwork and recordkeeping in hospitals. Conduct social research to advance knowledge in the social work field. Plan and conduct programs to combat social problems, prevent substance abuse, or improve community health and counseling services.

GOE Information—**Interest Area:** 10. Human Service. **Work Group:** 10.01. Counseling and Social Work. **Personality Type**—Social. Social occupations frequently involve working with, communicating with, and teaching people. These occupations often involve helping or providing service to others. **Work Values**—Social Service; Creativity; Autonomy; Responsibility; Achievement; Authority. **Skills**—Social Perceptiveness; Service Orientation; Negotiation; Coordination; Active Listening; Speaking. **Abilities**—*Cognitive:* Speed of Closure;

Problem Sensitivity; Written Expression; Originality; Inductive Reasoning; Oral Expression. *Psychomotor:* None met the criteria. *Physical:* None met the criteria. *Sensory:* Speech Recognition; Speech Clarity; Far Vision; Near Vision. **General Work Activities**—*Information Input:* Identifying Objects, Actions, and Events; Getting Information; Monitoring Processes, Materials, or Surroundings. *Mental Process:* Making Decisions and Solving Problems; Judging the Qualities of Things, Services, or Other People's Work; Updating and Using Relevant Knowledge. *Work Output:* Documenting or Recording Information; Interacting With Computers. *Interacting with Others:* Establishing and Maintaining Interpersonal Relationships; Resolving Conflicts and Negotiating with Others; Communicating with Persons Outside Organization. **Physical Work Conditions**—Indoors; Noisy; Disease or Infections; Sitting. **Other Job Characteristics**—Need to Be Exact or Accurate.

Experience—Job Zone 5. Extensive skill, knowledge, and experience are needed. **Job Preparation**—SVP 8.0 and above—four years to more than 10 years. **Knowledges**—Therapy and Counseling; Psychology; Philosophy and Theology; Sociology and Anthropology; Medicine and Dentistry; Customer and Personal Service. **Instructional Program**—Clinical/Medical Social Work.

Related SOC Job—21-1022 Medical and Public Health Social Workers. **Related OOH Job**—Social Workers. **Related DOT Job**—195.107-030 Social Worker, Medical.

21-1023.00 Mental Health and Substance Abuse Social Workers

- **Education/Training Required: Master's degree**
- **Employed: 120,140**
- **Annual Earnings: $34,410**
- **Growth: 26.7%**
- **Annual Job Openings: 15,000**

Assess and treat individuals with mental, emotional, or substance abuse problems, including abuse of alcohol, tobacco, and/or other drugs. Activities may include individual and group therapy, crisis intervention, case management, client advocacy, prevention, and education.

Counsel clients in individual and group sessions to assist them in dealing with substance abuse, mental and physical illness, poverty, unemployment, or physical abuse. Interview clients, review records, and confer with other professionals to evaluate mental or physical condition of client or patient. Collaborate with counselors, physicians, and nurses to plan and coordinate treatment, drawing on social work experience and patient needs. Monitor, evaluate, and record client progress with respect to treatment goals. Refer patient, client, or family to community resources for housing or treatment to assist in recovery from mental or physical illness, following through to ensure service efficacy. Counsel and aid family members to assist them in understanding, dealing with, and supporting the client or patient. Modify treatment plans according to changes in client status. Plan and conduct programs to prevent substance abuse, to combat social problems, or to improve health and counseling services in community. Supervise and direct other workers who provide services to clients or patients. Develop or advise on social policy and assist in community development. Conduct social research to advance knowledge in the social work field.

GOE Information—**Interest Area:** 10. Human Service. **Work Group:** 10.01. Counseling and Social Work. **Personality Type**—Social. Social occupations frequently involve working with, communicating with, and teaching people. These occupations often involve helping or providing service to others. **Work Values**—Social Service; Creativity; Autonomy; Responsibility; Achievement; Authority. **Skills**—Social Perceptiveness; Service Orientation; Negotiation; Persuasion; Active Listening; Judgment and Decision Making. **Abilities**—*Cognitive:* Problem Sensitivity; Originality; Oral Expression; Written Expression; Inductive Reasoning; Fluency of Ideas. *Psychomotor:* None met the criteria. *Physical:* None met the criteria. *Sensory:* Speech Recognition; Speech Clarity. **General Work Activities**—*Information Input:* Getting Information; Identifying Objects, Actions, and Events; Monitoring Processes, Materials, or Surroundings. *Mental Process:* Making Decisions and Solving Problems; Organizing, Planning, and Prioritizing; Updating and Using Relevant Knowledge. *Work Output:* Documenting or Recording Information; Interacting With Computers. *Interacting with Others:* Establishing and Maintaining Interpersonal Relationships; Assisting and Caring for Others; Resolving Conflicts and Negotiating with Others. **Physical Work Conditions**—Indoors; Noisy; Sitting. **Other Job Characteristics**—Need to Be Exact or Accurate.

Experience—Job Zone 5. Extensive skill, knowledge, and experience are needed. **Job Preparation**—SVP 8.0 and above—four years to more than 10 years. **Knowledges**—Psychology; Therapy and Counseling; Customer and Personal Service; Sociology and Anthropology. **Instructional Program**—Clinical/Medical Social Work.

Related SOC Job—21-1023 Mental Health and Substance Abuse Social Workers. **Related OOH Job**—Social Workers. **Related DOT Jobs**—195.107-034 Social Worker, Psychiatric; 195.167-050 Case Manager.

21-1029.99 Social Workers, All Other

- **Education/Training Required: Bachelor's degree**
- **Employed: 60,940**
- **Annual Earnings: $41,300**
- **Growth: 19.6%**
- **Annual Job Openings: 7,000**

All social workers not listed separately.

No task data available.

Note: The Department of Labor has not collected some data for this job, so it has fewer details than the other descriptions.

Related SOC Job—21-1029 Social Workers, All Other. **Related OOH Job**—Social Workers. **Related DOT Job**—No data available.

21-1091.00 Health Educators

- **Education/Training Required: Master's degree**
- **Employed: 51,970**
- **Annual Earnings: $39,730**
- **Growth: 22.5%**
- **Annual Job Openings: 8,000**

Promote, maintain, and improve individual and community health by assisting individuals and communities to adopt healthy behaviors. Collect and analyze data to identify community needs prior to planning, implementing, monitoring, and evaluating programs designed to encourage healthy lifestyles, policies, and environments. May also serve as a resource to assist individuals, other professionals, or the community and may administer fiscal resources for health education programs.

Document activities, recording information such as the numbers of applications completed, presentations conducted, and persons assisted. Develop and present health education and promotion programs such as training workshops, conferences, and school or community presentations. Develop and maintain cooperative working relationships with agencies and organizations interested in public health care. Prepare and distribute health education materials, including reports; bulletins; and visual aids such as films, videotapes, photographs, and posters. Develop operational plans and policies necessary to achieve health education objectives and services. Collaborate with health specialists and civic groups to determine community health needs and the availability of services and to develop goals for meeting needs. Maintain databases, mailing lists, telephone networks, and other information to facilitate the functioning of health education programs. Supervise professional and technical staff in implementing health programs, objectives, and goals. Design and conduct evaluations and diagnostic studies to assess the quality and performance of health education programs. Provide program information to the public by preparing and presenting press releases, conducting media campaigns, and/or maintaining program-related Web sites. Develop, prepare, and coordinate grant applications and grant-related activities to obtain funding for health education programs and related work. Provide guidance to agencies and organizations in the assessment of health education needs and in the development and delivery of health education programs. Develop and maintain health education libraries to provide resources for staff and community agencies. Develop, conduct, or coordinate health needs assessments and other public health surveys.

GOE Information—**Interest Area:** 05. Education and Training. **Work Group:** 05.06. Counseling, Health, and Fitness Education. **Personality Type**—Social. Social occupations frequently involve working with, communicating with, and teaching people. These occupations often involve helping or providing service to others. **Work Values**—Social Service; Authority; Creativity; Achievement; Social Status; Variety. **Skills**—Service Orientation; Social Perceptiveness; Monitoring; Learning Strategies; Instructing; Speaking. **Abilities**—*Cognitive:* Written Expression; Fluency of Ideas; Oral Expression; Originality; Category Flexibility; Deductive Reasoning. *Psychomotor:* Multilimb Coordination. *Physical:* None met the criteria. *Sensory:* Speech Clarity; Speech Recognition; Far Vision. **General Work Activities**—*Information Input:* Monitoring Processes, Materials, or Surroundings; Identifying Objects, Actions, and Events; Getting Information. *Mental Process:* Organizing, Planning, and Prioritizing; Thinking Creatively; Processing Information. *Work Output:* Documenting or Recording Information; Handling and Moving Objects. *Interacting with Others:* Establishing and Maintaining Interpersonal Relationships; Coaching and Developing Others; Communicating with Other Workers. **Physical Work Conditions**—Indoors; Disease or Infections; Sitting; Using Hands on Objects, Tools, or Controls. **Other Job Characteristics**—Need to Be Exact or Accurate; Repeat Same Tasks.

Experience—Job Zone 4. A minimum of two to four years of work-related skill, knowledge, or experience is needed. **Job Preparation**—SVP 7.0 to less than 8.0—two years to less than 10 years. **Knowledges**—Sociology and Anthropology; Customer and Personal Service; Education and Training; Personnel and Human Resources; Psychology; Therapy and Counseling. **Instructional Programs**—Community Health Services/Liaison/Counseling; Health Communications; International Public Health/International Health; Maternal and Child Health; Public Health Education and Promotion.

Related SOC Job—21-1091 Health Educators. **Related OOH Job**—Health Educators. **Related DOT Job**—079.117-014 Public Health Educator.

21-1092.00 Probation Officers and Correctional Treatment Specialists

- **Education/Training Required: Bachelor's degree**
- **Employed: 90,600**
- **Annual Earnings: $40,210**
- **Growth: 12.8%**
- **Annual Job Openings: 14,000**

Provide social services to assist in rehabilitation of law offenders in custody or on probation or parole. Make recommendations for actions involving formulation of rehabilitation plan and treatment of offender, including conditional release and education and employment stipulations.

Prepare and maintain case folder for each assigned inmate or offender. Write reports describing offenders' progress. Inform offenders or inmates of requirements of conditional release, such as office visits, restitution payments, or educational and employment stipulations. Discuss with offenders how such issues as drug and alcohol abuse and anger management problems might have played roles in their criminal behavior. Gather information about offenders' backgrounds by talking to offenders, their families and friends, and other people who have relevant information. Develop rehabilitation programs for assigned offenders or inmates, establishing rules of conduct, goals, and objectives. Develop liaisons and networks with other parole officers, community agencies, staff in correctional institutions, psychiatric facilities, and after-care agencies to make plans for helping offenders with life adjustments. Arrange for medical, mental health, or substance abuse treatment services according to individual needs and court orders. Provide offenders or inmates with assistance in matters concerning detainers, sentences in other jurisdictions, writs, and applications for social assistance. Arrange for post-release services such as employment, housing, counseling, education, and social activities. Recommend remedial action or initiate court action when terms of probation or parole are not complied with. Interview probationers and parolees regularly to evaluate their progress in accomplishing goals and maintaining the terms specified in their probation contracts and rehabilitation plans. Supervise people on community-based sentences, including people on electronically monitored home detention. Assess the suitability of penitentiary inmates for release under parole and statutory release programs and submit recommendations to parole boards. Investigate alleged parole violations, using interviews, surveillance, and search and seizure. Conduct prehearing and presentencing investigations and testify in court regarding offenders' backgrounds and recommended sentences and sentencing conditions.

GOE Information—Interest Area: 10. Human Service. **Work Group:** 10.01. Counseling and Social Work. **Personality Type**—Social. Social occupations frequently involve working with, communicating with, and teaching people. These occupations often involve helping or providing service to others. **Work Values**—Social Service; Supervision, Human Relations; Authority; Activity; Security; Autonomy. **Skills**—Social Perceptiveness; Persuasion; Negotiation; Management of Personnel Resources; Time Management; Monitoring. **Abilities**—*Cognitive:* Deductive Reasoning; Problem Sensitivity; Originality; Inductive Reasoning; Written Expression; Fluency of Ideas. *Psychomotor:* None met the criteria. *Physical:* Trunk Strength. *Sensory:* Speech Recognition; Near Vision. **General Work Activities**—*Information Input:* Identifying Objects, Actions, and Events; Getting Information; Monitoring Processes, Materials, or Surroundings. *Mental Process:* Organizing, Planning, and Prioritizing; Making Decisions and Solving Problems; Updating and Using Relevant

Knowledge. *Work Output:* Documenting or Recording Information; Interacting With Computers; Performing General Physical Activities. *Interacting with Others:* Establishing and Maintaining Interpersonal Relationships; Resolving Conflicts and Negotiating with Others; Communicating with Other Workers. **Physical Work Conditions**—More Often Indoors Than Outdoors; Very Hot or Cold; Disease or Infections; Sitting. **Other Job Characteristics**—Need to Be Exact or Accurate; Errors Have Important Consequences; Repeat Same Tasks.

Experience—Job Zone 4. A minimum of two to four years of work-related skill, knowledge, or experience is needed. **Job Preparation**—SVP 7.0 to less than 8.0—two years to less than 10 years. **Knowledges**—Therapy and Counseling; Psychology; Sociology and Anthropology; Philosophy and Theology; Law and Government; Public Safety and Security. **Instructional Program**—Social Work.

Related SOC Job—21-1092 Probation Officers and Correctional Treatment Specialists. **Related OOH Job**—Probation Officers and Correctional Treatment Specialists. **Related DOT Jobs**—166.267-022 Prisoner-Classification Interviewer; 195.107-042 Correctional-Treatment Specialist; 195.107-046 Probation-and-Parole Officer; 195.367-026 Preparole-Counseling Aide.

21-1093.00 Social and Human Service Assistants

- **Education/Training Required: Moderate-term on-the-job training**
- **Employed: 313,210**
- **Annual Earnings: $25,030**
- **Growth: 29.7%**
- **Annual Job Openings: 61,000**

Assist professionals from a wide variety of fields, such as psychology, rehabilitation, or social work, to provide client services, as well as support for families. May assist clients in identifying available benefits and social and community services and help clients obtain them. May assist social workers with developing, organizing, and conducting programs to prevent and resolve problems relevant to substance abuse, human relationships, rehabilitation, or adult daycare.

Provide information and refer individuals to public or private agencies or community services for assistance. Keep records and prepare reports for owner or management concerning visits with clients. Visit individuals in homes or attend group meetings to provide information on agency services, requirements, and procedures. Advise clients regarding food stamps, child care, food, money management, sanitation, or housekeeping. Submit reports and review reports or problems with superior. Oversee day-to-day group activities of residents in institution. Interview individuals and family members to compile information on social, educational, criminal, institutional, or drug history. Meet with youth groups to acquaint them with consequences of delinquent acts. Transport and accompany clients to shopping areas or to appointments, using automobile. Explain rules established by owner or management, such as sanitation and maintenance requirements and parking regulations. Observe and discuss meal preparation and suggest alternate methods of food preparation. Demonstrate use and care of equipment for tenant use. Consult with supervisor concerning programs for individual families. Monitor free, supplementary meal program to ensure cleanliness of facility and that eligibility guidelines are met for persons receiving meals. Observe clients' food selections and recommend alternate economical and nutritional food choices. Inform tenants of facilities such as laundries and playgrounds. Care for children in client's home during client's appointments. Assist in locating housing for displaced individuals. Assist clients with preparation of forms, such as tax or rent forms. Assist in planning of food budget, using charts and sample budgets.

GOE Information—Interest Area: 10. Human Service. **Work Group:** 10.01. Counseling and Social Work. **Personality Type**—Social. Social occupations frequently involve working with, communicating with, and teaching people. These occupations often involve helping or providing service to others. **Work Values**—Social Service; Authority; Supervision, Technical; Variety; Supervision, Human Relations; Advancement. **Skills**—Social Perceptiveness; Management of Financial Resources; Service Orientation; Speaking; Judgment and Decision Making; Active Listening. **Abilities**—*Cognitive:* Written Expression; Fluency of Ideas; Speed of Closure; Oral Comprehension; Memorization; Oral Expression. *Psychomotor:* None met the criteria. *Physical:* None met the criteria. *Sensory:* Speech Recognition; Hearing Sensitivity; Speech Clarity; Auditory Attention; Near Vision. **General Work Activities**—*Information Input:* Monitoring Processes, Materials, or Surroundings; Identifying Objects, Actions, and Events; Getting Information. *Mental Process:* Updating and Using Relevant Knowledge; Evaluating Information Against Standards; Organizing, Planning, and Prioritizing. *Work Output:* Handling and Moving Objects; Performing General Physical Activities; Documenting or Recording Information. *Interacting with Others:* Establishing and Maintaining Interpersonal Relationships; Resolving Conflicts and Negotiating with Others; Assisting and Caring for Others. **Physical Work Conditions**—Indoors; Noisy; Sitting. **Other Job Characteristics**—Need to Be Exact or Accurate; Repeat Same Tasks.

Experience—Job Zone 3. Previous work-related skill, knowledge, or experience is required. **Job Preparation**—SVP 6.0 to less than 7.0—more than one year and less than four years. **Knowledges**—Therapy and Counseling; Psychology; Philosophy and Theology; Sociology and Anthropology; Clerical Practices; Customer and Personal Service. **Instructional Program**—Mental and Social Health Services and Allied Professions, Other.

Related SOC Job—21-1093 Social and Human Service Assistants. **Related OOH Job**—Social and Human Service Assistants. **Related DOT Jobs**—195.367-010 Case Aide; 195.367-014 Management Aide; 195.367-022 Food-Management Aide; 195.367-034 Social-Services Aide.

21-1099.99 Community and Social Service Specialists, All Other

- **Education/Training Required: No data available**
- **Employed: 99,860**
- **Annual Earnings: $32,920**
- **Growth: 31.9%**
- **Annual Job Openings: 17,000**

All community and social service specialists not listed separately.

No task data available.

Note: The Department of Labor has not collected some data for this job, so it has fewer details than the other descriptions.

Related SOC Job—21-1099 Community and Social Service Specialists, All Other. **Related OOH Job**—None. **Related DOT Job**—No data available.

21-2000 Religious Workers

21-2011.00 Clergy

- **Education/Training Required: Master's degree**
- **Employed: 36,590**
- **Annual Earnings: $38,540**
- **Growth: 12.4%**
- **Annual Job Openings: 26,000**

Conduct religious worship and perform other spiritual functions associated with beliefs and practices of religious faith or denomination. Provide spiritual and moral guidance and assistance to members.

Pray and promote spirituality. Read from sacred texts such as the Bible, Torah, or Koran. Prepare and deliver sermons and other talks. Organize and lead regular religious services. Share information about religious issues by writing articles, giving speeches, or teaching. Instruct people who seek conversion to a particular faith. Visit people in homes, hospitals, and prisons to provide them with comfort and support. Counsel individuals and groups concerning their spiritual, emotional, and personal needs. Train leaders of church, community, and youth groups. Administer religious rites or ordinances. Study and interpret religious laws, doctrines, or traditions. Conduct special ceremonies such as weddings, funerals, and confirmations. Plan and lead religious education programs for their congregations. Respond to requests for assistance during emergencies or crises. Devise ways in which congregation membership can be expanded. Collaborate with committees and individuals to address financial and administrative issues pertaining to congregations. Prepare people for participation in religious ceremonies. Perform administrative duties such as overseeing building management, ordering supplies, contracting for services and repairs, and supervising the work of staff members and volunteers. Refer people to community support services, psychologists, and doctors as necessary. Participate in fundraising activities to support congregation activities and facilities. Organize and engage in interfaith, community, civic, educational, and recreational activities sponsored by or related to their religion.

GOE Information—Interest Area: 10. Human Service. **Work Group:** 10.02. Religious Work. **Personality Type**—Social. Social occupations frequently involve working with, communicating with, and teaching people. These occupations often involve helping or providing service to others. **Work Values**—Social Status; Social Service; Autonomy; Achievement; Recognition; Security. **Skills**—Management of Personnel Resources; Management of Financial Resources; Negotiation; Persuasion; Judgment and Decision Making; Service Orientation. **Abilities**—*Cognitive:* Memorization; Fluency of Ideas; Written Expression; Problem Sensitivity; Speed of Closure; Oral Expression. *Psychomotor:* Finger Dexterity. *Physical:* None met the criteria. *Sensory:* Speech Clarity; Speech Recognition; Far Vision; Depth Perception; Near Vision. **General Work Activities**—*Information Input:* Getting Information; Monitoring Processes, Materials, or Surroundings; Identifying Objects, Actions, and Events. *Mental Process:* Organizing, Planning, and Prioritizing; Developing Objectives and Strategies; Thinking Creatively. *Work Output:* Documenting or Recording Information; Interacting With Computers; Performing General Physical Activities. *Interacting with Others:* Establishing and Maintaining Interpersonal Relationships; Resolving Conflicts and Negotiating with Others; Assisting and Caring for Others. **Physical Work Conditions**—Indoors; Sitting. **Other Job Characteristics**—Need to Be Exact or Accurate; Errors Have Important Consequences.

Experience—Job Zone 5. Extensive skill, knowledge, and experience are needed. **Job Preparation**—SVP 8.0 and above—four years to more than 10 years. **Knowledges**—Philosophy and Theology; Therapy and Counseling; Sociology and Anthropology; Psychology; Customer and Personal Service; Public Safety and Security. **Instructional Programs**—Clinical Pastoral Counseling/Patient Counseling; Divinity/Ministry (BD, MDiv.); Pastoral Counseling and Specialized Ministries, Other; Pastoral Studies/Counseling; Philosophy; Pre-Theology/Pre-Ministerial Studies; Rabbinical Studies (M.H.L./Rav); Theological and Ministerial Studies, Other; Theological Studies and Religious Vocations, Other; Theology/Theological Studies; Youth Ministry.

Related SOC Job—21-2011 Clergy. **Related OOH Job**—Clergy. **Related DOT Job**—120.107-010 Clergy Member.

21-2021.00 Directors, Religious Activities and Education

- **Education/Training Required: Bachelor's degree**
- **Employed: 13,610**
- **Annual Earnings: $32,540**
- **Growth: 18.5%**
- **Annual Job Openings: 10,000**

Direct and coordinate activities of a denominational group to meet religious needs of students. Plan, direct, or coordinate church school programs designed to promote religious education among church membership. May provide counseling and guidance relative to marital, health, financial, and religious problems.

Select appropriate curricula and class structures for educational programs. Attend workshops, seminars, and conferences to obtain program ideas, information, and resources. Train and supervise religious education instructional staff. Analyze revenue and program cost data to determine budget priorities. Counsel individuals regarding interpersonal, health, financial, and religious problems. Participate in denominational activities aimed at goals such as promoting interfaith understanding or providing aid to new or small congregations. Plan and conduct conferences dealing with the interpretation of religious ideas and convictions. Visit congregation members' homes, or arrange for pastoral visits, to provide information and resources regarding religious education programs. Locate and distribute resources such as periodicals and curricula to enhance the effectiveness of educational programs. Schedule special events such as camps, conferences, meetings, seminars, and retreats. Interpret religious education activities to the public through speaking, leading discussions, and writing articles for local and national publications. Publicize programs through sources such as newsletters, bulletins, and mailings. Implement program plans by ordering needed materials, scheduling speakers, reserving space, and handling other administrative details. Identify and recruit potential volunteer workers. Develop and direct study courses and religious education programs within congregations. Confer with clergy members, congregation officials, and congregation organizations to encourage support of and participation in religious education activities. Collaborate with other ministry members to establish goals and objectives for religious education programs and to develop ways to encourage program participation. Analyze member participation and changes in congregation emphasis to determine needs for religious education.

GOE Information—**Interest Area:** 10. Human Service. **Work Group:** 10.02. Religious Work. **Personality Type**—Social. Social occupations frequently involve working with, communicating with, and teaching people. These occupations often involve helping or providing service to others. **Work Values**—Social Service; Social Status; Creativity; Achievement; Autonomy; Working Conditions. **Skills**—Management of Financial Resources; Management of Personnel Resources; Social Perceptiveness; Systems Analysis; Management of Material Resources; Service Orientation. **Abilities**—*Cognitive:* Oral Expression; Number Facility; Mathematical Reasoning; Fluency of Ideas; Oral Comprehension; Memorization. *Psychomotor:* None met the criteria. *Physical:* None met the criteria. *Sensory:* Speech Clarity. **General Work Activities**—*Information Input:* Getting Information; Monitoring Processes, Materials, or Surroundings; Identifying Objects, Actions, and Events. *Mental Process:* Organizing, Planning, and Prioritizing; Making Decisions and Solving Problems; Scheduling Work and Activities. *Work Output:* Documenting or Recording Information. *Interacting with Others:* Communicating with Other Workers; Communicating with Persons Outside Organization; Establishing and Maintaining Interpersonal Relationships. **Physical Work Conditions**—Indoors; Sitting. **Other Job Characteristics**—None met the criteria.

Experience—Job Zone 5. Extensive skill, knowledge, and experience are needed. **Job Preparation**—SVP 8.0 and above—four years to more than 10 years. **Knowledges**—Therapy and Counseling; Philosophy and Theology; Sociology and Anthropology; Economics and Accounting; Administration and Management; Psychology. **Instructional Programs**—Bible/Biblical Studies; Missions/Missionary Studies and Missiology; Philosophy; Religious Education; Youth Ministry.

Related SOC Job—21-2021 Directors, Religious Activities and Education. **Related OOH Job**—Directors, Religious Activities and Education. **Related DOT Jobs**—129.107-018 Director of Religious Activities; 129.107-022 Director, Religious Education.

21-2099.99 Religious Workers, All Other

- **Education/Training Required: Bachelor's degree**
- **Employed: 6,670**
- **Annual Earnings: $23,780**
- **Growth: 7.4%**
- **Annual Job Openings: 9,000**

All religious workers not listed separately.

No task data available.

Note: The Department of Labor has not collected some data for this job, so it has fewer details than the other descriptions.

Instructional Programs—Pastoral Studies/Counseling; Philosophy; Theological and Ministerial Studies, Other.

Related SOC Job—21-2099 Religious Workers, All Other. **Related OOH Job**—None. **Related DOT Jobs**—129.027-010 Cantor; 129.107-010 Christian Science Nurse; 129.107-014 Christian Science Practitioner; 129.107-026 Pastoral Assistant; 129.271-010 Mohel; 199.207-010 Dianetic Counselor.

23-0000

Legal Occupations

23-1000 Lawyers, Judges, and Related Workers

23-1011.00 Lawyers

- **Education/Training Required: First professional degree**
- **Employed: 529,190**
- **Annual Earnings: $98,930**
- **Growth: 15.0%**
- **Annual Job Openings: 40,000**

Represent clients in criminal and civil litigation and other legal proceedings, draw up legal documents, and manage or advise clients on legal transactions. May specialize in a single area or may practice broadly in many areas of law.

Advise clients concerning business transactions, claim liability, advisability of prosecuting or defending lawsuits, or legal rights and obligations. Interpret laws, rulings, and regulations for individuals and businesses. Analyze the probable outcomes of cases, using knowledge of legal precedents. Present and summarize cases to judges and juries. Gather evidence to formulate defense or to initiate legal actions by such means as interviewing clients and witnesses to ascertain the facts of a case. Evaluate findings and develop strategies and arguments in preparation for presentation of cases. Represent clients in court or before government agencies. Examine legal data to determine advisability of defending or prosecuting lawsuit. Select jurors, argue motions, meet with judges, and question witnesses during the course of a trial. Present evidence to defend clients or prosecute defendants in criminal or civil litigation. Study Constitution, statutes, decisions, regulations, and ordinances of quasi-judicial bodies to determine ramifications for cases. Prepare and draft legal documents, such as wills, deeds, patent applications, mortgages, leases, and contracts. Prepare legal briefs and opinions and file appeals in state and federal courts of appeal. Negotiate settlements of civil disputes. Confer with colleagues with specialties in appropriate areas of legal issue to establish and verify bases for legal proceedings. Search for and examine public and other legal records to write opinions or establish ownership. Supervise legal assistants. Perform administrative and management functions related to the practice of law. Act as agent, trustee, guardian, or executor for businesses or individuals. Probate wills and represent and advise executors and administrators of estates. Help develop federal and state programs, draft and interpret laws and legislation, and establish enforcement procedures. Work in environmental law, representing public interest groups, waste disposal companies, or construction firms in their dealings with state and federal agencies.

GOE Information—Interest Area: 12. Law and Public Safety. **Work Group:** 12.02. Legal Practice and Justice Administration. **Personality Type—**Enterprising. Enterprising occupations frequently involve starting up and carrying out projects. These occupations can involve leading people and making many decisions. They sometimes require risk taking and often deal with business. **Work Values—**Autonomy; Compensation; Ability Utilization; Social Service; Creativity; Recognition. **Skills—**Persuasion; Negotiation; Writing; Judgment and Decision Making; Critical Thinking; Speaking. **Abilities—***Cognitive:* Written Expression; Fluency of Ideas; Written Comprehension; Inductive Reasoning; Oral Expression; Deductive Reasoning. *Psychomotor:* None met the criteria. *Physical:* None met the criteria. *Sensory:* Speech Clarity; Speech Recognition; Near Vision; Far Vision. **General Work Activities—***Information Input:* Getting Information; Identifying Objects, Actions, and Events; Monitoring Processes, Materials, or Surroundings. *Mental Process:* Updating and Using Relevant Knowledge; Making Decisions and Solving Problems; Organizing, Planning, and Prioritizing. *Work Output:* Documenting or Recording Information; Interacting With Computers. *Interacting with Others:* Resolving Conflicts and Negotiating with Others; Communicating with Persons Outside Organization; Providing Consultation and Advice to Others. **Physical Work Conditions—**Indoors; Sitting. **Other Job Characteristics—**Need to Be Exact or Accurate; Errors Have Important Consequences.

Experience—Job Zone 5. Extensive skill, knowledge, and experience are needed. **Job Preparation—**SVP 8.0 and above—four years to more than 10 years. **Knowledges—**Law and Government; English Language; Personnel and Human Resources; Economics and Accounting; Psychology; Administration and Management. **Instructional Programs—**Advanced Legal Research/Studies, General (LL.M., M.C.L., M.L.I., M.S.L., J.S.D./S.J.D.); American/U.S. Law/Legal Studies/Jurisprudence (LL.M., M.C.J., J.S.D./S.J.D.); Banking, Corporate, Finance, and Securities Law (LL.M., J.S.D./S.J.D.); Canadian Law/Legal Studies/Jurisprudence (LL.M., M.C.J., J.S.D./S.J.D.); Comparative Law (LL.M., M.C.L., J.S.D./S.J.D.); Energy, Environment, and Natural Resources Law (LL.M., M.S., J.S.D./S.J.D.); Health Law (LL.M., M.J., J.S.D./S.J.D.); International Business, Trade, and Tax Law (LL.M., J.S.D./S.J.D.); International Law and Legal Studies (LL.M., J.S.D./S.J.D.); Law (LL.B., J.D.); Law, Legal Services, and Legal Studies, Other; Legal Research and Advanced Professional Studies, Other; Legal Studies, General; Programs for Foreign Lawyers (LL.M., M.C.L.); Tax Law/Taxation (LL.M., J.S.D./S.J.D.).

Related SOC Job—23-1011 Lawyers. **Related OOH Job—**Lawyers. **Related DOT Jobs—**110.107-010 Lawyer; 110.107-014 Lawyer, Criminal; 110.117-010 District Attorney; 110.117-014 Insurance Attorney; 110.117-018 Lawyer, Admiralty; 110.117-022 Lawyer, Corporation; 110.117-026 Lawyer, Patent; 110.117-030 Lawyer, Probate; 110.117-034 Lawyer, Real Estate; 110.117-038 Tax Attorney; 110.117-042 Title Attorney.

23-1021.00 Administrative Law Judges, Adjudicators, and Hearing Officers

- **Education/Training Required: Work experience plus degree**
- **Employed: 15,350**
- **Annual Earnings: $70,680**
- **Growth: 10.1%**
- **Annual Job Openings: 1,000**

Conduct hearings to decide or recommend decisions on claims concerning government programs or other government-related matters and prepare decisions. Determine penalties or the existence and the amount of liability or recommend the acceptance or rejection of claims or compromise settlements.

Prepare written opinions and decisions. Review and evaluate data on documents such as claim applications, birth or death certificates, and physician or employer records. Research and analyze laws, regulations, policies, and precedent decisions to prepare for hearings and to determine conclusions. Confer with individuals or organizations involved in cases in order to obtain relevant information. Recommend the acceptance or rejection of claims or compromise settlements according to laws, regulations, policies, and precedent decisions. Explain to claimants how they can appeal rulings that go against them. Monitor and direct the activities of trials and hearings to ensure that they are conducted fairly and that courts administer justice while safeguarding the legal rights of all involved parties.

Authorize payment of valid claims and determine method of payment. Conduct hearings to review and decide claims regarding issues such as social program eligibility, environmental protection, and enforcement of health and safety regulations. Rule on exceptions, motions, and admissibility of evidence. Determine existence and amount of liability according to current laws, administrative and judicial precedents, and available evidence. Issue subpoenas and administer oaths in preparation for formal hearings. Conduct studies of appeals procedures in field agencies to ensure adherence to legal requirements and to facilitate determination of cases.

GOE Information—Interest Area: 12. Law and Public Safety. **Work Group:** 12.02. Legal Practice and Justice Administration. **Personality Type**—Enterprising. Enterprising occupations frequently involve starting up and carrying out projects. These occupations can involve leading people and making many decisions. They sometimes require risk taking and often deal with business. **Work Values**—Autonomy; Working Conditions; Responsibility; Security; Authority; Social Service. **Skills**—Judgment and Decision Making; Reading Comprehension; Active Listening; Social Perceptiveness; Time Management; Critical Thinking. **Abilities**—*Cognitive:* Written Expression; Written Comprehension; Inductive Reasoning; Deductive Reasoning; Oral Expression; Oral Comprehension. *Psychomotor:* None met the criteria. *Physical:* None met the criteria. *Sensory:* Speech Clarity; Speech Recognition; Near Vision; Far Vision. **General Work Activities**—*Information Input:* Getting Information; Identifying Objects, Actions, and Events; Monitoring Processes, Materials, or Surroundings. *Mental Process:* Organizing, Planning, and Prioritizing; Evaluating Information Against Standards; Updating and Using Relevant Knowledge. *Work Output:* Documenting or Recording Information; Interacting With Computers. *Interacting with Others:* Establishing and Maintaining Interpersonal Relationships; Communicating with Persons Outside Organization; Communicating with Other Workers. **Physical Work Conditions**—Indoors; Sitting. **Other Job Characteristics**—Need to Be Exact or Accurate; Repeat Same Tasks.

Experience—Job Zone 5. Extensive skill, knowledge, and experience are needed. **Job Preparation**—SVP 8.0 and above—four years to more than 10 years. **Knowledges**—Law and Government; Medicine and Dentistry; Psychology; Customer and Personal Service; Therapy and Counseling; Biology. **Instructional Programs**—Law (LL.B., J.D.); Law, Legal Services, and Legal Studies, Other; Legal Studies, General.

Related SOC Job—23-1021 Administrative Law Judges, Adjudicators, and Hearing Officers. **Related OOH Job**—Judges, Magistrates, and Other Judicial Workers. **Related DOT Jobs**—119.107-010 Hearing Officer; 119.117-010 Appeals Reviewer, Veteran; 119.167-010 Adjudicator; 119.267-014 Appeals Referee; 169.267-010 Claims Adjudicator.

23-1022.00 Arbitrators, Mediators, and Conciliators

- **Education/Training Required: Work experience plus degree**
- **Employed: 5,780**
- **Annual Earnings: $54,360**
- **Growth: 15.5%**
- **Annual Job Openings: Fewer than 500**

Facilitate negotiation and conflict resolution through dialogue. Resolve conflicts outside of the court system by mutual consent of parties involved.

Use mediation techniques to facilitate communication between disputants, to further parties' understanding of different perspectives, and to guide parties toward mutual agreement. Set up appointments for parties to meet for mediation. Rule on exceptions, motions, and admissibility of evidence. Prepare written opinions and decisions regarding cases. Notify claimants of denied claims and appeal rights. Issue subpoenas and administer oaths to prepare for formal hearings. Authorize payment of valid claims. Organize and deliver public presentations about mediation to organizations such as community agencies and schools. Conduct studies of appeals procedures to ensure adherence to legal requirements and to facilitate disposition of cases. Arrange and conduct hearings to obtain information and evidence relative to disposition of claims. Determine existence and amount of liability according to evidence, laws, and administrative and judicial precedents. Review and evaluate information from documents such as claim applications, birth or death certificates, and physician or employer records. Analyze evidence and apply relevant laws, regulations, policies, and precedents to reach conclusions. Conduct initial meetings with disputants to outline the arbitration process, settle procedural matters such as fees, and determine details such as witness numbers and time requirements. Confer with disputants to clarify issues, identify underlying concerns, and develop an understanding of their respective needs and interests. Interview claimants, agents, or witnesses to obtain information about disputed issues. Participate in court proceedings. Prepare settlement agreements for disputants to sign. Recommend acceptance or rejection of compromise settlement offers. Research laws, regulations, policies, and precedent decisions to prepare for hearings.

GOE Information—Interest Area: 12. Law and Public Safety. **Work Group:** 12.02. Legal Practice and Justice Administration. **Personality Type**—Enterprising. Enterprising occupations frequently involve starting up and carrying out projects. These occupations can involve leading people and making many decisions. They sometimes require risk taking and often deal with business. **Work Values**—Autonomy; Working Conditions; Responsibility; Security; Authority; Social Service. **Skills**—Judgment and Decision Making; Active Listening; Critical Thinking; Writing; Reading Comprehension; Speaking. **Abilities**—*Cognitive:* Memorization; Written Comprehension; Oral Comprehension; Written Expression; Deductive Reasoning; Inductive Reasoning. *Psychomotor:* None met the criteria. *Physical:* None met the criteria. *Sensory:* Speech Clarity. **General Work Activities**—*Information Input:* Getting Information; Identifying Objects, Actions, and Events. *Mental Process:* Making Decisions and Solving Problems; Processing Information; Evaluating Information Against Standards. *Work Output:* Documenting or Recording Information. *Interacting with Others:* Communicating with Other Workers; Communicating with Persons Outside Organization; Resolving Conflicts and Negotiating with Others. **Physical Work Conditions**—Indoors; Sitting. **Other Job Characteristics**—Need to Be Exact or Accurate.

Experience—Job Zone 5. Extensive skill, knowledge, and experience are needed. **Job Preparation**—SVP 8.0 and above—four years to more than 10 years. **Knowledges**—Law and Government; Psychology; English Language; Administration and Management. **Instructional Programs**—Law (LL.B., J.D.); Law, Legal Services, and Legal Studies, Other; Legal Studies, General.

Related SOC Job—23-1022 Arbitrators, Mediators, and Conciliators. **Related OOH Job**—Judges, Magistrates, and Other Judicial Workers. **Related DOT Jobs**—169.107-010 Arbitrator; 169.207-010 Conciliator.

23-1023.00 Judges, Magistrate Judges, and Magistrates

- Education/Training Required: Work experience plus degree
- Employed: 25,330
- Annual Earnings: $97,570
- Growth: 6.9%
- Annual Job Openings: 1,000

Arbitrate, advise, adjudicate, or administer justice in a court of law. May sentence defendant in criminal cases according to government statutes. May determine liability of defendant in civil cases. May issue marriage licenses and perform wedding ceremonies.

Instruct juries on applicable laws, direct juries to deduce the facts from the evidence presented, and hear their verdicts. Sentence defendants in criminal cases on conviction by jury according to applicable government statutes. Rule on admissibility of evidence and methods of conducting testimony. Preside over hearings and listen to allegations made by plaintiffs to determine whether the evidence supports the charges. Read documents on pleadings and motions to ascertain facts and issues. Interpret and enforce rules of procedure or establish new rules in situations where there are no procedures already established by law. Monitor proceedings to ensure that all applicable rules and procedures are followed. Advise attorneys, juries, litigants, and court personnel regarding conduct, issues, and proceedings. Research legal issues and write opinions on the issues. Conduct preliminary hearings to decide issues such as whether there is reasonable and probable cause to hold defendants in felony cases. Write decisions on cases. Award compensation for damages to litigants in civil cases in relation to findings by juries or by the court. Settle disputes between opposing attorneys. Supervise other judges, court officers, and the court's administrative staff. Impose restrictions upon parties in civil cases until trials can be held. Rule on custody and access disputes and enforce court orders regarding custody and support of children. Grant divorces and divide assets between spouses. Participate in judicial tribunals to help resolve disputes. Perform wedding ceremonies.

GOE Information—Interest Area: 12. Law and Public Safety. **Work Group:** 12.02. Legal Practice and Justice Administration. **Personality Type—**Enterprising. Enterprising occupations frequently involve starting up and carrying out projects. These occupations can involve leading people and making many decisions. They sometimes require risk taking and often deal with business. **Work Values—**Responsibility; Autonomy; Social Status; Recognition; Authority; Security. **Skills—**Judgment and Decision Making; Persuasion; Negotiation; Critical Thinking; Active Listening; Reading Comprehension. **Abilities—***Cognitive:* Written Expression; Inductive Reasoning; Deductive Reasoning; Oral Comprehension; Written Comprehension; Memorization. *Psychomotor:* None met the criteria. *Physical:* None met the criteria. *Sensory:* Speech Clarity; Near Vision; Speech Recognition. **General Work Activities—***Information Input:* Getting Information; Identifying Objects, Actions, and Events; Monitoring Processes, Materials, or Surroundings. *Mental Process:* Making Decisions and Solving Problems; Judging the Qualities of Things, Services, or Other People's Work; Updating and Using Relevant Knowledge. *Work Output:* Documenting or Recording Information; Interacting With Computers. *Interacting with Others:* Performing for or Working with the Public; Resolving Conflicts and Negotiating with Others; Establishing and Maintaining Interpersonal Relationships. **Physical Work Conditions—**Indoors; Sitting. **Other Job Characteristics—**Need to Be Exact or Accurate; Errors Have Important Consequences.

Experience—Job Zone 5. Extensive skill, knowledge, and experience are needed. **Job Preparation—**SVP 8.0 and above—four years to more than 10 years. **Knowledges—**Law and Government; English Language; Philosophy and Theology; Therapy and Counseling; Psychology; Sociology and Anthropology. **Instructional Programs—**Law (LL.B., J.D.); Law, Legal Services, and Legal Studies, Other; Legal Studies, General.

Related SOC Job—23-1023 Judges, Magistrate Judges, and Magistrates. **Related OOH Job—**Judges, Magistrates, and Other Judicial Workers. **Related DOT Jobs—**111.107-010 Judge; 111.107-014 Magistrate.

23-2000 Legal Support Workers

23-2011.00 Paralegals and Legal Assistants

- Education/Training Required: Associate degree
- Employed: 217,700
- Annual Earnings: $41,170
- Growth: 29.7%
- Annual Job Openings: 28,000

Assist lawyers by researching legal precedent, investigating facts, or preparing legal documents. Conduct research to support a legal proceeding, to formulate a defense, or to initiate legal action.

Prepare legal documents, including briefs, pleadings, appeals, wills, contracts, and real estate closing statements. Prepare affidavits or other documents, maintain document file, and file pleadings with court clerk. Gather and analyze research data, such as statutes; decisions; and legal articles, codes, and documents. Investigate facts and law of cases to determine causes of action and to prepare cases. Call upon witnesses to testify at hearing. Direct and coordinate law office activity, including delivery of subpoenas. Arbitrate disputes between parties and assist in real estate closing process. Keep and monitor legal volumes to ensure that law library is up to date. Appraise and inventory real and personal property for estate planning.

GOE Information—Interest Area: 12. Law and Public Safety. **Work Group:** 12.03. Legal Support. **Personality Type—**Enterprising. Enterprising occupations frequently involve starting up and carrying out projects. These occupations can involve leading people and making many decisions. They sometimes require risk taking and often deal with business. **Work Values—**Working Conditions; Social Service; Advancement; Variety; Autonomy; Ability Utilization. **Skills—**Writing; Time Management; Active Listening; Speaking; Monitoring; Reading Comprehension. **Abilities—***Cognitive:* Flexibility of Closure; Written Expression; Fluency of Ideas; Written Comprehension; Inductive Reasoning; Category Flexibility. *Psychomotor:* None met the criteria. *Physical:* None met the criteria. *Sensory:* Near Vision; Speech Recognition; Speech Clarity; Far Vision; Auditory Attention. **General Work Activities—***Information Input:* Getting Information; Identifying Objects, Actions, and Events; Monitoring Processes, Materials, or Surroundings. *Mental Process:* Organizing, Planning, and Prioritizing; Processing Information; Updating and Using Relevant Knowledge. *Work Output:* Documenting or Recording Information; Interacting With Computers. *Interacting with Others:* Communicating with Other Workers; Establishing and Maintaining Interpersonal Relationships; Communicating with Persons Outside Organization. **Physical Work Conditions—**Indoors; Sitting; Repetitive Motions. **Other Job Characteristics—**Need to Be Exact or Accurate; Repeat Same Tasks.

Experience—Job Zone 3. Previous work-related skill, knowledge, or experience is required. **Job Preparation**—SVP 6.0 to less than 7.0—more than one year and less than four years. **Knowledges**—Clerical Practices; Law and Government; Computers and Electronics; Personnel and Human Resources; English Language; Customer and Personal Service. **Instructional Program**—Paralegal/Legal Assistant.

Related SOC Job—23-2011 Paralegals and Legal Assistants. **Related OOH Job**—Paralegals and Legal Assistants. **Related DOT Jobs**—119.167-014 Patent Agent; 119.267-022 Legal Investigator; 119.267-026 Paralegal.

23-2091.00 Court Reporters

- **Education/Training Required: Postsecondary vocational training**
- **Employed: 17,130**
- **Annual Earnings: $41,640**
- **Growth: 14.8%**
- **Annual Job Openings: 3,000**

Use verbatim methods and equipment to capture, store, retrieve, and transcribe pretrial and trial proceedings or other information. Includes stenocaptioners who operate computerized stenographic captioning equipment to provide captions of live or prerecorded broadcasts for hearing-impaired viewers.

Take notes in shorthand or use a stenotype or shorthand machine that prints letters on a paper tape. Provide transcripts of proceedings upon request of judges, lawyers, or the public. Record verbatim proceedings of courts, legislative assemblies, committee meetings, and other proceedings, using computerized recording equipment, electronic stenograph machines, or stenomasks. Transcribe recorded proceedings in accordance with established formats. Ask speakers to clarify inaudible statements. File a legible transcript of records of a court case with the court clerk's office. File and store shorthand notes of court session. Respond to requests during court sessions to read portions of the proceedings already recorded. Record depositions and other proceedings for attorneys. Verify accuracy of transcripts by checking copies against original records of proceedings and accuracy of rulings by checking with judges. Record symbols on computer disks or CD-ROM; then translate and display them as text in computer-aided transcription process.

GOE Information—Interest **Area:** 07. Government and Public Administration. **Work Group:** 07.04. Public Administration Clerical Support. **Personality Type**—Artistic. Artistic occupations frequently involve working with forms, designs, and patterns. They often require self-expression, and the work can be done without following a clear set of rules. **Work Values**—Working Conditions; Ability Utilization; Variety; Achievement; Recognition; Independence. **Skills**—Reading Comprehension; Active Listening; Equipment Selection; Operation and Control; Equipment Maintenance; Operation Monitoring. **Abilities**—*Cognitive:* Selective Attention; Memorization; Written Expression; Oral Comprehension; Written Comprehension. *Psychomotor:* Wrist-Finger Speed; Manual Dexterity. *Physical:* None met the criteria. *Sensory:* Speech Recognition; Near Vision; Auditory Attention. **General Work Activities**—*Information Input:* Getting Information; Identifying Objects, Actions, and Events; Monitoring Processes, Materials, or Surroundings. *Mental Process:* Updating and Using Relevant Knowledge; Organizing, Planning, and Prioritizing; Scheduling Work and Activities. *Work Output:* Documenting or Recording Information; Controlling Machines and Processes; Interacting With Computers. *Interacting with Others:* Communicating with Other Workers; Establishing and Maintaining

Interpersonal Relationships; Performing Administrative Activities. **Physical Work Conditions**—Indoors; Noisy; Sitting; Using Hands on Objects, Tools, or Controls; Repetitive Motions. **Other Job Characteristics**—Need to Be Exact or Accurate; Repeat Same Tasks.

Experience—Job Zone 3. Previous work-related skill, knowledge, or experience is required. **Job Preparation**—SVP 6.0 to less than 7.0—more than one year and less than four years. **Knowledges**—Clerical Practices; English Language; Law and Government; Computers and Electronics; Production and Processing; Customer and Personal Service. **Instructional Programs**—Communications Studies/Speech Communication and Rhetoric; Court Reporting/Court Reporter; English Composition; Journalism; Mass Communications/Media Studies.

Related SOC Job—23-2091 Court Reporters. **Related OOH Job**—Court Reporters. **Related DOT Jobs**—202.362-010 Shorthand Reporter; 202.362-014 Stenographer; 202.362-018 Stenographer, Print Shop; 202.362-022 Stenotype Operator; 202.382-010 Stenocaptioner; 203.362-026 Caption Writer.

23-2092.00 Law Clerks

- **Education/Training Required: Bachelor's degree**
- **Employed: 40,620**
- **Annual Earnings: $35,620**
- **Growth: 7.7%**
- **Annual Job Openings: 7,000**

Assist lawyers or judges by researching or preparing legal documents. May meet with clients or assist lawyers and judges in court.

Search for and study legal documents to investigate facts and law of cases, to determine causes of action, and to prepare cases. Research and analyze law sources to prepare drafts of briefs or arguments for review, approval, and use by attorney. Prepare affidavits of documents and maintain document files and case correspondence. Review and file pleadings, petitions, and other documents relevant to court actions. Prepare real estate closing statements and assist in closing process. Deliver or direct delivery of subpoenas to witnesses and parties to action. Serve copies of pleas to opposing counsel. Arrange transportation and accommodation for witnesses and jurors if required. Communicate and arbitrate disputes between parties. Appraise and inventory real and personal property for estate planning. Store, catalog, and maintain currency of legal volumes.

GOE Information—Interest Area: 12. Law and Public Safety. **Work Group:** 12.03. Legal Support. **Personality Type**—Enterprising. Enterprising occupations frequently involve starting up and carrying out projects. These occupations can involve leading people and making many decisions. They sometimes require risk taking and often deal with business. **Work Values**—Working Conditions; Advancement; Social Service; Variety; Activity; Social Status. **Skills**—Critical Thinking; Writing; Active Learning; Judgment and Decision Making; Time Management; Reading Comprehension. **Abilities**—*Cognitive:* Written Comprehension; Written Expression; Oral Comprehension; Oral Expression; Fluency of Ideas; Flexibility of Closure. *Psychomotor:* None met the criteria. *Physical:* None met the criteria. *Sensory:* Near Vision; Speech Recognition. **General Work Activities**—*Information Input:* Getting Information; Identifying Objects, Actions, and Events; Monitoring Processes, Materials, or Surroundings. *Mental Process:* Updating and Using Relevant Knowledge; Organizing, Planning, and Prioritizing; Analyzing Data or Information. *Work Output:* Documenting or Recording Information; Interacting With Computers. *Interacting with Others:*

Establishing and Maintaining Interpersonal Relationships; Communicating with Other Workers; Resolving Conflicts and Negotiating with Others. **Physical Work Conditions**—Indoors; Sitting. **Other Job Characteristics**—Need to Be Exact or Accurate; Repeat Same Tasks.

Experience—Job Zone 4. A minimum of two to four years of work-related skill, knowledge, or experience is needed. **Job Preparation**—SVP 7.0 to less than 8.0—two years to less than 10 years. **Knowledges**—Law and Government; Clerical Practices; English Language; Computers and Electronics; Economics and Accounting; Psychology. **Instructional Programs**—Law (LL.B., J.D.); Legal Studies, General.

Related SOC Job—23-2092 Law Clerks. **Related OOH Job**—Law Clerks. **Related DOT Job**—119.267-026 Paralegal.

23-2093.00 Title Examiners, Abstractors, and Searchers

- **Education/Training Required: Moderate-term on-the-job training**
- **Employed: 64,580**
- **Annual Earnings: $35,120**
- **Growth: 0.9%**
- **Annual Job Openings: 8,000**

Search real estate records, examine titles, or summarize pertinent legal or insurance details for a variety of purposes. May compile lists of mortgages, contracts, and other instruments pertaining to titles by searching public and private records for law firms, real estate agencies, or title insurance companies.

Prepare lists of all legal instruments applying to a specific piece of land and the buildings on it. Read search requests in order to ascertain types of title evidence required and to obtain descriptions of properties and names of involved parties. Examine documentation such as mortgages, liens, judgments, easements, plat books, maps, contracts, and agreements in order to verify factors such as properties' legal descriptions, ownership, or restrictions. Copy or summarize recorded documents, such as mortgages, trust deeds, and contracts, that affect property titles. Examine individual titles to determine if restrictions, such as delinquent taxes, will affect titles and limit property use. Prepare reports describing any title encumbrances encountered during searching activities and outlining actions needed to clear titles. Verify accuracy and completeness of land-related documents accepted for registration; prepare rejection notices when documents are not acceptable. Confer with real estate agents, lending institution personnel, buyers, sellers, contractors, surveyors, and courthouse personnel to exchange title-related information or to resolve problems. Enter into recordkeeping systems appropriate data needed to create new title records or update existing ones. Direct activities of workers who search records and examine titles, assigning, scheduling, and evaluating work and providing technical guidance as necessary. Obtain maps or drawings delineating properties from company title plants, county surveyors, and/or assessors' offices. Prepare and issue title commitments and title insurance policies based on information compiled from title searches. Summarize pertinent legal or insurance details or sections of statutes or case law from reference books so that they can be used in examinations or as proofs or ready reference. Retrieve and examine real estate closing files for accuracy and to ensure that information included is recorded and executed according to regulations. Prepare real estate closing statements, utilizing knowledge and expertise in real estate procedures.

GOE Information—Interest Area: 12. Law and Public Safety. **Work Group:** 12.03. Legal Support. **Personality Type**—Conventional. Conventional occupations frequently involve following set procedures and routines. These occupations can include working with data and details more than with ideas. Usually there is a clear line of authority to follow. **Work Values**—Independence; Company Policies and Practices; Supervision, Technical; Working Conditions; Advancement; Supervision, Human Relations. **Skills**—Writing; Critical Thinking; Management of Financial Resources; Reading Comprehension; Technology Design; Management of Material Resources. **Abilities**—*Cognitive:* Written Comprehension; Written Expression; Speed of Closure; Number Facility. *Psychomotor:* Wrist-Finger Speed. *Physical:* None met the criteria. *Sensory:* Near Vision. **General Work Activities**—*Information Input:* Getting Information; Monitoring Processes, Materials, or Surroundings; Identifying Objects, Actions, and Events. *Mental Process:* Organizing, Planning, and Prioritizing; Processing Information; Analyzing Data or Information. *Work Output:* Documenting or Recording Information; Interacting With Computers. *Interacting with Others:* Establishing and Maintaining Interpersonal Relationships; Monitoring and Controlling Resources; Performing for or Working with the Public. **Physical Work Conditions**—Indoors; Sitting; Repetitive Motions. **Other Job Characteristics**—Need to Be Exact or Accurate; Repeat Same Tasks.

Experience—Job Zone 3. Previous work-related skill, knowledge, or experience is required. **Job Preparation**—SVP 6.0 to less than 7.0—more than one year and less than four years. **Knowledges**—Clerical Practices; Law and Government; Geography; Customer and Personal Service; Computers and Electronics; English Language. **Instructional Programs**—Paralegal/Legal Assistant.

Related SOC Job—23-2093 Title Examiners, Abstractors, and Searchers. **Related OOH Job**—Title Examiners, Abstractors, and Searchers. **Related DOT Jobs**—119.167-018 Title Supervisor; 119.267-010 Abstractor; 119.287-010 Title Examiner; 162.267-010 Title Clerk; 209.367-046 Title Searcher.

23-2099.99 Legal Support Workers, All Other

- **Education/Training Required: Bachelor's degree**
- **Employed: 71,060**
- **Annual Earnings: $43,800**
- **Growth: 7.1%**
- **Annual Job Openings: 12,000**

All legal support workers not listed separately.

No task data available.

Note: The Department of Labor has not collected some data for this job, so it has fewer details than the other descriptions.

Related SOC Job—23-2099 Legal Support Workers, All Other. **Related OOH Job**—Paralegals and Legal Assistants. **Related DOT Jobs**—119.267-018 Contract Clerk; 119.367-010 Escrow Officer; 186.167-074 Closer.

25-0000

Education, Training, and Library Occupations

25-1000 Postsecondary Teachers

25-1011.00 Business Teachers, Postsecondary

- Education/Training Required: Master's degree
- Employed: 67,420
- Annual Earnings: $59,210
- Growth: 32.2%
- Annual Job Openings: 329,000

The job openings listed here are shared with 37 other postsecondary teaching occupations numbered 25-1021.00 through 25-1199.99.

Teach courses in business administration and management, such as accounting, finance, human resources, labor relations, marketing, and operations research.

Prepare and deliver lectures to undergraduate and/or graduate students on topics such as financial accounting, principles of marketing, and operations management. Evaluate and grade students' classwork, assignments, and papers. Compile, administer, and grade examinations or assign this work to others. Prepare course materials such as syllabi, homework assignments, and handouts. Maintain student attendance records, grades, and other required records. Initiate, facilitate, and moderate classroom discussions. Plan, evaluate, and revise curricula, course content, and course materials and methods of instruction. Keep abreast of developments in their field by reading current literature, talking with colleagues, and participating in professional organizations and conferences. Maintain regularly scheduled office hours to advise and assist students. Advise students on academic and vocational curricula and on career issues. Select and obtain materials and supplies such as textbooks. Collaborate with colleagues to address teaching and research issues. Collaborate with members of the business community to improve programs, to develop new programs, and to provide student access to learning opportunities such as internships. Participate in student recruitment, registration, and placement activities. Serve on academic or administrative committees that deal with institutional policies, departmental matters, and academic issues. Participate in campus and community events. Compile bibliographies of specialized materials for outside reading assignments. Perform administrative duties such as serving as department head. Supervise undergraduate and/or graduate teaching, internship, and research work. Conduct research in a particular field of knowledge and publish findings in professional journals, books, and/or electronic media. Act as advisers to student organizations. Provide professional consulting services to government and/or industry. Write grant proposals to procure external research funding.

GOE Information—Interest Area: 05. Education and Training. **Work Group:** 05.03. Postsecondary and Adult Teaching and Instructing. **Personality Type**—No data available. **Work Values**—No data available. **Skills**—Instructing; Learning Strategies; Writing; Monitoring; Active Learning; Speaking. **Abilities**—*Cognitive:* Written Expression; Written Comprehension; Oral Expression; Oral Comprehension; Deductive Reasoning; Mathematical Reasoning. *Psychomotor:* None met the criteria. *Physical:* None met the criteria. *Sensory:* Speech Clarity; Speech Recognition; Near Vision. **General Work Activities**—*Information Input:* Getting Information; Identifying Objects, Actions, and Events; Monitoring Processes, Materials, or Surroundings. *Mental Process:* Updating and Using Relevant Knowledge; Thinking Creatively; Organizing, Planning, and Prioritizing. *Work Output:* Interacting With Computers; Documenting or Recording Information. *Interacting with Others:* Teaching Others; Coaching and Developing Others; Establishing and Maintaining Interpersonal Relationships. **Physical Work Conditions**—Indoors; Sitting. **Other Job Characteristics**—Need to Be Exact or Accurate.

Experience—Job Zone 5. Extensive skill, knowledge, and experience are needed. **Job Preparation**—SVP 8.0 and above—four years to more than 10 years. **Knowledges**—Economics and Accounting; Education and Training; Sales and Marketing; Sociology and Anthropology; English Language; Personnel and Human Resources. **Instructional Programs**—Accounting; Actuarial Science; Business Administration/Management; Business Statistics; Business Teacher Education; Business/Commerce, General; Business/Corporate Communications; Entrepreneurship/Entrepreneurial Studies; Finance, General; Financial Planning and Services; Franchising and Franchise Operations; Human Resources Management/Personnel Administration, General; Insurance; International Business/Trade/Commerce; International Finance; International Marketing; Investments and Securities; Labor and Industrial Relations; Logistics and Materials Management; Management Science, General; Marketing Research; Marketing/Marketing Management, General; Operations Management and Supervision; Organizational Behavior Studies; Public Finance; Purchasing, Procurement/Acquisitions, and Contracts Management.

Related SOC Job—25-1011 Business Teachers, Postsecondary. **Related OOH Job**—Teachers—Postsecondary. **Related DOT Jobs**—090.222-010 Instructor, Business Education; 090.227-010 Faculty Member, College or University.

25-1021.00 Computer Science Teachers, Postsecondary

- Education/Training Required: Master's degree
- Employed: 38,520
- Annual Earnings: $54,270
- Growth: 32.2%
- Annual Job Openings: 329,000

The job openings listed here are shared with 37 other postsecondary teaching occupations numbered 25-1011.00 through 25-1199.99.

Teach courses in computer science. May specialize in a field of computer science, such as the design and function of computers or operations and research analysis.

Evaluate and grade students' classwork, laboratory work, assignments, and papers. Maintain student attendance records, grades, and other required records. Prepare and deliver lectures to undergraduate and/or graduate students on topics such as programming, data structures, and software design. Prepare course materials such as syllabi, homework assignments, and handouts. Compile, administer, and grade examinations or assign this work to others. Keep abreast of developments in their field by reading current literature, talking with colleagues, and participating in professional conferences. Initiate, facilitate, and moderate classroom discussions. Plan, evaluate, and revise curricula, course content, and course materials and methods of instruction. Supervise students' laboratory work. Maintain regularly scheduled office hours to advise and assist students. Select and obtain materials and supplies such as textbooks and laboratory equipment. Advise students on academic and vocational curricula and on career issues. Participate in student recruitment, registration, and placement activities. Collaborate with colleagues to address teaching and research issues. Serve on academic or administrative committees that deal with institutional policies, departmental matters, and academic issues. Act as advisers to student organizations. Supervise undergraduate and/or graduate teaching, internship, and research work. Perform administrative duties such as serving as department head. Conduct research in a particular field of knowledge and publish findings in professional journals, books, and/or electronic media. Direct research of other teachers or of graduate students working for advanced academic degrees. Provide professional consulting services to government and/or industry. Participate in campus and community events. Compile bibliographies of specialized materials for outside reading assignments. Write grant proposals to procure external research funding.

GOE Information—Interest Area: 05. Education and Training. **Work Group:** 05.03. Postsecondary and Adult Teaching and Instructing. **Personality Type—**Investigative. Investigative occupations frequently involve working with ideas and require an extensive amount of thinking. These occupations can involve searching for facts and figuring out problems mentally. **Work Values—**Authority; Social Service; Creativity; Ability Utilization; Achievement; Social Status. **Skills—**Programming; Instructing; Technology Design; Operations Analysis; Learning Strategies; Mathematics. **Abilities—***Cognitive:* Written Expression; Oral Expression; Written Comprehension; Mathematical Reasoning; Oral Comprehension; Memorization. *Psychomotor:* None met the criteria. *Physical:* None met the criteria. *Sensory:* Speech Clarity; Near Vision; Speech Recognition. **General Work Activities—***Information Input:* Getting Information; Identifying Objects, Actions, and Events; Monitoring Processes, Materials, or Surroundings. *Mental Process:* Updating and Using Relevant Knowledge; Thinking Creatively; Organizing, Planning, and Prioritizing. *Work Output:* Interacting With Computers; Documenting or Recording Information; Repairing and Maintaining Electronic Equipment. *Interacting with Others:* Teaching Others; Coaching and Developing Others; Interpreting the Meaning of Information for Others. **Physical Work Conditions—**Indoors; Sitting. **Other Job Characteristics—**Need to Be Exact or Accurate.

Experience—Job Zone 5. Extensive skill, knowledge, and experience are needed. **Job Preparation—**SVP 8.0 and above—four years to more than 10 years. **Knowledges—**Computers and Electronics; Education and Training; Telecommunications; Mathematics; English Language; Engineering and Technology. **Instructional Programs—**Computer and Information Sciences, General; Computer Programming/Programmer, General; Computer Science; Computer Systems Analysis/Analyst; Information Science/Studies.

Related SOC Job—25-1021 Computer Science Teachers, Postsecondary. **Related OOH Job—**Teachers—Postsecondary. **Related DOT Job—**090.227-010 Faculty Member, College or University.

25-1022.00 Mathematical Science Teachers, Postsecondary

- **Education/Training Required: Master's degree**
- **Employed: 44,660**
- **Annual Earnings: $53,820**
- **Growth: 32.2%**
- **Annual Job Openings: 329,000**

The job openings listed here are shared with 37 other postsecondary teaching occupations numbered 25-1011.00 through 25-1199.99.

Teach courses pertaining to mathematical concepts, statistics, and actuarial science and to the application of original and standardized mathematical techniques in solving specific problems and situations.

Evaluate and grade students' classwork, assignments, and papers. Compile, administer, and grade examinations or assign this work to others. Prepare and deliver lectures to undergraduate and/or graduate students on topics such as linear algebra, differential equations, and discrete mathematics. Prepare course materials such as syllabi, homework assignments, and handouts. Maintain student attendance records, grades, and other required records. Maintain regularly scheduled office hours to advise and assist students. Plan, evaluate, and revise curricula, course content, and course materials and methods of instruction. Initiate, facilitate, and moderate classroom discussions. Select and obtain materials and supplies such as textbooks. Keep abreast of developments in their field by reading current literature, talking with colleagues, and participating in professional conferences. Advise students on academic and vocational curricula and on career issues. Collaborate with colleagues to address teaching and research issues. Serve on academic or administrative committees that deal with institutional policies, departmental matters, and academic issues. Participate in student recruitment, registration, and placement activities. Perform administrative duties such as serving as department head. Conduct research in a particular field of knowledge and publish findings in books, professional journals, and/or electronic media. Supervise undergraduate and/or graduate teaching, internship, and research work. Act as advisers to student organizations. Participate in campus and community events. Write grant proposals to procure external research funding. Compile bibliographies of specialized materials for outside reading assignments. Provide professional consulting services to government and/or industry.

GOE Information—Interest Area: 05. Education and Training. **Work Group:** 05.03. Postsecondary and Adult Teaching and Instructing. **Personality Type—**Investigative. Investigative occupations frequently involve working with ideas and require an extensive amount of thinking. These occupations can involve searching for facts and figuring out problems mentally. **Work Values—**Authority; Social Service; Creativity; Ability Utilization; Achievement; Social Status. **Skills—**Mathematics; Instructing; Learning Strategies; Critical Thinking; Complex Problem Solving; Speaking. **Abilities—***Cognitive:* Mathematical Reasoning; Number Facility; Written Expression; Oral Expression; Written Comprehension; Deductive Reasoning. *Psychomotor:* None met the criteria. *Physical:* None met the criteria. *Sensory:* Speech Clarity; Speech Recognition; Near Vision. **General Work Activities—***Information Input:* Getting Information; Identifying Objects, Actions, and Events; Monitoring Processes, Materials, or Surroundings. *Mental Process:* Updating and Using Relevant Knowledge; Thinking Creatively; Organizing, Planning, and Prioritizing. *Work Output:* Interacting With Computers; Documenting or Recording Information. *Interacting with Others:* Teaching Others; Coaching and Developing Others; Establishing and Maintaining Interpersonal Relationships. **Physical Work Conditions—**Indoors; More Often Standing Than Sitting. **Other Job Characteristics—**Need to Be Exact or Accurate; Repeat Same Tasks.

Experience—Job Zone 5. Extensive skill, knowledge, and experience are needed. **Job Preparation—**SVP 8.0 and above—four years to more than 10 years. **Knowledges—**Mathematics; Education and Training; Physics; Computers and Electronics; English Language; Psychology. **Instructional Programs—**Algebra and Number Theory; Analysis and Functional Analysis; Applied Mathematics; Business Statistics; Geometry/Geometric Analysis; Logic; Mathematical Statistics and Probability; Mathematics and Statistics, Other; Mathematics, General; Mathematics, Other; Statistics, General; Topology and Foundations.

Related SOC Job—25-1022 Mathematical Science Teachers, Postsecondary. **Related OOH Job—**Teachers—Postsecondary. **Related DOT Job—**090.227-010 Faculty Member, College or University.

25-1031.00 Architecture Teachers, Postsecondary

- Education/Training Required: Master's degree
- Employed: 6,110
- Annual Earnings: $62,270
- Growth: 32.2%
- Annual Job Openings: 329,000

The job openings listed here are shared with 37 other postsecondary teaching occupations numbered 25-1011.00 through 25-1199.99.

Teach courses in architecture and architectural design, such as architectural environmental design, interior architecture/design, and landscape architecture.

Evaluate and grade students' work, including work performed in design studios. Prepare and deliver lectures to undergraduate and/or graduate students on topics such as architectural design methods, aesthetics and design, and structures and materials. Prepare course materials such as syllabi, homework assignments, and handouts. Initiate, facilitate, and moderate classroom discussions. Plan, evaluate, and revise curricula, course content, and course materials and methods of instruction. Keep abreast of developments in their field by reading current literature, talking with colleagues, and participating in professional conferences. Maintain student attendance records, grades, and other required records. Maintain regularly scheduled office hours to advise and assist students. Compile, administer, and grade examinations or assign this work to others. Conduct research in a particular field of knowledge and publish findings in professional journals, books, and/or electronic media. Supervise undergraduate and/or graduate teaching, internship, and research work. Advise students on academic and vocational curricula and on career issues. Collaborate with colleagues to address teaching and research issues. Compile bibliographies of specialized materials for outside reading assignments. Serve on academic or administrative committees that deal with institutional policies, departmental matters, and academic issues. Participate in student recruitment, registration, and placement activities. Select and obtain materials and supplies such as textbooks and laboratory equipment. Write grant proposals to procure external research funding. Provide professional consulting services to government and/or industry. Perform administrative duties such as serving as department head. Act as advisers to student organizations. Participate in campus and community events.

GOE Information—Interest Area: 05. Education and Training. **Work Group:** 05.03. Postsecondary and Adult Teaching and Instructing. **Personality Type—**No data available. **Work Values—**No data available. **Skills—**Instructing; Technology Design; Operations Analysis; Writing; Complex Problem Solving; Learning Strategies. **Abilities—** *Cognitive:* Written Expression; Originality; Written Comprehension; Oral Expression; Oral Comprehension; Fluency of Ideas. *Psychomotor:* None met the criteria. *Physical:* None met the criteria. *Sensory:* Speech Clarity; Far Vision; Near Vision; Speech Recognition. **General Work Activities—***Information Input:* Getting Information; Identifying Objects, Actions, and Events; Monitoring Processes, Materials, or Surroundings. *Mental Process:* Thinking Creatively; Updating and Using Relevant Knowledge; Organizing, Planning, and Prioritizing. *Work Output:* Interacting With Computers; Documenting or Recording Information; Drafting and Specifying Technical Devices. *Interacting with Others:* Teaching Others; Coaching and Developing Others; Establishing and Maintaining Interpersonal Relationships. **Physical Work Conditions—**Indoors; Sitting. **Other Job Characteristics—**Need to Be Exact or Accurate.

Experience—Job Zone 5. Extensive skill, knowledge, and experience are needed. **Job Preparation—**SVP 8.0 and above—four years to more than 10 years. **Knowledges—**Fine Arts; Design; Building and Construction; History and Archeology; Philosophy and Theology; Geography. **Instructional Programs—**Architectural Engineering; Architecture (BArch, BA/BS, MArch, MA/MS, PhD); City/Urban, Community, and Regional Planning; Environmental Design/Architecture; Interior Architecture; Landscape Architecture (BS, BSLA, BLA, MSLA, MLA, PhD); Teacher Education and Professional Development, Specific Subject Areas, Other.

Related SOC Job—25-1031 Architecture Teachers, Postsecondary. **Related OOH Job—**Teachers—Postsecondary. **Related DOT Job—**090.227-010 Faculty Member, College or University.

25-1032.00 Engineering Teachers, Postsecondary

- Education/Training Required: Master's degree
- Employed: 34,500
- Annual Earnings: $74,540
- Growth: 32.2%
- Annual Job Openings: 329,000

The job openings listed here are shared with 37 other postsecondary teaching occupations numbered 25-1011.00 through 25-1199.99.

Teach courses pertaining to the application of physical laws and principles of engineering for the development of machines, materials, instruments, processes, and services. Includes teachers of subjects such as chemical, civil, electrical, industrial, mechanical, mineral, and petroleum engineering. Includes both teachers primarily engaged in teaching and those who do a combination of both teaching and research.

Prepare and deliver lectures to undergraduate and/or graduate students on topics such as mechanics, hydraulics, and robotics. Keep abreast of developments in their field by reading current literature, talking with colleagues, and participating in professional conferences. Supervise undergraduate and/or graduate teaching, internship, and research work. Evaluate and grade students' classwork, laboratory work, assignments, and papers. Conduct research in a particular field of knowledge and publish findings in professional journals, books, and/or electronic media. Prepare course materials such as syllabi, homework assignments, and handouts. Compile, administer, and grade examinations or assign this work to others. Write grant proposals to procure external research funding. Supervise students' laboratory work. Initiate, facilitate, and moderate class discussions. Maintain regularly scheduled office hours to advise and assist students. Plan, evaluate, and revise curricula, course content, and course materials and methods of instruction. Advise students on academic and vocational curricula and on career issues. Maintain student attendance records, grades, and other required records. Collaborate with colleagues to address teaching and research issues. Select and obtain materials and supplies such as textbooks and laboratory equipment. Participate in student recruitment, registration, and placement activities. Serve on academic or administrative committees that deal with institutional policies, departmental matters, and academic issues. Perform administrative duties such as serving as department head. Provide professional consulting services to government and/or industry. Compile bibliographies of specialized materials for outside reading assignments. Act as advisers to student organizations. Participate in campus and community events.

GOE Information—Interest Area: 05. Education and Training. **Work Group:** 05.03. Postsecondary and Adult Teaching and Instructing.

Personality Type—Investigative. Investigative occupations frequently involve working with ideas and require an extensive amount of thinking. These occupations can involve searching for facts and figuring out problems mentally. **Work Values**—Authority; Social Service; Creativity; Ability Utilization; Achievement; Social Status. **Skills**—Science; Programming; Mathematics; Technology Design; Complex Problem Solving; Management of Financial Resources. **Abilities**—*Cognitive:* Oral Expression; Written Comprehension; Written Expression; Mathematical Reasoning; Number Facility; Oral Comprehension. *Psychomotor:* None met the criteria. *Physical:* None met the criteria. *Sensory:* Speech Clarity; Speech Recognition; Hearing Sensitivity; Far Vision; Visual Color Discrimination; Near Vision. **General Work Activities**—*Information Input:* Getting Information; Identifying Objects, Actions, and Events; Monitoring Processes, Materials, or Surroundings. *Mental Process:* Updating and Using Relevant Knowledge; Thinking Creatively; Analyzing Data or Information. *Work Output:* Interacting With Computers; Documenting or Recording Information; Drafting and Specifying Technical Devices. *Interacting with Others:* Teaching Others; Interpreting the Meaning of Information for Others; Coaching and Developing Others. **Physical Work Conditions**—Indoors; Sitting. **Other Job Characteristics**—Need to Be Exact or Accurate.

Experience—Job Zone 5. Extensive skill, knowledge, and experience are needed. **Job Preparation**—SVP 8.0 and above—four years to more than 10 years. **Knowledges**—Engineering and Technology; Design; Physics; Mathematics; Education and Training; Telecommunications. **Instructional Programs**—Aerospace, Aeronautical, and Astronautical Engineering; Agricultural/Biological Engineering and Bioengineering; Architectural Engineering; Biomedical/Medical Engineering; Ceramic Sciences and Engineering; Chemical Engineering; Civil Engineering, General; Civil Engineering, Other; Computer Engineering, General; Computer Engineering, Other; Computer Hardware Engineering; Computer Software Engineering; Construction Engineering; Electrical, Electronics, and Communications Engineering; Engineering Mechanics; Engineering Physics; Engineering Science; Engineering, General; Engineering, Other; Environmental/Environmental Health Engineering; Forest Engineering; Geological/Geophysical Engineering; Geotechnical Engineering; Industrial Engineering; Manufacturing Engineering; Materials Engineering; Materials Science; Mechanical Engineering; Metallurgical Engineering; Mining and Mineral Engineering; Naval Architecture and Marine Engineering; Nuclear Engineering; Ocean Engineering; Petroleum Engineering; Polymer/Plastics Engineering; Structural Engineering; Surveying Engineering; Systems Engineering; Teacher Education and Professional Development, Specific Subject Areas, Other; Textile Sciences and Engineering; Transportation and Highway Engineering; Water Resources Engineering.

Related SOC Job—25-1032 Engineering Teachers, Postsecondary. **Related OOH Job**—Teachers—Postsecondary. **Related DOT Job**—090.227-010 Faculty Member, College or University.

25-1041.00 Agricultural Sciences Teachers, Postsecondary

- **Education/Training Required: Master's degree**
- **Employed: 11,460**
- **Annual Earnings: $71,330**
- **Growth: 32.2%**
- **Annual Job Openings: 329,000**

The job openings listed here are shared with 37 other postsecondary teaching occupations numbered 25-1011.00 through 25-1199.99.

Teach courses in the agricultural sciences. Includes teachers of agronomy, dairy sciences, fisheries management, horticultural sciences, poultry sciences, range management, and agricultural soil conservation.

Prepare course materials such as syllabi, homework assignments, and handouts. Evaluate and grade students' classwork, laboratory work, assignments, and papers. Keep abreast of developments in their field by reading current literature, talking with colleagues, and participating in professional conferences. Prepare and deliver lectures to undergraduate and/or graduate students on topics such as crop production, plant genetics, and soil chemistry. Initiate, facilitate, and moderate classroom discussions. Conduct research in a particular field of knowledge and publish findings in professional journals, books, and/or electronic media. Supervise laboratory sessions and fieldwork and coordinate laboratory operations. Supervise undergraduate and/or graduate teaching, internship, and research work. Compile, administer, and grade examinations or assign this work to others. Advise students on academic and vocational curricula and on career issues. Plan, evaluate, and revise curricula, course content, and course materials and methods of instruction. Maintain student attendance records, grades, and other required records. Write grant proposals to procure external research funding. Collaborate with colleagues to address teaching and research issues. Maintain regularly scheduled office hours in order to advise and assist students. Participate in student recruitment, registration, and placement activities. Select and obtain materials and supplies such as textbooks and laboratory equipment. Act as advisers to student organizations. Participate in campus and community events. Serve on academic or administrative committees that deal with institutional policies, departmental matters, and academic issues. Provide professional consulting services to government and/or industry. Perform administrative duties such as serving as department head. Compile bibliographies of specialized materials for outside reading assignments.

GOE Information—**Interest Area:** 05. Education and Training. **Work Group:** 05.03. Postsecondary and Adult Teaching and Instructing. **Personality Type**—Investigative. Investigative occupations frequently involve working with ideas and require an extensive amount of thinking. These occupations can involve searching for facts and figuring out problems mentally. **Work Values**—Authority; Social Service; Creativity; Achievement; Social Status; Ability Utilization. **Skills**—Science; Management of Financial Resources; Writing; Instructing; Reading Comprehension; Active Learning. **Abilities**—*Cognitive:* Written Expression; Oral Comprehension; Oral Expression; Written Comprehension; Originality; Inductive Reasoning. *Psychomotor:* None met the criteria. *Physical:* None met the criteria. *Sensory:* Speech Clarity; Speech Recognition; Far Vision; Near Vision. **General Work Activities**—*Information Input:* Getting Information; Identifying Objects, Actions, and Events; Monitoring Processes, Materials, or Surroundings. *Mental Process:* Updating and Using Relevant Knowledge; Processing Information; Organizing, Planning, and Prioritizing. *Work Output:* Documenting or Recording Information; Interacting With Computers; Controlling Machines and Processes. *Interacting with Others:* Teaching Others; Interpreting the Meaning of Information for Others; Communicating with Persons Outside Organization. **Physical Work Conditions**—Indoors; Sitting. **Other Job Characteristics**—Need to Be Exact or Accurate.

Experience—Job Zone 5. Extensive skill, knowledge, and experience are needed. **Job Preparation**—SVP 8.0 and above—four years to more than 10 years. **Knowledges**—Food Production; Biology; Education and Training; Geography; Chemistry; English Language. **Instructional Programs**—Agribusiness/Agricultural Business Operations; Agricultural and Food Products Processing, General; Agricultural and Horticultural Plant Breeding; Agricultural Animal Breeding; Agricultural Business and Management, General; Agricultural Business and Management, Other; Agricultural Economics; Agricultural Mechanization, General; Agricultural Mechanization, Other; Agricultural Power Machinery Operation; Agricultural Production Operations, General; Agricultural Production Operations, Other; Agricultural Teacher Education; Agricultural/Farm Supplies Retailing and Wholesaling; Agriculture, Agricultural Operations, and Related Sciences, Other; Agriculture, General; Agriculture-Related Services, Other; Agronomy and Crop Science; Animal Health; Animal Nutrition; Animal Sciences, General; Animal Sciences, Other; Animal Training; Animal/Livestock Husbandry and Production; Applied Horticulture/Horticultural Operations, General; Aquaculture; Crop Production; Dairy Science; Equestrian/Equine Studies; Farm/Farm and Ranch Management; Food Science; Greenhouse Operations and Management; Horticultural Science; Horticultural Service Operations, Other; International Agriculture; Landscaping and Groundskeeping; Livestock Management; Ornamental Horticulture; Plant Nursery Operations and Management; Plant Protection and Integrated Pest Management; Plant Sciences, General; Plant Sciences, Other; Poultry Science; Range Science and Management; Soil Science and Agronomy, General; Turf and Turfgrass Management.

Related SOC Job—25-1041 Agricultural Sciences Teachers, Postsecondary. **Related OOH Job**—Teachers—Postsecondary. **Related DOT Job**—090.227-010 Faculty Member, College or University.

25-1042.00 Biological Science Teachers, Postsecondary

- **Education/Training Required: Master's degree**
- **Employed: 59,540**
- **Annual Earnings: $63,570**
- **Growth: 32.2%**
- **Annual Job Openings: 329,000**

The job openings listed here are shared with 37 other postsecondary teaching occupations numbered 25-1011.00 through 25-1199.99.

Teach courses in biological sciences.

Prepare and deliver lectures to undergraduate and/or graduate students on topics such as molecular biology, marine biology, and botany. Evaluate and grade students' classwork, laboratory work, assignments, and papers. Prepare course materials such as syllabi, homework assignments, and handouts. Compile, administer, and grade examinations or assign this work to others. Supervise students' laboratory work. Keep abreast of developments in their field by reading current literature, talking with colleagues, and participating in professional conferences. Maintain student attendance records, grades, and other required records. Initiate, facilitate, and moderate classroom discussions. Plan, evaluate, and revise curricula, course content, and course materials and methods of instruction. Advise students on academic and vocational curricula and on career issues. Maintain regularly scheduled office hours to advise and assist students. Supervise undergraduate and/or graduate teaching, internship, and research work. Select and obtain materials and supplies such as textbooks and laboratory equipment. Collaborate with colleagues to address teaching and research issues. Conduct research in a particular field of knowledge and publish findings in professional journals, books, and/or electronic media. Serve on academic or administrative

committees that deal with institutional policies, departmental matters, and academic issues. Participate in student recruitment, registration, and placement activities. Write grant proposals to procure external research funding. Perform administrative duties such as serving as department head. Act as advisers to student organizations. Compile bibliographies of specialized materials for outside reading assignments. Participate in campus and community events. Provide professional consulting services to government and/or industry.

GOE Information—**Interest Area:** 05. Education and Training. **Work Group:** 05.03. Postsecondary and Adult Teaching and Instructing. **Personality Type**—Investigative. Investigative occupations frequently involve working with ideas and require an extensive amount of thinking. These occupations can involve searching for facts and figuring out problems mentally. **Work Values**—Authority; Social Service; Creativity; Achievement; Social Status; Ability Utilization. **Skills**—Science; Instructing; Writing; Learning Strategies; Reading Comprehension; Speaking. **Abilities**—*Cognitive:* Written Expression; Oral Comprehension; Oral Expression; Written Comprehension; Category Flexibility; Inductive Reasoning. *Psychomotor:* None met the criteria. *Physical:* None met the criteria. *Sensory:* Speech Clarity; Speech Recognition; Near Vision. **General Work Activities**—*Information Input:* Getting Information; Identifying Objects, Actions, and Events; Monitoring Processes, Materials, or Surroundings. *Mental Process:* Updating and Using Relevant Knowledge; Thinking Creatively; Processing Information. *Work Output:* Documenting or Recording Information; Interacting With Computers. *Interacting with Others:* Teaching Others; Interpreting the Meaning of Information for Others; Communicating with Other Workers. **Physical Work Conditions**—Indoors; More Often Sitting Than Standing. **Other Job Characteristics**—Need to Be Exact or Accurate.

Experience—Job Zone 5. Extensive skill, knowledge, and experience are needed. **Job Preparation**—SVP 8.0 and above—four years to more than 10 years. **Knowledges**—Biology; Chemistry; Education and Training; Medicine and Dentistry; English Language; Physics. **Instructional Programs**—Anatomy; Animal Physiology; Biochemistry; Biological and Biomedical Sciences, Other; Biology/Biological Sciences, General; Biometry/Biometrics; Biophysics; Biotechnology; Botany/Plant Biology; Cell/Cellular Biology and Histology; Ecology; Ecology, Evolution, and Systematics, Other; Entomology; Evolutionary Biology; Immunology; Marine Biology and Biological Oceanography; Microbiology, General; Molecular Biology; Neuroscience; Nutrition Sciences; Parasitology; Pathology/Experimental Pathology; Pharmacology; Plant Genetics; Plant Pathology/Phytopathology; Plant Physiology; Radiation Biology/Radiobiology; Toxicology; Virology; Zoology/Animal Biology.

Related SOC Job—25-1042 Biological Science Teachers, Postsecondary. **Related OOH Job**—Teachers—Postsecondary. **Related DOT Job**—090.227-010 Faculty Member, College or University.

25-1043.00 Forestry and Conservation Science Teachers, Postsecondary

- **Education/Training Required: Master's degree**
- **Employed: 2,990**
- **Annual Earnings: $64,870**
- **Growth: 32.2%**
- **Annual Job Openings: 329,000**

The job openings listed here are shared with 37 other postsecondary teaching occupations numbered 25-1011.00 through 25-1199.99.

Teach courses in environmental and conservation science.

Conduct research in a particular field of knowledge and publish findings in books, professional journals, and/or electronic media. Keep abreast of developments in their field by reading current literature, talking with colleagues, and participating in professional conferences. Prepare and deliver lectures to undergraduate and/or graduate students on topics such as forest resource policy, forest pathology, and mapping. Evaluate and grade students' classwork, assignments, and papers. Write grant proposals to procure external research funding. Supervise undergraduate and/or graduate teaching, internship, and research work. Plan, evaluate, and revise curricula, course content, and course materials and methods of instruction. Prepare course materials such as syllabi, homework assignments, and handouts. Compile, administer, and grade examinations or assign this work to others. Advise students on academic and vocational curricula and on career issues. Initiate, facilitate, and moderate classroom discussions. Supervise students' laboratory work and fieldwork. Maintain student attendance records, grades, and other required records. Collaborate with colleagues to address teaching and research issues. Maintain regularly scheduled office hours in order to advise and assist students. Select and obtain materials and supplies such as textbooks and laboratory equipment. Participate in student recruitment, registration, and placement activities. Serve on academic or administrative committees that deal with institutional policies, departmental matters, and academic issues. Provide professional consulting services to government and/or industry. Perform administrative duties such as serving as department head. Compile bibliographies of specialized materials for outside reading assignments. Act as advisers to student organizations. Participate in campus and community events.

GOE Information—Interest Area: 05. Education and Training. **Work Group:** 05.03. Postsecondary and Adult Teaching and Instructing. **Personality Type**—Investigative. Investigative occupations frequently involve working with ideas and require an extensive amount of thinking. These occupations can involve searching for facts and figuring out problems mentally. **Work Values**—Authority; Social Service; Creativity; Achievement; Social Status; Ability Utilization. **Skills**—Science; Management of Financial Resources; Instructing; Writing; Management of Personnel Resources; Mathematics. **Abilities**—*Cognitive:* Written Expression; Written Comprehension; Oral Expression; Oral Comprehension; Inductive Reasoning; Originality. *Psychomotor:* None met the criteria. *Physical:* None met the criteria. *Sensory:* Speech Clarity; Speech Recognition; Near Vision; Far Vision. **General Work Activities**—*Information Input:* Getting Information; Identifying Objects, Actions, and Events; Monitoring Processes, Materials, or Surroundings. *Mental Process:* Thinking Creatively; Updating and Using Relevant Knowledge; Analyzing Data or Information. *Work Output:* Interacting With Computers; Documenting or Recording Information; Performing General Physical Activities. *Interacting with Others:* Communicating with Persons Outside Organization; Interpreting the Meaning of Information for Others; Teaching Others. **Physical Work Conditions**—Indoors; Sitting. **Other Job Characteristics**—Need to Be Exact or Accurate.

Experience—Job Zone 5. Extensive skill, knowledge, and experience are needed. **Job Preparation**—SVP 8.0 and above—four years to more than 10 years. **Knowledges**—Biology; Geography; Education and Training; Mathematics; English Language; Chemistry. **Instructional Program**—Science Teacher Education/General Science Teacher Education.

Related SOC Job—25-1043 Forestry and Conservation Science Teachers, Postsecondary. **Related OOH Job**—Teachers—Postsecondary. **Related DOT Job**—090.227-010 Faculty Member, College or University.

25-1051.00 Atmospheric, Earth, Marine, and Space Sciences Teachers, Postsecondary

- **Education/Training Required:** Master's degree
- **Employed:** 8,810
- **Annual Earnings:** $65,720
- **Growth:** 32.2%
- **Annual Job Openings:** 329,000

The job openings listed here are shared with 37 other postsecondary teaching occupations numbered 25-1011.00 through 25-1199.99.

Teach courses in the physical sciences, except chemistry and physics.

Conduct research in a particular field of knowledge and publish findings in professional journals, books, and/or electronic media. Write grant proposals to procure external research funding. Keep abreast of developments in their field by reading current literature, talking with colleagues, and participating in professional conferences. Supervise undergraduate and/or graduate teaching, internship, and research work. Prepare and deliver lectures to undergraduate and/or graduate students on topics such as structural geology, micrometeorology, and atmospheric thermodynamics. Supervise laboratory work and fieldwork. Evaluate and grade students' classwork, assignments, and papers. Prepare course materials such as syllabi, homework assignments, and handouts. Collaborate with colleagues to address teaching and research issues. Compile, administer, and grade examinations or assign this work to others. Plan, evaluate, and revise curricula, course content, and course materials and methods of instruction. Initiate, facilitate, and moderate classroom discussions. Maintain regularly scheduled office hours in order to advise and assist students. Advise students on academic and vocational curricula and on career issues. Maintain student attendance records, grades, and other required records. Participate in student recruitment, registration, and placement activities. Perform administrative duties such as serving as department head. Select and obtain materials and supplies such as textbooks and laboratory equipment. Serve on academic or administrative committees that deal with institutional policies, departmental matters, and academic issues. Compile bibliographies of specialized materials for outside reading assignments. Provide professional consulting services to government and/or industry. Act as advisers to student organizations. Participate in campus and community events.

GOE Information—Interest Area: 05. Education and Training. **Work Group:** 05.03. Postsecondary and Adult Teaching and Instructing. **Personality Type**—No data available. **Work Values**—No data available. **Skills**—Science; Programming; Management of Financial Resources; Mathematics; Complex Problem Solving; Instructing. **Abilities**—*Cognitive:* Written Expression; Oral Expression; Mathematical Reasoning; Oral Comprehension; Written Comprehension; Inductive Reasoning. *Psychomotor:* None met the criteria. *Physical:* None met the criteria. *Sensory:* Speech Clarity; Speech Recognition; Far Vision; Near Vision. **General Work Activities**—*Information Input:* Getting Information; Identifying Objects, Actions, and Events; Estimating the Needed Characteristics of Products, Events, or Information. *Mental Process:* Analyzing Data or Information; Thinking Creatively; Updating and Using Relevant Knowledge. *Work Output:* Documenting or Recording Information; Interacting With Computers. *Interacting with Others:* Interpreting the Meaning of Information for Others; Teaching Others; Communicating with Persons Outside Organization. **Physical Work Conditions**—Indoors; Sitting. **Other Job Characteristics**—Need to Be Exact or Accurate.

Experience—Job Zone 5. Extensive skill, knowledge, and experience are needed. **Job Preparation**—SVP 8.0 and above—four years to more than 10 years. **Knowledges**—Physics; Geography; Chemistry; Biology; Mathematics; Education and Training. **Instructional Programs**—Acoustics; Astronomy; Astrophysics; Atmospheric Chemistry and Climatology; Atmospheric Physics and Dynamics; Atmospheric Sciences and Meteorology, General; Atmospheric Sciences and Meteorology, Other; Atomic/Molecular Physics; Elementary Particle Physics; Geochemistry; Geochemistry and Petrology; Geological and Earth Sciences/Geosciences, Other; Geology/Earth Science, General; Geophysics and Seismology; Hydrology and Water Resources Science; Meteorology; Nuclear Physics; Oceanography, Chemical and Physical; Optics/Optical Sciences; Paleontology; Physics Teacher Education; Physics, Other; Planetary Astronomy and Science; Plasma and High-Temperature Physics; Science Teacher Education/General Science Teacher Education; Solid State and Low-Temperature Physics; Theoretical and Mathematical Physics.

Related SOC Job—25-1051 Atmospheric, Earth, Marine, and Space Sciences Teachers, Postsecondary. **Related OOH Job**—Teachers—Postsecondary. **Related DOT Job**—090.227-010 Faculty Member, College or University.

25-1052.00 Chemistry Teachers, Postsecondary

- **Education/Training Required: Master's degree**
- **Employed: 19,520**
- **Annual Earnings: $58,060**
- **Growth: 32.2%**
- **Annual Job Openings: 329,000**

The job openings listed here are shared with 37 other postsecondary teaching occupations numbered 25-1011.00 through 25-1199.99.

Teach courses pertaining to the chemical and physical properties and compositional changes of substances. Work may include instruction in the methods of qualitative and quantitative chemical analysis. Includes both teachers primarily engaged in teaching and those who do a combination of both teaching and research.

Prepare and deliver lectures to undergraduate and/or graduate students on topics such as organic chemistry, analytical chemistry, and chemical separation. Supervise students' laboratory work. Evaluate and grade students' classwork, laboratory performance, assignments, and papers. Compile, administer, and grade examinations or assign this work to others. Maintain student attendance records, grades, and other required records. Prepare course materials such as syllabi, homework assignments, and handouts. Maintain regularly scheduled office hours in order to advise and assist students. Plan, evaluate, and revise curricula, course content, and course materials and methods of instruction. Supervise undergraduate and/or graduate teaching, internship, and research work. Keep abreast of developments in their field by reading current literature, talking with colleagues, and participating in professional conferences. Initiate, facilitate, and moderate classroom discussions. Select and obtain materials and supplies such as textbooks and laboratory equipment. Conduct research in a particular field of knowledge and publish findings in professional journals, books, and/or electronic media. Advise students on academic and vocational curricula and on career issues. Collaborate with colleagues to address teaching and research issues. Serve on academic or administrative committees that deal with institutional policies, departmental matters, and academic issues. Write grant proposals to procure external research funding. Participate in student

recruitment, registration, and placement activities. Prepare and submit required reports related to instruction. Perform administrative duties such as serving as a department head. Act as advisers to student organizations. Compile bibliographies of specialized materials for outside reading assignments. Participate in campus and community events. Provide professional consulting services to government and/or industry.

GOE Information—**Interest Area:** 05. Education and Training. **Work Group:** 05.03. Postsecondary and Adult Teaching and Instructing. **Personality Type**—Investigative. Investigative occupations frequently involve working with ideas and require an extensive amount of thinking. These occupations can involve searching for facts and figuring out problems mentally. **Work Values**—Authority; Social Service; Creativity; Achievement; Social Status; Ability Utilization. **Skills**—Science; Mathematics; Instructing; Active Learning; Writing; Reading Comprehension. **Abilities**—*Cognitive:* Written Expression; Oral Expression; Oral Comprehension; Written Comprehension; Mathematical Reasoning; Memorization. *Psychomotor:* None met the criteria. *Physical:* None met the criteria. *Sensory:* Speech Clarity; Speech Recognition; Near Vision. **General Work Activities**—*Information Input:* Getting Information; Identifying Objects, Actions, and Events; Monitoring Processes, Materials, or Surroundings. *Mental Process:* Updating and Using Relevant Knowledge; Thinking Creatively; Processing Information. *Work Output:* Documenting or Recording Information; Interacting With Computers; Controlling Machines and Processes. *Interacting with Others:* Interpreting the Meaning of Information for Others; Teaching Others; Coaching and Developing Others. **Physical Work Conditions**—Indoors; Contaminants; Hazardous Conditions; Sitting. **Other Job Characteristics**—Need to Be Exact or Accurate; Errors Have Important Consequences.

Experience—Job Zone 5. Extensive skill, knowledge, and experience are needed. **Job Preparation**—SVP 8.0 and above—four years to more than 10 years. **Knowledges**—Chemistry; Biology; Physics; Education and Training; Mathematics; English Language. **Instructional Programs**—Analytical Chemistry; Chemical Physics; Chemistry, General; Chemistry, Other; Geochemistry; Inorganic Chemistry; Organic Chemistry; Physical and Theoretical Chemistry; Polymer Chemistry.

Related SOC Job—25-1052 Chemistry Teachers, Postsecondary. **Related OOH Job**—Teachers—Postsecondary. **Related DOT Job**—090.227-010 Faculty Member, College or University.

25-1053.00 Environmental Science Teachers, Postsecondary

- **Education/Training Required: Master's degree**
- **Employed: 4,340**
- **Annual Earnings: $60,880**
- **Growth: 32.2%**
- **Annual Job Openings: 329,000**

The job openings listed here are shared with 37 other postsecondary teaching occupations numbered 25-1011.00 through 25-1199.99.

Teach courses in environmental science.

Supervise undergraduate and/or graduate teaching, internship, and research work. Conduct research in a particular field of knowledge and publish findings in professional journals, books, and/or electronic media. Keep abreast of developments in their field by reading current literature, talking with colleagues, and participating in professional conferences. Evaluate and grade students' classwork, laboratory work, assignments, and papers. Write grant proposals to procure external research funding. Supervise students' laboratory work and fieldwork. Prepare course materials such as syllabi, homework assignments, and handouts. Plan, evaluate, and revise curricula, course content, and course materials and methods of instruction. Compile, administer, and grade examinations or assign this work to others. Initiate, facilitate, and moderate classroom discussions. Advise students on academic and vocational curricula and on career issues. Prepare and deliver lectures to undergraduate and/or graduate students on topics such as hazardous waste management, industrial safety, and environmental toxicology. Maintain student attendance records, grades, and other required records. Select and obtain materials and supplies such as textbooks and laboratory equipment. Maintain regularly scheduled office hours in order to advise and assist students. Collaborate with colleagues to address teaching and research issues. Perform administrative duties such as serving as department head. Participate in student recruitment, registration, and placement activities. Provide professional consulting services to government and/or industry. Serve on academic or administrative committees that deal with institutional policies, departmental matters, and academic issues. Compile bibliographies of specialized materials for outside reading assignments. Participate in campus and community events. Act as advisers to student organizations.

GOE Information—Interest Area: 05. Education and Training. **Work Group:** 05.03. Postsecondary and Adult Teaching and Instructing. **Personality Type—**No data available. **Work Values—**No data available. **Skills—**Science; Writing; Instructing; Reading Comprehension; Management of Financial Resources; Critical Thinking. **Abilities—***Cognitive:* Written Expression; Written Comprehension; Oral Comprehension; Oral Expression; Inductive Reasoning; Deductive Reasoning. *Psychomotor:* None met the criteria. *Physical:* None met the criteria. *Sensory:* Speech Clarity; Speech Recognition; Near Vision. **General Work Activities—***Information Input:* Getting Information; Identifying Objects, Actions, and Events; Monitoring Processes, Materials, or Surroundings. *Mental Process:* Analyzing Data or Information; Processing Information; Updating and Using Relevant Knowledge. *Work Output:* Documenting or Recording Information; Interacting With Computers. *Interacting with Others:* Teaching Others; Interpreting the Meaning of Information for Others; Communicating with Persons Outside Organization. **Physical Work Conditions—**Indoors; Sitting. **Other Job Characteristics—**Need to Be Exact or Accurate.

Experience—Job Zone 5. Extensive skill, knowledge, and experience are needed. **Job Preparation—**SVP 8.0 and above—four years to more than 10 years. **Knowledges—**Biology; Geography; Chemistry; Education and Training; Physics; History and Archeology. **Instructional Programs—**Environmental Science; Environmental Studies; Science Teacher Education/General Science Teacher Education.

Related SOC Job—25-1053 Environmental Science Teachers, Postsecondary. **Related OOH Job—**Teachers—Postsecondary. **Related DOT Job—**090.227-010 Faculty Member, College or University.

25-1054.00 Physics Teachers, Postsecondary

- **Education/Training Required: Master's degree**
- **Employed: 13,310**
- **Annual Earnings: $65,880**
- **Growth: 32.2%**
- **Annual Job Openings: 329,000**

The job openings listed here are shared with 37 other postsecondary teaching occupations numbered 25-1011.00 through 25-1199.99.

Teach courses pertaining to the laws of matter and energy. Includes both teachers primarily engaged in teaching and those who do a combination of both teaching and research.

Evaluate and grade students' classwork, laboratory work, assignments, and papers. Prepare and deliver lectures to undergraduate and/or graduate students on topics such as quantum mechanics, particle physics, and optics. Compile, administer, and grade examinations or assign this work to others. Maintain student attendance records, grades, and other required records. Supervise students' laboratory work. Prepare course materials such as syllabi, homework assignments, and handouts. Maintain regularly scheduled office hours to advise and assist students. Supervise undergraduate and/or graduate teaching, internship, and research work. Keep abreast of developments in their field by reading current literature, talking with colleagues, and participating in professional conferences. Plan, evaluate, and revise curricula, course content, and course materials and methods of instruction. Initiate, facilitate, and moderate classroom discussions. Conduct research in a particular field of knowledge and publish findings in professional journals, books, and/or electronic media. Advise students on academic and vocational curricula and on career issues. Select and obtain materials and supplies such as textbooks and laboratory equipment. Collaborate with colleagues to address teaching and research issues. Participate in student recruitment, registration, and placement activities. Serve on academic or administrative committees that deal with institutional policies, departmental matters, and academic issues. Write grant proposals to procure external research funding. Perform administrative duties such as serving as department head. Act as advisers to student organizations. Provide professional consulting services to government and/or industry. Compile bibliographies of specialized materials for outside reading assignments. Participate in campus and community events.

GOE Information—Interest Area: 05. Education and Training. **Work Group:** 05.03. Postsecondary and Adult Teaching and Instructing. **Personality Type—**Investigative. Investigative occupations frequently involve working with ideas and require an extensive amount of thinking. These occupations can involve searching for facts and figuring out problems mentally. **Work Values—**Authority; Social Service; Creativity; Achievement; Social Status; Ability Utilization. **Skills—**Science; Programming; Instructing; Mathematics; Learning Strategies; Critical Thinking. **Abilities—***Cognitive:* Written Expression; Oral Expression; Written Comprehension; Oral Comprehension; Mathematical Reasoning; Inductive Reasoning. *Psychomotor:* None met the criteria. *Physical:* None met the criteria. *Sensory:* Speech Clarity; Speech Recognition; Near Vision. **General Work Activities—***Information Input:* Getting Information; Identifying Objects, Actions, and Events; Monitoring Processes, Materials, or Surroundings. *Mental Process:* Updating and Using Relevant Knowledge; Thinking Creatively; Processing Information. *Work Output:* Interacting With Computers; Documenting or Recording Information. *Interacting with Others:* Teaching Others;

Interpreting the Meaning of Information for Others; Coaching and Developing Others. **Physical Work Conditions**—Indoors; Sitting. **Other Job Characteristics**—Need to Be Exact or Accurate.

Experience—Job Zone 5. Extensive skill, knowledge, and experience are needed. **Job Preparation**—SVP 8.0 and above—four years to more than 10 years. **Knowledges**—Physics; Mathematics; Education and Training; Chemistry; Engineering and Technology; Computers and Electronics. **Instructional Programs**—Acoustics; Atomic/Molecular Physics; Elementary Particle Physics; Nuclear Physics; Optics/Optical Sciences; Physics, General; Physics, Other; Plasma and High-Temperature Physics; Solid State and Low-Temperature Physics; Theoretical and Mathematical Physics.

Related SOC Job—25-1054 Physics Teachers, Postsecondary. **Related OOH Job**—Teachers—Postsecondary. **Related DOT Job**—090.227-010 Faculty Member, College or University.

25-1061.00 Anthropology and Archeology Teachers, Postsecondary

- Education/Training Required: **Master's degree**
- Employed: **5,320**
- Annual Earnings: **$60,710**
- Growth: **32.2%**
- Annual Job Openings: **329,000**

The job openings listed here are shared with 37 other postsecondary teaching occupations numbered 25-1011.00 through 25-1199.99.

Teach courses in anthropology or archeology.

Conduct research in a particular field of knowledge and publish findings in professional journals, books, and electronic media. Keep abreast of developments in their field by reading current literature, talking with colleagues, and participating in professional conferences. Prepare and deliver lectures to undergraduate and graduate students on topics such as research methods, urban anthropology, and language and culture. Evaluate and grade students' classwork, assignments, and papers. Initiate, facilitate, and moderate classroom discussions. Write grant proposals to procure external research funding. Supervise undergraduate and/or graduate teaching, internship, and research work. Prepare course materials such as syllabi, homework assignments, and handouts. Compile, administer, and grade examinations or assign this work to others. Supervise students' laboratory work or fieldwork. Plan, evaluate, and revise curricula, course content, and course materials and methods of instruction. Advise students on academic and vocational curricula, career issues, and laboratory and field research. Maintain student attendance records, grades, and other required records. Maintain regularly scheduled office hours in order to advise and assist students. Collaborate with colleagues to address teaching and research issues. Compile bibliographies of specialized materials for outside reading assignments. Perform administrative duties such as serving as department head. Select and obtain materials and supplies such as textbooks and laboratory equipment. Serve on academic or administrative committees that deal with institutional policies, departmental matters, and academic issues. Participate in student recruitment, registration, and placement activities. Participate in campus and community events. Provide professional consulting services to government and industry. Act as advisers to student organizations.

GOE Information—**Interest Area:** 05. Education and Training. **Work Group:** 05.03. Postsecondary and Adult Teaching and Instructing. **Personality Type**—Social. Social occupations frequently involve working with, communicating with, and teaching people. These occupations often involve helping or providing service to others. **Work Values**—Authority; Social Service; Creativity; Achievement; Social Status; Ability Utilization. **Skills**—Science; Writing; Critical Thinking; Instructing; Active Learning; Reading Comprehension. **Abilities**—*Cognitive:* Written Expression; Written Comprehension; Memorization; Oral Expression; Originality; Oral Comprehension. *Psychomotor:* None met the criteria. *Physical:* None met the criteria. *Sensory:* Speech Clarity; Near Vision; Speech Recognition; Far Vision. **General Work Activities**—*Information Input:* Getting Information; Identifying Objects, Actions, and Events; Monitoring Processes, Materials, or Surroundings. *Mental Process:* Processing Information; Thinking Creatively; Updating and Using Relevant Knowledge. *Work Output:* Documenting or Recording Information; Interacting With Computers. *Interacting with Others:* Teaching Others; Communicating with Persons Outside Organization; Interpreting the Meaning of Information for Others. **Physical Work Conditions**—Indoors; Sitting. **Other Job Characteristics**—Need to Be Exact or Accurate.

Experience—Job Zone 5. Extensive skill, knowledge, and experience are needed. **Job Preparation**—SVP 8.0 and above—four years to more than 10 years. **Knowledges**—Sociology and Anthropology; History and Archeology; Geography; Foreign Language; Philosophy and Theology; English Language. **Instructional Programs**—Anthropology; Archeology; Humanities/Humanistic Studies; Physical Anthropology; Social Science Teacher Education.

Related SOC Job—25-1061 Anthropology and Archeology Teachers, Postsecondary. **Related OOH Job**—Teachers—Postsecondary. **Related DOT Job**—090.227-010 Faculty Member, College or University.

25-1062.00 Area, Ethnic, and Cultural Studies Teachers, Postsecondary

- Education/Training Required: **Master's degree**
- Employed: **7,970**
- Annual Earnings: **$55,610**
- Growth: **32.2%**
- Annual Job Openings: **329,000**

The job openings listed here are shared with 37 other postsecondary teaching occupations numbered 25-1011.00 through 25-1199.99.

Teach courses pertaining to the culture and development of an area (e.g., Latin America), an ethnic group, or any other group (e.g., women's studies, urban affairs).

Keep abreast of developments in their field by reading current literature, talking with colleagues, and participating in professional conferences. Conduct research in a particular field of knowledge and publish findings in professional journals, books, and/or electronic media. Evaluate and grade students' classwork, assignments, and papers. Prepare course materials such as syllabi, homework assignments, and handouts. Prepare and deliver lectures to undergraduate and/or graduate students on topics such as race and ethnic relations, gender studies, and cross-cultural perspectives. Initiate, facilitate, and moderate classroom discussions. Compile, administer, and grade examinations or assign this work to others. Maintain regularly scheduled office hours in order to advise and assist students. Plan, evaluate, and revise curricula, course content, and course materials and methods of instruction. Maintain student attendance records, grades, and other required records. Advise students on academic and vocational curricula and on career issues. Supervise undergraduate and/or graduate teaching, internship, and research work. Select and obtain materials and supplies such as textbooks. Collaborate with colleagues to address teaching and research issues. Serve on academic or administrative committees that deal with institutional policies, departmental matters, and academic issues. Compile bibliographies of specialized materials for outside reading assignments. Write grant proposals to procure external research funding. Participate in campus and community events. Participate in student recruitment, registration, and placement activities. Act as advisers to student organizations. Incorporate experiential/site visit components into courses. Perform administrative duties such as serving as department head. Provide professional consulting services to government and/or industry.

GOE Information—Interest Area: 05. Education and Training. **Work Group:** 05.03. Postsecondary and Adult Teaching and Instructing. **Personality Type—**Social. Social occupations frequently involve working with, communicating with, and teaching people. These occupations often involve helping or providing service to others. **Work Values—**Authority; Social Service; Creativity; Achievement; Social Status; Ability Utilization. **Skills—**Writing; Critical Thinking; Instructing; Persuasion; Active Learning; Learning Strategies. **Abilities—***Cognitive:* Written Expression; Originality; Written Comprehension; Inductive Reasoning; Oral Expression; Oral Comprehension. *Psychomotor:* None met the criteria. *Physical:* None met the criteria. *Sensory:* Speech Clarity; Speech Recognition; Near Vision. **General Work Activities—***Information Input:* Getting Information; Identifying Objects, Actions, and Events; Monitoring Processes, Materials, or Surroundings. *Mental Process:* Updating and Using Relevant Knowledge; Organizing, Planning, and Prioritizing; Thinking Creatively. *Work Output:* Documenting or Recording Information; Interacting With Computers. *Interacting with Others:* Teaching Others; Establishing and Maintaining Interpersonal Relationships; Interpreting the Meaning of Information for Others. **Physical Work Conditions—**Indoors; Sitting. **Other Job Characteristics—**Need to Be Exact or Accurate.

Experience—Job Zone 5. Extensive skill, knowledge, and experience are needed. **Job Preparation—**SVP 8.0 and above—four years to more than 10 years. **Knowledges—**History and Archeology; Sociology and Anthropology; Foreign Language; Philosophy and Theology; Geography; Education and Training. **Instructional Programs—**African Studies; African-American/Black Studies; American Indian/Native American Studies; American/United States Studies/Civilization; Area Studies, Other; Area, Ethnic, Cultural, and Gender Studies, Other; Asian Studies/Civilization; Asian-American Studies; Balkans Studies; Baltic Studies; Canadian Studies; Caribbean Studies; Central/Middle and Eastern European Studies; Chinese Studies; Commonwealth Studies; East Asian Studies; Ethnic, Cultural Minority, and Gender Studies, Other; European Studies/Civilization; French Studies; Gay/Lesbian Studies; German Studies; Hispanic-American, Puerto Rican, and Mexican-American/Chicano Studies; Humanities/Humanistic Studies; Intercultural/Multicultural and Diversity Studies; Islamic Studies; Italian Studies; Japanese Studies; Jewish/Judaic Studies; Korean Studies; Latin American Studies; Near and Middle Eastern Studies; Pacific Area/Pacific Rim Studies; Polish Studies; Regional Studies (U.S., Canadian, Foreign); Religion/Religious Studies, Other; Russian Studies; Scandinavian Studies; Slavic Studies; Social Studies Teacher Education; South Asian Studies; Southeast Asian Studies; Spanish and Iberian Studies; Tibetan Studies; Ukraine Studies; Ural-Altaic and Central Asian Studies; Western European Studies; Women's Studies.

Related SOC Job—25-1062 Area, Ethnic, and Cultural Studies Teachers, Postsecondary. **Related OOH Job—**Teachers—Postsecondary. **Related DOT Job—**090.227-010 Faculty Member, College or University.

25-1063.00 Economics Teachers, Postsecondary

- **Education/Training Required: Master's degree**
- **Employed: 12,670**
- **Annual Earnings: $68,910**
- **Growth: 32.2%**
- **Annual Job Openings: 329,000**

The job openings listed here are shared with 37 other postsecondary teaching occupations numbered 25-1011.00 through 25-1199.99.

Teach courses in economics.

Prepare and deliver lectures to undergraduate and/or graduate students on topics such as econometrics, price theory, and macroeconomics. Prepare course materials such as syllabi, homework assignments, and handouts. Evaluate and grade students' classwork, assignments, and papers. Compile, administer, and grade examinations or assign this work to others. Keep abreast of developments in their field by reading current literature, talking with colleagues, and participating in professional conferences. Maintain student attendance records, grades, and other required records. Initiate, facilitate, and moderate classroom discussions. Maintain regularly scheduled office hours in order to advise and assist students. Select and obtain materials and supplies such as textbooks. Plan, evaluate, and revise curricula, course content, and course materials and methods of instruction. Conduct research in a particular field of knowledge and publish findings in professional journals, books, and/or electronic media. Supervise undergraduate and/or graduate teaching, internship, and research work. Advise students on academic and vocational curricula and on career issues. Serve on academic or administrative committees that deal with institutional policies, departmental matters, and academic issues. Collaborate with colleagues to address teaching and research issues. Compile bibliographies of specialized materials for outside reading assignments. Participate in student recruitment, registration, and placement activities. Perform administrative duties such as serving as department head. Write grant proposals to procure external research funding. Participate in campus and community events. Provide professional consulting services to government and/or industry. Act as advisers to student organizations.

GOE Information—Interest Area: 05. Education and Training. **Work Group:** 05.03. Postsecondary and Adult Teaching and Instructing. **Personality Type—**Social. Social occupations frequently involve working with, communicating with, and teaching people. These occupations often involve helping or providing service to others. **Work Values—**Authority; Social Service; Creativity; Achievement; Social Status; Ability Utilization. **Skills—**Mathematics; Writing; Instructing; Speaking; Reading Comprehension; Critical Thinking. **Abilities—***Cognitive:* Written Expression; Number Facility; Oral Expression; Mathematical Reasoning; Written Comprehension; Oral Comprehension. *Psychomotor:* None met the criteria. *Physical:* None met the criteria. *Sensory:* Speech Clarity; Speech Recognition; Far Vision; Hearing Sensitivity; Near Vision. **General Work Activities—***Information Input:* Getting Information; Identifying Objects, Actions, and Events; Estimating the Needed Characteristics of Products, Events, or Information. *Mental Process:* Thinking Creatively; Updating and Using Relevant Knowledge; Analyzing Data or Information. *Work Output:* Interacting With Computers; Documenting or Recording Information. *Interacting with Others:* Teaching Others; Interpreting the Meaning of Information for Others; Establishing and Maintaining Interpersonal Relationships. **Physical Work Conditions—**Indoors; Sitting. **Other Job Characteristics—**Need to Be Exact or Accurate.

Experience—Job Zone 5. Extensive skill, knowledge, and experience are needed. **Job Preparation**—SVP 8.0 and above—four years to more than 10 years. **Knowledges**—Economics and Accounting; History and Archeology; Mathematics; Education and Training; Philosophy and Theology; English Language. **Instructional Programs**—Applied Economics; Business/Managerial Economics; Development Economics and International Development; Econometrics and Quantitative Economics; Economics, General; Economics, Other; Humanities/Humanistic Studies; International Economics; Social Science Teacher Education.

Related SOC Job—25-1063 Economics Teachers, Postsecondary. **Related OOH Job**—Teachers—Postsecondary. **Related DOT Job**—090.227-010 Faculty Member, College or University.

25-1064.00 Geography Teachers, Postsecondary

- **Education/Training Required: Master's degree**
- **Employed: 4,250**
- **Annual Earnings: $57,870**
- **Growth: 32.2%**
- **Annual Job Openings: 329,000**

The job openings listed here are shared with 37 other postsecondary teaching occupations numbered 25-1011.00 through 25-1199.99.

Teach courses in geography.

Prepare and deliver lectures to undergraduate and/or graduate students on topics such as urbanization, environmental systems, and cultural geography. Evaluate and grade students' classwork, assignments, and papers. Compile, administer, and grade examinations or assign this work to others. Initiate, facilitate, and moderate classroom discussions. Maintain student attendance records, grades, and other required records. Prepare course materials such as syllabi, homework assignments, and handouts. Keep abreast of developments in their field by reading current literature, talking with colleagues, and participating in professional conferences. Supervise undergraduate and/or graduate teaching, internship, and research work. Plan, evaluate, and revise curricula, course content, and course materials and methods of instruction. Maintain regularly scheduled office hours to advise and assist students. Supervise students' laboratory work and fieldwork. Conduct research in a particular field of knowledge and publish findings in professional journals, books, and electronic media. Collaborate with colleagues to address teaching and research issues. Select and obtain materials and supplies such as textbooks. Advise students on academic and vocational curricula and on career issues. Serve on academic or administrative committees that deal with institutional policies, departmental matters, and academic issues. Participate in student recruitment, registration, and placement activities. Participate in campus and community events. Compile bibliographies of specialized materials for outside reading assignments. Perform administrative duties such as serving as department head. Write grant proposals to procure external research funding. Maintain geographic information systems laboratories, performing duties such as updating software. Perform spatial analysis and modeling, using geographic information system techniques. Act as advisers to student organizations. Provide professional consulting services to government and industry.

GOE Information—**Interest Area:** 05. Education and Training. **Work Group:** 05.03. Postsecondary and Adult Teaching and Instructing. **Personality Type**—No data available. **Work Values**—No data available. **Skills**—Science; Writing; Instructing; Learning Strategies;

Reading Comprehension; Critical Thinking. **Abilities**—*Cognitive:* Written Expression; Oral Expression; Written Comprehension; Oral Comprehension; Fluency of Ideas; Originality. *Psychomotor:* None met the criteria. *Physical:* None met the criteria. *Sensory:* Speech Clarity; Speech Recognition. **General Work Activities**—*Information Input:* Getting Information; Identifying Objects, Actions, and Events; Monitoring Processes, Materials, or Surroundings. *Mental Process:* Updating and Using Relevant Knowledge; Thinking Creatively; Organizing, Planning, and Prioritizing. *Work Output:* Documenting or Recording Information; Interacting With Computers. *Interacting with Others:* Teaching Others; Establishing and Maintaining Interpersonal Relationships; Communicating with Other Workers. **Physical Work Conditions**—Indoors; Sitting. **Other Job Characteristics**—Need to Be Exact or Accurate.

Experience—Job Zone 5. Extensive skill, knowledge, and experience are needed. **Job Preparation**—SVP 8.0 and above—four years to more than 10 years. **Knowledges**—Geography; Sociology and Anthropology; History and Archeology; Philosophy and Theology; Education and Training; Communications and Media. **Instructional Programs**—Geography; Geography Teacher Education; Humanities/Humanistic Studies.

Related SOC Job—25-1064 Geography Teachers, Postsecondary. **Related OOH Job**—Teachers—Postsecondary. **Related DOT Job**—090.227-010 Faculty Member, College or University.

25-1065.00 Political Science Teachers, Postsecondary

- **Education/Training Required: Master's degree**
- **Employed: 13,710**
- **Annual Earnings: $59,850**
- **Growth: 32.2%**
- **Annual Job Openings: 329,000**

The job openings listed here are shared with 37 other postsecondary teaching occupations numbered 25-1011.00 through 25-1199.99.

Teach courses in political science, international affairs, and international relations.

Initiate, facilitate, and moderate classroom discussions. Prepare and deliver lectures to undergraduate or graduate students on topics such as classical political thought, international relations, and democracy and citizenship. Evaluate and grade students' classwork, assignments, and papers. Compile, administer, and grade examinations or assign this work to others. Prepare course materials such as syllabi, homework assignments, and handouts. Keep abreast of developments in their field by reading current literature, talking with colleagues, and participating in professional conferences. Plan, evaluate, and revise curricula, course content, and course materials and methods of instruction. Maintain student attendance records, grades, and other required records. Maintain regularly scheduled office hours in order to advise and assist students. Advise students on academic and vocational curricula and on career issues. Select and obtain materials and supplies such as textbooks. Conduct research in a particular field of knowledge and publish findings in professional journals, books, and electronic media. Supervise undergraduate and graduate teaching, internship, and research work. Collaborate with colleagues to address teaching and research issues. Serve on academic or administrative committees that deal with institutional policies, departmental matters, and academic issues. Participate in student recruitment, registration, and placement activities. Participate in campus and community events. Compile bibliographies of specialized materials for outside reading assignments. Act as advisers to student organizations. Perform administrative duties such as serving as department head. Write grant proposals to procure external research funding. Provide professional consulting services to government and industry.

GOE Information—Interest Area: 05. Education and Training. **Work Group:** 05.03. Postsecondary and Adult Teaching and Instructing. **Personality Type**—Social. Social occupations frequently involve working with, communicating with, and teaching people. These occupations often involve helping or providing service to others. **Work Values**—Authority; Social Service; Creativity; Achievement; Social Status; Ability Utilization. **Skills**—Instructing; Writing; Persuasion; Learning Strategies; Reading Comprehension; Critical Thinking. **Abilities**—*Cognitive:* Written Expression; Oral Expression; Written Comprehension; Oral Comprehension; Memorization; Originality. *Psychomotor:* None met the criteria. *Physical:* None met the criteria. *Sensory:* Speech Clarity; Speech Recognition; Near Vision. **General Work Activities**—*Information Input:* Getting Information; Identifying Objects, Actions, and Events; Monitoring Processes, Materials, or Surroundings. *Mental Process:* Thinking Creatively; Updating and Using Relevant Knowledge; Analyzing Data or Information. *Work Output:* Documenting or Recording Information; Interacting With Computers. *Interacting with Others:* Teaching Others; Interpreting the Meaning of Information for Others; Communicating with Other Workers. **Physical Work Conditions**—Indoors; Sitting. **Other Job Characteristics**—Need to Be Exact or Accurate.

Experience—Job Zone 5. Extensive skill, knowledge, and experience are needed. **Job Preparation**—SVP 8.0 and above—four years to more than 10 years. **Knowledges**—History and Archeology; Philosophy and Theology; Sociology and Anthropology; Geography; Law and Government; Education and Training. **Instructional Programs**—American Government and Politics (United States); Humanities/Humanistic Studies; International Relations and Affairs; Political Science and Government, General; Political Science and Government, Other; Social Science Teacher Education.

Related SOC Job—25-1065 Political Science Teachers, Postsecondary. **Related OOH Job**—Teachers—Postsecondary. **Related DOT Job**—090.227-010 Faculty Member, College or University.

25-1066.00 Psychology Teachers, Postsecondary

- **Education/Training Required: Master's degree**
- **Employed: 30,240**
- **Annual Earnings: $56,370**
- **Growth: 32.2%**
- **Annual Job Openings: 329,000**

The job openings listed here are shared with 37 other postsecondary teaching occupations numbered 25-1011.00 through 25-1199.99.

Teach courses in psychology, such as child, clinical, and developmental psychology, and psychological counseling.

Prepare and deliver lectures to undergraduate and/or graduate students on topics such as abnormal psychology, cognitive processes, and work motivation. Evaluate and grade students' classwork, laboratory work, assignments, and papers. Initiate, facilitate, and moderate classroom discussions. Compile, administer, and grade examinations or assign this work to others. Keep abreast of developments in their field by reading current literature, talking with colleagues, and participating in professional conferences. Prepare

course materials such as syllabi, homework assignments, and handouts. Plan, evaluate, and revise curricula, course content, and course materials and methods of instruction. Maintain student attendance records, grades, and other required records. Supervise undergraduate and/or graduate teaching, internship, and research work. Maintain regularly scheduled office hours to advise and assist students. Conduct research in a particular field of knowledge and publish findings in professional journals, books, and electronic media. Advise students on academic and vocational curricula and on career issues. Select and obtain materials and supplies such as textbooks. Collaborate with colleagues to address teaching and research issues. Serve on academic or administrative committees that deal with institutional policies, departmental matters, and academic issues. Compile bibliographies of specialized materials for outside reading assignments. Participate in student recruitment, registration, and placement activities. Supervise students' laboratory work. Perform administrative duties such as serving as department head. Act as advisers to student organizations. Write grant proposals to procure external research funding. Participate in campus and community events. Provide professional consulting services to government and industry.

GOE Information—Interest Area: 05. Education and Training. **Work Group:** 05.03. Postsecondary and Adult Teaching and Instructing. **Personality Type**—Social. Social occupations frequently involve working with, communicating with, and teaching people. These occupations often involve helping or providing service to others. **Work Values**—Authority; Social Service; Creativity; Achievement; Social Status; Ability Utilization. **Skills**—Science; Learning Strategies; Instructing; Social Perceptiveness; Writing; Reading Comprehension. **Abilities**—*Cognitive:* Written Expression; Oral Expression; Written Comprehension; Oral Comprehension; Memorization; Deductive Reasoning. *Psychomotor:* None met the criteria. *Physical:* None met the criteria. *Sensory:* Speech Clarity; Speech Recognition; Near Vision. **General Work Activities**—*Information Input:* Getting Information; Identifying Objects, Actions, and Events; Monitoring Processes, Materials, or Surroundings. *Mental Process:* Updating and Using Relevant Knowledge; Thinking Creatively; Processing Information. *Work Output:* Documenting or Recording Information; Interacting With Computers. *Interacting with Others:* Teaching Others; Interpreting the Meaning of Information for Others; Coaching and Developing Others. **Physical Work Conditions**—Indoors; Sitting. **Other Job Characteristics**—Need to Be Exact or Accurate.

Experience—Job Zone 5. Extensive skill, knowledge, and experience are needed. **Job Preparation**—SVP 8.0 and above—four years to more than 10 years. **Knowledges**—Therapy and Counseling; Psychology; Sociology and Anthropology; Philosophy and Theology; Education and Training; English Language. **Instructional Programs**—Clinical Psychology; Cognitive Psychology and Psycholinguistics; Community Psychology; Comparative Psychology; Counseling Psychology; Developmental and Child Psychology; Educational Psychology; Experimental Psychology; Humanities/Humanistic Studies; Industrial and Organizational Psychology; Marriage and Family Therapy/Counseling; Personality Psychology; Physiological Psychology/Psychobiology; Psychology Teacher Education; Psychology, General; Psychology, Other; Psychometrics and Quantitative Psychology; School Psychology; Social Psychology; Social Science Teacher Education.

Related SOC Job—25-1066 Psychology Teachers, Postsecondary. **Related OOH Job**—Teachers—Postsecondary. **Related DOT Job**—090.227-010 Faculty Member, College or University.

25-1067.00 Sociology Teachers, Postsecondary

- **Education/Training Required: Master's degree**
- **Employed: 14,980**
- **Annual Earnings: $54,320**
- **Growth: 32.2%**
- **Annual Job Openings: 329,000**

The job openings listed here are shared with 37 other postsecondary teaching occupations numbered 25-1011.00 through 25-1199.99.

Teach courses in sociology.

Evaluate and grade students' classwork, assignments, and papers. Prepare and deliver lectures to undergraduate and graduate students on topics such as race and ethnic relations, measurement and data collection, and workplace social relations. Initiate, facilitate, and moderate classroom discussions. Prepare course materials such as syllabi, homework assignments, and handouts. Compile, administer, and grade examinations or assign this work to others. Keep abreast of developments in their field by reading current literature, talking with colleagues, and participating in professional conferences. Maintain student attendance records, grades, and other required records. Maintain regularly scheduled office hours in order to advise and assist students. Plan, evaluate, and revise curricula, course content, and course materials and methods of instruction. Advise students on academic and vocational curricula and on career issues. Collaborate with colleagues to address teaching and research issues. Conduct research in a particular field of knowledge and publish findings in professional journals, books, or electronic media. Select and obtain materials and supplies such as textbooks and laboratory equipment. Supervise undergraduate and graduate teaching, internship, and research work. Serve on academic or administrative committees that deal with institutional policies, departmental matters, and academic issues. Participate in student recruitment, registration, and placement activities. Perform administrative duties such as serving as department head. Supervise students' laboratory work and fieldwork. Write grant proposals to procure external research funding. Act as advisers to student organizations. Compile bibliographies of specialized materials for outside reading assignments. Participate in campus and community events. Provide professional consulting services to government and industry.

GOE Information—Interest Area: 05. Education and Training. **Work Group:** 05.03. Postsecondary and Adult Teaching and Instructing. **Personality Type—**Social. Social occupations frequently involve working with, communicating with, and teaching people. These occupations often involve helping or providing service to others. **Work Values—**Authority; Social Service; Creativity; Achievement; Social Status; Ability Utilization. **Skills—**Instructing; Learning Strategies; Writing; Science; Social Perceptiveness; Critical Thinking. **Abilities—***Cognitive:* Written Expression; Oral Expression; Written Comprehension; Oral Comprehension; Inductive Reasoning; Memorization. *Psychomotor:* None met the criteria. *Physical:* None met the criteria. *Sensory:* Speech Clarity; Speech Recognition; Near Vision. **General Work Activities—***Information Input:* Getting Information; Identifying Objects, Actions, and Events; Monitoring Processes, Materials, or Surroundings. *Mental Process:* Thinking Creatively; Updating and Using Relevant Knowledge; Organizing, Planning, and Prioritizing. *Work Output:* Interacting With Computers; Documenting or Recording Information. *Interacting with Others:* Teaching Others; Interpreting the Meaning of Information for Others; Coaching and Developing Others. **Physical Work Conditions—**Indoors; Sitting. **Other Job Characteristics—**Need to Be Exact or Accurate.

Experience—Job Zone 5. Extensive skill, knowledge, and experience are needed. **Job Preparation—**SVP 8.0 and above—four years to more than 10 years. **Knowledges—**Sociology and Anthropology; Philosophy and Theology; History and Archeology; Education and Training; English Language; Psychology. **Instructional Programs—**Humanities/Humanistic Studies; Social Science Teacher Education; Sociology.

Related SOC Job—25-1067 Sociology Teachers, Postsecondary. **Related OOH Job—**Teachers—Postsecondary. **Related DOT Job—**090.227-010 Faculty Member, College or University.

25-1069.99 Social Sciences Teachers, Postsecondary, All Other

- **Education/Training Required: Master's degree**
- **Employed: 6,330**
- **Annual Earnings: $60,040**
- **Growth: 32.2%**
- **Annual Job Openings: 329,000**

The job openings listed here are shared with 37 other postsecondary teaching occupations numbered 25-1011.00 through 25-1199.99.

All postsecondary social sciences teachers not listed separately.

No task data available.

Note: The Department of Labor has not collected some data for this job, so it has fewer details than the other descriptions.

Related SOC Job—25-1069 Social Sciences Teachers, Postsecondary, All Other. **Related OOH Job—**Teachers—Postsecondary. **Related DOT Job—**No data available.

25-1071.00 Health Specialties Teachers, Postsecondary

- **Education/Training Required: Master's degree**
- **Employed: 108,680**
- **Annual Earnings: $70,890**
- **Growth: 32.2%**
- **Annual Job Openings: 329,000**

The job openings listed here are shared with 37 other postsecondary teaching occupations numbered 25-1011.00 through 25-1199.99.

Teach courses in health specialties, such as veterinary medicine, dentistry, pharmacy, therapy, laboratory technology, and public health.

Initiate, facilitate, and moderate classroom discussions. Keep abreast of developments in their field by reading current literature, talking with colleagues, and participating in professional conferences. Compile, administer, and grade examinations or assign this work to others. Evaluate and grade students' classwork, assignments, and papers. Prepare course materials such as syllabi, homework assignments, and handouts. Prepare and deliver lectures to undergraduate or graduate students on topics such as public health, stress management, and worksite health promotion. Plan, evaluate, and revise curricula, course content, and course materials and methods of instruction. Supervise undergraduate or graduate teaching, internship, and research work. Conduct research in a particular field of knowledge and publish findings in professional journals, books, or electronic media. Collaborate with colleagues to address teaching and research issues. Supervise laboratory sessions. Maintain student attendance records, grades, and other required records. Maintain regularly scheduled office hours in order to advise and assist students. Advise students on academic and vocational curricula and on career issues. Participate in student recruitment, registration, and placement activities. Write grant proposals to procure external research funding. Serve on academic or administrative committees that deal with institutional policies, departmental matters, and academic issues. Select and obtain materials and supplies such as textbooks and laboratory equipment. Act as advisers to student organizations. Perform administrative duties such as serving as department head. Compile bibliographies of specialized materials for outside reading assignments. Provide professional consulting services to government and industry. Participate in campus and community events.

GOE Information—Interest Area: 05. Education and Training. **Work Group:** 05.03. Postsecondary and Adult Teaching and Instructing. **Personality Type**—Investigative. Investigative occupations frequently involve working with ideas and require an extensive amount of thinking. These occupations can involve searching for facts and figuring out problems mentally. **Work Values**—Authority; Social Service; Creativity; Achievement; Social Status; Ability Utilization. **Skills**—Science; Instructing; Writing; Learning Strategies; Reading Comprehension; Critical Thinking. **Abilities**—*Cognitive:* Written Expression; Oral Expression; Written Comprehension; Oral Comprehension; Inductive Reasoning; Originality. *Psychomotor:* None met the criteria. *Physical:* None met the criteria. *Sensory:* Speech Clarity; Speech Recognition; Near Vision. **General Work Activities**—*Information Input:* Identifying Objects, Actions, and Events; Getting Information; Monitoring Processes, Materials, or Surroundings. *Mental Process:* Updating and Using Relevant Knowledge; Analyzing Data or Information; Processing Information. *Work Output:* Documenting or Recording Information; Interacting With Computers; Handling and Moving Objects. *Interacting with Others:* Teaching Others; Establishing and Maintaining Interpersonal Relationships; Communicating with Other Workers. **Physical Work Conditions**—Indoors; Sitting. **Other Job Characteristics**—Need to Be Exact or Accurate.

Experience—Job Zone 5. Extensive skill, knowledge, and experience are needed. **Job Preparation**—SVP 8.0 and above—four years to more than 10 years. **Knowledges**—Biology; Medicine and Dentistry; Education and Training; Therapy and Counseling; Sociology and Anthropology; Psychology. **Instructional Programs**—Allied Health Diagnostic, Intervention, and Treatment Professions, Other; Art Therapy/Therapist; Asian Bodywork Therapy; Audiology/Audiologist and Hearing Sciences; Audiology/Audiologist and Speech-Language Pathology/Pathologist; Biostatistics; Blood Bank Technology Specialist; Cardiovascular Technology/Technologist; Chiropractic (DC); Clinical Laboratory Science/Medical Technology/Technologist; Clinical/Medical Laboratory Technician; Clinical/Medical Laboratory Technician/Assistant (Certificate); Communication Disorders, General; Cytotechnology/Cytotechnologist; Dance Therapy/Therapist; Dental Assisting/Assistant; Dental Clinical Sciences, General (MS, PhD); Dental Hygiene/Hygienist; Dental Laboratory Technology/Technician; Dental Services and Allied Professions, Other; Dentistry (DDS, DMD); Diagnostic Medical Sonography/Sonographer and Ultrasound Technician; Electrocardiograph Technology/Technologist; Electroneurodiagnostic/Electroencephalographic Technology/Technologist; Emergency Medical Technology/Technician (Paramedic); Environmental Health; Epidemiology; Health and Medical Assisting Services, Other; Health Occupations

Teacher Education; Health/Medical Physics; Health/Medical Preparatory Programs, Other; Hematology Technology/Technician; Hypnotherapy/Hypnotherapist; Massage Therapy/Therapeutic Massage; Medical Radiologic Technology/Science Radiation Therapist; Music Therapy/Therapist; Nuclear Medical Technology/Technologist; Occupational Health and Industrial Hygiene; Occupational Therapy Assistant; Occupational Therapy/Therapist; Orthotist/Prosthetist; Perfusion Technology/Perfusionist; Pharmacy (PharmD, BS/BPharm); Pharmacy Administration and Pharmacy Policy and Regulatory Affairs (MS, PhD); Pharmacy Technician; Pharmacy, Pharmaceutical Sciences, and Administration, Other; Physical Therapy Assistant; Physical Therapy/Therapist; Physician Assistant; Pre-Dentistry Studies; Pre-Medicine/Pre-Medical Studies; Pre-Nursing Studies; Pre-Pharmacy Studies; others.

Related SOC Job—25-1071 Health Specialties Teachers, Postsecondary. **Related OOH Job**—Teachers—Postsecondary. **Related DOT Job**—090.227-010 Faculty Member, College or University.

25-1072.00 Nursing Instructors and Teachers, Postsecondary

- Education/Training Required: Master's degree
- Employed: 37,020
- Annual Earnings: $53,160
- Growth: 32.2%
- Annual Job Openings: 329,000

The job openings listed here are shared with 37 other postsecondary teaching occupations numbered 25-1011.00 through 25-1199.99.

Demonstrate and teach patient care in classroom and clinical units to nursing students. Includes both teachers primarily engaged in teaching and those who do a combination of both teaching and research.

Initiate, facilitate, and moderate classroom discussions. Prepare and deliver lectures to undergraduate or graduate students on topics such as pharmacology, mental health nursing, and community health care practices. Keep abreast of developments in their field by reading current literature, talking with colleagues, and participating in professional conferences. Prepare course materials such as syllabi, homework assignments, and handouts. Supervise students' laboratory and clinical work. Evaluate and grade students' classwork, laboratory and clinic work, assignments, and papers. Collaborate with colleagues to address teaching and research issues. Plan, evaluate, and revise curricula, course content, and course materials and methods of instruction. Assess clinical education needs and patient and client teaching needs, utilizing a variety of methods. Compile, administer, and grade examinations or assign this work to others. Advise students on academic and vocational curricula and on career issues. Maintain student attendance records, grades, and other required records. Maintain regularly scheduled office hours to advise and assist students. Supervise undergraduate or graduate teaching, internship, and research work. Conduct research in a particular field of knowledge and publish findings in professional journals, books, and/or electronic media. Participate in student recruitment, registration, and placement activities. Serve on academic or administrative committees that deal with institutional policies, departmental matters, and academic issues. Coordinate training programs with area universities, clinics, hospitals, health agencies, and/or vocational schools. Compile bibliographies of specialized materials for outside reading assignments. Select and obtain materials and supplies such as textbooks and laboratory equipment. Participate in campus and community events. Write grant proposals to procure external research funding. Act as advisers to student organizations. Demonstrate patient care in clinical units of hospitals. Perform administrative duties such as serving as department head.

GOE Information—Interest Area: 05. Education and Training. **Work Group:** 05.03. Postsecondary and Adult Teaching and Instructing. **Personality Type**—Social. Social occupations frequently involve working with, communicating with, and teaching people. These occupations often involve helping or providing service to others. **Work Values**—Authority; Social Service; Achievement; Social Status; Ability Utilization; Autonomy. **Skills**—Science; Instructing; Social Perceptiveness; Writing; Learning Strategies; Reading Comprehension. **Abilities**—*Cognitive:* Written Expression; Written Comprehension; Oral Expression; Originality; Inductive Reasoning; Oral Comprehension. *Psychomotor:* None met the criteria. *Physical:* None met the criteria. *Sensory:* Speech Clarity; Speech Recognition; Near Vision; Far Vision. **General Work Activities**—*Information Input:* Getting Information; Identifying Objects, Actions, and Events; Monitoring Processes, Materials, or Surroundings. *Mental Process:* Updating and Using Relevant Knowledge; Organizing, Planning, and Prioritizing; Judging the Qualities of Things, Services, or Other People's Work. *Work Output:* Documenting or Recording Information; Interacting With Computers; Performing General Physical Activities. *Interacting with Others:* Teaching Others; Assisting and Caring for Others; Coaching and Developing Others. **Physical Work Conditions**—Indoors; Disease or Infections; Sitting. **Other Job Characteristics**—Need to Be Exact or Accurate; Errors Have Important Consequences.

Experience—Job Zone 5. Extensive skill, knowledge, and experience are needed. **Job Preparation**—SVP 8.0 and above—four years to more than 10 years. **Knowledges**—Therapy and Counseling; Sociology and Anthropology; Biology; Medicine and Dentistry; Philosophy and Theology; Psychology. **Instructional Programs**—Adult Health Nurse/Nursing; Family Practice Nurse/Nurse Practitioner; Maternal/Child Health Nurse/Nursing; Nurse Anesthetist; Nurse Midwife/Nursing Midwifery; Nursing—Registered Nurse Training (RN, ASN, BSN, MSN); Nursing Clinical Specialist; Nursing Science (MS, PhD); Nursing, Other; Pediatric Nurse/Nursing; Perioperative/Operating and Surgical Nurse/Nursing; Pre-Nursing Studies; Psychiatric/Mental Health Nurse/Nursing; Public Health/Community Nurse/Nursing.

Related SOC Job—25-1072 Nursing Instructors and Teachers, Postsecondary. **Related OOH Job**—Teachers—Postsecondary. **Related DOT Job**—075.124-018 Nurse, Instructor.

25-1081.00 Education Teachers, Postsecondary

- **Education/Training Required:** Master's degree
- **Employed:** 51,320
- **Annual Earnings:** $50,380
- **Growth:** 32.2%
- **Annual Job Openings:** 329,000

The job openings listed here are shared with 37 other postsecondary teaching occupations numbered 25-1011.00 through 25-1199.99.

Teach courses pertaining to education, such as counseling, curriculum, guidance, instruction, teacher education, and teaching English as a second language.

Prepare course materials such as syllabi, homework assignments, and handouts. Prepare and deliver lectures to undergraduate and/or graduate students on topics such as children's literature, learning and development, and reading instruction. Initiate, facilitate, and moderate classroom discussions. Evaluate and grade students' classwork, assignments, and papers. Plan, evaluate, and revise curricula, course content, and course materials and methods of instruction. Supervise students' fieldwork, internship, and research work. Keep abreast of developments in their field by reading current literature, talking with colleagues, and participating in professional conferences. Advise students on academic and vocational curricula and on career issues. Maintain regularly scheduled office hours to advise and assist students. Maintain student attendance records, grades, and other required records. Collaborate with colleagues to address teaching and research issues. Compile, administer, and grade examinations or assign this work to others. Conduct research in a particular field of knowledge and publish findings in professional journals, books, or electronic media. Select and obtain materials and supplies such as textbooks. Participate in student recruitment, registration, and placement activities. Advise and instruct teachers employed in school systems by providing activities such as in-service seminars. Serve on academic or administrative committees that deal with institutional policies, departmental matters, and academic issues. Compile bibliographies of specialized materials for outside reading assignments. Write grant proposals to procure external research funding. Participate in campus and community events. Perform administrative duties such as serving as department head. Act as advisers to student organizations. Provide professional consulting services to government and/or industry.

GOE Information—Interest Area: 05. Education and Training. **Work Group:** 05.03. Postsecondary and Adult Teaching and Instructing. **Personality Type**—No data available. **Work Values**—No data available. **Skills**—Instructing; Learning Strategies; Writing; Social Perceptiveness; Persuasion; Speaking. **Abilities**—*Cognitive:* Written Expression; Written Comprehension; Originality; Oral Expression; Oral Comprehension; Fluency of Ideas. *Psychomotor:* None met the criteria. *Physical:* None met the criteria. *Sensory:* Speech Clarity; Speech Recognition; Near Vision. **General Work Activities**—*Information Input:* Getting Information; Identifying Objects, Actions, and Events; Monitoring Processes, Materials, or Surroundings. *Mental Process:* Organizing, Planning, and Prioritizing; Thinking Creatively; Updating and Using Relevant Knowledge. *Work Output:* Documenting or Recording Information; Interacting With Computers. *Interacting with Others:* Establishing and Maintaining Interpersonal Relationships; Teaching Others; Coaching and Developing Others. **Physical Work Conditions**—Indoors; Sitting. **Other Job Characteristics**—Need to Be Exact or Accurate.

Experience—Job Zone 5. Extensive skill, knowledge, and experience are needed. **Job Preparation**—SVP 8.0 and above—four years to more than 10 years. **Knowledges**—Education and Training; Therapy and Counseling; Sociology and Anthropology; Philosophy and Theology; Psychology; English Language. **Instructional Programs**—Agricultural Teacher Education; Art Teacher Education; Biology Teacher Education; Business Teacher Education; Chemistry Teacher Education; Computer Teacher Education; Drama and Dance Teacher Education; Driver and Safety Teacher Education; Education, General; English/Language Arts Teacher Education; Family and Consumer Sciences/Home Economics Teacher Education; Foreign Language Teacher Education; French Language Teacher Education; Geography Teacher Education; German Language Teacher Education; Health Occupations Teacher Education; Health Teacher Education; History Teacher Education; Humanities/Humanistic Studies; Mathematics

Teacher Education; Music Teacher Education; Physical Education Teaching and Coaching; Physics Teacher Education; Reading Teacher Education; Sales and Marketing Operations/Marketing and Distribution Teacher Education; Science Teacher Education/General Science Teacher Education; Social Science Teacher Education; Social Studies Teacher Education; Spanish Language Teacher Education; Speech Teacher Education; Teacher Education and Professional Development, Specific Subject Areas, Other; Technical Teacher Education; Technology Teacher Education/Industrial Arts Teacher Education; Trade and Industrial Teacher Education.

Related SOC Job—25-1081 Education Teachers, Postsecondary. **Related OOH Job**—Teachers—Postsecondary. **Related DOT Job**—090.227-010 Faculty Member, College or University.

25-1082.00 Library Science Teachers, Postsecondary

- **Education/Training Required: Master's degree**
- **Employed: 3,960**
- **Annual Earnings: $53,810**
- **Growth: 32.2%**
- **Annual Job Openings: 329,000**

The job openings listed here are shared with 37 other postsecondary teaching occupations numbered 25-1011.00 through 25-1199.99.

Teach courses in library science.

Prepare course materials such as syllabi, homework assignments, and handouts. Prepare and deliver lectures to undergraduate or graduate students on topics such as collection development, archival methods, and indexing and abstracting. Evaluate and grade students' classwork, assignments, and papers. Keep abreast of developments in their field by reading current literature, talking with colleagues, and participating in professional conferences. Initiate, facilitate, and moderate classroom discussions. Plan, evaluate, and revise curricula, course content, and course materials and methods of instruction. Conduct research in a particular field of knowledge and publish findings in professional journals, books, and/or electronic media. Maintain student attendance records, grades, and other required records. Collaborate with colleagues to address teaching and research issues. Advise students on academic and vocational curricula and on career issues. Compile, administer, and grade examinations or assign this work to others. Supervise undergraduate or graduate teaching, internship, and research work. Maintain regularly scheduled office hours in order to advise and assist students. Write grant proposals to procure external research funding. Select and obtain materials and supplies such as textbooks. Serve on academic or administrative committees that deal with institutional policies, departmental matters, and academic issues. Compile bibliographies of specialized materials for outside reading assignments. Participate in student recruitment, registration, and placement activities. Perform administrative duties such as serving as department head. Participate in campus and community events. Act as advisers to student organizations. Provide professional consulting services to government and/or industry.

GOE Information—**Interest Area:** 05. Education and Training. **Work Group:** 05.03. Postsecondary and Adult Teaching and Instructing. **Personality Type**—No data available. **Work Values**—No data available. **Skills**—Writing; Instructing; Learning Strategies; Active Learning; Reading Comprehension; Monitoring. **Abilities**—*Cognitive:* Written Expression; Written Comprehension; Memorization; Oral Expression; Originality; Oral Comprehension. *Psychomotor:* None met the criteria. *Physical:* None met the criteria. *Sensory:* Speech Clarity; Far Vision; Near Vision; Speech Recognition. **General Work Activities**—*Information Input:* Getting Information; Identifying Objects, Actions, and Events; Monitoring Processes, Materials, or Surroundings. *Mental Process:* Updating and Using Relevant Knowledge; Thinking Creatively; Analyzing Data or Information. *Work Output:* Interacting With Computers; Documenting or Recording Information. *Interacting with Others:* Teaching Others; Interpreting the Meaning of Information for Others; Establishing and Maintaining Interpersonal Relationships. **Physical Work Conditions**—Indoors; Sitting. **Other Job Characteristics**—Need to Be Exact or Accurate.

Experience—Job Zone 5. Extensive skill, knowledge, and experience are needed. **Job Preparation**—SVP 8.0 and above—four years to more than 10 years. **Knowledges**—Education and Training; Sociology and Anthropology; English Language; Communications and Media; History and Archeology; Philosophy and Theology. **Instructional Programs**—Humanities/Humanistic Studies; Library Science/Librarianship; Teacher Education and Professional Development, Specific Subject Areas, Other.

Related SOC Job—25-1082 Library Science Teachers, Postsecondary. **Related OOH Job**—Teachers—Postsecondary. **Related DOT Job**—090.227-010 Faculty Member, College or University.

25-1111.00 Criminal Justice and Law Enforcement Teachers, Postsecondary

- **Education/Training Required: Master's degree**
- **Employed: 9,880**
- **Annual Earnings: $49,240**
- **Growth: 32.2%**
- **Annual Job Openings: 329,000**

The job openings listed here are shared with 37 other postsecondary teaching occupations numbered 25-1011.00 through 25-1199.99.

Teach courses in criminal justice, corrections, and law enforcement administration.

Initiate, facilitate, and moderate classroom discussions. Keep abreast of developments in their field by reading current literature, talking with colleagues, and participating in professional conferences. Evaluate and grade students' classwork, assignments, and papers. Compile, administer, and grade examinations or assign this work to others. Prepare and deliver lectures to undergraduate or graduate students on topics such as criminal law, defensive policing, and investigation techniques. Prepare course materials such as syllabi, homework assignments, and handouts. Conduct research in a particular field of knowledge and publish findings in professional journals, books, and/or electronic media. Plan, evaluate, and revise curricula, course content, and course materials and methods of instruction. Supervise undergraduate and/or graduate teaching, internship, and research work. Maintain student attendance records, grades, and other required records. Select and obtain materials and supplies such as textbooks. Advise students on academic and vocational curricula and on career issues. Maintain regularly scheduled office hours to advise and assist students. Collaborate with colleagues to address teaching and research issues. Write grant proposals to procure external research funding. Serve on academic or administrative committees that deal with institutional policies, departmental matters, and academic issues. Compile bibliographies of specialized materials for outside reading assignments. Participate in student recruitment, registration, and placement activities. Provide professional consulting services to government and/or industry. Perform administrative duties such as serving as department head. Participate in campus and community events. Act as advisers to student organizations.

GOE Information—Interest Area: 05. Education and Training. **Work Group:** 05.03. Postsecondary and Adult Teaching and Instructing. **Personality Type**—No data available. **Work Values**—No data available. **Skills**—Writing; Critical Thinking; Instructing; Active Learning; Persuasion; Reading Comprehension. **Abilities**—*Cognitive:* Written Expression; Written Comprehension; Oral Expression; Oral Comprehension; Inductive Reasoning; Deductive Reasoning. *Psychomotor:* None met the criteria. *Physical:* None met the criteria. *Sensory:* Speech Clarity; Near Vision; Speech Recognition. **General Work Activities**—*Information Input:* Getting Information; Identifying Objects, Actions, and Events; Monitoring Processes, Materials, or Surroundings. *Mental Process:* Updating and Using Relevant Knowledge; Thinking Creatively; Analyzing Data or Information. *Work Output:* Documenting or Recording Information; Interacting With Computers. *Interacting with Others:* Teaching Others; Interpreting the Meaning of Information for Others; Establishing and Maintaining Interpersonal Relationships. **Physical Work Conditions**—Indoors; Sitting. **Other Job Characteristics**—Need to Be Exact or Accurate.

Experience—Job Zone 5. Extensive skill, knowledge, and experience are needed. **Job Preparation**—SVP 8.0 and above—four years to more than 10 years. **Knowledges**—Sociology and Anthropology; Philosophy and Theology; History and Archeology; Law and Government; English Language; Education and Training. **Instructional Programs**—Corrections; Corrections Administration; Corrections and Criminal Justice, Other; Criminal Justice/Law Enforcement Administration; Criminal Justice/Police Science; Criminal Justice/Safety Studies; Criminalistics and Criminal Science; Forensic Science and Technology; Juvenile Corrections; Security and Loss Prevention Services; Teacher Education and Professional Development, Specific Subject Areas, Other.

Related SOC Job—25-1111 Criminal Justice and Law Enforcement Teachers, Postsecondary. **Related OOH Job**—Teachers—Postsecondary. **Related DOT Job**—090.227-010 Faculty Member, College or University.

25-1112.00 Law Teachers, Postsecondary

- **Education/Training Required: First professional degree**
- **Employed: 13,560**
- **Annual Earnings: $89,790**
- **Growth: 32.2%**
- **Annual Job Openings: 329,000**

The job openings listed here are shared with 37 other postsecondary teaching occupations numbered 25-1011.00 through 25-1199.99.

Teach courses in law.

Evaluate and grade students' classwork, assignments, papers, and oral presentations. Compile, administer, and grade examinations or assign this work to others. Prepare and deliver lectures to undergraduate or graduate students on topics such as civil procedure, contracts, and torts. Initiate, facilitate, and moderate classroom discussions. Prepare course materials such as syllabi, homework assignments, and handouts. Keep abreast of developments in their field by reading current literature, talking with colleagues, and participating in professional conferences. Plan, evaluate, and revise curricula, course content, and course materials and methods of instruction. Maintain regularly scheduled office hours to advise and assist students. Conduct research in a particular field of knowledge

and publish findings in professional journals, books, or electronic media. Advise students on academic and vocational curricula and on career issues. Supervise undergraduate and/or graduate teaching, internship, and research work. Select and obtain materials and supplies such as textbooks. Maintain student attendance records, grades, and other required records. Serve on academic or administrative committees that deal with institutional policies, departmental matters, and academic issues. Perform administrative duties such as serving as department head. Collaborate with colleagues to address teaching and research issues. Participate in student recruitment, registration, and placement activities. Compile bibliographies of specialized materials for outside reading assignments. Participate in campus and community events. Act as advisers to student organizations. Assign cases for students to hear and try. Provide professional consulting services to government or industry. Write grant proposals to procure external research funding.

GOE Information—Interest Area: 05. Education and Training. **Work Group:** 05.03. Postsecondary and Adult Teaching and Instructing. **Personality Type**—No data available. **Work Values**—No data available. **Skills**—Instructing; Critical Thinking; Writing; Reading Comprehension; Persuasion; Speaking. **Abilities**—*Cognitive:* Written Expression; Written Comprehension; Oral Expression; Oral Comprehension; Inductive Reasoning; Deductive Reasoning. *Psychomotor:* None met the criteria. *Physical:* None met the criteria. *Sensory:* Speech Clarity; Near Vision; Speech Recognition. **General Work Activities**—*Information Input:* Getting Information; Identifying Objects, Actions, and Events; Monitoring Processes, Materials, or Surroundings. *Mental Process:* Thinking Creatively; Updating and Using Relevant Knowledge; Organizing, Planning, and Prioritizing. *Work Output:* Documenting or Recording Information; Interacting With Computers. *Interacting with Others:* Teaching Others; Coaching and Developing Others; Establishing and Maintaining Interpersonal Relationships. **Physical Work Conditions**—Indoors; Sitting. **Other Job Characteristics**—Need to Be Exact or Accurate.

Experience—Job Zone 5. Extensive skill, knowledge, and experience are needed. **Job Preparation**—SVP 8.0 and above—four years to more than 10 years. **Knowledges**—Law and Government; English Language; Education and Training; History and Archeology; Philosophy and Theology; Communications and Media. **Instructional Program**—Law (LL.B., J.D.).

Related SOC Job—25-1112 Law Teachers, Postsecondary. **Related OOH Job**—Teachers—Postsecondary. **Related DOT Job**—090.227-010 Faculty Member, College or University.

25-1113.00 Social Work Teachers, Postsecondary

- **Education/Training Required: Master's degree**
- **Employed: 7,440**
- **Annual Earnings: $52,660**
- **Growth: 32.2%**
- **Annual Job Openings: 329,000**

The job openings listed here are shared with 37 other postsecondary teaching occupations numbered 25-1011.00 through 25-1199.99.

Teach courses in social work.

Initiate, facilitate, and moderate classroom discussions. Evaluate and grade students' classwork, assignments, and papers. Prepare and deliver lectures to undergraduate or graduate students on topics such as family behavior, child and adolescent mental health, and social intervention evaluation. Keep abreast of developments in their field by reading current literature, talking with colleagues, and participating in professional conferences. Supervise students' laboratory work and fieldwork. Conduct research in a particular field of knowledge and publish findings in professional journals, books, or electronic media. Prepare course materials such as syllabi, homework assignments, and handouts. Maintain regularly scheduled office hours to advise and assist students. Supervise undergraduate or graduate teaching, internship, and research work. Plan, evaluate, and revise curricula, course content, and course materials and methods of instruction. Collaborate with colleagues and with community agencies to address teaching and research issues. Compile, administer, and grade examinations or assign this work to others. Advise students on academic and vocational curricula and on career issues. Maintain student attendance records, grades, and other required records. Write grant proposals to procure external research funding. Serve on academic or administrative committees that deal with institutional policies, departmental matters, and academic issues. Perform administrative duties such as serving as department head. Compile bibliographies of specialized materials for outside reading assignments. Select and obtain materials and supplies such as textbooks and laboratory equipment. Participate in student recruitment, registration, and placement activities. Participate in campus and community events. Provide professional consulting services to government and industry. Act as advisers to student organizations.

GOE Information—Interest Area: 05. Education and Training. **Work Group:** 05.03. Postsecondary and Adult Teaching and Instructing. **Personality Type**—No data available. **Work Values**—No data available. **Skills**—Social Perceptiveness; Service Orientation; Instructing; Learning Strategies; Complex Problem Solving; Writing. **Abilities**—*Cognitive:* Written Expression; Oral Expression; Originality; Written Comprehension; Inductive Reasoning; Oral Comprehension. *Psychomotor:* None met the criteria. *Physical:* None met the criteria. *Sensory:* Speech Clarity; Speech Recognition; Near Vision. **General Work Activities**—*Information Input:* Getting Information; Identifying Objects, Actions, and Events; Monitoring Processes, Materials, or Surroundings. *Mental Process:* Updating and Using Relevant Knowledge; Judging the Qualities of Things, Services, or Other People's Work; Organizing, Planning, and Prioritizing. *Work Output:* Documenting or Recording Information; Interacting With Computers. *Interacting with Others:* Establishing and Maintaining Interpersonal Relationships; Teaching Others; Communicating with Other Workers. **Physical Work Conditions**—Indoors; Sitting. **Other Job Characteristics**—Need to Be Exact or Accurate.

Experience—Job Zone 5. Extensive skill, knowledge, and experience are needed. **Job Preparation**—SVP 8.0 and above—four years to more than 10 years. **Knowledges**—Therapy and Counseling; Sociology and Anthropology; Psychology; Education and Training; Philosophy and Theology; English Language. **Instructional Programs**—Clinical/Medical Social Work; Social Work; Teacher Education and Professional Development, Specific Subject Areas, Other.

Related SOC Job—25-1113 Social Work Teachers, Postsecondary. **Related OOH Job**—Teachers—Postsecondary. **Related DOT Job**—090.227-010 Faculty Member, College or University.

25-1121.00 Art, Drama, and Music Teachers, Postsecondary

- ● **Education/Training Required: Master's degree**
- ● **Employed: 69,260**
- ● **Annual Earnings: $51,240**
- ● **Growth: 32.2%**
- ● **Annual Job Openings: 329,000**

The job openings listed here are shared with 37 other postsecondary teaching occupations numbered 25-1011.00 through 25-1199.99.

Teach courses in drama; music; and the arts, including fine and applied art, such as painting and sculpture, or design and crafts.

Evaluate and grade students' classwork, performances, projects, assignments, and papers. Explain and demonstrate artistic techniques. Prepare students for performances, exams, or assessments. Prepare and deliver lectures to undergraduate or graduate students on topics such as acting techniques, fundamentals of music, and art history. Organize performance groups and direct their rehearsals. Prepare course materials such as syllabi, homework assignments, and handouts. Initiate, facilitate, and moderate classroom discussions. Keep abreast of developments in their field by reading current literature, talking with colleagues, and participating in professional conferences. Advise students on academic and vocational curricula and on career issues. Maintain student attendance records, grades, and other required records. Conduct research in a particular field of knowledge and publish findings in professional journals, books, or electronic media. Supervise undergraduate and/or graduate teaching, internship, and research work. Plan, evaluate, and revise curricula, course content, and course materials and methods of instruction. Maintain regularly scheduled office hours to advise and assist students. Compile, administer, and grade examinations or assign this work to others. Participate in student recruitment, registration, and placement activities. Select and obtain materials and supplies such as textbooks and performance pieces. Collaborate with colleagues to address teaching and research issues. Serve on academic or administrative committees that deal with institutional policies, departmental matters, and academic issues. Participate in campus and community events. Keep students informed of community events such as plays and concerts. Compile bibliographies of specialized materials for outside reading assignments. Display students' work in schools, galleries, and exhibitions. Perform administrative duties such as serving as department head. Act as advisers to student organizations. Write grant proposals to procure external research funding. Provide professional consulting services to government or industry.

GOE Information—Interest Area: 05. Education and Training. **Work Group:** 05.03. Postsecondary and Adult Teaching and Instructing. **Personality Type**—Artistic. Artistic occupations frequently involve working with forms, designs, and patterns. They often require self-expression, and the work can be done without following a clear set of rules. **Work Values**—Authority; Social Service; Creativity; Ability Utilization; Achievement; Autonomy. **Skills**—Instructing; Social Perceptiveness; Speaking; Persuasion; Active Listening; Learning Strategies. **Abilities**—*Cognitive:* Written Expression; Oral Expression; Originality; Written Comprehension; Fluency of Ideas; Oral Comprehension. *Psychomotor:* None met the criteria. *Physical:* None met the criteria. *Sensory:* Speech Clarity; Speech Recognition; Near Vision; Far Vision. **General Work Activities**—*Information Input:* Getting Information; Identifying Objects, Actions, and Events; Monitoring Processes, Materials, or Surroundings. *Mental Process:* Thinking Creatively; Organizing, Planning, and Prioritizing; Judging the Qualities of Things, Services, or Other People's Work. *Work*

Output: Documenting or Recording Information; Interacting With Computers; Performing General Physical Activities. *Interacting with Others:* Coaching and Developing Others; Teaching Others; Establishing and Maintaining Interpersonal Relationships. **Physical Work Conditions**—Indoors; Noisy; Sitting. **Other Job Characteristics**—Need to Be Exact or Accurate.

Experience—Job Zone 5. Extensive skill, knowledge, and experience are needed. **Job Preparation**—SVP 8.0 and above—four years to more than 10 years. **Knowledges**—Fine Arts; History and Archeology; Philosophy and Theology; Education and Training; Communications and Media; Sociology and Anthropology. **Instructional Programs**—Art History, Criticism, and Conservation; Art/Art Studies, General; Arts Management; Ceramic Arts and Ceramics; Cinematography and Film/Video Production; Commercial Photography; Conducting; Crafts/Craft Design, Folk Art, and Artisanry; Dance, General; Design and Applied Arts, Other; Design and Visual Communications, General; Directing and Theatrical Production; Drama and Dramatics/Theatre Arts, General; Dramatic/Theatre Arts and Stagecraft, Other; Fashion/Apparel Design; Fiber, Textile, and Weaving Arts; Film/Cinema Studies; Film/Video and Photographic Arts, Other; Fine Arts and Art Studies, Other; Fine/Studio Arts, General; Graphic Design; Humanities/Humanistic Studies; Industrial Design; Interior Design; Intermedia/Multimedia; Jazz/Jazz Studies; Metal and Jewelry Arts; Music History, Literature, and Theory; Music Management and Merchandising; Music Pedagogy; Music Performance, General; Music Theory and Composition; Music, Other; Musicology and Ethnomusicology; Painting; Photography; Piano and Organ; Playwriting and Screenwriting; Printmaking; Sculpture; Technical Theatre/Theatre Design and Technology; Theatre Literature, History, and Criticism; Theatre/Theatre Arts Management; Violin, Viola, Guitar, and Other Stringed Instruments; Visual and Performing Arts, General; Visual and Performing Arts, Other; Voice and Opera.

Related SOC Job—25-1121 Art, Drama, and Music Teachers, Postsecondary. **Related OOH Job**—Teachers—Postsecondary. **Related DOT Job**—090.227-010 Faculty Member, College or University.

25-1122.00 Communications Teachers, Postsecondary

- **Education/Training Required: Master's degree**
- **Employed: 22,320**
- **Annual Earnings: $50,890**
- **Growth: 32.2%**
- **Annual Job Openings: 329,000**

The job openings listed here are shared with 37 other postsecondary teaching occupations numbered 25-1011.00 through 25-1199.99.

Teach courses in communications, such as organizational communications, public relations, radio/television broadcasting, and journalism.

Evaluate and grade students' classwork, assignments, and papers. Prepare course materials such as syllabi, homework assignments, and handouts. Initiate, facilitate, and moderate classroom discussions. Prepare and deliver lectures to undergraduate or graduate students on topics such as public speaking, media criticism, and oral traditions. Compile, administer, and grade examinations or assign this work to others. Maintain student attendance records, grades, and other required records. Plan, evaluate, and revise curricula, course content, and course materials and methods of instruction. Maintain regularly scheduled office hours to advise and assist students. Keep abreast of developments in their field by reading current literature,

talking with colleagues, and participating in professional conferences. Advise students on academic and vocational curricula and on career issues. Supervise undergraduate or graduate teaching, internship, and research work. Select and obtain materials and supplies such as textbooks. Collaborate with colleagues to address teaching and research issues. Conduct research in a particular field of knowledge and publish findings in professional journals, books, or electronic media. Participate in student recruitment, registration, and placement activities. Serve on academic or administrative committees that deal with institutional policies, departmental matters, and academic issues. Compile bibliographies of specialized materials for outside reading assignments. Act as advisers to student organizations. Participate in campus and community events. Perform administrative duties such as serving as department head. Write grant proposals to procure external research funding. Provide professional consulting services to government or industry.

GOE Information—**Interest Area:** 05. Education and Training. **Work Group:** 05.03. Postsecondary and Adult Teaching and Instructing. **Personality Type**—No data available. **Work Values**—No data available. **Skills**—Instructing; Writing; Persuasion; Learning Strategies; Monitoring; Speaking. **Abilities**—*Cognitive:* Written Expression; Oral Expression; Written Comprehension; Oral Comprehension; Memorization; Inductive Reasoning. *Psychomotor:* None met the criteria. *Physical:* None met the criteria. *Sensory:* Speech Clarity; Speech Recognition. **General Work Activities**—*Information Input:* Getting Information; Identifying Objects, Actions, and Events; Monitoring Processes, Materials, or Surroundings. *Mental Process:* Updating and Using Relevant Knowledge; Organizing, Planning, and Prioritizing; Thinking Creatively. *Work Output:* Documenting or Recording Information; Interacting With Computers. *Interacting with Others:* Teaching Others; Establishing and Maintaining Interpersonal Relationships; Coaching and Developing Others. **Physical Work Conditions**—Indoors; Sitting. **Other Job Characteristics**—Need to Be Exact or Accurate.

Experience—Job Zone 5. Extensive skill, knowledge, and experience are needed. **Job Preparation**—SVP 8.0 and above—four years to more than 10 years. **Knowledges**—Communications and Media; Education and Training; Philosophy and Theology; English Language; Sociology and Anthropology; History and Archeology. **Instructional Programs**—Advertising; Broadcast Journalism; Communications Studies/Speech Communication and Rhetoric; Communications, Journalism, and Related Fields, Other; Digital Communications and Media/Multimedia; Health Communications; Humanities/Humanistic Studies; Journalism; Journalism, Other; Mass Communications/Media Studies; Political Communications; Public Relations/Image Management; Radio and Television.

Related SOC Job—25-1122 Communications Teachers, Postsecondary. **Related OOH Job**—Teachers—Postsecondary. **Related DOT Job**—090.227-010 Faculty Member, College or University.

25-1123.00 English Language and Literature Teachers, Postsecondary

- **Education/Training Required: Master's degree**
- **Employed: 58,710**
- **Annual Earnings: $49,480**
- **Growth: 32.2%**
- **Annual Job Openings: 329,000**

The job openings listed here are shared with 37 other postsecondary teaching occupations numbered 25-1011.00 through 25-1199.99.

Teach courses in English language and literature, including linguistics and comparative literature.

Initiate, facilitate, and moderate classroom discussions. Evaluate and grade students' classwork, assignments, and papers. Prepare course materials such as syllabi, homework assignments, and handouts. Prepare and deliver lectures to undergraduate and graduate students on topics such as poetry, novel structure, and translation and adaptation. Maintain student attendance records, grades, and other required records. Plan, evaluate, and revise curricula, course content, and course materials and methods of instruction. Compile, administer, and grade examinations or assign this work to others. Maintain regularly scheduled office hours in order to advise and assist students. Keep abreast of developments in their field by reading current literature, talking with colleagues, and participating in professional conferences. Select and obtain materials and supplies such as textbooks. Advise students on academic and vocational curricula and on career issues. Conduct research in a particular field of knowledge and publish findings in professional journals, books, or electronic media. Collaborate with colleagues to address teaching and research issues. Serve on academic or administrative committees that deal with institutional policies, departmental matters, and academic issues. Participate in campus and community events. Participate in student recruitment, registration, and placement activities. Compile bibliographies of specialized materials for outside reading assignments. Supervise undergraduate and/or graduate teaching, internship, and research work. Provide assistance to students in college writing centers. Perform administrative duties such as serving as department head. Recruit, train, and supervise student writing instructors. Act as advisers to student organizations. Write grant proposals to procure external research funding. Provide professional consulting services to government or industry.

GOE Information—Interest Area: 05. Education and Training. **Work Group:** 05.03. Postsecondary and Adult Teaching and Instructing. **Personality Type—**Artistic. Artistic occupations frequently involve working with forms, designs, and patterns. They often require self-expression, and the work can be done without following a clear set of rules. **Work Values—**Authority; Social Service; Creativity; Achievement; Ability Utilization; Autonomy. **Skills—**Instructing; Learning Strategies; Writing; Social Perceptiveness; Persuasion; Reading Comprehension. **Abilities—***Cognitive:* Written Expression; Written Comprehension; Originality; Fluency of Ideas; Oral Comprehension; Oral Expression. *Psychomotor:* None met the criteria. *Physical:* None met the criteria. *Sensory:* Speech Clarity; Speech Recognition; Near Vision. **General Work Activities—***Information Input:* Getting Information; Identifying Objects, Actions, and Events; Monitoring Processes, Materials, or Surroundings. *Mental Process:* Thinking Creatively; Organizing, Planning, and Prioritizing; Updating and Using Relevant Knowledge. *Work Output:* Documenting or Recording Information; Interacting With Computers. *Interacting with Others:* Teaching Others; Establishing and Maintaining Interpersonal Relationships; Coaching and Developing Others. **Physical Work Conditions—**Indoors; Sitting. **Other Job Characteristics—**Need to Be Exact or Accurate.

Experience—Job Zone 5. Extensive skill, knowledge, and experience are needed. **Job Preparation—**SVP 8.0 and above—four years to more than 10 years. **Knowledges—**Philosophy and Theology; English Language; History and Archeology; Education and Training; Sociology and Anthropology; Fine Arts. **Instructional Programs—**American Literature (Canadian); American Literature (United States); Comparative Literature; Creative Writing; English Composition; English Language and Literature, General; English Language and Literature/Letters, Other; English Literature (British and

Commonwealth); Humanities/Humanistic Studies; Technical and Business Writing.

Related SOC Job—25-1123 English Language and Literature Teachers, Postsecondary. **Related OOH Job—**Teachers—Postsecondary. **Related DOT Job—**090.227-010 Faculty Member, College or University.

25-1124.00 Foreign Language and Literature Teachers, Postsecondary

- **Education/Training Required: Master's degree**
- **Employed: 23,830**
- **Annual Earnings: $49,570**
- **Growth: 32.2%**
- **Annual Job Openings: 329,000**

The job openings listed here are shared with 37 other postsecondary teaching occupations numbered 25-1011.00 through 25-1199.99.

Teach courses in foreign (i.e., other than English) languages and literature.

Evaluate and grade students' classwork, assignments, and papers. Prepare course materials such as syllabi, homework assignments, and handouts. Initiate, facilitate, and moderate classroom discussions. Maintain student attendance records, grades, and other required records. Compile, administer, and grade examinations or assign this work to others. Plan, evaluate, and revise curricula, course content, and course materials and methods of instruction. Prepare and deliver lectures to undergraduate and graduate students on topics such as how to speak and write a foreign language and the cultural aspects of areas where a particular language is used. Maintain regularly scheduled office hours to advise and assist students. Select and obtain materials and supplies such as textbooks. Keep abreast of developments in their field by reading current literature, talking with colleagues, and participating in professional organizations and activities. Advise students on academic and vocational curricula and on career issues. Conduct research in a particular field of knowledge and publish findings in scholarly journals, books, and/or electronic media. Collaborate with colleagues to address teaching and research issues. Serve on academic or administrative committees that deal with institutional policies, departmental matters, and academic issues. Participate in student recruitment, registration, and placement activities. Compile bibliographies of specialized materials for outside reading assignments. Participate in campus and community events. Act as advisers to student organizations. Perform administrative duties such as serving as department head. Supervise undergraduate and graduate teaching, internship, and research work. Write grant proposals to procure external research funding. Provide professional consulting services to government or industry.

GOE Information—Interest Area: 05. Education and Training. **Work Group:** 05.03. Postsecondary and Adult Teaching and Instructing. **Personality Type—**Artistic. Artistic occupations frequently involve working with forms, designs, and patterns. They often require self-expression, and the work can be done without following a clear set of rules. **Work Values—**Authority; Social Service; Creativity; Achievement; Ability Utilization; Autonomy. **Skills—**Instructing; Learning Strategies; Writing; Persuasion; Speaking; Reading Comprehension. **Abilities—***Cognitive:* Written Expression; Oral Expression; Written Comprehension; Oral Comprehension; Memorization; Originality. *Psychomotor:* None met the criteria. *Physical:* None met the criteria. *Sensory:* Speech Clarity; Speech Recognition; Near Vision. **General Work Activities—***Information Input:* Getting Information; Identifying Objects, Actions, and Events;

Monitoring Processes, Materials, or Surroundings. *Mental Process:* Organizing, Planning, and Prioritizing; Thinking Creatively; Updating and Using Relevant Knowledge. *Work Output:* Documenting or Recording Information; Interacting With Computers. *Interacting with Others:* Teaching Others; Coaching and Developing Others; Establishing and Maintaining Interpersonal Relationships. **Physical Work Conditions**—Indoors; Sitting. **Other Job Characteristics**—Need to Be Exact or Accurate.

Experience—Job Zone 5. Extensive skill, knowledge, and experience are needed. **Job Preparation**—SVP 8.0 and above—four years to more than 10 years. **Knowledges**—Foreign Language; Philosophy and Theology; History and Archeology; Sociology and Anthropology; Geography; English Language. **Instructional Programs**—African Languages, Literatures, and Linguistics; Albanian Language and Literature; American Indian/Native American Languages, Literatures, and Linguistics; Ancient Near Eastern and Biblical Languages, Literatures, and Linguistics; Ancient/Classical Greek Language and Literature; Arabic Language and Literature; Australian/Oceanic/Pacific Languages, Literatures, and Linguistics; Bahasa Indonesian/Bahasa Malay Languages and Literatures; Baltic Languages, Literatures, and Linguistics; Bengali Language and Literature; Bulgarian Language and Literature; Burmese Language and Literature; Catalan Language and Literature; Celtic Languages, Literatures, and Linguistics; Chinese Language and Literature; Classics and Classical Languages, Literatures, and Linguistics, General; Classics and Classical Languages, Literatures, and Linguistics, Other; Czech Language and Literature; Danish Language and Literature; Dutch/Flemish Language and Literature; East Asian Languages, Literatures, and Linguistics, General; East Asian Languages, Literatures, and Linguistics, Other; Filipino/Tagalog Language and Literature; Finnish and Related Languages, Literatures, and Linguistics; Foreign Languages, Literatures, and Linguistics, Other; Foreign Languages/Modern Languages, General; French Language and Literature; German Language and Literature; Germanic Languages, Literatures, and Linguistics, General; Germanic Languages, Literatures, and Linguistics, Other; Hebrew Language and Literature; Hindi Language and Literature; Humanities/Humanistic Studies; Hungarian/Magyar Language and Literature; Iranian/Persian Languages, Literatures, and Linguistics; Italian Language and Literature; Japanese Language and Literature; Khmer/Cambodian Language and Literature; Korean Language and Literature; Language Interpretation and Translation; Lao/Laotian Language and Literature; Latin Language and Literature; Latin Teacher Education; Linguistics; others.

Related SOC Job—25-1124 Foreign Language and Literature Teachers, Postsecondary. **Related OOH Job**—Teachers—Postsecondary. **Related DOT Job**—090.227-010 Faculty Member, College or University.

25-1125.00 History Teachers, Postsecondary

- **Education/Training Required:** Master's degree
- **Employed:** 20,520
- **Annual Earnings:** $54,780
- **Growth:** 32.2%
- **Annual Job Openings:** 329,000

The job openings listed here are shared with 37 other postsecondary teaching occupations numbered 25-1011.00 through 25-1199.99.

Teach courses in human history and historiography.

Prepare and deliver lectures to undergraduate and/or graduate students on topics such as ancient history, postwar civilizations, and the history of third-world countries. Evaluate and grade students' classwork, assignments, and papers. Prepare course materials such as syllabi, homework assignments, and handouts. Compile, administer, and grade examinations or assign this work to others. Initiate, facilitate, and moderate classroom discussions. Keep abreast of developments in their field by reading current literature, talking with colleagues, and participating in professional conferences. Plan, evaluate, and revise curricula, course content, and course materials and methods of instruction. Maintain student attendance records, grades, and other required records. Maintain regularly scheduled office hours to advise and assist students. Conduct research in a particular field of knowledge and publish findings in professional journals, books, or electronic media. Select and obtain materials and supplies such as textbooks. Advise students on academic and vocational curricula and on career issues. Collaborate with colleagues to address teaching and research issues. Serve on academic or administrative committees that deal with institutional policies, departmental matters, and academic issues. Participate in campus and community events. Act as advisers to student organizations. Participate in student recruitment, registration, and placement activities. Compile bibliographies of specialized materials for outside reading assignments. Supervise undergraduate and graduate teaching, internship, and research work. Perform administrative duties such as serving as department head. Write grant proposals to procure external research funding. Provide professional consulting services to government, educational institutions, and industry.

GOE Information—**Interest Area:** 05. Education and Training. **Work Group:** 05.03. Postsecondary and Adult Teaching and Instructing. **Personality Type**—Social. Social occupations frequently involve working with, communicating with, and teaching people. These occupations often involve helping or providing service to others. **Work Values**—Authority; Social Service; Creativity; Achievement; Social Status; Ability Utilization. **Skills**—Writing; Instructing; Learning Strategies; Speaking; Persuasion; Reading Comprehension. **Abilities**—*Cognitive:* Written Expression; Written Comprehension; Memorization; Oral Expression; Oral Comprehension; Inductive Reasoning. *Psychomotor:* None met the criteria. *Physical:* None met the criteria. *Sensory:* Speech Clarity; Speech Recognition; Near Vision. **General Work Activities**—*Information Input:* Getting Information; Identifying Objects, Actions, and Events; Monitoring Processes, Materials, or Surroundings. *Mental Process:* Updating and Using Relevant Knowledge; Thinking Creatively; Organizing, Planning, and Prioritizing. *Work Output:* Documenting or Recording Information; Interacting With Computers. *Interacting with Others:* Interpreting the Meaning of Information for Others; Teaching Others; Establishing and Maintaining Interpersonal Relationships. **Physical Work Conditions**—Indoors; Sitting. **Other Job Characteristics**—Need to Be Exact or Accurate.

Experience—Job Zone 5. Extensive skill, knowledge, and experience are needed. **Job Preparation**—SVP 8.0 and above—four years to more than 10 years. **Knowledges**—History and Archeology; Philosophy and Theology; Geography; Sociology and Anthropology; Education and Training; English Language. **Instructional Programs**—American History (United States); Asian History; Canadian History; European History; History and Philosophy of Science and Technology; History, General; History, Other; Humanities/Humanistic Studies; Public/Applied History and Archival Administration.

Related SOC Job—25-1125 History Teachers, Postsecondary. **Related OOH Job**—Teachers—Postsecondary. **Related DOT Job**—090.227-010 Faculty Member, College or University.

25-1126.00 Philosophy and Religion Teachers, Postsecondary

- Education/Training Required: Master's degree
- Employed: 18,340
- Annual Earnings: $53,210
- Growth: 32.2%
- Annual Job Openings: 329,000

The job openings listed here are shared with 37 other postsecondary teaching occupations numbered 25-1011.00 through 25-1199.99.

Teach courses in philosophy, religion, and theology.

Evaluate and grade students' classwork, assignments, and papers. Initiate, facilitate, and moderate classroom discussions. Prepare and deliver lectures to undergraduate and graduate students on topics such as ethics, logic, and contemporary religious thought. Prepare course materials such as syllabi, homework assignments, and handouts. Compile, administer, and grade examinations or assign this work to others. Keep abreast of developments in their field by reading current literature, talking with colleagues, and participating in professional conferences. Maintain student attendance records, grades, and other required records. Plan, evaluate, and revise curricula, course content, and course materials and methods of instruction. Maintain regularly scheduled office hours to advise and assist students. Select and obtain materials and supplies such as textbooks. Advise students on academic and vocational curricula and on career issues. Conduct research in a particular field of knowledge and publish findings in professional journals, books, or electronic media. Perform administrative duties such as serving as department head. Serve on academic or administrative committees that deal with institutional policies, departmental matters, and academic issues. Collaborate with colleagues to address teaching and research issues. Participate in campus and community events. Participate in student recruitment, registration, and placement activities. Compile bibliographies of specialized materials for outside reading assignments. Supervise undergraduate and graduate teaching, internship, and research work. Act as advisers to student organizations. Write grant proposals to procure external research funding. Provide professional consulting services to government or industry.

GOE Information—Interest Area: 05. Education and Training. **Work Group:** 05.03. Postsecondary and Adult Teaching and Instructing. **Personality Type**—No data available. **Work Values**—No data available. **Skills**—Instructing; Writing; Critical Thinking; Reading Comprehension; Learning Strategies; Speaking. **Abilities**—*Cognitive:* Written Expression; Written Comprehension; Oral Expression; Oral Comprehension; Inductive Reasoning; Memorization. *Psychomotor:* None met the criteria. *Physical:* None met the criteria. *Sensory:* Speech Clarity; Speech Recognition; Near Vision. **General Work Activities**—*Information Input:* Getting Information; Identifying Objects, Actions, and Events; Monitoring Processes, Materials, or Surroundings. *Mental Process:* Thinking Creatively; Updating and Using Relevant Knowledge; Organizing, Planning, and Prioritizing. *Work Output:* Documenting or Recording Information; Interacting With Computers. *Interacting with Others:* Teaching Others; Interpreting the Meaning of Information for Others; Establishing and Maintaining Interpersonal Relationships. **Physical Work Conditions**—Indoors; Sitting. **Other Job Characteristics**—Need to Be Exact or Accurate.

Experience—Job Zone 5. Extensive skill, knowledge, and experience are needed. **Job Preparation**—SVP 8.0 and above—four years to more than 10 years. **Knowledges**—Philosophy and Theology; History and Archeology; Sociology and Anthropology; Education and Training;

Foreign Language; English Language. **Instructional Programs**—Bible/Biblical Studies; Buddhist Studies; Christian Studies; Divinity/Ministry (BD, MDiv.); Ethics; Hindu Studies; Humanities/Humanistic Studies; Missions/Missionary Studies and Missiology; Pastoral Counseling and Specialized Ministries, Other; Pastoral Studies/Counseling; Philosophy; Philosophy and Religion, Other; Philosophy, Other; Pre-Theology/Pre-Ministerial Studies; Rabbinical Studies (M.H.L./Rav); Religion/Religious Studies; Religious Education; Religious/Sacred Music; Talmudic Studies; Theological and Ministerial Studies, Other; Theological Studies and Religious Vocations, Other; Theology/Theological Studies.

Related SOC Job—25-1126 Philosophy and Religion Teachers, Postsecondary. **Related OOH Job**—Teachers—Postsecondary. **Related DOT Job**—090.227-010 Faculty Member, College or University.

25-1191.00 Graduate Teaching Assistants

- Education/Training Required: Master's degree
- Employed: 117,970
- Annual Earnings: $27,340
- Growth: 32.2%
- Annual Job Openings: 329,000

The job openings listed here are shared with 37 other postsecondary teaching occupations numbered 25-1011.00 through 25-1199.99.

Assist department chairperson, faculty members, or other professional staff members in college or university by performing teaching or teaching-related duties, such as teaching lower-level courses, developing teaching materials, preparing and giving examinations, and grading examinations or papers. Graduate assistants must be enrolled in a graduate school program. Graduate assistants who primarily perform non-teaching duties, such as laboratory research, should be reported in the occupational category related to the work performed.

Lead discussion sections, tutorials, and laboratory sections. Evaluate and grade examinations, assignments, and papers and record grades. Return assignments to students in accordance with established deadlines. Schedule and maintain regular office hours to meet with students. Inform students of the procedures for completing and submitting class work such as lab reports. Prepare and proctor examinations. Notify instructors of errors or problems with assignments. Meet with supervisors to discuss students' grades and to complete required grade-related paperwork. Copy and distribute classroom materials. Demonstrate use of laboratory equipment and enforce laboratory rules. Teach undergraduate-level courses. Complete laboratory projects prior to assigning them to students so that any needed modifications can be made. Develop teaching materials such as syllabi, visual aids, answer keys, supplementary notes, and course Web sites. Provide assistance to faculty members or staff with laboratory or field research. Arrange for supervisors to conduct teaching observations; meet with supervisors to receive feedback about teaching performance. Attend lectures given by the instructor whom they are assisting. Order or obtain materials needed for classes. Provide instructors with assistance in the use of audiovisual equipment. Assist faculty members or staff with student conferences.

GOE Information—Interest Area: 05. Education and Training. **Work Group:** 05.03. Postsecondary and Adult Teaching and Instructing. **Personality Type**—Social. Social occupations frequently involve working with, communicating with, and teaching people. These occupations often involve helping or providing service to others. **Work Values**—Social Service; Authority; Co-workers; Working Conditions; Creativity; Achievement. **Skills**—Learning Strategies; Instructing; Social Perceptiveness; Reading Comprehension; Time

Management; Writing. **Abilities**—*Cognitive:* Written Expression; Oral Comprehension; Oral Expression; Fluency of Ideas; Written Comprehension; Originality. *Psychomotor:* None met the criteria. *Physical:* None met the criteria. *Sensory:* Speech Clarity; Far Vision; Speech Recognition. **General Work Activities**—*Information Input:* Identifying Objects, Actions, and Events; Monitoring Processes, Materials, or Surroundings; Getting Information. *Mental Process:* Thinking Creatively; Updating and Using Relevant Knowledge; Processing Information. *Work Output:* Documenting or Recording Information; Interacting With Computers. *Interacting with Others:* Communicating with Other Workers; Interpreting the Meaning of Information to Others; Teaching Others. **Physical Work Conditions**—Indoors; Sitting. **Other Job Characteristics**—Need to Be Exact or Accurate.

Experience—Job Zone 5. Extensive skill, knowledge, and experience are needed. **Job Preparation**—SVP 8.0 and above—four years to more than 10 years. **Knowledges**—Education and Training; Sociology and Anthropology; English Language; Psychology; Philosophy and Theology; Computers and Electronics. **Instructional Programs**—Humanities/Humanistic Studies.

Related SOC Job—25-1191 Graduate Teaching Assistants. **Related OOH Job**—Teachers—Postsecondary. **Related DOT Job**—090.227-014 Graduate Assistant.

25-1192.00 Home Economics Teachers, Postsecondary

- Education/Training Required: Master's degree
- Employed: 4,010
- Annual Earnings: $48,720
- Growth: 32.2%
- Annual Job Openings: 329,000

The job openings listed here are shared with 37 other postsecondary teaching occupations numbered 25-1011.00 through 25-1199.99.

Teach courses in child care, family relations, finance, nutrition, and related subjects as pertaining to home management.

Evaluate and grade students' classwork, laboratory work, projects, assignments, and papers. Initiate, facilitate, and moderate classroom discussions. Prepare and deliver lectures to undergraduate or graduate students on topics such as food science, nutrition, and child care. Prepare course materials such as syllabi, homework assignments, and handouts. Keep abreast of developments in their field by reading current literature, talking with colleagues, and participating in professional conferences. Maintain student attendance records, grades, and other required records. Plan, evaluate, and revise curricula, course content, and course materials and methods of instruction. Compile, administer, and grade examinations or assign this work to others. Advise students on academic and vocational curricula and on career issues. Maintain regularly scheduled office hours to advise and assist students. Supervise undergraduate or graduate teaching, internship, and research work. Select and obtain materials and supplies such as textbooks. Conduct research in a particular field of knowledge and publish findings in professional journals, books, and/or electronic media. Collaborate with colleagues to address teaching and research issues. Act as advisers to student organizations. Participate in student recruitment, registration, and placement activities. Serve on academic or administrative committees that deal with institutional policies, departmental matters, and academic issues. Participate in campus and community events. Compile bibliographies of specialized materials for outside reading assignments. Perform administrative duties such as serving as department head. Write grant proposals to procure external research funding. Provide professional consulting services to government and industry.

GOE Information—**Interest Area:** 05. Education and Training. **Work Group:** 05.03. Postsecondary and Adult Teaching and Instructing. **Personality Type**—No data available. **Work Values**—No data available. **Skills**—Writing; Instructing; Learning Strategies; Service Orientation; Active Learning; Social Perceptiveness. **Abilities**—*Cognitive:* Written Expression; Oral Expression; Written Comprehension; Originality; Oral Comprehension; Memorization. *Psychomotor:* None met the criteria. *Physical:* None met the criteria. *Sensory:* Speech Clarity; Far Vision; Near Vision; Speech Recognition. **General Work Activities**—*Information Input:* Identifying Objects, Actions, and Events; Getting Information; Monitoring Processes, Materials, or Surroundings. *Mental Process:* Organizing, Planning, and Prioritizing; Updating and Using Relevant Knowledge; Processing Information. *Work Output:* Documenting or Recording Information; Interacting With Computers; Performing General Physical Activities. *Interacting with Others:* Teaching Others; Coaching and Developing Others; Establishing and Maintaining Interpersonal Relationships. **Physical Work Conditions**—Indoors; Sitting. **Other Job Characteristics**—Need to Be Exact or Accurate.

Experience—Job Zone 5. Extensive skill, knowledge, and experience are needed. **Job Preparation**—SVP 8.0 and above—four years to more than 10 years. **Knowledges**—Sociology and Anthropology; Philosophy and Theology; Education and Training; Therapy and Counseling; Psychology; English Language. **Instructional Programs**—Business Family and Consumer Sciences/Human Sciences; Child Care and Support Services Management; Family and Consumer Sciences/Human Sciences, General; Foodservice Systems Administration/Management; Human Development and Family Studies, General.

Related SOC Job—25-1192 Home Economics Teachers, Postsecondary. **Related OOH Job**—Teachers—Postsecondary. **Related DOT Jobs**—090.227-010 Faculty Member, College or University; 096.121-014 Home Economist.

25-1193.00 Recreation and Fitness Studies Teachers, Postsecondary

- Education/Training Required: Master's degree
- Employed: 16,530
- Annual Earnings: $45,890
- Growth: 32.2%
- Annual Job Openings: 329,000

The job openings listed here are shared with 37 other postsecondary teaching occupations numbered 25-1011.00 through 25-1199.99.

Teach courses pertaining to recreation, leisure, and fitness studies, including exercise physiology and facilities management.

Evaluate and grade students' classwork, assignments, and papers. Maintain student attendance records, grades, and other required records. Prepare and deliver lectures to undergraduate and graduate students on topics such as anatomy, therapeutic recreation, and conditioning theory. Prepare course materials such as syllabi, homework assignments, and handouts. Maintain regularly scheduled office hours to advise and assist students. Compile, administer, and grade examinations or assign this work to others. Plan, evaluate, and revise curricula, course content, and course materials and methods of instruction. Initiate, facilitate, and moderate classroom discussions.

Keep abreast of developments in their field by reading current literature, talking with colleagues, and participating in professional conferences. Advise students on academic and vocational curricula and on career issues. Participate in student recruitment, registration, and placement activities. Collaborate with colleagues to address teaching and research issues. Select and obtain materials and supplies such as textbooks. Participate in campus and community events. Serve on academic or administrative committees that deal with institutional policies, departmental matters, and academic issues. Compile bibliographies of specialized materials for outside reading assignments. Supervise undergraduate or graduate teaching, internship, and research work. Perform administrative duties such as serving as department heads. Prepare students to act as sports coaches. Conduct research in a particular field of knowledge and publish findings in professional journals, books, or electronic media. Act as advisers to student organizations. Write grant proposals to procure external research funding. Provide professional consulting services to government or industry.

GOE Information—Interest Area: 05. Education and Training. **Work Group:** 05.03. Postsecondary and Adult Teaching and Instructing. **Personality Type**—No data available. **Work Values**—No data available. **Skills**—Instructing; Learning Strategies; Science; Social Perceptiveness; Persuasion; Time Management. **Abilities**—*Cognitive:* Written Expression; Written Comprehension; Oral Expression; Originality; Oral Comprehension; Memorization. *Psychomotor:* None met the criteria. *Physical:* None met the criteria. *Sensory:* Speech Clarity; Speech Recognition; Near Vision. **General Work Activities**—*Information Input:* Getting Information; Identifying Objects, Actions, and Events; Monitoring Processes, Materials, or Surroundings. *Mental Process:* Organizing, Planning, and Prioritizing; Updating and Using Relevant Knowledge; Thinking Creatively. *Work Output:* Performing General Physical Activities; Documenting or Recording Information; Interacting With Computers. *Interacting with Others:* Coaching and Developing Others; Teaching Others; Establishing and Maintaining Interpersonal Relationships. **Physical Work Conditions**—More Often Outdoors Than Indoors; Standing. **Other Job Characteristics**—Need to Be Exact or Accurate.

Experience—Job Zone 5. Extensive skill, knowledge, and experience are needed. **Job Preparation**—SVP 8.0 and above—four years to more than 10 years. **Knowledges**—Education and Training; Psychology; Philosophy and Theology; Therapy and Counseling; Medicine and Dentistry; Personnel and Human Resources. **Instructional Programs**—Health and Physical Education, General; Parks, Recreation, and Leisure Studies; Sport and Fitness Administration/Management.

Related SOC Job—25-1193 Recreation and Fitness Studies Teachers, Postsecondary. **Related OOH Job**—Teachers—Postsecondary. **Related DOT Jobs**—090.227-010 Faculty Member, College or University; 099.224-010 Instructor, Physical Education.

25-1194.00 Vocational Education Teachers, Postsecondary

- **Education/Training Required: Work experience in a related occupation**
- **Employed: 105,980**
- **Annual Earnings: $41,750**
- **Growth: 32.2%**
- **Annual Job Openings: 329,000**

The job openings listed here are shared with 37 other postsecondary teaching occupations numbered 25-1011.00 through 25-1199.99.

Teach or instruct vocational or occupational subjects at the postsecondary level (but at less than the baccalaureate) to students who have graduated or left high school. Includes correspondence school instructors; industrial, commercial, and government training instructors; and adult education teachers and instructors who prepare persons to operate industrial machinery and equipment and transportation and communications equipment. Teaching may take place in public or private schools whose primary business is education or in a school associated with an organization whose primary business is other than education.

Supervise and monitor students' use of tools and equipment. Observe and evaluate students' work to determine progress, provide feedback, and make suggestions for improvement. Present lectures and conduct discussions to increase students' knowledge and competence, using visual aids such as graphs, charts, videotapes, and slides. Administer oral, written, or performance tests to measure progress and to evaluate training effectiveness. Prepare reports and maintain records such as student grades, attendance rolls, and training activity details. Supervise independent or group projects, field placements, laboratory work, or other training. Determine training needs of students or workers. Provide individualized instruction and tutorial or remedial instruction. Conduct on-the-job training, classes, or training sessions to teach and demonstrate principles, techniques, procedures, and methods of designated subjects. Develop curricula and plan course content and methods of instruction. Prepare outlines of instructional programs and training schedules and establish course goals. Integrate academic and vocational curricula so that students can obtain a variety of skills. Develop teaching aids such as instructional software, multimedia visual aids, or study materials. Select and assemble books, materials, supplies, and equipment for training, courses, or projects. Advise students on course selection, career decisions, and other academic and vocational concerns. Participate in conferences, seminars, and training sessions to keep abreast of developments in the field and integrate relevant information into training programs. Serve on faculty and school committees concerned with budgeting, curriculum revision, and course and diploma requirements. Review enrollment applications and correspond with applicants to obtain additional information. Arrange for lectures by experts in designated fields.

GOE Information—Interest Area: 05. Education and Training. **Work Group:** 05.03. Postsecondary and Adult Teaching and Instructing. **Personality Type**—Social. Social occupations frequently involve working with, communicating with, and teaching people. These occupations often involve helping or providing service to others. **Work Values**—Authority; Social Service; Creativity; Achievement; Responsibility; Working Conditions. **Skills**—Instructing; Learning Strategies; Social Perceptiveness; Service Orientation; Speaking; Time Management. **Abilities**—*Cognitive:* Oral Expression; Written Expression; Written Comprehension; Oral Comprehension; Originality; Fluency of Ideas. *Psychomotor:* None met the criteria. *Physical:* None met the criteria. *Sensory:* Speech Clarity; Far Vision; Speech Recognition; Near Vision. **General Work Activities**—*Information Input:* Monitoring Processes, Materials, or Surroundings; Getting Information; Identifying Objects, Actions, and Events. *Mental Process:* Updating and Using Relevant Knowledge; Organizing, Planning, and Prioritizing; Thinking Creatively. *Work Output:* Handling and Moving Objects; Documenting or Recording Information; Performing General Physical Activities. *Interacting with Others:* Teaching Others; Establishing and Maintaining Interpersonal Relationships; Coaching and Developing Others. **Physical Work Conditions**—Indoors; Standing; Using Hands on Objects, Tools, or Controls. **Other Job Characteristics**—Need to Be Exact or Accurate; Repeat Same Tasks.

Experience—Job Zone 4. A minimum of two to four years of work-related skill, knowledge, or experience is needed. **Job Preparation**—SVP 7.0 to less than 8.0—two years to less than 10 years. **Knowledges**—Education and Training; Psychology; Therapy and Counseling; Computers and Electronics; Sales and Marketing; Design. **Instructional Programs**—Agricultural Teacher Education; Business Teacher Education; Health Occupations Teacher Education; Sales and Marketing Operations/Marketing and Distribution Teacher Education; Teacher Education and Professional Development, Specific Subject Areas, Other; Technical Teacher Education; Technology Teacher Education/Industrial Arts Teacher Education; Trade and Industrial Teacher Education.

Related SOC Job—25-1194 Vocational Education Teachers, Postsecondary. **Related OOH Job**—Teachers—Postsecondary. **Related DOT Jobs**—075.127-010 Instructor, Psychiatric Aide; 097.221-010 Instructor, Vocational Training; 099.227-014 Instructor, Correspondence School; 099.227-018 Instructor, Ground Services; 166.221-010 Instructor, Technical Training; 166.227-010 Training Representative; 235.222-010 Private-Branch-Exchange Service Adviser; 239.227-010 Customer-Service-Representative Instructor; 375.227-010 Police-Academy Instructor; 378.227-010 Marksmanship Instructor; 522.264-010 Training Technician; others.

25-1199.99 Postsecondary Teachers, All Other

- **Education/Training Required: Master's degree**
- **Employed: 267,280**
- **Annual Earnings: $61,410**
- **Growth: 32.2%**
- **Annual Job Openings: 329,000**

The job openings listed here are shared with 37 other postsecondary teaching occupations numbered 25-1011.00 through 25-1194.00.

All postsecondary teachers not listed separately.

No task data available.

Note: The Department of Labor has not collected some data for this job, so it has fewer details than the other descriptions.

Related SOC Job—25-1199 Postsecondary Teachers, All Other. **Related OOH Job**—Teachers—Postsecondary. **Related DOT Job**—No data available.

25-2000 Primary, Secondary, and Special Education School Teachers

25-2011.00 Preschool Teachers, Except Special Education

- **Education/Training Required: Postsecondary vocational training**
- **Employed: 348,690**
- **Annual Earnings: $21,990**
- **Growth: 33.1%**
- **Annual Job Openings: 77,000**

Instruct children (normally up to 5 years of age) in activities designed to promote social, physical, and intellectual growth needed for primary school in preschool, day care center, or other child development facility. May be required to hold state certification.

Provide a variety of materials and resources for children to explore, manipulate, and use, both in learning activities and in imaginative play. Attend to children's basic needs by feeding them, dressing them, and changing their diapers. Establish and enforce rules for behavior and procedures for maintaining order. Read books to entire classes or to small groups. Teach basic skills such as color, shape, number, and letter recognition; personal hygiene; and social skills. Organize and lead activities designed to promote physical, mental, and social development, such as games, arts and crafts, music, storytelling, and field trips. Observe and evaluate children's performance, behavior, social development, and physical health. Meet with parents and guardians to discuss their children's progress and needs, determine their priorities for their children, and suggest ways that they can promote learning and development. Identify children showing signs of emotional, developmental, or health-related problems and discuss them with supervisors, parents or guardians, and child development specialists. Enforce all administration policies and rules governing students. Prepare materials and classrooms for class activities. Serve meals and snacks in accordance with nutritional guidelines. Teach proper eating habits and personal hygiene. Assimilate arriving children to the school environment by greeting them, helping them remove outerwear, and selecting activities of interest to them. Adapt teaching methods and instructional materials to meet students' varying needs and interests. Establish clear objectives for all lessons, units, and projects and communicate those objectives to children. Demonstrate activities to children. Arrange indoor and outdoor space to facilitate creative play, motor-skill activities, and safety. Plan and conduct activities for a balanced program of instruction, demonstration, and work time that provides students with opportunities to observe, question, and investigate. Maintain accurate and complete student records as required by laws, district policies, and administrative regulations.

GOE Information—Interest Area: 05. Education and Training. **Work Group:** 05.02. Preschool, Elementary, and Secondary Teaching and Instructing. **Personality Type**—Social. Social occupations frequently involve working with, communicating with, and teaching people. These occupations often involve helping or providing service to others. **Work Values**—Social Service; Authority; Creativity; Responsibility; Achievement; Autonomy. **Skills**—Learning Strategies; Social Perceptiveness; Writing; Negotiation; Instructing; Monitoring. **Abilities**—*Cognitive:* Originality; Oral Expression; Speed of Closure; Fluency of Ideas. *Psychomotor:* None met the criteria. *Physical:* Trunk Strength. *Sensory:* Speech Recognition; Hearing Sensitivity; Auditory Attention; Speech Clarity; Visual Color Discrimination. **General Work Activities**—*Information Input:* Getting Information; Identifying Objects, Actions, and Events; Monitoring Processes, Materials, or Surroundings. *Mental Process:* Organizing, Planning, and Prioritizing; Thinking Creatively; Making Decisions and Solving Problems. *Work Output:* Handling and Moving Objects; Performing General Physical Activities; Documenting or Recording Information. *Interacting with Others:* Establishing and Maintaining Interpersonal Relationships; Assisting and Caring for Others; Communicating with Other Workers. **Physical Work Conditions**—Indoors; Standing; Walking and Running; Bending or Twisting the Body. **Other Job Characteristics**—Need to Be Exact or Accurate.

Experience—Job Zone 3. Previous work-related skill, knowledge, or experience is required. **Job Preparation**—SVP 6.0 to less than 7.0—more than one year and less than four years. **Knowledges**—

Philosophy and Theology; Sociology and Anthropology; Customer and Personal Service; Psychology; Education and Training. **Instructional Programs**—Child Care and Support Services Management; Early Childhood Education and Teaching.

Related SOC Job—25-2011 Preschool Teachers, Except Special Education. **Related OOH Job**—Teachers—Preschool, Kindergarten, Elementary, Middle, and Secondary. **Related DOT Job**—092.227-018 Teacher, Preschool.

25-2012.00 Kindergarten Teachers, Except Special Education

- **Education/Training Required: Bachelor's degree**
- **Employed: 171,290**
- **Annual Earnings: $42,230**
- **Growth: 22.4%**
- **Annual Job Openings: 28,000**

Teach elemental natural and social science, personal hygiene, music, art, and literature to children from 4 to 6 years old. Promote physical, mental, and social development. May be required to hold state certification.

Teach basic skills such as color, shape, number, and letter recognition; personal hygiene; and social skills. Establish and enforce rules for behavior and policies and procedures to maintain order among students. Observe and evaluate children's performance, behavior, social development, and physical health. Instruct students individually and in groups, adapting teaching methods to meet students' varying needs and interests. Read books to entire classes or to small groups. Demonstrate activities to children. Provide a variety of materials and resources for children to explore, manipulate, and use, both in learning activities and in imaginative play. Plan and conduct activities for a balanced program of instruction, demonstration, and work time that provides students with opportunities to observe, question, and investigate. Confer with parents or guardians, other teachers, counselors, and administrators to resolve students' behavioral and academic problems. Prepare children for later grades by encouraging them to explore learning opportunities and to persevere with challenging tasks. Establish clear objectives for all lessons, units, and projects and communicate those objectives to children. Prepare and implement remedial programs for students requiring extra help. Meet with parents and guardians to discuss their children's progress and to determine their priorities for their children and their resource needs. Prepare objectives and outlines for courses of study, following curriculum guidelines or requirements of states and schools. Organize and lead activities designed to promote physical, mental, and social development such as games, arts and crafts, music, and storytelling. Guide and counsel students with adjustment or academic problems or special academic interests. Identify children showing signs of emotional, developmental, or health-related problems and discuss them with supervisors, parents or guardians, and child development specialists. Instruct and monitor students in the use and care of equipment and materials to prevent injuries and damage. Assimilate arriving children to the school environment by greeting them, helping them remove outerwear, and selecting activities of interest to them.

GOE Information—Interest Area: 05. Education and Training. **Work Group:** 05.02. Preschool, Elementary, and Secondary Teaching and Instructing. **Personality Type**—Social. Social occupations frequently involve working with, communicating with, and teaching people. These occupations often involve helping or providing service to others. **Work Values**—Social Service; Authority; Creativity;

Responsibility; Achievement; Autonomy. **Skills**—Instructing; Learning Strategies; Social Perceptiveness; Monitoring; Time Management; Writing. **Abilities**—*Cognitive:* Originality; Fluency of Ideas; Problem Sensitivity; Oral Expression; Written Expression; Oral Comprehension. *Psychomotor:* None met the criteria. *Physical:* None met the criteria. *Sensory:* Speech Recognition; Speech Clarity; Hearing Sensitivity; Visual Color Discrimination; Far Vision; Auditory Attention. **General Work Activities**—*Information Input:* Monitoring Processes, Materials, or Surroundings; Identifying Objects, Actions, and Events; Getting Information. *Mental Process:* Organizing, Planning, and Prioritizing; Updating and Using Relevant Knowledge; Thinking Creatively. *Work Output:* Documenting or Recording Information; Handling and Moving Objects; Interacting With Computers. *Interacting with Others:* Establishing and Maintaining Interpersonal Relationships; Coaching and Developing Others; Teaching Others. **Physical Work Conditions**—Indoors; Disease or Infections; Standing. **Other Job Characteristics**—Need to Be Exact or Accurate.

Experience—Job Zone 4. A minimum of two to four years of work-related skill, knowledge, or experience is needed. **Job Preparation**—SVP 7.0 to less than 8.0—two years to less than 10 years. **Knowledges**—History and Archeology; Geography; Sociology and Anthropology; Philosophy and Theology; Education and Training; Psychology. **Instructional Program**—Early Childhood Education and Teaching.

Related SOC Job—25-2012 Kindergarten Teachers, Except Special Education. **Related OOH Job**—Teachers—Preschool, Kindergarten, Elementary, Middle, and Secondary. **Related DOT Job**—092.227-014 Teacher, Kindergarten.

25-2021.00 Elementary School Teachers, Except Special Education

- **Education/Training Required: Bachelor's degree**
- **Employed: 1,486,650**
- **Annual Earnings: $44,040**
- **Growth: 18.2%**
- **Annual Job Openings: 203,000**

Teach pupils in public or private schools at the elementary level basic academic, social, and other formative skills.

Establish and enforce rules for behavior and procedures for maintaining order among the students for whom they are responsible. Observe and evaluate students' performance, behavior, social development, and physical health. Prepare materials and classrooms for class activities. Adapt teaching methods and instructional materials to meet students' varying needs and interests. Plan and conduct activities for a balanced program of instruction, demonstration, and work time that provides students with opportunities to observe, question, and investigate. Instruct students individually and in groups, using various teaching methods such as lectures, discussions, and demonstrations. Establish clear objectives for all lessons, units, and projects and communicate those objectives to students. Assign and grade classwork and homework. Read books to entire classes or small groups. Prepare, administer, and grade tests and assignments in order to evaluate students' progress. Confer with parents or guardians, teachers, counselors, and administrators to resolve students' behavioral and academic problems. Meet with parents and guardians to discuss their children's progress and to determine their priorities for their children and their resource needs. Prepare students for later grades by encouraging them to explore learning opportunities and to persevere with challenging tasks. Maintain accurate and complete student records as required by laws, district policies, and administrative regulations. Guide and counsel students with adjustment or academic problems or special academic interests. Prepare and implement remedial programs for students requiring extra help. Prepare objectives and outlines for courses of study, following curriculum guidelines or requirements of states and schools. Provide a variety of materials and resources for children to explore, manipulate, and use, both in learning activities and in imaginative play. Enforce administration policies and rules governing students. Confer with other staff members to plan and schedule lessons promoting learning, following approved curricula.

GOE Information—Interest Area: 05. Education and Training. **Work Group:** 05.02. Preschool, Elementary, and Secondary Teaching and Instructing. **Personality Type**—Social. Social occupations frequently involve working with, communicating with, and teaching people. These occupations often involve helping or providing service to others. **Work Values**—Authority; Social Service; Creativity; Responsibility; Achievement; Autonomy. **Skills**—Instructing; Learning Strategies; Monitoring; Social Perceptiveness; Persuasion; Speaking. **Abilities**—*Cognitive:* Originality; Fluency of Ideas; Oral Expression; Written Expression; Written Comprehension; Oral Comprehension. *Psychomotor:* None met the criteria. *Physical:* Trunk Strength. *Sensory:* Speech Clarity; Speech Recognition; Far Vision; Hearing Sensitivity; Visual Color Discrimination; Auditory Attention. **General Work Activities**—*Information Input:* Getting Information; Identifying Objects, Actions, and Events; Monitoring Processes, Materials, or Surroundings. *Mental Process:* Organizing, Planning, and Prioritizing; Thinking Creatively; Updating and Using Relevant Knowledge. *Work Output:* Documenting or Recording Information; Handling and Moving Objects; Interacting With Computers. *Interacting with Others:* Establishing and Maintaining Interpersonal Relationships; Coaching and Developing Others; Teaching Others. **Physical Work Conditions**—Indoors; Noisy; Disease or Infections; Standing. **Other Job Characteristics**—Need to Be Exact or Accurate.

Experience—Job Zone 4. A minimum of two to four years of work-related skill, knowledge, or experience is needed. **Job Preparation**—SVP 7.0 to less than 8.0—two years to less than 10 years. **Knowledges**—Geography; History and Archeology; Sociology and Anthropology; Education and Training; Therapy and Counseling; Philosophy and Theology. **Instructional Programs**—Elementary Education and Teaching; Teacher Education, Multiple Levels.

Related SOC Job—25-2021 Elementary School Teachers, Except Special Education. **Related OOH Job**—Teachers—Preschool, Kindergarten, Elementary, Middle, and Secondary. **Related DOT Job**—092.227-010 Teacher, Elementary School.

25-2022.00 Middle School Teachers, Except Special and Vocational Education

- **Education/Training Required:** Bachelor's degree
- **Employed:** 637,340
- **Annual Earnings:** $44,640
- **Growth:** 13.7%
- **Annual Job Openings:** 83,000

Teach students in public or private schools in one or more subjects at the middle, intermediate, or junior high level, which falls between elementary and senior high school as defined by applicable state laws and regulations.

Establish and enforce rules for behavior and procedures for maintaining order among the students for whom they are responsible. Adapt teaching methods and instructional materials to meet students' varying needs and interests. Instruct through lectures, discussions, and demonstrations in one or more subjects such as English, mathematics, or social studies. Prepare, administer, and grade tests and assignments to evaluate students' progress. Establish clear objectives for all lessons, units, and projects and communicate these objectives to students. Plan and conduct activities for a balanced program of instruction, demonstration, and work time that provides students with opportunities to observe, question, and investigate. Maintain accurate, complete, and correct student records as required by laws, district policies, and administrative regulations. Observe and evaluate students' performance, behavior, social development, and physical health. Assign lessons and correct homework. Prepare materials and classrooms for class activities. Enforce all administration policies and rules governing students. Confer with parents or guardians, other teachers, counselors, and administrators to resolve students' behavioral and academic problems. Prepare students for later grades by encouraging them to explore learning opportunities and to persevere with challenging tasks. Prepare objectives and outlines for courses of study, following curriculum guidelines or requirements of states and schools. Guide and counsel students with adjustment or academic problems or special academic interests. Meet with parents and guardians to discuss their children's progress and to determine their priorities for their children and their resource needs. Meet with other professionals to discuss individual students' needs and progress. Prepare and implement remedial programs for students requiring extra help. Prepare for assigned classes and show written evidence of preparation upon request of immediate supervisors. Instruct and monitor students in the use and care of equipment and materials to prevent injury and damage.

GOE Information—Interest Area: 05. Education and Training. **Work Group:** 05.02. Preschool, Elementary, and Secondary Teaching and Instructing. **Personality Type**—Social. Social occupations frequently involve working with, communicating with, and teaching people. These occupations often involve helping or providing service to others. **Work Values**—Social Service; Authority; Creativity; Responsibility; Achievement; Ability Utilization. **Skills**—Learning Strategies; Instructing; Social Perceptiveness; Monitoring; Time Management; Persuasion. **Abilities**—*Cognitive:* Originality; Written Expression; Oral Expression; Problem Sensitivity; Number Facility; Written Comprehension. *Psychomotor:* None met the criteria. *Physical:* None met the criteria. *Sensory:* Speech Clarity; Speech Recognition; Far Vision; Hearing Sensitivity; Auditory Attention; Visual Color Discrimination. **General Work Activities**—*Information Input:* Monitoring Processes, Materials, or Surroundings; Identifying Objects, Actions, and Events; Getting Information. *Mental Process:* Organizing, Planning, and Prioritizing; Updating and Using Relevant Knowledge; Thinking Creatively. *Work Output:* Documenting or Recording Information; Interacting With Computers; Handling and Moving Objects. *Interacting with Others:* Coaching and Developing Others; Establishing and Maintaining Interpersonal Relationships; Teaching Others. **Physical Work Conditions**—Indoors; Noisy; Standing. **Other Job Characteristics**—Need to Be Exact or Accurate.

Experience—Job Zone 4. A minimum of two to four years of work-related skill, knowledge, or experience is needed. **Job Preparation**—SVP 7.0 to less than 8.0—two years to less than 10 years. **Knowledges**—Sociology and Anthropology; Education and Training; History and Archeology; Philosophy and Theology; Geography; Therapy and Counseling. **Instructional Programs**—Art Teacher Education; Computer Teacher Education; English/Language Arts

Teacher Education; Family and Consumer Sciences/Home Economics Teacher Education; Foreign Language Teacher Education; Health Occupations Teacher Education; Health Teacher Education; History Teacher Education; Junior High/Intermediate/Middle School Education and Teaching; Mathematics Teacher Education; Music Teacher Education; Physical Education Teaching and Coaching; Reading Teacher Education; Science Teacher Education/General Science Teacher Education; Social Science Teacher Education; Social Studies Teacher Education; Teacher Education and Professional Development, Specific Subject Areas, Other; Technology Teacher Education/Industrial Arts Teacher Education.

Related SOC Job—25-2022 Middle School Teachers, Except Special and Vocational Education. **Related OOH Job**—Teachers—Preschool, Kindergarten, Elementary, Middle, and Secondary. **Related DOT Jobs**—091.227-010 Teacher, Secondary School; 099.224-010 Instructor, Physical Education.

25-2023.00 Vocational Education Teachers, Middle School

- **Education/Training Required: Work experience plus degree**
- **Employed: 15,380**
- **Annual Earnings: $43,820**
- **Growth: –0.9%**
- **Annual Job Openings: 2,000**

Teach or instruct vocational or occupational subjects at the middle school level.

Establish and enforce rules for behavior and procedures for maintaining order among the students for whom they are responsible. Instruct and monitor students in the use and care of equipment and materials to prevent injuries and damage. Instruct students individually and in groups, using various teaching methods such as lectures, discussions, and demonstrations. Maintain accurate and complete student records as required by laws, district policies, and administrative regulations. Prepare materials and classrooms for class activities. Establish clear objectives for all lessons, units, and projects and communicate those objectives to students. Plan and conduct activities for a balanced program of instruction, demonstration, and work time that provides students with opportunities to observe, question, and investigate. Adapt teaching methods and instructional materials to meet students' varying needs and interests. Prepare, administer, and grade tests and assignments to evaluate students' progress. Assign and grade classwork and homework. Enforce all administration policies and rules governing students. Observe and evaluate students' performance, behavior, social development, and physical health. Use computers, audiovisual aids, and other equipment and materials to supplement presentations. Prepare objectives and outlines for courses of study, following curriculum guidelines or requirements of states and schools. Prepare students for later educational experiences by encouraging them to explore learning opportunities and to persevere with challenging tasks. Meet with parents and guardians to discuss their children's progress and to determine their priorities for their children and their resource needs. Confer with parents or guardians, other teachers, counselors, and administrators to resolve students' behavioral and academic problems. Guide and counsel students with adjustment or academic problems or special academic interests. Prepare for assigned classes and show written evidence of preparation upon request of immediate supervisors. Prepare and implement remedial programs for students requiring extra help.

GOE Information—**Interest Area:** 05. Education and Training. **Work Group:** 05.02. Preschool, Elementary, and Secondary Teaching and Instructing. **Personality Type**—Social. Social occupations frequently involve working with, communicating with, and teaching people. These occupations often involve helping or providing service to others. **Work Values**—Social Service; Authority; Creativity; Responsibility; Achievement; Ability Utilization. **Skills**—Learning Strategies; Management of Financial Resources; Social Perceptiveness; Instructing; Time Management; Management of Material Resources. **Abilities**—*Cognitive:* Written Expression; Originality; Problem Sensitivity; Oral Expression; Number Facility; Written Comprehension. *Psychomotor:* None met the criteria. *Physical:* Trunk Strength. *Sensory:* Speech Clarity; Hearing Sensitivity; Visual Color Discrimination; Auditory Attention; Speech Recognition; Far Vision. **General Work Activities**—*Information Input:* Identifying Objects, Actions, and Events; Getting Information; Monitoring Processes, Materials, or Surroundings. *Mental Process:* Organizing, Planning, and Prioritizing; Updating and Using Relevant Knowledge; Thinking Creatively. *Work Output:* Handling and Moving Objects; Interacting With Computers; Performing General Physical Activities. *Interacting with Others:* Establishing and Maintaining Interpersonal Relationships; Teaching Others; Coaching and Developing Others. **Physical Work Conditions**—Indoors; Noisy; Standing; Using Hands on Objects, Tools, or Controls. **Other Job Characteristics**—Need to Be Exact or Accurate; Repeat Same Tasks.

Experience—Job Zone 4. A minimum of two to four years of work-related skill, knowledge, or experience is needed. **Job Preparation**—SVP 7.0 to less than 8.0—two years to less than 10 years. **Knowledges**—Education and Training; Psychology; Sociology and Anthropology; History and Archeology; Therapy and Counseling; Clerical Practices. **Instructional Programs**—Technology Education/Industrial Arts; Technology Teacher Education/Industrial Arts Teacher Education.

Related SOC Job—25-2023 Vocational Education Teachers, Middle School. **Related OOH Job**—Teachers—Preschool, Kindergarten, Elementary, Middle, and Secondary. **Related DOT Job**—091.221-010 Teacher, Industrial Arts.

25-2031.00 Secondary School Teachers, Except Special and Vocational Education

- **Education/Training Required: Bachelor's degree**
- **Employed: 1,015,740**
- **Annual Earnings: $46,060**
- **Growth: 14.4%**
- **Annual Job Openings: 107,000**

Instruct students in secondary public or private schools in one or more subjects at the secondary level, such as English, mathematics, or social studies. May be designated according to subject matter specialty, such as typing instructors, commercial teachers, or English teachers.

Establish and enforce rules for behavior and procedures for maintaining order among the students for whom they are responsible. Instruct through lectures, discussions, and demonstrations in one or more subjects such as English, mathematics, or social studies. Establish clear objectives for all lessons, units, and projects and communicate those objectives to students. Prepare, administer, and grade tests and assignments to evaluate students' progress. Prepare materials and classrooms for class activities. Adapt teaching methods and instructional materials to meet students' varying needs and interests. Assign and grade classwork and homework. Maintain accurate and complete student records as required by laws, district policies, and administrative regulations. Enforce all administration policies and rules governing students. Observe and evaluate students' performance, behavior, social development, and physical health. Plan and conduct activities for a balanced program of instruction, demonstration, and work time that provides students with opportunities to observe, question, and investigate. Prepare students for later grades by encouraging them to explore learning opportunities and to persevere with challenging tasks. Guide and counsel students with adjustment and/or academic problems or special academic interests. Instruct and monitor students in the use and care of equipment and materials to prevent injuries and damage. Prepare for assigned classes and show written evidence of preparation upon request of immediate supervisors. Meet with parents and guardians to discuss their children's progress and to determine their priorities for their children and their resource needs. Confer with parents or guardians, other teachers, counselors, and administrators in order to resolve students' behavioral and academic problems. Use computers, audiovisual aids, and other equipment and materials to supplement presentations. Prepare objectives and outlines for courses of study, following curriculum guidelines or requirements of states and schools. Meet with other professionals to discuss individual students' needs and progress.

GOE Information—Interest Area: 05. Education and Training. Work Group: 05.02. Preschool, Elementary, and Secondary Teaching and Instructing. Personality Type—Social. Social occupations frequently involve working with, communicating with, and teaching people. These occupations often involve helping or providing service to others. Work Values—Social Service; Authority; Creativity; Responsibility; Achievement; Ability Utilization. Skills—Learning Strategies; Persuasion; Social Perceptiveness; Instructing; Monitoring; Time Management. Abilities—*Cognitive:* Originality; Oral Expression; Number Facility; Written Expression; Fluency of Ideas; Oral Comprehension. *Psychomotor:* None met the criteria. *Physical:* Trunk Strength. *Sensory:* Speech Clarity; Far Vision; Speech Recognition; Hearing Sensitivity; Auditory Attention; Visual Color Discrimination. General Work Activities—*Information Input:* Identifying Objects, Actions, and Events; Getting Information; Monitoring Processes, Materials, or Surroundings. *Mental Process:* Organizing, Planning, and Prioritizing; Updating and Using Relevant Knowledge; Making Decisions and Solving Problems. *Work Output:* Interacting With Computers; Documenting or Recording Information; Handling and Moving Objects. *Interacting with Others:* Establishing and Maintaining Interpersonal Relationships; Communicating with Other Workers; Coaching and Developing Others. Physical Work Conditions—Indoors; Noisy; Standing. Other Job Characteristics—Need to Be Exact or Accurate.

Experience—Job Zone 4. A minimum of two to four years of work-related skill, knowledge, or experience is needed. Job Preparation—SVP 7.0 to less than 8.0—two years to less than 10 years. Knowledges—Education and Training; History and Archeology; Philosophy and Theology; Sociology and Anthropology; Geography; Therapy and Counseling. Instructional Programs—Agricultural Teacher Education; Art Teacher Education; Biology Teacher Education; Business Teacher Education; Chemistry Teacher Education; Computer Teacher Education; Drama and Dance Teacher Education; Driver and Safety Teacher Education; English/Language Arts Teacher Education; Family and Consumer Sciences/Home Economics Teacher Education; Foreign Language Teacher Education; French Language Teacher Education; Geography Teacher Education; German Language Teacher Education; Health Occupations Teacher Education; Health Teacher Education; History Teacher Education; Junior High/Intermediate/Middle School Education and Teaching; Latin Teacher Education; Mathematics Teacher Education; Music Teacher Education; Physical Education Teaching and Coaching; Physics Teacher Education; Reading Teacher Education; Sales and

Marketing Operations/Marketing and Distribution Teacher Education; Science Teacher Education/General Science Teacher Education; Secondary Education and Teaching; Social Science Teacher Education; Social Studies Teacher Education; Spanish Language Teacher Education; Speech Teacher Education; Teacher Education and Professional Development, Specific Subject Areas, Other; Teacher Education, Multiple Levels; Technology Teacher Education/Industrial Arts Teacher Education.

Related SOC Job—25-2031 Secondary School Teachers, Except Special and Vocational Education. Related OOH Job—Teachers—Preschool, Kindergarten, Elementary, Middle, and Secondary. Related DOT Jobs—091.227-010 Teacher, Secondary School; 099.224-010 Instructor, Physical Education; 099.227-022 Instructor, Military Science.

25-2032.00 Vocational Education Teachers, Secondary School

- **Education/Training Required: Work experience plus degree**
- **Employed: 96,600**
- **Annual Earnings: $47,090**
- **Growth: 9.1%**
- **Annual Job Openings: 10,000**

Teach or instruct vocational or occupational subjects at the secondary school level.

Prepare materials and classroom for class activities. Maintain accurate and complete student records as required by law, district policy, and administrative regulations. Instruct students individually and in groups, using various teaching methods such as lectures, discussions, and demonstrations. Observe and evaluate students' performance, behavior, social development, and physical health. Establish and enforce rules for behavior and procedures for maintaining order among the students for whom they are responsible. Instruct and monitor students the in use and care of equipment and materials to prevent injury and damage. Plan and conduct activities for a balanced program of instruction, demonstration, and work time that provides students with opportunities to observe, question, and investigate. Prepare, administer, and grade tests and assignments to evaluate students' progress. Enforce all administration policies and rules governing students. Assign and grade classwork and homework. Instruct students in the knowledge and skills required in a specific occupation or occupational field, using a systematic plan of lectures; discussions; audiovisual presentations; and laboratory, shop, and field studies. Establish clear objectives for all lessons, units, and projects and communicate those objectives to students. Use computers, audiovisual aids, and other equipment and materials to supplement presentations. Plan and supervise work-experience programs in businesses, industrial shops, and school laboratories. Prepare students for later grades by encouraging them to explore learning opportunities and to persevere with challenging tasks. Confer with parents or guardians, other teachers, counselors, and administrators in order to resolve students' behavioral and academic problems. Guide and counsel students with adjustment or academic problems or special academic interests. Prepare objectives and outlines for courses of study, following curriculum guidelines or requirements of states and schools. Keep informed about trends in education and subject matter specialties.

GOE Information—Interest Area: 05. Education and Training. Work Group: 05.02. Preschool, Elementary, and Secondary Teaching and Instructing. Personality Type—Social. Social occupations frequently involve working with, communicating with, and teaching people. These occupations often involve helping or providing service to others. **Work Values**—Social Service; Authority; Creativity; Responsibility; Achievement; Ability Utilization. **Skills**— Management of Financial Resources; Learning Strategies; Social Perceptiveness; Instructing; Management of Material Resources; Persuasion. **Abilities**—*Cognitive:* Originality; Oral Expression; Written Expression; Written Comprehension; Fluency of Ideas; Category Flexibility. *Psychomotor:* Response Orientation; Arm-Hand Steadiness. *Physical:* Trunk Strength. *Sensory:* Hearing Sensitivity; Speech Clarity; Far Vision; Visual Color Discrimination; Speech Recognition; Auditory Attention. **General Work Activities**— *Information Input:* Monitoring Processes, Materials, or Surroundings; Getting Information; Identifying Objects, Actions, and Events. *Mental Process:* Updating and Using Relevant Knowledge; Organizing, Planning, and Prioritizing; Scheduling Work and Activities. *Work Output:* Interacting With Computers; Documenting or Recording Information; Handling and Moving Objects. *Interacting with Others:* Teaching Others; Establishing and Maintaining Interpersonal Relationships; Coaching and Developing Others. **Physical Work Conditions**—Indoors; Noisy; Standing; Using Hands on Objects, Tools, or Controls. **Other Job Characteristics**—Need to Be Exact or Accurate.

Experience—Job Zone 4. A minimum of two to four years of work-related skill, knowledge, or experience is needed. **Job Preparation**— SVP 7.0 to less than 8.0—two years to less than 10 years. **Knowledges**—Education and Training; Therapy and Counseling; Sociology and Anthropology; Psychology; Design; Clerical Practices. **Instructional Programs**—Technology Education/Industrial Arts; Technology Teacher Education/Industrial Arts Teacher Education.

Related SOC Job—25-2032 Vocational Education Teachers, Secondary School. **Related OOH Job**—Teachers—Preschool, Kindergarten, Elementary, Middle, and Secondary. **Related DOT Job**—091.221-010 Teacher, Industrial Arts.

25-2041.00 Special Education Teachers, Preschool, Kindergarten, and Elementary School

- **Education/Training Required: Bachelor's degree**
- **Employed: 214,060**
- **Annual Earnings: $44,630**
- **Growth: 23.3%**
- **Annual Job Openings: 18,000**

Teach elementary and preschool school subjects to educationally and physically handicapped students. Includes teachers who specialize and work with audibly and visually handicapped students and those who teach basic academic and life processes skills to the mentally impaired.

Instruct students in academic subjects, using a variety of techniques such as phonetics, multisensory learning, and repetition to reinforce learning and to meet students' varying needs and interests. Employ special educational strategies and techniques during instruction to improve the development of sensory- and perceptual-motor skills, language, cognition, and memory. Teach socially acceptable behavior, employing techniques such as behavior modification and positive reinforcement. Modify the general education curriculum for special-needs students based upon a variety of instructional techniques and technologies. Meet with parents and guardians to discuss their children's progress and to determine their priorities for their children and their resource needs. Plan and conduct activities for a balanced program of instruction, demonstration, and work time that

provides students with opportunities to observe, question, and investigate. Establish and enforce rules for behavior and policies and procedures to maintain order among the students for whom they are responsible. Confer with parents, administrators, testing specialists, social workers, and professionals to develop individual educational plans designed to promote students' educational, physical, and social development. Maintain accurate and complete student records and prepare reports on children and activities as required by laws, district policies, and administrative regulations. Establish clear objectives for all lessons, units, and projects and communicate those objectives to students. Develop and implement strategies to meet the needs of students with a variety of handicapping conditions. Prepare classrooms for class activities and provide a variety of materials and resources for children to explore, manipulate, and use, both in learning activities and imaginative play. Confer with parents or guardians, teachers, counselors, and administrators to resolve students' behavioral and academic problems. Observe and evaluate students' performance, behavior, social development, and physical health. Teach students personal development skills such as goal setting, independence, and self-advocacy.

GOE Information—**Interest Area:** 05. Education and Training. **Work Group:** 05.02. Preschool, Elementary, and Secondary Teaching and Instructing. **Personality Type**—Social. Social occupations frequently involve working with, communicating with, and teaching people. These occupations often involve helping or providing service to others. **Work Values**—Social Service; Authority; Creativity; Achievement; Responsibility; Ability Utilization. **Skills**—Learning Strategies; Instructing; Social Perceptiveness; Monitoring; Negotiation; Time Management. **Abilities**—*Cognitive:* Written Expression; Originality; Fluency of Ideas; Written Comprehension; Oral Comprehension; Oral Expression. *Psychomotor:* None met the criteria. *Physical:* Trunk Strength. *Sensory:* Speech Clarity; Speech Recognition; Hearing Sensitivity; Far Vision; Auditory Attention; Visual Color Discrimination. **General Work Activities**—*Information Input:* Monitoring Processes, Materials, or Surroundings; Identifying Objects, Actions, and Events; Getting Information. *Mental Process:* Organizing, Planning, and Prioritizing; Updating and Using Relevant Knowledge; Making Decisions and Solving Problems. *Work Output:* Documenting or Recording Information; Interacting With Computers; Performing General Physical Activities. *Interacting with Others:* Establishing and Maintaining Interpersonal Relationships; Teaching Others; Coaching and Developing Others. **Physical Work Conditions**—Indoors; Noisy; Standing. **Other Job Characteristics**— Need to Be Exact or Accurate.

Experience—Job Zone 4. A minimum of two to four years of work-related skill, knowledge, or experience is needed. **Job Preparation**— SVP 7.0 to less than 8.0—two years to less than 10 years. **Knowledges**—Psychology; History and Archeology; Therapy and Counseling; Geography; Philosophy and Theology; Sociology and Anthropology. **Instructional Programs**—Education/Teaching of Individuals with Autism; Education/Teaching of Individuals with Emotional Disturbances; Education/Teaching of Individuals with Hearing Impairments, Including Deafness; Education/Teaching of Individuals with Mental Retardation; Education/Teaching of Individuals with Multiple Disabilities; Education/Teaching of Individuals with Orthopedic and Other Physical Health Impairments; Education/Teaching of Individuals with Specific Learning Disabilities; Education/Teaching of Individuals with Speech or Language Impairments; Education/Teaching of Individuals with Traumatic Brain Injuries; Education/Teaching of Individuals with Vision Impairments, Including Blindness; Special Education and Teaching, Other; Special Education, General.

Related SOC Job—25-2041 Special Education Teachers, Preschool, Kindergarten, and Elementary School. **Related OOH Job**—Teachers—Special Education. **Related DOT Jobs**—094.224-010 Teacher, Hearing Impaired; 094.224-014 Teacher, Physically Impaired; 094.224-018 Teacher, Visually Impaired; 094.227-010 Teacher, Emotionally Impaired; 094.227-022 Teacher, Mentally Impaired; 094.227-030 Teacher, Learning Disabled; 094.267-010 Evaluator; 099.227-042 Teacher, Resource; 195.227-018 Teacher, Home Therapy.

25-2042.00 Special Education Teachers, Middle School

- **Education/Training Required: Bachelor's degree**
- **Employed: 103,480**
- **Annual Earnings: $45,490**
- **Growth: 19.9%**
- **Annual Job Openings: 8,000**

Teach middle school subjects to educationally and physically handicapped students. Includes teachers who specialize and work with audibly and visually handicapped students and those who teach basic academic and life processes skills to the mentally impaired.

Establish and enforce rules for behavior and policies and procedures to maintain order among students. Maintain accurate and complete student records and prepare reports on children and activities as required by laws, district policies, and administrative regulations. Prepare materials and classrooms for class activities. Confer with parents, administrators, testing specialists, social workers, and professionals to develop individual educational plans designed to promote students' educational, physical, and social development. Develop and implement strategies to meet the needs of students with a variety of handicapping conditions. Teach socially acceptable behavior, employing techniques such as behavior modification and positive reinforcement. Modify the general education curriculum for special-needs students based upon a variety of instructional techniques and instructional technology. Employ special educational strategies and techniques during instruction to improve the development of sensory- and perceptual-motor skills, language, cognition, and memory. Confer with parents or guardians, other teachers, counselors, and administrators to resolve students' behavioral and academic problems. Instruct through lectures, discussions, and demonstrations in one or more subjects such as English, mathematics, or social studies. Coordinate placement of students with special needs into mainstream classes. Meet with parents and guardians to discuss their children's progress and to determine their priorities for their children and their resource needs. Guide and counsel students with adjustment or academic problems or special academic interests. Prepare, administer, and grade tests and assignments to evaluate students' progress. Observe and evaluate students' performance, behavior, social development, and physical health. Establish clear objectives for all lessons, units, and projects and communicate those objectives to students. Teach students personal development skills such as goal setting, independence, and self-advocacy. Plan and conduct activities for a balanced program of instruction, demonstration, and work time that provides students with opportunities to observe, question, and investigate.

GOE Information—**Interest Area:** 05. Education and Training. **Work Group:** 05.02. Preschool, Elementary, and Secondary Teaching and Instructing. **Personality Type**—Social. Social occupations frequently involve working with, communicating with, and teaching people. These occupations often involve helping or providing service to others. **Work Values**—Social Service; Authority; Creativity; Achievement; Responsibility; Ability Utilization. **Skills**—Learning Strategies; Social Perceptiveness; Instructing; Monitoring; Persuasion; Negotiation. **Abilities**—*Cognitive:* Originality; Written Expression; Written Comprehension; Oral Expression; Number Facility; Fluency of Ideas. *Psychomotor:* None met the criteria. *Physical:* None met the criteria. *Sensory:* Speech Clarity; Speech Recognition; Hearing Sensitivity; Far Vision; Visual Color Discrimination; Auditory Attention. **General Work Activities**—*Information Input:* Monitoring Processes, Materials, or Surroundings; Getting Information; Identifying Objects, Actions, and Events. *Mental Process:* Organizing, Planning, and Prioritizing; Updating and Using Relevant Knowledge; Making Decisions and Solving Problems. *Work Output:* Documenting or Recording Information; Interacting With Computers; Handling and Moving Objects. *Interacting with Others:* Establishing and Maintaining Interpersonal Relationships; Teaching Others; Coaching and Developing Others. **Physical Work Conditions**—Indoors; Noisy; Standing. **Other Job Characteristics**—Need to Be Exact or Accurate.

Experience—Job Zone 4. A minimum of two to four years of work-related skill, knowledge, or experience is needed. **Job Preparation**—SVP 7.0 to less than 8.0–two years to less than 10 years. **Knowledges**—Geography; History and Archeology; Psychology; Therapy and Counseling; Sociology and Anthropology; Education and Training. **Instructional Program**—Special Education, General.

Related SOC Job—25-2042 Special Education Teachers, Middle School. **Related OOH Job**—Teachers—Special Education. **Related DOT Jobs**—094.224-010 Teacher, Hearing Impaired; 094.224-014 Teacher, Physically Impaired; 094.224-018 Teacher, Visually Impaired; 094.227-010 Teacher, Emotionally Impaired; 094.227-022 Teacher, Mentally Impaired; 094.227-026 Teacher, Vocational Training; 094.227-030 Teacher, Learning Disabled; 099.227-042 Teacher, Resource.

25-2043.00 Special Education Teachers, Secondary School

- **Education/Training Required: Bachelor's degree**
- **Employed: 136,290**
- **Annual Earnings: $46,820**
- **Growth: 17.9%**
- **Annual Job Openings: 11,000**

Teach secondary school subjects to educationally and physically handicapped students. Includes teachers who specialize and work with audibly and visually handicapped students and those who teach basic academic and life processes skills to the mentally impaired.

Maintain accurate and complete student records and prepare reports on children and activities as required by laws, district policies, and administrative regulations. Prepare materials and classrooms for class activities. Teach socially acceptable behavior, employing techniques such as behavior modification and positive reinforcement. Establish and enforce rules for behavior and policies and procedures to maintain order among students. Confer with parents, administrators, testing specialists, social workers, and professionals to develop individual educational plans designed to promote students' educational, physical, and social development. Instruct through lectures, discussions, and demonstrations in one or more subjects such as English, mathematics, or social studies. Employ special educational strategies and techniques during instruction to improve the development of sensory- and perceptual-motor skills, language, cognition, and memory. Plan and conduct activities for a balanced program of instruction, demonstration, and work time that provides students with opportunities to observe, question, and investigate. Prepare students for later grades by encouraging them to explore learning opportunities and to persevere with challenging tasks. Teach personal development skills such as goal setting, independence, and self-advocacy. Establish clear objectives for all lessons, units, and projects and communicate those objectives to students. Develop and implement strategies to meet the needs of students with a variety of handicapping conditions. Modify the general education curriculum for special-needs students based upon a variety of instructional techniques and technologies. Meet with other professionals to discuss individual students' needs and progress. Confer with parents or guardians, other teachers, counselors, and administrators to resolve students' behavioral and academic problems. Meet with parents and guardians to discuss their children's progress and to determine their priorities for their children and their resource needs. Guide and counsel students with adjustment or academic problems or special academic interests.

GOE Information—Interest Area: 05. Education and Training. **Work Group:** 05.02. Preschool, Elementary, and Secondary Teaching and Instructing. **Personality Type—**Social. Social occupations frequently involve working with, communicating with, and teaching people. These occupations often involve helping or providing service to others. **Work Values—**Social Service; Authority; Creativity; Achievement; Responsibility; Ability Utilization. **Skills—**Learning Strategies; Social Perceptiveness; Negotiation; Instructing; Persuasion; Service Orientation. **Abilities—***Cognitive:* Originality; Written Expression; Fluency of Ideas; Inductive Reasoning; Oral Expression; Problem Sensitivity. *Psychomotor:* None met the criteria. *Physical:* None met the criteria. *Sensory:* Speech Clarity; Speech Recognition. **General Work Activities—***Information Input:* Identifying Objects, Actions, and Events; Monitoring Processes, Materials, or Surroundings; Getting Information. *Mental Process:* Organizing, Planning, and Prioritizing; Updating and Using Relevant Knowledge; Thinking Creatively. *Work Output:* Documenting or Recording Information; Interacting With Computers. *Interacting with Others:* Establishing and Maintaining Interpersonal Relationships; Coaching and Developing Others; Communicating with Other Workers. **Physical Work Conditions—**Indoors; Noisy; Standing. **Other Job Characteristics—**Need to Be Exact or Accurate.

Experience—Job Zone 4. A minimum of two to four years of work-related skill, knowledge, or experience is needed. **Job Preparation—**SVP 7.0 to less than 8.0—two years to less than 10 years. **Knowledges—**Therapy and Counseling; History and Archeology; Geography; Psychology; Philosophy and Theology; Sociology and Anthropology. **Instructional Program—**Special Education, General.

Related SOC Job—25-2043 Special Education Teachers, Secondary School. **Related OOH Job—**Teachers—Special Education. **Related DOT Jobs—**094.107-010 Work-Study Coordinator, Special Education; 094.224-010 Teacher, Hearing Impaired; 094.224-014 Teacher, Physically Impaired; 094.224-018 Teacher, Visually Impaired; 094.227-010 Teacher, Emotionally Impaired; 094.227-022 Teacher, Mentally Impaired; 094.227-026 Teacher, Vocational Training; 094.227-030 Teacher, Learning Disabled; 099.227-042 Teacher, Resource.

25-3000 Other Teachers and Instructors

25-3011.00 Adult Literacy, Remedial Education, and GED Teachers and Instructors

- **Education/Training Required: Bachelor's degree**
- **Employed: 66,070**
- **Annual Earnings: $41,270**
- **Growth: 15.6%**
- **Annual Job Openings: 27,000**

Teach or instruct out-of-school youths and adults in remedial education classes, preparatory classes for the General Educational Development test, literacy, or English as a Second Language. Teaching may or may not take place in a traditional educational institution.

Adapt teaching methods and instructional materials to meet students' varying needs, abilities, and interests. Observe and evaluate students' work to determine progress and make suggestions for improvement. Instruct students individually and in groups, using various teaching methods such as lectures, discussions, and demonstrations. Plan and conduct activities for a balanced program of instruction, demonstration, and work time that provides students with opportunities to observe, question, and investigate. Maintain accurate and complete student records as required by laws or administrative policies. Prepare materials and classrooms for class activities. Establish clear objectives for all lessons, units, and projects and communicate those objectives to students. Conduct classes, workshops, and demonstrations to teach principles, techniques, or methods in subjects such as basic English language skills, life skills, and workforce entry skills. Prepare students for further education by encouraging them to explore learning opportunities and to persevere with challenging tasks. Establish and enforce rules for behavior and procedures for maintaining order among the students for whom they are responsible. Provide information, guidance, and preparation for the General Equivalency Diploma (GED) examination. Assign and grade classwork and homework. Observe students to determine qualifications, limitations, abilities, interests, and other individual characteristics. Register, orient, and assess new students according to standards and procedures. Prepare and implement remedial programs for students requiring extra help. Prepare and administer written, oral, and performance tests and issue grades in accordance with performance. Use computers, audiovisual aids, and other equipment and materials to supplement presentations. Prepare objectives and outlines for courses of study, following curriculum guidelines or requirements of states and schools. Guide and counsel students with adjustment or academic problems or special academic interests. Enforce administration policies and rules governing students.

GOE Information—Interest Area: 05. Education and Training. **Work Group:** 05.03. Postsecondary and Adult Teaching and Instructing. **Personality Type—**Social. Social occupations frequently involve working with, communicating with, and teaching people. These occupations often involve helping or providing service to others. **Work Values—**Authority; Social Service; Creativity; Achievement; Responsibility; Working Conditions. **Skills—**Instructing; Learning Strategies; Social Perceptiveness; Service Orientation; Persuasion; Speaking. **Abilities—***Cognitive:* Originality; Written Expression; Written Comprehension; Oral Expression; Number Facility; Fluency of Ideas. *Psychomotor:* None met the criteria. *Physical:* None met the criteria. *Sensory:* Speech Clarity; Far Vision; Speech Recognition; Hearing Sensitivity; Auditory Attention. **General Work Activities—** *Information Input:* Monitoring Processes, Materials, or Surroundings; Identifying Objects, Actions, and Events; Getting Information. *Mental Process:* Organizing, Planning, and Prioritizing; Updating and Using Relevant Knowledge; Thinking Creatively. *Work Output:* Documenting or Recording Information; Interacting With Computers. *Interacting with Others:* Establishing and Maintaining Interpersonal Relationships; Teaching Others; Coaching and Developing Others. **Physical Work Conditions—**Indoors; More Often Standing Than Sitting. **Other Job Characteristics—**Need to Be Exact or Accurate.

Experience—Job Zone 4. A minimum of two to four years of work-related skill, knowledge, or experience is needed. **Job Preparation—** SVP 7.0 to less than 8.0—two years to less than 10 years. **Knowledges—**Education and Training; History and Archeology; Sociology and Anthropology; Therapy and Counseling; Geography; English Language. **Instructional Programs—**Adult and Continuing Education and Teaching; Adult Literacy Tutor/Instructor; Bilingual and Multilingual Education; Multicultural Education; Teaching English as a Second or Foreign Language/ESL Language Instructor.

Related SOC Job—25-3011 Adult Literacy, Remedial Education, and GED Teachers and Instructors. **Related OOH Job—**Teachers—Adult Literacy and Remedial Education. **Related DOT Job—**099.227-030 Teacher, Adult Education.

25-3021.00 Self-Enrichment Education Teachers

- **Education/Training Required: Work experience in a related occupation**
- **Employed: 141,650**
- **Annual Earnings: $32,360**
- **Growth: 25.3%**
- **Annual Job Openings: 74,000**

Teach or instruct courses other than those that normally lead to an occupational objective or degree. Courses may include self-improvement, non-vocational, and nonacademic subjects. Teaching may or may not take place in a traditional educational institution.

Adapt teaching methods and instructional materials to meet students' varying needs and interests. Conduct classes, workshops, and demonstrations and provide individual instruction to teach topics and skills such as cooking, dancing, writing, physical fitness, photography, personal finance, and flying. Monitor students' performance to make suggestions for improvement and to ensure that they satisfy course standards, training requirements, and objectives. Observe students to determine qualifications, limitations, abilities, interests, and other individual characteristics. Instruct students individually and in groups, using various teaching methods such as lectures, discussions, and demonstrations. Establish clear objectives for all lessons, units, and projects and communicate those objectives to students. Instruct and monitor students in use and care of equipment and materials to prevent injury and damage. Prepare students for further development by encouraging them to explore learning opportunities and to persevere with challenging tasks. Prepare materials and classrooms for class activities. Enforce policies and rules governing students. Plan and conduct activities for a balanced program of instruction, demonstration, and work time that provides students with opportunities to observe, question, and investigate. Prepare instructional program objectives, outlines, and lesson plans.

Maintain accurate and complete student records as required by administrative policy. Participate in publicity planning and student recruitment. Plan and supervise class projects, field trips, visits by guest speakers, contests, or other experiential activities and guide students in learning from those activities. Attend professional meetings, conferences, and workshops in order to maintain and improve professional competence. Meet with other instructors to discuss individual students and their progress. Confer with other teachers and professionals to plan and schedule lessons promoting learning and development. Attend staff meetings and serve on committees as required. Prepare and administer written, oral, and performance tests and issue grades in accordance with performance.

GOE Information—Interest Area: 05. Education and Training. **Work Group:** 05.03. Postsecondary and Adult Teaching and Instructing. **Personality Type—**Social. Social occupations frequently involve working with, communicating with, and teaching people. These occupations often involve helping or providing service to others. **Work Values—**Authority; Social Service; Creativity; Achievement; Responsibility; Working Conditions. **Skills—**Instructing; Learning Strategies; Social Perceptiveness; Service Orientation; Monitoring; Speaking. **Abilities—***Cognitive:* Originality; Written Expression; Oral Expression; Oral Comprehension; Selective Attention. *Psychomotor:* None met the criteria. *Physical:* None met the criteria. *Sensory:* Speech Clarity; Speech Recognition. **General Work Activities—***Information Input:* Getting Information; Monitoring Processes, Materials, or Surroundings; Identifying Objects, Actions, and Events. *Mental Process:* Thinking Creatively; Organizing, Planning, and Prioritizing; Making Decisions and Solving Problems. *Work Output:* Performing General Physical Activities; Handling and Moving Objects; Documenting or Recording Information. *Interacting with Others:* Coaching and Developing Others; Teaching Others; Performing for or Working with the Public. **Physical Work Conditions—**Indoors; Standing. **Other Job Characteristics—**Need to Be Exact or Accurate.

Experience—Job Zone 3. Previous work-related skill, knowledge, or experience is required. **Job Preparation—**SVP 6.0 to less than 7.0— more than one year and less than four years. **Knowledges—**Fine Arts; Education and Training; Psychology; Customer and Personal Service; Sales and Marketing; Administration and Management. **Instructional Program—**Adult and Continuing Education and Teaching.

Related SOC Job—25-3021 Self-Enrichment Education Teachers. **Related OOH Job—**Teachers—Self-Enrichment Education. **Related DOT Jobs—**097.227-010 Instructor, Flying II; 099.223-010 Instructor, Driving; 099.224-014 Teacher, Adventure Education; 099.227-026 Instructor, Modeling; 099.227-030 Teacher, Adult Education; 099.227-038 Teacher; 149.021-010 Teacher, Art; 150.027-014 Teacher, Drama; 151.027-014 Instructor, Dancing; 152.021-010 Teacher, Music; 159.227-010 Instructor, Bridge; 169.127-010 Civil Preparedness Training Officer.

25-3099.99 Teachers and Instructors, All Other

- **Education/Training Required: Bachelor's degree**
- **Employed: 530,670**
- **Annual Earnings: $27,130**
- **Growth: 14.9%**
- **Annual Job Openings: 169,000**

All teachers and instructors not listed separately.

No task data available.

Note: The Department of Labor has not collected some data for this job, so it has fewer details than the other descriptions.

Related SOC Job—25-3099 Teachers and Instructors, All Other. **Related OOH Job**—None. **Related DOT Jobs**—076.224-014 Orientation And Mobility Therapist For The Blind; 090.227-018 Instructor, Extension Work; 099.227-034 Tutor.

25-4000 Librarians, Curators, and Archivists

25-4011.00 Archivists

- Education/Training Required: Master's degree
- Employed: 5,410
- Annual Earnings: $37,420
- Growth: 13.4%
- Annual Job Openings: 1,000

Appraise, edit, and direct safekeeping of permanent records and historically valuable documents. Participate in research activities based on archival materials.

Create and maintain accessible, retrievable computer archives and databases, incorporating current advances in electric information storage technology. Organize archival records and develop classification systems to facilitate access to archival materials. Authenticate and appraise historical documents and archival materials. Provide reference services and assistance for users needing archival materials. Direct activities of workers who assist in arranging, cataloguing, exhibiting, and maintaining collections of valuable materials. Prepare archival records, such as document descriptions, to allow easy access to information. Preserve records, documents, and objects, copying records to film, videotape, audiotape, disk, or computer formats as necessary. Establish and administer policy guidelines concerning public access and use of materials. Locate new materials and direct their acquisition and display. Research and record the origins and historical significance of archival materials. Specialize in an area of history or technology, researching topics or items relevant to collections to determine what should be retained or acquired. Coordinate educational and public outreach programs such as tours, workshops, lectures, and classes. Select and edit documents for publication and display, applying knowledge of subject, literary expression, and presentation techniques.

GOE Information—**Interest Area:** 05. Education and Training. **Work Group:** 05.05. Archival and Museum Services. **Personality Type**— Investigative. Investigative occupations frequently involve working with ideas and require an extensive amount of thinking. These occupations can involve searching for facts and figuring out problems mentally. **Work Values**—Working Conditions; Authority; Creativity; Autonomy; Ability Utilization; Co-workers. **Skills**—Programming; Writing; Reading Comprehension; Persuasion; Operations Analysis; Quality Control Analysis. **Abilities**—*Cognitive:* Category Flexibility; Written Expression; Written Comprehension; Oral Expression; Number Facility; Originality. *Psychomotor:* None met the criteria. *Physical:* None met the criteria. *Sensory:* Near Vision; Visual Color Discrimination; Far Vision. **General Work Activities**—*Information Input:* Getting Information; Identifying Objects, Actions, and Events; Monitoring Processes, Materials, or Surroundings. *Mental Process:* Organizing, Planning, and Prioritizing; Making Decisions and Solving Problems; Updating and Using Relevant Knowledge. *Work Output:* Documenting or Recording Information; Handling and Moving Objects; Interacting With Computers. *Interacting with Others:* Communicating with Persons Outside Organization; Establishing and Maintaining Interpersonal Relationships; Communicating with Other Workers. **Physical Work Conditions**— Indoors; Sitting. **Other Job Characteristics**—Need to Be Exact or Accurate.

Experience—Job Zone 4. A minimum of two to four years of work-related skill, knowledge, or experience is needed. **Job Preparation**— SVP 7.0 to less than 8.0—two years to less than 10 years. **Knowledges**—Clerical Practices; History and Archeology; Computers and Electronics; English Language; Administration and Management; Customer and Personal Service. **Instructional Programs**—Art History, Criticism and Conservation; Cultural Resource Management and Policy Analysis; Historic Preservation and Conservation; Historic Preservation and Conservation, Other; History, General; Museology/Museum Studies; Public/Applied History and Archival Administration.

Related SOC Job—25-4011 Archivists. **Related OOH Job**—Archivists, Curators, and Museum Technicians. **Related DOT Job**—101.167-010 Archivist.

25-4012.00 Curators

- Education/Training Required: Master's degree
- Employed: 8,790
- Annual Earnings: $45,240
- Growth: 15.7%
- Annual Job Openings: 1,000

Administer affairs of museum and conduct research programs. Direct instructional, research, and public service activities of institution.

Plan and organize the acquisition, storage, and exhibition of collections and related materials, including the selection of exhibition themes and designs. Develop and maintain an institution's registration, cataloging, and basic recordkeeping systems, using computer databases. Provide information from the institution's holdings to other curators and to the public. Inspect premises to assess the need for repairs and to ensure that climate and pest-control issues are addressed. Train and supervise curatorial, fiscal, technical, research, and clerical staff, as well as volunteers or interns. Negotiate and authorize purchase, sale, exchange, or loan of collections. Plan and conduct special research projects in area of interest or expertise. Conduct or organize tours, workshops, and instructional sessions to acquaint individuals with an institution's facilities and materials. Confer with the board of directors to formulate and interpret policies, to determine budget requirements, and to plan overall operations. Attend meetings, conventions, and civic events to promote use of institution's services, to seek financing, and to maintain community alliances. Schedule events and organize details, including refreshment, entertainment, decorations, and the collection of any fees. Write and review grant proposals, journal articles, institutional reports, and publicity materials. Study, examine, and test acquisitions to authenticate their origin, composition, and history and to assess their current value. Arrange insurance coverage for objects on loan or for special exhibits and recommend changes in coverage for the entire collection. Establish specifications for reproductions and oversee their manufacture or select items from commercially available replica sources.

GOE Information—**Interest Area:** 05. Education and Training. **Work Group:** 05.05. Archival and Museum Services. **Personality Type**— Artistic. Artistic occupations frequently involve working with forms, designs, and patterns. They often require self-expression, and the work can be done without following a clear set of rules. **Work Values**—Authority; Creativity; Working Conditions; Responsibility; Co-workers; Social Service. **Skills**—Management of Financial Resources; Management of Personnel Resources; Writing; Time Management; Speaking; Persuasion. **Abilities**—*Cognitive:* Visualization; Written Expression; Number Facility; Fluency of Ideas; Mathematical Reasoning; Written Comprehension. *Psychomotor:* Arm-Hand Steadiness; Finger Dexterity; Manual Dexterity; Multilimb Coordination. *Physical:* Extent Flexibility; Static Strength; Trunk Strength. *Sensory:* Visual Color Discrimination; Far Vision; Near Vision; Speech Recognition; Speech Clarity; Auditory Attention. **General Work Activities**—*Information Input:* Getting Information; Identifying Objects, Actions, and Events; Monitoring Processes, Materials, or Surroundings. *Mental Process:* Organizing, Planning, and Prioritizing; Thinking Creatively; Judging the Qualities of Things, Services, or Other People's Work. *Work Output:* Handling and Moving Objects; Performing General Physical Activities; Documenting or Recording Information. *Interacting with Others:* Communicating with Other Workers; Establishing and Maintaining Interpersonal Relationships; Communicating with Persons Outside Organization. **Physical Work Conditions**—Indoors; Sitting. **Other Job Characteristics**—Need to Be Exact or Accurate.

Experience—Job Zone 4. A minimum of two to four years of work-related skill, knowledge, or experience is needed. **Job Preparation**—SVP 7.0 to less than 8.0—two years to less than 10 years. **Knowledges**—Fine Arts; History and Archeology; Clerical Practices; Philosophy and Theology; Sociology and Anthropology; Geography. **Instructional Programs**—Art History, Criticism, and Conservation; History, General; Museology/Museum Studies; Public/Applied History and Archival Administration.

Related SOC Job—25-4012 Curators. **Related OOH Job**—Archivists, Curators, and Museum Technicians. **Related DOT Jobs**—099.167-030 Educational Resource Coordinator; 102.017-010 Curator; 102.117-010 Supervisor, Historic Sites; 102.117-014 Director, Museum-or-Zoo; 102.167-014 Historic-Site Administrator; 102.167-018 Registrar, Museum; 109.067-014 Research Associate.

25-4013.00 Museum Technicians and Conservators

- **Education/Training Required: Bachelor's degree**
- **Employed: 9,370**
- **Annual Earnings: $34,090**
- **Growth: 14.1%**
- **Annual Job Openings: 2,000**

Prepare specimens, such as fossils, skeletal parts, lace, and textiles, for museum collection and exhibits. May restore documents or install, arrange, and exhibit materials.

Install, arrange, assemble, and prepare artifacts for exhibition, ensuring the artifacts' safety, reporting their status and condition, and identifying and correcting any problems with the setup. Coordinate exhibit installations, assisting with design; constructing displays, dioramas, display cases, and models; and ensuring the availability of necessary materials. Determine whether objects need repair and choose the safest and most effective method of repair. Clean objects, such as paper, textiles, wood, metal, glass, rock, pottery, and furniture, using cleansers, solvents, soap solutions, and polishes. Prepare artifacts for storage and shipping. Supervise and work with volunteers. Present public programs and tours. Specialize in particular materials or types of object, such as documents and books, paintings,

decorative arts, textiles, metals, or architectural materials. Recommend preservation procedures, such as control of temperature and humidity, to curatorial and building staff. Classify and assign registration numbers to artifacts and supervise inventory control. Direct and supervise curatorial and technical staff in the handling, mounting, care, and storage of art objects. Perform on-site fieldwork, which may involve interviewing people, inspecting and identifying artifacts, note-taking, viewing sites and collections, and repainting exhibition spaces. Repair, restore, and reassemble artifacts, designing and fabricating missing or broken parts, to restore them to their original appearance and prevent deterioration. Prepare reports on the operation of conservation laboratories, documenting the condition of artifacts, treatment options, and the methods of preservation and repair used. Study object documentation or conduct standard chemical and physical tests to ascertain the object's age, composition, original appearance, need for treatment or restoration, and appropriate preservation method. Cut and weld metal sections in reconstruction or renovation of exterior structural sections and accessories of exhibits. Perform tests and examinations to establish storage and conservation requirements, policies, and procedures.

GOE Information—**Interest Area:** 05. Education and Training. **Work Group:** 05.05. Archival and Museum Services. **Personality Type**—Artistic. Artistic occupations frequently involve working with forms, designs, and patterns. They often require self-expression, and the work can be done without following a clear set of rules. **Work Values**—Working Conditions; Co-workers; Ability Utilization; Achievement; Moral Values; Creativity. **Skills**—Management of Material Resources; Repairing; Installation; Technology Design; Equipment Maintenance; Time Management. **Abilities**—*Cognitive:* Visualization; Category Flexibility; Originality; Inductive Reasoning; Deductive Reasoning; Fluency of Ideas. *Psychomotor:* Arm-Hand Steadiness; Manual Dexterity; Finger Dexterity. *Physical:* Trunk Strength. *Sensory:* Speech Clarity; Near Vision. **General Work Activities**—*Information Input:* Monitoring Processes, Materials, or Surroundings; Identifying Objects, Actions, and Events; Getting Information. *Mental Process:* Organizing, Planning, and Prioritizing; Updating and Using Relevant Knowledge; Processing Information. *Work Output:* Handling and Moving Objects; Performing General Physical Activities; Documenting or Recording Information. *Interacting with Others:* Establishing and Maintaining Interpersonal Relationships; Communicating with Other Workers; Communicating with Persons Outside Organization. **Physical Work Conditions**—Indoors; Standing; Using Hands on Objects, Tools, or Controls. **Other Job Characteristics**—Need to Be Exact or Accurate.

Experience—Job Zone 3. Previous work-related skill, knowledge, or experience is required. **Job Preparation**—SVP 6.0 to less than 7.0—more than one year and less than four years. **Knowledges**—History and Archeology; Fine Arts; Sociology and Anthropology; Design; Clerical Practices; Education and Training. **Instructional Programs**—Art History, Criticism, and Conservation; Museology/Museum Studies; Public/Applied History and Archival Administration.

Related SOC Job—25-4013 Museum Technicians and Conservators. **Related OOH Job**—Archivists, Curators, and Museum Technicians. **Related DOT Jobs**—055.381-010 Conservator, Artifacts; 102.167-010 Art Conservator; 102.261-010 Conservation Technician; 102.361-010 Restorer, Lace and Textiles; 102.361-014 Restorer, Ceramic; 102.367-010 Fine Arts Packer; 102.381-010 Museum Technician; 109.267-010 Research Assistant I; 109.281-010 Armorer Technician; 109.361-010 Restorer, Paper-and-Prints; 779.381-018 Repairer, Art Objects; 899.384-010 Transportation-Equipment-Maintenance Worker; 979.361-010 Document Restorer.

25-4021.00 Librarians

- **Education/Training Required: Master's degree**
- **Employed: 146,740**
- **Annual Earnings: $47,400**
- **Growth: 4.9%**
- **Annual Job Openings: 8,000**

Administer libraries and perform related library services. Work in a variety of settings, including public libraries, schools, colleges and universities, museums, corporations, government agencies, law firms, non-profit organizations, and healthcare providers. Tasks may include selecting, acquiring, cataloguing, classifying, circulating, and maintaining library materials and furnishing reference, bibliographical, and readers' advisory services. May perform in-depth, strategic research and synthesize, analyze, edit, and filter information. May set up or work with databases and information systems to catalogue and access information.

Search standard reference materials, including online sources and the Internet, to answer patrons' reference questions. Analyze patrons' requests to determine needed information and assist in furnishing or locating that information. Teach library patrons to search for information by using databases. Keep records of circulation and materials. Supervise budgeting, planning, and personnel activities. Check books in and out of the library. Explain use of library facilities, resources, equipment, and services and provide information about library policies. Review and evaluate resource material, such as book reviews and catalogs, to select and order print, audiovisual, and electronic resources. Code, classify, and catalog books, publications, films, audiovisual aids, and other library materials based on subject matter or standard library classification systems. Locate unusual or unique information in response to specific requests. Direct and train library staff in duties such as receiving, shelving, researching, cataloging, and equipment use. Respond to customer complaints, taking action as necessary. Organize collections of books, publications, documents, audiovisual aids, and other reference materials for convenient access. Develop library policies and procedures. Evaluate materials to determine outdated or unused items to be discarded. Develop information access aids such as indexes and annotated bibliographies, Web pages, electronic pathfinders, and online tutorials. Plan and deliver client-centered programs and services such as special services for corporate clients, storytelling for children, newsletters, or programs for special groups. Compile lists of books, periodicals, articles, and audiovisual materials on particular subjects. Arrange for interlibrary loans of materials not available in a particular library. Assemble and arrange display materials. Confer with teachers, parents, and community organizations to develop, plan, and conduct programs in reading, viewing, and communication skills. Compile lists of overdue materials and notify borrowers that their materials are overdue.

GOE Information—**Interest Area:** 05. Education and Training. **Work Group:** 05.04. Library Services. **Personality Type**—Artistic. Artistic occupations frequently involve working with forms, designs, and patterns. They often require self-expression, and the work can be done without following a clear set of rules. **Work Values**—Working Conditions; Authority; Social Service; Co-workers; Responsibility; Autonomy. **Skills**—Management of Financial Resources; Management of Material Resources; Learning Strategies; Persuasion; Service Orientation; Systems Evaluation. **Abilities**—*Cognitive:* Flexibility of Closure; Memorization; Category Flexibility; Fluency of Ideas; Number Facility; Written Comprehension. *Psychomotor:* Finger Dexterity; Manual Dexterity. *Physical:* Static Strength; Trunk Strength. *Sensory:* Far Vision; Near Vision; Speech Recognition;

Speech Clarity; Visual Color Discrimination. **General Work Activities**—*Information Input:* Getting Information; Identifying Objects, Actions, and Events; Monitoring Processes, Materials, or Surroundings. *Mental Process:* Updating and Using Relevant Knowledge; Organizing, Planning, and Prioritizing; Processing Information. *Work Output:* Handling and Moving Objects; Interacting With Computers; Documenting or Recording Information. *Interacting with Others:* Establishing and Maintaining Interpersonal Relationships; Communicating with Other Workers; Teaching Others. **Physical Work Conditions**—Indoors; Sitting; Using Hands on Objects, Tools, or Controls; Repetitive Motions. **Other Job Characteristics**—Need to Be Exact or Accurate; Automation; Repeat Same Tasks.

Experience—Job Zone 5. Extensive skill, knowledge, and experience are needed. **Job Preparation**—SVP 8.0 and above—four years to more than 10 years. **Knowledges**—Customer and Personal Service; Communications and Media; Clerical Practices; Personnel and Human Resources; English Language; Computers and Electronics. **Instructional Programs**—Library Science, Other; Library Science/Librarianship; School Librarian/School Library Media Specialist.

Related SOC Job—25-4021 Librarians. **Related OOH Job**—Librarians. **Related DOT Jobs**—100.117-010 Library Director; 100.127-010 Chief Librarian, Branch or Department; 100.127-014 Librarian; 100.167-010 Audiovisual Librarian; 100.167-014 Bookmobile Librarian; 100.167-018 Children's Librarian; 100.167-022 Institution Librarian; 100.167-026 Librarian, Special Library; 100.167-030 Media Specialist, School Library; 100.167-034 Young-Adult Librarian; 100.167-038 News Librarian; 100.267-010 Acquisitions Librarian; 100.267-014 Librarian, Special Collections; 100.367-022 Music Librarian; others.

25-4031.00 Library Technicians

- **Education/Training Required: Short-term on-the-job training**
- **Employed: 115,770**
- **Annual Earnings: $25,650**
- **Growth: 13.4%**
- **Annual Job Openings: 25,000**

Assist librarians by helping readers in the use of library catalogs, databases, and indexes to locate books and other materials and by answering questions that require only brief consultation of standard reference. Compile records; sort and shelve books; remove or repair damaged books; register patrons; check materials in and out of the circulation process. Replace materials in shelving area (stacks) or files. Includes bookmobile drivers who operate bookmobiles or light trucks that pull trailers to specific locations on a predetermined schedule and assist with providing services in mobile libraries.

Reserve, circulate, renew, and discharge books and other materials. Enter and update patrons' records on computers. Provide assistance to teachers and students by locating materials and helping to complete special projects. Guide patrons in finding and using library resources, including reference materials, audiovisual equipment, computers, and electronic resources. Answer routine reference inquiries and refer patrons needing further assistance to librarians. Train other staff, volunteers, or student assistants, and schedule and supervise their work. Sort books, publications, and other items according to procedure and return them to shelves, files, or other designated storage areas. Conduct reference searches, using printed materials and in-house and online databases. Deliver and retrieve items throughout the library by hand or using pushcart. Take actions to halt disruption of library activities by problem patrons. Process interlibrary loans for patrons. Process print and non-print library materials to prepare them for inclusion in library collections. Retrieve information from central databases for storage in a library's computer. Organize and maintain periodicals and reference materials. Compile and maintain records relating to circulation, materials, and equipment. Collect fines and respond to complaints about fines. Issue identification cards to borrowers. Verify bibliographical data for materials, including author, title, publisher, publication date, and edition. Review subject matter of materials to be classified and select classification numbers and headings according to classification systems. Send out notices about lost or overdue books. Prepare order slips for materials to be acquired, checking prices and figuring costs. Design, customize, and maintain databases, Web pages, and local area networks. Operate and maintain audiovisual equipment such as projectors, tape recorders, and videocassette recorders. File catalog cards according to system used. Prepare volumes for binding. Conduct children's programs and other specialized programs such as library tours. Compose explanatory summaries of contents of books and other reference materials.

GOE Information—Interest Area: 05. Education and Training. **Work Group:** 05.04. Library Services. **Personality Type—**Conventional. Conventional occupations frequently involve following set procedures and routines. These occupations can include working with data and details more than with ideas. Usually there is a clear line of authority to follow. **Work Values—**Working Conditions; Social Service; Co-workers; Authority; Moral Values; Advancement. **Skills—**Service Orientation; Reading Comprehension; Instructing; Writing; Active Listening; Learning Strategies. **Abilities—***Cognitive:* Category Flexibility; Fluency of Ideas; Memorization; Flexibility of Closure; Written Expression; Information Ordering. *Psychomotor:* Manual Dexterity; Arm-Hand Steadiness; Finger Dexterity. *Physical:* Static Strength. *Sensory:* Near Vision; Speech Clarity; Speech Recognition; Visual Color Discrimination. **General Work Activities—***Information Input:* Getting Information; Identifying Objects, Actions, and Events; Monitoring Processes, Materials, or Surroundings. *Mental Process:* Processing Information; Updating and Using Relevant Knowledge; Organizing, Planning, and Prioritizing. *Work Output:* Handling and Moving Objects; Interacting With Computers; Documenting or Recording Information. *Interacting with Others:* Establishing and Maintaining Interpersonal Relationships; Performing for or Working with the Public; Communicating with Other Workers. **Physical Work Conditions—**Indoors; Sitting; Using Hands on Objects, Tools, or Controls; Repetitive Motions. **Other Job Characteristics—**Need to Be Exact or Accurate; Repeat Same Tasks; Automation.

Experience—Job Zone 3. Previous work-related skill, knowledge, or experience is required. **Job Preparation—**SVP 6.0 to less than 7.0—more than one year and less than four years. **Knowledges—**Clerical Practices; Computers and Electronics; Customer and Personal Service; English Language; Education and Training; Administration and Management. **Instructional Program—**Library Assistant.

Related SOC Job—25-4031 Library Technicians. **Related OOH Job—**Library Technicians. **Related DOT Jobs—**100.367-010 Bibliographer; 100.367-014 Classifier; 100.367-018 Library Technical Assistant; 100.387-010 Catalog Librarian.

25-9000 Other Education, Training, and Library Occupations

25-9011.00 Audio-Visual Collections Specialists

- **Education/Training Required: Moderate-term on-the-job training**
- **Employed: 6,910**
- **Annual Earnings: $40,260**
- **Growth: 18.6%**
- **Annual Job Openings: 1,000**

Prepare, plan, and operate audiovisual teaching aids for use in education. May record, catalogue, and file audiovisual materials.

Set up, adjust, and operate audiovisual equipment such as cameras, film and slide projectors, and recording equipment for meetings, events, classes, seminars, and videoconferences. Offer presentations and workshops on the role of multimedia in effective presentations. Attend conventions and conferences, read trade journals, and communicate with industry insiders to keep abreast of industry developments. Instruct users in the selection, use, and design of audiovisual materials and assist them in the preparation of instructional materials and the rehearsal of presentations. Maintain hardware and software, including computers, scanners, color copiers, and color laser printers. Confer with teachers to select course materials and to determine which training aids are best suited to particular grade levels. Perform simple maintenance tasks such as cleaning monitors and lenses and changing batteries and light bulbs. Develop manuals, texts, workbooks, or related materials for use in conjunction with production materials. Determine formats, approaches, content, levels, and mediums necessary to meet production objectives effectively and within budgetary constraints. Direct and coordinate activities of assistants and other personnel during production. Acquire, catalog, and maintain collections of audiovisual material such as films, videotapes and audiotapes, photographs, and software programs. Narrate presentations and productions. Construct and position properties, sets, lighting equipment, and other equipment. Develop preproduction ideas and incorporate them into outlines, scripts, storyboards, and graphics. Plan and prepare audiovisual teaching aids and methods for use in school systems. Produce rough and finished graphics and graphic designs. Locate and secure settings, properties, effects, and other production necessities.

GOE Information—Interest Area: 05. Education and Training. **Work Group:** 05.05. Archival and Museum Services. **Personality Type—**Conventional. Conventional occupations frequently involve following set procedures and routines. These occupations can include working with data and details more than with ideas. Usually there is a clear line of authority to follow. **Work Values—**Working Conditions; Authority; Co-workers; Ability Utilization; Social Service; Creativity. **Skills—**Troubleshooting; Installation; Technology Design; Instructing; Equipment Selection; Operations Analysis. **Abilities—***Cognitive:* Written Expression; Visualization; Category Flexibility; Oral Expression; Fluency of Ideas; Written Comprehension. *Psychomotor:* Control Precision. *Physical:* None met the criteria. *Sensory:* Far Vision; Speech Clarity; Near Vision. **General Work Activities—***Information Input:* Identifying Objects, Actions, and Events; Monitoring Processes, Materials, or Surroundings;

Getting Information. *Mental Process:* Updating and Using Relevant Knowledge; Thinking Creatively; Organizing, Planning, and Prioritizing. *Work Output:* Interacting With Computers; Controlling Machines and Processes; Handling and Moving Objects. *Interacting with Others:* Communicating with Other Workers; Performing for or Working with the Public; Establishing and Maintaining Interpersonal Relationships. **Physical Work Conditions**—Indoors; Sitting; Using Hands on Objects, Tools, or Controls. **Other Job Characteristics**—Need to Be Exact or Accurate.

Experience—Job Zone 5. Extensive skill, knowledge, and experience are needed. **Job Preparation**—SVP 8.0 and above—four years to more than 10 years. **Knowledges**—Education and Training; Communications and Media; Computers and Electronics; Telecommunications; Customer and Personal Service; Clerical Practices. **Instructional Program**—No related CIP programs.

Related SOC Job—25-9011 Audio-Visual Collections Specialists. **Related OOH Job**—Audio-Visual Collections Specialists. **Related DOT Jobs**—099.167-018 Audiovisual specialist; 149.061-010 Audiovisual Production Specialist.

25-9021.00 Farm and Home Management Advisors

- Education/Training Required: Bachelor's degree
- Employed: 12,620
- Annual Earnings: $41,890
- Growth: 7.7%
- Annual Job Openings: 2,000

Advise, instruct, and assist individuals and families engaged in agriculture, agricultural-related processes, or home economics activities. Demonstrate procedures and apply research findings to solve problems; instruct and train in product development, sales, and the utilization of machinery and equipment to promote general welfare. Includes county agricultural agents, feed and farm management advisers, home economists, and extension service advisors.

Collaborate with producers to diagnose and prevent management and production problems. Conduct classes or deliver lectures on subjects such as nutrition, home management, and farming techniques. Advise farmers and demonstrate techniques in areas such as feeding and health maintenance of livestock, growing and harvesting practices, and financial planning. Research information requested by farmers. Prepare and distribute leaflets, pamphlets, and visual aids for educational and informational purposes. Collect and evaluate data to determine community program needs. Maintain records of services provided and the effects of advice given. Schedule and make regular visits to farmers. Collaborate with social service and health care professionals to advise individuals and families on home management practices such as budget planning, meal preparation, and time management. Organize, advise, and participate in community activities and organizations such as county and state fair events and 4-H clubs. Conduct field demonstrations of new products, techniques, or services. Conduct agricultural research, analyze data, and prepare research reports. Act as an advocate for farmers or farmers' groups. Provide direct assistance to farmers by performing activities such as purchasing or selling products and supplies, supervising properties, and collecting soil and herbage samples for testing. Set and monitor production targets.

GOE Information—**Interest Area:** 05. Education and Training. **Work Group:** 05.03. Postsecondary and Adult Teaching and Instructing. **Personality Type**—Social. Social occupations frequently involve working with, communicating with, and teaching people. These occupations often involve helping or providing service to others. **Work Values**—Social Service; Creativity; Authority; Autonomy; Responsibility; Achievement. **Skills**—Management of Financial Resources; Science; Service Orientation; Learning Strategies; Management of Personnel Resources; Writing. **Abilities**—*Cognitive:* Fluency of Ideas; Originality; Number Facility; Mathematical Reasoning; Written Expression; Inductive Reasoning. *Psychomotor:* Multilimb Coordination; Control Precision. *Physical:* None met the criteria. *Sensory:* Speech Clarity; Speech Recognition; Depth Perception; Far Vision; Visual Color Discrimination; Hearing Sensitivity. **General Work Activities**—*Information Input:* Getting Information; Identifying Objects, Actions, and Events; Monitoring Processes, Materials, or Surroundings. *Mental Process:* Organizing, Planning, and Prioritizing; Updating and Using Relevant Knowledge; Scheduling Work and Activities. *Work Output:* Interacting With Computers; Documenting or Recording Information; Performing General Physical Activities. *Interacting with Others:* Communicating with Persons Outside Organization; Establishing and Maintaining Interpersonal Relationships; Teaching Others. **Physical Work Conditions**—Indoors; Sitting. **Other Job Characteristics**—Need to Be Exact or Accurate.

Experience—Job Zone 5. Extensive skill, knowledge, and experience are needed. **Job Preparation**—SVP 8.0 and above—four years to more than 10 years. **Knowledges**—Food Production; Education and Training; Biology; Sociology and Anthropology; Customer and Personal Service; Psychology. **Instructional Programs**—Adult Development and Aging; Agricultural and Extension Education Services; Animal Nutrition; Animal/Livestock Husbandry and Production; Apparel and Textiles, General; Business Family and Consumer Sciences/Human Sciences; Child Development; Consumer Economics; Consumer Merchandising or Retailing Management; Consumer Services and Advocacy; Crop Production; Family and Community Services; Family and Consumer Economics and Related Services, Other; Family and Consumer Sciences/Human Sciences, General; Family and Consumer Sciences/Human Sciences, Other; Family Resource Management Studies, General; Family Systems; Farm/Farm and Ranch Management; Home Furnishings and Equipment Installers; Housing and Human Environments, General; Housing and Human Environments, Other; Human Development, Family Studies, and Related Services, Other.

Related SOC Job—25-9021 Farm and Home Management Advisors. **Related OOH Job**—Farm and Home Management Advisors. **Related DOT Jobs**—096.121-010 County Home-Demonstration Agent; 096.127-010 County-Agricultural Agent; 096.127-014 Extension Service Specialist; 096.127-018 Feed and Farm Management Adviser; 096.127-022 Four-H Club Agent.

25-9031.00 Instructional Coordinators

- Education/Training Required: Master's degree
- Employed: 112,880
- Annual Earnings: $50,430
- Growth: 27.5%
- Annual Job Openings: 15,000

Develop instructional material, coordinate educational content, and incorporate current technology in specialized fields that provide guidelines to educators and instructors for developing curricula and conducting courses.

Conduct or participate in workshops, committees, and conferences designed to promote the intellectual, social, and physical welfare of students. Plan and conduct teacher training programs and conferences dealing with new classroom procedures, instructional materials and equipment, and teaching aids. Advise teaching and administrative staff in curriculum development, use of materials and equipment, and implementation of state and federal programs and procedures. Recommend, order, or authorize purchase of instructional materials, supplies, equipment, and visual aids designed to meet student educational needs and district standards. Interpret and enforce provisions of state education codes and rules and regulations of state education boards. Confer with members of educational committees and advisory groups to obtain knowledge of subject areas and to relate curriculum materials to specific subjects, individual student needs, and occupational areas. Organize production and design of curriculum materials. Research, evaluate, and prepare recommendations on curricula, instructional methods, and materials for school systems. Observe work of teaching staff to evaluate performance and to recommend changes that could strengthen teaching skills. Develop instructional materials to be used by educators and instructors. Prepare grant proposals, budgets, and program policies and goals or assist in their preparation. Develop tests, questionnaires, and procedures that measure the effectiveness of curricula and use these tools to determine whether program objectives are being met. Update the content of educational programs to ensure that students are being trained with equipment and processes that are technologically current. Address public audiences to explain program objectives and to elicit support. Advise and teach students. Prepare or approve manuals, guidelines, and reports on state educational policies and practices for distribution to school districts. Develop classroom-based and distance-learning training courses, using needs assessments and skill level analyses. Inspect instructional equipment to determine if repairs are needed and authorize necessary repairs.

GOE Information—Interest Area: 05. Education and Training. **Work Group:** 05.01. Managerial Work in Education. **Personality Type—** Social. Social occupations frequently involve working with, communicating with, and teaching people. These occupations often involve helping or providing service to others. **Work Values—**Authority; Creativity; Autonomy; Responsibility; Achievement; Social Service. **Skills—**Management of Financial Resources; Learning Strategies; Social Perceptiveness; Monitoring; Coordination; Time Management. **Abilities—***Cognitive:* Written Expression; Originality; Fluency of Ideas; Oral Expression; Number Facility; Mathematical Reasoning. *Psychomotor:* None met the criteria. *Physical:* None met the criteria. *Sensory:* Speech Clarity; Speech Recognition; Hearing Sensitivity; Far Vision; Visual Color Discrimination. **General Work Activities—** *Information Input:* Getting Information; Identifying Objects, Actions, and Events; Monitoring Processes, Materials, or Surroundings. *Mental Process:* Updating and Using Relevant Knowledge; Organizing, Planning, and Prioritizing; Making Decisions and Solving Problems. *Work Output:* Documenting or Recording Information; Interacting With Computers. *Interacting with Others:* Providing Consultation and Advice to Others; Coaching and Developing Others; Communicating with Other Workers. **Physical Work Conditions—**Indoors; Sitting. **Other Job Characteristics—**Need to Be Exact or Accurate.

Experience—Job Zone 5. Extensive skill, knowledge, and experience are needed. **Job Preparation—**SVP 8.0 and above—four years to more than 10 years. **Knowledges—**Education and Training; Personnel and Human Resources; English Language; Sociology and Anthropology; Communications and Media; Psychology. **Instructional Programs—** Curriculum and Instruction; Educational/Instructional Media Design.

Related SOC Job—25-9031 Instructional Coordinators. **Related OOH Job—**Instructional Coordinators. **Related DOT Jobs—**094.167-010 Supervisor, Special Education; 099.117-026 Supervisor, Education; 099.167-014 Consultant, Education; 099.167-018 Audiovisual Specialist; 099.167-022 Educational Specialist; 099.167-026 Music Supervisor.

25-9041.00 Teacher Assistants

- **Education/Training Required: Short-term on-the-job training**
- **Employed: 1,260,400**
- **Annual Earnings: $20,090**
- **Growth: 14.1%**
- **Annual Job Openings: 252,000**

Perform duties that are instructional in nature or deliver direct services to students or parents. Serve in a position for which a teacher or another professional has ultimate responsibility for the design and implementation of educational programs and services.

Provide extra assistance to students with special needs, such as non-English-speaking students or those with physical and mental disabilities. Tutor and assist children individually or in small groups to help them master assignments and to reinforce learning concepts presented by teachers. Supervise students in classrooms, halls, cafeterias, school yards, and gymnasiums or on field trips. Enforce administration policies and rules governing students. Observe students' performance and record relevant data to assess progress. Discuss assigned duties with classroom teachers to coordinate instructional efforts. Instruct and monitor students in the use and care of equipment and materials to prevent injuries and damage. Present subject matter to students under the direction and guidance of teachers, using lectures, discussions, or supervised role-playing methods. Organize and label materials and display students' work in a manner appropriate for their eye levels and perceptual skills. Distribute tests and homework assignments and collect them when they are completed. Type, file, and duplicate materials. Distribute teaching materials such as textbooks, workbooks, papers, and pencils to students. Use computers, audiovisual aids, and other equipment and materials to supplement presentations. Attend staff meetings and serve on committees as required. Prepare lesson materials, bulletin board displays, exhibits, equipment, and demonstrations. Carry out therapeutic regimens such as behavior modification and personal development programs under the supervision of special education instructors, psychologists, or speech-language pathologists. Provide disabled students with assistive devices, supportive technology, and assistance accessing facilities such as restrooms. Assist in bus loading and unloading. Take class attendance and maintain attendance records. Grade homework and tests, and compute and record results, using answer sheets or electronic marking devices. Organize and supervise games and other recreational activities to promote physical, mental, and social development.

GOE Information—Interest Area: 05. Education and Training. **Work Group:** 05.02. Preschool, Elementary, and Secondary Teaching and Instructing. **Personality Type—**Social. Social occupations frequently involve working with, communicating with, and teaching people. These occupations often involve helping or providing service to others. **Work Values—**Social Service; Authority; Co-workers; Working Conditions; Achievement; Supervision, Human Relations. **Skills—** Social Perceptiveness; Learning Strategies; Instructing; Persuasion; Active Listening; Negotiation. **Abilities—***Cognitive:* Originality; Oral Comprehension. *Psychomotor:* None met the criteria. *Physical:* None met the criteria. *Sensory:* Speech Clarity; Far Vision; Speech Recognition; Hearing Sensitivity. **General Work Activities—** *Information Input:* Monitoring Processes, Materials, or Surroundings; Getting Information; Identifying Objects, Actions, and Events. *Mental Process:* Organizing, Planning, and Prioritizing; Updating and Using Relevant Knowledge; Thinking Creatively. *Work Output:* Documenting or Recording Information; Interacting With Computers; Performing General Physical Activities. *Interacting with Others:* Establishing and Maintaining Interpersonal Relationships; Communicating with Other Workers; Assisting and Caring for Others. **Physical Work Conditions—**Indoors; Noisy; Standing. **Other Job Characteristics—**Need to Be Exact or Accurate.

Experience—Job Zone 3. Previous work-related skill, knowledge, or experience is required. **Job Preparation—**SVP 6.0 to less than 7.0— more than one year and less than four years. **Knowledges—** Geography; History and Archeology; Psychology; Therapy and Counseling; Sociology and Anthropology; English Language. **Instructional Programs—**Teacher Assistant/aide; Teaching Assistant/Aides, Other.

Related SOC Job—25-9041 Teacher Assistants. **Related OOH Job—** Teacher Assistants. **Related DOT Job—**099.327-010 Teacher Aide I.

25-9099.99 Education, Training, and Library Workers, All Other

- **Education/Training Required: No data available**
- **Employed: 72,450**
- **Annual Earnings: $29,880**
- **Growth: 20.5%**
- **Annual Job Openings: 9,000**

All education, training, and library workers not listed separately.

No task data available.

Note: The Department of Labor has not collected some data for this job, so it has fewer details than the other descriptions.

Related SOC Job—25-9099 Education, Training, and Library Workers, All Other. **Related OOH Job—**None. **Related DOT Jobs—**109.267-014 Research Worker, Encyclopedia; 109.364-010 Craft Demonstrator; 249.367-074 Teacher Aide II; 249.367-086 Satellite-Instruction Facilitator.

27-0000

Arts, Design, Entertainment, Sports, and Media Occupations

27-1000 Art and Design Workers

27-1011.00 Art Directors

- Education/Training Required: Work experience plus degree
- Employed: 29,350
- Annual Earnings: $63,950
- Growth: 11.5%
- Annual Job Openings: 10,000

Formulate design concepts and presentation approaches and direct workers engaged in art work, layout design, and copy writing for visual communications media, such as magazines, books, newspapers, and packaging.

Formulate basic layout design or presentation approach and specify material details, such as style and size of type, photographs, graphics, animation, video, and sound. Review and approve proofs of printed copy and art and copy materials developed by staff members. Manage own accounts and projects, working within budget and scheduling requirements. Confer with creative, art, copy-writing, or production department heads to discuss client requirements and presentation concepts and to coordinate creative activities. Present final layouts to clients for approval. Confer with clients to determine objectives; budget; background information; and presentation approaches, styles, and techniques. Hire, train, and direct staff members who develop design concepts into art layouts or who prepare layouts for printing. Work with creative directors to develop design solutions. Review illustrative material to determine if it conforms to standards and specifications. Attend photo shoots and printing sessions to ensure that the products needed are obtained. Create custom illustrations or other graphic elements. Mark up, paste, and complete layouts and write typography instructions to prepare materials for typesetting or printing. Negotiate with printers and estimators to determine what services will be performed. Conceptualize and help design interfaces for multimedia games, products, and devices. Prepare detailed storyboards showing sequence and timing of story development for television production.

GOE Information—Interest Area: 03. Arts and Communication. Work Group: 03.01. Managerial Work in Arts and Communication. Personality Type—Artistic. Artistic occupations frequently involve working with forms, designs, and patterns. They often require self-expression, and the work can be done without following a clear set of rules. Work Values—Creativity; Ability Utilization; Autonomy; Authority; Achievement; Recognition. Skills—Management of Financial Resources; Coordination; Negotiation; Operations Analysis; Persuasion; Service Orientation. Abilities—*Cognitive:* Originality; Fluency of Ideas; Visualization; Category Flexibility; Speed of Closure; Written Expression. *Psychomotor:* Arm-Hand Steadiness; Finger Dexterity; Manual Dexterity. *Physical:* None met the criteria. *Sensory:* Visual Color Discrimination; Far Vision; Near Vision; Speech Recognition; Speech Clarity. General Work Activities—*Information Input:* Getting Information; Identifying Objects, Actions, and Events; Estimating the Needed Characteristics of Products, Events, or Information. *Mental Process:* Thinking Creatively; Updating and Using Relevant Knowledge; Organizing, Planning, and Prioritizing. *Work Output:* Interacting With Computers; Documenting or Recording Information. *Interacting with Others:* Providing Consultation and Advice to Others; Establishing and Maintaining Interpersonal Relationships; Communicating with Other Workers. Physical Work Conditions—Indoors; Sitting; Using Hands on Objects, Tools, or Controls; Repetitive Motions. Other Job Characteristics—Need to Be Exact or Accurate.

Experience—Job Zone 4. A minimum of two to four years of work-related skill, knowledge, or experience is needed. Job Preparation—SVP 7.0 to less than 8.0—two years to less than 10 years. Knowledges—Design; Fine Arts; Communications and Media; Production and Processing; Computers and Electronics; Education and Training. Instructional Programs—Graphic Design; Intermedia/Multimedia.

Related SOC Job—27-1011 Art Directors. Related OOH Job—Artists and Related Workers. Related DOT Jobs—141.031-010 Art Director; 141.067-010 Creative Director; 141.137-010 Production Manager, Advertising.

27-1012.00 Craft Artists

- Education/Training Required: Associate degree
- Employed: 4,300
- Annual Earnings: $22,430
- Growth: 10.6%
- Annual Job Openings: 1,000

Create or reproduce hand-made objects for sale and exhibition, using a variety of techniques such as welding, weaving, pottery, and needlecraft.

Create functional or decorative objects by hand, using a variety of methods and materials. Cut, shape, fit, join, mold, or otherwise process materials, using hand tools, power tools, or machinery. Attend craft shows to market products. Select materials for use based on strength, color, texture, balance, weight, size, malleability, and other characteristics. Apply finishes to objects being crafted. Develop concepts or creative ideas for craft objects. Set specifications for materials, dimensions, and finishes. Confer with customers to assess customer needs or obtain feedback. Fabricate patterns or templates to guide craft production. Create prototypes or models of objects to be crafted. Sketch or draw objects to be crafted. Advertise products and work, using media such as Internet advertising and brochures. Develop product packaging, display, and pricing strategies. Research craft trends, venues, and customer buying patterns in order to inspire designs and marketing strategies. Develop designs, using specialized computer software.

GOE Information—Interest Area: 03. Arts and Communication. Work Group: 03.04. Studio Art. Personality Type—No data available. Work Values—No data available. Skills—Management of Financial Resources; Management of Material Resources; Repairing; Equipment Selection; Operations Analysis; Equipment Maintenance. Abilities—*Cognitive:* Originality; Visualization; Fluency of Ideas; Number Facility; Category Flexibility. *Psychomotor:* Arm-Hand Steadiness; Multilimb Coordination; Manual Dexterity; Finger Dexterity; Wrist-Finger Speed; Reaction Time. *Physical:* Extent Flexibility; Static Strength; Trunk Strength. *Sensory:* Visual Color Discrimination; Depth Perception; Hearing Sensitivity; Far Vision; Speech Recognition. General Work Activities—*Information Input:* Getting Information; Monitoring Processes, Materials, or Surroundings; Inspecting Equipment, Structures, or Materials. *Mental Process:* Thinking Creatively; Organizing, Planning, and Prioritizing; Making Decisions and Solving Problems. *Work Output:* Handling and Moving Objects; Controlling Machines and Processes; Performing General Physical Activities. *Interacting with Others:* Performing for or Working with the Public; Monitoring and Controlling Resources; Communicating with Persons Outside Organization. Physical Work Conditions—Indoors; Contaminants; Standing; Using Hands on Objects, Tools, or Controls; Repetitive Motions. Other Job Characteristics—Need to Be Exact or Accurate; Repeat Same Tasks.

Experience—Job Zone 2. Some previous work-related skill, knowledge, or experience may be helpful in these occupations, but usually is not needed. **Job Preparation**—SVP 4.0 to less than 6.0—six months to less than two years. **Knowledges**—Fine Arts; Sales and Marketing; Production and Processing; Design; Mechanical Devices; Clerical Practices. **Instructional Programs**—Art/Art Studies, General; Ceramic Arts and Ceramics; Crafts/Craft Design, Folk Art and Artisanry; Drawing; Fiber, Textile, and Weaving Arts; Metal and Jewelry Arts; Painting; Printmaking; Sculpture.

Related SOC Job—27-1012 Craft Artists. **Related OOH Job**—Artists and Related Workers. **Related DOT Job**—199.261-010 Taxidermist.

27-1013.00 Fine Artists, Including Painters, Sculptors, and Illustrators

- **Education/Training Required: Long-term on-the-job training**
- **Employed: 10,390**
- **Annual Earnings: $41,280**
- **Growth: 10.2%**
- **Annual Job Openings: 4,000**

Create original artwork, using any of a wide variety of mediums and techniques such as painting and sculpture.

Use materials such as pens and ink, watercolors, charcoal, oil, or computer software to create artwork. Integrate and develop visual elements, such as line, space, mass, color, and perspective, to produce desired effects such as the illustration of ideas, emotions, or moods. Confer with clients, editors, writers, art directors, and other interested parties regarding the nature and content of artwork to be produced. Submit preliminary or finished artwork or project plans to clients for approval, incorporating changes as necessary. Maintain portfolios of artistic work to demonstrate styles, interests, and abilities. Create finished artwork as decoration or to elucidate or substitute for spoken or written messages. Cut, bend, laminate, arrange, and fasten individual or mixed raw and manufactured materials and products to form works of art. Monitor events, trends, and other circumstances; research specific subject areas; attend art exhibitions; and read art publications to develop ideas and keep current on art world activities. Study different techniques to learn how to apply them to artistic endeavors. Render drawings, illustrations, and sketches of buildings, manufactured products, or models, working from sketches, blueprints, memory, models, or reference materials. Create sculptures, statues, and other three-dimensional artwork by using abrasives and tools to shape, carve, and fabricate materials such as clay, stone, wood, or metal. Create sketches, profiles, or likenesses of posed subjects or photographs, using any combination of freehand drawing, mechanical assembly kits, and computer imaging. Study styles, techniques, colors, textures, and materials used in works undergoing restoration to ensure consistency during the restoration process. Develop project budgets for approval, estimating timelines and material costs. Shade and fill in sketch outlines and backgrounds, using a variety of media such as watercolors, markers, and transparent washes, labeling designated colors when necessary. Collaborate with engineers, mechanics, and other technical experts as necessary to build and install creations.

GOE Information—**Interest Area:** 03. Arts and Communication. **Work Group:** 03.04. Studio Art. **Personality Type**—Artistic. Artistic occupations frequently involve working with forms, designs, and patterns. They often require self-expression, and the work can be done without following a clear set of rules. **Work Values**—Creativity; Ability Utilization; Independence; Achievement; Autonomy; Recognition. **Skills**—Management of Financial Resources; Equipment Selection; Operations Analysis; Repairing; Equipment Maintenance; Complex Problem Solving. **Abilities**—*Cognitive:* Originality; Visualization; Fluency of Ideas; Selective Attention; Category Flexibility; Perceptual Speed. *Psychomotor:* Manual Dexterity; Arm-Hand Steadiness; Finger Dexterity; Control Precision; Multilimb Coordination. *Physical:* Static Strength; Trunk Strength. *Sensory:* Visual Color Discrimination; Far Vision; Depth Perception; Speech Recognition; Auditory Attention. **General Work Activities**—*Information Input:* Getting Information; Monitoring Processes, Materials, or Surroundings; Identifying Objects, Actions, and Events. *Mental Process:* Thinking Creatively; Organizing, Planning, and Prioritizing; Making Decisions and Solving Problems. *Work Output:* Handling and Moving Objects; Performing General Physical Activities; Controlling Machines and Processes. *Interacting with Others:* Communicating with Persons Outside Organization; Influencing Others or Selling; Establishing and Maintaining Interpersonal Relationships. **Physical Work Conditions**—Indoors; Contaminants; Standing; Using Hands on Objects, Tools, or Controls; Repetitive Motions. **Other Job Characteristics**—Need to Be Exact or Accurate.

Experience—Job Zone 3. Previous work-related skill, knowledge, or experience is required. **Job Preparation**—SVP 6.0 to less than 7.0—more than one year and less than four years. **Knowledges**—Fine Arts; Design; Sales and Marketing; Production and Processing; Economics and Accounting; Communications and Media. **Instructional Programs**—Art/Art Studies, General; Ceramic Arts and Ceramics; Drawing; Fine Arts and Art Studies, Other; Fine/Studio Arts, General; Intermedia/Multimedia; Medical Illustration/Medical Illustrator; Painting; Printmaking; Sculpture.

Related SOC Job—27-1013 Fine Artists, Including Painters, Sculptors, and Illustrators. **Related OOH Job**—Artists and Related Workers. **Related DOT Jobs**—102.261-014 Paintings Restorer; 141.061-010 Cartoonist; 141.061-014 Fashion Artist; 141.061-022 Illustrator; 141.061-026 Illustrator, Medical and Scientific; 141.061-030 Illustrator, Set; 141.061-034 Police Artist; 141.081-010 Cartoonist, Motion Pictures; 144.061-010 Painter; 144.061-014 Printmaker; 144.061-018 Sculptor; 149.041-010 Quick Sketch Artist; 149.051-010 Silhouette Artist; 149.261-010 Exhibit Artist; 970.281-014 Delineator; 970.361-018 Artist, Suspect.

27-1014.00 Multi-Media Artists and Animators

- **Education/Training Required: Bachelor's degree**
- **Employed: 23,790**
- **Annual Earnings: $50,290**
- **Growth: 14.1%**
- **Annual Job Openings: 14,000**

Create special effects, animation, or other visual images, using film, video, computers, or other electronic tools and media, for use in products or creations such as computer games, movies, music videos, and commercials.

Design complex graphics and animation, using independent judgment, creativity, and computer equipment. Create two-dimensional and three-dimensional images depicting objects in motion or illustrating a process, using computer animation or modeling programs. Make objects or characters appear lifelike by manipulating light, color, texture, shadow, and transparency or manipulating static images to give the illusion of motion. Apply story development, directing, cinematography, and editing to animation to create storyboards that show the flow of the animation and map out key scenes and characters. Assemble, typeset, scan, and produce digital camera-ready art or film negatives and printer's proofs. Script, plan, and create animated narrative sequences under tight deadlines, using computer software and hand-drawing techniques. Create basic designs, drawings, and illustrations for product labels, cartons, direct mail, or television. Create pen-and-paper images to be scanned, edited, colored, textured, or animated by computer. Develop briefings, brochures, multimedia presentations, Web pages, promotional products, technical illustrations, and computer artwork for use in products, technical manuals, literature, newsletters, and slide shows. Use models to simulate the behavior of animated objects in the finished sequence. Create and install special effects as required by the script, mixing chemicals and fabricating needed parts from wood, metal, plaster, and clay. Participate in design and production of multimedia campaigns, handling budgeting and scheduling and assisting with such responsibilities as production coordination, background design, and progress tracking. Convert real objects to animated objects through modeling, using techniques such as optical scanning. Implement and maintain configuration control systems.

GOE Information—Interest Area: 03. Arts and Communication. **Work Group:** 03.09. Media Technology. **Personality Type—**No data available. **Work Values—**No data available. **Skills—**Operations Analysis; Technology Design; Time Management; Judgment and Decision Making; Active Listening; Reading Comprehension. **Abilities—***Cognitive:* Originality; Visualization; Fluency of Ideas; Perceptual Speed; Selective Attention; Number Facility. *Psychomotor:* Arm-Hand Steadiness; Manual Dexterity; Finger Dexterity; Control Precision. *Physical:* None met the criteria. *Sensory:* Visual Color Discrimination; Far Vision. **General Work Activities—***Information Input:* Getting Information; Identifying Objects, Actions, and Events; Monitoring Processes, Materials, or Surroundings. *Mental Process:* Updating and Using Relevant Knowledge; Thinking Creatively; Making Decisions and Solving Problems. *Work Output:* Interacting With Computers; Documenting or Recording Information. *Interacting with Others:* Establishing and Maintaining Interpersonal Relationships; Communicating with Other Workers; Communicating with Persons Outside Organization. **Physical Work Conditions—**Indoors; Sitting; Using Hands on Objects, Tools, or Controls; Repetitive Motions. **Other Job Characteristics—**Repeat Same Tasks; Need to Be Exact or Accurate.

Experience—Job Zone 4. A minimum of two to four years of work-related skill, knowledge, or experience is needed. **Job Preparation—**SVP 7.0 to less than 8.0—two years to less than 10 years. **Knowledges—**Fine Arts; Design; Computers and Electronics; Communications and Media; English Language. **Instructional Programs—**Animation, Interactive Technology, Video Graphics, and Special Effects; Drawing; Graphic Design; Intermedia/Multimedia; Painting; Printmaking; Web Page, Digital/Multimedia, and Information Resources Design.

Related SOC Job—27-1014 Multi-Media Artists and Animators. **Related OOH Job—**Artists and Related Workers. **Related DOT Job—**141.081-010 Cartoonist, Motion Pictures.

27-1019.99 Artists and Related Workers, All Other

- **Education/Training Required: Long-term on-the-job training**
- **Employed: 5,290**
- **Annual Earnings: $31,230**
- **Growth: 10.0%**
- **Annual Job Openings: 1,000**

All artists and related workers not listed separately.

No task data available.

Note: The Department of Labor has not collected some data for this job, so it has fewer details than the other descriptions.

Related SOC Job—27-1019 Artists and Related Workers, All Other. **Related OOH Job—**None. **Related DOT Job—**191.287-014 Appraiser, Art.

27-1021.00 Commercial and Industrial Designers

- **Education/Training Required: Bachelor's degree**
- **Employed: 31,650**
- **Annual Earnings: $52,200**
- **Growth: 10.8%**
- **Annual Job Openings: 7,000**

Develop and design manufactured products, such as cars, home appliances, and children's toys. Combine artistic talent with research on product use, marketing, and materials to create the most functional and appealing product design.

Prepare sketches of ideas, detailed drawings, illustrations, artwork, or blueprints, using drafting instruments, paints and brushes, or computer-aided design equipment. Direct and coordinate the fabrication of models or samples and the drafting of working drawings and specification sheets from sketches. Modify and refine designs, using working models, to conform with customer specifications, production limitations, or changes in design trends. Coordinate the look and function of product lines. Confer with engineering, marketing, production, or sales departments, or with customers, to establish and evaluate design concepts for manufactured products. Present designs and reports to customers or design committees for approval and discuss need for modification. Evaluate feasibility of design ideas based on factors such as appearance, safety, function, serviceability, budget, production costs/methods, and market characteristics. Read publications, attend showings, and study competing products and design styles and motifs to obtain perspective and generate design concepts. Research production specifications, costs, production materials, and manufacturing methods and provide cost estimates and itemized production requirements. Design graphic material for use as ornamentation, illustration, or advertising on manufactured materials and packaging or containers. Develop manufacturing procedures and monitor the manufacture of their designs in a factory to improve operations and product quality. Supervise assistants' work throughout the design process. Fabricate models or samples in paper, wood, glass, fabric, plastic, metal, or other materials, using hand or power tools. Investigate product characteristics such as the product's safety and handling qualities; its market appeal; how efficiently it can be produced; and ways of distributing, using, and maintaining it. Develop industrial standards and regulatory guidelines. Participate in new product planning or market research, including studying the potential need for new products. Advise corporations on issues involving corporate image projects or problems.

GOE Information—Interest Area: 03. Arts and Communication. **Work Group:** 03.05. Design. **Personality Type—**Artistic. Artistic occupations frequently involve working with forms, designs, and patterns. They often require self-expression, and the work can be done without following a clear set of rules. **Work Values—**Creativity; Ability Utilization; Achievement; Recognition; Autonomy; Working Conditions. **Skills—**Technology Design; Operations Analysis; Quality

Control Analysis; Troubleshooting; Installation; Systems Evaluation. **Abilities**—*Cognitive:* Originality; Fluency of Ideas; Visualization; Number Facility; Mathematical Reasoning; Information Ordering. *Psychomotor:* Finger Dexterity. *Physical:* None met the criteria. *Sensory:* Visual Color Discrimination; Far Vision; Depth Perception; Speech Clarity; Near Vision; Speech Recognition. **General Work Activities**—*Information Input:* Monitoring Processes, Materials, or Surroundings; Getting Information; Identifying Objects, Actions, and Events. *Mental Process:* Thinking Creatively; Updating and Using Relevant Knowledge; Organizing, Planning, and Prioritizing. *Work Output:* Drafting and Specifying Technical Devices; Interacting With Computers; Documenting or Recording Information. *Interacting with Others:* Communicating with Other Workers; Establishing and Maintaining Interpersonal Relationships; Providing Consultation and Advice to Others. **Physical Work Conditions**—Indoors; Sitting; Using Hands on Objects, Tools, or Controls; Repetitive Motions. **Other Job Characteristics**—Need to Be Exact or Accurate; Repeat Same Tasks.

Experience—Job Zone 4. A minimum of two to four years of work-related skill, knowledge, or experience is needed. **Job Preparation**—SVP 7.0 to less than 8.0—two years to less than 10 years. **Knowledges**—Design; Engineering and Technology; Mathematics; Production and Processing; Physics; Mechanical Devices. **Instructional Programs**—Commercial and Advertising Art; Design and Applied Arts, Other; Design and Visual Communications, General; Industrial Design.

Related SOC Job—27-1021 Commercial and Industrial Designers. **Related OOH Job**—Commercial and Industrial Designers. **Related DOT Jobs**—141.061-038 Commercial Designer; 142.061-010 Bank-Note Designer; 142.061-014 Cloth Designer; 142.061-022 Furniture Designer; 142.061-026 Industrial Designer; 142.061-030 Memorial Designer; 142.061-034 Ornamental-Metalwork Designer; 142.061-038 Safety-Clothing-and-Equipment Developer; 142.061-054 Stained Glass Artist; 142.081-018 Package Designer.

27-1022.00 Fashion Designers

- **Education/Training Required: Bachelor's degree**
- **Employed: 12,980**
- **Annual Earnings: $60,860**
- **Growth: 8.4%**
- **Annual Job Openings: 2,000**

Design clothing and accessories. Create original garments or design garments that follow well-established fashion trends. May develop the line of color and kinds of materials.

Identify target markets for designs, looking at factors such as age, gender, and socioeconomic status. Provide sample garments to agents and sales representatives and arrange for showings of sample garments at sales meetings or fashion shows. Purchase new or used clothing and accessory items as needed to complete designs. Read scripts and consult directors and other production staff in order to develop design concepts and plan productions. Research the styles and periods of clothing needed for film or theatrical productions. Sew together sections of material to form mockups or samples of garments or articles, using sewing equipment. Test fabrics or oversee testing so that garment care labels can be created. Direct and coordinate workers involved in drawing and cutting patterns and constructing samples or finished garments. Sketch rough and detailed drawings of apparel or accessories and write specifications such as color schemes, construction, material types, and accessory requirements. Visit textile showrooms to keep up to date on the latest fabrics. Determine prices for styles. Confer with sales and management executives or with clients to discuss design ideas. Design custom clothing and accessories for individuals; retailers; or theatrical, television, or film productions. Adapt other designers' ideas for the mass market. Collaborate with other designers to coordinate special products and designs. Draw patterns for articles designed; then cut patterns and cut material according to patterns, using measuring instruments and scissors. Develop a group of products or accessories and market them through venues such as boutiques or mail-order catalogs. Examine sample garments on and off models; then modify designs to achieve desired effects. Select materials and production techniques to be used for products. Attend fashion shows and review garment magazines and manuals to gather information about fashion trends and consumer preferences.

GOE Information—**Interest Area:** 03. Arts and Communication. **Work Group:** 03.05. Design. **Personality Type**—Artistic. Artistic occupations frequently involve working with forms, designs, and patterns. They often require self-expression, and the work can be done without following a clear set of rules. **Work Values**—Creativity; Ability Utilization; Achievement; Recognition; Responsibility; Autonomy. **Skills**—Systems Analysis; Operations Analysis; Management of Financial Resources; Systems Evaluation; Management of Material Resources; Persuasion. **Abilities**—*Cognitive:* Originality; Fluency of Ideas; Visualization; Time Sharing; Number Facility; Oral Expression. *Psychomotor:* Wrist-Finger Speed; Arm-Hand Steadiness; Finger Dexterity; Manual Dexterity; Multilimb Coordination; Control Precision. *Physical:* None met the criteria. *Sensory:* Visual Color Discrimination; Auditory Attention. **General Work Activities**—*Information Input:* Getting Information; Identifying Objects, Actions, and Events; Estimating the Needed Characteristics of Products, Events, or Information. *Mental Process:* Thinking Creatively; Judging the Qualities of Things, Services, or Other People's Work; Updating and Using Relevant Knowledge. *Work Output:* Drafting and Specifying Technical Devices; Handling and Moving Objects; Controlling Machines and Processes. *Interacting with Others:* Communicating with Other Workers; Establishing and Maintaining Interpersonal Relationships; Communicating with Persons Outside Organization. **Physical Work Conditions**—Indoors; Sitting; Using Hands on Objects, Tools, or Controls. **Other Job Characteristics**—None met the criteria.

Experience—Job Zone 3. Previous work-related skill, knowledge, or experience is required. **Job Preparation**—SVP 6.0 to less than 7.0—more than one year and less than four years. **Knowledges**—Fine Arts; Design; Sales and Marketing; Education and Training. **Instructional Programs**—Apparel and Textile Manufacture; Fashion and Fabric Consultant; Fashion/Apparel Design; Textile Science.

Related SOC Job—27-1022 Fashion Designers. **Related OOH Job**—Fashion Designers. **Related DOT Jobs**—142.061-018 Fashion Designer; 142.081-014 Fur Designer; 142.281-010 Copyist.

27-1023.00 Floral Designers

- **Education/Training Required: Moderate-term on-the-job training**
- **Employed: 63,920**
- **Annual Earnings: $21,060**
- **Growth: 10.3%**
- **Annual Job Openings: 14,000**

Design, cut, and arrange live, dried, or artificial flowers and foliage.

Confer with clients regarding price and type of arrangement desired and the date, time, and place of delivery. Plan arrangement according to client's requirements, utilizing knowledge of design and properties of materials, or select appropriate standard design pattern. Water plants and cut, condition, and clean flowers and foliage for storage. Select flora and foliage for arrangements, working with numerous combinations to synthesize and develop new creations. Order and purchase flowers and supplies from wholesalers and growers. Wrap and price completed arrangements. Trim material and arrange bouquets, wreaths, terrariums, and other items, using trimmers, shapers, wire, pins, floral tape, foam, and other materials. Perform office and retail service duties such as keeping financial records, serving customers, answering telephones, selling giftware items, and receiving payment. Inform customers about the care, maintenance, and handling of various flowers and foliage, indoor plants, and other items. Decorate or supervise the decoration of buildings, halls, churches, or other facilities for parties, weddings, and other occasions. Perform general cleaning duties in the store to ensure the shop is clean and tidy. Unpack stock as it comes into the shop. Create and change in-store and window displays, designs, and looks to enhance a shop's image. Conduct classes or demonstrations or train other workers. Grow flowers for use in arrangements or for sale in shop.

GOE Information—Interest Area: 03. Arts and Communication. **Work Group:** 03.05. Design. **Personality Type—**Artistic. Artistic occupations frequently involve working with forms, designs, and patterns. They often require self-expression, and the work can be done without following a clear set of rules. **Work Values—**Creativity; Achievement; Ability Utilization; Autonomy; Recognition; Independence. **Skills—**Management of Material Resources; Management of Financial Resources; Management of Personnel Resources; Service Orientation; Social Perceptiveness; Operations Analysis. **Abilities—***Cognitive:* Visualization; Originality; Fluency of Ideas; Category Flexibility; Oral Expression. *Psychomotor:* Arm-Hand Steadiness; Manual Dexterity; Multilimb Coordination. *Physical:* Trunk Strength. *Sensory:* Visual Color Discrimination. **General Work Activities—***Information Input:* Getting Information; Identifying Objects, Actions, and Events; Monitoring Processes, Materials, or Surroundings. *Mental Process:* Thinking Creatively; Organizing, Planning, and Prioritizing; Processing Information. *Work Output:* Handling and Moving Objects; Performing General Physical Activities; Operating Vehicles or Equipment. *Interacting with Others:* Performing for or Working with the Public; Influencing Others or Selling; Establishing and Maintaining Interpersonal Relationships. **Physical Work Conditions—**Indoors; Standing; Using Hands on Objects, Tools, or Controls; Repetitive Motions. **Other Job Characteristics—**Need to Be Exact or Accurate.

Experience—Job Zone 2. Some previous work-related skill, knowledge, or experience may be helpful in these occupations, but usually is not needed. **Job Preparation—**SVP 4.0 to less than 6.0—six months to less than two years. **Knowledges—**Fine Arts; Sales and Marketing; Customer and Personal Service; Design; Production and Processing; Personnel and Human Resources. **Instructional Program—**Floriculture/Floristry Operations and Management.

Related SOC Job—27-1023 Floral Designers. **Related OOH Job—**Floral Designers. **Related DOT Jobs—**142.081-010 Floral Designer; 899.364-014 Artificial-Foliage Arranger.

27-1024.00 Graphic Designers

- **Education/Training Required: Bachelor's degree**
- **Employed: 178,530**
- **Annual Earnings: $38,390**
- **Growth: 15.2%**
- **Annual Job Openings: 35,000**

Design or create graphics to meet specific commercial or promotional needs, such as packaging, displays, or logos. May use a variety of media to achieve artistic or decorative effects.

Create designs, concepts, and sample layouts based on knowledge of layout principles and esthetic design concepts. Determine size and arrangement of illustrative material and copy and select style and size of type. Use computer software to generate new images. Mark up, paste, and assemble final layouts to prepare layouts for printer. Draw and print charts, graphs, illustrations, and other artwork, using computer. Review final layouts and suggest improvements as needed. Confer with clients to discuss and determine layout design. Develop graphics and layouts for product illustrations, company logos, and Internet Web sites. Key information into computer equipment to create layouts for client or supervisor. Prepare illustrations or rough sketches of material, discussing them with clients or supervisors and making necessary changes. Study illustrations and photographs to plan presentation of materials, products, or services. Prepare notes and instructions for workers who assemble and prepare final layouts for printing. Develop negatives and prints to produce layout photographs, using negative and print developing equipment and tools. Photograph layouts, using camera, to make layout prints for supervisors or clients. Produce still and animated graphics for on-air and taped portions of television news broadcasts, using electronic video equipment.

GOE Information—Interest Area: 03. Arts and Communication. **Work Group:** 03.05. Design. **Personality Type—**Artistic. Artistic occupations frequently involve working with forms, designs, and patterns. They often require self-expression, and the work can be done without following a clear set of rules. **Work Values—**Creativity; Ability Utilization; Achievement; Recognition; Working Conditions; Variety. **Skills—**Persuasion; Operations Analysis; Troubleshooting; Time Management; Complex Problem Solving; Quality Control Analysis. **Abilities—***Cognitive:* Originality; Visualization; Fluency of Ideas; Category Flexibility; Information Ordering; Inductive Reasoning. *Psychomotor:* Finger Dexterity; Arm-Hand Steadiness; Manual Dexterity. *Physical:* None met the criteria. *Sensory:* Visual Color Discrimination; Near Vision; Far Vision. **General Work Activities—***Information Input:* Getting Information; Identifying Objects, Actions, and Events; Estimating the Needed Characteristics of Products, Events, or Information. *Mental Process:* Thinking Creatively; Updating and Using Relevant Knowledge; Organizing, Planning, and Prioritizing. *Work Output:* Interacting With Computers; Drafting and Specifying Technical Devices; Documenting or Recording Information. *Interacting with Others:* Establishing and Maintaining Interpersonal Relationships; Communicating with Persons Outside Organization; Communicating with Other Workers. **Physical Work Conditions—**Indoors; Sitting; Using Hands on Objects, Tools, or Controls; Repetitive Motions. **Other Job Characteristics—**Need to Be Exact or Accurate; Repeat Same Tasks.

Experience—Job Zone 4. A minimum of two to four years of work-related skill, knowledge, or experience is needed. **Job Preparation—**SVP 7.0 to less than 8.0—two years to less than 10 years. **Knowledges—**Fine Arts; Design; Communications and Media; Sales and Marketing; Computers and Electronics; Clerical Practices. **Instructional Programs—**Agricultural Communications/Journalism; Commercial and Advertising Art; Computer Graphics; Design and Visual Communications, General; Graphic Design; Industrial Design; Web Page, Digital/Multimedia, and Information Resources Design.

Related SOC Job—27-1024 Graphic Designers. **Related OOH Job—**Graphic Designers. **Related DOT Job—**141.061-018 Graphic Designer.

27-1025.00 Interior Designers

- Education/Training Required: Bachelor's degree
- Employed: 50,020
- Annual Earnings: $41,350
- Growth: 15.5%
- Annual Job Openings: 10,000

Plan, design, and furnish interiors of residential, commercial, or industrial buildings. Formulate design that is practical, aesthetic, and conducive to intended purposes, such as raising productivity, selling merchandise, or improving lifestyle. May specialize in a particular field, style, or phase of interior design.

Estimate material requirements and costs and present design to client for approval. Confer with client to determine factors affecting planning interior environments, such as budget, architectural preferences, and purpose and function. Advise client on interior design factors such as space planning, layout, and utilization of furnishings or equipment and color coordination. Select or design and purchase furnishings, artwork, and accessories. Formulate environmental plan to be practical, esthetic, and conducive to intended purposes such as raising productivity or selling merchandise. Subcontract fabrication, installation, and arrangement of carpeting, fixtures, accessories, draperies, paint and wall coverings, artwork, furniture, and related items. Render design ideas in form of paste-ups or drawings. Plan and design interior environments for boats, planes, buses, trains, and other enclosed spaces.

GOE Information—Interest Area: 03. Arts and Communication. **Work Group:** 03.05. Design. **Personality Type**—Artistic. Artistic occupations frequently involve working with forms, designs, and patterns. They often require self-expression, and the work can be done without following a clear set of rules. **Work Values**—Creativity; Recognition; Ability Utilization; Achievement; Autonomy; Responsibility. **Skills**—Installation; Persuasion; Management of Financial Resources; Negotiation; Active Learning; Mathematics. **Abilities**—*Cognitive:* Originality; Visualization; Fluency of Ideas; Deductive Reasoning; Mathematical Reasoning; Speed of Closure. *Psychomotor:* None met the criteria. *Physical:* None met the criteria. *Sensory:* Visual Color Discrimination; Depth Perception; Far Vision; Speech Recognition. **General Work Activities**—*Information Input:* Identifying Objects, Actions, and Events; Getting Information; Monitoring Processes, Materials, or Surroundings. *Mental Process:* Thinking Creatively; Organizing, Planning, and Prioritizing; Updating and Using Relevant Knowledge. *Work Output:* Interacting With Computers; Drafting and Specifying Technical Devices; Documenting or Recording Information. *Interacting with Others:* Influencing Others or Selling; Communicating with Other Workers; Establishing and Maintaining Interpersonal Relationships. **Physical Work Conditions**—Indoors; Sitting. **Other Job Characteristics**—Need to Be Exact or Accurate.

Experience—Job Zone 3. Previous work-related skill, knowledge, or experience is required. **Job Preparation**—SVP 6.0 to less than 7.0—more than one year and less than four years. **Knowledges**—Design; Sales and Marketing; Building and Construction; Administration and Management; Clerical Practices; Fine Arts. **Instructional Programs**—Facilities Planning and Management; Interior Architecture; Interior Design; Textile Science.

Related SOC Job—27-1025 Interior Designers. **Related OOH Job**—Interior Designers. **Related DOT Jobs**—141.051-010 Color Expert; 142.051-014 Interior Designer.

27-1026.00 Merchandise Displayers and Window Trimmers

- Education/Training Required: Moderate-term on-the-job training
- Employed: 64,320
- Annual Earnings: $22,590
- Growth: 10.3%
- Annual Job Openings: 13,000

Plan and erect commercial displays, such as those in windows and interiors of retail stores and at trade exhibitions.

Take photographs of displays and signage. Plan and erect commercial displays to entice and appeal to customers. Place prices and descriptive signs on backdrops, fixtures, merchandise, or floor. Change or rotate window displays, interior display areas, and signage to reflect changes in inventory or promotion. Obtain plans from display designers or display managers and discuss their implementation with clients or supervisors. Develop ideas or plans for merchandise displays or window decorations. Consult with advertising and sales staff to determine type of merchandise to be featured and time and place for each display. Arrange properties, furniture, merchandise, backdrops, and other accessories as shown in prepared sketches. Construct or assemble displays and display components from fabric, glass, paper, and plastic according to specifications, using hand tools and woodworking power tools. Collaborate with others to obtain products and other display items. Use computers to produce signage. Dress mannequins for displays. Maintain props and mannequins, inspecting them for imperfections and applying preservative coatings as necessary. Select themes, lighting, colors, and props to be used. Attend training sessions and corporate planning meetings to obtain new ideas for product launches. Instruct sales staff in color-coordination of clothing racks and counter displays. Store, pack, and maintain records of props and display items. Prepare sketches, floor plans, or models of proposed displays. Cut out designs on cardboard, hardboard, and plywood according to motif of event. Install booths, exhibits, displays, carpets, and drapes as guided by floor plan of building and specifications. Install decorations such as flags, banners, festive lights, and bunting on or in building, street, exhibit hall, or booth. Create and enhance mannequin faces by mixing and applying paint and attaching measured eyelash strips, using artist's brush, airbrush, pins, ruler, and scissors.

GOE Information—Interest Area: 03. Arts and Communication. **Work Group:** 03.05. Design. **Personality Type**—Artistic. Artistic occupations frequently involve working with forms, designs, and patterns. They often require self-expression, and the work can be done without following a clear set of rules. **Work Values**—Creativity; Ability Utilization; Achievement; Working Conditions; Recognition; Independence. **Skills**—Persuasion; Negotiation; Management of Personnel Resources; Coordination; Management of Financial Resources. **Abilities**—*Cognitive:* Visualization; Originality; Fluency of Ideas; Oral Comprehension. *Psychomotor:* Speed of Limb Movement; Arm-Hand Steadiness; Finger Dexterity; Manual Dexterity; Multilimb Coordination. *Physical:* Extent Flexibility; Gross Body Equilibrium; Gross Body Coordination; Stamina; Static Strength; Trunk Strength. *Sensory:* Far Vision; Visual Color Discrimination; Speech Recognition. **General Work Activities**—*Information Input:* Identifying Objects, Actions, and Events; Getting Information; Monitoring Processes, Materials, or Surroundings. *Mental Process:* Thinking Creatively; Making Decisions and Solving Problems; Organizing, Planning, and Prioritizing. *Work Output:* Handling and Moving Objects; Performing General Physical Activities. *Interacting* *with Others:* Establishing and Maintaining Interpersonal Relationships; Communicating with Persons Outside Organization; Communicating with Other Workers. **Physical Work Conditions**—Indoors; Contaminants; Walking and Running; Using Hands on Objects, Tools, or Controls; Bending or Twisting the Body; Repetitive Motions. **Other Job Characteristics**—Need to Be Exact or Accurate; Errors Have Important Consequences.

Experience—Job Zone 2. Some previous work-related skill, knowledge, or experience may be helpful in these occupations, but usually is not needed. **Job Preparation**—SVP 4.0 to less than 6.0—six months to less than two years. **Knowledges**—Sales and Marketing; Design; Administration and Management; Computers and Electronics; Customer and Personal Service. **Instructional Program**—No related CIP programs.

Related SOC Job—27-1026 Merchandise Displayers and Window Trimmers. **Related OOH Job**—Merchandise Displayers and Window Trimmers. **Related DOT Jobs**—142.031-014 Manager, Display; 298.081-010 Displayer, Merchandise; 298.381-010 Decorator.

27-1027.00 Set and Exhibit Designers

- **Education/Training Required: Bachelor's degree**
- **Employed: 8,380**
- **Annual Earnings: $37,390**
- **Growth: 9.3%**
- **Annual Job Openings: 2,000**

Design special exhibits and movie, television, and theater sets. May study scripts, confer with directors, and conduct research to determine appropriate architectural styles.

Examine objects to be included in exhibits to plan where and how to display them. Acquire, or arrange for acquisition of, specimens or graphics required to complete exhibits. Prepare rough drafts and scale working drawings of sets, including floor plans, scenery, and properties to be constructed. Confer with clients and staff to gather information about exhibit space, proposed themes and content, timelines, budgets, materials, and promotion requirements. Estimate set- or exhibit-related costs, including materials, construction, and rental of props or locations. Develop set designs based on evaluation of scripts, budgets, research information, and available locations. Direct and coordinate construction, erection, or decoration activities to ensure that sets or exhibits meet design, budget, and schedule requirements. Inspect installed exhibits for conformance to specifications and satisfactory operation of special effects components. Plan for location-specific issues such as space limitations, traffic flow patterns, and safety concerns. Submit plans for approval and adapt plans to serve intended purposes or to conform to budget or fabrication restrictions. Prepare preliminary renderings of proposed exhibits, including detailed construction, layout, and material specifications and diagrams relating to aspects such as special effects and lighting. Select and purchase lumber and hardware necessary for set construction. Collaborate with those in charge of lighting and sound so that those production aspects can be coordinated with set designs or exhibit layouts. Research architectural and stylistic elements appropriate to the time period to be depicted, consulting experts for information as necessary. Design and produce displays and materials that can be used to decorate windows, interior displays, or event locations such as streets and fairgrounds. Coordinate the removal of sets, props, and exhibits after productions or events are complete. Select set props such as furniture, pictures, lamps, and rugs. Confer with conservators to determine how to handle an exhibit's environmental aspects, such as lighting, temperature, and humidity, so that objects will be protected and exhibits will be enhanced.

GOE Information—**Interest Area:** 03. Arts and Communication. **Work Group:** 03.05. Design. **Personality Type**—Artistic. Artistic occupations frequently involve working with forms, designs, and patterns. They often require self-expression, and the work can be done without following a clear set of rules. **Work Values**—Creativity; Ability Utilization; Achievement; Autonomy; Recognition; Variety. **Skills**—Persuasion; Installation; Management of Material Resources; Management of Personnel Resources; Operations Analysis; Negotiation. **Abilities**—*Cognitive:* Visualization; Spatial Orientation; Originality; Fluency of Ideas; Time Sharing; Number Facility. *Psychomotor:* Wrist-Finger Speed; Arm-Hand Steadiness; Manual Dexterity; Finger Dexterity. *Physical:* Extent Flexibility. *Sensory:* Visual Color Discrimination; Far Vision; Near Vision. **General Work Activities**—*Information Input:* Getting Information; Identifying Objects, Actions, and Events; Monitoring Processes, Materials, or Surroundings. *Mental Process:* Organizing, Planning, and Prioritizing; Thinking Creatively; Updating and Using Relevant Knowledge. *Work Output:* Handling and Moving Objects; Performing General Physical Activities; Drafting and Specifying Technical Devices. *Interacting with Others:* Coordinating the Work and Activities of Others; Establishing and Maintaining Interpersonal Relationships; Communicating with Other Workers. **Physical Work Conditions**—Indoors; Sitting; Using Hands on Objects, Tools, or Controls. **Other Job Characteristics**—Need to Be Exact or Accurate; Repeat Same Tasks.

Experience—Job Zone 4. A minimum of two to four years of work-related skill, knowledge, or experience is needed. **Job Preparation**—SVP 7.0 to less than 8.0—two years to less than 10 years. **Knowledges**—Fine Arts; Design; History and Archeology; Communications and Media; Sociology and Anthropology; Computers and Electronics. **Instructional Programs**—Design and Applied Arts, Other; Design and Visual Communications, General; Illustration; Technical Theatre/Theatre Design and Technology.

Related SOC Job—27-1027 Set and Exhibit Designers. **Related OOH Job**—Set and Exhibit Designers. **Related DOT Jobs**—142.051-010 Display Designer; 142.061-042 Set Decorator; 142.061-046 Set Designer; 142.061-050 Set Designer; 142.061-058 Exhibit Designer; 142.061-062 Art Director; 149.031-010 Supervisor, Scenic Arts.

27-1029.99 Designers, All Other

- **Education/Training Required: No data available**
- **Employed: 12,410**
- **Annual Earnings: $43,600**
- **Growth: 13.6%**
- **Annual Job Openings: 2,000**

All designers not listed separately.

No task data available.

Note: The Department of Labor has not collected some data for this job, so it has fewer details than the other descriptions.

Related SOC Job—27-1029 Designers, All Other. **Related OOH Job**—None. **Related DOT Job**—No data available.

27-2000 Entertainers and Performers, Sports and Related Workers

27-2011.00 Actors

- **Education/Training Required: Long-term on-the-job training**
- **Employed: 59,590**
- **Annual Earnings: No data available**
- **Growth: 16.1%**
- **Annual Job Openings: 11,000**

Play parts in stage, television, radio, video, or motion picture productions for entertainment, information, or instruction. Interpret serious or comic role by speech, gesture, and body movement to entertain or inform audience. May dance and sing.

Study and rehearse roles from scripts to interpret, learn and memorize lines, stunts, and cues as directed. Work closely with directors, other actors, and playwrights to find the interpretation most suited to the role. Learn about characters in scripts and their relationships to each other to develop role interpretations. Collaborate with other actors as part of an ensemble. Perform humorous and serious interpretations of emotions, actions, and situations, using body movements, facial expressions, and gestures. Attend auditions and casting calls to audition for roles. Portray and interpret roles, using speech, gestures, and body movements to entertain, inform, or instruct radio, film, television, or live audiences. Work with other crewmembers responsible for lighting, costumes, makeup, and props. Sing or dance during dramatic or comedic performances. Read from scripts or books to narrate action or to inform or entertain audiences, utilizing few or no stage props. Promote productions using means such as interviews about plays or movies. Write original or adapted material for dramas, comedies, puppet shows, narration, or other performances. Prepare and perform action stunts for motion picture, television, or stage productions. Tell jokes; perform comic dances, songs, and skits; impersonate mannerisms and voices of others; contort face; and use other devices to amuse audiences. Introduce performances and performers to stimulate excitement and coordinate smooth transition of acts during events. Manipulate strings, wires, rods, or fingers to animate puppets or dummies in synchronization with talking, singing, or recorded programs. Dress in comical clown costumes and makeup and perform comedy routines to entertain audiences. Perform original and stock tricks of illusion to entertain and mystify audiences, occasionally including audience members as participants. Construct puppets and ventriloquist dummies and sew accessory clothing, using hand tools and machines.

GOE Information—Interest Area: 03. Arts and Communication. **Work Group:** 03.06. Drama. **Personality Type**—Artistic. Artistic occupations frequently involve working with forms, designs, and patterns. They often require self-expression, and the work can be done without following a clear set of rules. **Work Values**—Ability Utilization; Recognition; Creativity; Variety; Achievement; Social Status. **Skills**—Social Perceptiveness; Speaking; Active Listening; Persuasion; Coordination; Judgment and Decision Making. **Abilities**—*Cognitive:* Memorization; Fluency of Ideas; Originality; Written Expression; Oral Expression; Oral Comprehension. *Psychomotor:* None met the criteria. *Physical:* Gross Body Coordination. *Sensory:* Speech Clarity. **General Work Activities**—*Information Input:* Identifying Objects, Actions, and Events; Getting Information; Monitoring Processes, Materials, or Surroundings. *Mental Process:* Thinking Creatively; Organizing, Planning, and Prioritizing; Judging the Qualities of Things, Services, or Other People's Work. *Work Output:* Performing General Physical Activities; Handling and Moving Objects; Documenting or Recording Information. *Interacting with Others:* Performing for or Working with the Public; Establishing and Maintaining Interpersonal Relationships; Communicating with Other Workers. **Physical Work Conditions**—Indoors; Standing. **Other Job Characteristics**—Need to Be Exact or Accurate.

Experience—Job Zone 2. Some previous work-related skill, knowledge, or experience may be helpful in these occupations, but usually is not needed. **Job Preparation**—SVP 4.0 to less than 6.0—six months to less than two years. **Knowledges**—Fine Arts; Communications and Media; Sociology and Anthropology; History and Archeology; Psychology; English Language. **Instructional Programs**—Acting; Directing and Theatrical Production; Drama and Dramatics/Theatre Arts, General; Dramatic/Theatre Arts and Stagecraft, Other; Theatre/Theatre Arts Management.

Related SOC Job—27-2011 Actors. **Related OOH Job**—Actors, Producers, and Directors. **Related DOT Jobs**—150.047-010 Actor; 150.147-010 Narrator; 159.041-010 Magician; 159.041-014 Puppeteer; 159.044-010 Ventriloquist; 159.047-010 Clown; 159.047-014 Comedian; 159.047-018 Impersonator; 159.047-022 Mime; 159.247-010 Acrobat; 159.247-014 Aerialist; 159.341-010 Juggler; 159.341-014 Stunt Performer; 159.347-014 Aquatic Performer; 159.347-018 Thrill Performer; 159.347-022 Wire Walker; 159.367-010 Ring Conductor; 159.647-010 Amusement Park Entertainer; 159.647-014 Extra; 159.647-022 Show Girl; others.

27-2012.00 Producers and Directors

- **Education/Training Required: Work experience plus degree**
- **Employed: 59,070**
- **Annual Earnings: $53,860**
- **Growth: 16.6%**
- **Annual Job Openings: 11,000**

The job openings listed here are shared with 27-2012.01 Producers, 27-2012.02 Directors—Stage, Motion Pictures, Television, and Radio, 27-2012.03 Program Directors, 27-2012.04 Talent Directors, and 27-2012.05 Technical Directors/Managers.

Produce or direct stage, television, radio, video, or motion picture productions for entertainment, information, or instruction. Responsible for creative decisions, such as interpretation of script, choice of guests, set design, sound, special effects, and choreography.

No task data available.

GOE Information—Interest Area: 03. Arts and Communication. **Work Group:** 03.01. Managerial Work in Arts and Communication. **Note:** The Department of Labor has not collected some data for this job, so it has fewer details than the other descriptions.

Instructional Programs—Cinematography and Film/Video Production; Directing and Theatrical Production; Drama and Dramatics/Theatre Arts, General; Dramatic/Theatre Arts and Stagecraft, Other; Film/Cinema Studies; Radio and Television; Theatre/Theatre Arts Management.

Related SOC Job—27-2012 Producers and Directors. **Related OOH Job**—Actors, Producers, and Directors. **Related DOT Job**—No data available.

27-2012.01 Producers

- **Education/Training Required:** Work experience plus degree
- **Employed:** 59,070
- **Annual Earnings:** $53,860
- **Growth:** 16.6%
- **Annual Job Openings:** 11,000

The job openings listed here are shared with 27-2012.00 Producers and Directors, 27-2012.02 Directors—Stage, Motion Pictures, Television, and Radio, 27-2012.03 Program Directors, 27-2012.04 Talent Directors, and 27-2012.05 Technical Directors/Managers.

Plan and coordinate various aspects of radio, television, stage, or motion picture production, such as selecting script; coordinating writing, directing, and editing; and arranging financing.

Coordinate the activities of writers, directors, managers, and other personnel throughout the production process. Monitor post-production processes to ensure accurate completion of all details. Perform management activities such as budgeting, scheduling, planning, and marketing. Determine production size, content, and budget, establishing details such as production schedules and management policies. Compose and edit scripts or provide screenwriters with story outlines from which scripts can be written. Conduct meetings with staff to discuss production progress and to ensure production objectives are attained. Resolve personnel problems that arise during the production process by acting as liaisons between dissenting parties when necessary. Produce shows for special occasions, such as holidays or testimonials. Edit and write news stories from information collected by reporters. Write and submit proposals to bid on contracts for projects. Hire directors, principal cast members, and key production staff members. Arrange financing for productions. Select plays, scripts, books, or ideas to be produced. Review film, recordings, or rehearsals to ensure conformance to production and broadcast standards. Perform administrative duties such as preparing operational reports, distributing rehearsal call sheets and script copies, and arranging for rehearsal quarters. Obtain and distribute costumes, props, music, and studio equipment needed to complete productions. Negotiate contracts with artistic personnel, often in accordance with collective bargaining agreements. Maintain knowledge of minimum wages and working conditions established by unions or associations of actors and technicians. Plan and coordinate the production of musical recordings, selecting music and directing performers. Negotiate with parties, including independent producers and the distributors and broadcasters who will be handling completed productions. Develop marketing plans for finished products, collaborating with sales associates to supervise product distribution. Determine and direct the content of radio programming.

GOE Information—Interest Area: 03. Arts and Communication. **Work Group:** 03.01. Managerial Work in Arts and Communication. **Personality Type—**Artistic. Artistic occupations frequently involve working with forms, designs, and patterns. They often require self-expression, and the work can be done without following a clear set of rules. **Work Values—**Authority; Creativity; Recognition; Responsibility; Autonomy; Achievement. **Skills—**Monitoring; Management of Personnel Resources; Writing; Negotiation; Management of Financial Resources; Coordination. **Abilities—***Cognitive:* Written Expression; Fluency of Ideas; Originality; Oral Expression; Number Facility; Written Comprehension. *Psychomotor:* None met the criteria. *Physical:* None met the criteria. *Sensory:* Speech Recognition; Hearing Sensitivity; Speech Clarity; Near Vision; Far Vision; Auditory Attention. **General Work Activities—***Information Input:* Getting Information; Identifying Objects, Actions, and Events; Monitoring Processes, Materials, or Surroundings. *Mental Process:*

Organizing, Planning, and Prioritizing; Thinking Creatively; Updating and Using Relevant Knowledge. *Work Output:* Interacting With Computers; Documenting or Recording Information; Controlling Machines and Processes. *Interacting with Others:* Communicating with Persons Outside Organization; Establishing and Maintaining Interpersonal Relationships; Communicating with Other Workers. **Physical Work Conditions—**Indoors; Sitting. **Other Job Characteristics—**Need to Be Exact or Accurate; Errors Have Important Consequences; Repeat Same Tasks.

Experience—Job Zone 4. A minimum of two to four years of work-related skill, knowledge, or experience is needed. **Job Preparation—**SVP 7.0 to less than 8.0—two years to less than 10 years. **Knowledges—**Communications and Media; Fine Arts; Clerical Practices; Sales and Marketing; Administration and Management; Telecommunications. **Instructional Programs—**Cinematography and Film/Video Production; Directing and Theatrical Production; Drama and Dramatics/Theatre Arts, General; Dramatic/Theatre Arts and Stagecraft, Other; Film/Cinema Studies; Radio and Television; Theatre/Theatre Arts Management.

Related SOC Job—27-2012 Producers and Directors. **Related OOH Job—**Actors, Producers, and Directors. **Related DOT Jobs—**159.117-010 Producer; 187.167-174 Producer; 187.167-178 Producer; 187.167-182 Producer, Assistant; 962.167-014 Program Assistant.

27-2012.02 Directors—Stage, Motion Pictures, Television, and Radio

- **Education/Training Required:** Work experience plus degree
- **Employed:** 59,070
- **Annual Earnings:** $53,860
- **Growth:** 16.6%
- **Annual Job Openings:** 11,000

The job openings listed here are shared with 27-2012.00 Producers and Directors, 27-2012.01 Producers, 27-2012.03 Program Directors, 27-2012.04 Talent Directors, and 27-2012.05 Technical Directors/Managers.

Interpret script, conduct rehearsals, and direct activities of cast and technical crew for stage, motion pictures, television, or radio programs.

Direct live broadcasts, films and recordings, or non-broadcast programming for public entertainment or education. Supervise and coordinate the work of camera, lighting, design, and sound crew members. Study and research scripts to determine how they should be directed. Cut and edit film or tape to integrate component parts into desired sequences. Collaborate with film and sound editors during the post-production process as films are edited and soundtracks are added. Confer with technical directors, managers, crew members, and writers to discuss details of production, such as photography, script, music, sets, and costumes. Plan details such as framing, composition, camera movement, sound, and actor movement for each shot or scene. Communicate to actors the approach, characterization, and movement needed for each scene in such a way that rehearsals and takes are minimized. Establish pace of programs and sequences of scenes according to time requirements and cast and set accessibility. Choose settings and locations for films and determine how scenes will be shot in these settings. Identify and approve equipment and elements required for productions, such as scenery, lights, props, costumes, choreography, and music. Compile scripts, program notes, and other material related to productions. Perform producers' duties such as securing financial backing, establishing and administering budgets, and recruiting cast and crew. Select plays or scripts for production and determine how material should be interpreted and performed. Compile cue words and phrases; cue announcers, cast members, and technicians during performances. Consult with writers, producers, or actors about script changes or "workshop" scripts, through rehearsal with writers and actors, to create final drafts. Collaborate with producers to hire crew members such as art directors, cinematographers, and costumer designers. Review film daily to check on work in progress and to plan for future filming. Interpret stage-set diagrams to determine stage layouts and supervise placement of equipment and scenery. Hold auditions for parts or negotiate contracts with actors determined suitable for specific roles, working in conjunction with producers.

GOE Information—Interest Area: 03. Arts and Communication. **Work Group:** 03.06. Drama. **Personality Type—**Artistic. Artistic occupations frequently involve working with forms, designs, and patterns. They often require self-expression, and the work can be done without following a clear set of rules. **Work Values—**Authority; Creativity; Recognition; Responsibility; Achievement; Autonomy. **Skills—**Management of Personnel Resources; Time Management; Judgment and Decision Making; Operations Analysis; Active Listening; Speaking. **Abilities—***Cognitive:* Originality; Fluency of Ideas; Number Facility; Visualization; Written Expression; Time Sharing. *Psychomotor:* Reaction Time. *Physical:* None met the criteria. *Sensory:* Speech Clarity; Visual Color Discrimination; Hearing Sensitivity; Far Vision; Speech Recognition; Depth Perception. **General Work Activities—***Information Input:* Getting Information; Monitoring Processes, Materials, or Surroundings; Identifying Objects, Actions, and Events. *Mental Process:* Thinking Creatively; Organizing, Planning, and Prioritizing; Updating and Using Relevant Knowledge. *Work Output:* Controlling Machines and Processes; Handling and Moving Objects; Documenting or Recording Information. *Interacting with Others:* Communicating with Other Workers; Establishing and Maintaining Interpersonal Relationships; Communicating with Persons Outside Organization. **Physical Work Conditions—**More Often Outdoors Than Indoors; Noisy; Sitting; Using Hands on Objects, Tools, or Controls. **Other Job Characteristics—**Need to Be Exact or Accurate; Errors Have Important Consequences.

Experience—Job Zone 4. A minimum of two to four years of work-related skill, knowledge, or experience is needed. **Job Preparation—**SVP 7.0 to less than 8.0—two years to less than 10 years. **Knowledges—**Communications and Media; Telecommunications; Fine Arts; Geography; Computers and Electronics; Education and Training. **Instructional Programs—**Cinematography and Film/Video Production; Directing and Theatrical Production; Drama and Dramatics/Theatre Arts, General; Dramatic/Theatre Arts and Stagecraft, Other; Film/Cinema Studies; Radio and Television; Theatre/Theatre Arts Management.

Related SOC Job—27-2012 Producers and Directors. **Related OOH Job—**Actors, Producers, and Directors. **Related DOT Jobs—**139.167-010 Program Coordinator; 150.027-010 Dramatic Coach; 150.067-010 Director, Stage; 159.067-010 Director, Motion Picture; 159.067-014 Director, Television; 159.167-014 Director, Radio; 159.167-018 Manager, Stage.

27-2012.03 Program Directors

- Education/Training Required: Work experience plus degree
- Employed: 59,070
- Annual Earnings: $53,860
- Growth: 16.6%
- Annual Job Openings: 11,000

The job openings listed here are shared with 27-2012.00 Producers and Directors, 27-2012.01 Producers, 27-2012.02 Directors—Stage, Motion Pictures, Television, and Radio, 27-2012.04 Talent Directors, and 27-2012.05 Technical Directors/Managers.

Direct and coordinate activities of personnel engaged in preparation of radio or television station program schedules and programs such as sports or news.

Plan and schedule programming and event coverage based on broadcast length; time availability; and other factors such as community needs, ratings data, and viewer demographics. Monitor and review programming to ensure that schedules are met, guidelines are adhered to, and performances are of adequate quality. Direct and coordinate activities of personnel engaged in broadcast news, sports, or programming. Check completed program logs for accuracy and conformance with FCC rules and regulations and resolve program log inaccuracies. Establish work schedules and assign work to staff members. Coordinate activities between departments such as news and programming. Perform personnel duties such as hiring staff and evaluating work performance. Evaluate new and existing programming for suitability and to assess the need for changes, using information such as audience surveys and feedback. Develop budgets for programming and broadcasting activities and monitor expenditures to ensure that they remain within budgetary limits. Confer with directors and production staff to discuss issues such as production and casting problems, budgets, policies, and news coverage. Select, acquire, and maintain programs, music, films, and other needed materials and obtain legal clearances for their use as necessary. Monitor network transmissions for advisories concerning daily program schedules, program content, special feeds, or program changes. Develop promotions for current programs and specials. Prepare copy and edit tape so that material is ready for broadcasting. Develop ideas for programs and features that a station could produce. Participate in the planning and execution of fundraising activities. Review information about programs and schedules to ensure accuracy and provide such information to local media outlets as necessary. Read news, read or record public service and promotional announcements, and otherwise participate as a member of an on-air shift as required. Operate and maintain on-air and production audio equipment. Direct setup of remote facilities and install or cancel programs at remote stations.

GOE Information—Interest Area: 03. Arts and Communication. **Work Group:** 03.01. Managerial Work in Arts and Communication. **Personality Type—**Enterprising. Enterprising occupations frequently involve starting up and carrying out projects. These occupations can involve leading people and making many decisions. They sometimes require risk taking and often deal with business. **Work Values—**Authority; Creativity; Variety; Autonomy; Responsibility; Recognition. **Skills—**Management of Financial Resources; Operations Analysis; Management of Personnel Resources; Coordination; Time Management; Writing. **Abilities—***Cognitive:* Mathematical Reasoning; Originality; Number Facility; Written Expression; Fluency of Ideas; Time Sharing. *Psychomotor:* None met the criteria. *Physical:* None met the criteria. *Sensory:* Far Vision; Speech Clarity; Near Vision; Speech Recognition. **General Work Activities—***Information Input:* Getting Information; Identifying Objects, Actions, and Events; Estimating the Needed Characteristics of Products, Events, or Information. *Mental Process:* Organizing, Planning, and Prioritizing; Thinking Creatively; Updating and Using Relevant Knowledge. *Work Output:* Documenting or Recording Information; Interacting With Computers; Controlling Machines and Processes. *Interacting with Others:* Communicating with Persons Outside Organization; Communicating with Other Workers; Establishing and Maintaining Interpersonal Relationships. **Physical Work Conditions—**Indoors;

Noisy; Sitting. **Other Job Characteristics**—Need to Be Exact or Accurate; Repeat Same Tasks; Errors Have Important Consequences.

Experience—Job Zone 4. A minimum of two to four years of work-related skill, knowledge, or experience is needed. **Job Preparation**—SVP 7.0 to less than 8.0—two years to less than 10 years. **Knowledges**—Telecommunications; Communications and Media; Computers and Electronics; Clerical Practices; Personnel and Human Resources; Customer and Personal Service. **Instructional Programs**—Cinematography and Film/Video Production; Directing and Theatrical Production; Drama and Dramatics/Theatre Arts, General; Dramatic/Theatre Arts and Stagecraft, Other; Film/Cinema Studies; Radio and Television; Theatre/Theatre Arts Management.

Related SOC Job—27-2012 Producers and Directors. **Related OOH Job**—Actors, Producers, and Directors. **Related DOT Jobs**—169.167-070 Director, Educational Programming; 184.117-010 Director, Public Service; 184.167-014 Director, News; 184.167-022 Director, Operations, Broadcast; 184.167-030 Director, Program; 184.167-034 Director, Sports; 194.162-010 Program Director, Cable Television.

27-2012.04 Talent Directors

- **Education/Training Required: Long-term on-the-job training**
- **Employed: 59,070**
- **Annual Earnings: $53,860**
- **Growth: 16.6%**
- **Annual Job Openings: 11,000**

The job openings listed here are shared with 27-2012.00 Producers and Directors, 27-2012.01 Producers, 27-2012.02 Directors—Stage, Motion Pictures, Television, and Radio, 27-2012.03 Program Directors, and 27-2012.05 Technical Directors/Managers.

Audition and interview performers to select most appropriate talent for parts in stage, television, radio, or motion picture productions.

Review performer information such as photos, resumes, voice tapes, videos, and union membership to decide whom to audition for parts. Read scripts and confer with producers to determine the types and numbers of performers required for a given production. Select performers for roles or submit lists of suitable performers to producers or directors for final selection. Serve as liaisons between directors, actors, and agents. Audition and interview performers to match their attributes to specific roles or to increase the pool of available acting talent. Maintain talent files that include information such as performers' specialties, past performances, and availability. Prepare actors for auditions by providing scripts and information about roles and casting requirements. Attend or view productions to maintain knowledge of available actors. Negotiate contract agreements with performers, with agents, or between performers and agents or production companies. Contact agents and actors to provide notification of audition and performance opportunities and to set up audition times. Hire and supervise workers who help locate people with specified attributes and talents. Arrange for or design screen tests or auditions for prospective performers. Locate performers or extras for crowd and background scenes and stand-ins or photo doubles for actors by direct contact or through agents.

GOE Information—Interest Area: 03. Arts and Communication. **Work Group:** 03.07. Music. **Personality Type**—Artistic. Artistic occupations frequently involve working with forms, designs, and patterns. They often require self-expression, and the work can be done without following a clear set of rules. **Work Values**—Authority; Responsibility; Autonomy; Creativity; Variety; Working Conditions. **Skills**—Management of Financial Resources; Management of Personnel Resources; Persuasion; Social Perceptiveness; Negotiation;

Judgment and Decision Making. **Abilities**—*Cognitive:* Fluency of Ideas; Written Expression; Originality; Category Flexibility; Oral Expression; Number Facility. *Psychomotor:* None met the criteria. *Physical:* None met the criteria. *Sensory:* Auditory Attention; Speech Recognition; Speech Clarity; Visual Color Discrimination. **General Work Activities**—*Information Input:* Getting Information; Identifying Objects, Actions, and Events; Monitoring Processes, Materials, or Surroundings. *Mental Process:* Making Decisions and Solving Problems; Organizing, Planning, and Prioritizing; Thinking Creatively. *Work Output:* Documenting or Recording Information; Interacting With Computers. *Interacting with Others:* Communicating with Persons Outside Organization; Communicating with Other Workers; Coordinating the Work and Activities of Others. **Physical Work Conditions**—Indoors; Noisy; Sitting. **Other Job Characteristics**—Need to Be Exact or Accurate; Errors Have Important Consequences.

Experience—Job Zone 4. A minimum of two to four years of work-related skill, knowledge, or experience is needed. **Job Preparation**—SVP 7.0 to less than 8.0—two years to less than 10 years. **Knowledges**—Fine Arts; Communications and Media; Clerical Practices; Computers and Electronics; Sales and Marketing; Telecommunications. **Instructional Programs**—Cinematography and Film/Video Production; Directing and Theatrical Production; Drama and Dramatics/Theatre Arts, General; Dramatic/Theatre Arts and Stagecraft, Other; Film/Cinema Studies; Radio and Television; Theatre/Theatre Arts Management.

Related SOC Job—27-2012 Producers and Directors. **Related OOH Job**—Actors, Producers, and Directors. **Related DOT Jobs**—159.167-010 Artist and Repertoire Manager; 159.267-010 Director, Casting; 166.167-010 Contestant Coordinator.

27-2012.05 Technical Directors/Managers

- **Education/Training Required: Long-term on-the-job training**
- **Employed: 59,070**
- **Annual Earnings: $53,860**
- **Growth: 16.6%**
- **Annual Job Openings: 11,000**

The job openings listed here are shared with 27-2012.00 Producers and Directors, 27-2012.01 Producers, 27-2012.02 Directors—Stage, Motion Pictures, Television, and Radio, 27-2012.03 Program Directors, and 27-2012.04 Talent Directors.

Coordinate activities of technical departments, such as taping, editing, engineering, and maintenance, to produce radio or television programs.

Direct technical aspects of newscasts and other productions, checking and switching between video sources and taking responsibility for the on-air product, including camera shots and graphics. Test equipment to ensure proper operation. Monitor broadcasts to ensure that programs conform to station or network policies and regulations. Observe pictures through monitors and direct camera and video staff concerning shading and composition. Act as liaisons between engineering and production departments. Supervise and assign duties to workers engaged in technical control and production of radio and television programs. Schedule use of studio and editing facilities for producers and engineering and maintenance staff. Confer with operations directors to formulate and maintain fair and attainable technical policies for programs. Operate equipment to produce programs or broadcast live programs from remote locations. Train workers in use of equipment such as switchers, cameras, monitors, microphones, and lights. Switch between video sources in a studio or on multi-camera remotes, using equipment such as switchers, video slide projectors, and video effects generators. Set up and execute video transitions and special effects such as fades, dissolves, cuts, keys, and supers, using computers to manipulate pictures as necessary. Collaborate with promotions directors to produce on-air station promotions. Discuss filter options, lens choices, and the visual effects of objects being filmed with photography directors and video operators. Follow instructions from production managers and directors during productions, such as commands for camera cuts, effects, graphics, and takes.

GOE Information—Interest Area: 03. Arts and Communication. **Work Group:** 03.01. Managerial Work in Arts and Communication. **Personality Type**—Realistic. Realistic occupations frequently involve work activities that include practical, hands-on problems and solutions. They often deal with plants; animals; and real-world materials like wood, tools, and machinery. Many of the occupations require working outside and do not involve a lot of paperwork or working closely with others. **Work Values**—Authority; Autonomy; Creativity; Variety; Ability Utilization; Responsibility. **Skills**—Operation and Control; Operation Monitoring; Monitoring; Systems Analysis; Time Management; Troubleshooting. **Abilities**—*Cognitive:* Fluency of Ideas; Originality; Time Sharing; Visualization; Perceptual Speed; Written Expression. *Psychomotor:* Response Orientation; Reaction Time; Control Precision; Arm-Hand Steadiness. *Physical:* None met the criteria. *Sensory:* Visual Color Discrimination; Far Vision; Auditory Attention; Speech Recognition; Depth Perception; Hearing Sensitivity. **General Work Activities**—*Information Input:* Monitoring Processes, Materials, or Surroundings; Getting Information; Estimating the Needed Characteristics of Products, Events, or Information. *Mental Process:* Organizing, Planning, and Prioritizing; Making Decisions and Solving Problems; Updating and Using Relevant Knowledge. *Work Output:* Documenting or Recording Information; Drafting and Specifying Technical Devices; Interacting With Computers. *Interacting with Others:* Communicating with Other Workers; Communicating with Persons Outside Organization; Guiding, Directing, and Motivating Subordinates. **Physical Work Conditions**—Indoors; Noisy; Sitting; Using Hands on Objects, Tools, or Controls. **Other Job Characteristics**—Need to Be Exact or Accurate; Repeat Same Tasks.

Experience—Job Zone 3. Previous work-related skill, knowledge, or experience is required. **Job Preparation**—SVP 6.0 to less than 7.0—more than one year and less than four years. **Knowledges**—Communications and Media; Telecommunications; Computers and Electronics; Philosophy and Theology; Engineering and Technology; Sales and Marketing. **Instructional Programs**—Cinematography and Film/Video Production; Directing and Theatrical Production; Drama and Dramatics/Theatre Arts, General; Dramatic/Theatre Arts and Stagecraft, Other; Film/Cinema Studies; Radio and Television; Theatre/Theatre Arts Management.

Related SOC Job—27-2012 Producers and Directors. **Related OOH Job**—Actors, Producers, and Directors. **Related DOT Jobs**—184.162-010 Manager, Production; 962.162-010 Director, Technical.

27-2021.00 Athletes and Sports Competitors

- **Education/Training Required: Long-term on-the-job training**
- **Employed: 12,230**
- **Annual Earnings: $39,930**
- **Growth: 21.1%**
- **Annual Job Openings: 6,000**

Compete in athletic events.

Lead teams by serving as captains. Receive instructions from coaches and other sports staff prior to events and discuss their performance afterwards. Participate in athletic events and competitive sports according to established rules and regulations. Maintain optimum physical fitness levels by training regularly, following nutrition plans, and consulting with health professionals. Exercise and practice under the direction of athletic trainers or professional coaches to develop skills, improve physical condition, and prepare for competitions. Attend scheduled practice and training sessions. Assess performance following athletic competition, identifying strengths and weaknesses and making adjustments to improve future performance. Maintain equipment used in a particular sport. Represent teams or professional sports clubs, performing such activities as meeting with members of the media, making speeches, or participating in charity events.

GOE Information—Interest Area: 09. Hospitality, Tourism, and Recreation. **Work Group:** 09.06. Sports. **Personality Type**—Enterprising. Enterprising occupations frequently involve starting up and carrying out projects. These occupations can involve leading people and making many decisions. They sometimes require risk taking and often deal with business. **Work Values**—Recognition; Ability Utilization; Social Status; Compensation; Achievement; Co-workers. **Skills**—None met the criteria. **Abilities**—*Cognitive:* Spatial Orientation; Time Sharing; Visualization; Selective Attention; Memorization. *Psychomotor:* Speed of Limb Movement; Reaction Time; Multilimb Coordination; Response Orientation; Rate Control; Wrist-Finger Speed. *Physical:* Dynamic Flexibility; Explosive Strength; Stamina; Dynamic Strength; Gross Body Coordination; Trunk Strength. *Sensory:* Depth Perception; Glare Sensitivity; Peripheral Vision; Auditory Attention; Far Vision. **General Work Activities**—*Information Input:* Monitoring Processes, Materials, or Surroundings; Getting Information. *Mental Process:* None met the criteria. *Work Output:* Performing General Physical Activities; Handling and Moving Objects. *Interacting with Others:* Performing for or Working with the Public; Communicating with Persons Outside Organization; Establishing and Maintaining Interpersonal Relationships. **Physical Work Conditions**—More Often Outdoors Than Indoors; Minor Burns, Cuts, Bites, or Stings; Standing; Walking and Running; Bending or Twisting the Body. **Other Job Characteristics**—None met the criteria.

Experience—Job Zone 3. Previous work-related skill, knowledge, or experience is required. **Job Preparation**—SVP 6.0 to less than 7.0—more than one year and less than four years. **Knowledges**—Biology; Medicine and Dentistry. **Instructional Program**—Health and Physical Education, General.

Related SOC Job—27-2021 Athletes and Sports Competitors. **Related OOH Job**—Athletes, Coaches, Umpires, and Related Workers. **Related DOT Jobs**—153.243-010 Automobile Racer; 153.243-014 Motorcycle Racer; 153.244-010 Jockey; 153.244-014 Sulky Driver; 153.341-010 Professional Athlete; 159.344-010 Equestrian; 159.344-014 Rodeo Performer; 159.344-018 Show-Horse Driver.

27-2022.00 Coaches and Scouts

- **Education/Training Required: Long-term on-the-job training**
- **Employed: 145,440**
- **Annual Earnings: $25,990**
- **Growth: 20.4%**
- **Annual Job Openings: 63,000**

Instruct or coach groups or individuals in the fundamentals of sports. Demonstrate techniques and methods of participation. May evaluate athletes' strengths and weaknesses as possible recruits or to improve the athletes' technique to prepare them for competition.

Plan, organize, and conduct practice sessions. Provide training direction, encouragement, and motivation to prepare athletes for games, competitive events, or tours. Identify and recruit potential athletes, arranging and offering incentives such as athletic scholarships. Plan strategies and choose team members for individual games or sports seasons. Plan and direct physical conditioning programs that will enable athletes to achieve maximum performance. Adjust coaching techniques based on the strengths and weaknesses of athletes. File scouting reports that detail player assessments, provide recommendations on athlete recruitment, and identify locations and individuals to be targeted for future recruitment efforts. Keep records of athlete, team, and opposing team performance. Instruct individuals or groups in sports rules, game strategies, and performance principles such as specific ways of moving the body, hands, and feet in order to achieve desired results. Analyze the strengths and weaknesses of opposing teams to develop game strategies. Evaluate athletes' skills and review performance records to determine their fitness and potential in a particular area of athletics. Keep abreast of changing rules, techniques, technologies, and philosophies relevant to their sport. Monitor athletes' use of equipment to ensure safe and proper use. Explain and enforce safety rules and regulations. Develop and arrange competition schedules and programs. Serve as organizer, leader, instructor, or referee for outdoor and indoor games such as volleyball, football, and soccer. Explain and demonstrate the use of sports and training equipment, such as trampolines or weights. Perform activities that support a team or a specific sport, such as meeting with media representatives and appearing at fundraising events. Arrange and conduct sports-related activities such as training camps, skill-improvement courses, clinics, or pre-season try-outs. Select, acquire, store, and issue equipment and other materials as necessary. Negotiate with professional athletes or their representatives to obtain services and arrange contracts.

GOE Information—Interest Area: 09. Hospitality, Tourism, and Recreation. **Work Group:** 09.06. Sports. **Personality Type—** Enterprising. Enterprising occupations frequently involve starting up and carrying out projects. These occupations can involve leading people and making many decisions. They sometimes require risk taking and often deal with business. **Work Values—**Authority; Responsibility; Recognition; Autonomy; Creativity; Achievement. **Skills—**Management of Personnel Resources; Social Perceptiveness; Persuasion; Management of Financial Resources; Negotiation; Instructing. **Abilities—***Cognitive:* Visualization; Fluency of Ideas; Memorization; Speed of Closure; Originality; Category Flexibility. *Psychomotor:* Multilimb Coordination; Arm-Hand Steadiness; Manual Dexterity. *Physical:* Gross Body Coordination; Dynamic Strength; Gross Body Equilibrium; Static Strength; Stamina; Trunk Strength. *Sensory:* Speech Clarity; Speech Recognition; Depth Perception; Auditory Attention; Hearing Sensitivity; Far Vision. **General Work Activities—***Information Input:* Getting Information; Identifying Objects, Actions, and Events; Monitoring Processes, Materials, or Surroundings. *Mental Process:* Making Decisions and Solving Problems; Organizing, Planning, and Prioritizing; Scheduling Work and Activities. *Work Output:* Performing General Physical Activities; Handling and Moving Objects; Documenting or Recording Information. *Interacting with Others:* Coaching and Developing Others; Establishing and Maintaining Interpersonal Relationships; Coordinating the Work and Activities of Others. **Physical Work Conditions—**More Often Indoors Than Outdoors; Noisy; Standing; Walking and Running. **Other Job Characteristics—**Need to Be Exact or Accurate.

Experience—Job Zone 5. Extensive skill, knowledge, and experience are needed. **Job Preparation—**SVP 8.0 and above—four years to more than 10 years. **Knowledges—**Psychology; Education and Training; Therapy and Counseling; Sales and Marketing; Personnel and Human Resources; Sociology and Anthropology. **Instructional Programs—**Health and Physical Education, General; Physical Education Teaching and Coaching; Sport and Fitness Administration/Management.

Related SOC Job—27-2022 Coaches and Scouts. **Related OOH Job—**Athletes, Coaches, Umpires, and Related Workers. **Related DOT Jobs—**153.117-010 Head Coach; 153.117-018 Scout, Professional Sports; 153.227-010 Coach, Professional Athletes.

27-2023.00 Umpires, Referees, and Other Sports Officials

- **Education/Training Required: Long-term on-the-job training**
- **Employed: 12,800**
- **Annual Earnings: $21,610**
- **Growth: 19.0%**
- **Annual Job Openings: 6,000**

Officiate at competitive athletic or sporting events. Detect infractions of rules and decide penalties according to established regulations.

Officiate at sporting events, games, or competitions to maintain standards of play and to ensure that game rules are observed. Judge performances in sporting competitions in order to award points, impose scoring penalties, and determine results. Inspect sporting equipment or examine participants to ensure compliance with event and safety regulations. Keep track of event times, including race times and elapsed time during game segments, starting or stopping play when necessary. Signal participants or other officials to make them aware of infractions or to otherwise regulate play or competition. Verify scoring calculations before competition winners are announced. Resolve claims of rule infractions or complaints by participants and assess any necessary penalties according to regulations. Start races and competitions. Teach and explain the rules and regulations governing a specific sport. Verify credentials of participants in sporting events and make other qualifying determinations such as starting order or handicap number. Confer with other sporting officials, coaches, players, and facility managers to provide information, coordinate activities, and discuss problems. Report to regulating organizations regarding sporting activities, complaints made, and actions taken or needed such as fines or other disciplinary actions. Compile scores and other athletic records. Direct participants to assigned areas such as starting blocks or penalty areas. Research and study players and teams to anticipate issues that might arise in future engagements.

GOE Information—Interest Area: 09. Hospitality, Tourism, and Recreation. **Work Group:** 09.06. Sports. **Personality Type—** Enterprising. Enterprising occupations frequently involve starting up and carrying out projects. These occupations can involve leading people and making many decisions. They sometimes require risk taking and often deal with business. **Work Values—**Authority; Responsibility; Ability Utilization; Achievement; Autonomy; Recognition. **Skills—**Judgment and Decision Making; Negotiation; Persuasion; Monitoring; Social Perceptiveness; Active Listening. **Abilities—***Cognitive:* Perceptual Speed; Flexibility of Closure; Selective Attention; Speed of Closure; Time Sharing; Problem Sensitivity. *Psychomotor:* None met the criteria. *Physical:* Gross Body Coordination; Stamina; Trunk Strength. *Sensory:* Far Vision; Auditory Attention; Visual Color Discrimination; Hearing Sensitivity; Speech Clarity. **General Work Activities—***Information Input:* Getting

Information; Identifying Objects, Actions, and Events; Monitoring Processes, Materials, or Surroundings. *Mental Process:* Evaluating Information Against Standards; Making Decisions and Solving Problems; Updating and Using Relevant Knowledge. *Work Output:* Performing General Physical Activities; Documenting or Recording Information. *Interacting with Others:* Resolving Conflicts and Negotiating with Others; Establishing and Maintaining Interpersonal Relationships; Coaching and Developing Others. **Physical Work Conditions**—Outdoors; Noisy; Standing; Walking and Running. **Other Job Characteristics**—Need to Be Exact or Accurate; Repeat Same Tasks.

Experience—Job Zone 3. Previous work-related skill, knowledge, or experience is required. **Job Preparation**—SVP 6.0 to less than 7.0—more than one year and less than four years. **Knowledges**—Psychology. **Instructional Program**—No related CIP programs.

Related SOC Job—27-2023 Umpires, Referees, and Other Sports Officials. **Related OOH Job**—Athletes, Coaches, Umpires, and Related Workers. **Related DOT Jobs**—153.117-022 Steward, Racetrack; 153.167-010 Paddock Judge; 153.167-014 Pit Steward; 153.167-018 Racing Secretary and Handicapper; 153.267-010 Horse-Race Starter; 153.267-014 Patrol Judge; 153.267-018 Umpire; 153.287-010 Hoof and Shoe Inspector; 153.367-010 Clocker; 153.367-014 Horse-Race Timer; 153.384-010 Marshal; 153.387-010 Identifier, Horse; 153.387-014 Scorer; 153.467-010 Clerk-of-Scales; 153.667-010 Starter; 219.267-010 Handicapper, Harness Racing; 349.367-010 Kennel Manager, Dog Track; others.

27-2031.00 Dancers

- **Education/Training Required: Long-term on-the-job training**
- **Employed: 16,240**
- **Annual Earnings: No data available**
- **Growth: 16.8%**
- **Annual Job Openings: 4,000**

Perform dances. May also sing or act.

Train, exercise, and attend dance classes to maintain high levels of technical proficiency, physical ability, and physical fitness. Study and practice dance moves required in roles. Harmonize body movements to rhythm of musical accompaniment. Perform classical, modern, or acrobatic dances in productions, expressing stories, rhythm, and sound with their bodies. Collaborate with choreographers to refine or modify dance steps. Coordinate dancing with that of partners or dance ensembles. Attend costume fittings, photography sessions, and makeup calls associated with dance performances. Audition for dance roles or for membership in dance companies. Develop self-understanding of physical capabilities and limitations and choose dance styles accordingly. Monitor the field of dance to remain aware of current trends and innovations. Teach dance students. Devise and choreograph dance for self or others. Perform in productions, singing or acting in addition to dancing if required.

GOE Information—**Interest Area:** 03. Arts and Communication. **Work Group:** 03.08. Dance. **Personality Type**—Artistic. Artistic occupations frequently involve working with forms, designs, and patterns. They often require self-expression, and the work can be done without following a clear set of rules. **Work Values**—Ability Utilization; Recognition; Achievement; Creativity; Moral Values; Social Status. **Skills**—Negotiation; Instructing; Social Perceptiveness; Time Management; Monitoring; Active Listening. **Abilities**—*Cognitive:* Memorization; Originality; Fluency of Ideas; Visualization; Perceptual Speed; Speed of Closure. *Psychomotor:* Multilimb Coordination; Speed of Limb Movement; Arm-Hand Steadiness.

Physical: Gross Body Coordination; Dynamic Flexibility; Gross Body Equilibrium; Dynamic Strength; Stamina; Extent Flexibility. *Sensory:* Hearing Sensitivity; Far Vision; Speech Clarity. **General Work Activities**—*Information Input:* Getting Information; Identifying Objects, Actions, and Events. *Mental Process:* Thinking Creatively; Organizing, Planning, and Prioritizing; Updating and Using Relevant Knowledge. *Work Output:* Performing General Physical Activities; Handling and Moving Objects. *Interacting with Others:* Performing for or Working with the Public; Establishing and Maintaining Interpersonal Relationships; Coaching and Developing Others. **Physical Work Conditions**—Indoors; Standing; Walking and Running; Keeping or Regaining Balance; Bending or Twisting the Body; Repetitive Motions. **Other Job Characteristics**—Need to Be Exact or Accurate; Repeat Same Tasks.

Experience—Job Zone 3. Previous work-related skill, knowledge, or experience is required. **Job Preparation**—SVP 6.0 to less than 7.0—more than one year and less than four years. **Knowledges**—Fine Arts; Communications and Media. **Instructional Programs**—Ballet; Dance, General; Dance, Other.

Related SOC Job—27-2031 Dancers. **Related OOH Job**—Dancers and Choreographers. **Related DOT Job**—151.047-010 Dancer.

27-2032.00 Choreographers

- **Education/Training Required: Work experience in a related occupation**
- **Employed: 16,150**
- **Annual Earnings: $32,950**
- **Growth: 16.8%**
- **Annual Job Openings: 4,000**

Create and teach dance. May direct and stage presentations.

Direct rehearsals to instruct dancers in how to use dance steps and in techniques to achieve desired effects. Read and study storylines and musical scores to determine how to translate ideas and moods into dance movements. Design dances for individual dancers, dance companies, musical theatre, opera, fashion shows, film, television productions, and special events and for dancers ranging from beginners to professionals. Choose the music, sound effects, or spoken narrative to accompany a dance. Advise dancers on how to stand and move properly, teaching correct dance techniques to help prevent injuries. Coordinate production music with music directors. Audition performers for one or more dance parts. Direct and stage dance presentations for various forms of entertainment. Develop ideas for creating dances, keeping notes and sketches to record influences. Train, exercise, and attend dance classes to maintain high levels of technical proficiency, physical ability, and physical fitness. Teach students, dancers, and other performers about rhythm and interpretive movement. Assess students' dancing abilities to determine where improvement or change is needed. Experiment with different types of dancers, steps, dances, and placements, testing ideas informally to get feedback from dancers. Seek influences from other art forms such as theatre, the visual arts, and architecture. Design sets, lighting, costumes, and other artistic elements of productions in collaboration with cast members. Record dance movements and their technical aspects, using a technical understanding of the patterns and formations of choreography. Re-stage traditional dances and works in dance companies' repertoires, developing new interpretations. Manage dance schools or assist in their management.

GOE Information—**Interest Area:** 03. Arts and Communication. **Work Group:** 03.08. Dance. **Personality Type**—Artistic. Artistic occupations frequently involve working with forms, designs, and patterns. They often require self-expression, and the work can be done without following a clear set of rules. **Work Values**—Creativity; Authority; Responsibility; Ability Utilization; Autonomy; Recognition. **Skills**—Management of Personnel Resources; Instructing; Time Management; Persuasion; Negotiation; Speaking. **Abilities**—*Cognitive:* Originality; Fluency of Ideas; Visualization; Time Sharing; Memorization; Oral Expression. *Psychomotor:* Speed of Limb Movement; Multilimb Coordination; Arm-Hand Steadiness. *Physical:* Gross Body Coordination; Gross Body Equilibrium; Stamina; Dynamic Strength; Extent Flexibility; Dynamic Flexibility. *Sensory:* Speech Clarity; Visual Color Discrimination; Far Vision. **General Work Activities**—*Information Input:* Getting Information; Identifying Objects, Actions, and Events; Monitoring Processes, Materials, or Surroundings. *Mental Process:* Thinking Creatively; Organizing, Planning, and Prioritizing; Scheduling Work and Activities. *Work Output:* Performing General Physical Activities; Handling and Moving Objects; Documenting or Recording Information. *Interacting with Others:* Guiding, Directing, and Motivating Subordinates; Coaching and Developing Others; Coordinating the Work and Activities of Others. **Physical Work Conditions**—Indoors; Standing; Walking and Running; Keeping or Regaining Balance; Bending or Twisting the Body; Repetitive Motions. **Other Job Characteristics**—Need to Be Exact or Accurate; Repeat Same Tasks.

Experience—Job Zone 4. A minimum of two to four years of work-related skill, knowledge, and experience is needed. **Job Preparation**—SVP 7.0 to less than 8.0—two years to less than 10 years. **Knowledges**—Fine Arts; History and Archeology; Philosophy and Theology; Sociology and Anthropology; Communications and Media; Education and Training. **Instructional Programs**—Dance, General; Dance, Other.

Related SOC Job—27-2032 Choreographers. **Related OOH Job**—Dancers and Choreographers. **Related DOT Job**—151.027-010 Choreographer.

27-2041.00 Music Directors and Composers

- **Education/Training Required: Master's degree**
- **Employed: 8,610**
- **Annual Earnings: $34,810**
- **Growth: 10.4%**
- **Annual Job Openings: 11,000**

The job openings listed here are shared with 27-2041.01 Music Directors and 27-2041.04 Music Composers and Arrangers.

Conduct, direct, plan, and lead instrumental or vocal performances by musical groups such as orchestras, choirs, and glee clubs. Includes arrangers, composers, choral directors, and orchestrators.

No task data available.

GOE Information—**Interest Area:** 03. Arts and Communication. **Work Group:** 03.07. Music. **Note:** The Department of Labor has not collected some data for this job, so it has fewer details than the other descriptions.

Instructional Programs—Conducting; Music Management and Merchandising; Music Performance, General; Music Theory and Composition; Music, Other; Musicology and Ethnomusicology; Religious/Sacred Music; Voice and Opera.

Related SOC Job—27-2041 Music Directors and Composers. **Related OOH Job**—Musicians, Singers, and Related Workers. **Related DOT Job**—No data available.

27-2041.01 Music Directors

- **Education/Training Required: Master's degree**
- **Employed: 8,610**
- **Annual Earnings: $34,810**
- **Growth: 10.4%**
- **Annual Job Openings: 11,000**

The job openings listed here are shared with 27-2041.00 Music Directors and Composers and 27-2041.04 Music Composers and Arrangers.

Direct and conduct instrumental or vocal performances by musical groups such as orchestras or choirs.

Coordinate and organize tours or hire touring companies to arrange concert dates, venues, accommodations, and transportation for longer tours. Position members within groups to obtain balance among instrumental or vocal sections. Study scores to learn the music in detail and to develop interpretations. Use gestures to shape the music being played, communicating desired tempo, phrasing, tone, color, pitch, volume, and other performance aspects. Collaborate with music librarians to ensure availability of scores. Meet with composers to discuss interpretations of their work. Perform administrative tasks such as applying for grants, developing budgets, negotiating contracts, and designing and printing programs and other promotional materials. Confer with clergy to select music for church services. Plan and implement fundraising and promotional activities. Assign and review staff work in such areas as scoring, arranging, and copying music and vocal coaching. Plan and schedule rehearsals and performances and arrange details such as locations, accompanists, and instrumentalists. Transcribe musical compositions and melodic lines to adapt them to a particular group or to create a particular musical style. Engage services of composers to write scores. Direct groups at rehearsals and live or recorded performances to achieve desired effects such as tonal and harmonic balance dynamics, rhythm, and tempo. Consider such factors as ensemble size and abilities, availability of scores, and the need for musical variety to select music to be performed. Conduct guest soloists in addition to ensemble members. Audition and select performers for musical presentations. Meet with soloists and concertmasters to discuss and prepare for performances.

GOE Information—**Interest Area:** 03. Arts and Communication. **Work Group:** 03.07. Music. **Personality Type**—Artistic. Artistic occupations frequently involve working with forms, designs, and patterns. They often require self-expression, and the work can be done without following a clear set of rules. **Work Values**—Creativity; Authority; Ability Utilization; Responsibility; Autonomy; Recognition. **Skills**—Management of Personnel Resources; Coordination; Time Management; Systems Analysis; Operations Analysis; Instructing. **Abilities**—*Cognitive:* Originality; Oral Expression; Fluency of Ideas; Written Expression; Flexibility of Closure; Oral Comprehension. *Psychomotor:* Wrist-Finger Speed. *Physical:* Extent Flexibility. *Sensory:* Sound Localization; Hearing Sensitivity; Auditory Attention; Speech Clarity. **General Work Activities**—*Information Input:* Getting Information; Identifying Objects, Actions, and Events; Monitoring Processes, Materials, or Surroundings. *Mental Process:* Organizing, Planning, and Prioritizing; Thinking Creatively; Scheduling Work and Activities. *Work Output:* None met the criteria. *Interacting with Others:* Coordinating the Work and Activities of Others; Establishing and Maintaining Interpersonal Relationships; Guiding, Directing, and Motivating Subordinates. **Physical Work Conditions**—Indoors; More Often Standing Than Sitting. **Other Job Characteristics**—Need to Be Exact or Accurate.

Experience—Job Zone 5. Extensive skill, knowledge, and experience are needed. **Job Preparation**—SVP 8.0 and above—four years to more than 10 years. **Knowledges**—Fine Arts; Personnel and Human Resources; Administration and Management. **Instructional Programs**—Conducting; Music Management and Merchandising; Music Performance, General; Music Theory and Composition; Music, Other; Musicology and Ethnomusicology; Religious/Sacred Music; Voice and Opera.

Related SOC Job—27-2041 Music Directors and Composers. **Related OOH Job**—Musicians, Singers, and Related Workers. **Related DOT Jobs**—152.047-010 Choral Director; 152.047-014 Conductor, Orchestra; 152.047-018 Director, Music.

27-2041.04 Music Composers and Arrangers

- **Education/Training Required: Work experience plus degree**
- **Employed: 8,610**
- **Annual Earnings: $34,810**
- **Growth: 10.4%**
- **Annual Job Openings: 11,000**

The job openings listed here are shared with 27-2041.00 Music Directors and Composers and 27-2041.01 Music Directors.

Write and transcribe musical scores.

Determine voices, instruments, harmonic structures, rhythms, tempos, and tone balances required to achieve the effects desired in a musical composition. Experiment with different sounds and types and pieces of music, using synthesizers and computers as necessary to test and evaluate ideas. Explore and develop musical ideas based on sources such as imagination or sounds in the environment. Fill in details of orchestral sketches, such as adding vocal parts to scores. Rewrite original musical scores in different musical styles by changing rhythms, harmonies, or tempos. Create original musical forms or write within circumscribed musical forms such as sonatas, symphonies, or operas. Use computers and synthesizers to compose, orchestrate, and arrange music. Score compositions so that they are consistent with instrumental and vocal capabilities such as ranges and keys, using knowledge of music theory. Write changes directly into compositions or use computer software to make changes. Transcribe ideas for musical compositions into musical notation, using instruments, pen and paper, or computers. Write music for commercial media, including advertising jingles or film soundtracks. Transpose music from one voice or instrument to another to accommodate particular musicians. Collaborate with other colleagues, such as copyists, to complete final scores. Study films or scripts to determine how musical scores can be used to create desired effects or moods. Accept commissions to create music for special occasions. Write musical scores for orchestras, bands, choral groups, or individual instrumentalists or vocalists, using knowledge of music theory and of instrumental and vocal capabilities. Study original pieces of music to become familiar with them prior to making any changes. Guide musicians during rehearsals, performances, or recording sessions. Copy parts from scores for individual performers. Confer with producers and directors to define the nature and placement of film or television music. Apply elements of music theory to create musical and tonal structures, including harmonies and melodies.

GOE Information—Interest Area: 03. Arts and Communication. **Work Group:** 03.07. Music. **Personality Type**—Artistic. Artistic occupations frequently involve working with forms, designs, and patterns. They often require self-expression, and the work can be done without following a clear set of rules. **Work Values**—Creativity; Ability Utilization; Autonomy; Independence; Responsibility; Achievement. **Skills**—None met the criteria. **Abilities**—*Cognitive:* Originality; Fluency of Ideas; Written Expression. *Psychomotor:* None met the criteria. *Physical:* None met the criteria. *Sensory:* Hearing Sensitivity; Sound Localization; Auditory Attention. **General Work Activities**—*Information Input:* Identifying Objects, Actions, and Events; Getting Information. *Mental Process:* Thinking Creatively; Judging the Qualities of Things, Services, or Other People's Work; Making Decisions and Solving Problems. *Work Output:* Documenting or Recording Information. *Interacting with Others:* Interpreting the Meaning of Information for Others; Communicating with Persons Outside Organization. **Physical Work Conditions**—Indoors; Sitting. **Other Job Characteristics**—None met the criteria.

Experience—Job Zone 4. A minimum of two to four years of work-related skill, knowledge, or experience is needed. **Job Preparation**—SVP 7.0 to less than 8.0—two years to less than 10 years. **Knowledges**—Fine Arts. **Instructional Programs**—Conducting; Music Management and Merchandising; Music Performance, General; Music Theory and Composition; Music, Other; Musicology and Ethnomusicology; Religious/Sacred Music; Voice and Opera.

Related SOC Job—27-2041 Music Directors and Composers. **Related OOH Job**—Musicians, Singers, and Related Workers. **Related DOT Jobs**—152.067-010 Arranger; 152.067-014 Composer; 152.067-022 Orchestrator; 152.267-010 Copyist.

27-2042.00 Musicians and Singers

- **Education/Training Required: Long-term on-the-job training**
- **Employed: 50,410**
- **Annual Earnings: No data available**
- **Growth: 14.0%**
- **Annual Job Openings: 37,000**

The job openings listed here are shared with 27-2042.01 Singers and 27-2042.02 Musicians, Instrumental.

Play one or more musical instruments or entertain by singing songs in recital; in accompaniment; or as a member of an orchestra, band, or other musical group. Musical performers may entertain on stage, radio, TV, film, or video or record in studios.

No task data available.

GOE Information—Interest Area: 03. Arts and Communication. **Work Group:** 03.07. Music. **Note:** The Department of Labor has not collected some data for this job, so it has fewer details than the other descriptions.

Instructional Programs—Jazz/Jazz Studies; Music Pedagogy; Music Performance, General; Music, General; Music, Other; Piano and Organ; Violin, Viola, Guitar, and Other Stringed Instruments; Voice and Opera.

Related SOC Job—27-2042 Musicians and Singers. **Related OOH Job**—Musicians, Singers, and Related Workers. **Related DOT Job**—No data available.

27-2042.01 Singers

- **Education/Training Required: Long-term on-the-job training**
- **Employed: 50,410**
- **Annual Earnings: No data available**
- **Growth: 14.0%**
- **Annual Job Openings: 37,000**

The job openings listed here are shared with 27-2042.00 Musicians and Singers and 27-2042.02 Musicians, Instrumental.

Sing songs on stage, radio, or television or in motion pictures.

Perform before live audiences or in television, radio, or movie productions. Sing as a soloist or as a member of a vocal group. Make or participate in recordings. Learn acting, dancing, and other skills required for dramatic singing roles. Compose songs or create vocal arrangements. Collaborate with a manager or agent who handles administrative details, finds work, and negotiates contracts. Research particular roles to find out more about a character or the time and place in which a piece is set. Sing a cappella or with musical accompaniment. Practice singing exercises and study with vocal coaches to develop their voices and skills and to rehearse for upcoming roles. Observe choral leaders or prompters for cues or directions in vocal presentation. Memorize musical selections and routines or sing following printed text, musical notation, or customer instructions. Interpret or modify music, applying knowledge of harmony, melody, rhythm, and voice production to individualize presentations and maintain audience interest. Seek out and learn new music that is suitable for live performance or recording.

GOE Information—Interest Area: 03. Arts and Communication. **Work Group:** 03.07. Music. **Personality Type—**Artistic. Artistic occupations frequently involve working with forms, designs, and patterns. They often require self-expression, and the work can be done without following a clear set of rules. **Work Values—**Ability Utilization; Achievement; Recognition; Creativity; Autonomy; Moral Values. **Skills—**None met the criteria. **Abilities—***Cognitive:* Memorization; Originality. *Psychomotor:* None met the criteria. *Physical:* None met the criteria. *Sensory:* Hearing Sensitivity; Sound Localization; Auditory Attention; Speech Clarity. **General Work Activities—***Information Input:* Getting Information. *Mental Process:* Thinking Creatively; Organizing, Planning, and Prioritizing. *Work Output:* None met the criteria. *Interacting with Others:* Performing for or Working with the Public; Communicating with Persons Outside Organization; Establishing and Maintaining Interpersonal Relationships. **Physical Work Conditions—**Indoors; More Often Standing Than Sitting. **Other Job Characteristics—**None met the criteria.

Experience—Job Zone 2. Some previous work-related skill, knowledge, or experience may be helpful in these occupations, but usually is not needed. **Job Preparation—**SVP 4.0 to less than 6.0—six months to less than two years. **Knowledges—**Fine Arts. **Instructional Programs—**Jazz/Jazz Studies; Music Performance, General; Music, General; Music, Other; Voice and Opera.

Related SOC Job—27-2042 Musicians and Singers. **Related OOH Job—**Musicians, Singers, and Related Workers. **Related DOT Jobs—**152.047-022 Singer; 230.647-010 Singing Messenger.

27-2042.02 Musicians, Instrumental

- **Education/Training Required: Long-term on-the-job training**
- **Employed: 50,410**
- **Annual Earnings: No data available**
- **Growth: 14.0%**
- **Annual Job Openings: 37,000**

The job openings listed here are shared with 27-2042.00 Musicians and Singers and 27-2042.01 Singers.

Play one or more musical instruments in recital; in accompaniment; or as members of an orchestra, band, or other musical group.

Practice musical instrument performances, individually or in rehearsal with other musicians, to master individual pieces of music and to maintain and improve skills. Perform before live audiences. Specialize in playing a specific family of instruments or a particular type of music. Play musical instruments as soloists or as members or guest artists of musical groups such as orchestras, ensembles, or bands. Play from memory or by following scores. Sight-read musical parts during rehearsals. Audition for orchestras, bands, or other musical groups. Provide the musical background for live shows such as ballets, operas, musical theatre, and cabarets. Transpose music to alternate keys or to fit individual styles or purposes. Promote their own or their group's music by participating in media interviews and other activities. Make or participate in recordings in music studios. Direct bands or orchestras. Teach music for specific instruments. Compose original music such as popular songs, symphonies, or sonatas. Improvise music during performances.

GOE Information—Interest Area: 03. Arts and Communication. **Work Group:** 03.07. Music. **Personality Type—**Artistic. Artistic occupations frequently involve working with forms, designs, and patterns. They often require self-expression, and the work can be done without following a clear set of rules. **Work Values—**Ability Utilization; Achievement; Creativity; Recognition; Moral Values; Autonomy. **Skills—**Coordination; Active Listening; Equipment Maintenance; Monitoring; Equipment Selection; Active Learning. **Abilities—***Cognitive:* Originality; Selective Attention; Time Sharing; Perceptual Speed; Fluency of Ideas; Speed of Closure. *Psychomotor:* Multilimb Coordination; Wrist-Finger Speed; Manual Dexterity; Arm-Hand Steadiness; Finger Dexterity. *Physical:* Static Strength. *Sensory:* Hearing Sensitivity; Auditory Attention; Far Vision. **General Work Activities—***Information Input:* Identifying Objects, Actions, and Events; Monitoring Processes, Materials, or Surroundings; Getting Information. *Mental Process:* Thinking Creatively; Making Decisions and Solving Problems; Organizing, Planning, and Prioritizing. *Work Output:* Handling and Moving Objects; Performing General Physical Activities; Documenting or Recording Information. *Interacting with Others:* Performing for or Working with the Public; Establishing and Maintaining Interpersonal Relationships; Coordinating the Work and Activities of Others. **Physical Work Conditions—**Indoors; Noisy; Sitting; Using Hands on Objects, Tools, or Controls; Repetitive Motions. **Other Job Characteristics—**Need to Be Exact or Accurate; Repeat Same Tasks.

Experience—Job Zone 4. A minimum of two to four years of work-related skill, knowledge, or experience is needed. **Job Preparation—**SVP 7.0 to less than 8.0—two years to less than 10 years. **Knowledges—**Fine Arts; Psychology; Education and Training. **Instructional Programs—**Jazz/Jazz Studies; Music Pedagogy; Music Performance, General; Music, General; Music, Other; Piano and Organ; Violin, Viola, Guitar, and Other Stringed Instruments.

Related SOC Job—27-2042 Musicians and Singers. **Related OOH Job**—Musicians, Singers, and Related Workers. **Related DOT Job**—152.041-010 Musician, Instrumental.

27-2099.99 Entertainers and Performers, Sports and Related Workers, All Other

- **Education/Training Required: Long-term on-the-job training**
- **Employed: 68,540**
- **Annual Earnings: No data available**
- **Growth: 21.0%**
- **Annual Job Openings: 17,000**

All entertainers and performers, sports and related workers not listed separately.

No task data available.

Note: The Department of Labor has not collected some data for this job, so it has fewer details than the other descriptions.

Related SOC Job—27-2099 Entertainers and Performers, Sports and Related Workers, All Other. **Related OOH Job**—None. **Related DOT Jobs**—152.367-010 Prompter; 159.207-010 Astrologer; 159.647-018 Psychic Reader.

27-3000 Media and Communication Workers

27-3011.00 Radio and Television Announcers

- **Education/Training Required: Moderate-term on-the-job training**
- **Employed: 41,090**
- **Annual Earnings: $24,120**
- **Growth: –6.5%**
- **Annual Job Openings: 8,000**

Talk on radio or television. May interview guests, act as master of ceremonies, read news flashes, identify station by giving call letters, or announce song title and artist.

Prepare and deliver news, sports, and/or weather reports, gathering and rewriting material so that it will convey required information and fit specific time slots. Read news flashes to inform audiences of important events. Identify stations and introduce or close shows, using memorized or read scripts or ad-libs. Select program content, in conjunction with producers and assistants, based on factors such as program specialties, audience tastes, or requests from the public. Study background information to prepare for programs or interviews. Comment on music and other matters, such as weather or traffic conditions. Interview show guests about their lives, their work, or topics of current interest. Discuss various topics over the telephone with viewers or listeners. Host civic, charitable, or promotional events that are broadcast over television or radio. Make promotional appearances at public or private events to represent their employers. Operate control consoles. Announce musical selections, station breaks, commercials, or public service information and accept requests from listening audience. Keep daily program logs to provide information on all elements aired during broadcast, such as musical selections and station promotions. Record commercials for later

broadcast. Locate guests to appear on talk or interview shows. Describe or demonstrate products that viewers may purchase through specific shows or in stores. Coordinate games, contests, or other on-air competitions, performing such duties as asking questions and awarding prizes. Attend press conferences to gather information for broadcast. Provide commentary and conduct interviews during sporting events, parades, conventions, and other events. Give network cues permitting selected stations to receive programs. Moderate panels or discussion shows on topics such as current affairs, art, or education.

GOE Information—Interest Area: 03. Arts and Communication. **Work Group:** 03.06. Drama. **Personality Type**—Artistic. Artistic occupations frequently involve working with forms, designs, and patterns. They often require self-expression, and the work can be done without following a clear set of rules. **Work Values**—Recognition; Working Conditions; Creativity; Variety; Social Status; Ability Utilization. **Skills**—Speaking; Writing; Social Perceptiveness; Time Management; Monitoring; Active Listening. **Abilities**—*Cognitive:* Memorization; Originality; Fluency of Ideas; Time Sharing; Speed of Closure; Oral Expression. *Psychomotor:* None met the criteria. *Physical:* None met the criteria. *Sensory:* Speech Clarity; Speech Recognition. **General Work Activities**—*Information Input:* Identifying Objects, Actions, and Events; Getting Information; Monitoring Processes, Materials, or Surroundings. *Mental Process:* Thinking Creatively; Updating and Using Relevant Knowledge; Organizing, Planning, and Prioritizing. *Work Output:* Documenting or Recording Information; Interacting With Computers; Controlling Machines and Processes. *Interacting with Others:* Performing for or Working with the Public; Communicating with Persons Outside Organization; Establishing and Maintaining Interpersonal Relationships. **Physical Work Conditions**—Indoors; Sitting; Using Hands on Objects, Tools, or Controls. **Other Job Characteristics**—Need to Be Exact or Accurate; Repeat Same Tasks.

Experience—Job Zone 3. Previous work-related skill, knowledge, or experience is required. **Job Preparation**—SVP 6.0 to less than 7.0—more than one year and less than four years. **Knowledges**—Communications and Media; Telecommunications; Fine Arts; History and Archeology; Computers and Electronics; Geography. **Instructional Programs**—Broadcast Journalism; Radio and Television.

Related SOC Job—27-3011 Radio and Television Announcers. **Related OOH Job**—Announcers. **Related DOT Jobs**—159.147-010 Announcer; 159.147-014 Disc Jockey; 159.147-018 Show Host/Hostess.

27-3012.00 Public Address System and Other Announcers

- **Education/Training Required: Associate degree**
- **Employed: 8,150**
- **Annual Earnings: $23,290**
- **Growth: 3.8%**
- **Annual Job Openings: 2,000**

Make announcements over loudspeaker at sporting or other public events. May act as master of ceremonies or disc jockey at weddings, parties, clubs, or other gathering places.

Greet attendees and serve as masters of ceremonies at banquets, store openings, and other events. Preview any music intended to be broadcast over the public address system. Inform patrons of coming events at a specific venue. Meet with event directors to review schedules and exchange information about details, such as national anthem performers and starting lineups. Announce programs and player substitutions or other changes to patrons. Read prepared scripts describing acts or tricks presented during performances. Improvise commentary on items of interest, such as background and history of an event or past records of participants. Instruct and calm crowds during emergencies. Learn to pronounce the names of players, coaches, institutional personnel, officials, and other individuals involved in an event. Study the layout of an event venue in order to be able to give accurate directions in the event of an emergency. Review and announce crowd control procedures before the beginning of each event. Provide running commentaries of event activities, such as play-by-play descriptions or explanations of official decisions. Organize team information, such as statistics and tournament records, to ensure accessibility for use during events. Furnish information concerning plays to scoreboard operators.

GOE Information—Interest Area: 03. Arts and Communication. **Work Group:** 03.06. Drama. **Personality Type—**Social. Social occupations frequently involve working with, communicating with, and teaching people. These occupations often involve helping or providing service to others. **Work Values—**Recognition; Creativity; Variety; Social Status; Working Conditions; Responsibility. **Skills—**Management of Material Resources; Social Perceptiveness; Operation and Control; Equipment Selection; Installation; Operation Monitoring. **Abilities—**Cognitive: Time Sharing; Fluency of Ideas; Speed of Closure; Flexibility of Closure; Oral Expression; Written Expression. Psychomotor: Control Precision; Multilimb Coordination; Arm-Hand Steadiness; Manual Dexterity. Physical: None met the criteria. Sensory: Auditory Attention; Speech Clarity; Hearing Sensitivity; Far Vision; Speech Recognition; Visual Color Discrimination. **General Work Activities—**Information Input: Monitoring Processes, Materials, or Surroundings; Identifying Objects, Actions, and Events; Inspecting Equipment, Structures, or Materials. Mental Process: Thinking Creatively; Updating and Using Relevant Knowledge; Making Decisions and Solving Problems. Work Output: Handling and Moving Objects; Performing General Physical Activities; Controlling Machines and Processes. Interacting with Others: Performing for or Working with the Public; Communicating with Persons Outside Organization; Establishing and Maintaining Interpersonal Relationships. **Physical Work Conditions—**Indoors; Standing; Using Hands on Objects, Tools, or Controls. **Other Job Characteristics—**Need to Be Exact or Accurate.

Experience—Job Zone 2. Some previous work-related skill, knowledge, or experience may be helpful in these occupations, but usually is not needed. **Job Preparation—**SVP 4.0 to less than 6.0—six months to less than two years. **Knowledges—**Sales and Marketing; Computers and Electronics; Customer and Personal Service; Communications and Media. **Instructional Program—**Communications Studies/Speech Communication and Rhetoric.

Related SOC Job—27-3012 Public Address System and Other Announcers. **Related OOH Job—**Announcers. **Related DOT Job—**159.347-010 Announcer.

27-3021.00 Broadcast News Analysts

- **Education/Training Required: Bachelor's degree**
- **Employed: 6,680**
- **Annual Earnings: $42,810**
- **Growth: 4.3%**
- **Annual Job Openings: 1,000**

Analyze, interpret, and broadcast news received from various sources.

Analyze and interpret news and information received from various sources in order to be able to broadcast the information. Write commentaries, columns, or scripts, using computers. Examine news items of local, national, and international significance to determine topics to address or obtain assignments from editorial staff members. Coordinate and serve as an anchor on news broadcast programs. Edit news material to ensure that it fits within available time or space. Select material most pertinent to presentation and organize this material into appropriate formats. Gather information and develop perspectives about news subjects through research, interviews, observation, and experience. Present news stories and introduce in-depth videotaped segments or live transmissions from on-the-scene reporters.

GOE Information—Interest Area: 03. Arts and Communication. **Work Group:** 03.03. News, Broadcasting, and Public Relations. **Personality Type—**Artistic. Artistic occupations frequently involve working with forms, designs, and patterns. They often require self-expression, and the work can be done without following a clear set of rules. **Work Values—**Creativity; Recognition; Achievement; Social Status; Working Conditions; Variety. **Skills—**Writing; Time Management; Management of Personnel Resources; Speaking; Social Perceptiveness; Reading Comprehension. **Abilities—**Cognitive: Written Expression; Fluency of Ideas; Speed of Closure; Perceptual Speed; Originality; Written Comprehension. Psychomotor: None met the criteria. Physical: None met the criteria. Sensory: Speech Clarity; Speech Recognition; Far Vision; Hearing Sensitivity; Near Vision; Auditory Attention. **General Work Activities—**Information Input: Getting Information; Identifying Objects, Actions, and Events; Monitoring Processes, Materials, or Surroundings. Mental Process: Updating and Using Relevant Knowledge; Thinking Creatively; Processing Information. Work Output: Documenting or Recording Information; Interacting With Computers. Interacting with Others: Communicating with Persons Outside Organization; Performing for or Working with the Public; Establishing and Maintaining Interpersonal Relationships. **Physical Work Conditions—**Indoors; Noisy; Sitting; Repetitive Motions. **Other Job Characteristics—**Need to Be Exact or Accurate; Repeat Same Tasks.

Experience—Job Zone 4. A minimum of two to four years of work-related skill, knowledge, or experience is needed. **Job Preparation—**SVP 7.0 to less than 8.0—two years to less than 10 years. **Knowledges—**Communications and Media; Telecommunications; English Language; Geography; Sociology and Anthropology; History and Archeology. **Instructional Programs—**Broadcast Journalism; Journalism; Political Communications; Radio and Television.

Related SOC Job—27-3021 Broadcast News Analysts. **Related OOH Job—**News Analysts, Reporters, and Correspondents. **Related DOT Jobs—**131.067-010 Columnist/Commentator; 131.262-010 Newscaster.

27-3022.00 Reporters and Correspondents

- **Education/Training Required: Bachelor's degree**
- **Employed: 52,920**
- **Annual Earnings: $32,270**
- **Growth: 4.9%**
- **Annual Job Openings: 4,000**

Collect and analyze facts about newsworthy events by interview, investigation, or observation. Report and write stories for newspaper, news magazine, radio, or television.

Report and write news stories for publication or broadcast, describing the background and details of events. Arrange interviews with people who can provide information about a particular story. Review copy and correct errors in content, grammar, and punctuation, following prescribed editorial style and formatting guidelines. Review and evaluate notes taken about event aspects to isolate pertinent facts and details. Determine a story's emphasis, length, and format and organize material accordingly. Research and analyze background information related to stories in order to be able to provide complete and accurate information. Gather information about events through research; interviews; experience; and attendance at political, news, sports, artistic, social, and other functions. Investigate breaking news developments such as disasters, crimes, and human interest stories. Research and report on specialized fields such as medicine, science and technology, politics, foreign affairs, sports, arts, consumer affairs, business, religion, crime, or education. Check reference materials such as books, news files, and public records to obtain relevant facts. Receive assignments or evaluate leads and tips to develop story ideas. Discuss issues with editors in order to establish priorities and positions. Revise work to meet editorial approval or to fit time or space requirements. Photograph or videotape news events or request that a photographer be assigned to provide such coverage. Develop ideas and material for columns or commentaries by analyzing and interpreting news, current issues, and personal experiences. Transmit news stories or reporting information from remote locations, using equipment such as satellite phones, telephones, fax machines, or modems. Present live or recorded commentary via broadcast media. Conduct taped or filmed interviews or narratives. Edit or assist in editing videos for broadcast. Write columns, editorials, commentaries, or reviews that interpret events or offer opinions. Write reviews of literary, musical, and other artwork based on knowledge, judgment, and experience.

GOE Information—Interest Area: 03. Arts and Communication. **Work Group:** 03.03. News, Broadcasting, and Public Relations. **Personality Type—**Artistic. Artistic occupations frequently involve working with forms, designs, and patterns. They often require self-expression, and the work can be done without following a clear set of rules. **Work Values—**Creativity; Recognition; Advancement; Ability Utilization; Variety; Achievement. **Skills—**Writing; Active Listening; Reading Comprehension; Speaking; Critical Thinking; Active Learning. **Abilities—***Cognitive:* Written Expression; Fluency of Ideas; Originality; Written Comprehension; Oral Comprehension; Speed of Closure. *Psychomotor:* None met the criteria. *Physical:* None met the criteria. *Sensory:* Speech Recognition; Speech Clarity; Near Vision. **General Work Activities—***Information Input:* Getting Information; Identifying Objects, Actions, and Events; Monitoring Processes, Materials, or Surroundings. *Mental Process:* Thinking Creatively; Organizing, Planning, and Prioritizing; Updating and Using Relevant Knowledge. *Work Output:* Documenting or Recording Information; Interacting With Computers. *Interacting with Others:* Communicating with Persons Outside Organization; Establishing and Maintaining Interpersonal Relationships; Performing for or Working with the Public. **Physical Work Conditions—**More Often Indoors Than Outdoors; Noisy; Sitting. **Other Job Characteristics—**Need to Be Exact or Accurate; Errors Have Important Consequences.

Experience—Job Zone 4. A minimum of two to four years of work-related skill, knowledge, or experience is needed. **Job Preparation—**SVP 7.0 to less than 8.0—two years to less than 10 years. **Knowledges—**Communications and Media; English Language; Geography; Sociology and Anthropology; Clerical Practices; Computers and Electronics. **Instructional Programs—**Agricultural Communications/Journalism; Broadcast Journalism; Journalism; Journalism, Other; Mass Communications/Media Studies; Photojournalism; Political Communications.

Related SOC Job—27-3022 Reporters and Correspondents. **Related OOH Job—**News Analysts, Reporters, and Correspondents. **Related DOT Jobs—**131.262-014 Newswriter; 131.262-018 Reporter.

27-3031.00 Public Relations Specialists

- **Education/Training Required: Bachelor's degree**
- **Employed: 191,430**
- **Annual Earnings: $45,020**
- **Growth: 22.9%**
- **Annual Job Openings: 38,000**

Engage in promoting or creating good will for individuals, groups, or organizations by writing or selecting favorable publicity material and releasing it through various communications media. May prepare and arrange displays and make speeches.

Prepare or edit organizational publications for internal and external audiences, including employee newsletters and stockholders' reports. Respond to requests for information from the media or designate another appropriate spokesperson or information source. Establish and maintain cooperative relationships with representatives of community, consumer, employee, and public interest groups. Plan and direct development and communication of informational programs to maintain favorable public and stockholder perceptions of an organization's accomplishments and agenda. Confer with production and support personnel to produce or coordinate production of advertisements and promotions. Arrange public appearances, lectures, contests, or exhibits for clients to increase product and service awareness and to promote goodwill. Study the objectives, promotional policies, and needs of organizations to develop public relations strategies that will influence public opinion or promote ideas, products, and services. Consult with advertising agencies or staff to arrange promotional campaigns in all types of media for products, organizations, or individuals. Confer with other managers to identify trends and key group interests and concerns or to provide advice on business decisions. Coach client representatives in effective communication with the public and with employees. Prepare and deliver speeches to further public relations objectives. Purchase advertising space and time as required to promote client's product or agenda. Plan and conduct market and public opinion research to test products or determine potential for product success, communicating results to client or management.

GOE Information—Interest Area: 03. Arts and Communication. **Work Group:** 03.03. News, Broadcasting, and Public Relations. **Personality Type—**Enterprising. Enterprising occupations frequently involve starting up and carrying out projects. These occupations can involve leading people and making many decisions. They sometimes require risk taking and often deal with business. **Work Values—**Creativity; Recognition; Ability Utilization; Achievement; Variety; Compensation. **Skills—**Service Orientation; Persuasion; Management of Financial Resources; Negotiation; Social Perceptiveness. **Abilities—***Cognitive:* Fluency of Ideas; Problem Sensitivity; Written Expression; Originality; Oral Expression; Inductive Reasoning. *Psychomotor:* None met the criteria. *Physical:* None met the criteria. *Sensory:* Speech Clarity; Speech Recognition; Near Vision. **General Work Activities—***Information Input:* Getting Information; Identifying Objects, Actions, and Events; Monitoring Processes, Materials, or Surroundings. *Mental Process:* Organizing, Planning, and Prioritizing; Updating and Using Relevant Knowledge; Thinking Creatively. *Work Output:* Interacting With Computers; Documenting or Recording Information. *Interacting with Others:* Communicating with Persons Outside Organization; Communicating with Other

Workers; Establishing and Maintaining Interpersonal Relationships. **Physical Work Conditions**—Indoors; Sitting. **Other Job Characteristics**—Need to Be Exact or Accurate.

Experience—Job Zone 4. A minimum of two to four years of work-related skill, knowledge, or experience is needed. **Job Preparation**—SVP 7.0 to less than 8.0—two years to less than 10 years. **Knowledges**—Sales and Marketing; Communications and Media; Customer and Personal Service; Sociology and Anthropology; Administration and Management; Clerical Practices. **Instructional Programs**—Communications Studies/Speech Communication and Rhetoric; Family and Consumer Sciences/Human Sciences Communications; Health Communications; Political Communications; Public Relations/Image Management.

Related SOC Job—27-3031 Public Relations Specialists. **Related OOH Job**—Public Relations Specialists. **Related DOT Jobs**—165.017-010 Lobbyist; 165.167-010 Sales-Service Promoter.

27-3041.00 Editors

- **Education/Training Required: Bachelor's degree**
- **Employed: 96,270**
- **Annual Earnings: $45,510**
- **Growth: 14.8%**
- **Annual Job Openings: 16,000**

Perform variety of editorial duties, such as laying out, indexing, and revising content of written materials, in preparation for final publication.

Prepare, rewrite, and edit copy to improve readability or supervise others who do this work. Read copy or proof to detect and correct errors in spelling, punctuation, and syntax. Allocate print space for story text, photos, and illustrations according to space parameters and copy significance, using knowledge of layout principles. Plan the contents of publications according to the publication's style, editorial policy, and publishing requirements. Verify facts, dates, and statistics, using standard reference sources. Review and approve proofs submitted by composing room prior to publication production. Develop story or content ideas, considering reader or audience appeal. Oversee publication production, including artwork, layout, computer typesetting, and printing, ensuring adherence to deadlines and budget requirements. Confer with management and editorial staff members regarding placement and emphasis of developing news stories. Assign topics, events, and stories to individual writers or reporters for coverage. Read, evaluate, and edit manuscripts or other materials submitted for publication and confer with authors regarding changes in content, style or organization, or publication. Monitor news-gathering operations to ensure utilization of all news sources, such as press releases, telephone contacts, radio, television, wire services, and other reporters. Meet frequently with artists, typesetters, layout personnel, marketing directors, and production managers to discuss projects and resolve problems. Supervise and coordinate work of reporters and other editors. Make manuscript acceptance or revision recommendations to the publisher. Select local, state, national, and international news items received from wire services based on assessment of items' significance and interest value. Interview and hire writers and reporters or negotiate contracts, royalties, and payments for authors or freelancers. Direct the policies and departments of newspapers, magazines, and other publishing establishments. Arrange for copyright permissions. Read material to determine index items and arrange them alphabetically or topically, indicating page or chapter location.

GOE Information—**Interest Area:** 03. Arts and Communication. **Work Group:** 03.02. Writing and Editing. **Personality Type**—Artistic. Artistic occupations frequently involve working with forms, designs, and patterns. They often require self-expression, and the work can be done without following a clear set of rules. **Work Values**—Creativity; Recognition; Ability Utilization; Responsibility; Achievement; Autonomy. **Skills**—Writing; Reading Comprehension; Active Listening; Persuasion; Time Management; Critical Thinking. **Abilities**—*Cognitive:* Written Expression; Originality; Fluency of Ideas; Written Comprehension; Visualization; Memorization. *Psychomotor:* None met the criteria. *Physical:* None met the criteria. *Sensory:* Near Vision; Speech Clarity; Speech Recognition. **General Work Activities**—*Information Input:* Getting Information; Identifying Objects, Actions, and Events; Monitoring Processes, Materials, or Surroundings. *Mental Process:* Organizing, Planning, and Prioritizing; Thinking Creatively; Processing Information. *Work Output:* Documenting or Recording Information; Interacting With Computers. *Interacting with Others:* Communicating with Persons Outside Organization; Establishing and Maintaining Interpersonal Relationships; Communicating with Other Workers. **Physical Work Conditions**—Indoors; Sitting; Using Hands on Objects, Tools, or Controls; Repetitive Motions. **Other Job Characteristics**—Need to Be Exact or Accurate; Repeat Same Tasks; Errors Have Important Consequences.

Experience—Job Zone 4. A minimum of two to four years of work-related skill, knowledge, or experience is needed. **Job Preparation**—SVP 7.0 to less than 8.0—two years to less than 10 years. **Knowledges**—Communications and Media; History and Archeology; Geography; English Language; Sales and Marketing; Clerical Practices. **Instructional Programs**—Broadcast Journalism; Business/Corporate Communications; Communications, Journalism, and Related Fields, Other; Creative Writing; Family and Consumer Sciences/Human Sciences Communications; Journalism; Mass Communications/Media Studies; Publishing; Technical and Business Writing.

Related SOC Job—27-3041 Editors. **Related OOH Job**—Writers and Editors. **Related DOT Jobs**—131.267-022 Script Reader; 132.017-010 Editor, Managing, Newspaper; 132.017-014 Editor, Newspaper; 132.037-010 Continuity Director; 132.037-014 Editor, City; 132.037-018 Editor, Department; 132.037-022 Editor, Publications; 132.037-026 Story Editor; 132.067-010 Bureau Chief; 132.067-014 Editor, Book; 132.067-018 Editor, Dictionary; 132.067-022 Editor, Greeting Card; 132.067-026 Editor, News; 132.067-030 Program Proposals Coordinator; 132.132-010 Assignment Editor; 132.267-010 Editor, Telegraph; others.

27-3042.00 Technical Writers

- **Education/Training Required: Bachelor's degree**
- **Employed: 46,250**
- **Annual Earnings: $55,160**
- **Growth: 23.2%**
- **Annual Job Openings: 5,000**

Write technical materials, such as equipment manuals, appendices, or operating and maintenance instructions. May assist in layout work.

Organize material and complete writing assignment according to set standards regarding order, clarity, conciseness, style, and terminology. Maintain records and files of work and revisions. Edit, standardize, or make changes to material prepared by other writers or establishment personnel. Confer with customer representatives, vendors, plant executives, or publisher to establish technical specifications and to determine subject material to be developed for publication. Review published materials and recommend revisions or changes in scope, format, content, and methods of reproduction and binding. Select photographs, drawings, sketches, diagrams, and charts to illustrate material. Study drawings, specifications, mockups, and product samples to integrate and delineate technology, operating procedure, and production sequence and detail. Interview production and engineering personnel and read journals and other material to become familiar with product technologies and production methods. Observe production, developmental, and experimental activities to determine operating procedure and detail. Arrange for typing, duplication, and distribution of material. Assist in laying out material for publication. Analyze developments in specific field to determine need for revisions in previously published materials and development of new material. Review manufacturer's and trade catalogs, drawings, and other data relative to operation, maintenance, and service of equipment. Draw sketches to illustrate specified materials or assembly sequence.

GOE Information—Interest Area: 03. Arts and Communication. **Work Group:** 03.02. Writing and Editing. **Personality Type—** Artistic. Artistic occupations frequently involve working with forms, designs, and patterns. They often require self-expression, and the work can be done without following a clear set of rules. **Work Values—**Creativity; Ability Utilization; Achievement; Responsibility; Recognition; Social Status. **Skills—**Writing; Technology Design; Active Listening; Quality Control Analysis; Coordination; Reading Comprehension. **Abilities—***Cognitive:* Written Expression; Written Comprehension; Fluency of Ideas; Oral Expression; Originality; Visualization. *Psychomotor:* None met the criteria. *Physical:* None met the criteria. *Sensory:* Near Vision. **General Work Activities—** *Information Input:* Getting Information; Monitoring Processes, Materials, or Surroundings; Identifying Objects, Actions, and Events. *Mental Process:* Updating and Using Relevant Knowledge; Thinking Creatively; Organizing, Planning, and Prioritizing. *Work Output:* Documenting or Recording Information; Interacting With Computers; Drafting and Specifying Technical Devices. *Interacting with Others:* Communicating with Other Workers; Coordinating the Work and Activities of Others; Establishing and Maintaining Interpersonal Relationships. **Physical Work Conditions—**Indoors; Sitting; Using Hands on Objects, Tools, or Controls; Repetitive Motions. **Other Job Characteristics—**Need to Be Exact or Accurate; Repeat Same Tasks; Errors Have Important Consequences.

Experience—Job Zone 4. A minimum of two to four years of work-related skill, knowledge, or experience is needed. **Job Preparation—** SVP 7.0 to less than 8.0—two years to less than 10 years. **Knowledges—**Communications and Media; Clerical Practices; English Language; Computers and Electronics; Education and Training; Engineering and Technology. **Instructional Programs—** Business/Corporate Communications; Communications Studies/ Speech Communication and Rhetoric; Technical and Business Writing.

Related SOC Job—27-3042 Technical Writers. **Related OOH Job—** Writers and Editors. **Related DOT Jobs—**019.267-010 Specification Writer; 131.267-026 Writer, Technical Publications; 132.017-018 Editor, Technical and Scientific Publications.

27-3043.00 Writers and Authors

- **Education/Training Required: Bachelor's degree**
- **Employed: 43,020**
- **Annual Earnings: $46,420**
- **Growth: 17.7%**
- **Annual Job Openings: 14,000**

The job openings listed here are shared with 27-3043.04 Copy Writers and 27-3043.05 Poets, Lyricists, and Creative Writers.

Originate and prepare written material, such as scripts, stories, advertisements, and other material.

No task data available.

GOE Information—Interest Area: 03. Arts and Communication. **Work Group:** 03.02. Writing and Editing. **Note:** The Department of Labor has not collected some data for this job, so it has fewer details than the other descriptions.

Instructional Programs—Broadcast Journalism; Business/Corporate Communications; Communications, Journalism, and Related Fields, Other; Creative Writing; English Composition; Family and Consumer Sciences/Human Sciences Communications; Journalism; Mass Communications/Media Studies; Playwriting and Screenwriting; Technical and Business Writing.

Related SOC Job—27-3043 Writers and Authors. **Related OOH Job—** Writers and Editors. **Related DOT Job—**No data available.

27-3043.04 Copy Writers

- **Education/Training Required: Bachelor's degree**
- **Employed: 43,020**
- **Annual Earnings: $46,420**
- **Growth: 17.7%**
- **Annual Job Openings: 14,000**

The job openings listed here are shared with 27-3043.00 Writers and Authors and Poets, Lyricists, and Creative Writers.

Write advertising copy for use by publication or broadcast media to promote sale of goods and services.

Write advertising copy for use by publication, broadcast, or Internet media to promote the sale of goods and services. Present drafts and ideas to clients. Discuss with the client the product, advertising themes and methods, and any changes that should be made in advertising copy. Consult with sales, media, and marketing representatives to obtain information on product or service and discuss style and length of advertising copy. Vary language and tone of messages based on product and medium. Edit or rewrite existing copy as necessary and submit copy for approval by supervisor. Write to customers in their terms and on their level so that the advertiser's sales message is more readily received. Write articles; bulletins; sales letters; speeches; and other related informative, marketing, and promotional material. Invent names for products and write the slogans that appear on packaging, brochures, and other promotional material. Review advertising trends, consumer surveys, and other data regarding marketing of goods and services to determine the best way to promote products. Develop advertising campaigns for a wide range of clients, working with an advertising agency's creative director and art director to determine the best way to present advertising information. Conduct research and interviews to determine which of a product's selling features should be promoted.

GOE Information—Interest Area: 03. Arts and Communication. **Work Group:** 03.02. Writing and Editing. **Personality Type—** Artistic. Artistic occupations frequently involve working with forms, designs, and patterns. They often require self-expression, and the work can be done without following a clear set of rules. **Work Values—**Creativity; Recognition; Advancement; Ability Utilization; Responsibility; Working Conditions. **Skills—**Persuasion; Technology Design; Time Management; Equipment Selection; Quality Control Analysis; Negotiation. **Abilities—***Cognitive:* Fluency of Ideas; Originality; Written Expression; Oral Comprehension; Oral Expression; Inductive Reasoning. *Psychomotor:* None met the criteria. *Physical:* None met the criteria. *Sensory:* Near Vision; Speech Recognition; Speech Clarity. **General Work Activities—***Information Input:* Getting Information; Identifying Objects, Actions, and Events; Monitoring Processes, Materials, or Surroundings. *Mental Process:* Thinking Creatively; Organizing, Planning, and Prioritizing; Updating and Using Relevant Knowledge. *Work Output:* Interacting With Computers; Documenting or Recording Information. *Interacting with Others:* Communicating with Persons Outside Organization; Communicating with Other Workers; Establishing and Maintaining Interpersonal Relationships. **Physical Work Conditions—**Indoors; Sitting; Using Hands on Objects, Tools, or Controls; Repetitive Motions. **Other Job Characteristics—**Need to Be Exact or Accurate; Repeat Same Tasks.

Experience—Job Zone 4. A minimum of two to four years of work-related skill, knowledge, or experience is needed. **Job Preparation—** SVP 7.0 to less than 8.0—two years to less than 10 years. **Knowledges—**Sales and Marketing; Communications and Media; Sociology and Anthropology; English Language; Computers and Electronics; Psychology. **Instructional Programs—**Communications Studies/Speech Communication and Rhetoric; English Composition; Journalism; Mass Communications/Media Studies.

Related SOC Job—27-3043 Writers and Authors. **Related OOH Job—** Writers and Editors. **Related DOT Job—**131.067-014 Copy Writer.

27-3043.05 Poets, Lyricists, and Creative Writers

- Education/Training Required: Bachelor's degree
- Employed: 43,020
- Annual Earnings: $46,420
- Growth: 17.7%
- Annual Job Openings: 14,000

The job openings listed here are shared with 27-3043.00 Writers and Authors and 27-3043.04 Copy Writers.

Create original written works, such as scripts, essays, prose, poetry, or song lyrics, for publication or performance.

Revise written material to meet personal standards and to satisfy needs of clients, publishers, directors, or producers. Choose subject matter and suitable form to express personal feelings and experiences or ideas or to narrate stories or events. Plan project arrangements or outlines and organize material accordingly. Prepare works in appropriate format for publication and send them to publishers or producers. Follow appropriate procedures to get copyrights for completed work. Write fiction or nonfiction prose such as short stories, novels, biographies, articles, descriptive or critical analyses, and essays. Develop factors such as themes, plots, characterizations, psychological analyses, historical environments, action, and dialogue to create material. Confer with clients, editors, publishers, or producers to dis-

cuss changes or revisions to written material. Conduct research to obtain factual information and authentic detail, using sources such as newspaper accounts, diaries, and interviews. Write narrative, dramatic, lyric, or other types of poetry for publication. Attend book launches and publicity events or conduct public readings. Write words to fit musical compositions, including lyrics for operas, musical plays, and choral works. Adapt text to accommodate musical requirements of composers and singers. Teach writing classes. Write humorous material for publication or for performances such as comedy routines, gags, and comedy shows. Collaborate with other writers on specific projects.

GOE Information—Interest Area: 03. Arts and Communication. **Work Group:** 03.02. Writing and Editing. **Personality Type—** Artistic. Artistic occupations frequently involve working with forms, designs, and patterns. They often require self-expression, and the work can be done without following a clear set of rules. **Work Values—**Creativity; Ability Utilization; Recognition; Independence; Achievement; Autonomy. **Skills—**Writing; Social Perceptiveness; Persuasion; Management of Financial Resources; Active Listening; Reading Comprehension. **Abilities—***Cognitive:* Originality; Written Expression; Fluency of Ideas; Written Comprehension; Deductive Reasoning; Visualization. *Psychomotor:* Finger Dexterity; Arm-Hand Steadiness. *Physical:* None met the criteria. *Sensory:* Speech Clarity; Hearing Sensitivity; Speech Recognition; Near Vision; Far Vision. **General Work Activities—***Information Input:* Getting Information; Identifying Objects, Actions, and Events; Monitoring Processes, Materials, or Surroundings. *Mental Process:* Thinking Creatively; Organizing, Planning, and Prioritizing; Updating and Using Relevant Knowledge. *Work Output:* Documenting or Recording Information; Interacting With Computers. *Interacting with Others:* Interpreting the Meaning of Information to Others; Establishing and Maintaining Interpersonal Relationships; Communicating with Persons Outside Organization. **Physical Work Conditions—**Indoors; Sitting; Using Hands on Objects, Tools, or Controls; Repetitive Motions. **Other Job Characteristics—**Need to Be Exact or Accurate; Repeat Same Tasks.

Experience—Job Zone 4. A minimum of two to four years of work-related skill, knowledge, or experience is needed. **Job Preparation—** SVP 7.0 to less than 8.0—two years to less than 10 years. **Knowledges—**Fine Arts; Communications and Media; Philosophy and Theology; Sociology and Anthropology; Sales and Marketing; English Language. **Instructional Programs—**Communications Studies/Speech Communication and Rhetoric; Creative Writing; English Composition; Family and Consumer Sciences/Human Sciences Communications; Mass Communications/Media Studies; Playwriting and Screenwriting.

Related SOC Job—27-3043 Writers and Authors. **Related OOH Job—** Writers and Editors. **Related DOT Jobs—**052.067-010 Biographer; 131.067-010 Columnist/Commentator; 131.067-018 Critic; 131.067-022 Editorial Writer; 131.067-026 Humorist; 131.067-030 Librettist; 131.067-034 Lyricist; 131.067-038 Playwright; 131.067-042 Poet; 131.067-046 Writer, Prose, Fiction and Nonfiction; 131.067-050 Screen Writer; 131.087-010 Continuity Writer; 139.087-010 Crossword-Puzzle Maker.

27-3091.00 Interpreters and Translators

- Education/Training Required: Long-term on-the-job training
- Employed: 29,240
- Annual Earnings: $34,800
- Growth: 19.9%
- Annual Job Openings: 4,000

Translate or interpret written, oral, or sign language text into another language for others.

Follow ethical codes that protect the confidentiality of information. Identify and resolve conflicts related to the meanings of words, concepts, practices, or behaviors. Proofread, edit, and revise translated materials. Translate messages simultaneously or consecutively into specified languages orally or by using hand signs, maintaining message content, context, and style as much as possible. Check translations of technical terms and terminology to ensure that they are accurate and remain consistent throughout translation revisions. Read written materials such as legal documents, scientific works, or news reports and rewrite material into specified languages. Refer to reference materials such as dictionaries, lexicons, encyclopedias, and computerized terminology banks as needed to ensure translation accuracy. Compile terminology and information to be used in translations, including technical terms such as those for legal or medical material. Adapt translations to students' cognitive and grade levels, collaborating with educational team members as necessary. Listen to speakers' statements to determine meanings and to prepare translations, using electronic listening systems as necessary. Check original texts or confer with authors to ensure that translations retain the content, meaning, and feeling of the original material. Compile information about the content and context of information to be translated, as well as details of the groups for whom translation or interpretation is being performed. Discuss translation requirements with clients and determine any fees to be charged for services provided. Adapt software and accompanying technical documents to another language and culture. Educate students, parents, staff, and teachers about the roles and functions of educational interpreters. Train and supervise other translators/interpreters. Travel with or guide tourists who speak another language.

GOE Information—Interest Area: 03. Arts and Communication. **Work Group:** 03.03. News, Broadcasting, and Public Relations. **Personality Type—**Artistic. Artistic occupations frequently involve working with forms, designs, and patterns. They often require self-expression, and the work can be done without following a clear set of rules. **Work Values—**Social Service; Ability Utilization; Achievement; Working Conditions; Autonomy; Social Status. **Skills—**Social Perceptiveness; Speaking; Active Listening; Writing; Reading Comprehension. **Abilities—***Cognitive:* Written Expression; Written Comprehension; Selective Attention; Oral Expression; Speed of Closure; Oral Comprehension. *Psychomotor:* Finger Dexterity. *Physical:* None met the criteria. *Sensory:* Speech Recognition; Speech Clarity; Hearing Sensitivity; Auditory Attention; Far Vision; Near Vision. **General Work Activities—***Information Input:* Identifying Objects, Actions, and Events; Getting Information; Monitoring Processes, Materials, or Surroundings. *Mental Process:* Updating and Using Relevant Knowledge; Thinking Creatively; Analyzing Data or Information. *Work Output:* Documenting or Recording Information; Interacting With Computers; Performing General Physical Activities. *Interacting with Others:* Interpreting the Meaning of Information for Others; Communicating with Other Workers; Establishing and Maintaining Interpersonal Relationships. **Physical Work Conditions—**Indoors; Sitting; Repetitive Motions. **Other Job Characteristics—**Need to Be Exact or Accurate; Repeat Same Tasks.

Experience—Job Zone 4. A minimum of two to four years of work-related skill, knowledge, or experience is needed. **Job Preparation—**SVP 7.0 to less than 8.0—two years to less than 10 years.

Knowledges—Foreign Language; English Language; Geography; Sociology and Anthropology; Computers and Electronics; Communications and Media. **Instructional Programs—**African Languages, Literatures, and Linguistics; Albanian Language and Literature; American Indian/Native American Languages, Literatures, and Linguistics; American Sign Language (ASL); American Sign Language, Other; Ancient Near Eastern and Biblical Languages, Literatures, and Linguistics; Ancient/Classical Greek Language and Literature; Arabic Language and Literature; Australian/Oceanic/Pacific Languages, Literatures, and Linguistics; Bahasa Indonesian/Bahasa Malay Languages and Literatures; Baltic Languages, Literatures, and Linguistics; Bengali Language and Literature; Bulgarian Language and Literature; Burmese Language and Literature; Catalan Language and Literature; Celtic Languages, Literatures, and Linguistics; Chinese Language and Literature; Classics and Classical Languages, Literatures, and Linguistics, General; Classics and Classical Languages, Literatures, and Linguistics, Other; Czech Language and Literature; Danish Language and Literature; Dutch/Flemish Language and Literature; East Asian Languages, Literatures, and Linguistics, General; East Asian Languages, Literatures, and Linguistics, Other; Education/Teaching of Individuals with Hearing Impairments, Including Deafness; Filipino/Tagalog Language and Literature; Finnish and Related Languages, Literatures, and Linguistics; Foreign Languages, Literatures, and Linguistics, Other; Foreign Languages/Modern Languages, General; French Language and Literature; German Language and Literature; Germanic Languages, Literatures, and Linguistics, General; Germanic Languages, Literatures, and Linguistics, Other; Hebrew Language and Literature; Hindi Language and Literature; Hungarian/Magyar Language and Literature; Iranian/Persian Languages, Literatures, and Linguistics; Italian Language and Literature; Japanese Language and Literature; Khmer/Cambodian Language and Literature; Korean Language and Literature; Language Interpretation and Translation; Lao/Laotian Language and Literature; others.

Related SOC Job—27-3091 Interpreters and Translators. **Related OOH Job—**Interpreters and Translators. **Related DOT Jobs—**137.267-010 Interpreter; 137.267-014 Interpreter, Deaf; 137.267-018 Translator.

27-3099.99 Media and Communication Workers, All Other

- **Education/Training Required: Long-term on-the-job training**
- **Employed: 25,660**
- **Annual Earnings: $41,890**
- **Growth: 15.7%**
- **Annual Job Openings: 5,000**

All media and communication workers not listed separately.

No task data available.

Note: The Department of Labor has not collected some data for this job, so it has fewer details than the other descriptions.

Related SOC Job—27-3099 Media and Communication Workers, All Other. **Related OOH Job—**None. **Related DOT Jobs—**131.087-014 Reader; 199.267-038 Graphologist.

27-4000 Media and Communication Equipment Workers

27-4011.00 Audio and Video Equipment Technicians

- **Education/Training Required: Long-term on-the-job training**
- **Employed: 40,390**
- **Annual Earnings: $32,940**
- **Growth: 18.1%**
- **Annual Job Openings: 5,000**

Set up or set up and operate audio and video equipment, including microphones, sound speakers, video screens, projectors, video monitors, recording equipment, connecting wires and cables, sound and mixing boards, and related electronic equipment for concerts, sports events, meetings and conventions, presentations, and news conferences. May also set up and operate associated spotlights and other custom lighting systems.

Notify supervisors when major equipment repairs are needed. Monitor incoming and outgoing pictures and sound feeds to ensure quality; notify directors of any possible problems. Mix and regulate sound inputs and feeds or coordinate audio feeds with television pictures. Install, adjust, and operate electronic equipment used to record, edit, and transmit radio and television programs, cable programs, and motion pictures. Design layouts of audio and video equipment and perform upgrades and maintenance. Perform minor repairs and routine cleaning of audio and video equipment. Diagnose and resolve media system problems in classrooms. Switch sources of video input from one camera or studio to another, from film to live programming, or from network to local programming. Meet with directors and senior members of camera crews to discuss assignments and determine filming sequences, camera movements, and picture composition. Construct and position properties, sets, lighting equipment, and other equipment. Compress, digitize, duplicate, and store audio and video data. Obtain, set up, and load videotapes for scheduled productions or broadcasts. Edit videotapes by erasing and removing portions of programs and adding video or sound as required. Direct and coordinate activities of assistants and other personnel during production. Plan and develop pre-production ideas into outlines, scripts, storyboards, and graphics, using own ideas or specifications of assignments. Maintain inventories of audiotapes and videotapes and related supplies. Determine formats, approaches, content, levels, and media to effectively meet objectives within budgetary constraints, utilizing research, knowledge, and training. Record and edit audio material such as movie soundtracks, using audio recording and editing equipment. Inform users of audiotaping and videotaping service policies and procedures. Obtain and preview musical performance programs prior to events to become familiar with the order and approximate times of pieces. Produce rough and finished graphics and graphic designs. Locate and secure settings, properties, effects, and other production necessities.

GOE Information—Interest Area: 03. Arts and Communication. **Work Group:** 03.09. Media Technology. **Personality Type—** Conventional. Conventional occupations frequently involve following set procedures and routines. These occupations can include working with data and details more than with ideas. Usually there is a clear line of authority to follow. **Work Values—**Working Conditions; Authority; Co-workers; Ability Utilization; Social Service; Creativity. **Skills—**Installation; Operation and Control; Equipment Maintenance; Troubleshooting; Operation Monitoring; Repairing. **Abilities—***Cognitive:* Time Sharing; Originality; Visualization; Perceptual Speed; Written Expression; Fluency of Ideas. *Psychomotor:* Control Precision; Response Orientation; Reaction Time; Manual Dexterity; Arm-Hand Steadiness; Finger Dexterity. *Physical:* Static Strength; Extent Flexibility; Trunk Strength. *Sensory:* Sound Localization; Visual Color Discrimination; Auditory Attention; Hearing Sensitivity; Glare Sensitivity; Far Vision. **General Work Activities—***Information Input:* Monitoring Processes, Materials, or Surroundings; Identifying Objects, Actions, and Events; Inspecting Equipment, Structures, or Materials. *Mental Process:* Updating and Using Relevant Knowledge; Thinking Creatively; Organizing, Planning, and Prioritizing. *Work Output:* Controlling Machines and Processes; Handling and Moving Objects; Interacting With Computers. *Interacting with Others:* Communicating with Other Workers; Establishing and Maintaining Interpersonal Relationships; Communicating with Persons Outside Organization. **Physical Work Conditions—**Indoors; Standing; Using Hands on Objects, Tools, or Controls. **Other Job Characteristics—**Need to Be Exact or Accurate; Repeat Same Tasks.

Experience—Job Zone 3. Previous work-related skill, knowledge, or experience is required. **Job Preparation—**SVP 6.0 to less than 7.0— more than one year and less than four years. **Knowledges—** Computers and Electronics; Telecommunications; Engineering and Technology; Communications and Media; Mechanical Devices; Physics. **Instructional Programs—**Agricultural Communications/ Journalism; Photographic and Film/Video Technology/Technician and Assistant; Recording Arts Technology/Technician.

Related SOC Job—27-4011 Audio and Video Equipment Technicians. **Related OOH Job—**Broadcast and Sound Engineering Technicians and Radio Operators. **Related DOT Jobs—**159.042-010 Laserist; 194.262-014 Sound Controller; 962.261-010 Planetarium Technician; 962.261-014 Stage Technician; 962.267-010 Sight-Effects Specialist; 962.281-018 Special Effects Specialist; 962.362-010 Communications Technician; 962.362-014 Light Technician; 962.381-014 Lighting-Equipment Operator.

27-4012.00 Broadcast Technicians

- **Education/Training Required: Associate degree**
- **Employed: 30,730**
- **Annual Earnings: $30,410**
- **Growth: 9.8%**
- **Annual Job Openings: 4,000**

Set up, operate, and maintain the electronic equipment used to transmit radio and television programs. Control audio equipment to regulate volume level and quality of sound during radio and television broadcasts. Operate radio transmitter to broadcast radio and television programs.

Maintain programming logs as required by station management and the Federal Communications Commission. Control audio equipment to regulate the volume and sound quality during radio and television broadcasts. Monitor strength, clarity, and reliability of incoming and outgoing signals and adjust equipment as necessary to maintain quality broadcasts. Regulate the fidelity, brightness, and contrast of video transmissions, using video console control panels. Observe monitors and converse with station personnel to determine audio and video levels and to ascertain that programs are airing. Preview scheduled programs to ensure that signals are functioning and programs are ready for transmission. Select sources from which programming will be received or through which programming will be transmitted. Report equipment problems, ensure that repairs are made; make emergency repairs to equipment when necessary and possible. Record sound onto tape or film for radio or television, checking its quality and making adjustments where necessary. Align antennae with receiving dishes to obtain the clearest signal for transmission of broadcasts from field locations. Substitute programs in cases where signals fail. Organize recording sessions and prepare areas such as radio booths and television stations for recording. Perform preventive and minor equipment maintenance, using hand tools. Instruct trainees in how to use television production equipment, how to film events, and how to copy and edit graphics or sound onto videotape. Schedule programming or read television programming logs to determine which programs are to be recorded or aired. Edit broadcast material electronically, using computers. Give technical directions to other personnel during filming. Set up and operate portable field transmission equipment outside the studio. Determine the number, type, and approximate location of microphones needed for best sound recording or transmission quality and position them appropriately. Design and modify equipment to employer specifications. Prepare reports outlining past and future programs, including content.

GOE Information—Interest Area: 03. Arts and Communication. **Work Group:** 03.09. Media Technology. **Personality Type—**Realistic. Realistic occupations frequently involve work activities that include practical, hands-on problems and solutions. They often deal with plants; animals; and real-world materials like wood, tools, and machinery. Many of the occupations require working outside and do not involve a lot of paperwork or working closely with others. **Work Values—**Variety; Advancement; Working Conditions; Recognition; Supervision, Human Relations; Company Policies and Practices. **Skills—**Operation Monitoring; Operation and Control; Troubleshooting; Installation; Equipment Maintenance; Repairing. **Abilities—***Cognitive:* Perceptual Speed; Time Sharing; Selective Attention; Fluency of Ideas; Speed of Closure; Visualization. *Psychomotor:* Control Precision; Response Orientation; Reaction Time; Finger Dexterity; Rate Control; Manual Dexterity. *Physical:* Static Strength. *Sensory:* Visual Color Discrimination; Hearing Sensitivity; Far Vision; Auditory Attention; Speech Recognition; Depth Perception. **General Work Activities—***Information Input:* Monitoring Processes, Materials, or Surroundings; Identifying Objects, Actions, and Events; Getting Information. *Mental Process:* Updating and Using Relevant Knowledge; Organizing, Planning, and Prioritizing; Making Decisions and Solving Problems. *Work Output:* Controlling Machines and Processes; Documenting or Recording Information; Interacting With Computers. *Interacting with Others:* Establishing and Maintaining Interpersonal Relationships; Communicating with Other Workers; Teaching Others. **Physical Work Conditions—**Indoors; Noisy; Sitting; Using Hands on Objects, Tools, or Controls. **Other Job Characteristics—**Need to Be Exact or Accurate; Repeat Same Tasks; Errors Have Important Consequences; Pace Determined by Speed of Equipment.

Experience—Job Zone 3. Previous work-related skill, knowledge, or experience is required. **Job Preparation—**SVP 6.0 to less than 7.0— more than one year and less than four years. **Knowledges—**Telecommunications; Communications and Media; Engineering and Technology; Computers and Electronics; Mechanical Devices; Production and Processing. **Instructional Programs—**Audiovisual Communications Technologies/Technicians, Other; Communications Technology/Technician; Radio and Television Broadcasting Technology/Technician.

Related SOC Job—27-4012 Broadcast Technicians. **Related OOH Job—**Broadcast and Sound Engineering Technicians and Radio Operators. **Related DOT Jobs—**193.167-014 Field Supervisor, Broadcast; 193.262-018 Field Engineer; 193.262-038 Transmitter Operator; 194.062-010 Television Technician; 194.122-010 Access Coordinator, Cable Television; 194.262-010 Audio Operator; 194.262-022 Master Control Operator; 194.282-010 Video Operator; 194.362-018 Telecine Operator; 194.362-022 Technician, News Gathering; 194.381-010 Technical Testing Engineer; 194.382-018 Videotape Operator.

27-4013.00 Radio Operators

- **Education/Training Required: Moderate-term on-the-job training**
- **Employed: 1,190**
- **Annual Earnings: $36,230**
- **Growth: −12.9%**
- **Annual Job Openings: Fewer than 500**

Receive and transmit communications, using radiotelegraph or radiotelephone equipment in accordance with government regulations. May repair equipment.

Coordinate radio-related aspects of locating and contacting airplanes and ships that are missing or in distress. Operate radio equipment to communicate with ships, aircraft, mining crews, offshore oil rigs, logging camps, and other remote operations. Turn controls or throw switches to activate power, adjust voice volume and modulation, and set transmitters on specified frequencies. Maintain station logs of messages transmitted and received for activities such as flight testing and fire locations. Conduct periodic equipment inspections and routine tests to ensure that operations standards are met. Review applicable regulations regarding radio communications and report violations. Repair radio equipment as necessary, using electronic testing equipment, hand tools, and power tools. Determine and obtain bearings of sources from which signals originate, using direction-finding procedures and equipment. Examine and operate new equipment prior to installation to ensure that it performs properly. Operate sound-recording equipment to record signals and preserve broadcasts for purposes such as analysis by intelligence personnel. Send, receive, and interpret coded messages. Set up antennas and mobile communication units during military field exercises. Broadcast weather reports and warnings. Communicate with receiving operators to exchange transmission instructions. Monitor emergency frequencies to detect distress calls and respond by dispatching emergency equipment.

GOE Information—Interest Area: 03. Arts and Communication. **Work Group:** 03.09. Media Technology. **Personality Type—**Realistic. Realistic occupations frequently involve work activities that include practical, hands-on problems and solutions. They often deal with plants; animals; and real-world materials like wood, tools, and machinery. Many of the occupations require working outside and do not involve a lot of paperwork or working closely with others. **Work Values—**Supervision, Human Relations; Achievement; Independence; Company Policies and Practices; Supervision, Technical; Variety. **Skills—**Operation Monitoring; Operation and Control. **Abilities—***Cognitive:* Time Sharing; Oral Expression; Flexibility of Closure; Speed of Closure; Selective Attention; Written Comprehension. *Psychomotor:* Response Orientation; Reaction Time; Control Precision. *Physical:* None met the criteria. *Sensory:* Sound Localization; Auditory Attention; Hearing Sensitivity; Speech Clarity; Speech Recognition. **General Work Activities—***Information Input:* Getting Information; Monitoring Processes, Materials, or Surroundings; Identifying Objects, Actions, and Events. *Mental*

Process: Processing Information; Updating and Using Relevant Knowledge; Making Decisions and Solving Problems. *Work Output:* Documenting or Recording Information; Repairing and Maintaining Electronic Equipment; Controlling Machines and Processes. *Interacting with Others:* Communicating with Other Workers; Interpreting the Meaning of Information for Others. **Physical Work Conditions**—Indoors; Sitting; Using Hands on Objects, Tools, or Controls. **Other Job Characteristics**—Need to Be Exact or Accurate; Errors Have Important Consequences; Repeat Same Tasks.

Experience—Job Zone 3. Previous work-related skill, knowledge, or experience is required. **Job Preparation**—SVP 6.0 to less than 7.0— more than one year and less than four years. **Knowledges**— Telecommunications; Computers and Electronics; Communications and Media. **Instructional Program**—Communications Systems Installation and Repair Technology.

Related SOC Job—27-4013 Radio Operators. **Related OOH Job**— Broadcast and Sound Engineering Technicians and Radio Operators. **Related DOT Jobs**—193.162-022 Airline-Radio Operator, Chief; 193.262-010 Airline-Radio Operator; 193.262-014 Dispatcher; 193.262-022 Radio Officer; 193.262-026 Radio Station Operator; 193.262-030 Radiotelegraph Operator; 193.262-034 Radiotelephone Operator; 193.362-010 Photoradio Operator; 193.362-014 Radio-Intelligence Operator; 193.382-010 Electronic Intelligence Operations Specialist.

27-4014.00 Sound Engineering Technicians

- **Education/Training Required: Postsecondary vocational training**
- **Employed: 12,680**
- **Annual Earnings: $38,390**
- **Growth: 18.4%**
- **Annual Job Openings: 2,000**

Operate machines and equipment to record, synchronize, mix, or reproduce music, voices, or sound effects in sporting arenas, theater productions, recording studios, or movie and video productions.

Confer with producers, performers, and others in order to determine and achieve the desired sound for a production such as a musical recording or a film. Set up, test, and adjust recording equipment for recording sessions and live performances; tear down equipment after event completion. Regulate volume level and sound quality during recording sessions, using control consoles. Prepare for recording sessions by performing activities such as selecting and setting up microphones. Report equipment problems and ensure that required repairs are made. Mix and edit voices, music, and taped sound effects for live performances and for prerecorded events, using sound mixing boards. Synchronize and equalize prerecorded dialogue, music, and sound effects with visual action of motion pictures or television productions, using control consoles. Record speech, music, and other sounds on recording media, using recording equipment. Reproduce and duplicate sound recordings from original recording media, using sound editing and duplication equipment. Separate instruments, vocals, and other sounds; then combine sounds later during the mixing or post-production stage. Keep logs of recordings. Create musical instrument digital interface programs for music projects, commercials, or film post-production.

GOE Information—**Interest Area:** 03. Arts and Communication. **Work Group:** 03.09. Media Technology. **Personality Type**—Realistic. Realistic occupations frequently involve work activities that include practical, hands-on problems and solutions. They often deal with plants; animals; and real-world materials like wood, tools, and

machinery. Many of the occupations require working outside and do not involve a lot of paperwork or working closely with others. **Work Values**—Working Conditions; Creativity; Authority; Moral Values; Company Policies and Practices; Independence. **Skills**—Technology Design; Operation Monitoring; Operation and Control; Installation; Equipment Maintenance; Troubleshooting. **Abilities**—*Cognitive:* Originality; Fluency of Ideas; Perceptual Speed; Speed of Closure; Selective Attention; Flexibility of Closure. *Psychomotor:* Response Orientation; Control Precision; Multilimb Coordination; Wrist-Finger Speed; Reaction Time; Finger Dexterity. *Physical:* Static Strength; Trunk Strength. *Sensory:* Hearing Sensitivity; Auditory Attention; Sound Localization; Depth Perception; Far Vision; Speech Recognition. **General Work Activities**—*Information Input:* Monitoring Processes, Materials, or Surroundings; Getting Information; Identifying Objects, Actions, and Events. *Mental Process:* Updating and Using Relevant Knowledge; Making Decisions and Solving Problems; Organizing, Planning, and Prioritizing. *Work Output:* Repairing and Maintaining Electronic Equipment; Interacting With Computers; Handling and Moving Objects. *Interacting with Others:* Communicating with Other Workers; Establishing and Maintaining Interpersonal Relationships; Providing Consultation and Advice to Others. **Physical Work Conditions**— Indoors; Noisy; Sitting; Using Hands on Objects, Tools, or Controls; Repetitive Motions. **Other Job Characteristics**—Need to Be Exact or Accurate; Repeat Same Tasks.

Experience—Job Zone 3. Previous work-related skill, knowledge, or experience is required. **Job Preparation**—SVP 6.0 to less than 7.0— more than one year and less than four years. **Knowledges**—Fine Arts; Communications and Media; Telecommunications; Computers and Electronics; Customer and Personal Service; Production and Processing. **Instructional Programs**—Communications Technology/Technician; Recording Arts Technology/Technician.

Related SOC Job—27-4014 Sound Engineering Technicians. **Related OOH Job**—Broadcast and Sound Engineering Technicians and Radio Operators. **Related DOT Jobs**—194.262-018 Sound Mixer; 194.362-010 Recording Engineer; 194.362-014 Rerecording Mixer; 194.382-014 Tape Transferrer; 962.167-010 Manager, Sound Effects; 962.281-014 Sound-Effects Technician; 962.382-010 Recordist.

27-4021.00 Photographers

- **Education/Training Required: Long-term on-the-job training**
- **Employed: 58,260**
- **Annual Earnings: $26,100**
- **Growth: 12.3%**
- **Annual Job Openings: 23,000**

Photograph persons, subjects, merchandise, or other commercial products. May develop negatives and produce finished prints.

Take pictures of individuals, families, and small groups, either in studio or on location. Adjust apertures, shutter speeds, and camera focus based on a combination of factors such as lighting, field depth, subject motion, film type, and film speed. Use traditional or digital cameras, along with a variety of equipment such as tripods, filters, and flash attachments. Create artificial light, using flashes and reflectors. Determine desired images and picture composition; select and adjust subjects, equipment, and lighting to achieve desired effects. Scan photographs into computers for editing, storage, and electronic transmission. Test equipment prior to use to ensure that it is in good working order. Review sets of photographs to select the best work. Estimate or measure light levels, distances, and numbers of exposures needed, using measuring devices and formulas. Manipulate and enhance scanned or digital images to create desired effects, using computers and specialized software. Perform maintenance tasks necessary to keep equipment working properly. Perform general office duties such as scheduling appointments, keeping books, and ordering supplies. Consult with clients or advertising staff and study assignments to determine project goals, locations, and equipment needs. Select and assemble equipment and required background properties according to subjects, materials, and conditions. Enhance, retouch, and resize photographs and negatives, using airbrushing and other techniques. Set up, mount, or install photographic equipment and cameras. Produce computer-readable digital images from film, using flatbed scanners and photofinishing laboratories. Develop and print exposed film, using chemicals, touchup tools, and developing and printing equipment, or send film to photofinishing laboratories for processing. Direct activities of workers who are setting up photographic equipment. Employ a variety of specialized photographic materials and techniques, including infrared and ultraviolet films, macro-photography, photogrammetry, and sensitometry. Engage in research to develop new photographic procedures and materials.

GOE Information—Interest Area: 03. Arts and Communication. **Work Group:** 03.09. Media Technology. **Personality Type**—Artistic. Artistic occupations frequently involve working with forms, designs, and patterns. They often require self-expression, and the work can be done without following a clear set of rules. **Work Values**—Creativity; Ability Utilization; Achievement; Autonomy; Recognition; Independence. **Skills**—Persuasion; Equipment Maintenance; Management of Financial Resources; Operation Monitoring; Service Orientation; Monitoring. **Abilities**—*Cognitive:* Spatial Orientation; Fluency of Ideas; Originality; Visualization; Memorization; Speed of Closure. *Psychomotor:* Rate Control; Reaction Time; Response Orientation; Wrist-Finger Speed; Arm-Hand Steadiness; Control Precision. *Physical:* Gross Body Coordination; Extent Flexibility; Static Strength; Trunk Strength. *Sensory:* Night Vision; Glare Sensitivity; Peripheral Vision; Visual Color Discrimination; Far Vision; Depth Perception. **General Work Activities**—*Information Input:* Identifying Objects, Actions, and Events; Monitoring Processes, Materials, or Surroundings; Inspecting Equipment, Structures, or Materials. *Mental Process:* Thinking Creatively; Updating and Using Relevant Knowledge; Making Decisions and Solving Problems. *Work Output:* Handling and Moving Objects; Performing General Physical Activities; Interacting With Computers. *Interacting with Others:* Establishing and Maintaining Interpersonal Relationships; Influencing Others or Selling; Communicating with Other Workers. **Physical Work Conditions**—More Often Indoors Than Outdoors; Sitting; Using Hands on Objects, Tools, or Controls. **Other Job Characteristics**—Need to Be Exact or Accurate; Pace Determined by Speed of Equipment; Repeat Same Tasks; Errors Have Important Consequences.

Experience—Job Zone 3. Previous work-related skill, knowledge, or experience is required. **Job Preparation**—SVP 6.0 to less than 7.0—more than one year and less than four years. **Knowledges**—Sales and Marketing; Fine Arts; Clerical Practices; Customer and Personal Service; Production and Processing; Communications and Media. **Instructional Programs**—Art/Art Studies, General; Commercial Photography; Film/Video and Photographic Arts, Other; Photography; Photojournalism.

Related SOC Job—27-4021 Photographers. **Related OOH Job**—Photographers. **Related DOT Jobs**—029.280-010 Photo-Optics Technician; 143.062-014 Photographer, Aerial; 143.062-018 Photographer, Apprentice; 143.062-026 Photographer, Scientific; 143.062-030 Photographer, Still; 143.062-034 Photojournalist; 143.362-010 Biological Photographer; 143.362-014 Ophthalmic Photographer; 143.382-014 Photographer, Finish.

27-4031.00 Camera Operators, Television, Video, and Motion Picture

- **Education/Training Required: Moderate-term on-the-job training**
- **Employed: 22,530**
- **Annual Earnings: $41,610**
- **Growth: 14.2%**
- **Annual Job Openings: 4,000**

Operate television, video, or motion picture camera to photograph images or scenes for various purposes, such as TV broadcasts, advertising, video production, or motion pictures.

Operate television or motion picture cameras to record scenes for television broadcasts, advertising, or motion pictures. Compose and frame each shot, applying the technical aspects of light, lenses, film, filters, and camera settings to achieve the effects sought by directors. Operate zoom lenses, changing images according to specifications and rehearsal instructions. Use cameras in any of several different camera mounts, such as stationary, track-mounted, or crane-mounted. Test, clean, and maintain equipment to ensure proper working condition. Adjust positions and controls of cameras, printers, and related equipment to change focus, exposure, and lighting. Gather and edit raw footage on location to send to television affiliates for broadcast, using electronic news-gathering or film-production equipment. Confer with directors, sound and lighting technicians, electricians, and other crew members to discuss assignments and determine filming sequences, desired effects, camera movements, and lighting requirements. Observe sets or locations for potential problems and to determine filming and lighting requirements. Instruct camera operators regarding camera setups, angles, distances, movement, and variables and cues for starting and stopping filming. Select and assemble cameras, accessories, equipment, and film stock to be used during filming, using knowledge of filming techniques, requirements, and computations. Label and record contents of exposed film and note details on report forms. Read charts and compute ratios to determine variables such as lighting, shutter angles, filter factors, and camera distances. Set up cameras, optical printers, and related equipment to produce photographs and special effects. View films to resolve problems of exposure control, subject and camera movement, changes in subject distance, and related variables. Reload camera magazines with fresh raw film stock. Read and analyze work orders and specifications to determine locations of subject material, work procedures, sequences of operations, and machine setups. Receive raw film stock and maintain film inventories.

GOE Information—Interest Area: 03. Arts and Communication. **Work Group:** 03.09. Media Technology. **Personality Type**—Artistic. Artistic occupations frequently involve working with forms, designs, and patterns. They often require self-expression, and the work can be done without following a clear set of rules. **Work Values**—Ability Utilization; Recognition; Variety; Creativity; Achievement; Working Conditions. **Skills**—Operation Monitoring; Equipment Maintenance; Operation and Control; Troubleshooting; Equipment Selection; Active Listening. **Abilities**—*Cognitive:* Spatial Orientation; Perceptual Speed; Visualization; Selective Attention; Memorization; Originality. *Psychomotor:* Rate Control; Response Orientation; Control Precision; Reaction Time; Arm-Hand Steadiness; Multilimb Coordination. *Physical:* Extent Flexibility; Static Strength; Trunk Strength. *Sensory:* Glare Sensitivity; Far Vision; Depth Perception; Visual Color Discrimination; Hearing Sensitivity; Auditory Attention. **General Work Activities**—*Information Input:* Identifying Objects, Actions, and Events; Getting Information; Monitoring Processes, Materials, or Surroundings. *Mental Process:* Thinking Creatively; Updating and Using Relevant Knowledge; Organizing, Planning, and Prioritizing. *Work Output:* Handling and Moving Objects; Performing General Physical Activities; Controlling Machines and Processes. *Interacting with Others:* Establishing and Maintaining Interpersonal Relationships; Performing for or Working with the Public; Communicating with Persons Outside Organization. **Physical Work Conditions**—More Often Indoors Than Outdoors; Very Bright or Dim Lighting; Standing; Using Hands on Objects, Tools, or Controls. **Other Job Characteristics**—Need to Be Exact or Accurate; Errors Have Important Consequences; Repeat Same Tasks.

Experience—Job Zone 3. Previous work-related skill, knowledge, or experience is required. **Job Preparation**—SVP 6.0 to less than 7.0—more than one year and less than four years. **Knowledges**—Communications and Media; Telecommunications; Computers and Electronics; Engineering and Technology; Clerical Practices; Production and Processing; Education and Training. **Instructional Programs**—Audiovisual Communications Technologies/Technicians, Other; Cinematography and Film/Video Production; Radio and Television Broadcasting Technology/Technician.

Related SOC Job—27-4031 Camera Operators, Television, Video, and Motion Picture. **Related OOH Job**—Television, Video, and Motion Picture Camera Operators and Editors. **Related DOT Jobs**—143.062-010 Director of Photography; 143.062-022 Camera Operator; 143.260-010 Optical-Effects-Camera Operator; 143.382-010 Camera Operator, Animation; 976.382-010 Camera Operator, Title.

27-4032.00 Film and Video Editors

- **Education/Training Required: Bachelor's degree**
- **Employed: 15,200**
- **Annual Earnings: $46,930**
- **Growth: 18.6%**
- **Annual Job Openings: 3,000**

Edit motion picture soundtracks, film, and video.

Cut shot sequences to different angles at specific points in scenes, making each individual cut as fluid and seamless as possible. Study scripts to become familiar with production concepts and requirements. Edit films and videotapes to insert music, dialogue, and sound effects; to arrange films into sequences; and to correct errors, using editing equipment. Select and combine the most effective shots of each scene to form a logical and smoothly running story. Mark frames where a particular shot or piece of sound is to begin or end. Determine the specific audio and visual effects and music necessary to complete films. Verify key numbers and time codes on materials. Organize and string together raw footage into a continuous whole according to scripts or the instructions of directors and producers. Review assembled films or edited videotapes on screens or monitors to determine if corrections are necessary. Program computerized graphic effects. Review footage sequence by sequence to become familiar with it before assembling it into a final product. Set up and operate computer editing systems, electronic titling systems, video switching equipment, and digital video effects units to produce a final product. Record needed sounds or obtain them from sound effects libraries. Confer with producers and directors concerning layout or editing approaches needed to increase dramatic or entertainment value of productions. Manipulate plot, score, sound, and graphics to make the parts into a continuous whole, working closely with people in audio, visual, music, optical, or special effects departments. Supervise and coordinate activities of workers engaged in film editing, assembling, and recording activities. Trim film segments to specified lengths and reassemble segments in sequences that present stories with maximum effect. Develop post-production models for films. Piece sounds together to develop film soundtracks. Conduct film screenings for directors and members of production staffs. Collaborate with music editors to select appropriate passages of music and develop production scores. Discuss the sound requirements of pictures with sound effects editors.

GOE Information—**Interest Area:** 03. Arts and Communication. **Work Group:** 03.09. Media Technology. **Personality Type**—Artistic. Artistic occupations frequently involve working with forms, designs, and patterns. They often require self-expression, and the work can be done without following a clear set of rules. **Work Values**—Creativity; Recognition; Authority; Social Status; Autonomy; Variety. **Skills**—Operation and Control; Equipment Selection; Equipment Maintenance; Operations Analysis; Installation; Troubleshooting. **Abilities**—*Cognitive:* Visualization; Originality; Fluency of Ideas; Perceptual Speed; Information Ordering; Category Flexibility. *Psychomotor:* Reaction Time; Arm-Hand Steadiness; Control Precision; Finger Dexterity; Manual Dexterity. *Physical:* None met the criteria. *Sensory:* Hearing Sensitivity; Visual Color Discrimination; Far Vision; Auditory Attention; Speech Recognition; Depth Perception. **General Work Activities**—*Information Input:* Getting Information; Identifying Objects, Actions, and Events; Monitoring Processes, Materials, or Surroundings. *Mental Process:* Organizing, Planning, and Prioritizing; Thinking Creatively; Updating and Using Relevant Knowledge. *Work Output:* Interacting With Computers; Handling and Moving Objects; Controlling Machines and Processes. *Interacting with Others:* Establishing and Maintaining Interpersonal Relationships; Providing Consultation and Advice to Others; Performing for or Working with the Public. **Physical Work Conditions**—Indoors; Sitting; Using Hands on Objects, Tools, or Controls; Repetitive Motions. **Other Job Characteristics**—Need to Be Exact or Accurate; Errors Have Important Consequences; Repeat Same Tasks.

Experience—Job Zone 3. Previous work-related skill, knowledge, or experience is required. **Job Preparation**—SVP 6.0 to less than 7.0—more than one year and less than four years. **Knowledges**—Fine Arts; Communications and Media; Design; Computers and Electronics; Education and Training; Telecommunications. **Instructional Programs**—Audiovisual Communications Technologies/Technicians, Other; Cinematography and Film/Video Production; Communications Technology/Technician; Photojournalism; Radio and Television; Radio and Television Broadcasting Technology/Technician.

Related SOC Job—27-4032 Film and Video Editors. **Related OOH Job**—Television, Video, and Motion Picture Camera Operators and Editors. **Related DOT Jobs**—962.132-010 Supervising Film-or-Videotape Editor; 962.262-010 Film or Videotape Editor; 962.361-010 Optical-Effects Layout Person; 962.382-014 Sound Cutter.

27-4099.99 Media and Communication Equipment Workers, All Other

- **Education/Training Required:** Moderate-term on-the-job training
- **Employed:** 17,200
- **Annual Earnings:** $47,740
- **Growth:** 17.0%
- **Annual Job Openings:** 3,000

All media and communication equipment workers not listed separately.

No task data available.

Note: The Department of Labor has not collected some data for this job, so it has fewer details than the other descriptions.

Related SOC Job—27-4099 Media and Communication Equipment Workers, All Other. **Related OOH Job**—None. **Related DOT Job**—No data available.

29-0000

Healthcare Practitioners and Technical Occupations

29-1000 Health Diagnosing and Treating Practitioners

29-1011.00 Chiropractors

- Education/Training Required: First professional degree
- Employed: 24,290
- Annual Earnings: $67,200
- Growth: 22.4%
- Annual Job Openings: 4,000

Adjust spinal column and other articulations of the body to correct abnormalities of the human body believed to be caused by interference with the nervous system. Examine patient to determine nature and extent of disorder. Manipulate spine or other involved area. May utilize supplementary measures, such as exercise, rest, water, light, heat, and nutritional therapy.

Perform a series of manual adjustments to the spine, or other articulations of the body, to correct the musculoskeletal system. Evaluate the functioning of the neuromuscularskeletal system and the spine, using systems of chiropractic diagnosis. Diagnose health problems by reviewing patients' health and medical histories; questioning, observing, and examining patients; and interpreting X rays. Maintain accurate case histories of patients. Advise patients about recommended courses of treatment. Obtain and record patients' medical histories. Analyze X rays to locate the sources of patients' difficulties and to rule out fractures or diseases as sources of problems. Counsel patients about nutrition, exercise, sleeping habits, stress management, and other matters. Arrange for diagnostic X rays to be taken. Consult with and refer patients to appropriate health practitioners when necessary. Suggest and apply the use of supports such as straps, tapes, bandages, and braces if necessary.

GOE Information—Interest Area: 08. Health Science. Work Group: 08.04. Health Specialties. Personality Type—Investigative. Investigative occupations frequently involve working with ideas and require an extensive amount of thinking. These occupations can involve searching for facts and figuring out problems mentally. Work Values—Social Service; Responsibility; Autonomy; Recognition; Social Status; Compensation. Skills—Science; Social Perceptiveness; Management of Financial Resources; Persuasion; Service Orientation; Reading Comprehension. Abilities—*Cognitive:* Problem Sensitivity; Inductive Reasoning; Deductive Reasoning; Oral Expression; Speed of Closure; Oral Comprehension. *Psychomotor:* Arm-Hand Steadiness; Manual Dexterity; Multilimb Coordination; Finger Dexterity; Control Precision. *Physical:* Dynamic Strength; Static Strength; Extent Flexibility; Trunk Strength. *Sensory:* Speech Recognition; Visual Color Discrimination. General Work Activities—*Information Input:* Identifying Objects, Actions, and Events; Getting Information; Monitoring Processes, Materials, or Surroundings. *Mental Process:* Updating and Using Relevant Knowledge; Making Decisions and Solving Problems; Processing Information. *Work Output:* Handling and Moving Objects; Performing General Physical Activities; Documenting or Recording Information. *Interacting with Others:* Assisting and Caring for Others; Performing for or Working with the Public; Establishing and Maintaining Interpersonal Relationships. Physical Work Conditions—Indoors; Disease or Infections; Standing; Using Hands on Objects, Tools, or Controls; Bending or Twisting the Body; Repetitive Motions. Other Job Characteristics—Need to Be Exact or Accurate; Repeat Same Tasks; Errors Have Important Consequences.

Experience—Job Zone 5. Extensive skill, knowledge, and experience are needed. Job Preparation—SVP 8.0 and above—four years to more than 10 years. Knowledges—Medicine and Dentistry; Therapy and Counseling; Biology; Psychology; Sales and Marketing; Customer and Personal Service. Instructional Program—Chiropractic (DC).

Related SOC Job—29-1011 Chiropractors. Related OOH Job—Chiropractors. Related DOT Job—079.101-010 Chiropractor.

29-1021.00 Dentists, General

- Education/Training Required: First professional degree
- Employed: 86,270
- Annual Earnings: $125,300
- Growth: 13.5%
- Annual Job Openings: 7,000

Diagnose and treat diseases, injuries, and malformations of teeth and gums and related oral structures. May treat diseases of nerve, pulp, and other dental tissues affecting vitality of teeth.

Use masks, gloves, and safety glasses to protect themselves and their patients from infectious diseases. Administer anesthetics to limit the amount of pain experienced by patients during procedures. Examine teeth, gums, and related tissues, using dental instruments, X rays, and other diagnostic equipment, to evaluate dental health, diagnose diseases or abnormalities, and plan appropriate treatments. Formulate plan of treatment for patient's teeth and mouth tissue. Use air turbine and hand instruments, dental appliances, and surgical implements. Advise and instruct patients regarding preventive dental care, the causes and treatment of dental problems, and oral health care services. Design, make, and fit prosthodontic appliances such as space maintainers, bridges, and dentures or write fabrication instructions or prescriptions for denturists and dental technicians. Diagnose and treat diseases, injuries, and malformations of teeth, gums, and related oral structures and provide preventive and corrective services. Fill pulp chamber and canal with endodontic materials. Write prescriptions for antibiotics and other medications. Analyze and evaluate dental needs to determine changes and trends in patterns of dental disease. Treat exposure of pulp by pulp capping, removal of pulp from pulp chamber, or root canal, using dental instruments. Eliminate irritating margins of fillings and correct occlusions, using dental instruments. Perform oral and periodontal surgery on the jaw or mouth. Remove diseased tissue, using surgical instruments. Apply fluoride and sealants to teeth. Manage business, employing and supervising staff and handling paperwork and insurance claims. Bleach, clean, or polish teeth to restore natural color. Plan, organize, and maintain dental health programs. Produce and evaluate dental health educational materials.

GOE Information—Interest Area: 08. Health Science. Work Group: 08.03. Dentistry. Personality Type—Investigative. Investigative occupations frequently involve working with ideas and require an extensive amount of thinking. These occupations can involve searching for facts and figuring out problems mentally. Work Values—Social Service; Social Status; Responsibility; Recognition; Ability Utilization; Achievement. Skills—Science; Management of Financial Resources; Management of Material Resources; Complex Problem Solving; Equipment Selection; Management of Personnel Resources. Abilities—*Cognitive:* Inductive Reasoning; Problem Sensitivity; Originality; Flexibility of Closure; Deductive Reasoning; Fluency of Ideas. *Psychomotor:* Control Precision; Arm-Hand Steadiness; Finger Dexterity; Response Orientation; Manual Dexterity; Wrist-Finger Speed. *Physical:* Extent Flexibility. *Sensory:* Near Vision; Depth Perception; Visual Color Discrimination; Speech Recognition;

Hearing Sensitivity; Far Vision. **General Work Activities—** *Information Input:* Identifying Objects, Actions, and Events; Getting Information; Monitoring Processes, Materials, or Surroundings. *Mental Process:* Making Decisions and Solving Problems; Updating and Using Relevant Knowledge; Organizing, Planning, and Prioritizing. *Work Output:* Controlling Machines and Processes; Documenting or Recording Information; Handling and Moving Objects. *Interacting with Others:* Assisting and Caring for Others; Performing for or Working with the Public; Providing Consultation and Advice to Others. **Physical Work Conditions—**Indoors; Contaminants; Radiation; Disease or Infections; Sitting; Using Hands on Objects, Tools, or Controls. **Other Job Characteristics—**Need to Be Exact or Accurate; Errors Have Important Consequences; Repeat Same Tasks.

Experience—Job Zone 5. Extensive skill, knowledge, and experience are needed. **Job Preparation—**SVP 8.0 and above—four years to more than 10 years. **Knowledges—**Medicine and Dentistry; Biology; Psychology; Personnel and Human Resources; Chemistry; Economics and Accounting. **Instructional Programs—**Advanced General Dentistry (Cert, MS, PhD); Dental Public Health and Education (Cert, MS/MPH, PhD/DPH); Dental Public Health Specialty; Dentistry (DDS, DMD); Pediatric Dentistry/Pedodontics (Cert, MS, PhD); Pedodontics Specialty.

Related SOC Job—29-1021 Dentists, General. **Related OOH Job—** Dentists. **Related DOT Jobs—**072.101-010 Dentist; 072.101-014 Endodontist; 072.101-026 Pediatric Dentist; 072.101-030 Periodontist; 072.101-038 Public-Health Dentist.

29-1022.00 Oral and Maxillofacial Surgeons

- **Education/Training Required: First professional degree**
- **Employed: 5,120**
- **Annual Earnings: more than $145,600**
- **Growth: 16.2%**
- **Annual Job Openings: Fewer than 500**

Perform surgery on mouth, jaws, and related head and neck structure to execute difficult and multiple extractions of teeth, to remove tumors and other abnormal growths, to correct abnormal jaw relations by mandibular or maxillary revision, to prepare mouth for insertion of dental prosthesis, or to treat fractured jaws.

Administer general and local anesthetics. Remove impacted, damaged, and non-restorable teeth. Evaluate the position of the wisdom teeth in order to determine whether problems exist currently or might occur in the future. Collaborate with other professionals such as restorative dentists and orthodontists in order to plan treatment. Perform surgery to prepare the mouth for dental implants and to aid in the regeneration of deficient bone and gum tissues. Remove tumors and other abnormal growths of the oral and facial regions, using surgical instruments. Treat infections of the oral cavity, salivary glands, jaws, and neck. Treat problems affecting the oral mucosa such as mouth ulcers and infections. Provide emergency treatment of facial injuries, including facial lacerations, intra-oral lacerations, and fractured facial bones. Perform surgery on the mouth and jaws in order to treat conditions such as cleft lip and palate and jaw growth problems. Restore form and function by moving skin, bone, nerves, and other tissues from other parts of the body in order to reconstruct the jaws and face. Perform minor cosmetic procedures such as chin and cheekbone enhancements and minor facial rejuvenation procedures including the use of Botox and laser technology. Treat snoring problems, using laser surgery.

GOE Information—Interest Area: 08. Health Science. **Work Group:** 08.03. Dentistry. **Personality Type—**Investigative. Investigative occupations frequently involve working with ideas and require an extensive amount of thinking. These occupations can involve searching for facts and figuring out problems mentally. **Work Values—**Social Service; Social Status; Recognition; Responsibility; Achievement; Compensation. **Skills—**Science; Management of Financial Resources; Equipment Selection; Management of Personnel Resources; Service Orientation; Complex Problem Solving. **Abilities—***Cognitive:* Problem Sensitivity; Inductive Reasoning; Deductive Reasoning; Originality; Written Comprehension; Flexibility of Closure. *Psychomotor:* Manual Dexterity; Control Precision; Arm-Hand Steadiness; Finger Dexterity; Wrist-Finger Speed; Multilimb Coordination. *Physical:* Extent Flexibility; Static Strength; Trunk Strength. *Sensory:* Visual Color Discrimination; Near Vision; Depth Perception; Far Vision; Speech Recognition; Speech Clarity. **General Work Activities—***Information Input:* Identifying Objects, Actions, and Events; Getting Information; Monitoring Processes, Materials, or Surroundings. *Mental Process:* Making Decisions and Solving Problems; Updating and Using Relevant Knowledge; Processing Information. *Work Output:* Documenting or Recording Information; Handling and Moving Objects; Controlling Machines and Processes. *Interacting with Others:* Assisting and Caring for Others; Performing for or Working with the Public; Establishing and Maintaining Interpersonal Relationships. **Physical Work Conditions—**Indoors; Disease or Infections; Standing; Using Hands on Objects, Tools, or Controls; Bending or Twisting the Body; Repetitive Motions. **Other Job Characteristics—**Need to Be Exact or Accurate; Errors Have Important Consequences; Repeat Same Tasks.

Experience—Job Zone 5. Extensive skill, knowledge, and experience are needed. **Job Preparation—**SVP 8.0 and above—four years to more than 10 years. **Knowledges—**Medicine and Dentistry; Biology; Therapy and Counseling; Chemistry; Psychology; Personnel and Human Resources. **Instructional Programs—**Dental/Oral Surgery Specialty; Oral/Maxillofacial Surgery (Cert, MS, PhD).

Related SOC Job—29-1022 Oral and Maxillofacial Surgeons. **Related OOH Job—**Dentists. **Related DOT Job—**072.101-018 Oral and Maxillofacial Surgeon.

29-1023.00 Orthodontists

- **Education/Training Required: First professional degree**
- **Employed: 4,820**
- **Annual Earnings: more than $145,600**
- **Growth: 12.8%**
- **Annual Job Openings: 1,000**

Examine, diagnose, and treat dental malocclusions and oral cavity anomalies. Design and fabricate appliances to realign teeth and jaws to produce and maintain normal function and to improve appearance.

Fit dental appliances in patients' mouths to alter the position and relationship of teeth and jaws and to realign teeth. Study diagnostic records such as medical/dental histories, plaster models of the teeth, photos of a patient's face and teeth, and X rays to develop patient treatment plans. Diagnose teeth and jaw or other dental-facial abnormalities. Examine patients to assess abnormalities of jaw development, tooth position, and other dental-facial structures. Prepare diagnostic and treatment records. Adjust dental appliances periodically to produce and maintain normal function. Provide patients with proposed treatment plans and cost estimates. Instruct dental officers and technical assistants in orthodontic procedures and techniques. Coordinate orthodontic services with other dental and medical services. Design and fabricate appliances, such as space maintainers, retainers, and labial and lingual arch wires.

GOE Information—Interest Area: 08. Health Science. **Work Group:** 08.03. Dentistry. **Personality Type**—Investigative. Investigative occupations frequently involve working with ideas and require an extensive amount of thinking. These occupations can involve searching for facts and figuring out problems mentally. **Work Values**—Social Service; Social Status; Responsibility; Recognition; Ability Utilization; Achievement. **Skills**—Management of Financial Resources; Management of Personnel Resources; Equipment Selection; Management of Material Resources; Technology Design; Judgment and Decision Making. **Abilities**—*Cognitive:* Problem Sensitivity; Inductive Reasoning; Written Expression; Visualization; Perceptual Speed; Fluency of Ideas. *Psychomotor:* Control Precision; Finger Dexterity; Manual Dexterity; Arm-Hand Steadiness; Multilimb Coordination. *Physical:* None met the criteria. *Sensory:* Visual Color Discrimination; Far Vision; Near Vision; Speech Clarity; Speech Recognition. **General Work Activities**—*Information Input:* Getting Information; Identifying Objects, Actions, and Events; Monitoring Processes, Materials, or Surroundings. *Mental Process:* Making Decisions and Solving Problems; Updating and Using Relevant Knowledge; Processing Information. *Work Output:* Handling and Moving Objects; Documenting or Recording Information; Controlling Machines and Processes. *Interacting with Others:* Performing for or Working with the Public; Establishing and Maintaining Interpersonal Relationships; Assisting and Caring for Others. **Physical Work Conditions**—Indoors; Disease or Infections; Sitting; Using Hands on Objects, Tools, or Controls; Bending or Twisting the Body; Repetitive Motions. **Other Job Characteristics**—Need to Be Exact or Accurate; Repeat Same Tasks.

Experience—Job Zone 5. Extensive skill, knowledge, and experience are needed. **Job Preparation**—SVP 8.0 and above—four years to more than 10 years. **Knowledges**—Medicine and Dentistry; Biology; Sales and Marketing; Economics and Accounting; Personnel and Human Resources; Customer and Personal Service. **Instructional Programs**—Orthodontics Specialty; Orthodontics/Orthodontology (Cert, MS, PhD).

Related SOC Job—29-1023 Orthodontists. **Related OOH Job**—Dentists. **Related DOT Job**—072.101-022 Orthodontist.

29-1024.00 Prosthodontists

- ● **Education/Training Required: First professional degree**
- ● **Employed: 560**
- ● **Annual Earnings: more than $145,600**
- ● **Growth: 13.6%**
- ● **Annual Job Openings: Fewer than 500**

Construct oral prostheses to replace missing teeth and other oral structures to correct natural and acquired deformation of mouth and jaws; to restore and maintain oral function, such as chewing and speaking; and to improve appearance.

Replace missing teeth and associated oral structures with permanent fixtures, such as crowns and bridges, or removable fixtures, such as dentures. Fit prostheses to patients, making any necessary adjustments and modifications. Design and fabricate dental prostheses or supervise dental technicians and laboratory bench workers who construct the devices. Measure and take impressions of patients' jaws and teeth to determine the shape and size of dental prostheses, using face bows, dental articulators, recording devices, and other materials.

Collaborate with general dentists, specialists, and other health professionals to develop solutions to dental and oral health concerns. Repair, reline, and/or rebase dentures. Restore function and aesthetics to traumatic injury victims or to individuals with diseases or birth defects. Use bonding technology on the surface of the teeth to change tooth shape or to close gaps. Treat facial pain and jaw joint problems. Place veneers onto teeth to conceal defects. Bleach discolored teeth to brighten and whiten them.

GOE Information—Interest Area: 08. Health Science. **Work Group:** 08.03. Dentistry. **Personality Type**—Investigative. Investigative occupations frequently involve working with ideas and require an extensive amount of thinking. These occupations can involve searching for facts and figuring out problems mentally. **Work Values**—Social Service; Responsibility; Ability Utilization; Achievement; Autonomy; Social Status. **Skills**—Management of Financial Resources; Science; Social Perceptiveness; Reading Comprehension; Active Learning; Equipment Selection. **Abilities**—*Cognitive:* Visualization; Fluency of Ideas; Originality; Deductive Reasoning; Oral Expression; Inductive Reasoning. *Psychomotor:* Arm-Hand Steadiness; Finger Dexterity; Manual Dexterity; Control Precision; Multilimb Coordination. *Physical:* Extent Flexibility. *Sensory:* Near Vision; Visual Color Discrimination; Speech Recognition; Far Vision; Speech Clarity. **General Work Activities**—*Information Input:* Monitoring Processes, Materials, or Surroundings; Getting Information; Identifying Objects, Actions, and Events. *Mental Process:* Making Decisions and Solving Problems; Updating and Using Relevant Knowledge; Organizing, Planning, and Prioritizing. *Work Output:* Documenting or Recording Information; Controlling Machines and Processes; Handling and Moving Objects. *Interacting with Others:* Performing for or Working with the Public; Assisting and Caring for Others; Establishing and Maintaining Interpersonal Relationships. **Physical Work Conditions**—Indoors; Noisy; Contaminants; Disease or Infections; Hazardous Equipment; Using Hands on Objects, Tools, or Controls. **Other Job Characteristics**—Need to Be Exact or Accurate; Errors Have Important Consequences; Repeat Same Tasks.

Experience—Job Zone 5. Extensive skill, knowledge, and experience are needed. **Job Preparation**—SVP 8.0 and above—four years to more than 10 years. **Knowledges**—Medicine and Dentistry; Biology; Chemistry; Psychology; Sales and Marketing; Engineering and Technology. **Instructional Programs**—Prosthodontics Specialty; Prosthodontics/Prosthodontology (Cert, MS, PhD).

Related SOC Job—29-1024 Prosthodontists. **Related OOH Job**—Dentists. **Related DOT Job**—072.101-034 Prosthodontist.

29-1029.99 Dentists, All Other Specialists

- ● **Education/Training Required: First professional degree**
- ● **Employed: 3,480**
- ● **Annual Earnings: $94,600**
- ● **Growth: 12.2%**
- ● **Annual Job Openings: Fewer than 500**

All dentists not listed separately.

No task data available.

Note: The Department of Labor has not collected some data for this job, so it has fewer details than the other descriptions.

Related SOC Job—29-1029 Dentists, All Other Specialists. **Related OOH Job**—Dentists. **Related DOT Job**—072.061-010 Oral Pathologist.

29-1031.00 Dietitians and Nutritionists

- **Education/Training Required: Bachelor's degree**
- **Employed: 48,850**
- **Annual Earnings: $44,940**
- **Growth: 18.3%**
- **Annual Job Openings: 4,000**

Plan and conduct food service or nutritional programs to assist in the promotion of health and control of disease. May supervise activities of a department providing quantity food services, counsel individuals, or conduct nutritional research.

Assess nutritional needs, diet restrictions, and current health plans to develop and implement dietary-care plans and provide nutritional counseling. Consult with physicians and health care personnel to determine nutritional needs and diet restrictions of patient or client. Advise patients and their families on nutritional principles, dietary plans and diet modifications, and food selection and preparation. Counsel individuals and groups on basic rules of good nutrition, healthy eating habits, and nutrition monitoring to improve their quality of life. Monitor food service operations to ensure conformance to nutritional, safety, sanitation, and quality standards. Coordinate recipe development and standardization and develop new menus for independent food service operations. Develop policies for food service or nutritional programs to assist in health promotion and disease control. Inspect meals served for conformance to prescribed diets and standards of palatability and appearance. Develop curriculum and prepare manuals, visual aids, course outlines, and other materials used in teaching. Prepare and administer budgets for food, equipment, and supplies. Purchase food in accordance with health and safety codes. Select, train, and supervise workers who plan, prepare, and serve meals. Manage quantity food service departments or clinical and community nutrition services. Coordinate diet counseling services. Advise food service managers and organizations on sanitation, safety procedures, menu development, budgeting, and planning to assist with the establishment, operation, and evaluation of food service facilities and nutrition programs. Organize, develop, analyze, test, and prepare special meals such as low-fat, low-cholesterol, and chemical-free meals. Plan, conduct, and evaluate dietary, nutritional, and epidemiological research. Plan and conduct training programs in dietetics, nutrition, and institutional management and administration for medical students, health-care personnel, and the general public. Make recommendations regarding public policy, such as nutrition labeling, food fortification, and nutrition standards for school programs.

GOE Information—Interest Area: 08. Health Science. **Work Group:** 08.09. Health Protection and Promotion. **Personality Type—** Investigative. Investigative occupations frequently involve working with ideas and require an extensive amount of thinking. These occupations can involve searching for facts and figuring out problems mentally. **Work Values—**Social Service; Authority; Creativity; Ability Utilization; Achievement; Social Status. **Skills—**Science; Social Perceptiveness; Writing; Instructing; Speaking; Reading Comprehension. **Abilities—***Cognitive:* Written Expression; Category Flexibility; Deductive Reasoning; Speed of Closure; Written Comprehension; Mathematical Reasoning. *Psychomotor:* None met the criteria. *Physical:* None met the criteria. *Sensory:* Speech Clarity; Far Vision; Near Vision; Speech Recognition; Visual Color Discrimination. **General Work Activities—***Information Input:* Identifying Objects, Actions, and Events; Getting Information; Monitoring Processes, Materials, or Surroundings. *Mental Process:* Updating and Using Relevant Knowledge; Organizing, Planning, and

Prioritizing; Analyzing Data or Information. *Work Output:* Documenting or Recording Information; Interacting With Computers. *Interacting with Others:* Communicating with Other Workers; Establishing and Maintaining Interpersonal Relationships; Teaching Others. **Physical Work Conditions—**Indoors; More Often Sitting Than Standing. **Other Job Characteristics—**Need to Be Exact or Accurate.

Experience—Job Zone 5. Extensive skill, knowledge, and experience are needed. **Job Preparation—**SVP 8.0 and above—four years to more than 10 years. **Knowledges—**Food Production; Therapy and Counseling; Sociology and Anthropology; Medicine and Dentistry; Philosophy and Theology; Psychology. **Instructional Programs—** Clinical Nutrition/Nutritionist (NR); Dietetic and Clinical Nutrition Services, Other; Dietetics/Dietician (RD); Foods, Nutrition, and Related Services, Other; Foods, Nutrition, and Wellness Studies, General; Foodservice Systems Administration/Management; Human Nutrition; Nutrition Sciences.

Related SOC Job—29-1031 Dietitians and Nutritionists. **Related OOH Job—**Dietitians and Nutritionists. **Related DOT Jobs—**077.061-010 Dietitian, Research; 077.117-010 Dietitian, Chief; 077.127-010 Community Dietitian; 077.127-014 Dietitian, Clinical; 077.127-018 Dietitian, Consultant; 077.127-022 Dietitian, Teaching.

29-1041.00 Optometrists

- **Education/Training Required: First professional degree**
- **Employed: 23,720**
- **Annual Earnings: $88,040**
- **Growth: 19.7%**
- **Annual Job Openings: 2,000**

Diagnose, manage, and treat conditions and diseases of the human eye and visual system. Examine eyes and visual system, diagnose problems or impairments, prescribe corrective lenses, and provide treatment. May prescribe therapeutic drugs to treat specific eye conditions.

Examine eyes, using observation, instruments, and pharmaceutical agents, to determine visual acuity and perception, focus, and coordination and to diagnose diseases and other abnormalities such as glaucoma or color-blindness. Analyze test results and develop a treatment plan. Prescribe, supply, fit, and adjust eyeglasses, contact lenses, and other vision aids. Prescribe medications to treat eye diseases if state laws permit. Educate and counsel patients on contact lens care, visual hygiene, lighting arrangements, and safety factors. Consult with and refer patients to ophthalmologist or other health care practitioner if additional medical treatment is determined necessary. Remove foreign bodies from the eye. Provide patients undergoing eye surgeries, such as cataract and laser vision correction, with pre- and post-operative care. Prescribe therapeutic procedures to correct or conserve vision. Provide vision therapy and low vision rehabilitation.

GOE Information—Interest Area: 08. Health Science. **Work Group:** 08.04. Health Specialties. **Personality Type—**Investigative. Investigative occupations frequently involve working with ideas and require an extensive amount of thinking. These occupations can involve searching for facts and figuring out problems mentally. **Work Values—**Social Service; Responsibility; Social Status; Recognition; Ability Utilization; Autonomy. **Skills—**Science; Judgment and Decision Making; Management of Personnel Resources; Active Listening; Reading Comprehension; Persuasion. **Abilities—***Cognitive:* Inductive Reasoning; Speed of Closure; Problem Sensitivity; Flexibility of Closure; Deductive Reasoning; Oral Expression. *Psychomotor:* Arm-Hand Steadiness; Control Precision; Manual

Dexterity; Finger Dexterity; Multilimb Coordination. *Physical:* Trunk Strength. *Sensory:* Near Vision; Depth Perception; Far Vision; Visual Color Discrimination; Speech Recognition. **General Work Activities**—*Information Input:* Identifying Objects, Actions, and Events; Getting Information; Monitoring Processes, Materials, or Surroundings. *Mental Process:* Making Decisions and Solving Problems; Evaluating Information Against Standards; Processing Information. *Work Output:* Handling and Moving Objects; Documenting or Recording Information; Interacting With Computers. *Interacting with Others:* Performing for or Working with the Public; Establishing and Maintaining Interpersonal Relationships; Teaching Others. **Physical Work Conditions**—Indoors; Disease or Infections; Sitting; Using Hands on Objects, Tools, or Controls; Repetitive Motions. **Other Job Characteristics**—Need to Be Exact or Accurate; Errors Have Important Consequences.

Experience—Job Zone 5. Extensive skill, knowledge, and experience are needed. **Job Preparation**—SVP 8.0 and above—four years to more than 10 years. **Knowledges**—Medicine and Dentistry; Biology; Psychology; Sales and Marketing; Economics and Accounting; Personnel and Human Resources. **Instructional Program**—Optometry (OD).

Related SOC Job—29-1041 Optometrists. **Related OOH Job**—Optometrists. **Related DOT Job**—079.101-018 Optometrist.

29-1051.00 Pharmacists

- **Education/Training Required: First professional degree**
- **Employed: 229,740**
- **Annual Earnings: $89,820**
- **Growth: 24.6%**
- **Annual Job Openings: 16,000**

Compound and dispense medications, following prescriptions issued by physicians, dentists, or other authorized medical practitioners.

Review prescriptions to assure accuracy, to ascertain the needed ingredients, and to evaluate their suitability. Provide information and advice regarding drug interactions, side effects, dosage and proper medication storage. Analyze prescribing trends to monitor patient compliance and to prevent excessive usage or harmful interactions. Order and purchase pharmaceutical supplies, medical supplies, and drugs, maintaining stock and storing and handling it properly. Maintain records, such as pharmacy files; patient profiles; charge system files; inventories; control records for radioactive nuclei; and registries of poisons, narcotics, and controlled drugs. Provide specialized services to help patients manage conditions such as diabetes, asthma, smoking cessation, or high blood pressure. Advise customers on the selection of medication brands, medical equipment, and health-care supplies. Collaborate with other health care professionals to plan, monitor, review, and evaluate the quality and effectiveness of drugs and drug regimens, providing advice on drug applications and characteristics. Compound and dispense medications as prescribed by doctors and dentists by calculating, weighing, measuring, and mixing ingredients or oversee these activities. Offer health promotion and prevention activities, for example, training people to use devices such as blood pressure or diabetes monitors. Refer patients to other health professionals and agencies when appropriate. Prepare sterile solutions and infusions for use in surgical procedures, emergency rooms, or patients' homes. Plan, implement, and maintain procedures for mixing, packaging, and labeling pharmaceuticals according to policy and legal requirements to ensure quality, security, and proper disposal. Assay radiopharmaceuticals, verify rates of disintegration, and calculate the volume required to produce

the desired results to ensure proper dosages. Manage pharmacy operations, hiring and supervising staff, performing administrative duties, and buying and selling non-pharmaceutical merchandise. Work in hospitals, clinics, or for Health Management Organizations (HMOs), dispensing prescriptions, serving as a medical team consultant, or specializing in specific drug therapy areas such as oncology or nuclear pharmacotherapy.

GOE Information—**Interest Area:** 08. Health Science. **Work Group:** 08.02. Medicine and Surgery. **Personality Type**—Investigative. Investigative occupations frequently involve working with ideas and require an extensive amount of thinking. These occupations can involve searching for facts and figuring out problems mentally. **Work Values**—Social Service; Authority; Social Status; Ability Utilization; Working Conditions; Security. **Skills**—Science; Reading Comprehension; Social Perceptiveness; Active Listening; Instructing; Mathematics. **Abilities**—*Cognitive:* Problem Sensitivity; Written Expression; Oral Comprehension; Mathematical Reasoning; Deductive Reasoning; Oral Expression. *Psychomotor:* Arm-Hand Steadiness. *Physical:* None met the criteria. *Sensory:* Near Vision; Speech Recognition; Visual Color Discrimination. **General Work Activities**—*Information Input:* Identifying Objects, Actions, and Events; Monitoring Processes, Materials, or Surroundings; Getting Information. *Mental Process:* Updating and Using Relevant Knowledge; Making Decisions and Solving Problems; Processing Information. *Work Output:* Documenting or Recording Information; Interacting With Computers; Controlling Machines and Processes. *Interacting with Others:* Establishing and Maintaining Interpersonal Relationships; Assisting and Caring for Others; Performing for or Working with the Public. **Physical Work Conditions**—Indoors; Disease or Infections; Standing; Repetitive Motions. **Other Job Characteristics**—Need to Be Exact or Accurate; Errors Have Important Consequences; Repeat Same Tasks.

Experience—Job Zone 5. Extensive skill, knowledge, and experience are needed. **Job Preparation**—SVP 8.0 and above—four years to more than 10 years. **Knowledges**—Medicine and Dentistry; Chemistry; Therapy and Counseling; Biology; Psychology; Customer and Personal Service. **Instructional Programs**—Clinical and Industrial Drug Development (MS, PhD); Clinical, Hospital, and Managed Care Pharmacy (MS, PhD); Industrial and Physical Pharmacy and Cosmetic Sciences (MS, PhD); Medicinal and Pharmaceutical Chemistry (MS, PhD); Natural Products Chemistry and Pharmacognosy (MS, PhD); Pharmaceutics and Drug Design (MS, PhD); Pharmacoeconomics/Pharmaceutical Economics (MS, PhD); Pharmacy (PharmD, BS/BPharm); Pharmacy Administration and Pharmacy Policy and Regulatory Affairs (MS, PhD); Pharmacy, Pharmaceutical Sciences, and Administration, Other.

Related SOC Job—29-1051 Pharmacists. **Related OOH Job**—Pharmacists. **Related DOT Jobs**—074.161-010 Pharmacist; 074.161-014 Radiopharmacist; 074.167-010 Director, Pharmacy Services.

29-1061.00 Anesthesiologists

- **Education/Training Required: First professional degree**
- **Employed: 27,970**
- **Annual Earnings: more than $145,600**
- **Growth: 24.0%**
- **Annual Job Openings: 41,000**

Administer anesthetics during surgery or other medical procedures.

Administer anesthetic or sedation during medical procedures, using local, intravenous, spinal, or caudal methods. Monitor patient before, during, and after anesthesia and counteract adverse reactions or complications. Provide and maintain life support and airway management and help prepare patients for emergency surgery. Record type and amount of anesthesia and patient condition throughout procedure. Examine patient; obtain medical history; and use diagnostic tests to determine risk during surgical, obstetrical, and other medical procedures. Position patient on operating table to maximize patient comfort and surgical accessibility. Decide when patients have recovered or stabilized enough to be sent to another room or ward or to be sent home following outpatient surgery. Coordinate administration of anesthetics with surgeons during operation. Confer with other medical professionals to determine type and method of anesthetic or sedation to render patient insensible to pain. Coordinate and direct work of nurses, medical technicians, and other health care providers. Order laboratory tests, X rays, and other diagnostic procedures. Diagnose illnesses, using examinations, tests, and reports. Manage anesthesiological services, coordinating them with other medical activities and formulating plans and procedures. Provide medical care and consultation in many settings, prescribing medication and treatment and referring patients for surgery. Inform students and staff of types and methods of anesthesia administration, signs of complications, and emergency methods to counteract reactions. Schedule and maintain use of surgical suite, including operating, wash-up, and waiting rooms and anesthetic and sterilizing equipment. Instruct individuals and groups on ways to preserve health and prevent disease. Conduct medical research to aid in controlling and curing disease, to investigate new medications, and to develop and test new medical techniques.

GOE Information—Interest Area: 08. Health Science. **Work Group:** 08.02. Medicine and Surgery. **Personality Type**—Investigative. Investigative occupations frequently involve working with ideas and require an extensive amount of thinking. These occupations can involve searching for facts and figuring out problems mentally. **Work Values**—Social Service; Social Status; Compensation; Ability Utilization; Achievement; Recognition. **Skills**—Operation Monitoring; Science; Operation and Control; Judgment and Decision Making; Monitoring; Complex Problem Solving. **Abilities**—*Cognitive:* Problem Sensitivity; Inductive Reasoning; Perceptual Speed; Deductive Reasoning; Flexibility of Closure; Number Facility. *Psychomotor:* Arm-Hand Steadiness; Response Orientation; Finger Dexterity; Control Precision; Manual Dexterity; Multilimb Coordination. *Physical:* Static Strength; Trunk Strength. *Sensory:* Speech Recognition; Speech Clarity; Visual Color Discrimination; Hearing Sensitivity; Near Vision; Auditory Attention. **General Work Activities**—*Information Input:* Monitoring Processes, Materials, or Surroundings; Identifying Objects, Actions, and Events; Inspecting Equipment, Structures, or Materials. *Mental Process:* Updating and Using Relevant Knowledge; Making Decisions and Solving Problems; Analyzing Data or Information. *Work Output:* Controlling Machines and Processes; Documenting or Recording Information; Handling and Moving Objects. *Interacting with Others:* Assisting and Caring for Others; Performing for or Working with the Public; Providing Consultation and Advice to Others. **Physical Work Conditions**—Indoors; Contaminants; Radiation; Disease or Infections; Standing; Using Hands on Objects, Tools, or Controls. **Other Job Characteristics**—Need to Be Exact or Accurate; Errors Have Important Consequences; Repeat Same Tasks.

Experience—Job Zone 5. Extensive skill, knowledge, and experience are needed. **Job Preparation**—SVP 8.0 and above—four years to more than 10 years. **Knowledges**—Medicine and Dentistry; Biology; Chemistry; Psychology; Physics; Therapy and Counseling. **Instructional Programs**—Anesthesiology; Critical Care Anesthesiology; Medicine (MD).

Related SOC Job—29-1061 Anesthesiologists. **Related OOH Job**—Physicians and Surgeons. **Related DOT Job**—070.101-010 Anesthesiologist.

29-1062.00 Family and General Practitioners

- **Education/Training Required:** First professional degree
- **Employed:** 112,150
- **Annual Earnings:** $140,400
- **Growth:** 24.0%
- **Annual Job Openings:** 41,000

Diagnose, treat, and help prevent diseases and injuries that commonly occur in the general population.

Prescribe or administer treatment, therapy, medication, vaccination, and other specialized medical care to treat or prevent illness, disease, or injury. Order, perform, and interpret tests and analyze records, reports, and examination information to diagnose patients' condition. Monitor the patients' conditions and progress and re-evaluate treatments as necessary. Explain procedures and discuss test results or prescribed treatments with patients. Collect, record, and maintain patient information, such as medical history, reports, and examination results. Advise patients and community members concerning diet, activity, hygiene, and disease prevention. Refer patients to medical specialists or other practitioners when necessary. Direct and coordinate activities of nurses, students, assistants, specialists, therapists, and other medical staff. Coordinate work with nurses, social workers, rehabilitation therapists, pharmacists, psychologists, and other health care providers. Deliver babies. Operate on patients to remove, repair, or improve functioning of diseased or injured body parts and systems. Plan, implement, or administer health programs or standards in hospital, business, or community for information, prevention, or treatment of injury or illness. Prepare reports for government or management of birth, death, and disease statistics; workforce evaluations; or medical status of individuals. Conduct research to study anatomy and develop or test medications, treatments, or procedures to prevent or control disease or injury.

GOE Information—Interest Area: 08. Health Science. **Work Group:** 08.02. Medicine and Surgery. **Personality Type**—Investigative. Investigative occupations frequently involve working with ideas and require an extensive amount of thinking. These occupations can involve searching for facts and figuring out problems mentally. **Work Values**—Social Service; Social Status; Recognition; Ability Utilization; Responsibility; Achievement. **Skills**—Science; Social Perceptiveness; Reading Comprehension; Complex Problem Solving; Service Orientation; Persuasion. **Abilities**—*Cognitive:* Problem Sensitivity; Inductive Reasoning; Flexibility of Closure; Speed of Closure; Written Comprehension; Oral Comprehension. *Psychomotor:* Manual Dexterity; Arm-Hand Steadiness; Finger Dexterity. *Physical:* None met the criteria. *Sensory:* Hearing Sensitivity; Speech Recognition; Speech Clarity; Near Vision. **General Work Activities**—*Information Input:* Identifying Objects, Actions, and Events; Getting Information; Monitoring Processes, Materials, or Surroundings. *Mental Process:* Making Decisions and Solving Problems; Updating and Using Relevant Knowledge; Processing Information. *Work Output:* Documenting or Recording Information. *Interacting with Others:* Assisting and Caring for Others; Performing for or Working with the Public; Establishing and Maintaining Interpersonal Relationships. **Physical Work Conditions**—Indoors; Disease or Infections; Standing; Using Hands on Objects, Tools, or Controls. **Other Job Characteristics**—Need to Be Exact or Accurate; Errors Have Important Consequences.

Experience—Job Zone 5. Extensive skill, knowledge, and experience are needed. Job Preparation—SVP 8.0 and above—four years to more than 10 years. Knowledges—Medicine and Dentistry; Therapy and Counseling; Biology; Psychology; Sociology and Anthropology; Chemistry. Instructional Programs—Family Medicine; Medicine (MD); Osteopathic Medicine/Osteopathy (DO).

Related SOC Job—29-1062 Family and General Practitioners. Related OOH Job—Physicians and Surgeons. Related DOT Jobs—070.101-022 General Practitioner; 070.101-026 Family Practitioner; 070.101-046 Public Health Physician; 070.101-078 Physician, Occupational; 070.101-082 Police Surgeon.

29-1063.00 Internists, General

- Education/Training Required: First professional degree
- Employed: 48,210
- Annual Earnings: more than $145,600
- Growth: 24.0%
- Annual Job Openings: 41,000

Diagnose and provide non-surgical treatment of diseases and injuries of internal organ systems. Provide care mainly for adults who have a wide range of problems associated with the internal organs.

Treat internal disorders, such as hypertension; heart disease; diabetes; and problems of the lung, brain, kidney, and gastrointestinal tract. Analyze records, reports, test results, or examination information to diagnose medical condition of patient. Prescribe or administer medication, therapy, and other specialized medical care to treat or prevent illness, disease, or injury. Provide and manage long-term, comprehensive medical care, including diagnosis and non-surgical treatment of diseases, for adult patients in an office or hospital. Manage and treat common health problems, such as infections, influenza and pneumonia, as well as serious, chronic, and complex illnesses, in adolescents, adults, and the elderly. Monitor patients' conditions and progress and re-evaluate treatments as necessary. Collect, record, and maintain patient information, such as medical history, reports, and examination results. Make diagnoses when different illnesses occur together or in situations where the diagnosis may be obscure. Explain procedures and discuss test results or prescribed treatments with patients. Advise patients and community members concerning diet, activity, hygiene, and disease prevention. Refer patient to medical specialist or other practitioner when necessary. Immunize patients to protect them from preventable diseases. Advise surgeon of a patient's risk status and recommend appropriate intervention to minimize risk. Direct and coordinate activities of nurses, students, assistants, specialists, therapists, and other medical staff. Provide consulting services to other doctors caring for patients with special or difficult problems. Operate on patients to remove, repair, or improve functioning of diseased or injured body parts and systems. Plan, implement, or administer health programs in hospitals, businesses, or communities for prevention and treatment of injuries or illnesses. Conduct research to develop or test medications, treatments, or procedures to prevent or control disease or injury. Prepare government or organizational reports on birth, death, and disease statistics; workforce evaluations; or the medical status of individuals.

GOE Information—Interest Area: 08. Health Science. Work Group: 08.02. Medicine and Surgery. Personality Type—Investigative. Investigative occupations frequently involve working with ideas and require an extensive amount of thinking. These occupations can involve searching for facts and figuring out problems mentally. Work Values—Social Service; Social Status; Recognition; Ability Utilization; Responsibility; Achievement. Skills—Science; Judgment and Decision Making; Complex Problem Solving; Social Perceptiveness; Persuasion; Service Orientation. Abilities—*Cognitive:* Problem Sensitivity; Inductive Reasoning; Written Comprehension; Written Expression; Deductive Reasoning; Oral Comprehension. *Psychomotor:* Finger Dexterity; Manual Dexterity. *Physical:* None met the criteria. *Sensory:* Hearing Sensitivity; Speech Recognition; Visual Color Discrimination; Speech Clarity; Near Vision. General Work Activities—*Information Input:* Monitoring Processes, Materials, or Surroundings; Identifying Objects, Actions, and Events; Getting Information. *Mental Process:* Making Decisions and Solving Problems; Updating and Using Relevant Knowledge; Processing Information. *Work Output:* Documenting or Recording Information; Interacting With Computers; Performing General Physical Activities. *Interacting with Others:* Assisting and Caring for Others; Establishing and Maintaining Interpersonal Relationships; Providing Consultation and Advice to Others. Physical Work Conditions—Indoors; Disease or Infections; Standing. Other Job Characteristics—Need to Be Exact or Accurate; Errors Have Important Consequences.

Experience—Job Zone 5. Extensive skill, knowledge, and experience are needed. Job Preparation—SVP 8.0 and above—four years to more than 10 years. Knowledges—Medicine and Dentistry; Biology; Therapy and Counseling; Psychology; Chemistry; Education and Training. Instructional Programs—Cardiology; Critical Care Medicine; Endocrinology and Metabolism; Gastroenterology; Geriatric Medicine; Hematology; Infectious Disease; Internal Medicine; Medicine (MD); Nephrology; Neurology; Nuclear Medicine; Oncology; Pulmonary Disease; Rheumatology.

Related SOC Job—29-1063 Internists, General. Related OOH Job—Physicians and Surgeons. Related DOT Job—070.101-042 Internist.

29-1064.00 Obstetricians and Gynecologists

- Education/Training Required: First professional degree
- Employed: 21,910
- Annual Earnings: more than $145,600
- Growth: 24.0%
- Annual Job Openings: 41,000

Diagnose, treat, and help prevent diseases of women, especially those affecting the reproductive system and the process of childbirth.

Care for and treat women during prenatal, natal, and post-natal periods. Explain procedures and discuss test results or prescribed treatments with patients. Treat diseases of female organs. Monitor patients' condition and progress and re-evaluate treatments as necessary. Perform cesarean sections or other surgical procedures as needed to preserve patients' health and deliver babies safely. Prescribe or administer therapy, medication, and other specialized medical care to treat or prevent illness, disease, or injury. Analyze records, reports, test results, or examination information to diagnose medical condition of patient. Collect, record, and maintain patient information, such as medical histories, reports, and examination results. Advise patients and community members concerning diet, activity, hygiene, and disease prevention. Refer patient to medical specialist or other practitioner when necessary. Consult with, or provide consulting services to, other physicians. Direct and coordinate activities of nurses, students, assistants, specialists, therapists, and other medical staff. Plan, implement, or administer health programs in hospitals, businesses, or communities for prevention and treatment of injuries or illnesses. Prepare government and organizational reports on birth, death, and disease statistics; workforce evaluations; or the medical status of individuals. Conduct research to develop or test medications, treatments, or procedures to prevent or control disease or injury.

GOE Information—Interest Area: 08. Health Science. **Work Group:** 08.02. Medicine and Surgery. **Personality Type—**Investigative. Investigative occupations frequently involve working with ideas and require an extensive amount of thinking. These occupations can involve searching for facts and figuring out problems mentally. **Work Values—**Social Service; Social Status; Recognition; Ability Utilization; Responsibility; Achievement. **Skills—**Science; Judgment and Decision Making; Reading Comprehension; Active Learning; Complex Problem Solving; Social Perceptiveness. **Abilities—***Cognitive:* Problem Sensitivity; Inductive Reasoning; Oral Expression; Oral Comprehension; Deductive Reasoning; Written Comprehension. *Psychomotor:* Manual Dexterity; Arm-Hand Steadiness; Finger Dexterity; Multilimb Coordination; Control Precision. *Physical:* Trunk Strength. *Sensory:* Speech Recognition; Hearing Sensitivity; Speech Clarity; Far Vision; Near Vision; Visual Color Discrimination. **General Work Activities—***Information Input:* Monitoring Processes, Materials, or Surroundings; Identifying Objects, Actions, and Events; Getting Information. *Mental Process:* Making Decisions and Solving Problems; Updating and Using Relevant Knowledge; Processing Information. *Work Output:* Documenting or Recording Information; Controlling Machines and Processes; Handling and Moving Objects. *Interacting with Others:* Assisting and Caring for Others; Interpreting the Meaning of Information for Others; Establishing and Maintaining Interpersonal Relationships. **Physical Work Conditions—**Indoors; Disease or Infections; Standing; Using Hands on Objects, Tools, or Controls. **Other Job Characteristics—**Need to Be Exact or Accurate; Errors Have Important Consequences.

Experience—Job Zone 5. Extensive skill, knowledge, and experience are needed. **Job Preparation—**SVP 8.0 and above—four years to more than 10 years. **Knowledges—**Medicine and Dentistry; Therapy and Counseling; Biology; Psychology; Sociology and Anthropology; Chemistry. **Instructional Programs—**Medicine (MD); Neonatal-Perinatal Medicine; Obstetrics and Gynecology.

Related SOC Job—29-1064 Obstetricians and Gynecologists. **Related OOH Job—**Physicians and Surgeons. **Related DOT Jobs—**070.101-034 Gynecologist; 070.101-054 Obstetrician.

29-1065.00 Pediatricians, General

- **Education/Training Required: First professional degree**
- **Employed: 26,400**
- **Annual Earnings: $136,600**
- **Growth: 24.0%**
- **Annual Job Openings: 41,000**

Diagnose, treat, and help prevent children's diseases and injuries.

Examine patients or order, perform, and interpret diagnostic tests to obtain information on medical condition and determine diagnosis. Examine children regularly to assess their growth and development. Prescribe or administer treatment, therapy, medication, vaccination, and other specialized medical care to treat or prevent illness, disease,

or injury in infants and children. Collect, record, and maintain patient information, such as medical history, reports, and examination results. Advise patients, parents or guardians, and community members concerning diet, activity, hygiene, and disease prevention. Treat children who have minor illnesses, acute and chronic health problems, and growth and development concerns. Explain procedures and discuss test results or prescribed treatments with patients and parents or guardians. Monitor patients' condition and progress and re-evaluate treatments as necessary. Plan and execute medical care programs to aid in the mental and physical growth and development of children and adolescents. Refer patient to medical specialist or other practitioner when necessary. Direct and coordinate activities of nurses, students, assistants, specialists, therapists, and other medical staff. Provide consulting services to other physicians. Plan, implement, or administer health programs or standards in hospital, business, or community for information, prevention, or treatment of injury or illness. Operate on patients to remove, repair, or improve functioning of diseased or injured body parts and systems. Conduct research to study anatomy and develop or test medications, treatments, or procedures to prevent or control disease or injury. Prepare reports for government or management of birth, death, and disease statistics; workforce evaluations; or medical status of individuals.

GOE Information—Interest Area: 08. Health Science. **Work Group:** 08.02. Medicine and Surgery. **Personality Type—**Investigative. Investigative occupations frequently involve working with ideas and require an extensive amount of thinking. These occupations can involve searching for facts and figuring out problems mentally. **Work Values—**Social Service; Social Status; Recognition; Ability Utilization; Responsibility; Achievement. **Skills—**Science; Social Perceptiveness; Active Learning; Persuasion; Critical Thinking; Management of Financial Resources. **Abilities—***Cognitive:* Problem Sensitivity; Inductive Reasoning; Written Expression; Written Comprehension; Oral Comprehension; Flexibility of Closure. *Psychomotor:* Arm-Hand Steadiness; Finger Dexterity. *Physical:* None met the criteria. *Sensory:* Hearing Sensitivity; Speech Recognition; Visual Color Discrimination; Speech Clarity; Near Vision. **General Work Activities—***Information Input:* Getting Information; Identifying Objects, Actions, and Events; Monitoring Processes, Materials, or Surroundings. *Mental Process:* Making Decisions and Solving Problems; Updating and Using Relevant Knowledge; Analyzing Data or Information. *Work Output:* Documenting or Recording Information; Interacting With Computers. *Interacting with Others:* Assisting and Caring for Others; Establishing and Maintaining Interpersonal Relationships; Interpreting the Meaning of Information for Others. **Physical Work Conditions—**Indoors; Disease or Infections; Standing; Using Hands on Objects, Tools, or Controls. **Other Job Characteristics—**Need to Be Exact or Accurate; Errors Have Important Consequences.

Experience—Job Zone 5. Extensive skill, knowledge, and experience are needed. **Job Preparation—**SVP 8.0 and above—four years to more than 10 years. **Knowledges—**Medicine and Dentistry; Therapy and Counseling; Biology; Psychology; Chemistry; Sociology and Anthropology. **Instructional Programs—**Child/Pediatric Neurology; Family Medicine; Medicine (MD); Neonatal-Perinatal Medicine; Pediatric Cardiology; Pediatric Endocrinology; Pediatric Hemato-Oncology; Pediatric Nephrology; Pediatric Orthopedics; Pediatric Surgery; Pediatrics.

Related SOC Job—29-1065 Pediatricians, General. **Related OOH Job—**Physicians and Surgeons. **Related DOT Job—**070.101-066 Pediatrician.

29-1066.00 Psychiatrists

- **Education/Training Required: First professional degree**
- **Employed: 23,450**
- **Annual Earnings: more than $145,600**
- **Growth: 24.0%**
- **Annual Job Openings: 41,000**

Diagnose, treat, and help prevent disorders of the mind.

Analyze and evaluate patient data and test findings to diagnose nature and extent of mental disorder. Prescribe, direct, and administer psychotherapeutic treatments or medications to treat mental, emotional, or behavioral disorders. Collaborate with physicians, psychologists, social workers, psychiatric nurses, or other professionals to discuss treatment plans and progress. Gather and maintain patient information and records, including social and medical history obtained from patients, relatives, and other professionals. Counsel outpatients and other patients during office visits. Design individualized care plans, using a variety of treatments. Examine or conduct laboratory or diagnostic tests on patient to provide information on general physical condition and mental disorder. Advise and inform guardians, relatives, and significant others of patients' conditions and treatment. Review and evaluate treatment procedures and outcomes of other psychiatrists and medical professionals. Teach, conduct research, and publish findings to increase understanding of mental, emotional, and behavioral states and disorders. Prepare and submit case reports and summaries to government and mental health agencies. Serve on committees to promote and maintain community mental health services and delivery systems.

GOE Information—Interest Area: 08. Health Science. **Work Group:** 08.02. Medicine and Surgery. **Personality Type**—Investigative. Investigative occupations frequently involve working with ideas and require an extensive amount of thinking. These occupations can involve searching for facts and figuring out problems mentally. **Work Values**—Social Service; Responsibility; Ability Utilization; Achievement; Autonomy; Social Status. **Skills**—Social Perceptiveness; Science; Persuasion; Systems Analysis; Active Learning; Active Listening. **Abilities**—*Cognitive:* Inductive Reasoning; Problem Sensitivity; Written Expression; Deductive Reasoning; Oral Comprehension; Oral Expression. *Psychomotor:* None met the criteria. *Physical:* None met the criteria. *Sensory:* Speech Recognition; Speech Clarity; Near Vision. **General Work Activities**—*Information Input:* Monitoring Processes, Materials, or Surroundings; Getting Information; Identifying Objects, Actions, and Events. *Mental Process:* Making Decisions and Solving Problems; Updating and Using Relevant Knowledge; Judging the Qualities of Things, Services, or Other People's Work. *Work Output:* Documenting or Recording Information; Interacting With Computers. *Interacting with Others:* Establishing and Maintaining Interpersonal Relationships; Assisting and Caring for Others; Teaching Others. **Physical Work Conditions**—Indoors; Disease or Infections; Sitting. **Other Job Characteristics**—Errors Have Important Consequences; Need to Be Exact or Accurate.

Experience—Job Zone 5. Extensive skill, knowledge, and experience are needed. **Job Preparation**—SVP 8.0 and above—four years to more than 10 years. **Knowledges**—Therapy and Counseling; Medicine and Dentistry; Psychology; Biology; Philosophy and Theology; Sociology and Anthropology. **Instructional Programs**—Child Psychiatry; Medicine (MD); Psychiatry; Psychical Medical and Rehabilitation/Psychiatry.

Related SOC Job—29-1066 Psychiatrists. **Related OOH Job**—Physicians and Surgeons. **Related DOT Job**—070.107-014 Psychiatrist.

29-1067.00 Surgeons

- **Education/Training Required: First professional degree**
- **Employed: 52,930**
- **Annual Earnings: more than $145,600**
- **Growth: 24.0%**
- **Annual Job Openings: 41,000**

Treat diseases, injuries, and deformities by invasive methods, such as manual manipulation, or by using instruments and appliances.

Analyze patient's medical history, medication allergies, physical condition, and examination results to verify operation's necessity and to determine best procedure. Operate on patients to correct deformities, repair injuries, prevent and treat diseases, or improve or restore patients' functions. Follow established surgical techniques during the operation. Prescribe preoperative and postoperative treatments and procedures, such as sedatives, diets, antibiotics, and preparation and treatment of the patient's operative area. Examine patient to provide information on medical condition and surgical risk. Diagnose bodily disorders and orthopedic conditions and provide treatments, such as medicines and surgeries, in clinics, hospital wards, and operating rooms. Direct and coordinate activities of nurses, assistants, specialists, residents, and other medical staff. Provide consultation and surgical assistance to other physicians and surgeons. Refer patient to medical specialist or other practitioners when necessary. Examine instruments, equipment, and operating room to ensure sterility. Prepare case histories. Manage surgery services, including planning, scheduling and coordination, determination of procedures, and procurement of supplies and equipment. Conduct research to develop and test surgical techniques that can improve operating procedures and outcomes.

GOE Information—Interest Area: 08. Health Science. **Work Group:** 08.02. Medicine and Surgery. **Personality Type**—Investigative. Investigative occupations frequently involve working with ideas and require an extensive amount of thinking. These occupations can involve searching for facts and figuring out problems mentally. **Work Values**—Social Service; Social Status; Recognition; Ability Utilization; Achievement; Authority. **Skills**—Science; Reading Comprehension; Judgment and Decision Making; Management of Financial Resources; Complex Problem Solving; Critical Thinking. **Abilities**—*Cognitive:* Problem Sensitivity; Inductive Reasoning; Selective Attention; Deductive Reasoning; Oral Comprehension; Flexibility of Closure. *Psychomotor:* Manual Dexterity; Arm-Hand Steadiness; Finger Dexterity; Control Precision; Response Orientation; Multilimb Coordination. *Physical:* Extent Flexibility; Static Strength; Trunk Strength. *Sensory:* Speech Clarity; Near Vision; Speech Recognition; Visual Color Discrimination; Far Vision; Hearing Sensitivity. **General Work Activities**—*Information Input:* Monitoring Processes, Materials, or Surroundings; Identifying Objects, Actions, and Events; Getting Information. *Mental Process:* Making Decisions and Solving Problems; Updating and Using Relevant Knowledge; Processing Information. *Work Output:* Documenting or Recording Information; Handling and Moving Objects; Controlling Machines and Processes. *Interacting with Others:* Assisting and Caring for Others; Performing for or Working with the Public; Establishing and Maintaining Interpersonal Relationships. **Physical Work Conditions**—Indoors; Contaminants; Radiation; Disease or Infections; Standing; Using Hands on Objects, Tools, or Controls. **Other Job Characteristics**—Need to Be Exact or Accurate; Errors Have Important Consequences; Repeat Same Tasks.

Experience—Job Zone 5. Extensive skill, knowledge, and experience are needed. **Job Preparation**—SVP 8.0 and above—four years to more than 10 years. **Knowledges**—Medicine and Dentistry; Biology; Therapy and Counseling; Psychology; Chemistry; Customer and Personal Service. **Instructional Programs**—Adult Reconstructive Orthopedics (Orthopedic Surgery); Colon and Rectal Surgery; Critical Care Surgery; General Surgery; Hand Surgery; Medicine (MD); Neurological Surgery/Neurosurgery; Orthopedic Surgery of the Spine; Orthopedics/Orthopedic Surgery; Otolaryngology; Pediatric Orthopedics; Pediatric Surgery; Plastic Surgery; Sports Medicine; Thoracic Surgery; Urology; Vascular Surgery.

Related SOC Job—29-1067 Surgeons. **Related OOH Job**—Physicians and Surgeons. **Related DOT Job**—070.101-094 Surgeon.

29-1069.99 Physicians and Surgeons, All Other

- **Education/Training Required: First professional degree**
- **Employed: 180,210**
- **Annual Earnings: $143,480**
- **Growth: 24.0%**
- **Annual Job Openings: 41,000**

All physicians and surgeons not listed separately.

No task data available.

Note: The Department of Labor has not collected some data for this job, so it has fewer details than the other descriptions.

Related SOC Job—29-1069 Physicians and Surgeons, All Other. **Related OOH Job**—Physicians and Surgeons. **Related DOT Jobs**—070.061-010 Pathologist; 070.101-014 Cardiologist; 070.101-018 Dermatologist; 070.101-050 Neurologist; 070.101-058 Ophthalmologist; 070.101-062 Otolaryngologist; 070.101-070 Physiatrist; 070.101-086 Proctologist; 070.101-098 Urologist; 070.101-102 Allergist-Immunologist; 071.101-010 Osteopathic Physician.

29-1071.00 Physician Assistants

- **Education/Training Required: Bachelor's degree**
- **Employed: 63,350**
- **Annual Earnings: $72,030**
- **Growth: 49.6%**
- **Annual Job Openings: 10,000**

Under the supervision of a physician, provide healthcare services typically performed by a physician. Conduct complete physicals, provide treatment, and counsel patients. May, in some cases, prescribe medication. Must graduate from an accredited educational program for physician assistants.

Examine patients to obtain information about their physical condition. Make tentative diagnoses and decisions about management and treatment of patients. Interpret diagnostic test results for deviations from normal. Obtain, compile, and record patient medical data, including health history, progress notes, and results of physical examination. Administer or order diagnostic tests, such as X-ray, electrocardiogram, and laboratory tests. Prescribe therapy or medication with physician approval. Perform therapeutic procedures, such as injections, immunizations, suturing and wound care, and infection management. Instruct and counsel patients about prescribed therapeutic regimens, normal growth and development, family planning, emotional problems of daily living, and health maintenance. Provide physicians with assistance during surgery or complicated medical procedures. Supervise and coordinate activities of technicians and technical assistants. Visit and observe patients on hospital rounds or house calls, updating charts, ordering therapy, and reporting back to physician. Order medical and laboratory supplies and equipment.

GOE Information—**Interest Area:** 08. Health Science. **Work Group:** 08.02. Medicine and Surgery. **Personality Type**—Investigative. Investigative occupations frequently involve working with ideas and require an extensive amount of thinking. These occupations can involve searching for facts and figuring out problems mentally. **Work Values**—Social Service; Achievement; Co-workers; Ability Utilization; Activity; Social Status. **Skills**—Science; Social Perceptiveness; Reading Comprehension; Critical Thinking; Active Listening; Instructing. **Abilities**—*Cognitive:* Inductive Reasoning; Problem Sensitivity; Speed of Closure; Flexibility of Closure; Oral Expression; Written Expression. *Psychomotor:* Arm-Hand Steadiness. *Physical:* Trunk Strength. *Sensory:* Near Vision; Speech Recognition. **General Work Activities**—*Information Input:* Identifying Objects, Actions, and Events; Monitoring Processes, Materials, or Surroundings; Getting Information. *Mental Process:* Updating and Using Relevant Knowledge; Making Decisions and Solving Problems; Processing Information. *Work Output:* Documenting or Recording Information; Interacting With Computers; Performing General Physical Activities. *Interacting with Others:* Assisting and Caring for Others; Establishing and Maintaining Interpersonal Relationships; Communicating with Other Workers. **Physical Work Conditions**—Indoors; Disease or Infections; Standing. **Other Job Characteristics**—Need to Be Exact or Accurate; Errors Have Important Consequences.

Experience—Job Zone 4. A minimum of two to four years of work-related skill, knowledge, or experience is needed. **Job Preparation**—SVP 7.0 to less than 8.0—two years to less than 10 years. **Knowledges**—Medicine and Dentistry; Biology; Therapy and Counseling; Psychology; Chemistry; Customer and Personal Service. **Instructional Program**—Physician Assistant.

Related SOC Job—29-1071 Physician Assistants. **Related OOH Job**—Physician Assistants. **Related DOT Jobs**—079.364-018 Physician Assistant; 079.367-018 Medical-Service Technician.

29-1081.00 Podiatrists

- **Education/Training Required: First professional degree**
- **Employed: 8,290**
- **Annual Earnings: $100,550**
- **Growth: 16.2%**
- **Annual Job Openings: 1,000**

Diagnose and treat diseases and deformities of the human foot.

Treat bone, muscle, and joint disorders affecting the feet. Diagnose diseases and deformities of the foot, using medical histories, physical examinations, X rays, and laboratory test results. Prescribe medications, corrective devices, physical therapy, or surgery. Treat conditions such as corns, calluses, ingrown nails, tumors, shortened tendons, bunions, cysts, and abscesses by surgical methods. Advise patients about treatments and foot care techniques necessary for prevention of future problems. Refer patients to physicians when symptoms indicative of systemic disorders, such as arthritis or diabetes, are observed in feet and legs. Correct deformities by means of plaster casts and strapping. Make and fit prosthetic appliances. Perform administrative duties such as hiring employees, ordering supplies, and keeping records. Educate the public about the benefits of foot care through techniques such as speaking engagements, advertising, and other forums. Treat deformities, using mechanical methods, such as whirlpool or paraffin baths, and electrical methods, such as shortwave and low-voltage currents.

GOE Information—Interest Area: 08. Health Science. Work Group: 08.04. Health Specialties. Personality Type—Social. Social occupations frequently involve working with, communicating with, and teaching people. These occupations often involve helping or providing service to others. Work Values—Social Service; Responsibility; Recognition; Autonomy; Social Status; Ability Utilization. Skills—Science; Active Listening; Complex Problem Solving; Management of Financial Resources; Reading Comprehension; Active Learning. Abilities—*Cognitive:* Problem Sensitivity; Inductive Reasoning; Flexibility of Closure; Speed of Closure; Written Comprehension; Deductive Reasoning. *Psychomotor:* Manual Dexterity; Arm-Hand Steadiness; Control Precision; Finger Dexterity; Multilimb Coordination. *Physical:* None met the criteria. *Sensory:* Speech Clarity; Speech Recognition; Far Vision; Visual Color Discrimination; Hearing Sensitivity; Near Vision. General Work Activities—*Information Input:* Identifying Objects, Actions, and Events; Monitoring Processes, Materials, or Surroundings; Getting Information. *Mental Process:* Making Decisions and Solving Problems; Updating and Using Relevant Knowledge; Organizing, Planning, and Prioritizing. *Work Output:* Documenting or Recording Information; Handling and Moving Objects; Controlling Machines and Processes. *Interacting with Others:* Establishing and Maintaining Interpersonal Relationships; Assisting and Caring for Others; Interpreting the Meaning of Information for Others. Physical Work Conditions—Indoors; Contaminants; Disease or Infections; Sitting; Using Hands on Objects, Tools, or Controls; Repetitive Motions. Other Job Characteristics—Need to Be Exact or Accurate; Errors Have Important Consequences; Repeat Same Tasks.

Experience—Job Zone 5. Extensive skill, knowledge, and experience are needed. Job Preparation—SVP 8.0 and above—four years to more than 10 years. Knowledges—Medicine and Dentistry; Biology; Therapy and Counseling; Sales and Marketing; Chemistry; Customer and Personal Service. Instructional Program—Podiatric Medicine/Podiatry (DPM).

Related SOC Job—29-1081 Podiatrists. Related OOH Job—Podiatrists. Related DOT Job—079.101-022 Podiatrist.

29-1111.00 Registered Nurses

- **Education/Training Required: Associate degree**
- **Employed: 2,368,070**
- **Annual Earnings: $54,670**
- **Growth: 29.4%**
- **Annual Job Openings: 229,000**

Assess patient health problems and needs, develop and implement nursing care plans, and maintain medical records. Administer nursing care to ill, injured, convalescent, or disabled patients. May advise patients on health maintenance and disease prevention or provide case management. Licensing or registration required. Includes advance practice nurses, such as nurse practitioners, clinical nurse specialists, certified nurse midwives, and certified registered nurse anesthetists. Advanced practice nursing is practiced by RNs who have specialized formal, post-basic education and who function in highly autonomous and specialized roles.

Maintain accurate, detailed reports and records. Monitor, record, and report symptoms and changes in patients' conditions. Record patients' medical information and vital signs. Modify patient treatment plans as indicated by patients' responses and conditions. Consult and coordinate with health care team members to assess, plan, implement, and evaluate patient care plans. Order, interpret, and evaluate diagnostic tests to identify and assess patient's condition. Monitor all aspects of patient care, including diet and physical activity. Direct and supervise less-skilled nursing or health care personnel or supervise a particular unit. Prepare patients for, and assist with, examinations and treatments. Observe nurses and visit patients to ensure proper nursing care. Assess the needs of individuals, families, or communities, including assessment of individuals' home or work environments, to identify potential health or safety problems. Instruct individuals, families, and other groups on topics such as health education, disease prevention, and childbirth; develop health improvement programs. Prepare rooms, sterile instruments, equipment, and supplies and ensure that stock of supplies is maintained. Inform physician of patient's condition during anesthesia. Deliver infants and provide prenatal and postpartum care and treatment under obstetrician's supervision. Administer local, inhalation, intravenous, and other anesthetics. Provide health care, first aid, immunizations, and assistance in convalescence and rehabilitation in locations such as schools, hospitals, and industry. Conduct specified laboratory tests. Perform physical examinations, make tentative diagnoses, and treat patients en route to hospitals or at disaster site triage centers. Hand items to surgeons during operations. Prescribe or recommend drugs; medical devices; or other forms of treatment, such as physical therapy, inhalation therapy, or related therapeutic procedures. Direct and coordinate infection control programs, advising and consulting with specified personnel about necessary precautions. Perform administrative and managerial functions, such as taking responsibility for a unit's staff, budget, planning, and long-range goals.

GOE Information—Interest Area: 08. Health Science. Work Group: 08.02. Medicine and Surgery. Personality Type—Social. Social occupations frequently involve working with, communicating with, and teaching people. These occupations often involve helping or providing service to others. Work Values—Social Service; Co-workers; Ability Utilization; Achievement; Activity; Social Status. Skills—Social Perceptiveness; Service Orientation; Science; Time Management; Monitoring; Instructing. Abilities—*Cognitive:* Problem Sensitivity; Inductive Reasoning; Flexibility of Closure; Speed of Closure; Deductive Reasoning; Oral Expression. *Psychomotor:* Arm-Hand Steadiness; Manual Dexterity. *Physical:* Extent Flexibility; Gross Body Coordination; Static Strength; Trunk Strength. *Sensory:* Speech Recognition; Near Vision; Auditory Attention; Speech Clarity. General Work Activities—*Information Input:* Identifying Objects, Actions, and Events; Monitoring Processes, Materials, or Surroundings; Getting Information. *Mental Process:* Updating and Using Relevant Knowledge; Organizing, Planning, and Prioritizing; Making Decisions and Solving Problems. *Work Output:* Documenting or Recording Information; Handling and Moving Objects; Performing General Physical Activities. *Interacting with Others:* Assisting and Caring for Others; Establishing and Maintaining Interpersonal Relationships; Performing for or Working with the Public. Physical Work Conditions—Indoors; Noisy; Contaminants; Disease or Infections; Standing; Using Hands on Objects, Tools, or Controls. Other Job Characteristics—Need to Be Exact or Accurate; Errors Have Important Consequences; Repeat Same Tasks.

Experience—Job Zone 3. Previous work-related skill, knowledge, or experience is required. Job Preparation—SVP 6.0 to less than 7.0—more than one year and less than four years. Knowledges—Medicine and Dentistry; Psychology; Therapy and Counseling; Biology; Sociology and Anthropology; Philosophy and Theology. Instructional Programs—Adult Health Nurse/Nursing; Critical Care Nursing; Family Practice Nurse/Nurse Practitioner; Maternal/Child Health Nurse/Nursing; Nurse Anesthetist; Nurse Midwife/Nursing Midwifery; Nursing—Registered Nurse Training (RN, ASN, BSN, MSN); Nursing Clinical Specialist; Nursing Science (MS, PhD);

Nursing, Other; Occupational and Environmental Health Nursing; Pediatric Nurse/Nursing; Perioperative/Operating Room and Surgical Nurse/Nursing; Psychiatric/Mental Health Nurse/Nursing; Public Health/Community Nurse/Nursing.

Related SOC Job—29-1111 Registered Nurses. **Related OOH Job**—Registered Nurses. **Related DOT Jobs**—075.124-010 Nurse, School; 075.124-014 Nurse, Community Health; 075.127-014 Nurse, Consultant; 075.127-026 Nurse Supervisor, Community-Health Nursing; 075.127-030 Nurse Supervisor, Evening-or-Night; 075.127-034 Nurse, Infection Control; 075.137-010 Nurse Supervisor, Occupational Health Nursing; 075.137-014 Nurse, Head; 075.167-010 Nurse, Supervisor; 075.264-010 Nurse Practitioner; 075.264-014 Nurse-Midwife; 075.364-010 Nurse, General Duty; 075.371-010 Nurse Anesthetist; others.

29-1121.00 Audiologists

- **Education/Training Required: Master's degree**
- **Employed: 10,330**
- **Annual Earnings: $53,490**
- **Growth: 9.1%**
- **Annual Job Openings: Fewer than 500**

Assess and treat persons with hearing and related disorders. May fit hearing aids and provide auditory training. May perform research related to hearing problems.

Evaluate hearing and speech/language disorders to determine diagnoses and courses of treatment. Administer hearing or speech/language evaluations, tests, or examinations to patients to collect information on type and degree of impairment, using specialized instruments and electronic equipment. Fit and dispense assistive devices, such as hearing aids. Maintain client records at all stages, including initial evaluation and discharge. Refer clients to additional medical or educational services if needed. Counsel and instruct clients in techniques to improve hearing or speech impairment, including sign language or lip-reading. Monitor clients' progress and discharge them from treatment when goals have been attained. Plan and conduct treatment programs for clients' hearing or speech problems, consulting with physicians, nurses, psychologists, and other health care personnel as necessary. Recommend assistive devices according to clients' needs or nature of impairments. Participate in conferences or training to update or share knowledge of new hearing or speech disorder treatment methods or technologies. Instruct clients, parents, teachers, or employers in how to avoid behavior patterns that lead to miscommunication. Examine and clean patients' ear canals. Advise educators or other medical staff on speech or hearing topics. Educate and supervise audiology students and health care personnel. Fit and tune cochlear implants, providing rehabilitation for adjustment to listening with implant amplification systems. Work with multi-disciplinary teams to assess and rehabilitate recipients of implanted hearing devices. Develop and supervise hearing screening programs. Conduct or direct research on hearing or speech topics and report findings to help in the development of procedures, technology, or treatments. Measure noise levels in workplaces and conduct hearing protection programs in industry, schools, and communities.

GOE Information—**Interest Area:** 08. Health Science. **Work Group:** 08.07. Medical Therapy. **Personality Type**—Social. Social occupations frequently involve working with, communicating with, and teaching people. These occupations often involve helping or providing service to others. **Work Values**—Social Service; Authority; Creativity; Achievement; Co-workers; Ability Utilization. **Skills**—

Social Perceptiveness; Science; Service Orientation; Persuasion; Equipment Selection; Reading Comprehension. **Abilities**—*Cognitive:* Inductive Reasoning; Problem Sensitivity; Written Expression; Oral Expression; Flexibility of Closure; Deductive Reasoning. *Psychomotor:* Finger Dexterity; Manual Dexterity; Arm-Hand Steadiness. *Physical:* None met the criteria. *Sensory:* Hearing Sensitivity; Auditory Attention; Speech Recognition; Far Vision; Speech Clarity. **General Work Activities**—*Information Input:* Identifying Objects, Actions, and Events; Getting Information; Monitoring Processes, Materials, or Surroundings. *Mental Process:* Updating and Using Relevant Knowledge; Making Decisions and Solving Problems; Processing Information. *Work Output:* Documenting or Recording Information; Interacting With Computers; Handling and Moving Objects. *Interacting with Others:* Performing for or Working with the Public; Establishing and Maintaining Interpersonal Relationships; Assisting and Caring for Others. **Physical Work Conditions**—Indoors; Disease or Infections; Sitting; Using Hands on Objects, Tools, or Controls. **Other Job Characteristics**—Need to Be Exact or Accurate; Repeat Same Tasks.

Experience—Job Zone 5. Extensive skill, knowledge, and experience are needed. **Job Preparation**—SVP 8.0 and above—four years to more than 10 years. **Knowledges**—Therapy and Counseling; Medicine and Dentistry; Psychology; Customer and Personal Service; Sales and Marketing; English Language. **Instructional Programs**—Audiology/Audiologist and Hearing Sciences; Audiology/Audiologist and Speech-Language Pathology/Pathologist; Communication Disorders Sciences and Services, Other; Communication Disorders, General.

Related SOC Job—29-1121 Audiologists. **Related OOH Job**—Audiologists. **Related DOT Jobs**—076.101-010 Audiologist; 076.101-014 Director, Speech-and-Hearing Clinic; 079.131-010 Director, Speech-And-Hearing Clinic.

29-1122.00 Occupational Therapists

- **Education/Training Required: Master's degree**
- **Employed: 87,430**
- **Annual Earnings: $56,860**
- **Growth: 33.6%**
- **Annual Job Openings: 7,000**

Assess, plan, organize, and participate in rehabilitative programs that help restore vocational, homemaking, and daily living skills, as well as general independence, to disabled persons.

Complete and maintain necessary records. Evaluate patients' progress and prepare reports that detail progress. Test and evaluate patients' physical and mental abilities and analyze medical data to determine realistic rehabilitation goals for patients. Select activities that will help individuals learn work and life-management skills within limits of their mental and physical capabilities. Plan, organize, and conduct occupational therapy programs in hospital, institutional, or community settings to help rehabilitate those impaired because of illness, injury or psychological or developmental problems. Recommend changes in patients' work or living environments consistent with their needs and capabilities. Consult with rehabilitation team to select activity programs and coordinate occupational therapy with other therapeutic activities. Help clients improve decisionmaking, abstract reasoning, memory, sequencing, coordination, and perceptual skills, using computer programs. Develop and participate in health promotion programs, group activities, or discussions to promote client health, facilitate social adjustment, alleviate stress, and prevent physical or mental disability. Provide training and supervision in therapy techniques and objectives for students and nurses and other medical staff. Design and create, or requisition, special supplies and equipment, such as splints, braces, and computer-aided adaptive equipment. Plan and implement programs and social activities to help patients learn work and school skills and adjust to handicaps. Lay out materials such as puzzles, scissors, and eating utensils for use in therapy; clean and repair these tools after therapy sessions. Advise on health risks in the workplace and on health-related transition to retirement. Conduct research in occupational therapy. Provide patients with assistance in locating and holding jobs.

GOE Information—Interest Area: 08. Health Science. **Work Group:** 08.07. Medical Therapy. **Personality Type**—Social. Social occupations frequently involve working with, communicating with, and teaching people. These occupations often involve helping or providing service to others. **Work Values**—Social Service; Achievement; Co-workers; Ability Utilization; Authority; Social Status. **Skills**—Social Perceptiveness; Service Orientation; Science; Technology Design; Reading Comprehension; Coordination. **Abilities**—*Cognitive:* Problem Sensitivity; Inductive Reasoning; Speed of Closure; Originality; Deductive Reasoning; Oral Expression. *Psychomotor:* Finger Dexterity; Manual Dexterity. *Physical:* Trunk Strength. *Sensory:* Speech Recognition; Speech Clarity; Far Vision; Near Vision. **General Work Activities**—*Information Input:* Identifying Objects, Actions, and Events; Monitoring Processes, Materials, or Surroundings; Getting Information. *Mental Process:* Updating and Using Relevant Knowledge; Making Decisions and Solving Problems; Organizing, Planning, and Prioritizing. *Work Output:* Handling and Moving Objects; Documenting or Recording Information; Performing General Physical Activities. *Interacting with Others:* Establishing and Maintaining Interpersonal Relationships; Assisting and Caring for Others; Communicating with Other Workers. **Physical Work Conditions**—Indoors; Disease or Infections; Standing. **Other Job Characteristics**—Need to Be Exact or Accurate.

Experience—Job Zone 4. A minimum of two to four years of work-related skill, knowledge, or experience is needed. **Job Preparation**—SVP 7.0 to less than 8.0—two years to less than 10 years. **Knowledges**—Therapy and Counseling; Psychology; Medicine and Dentistry; Customer and Personal Service; Biology; Sociology and Anthropology. **Instructional Program**—Occupational Therapy/Therapist.

Related SOC Job—29-1122 Occupational Therapists. **Related OOH Job**—Occupational Therapists. **Related DOT Jobs**—076.121-010 Occupational Therapist; 076.167-010 Industrial Therapist.

29-1123.00 Physical Therapists

- **Education/Training Required: Master's degree**
- **Employed: 151,280**
- **Annual Earnings: $63,080**
- **Growth: 36.7%**
- **Annual Job Openings: 13,000**

Assess, plan, organize, and participate in rehabilitative programs that improve mobility, relieve pain, increase strength, and decrease or prevent deformity of patients suffering from disease or injury.

Plan, prepare, and carry out individually designed programs of physical treatment to maintain, improve, or restore physical functioning; alleviate pain; and prevent physical dysfunction in patients. Perform and document an initial exam, evaluating data to identify problems and determine a diagnosis prior to intervention. Evaluate effects of treatment at various stages and adjust treatments to achieve maximum benefit. Administer manual exercises, massage, or traction to help relieve pain, increase patient strength, or decrease or prevent deformity or crippling. Instruct patient and family in treatment procedures to be continued at home. Confer with the patient, medical practitioners, and appropriate others to plan, implement, and assess the intervention program. Review physician's referral and patient's medical records to help determine diagnosis and physical therapy treatment required. Obtain patients' informed consent to proposed interventions. Record prognosis, treatment, response, and progress in patient's chart or enter information into computer. Discharge patient from physical therapy when goals or projected outcomes have been attained and provide for appropriate follow-up care or referrals. Test and measure patient's strength, motor development and function, sensory perception, functional capacity, and respiratory and circulatory efficiency and record data. Identify and document goals, anticipated progress, and plans for reevaluation. Provide information to the patient about the proposed intervention, its material risks and expected benefits, and any reasonable alternatives. Inform patients when diagnosis reveals findings outside physical therapy and refer to appropriate practitioners. Direct, supervise, assess, and communicate with supportive personnel. Administer treatment involving application of physical agents, using equipment, moist packs, ultraviolet and infrared lamps, and ultrasound machines. Teach physical therapy students as well as those in other health professions. Evaluate, fit, and adjust prosthetic and orthotic devices and recommend modification to orthotist. Provide educational information about physical therapy and physical therapists, injury prevention, ergonomics, and ways to promote health.

GOE Information—Interest Area: 08. Health Science. **Work Group:** 08.07. Medical Therapy. **Personality Type**—Social. Social occupations frequently involve working with, communicating with, and teaching people. These occupations often involve helping or providing service to others. **Work Values**—Social Service; Achievement; Co-workers; Ability Utilization; Authority; Social Status. **Skills**—Science; Reading Comprehension; Social Perceptiveness; Instructing; Learning Strategies; Service Orientation. **Abilities**—*Cognitive:* Problem Sensitivity; Speed of Closure; Deductive Reasoning; Written Comprehension; Inductive Reasoning; Written Expression. *Psychomotor:* Manual Dexterity; Multilimb Coordination; Arm-Hand Steadiness; Finger Dexterity; Control Precision. *Physical:* Dynamic Strength; Extent Flexibility; Gross Body Coordination; Stamina; Static Strength; Trunk Strength. *Sensory:* Speech Recognition; Far Vision; Near Vision. **General Work Activities**—*Information Input:* Identifying Objects, Actions, and Events; Monitoring Processes, Materials, or Surroundings; Getting Information. *Mental Process:* Organizing, Planning, and Prioritizing; Updating and Using Relevant Knowledge; Analyzing Data or Information. *Work Output:* Handling and Moving Objects; Performing General Physical Activities; Documenting or Recording Information. *Interacting with Others:* Assisting and Caring for Others; Establishing and Maintaining Interpersonal Relationships; Communicating with Other Workers. **Physical Work Conditions**—Indoors; Contaminants; Disease or Infections; Standing; Walking and Running; Bending or Twisting the Body. **Other Job Characteristics**—Need to Be Exact or Accurate; Errors Have Important Consequences.

Experience—Job Zone 5. Extensive skill, knowledge, and experience are needed. **Job Preparation**—SVP 8.0 and above—four years to more than 10 years. **Knowledges**—Therapy and Counseling; Medicine and Dentistry; Psychology; Biology; Sociology and Anthropology; Customer and Personal Service. **Instructional Programs**—Kinesiotherapy/Kinesiotherapist; Physical Therapy/Therapist.

Related SOC Job—29-1123 Physical Therapists. **Related OOH Job**—Physical Therapists. **Related DOT Job**—076.121-014 Physical Therapist.

29-1124.00 Radiation Therapists

- **Education/Training Required: Associate degree**
- **Employed: 14,120**
- **Annual Earnings: $62,340**
- **Growth: 26.3%**
- **Annual Job Openings: 1,000**

Provide radiation therapy to patients as prescribed by a radiologist according to established practices and standards. Duties may include reviewing prescription and diagnosis; acting as liaison with physician and supportive care personnel; preparing equipment, such as immobilization, treatment, and protection devices; and maintaining records, reports, and files. May assist in dosimetry procedures and tumor localization.

Administer prescribed doses of radiation to specific body parts, using radiation therapy equipment according to established practices and standards. Position patients for treatment with accuracy according to prescription. Enter data into computer and set controls to operate and adjust equipment and regulate dosage. Follow principles of radiation protection for patient, self, and others. Maintain records, reports and files as required, including such information as radiation dosages, equipment settings, and patients' reactions. Review prescription, diagnosis, patient chart, and identification. Conduct most treatment sessions independently in accordance with the long-term treatment plan and under the general direction of the patient's physician. Check radiation therapy equipment to ensure proper operation. Observe and reassure patients during treatment and report unusual reactions to physician or turn equipment off if unexpected adverse reactions occur. Check for side effects such as skin irritation, nausea, and hair loss to assess patients' reaction to treatment. Educate, prepare, and reassure patients and their families by answering questions, providing physical assistance, and reinforcing physicians' advice regarding treatment reactions and post-treatment care. Calculate actual treatment dosages delivered during each session. Prepare and construct equipment, such as immobilization, treatment, and protection devices. Photograph treated area of patient and process film. Help physicians, radiation oncologists, and clinical physicists to prepare physical and technical aspects of radiation treatment plans, using information about patient condition and anatomy. Train and supervise student or subordinate radiotherapy technologists. Provide assistance to other health care personnel during dosimetry procedures and tumor localization. Implement appropriate follow-up care plans. Act as liaison with physicist and supportive care personnel. Store, sterilize, or prepare the special applicators containing the radioactive substance implanted by the physician. Assist in the preparation of sealed radioactive materials, such as cobalt, radium, cesium, and isotopes, for use in radiation treatments.

GOE Information—**Interest Area:** 08. Health Science. **Work Group:** 08.07. Medical Therapy. **Personality Type**—Social. Social occupations frequently involve working with, communicating with, and teaching people. These occupations often involve helping or providing service to others. **Work Values**—Social Service; Co-workers; Ability Utilization; Security; Achievement; Moral Values. **Skills**—Operation Monitoring; Operation and Control; Technology Design; Time Management; Science; Management of Personnel Resources. **Abilities**—*Cognitive:* Problem Sensitivity; Perceptual Speed; Memorization; Number Facility; Mathematical Reasoning; Written Comprehension. *Psychomotor:* Reaction Time; Response Orientation; Arm-Hand Steadiness; Control Precision; Manual Dexterity. *Physical:* Extent Flexibility; Trunk Strength. *Sensory:* Visual Color Discrimination; Speech Recognition; Near Vision; Speech Clarity; Depth Perception; Hearing Sensitivity. **General Work Activities**—*Information Input:* Monitoring Processes, Materials, or Surroundings; Identifying Objects, Actions, and Events; Inspecting Equipment, Structures, or Materials. *Mental Process:* Updating and Using Relevant Knowledge; Processing Information; Evaluating Information Against Standards. *Work Output:* Handling and Moving Objects; Controlling Machines and Processes; Documenting or Recording Information. *Interacting with Others:* Assisting and Caring for Others; Establishing and Maintaining Interpersonal Relationships; Performing for or Working with the Public. **Physical Work Conditions**—Indoors; Disease or Infections; Standing; Walking and Running; Using Hands on Objects, Tools, or Controls; Repetitive Motions. **Other Job Characteristics**—Need to Be Exact or Accurate; Repeat Same Tasks; Errors Have Important Consequences; Pace Determined by Speed of Equipment.

Experience—Job Zone 3. Previous work-related skill, knowledge, or experience is required. **Job Preparation**—SVP 6.0 to less than 7.0—more than one year and less than four years. **Knowledges**—Medicine and Dentistry; Biology; Physics; Psychology; Therapy and Counseling; Customer and Personal Service. **Instructional Program**—Medical Radiologic Technology/Science Radiation Therapist.

Related SOC Job—29-1124 Radiation Therapists. **Related OOH Job**—Radiation Therapists. **Related DOT Job**—078.361-034 Radiation Therapist.

29-1125.00 Recreational Therapists

- **Education/Training Required: Bachelor's degree**
- **Employed: 23,260**
- **Annual Earnings: $33,480**
- **Growth: 5.7%**
- **Annual Job Openings: 3,000**

Plan, direct, or coordinate medically approved recreation programs for patients in hospitals, nursing homes, or other institutions. Activities include sports, trips, dramatics, social activities, and arts and crafts. May assess a patient condition and recommend appropriate recreational activity.

Observe, analyze, and record patients' participation, reactions, and progress during treatment sessions, modifying treatment programs as needed. Develop treatment plan to meet needs of patient, based on needs assessment, patient interests, and objectives of therapy. Encourage clients with special needs and circumstances to acquire new skills and get involved in health-promoting leisure activities, such as sports, games, arts and crafts, and gardening. Counsel and encourage patients to develop leisure activities. Confer with members of treatment team to plan and evaluate therapy programs. Conduct therapy sessions to improve patients' mental and physical well-being. Instruct patient in activities and techniques, such as sports, dance, music, art, or relaxation techniques, designed to meet their specific physical or psychological needs. Obtain information from medical records, medical staff, family members, and the patients themselves to assess patients' capabilities, needs, and interests. Plan, organize, direct, and participate in treatment programs and activities to facilitate patients' rehabilitation, help them integrate into the community, and prevent further medical problems. Prepare and submit reports and charts to treatment team to reflect patients' reactions and evidence of progress or regression.

GOE Information—Interest Area: 08. Health Science. **Work Group:** 08.07. Medical Therapy. **Personality Type**—Social. Social occupations frequently involve working with, communicating with, and teaching people. These occupations often involve helping or providing service to others. **Work Values**—Social Service; Co-workers; Creativity; Achievement; Social Status; Authority. **Skills**—Social Perceptiveness; Writing; Persuasion; Instructing; Learning Strategies; Service Orientation. **Abilities**—*Cognitive:* Originality; Written Expression; Memorization; Problem Sensitivity; Fluency of Ideas; Oral Expression. *Psychomotor:* Reaction Time; Multilimb Coordination. *Physical:* Gross Body Coordination; Stamina; Trunk Strength; Static Strength. *Sensory:* Speech Recognition. **General Work Activities**—*Information Input:* Monitoring Processes, Materials, or Surroundings; Getting Information; Identifying Objects, Actions, and Events. *Mental Process:* Organizing, Planning, and Prioritizing; Thinking Creatively; Making Decisions and Solving Problems. *Work Output:* Documenting or Recording Information; Handling and Moving Objects; Performing General Physical Activities. *Interacting with Others:* Assisting and Caring for Others; Establishing and Maintaining Interpersonal Relationships; Communicating with Other Workers. **Physical Work Conditions**—Indoors; Disease or Infections; Standing. **Other Job Characteristics**—Need to Be Exact or Accurate; Errors Have Important Consequences.

Experience—Job Zone 4. A minimum of two to four years of work-related skill, knowledge, or experience is needed. **Job Preparation**—SVP 7.0 to less than 8.0—two years to less than 10 years. **Knowledges**—Psychology; Therapy and Counseling; Fine Arts; Sociology and Anthropology; Philosophy and Theology; Customer and Personal Service. **Instructional Program**—Therapeutic Recreation/Recreational Therapy.

Related SOC Job—29-1125 Recreational Therapists. **Related OOH Job**—Recreational Therapists. **Related DOT Jobs**—076.124-014 Recreational Therapist; 076.124-018 Horticultural Therapist; 076.127-010 Art Therapist; 076.127-014 Music Therapist; 076.127-018 Dance Therapist.

29-1126.00 Respiratory Therapists

- **Education/Training Required: Associate degree**
- **Employed: 95,320**
- **Annual Earnings: $45,140**
- **Growth: 28.4%**
- **Annual Job Openings: 7,000**

Assess, treat, and care for patients with breathing disorders. Assume primary responsibility for all respiratory care modalities, including the supervision of respiratory therapy technicians. Initiate and conduct therapeutic procedures; maintain patient records; and select, assemble, check, and operate equipment.

Set up and operate devices such as mechanical ventilators, therapeutic gas administration apparatus, environmental control systems, and aerosol generators, following specified parameters of treatment. Provide emergency care, including artificial respiration, external cardiac massage, and assistance with cardiopulmonary resuscitation. Determine requirements for treatment, such as type, method, and duration of therapy; precautions to be taken; and medication and dosages, compatible with physicians' orders. Monitor patient's physiological responses to therapy, such as vital signs, arterial blood gases, and blood chemistry changes, and consult with physician if adverse reactions occur. Read prescription, measure arterial blood gases, and review patient information to assess patient condition. Work as part of a team of physicians, nurses, and other health care professionals to manage patient care. Enforce safety rules and ensure careful adherence to physicians' orders. Maintain charts that contain patients' pertinent identification and therapy information. Inspect, clean, test, and maintain respiratory therapy equipment to ensure equipment is functioning safely and efficiently, ordering repairs when necessary. Educate patients and their families about their conditions and teach appropriate disease management techniques, such as breathing exercises and the use of medications and respiratory equipment. Explain treatment procedures to patients to gain cooperation and allay fears. Relay blood analysis results to a physician. Perform pulmonary function and adjust equipment to obtain optimum results in therapy. Perform bronchopulmonary drainage and assist or instruct patients in performance of breathing exercises. Demonstrate respiratory care procedures to trainees and other health care personnel. Teach, train, supervise, and utilize the assistance of students, respiratory therapy technicians, and assistants. Make emergency visits to resolve equipment problems. Use a variety of testing techniques to assist doctors in cardiac and pulmonary research and to diagnose disorders. Conduct tests, such as electrocardiograms (EKGs), stress testing, and lung capacity tests, to evaluate patients' cardiopulmonary functions.

GOE Information—Interest Area: 08. Health Science. **Work Group:** 08.07. Medical Therapy. **Personality Type**—Investigative. Investigative occupations frequently involve working with ideas and require an extensive amount of thinking. These occupations can involve searching for facts and figuring out problems mentally. **Work Values**—Social Service; Co-workers; Achievement; Social Status; Ability Utilization; Authority. **Skills**—Science; Operation Monitoring; Mathematics; Instructing; Active Learning; Reading Comprehension. **Abilities**—*Cognitive:* Speed of Closure; Inductive Reasoning; Problem Sensitivity; Flexibility of Closure; Oral Expression; Written Comprehension. *Psychomotor:* Control Precision; Response Orientation; Manual Dexterity; Arm-Hand Steadiness; Reaction Time; Finger Dexterity. *Physical:* Trunk Strength; Dynamic Strength; Static Strength. *Sensory:* Hearing Sensitivity; Speech Recognition; Auditory Attention; Visual Color Discrimination; Speech Clarity; Far Vision. **General Work Activities**—*Information Input:* Getting Information; Identifying Objects, Actions, and Events; Monitoring Processes, Materials, or Surroundings. *Mental Process:* Making Decisions and Solving Problems; Updating and Using Relevant Knowledge; Organizing, Planning, and Prioritizing. *Work Output:* Documenting or Recording Information; Controlling Machines and Processes; Performing General Physical Activities. *Interacting with Others:* Assisting and Caring for Others; Establishing and Maintaining Interpersonal Relationships; Communicating with Other Workers. **Physical Work Conditions**—Indoors; Disease or Infections; Standing. **Other Job Characteristics**—Need to Be Exact or Accurate; Errors Have Important Consequences.

Experience—Job Zone 3. Previous work-related skill, knowledge, or experience is required. **Job Preparation**—SVP 6.0 to less than 7.0—more than one year and less than four years. **Knowledges**—Medicine and Dentistry; Biology; Psychology; Customer and Personal Service; Therapy and Counseling; Chemistry. **Instructional Program**—Respiratory Therapy/Therapist.

Related SOC Job—29-1126 Respiratory Therapists. **Related OOH Job**—Respiratory Therapists. **Related DOT Job**—076.361-014 Respiratory Therapist.

29-1127.00 Speech-Language Pathologists

- **Education/Training Required: Master's degree**
- **Employed: 94,660**
- **Annual Earnings: $54,880**
- **Growth: 14.6%**
- **Annual Job Openings: 5,000**

Assess and treat persons with speech, language, voice, and fluency disorders. May select alternative communication systems and teach their use. May perform research related to speech and language problems.

Monitor patients' progress and adjust treatments accordingly. Evaluate hearing and speech/language test results and medical or background information to diagnose and plan treatment for speech, language, fluency, voice, and swallowing disorders. Administer hearing or speech and language evaluations, tests, or examinations to patients to collect information on type and degree of impairments, using written and oral tests and special instruments. Record information on the initial evaluation, treatment, progress, and discharge of clients. Develop and implement treatment plans for problems such as stuttering, delayed language, swallowing disorders, and inappropriate pitch or harsh voice problems, based on own assessments and recommendations of physicians, psychologists, or social workers. Develop individual or group programs in schools to deal with speech or language problems. Instruct clients in techniques for more effective communication, including sign language, lip reading, and voice improvement. Teach clients to control or strengthen tongue, jaw, face muscles, and breathing mechanisms. Develop speech exercise programs to reduce disabilities. Consult with and advise educators or medical staff on speech or hearing topics, such as communication strategies or speech and language stimulation. Instruct patients and family members in strategies to cope with or avoid communication-related misunderstandings. Design, develop, and employ alternative diagnostic or communication devices and strategies. Conduct lessons and direct educational or therapeutic games to assist teachers dealing with speech problems. Refer clients to additional medical or educational services if needed. Participate in conferences or training, or publish research results, to share knowledge of new hearing or speech disorder treatment methods or technologies. Communicate with non-speaking students, using sign language or computer technology. Provide communication instruction to dialect speakers or students with limited English proficiency. Use computer applications to identify and assist with communication disabilities.

GOE Information—**Interest Area:** 08. Health Science. **Work Group:** 08.07. Medical Therapy. **Personality Type**—Social. Social occupations frequently involve working with, communicating with, and teaching people. These occupations often involve helping or providing service to others. **Work Values**—Social Service; Authority; Creativity; Achievement; Co-workers; Ability Utilization. **Skills**—Instructing; Learning Strategies; Social Perceptiveness; Speaking; Monitoring; Service Orientation. **Abilities**—*Cognitive:* Flexibility of Closure; Inductive Reasoning; Originality; Fluency of Ideas; Problem Sensitivity; Deductive Reasoning. *Psychomotor:* Finger Dexterity. *Physical:* None met the criteria. *Sensory:* Speech Recognition; Hearing Sensitivity; Auditory Attention; Speech Clarity; Far Vision; Near Vision. **General Work Activities**—*Information Input:* Getting Information; Identifying Objects, Actions, and Events; Monitoring Processes, Materials, or Surroundings. *Mental Process:* Making Decisions and Solving Problems; Organizing, Planning, and Prioritizing; Updating and Using Relevant Knowledge. *Work Output:* Documenting or Recording Information; Interacting With Computers. *Interacting with Others:* Establishing and Maintaining Interpersonal Relationships; Communicating with Other Workers; Performing for or Working with the Public. **Physical Work Conditions**—Indoors; Disease or Infections; Sitting. **Other Job Characteristics**—Need to Be Exact or Accurate.

Experience—Job Zone 5. Extensive skill, knowledge, and experience are needed. **Job Preparation**—SVP 8.0 and above—four years to more than 10 years. **Knowledges**—Therapy and Counseling; Psychology; Education and Training; Sociology and Anthropology; Medicine and Dentistry; English Language. **Instructional Programs**—Audiology/Audiologist and Speech-Language Pathology/Pathologist; Communication Disorders Sciences and Services, Other; Communication Disorders, General; Speech-Language Pathology/ Pathologist.

Related SOC Job—29-1127 Speech-Language Pathologists. **Related OOH Job**—Speech-Language Pathologists. **Related DOT Jobs**—076.101-014 Director, Speech-and-Hearing Clinic; 076.104-010 Voice Pathologist; 076.107-010 Speech Pathologist.

29-1129.99 Therapists, All Other

- **Education/Training Required: No data available**
- **Employed: 9,730**
- **Annual Earnings: $42,070**
- **Growth: 15.0%**
- **Annual Job Openings: 2,000**

All therapists not listed separately.

No task data available.

Note: The Department of Labor has not collected some data for this job, so it has fewer details than the other descriptions.

Related SOC Job—29-1129 Therapists, All Other. **Related OOH Job**—None. **Related DOT Jobs**—076.121-018 Exercise Physiologist; 076.124-010 Manual-Arts Therapist; 076.224-018 Movement Therapist; 076.264-010 Physical-Integration Practitioner; 076.361-010 Corrective Therapist; 079.157-010 Hypnotherapist.

29-1131.00 Veterinarians

- **Education/Training Required: First professional degree**
- **Employed: 47,870**
- **Annual Earnings: $68,910**
- **Growth: 17.4%**
- **Annual Job Openings: 8,000**

Diagnose and treat diseases and dysfunctions of animals. May engage in a particular function, such as research and development, consultation, administration, technical writing, sale or production of commercial products, or rendering of technical services to commercial firms or other organizations. Includes veterinarians who inspect livestock.

Examine animals to detect and determine the nature of diseases or injuries. Treat sick or injured animals by prescribing medication, setting bones, dressing wounds, or performing surgery. Inoculate animals against various diseases such as rabies and distemper. Collect body tissue, feces, blood, urine, or other body fluids for examination and analysis. Operate diagnostic equipment such as radiographic and ultrasound equipment and interpret the resulting images. Advise animal owners regarding sanitary measures, feeding, and general care necessary to promote health of animals. Educate the public about diseases that can be spread from animals to humans. Train and supervise workers who handle and care for animals. Provide care to a wide range of animals or specialize in a particular species, such as horses or exotic birds. Euthanize animals. Establish and conduct quarantine and testing procedures that prevent the spread of diseases to other animals or to humans and that comply with applicable government regulations. Conduct postmortem studies and analyses to determine the causes of animals' deaths. Perform administrative duties such as scheduling appointments, accepting payments from clients, and maintaining business records. Drive mobile clinic vans to farms so that health problems can be treated or prevented. Direct the overall operations of animal hospitals, clinics, or mobile services to farms. Specialize in a particular type of treatment such as dentistry, pathology, nutrition, surgery, microbiology, or internal medicine. Inspect and test horses, sheep, poultry, and other animals to detect the presence of communicable diseases. Research diseases to which animals could be susceptible. Plan and execute animal nutrition and reproduction programs. Inspect animal housing facilities to determine their cleanliness and adequacy. Determine the effects of drug therapies, antibiotics, or new surgical techniques by testing them on animals.

GOE Information—Interest Area: 08. Health Science. Work Group: 08.05. Animal Care. Personality Type—Investigative. Investigative occupations frequently involve working with ideas and require an extensive amount of thinking. These occupations can involve searching for facts and figuring out problems mentally. Work Values—Recognition; Ability Utilization; Responsibility; Achievement; Autonomy; Social Status. Skills—Science; Management of Financial Resources; Reading Comprehension; Judgment and Decision Making; Complex Problem Solving; Management of Personnel Resources. Abilities—Cognitive: Inductive Reasoning; Problem Sensitivity; Deductive Reasoning; Written Comprehension; Mathematical Reasoning; Oral Expression. Psychomotor: Manual Dexterity; Arm-Hand Steadiness; Finger Dexterity; Control Precision; Reaction Time; Multilimb Coordination. Physical: Static Strength; Extent Flexibility; Trunk Strength. Sensory: Visual Color Discrimination; Speech Recognition; Hearing Sensitivity; Far Vision; Speech Clarity; Depth Perception. General Work Activities—Information Input: Monitoring Processes, Materials, or Surroundings; Identifying Objects, Actions, and Events; Getting Information. Mental Process: Making Decisions and Solving Problems; Updating and Using Relevant Knowledge; Analyzing Data or Information. Work Output: Handling and Moving Objects; Documenting or Recording Information; Performing General Physical Activities. Interacting with Others: Assisting and Caring for Others; Performing for or Working with the Public; Establishing and Maintaining Interpersonal Relationships. Physical Work Conditions—Indoors; Noisy; Contaminants; Disease or Infections; Standing; Using Hands on Objects, Tools, or Controls. Other Job Characteristics—Need to Be Exact or Accurate; Errors Have Important Consequences; Repeat Same Tasks.

Experience—Job Zone 5. Extensive skill, knowledge, and experience are needed. Job Preparation—SVP 8.0 and above—four years to more than 10 years. Knowledges—Biology; Medicine and Dentistry; Chemistry; Therapy and Counseling; Sales and Marketing; Customer and Personal Service. Instructional Programs—Comparative and Laboratory Animal Medicine (Cert, MS, PhD); Laboratory Animal Medicine; Large Animal/Food Animal and Equine Surgery and Medicine (Cert, MS, PhD); Small/Companion Animal Surgery and Medicine (Cert, MS, PhD); Theriogenology; Veterinary Anatomy (Cert, MS, PhD); Veterinary Anesthesiology; Veterinary Biomedical and Clinical Sciences, Other (Cert, MS. PhD); Veterinary Dentistry; Veterinary Dermatology; Veterinary Emergency and Critical Care Medicine; Veterinary Infectious Diseases (Cert, MS, PhD); Veterinary Internal Medicine (DVM); Veterinary

Microbiology; Veterinary Microbiology and Immunobiology (Cert, MS, PhD); Veterinary Nutrition; Veterinary Ophthalmology; Veterinary Pathology; Veterinary Pathology and Pathobiology (Cert, MS, PhD); Veterinary Physiology (Cert, MS, PhD); Veterinary Practice; Veterinary Preventive Medicine; Veterinary Preventive Medicine, Epidemiology, and Public Health (Cert, MS, PhD); Veterinary Radiology; Veterinary Residency Programs, Other; Veterinary Sciences/Veterinary Clinical Sciences, General (Cert, MS, PhD); Veterinary Surgery; Veterinary Toxicology; Veterinary Toxicology and Pharmacology (Cert, MS, PhD); Zoological Medicine.

Related SOC Job—29-1131 Veterinarians. Related OOH Job—Veterinarians. Related DOT Jobs—073.061-010 Veterinarian, Laboratory Animal Care; 073.061-014 Veterinary Anatomist; 073.061-018 Veterinary Microbiologist; 073.061-022 Veterinary Epidemiologist; 073.061-026 Veterinary Parasitologist; 073.061-030 Veterinary Pathologist; 073.061-034 Veterinary Pharmacologist; 073.061-038 Veterinary Physiologist; 073.101-010 Veterinarian; 073.101-014 Veterinarian, Poultry; 073.101-018 Zoo Veterinarian; 073.161-010 Veterinary Livestock Inspector; 073.261-010 Veterinary Virus-Serum Inspector; others.

29-1199.99 Health Diagnosing and Treating Practitioners, All Other

- Education/Training Required: No data available
- Employed: 57,880
- Annual Earnings: $57,480
- Growth: 17.4%
- Annual Job Openings: 6,000

All health diagnosing and treating practitioners not listed separately.

No task data available.

Note: The Department of Labor has not collected some data for this job, so it has fewer details than the other descriptions.

Related SOC Job—29-1199 Health Diagnosing and Treating Practitioners, All Other. Related OOH Job—None. Related DOT Jobs—070.101-090 Radiologist; 079.101-014 Doctor, Naturopathic; 079.271-010 Acupuncturist; 079.271-014 Acupressurist.

29-2000 Health Technologists and Technicians

29-2011.00 Medical and Clinical Laboratory Technologists

- Education/Training Required: Bachelor's degree
- Employed: 155,250
- Annual Earnings: $47,710
- Growth: 20.5%
- Annual Job Openings: 14,000

Perform complex medical laboratory tests for diagnosis, treatment, and prevention of disease. May train or supervise staff.

Analyze laboratory findings to check the accuracy of the results. Conduct chemical analysis of body fluids, including blood, urine, and spinal fluid, to determine presence of normal and abnormal components. Operate, calibrate, and maintain equipment used in quantitative and qualitative analysis, such as spectrophotometers, calorimeters, flame photometers, and computer-controlled analyzers. Enter data from analysis of medical tests and clinical results into computer for storage. Analyze samples of biological material for chemical content or reaction. Establish and monitor programs to ensure the accuracy of laboratory results. Set up, clean, and maintain laboratory equipment. Provide technical information about test results to physicians, family members, and researchers. Supervise, train, and direct lab assistants, medical and clinical laboratory technicians and technologists, and other medical laboratory workers engaged in laboratory testing. Develop, standardize, evaluate, and modify procedures, techniques, and tests used in the analysis of specimens and in medical laboratory experiments. Cultivate, isolate, and assist in identifying microbial organisms and perform various tests on these microorganisms. Study blood samples to determine the number of cells and their morphology, as well as the blood group, type, and compatibility for transfusion purposes, using microscopic technique. Obtain, cut, stain, and mount biological material on slides for microscopic study and diagnosis, following standard laboratory procedures. Select and prepare specimen and media for cell culture, using aseptic technique and knowledge of medium components and cell requirements. Conduct medical research under direction of microbiologist or biochemist. Harvest cell cultures at optimum time based on knowledge of cell cycle differences and culture conditions.

GOE Information—Interest Area: 08. Health Science. **Work Group:** 08.06. Medical Technology. **Personality Type—**Investigative. Investigative occupations frequently involve working with ideas and require an extensive amount of thinking. These occupations can involve searching for facts and figuring out problems mentally. **Work Values—**Ability Utilization; Variety; Activity; Achievement; Social Status; Social Service. **Skills—**Equipment Maintenance; Operation Monitoring; Quality Control Analysis; Science; Operation and Control; Repairing. **Abilities—***Cognitive:* Flexibility of Closure; Inductive Reasoning; Problem Sensitivity; Category Flexibility; Oral Comprehension; Perceptual Speed. *Psychomotor:* Arm-Hand Steadiness; Finger Dexterity; Rate Control; Wrist-Finger Speed; Control Precision; Reaction Time. *Physical:* Static Strength; Trunk Strength. *Sensory:* Near Vision; Visual Color Discrimination; Depth Perception; Hearing Sensitivity; Far Vision; Speech Clarity. **General Work Activities—***Information Input:* Identifying Objects, Actions, and Events; Monitoring Processes, Materials, or Surroundings; Inspecting Equipment, Structures, or Materials. *Mental Process:* Updating and Using Relevant Knowledge; Processing Information; Making Decisions and Solving Problems. *Work Output:* Documenting or Recording Information; Handling and Moving Objects; Controlling Machines and Processes. *Interacting with Others:* Establishing and Maintaining Interpersonal Relationships; Communicating with Other Workers; Coordinating the Work and Activities of Others. **Physical Work Conditions—**Indoors; Contaminants; Disease or Infections; Hazardous Conditions; Using Hands on Objects, Tools, or Controls; Repetitive Motions. **Other Job Characteristics—**Need to Be Exact or Accurate; Repeat Same Tasks; Errors Have Important Consequences; Automation; Pace Determined by Speed of Equipment.

Experience—Job Zone 4. A minimum of two to four years of work-related skill, knowledge, or experience is needed. **Job Preparation—**SVP 7.0 to less than 8.0—two years to less than 10 years. **Knowledges—**Biology; Chemistry; Mechanical Devices; Public Safety and Security; Computers and Electronics; Medicine and Dentistry. **Instructional Programs—**Clinical Laboratory Science/Medical Technology/Technologist; Clinical/Medical Laboratory Science and Allied Professions, Other; Cytogenetics/Genetics/Clinical Genetics Technology/Technologists; Cytotechnology/Cytotechnologist; Histologic Technology/Histotechnologist; Renal/Dialysis Technologist/Technician.

Related SOC Job—29-2011 Medical and Clinical Laboratory Technologists. **Related OOH Job—**Clinical Laboratory Technologists and Technicians. **Related DOT Jobs—**078.121-010 Medical Technologist, Teaching Supervisor; 078.161-010 Medical Technologist, Chief; 078.261-010 Biochemistry Technologist; 078.261-014 Microbiology Technologist; 078.261-026 Cytogenetic Technologist; 078.261-030 Histotechnologist; 078.261-038 Medical Technologist; 078.261-046 Immunohematologist; 078.281-010 Cytotechnologist.

29-2012.00 Medical and Clinical Laboratory Technicians

- **Education/Training Required: Associate degree**
- **Employed: 142,330**
- **Annual Earnings: $31,700**
- **Growth: 25.0%**
- **Annual Job Openings: 14,000**

Perform routine medical laboratory tests for the diagnosis, treatment, and prevention of disease. May work under the supervision of a medical technologist.

Conduct chemical analyses of body fluids, such as blood and urine, using microscope or automatic analyzer to detect abnormalities or diseases, and enter findings into computer. Set up, adjust, maintain, and clean medical laboratory equipment. Analyze the results of tests and experiments to ensure conformity to specifications, using special mechanical and electrical devices. Analyze and record test data to issue reports that use charts, graphs and narratives. Conduct blood tests for transfusion purposes and perform blood counts. Perform medical research to further control and cure disease. Obtain specimens, cultivating, isolating, and identifying microorganisms for analysis. Examine cells stained with dye to locate abnormalities. Collect blood or tissue samples from patients, observing principles of asepsis to obtain blood sample. Consult with a pathologist to determine a final diagnosis when abnormal cells are found. Inoculate fertilized eggs, broths, or other bacteriological media with organisms. Cut, stain, and mount tissue samples for examination by pathologists. Supervise and instruct other technicians and laboratory assistants. Prepare standard volumetric solutions and reagents to be combined with samples, following standardized formulas or experimental procedures. Prepare vaccines and serums by standard laboratory methods, testing for virus inactivity and sterility. Test raw materials, processes, and finished products to determine quality and quantity of materials or characteristics of a substance.

GOE Information—Interest Area: 08. Health Science. **Work Group:** 08.06. Medical Technology. **Personality Type—**Realistic. Realistic occupations frequently involve work activities that include practical, hands-on problems and solutions. They often deal with plants; animals; and real-world materials like wood, tools, and machinery. Many of the occupations require working outside and do not involve a lot of paperwork or working closely with others. **Work Values—**Ability Utilization; Co-workers; Activity; Security; Achievement; Social Service. **Skills—**Science; Equipment Maintenance; Troubleshooting; Operation Monitoring; Quality Control Analysis; Operation and Control. **Abilities—***Cognitive:* Flexibility of Closure; Inductive Reasoning; Written Comprehension; Problem Sensitivity; Written

Expression; Memorization. *Psychomotor:* Arm-Hand Steadiness; Finger Dexterity; Control Precision; Rate Control; Reaction Time; Manual Dexterity. *Physical:* Trunk Strength. *Sensory:* Visual Color Discrimination; Near Vision; Far Vision; Depth Perception; Hearing Sensitivity; Speech Clarity. **General Work Activities**—*Information Input:* Monitoring Processes, Materials, or Surroundings; Identifying Objects, Actions, and Events; Inspecting Equipment, Structures, or Materials. *Mental Process:* Updating and Using Relevant Knowledge; Processing Information; Evaluating Information Against Standards. *Work Output:* Documenting or Recording Information; Handling and Moving Objects; Controlling Machines and Processes. *Interacting with Others:* Communicating with Other Workers; Assisting and Caring for Others; Establishing and Maintaining Interpersonal Relationships. **Physical Work Conditions**—Indoors; Disease or Infections; Standing; Walking and Running; Using Hands on Objects, Tools, or Controls. **Other Job Characteristics**—Need to Be Exact or Accurate; Errors Have Important Consequences; Repeat Same Tasks.

Experience—Job Zone 2. Some previous work-related skill, knowledge, or experience may be helpful in these occupations, but usually is not needed. **Job Preparation**—SVP 4.0 to less than 6.0—six months to less than two years. **Knowledges**—Medicine and Dentistry; Therapy and Counseling; Biology; Clerical Practices. **Instructional Programs**—Blood Bank Technology Specialist; Clinical/Medical Laboratory Technician; Clinical/Medical Laboratory Technician/ Assistant (Certificate); Hematology Technology/Technician; Histologic Technician.

Related SOC Job—29-2012 Medical and Clinical Laboratory Technicians. **Related OOH Job**—Clinical Laboratory Technologists and Technicians. **Related DOT Jobs**—078.367-014 Specimen Processor; 078.381-014 Medical-Laboratory Technician; 078.687-010 Laboratory Assistant, Blood and Plasma; 559.361-010 Laboratory Technician, Pharmaceutical.

29-2021.00 Dental Hygienists

- Education/Training Required: Associate degree
- Employed: 161,140
- Annual Earnings: $60,890
- Growth: 43.3%
- Annual Job Openings: 17,000

Clean teeth and examine oral areas, head, and neck for signs of oral disease. May educate patients on oral hygiene, take and develop X rays, or apply fluoride or sealants.

Clean calcareous deposits, accretions, and stains from teeth and beneath margins of gums, using dental instruments. Feel and visually examine gums for sores and signs of disease. Chart conditions of decay and disease for diagnosis and treatment by dentist. Feel lymph nodes under patient's chin to detect swelling or tenderness that could indicate presence of oral cancer. Apply fluorides and other cavity-preventing agents to arrest dental decay. Examine gums, using probes, to locate periodontal recessed gums and signs of gum disease. Expose and develop X-ray film. Provide clinical services and health education to improve and maintain oral health of schoolchildren. Remove excess cement from coronal surfaces of teeth. Make impressions for study casts. Place, carve, and finish amalgam restorations. Administer local anesthetic agents. Conduct dental health clinics for community groups to augment services of dentist. Remove sutures and dressings. Place and remove rubber dams, matrices, and temporary restorations.

GOE Information—Interest Area: 08. Health Science. **Work Group:** 08.03. Dentistry. **Personality Type**—Social. Social occupations frequently involve working with, communicating with, and teaching people. These occupations often involve helping or providing service to others. **Work Values**—Social Service; Co-workers; Security; Social Status; Authority; Ability Utilization. **Skills**—Active Learning; Time Management; Persuasion; Reading Comprehension; Science; Social Perceptiveness. **Abilities**—*Cognitive:* Problem Sensitivity; Flexibility of Closure; Inductive Reasoning; Speed of Closure; Oral Expression; Selective Attention. *Psychomotor:* Control Precision; Finger Dexterity; Manual Dexterity; Arm-Hand Steadiness; Multilimb Coordination. *Physical:* Extent Flexibility. *Sensory:* Near Vision; Visual Color Discrimination; Speech Clarity; Speech Recognition. **General Work Activities**—*Information Input:* Identifying Objects, Actions, and Events; Getting Information; Monitoring Processes, Materials, or Surroundings. *Mental Process:* Updating and Using Relevant Knowledge; Organizing, Planning, and Prioritizing; Making Decisions and Solving Problems. *Work Output:* Documenting or Recording Information; Handling and Moving Objects; Interacting With Computers. *Interacting with Others:* Establishing and Maintaining Interpersonal Relationships; Assisting and Caring for Others; Performing for or Working with the Public. **Physical Work Conditions**—Indoors; Radiation; Disease or Infections; Sitting; Using Hands on Objects, Tools, or Controls; Repetitive Motions. **Other Job Characteristics**—Need to Be Exact or Accurate; Repeat Same Tasks; Errors Have Important Consequences.

Experience—Job Zone 3. Previous work-related skill, knowledge, or experience is required. **Job Preparation**—SVP 6.0 to less than 7.0— more than one year and less than four years. **Knowledges**—Biology; Medicine and Dentistry; Chemistry; Psychology; Sales and Marketing; Therapy and Counseling. **Instructional Program**—Dental Hygiene/Hygienist.

Related SOC Job—29-2021 Dental Hygienists. **Related OOH Job**— Dental Hygienists. **Related DOT Job**—078.361-010 Dental Hygienist.

29-2031.00 Cardiovascular Technologists and Technicians

- Education/Training Required: Associate degree
- Employed: 43,560
- Annual Earnings: $40,420
- Growth: 32.6%
- Annual Job Openings: 5,000

Conduct tests on pulmonary or cardiovascular systems of patients for diagnostic purposes. May conduct or assist in electrocardiograms, cardiac catheterizations, pulmonary-functions, lung capacity, and similar tests.

Monitor patients' blood pressure and heart rate, using electrocardiogram (EKG) equipment, during diagnostic and therapeutic procedures to notify the physician if something appears wrong. Monitor patients' comfort and safety during tests, alerting physicians to abnormalities or changes in patient responses. Explain testing procedures to patient to obtain cooperation and reduce anxiety. Prepare reports of diagnostic procedures for interpretation by physician. Observe gauges, recorder, and video screens of data analysis system during imaging of cardiovascular system. Conduct electrocardiogram (EKG), phonocardiogram, echocardiogram, stress testing, or other cardiovascular tests to record patients' cardiac activity, using specialized electronic test equipment, recording devices, and laboratory instruments. Obtain and record patient identification, medical history, or test results. Prepare and position patients for testing. Attach electrodes to the patients' chests, arms, and legs; connect electrodes to leads from the electrocardiogram (EKG) machine; and operate the EKG machine to obtain a reading. Adjust equipment and controls according to physicians' orders or established protocol. Check, test, and maintain cardiology equipment, making minor repairs when necessary, to ensure proper operation. Supervise and train other cardiology technologists and students. Assist physicians in diagnosis and treatment of cardiac and peripheral vascular treatments, for example, assisting with balloon angioplasties to treat blood vessel blockages. Operate diagnostic imaging equipment to produce contrast-enhanced radiographs of heart and cardiovascular system. Inject contrast medium into patients' blood vessels. Observe ultrasound display screen and listen to signals to record vascular information such as blood pressure, limb volume changes, oxygen saturation, and cerebral circulation. Assess cardiac physiology and calculate valve areas from blood flow velocity measurements. Compare measurements of heart wall thickness and chamber sizes to standard norms to identify abnormalities. Activate fluoroscope and camera to produce images used to guide catheter through cardiovascular system.

GOE Information—Interest Area: 08. Health Science. **Work Group:** 08.06. Medical Technology. **Personality Type—**Investigative. Investigative occupations frequently involve working with ideas and require an extensive amount of thinking. These occupations can involve searching for facts and figuring out problems mentally. **Work Values—**Social Service; Social Status; Recognition; Compensation; Company Policies and Practices; Ability Utilization. **Skills—**Operation Monitoring; Science; Equipment Maintenance; Instructing; Service Orientation; Operation and Control. **Abilities—***Cognitive:* Perceptual Speed; Problem Sensitivity; Number Facility; Speed of Closure; Written Comprehension; Time Sharing. *Psychomotor:* Reaction Time; Arm-Hand Steadiness; Response Orientation; Control Precision; Multilimb Coordination. *Physical:* Static Strength. *Sensory:* Speech Recognition; Hearing Sensitivity; Far Vision; Visual Color Discrimination; Near Vision; Auditory Attention. **General Work Activities—***Information Input:* Monitoring Processes, Materials, or Surroundings; Identifying Objects, Actions, and Events; Inspecting Equipment, Structures, or Materials. *Mental Process:* Updating and Using Relevant Knowledge; Organizing, Planning, and Prioritizing; Making Decisions and Solving Problems. *Work Output:* Handling and Moving Objects; Documenting or Recording Information; Interacting With Computers. *Interacting with Others:* Assisting and Caring for Others; Establishing and Maintaining Interpersonal Relationships; Performing for or Working with the Public. **Physical Work Conditions—**Indoors; Radiation; Disease or Infections; Standing; Walking and Running; Using Hands on Objects, Tools, or Controls. **Other Job Characteristics—**Need to Be Exact or Accurate; Repeat Same Tasks; Errors Have Important Consequences.

Experience—Job Zone 3. Previous work-related skill, knowledge, or experience is required. **Job Preparation—**SVP 6.0 to less than 7.0—more than one year and less than four years. **Knowledges—**Medicine and Dentistry; Customer and Personal Service; Psychology; Physics; Biology; Therapy and Counseling. **Instructional Programs—**Cardiopulmonary Technology/Technologist; Cardiovascular Technology/Technologist; Electrocardiograph Technology/Technician; Perfusion Technology/Perfusionist.

Related SOC Job—29-2031 Cardiovascular Technologists and Technicians. **Related OOH Job—**Cardiovascular Technologists and Technicians. **Related DOT Jobs—**078.161-014 Cardiopulmonary Technologist, Chief; 078.262-010 Pulmonary-Function Technician; 078.264-010 Holter Scanning Technician; 078.362-018 Electrocardiograph Technician; 078.362-030 Cardiopulmonary

Technologist; 078.362-034 Perfusionist; 078.362-050 Special Procedures Technologist, Cardiac Catheterization; 078.362-062 Stress Test Technician; 078.364-014 Echocardiograph Technician; 078.365-010 Cardiac Monitor Technician; 078.367-010 Cardiac Monitor Technician.

29-2032.00 Diagnostic Medical Sonographers

- **Education/Training Required: Associate degree**
- **Employed: 43,590**
- **Annual Earnings: $54,370**
- **Growth: 34.8%**
- **Annual Job Openings: 5,000**

Produce ultrasonic recordings of internal organs for use by physicians.

Decide which images to include, looking for differences between healthy and pathological areas. Observe screen during scan to ensure that image produced is satisfactory for diagnostic purposes, making adjustments to equipment as required. Observe and care for patients throughout examinations to ensure their safety and comfort. Provide sonogram and oral or written summary of technical findings to physician for use in medical diagnosis. Operate ultrasound equipment to produce and record images of the motion, shape, and composition of blood, organs, tissues, and bodily masses such as fluid accumulations. Select appropriate equipment settings and adjust patient positions to obtain the best sites and angles. Determine whether scope of exam should be extended based on findings. Process and code film from procedures and complete appropriate documentation. Obtain and record accurate patient history, including prior test results and information from physical examinations. Prepare patient for exam by explaining procedure, transferring them to ultrasound table, scrubbing skin and applying gel, and positioning them properly. Record and store suitable images, using camera unit connected to the ultrasound equipment. Coordinate work with physicians and other health care team members, including providing assistance during invasive procedures. Maintain records that include patient information; sonographs and interpretations; files of correspondence, publications, and regulations; or quality assurance records such as pathology, biopsy, or post-operative reports. Perform legal and ethical duties, including preparing safety and accident reports, obtaining written consent from patient to perform invasive procedures, and reporting symptoms of abuse and neglect. Supervise and train students and other medical sonographers. Maintain stock and supplies, preparing supplies for special examinations and ordering supplies when necessary. Clean, check, and maintain sonographic equipment, submitting maintenance requests or performing minor repairs as necessary. Perform clerical duties such as scheduling exams and special procedures, keeping records, and archiving computerized images.

GOE Information—Interest Area: 08. Health Science. **Work Group:** 08.06. Medical Technology. **Personality Type—**No data available. **Work Values—**No data available. **Skills—**Operation and Control; Social Perceptiveness; Reading Comprehension; Science; Learning Strategies; Instructing. **Abilities—***Cognitive:* Flexibility of Closure; Problem Sensitivity; Speed of Closure; Perceptual Speed; Inductive Reasoning; Written Expression. *Psychomotor:* Control Precision; Response Orientation; Reaction Time; Manual Dexterity; Wrist-Finger Speed; Multilimb Coordination. *Physical:* Extent Flexibility; Static Strength; Trunk Strength. *Sensory:* Near Vision; Depth Perception; Visual Color Discrimination; Far Vision; Speech Recognition. **General Work Activities—***Information Input:*

Identifying Objects, Actions, and Events; Monitoring Processes, Materials, or Surroundings; Getting Information. *Mental Process:* Organizing, Planning, and Prioritizing; Updating and Using Relevant Knowledge; Making Decisions and Solving Problems. *Work Output:* Handling and Moving Objects; Controlling Machines and Processes; Documenting or Recording Information. *Interacting with Others:* Assisting and Caring for Others; Establishing and Maintaining Interpersonal Relationships; Communicating with Other Workers. **Physical Work Conditions**—Indoors; Cramped Work Space, Awkward Positions; Disease or Infections; Using Hands on Objects, Tools, or Controls; Bending or Twisting the Body; Repetitive Motions. **Other Job Characteristics**—Need to Be Exact or Accurate; Repeat Same Tasks; Errors Have Important Consequences.

Experience—Job Zone 3. Previous work-related skill, knowledge, or experience is required. **Job Preparation**—SVP 6.0 to less than 7.0—more than one year and less than four years. **Knowledges**—Medicine and Dentistry; Biology; Physics; Therapy and Counseling; Education and Training; Clerical Practices. **Instructional Programs**—Allied Health Diagnostic, Intervention, and Treatment Professions, Other; Diagnostic Medical Sonography/Sonographer and Ultrasound Technician.

Related SOC Job—29-2032 Diagnostic Medical Sonographers. **Related OOH Job**—Diagnostic Medical Sonographers. **Related DOT Job**—078.364-010 Ultrasound Technologist.

29-2033.00 Nuclear Medicine Technologists

- **Education/Training Required: Associate degree**
- **Employed: 18,280**
- **Annual Earnings: $59,670**
- **Growth: 21.5%**
- **Annual Job Openings: 2,000**

Prepare, administer, and measure radioactive isotopes in therapeutic, diagnostic, and tracer studies, utilizing a variety of radioisotope equipment. Prepare stock solutions of radioactive materials and calculate doses to be administered by radiologists. Subject patients to radiation. Execute blood volume, red cell survival, and fat absorption studies, following standard laboratory techniques.

Calculate, measure, and record radiation dosage or radiopharmaceuticals received, used, and disposed, using computer and following physician's prescription. Detect and map radiopharmaceuticals in patients' bodies, using a camera to produce photographic or computer images. Explain test procedures and safety precautions to patients and provide them with assistance during test procedures. Administer radiopharmaceuticals or radiation to patients to detect or treat diseases, using radioisotope equipment, under direction of physician. Produce a computer-generated or film image for interpretation by a physician. Process cardiac function studies, using computer. Dispose of radioactive materials and store radiopharmaceuticals, following radiation safety procedures. Record and process results of procedures. Prepare stock radiopharmaceuticals, adhering to safety standards that minimize radiation exposure to workers and patients. Maintain and calibrate radioisotope and laboratory equipment. Gather information on patients' illnesses and medical history to guide the choice of diagnostic procedures for therapy. Measure glandular activity, blood volume, red cell survival, and radioactivity of patient, using scanners, Geiger counters, scintillometers, and other laboratory equipment. Train and supervise student or subordinate nuclear medicine technologists. Position radiation fields, radiation beams, and patient to allow for most effective treatment of

patient's disease, using computer. Add radioactive substances to biological specimens, such as blood, urine, and feces, to determine therapeutic drug or hormone levels. Develop treatment procedures for nuclear medicine treatment programs.

GOE Information—Interest Area: 08. Health Science. **Work Group:** 08.06. Medical Technology. **Personality Type**—Investigative. Investigative occupations frequently involve working with ideas and require an extensive amount of thinking. These occupations can involve searching for facts and figuring out problems mentally. **Work Values**—Social Service; Ability Utilization; Variety; Achievement; Social Status; Co-workers. **Skills**—Science; Operation Monitoring; Operation and Control; Quality Control Analysis; Social Perceptiveness; Service Orientation. **Abilities**—*Cognitive:* Problem Sensitivity; Perceptual Speed; Number Facility; Mathematical Reasoning; Written Comprehension; Oral Comprehension. *Psychomotor:* Arm-Hand Steadiness; Response Orientation; Reaction Time; Finger Dexterity; Control Precision; Manual Dexterity. *Physical:* Trunk Strength; Static Strength. *Sensory:* Visual Color Discrimination; Hearing Sensitivity; Far Vision; Speech Recognition; Depth Perception; Near Vision. **General Work Activities**—*Information Input:* Monitoring Processes, Materials, or Surroundings; Inspecting Equipment, Structures, or Materials; Identifying Objects, Actions, and Events. *Mental Process:* Updating and Using Relevant Knowledge; Organizing, Planning, and Prioritizing. *Work Output:* Handling and Moving Objects; Documenting or Recording Information; Interacting With Computers. *Interacting with Others:* Assisting and Caring for Others; Performing for or Working with the Public; Establishing and Maintaining Interpersonal Relationships. **Physical Work Conditions**—Indoors; Contaminants; Radiation; Disease or Infections; Standing; Using Hands on Objects, Tools, or Controls. **Other Job Characteristics**—Need to Be Exact or Accurate; Errors Have Important Consequences; Repeat Same Tasks.

Experience—Job Zone 3. Previous work-related skill, knowledge, or experience is required. **Job Preparation**—SVP 6.0 to less than 7.0—more than one year and less than four years. **Knowledges**—Medicine and Dentistry; Biology; Physics; Chemistry; Customer and Personal Service; Computers and Electronics. **Instructional Programs**—Nuclear Medical Technology/Technologist; Radiation Protection/Health Physics Technician.

Related SOC Job—29-2033 Nuclear Medicine Technologists. **Related OOH Job**—Nuclear Medicine Technologists. **Related DOT Jobs**—078.131-010 Chief Technologist, Nuclear Medicine; 078.261-034 Medical Radiation Dosimetrist; 078.361-018 Nuclear Medicine Technologist.

29-2034.00 Radiologic Technologists and Technicians

- **Education/Training Required: Associate degree**
- **Employed: 184,580**
- **Annual Earnings: $45,950**
- **Growth: 23.2%**
- **Annual Job Openings: 17,000**

The job openings listed here are shared with 29-2034.01 Radiologic Technologists and 29-2034.02 Radiologic Technicians.

Take X rays and CAT scans or administer nonradioactive materials into patient's bloodstream for diagnostic purposes. Includes technologists who specialize in other modalities, such as computed tomography and magnetic resonance. Includes workers whose primary duties are to demonstrate portions of the human body on X-ray film or fluoroscopic screen.

No task data available.

GOE Information—Interest Area: 08. Health Science. Work Group: 08.06. Medical Technology. Note: The Department of Labor has not collected some data for this job, so it has fewer details than the other descriptions.

Instructional Programs—Allied Health Diagnostic, Intervention, and Treatment Professions, Other; Medical Radiologic Technology/Science Radiation Therapist; Radiologic Technology/Science Radiographer.

Related SOC Job—29-2034 Radiologic Technologists and Technicians. Related OOH Job—Radiologic Technologists and Technicians. Related DOT Job—No data available.

29-2034.01 Radiologic Technologists

- **Education/Training Required: Associate degree**
- **Employed: 184,580**
- **Annual Earnings: $45,950**
- **Growth: 23.2%**
- **Annual Job Openings: 17,000**

The job openings listed here are shared with 29-2034.00 Radiologic Technologists and Technicians and 29-2034.02 Radiologic Technicians.

Take X rays and Computerized Axial Tomography (CAT or CT) scans or administer nonradioactive materials into patient's bloodstream for diagnostic purposes. Includes technologists who specialize in other modalities, such as computed tomography, ultrasound, and magnetic resonance.

Review and evaluate developed X rays, videotape, or computer-generated information to determine if images are satisfactory for diagnostic purposes. Use radiation safety measures and protection devices to comply with government regulations and to ensure safety of patients and staff. Explain procedures and observe patients to ensure safety and comfort during scan. Operate or oversee operation of radiologic and magnetic imaging equipment to produce images of the body for diagnostic purposes. Position and immobilize patient on examining table. Position imaging equipment and adjust controls to set exposure time and distance according to specification of examination. Key commands and data into computer to document and specify scan sequences, adjust transmitters and receivers, or photograph certain images. Monitor video display of area being scanned and adjust density or contrast to improve picture quality. Monitor patients' conditions and reactions, reporting abnormal signs to physician. Prepare and administer oral or injected contrast media to patients. Set up examination rooms, ensuring that all necessary equipment is ready. Take thorough and accurate patient medical histories. Remove and process film. Record, process, and maintain patient data and treatment records and prepare reports. Coordinate work with clerical personnel or other technologists. Demonstrate new equipment, procedures, and techniques to staff and provide technical assistance. Provide assistance in dressing or changing seriously ill, injured, or disabled patients. Move ultrasound scanner over patient's body and watch pattern produced on video screen. Measure thickness of section to be radiographed, using instruments similar to measuring tapes. Operate fluoroscope to aid physician to view and guide wire or catheter through blood vessels to area of interest. Assign duties to radiologic staff to maintain patient flows and achieve production goals. Collaborate with other medical team members, such as physicians and nurses, to conduct angiography or special vascular procedures. Perform administrative duties such as developing departmental operating budget, coordinating purchases of supplies and equipment, and preparing work schedules.

GOE Information—Interest Area: 08. Health Science. Work Group: 08.06. Medical Technology. Personality Type—Realistic. Realistic occupations frequently involve work activities that include practical, hands-on problems and solutions. They often deal with plants; animals; and real-world materials like wood, tools, and machinery. Many of the occupations require working outside and do not involve a lot of paperwork or working closely with others. Work Values—Social Service; Ability Utilization; Authority; Co-workers; Security; Achievement. Skills—Operation Monitoring; Social Perceptiveness; Instructing; Reading Comprehension; Service Orientation; Active Listening. Abilities—*Cognitive:* Speed of Closure; Flexibility of Closure; Perceptual Speed; Memorization; Inductive Reasoning; Problem Sensitivity. *Psychomotor:* Rate Control; Control Precision; Reaction Time; Arm-Hand Steadiness; Finger Dexterity; Multilimb Coordination. *Physical:* Static Strength; Extent Flexibility; Trunk Strength. *Sensory:* Depth Perception; Far Vision; Visual Color Discrimination; Near Vision; Hearing Sensitivity; Speech Recognition. General Work Activities—*Information Input:* Identifying Objects, Actions, and Events; Monitoring Processes, Materials, or Surroundings; Getting Information. *Mental Process:* Updating and Using Relevant Knowledge; Making Decisions and Solving Problems; Processing Information. *Work Output:* Handling and Moving Objects; Performing General Physical Activities; Controlling Machines and Processes. *Interacting with Others:* Assisting and Caring for Others; Performing for or Working with the Public; Establishing and Maintaining Interpersonal Relationships. Physical Work Conditions—Indoors; Disease or Infections; Standing; Walking and Running; Using Hands on Objects, Tools, or Controls; Repetitive Motions. Other Job Characteristics—Need to Be Exact or Accurate; Repeat Same Tasks; Errors Have Important Consequences.

Experience—Job Zone 3. Previous work-related skill, knowledge, or experience is required. Job Preparation—SVP 6.0 to less than 7.0—more than one year and less than four years. Knowledges—Medicine and Dentistry; Biology; Physics; Psychology; Chemistry; Customer and Personal Service. Instructional Programs—Allied Health Diagnostic, Intervention, and Treatment Professions, Other; Medical Radiologic Technology/Science Radiation Therapist; Radiologic Technology/Science Radiographer.

Related SOC Job—29-2034 Radiologic Technologists and Technicians. Related OOH Job—Radiologic Technologists and Technicians. Related DOT Jobs—078.162-010 Radiologic Technologist, Chief; 078.362-026 Radiologic Technologist; 078.362-046 Special Procedures Technologist, Angiogram; 078.362-054 Special Procedures Technologist, CT Scan; 078.362-058 Special Procedures Technologist, Magnetic Resonance Imaging (MRI); 078.364-010 Ultrasound Technologist.

29-2034.02 Radiologic Technicians

- **Education/Training Required: Associate degree**
- **Employed: 184,580**
- **Annual Earnings: $45,950**
- **Growth: 23.2%**
- **Annual Job Openings: 17,000**

The job openings listed here are shared with 29-2034.00 Radiologic Technologists and Technicians and 29-2034.01 Radiologic Technologists.

Maintain and use equipment and supplies necessary to demonstrate portions the human body on X-ray film or fluoroscopic screen for diagnostic purposes.

Use beam-restrictive devices and patient-shielding techniques to minimize radiation exposure to patient and staff. Position X-ray equipment and adjust controls to set exposure factors, such as time and distance. Position patient on examining table and set up and adjust equipment to obtain optimum view of specific body area as requested by physician. Determine patients' X-ray needs by reading requests or instructions from physicians. Make exposures necessary for the requested procedures, rejecting and repeating work that does not meet established standards. Process exposed radiographs, using film processors or computer-generated methods. Explain procedures to patients to reduce anxieties and obtain cooperation. Perform procedures such as linear tomography; mammography; sonograms; joint and cyst aspirations; routine contrast studies; routine fluoroscopy; and examinations of the head, trunk, and extremities under supervision of physician. Prepare and set up X-ray room for patient. Assure that sterile supplies, contrast materials, catheters, and other required equipment are present and in working order, requisitioning materials as necessary. Maintain records of patients examined, examinations performed, views taken, and technical factors used. Provide assistance to physicians or other technologists in the performance of more complex procedures. Monitor equipment operation and report malfunctioning equipment to supervisor. Provide students and other technologists with suggestions of additional views, alternate positioning, or improved techniques to ensure the images produced are of the highest quality. Coordinate work of other technicians or technologists when procedures require more than one person. Assist with on-the-job training of new employees and students and provide input to supervisors regarding training performance. Maintain a current file of examination protocols. Operate mobile X-ray equipment in operating room, in emergency room, or at patient's bedside. Provide assistance in radiopharmaceutical administration, monitoring patients' vital signs and notifying the radiologist of any relevant changes.

GOE Information—Interest Area: 08. Health Science. Work Group: 08.06. Medical Technology. Personality Type—Realistic. Realistic occupations frequently involve work activities that include practical, hands-on problems and solutions. They often deal with plants; animals; and real-world materials like wood, tools, and machinery. Many of the occupations require working outside and do not involve a lot of paperwork or working closely with others. Work Values—Social Service; Co-workers; Moral Values; Security. Skills—Science; Operation Monitoring; Operation and Control; Service Orientation; Equipment Selection; Negotiation. Abilities—*Cognitive:* Time Sharing; Oral Comprehension; Flexibility of Closure; Problem Sensitivity; Written Comprehension; Oral Expression. *Psychomotor:* Control Precision; Arm-Hand Steadiness; Reaction Time; Multilimb Coordination; Manual Dexterity. *Physical:* Extent Flexibility; Static Strength; Gross Body Coordination; Stamina; Trunk Strength. *Sensory:* Depth Perception; Near Vision; Speech Recognition. General Work Activities—*Information Input:* Monitoring Processes, Materials, or Surroundings; Getting Information; Identifying Objects, Actions, and Events. *Mental Process:* Updating and Using Relevant Knowledge; Making Decisions and Solving Problems; Processing Information. *Work Output:* Handling and Moving Objects; Controlling Machines and Processes; Performing General Physical Activities. *Interacting with Others:* Assisting and Caring for Others; Establishing and Maintaining Interpersonal Relationships; Performing for or Working with the Public. Physical Work Conditions—Indoors; Radiation; Disease or Infections; Standing; Walking and Running; Using Hands on Objects, Tools, or Controls. Other Job Characteristics—Need to Be Exact or Accurate; Repeat Same Tasks; Errors Have Important Consequences; Automation.

Experience—Job Zone 3. Previous work-related skill, knowledge, or experience is required. Job Preparation—SVP 6.0 to less than 7.0— more than one year and less than four years. Knowledges—Medicine and Dentistry; Clerical Practices; Psychology; Physics; Biology; Chemistry. Instructional Programs—Allied Health Diagnostic, Intervention, and Treatment Professions, Other; Medical Radiologic Technology/Science Radiation Therapist; Radiologic Technology/ Science Radiographer.

Related SOC Job—29-2034 Radiologic Technologists and Technicians. Related OOH Job—Radiologic Technologists and Technicians. Related DOT Job—078.362-026 Radiologic Technologist.

29-2041.00 Emergency Medical Technicians and Paramedics

- **Education/Training Required: Postsecondary vocational training**
- **Employed: 196,880**
- **Annual Earnings: $26,080**
- **Growth: 27.3%**
- **Annual Job Openings: 21,000**

Assess injuries, administer emergency medical care, and extricate trapped individuals. Transport injured or sick persons to medical facilities.

Administer first-aid treatment and life-support care to sick or injured persons in prehospital setting. Operate equipment such as electrocardiograms (EKGs), external defibrillators, and bag-valve mask resuscitators in advanced life-support environments. Assess nature and extent of illness or injury to establish and prioritize medical procedures. Maintain vehicles and medical and communication equipment and replenish first-aid equipment and supplies. Observe, record, and report to physician the patient's condition or injury, the treatment provided, and reactions to drugs and treatment. Perform emergency diagnostic and treatment procedures, such as stomach suction, airway management, or heart monitoring, during ambulance ride. Administer drugs, orally or by injection, and perform intravenous procedures under a physician's direction. Comfort and reassure patients. Coordinate work with other emergency medical team members and police and fire department personnel. Communicate with dispatchers and treatment center personnel to provide information about situation, to arrange reception of victims, and to receive instructions for further treatment. Immobilize patient for placement on stretcher and ambulance transport, using backboard or other spinal immobilization device. Decontaminate ambulance interior following treatment of patient with infectious disease and report case to proper authorities. Drive mobile intensive care unit to specified location, following instructions from emergency medical dispatcher. Coordinate with treatment center personnel to obtain patients' vital statistics and medical history, to determine the circumstances of the emergency, and to administer emergency treatment.

GOE Information—Interest Area: 12. Law and Public Safety. Work Group: 12.06. Emergency Responding. Personality Type—Social. Social occupations frequently involve working with, communicating with, and teaching people. These occupations often involve helping or providing service to others. Work Values—Social Service; Achievement; Co-workers; Variety; Ability Utilization; Social Status. Skills—Equipment Maintenance; Operation Monitoring; Service Orientation; Social Perceptiveness; Operation and Control; Coordination. Abilities—*Cognitive:* Speed of Closure; Spatial Orientation; Time Sharing; Problem Sensitivity; Flexibility of Closure; Perceptual Speed. *Psychomotor:* Reaction Time; Rate Control;

Response Orientation; Manual Dexterity; Speed of Limb Movement; Control Precision. *Physical:* Stamina; Extent Flexibility; Static Strength; Explosive Strength; Gross Body Equilibrium; Gross Body Coordination. *Sensory:* Glare Sensitivity; Night Vision; Peripheral Vision; Auditory Attention; Hearing Sensitivity; Depth Perception. **General Work Activities**—*Information Input:* Identifying Objects, Actions, and Events; Monitoring Processes, Materials, or Surroundings; Getting Information. *Mental Process:* Making Decisions and Solving Problems; Updating and Using Relevant Knowledge; Processing Information. *Work Output:* Performing General Physical Activities; Handling and Moving Objects; Documenting or Recording Information. *Interacting with Others:* Assisting and Caring for Others; Performing for or Working with the Public; Establishing and Maintaining Interpersonal Relationships. **Physical Work Conditions**—Outdoors; Noisy; Very Bright or Dim Lighting; Contaminants; Cramped Work Space, Awkward Positions; Disease or Infections. **Other Job Characteristics**—Errors Have Important Consequences; Need to Be Exact or Accurate; Repeat Same Tasks.

Experience—Job Zone 2. Some previous work-related skill, knowledge, or experience may be helpful in these occupations, but usually is not needed. **Job Preparation**—SVP 4.0 to less than 6.0—six months to less than two years. **Knowledges**—Medicine and Dentistry; Therapy and Counseling; Customer and Personal Service; Chemistry; Psychology; Biology. **Instructional Programs**—Emergency Medical Technology/Technician (Ambulance); Emergency Medical Technology/Technician (Paramedic).

Related SOC Job—29-2041 Emergency Medical Technicians and Paramedics. **Related OOH Job**—Emergency Medical Technicians and Paramedics. **Related DOT Jobs**—079.364-026 Paramedic; 079.374-010 Emergency Medical Technician.

29-2051.00 Dietetic Technicians

- **Education/Training Required: Moderate-term on-the-job training**
- **Employed: 23,780**
- **Annual Earnings: $23,470**
- **Growth: 19.1%**
- **Annual Job Openings: 3,000**

Assist dietitians in the provision of food service and nutritional programs. Under the supervision of dietitians, may plan and produce meals based on established guidelines, teach principles of food and nutrition, or counsel individuals.

Observe patient food intake and report progress and dietary problems to dietician. Prepare a major meal, following recipes and determining group food quantities. Analyze menus and recipes, standardize recipes, and test new products. Supervise food production and service or assist dietitians and nutritionists in food service supervision and planning. Obtain and evaluate dietary histories of individuals to plan nutritional programs. Plan menus and diets or guide individuals and families in food selection, preparation, and menu planning based upon nutritional needs and established guidelines. Determine food and beverage costs and assist in implementing cost control procedures. Develop job specifications, job descriptions, and work schedules. Select, schedule, and conduct orientation and in-service education programs. Provide dietitians with assistance researching food, nutrition, and food service systems. Deliver speeches on diet, nutrition, and health to promote healthy eating habits and illness prevention and treatment. Refer patients to other relevant services to provide continuity of care.

GOE Information—**Interest Area:** 08. Health Science. **Work Group:** 08.09. Health Protection and Promotion. **Personality Type**—Social. Social occupations frequently involve working with, communicating with, and teaching people. These occupations often involve helping or providing service to others. **Work Values**—Social Service; Co-workers; Working Conditions; Authority; Variety; Supervision, Technical. **Skills**—Social Perceptiveness. **Abilities**—*Cognitive:* Oral Expression; Fluency of Ideas; Category Flexibility; Deductive Reasoning; Written Expression; Originality. *Psychomotor:* None met the criteria. *Physical:* None met the criteria. *Sensory:* Speech Clarity; Speech Recognition. **General Work Activities**—*Information Input:* Identifying Objects, Actions, and Events; Getting Information; Inspecting Equipment, Structures, or Materials. *Mental Process:* Organizing, Planning, and Prioritizing; Making Decisions and Solving Problems; Evaluating Information Against Standards. *Work Output:* Handling and Moving Objects; Performing General Physical Activities; Controlling Machines and Processes. *Interacting with Others:* Establishing and Maintaining Interpersonal Relationships; Communicating with Other Workers; Assisting and Caring for Others. **Physical Work Conditions**—Indoors; Disease or Infections; Minor Burns, Cuts, Bites, or Stings; Standing; Walking and Running; Repetitive Motions. **Other Job Characteristics**—Need to Be Exact or Accurate; Repeat Same Tasks.

Experience—Job Zone 3. Previous work-related skill, knowledge, or experience is required. **Job Preparation**—SVP 6.0 to less than 7.0—more than one year and less than four years. **Knowledges**—Food Production; Medicine and Dentistry. **Instructional Programs**—Dietitian Assistant; Dietetic Technician (DTR); Dietetics/Dietician (RD); Foods, Nutrition, and Wellness Studies, General; Nutrition Sciences.

Related SOC Job—29-2051 Dietetic Technicians. **Related OOH Job**—Dietetic Technicians. **Related DOT Job**—077.124-010 Dietetic Technician.

29-2052.00 Pharmacy Technicians

- **Education/Training Required: Moderate-term on-the-job training**
- **Employed: 266,790**
- **Annual Earnings: $24,390**
- **Growth: 28.6%**
- **Annual Job Openings: 35,000**

Prepare medications under the direction of a pharmacist. May measure, mix, count out, label, and record amounts and dosages of medications.

Receive written prescription or refill requests and verify that information is complete and accurate. Maintain proper storage and security conditions for drugs. Answer telephones, responding to questions or requests. Fill bottles with prescribed medications and type and affix labels. Assist customers by answering simple questions, locating items, or referring them to the pharmacist for medication information. Price and file prescriptions that have been filled. Clean and help maintain equipment and work areas and sterilize glassware according to prescribed methods. Establish and maintain patient profiles, including lists of medications taken by individual patients. Order, label, and count stock of medications, chemicals, and supplies and enter inventory data into computer. Receive and store incoming supplies, verify quantities against invoices, and inform supervisors of stock needs and shortages. Transfer medication from vials to the appropriate number of sterile disposable syringes, using aseptic techniques. Under pharmacist supervision, add measured drugs or nutrients to intravenous solutions under sterile conditions to prepare intravenous (IV) packs. Supply and monitor robotic machines that dispense medicine into containers and label the containers. Prepare and process medical insurance claim forms and records. Mix pharmaceutical preparations according to written prescriptions. Operate cash registers to accept payment from customers. Compute charges for medication and equipment dispensed to hospital patients and enter data in computer. Deliver medications and pharmaceutical supplies to patients, nursing stations, or surgery. Price stock and mark items for sale. Maintain and merchandise home health-care products and services.

GOE Information—Interest Area: 08. Health Science. Work Group: 08.02. Medicine and Surgery. Personality Type—Conventional. Conventional occupations frequently involve following set procedures and routines. These occupations can include working with data and details more than with ideas. Usually there is a clear line of authority to follow. Work Values—Working Conditions; Social Service; Co-workers; Activity; Security. Skills—Service Orientation; Active Listening; Instructing; Mathematics; Speaking; Active Learning. Abilities—*Cognitive:* Information Ordering; Oral Expression; Oral Comprehension. *Psychomotor:* Arm-Hand Steadiness. *Physical:* Extent Flexibility; Trunk Strength. *Sensory:* Near Vision; Speech Recognition. General Work Activities—*Information Input:* Getting Information; Identifying Objects, Actions, and Events; Monitoring Processes, Materials, or Surroundings. *Mental Process:* Organizing, Planning, and Prioritizing; Making Decisions and Solving Problems; Processing Information. *Work Output:* Handling and Moving Objects; Interacting With Computers. *Interacting with Others:* Establishing and Maintaining Interpersonal Relationships; Performing for or Working with the Public; Communicating with Other Workers. Physical Work Conditions—Indoors; Standing; Using Hands on Objects, Tools, or Controls; Repetitive Motions. Other Job Characteristics—Need to Be Exact or Accurate; Repeat Same Tasks.

Experience—Job Zone 2. Some previous work-related skill, knowledge, or experience may be helpful in these occupations, but usually is not needed. Job Preparation—SVP 4.0 to less than 6.0—six months to less than two years. Knowledges—Medicine and Dentistry; Chemistry; Customer and Personal Service; Mathematics; Clerical Practices; Computers and Electronics. Instructional Program—Pharmacy Technician.

Related SOC Job—29-2052 Pharmacy Technicians. Related OOH Job—Pharmacy Technicians. Related DOT Jobs—074.381-010 Pharmacist Assistant; 074.382-010 Pharmacy Technician.

29-2053.00 Psychiatric Technicians

- Education/Training Required: Moderate-term on-the-job training
- Employed: 62,040
- Annual Earnings: $26,770
- Growth: 3.2%
- Annual Job Openings: 6,000

Care for mentally impaired or emotionally disturbed individuals, following physician instructions and hospital procedures. Monitor patients' physical and emotional well-being and report to medical staff. May participate in rehabilitation and treatment programs, help with personal hygiene, and administer oral medications and hypodermic injections.

Monitor patients' physical and emotional well-being and report unusual behavior or physical ailments to medical staff. Provide nursing, psychiatric, and personal care to mentally ill, emotionally disturbed, or mentally retarded patients. Observe and influence patients' behavior, communicating and interacting with them and teaching, counseling, and befriending them. Take and record measures of patients' physical condition, using devices such as thermometers and blood pressure gauges. Encourage patients to develop work skills and to participate in social, recreational, and other therapeutic activities that enhance interpersonal skills and develop social relationships. Collaborate with or assist doctors, psychologists, or rehabilitation therapists in working with mentally ill, emotionally disturbed, or developmentally disabled patients to treat patients, rehabilitate them, and return them to the community. Develop and teach strategies to promote client wellness and independence. Restrain violent, potentially violent, or suicidal patients by verbal or physical means as required. Aid patients in performing tasks such as bathing and keeping beds, clothing, and living areas clean. Administer oral medications and hypodermic injections, following physician's prescriptions and hospital procedures. Issue medications from dispensary and maintain records in accordance with specified procedures. Interview new patients to complete admission forms, to assess their mental health status, and to obtain their mental health and treatment history. Lead prescribed individual or group therapy sessions as part of specific therapeutic procedures. Contact patients' relatives to arrange family conferences.

GOE Information—Interest Area: 08. Health Science. Work Group: 08.08. Patient Care and Assistance. Personality Type—Social. Social occupations frequently involve working with, communicating with, and teaching people. These occupations often involve helping or providing service to others. Work Values—Social Service; Co-workers; Supervision, Human Relations; Security; Company Policies and Practices; Advancement. Skills—Social Perceptiveness; Service Orientation; Writing; Active Listening; Learning Strategies; Instructing. Abilities—*Cognitive:* Problem Sensitivity; Oral Expression; Originality; Oral Comprehension; Selective Attention; Perceptual Speed. *Psychomotor:* Response Orientation; Speed of Limb Movement; Reaction Time; Multilimb Coordination; Arm-Hand Steadiness. *Physical:* Explosive Strength; Gross Body Coordination; Stamina; Static Strength; Dynamic Strength; Extent Flexibility. *Sensory:* Speech Recognition; Visual Color Discrimination; Hearing Sensitivity; Speech Clarity. General Work Activities—*Information Input:* Identifying Objects, Actions, and Events; Monitoring Processes, Materials, or Surroundings; Getting Information. *Mental Process:* Organizing, Planning, and Prioritizing; Updating and Using Relevant Knowledge; Making Decisions and Solving Problems. *Work Output:* Documenting or Recording Information; Performing General Physical Activities; Handling and Moving Objects. *Interacting with Others:* Resolving Conflicts and Negotiating with Others; Establishing and Maintaining Interpersonal Relationships; Communicating with Other Workers. Physical Work Conditions—Indoors; Noisy; Contaminants; Disease or Infections; Standing; Bending or Twisting the Body. Other Job Characteristics—Need to Be Exact or Accurate; Repeat Same Tasks; Errors Have Important Consequences.

Experience—Job Zone 3. Previous work-related skill, knowledge, or experience is required. Job Preparation—SVP 6.0 to less than 7.0—more than one year and less than four years. Knowledges—Psychology; Therapy and Counseling; Sociology and Anthropology; Medicine and Dentistry; Public Safety and Security; Therapy and Counseling. Instructional Program—Psychiatric/Mental Health Services Technician.

Related SOC Job—29-2053 Psychiatric Technicians. Related OOH Job—Psychiatric Technicians. Related DOT Job—079.374-026 Psychiatric Technician.

29-2054.00 Respiratory Therapy Technicians

- **Education/Training Required:** Postsecondary vocational training
- **Employed:** 22,060
- **Annual Earnings:** $38,200
- **Growth:** 3.3%
- **Annual Job Openings:** 2,000

Provide specific, well-defined respiratory care procedures under the direction of respiratory therapists and physicians.

Use ventilators and various oxygen devices and aerosol and breathing treatments in the provision of respiratory therapy. Work with patients in areas such as the emergency room, neonatal or pediatric intensive care, and surgical intensive care, treating conditions including emphysema, chronic bronchitis, asthma, cystic fibrosis, and pneumonia. Read and evaluate physicians' orders and patients' chart information to determine patients' condition and treatment protocols. Keep records of patients' therapy, completing all necessary forms. Set equipment controls to regulate the flow of oxygen, gases, mists, or aerosols. Assess patients' response to treatments and modify treatments according to protocol if necessary. Provide respiratory care involving the application of well-defined therapeutic techniques under the supervision of a respiratory therapist and a physician. Prepare and test devices such as mechanical ventilators, therapeutic gas administration apparatus, environmental control systems, aerosol generators, and electrocardiogram (EKG) machines. Monitor patients during treatment and report any unusual reactions to the respiratory therapist. Explain treatment procedures to patients. Clean, sterilize, check, and maintain respiratory therapy equipment. Perform diagnostic procedures to assess the severity of respiratory dysfunction in patients. Follow and enforce safety rules applying to equipment. Administer breathing and oxygen procedures such as intermittent positive pressure breathing treatments, ultrasonic nebulizer treatments, and incentive spirometer treatments. Recommend and review bedside procedures, X rays, and laboratory tests. Interview and examine patients to collect clinical data. Teach patients how to use respiratory equipment at home. Teach or oversee other workers who provide respiratory care services.

GOE Information—Interest Area: 08. Health Science. **Work Group:** 08.07. Medical Therapy. **Personality Type—**No data available. **Work Values—**No data available. **Skills—**Operation Monitoring; Operation and Control; Troubleshooting; Equipment Maintenance; Time Management; Technology Design. **Abilities—***Cognitive:* Perceptual Speed; Speed of Closure; Problem Sensitivity; Flexibility of Closure; Inductive Reasoning; Time Sharing. *Psychomotor:* Reaction Time; Response Orientation; Control Precision; Arm-Hand Steadiness; Manual Dexterity; Finger Dexterity. *Physical:* Extent Flexibility; Stamina; Static Strength; Gross Body Coordination; Trunk Strength. *Sensory:* Auditory Attention; Hearing Sensitivity; Visual Color Discrimination; Speech Recognition; Speech Clarity; Near Vision. **General Work Activities—***Information Input:* Monitoring Processes, Materials, or Surroundings; Identifying Objects, Actions, and Events; Inspecting Equipment, Structures, or Materials. *Mental Process:* Making Decisions and Solving Problems; Updating and Using Relevant Knowledge; Processing Information. *Work Output:* Controlling Machines and Processes; Handling and Moving Objects; Documenting or Recording Information. *Interacting with Others:* Assisting and Caring for Others; Establishing and Maintaining Interpersonal Relationships; Communicating with Other Workers. **Physical Work Conditions—**Indoors; Contaminants; Disease or Infections; Standing; Walking and Running; Using Hands on Objects, Tools, or Controls. **Other Job Characteristics—**Errors Have Important Consequences; Need to Be Exact or Accurate; Repeat Same Tasks.

Experience—Job Zone 3. Previous work-related skill, knowledge, or experience is required. **Job Preparation—**SVP 6.0 to less than 7.0—more than one year and less than four years. **Knowledges—**Medicine and Dentistry; Psychology; Biology; Chemistry; Physics; Customer and Personal Service. **Instructional Programs—**Respiratory Therapy Technician; Respiratory Therapy/Therapist.

Related SOC Job—29-2054 Respiratory Therapy Technicians. **Related OOH Job—**Respiratory Therapists. **Related DOT Job—**No data available.

29-2055.00 Surgical Technologists

- **Education/Training Required:** Postsecondary vocational training
- **Employed:** 83,680
- **Annual Earnings:** $34,830
- **Growth:** 29.5%
- **Annual Job Openings:** 12,000

Assist in operations under the supervision of surgeons, registered nurses, or other surgical personnel. May help set up operating room; prepare and transport patients for surgery; adjust lights and equipment; pass instruments and other supplies to surgeons and surgeon's assistants; hold retractors; cut sutures; and help count sponges, needles, supplies, and instruments.

Count sponges, needles, and instruments before and after operation. Hand instruments and supplies to surgeons and surgeons' assistants, hold retractors and cut sutures, and perform other tasks as directed by surgeon during operation. Scrub arms and hands and assist the surgical team in scrubbing and putting on gloves, masks, and surgical clothing. Position patients on the operating table and cover them with sterile surgical drapes to prevent exposure. Provide technical assistance to surgeons, surgical nurses, and anesthesiologists. Wash and sterilize equipment, using germicides and sterilizers. Prepare, care for, and dispose of tissue specimens taken for laboratory analysis. Clean and restock the operating room, placing equipment and supplies and arranging instruments according to instruction. Prepare dressings or bandages and apply or assist with their application following surgery. Operate, assemble, adjust, or monitor sterilizers, lights, suction machines, and diagnostic equipment to ensure proper operation. Monitor and continually assess operating room conditions, including patient and surgical team needs. Observe patients' vital signs to assess physical condition. Maintain supply of fluids, such as plasma, saline, blood, and glucose, for use during operations. Maintain files and records of surgical procedures.

GOE Information—Interest Area: 08. Health Science. **Work Group:** 08.02. Medicine and Surgery. **Personality Type—**Realistic. Realistic occupations frequently involve work activities that include practical, hands-on problems and solutions. They often deal with plants; animals; and real-world materials like wood, tools, and machinery. Many of the occupations require working outside and do not involve a lot of paperwork or working closely with others. **Work Values—**Social Service; Security; Supervision, Human Relations; Co-workers; Company Policies and Practices; Moral Values. **Skills—**Troubleshooting; Equipment Selection; Instructing; Operation Monitoring; Science; Reading Comprehension. **Abilities—***Cognitive:* Time Sharing; Problem Sensitivity; Selective Attention; Spatial

Orientation; Speed of Closure; Written Expression. *Psychomotor:* Arm-Hand Steadiness; Response Orientation; Manual Dexterity; Reaction Time; Finger Dexterity; Control Precision. *Physical:* Static Strength; Gross Body Coordination; Trunk Strength. *Sensory:* Speech Recognition; Near Vision; Auditory Attention; Visual Color Discrimination; Depth Perception; Speech Clarity. **General Work Activities**—*Information Input:* Monitoring Processes, Materials, or Surroundings; Identifying Objects, Actions, and Events; Getting Information. *Mental Process:* Updating and Using Relevant Knowledge; Making Decisions and Solving Problems; Organizing, Planning, and Prioritizing. *Work Output:* Handling and Moving Objects; Performing General Physical Activities; Repairing and Maintaining Mechanical Equipment. *Interacting with Others:* Assisting and Caring for Others; Establishing and Maintaining Interpersonal Relationships; Communicating with Other Workers. **Physical Work Conditions**—Indoors; Contaminants; Disease or Infections; Hazardous Conditions; Standing; Using Hands on Objects, Tools, or Controls. **Other Job Characteristics**—Need to Be Exact or Accurate; Errors Have Important Consequences.

Experience—Job Zone 3. Previous work-related skill, knowledge, or experience is required. **Job Preparation**—SVP 6.0 to less than 7.0— more than one year and less than four years. **Knowledges**—Medicine and Dentistry; Chemistry; Philosophy and Theology; Psychology; Customer and Personal Service; Therapy and Counseling. **Instructional Programs**—Pathology/Pathologist Assistant ; Surgical Technology/Technologist.

Related SOC Job—29-2055 Surgical Technologists. **Related OOH Job**—Surgical Technologists. **Related DOT Job**—079.374-022 Surgical Technician.

29-2056.00 Veterinary Technologists and Technicians

- **Education/Training Required: Associate degree**
- **Employed: 63,860**
- **Annual Earnings: $25,670**
- **Growth: 35.3%**
- **Annual Job Openings: 9,000**

Perform medical tests in a laboratory environment for use in the treatment and diagnosis of diseases in animals. Prepare vaccines and serums for prevention of diseases. Prepare tissue samples; take blood samples; and execute laboratory tests, such as urinalysis and blood counts. Clean and sterilize instruments and materials and maintain equipment and machines.

Administer anesthesia to animals, under the direction of a veterinarian, and monitor animals' responses to anesthetics so that dosages can be adjusted. Care for and monitor the condition of animals recovering from surgery. Prepare and administer medications, vaccines, serums, and treatments as prescribed by veterinarians. Perform laboratory tests on blood, urine, and feces, such as urinalyses and blood counts, to assist in the diagnosis and treatment of animal health problems. Administer emergency first aid, such as performing emergency resuscitation or other life-saving procedures. Collect, prepare, and label samples for laboratory testing, culture, or microscopic examination. Clean and sterilize instruments, equipment, and materials. Provide veterinarians with the correct equipment and instruments as needed. Fill prescriptions, measuring medications and labeling containers. Prepare animals for surgery, performing such tasks as shaving surgical areas. Take animals into treatment areas and assist with physical examinations by performing such duties as obtaining temperature, pulse, and respiration data. Observe the

behavior and condition of animals and monitor their clinical symptoms. Take and develop diagnostic radiographs, using X-ray equipment. Maintain laboratory, research, and treatment records, as well as inventories of pharmaceuticals, equipment, and supplies. Give enemas and perform catheterizations, ear flushes, intravenous feedings, and gavages. Prepare treatment rooms for surgery. Maintain instruments, equipment, and machinery to ensure proper working condition. Perform dental work such as cleaning, polishing, and extracting teeth. Clean kennels, animal holding areas, surgery suites, examination rooms, and animal loading/unloading facilities to control the spread of disease. Provide information and counseling regarding issues such as animal health care, behavior problems, and nutrition. Provide assistance with animal euthanasia and the disposal of remains. Dress and suture wounds and apply splints and other protective devices. Perform a variety of office, clerical, and accounting duties, such as reception, billing, bookkeeping, or selling products.

GOE Information—**Interest Area:** 08. Health Science. **Work Group:** 08.05. Animal Care. **Personality Type**—No data available. **Work Values**—No data available. **Skills**—Science; Operation Monitoring; Instructing; Equipment Maintenance; Social Perceptiveness; Operation and Control. **Abilities**—*Cognitive:* Speed of Closure; Oral Comprehension; Inductive Reasoning; Category Flexibility; Memorization; Information Ordering. *Psychomotor:* Arm-Hand Steadiness; Manual Dexterity; Control Precision. *Physical:* None met the criteria. *Sensory:* None met the criteria. **General Work Activities**—*Information Input:* Monitoring Processes, Materials, or Surroundings; Identifying Objects, Actions, and Events; Getting Information. *Mental Process:* Updating and Using Relevant Knowledge; Making Decisions and Solving Problems; Organizing, Planning, and Prioritizing. *Work Output:* Handling and Moving Objects; Performing General Physical Activities; Documenting or Recording Information. *Interacting with Others:* Establishing and Maintaining Interpersonal Relationships; Assisting and Caring for Others; Performing for or Working with the Public. **Physical Work Conditions**—Indoors; Contaminants; Radiation; Disease or Infections; Minor Burns, Cuts, Bites, or Stings; Standing. **Other Job Characteristics**—Errors Have Important Consequences; Need to Be Exact or Accurate; Repeat Same Tasks.

Experience—Job Zone 3. Previous work-related skill, knowledge, or experience is required. **Job Preparation**—SVP 6.0 to less than 7.0— more than one year and less than four years. **Knowledges**—Biology; Medicine and Dentistry; Chemistry; Sales and Marketing; Customer and Personal Service; Mathematics. **Instructional Program**— Veterinary/Animal Health Technology/Technician and Veterinary Assistant.

Related SOC Job—29-2056 Veterinary Technologists and Technicians. **Related OOH Job**—Veterinary Technologists and Technicians. **Related DOT Job**—079.361-014 Veterinary Technician.

29-2061.00 Licensed Practical and Licensed Vocational Nurses

- **Education/Training Required: Postsecondary vocational training**
- **Employed: 710,020**
- **Annual Earnings: $35,230**
- **Growth: 17.1%**
- **Annual Job Openings: 84,000**

Care for ill, injured, convalescent, or disabled persons in hospitals, nursing homes, clinics, private homes, group homes, and similar institutions. May work under the supervision of a registered nurse. Licensing required.

Observe patients, charting and reporting changes in patients' conditions, such as adverse reactions to medication or treatment, and taking any necessary action. Administer prescribed medications or start intravenous fluids and note times and amounts on patients' charts. Answer patients' calls and determine how to assist them. Measure and record patients' vital signs, such as height, weight, temperature, blood pressure, pulse, and respiration. Provide basic patient care and treatments, such as taking temperatures or blood pressures, dressing wounds, treating bedsores, giving enemas or douches, rubbing with alcohol, massaging, or performing catheterizations. Help patients with bathing, dressing, maintaining personal hygiene, moving in bed, or standing and walking. Supervise nurses' aides and assistants. Work as part of a health care team to assess patient needs, plan and modify care, and implement interventions. Record food and fluid intake and output. Evaluate nursing intervention outcomes, conferring with other health care team members as necessary. Assemble and use equipment such as catheters, tracheotomy tubes, and oxygen suppliers. Collect samples such as blood, urine, and sputum from patients and perform routine laboratory tests on samples. Prepare patients for examinations, tests, or treatments and explain procedures. Prepare food trays and examine them for conformance to prescribed diet. Apply compresses, ice bags, and hot water bottles. Clean rooms and make beds. Inventory and requisition supplies and instruments. Provide medical treatment and personal care to patients in private home settings, such as cooking, keeping rooms orderly, seeing that patients are comfortable and in good spirits, and instructing family members in simple nursing tasks. Sterilize equipment and supplies, using germicides, sterilizer, or autoclave. Assist in delivery, care, and feeding of infants. Wash and dress bodies of deceased persons. Make appointments, keep records, and perform other clerical duties in doctors' offices and clinics. Set up equipment and prepare medical treatment rooms.

GOE Information—Interest Area: 08. Health Science. **Work Group:** 08.08. Patient Care and Assistance. **Personality Type—**Social. Social occupations frequently involve working with, communicating with, and teaching people. These occupations often involve helping or providing service to others. **Work Values—**Social Service; Co-workers; Achievement; Ability Utilization; Activity; Social Status. **Skills—**Science; Operation Monitoring; Service Orientation; Judgment and Decision Making; Active Listening; Management of Personnel Resources. **Abilities—***Cognitive:* Speed of Closure; Problem Sensitivity; Perceptual Speed; Inductive Reasoning; Memorization; Deductive Reasoning. *Psychomotor:* Manual Dexterity; Arm-Hand Steadiness; Finger Dexterity. *Physical:* Trunk Strength; Extent Flexibility. *Sensory:* Speech Recognition; Hearing Sensitivity; Visual Color Discrimination; Depth Perception; Near Vision; Auditory Attention. **General Work Activities—***Information Input:* Monitoring Processes, Materials, or Surroundings; Identifying Objects, Actions, and Events; Getting Information. *Mental Process:* Updating and Using Relevant Knowledge; Making Decisions and Solving Problems; Organizing, Planning, and Prioritizing. *Work Output:* Documenting or Recording Information; Repairing and Maintaining Electronic Equipment; Performing General Physical Activities. *Interacting with Others:* Assisting and Caring for Others; Teaching Others; Establishing and Maintaining Interpersonal Relationships. **Physical Work Conditions—**Indoors; Disease or Infections; Standing; Walking and Running. **Other Job Characteristics—**Need to Be Exact or Accurate; Errors Have Important Consequences; Repeat Same Tasks.

Experience—Job Zone 3. Previous work-related skill, knowledge, or experience is required. **Job Preparation—**SVP 6.0 to less than 7.0—more than one year and less than four years. **Knowledges—**Psychology; Therapy and Counseling; Medicine and Dentistry;

Customer and Personal Service; Philosophy and Theology; Sociology and Anthropology. **Instructional Program—**Licensed Practical Nurse Training (LPN, Cert, Dipl, AAS).

Related SOC Job—29-2061 Licensed Practical and Licensed Vocational Nurses. **Related OOH Job**—Licensed Practical and Licensed Vocational Nurses. **Related DOT Job**—079.374-014 Nurse, Licensed Practical.

29-2071.00 Medical Records and Health Information Technicians

- **Education/Training Required: Associate degree**
- **Employed: 160,450**
- **Annual Earnings: $26,690**
- **Growth: 28.9%**
- **Annual Job Openings: 14,000**

Compile, process, and maintain medical records of hospital and clinic patients in a manner consistent with medical, administrative, ethical, legal, and regulatory requirements of the health care system. Process, maintain, compile, and report patient information for health requirements and standards.

Protect the security of medical records to ensure that confidentiality is maintained. Process patient admission and discharge documents. Review records for completeness, accuracy, and compliance with regulations. Compile and maintain patients' medical records to document condition and treatment and to provide data for research or cost control and care improvement efforts. Enter data such as demographic characteristics, history and extent of disease, diagnostic procedures, and treatment into computer. Release information to persons and agencies according to regulations. Plan, develop, maintain, and operate a variety of health record indexes and storage and retrieval systems to collect, classify, store, and analyze information. Manage the department and supervise clerical workers, directing and controlling activities of personnel in the medical records department. Transcribe medical reports. Identify, compile, abstract, and code patient data, using standard classification systems. Resolve or clarify codes and diagnoses with conflicting, missing, or unclear information by consulting with doctors or others or by participating in the coding team's regular meetings. Train medical records staff. Assign the patient to diagnosis-related groups (DRGs), using appropriate computer software. Post medical insurance billings. Process and prepare business and government forms. Contact discharged patients, their families, and physicians to maintain registry with follow-up information, such as quality of life and length of survival of cancer patients. Prepare statistical reports, narrative reports, and graphic presentations of information such as tumor registry data for use by hospital staff, researchers, or other users. Consult classification manuals to locate information about disease processes. Compile medical care and census data for statistical reports on diseases treated, surgery performed, or use of hospital beds. Develop in-service educational materials.

GOE Information—Interest Area: 08. Health Science. **Work Group:** 08.06. Medical Technology. **Personality Type—**Conventional. Conventional occupations frequently involve following set procedures and routines. These occupations can include working with data and details more than with ideas. Usually there is a clear line of authority to follow. **Work Values—**Working Conditions; Moral Values; Activity; Security; Supervision, Human Relations; Independence. **Skills—**Systems Evaluation; Active Listening; Reading Comprehension; Instructing; Critical Thinking; Time Management.

Abilities—*Cognitive:* Category Flexibility; Perceptual Speed; Information Ordering; Written Expression; Memorization; Written Comprehension. *Psychomotor:* None met the criteria. *Physical:* None met the criteria. *Sensory:* Near Vision; Speech Recognition. **General Work Activities**—*Information Input:* Getting Information; Monitoring Processes, Materials, or Surroundings; Identifying Objects, Actions, and Events. *Mental Process:* Updating and Using Relevant Knowledge; Evaluating Information Against Standards; Organizing, Planning, and Prioritizing. *Work Output:* Handling and Moving Objects; Interacting With Computers; Documenting or Recording Information. *Interacting with Others:* Communicating with Other Workers; Establishing and Maintaining Interpersonal Relationships; Communicating with Persons Outside Organization. **Physical Work Conditions**—Indoors; Noisy; Sitting; Using Hands on Objects, Tools, or Controls; Repetitive Motions. **Other Job Characteristics**—Need to Be Exact or Accurate; Repeat Same Tasks; Automation.

Experience—Job Zone 3. Previous work-related skill, knowledge, or experience is required. **Job Preparation**—SVP 6.0 to less than 7.0—more than one year and less than four years. **Knowledges**—Clerical Practices; Personnel and Human Resources; Administration and Management; Computers and Electronics. **Instructional Programs**—Health Information/Medical Records Technology/Technician; Medical Insurance Coding Specialist/Coder.

Related SOC Job—29-2071 Medical Records and Health Information Technicians. **Related OOH Job**—Medical Records and Health Information Technicians. **Related DOT Jobs**—079.262-014 Medical Record Coder; 079.362-014 Medical Record Technician; 079.362-018 Tumor Registrar; 169.167-046 Public Health Registrar; 245.362-010 Medical-Record Clerk.

29-2081.00 Opticians, Dispensing

- **Education/Training Required: Long-term on-the-job training**
- **Employed: 70,090**
- **Annual Earnings: $29,000**
- **Growth: 13.6%**
- **Annual Job Openings: 6,000**

Design, measure, fit, and adapt lenses and frames for client according to written optical prescription or specification. Assist client with selecting frames. Measure customer for size of eyeglasses and coordinate frames with facial and eye measurements and optical prescription. Prepare work order for optical laboratory containing instructions for grinding and mounting lenses in frames. Verify exactness of finished lens spectacles. Adjust frame and lens position to fit client. May shape or reshape frames.

Measure clients' bridge and eye size, temple length, vertex distance, pupillary distance, and optical centers of eyes, using measuring devices. Verify that finished lenses are ground to specifications. Prepare work orders and instructions for grinding lenses and fabricating eyeglasses. Assist clients in selecting frames according to style and color and ensure that frames are coordinated with facial and eye measurements and optical prescriptions. Maintain records of customer prescriptions, work orders, and payments. Perform administrative duties such as tracking inventory and sales, submitting patient insurance information, and performing simple bookkeeping. Recommend specific lenses, lens coatings, and frames to suit client needs. Sell goods such as contact lenses, spectacles, sunglasses, and other goods related to eyes in general. Heat, shape, or bend plastic or metal frames to adjust eyeglasses to fit clients, using pliers and hands. Evaluate prescriptions in conjunction with clients' vocational and avocational visual requirements. Instruct clients in how to wear and care for eyeglasses. Determine clients' current lens prescriptions, when necessary, using lensometers or lens analyzers and clients' eyeglasses. Show customers how to insert, remove, and care for their contact lenses. Repair damaged frames. Obtain a customer's previous record or verify a prescription with the examining optometrist or ophthalmologist. Arrange and maintain displays of optical merchandise. Fabricate lenses to meet prescription specifications. Grind lens edges or apply coatings to lenses. Assemble eyeglasses by cutting and edging lenses and fitting the lenses into frames. Supervise the training of student opticians.

GOE Information—Interest Area: 08. Health Science. **Work Group:** 08.06. Medical Technology. **Personality Type**—Enterprising. Enterprising occupations frequently involve starting up and carrying out projects. These occupations can involve leading people and making many decisions. They sometimes require risk taking and often deal with business. **Work Values**—Social Service; Social Status; Achievement; Responsibility; Authority; Security. **Skills**—Persuasion; Service Orientation; Technology Design; Speaking; Equipment Selection; Mathematics. **Abilities**—*Cognitive:* Oral Expression; Written Expression; Written Comprehension; Oral Comprehension. *Psychomotor:* Finger Dexterity; Arm-Hand Steadiness; Manual Dexterity. *Physical:* None met the criteria. *Sensory:* Near Vision; Speech Recognition. **General Work Activities**—*Information Input:* Getting Information; Monitoring Processes, Materials, or Surroundings; Identifying Objects, Actions, and Events. *Mental Process:* Updating and Using Relevant Knowledge; Processing Information; Making Decisions and Solving Problems. *Work Output:* Documenting or Recording Information; Handling and Moving Objects; Interacting With Computers. *Interacting with Others:* Performing for or Working with the Public; Assisting and Caring for Others; Communicating with Other Workers. **Physical Work Conditions**—Indoors; Standing; Using Hands on Objects, Tools, or Controls. **Other Job Characteristics**—Need to Be Exact or Accurate; Repeat Same Tasks.

Experience—Job Zone 3. Previous work-related skill, knowledge, or experience is required. **Job Preparation**—SVP 6.0 to less than 7.0—more than one year and less than four years. **Knowledges**—Sales and Marketing; Customer and Personal Service; Production and Processing; Clerical Practices; Economics and Accounting; Psychology. **Instructional Program**—Opticianry/Ophthalmic Dispensing Optician.

Related SOC Job—29-2081 Opticians, Dispensing. **Related OOH Job**—Opticians, Dispensing. **Related DOT Jobs**—299.361-010 Optician, Dispensing; 299.361-014 Optician Apprentice, Dispensing.

29-2091.00 Orthotists and Prosthetists

- **Education/Training Required: Bachelor's degree**
- **Employed: 5,190**
- **Annual Earnings: $53,760**
- **Growth: 18.0%**
- **Annual Job Openings: Fewer than 500**

Assist patients with disabling conditions of limbs and spine or with partial or total absence of limb by fitting and preparing orthopedic braces or prostheses.

Examine, interview, and measure patients in order to determine their appliance needs and to identify factors that could affect appliance fit. Fit, test, and evaluate devices on patients and make adjustments for proper fit, function, and comfort. Instruct patients in the use and care of orthoses and prostheses. Design orthopedic and prosthetic devices based on physicians' prescriptions and examination and measurement of patients. Maintain patients' records. Make and modify plaster casts of areas that will be fitted with prostheses or orthoses for use in the device construction process. Select materials and components to be used, based on device design. Confer with physicians to formulate specifications and prescriptions for orthopedic or prosthetic devices. Repair, rebuild, and modify prosthetic and orthopedic appliances. Construct and fabricate appliances or supervise others who are constructing the appliances. Train and supervise orthopedic and prosthetic assistants and technicians and other support staff. Update skills and knowledge by attending conferences and seminars. Show and explain orthopedic and prosthetic appliances to healthcare workers. Research new ways to construct and use orthopedic and prosthetic devices. Publish research findings and present them at conferences and seminars.

GOE Information—Interest Area: 08. Health Science. **Work Group:** 08.06. Medical Technology. **Personality Type**—Social. Social occupations frequently involve working with, communicating with, and teaching people. These occupations often involve helping or providing service to others. **Work Values**—Social Service; Achievement; Ability Utilization; Recognition; Authority; Social Status. **Skills**—Technology Design; Management of Financial Resources; Management of Material Resources; Service Orientation; Management of Personnel Resources; Operations Analysis. **Abilities**—*Cognitive:* Visualization; Written Expression; Inductive Reasoning; Originality; Category Flexibility; Oral Expression. *Psychomotor:* Manual Dexterity; Finger Dexterity; Multilimb Coordination; Arm-Hand Steadiness; Control Precision. *Physical:* None met the criteria. *Sensory:* Visual Color Discrimination; Near Vision; Speech Recognition; Auditory Attention. **General Work Activities**—*Information Input:* Monitoring Processes, Materials, or Surroundings; Identifying Objects, Actions, and Events; Getting Information. *Mental Process:* Updating and Using Relevant Knowledge; Making Decisions and Solving Problems; Thinking Creatively. *Work Output:* Documenting or Recording Information; Handling and Moving Objects; Drafting and Specifying Technical Devices. *Interacting with Others:* Performing for or Working with the Public; Assisting and Caring for Others; Establishing and Maintaining Interpersonal Relationships. **Physical Work Conditions**—Indoors; Noisy; Contaminants; Disease or Infections; Hazardous Equipment; Using Hands on Objects, Tools, or Controls. **Other Job Characteristics**—Need to Be Exact or Accurate; Errors Have Important Consequences.

Experience—Job Zone 5. Extensive skill, knowledge, and experience are needed. **Job Preparation**—SVP 8.0 and above—four years to more than 10 years. **Knowledges**—Engineering and Technology; Medicine and Dentistry; Design; Therapy and Counseling; Psychology; Production and Processing. **Instructional Programs**—Assistive/Augmentative Technology and Rehabiliation Engineering; Orthotist/Prosthetist.

Related SOC Job—29-2091 Orthotists and Prosthetists. **Related OOH Job**—Orthotists and Prosthetists. **Related DOT Jobs**—078.261-018 Orthotist; 078.261-022 Prosthetist; 078.361-022 Orthotics Assistant; 078.361-026 Prosthetics Assistant; 078.664-010 Orthopedic Assistant.

29-2099.99 Health Technologists and Technicians, All Other

- **Education/Training Required: No data available**
- **Employed: 71,140**
- **Annual Earnings: $34,300**
- **Growth: 22.9%**
- **Annual Job Openings: 8,000**

All health technologists and technicians not listed separately.

No task data available.

Note: The Department of Labor has not collected some data for this job, so it has fewer details than the other descriptions.

Related SOC Job—29-2099 Health Technologists and Technicians, All Other. **Related OOH Job**—None. **Related DOT Jobs**—078.361-038 Ophthalmic Technician; 078.362-010 Audiometrist; 078.362-014 Dialysis Technician; 078.362-022 Electroencephalographic Technologist; 078.362-038 Electromyographic Technician; 078.362-042 Polysomnographic Technician; 078.384-010 Cephalometric Analyst; 079.364-014 Optometric Assistant; 079.364-641 Health Care Sanitary Technician; 079.371-014 Orthoptist; 354.677-010 First-Aid Attendant.

29-9000 Other Healthcare Practitioners and Technical Occupations

29-9011.00 Occupational Health and Safety Specialists

- **Education/Training Required: Master's degree**
- **Employed: 35,460**
- **Annual Earnings: $53,710**
- **Growth: 12.4%**
- **Annual Job Openings: 3,000**

Review, evaluate, and analyze work environments and design programs and procedures to control, eliminate, and prevent disease or injury caused by chemical, physical, and biological agents or ergonomic factors. May conduct inspections and enforce adherence to laws and regulations governing the health and safety of individuals. May be employed in the public or private sector.

Order suspension of activities that pose threats to workers' health and safety. Recommend measures to help protect workers from potentially hazardous work methods, processes, or materials. Investigate accidents to identify causes and to determine how such accidents might be prevented in the future. Investigate the adequacy of ventilation, exhaust equipment, lighting, and other conditions that could affect employee health, comfort, or performance. Develop and maintain hygiene programs such as noise surveys, continuous atmosphere monitoring, ventilation surveys, and asbestos management plans. Inspect and evaluate workplace environments, equipment, and practices to ensure compliance with safety standards and government regulations. Collaborate with engineers and physicians to institute control and remedial measures for hazardous and potentially hazardous conditions or equipment. Conduct safety training and education programs and demonstrate the use of safety equipment. Provide new-employee health and safety orientations and develop materials for these presentations. Collect samples of dust, gases, vapors, and other potentially toxic materials for analysis. Investigate health-related complaints and inspect facilities to ensure that they comply with public health legislation and regulations. Coordinate "right-to-know" programs regarding hazardous chemicals and other substances. Maintain and update emergency response plans and procedures. Develop and maintain medical monitoring programs for employees. Conduct audits at hazardous waste sites or industrial sites and participate in hazardous waste site investigations.

Inspect specified areas to ensure the presence of fire prevention equipment, safety equipment, and first-aid supplies. Collect samples of hazardous materials or arrange for sample collection. Maintain inventories of hazardous materials and hazardous wastes, using waste tracking systems to ensure that materials are handled properly. Prepare hazardous, radioactive, and mixed waste samples for transportation and storage by treating, compacting, packaging, and labeling them.

GOE Information—Interest Area: 07. Government and Public Administration. **Work Group:** 07.03. Regulations Enforcement. **Personality Type**—Social. Social occupations frequently involve working with, communicating with, and teaching people. These occupations often involve helping or providing service to others. **Work Values**—Autonomy; Creativity; Recognition; Authority; Variety; Ability Utilization. **Skills**—Science; Management of Financial Resources; Technology Design; Persuasion; Systems Analysis; Management of Material Resources. **Abilities**—*Cognitive:* Problem Sensitivity; Written Expression; Flexibility of Closure; Deductive Reasoning; Originality; Inductive Reasoning. *Psychomotor:* Finger Dexterity. *Physical:* None met the criteria. *Sensory:* Hearing Sensitivity; Far Vision; Visual Color Discrimination; Speech Clarity; Auditory Attention; Depth Perception. **General Work Activities**—*Information Input:* Getting Information; Monitoring Processes, Materials, or Surroundings; Identifying Objects, Actions, and Events. *Mental Process:* Organizing, Planning, and Prioritizing; Updating and Using Relevant Knowledge; Processing Information. *Work Output:* Documenting or Recording Information; Interacting With Computers; Drafting and Specifying Technical Devices. *Interacting with Others:* Communicating with Other Workers; Providing Consultation and Advice to Others; Establishing and Maintaining Interpersonal Relationships. **Physical Work Conditions**—More Often Indoors than Outdoors; Noisy; Contaminants; Sitting. **Other Job Characteristics**—Need to Be Exact or Accurate; Errors Have Important Consequences.

Experience—Job Zone 4. A minimum of two to four years of work-related skill, knowledge, and experience is needed. **Job Preparation**—SVP 7.0 to less than 8.0—two years to less than 10 years. **Knowledges**—Chemistry; Biology; Physics; Engineering and Technology; Public Safety and Security; Education and Training. **Instructional Programs**—Environmental Health; Industrial Safety Technology/Technician; Occupational Health and Industrial Hygiene; Occupational Safety and Health Technology/Technician; Quality Control and Safety Technologies/Technicians, Other.

Related SOC Job—29-9011 Occupational Health and Safety Specialists. **Related OOH Job**—Occupational Health and Safety Specialists and Technicians. **Related DOT Jobs**—079.117-018 Sanitarian; 079.161-010 Industrial Hygienist; 168.161-014 Industrial-Safety-And-Health Technician; 168.167-018 Health Officer, Field; 168.167-042 Inspector, Health Care Facilities; 168.167-062 Occupational-Safety-And-Health Inspector; 168.167-078 Safety Inspector; 168.167-086 Safety Manager; 168.261-010 Radiation-Protection Specialist; 168.264-014 Safety Inspector; 168.267-030 Dining-Service Inspector; 168.267-042 Food And Drug Inspector; 168.267-046 Inspector, Furniture And Bedding; others.

29-9012.00 Occupational Health and Safety Technicians

- **Education/Training Required: Associate degree**
- **Employed: 9,510**
- **Annual Earnings: $43,150**
- **Growth: 17.1%**
- **Annual Job Openings: 1,000**

Collect data on work environments for analysis by occupational health and safety specialists. Implement and conduct evaluation of programs designed to limit chemical, physical, biological, and ergonomic risks to workers.

Maintain all required records and documentation. Supply, operate, and maintain personal protective equipment. Verify that safety equipment such as hearing protection and respirators is available to employees and monitor their use of such equipment to ensure proper fit and use. Prepare and calibrate equipment used to collect and analyze samples. Evaluate situations where a worker has refused to work on the grounds that danger or potential harm exists and determine how such situations should be handled. Test workplaces for environmental hazards such as exposure to radiation, chemical and biological hazards, and excessive noise. Prepare and review specifications and orders for the purchase of safety equipment, ensuring that proper features are present and that items conform to health and safety standards. Report the results of environmental contaminant analyses and recommend corrective measures to be applied. Review physicians' reports and conduct worker studies to determine whether specific instances of disease or illness are job-related. Examine credentials, licenses, or permits to ensure compliance with licensing requirements. Conduct fire drills and inspect fire suppression systems and portable fire systems to ensure that they are in working order. Educate the public about health issues and enforce health legislation to prevent disease, to promote health, and to help people understand health protection procedures and regulations. Provide consultation to organizations or agencies on the application of safety principles, practices, and techniques in the workplace. Conduct interviews to obtain information and evidence regarding communicable diseases or violations of health and sanitation regulations. Review records and reports concerning laboratory results, staffing, floor plans, fire inspections, and sanitation to gather information for the development and enforcement of safety activities. Prepare documents to be used in legal proceedings, testifying in such proceedings when necessary. Plan emergency response drills. Maintain logbooks of daily activities, including areas visited and activities performed.

GOE Information—Interest Area: 07. Government and Public Administration. **Work Group:** 07.03. Regulations Enforcement. **Personality Type**—No data available. **Work Values**—No data available. **Skills**—Science; Persuasion; Technology Design; Operations Analysis; Negotiation; Management of Personnel Resources. **Abilities**—*Cognitive:* Flexibility of Closure; Written Expression; Perceptual Speed; Problem Sensitivity; Number Facility; Fluency of Ideas. *Psychomotor:* Multilimb Coordination; Control Precision. *Physical:* None met the criteria. *Sensory:* Speech Clarity; Far Vision; Depth Perception; Hearing Sensitivity; Auditory Attention; Visual Color Discrimination. **General Work Activities**—*Information Input:* Getting Information; Inspecting Equipment, Structures, or Materials; Monitoring Processes, Materials, or Surroundings. *Mental Process:* Organizing, Planning, and Prioritizing; Updating and Using Relevant

Knowledge; Evaluating Information Against Standards. *Work Output:* Documenting or Recording Information; Performing General Physical Activities; Interacting With Computers. *Interacting with Others:* Establishing and Maintaining Interpersonal Relationships; Communicating with Other Workers; Teaching Others. **Physical Work Conditions**—More Often Outdoors Than Indoors; Noisy; Hazardous Conditions; Hazardous Equipment; Standing. **Other Job Characteristics**—Need to Be Exact or Accurate.

Experience—Job Zone 3. Previous work-related skill, knowledge, or experience is required. **Job Preparation**—SVP 6.0 to less than 7.0—more than one year and less than four years. **Knowledge**—Building and Construction; Education and Training; Chemistry; Public Safety and Security; Engineering and Technology; Physics. **Instructional Programs**—Environmental Health; Occupational Health and Industrial Hygiene; Radiation Protection/Health Physics Technician.

Related SOC Job—29-9012 Occupational Health and Safety Technicians. **Related OOH Job**—Occupational Health and Safety Specialists and Technicians. **Related DOT Job**—199.167-010 Radiation Monitor.

29-9091.00 Athletic Trainers

- Education/Training Required: Bachelor's degree
- Employed: 15,110
- Annual Earnings: $34,260
- Growth: 29.3%
- Annual Job Openings: 1,000

Evaluate, advise, and treat athletes to assist recovery from injury, avoid injury, or maintain peak physical fitness.

Conduct an initial assessment of an athlete's injury or illness to provide emergency or continued care and to determine whether they should be referred to physicians for definitive diagnosis and treatment. Care for athletic injuries, using physical therapy equipment, techniques, and medication. Evaluate athletes' readiness to play and provide participation clearances when necessary and warranted. Apply protective or injury preventive devices such as tape, bandages, or braces to body parts such as ankles, fingers, or wrists. Assess and report the progress of recovering athletes to coaches and physicians. Collaborate with physicians to develop and implement comprehensive rehabilitation programs for athletic injuries. Advise athletes on the proper use of equipment. Plan and implement comprehensive athletic injury and illness prevention programs. Develop training programs and routines designed to improve athletic performance. Travel with athletic teams to be available at sporting events. Instruct coaches, athletes, parents, medical personnel, and community members in the care and prevention of athletic injuries. Inspect playing fields to locate any items that could injure players. Conduct research and provide instruction on subject matter related to athletic training or sports medicine. Recommend special diets to improve athletes' health, increase their stamina, or alter their weight. Massage body parts to relieve soreness, strains, and bruises. Confer with coaches to select protective equipment. Accompany injured athletes to hospitals. Perform team-support duties such as running errands, maintaining equipment, and stocking supplies. Lead stretching exercises for team members prior to games and practices.

GOE Information—Interest Area: 08. Health Science. **Work Group:** 08.09. Health Protection and Promotion. **Personality Type—**Social. Social occupations frequently involve working with, communicating with, and teaching people. These occupations often involve helping or providing service to others. **Work Values—**Social Service; Authority; Variety; Creativity; Autonomy; Advancement. **Skills—**Social Perceptiveness; Science; Management of Material Resources; Management of Financial Resources; Time Management; Management of Personnel Resources. **Abilities—***Cognitive:* Inductive Reasoning; Problem Sensitivity; Originality; Deductive Reasoning; Information Ordering; Category Flexibility. *Psychomotor:* Manual Dexterity; Multilimb Coordination; Arm-Hand Steadiness. *Physical:* Extent Flexibility; Stamina; Gross Body Coordination; Trunk Strength; Static Strength. *Sensory:* Speech Clarity; Speech Recognition. **General Work Activities—***Information Input:* Monitoring Processes, Materials, or Surroundings; Identifying Objects, Actions, and Events; Getting Information. *Mental Process:* Updating and Using Relevant Knowledge; Making Decisions and Solving Problems; Organizing, Planning, and Prioritizing. *Work Output:* Handling and Moving Objects; Performing General Physical Activities; Documenting or Recording Information. *Interacting with Others:* Assisting and Caring for Others; Coaching and Developing Others; Establishing and Maintaining Interpersonal Relationships. **Physical Work Conditions—**More Often Indoors Than Outdoors; Very Hot or Cold; Contaminants; Disease or Infections; Standing. **Other Job Characteristics—**Need to Be Exact or Accurate; Errors Have Important Consequences.

Experience—Job Zone 5. Extensive skill, knowledge, and experience are needed. **Job Preparation—**SVP 8.0 and above—four years to more than 10 years. **Knowledges—**Therapy and Counseling; Medicine and Dentistry; Biology; Psychology; Sociology and Anthropology; Education and Training. **Instructional Program—**Athletic Training/Trainer.

Related SOC Job—29-9091 Athletic Trainers. **Related OOH Job—**Athletic Trainers. **Related DOT Job—**153.224-010 Athletic Trainer.

29-9099.99 Healthcare Practitioners and Technical Workers, All Other

- Education/Training Required: No data available
- Employed: 50,880
- Annual Earnings: $33,520
- Growth: 23.8%
- Annual Job Openings: 5,000

All healthcare practitioners and technical workers not listed separately.

No task data available.

Note: The Department of Labor has not collected some data for this job, so it has fewer details than the other descriptions.

Related SOC Job—29-9099 Healthcare Practitioners and Technical Workers, All Other. **Related OOH Job—**None. **Related DOT Jobs—**078.261-042 Pheresis Specialist; 079.151-010 Transplant Coordinator; 079.262-010 Utilization-Review Coordinator; 079.267-010 Utilization-Review Coordinator.

31-0000

Healthcare Support Occupations

31-1000 Nursing, Psychiatric, and Home Health Aides

31-1011.00 Home Health Aides

- **Education/Training Required: Short-term on-the-job training**
- **Employed: 663,280**
- **Annual Earnings: $18,800**
- **Growth: 56.0%**
- **Annual Job Openings: 170,000**

Provide routine, personal healthcare, such as bathing, dressing, or grooming, to elderly, convalescent, or disabled persons in the home of patients or in a residential care facility.

Maintain records of patient care, condition, progress, or problems to report and discuss observations with supervisor or case manager. Provide patients with help moving in and out of beds, baths, wheelchairs, or automobiles and with dressing and grooming. Provide patients and families with emotional support and instruction in areas such as caring for infants, preparing healthy meals, living independently, or adapting to disability or illness. Change bed linens, wash and iron patients' laundry, and clean patients' quarters. Entertain, converse with, or read aloud to patients to keep them mentally healthy and alert. Plan, purchase, prepare, or serve meals to patients or other family members according to prescribed diets. Direct patients in simple prescribed exercises or in the use of braces or artificial limbs. Check patients' pulse, temperature, and respiration. Change dressings. Perform a variety of duties as requested by client, such as obtaining household supplies or running errands. Accompany clients to doctors' offices and on other trips outside the home, providing transportation, assistance, and companionship. Administer prescribed oral medications under written direction of physician or as directed by home care nurse and aide. Care for children who are disabled or who have sick or disabled parents. Massage patients and apply preparations and treatments such as liniment, alcohol rubs, and heat-lamp stimulation.

GOE Information—Interest Area: 08. Health Science. **Work Group:** 08.08. Patient Care and Assistance. **Personality Type**—Social. Social occupations frequently involve working with, communicating with, and teaching people. These occupations often involve helping or providing service to others. **Work Values**—Social Service; Variety. **Skills**—Social Perceptiveness. **Abilities**—*Cognitive:* Flexibility of Closure; Time Sharing; Perceptual Speed; Oral Expression; Speed of Closure. *Psychomotor:* Response Orientation; Reaction Time; Multilimb Coordination; Arm-Hand Steadiness; Finger Dexterity; Control Precision. *Physical:* Static Strength; Gross Body Coordination; Trunk Strength; Stamina; Dynamic Strength; Extent Flexibility. *Sensory:* Speech Recognition; Depth Perception; Hearing Sensitivity; Far Vision; Speech Clarity. **General Work Activities**—*Information Input:* Monitoring Processes, Materials, or Surroundings; Identifying Objects, Actions, and Events; Getting Information. *Mental Process:* Organizing, Planning, and Prioritizing; Making Decisions and Solving Problems; Updating and Using Relevant Knowledge. *Work Output:* Documenting or Recording Information; Handling and Moving Objects; Performing General Physical Activities. *Interacting with Others:* Assisting and Caring for Others; Establishing and Maintaining Interpersonal Relationships; Communicating with Other Workers. **Physical Work Conditions**—Indoors; Disease or Infections; Standing; Walking and Running; Repetitive Motions. **Other Job Characteristics**—Need to Be Exact or Accurate; Errors Have Important Consequences.

Experience—Job Zone 2. Some previous work-related skill, knowledge, or experience may be helpful in these occupations, but usually is not needed. **Job Preparation**—SVP 4.0 to less than 6.0—six months to less than two years. **Knowledges**—Medicine and Dentistry; Therapy and Counseling; Psychology. **Instructional Program**—Home Health Aide/Home Attendant.

Related SOC Job—31-1011 Home Health Aides. **Related OOH Job**—Nursing, Psychiatric, and Home Health Aides. **Related DOT Job**—354.377-014 Home Attendant.

31-1012.00 Nursing Aides, Orderlies, and Attendants

- **Education/Training Required: Short-term on-the-job training**
- **Employed: 1,391,430**
- **Annual Earnings: $21,440**
- **Growth: 22.3%**
- **Annual Job Openings: 307,000**

Provide basic patient care under direction of nursing staff. Perform duties such as feeding, bathing, dressing, grooming, or moving patients or changing linens.

Turn and reposition bedridden patients, alone or with assistance, to prevent bedsores. Answer patients' call signals. Feed patients who are unable to feed themselves. Observe patients' conditions, measuring and recording food and liquid intake and output and vital signs, and report changes to professional staff. Provide patient care by supplying and emptying bedpans, applying dressings, and supervising exercise routines. Provide patients with help walking, exercising, and moving in and out of bed. Bathe, groom, shave, dress, or drape patients to prepare them for surgery, treatment, or examination. Collect specimens such as urine, feces, or sputum. Prepare, serve, and collect food trays. Clean rooms and change linens. Transport patients to treatment units, using a wheelchair or stretcher. Deliver messages, documents, and specimens. Answer phones and direct visitors. Administer medications and treatments, such as catheterizations, suppositories, irrigations, enemas, massages, and douches, as directed by a physician or nurse. Restrain patients if necessary. Maintain inventory by storing, preparing, sterilizing, and issuing supplies such as dressing packs and treatment trays. Explain medical instructions to patients and family members. Perform clerical duties such as processing documents and scheduling appointments. Work as part of a medical team that examines and treats clinic outpatients. Set up equipment such as oxygen tents, portable X-ray machines, and overhead irrigation bottles.

GOE Information—Interest Area: 08. Health Science. **Work Group:** 08.08. Patient Care and Assistance. **Personality Type**—Social. Social occupations frequently involve working with, communicating with, and teaching people. These occupations often involve helping or providing service to others. **Work Values**—Social Service; Co-workers; Supervision, Technical; Security; Supervision, Human Relations; Variety. **Skills**—Social Perceptiveness; Operation Monitoring; Time Management; Service Orientation; Monitoring; Instructing. **Abilities**—*Cognitive:* Speed of Closure; Perceptual Speed; Flexibility of Closure; Oral Comprehension; Selective Attention; Oral Expression. *Psychomotor:* Arm-Hand Steadiness; Reaction Time; Response Orientation; Multilimb Coordination; Finger Dexterity; Manual Dexterity. *Physical:* Static Strength; Extent Flexibility; Gross Body Coordination; Trunk Strength; Dynamic Strength; Stamina. *Sensory:* Speech Recognition; Visual Color Discrimination; Depth Perception; Hearing Sensitivity; Auditory Attention; Near Vision.

General Work Activities—*Information Input:* Monitoring Processes, Materials, or Surroundings; Identifying Objects, Actions, and Events; Getting Information. *Mental Process:* Organizing, Planning, and Prioritizing; Thinking Creatively; Judging the Qualities of Things, Services, or Other People's Work. *Work Output:* Performing General Physical Activities; Handling and Moving Objects; Documenting or Recording Information. *Interacting with Others:* Assisting and Caring for Others; Establishing and Maintaining Interpersonal Relationships; Teaching Others. **Physical Work Conditions—** Indoors; Disease or Infections; Standing; Walking and Running; Using Hands on Objects, Tools, or Controls; Bending or Twisting the Body. **Other Job Characteristics—**Need to Be Exact or Accurate; Errors Have Important Consequences; Repeat Same Tasks.

Experience—Job Zone 2. Some previous work-related skill, knowledge, or experience may be helpful in these occupations, but usually is not needed. **Job Preparation**—SVP 4.0 to less than 6.0—six months to less than two years. **Knowledges**—Psychology; Medicine and Dentistry; Customer and Personal Service; Chemistry; English Language; Education and Training. **Instructional Programs**—Health Aide; Nurse/Nursing Assistant/Aide.

Related SOC Job—31-1012 Nursing Aides, Orderlies, and Attendants. **Related OOH Job**—Nursing, Psychiatric, and Home Health Aides. **Related DOT Jobs**—354.374-010 Nurse, Practical; 355.374-014 Certified Medication Technician; 355.674-014 Nurse Assistant; 355.674-018 Orderly.

31-1013.00 Psychiatric Aides

- Education/Training Required: Short-term on-the-job training
- Employed: 56,150
- Annual Earnings: $22,920
- Growth: 2.3%
- Annual Job Openings: 10,000

Assist mentally impaired or emotionally disturbed patients, working under direction of nursing and medical staff.

Monitor patients in order to detect unusual behavior and report observations to professional staff. Provide mentally impaired or emotionally disturbed patients with routine physical, emotional, psychological, or rehabilitation care under the direction of nursing and medical staff. Record and maintain records of patient condition and activity, including vital signs, eating habits, and behavior. Work as part of a team that may include psychiatrists, psychologists, psychiatric nurses, and social workers. Aid patients in becoming accustomed to hospital routine. Perform nursing duties such as administering medications, measuring vital signs, collecting specimens, and drawing blood samples. Organize, supervise, and encourage patient participation in social, educational, and recreational activities. Serve meals and feed patients needing assistance or persuasion. Restrain or aid patients as necessary to prevent injury. Interview patients upon admission and record information. Provide patients with assistance in bathing, dressing, and grooming, demonstrating these skills as necessary. Participate in recreational activities with patients, including card games, sports, or television viewing. Maintain patients' restrictions to assigned areas. Accompany patients to and from wards for medical and dental treatments, shopping trips, and religious and recreational events. Clean and disinfect rooms and furnishings to maintain a safe and orderly environment.

GOE Information—Interest Area: 08. Health Science. **Work Group:** 08.08. Patient Care and Assistance. **Personality Type**—Social. Social occupations frequently involve working with, communicating with,

and teaching people. These occupations often involve helping or providing service to others. **Work Values**—Social Service; Co-workers; Supervision, Human Relations; Supervision, Technical; Security; Variety. **Skills**—Social Perceptiveness; Persuasion; Negotiation; Service Orientation; Learning Strategies; Writing. **Abilities**—*Cognitive:* Problem Sensitivity; Speed of Closure; Memorization; Oral Expression; Oral Comprehension; Inductive Reasoning. *Psychomotor:* Arm-Hand Steadiness; Multilimb Coordination. *Physical:* Static Strength; Trunk Strength. *Sensory:* Speech Recognition; Speech Clarity; Auditory Attention. **General Work Activities—***Information Input:* Monitoring Processes, Materials, or Surroundings; Identifying Objects, Actions, and Events; Getting Information. *Mental Process:* Making Decisions and Solving Problems; Updating and Using Relevant Knowledge; Judging the Qualities of Things, Services, or Other People's Work. *Work Output:* Documenting or Recording Information; Performing General Physical Activities; Operating Vehicles or Equipment. *Interacting with Others:* Assisting and Caring for Others; Establishing and Maintaining Interpersonal Relationships; Resolving Conflicts and Negotiating with Others. **Physical Work Conditions**—Indoors; Noisy; Disease or Infections; Standing; Walking and Running. **Other Job Characteristics**—Need to Be Exact or Accurate; Errors Have Important Consequences; Repeat Same Tasks.

Experience—Job Zone 2. Some previous work-related skill, knowledge, or experience may be helpful in these occupations, but usually is not needed. **Job Preparation**—SVP 4.0 to less than 6.0—six months to less than two years. **Knowledges**—Psychology; Therapy and Counseling; Philosophy and Theology; Medicine and Dentistry; Sociology and Anthropology; Public Safety and Security. **Instructional Programs**—Health Aide; Psychiatric/Mental Health Services Technician.

Related SOC Job—31-1013 Psychiatric Aides. **Related OOH Job**—Nursing, Psychiatric, and Home Health Aides. **Related DOT Jobs**—355.377-014 Psychiatric Aide; 355.377-018 Mental-Retardation Aide.

31-2000 Occupational and Physical Therapist Assistants and Aides

31-2011.00 Occupational Therapist Assistants

- Education/Training Required: Associate degree
- Employed: 22,160
- Annual Earnings: $39,750
- Growth: 34.1%
- Annual Job Openings: 2,000

Assist occupational therapists in providing occupational therapy treatments and procedures. May, in accordance with state laws, assist in development of treatment plans, carry out routine functions, direct activity programs, and document the progress of treatments. Generally requires formal training.

Observe and record patients' progress, attitudes, and behavior and maintain this information in client records. Maintain and promote a positive attitude toward clients and their treatment programs. Monitor patients' performance in therapy activities, providing encouragement. Select therapy activities to fit patients' needs and capabilities. Instruct, or assist in instructing, patients and families in home programs, basic living skills, and the care and use of adaptive equipment. Evaluate the daily living skills and capacities of physically, developmentally, or emotionally disabled clients. Aid patients in dressing and grooming themselves. Implement, or assist occupational therapists with implementing, treatment plans designed to help clients function independently. Report to supervisors, verbally or in writing, on patients' progress, attitudes, and behavior. Alter treatment programs to obtain better results if treatment is not having the intended effect. Work under the direction of occupational therapists to plan, implement, and administer educational, vocational, and recreational programs that restore and enhance performance in individuals with functional impairments. Design, fabricate, and repair assistive devices and make adaptive changes to equipment and environments. Assemble, clean, and maintain equipment and materials for patient use. Teach patients how to deal constructively with their emotions. Perform clerical duties such as scheduling appointments, collecting data, and documenting health insurance billings. Transport patients to and from the occupational therapy work area. Demonstrate therapy techniques such as manual and creative arts or games. Order any needed educational or treatment supplies. Assist educational specialists or clinical psychologists in administering situational or diagnostic tests to measure client's abilities or progress.

GOE Information—Interest Area: 08. Health Science. **Work Group:** 08.07. Medical Therapy. **Personality Type—**Social. Social occupations frequently involve working with, communicating with, and teaching people. These occupations often involve helping or providing service to others. **Work Values—**Social Service; Security; Achievement; Co-workers; Supervision, Human Relations; Recognition. **Skills—**Social Perceptiveness; Operations Analysis; Persuasion; Service Orientation; Writing; Time Management. **Abilities—***Cognitive:* Oral Expression; Number Facility; Originality; Oral Comprehension; Category Flexibility; Problem Sensitivity. *Psychomotor:* Response Orientation; Reaction Time; Multilimb Coordination; Arm-Hand Steadiness; Finger Dexterity. *Physical:* Extent Flexibility; Gross Body Coordination; Stamina; Static Strength; Trunk Strength. *Sensory:* Speech Recognition; Auditory Attention; Hearing Sensitivity; Speech Clarity; Far Vision. **General Work Activities—***Information Input:* Getting Information; Monitoring Processes, Materials, or Surroundings; Identifying Objects, Actions, and Events. *Mental Process:* Organizing, Planning, and Prioritizing; Thinking Creatively; Making Decisions and Solving Problems. *Work Output:* Documenting or Recording Information; Performing General Physical Activities; Handling and Moving Objects. *Interacting with Others:* Assisting and Caring for Others; Establishing and Maintaining Interpersonal Relationships; Communicating with Other Workers. **Physical Work Conditions—**Indoors; Disease or Infections; Standing; Walking and Running; Using Hands on Objects, Tools, or Controls; Bending or Twisting the Body. **Other Job Characteristics—**Need to Be Exact or Accurate; Repeat Same Tasks.

Experience—Job Zone 3. Previous work-related skill, knowledge, or experience is required. **Job Preparation—**SVP 6.0 to less than 7.0—more than one year and less than four years. **Knowledges—**Therapy and Counseling; Psychology; Sociology and Anthropology; Philosophy and Theology; Medicine and Dentistry; Biology. **Instructional Program—**Occupational Therapy Assistant.

Related SOC Job—31-2011 Occupational Therapist Assistants. **Related OOH Job—**Occupational Therapist Assistants and Aides. **Related DOT Job—**076.364-010 Occupational Therapy Assistant.

31-2012.00 Occupational Therapist Aides

- **Education/Training Required: Short-term on-the-job training**
- **Employed: 6,220**
- **Annual Earnings: $24,310**
- **Growth: 26.3%**
- **Annual Job Openings: Fewer than 500**

Under close supervision of an occupational therapist or occupational therapy assistant, perform only delegated, selected, or routine tasks in specific situations. These duties include preparing patient and treatment room.

Encourage patients and attend to their physical needs to facilitate the attainment of therapeutic goals. Report to supervisors or therapists, verbally or in writing, on patients' progress, attitudes, attendance, and accomplishments. Observe patients' attendance, progress, attitudes, and accomplishments and record and maintain information in client records. Manage intra-departmental infection control and equipment security. Evaluate the living skills and capacities of physically, developmentally, or emotionally disabled clients. Prepare and maintain work area, materials, and equipment and maintain inventory of treatment and educational supplies. Instruct patients and families in work, social, and living skills; the care and use of adaptive equipment; and other skills to facilitate home and work adjustment to disability. Supervise patients in choosing and completing work details or arts and crafts projects. Assist occupational therapists in planning, implementing, and administering therapy programs to restore, reinforce, and enhance performance, using selected activities and special equipment. Perform clerical, administrative, and secretarial duties such as answering phones, restocking and ordering supplies, filling out paperwork, and scheduling appointments. Demonstrate therapy techniques, such as manual and creative arts and games. Transport patients to and from the occupational therapy work area. Adjust and repair assistive devices and make adaptive changes to other equipment and to environments. Assist educational specialists or clinical psychologists in administering situational or diagnostic tests to measure client's abilities or progress. Accompany patients on outings, providing transportation when necessary.

GOE Information—Interest Area: 08. Health Science. **Work Group:** 08.07. Medical Therapy. **Personality Type—**Social. Social occupations frequently involve working with, communicating with, and teaching people. These occupations often involve helping or providing service to others. **Work Values—**Social Service; Security; Achievement; Co-workers; Supervision, Human Relations; Recognition. **Skills—**Service Orientation; Learning Strategies; Social Perceptiveness; Coordination; Equipment Maintenance; Technology Design. **Abilities—***Cognitive:* Written Expression; Time Sharing; Oral Comprehension; Selective Attention; Category Flexibility; Inductive Reasoning. *Psychomotor:* Multilimb Coordination; Arm-Hand Steadiness; Manual Dexterity; Finger Dexterity. *Physical:* Gross Body Equilibrium; Static Strength; Gross Body Coordination; Extent Flexibility; Trunk Strength; Stamina. *Sensory:* Speech Recognition. **General Work Activities—***Information Input:* Identifying Objects, Actions, and Events; Monitoring Processes, Materials, or Surroundings; Getting Information. *Mental Process:* Organizing, Planning, and Prioritizing; Making Decisions and Solving Problems; Updating and Using Relevant Knowledge. *Work Output:* Handling and Moving Objects; Performing General Physical Activities; Documenting or Recording Information. *Interacting with Others:* Assisting and Caring for Others; Establishing and Maintaining Interpersonal Relationships; Communicating with Other Workers. **Physical Work Conditions—**Indoors; Noisy; Contaminants; Disease or Infections; Standing; Walking and Running. **Other Job Characteristics**—Need to Be Exact or Accurate; Errors Have Important Consequences; Repeat Same Tasks.

Experience—Job Zone 2. Some previous work-related skill, knowledge, or experience may be helpful in these occupations, but usually is not needed. **Job Preparation**—SVP 4.0 to less than 6.0—six months to less than two years. **Knowledges**—Therapy and Counseling; Medicine and Dentistry; Psychology; Biology; Education and Training; Customer and Personal Service. **Instructional Program**—Occupational Therapy Assistant.

Related SOC Job—31-2012 Occupational Therapist Aides. **Related OOH Job**—Occupational Therapist Assistants and Aides. **Related DOT Job**—355.377-010 Occupational Therapy Aide.

31-2021.00 Physical Therapist Assistants

- Education/Training Required: Associate degree
- Employed: 58,670
- Annual Earnings: $39,490
- Growth: 44.2%
- Annual Job Openings: 7,000

Assist physical therapists in providing physical therapy treatments and procedures. May, in accordance with state laws, assist in the development of treatment plans, carry out routine functions, document the progress of treatment, and modify specific treatments in accordance with patient status and within the scope of treatment plans established by a physical therapist. Generally requires formal training.

Instruct, motivate, safeguard, and assist patients as they practice exercises and functional activities. Confer with physical therapy staff or others to discuss and evaluate patient information for planning, modifying, and coordinating treatment. Administer active and passive manual therapeutic exercises; therapeutic massage; and heat, light, sound, water, and electrical modality treatments such as ultrasound. Observe patients during treatments to compile and evaluate data on patients' responses and progress and report to physical therapist. Measure patients' range of joint motion, body parts, and vital signs to determine effects of treatments or for patient evaluations. Secure patients into or onto therapy equipment. Fit patients for orthopedic braces, prostheses, and supportive devices such as crutches. Train patients in the use of orthopedic braces, prostheses, or supportive devices. Transport patients to and from treatment areas, lifting and transferring them according to positioning requirements. Monitor operation of equipment and record use of equipment and administration of treatment. Clean work area and check and store equipment after treatment. Assist patients to dress; undress; or put on and remove supportive devices such as braces, splints, and slings. Administer traction to relieve neck and back pain, using intermittent and static traction equipment. Perform clerical duties, such as taking inventory, ordering supplies, answering telephone, taking messages, and filling out forms. Prepare treatment areas and electrotherapy equipment for use by physiotherapists. Perform postural drainage, percussions, and vibrations and teach deep breathing exercises to treat respiratory conditions.

GOE Information—Interest Area: 08. Health Science. **Work Group:** 08.07. Medical Therapy. **Personality Type**—Social. Social occupations frequently involve working with, communicating with, and teaching people. These occupations often involve helping or providing service to others. **Work Values**—Social Service; Security; Achievement; Co-workers; Supervision, Human Relations; Working Conditions. **Skills**—Science; Social Perceptiveness; Service

Orientation; Writing; Time Management; Instructing. **Abilities**—*Cognitive:* Time Sharing; Oral Comprehension; Oral Expression; Information Ordering; Problem Sensitivity; Deductive Reasoning. *Psychomotor:* Multilimb Coordination; Arm-Hand Steadiness; Manual Dexterity. *Physical:* Static Strength; Dynamic Strength; Extent Flexibility; Gross Body Coordination; Gross Body Equilibrium; Trunk Strength. *Sensory:* Speech Clarity; Speech Recognition. **General Work Activities**—*Information Input:* Monitoring Processes, Materials, or Surroundings; Identifying Objects, Actions, and Events; Getting Information. *Mental Process:* Updating and Using Relevant Knowledge; Making Decisions and Solving Problems; Organizing, Planning, and Prioritizing. *Work Output:* Handling and Moving Objects; Performing General Physical Activities; Documenting or Recording Information. *Interacting with Others:* Assisting and Caring for Others; Performing for or Working with the Public; Establishing and Maintaining Interpersonal Relationships. **Physical Work Conditions**—Indoors; Disease or Infections; Standing; Walking and Running; Using Hands on Objects, Tools, or Controls; Bending or Twisting the Body. **Other Job Characteristics**—Need to Be Exact or Accurate; Errors Have Important Consequences.

Experience—Job Zone 3. Previous work-related skill, knowledge, or experience is required. **Job Preparation**—SVP 6.0 to less than 7.0—more than one year and less than four years. **Knowledges**—Therapy and Counseling; Psychology; Medicine and Dentistry; Education and Training; Sociology and Anthropology; Biology. **Instructional Program**—Physical Therapy Assistant.

Related SOC Job—31-2021 Physical Therapist Assistants. **Related OOH Job**—Physical Therapist Assistants and Aides. **Related DOT Job**—076.224-010 Physical Therapist Assistant.

31-2022.00 Physical Therapist Aides

- Education/Training Required: Short-term on-the-job training
- Employed: 41,930
- Annual Earnings: $21,510
- Growth: 34.4%
- Annual Job Openings: 5,000

Under close supervision of a physical therapist or physical therapy assistant, perform only delegated, selected, or routine tasks in specific situations. These duties include preparing the patient and the treatment area.

Clean and organize work area and disinfect equipment after treatment. Observe patients during treatment to compile and evaluate data on patients' responses and progress and report to physical therapist. Instruct, motivate, safeguard, and assist patients practicing exercises and functional activities under direction of medical staff. Secure patients into or onto therapy equipment. Transport patients to and from treatment areas, using wheelchairs or providing standing support. Confer with physical therapy staff or others to discuss and evaluate patient information for planning, modifying, and coordinating treatment. Record treatment given and equipment used. Perform clerical duties, such as taking inventory, ordering supplies, answering telephone, taking messages, and filling out forms. Maintain equipment and furniture to keep it in good working condition, including performing the assembly and disassembly of equipment and accessories. Administer active and passive manual therapeutic exercises; therapeutic massage; and heat, light, sound, water, or electrical modality treatments such as ultrasound. Change linens, such as bed sheets and pillowcases. Arrange treatment supplies to keep them in order. Assist patients to dress; undress; and put on and remove supportive devices, such as braces, splints, and slings. Measure patient's range of joint motion, body parts, and vital signs to determine effects of treatments or for patient evaluations. Train patients to use orthopedic braces, prostheses, or supportive devices. Fit patients for orthopedic braces, prostheses, or supportive devices, adjusting fit as needed. Participate in patient care tasks, such as assisting with passing food trays, feeding residents, or bathing residents on bed rest. Administer traction to relieve neck and back pain, using intermittent and static traction equipment.

GOE Information—Interest Area: 08. Health Science. **Work Group:** 08.07. Medical Therapy. **Personality Type—**Social. Social occupations frequently involve working with, communicating with, and teaching people. These occupations often involve helping or providing service to others. **Work Values—**Social Service; Security; Achievement; Co-workers; Supervision, Human Relations; Working Conditions. **Skills—**Social Perceptiveness; Service Orientation; Operation Monitoring; Equipment Maintenance; Time Management; Learning Strategies. **Abilities—***Cognitive:* Perceptual Speed. *Psychomotor:* Multilimb Coordination; Arm-Hand Steadiness. *Physical:* Static Strength; Extent Flexibility; Trunk Strength. *Sensory:* Hearing Sensitivity; Depth Perception; Speech Recognition. **General Work Activities—***Information Input:* Monitoring Processes, Materials, or Surroundings; Identifying Objects, Actions, and Events; Getting Information. *Mental Process:* Organizing, Planning, and Prioritizing; Updating and Using Relevant Knowledge; Judging the Qualities of Things, Services, or Other People's Work. *Work Output:* Handling and Moving Objects; Documenting or Recording Information; Performing General Physical Activities. *Interacting with Others:* Assisting and Caring for Others; Establishing and Maintaining Interpersonal Relationships; Performing for or Working with the Public. **Physical Work Conditions—**Indoors; Disease or Infections; Standing; Walking and Running; Using Hands on Objects, Tools, or Controls; Repetitive Motions. **Other Job Characteristics—**Need to Be Exact or Accurate; Errors Have Important Consequences.

Experience—Job Zone 2. Some previous work-related skill, knowledge, or experience may be helpful in these occupations, but usually is not needed. **Job Preparation—**SVP 4.0 to less than 6.0—six months to less than two years. **Knowledges—**Psychology; Medicine and Dentistry; Therapy and Counseling; Customer and Personal Service; Clerical Practices; Education and Training. **Instructional Program—**Physical Therapy Assistant.

Related SOC Job—31-2022 Physical Therapist Aides. **Related OOH Job—**Physical Therapist Assistants and Aides. **Related DOT Job—**355.354-010 Physical Therapy Aide.

31-9000 Other Healthcare Support Occupations

31-9011.00 Massage Therapists

- **Education/Training Required: Postsecondary vocational training**
- **Employed: 37,670**
- **Annual Earnings: $32,890**
- **Growth: 23.6%**
- **Annual Job Openings: 12,000**

Massage customers for hygienic or remedial purposes.

Confer with clients about their medical histories and any problems with stress or pain to determine whether massage would be helpful. Apply finger and hand pressure to specific points of the body.

Massage and knead the muscles and soft tissues of the human body to provide courses of treatment for medical conditions and injuries or wellness maintenance. Maintain treatment records. Provide clients with guidance and information about techniques for postural improvement and stretching, strengthening, relaxation, and rehabilitative exercises. Assess clients' soft tissue condition, joint quality and function, muscle strength, and range of motion. Develop and propose client treatment plans that specify which types of massage are to be used. Refer clients to other types of therapists when necessary. Use complementary aids, such as infrared lamps, wet compresses, ice, and whirlpool baths, to promote clients' recovery, relaxation, and well-being. Treat clients in own offices or travel to clients' offices and homes. Consult with other health care professionals such as physiotherapists, chiropractors, physicians, and psychologists to develop treatment plans for clients. Prepare and blend oils and apply the blends to clients' skin.

GOE Information—Interest Area: 08. Health Science. **Work Group:** 08.07. Medical Therapy. **Personality Type—**No data available. **Work Values—**No data available. **Skills—**Service Orientation; Active Listening. **Abilities—***Cognitive:* Selective Attention; Inductive Reasoning; Problem Sensitivity; Fluency of Ideas; Oral Expression; Deductive Reasoning. *Psychomotor:* Multilimb Coordination; Manual Dexterity; Arm-Hand Steadiness; Finger Dexterity; Control Precision. *Physical:* Dynamic Strength; Stamina; Trunk Strength; Extent Flexibility; Static Strength. *Sensory:* Speech Recognition. **General Work Activities—***Information Input:* Monitoring Processes, Materials, or Surroundings; Identifying Objects, Actions, and Events; Getting Information. *Mental Process:* Updating and Using Relevant Knowledge; Thinking Creatively; Making Decisions and Solving Problems. *Work Output:* Handling and Moving Objects; Performing General Physical Activities; Documenting or Recording Information. *Interacting with Others:* Performing for or Working with the Public; Assisting and Caring for Others; Establishing and Maintaining Interpersonal Relationships. **Physical Work Conditions—**Indoors; Standing; Using Hands on Objects, Tools, or Controls; Repetitive Motions. **Other Job Characteristics—**Need to Be Exact or Accurate; Repeat Same Tasks.

Experience—Job Zone 3. Previous work-related skill, knowledge, or experience is required. **Job Preparation—**SVP 6.0 to less than 7.0—more than one year and less than four years. **Knowledges—**Therapy and Counseling; Psychology; Sales and Marketing; Medicine and Dentistry; Chemistry; English Language. **Instructional Programs—**Asian Bodywork Therapy; Massage Therapy/Therapeutic Massage; Somatic Bodywork; Somatic Bodywork and Related Therapeutic Services, Other.

Related SOC Job—31-9011 Massage Therapists. **Related OOH Job—**Massage Therapists. **Related DOT Job—**334.374-010 Masseur/Masseuse.

31-9091.00 Dental Assistants

- **Education/Training Required: Moderate-term on-the-job training**
- **Employed: 270,720**
- **Annual Earnings: $29,520**
- **Growth: 42.7%**
- **Annual Job Openings: 45,000**

Assist dentist, set up patient and equipment, and keep records.

Prepare patient, sterilize and disinfect instruments, set up instrument trays, prepare materials, and assist dentist during dental procedures.

Expose dental diagnostic X rays. Record treatment information in patient records. Take and record medical and dental histories and vital signs of patients. Provide postoperative instructions prescribed by dentist. Assist dentist in management of medical and dental emergencies. Pour, trim, and polish study casts. Instruct patients in oral hygiene and plaque control programs. Make preliminary impressions for study casts and occlusal registrations for mounting study casts. Clean and polish removable appliances. Clean teeth, using dental instruments. Apply protective coating of fluoride to teeth. Fabricate temporary restorations and custom impressions from preliminary impressions. Schedule appointments, prepare bills, and receive payment for dental services; complete insurance forms; and maintain records, manually or using computer.

GOE Information—Interest Area: 08. Health Science. **Work Group:** 08.03. Dentistry. **Personality Type—**Social. Social occupations frequently involve working with, communicating with, and teaching people. These occupations often involve helping or providing service to others. **Work Values—**Social Service; Working Conditions; Security; Co-workers; Recognition; Compensation. **Skills—**Equipment Maintenance; Social Perceptiveness; Operation and Control; Management of Material Resources; Operation Monitoring; Equipment Selection. **Abilities—***Cognitive:* Time Sharing; Flexibility of Closure; Memorization; Oral Comprehension; Speed of Closure; Perceptual Speed. *Psychomotor:* Manual Dexterity; Arm-Hand Steadiness; Finger Dexterity; Control Precision; Multilimb Coordination. *Physical:* Extent Flexibility; Trunk Strength. *Sensory:* Depth Perception; Near Vision; Speech Recognition; Visual Color Discrimination. **General Work Activities—***Information Input:* Identifying Objects, Actions, and Events; Monitoring Processes, Materials, or Surroundings; Getting Information. *Mental Process:* Organizing, Planning, and Prioritizing; Updating and Using Relevant Knowledge; Processing Information. *Work Output:* Handling and Moving Objects; Documenting or Recording Information; Controlling Machines and Processes. *Interacting with Others:* Assisting and Caring for Others; Communicating with Other Workers; Coordinating the Work and Activities of Others. **Physical Work Conditions—**Indoors; Contaminants; Disease or Infections; Using Hands on Objects, Tools, or Controls; Bending or Twisting the Body; Repetitive Motions. **Other Job Characteristics—**Need to Be Exact or Accurate; Repeat Same Tasks.

Experience—Job Zone 2. Some previous work-related skill, knowledge, or experience may be helpful in these occupations, but usually is not needed. **Job Preparation—**SVP 4.0 to less than 6.0—six months to less than two years. **Knowledges—**Medicine and Dentistry; Chemistry; Clerical Practices; Customer and Personal Service; Psychology; Computers and Electronics. **Instructional Program—**Dental Assisting/Assistant.

Related SOC Job—31-9091 Dental Assistants. **Related OOH Job—**Dental Assistants. **Related DOT Job—**079.361-018 Dental Assistant.

31-9092.00 Medical Assistants

- **Education/Training Required: Moderate-term on-the-job training**
- **Employed: 382,720**
- **Annual Earnings: $25,350**
- **Growth: 52.1%**
- **Annual Job Openings: 93,000**

Perform administrative and certain clinical duties under the direction of physician. Administrative duties may include scheduling appointments, maintaining medical records, billing, and coding for insurance purposes.

Clinical duties may include taking and recording vital signs and medical histories, preparing patients for examination, drawing blood, and administering medications as directed by physician.

Interview patients to obtain medical information and measure their vital signs, weight, and height. Show patients to examination rooms and prepare them for the physician. Record patients' medical history, vital statistics, and information such as test results in medical records. Prepare and administer medications as directed by a physician. Collect blood, tissue, or other laboratory specimens; log the specimens; and prepare them for testing. Explain treatment procedures, medications, diets, and physicians' instructions to patients. Help physicians examine and treat patients, handing them instruments and materials or performing such tasks as giving injections or removing sutures. Authorize drug refills and provide prescription information to pharmacies. Prepare treatment rooms for patient examinations, keeping the rooms neat and clean. Clean and sterilize instruments and dispose of contaminated supplies. Schedule appointments for patients. Change dressings on wounds. Greet and log in patients arriving at office or clinic. Contact medical facilities or departments to schedule patients for tests or admission. Perform general office duties such as answering telephones, taking dictation, or completing insurance forms. Inventory and order medical, lab, or office supplies and equipment. Perform routine laboratory tests and sample analyses. Set up medical laboratory equipment. Keep financial records and perform other bookkeeping duties, such as handling credit and collections and mailing monthly statements to patients. Operate X-ray, electrocardiogram (EKG), and other equipment to administer routine diagnostic tests. Give physiotherapy treatments such as diathermy, galvanics, and hydrotherapy.

GOE Information—Interest Area: 08. Health Science. **Work Group:** 08.02. Medicine and Surgery. **Personality Type—**Social. Social occupations frequently involve working with, communicating with, and teaching people. These occupations often involve helping or providing service to others. **Work Values—**Social Service; Co-workers; Supervision, Human Relations; Compensation; Variety; Security. **Skills—**Social Perceptiveness; Service Orientation; Instructing; Operation Monitoring; Active Listening; Operation and Control. **Abilities—***Cognitive:* Oral Comprehension; Written Comprehension; Oral Expression; Memorization; Written Expression; Time Sharing. *Psychomotor:* Arm-Hand Steadiness; Multilimb Coordination; Manual Dexterity; Control Precision; Finger Dexterity. *Physical:* Trunk Strength. *Sensory:* Speech Recognition; Near Vision. **General Work Activities—***Information Input:* Identifying Objects, Actions, and Events; Monitoring Processes, Materials, or Surroundings; Getting Information. *Mental Process:* Updating and Using Relevant Knowledge; Evaluating Information Against Standards; Making Decisions and Solving Problems. *Work Output:* Documenting or Recording Information; Handling and Moving Objects; Performing General Physical Activities. *Interacting with Others:* Assisting and Caring for Others; Establishing and Maintaining Interpersonal Relationships; Communicating with Other Workers. **Physical Work Conditions—**Indoors; Disease or Infections; Standing; Walking and Running; Using Hands on Objects, Tools, or Controls. **Other Job Characteristics—**Need to Be Exact or Accurate; Repeat Same Tasks.

Experience—Job Zone 3. Previous work-related skill, knowledge, or experience is required. **Job Preparation—**SVP 6.0 to less than 7.0—more than one year and less than four years. **Knowledges—**Medicine and Dentistry; Therapy and Counseling; Customer and Personal Service; Clerical Practices; Psychology; English Language. **Instructional Programs—**Anesthesiologist Assistant; Chiropractic Assistant/Technician; Health and Medical Assisting Services, Other; Medical Administrative/Executive Assistant and Medical Secretary;

Medical Insurance Coding Specialist/Coder; Medical Office Assistant/Specialist; Medical Office Management/Administration; Medical Reception/Receptionist; Medical/Clinical Assistant; Ophthalmic Technician/Technologist; Optometric Technician/Assistant; Orthoptics/Orthoptist.

Related SOC Job—31-9092 Medical Assistants. **Related OOH Job**—Medical Assistants. **Related DOT Jobs**—079.362-010 Medical Assistant; 079.364-010 Chiropractor Assistant; 079.374-018 Podiatric Assistant.

31-9093.00 Medical Equipment Preparers

- Education/Training Required: Short-term on-the-job training
- Employed: 41,790
- Annual Earnings: $24,880
- Growth: 20.0%
- Annual Job Openings: 8,000

Prepare, sterilize, install, or clean laboratory or healthcare equipment. May perform routine laboratory tasks and operate or inspect equipment.

Organize and assemble routine and specialty surgical instrument trays and other sterilized supplies, filling special requests as needed. Clean instruments to prepare them for sterilization. Operate and maintain steam autoclaves, keeping records of loads completed, items in loads, and maintenance procedures performed. Record sterilizer test results. Disinfect and sterilize equipment such as respirators, hospital beds, and oxygen and dialysis equipment, using sterilizers, aerators, and washers. Start equipment and observe gauges and equipment operation to detect malfunctions and to ensure equipment is operating to prescribed standards. Examine equipment to detect leaks, worn or loose parts, or other indications of disrepair. Report defective equipment to appropriate supervisors or staff. Check sterile supplies to ensure that they are not outdated. Maintain records of inventory and equipment usage. Attend hospital in-service programs related to areas of work specialization. Purge wastes from equipment by connecting equipment to water sources and flushing water through systems. Deliver equipment to specified hospital locations or to patients' residences. Assist hospital staff with patient care duties such as providing transportation or setting up traction. Install and set up medical equipment, using hand tools.

GOE Information—**Interest Area:** 08. Health Science. **Work Group:** 08.06. Medical Technology. **Personality Type**—Realistic. Realistic occupations frequently involve work activities that include practical, hands-on problems and solutions. They often deal with plants; animals; and real-world materials like wood, tools, and machinery. Many of the occupations require working outside and do not involve a lot of paperwork or working closely with others. **Work Values**—Independence; Supervision, Technical; Moral Values; Security; Supervision, Human Relations. **Skills**—Operation Monitoring; Management of Material Resources; Equipment Maintenance; Quality Control Analysis; Service Orientation; Operation and Control. **Abilities**—*Cognitive:* Perceptual Speed. *Psychomotor:* Manual Dexterity; Arm-Hand Steadiness; Control Precision; Finger Dexterity. *Physical:* Trunk Strength; Static Strength. *Sensory:* None met the criteria. **General Work Activities**—*Information Input:* Monitoring Processes, Materials, or Surroundings; Inspecting Equipment, Structures, or Materials; Identifying Objects, Actions, and Events. *Mental Process:* Updating and Using Relevant Knowledge; Evaluating Information Against Standards; Making Decisions and Solving Problems. *Work Output:* Handling and Moving Objects; Controlling Machines and Processes; Documenting or Recording Information. *Interacting with Others:* Assisting and Caring for Others; Communicating with Other Workers; Establishing and Maintaining

Interpersonal Relationships. **Physical Work Conditions**—Indoors; Contaminants; Disease or Infections; Standing; Using Hands on Objects, Tools, or Controls; Repetitive Motions. **Other Job Characteristics**—Need to Be Exact or Accurate; Errors Have Important Consequences; Repeat Same Tasks; Pace Determined by Speed of Equipment.

Experience—Job Zone 2. Some previous work-related skill, knowledge, or experience may be helpful in these occupations, but usually is not needed. **Job Preparation**—SVP 4.0 to less than 6.0—six months to less than two years. **Knowledges**—Chemistry; Biology; Medicine and Dentistry; Production and Processing; Education and Training; Customer and Personal Service. **Instructional Programs**—Health and Medical Assisting Services, Other; Medical/Clinical Assistant.

Related SOC Job—31-9093 Medical Equipment Preparers. **Related OOH Job**—Medical Equipment Preparers. **Related DOT Jobs**—355.674-022 Respiratory-Therapy Aide; 359.363-010 Health-Equipment Servicer; 599.584-010 Reuse Technician.

31-9094.00 Medical Transcriptionists

- Education/Training Required: Postsecondary vocational training
- Employed: 90,380
- Annual Earnings: $29,080
- Growth: 23.3%
- Annual Job Openings: 20,000

Use transcribing machines with headset and foot pedal to listen to recordings by physicians and other healthcare professionals dictating a variety of medical reports, such as emergency room visits, diagnostic imaging studies, operations, chart reviews, and final summaries. Transcribe dictated reports and translate medical jargon and abbreviations into their expanded forms. Edit as necessary and return reports in either printed or electronic form to the dictator for review and signature or correction.

Transcribe dictation for a variety of medical reports such as patient histories, physical examinations, emergency room visits, operations, chart reviews, consultation, or discharge summaries. Review and edit transcribed reports or dictated material for spelling, grammar, clarity, consistency, and proper medical terminology. Distinguish between homonyms and recognize inconsistencies and mistakes in medical terms, referring to dictionaries; drug references; and other sources on anatomy, physiology, and medicine. Return dictated reports in printed or electronic form for physicians' review, signature, and corrections and for inclusion in patients' medical records. Translate medical jargon and abbreviations into their expanded forms to ensure the accuracy of patient and healthcare facility records. Take dictation, using either shorthand or a stenotype machine or using headsets and transcribing machines; then convert dictated materials or rough notes to written form. Identify mistakes in reports and check with doctors to obtain the correct information. Perform data entry and data retrieval services, providing data for inclusion in medical records and for transmission to physicians. Produce medical reports, correspondence, records, patient-care information, statistics, medical research, and administrative material. Answer inquiries concerning the progress of medical cases within the limits of confidentiality laws. Set up and maintain medical files and databases, including records such as X-ray, lab, and procedure reports; medical histories; diagnostic workups; admission and discharge summaries; and clinical resumes. Perform a variety of clerical and office tasks, such as handling incoming and outgoing mail, completing and submitting insurance claims, typing, filing, and operating office machines. Decide which information should be included or excluded in reports. Receive patients, schedule appointments, and maintain patient records. Receive and screen telephone calls and visitors.

GOE Information—Interest Area: 08. Health Science. **Work Group:** 08.02. Medicine and Surgery. **Personality Type—**No data available. **Work Values—**No data available. **Skills—**Active Listening; Reading Comprehension; Time Management; Writing. **Abilities—***Cognitive:* Written Expression; Perceptual Speed; Oral Comprehension; Written Comprehension; Selective Attention; Flexibility of Closure. *Psychomotor:* Finger Dexterity. *Physical:* None met the criteria. *Sensory:* Speech Recognition. **General Work Activities—***Information Input:* Getting Information; Identifying Objects, Actions, and Events; Monitoring Processes, Materials, or Surroundings. *Mental Process:* Updating and Using Relevant Knowledge; Processing Information; Organizing, Planning, and Prioritizing. *Work Output:* Documenting or Recording Information; Interacting With Computers. *Interacting with Others:* Establishing and Maintaining Interpersonal Relationships; Communicating with Other Workers; Interpreting the Meaning of Information for Others. **Physical Work Conditions—**Indoors; Sitting; Using Hands on Objects, Tools, or Controls; Repetitive Motions. **Other Job Characteristics—**Need to Be Exact or Accurate; Repeat Same Tasks; Automation; Pace Determined by Speed of Equipment.

Experience—Job Zone 3. Previous work-related skill, knowledge, or experience is required. **Job Preparation—**SVP 6.0 to less than 7.0— more than one year and less than four years. **Knowledges—**Clerical Practices; English Language; Medicine and Dentistry; Computers and Electronics. **Instructional Program—**Medical Transcription/ Transcriptionist.

Related SOC Job—31-9094 Medical Transcriptionists. **Related OOH Job—**Medical Transcriptionists. **Related DOT Job—**203.582-058 Transcribing-Machine Operator.

31-9095.00 Pharmacy Aides

- **Education/Training Required: Short-term on-the-job training**
- **Employed: 46,610**
- **Annual Earnings: $18,900**
- **Growth: 17.4%**
- **Annual Job Openings: 9,000**

Record drugs delivered to the pharmacy, store incoming merchandise, and inform the supervisor of stock needs. May operate cash register and accept prescriptions for filling.

Accept prescriptions for filling, gathering and processing necessary information. Answer telephone inquiries, referring callers to pharmacist when necessary. Prepare solid and liquid dosage medications for dispensing into bottles and unit dose packaging. Greet customers and help them locate merchandise. Unpack, sort, count, and label incoming merchandise, including items requiring special handling or refrigeration. Prepare prescription labels by typing or operating a computer and printer. Receive, store, and inventory pharmaceutical supplies, notifying pharmacist when levels are low. Operate cash register to process cash and credit sales. Restock storage areas, replenishing items on shelves. Perform clerical tasks such as filing, compiling and maintaining prescription records, and composing letters. Maintain and clean equipment, work areas, and shelves. Provide customers with information about the uses and effects of drugs. Prepare, maintain, and record records of inventories, receipts, purchases, and deliveries, using a variety of computer screen formats. Process medical insurance claims, posting bill amounts and calculating co-payments. Compound, package, and label pharmaceutical

products under direction of pharmacist. Operate capsule- and tablet-counting machine that automatically distributes a certain number of capsules or tablets into smaller containers. Calculate anticipated drug usage for a prescribed period. Deliver medication to treatment areas, living units, residences, and clinics, using various means of transportation.

GOE Information—Interest Area: 08. Health Science. **Work Group:** 08.02. Medicine and Surgery. **Personality Type—**No data available. **Work Values—**No data available. **Skills—**Operation and Control; Service Orientation; Judgment and Decision Making; Systems Evaluation; Active Learning; Learning Strategies. **Abilities—***Cognitive:* Oral Comprehension; Memorization; Oral Expression; Problem Sensitivity; Time Sharing. *Psychomotor:* None met the criteria. *Physical:* Extent Flexibility; Trunk Strength. *Sensory:* Near Vision. **General Work Activities—***Information Input:* Identifying Objects, Actions, and Events; Getting Information; Monitoring Processes, Materials, or Surroundings. *Mental Process:* Updating and Using Relevant Knowledge; Organizing, Planning, and Prioritizing; Judging the Qualities of Things, Services, or Other People's Work. *Work Output:* Interacting With Computers; Handling and Moving Objects; Performing General Physical Activities. *Interacting with Others:* Establishing and Maintaining Interpersonal Relationships; Performing for or Working with the Public; Resolving Conflicts and Negotiating with Others. **Physical Work Conditions—**Indoors; Disease or Infections; Standing; Walking and Running; Using Hands on Objects, Tools, or Controls; Repetitive Motions. **Other Job Characteristics—**Need to Be Exact or Accurate; Repeat Same Tasks; Errors Have Important Consequences.

Experience—Job Zone 2. Some previous work-related skill, knowledge, or experience may be helpful in these occupations, but usually is not needed. **Job Preparation—**SVP 4.0 to less than 6.0—six months to less than two years. **Knowledges—**Medicine and Dentistry; Clerical Practices; Customer and Personal Service; Chemistry; Economics and Accounting; Computers and Electronics. **Instructional Program—**Pharmacy Technician.

Related SOC Job—31-9095 Pharmacy Aides. **Related OOH Job—**Pharmacy Aides. **Related DOT Job—**074.381-010 Pharmacist Assistant.

31-9096.00 Veterinary Assistants and Laboratory Animal Caretakers

- **Education/Training Required: Short-term on-the-job training**
- **Employed: 69,890**
- **Annual Earnings: $19,610**
- **Growth: 21.0%**
- **Annual Job Openings: 14,000**

Feed, water, and examine pets and other nonfarm animals for signs of illness, disease, or injury in laboratories and animal hospitals and clinics. Clean and disinfect cages and work areas and sterilize laboratory and surgical equipment. May provide routine post-operative care, administer medication orally or topically, or prepare samples for laboratory examination under the supervision of veterinary or laboratory animal technologists or technicians, veterinarians, or scientists.

Monitor animals recovering from surgery and notify veterinarians of any unusual changes or symptoms. Administer anesthetics during surgery and monitor the effects on animals. Clean, maintain, and sterilize instruments and equipment. Administer medication, immunizations, and blood plasma to animals as prescribed by veterinarians. Provide emergency first aid to sick or injured animals. Clean and maintain kennels, animal holding areas, examination and operating rooms, and animal loading/unloading facilities to control the spread of disease. Hold or restrain animals during veterinary procedures. Perform routine laboratory tests or diagnostic tests such as taking and developing X rays. Fill medication prescriptions. Collect laboratory specimens such as blood, urine, and feces for testing. Examine animals to detect behavioral changes or clinical symptoms that could indicate illness or injury. Assist veterinarians in examining animals to determine the nature of illnesses or injuries. Prepare surgical equipment and pass instruments and materials to veterinarians during surgical procedures. Perform enemas, catheterization, ear flushes, intravenous feedings, and gavages. Prepare feed for animals according to specific instructions such as diet lists and schedules. Exercise animals and provide them with companionship. Record information relating to animal genealogy, feeding schedules, appearance, behavior, and breeding. Educate and advise clients on animal health care, nutrition, and behavior problems. Perform hygiene-related duties such as clipping animals' claws and cleaning and polishing teeth. Prepare examination or treatment rooms by stocking them with appropriate supplies. Provide assistance with euthanasia of animals and disposal of corpses. Perform office reception duties such as scheduling appointments and helping customers. Dust, spray, or bathe animals to control insect pests. Write reports, maintain research information, and perform clerical duties. Perform accounting duties, including bookkeeping, billing customers for services, and maintaining inventories. Assist professional personnel with research projects in commercial, public health, or research laboratories.

GOE Information—Interest Area: 08. Health Science. **Work Group:** 08.05. Animal Care. **Personality Type**—Realistic. Realistic occupations frequently involve work activities that include practical, hands-on problems and solutions. They often deal with plants; animals; and real-world materials like wood, tools, and machinery. Many of the occupations require working outside and do not involve a lot of paperwork or working closely with others. **Work Values**—Supervision, Technical; Variety. **Skills**—Science; Operation Monitoring; Active Listening; Reading Comprehension; Instructing; Equipment Maintenance. **Abilities**—*Cognitive:* Problem Sensitivity; Inductive Reasoning; Oral Expression; Speed of Closure; Oral Comprehension. *Psychomotor:* Manual Dexterity; Arm-Hand Steadiness; Multilimb Coordination; Control Precision; Finger Dexterity. *Physical:* Extent Flexibility; Static Strength; Gross Body Coordination; Trunk Strength. *Sensory:* Speech Clarity; Speech Recognition. **General Work Activities**—*Information Input:* Identifying Objects, Actions, and Events; Monitoring Processes, Materials, or Surroundings; Getting Information. *Mental Process:* Updating and Using Relevant Knowledge; Organizing, Planning, and Prioritizing; Making Decisions and Solving Problems. *Work Output:* Handling and Moving Objects; Performing General Physical Activities; Documenting or Recording Information. *Interacting with Others:* Assisting and Caring for Others; Establishing and Maintaining Interpersonal Relationships; Communicating with Other Workers. **Physical Work Conditions**—Indoors; Disease or Infections; Minor Burns, Cuts, Bites, or Stings; Standing; Walking and Running; Using Hands on Objects, Tools, or Controls. **Other Job Characteristics**—Need to Be Exact or Accurate; Errors Have Important Consequences; Repeat Same Tasks.

Experience—Job Zone 2. Some previous work-related skill, knowledge, or experience may be helpful in these occupations, but usually is not needed. **Job Preparation**—SVP 4.0 to less than 6.0–six months to less than two years. **Knowledges**—Medicine and Dentistry; Biology; Chemistry; Clerical Practices. **Instructional Program**—Veterinary/Animal Health Technology/Technician and Veterinary Assistant.

Related SOC Job—31-9096 Veterinary Assistants and Laboratory Animal Caretakers. **Related OOH Job**—Veterinary Assistants and Laboratory Animal Caretakers. **Related DOT Job**—079.361-014 Veterinary Technician.

31-9099.99 Healthcare Support Workers, All Other

- **Education/Training Required: Short-term on-the-job training**
- **Employed: 184,200**
- **Annual Earnings: $26,020**
- **Growth: 20.9%**
- **Annual Job Openings: 38,000**

All healthcare support workers not listed separately.

No task data available.

Note: The Department of Labor has not collected some data for this job, so it has fewer details than the other descriptions.

Related SOC Job—31-9099 Healthcare Support Workers, All Other. **Related OOH Job**—None. **Related DOT Jobs**—079.364-022 Phlebotomist; 354.377-010 Birth Attendant; 355.667-010 Morgue Attendant; 355.677-014 Transporter, Patients.

33-0000

Protective Service Occupations

33-1000 First-Line Supervisors/ Managers, Protective Service Workers

33-1011.00 First-Line Supervisors/ Managers of Correctional Officers

- Education/Training Required: Work experience in a related occupation
- Employed: 37,530
- Annual Earnings: $48,570
- Growth: 9.4%
- Annual Job Openings: 2,000

Supervise and coordinate activities of correctional officers and jailers.

Take, receive, and check periodic inmate counts. Maintain order, discipline, and security within assigned areas in accordance with relevant rules, regulations, policies, and laws. Respond to emergencies such as escapes. Maintain knowledge of, comply with, and enforce all institutional policies, rules, procedures, and regulations. Supervise and direct the work of correctional officers to ensure the safe custody, discipline, and welfare of inmates. Restrain, secure, and control offenders, using chemical agents, firearms, and other weapons of force as necessary. Supervise and perform searches of inmates and their quarters to locate contraband items. Monitor behavior of subordinates to ensure alert, courteous, and professional behavior toward inmates, parolees, fellow employees, visitors, and the public. Complete administrative paperwork and supervise the preparation and maintenance of records, forms, and reports. Instruct employees and provide on-the-job training. Conduct roll calls of correctional officers. Supervise activities such as searches, shakedowns, riot control, and institutional tours. Carry injured offenders or employees to safety and provide emergency first aid when necessary. Supervise and provide security for offenders performing tasks such as construction, maintenance, laundry, food service, and other industrial or agricultural operations. Develop work and security procedures. Set up employee work schedules. Resolve problems between inmates. Read and review offender information to identify issues that require special attention. Rate behavior of inmates, promoting acceptable attitudes and behaviors to those with low ratings. Transfer and transport offenders on foot or by driving vehicles such as trailers, vans, and buses. Examine incoming and outgoing mail to ensure conformance with regulations. Convey correctional officers' and inmates' complaints to superiors.

GOE Information—Interest Area: 12. Law and Public Safety. **Work Group:** 12.01. Managerial Work in Law and Public Safety. **Personality Type**—No data available. **Work Values**—No data available. **Skills**—Management of Personnel Resources; Social Perceptiveness; Negotiation; Persuasion; Monitoring; Service Orientation. **Abilities**—*Cognitive:* Flexibility of Closure; Perceptual Speed; Selective Attention; Problem Sensitivity; Written Expression; Time Sharing. *Psychomotor:* Response Orientation; Reaction Time; Multilimb Coordination; Arm-Hand Steadiness; Manual Dexterity. *Physical:* Static Strength; Explosive Strength; Stamina; Gross Body Coordination; Gross Body Equilibrium; Trunk Strength. *Sensory:* Auditory Attention; Depth Perception; Far Vision; Hearing Sensitivity; Speech Recognition; Speech Clarity. **General Work Activities**—*Information Input:* Monitoring Processes, Materials, or Surroundings; Identifying Objects, Actions, and Events; Getting Information. *Mental Process:* Making Decisions and Solving Problems; Organizing, Planning, and Prioritizing; Evaluating Information Against Standards. *Work Output:* Documenting or Recording Information; Performing General Physical Activities; Handling and Moving Objects. *Interacting with Others:* Resolving Conflicts and Negotiating with Others; Guiding, Directing, and Motivating Subordinates; Coaching and Developing Others. **Physical Work Conditions**—More Often Indoors Than Outdoors; Noisy; Very Bright or Dim Lighting; Contaminants; Disease or Infections. **Other Job Characteristics**—Repeat Same Tasks; Need to Be Exact or Accurate.

Experience—Job Zone 3. Previous work-related skill, knowledge, or experience is required. **Job Preparation**—SVP 6.0 to less than 7.0— more than one year and less than four years. **Knowledges**—Public Safety and Security; Psychology; Therapy and Counseling; Personnel and Human Resources; Clerical Practices; Administration and Management. **Instructional Programs**—Corrections; Corrections Administration.

Related SOC Job—33-1011 First-Line Supervisors/Managers of Correctional Officers. **Related OOH Job**—Correctional Officers. **Related DOT Jobs**—372.137-010 Correction Officer, Head; 372.167-018 Jailer, Chief.

33-1012.00 First-Line Supervisors/ Managers of Police and Detectives

- Education/Training Required: Work experience in a related occupation
- Employed: 91,320
- Annual Earnings: $65,570
- Growth: 15.5%
- Annual Job Openings: 9,000

Supervise and coordinate activities of members of police force.

Explain police operations to subordinates to assist them in performing their job duties. Inform personnel of changes in regulations and policies, implications of new or amended laws, and new techniques of police work. Supervise and coordinate the investigation of criminal cases, offering guidance and expertise to investigators and ensuring that procedures are conducted in accordance with laws and regulations. Investigate and resolve personnel problems within organization and charges of misconduct against staff. Train staff in proper police work procedures. Maintain logs; prepare reports; and direct the preparation, handling, and maintenance of departmental records. Monitor and evaluate the job performance of subordinates and authorize promotions and transfers. Direct collection, preparation, and handling of evidence and personal property of prisoners. Develop, implement, and revise departmental policies and procedures. Conduct raids and order detention of witnesses and suspects for questioning. Prepare work schedules and assign duties to subordinates. Discipline staff for violation of department rules and regulations. Cooperate with court personnel and officials from other law enforcement agencies and testify in court as necessary. Review contents of written orders to ensure adherence to legal requirements. Inspect facilities, supplies, vehicles, and equipment to ensure conformance to standards. Prepare news releases and respond to police correspondence. Requisition and issue equipment and supplies. Meet with civic, educational, and community groups to develop community programs and events and to discuss law enforcement subjects. Direct release or transfer of prisoners. Prepare budgets and manage expenditures of department funds.

GOE Information—Interest Area: 12. Law and Public Safety. **Work Group:** 12.01. Managerial Work in Law and Public Safety. **Personality Type**—Enterprising. Enterprising occupations frequently involve starting up and carrying out projects. These occupations can involve leading people and making many decisions. They sometimes require risk taking and often deal with business. **Work Values**—Authority; Social Status; Responsibility; Social Service; Achievement; Autonomy. **Skills**—Management of Personnel Resources; Persuasion; Negotiation; Social Perceptiveness; Service Orientation; Monitoring. **Abilities**—*Cognitive:* Spatial Orientation; Speed of Closure; Memorization; Time Sharing; Flexibility of Closure; Written Expression. *Psychomotor:* Reaction Time; Response Orientation; Rate Control; Multilimb Coordination; Speed of Limb Movement; Control Precision. *Physical:* Stamina; Static Strength; Gross Body Coordination; Extent Flexibility; Trunk Strength. *Sensory:* Night Vision; Glare Sensitivity; Peripheral Vision; Sound Localization; Far Vision; Depth Perception. **General Work Activities**—*Information Input:* Monitoring Processes, Materials, or Surroundings; Getting Information; Identifying Objects, Actions, and Events. *Mental Process:* Making Decisions and Solving Problems; Updating and Using Relevant Knowledge; Organizing, Planning, and Prioritizing. *Work Output:* Documenting or Recording Information; Performing General Physical Activities; Operating Vehicles or Equipment. *Interacting with Others:* Guiding, Directing, and Motivating Subordinates; Performing for or Working with the Public; Resolving Conflicts and Negotiating with Others. **Physical Work Conditions**—More Often Outdoors Than Indoors; Very Hot or Cold; Very Bright or Dim Lighting; Hazardous Equipment; Sitting. **Other Job Characteristics**—Need to Be Exact or Accurate; Errors Have Important Consequences; Repeat Same Tasks.

Experience—Job Zone 4. A minimum of two to four years of work-related skill, knowledge, or experience is needed. **Job Preparation**—SVP 7.0 to less than 8.0—two years to less than 10 years. **Knowledges**—Public Safety and Security; Psychology; Law and Government; Personnel and Human Resources; Education and Training; Telecommunications. **Instructional Programs**—Corrections; Criminal Justice/Law Enforcement Administration; Criminal Justice/Safety Studies.

Related SOC Job—33-1012 First-Line Supervisors/Managers of Police and Detectives. **Related OOH Job**—Police and Detectives. **Related DOT Jobs**—375.133-010 Police Sergeant, Precinct I; 375.137-010 Commander, Identification and Records; 375.137-014 Desk Officer; 375.137-018 Police Lieutenant, Community Relations; 375.137-026 Traffic Sergeant; 375.137-030 Commander, Police Reserves; 375.137-034 Commanding Officer, Police; 375.163-010 Commanding Officer, Motorized Squad; 375.167-010 Commanding Officer, Homicide Squad; 375.167-014 Commanding Officer, Investigation Division; 375.167-022 Detective Chief; others.

33-1021.00 First-Line Supervisors/ Managers of Fire Fighting and Prevention Workers

- **Education/Training Required: Work experience in a related occupation**
- **Employed: 53,490**
- **Annual Earnings: $60,840**
- **Growth: 21.1%**
- **Annual Job Openings: 4,000**

The job openings listed here are shared with 33-1021.01 Municipal Fire Fighting and Prevention Supervisors and 33-1021.02 Forest Fire Fighting and Prevention Supervisors.

Supervise and coordinate activities of workers engaged in fire fighting and fire prevention and control.

No task data available.

GOE Information—Interest Area: 12. Law and Public Safety. **Work Group:** 12.01. Managerial Work in Law and Public Safety. **Note:** The Department of Labor has not collected some data for this job, so it has fewer details than the other descriptions.

Instructional Programs—Fire Protection and Safety Technology/Technician; Fire Services Administration.

Related SOC Job—33-1021 First-Line Supervisors/Managers of Fire Fighting and Prevention Workers. **Related OOH Job**—Fire Fighting Occupations. **Related DOT Job**—No data available.

33-1021.01 Municipal Fire Fighting and Prevention Supervisors

- **Education/Training Required: Work experience in a related occupation**
- **Employed: 53,490**
- **Annual Earnings: $60,840**
- **Growth: 21.1%**
- **Annual Job Openings: 4,000**

The job openings listed here are shared with 33-1021.00 First-Line Supervisors/Managers of Fire Fighting and Prevention Workers and 33-1021.02 Forest Fire Fighting and Prevention Supervisors.

Supervise fire fighters who control and extinguish municipal fires, protect life and property, and conduct rescue efforts.

Assign firefighters to jobs at strategic locations to facilitate rescue of persons and maximize application of extinguishing agents. Provide emergency medical services as required and perform light to heavy rescue functions at emergencies. Assess nature and extent of fire, condition of building, danger to adjacent buildings, and water supply status to determine crew or company requirements. Instruct and drill fire department personnel in assigned duties, including firefighting, medical care, hazardous materials response, fire prevention, and related subjects. Evaluate the performance of assigned firefighting personnel. Direct the training of firefighters, assigning of instructors to training classes, and providing of supervisors with reports on training progress and status. Prepare activity reports listing fire call locations, actions taken, fire types and probable causes, damage estimates, and situation dispositions. Maintain required maps and records. Attend in-service training classes to remain current in knowledge of codes, laws, ordinances, and regulations. Evaluate fire station procedures to ensure efficiency and enforcement of departmental regulations. Direct firefighters in station maintenance duties and participate in these duties. Compile and maintain equipment and personnel records, including accident reports. Direct investigation of cases of suspected arson, hazards, and false alarms and submit reports outlining findings. Recommend personnel actions related to disciplinary procedures, performance, leaves of absence, and grievances. Supervise and participate in the inspection of properties to ensure that they are in compliance with applicable fire codes, ordinances, laws, regulations, and standards. Write and submit proposals for repair, modification, or replacement of firefighting equipment. Coordinate the distribution of fire prevention promotional materials. Identify corrective actions needed to bring properties into compliance with applicable fire codes and ordinances and conduct follow-up inspections to see if corrective actions have been taken. Participate in creating fire safety guidelines and evacuation schemes for non-residential buildings.

GOE Information—Interest Area: 12. Law and Public Safety. Work Group: 12.01. Managerial Work in Law and Public Safety. Personality Type—Realistic. Realistic occupations frequently involve work activities that include practical, hands-on problems and solutions. They often deal with plants; animals; and real-world materials like wood, tools, and machinery. Many of the occupations require working outside and do not involve a lot of paperwork or working closely with others. Work Values—Authority; Social Status; Achievement; Co-workers; Responsibility; Social Service. Skills— Equipment Maintenance; Management of Personnel Resources; Service Orientation; Operation Monitoring; Management of Material Resources; Coordination. Abilities—Cognitive: Spatial Orientation; Speed of Closure; Flexibility of Closure; Problem Sensitivity; Selective Attention; Inductive Reasoning. Psychomotor: Reaction Time; Multilimb Coordination; Control Precision; Manual Dexterity; Arm-Hand Steadiness. Physical: Static Strength; Stamina; Gross Body Coordination; Dynamic Strength; Extent Flexibility. Sensory: Auditory Attention; Speech Clarity; Depth Perception; Far Vision; Speech Recognition. General Work Activities—Information Input: Monitoring Processes, Materials, or Surroundings; Identifying Objects, Actions, and Events; Inspecting Equipment, Structures, or Materials. Mental Process: Making Decisions and Solving Problems; Updating and Using Relevant Knowledge; Organizing, Planning, and Prioritizing. Work Output: Performing General Physical Activities; Handling and Moving Objects; Documenting or Recording Information. Interacting with Others: Assisting and Caring for Others; Resolving Conflicts and Negotiating with Others; Establishing and Maintaining Interpersonal Relationships. Physical Work Conditions—More Often Outdoors Than Indoors; Noisy; Contaminants; Disease or Infections; Hazardous Equipment. Other Job Characteristics—Need to Be Exact or Accurate; Errors Have Important Consequences; Repeat Same Tasks.

Experience—Job Zone 3. Previous work-related skill, knowledge, or experience is required. Job Preparation—SVP 6.0 to less than 7.0— more than one year and less than four years. Knowledges—Public Safety and Security; Building and Construction; Medicine and Dentistry; Education and Training; Customer and Personal Service; Mechanical Devices. Instructional Programs—Fire Protection and Safety Technology/Technician; Fire Services Administration.

Related SOC Job—33-1021 First-Line Supervisors/Managers of Fire Fighting and Prevention Workers. Related OOH Job—Fire Fighting Occupations. Related DOT Jobs—373.134-010 Fire Captain; 373.167-010 Battalion Chief; 373.167-014 Captain, Fire-Prevention Bureau; 373.167-018 Fire Marshal.

33-1021.02 Forest Fire Fighting and Prevention Supervisors

- Education/Training Required: Work experience in a related occupation
- Employed: 53,490
- Annual Earnings: $60,840
- Growth: 21.1%
- Annual Job Openings: 4,000

The job openings listed here are shared with 33-1021.00 First-Line Supervisors/Managers of Fire Fighting and Prevention Workers and 33-1021.01 Municipal Fire Fighting and Prevention Supervisors.

Supervise fire fighters who control and suppress fires in forests or vacant public land.

Communicate fire details to superiors, subordinates, and interagency dispatch centers, using two-way radios. Serve as working leader of an engine, hand, helicopter, or prescribed fire crew of three or more fire-fighters. Maintain fire suppression equipment in good condition, checking equipment periodically to ensure that it is ready for use. Evaluate size, location, and condition of forest fires in order to request and dispatch crews and position equipment so fires can be contained safely and effectively. Operate wildland fire engines and hoselays. Direct and supervise prescribed burn projects and prepare post-burn reports analyzing burn conditions and results. Monitor prescribed burns to ensure that they are conducted safely and effectively. Identify staff training and development needs to ensure that appropriate training can be arranged. Maintain knowledge of forest fire laws and fire prevention techniques and tactics. Recommend equipment modifications or new equipment purchases. Perform administrative duties such as compiling and maintaining records, completing forms, preparing reports, and composing correspondence. Recruit and hire forest fire-fighting personnel. Train workers in such skills as parachute jumping, fire suppression, aerial observation, and radio communication, both in the classroom and on the job. Review and evaluate employee performance. Observe fires and crews from air to determine fire-fighting force requirements and to note changing conditions that will affect fire-fighting efforts. Inspect all stations, uniforms, equipment, and recreation areas to ensure compliance with safety standards, taking corrective action as necessary. Schedule employee work assignments and set work priorities. Regulate open burning by issuing burning permits, inspecting problem sites, issuing citations for violations of laws and ordinances, and educating the public in proper burning practices. Direct investigations of suspected arsons in wildfires, working closely with other investigating agencies. Monitor fire suppression expenditures to ensure that they are necessary and reasonable.

GOE Information—Interest Area: 12. Law and Public Safety. Work Group: 12.01. Managerial Work in Law and Public Safety. Personality Type—Realistic. Realistic occupations frequently involve work activities that include practical, hands-on problems and solutions. They often deal with plants; animals; and real-world materials like wood, tools, and machinery. Many of the occupations require working outside and do not involve a lot of paperwork or working closely with others. Work Values—Authority; Social Status; Responsibility; Achievement; Autonomy; Co-workers. Skills— Equipment Maintenance; Repairing; Operation Monitoring; Management of Personnel Resources; Operation and Control; Management of Material Resources. Abilities—Cognitive: Spatial Orientation; Visualization; Flexibility of Closure; Fluency of Ideas; Speed of Closure; Originality. Psychomotor: Reaction Time; Control Precision; Speed of Limb Movement; Multilimb Coordination; Rate Control; Response Orientation. Physical: Dynamic Strength; Stamina; Static Strength; Gross Body Coordination; Extent Flexibility; Trunk Strength. Sensory: Glare Sensitivity; Far Vision; Depth Perception; Auditory Attention; Hearing Sensitivity; Visual Color Discrimination. General Work Activities—Information Input: Monitoring Processes, Materials, or Surroundings; Identifying Objects, Actions, and Events; Getting Information. Mental Process: Updating and Using Relevant Knowledge; Making Decisions and Solving Problems; Processing Information. Work Output: Performing General Physical Activities; Handling and Moving Objects; Operating Vehicles or Equipment. Interacting with Others: Communicating with Other Workers; Communicating with Persons Outside Organization; Establishing and Maintaining Interpersonal Relationships. Physical Work Conditions—Outdoors; Noisy; Very Hot or Cold; Hazardous Equipment; Minor Burns, Cuts, Bites, or Stings; Standing. Other Job Characteristics—Need to Be Exact or Accurate; Errors Have Important Consequences; Repeat Same Tasks.

Experience—Job Zone 3. Previous work-related skill, knowledge, or experience is required. **Job Preparation**—SVP 6.0 to less than 7.0—more than one year and less than four years. **Knowledges**—Public Safety and Security; Building and Construction; Customer and Personal Service; Personnel and Human Resources; Mechanical Devices; Transportation. **Instructional Programs**—Fire Protection and Safety Technology/Technician; Fire Services Administration.

Related SOC Job—33-1021 First-Line Supervisors/Managers of Fire Fighting and Prevention Workers. **Related OOH Job**—Fire Fighting Occupations. **Related DOT Job**—452.134-010 Smoke Jumper Supervisor.

33-1099.99 First-Line Supervisors/ Managers, Protective Service Workers, All Other

- **Education/Training Required: Work experience in a related occupation**
- **Employed: 49,330**
- **Annual Earnings: $41,150**
- **Growth: 8.7%**
- **Annual Job Openings: 5,000**

All protective service supervisors not listed separately above.

No task data available.

Note: The Department of Labor has not collected some data for this job, so it has fewer details than the other descriptions.

Related SOC Job—33-1099 First-Line Supervisors/Managers, Protective Service Workers, All Other. **Related OOH Job**—None. **Related DOT Jobs**—372.167-014 Guard, Chief; 376.137-010 Manager, Internal Security.

33-2000 Fire Fighting and Prevention Workers

33-2011.00 Fire Fighters

- **Education/Training Required: Long-term on-the-job training**
- **Employed: 282,180**
- **Annual Earnings: $39,090**
- **Growth: 24.3%**
- **Annual Job Openings: 21,000**

The job openings listed here are shared with 33-2011.01 Municipal Fire Fighters and 33-2011.02 Forest Fire Fighters.

Control and extinguish fires or respond to emergency situations where life, property, or the environment is at risk. Duties may include fire prevention, emergency medical service, hazardous material response, search and rescue, and disaster management.

No task data available.

GOE Information—Interest Area: 12. Law and Public Safety. **Work Group:** 12.06. Emergency Responding. **Note:** The Department of Labor has not collected some data for this job, so it has fewer details than the other descriptions.

Instructional Programs—Fire Protection, Other; Fire Science/Firefighting.

Related SOC Job—33-2011 Fire Fighters. **Related OOH Job**—Fire Fighting Occupations. **Related DOT Job**—No data available.

33-2011.01 Municipal Fire Fighters

- **Education/Training Required: Long-term on-the-job training**
- **Employed: 282,180**
- **Annual Earnings: $39,090**
- **Growth: 24.3%**
- **Annual Job Openings: 21,000**

The job openings listed here are shared with 33-2011.00 Fire Fighters and 33-2011.02 Forest Fire Fighters.

Control and extinguish municipal fires, protect life and property, and conduct rescue efforts.

Administer first aid and cardiopulmonary resuscitation to injured persons. Rescue victims from burning buildings and accident sites. Search burning buildings to locate fire victims. Drive and operate fire fighting vehicles and equipment. Move toward the source of a fire, using knowledge of types of fires, construction design, building materials, and physical layout of properties. Dress with equipment such as fire-resistant clothing and breathing apparatus. Position and climb ladders to gain access to upper levels of buildings or to rescue individuals from burning structures. Take action to contain hazardous chemicals that might catch fire, leak, or spill. Assess fires and situations and report conditions to superiors to receive instructions, using two-way radios. Respond to fire alarms and other calls for assistance, such as automobile and industrial accidents. Operate pumps connected to high-pressure hoses. Select and attach hose nozzles, depending on fire type, and direct streams of water or chemicals onto fires. Create openings in buildings for ventilation or entrance, using axes, chisels, crowbars, electric saws, or core cutters. Inspect fire sites after flames have been extinguished to ensure that there is no further danger. Lay hose lines and connect them to water supplies. Protect property from water and smoke, using waterproof salvage covers, smoke ejectors, and deodorants. Participate in physical training activities to maintain a high level of physical fitness. Salvage property by removing broken glass, pumping out water, and ventilating buildings to remove smoke. Participate in fire drills and demonstrations of fire fighting techniques. Clean and maintain fire stations and fire fighting equipment and apparatus. Collaborate with police to respond to accidents, disasters, and arson investigation calls. Establish firelines to prevent unauthorized persons from entering areas near fires. Inform and educate the public on fire prevention. Inspect buildings for fire hazards and compliance with fire prevention ordinances, testing and checking smoke alarms and fire suppression equipment as necessary.

GOE Information—Interest Area: 12. Law and Public Safety. **Work Group:** 12.06. Emergency Responding. **Personality Type**—Realistic. Realistic occupations frequently involve work activities that include practical, hands-on problems and solutions. They often deal with plants; animals; and real-world materials like wood, tools, and machinery. Many of the occupations require working outside and do not involve a lot of paperwork or working closely with others. **Work Values**—Social Status; Achievement; Social Service; Co-workers; Supervision, Technical; Supervision, Human Relations. **Skills**—Equipment Maintenance; Service Orientation; Equipment Selection; Operation Monitoring; Social Perceptiveness; Coordination. **Abilities**—*Cognitive:* Spatial Orientation; Flexibility of Closure; Speed of Closure; Selective Attention; Perceptual Speed; Inductive Reasoning. *Psychomotor:* Speed of Limb Movement; Response Orientation; Reaction Time; Multilimb Coordination; Manual

Dexterity; Rate Control. *Physical:* Static Strength; Dynamic Strength; Stamina; Trunk Strength; Explosive Strength; Gross Body Coordination. *Sensory:* Sound Localization; Peripheral Vision; Night Vision; Glare Sensitivity; Auditory Attention; Depth Perception. **General Work Activities—***Information Input:* Identifying Objects, Actions, and Events; Monitoring Processes, Materials, or Surroundings; Getting Information. *Mental Process:* Updating and Using Relevant Knowledge; Making Decisions and Solving Problems; Judging the Qualities of Things, Services, or Other People's Work. *Work Output:* Handling and Moving Objects; Performing General Physical Activities; Operating Vehicles or Equipment. *Interacting with Others:* Communicating with Other Workers; Establishing and Maintaining Interpersonal Relationships; Assisting and Caring for Others. **Physical Work Conditions—**More Often Outdoors Than Indoors; Noisy; Contaminants; Disease or Infections; Hazardous Equipment. **Other Job Characteristics—**Need to Be Exact or Accurate; Errors Have Important Consequences; Repeat Same Tasks.

Experience—Job Zone 3. Previous work-related skill, knowledge, or experience is required. **Job Preparation—**SVP 6.0 to less than 7.0—more than one year and less than four years. **Knowledges—**Medicine and Dentistry; Customer and Personal Service; Physics; Building and Construction; Chemistry; Public Safety and Security. **Instructional Programs—**Fire Protection, Other; Fire Science/Firefighting.

Related SOC Job—33-2011 Fire Fighters. **Related OOH Job—**Fire Fighting Occupations. **Related DOT Jobs—**373.363-010 Fire Chief's Aide; 373.364-010 Fire Fighter; 373.364-640 Fire Apparatus Engineer; 373.364-641 Fire Engineer; 373.663-010 Fire Fighter, Crash, Fire, and Rescue; 379.374-580 Fire Medic.

33-2011.02 Forest Fire Fighters

- **Education/Training Required: Long-term on-the-job training**
- **Employed: 282,180**
- **Annual Earnings: $39,090**
- **Growth: 24.3%**
- **Annual Job Openings: 21,000**

The job openings listed here are shared with 33-2011.00 Fire Fighters and 33-2011.01 Municipal Fire Fighters.

Control and suppress fires in forests or vacant public land.

Maintain contact with fire dispatchers at all times to notify them of the need for additional firefighters and supplies or to detail any difficulties encountered. Rescue fire victims and administer emergency medical aid. Collaborate with other firefighters as a member of a firefighting crew. Patrol burned areas after fires to locate and eliminate hot spots that may restart fires. Extinguish flames and embers to suppress fires, using shovels or engine- or hand-driven water or chemical pumps. Fell trees, cut and clear brush, and dig trenches to create firelines, using axes, chainsaws, or shovels. Maintain knowledge of current firefighting practices by participating in drills and by attending seminars, conventions, and conferences. Operate pumps connected to high-pressure hoses. Participate in physical training to maintain high levels of physical fitness. Establish water supplies, connect hoses, and direct water onto fires. Maintain fire equipment and firehouse living quarters. Inform and educate the public about fire prevention. Take action to contain any hazardous chemicals that could catch fire, leak, or spill. Organize fire caches, positioning equipment for the most effective response. Transport personnel and cargo to and from fire areas. Participate in fire prevention and inspection programs. Perform forest maintenance and improvement tasks such as cutting brush, planting trees, building trails, and marking timber. Test and maintain tools, equipment, jump gear, and para-

chutes to ensure readiness for fire-suppression activities. Observe forest areas from fire lookout towers to spot potential problems. Orient self in relation to fire, using compass and map, and collect supplies and equipment dropped by parachute. Serve as fully trained lead helicopter crewmember and as helispot manager. Drop weighted paper streamers from aircraft to determine the speed and direction of the wind at fire sites.

GOE Information—Interest Area: 12. Law and Public Safety. **Work Group:** 12.06. Emergency Responding. **Personality Type—**Realistic. Realistic occupations frequently involve work activities that include practical, hands-on problems and solutions. They often deal with plants; animals; and real-world materials like wood, tools, and machinery. Many of the occupations require working outside and do not involve a lot of paperwork or working closely with others. **Work Values—**Achievement; Co-workers; Social Status; Supervision, Technical; Supervision, Human Relations; Ability Utilization. **Skills—**Management of Personnel Resources; Repairing; Equipment Maintenance; Operation Monitoring; Systems Analysis; Operation and Control. **Abilities—***Cognitive:* Spatial Orientation; Speed of Closure; Flexibility of Closure; Problem Sensitivity; Time Sharing; Selective Attention. *Psychomotor:* Speed of Limb Movement; Response Orientation; Reaction Time; Manual Dexterity; Control Precision; Multilimb Coordination. *Physical:* Static Strength; Gross Body Equilibrium; Stamina; Dynamic Strength; Extent Flexibility; Gross Body Coordination. *Sensory:* Glare Sensitivity; Auditory Attention; Depth Perception; Far Vision; Speech Clarity; Speech Recognition. **General Work Activities—***Information Input:* Identifying Objects, Actions, and Events; Monitoring Processes, Materials, or Surroundings; Inspecting Equipment, Structures, or Materials. *Mental Process:* Making Decisions and Solving Problems; Updating and Using Relevant Knowledge; Developing Objectives and Strategies. *Work Output:* Performing General Physical Activities; Handling and Moving Objects; Controlling Machines and Processes. *Interacting with Others:* Establishing and Maintaining Interpersonal Relationships; Assisting and Caring for Others; Coordinating the Work and Activities of Others. **Physical Work Conditions—**Outdoors; Very Hot or Cold; Contaminants; Hazardous Conditions; Minor Burns, Cuts, Bites, or Stings; Using Hands on Objects, Tools, or Controls. **Other Job Characteristics—**Errors Have Important Consequences; Repeat Same Tasks; Need to Be Exact or Accurate.

Experience—Job Zone 2. Some previous work-related skill, knowledge, or experience may be helpful in these occupations, but usually is not needed. **Job Preparation—**SVP 4.0 to less than 6.0—six months to less than two years. **Knowledges—**Geography; Customer and Personal Service; Mechanical Devices; Education and Training; Public Safety and Security; Psychology. **Instructional Programs—**Fire Protection, Other; Fire Science/Firefighting.

Related SOC Job—33-2011 Fire Fighters. **Related OOH Job—**Fire Fighting Occupations. **Related DOT Jobs—**452.364-014 Smoke Jumper; 452.687-014 Forest-Fire Fighter; 452.687-640 Wildland Fire Fighter Specialist.

33-2021.00 Fire Inspectors and Investigators

- **Education/Training Required: Moderate-term on-the-job training**
- **Employed: 12,820**
- **Annual Earnings: $47,090**
- **Growth: –5.5%**
- **Annual Job Openings: Fewer than 500**

The job openings listed here are shared with 33-2021.01 Fire Inspectors and 33-2021.02 Fire Investigators.

Inspect buildings to detect fire hazards and enforce local ordinances and state laws. Investigate and gather facts to determine cause of fires and explosions.

No task data available.

Note: The Department of Labor has not collected some data for this job, so it has fewer details than the other descriptions.

Instructional Programs—Fire Protection and Safety Technology/Technician; Fire Science/Firefighting.

Related SOC Job—33-2021 Fire Inspectors and Investigators. **Related OOH Job**—Fire Fighting Occupations. **Related DOT Job**—No data available.

33-2021.01 Fire Inspectors

- **Education/Training Required: Moderate-term on-the-job training**
- **Employed: 12,820**
- **Annual Earnings: $47,090**
- **Growth: –5.5%**
- **Annual Job Openings: Fewer than 500**

The job openings listed here are shared with 33-2021.00 Fire Inspectors and Investigators and 33-2021.02 Fire Investigators.

Inspect buildings and equipment to detect fire hazards and enforce state and local regulations.

Inspect buildings to locate hazardous conditions and fire code violations such as accumulations of combustible material, electrical wiring problems, and inadequate or non-functional fire exits. Identify corrective actions necessary to bring properties into compliance with applicable fire codes, laws, regulations, and standards and explain these measures to property owners or their representatives. Conduct inspections and acceptance testing of newly installed fire protection systems. Inspect and test fire protection or fire detection systems to verify that such systems are installed in accordance with appropriate laws, codes, ordinances, regulations, and standards. Conduct fire code compliance follow-ups to ensure that corrective actions have been taken in cases where violations were found. Inspect properties that store, handle, and use hazardous materials to ensure compliance with laws, codes, and regulations; issue hazardous materials permits to facilities found in compliance. Write detailed reports of fire inspections performed, fire code violations observed, and corrective recommendations offered. Review blueprints and plans for new or remodeled buildings to ensure the structures meet fire safety codes. Develop or review fire exit plans. Attend training classes to maintain current knowledge of fire prevention, safety, and firefighting procedures. Present and explain fire code requirements and fire prevention information to architects, contractors, attorneys, engineers, developers, fire service personnel, and the general public. Conduct fire exit drills to monitor and evaluate evacuation procedures. Inspect liquefied petroleum installations, storage containers, and transportation and delivery systems for compliance with fire laws. Search for clues as to the cause of a fire after the fire is completely extinguished. Develop and coordinate fire prevention programs such as false alarm billing, fire inspection reporting, and hazardous materials management. Testify in court regarding fire code and fire safety issues. Recommend changes to fire prevention, inspection, and fire code endorsement procedures.

GOE Information—Interest Area: 07. Government and Public Administration. **Work Group:** 07.03. Regulations Enforcement. **Personality Type**—Conventional. Conventional occupations frequently involve following set procedures and routines. These occupations can include working with data and details more than with ideas. Usually there is a clear line of authority to follow. **Work Values**—Achievement; Social Status; Security; Authority; Supervision, Technical; Ability Utilization. **Skills**—Persuasion; Science; Service Orientation; Negotiation; Operations Analysis; Operation Monitoring. **Abilities**—*Cognitive:* Flexibility of Closure; Inductive Reasoning; Written Expression; Problem Sensitivity; Written Comprehension; Category Flexibility. *Psychomotor:* None met the criteria. *Physical:* None met the criteria. *Sensory:* Speech Clarity; Auditory Attention; Far Vision; Near Vision. **General Work Activities**—*Information Input:* Identifying Objects, Actions, and Events; Inspecting Equipment, Structures, or Materials; Monitoring Processes, Materials, or Surroundings. *Mental Process:* Updating and Using Relevant Knowledge; Organizing, Planning, and Prioritizing; Processing Information. *Work Output:* Documenting or Recording Information; Performing General Physical Activities; Handling and Moving Objects. *Interacting with Others:* Establishing and Maintaining Interpersonal Relationships; Performing for or Working with the Public; Communicating with Persons Outside Organization. **Physical Work Conditions**—More Often Outdoors Than Indoors; Noisy; Very Hot or Cold; Very Bright or Dim Lighting; Hazardous Equipment. **Other Job Characteristics**—Need to Be Exact or Accurate; Errors Have Important Consequences; Repeat Same Tasks.

Experience—Job Zone 3. Previous work-related skill, knowledge, or experience is required. **Job Preparation**—SVP 6.0 to less than 7.0—more than one year and less than four years. **Knowledges**—Public Safety and Security; Building and Construction; Customer and Personal Service; Physics; Design; Law and Government. **Instructional Programs**—Fire Protection and Safety Technology/Technician; Fire Science/Firefighting.

Related SOC Job—33-2021 Fire Inspectors and Investigators. **Related OOH Job**—Fire Fighting Occupations. **Related DOT Jobs**—168.267-010 Building Inspector; 373.267-010 Fire Inspector; 373.367-010 Fire Inspector; 379.687-010 Fire-Extinguisher-Sprinkler Inspector.

33-2021.02 Fire Investigators

- **Education/Training Required: Bachelor's degree**
- **Employed: 12,820**
- **Annual Earnings: $47,090**
- **Growth: –5.5%**
- **Annual Job Openings: Fewer than 500**

The job openings listed here are shared with 33-2021.00 Fire Inspectors and Investigators and 33-2021.01 Fire Inspectors.

Conduct investigations to determine causes of fires and explosions.

Package collected pieces of evidence in securely closed containers such as bags, crates, or boxes to protect them. Examine fire sites and collect evidence such as glass, metal fragments, charred wood, and accelerant residue for use in determining the cause of a fire. Instruct children about the dangers of fire. Analyze evidence and other information to determine probable cause of fire or explosion. Photograph damage and evidence related to causes of fires or explosions to document investigation findings. Subpoena and interview witnesses, property owners, and building occupants to obtain information and sworn testimony. Swear out warrants and arrest and process suspected arsonists. Testify in court cases involving fires, suspected arson, and false alarms. Prepare and maintain reports of investigation results and records of convicted arsonists and arson suspects. Test sites and materials to establish facts such as burn patterns and flash points of materials, using test equipment. Conduct internal investigation to determine negligence and violation of laws and regulations by fire department employees. Dust evidence or portions of fire scenes for latent fingerprints.

GOE Information—Interest Area: 12. Law and Public Safety. **Work Group:** 12.04. Law Enforcement and Public Safety. **Personality Type—**Investigative. Investigative occupations frequently involve working with ideas and require an extensive amount of thinking. These occupations can involve searching for facts and figuring out problems mentally. **Work Values—**Achievement; Ability Utilization; Responsibility; Social Status; Variety; Security. **Skills—**Management of Personnel Resources; Equipment Maintenance; Science; Judgment and Decision Making; Operation and Control; Repairing. **Abilities—** *Cognitive:* Flexibility of Closure; Inductive Reasoning; Problem Sensitivity; Deductive Reasoning; Visualization; Category Flexibility. *Psychomotor:* Reaction Time; Multilimb Coordination; Arm-Hand Steadiness; Control Precision; Manual Dexterity; Finger Dexterity. *Physical:* Static Strength. *Sensory:* Near Vision; Far Vision; Visual Color Discrimination; Speech Clarity; Auditory Attention; Speech Recognition. **General Work Activities—***Information Input:* Identifying Objects, Actions, and Events; Monitoring Processes, Materials, or Surroundings; Inspecting Equipment, Structures, or Materials. *Mental Process:* Updating and Using Relevant Knowledge; Processing Information; Making Decisions and Solving Problems. *Work Output:* Handling and Moving Objects; Performing General Physical Activities; Documenting or Recording Information. *Interacting with Others:* Communicating with Persons Outside Organization; Establishing and Maintaining Interpersonal Relationships; Performing for or Working with the Public. **Physical Work Conditions—**Indoors; Noisy; Contaminants; Hazardous Conditions; Hazardous Equipment; Using Hands on Objects, Tools, or Controls. **Other Job Characteristics—**Need to Be Exact or Accurate; Repeat Same Tasks; Errors Have Important Consequences.

Experience—Job Zone 3. Previous work-related skill, knowledge, or experience is required. **Job Preparation—**SVP 6.0 to less than 7.0— more than one year and less than four years. **Knowledges—**Building and Construction; Public Safety and Security; Physics; Chemistry; Mechanical Devices; Psychology. **Instructional Programs—**Fire Protection and Safety Technology/Technician; Fire Science/ Firefighting.

Related SOC Job—33-2021 Fire Inspectors and Investigators. **Related OOH Job—**Fire Fighting Occupations. **Related DOT Jobs—**373.267- 014 Fire Marshal; 373.267-018 Fire-Investigation Lieutenant; 373.267- 640 Arson And Bomb Investigator.

33-2022.00 Forest Fire Inspectors and Prevention Specialists

- **Education/Training Required: Moderate-term on-the-job training**
- **Employed: 1,720**
- **Annual Earnings: $34,270**
- **Growth: –3.1%**
- **Annual Job Openings: Fewer than 500**

Enforce fire regulations and inspect for forest fire hazards. Report forest fires and weather conditions.

Relay messages about emergencies, accidents, locations of crew and personnel, and fire hazard conditions. Direct crews working on fire-lines during forest fires. Estimate sizes and characteristics of fires and report findings to base camps by radio or telephone. Administer regulations regarding sanitation, fire prevention, violation corrections, and related forest regulations. Extinguish smaller fires with portable extinguishers, shovels, and axes. Locate forest fires on area maps, using azimuth sighters and known landmarks. Maintain records and logbooks. Examine and inventory firefighting equipment such as axes, fire hoses, shovels, pumps, buckets, and fire extinguishers to determine amount and condition. Direct maintenance and repair of firefighting equipment or requisition new equipment. Restrict public access and recreational use of forest lands during critical fire seasons. Patrol assigned areas, looking for forest fires, hazardous conditions, and weather phenomena. Compile and report meteorological data, such as temperature, relative humidity, wind direction and velocity, and types of cloud formations. Inspect campsites to ensure that campers are in compliance with forest use regulations. Inspect forest tracts and logging areas for fire hazards such as accumulated wastes or mishandling of combustibles and recommend appropriate fire prevention measures.

GOE Information—Interest Area: 07. Government and Public Administration. **Work Group:** 07.03. Regulations Enforcement. **Personality Type—**Realistic. Realistic occupations frequently involve work activities that include practical, hands-on problems and solutions. They often deal with plants; animals; and real-world materials like wood, tools, and machinery. Many of the occupations require working outside and do not involve a lot of paperwork or working closely with others. **Work Values—**Achievement; Authority; Ability Utilization; Social Status; Responsibility; Variety. **Skills—** Management of Personnel Resources; Equipment Maintenance; Service Orientation; Repairing; Science; Technology Design. **Abilities—***Cognitive:* Flexibility of Closure; Perceptual Speed; Speed of Closure; Problem Sensitivity; Originality; Time Sharing. *Psychomotor:* Multilimb Coordination; Arm-Hand Steadiness; Control Precision. *Physical:* Trunk Strength. *Sensory:* Depth Perception; Far Vision; Visual Color Discrimination; Speech Clarity. **General Work Activities—***Information Input:* Identifying Objects, Actions, and Events; Monitoring Processes, Materials, or Surroundings; Getting Information. *Mental Process:* Scheduling Work and Activities; Developing Objectives and Strategies; Updating and Using Relevant Knowledge. *Work Output:* Performing General Physical Activities; Documenting or Recording Information; Handling and Moving Objects. *Interacting with Others:* Performing for or Working with the Public; Establishing and Maintaining Interpersonal Relationships; Resolving Conflicts and Negotiating with Others. **Physical Work Conditions—**More Often Outdoors Than Indoors; Very Hot or Cold. **Other Job Characteristics—**Need to Be Exact or Accurate.

Experience—Job Zone 3. Previous work-related skill, knowledge, or experience is required. **Job Preparation—**SVP 6.0 to less than 7.0— more than one year and less than four years. **Knowledges—** Geography; Education and Training; Law and Government; Biology; Public Safety and Security; Telecommunications. **Instructional Program—**Fire Science/Firefighting.

Related SOC Job—33-2022 Forest Fire Inspectors and Prevention Specialists. **Related OOH Job—**Fire Fighting Occupations. **Related DOT Jobs—**452.167-010 Fire Warden; 452.367-010 Fire Lookout; 452.367-014 Fire Ranger.

33-3000 Law Enforcement Workers

33-3011.00 Bailiffs

- **Education/Training Required:** Moderate-term on-the-job training
- **Employed:** 17,160
- **Annual Earnings:** $33,800
- **Growth:** 13.2%
- **Annual Job Openings:** 2,000

Maintain order in courts of law.

Collect and retain unauthorized firearms from persons entering courtroom. Maintain order in courtroom during trial and guard jury from outside contact. Guard lodging of sequestered jury. Provide jury escort to restaurant and other areas outside of courtroom to prevent jury contact with public. Enforce courtroom rules of behavior and warn persons not to smoke or disturb court procedure. Report need for police or medical assistance to sheriff's office. Check courtroom for security and cleanliness and assure availability of sundry supplies for use of judge. Announce entrance of judge. Stop people from entering courtroom while judge charges jury.

GOE Information—Interest Area: 12. Law and Public Safety. **Work Group:** 12.04. Law Enforcement and Public Safety. **Personality Type**—Social. Social occupations frequently involve working with, communicating with, and teaching people. These occupations often involve helping or providing service to others. **Work Values**—Security; Supervision, Human Relations; Authority; Company Policies and Practices; Supervision, Technical; Co-workers. **Skills**—Persuasion; Social Perceptiveness; Active Listening. **Abilities**—*Cognitive:* Selective Attention; Problem Sensitivity. *Psychomotor:* Reaction Time; Response Orientation. *Physical:* Static Strength; Gross Body Coordination; Stamina; Trunk Strength. *Sensory:* Speech Clarity. **General Work Activities**—*Information Input:* Monitoring Processes, Materials, or Surroundings; Identifying Objects, Actions, and Events; Getting Information. *Mental Process:* Making Decisions and Solving Problems; Judging the Qualities of Things, Services, or Other People's Work; Processing Information. *Work Output:* Performing General Physical Activities; Handling and Moving Objects; Documenting or Recording Information. *Interacting with Others:* Resolving Conflicts and Negotiating with Others; Performing for or Working with the Public; Communicating with Persons Outside Organization. **Physical Work Conditions**—Indoors; Contaminants; Disease or Infections; Sitting. **Other Job Characteristics**—Need to Be Exact or Accurate; Repeat Same Tasks.

Experience—Job Zone 2. Some previous work-related skill, knowledge, or experience may be helpful in these occupations, but usually is not needed. **Job Preparation**—SVP 4.0 to less than 6.0—six months to less than two years. **Knowledges**—Public Safety and Security; Law and Government; Philosophy and Theology; Customer and Personal Service; Psychology; Sociology and Anthropology. **Instructional Program**—Criminal Justice/Police Science.

Related SOC Job—33-3011 Bailiffs. **Related OOH Job**—Correctional Officers. **Related DOT Job**—377.667-010 Bailiff.

33-3012.00 Correctional Officers and Jailers

- **Education/Training Required:** Moderate-term on-the-job training
- **Employed:** 411,080
- **Annual Earnings:** $34,090
- **Growth:** 6.7%
- **Annual Job Openings:** 54,000

Guard inmates in penal or rehabilitative institution in accordance with established regulations and procedures. May guard prisoners in transit between jail, courtroom, prison, or other point. Includes deputy sheriffs and police who spend the majority of their time guarding prisoners in correctional institutions.

Monitor conduct of prisoners according to established policies, regulations, and procedures to prevent escape or violence. Inspect conditions of locks, window bars, grills, doors, and gates at correctional facilities to ensure that they will prevent escapes. Search prisoners, cells, and vehicles for weapons, valuables, or drugs. Guard facility entrances to screen visitors. Search for and recapture escapees. Inspect mail for the presence of contraband. Take prisoners into custody and escort to locations within and outside of facility, such as visiting room, courtroom, or airport. Record information such as prisoner identification, charges, and incidences of inmate disturbance. Use weapons, handcuffs, and physical force to maintain discipline and order among prisoners. Conduct fire, safety, and sanitation inspections. Provide to supervisors oral and written reports of the quality and quantity of work performed by inmates, inmate disturbances and rule violations, and unusual occurrences. Settle disputes between inmates. Drive passenger vehicles and trucks used to transport inmates to other institutions, courtrooms, hospitals, and work sites. Arrange daily schedules for prisoners, including library visits, work assignments, family visits, and counseling appointments. Assign duties to inmates, providing instructions as needed. Issue clothing, tools, and other authorized items to inmates. Serve meals and distribute commissary items to prisoners. Investigate crimes that have occurred within an institution or assist police in their investigations of crimes and inmates. Maintain records of prisoners' identification and charges. Supervise and coordinate work of other correctional service officers. Sponsor inmate recreational activities such as newspapers and self-help groups.

GOE Information—Interest Area: 12. Law and Public Safety. **Work Group:** 12.04. Law Enforcement and Public Safety. **Personality Type**—Realistic. Realistic occupations frequently involve work activities that include practical, hands-on problems and solutions. They often deal with plants; animals; and real-world materials like wood, tools, and machinery. Many of the occupations require working outside and do not involve a lot of paperwork or working closely with others. **Work Values**—Security; Authority; Supervision, Human Relations; Company Policies and Practices; Co-workers; Supervision, Technical. **Skills**—Social Perceptiveness; Persuasion; Negotiation; Writing; Speaking; Monitoring. **Abilities**—*Cognitive:* Spatial Orientation; Flexibility of Closure; Time Sharing; Speed of Closure; Selective Attention; Perceptual Speed. *Psychomotor:* Reaction Time; Response Orientation; Speed of Limb Movement; Multilimb Coordination; Manual Dexterity; Arm-Hand Steadiness. *Physical:* Explosive Strength; Static Strength; Stamina; Dynamic Strength; Gross Body Coordination; Gross Body Equilibrium. *Sensory:* Sound Localization; Peripheral Vision; Glare Sensitivity; Night Vision; Far Vision; Auditory Attention. **General Work Activities**—*Information*

Input: Monitoring Processes, Materials, or Surroundings; Identifying Objects, Actions, and Events; Inspecting Equipment, Structures, or Materials. *Mental Process:* Making Decisions and Solving Problems; Updating and Using Relevant Knowledge; Evaluating Information Against Standards. *Work Output:* Documenting or Recording Information; Performing General Physical Activities; Handling and Moving Objects. *Interacting with Others:* Establishing and Maintaining Interpersonal Relationships; Communicating with Other Workers; Resolving Conflicts and Negotiating with Others. **Physical Work Conditions**—More Often Indoors Than Outdoors; Noisy; Contaminants; Disease or Infections; Standing. **Other Job Characteristics**—Need to Be Exact or Accurate; Repeat Same Tasks; Errors Have Important Consequences.

Experience—Job Zone 3. Previous work-related skill, knowledge, or experience is required. **Job Preparation**—SVP 6.0 to less than 7.0—more than one year and less than four years. **Knowledges**—Psychology; Public Safety and Security; Law and Government; Philosophy and Theology; Sociology and Anthropology; Therapy and Counseling. **Instructional Programs**—Corrections; Corrections and Criminal Justice, Other; Juvenile Corrections.

Related SOC Job—33-3012 Correctional Officers and Jailers. **Related OOH Job**—Correctional Officers. **Related DOT Jobs**—372.367-014 Jailer; 372.567-014 Guard, Immigration; 372.667-018 Correction Officer; 372.677-010 Patrol Conductor; 375.367-010 Police Officer II.

33-3021.00 Detectives and Criminal Investigators

- **Education/Training Required: Work experience in a related occupation**
- **Employed: 85,270**
- **Annual Earnings: $55,790**
- **Growth: 16.3%**
- **Annual Job Openings: 9,000**

The job openings listed here are shared with 33-3021.01 Police Detectives, 33-3021.02 Police Identification and Records Officers, 33-3021.03 Criminal Investigators and Special Agents, and 33-3021.05 Immigration and Customs Inspectors.

Conduct investigations related to suspected violations of federal, state, or local laws to prevent or solve crimes.

No task data available.

GOE Information—Interest Area: 12. Law and Public Safety. **Work Group:** 12.04. Law Enforcement and Public Safety. **Note:** The Department of Labor has not collected some data for this job, so it has fewer details than the other descriptions.

Instructional Programs—Criminal Justice/Police Science; Criminalistics and Criminal Science.

Related SOC Job—33-3021 Detectives and Criminal Investigators. **Related OOH Job**—Police and Detectives. **Related DOT Job**—No data available.

33-3021.01 Police Detectives

- **Education/Training Required: Work experience in a related occupation**
- **Employed: 85,270**
- **Annual Earnings: $55,790**
- **Growth: 16.3%**
- **Annual Job Openings: 9,000**

The job openings listed here are shared with 33-3021.00 Detectives and Criminal Investigators, 33-3021.02 Police Identification and Records Officers, 33-3021.03 Criminal Investigators and Special Agents, and 33-3021.05 Immigration and Customs Inspectors.

Conduct investigations to prevent crimes or solve criminal cases.

Examine crime scenes to obtain clues and evidence, such as loose hairs, fibers, clothing, or weapons. Secure deceased body and obtain evidence from it, preventing bystanders from tampering with it prior to medical examiner's arrival. Obtain evidence from suspects. Provide testimony as a witness in court. Analyze completed police reports to determine what additional information and investigative work is needed. Prepare charges, responses to charges, or information for court cases according to formalized procedures. Note, mark, and photograph location of objects found, such as footprints, tire tracks, bullets, and bloodstains, and take measurements of the scene. Obtain facts or statements from complainants, witnesses, and accused persons and record interviews, using recording device. Obtain summary of incident from officer in charge at crime scene, taking care to avoid disturbing evidence. Examine records and governmental agency files to find identifying data about suspects. Prepare and serve search and arrest warrants. Block or rope off scene and check perimeter to ensure that entire scene is secured. Summon medical help for injured individuals and alert medical personnel to take statements from them. Provide information to lab personnel concerning the source of an item of evidence and tests to be performed. Monitor conditions of victims who are unconscious so that arrangements can be made to take statements if consciousness is regained. Secure persons at scene, keeping witnesses from conversing or leaving the scene before investigators arrive. Preserve, process, and analyze items of evidence obtained from crime scenes and suspects, placing them in proper containers and destroying evidence no longer needed. Record progress of investigation, maintain informational files on suspects, and submit reports to commanding officer or magistrate to authorize warrants. Organize scene search, assigning specific tasks and areas of search to individual officers and obtaining adequate lighting as necessary. Take photographs from all angles of relevant parts of a crime scene, including entrance and exit routes and streets and intersections.

GOE Information—Interest Area: 12. Law and Public Safety. **Work Group:** 12.04. Law Enforcement and Public Safety. **Personality Type**—Enterprising. Enterprising occupations frequently involve starting up and carrying out projects. These occupations can involve leading people and making many decisions. They sometimes require risk taking and often deal with business. **Work Values**—Variety; Responsibility; Ability Utilization; Achievement; Social Status; Social Service. **Skills**—Persuasion; Negotiation; Social Perceptiveness; Coordination; Speaking; Active Listening. **Abilities**—*Cognitive:* Speed of Closure; Flexibility of Closure; Fluency of Ideas; Spatial Orientation; Memorization; Time Sharing. *Psychomotor:* Response Orientation; Reaction Time; Multilimb Coordination; Arm-Hand Steadiness; Control Precision; Manual Dexterity. *Physical:* Static Strength; Gross Body Coordination; Stamina. *Sensory:* Speech Recognition; Auditory Attention; Depth Perception; Near Vision; Visual Color Discrimination; Speech Clarity. **General Work Activities**—*Information Input:* Getting Information; Identifying Objects, Actions, and Events; Monitoring Processes, Materials, or Surroundings. *Mental Process:* Making Decisions and Solving Problems; Updating and Using Relevant Knowledge; Organizing, Planning, and Prioritizing. *Work Output:* Performing General Physical Activities; Documenting or Recording Information; Interacting With Computers. *Interacting with Others:* Communicating with Persons Outside Organization; Performing for or Working with the Public; Establishing and Maintaining Interpersonal Relationships. **Physical Work Conditions**—More

Often Indoors Than Outdoors; Very Hot or Cold; Sitting. **Other Job Characteristics**—Need to Be Exact or Accurate; Errors Have Important Consequences; Repeat Same Tasks.

Experience—Job Zone 4. A minimum of two to four years of work-related skill, knowledge, or experience is needed. **Job Preparation**—SVP 7.0 to less than 8.0—two years to less than 10 years. **Knowledges**—Public Safety and Security; Law and Government; Psychology; Therapy and Counseling; Philosophy and Theology; Education and Training. **Instructional Programs**—Criminal Justice/Police Science; Criminalistics and Criminal Science.

Related SOC Job—33-3021 Detectives and Criminal Investigators. **Related OOH Job**—Police and Detectives. **Related DOT Jobs**—375.267-010 Detective; 375.267-014 Detective, Narcotics and Vice; 375.267-018 Investigator, Narcotics; 375.267-022 Investigator, Vice; 375.267-034 Investigator, Internal Affairs.

33-3021.02 Police Identification and Records Officers

- **Education/Training Required: Work experience in a related occupation**
- **Employed: 85,270**
- **Annual Earnings: $55,790**
- **Growth: 16.3%**
- **Annual Job Openings: 9,000**

The job openings listed here are shared with 33-3021.00 Detectives and Criminal Investigators, 33-3021.01 Police Detectives, 33-3021.03 Criminal Investigators and Special Agents, and 33-3021.05 Immigration and Customs Inspectors.

Collect evidence at crime scene, classify and identify fingerprints, and photograph evidence for use in criminal and civil cases.

Photograph crime or accident scenes for evidence records. Analyze and process evidence at crime scenes and in the laboratory, wearing protective equipment and using powders and chemicals. Look for trace evidence, such as fingerprints, hairs, fibers, or shoe impressions, using alternative light sources when necessary. Dust selected areas of crime scene and lift latent fingerprints, adhering to proper preservation procedures. Testify in court and present evidence. Package, store, and retrieve evidence. Serve as technical advisor and coordinate with other law enforcement workers to exchange information on crime scene collection activities. Perform emergency work during off-hours. Submit evidence to supervisors. Process film and prints from crime or accident scenes. Identify, classify, and file fingerprints, using systems such as the Henry Classification system.

GOE Information—**Interest Area:** 12. Law and Public Safety. **Work Group:** 12.04. Law Enforcement and Public Safety. **Personality Type**—Conventional. Conventional occupations frequently involve following set procedures and routines. These occupations can include working with data and details more than with ideas. Usually there is a clear line of authority to follow. **Work Values**—Supervision, Human Relations; Supervision, Technical; Advancement; Co-workers; Company Policies and Practices; Security. **Skills**—Persuasion; Judgment and Decision Making; Negotiation; Service Orientation; Social Perceptiveness; Critical Thinking. **Abilities**—*Cognitive:* Flexibility of Closure; Spatial Orientation; Speed of Closure; Time Sharing; Selective Attention; Memorization. *Psychomotor:* Arm-Hand Steadiness; Response Orientation; Finger Dexterity; Reaction Time; Manual Dexterity; Control Precision. *Physical:* Gross Body Coordination; Extent Flexibility; Stamina; Static Strength; Trunk

Strength. *Sensory:* Glare Sensitivity; Night Vision; Near Vision; Visual Color Discrimination; Far Vision; Speech Recognition. **General Work Activities**—*Information Input:* Identifying Objects, Actions, and Events; Getting Information; Monitoring Processes, Materials, or Surroundings. *Mental Process:* Evaluating Information Against Standards; Updating and Using Relevant Knowledge; Making Decisions and Solving Problems. *Work Output:* Handling and Moving Objects; Documenting or Recording Information; Performing General Physical Activities. *Interacting with Others:* Performing for or Working with the Public; Resolving Conflicts and Negotiating with Others; Communicating with Other Workers. **Physical Work Conditions**—More Often Outdoors Than Indoors; Noisy; Very Hot or Cold; Contaminants; Using Hands on Objects, Tools, or Controls. **Other Job Characteristics**—Need to Be Exact or Accurate; Errors Have Important Consequences; Repeat Same Tasks.

Experience—Job Zone 3. Previous work-related skill, knowledge, or experience is required. **Job Preparation**—SVP 6.0 to less than 7.0—more than one year and less than four years. **Knowledges**—Law and Government; Public Safety and Security; Customer and Personal Service; Telecommunications; Psychology; Computers and Electronics. **Instructional Programs**—Criminal Justice/Police Science; Criminalistics and Criminal Science.

Related SOC Job—33-3021 Detectives and Criminal Investigators. **Related OOH Job**—Police and Detectives. **Related DOT Jobs**—375.384-010 Police Officer, Identification and Records; 375.387-010 Fingerprint Classifier.

33-3021.03 Criminal Investigators and Special Agents

- **Education/Training Required: Work experience in a related occupation**
- **Employed: 85,270**
- **Annual Earnings: $55,790**
- **Growth: 16.3%**
- **Annual Job Openings: 9,000**

The job openings listed here are shared with 33-3021.00 Detectives and Criminal Investigators, 33-3021.01 Police Detectives, 33-3021.02 Police Identification and Records Officers, and 33-3021.05 Immigration and Customs Inspectors.

Investigate alleged or suspected criminal violations of federal, state, or local laws to determine if evidence is sufficient to recommend prosecution.

Record evidence and documents, using equipment such as cameras and photocopy machines. Obtain and verify evidence by interviewing and observing suspects and witnesses or by analyzing records. Examine records to locate links in chains of evidence or information. Prepare reports that detail investigation findings. Determine scope, timing, and direction of investigations. Collaborate with other offices and agencies to exchange information and coordinate activities. Testify before grand juries concerning criminal activity investigations. Analyze evidence in laboratories or in the field. Investigate organized crime, public corruption, financial crime, copyright infringement, civil rights violations, bank robbery, extortion, kidnapping, and other violations of federal or state statutes. Identify case issues and evidence needed, based on analysis of charges, complaints, or allegations of law violations. Obtain and use search and arrest warrants. Serve subpoenas or other official papers. Collaborate with other authorities on activities such as surveillance, transcription, and research. Develop relationships with informants to obtain information related to cases. Search for and collect evidence such as fingerprints, using investigative equipment. Collect and record physical information about arrested suspects, including fingerprints, height and weight measurements, and photographs. Compare crime scene fingerprints with those from suspects or fingerprint files to identify perpetrators, using computers. Administer counter-terrorism and counter-narcotics reward programs. Provide protection for individuals such as government leaders, political candidates, and visiting foreign dignitaries. Perform undercover assignments and maintain surveillance, including monitoring authorized wiretaps. Manage security programs designed to protect personnel, facilities, and information. Issue security clearances.

GOE Information—Interest Area: 12. Law and Public Safety. **Work Group:** 12.04. Law Enforcement and Public Safety. **Personality Type**—Enterprising. Enterprising occupations frequently involve starting up and carrying out projects. These occupations can involve leading people and making many decisions. They sometimes require risk taking and often deal with business. **Work Values**—Achievement; Social Status; Ability Utilization; Security; Supervision, Human Relations; Authority. **Skills**—Negotiation; Programming; Judgment and Decision Making; Operations Analysis; Service Orientation; Persuasion. **Abilities**—*Cognitive:* Flexibility of Closure; Problem Sensitivity; Inductive Reasoning; Speed of Closure; Selective Attention; Category Flexibility. *Psychomotor:* Response Orientation; Rate Control; Reaction Time; Control Precision; Multilimb Coordination; Arm-Hand Steadiness. *Physical:* Trunk Strength. *Sensory:* Far Vision; Speech Recognition; Visual Color Discrimination; Auditory Attention; Speech Clarity; Near Vision. **General Work Activities**—*Information Input:* Identifying Objects, Actions, and Events; Getting Information; Estimating the Needed Characteristics of Products, Events, or Information. *Mental Process:* Analyzing Data or Information; Making Decisions and Solving Problems; Updating and Using Relevant Knowledge. *Work Output:* Documenting or Recording Information; Performing General Physical Activities; Interacting With Computers. *Interacting with Others:* Communicating with Persons Outside Organization; Establishing and Maintaining Interpersonal Relationships; Performing for or Working with the Public. **Physical Work Conditions**—More Often Outdoors Than Indoors; Noisy; Very Hot or Cold; Standing. **Other Job Characteristics**—Need to Be Exact or Accurate; Repeat Same Tasks; Errors Have Important Consequences.

Experience—Job Zone 4. A minimum of two to four years of work-related skill, knowledge, or experience is needed. **Job Preparation**—SVP 7.0 to less than 8.0—two years to less than 10 years. **Knowledges**—Law and Government; Psychology; Geography; Public Safety and Security; Clerical Practices; Telecommunications. **Instructional Programs**—Criminal Justice/Police Science; Criminalistics and Criminal Science.

Related SOC Job—33-3021 Detectives and Criminal Investigators. **Related OOH Job**—Police and Detectives. **Related DOT Jobs**—195.267-022 Child Support Officer; 375.167-042 Special Agent; 375.267-038 Police Officer III; 377.264-010 Identification Officer.

33-3021.05 Immigration and Customs Inspectors

- **Education/Training Required:** Work experience in a related occupation
- **Employed:** 85,270
- **Annual Earnings:** $55,790
- **Growth:** 16.3%
- **Annual Job Openings:** 9,000

The job openings listed here are shared with 33-3021.00 Detectives and Criminal Investigators, 33-3021.01 Police Detectives, 33-3021.02 Police Identification and Records Officers, and 33-3021.03 Criminal Investigators and Special Agents.

Investigate and inspect persons, common carriers, goods, and merchandise arriving in or departing from the United States or moving between states to detect violations of immigration and customs laws and regulations.

Examine immigration applications, visas, and passports and interview persons to determine eligibility for admission, residence, and travel in U.S. Detain persons found to be in violation of customs or immigration laws and arrange for legal action such as deportation. Locate and seize contraband or undeclared merchandise and vehicles, aircraft, or boats that contain such merchandise. Interpret and explain laws and regulations to travelers, prospective immigrants, shippers, and manufacturers. Inspect cargo, baggage, and personal articles entering or leaving U.S. for compliance with revenue laws and U.S. Customs Service regulations. Record and report job-related activities, findings, transactions, violations, discrepancies, and decisions. Institute civil and criminal prosecutions and cooperate with other law enforcement agencies in the investigation and prosecution of those in violation of immigration or customs laws. Testify regarding decisions at immigration appeals or in federal court. Determine duty and taxes to be paid on goods. Collect samples of merchandise for examination, appraisal, or testing. Investigate applications for duty refunds and petition for remission or mitigation of penalties when warranted.

GOE Information—Interest Area: 07. Government and Public Administration. **Work Group:** 07.03. Regulations Enforcement. **Personality Type**—Conventional. Conventional occupations frequently involve following set procedures and routines. These occupations can include working with data and details more than with ideas. Usually there is a clear line of authority to follow. **Work Values**—Supervision, Technical; Supervision, Human Relations; Advancement; Security; Company Policies and Practices; Authority. **Skills**—Persuasion; Negotiation; Speaking; Social Perceptiveness; Operations Analysis; Equipment Selection. **Abilities**—*Cognitive:* Problem Sensitivity; Inductive Reasoning; Flexibility of Closure; Deductive Reasoning; Written Expression; Oral Expression. *Psychomotor:* Reaction Time; Multilimb Coordination; Control Precision; Manual Dexterity; Arm-Hand Steadiness. *Physical:* Static Strength; Stamina; Extent Flexibility. *Sensory:* Speech Recognition; Speech Clarity; Far Vision; Visual Color Discrimination; Depth Perception; Near Vision. **General Work Activities**—*Information Input:* Getting Information; Identifying Objects, Actions, and Events; Monitoring Processes, Materials, or Surroundings. *Mental Process:* Updating and Using Relevant Knowledge; Making Decisions and Solving Problems; Processing Information. *Work Output:* Handling and Moving Objects; Performing General Physical Activities; Documenting or Recording Information. *Interacting with Others:* Establishing and Maintaining Interpersonal Relationships; Communicating with Other Workers; Performing for or Working with the Public. **Physical Work Conditions**—More Often Outdoors Than Indoors; Noisy; Contaminants; Radiation; Hazardous Equipment. **Other Job Characteristics**—Need to Be Exact or Accurate; Repeat Same Tasks; Errors Have Important Consequences.

Experience—Job Zone 4. A minimum of two to four years of work-related skill, knowledge, or experience is needed. **Job Preparation**—SVP 7.0 to less than 8.0—two years to less than 10 years. **Knowledges**—Public Safety and Security; Law and Government; Foreign Language; Geography; Customer and Personal Service; Philosophy and Theology. **Instructional Programs**—Criminal Justice/Police Science; Criminalistics and Criminal Science.

Related SOC Job—33-3021 Detectives and Criminal Investigators. Related OOH Job—Police and Detectives. Related DOT Jobs—168.167-022 Immigration Inspector; 168.267-018 Customs Import Specialist; 168.267-022 Customs Inspector; 168.387-010 Opener-Verifier-Packer, Customs; 188.167-090 Special Agent, Customs.

33-3031.00 Fish and Game Wardens

- Education/Training Required: Long-term on-the-job training
- Employed: 6,300
- Annual Earnings: $42,850
- Growth: 10.5%
- Annual Job Openings: 1,000

Patrol assigned area to prevent fish and game law violations. Investigate reports of damage to crops or property by wildlife. Compile biological data.

Patrol assigned areas by car, boat, airplane, or horse or on foot to enforce game, fish, or boating laws and to manage wildlife programs, lakes, or land. Investigate hunting accidents and reports of fish and game law violations and issue warnings or citations and file reports as necessary. Serve warrants, make arrests, and compile and present evidence for court actions. Protect and preserve native wildlife, plants, and ecosystems. Promote and provide hunter and trapper safety training. Seize equipment used in fish and game law violations and arrange for disposition of fish or game illegally taken or possessed. Provide assistance to other local law enforcement agencies as required. Address schools, civic groups, sporting clubs, and the media to disseminate information concerning wildlife conservation and regulations. Recommend revisions or changes in hunting and trapping regulations or seasons and in animal management programs so that wildlife balances and habitats can be maintained. Inspect commercial operations relating to fish and wildlife, recreation, and protected areas. Collect and report information on populations and conditions of fish and wildlife in their habitats, availability of game food and cover, and suspected pollution. Survey areas and compile figures of bag counts of hunters to determine the effectiveness of control measures. Participate in search-and-rescue operations and in firefighting efforts. Investigate crop, property, or habitat damage or destruction or instances of water pollution to determine causes and to advise property owners of preventive measures. Design and implement control measures to prevent or counteract damage caused by wildlife or people. Document and detail the extent of crop, property, or habitat damage and make financial loss estimates and compensation recommendations. Supervise the activities of seasonal workers. Issue licenses, permits, and other documentation. Provide advice and information to park and reserve visitors. Perform facilities maintenance work such as constructing or repairing structures and controlling weeds and pests.

GOE Information—Interest Area: 07. Government and Public Administration. Work Group: 07.03. Regulations Enforcement. Personality Type—Realistic. Realistic occupations frequently involve work activities that include practical, hands-on problems and solutions. They often deal with plants; animals; and real-world materials like wood, tools, and machinery. Many of the occupations require working outside and do not involve a lot of paperwork or working closely with others. Work Values—Responsibility; Authority; Variety; Security; Social Status; Creativity. Skills—Persuasion; Equipment Maintenance; Social Perceptiveness; Speaking; Science; Writing. Abilities—*Cognitive:* Spatial Orientation; Flexibility of Closure; Fluency of Ideas; Problem Sensitivity; Speed of Closure; Originality. *Psychomotor:* Response Orientation; Rate Control; Reaction Time; Multilimb Coordination; Control Precision; Manual Dexterity.

Physical: Gross Body Equilibrium; Stamina; Static Strength; Dynamic Strength; Gross Body Coordination; Trunk Strength. *Sensory:* Glare Sensitivity; Sound Localization; Night Vision; Peripheral Vision; Depth Perception; Far Vision. General Work Activities—*Information Input:* Getting Information; Identifying Objects, Actions, and Events; Monitoring Processes, Materials, or Surroundings. *Mental Process:* Evaluating Information Against Standards; Organizing, Planning, and Prioritizing; Making Decisions and Solving Problems. *Work Output:* Performing General Physical Activities; Handling and Moving Objects; Operating Vehicles or Equipment. *Interacting with Others:* Communicating with Persons Outside Organization; Establishing and Maintaining Interpersonal Relationships; Performing for or Working with the Public. Physical Work Conditions—Outdoors; Very Hot or Cold; Very Bright or Dim Lighting; Contaminants; Hazardous Equipment; Minor Burns, Cuts, Bites, or Stings. Other Job Characteristics—Errors Have Important Consequences; Need to Be Exact or Accurate.

Experience—Job Zone 4. A minimum of two to four years of work-related skill, knowledge, or experience is needed. Job Preparation—SVP 7.0 to less than 8.0—two years to less than 10 years. Knowledges—Biology; Law and Government; Public Safety and Security; Geography; Psychology; Sociology and Anthropology. Instructional Programs—Fishing and Fisheries Sciences and Management; Natural Resource Economics; Wildlife and Wildlands Science and Management.

Related SOC Job—33-3031 Fish and Game Wardens. Related OOH Job—Police and Detectives. Related DOT Jobs—379.167-010 Fish and Game Warden; 379.267-010 Wildlife Control Agent.

33-3041.00 Parking Enforcement Workers

- Education/Training Required: Short-term on-the-job training
- Employed: 10,140
- Annual Earnings: $29,070
- Growth: 15.1%
- Annual Job Openings: 1,000

Patrol assigned area, such as public parking lot or section of city, to issue tickets to overtime parking violators and illegally parked vehicles.

Patrol an assigned area by vehicle or on foot to ensure public compliance with existing parking ordinance. Maintain close communications with dispatching personnel, using two-way radios or cell phones. Write warnings and citations for illegally parked vehicles. Mark tires of parked vehicles with chalk, record time of marking, and return at regular intervals to ensure that parking time limits are not exceeded. Respond to and make radio dispatch calls regarding parking violations and complaints. Train new or temporary staff. Identify vehicles in violation of parking codes, checking with dispatchers when necessary to confirm identities or to determine whether vehicles need to be booted or towed. Perform simple vehicle maintenance procedures such as checking oil and gas; report mechanical problems to supervisors. Observe and report hazardous conditions such as missing traffic signals or signs and street markings that need to be repainted. Investigate and answer complaints regarding contested parking citations, determining their validity and routing them appropriately. Maintain assigned equipment and supplies such as handheld citation computers, citation books, rain gear, tire-marking chalk, and street cones. Provide information to the public regarding parking regulations and facilities and the location of streets, buildings, and points of interest. Appear in court at hearings regarding contested traffic citations. Make arrangements for illegally parked or abandoned vehicles to be towed and direct tow-truck drivers to the correct vehicles. Perform traffic control duties such as setting up barricades and temporary signs, placing bags on parking meters to limit their use, or directing traffic. Provide assistance to motorists needing help with problems such as flat tires, keys locked in cars, or dead batteries. Enter and retrieve information pertaining to vehicle registration, identification, and status, using handheld computers. Collect coins deposited in meters. Prepare and maintain required records, including logs of parking enforcement activities and records of contested citations.

GOE Information—Interest Area: 12. Law and Public Safety. **Work Group:** 12.04. Law Enforcement and Public Safety. **Personality Type**—Conventional. Conventional occupations frequently involve following set procedures and routines. These occupations can include working with data and details more than with ideas. Usually there is a clear line of authority to follow. **Work Values**—Independence; Supervision, Technical; Security; Supervision, Human Relations. **Skills**—Writing; Speaking; Active Listening; Equipment Maintenance; Service Orientation; Negotiation. **Abilities**—*Cognitive:* Spatial Orientation. *Psychomotor:* Response Orientation; Multilimb Coordination; Control Precision; Reaction Time. *Physical:* Gross Body Coordination; Trunk Strength; Static Strength. *Sensory:* Glare Sensitivity; Far Vision; Depth Perception. **General Work Activities**—*Information Input:* Identifying Objects, Actions, and Events; Monitoring Processes, Materials, or Surroundings; Getting Information. *Mental Process:* Evaluating Information Against Standards; Organizing, Planning, and Prioritizing; Making Decisions and Solving Problems. *Work Output:* Performing General Physical Activities; Documenting or Recording Information. *Interacting with Others:* Performing for or Working with the Public; Establishing and Maintaining Interpersonal Relationships; Communicating with Other Workers. **Physical Work Conditions**—Outdoors; Very Hot or Cold; More Often Sitting Than Standing; Walking and Running; Repetitive Motions. **Other Job Characteristics**—Need to Be Exact or Accurate; Repeat Same Tasks.

Experience—Job Zone 2. Some previous work-related skill, knowledge, or experience may be helpful in these occupations, but usually is not needed. **Job Preparation**—SVP 4.0 to less than 6.0—six months to less than two years. **Knowledges**—Law and Government; Public Safety and Security; Customer and Personal Service; Geography; Transportation; Psychology. **Instructional Program**—Protective Services, Other.

Related SOC Job—33-3041 Parking Enforcement Workers. **Related OOH Job**—Parking Enforcement Workers. **Related DOT Job**—375.587-010 Parking Enforcement Officer.

33-3051.00 Police and Sheriff's Patrol Officers

- **Education/Training Required: Long-term on-the-job training**
- **Employed: 624,130**
- **Annual Earnings: $46,290**
- **Growth: 15.5%**
- **Annual Job Openings: 47,000**

The job openings listed here are shared with 33-3051.01 Police Patrol Officers and 33-3051.03 Sheriffs and Deputy Sheriffs.

Maintain order, enforce laws and ordinances, and protect life and property in an assigned patrol district. Perform combination of following duties: Patrol a specific area on foot or in a vehicle, direct traffic, issue traffic summonses, investigate accidents, apprehend and arrest suspects, or serve legal processes of courts.

No task data available.

GOE Information—Interest Area: 12. Law and Public Safety. **Work Group:** 12.04. Law Enforcement and Public Safety. **Note:** The Department of Labor has not collected some data for this job, so it has fewer details than the other descriptions.

Instructional Programs—Criminal Justice/Police Science; Criminalistics and Criminal Science.

Related SOC Job—33-3051 Police and Sheriff's Patrol Officers. **Related OOH Job**—Police and Detectives. **Related DOT Job**—No data available.

33-3051.01 Police Patrol Officers

- **Education/Training Required: Long-term on-the-job training**
- **Employed: 624,130**
- **Annual Earnings: $46,290**
- **Growth: 15.5%**
- **Annual Job Openings: 47,000**

The job openings listed here are shared with 33-3051.00 Police and Sheriff's Patrol Officers and 33-3051.03 Sheriffs and Deputy Sheriffs.

Patrol assigned area to enforce laws and ordinances, regulate traffic, control crowds, prevent crime, and arrest violators.

Provide for public safety by maintaining order, responding to emergencies, protecting people and property, enforcing motor vehicle and criminal laws, and promoting good community relations. Identify, pursue, and arrest suspects and perpetrators of criminal acts. Record facts to prepare reports that document incidents and activities. Review facts of incidents to determine if criminal act or statute violations were involved. Render aid to accident victims and other persons requiring first aid for physical injuries. Testify in court to present evidence or act as witness in traffic and criminal cases. Evaluate complaint and emergency-request information to determine response requirements. Patrol specific area on foot, horseback, or motorized conveyance, responding promptly to calls for assistance. Monitor, note, report, and investigate suspicious persons and situations, safety hazards, and unusual or illegal activity in patrol area. Investigate traffic accidents and other accidents to determine causes and to determine if a crime has been committed. Photograph or draw diagrams of crime or accident scenes and interview principals and eyewitnesses. Monitor traffic to ensure that motorists observe traffic regulations and exhibit safe driving procedures. Relay complaint and emergency-request information to appropriate agency dispatchers. Issue citations or warnings to violators of motor vehicle ordinances. Direct traffic flow and reroute traffic in case of emergencies. Inform citizens of community services and recommend options to facilitate longer-term problem resolution. Provide road information to assist motorists. Process prisoners and prepare and maintain records of prisoner bookings and prisoner status during booking and pre-trial process. Inspect public establishments to ensure compliance with rules and regulations. Act as official escorts, such as when leading funeral processions or firefighters.

GOE Information—Interest Area: 12. Law and Public Safety. **Work Group:** 12.04. Law Enforcement and Public Safety. **Personality Type**—Social. Social occupations frequently involve working with, communicating with, and teaching people. These occupations often involve helping or providing service to others. **Work Values**—Variety; Security; Social Service; Social Status; Supervision, Human Relations; Authority. **Skills**—Persuasion; Negotiation; Judgment and Decision Making; Social Perceptiveness; Service Orientation; Active Listening. **Abilities**—*Cognitive:* Spatial Orientation; Time Sharing; Speed of

Closure; Flexibility of Closure; Perceptual Speed; Memorization. *Psychomotor:* Reaction Time; Rate Control; Response Orientation; Speed of Limb Movement; Multilimb Coordination; Control Precision. *Physical:* Explosive Strength; Stamina; Gross Body Equilibrium; Gross Body Coordination; Static Strength; Dynamic Strength. *Sensory:* Night Vision; Sound Localization; Peripheral Vision; Glare Sensitivity; Far Vision; Auditory Attention. **General Work Activities**—*Information Input:* Identifying Objects, Actions, and Events; Monitoring Processes, Materials, or Surroundings; Getting Information. *Mental Process:* Making Decisions and Solving Problems; Evaluating Information Against Standards; Updating and Using Relevant Knowledge. *Work Output:* Performing General Physical Activities; Documenting or Recording Information; Operating Vehicles or Equipment. *Interacting with Others:* Resolving Conflicts and Negotiating with Others; Performing for or Working with the Public; Communicating with Persons Outside Organization. **Physical Work Conditions**—Outdoors; Noisy; Very Hot or Cold; Contaminants; Hazardous Equipment; Using Hands on Objects, Tools, or Controls. **Other Job Characteristics**—Need to Be Exact or Accurate; Errors Have Important Consequences; Repeat Same Tasks.

Experience—Job Zone 3. Previous work-related skill, knowledge, or experience is required. **Job Preparation**—SVP 6.0 to less than 7.0— more than one year and less than four years. **Knowledges**—Public Safety and Security; Law and Government; Psychology; Customer and Personal Service; Telecommunications. **Instructional Programs**—Criminal Justice/Police Science; Criminalistics and Criminal Science.

Related SOC Job—33-3051 Police and Sheriff's Patrol Officers. **Related OOH Job**—Police and Detectives. **Related DOT Jobs**— 168.167-010 Customs Patrol Officer; 169.167-042 Park Ranger; 372.363-010 Protective Officer; 375.163-014 Pilot, Highway Patrol; 375.263-010 Accident-Prevention-Squad Police Officer; 375.263-014 Police Officer I; 375.263-018 State-Highway Police Officer; 375.264-010 Police Officer, Crime Prevention; 375.267-030 Police Inspector II; 375.267-042 Police Officer, Safety Instruction; 375.363-010 Border Guard; 375.367-014 Complaint Evaluation Officer; 375.367-018 Police Officer, Booking; others.

33-3051.03 Sheriffs and Deputy Sheriffs

- **Education/Training Required: Long-term on-the-job training**
- **Employed: 624,130**
- **Annual Earnings: $46,290**
- **Growth: 15.5%**
- **Annual Job Openings: 47,000**

The job openings listed here are shared with 33-3051.00 Police and Sheriff's Patrol Officers and 33-3051.01 Police Patrol Officers.

Enforce law and order in rural or unincorporated districts or serve legal processes of courts. May patrol courthouse, guard court or grand jury, or escort defendants.

Drive vehicles or patrol specific areas to detect law violators, issue citations, and make arrests. Investigate illegal or suspicious activities. Verify that the proper legal charges have been made against law offenders. Execute arrest warrants, locating and taking persons into custody. Record daily activities and submit logs and other related reports and paperwork to appropriate authorities. Patrol and guard courthouses, grand jury rooms, or assigned areas to provide security, enforce laws, maintain order, and arrest violators. Notify patrol units to take violators into custody or to provide needed assistance or medical aid. Place people in protective custody. Serve statements of claims, subpoenas, summonses, jury summonses, orders to pay

alimony, and other court orders. Take control of accident scenes to maintain traffic flow, to assist accident victims, and to investigate causes. Question individuals entering secured areas to determine their business, directing and rerouting individuals as necessary. Transport or escort prisoners and defendants en route to courtrooms, prisons or jails, attorneys' offices, or medical facilities. Locate and confiscate real or personal property, as directed by court order. Manage jail operations and tend to jail inmates.

GOE Information—**Interest Area:** 12. Law and Public Safety. **Work Group:** 12.04. Law Enforcement and Public Safety. **Personality Type**—Social. Social occupations frequently involve working with, communicating with, and teaching people. These occupations often involve helping or providing service to others. **Work Values**— Authority; Security; Variety; Responsibility; Social Status; Social Service. **Skills**—Negotiation; Persuasion; Social Perceptiveness; Service Orientation; Complex Problem Solving; Judgment and Decision Making. **Abilities**—*Cognitive:* Inductive Reasoning; Perceptual Speed; Problem Sensitivity; Originality; Selective Attention; Flexibility of Closure. *Psychomotor:* Response Orientation; Reaction Time; Rate Control; Multilimb Coordination; Arm-Hand Steadiness; Manual Dexterity. *Physical:* Explosive Strength; Static Strength; Stamina; Gross Body Equilibrium; Gross Body Coordination; Extent Flexibility. *Sensory:* Hearing Sensitivity; Depth Perception; Far Vision; Auditory Attention; Visual Color Discrimination; Speech Clarity. **General Work Activities**— *Information Input:* Getting Information; Monitoring Processes, Materials, or Surroundings; Identifying Objects, Actions, and Events. *Mental Process:* Making Decisions and Solving Problems; Updating and Using Relevant Knowledge; Processing Information. *Work Output:* Documenting or Recording Information; Operating Vehicles or Equipment; Performing General Physical Activities. *Interacting with Others:* Resolving Conflicts and Negotiating with Others; Establishing and Maintaining Interpersonal Relationships; Performing for or Working with the Public. **Physical Work Conditions**—More Often Outdoors Than Indoors; Very Hot or Cold; Contaminants; Disease or Infections; Sitting. **Other Job Characteristics**—Need to Be Exact or Accurate; Errors Have Important Consequences; Repeat Same Tasks.

Experience—Job Zone 3. Previous work-related skill, knowledge, or experience is required. **Job Preparation**—SVP 6.0 to less than 7.0— more than one year and less than four years. **Knowledges**—Public Safety and Security; Law and Government; Telecommunications; Psychology; Therapy and Counseling; Customer and Personal Service. **Instructional Programs**—Criminal Justice/Police Science; Criminalistics and Criminal Science.

Related SOC Job—33-3051 Police and Sheriff's Patrol Officers. **Related OOH Job**—Police and Detectives. **Related DOT Jobs**— 377.263-010 Sheriff, Deputy; 377.363-010 Deputy Sheriff, Grand Jury; 377.667-014 Deputy Sheriff, Building Guard; 377.667-018 Deputy Sheriff, Civil Division.

33-3052.00 Transit and Railroad Police

- **Education/Training Required: Long-term on-the-job training**
- **Employed: 5,090**
- **Annual Earnings: $48,850**
- **Growth: 9.2%**
- **Annual Job Openings: Fewer than 500**

Protect and police railroad and transit property, employees, or passengers.

Patrol railroad yards, cars, stations, and other facilities to protect company property and shipments and to maintain order. Examine credentials of unauthorized persons attempting to enter secured areas. Apprehend or remove trespassers or thieves from railroad property or coordinate with law enforcement agencies in apprehensions and removals. Prepare reports documenting investigation activities and results. Investigate or direct investigations of freight theft, suspicious damage or loss of passengers' valuables, and other crimes on railroad property. Direct security activities at derailments, fires, floods, and strikes involving railroad property. Direct and coordinate the daily activities and training of security staff. Interview neighbors, associates, and former employers of job applicants to verify personal references and to obtain work history data. Record and verify seal numbers from boxcars containing frequently pilfered items, such as cigarettes and liquor, to detect tampering. Plan and implement special safety and preventive programs, such as fire and accident prevention. Seal empty boxcars by twisting nails in door hasps, using nail twisters.

GOE Information—Interest Area: 12. Law and Public Safety. **Work Group:** 12.04. Law Enforcement and Public Safety. **Personality Type**—Enterprising. Enterprising occupations frequently involve starting up and carrying out projects. These occupations can involve leading people and making many decisions. They sometimes require risk taking and often deal with business. **Work Values**—Authority; Responsibility; Creativity; Variety; Security; Achievement. **Skills**—Persuasion; Service Orientation; Social Perceptiveness; Negotiation; Active Listening; Writing. **Abilities**—*Cognitive:* Spatial Orientation; Speed of Closure; Flexibility of Closure; Perceptual Speed; Inductive Reasoning; Problem Sensitivity. *Psychomotor:* Response Orientation; Reaction Time; Rate Control; Multilimb Coordination; Control Precision; Arm-Hand Steadiness. *Physical:* Explosive Strength; Stamina; Dynamic Strength; Static Strength; Gross Body Equilibrium; Gross Body Coordination. *Sensory:* Night Vision; Glare Sensitivity; Peripheral Vision; Sound Localization; Far Vision; Depth Perception. **General Work Activities**—*Information Input:* Identifying Objects, Actions, and Events; Monitoring Processes, Materials, or Surroundings; Getting Information. *Mental Process:* Updating and Using Relevant Knowledge; Making Decisions and Solving Problems; Processing Information. *Work Output:* Performing General Physical Activities; Handling and Moving Objects; Documenting or Recording Information. *Interacting with Others:* Establishing and Maintaining Interpersonal Relationships; Resolving Conflicts and Negotiating with Others; Performing for or Working with the Public. **Physical Work Conditions**—More Often Indoors Than Outdoors; Noisy; Very Hot or Cold; Very Bright or Dim Lighting; Hazardous Conditions. **Other Job Characteristics**—Need to Be Exact or Accurate; Errors Have Important Consequences; Repeat Same Tasks.

Experience—Job Zone 3. Previous work-related skill, knowledge, or experience is required. **Job Preparation**—SVP 6.0 to less than 7.0—more than one year and less than four years. **Knowledges**—Public Safety and Security; Transportation; Telecommunications; English Language; Law and Government; Geography. **Instructional Programs**—Protective Services, Other; Security and Loss Prevention Services.

Related SOC Job—33-3052 Transit and Railroad Police. **Related OOH Job**—Police and Detectives. **Related DOT Jobs**—372.267-010 Special Agent; 376.167-010 Special Agent-in-Charge; 376.667-018 Patroller.

33-9000 Other Protective Service Workers

33-9011.00 Animal Control Workers

- **Education/Training Required: Moderate-term on-the-job training**
- **Employed: 13,940**
- **Annual Earnings: $26,780**
- **Growth: 14.4%**
- **Annual Job Openings: 4,000**

Handle animals for the purpose of investigations of mistreatment or control of abandoned, dangerous, or unattended animals.

Investigate reports of animal attacks or animal cruelty, interviewing witnesses, collecting evidence, and writing reports. Capture and remove stray, uncontrolled, or abused animals from undesirable conditions, using nets, nooses, or tranquilizer darts as necessary. Examine animals for injuries or malnutrition and arrange for any necessary medical treatment. Remove captured animals from animal-control service vehicles and place animals in shelter cages or other enclosures. Euthanize rabid, unclaimed, or severely injured animals. Supply animals with food, water, and personal care. Clean facilities and equipment such as dog pens and animal control trucks. Prepare for prosecutions related to animal treatment and give evidence in court. Contact animal owners to inform them that their pets are at animal holding facilities. Educate the public about animal welfare and animal control laws and regulations. Write reports of activities and maintain files of impoundments and dispositions of animals. Issue warnings or citations in connection with animal-related offenses or contact police to report violations and request arrests. Answer inquiries from the public concerning animal control operations. Examine animal licenses and inspect establishments housing animals for compliance with laws. Organize the adoption of unclaimed animals. Train police officers in dog handling and training techniques for tracking, crowd control, and narcotics and bomb detection.

GOE Information—Interest Area: 12. Law and Public Safety. **Work Group:** 12.05. Safety and Security. **Personality Type**—Social. Social occupations frequently involve working with, communicating with, and teaching people. These occupations often involve helping or providing service to others. **Work Values**—Authority; Supervision, Technical; Social Service; Variety; Security. **Skills**—Negotiation; Active Listening; Writing; Reading Comprehension; Equipment Maintenance; Social Perceptiveness. **Abilities**—*Cognitive:* Time Sharing; Inductive Reasoning; Originality; Oral Expression; Written Expression; Oral Comprehension. *Psychomotor:* Manual Dexterity; Multilimb Coordination; Arm-Hand Steadiness; Control Precision. *Physical:* Static Strength. *Sensory:* Far Vision; Depth Perception; Auditory Attention; Speech Recognition. **General Work Activities**—*Information Input:* Identifying Objects, Actions, and Events; Getting Information; Monitoring Processes, Materials, or Surroundings. *Mental Process:* Making Decisions and Solving Problems; Updating and Using Relevant Knowledge; Evaluating Information Against Standards. *Work Output:* Handling and Moving Objects; Performing General Physical Activities; Documenting or Recording Information. *Interacting with Others:* Communicating with Persons Outside Organization; Performing for or Working with the Public; Resolving Conflicts and Negotiating with Others. **Physical Work Conditions**—More Often Outdoors Than Indoors; Contaminants; Disease or Infections; Minor Burns, Cuts, Bites, or Stings; Using Hands on

Objects, Tools, or Controls. **Other Job Characteristics**—Errors Have Important Consequences; Need to Be Exact or Accurate; Repeat Same Tasks.

Experience—Job Zone 2. Some previous work-related skill, knowledge, or experience may be helpful in these occupations, but usually is not needed. **Job Preparation**—SVP 4.0 to less than 6.0–six months to less than two years. **Knowledges**—Public Safety and Security; Law and Government; Biology; Customer and Personal Service; Telecommunications; Education and Training. **Instructional Program**—Protective Services, Other.

Related SOC Job—33-9011 Animal Control Workers. **Related OOH Job**—Animal Control Workers. **Related DOT Jobs**—379.137-010 Supervisor, Animal Cruelty Investigation; 379.227-010 Instructor-Trainer, Canine Service; 379.263-010 Animal Treatment Investigator; 379.673-010 Dog Catcher.

33-9021.00 Private Detectives and Investigators

- Education/Training Required: Work experience in a related occupation
- Employed: 33,720
- Annual Earnings: $32,650
- Growth: 17.7%
- Annual Job Openings: 7,000

Detect occurrences of unlawful acts or infractions of rules in private establishment or seek, examine, and compile information for client.

Question persons to obtain evidence for cases of divorce, child custody, or missing persons or information about individuals' character or financial status. Conduct private investigations on a paid basis. Confer with establishment officials, security departments, police, or postal officials to identify problems, provide information, and receive instructions. Observe and document activities of individuals to detect unlawful acts or to obtain evidence for cases, using binoculars and still or video cameras. Investigate companies' financial standings or locate funds stolen by embezzlers, using accounting skills. Monitor industrial or commercial properties to enforce conformance to establishment rules and to protect people or property. Search computer databases, credit reports, public records, tax and legal filings, and other resources to locate persons or to compile information for investigations. Write reports and case summaries to document investigations. Count cash and review transactions, sales checks, and register tapes to verify amounts and to identify shortages. Perform undercover operations such as evaluating the performance and honesty of employees by posing as customers or employees. Expose fraudulent insurance claims or stolen funds. Alert appropriate personnel to suspects' locations. Conduct background investigations of individuals, such as pre-employment checks, to obtain information about an individual's character, financial status, or personal history. Testify at hearings and court trials to present evidence. Warn troublemakers causing problems on establishment premises and eject them from premises when necessary. Obtain and analyze information on suspects, crimes, and disturbances to solve cases, to identify criminal activity, and to gather information for court cases. Apprehend suspects and release them to law enforcement authorities or security personnel.

GOE Information—**Interest Area:** 12. Law and Public Safety. **Work Group:** 12.05. Safety and Security. **Personality Type**—Enterprising. Enterprising occupations frequently involve starting up and carrying

out projects. These occupations can involve leading people and making many decisions. They sometimes require risk taking and often deal with business. **Work Values**—Ability Utilization; Responsibility; Achievement; Creativity; Authority; Social Status. **Skills**—Systems Evaluation; Systems Analysis; Persuasion; Writing; Active Listening; Speaking. **Abilities**—*Cognitive:* Speed of Closure; Fluency of Ideas; Inductive Reasoning; Written Expression; Selective Attention; Flexibility of Closure. *Psychomotor:* Speed of Limb Movement; Reaction Time; Response Orientation. *Physical:* Explosive Strength; Stamina; Static Strength; Gross Body Coordination; Extent Flexibility. *Sensory:* Night Vision; Sound Localization; Peripheral Vision; Far Vision; Auditory Attention; Near Vision. **General Work Activities**—*Information Input:* Getting Information; Identifying Objects, Actions, and Events; Monitoring Processes, Materials, or Surroundings. *Mental Process:* Analyzing Data or Information; Judging the Qualities of Things, Services, or Other People's Work; Making Decisions and Solving Problems. *Work Output:* Documenting or Recording Information; Performing General Physical Activities. *Interacting with Others:* Communicating with Other Workers; Assisting and Caring for Others; Communicating with Persons Outside Organization. **Physical Work Conditions**—More Often Indoors Than Outdoors; Standing; Walking and Running. **Other Job Characteristics**—Need to Be Exact or Accurate; Errors Have Important Consequences.

Experience—Job Zone 2. Some previous work-related skill, knowledge, or experience may be helpful in these occupations, but usually is not needed. **Job Preparation**—SVP 4.0 to less than 6.0–six months to less than two years. **Knowledges**—Public Safety and Security; Law and Government. **Instructional Program**—Criminal Justice/Police Science.

Related SOC Job—33-9021 Private Detectives and Investigators. **Related OOH Job**—Private Detectives and Investigators. **Related DOT Jobs**—186.267-010 Bonding Agent; 241.367-026 Skip Tracer; 376.267-010 Investigator, Cash Shortage; 376.267-014 Investigator, Fraud; 376.267-018 Investigator, Private; 376.267-022 Shopping Investigator; 376.367-010 Alarm Investigator; 376.367-014 Detective I; 376.367-018 House Officer; 376.367-022 Investigator; 376.367-026 Undercover Operator; 376.667-014 Detective II.

33-9031.00 Gaming Surveillance Officers and Gaming Investigators

- Education/Training Required: Moderate-term on-the-job training
- Employed: 8,730
- Annual Earnings: $25,870
- Growth: 24.5%
- Annual Job Openings: 2,000

Act as oversight and security agent for management and customers. Observe casino or casino hotel operation for irregular activities such as cheating or theft by either employees or patrons. May utilize one-way mirrors above the casino floor and cashier's cage and from desk. Use of audio/video equipment is also common to observe operation of the business. Usually required to provide verbal and written reports of all violations and suspicious behavior to supervisor.

Observe casino or casino hotel operations for irregular activities such as cheating or theft by employees or patrons, using audio and video equipment and one-way mirrors. Report all violations and suspicious behaviors to supervisors verbally or in writing. Monitor establishment activities to ensure adherence to all state gaming regulations and company policies and procedures. Act as oversight or security agents for management or customers. Supervise or train surveillance observers.

GOE Information—Interest Area: 12. Law and Public Safety. **Work Group:** 12.05. Safety and Security. **Personality Type**—No data available. **Work Values**—No data available. **Skills**—Management of Personnel Resources; Active Listening; Writing; Negotiation; Learning Strategies; Social Perceptiveness. **Abilities**—*Cognitive:* Selective Attention; Speed of Closure; Perceptual Speed; Problem Sensitivity; Time Sharing; Flexibility of Closure. *Psychomotor:* None met the criteria. *Physical:* None met the criteria. *Sensory:* Far Vision. **General Work Activities**—*Information Input:* Monitoring Processes, Materials, or Surroundings; Identifying Objects, Actions, and Events; Inspecting Equipment, Structures, or Materials. *Mental Process:* Evaluating Information Against Standards; Updating and Using Relevant Knowledge; Organizing, Planning, and Prioritizing. *Work Output:* Documenting or Recording Information; Handling and Moving Objects; Repairing and Maintaining Electronic Equipment. *Interacting with Others:* Communicating with Other Workers; Coaching and Developing Others; Coordinating the Work and Activities of Others. **Physical Work Conditions**—Indoors; Contaminants; Sitting; Using Hands on Objects, Tools, or Controls; Repetitive Motions. **Other Job Characteristics**—Need to Be Exact or Accurate; Repeat Same Tasks.

Experience—Job Zone 2. Some previous work-related skill, knowledge, or experience may be helpful in these occupations, but usually is not needed. **Job Preparation**—SVP 4.0 to less than 6.0—six months to less than two years. **Knowledges**—Public Safety and Security; Computers and Electronics; Telecommunications; Law and Government; Clerical Practices; Education and Training. **Instructional Program**—No related CIP programs.

Related SOC Job—33-9031 Gaming Surveillance Officers and Gaming Investigators. **Related OOH Job**—Security Guards and Gaming Surveillance Officers. **Related DOT Jobs**—343.367-014 Gambling Monitor; 379.367-010 Surveillance-System Monitor.

33-9032.00 Security Guards

- **Education/Training Required: Short-term on-the-job training**
- **Employed: 994,220**
- **Annual Earnings: $20,760**
- **Growth: 12.6%**
- **Annual Job Openings: 230,000**

Guard, patrol, or monitor premises to prevent theft, violence, or infractions of rules.

Patrol industrial or commercial premises to prevent and detect signs of intrusion and ensure security of doors, windows, and gates. Answer alarms and investigate disturbances. Monitor and authorize entrance and departure of employees, visitors, and other persons to guard against theft and maintain security of premises. Write reports of daily activities and irregularities such as equipment or property damage, theft, presence of unauthorized persons, or unusual occurrences. Call police or fire departments in cases of emergency, such as fire or presence of unauthorized persons. Circulate among visitors, patrons, or employees to preserve order and protect property. Answer telephone calls to take messages, answer questions, and provide information during non-business hours or when switchboard is closed. Warn persons of rule infractions or violations and apprehend or evict violators from premises, using force when necessary. Operate detecting devices to screen individuals and prevent passage of prohibited articles into restricted areas. Escort or drive motor vehicle to transport individuals to specified locations or to provide personal protection. Inspect and adjust security systems, equipment, or machinery to ensure operational use and to detect evidence of tampering. Drive or guard armored vehicle to transport money and valuables to prevent theft and ensure safe delivery. Monitor and adjust controls that regulate building systems, such as air conditioning, furnace, or boiler.

GOE Information—Interest Area: 12. Law and Public Safety. **Work Group:** 12.05. Safety and Security. **Personality Type**—Social. Social occupations frequently involve working with, communicating with, and teaching people. These occupations often involve helping or providing service to others. **Work Values**—Social Service; Authority; Supervision, Human Relations; Supervision, Technical. **Skills**—Social Perceptiveness; Negotiation; Speaking; Equipment Maintenance; Learning Strategies; Writing. **Abilities**—*Cognitive:* Flexibility of Closure; Selective Attention; Perceptual Speed; Problem Sensitivity; Speed of Closure; Memorization. *Psychomotor:* Response Orientation; Reaction Time; Arm-Hand Steadiness. *Physical:* Explosive Strength; Stamina; Static Strength; Gross Body Coordination; Trunk Strength. *Sensory:* Sound Localization; Far Vision; Hearing Sensitivity; Auditory Attention; Depth Perception; Speech Recognition. **General Work Activities**—*Information Input:* Monitoring Processes, Materials, or Surroundings; Identifying Objects, Actions, and Events; Getting Information. *Mental Process:* Making Decisions and Solving Problems; Organizing, Planning, and Prioritizing; Updating and Using Relevant Knowledge. *Work Output:* Documenting or Recording Information; Performing General Physical Activities. *Interacting with Others:* Communicating with Other Workers; Resolving Conflicts and Negotiating with Others; Performing for or Working with the Public. **Physical Work Conditions**—More Often Outdoors Than Indoors; Noisy; Very Hot or Cold; More Often Sitting Than Standing. **Other Job Characteristics**—Need to Be Exact or Accurate; Repeat Same Tasks.

Experience—Job Zone 2. Some previous work-related skill, knowledge, or experience may be helpful in these occupations, but usually is not needed. **Job Preparation**—SVP 4.0 to less than 6.0—six months to less than two years. **Knowledges**—Public Safety and Security; Customer and Personal Service; Telecommunications; Law and Government; Clerical Practices; Transportation. **Instructional Programs**—Securities Services Administration/Management; Security and Loss Prevention Services.

Related SOC Job—33-9032 Security Guards. **Related OOH Job**—Security Guards and Gaming Surveillance Officers. **Related DOT Jobs**—372.563-010 Armored-Car Guard and Driver; 372.567-010 Armored-Car Guard; 372.667-010 Airline Security Representative; 372.667-014 Bodyguard; 372.667-030 Gate Guard; 372.667-034 Guard, Security; 372.667-038 Merchant Patroller; 376.667-010 Bouncer; 379.667-010 Golf-Course Ranger.

33-9091.00 Crossing Guards

- **Education/Training Required: Short-term on-the-job training**
- **Employed: 69,390**
- **Annual Earnings: $20,050**
- **Growth: 19.7%**
- **Annual Job Openings: 26,000**

Guide or control vehicular or pedestrian traffic at such places as streets, schools, railroad crossings, or construction sites.

Monitor traffic flow to locate safe gaps through which pedestrians can cross streets. Direct or escort pedestrians across streets, stopping traffic as necessary. Guide or control vehicular or pedestrian traffic at such places as street and railroad crossings and construction sites. Communicate traffic and crossing rules and other information to students and adults. Report unsafe behavior of children to school officials. Record license numbers of vehicles disregarding traffic signals and report infractions to appropriate authorities. Direct traffic movement or warn of hazards, using signs, flags, lanterns, and hand signals. Learn the location and purpose of street traffic signs within assigned patrol areas. Stop speeding vehicles to warn drivers of traffic laws. Distribute traffic control signs and markers at designated points. Discuss traffic routing plans and control point locations with superiors. Inform drivers of detour routes through construction sites.

GOE Information—Interest Area: 12. Law and Public Safety. **Work Group:** 12.05. Safety and Security. **Personality Type**—Social. Social occupations frequently involve working with, communicating with, and teaching people. These occupations often involve helping or providing service to others. **Work Values**—Independence; Social Service; Supervision, Technical; Authority; Moral Values. **Skills**—None met the criteria. **Abilities**—*Cognitive:* Time Sharing; Problem Sensitivity; Selective Attention. *Psychomotor:* Speed of Limb Movement; Reaction Time; Manual Dexterity; Arm-Hand Steadiness. *Physical:* Stamina; Trunk Strength; Gross Body Coordination. *Sensory:* Far Vision; Speech Clarity. **General Work Activities**—*Information Input:* Getting Information; Monitoring Processes, Materials, or Surroundings; Estimating Needed Characteristics of Products, Events, or Information. *Mental Process:* Making Decisions and Solving Problems; Organizing, Planning, and Prioritizing; Thinking Creatively. *Work Output:* Performing General Physical Activities; Handling and Moving Objects. *Interacting with Others:* Performing for or Working with the Public; Assisting and Caring for Others; Establishing and Maintaining Interpersonal Relationships. **Physical Work Conditions**—Outdoors; Contaminants; Hazardous Equipment; Standing; Walking and Running; Using Hands on Objects, Tools, or Controls. **Other Job Characteristics**—Need to Be Exact or Accurate; Errors Have Important Consequences.

Experience—Job Zone 1. No previous work-related skill, knowledge, or experience is needed. **Job Preparation**—SVP below 4.0—less than six months. **Knowledges**—Public Safety and Security. **Instructional Programs**—Protective Services, Other; Security and Loss Prevention Services.

Related SOC Job—33-9091 Crossing Guards. **Related OOH Job**—Crossing Guards. **Related DOT Jobs**—371.567-010 Guard, School-Crossing; 371.667-010 Crossing Tender; 372.667-022 Flagger.

33-9092.00 Lifeguards, Ski Patrol, and Other Recreational Protective Service Workers

- **Education/Training Required:** Short-term on-the-job training
- **Employed:** 107,620
- **Annual Earnings:** $16,910
- **Growth:** 20.4%
- **Annual Job Openings:** 49,000

Monitor recreational areas, such as pools, beaches, or ski slopes, to provide assistance and protection to participants.

Rescue distressed persons, using rescue techniques and equipment. Contact emergency medical personnel in case of serious injury. Patrol or monitor recreational areas such as trails, slopes, and swimming areas on foot, in vehicles, or from towers. Examine injured persons and administer first aid or cardiopulmonary resuscitation if necessary, utilizing training and medical supplies and equipment. Instruct participants in skiing, swimming, or other recreational activities and provide safety precaution information. Warn recreational participants of inclement weather, unsafe areas, or illegal conduct. Complete and maintain records of weather and beach conditions, emergency medical treatments performed, and other relevant incident information. Inspect recreational equipment, such as rope tows, T-bars, J-bars, and chair lifts, for safety hazards and damage or wear. Provide assistance with staff selection, training, and supervision. Inspect recreational facilities for cleanliness. Observe activities in assigned areas, using binoculars to detect hazards, disturbances, or safety infractions. Provide assistance in the safe use of equipment such as ski lifts. Operate underwater recovery units. Participate in recreational demonstrations to entertain resort guests.

GOE Information—Interest Area: 12. Law and Public Safety. **Work Group:** 12.05. Safety and Security. **Personality Type**—Realistic. Realistic occupations frequently involve work activities that include practical, hands-on problems and solutions. They often deal with plants; animals; and real-world materials like wood, tools, and machinery. Many of the occupations require working outside and do not involve a lot of paperwork or working closely with others. **Work Values**—Social Service; Authority; Supervision, Technical; Variety; Achievement; Social Status. **Skills**—Monitoring; Social Perceptiveness; Equipment Maintenance; Operation Monitoring; Instructing; Service Orientation. **Abilities**—*Cognitive:* Flexibility of Closure; Speed of Closure; Time Sharing; Selective Attention; Oral Expression; Problem Sensitivity. *Psychomotor:* Multilimb Coordination. *Physical:* Stamina; Gross Body Coordination; Static Strength; Trunk Strength. *Sensory:* Far Vision; Auditory Attention; Speech Recognition; Speech Clarity. **General Work Activities**—*Information Input:* Identifying Objects, Actions, and Events; Monitoring Processes, Materials, or Surroundings; Inspecting Equipment, Structures, or Materials. *Mental Process:* Making Decisions and Solving Problems; Processing Information; Updating and Using Relevant Knowledge. *Work Output:* Performing General Physical Activities; Documenting or Recording Information. *Interacting with Others:* Assisting and Caring for Others; Communicating with Other Workers; Establishing and Maintaining Interpersonal Relationships. **Physical Work Conditions**—Indoors; Noisy; Sitting. **Other Job Characteristics**—Errors Have Important Consequences; Need to Be Exact or Accurate.

Experience—Job Zone 1. No previous work-related skill, knowledge, or experience is needed. **Job Preparation**—SVP below 4.0—less than six months. **Knowledges**—Medicine and Dentistry; Chemistry; Customer and Personal Service; Psychology; Public Safety and Security; Education and Training. **Instructional Program**—Protective Services, Other.

Related SOC Job—33-9092 Lifeguards, Ski Patrol, and Other Recreational Protective Service Workers. **Related OOH Job**—Lifeguards, Ski Patrol, and Other Recreational Protective Services. **Related DOT Jobs**—379.364-014 Beach Lifeguard; 379.664-010 Ski Patroller; 379.667-014 Lifeguard.

33-9099.01 Transportation Security Screeners

- **Education/Training Required: Work experience in a related occupation**
- **Employed: 141,480**
- **Annual Earnings: $30,720**
- **Growth: 9.6%**
- **Annual Job Openings: 53,000**

The job openings listed here are shared with 33-9099.99 Protective Service Workers, All Other.

Inspect baggage or cargo and screen passengers to detect and prevent potentially dangerous objects from being transported into secure areas or onto aircraft.

Watch for potentially dangerous persons whose pictures are posted at checkpoints. Locate suspicious bags pictured in printouts sent from remote monitoring areas and set these bags aside for inspection. Monitor passenger flow through screening checkpoints to ensure order and efficiency. Notify supervisors or other appropriate personnel when security breaches occur. Record information about any baggage that sets off alarms in monitoring equipment. Send checked baggage through automated screening machines and set bags aside for searching or rescreening as indicated by equipment. Ask passengers to remove shoes and divest themselves of metal objects prior to walking through metal detectors. View images of checked bags and cargo, using remote screening equipment, and alert baggage screeners or handlers to any possible problems. Perform pat-down or hand-held wand searches of passengers who have triggered machine alarms, who are unable to pass through metal detectors, or who have been randomly identified for such searches. Search carry-on or checked baggage by hand when it is suspected to contain prohibited items such as weapons. Test baggage for any explosive materials, using equipment such as explosive detection machines or chemical swab systems. Challenge suspicious people, requesting their badges and asking what their business is in a particular areas. Follow those who breach security until police or other security personnel arrive to apprehend them. Patrol work areas to detect any suspicious items. Provide directions and respond to passenger inquiries. Contact police directly in cases of urgent security issues, using phones or two-way radios. Inspect checked baggage for signs of tampering. Close entry areas following security breaches or reopen areas after receiving notification that the airport is secure. Contact leads or supervisors to discuss objects of concern that are not on prohibited object lists. Check passengers' tickets to ensure that they are valid and to determine whether passengers have designations that require special handling, such as providing photo identification.

GOE Information—Interest Area: 12. Law and Public Safety. **Work Group:** 12.05. Safety and Security. **Note:** The Department of Labor has not collected some data for this job, so it has fewer details than the other descriptions.

Instructional Program—No related CIP programs; this job is learned through work experience in a related occupation.

Related SOC Job—33-9099 Protective Service Workers, All Other. **Related OOH Job**—Security Guards and Gaming Surveillance Officers. **Related DOT Job**—No data available.

33-9099.99 Protective Service Workers, All Other

- **Education/Training Required: No data available**
- **Employed: 141,480**
- **Annual Earnings: $30,720**
- **Growth: 9.6%**
- **Annual Job Openings: 53,000**

The job openings listed here are shared with 33-9099.01 Transportation Security Screeners.

All protective service workers not listed separately.

No task data available.

Note: The Department of Labor has not collected some data for this job, so it has fewer details than the other descriptions.

Related SOC Job—33-9099 Protective Service Workers, All Other. **Related OOH Job**—None. **Related DOT Jobs**—199.267-026 Polygraph Examiner; 372.367-010 Community Service Officer, Patrol; 372.667-042 School Bus Monitor; 377.267-010 Deputy United States Marshal; 379.367-010 Surveillance-System Monitor.

35-0000

Food Preparation and Serving Related Occupations

35-1000 Supervisors, Food Preparation and Serving Workers

35-1011.00 Chefs and Head Cooks

- Education/Training Required: Work experience in a related occupation
- Employed: 115,850
- Annual Earnings: $32,330
- Growth: 16.7%
- Annual Job Openings: 11,000

Direct the preparation, seasoning, and cooking of salads, soups, fish, meats, vegetables, desserts, or other foods. May plan and price menu items, order supplies, and keep records and accounts. May participate in cooking.

Check the quality of raw and cooked food products to ensure that standards are met. Monitor sanitation practices to ensure that employees follow standards and regulations. Check the quantity and quality of received products. Order or requisition food and other supplies needed to ensure efficient operation. Supervise and coordinate activities of cooks and workers engaged in food preparation. Inspect supplies, equipment, and work areas to ensure conformance to established standards. Determine how food should be presented and create decorative food displays. Instruct cooks and other workers in the preparation, cooking, garnishing, and presentation of food. Estimate amounts and costs of required supplies, such as food and ingredients. Collaborate with other personnel to plan and develop recipes and menus, taking into account such factors as seasonal availability of ingredients and the likely number of customers. Analyze recipes to assign prices to menu items based on food, labor, and overhead costs. Prepare and cook foods of all types, either on a regular basis or for special guests or functions. Determine production schedules and staff requirements necessary to ensure timely delivery of services. Recruit and hire staff, including cooks and other kitchen workers. Meet with customers to discuss menus for special occasions such as weddings, parties, and banquets. Demonstrate new cooking techniques and equipment to staff. Meet with sales representatives to negotiate prices and order supplies. Arrange for equipment purchases and repairs. Record production and operational data on specified forms. Plan, direct, and supervise the food preparation and cooking activities of multiple kitchens or restaurants in an establishment such as a restaurant chain, hospital, or hotel. Coordinate planning, budgeting, and purchasing for all the food operations within establishments such as clubs, hotels, or restaurant chains.

GOE Information—Interest Area: 09. Hospitality, Tourism, and Recreation. Work Group: 09.04. Food and Beverage Preparation. Personality Type—Enterprising. Enterprising occupations frequently involve starting up and carrying out projects. These occupations can involve leading people and making many decisions. They sometimes require risk taking and often deal with business. Work Values—Authority; Responsibility; Creativity; Autonomy; Co-workers; Achievement. Skills—Management of Financial Resources; Equipment Maintenance; Repairing; Management of Personnel Resources; Service Orientation; Negotiation. Abilities—*Cognitive:* Originality; Number Facility; Visualization; Mathematical Reasoning; Fluency of Ideas; Time Sharing. *Psychomotor:* Arm-Hand Steadiness; Manual Dexterity; Multilimb Coordination; Control Precision; Finger Dexterity. *Physical:* Stamina; Trunk Strength; Extent Flexibility. *Sensory:* Visual Color Discrimination; Speech Recognition; Auditory Attention; Hearing Sensitivity; Speech Clarity. **General**

Work Activities—*Information Input:* Identifying Objects, Actions, and Events; Getting Information; Monitoring Processes, Materials, or Surroundings. *Mental Process:* Organizing, Planning, and Prioritizing; Making Decisions and Solving Problems; Thinking Creatively. *Work Output:* Handling and Moving Objects; Performing General Physical Activities; Controlling Machines and Processes. *Interacting with Others:* Monitoring and Controlling Resources; Establishing and Maintaining Interpersonal Relationships; Guiding, Directing, and Motivating Subordinates. **Physical Work Conditions**—Minor Burns, Cuts, Bites, or Stings; Standing; Walking and Running; Using Hands on Objects, Tools, or Controls; Bending or Twisting the Body; Repetitive Motions. **Other Job Characteristics**—Need to Be Exact or Accurate; Repeat Same Tasks; Pace Determined by Speed of Equipment.

Experience—Job Zone 3. Previous work-related skill, knowledge, or experience is required. Job Preparation—SVP 6.0 to less than 7.0— more than one year and less than four years. Knowledges—Food Production; Production and Processing; Administration and Management; Chemistry; Education and Training; Personnel and Human Resources. Instructional Programs—Baking and Pastry Arts/Baker/Pastry Chef; Cooking and Related Culinary Arts, General; Culinary Arts/Chef Training.

Related SOC Job—35-1011 Chefs and Head Cooks. Related OOH Job— Chefs, Cooks, and Food Preparation Workers. Related DOT Jobs— 313.131-010 Baker, Head; 313.131-014 Chef; 313.131-018 Cook, Head, School Cafeteria; 313.131-022 Pastry Chef; 313.131-026 Sous Chef; 313.361-010 Baker, Second; 313.361-038 Pie Maker; 313.381-010 Baker; 313.381-018 Cook Apprentice, Pastry; 313.381-026 Cook, Pastry; 315.131-010 Cook, Chief; 315.131-014 Pastry Chef; 315.137-010 Chef, Passenger Vessel; 315.137-014 Sous Chef.

35-1012.00 First-Line Supervisors/ Managers of Food Preparation and Serving Workers

- Education/Training Required: Work experience in a related occupation
- Employed: 748,550
- Annual Earnings: $26,050
- Growth: 16.6%
- Annual Job Openings: 187,000

Supervise workers engaged in preparing and serving food.

Compile and balance cash receipts at the end of the day or shift. Resolve customer complaints regarding food service. Inspect supplies, equipment, and work areas to ensure efficient service and conformance to standards. Train workers in food preparation and in service, sanitation, and safety procedures. Control inventories of food, equipment, smallware, and liquor and report shortages to designated personnel. Observe and evaluate workers and work procedures to ensure quality standards and service. Assign duties, responsibilities, and workstations to employees in accordance with work requirements. Estimate ingredients and supplies required to prepare a recipe. Perform personnel actions such as hiring and firing staff, consulting with other managers as necessary. Analyze operational problems, such as theft and wastage, and establish procedures to alleviate these problems. Specify food portions and courses, production and time sequences, and workstation and equipment arrangements. Recommend measures for improving work procedures and worker performance to increase service quality and enhance job safety. Greet and seat guests and present menus and wine lists. Present bills and accept payments. Forecast staff, equipment, and supply requirements based on a master menu. Record production and operational data on specified forms. Perform serving duties such as carving meat, preparing flambé dishes, or serving wine and liquor. Purchase or requisition supplies and equipment needed to ensure quality and timely delivery of services. Collaborate with other personnel to plan menus, serving arrangements, and related details. Supervise and check the assembly of regular and special diet trays and the delivery of food trolleys to hospital patients. Schedule parties and take reservations. Develop departmental objectives, budgets, policies, procedures, and strategies. Develop equipment maintenance schedules and arrange for repairs. Evaluate new products for usefulness and suitability.

GOE Information—Interest Area: 09. Hospitality, Tourism, and Recreation. **Work Group:** 09.01. Managerial Work in Hospitality and Tourism. **Personality Type**—Enterprising. Enterprising occupations frequently involve starting up and carrying out projects. These occupations can involve leading people and making many decisions. They sometimes require risk taking and often deal with business. **Work Values**—Authority; Responsibility; Co-workers; Creativity; Autonomy; Social Service. **Skills**—Management of Financial Resources; Equipment Maintenance; Management of Personnel Resources; Operation Monitoring; Management of Material Resources; Monitoring. **Abilities**—*Cognitive:* Time Sharing; Memorization; Deductive Reasoning; Information Ordering; Problem Sensitivity; Oral Expression. *Psychomotor:* Arm-Hand Steadiness. *Physical:* Extent Flexibility; Trunk Strength. *Sensory:* Speech Recognition. **General Work Activities**—*Information Input:* Identifying Objects, Actions, and Events; Getting Information; Monitoring Processes, Materials, or Surroundings. *Mental Process:* Making Decisions and Solving Problems; Organizing, Planning, and Prioritizing; Processing Information. *Work Output:* Handling and Moving Objects; Interacting With Computers; Performing General Physical Activities. *Interacting with Others:* Establishing and Maintaining Interpersonal Relationships; Communicating with Other Workers; Performing for or Working with the Public. **Physical Work Conditions**—Indoors; Minor Burns, Cuts, Bites, or Stings; Standing; Walking and Running; Using Hands on Objects, Tools, or Controls; Repetitive Motions. **Other Job Characteristics**—Need to Be Exact or Accurate; Repeat Same Tasks; Errors Have Important Consequences.

Experience—Job Zone 2. Some previous work-related skill, knowledge, or experience may be helpful in these occupations, but usually is not needed. **Job Preparation**—SVP 4.0 to less than 6.0—six months to less than two years. **Knowledges**—Food Production; Administration and Management; Customer and Personal Service; Sales and Marketing; Economics and Accounting; Production and Processing. **Instructional Programs**—Cooking and Related Culinary Arts, General; Foodservice Systems Administration/Management; Restaurant, Culinary, and Catering Management/Manager.

Related SOC Job—35-1012 First-Line Supervisors/Managers of Food Preparation and Serving Workers. **Related OOH Job**—First-Line Supervisors/Managers of Food Preparation and Serving Workers. **Related DOT Jobs**—310.137-018 Steward/Stewardess; 310.137-022 Steward/Stewardess, Banquet; 310.137-026 Steward/Stewardess, Railroad Dining Car; 311.137-010 Counter Supervisor; 311.137-014 Waiter/Waitress, Banquet, Head; 311.137-018 Waiter/Waitress, Captain; 311.137-022 Waiter/Waitress, Head; 318.137-010 Kitchen Steward/Stewardess; 319.137-010 Food-Service Supervisor; 319.137-022 Supervisor, Commissary Production; 319.137-026 Supervisor, Kosher Dietary Service; 319.137-030 Kitchen Supervisor; others.

35-2000 Cooks and Food Preparation Workers

35-2011.00 Cooks, Fast Food

- **Education/Training Required: Short-term on-the-job training**
- **Employed: 631,190**
- **Annual Earnings: $15,080**
- **Growth: 16.4%**
- **Annual Job Openings: 174,000**

Prepare and cook food in a fast food restaurant with a limited menu. Duties of the cooks are limited to preparation of a few basic items and normally involve operating large-volume single-purpose cooking equipment.

Maintain sanitation, health, and safety standards in work areas. Clean food preparation areas, cooking surfaces, and utensils. Operate large-volume cooking equipment such as grills, deep-fat fryers, or griddles. Verify that prepared food meets requirements for quality and quantity. Read food order slips or receive verbal instructions as to food required by patron and prepare and cook food according to instructions. Take food and drink orders and receive payment from customers. Wash, cut, and prepare foods designated for cooking. Measure ingredients required for specific food items being prepared. Cook and package batches of food, such as hamburgers and fried chicken, which are prepared to order or kept warm until sold. Cook the exact number of items ordered by each customer, working on several different orders simultaneously. Serve orders to customers at windows, counters, or tables. Clean, stock, and restock workstations and display cases. Prepare specialty foods such as pizzas, fish and chips, sandwiches, and tacos, following specific methods that usually require short preparation time. Prepare dough, following recipe. Schedule activities and equipment use with managers, using information about daily menus to help coordinate cooking times. Prepare and serve beverages such as coffee and fountain drinks. Mix ingredients such as pancake or waffle batters. Order and take delivery of supplies. Pre-cook items such as bacon to prepare them for later use.

GOE Information—Interest Area: 09. Hospitality, Tourism, and Recreation. **Work Group:** 09.04. Food and Beverage Preparation. **Personality Type**—Realistic. Realistic occupations frequently involve work activities that include practical, hands-on problems and solutions. They often deal with plants; animals; and real-world materials like wood, tools, and machinery. Many of the occupations require working outside and do not involve a lot of paperwork or working closely with others. **Work Values**—Moral Values; Supervision, Technical; Co-workers; Activity. **Skills**—Systems Analysis; Systems Evaluation; Installation; Management of Material Resources; Equipment Maintenance; Management of Financial Resources. **Abilities**—*Cognitive:* Time Sharing. *Psychomotor:* Manual Dexterity; Arm-Hand Steadiness. *Physical:* Stamina; Trunk Strength; Static Strength. *Sensory:* None met the criteria. **General Work Activities**—*Information Input:* Monitoring Processes, Materials, or Surroundings; Getting Information; Identifying Objects, Actions, and Events. *Mental Process:* Organizing, Planning, and Prioritizing; Scheduling Work and Activities; Judging the Qualities of Things, Services, or Other People's Work. *Work Output:* Handling and Moving Objects; Performing General Physical Activities; Controlling Machines and Processes. *Interacting with Others:* Establishing and Maintaining Interpersonal Relationships; Communicating with Other Workers; Teaching Others. **Physical Work Conditions**—Indoors; Minor Burns, Cuts, Bites, or Stings; Standing; Walking and Running; Using Hands on Objects, Tools, or Controls; Repetitive Motions. **Other Job Characteristics**—Need to Be Exact or Accurate; Pace Determined by Speed of Equipment.

Experience—Job Zone 1. No previous work-related skill, knowledge, or experience is needed. **Job Preparation**—SVP below 4.0—less than six months. **Knowledges**—Food Production; Sales and Marketing; Administration and Management; Personnel and Human Resources; Customer and Personal Service; Economics and Accounting. **Instructional Programs**—Food Preparation/Professional Cooking/Kitchen Assistant; Institutional Food Worker.

Related SOC Job—35-2011 Cooks, Fast Food. **Related OOH Job**—Chefs, Cooks, and Food Preparation Workers. **Related DOT Jobs**—313.361-026 Cook, Specialty; 313.374-010 Cook, Fast Food; 313.381-014 Baker, Pizza.

35-2012.00 Cooks, Institution and Cafeteria

- **Education/Training Required: Moderate-term on-the-job training**
- **Employed: 393,500**
- **Annual Earnings: $19,640**
- **Growth: 1.4%**
- **Annual Job Openings: 98,000**

Prepare and cook large quantities of food for institutions, such as schools, hospitals, or cafeterias.

Clean and inspect galley equipment, kitchen appliances, and work areas to ensure cleanliness and functional operation. Apportion and serve food to facility residents, employees, or patrons. Cook food-stuffs according to menus, special dietary or nutritional restrictions, and numbers of portions to be served. Clean, cut, and cook meat, fish, and poultry. Monitor use of government food commodities to ensure that proper procedures are followed. Wash pots, pans, dishes, utensils, and other cooking equipment. Compile and maintain records of food use and expenditures. Direct activities of one or more workers who assist in preparing and serving meals. Bake breads, rolls, and other pastries. Train new employees. Take inventory of supplies and equipment. Monitor menus and spending to ensure that meals are prepared economically. Plan menus that are varied, nutritionally balanced, and appetizing, taking advantage of foods in season and local availability. Requisition food supplies, kitchen equipment, and appliances based on estimates of future needs. Determine meal prices based on calculations of ingredient prices.

GOE Information—**Interest Area:** 09. Hospitality, Tourism, and Recreation. **Work Group:** 09.04. Food and Beverage Preparation. **Personality Type**—Realistic. Realistic occupations frequently involve work activities that include practical, hands-on problems and solutions. They often deal with plants; animals; and real-world materials like wood, tools, and machinery. Many of the occupations require working outside and do not involve a lot of paperwork or working closely with others. **Work Values**—Supervision, Technical; Co-workers; Authority. **Skills**—Instructing; Service Orientation; Equipment Selection; Social Perceptiveness; Operation Monitoring. **Abilities**—*Cognitive:* Number Facility; Time Sharing; Mathematical Reasoning. *Psychomotor:* Manual Dexterity; Multilimb Coordination; Arm-Hand Steadiness. *Physical:* Stamina; Trunk Strength; Static Strength; Extent Flexibility. *Sensory:* Hearing Sensitivity; Auditory Attention; Visual Color Discrimination. **General Work Activities**—*Information Input:* Identifying Objects, Actions, and Events; Getting Information;

Monitoring Processes, Materials, or Surroundings. *Mental Process:* Organizing, Planning, and Prioritizing; Updating and Using Relevant Knowledge; Processing Information. *Work Output:* Handling and Moving Objects; Performing General Physical Activities; Controlling Machines and Processes. *Interacting with Others:* Establishing and Maintaining Interpersonal Relationships; Performing for or Working with the Public; Communicating with Other Workers. **Physical Work Conditions**—Indoors; Very Hot or Cold; Minor Burns, Cuts, Bites, or Stings; Standing; Walking and Running; Repetitive Motions. **Other Job Characteristics**—Need to Be Exact or Accurate; Repeat Same Tasks.

Experience—Job Zone 2. Some previous work-related skill, knowledge, or experience may be helpful in these occupations, but usually is not needed. **Job Preparation**—SVP 4.0 to less than 6.0—six months to less than two years. **Knowledges**—Food Production; Public Safety and Security; Production and Processing. **Instructional Programs**—Cooking and Related Culinary Arts, General; Culinary Arts and Related Services, Other; Food Preparation/Professional Cooking/Kitchen Assistant; Foodservice Systems Administration/Management; Institutional Food Worker.

Related SOC Job—35-2012 Cooks, Institution and Cafeteria. **Related OOH Job**—Chefs, Cooks, and Food Preparation Workers. **Related DOT Jobs**—313.381-030 Cook, School Cafeteria; 315.361-010 Cook; 315.371-010 Cook, Mess; 315.381-010 Cook; 315.381-022 Cook, Third; 315.381-026 Second Cook and Baker.

35-2013.00 Cooks, Private Household

- **Education/Training Required: Long-term on-the-job training**
- **Employed: 830**
- **Annual Earnings: $20,820**
- **Growth: –5.6%**
- **Annual Job Openings: 2,000**

Prepare meals in private homes.

Plan menus according to employers' needs and diet restrictions. Shop for or order food and kitchen supplies and equipment. Peel, wash, trim, and cook vegetables and meats and bake breads and pastries. Prepare meals in private homes according to employers' recipes or tastes, handling all meals for the family and possibly for other household staff. Stock, organize, and clean kitchens and cooking utensils. Specialize in preparing fancy dishes or food for special diets. Create and explore new cuisines. Direct the operation and organization of kitchens and all food-related activities, including the presentation and serving of food. Plan and prepare food for parties, holiday meals, luncheons, special functions, and other social events. Serve meals and snacks to employing families and their guests. Travel with employers to vacation homes to provide meal preparation at those locations.

GOE Information—**Interest Area:** 09. Hospitality, Tourism, and Recreation. **Work Group:** 09.04. Food and Beverage Preparation. **Personality Type**—No data available. **Work Values**—No data available. **Skills**—Management of Financial Resources; Management of Material Resources; Time Management; Equipment Selection; Service Orientation; Quality Control Analysis. **Abilities**—*Cognitive:* Originality; Fluency of Ideas; Category Flexibility; Number Facility. *Psychomotor:* Manual Dexterity; Wrist-Finger Speed; Multilimb Coordination; Arm-Hand Steadiness; Finger Dexterity. *Physical:* Extent Flexibility; Dynamic Strength; Static Strength; Trunk Strength. *Sensory:* Hearing Sensitivity; Visual Color Discrimination; Depth Perception. **General Work Activities**—*Information Input:*

Getting Information; Identifying Objects, Actions, and Events; Monitoring Processes, Materials, or Surroundings. *Mental Process:* Organizing, Planning, and Prioritizing; Thinking Creatively; Updating and Using Relevant Knowledge. *Work Output:* Handling and Moving Objects; Performing General Physical Activities; Interacting With Computers. *Interacting with Others:* Monitoring and Controlling Resources; Establishing and Maintaining Interpersonal Relationships; Influencing Others or Selling. **Physical Work Conditions**—Indoors; Minor Burns, Cuts, Bites, or Stings; Standing; Using Hands on Objects, Tools, or Controls; Repetitive Motions. **Other Job Characteristics**—Need to Be Exact or Accurate.

Experience—Job Zone 3. Previous work-related skill, knowledge, or experience is required. **Job Preparation**—SVP 6.0 to less than 7.0—more than one year and less than four years. **Knowledges**—Sales and Marketing; Food Production; Production and Processing; Customer and Personal Service; Clerical Practices; Economics and Accounting. **Instructional Programs**—Culinary Arts/Chef Training; Food Preparation/Professional Cooking/Kitchen Assistant.

Related SOC Job—35-2013 Cooks, Private Household. **Related OOH Job**—Chefs, Cooks, and Food Preparation Workers. **Related DOT Job**—305.281-010 Cook.

35-2014.00 Cooks, Restaurant

- **Education/Training Required: Long-term on-the-job training**
- **Employed: 791,450**
- **Annual Earnings: $19,840**
- **Growth: 16.6%**
- **Annual Job Openings: 207,000**

Prepare, season, and cook soups, meats, vegetables, desserts, or other food-stuffs in restaurants. May order supplies, keep records and accounts, price items on menu, or plan menu.

Inspect food preparation and serving areas to ensure observance of safe, sanitary food-handling practices. Turn or stir foods to ensure even cooking. Season and cook food according to recipes or personal judgment and experience. Observe and test foods to determine if they have been cooked sufficiently, using methods such as tasting them, smelling them, or piercing them with utensils. Weigh, measure, and mix ingredients according to recipes or personal judgment, using various kitchen utensils and equipment. Portion, arrange, and garnish food and serve food to waiters or patrons. Regulate temperature of ovens, broilers, grills, and roasters. Substitute for or assist other cooks during emergencies or rush periods. Bake, roast, broil, and steam meats, fish, vegetables, and other foods. Wash, peel, cut, and seed fruits and vegetables to prepare them for consumption. Estimate expected food consumption, requisition or purchase supplies, or procure food from storage. Carve and trim meats such as beef, veal, ham, pork, and lamb for hot or cold service or for sandwiches. Coordinate and supervise work of kitchen staff. Consult with supervisory staff to plan menus, taking into consideration factors such as costs and special event needs. Butcher and dress animals, fowl, or shellfish or cut and bone meat prior to cooking. Prepare relishes and hors d'oeuvres. Bake breads, rolls, cakes, and pastries. Keep records and accounts. Plan and price menu items.

GOE Information—**Interest Area:** 09. Hospitality, Tourism, and Recreation. **Work Group:** 09.04. Food and Beverage Preparation. **Personality Type**—Realistic. Realistic occupations frequently involve work activities that include practical, hands-on problems and solutions. They often deal with plants; animals; and real-world materials like wood, tools, and machinery. Many of the occupations require

working outside and do not involve a lot of paperwork or working closely with others. **Work Values**—Creativity; Co-workers; Authority; Responsibility; Social Service; Moral Values. **Skills**—Equipment Maintenance. **Abilities**—*Cognitive:* Time Sharing; Originality; Perceptual Speed; Information Ordering; Memorization; Fluency of Ideas. *Psychomotor:* Manual Dexterity; Wrist-Finger Speed; Multilimb Coordination; Control Precision; Arm-Hand Steadiness. *Physical:* Extent Flexibility; Trunk Strength. *Sensory:* Speech Clarity. **General Work Activities**—*Information Input:* Identifying Objects, Actions, and Events; Getting Information; Monitoring Processes, Materials, or Surroundings. *Mental Process:* Organizing, Planning, and Prioritizing; Judging the Qualities of Things, Services, or Other People's Work; Processing Information. *Work Output:* Handling and Moving Objects; Performing General Physical Activities; Controlling Machines and Processes. *Interacting with Others:* Establishing and Maintaining Interpersonal Relationships; Coordinating the Work and Activities of Others; Teaching Others. **Physical Work Conditions**—Indoors; Very Hot or Cold; Minor Burns, Cuts, Bites, or Stings; Standing; Using Hands on Objects, Tools, or Controls; Repetitive Motions. **Other Job Characteristics**—Need to Be Exact or Accurate.

Experience—Job Zone 2. Some previous work-related skill, knowledge, or experience may be helpful in these occupations, but usually is not needed. **Job Preparation**—SVP 4.0 to less than 6.0—six months to less than two years. **Knowledges**—Food Production; Production and Processing; Customer and Personal Service. **Instructional Programs**—Cooking and Related Culinary Arts, General; Culinary Arts/Chef Training.

Related SOC Job—35-2014 Cooks, Restaurant. **Related OOH Job**—Chefs, Cooks, and Food Preparation Workers. **Related DOT Jobs**—313.281-010 Chef De Froid; 313.361-014 Cook; 313.361-018 Cook Apprentice; 313.361-030 Cook, Specialty, Foreign Food; 313.361-034 Garde Manger; 313.381-022 Cook, Barbecue; 313.381-034 Ice-Cream Chef; 315.361-022 Cook, Station; 315.381-014 Cook, Larder; 315.381-018 Cook, Railroad.

35-2015.00 Cooks, Short Order

- **Education/Training Required: Short-term on-the-job training**
- **Employed: 203,350**
- **Annual Earnings: $17,230**
- **Growth: 11.8%**
- **Annual Job Openings: 58,000**

Prepare and cook to order a variety of foods that require only a short preparation time. May take orders from customers and serve patrons at counters or tables.

Clean food preparation equipment, work areas, and counters or tables. Plan work on orders so that items served together are finished at the same time. Grill, cook, and fry foods such as french fries, eggs, and pancakes. Take orders from customers and cook foods requiring short preparation times according to customer requirements. Grill and garnish hamburgers or other meats such as steaks and chops. Complete orders from steam tables, placing food on plates and serving customers at tables or counters. Perform simple food preparation tasks such as making sandwiches, carving meats, and brewing coffee. Order supplies and stock them on shelves. Accept payments and make change or write charge slips as necessary.

GOE Information—**Interest Area:** 09. Hospitality, Tourism, and Recreation. **Work Group:** 09.04. Food and Beverage Preparation. **Personality Type**—Realistic. Realistic occupations frequently involve work activities that include practical, hands-on problems and solutions. They often deal with plants; animals; and real-world materials like wood, tools, and machinery. Many of the occupations require working outside and do not involve a lot of paperwork or working closely with others. **Work Values**—Moral Values; Social Service; Co-workers; Activity. **Skills**—Troubleshooting; Management of Personnel Resources; Time Management; Judgment and Decision Making; Operation and Control; Instructing. **Abilities**—*Cognitive:* Time Sharing; Perceptual Speed. *Psychomotor:* Wrist-Finger Speed; Reaction Time; Manual Dexterity; Multilimb Coordination; Arm-Hand Steadiness; Control Precision. *Physical:* Extent Flexibility; Trunk Strength; Static Strength. *Sensory:* Speech Recognition; Visual Color Discrimination; Auditory Attention. **General Work Activities**—*Information Input:* Getting Information; Identifying Objects, Actions, and Events; Monitoring Processes, Materials, or Surroundings. *Mental Process:* Organizing, Planning, and Prioritizing; Making Decisions and Solving Problems. *Work Output:* Handling and Moving Objects; Performing General Physical Activities. *Interacting with Others:* Establishing and Maintaining Interpersonal Relationships; Performing for or Working with the Public; Assisting and Caring for Others. **Physical Work Conditions**—Indoors; Very Hot or Cold; Minor Burns, Cuts, Bites, or Stings; Standing; Using Hands on Objects, Tools, or Controls; Repetitive Motions. **Other Job Characteristics**—Need to Be Exact or Accurate.

Experience—Job Zone 1. No previous work-related skill, knowledge, or experience is needed. **Job Preparation**—SVP below 4.0—less than six months. **Knowledges**—Food Production; Production and Processing. **Instructional Programs**—Food Preparation/Professional Cooking/Kitchen Assistant; Institutional Food Worker.

Related SOC Job—35-2015 Cooks, Short Order. **Related OOH Job**—Chefs, Cooks, and Food Preparation Workers. **Related DOT Job**—313.374-014 Cook, Short Order.

35-2019.99 Cooks, All Other

- **Education/Training Required: No data available**
- **Employed: 12,100**
- **Annual Earnings: $21,800**
- **Growth: 5.7%**
- **Annual Job Openings: 3,000**

All cooks not listed separately.

No task data available.

Note: The Department of Labor has not collected some data for this job, so it has fewer details than the other descriptions.

Related SOC Job—35-2019 Cooks, All Other. **Related OOH Job**—None. **Related DOT Job**—No data available.

35-2021.00 Food Preparation Workers

- **Education/Training Required: Short-term on-the-job training**
- **Employed: 880,360**
- **Annual Earnings: $17,040**
- **Growth: 19.7%**
- **Annual Job Openings: 294,000**

Perform a variety of food preparation duties other than cooking, such as preparing cold foods and shellfish, slicing meat, and brewing coffee or tea.

Clean work areas, equipment, utensils, dishes, and silverware. Store food in designated containers and storage areas to prevent spoilage.

Prepare a variety of foods according to customers' orders or supervisors' instructions, following approved procedures. Package take-out foods or serve food to customers. Portion and wrap the food or place it directly on plates for service to patrons. Place food trays over food warmers for immediate service or store them in refrigerated storage cabinets. Inform supervisors when supplies are getting low or equipment is not working properly. Weigh or measure ingredients. Assist cooks and kitchen staff with various tasks as needed and provide cooks with needed items. Wash, peel, and cut various foods to prepare for cooking or serving. Receive and store food supplies, equipment, and utensils in refrigerators, cupboards, and other storage areas. Stock cupboards and refrigerators and tend salad bars and buffet meals. Remove trash and clean kitchen garbage containers. Prepare and serve a variety of beverages such as coffee, tea, and soft drinks. Carry food supplies, equipment, and utensils to and from storage and work areas. Make special dressings and sauces as condiments for sandwiches. Scrape leftovers from dishes into garbage containers. Use manual or electric appliances to clean, peel, slice, and trim foods. Stir and strain soups and sauces. Distribute food to waiters and waitresses to serve to customers. Keep records of the quantities of food used. Load dishes, glasses, and tableware into dishwashing machines. Butcher and clean fowl, fish, poultry, and shellfish to prepare for cooking or serving. Cut, slice, or grind meat, poultry, and seafood to prepare for cooking. Work on assembly lines adding cutlery, napkins, food, and other items to trays in hospitals, cafeterias, airline kitchens, and similar establishments. Mix ingredients for green salads, molded fruit salads, vegetable salads, and pasta salads. Distribute menus to hospital patients, collect diet sheets, and deliver food trays and snacks to nursing units or directly to patients.

GOE Information—Interest Area: 09. Hospitality, Tourism, and Recreation. **Work Group:** 09.04. Food and Beverage Preparation. **Personality Type**—Realistic. Realistic occupations frequently involve work activities that include practical, hands-on problems and solutions. They often deal with plants; animals; and real-world materials like wood, tools, and machinery. Many of the occupations require working outside and do not involve a lot of paperwork or working closely with others. **Work Values**—Co-workers; Supervision, Technical. **Skills**—None met the criteria. **Abilities**—*Cognitive:* Perceptual Speed; Time Sharing; Visualization. *Psychomotor:* Wrist-Finger Speed; Speed of Limb Movement; Manual Dexterity; Arm-Hand Steadiness; Control Precision. *Physical:* Extent Flexibility; Static Strength; Trunk Strength. *Sensory:* Auditory Attention; Visual Color Discrimination; Hearing Sensitivity. **General Work Activities**—*Information Input:* Identifying Objects, Actions, and Events; Monitoring Processes, Materials, or Surroundings; Getting Information. *Mental Process:* Updating and Using Relevant Knowledge; Judging the Qualities of Things, Services, or Other People's Work. *Work Output:* Handling and Moving Objects; Performing General Physical Activities; Controlling Machines and Processes. *Interacting with Others:* Establishing and Maintaining Interpersonal Relationships; Performing for or Working with the Public; Communicating with Other Workers. **Physical Work Conditions**—Indoors; Minor Burns, Cuts, Bites, or Stings; Standing; Walking and Running; Using Hands on Objects, Tools, or Controls; Repetitive Motions. **Other Job Characteristics**—Need to Be Exact or Accurate.

Experience—Job Zone 1. No previous work-related skill, knowledge, or experience is needed. **Job Preparation**—SVP below 4.0—less than six months. **Knowledges**—Food Production; Production and Processing; Sales and Marketing; Customer and Personal Service; Administration and Management. **Instructional Programs**—Cooking and Related Culinary Arts, General; Food Preparation/Professional Cooking/Kitchen Assistant; Institutional Food Worker.

Related SOC Job—35-2021 Food Preparation Workers. **Related OOH Job**—Chefs, Cooks, and Food Preparation Workers. **Related DOT Jobs**—311.674-014 Raw Shellfish Preparer; 313.684-010 Baker Helper; 313.687-010 Cook Helper, Pastry; 316.661-010 Carver; 316.684-010 Butcher, Chicken and Fish; 316.684-014 Deli Cutter-Slicer; 317.384-010 Salad Maker; 317.664-010 Sandwich Maker; 317.684-010 Coffee Maker; 317.684-014 Pantry Goods Maker; 317.687-010 Cook Helper; 319.484-010 Food Assembler, Kitchen; 319.677-010 Caterer Helper.

35-3000 Food and Beverage Serving Workers

35-3011.00 Bartenders

- **Education/Training Required: Short-term on-the-job training**
- **Employed: 480,010**
- **Annual Earnings: $15,850**
- **Growth: 14.8%**
- **Annual Job Openings: 82,000**

Mix and serve drinks to patrons, directly or through waitstaff.

Collect money for drinks served. Check identification of customers to verify age requirements for purchase of alcohol. Balance cash receipts. Attempt to limit problems and liability related to customers' excessive drinking by taking steps such as persuading customers to stop drinking or ordering taxis or other transportation for intoxicated patrons. Clean glasses, utensils, and bar equipment. Take beverage orders from serving staff or directly from patrons. Serve wine and bottled or draft beer. Clean bars, work areas, and tables. Mix ingredients, such as liquor, soda, water, sugar, and bitters, to prepare cocktails and other drinks. Serve snacks or food items to customers seated at the bar. Order or requisition liquors and supplies. Ask customers who become loud and obnoxious to leave or physically remove them. Slice and pit fruit for garnishing drinks. Arrange bottles and glasses to make attractive displays. Plan, organize, and control the operations of a cocktail lounge or bar. Supervise the work of bar staff and other bartenders. Plan bar menus. Prepare appetizers such as pickles, cheese, and cold meats. Create drink recipes.

GOE Information—Interest Area: 09. Hospitality, Tourism, and Recreation. **Work Group:** 09.05. Food and Beverage Service. **Personality Type**—Enterprising. Enterprising occupations frequently involve starting up and carrying out projects. These occupations can involve leading people and making many decisions. They sometimes require risk taking and often deal with business. **Work Values**—Social Service; Supervision, Technical; Co-workers. **Skills**—None met the criteria. **Abilities**—*Cognitive:* Memorization; Problem Sensitivity; Time Sharing; Originality. *Psychomotor:* Manual Dexterity; Arm-Hand Steadiness; Multilimb Coordination. *Physical:* Static Strength; Gross Body Coordination; Extent Flexibility; Trunk Strength. *Sensory:* Speech Recognition. **General Work Activities**—*Information Input:* Identifying Objects, Actions, and Events; Getting Information; Monitoring Processes, Materials, or Surroundings. *Mental Process:* Judging the Qualities of Things, Services, or Other People's Work; Making Decisions and Solving Problems; Updating and Using Relevant Knowledge. *Work Output:* Handling and Moving Objects; Performing General Physical Activities. *Interacting with Others:* Performing for or Working with the Public; Establishing and Maintaining Interpersonal Relationships; Communicating with Persons Outside Organization. **Physical Work Conditions**—Indoors; Standing; Walking and Running; Using Hands on Objects, Tools, or

Controls; Repetitive Motions. **Other Job Characteristics**—Need to Be Exact or Accurate.

Experience—Job Zone 2. Some previous work-related skill, knowledge, or experience may be helpful in these occupations, but usually is not needed. **Job Preparation**—SVP 4.0 to less than 6.0–six months to less than two years. **Knowledges**—Food Production; Psychology; Customer and Personal Service; Sales and Marketing; Production and Processing. **Instructional Program**—Bartending/Bartender.

Related SOC Job—35-3011 Bartenders. **Related OOH Job**—Food and Beverage Serving and Related Workers. **Related DOT Jobs**—312.474-010 Bartender; 312.477-010 Bar Attendant; 312.677-010 Taproom Attendant.

35-3021.00 Combined Food Preparation and Serving Workers, Including Fast Food

- **Education/Training Required: Short-term on-the-job training**
- **Employed: 2,298,010**
- **Annual Earnings: $14,790**
- **Growth: 17.1%**
- **Annual Job Openings: 751,000**

Perform duties that combine food preparation and food service.

Accept payment from customers and make change as necessary. Request and record customer orders and compute bills, using cash registers, multicounting machines, or pencil and paper. Clean and organize eating and service areas. Serve customers in eating places that specialize in fast service and inexpensive carry-out food. Prepare and serve cold drinks or frozen milk drinks or desserts, using drink-dispensing, milkshake, or frozen custard machines. Select food items from serving or storage areas and place them in dishes, on serving trays, or in takeout bags. Prepare simple foods and beverages such as sandwiches, salads, and coffee. Notify kitchen personnel of shortages or special orders. Cook or reheat food items such as french fries. Wash dishes, glassware, and silverware after meals. Collect and return dirty dishes to the kitchen for washing. Relay food orders to cooks. Distribute food to servers. Serve food and beverages to guests at banquets or other social functions. Provide caterers with assistance in food preparation or service. Pack food, dishes, utensils, tablecloths, and accessories for transportation from catering or food preparation establishments to locations designated by customers. Arrange tables and decorations according to instructions.

GOE Information—Interest Area: 09. Hospitality, Tourism, and Recreation. **Work Group:** 09.05. Food and Beverage Service. **Personality Type**—Realistic. Realistic occupations frequently involve work activities that include practical, hands-on problems and solutions. They often deal with plants; animals; and real-world materials like wood, tools, and machinery. Many of the occupations require working outside and do not involve a lot of paperwork or working closely with others. **Work Values**—Moral Values; Co-workers. **Skills**—None met the criteria. **Abilities**—*Cognitive:* None met the criteria. *Psychomotor:* Multilimb Coordination. *Physical:* Extent Flexibility; Trunk Strength. *Sensory:* None met the criteria. **General Work Activities**—*Information Input:* Identifying Objects, Actions, and Events; Getting Information; Monitoring Processes, Materials, or Surroundings. *Mental Process:* Organizing, Planning, and Prioritizing; Thinking Creatively. *Work Output:* Handling and Moving Objects; Performing General Physical Activities. *Interacting with Others:* Performing for or Working with the Public; Establishing and Maintaining Interpersonal Relationships; Coordinating the Work and Activities of Others. **Physical Work Conditions**—Indoors; Minor

Burns, Cuts, Bites, or Stings; Standing; Walking and Running; Using Hands on Objects, Tools, or Controls; Repetitive Motions. **Other Job Characteristics**—Need to Be Exact or Accurate; Repeat Same Tasks.

Experience—Job Zone 1. No previous work-related skill, knowledge, or experience is needed. **Job Preparation**—SVP below 4.0—less than six months. **Knowledges**—Food Production; Sales and Marketing; Economics and Accounting; Production and Processing; Customer and Personal Service; Personnel and Human Resources. **Instructional Programs**—Food Preparation/Professional Cooking/Kitchen Assistant; Institutional Food Worker.

Related SOC Job—35-3021 Combined Food Preparation and Serving Workers, Including Fast Food. **Related OOH Job**—Food and Beverage Serving and Related Workers. **Related DOT Job**—311.472-010 Fast-Foods Worker.

35-3022.00 Counter Attendants, Cafeteria, Food Concession, and Coffee Shop

- **Education/Training Required: Short-term on-the-job training**
- **Employed: 501,390**
- **Annual Earnings: $15,820**
- **Growth: 17.5%**
- **Annual Job Openings: 199,000**

Serve food to diners at counter or from a steam table.

Scrub and polish counters, steam tables, and other equipment and clean glasses, dishes, and fountain equipment. Serve food, beverages, or desserts to customers in such settings as take-out counters of restaurants or lunchrooms, business or industrial establishments, hotel rooms, and cars. Replenish foods at serving stations. Take customers' orders and write ordered items on tickets, giving ticket stubs to customers when needed to identify filled orders. Prepare food such as sandwiches, salads, and ice cream dishes, using standard formulas or following directions. Wrap menu item such as sandwiches, hot entrees, and desserts for serving or for takeout. Prepare bills for food, using cash registers, calculators, or adding machines, and accept payment or make change. Deliver orders to kitchens and pick up and serve food when it is ready. Serve salads, vegetables, meat, breads, and cocktails; ladle soups and sauces; portion desserts; and fill beverage cups and glasses. Add relishes and garnishes to food orders according to instructions. Carve meat. Order items needed to replenish supplies. Set up dining areas for meals and clear them following meals. Brew coffee and tea and fill containers with requested beverages. Balance receipts and payments in cash registers. Arrange reservations for patrons of dining establishments.

GOE Information—**Interest Area:** 09. Hospitality, Tourism, and Recreation. **Work Group:** 09.05. Food and Beverage Service. **Personality Type**—Social. Social occupations frequently involve working with, communicating with, and teaching people. These occupations often involve helping or providing service to others. **Work Values**—Social Service; Supervision, Technical; Co-workers; Moral Values. **Skills**—None met the criteria. **Abilities**—*Cognitive:* Time Sharing. *Psychomotor:* Manual Dexterity; Arm-Hand Steadiness. *Physical:* Extent Flexibility; Trunk Strength. *Sensory:* Speech Recognition. **General Work Activities**—*Information Input:* Identifying Objects, Actions, and Events. *Mental Process:* Thinking Creatively; Organizing, Planning, and Prioritizing; Making Decisions and Solving Problems. *Work Output:* Handling and Moving Objects; Performing General Physical Activities; Controlling Machines and

Processes. *Interacting with Others:* Performing for or Working with the Public; Establishing and Maintaining Interpersonal Relationships; Communicating with Other Workers. **Physical Work Conditions**—Indoors; Noisy; Standing; Walking and Running; Using Hands on Objects, Tools, or Controls; Repetitive Motions. **Other Job Characteristics**—Need to Be Exact or Accurate.

Experience—Job Zone 1. No previous work-related skill, knowledge, or experience is needed. **Job Preparation**—SVP below 4.0—less than six months. **Knowledges**—Food Production; Sales and Marketing. **Instructional Program**—Food Service, Waiter/Waitress, and Dining Room Management/Manager.

Related SOC Job—35-3022 Counter Attendants, Cafeteria, Food Concession, and Coffee Shop. **Related OOH Job**—Food and Beverage Serving and Related Workers. **Related DOT Jobs**—311.477-014 Counter Attendant, Lunchroom or Coffee Shop; 311.477-038 Waiter/Waitress, Take Out; 311.674-010 Canteen Operator; 311.677-014 Counter Attendant, Cafeteria; 319.474-010 Fountain Server.

35-3031.00 Waiters and Waitresses

- **Education/Training Required: Short-term on-the-job training**
- **Employed: 2,274,770**
- **Annual Earnings: $14,200**
- **Growth: 16.7%**
- **Annual Job Openings: 800,000**

Take orders and serve food and beverages to patrons at tables in dining establishment.

Check patrons' identification to ensure that they meet minimum age requirements for consumption of alcoholic beverages. Collect payments from customers. Write patrons' food orders on order slips, memorize orders, or enter orders into computers for transmittal to kitchen staff. Take orders from patrons for food or beverages. Check with customers to ensure that they are enjoying their meals and take action to correct any problems. Prepare checks that itemize and total meal costs and sales taxes. Serve food or beverages to patrons and prepare or serve specialty dishes at tables as required. Remove dishes and glasses from tables or counters and take them to kitchen for cleaning. Present menus to patrons and answer questions about menu items, making recommendations upon request. Inform customers of daily specials. Clean tables or counters after patrons have finished dining. Prepare hot, cold, and mixed drinks for patrons and chill bottles of wine. Explain how various menu items are prepared, describing ingredients and cooking methods. Prepare tables for meals, including setting up items such as linens, silverware, and glassware. Perform food preparation duties such as preparing salads, appetizers, and cold dishes; portioning desserts; and brewing coffee. Stock service areas with supplies such as coffee, food, tableware, and linens. Garnish and decorate dishes in preparation for serving. Fill salt, pepper, sugar, cream, condiment, and napkin containers. Escort customers to their tables. Describe and recommend wines to customers. Bring wine selections to tables with appropriate glasses and pour the wines for customers.

GOE Information—**Interest Area:** 09. Hospitality, Tourism, and Recreation. **Work Group:** 09.05. Food and Beverage Service. **Personality Type**—Social. Social occupations frequently involve working with, communicating with, and teaching people. These occupations often involve helping or providing service to others. **Work Values**—Social Service; Supervision, Technical; Co-workers. **Skills**—Service Orientation. **Abilities**—*Cognitive:* Memorization; Time Sharing. *Psychomotor:* Manual Dexterity; Arm-Hand Steadiness;

Multilimb Coordination. *Physical:* Gross Body Coordination; Extent Flexibility; Stamina; Trunk Strength. *Sensory:* Speech Recognition. **General Work Activities**—*Information Input:* Identifying Objects, Actions, and Events; Getting Information; Monitoring Processes, Materials, or Surroundings. *Mental Process:* Organizing, Planning, and Prioritizing; Processing Information; Making Decisions and Solving Problems. *Work Output:* Handling and Moving Objects; Performing General Physical Activities. *Interacting with Others:* Performing for or Working with the Public; Establishing and Maintaining Interpersonal Relationships; Communicating with Other Workers. **Physical Work Conditions**—Indoors; Minor Burns, Cuts, Bites, or Stings; Standing; Walking and Running; Using Hands on Objects, Tools, or Controls; Repetitive Motions. **Other Job Characteristics**—Need to Be Exact or Accurate.

Experience—Job Zone 1. No previous work-related skill, knowledge, or experience is needed. **Job Preparation**—SVP below 4.0—less than six months. **Knowledges**—Food Production; Sales and Marketing; Customer and Personal Service; Psychology; Personnel and Human Resources; Production and Processing. **Instructional Program**—Food Service, Waiter/Waitress, and Dining Room Management/Manager.

Related SOC Job—35-3031 Waiters and Waitresses. **Related OOH Job**—Food and Beverage Serving and Related Workers. **Related DOT Jobs**—310.357-010 Wine Steward/Stewardess; 311.477-018 Waiter/Waitress, Bar; 311.477-022 Waiter/Waitress, Dining Car; 311.477-026 Waiter/Waitress, Formal; 311.477-030 Waiter/Waitress, Informal; 311.674-018 Waiter/Waitress, Buffet; 350.677-010 Mess Attendant; 350.677-026 Steward/Stewardess, Wine; 350.677-030 Waiter/Waitress; 352.677-018 Waiter/Waitress, Club.

35-3041.00 Food Servers, Nonrestaurant

- **Education/Training Required:** Short-term on-the-job training
- **Employed:** 188,750
- **Annual Earnings:** $17,210
- **Growth:** 8.8%
- **Annual Job Openings:** 45,000

Serve food to patrons outside of a restaurant environment, such as in hotels, hospital rooms, or cars.

Monitor food distribution, ensuring that meals are delivered to the correct recipients and that guidelines such as those for special diets are followed. Clean and sterilize dishes, kitchen utensils, equipment, and facilities. Examine trays to ensure that they contain required items. Place food servings on plates and trays according to orders or instructions. Load trays with accessories such as eating utensils, napkins, and condiments. Take food orders and relay orders to kitchens or serving counters so they can be filled. Stock service stations with items such as ice, napkins, and straws. Remove trays and stack dishes for return to kitchen after meals are finished. Prepare food items such as sandwiches, salads, soups, and beverages. Monitor food preparation and serving techniques to ensure that proper procedures are followed. Carry food, silverware, and linen on trays or use carts to carry trays. Determine where patients or patrons would like to eat their meals and help them get situated. Record amounts and types of special food items served to customers. Total checks, present them to customers, and accept payment for services.

GOE Information—**Interest Area:** 09. Hospitality, Tourism, and Recreation. **Work Group:** 09.05. Food and Beverage Service. **Personality Type**—Social. Social occupations frequently involve working with, communicating with, and teaching people. These occupations often involve helping or providing service to others.

Work Values—Social Service; Supervision, Technical; Co-workers; Moral Values. **Skills**—Operation Monitoring. **Abilities**—*Cognitive:* None met the criteria. *Psychomotor:* Arm-Hand Steadiness; Manual Dexterity. *Physical:* Trunk Strength. *Sensory:* None met the criteria. **General Work Activities**—*Information Input:* Identifying Objects, Actions, and Events; Getting Information; Monitoring Processes, Materials, or Surroundings. *Mental Process:* Organizing, Planning, and Prioritizing; Updating and Using Relevant Knowledge; Processing Information. *Work Output:* Handling and Moving Objects; Performing General Physical Activities; Controlling Machines and Processes. *Interacting with Others:* Establishing and Maintaining Interpersonal Relationships; Assisting and Caring for Others; Communicating with Other Workers. **Physical Work Conditions**—Indoors; Disease or Infections; Standing; Walking and Running; Using Hands on Objects, Tools, or Controls; Repetitive Motions. **Other Job Characteristics**—Need to Be Exact or Accurate; Repeat Same Tasks.

Experience—Job Zone 1. No previous work-related skill, knowledge, or experience is needed. **Job Preparation**—SVP below 4.0—less than six months. **Knowledges**—Food Production; Customer and Personal Service. **Instructional Program**—Food Service, Waiter/Waitress, and Dining Room Management/Manager.

Related SOC Job—35-3041 Food Servers, Nonrestaurant. **Related OOH Job**—Food and Beverage Serving and Related Workers. **Related DOT Jobs**—311.477-010 Car Hop; 311.477-034 Waiter/Waitress, Room Service; 319.677-014 Food-Service Worker, Hospital.

35-9000 Other Food Preparation and Serving Related Workers

35-9011.00 Dining Room and Cafeteria Attendants and Bartender Helpers

- **Education/Training Required:** Short-term on-the-job training
- **Employed:** 391,320
- **Annual Earnings:** $15,040
- **Growth:** 15.6%
- **Annual Job Openings:** 174,000

Facilitate food service. Clean tables; carry dirty dishes; replace soiled table linens; set tables; replenish supply of clean linens, silverware, glassware, and dishes; supply service bar with food; and serve water, butter, and coffee to patrons.

Wipe tables and seats with dampened cloths and replace dirty tablecloths. Set tables with clean linens, condiments, and other supplies. Scrape and stack dirty dishes and carry dishes and other tableware to kitchens for cleaning. Clean up spilled food, drink, and broken dishes and remove empty bottles and trash. Perform serving, cleaning, and stocking duties in establishments such as cafeterias or dining rooms to facilitate customer service. Maintain adequate supplies of items such as clean linens, silverware, glassware, dishes, and trays. Fill beverage and ice dispensers. Serve ice water, coffee, rolls, and butter to patrons. Stock cabinets and serving areas with condiments and refill condiment containers as necessary. Locate items requested by customers. Carry food, dishes, trays, and silverware from kitchens and supply departments to serving counters. Serve food to customers when waiters and waitresses need assistance. Clean and polish counters, shelves, walls, furniture, and equipment in food service areas and other areas of restaurants and mop and vacuum floors. Carry trays from food counters to tables for cafeteria patrons. Replenish supplies of food and equipment at steam tables and service bars. Run cash registers. Garnish foods and position them on tables to make them visible and accessible. Wash glasses and other serving equipment at bars. Carry linens to and from laundry areas. Stock refrigerating units with wines and bottled beer and replace empty beer kegs. Mix and prepare flavors for mixed drinks. Slice and pit fruit used to garnish drinks. Stock vending machines with food.

GOE Information—Interest Area: 09. Hospitality, Tourism, and Recreation. **Work Group:** 09.05. Food and Beverage Service. **Personality Type**—Realistic. Realistic occupations frequently involve work activities that include practical, hands-on problems and solutions. They often deal with plants; animals; and real-world materials like wood, tools, and machinery. Many of the occupations require working outside and do not involve a lot of paperwork or working closely with others. **Work Values**—Supervision, Technical; Social Service; Co-workers; Moral Values. **Skills**—None met the criteria. **Abilities**—*Cognitive:* None met the criteria. *Psychomotor:* Speed of Limb Movement; Manual Dexterity; Multilimb Coordination; Arm-Hand Steadiness; Finger Dexterity. *Physical:* Static Strength; Extent Flexibility; Stamina; Dynamic Strength; Trunk Strength; Gross Body Coordination. *Sensory:* Auditory Attention. **General Work Activities**—*Information Input:* Identifying Objects, Actions, and Events; Monitoring Processes, Materials, or Surroundings. *Mental Process:* Judging the Qualities of Things, Services, or Other People's Work. *Work Output:* Handling and Moving Objects; Performing General Physical Activities. *Interacting with Others:* Performing for or Working with the Public; Establishing and Maintaining Interpersonal Relationships; Assisting and Caring for Others. **Physical Work Conditions**—Indoors; Noisy; Standing; Walking and Running; Using Hands on Objects, Tools, or Controls; Repetitive Motions. **Other Job Characteristics**—Need to Be Exact or Accurate.

Experience—Job Zone 1. No previous work-related skill, knowledge, or experience is needed. **Job Preparation**—SVP below 4.0—less than six months. **Knowledges**—Food Production; Customer and Personal Service; Psychology. **Instructional Program**—Food Service, Waiter/Waitress, and Dining Room Management/Manager.

Related SOC Job—35-9011 Dining Room and Cafeteria Attendants and Bartender Helpers. **Related OOH Job**—Food and Beverage Serving and Related Workers. **Related DOT Jobs**—311.677-010 Cafeteria Attendant; 311.677-018 Dining Room Attendant; 312.687-010 Bartender Helper; 319.687-010 Counter-Supply Worker.

35-9021.00 Dishwashers

- **Education/Training Required:** Short-term on-the-job training
- **Employed:** 498,620
- **Annual Earnings:** $15,490
- **Growth:** 15.8%
- **Annual Job Openings:** 164,000

Clean dishes, kitchen, food preparation equipment, or utensils.

Wash dishes, glassware, flatware, pots, and pans by hand or using dishwashers . Place clean dishes, utensils, and cooking equipment in storage areas. Maintain kitchen work areas, equipment, and utensils in clean and orderly condition. Stock supplies such as food and utensils in serving stations, cupboards, refrigerators, and salad bars. Sweep and scrub floors. Clean garbage cans with water or steam. Sort and remove trash, placing it in designated pickup areas. Clean and prepare various foods for cooking or serving. Set up banquet tables.

Transfer supplies and equipment between storage and work areas by hand or using hand trucks. Receive and store supplies. Prepare and package individual place settings. Load or unload trucks that deliver or pick up food and supplies.

GOE Information—Interest Area: 09. Hospitality, Tourism, and Recreation. **Work Group:** 09.04. Food and Beverage Preparation. **Personality Type**—Realistic. Realistic occupations frequently involve work activities that include practical, hands-on problems and solutions. They often deal with plants; animals; and real-world materials like wood, tools, and machinery. Many of the occupations require working outside and do not involve a lot of paperwork or working closely with others. **Work Values**—Moral Values; Co-workers. **Skills**—Equipment Maintenance; Installation; Operation Monitoring; Repairing. **Abilities**—*Cognitive:* None met the criteria. *Psychomotor:* Manual Dexterity; Rate Control; Speed of Limb Movement; Response Orientation; Reaction Time; Multilimb Coordination. *Physical:* Extent Flexibility; Stamina; Static Strength; Dynamic Strength; Gross Body Coordination; Trunk Strength. *Sensory:* None met the criteria. **General Work Activities**—*Information Input:* Getting Information; Identifying Objects, Actions, and Events; Monitoring Processes, Materials, or Surroundings. *Mental Process:* Thinking Creatively; Judging the Qualities of Things, Services, or Other People's Work; Organizing, Planning, and Prioritizing. *Work Output:* Handling and Moving Objects; Controlling Machines and Processes; Performing General Physical Activities. *Interacting with Others:* Establishing and Maintaining Interpersonal Relationships; Communicating with Other Workers; Performing for or Working with the Public. **Physical Work Conditions**—Minor Burns, Cuts, Bites, or Stings; Standing; Walking and Running; Using Hands on Objects, Tools, or Controls; Bending or Twisting the Body; Repetitive Motions. **Other Job Characteristics**—Pace Determined by Speed of Equipment; Need to Be Exact or Accurate.

Experience—Job Zone 1. No previous work-related skill, knowledge, or experience is needed. **Job Preparation**—SVP below 4.0—less than six months. **Knowledges**—Food Production; Transportation. **Instructional Program**—Food Preparation/Professional Cooking/Kitchen Assistant.

Related SOC Job—35-9021 Dishwashers. **Related OOH Job**—Food and Beverage Serving and Related Workers. **Related DOT Jobs**—318.687-010 Kitchen Helper; 318.687-014 Scullion; 318.687-018 Silver Wrapper.

35-9031.00 Hosts and Hostesses, Restaurant, Lounge, and Coffee Shop

- **Education/Training Required:** Short-term on-the-job training
- **Employed:** 328,930
- **Annual Earnings:** $15,840
- **Growth:** 16.3%
- **Annual Job Openings:** 116,000

Welcome patrons, seat them at tables or in lounge, and help ensure quality of facilities and service.

Provide guests with menus. Greet guests and seat them at tables or in waiting areas. Assign patrons to tables suitable for their needs. Inspect dining and serving areas to ensure cleanliness and proper setup. Speak with patrons to ensure satisfaction with food and service and to respond to complaints. Receive and record patrons' dining reservations. Maintain contact with kitchen staff, management, serving staff, and customers to ensure that dining details are handled properly and customers' concerns are addressed. Inform patrons of establishment specialties and features. Direct patrons to coatrooms and waiting areas such as lounges. Operate cash registers to accept payments for food and beverages. Prepare cash receipts after establishments close and make bank deposits. Supervise and coordinate activities of dining room staff to ensure that patrons receive prompt and courteous service. Prepare staff work schedules. Order or requisition supplies and equipment for tables and serving stations. Hire, train, and supervise food and beverage service staff. Plan parties or other special events and services. Confer with other staff to help plan establishments' menus. Perform marketing and advertising services.

GOE Information—Interest Area: 09. Hospitality, Tourism, and Recreation. **Work Group:** 09.05. Food and Beverage Service. **Personality Type—**Enterprising. Enterprising occupations frequently involve starting up and carrying out projects. These occupations can involve leading people and making many decisions. They sometimes require risk taking and often deal with business. **Work Values—**Supervision, Technical; Social Service; Co-workers; Authority. **Skills—**None met the criteria. **Abilities—***Cognitive:* Time Sharing. *Psychomotor:* None met the criteria. *Physical:* Trunk Strength. *Sensory:* Speech Recognition. **General Work Activities—***Information Input:* Identifying Objects, Actions, and Events; Monitoring Processes, Materials, or Surroundings; Getting Information. *Mental Process:* None met the criteria. *Work Output:* Handling and Moving Objects; Performing General Physical Activities. *Interacting with Others:* Establishing and Maintaining Interpersonal Relationships; Performing for or Working with the Public; Assisting and Caring for Others. **Physical Work Conditions—**Indoors; Standing; Walking and Running. **Other Job Characteristics—**Need to Be Exact or Accurate.

Experience—Job Zone 1. No previous work-related skill, knowledge, or experience is needed. **Job Preparation—**SVP below 4.0—less than six months. **Knowledges—**Food Production; Sales and Marketing. **Instructional Program—**Food Service, Waiter/Waitress, and Dining Room Management/Manager.

Related SOC Job—35-9031 Hosts and Hostesses, Restaurant, Lounge, and Coffee Shop. **Related OOH Job—**Food and Beverage Serving and Related Workers. **Related DOT Job—**310.137-010 Host/Hostess, Restaurant.

35-9099.99 Food Preparation and Serving Related Workers, All Other

- **Education/Training Required: No data available**
- **Employed: 58,730**
- **Annual Earnings: $17,440**
- **Growth: 16.7%**
- **Annual Job Openings: 28,000**

All food preparation and serving related workers not listed separately.

No task data available.

Note: The Department of Labor has not collected some data for this job, so it has fewer details than the other descriptions.

Related SOC Job—35-9099 Food Preparation and Serving Related Workers, All Other. **Related OOH Job—**Food and Beverage Serving and Related Workers. **Related DOT Jobs—**211.482-018 Food-And-Beverage Checker; 319.464-010 Automat-Car Attendant; 319.464-014 Vending-Machine Attendant; 319.467-010 Food Order Expediter; 319.567-010 Mini Bar Attendant.

37-0000 Building and Grounds Cleaning and Maintenance Occupations

37-1000 Supervisors, Building and Grounds Cleaning and Maintenance Workers

37-1011.00 First-Line Supervisors/Managers of Housekeeping and Janitorial Workers

- **Education/Training Required:** Work experience in a related occupation
- **Employed:** 186,870
- **Annual Earnings:** $30,330
- **Growth:** 19.0%
- **Annual Job Openings:** 21,000

Supervise work activities of cleaning personnel in hotels, hospitals, offices, and other establishments.

Direct activities for stopping the spread of infections in facilities such as hospitals. Inspect work performed to ensure that it meets specifications and established standards. Plan and prepare employee work schedules. Perform or assist with cleaning duties as necessary. Investigate complaints about service and equipment and take corrective action. Coordinate activities with other departments to ensure that services are provided in an efficient and timely manner. Check equipment to ensure that it is in working order. Inspect and evaluate the physical condition of facilities to determine the type of work required. Select the most suitable cleaning materials for different types of linens, furniture, flooring, and surfaces. Instruct staff in work policies and procedures and the use and maintenance of equipment. Issue supplies and equipment to workers. Forecast necessary levels of staffing and stock at different times to facilitate effective scheduling and ordering. Inventory stock to ensure that supplies and equipment are available in adequate amounts. Evaluate employee performance and recommend personnel actions such as promotions, transfers, and dismissals. Confer with staff to resolve performance and personnel problems and to discuss company policies. Establish and implement operational standards and procedures for the departments they supervise. Recommend or arrange for additional services such as painting, repair work, renovations, and the replacement of furnishings and equipment. Select and order or purchase new equipment, supplies, and furnishings. Recommend changes that could improve service and increase operational efficiency. Maintain required records of work hours, budgets, payrolls, and other information. Screen job applicants and hire new employees. Supervise in-house services such as laundries, maintenance and repair, dry cleaning, and valet services. Advise managers, desk clerks, or admitting personnel of rooms ready for occupancy. Perform financial tasks such as estimating costs and preparing and managing budgets. Prepare activity and personnel reports and reports containing information such as occupancy, hours worked, facility usage, work performed, and departmental expenses.

GOE Information—Interest Area: 04. Business and Administration. **Work Group:** 04.02. Managerial Work in Business Detail. **Personality Type—**Enterprising. Enterprising occupations frequently involve starting up and carrying out projects. These occupations can involve leading people and making many decisions. They sometimes require risk taking and often deal with business. **Work Values—**Authority; Co-workers; Autonomy; Responsibility; Activity; Creativity. **Skills—**Management of Personnel Resources; Monitoring; Service Orientation; Equipment Maintenance; Systems Evaluation; Writing. **Abilities—***Cognitive:* None met the criteria. *Psychomotor:* None met the criteria. *Physical:* None met the criteria. *Sensory:* None met the criteria. **General Work Activities—***Information Input:* Identifying Objects, Actions, and Events; Getting Information; Inspecting Equipment, Structures, or Materials. *Mental Process:* Organizing, Planning, and Prioritizing; Scheduling Work and Activities; Processing Information. *Work Output:* Handling and Moving Objects; Repairing and Maintaining Mechanical Equipment; Controlling Machines and Processes. *Interacting with Others:* Establishing and Maintaining Interpersonal Relationships; Coordinating the Work and Activities of Others; Resolving Conflicts and Negotiating with Others. **Physical Work Conditions—**Indoors; Contaminants; Disease or Infections; Standing; Walking and Running. **Other Job Characteristics—**Need to Be Exact or Accurate; Errors Have Important Consequences.

Experience—Job Zone 3. Previous work-related skill, knowledge, or experience is required. **Job Preparation—**SVP 6.0 to less than 7.0—more than one year and less than four years. **Knowledges—**Chemistry; Building and Construction; Public Safety and Security; Administration and Management; Mechanical Devices; Physics. **Instructional Program—**No related CIP programs.

Related SOC Job—37-1011 First-Line Supervisors/Managers of Housekeeping and Janitorial Workers. **Related OOH Job—**Building Cleaning Workers. **Related DOT Jobs—**187.167-046 Executive Housekeeper; 301.137-010 Housekeeper, Home; 309.137-010 Butler; 321.137-010 Housekeeper; 381.137-010 Supervisor, Janitorial Services; 382.137-010 Supervisor, Maintenance; 389.137-010 Supervisor, Home Restoration Service.

37-1012.00 First-Line Supervisors/Managers of Landscaping, Lawn Service, and Groundskeeping Workers

- **Education/Training Required:** Work experience in a related occupation
- **Employed:** 106,280
- **Annual Earnings:** $36,320
- **Growth:** 17.8%
- **Annual Job Openings:** 14,000

Plan, organize, direct, or coordinate activities of workers engaged in landscaping or groundskeeping activities, such as planting and maintaining ornamental trees, shrubs, flowers, and lawns and applying fertilizers, pesticides, and other chemicals, according to contract specifications. May also coordinate activities of workers engaged in terracing hillsides, building retaining walls, constructing pathways, installing patios, and similar activities in following a landscape design plan. Work may involve reviewing contracts to ascertain service, machine, and work force requirements; answering inquiries from potential customers regarding methods, material, and price ranges; and preparing estimates according to labor, material, and machine costs.

Establish and enforce operating procedures and work standards that will ensure adequate performance and personnel safety. Inspect completed work to ensure conformance to specifications, standards, and contract requirements. Direct activities of workers who perform duties such as landscaping, cultivating lawns, or pruning trees and shrubs. Schedule work for crews depending on work priorities, crew and equipment availability, and weather conditions. Plant and maintain vegetation through activities such as mulching, fertilizing, watering, mowing, and pruning. Monitor project activities to ensure that instructions are followed, deadlines are met, and schedules are maintained. Train workers in tasks such as transplanting and pruning trees and shrubs, finishing cement, using equipment, and caring for turf. Provide workers with assistance in performing duties as necessary to meet deadlines. Inventory supplies of tools, equipment, and materials to ensure that sufficient supplies are available and items are in usable condition. Confer with other supervisors to coordinate work activities with those of other departments or units. Perform personnel-related activities such as hiring workers, evaluating staff performance, and taking disciplinary actions when performance problems occur. Direct or perform mixing and application of fertilizers, insecticides, herbicides, and fungicides. Review contracts or work assignments to determine service, machine, and workforce requirements for jobs. Maintain required records such as personnel information and project records. Prepare and maintain required records such as work activity and personnel reports. Order the performance of corrective work when problems occur and recommend procedural changes to avoid such problems. Identify diseases and pests affecting landscaping and order appropriate treatments. Investigate work-related complaints to verify problems and to determine responses. Direct and assist workers engaged in the maintenance and repair of equipment such as power tools and motorized equipment. Install and maintain landscaped areas, performing tasks such as removing snow, pouring cement curbs, and repairing sidewalks.

GOE Information—Interest Area: 01. Agriculture and Natural Resources. **Work Group:** 01.01. Managerial Work in Agriculture and Natural Resources. **Personality Type—**Realistic. Realistic occupations frequently involve work activities that include practical, hands-on problems and solutions. They often deal with plants; animals; and real-world materials like wood, tools, and machinery. Many of the occupations require working outside and do not involve a lot of paperwork or working closely with others. **Work Values—**Authority; Autonomy; Responsibility; Creativity; Social Service; Co-workers. **Skills—**Repairing; Equipment Maintenance; Systems Analysis; Management of Personnel Resources; Operations Analysis; Monitoring. **Abilities—***Cognitive:* Time Sharing; Perceptual Speed; Originality; Visualization; Fluency of Ideas. *Psychomotor:* Rate Control; Multilimb Coordination; Response Orientation; Manual Dexterity; Arm-Hand Steadiness; Reaction Time. *Physical:* Static Strength; Stamina; Trunk Strength; Extent Flexibility. *Sensory:* Depth Perception; Visual Color Discrimination; Auditory Attention; Hearing Sensitivity; Far Vision. **General Work Activities—***Information Input:* Identifying Objects, Actions, and Events; Monitoring Processes, Materials, or Surroundings; Getting Information. *Mental Process:* Organizing, Planning, and Prioritizing; Updating and Using Relevant Knowledge; Thinking Creatively. *Work Output:* Handling and Moving Objects; Performing General Physical Activities; Controlling Machines and Processes. *Interacting with Others:* Coordinating the Work and Activities of Others; Guiding, Directing, and Motivating Subordinates; Establishing and Maintaining Interpersonal Relationships. **Physical Work Conditions—**Outdoors; Noisy; Contaminants; Minor Burns, Cuts, Bites, or Stings; Standing. **Other Job Characteristics—**Need to Be Exact or Accurate; Errors Have Important Consequences.

Experience—Job Zone 2. Some previous work-related skill, knowledge, or experience may be helpful in these occupations, but usually is not needed. **Job Preparation—**SVP 4.0 to less than 6.0—six months to less than two years. **Knowledges—**Mechanical Devices; Building and Construction; Education and Training; Design; Biology; Chemistry. **Instructional Programs—**Landscaping and Groundskeeping; Ornamental Horticulture; Turf and Turfgrass Management.

Related SOC Job—37-1012 First-Line Supervisors/Managers of Landscaping, Lawn Service, and Groundskeeping Workers. **Related OOH Job—**Grounds Maintenance Workers. **Related DOT Jobs—**406.134-010 Supervisor, Cemetery Workers; 406.134-014 Supervisor, Landscape; 406.137-010 Greenskeeper I; 406.137-014 Superintendent, Greens; 408.131-010 Supervisor, Spray, Lawn and Tree Service; 408.137-014 Supervisor, Tree-Trimming.

37-2000 Building Cleaning and Pest Control Workers

37-2011.00 Janitors and Cleaners, Except Maids and Housekeeping Cleaners

- **Education/Training Required: Short-term on-the-job training**
- **Employed: 2,107,360**
- **Annual Earnings: $19,390**
- **Growth: 18.5%**
- **Annual Job Openings: 528,000**

Keep buildings in clean and orderly condition. Perform heavy cleaning duties, such as cleaning floors, shampooing rugs, washing walls and glass, and removing rubbish. Duties may include tending furnace and boiler, performing routine maintenance activities, notifying management of need for repairs, and cleaning snow or debris from sidewalk.

Monitor building security and safety by performing such tasks as locking doors after operating hours and checking electrical appliance use to ensure that hazards are not created. Service, clean, and supply restrooms. Gather and empty trash. Clean building floors by sweeping, mopping, scrubbing, or vacuuming them. Follow procedures for the use of chemical cleaners and power equipment to prevent damage to floors and fixtures. Mix water and detergents or acids in containers to prepare cleaning solutions according to specifications. Strip, seal, finish, and polish floors. Notify managers concerning the need for major repairs or additions to building operating systems. Requisition supplies and equipment needed for cleaning and maintenance duties. Clean windows, glass partitions, and mirrors, using soapy water or other cleaners, sponges, and squeegees. Steam-clean or shampoo carpets. Set up, arrange, and remove decorations, tables, chairs, ladders, and scaffolding to prepare facilities for events such as banquets and meetings. Clean and polish furniture and fixtures. Dust furniture, walls, machines, and equipment. Move heavy furniture, equipment, and supplies, either manually or by using hand trucks. Remove snow from sidewalks, driveways, and parking areas, using snowplows, snowblowers, and snow shovels, and spread snow-melting chemicals. Clean laboratory equipment, such as glassware and metal instruments, using solvents, brushes, rags, and power cleaning equipment. Spray insecticides and fumigants to prevent insect and rodent infestation. Make adjustments and minor repairs to heating, cooling, ventilating, plumbing, and electrical systems. Drive vehicles required to perform or travel to cleaning work, including vans, industrial trucks, or industrial vacuum cleaners. Mow and trim lawns and shrubbery, using mowers and hand and power trimmers, and clear debris from grounds. Clean and restore building interiors damaged by fire, smoke, or water, using commercial cleaning equipment. Clean chimneys, flues, and connecting pipes, using power and hand tools.

GOE Information—Interest Area: 09. Hospitality, Tourism, and Recreation. **Work Group:** 09.03. Hospitality and Travel Services. **Personality Type—**Realistic. Realistic occupations frequently involve work activities that include practical, hands-on problems and solutions. They often deal with plants; animals; and real-world materials like wood, tools, and machinery. Many of the occupations require working outside and do not involve a lot of paperwork or working closely with others. **Work Values**—Independence; Moral Values. **Skills**—Equipment Maintenance; Repairing. **Abilities**—*Cognitive:* None met the criteria. *Psychomotor:* Multilimb Coordination; Arm-Hand Steadiness; Manual Dexterity. *Physical:* Extent Flexibility; Static Strength; Trunk Strength; Stamina; Gross Body Coordination. *Sensory:* None met the criteria. **General Work Activities**—*Information Input:* Monitoring Processes, Materials, or Surroundings; Inspecting Equipment, Structures, or Materials; Identifying Objects, Actions, and Events. *Mental Process:* Organizing, Planning, and Prioritizing; Updating and Using Relevant Knowledge; Scheduling Work and Activities. *Work Output:* Handling and Moving Objects; Performing General Physical Activities; Controlling Machines and Processes. *Interacting with Others:* Establishing and Maintaining Interpersonal Relationships; Communicating with Other Workers; Performing for or Working with the Public. **Physical Work Conditions**—Indoors; Contaminants; Standing; Walking and Running; Using Hands on Objects, Tools, or Controls; Bending or Twisting the Body. **Other Job Characteristics**—Need to Be Exact or Accurate.

Experience—Job Zone 1. No previous work-related skill, knowledge, or experience is needed. **Job Preparation**—SVP below 4.0—less than six months. **Knowledges**—Chemistry; Public Safety and Security. **Instructional Program**—No related CIP programs.

Related SOC Job—37-2011 Janitors and Cleaners, Except Maids and Housekeeping Cleaners. **Related OOH Job**—Building Cleaning Workers. **Related DOT Jobs**—358.687-010 Change-House Attendant; 381.687-014 Cleaner, Commercial or Institutional; 381.687-018 Cleaner, Industrial; 381.687-022 Cleaner, Laboratory Equipment; 381.687-026 Cleaner, Wall; 381.687-030 Patch Worker; 381.687-034 Waxer, Floor; 382.664-010 Janitor; 389.664-010 Cleaner, Home Restoration Service; 389.667-010 Sexton; 389.683-010 Sweeper-Cleaner, Industrial; 389.684-560 Multi-Story Window/Building Exterior Cleaner; 389.687-014 Cleaner, Window; 891.684-018 Swimming-Pool Servicer; others.

37-2012.00 Maids and Housekeeping Cleaners

- **Education/Training Required: Short-term on-the-job training**
- **Employed: 893,820**
- **Annual Earnings: $17,080**
- **Growth: 11.6%**
- **Annual Job Openings: 314,000**

Perform any combination of light cleaning duties to maintain private households or commercial establishments, such as hotels, restaurants, and hospitals, in a clean and orderly manner. Duties include making beds, replenishing linens, cleaning rooms and halls, and vacuuming.

Clean rooms, hallways, lobbies, lounges, restrooms, corridors, elevators, stairways, locker rooms, and other work areas so that health standards are met. Carry linens, towels, toilet items, and cleaning supplies, using wheeled carts. Empty wastebaskets, empty and clean ashtrays, and transport other trash and waste to disposal areas. Replenish supplies such as drinking glasses, linens, writing supplies, and bathroom items. Keep storage areas and carts well stocked, clean, and tidy. Dust and polish furniture and equipment. Sweep, scrub, wax, and polish floors, using brooms, mops, and powered scrubbing and waxing machines. Clean rugs, carpets, upholstered furniture, and draperies, using vacuum cleaners and shampooers. Wash windows, walls, ceilings, and woodwork, waxing and polishing as necessary. Hang draperies and dust window blinds. Disinfect equipment and supplies, using germicides or steam-operated sterilizers. Observe precautions required to protect hotel and guest property and report damage, theft, and found articles to supervisors. Care for children or elderly persons by overseeing their activities; providing companionship; and assisting them with dressing, bathing, eating, and other needs. Wash dishes and clean kitchens, cooking utensils, and silverware. Remove debris from driveways, garages, and swimming pool areas. Sort clothing and other articles, load washing machines, and iron and fold dried items. Run errands such as taking laundry to the cleaners and buying groceries. Sort, count, and mark clean linens and store them in linen closets. Polish silver accessories and metalwork such as fixtures and fittings. Prepare rooms for meetings and arrange decorations, media equipment, and furniture for social or business functions. Purchase or order groceries and household supplies to keep kitchens stocked and record expenditures. Request repair services and wait for repair workers to arrive. Replace light bulbs. Assign duties to other staff and give instructions regarding work methods and routines. Plan menus and cook and serve meals and refreshments, following employer's instructions or own methods.

GOE Information—**Interest Area:** 09. Hospitality, Tourism, and Recreation. **Work Group:** 09.03. Hospitality and Travel Services. **Personality Type**—Realistic. Realistic occupations frequently involve work activities that include practical, hands-on problems and solutions. They often deal with plants; animals; and real-world materials like wood, tools, and machinery. Many of the occupations require working outside and do not involve a lot of paperwork or working closely with others. **Work Values**—Independence; Moral Values; Social Service; Activity. **Skills**—None met the criteria. **Abilities**—*Cognitive:* None met the criteria. *Psychomotor:* Arm-Hand Steadiness. *Physical:* Extent Flexibility; Gross Body Coordination; Trunk Strength; Stamina; Static Strength. *Sensory:* None met the criteria. **General Work Activities**—*Information Input:* Getting Information; Monitoring Processes, Materials, or Surroundings; Identifying Objects, Actions, and Events. *Mental Process:* Organizing, Planning, and Prioritizing; Judging the Qualities of Things, Services, or Other People's Work. *Work Output:* Handling and Moving Objects; Performing General Physical Activities. *Interacting with Others:* Establishing and Maintaining Interpersonal Relationships; Performing for or Working with the Public; Coaching and Developing Others. **Physical Work Conditions**—Indoors; Contaminants; Standing; Walking and Running; Bending or Twisting the Body; Repetitive Motions. **Other Job Characteristics**—Need to Be Exact or Accurate.

Experience—Job Zone 1. No previous work-related skill, knowledge, or experience is needed. **Job Preparation**—SVP below 4.0—less than six months. **Knowledges**—Chemistry. **Instructional Program**—No related CIP programs.

Related SOC Job—37-2012 Maids and Housekeeping Cleaners. **Related OOH Job**—Building Cleaning Workers. **Related DOT Jobs**—301.474-010 House Worker, General; 301.687-010 Caretaker; 301.687-014 Day Worker; 302.685-010 Laundry Worker, Domestic; 302.687-010 Ironer; 309.674-010 Butler, Second; 323.687-010 Cleaner, Hospital; 323.687-014 Cleaner, Housekeeping; 323.687-018 Housecleaner; 381.684-560 Housekeeper, Commercial, Residential, or Industrial.

37-2019.99 Building Cleaning Workers, All Other

- **Education/Training Required: No data available**
- **Employed: 15,610**
- **Annual Earnings: $23,400**
- **Growth: 19.8%**
- **Annual Job Openings: 3,000**

All building cleaning workers not listed separately.

No task data available.

Note: The Department of Labor has not collected some data for this job, so it has fewer details than the other descriptions.

Related SOC Job—37-2019 Building Cleaning Workers, All Other. **Related OOH Job**—None. **Related DOT Jobs**—369.384-014 Rug Cleaner, Hand; 389.687-010 Air Purifier Servicer; 389.687-018 Light-Fixture Servicer.

37-2021.00 Pest Control Workers

- **Education/Training Required: Moderate-term on-the-job training**
- **Employed: 62,400**
- **Annual Earnings: $27,170**
- **Growth: 18.4%**
- **Annual Job Openings: 4,000**

Spray or release chemical solutions or toxic gases and set traps to kill pests and vermin, such as mice, termites, and roaches, that infest buildings and surrounding areas.

Record work activities performed. Inspect premises to identify infestation source and extent of damage to property, wall and roof porosity, and access to infested locations. Spray or dust chemical solutions, powders, or gases into rooms; onto clothing, furnishings, or wood; and over marshlands, ditches, and catch-basins. Clean work site after completion of job. Direct or assist other workers in treatment and extermination processes to eliminate and control rodents, insects, and weeds. Drive truck equipped with power spraying equipment. Measure area dimensions requiring treatment, using rule; calculate fumigant requirements; and estimate cost for service. Post warning signs and lock building doors to secure area to be fumigated. Cut or bore openings in building or surrounding concrete, access infested areas, insert nozzle, and inject pesticide to impregnate ground. Study preliminary reports and diagrams of infested area and determine treatment type required to eliminate and prevent recurrence of infestation. Dig up and burn or spray weeds with herbicides. Set mechanical traps and place poisonous paste or bait in sewers, burrows, and ditches. Clean and remove blockages from infested areas to facilitate spraying procedure and provide drainage, using broom, mop, shovel, and rake. Position and fasten edges of tarpaulins over building and tape vents to ensure airtight environment and check for leaks.

GOE Information—Interest Area: 01. Agriculture and Natural Resources. **Work Group:** 01.05. Nursery, Groundskeeping, and Pest Control. **Personality Type**—Realistic. Realistic occupations frequently involve work activities that include practical, hands-on problems and solutions. They often deal with plants; animals; and real-world materials like wood, tools, and machinery. Many of the occupations require working outside and do not involve a lot of paperwork or working closely with others. **Work Values**—Independence; Supervision, Technical; Social Service. **Skills**—Persuasion; Service Orientation; Equipment Selection; Social Perceptiveness; Active Learning; Management of Material Resources. **Abilities**—*Cognitive:* Spatial Orientation; Flexibility of Closure; Number Facility; Perceptual Speed; Time Sharing; Mathematical Reasoning. *Psychomotor:* Response Orientation; Speed of Limb Movement; Multilimb Coordination; Control Precision; Reaction Time; Manual Dexterity. *Physical:* Extent Flexibility; Gross Body Equilibrium; Trunk Strength; Dynamic Strength; Gross Body Coordination; Stamina. *Sensory:* Glare Sensitivity; Depth Perception; Hearing Sensitivity; Visual Color Discrimination; Far Vision; Speech Recognition. **General Work Activities**—*Information Input:* Monitoring Processes, Materials, or Surroundings; Identifying Objects, Actions, and Events; Inspecting Equipment, Structures, or Materials. *Mental Process:* Updating and Using Relevant Knowledge; Evaluating Information Against Standards; Making Decisions and Solving Problems. *Work Output:* Performing General Physical Activities; Handling and Moving Objects; Repairing and Maintaining Mechanical Equipment. *Interacting with Others:* Communicating with Persons Outside Organization; Performing for or Working with the Public; Establishing and Maintaining Interpersonal Relationships. **Physical Work Conditions**—More Often Outdoors Than Indoors; Very Hot or Cold; Contaminants; Hazardous Conditions; Using Hands on Objects, Tools, or Controls. **Other Job Characteristics**—Need to Be Exact or Accurate; Errors Have Important Consequences.

Experience—Job Zone 2. Some previous work-related skill, knowledge, or experience may be helpful in these occupations, but usually is not needed. **Job Preparation**—SVP 4.0 to less than 6.0—six months to less than two years. **Knowledges**—Sales and Marketing; Chemistry; Biology; Customer and Personal Service; Education and Training; Building and Construction. **Instructional Program**—Agricultural/Farm Supplies Retailing and Wholesaling.

Related SOC Job—37-2021 Pest Control Workers. **Related OOH Job**—Pest Control Workers. **Related DOT Jobs**—379.687-014 Mosquito Sprayer; 383.361-010 Fumigator; 383.364-010 Exterminator, Termite; 383.684-010 Exterminator Helper; 383.687-010 Exterminator Helper, Termite; 389.684-010 Exterminator.

37-3000 Grounds Maintenance Workers

37-3011.00 Landscaping and Groundskeeping Workers

- **Education/Training Required: Short-term on-the-job training**
- **Employed: 896,690**
- **Annual Earnings: $20,670**
- **Growth: 19.5%**
- **Annual Job Openings: 243,000**

Landscape or maintain grounds of property, using hand or power tools or equipment. Workers typically perform a variety of tasks, which may include any combination of the following: sod laying, mowing, trimming, planting, watering, fertilizing, digging, raking, sprinkler installation, and installation of mortarless segmental concrete masonry wall units.

Operate powered equipment such as mowers, tractors, twin-axle vehicles, snowblowers, chain saws, electric clippers, sod cutters, and pruning saws. Mow and edge lawns, using power mowers and edgers.

Shovel snow from walks, driveways, and parking lots and spread salt in those areas. Care for established lawns by mulching; aerating; weeding; grubbing and removing thatch; and trimming and edging around flower beds, walks, and walls. Use hand tools such as shovels, rakes, pruning saws, saws, hedge and brush trimmers, and axes. Prune and trim trees, shrubs, and hedges, using shears, pruners, or chain saws. Maintain and repair tools; equipment; and structures such as buildings, greenhouses, fences, and benches, using hand and power tools. Gather and remove litter. Mix and spray or spread fertilizers, herbicides, or insecticides onto grass, shrubs, and trees, using hand or automatic sprayers or spreaders. Provide proper upkeep of sidewalks, driveways, parking lots, fountains, planters, burial sites, and other grounds features. Water lawns, trees, and plants, using portable sprinkler systems, hoses, or watering cans. Trim and pick flowers and clean flowerbeds. Rake, mulch, and compost leaves. Plant seeds, bulbs, foliage, flowering plants, grass, ground covers, trees, and shrubs and apply mulch for protection, using gardening tools. Follow planned landscaping designs to determine where to lay sod, sow grass, or plant flowers and foliage. Decorate gardens with stones and plants. Maintain irrigation systems, including winterizing the systems and starting them up in spring. Care for natural turf fields, making sure the underlying soil has the required composition to allow proper drainage and to support the grasses used on the fields. Use irrigation methods to adjust the amount of water consumption and to prevent waste. Haul or spread topsoil and spread straw over seeded soil to hold soil in place. Advise customers on plant selection and care. Care for artificial turf fields, periodically removing the turf and replacing cushioning pads and vacuuming and disinfecting the turf after use to prevent the growth of harmful bacteria.

GOE Information—Interest Area: 01. Agriculture and Natural Resources. **Work Group:** 01.05. Nursery, Groundskeeping, and Pest Control. **Personality Type—**Realistic. Realistic occupations frequently involve work activities that include practical, hands-on problems and solutions. They often deal with plants; animals; and real-world materials like wood, tools, and machinery. Many of the occupations require working outside and do not involve a lot of paperwork or working closely with others. **Work Values—**Moral Values; Independence. **Skills—**Equipment Maintenance; Repairing; Operation Monitoring; Installation; Troubleshooting. **Abilities—**Cognitive: Visualization; Selective Attention. Psychomotor: Multilimb Coordination; Control Precision; Rate Control; Reaction Time; Manual Dexterity; Arm-Hand Steadiness. Physical: Static Strength; Extent Flexibility; Gross Body Coordination; Gross Body Equilibrium; Stamina; Trunk Strength. Sensory: Depth Perception; Visual Color Discrimination; Auditory Attention. **General Work Activities—**Information Input: Monitoring Processes, Materials, or Surroundings; Inspecting Equipment, Structures, or Materials; Identifying Objects, Actions, and Events. Mental Process: Organizing, Planning, and Prioritizing; Updating and Using Relevant Knowledge; Making Decisions and Solving Problems. Work Output: Performing General Physical Activities; Handling and Moving Objects; Controlling Machines and Processes. Interacting with Others: Establishing and Maintaining Interpersonal Relationships; Communicating with Other Workers; Coordinating the Work and Activities of Others. **Physical Work Conditions—**Outdoors; Noisy; Very Hot or Cold; Contaminants; Standing; Using Hands on Objects, Tools, or Controls. **Other Job Characteristics—**Pace Determined by Speed of Equipment.

Experience—Job Zone 1. No previous work-related skill, knowledge, or experience is needed. **Job Preparation—**SVP below 4.0—less than six months. **Knowledges—**Mechanical Devices. **Instructional Programs—**Landscaping and Groundskeeping; Turf and Turfgrass Management.

Related SOC Job—37-3011 Landscaping and Groundskeeping Workers. **Related OOH Job—**Grounds Maintenance Workers. **Related DOT Jobs—**301.687-018 Yard Worker; 405.684-014 Horticultural Worker I; 405.687-010 Flower Picker; 405.687-018 Transplanter, Orchid; 406.683-010 Greenskeeper II; 406.684-014 Groundskeeper, Industrial-Commercial; 406.687-010 Landscape Specialist; 408.161-010 Landscape Gardener; 408.364-010 Plant-Care Worker; 408.364-640 Landscape Technician; 408.684-010 Lawn-Service Worker; 408.684-640 Landscape Management Technician; 408.687-014 Laborer, Landscape; 408.687-018 Tree-Surgeon Helper II; others.

37-3012.00 Pesticide Handlers, Sprayers, and Applicators, Vegetation

- **Education/Training Required:** Moderate-term on-the-job training
- **Employed:** 25,770
- **Annual Earnings:** $26,120
- **Growth:** 16.6%
- **Annual Job Openings:** 6,000

Mix or apply pesticides, herbicides, fungicides, or insecticides through sprays, dusts, vapors, soil incorporation, or chemical application on trees, shrubs, lawns, or botanical crops. Usually requires specific training and state or federal certification.

Fill sprayer tanks with water and chemicals according to formulas. Mix pesticides, herbicides, and fungicides for application to trees, shrubs, lawns, or botanical crops. Cover areas to specified depths with pesticides, applying knowledge of weather conditions, droplet sizes, elevation-to-distance ratios, and obstructions. Lift, push, and swing nozzles, hoses, and tubes to direct spray over designated areas. Start motors and engage machinery such as sprayer agitators and pumps or portable spray equipment. Connect hoses and nozzles selected according to terrain, distribution pattern requirements, types of infestations, and velocities. Clean and service machinery to ensure operating efficiency, using water, gasoline, lubricants, and hand tools. Provide driving instructions to truck drivers to ensure complete coverage of designated areas, using hand and horn signals. Plant grass with seed spreaders and operate straw blowers to cover seeded areas with mixtures of asphalt and straw.

GOE Information—Interest Area: 01. Agriculture and Natural Resources. **Work Group:** 01.05. Nursery, Groundskeeping, and Pest Control. **Personality Type—**Realistic. Realistic occupations frequently involve work activities that include practical, hands-on problems and solutions. They often deal with plants; animals; and real-world materials like wood, tools, and machinery. Many of the occupations require working outside and do not involve a lot of paperwork or working closely with others. **Work Values—**Independence; Supervision, Technical. **Skills—**Repairing; Equipment Maintenance; Operation Monitoring; Management of Material Resources; Installation; Troubleshooting. **Abilities—**Cognitive: Number Facility. Psychomotor: Rate Control; Multilimb Coordination; Manual Dexterity; Control Precision; Arm-Hand Steadiness; Finger Dexterity. Physical: Stamina; Static Strength; Trunk Strength. Sensory: Depth Perception; Visual Color Discrimination. **General Work Activities—**Information Input: Monitoring Processes, Materials, or Surroundings; Identifying Objects, Actions, and Events; Getting Information. Mental Process: Updating and Using Relevant Knowledge; Organizing, Planning, and Prioritizing; Scheduling Work and Activities. Work Output: Handling and Moving Objects; Performing General Physical Activities; Controlling Machines and Processes. Interacting with Others: Performing for or Working with the Public; Establishing and Maintaining Interpersonal Relationships; Communicating with Other Workers. **Physical Work Conditions**—Outdoors; Noisy; Contaminants; Hazardous Conditions; Using Hands on Objects, Tools, or Controls; Repetitive Motions. **Other Job Characteristics**—Need to Be Exact or Accurate; Errors Have Important Consequences; Repeat Same Tasks.

Experience—Job Zone 3. Previous work-related skill, knowledge, or experience is required. **Job Preparation**—SVP 6.0 to less than 7.0—more than one year and less than four years. **Knowledges**—Biology; Chemistry; Mechanical Devices; Customer and Personal Service; Transportation; Public Safety and Security. **Instructional Programs**—Landscaping and Groundskeeping; Plant Nursery Operations and Management; Turf and Turfgrass Management.

Related SOC Job—37-3012 Pesticide Handlers, Sprayers, and Applicators, Vegetation. **Related OOH Job**—Grounds Maintenance Workers. **Related DOT Jobs**—408.381-014 Weed Inspector; 408.381-560 Agricultural Service Worker; 408.662-010 Hydro-Sprayer Operator; 408.684-014 Sprayer, Hand.

37-3013.00 Tree Trimmers and Pruners

- **Education/Training Required: Short-term on-the-job training**
- **Employed: 29,790**
- **Annual Earnings: $27,920**
- **Growth: 16.5%**
- **Annual Job Openings: 11,000**

Cut away dead or excess branches from trees or shrubs to maintain right-of-way for roads, sidewalks, or utilities or to improve appearance, health, and value of tree. Prune or treat trees or shrubs, using handsaws, pruning hooks, shears, and clippers. May use truck-mounted lifts and power pruners. May fill cavities in trees to promote healing and prevent deterioration.

Supervise others engaged in tree-trimming work and train lower-level employees. Transplant and remove trees and shrubs and prepare trees for moving. Climb trees, using climbing hooks and belts, or climb ladders to gain access to work areas. Operate boom trucks, loaders, stump chippers, brush chippers, tractors, power saws, trucks, sprayers, and other equipment and tools. Operate shredding and chipping equipment and feed limbs and brush into the machines. Remove broken limbs from wires, using hooked extension poles. Prune, cut down, fertilize, and spray trees as directed by tree surgeons. Spray trees to treat diseased or unhealthy trees, including mixing chemicals and calibrating spray equipment. Clean, sharpen, and lubricate tools and equipment. Trim, top, and reshape trees to achieve attractive shapes or to remove low-hanging branches. Cable, brace, tie, bolt, stake, and guy trees and branches to provide support. Clear sites, streets, and grounds of woody and herbaceous materials, such as tree stumps and fallen trees and limbs. Collect debris and refuse from tree trimming and removal operations into piles, using shovels, rakes, or other tools. Load debris and refuse onto trucks and haul it away for disposal. Inspect trees to determine if they have diseases or pest problems. Cut away dead and excess branches from trees or clear branches around power lines, using climbing equipment or buckets of extended truck booms and/or chain saws, hooks, hand saws, shears, and clippers. Apply tar or other protective substances to cut surfaces to seal surfaces and to protect them from fungi and insects. Split logs or wooden blocks into bolts, pickets, posts, or stakes, using hand tools such as ax wedges, sledgehammers, and mallets. Trim jagged stumps, using saws or pruning shears. Water,

root-feed, and fertilize trees. Harvest tanbark by cutting rings and slits in bark and stripping bark from trees, using spuds or axes. Install lightning protection on trees. Plan and develop budgets for tree work and estimate the monetary value of trees. Provide information to the public regarding trees, such as advice on tree care.

GOE Information—**Interest Area:** 01. Agriculture and Natural Resources. **Work Group:** 01.05. Nursery, Groundskeeping, and Pest Control. **Personality Type**—Realistic. Realistic occupations frequently involve work activities that include practical, hands-on problems and solutions. They often deal with plants; animals; and real-world materials like wood, tools, and machinery. Many of the occupations require working outside and do not involve a lot of paperwork or working closely with others. **Work Values**—Moral Values; Independence. **Skills**—Operation and Control. **Abilities**—*Cognitive:* None met the criteria. *Psychomotor:* Multilimb Coordination; Speed of Limb Movement; Wrist-Finger Speed; Manual Dexterity; Arm-Hand Steadiness. *Physical:* Explosive Strength; Dynamic Flexibility; Dynamic Strength; Extent Flexibility; Gross Body Coordination; Static Strength. *Sensory:* None met the criteria. **General Work Activities**—*Information Input:* Getting Information. *Mental Process:* None met the criteria. *Work Output:* Performing General Physical Activities; Handling and Moving Objects; Controlling Machines and Processes. *Interacting with Others:* None met the criteria. **Physical Work Conditions**—Outdoors; High Places; Minor Burns, Cuts, Bites, or Stings; Standing; Using Hands on Objects, Tools, or Controls; Repetitive Motions. **Other Job Characteristics**—None met the criteria.

Experience—Job Zone 2. Some previous work-related skill, knowledge, or experience may be helpful in these occupations, but usually is not needed. **Job Preparation**—SVP 4.0 to less than 6.0—six months to less than two years. **Knowledges**—Biology; Chemistry; Mechanical Devices. **Instructional Program**—Horticultural Service Operations, Other.

Related SOC Job—37-3013 Tree Trimmers and Pruners. **Related OOH Job**—Grounds Maintenance Workers. **Related DOT Jobs**—403.687-022 Vine Pruner; 408.181-010 Tree Surgeon; 408.664-010 Tree Trimmer; 408.667-010 Tree-Trimmer Helper; 408.684-018 Tree Pruner; 454.687-014 Laborer, Tanbark; 459.687-010 Laborer, Brush Clearing.

37-3019.99 Grounds Maintenance Workers, All Other

- **Education/Training Required: No data available**
- **Employed: 17,960**
- **Annual Earnings: $20,890**
- **Growth: 26.3%**
- **Annual Job Openings: 5,000**

All grounds maintenance workers not listed separately.

No task data available.

Note: The Department of Labor has not collected some data for this job, so it has fewer details than the other descriptions.

Related SOC Job—37-3019 Grounds Maintenance Workers, All Other. **Related OOH Job**—Grounds Maintenance Workers. **Related DOT Jobs**—329.683-010 Attendant, Campground; 406.381-010 Gardener, Special Effects And Instruction Models; 406.684-010 Cemetery Worker; 406.684-018 Garden Worker; 454.684-022 River.

39-0000

Personal Care and Service Occupations

39-1000 Supervisors, Personal Care and Service Workers

39-1011.00 Gaming Supervisors

- **Education/Training Required: Work experience in a related occupation**
- **Employed:** 24,180
- **Annual Earnings:** $40,300
- **Growth:** 16.3%
- **Annual Job Openings:** 8,000

Supervise gaming operations and personnel in an assigned area. Circulate among tables and observe operations. Ensure that stations and games are covered for each shift. May explain and interpret operating rules of house to patrons. May plan and organize activities and create friendly atmosphere for guests in hotels/casinos. May adjust service complaints.

Monitor game operations to ensure that house rules are followed, that tribal, state, and federal regulations are adhered to, and that employees provide prompt and courteous service. Observe gamblers' behavior for signs of cheating such as marking, switching, or counting cards; notify security staff of suspected cheating. Maintain familiarity with the games at a facility and with strategies and tricks used by cheaters at such games. Perform paperwork required for monetary transactions. Resolve customer and employee complaints. Greet customers and ask about the quality of service they are receiving. Establish and maintain banks and table limits for each game. Report customer-related incidents occurring in gaming areas to supervisors. Monitor stations and games and move dealers from game to game to ensure adequate staffing. Explain and interpret house rules, such as game rules and betting limits, for patrons. Supervise the distribution of complimentary meals, hotel rooms, discounts, and other items given to players based on length of play and amount bet. Evaluate workers' performance and prepare written performance evaluations. Monitor patrons for signs of compulsive gambling, offering assistance if necessary. Record, issue receipts for, and pay off bets. Monitor and verify the counting, wrapping, weighing, and distribution of currency and coins. Direct workers compiling summary sheets for each race or event to record amounts wagered and amounts to be paid to winners. Determine how many gaming tables to open each day and schedule staff accordingly. Establish policies on types of gambling offered, odds, and extension of credit. Interview, hire, and train workers. Provide fire protection and first-aid assistance when necessary. Review operational expenses, budget estimates, betting accounts, and collection reports for accuracy.

GOE Information—Interest Area: 09. Hospitality, Tourism, and Recreation. **Work Group:** 09.01. Managerial Work in Hospitality and Tourism. **Personality Type—**Enterprising. Enterprising occupations frequently involve starting up and carrying out projects. These occupations can involve leading people and making many decisions. They sometimes require risk taking and often deal with business. **Work Values—**Authority; Responsibility; Social Service; Creativity; Autonomy; Working Conditions. **Skills—**Management of Personnel Resources; Instructing; Service Orientation; Social Perceptiveness; Monitoring; Mathematics. **Abilities—***Cognitive:* Speed of Closure; Selective Attention; Flexibility of Closure; Perceptual Speed; Problem Sensitivity; Number Facility. *Psychomotor:* None met the criteria. *Physical:* Trunk Strength. *Sensory:* Auditory Attention; Far Vision; Speech Clarity; Speech Recognition. **General Work Activities—***Information Input:* Monitoring Processes, Materials, or Surroundings; Identifying Objects, Actions, and Events; Getting Information.

Mental Process: Evaluating Information Against Standards; Organizing, Planning, and Prioritizing; Judging the Qualities of Things, Services, or Other People's Work. *Work Output:* Documenting or Recording Information; Interacting With Computers; Performing General Physical Activities. *Interacting with Others:* Guiding, Directing, and Motivating Subordinates; Performing for or Working with the Public; Communicating with Other Workers. **Physical Work Conditions—**Indoors; Noisy; Contaminants; Standing; Walking and Running. **Other Job Characteristics—**Need to Be Exact or Accurate; Repeat Same Tasks.

Experience—Job Zone 2. Some previous work-related skill, knowledge, or experience may be helpful in these occupations, but usually is not needed. **Job Preparation—**SVP 4.0 to less than 6.0—six months to less than two years. **Knowledges—**Customer and Personal Service; Psychology; Education and Training; Mathematics; Sales and Marketing; Personnel and Human Resources. **Instructional Program—**No related CIP programs.

Related SOC Job—39-1011 Gaming Supervisors. **Related OOH Job—**Gaming Services Occupations. **Related DOT Job—**No data available.

39-1012.00 Slot Key Persons

- **Education/Training Required: Postsecondary vocational training**
- **Employed:** 14,700
- **Annual Earnings:** $22,120
- **Growth:** 23.0%
- **Annual Job Openings:** 5,000

Coordinate/supervise functions of slot department workers to provide service to patrons. Handle and settle complaints of players. Verify and pay off jackpots. Reset slot machines after payoffs. Make minor repairs or adjustments to slot machines. Recommend removal of slot machines for repair. Report hazards and enforces safety rules.

Monitor payment of hand-delivered jackpots to ensure promptness. Monitor functioning of slot machine coin dispensers and fill coin hoppers when necessary. Respond to and resolve patrons' complaints. Patrol assigned areas to ensure that players are following rules and that machines are functioning correctly. Reset slot machines after payoffs. Perform minor repairs or make adjustments to slot machines, resolving problems such as machine tilts and coin jams. Record the specifics of malfunctioning machines and document malfunctions needing repair. Exchange currency for customers, converting currency into requested combinations of bills and coins. Answer patrons' questions about gaming machine functions and payouts. Attach "out of order" signs to malfunctioning machines and notify technicians when machines need to be repaired or removed. Enforce safety rules and report or remove safety hazards as well as guests who are underage, intoxicated, disruptive, or cheating. Coordinate and oversee the work of slot department workers, including change runners and slot technicians.

GOE Information—Interest Area: 09. Hospitality, Tourism, and Recreation. **Work Group:** 09.02. Recreational Services. **Personality Type—**No data available. **Work Values—**No data available. **Skills—**Repairing; Equipment Maintenance; Social Perceptiveness; Service Orientation; Operation Monitoring; Management of Personnel Resources. **Abilities—***Cognitive:* Selective Attention. *Psychomotor:* Arm-Hand Steadiness; Manual Dexterity. *Physical:* Extent Flexibility; Trunk Strength. *Sensory:* Auditory Attention; Far Vision. **General Work Activities—***Information Input:* Getting Information; Identifying Objects, Actions, and Events; Monitoring Processes,

Materials, or Surroundings. *Mental Process:* Evaluating Information Against Standards; Making Decisions and Solving Problems; Updating and Using Relevant Knowledge. *Work Output:* Handling and Moving Objects; Performing General Physical Activities; Repairing and Maintaining Electronic Equipment. *Interacting with Others:* Communicating with Other Workers; Performing for or Working with the Public; Establishing and Maintaining Interpersonal Relationships. **Physical Work Conditions**—Indoors; Noisy; Contaminants; Standing; Walking and Running; Using Hands on Objects, Tools, or Controls. **Other Job Characteristics**—Need to Be Exact or Accurate; Repeat Same Tasks; Errors Have Important Consequences.

Experience—Job Zone 2. Some previous work-related skill, knowledge, or experience may be helpful in these occupations, but usually is not needed. **Job Preparation**—SVP 4.0 to less than 6.0—six months to less than two years. **Knowledges**—Customer and Personal Service; Sales and Marketing; Administration and Management; Public Safety and Security. **Instructional Program**—No related CIP programs.

Related SOC Job—39-1012 Slot Key Persons. **Related OOH Job**—Gaming Services Occupations. **Related DOT Job**—343.137-014 Supervisor, Cardroom.

39-1021.00 First-Line Supervisors/ Managers of Personal Service Workers

- **Education/Training Required: Work experience in a related occupation**
- **Employed: 125,760**
- **Annual Earnings: $31,390**
- **Growth: 18.3%**
- **Annual Job Openings: 20,000**

Supervise and coordinate activities of personal service workers such as flight attendants, hairdressers, or caddies.

Requisition necessary supplies, equipment, and services. Inform workers about interests and special needs of specific groups. Participate in continuing education to stay abreast of industry trends and developments. Meet with managers and other supervisors to stay informed of changes affecting operations. Collaborate with staff members to plan and develop programs of events, schedules of activities, or menus. Direct marketing, advertising, and other customer recruitment efforts. Train workers in proper operational procedures and functions and explain company policies. Furnish customers with information on events and activities. Resolve customer complaints regarding worker performance and services rendered. Analyze and record personnel and operational data and write related activity reports. Observe and evaluate workers' appearance and performance to ensure quality service and compliance with specifications. Recruit and hire staff members. Inspect work areas and operating equipment to ensure conformance to established standards in areas such as cleanliness and maintenance. Direct and coordinate the activities of workers such as flight attendants, hotel staff, or hair stylists. Assign work schedules, following work requirements, to ensure quality and timely delivery of service. Apply customer/guest feedback to service improvement efforts. Take disciplinary action to address performance problems.

GOE Information—**Interest Area:** 09. Hospitality, Tourism, and Recreation. **Work Group:** 09.01. Managerial Work in Hospitality and Tourism. **Personality Type**—Enterprising. Enterprising occupations

frequently involve starting up and carrying out projects. These occupations can involve leading people and making many decisions. They sometimes require risk taking and often deal with business. **Work Values**—Authority; Autonomy; Working Conditions; Co-workers; Responsibility; Activity. **Skills**—Management of Personnel Resources; Service Orientation; Coordination; Systems Evaluation; Management of Material Resources; Systems Analysis. **Abilities**—*Cognitive:* Time Sharing; Fluency of Ideas; Speed of Closure; Written Expression; Information Ordering; Perceptual Speed. *Psychomotor:* None met the criteria. *Physical:* None met the criteria. *Sensory:* Far Vision. **General Work Activities**—*Information Input:* Getting Information; Identifying Objects, Actions, and Events; Monitoring Processes, Materials, or Surroundings. *Mental Process:* Organizing, Planning, and Prioritizing; Scheduling Work and Activities; Judging the Qualities of Things, Services, or Other People's Work. *Work Output:* None met the criteria. *Interacting with Others:* Coordinating the Work and Activities of Others; Communicating with Other Workers; Establishing and Maintaining Interpersonal Relationships. **Physical Work Conditions**—Indoors; More Often Standing Than Sitting. **Other Job Characteristics**—Need to Be Exact or Accurate.

Experience—Job Zone 3. Previous work-related skill, knowledge, or experience is required. **Job Preparation**—SVP 6.0 to less than 7.0—more than one year and less than four years. **Knowledges**—Administration and Management; Personnel and Human Resources; Customer and Personal Service. **Instructional Program**—No related CIP programs.

Related SOC Job—39-1021 First-Line Supervisors/Managers of Personal Service Workers. **Related OOH Job**—First-Line Supervisors/Managers of Personal Service Workers. **Related DOT Jobs**—321.137-014 Inspector; 323.137-010 Supervisor, Housecleaner; 324.137-010 Baggage Porter, Head; 324.137-014 Bell Captain; 329.137-010 Superintendent, Service; 341.137-010 Caddie Supervisor; 342.137-010 Supervisor, Rides; 344.137-010 Usher, Head; 350.137-018 Steward/Stewardess, Chief, Passenger Ship; 350.137-022 Steward/Stewardess, Second; 350.137-026 Steward/Stewardess, Third; 352.137-010 Supervisor, Airplane-Flight Attendant; 353.137-010 Guide, Chief Airport; 358.137-010 Checkroom Chief; others.

39-2000 Animal Care and Service Workers

39-2011.00 Animal Trainers

- **Education/Training Required: Moderate-term on-the-job training**
- **Employed: 8,320**
- **Annual Earnings: $24,800**
- **Growth: 20.3%**
- **Annual Job Openings: 3,000**

Train animals for riding, harness, security, performance, or obedience or assisting persons with disabilities. Accustom animals to human voice and contact and condition animals to respond to commands. Train animals according to prescribed standards for show or competition. May train animals to carry pack loads or work as part of pack team.

Observe animals' physical conditions to detect illness or unhealthy conditions requiring medical care. Cue or signal animals during performances. Administer prescribed medications to animals. Evaluate animals to determine their temperaments, abilities, and aptitude for training. Feed and exercise animals and provide other general care such as cleaning and maintaining holding and performance areas. Talk to and interact with animals in order to familiarize them to human voices and contact. Conduct training programs to develop and maintain desired animal behaviors for competition, entertainment, obedience, security, riding, and related areas. Keep records documenting animal health, diet, and behavior. Advise animal owners regarding the purchase of specific animals. Instruct jockeys in handling specific horses during races. Train horses or other equines for riding, harness, show, racing, or other work, using knowledge of breed characteristics, training methods, performance standards, and the peculiarities of each animal. Use oral, spur, rein, and hand commands to condition horses to carry riders or to pull horse-drawn equipment. Place tack or harnesses on horses to accustom horses to the feel of equipment. Train dogs in human-assistance or property protection duties. Retrain horses to break bad habits, such as kicking, bolting, and resisting bridling and grooming. Train and rehearse animals, according to scripts, for motion picture, television, film, stage, or circus performances. Organize and conduct animal shows. Arrange for mating of stallions and mares and assist mares during foaling.

GOE Information—Interest Area: 08. Health Science. **Work Group:** 08.05. Animal Care. **Personality Type—**Social. Social occupations frequently involve working with, communicating with, and teaching people. These occupations often involve helping or providing service to others. **Work Values—**Responsibility; Independence; Creativity; Autonomy; Compensation. **Skills—**Management of Financial Resources; Persuasion; Instructing; Service Orientation; Learning Strategies; Monitoring. **Abilities—**Cognitive: Problem Sensitivity; Originality; Fluency of Ideas; Speed of Closure; Time Sharing; Memorization. Psychomotor: Response Orientation; Rate Control; Speed of Limb Movement; Multilimb Coordination; Reaction Time; Control Precision. Physical: Dynamic Strength; Stamina; Extent Flexibility; Gross Body Coordination; Static Strength; Trunk Strength. Sensory: Depth Perception; Hearing Sensitivity; Far Vision; Visual Color Discrimination; Auditory Attention; Speech Clarity. **General Work Activities—**Information Input: Identifying Objects, Actions, and Events; Monitoring Processes, Materials, or Surroundings; Getting Information. Mental Process: Updating and Using Relevant Knowledge; Thinking Creatively; Judging the Qualities of Things, Services, or Other People's Work. Work Output: Handling and Moving Objects; Performing General Physical Activities; Documenting or Recording Information. Interacting with Others: Establishing and Maintaining Interpersonal Relationships; Teaching Others; Performing for or Working with the Public. **Physical Work Conditions—**Outdoors; Noisy; Standing; Walking and Running; Using Hands on Objects, Tools, or Controls; Repetitive Motions. **Other Job Characteristics—**None met the criteria.

Experience—Job Zone 2. Some previous work-related skill, knowledge, or experience may be helpful in these occupations, but usually is not needed. **Job Preparation—**SVP 4.0 to less than 6.0—six months to less than two years. **Knowledges—**Sales and Marketing; Biology; Customer and Personal Service; Economics and Accounting; Communications and Media; Clerical Practices. **Instructional Programs—**Animal Training; Equestrian/Equine Studies.

Related SOC Job—39-2011 Animal Trainers. **Related OOH Job—**Animal Care and Service Workers. **Related DOT Jobs—**159.224-010 Animal Trainer; 419.224-010 Horse Trainer.

39-2021.00 Nonfarm Animal Caretakers

- **Education/Training Required: Short-term on-the-job training**
- **Employed: 100,550**
- **Annual Earnings: $17,720**
- **Growth: 25.6%**
- **Annual Job Openings: 31,000**

Feed, water, groom, bathe, exercise, or otherwise care for pets and other nonfarm animals, such as dogs, cats, ornamental fish or birds, zoo animals, and mice. Work in settings such as kennels, animal shelters, zoos, circuses, and aquariums. May keep records of feedings, treatments, and animals received or discharged. May clean, disinfect, and repair cages, pens, or fish tanks.

Feed and water animals according to schedules and feeding instructions. Clean, organize, and disinfect animal quarters such as pens, stables, cages, and yards and animal equipment such as saddles and bridles. Answer telephones and schedule appointments. Examine and observe animals to detect signs of illness, disease, or injury. Respond to questions from patrons and provide information about animals, such as behavior, habitat, breeding habits, or facility activities. Provide treatment to sick or injured animals or contact veterinarians to secure treatment. Collect and record animal information such as weight, size, physical condition, treatments received, medications given, and food intake. Perform animal grooming duties such as washing, brushing, clipping, and trimming coats; cutting nails; and cleaning ears. Exercise animals to maintain their physical and mental health. Order, unload, and store feed and supplies. Mix food, liquid formulas, medications, or food supplements according to instructions, prescriptions, and knowledge of animal species. Clean and disinfect surgical equipment. Discuss with clients their pets' grooming needs. Observe and caution children petting and feeding animals in designated areas to ensure the safety of humans and animals. Find homes for stray or unwanted animals. Adjust controls to regulate specified temperature and humidity of animal quarters, nurseries, or exhibit areas. Anesthetize and inoculate animals, according to instructions. Transfer animals between enclosures to facilitate breeding, birthing, shipping, or rearrangement of exhibits. Install, maintain, and repair animal care facility equipment such as infrared lights, feeding devices, and cages. Train animals to perform certain tasks. Teach obedience classes. Sell pet food and supplies. Saddle and shoe animals.

GOE Information—Interest Area: 08. Health Science. **Work Group:** 08.05. Animal Care. **Personality Type—**Realistic. Realistic occupations frequently involve work activities that include practical, hands-on problems and solutions. They often deal with plants; animals; and real-world materials like wood, tools, and machinery. Many of the occupations require working outside and do not involve a lot of paperwork or working closely with others. **Work Values—**Independence; Supervision, Technical; Activity. **Skills—**Time Management; Management of Financial Resources; Social Perceptiveness; Equipment Maintenance; Management of Material Resources. **Abilities—**Cognitive: Speed of Closure. Psychomotor: Arm-Hand Steadiness; Multilimb Coordination; Control Precision. Physical: Static Strength; Stamina; Trunk Strength; Gross Body Coordination; Extent Flexibility. Sensory: Depth Perception; Speech Recognition; Far Vision; Auditory Attention. **General Work Activities—**Information Input: Identifying Objects, Actions, and Events; Monitoring Processes, Materials, or Surroundings; Getting Information. Mental Process: Organizing, Planning, and Prioritizing; Updating and Using Relevant Knowledge; Making Decisions and

Solving Problems. *Work Output:* Handling and Moving Objects; Performing General Physical Activities; Documenting or Recording Information. *Interacting with Others:* Performing for or Working with the Public; Establishing and Maintaining Interpersonal Relationships; Resolving Conflicts and Negotiating with Others. **Physical Work Conditions**—More Often Outdoors Than Indoors; Noisy; Contaminants; Minor Burns, Cuts, Bites, or Stings; Standing. **Other Job Characteristics**—Need to Be Exact or Accurate.

Experience—Job Zone 2. Some previous work-related skill, knowledge, or experience may be helpful in these occupations, but usually is not needed. **Job Preparation**—SVP 4.0 to less than 6.0—six months to less than two years. **Knowledges**—Customer and Personal Service. **Instructional Programs**—Agricultural/Farm Supplies Retailing and Wholesaling; Dog/Pet/Animal Grooming.

Related SOC Job—39-2021 Nonfarm Animal Caretakers. **Related OOH Job**—Animal Care and Service Workers. **Related DOT Jobs**—153.674-010 Exerciser, Horse; 153.674-014 Lead Pony Rider; 410.674-010 Animal Caretaker; 410.674-022 Stable Attendant; 412.674-010 Animal Keeper; 412.674-014 Animal-Nursery Worker; 418.381-010 Horseshoer; 418.674-010 Dog Groomer; 418.677-010 Dog Bather; 449.674-010 Aquarist.

39-3000 Entertainment Attendants and Related Workers

39-3011.00 Gaming Dealers

- **Education/Training Required:** Postsecondary vocational training
- **Employed:** 82,320
- **Annual Earnings:** $14,260
- **Growth:** 28.0%
- **Annual Job Openings:** 11,000

Operate table games. Stand or sit behind table and operate games of chance by dispensing the appropriate number of cards or blocks to players or operating other gaming equipment. Compare the house's hand against players' hands and pay off or collect players' money or chips.

Exchange paper currency for playing chips or coin money. Pay winnings or collect losing bets as established by the rules and procedures of a specific game. Deal cards to house hands and compare these with players' hands to determine winners, as in blackjack. Conduct gambling games such as dice, roulette, cards, or keno, following all applicable rules and regulations. Check to ensure that all players have placed bets before play begins. Stand behind a gaming table and deal the appropriate number of cards to each player. Inspect cards and equipment to be used in games to ensure that they are in good condition. Start and control games and gaming equipment and announce winning numbers or colors. Open and close cash floats and game tables. Compute amounts of players' wins or losses or scan winning tickets presented by patrons to calculate the amount of money won. Apply rule variations to card games such as poker, in which players bet on the value of their hands. Receive, verify, and record patrons' cash wagers. Answer questions about game rules and casino policies. Refer patrons to gaming cashiers to collect winnings. Work as part of a team of dealers in games such as baccarat or craps. Participate in games for gambling establishments to provide the minimum complement of players at a table. Seat patrons at gaming tables. Prepare collection reports for submission to supervisors. Monitor gambling tables and supervise staff. Train new dealers.

GOE Information—**Interest Area:** 09. Hospitality, Tourism, and Recreation. **Work Group:** 09.02. Recreational Services. **Personality Type**—Enterprising. Enterprising occupations frequently involve starting up and carrying out projects. These occupations can involve leading people and making many decisions. They sometimes require risk taking and often deal with business. **Work Values**—Supervision, Technical; Co-workers. **Skills**—Service Orientation; Speaking; Mathematics. **Abilities**—*Cognitive:* Perceptual Speed; Speed of Closure; Number Facility; Selective Attention; Flexibility of Closure. *Psychomotor:* Manual Dexterity; Arm-Hand Steadiness. *Physical:* Trunk Strength; Extent Flexibility. *Sensory:* Hearing Sensitivity; Auditory Attention; Visual Color Discrimination. **General Work Activities**—*Information Input:* Monitoring Processes, Materials, or Surroundings; Identifying Objects, Actions, and Events; Getting Information. *Mental Process:* Judging the Qualities of Things, Services, or Other People's Work; Updating and Using Relevant Knowledge; Evaluating Information Against Standards. *Work Output:* Handling and Moving Objects; Performing General Physical Activities. *Interacting with Others:* Performing for or Working with the Public; Communicating with Other Workers; Establishing and Maintaining Interpersonal Relationships. **Physical Work Conditions**—Indoors; Noisy; Standing; Using Hands on Objects, Tools, or Controls; Bending or Twisting the Body; Repetitive Motions. **Other Job Characteristics**—Need to Be Exact or Accurate; Repeat Same Tasks.

Experience—Job Zone 2. Some previous work-related skill, knowledge, or experience may be helpful in these occupations, but usually is not needed. **Job Preparation**—SVP 4.0 to less than 6.0—six months to less than two years. **Knowledges**—Psychology; Mathematics; Customer and Personal Service; Sales and Marketing. **Instructional Program**—No related CIP programs.

Related SOC Job—39-3011 Gaming Dealers. **Related OOH Job**—Gaming Services Occupations. **Related DOT Job**—343.464-010 Gambling Dealer.

39-3012.00 Gaming and Sports Book Writers and Runners

- **Education/Training Required:** Postsecondary vocational training
- **Employed:** 19,290
- **Annual Earnings:** $18,440
- **Growth:** 22.1%
- **Annual Job Openings:** 2,000

Assist in the operation of games such as keno and bingo. Scan winning tickets presented by patrons, calculate amount of winnings, and pay patrons. May operate keno and bingo equipment. May start gaming equipment that randomly selects numbers. May announce number selected until total numbers specified for each game are selected. May pick up tickets from players; collect bets; and receive, verify, and record patrons' cash wagers.

Compute and verify amounts won and lost; then pay out winnings or refer patrons to workers such as gaming cashiers so that winnings can be collected. Collect bets in the form of cash or chips, verifying and recording amounts. Collect cards or tickets from players. Answer questions about game rules and casino policies. Compare the house hand with players' hands in order to determine the winner. Check to ensure that all players have placed their bets before play begins. Conduct gambling tables or games such as dice, roulette, cards, or keno and ensure that game rules are followed. Inspect cards and equipment to be used in games to ensure they are in proper condition. Pay off or move bets as established by game rules and procedures. Prepare collection reports for submission to supervisors. Exchange paper currency for playing chips or coins. Open and close cash floats and game tables. Start gaming equipment that randomly selects numbered balls and announce winning numbers and colors. Record the number of tickets cashed and the amount paid out after each race or event. Operate games in which players bet that a ball will come to rest in a particular slot on a rotating wheel, performing actions such as spinning the wheel and releasing the ball. Supervise staff and games and mediate disputes. Push dice to shooters and retrieve thrown dice. Deliver tickets, cards, and money to bingo callers. Participate in games for gambling establishments to provide the minimum complement of players at a table. Sell food, beverages, and tobacco to players. Take the house percentage from each pot. Seat patrons at gaming tables.

GOE Information—Interest Area: 09. Hospitality, Tourism, and Recreation. Work Group: 09.02. Recreational Services. Personality Type—Enterprising. Enterprising occupations frequently involve starting up and carrying out projects. These occupations can involve leading people and making many decisions. They sometimes require risk taking and often deal with business. Work Values—Supervision, Technical; Co-workers. Skills—None met the criteria. Abilities—Cognitive: Mathematical Reasoning; Selective Attention; Perceptual Speed; Number Facility; Time Sharing. Psychomotor: Arm-Hand Steadiness; Finger Dexterity. Physical: None met the criteria. Sensory: None met the criteria. General Work Activities—Information Input: Monitoring Processes, Materials, or Surroundings; Identifying Objects, Actions, and Events; Getting Information. Mental Process: Processing Information; Judging the Qualities of Things, Services, or Other People's Work; Evaluating Information Against Standards. Work Output: Handling and Moving Objects; Performing General Physical Activities; Interacting With Computers. Interacting with Others: Performing for or Working with the Public; Establishing and Maintaining Interpersonal Relationships; Resolving Conflicts and Negotiating with Others. Physical Work Conditions—Indoors; Noisy; Sitting; Using Hands on Objects, Tools, or Controls; Repetitive Motions. Other Job Characteristics—Need to Be Exact or Accurate; Repeat Same Tasks; Errors Have Important Consequences; Pace Determined by Speed of Equipment.

Experience—Job Zone 2. Some previous work-related skill, knowledge, or experience may be helpful in these occupations, but usually is not needed. Job Preparation—SVP 4.0 to less than 6.0–six months to less than two years. Knowledges—Customer and Personal Service; Sales and Marketing; Psychology; Public Safety and Security; Mathematics; Computers and Electronics. Instructional Program—No related CIP programs.

Related SOC Job—39-3012 Gaming and Sports Book Writers and Runners. Related OOH Job—Gaming Services Occupations. Related DOT Jobs—343.467-010 Cardroom Attendant I; 343.467-022 Keno Writer.

39-3019.99 Gaming Service Workers, All Other

- Education/Training Required: No data available
- Employed: No data available
- Annual Earnings: $21,560
- Growth: 26.3%
- Annual Job Openings: 2,000

All gaming service workers not listed separately.

No task data available.

Note: The Department of Labor has not collected some data for this job, so it has fewer details than the other descriptions.

Related SOC Job—39-3019 Gaming Service Workers, All Other. Related OOH Job—Gaming Services Occupations. Related DOT Job—343.367-010 Card Player.

39-3021.00 Motion Picture Projectionists

- Education/Training Required: Short-term on-the-job training
- Employed: 10,230
- Annual Earnings: $16,780
- Growth: –9.9%
- Annual Job Openings: 4,000

Set up and operate motion picture projection and related sound reproduction equipment.

Insert film into top magazine reel or thread film through a series of sprockets and guide rollers, attaching the end to a take-up reel. Start projectors and open shutters to project images onto screens. Monitor operations to ensure that standards for sound and image projection quality are met. Operate equipment to show films in a number of theaters simultaneously. Splice separate film reels, advertisements, and movie trailers together to form a feature-length presentation on one continuous reel. Inspect movie films to ensure that they are complete and in good condition. Set up and adjust picture projectors and screens to achieve proper size, illumination, and focus of images and proper volume and tone of sound. Perform regular maintenance tasks such as rotating or replacing xenon bulbs, cleaning lenses, lubricating machinery, and keeping electrical contacts clean and tight. Inspect projection equipment prior to operation to ensure proper working order. Splice and rewind film onto reels automatically or by hand to repair faulty or broken sections of film. Remove film splicing to prepare films for shipment after showings and return films to their sources. Perform minor repairs such as replacing worn sprockets or notify maintenance personnel of the need for major repairs. Open and close facilities according to rules and schedules. Observe projector operation to anticipate need to transfer operations from one projector to another. Set up and inspect curtain and screen controls. Project motion pictures onto back screens for inclusion in scenes within film or stage productions. Remove full take-up reels and run film through rewinding machines to rewind projected films so they may be shown again. Operate special-effects equipment, such as stereopticons, to project pictures onto screens. Coordinate equipment operation with presentation of supplemental material, such as music, oral commentaries, or sound effects. Install and connect auxiliary equipment, such as microphones, amplifiers, disc playback machines, and lights. Prepare film inspection reports, attendance sheets, and log books.

GOE Information—Interest Area: 09. Hospitality, Tourism, and Recreation. Work Group: 09.02. Recreational Services. Personality Type—Realistic. Realistic occupations frequently involve work activities that include practical, hands-on problems and solutions. They often deal with plants; animals; and real-world materials like wood, tools, and machinery. Many of the occupations require working outside and do not involve a lot of paperwork or working closely with others. Work Values—Independence; Moral Values; Working Conditions; Supervision, Technical; Supervision, Human Relations. Skills—Equipment Maintenance; Repairing; Operation Monitoring; Troubleshooting; Operation and Control; Installation. Abilities—Cognitive: Visualization; Perceptual Speed; Selective Attention.

Psychomotor: Rate Control; Reaction Time; Arm-Hand Steadiness; Control Precision; Manual Dexterity; Multilimb Coordination. *Physical:* None met the criteria. *Sensory:* Visual Color Discrimination; Far Vision; Hearing Sensitivity; Depth Perception; Auditory Attention. **General Work Activities**—*Information Input:* Monitoring Processes, Materials, or Surroundings; Inspecting Equipment, Structures, or Materials; Identifying Objects, Actions, and Events. *Mental Process:* Making Decisions and Solving Problems; Organizing, Planning, and Prioritizing; Updating and Using Relevant Knowledge. *Work Output:* Handling and Moving Objects; Controlling Machines and Processes; Repairing and Maintaining Mechanical Equipment. *Interacting with Others:* Communicating with Other Workers; Establishing and Maintaining Interpersonal Relationships; Performing for or Working with the Public. **Physical Work Conditions**—Indoors; Noisy; Standing; Walking and Running; Using Hands on Objects, Tools, or Controls; Repetitive Motions. **Other Job Characteristics**—Need to Be Exact or Accurate; Repeat Same Tasks; Pace Determined by Speed of Equipment; Automation; Errors Have Important Consequences.

Experience—Job Zone 2. Some previous work-related skill, knowledge, or experience may be helpful in these occupations, but usually is not needed. **Job Preparation**—SVP 4.0 to less than 6.0—six months to less than two years. **Knowledges**—Mechanical Devices. **Instructional Program**—No related CIP programs.

Related SOC Job—39-3021 Motion Picture Projectionists. **Related OOH Job**—Motion Picture Projectionists. **Related DOT Jobs**—960.362-010 Motion-Picture Projectionist; 960.382-010 Audiovisual Technician.

39-3031.00 Ushers, Lobby Attendants, and Ticket Takers

- Education/Training Required: Short-term on-the-job training
- Employed: 102,330
- Annual Earnings: $15,400
- Growth: 10.6%
- Annual Job Openings: 45,000

Assist patrons at entertainment events by performing duties such as collecting admission tickets and passes from patrons, assisting in finding seats, searching for lost articles, and locating such facilities as restrooms and telephones.

Sell and collect admission tickets and passes from patrons at entertainment events. Greet patrons attending entertainment events. Examine tickets or passes to verify authenticity, using criteria such as color and date issued. Guide patrons to exits or provide other instructions or assistance in case of emergency. Maintain order and ensure adherence to safety rules. Provide assistance with patrons' special needs, such as helping those with wheelchairs. Direct patrons to restrooms, concession stands, and telephones. Refuse admittance to undesirable persons or persons without tickets or passes. Settle seating disputes and help solve other customer concerns. Assist patrons in finding seats, lighting the way with flashlights if necessary. Search for lost articles or for parents of lost children. Count and record number of tickets collected. Operate refreshment stands during intermission or obtain refreshments for press box patrons during performances. Verify credentials of patrons desiring entrance into press-box and permit only authorized persons to enter. Distribute programs to patrons. Schedule and manage volunteer usher corps. Work with others to change advertising displays. Manage inventory and sale of artist merchandise. Give door checks to patrons who are temporarily leaving establishments. Manage informational kiosk and display of event signs and posters. Page individuals wanted at the box office.

GOE Information—**Interest Area:** 09. Hospitality, Tourism, and Recreation. **Work Group:** 09.02. Recreational Services. **Personality Type**—Social. Social occupations frequently involve working with, communicating with, and teaching people. These occupations often involve helping or providing service to others. **Work Values**—Social Service; Co-workers; Supervision, Technical. **Skills**—None met the criteria. **Abilities**—*Cognitive:* None met the criteria. *Psychomotor:* None met the criteria. *Physical:* Trunk Strength. *Sensory:* None met the criteria. **General Work Activities**—*Information Input:* Getting Information. *Mental Process:* Organizing, Planning, and Prioritizing; Updating and Using Relevant Knowledge; Judging the Qualities of Things, Services, or Other People's Work. *Work Output:* Handling and Moving Objects; Performing General Physical Activities; Interacting With Computers. *Interacting with Others:* Establishing and Maintaining Interpersonal Relationships; Communicating with Other Workers; Assisting and Caring for Others. **Physical Work Conditions**—Indoors; Standing; Using Hands on Objects, Tools, or Controls; Repetitive Motions. **Other Job Characteristics**—Need to Be Exact or Accurate; Repeat Same Tasks.

Experience—Job Zone 1. No previous work-related skill, knowledge, or experience is needed. **Job Preparation**—SVP below 4.0—less than six months. **Knowledges**—Food Production; History and Archeology. **Instructional Program**—No related CIP programs.

Related SOC Job—39-3031 Ushers, Lobby Attendants, and Ticket Takers. **Related OOH Job**—Ushers, Lobby Attendants, and Ticket Takers. **Related DOT Jobs**—344.667-010 Ticket Taker; 344.677-010 Press-Box Custodian; 344.677-014 Usher; 349.673-010 Drive-in Theater Attendant; 349.677-018 Children's Attendant.

39-3091.00 Amusement and Recreation Attendants

- Education/Training Required: Short-term on-the-job training
- Employed: 232,030
- Annual Earnings: $15,920
- Growth: 28.0%
- Annual Job Openings: 130,000

Perform variety of attending duties at amusement or recreation facility. May schedule use of recreation facilities, maintain and provide equipment to participants of sporting events or recreational pursuits, or operate amusement concessions and rides.

Provide information about facilities, entertainment options, and rules and regulations. Record details of attendance, sales, receipts, reservations, or repair activities. Monitor activities to ensure adherence to rules and safety procedures or arrange for the removal of unruly patrons. Sell tickets and collect fees from customers. Clean sporting equipment, vehicles, rides, booths, facilities, or grounds. Keep informed of shut-down and emergency evacuation procedures. Operate machines to clean, smooth, and prepare the ice surfaces of rinks for activities such as skating, hockey, and curling. Announce or describe amusement park attractions to patrons to entice customers to games and other entertainment. Fasten safety devices for patrons or provide them with directions for fastening devices. Inspect equipment to detect wear and damage and perform minor repairs, adjustments, or maintenance tasks such as oiling parts. Operate, drive, or explain the use of mechanical riding devices or other automatic equipment in amusement parks, carnivals, or recreation areas. Rent, sell, or issue sporting equipment and supplies such as bowling shoes, golf balls, swimming suits, and beach chairs. Verify, collect, or punch tickets before admitting patrons to venues such as amusement parks and rides. Direct patrons to rides, seats, or attractions. Tend amusement booths in parks, carnivals, or stadiums, performing duties such as conducting games, photographing patrons, and awarding prizes. Provide assistance to patrons entering or exiting amusement rides, boats, or ski lifts or mounting or dismounting animals. Sell and serve refreshments to customers. Schedule the use of recreation facilities such as golf courses, tennis courts, bowling alleys, and softball diamonds. Maintain inventories of equipment, storing and retrieving items and assembling and disassembling equipment as necessary.

GOE Information—Interest Area: 09. Hospitality, Tourism, and Recreation. **Work Group:** 09.02. Recreational Services. **Personality Type—Realistic.** Realistic occupations frequently involve work activities that include practical, hands-on problems and solutions. They often deal with plants; animals; and real-world materials like wood, tools, and machinery. Many of the occupations require working outside and do not involve a lot of paperwork or working closely with others. **Work Values—**Social Service; Supervision, Technical; Co-workers; Moral Values. **Skills—**None met the criteria. **Abilities—***Cognitive:* Oral Expression; Problem Sensitivity. *Psychomotor:* Multilimb Coordination; Control Precision. *Physical:* None met the criteria. *Sensory:* Speech Clarity. **General Work Activities—***Information Input:* Getting Information; Inspecting Equipment, Structures, or Materials; Monitoring Processes, Materials, or Surroundings. *Mental Process:* Evaluating Information Against Standards; Organizing, Planning, and Prioritizing; Updating and Using Relevant Knowledge. *Work Output:* Performing General Physical Activities; Handling and Moving Objects. *Interacting with Others:* Establishing and Maintaining Interpersonal Relationships; Communicating with Other Workers; Performing for or Working with the Public. **Physical Work Conditions—**More Often Indoors Than Outdoors; Noisy; Sitting; Using Hands on Objects, Tools, or Controls. **Other Job Characteristics—**None met the criteria.

Experience—Job Zone 1. No previous work-related skill, knowledge, or experience is needed. **Job Preparation—**SVP below 4.0—less than six months. **Knowledges—**Customer and Personal Service; Public Safety and Security. **Instructional Program—**No related CIP programs.

Related SOC Job—39-3091 Amusement and Recreation Attendants. **Related OOH Job—**Amusement and Recreation Attendants. **Related DOT Jobs—**195.367-030 Recreation Aide; 340.367-010 Desk Clerk, Bowling Floor; 340.477-010 Racker; 341.367-010 Recreation-Facility Attendant; 341.464-010 Skate-Shop Attendant; 341.665-010 Ski-Tow Operator; 341.677-010 Caddie; 341.683-010 Golf-Range Attendant; 342.357-010 Weight Guesser; 342.657-010 Barker; 342.657-014 Game Attendant; 342.663-010 Ride Operator; 342.665-010 Fun-House Operator; 342.667-010 Wharf Attendant; 342.667-014 Attendant, Arcade; 342.677-010 Ride Attendant; 343.467-014 Floor Attendant; others.

39-3092.00 Costume Attendants

- **Education/Training Required: Short-term on-the-job training**
- **Employed: 3,900**
- **Annual Earnings: $25,360**
- **Growth: 23.4%**
- **Annual Job Openings: 2,000**

Select, fit, and take care of costumes for cast members and aid entertainers.

Distribute costumes and related equipment and keep records of item status. Arrange costumes in order of use to facilitate quick-change procedures for performances. Return borrowed or rented items when productions are complete and return other items to storage. Clean and press costumes before and after performances and perform any minor repairs. Assign lockers to employees and maintain locker rooms, dressing rooms, wig rooms, and costume storage and laundry areas. Provide assistance to cast members in wearing costumes or assign cast dressers to assist specific cast members with costume changes. Design and construct costumes or send them to tailors for construction, major repairs, or alterations. Purchase, rent, or requisition costumes and other wardrobe necessities. Check the appearance of costumes on stage and under lights to determine whether desired effects are being achieved. Inventory stock to determine types and conditions of available costuming. Collaborate with production designers, costume designers, and other production staff to discuss and execute costume design details. Monitor, maintain, and secure inventories of costumes, wigs, and makeup, providing keys or access to assigned directors, costume designers, and wardrobe mistresses/masters. Create worksheets for dressing lists, show notes, and costume checks. Direct the work of wardrobe crews during dress rehearsals and performances. Examine costume fit on cast members and sketch or write notes for alterations. Review scripts or other production information to determine a story's locale and period, as well as the number of characters and required costumes. Recommend vendors and monitor their work. Study books, pictures, and examples of period clothing to determine styles worn during specific periods in history. Provide managers with budget recommendations and take responsibility for budgetary line items related to costumes, storage, and makeup needs. Participate in the hiring, training, scheduling, and supervision of alteration workers. Care for non-clothing items such as flags, table skirts, and draperies.

GOE Information—Interest Area: 03. Arts and Communication. **Work Group:** 03.06. Drama. **Personality Type—Artistic.** Artistic occupations frequently involve working with forms, designs, and patterns. They often require self-expression, and the work can be done without following a clear set of rules. **Work Values—**Creativity; Social Service; Autonomy; Variety; Responsibility; Moral Values. **Skills—**Management of Financial Resources; Coordination; Operations Analysis; Negotiation; Social Perceptiveness; Service Orientation. **Abilities—***Cognitive:* Originality. *Psychomotor:* Arm-Hand Steadiness; Manual Dexterity; Finger Dexterity; Control Precision. *Physical:* None met the criteria. *Sensory:* Visual Color Discrimination; Far Vision. **General Work Activities—***Information Input:* Monitoring Processes, Materials, or Surroundings; Getting Information; Identifying Objects, Actions, and Events. *Mental Process:* Organizing, Planning, and Prioritizing; Thinking Creatively; Making Decisions and Solving Problems. *Work Output:* Handling and Moving Objects; Performing General Physical Activities; Documenting or Recording Information. *Interacting with Others:* Establishing and Maintaining Interpersonal Relationships; Assisting and Caring for Others; Communicating with Other Workers. **Physical Work Conditions—**Indoors; Contaminants; Standing; Walking and Running; Using Hands on Objects, Tools, or Controls. **Other Job Characteristics—**Need to Be Exact or Accurate.

Experience—Job Zone 2. Some previous work-related skill, knowledge, or experience may be helpful in these occupations, but usually is not needed. **Job Preparation—**SVP 4.0 to less than 6.0—six months to less than two years. **Knowledges—**Fine Arts; Customer and Personal Service; Sociology and Anthropology; Psychology. **Instructional Program—**No related CIP programs.

Related SOC Job—39-3092 Costume Attendants. **Related OOH Job**—Costume Attendants. **Related DOT Jobs**—346.261-010 Costumer; 346.361-010 Wardrobe Supervisor.

39-3093.00 Locker Room, Coatroom, and Dressing Room Attendants

- **Education/Training Required: Short-term on-the-job training**
- **Employed: 20,340**
- **Annual Earnings: $17,940**
- **Growth: 17.3%**
- **Annual Job Openings: 12,000**

Provide personal items to patrons or customers in locker rooms, dressing rooms, or coatrooms.

Assign dressing room facilities, locker space, or clothing containers to patrons of athletic or bathing establishments. Answer customer inquiries or explain cost, availability, policies, and procedures of facilities. Check supplies to ensure adequate availability and order new supplies when necessary. Refer guest problems or complaints to supervisors. Clean and polish footwear, using brushes, sponges, cleaning fluid, polishes, waxes, liquid or sole dressing, and daubers. Report and document safety hazards, potentially hazardous conditions, and unsafe practices and procedures. Operate washing machines and dryers to clean soiled apparel and towels. Monitor patrons' facility use to ensure that rules and regulations are followed and safety and order are maintained. Procure beverages, food, and other items as requested. Activate emergency action plans and administer first aid as necessary. Store personal possessions for patrons, issue claim checks for articles stored, and return articles on receipt of checks. Provide towels and sheets to clients in public baths, steam rooms, and restrooms. Collect soiled linen or clothing for laundering. Operate controls that regulate temperatures or room environments. Attend to needs of athletic teams in clubhouses. Provide assistance to patrons by performing duties such as opening doors and carrying bags. Stencil identifying information on equipment. Maintain inventories of clothing or uniforms, accessories, equipment, or linens. Issue gym clothes, uniforms, towels, athletic equipment, and special athletic apparel. Maintain a lost-and-found collection. Set up various apparatus or athletic equipment. Provide or arrange for services such as clothes pressing, cleaning, and repair.

GOE Information—Interest Area: 09. Hospitality, Tourism, and Recreation. **Work Group:** 09.02. Recreational Services. **Personality Type**—Social. Social occupations frequently involve working with, communicating with, and teaching people. These occupations often involve helping or providing service to others. **Work Values**—Social Service; Working Conditions; Variety. **Skills**—Service Orientation. **Abilities**—*Cognitive:* None met the criteria. *Psychomotor:* None met the criteria. *Physical:* Extent Flexibility; Trunk Strength. *Sensory:* None met the criteria. **General Work Activities**—*Information Input:* Monitoring Processes, Materials, or Surroundings. *Mental Process:* None met the criteria. *Work Output:* None met the criteria. *Interacting with Others:* Establishing and Maintaining Interpersonal Relationships; Performing for or Working with the Public. **Physical Work Conditions**—Indoors; Standing; Walking and Running; Using Hands on Objects, Tools, or Controls; Bending or Twisting the Body; Repetitive Motions. **Other Job Characteristics**—Need to Be Exact or Accurate.

Experience—Job Zone 1. No previous work-related skill, knowledge, or experience is needed. **Job Preparation**—SVP below 4.0—less than

six months. **Knowledges**—Customer and Personal Service. **Instructional Program**—No related CIP programs.

Related SOC Job—39-3093 Locker Room, Coatroom, and Dressing Room Attendants. **Related OOH Job**—Locker Room, Coatroom and Dressing Room Attendants. **Related DOT Jobs**—324.577-010 Room-Service Clerk; 324.677-014 Doorkeeper; 329.467-010 Attendant, Lodging Facilities; 329.677-010 Porter, Marina; 334.677-010 Rubber; 335.677-010 Cooling-Room Attendant; 335.677-014 Hot-Room Attendant; 346.667-010 Jockey-Room Custodian; 346.677-010 Jockey Valet; 346.677-014 Riding-Silks Custodian; 346.677-018 Second; 358.677-010 Checkroom Attendant; 358.677-014 Locker-Room Attendant; 358.677-018 Rest Room Attendant; 359.367-014 Weight-Reduction Specialist; others.

39-3099.99 Entertainment Attendants and Related Workers, All Other

- **Education/Training Required: No data available**
- **Employed: 37,640**
- **Annual Earnings: No data available**
- **Growth: 20.0%**
- **Annual Job Openings: 19,000**

All entertainment attendants and related workers not listed separately.

No task data available.

Note: The Department of Labor has not collected some data for this job, so it has fewer details than the other descriptions.

Related SOC Job—39-3099 Entertainment Attendants and Related Workers, All Other. **Related OOH Job**—Gaming Services Occupations. **Related DOT Job**—No data available.

39-4000 Funeral Service Workers

39-4011.00 Embalmers

- **Education/Training Required: Postsecondary vocational training**
- **Employed: 9,840**
- **Annual Earnings: $36,960**
- **Growth: 15.6%**
- **Annual Job Openings: 2,000**

Prepare bodies for interment in conformity with legal requirements.

Conform to laws of health and sanitation and ensure that legal requirements concerning embalming are met. Apply cosmetics to impart lifelike appearance to the deceased. Incise stomach and abdominal walls and probe internal organs, using trocar, to withdraw blood and waste matter from organs. Close incisions, using needles and sutures. Reshape or reconstruct disfigured or maimed bodies when necessary, using derma-surgery techniques and materials such as clay, cotton, plaster of paris, and wax. Make incisions in arms or thighs and drain blood from circulatory system and replace it with embalming fluid, using pump. Dress bodies and place them in caskets. Join lips, using needles and thread or wire. Conduct interviews to arrange for the preparation of obituary notices, to assist with the selection of caskets or urns, and to determine the location and time of burials or cremations. Perform the duties of funeral directors, including coordinating funeral activities. Attach trocar to pump-tube, start pump, and repeat probing to force embalming fluid into organs. Perform special procedures necessary for remains that are to be transported to other states or overseas or where death was caused by infectious disease. Maintain records such as itemized lists of clothing or valuables delivered with body and names of persons embalmed. Insert convex celluloid or cotton between eyeballs and eyelids to prevent slipping and sinking of eyelids. Wash and dry bodies, using germicidal soap and towels or hot air dryers. Arrange for transporting the deceased to another state for interment. Supervise funeral attendants and other funeral home staff. Pack body orifices with cotton saturated with embalming fluid to prevent escape of gases or waste matter. Assist with placing caskets in hearses and organize cemetery processions. Serve as pallbearers, attend visiting rooms, and provide other assistance to the bereaved. Direct casket and floral display placement and arrange guest seating. Arrange funeral home equipment and perform general maintenance. Assist coroners at death scenes or at autopsies, file police reports, and testify at inquests or in court if employed by a coroner.

GOE Information—Interest Area: 08. Health Science. Work Group: 08.09. Health Protection and Promotion. Personality Type—Realistic. Realistic occupations frequently involve work activities that include practical, hands-on problems and solutions. They often deal with plants; animals; and real-world materials like wood, tools, and machinery. Many of the occupations require working outside and do not involve a lot of paperwork or working closely with others. Work Values—Independence; Social Service; Security; Autonomy; Supervision, Technical. Skills—Service Orientation; Science; Management of Financial Resources; Management of Material Resources; Social Perceptiveness; Equipment Maintenance. Abilities—Cognitive: Visualization; Problem Sensitivity. Psychomotor: Arm-Hand Steadiness; Manual Dexterity; Control Precision; Finger Dexterity; Multilimb Coordination. Physical: Static Strength; Trunk Strength. Sensory: Visual Color Discrimination; Near Vision. General Work Activities—Information Input: Monitoring Processes, Materials, or Surroundings; Getting Information; Identifying Objects, Actions, and Events. Mental Process: Updating and Using Relevant Knowledge; Making Decisions and Solving Problems; Processing Information. Work Output: Handling and Moving Objects; Performing General Physical Activities; Documenting or Recording Information. Interacting with Others: Assisting and Caring for Others; Performing for or Working with the Public; Establishing and Maintaining Interpersonal Relationships. Physical Work Conditions—Indoors; Contaminants; Disease or Infections; Hazardous Conditions; Standing; Using Hands on Objects, Tools, or Controls. Other Job Characteristics—Need to Be Exact or Accurate; Errors Have Important Consequences; Repeat Same Tasks.

Experience—Job Zone 3. Previous work-related skill, knowledge, or experience is required. Job Preparation—SVP 6.0 to less than 7.0—more than one year and less than four years. Knowledges—Chemistry; Biology; Customer and Personal Service; Philosophy and Theology; Therapy and Counseling; Medicine and Dentistry. Instructional Programs—Funeral Service and Mortuary Science, General; Mortuary Science and Embalming/Embalmer.

Related SOC Job—39-4011 Embalmers. Related OOH Job—Embalmers. Related DOT Jobs—338.371-010 Embalmer Apprentice; 338.371-014 Embalmer.

39-4021.00 Funeral Attendants

- **Education/Training Required: Short-term on-the-job training**
- **Employed: 30,220**
- **Annual Earnings: $19,720**
- **Growth: 20.8%**
- **Annual Job Openings: 8,000**

Perform variety of tasks during funeral, such as placing casket in parlor or chapel prior to service, arranging floral offerings or lights around casket, directing or escorting mourners, closing casket, and issuing and storing funeral equipment.

Perform a variety of tasks during funerals to assist funeral directors and to ensure that services run smoothly and as planned. Greet people at the funeral home. Offer assistance to mourners as they enter or exit limousines. Close caskets at appropriate point in services. Transfer the deceased to funeral homes. Obtain burial permits and register deaths. Direct or escort mourners to parlors or chapels in which wakes or funerals are being held. Place caskets in parlors or chapels prior to wakes or funerals. Clean and drive funeral vehicles such as cars or hearses in funeral processions. Carry flowers to hearses or limousines for transportation to places of interment. Clean funeral parlors and chapels. Arrange floral offerings or lights around caskets. Provide advice to mourners on how to make charitable donations in honor of the deceased. Perform general maintenance duties for funeral homes. Issue and store funeral equipment. Assist with cremations and with the processing and packaging of cremated remains. Act as pallbearers.

GOE Information—Interest Area: 10. Human Service. Work Group: 10.03. Child/Personal Care and Services. Personality Type—Social. Social occupations frequently involve working with, communicating with, and teaching people. These occupations often involve helping or providing service to others. Work Values—Social Service; Security. Skills—Social Perceptiveness. Abilities—Cognitive: None met the criteria. Psychomotor: Multilimb Coordination. Physical: Static Strength; Trunk Strength. Sensory: None met the criteria. General Work Activities—Information Input: Getting Information; Identifying Objects, Actions, and Events; Monitoring Processes, Materials, or Surroundings. Mental Process: Making Decisions and Solving Problems; Judging the Qualities of Things, Services, or Other People's Work; Organizing, Planning, and Prioritizing. Work Output: Handling and Moving Objects; Performing General Physical Activities; Operating Vehicles or Equipment. Interacting with Others: Assisting and Caring for Others; Performing for or Working with the Public; Establishing and Maintaining Interpersonal Relationships. Physical Work Conditions—More Often Indoors Than Outdoors; Standing. Other Job Characteristics—Need to Be Exact or Accurate.

Experience—Job Zone 2. Some previous work-related skill, knowledge, or experience may be helpful in these occupations, but usually is not needed. Job Preparation—SVP 4.0 to less than 6.0—six months to less than two years. Knowledges—Philosophy and Theology; Customer and Personal Service; Transportation; Psychology; Law and Government; Clerical Practices. Instructional Program—Funeral Service and Mortuary Science, General.

Related SOC Job—39-4021 Funeral Attendants. Related OOH Job—Funeral Attendants. Related DOT Jobs—359.677-014 Funeral Attendant; 359.687-010 Pallbearer.

39-5000 Personal Appearance Workers

39-5011.00 Barbers

- Education/Training Required: Postsecondary vocational training
- Employed: 13,630
- Annual Earnings: $21,760
- Growth: 8.2%
- Annual Job Openings: 5,000

Provide barbering services, such as cutting, trimming, shampooing, and styling hair; trimming beards; or giving shaves.

Clean and sterilize scissors, combs, clippers, and other instruments. Cut and trim hair according to clients' instructions and current hairstyles, using clippers, combs, hand-held blow driers, and scissors. Drape and pin protective cloths around customers' shoulders. Question patrons regarding desired services and haircut styles. Clean workstations and sweep floors. Record services provided on cashiers' tickets or receive payment from customers. Order supplies. Shape and trim beards and moustaches, using scissors. Stay informed of the latest styles and hair care techniques. Suggest treatments to alleviate hair problems. Shampoo hair. Keep card files on clientele, recording notes of work done, products used, and fees charged after each visit. Perform clerical and administrative duties such as keeping records, paying bills, and hiring and supervising personnel. Curl, color, or straighten hair, using special chemical solutions and equipment. Apply lather and shave beards or neck and temple hair contours, using razors. Measure, fit, and groom hairpieces. Recommend and sell lotions, tonics, or other cosmetic supplies. Provide face, neck, and scalp massages. Provide skin care and nail treatments. Identify hair problems by using microscopes and testing devices or by sending clients' hair samples out to independent laboratories for analysis.

GOE Information—Interest Area: 09. Hospitality, Tourism, and Recreation. Work Group: 09.07. Barber and Beauty Services. Personality Type—Realistic. Realistic occupations frequently involve work activities that include practical, hands-on problems and solutions. They often deal with plants; animals; and real-world materials like wood, tools, and machinery. Many of the occupations require working outside and do not involve a lot of paperwork or working closely with others. Work Values—Social Service; Autonomy; Moral Values; Recognition; Creativity; Independence. Skills—Management of Financial Resources; Management of Material Resources. Abilities—*Cognitive:* Selective Attention; Originality; Visualization. *Psychomotor:* Arm-Hand Steadiness; Manual Dexterity; Control Precision; Finger Dexterity. *Physical:* Trunk Strength. *Sensory:* None met the criteria. General Work Activities—*Information Input:* Getting Information; Identifying Objects, Actions, and Events; Inspecting Equipment, Structures, or Materials. *Mental Process:* Thinking Creatively; Organizing, Planning, and Prioritizing; Updating and Using Relevant Knowledge. *Work Output:* Controlling Machines and Processes; Performing General Physical Activities; Handling and Moving Objects. *Interacting with Others:* Performing for or Working with the Public; Establishing and Maintaining Interpersonal Relationships; Communicating with Persons Outside Organization. Physical Work Conditions—Indoors; Standing; Using Hands on Objects, Tools, or Controls; Repetitive Motions. Other Job Characteristics—Need to Be Exact or Accurate.

Experience—Job Zone 3. Previous work-related skill, knowledge, or experience is required. Job Preparation—SVP 6.0 to less than 7.0—

more than one year and less than four years. Knowledges—Customer and Personal Service; Sales and Marketing. Instructional Programs—Barbering/Barber; Cosmetology, Barber/Styling, and Nail Instructor; Hair Styling/Stylist and Hair Design; Salon/Beauty Salon Management/Manager.

Related SOC Job—39-5011 Barbers. Related OOH Job—Barbers, Cosmetologists, and Other Personal Appearance Workers. Related DOT Jobs—330.371-010 Barber; 330.371-014 Barber Apprentice.

39-5012.00 Hairdressers, Hairstylists, and Cosmetologists

- Education/Training Required: Postsecondary vocational training
- Employed: 338,910
- Annual Earnings: $20,610
- Growth: 16.1%
- Annual Job Openings: 59,000

Provide beauty services, such as shampooing, cutting, coloring, and styling hair and massaging and treating scalp. May also apply makeup, dress wigs, perform hair removal, and provide nail and skin care services.

Keep work stations clean and sanitize tools such as scissors and combs. Cut, trim, and shape hair or hairpieces based on customers' instructions, hair type, and facial features, using clippers, scissors, trimmers, and razors. Analyze patrons' hair and other physical features to determine and recommend beauty treatment or suggest hairstyles. Schedule client appointments. Bleach, dye, or tint hair, using applicator or brush. Update and maintain customer information records, such as beauty services provided. Shampoo, rinse, condition, and dry hair and scalp or hairpieces with water, liquid soap, or other solutions. Operate cash registers to receive payments from patrons. Demonstrate and sell hair care products and cosmetics. Apply water, setting, straightening, or waving solutions to hair and use curlers, rollers, hot combs, and curling irons to press and curl hair. Develop new styles and techniques. Comb, brush, and spray hair or wigs to set style. Shape eyebrows and remove facial hair, using depilatory cream, tweezers, electrolysis, or wax. Administer therapeutic medication and advise patron to seek medical treatment for chronic or contagious scalp conditions. Massage and treat scalp for hygienic and remedial purposes, using hands, fingers, or vibrating equipment. Shave, trim, and shape beards and moustaches. Train or supervise other hairstylists, hairdressers, and assistants. Recommend and explain the use of cosmetics, lotions, and creams to soften and lubricate skin and enhance and restore natural appearance. Give facials to patrons, using special compounds such as lotions and creams. Clean, shape, and polish fingernails and toenails, using files and nail polish. Apply artificial fingernails. Attach wigs or hairpieces to model heads and dress wigs and hairpieces according to instructions, samples, sketches, or photographs.

GOE Information—Interest Area: 09. Hospitality, Tourism, and Recreation. Work Group: 09.07. Barber and Beauty Services. Personality Type—Enterprising. Enterprising occupations frequently involve starting up and carrying out projects. These occupations can involve leading people and making many decisions. They sometimes require risk taking and often deal with business. Work Values—Social Service; Creativity; Achievement; Autonomy; Recognition; Moral Values. Skills—Science; Management of Financial Resources; Operations Analysis; Equipment Selection; Learning Strategies; Social Perceptiveness. Abilities—*Cognitive:* Visualization; Fluency of Ideas; Time Sharing; Originality; Flexibility of Closure; Perceptual

Speed. *Psychomotor:* Arm-Hand Steadiness; Manual Dexterity; Finger Dexterity; Multilimb Coordination; Control Precision. *Physical:* Extent Flexibility; Trunk Strength. *Sensory:* Visual Color Discrimination; Speech Recognition. **General Work Activities—** *Information Input:* Getting Information; Identifying Objects, Actions, and Events; Monitoring Processes, Materials, or Surroundings. *Mental Process:* Thinking Creatively; Updating and Using Relevant Knowledge; Organizing, Planning, and Prioritizing. *Work Output:* Handling and Moving Objects; Performing General Physical Activities; Documenting or Recording Information. *Interacting with Others:* Performing for or Working with the Public; Providing Consultation and Advice to Others; Establishing and Maintaining Interpersonal Relationships. **Physical Work Conditions—**Indoors; Contaminants; Minor Burns, Cuts, Bites, or Stings; Standing; Using Hands on Objects, Tools, or Controls; Repetitive Motions. **Other Job Characteristics—**Need to Be Exact or Accurate; Repeat Same Tasks.

Experience—Job Zone 3. Previous work-related skill, knowledge, or experience is required. **Job Preparation**—SVP 6.0 to less than 7.0— more than one year and less than four years. **Knowledges—** Chemistry; Sales and Marketing; Customer and Personal Service. **Instructional Programs—**Cosmetology and Related Personal Grooming Arts, Other; Cosmetology, Barber/Styling, and Nail Instructor; Cosmetology/Cosmetologist, General; Electrolysis/ Electrology and Electrolysis Technician; Hair Styling/Stylist and Hair Design; Make-Up Artist/Specialist; Permanent Cosmetics/Makeup and Tattooing; Salon/Beauty Salon Management/Manager.

Related SOC Job—39-5012 Hairdressers, Hairstylists, and Cosmetologists. **Related OOH Job**—Barbers, Cosmetologists, and Other Personal Appearance Workers. **Related DOT Jobs**—332.271-010 Cosmetologist; 332.271-014 Cosmetologist Apprentice; 332.271-018 Hair Stylist; 332.361-010 Wig Dresser; 339.361-010 Mortuary Beautician.

39-5091.00 Makeup Artists, Theatrical and Performance

- **Education/Training Required: Postsecondary vocational training**
- **Employed: 1,070**
- **Annual Earnings: $23,480**
- **Growth: 13.2%**
- **Annual Job Openings: Fewer than 500**

Apply makeup to performers to reflect period, setting, and situation of their role.

Analyze a script, noting events that affect each character's appearance, so that plans can be made for each scene. Apply makeup to enhance or alter the appearance of people appearing in productions such as movies. Assess performers' skin type to ensure that makeup will not cause breakouts or skin irritations. Attach prostheses to performers and apply makeup to create special features or effects such as scars, aging, or illness. Cleanse and tone the skin to prepare it for makeup application. Confer with stage or motion picture officials and performers in order to determine desired effects. Design rubber or plastic prostheses that can be used to change performers' appearances. Duplicate work precisely to replicate characters' appearances on a daily basis. Evaluate environmental characteristics such as venue size and lighting plans to determine makeup requirements. Alter or maintain makeup during productions as necessary to compensate for lighting changes or to achieve continuity of effect. Provide performers with makeup removal assistance after performances have been completed. Requisition or acquire needed materials for special effects, including wigs, beards, and special cosmetics. Select desired makeup shades from stock or mix oil, grease, and coloring to achieve specific color effects. Study production information such as character descriptions, period settings, and situations to determine makeup requirements. Write makeup sheets and take photos to document specific looks and the products that were used to achieve the looks. Advise hairdressers on the hairstyles required for character parts. Wash and reset wigs. Establish budgets and work within budgetary limits. Examine sketches, photographs, and plaster models in order to obtain desired character image depiction. Create character drawings or models, based upon independent research, in order to augment period production files. Demonstrate products to clients and provide instruction in makeup application.

GOE Information—Interest Area: 03. Arts and Communication. **Work Group:** 03.06. Drama. **Personality Type**—Artistic. Artistic occupations frequently involve working with forms, designs, and patterns. They often require self-expression, and the work can be done without following a clear set of rules. **Work Values—**Social Service; Creativity; Recognition; Ability Utilization; Achievement; Autonomy. **Skills—**None met the criteria. **Abilities—***Cognitive:* Originality; Visualization; Fluency of Ideas; Information Ordering; Memorization. *Psychomotor:* Arm-Hand Steadiness; Wrist-Finger Speed; Manual Dexterity; Finger Dexterity; Multilimb Coordination. *Physical:* Trunk Strength. *Sensory:* Visual Color Discrimination. **General Work Activities—***Information Input:* Getting Information; Identifying Objects, Actions, and Events; Monitoring Processes, Materials, or Surroundings. *Mental Process:* Thinking Creatively; Judging the Qualities of Things, Services, or Other People's Work; Organizing, Planning, and Prioritizing. *Work Output:* Handling and Moving Objects; Drafting and Specifying Technical Devices; Performing General Physical Activities. *Interacting with Others:* Assisting and Caring for Others; Communicating with Other Workers; Establishing and Maintaining Interpersonal Relationships. **Physical Work Conditions—**Indoors; More Often Standing Than Sitting; Using Hands on Objects, Tools, or Controls. **Other Job Characteristics—**Need to Be Exact or Accurate.

Experience—Job Zone 2. Some previous work-related skill, knowledge, or experience may be helpful in these occupations, but usually is not needed. **Job Preparation**—SVP 4.0 to less than 6.0—six months to less than two years. **Knowledges—**Fine Arts; Sociology and Anthropology. **Instructional Programs—**Cosmetology/ Cosmetologist, General; Makeup Artist/Specialist; Permanent Cosmetics/Makeup and Tattooing.

Related SOC Job—39-5091 Makeup Artists, Theatrical and Performance. **Related OOH Job**—Barbers, Cosmetologists, and Other Personal Appearance Workers. **Related DOT Jobs**—333.071-010 Make-Up Artist; 333.271-010 Body-Make-Up Artist.

39-5092.00 Manicurists and Pedicurists

- **Education/Training Required: Postsecondary vocational training**
- **Employed: 42,960**
- **Annual Earnings: $18,280**
- **Growth: 21.0%**
- **Annual Job Openings: 12,000**

Clean and shape customers' fingernails and toenails. May polish or decorate nails.

Clean and sanitize tools and work environment. Schedule client appointments and accept payments. Remove previously applied nail polish, using liquid remover and swabs. Clean customers' nails in soapy water, using swabs, files, and orange sticks. Shape and smooth ends of nails, using scissors, files, and emery boards. Apply undercoat and clear or colored polish onto nails with brush. Advise clients on nail care and use of products and colors. Assess the condition of clients' hands, remove dead skin from the hands, and massage them. Soften nail cuticles with water and oil; push back cuticles, using cuticle knife; and trim cuticles, using scissors or nippers. Brush powder and solvent onto nails and paper forms to maintain nail appearance and to extend nails; then remove forms and shape and smooth nail edges, using rotary abrasive wheel. Maintain supply inventories and records of client services. Treat nails to repair or improve strength and resilience by wrapping or provide treatment to nail biters. Roughen surfaces of fingernails, using abrasive wheel. Promote and sell nail care products. Attach paper forms to tips of customers' fingers to support and shape artificial nails. Polish nails, using powdered polish and buffer. Whiten underside of nails with white paste or pencil. Decorate clients' nails by piercing them or attaching ornaments or designs.

GOE Information—Interest Area: 09. Hospitality, Tourism, and Recreation. **Work Group:** 09.07. Barber and Beauty Services. **Personality Type—**Enterprising. Enterprising occupations frequently involve starting up and carrying out projects. These occupations can involve leading people and making many decisions. They sometimes require risk taking and often deal with business. **Work Values—**Social Service; Moral Values; Autonomy; Independence. **Skills—**Management of Financial Resources; Time Management. **Abilities—***Cognitive:* None met the criteria. *Psychomotor:* Arm-Hand Steadiness; Finger Dexterity; Manual Dexterity; Multilimb Coordination. *Physical:* None met the criteria. *Sensory:* Speech Recognition; Visual Color Discrimination. **General Work Activities—***Information Input:* Monitoring Processes, Materials, or Surroundings; Getting Information; Inspecting Equipment, Structures, or Materials. *Mental Process:* Organizing, Planning, and Prioritizing; Updating and Using Relevant Knowledge; Scheduling Work and Activities. *Work Output:* Handling and Moving Objects. *Interacting with Others:* Performing for or Working with the Public; Establishing and Maintaining Interpersonal Relationships; Assisting and Caring for Others. **Physical Work Conditions—**Indoors; Contaminants; Hazardous Conditions; Sitting; Using Hands on Objects, Tools, or Controls; Repetitive Motions. **Other Job Characteristics—**Need to Be Exact or Accurate; Repeat Same Tasks.

Experience—Job Zone 3. Previous work-related skill, knowledge, or experience is required. **Job Preparation—**SVP 6.0 to less than 7.0—more than one year and less than four years. **Knowledges—**Sales and Marketing; Chemistry; Customer and Personal Service. **Instructional Programs—**Cosmetology/Cosmetologist, General; Nail Technician/Specialist and Manicurist.

Related SOC Job—39-5092 Manicurists and Pedicurists. **Related OOH Job—**Barbers, Cosmetologists, and Other Personal Appearance Workers. **Related DOT Jobs—**331.674-010 Manicurist; 331.674-014 Fingernail Former.

39-5093.00 Shampooers

- **Education/Training Required: Short-term on-the-job training**
- **Employed: 16,040**
- **Annual Earnings: $15,570**
- **Growth: 13.1%**
- **Annual Job Openings: 5,000**

Shampoo and rinse customers' hair.

Massage, shampoo, and condition patron's hair and scalp to clean them and remove excess oil. Treat scalp conditions and hair loss, using specialized lotions, shampoos, or equipment such as infrared lamps or vibrating equipment. Advise patrons with chronic or potentially contagious scalp conditions to seek medical treatment. Maintain treatment records.

GOE Information—Interest Area: 09. Hospitality, Tourism, and Recreation. **Work Group:** 09.07. Barber and Beauty Services. **Note:** The Department of Labor has not collected some data for this job, so it has fewer details than the other descriptions.

Instructional Program—Hairstyling/Stylist and Hair Design.

Related SOC Job—39-5093 Shampooers. **Related OOH Job—**Barbers, Cosmetologists, and Other Personal Appearance Workers. **Related DOT Job—**332.271-010 Cosmetologist.

39-5094.00 Skin Care Specialists

- **Education/Training Required: Postsecondary vocational training**
- **Employed: 22,740**
- **Annual Earnings: $23,340**
- **Growth: 20.4%**
- **Annual Job Openings: 6,000**

Provide skin care treatments to face and body to enhance an individual's appearance.

Sterilize equipment and clean work areas. Keep records of client needs and preferences and the services provided. Demonstrate how to clean and care for skin properly and recommend skin-care regimens. Examine clients' skin, using magnifying lamps or visors when necessary, to evaluate skin condition and appearance. Select and apply cosmetic products such as creams, lotions, and tonics. Cleanse clients' skin with water, creams, or lotions. Treat the facial skin to maintain and improve its appearance, using specialized techniques and products such as peels and masks. Refer clients to medical personnel for treatment of serious skin problems. Determine which products or colors will improve clients' skin quality and appearance. Perform simple extractions to remove blackheads. Provide facial and body massages. Remove body and facial hair by applying wax. Apply chemical peels in order to reduce fine lines and age spots. Advise clients about colors and types of makeup and instruct them in makeup application techniques. Sell makeup to clients. Collaborate with plastic surgeons and dermatologists to provide patients with preoperative and postoperative skin care. Give manicures and pedicures and apply artificial nails. Tint eyelashes and eyebrows.

GOE Information—Interest Area: 09. Hospitality, Tourism, and Recreation. **Work Group:** 09.07. Barber and Beauty Services. **Personality Type—**No data available. **Work Values—**No data available. **Skills—**Service Orientation; Equipment Selection; Time Management; Equipment Maintenance; Social Perceptiveness; Science. **Abilities—***Cognitive:* Oral Expression; Originality; Category Flexibility; Inductive Reasoning; Fluency of Ideas; Oral Comprehension. *Psychomotor:* Arm-Hand Steadiness; Finger Dexterity; Manual Dexterity; Control Precision. *Physical:* None met the criteria. *Sensory:* Visual Color Discrimination; Near Vision; Speech Recognition. **General Work Activities—***Information Input:* Identifying Objects, Actions, and Events; Getting Information; Monitoring Processes, Materials, or Surroundings. *Mental Process:* Updating and Using Relevant Knowledge; Thinking Creatively; Organizing, Planning, and Prioritizing. *Work Output:* Handling and Moving Objects; Performing General Physical Activities;

Documenting or Recording Information. *Interacting with Others:* Establishing and Maintaining Interpersonal Relationships; Influencing Others or Selling; Assisting and Caring for Others. **Physical Work Conditions**—Indoors; Standing; Using Hands on Objects, Tools, or Controls; Bending or Twisting the Body; Repetitive Motions. **Other Job Characteristics**—Need to Be Exact or Accurate; Repeat Same Tasks.

Experience—Job Zone 3. Previous work-related skill, knowledge, or experience is required. **Job Preparation**—SVP 6.0 to less than 7.0— more than one year and less than four years. **Knowledges**—Sales and Marketing; Customer and Personal Service; Chemistry. **Instructional Programs**—Cosmetology/Cosmetologist, General; Facial Treatment Specialist/Facialist.

Related SOC Job—39-5094 Skin Care Specialists. **Related OOH Job**—Barbers, Cosmetologists, and Other Personal Appearance Workers. **Related DOT Job**—No data available.

39-6000 Transportation, Tourism, and Lodging Attendants

39-6011.00 Baggage Porters and Bellhops

- Education/Training Required: Short-term on-the-job training
- Employed: 51,300
- Annual Earnings: $17,590
- Growth: 14.0%
- Annual Job Openings: 5,000

Handle baggage for travelers at transportation terminals or for guests at hotels or similar establishments.

Transfer luggage, trunks, and packages to and from rooms, loading areas, vehicles, or transportation terminals by hand or using baggage carts. Supply guests or travelers with directions, travel information, and other information such as available services and points of interest. Receive and mark baggage by completing and attaching claim checks. Greet incoming guests and escort them to their rooms. Assist physically challenged travelers and other guests with special needs. Act as part of the security team at transportation terminals, hotels, or similar establishments. Deliver messages and room service orders and run errands for guests. Explain the operation of room features such as locks, ventilation systems, and televisions. Arrange for shipments of baggage, express mail, and parcels by providing weighing and billing services. Maintain clean lobbies or entrance areas for travelers or guests. Transport guests about premises and local areas or arrange for transportation. Compute and complete charge slips for services rendered and maintain records. Page guests in hotel lobbies, dining rooms, or other areas. Pick up and return items for laundry and valet service. Inspect guests' rooms to ensure that they are adequately stocked, orderly, and comfortable. Complete baggage insurance forms. Set up conference rooms, display tables, racks, or shelves and arrange merchandise displays for sales personnel.

GOE Information—Interest Area: 09. Hospitality, Tourism, and Recreation. **Work Group:** 09.03. Hospitality and Travel Services. **Personality Type**—Enterprising. Enterprising occupations frequently involve starting up and carrying out projects. These occupations can involve leading people and making many decisions. They sometimes require risk taking and often deal with business. **Work Values**—

Social Service; Independence; Supervision, Technical. **Skills**—Social Perceptiveness. **Abilities**—*Cognitive:* Selective Attention; Oral Expression. *Psychomotor:* Manual Dexterity; Multilimb Coordination. *Physical:* Static Strength; Stamina; Extent Flexibility; Gross Body Coordination; Dynamic Strength; Trunk Strength. *Sensory:* Speech Recognition. **General Work Activities**—*Information Input:* Identifying Objects, Actions, and Events; Monitoring Processes, Materials, or Surroundings; Getting Information. *Mental Process:* Processing Information; Updating and Using Relevant Knowledge; Judging the Qualities of Things, Services, or Other People's Work. *Work Output:* Handling and Moving Objects; Performing General Physical Activities. *Interacting with Others:* Performing for or Working with the Public; Establishing and Maintaining Interpersonal Relationships; Assisting and Caring for Others. **Physical Work Conditions**—Outdoors; Very Hot or Cold; Very Bright or Dim Lighting; Standing; Walking and Running; Repetitive Motions. **Other Job Characteristics**—Need to Be Exact or Accurate; Automation.

Experience—Job Zone 1. No previous work-related skill, knowledge, or experience is needed. **Job Preparation**—SVP below 4.0—less than six months. **Knowledges**—Transportation; Public Safety and Security. **Instructional Program**—No related CIP programs.

Related SOC Job—39-6011 Baggage Porters and Bellhops. **Related OOH Job**—Baggage Porters and Bellhops. **Related DOT Jobs**—324.477-010 Porter, Baggage; 324.677-010 Bellhop; 357.477-010 Baggage Checker; 357.677-010 Porter.

39-6012.00 Concierges

- Education/Training Required: Moderate-term on-the-job training
- Employed: 16,810
- Annual Earnings: $23,510
- Growth: 16.0%
- Annual Job Openings: 2,000

Assist patrons at hotel, apartment, or office building with personal services. May take messages; arrange or give advice on transportation, business services, or entertainment; or monitor guest requests for housekeeping and maintenance.

Make dining and other reservations for patrons and obtain tickets for events. Provide information about local features such as shopping, dining, nightlife, and recreational destinations. Make travel arrangements for sightseeing and other tours. Receive, store, and deliver luggage and mail. Perform office duties on a temporary basis when needed. Pick up and deliver items or run errands for guests. Carry out unusual requests such as searching for hard-to-find items and arranging for exotic services such as hot-air balloon rides. Arrange for the replacement of items lost by travelers. Arrange for interpreters or translators when patrons require such services. Plan special events, parties, and meetings, which may include booking musicians or celebrities to appear.

GOE Information—Interest Area: 09. Hospitality, Tourism, and Recreation. **Work Group:** 09.03. Hospitality and Travel Services. **Personality Type**—No data available. **Work Values**—No data available. **Skills**—Service Orientation; Management of Personnel Resources; Social Perceptiveness; Persuasion; Critical Thinking; Learning Strategies. **Abilities**—*Cognitive:* Memorization; Fluency of Ideas; Oral Expression; Originality; Oral Comprehension. *Psychomotor:* None met the criteria. *Physical:* Trunk Strength. *Sensory:* Speech Recognition; Speech Clarity. **General Work Activities**—*Information Input:* Identifying Objects, Actions, and Events; Getting

Information; Monitoring Processes, Materials, or Surroundings. *Mental Process:* Updating and Using Relevant Knowledge; Organizing, Planning, and Prioritizing; Judging the Qualities of Things, Services, or Other People's Work. *Work Output:* Documenting or Recording Information; Interacting With Computers; Handling and Moving Objects. *Interacting with Others:* Performing for or Working with the Public; Establishing and Maintaining Interpersonal Relationships; Communicating with Persons Outside Organization. **Physical Work Conditions**—Indoors; Noisy; Standing; Repetitive Motions. **Other Job Characteristics**—Need to Be Exact or Accurate; Repeat Same Tasks.

Experience—Job Zone 2. Some previous work-related skill, knowledge, or experience may be helpful in these occupations, but usually is not needed. **Job Preparation**—SVP 4.0 to less than 6.0—six months to less than two years. **Knowledges**—Customer and Personal Service; Philosophy and Theology; Clerical Practices; Psychology; Communications and Media; Public Safety and Security. **Instructional Program**—No related CIP programs.

Related SOC Job—39-6012 Concierges. **Related OOH Job**—Concierges. **Related DOT Job**—No data available.

39-6021.00 Tour Guides and Escorts

- **Education/Training Required: Moderate-term on-the-job training**
- **Employed: 28,320**
- **Annual Earnings: $19,990**
- **Growth: 16.6%**
- **Annual Job Openings: 5,000**

Escort individuals or groups on sightseeing tours or through places of interest such as industrial establishments, public buildings, and art galleries.

Conduct educational activities for schoolchildren. Escort individuals or groups on cruises; on sightseeing tours; or through places of interest such as industrial establishments, public buildings, and art galleries. Describe tour points of interest to group members and respond to questions. Monitor visitors' activities to ensure compliance with establishment or tour regulations and safety practices. Greet and register visitors and issue any required identification badges or safety devices. Distribute brochures, show audiovisual presentations, and explain establishment processes and operations at tour sites. Provide directions and other pertinent information to visitors. Provide for physical safety of groups, performing such activities as providing first aid and directing emergency evacuations. Research environmental conditions and clients' skill and ability levels to plan expeditions, instruction, and commentary that are appropriate. Provide information about wildlife varieties and habitats, as well as any relevant regulations, such as those pertaining to hunting and fishing. Collect fees and tickets from group members. Teach skills, such as proper climbing methods, and demonstrate and advise on the use of equipment. Select travel routes and sites to be visited based on knowledge of specific areas. Solicit tour patronage and sell souvenirs. Speak foreign languages to communicate with foreign visitors. Assemble and check the required supplies and equipment prior to departure. Perform clerical duties such as filing, typing, operating switchboards, and routing mail and messages. Drive motor vehicles to transport visitors to establishments and tour site locations.

GOE Information—**Interest Area:** 09. Hospitality, Tourism, and Recreation. **Work Group:** 09.03. Hospitality and Travel Services. **Personality Type**—Social. Social occupations frequently involve working with, communicating with, and teaching people. These occupations often involve helping or providing service to others. **Work Values**—Social Service; Authority; Variety; Supervision, Technical. **Skills**—Speaking; Reading Comprehension; Active Listening; Social Perceptiveness. **Abilities**—*Cognitive:* Oral Expression; Memorization. *Psychomotor:* None met the criteria. *Physical:* Trunk Strength. *Sensory:* Speech Recognition; Speech Clarity; Far Vision. **General Work Activities**—*Information Input:* Getting Information; Identifying Objects, Actions, and Events; Monitoring Processes, Materials, or Surroundings. *Mental Process:* Updating and Using Relevant Knowledge; Thinking Creatively; Organizing, Planning, and Prioritizing. *Work Output:* Handling and Moving Objects; Performing General Physical Activities. *Interacting with Others:* Performing for or Working with the Public; Establishing and Maintaining Interpersonal Relationships; Communicating with Persons Outside Organization. **Physical Work Conditions**—Standing. **Other Job Characteristics**—Need to Be Exact or Accurate.

Experience—Job Zone 3. Previous work-related skill, knowledge, or experience is required. **Job Preparation**—SVP 6.0 to less than 7.0—more than one year and less than four years. **Knowledges**—History and Archeology; Fine Arts; Philosophy and Theology; Sociology and Anthropology; Customer and Personal Service; Communications and Media. **Instructional Program**—Tourism and Travel Services Management.

Related SOC Job—39-6021 Tour Guides and Escorts. **Related OOH Job**—Tour Guides and Escorts. **Related DOT Jobs**—109.367-010 Museum Attendant; 353.363-010 Guide, Sightseeing; 353.367-010 Guide; 353.367-014 Guide, Establishment; 353.367-018 Guide, Plant; 353.367-022 Page; 353.667-010 Escort.

39-6022.00 Travel Guides

- **Education/Training Required: Moderate-term on-the-job training**
- **Employed: 3,120**
- **Annual Earnings: $29,240**
- **Growth: 9.6%**
- **Annual Job Openings: 1,000**

Plan, organize, and conduct long-distance cruises, tours, and expeditions for individuals and groups.

Verify amounts and quality of equipment prior to expeditions or tours. Arrange for tour or expedition details such as accommodations, transportation, equipment, and the availability of medical personnel. Attend to special needs of tour participants. Give advice on sightseeing and shopping. Lead individuals or groups to tour site locations and describe points of interest. Plan tour itineraries, applying knowledge of travel routes and destination sites. Administer first aid to injured group participants. Pilot airplanes or drive land and water vehicles to transport tourists to activity/tour sites. Explain hunting and fishing laws to groups to ensure compliance. Instruct novices in climbing techniques, mountaineering, and wilderness survival and demonstrate use of hunting, fishing, and climbing equipment. Evaluate services received on the tour and report findings to tour organizers. Pay bills and record checks issued. Provide tourists with assistance in obtaining permits and documents such as visas, passports, and health certificates and in converting currency. Set up camps and prepare meals for tour group members. Sell or rent equipment, clothing, and supplies related to expeditions. Resolve any problems with itineraries, service, or accommodations. Sell travel packages.

GOE Information—Interest Area: 09. Hospitality, Tourism, and Recreation. **Work Group:** 09.03. Hospitality and Travel Services. **Personality Type**—Enterprising. Enterprising occupations frequently involve starting up and carrying out projects. These occupations can involve leading people and making many decisions. They sometimes require risk taking and often deal with business. **Work Values**— Social Service; Variety; Creativity; Autonomy; Authority; Recognition. **Skills**—Management of Material Resources; Service Orientation; Operation and Control. **Abilities**—*Cognitive:* Spatial Orientation; Memorization; Time Sharing; Mathematical Reasoning; Oral Comprehension; Number Facility. *Psychomotor:* Reaction Time; Rate Control; Response Orientation; Multilimb Coordination. *Physical:* Stamina; Explosive Strength; Gross Body Coordination; Trunk Strength; Static Strength. *Sensory:* Glare Sensitivity; Night Vision; Peripheral Vision; Auditory Attention; Depth Perception; Speech Clarity. **General Work Activities**—*Information Input:* Getting Information; Identifying Objects, Actions, and Events; Estimating the Needed Characteristics of Products, Events, or Information. *Mental Process:* Scheduling Work and Activities; Organizing, Planning, and Prioritizing; Making Decisions and Solving Problems. *Work Output:* Performing General Physical Activities; Operating Vehicles or Equipment; Handling and Moving Objects. *Interacting with Others:* Performing for or Working with the Public; Assisting and Caring for Others; Communicating with Persons Outside Organization. **Physical Work Conditions**—More Often Outdoors Than Indoors; More Often Standing Than Sitting; Walking and Running. **Other Job Characteristics**—None met the criteria.

Experience—Job Zone 2. Some previous work-related skill, knowledge, or experience may be helpful in these occupations, but usually is not needed. **Job Preparation**—SVP 4.0 to less than 6.0—six months to less than two years. **Knowledges**—Geography; Transportation; Medicine and Dentistry; Sales and Marketing; Communications and Media; Customer and Personal Service. **Instructional Program**—Selling Skills and Sales Operations.

Related SOC Job—39-6022 Travel Guides. **Related OOH Job**—Travel Guides. **Related DOT Jobs**—353.161-010 Guide, Hunting and Fishing; 353.164-010 Guide, Alpine; 353.167-010 Guide, Travel; 353.364-010 Dude Wrangler.

39-6031.00 Flight Attendants

- Education/Training Required: Long-term on-the-job training
- Employed: 99,590
- Annual Earnings: $46,680
- Growth: 16.3%
- Annual Job Openings: 7,000

Provide personal services to ensure the safety and comfort of airline passengers during flight. Greet passengers, verify tickets, explain use of safety equipment, and serve food or beverages.

Direct and assist passengers in the event of an emergency, such as directing passengers to evacuate a plane following an emergency landing. Announce and demonstrate safety and emergency procedures such as the use of oxygen masks, seat belts, and life jackets. Walk aisles of planes to verify that passengers have complied with federal regulations prior to takeoffs and landings. Verify that first aid kits and other emergency equipment, including fire extinguishers and oxygen bottles, are in working order. Administer first aid to passengers in distress. Attend preflight briefings concerning weather, altitudes, routes, emergency procedures, crew coordination, lengths of flights, food and beverage services offered, and numbers of passengers. Prepare passengers and aircraft for landing, following

procedures. Determine special assistance needs of passengers such as small children, the elderly, or disabled persons. Check to ensure that food, beverages, blankets, reading material, emergency equipment, and other supplies are aboard and are in adequate supply. Reassure passengers when situations such as turbulence are encountered. Announce flight delays and descent preparations. Inspect passenger tickets to verify information and to obtain destination information. Answer passengers' questions about flights, aircraft, weather, travel routes and services, arrival times, and schedules. Assist passengers while entering or disembarking the aircraft. Inspect and clean cabins, checking for any problems and making sure that cabins are in order. Greet passengers boarding aircraft and direct them to assigned seats. Conduct periodic trips through the cabin to ensure passenger comfort and to distribute reading material, headphones, pillows, playing cards, and blankets. Take inventory of headsets, alcoholic beverages, and money collected. Operate audio and video systems. Assist passengers in placing carry-on luggage in overhead, garment, or underseat storage. Prepare reports showing places of departure and destination, passenger ticket numbers, meal and beverage inventories, the conditions of cabin equipment, and any problems encountered by passengers.

GOE Information—Interest Area: 09. Hospitality, Tourism, and Recreation. **Work Group:** 09.03. Hospitality and Travel Services. **Personality Type**—Enterprising. Enterprising occupations frequently involve starting up and carrying out projects. These occupations can involve leading people and making many decisions. They sometimes require risk taking and often deal with business. **Work Values**— Social Service; Supervision, Technical; Co-workers; Supervision, Human Relations; Company Policies and Practices; Compensation. **Skills**—Service Orientation; Social Perceptiveness; Critical Thinking; Reading Comprehension; Negotiation; Coordination. **Abilities**— *Cognitive:* Selective Attention; Flexibility of Closure; Perceptual Speed; Oral Expression; Problem Sensitivity; Speed of Closure. *Psychomotor:* Speed of Limb Movement; Multilimb Coordination; Manual Dexterity; Arm-Hand Steadiness; Finger Dexterity. *Physical:* Gross Body Equilibrium; Extent Flexibility; Gross Body Coordination; Stamina; Static Strength; Trunk Strength. *Sensory:* Auditory Attention; Speech Clarity; Speech Recognition; Far Vision; Visual Color Discrimination; Depth Perception. **General Work Activities**—*Information Input:* Monitoring Processes, Materials, or Surroundings; Inspecting Equipment, Structures, or Materials; Identifying Objects, Actions, and Events. *Mental Process:* Making Decisions and Solving Problems; Updating and Using Relevant Knowledge; Evaluating Information Against Standards. *Work Output:* Handling and Moving Objects; Performing General Physical Activities; Documenting or Recording Information. *Interacting with Others:* Performing for or Working with the Public; Assisting and Caring for Others; Resolving Conflicts and Negotiating with Others. **Physical Work Conditions**—Indoors; Noisy; Contaminants; Disease or Infections; High Places; Standing. **Other Job Characteristics**— Errors Have Important Consequences; Need to Be Exact or Accurate.

Experience—Job Zone 2. Some previous work-related skill, knowledge, or experience may be helpful in these occupations, but usually is not needed. **Job Preparation**—SVP 4.0 to less than 6.0—six months to less than two years. **Knowledges**—Customer and Personal Service; Psychology; Transportation; Geography; Philosophy and Theology; Public Safety and Security. **Instructional Program**—Airline Flight Attendant.

Related SOC Job—39-6031 Flight Attendants. **Related OOH Job**— Flight Attendants. **Related DOT Jobs**—352.367-010 Airplane-Flight Attendant; 352.367-014 Flight Attendant, Ramp.

39-6032.00 Transportation Attendants, Except Flight Attendants and Baggage Porters

- **Education/Training Required:** Short-term on-the-job training
- **Employed:** 24,810
- **Annual Earnings:** $19,290
- **Growth:** 15.9%
- **Annual Job Openings:** 2,000

Provide services to ensure the safety and comfort of passengers aboard ships, buses, or trains or within the station or terminal. Perform duties such as greeting passengers, explaining the use of safety equipment, serving meals or beverages, or answering questions related to travel.

Distribute sports and game equipment, magazines, newspapers, pillows, blankets, and other items to passengers and guests. Provide customers with information on routes, gates, prices, timetables, or terminals and concourses. Provide boarding assistance to elderly, sick, or injured people. Issue and collect passenger boarding passes and transfers, tearing or punching tickets as necessary to prevent reuse. Greet passengers boarding transportation equipment and announce routes and stops. Explain and demonstrate safety procedures and safety equipment use. Determine or facilitate seating arrangements. Count and verify tickets and seat reservations and record numbers of passengers boarding and disembarking. Collect fares from passengers and provide change in return. Transport baggage or coordinate transportation between assigned rooms, terminals, or platforms. Serve food and beverages. Perform equipment safety checks prior to departure. Inspect kitchens and dining areas to ensure adherence to sanitation requirements. Clean rooms and bathroom facilities, change linens, and replenish supplies in washrooms. Adjust window shades and seat cushions at the request of passengers. Signal transportation operators to stop or to proceed. Respond to passengers' questions, requests, or complaints. Open and close doors for passengers.

GOE Information—Interest Area: 09. Hospitality, Tourism, and Recreation. **Work Group:** 09.03. Hospitality and Travel Services. **Personality Type**—Enterprising. Enterprising occupations frequently involve starting up and carrying out projects. These occupations can involve leading people and making many decisions. They sometimes require risk taking and often deal with business. **Work Values**—Social Service; Supervision, Technical; Co-workers; Security. **Skills**—Service Orientation. **Abilities**—*Cognitive:* Memorization. *Psychomotor:* Reaction Time. *Physical:* Gross Body Equilibrium; Static Strength; Extent Flexibility. *Sensory:* None met the criteria. **General Work Activities**—*Information Input:* Monitoring Processes, Materials, or Surroundings; Getting Information; Inspecting Equipment, Structures, or Materials. *Mental Process:* Organizing, Planning, and Prioritizing; Analyzing Data or Information; Scheduling Work and Activities. *Work Output:* Performing General Physical Activities; Handling and Moving Objects; Documenting or Recording Information. *Interacting with Others:* Performing for or Working with the Public; Assisting and Caring for Others; Establishing and Maintaining Interpersonal Relationships. **Physical Work Conditions**—Indoors; Standing; Walking and Running; Bending or Twisting the Body. **Other Job Characteristics**—None met the criteria.

Experience—Job Zone 1. No previous work-related skill, knowledge, or experience is needed. **Job Preparation**—SVP below 4.0—less than six months. **Knowledges**—Customer and Personal Service; Transportation. **Instructional Program**—Selling Skills and Sales Operations.

Related SOC Job—39-6032 Transportation Attendants, Except Flight Attendants and Baggage Porters. **Related OOH Job**—Transportation Attendants, Except Flight Attendants and Baggage Porters. **Related DOT Jobs**—350.677-014 Passenger Attendant; 350.677-018 Steward/Stewardess, Bath; 350.677-022 Steward/Stewardess; 351.677-010 Service Attendant, Sleeping Car; 352.577-010 Bus Attendant; 352.677-010 Passenger Service Representative I; 910.367-026 Passenger Representative; 910.667-014 Conductor; 910.677-010 Passenger Service Representative II.

39-9000 Other Personal Care and Service Workers

39-9011.00 Child Care Workers

- **Education/Training Required:** Short-term on-the-job training
- **Employed:** 557,680
- **Annual Earnings:** $17,050
- **Growth:** 13.8%
- **Annual Job Openings:** 439,000

The job openings listed here are shared with 39-9011.01 Nannies.

Attend to children at schools, businesses, private households, and child care institutions. Perform a variety of tasks, such as dressing, feeding, bathing, and overseeing play.

Support children's emotional and social development, encouraging understanding of others and positive self-concepts. Care for children in institutional setting, such as group homes, nursery schools, private businesses, or schools for the handicapped. Sanitize toys and play equipment. Discipline children and recommend or initiate other measures to control behavior, such as caring for own clothing and picking up toys and books. Identify signs of emotional or developmental problems in children and bring them to parents' or guardians' attention. Observe and monitor children's play activities. Keep records on individual children, including daily observations and information about activities, meals served, and medications administered. Instruct children in health and personal habits such as eating, resting, and toilet habits. Read to children and teach them simple painting, drawing, handicrafts, and songs. Organize and participate in recreational activities, such as games. Assist in preparing food for children, serve meals and refreshments to children, and regulate rest periods. Organize and store toys and materials to ensure order in activity areas. Operate in-house daycare centers within businesses. Sterilize bottles and prepare formulas. Provide counseling or therapy to mentally disturbed, delinquent, or handicapped children. Dress children and change diapers. Help children with homework and school work. Perform housekeeping duties such as laundry, cleaning, dishwashing, and changing of linens. Accompany children to and from school, on outings, and to medical appointments. Place or hoist children into baths or pools.

GOE Information—Interest Area: 10. Human Service. **Work Group:** 10.03. Child/Personal Care and Services. **Personality Type**—Social. Social occupations frequently involve working with, communicating with, and teaching people. These occupations often involve helping or providing service to others. **Work Values**—Social Service; Activity; Variety; Co-workers; Authority; Security. **Skills**—Negotiation; Social Perceptiveness; Learning Strategies; Service Orientation; Persuasion; Monitoring. **Abilities**—*Cognitive:* Fluency of Ideas; Originality; Time Sharing; Flexibility of Closure; Inductive Reasoning; Problem Sensitivity. *Psychomotor:* None met the criteria. *Physical:* Extent

Flexibility; Static Strength; Trunk Strength. *Sensory:* Hearing Sensitivity; Speech Recognition; Speech Clarity; Far Vision. **General Work Activities**—*Information Input:* Monitoring Processes, Materials, or Surroundings; Getting Information; Identifying Objects, Actions, and Events. *Mental Process:* Organizing, Planning, and Prioritizing; Thinking Creatively; Making Decisions and Solving Problems. *Work Output:* Performing General Physical Activities; Documenting or Recording Information. *Interacting with Others:* Assisting and Caring for Others; Establishing and Maintaining Interpersonal Relationships; Communicating with Other Workers. **Physical Work Conditions**—Indoors; Noisy; Disease or Infections; Standing. **Other Job Characteristics**—Need to Be Exact or Accurate.

Experience—Job Zone 2. Some previous work-related skill, knowledge, or experience may be helpful in these occupations, but usually is not needed. **Job Preparation**—SVP 4.0 to less than 6.0—six months to less than two years. **Knowledges**—Sociology and Anthropology; Psychology; Public Safety and Security. **Instructional Program**—Child Care Provider/Assistant.

Related SOC Job—39-9011 Child Care Workers. **Related OOH Job**—Child Care Workers. **Related DOT Jobs**—099.227-010 Children's Tutor; 301.677-010 Child Monitor; 309.677-014 Foster Parent; 355.674-010 Child-Care Attendant, School; 359.342-540 Child Care Development Specialist; 359.677-010 Attendant, Children's Institution; 359.677-018 Nursery School Attendant; 359.677-026 Playroom Attendant.

39-9011.01 Nannies

- **Education/Training Required: Short-term on-the-job training**
- **Employed: 557,680**
- **Annual Earnings: $17,050**
- **Growth: 13.8%**
- **Annual Job Openings: 439,000**

The job openings listed here are shared with 39-9011.00 Child Care Workers.

Care for children in private households and provide support and expertise to parents in satisfying children's physical, emotional, intellectual, and social needs. Duties may include meal planning and preparation, laundry and clothing care, organization of play activities and outings, discipline, intellectual stimulation, language activities, and transportation.

Perform first aid or CPR when required. Regulate children's rest periods and nap schedules. Meet regularly with parents to discuss children's activities and development. Help prepare and serve nutritionally balanced meals and snacks for children. Instruct children in safe behavior, such as seeking adult assistance when crossing the street and avoiding contact or play with unsafe objects. Organize and conduct age-appropriate recreational activities, such as games, arts and crafts, sports, walks, and play dates. Observe children's behavior for irregularities, take temperature, transport children to doctor, or administer medications as directed to maintain children's health. Model appropriate social behaviors and encourage concern for others to cultivate development of interpersonal relationships and communication skills. Work with parents to develop and implement discipline programs to promote desirable child behavior. Help develop or monitor family schedule. Supervise and assist with homework. Assign appropriate chores and praise targeted behaviors to encourage development of self-control, self-confidence, and responsibility. Transport children to schools, social outings, and medical appointments. Perform housekeeping and cleaning duties related to children's care. Instruct and assist children in the development of

health and personal habits, such as eating, resting, and toilet behavior. Keep records of play, meal schedules, and bill payment. Teach and perform age-appropriate activities such as lap play, reading, and arts and crafts to encourage intellectual development of children. Remove hazards and develop appropriate boundaries and rules to create a safe environment for children.

GOE Information—**Interest Area:** 10. Human Service. **Work Group:** 10.03. Child/Personal Care and Services. **Personality Type**—Social. Social occupations frequently involve working with, communicating with, and teaching people. These occupations often involve helping or providing service to others. **Work Values**—No data available. **Skills**—Negotiation; Management of Financial Resources; Social Perceptiveness; Time Management; Persuasion; Instructing. **Abilities**—*Cognitive:* Spatial Orientation; Fluency of Ideas; Flexibility of Closure; Originality; Memorization; Problem Sensitivity. *Psychomotor:* Response Orientation; Multilimb Coordination; Arm-Hand Steadiness; Control Precision; Manual Dexterity. *Physical:* Extent Flexibility; Static Strength; Gross Body Coordination; Stamina; Trunk Strength. *Sensory:* Peripheral Vision; Hearing Sensitivity; Speech Recognition; Depth Perception; Auditory Attention; Far Vision. **General Work Activities**—*Information Input:* Identifying Objects, Actions, and Events; Getting Information; Monitoring Processes, Materials, or Surroundings. *Mental Process:* Organizing, Planning, and Prioritizing; Updating and Using Relevant Knowledge; Scheduling Work and Activities. *Work Output:* Handling and Moving Objects; Performing General Physical Activities; Operating Vehicles or Equipment. *Interacting with Others:* Assisting and Caring for Others; Establishing and Maintaining Interpersonal Relationships; Coaching and Developing Others. **Physical Work Conditions**—More Often Indoors Than Outdoors; Disease or Infections; Standing; Using Hands on Objects, Tools, or Controls. **Other Job Characteristics**—Errors Have Important Consequences; Need to Be Exact or Accurate.

Experience—Job Zone 3. Previous work-related skill, knowledge, or experience is required. **Job Preparation**—SVP 6.0 to less than 7.0—more than one year and less than four years. **Knowledges**—Philosophy and Theology; Medicine and Dentistry; Geography; Therapy and Counseling; Sociology and Anthropology; Psychology. **Instructional Program**—No related CIP programs.

Related SOC Job—39-9011 Child Care Workers. **Related OOH Job**—Child Care Workers. **Related DOT Job**—No data available.

39-9021.00 Personal and Home Care Aides

- **Education/Training Required: Short-term on-the-job training**
- **Employed: 566,860**
- **Annual Earnings: $17,340**
- **Growth: 41.0%**
- **Annual Job Openings: 230,000**

Assist elderly or disabled adults with daily living activities at the person's home or in a daytime non-residential facility. Duties performed at a place of residence may include keeping house (making beds, doing laundry, washing dishes) and preparing meals. May provide meals and supervised activities at non-residential care facilities. May advise families, the elderly, and disabled on such things as nutrition, cleanliness, and household utilities.

Perform health care–related tasks, such as monitoring vital signs and medication, under the direction of registered nurses and physiotherapists. Administer bedside and personal care, such as ambulation and personal hygiene assistance. Prepare and maintain records of client progress and services performed, reporting changes in client condition to manager or supervisor. Perform housekeeping duties, such as cooking, cleaning, washing clothes and dishes, and running errands. Care for individuals and families during periods of incapacitation, family disruption, or convalescence, providing companionship, personal care, and help in adjusting to new lifestyles. Instruct and advise clients on issues such as household cleanliness, utilities, hygiene, nutrition, and infant care. Plan, shop for, and prepare nutritious meals or assist families in planning, shopping for, and preparing nutritious meals. Participate in case reviews, consulting with the team caring for the client, to evaluate the client's needs and plan for continuing services. Transport clients to locations outside the home, such as to physicians' offices or on outings, using a motor vehicle. Train family members to provide bedside care. Provide clients with communication assistance, typing their correspondence and obtaining information for them.

GOE Information—Interest Area: 10. Human Service. **Work Group:** 10.03. Child/Personal Care and Services. **Personality Type**—Social. Social occupations frequently involve working with, communicating with, and teaching people. These occupations often involve helping or providing service to others. **Work Values**—Social Service; Authority; Variety; Independence; Supervision, Technical. **Skills**—Social Perceptiveness; Persuasion; Service Orientation; Learning Strategies; Monitoring; Coordination. **Abilities**—*Cognitive:* Problem Sensitivity; Oral Comprehension; Oral Expression. *Psychomotor:* Control Precision; Multilimb Coordination; Arm-Hand Steadiness. *Physical:* Static Strength; Trunk Strength; Stamina; Extent Flexibility. *Sensory:* Speech Recognition; Depth Perception; Speech Clarity; Far Vision. **General Work Activities**—*Information Input:* Monitoring Processes, Materials, or Surroundings; Identifying Objects, Actions, and Events; Getting Information. *Mental Process:* Making Decisions and Solving Problems; Organizing, Planning, and Prioritizing; Updating and Using Relevant Knowledge. *Work Output:* Documenting or Recording Information; Performing General Physical Activities. *Interacting with Others:* Assisting and Caring for Others; Establishing and Maintaining Interpersonal Relationships; Communicating with Other Workers. **Physical Work Conditions**—Disease or Infections; Standing. **Other Job Characteristics**—Errors Have Important Consequences; Need to Be Exact or Accurate.

Experience—Job Zone 2. Some previous work-related skill, knowledge, or experience may be helpful in these occupations, but usually is not needed. **Job Preparation**—SVP 4.0 to less than 6.0—six months to less than two years. **Knowledges**—Customer and Personal Service. **Instructional Program**—No related CIP programs.

Related SOC Job—39-9021 Personal and Home Care Aides. **Related OOH Job**—Personal and Home Care Aides. **Related DOT Jobs**—309.354-010 Homemaker; 309.674-014 Personal Attendant; 309.677-010 Companion; 359.573-010 Blind Aide.

39-9031.00 Fitness Trainers and Aerobics Instructors

- **Education/Training Required: Postsecondary vocational training**
- **Employed: 189,220**
- **Annual Earnings: $25,840**
- **Growth: 27.1%**
- **Annual Job Openings: 50,000**

Instruct or coach groups or individuals in exercise activities and the fundamentals of sports. Demonstrate techniques and methods of participa-
tion. Observe participants and inform them of corrective measures necessary to improve their skills.

Explain and enforce safety rules and regulations governing sports, recreational activities, and the use of exercise equipment. Offer alternatives during classes to accommodate different levels of fitness. Plan routines, choose appropriate music, and choose different movements for each set of muscles, depending on participants' capabilities and limitations. Observe participants and inform them of corrective measures necessary for skill improvement. Teach proper breathing techniques used during physical exertion. Teach and demonstrate use of gymnastic and training equipment such as trampolines and weights. Instruct participants in maintaining exertion levels to maximize benefits from exercise routines. Maintain fitness equipment. Conduct therapeutic, recreational, or athletic activities. Monitor participants' progress and adapt programs as needed. Evaluate individuals' abilities, needs, and physical conditions and develop suitable training programs to meet any special requirements. Plan physical education programs to promote development of participants' physical attributes and social skills. Provide students with information and resources regarding nutrition, weight control, and lifestyle issues. Administer emergency first aid, wrap injuries, treat minor chronic disabilities, or refer injured persons to physicians. Advise clients about proper clothing and shoes. Wrap ankles, fingers, wrists, or other body parts with synthetic skin, gauze, or adhesive tape to support muscles and ligaments. Teach individual and team sports to participants through instruction and demonstration, utilizing knowledge of sports techniques and of participants' physical capabilities. Promote health clubs through membership sales and record member information. Organize, lead, and referee indoor and outdoor games such as volleyball, baseball, and basketball. Maintain equipment inventories and select, store, or issue equipment as needed. Organize and conduct competitions and tournaments. Advise participants in use of heat or ultraviolet treatments and hot baths. Massage body parts to relieve soreness, strains, and bruises.

GOE Information—Interest Area: 05. Education and Training. **Work Group:** 05.06. Counseling, Health, and Fitness Education. **Personality Type**—Social. Social occupations frequently involve working with, communicating with, and teaching people. These occupations often involve helping or providing service to others. **Work Values**—Creativity; Authority; Social Service; Responsibility; Achievement; Social Status. **Skills**—Instructing; Equipment Selection; Monitoring; Service Orientation; Coordination; Social Perceptiveness. **Abilities**—*Cognitive:* Originality; Memorization; Fluency of Ideas; Oral Expression; Deductive Reasoning. *Psychomotor:* Speed of Limb Movement; Multilimb Coordination. *Physical:* Stamina; Gross Body Coordination; Dynamic Strength; Dynamic Flexibility; Static Strength; Extent Flexibility. *Sensory:* Speech Clarity. **General Work Activities**—*Information Input:* Monitoring Processes, Materials, or Surroundings; Identifying Objects, Actions, and Events; Getting Information. *Mental Process:* Updating and Using Relevant Knowledge; Thinking Creatively; Making Decisions and Solving Problems. *Work Output:* Performing General Physical Activities; Handling and Moving Objects; Documenting or Recording Information. *Interacting with Others:* Coaching and Developing Others; Performing for or Working with the Public; Assisting and Caring for Others. **Physical Work Conditions**—Indoors; Standing; Walking and Running; Repetitive Motions. **Other Job Characteristics**—None met the criteria.

Experience—Job Zone 3. Previous work-related skill, knowledge, or experience is required. **Job Preparation**—SVP 6.0 to less than 7.0—more than one year and less than four years. **Knowledges**—Customer and Personal Service; Psychology; Education and Training; Sociology and Anthropology; Sales and Marketing; Personnel and Human Resources. **Instructional Programs**—Health and Physical Education, General; Physical Education Teaching and Coaching; Sport and Fitness Administration/Management.

Related SOC Job—39-9031 Fitness Trainers and Aerobics Instructors. **Related OOH Job**—Fitness Workers. **Related DOT Jobs**—099.224-010 Instructor, Physical Education; 153.227-014 Instructor, Physical; 153.227-018 Instructor, Sports.

39-9032.00 Recreation Workers

- **Education/Training Required: Bachelor's degree**
- **Employed: 264,840**
- **Annual Earnings: $20,110**
- **Growth: 17.3%**
- **Annual Job Openings: 69,000**

Conduct recreation activities with groups in public, private, or volunteer agencies or recreation facilities. Organize and promote activities such as arts and crafts, sports, games, music, dramatics, social recreation, camping, and hobbies, taking into account the needs and interests of individual members.

Enforce rules and regulations of recreational facilities to maintain discipline and ensure safety. Organize, lead, and promote interest in recreational activities such as arts, crafts, sports, games, camping, and hobbies. Manage the daily operations of recreational facilities. Administer first aid according to prescribed procedures and notify emergency medical personnel when necessary. Ascertain and interpret group interests, evaluate equipment and facilities, and adapt activities to meet participant needs. Greet new arrivals to activities, introducing them to other participants, explaining facility rules, and encouraging participation. Complete and maintain time and attendance forms and inventory lists. Explain principles, techniques, and safety procedures to participants in recreational activities and demonstrate use of materials and equipment. Evaluate recreation areas, facilities, and services to determine if they are producing desired results. Confer with management to discuss and resolve participant complaints. Supervise and coordinate the work activities of personnel, such as training staff members and assigning work duties. Meet and collaborate with agency personnel, community organizations, and other professional personnel to plan balanced recreational programs for participants. Schedule maintenance and use of facilities. Direct special activities or events such as aquatics, gymnastics, or performing arts. Meet with staff to discuss rules, regulations, and work-related problems. Provide for entertainment and set up related decorations and equipment. Encourage participants to develop their own activities and leadership skills through group discussions. Serve as liaison between park or recreation administrators and activity instructors. Evaluate staff performance, recording evaluations on appropriate forms. Oversee the purchase, planning, design, construction, and upkeep of recreation facilities and areas.

GOE Information—**Interest Area:** 09. Hospitality, Tourism, and Recreation. **Work Group:** 09.02. Recreational Services. **Personality Type**—Social. Social occupations frequently involve working with, communicating with, and teaching people. These occupations often involve helping or providing service to others. **Work Values**—Social Service; Creativity; Autonomy; Co-workers; Authority; Variety. **Skills**—Management of Financial Resources; Management of Personnel Resources; Service Orientation; Management of Material Resources; Social Perceptiveness; Time Management. **Abilities**—*Cognitive:* Memorization; Originality; Time Sharing; Fluency of Ideas; Information Ordering; Oral Expression. *Psychomotor:* Multilimb

Coordination. *Physical:* Trunk Strength. *Sensory:* Speech Clarity; Speech Recognition; Far Vision. **General Work Activities**—*Information Input:* Getting Information; Identifying Objects, Actions, and Events; Monitoring Processes, Materials, or Surroundings. *Mental Process:* Organizing, Planning, and Prioritizing; Thinking Creatively; Scheduling Work and Activities. *Work Output:* Handling and Moving Objects; Performing General Physical Activities; Interacting With Computers. *Interacting with Others:* Establishing and Maintaining Interpersonal Relationships; Communicating with Persons Outside Organization; Communicating with Other Workers. **Physical Work Conditions**—Indoors; Noisy; More Often Standing Than Sitting; Using Hands on Objects, Tools, or Controls. **Other Job Characteristics**—Need to Be Exact or Accurate.

Experience—Job Zone 4. A minimum of two to four years of work-related skill, knowledge, or experience is needed. **Job Preparation**—SVP 7.0 to less than 8.0—two years to less than 10 years. **Knowledges**—Psychology; Customer and Personal Service; Therapy and Counseling; Sociology and Anthropology; Sales and Marketing; Clerical Practices. **Instructional Programs**—Health and Physical Education/Fitness, Other; Parks, Recreation, and Leisure Facilities Management; Parks, Recreation, and Leisure Studies; Parks, Recreation, Leisure, and Fitness Studies, Other; Sport and Fitness Administration/Management.

Related SOC Job—39-9032 Recreation Workers. **Related OOH Job**—Recreation Workers. **Related DOT Jobs**—159.124-010 Counselor, Camp; 187.167-238 Recreation Supervisor; 195.167-026 Director, Recreation Center; 195.227-010 Program Aide, Group Work; 195.227-014 Recreation Leader; 352.167-010 Director, Social.

39-9041.00 Residential Advisors

- **Education/Training Required: Moderate-term on-the-job training**
- **Employed: 50,490**
- **Annual Earnings: $21,850**
- **Growth: 28.9%**
- **Annual Job Openings: 22,000**

Coordinate activities for residents of boarding schools, college fraternities or sororities, college dormitories, or similar establishments. Order supplies and determine need for maintenance, repairs, and furnishings. May maintain household records and assign rooms. May refer residents to counseling resources if needed.

Enforce rules and regulations to ensure the smooth and orderly operation of dormitory programs. Provide emergency first aid and summon medical assistance when necessary. Mediate interpersonal problems between residents. Administer, coordinate, or recommend disciplinary and corrective actions. Communicate with other staff to resolve problems with individual students. Counsel students in the handling of issues such as family, financial, and educational problems. Make regular rounds to ensure that residents and areas are safe and secure. Observe students to detect and report unusual behavior. Determine the need for facility maintenance and repair and notify appropriate personnel. Collaborate with counselors to develop counseling programs that address the needs of individual students. Develop program plans for individuals or assist in plan development. Hold regular meetings with each assigned unit. Direct and participate in on- and off-campus recreational activities for residents of institutions, boarding schools, fraternities or sororities, children's homes, or similar establishments. Assign rooms to students. Provide requested information on students' progress and the development of case plans. Confer with medical personnel to better understand the backgrounds and needs of individual residents. Answer telephones and route calls or deliver messages. Supervise participants in work-study programs. Process contract cancellations for students who are unable to follow residence hall policies and procedures. Sort and distribute mail. Supervise the activities of housekeeping personnel. Order supplies for facilities. Supervise students' housekeeping work to ensure that it is done properly. Chaperone group-sponsored trips and social functions. Compile information such as residents' daily activities and the quantities of supplies used to prepare required reports. Accompany and supervise students during meals. Provide transportation or escort for expeditions such as shopping trips or visits to doctors or dentists. Inventory, pack, and remove items left behind by former residents.

GOE Information—Interest Area: 10. Human Service. **Work Group:** 10.01. Counseling and Social Work. **Personality Type**—Social. Social occupations frequently involve working with, communicating with, and teaching people. These occupations often involve helping or providing service to others. **Work Values**—Social Service; Supervision, Human Relations; Working Conditions; Authority; Autonomy; Creativity. **Skills**—Social Perceptiveness; Monitoring; Management of Personnel Resources; Persuasion; Time Management; Service Orientation. **Abilities**—*Cognitive:* Originality; Oral Expression; Fluency of Ideas; Oral Comprehension; Problem Sensitivity; Number Facility. *Psychomotor:* None met the criteria. *Physical:* None met the criteria. *Sensory:* Speech Recognition; Hearing Sensitivity; Speech Clarity. **General Work Activities**—*Information Input:* Getting Information; Monitoring Processes, Materials, or Surroundings; Identifying Objects, Actions, and Events. *Mental Process:* Organizing, Planning, and Prioritizing; Making Decisions and Solving Problems; Scheduling Work and Activities. *Work Output:* Documenting or Recording Information; Interacting With Computers. *Interacting with Others:* Establishing and Maintaining Interpersonal Relationships; Communicating with Other Workers; Resolving Conflicts and Negotiating with Others. **Physical Work Conditions**—Indoors; Noisy; Sitting. **Other Job Characteristics**—Need to Be Exact or Accurate.

Experience—Job Zone 3. Previous work-related skill, knowledge, or experience is required. **Job Preparation**—SVP 6.0 to less than 7.0—more than one year and less than four years. **Knowledges**—Therapy and Counseling; Philosophy and Theology; Sociology and Anthropology; Psychology; Personnel and Human Resources; Customer and Personal Service. **Instructional Program**—Hotel/Motel Administration/Management.

Related SOC Job—39-9041 Residential Advisors. **Related OOH Job**—Residential Advisors. **Related DOT Job**—187.167-186 Residence Supervisor.

39-9099.99 Personal Care and Service Workers, All Other

- **Education/Training Required: Short-term on-the-job training**
- **Employed: 60,260**
- **Annual Earnings: $18,520**
- **Growth: 15.9%**
- **Annual Job Openings: 30,000**

All personal care and service workers not listed separately.

No task data available.

Note: The Department of Labor has not collected some data for this job, so it has fewer details than the other descriptions.

Related SOC Job—39-9099 Personal Care and Service Workers, All Other. **Related OOH Job**—None. **Related DOT Jobs**—143.457-010 Photographer; 309.367-010 House Sitter; 339.371-010 Electrologist; 339.371-014 Scalp-Treatment Operator; 339.571-010 Tattoo Artist; 346.374-010 Costumer Assistant; 346.674-010 Dresser; 349.667-010 Host/Hostess, Dance Hall; 349.667-014 Host/Hostess, Head; 352.377-010 Host/Hostess, Ground; 352.667-014 Parlor Chaperone; 352.677-014 Receptionist, Airline Lounge; 355.687-014 Graves Registration Specialist; 359.367-010 Escort; 359.667-010 Chaperon; others.

41-0000
Sales and Related Occupations

41-1000 Supervisors, Sales Workers

41-1011.00 First-Line Supervisors/ Managers of Retail Sales Workers

- **Education/Training Required: Work experience in a related occupation**
- **Employed: 1,083,890**
- **Annual Earnings: $32,840**
- **Growth: 3.8%**
- **Annual Job Openings: 229,000**

Directly supervise sales workers in a retail establishment or department. Duties may include management functions, such as purchasing, budgeting, accounting, and personnel work, in addition to supervisory duties.

Provide customer service by greeting and assisting customers and responding to customer inquiries and complaints. Assign employees to specific duties. Monitor sales activities to ensure that customers receive satisfactory service and quality goods. Direct and supervise employees engaged in sales, inventory-taking, reconciling cash receipts, or performing services for customers. Inventory stock and reorder when inventory drops to a specified level. Keep records of purchases, sales, and requisitions. Enforce safety, health, and security rules. Examine products purchased for resale or received for storage to assess the condition of each product or item. Hire, train, and evaluate personnel in sales or marketing establishments, promoting or firing workers when appropriate. Perform work activities of subordinates, such as cleaning and organizing shelves and displays and selling merchandise. Establish and implement policies, goals, objectives, and procedures for their department. Instruct staff on how to handle difficult and complicated sales. Formulate pricing policies for merchandise according to profitability requirements. Estimate consumer demand and determine the types and amounts of goods to be sold. Examine merchandise to ensure that it is correctly priced and displayed and that it functions as advertised. Plan and prepare work schedules and keep records of employees' work schedules and time cards. Review inventory and sales records to prepare reports for management and budget departments. Plan and coordinate advertising campaigns and sales promotions and prepare merchandise displays and advertising copy. Confer with company officials to develop methods and procedures to increase sales, expand markets, and promote business. Establish credit policies and operating procedures. Plan budgets and authorize payments and merchandise returns.

GOE Information—**Interest Area:** 14. Retail and Wholesale Sales and Service. **Work Group:** 14.01. Managerial Work in Retail/Wholesale Sales and Service. **Personality Type**—Enterprising. Enterprising occupations frequently involve starting up and carrying out projects. These occupations can involve leading people and making many decisions. They sometimes require risk taking and often deal with business. **Work Values**—Authority; Responsibility; Creativity; Autonomy; Working Conditions; Variety. **Skills**—Management of Personnel Resources; Management of Financial Resources; Persuasion; Repairing; Equipment Maintenance; Monitoring. **Abilities**—*Cognitive:* Mathematical Reasoning; Number Facility; Originality; Time Sharing; Memorization; Written Expression. *Psychomotor:* Manual Dexterity. *Physical:* Extent Flexibility; Trunk Strength; Stamina; Static Strength. *Sensory:* Speech Recognition; Far Vision; Speech Clarity; Near Vision. **General Work Activities**—*Information Input:* Inspecting Equipment, Structures, or Materials; Getting Information; Monitoring Processes, Materials, or Surroundings. *Mental Process:* Organizing, Planning, and Prioritizing; Thinking Creatively; Updating and Using Relevant Knowledge. *Work Output:* Handling and Moving Objects; Performing General Physical Activities; Documenting or Recording Information. *Interacting with Others:* Establishing and Maintaining Interpersonal Relationships; Communicating with Other Workers; Performing for or Working with the Public. **Physical Work Conditions**—Indoors; Hazardous Equipment; Standing; Walking and Running; Using Hands on Objects, Tools, or Controls. **Other Job Characteristics**—Need to Be Exact or Accurate.

Experience—Job Zone 2. Some previous work-related skill, knowledge, or experience may be helpful in these occupations, but usually is not needed. **Job Preparation**—SVP 4.0 to less than 6.0–six months to less than two years. **Knowledges**—Sales and Marketing; Personnel and Human Resources; Administration and Management; Customer and Personal Service; Economics and Accounting; Public Safety and Security. **Instructional Programs**—Business, Management, Marketing, and Related Support Services; Consumer Merchandising or Retailing Management; E-Commerce/Electronic Commerce; Floriculture/Floristry Operations and Management; Retailing and Retail Operations; Selling Skills and Sales Operations; Special Products Marketing Operations; Specialized Merchandising, Sales, and Related Marketing Operations, Other.

Related SOC Job—41-1011 First-Line Supervisors/Managers of Retail Sales Workers. **Related OOH Job**—Sales Worker Supervisors. **Related DOT Jobs**—185.167-010 Commissary Manager; 185.167-014 Manager, Automobile Service Station; 185.167-022 Manager, Food Concession; 185.167-026 Manager, Machinery-or-Equipment, Rental and Leasing; 185.167-038 Manager, Parts; 185.167-046 Manager, Retail Store; 185.167-066 Vending-Stand Supervisor; 299.137-010 Manager, Department; 299.137-022 Supervisor, Ice Storage, Sale, and Delivery; 299.137-026 Supervisor, Marina Sales and Service.

41-1012.00 First-Line Supervisors/ Managers of Non-Retail Sales Workers

- **Education/Training Required: Work experience in a related occupation**
- **Employed: 294,010**
- **Annual Earnings: $61,970**
- **Growth: 1.9%**
- **Annual Job Openings: 38,000**

Directly supervise and coordinate activities of sales workers other than retail sales workers. May perform duties such as budgeting, accounting, and personnel work in addition to supervisory duties.

Listen to and resolve customer complaints regarding services, products, or personnel. Monitor sales staff performance to ensure that goals are met. Hire, train, and evaluate personnel. Confer with company officials to develop methods and procedures to increase sales, expand markets, and promote business. Direct and supervise employees engaged in sales, inventory-taking, reconciling cash receipts, or performing specific services such as pumping gasoline for customers. Provide staff with assistance in performing difficult or complicated duties. Plan and prepare work schedules and assign employees to specific duties. Attend company meetings to exchange product information and coordinate work activities with other departments. Prepare sales and inventory reports for management and budget departments.

Formulate pricing policies on merchandise according to profitability requirements. Examine merchandise to ensure correct pricing and display and ensure that it functions as advertised. Analyze details of sales territories to assess their growth potential and to set quotas. Visit retailers and sales representatives to promote products and gather information. Keep records pertaining to purchases, sales, and requisitions. Coordinate sales promotion activities and prepare merchandise displays and advertising copy. Prepare rental or lease agreements, specifying charges and payment procedures for use of machinery, tools, or other items. Inventory stock and reorder when inventories drop to specified levels. Examine products purchased for resale or received for storage to determine product condition.

GOE Information—Interest Area: 14. Retail and Wholesale Sales and Service. **Work Group:** 14.01. Managerial Work in Retail/Wholesale Sales and Service. **Personality Type—Enterprising.** Enterprising occupations frequently involve starting up and carrying out projects. These occupations can involve leading people and making many decisions. They sometimes require risk taking and often deal with business. **Work Values—**Authority; Responsibility; Creativity; Autonomy; Working Conditions; Variety. **Skills—**Management of Personnel Resources; Negotiation; Persuasion; Time Management; Social Perceptiveness; Monitoring. **Abilities—***Cognitive:* Mathematical Reasoning; Number Facility; Originality; Written Expression; Fluency of Ideas; Oral Expression. *Psychomotor:* Finger Dexterity. *Physical:* None met the criteria. *Sensory:* Speech Recognition; Speech Clarity; Far Vision. **General Work Activities—***Information Input:* Getting Information; Identifying Objects, Actions, and Events; Monitoring Processes, Materials, or Surroundings. *Mental Process:* Organizing, Planning, and Prioritizing; Thinking Creatively; Updating and Using Relevant Knowledge. *Work Output:* Interacting With Computers; Documenting or Recording Information. *Interacting with Others:* Establishing and Maintaining Interpersonal Relationships; Monitoring and Controlling Resources; Communicating with Other Workers. **Physical Work Conditions—**Indoors; Noisy. **Other Job Characteristics—**Need to Be Exact or Accurate; Repeat Same Tasks.

Experience—Job Zone 4. A minimum of two to four years of work-related skill, knowledge, or experience is needed. **Job Preparation—**SVP 7.0 to less than 8.0—two years to less than 10 years. **Knowledges—**Sales and Marketing; Economics and Accounting; Personnel and Human Resources; Administration and Management; Education and Training; Customer and Personal Service. **Instructional Programs—**Business, Management, Marketing, and Related Support Services; General Merchandising, Sales, and Related Marketing Operations, Other; Special Products Marketing Operations; Specialized Merchandising, Sales, and Related Marketing Operations, Other.

Related SOC Job—41-1012 First-Line Supervisors/Managers of Non-Retail Sales Workers. **Related OOH Job—**Sales Worker Supervisors. **Related DOT Jobs—**163.167-014 Manager, Circulation; 166.167-046 Special Agent; 169.167-038 Order Department Supervisor; 180.167-010 Artificial-Breeding Distributor; 185.157-018 Wholesaler II; 185.167-030 Manager, Meat Sales and Storage; 185.167-038 Manager, Parts; 185.167-050 Manager, Textile Conversion; 185.167-054 Manager, Tobacco Warehouse; 185.167-070 Wholesaler I; 186.167-034 Manager, Insurance Office; 187.167-098 Manager, Employment Agency; 187.167-138 Manager, Sales; others.

41-2000 Retail Sales Workers

41-2011.00 Cashiers

- **Education/Training Required: Short-term on-the-job training**
- **Employed: 3,481,420**
- **Annual Earnings: $16,260**
- **Growth: 3.1%**
- **Annual Job Openings: 1,211,000**

Receive and disburse money in establishments other than financial institutions. Usually involves use of electronic scanners, cash registers, or related equipment. Often involved in processing credit or debit card transactions and validating checks.

Receive payment by cash, check, credit cards, vouchers, or automatic debits. Issue receipts, refunds, credits, or change due to customers. Count money in cash drawers at the beginning of shifts to ensure that amounts are correct and that there is adequate change. Greet customers entering establishments. Maintain clean and orderly checkout areas. Establish or identify prices of goods, services, or admission and tabulate bills, using calculators, cash registers, or optical price scanners. Issue trading stamps and redeem food stamps and coupons. Resolve customer complaints. Answer customers' questions and provide information on procedures or policies. Cash checks for customers. Weigh items sold by weight to determine prices. Compute and record totals of transactions. Calculate total payments received during a time period and reconcile this with total sales. Sell tickets and other items to customers. Keep periodic balance sheets of amounts and numbers of transactions. Bag, box, wrap, or gift-wrap merchandise and prepare packages for shipment. Sort, count, and wrap currency and coins. Process merchandise returns and exchanges. Pay company bills by cash, vouchers, or checks. Stock shelves and mark prices on shelves and items. Request information or assistance, using paging systems. Compile and maintain non-monetary reports and records. Monitor checkout stations to ensure that they have adequate cash available and that they are staffed appropriately. Post charges against guests' or patients' accounts. Offer customers carry-out service at the completion of transactions.

GOE Information—Interest Area: 14. Retail and Wholesale Sales and Service. **Work Group:** 14.06. Customer Service. **Personality Type—**Conventional. Conventional occupations frequently involve following set procedures and routines. These occupations can include working with data and details more than with ideas. Usually there is a clear line of authority to follow. **Work Values—**Supervision, Technical; Co-workers; Social Service; Supervision, Human Relations; Advancement. **Skills—**Social Perceptiveness. **Abilities—***Cognitive:* Speed of Closure; Memorization; Number Facility; Perceptual Speed; Time Sharing; Oral Expression. *Psychomotor:* Wrist-Finger Speed; Manual Dexterity; Multilimb Coordination; Arm-Hand Steadiness. *Physical:* Extent Flexibility; Trunk Strength; Static Strength. *Sensory:* Speech Recognition; Speech Clarity; Auditory Attention. **General Work Activities—***Information Input:* Identifying Objects, Actions, and Events; Getting Information; Monitoring Processes, Materials, or Surroundings. *Mental Process:* Processing Information; Updating and Using Relevant Knowledge; Organizing, Planning, and Prioritizing. *Work Output:* Handling and Moving Objects; Interacting With Computers; Controlling Machines and Processes. *Interacting with Others:* Establishing and Maintaining Interpersonal Relationships; Performing for or Working with the Public; Assisting and Caring for Others. **Physical Work Conditions—**Indoors; Standing; Walking and Running; Using Hands on Objects, Tools, or Controls; Bending or

Twisting the Body; Repetitive Motions. **Other Job Characteristics**—Need to Be Exact or Accurate; Repeat Same Tasks.

Experience—Job Zone 1. No previous work-related skill, knowledge, or experience is needed. **Job Preparation**—SVP below 4.0—less than six months. **Knowledges**—Education and Training; Customer and Personal Service; Administration and Management; Mathematics; Public Safety and Security; English Language. **Instructional Program**—Retailing and Retail Operations.

Related SOC Job—41-2011 Cashiers. **Related OOH Job**—Cashiers. **Related DOT Jobs**—211.367-010 Paymaster of Purses; 211.462-010 Cashier II; 211.462-014 Cashier-Checker; 211.462-018 Cashier-Wrapper; 211.462-026 Check Cashier; 211.462-030 Drivers'-Cash Clerk; 211.462-034 Teller; 211.462-038 Toll Collector; 211.467-010 Cashier, Courtesy Booth; 211.467-014 Money Counter; 211.467-018 Parimutuel-Ticket Cashier; 211.467-022 Parimutuel-Ticket Seller; 211.467-026 Sheet Writer; 211.467-030 Ticket Seller; 211.482-010 Cashier, Tube Room; 211.482-014 Food Checker; others.

41-2012.00 Gaming Change Persons and Booth Cashiers

- **Education/Training Required:** Short-term on-the-job training
- **Employed:** 28,590
- **Annual Earnings:** $20,050
- **Growth:** 18.5%
- **Annual Job Openings:** 11,000

Exchange coins and tokens for patrons' money. May issue payoffs and obtain customer's signature on receipt when winnings exceed the amount held in the slot machine. May operate a booth in the slot machine area and furnish change persons with money bank at the start of the shift or count and audit money in drawers.

Count money and audit money drawers. Keep accurate records of monetary exchanges, authorization forms, and transaction reconciliations. Exchange money, credit, and casino chips and make change for customers. Work in and monitor an assigned area on the casino floor where slot machines are located. Listen for jackpot alarm bells and issue payoffs to winners. Maintain cage security according to rules. Obtain customers' signatures on receipts when winnings exceed the amount held in a slot machine. Reconcile daily summaries of transactions to balance books. Sell gambling chips, tokens, or tickets to patrons or to other workers for resale to patrons. Calculate the value of chips won or lost by players. Furnish change persons with a money bank at the start of each shift. Accept credit applications and verify credit references to provide check-cashing authorization or to establish house credit accounts.

GOE Information—**Interest Area:** 14. Retail and Wholesale Sales and Service. **Work Group:** 14.06. Customer Service. **Personality Type**—No data available. **Work Values**—No data available. **Skills**—None met the criteria. **Abilities**—*Cognitive:* Number Facility; Selective Attention; Speed of Closure. *Psychomotor:* Manual Dexterity. *Physical:* Trunk Strength. *Sensory:* Auditory Attention; Hearing Sensitivity; Visual Color Discrimination; Far Vision. **General Work Activities**—*Information Input:* Identifying Objects, Actions, and Events; Getting Information; Monitoring Processes, Materials, or Surroundings. *Mental Process:* Making Decisions and Solving Problems; Processing Information; Evaluating Information Against Standards. *Work Output:* Documenting or Recording Information; Repairing and Maintaining Mechanical Equipment; Handling and Moving Objects. *Interacting with Others:* Performing for or Working with the Public; Communicating with Other Workers; Establishing and Maintaining

Interpersonal Relationships. **Physical Work Conditions**—Indoors; Noisy; Standing; Walking and Running; Using Hands on Objects, Tools, or Controls; Bending or Twisting the Body. **Other Job Characteristics**—Need to Be Exact or Accurate; Repeat Same Tasks; Errors Have Important Consequences.

Experience—Job Zone 2. Some previous work-related skill, knowledge, or experience may be helpful in these occupations, but usually is not needed. **Job Preparation**—SVP 4.0 to less than 6.0—six months to less than two years. **Knowledges**—Customer and Personal Service; Sales and Marketing; Economics and Accounting; Engineering and Technology; Public Safety and Security; Administration and Management. **Instructional Program**—Retailing and Retail Operations.

Related SOC Job—41-2012 Gaming Change Persons and Booth Cashiers. **Related OOH Job**—Cashiers. **Related DOT Job**—211.467-034 Change Person.

41-2021.00 Counter and Rental Clerks

- **Education/Training Required:** Short-term on-the-job training
- **Employed:** 473,090
- **Annual Earnings:** $18,970
- **Growth:** 23.1%
- **Annual Job Openings:** 126,000

Receive orders for repairs, rentals, and services. May describe available options, compute cost, and accept payment.

Compute charges for merchandise or services and receive payments. Prepare merchandise for display or for purchase or rental. Recommend and provide advice on a wide variety of products and services. Answer telephones to provide information and receive orders. Greet customers and discuss the type, quality, and quantity of merchandise sought for rental. Keep records of transactions and of the number of customers entering an establishment. Prepare rental forms, obtaining customer signature and other information, such as required licenses. Receive, examine, and tag articles to be altered, cleaned, stored, or repaired. Inspect and adjust rental items to meet needs of customer. Explain rental fees, policies, and procedures. Reserve items for requested times and keep records of items rented. Receive orders for services, such as rentals, repairs, dry cleaning, and storage. Rent items, arrange for provision of services to customers, and accept returns. Provide information about rental items, such as availability, operation, or description. Advise customers on use and care of merchandise. Allocate equipment to participants in sporting events or recreational activities.

GOE Information—**Interest Area:** 14. Retail and Wholesale Sales and Service. **Work Group:** 14.06. Customer Service. **Personality Type**—Conventional. Conventional occupations frequently involve following set procedures and routines. These occupations can include working with data and details more than with ideas. Usually there is a clear line of authority to follow. **Work Values**—Supervision, Technical; Social Service; Working Conditions; Co-workers; Advancement; Supervision, Human Relations. **Skills**—None met the criteria. **Abilities**—*Cognitive:* None met the criteria. *Psychomotor:* None met the criteria. *Physical:* Trunk Strength. *Sensory:* None met the criteria. **General Work Activities**—*Information Input:* Identifying Objects, Actions, and Events; Monitoring Processes, Materials, or Surroundings; Getting Information. *Mental Process:* Updating and Using Relevant Knowledge; Evaluating Information Against Standards; Judging the Qualities of Things, Services, or Other People's Work. *Work Output:* None met the criteria. *Interacting with*

Others: Performing for or Working with the Public; Establishing and Maintaining Interpersonal Relationships; Coaching and Developing Others. **Physical Work Conditions**—Indoors; Noisy; Minor Burns, Cuts, Bites, or Stings; Standing; Walking and Running; Using Hands on Objects, Tools, or Controls. **Other Job Characteristics**—Need to Be Exact or Accurate; Repeat Same Tasks.

Experience—Job Zone 1. No previous work-related skill, knowledge, or experience is needed. **Job Preparation**—SVP below 4.0—less than six months. **Knowledges**—Food Production; Administration and Management; Sales and Marketing; Personnel and Human Resources. **Instructional Program**—Selling Skills and Sales Operations.

Related SOC Job—41-2021 Counter and Rental Clerks. **Related OOH Job**—Counter and Rental Clerks. **Related DOT Jobs**—216.482-030 Laundry Pricing Clerk; 249.362-010 Counter Clerk; 249.366-010 Counter Clerk; 290.477-010 Coupon-Redemption Clerk; 290.477-018 Sales Clerk, Food; 295.357-010 Apparel-Rental Clerk; 295.357-014 Tool-and-Equipment-Rental Clerk; 295.357-018 Furniture-Rental Consultant; 295.367-010 Airplane-Charter Clerk; 295.367-014 Baby-Stroller and Wheelchair Rental Clerk; 295.367-026 Storage-Facility Rental Clerk; 295.467-010 Bicycle-Rental Clerk; 295.467-014 Boat-Rental Clerk; others.

41-2022.00 Parts Salespersons

- **Education/Training Required: Moderate-term on-the-job training**
- **Employed: 235,190**
- **Annual Earnings: $26,450**
- **Growth: −6.6%**
- **Annual Job Openings: 28,000**

Sell spare and replacement parts and equipment in repair shop or parts store.

Read catalogs, microfiche viewers, or computer displays to determine replacement part stock numbers and prices. Determine replacement parts required according to inspections of old parts, customer requests, or customers' descriptions of malfunctions. Receive and fill telephone orders for parts. Fill customer orders from stock. Prepare sales slips or sales contracts. Receive payment or obtain credit authorization. Take inventory of stock. Advise customers on substitution or modification of parts when identical replacements are not available. Examine returned parts for defects and exchange defective parts or refund money. Mark and store parts in stockrooms according to prearranged systems. Discuss use and features of various parts, based on knowledge of machines or equipment. Demonstrate equipment to customers and explain functioning of equipment. Place new merchandise on display. Measure parts, using precision measuring instruments, to determine whether similar parts may be machined to required sizes. Repair parts or equipment.

GOE Information—**Interest Area:** 14. Retail and Wholesale Sales and Service. **Work Group:** 14.03. General Sales. **Personality Type**—Enterprising. Enterprising occupations frequently involve starting up and carrying out projects. These occupations can involve leading people and making many decisions. They sometimes require risk taking and often deal with business. **Work Values**—Supervision, Technical; Social Service; Working Conditions; Co-workers; Advancement; Supervision, Human Relations. **Skills**—Service Orientation; Management of Personnel Resources; Negotiation; Social Perceptiveness; Management of Financial Resources; Equipment Selection. **Abilities**—*Cognitive:* Speed of Closure; Category Flexibility; Flexibility of Closure; Memorization; Perceptual

Speed; Oral Expression. *Psychomotor:* Arm-Hand Steadiness; Finger Dexterity. *Physical:* Extent Flexibility; Static Strength; Trunk Strength. *Sensory:* Speech Recognition; Near Vision; Hearing Sensitivity; Visual Color Discrimination; Far Vision; Auditory Attention. **General Work Activities**—*Information Input:* Getting Information; Monitoring Processes, Materials, or Surroundings; Identifying Objects, Actions, and Events. *Mental Process:* Updating and Using Relevant Knowledge; Judging the Qualities of Things, Services, or Other People's Work; Organizing, Planning, and Prioritizing. *Work Output:* Handling and Moving Objects; Interacting With Computers; Performing General Physical Activities. *Interacting with Others:* Establishing and Maintaining Interpersonal Relationships; Performing for or Working with the Public; Communicating with Persons Outside Organization. **Physical Work Conditions**—Indoors; Noisy; Contaminants; Standing; Repetitive Motions. **Other Job Characteristics**—Need to Be Exact or Accurate; Repeat Same Tasks.

Experience—Job Zone 2. Some previous work-related skill, knowledge, or experience may be helpful in these occupations, but usually is not needed. **Job Preparation**—SVP 4.0 to less than 6.0—six months to less than two years. **Knowledges**—Sales and Marketing; Customer and Personal Service; Mechanical Devices; Computers and Electronics; Production and Processing; Mathematics. **Instructional Programs**—Selling Skills and Sales Operations; Vehicle Parts and Accessories Marketing Operations.

Related SOC Job—41-2022 Parts Salespersons. **Related OOH Job**—Parts Salespersons. **Related DOT Job**—279.357-062 Salesperson, Parts.

41-2031.00 Retail Salespersons

- **Education/Training Required: Short-term on-the-job training**
- **Employed: 4,344,770**
- **Annual Earnings: $19,140**
- **Growth: 17.3%**
- **Annual Job Openings: 1,350,000**

Sell merchandise, such as furniture, motor vehicles, appliances, or apparel, in a retail establishment.

Greet customers and ascertain what each customer wants or needs. Open and close cash registers, performing tasks such as counting money; separating charge slips, coupons, and vouchers; balancing cash drawers; and making deposits. Maintain knowledge of current sales and promotions, policies regarding payment and exchanges, and security practices. Compute sales prices and total purchases and receive and process cash or credit payment. Watch for and recognize security risks and thefts and know how to prevent or handle these situations. Maintain records related to sales. Recommend, select, and help locate or obtain merchandise based on customer needs and desires. Answer questions regarding the store and its merchandise. Describe merchandise and explain use, operation, and care of merchandise to customers. Prepare sales slips or sales contracts. Ticket, arrange, and display merchandise to promote sales. Place special orders or call other stores to find desired items. Demonstrate use or operation of merchandise. Clean shelves, counters, and tables. Exchange merchandise for customers and accept returns. Bag or package purchases and wrap gifts. Help customers try on or fit merchandise. Inventory stock and requisition new stock. Prepare merchandise for purchase or rental. Sell or arrange for delivery, insurance, financing, or service contracts for merchandise. Estimate and quote trade-in allowances. Estimate cost of repair or alteration of merchandise. Estimate quantity and cost of merchandise required, such as paint or floor covering. Rent merchandise to customers.

GOE Information—Interest Area: 14. Retail and Wholesale Sales and Service. **Work Group:** 14.03. General Sales. **Personality Type—**Enterprising. Enterprising occupations frequently involve starting up and carrying out projects. These occupations can involve leading people and making many decisions. They sometimes require risk taking and often deal with business. **Work Values—**Supervision, Technical; Advancement; Social Service; Co-workers; Working Conditions; Supervision, Human Relations. **Skills—**None met the criteria. **Abilities—***Cognitive:* Memorization. *Psychomotor:* None met the criteria. *Physical:* Trunk Strength. *Sensory:* Speech Recognition; Far Vision. **General Work Activities—***Information Input:* Monitoring Processes, Materials, or Surroundings; Identifying Objects, Actions, and Events; Getting Information. *Mental Process:* Updating and Using Relevant Knowledge; Organizing, Planning, and Prioritizing; Thinking Creatively. *Work Output:* Handling and Moving Objects; Performing General Physical Activities; Interacting With Computers. *Interacting with Others:* Performing for or Working with the Public; Establishing and Maintaining Interpersonal Relationships; Influencing Others or Selling. **Physical Work Conditions—**Indoors; Standing; Walking and Running; Using Hands on Objects, Tools, or Controls; Repetitive Motions. **Other Job Characteristics—**Need to Be Exact or Accurate; Repeat Same Tasks.

Experience—Job Zone 2. Some previous work-related skill, knowledge, or experience may be helpful in these occupations, but usually is not needed. **Job Preparation—**SVP 4.0 to less than 6.0—six months to less than two years. **Knowledges—**Sales and Marketing; Customer and Personal Service; Administration and Management; Personnel and Human Resources; Education and Training; Clerical Practices. **Instructional Programs—**Floriculture/Floristry Operations and Management; Retailing and Retail Operations; Sales, Distribution, and Marketing Operations, General; Selling Skills and Sales Operations.

Related SOC Job—41-2031 Retail Salespersons. **Related OOH Job—**Retail Salespersons. **Related DOT Jobs—**260.357-026 Salesperson, Flowers; 261.351-010 Salesperson, Wigs; 261.354-010 Salesperson, Corsets; 261.357-042 Salesperson, Furs; 261.357-046 Salesperson, Infants' and Children's Wear; 261.357-050 Salesperson, Men's and Boys' Clothing; 261.357-054 Salesperson, Men's Furnishings; 261.357-058 Salesperson, Millinery; 261.357-062 Salesperson, Shoes; 261.357-066 Salesperson, Women's Apparel and Accessories; 261.357-070 Salesperson, Yard Goods; others.

41-3000 Sales Representatives, Services

41-3011.00 Advertising Sales Agents

- **Education/Training Required: Moderate-term on-the-job training**
- **Employed: 153,890**
- **Annual Earnings: $41,770**
- **Growth: 16.3%**
- **Annual Job Openings: 24,000**

Sell or solicit advertising, including graphic art, advertising space in publications, custom-made signs, or TV and radio advertising time. May obtain leases for outdoor advertising sites or persuade retailer to use sales promotion display items.

Prepare and deliver sales presentations to new and existing customers to sell new advertising programs and to protect and increase existing advertising. Explain to customers how specific types of advertising will help promote their products or services in the most effective way possible. Maintain assigned account bases while developing new accounts. Process all correspondence and paperwork related to accounts. Deliver advertising or illustration proofs to customers for approval. Draw up contracts for advertising work and collect payments due. Locate and contact potential clients to offer advertising services. Provide clients with estimates of the costs of advertising products or services. Recommend appropriate sizes and formats for advertising, depending on medium being used. Inform customers of available options for advertisement artwork and provide samples. Obtain and study information about clients' products, needs, problems, advertising history, and business practices to offer effective sales presentations and appropriate product assistance. Determine advertising medium to be used and prepare sample advertisements within the selected medium for presentation to customers. Consult with company officials, sales departments, and advertising agencies to develop promotional plans. Prepare promotional plans, sales literature, media kits, and sales contracts, using computer. Identify new advertising markets and propose products to serve them. Write copy as part of layout. Attend sales meetings, industry trade shows, and training seminars to gather information, promote products, expand network of contacts, and increase knowledge. Gather all relevant material for bid processes and coordinate bidding and contract approval. Arrange for commercial taping sessions and accompany clients to sessions. Write sales outlines for use by staff.

GOE Information—Interest Area: 14. Retail and Wholesale Sales and Service. **Work Group:** 14.03. General Sales. **Personality Type—**Enterprising. Enterprising occupations frequently involve starting up and carrying out projects. These occupations can involve leading people and making many decisions. They sometimes require risk taking and often deal with business. **Work Values—**Creativity; Variety; Working Conditions; Ability Utilization; Achievement; Autonomy. **Skills—**Negotiation; Management of Financial Resources; Persuasion; Speaking; Social Perceptiveness; Service Orientation. **Abilities—***Cognitive:* Written Expression; Fluency of Ideas; Originality; Oral Expression; Written Comprehension; Inductive Reasoning. *Psychomotor:* None met the criteria. *Physical:* None met the criteria. *Sensory:* Speech Recognition; Speech Clarity; Near Vision. **General Work Activities—***Information Input:* Getting Information; Identifying Objects, Actions, and Events; Monitoring Processes, Materials, or Surroundings. *Mental Process:* Organizing, Planning, and Prioritizing; Thinking Creatively; Updating and Using Relevant Knowledge. *Work Output:* Interacting With Computers. *Interacting with Others:* Influencing Others or Selling; Communicating with Persons Outside Organization; Establishing and Maintaining Interpersonal Relationships. **Physical Work Conditions—**More Often Outdoors Than Indoors; Standing. **Other Job Characteristics—**Need to Be Exact or Accurate.

Experience—Job Zone 3. Previous work-related skill, knowledge, or experience is required. **Job Preparation—**SVP 6.0 to less than 7.0—more than one year and less than four years. **Knowledges—**Sales and Marketing; Economics and Accounting; Communications and Media; Customer and Personal Service; English Language; Transportation. **Instructional Program—**Advertising.

Related SOC Job—41-3011 Advertising Sales Agents. **Related OOH Job—**Advertising Sales Agents. **Related DOT Jobs—**254.251-010 Sales Representative, Graphic Art; 254.257-010 Sales Representative, Signs and Displays; 254.357-010 Leasing Agent, Outdoor Advertising; 254.357-014 Sales Representative, Advertising; 254.357-022 Sales Representative, Signs; 259.357-018 Sales Representative, Radio and Television Time; 269.357-018 Sales-Promotion Representative.

41-3021.00 Insurance Sales Agents

- Education/Training Required: Bachelor's degree
- Employed: 299,470
- Annual Earnings: $42,340
- Growth: 6.6%
- Annual Job Openings: 44,000

Sell life, property, casualty, health, automotive, or other types of insurance. May refer clients to independent brokers, work as independent broker, or be employed by an insurance company.

Call on policyholders to deliver and explain policy, to analyze insurance program and suggest additions or changes, or to change beneficiaries. Calculate premiums and establish payment method. Customize insurance programs to suit individual customers, often covering a variety of risks. Sell various types of insurance policies to businesses and individuals on behalf of insurance companies, including automobile, fire, life, property, medical, and dental insurance or specialized policies such as marine, farm/crop, and medical malpractice. Interview prospective clients to obtain data about their financial resources and needs and the physical condition of the person or property to be insured and to discuss any existing coverage. Seek out new clients and develop clientele by networking to find new customers and generate lists of prospective clients. Explain features, advantages, and disadvantages of various policies to promote sale of insurance plans. Contact underwriter and submit forms to obtain binder coverage. Ensure that policy requirements are fulfilled, including any necessary medical examinations and the completion of appropriate forms. Confer with clients to obtain and provide information when claims are made on a policy. Perform administrative tasks, such as maintaining records and handling policy renewals. Select company that offers type of coverage requested by client to underwrite policy. Monitor insurance claims to ensure that they are settled equitably for both the client and the insurer. Develop marketing strategies to compete with other individuals or companies who sell insurance. Attend meetings, seminars, and programs to learn about new products and services, learn new skills, and receive technical assistance in developing new accounts. Inspect property, examining its general condition, type of construction, age, and other characteristics, to decide if it is a good insurance risk. Install bookkeeping systems and resolve system problems. Plan and oversee incorporation of insurance program into bookkeeping system of company. Explain necessary bookkeeping requirements for customer to implement and provide group insurance program.

GOE Information—Interest Area: 06. Finance and Insurance. **Work Group:** 06.05. Finance/Insurance Sales and Support. **Personality Type**—Enterprising. Enterprising occupations frequently involve starting up and carrying out projects. These occupations can involve leading people and making many decisions. They sometimes require risk taking and often deal with business. **Work Values**—Working Conditions; Advancement; Responsibility; Autonomy; Social Service; Supervision, Technical. **Skills**—Persuasion; Time Management; Negotiation; Judgment and Decision Making; Service Orientation; Speaking. **Abilities**—*Cognitive:* Number Facility; Mathematical Reasoning; Memorization; Deductive Reasoning; Speed of Closure; Oral Expression. *Psychomotor:* None met the criteria. *Physical:* None met the criteria. *Sensory:* Near Vision; Speech Recognition; Far Vision; Speech Clarity. **General Work Activities**—*Information Input:* Getting Information; Identifying Objects, Actions, and Events; Monitoring Processes, Materials, or Surroundings. *Mental Process:* Processing Information; Making Decisions and Solving Problems; Updating and Using Relevant Knowledge. *Work Output:* Documenting or Recording Information; Interacting With

Computers. *Interacting with Others:* Establishing and Maintaining Interpersonal Relationships; Communicating with Persons Outside Organization; Resolving Conflicts and Negotiating with Others. **Physical Work Conditions**—Indoors; Sitting. **Other Job Characteristics**—Need to Be Exact or Accurate; Repeat Same Tasks.

Experience—Job Zone 3. Previous work-related skill, knowledge, or experience is required. **Job Preparation**—SVP 6.0 to less than 7.0—more than one year and less than four years. **Knowledges**—Sales and Marketing; Customer and Personal Service; Economics and Accounting; Computers and Electronics; Clerical Practices; Law and Government. **Instructional Program**—Insurance.

Related SOC Job—41-3021 Insurance Sales Agents. **Related OOH Job**—Insurance Sales Agents. **Related DOT Jobs**—169.167-050 Special Agent, Group Insurance; 186.167-010 Estate Planner; 239.267-010 Placer; 250.257-010 Sales Agent, Insurance.

41-3031.00 Securities, Commodities, and Financial Services Sales Agents

- Education/Training Required: Bachelor's degree
- Employed: 251,710
- Annual Earnings: $67,130
- Growth: 11.5%
- Annual Job Openings: 37,000

The job openings listed here are shared with 41-3031.01 Sales Agents, Securities and Commodities and 41-3031.02 Sales Agents, Financial Services.

Buy and sell securities in investment and trading firms or call upon businesses and individuals to sell financial services. Provide financial services, such as loan, tax, and securities counseling. May advise securities customers about such things as stocks, bonds, and market conditions.

No task data available.

GOE Information—Interest Area: 06. Finance and Insurance. **Work Group:** 06.05. Finance/Insurance Sales and Support. **Note:** The Department of Labor has not collected some data for this job, so it has fewer details than the other descriptions.

Instructional Programs—Financial Planning and Services; Investments and Securities.

Related SOC Job—41-3031 Securities, Commodities, and Financial Services Sales Agents. **Related OOH Job**—Securities, Commodities, and Financial Services Sales Agents. **Related DOT Job**—No data available.

41-3031.01 Sales Agents, Securities and Commodities

- Education/Training Required: Bachelor's degree
- Employed: 251,710
- Annual Earnings: $67,130
- Growth: 11.5%
- Annual Job Openings: 37,000

The job openings listed here are shared with 41-3031.00 Securities, Commodities, and Financial Services Sales Agents and 41-3031.02 Sales Agents, Financial Services.

Buy and sell securities in investment and trading firms and develop and implement financial plans for individuals, businesses, and organizations.

Complete sales order tickets and submit for processing of client requested transactions. Interview clients to determine clients' assets, liabilities, cash flow, insurance coverage, tax status, and financial objectives. Record transactions accurately and keep clients informed about transactions. Develop financial plans based on analysis of clients' financial status and discuss financial options with clients. Review all securities transactions to ensure accuracy of information and ensure that trades conform to regulations of governing agencies. Offer advice on the purchase or sale of particular securities. Relay buy or sell orders to securities exchanges or to firm trading departments. Identify potential clients, using advertising campaigns, mailing lists, and personal contacts. Review financial periodicals, stock and bond reports, business publications, and other material to identify potential investments for clients and to keep abreast of trends affecting market conditions. Contact prospective customers to determine customer needs, present information, and explain available services. Prepare documents needed to implement plans selected by clients. Analyze market conditions to determine optimum times to execute securities transactions. Explain stock market terms and trading practices to clients. Inform and advise concerned parties regarding fluctuations and securities transactions affecting plans or accounts. Calculate costs for billings and commissions purposes. Supply the latest price quotes on any security, as well as information on the activities and financial positions of the corporations issuing these securities. Prepare financial reports to monitor client or corporate finances. Read corporate reports and calculate ratios to determine best prospects for profit on stock purchases and to monitor client accounts.

GOE Information—Interest Area: 06. Finance and Insurance. **Work Group:** 06.05. Finance/Insurance Sales and Support. **Personality Type**—Enterprising. Enterprising occupations frequently involve starting up and carrying out projects. These occupations can involve leading people and making many decisions. They sometimes require risk taking and often deal with business. **Work Values**—Recognition; Compensation; Responsibility; Working Conditions; Autonomy; Social Status. **Skills**—Management of Financial Resources; Persuasion; Social Perceptiveness; Negotiation; Judgment and Decision Making; Service Orientation. **Abilities**—*Cognitive:* Number Facility; Mathematical Reasoning; Fluency of Ideas; Deductive Reasoning; Originality; Oral Expression. *Psychomotor:* None met the criteria. *Physical:* None met the criteria. *Sensory:* Speech Recognition; Speech Clarity; Near Vision. **General Work Activities**—*Information Input:* Identifying Objects, Actions, and Events; Getting Information; Monitoring Processes, Materials, or Surroundings. *Mental Process:* Organizing, Planning, and Prioritizing; Updating and Using Relevant Knowledge; Making Decisions and Solving Problems. *Work Output:* Interacting With Computers; Documenting or Recording Information. *Interacting with Others:* Influencing Others or Selling; Communicating with Persons Outside Organization; Establishing and Maintaining Interpersonal Relationships. **Physical Work Conditions**—Indoors; Sitting. **Other Job Characteristics**—Need to Be Exact or Accurate; Errors Have Important Consequences; Repeat Same Tasks; Automation.

Experience—Job Zone 4. A minimum of two to four years of work-related skill, knowledge, or experience is needed. **Job Preparation**—SVP 7.0 to less than 8.0—two years to less than 10 years. **Knowledges**—Customer and Personal Service; Economics and Accounting; Sales and Marketing; Clerical Practices; Law and Government; Mathematics. **Instructional Programs**—Financial Planning and Services; Investments and Securities.

Related SOC Job—41-3031 Securities, Commodities, and Financial Services Sales Agents. **Related OOH Job**—Securities, Commodities, and Financial Services Sales Agents. **Related DOT Jobs**—162.157-010

Broker-and-Market Operator, Grain; 162.167-034 Floor Broker; 162.167-038 Securities Trader; 250.257-014 Financial Planner; 250.257-018 Registered Representative.

41-3031.02 Sales Agents, Financial Services

- **Education/Training Required:** Bachelor's degree
- **Employed:** 251,710
- **Annual Earnings:** $67,130
- **Growth:** 11.5%
- **Annual Job Openings:** 37,000

The job openings listed here are shared with 41-3031.00 Securities, Commodities, and Financial Services Sales Agents and 41-3031.01 Sales Agents, Securities and Commodities.

Sell financial services such as loan, tax, and securities counseling to customers of financial institutions and business establishments.

Determine customers' financial services needs and prepare proposals to sell services that address these needs. Contact prospective customers to present information and explain available services. Sell services and equipment, such as trusts, investments, and check processing services. Prepare forms or agreements to complete sales. Develop prospects from current commercial customers, referral leads, and sales and trade meetings. Review business trends in order to advise customers regarding expected fluctuations. Make presentations on financial services to groups to attract new clients. Evaluate costs and revenue of agreements to determine continued profitability.

GOE Information—Interest Area: 06. Finance and Insurance. **Work Group:** 06.05. Finance/Insurance Sales and Support. **Personality Type**—Enterprising. Enterprising occupations frequently involve starting up and carrying out projects. These occupations can involve leading people and making many decisions. They sometimes require risk taking and often deal with business. **Work Values**—Recognition; Compensation; Working Conditions; Responsibility; Autonomy; Social Status. **Skills**—Persuasion; Management of Financial Resources; Service Orientation; Negotiation; Speaking; Monitoring. **Abilities**—*Cognitive:* Number Facility; Fluency of Ideas; Mathematical Reasoning; Deductive Reasoning; Written Expression; Originality. *Psychomotor:* None met the criteria. *Physical:* None met the criteria. *Sensory:* Speech Clarity; Speech Recognition; Far Vision; Near Vision. **General Work Activities**—*Information Input:* Getting Information; Identifying Objects, Actions, and Events; Monitoring Processes, Materials, or Surroundings. *Mental Process:* Making Decisions and Solving Problems; Organizing, Planning, and Prioritizing; Updating and Using Relevant Knowledge. *Work Output:* Documenting or Recording Information; Interacting With Computers. *Interacting with Others:* Influencing Others or Selling; Performing for or Working with the Public; Establishing and Maintaining Interpersonal Relationships. **Physical Work Conditions**—Indoors; Sitting. **Other Job Characteristics**—Need to Be Exact or Accurate; Automation; Repeat Same Tasks.

Experience—Job Zone 4. A minimum of two to four years of work-related skill, knowledge, or experience is needed. **Job Preparation**—SVP 7.0 to less than 8.0—two years to less than 10 years. **Knowledges**—Sales and Marketing; Economics and Accounting; Customer and Personal Service; Law and Government; Mathematics; Personnel and Human Resources. **Instructional Programs**—Business and Personal/Financial Services Marketing Operations; Financial Planning and Services; Investments and Securities.

Related SOC Job—41-3031 Securities, Commodities, and Financial Services Sales Agents. **Related OOH Job**—Securities, Commodities, and Financial Services Sales Agents. **Related DOT Jobs**—250.257-022 Sales Representative, Financial Services; 250.357-026 Sales Agent, Financial-Report Service.

41-3041.00 Travel Agents

- Education/Training Required: Postsecondary vocational training
- Employed: 88,590
- Annual Earnings: $28,670
- Growth: −6.1%
- Annual Job Openings: 4,000

Plan and sell transportation and accommodations for travel agency customers. Determine destination, modes of transportation, travel dates, costs, and accommodations required.

Collect payment for transportation and accommodations from customer. Converse with customer to determine destination, mode of transportation, travel dates, financial considerations, and accommodations required. Compute cost of travel and accommodations, using calculator, computer, carrier tariff books, and hotel rate books, or quote package tour's costs. Book transportation and hotel reservations, using computer terminal or telephone. Plan, describe, arrange, and sell itinerary tour packages and promotional travel incentives offered by various travel carriers. Provide customer with brochures and publications containing travel information, such as local customs, points of interest, or foreign country regulations. Print or request transportation carrier tickets, using computer printer system or system link to travel carrier.

GOE Information—Interest Area: 09. Hospitality, Tourism, and Recreation. **Work Group:** 09.03. Hospitality and Travel Services. **Personality Type**—Enterprising. Enterprising occupations frequently involve starting up and carrying out projects. These occupations can involve leading people and making many decisions. They sometimes require risk taking and often deal with business. **Work Values**—Social Service; Working Conditions; Autonomy; Recognition; Variety; Creativity. **Skills**—Service Orientation; Persuasion; Active Listening; Speaking; Negotiation; Time Management. **Abilities**—*Cognitive:* Fluency of Ideas; Time Sharing; Originality; Memorization; Oral Expression; Deductive Reasoning. *Psychomotor:* None met the criteria. *Physical:* None met the criteria. *Sensory:* Speech Recognition; Near Vision; Auditory Attention. **General Work Activities**—*Information Input:* Getting Information; Identifying Objects, Actions, and Events; Estimating the Needed Characteristics of Products, Events, or Information. *Mental Process:* Organizing, Planning, and Prioritizing; Updating and Using Relevant Knowledge; Processing Information. *Work Output:* Documenting or Recording Information; Interacting With Computers. *Interacting with Others:* Performing for or Working with the Public; Establishing and Maintaining Interpersonal Relationships; Communicating with Persons Outside Organization. **Physical Work Conditions**—Indoors; Sitting. **Other Job Characteristics**—Need to Be Exact or Accurate; Automation; Errors Have Important Consequences; Repeat Same Tasks.

Experience—Job Zone 3. Previous work-related skill, knowledge, or experience is required. **Job Preparation**—SVP 6.0 to less than 7.0—more than one year and less than four years. **Knowledges**—Geography; Sales and Marketing; Clerical Practices; Transportation; Economics and Accounting; Customer and Personal Service. **Instructional Programs**—Selling Skills and Sales Operations; Tourism and Travel Services Marketing Operations.

Related SOC Job—41-3041 Travel Agents. **Related OOH Job**—Travel Agents. **Related DOT Job**—252.152-010 Travel Agent.

41-3099.99 Sales Representatives, Services, All Other

- Education/Training Required: No data available
- Employed: 439,450
- Annual Earnings: $46,790
- Growth: 18.7%
- Annual Job Openings: 61,000

All services sales representatives not listed separately.

No task data available.

Note: The Department of Labor has not collected some data for this job, so it has fewer details than the other descriptions.

Related SOC Job—41-3099 Sales Representatives, Services, All Other. **Related OOH Job**—None. **Related DOT Jobs**—165.157-010 Song Plugger; 236.252-010 Representative, Personal Service; 250.357-022 Sales Representative; 251.157-014 Sales Representative, Data Processing Services; 251.257-014 Sales Agent, Psychological Tests And Industrial Relations; 251.357-010 Sales Agent, Business Services; 251.357-018 Sales Agent, Pest Control Service; 251.357-022 Sales Representative, Franchise; 251.357-026 Sales Representative, Herbicide Service; 252.257-010 Traffic Agent; 252.357-010 Crating-And-Moving Estimator; others.

41-4000 Sales Representatives, Wholesale and Manufacturing

41-4011.00 Sales Representatives, Wholesale and Manufacturing, Technical and Scientific Products

- Education/Training Required: Associate degree
- Employed: 379,890
- Annual Earnings: $60,760
- Growth: 14.4%
- Annual Job Openings: 47,000

Sell goods for wholesalers or manufacturers where technical or scientific knowledge is required in such areas as biology, engineering, chemistry, and electronics, normally obtained from at least 2 years of postsecondary education.

Contact new and existing customers to discuss their needs and to explain how these needs could be met by specific products and services. Answer customers' questions about products, prices, availability, product uses, and credit terms. Quote prices, credit terms, and other bid specifications. Emphasize product features based on analyses of customers' needs and on technical knowledge of product capabilities and limitations. Maintain customer records, using automated systems. Negotiate prices and terms of sales and service agreements. Identify prospective customers by using business directories, following leads from existing clients, participating in organizations and clubs, and attending trade shows and conferences. Prepare sales contracts for orders obtained and submit orders for processing. Select the correct products or assist customers in making product selections based on customers' needs, product specifications, and applicable regulations. Collaborate with colleagues to exchange information such as selling strategies and marketing information. Prepare sales presentations and proposals that explain product specifications and applications. Provide customers with ongoing technical support. Demonstrate and explain the operation and use of products. Inform customers of estimated delivery schedules, service contracts, warranties, or other information pertaining to purchased products. Attend sales and trade meetings and read related publications to obtain information about market conditions, business trends, and industry developments. Visit establishments to evaluate needs and to promote product or service sales. Complete expense reports, sales reports, and other paperwork. Initiate sales campaigns and follow marketing plan guidelines to meet sales and production expectations. Recommend ways for customers to alter product usage to improve production. Complete product and development training as required. Provide feedback to company's product design team so that products can be tailored to clients' needs. Arrange for installation and test-operation of machinery.

GOE Information—Interest Area: 14. Retail and Wholesale Sales and Service. **Work Group:** 14.02. Technical Sales. **Personality Type—** Enterprising. Enterprising occupations frequently involve starting up and carrying out projects. These occupations can involve leading people and making many decisions. They sometimes require risk taking and often deal with business. **Work Values—**Autonomy; Recognition; Variety; Compensation; Creativity; Achievement. **Skills—**Persuasion; Negotiation; Management of Financial Resources; Service Orientation; Science; Coordination. **Abilities—***Cognitive:* Fluency of Ideas; Originality; Memorization; Number Facility; Oral Expression; Oral Comprehension. *Psychomotor:* None met the criteria. *Physical:* None met the criteria. *Sensory:* Speech Clarity; Speech Recognition; Far Vision. **General Work Activities—***Information Input:* Getting Information; Monitoring Processes, Materials, or Surroundings; Identifying Objects, Actions, and Events. *Mental Process:* Making Decisions and Solving Problems; Updating and Using Relevant Knowledge; Organizing, Planning, and Prioritizing. *Work Output:* Documenting or Recording Information; Interacting With Computers. *Interacting with Others:* Influencing Others or Selling; Communicating with Persons Outside Organization; Establishing and Maintaining Interpersonal Relationships. **Physical Work Conditions—**Indoors; Sitting. **Other Job Characteristics—**Need to Be Exact or Accurate.

Experience—Job Zone 4. A minimum of two to four years of work-related skill, knowledge, or experience is needed. **Job Preparation—** SVP 7.0 to less than 8.0—two years to less than 10 years. **Knowledges—**Sales and Marketing; Customer and Personal Service; Administration and Management; Production and Processing; Computers and Electronics; Transportation. **Instructional Programs—**Business, Management, Marketing, and Related Support Services; Selling Skills and Sales Operations.

Related SOC Job—41-4011 Sales Representatives, Wholesale and Manufacturing, Technical and Scientific Products. **Related OOH Job—**Sales Representatives, Wholesale and Manufacturing. **Related DOT Jobs—**259.257-014 Sales Representative, Electroplating; 262.157-010 Pharmaceutical Detailer; 262.357-010 Sales Representative, Chemicals and Drugs; 262.357-022 Sales Representative, Water-Treatment Chemicals; 271.257-010 Sales Representative, Communication Equipment; 271.352-010 Sales Representative, Radiographic-Inspection Equipment and Services; 271.352-014 Sales Representative, Ultrasonic Equipment; 271.357-010 Sales Representative, Electronics Parts; others.

41-4012.00 Sales Representatives, Wholesale and Manufacturing, Except Technical and Scientific Products

- **Education/Training Required:** Moderate-term on-the-job training
- **Employed:** 1,436,800
- **Annual Earnings:** $47,380
- **Growth:** 12.9%
- **Annual Job Openings:** 169,000

Sell goods for wholesalers or manufacturers to businesses or groups of individuals. Work requires substantial knowledge of items sold.

Answer customers' questions about products, prices, availability, product uses, and credit terms. Recommend products to customers based on customers' needs and interests. Contact regular and prospective customers to demonstrate products, explain product features, and solicit orders. Estimate or quote prices, credit or contract terms, warranties, and delivery dates. Consult with clients after sales or contract signings to resolve problems and to provide ongoing support. Prepare drawings, estimates, and bids that meet specific customer needs. Provide customers with product samples and catalogs. Identify prospective customers by using business directories, following leads from existing clients, participating in organizations and clubs, and attending trade shows and conferences. Arrange and direct delivery and installation of products and equipment. Monitor market conditions; product innovations; and competitors' products, prices, and sales. Negotiate details of contracts and payments and prepare sales contracts and order forms. Perform administrative duties, such as preparing sales budgets and reports, keeping sales records, and filing expense account reports. Obtain credit information about prospective customers. Forward orders to manufacturers. Check stock levels and reorder merchandise as necessary. Plan, assemble, and stock product displays in retail stores or make recommendations to retailers regarding product displays, promotional programs, and advertising. Negotiate with retail merchants to improve product exposure such as shelf positioning and advertising. Train customers' employees to operate and maintain new equipment. Buy products from manufacturers or brokerage firms and distribute them to wholesale and retail clients.

GOE Information—Interest Area: 14. Retail and Wholesale Sales and Service. **Work Group:** 14.03. General Sales. **Personality Type—** Enterprising. Enterprising occupations frequently involve starting up and carrying out projects. These occupations can involve leading people and making many decisions. They sometimes require risk taking and often deal with business. **Work Values—**Autonomy; Recognition; Variety; Compensation; Creativity; Supervision, Technical. **Skills—**Negotiation; Persuasion; Service Orientation; Management of Financial Resources; Time Management; Operations Analysis. **Abilities—***Cognitive:* Written Expression; Written Comprehension; Category Flexibility; Originality; Fluency of Ideas; Deductive Reasoning. *Psychomotor:* None met the criteria. *Physical:* None met the criteria. *Sensory:* Speech Recognition; Speech Clarity. **General Work Activities—***Information Input:* Getting Information; Identifying Objects, Actions, and Events; Monitoring Processes, Materials, or Surroundings. *Mental Process:* Organizing, Planning, and Prioritizing; Processing Information; Updating and Using Relevant Knowledge. *Work Output:* Handling and Moving Objects; Interacting With Computers; Performing General Physical Activities. *Interacting with Others:* Establishing and Maintaining Interpersonal

Relationships; Influencing Others or Selling; Communicating with Persons Outside Organization. **Physical Work Conditions—** Outdoors; Noisy; Contaminants; More Often Standing Than Sitting; Walking and Running. **Other Job Characteristics—**Need to Be Exact or Accurate.

Experience—Job Zone 3. Previous work-related skill, knowledge, or experience is required. **Job Preparation—**SVP 6.0 to less than 7.0— more than one year and less than four years. **Knowledges—**Sales and Marketing; Economics and Accounting; Customer and Personal Service; Administration and Management; Transportation; Production and Processing. **Instructional Programs—**Apparel and Accessories Marketing Operations; Business, Management, Marketing, and Related Support Services; Fashion Merchandising; General Merchandising, Sales, and Related Marketing Operations, Other; Sales, Distribution, and Marketing Operations, General; Specialized Merchandising, Sales, and Related Marketing Operations, Other; Special Products Marketing Operations.

Related SOC Job—41-4012 Sales Representatives, Wholesale and Manufacturing, Except Technical and Scientific Products. **Related OOH Job—**Sales Representatives, Wholesale and Manufacturing. **Related DOT Jobs—**162.157-026 Commission Agent, Livestock; 260.257-010 Sales Representative, Livestock; 260.357-010 Commission Agent, Agricultural Produce; 260.357-014 Sales Representative, Food Products; 260.357-018 Sales Representative, Malt Liquors; 260.357-022 Sales Representative, Tobacco Products and Smoking Supplies; 261.357-010 Sales Representative, Apparel Trimmings; 261.357-014 Sales Representative, Canvas Products; 261.357-018 Sales Representative, Footwear; others.

41-9000 Other Sales and Related Workers

41-9011.00 Demonstrators and Product Promoters

- **Education/Training Required: Moderate-term on-the-job training**
- **Employed: 86,050**
- **Annual Earnings: $20,730**
- **Growth: 16.5%**
- **Annual Job Openings: 32,000**

Demonstrate merchandise and answer questions for the purpose of creating public interest in buying the product. May sell demonstrated merchandise.

Demonstrate and explain products, methods, or services to persuade customers to purchase products or utilize services. Identify interested and qualified customers in order to provide them with additional information. Keep areas neat while working and return items to correct locations following demonstrations. Practice demonstrations to ensure that they will run smoothly. Prepare and alter presentation contents to target specific audiences. Learn about competitors' products and consumers' interests and concerns in order to answer questions and provide more complete information. Recommend product or service improvements to employers. Wear costumes or signboards and walk in public to promote merchandise, services, or events. Write articles and pamphlets about products.

Suggest specific product purchases to meet customers' needs. Train demonstrators to present a company's products or services. Set up and arrange displays and demonstration areas to attract the attention of prospective customers. Provide product samples, coupons, informational brochures, and other incentives to persuade people to buy products. Record and report demonstration-related information such as the number of questions asked by the audience and the number of coupons distributed. Sell products being promoted and keep records of sales. Stock shelves with products. Give tours of plants where specific products are made. Develop lists of prospective clients from sources such as newspaper items, company records, local merchants, and customers. Contact businesses and civic establishments to arrange to exhibit and sell merchandise. Visit trade shows, stores, community organizations, and other venues to demonstrate products or services, and to answer questions from potential customers. Transport, assemble, and disassemble materials used in presentations. Instruct customers in alteration of products. Provide product information, using lectures, films, charts, or slide shows. Collect fees or accept donations. Work as part of a team of demonstrators to accommodate large crowds. Research and investigate products to be presented to prepare for demonstrations.

GOE Information—Interest Area: 14. Retail and Wholesale Sales and Service. **Work Group:** 14.04. Personal Soliciting. **Personality Type—**Enterprising. Enterprising occupations frequently involve starting up and carrying out projects. These occupations can involve leading people and making many decisions. They sometimes require risk taking and often deal with business. **Work Values—**Independence; Variety; Social Service; Supervision, Technical. **Skills—**Persuasion; Speaking; Social Perceptiveness; Systems Evaluation; Writing; Learning Strategies. **Abilities—***Cognitive:* Fluency of Ideas; Memorization; Originality; Written Expression; Oral Expression; Written Comprehension. *Psychomotor:* None met the criteria. *Physical:* None met the criteria. *Sensory:* Speech Clarity; Auditory Attention. **General Work Activities—***Information Input:* Identifying Objects, Actions, and Events; Getting Information. *Mental Process:* Organizing, Planning, and Prioritizing; Scheduling Work and Activities; Judging the Qualities of Things, Services, or Other People's Work. *Work Output:* Handling and Moving Objects; Performing General Physical Activities; Documenting or Recording Information. *Interacting with Others:* Communicating with Persons Outside Organization; Establishing and Maintaining Interpersonal Relationships; Performing for or Working with the Public. **Physical Work Conditions—**More Often Indoors Than Outdoors; Standing; Walking and Running; Using Hands on Objects, Tools, or Controls. **Other Job Characteristics—**None met the criteria.

Experience—Job Zone 1. No previous work-related skill, knowledge, or experience is needed. **Job Preparation—**SVP below 4.0—less than six months. **Knowledges—**Sales and Marketing; Communications and Media; Education and Training; Economics and Accounting; English Language; Clerical Practices. **Instructional Program—**Retailing and Retail Operations.

Related SOC Job—41-9011 Demonstrators and Product Promoters. **Related OOH Job—**Demonstrators, Product Promoters, and Models. **Related DOT Jobs—**279.357-010 Sales Exhibitor; 293.357-018 Goodwill Ambassador; 297.354-010 Demonstrator; 297.354-014 Demonstrator, Knitting; 297.357-010 Demonstrator, Electric-Gas Appliances; 297.367-010 Exhibit-Display Representative; 297.451-010 Instructor, Painting; 297.454-010 Demonstrator, Sewing Techniques; 299.687-014 Sandwich-Board Carrier.

41-9012.00 Models

- **Education/Training Required: Moderate-term on-the-job training**
- **Employed: 1,430**
- **Annual Earnings: $22,700**
- **Growth: 15.7%**
- **Annual Job Openings: 1,000**

Model garments and other apparel to display clothing before prospective buyers at fashion shows, private showings, or retail establishments or before photographer. May pose for photos to be used for advertising purposes. May pose as subject for paintings, sculptures, and other types of artistic expression.

Display clothing and merchandise in commercials, advertisements, or fashion shows. Work closely with photographers, fashion coordinators, directors, producers, stylists, makeup artists, other models, and clients to produce the desired looks and to finish photo shoots on schedule. Report job completions to agencies and obtain information about future appointments. Record rates of pay and durations of jobs on vouchers. Wear character costumes and impersonate characters portrayed to amuse children and adults. Make many quick changes backstage during fashion shows and yet maintain poised appearance before audiences. Inform prospective purchasers about models, numbers, and prices of garments; the garments' designers; and where garments can be purchased. Hand out samples or gifts, demonstrate products, and converse with children and adults while dressed in costume. Assemble and maintain portfolios, print composite cards, and travel to go-sees to obtain jobs. Stand, turn, and walk to demonstrate features of garments for observers at fashion shows, private showings, and retail establishments. Promote products and services in television commercials, on film, or in videos. Pose for artists and photographers. Pose as directed or strike suitable interpretive poses for promoting and selling merchandise or fashions during appearances, filming, or photo sessions. Gather information from agents concerning the pay, dates, times, provisions, and lengths of jobs. Dress in sample or completed garments and select accessories. Apply makeup to face and style hair to enhance appearance, considering such factors as color, camera techniques, and facial features. Follow strict routines of diet, sleep, and exercise to maintain appearance.

GOE Information—Interest Area: 14. Retail and Wholesale Sales and Service. **Work Group:** 14.04. Personal Soliciting. **Personality Type—** Artistic. Artistic occupations frequently involve working with forms, designs, and patterns. They often require self-expression, and the work can be done without following a clear set of rules. **Work Values—** Recognition; Compensation; Social Status. **Skills—** None met the criteria. **Abilities—** *Cognitive:* None met the criteria. *Psychomotor:* None met the criteria. *Physical:* Gross Body Coordination. *Sensory:* None met the criteria. **General Work Activities—** *Information Input:* None met the criteria. *Mental Process:* Organizing, Planning, and Prioritizing; Thinking Creatively. *Work Output:* Performing General Physical Activities. *Interacting with Others:* Performing for or Working with the Public; Establishing and Maintaining Interpersonal Relationships; Communicating with Persons Outside Organization. **Physical Work Conditions—** Indoors; Standing; Walking and Running. **Other Job Characteristics—** None met the criteria.

Experience— Job Zone 1. No previous work-related skill, knowledge, or experience is needed. **Job Preparation—** SVP below 4.0—less than six months. **Knowledges—** Fine Arts; Sales and Marketing; Communications and Media. **Instructional Program—** Fashion Modeling.

Related SOC Job— 41-9012 Models. **Related OOH Job—** Demonstrators, Product Promoters, and Models. **Related DOT Jobs—** 297.667-014 Model; 299.647-010 Impersonator, Character; 961.367-010 Model, Photographers'; 961.667-010 Model, Artists'.

41-9021.00 Real Estate Brokers

- **Education/Training Required: Work experience in a related occupation**
- **Employed: 41,760**
- **Annual Earnings: $57,190**
- **Growth: 7.8%**
- **Annual Job Openings: 12,000**

Operate real estate office or work for commercial real estate firm, overseeing real estate transactions. Other duties usually include selling real estate or renting properties and arranging loans.

Sell, for a fee, real estate owned by others. Obtain agreements from property owners to place properties for sale with real estate firms. Monitor fulfillment of purchase contract terms to ensure that they are handled in a timely manner. Compare a property with similar properties that have recently sold to determine its competitive market price. Act as an intermediary in negotiations between buyers and sellers over property prices and settlement details and during the closing of sales. Generate lists of properties for sale, their locations and descriptions, and available financing options, using computers. Maintain knowledge of real estate law; local economies; fair housing laws; and types of available mortgages, financing options, and government programs. Check work completed by loan officers, attorneys, and other professionals to ensure that it is performed properly. Arrange for financing of property purchases. Appraise property values, assessing income potential when relevant. Maintain awareness of current income tax regulations, local zoning, building and tax laws, and growth possibilities of the area where a property is located. Manage and operate real estate offices, handling associated business details. Supervise agents who handle real estate transactions. Rent properties or manage rental properties. Arrange for title searches of properties being sold. Give buyers virtual tours of properties in which they are interested, using computers. Review property details to ensure that environmental regulations are met. Develop, sell, or lease property used for industry or manufacturing. Maintain working knowledge of various factors that determine a farm's capacity to produce, including agricultural variables and proximity to market centers and transportation facilities.

GOE Information—Interest Area: 14. Retail and Wholesale Sales and Service. **Work Group:** 14.03. General Sales. **Personality Type—** No data available. **Work Values—** No data available. **Skills—** Management of Financial Resources; Negotiation; Judgment and Decision Making; Persuasion; Mathematics; Active Listening. **Abilities—** *Cognitive:* Written Comprehension; Deductive Reasoning; Oral Comprehension; Mathematical Reasoning; Oral Expression; Written Expression. *Psychomotor:* None met the criteria. *Physical:* None met the criteria. *Sensory:* Speech Recognition; Near Vision. **General Work Activities—** *Information Input:* Getting Information; Identifying Objects, Actions, and Events; Monitoring Processes, Materials, or Surroundings. *Mental Process:* Organizing, Planning, and Prioritizing; Making Decisions and Solving Problems; Scheduling Work and Activities. *Work Output:* Documenting or Recording Information; Interacting With Computers; Operating Vehicles or Equipment. *Interacting with Others:* Communicating with Persons Outside Organization; Resolving Conflicts and Negotiating with Others; Performing for or Working with the Public. **Physical Work**

Conditions—More Often Indoors Than Outdoors; Sitting. **Other Job Characteristics**—Need to Be Exact or Accurate; Repeat Same Tasks.

Experience—Job Zone 3. Previous work-related skill, knowledge, or experience is required. **Job Preparation**—SVP 6.0 to less than 7.0—more than one year and less than four years. **Knowledges**—Sales and Marketing; Law and Government; Customer and Personal Service; Building and Construction; Personnel and Human Resources; Economics and Accounting; Administration and Management. **Instructional Program**—Real Estate.

Related SOC Job—41-9021 Real Estate Brokers. **Related OOH Job**—Real Estate Brokers and Sales Agents. **Related DOT Job**—250.357-018 Real-Estate Broker (UR).

41-9022.00 Real Estate Sales Agents

- **Education/Training Required: Postsecondary vocational training**
- **Employed: 150,200**
- **Annual Earnings: $39,240**
- **Growth: 14.7%**
- **Annual Job Openings: 41,000**

Rent, buy, or sell property for clients. Perform duties such as studying property listings, interviewing prospective clients, accompanying clients to property site, discussing conditions of sale, and drawing up real estate contracts. Includes agents who represent buyer.

Present purchase offers to sellers for consideration. Confer with escrow companies, lenders, home inspectors, and pest control operators to ensure that terms and conditions of purchase agreements are met before closing dates. Interview clients to determine what kinds of properties they are seeking. Prepare documents such as representation contracts, purchase agreements, closing statements, deeds, and leases. Coordinate property closings, overseeing signing of documents and disbursement of funds. Act as an intermediary in negotiations between buyers and sellers, generally representing one or the other. Promote sales of properties through advertisements, open houses, and participation in multiple listing services. Compare a property with similar properties that have recently sold to determine its competitive market price. Coordinate appointments to show homes to prospective buyers. Generate lists of properties that are compatible with buyers' needs and financial resources. Display commercial, industrial, agricultural, and residential properties to clients and explain their features. Arrange for title searches to determine whether clients have clear property titles. Review plans for new construction with clients, enumerating and recommending available options and features. Answer clients' questions regarding construction work, financing, maintenance, repairs, and appraisals. Accompany buyers during visits to and inspections of property, advising them on the suitability and value of the homes they are visiting. Inspect condition of premises and arrange for necessary maintenance or notify owners of maintenance needs. Advise sellers on how to make homes more appealing to potential buyers. Arrange meetings between buyers and sellers when details of transactions need to be negotiated. Advise clients on market conditions, prices, mortgages, legal requirements, and related matters. Evaluate mortgage options to help clients obtain financing at the best prevailing rates and terms. Review property listings, trade journals, and relevant literature and attend conventions, seminars, and staff and association meetings to remain knowledgeable about real estate markets.

GOE Information—Interest Area: 14. Retail and Wholesale Sales and Service. **Work Group:** 14.03. General Sales. **Personality Type**—

Enterprising. Enterprising occupations frequently involve starting up and carrying out projects. These occupations can involve leading people and making many decisions. They sometimes require risk taking and often deal with business. **Work Values**—Responsibility; Recognition; Compensation; Variety; Autonomy; Social Status. **Skills**—Negotiation; Coordination; Service Orientation; Speaking; Time Management; Management of Financial Resources. **Abilities**—*Cognitive:* Mathematical Reasoning; Memorization; Fluency of Ideas; Flexibility of Closure; Oral Expression; Speed of Closure. *Psychomotor:* None met the criteria. *Physical:* None met the criteria. *Sensory:* Near Vision; Speech Recognition; Far Vision; Speech Clarity; Visual Color Discrimination; Depth Perception. **General Work Activities**—*Information Input:* Getting Information; Identifying Objects, Actions, and Events; Monitoring Processes, Materials, or Surroundings. *Mental Process:* Updating and Using Relevant Knowledge; Organizing, Planning, and Prioritizing; Making Decisions and Solving Problems. *Work Output:* Interacting With Computers; Documenting or Recording Information. *Interacting with Others:* Performing for or Working with the Public; Resolving Conflicts and Negotiating with Others; Communicating with Persons Outside Organization. **Physical Work Conditions**—More Often Indoors Than Outdoors; Sitting. **Other Job Characteristics**—Need to Be Exact or Accurate; Errors Have Important Consequences.

Experience—Job Zone 2. Some previous work-related skill, knowledge, or experience may be helpful in these occupations, but usually is not needed. **Job Preparation**—SVP 4.0 to less than 6.0—six months to less than two years. **Knowledges**—Sales and Marketing; Clerical Practices; Customer and Personal Service; Law and Government; Economics and Accounting; Building and Construction. **Instructional Program**—Real Estate.

Related SOC Job—41-9022 Real Estate Sales Agents. **Related OOH Job**—Real Estate Brokers and Sales Agents. **Related DOT Jobs**—250.157-010 Superintendent, Sales; 250.357-010 Building Consultant; 250.357-014 Leasing Agent, Residence; 250.357-018 Real-Estate Broker (UR).

41-9031.00 Sales Engineers

- **Education/Training Required: Bachelor's degree**
- **Employed: 69,790**
- **Annual Earnings: $74,200**
- **Growth: 14.0%**
- **Annual Job Openings: 8,000**

Sell business goods or services, the selling of which requires a technical background equivalent to a baccalaureate degree in engineering.

Plan and modify product configurations to meet customer needs. Confer with customers and engineers to assess equipment needs and to determine system requirements. Collaborate with sales teams to understand customer requirements, to promote the sale of company products, and to provide sales support. Secure and renew orders and arrange delivery. Develop, present, or respond to proposals for specific customer requirements, including request for proposal responses and industry-specific solutions. Sell products requiring extensive technical expertise and support for installation and use, such as material handling equipment, numerical-control machinery, and computer systems. Diagnose problems with installed equipment. Prepare and deliver technical presentations that explain products or services to customers and prospective customers. Recommend improved materials or machinery to customers, documenting how such changes will lower costs or increase production. Provide technical and non-technical support and services to clients or other staff members regarding the use, operation, and maintenance of equipment. Research and identify potential customers for products or services. Visit prospective buyers at commercial, industrial, or other establishments to show samples or catalogs and to inform them about product pricing, availability, and advantages. Create sales or service contracts for products or services. Arrange for demonstrations or trial installations of equipment. Keep informed on industry news and trends; products; services; competitors; relevant information about legacy, existing, and emerging technologies; and the latest product-line developments. Attend company training seminars to become familiar with product lines. Provide information needed for the development of custom-made machinery. Develop sales plans to introduce products in new markets. Write technical documentation for products. Identify resale opportunities and support them to achieve sales plans. Document account activities, generate reports, and keep records of business transactions with customers and suppliers.

GOE Information—Interest Area: 14. Retail and Wholesale Sales and Service. **Work Group:** 14.02. Technical Sales. **Personality Type—** Enterprising. Enterprising occupations frequently involve starting up and carrying out projects. These occupations can involve leading people and making many decisions. They sometimes require risk taking and often deal with business. **Work Values—**Ability Utilization; Creativity; Recognition; Variety; Advancement; Responsibility. **Skills—**Operations Analysis; Science; Systems Evaluation; Programming; Technology Design; Installation. **Abilities—***Cognitive:* Oral Expression; Fluency of Ideas; Mathematical Reasoning; Number Facility; Written Expression; Originality. *Psychomotor:* None met the criteria. *Physical:* None met the criteria. *Sensory:* Speech Recognition; Speech Clarity; Far Vision; Visual Color Discrimination; Depth Perception; Auditory Attention. **General Work Activities—** *Information Input:* Getting Information; Identifying Objects, Actions, and Events; Monitoring Processes, Materials, or Surroundings. *Mental Process:* Updating and Using Relevant Knowledge; Thinking Creatively; Organizing, Planning, and Prioritizing. *Work Output:* Interacting With Computers; Drafting and Specifying Technical Devices; Documenting or Recording Information. *Interacting with Others:* Influencing Others or Selling; Communicating with Persons Outside Organization; Communicating with Other Workers. **Physical Work Conditions—**Indoors; Sitting; Repetitive Motions. **Other Job Characteristics—**Need to Be Exact or Accurate; Repeat Same Tasks.

Experience—Job Zone 4. A minimum of two to four years of work-related skill, knowledge, or experience is needed. **Job Preparation—** SVP 7.0 to less than 8.0—two years to less than 10 years. **Knowledges—**Sales and Marketing; Engineering and Technology; Design; Physics; Computers and Electronics; Customer and Personal Service. **Instructional Program—**Selling Skills and Sales Operations.

Related SOC Job—41-9031 Sales Engineers. **Related OOH Job—**Sales Engineers. **Related DOT Jobs—**002.151-010 Sales Engineer, Aeronautical Products; 003.151-010 Sales-Engineer, Electrical Products; 003.151-014 Sales-Engineer, Electronics Products and Systems; 006.151-010 Sales Engineer, Ceramic Products; 007.151-010 Sales Engineer, Mechanical Equipment; 008.151-010 Chemical-Equipment Sales Engineer; 010.151-010 Sales Engineer, Mining-and-Oil-Well Equipment and Services; 013.151-010 Sales Engineer, Agricultural Equipment; 014.151-010 Sales Engineer, Marine Equipment; others.

41-9041.00 Telemarketers

- **Education/Training Required: Short-term on-the-job training**
- **Employed: 400,860**
- **Annual Earnings: $20,360**
- **Growth: −10.0%**
- **Annual Job Openings: 156,000**

Solicit orders for goods or services over the telephone.

Contact businesses or private individuals by telephone to solicit sales for goods or services or to request donations for charitable causes. Deliver prepared sales talks, reading from scripts that describe products or services, to persuade potential customers to purchase a product or service or to make a donation. Explain products or services and prices and answer questions from customers. Obtain customer information such as name, address, and payment method and enter orders into computers. Record names, addresses, purchases, and reactions of prospects contacted. Adjust sales scripts to better target the needs and interests of specific individuals. Obtain names and telephone numbers of potential customers from sources such as telephone directories, magazine reply cards, and lists purchased from other organizations. Answer telephone calls from potential customers who have been solicited through advertisements. Telephone or write letters to respond to correspondence from customers or to follow up initial sales contacts. Maintain records of contacts, accounts, and orders. Schedule appointments for sales representatives to meet with prospective customers or for customers to attend sales presentations. Conduct client or market surveys to obtain information about potential customers.

GOE Information—Interest Area: 14. Retail and Wholesale Sales and Service. **Work Group:** 14.04. Personal Soliciting. **Personality Type—** Enterprising. Enterprising occupations frequently involve starting up and carrying out projects. These occupations can involve leading people and making many decisions. They sometimes require risk taking and often deal with business. **Work Values—**Independence. **Skills—**Persuasion; Negotiation; Speaking; Active Listening; Service Orientation. **Abilities—***Cognitive:* Oral Expression. *Psychomotor:* None met the criteria. *Physical:* None met the criteria. *Sensory:* Speech Clarity; Speech Recognition. **General Work Activities—***Information Input:* Getting Information; Identifying Objects, Actions, and Events. *Mental Process:* Updating and Using Relevant Knowledge; Processing Information; Making Decisions and Solving Problems. *Work Output:* Interacting With Computers; Documenting or Recording Information. *Interacting with Others:* Influencing Others or Selling; Establishing and Maintaining Interpersonal Relationships; Communicating with Persons Outside Organization. **Physical Work Conditions—**Indoors; Noisy; Sitting; Using Hands on Objects, Tools, or Controls; Repetitive Motions. **Other Job Characteristics—**Need to Be Exact or Accurate; Repeat Same Tasks; Automation.

Experience—Job Zone 2. Some previous work-related skill, knowledge, or experience may be helpful in these occupations, but usually is not needed. **Job Preparation—**SVP 4.0 to less than 6.0—six months to less than two years. **Knowledges—**Sales and Marketing; Communications and Media; English Language. **Instructional Programs—**Sales, Distribution, and Marketing Operations, General; Selling Skills and Sales Operations.

Related SOC Job—41-9041 Telemarketers. **Related OOH Job—** Telemarketers. **Related DOT Job—**299.357-014 Telephone Solicitor.

41-9091.00 Door-To-Door Sales Workers, News and Street Vendors, and Related Workers

- Education/Training Required: Short-term on-the-job training
- Employed: 10,970
- Annual Earnings: $20,450
- Growth: −7.4%
- Annual Job Openings: 56,000

Sell goods or services door-to-door or on the street.

Contact customers to persuade them to purchase merchandise or services. Circulate among potential customers or travel by foot, truck, automobile, or bicycle to deliver or sell merchandise or services. Explain products or services and prices and demonstrate use of products. Deliver merchandise and collect payment. Develop prospect lists. Distribute product samples or literature that details products or services. Order or purchase supplies. Stock carts or stands. Answer questions about product features and benefits. Set up and display sample merchandise at parties or stands. Arrange buying parties, and solicit sponsorship of such parties, in order to sell merchandise. Write and record orders for merchandise or enter orders into computers.

GOE Information—Interest Area: 14. Retail and Wholesale Sales and Service. **Work Group:** 14.04. Personal Soliciting. **Personality Type—** Enterprising. Enterprising occupations frequently involve starting up and carrying out projects. These occupations can involve leading people and making many decisions. They sometimes require risk taking and often deal with business. **Work Values—**Independence. **Skills—**Persuasion. **Abilities—**Cognitive: Number Facility. *Psychomotor:* None met the criteria. *Physical:* None met the criteria. *Sensory:* Speech Clarity. **General Work Activities—***Information Input:* Getting Information. *Mental Process:* Thinking Creatively; Updating and Using Relevant Knowledge. *Work Output:* Performing General Physical Activities; Handling and Moving Objects; Documenting or Recording Information. *Interacting with Others:* Influencing Others or Selling; Communicating with Persons Outside Organization; Performing for or Working with the Public. **Physical Work Conditions—**More Often Outdoors Than Indoors; More Often Standing Than Sitting; Walking and Running. **Other Job Characteristics—**None met the criteria.

Experience—Job Zone 1. No previous work-related skill, knowledge, or experience is needed. **Job Preparation—**SVP below 4.0—less than six months. **Knowledges—**Sales and Marketing; Economics and Accounting; Communications and Media. **Instructional Program—** Selling Skills and Sales Operations.

Related SOC Job—41-9091 Door-To-Door Sales Workers, News and Street Vendors, and Related Workers. **Related OOH Job—**Door-To-Door Sales Workers, News and Street Vendors, and Related Workers. **Related DOT Jobs—**279.357-038 Salesperson-Demonstrator, Party Plan; 291.357-010 Sales Representative, Door-To-Door; 291.454-010 Lei Seller; 291.457-010 Cigarette Vendor; 291.457-014 Lounge-Car Attendant; 291.457-018 Peddler; 291.457-022 Vendor; 292.457-010 Newspaper Carrier.

41-9099.99 Sales and Related Workers, All Other

- Education/Training Required: No data available
- Employed: 178,480
- Annual Earnings: $32,800
- Growth: 18.4%
- Annual Job Openings: 53,000

All sales and related workers not listed separately.

No task data available.

Note: The Department of Labor has not collected some data for this job, so it has fewer details than the other descriptions.

Related SOC Job—41-9099 Sales and Related Workers, All Other. **Related OOH Job—**None. **Related DOT Jobs—**191.157-010 Pawnbroker; 191.287-010 Appraiser; 259.357-034 Ticket Broker; 294.257-010 Auctioneer; 296.357-010 Personal Shopper; 296.367-010 Automobile Locator; 296.367-014 Comparison Shopper; 299.357-018 Wedding Consultant; 299.364-010 Drapery And Upholstery Measurer; 299.364-014 Gift Wrapper; 299.367-010 Customer-Service Clerk; 299.387-010 Drapery And Upholstery Estimator; 299.387-018 Stamp Classifier; 299.667-014 Stock Checker, Apparel; 869.367-014 Measurer.

43-0000

Office and Administrative Support Occupations

43-1000 Supervisors, Office and Administrative Support Workers

43-1011.00 First-Line Supervisors/ Managers of Office and Administrative Support Workers

- Education/Training Required: Work experience in a related occupation
- Employed: 1,352,130
- Annual Earnings: $42,400
- Growth: 8.1%
- Annual Job Openings: 167,000

Supervise and coordinate the activities of clerical and administrative support workers.

Resolve customer complaints and answer customers' questions regarding policies and procedures. Supervise the work of office, administrative, or customer service employees to ensure adherence to quality standards, deadlines, and proper procedures, correcting errors or problems. Provide employees with guidance in handling difficult or complex problems and in resolving escalated complaints or disputes. Implement corporate and departmental policies, procedures, and service standards in conjunction with management. Discuss job performance problems with employees to identify causes and issues and to work on resolving problems. Train and instruct employees in job duties and company policies or arrange for training to be provided. Evaluate employees' job performance and conformance to regulations and recommend appropriate personnel action. Recruit, interview, and select employees. Review records and reports pertaining to activities such as production, payroll, and shipping to verify details, monitor work activities, and evaluate performance. Interpret and communicate work procedures and company policies to staff. Prepare and issue work schedules, deadlines, and duty assignments of office or administrative staff. Maintain records pertaining to inventory, personnel, orders, supplies, and machine maintenance. Compute figures such as balances, totals, and commissions. Research, compile, and prepare reports, manuals, correspondence, and other information required by management or governmental agencies. Coordinate activities with other supervisory personnel and with other work units or departments. Analyze financial activities of establishments or departments and provide input into budget planning and preparation processes. Develop or update procedures, policies, and standards. Make recommendations to management concerning such issues as staffing decisions and procedural changes. Consult with managers and other personnel to resolve problems in areas such as equipment performance, output quality, and work schedules. Participate in the work of subordinates to facilitate productivity or to overcome difficult aspects of work.

GOE Information—Interest Area: 04. Business and Administration. Work Group: 04.02. Managerial Work in Business Detail. Personality Type—Enterprising. Enterprising occupations frequently involve starting up and carrying out projects. These occupations can involve leading people and making many decisions. They sometimes require risk taking and often deal with business. Work Values—Authority; Autonomy; Creativity; Social Service; Responsibility; Working Conditions. Skills—Management of Personnel Resources; Management of Financial Resources; Negotiation; Management of Material Resources; Persuasion; Monitoring. Abilities—*Cognitive:* Memorization; Number Facility; Mathematical Reasoning; Written

Expression; Oral Expression; Perceptual Speed. *Psychomotor:* Wrist-Finger Speed. *Physical:* Extent Flexibility. *Sensory:* Speech Clarity; Speech Recognition; Near Vision. General Work Activities— *Information Input:* Getting Information; Identifying Objects, Actions, and Events; Monitoring Processes, Materials, or Surroundings. *Mental Process:* Organizing, Planning, and Prioritizing; Updating and Using Relevant Knowledge; Making Decisions and Solving Problems. *Work Output:* Documenting or Recording Information; Interacting With Computers. *Interacting with Others:* Establishing and Maintaining Interpersonal Relationships; Communicating with Other Workers; Guiding, Directing, and Motivating Subordinates. Physical Work Conditions—Indoors; Noisy; Sitting. Other Job Characteristics— Need to Be Exact or Accurate; Repeat Same Tasks.

Experience—Job Zone 3. Previous work-related skill, knowledge, or experience is required. Job Preparation—SVP 6.0 to less than 7.0— more than one year and less than four years. Knowledges— Administration and Management; Clerical Practices; Economics and Accounting; Personnel and Human Resources; Customer and Personal Service; Education and Training. Instructional Programs— Agricultural Business Technology; Customer Service Management; Medical Staff Services Technology/Technician; Medical/Health Management and Clinical Assistant/Specialist; Office Management and Supervision.

Related SOC Job—43-1011 First-Line Supervisors/Managers of Office and Administrative Support Workers. Related OOH Job—Office and Administrative Support Worker Supervisors and Managers. Related DOT Jobs—109.137-010 Shelving Supervisor; 168.167-058 Manager, Customer Service; 168.167-070 Regulatory Administrator; 202.132-010 Supervisor, Steno Pool; 203.132-010 Supervisor, Telegraphic-Typewriter Operators; 203.132-014 Supervisor, Transcribing Operators; 203.137-010 Supervisor, Word Processing; 203.137-014 Typing Section Chief; 205.137-014 Supervisor, Survey Workers; 205.162-010 Admitting Officer; 206.137-010 Supervisor, Files; 207.137-010 Chief Clerk, Print Shop; others.

43-2000 Communications Equipment Operators

43-2011.00 Switchboard Operators, Including Answering Service

- Education/Training Required: Short-term on-the-job training
- Employed: 194,980
- Annual Earnings: $22,060
- Growth: –8.8%
- Annual Job Openings: 34,000

Operate telephone business systems equipment or switchboards to relay incoming, outgoing, and interoffice calls. May supply information to callers and record messages.

Operate communication systems, such as telephone, switchboard, intercom, two-way radio, or public address. Answer incoming calls, greeting callers, providing information, transferring calls, and taking messages as necessary. Route emergency calls appropriately. Page individuals to inform them of telephone calls, using paging and interoffice communication equipment. Relay and route written and verbal messages. Place telephone calls or arrange conference calls as instructed. Perform clerical duties, such as typing, proofreading, accepting orders, scheduling appointments, and sorting mail.

Monitor alarm systems to ensure that secure conditions are maintained. Contact security staff members when necessary, using radiotelephones. Keep records of calls placed and charges incurred. Record messages, suggesting rewording for clarity and conciseness. Stamp messages with time and date and file them appropriately. Answer simple questions about clients' businesses, using reference files. Complete forms for sales orders.

GOE Information—Interest Area: 04. Business and Administration. **Work Group:** 04.08. Clerical Machine Operation. **Personality Type—**Conventional. Conventional occupations frequently involve following set procedures and routines. These occupations can include working with data and details more than with ideas. Usually there is a clear line of authority to follow. **Work Values—** Independence; Activity; Supervision, Technical; Supervision, Human Relations; Moral Values; Working Conditions. **Skills—**None met the criteria. **Abilities—***Cognitive:* None met the criteria. *Psychomotor:* None met the criteria. *Physical:* None met the criteria. *Sensory:* Speech Recognition; Speech Clarity; Hearing Sensitivity. **General Work Activities—***Information Input:* Getting Information; Identifying Objects, Actions, and Events; Monitoring Processes, Materials, or Surroundings. *Mental Process:* Updating and Using Relevant Knowledge; Processing Information; Organizing, Planning, and Prioritizing. *Work Output:* Interacting With Computers; Documenting or Recording Information. *Interacting with Others:* Establishing and Maintaining Interpersonal Relationships; Performing for or Working with the Public; Communicating with Persons Outside Organization. **Physical Work Conditions—**Indoors; Sitting; Using Hands on Objects, Tools, or Controls; Repetitive Motions. **Other Job Characteristics—**Need to Be Exact or Accurate; Repeat Same Tasks.

Experience—Job Zone 2. Some previous work-related skill, knowledge, or experience may be helpful in these occupations, but usually is not needed. **Job Preparation—**SVP 4.0 to less than 6.0—six months to less than two years. **Knowledges—**Clerical Practices; Customer and Personal Service; English Language. **Instructional Program—**Receptionist.

Related SOC Job—43-2011 Switchboard Operators, Including Answering Service. **Related OOH Job—**Communications Equipment Operators. **Related DOT Jobs—**235.562-014 Switchboard Operator, Police District; 235.662-014 Communication-Center Operator; 235.662-022 Telephone Operator; 235.662-026 Telephone-Answering-Service Operator; 239.362-010 Telephone Clerk, Telegraph Office.

43-2021.00 Telephone Operators

- **Education/Training Required: Short-term on-the-job training**
- **Employed: 29,290**
- **Annual Earnings: $31,380**
- **Growth: –35.7%**
- **Annual Job Openings: 3,000**

Provide information by accessing alphabetical and geographical directories. Assist customers with special billing requests, such as charges to a third party and credits or refunds for incorrectly dialed numbers or bad connections. May handle emergency calls and assist children or people with physical disabilities to make telephone calls.

Observe signal lights on switchboards and dial or press buttons to make connections. Interrupt busy lines if an emergency warrants. Keep records of calls placed and received and of related toll charges. Monitor automated systems for placing collect calls and intervene for callers needing assistance.

Offer special assistance to persons such as those who are unable to dial or those who are in emergency situations.

Operate telephone switchboards and systems to advance and complete connections, including those for local, long distance, pay telephone, mobile, person-to-person, and emergency calls. Listen to customer requests, referring to alphabetical or geographical directories to answer questions and provide telephone information. Calculate and quote charges for services such as long-distance connections. Set up conference calls in different locations and time zones. Provide relay service for hearing-impaired users. Perform clerical duties such as typing, proofreading, and sorting mail. Suggest and check alternate spellings, locations, or listing formats for customers lacking details or complete information. Consult charts to determine charges for pay-telephone calls, requesting coin deposits for calls as necessary. Operate paging systems or other systems of bells or buzzers to notify recipients of incoming calls. Promote company products, services, and savings plans when appropriate. Provide assistance for customers with special billing requests. Record messages to be used on telephone systems. Update directory information. Insert tickets in calculagraphs (time-stamping devices) to record times of toll calls.

GOE Information—Interest Area: 03. Arts and Communication. **Work Group:** 03.10. Communications Technology. **Personality Type—**Conventional. Conventional occupations frequently involve following set procedures and routines. These occupations can include working with data and details more than with ideas. Usually there is a clear line of authority to follow. **Work Values—**Supervision, Technical; Independence; Social Service; Supervision, Human Relations; Activity; Company Policies and Practices. **Skills—**None met the criteria. **Abilities—***Cognitive:* None met the criteria. *Psychomotor:* Wrist-Finger Speed; Reaction Time. *Physical:* None met the criteria. *Sensory:* Speech Recognition. **General Work Activities—***Information Input:* Getting Information. *Mental Process:* Processing Information. *Work Output:* Handling and Moving Objects. *Interacting with Others:* Communicating with Persons Outside Organization; Assisting and Caring for Others; Performing for or Working with the Public. **Physical Work Conditions—**Indoors; Sitting; Using Hands on Objects, Tools, or Controls. **Other Job Characteristics—**Need to Be Exact or Accurate.

Experience—Job Zone 1. No previous work-related skill, knowledge, or experience is needed. **Job Preparation—**SVP below 4.0—less than six months. **Knowledges—**Telecommunications. **Instructional Programs—**Customer Service Support/Call Center/Teleservice Operation; Receptionist.

Related SOC Job—43-2021 Telephone Operators. **Related OOH Job—**Communications Equipment Operators. **Related DOT Jobs—**235.462-010 Central-Office Operator; 235.662-018 Directory-Assistance Operator.

43-2099.99 Communications Equipment Operators, All Other

- **Education/Training Required: Short-term on-the-job training**
- **Employed: 3,870**
- **Annual Earnings: $32,540**
- **Growth: –10.8%**
- **Annual Job Openings: 1,000**

All communications equipment operators not listed separately.

No task data available.

Note: The Department of Labor has not collected some data for this job, so it has fewer details than the other descriptions.

Related SOC Job—43-2099 Communications Equipment Operators, All Other. **Related OOH Job**—Communications Equipment Operators. **Related DOT Jobs**—203.562-010 Wire-Transfer Clerk; 235.562-010 Clerk, Route; 236.562-010 Telegrapher; 236.562-014 Telegrapher Agent; 237.367-034 Pay-Station Attendant; 239.382-010 Wire-Photo Operator, News.

43-3000 Financial Clerks

43-3011.00 Bill and Account Collectors

- **Education/Training Required: Short-term on-the-job training**
- **Employed: 431,280**
- **Annual Earnings: $28,160**
- **Growth: 21.4%**
- **Annual Job Openings: 85,000**

Locate and notify customers of delinquent accounts by mail, telephone, or personal visit to solicit payment. Duties include receiving payment and posting amount to customer's account, preparing statements to credit department if customer fails to respond, initiating repossession proceedings or service disconnection, and keeping records of collection and status of accounts.

Receive payments and post amounts paid to customer accounts. Locate and monitor overdue accounts, using computers and a variety of automated systems. Record information about financial status of customers and status of collection efforts. Locate and notify customers of delinquent accounts by mail, telephone, or personal visits to solicit payment. Confer with customers by telephone or in person to determine reasons for overdue payments and to review the terms of sales, service, or credit contracts. Advise customers of necessary actions and strategies for debt repayment. Persuade customers to pay amounts due on credit accounts, damage claims, or nonpayable checks or to return merchandise. Sort and file correspondence and perform miscellaneous clerical duties such as answering correspondence and writing reports. Perform various administrative functions for assigned accounts, such as recording address changes and purging the records of deceased customers. Arrange for debt repayment or establish repayment schedules based on customers' financial situations. Negotiate credit extensions when necessary. Trace delinquent customers to new addresses by inquiring at post offices, telephone companies, or credit bureaus or through the questioning of neighbors. Notify credit departments, order merchandise repossession or service disconnection, and turn over account records to attorneys when customers fail to respond to collection attempts. Drive vehicles to visit customers, return merchandise to creditors, or deliver bills.

GOE Information—Interest Area: 06. Finance and Insurance. **Work Group:** 06.04. Finance/Insurance Customer Service. **Personality Type**—Conventional. Conventional occupations frequently involve following set procedures and routines. These occupations can include working with data and details more than with ideas. Usually there is a clear line of authority to follow. **Work Values**—Supervision, Human Relations; Supervision, Technical; Authority; Variety; Advancement; Activity. **Skills**—Management of Financial Resources; Management of Personnel Resources; Speaking; Social Perceptiveness; Time Management; Persuasion. **Abilities**—*Cognitive:* Written Expression; Time Sharing; Oral Expression; Written Comprehension; Oral Comprehension. *Psychomotor:* None met the

criteria. *Physical:* None met the criteria. *Sensory:* Speech Recognition; Near Vision. **General Work Activities**—*Information Input:* Getting Information; Identifying Objects, Actions, and Events; Monitoring Processes, Materials, or Surroundings. *Mental Process:* Processing Information; Updating and Using Relevant Knowledge; Organizing, Planning, and Prioritizing. *Work Output:* Documenting or Recording Information; Interacting With Computers. *Interacting with Others:* Establishing and Maintaining Interpersonal Relationships; Resolving Conflicts and Negotiating with Others; Communicating with Persons Outside Organization. **Physical Work Conditions**—Indoors; Sitting; Using Hands on Objects, Tools, or Controls; Repetitive Motions. **Other Job Characteristics**—Need to Be Exact or Accurate; Repeat Same Tasks.

Experience—Job Zone 3. Previous work-related skill, knowledge, or experience is required. **Job Preparation**—SVP 6.0 to less than 7.0—more than one year and less than four years. **Knowledges**—Clerical Practices; Economics and Accounting; Customer and Personal Service; Law and Government; Computers and Electronics; Personnel and Human Resources. **Instructional Program**—Banking and Financial Support Services.

Related SOC Job—43-3011 Bill and Account Collectors. **Related OOH Job**—Bill and Account Collectors. **Related DOT Jobs**—241.357-010 Collection Clerk; 241.367-010 Collector; 241.367-022 Repossessor.

43-3021.00 Billing and Posting Clerks and Machine Operators

- **Education/Training Required: Moderate-term on-the-job training**
- **Employed: 513,020**
- **Annual Earnings: $27,780**
- **Growth: 3.4%**
- **Annual Job Openings: 70,000**

The job openings listed here are shared with 43-3021.01 Statement Clerks, 43-3021.02 Billing, Cost, and Rate Clerks, and 43-3021.03 Billing, Posting, and Calculating Machine Operators.

Compile, compute, and record billing, accounting, statistical, and other numerical data for billing purposes. Prepare billing invoices for services rendered or for delivery or shipment of goods.

No task data available.

GOE Information—Interest Area: 04. Business and Administration. **Work Group:** 04.06. Mathematical Clerical Support. **Note:** The Department of Labor has not collected some data for this job, so it has fewer details than the other descriptions.

Instructional Program—Accounting Technology/Technician and Bookkeeping.

Related SOC Job—43-3021 Billing and Posting Clerks and Machine Operators. **Related OOH Job**—Billing and Posting Clerks and Machine Operators. **Related DOT Job**—No data available.

43-3021.01 Statement Clerks

- **Education/Training Required: Moderate-term on-the-job training**
- **Employed: 513,020**
- **Annual Earnings: $27,780**
- **Growth: 3.4%**
- **Annual Job Openings: 70,000**

The job openings listed here are shared with 43-3021.00 Billing and Posting Clerks and Machine Operators, 43-3021.02 Billing, Cost, and Rate Clerks, and 43-3021.03 Billing, Posting, and Calculating Machine Operators.

Prepare and distribute bank statements to customers, answer inquiries, and reconcile discrepancies in records and accounts.

Encode and cancel checks, using bank machines. Take orders for imprinted checks. Compare previously prepared bank statements with canceled checks and reconcile discrepancies. Verify signatures and required information on checks. Post stop-payment notices to prevent payment of protested checks. Maintain files of canceled checks and customers' signatures. Match statements with batches of canceled checks by account numbers. Weigh envelopes containing statements to determine correct postage and affix postage, using stamps or metering equipment. Load machines with statements, cancelled checks, and envelopes to prepare statements for distribution to customers or stuff envelopes by hand. Retrieve checks returned to customers in error, adjusting customer accounts and answering inquiries about errors as necessary. Route statements for mailing or over-the-counter delivery to customers. Monitor equipment to ensure proper operation. Fix minor problems, such as equipment jams, and notify repair personnel of major equipment problems.

GOE Information—Interest Area: 04. Business and Administration. **Work Group:** 04.06. Mathematical Clerical Support. **Personality Type**—Conventional. Conventional occupations frequently involve following set procedures and routines. These occupations can include working with data and details more than with ideas. Usually there is a clear line of authority to follow. **Work Values**—Working Conditions; Supervision, Human Relations; Supervision, Technical; Advancement; Activity; Social Service. **Skills**—Critical Thinking. **Abilities**—*Cognitive:* Perceptual Speed; Number Facility. *Psychomotor:* None met the criteria. *Physical:* None met the criteria. *Sensory:* None met the criteria. **General Work Activities**—*Information Input:* Getting Information. *Mental Process:* Organizing, Planning, and Prioritizing; Updating and Using Relevant Knowledge; Processing Information. *Work Output:* Interacting With Computers. *Interacting with Others:* Establishing and Maintaining Interpersonal Relationships; Communicating with Other Workers; Performing Administrative Activities. **Physical Work Conditions**—Indoors; Sitting; Repetitive Motions. **Other Job Characteristics**—Repeat Same Tasks; Need to Be Exact or Accurate.

Experience—Job Zone 2. Some previous work-related skill, knowledge, or experience may be helpful in these occupations, but usually is not needed. **Job Preparation**—SVP 4.0 to less than 6.0—six months to less than two years. **Knowledges**—Economics and Accounting; Clerical Practices; Administration and Management; Mathematics. **Instructional Program**—Accounting Technology/Technician and Bookkeeping.

Related SOC Job—43-3021 Billing and Posting Clerks and Machine Operators. **Related OOH Job**—Billing and Posting Clerks and Machine Operators. **Related DOT Job**—214.362-046 Statement Clerk.

43-3021.02 Billing, Cost, and Rate Clerks

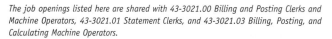

- Education/Training Required: Moderate-term on-the-job training
- Employed: 513,020
- Annual Earnings: $27,780
- Growth: 3.4%
- Annual Job Openings: 70,000

The job openings listed here are shared with 43-3021.00 Billing and Posting Clerks and Machine Operators, 43-3021.01 Statement Clerks, and 43-3021.03 Billing, Posting, and Calculating Machine Operators.

Compile data, compute fees and charges, and prepare invoices for billing purposes. Duties include computing costs and calculating rates for goods, services, and shipment of goods; posting data; and keeping other relevant records. May involve use of computer or typewriter, calculator, and adding and bookkeeping machines.

Verify accuracy of billing data and revise any errors. Operate typing, adding, calculating, and billing machines. Prepare itemized statements, bills, or invoices and record amounts due for items purchased or services rendered. Review documents such as purchase orders, sales tickets, charge slips, or hospital records to compute fees and charges due. Perform bookkeeping work, including posting data and keeping other records concerning costs of goods and services and the shipment of goods. Keep records of invoices and support documents. Resolve discrepancies in accounting records. Type billing documents, shipping labels, credit memorandums, and credit forms, using typewriters or computers. Contact customers to obtain or relay account information. Compute credit terms, discounts, shipment charges, and rates for goods and services to complete billing documents. Answer mail and telephone inquiries regarding rates, routing, and procedures. Track accumulated hours and dollar amounts charged to each client job to calculate client fees for professional services such as legal and accounting services. Review compiled data on operating costs and revenues to set rates. Compile reports of cost factors, such as labor, production, storage, and equipment. Consult sources such as rate books, manuals, and insurance company representatives to determine specific charges and information such as rules, regulations, and government tax and tariff information. Update manuals when rates, rules, or regulations are amended. Estimate market value of products or services.

GOE Information—Interest Area: 04. Business and Administration. **Work Group:** 04.06. Mathematical Clerical Support. **Personality Type**—Conventional. Conventional occupations frequently involve following set procedures and routines. These occupations can include working with data and details more than with ideas. Usually there is a clear line of authority to follow. **Work Values**—Working Conditions; Independence; Advancement; Supervision, Technical; Activity; Supervision, Human Relations. **Skills**—Writing; Active Listening; Service Orientation; Reading Comprehension; Instructing; Social Perceptiveness. **Abilities**—*Cognitive:* Number Facility; Mathematical Reasoning; Category Flexibility. *Psychomotor:* None met the criteria. *Physical:* None met the criteria. *Sensory:* Speech Recognition; Near Vision. **General Work Activities**—*Information Input:* Getting Information; Identifying Objects, Actions, and Events; Monitoring Processes, Materials, or Surroundings. *Mental Process:* Organizing, Planning, and Prioritizing; Processing Information; Updating and Using Relevant Knowledge. *Work Output:* Interacting With Computers; Documenting or Recording Information. *Interacting with Others:* Establishing and Maintaining Interpersonal Relationships; Communicating with Other Workers; Performing Administrative Activities. **Physical Work Conditions**—Indoors; Sitting. **Other Job Characteristics**—Need to Be Exact or Accurate; Repeat Same Tasks.

Experience—Job Zone 3. Previous work-related skill, knowledge, or experience is required. **Job Preparation**—SVP 6.0 to less than 7.0—more than one year and less than four years. **Knowledges**—Clerical Practices; Economics and Accounting; Computers and Electronics; Customer and Personal Service; Mathematics; English Language. **Instructional Program**—Accounting Technology/Technician and Bookkeeping.

Related SOC Job—43-3021 Billing and Posting Clerks and Machine Operators. **Related OOH Job**—Billing and Posting Clerks and Machine Operators. **Related DOT Jobs**—184.387-010 Wharfinger; 191.367-010 Personal Property Assessor; 214.267-010 Rate Analyst, Freight; 214.362-010 Demurrage Clerk; 214.362-014 Documentation-Billing Clerk; 214.362-022 Insurance Clerk; 214.362-026 Invoice-Control Clerk; 214.362-038 Traffic-Rate Clerk; 214.362-042 Billing Clerk; 214.382-014 Billing Typist; 214.382-018 C.O.D. Clerk; 214.382-022 Interline Clerk; 214.382-026 Revising Clerk; 214.382-030 Settlement Clerk; 214.387-010 Billing-Control Clerk; 214.387-014 Rate Reviewer; others.

43-3021.03 Billing, Posting, and Calculating Machine Operators

- **Education/Training Required: Moderate-term on-the-job training**
- **Employed: 513,020**
- **Annual Earnings: $27,780**
- **Growth: 3.4%**
- **Annual Job Openings: 70,000**

The job openings listed here are shared with 43-3021.00 Billing and Posting Clerks and Machine Operators, 43-3021.01 Statement Clerks, and 43-3021.02 Billing, Cost, and Rate Clerks.

Operate machines that automatically perform mathematical processes, such as addition, subtraction, multiplication, and division, to calculate and record billing, accounting, statistical, and other numerical data. Duties include operating special billing machines to prepare statements, bills, and invoices and operating bookkeeping machines to copy and post data, make computations, and compile records of transactions.

Enter into machines all information needed for bill generation. Train other calculating machine operators and review their work. Operate special billing machines to prepare statements, bills, and invoices. Operate bookkeeping machines to copy and post data, make computations, and compile records of transactions. Reconcile and post receipts for cash received by various departments. Prepare transmittal reports for changes to assessment and tax rolls; redemption file changes; and warrants, deposits, and invoices. Encode and add amounts of transaction documents, such as checks or money orders, using encoding machines. Balance and reconcile batch control totals with source documents or computer listings to locate errors, encode correct amounts, or prepare correction records. Compute payroll and retirement amounts, applying knowledge of payroll deductions, actuarial tables, disability factors, and survivor allowances. Maintain ledgers and registers, posting charges and refunds to individual funds and computing and verifying balances. Compute monies due on personal and real property, inventories, redemption payments, and other amounts, applying specialized knowledge of tax rates, formulas, interest rates, and other relevant information. Verify and post to ledgers purchase orders, reports of goods received, invoices, paid vouchers, and other information. Assign purchase order numbers to invoices, requisitions, and formal and informal bids. Verify completeness and accuracy of original documents such as business property statements, tax rolls, invoices, bonds and coupons, and redemption certificates. Bundle sorted documents to prepare those drawn on other banks for collection. Transcribe data from office records, using specified forms, billing machines, and transcribing machines. Sort and list items for proof or collection. Send completed bills to billing clerks for information verification. Transfer data from machines, such as encoding machines, to computers. Sort and micro-

film transaction documents, such as checks, using sorting machines. Observe operation of sorters to locate documents that machines cannot read and manually record amounts of these documents.

GOE Information—Interest Area: 04. Business and Administration. **Work Group:** 04.08. Clerical Machine Operation. **Personality Type**—Conventional. Conventional occupations frequently involve following set procedures and routines. These occupations can include working with data and details more than with ideas. Usually there is a clear line of authority to follow. **Work Values**—Independence; Supervision, Technical; Supervision, Human Relations; Advancement; Activity; Working Conditions. **Skills**—Speaking; Active Listening; Writing. **Abilities**—*Cognitive:* Mathematical Reasoning; Number Facility; Deductive Reasoning; Written Expression; Oral Expression; Written Comprehension. *Psychomotor:* None met the criteria. *Physical:* None met the criteria. *Sensory:* Near Vision; Speech Recognition. **General Work Activities**—*Information Input:* Getting Information; Identifying Objects, Actions, and Events; Monitoring Processes, Materials, or Surroundings. *Mental Process:* Organizing, Planning, and Prioritizing; Updating and Using Relevant Knowledge; Processing Information. *Work Output:* Interacting With Computers; Documenting or Recording Information. *Interacting with Others:* Establishing and Maintaining Interpersonal Relationships; Communicating with Other Workers; Communicating with Persons Outside Organization. **Physical Work Conditions**—Indoors; Noisy; Contaminants; Sitting; Using Hands on Objects, Tools, or Controls; Repetitive Motions. **Other Job Characteristics**—Repeat Same Tasks; Need to Be Exact or Accurate.

Experience—Job Zone 2. Some previous work-related skill, knowledge, or experience may be helpful in these occupations, but usually is not needed. **Job Preparation**—SVP 4.0 to less than 6.0—six months to less than two years. **Knowledges**—Economics and Accounting; Clerical Practices; Personnel and Human Resources. **Instructional Program**—Accounting Technology/Technician and Bookkeeping.

Related SOC Job—43-3021 Billing and Posting Clerks and Machine Operators. **Related OOH Job**—Billing and Posting Clerks and Machine Operators. **Related DOT Jobs**—214.462-010 Accounts-Adjustable Clerk; 214.482-010 Billing-Machine Operator; 216.482-018 Audit-Machine Operator; 216.482-022 Calculating-Machine Operator; 217.382-010 Proof-Machine Operator; 219.382-010 Check Writer.

43-3031.00 Bookkeeping, Accounting, and Auditing Clerks

- **Education/Training Required: Moderate-term on-the-job training**
- **Employed: 1,815,340**
- **Annual Earnings: $29,490**
- **Growth: 5.9%**
- **Annual Job Openings: 291,000**

Compute, classify, and record numerical data to keep financial records complete. Perform any combination of routine calculating, posting, and verifying duties to obtain primary financial data for use in maintaining accounting records. May also check the accuracy of figures, calculations, and postings pertaining to business transactions recorded by other workers.

Operate computers programmed with accounting software to record, store, and analyze information. Check figures, postings, and documents for correct entry, mathematical accuracy, and proper codes. Comply with federal, state, and company policies, procedures, and regulations. Debit, credit, and total accounts on computer spreadsheets and databases, using specialized accounting software. Classify, record, and summarize numerical and financial data to compile and keep financial records, using journals and ledgers or computers. Calculate, prepare, and issue bills, invoices, account statements, and other financial statements according to established procedures. Code documents according to company procedures. Compile statistical, financial, accounting, or auditing reports and tables pertaining to such matters as cash receipts, expenditures, accounts payable and receivable, and profits and losses. Operate 10-key calculators, typewriters, and copy machines to perform calculations and produce documents. Access computerized financial information to answer general questions as well as those related to specific accounts. Reconcile or note and report discrepancies found in records. Perform financial calculations such as amounts due, interest charges, balances, discounts, equity, and principal. Perform general office duties such as filing, answering telephones, and handling routine correspondence. Prepare bank deposits by compiling data from cashiers; verifying and balancing receipts; and sending cash, checks, or other forms of payment to banks. Receive, record, and bank cash, checks, and vouchers. Calculate and prepare checks for utilities, taxes, and other payments. Compare computer printouts to manually maintained journals to determine if they match. Reconcile records of bank transactions. Prepare trial balances of books. Monitor status of loans and accounts to ensure that payments are up to date. Transfer details from separate journals to general ledgers or data-processing sheets. Compile budget data and documents based on estimated revenues and expenses and previous budgets. Calculate costs of materials, overhead, and other expenses, based on estimates, quotations, and price lists.

GOE Information—**Interest Area:** 04. Business and Administration. **Work Group:** 04.06. Mathematical Clerical Support. **Personality Type**—Conventional. Conventional occupations frequently involve following set procedures and routines. These occupations can include working with data and details more than with ideas. Usually there is a clear line of authority to follow. **Work Values**—Independence; Working Conditions; Advancement; Autonomy; Company Policies and Practices; Activity. **Skills**—Management of Financial Resources; Mathematics; Time Management; Critical Thinking; Active Learning; Instructing. **Abilities**—*Cognitive:* Mathematical Reasoning; Number Facility; Category Flexibility; Perceptual Speed; Information Ordering; Time Sharing. *Psychomotor:* None met the criteria. *Physical:* None met the criteria. *Sensory:* Near Vision; Speech Recognition. **General Work Activities**—*Information Input:* Getting Information; Identifying Objects, Actions, and Events; Monitoring Processes, Materials, or Surroundings. *Mental Process:* Organizing, Planning, and Prioritizing; Processing Information; Analyzing Data or Information. *Work Output:* Interacting With Computers; Documenting or Recording Information. *Interacting with Others:* Establishing and Maintaining Interpersonal Relationships; Communicating with Other Workers; Performing Administrative Activities. **Physical Work Conditions**—Indoors; Sitting; Repetitive Motions. **Other Job Characteristics**—Need to Be Exact or Accurate; Repeat Same Tasks; Automation.

Experience—Job Zone 3. Previous work-related skill, knowledge, or experience is required. **Job Preparation**—SVP 6.0 to less than 7.0—more than one year and less than four years. **Knowledges**—Clerical Practices; Economics and Accounting; Mathematics; Computers and Electronics. **Instructional Programs**—Accounting and Related Services, Other; Accounting Technology/Technician and Bookkeeping.

Related SOC Job—43-3031 Bookkeeping, Accounting, and Auditing Clerks. **Related OOH Job**—Bookkeeping, Accounting, and Auditing Clerks. **Related DOT Jobs**—210.362-010 Distribution-Accounting Clerk; 210.367-010 Account-Information Clerk; 210.367-014 Foreign-Exchange-Position Clerk; 210.382-010 Audit Clerk; 210.382-014 Bookkeeper; 210.382-030 Classification-Control Clerk; 210.382-038 Credit-Card Clerk; 210.382-042 Fixed-Capital Clerk; 210.382-046 General-Ledger Bookkeeper; 210.382-050 Mortgage-Loan-Computation Clerk; 210.382-054 Night Auditor; 210.382-062 Securities Clerk; 216.362-014 Collection Clerk; 216.362-022 Food-and-Beverage Controller; others.

43-3041.00 Gaming Cage Workers

- **Education/Training Required: Short-term on-the-job training**
- **Employed: 18,730**
- **Annual Earnings: $22,380**
- **Growth: 17.0%**
- **Annual Job Openings: 2,000**

In a gaming establishment, conduct financial transactions for patrons. May reconcile daily summaries of transactions to balance books. Accept patron's credit application and verify credit references to provide check-cashing authorization or to establish house credit accounts. May sell gambling chips, tokens, or tickets to patrons or to other workers for resale to patrons. May convert gaming chips, tokens, or tickets to currency upon patron's request. May use a cash register or computer to record transaction.

Follow all gaming regulations. Maintain confidentiality of customers' transactions. Count funds and reconcile daily summaries of transactions to balance books. Convert gaming checks, coupons, tokens, and coins to currency for gaming patrons. Maintain cage security. Determine cash requirements for windows and order all necessary currency, coins, and chips. Verify accuracy of reports such as authorization forms, transaction reconciliations, and exchange summary reports. Cash checks and process credit card advances for patrons. Sell gambling chips, tokens, or tickets to patrons or to other workers for resale to patrons. Perform removal and rotation of cash, coin, and chip inventories as necessary. Supply currency, coins, chips, and gaming checks to other departments as needed. Provide assistance in the training and orientation of new cashiers. Provide customers with information about casino operations. Record casino exchange transactions, using cash registers. Prepare bank deposits, balancing assigned funds as necessary. Prepare reports, including assignment of company funds and recording of department revenues. Establish new computer accounts.

GOE Information—**Interest Area:** 14. Retail and Wholesale Sales and Service. **Work Group:** 14.06. Customer Service. **Personality Type**—No data available. **Work Values**—No data available. **Skills**—Service Orientation; Management of Personnel Resources; Instructing; Management of Material Resources. **Abilities**—*Cognitive:* Number Facility; Perceptual Speed; Selective Attention; Mathematical Reasoning; Oral Expression. *Psychomotor:* None met the criteria. *Physical:* Trunk Strength; Extent Flexibility. *Sensory:* None met the criteria. **General Work Activities**—*Information Input:* Identifying Objects, Actions, and Events; Monitoring Processes, Materials, or Surroundings; Getting Information. *Mental Process:* Processing Information; Making Decisions and Solving Problems; Updating and Using Relevant Knowledge. *Work Output:* Documenting or Recording Information; Handling and Moving Objects; Interacting With Computers. *Interacting with Others:* Performing for or Working with the Public; Establishing and Maintaining Interpersonal

Relationships; Communicating with Other Workers. **Physical Work Conditions**—Indoors; Noisy; Standing; Using Hands on Objects, Tools, or Controls; Bending or Twisting the Body; Repetitive Motions. **Other Job Characteristics**—Need to Be Exact or Accurate; Repeat Same Tasks; Errors Have Important Consequences.

Experience—Job Zone 2. Some previous work-related skill, knowledge, or experience may be helpful in these occupations, but usually is not needed. **Job Preparation**—SVP 4.0 to less than 6.0—six months to less than two years. **Knowledges**—Customer and Personal Service; Economics and Accounting; Mathematics; Public Safety and Security. **Instructional Program**—Accounting Technology/Technician and Bookkeeping.

Related SOC Job—43-3041 Gaming Cage Workers. **Related OOH Job**—Gaming Cage Workers. **Related DOT Job**—211.462-022 Cashier, Gambling.

43-3051.00 Payroll and Timekeeping Clerks

- **Education/Training Required: Moderate-term on-the-job training**
- **Employed: 205,600**
- **Annual Earnings: $31,360**
- **Growth: 17.3%**
- **Annual Job Openings: 36,000**

Compile and post employee time and payroll data. May compute employees' time worked, production, and commission. May compute and post wages and deductions. May prepare paychecks.

Process and issue employee paychecks and statements of earnings and deductions. Compute wages and deductions and enter data into computers. Compile employee time, production, and payroll data from time sheets and other records. Review time sheets, work charts, wage computation, and other information to detect and reconcile payroll discrepancies. Verify attendance, hours worked, and pay adjustments and post information onto designated records. Record employee information, such as exemptions, transfers, and resignations, to maintain and update payroll records. Keep informed about changes in tax and deduction laws that apply to the payroll process. Issue and record adjustments to pay related to previous errors or retroactive increases. Provide information to employees and managers on payroll matters, tax issues, benefit plans, and collective agreement provisions. Complete time sheets showing employees' arrival and departure times. Post relevant work hours to client files to bill clients properly. Distribute and collect timecards each pay period. Complete, verify, and process forms and documentation for administration of benefits such as pension plans and unemployment and medical insurance. Prepare and balance period-end reports and reconcile issued payrolls to bank statements. Compile statistical reports, statements, and summaries related to pay and benefits accounts and submit them to appropriate departments. Coordinate special programs, such as United Way campaigns, that involve payroll deductions.

GOE Information—Interest Area: 04. Business and Administration. **Work Group:** 04.06. Mathematical Clerical Support. **Personality Type**—Conventional. Conventional occupations frequently involve following set procedures and routines. These occupations can include working with data and details more than with ideas. Usually there is a clear line of authority to follow. **Work Values**—Working

Conditions; Independence; Supervision, Technical; Advancement; Supervision, Human Relations; Co-workers. **Skills**—Mathematics; Time Management; Active Listening; Writing; Speaking; Learning Strategies. **Abilities**—*Cognitive:* Mathematical Reasoning; Number Facility; Written Comprehension; Oral Expression; Deductive Reasoning. *Psychomotor:* None met the criteria. *Physical:* None met the criteria. *Sensory:* Near Vision. **General Work Activities**—*Information Input:* Getting Information; Identifying Objects, Actions, and Events; Monitoring Processes, Materials, or Surroundings. *Mental Process:* Processing Information; Organizing, Planning, and Prioritizing; Updating and Using Relevant Knowledge. *Work Output:* Documenting or Recording Information; Interacting With Computers. *Interacting with Others:* Establishing and Maintaining Interpersonal Relationships; Performing Administrative Activities; Communicating with Other Workers. **Physical Work Conditions**—Indoors; Noisy; Sitting; Repetitive Motions. **Other Job Characteristics**—Need to Be Exact or Accurate; Repeat Same Tasks.

Experience—Job Zone 3. Previous work-related skill, knowledge, or experience is required. **Job Preparation**—SVP 6.0 to less than 7.0—more than one year and less than four years. **Knowledges**—Clerical Practices; Economics and Accounting; Administration and Management; Personnel and Human Resources; Mathematics; Customer and Personal Service. **Instructional Program**—Accounting Technology/Technician and Bookkeeping.

Related SOC Job—43-3051 Payroll and Timekeeping Clerks. **Related OOH Job**—Payroll and Timekeeping Clerks. **Related DOT Jobs**—215.362-018 Flight-Crew-Time Clerk; 215.362-022 Timekeeper; 215.382-014 Payroll Clerk.

43-3061.00 Procurement Clerks

- **Education/Training Required: Short-term on-the-job training**
- **Employed: 71,390**
- **Annual Earnings: $32,210**
- **Growth: –2.7%**
- **Annual Job Openings: 10,000**

Compile information and records to draw up purchase orders for procurement of materials and services.

Prepare purchase orders and send copies to suppliers and to departments originating requests. Determine if inventory quantities are sufficient for needs, ordering more materials when necessary. Respond to customer and supplier inquiries about order status, changes, or cancellations. Perform buying duties when necessary. Contact suppliers to schedule or expedite deliveries and to resolve shortages, missed or late deliveries, and other problems. Review requisition orders to verify accuracy, terminology, and specifications. Prepare, maintain, and review purchasing files, reports, and price lists. Compare prices, specifications, and delivery dates to determine the best bid among potential suppliers. Track the status of requisitions, contracts, and orders. Calculate costs of orders and charge or forward invoices to appropriate accounts. Check shipments when they arrive to ensure that orders have been filled correctly and that goods meet specifications. Compare suppliers' bills with bids and purchase orders to verify accuracy. Approve bills for payment. Locate suppliers, using sources such as catalogs and the Internet, and interview them to gather information about products to be ordered. Maintain knowledge of all organizational and governmental rules affecting purchases and provide information about these rules to organization staff members and to vendors. Monitor in-house inventory movement and complete inventory transfer forms for bookkeeping purposes. Monitor contractor performance, recommending contract modifications when necessary. Prepare invitation-of-bid forms and mail forms to supplier firms or distribute forms for public posting.

GOE Information—Interest Area: 04. Business and Administration. **Work Group:** 04.07. Records and Materials Processing. **Personality Type**—Conventional. Conventional occupations frequently involve following set procedures and routines. These occupations can include working with data and details more than with ideas. Usually there is a clear line of authority to follow. **Work Values**—Supervision, Technical; Working Conditions; Independence; Advancement; Co-workers; Recognition. **Skills**—Management of Financial Resources; Management of Material Resources; Operations Analysis; Time Management; Monitoring; Service Orientation. **Abilities**—*Cognitive:* Mathematical Reasoning; Oral Comprehension; Written Expression; Written Comprehension; Oral Expression; Deductive Reasoning. *Psychomotor:* None met the criteria. *Physical:* None met the criteria. *Sensory:* Near Vision. **General Work Activities**—*Information Input:* Identifying Objects, Actions, and Events; Monitoring Processes, Materials, or Surroundings; Getting Information. *Mental Process:* Organizing, Planning, and Prioritizing; Processing Information; Updating and Using Relevant Knowledge. *Work Output:* Interacting With Computers; Documenting or Recording Information. *Interacting with Others:* Establishing and Maintaining Interpersonal Relationships; Communicating with Other Workers; Communicating with Persons Outside Organization. **Physical Work Conditions**—Indoors; Noisy; Sitting; Repetitive Motions. **Other Job Characteristics**—Need to Be Exact or Accurate; Repeat Same Tasks.

Experience—Job Zone 3. Previous work-related skill, knowledge, or experience is required. **Job Preparation**—SVP 6.0 to less than 7.0—more than one year and less than four years. **Knowledges**—Clerical Practices; Administration and Management; Customer and Personal Service; Mathematics; Communications and Media; Economics and Accounting. **Instructional Program**—General Office Occupations and Clerical Services.

Related SOC Job—43-3061 Procurement Clerks. **Related OOH Job**—Procurement Clerks. **Related DOT Jobs**—249.367-066 Procurement Clerk; 976.567-010 Film-Replacement Orderer.

43-3071.00 Tellers

- **Education/Training Required: Short-term on-the-job training**
- **Employed: 599,220**
- **Annual Earnings: $21,300**
- **Growth: 6.8%**
- **Annual Job Openings: 108,000**

Receive and pay out money. Keep records of money and negotiable instruments involved in a financial institution's various transactions.

Balance currency, coin, and checks in cash drawers at ends of shifts and calculate daily transactions, using computers, calculators, or adding machines. Cash checks and pay out money after verifying that signatures are correct, that written and numerical amounts agree, and that accounts have sufficient funds. Receive checks and cash for deposit, verify amounts, and check accuracy of deposit slips. Examine checks for endorsements and to verify other information such as dates, bank names, identification of the persons receiving payments, and the legality of the documents. Enter customers' trans-

actions into computers to record transactions and issue computer-generated receipts. Count currency, coins, and checks received, by hand or using currency-counting machine, to prepare them for deposit or shipment to branch banks or the Federal Reserve Bank. Identify transaction mistakes when debits and credits do not balance. Prepare and verify cashier's checks. Arrange monies received in cash boxes and coin dispensers according to denomination. Process transactions such as term deposits, retirement savings plan contributions, automated teller transactions, night deposits, and mail deposits. Receive mortgage, loan, or public utility bill payments, verifying payment dates and amounts due. Resolve problems or discrepancies concerning customers' accounts. Explain, promote, or sell products or services such as travelers' checks, savings bonds, money orders, and cashier's checks, using computerized information about customers to tailor recommendations. Perform clerical tasks such as typing, filing, and microfilm photography. Monitor bank vaults to ensure cash balances are correct. Order a supply of cash to meet daily needs. Sort and file deposit slips and checks. Receive and count daily inventories of cash, drafts, and travelers' checks. Process and maintain records of customer loans. Count, verify, and post armored car deposits. Carry out special services for customers, such as ordering bank cards and checks. Compute financial fees, interest, and service charges. Obtain and process information required for the provision of services, such as opening accounts, savings plans, and purchasing bonds.

GOE Information—Interest Area: 06. Finance and Insurance. **Work Group:** 06.04. Finance/Insurance Customer Service. **Personality Type**—Conventional. Conventional occupations frequently involve following set procedures and routines. These occupations can include working with data and details more than with ideas. Usually there is a clear line of authority to follow. **Work Values**—Working Conditions; Co-workers; Supervision, Technical; Social Service; Supervision, Human Relations; Security. **Skills**—Service Orientation; Mathematics. **Abilities**—*Cognitive:* Number Facility; Perceptual Speed; Oral Expression; Oral Comprehension; Selective Attention; Mathematical Reasoning. *Psychomotor:* Wrist-Finger Speed; Manual Dexterity. *Physical:* None met the criteria. *Sensory:* Near Vision. **General Work Activities**—*Information Input:* Getting Information; Identifying Objects, Actions, and Events; Monitoring Processes, Materials, or Surroundings. *Mental Process:* Evaluating Information Against Standards; Processing Information; Updating and Using Relevant Knowledge. *Work Output:* Interacting With Computers; Documenting or Recording Information; Handling and Moving Objects. *Interacting with Others:* Performing for or Working with the Public; Establishing and Maintaining Interpersonal Relationships; Communicating with Other Workers. **Physical Work Conditions**—Indoors; More Often Standing Than Sitting; Using Hands on Objects, Tools, or Controls; Repetitive Motions. **Other Job Characteristics**—Need to Be Exact or Accurate; Repeat Same Tasks.

Experience—Job Zone 2. Some previous work-related skill, knowledge, or experience may be helpful in these occupations, but usually is not needed. **Job Preparation**—SVP 4.0 to less than 6.0—six months to less than two years. **Knowledges**—Customer and Personal Service; Sales and Marketing; English Language; Clerical Practices. **Instructional Program**—Banking and Financial Support Services.

Related SOC Job—43-3071 Tellers. **Related OOH Job**—Tellers. **Related DOT Jobs**—211.362-014 Foreign Banknote Teller-Trader; 211.362-018 Teller; 211.382-010 Teller, Vault; 219.462-010 Coupon Clerk.

43-4000 Information and Record Clerks

43-4011.00 Brokerage Clerks

- **Education/Training Required: Moderate-term on-the-job training**
- **Employed: 70,110**
- **Annual Earnings: $35,450**
- **Growth: 7.5%**
- **Annual Job Openings: 17,000**

Perform clerical duties involving the purchase or sale of securities. Duties include writing orders for stock purchases and sales, computing transfer taxes, verifying stock transactions, accepting and delivering securities, tracking stock price fluctuations, computing equity, distributing dividends, and keeping records of daily transactions and holdings.

Correspond with customers and confer with co-workers to answer inquiries, discuss market fluctuations, and resolve account problems. Record and document security transactions, such as purchases, sales, conversions, redemptions, and payments, using computers, accounting ledgers, and certificate records. Schedule and coordinate transfer and delivery of security certificates between companies, departments, and customers. Prepare forms, such as receipts, withdrawal orders, transmittal papers, and transfer confirmations, based on transaction requests from stockholders. File, type, and operate standard office machines. Monitor daily stock prices and compute fluctuations to determine the need for additional collateral to secure loans. Prepare reports summarizing daily transactions and earnings for individual customer accounts. Compute total holdings, dividends, interest, transfer taxes, brokerage fees, and commissions and allocate appropriate payments to customers. Verify ownership and transaction information and dividend distribution instructions to ensure conformance with governmental regulations, using stock records and reports.

GOE Information—Interest Area: 04. Business and Administration. **Work Group:** 04.06. Mathematical Clerical Support. **Personality Type—**Conventional. Conventional occupations frequently involve following set procedures and routines. These occupations can include working with data and details more than with ideas. Usually there is a clear line of authority to follow. **Work Values—**Working Conditions; Activity; Co-workers; Supervision, Human Relations; Supervision, Technical; Advancement. **Skills—**Service Orientation; Mathematics; Speaking; Active Listening; Systems Evaluation; Active Learning. **Abilities—***Cognitive:* Number Facility; Mathematical Reasoning; Written Comprehension; Deductive Reasoning; Written Expression; Oral Expression. *Psychomotor:* Finger Dexterity. *Physical:* None met the criteria. *Sensory:* Speech Recognition; Speech Clarity; Near Vision. **General Work Activities—***Information Input:* Identifying Objects, Actions, and Events; Getting Information; Monitoring Processes, Materials, or Surroundings. *Mental Process:* Updating and Using Relevant Knowledge; Organizing, Planning, and Prioritizing; Processing Information. *Work Output:* Interacting With Computers; Documenting or Recording Information. *Interacting with Others:* Establishing and Maintaining Interpersonal Relationships; Communicating with Other Workers; Communicating with Persons Outside Organization. **Physical Work Conditions—**Indoors; Sitting; Repetitive Motions. **Other Job Characteristics—**Need to Be Exact or Accurate; Repeat Same Tasks; Errors Have Important Consequences.

Experience—Job Zone 3. Previous work-related skill, knowledge, or experience is required. **Job Preparation—**SVP 6.0 to less than 7.0—

more than one year and less than four years. **Knowledges—**Clerical Practices; Economics and Accounting; Customer and Personal Service; Sales and Marketing; Computers and Electronics; Mathematics. **Instructional Program—**Accounting Technology/ Technician and Bookkeeping.

Related SOC Job—43-4011 Brokerage Clerks. **Related OOH Job—**Brokerage Clerks. **Related DOT Jobs—**216.362-046 Transfer Clerk; 216.382-046 Margin Clerk II; 216.482-034 Dividend Clerk; 219.362-018 Brokerage Clerk II; 219.362-054 Securities Clerk; 219.482-010 Brokerage Clerk I.

43-4021.00 Correspondence Clerks

- **Education/Training Required: Short-term on-the-job training**
- **Employed: 17,990**
- **Annual Earnings: $28,420**
- **Growth: –6.9%**
- **Annual Job Openings: 5,000**

Compose letters in reply to requests for merchandise, damage claims, credit and other information, delinquent accounts, incorrect billings, or unsatisfactory services. Duties may include gathering data to formulate reply and typing correspondence.

Prepare documents and correspondence such as damage claims, credit and billing inquiries, invoices, and service complaints. Compile data from records to prepare periodic reports. Present clear and concise explanations of governing rules and regulations. Read incoming correspondence to ascertain nature of writers' concerns and to determine disposition of correspondence. Type acknowledgment letters to persons sending correspondence. Review correspondence for format and typographical accuracy, assemble the information into a prescribed form with the correct number of copies, and submit it to an authorized official for signature. Maintain files and control records to show correspondence activities. Gather records pertinent to specific problems, review them for completeness and accuracy, and attach records to correspondence as necessary. Complete form letters in response to requests or problems identified by correspondence. Route correspondence to other departments for reply. Compose letters in reply to correspondence concerning such items as requests for merchandise, damage claims, credit information requests, delinquent accounts, incorrect billing, or unsatisfactory service. Ensure that money collected is properly recorded and secured. Respond to internal and external requests for the release of information contained in medical records, copying medical records and selective extracts in accordance with laws and regulations. Compute costs of records furnished to requesters and write letters to obtain payment. Compose correspondence requesting medical information and records. Prepare records for shipment by certified mail. Obtain written authorization to access required medical information. Confer with company personnel regarding feasibility of complying with writers' requests. Submit completed documents to typists for typing in final form and instruct typists in matters such as format, addresses, addressees, and the necessary number of copies. Process orders for goods requested in correspondence. Compile data pertinent to manufacture of special products for customers.

GOE Information—Interest Area: 04. Business and Administration. **Work Group:** 04.07. Records and Materials Processing. **Personality Type—**Conventional. Conventional occupations frequently involve following set procedures and routines. These occupations can include working with data and details more than with ideas. Usually there is a clear line of authority to follow. **Work Values—**Working Conditions; Social Service; Supervision, Human Relations; Company

Policies and Practices; Supervision, Technical; Activity. **Skills—** Writing; Instructing; Reading Comprehension; Learning Strategies; Active Listening; Critical Thinking. **Abilities—***Cognitive:* Written Expression; Speed of Closure; Number Facility; Mathematical Reasoning; Memorization; Selective Attention. *Psychomotor:* Finger Dexterity. *Physical:* None met the criteria. *Sensory:* Speech Recognition; Near Vision. **General Work Activities—***Information Input:* Getting Information; Identifying Objects, Actions, and Events. *Mental Process:* Organizing, Planning, and Prioritizing; Processing Information; Updating and Using Relevant Knowledge. *Work Output:* Interacting With Computers; Documenting or Recording Information. *Interacting with Others:* Establishing and Maintaining Interpersonal Relationships; Communicating with Other Workers; Resolving Conflicts and Negotiating with Others. **Physical Work Conditions—**Indoors; Sitting; Repetitive Motions. **Other Job Characteristics—**Repeat Same Tasks; Need to Be Exact or Accurate; Automation.

Experience—Job Zone 2. Some previous work-related skill, knowledge, or experience may be helpful in these occupations, but usually is not needed. **Job Preparation—**SVP 4.0 to less than 6.0—six months to less than two years. **Knowledges—**Clerical Practices; Economics and Accounting; Therapy and Counseling; Personnel and Human Resources; Medicine and Dentistry; Customer and Personal Service. **Instructional Program—**General Office Occupations and Clerical Services.

Related SOC Job—43-4021 Correspondence Clerks. **Related OOH Job—**Correspondence Clerks. **Related DOT Jobs—**209.362-034 Correspondence Clerk; 209.367-018 Correspondence-Review Clerk; 209.387-034 Suggestion Clerk; 221.367-062 Sales Correspondent.

43-4031.00 Court, Municipal, and License Clerks

- **Education/Training Required: Short-term on-the-job training**
- **Employed: 102,060**
- **Annual Earnings: $29,320**
- **Growth: 18.6%**
- **Annual Job Openings: 13,000**

The job openings listed here are shared with 43-4031.01 Court Clerks, 43-4031.02 Municipal Clerks, and 43-4031.03 License Clerks.

Perform clerical duties in courts of law, municipalities, and governmental licensing agencies and bureaus. May prepare docket of cases to be called, secure information for judges and court, prepare draft agendas or bylaws for town or city council, answer official correspondence, keep fiscal records and accounts, issue licenses or permits, record data, administer tests, or collect fees.

No task data available.

GOE Information—Interest Area: 07. Government and Public Administration. **Work Group:** 07.04. Public Administration Clerical Support. **Note:** The Department of Labor has not collected some data for this job, so it has fewer details than the other descriptions.

Instructional Program—General Office Occupations and Clerical Services.

Related SOC Job—43-4031 Court, Municipal, and License Clerks. **Related OOH Job—**Court, Municipal, and License Clerks. **Related DOT Job—**No data available.

43-4031.01 Court Clerks

- **Education/Training Required: Short-term on-the-job training**
- **Employed: 102,060**
- **Annual Earnings: $29,320**
- **Growth: 18.6%**
- **Annual Job Openings: 13,000**

The job openings listed here are shared with 43-4031.00 Court, Municipal, and License Clerks, 43-4031.02 Municipal Clerks, and 43-4031.03 License Clerks.

Perform clerical duties in court of law; prepare docket of cases to be called; secure information for judges; and contact witnesses, attorneys, and litigants to obtain information for court.

Prepare dockets or calendars of cases to be called, using typewriters or computers. Record case dispositions, court orders, and arrangements made for payment of court fees. Answer inquiries from the general public regarding judicial procedures, court appearances, trial dates, adjournments, outstanding warrants, summonses, subpoenas, witness fees, and payment of fines. Prepare and issue orders of the court, including probation orders, release documentation, sentencing information, and summonses. Prepare documents recording the outcomes of court proceedings. Instruct parties about timing of court appearances. Explain procedures or forms to parties in cases or to the general public. Search files and contact witnesses, attorneys, and litigants to obtain information for the court. Follow procedures to secure courtrooms and exhibits such as money, drugs, and weapons. Amend indictments when necessary and endorse indictments with pertinent information. Read charges and related information to the court and, if necessary, record defendants' pleas. Swear in jury members, interpreters, witnesses, and defendants. Collect court fees or fines and record amounts collected. Direct support staff in handling of paperwork processed by clerks' offices. Examine legal documents submitted to courts for adherence to laws or court procedures. Prepare and mark all applicable court exhibits and evidence. Record court proceedings, using recording equipment, or record minutes of court proceedings, using stenotype machines or shorthand. Prepare courtrooms with paper, pens, water, easels, and electronic equipment and ensure that recording equipment is working. Conduct roll calls and poll jurors. Meet with judges, lawyers, parole officers, police, and social agency officials to coordinate the functions of the court. Open courts, calling them to order and announcing judges.

GOE Information—Interest Area: 07. Government and Public Administration. **Work Group:** 07.04. Public Administration Clerical Support. **Personality Type—**Conventional. Conventional occupations frequently involve following set procedures and routines. These occupations can include working with data and details more than with ideas. Usually there is a clear line of authority to follow. **Work Values—**Working Conditions; Supervision, Human Relations; Activity; Security; Company Policies and Practices; Authority. **Skills—**Active Listening; Instructing; Service Orientation; Writing; Coordination; Critical Thinking. **Abilities—***Cognitive:* Written Expression; Written Comprehension; Oral Expression; Oral Comprehension; Selective Attention; Time Sharing. *Psychomotor:* None met the criteria. *Physical:* None met the criteria. *Sensory:* Near Vision; Speech Recognition; Speech Clarity. **General Work Activities—***Information Input:* Getting Information; Identifying Objects, Actions, and Events; Monitoring Processes, Materials, or Surroundings. *Mental Process:* Organizing, Planning, and Prioritizing; Updating and Using Relevant Knowledge; Processing Information. *Work Output:* Documenting or Recording Information; Interacting With Computers; Handling and Moving Objects. *Interacting with Others:* Establishing and Maintaining Interpersonal Relationships;

Communicating with Persons Outside Organization; Performing for or Working with the Public. **Physical Work Conditions**—Indoors; Noisy; Sitting; Using Hands on Objects, Tools, or Controls; Repetitive Motions. **Other Job Characteristics**—Need to Be Exact or Accurate; Repeat Same Tasks; Automation; Errors Have Important Consequences.

Experience—Job Zone 2. Some previous work-related skill, knowledge, or experience may be helpful in these occupations, but usually is not needed. **Job Preparation**—SVP 4.0 to less than 6.0—six months to less than two years. **Knowledges**—Clerical Practices; Law and Government; Computers and Electronics; Customer and Personal Service. **Instructional Program**—General Office Occupations and Clerical Services.

Related SOC Job—43-4031 Court, Municipal, and License Clerks. **Related OOH Job**—Court, Municipal, and License Clerks. **Related DOT Job**—243.362-010 Court Clerk.

43-4031.02 Municipal Clerks

- **Education/Training Required: Short-term on-the-job training**
- **Employed: 102,060**
- **Annual Earnings: $29,320**
- **Growth: 18.6%**
- **Annual Job Openings: 13,000**

The job openings listed here are shared with 43-4031.00 Court, Municipal, and License Clerks, 43-4031.01 Court Clerks, and 43-4031.03 License Clerks.

Draft agendas and bylaws for town or city council, record minutes of council meetings, answer official correspondence, keep fiscal records and accounts, and prepare reports on civic needs.

Participate in the administration of municipal elections, including preparation and distribution of ballots, appointment and training of election officers, and tabulation and certification of results. Record and edit the minutes of meetings; then distribute them to appropriate officials and staff members. Plan and direct the maintenance, filing, safekeeping, and computerization of all municipal documents. Issue public notification of all official activities and meetings. Maintain and update documents such as municipal codes and city charters. Prepare meeting agendas and packets of related information. Prepare ordinances, resolutions, and proclamations so that they can be executed, recorded, archived, and distributed. Respond to requests for information from the public, other municipalities, state officials, and state and federal legislative offices. Maintain fiscal records and accounts. Perform budgeting duties, including assisting in budget preparation, expenditure review, and budget administration. Perform general office duties such as taking and transcribing dictation, typing and proofreading correspondence, distributing and filing official forms, and scheduling appointments. Coordinate and maintain office-tracking systems for correspondence and follow-up actions. Research information in the municipal archives upon request of public officials and private citizens. Perform contract administration duties, assisting with bid openings and the awarding of contracts. Collaborate with other staff to assist in the development and implementation of goals, objectives, policies, and priorities. Represent municipalities at community events and serve as liaisons on community committees. Serve as a notary of the public. Issue various permits and licenses, including marriage, fishing, hunting, and dog licenses, and collect appropriate fees. Provide assistance to persons with disabilities in reaching less-accessible areas of municipal facilities. Process claims against the municipality, maintaining files and log of claims, and coordinate claim response and handling with municipal claims administrators.

GOE Information—Interest Area: 07. Government and Public Administration. **Work Group:** 07.04. Public Administration Clerical Support. **Personality Type**—Conventional. Conventional occupations frequently involve following set procedures and routines. These occupations can include working with data and details more than with ideas. Usually there is a clear line of authority to follow. **Work Values**—Working Conditions; Supervision, Human Relations; Company Policies and Practices; Security; Supervision, Technical; Social Service. **Skills**—Service Orientation; Management of Financial Resources; Writing; Social Perceptiveness; Active Listening; Management of Personnel Resources. **Abilities**—*Cognitive:* Written Expression; Written Comprehension; Oral Expression; Oral Comprehension; Mathematical Reasoning. *Psychomotor:* None met the criteria. *Physical:* None met the criteria. *Sensory:* Near Vision; Speech Recognition. **General Work Activities**—*Information Input:* Getting Information; Identifying Objects, Actions, and Events; Monitoring Processes, Materials, or Surroundings. *Mental Process:* Organizing, Planning, and Prioritizing; Updating and Using Relevant Knowledge; Processing Information. *Work Output:* Documenting or Recording Information; Interacting With Computers; Handling and Moving Objects. *Interacting with Others:* Performing for or Working with the Public; Communicating with Persons Outside Organization; Communicating with Other Workers. **Physical Work Conditions**—Indoors; Sitting. **Other Job Characteristics**—Repeat Same Tasks; Need to Be Exact or Accurate.

Experience—Job Zone 3. Previous work-related skill, knowledge, or experience is required. **Job Preparation**—SVP 6.0 to less than 7.0—more than one year and less than four years. **Knowledges**—Clerical Practices; Law and Government; English Language; Economics and Accounting; Personnel and Human Resources; Administration and Management. **Instructional Program**—General Office Occupations and Clerical Services.

Related SOC Job—43-4031 Court, Municipal, and License Clerks. **Related OOH Job**—Court, Municipal, and License Clerks. **Related DOT Job**—243.367-018 Town Clerk.

43-4031.03 License Clerks

- **Education/Training Required: Short-term on-the-job training**
- **Employed: 102,060**
- **Annual Earnings: $29,320**
- **Growth: 18.6%**
- **Annual Job Openings: 13,000**

The job openings listed here are shared with 43-4031.00 Court, Municipal, and License Clerks, 43-4031.01 Court Clerks, and 43-4031.02 Municipal Clerks.

Issue licenses or permits to qualified applicants. Obtain necessary information, record data, advise applicants on requirements, collect fees, and issue licenses. May conduct oral, written, visual, or performance testing.

Collect prescribed fees for licenses. Code information on license applications for entry into computers. Evaluate information on applications to verify completeness and accuracy and to determine whether applicants are qualified to obtain desired licenses. Answer questions and provide advice to the public regarding licensing policies, procedures, and regulations. Maintain records of applications made and licensing fees collected. Question applicants to obtain required information, such as name, address, and age, and record data on prescribed forms. Update operational records and licensing information, using computer terminals. Inform customers by mail or telephone of additional steps they need to take to obtain licenses. Perform routine data entry and other office support activities, including creating, sorting, photocopying, distributing, and filing documents. Stock counters with adequate supplies of forms, film, licenses, and other required materials. Enforce canine licensing regulations, contacting non-compliant owners in person or by mail to inform them of the required regulations and potential enforcement actions. Assemble photographs with printed license information to produce completed documents. Prepare bank deposits and take them to banks. Operate specialized photographic equipment to obtain photographs for drivers' licenses and photo identification cards. Instruct customers in the completion of drivers' license application forms and other forms such as voter registration cards and organ donor forms. Conduct and score oral, visual, written, or performance tests to determine applicant qualifications and notify applicants of their scores. Send by mail drivers' licenses to out-of-county or out-of-state applicants. Perform record checks on past and current licensees as required by investigations. Respond to correspondence from insurance companies regarding the licensure of agents, brokers, and adjusters. Prepare lists of overdue accounts and license suspensions and issuances. Train other workers and coordinate their work as necessary.

GOE Information—Interest Area: 07. Government and Public Administration. **Work Group:** 07.04. Public Administration Clerical Support. **Personality Type**—Conventional. Conventional occupations frequently involve following set procedures and routines. These occupations can include working with data and details more than with ideas. Usually there is a clear line of authority to follow. **Work Values**—Supervision, Human Relations; Supervision, Technical; Social Service; Working Conditions; Activity; Company Policies and Practices. **Skills**—Instructing; Service Orientation; Reading Comprehension; Active Listening; Writing; Speaking. **Abilities**—*Cognitive:* Written Expression. *Psychomotor:* None met the criteria. *Physical:* None met the criteria. *Sensory:* None met the criteria. **General Work Activities**—*Information Input:* Getting Information; Identifying Objects, Actions, and Events; Monitoring Processes, Materials, or Surroundings. *Mental Process:* Updating and Using Relevant Knowledge; Processing Information; Organizing, Planning, and Prioritizing. *Work Output:* Interacting With Computers; Documenting or Recording Information. *Interacting with Others:* Performing for or Working with the Public; Establishing and Maintaining Interpersonal Relationships; Communicating with Other Workers. **Physical Work Conditions**—Indoors; Noisy; Sitting; Using Hands on Objects, Tools, or Controls; Repetitive Motions. **Other Job Characteristics**—Need to Be Exact or Accurate; Repeat Same Tasks.

Experience—Job Zone 2. Some previous work-related skill, knowledge, or experience may be helpful in these occupations, but usually is not needed. **Job Preparation**—SVP 4.0 to less than 6.0—six months to less than two years. **Knowledges**—Clerical Practices; Customer and Personal Service; Law and Government; Computers and Electronics; Personnel and Human Resources. **Instructional Program**—General Office Occupations and Clerical Services.

Related SOC Job—43-4031 Court, Municipal, and License Clerks. **Related OOH Job**—Court, Municipal, and License Clerks. **Related DOT Jobs**—205.367-034 License Clerk; 249.367-030 Dog Licenser; 379.137-014 Supervisor, Dog License Officer.

43-4041.00 Credit Authorizers, Checkers, and Clerks

- **Education/Training Required: Short-term on-the-job training**
- **Employed: 65,410**
- **Annual Earnings: $29,330**
- **Growth: –41.2%**
- **Annual Job Openings: 5,000**

The job openings listed here are shared with 43-4041.01 Credit Authorizers and 43-4041.02 Credit Checkers.

Authorize credit charges against customers' accounts. Investigate history and credit standing of individuals or business establishments applying for credit. May interview applicants to obtain personal and financial data, determine creditworthiness, process applications, and notify customers of acceptance or rejection of credit.

No task data available.

GOE Information—Interest Area: 06. Finance and Insurance. **Work Group:** 06.03. Finance/Insurance Records Processing. **Note:** The Department of Labor has not collected some data for this job, so it has fewer details than the other descriptions.

Instructional Program—Banking and Financial Support Services.

Related SOC Job—43-4041 Credit Authorizers, Checkers, and Clerks. **Related OOH Job**—Credit Authorizers, Checkers, and Clerks. **Related DOT Job**—No data available.

43-4041.01 Credit Authorizers

- **Education/Training Required: Short-term on-the-job training**
- **Employed: 65,410**
- **Annual Earnings: $29,330**
- **Growth: –41.2%**
- **Annual Job Openings: 5,000**

The job openings listed here are shared with 43-4041.00 Credit Authorizers, Checkers, and Clerks and 43-4041.02 Credit Checkers.

Authorize credit charges against customers' accounts.

Keep records of customers' charges and payments. Evaluate customers' computerized credit records and payment histories to decide whether to approve new credit, based on predetermined standards. File sales slips in customers' ledgers for billing purposes. Receive charge slips or credit applications by mail or receive information from salespeople or merchants by telephone. Mail charge statements to customers. Prepare credit cards or charge account plates.

GOE Information—Interest Area: 06. Finance and Insurance. **Work Group:** 06.03. Finance/Insurance Records Processing. **Personality Type**—Conventional. Conventional occupations frequently involve following set procedures and routines. These occupations can include working with data and details more than with ideas. Usually there is a clear line of authority to follow. **Work Values**—Working Conditions; Supervision, Human Relations; Supervision, Technical; Security; Independence; Advancement. **Skills**—Management of Personnel Resources; Management of Financial Resources; Service Orientation; Negotiation; Persuasion; Speaking. **Abilities**—*Cognitive:* Written Expression; Number Facility; Speed of Closure; Category Flexibility; Inductive Reasoning; Mathematical Reasoning. *Psychomotor:* None met the criteria. *Physical:* None met the criteria. *Sensory:* Speech Recognition. **General Work Activities**—*Information Input:* Getting Information; Identifying Objects, Actions, and Events;

Estimating the Needed Characteristics of Products, Events, or Information. *Mental Process:* Organizing, Planning, and Prioritizing; Updating and Using Relevant Knowledge; Processing Information. *Work Output:* Documenting or Recording Information; Interacting With Computers. *Interacting with Others:* Establishing and Maintaining Interpersonal Relationships; Communicating with Other Workers; Communicating with Persons Outside Organization. **Physical Work Conditions**—Indoors; Very Bright or Dim Lighting; Sitting; Repetitive Motions. **Other Job Characteristics**—Need to Be Exact or Accurate; Repeat Same Tasks.

Experience—Job Zone 3. Previous work-related skill, knowledge, or experience is required. **Job Preparation**—SVP 6.0 to less than 7.0—more than one year and less than four years. **Knowledges**—Economics and Accounting; Administration and Management; Clerical Practices; Sales and Marketing; Law and Government; Customer and Personal Service. **Instructional Program**—Banking and Financial Support Services.

Related SOC Job—43-4041 Credit Authorizers, Checkers, and Clerks. **Related OOH Job**—Credit Authorizers, Checkers, and Clerks. **Related DOT Job**—249.367-022 Credit Authorizer.

43-4041.02 Credit Checkers

- Education/Training Required: Short-term on-the-job training
- Employed: 65,410
- Annual Earnings: $29,330
- Growth: –41.2%
- Annual Job Openings: 5,000

The job openings listed here are shared with 43-4041.00 Credit Authorizers, Checkers, and Clerks and 43-4041.01 Credit Authorizers.

Investigate history and credit standing of individuals or business establishments applying for credit. Telephone or write to credit departments of business and service establishments to obtain information about applicant's credit standing.

Compile and analyze credit information gathered by investigation. Obtain information about potential creditors from banks, credit bureaus, and other credit services and provide reciprocal information if requested. Interview credit applicants by telephone or in person to obtain personal and financial data needed to complete credit report. Prepare reports of findings and recommendations, using typewriters or computers. Contact former employers and other acquaintances to verify applicants' references, employment, health history, and social behavior. Examine city directories and public records to verify residence, property ownership, bankruptcies, liens, arrest record, or unpaid taxes of applicants. Relay credit report information to subscribers by mail or by telephone.

GOE Information—Interest Area: 06. Finance and Insurance. **Work Group:** 06.03. Finance/Insurance Records Processing. **Personality Type**—Conventional. Conventional occupations frequently involve following set procedures and routines. These occupations can include working with data and details more than with ideas. Usually there is a clear line of authority to follow. **Work Values**—Working Conditions; Supervision, Human Relations; Supervision, Technical; Advancement; Activity; Co-workers. **Skills**—Reading Comprehension; Speaking; Critical Thinking; Writing; Active Listening; Time Management. **Abilities**—*Cognitive:* Written Expression; Written Comprehension; Oral Expression; Inductive Reasoning; Oral Comprehension; Selective Attention. *Psychomotor:* None met the criteria. *Physical:* None met the criteria. *Sensory:* Speech Recognition. **General Work Activities**—*Information Input:* Getting Information;

Monitoring Processes, Materials, or Surroundings. *Mental Process:* Updating and Using Relevant Knowledge; Making Decisions and Solving Problems; Organizing, Planning, and Prioritizing. *Work Output:* Interacting With Computers; Documenting or Recording Information. *Interacting with Others:* Communicating with Persons Outside Organization; Establishing and Maintaining Interpersonal Relationships; Interpreting the Meaning of Information for Others. **Physical Work Conditions**—Indoors; Noisy; Sitting; Repetitive Motions. **Other Job Characteristics**—Need to Be Exact or Accurate; Repeat Same Tasks; Errors Have Important Consequences; Automation.

Experience—Job Zone 2. Some previous work-related skill, knowledge, or experience may be helpful in these occupations, but usually is not needed. **Job Preparation**—SVP 4.0 to less than 6.0—six months to less than two years. **Knowledges**—Clerical Practices; Economics and Accounting; Sales and Marketing; Law and Government; Customer and Personal Service; English Language. **Instructional Program**—Banking and Financial Support Services.

Related SOC Job—43-4041 Credit Authorizers, Checkers, and Clerks. **Related OOH Job**—Credit Authorizers, Checkers, and Clerks. **Related DOT Jobs**—209.362-018 Credit Reference Clerk; 237.367-014 Call-Out Operator; 241.267-030 Investigator.

43-4051.00 Customer Service Representatives

- Education/Training Required: Moderate-term on-the-job training
- Employed: 2,067,700
- Annual Earnings: $27,490
- Growth: 22.8%
- Annual Job Openings: 510,000

Interact with customers to provide information in response to inquiries about products and services and to handle and resolve complaints.

Confer with customers by telephone or in person to provide information about products and services, to take orders or cancel accounts, or to obtain details of complaints. Keep records of customer interactions and transactions, recording details of inquiries, complaints, and comments, as well as actions taken. Resolve customers' service or billing complaints by performing activities such as exchanging merchandise, refunding money, and adjusting bills. Check to ensure that appropriate changes were made to resolve customers' problems. Contact customers to respond to inquiries or to notify them of claim investigation results and any planned adjustments. Refer unresolved customer grievances to designated departments for further investigation. Determine charges for services requested, collect deposits or payments, or arrange for billing. Complete contract forms, prepare change of address records, and issue service discontinuance orders, using computers. Obtain and examine all relevant information to assess validity of complaints and to determine possible causes, such as extreme weather conditions, that could increase utility bills. Solicit sale of new or additional services or products. Review insurance policy terms to determine whether a particular loss is covered by insurance. Review claims adjustments with dealers, examining parts claimed to be defective and approving or disapproving dealers' claims. Compare disputed merchandise with original requisitions and information from invoices and prepare invoices for returned goods. Order tests that could determine the causes of product malfunctions. Recommend improvements in products, packaging, shipping, service, or billing methods and procedures to prevent future problems.

GOE Information—Interest Area: 14. Retail and Wholesale Sales and Service. Work Group: 14.06. Customer Service. Personality Type—Conventional. Conventional occupations frequently involve following set procedures and routines. These occupations can include working with data and details more than with ideas. Usually there is a clear line of authority to follow. Work Values—Supervision, Technical; Working Conditions; Supervision, Human Relations; Social Service; Advancement; Security. Skills—Service Orientation; Monitoring; Reading Comprehension; Active Listening; Social Perceptiveness; Time Management. Abilities—*Cognitive:* Fluency of Ideas; Flexibility of Closure; Memorization; Perceptual Speed; Speed of Closure; Mathematical Reasoning. *Psychomotor:* Finger Dexterity. *Physical:* None met the criteria. *Sensory:* Speech Recognition; Auditory Attention; Speech Clarity; Near Vision. General Work Activities—*Information Input:* Monitoring Processes, Materials, or Surroundings; Getting Information; Identifying Objects, Actions, and Events. *Mental Process:* Updating and Using Relevant Knowledge; Making Decisions and Solving Problems; Processing Information. *Work Output:* Interacting With Computers; Documenting or Recording Information. *Interacting with Others:* Establishing and Maintaining Interpersonal Relationships; Resolving Conflicts and Negotiating with Others; Communicating with Other Workers. Physical Work Conditions—Indoors; Sitting; Using Hands on Objects, Tools, or Controls; Repetitive Motions. Other Job Characteristics—Need to Be Exact or Accurate; Repeat Same Tasks.

Experience—Job Zone 2. Some previous work-related skill, knowledge, or experience may be helpful in these occupations, but usually is not needed. Job Preparation—SVP 4.0 to less than 6.0—six months to less than two years. Knowledges—Customer and Personal Service; Clerical Practices; Sales and Marketing; Administration and Management; Computers and Electronics. Instructional Programs—Customer Service Support/Call Center/Teleservice Operation; Receptionist.

Related SOC Job—43-4051 Customer Service Representatives. Related OOH Job—Customer Service Representatives. Related DOT Jobs—191.167-022 Service Representative; 209.587-042 Return-To-Factory Clerk; 221.387-014 Complaint Clerk; 239.362-014 Customer Service Representative; 241.267-034 Investigator, Utility-Bill Complaints; 241.367-014 Customer-Complaint Clerk; 241.367-034 Tire Adjuster; 241.387-010 Claims Clerk.

43-4061.00 Eligibility Interviewers, Government Programs

- Education/Training Required: Moderate-term on-the-job training
- Employed: 85,550
- Annual Earnings: $33,740
- Growth: –9.4%
- Annual Job Openings: 10,000

Determine eligibility of persons applying to receive assistance from government programs and agency resources, such as welfare, unemployment benefits, social security, and public housing.

Answer applicants' questions about benefits and claim procedures. Interview benefits recipients at specified intervals to certify their eligibility for continuing benefits. Interpret and explain information such as eligibility requirements, application details, payment methods, and applicants' legal rights. Initiate procedures to grant, modify, deny, or terminate assistance or refer applicants to other agencies for assistance. Compile, record, and evaluate personal and financial data to verify completeness and accuracy and to determine eligibility status. Interview and investigate applicants for public assistance to gather information pertinent to their applications. Check with employers or other references to verify answers and obtain further information. Keep records of assigned cases and prepare required reports. Schedule benefits claimants for adjudication interviews to address questions of eligibility. Prepare applications and forms for applicants for such purposes as school enrollment, employment, and medical services. Refer applicants to job openings or to interviews with other staff in accordance with administrative guidelines or office procedures. Provide social workers with pertinent information gathered during applicant interviews. Compute and authorize amounts of assistance for programs such as grants, monetary payments, and food stamps. Monitor the payments of benefits throughout the duration of a claim. Provide applicants with assistance in completing application forms such as those for job referrals or unemployment compensation claims. Investigate claimants for the possibility of fraud or abuse. Conduct annual, interim, and special housing reviews and home visits to ensure conformance to regulations.

GOE Information—Interest Area: 10. Human Service. Work Group: 10.04. Client Interviewing. Personality Type—Conventional. Conventional occupations frequently involve following set procedures and routines. These occupations can include working with data and details more than with ideas. Usually there is a clear line of authority to follow. Work Values—Social Service; Supervision, Technical; Security; Authority; Supervision, Human Relations; Advancement. Skills—Service Orientation; Speaking; Active Listening; Social Perceptiveness; Writing; Active Learning. Abilities—*Cognitive:* Written Expression; Written Comprehension; Oral Expression. *Psychomotor:* None met the criteria. *Physical:* None met the criteria. *Sensory:* None met the criteria. General Work Activities—*Information Input:* Getting Information; Identifying Objects, Actions, and Events; Monitoring Processes, Materials, or Surroundings. *Mental Process:* Organizing, Planning, and Prioritizing; Updating and Using Relevant Knowledge; Scheduling Work and Activities. *Work Output:* Documenting or Recording Information; Interacting With Computers. *Interacting with Others:* Establishing and Maintaining Interpersonal Relationships; Performing for or Working with the Public; Performing Administrative Activities. Physical Work Conditions—Indoors; Contaminants; Sitting; Using Hands on Objects, Tools, or Controls; Repetitive Motions. Other Job Characteristics—Repeat Same Tasks; Need to Be Exact or Accurate; Automation.

Experience—Job Zone 3. Previous work-related skill, knowledge, or experience is required. Job Preparation—SVP 6.0 to less than 7.0—more than one year and less than four years. Knowledges—Clerical Practices; Customer and Personal Service; Law and Government; Psychology; Sociology and Anthropology; Computers and Electronics. Instructional Program—Community Organization and Advocacy.

Related SOC Job—43-4061 Eligibility Interviewers, Government Programs. Related OOH Job—Interviewers. Related DOT Jobs—168.267-038 Eligibility-and-Occupancy Interviewer; 169.167-018 Contact Representative; 169.367-010 Employment-and-Claims Aide; 195.267-010 Eligibility Worker; 195.267-018 Patient-Resources-and-Reimbursement Agent; 205.367-046 Rehabilitation Clerk.

43-4071.00 File Clerks

- **Education/Training Required: Short-term on-the-job training**
- **Employed: 229,830**
- **Annual Earnings: $21,430**
- **Growth: –36.3%**
- **Annual Job Openings: 50,000**

File correspondence, cards, invoices, receipts, and other records in alphabetical or numerical order or according to the filing system used. Locate and remove material from file when requested.

Keep records of materials filed or removed, using logbooks or computers. Add new material to file records and create new records as necessary. Perform general office duties such as typing, operating office machines, and sorting mail. Track materials removed from files to ensure that borrowed files are returned. Gather materials to be filed from departments and employees. Sort or classify information according to guidelines such as content; purpose; user criteria; or chronological, alphabetical, or numerical order. Find and retrieve information from files in response to requests from authorized users. Scan or read incoming materials to determine how and where they should be classified or filed. Place materials into storage receptacles, such as file cabinets, boxes, bins, or drawers, according to classification and identification information. Assign and record or stamp identification numbers or codes to index materials for filing. Answer questions about records and files. Modify and improve filing systems or implement new filing systems. Perform periodic inspections of materials or files to ensure correct placement, legibility, and proper condition. Eliminate outdated or unnecessary materials, destroying them or transferring them to inactive storage according to file maintenance guidelines or legal requirements. Enter document identification codes into systems to determine locations of documents to be retrieved. Operate mechanized files that rotate to bring needed records to a particular location. Design forms related to filing systems. Retrieve documents stored in microfilm or microfiche and place them in viewers for reading.

GOE Information—Interest Area: 04. Business and Administration. **Work Group:** 04.07. Records and Materials Processing. **Personality Type—**Conventional. Conventional occupations frequently involve following set procedures and routines. These occupations can include working with data and details more than with ideas. Usually there is a clear line of authority to follow. **Work Values—**Moral Values; Working Conditions; Supervision, Human Relations; Independence; Company Policies and Practices; Supervision, Technical. **Skills—**Service Orientation. **Abilities—***Cognitive:* Category Flexibility; Flexibility of Closure; Perceptual Speed; Memorization; Oral Comprehension. *Psychomotor:* Wrist-Finger Speed; Finger Dexterity. *Physical:* None met the criteria. *Sensory:* Near Vision; Speech Recognition. **General Work Activities—***Information Input:* Getting Information; Monitoring Processes, Materials, or Surroundings; Identifying Objects, Actions, and Events. *Mental Process:* Organizing, Planning, and Prioritizing; Updating and Using Relevant Knowledge; Processing Information. *Work Output:* Handling and Moving Objects; Documenting or Recording Information; Interacting With Computers. *Interacting with Others:* Establishing and Maintaining Interpersonal Relationships; Performing Administrative Activities; Communicating with Other Workers. **Physical Work Conditions—**Indoors; Sitting; Using Hands on Objects, Tools, or Controls; Repetitive Motions. **Other Job Characteristics—**Need to Be Exact or Accurate; Repeat Same Tasks.

Experience—Job Zone 3. Previous work-related skill, knowledge, or experience is required. **Job Preparation—**SVP 6.0 to less than 7.0—

more than one year and less than four years. **Knowledges—**Clerical Practices; Computers and Electronics; English Language. **Instructional Program—**General Office Occupations and Clerical Services.

Related SOC Job—43-4071 File Clerks. **Related OOH Job—**File Clerks. **Related DOT Jobs—**206.367-014 File Clerk II; 206.367-018 Tape Librarian; 206.387-010 Classification Clerk; 206.387-014 Fingerprint Clerk II; 206.387-022 Record Clerk; 206.387-034 File Clerk I.

43-4081.00 Hotel, Motel, and Resort Desk Clerks

- **Education/Training Required: Short-term on-the-job training**
- **Employed: 207,190**
- **Annual Earnings: $17,810**
- **Growth: 17.2%**
- **Annual Job Openings: 62,000**

Accommodate hotel, motel, and resort patrons by registering and assigning rooms to guests, issuing room keys, transmitting and receiving messages, keeping records of occupied rooms and guests' accounts, making and confirming reservations, and presenting statements to and collecting payments from departing guests.

Greet, register, and assign rooms to guests of hotels or motels. Verify customers' credit and establish how the customer will pay for the accommodation. Keep records of room availability and guests' accounts manually or using computers. Compute bills, collect payments, and make change for guests. Perform simple bookkeeping activities, such as balancing cash accounts. Issue room keys and escort instructions to bellhops. Review accounts and charges with guests during the checkout process. Post charges, such as those for rooms, food, liquor, or telephone calls, to ledgers manually or by using computers. Transmit and receive messages, using telephones or telephone switchboards. Contact housekeeping or maintenance staff when guests report problems. Make and confirm reservations. Answer inquiries pertaining to hotel services; registration of guests; and shopping, dining, entertainment, and travel directions. Record guest comments or complaints, referring customers to managers as necessary. Advise housekeeping staff when rooms have been vacated and are ready for cleaning. Arrange tours, taxis, or restaurant reservations for customers. Deposit guests' valuables in hotel safes or safe-deposit boxes. Date-stamp, sort, and rack incoming mail and messages.

GOE Information—Interest Area: 09. Hospitality, Tourism, and Recreation. **Work Group:** 09.03. Hospitality and Travel Services. **Personality Type—**Conventional. Conventional occupations frequently involve following set procedures and routines. These occupations can include working with data and details more than with ideas. Usually there is a clear line of authority to follow. **Work Values—**Social Service; Working Conditions; Supervision, Human Relations; Supervision, Technical; Co-workers; Company Policies and Practices. **Skills—**Service Orientation; Critical Thinking. **Abilities—***Cognitive:* Number Facility; Time Sharing; Speed of Closure; Mathematical Reasoning; Oral Expression. *Psychomotor:* None met the criteria. *Physical:* Trunk Strength. *Sensory:* Speech Recognition; Speech Clarity; Near Vision; Far Vision. **General Work Activities—***Information Input:* Getting Information; Identifying Objects, Actions, and Events; Monitoring Processes, Materials, or Surroundings. *Mental Process:* Making Decisions and Solving Problems; Organizing, Planning, and Prioritizing; Processing Information. *Work Output:* Interacting With Computers; Documenting or Recording Information. *Interacting with Others:* Performing for or Working with the Public; Establishing and Maintaining Interpersonal

Relationships; Assisting and Caring for Others. **Physical Work Conditions**—Indoors; Standing; Using Hands on Objects, Tools, or Controls; Repetitive Motions. **Other Job Characteristics**—Repeat Same Tasks; Need to Be Exact or Accurate.

Experience—Job Zone 2. Some previous work-related skill, knowledge, or experience may be helpful in these occupations, but usually is not needed. **Job Preparation**—SVP 4.0 to less than 6.0—six months to less than two years. **Knowledges**—Customer and Personal Service; Clerical Practices; Sales and Marketing; Economics and Accounting; Computers and Electronics; Administration and Management. **Instructional Program**—Selling Skills and Sales Operations.

Related SOC Job—43-4081 Hotel, Motel, and Resort Desk Clerks. **Related OOH Job**—Hotel, Motel, and Resort Desk Clerks. **Related DOT Jobs**—238.162-900 Hotel Associate; 238.367-038 Hotel Clerk.

43-4111.00 Interviewers, Except Eligibility and Loan

- **Education/Training Required: Short-term on-the-job training**
- **Employed: 201,790**
- **Annual Earnings: $25,110**
- **Growth: 26.0%**
- **Annual Job Openings: 43,000**

Interview persons by telephone, by mail, in person, or by other means for the purpose of completing forms, applications, or questionnaires. Ask specific questions, record answers, and assist persons with completing form. May sort, classify, and file forms.

Ask questions in accordance with instructions to obtain various specified information such as person's name, address, age, religious preference, and state of residency. Identify and resolve inconsistencies in interviewees' responses by means of appropriate questioning or explanation. Compile, record, and code results and data from interview or survey, using computer or specified form. Review data obtained from interview for completeness and accuracy. Contact individuals to be interviewed at home, place of business, or field location by telephone, by mail, or in person. Assist individuals in filling out applications or questionnaires. Ensure payment for services by verifying benefits with the person's insurance provider or working out financing options. Identify and report problems in obtaining valid data. Explain survey objectives and procedures to interviewees and interpret survey questions to help interviewees' comprehension. Perform patient services, such as answering the telephone and assisting patients with financial and medical questions. Prepare reports to provide answers in response to specific problems. Locate and list addresses and households. Perform other office duties as needed, such as telemarketing and customer service inquiries, billing patients, and receiving payments. Meet with supervisor daily to submit completed assignments and discuss progress. Collect and analyze data, such as studying old records; tallying the number of outpatients entering each day or week; or participating in federal, state, or local population surveys as a census enumerator.

GOE Information—Interest Area: 10. Human Service. **Work Group:** 10.04. Client Interviewing. **Personality Type**—Conventional. Conventional occupations frequently involve following set procedures and routines. These occupations can include working with data and details more than with ideas. Usually there is a clear line of authority to follow. **Work Values**—Independence; Supervision, Technical. **Skills**—Service Orientation; Speaking; Social Perceptiveness; Active Listening. **Abilities**—*Cognitive:* Written

Expression; Oral Expression; Oral Comprehension; Speed of Closure; Category Flexibility; Selective Attention. *Psychomotor:* None met the criteria. *Physical:* None met the criteria. *Sensory:* Speech Recognition; Speech Clarity. **General Work Activities**—*Information Input:* Getting Information; Identifying Objects, Actions, and Events; Monitoring Processes, Materials, or Surroundings. *Mental Process:* Updating and Using Relevant Knowledge; Organizing, Planning, and Prioritizing; Processing Information. *Work Output:* Documenting or Recording Information; Interacting With Computers; Handling and Moving Objects. *Interacting with Others:* Establishing and Maintaining Interpersonal Relationships; Communicating with Other Workers; Assisting and Caring for Others. **Physical Work Conditions**—Indoors; Sitting; Using Hands on Objects, Tools, or Controls; Repetitive Motions. **Other Job Characteristics**—Need to Be Exact or Accurate; Repeat Same Tasks; Automation.

Experience—Job Zone 3. Previous work-related skill, knowledge, or experience is required. **Job Preparation**—SVP 6.0 to less than 7.0—more than one year and less than four years. **Knowledges**—Therapy and Counseling; Customer and Personal Service; Sales and Marketing; Psychology; Medicine and Dentistry; Education and Training. **Instructional Program**—Receptionist.

Related SOC Job—43-4111 Interviewers, Except Eligibility and Loan. **Related OOH Job**—Interviewers. **Related DOT Jobs**—205.362-018 Hospital-Admitting Clerk; 205.367-014 Charge-Account Clerk; 205.367-026 Creel Clerk; 205.367-042 Registration Clerk; 205.367-054 Survey Worker; 205.367-058 Traffic Checker.

43-4121.00 Library Assistants, Clerical

- **Education/Training Required: Short-term on-the-job training**
- **Employed: 104,650**
- **Annual Earnings: $21,140**
- **Growth: 12.5%**
- **Annual Job Openings: 26,000**

Compile records; sort and shelve books; and issue and receive library materials such as pictures, cards, slides, and microfilm. Locate library materials for loan and replace material in shelving area, stacks, or files according to identification number and title. Register patrons to permit them to borrow books, periodicals, and other library materials.

Lend and collect books, periodicals, videotapes, and other materials at circulation desks. Enter and update patrons' records on computers. Process new materials, including books, audiovisual materials, and computer software. Sort books, publications, and other items according to established procedure and return them to shelves, files, or other designated storage areas. Locate library materials for patrons, including books, periodicals, tape cassettes, Braille volumes, and pictures. Instruct patrons on how to use reference sources, card catalogs, and automated information systems. Inspect returned books for condition and due-date status and compute any applicable fines. Answer routine inquiries and refer patrons in need of professional assistance to librarians. Maintain records of items received, stored, issued, and returned and file catalog cards according to system used. Perform clerical activities such as filing, typing, word processing, photocopying and mailing out material, and mail sorting. Provide assistance to librarians in the maintenance of collections of books, periodicals, magazines, newspapers, and audiovisual and other materials. Take action to deal with disruptive or problem patrons. Classify and catalog items according to content and purpose. Register new patrons and issue borrower identification cards that permit patrons to borrow books and other materials. Send out notices and accept fine payments for lost or overdue books. Operate small branch libraries under the direction of off-site librarian supervisors. Prepare, store, and retrieve classification and catalog information, lecture notes, or other information related to stored documents, using computers. Schedule and supervise clerical workers, volunteers, and student assistants. Operate and maintain audiovisual equipment. Review records, such as microfilm and issue cards, to identify titles of overdue materials and delinquent borrowers. Select substitute titles when requested materials are unavailable, following criteria such as age, education, and interests. Repair books, using mending tape, paste, and brushes.

GOE Information—Interest Area: 05. Education and Training. **Work Group:** 05.04. Library Services. **Personality Type—**Conventional. Conventional occupations frequently involve following set procedures and routines. These occupations can include working with data and details more than with ideas. Usually there is a clear line of authority to follow. **Work Values—**Supervision, Technical; Working Conditions; Social Service; Supervision, Human Relations; Moral Values; Security. **Skills—**Service Orientation; Reading Comprehension; Writing. **Abilities—***Cognitive:* Category Flexibility; Flexibility of Closure; Memorization; Speed of Closure; Perceptual Speed; Information Ordering. *Psychomotor:* Finger Dexterity; Arm-Hand Steadiness; Manual Dexterity. *Physical:* Static Strength; Trunk Strength. *Sensory:* Far Vision; Near Vision; Speech Recognition; Visual Color Discrimination. **General Work Activities—***Information Input:* Getting Information; Monitoring Processes, Materials, or Surroundings; Identifying Objects, Actions, and Events. *Mental Process:* Organizing, Planning, and Prioritizing; Updating and Using Relevant Knowledge; Processing Information. *Work Output:* Handling and Moving Objects; Interacting With Computers; Documenting or Recording Information. *Interacting with Others:* Establishing and Maintaining Interpersonal Relationships; Communicating with Other Workers; Performing for or Working with the Public. **Physical Work Conditions—**Indoors; Sitting; Using Hands on Objects, Tools, or Controls; Repetitive Motions. **Other Job Characteristics—**Need to Be Exact or Accurate; Repeat Same Tasks; Automation.

Experience—Job Zone 3. Previous work-related skill, knowledge, or experience is required. **Job Preparation—**SVP 6.0 to less than 7.0— more than one year and less than four years. **Knowledges—**Clerical Practices; Computers and Electronics; Customer and Personal Service. **Instructional Program—**Library Assistant.

Related SOC Job—43-4121 Library Assistants, Clerical. **Related OOH Job—**Library Assistants, Clerical. **Related DOT Jobs—**209.387-026 Library Clerk, Talking Books; 222.367-026 Film-or-Tape Librarian; 222.587-014 Braille-and-Talking Books Clerk; 249.363-010 Bookmobile Driver; 249.365-010 Registration Clerk; 249.367-046 Library Assistant; 249.687-014 Page.

43-4131.00 Loan Interviewers and Clerks

- **Education/Training Required: Short-term on-the-job training**
- **Employed: 231,700**
- **Annual Earnings: $30,200**
- **Growth: –0.6%**
- **Annual Job Openings: 36,000**

Interview loan applicants to elicit information; investigate applicants' backgrounds and verify references; prepare loan request papers; and forward findings, reports, and documents to appraisal department. Review loan papers to ensure completeness and complete transactions between loan establishment, borrowers, and sellers upon approval of loan.

Verify and examine information and accuracy of loan application and closing documents. Interview loan applicants to obtain personal and financial data and to assist in completing applications. Assemble and compile documents for loan closings, such as title abstracts, insurance forms, loan forms, and tax receipts. Answer questions and advise customers regarding loans and transactions. Contact customers by mail, by telephone, or in person concerning acceptance or rejection of applications. Record applications for loan and credit, loan information, and disbursements of funds, using computers. Prepare and type loan applications, closing documents, legal documents, letters, forms, government notices, and checks, using computers. Present loan and repayment schedules to customers. Calculate, review, and correct errors on interest, principal, payment, and closing costs, using computers or calculators. Check value of customer collateral to be held as loan security. Contact credit bureaus, employers, and other sources to check applicants' credit and personal references. File and maintain loan records. Schedule and conduct closings of mortgage transactions. Accept payment on accounts. Submit loan applications with recommendation for underwriting approval. Order property insurance or mortgage insurance policies to ensure protection against loss on mortgaged property. Review customer accounts to determine whether payments are made on time and that other loan terms are being followed. Establish credit limits and grant extensions of credit on overdue accounts.

GOE Information—Interest Area: 06. Finance and Insurance. **Work Group:** 06.04. Finance/Insurance Customer Service. **Personality Type—**Conventional. Conventional occupations frequently involve following set procedures and routines. These occupations can include working with data and details more than with ideas. Usually there is a clear line of authority to follow. **Work Values—**Working Conditions; Advancement; Social Service; Co-workers; Supervision, Human Relations; Supervision, Technical. **Skills—**Service Orientation; Learning Strategies; Time Management; Mathematics; Speaking; Persuasion. **Abilities—***Cognitive:* Number Facility; Mathematical Reasoning; Written Expression; Deductive Reasoning; Oral Expression; Speed of Closure. *Psychomotor:* Finger Dexterity. *Physical:* None met the criteria. *Sensory:* Speech Recognition; Hearing Sensitivity; Near Vision; Speech Clarity. **General Work Activities—***Information Input:* Identifying Objects, Actions, and Events; Getting Information; Monitoring Processes, Materials, or Surroundings. *Mental Process:* Processing Information; Updating and Using Relevant Knowledge; Making Decisions and Solving Problems. *Work Output:* Documenting or Recording Information; Interacting With Computers. *Interacting with Others:* Communicating with Persons Outside Organization; Performing for or Working with the Public; Interpreting the Meaning of Information to Others. **Physical Work Conditions—**Indoors; Sitting. **Other Job Characteristics—**Need to Be Exact or Accurate; Repeat Same Tasks; Automation.

Experience—Job Zone 3. Previous work-related skill, knowledge, or experience is required. **Job Preparation—**SVP 6.0 to less than 7.0— more than one year and less than four years. **Knowledges—**Economics and Accounting; Clerical Practices; Mathematics; Customer and Personal Service; Law and Government. **Instructional Program—**Banking and Financial Support Services.

Related SOC Job—43-4131 Loan Interviewers and Clerks. **Related OOH Job—**Interviewers. **Related DOT Jobs—**205.367-022 Credit Clerk; 219.362-038 Mortgage-Closing Clerk; 219.367-046 Disbursement Clerk; 241.367-018 Loan Interviewer, Mortgage; 249.362-014 Mortgage Clerk; 249.362-018 Mortgage Loan Closer; 249.362-022 Mortgage Loan Processor.

43-4141.00 New Accounts Clerks

- **Education/Training Required: Work experience in a related occupation**
- **Employed: 82,450**
- **Annual Earnings: $27,420**
- **Growth: 1.7%**
- **Annual Job Openings: 7,000**

Interview persons desiring to open bank accounts. Explain banking services available to prospective customers and assist them in preparing application form.

Answer customers' questions and explain available services such as deposit accounts, bonds, and securities. Compile information about new accounts, enter account information into computers, and file related forms or other documents. Refer customers to appropriate bank personnel to meet their financial needs. Interview customers to obtain information needed for opening accounts or renting safe-deposit boxes. Inform customers of procedures for applying for services such as ATM cards, direct deposit of checks, and certificates of deposit. Obtain credit records from reporting agencies. Collect and record customer deposits and fees and issue receipts using computers. Investigate and correct errors upon customers' request according to customer and bank records. Perform teller duties as required. Execute wire transfers of funds. Duplicate records for distribution to branch offices. Issue initial and replacement safe-deposit keys to customers and admit customers to vaults. Perform foreign currency transactions and sell traveler's checks. Schedule repairs for locks on safe-deposit boxes.

GOE Information—Interest Area: 06. Finance and Insurance. **Work Group:** 06.04. Finance/Insurance Customer Service. **Personality Type**—Conventional. Conventional occupations frequently involve following set procedures and routines. These occupations can include working with data and details more than with ideas. Usually there is a clear line of authority to follow. **Work Values**—Working Conditions; Social Service; Supervision, Technical; Co-workers; Supervision, Human Relations; Advancement. **Skills**—Service Orientation; Active Listening; Critical Thinking; Social Perceptiveness; Writing; Speaking. **Abilities**—*Cognitive:* Number Facility; Oral Expression; Speed of Closure; Written Comprehension. *Psychomotor:* None met the criteria. *Physical:* None met the criteria. *Sensory:* Speech Recognition; Near Vision. **General Work Activities**—*Information Input:* Getting Information; Identifying Objects, Actions, and Events; Monitoring Processes, Materials, or Surroundings. *Mental Process:* Processing Information; Organizing, Planning, and Prioritizing; Judging the Qualities of Things, Services, or Other People's Work. *Work Output:* Interacting With Computers; Documenting or Recording Information. *Interacting with Others:* Establishing and Maintaining Interpersonal Relationships; Performing for or Working with the Public; Communicating with Other Workers. **Physical Work Conditions**—Indoors; Noisy; Sitting. **Other Job Characteristics**—Need to Be Exact or Accurate; Repeat Same Tasks; Automation.

Experience—Job Zone 2. Some previous work-related skill, knowledge, or experience may be helpful in these occupations, but usually is not needed. **Job Preparation**—SVP 4.0 to less than 6.0—six months to less than two years. **Knowledges**—Sales and Marketing; Customer and Personal Service; Economics and Accounting; Mathematics; Clerical Practices; Law and Government. **Instructional Program**—Banking and Financial Support Services.

Related SOC Job—43-4141 New Accounts Clerks. **Related OOH Job**—New Account Clerks. **Related DOT Jobs**—205.362-026 Customer Service Representative; 295.367-022 Safe-Deposit-Box Rental Clerk.

43-4151.00 Order Clerks

- **Education/Training Required: Short-term on-the-job training**
- **Employed: 259,760**
- **Annual Earnings: $25,570**
- **Growth: –21.4%**
- **Annual Job Openings: 48,000**

Receive and process incoming orders for materials; merchandise; classified ads; or services such as repairs, installations, or rental of facilities. Duties include informing customers of receipt, prices, shipping dates, and delays; preparing contracts; and handling complaints.

Obtain customers' names, addresses, and billing information; product numbers; and specifications of items to be purchased and enter this information on order forms. Prepare invoices, shipping documents, and contracts. Inform customers by mail or telephone of order information, such as unit prices, shipping dates, and any anticipated delays. Receive and respond to customer complaints. Verify customer and order information for correctness, checking it against previously obtained information as necessary. Direct specified departments or units to prepare and ship orders to designated locations. Check inventory records to determine availability of requested merchandise. Review orders for completeness according to reporting procedures and forward incomplete orders for further processing. Attempt to sell additional merchandise or services to prospective or current customers by telephone or through visits. File copies of orders received or post orders on records. Compute total charges for merchandise or services and shipping charges. Confer with production, sales, shipping, warehouse, or common carrier personnel to expedite or trace shipments. Recommend merchandise or services that will meet customers' needs. Adjust inventory records to reflect product movement. Collect payment for merchandise, record transactions, and send items such as checks or money orders for further processing. Inspect outgoing work for compliance with customers' specifications. Notify departments when supplies of specific items are low or when orders would deplete available supplies. Recommend type of packing or labeling needed on order. Calculate and compile order-related statistics and prepare reports for management.

GOE Information—Interest Area: 14. Retail and Wholesale Sales and Service. **Work Group:** 14.06. Customer Service. **Personality Type**—Conventional. Conventional occupations frequently involve following set procedures and routines. These occupations can include working with data and details more than with ideas. Usually there is a clear line of authority to follow. **Work Values**—Supervision, Technical; Advancement; Supervision, Human Relations; Social Service; Co-workers; Activity. **Skills**—Service Orientation; Active Listening. **Abilities**—*Cognitive:* Number Facility; Flexibility of Closure; Speed of Closure; Perceptual Speed; Oral Expression; Time Sharing. *Psychomotor:* Finger Dexterity. *Physical:* Trunk Strength. *Sensory:* Speech Recognition; Near Vision; Auditory Attention; Speech Clarity. **General Work Activities**—*Information Input:* Getting Information; Identifying Objects, Actions, and Events; Monitoring Processes, Materials, or Surroundings. *Mental Process:* Updating and Using Relevant Knowledge; Organizing, Planning, and Prioritizing; Making Decisions and Solving Problems. *Work Output:* Interacting With Computers; Documenting or Recording Information. *Interacting with Others:* Establishing and Maintaining Interpersonal Relationships; Communicating with Other Workers; Performing

Administrative Activities. **Physical Work Conditions**—Indoors; Very Hot or Cold; Contaminants; Sitting. **Other Job Characteristics**—Repeat Same Tasks; Need to Be Exact or Accurate.

Experience—Job Zone 2. Some previous work-related skill, knowledge, or experience may be helpful in these occupations, but usually is not needed. **Job Preparation**—SVP 4.0 to less than 6.0—six months to less than two years. **Knowledges**—Customer and Personal Service; Sales and Marketing; Clerical Practices; Building and Construction; Production and Processing; Economics and Accounting. **Instructional Program**—General Office Occupations and Clerical Services.

Related SOC Job—43-4151 Order Clerks. **Related OOH Job**—Order Clerks. **Related DOT Jobs**—209.387-018 Contact Clerk; 209.567-014 Order Clerk, Food and Beverage; 245.367-026 Order-Control Clerk, Blood Bank; 247.367-010 Classified-Ad Clerk I; 247.387-010 Advertising Clerk; 247.387-018 Advertising-Space Clerk; 247.387-022 Classified-Ad Clerk II; 249.362-026 Order Clerk; 249.367-042 Gas-Distribution-and-Emergency Clerk; 295.367-018 Film-Rental Clerk; 659.462-010 Electrotype Servicer.

43-4161.00 Human Resources Assistants, Except Payroll and Timekeeping

- **Education/Training Required: Short-term on-the-job training**
- **Employed: 161,870**
- **Annual Earnings: $32,730**
- **Growth: 16.7%**
- **Annual Job Openings: 28,000**

Compile and keep personnel records. Record data for each employee, such as address, weekly earnings, absences, amount of sales or production, supervisory reports on ability, and date of and reason for termination. Compile and type reports from employment records. File employment records. Search employee files and furnish information to authorized persons.

Explain company personnel policies, benefits, and procedures to employees or job applicants. Process, verify, and maintain documentation relating to personnel activities such as staffing, recruitment, training, grievances, performance evaluations, and classifications. Record data for each employee, including such information as addresses, weekly earnings, absences, amount of sales or production, supervisory reports on performance, and dates of and reasons for terminations. Process and review employment applications to evaluate qualifications or eligibility of applicants. Answer questions regarding examinations, eligibility, salaries, benefits, and other pertinent information. Examine employee files to answer inquiries and provide information for personnel actions. Gather personnel records from other departments or employees. Search employee files to obtain information for authorized persons and organizations such as credit bureaus and finance companies. Interview job applicants to obtain and verify information used to screen and evaluate them. Request information from law enforcement officials, previous employers, and other references to determine applicants' employment acceptability. Compile and prepare reports and documents pertaining to personnel activities. Inform job applicants of their acceptance or rejection of employment. Select applicants meeting specified job requirements and refer them to hiring personnel. Arrange for in-house and external training activities. Arrange for advertising or posting of job vacancies and notify eligible workers of position availability. Provide assistance in administering employee benefit programs and worker's

compensation plans. Prepare badges, passes, and identification cards and perform other security-related duties. Administer and score applicant and employee aptitude, personality, and interest assessment instruments.

GOE Information—**Interest Area:** 04. Business and Administration. **Work Group:** 04.07. Records and Materials Processing. **Personality Type**—Conventional. Conventional occupations frequently involve following set procedures and routines. These occupations can include working with data and details more than with ideas. Usually there is a clear line of authority to follow. **Work Values**—Working Conditions; Supervision, Human Relations; Supervision, Technical; Social Service; Company Policies and Practices; Activity. **Skills**—Active Listening; Writing; Management of Personnel Resources; Speaking; Management of Financial Resources; Reading Comprehension. **Abilities**—*Cognitive:* Category Flexibility; Flexibility of Closure; Speed of Closure; Memorization; Written Comprehension; Mathematical Reasoning. *Psychomotor:* None met the criteria. *Physical:* None met the criteria. *Sensory:* Speech Recognition; Near Vision; Far Vision; Speech Clarity. **General Work Activities**—*Information Input:* Getting Information; Monitoring Processes, Materials, or Surroundings; Identifying Objects, Actions, and Events. *Mental Process:* Organizing, Planning, and Prioritizing; Evaluating Information Against Standards; Processing Information. *Work Output:* Documenting or Recording Information; Interacting With Computers. *Interacting with Others:* Establishing and Maintaining Interpersonal Relationships; Communicating with Other Workers; Performing Administrative Activities. **Physical Work Conditions**—Indoors; Noisy; Sitting. **Other Job Characteristics**—Need to Be Exact or Accurate; Repeat Same Tasks.

Experience—Job Zone 3. Previous work-related skill, knowledge, or experience is required. **Job Preparation**—SVP 6.0 to less than 7.0—more than one year and less than four years. **Knowledges**—Clerical Practices; Personnel and Human Resources; Customer and Personal Service; Computers and Electronics; Economics and Accounting; Education and Training. **Instructional Program**—General Office Occupations and Clerical Services.

Related SOC Job—43-4161 Human Resources Assistants, Except Payroll and Timekeeping. **Related OOH Job**—Human Resources Assistants, Except Payroll and Timekeeping. **Related DOT Jobs**—205.362-010 Civil-Service Clerk; 205.362-014 Employment Clerk; 205.362-022 Identification Clerk; 205.367-062 Referral Clerk, Temporary Help Agency; 205.567-010 Benefits Clerk II; 209.362-026 Personnel Clerk; 241.267-010 Agent-Contract Clerk; 249.367-090 Assignment Clerk.

43-4171.00 Receptionists and Information Clerks

- **Education/Training Required: Short-term on-the-job training**
- **Employed: 1,088,400**
- **Annual Earnings: $22,150**
- **Growth: 21.7%**
- **Annual Job Openings: 299,000**

Answer inquiries and obtain information for general public, customers, visitors, and other interested parties. Provide information regarding activities conducted at establishment and location of departments, offices, and employees within organization.

Operate telephone switchboard to answer, screen, and forward calls, providing information, taking messages, and scheduling appointments. Receive payment and record receipts for services. Perform administrative support tasks such as proofreading, transcribing handwritten information, and operating calculators or computers to work with pay records, invoices, balance sheets, and other documents. Greet persons entering establishment, determine nature and purpose of visit, and direct or escort them to specific destinations. Hear and resolve complaints from customers and public. File and maintain records. Transmit information or documents to customers, using computer, mail, or facsimile machine. Schedule appointments and maintain and update appointment calendars. Analyze data to determine answers to questions from customers or members of the public. Provide information about establishment such as location of departments or offices, employees within the organization, or services provided. Keep a current record of staff members' whereabouts and availability. Collect, sort, distribute, and prepare mail, messages, and courier deliveries. Calculate and quote rates for tours, stocks, insurance policies, or other products and services. Take orders for merchandise or materials and send them to the proper departments to be filled. Process and prepare memos, correspondence, travel vouchers, or other documents. Schedule space and equipment for special programs and prepare lists of participants. Enroll individuals to participate in programs and notify them of their acceptance. Conduct tours or deliver talks describing features of public facility such as a historic site or national park. Perform duties such as taking care of plants and straightening magazines to maintain lobby or reception area.

GOE Information—Interest Area: 14. Retail and Wholesale Sales and Service. **Work Group:** 14.06. Customer Service. **Personality Type—** Conventional. Conventional occupations frequently involve following set procedures and routines. These occupations can include working with data and details more than with ideas. Usually there is a clear line of authority to follow. **Work Values—**Supervision, Technical; Social Service; Working Conditions; Company Policies and Practices; Activity; Supervision, Human Relations. **Skills—** Service Orientation; Active Listening; Social Perceptiveness; Writing; Reading Comprehension; Speaking. **Abilities—***Cognitive:* Memorization; Oral Expression; Speed of Closure. *Psychomotor:* None met the criteria. *Physical:* None met the criteria. *Sensory:* Speech Recognition; Speech Clarity. **General Work Activities—***Information Input:* Getting Information; Monitoring Processes, Materials, or Surroundings; Identifying Objects, Actions, and Events. *Mental Process:* Organizing, Planning, and Prioritizing; Updating and Using Relevant Knowledge; Making Decisions and Solving Problems. *Work Output:* Interacting With Computers; Handling and Moving Objects; Documenting or Recording Information. *Interacting with Others:* Establishing and Maintaining Interpersonal Relationships; Communicating with Other Workers; Communicating with Persons Outside Organization. **Physical Work Conditions—**Indoors; Sitting; Repetitive Motions. **Other Job Characteristics—**Need to Be Exact or Accurate; Repeat Same Tasks.

Experience—Job Zone 2. Some previous work-related skill, knowledge, or experience may be helpful in these occupations, but usually is not needed. **Job Preparation—**SVP 4.0 to less than 6.0—six months to less than two years. **Knowledges—**Clerical Practices; Customer and Personal Service; Computers and Electronics. **Instructional Programs—**General Office Occupations and Clerical Services; Health Unit Coordinator/Ward Clerk; Medical Reception/Receptionist; Receptionist.

Related SOC Job—43-4171 Receptionists and Information Clerks. **Related OOH Job—**Receptionists and Information Clerks. **Related**

DOT Jobs—203.362-014 Credit Reporting Clerk; 205.367-038 Registrar; 237.267-010 Information Clerk, Automobile Club; 237.367-010 Appointment Clerk; 237.367-018 Information Clerk; 237.367-022 Information Clerk; 237.367-038 Receptionist; 237.367-042 Referral-and-Information Aide; 237.367-046 Telephone Quotation Clerk; 238.367-022 Space Scheduler; 238.367-034 Scheduler; 239.367-034 Utility Clerk; 249.262-010 Policyholder-Information Clerk; 249.367-082 Park Aide.

43-4181.00 Reservation and Transportation Ticket Agents and Travel Clerks

- **Education/Training Required: Short-term on-the-job training**
- **Employed: 160,120**
- **Annual Earnings: $28,120**
- **Growth: 2.4%**
- **Annual Job Openings: 30,000**

Make and confirm reservations and sell tickets to passengers and for large hotel or motel chains. May check baggage and direct passengers to designated concourse, pier, or track; make reservations; deliver tickets; arrange for visas; contact individuals and groups to inform them of package tours; or provide tourists with travel information, such as points of interest, restaurants, rates, and emergency service.

Plan routes, itineraries, and accommodation details and compute fares and fees, using schedules, rate books, and computers. Make and confirm reservations for transportation and accommodations, using telephones, faxes, mail, and computers. Prepare customer invoices and accept payment. Answer inquiries regarding such information as schedules, accommodations, procedures, and policies. Assemble and issue required documentation such as tickets, travel insurance policies, and itineraries. Determine whether space is available on travel dates requested by customers and assign requested spaces when available. Inform clients of essential travel information such as travel times, transportation connections, and medical and visa requirements. Maintain computerized inventories of available passenger space and provide information on space reserved or available. Confer with customers to determine their service requirements and travel preferences. Examine passenger documentation to determine destinations and to assign boarding passes. Provide boarding or disembarking assistance to passengers needing special assistance. Check baggage and cargo and direct passengers to designated locations for loading. Announce arrival and departure information, using public-address systems. Trace lost, delayed, or misdirected baggage for customers. Promote particular destinations, tour packages, and other travel services. Provide clients with assistance in preparing required travel documents and forms. Open and close information facilities and keep them clean during operation. Provide customers with travel suggestions and information such as guides, directories, brochures, and maps. Contact customers or travel agents to advise them of travel conveyance changes or to confirm reservations. Contact motel, hotel, resort, and travel operators to obtain current advertising literature.

GOE Information—Interest Area: 09. Hospitality, Tourism, and Recreation. **Work Group:** 09.03. Hospitality and Travel Services. **Personality Type—**Conventional. Conventional occupations frequently involve following set procedures and routines. These occupations can include working with data and details more than with ideas. Usually there is a clear line of authority to follow. **Work Values—**Social Service; Working Conditions; Supervision, Human

Relations; Supervision, Technical; Company Policies and Practices; Activity. **Skills**—Service Orientation; Instructing; Operation and Control; Operation Monitoring; Active Listening; Speaking. **Abilities**—*Cognitive:* Memorization; Number Facility; Mathematical Reasoning; Oral Expression; Fluency of Ideas; Speed of Closure. *Psychomotor:* Wrist-Finger Speed. *Physical:* Trunk Strength. *Sensory:* Near Vision; Auditory Attention; Speech Clarity. **General Work Activities**—*Information Input:* Getting Information; Identifying Objects, Actions, and Events; Monitoring Processes, Materials, or Surroundings. *Mental Process:* Making Decisions and Solving Problems; Updating and Using Relevant Knowledge; Processing Information. *Work Output:* Interacting With Computers; Documenting or Recording Information; Handling and Moving Objects. *Interacting with Others:* Establishing and Maintaining Interpersonal Relationships; Performing for or Working with the Public; Resolving Conflicts and Negotiating with Others. **Physical Work Conditions**—Indoors; Noisy; Sitting; Using Hands on Objects, Tools, or Controls; Repetitive Motions. **Other Job Characteristics**—Repeat Same Tasks; Need to Be Exact or Accurate.

Experience—Job Zone 2. Some previous work-related skill, knowledge, or experience may be helpful in these occupations, but usually is not needed. **Job Preparation**—SVP 4.0 to less than 6.0—six months to less than two years. **Knowledges**—Customer and Personal Service; Transportation; Sales and Marketing; Clerical Practices; Public Safety and Security. **Instructional Programs**—Hospitality/Travel Services Sales Operations; Selling Skills and Sales Operations; Tourism and Travel Services Marketing Operations; Tourism Promotion Operations.

Related SOC Job—43-4181 Reservation and Transportation Ticket Agents and Travel Clerks. **Related OOH Job**—Reservation and Transportation Ticket Agents and Travel Clerks. **Related DOT Jobs**—214.362-030 Rate Clerk, Passenger; 237.367-050 Tourist-Information Assistant; 238.167-010 Travel Clerk; 238.167-014 Travel Counselor, Automobile Club; 238.362-014 Reservation Clerk; 238.367-010 Gate Agent; 238.367-014 Reservation Clerk; 238.367-018 Reservations Agent; 238.367-026 Ticket Agent; 238.367-030 Travel Clerk; 248.382-010 Ticketing Clerk.

43-4199.99 Information and Record Clerks, All Other

- **Education/Training Required: Short-term on-the-job training**
- **Employed: 288,730**
- **Annual Earnings: $33,610**
- **Growth: –8.6%**
- **Annual Job Openings: 46,000**

All information and record clerks not listed separately.

No task data available.

Note: The Department of Labor has not collected some data for this job, so it has fewer details than the other descriptions.

Related SOC Job—43-4199 Information and Record Clerks, All Other. **Related OOH Job**—None. **Related DOT Jobs**—214.362-034 Tariff Inspector; 241.367-038 Investigator, Dealer Accounts; 249.387-018 Pedigree Tracer.

43-5000 Material Recording, Scheduling, Dispatching, and Distributing Workers

43-5011.00 Cargo and Freight Agents

- **Education/Training Required: Moderate-term on-the-job training**
- **Employed: 78,730**
- **Annual Earnings: $35,860**
- **Growth: –5.6%**
- **Annual Job Openings: 12,000**

Expedite and route movement of incoming and outgoing cargo and freight shipments in airline, train, and trucking terminals and shipping docks. Take orders from customers and arrange pickup of freight and cargo for delivery to loading platform. Prepare and examine bills of lading to determine shipping charges and tariffs.

Negotiate and arrange transport of goods with shipping or freight companies. Notify consignees, passengers, or customers of the arrival of freight or baggage and arrange for delivery. Advise clients on transportation and payment methods. Prepare manifests showing baggage, mail, and freight weights and number of passengers on airplanes and transmit data to destinations. Determine method of shipment and prepare bills of lading, invoices, and other shipping documents. Check import/export documentation to determine cargo contents and classify goods into different fee or tariff groups, using a tariff coding system. Estimate freight or postal rates and record shipment costs and weights. Enter shipping information into a computer by hand or by using a hand-held scanner that reads bar codes on goods. Retrieve stored items and trace lost shipments as necessary. Pack goods for shipping, using tools such as staplers, strapping machines, and hammers. Direct delivery trucks to shipping doors or designated marshalling areas and help load and unload goods safely. Inspect and count items received and check them against invoices or other documents, recording shortages and rejecting damaged goods. Install straps, braces, and padding to loads to prevent shifting or damage during shipment. Keep records of all goods shipped, received, and stored. Coordinate and supervise activities of workers engaged in packing and shipping merchandise. Arrange insurance coverage for goods. Direct or participate in cargo loading to ensure completeness of load and even distribution of weight. Open cargo containers and unwrap contents, using steel cutters, crowbars, or other hand tools. Attach address labels, identification codes, and shipping instructions to containers. Contact vendors or claims adjustment departments to resolve problems with shipments or contact service depots to arrange for repairs. Route received goods to first available flight or to appropriate storage areas or departments, using forklifts, handtrucks, or other equipment. Maintain a supply of packing materials.

GOE Information—**Interest Area:** 16. Transportation, Distribution, and Logistics. **Work Group:** 16.07. Transportation Support Work. **Personality Type**—Conventional. Conventional occupations frequently involve following set procedures and routines. These occupations can include working with data and details more than with ideas. Usually there is a clear line of authority to follow. **Work Values**—Supervision, Technical; Supervision, Human Relations; Company Policies and Practices; Moral Values; Advancement. **Skills**—Negotiation; Instructing; Service Orientation; Monitoring; Writing; Speaking. **Abilities**—*Cognitive:* Mathematical Reasoning; Perceptual

Speed; Written Expression; Selective Attention; Number Facility; Oral Comprehension. *Psychomotor:* None met the criteria. *Physical:* None met the criteria. *Sensory:* None met the criteria. **General Work Activities**—*Information Input:* Monitoring Processes, Materials, or Surroundings; Getting Information; Identifying Objects, Actions, and Events. *Mental Process:* Making Decisions and Solving Problems; Organizing, Planning, and Prioritizing; Processing Information. *Work Output:* Interacting With Computers; Documenting or Recording Information. *Interacting with Others:* Establishing and Maintaining Interpersonal Relationships; Resolving Conflicts and Negotiating with Others; Communicating with Other Workers. **Physical Work Conditions**—Indoors; Sitting; Repetitive Motions. **Other Job Characteristics**—Need to Be Exact or Accurate; Repeat Same Tasks; Errors Have Important Consequences.

Experience—Job Zone 2. Some previous work-related skill, knowledge, or experience may be helpful in these occupations, but usually is not needed. **Job Preparation**—SVP 4.0 to less than 6.0—six months to less than two years. **Knowledges**—Transportation; Geography; Customer and Personal Service; Clerical Practices; Administration and Management; Computers and Electronics. **Instructional Program**—General Office Occupations and Clerical Services.

Related SOC Job—43-5011 Cargo and Freight Agents. **Related OOH Job**—Cargo and Freight Agents. **Related DOT Jobs**—248.362-640 Transportation Clerk; 248.367-018 Cargo Agent; 912.367-014 Transportation Agent.

43-5021.00 Couriers and Messengers

- **Education/Training Required: Short-term on-the-job training**
- **Employed: 106,520**
- **Annual Earnings: $20,870**
- **Growth: –8.6%**
- **Annual Job Openings: 24,000**

Pick up and carry messages, documents, packages, and other items between offices or departments within an establishment or to other business concerns, traveling by foot, bicycle, motorcycle, automobile, or public conveyance.

Walk, ride bicycles, drive vehicles, or use public conveyances in order to reach destinations to deliver messages or materials. Load vehicles with listed goods, ensuring goods are loaded correctly and taking precautions with hazardous goods. Receive messages or materials to be delivered and information on recipients, such as names, addresses, telephone numbers, and delivery instructions, communicated via telephone, two-way radio, or in person. Unload and sort items collected along delivery routes. Plan and follow the most efficient routes for delivering goods. Deliver messages and items such as newspapers, documents, and packages between establishment departments and to other establishments and private homes. Sort items to be delivered according to the delivery route. Obtain signatures and payments or arrange for recipients to make payments. Record information such as items received and delivered and recipients' responses to messages. Check with home offices after completed deliveries to confirm deliveries and collections and to receive instructions for other deliveries. Perform routine maintenance on delivery vehicles, such as monitoring fluid levels and replenishing fuel. Call by telephone to deliver verbal messages. Open, sort, and distribute incoming mail. Perform general office or clerical work such as filing materials, operating duplicating machines, or running errands. Collect, seal, and stamp outgoing mail, using postage meters and envelope sealers. Unload goods from large trucks and load them onto smaller delivery vehicles.

GOE Information—**Interest Area:** 16. Transportation, Distribution, and Logistics. **Work Group:** 16.06. Other Services Requiring Driving. **Personality Type**—Realistic. Realistic occupations frequently involve work activities that include practical, hands-on problems and solutions. They often deal with plants; animals; and real-world materials like wood, tools, and machinery. Many of the occupations require working outside and do not involve a lot of paperwork or working closely with others. **Work Values**—Independence; Social Service. **Skills**—Equipment Maintenance; Operation and Control. **Abilities**—*Cognitive:* Spatial Orientation; Time Sharing; Perceptual Speed. *Psychomotor:* Response Orientation; Speed of Limb Movement; Multilimb Coordination; Rate Control; Reaction Time; Control Precision. *Physical:* Stamina; Static Strength; Gross Body Coordination; Extent Flexibility; Dynamic Strength; Trunk Strength. *Sensory:* Sound Localization; Glare Sensitivity; Depth Perception; Speech Recognition; Visual Color Discrimination. **General Work Activities**—*Information Input:* Getting Information; Identifying Objects, Actions, and Events; Monitoring Processes, Materials, or Surroundings. *Mental Process:* Organizing, Planning, and Prioritizing; Updating and Using Relevant Knowledge; Analyzing Data or Information. *Work Output:* Handling and Moving Objects; Performing General Physical Activities; Documenting or Recording Information. *Interacting with Others:* Establishing and Maintaining Interpersonal Relationships; Communicating with Persons Outside Organization; Performing for or Working with the Public. **Physical Work Conditions**—Outdoors; Very Hot or Cold; Standing; Walking and Running; Using Hands on Objects, Tools, or Controls; Repetitive Motions. **Other Job Characteristics**—Need to Be Exact or Accurate.

Experience—Job Zone 2. Some previous work-related skill, knowledge, or experience may be helpful in these occupations, but usually is not needed. **Job Preparation**—SVP 4.0 to less than 6.0—six months to less than two years. **Knowledges**—Transportation. **Instructional Program**—No related CIP programs.

Related SOC Job—43-5021 Couriers and Messengers. **Related OOH Job**—Couriers and Messengers. **Related DOT Jobs**—215.563-010 Caller; 230.663-010 Deliverer, Outside; 239.567-010 Office Helper; 239.677-010 Messenger, Copy; 239.687-010 Route Aide; 239.687-014 Tube Operator; 299.477-010 Deliverer, Merchandise.

43-5031.00 Police, Fire, and Ambulance Dispatchers

- **Education/Training Required: Moderate-term on-the-job training**
- **Employed: 94,060**
- **Annual Earnings: $30,060**
- **Growth: 15.9%**
- **Annual Job Openings: 12,000**

Receive complaints from public concerning crimes and police emergencies. Broadcast orders to police patrol units in vicinity of complaint to investigate. Operate radio, telephone, or computer equipment to receive reports of fires and medical emergencies and relay information or orders to proper officials.

Determine response requirements and relative priorities of situations and dispatch units in accordance with established procedures. Record details of calls, dispatches, and messages. Question callers to determine their locations and the nature of their problems to determine type of response needed. Enter, update, and retrieve information from teletype networks and computerized data systems regarding such things as wanted persons, stolen property, vehicle registration, and stolen vehicles. Scan status charts and computer screens and contact emergency response field units to determine emergency units available for dispatch. Relay information and messages to and from emergency sites, to law enforcement agencies, and to all other individuals or groups requiring notification. Receive incoming telephone or alarm system calls regarding emergency and non-emergency police and fire service, emergency ambulance service, information, and after-hours calls for departments within a city. Maintain access to, and security of, highly sensitive materials. Observe alarm registers and scan maps to determine whether a specific emergency is in the dispatch service area. Maintain files of information relating to emergency calls such as personnel rosters and emergency call-out and pager files. Monitor various radio frequencies such as those used by public works departments, school security, and civil defense to keep apprised of developing situations. Learn material and pass required tests for certification. Read and effectively interpret small-scale maps and information from a computer screen to determine locations and provide directions. Answer routine inquiries and refer calls not requiring dispatches to appropriate departments and agencies. Provide emergency medical instructions to callers. Monitor alarm systems to detect emergencies such as fires and illegal entry into establishments. Test and adjust communication and alarm systems and report malfunctions to maintenance units. Operate and maintain mobile dispatch vehicles and equipment.

GOE Information—Interest Area: 03. Arts and Communication. **Work Group:** 03.10. Communications Technology. **Personality Type**—Social. Social occupations frequently involve working with, communicating with, and teaching people. These occupations often involve helping or providing service to others. **Work Values**—Social Service; Authority; Supervision, Technical; Supervision, Human Relations; Security; Recognition. **Skills**—Active Listening; Speaking; Social Perceptiveness; Judgment and Decision Making; Critical Thinking; Service Orientation. **Abilities**—*Cognitive:* Perceptual Speed; Speed of Closure; Time Sharing; Flexibility of Closure; Memorization; Selective Attention. *Psychomotor:* Reaction Time; Response Orientation; Finger Dexterity; Arm-Hand Steadiness. *Physical:* None met the criteria. *Sensory:* Speech Recognition; Auditory Attention; Hearing Sensitivity; Speech Clarity; Near Vision; Visual Color Discrimination. **General Work Activities**—*Information Input:* Getting Information; Identifying Objects, Actions, and Events; Monitoring Processes, Materials, or Surroundings. *Mental Process:* Processing Information; Updating and Using Relevant Knowledge; Making Decisions and Solving Problems. *Work Output:* Documenting or Recording Information; Interacting With Computers. *Interacting with Others:* Performing for or Working with the Public; Resolving Conflicts and Negotiating with Others; Communicating with Persons Outside Organization. **Physical Work Conditions**—Indoors; Noisy; Sitting; Using Hands on Objects, Tools, or Controls; Repetitive Motions. **Other Job Characteristics**—Need to Be Exact or Accurate; Repeat Same Tasks; Errors Have Important Consequences.

Experience—Job Zone 2. Some previous work-related skill, knowledge, or experience may be helpful in these occupations, but usually is not needed. **Job Preparation**—SVP 4.0 to less than 6.0—six months to less than two years. **Knowledges**—Telecommunications; Customer and Personal Service; Clerical Practices; Public Safety and Security; Law and Government; Computers and Electronics. **Instructional Program**—No related CIP programs.

Related SOC Job—43-5031 Police, Fire, and Ambulance Dispatchers. **Related OOH Job**—Dispatchers. **Related DOT Jobs**—379.162-010 Alarm Operator; 379.362-010 Dispatcher, Radio; 379.362-014 Protective-Signal Operator; 379.362-018 Telecommunicator.

43-5032.00 Dispatchers, Except Police, Fire, and Ambulance

- **Education/Training Required: Moderate-term on-the-job training**
- **Employed: 172,550**
- **Annual Earnings: $31,390**
- **Growth: 5.7%**
- **Annual Job Openings: 19,000**

Schedule and dispatch workers, work crews, equipment, or service vehicles for conveyance of materials, freight, or passengers or for normal installation, service, or emergency repairs rendered outside the place of business. Duties may include using radio, telephone, or computer to transmit assignments and compiling statistics and reports on work progress.

Schedule and dispatch workers, work crews, equipment, or service vehicles to appropriate locations according to customer requests, specifications, or needs, using radios or telephones. Arrange for necessary repairs to restore service and schedules. Relay work orders, messages, and information to or from work crews, supervisors, and field inspectors, using telephones or two-way radios. Confer with customers or supervising personnel to address questions, problems, and requests for service or equipment. Prepare daily work and run schedules. Receive or prepare work orders. Oversee all communications within specifically assigned territories. Monitor personnel or equipment locations and utilization to coordinate service and schedules. Record and maintain files and records of customer requests, work or services performed, charges, expenses, inventory, and other dispatch information. Determine types or amounts of equipment, vehicles, materials, or personnel required according to work orders or specifications. Advise personnel about traffic problems such as construction areas, accidents, congestion, weather conditions, and other hazards. Ensure timely and efficient movement of trains according to train orders and schedules. Order supplies and equipment and issue them to personnel.

GOE Information—Interest Area: 03. Arts and Communication. **Work Group:** 03.10. Communications Technology. **Personality Type**—Conventional. Conventional occupations frequently involve following set procedures and routines. These occupations can include working with data and details more than with ideas. Usually there is a clear line of authority to follow. **Work Values**—Supervision, Technical; Authority. **Skills**—Operations Analysis; Service Orientation; Management of Personnel Resources; Systems Evaluation; Systems Analysis; Judgment and Decision Making. **Abilities**—*Cognitive:* Time Sharing; Information Ordering; Oral Expression; Selective Attention; Problem Sensitivity; Deductive Reasoning. *Psychomotor:* None met the criteria. *Physical:* None met the criteria. *Sensory:* Speech Recognition; Auditory Attention; Speech Clarity. **General Work Activities**—*Information Input:* Getting Information; Monitoring Processes, Materials, or Surroundings; Identifying Objects, Actions, and Events. *Mental Process:* Processing Information; Making Decisions and Solving Problems; Organizing, Planning, and Prioritizing. *Work Output:* Documenting or Recording Information; Interacting With Computers. *Interacting with Others:* Communicating with Other Workers; Establishing and Maintaining Interpersonal Relationships; Performing Administrative Activities. **Physical Work Conditions**—Indoors; Noisy; Sitting; Using Hands on Objects, Tools, or Controls; Repetitive Motions. **Other Job Characteristics**—Repeat Same Tasks; Need to Be Exact or Accurate; Automation.

Experience—Job Zone 2. Some previous work-related skill, knowledge, or experience may be helpful in these occupations, but usually is not needed. **Job Preparation**—SVP 4.0 to less than 6.0—six months to less than two years. **Knowledges**—Transportation; Clerical Practices; Public Safety and Security; Communications and Media; Computers and Electronics; Customer and Personal Service. **Instructional Program**—No related CIP programs.

Related SOC Job—43-5032 Dispatchers, Except Police, Fire, and Ambulance. **Related OOH Job**—Dispatchers. **Related DOT Jobs**—215.167-010 Car Clerk, Pullman; 215.367-018 Taxicab Coordinator; 221.362-014 Dispatcher, Relay; 221.367-070 Service Clerk; 221.367-082 Work-Order-Sorting Clerk; 239.167-014 Dispatcher; 239.367-014 Dispatcher, Maintenance Service; 239.367-022 Receiver-Dispatcher; 239.367-030 Dispatcher, Street Department; 248.367-026 Dispatcher, Ship Pilot; 249.167-014 Dispatcher, Motor Vehicle; 249.167-070 Routing Clerk; 372.167-010 Dispatcher, Security Guard; 910.167-014 Train Dispatcher, Assistant Chief; others.

43-5041.00 Meter Readers, Utilities

- **Education/Training Required: Short-term on-the-job training**
- **Employed: 46,920**
- **Annual Earnings: $29,310**
- **Growth: –44.9%**
- **Annual Job Openings: 8,000**

Read meter and record consumption of electricity, gas, water, or steam.

Read electric, gas, water, or steam consumption meters and enter data in route books or handheld computers. Walk or drive vehicles along established routes to take readings of meter dials. Upload into office computers all information collected on hand-held computers during meter rounds or return route books or hand-hand computers to business offices so that data can be compiled. Verify readings in cases where consumption appears to be abnormal and record possible reasons for fluctuations. Inspect meters for unauthorized connections, defects, and damage such as broken seals. Report to service departments any problems such as meter irregularities, damaged equipment, or impediments to meter access, including dogs. Answer customers' questions about services and charges or direct them to customer service centers. Update client address and meter location information. Leave messages to arrange different times to read meters in cases in which meters are not accessible. Connect and disconnect utility services at specific locations. Collect past-due bills. Report lost or broken keys.

GOE Information—Interest Area: 04. Business and Administration. **Work Group:** 04.07. Records and Materials Processing. **Personality Type**—Conventional. Conventional occupations frequently involve following set procedures and routines. These occupations can include working with data and details more than with ideas. Usually there is a clear line of authority to follow. **Work Values**—Independence; Supervision, Technical; Supervision, Human Relations; Company Policies and Practices; Security; Moral Values. **Skills**—Repairing; Operation Monitoring; Installation; Systems Evaluation; Management of Personnel Resources; Management of Material Resources. **Abilities**—*Cognitive:* Spatial Orientation; Perceptual Speed. *Psychomotor:* Response Orientation; Reaction Time; Speed of Limb Movement; Multilimb Coordination; Rate Control; Control Precision. *Physical:* Extent Flexibility; Gross Body Coordination; Static Strength; Trunk Strength. *Sensory:* Glare Sensitivity; Visual Color Discrimination; Depth Perception; Hearing Sensitivity; Far Vision; Auditory Attention. **General Work Activities**—*Information Input:* Monitoring Processes, Materials, or Surroundings; Identifying Objects, Actions, and Events; Inspecting Equipment, Structures, or Materials. *Mental Process:* Making Decisions and Solving Problems; Organizing, Planning, and Prioritizing; Processing Information. *Work Output:* Performing General Physical Activities; Documenting or Recording Information; Operating Vehicles or Equipment. *Interacting with Others:* Performing for or Working with the Public; Communicating with Other Workers; Communicating with Persons Outside Organization. **Physical Work Conditions**—Outdoors; Minor Burns, Cuts, Bites, or Stings; Standing; Walking and Running; Using Hands on Objects, Tools, or Controls; Repetitive Motions. **Other Job Characteristics**—Need to Be Exact or Accurate; Repeat Same Tasks.

Experience—Job Zone 2. Some previous work-related skill, knowledge, or experience may be helpful in these occupations, but usually is not needed. **Job Preparation**—SVP 4.0 to less than 6.0—six months to less than two years. **Knowledges**—Transportation; Public Safety and Security. **Instructional Program**—No related CIP programs.

Related SOC Job—43-5041 Meter Readers, Utilities. **Related OOH Job**—Meter Readers, Utilities. **Related DOT Job**—209.567-010 Meter Reader.

43-5051.00 Postal Service Clerks

- **Education/Training Required: Short-term on-the-job training**
- **Employed: 78,710**
- **Annual Earnings: $48,310**
- **Growth: 0.0%**
- **Annual Job Openings: 4,000**

Perform any combination of tasks in a post office, such as receiving letters and parcels; selling postage and revenue stamps, postal cards, and stamped envelopes; filling out and selling money orders; placing mail in pigeonholes of mail rack or in bags according to state, address, or other scheme; and examining mail for correct postage.

Keep money drawers in order and record and balance daily transactions. Weigh letters and parcels; compute mailing costs based on type, weight, and destination; and affix correct postage. Obtain signatures from recipients of registered or special delivery mail. Register, certify, and insure letters and parcels. Sell and collect payment for products such as stamps, prepaid mail envelopes, and money orders. Check mail to ensure correct postage and that packages and letters are in proper condition for mailing. Answer questions regarding mail regulations and procedures, postage rates, and post office boxes. Complete forms regarding changes of address or theft or loss of mail or for special services such as registered or priority mail. Provide assistance to the public in complying with federal regulations of Postal Service and other federal agencies. Sort incoming and outgoing mail according to type and destination by hand or by operating electronic mail-sorting and scanning devices. Cash money orders. Rent post office boxes to customers. Put undelivered parcels away, retrieve them when customers come to claim them, and complete any related documentation. Provide customers with assistance in filing claims for mail theft or lost or damaged mail. Respond to complaints regarding mail theft, delivery problems, and lost or damaged mail, filling out forms and making appropriate referrals for investigation. Receive letters and parcels and place mail into bags. Feed mail into postage-canceling devices or hand-stamp mail to cancel postage. Transport mail from one workstation to another. Set postage meters and calibrate them to ensure correct operation. Post announcements or government information on public bulletin boards.

GOE Information—Interest Area: 04. Business and Administration. Work Group: 04.07. Records and Materials Processing. Personality Type—Conventional. Conventional occupations frequently involve following set procedures and routines. These occupations can include working with data and details more than with ideas. Usually there is a clear line of authority to follow. Work Values—Supervision, Technical; Security; Supervision, Human Relations; Social Service; Company Policies and Practices; Compensation. Skills—Service Orientation. Abilities—*Cognitive:* Number Facility; Perceptual Speed; Time Sharing; Selective Attention. *Psychomotor:* Manual Dexterity; Multilimb Coordination; Arm-Hand Steadiness; Finger Dexterity. *Physical:* Extent Flexibility; Static Strength; Gross Body Coordination; Trunk Strength. *Sensory:* Hearing Sensitivity; Speech Recognition; Auditory Attention. General Work Activities— *Information Input:* Identifying Objects, Actions, and Events; Getting Information; Monitoring Processes, Materials, or Surroundings. *Mental Process:* Updating and Using Relevant Knowledge; Processing Information; Organizing, Planning, and Prioritizing. *Work Output:* Handling and Moving Objects; Performing General Physical Activities; Documenting or Recording Information. *Interacting with Others:* Performing for or Working with the Public; Establishing and Maintaining Interpersonal Relationships; Communicating with Other Workers. Physical Work Conditions—Indoors; Noisy; Contaminants; Standing; Bending or Twisting the Body; Repetitive Motions. Other Job Characteristics—Need to Be Exact or Accurate.

Experience—Job Zone 2. Some previous work-related skill, knowledge, or experience may be helpful in these occupations, but usually is not needed. Job Preparation—SVP 4.0 to less than 6.0—six months to less than two years. Knowledges—Sales and Marketing; Transportation; Clerical Practices; Public Safety and Security; Customer and Personal Service; Production and Processing. Instructional Program—General Office Occupations and Clerical Services.

Related SOC Job—43-5051 Postal Service Clerks. Related OOH Job— Postal Service Workers. Related DOT Jobs—209.687-014 Mail Handler; 243.367-014 Post-Office Clerk.

43-5052.00 Postal Service Mail Carriers

- Education/Training Required: Short-term on-the-job training
- Employed: 347,180
- Annual Earnings: $46,330
- Growth: 0.0%
- Annual Job Openings: 19,000

Sort mail for delivery. Deliver mail on established route by vehicle or on foot.

Obtain signed receipts for registered, certified, and insured mail; collect associated charges; and complete any necessary paperwork. Sort mail for delivery, arranging it in delivery sequence. Deliver mail to residences and business establishments along specified routes by walking or driving, using a combination of satchels, carts, cars, and small trucks. Return to the post office with mail collected from homes, businesses, and public mailboxes. Turn in money and receipts collected along mail routes. Sign for cash-on-delivery and registered mail before leaving the post office. Record address changes and redirect mail for those addresses. Hold mail for customers who are away from delivery locations. Bundle mail in preparation for delivery or transportation to relay boxes. Leave notices telling patrons where to collect mail that could not be delivered. Meet schedules for the collection and return of mail. Return incorrectly addressed mail to

senders. Maintain accurate records of deliveries. Answer customers' questions about postal services and regulations. Provide customers with change of address cards and other forms. Report any unusual circumstances concerning mail delivery, including the condition of street letter boxes. Register, certify, and insure parcels and letters. Travel to post offices to pick up the mail for routes or pick up mail from postal relay boxes. Enter change of address orders into computers that process forwarding address stickers. Complete forms that notify publishers of address changes. Sell stamps and money orders.

GOE Information—Interest Area: 16. Transportation, Distribution, and Logistics. Work Group: 16.06. Other Services Requiring Driving. Personality Type—Conventional. Conventional occupations frequently involve following set procedures and routines. These occupations can include working with data and details more than with ideas. Usually there is a clear line of authority to follow. Work Values—Independence; Security; Supervision, Human Relations; Social Service; Company Policies and Practices; Supervision, Technical. Skills—None met the criteria. Abilities—*Cognitive:* Perceptual Speed; Time Sharing. *Psychomotor:* Control Precision; Multilimb Coordination; Manual Dexterity; Arm-Hand Steadiness; Finger Dexterity. *Physical:* Stamina; Extent Flexibility; Static Strength; Trunk Strength. *Sensory:* Depth Perception; Far Vision. General Work Activities—*Information Input:* Getting Information; Identifying Objects, Actions, and Events; Inspecting Equipment, Structures, or Materials. *Mental Process:* Updating and Using Relevant Knowledge; Processing Information; Organizing, Planning, and Prioritizing. *Work Output:* Handling and Moving Objects; Performing General Physical Activities; Operating Vehicles or Equipment. *Interacting with Others:* Performing for or Working with the Public; Communicating with Other Workers; Establishing and Maintaining Interpersonal Relationships. Physical Work Conditions—Outdoors; Very Hot or Cold; Contaminants; Standing; Using Hands on Objects, Tools, or Controls; Repetitive Motions. Other Job Characteristics— Need to Be Exact or Accurate; Repeat Same Tasks.

Experience—Job Zone 2. Some previous work-related skill, knowledge, or experience may be helpful in these occupations, but usually is not needed. Job Preparation—SVP 4.0 to less than 6.0—six months to less than two years. Knowledges—Transportation; Public Safety and Security; Customer and Personal Service. Instructional Program—General Office Occupations and Clerical Services.

Related SOC Job—43-5052 Postal Service Mail Carriers. Related OOH Job—Postal Service Workers. Related DOT Jobs—230.363-010 Rural Mail Carrier; 230.367-010 Mail Carrier.

43-5053.00 Postal Service Mail Sorters, Processors, and Processing Machine Operators

- Education/Training Required: Short-term on-the-job training
- Employed: 208,600
- Annual Earnings: $43,420
- Growth: 0.0%
- Annual Job Openings: 11,000

Prepare incoming and outgoing mail for distribution. Examine, sort, and route mail by state, type of mail, or other scheme. Load, operate, and occasionally adjust and repair mail-processing, -sorting, and -canceling machinery. Keep records of shipments, pouches, and sacks and perform other duties related to mail handling within the postal service. Must complete a competitive exam.

Direct items according to established routing schemes, using computer-controlled keyboards or voice recognition equipment. Bundle, label, and route sorted mail to designated areas depending on destinations and according to established procedures and deadlines. Serve the public at counters or windows, such as by selling stamps and weighing parcels. Supervise other mail sorters. Train new workers. Distribute incoming mail into the correct boxes or pigeonholes. Operate various types of equipment, such as computer scanning equipment, addressographs, mimeographs, optical character readers, and bar-code sorters. Search directories to find correct addresses for redirected mail. Clear jams in sorting equipment. Open and label mail containers. Check items to ensure that addresses are legible and correct, that sufficient postage has been paid or the appropriate documentation is attached, and that items are in a suitable condition for processing. Rewrap soiled or broken parcels. Weigh articles to determine required postage. Move containers of mail, using equipment such as forklifts and automated "trains." Sort odd-sized mail by hand, sort mail that other workers have been unable to sort, and segregate items requiring special handling. Accept and check containers of mail from large-volume mailers, couriers, and contractors. Load and unload mail trucks, sometimes lifting containers of mail onto equipment that transports items to sorting stations. Cancel letter or parcel post stamps by hand. Dump sacks of mail onto conveyors for culling and sorting.

GOE Information—Interest Area: 04. Business and Administration. **Work Group:** 04.07. Records and Materials Processing. **Personality Type**—No data available. **Work Values**—No data available. **Skills**—None met the criteria. **Abilities**—*Cognitive:* None met the criteria. *Psychomotor:* Rate Control; Manual Dexterity; Multilimb Coordination; Reaction Time; Control Precision; Finger Dexterity. *Physical:* Static Strength; Extent Flexibility; Trunk Strength. *Sensory:* Depth Perception. **General Work Activities**—*Information Input:* Getting Information; Identifying Objects, Actions, and Events; Inspecting Equipment, Structures, or Materials. *Mental Process:* Organizing, Planning, and Prioritizing; Updating and Using Relevant Knowledge; Processing Information. *Work Output:* Handling and Moving Objects; Performing General Physical Activities; Controlling Machines and Processes. *Interacting with Others:* Establishing and Maintaining Interpersonal Relationships; Assisting and Caring for Others; Communicating with Other Workers. **Physical Work Conditions**—Indoors; Noisy; Contaminants; Standing; Using Hands on Objects, Tools, or Controls; Repetitive Motions. **Other Job Characteristics**—Need to Be Exact or Accurate; Repeat Same Tasks; Automation; Pace Determined by Speed of Equipment.

Experience—Job Zone 2. Some previous work-related skill, knowledge, or experience may be helpful in these occupations, but usually is not needed. **Job Preparation**—SVP 4.0 to less than 6.0—six months to less than two years. **Knowledges**—Public Safety and Security; Geography. **Instructional Program**—General Office Occupations and Clerical Services.

Related SOC Job—43-5053 Postal Service Mail Sorters, Processors, and Processing Machine Operators. **Related OOH Job**—Postal Service Workers. **Related DOT Job**—209.687-014 Mail Handler.

43-5061.00 Production, Planning, and Expediting Clerks

- **Education/Training Required: Short-term on-the-job training**
- **Employed: 287,980**
- **Annual Earnings: $37,590**
- **Growth: 7.7%**
- **Annual Job Openings: 24,000**

Coordinate and expedite the flow of work and materials within or between departments of an establishment according to production schedule. Duties include reviewing and distributing production, work, and shipment schedules; conferring with department supervisors to determine progress of work and completion dates; and compiling reports on progress of work, inventory levels, costs, and production problems.

Examine documents, materials, and products and monitor work processes to assess completeness, accuracy, and conformance to standards and specifications. Review documents such as production schedules, work orders, and staffing tables to determine personnel and materials requirements and material priorities. Revise production schedules when required due to design changes, labor or material shortages, backlogs, or other interruptions, collaborating with management, marketing, sales, production, and engineering. Confer with department supervisors and other personnel to assess progress and discuss needed changes. Confer with establishment personnel, vendors, and customers to coordinate production and shipping activities and to resolve complaints or eliminate delays. Record production data, including volume produced, consumption of raw materials, and quality control measures. Requisition and maintain inventories of materials and supplies necessary to meet production demands. Calculate figures such as required amounts of labor and materials, manufacturing costs, and wages, using pricing schedules, adding machines, calculators, or computers. Distribute production schedules and work orders to departments. Compile information, such as production rates and progress, materials inventories, materials used, and customer information, so that status reports can be completed. Arrange for delivery, assembly, and distribution of supplies and parts to expedite flow of materials and meet production schedules. Contact suppliers to verify shipment details. Maintain files such as maintenance records, bills of lading, and cost reports. Plan production commitments and timetables for business units, specific programs, or jobs, using sales forecasts. Establish and prepare product construction directions and locations and information on required tools, materials, and equipment; numbers of workers needed; and cost projections. Compile and prepare documentation related to production sequences; transportation; personnel schedules; and purchase, maintenance, and repair orders. Provide documentation and information to account for delays, difficulties, and changes to cost estimates.

GOE Information—Interest Area: 04. Business and Administration. **Work Group:** 04.07. Records and Materials Processing. **Personality Type**—Conventional. Conventional occupations frequently involve following set procedures and routines. These occupations can include working with data and details more than with ideas. Usually there is a clear line of authority to follow. **Work Values**—Supervision, Technical; Supervision, Human Relations; Advancement; Activity; Company Policies and Practices; Co-workers. **Skills**—Management of Material Resources; Management of Financial Resources; Systems Evaluation; Operations Analysis; Negotiation; Persuasion. **Abilities**—*Cognitive:* Number Facility; Written Expression; Flexibility of Closure; Originality; Written Comprehension; Oral Comprehension. *Psychomotor:* None met the criteria. *Physical:* None met the criteria. *Sensory:* Speech Recognition. **General Work Activities**—*Information Input:* Monitoring Processes, Materials, or Surroundings; Identifying Objects, Actions, and Events; Getting Information. *Mental Process:* Organizing, Planning, and Prioritizing; Scheduling Work and Activities; Updating and Using Relevant Knowledge. *Work Output:* Interacting With Computers; Documenting or Recording Information. *Interacting with Others:* Establishing and Maintaining Interpersonal Relationships; Communicating with Other Workers; Coordinating the Work and Activities of Others. **Physical Work Conditions**—Indoors; Noisy; Contaminants; Sitting. **Other Job Characteristics**—Need to Be Exact or Accurate; Repeat Same Tasks; Errors Have Important Consequences.

Experience—Job Zone 2. Some previous work-related skill, knowledge, or experience may be helpful in these occupations, but usually is not needed. **Job Preparation**—SVP 4.0 to less than 6.0—six months to less than two years. **Knowledges**—Production and Processing; Clerical Practices; Computers and Electronics; Administration and Management; Mathematics; Customer and Personal Service. **Instructional Program**—Parts, Warehousing, and Inventory Management Operations.

Related SOC Job—43-5061 Production, Planning, and Expediting Clerks. **Related OOH Job**—Production, Planning, and Expediting Clerks. **Related DOT Jobs**—199.382-010 Television-Schedule Coordinator; 215.362-010 Crew Scheduler; 215.362-014 Dispatcher Clerk; 215.367-010 Assignment Clerk; 215.367-014 Personnel Scheduler; 219.362-030 Extension Clerk; 219.387-010 Assignment Clerk; 221.162-010 Production Scheduler, Paperboard Products; 221.167-010 Copy Cutter; 221.167-014 Material Coordinator; 221.167-018 Production Coordinator; 221.167-022 Retort-Load Expediter; 221.167-026 Customer Services Coordinator; 221.362-018 Estimator, Paperboard Boxes; others.

43-5071.00 Shipping, Receiving, and Traffic Clerks

- **Education/Training Required: Short-term on-the-job training**
- **Employed: 759,910**
- **Annual Earnings: $25,180**
- **Growth: 3.7%**
- **Annual Job Openings: 121,000**

Verify and keep records on incoming and outgoing shipments. Prepare items for shipment. Duties include assembling, addressing, stamping, and shipping merchandise or material; receiving, unpacking, verifying, and recording incoming merchandise or material; and arranging for the transportation of products.

Examine contents and compare with records such as manifests, invoices, or orders to verify accuracy of incoming or outgoing shipment. Prepare documents such as work orders, bills of lading, and shipping orders to route materials. Determine shipping method for materials, using knowledge of shipping procedures, routes, and rates. Record shipment data such as weight, charges, space availability, and damages and discrepancies for reporting, accounting, and recordkeeping purposes. Contact carrier representative to make arrangements and to issue instructions for shipping and delivery of materials. Confer and correspond with establishment representatives to rectify problems such as damages, shortages, and nonconformance to specifications. Requisition and store shipping materials and supplies to maintain inventory of stock. Deliver or route materials to departments, using work devices such as handtruck, conveyor, or sorting bins. Compute amounts such as space available and shipping, storage, and demurrage charges, using calculator or price list. Pack, seal, label, and affix postage to prepare materials for shipping, using work devices such as hand tools, power tools, and postage meter.

GOE Information—Interest Area: 04. Business and Administration. **Work Group:** 04.07. Records and Materials Processing. **Personality Type**—Conventional. Conventional occupations frequently involve following set procedures and routines. These occupations can include working with data and details more than with ideas. Usually there is a clear line of authority to follow. **Work Values**—Moral Values; Supervision, Human Relations; Supervision, Technical; Advancement. **Skills**—Mathematics; Learning Strategies; Management of Financial Resources; Negotiation; Speaking; Time Management.

Abilities—*Cognitive:* Perceptual Speed; Number Facility; Time Sharing. *Psychomotor:* Manual Dexterity; Multilimb Coordination. *Physical:* Extent Flexibility; Static Strength; Gross Body Coordination; Trunk Strength. *Sensory:* Speech Recognition. **General Work Activities**—*Information Input:* Getting Information; Monitoring Processes, Materials, or Surroundings; Identifying Objects, Actions, and Events. *Mental Process:* Making Decisions and Solving Problems; Organizing, Planning, and Prioritizing; Updating and Using Relevant Knowledge. *Work Output:* Handling and Moving Objects; Interacting With Computers; Performing General Physical Activities. *Interacting with Others:* Establishing and Maintaining Interpersonal Relationships; Communicating with Other Workers; Performing Administrative Activities. **Physical Work Conditions**—Indoors; Noisy; Contaminants; Sitting; Walking and Running; Using Hands on Objects, Tools, or Controls. **Other Job Characteristics**—Need to Be Exact or Accurate; Repeat Same Tasks.

Experience—Job Zone 2. Some previous work-related skill, knowledge, or experience may be helpful in these occupations, but usually is not needed. **Job Preparation**—SVP 4.0 to less than 6.0—six months to less than two years. **Knowledges**—Clerical Practices; Production and Processing; Transportation; Computers and Electronics; Education and Training; Customer and Personal Service. **Instructional Programs**—General Office Occupations and Clerical Services; Traffic, Customs, and Transportation Clerk/Technician.

Related SOC Job—43-5071 Shipping, Receiving, and Traffic Clerks. **Related OOH Job**—Shipping, Receiving, and Traffic Clerks. **Related DOT Jobs**—209.367-042 Reconsignment Clerk; 214.587-014 Traffic Clerk; 219.367-022 Paper-Control Clerk; 219.367-030 Shipping-Order Clerk; 221.367-022 Industrial-Order Clerk; 222.367-066 Truckload Checker; 222.387-014 Car Checker; 222.387-022 Gun-Repair Clerk; 222.387-050 Shipping and Receiving Clerk; 222.567-010 Grain Elevator Clerk; 222.567-014 Ship Runner; 222.587-018 Distributing Clerk; 222.587-034 Route-Delivery Clerk; 222.587-058 Vault Worker; 222.687-022 Routing Clerk; 222.687-030 Shipping Checker; others.

43-5081.00 Stock Clerks and Order Fillers

- **Education/Training Required: Short-term on-the-job training**
- **Employed: 1,625,430**
- **Annual Earnings: $20,100**
- **Growth: –7.3%**
- **Annual Job Openings: 351,000**

The job openings listed here are shared with 43-5081.01 Stock Clerks, Sales Floor, 43-5081.02 Marking Clerks, 43-5081.03 Stock Clerks—Stockroom, Warehouse, or Storage Yard, 43-5081.04 Order Fillers, Wholesale and Retail Sales.

Receive, store, and issue sales floor merchandise, materials, equipment, and other items from stockroom, warehouse, or storage yard to fill shelves, racks, tables, or customers' orders. May mark prices on merchandise and set up sales displays.

No task data available.

GOE Information—Interest Area: 04. Business and Administration. **Work Group:** 04.07. Records and Materials Processing. **Note:** The Department of Labor has not collected some data for this job, so it has fewer details than the other descriptions.

Instructional Program—Retailing and Retail Operations.

Related SOC Job—43-5081 Stock Clerks and Order Fillers. **Related OOH Job**—Stock Clerks and Order Fillers. **Related DOT Job**—No data available.

43-5081.01 Stock Clerks, Sales Floor

- Education/Training Required: Short-term on-the-job training
- Employed: 1,625,430
- Annual Earnings: $20,100
- Growth: –7.3%
- Annual Job Openings: 351,000

The job openings listed here are shared with 43-5081.00 Stock Clerks and Order Fillers, 43-5081.02 Marking Clerks, 43-5081.03 Stock Clerks—Stockroom, Warehouse, or Storage Yard, 43-5081.04 Order Fillers, Wholesale and Retail Sales.

Receive, store, and issue sales floor merchandise. Stock shelves, racks, cases, bins, and tables with merchandise and arrange merchandise displays to attract customers. May periodically take physical count of stock or check and mark merchandise.

Answer customers' questions about merchandise and advise customers on merchandise selection. Itemize and total customer merchandise selection at checkout counter, using cash register, and accept cash or charge card for purchases. Take inventory or examine merchandise to identify items to be reordered or replenished. Pack customer purchases in bags or cartons. Stock shelves, racks, cases, bins, and tables with new or transferred merchandise. Receive, open, unpack, and issue sales floor merchandise. Clean display cases, shelves, and aisles. Compare merchandise invoices to items actually received to ensure that shipments are correct. Requisition merchandise from supplier based on available space, merchandise on hand, customer demand, or advertised specials. Transport packages to customers' vehicles. Stamp, attach, or change price tags on merchandise, referring to price list. Design and set up advertising signs and displays of merchandise on shelves, counters, or tables to attract customers and promote sales.

GOE Information—Interest Area: 04. Business and Administration. Work Group: 04.07. Records and Materials Processing. Personality Type—Realistic. Realistic occupations frequently involve work activities that include practical, hands-on problems and solutions. They often deal with plants; animals; and real-world materials like wood, tools, and machinery. Many of the occupations require working outside and do not involve a lot of paperwork or working closely with others. Work Values—Independence; Supervision, Technical; Advancement; Moral Values; Activity. Skills—None met the criteria. Abilities—*Cognitive:* None met the criteria. *Psychomotor:* Multilimb Coordination; Manual Dexterity. *Physical:* Extent Flexibility; Trunk Strength; Static Strength. *Sensory:* None met the criteria. General Work Activities—*Information Input:* Identifying Objects, Actions, and Events; Getting Information; Inspecting Equipment, Structures, or Materials. *Mental Process:* Updating and Using Relevant Knowledge; Organizing, Planning, and Prioritizing; Judging the Qualities of Things, Services, or Other People's Work. *Work Output:* Handling and Moving Objects; Performing General Physical Activities; Controlling Machines and Processes. *Interacting with Others:* Establishing and Maintaining Interpersonal Relationships; Performing for or Working with the Public; Communicating with Other Workers. Physical Work Conditions—Indoors; Standing; Walking and Running; Kneeling, Crouching, Stooping, or Crawling; Using Hands on Objects, Tools, or Controls; Bending or Twisting the Body. Other Job Characteristics—Need to Be Exact or Accurate; Repeat Same Tasks.

Experience—Job Zone 1. No previous work-related skill, knowledge, or experience is needed. Job Preparation—SVP below 4.0—less than six months. Knowledges—Administration and Management. Instructional Program—Retailing and Retail Operations.

Related SOC Job—43-5081 Stock Clerks and Order Fillers. Related OOH Job—Stock Clerks and Order Fillers. Related DOT Jobs—

299.367-014 Stock Clerk; 299.677-014 Sales Attendant, Building Materials.

43-5081.02 Marking Clerks

- Education/Training Required: Short-term on-the-job training
- Employed: 1,625,430
- Annual Earnings: $20,100
- Growth: –7.3%
- Annual Job Openings: 351,000

The job openings listed here are shared with 43-5081.00 Stock Clerks and Order Fillers, 43-5081.01 Stock Clerks, Sales Floor, 43-5081.03 Stock Clerks—Stockroom, Warehouse, or Storage Yard, 43-5081.04 Order Fillers, Wholesale and Retail Sales.

Print and attach price tickets to articles of merchandise using one or several methods, such as marking price on tickets by hand or using ticket-printing machine.

Put price information on tickets, marking by hand or using ticket-printing machine. Compare printed price tickets with entries on purchase orders to verify accuracy and notify supervisor of discrepancies. Pin, paste, sew, tie, or staple tickets, tags, or labels to article. Record number and types of articles marked and pack articles in boxes. Mark selling price by hand on boxes containing merchandise. Record price, buyer, and grade of product on tickets attached to products auctioned. Keep records of production, returned goods, and related transactions. Indicate item size, style, color, and inspection results on tags, tickets, and labels, using rubber stamp or writing instrument. Change the price of books in a warehouse.

GOE Information—Interest Area: 04. Business and Administration. Work Group: 04.07. Records and Materials Processing. Personality Type—Conventional. Conventional occupations frequently involve following set procedures and routines. These occupations can include working with data and details more than with ideas. Usually there is a clear line of authority to follow. Work Values—Independence; Moral Values; Supervision, Technical. Skills—Monitoring; Instructing; Mathematics; Management of Financial Resources; Learning Strategies. Abilities—*Cognitive:* None met the criteria. *Psychomotor:* Manual Dexterity; Arm-Hand Steadiness. *Physical:* Trunk Strength. *Sensory:* None met the criteria. General Work Activities—*Information Input:* Estimating the Needed Characteristics of Products, Events, or Information. *Mental Process:* Organizing, Planning, and Prioritizing; Updating and Using Relevant Knowledge; Processing Information. *Work Output:* Handling and Moving Objects; Performing General Physical Activities; Interacting With Computers. *Interacting with Others:* Establishing and Maintaining Interpersonal Relationships; Communicating with Other Workers; Coordinating the Work and Activities of Others. Physical Work Conditions—Indoors; Standing; Walking and Running; Using Hands on Objects, Tools, or Controls; Bending or Twisting the Body; Repetitive Motions. Other Job Characteristics—Need to Be Exact or Accurate; Repeat Same Tasks.

Experience—Job Zone 2. Some previous work-related skill, knowledge, or experience may be helpful in these occupations, but usually is not needed. Job Preparation—SVP 4.0 to less than 6.0—six months to less than two years. Knowledges—Production and Processing; Sales and Marketing; Mathematics; Education and Training. Instructional Program—Retailing and Retail Operations.

Related SOC Job—43-5081 Stock Clerks and Order Fillers. Related OOH Job—Stock Clerks and Order Fillers. Related DOT Jobs—209.587-034 Marker; 216.567-010 Ticket Marker; 222.387-054 Sorter-Pricer; 229.587-018 Ticketer.

43-5081.03 Stock Clerks—Stockroom, Warehouse, or Storage Yard

- **Education/Training Required: Short-term on-the-job training**
- **Employed: 1,625,430**
- **Annual Earnings: $20,100**
- **Growth: –7.3%**
- **Annual Job Openings: 351,000**

The job openings listed here are shared with 43-5081.00 Stock Clerks and Order Fillers, 43-5081.01 Stock Clerks, Sales Floor, 43-5081.02 Marking Clerks, 43-5081.04 Order Fillers, Wholesale and Retail Sales.

Receive, store, and issue materials, equipment, and other items from stockroom, warehouse, or storage yard. Keep records and compile stock reports.

Receive and count stock items and record data manually or by using computer. Pack and unpack items to be stocked on shelves in stockrooms, warehouses, or storage yards. Verify inventory computations by comparing them to physical counts of stock and investigate discrepancies or adjust errors. Store items in an orderly and accessible manner in warehouses, tool rooms, supply rooms, or other areas. Mark stock items, using identification tags, stamps, electric marking tools, or other labeling equipment. Clean and maintain supplies, tools, equipment, and storage areas to ensure compliance with safety regulations. Determine proper storage methods, identification, and stock location based on turnover, environmental factors, and physical capabilities of facilities. Keep records on the use and damage of stock or stock handling equipment. Examine and inspect stock items for wear or defects, reporting any damage to supervisors. Provide assistance or direction to other stockroom, warehouse, or storage yard workers. Dispose of damaged or defective items or return them to vendors. Drive trucks to pick up incoming stock or to deliver parts to designated locations. Prepare and maintain records and reports of inventories, price lists, shortages, shipments, expenditures, and goods used or issued. Sell materials, equipment, and other items from stock in retail settings. Issue or distribute materials, products, parts, and supplies to customers or co-workers based on information from incoming requisitions. Advise retail customers or internal users on the appropriateness of parts, supplies, or materials requested. Purchase new or additional stock or prepare documents that provide for such purchases. Compile, review, and maintain data from contracts, purchase orders, requisitions, and other documents to assess supply needs. Confer with engineering and purchasing personnel and vendors regarding stock procurement and availability. Determine sequence and release of backorders according to stock availability. Prepare products, supplies, equipment, or other items for use by adjusting, repairing, or assembling them as necessary.

GOE Information—Interest Area: 04. Business and Administration. **Work Group:** 04.07. Records and Materials Processing. **Personality Type**—Conventional. Conventional occupations frequently involve following set procedures and routines. These occupations can include working with data and details more than with ideas. Usually there is a clear line of authority to follow. **Work Values**—Moral Values; Supervision, Technical; Independence; Supervision, Human Relations. **Skills**—None met the criteria. **Abilities**—*Cognitive:* None met the criteria. *Psychomotor:* Multilimb Coordination; Manual Dexterity; Arm-Hand Steadiness. *Physical:* Extent Flexibility; Static Strength; Stamina; Trunk Strength. *Sensory:* Depth Perception; Far Vision. **General Work Activities**—*Information Input:* Getting Information; Identifying Objects, Actions, and Events; Monitoring Processes, Materials, or Surroundings. *Mental Process:* Organizing,

Planning, and Prioritizing; Processing Information. *Work Output:* Handling and Moving Objects; Performing General Physical Activities; Controlling Machines and Processes. *Interacting with Others:* Establishing and Maintaining Interpersonal Relationships; Performing for or Working with the Public; Communicating with Other Workers. **Physical Work Conditions**—Indoors; Standing; Walking and Running; Using Hands on Objects, Tools, or Controls; Bending or Twisting the Body; Repetitive Motions. **Other Job Characteristics**—Need to Be Exact or Accurate; Repeat Same Tasks.

Experience—Job Zone 1. No previous work-related skill, knowledge, or experience is needed. **Job Preparation**—SVP below 4.0—less than six months. **Knowledges**—Food Production; Production and Processing. **Instructional Program**—Retailing and Retail Operations.

Related SOC Job—43-5081 Stock Clerks and Order Fillers. **Related OOH Job**—Stock Clerks and Order Fillers. **Related DOT Jobs**—219.367-018 Merchandise Distributor; 219.387-026 Space-and-Storage Clerk; 219.387-030 Stock Control Clerk; 221.587-018 Odd-Piece Checker; 221.587-022 Outsole Scheduler; 222.367-014 Cut-File Clerk; 222.367-038 Magazine Keeper; 222.367-042 Parts Clerk; 222.367-050 Prescription Clerk, Lens-and-Frames; 222.367-062 Tool-Crib Attendant; 222.387-018 Fuel-Oil Clerk; 222.387-026 Inventory Clerk; 222.387-030 Linen-Room Attendant; 222.387-034 Material Clerk; 222.387-042 Property Custodian; others.

43-5081.04 Order Fillers, Wholesale and Retail Sales

- **Education/Training Required: Short-term on-the-job training**
- **Employed: 1,625,430**
- **Annual Earnings: $20,100**
- **Growth: –7.3%**
- **Annual Job Openings: 351,000**

The job openings listed here are shared with 43-5081.00 Stock Clerks and Order Fillers, 43-5081.01 Stock Clerks, Sales Floor, 43-5081.02 Marking Clerks, and 43-5081.03 Stock Clerks—Stockroom, Warehouse, or Storage Yard.

Fill customers' mail and telephone orders from stored merchandise in accordance with specifications on sales slips or order forms. Duties include computing prices of items; completing order receipts; keeping records of outgoing orders; and requisitioning additional materials, supplies, and equipment.

Read orders to ascertain catalog numbers, sizes, colors, and quantities of merchandise. Obtain merchandise from bins or shelves. Compute prices of items or groups of items. Complete order receipts. Keep records of outgoing orders. Place merchandise on conveyors leading to wrapping areas. Requisition additional materials, supplies, and equipment.

GOE Information—Interest Area: 04. Business and Administration. **Work Group:** 04.07. Records and Materials Processing. **Personality Type**—Conventional. Conventional occupations frequently involve following set procedures and routines. These occupations can include working with data and details more than with ideas. Usually there is a clear line of authority to follow. **Work Values**—Moral Values. **Skills**—None met the criteria. **Abilities**—*Cognitive:* None met the criteria. *Psychomotor:* Manual Dexterity. *Physical:* Extent Flexibility; Trunk Strength. *Sensory:* None met the criteria. **General Work Activities**—*Information Input:* Identifying Objects, Actions, and Events; Getting Information. *Mental Process:* Processing Information; Evaluating Information Against Standards; Updating and Using Relevant Knowledge. *Work Output:* Handling and Moving

Objects; Interacting With Computers. *Interacting with Others:* Communicating with Persons Outside Organization; Establishing and Maintaining Interpersonal Relationships; Influencing Others or Selling. **Physical Work Conditions**—Indoors; Noisy; Contaminants; Standing; Using Hands on Objects, Tools, or Controls; Repetitive Motions. **Other Job Characteristics**—Need to Be Exact or Accurate; Repeat Same Tasks.

Experience—Job Zone 2. Some previous work-related skill, knowledge, or experience may be helpful in these occupations, but usually is not needed. **Job Preparation**—SVP 4.0 to less than 6.0—six months to less than two years. **Knowledges**—Sales and Marketing; Production and Processing. **Instructional Program**—Retailing and Retail Operations.

Related SOC Job—43-5081 Stock Clerks and Order Fillers. **Related OOH Job**—Stock Clerks and Order Fillers. **Related DOT Jobs**—222.487-014 Order Filler; 299.387-014 Stamp Analyst.

43-5111.00 Weighers, Measurers, Checkers, and Samplers, Recordkeeping

- **Education/Training Required: Short-term on-the-job training**
- **Employed: 79,050**
- **Annual Earnings: $25,310**
- **Growth: –11.3%**
- **Annual Job Openings: 7,000**

Weigh, measure, and check materials, supplies, and equipment for the purpose of keeping relevant records. Duties are primarily clerical by nature.

Collect or prepare measurement, weight, or identification labels and attach them to products. Document quantity, quality, type, weight, test result data, and value of materials or products to maintain shipping, receiving, and production records and files. Compare product labels, tags, or tickets; shipping manifests; purchase orders; and bills of lading to verify accuracy of shipment contents, quality specifications, or weights. Count or estimate quantities of materials, parts, or products received or shipped. Weigh or measure materials, equipment, or products to maintain relevant records, using volume meters, scales, rules, or calipers. Communicate with customers and vendors to exchange information regarding products, materials, and services. Compute product totals and charges for shipments. Collect product samples and prepare them for laboratory analysis or testing. Unload or unpack incoming shipments. Operate scalehouse computers to obtain weight information about incoming shipments such as those from waste haulers. Fill orders for products and samples, following order tickets, and forward or mail items. Sort products or materials into predetermined sequences or groupings for display, packing, shipping, or storage. Maintain financial records, such as accounts of daily collections and billings and records of receipts issued. Signal or instruct other workers to weigh, move, or check products. Store samples of finished products in labeled cartons and record their location. Remove from stock products or loads not meeting quality standards and notify supervisors or appropriate departments of discrepancies or shortages. Maintain, monitor, and clean work areas, such as recycling collection sites, drop boxes, counters and windows, and areas around scale houses. Inspect incoming loads of waste to identify contents and to screen for the presence of specific regulated or hazardous wastes. Examine products or materials, parts, subassemblies, and packaging for damage, defects, or shortages, using specification sheets, gauges, and standards charts. Transport materials, products, or samples to processing, shipping, or storage areas manually or by using conveyors, pumps, or hand trucks.

GOE Information—Interest Area: 04. Business and Administration. **Work Group:** 04.07. Records and Materials Processing. **Personality Type**—Conventional. Conventional occupations frequently involve following set procedures and routines. These occupations can include working with data and details more than with ideas. Usually there is a clear line of authority to follow. **Work Values**—Supervision, Technical; Moral Values; Supervision, Human Relations; Independence. **Skills**—Reading Comprehension; Management of Financial Resources; Writing; Negotiation; Science; Social Perceptiveness. **Abilities**—*Cognitive:* Selective Attention; Flexibility of Closure; Mathematical Reasoning; Perceptual Speed; Number Facility; Category Flexibility. *Psychomotor:* Finger Dexterity; Arm-Hand Steadiness. *Physical:* Stamina. *Sensory:* Auditory Attention; Far Vision; Speech Recognition; Visual Color Discrimination. **General Work Activities**—*Information Input:* Identifying Objects, Actions, and Events; Monitoring Processes, Materials, or Surroundings; Getting Information. *Mental Process:* Processing Information; Analyzing Data or Information; Updating and Using Relevant Knowledge. *Work Output:* Interacting With Computers; Documenting or Recording Information; Performing General Physical Activities. *Interacting with Others:* Establishing and Maintaining Interpersonal Relationships; Communicating with Other Workers; Coordinating the Work and Activities of Others. **Physical Work Conditions**—Indoors; Noisy; Contaminants; Hazardous Equipment; Sitting; Using Hands on Objects, Tools, or Controls. **Other Job Characteristics**—Repeat Same Tasks; Need to Be Exact or Accurate; Errors Have Important Consequences.

Experience—Job Zone 2. Some previous work-related skill, knowledge, or experience may be helpful in these occupations, but usually is not needed. **Job Preparation**—SVP 4.0 to less than 6.0—six months to less than two years. **Knowledges**—Clerical Practices; Production and Processing; Customer and Personal Service. **Instructional Program**—General Office Occupations and Clerical Services.

Related SOC Job—43-5111 Weighers, Measurers, Checkers, and Samplers, Recordkeeping. **Related OOH Job**—Weighers, Measurers, Checkers, and Samplers, Recordkeeping. **Related DOT Jobs**—206.587-010 Brand Recorder; 209.587-046 Sample Clerk, Paper; 216.462-010 Booking Prizer; 219.367-010 Checker, Dump Grounds; 221.467-010 Gin Clerk; 221.482-018 Ticket Worker; 221.487-010 Lumber Scaler; 221.587-010 Checker; 221.587-026 Recorder; 221.587-030 Tallier; 221.587-034 Tare Weigher; 221.587-046 Wheel-Press Clerk; 221.687-014 Ticket Puller; 222.367-010 Cargo Checker; 222.387-010 Aircraft-Shipping Checker; 222.387-066 Sample Clerk; 222.387-074 Shipping-and-Receiving Weigher; others.

43-6000 Secretaries and Administrative Assistants

43-6011.00 Executive Secretaries and Administrative Assistants

- **Education/Training Required: Moderate-term on-the-job training**
- **Employed: 1,442,040**
- **Annual Earnings: $35,960**
- **Growth: 12.4%**
- **Annual Job Openings: 218,000**

Provide high-level administrative support by conducting research; preparing statistical reports; handling information requests; and performing clerical functions such as preparing correspondence, receiving visitors, arranging conference calls, and scheduling meetings. May also train and supervise lower-level clerical staff.

Manage and maintain executives' schedules. Prepare invoices, reports, memos, letters, financial statements, and other documents, using word-processing, spreadsheet, database, or presentation software. Open, sort, and distribute incoming correspondence, including faxes and e-mail. Read and analyze incoming memos, submissions, and reports to determine their significance and plan their distribution. File and retrieve corporate documents, records, and reports. Greet visitors and determine whether they should be given access to specific individuals. Prepare responses to correspondence containing routine inquiries. Perform general office duties such as ordering supplies, maintaining records management systems, and performing basic bookkeeping work. Prepare agendas and make arrangements for committee, board, and other meetings. Make travel arrangements for executives. Conduct research, compile data, and prepare papers for consideration and presentation by executives, committees, and boards of directors. Compile, transcribe, and distribute minutes of meetings. Attend meetings to record minutes. Coordinate and direct office services, such as records and budget preparation, personnel, and housekeeping, to aid executives. Meet with individuals, special-interest groups, and others on behalf of executives, committees, and boards of directors. Set up and oversee administrative policies and procedures for offices or organizations. Supervise and train other clerical staff. Review operating practices and procedures to determine whether improvements can be made in areas such as workflow, reporting procedures, or expenditures. Interpret administrative and operating policies and procedures for employees.

GOE Information—Interest Area: 04. Business and Administration. **Work Group:** 04.04. Secretarial Support. **Personality Type—**Conventional. Conventional occupations frequently involve following set procedures and routines. These occupations can include working with data and details more than with ideas. Usually there is a clear line of authority to follow. **Work Values—**Social Service; Working Conditions; Company Policies and Practices; Supervision, Human Relations; Advancement; Supervision, Technical. **Skills—**Writing; Active Listening; Management of Financial Resources; Speaking; Time Management. **Abilities—***Cognitive:* Written Expression; Time Sharing; Speed of Closure; Oral Comprehension; Information Ordering; Category Flexibility. *Psychomotor:* None met the criteria. *Physical:* None met the criteria. *Sensory:* Speech Recognition; Near Vision; Speech Clarity. **General Work Activities—***Information Input:* Getting Information; Identifying Objects, Actions, and Events; Monitoring Processes, Materials, or Surroundings. *Mental Process:* Organizing, Planning, and Prioritizing; Updating and Using Relevant Knowledge; Scheduling Work and Activities. *Work Output:* Interacting With Computers; Documenting or Recording Information. *Interacting with Others:* Establishing and Maintaining Interpersonal Relationships; Communicating with Other Workers; Performing Administrative Activities. **Physical Work Conditions—**Indoors; Sitting; Repetitive Motions. **Other Job Characteristics—**Need to Be Exact or Accurate; Repeat Same Tasks.

Experience—Job Zone 3. Previous work-related skill, knowledge, or experience is required. **Job Preparation—**SVP 6.0 to less than 7.0—more than one year and less than four years. **Knowledges—**Clerical Practices; Customer and Personal Service; English Language; Computers and Electronics; Communications and Media; Personnel and Human Resources. **Instructional Programs—**Administrative Assistant and Secretarial Science, General; Executive

Assistant/Executive Secretary; Medical Administrative/Executive Assistant and Medical Secretary.

Related SOC Job—43-6011 Executive Secretaries and Administrative Assistants. **Related OOH Job—**Secretaries and Administrative Assistants. **Related DOT Jobs—**169.167-010 Administrative Assistant; 169.167-014 Administrative Secretary.

43-6012.00 Legal Secretaries

- **Education/Training Required: Postsecondary vocational training**
- **Employed: 265,000**
- **Annual Earnings: $37,750**
- **Growth: 17.4%**
- **Annual Job Openings: 41,000**

Perform secretarial duties, utilizing legal terminology, procedures, and documents. Prepare legal papers and correspondence, such as summonses, complaints, motions, and subpoenas. May also assist with legal research.

Prepare and process legal documents and papers, such as summonses, subpoenas, complaints, appeals, motions, and pretrial agreements. Mail, fax, or arrange for delivery of legal correspondence to clients, witnesses, and court officials. Receive and place telephone calls. Schedule and make appointments. Make photocopies of correspondence, documents, and other printed matter. Organize and maintain law libraries, documents, and case files. Assist attorneys in collecting information such as employment, medical, and other records. Attend legal meetings, such as client interviews, hearings, or depositions, and take notes. Draft and type office memos. Review legal publications and perform database searches to identify laws and court decisions relevant to pending cases. Submit articles and information from searches to attorneys for review and approval for use. Complete various forms such as accident reports, trial and courtroom requests, and applications for clients.

GOE Information—Interest Area: 04. Business and Administration. **Work Group:** 04.04. Secretarial Support. **Personality Type—**Conventional. Conventional occupations frequently involve following set procedures and routines. These occupations can include working with data and details more than with ideas. Usually there is a clear line of authority to follow. **Work Values—**Working Conditions; Activity; Company Policies and Practices; Supervision, Technical; Compensation; Security. **Skills—**Writing; Time Management; Reading Comprehension; Social Perceptiveness; Judgment and Decision Making; Active Listening. **Abilities—***Cognitive:* Written Expression; Written Comprehension; Oral Comprehension; Time Sharing; Oral Expression; Speed of Closure. *Psychomotor:* None met the criteria. *Physical:* None met the criteria. *Sensory:* Near Vision; Speech Recognition. **General Work Activities—***Information Input:* Getting Information; Monitoring Processes, Materials, or Surroundings. *Mental Process:* Organizing, Planning, and Prioritizing; Updating and Using Relevant Knowledge; Scheduling Work and Activities. *Work Output:* Interacting With Computers; Documenting or Recording Information. *Interacting with Others:* Performing Administrative Activities; Establishing and Maintaining Interpersonal Relationships; Communicating with Persons Outside Organization. **Physical Work Conditions—**Indoors; Sitting; Repetitive Motions. **Other Job Characteristics—**Need to Be Exact or Accurate; Repeat Same Tasks; Errors Have Important Consequences.

Experience—Job Zone 3. Previous work-related skill, knowledge, or experience is required. **Job Preparation—**SVP 6.0 to less than 7.0—

more than one year and less than four years. **Knowledges**—Clerical Practices; Law and Government; Economics and Accounting; Customer and Personal Service; Computers and Electronics; English Language. **Instructional Program**—Legal Administrative Assistant/Secretary.

Related SOC Job—43-6012 Legal Secretaries. **Related OOH Job**—Secretaries and Administrative Assistants. **Related DOT Job**—201.362-010 Legal Secretary.

43-6013.00 Medical Secretaries

- **Education/Training Required: Postsecondary vocational training**
- **Employed: 381,020**
- **Annual Earnings: $27,320**
- **Growth: 17.0%**
- **Annual Job Openings: 55,000**

Perform secretarial duties, utilizing specific knowledge of medical terminology and hospital, clinic, or laboratory procedures. Duties include scheduling appointments; billing patients; and compiling and recording medical charts, reports, and correspondence.

Schedule and confirm patient diagnostic appointments, surgeries, and medical consultations. Compile and record medical charts, reports, and correspondence, using typewriter or personal computer. Answer telephones and direct calls to appropriate staff. Receive and route messages and documents such as laboratory results to appropriate staff. Greet visitors, ascertain purpose of visit, and direct them to appropriate staff. Interview patients to complete documents, case histories, and forms such as intake and insurance forms. Maintain medical records, technical library, and correspondence files. Operate office equipment such as voice mail messaging systems and use word-processing, spreadsheet, and other software applications to prepare reports, invoices, financial statements, letters, case histories, and medical records. Transmit correspondence and medical records by mail, e-mail, or fax. Perform various clerical and administrative functions, such as ordering and maintaining an inventory of supplies. Arrange hospital admissions for patients. Transcribe recorded messages and practitioners' diagnoses and recommendations into patients' medical records. Perform bookkeeping duties, such as credits and collections, preparing and sending financial statements and bills, and keeping financial records. Complete insurance and other claim forms. Prepare correspondence and assist physicians or medical scientists with preparation of reports, speeches, articles, and conference proceedings.

GOE Information—Interest Area: 04. Business and Administration. **Work Group:** 04.04. Secretarial Support. **Personality Type**—Conventional. Conventional occupations frequently involve following set procedures and routines. These occupations can include working with data and details more than with ideas. Usually there is a clear line of authority to follow. **Work Values**—Working Conditions; Activity; Company Policies and Practices; Supervision, Technical; Security; Supervision, Human Relations. **Skills**—Social Perceptiveness; Writing; Management of Material Resources; Active Listening; Reading Comprehension; Speaking. **Abilities**—*Cognitive:* Category Flexibility; Information Ordering; Number Facility; Time Sharing; Written Comprehension. *Psychomotor:* None met the criteria. *Physical:* None met the criteria. *Sensory:* Near Vision; Speech Recognition; Auditory Attention. **General Work Activities**—*Information Input:* Getting Information; Monitoring Processes, Materials, or Surroundings; Identifying Objects, Actions, and Events. *Mental Process:* Organizing, Planning, and Prioritizing; Processing

Information; Updating and Using Relevant Knowledge. *Work Output:* Documenting or Recording Information; Interacting With Computers; Handling and Moving Objects. *Interacting with Others:* Establishing and Maintaining Interpersonal Relationships; Assisting and Caring for Others; Communicating with Other Workers. **Physical Work Conditions**—Noisy; Disease or Infections; Sitting; Using Hands on Objects, Tools, or Controls. **Other Job Characteristics**—Need to Be Exact or Accurate; Errors Have Important Consequences; Repeat Same Tasks.

Experience—Job Zone 2. Some previous work-related skill, knowledge, or experience may be helpful in these occupations, but usually is not needed. **Job Preparation**—SVP 4.0 to less than 6.0—six months to less than two years. **Knowledges**—Telecommunications; Clerical Practices; Customer and Personal Service; Communications and Media; Computers and Electronics; English Language. **Instructional Programs**—Medical Administrative/Executive Assistant and Medical Secretary; Medical Insurance Specialist/Medical Biller; Medical Office Assistant/Specialist.

Related SOC Job—43-6013 Medical Secretaries. **Related OOH Job**—Secretaries and Administrative Assistants. **Related DOT Job**—201.362-014 Medical Secretary.

43-6014.00 Secretaries, Except Legal, Medical, and Executive

- **Education/Training Required: Moderate-term on-the-job training**
- **Employed: 1,744,380**
- **Annual Earnings: $26,670**
- **Growth: −2.5%**
- **Annual Job Openings: 231,000**

Perform routine clerical and administrative functions such as drafting correspondence, scheduling appointments, organizing and maintaining paper and electronic files, or providing information to callers.

Operate office equipment such as fax machines, copiers, and phone systems and use computers for spreadsheet, word-processing, database management, and other applications. Answer telephones and give information to callers, take messages, or transfer calls to appropriate individuals. Greet visitors and callers, handle their inquiries, and direct them to the appropriate persons according to their needs. Set up and maintain paper and electronic filing systems for records, correspondence, and other material. Locate and attach appropriate files to incoming correspondence requiring replies. Open, read, route, and distribute incoming mail and other material and prepare answers to routine letters. Complete forms in accordance with company procedures. Make copies of correspondence and other printed material. Review work done by others to check for correct spelling and grammar, ensure that company format policies are followed, and recommend revisions. Compose, type, and distribute meeting notes, routine correspondence, and reports. Learn to operate new office technologies as they are developed and implemented. Maintain scheduling and event calendars. Schedule and confirm appointments for clients, customers, or supervisors. Manage projects and contribute to committee and team work. Mail newsletters, promotional material, and other information. Order and dispense supplies. Conduct searches to find needed information, using such sources as the Internet. Provide services to customers, such as order placement and account information. Collect and disburse funds from cash accounts and keep records of collections and disbursements. Prepare and mail checks. Establish work procedures and schedules and keep track of the daily work of clerical staff. Coordinate conferences and meetings. Take dictation in shorthand or by machine and transcribe information. Arrange conferences, meetings, and travel reservations for office personnel. Operate electronic mail systems and coordinate the flow of information both internally and with other organizations. Supervise other clerical staff and provide training and orientation to new staff.

GOE Information—Interest Area: 04. Business and Administration. **Work Group:** 04.04. Secretarial Support. **Personality Type—** Conventional. Conventional occupations frequently involve following set procedures and routines. These occupations can include working with data and details more than with ideas. Usually there is a clear line of authority to follow. **Work Values—**Working Conditions; Activity; Company Policies and Practices; Supervision, Technical; Moral Values; Supervision, Human Relations. **Skills—** Writing; Active Listening; Social Perceptiveness. **Abilities—***Cognitive:* Written Expression; Time Sharing; Information Ordering; Category Flexibility; Oral Expression. *Psychomotor:* None met the criteria. *Physical:* None met the criteria. *Sensory:* Speech Recognition; Near Vision. **General Work Activities—***Information Input:* Getting Information; Identifying Objects, Actions, and Events; Monitoring Processes, Materials, or Surroundings. *Mental Process:* Organizing, Planning, and Prioritizing; Updating and Using Relevant Knowledge; Processing Information. *Work Output:* Interacting With Computers; Documenting or Recording Information; Handling and Moving Objects. *Interacting with Others:* Establishing and Maintaining Interpersonal Relationships; Communicating with Other Workers; Communicating with Persons Outside Organization. **Physical Work Conditions—**Indoors; Sitting; Repetitive Motions. **Other Job Characteristics—**Need to Be Exact or Accurate; Repeat Same Tasks.

Experience—Job Zone 2. Some previous work-related skill, knowledge, or experience may be helpful in these occupations, but usually is not needed. **Job Preparation—**SVP 4.0 to less than 6.0—six months to less than two years. **Knowledges—**Clerical Practices; Customer and Personal Service; Computers and Electronics; Economics and Accounting; English Language; Personnel and Human Resources. **Instructional Programs—**Administrative Assistant and Secretarial Science, General; Executive Assistant/Executive Secretary.

Related SOC Job—43-6014 Secretaries, Except Legal, Medical, and Executive. **Related OOH Job—**Secretaries and Administrative Assistants. **Related DOT Jobs—**201.162-010 Social Secretary; 201.362-018 Membership Secretary; 201.362-022 School Secretary; 201.362-026 Script Supervisor; 201.362-030 Secretary; 219.362-074 Trust Operations Assistant.

43-9000 Other Office and Administrative Support Workers

43-9011.00 Computer Operators

- **Education/Training Required: Moderate-term on-the-job training**
- **Employed: 129,160**
- **Annual Earnings: $32,070**
- **Growth: –32.6%**
- **Annual Job Openings: 13,000**

Monitor and control electronic computer and peripheral electronic data processing equipment to process business, scientific, engineering, and other data according to operating instructions. May enter commands at a computer terminal and set controls on computer and peripheral devices. Monitor and respond to operating and error messages.

Enter commands, using computer terminal, and activate controls on computer and peripheral equipment to integrate and operate equipment. Monitor the system for equipment failure or errors in performance. Notify supervisor or computer maintenance technicians of equipment malfunctions. Respond to program error messages by finding and correcting problems or terminating the program. Read job setup instructions to determine equipment to be used, order of use, material such as disks and paper to be loaded, and control settings. Operate spreadsheet programs and other types of software to load and manipulate data and to produce reports. Retrieve, separate, and sort program output as needed and send data to specified users. Load peripheral equipment with selected materials for operating runs or oversee loading of peripheral equipment by peripheral equipment operators. Answer telephone calls to assist computer users encountering problems. Record information such as computer operating time, problems that occurred, and actions taken. Oversee the operation of computer hardware systems, including coordinating and scheduling the use of computer terminals and networks to ensure efficient use. Clear equipment at end of operating run and review schedule to determine next assignment. Type command on keyboard to transfer encoded data from memory unit to magnetic tape and assist in labeling, classifying, cataloging, and maintaining tapes. Supervise and train peripheral equipment operators and computer operator trainees. Help programmers and systems analysts test and debug new programs.

GOE Information—Interest Area: 11. Information Technology. **Work Group:** 11.02. Information Technology Specialties. **Personality Type—**Conventional. Conventional occupations frequently involve following set procedures and routines. These occupations can include working with data and details more than with ideas. Usually there is a clear line of authority to follow. **Work Values—**Working Conditions; Supervision, Human Relations; Independence; Recognition; Company Policies and Practices; Supervision, Technical. **Skills—**Troubleshooting; Systems Evaluation; Service Orientation; Critical Thinking; Instructing; Management of Financial Resources. **Abilities—***Cognitive:* Oral Expression; Written Comprehension; Oral Comprehension; Information Ordering; Flexibility of Closure; Deductive Reasoning. *Psychomotor:* None met the criteria. *Physical:* None met the criteria. *Sensory:* Near Vision. **General Work Activities—***Information Input:* Getting Information; Identifying Objects, Actions, and Events; Monitoring Processes, Materials, or Surroundings. *Mental Process:* Updating and Using Relevant Knowledge; Organizing, Planning, and Prioritizing; Processing Information. *Work Output:* Documenting or Recording Information; Interacting With Computers. *Interacting with Others:* Communicating with Other Workers; Establishing and Maintaining Interpersonal Relationships; Providing Consultation and Advice to Others. **Physical Work Conditions—**Indoors; Sitting; Using Hands on Objects, Tools, or Controls; Repetitive Motions. **Other Job Characteristics—**Need to Be Exact or Accurate; Repeat Same Tasks; Errors Have Important Consequences; Automation.

Experience—Job Zone 3. Previous work-related skill, knowledge, or experience is required. **Job Preparation—**SVP 6.0 to less than 7.0— more than one year and less than four years. **Knowledges—** Computers and Electronics; Sales and Marketing; Clerical Practices; Telecommunications; Administration and Management; Customer and Personal Service. **Instructional Program—**Data Processing and Data Processing Technology/Technician.

Related SOC Job—43-9011 Computer Operators. **Related OOH Job**—Computer Operators. **Related DOT Jobs**—213.362-010 Computer Operator; 213.382-010 Computer Peripheral Equipment Operator; 213.582-010 Digitizer Operator.

43-9021.00 Data Entry Keyers

- **Education/Training Required: Moderate-term on-the-job training**
- **Employed: 296,700**
- **Annual Earnings: $23,810**
- **Growth: –0.7%**
- **Annual Job Openings: 85,000**

Operate data entry device, such as keyboard or photo-composing perforator. Duties may include verifying data and preparing materials for printing.

Read source documents such as canceled checks, sales reports, or bills and enter data in specific data fields or onto tapes or disks for subsequent entry, using keyboards or scanners. Compile, sort, and verify the accuracy of data before it is entered. Compare data with source documents or re-enter data in verification format to detect errors. Store completed documents in appropriate locations. Locate and correct data entry errors or report them to supervisors. Maintain logs of activities and completed work. Select materials needed to complete work assignments. Load machines with required input or output media such as paper, cards, disks, tape, or Braille media. Resolve garbled or indecipherable messages, using cryptographic procedures and equipment.

GOE Information—Interest Area: 04. Business and Administration. **Work Group:** 04.08. Clerical Machine Operation. **Personality Type**—Conventional. Conventional occupations frequently involve following set procedures and routines. These occupations can include working with data and details more than with ideas. Usually there is a clear line of authority to follow. **Work Values**—Independence; Moral Values; Activity; Supervision, Human Relations; Supervision, Technical. **Skills**—Service Orientation; Social Perceptiveness. **Abilities**—*Cognitive:* Flexibility of Closure; Speed of Closure; Perceptual Speed; Memorization; Number Facility; Selective Attention. *Psychomotor:* Wrist-Finger Speed; Finger Dexterity. *Physical:* None met the criteria. *Sensory:* Near Vision; Speech Recognition; Auditory Attention; Far Vision. **General Work Activities**—*Information Input:* Getting Information; Identifying Objects, Actions, and Events; Monitoring Processes, Materials, or Surroundings. *Mental Process:* Processing Information; Updating and Using Relevant Knowledge; Organizing, Planning, and Prioritizing. *Work Output:* Documenting or Recording Information; Interacting With Computers; Handling and Moving Objects. *Interacting with Others:* Establishing and Maintaining Interpersonal Relationships; Communicating with Other Workers; Coaching and Developing Others. **Physical Work Conditions**—Indoors; Noisy; Sitting; Using Hands on Objects, Tools, or Controls; Repetitive Motions. **Other Job Characteristics**—Need to Be Exact or Accurate; Repeat Same Tasks; Automation.

Experience—Job Zone 2. Some previous work-related skill, knowledge, or experience may be helpful in these occupations, but usually is not needed. **Job Preparation**—SVP 4.0 to less than 6.0—six months to less than two years. **Knowledges**—Clerical Practices; Economics and Accounting; Computers and Electronics; Customer and Personal Service; Personnel and Human Resources; Administration and Management. **Instructional Programs**—Business/Office Automation/Technology/Data Entry; Data Entry/Microcomputer

Applications; Graphic and Printing Equipment Operator, General Production.

Related SOC Job—43-9021 Data Entry Keyers. **Related OOH Job**—Data Entry and Information Processing Workers. **Related DOT Jobs**—203.382-018 Magnetic-Tape-Composer Operator; 203.382-026 Varitype Operator; 203.582-010 Braille Operator; 203.582-014 Braille Typist; 203.582-018 Cryptographic-Machine Operator; 203.582-038 Perforator Typist; 203.582-042 Photocomposing-Perforator-Machine Operator; 203.582-046 Photocomposition-Keyboard Operator; 203.582-054 Data Entry Clerk; 203.582-062 Typesetter-Perforator Operator.

43-9022.00 Word Processors and Typists

- **Education/Training Required: Moderate-term on-the-job training**
- **Employed: 153,580**
- **Annual Earnings: $29,020**
- **Growth: –15.3%**
- **Annual Job Openings: 30,000**

Use word processor/computer or typewriter to type letters, reports, forms, or other material from rough draft, corrected copy, or voice recording. May perform other clerical duties as assigned.

Check completed work for spelling, grammar, punctuation, and format. Perform other clerical duties such as answering telephone, sorting and distributing mail, running errands, or sending faxes. Gather, register, and arrange the material to be typed, following instructions. File and store completed documents on computer hard drive or disk and maintain a computer filing system to store, retrieve, update, and delete documents. Type correspondence, reports, text, and other written material from rough drafts, corrected copies, voice recordings, dictation, or previous versions, using a computer, word processor, or typewriter. Print and make copies of work. Keep records of work performed. Compute and verify totals on report forms, requisitions, or bills, using adding machine or calculator. Collate pages of reports and other documents prepared. Electronically sort and compile text and numerical data, retrieving, updating, and merging documents as required. Reformat documents, moving paragraphs or columns. Search for specific sets of stored, typed characters in order to make changes. Adjust settings for format, page layout, line spacing, and other style requirements. Address envelopes or prepare envelope labels, using typewriter or computer. Operate and resupply printers and computers, changing print wheels or fluid cartridges; adding paper; and loading blank tapes, cards, or disks into equipment. Transmit work electronically to other locations. Work with technical material, preparing statistical reports, planning and typing statistical tables, and combining and rearranging material from different sources. Use data entry devices, such as optical scanners, to input data into computers for revision or editing. Transcribe stenotyped notes of court proceedings.

GOE Information—Interest Area: 04. Business and Administration. **Work Group:** 04.08. Clerical Machine Operation. **Personality Type**—Conventional. Conventional occupations frequently involve following set procedures and routines. These occupations can include working with data and details more than with ideas. Usually there is a clear line of authority to follow. **Work Values**—Working Conditions; Independence; Company Policies and Practices; Moral Values; Supervision, Human Relations; Activity. **Skills**—Installation; Social Perceptiveness; Equipment Selection; Writing; Learning Strategies; Speaking. **Abilities**—*Cognitive:* Perceptual Speed. *Psychomotor:* Wrist-Finger Speed. *Physical:* None met the criteria.

Sensory: Near Vision. **General Work Activities—***Information Input:* Getting Information; Identifying Objects, Actions, and Events; Monitoring Processes, Materials, or Surroundings. *Mental Process:* Organizing, Planning, and Prioritizing; Thinking Creatively; Updating and Using Relevant Knowledge. *Work Output:* Interacting With Computers; Documenting or Recording Information. *Interacting with Others:* Establishing and Maintaining Interpersonal Relationships; Performing Administrative Activities; Communicating with Other Workers. **Physical Work Conditions—**Indoors; Sitting. **Other Job Characteristics—**Need to Be Exact or Accurate; Repeat Same Tasks.

Experience—Job Zone 2. Some previous work-related skill, knowledge, or experience may be helpful in these occupations, but usually is not needed. **Job Preparation—**SVP 4.0 to less than 6.0—six months to less than two years. **Knowledges—**Clerical Practices; Computers and Electronics; Customer and Personal Service; English Language. **Instructional Programs—**General Office Occupations and Clerical Services; Word Processing.

Related SOC Job—43-9022 Word Processors and Typists. **Related OOH Job—**Data Entry and Information Processing Workers. **Related DOT Jobs—**203.362-010 Clerk-Typist; 203.382-030 Word Processing Machine Operator; 203.582-050 Telegraphic-Typewriter Operator; 203.582-058 Transcribing-Machine Operator; 203.582-066 Typist; 203.582-078 Notereader; 209.382-010 Continuity Clerk; 209.587-010 Addresser.

43-9031.00 Desktop Publishers

- **Education/Training Required: Postsecondary vocational training**
- **Employed: 29,910**
- **Annual Earnings: $32,800**
- **Growth: 23.2%**
- **Annual Job Openings: 8,000**

Format typescript and graphic elements, using computer software to produce publication-ready material.

Check preliminary and final proofs for errors and make necessary corrections. Operate desktop publishing software and equipment to design, lay out, and produce camera-ready copy. View monitors for visual representation of work in progress and for instructions and feedback throughout process, making modifications as necessary. Enter text into computer keyboard and select the size and style of type, column width, and appropriate spacing for printed materials. Store copies of publications on paper, magnetic tape, film, or diskette. Position text and art elements from a variety of databases in a visually appealing way to design print or Web pages, using knowledge of type styles and size and layout patterns. Enter digitized data into electronic prepress system computer memory, using scanner, camera, keyboard, or mouse. Edit graphics and photos, using pixel or bitmap editing, airbrushing, masking, or image retouching. Import text and art elements such as electronic clip art or electronic files from photographs that have been scanned or produced with a digital camera, using computer software. Prepare sample layouts for approval, using computer software. Study layout or other design instructions to determine work to be done and sequence of operations. Load floppy disks or tapes containing information into system. Convert various types of files for printing or for the Internet, using computer software. Enter data, such as coordinates of images and color specifications, into system to retouch and make color corrections. Select number of colors and determine color separations. Transmit, deliver, or mail publication master to printer for produc-

tion into film and plates. Collaborate with graphic artists, editors, and writers to produce master copies according to design specifications. Create special effects such as vignettes, mosaics, and image combining and add elements such as sound and animation to electronic publications.

GOE Information—Interest Area: 13. Manufacturing. **Work Group:** 13.08. Graphic Arts Production. **Personality Type—**Realistic. Realistic occupations frequently involve work activities that include practical, hands-on problems and solutions. They often deal with plants; animals; and real-world materials like wood, tools, and machinery. Many of the occupations require working outside and do not involve a lot of paperwork or working closely with others. **Work Values—**Working Conditions; Independence; Supervision, Human Relations; Supervision, Technical; Variety; Moral Values. **Skills—**Operation and Control; Operations Analysis; Time Management; Service Orientation; Active Listening; Writing. **Abilities—***Cognitive:* Visualization; Fluency of Ideas; Originality; Flexibility of Closure; Category Flexibility; Written Expression. *Psychomotor:* Finger Dexterity; Arm-Hand Steadiness. *Physical:* None met the criteria. *Sensory:* Visual Color Discrimination; Near Vision; Speech Recognition; Far Vision. **General Work Activities—***Information Input:* Getting Information; Identifying Objects, Actions, and Events; Monitoring Processes, Materials, or Surroundings. *Mental Process:* Organizing, Planning, and Prioritizing; Thinking Creatively; Updating and Using Relevant Knowledge. *Work Output:* Interacting With Computers; Documenting or Recording Information. *Interacting with Others:* Establishing and Maintaining Interpersonal Relationships; Communicating with Other Workers; Communicating with Persons Outside Organization. **Physical Work Conditions—**Indoors; Sitting; Repetitive Motions. **Other Job Characteristics—**Need to Be Exact or Accurate; Repeat Same Tasks.

Experience—Job Zone 3. Previous work-related skill, knowledge, or experience is required. **Job Preparation—**SVP 6.0 to less than 7.0—more than one year and less than four years. **Knowledges—**Computers and Electronics; Production and Processing; English Language. **Instructional Program—**Prepress/Desktop Publishing and Digital Imaging Design.

Related SOC Job—43-9031 Desktop Publishers. **Related OOH Job—**Desktop Publishers. **Related DOT Job—**979.282-010 Electronic Prepress System Operator.

43-9041.00 Insurance Claims and Policy Processing Clerks

- **Education/Training Required: Moderate-term on-the-job training**
- **Employed: 239,120**
- **Annual Earnings: $30,130**
- **Growth: 4.5%**
- **Annual Job Openings: 36,000**

The job openings listed here are shared with 43-9041.01 Insurance Claims Clerks and 43-9041.02 Insurance Policy Processing Clerks.

Process new insurance policies, modifications to existing policies, and claims forms. Obtain information from policyholders to verify the accuracy and completeness of information on claims forms, applications and related documents, and company records. Update existing policies and company records to reflect changes requested by policyholders and insurance company representatives.

No task data available.

GOE Information—**Interest Area:** 06. Finance and Insurance. **Work Group:** 06.03. Finance/Insurance Records Processing. **Note:** The Department of Labor has not collected some data for this job, so it has fewer details than the other descriptions. **Instructional Program**—General Office Occupations and Clerical Services.

Related SOC Job—43-9041 Insurance Claims and Policy Processing Clerks. **Related OOH Job**—Insurance Claims and Policy Processing Clerks. **Related DOT Job**—No data available.

43-9041.01 Insurance Claims Clerks

- **Education/Training Required: Moderate-term on-the-job training**
- **Employed: 239,120**
- **Annual Earnings: $30,130**
- **Growth: 4.5%**
- **Annual Job Openings: 36,000**

The job openings listed here are shared with 43-9041.00 Insurance Claims and Policy Processing Clerks and 43-9041.02 Insurance Policy Processing Clerks.

Obtain information from insured or designated persons for purpose of settling claim with insurance carrier.

Review insurance policy to determine coverage. Prepare and review insurance-claim forms and related documents for completeness. Provide customer service, such as giving limited instructions on how to proceed with claims or providing referrals to auto repair facilities or local contractors. Organize and work with detailed office or warehouse records, using computers to enter, access, search, and retrieve data. Post or attach information to claim file. Pay small claims. Transmit claims for payment or further investigation. Contact insured or other involved persons to obtain missing information. Calculate amount of claim. Apply insurance rating systems.

GOE Information—**Interest Area:** 06. Finance and Insurance. **Work Group:** 06.03. Finance/Insurance Records Processing. **Personality Type**—Conventional. Conventional occupations frequently involve following set procedures and routines. These occupations can include working with data and details more than with ideas. Usually there is a clear line of authority to follow. **Work Values**—Supervision, Human Relations; Working Conditions; Moral Values; Advancement; Independence; Company Policies and Practices. **Skills**—Service Orientation. **Abilities**—*Cognitive:* Number Facility; Written Comprehension; Oral Expression; Written Expression; Mathematical Reasoning. *Psychomotor:* None met the criteria. *Physical:* None met the criteria. *Sensory:* Speech Recognition; Near Vision; Speech Clarity. **General Work Activities**—*Information Input:* Identifying Objects, Actions, and Events; Getting Information. *Mental Process:* Processing Information; Evaluating Information Against Standards; Organizing, Planning, and Prioritizing. *Work Output:* Documenting or Recording Information; Interacting With Computers. *Interacting with Others:* Establishing and Maintaining Interpersonal Relationships; Communicating with Other Workers; Communicating with Persons Outside Organization. **Physical Work Conditions**—Indoors; Sitting; Repetitive Motions. **Other Job Characteristics**—Need to Be Exact or Accurate; Repeat Same Tasks; Errors Have Important Consequences.

Experience—Job Zone 2. Some previous work-related skill, knowledge, or experience may be helpful in these occupations, but usually is not needed. **Job Preparation**—SVP 4.0 to less than 6.0—six months to less than two years. **Knowledges**—Clerical Practices; Customer and Personal Service; Computers and Electronics; Economics and Accounting; Law and Government. **Instructional Program**—General Office Occupations and Clerical Services.

Related SOC Job—43-9041 Insurance Claims and Policy Processing Clerks. **Related OOH Job**—Insurance Claims and Policy Processing Clerks. **Related DOT Jobs**—205.367-018 Claims Clerk II; 241.362-010 Claims Clerk I.

43-9041.02 Insurance Policy Processing Clerks

- **Education/Training Required: Moderate-term on-the-job training**
- **Employed: 239,120**
- **Annual Earnings: $30,130**
- **Growth: 4.5%**
- **Annual Job Openings: 36,000**

The job openings listed here are shared with 43-9041.00 Insurance Claims and Policy Processing Clerks and 43-9041.01 Insurance Claims Clerks.

Process applications for, changes to, reinstatement of, and cancellation of insurance policies. Duties include reviewing insurance applications to ensure that all questions have been answered, compiling data on insurance policy changes, changing policy records to conform to insured party's specifications, compiling data on lapsed insurance policies to determine automatic reinstatement according to company policies, canceling insurance policies as requested by agents, and verifying the accuracy of insurance company records.

Modify, update, and process existing policies and claims to reflect any change in beneficiary, amount of coverage, or type of insurance. Process and record new insurance policies and claims. Review and verify data, such as age, name, address, and principal sum and value of property, on insurance applications and policies. Organize and work with detailed office or warehouse records, maintaining files for each policyholder, including policies that are to be reinstated or cancelled. Examine letters from policyholders or agents, original insurance applications, and other company documents to determine whether changes are needed and effects of changes. Correspond with insured or agent to obtain information or inform them of account status or changes. Transcribe data to worksheets and enter data into computer for use in preparing documents and adjusting accounts. Notify insurance agent and accounting department of policy cancellation. Interview clients and take their calls to provide customer service and obtain information on claims. Compare information from application to criteria for policy reinstatement and approve reinstatement when criteria are met. Process, prepare, and submit business or government forms, such as submitting applications for coverage to insurance carriers. Collect initial premiums and issue receipts. Calculate premiums, refunds, commissions, adjustments, and new reserve requirements, using insurance rate standards. Obtain computer printout of policy cancellations or retrieve cancellation cards from file. Compose business correspondence for supervisors, managers, and professionals. Check computations of interest accrued, premiums due, and settlement surrender on loan values.

GOE Information—**Interest Area:** 06. Finance and Insurance. **Work Group:** 06.03. Finance/Insurance Records Processing. **Personality Type**—Conventional. Conventional occupations frequently involve following set procedures and routines. These occupations can include working with data and details more than with ideas. Usually there is a clear line of authority to follow. **Work Values**—Working Conditions; Supervision, Human Relations; Supervision, Technical; Advancement; Co-workers; Company Policies and Practices. **Skills**—Critical Thinking; Social Perceptiveness; Service Orientation; Learning Strategies; Active Learning; Mathematics. **Abilities**—*Cognitive:* Mathematical Reasoning; Number Facility; Speed of

Closure; Deductive Reasoning; Written Expression; Written Comprehension. *Psychomotor:* None met the criteria. *Physical:* None met the criteria. *Sensory:* Near Vision; Speech Recognition. **General Work Activities**—*Information Input:* Getting Information; Identifying Objects, Actions, and Events; Monitoring Processes, Materials, or Surroundings. *Mental Process:* Organizing, Planning, and Prioritizing; Updating and Using Relevant Knowledge; Making Decisions and Solving Problems. *Work Output:* Interacting With Computers; Documenting or Recording Information. *Interacting with Others:* Communicating with Other Workers; Establishing and Maintaining Interpersonal Relationships; Communicating with Persons Outside Organization. **Physical Work Conditions**—Sitting; Repetitive Motions. **Other Job Characteristics**—Need to Be Exact or Accurate; Repeat Same Tasks; Automation.

Experience—Job Zone 2. Some previous work-related skill, knowledge, or experience may be helpful in these occupations, but usually is not needed. **Job Preparation**—SVP 4.0 to less than 6.0—six months to less than two years. **Knowledges**—Clerical Practices; Customer and Personal Service; Computers and Electronics; Sales and Marketing; Economics and Accounting; Production and Processing. **Instructional Program**—General Office Occupations and Clerical Services.

Related SOC Job—43-9041 Insurance Claims and Policy Processing Clerks. **Related OOH Job**—Insurance Claims and Policy Processing Clerks. **Related DOT Jobs**—203.382-014 Cancellation Clerk; 209.382-014 Special-Certificate Dictator; 209.687-018 Reviewer; 219.362-042 Policy-Change Clerk; 219.362-050 Revival Clerk; 219.482-014 Insurance Checker.

43-9051.00 Mail Clerks and Mail Machine Operators, Except Postal Service

- **Education/Training Required: Short-term on-the-job training**
- **Employed: 148,330**
- **Annual Earnings: $22,870**
- **Growth: –37.1%**
- **Annual Job Openings: 33,000**

Prepare incoming and outgoing mail for distribution. Use hand or mail-handling machines to time-stamp, open, read, sort, and route incoming mail and address, seal, stamp, fold, stuff, and affix postage to outgoing mail or packages. Duties may also include keeping necessary records and completed forms.

Release packages or letters to customers upon presentation of written notices or other identification. Sell mail products and accept payment for products and mailing charges. Place incoming or outgoing letters or packages into sacks or bins based on destination or type and place identifying tags on sacks or bins. Lift and unload containers of mail or parcels onto equipment for transportation to sortation stations. Inspect mail machine output for defects; determine how to eliminate causes of any defects. Use equipment such as forklifts and automated "trains" to move containers of mail. Remove containers of sorted mail/parcels and transfer them to designated areas according to established procedures. Operate computer-controlled keyboards or voice recognition equipment to direct items according to established routing schemes. Wrap packages or bundles by hand or by using tying machines. Accept and check containers of mail or parcels from large-volume mailers, couriers, and contractors. Start machines that automatically feed plates, stencils, or tapes through mechanisms and observe machine operations to detect any malfunctions. Sort and

route incoming mail and collect outgoing mail, using carts as necessary. Insert material for printing or addressing into loading racks on machines; select type or die sizes; and position plates, stencils, or tapes in machine magazines. Affix postage to packages or letters by hand or stamp materials, using postage meters. Adjust guides, rollers, loose card inserters, weighing machines, and tying arms, using rules and hand tools. Contact delivery or courier services to arrange delivery of letters and parcels. Fold letters or circulars and insert them in envelopes. Stamp dates and times of receipt of incoming mail. Operate embossing machines or typewriters to make corrections, additions, and changes to address plates. Remove from machines printed materials such as labeled articles, postmarked envelopes or tape, and folded sheets. Seal or open envelopes by hand or by using machines. Mail merchandise samples or promotional literature in response to requests. Determine manner in which mail is to be sent and prepare it for delivery to mailing facilities. Read production orders to determine types and sizes of items scheduled for printing and mailing. Add ink, fill paste reservoirs, and change machine ribbons when necessary.

GOE Information—**Interest Area:** 04. Business and Administration. **Work Group:** 04.08. Clerical Machine Operation. **Personality Type**—Conventional. Conventional occupations frequently involve following set procedures and routines. These occupations can include working with data and details more than with ideas. Usually there is a clear line of authority to follow. **Work Values**—Supervision, Technical; Independence; Moral Values; Supervision, Human Relations; Activity; Security. **Skills**—None met the criteria. **Abilities**—*Cognitive:* Perceptual Speed. *Psychomotor:* Wrist-Finger Speed; Manual Dexterity; Multilimb Coordination. *Physical:* Extent Flexibility. *Sensory:* None met the criteria. **General Work Activities**—*Information Input:* None met the criteria. *Mental Process:* None met the criteria. *Work Output:* Handling and Moving Objects; Performing General Physical Activities; Controlling Machines and Processes. *Interacting with Others:* None met the criteria. **Physical Work Conditions**—Indoors; More Often Standing Than Sitting; Using Hands on Objects, Tools, or Controls; Repetitive Motions. **Other Job Characteristics**—None met the criteria.

Experience—Job Zone 1. No previous work-related skill, knowledge, or experience is needed. **Job Preparation**—SVP below 4.0—less than six months. **Knowledges**—Geography; Fine Arts. **Instructional Program**—General Office Occupations and Clerical Services.

Related SOC Job—43-9051 Mail Clerks and Mail Machine Operators, Except Postal Service. **Related OOH Job**—Mail Clerks and Mail Machine Operators, Except Postal Service. **Related DOT Jobs**—208.462-010 Mailing-Machine Operator; 208.582-010 Addressing-Machine Operator; 208.685-014 Folding-Machine Operator; 208.685-018 Inserting-Machine Operator; 208.685-026 Sealing-and-Canceling-Machine Operator; 208.685-034 Wing-Mailer-Machine Operator; 209.587-018 Direct-Mail Clerk; 209.687-026 Mail Clerk; 222.367-022 Express Clerk; 222.387-038 Parcel Post Clerk; 222.567-018 Slot-Tag Inserter; 222.587-030 Mailer; 222.587-032 Mailer Apprentice; 249.687-010 Office Copy Selector.

43-9061.00 Office Clerks, General

- **Education/Training Required: Short-term on-the-job training**
- **Employed: 2,997,370**
- **Annual Earnings: $23,070**
- **Growth: 8.4%**
- **Annual Job Openings: 695,000**

Perform duties too varied and diverse to be classified in any specific office clerical occupation requiring limited knowledge of office management systems and procedures. Clerical duties may be assigned in accordance with the office procedures of individual establishments and may include a combination of answering telephones, bookkeeping, typing or word processing, stenography, office machine operation, and filing.

Collect, count, and disburse money; do basic bookkeeping; and complete banking transactions. Communicate with customers, employees, and other individuals to answer questions, disseminate or explain information, take orders, and address complaints. Answer telephones, direct calls, and take messages. Compile, copy, sort, and file records of office activities, business transactions, and other activities. Complete and mail bills, contracts, policies, invoices, or checks. Operate office machines such as photocopiers and scanners, facsimile machines, voice mail systems, and personal computers. Compute, record, and proofread data and other information, such as records or reports. Maintain and update filing, inventory, mailing, and database systems, either manually or using a computer. Open, sort, and route incoming mail; answer correspondence; and prepare outgoing mail. Review files, records, and other documents to obtain information to respond to requests. Deliver messages and run errands. Inventory and order materials, supplies, and services. Complete work schedules, manage calendars, and arrange appointments. Process and prepare documents such as business or government forms and expense reports. Monitor and direct the work of lower-level clerks. Type, format, proofread, and edit correspondence and other documents from notes or dictating machines, using computers or typewriters. Count, weigh, measure, or organize materials. Train other staff members to perform work activities, such as using computer applications. Prepare meeting agendas, attend meetings, and record and transcribe minutes. Troubleshoot problems involving office equipment, such as computer hardware and software. Make travel arrangements for office personnel.

GOE Information—Interest Area: 04. Business and Administration. **Work Group:** 04.07. Records and Materials Processing. **Personality Type**—Conventional. Conventional occupations frequently involve following set procedures and routines. These occupations can include working with data and details more than with ideas. Usually there is a clear line of authority to follow. **Work Values—**Advancement; Supervision, Technical; Co-workers; Working Conditions; Supervision, Human Relations; Activity. **Skills—**None met the criteria. **Abilities—***Cognitive:* Number Facility; Time Sharing; Mathematical Reasoning; Perceptual Speed; Oral Expression; Written Expression. *Psychomotor:* Wrist-Finger Speed; Manual Dexterity. *Physical:* None met the criteria. *Sensory:* Speech Recognition; Near Vision; Far Vision. **General Work Activities—***Information Input:* Getting Information; Identifying Objects, Actions, and Events; Monitoring Processes, Materials, or Surroundings. *Mental Process:* Organizing, Planning, and Prioritizing; Processing Information; Updating and Using Relevant Knowledge. *Work Output:* Interacting With Computers; Documenting or Recording Information. *Interacting with Others:* Establishing and Maintaining Interpersonal Relationships; Communicating with Other Workers; Performing for or Working with the Public. **Physical Work Conditions—**Indoors; Sitting; Using Hands on Objects, Tools, or Controls. **Other Job Characteristics—**Need to Be Exact or Accurate; Repeat Same Tasks.

Experience—Job Zone 2. Some previous work-related skill, knowledge, or experience may be helpful in these occupations, but usually is not needed. **Job Preparation—**SVP 4.0 to less than 6.0—six months to less than two years. **Knowledges—**Clerical Practices; Economics and Accounting; Customer and Personal Service; Personnel and Human Resources; Mathematics; Computers and Electronics.

Instructional Program—General Office Occupations and Clerical Services.

Related SOC Job—43-9061 Office Clerks, General. **Related OOH Job—**Office Clerks, General. **Related DOT Jobs—**162.167-026 Prize Coordinator; 199.267-018 Examination Proctor; 205.367-010 Admissions Evaluator; 205.367-030 Election Clerk; 209.362-010 Circulation Clerk; 209.362-014 Control Clerk, Auditing; 209.362-022 Identification Clerk; 209.362-030 Congressional-District Aide; 209.367-010 Agent-Licensing Clerk; 209.367-026 Fingerprint Clerk I; 209.367-034 Lost-Charge-Card Clerk; 209.367-038 News Assistant; 209.367-050 Trip Follower; 209.367-054 Yard Clerk; 209.382-022 Traffic Clerk; others.

43-9071.00 Office Machine Operators, Except Computer

- **Education/Training Required: Short-term on-the-job training**
- **Employed: 87,900**
- **Annual Earnings: $23,990**
- **Growth: −21.9%**
- **Annual Job Openings: 19,000**

Operate one or more of a variety of office machines, such as photocopying, photographic, and duplicating machines or other office machines.

Operate auxiliary machines such as collators; pad- and tablet-making machines; staplers; and paper-punching, -folding, -cutting, and -perforating machines. Compute prices for services and receive payment or provide supervisors with billing information. Complete records of production, including work volumes and outputs, materials used, and any backlogs. Prepare and process papers for use in scanning, microfilming, and microfiche. Deliver completed work. Set up and adjust machines, regulating factors such as speed, ink flow, focus, and number of copies. Move heat units and clamping frames over screen beds to form Braille impressions on pages; then raise frames to release individual copies. Sort, assemble, and proof completed work. Clean and file master copies or plates. Cut copies apart and write identifying information, such as page numbers or titles, on copies. Monitor machine operation and make adjustments as necessary to ensure proper operation. File and store completed documents. Load machines with materials such as blank paper or film. Maintain stock of supplies and requisition any needed items. Operate office machines such as high-speed business photocopiers; reader/scanners; addressing machines; stencil-cutting machines; microfilm reader/printers; and folding and inserting, bursting, and binder machines. Read job orders to determine the type of work to be done, the quantities to be produced, and the materials needed. Place original copies in feed trays, feed originals into feed rolls, or position originals on tables beneath camera lenses. Clean machines, perform minor repairs, and report major repair needs.

GOE Information—Interest Area: 04. Business and Administration. **Work Group:** 04.08. Clerical Machine Operation. **Personality Type**—Conventional. Conventional occupations frequently involve following set procedures and routines. These occupations can include working with data and details more than with ideas. Usually there is a clear line of authority to follow. **Work Values—**Independence; Supervision, Technical; Moral Values; Supervision, Human Relations. **Skills—**Repairing. **Abilities—***Cognitive:* None met the criteria. *Psychomotor:* Wrist-Finger Speed; Control Precision. *Physical:* None met the criteria. *Sensory:* Visual Color Discrimination. **General Work Activities—***Information Input:* None met the criteria. *Mental Process:* None met the criteria. *Work Output:* Handling and

Moving Objects; Performing General Physical Activities; Controlling Machines and Processes. *Interacting with Others:* None met the criteria. **Physical Work Conditions**—Indoors; Standing; Using Hands on Objects, Tools, or Controls; Repetitive Motions. **Other Job Characteristics**—None met the criteria.

Experience—Job Zone 1. No previous work-related skill, knowledge, or experience is needed. **Job Preparation**—SVP below 4.0—less than six months. **Knowledges**—Food Production; Fine Arts. **Instructional Programs**—Agricultural Business Technology; General Office Occupations and Clerical Services.

Related SOC Job—43-9071 Office Machine Operators, Except Computer. **Related OOH Job**—Office Machine Operators, Except Computer. **Related DOT Jobs**—207.682-010 Duplicating-Machine Operator I; 207.682-014 Duplicating-Machine Operator II; 207.682-018 Offset-Duplicating-Machine Operator; 207.685-010 Braille-Duplicating-Machine Operator; 207.685-014 Photocopying-Machine Operator; 207.685-018 Photographic-Machine Operator.

43-9081.00 Proofreaders and Copy Markers

- **Education/Training Required: Short-term on-the-job training**
- **Employed: 18,070**
- **Annual Earnings: $25,590**
- **Growth: 1.7%**
- **Annual Job Openings: 5,000**

Read transcript or proof type setup to detect and mark for correction any grammatical, typographical, or compositional errors.

Correct or record omissions, errors, or inconsistencies found. Mark copy to indicate and correct errors in type, arrangement, grammar, punctuation, or spelling, using standard printers' marks. Read corrected copies or proofs to ensure that all corrections have been made. Compare information or figures on one record against same data on other records, or with original copy, to detect errors. Consult reference books or secure aid of readers to check references with rules of grammar and composition. Route proofs with marked corrections to authors, editors, typists, or typesetters for correction or reprinting. Measure dimensions, spacing, and positioning of page elements (copy and illustrations) to verify conformance to specifications, using printer's ruler. Read proof sheets aloud, calling out punctuation marks and spelling unusual words and proper names.

GOE Information—**Interest Area:** 06. Finance and Insurance. **Work Group:** 06.03. Finance/Insurance Records Processing. **Personality Type**—Conventional. Conventional occupations frequently involve following set procedures and routines. These occupations can include working with data and details more than with ideas. Usually there is a clear line of authority to follow. **Work Values**—Working Conditions; Independence; Moral Values; Supervision, Human Relations; Company Policies and Practices; Supervision, Technical. **Skills**—Writing; Reading Comprehension; Active Listening; Critical Thinking; Operations Analysis; Monitoring. **Abilities**—*Cognitive:* Written Expression; Written Comprehension; Perceptual Speed. *Psychomotor:* None met the criteria. *Physical:* None met the criteria. *Sensory:* Near Vision. **General Work Activities**—*Information Input:* Getting Information; Identifying Objects, Actions, and Events; Monitoring Processes, Materials, or Surroundings. *Mental Process:* Thinking Creatively; Organizing, Planning, and Prioritizing; Updating and Using Relevant Knowledge. *Work Output:* Interacting With Computers; Documenting or Recording Information.

Interacting with Others: Establishing and Maintaining Interpersonal Relationships; Communicating with Other Workers; Teaching Others. **Physical Work Conditions**—Indoors; Sitting; Using Hands on Objects, Tools, or Controls; Repetitive Motions. **Other Job Characteristics**—Need to Be Exact or Accurate; Repeat Same Tasks; Errors Have Important Consequences.

Experience—Job Zone 4. A minimum of two to four years of work-related skill, knowledge, or experience is needed. **Job Preparation**—SVP 7.0 to less than 8.0—two years to less than 10 years. **Knowledges**—Philosophy and Theology; Communications and Media; Geography; English Language; Clerical Practices; Personnel and Human Resources. **Instructional Program**—Graphic and Printing Equipment Operator, General Production.

Related SOC Job—43-9081 Proofreaders and Copy Markers. **Related OOH Job**—Proofreaders and Copy Markers. **Related DOT Jobs**—209.367-014 Braille Proofreader; 209.387-030 Proofreader; 209.667-010 Copy Holder; 209.687-010 Checker II; 247.667-010 Production Proofreader.

43-9111.00 Statistical Assistants

- **Education/Training Required: Moderate-term on-the-job training**
- **Employed: 18,700**
- **Annual Earnings: $28,950**
- **Growth: 5.7%**
- **Annual Job Openings: 1,000**

Compile and compute data according to statistical formulas for use in statistical studies. May perform actuarial computations and compile charts and graphs for use by actuaries. Includes actuarial clerks.

Compute and analyze data, using statistical formulas and computers or calculators. Enter data into computers for use in analyses and reports. Compile statistics from source materials, such as production and sales records, quality-control and test records, time sheets, and survey sheets. Compile reports, charts, and graphs that describe and interpret findings of analyses. Check source data to verify its completeness and accuracy. Participate in the publication of data and information. Discuss data presentation requirements with clients. File data and related information and maintain and update databases. Select statistical tests for analyzing data. Organize paperwork such as survey forms and reports for distribution and for analysis. Code data as necessary prior to computer entry, using lists of codes. Check survey responses for errors such as the use of pens instead of pencils and set aside response forms that cannot be used. Interview people and keep track of their responses. Send out surveys.

GOE Information—**Interest Area:** 15. Scientific Research, Engineering, and Mathematics. **Work Group:** 15.06. Mathematics and Data Analysis. **Personality Type**—Conventional. Conventional occupations frequently involve following set procedures and routines. These occupations can include working with data and details more than with ideas. Usually there is a clear line of authority to follow. **Work Values**—Independence; Working Conditions; Advancement. **Skills**—Mathematics; Operations Analysis; Quality Control Analysis; Complex Problem Solving; Programming; Monitoring. **Abilities**—*Cognitive:* Mathematical Reasoning; Number Facility; Fluency of Ideas; Memorization; Category Flexibility; Written Expression. *Psychomotor:* Finger Dexterity. *Physical:* None met the criteria. *Sensory:* Far Vision; Near Vision; Speech Recognition; Speech Clarity. **General Work Activities**—*Information*

Input: Getting Information; Identifying Objects, Actions, and Events; Monitoring Processes, Materials, or Surroundings. *Mental Process:* Processing Information; Analyzing Data or Information; Organizing, Planning, and Prioritizing; Updating and Using Relevant Knowledge. *Work Output:* Interacting With Computers; Documenting or Recording Information. *Interacting with Others:* Establishing and Maintaining Interpersonal Relationships; Communicating with Other Workers; Providing Consultation and Advice to Others. **Physical Work Conditions**—Indoors; Sitting. **Other Job Characteristics**—Need to Be Exact or Accurate; Repeat Same Tasks.

Experience—Job Zone 3. Previous work-related skill, knowledge, or experience is required. **Job Preparation**—SVP 6.0 to less than 7.0—more than one year and less than four years. **Knowledges**—Mathematics; Clerical Practices; Computers and Electronics; Administration and Management; Customer and Personal Service; Communications and Media. **Instructional Program**—Accounting Technology/Technician and Bookkeeping.

Related SOC Job—43-9111 Statistical Assistants. **Related OOH Job**—Statistical Assistants. **Related DOT Jobs**—209.387-014 Compiler; 214.487-010 Chart Calculator; 216.382-062 Statistical Clerk; 216.382-066 Statistical Clerk, Advertising; 219.387-022 Planimeter Operator; 221.382-010 Chart Clerk; 221.584-010 Chart Changer.

43-9199.99 Office and Administrative Support Workers, All Other

- **Education/Training Required: No data available**
- **Employed: 287,270**
- **Annual Earnings: $26,040**
- **Growth: 10.0%**
- **Annual Job Openings: 63,000**

All office and administrative support workers not listed separately.

No task data available.

Note: The Department of Labor has not collected some data for this job, so it has fewer details than the other descriptions.

Related SOC Job—43-9199 Office and Administrative Support Workers, All Other. **Related OOH Job**—None. **Related DOT Jobs**—206.367-010 Engineering-Document-Control Clerk; 208.582-014 Embossing-Machine Operator I; 208.682-010 Embossing-Machine Operator II; 208.685-010 Collator Operator; 208.685-022 Microfilm Mounter; 211.362-010 Cashier I; 216.587-010 Booking Clerk; 216.685-010 Gas Usage Meter Clerk; 217.485-010 Currency Counter; 217.585-010 Coin-Counter-And-Wrapper; 219.367-014 Insurance Clerk; 221.362-010 Aircraft-Log Clerk; 221.362-026 Railroad-Maintenance Clerk; 229.267-010 Parts Cataloger; others.

45-0000

Farming, Fishing, and Forestry Occupations

45-1000 Supervisors, Farming, Fishing, and Forestry Workers

45-1011.00 First-Line Supervisors/ Managers of Farming, Fishing, and Forestry Workers

- **Education/Training Required: Work experience in a related occupation**
- **Employed: 19,750**
- **Annual Earnings: $36,030**
- **Growth: 3.6%**
- **Annual Job Openings: No data available.**

The job openings listed here are shared with 45-1011.05 First-Line Supervisors/Managers of Logging Workers, 45-1011.06 First-Line Supervisors/Managers of Aquacultural Workers, 45-1011.07 First-Line Supervisors/Managers of Agricultural Crop and Horticultural Workers, and 45-1011.08 First-Line Supervisors/Managers of Animal Husbandry and Animal Care Workers.

Directly supervise and coordinate the activities of agricultural, forestry, aquacultural, and related workers.

No task data available.

GOE Information—Interest Area: 01. Agriculture and Natural Resources. **Work Group:** 01.01. Managerial Work in Agriculture and Natural Resources. **Note:** The Department of Labor has not collected some data for this job, so it has fewer details than the other descriptions.

Instructional Programs—Agricultural Animal Breeding; Agricultural Business and Management, Other; Agricultural Production Operations, General; Agricultural Production Operations, Other; Agriculture, Agricultural Operations, and Related Sciences, Other; Agronomy and Crop Science; Animal Nutrition; Animal Sciences, General; Animal/Livestock Husbandry and Production; Aquaculture; Crop Production; Dairy Husbandry and Production; Dairy Science; Farm/Farm and Ranch Management; Fishing and Fisheries Sciences and Management; Horse Husbandry/Equine Science and Management; Livestock Management; Plant Sciences, General; Poultry Science; Range Science and Management.

Related SOC Job—45-1011 First-Line Supervisors/Managers of Farming, Fishing, and Forestry Workers. **Related OOH Job—**Supervisors, Farming, Fishing, and Forestry Workers. **Related DOT Job—**No data available.

45-1011.05 First-Line Supervisors/ Managers of Logging Workers

- **Education/Training Required: Bachelor's degree**
- **Employed: 19,750**
- **Annual Earnings: $36,030**
- **Growth: 3.6%**
- **Annual Job Openings: 11,000**

The job openings listed here are shared with 45-1011.00 First-Line Supervisors/Managers of Farming, Fishing, and Forestry Workers, 45-1011.06 First-Line Supervisors/Managers of Aquacultural Workers, 45-1011.07 First-Line Supervisors/Managers of Agricultural Crop and Horticultural Workers, and 45-1011.08 First-Line Supervisors/Managers of Animal Husbandry and Animal Care Workers.

Directly supervise and coordinate activities of logging workers.

Monitor workers to ensure that safety regulations are followed, warning or disciplining those who violate safety regulations. Plan and schedule logging operations such as felling and bucking trees and grading, sorting, yarding, or loading logs. Change logging operations or methods to eliminate unsafe conditions. Monitor logging operations to identify and solve problems; improve work methods; and ensure compliance with safety, company, and government regulations. Train workers in tree felling and bucking, operation of tractors and loading machines, yarding and loading techniques, and safety regulations. Determine logging operation methods, crew sizes, and equipment requirements, conferring with mill, company, and forestry officials as necessary. Assign to workers duties such as trees to be cut; cutting sequences and specifications; and loading of trucks, railcars, or rafts. Supervise and coordinate the activities of workers engaged in logging operations and silvicultural operations. Coordinate the selection and movement of logs from storage areas according to transportation schedules or production requirements. Communicate with forestry personnel regarding forest harvesting and forest management plans, procedures, and schedules. Schedule work crews, equipment, and transportation for several different work locations. Coordinate the dismantling and moving of equipment and its setup at new worksites. Prepare production and personnel time records for management.

GOE Information—Interest Area: 01. Agriculture and Natural Resources. **Work Group:** 01.01. Managerial Work in Agriculture and Natural Resources. **Personality Type—**Realistic. Realistic occupations frequently involve work activities that include practical, hands-on problems and solutions. They often deal with plants; animals; and real-world materials like wood, tools, and machinery. Many of the occupations require working outside and do not involve a lot of paperwork or working closely with others. **Work Values—**Authority; Responsibility; Autonomy; Creativity; Activity; Variety. **Skills—**Repairing; Equipment Maintenance; Troubleshooting; Installation; Operation Monitoring; Systems Analysis. **Abilities—***Cognitive:* Spatial Orientation; Number Facility; Visualization; Perceptual Speed; Selective Attention; Time Sharing. *Psychomotor:* Reaction Time; Rate Control; Response Orientation; Multilimb Coordination; Wrist-Finger Speed; Control Precision. *Physical:* Dynamic Strength; Static Strength; Stamina; Trunk Strength; Gross Body Coordination; Extent Flexibility. *Sensory:* Peripheral Vision; Depth Perception; Sound Localization; Hearing Sensitivity; Far Vision; Auditory Attention. **General Work Activities—***Information Input:* Monitoring Processes, Materials, or Surroundings; Getting Information; Inspecting Equipment, Structures, or Materials. *Mental Process:* Making Decisions and Solving Problems; Judging the Qualities of Things, Services, or Other People's Work; Organizing, Planning, and Prioritizing. *Work Output:* Handling and Moving Objects; Performing General Physical Activities; Repairing and Maintaining Mechanical Equipment. *Interacting with Others:* Monitoring and Controlling Resources; Guiding, Directing, and Motivating Subordinates; Resolving Conflicts and Negotiating with Others. **Physical Work Conditions—**Outdoors; Noisy; Very Hot or Cold; Contaminants; Hazardous Equipment; Minor Burns, Cuts, Bites, or stings. **Other Job Characteristics—**Need to Be Exact or Accurate; Repeat Same Tasks; Errors Have Important Consequences; Pace Determined by Speed of Equipment; Automation.

Experience—Job Zone 2. Some previous work-related skill, knowledge, or experience may be helpful in these occupations, but usually is not needed. **Job Preparation—**SVP 4.0 to less than 6.0—six months to less than two years. **Knowledges—**Mechanical Devices; Production and Processing; Economics and Accounting; Administration and Management; Building and Construction; Transportation.

Instructional Programs—Agricultural Business and Management, Other; Farm/Farm and Ranch Management.

Related SOC Job—45-1011 First-Line Supervisors/Managers of Farming, Fishing, and Forestry Workers. **Related OOH Job**—Supervisors, Farming, Fishing, and Forestry Workers. **Related DOT Jobs**—183.167-038 Superintendent, Logging; 454.134-010 Supervisor, Felling-Bucking; 455.134-010 Supervisor, Log Sorting; 459.133-010 Supervisor, Logging; 459.137-010 Woods Boss; 921.131-010 Hook Tender.

45-1011.06 First-Line Supervisors/ Managers of Aquacultural Workers

- **Education/Training Required: Associate degree**
- **Employed: 19,750**
- **Annual Earnings: $36,030**
- **Growth: 3.6%**
- **Annual Job Openings: 11,000**

The job openings listed here are shared with 45-1011.00 First-Line Supervisors/Managers of Farming, Fishing, and Forestry Workers, 45-1011.05 First-Line Supervisors/Managers of Logging Workers, 45-1011.07 First-Line Supervisors/Managers of Agricultural Crop and Horticultural Workers, and 45-1011.08 First-Line Supervisors/Managers of Animal Husbandry and Animal Care Workers.

Directly supervise and coordinate activities of aquacultural workers.

Engage in the same fishery work as workers supervised. Requisition supplies. Assign to workers duties such as fertilizing and incubating spawn; feeding and transferring fish; and planting, cultivating, and harvesting shellfish beds. Perform both supervisory and management functions such as accounting, marketing, and personnel work. Confer with managers to determine times and places of seed planting, and cultivating, feeding, or harvesting of fish or shellfish. Maintain workers' time records. Record the numbers and types of fish or shellfish reared, harvested, released, sold, and shipped. Interview and select new employees. Train workers in spawning, rearing, cultivating, and harvesting methods and in the use of equipment. Supervise the artificial spawning of various salmon and trout species. Direct workers to correct problems such as disease, quality of seed distribution, or adequacy of cultivation. Prepare or direct the preparation of fish food and specify medications to be added to food and water to treat fish for diseases. Plan work schedules according to personnel and equipment availability, tidal levels, feeding schedules, or transfer and harvest needs. Observe fish and beds or ponds to detect diseases, monitor fish growth, determine quality of fish, or determine completeness of harvesting. Direct and monitor worker activities such as treatment and rearing of fingerlings, maintenance of equipment, and harvesting of fish or shellfish. Select and ship eggs to other hatcheries.

GOE Information—Interest Area: 01. Agriculture and Natural Resources. **Work Group:** 01.01. Managerial Work in Agriculture and Natural Resources. **Personality Type**—Realistic. Realistic occupations frequently involve work activities that include practical, hands-on problems and solutions. They often deal with plants; animals; and real-world materials like wood, tools, and machinery. Many of the occupations require working outside and do not involve a lot of paperwork or working closely with others. **Work Values**—Authority; Responsibility; Autonomy; Creativity; Activity; Achievement. **Skills**—Management of Personnel Resources; Systems Analysis; Management of Material Resources; Operation and Control; Systems Evaluation.

Abilities—*Cognitive:* Spatial Orientation; Speed of Closure; Number Facility; Flexibility of Closure; Memorization; Perceptual Speed. *Psychomotor:* Wrist-Finger Speed; Manual Dexterity; Arm-Hand Steadiness; Control Precision. *Physical:* Gross Body Coordination; Static Strength; Extent Flexibility; Trunk Strength. *Sensory:* Depth Perception; Far Vision; Visual Color Discrimination. **General Work Activities**—*Information Input:* Monitoring Processes, Materials, or Surroundings; Identifying Objects, Actions, and Events; Getting Information. *Mental Process:* Scheduling Work and Activities; Organizing, Planning, and Prioritizing; Updating and Using Relevant Knowledge; Making Decisions and Solving Problems.. *Work Output:* Performing General Physical Activities; Documenting or Recording Information; Handling and Moving Objects. *Interacting with Others:* Communicating with Other Workers; Coordinating the Work and Activities of Others; Establishing and Maintaining Interpersonal Relationships. **Physical Work Conditions**—More Often Outdoors Than Indoors; More Often Sitting Than Standing; Walking and Running; Using Hands on Objects, Tools, or Controls. **Other Job Characteristics**—Need to Be Exact or Accurate.

Experience—Job Zone 3. Previous work-related skill, knowledge, or experience is required. **Job Preparation**—SVP 6.0 to less than 7.0—more than one year and less than four years. **Knowledges**—Food Production; Biology; Personnel and Human Resources; Production and Processing; Administration and Management. **Instructional Programs**—Agricultural Business and Management, Other; Aquaculture; Fishing and Fisheries Sciences and Management.

Related SOC Job—45-1011 First-Line Supervisors/Managers of Farming, Fishing, and Forestry Workers. **Related OOH Job**—Supervisors, Farming, Fishing, and Forestry Workers. **Related DOT Jobs**—446.133-010 Supervisor, Shellfish Farming; 446.134-010 Supervisor, Fish Hatchery.

45-1011.07 First-Line Supervisors/ Managers of Agricultural Crop and Horticultural Workers

- **Education/Training Required: Associate degree**
- **Employed: 19,750**
- **Annual Earnings: $36,030**
- **Growth: 3.6%**
- **Annual Job Openings: 11,000**

The job openings listed here are shared with 45-1011.00 First-Line Supervisors/Managers of Farming, Fishing, and Forestry Workers, 45-1011.05 First-Line Supervisors/Managers of Logging Workers, 45-1011.06 First-Line Supervisors/Managers of Aquacultural Workers, and 45-1011.08 First-Line Supervisors/Managers of Animal Husbandry and Animal Care Workers.

Directly supervise and coordinate activities of agricultural crop or horticultural workers.

Prepare and maintain time and payroll reports, as well as details of personnel actions such as performance evaluations, hires, promotions, and disciplinary actions. Monitor and oversee construction projects such as horticultural buildings and irrigation systems. Calculate and monitor budgets for maintenance and development of collections, grounds, and infrastructure. Perform hardscape activities, including installation and repair of irrigation systems, resurfacing and grading of paths, rockwork, or erosion control. Prepare reports regarding farm conditions, crop yields, machinery breakdowns, or labor problems. Requisition and purchase supplies such as insecticides, machine parts or lubricants, and tools. Investigate grievances and settle disputes to maintain harmony among workers. Issue equipment such as farm implements, machinery, ladders, or containers to workers and collect equipment when work is complete. Confer with managers to evaluate weather and soil conditions; to develop plans and procedures; and to discuss issues such as changes in fertilizers, herbicides, or cultivating techniques. Estimate labor requirements for jobs and plan work schedules accordingly. Inspect crops, fields, and plant stock to determine conditions and need for cultivating, spraying, weeding, or harvesting. Observe workers to detect inefficient and unsafe work procedures or to identify problems, initiating corrective action as necessary. Read inventory records, customer orders, and shipping schedules to determine required activities. Assign duties such as cultivation, irrigation, and harvesting of crops or plants; product packaging and grading; and equipment maintenance. Drive and operate farm machinery such as trucks, tractors, or self-propelled harvesters to transport workers and supplies or to cultivate and harvest fields. Perform the same horticultural or agricultural duties as subordinates. Review employees' work to evaluate quality and quantity. Inspect facilities to determine maintenance needs. Recruit, hire, and discharge workers. Train workers in techniques such as planting, harvesting, weeding, and insect identification and in the use of safety measures. Arrange for transportation, equipment, and living quarters for seasonal workers. Contract with seasonal workers and farmers to provide employment. Direct or assist with the adjustment and repair of farm equipment and machinery.

GOE Information—Interest Area: 01. Agriculture and Natural Resources. Work Group: 01.01. Managerial Work in Agriculture and Natural Resources. Personality Type—Realistic. Realistic occupations frequently involve work activities that include practical, hands-on problems and solutions. They often deal with plants; animals; and real-world materials like wood, tools, and machinery. Many of the occupations require working outside and do not involve a lot of paperwork or working closely with others. Work Values—Authority; Responsibility; Autonomy; Creativity; Variety; Activity. Skills—Management of Personnel Resources; Management of Material Resources; Systems Analysis; Systems Evaluation; Operation Monitoring; Equipment Maintenance. Abilities—*Cognitive:* Spatial Orientation; Number Facility; Mathematical Reasoning; Oral Expression. *Psychomotor:* Control Precision; Multilimb Coordination; Wrist-Finger Speed; Manual Dexterity. *Physical:* Trunk Strength. *Sensory:* None met the criteria. General Work Activities—*Information Input:* Getting Information; Identifying Objects, Actions, and Events; Monitoring Processes, Materials, or Surroundings. *Mental Process:* Scheduling Work and Activities; Making Decisions and Solving Problems; Organizing, Planning, and Prioritizing. *Work Output:* Performing General Physical Activities; Handling and Moving Objects; Operating Vehicles or Equipment. *Interacting with Others:* Communicating with Other Workers; Coordinating the Work and Activities of Others; Guiding, Directing, and Motivating Subordinates. Physical Work Conditions—Outdoors; Standing; Using Hands on Objects, Tools, or Controls. Other Job Characteristics—Need to Be Exact or Accurate.

Experience—Job Zone 3. Previous work-related skill, knowledge, or experience is required. Job Preparation—SVP 6.0 to less than 7.0—more than one year and less than four years. Knowledges—Food Production; Biology; Personnel and Human Resources; Administration and Management; Chemistry; Mechanical Devices. Instructional Programs—Agricultural Business and Management, Other; Agricultural Production Operations, General; Agricultural Production Operations, Other; Agriculture, Agricultural Operations, and Related Sciences, Other; Agronomy and Crop Science; Crop Production; Farm/Farm and Ranch Management; Plant Sciences, General.

Related SOC Job—45-1011 First-Line Supervisors/Managers of Farming, Fishing, and Forestry Workers. Related OOH Job—Supervisors, Farming, Fishing, and Forestry Workers. Related DOT Jobs—180.167-014 Field Supervisor, Seed Production; 180.167-022 Group Leader; 180.167-050 Migrant Leader; 401.137-010 Supervisor, Area; 401.137-014 Supervisor, Detasseling Crew; 402.131-010 Supervisor, Vegetable Farming; 403.131-010 Supervisor, Tree-Fruit-and-Nut Farming; 403.131-014 Supervisor, Vine-Fruit Farming; 404.131-010 Supervisor, Field-Crop Farming; 404.131-014 Supervisor, Shed Workers; 405.131-010 Supervisor, Horticultural-Specialty Farming; 405.137-010 Supervisor, Rose-Grading; others.

45-1011.08 First-Line Supervisors/ Managers of Animal Husbandry and Animal Care Workers

- **Education/Training Required: Associate degree**
- **Employed: 19,750**
- **Annual Earnings: $36,030**
- **Growth: 3.6%**
- **Annual Job Openings: 11,000**

The job openings listed here are shared with 45-1011.00 First-Line Supervisors/Managers of Farming, Fishing, and Forestry Workers, 45-1011.05 First-Line Supervisors/Managers of Logging Workers, 45-1011.06 First-Line Supervisors/Managers of Aquacultural Workers, and 45-1011.07 First-Line Supervisors/Managers of Agricultural Crop and Horticultural Workers.

Directly supervise and coordinate activities of animal husbandry or animal care workers.

Study feed, weight, health, genetic, or milk production records to determine feed formulas and rations and breeding schedules. Inspect buildings, fences, fields or ranges, supplies, and equipment in order to determine work to be performed. Monitor animal care, maintenance, or breeding or packing and transfer activities to ensure work is done correctly. Train workers in animal care procedures, maintenance duties, and safety precautions. Perform the same animal care duties as subordinates. Observe animals for signs of illness, injury, or unusual behavior, notifying veterinarians or managers as warranted. Plan budgets and arrange for purchase of animals, feed, or supplies. Direct and assist workers in maintenance and repair of facilities. Recruit, hire, and pay workers. Confer with managers to determine production requirements, conditions of equipment and supplies, and work schedules. Transport or arrange for transport of animals, equipment, food, animal feed, and other supplies to and from worksites. Treat animal illnesses or injuries, following experience or instructions of veterinarians. Inseminate livestock artificially to produce desired offspring. Investigate complaints of animal neglect or cruelty and follow up on complaints appearing to require prosecution. Monitor eggs and adjust incubator thermometers and gauges to facilitate hatching progress and to maintain specified conditions. Operate euthanasia equipment to destroy animals. Prepare reports concerning facility activities, employees' time records, and animal treatment. Assign tasks such as feeding and treatment of animals, and cleaning and maintenance of animal quarters. Establish work schedules and procedures.

GOE Information—Interest Area: 01. Agriculture and Natural Resources. Work Group: 01.01. Managerial Work in Agriculture and Natural Resources. Personality Type—Realistic. Realistic occupations frequently involve work activities that include practical, hands-on problems and solutions. They often deal with plants; animals; and real-world materials like wood, tools, and machinery. Many of the occupations require working outside and do not involve a lot of paperwork or working closely with others. **Work Values**—Authority; Responsibility; Autonomy; Activity; Variety; Creativity. **Skills**—Management of Personnel Resources; Management of Financial Resources; Management of Material Resources; Systems Evaluation; Systems Analysis; Instructing. **Abilities**—*Cognitive:* Spatial Orientation; Number Facility; Memorization; Speed of Closure; Problem Sensitivity; Perceptual Speed. *Psychomotor:* Wrist-Finger Speed; Manual Dexterity; Control Precision; Reaction Time; Arm-Hand Steadiness; Multilimb Coordination. *Physical:* Gross Body Coordination; Static Strength; Extent Flexibility; Trunk Strength. *Sensory:* Peripheral Vision; Depth Perception; Auditory Attention. **General Work Activities**—*Information Input:* Identifying Objects, Actions, and Events; Getting Information; Monitoring Processes, Materials, or Surroundings. *Mental Process:* Scheduling Work and Activities; Organizing, Planning, and Prioritizing; Updating and Using Relevant Knowledge. *Work Output:* Performing General Physical Activities; Handling and Moving Objects; Documenting or Recording Information. *Interacting with Others:* Communicating with Other Workers; Establishing and Maintaining Interpersonal Relationships; Coordinating the Work and Activities of Others. **Physical Work Conditions**—More Often Outdoors Than Indoors; Contaminants; Standing; Walking and Running; Using Hands on Objects, Tools, or Controls. **Other Job Characteristics**—Need to Be Exact or Accurate.

Experience—Job Zone 3. Previous work-related skill, knowledge, or experience is required. **Job Preparation**—SVP 6.0 to less than 7.0—more than one year and less than four years. **Knowledges**—Biology; Food Production; Medicine and Dentistry; Personnel and Human Resources; Administration and Management. **Instructional Programs**—Agricultural Animal Breeding; Agriculture, Agricultural Operations, and Related Sciences, Other; Animal Nutrition; Animal Sciences, General; Livestock Management; Poultry Science.

Related SOC Job—45-1011 First-Line Supervisors/Managers of Farming, Fishing, and Forestry Workers. **Related OOH Job**—Supervisors, Farming, Fishing, and Forestry Workers. **Related DOT Jobs**—180.167-038 Manager, Game Preserve; 187.167-218 Manager, Animal Shelter; 410.131-010 Barn Boss; 410.131-014 Supervisor, Artificial Breeding Ranch; 410.131-018 Supervisor, Dairy Farm; 410.131-022 Supervisor, Stock Ranch; 410.134-010 Supervisor, Livestock-Yard; 410.134-014 Supervisor, Wool-Shearing; 410.134-018 Supervisor, Kennel; 410.134-022 Supervisor, Research Dairy Farm; 410.137-010 Camp Tender; 410.137-014 Top Screw; 410.137-018 Supervisor, Animal Maintenance; others.

45-1012.00 Farm Labor Contractors

- **Education/Training Required:** Work experience in a related occupation
- **Employed:** 2,310
- **Annual Earnings:** $19,810
- **Growth:** 3.6%
- **Annual Job Openings:** 11,000

Recruit, hire, furnish, and supervise seasonal or temporary agricultural laborers for a fee. May transport, house, and provide meals for workers.

Recruit and hire agricultural workers. Pay wages of contracted farm laborers. Employ foremen to deal directly with workers when recruiting, hiring, instructing, assigning tasks, and enforcing work rules. Direct and transport workers to appropriate worksites. Provide check-cashing services to employees. Provide food, drinking water, and field sanitation facilities to contracted workers. Furnish tools for employee use. Supervise the work of contracted employees.

GOE Information—**Interest Area:** 01. Agriculture and Natural Resources. **Work Group:** 01.01. Managerial Work in Agriculture and Natural Resources. **Note:** The Department of Labor has not collected some data for this job, so it has fewer details than the other descriptions.

Instructional Program—No related CIP programs.

Related SOC Job—45-1012 Farm Labor Contractors. **Related OOH Job**—Supervisors, Farming, Fishing, and Forestry Workers. **Related DOT Job**—409.117-010 Harvest Contractor.

45-2000 Agricultural Workers

45-2011.00 Agricultural Inspectors

- **Education/Training Required:** Work experience in a related occupation
- **Employed:** 11,730
- **Annual Earnings:** $32,840
- **Growth:** 6.8%
- **Annual Job Openings:** 3,000

Inspect agricultural commodities, processing equipment, and facilities and fish and logging operations to ensure compliance with regulations and laws governing health, quality, and safety.

Set standards for the production of meat and poultry products and for food ingredients, additives, and compounds used to prepare and package products. Direct and monitor the quarantine and treatment or destruction of plants and plant products. Monitor the operations and sanitary conditions of slaughtering and meat processing plants. Verify that transportation and handling procedures meet regulatory requirements. Take emergency actions such as closing production facilities if product safety is compromised. Set labeling standards and approve labels for meat and poultry products. Review and monitor foreign product inspection systems in countries of origin to ensure equivalence to the U.S. system. Inspect the cleanliness and practices of establishment employees. Advise farmers and growers of development programs or new equipment and techniques to aid in quality production. Inspect livestock to determine effectiveness of medication and feeding programs. Provide consultative services in areas such as equipment and product evaluation, plant construction and layout, and food safety systems. Monitor the grading performed by company employees to verify conformance to standards. Write reports of findings and recommendations and advise farmers, growers, or processors of corrective action to be taken. Inspect and test horticultural products or livestock to detect harmful diseases, chemical residues, and infestations and to determine the quality of products or animals. Examine, weigh, and measure commodities such as poultry, eggs, meat, and seafood to certify qualities, grades, and weights. Label and seal graded products and issue official grading certificates. Interpret and enforce government acts and regulations and explain required standards to agricultural workers. Inspect food products and processing procedures to determine whether products are safe to eat. Inspect agricultural commodities and related operations, as well as fish and logging operations, for compliance with laws and regulations governing health, quality, and safety. Testify in legal proceedings. Collect samples from animals, plants, or products and route them to laboratories for microbiological assessment, ingredient verification, and other testing.

GOE Information—**Interest Area:** 07. Government and Public Administration. **Work Group:** 07.03. Regulations Enforcement.

Personality Type—Realistic. Realistic occupations frequently involve work activities that include practical, hands-on problems and solutions. They often deal with plants; animals; and real-world materials like wood, tools, and machinery. Many of the occupations require working outside and do not involve a lot of paperwork or working closely with others. **Work Values**—Responsibility; Autonomy; Independence; Security; Supervision, Technical; Variety. **Skills**—Quality Control Analysis; Science; Operation Monitoring; Systems Evaluation; Writing; Systems Analysis. **Abilities**—*Cognitive:* Written Expression; Spatial Orientation; Problem Sensitivity; Memorization; Speed of Closure; Flexibility of Closure. *Psychomotor:* Wrist-Finger Speed; Manual Dexterity; Arm-Hand Steadiness. *Physical:* Gross Body Coordination; Extent Flexibility; Trunk Strength. *Sensory:* Speech Clarity; Visual Color Discrimination; Near Vision. **General Work Activities**—*Information Input:* Identifying Objects, Actions, and Events; Inspecting Equipment, Structures, or Materials; Getting Information. *Mental Process:* Evaluating Information Against Standards; Judging the Qualities of Things, Services, or Other People's Work; Making Decisions and Solving Problems. *Work Output:* Documenting or Recording Information; Handling and Moving Objects; Performing General Physical Activities. *Interacting with Others:* Providing Consultation and Advice to Others; Communicating with Persons Outside Organization; Interpreting the Meaning of Information for Others. **Physical Work Conditions**—More Often Outdoors Than Indoors; Standing; Walking and Running; Using Hands on Objects, Tools, or Controls. **Other Job Characteristics**—Need to Be Exact or Accurate; Errors Have Important Consequences.

Experience—Job Zone 4. A minimum of two to four years of work-related skill, knowledge, or experience is needed. **Job Preparation**—SVP 7.0 to less than 8.0—two years to less than 10 years. **Knowledges**—Food Production; Biology; Production and Processing; Law and Government. **Instructional Program**—Agricultural and Food Products Processing, General.

Related SOC Job—45-2011 Agricultural Inspectors. **Related OOH Job**—Agricultural Workers. **Related DOT Jobs**—168.287-010 Inspector, Agricultural Commodities; 411.267-010 Field Service Technician, Poultry.

45-2021.00 Animal Breeders

- **Education/Training Required:** Moderate-term on-the-job training
- **Employed:** 1,860
- **Annual Earnings:** $26,820
- **Growth:** 5.6%
- **Annual Job Openings:** 1,000

Breed animals, including cattle, goats, horses, sheep, swine, poultry, dogs, cats, or pet birds. Select and breed animals according to their genealogy, characteristics, and offspring. May require a knowledge of artificial insemination techniques and equipment use. May involve keeping records on heats, birth intervals, or pedigree.

Feed and water animals and clean and disinfect pens, cages, yards, and hutches. Examine animals to detect symptoms of illness or injury. Place vaccines in drinking water, inject vaccines, or dust air with vaccine powder to protect animals from diseases. Select animals to be bred and semen specimens to be used according to knowledge of animals, genealogies, traits, and desired offspring characteristics. Treat minor injuries and ailments and contact veterinarians to obtain treatment for animals with serious illnesses or injuries. Observe animals in heat to detect approach of estrus and exercise animals to induce or hasten estrus if necessary. Record animal characteristics such as weights, growth patterns, and diets. Exhibit animals at shows. Build hutches, pens, and fenced yards. Clip or shear hair on animals. Attach rubber collecting sheaths to genitals of tethered bull and stimulate animal's organ to induce ejaculation. Package and label semen to be used for artificial insemination, recording information such as the date, source, quality, and concentration. Prepare containers of semen for freezing and storage or shipment, placing them in dry ice or liquid nitrogen. Maintain logs of semen specimens used and animals bred. Arrange for sale of animals and eggs to hospitals, research centers, pet shops, and food-processing plants. Measure specified amounts of semen into calibrated syringes and insert syringes into inseminating guns. Inject prepared animal semen into female animals for breeding purposes by inserting nozzle of syringe into vagina and depressing syringe plunger. Adjust controls to maintain specific building temperatures required for animals' health and safety. Examine semen microscopically to assess and record density and motility of gametes and dilute semen with prescribed diluents according to formulas. Brand, tattoo, or tag animals to allow animal identification. Perform procedures such as animal dehorning or castration.

GOE Information—**Interest Area:** 08. Health Science. **Work Group:** 08.05. Animal Care. **Personality Type**—Realistic. Realistic occupations frequently involve work activities that include practical, hands-on problems and solutions. They often deal with plants; animals; and real-world materials like wood, tools, and machinery. Many of the occupations require working outside and do not involve a lot of paperwork or working closely with others. **Work Values**—Responsibility; Independence; Autonomy; Creativity; Activity; Compensation. **Skills**—Management of Financial Resources; Equipment Maintenance; Repairing; Monitoring; Quality Control Analysis; Science. **Abilities**—*Cognitive:* Perceptual Speed; Number Facility; Category Flexibility; Speed of Closure; Visualization. *Psychomotor:* Multilimb Coordination; Arm-Hand Steadiness; Manual Dexterity; Finger Dexterity; Control Precision. *Physical:* Dynamic Strength; Static Strength; Trunk Strength; Gross Body Coordination; Extent Flexibility. *Sensory:* Depth Perception; Visual Color Discrimination; Far Vision; Auditory Attention. **General Work Activities**—*Information Input:* Identifying Objects, Actions, and Events; Monitoring Processes, Materials, or Surroundings; Getting Information. *Mental Process:* Organizing, Planning, and Prioritizing; Judging the Qualities of Things, Services, or Other People's Work; Making Decisions and Solving Problems. *Work Output:* Handling and Moving Objects; Performing General Physical Activities; Interacting With Computers. *Interacting with Others:* Influencing Others or Selling; Establishing and Maintaining Interpersonal Relationships; Monitoring and Controlling Resources. **Physical Work Conditions**—Outdoors; Noisy; Very Hot or Cold; Contaminants; Standing; Using Hands on Objects, Tools, or Controls. **Other Job Characteristics**—Need to Be Exact or Accurate.

Experience—Job Zone 3. Previous work-related skill, knowledge, or experience is required. **Job Preparation**—SVP 6.0 to less than 7.0—more than one year and less than four years. **Knowledges**—Biology; Sales and Marketing; Production and Processing; Food Production; Medicine and Dentistry; Transportation. **Instructional Programs**—Animal/Livestock Husbandry and Production; Horse Husbandry/Equine Science and Management.

Related SOC Job—45-2021 Animal Breeders. **Related OOH Job**—Agricultural Workers. **Related DOT Jobs**—410.161-010 Animal Breeder; 410.161-014 Fur Farmer; 410.161-018 Livestock Rancher; 410.161-022 Hog-Confinement-System Manager; 411.161-010 Canary Breeder; 411.161-014 Poultry Breeder; 413.161-014 Reptile Farmer.

45-2041.00 Graders and Sorters, Agricultural Products

- **Education/Training Required:** Work experience in a related occupation
- **Employed:** 45,010
- **Annual Earnings:** $16,770
- **Growth:** 7.9%
- **Annual Job Openings:** 4,000

Grade, sort, or classify unprocessed food and other agricultural products by size, weight, color, or condition.

Grade and sort products according to factors such as color, species, length, width, appearance, feel, smell, and quality to ensure correct processing and usage. Separate fiber tufts between fingers to assess strength, uniformity, and cohesive quality of fibers. Discard inferior or defective products and foreign matter and place acceptable products in containers for further processing. Weigh products or estimate their weight visually or by feel. Place products in containers according to grade and mark grades on containers. Record grade or identification numbers on tags or on shipping, receiving, or sales sheets. Examine product fibers through microscopes to determine maturity and spirality of fibers.

GOE Information—Interest Area: 13. Manufacturing. **Work Group:** 13.07. Production Quality Control. **Personality Type—Realistic.** Realistic occupations frequently involve work activities that include practical, hands-on problems and solutions. They often deal with plants; animals; and real-world materials like wood, tools, and machinery. Many of the occupations require working outside and do not involve a lot of paperwork or working closely with others. **Work Values—Independence; Supervision, Technical; Moral Values; Supervision, Human Relations; Responsibility; Activity. Skills—None met the criteria. Abilities—***Cognitive:* Perceptual Speed; Speed of Closure; Category Flexibility; Flexibility of Closure; Selective Attention; Number Facility. *Psychomotor:* Speed of Limb Movement; Wrist-Finger Speed; Manual Dexterity; Arm-Hand Steadiness; Finger Dexterity; Reaction Time. *Physical:* Extent Flexibility. *Sensory:* Visual Color Discrimination. **General Work Activities—***Information Input:* Identifying Objects, Actions, and Events; Inspecting Equipment, Structures, or Materials; Getting Information. *Mental Process:* Judging the Qualities of Things, Services, or Other People's Work; Evaluating Information Against Standards; Processing Information. *Work Output:* Handling and Moving Objects; Performing General Physical Activities. *Interacting with Others:* None met the criteria. **Physical Work Conditions—**Indoors; Standing; Using Hands on Objects, Tools, or Controls; Repetitive Motions. **Other Job Characteristics—**Need to Be Exact or Accurate; Repeat Same Tasks.

Experience—Job Zone 1. No previous work-related skill, knowledge, or experience is needed. **Job Preparation—**SVP below 4.0—less than six months. **Knowledges—**Production and Processing. **Instructional Program—**Agricultural/Farm Supplies Retailing and Wholesaling.

Related SOC Job—45-2041 Graders and Sorters, Agricultural Products. **Related OOH Job—**Agricultural Workers. **Related DOT Jobs—**409.687-010 Inspector-Grader, Agricultural Establishment; 410.687-026 Wool-Fleece Sorter; 411.687-010 Chick Grader; 411.687-014 Chick Sexer; 429.387-010 Cotton Classer; 429.587-010 Cotton Classer Aide; 446.687-010 Clam Sorter; 522.384-010 Fish Roe Technician; 529.687-074 Egg Candler; 529.687-186 Sorter, Agricultural Produce; 589.387-014 Wool Sorter; 589.687-054 Wool-Fleece Grader.

45-2091.00 Agricultural Equipment Operators

- **Education/Training Required:** Moderate-term on-the-job training
- **Employed:** 19,940
- **Annual Earnings:** $19,460
- **Growth:** –0.1%
- **Annual Job Openings:** 12,000

Drive and control farm equipment to till soil and to plant, cultivate, and harvest crops. May perform tasks such as crop baling or hay bucking. May operate stationary equipment to perform post-harvest tasks, such as husking, shelling, threshing, and ginning.

Walk beside or ride on planting machines while inserting plants in planter mechanisms at specified intervals. Position boxes or attach bags at discharge ends of machinery to catch products, removing and closing full containers. Observe and listen to machinery operation to detect equipment malfunctions. Operate or tend equipment used in agricultural production, such as tractors, combines, and irrigation equipment. Operate towed machines such as seed drills or manure spreaders to plant, fertilize, dust, and spray crops. Guide products on conveyors to regulate flow through machines and to discard diseased or rotten products. Weigh crop-filled containers and record weights and other identifying information. Mix specified materials or chemicals and dump solutions, powders, or seeds into planter or sprayer machinery. Spray fertilizer or pesticide solutions to control insects, fungus and weed growth, and diseases, using hand sprayers. Adjust, repair, and service farm machinery and notify supervisors when machinery malfunctions. Irrigate soil, using portable pipes or ditch systems, and maintain ditches or pipes and pumps. Direct and monitor the activities of work crews engaged in planting, weeding, or harvesting activities. Manipulate controls to set, activate, and adjust mechanisms on machinery. Drive trucks to haul crops, supplies, tools, or farm workers. Load and unload crops or containers of materials manually or using conveyors, handtrucks, forklifts, or transfer augers. Load hoppers, containers, or conveyors to feed machines with products, using forklifts, transfer augers, suction gates, shovels, or pitchforks.

GOE Information—Interest Area: 01. Agriculture and Natural Resources. **Work Group:** 01.04. General Farming. **Personality Type—Realistic.** Realistic occupations frequently involve work activities that include practical, hands-on problems and solutions. They often deal with plants; animals; and real-world materials like wood, tools, and machinery. Many of the occupations require working outside and do not involve a lot of paperwork or working closely with others. **Work Values—Moral Values; Independence; Authority; Variety. Skills—Repairing; Equipment Maintenance; Operation and Control; Operation Monitoring; Systems Analysis; Science. Abilities—***Cognitive:* Spatial Orientation; Information Ordering; Time Sharing; Visualization; Number Facility. *Psychomotor:* Multilimb Coordination; Control Precision; Rate Control; Response Orientation; Manual Dexterity; Reaction Time. *Physical:* Explosive Strength; Static Strength; Dynamic Strength; Stamina; Dynamic Flexibility; Extent Flexibility. *Sensory:* Hearing Sensitivity; Peripheral Vision; Sound Localization; Far Vision; Visual Color Discrimination. **General Work Activities—***Information Input:* Inspecting Equipment, Structures, or Materials; Monitoring Processes, Materials, or Surroundings; Identifying Objects, Actions, and Events. *Mental Process:* None met the criteria. *Work Output:* Performing General Physical Activities; Handling and Moving Objects; Controlling Machines and Processes. *Interacting with Others:* Coordinating the Work and Activities of

Others. **Physical Work Conditions**—Outdoors; Very Hot or Cold; Contaminants; Hazardous Equipment; Minor Burns, Cuts, Bites, or Stings; Using Hands on Objects, Tools, or Controls. **Other Job Characteristics**—Errors Have Important Consequences; Pace Determined by Speed of Equipment.

Experience—Job Zone 2. Some previous work-related skill, knowledge, or experience may be helpful in these occupations, but usually is not needed. **Job Preparation**—SVP 4.0 to less than 6.0—six months to less than two years. **Knowledges**—Food Production; Mechanical Devices; Chemistry. **Instructional Program**—Agricultural Power Machinery Operation.

Related SOC Job—45-2091 Agricultural Equipment Operators. **Related OOH Job**—Agricultural Workers. **Related DOT Jobs**—401.683-010 Farmworker, Grain I; 401.683-014 Farmworker, Rice; 402.663-010 Farmworker, Vegetable I; 403.683-010 Farmworker, Fruit I; 404.663-010 Farmworker, Field Crop I; 404.685-010 Seed-Potato Arranger; 405.683-010 Farmworker, Bulbs; 405.683-014 Growth-Media Mixer, Mushroom; 407.663-010 Farmworker, Diversified Crops I; 409.683-010 Farm-Machine Operator; 409.683-014 Field Hauler; 409.685-010 Farm-Machine Tender; 409.686-010 Farmworker, Machine; 421.683-010 Farmworker, General I; others.

45-2092.00 Farmworkers and Laborers, Crop, Nursery, and Greenhouse

- **Education/Training Required: Short-term on-the-job training**
- **Employed: 227,750**
- **Annual Earnings: $16,450**
- **Growth: −2.7%**
- **Annual Job Openings: 121,000**

The job openings listed here are shared with 45-2092.01 Nursery Workers and 45-2092.02 Farmworkers and Laborers, Crop.

Manually plant, cultivate, and harvest vegetables, fruits, nuts, horticultural specialties, and field crops. Use hand tools, such as shovels, trowels, hoes, tampers, pruning hooks, shears, and knives. Duties may include tilling soil and applying fertilizers; transplanting, weeding, thinning, or pruning crops; applying pesticides; and cleaning, grading, sorting, packing, and loading harvested products. May construct trellises, repair fences and farm buildings, or participate in irrigation activities.

No task data available.

GOE Information—**Interest Area:** 01. Agriculture and Natural Resources. **Work Group:** 01.04. General Farming. **Note:** The Department of Labor has not collected some data for this job, so it has fewer details than the other descriptions.

Instructional Program—Agricultural Production Operations, General.

Related SOC Job—45-2092 Farmworkers and Laborers, Crop, Nursery, and Greenhouse. **Related OOH Job**—Agricultural Workers. **Related DOT Job**—No data available.

45-2092.01 Nursery Workers

- **Education/Training Required: Short-term on-the-job training**
- **Employed: 227,750**
- **Annual Earnings: $16,450**
- **Growth: −2.7%**
- **Annual Job Openings: 121,000**

The job openings listed here are shared with 45-2092.00 Farmworkers and Laborers, Crop, Nursery, and Greenhouse and 45-2092.02 Farmworkers and Laborers, Crop.

Work in nursery facilities or at customer location planting, cultivating, harvesting, and transplanting trees, shrubs, or plants.

Trap and destroy pests such as moles, gophers, and mice, using pesticides. Sell and deliver plants and flowers to customers. Harvest plants and transplant or pot and label them. Record information about plants and plant growth. Provide information and advice to the public regarding the selection, purchase, and care of products. Maintain inventory, ordering materials as required. Operate tractors and other machinery and equipment to fertilize, cultivate, harvest, and spray fields and plants. Cut, roll, and stack sod. Dig, cut, and transplant seedlings, cuttings, trees, and shrubs. Fold and staple corrugated forms to make boxes used for packing horticultural products. Dig, rake, and screen soil and fill cold frames and hot beds in preparation for planting. Dip cut flowers into disinfectant, count them into bunches, and place them in boxes to prepare them for storage and shipping. Feel plants' leaves and note their coloring to detect the presence of insects or disease. Fill growing tanks with water. Graft plants and trees into different rootstock to reduce disease by inserting and tying buds into incisions in rootstock. Inspect plants and bud ties to assess quality. Move containerized shrubs, plants, and trees, using wheelbarrows or tractors. Plant, spray, weed, fertilize, and water plants, shrubs, and trees, using hand tools and gardening tools. Regulate greenhouse conditions and indoor and outdoor irrigation systems. Sow grass seed or plant plugs of grass. Clean work areas and maintain grounds and landscaping. Haul and spread topsoil, fertilizer, peat moss, and other materials to condition soil, using wheelbarrows or carts and shovels. Tie and bunch flowers, plants, shrubs, and trees; wrap their roots; and pack them into boxes to fill orders. Maintain and repair irrigation and climate control systems.

GOE Information—**Interest Area:** 01. Agriculture and Natural Resources. **Work Group:** 01.05. Nursery, Groundskeeping, and Pest Control. **Personality Type**—Realistic. Realistic occupations frequently involve work activities that include practical, hands-on problems and solutions. They often deal with plants; animals; and real-world materials like wood, tools, and machinery. Many of the occupations require working outside and do not involve a lot of paperwork or working closely with others. **Work Values**—Moral Values; Supervision, Technical; Independence; Supervision, Human Relations. **Skills**—None met the criteria. **Abilities**—*Cognitive:* Spatial Orientation; Flexibility of Closure; Visualization. *Psychomotor:* Speed of Limb Movement; Wrist-Finger Speed; Manual Dexterity; Arm-Hand Steadiness; Multilimb Coordination; Control Precision. *Physical:* Dynamic Flexibility; Dynamic Strength; Extent Flexibility; Static Strength; Trunk Strength; Stamina. *Sensory:* None met the criteria. **General Work Activities**—*Information Input:* Inspecting Equipment, Structures, or Materials. *Mental Process:* Organizing, Planning, and Prioritizing; Judging the Qualities of Things, Services, or Other People's Work. *Work Output:* Performing General Physical Activities; Handling and Moving Objects. *Interacting with Others:* Communicating with Persons Outside Organization. **Physical Work Conditions**—Outdoors; Minor Burns, Cuts, Bites, or Stings; Standing; Kneeling, Crouching, Stooping, or Crawling; Using Hands on Objects, Tools, or Controls; Bending or Twisting the Body. **Other Job Characteristics**—None met the criteria.

Experience—Job Zone 1. No previous work-related skill, knowledge, or experience is needed. **Job Preparation**—SVP below 4.0—less than six months. **Knowledges**—Biology. **Instructional Program**—Agricultural Production Operations, General.

Related SOC Job—45-2092 Farmworkers and Laborers, Crop, Nursery, and Greenhouse. **Related OOH Job**—Agricultural Workers. **Related DOT Jobs**—405.684-010 Budder; 405.687-014 Horticultural Worker II.

45-2092.02 Farmworkers and Laborers, Crop

- **Education/Training Required: Short-term on-the-job training**
- **Employed: 227,750**
- **Annual Earnings: $16,450**
- **Growth: −2.7%**
- **Annual Job Openings: 121,000**

The job openings listed here are shared with 45-2092.00 Farmworkers and Laborers, Crop, Nursery, and Greenhouse and 45-2092.01 Nursery Workers.

Manually plant, cultivate, and harvest vegetables, fruits, nuts, and field crops. Use hand tools, such as shovels, trowels, hoes, tampers, pruning hooks, shears, and knives. Duties may include tilling soil and applying fertilizers; transplanting, weeding, thinning, or pruning crops; applying pesticides; cleaning, packing, and loading harvested products. May construct trellises, repair fences and farm buildings, or participate in irrigation activities.

Identify plants, pests, and weeds to determine the selection and application of pesticides and fertilizers. Apply pesticides, herbicides, or fertilizers to crops. Repair and maintain farm vehicles, implements, and mechanical equipment. Record information about crops, such as pesticide use, yields, or costs. Direct and monitor the work of casual and seasonal help during planting and harvesting. Clear and maintain irrigation ditches. Set up and operate irrigation equipment. Repair farm buildings, fences, and other structures. Participate in the inspection, grading, sorting, storage, and post-harvest treatment of crops. Harvest fruits and vegetables by hand. Operate tractors, tractor-drawn machinery, and self-propelled machinery to plow, harrow, and fertilize soil or to plant, cultivate, spray, and harvest crops. Inform farmers or farm managers of crop progress. Dig and plant seeds or transplant seedlings by hand. Load agricultural products into trucks and drive trucks to market or storage facilities.

GOE Information—Interest Area: 01. Agriculture and Natural Resources. **Work Group:** 01.04. General Farming. **Personality Type**—Realistic. Realistic occupations frequently involve work activities that include practical, hands-on problems and solutions. They often deal with plants; animals; and real-world materials like wood, tools, and machinery. Many of the occupations require working outside and do not involve a lot of paperwork or working closely with others. **Work Values**—Independence; Moral Values; Variety. **Skills**—Repairing; Operation and Control; Equipment Maintenance; Operation Monitoring; Installation. **Abilities**—*Cognitive:* Spatial Orientation; Information Ordering; Time Sharing. *Psychomotor:* Response Orientation; Rate Control; Multilimb Coordination; Control Precision; Reaction Time; Wrist-Finger Speed. *Physical:* Static Strength; Explosive Strength; Extent Flexibility; Dynamic Strength; Trunk Strength; Dynamic Flexibility. *Sensory:* Sound Localization; Hearing Sensitivity; Peripheral Vision; Depth Perception; Night Vision; Glare Sensitivity. **General Work Activities**—*Information Input:* Identifying Objects, Actions, and Events; Monitoring Processes, Materials, or Surroundings; Estimating the Needed Characteristics of Products, Events, or Information. *Mental Process:* Organizing, Planning, and Prioritizing; Making Decisions and Solving Problems; Judging the Qualities of Things, Services, or Other People's Work. *Work Output:* Performing General Physical Activities; Handling and Moving Objects; Repairing and Maintaining

Mechanical Equipment. *Interacting with Others:* Coordinating the Work and Activities of Others; Monitoring and Controlling Resources; Establishing and Maintaining Interpersonal Relationships. **Physical Work Conditions**—Outdoors; Contaminants; Hazardous Equipment; Standing; Walking and Running; Using Hands on Objects, Tools, or Controls. **Other Job Characteristics**—None met the criteria.

Experience—Job Zone 1. No previous work-related skill, knowledge, or experience is needed. **Job Preparation**—SVP below 4.0–less than six months. **Knowledges**—Food Production; Building and Construction; Mechanical Devices; Chemistry; Biology; Transportation. **Instructional Program**—Crop Production.

Related SOC Job—45-2092 Farmworkers and Laborers, Crop, Nursery, and Greenhouse. **Related OOH Job**—Agricultural Workers. **Related DOT Jobs**—401.687-010 Farmworker, Grain II; 402.687-010 Farmworker, Vegetable II; 402.687-014 Harvest Worker, Vegetable; 403.687-010 Farmworker, Fruit II; 403.687-014 Fig Caprifier; 403.687-018 Harvest Worker, Fruit; 404.686-010 Seed Cutter; 404.687-010 Farmworker, Field Crop II; 404.687-014 Harvest Worker, Field Crop; 407.687-010 Farmworker, Diversified Crops II; 409.684-010 Irrigator, Valve Pipe; 409.685-014 Irrigator, Sprinkling System; 409.687-014 Irrigator, Gravity Flow; 409.687-018 Weeder-Thinner; others.

45-2093.00 Farmworkers, Farm and Ranch Animals

- **Education/Training Required: Short-term on-the-job training**
- **Employed: 49,740**
- **Annual Earnings: $18,220**
- **Growth: 0.9%**
- **Annual Job Openings: 16,000**

Attend to live farm, ranch, or aquacultural animals that may include cattle, sheep, swine, goats, horses and other equines, poultry, finfish, shellfish, and bees. Attend to animals produced for animal products, such as meat, fur, skins, feathers, eggs, milk, and honey. Duties may include feeding, watering, herding, grazing, castrating, branding, debeaking, weighing, catching, and loading animals. May maintain records on animals; examine animals to detect diseases and injuries; assist in birth deliveries; and administer medications, vaccinations, or insecticides as appropriate. May clean and maintain animal housing areas.

Provide medical treatment, such as administering medications and vaccinations, or arrange for veterinarians to provide more extensive treatment. Mix feed, additives, and medicines in prescribed portions. Perform duties related to livestock reproduction, such as breeding animals within appropriate timeframes, performing artificial inseminations, and helping with animal births. Feed and water livestock and monitor food and water supplies. Patrol grazing lands on horseback or using all-terrain vehicles. Clean stalls, pens, and equipment, using disinfectant solutions, brushes, shovels, water hoses, or pumps. Drive trucks, tractors, and other equipment to distribute feed to animals. Examine animals to detect illness, injury, or disease and to check physical characteristics, such as rate of weight gain. Groom, clip, trim, and/or castrate animals; dock ears and tails; or shear coats to collect hair. Herd livestock to pastures for grazing or to scales, trucks, or other enclosures. Mark livestock to identify ownership and grade, using brands, tags, paint, or tattoos. Milk animals such as cows and goats by hand or using milking machines. Trim and shear poultry beaks, toes, and wings, using debeaking machines, heated hand shears, or hot wires. Segregate animals according to weight, age, color, and physical condition. Order food for animals and arrange for its delivery. Move equipment, poultry, or livestock from one location to another manually or using trucks or carts. Maintain growth, feeding, production, and cost records. Inspect, maintain, and repair equipment, machinery, buildings, pens, yards, and fences. Collect, inspect, and place eggs in incubators; operate machines for egg washing, candling, and grading; and pack eggs in cartons. Spray livestock with disinfectants and insecticides or dip or bathe animals. Shift animals between grazing areas to ensure that they have sufficient access to food. Protect herds from predators, using trained dogs.

GOE Information—Interest Area: 01. Agriculture and Natural Resources. **Work Group:** 01.04. General Farming. **Personality Type**—Realistic. Realistic occupations frequently involve work activities that include practical, hands-on problems and solutions. They often deal with plants; animals; and real-world materials like wood, tools, and machinery. Many of the occupations require working outside and do not involve a lot of paperwork or working closely with others. **Work Values**—Moral Values; Independence; Variety. **Skills**—Repairing; Equipment Maintenance. **Abilities**—*Cognitive:* Number Facility. *Psychomotor:* Multilimb Coordination; Speed of Limb Movement; Manual Dexterity; Reaction Time; Rate Control; Wrist-Finger Speed. *Physical:* Static Strength; Explosive Strength; Dynamic Flexibility; Dynamic Strength; Trunk Strength; Gross Body Coordination. *Sensory:* None met the criteria. **General Work Activities**—*Information Input:* Monitoring Processes, Materials, or Surroundings; Inspecting Equipment, Structures, or Materials; Getting Information. *Mental Process:* Judging the Qualities of Things, Services, or Other People's Work; Updating and Using Relevant Knowledge; Making Decisions and Solving Problems. *Work Output:* Handling and Moving Objects; Performing General Physical Activities; Controlling Machines and Processes. *Interacting with Others:* None met the criteria. **Physical Work Conditions**—Outdoors; Minor Burns, Cuts, Bites, or Stings; Standing; Walking and Running; Kneeling, Crouching, Stooping, or Crawling; Bending or Twisting the Body. **Other Job Characteristics**—None met the criteria.

Experience—Job Zone 1. No previous work-related skill, knowledge, or experience is needed. **Job Preparation**—SVP below 4.0—less than six months. **Knowledges**—Food Production; Biology. **Instructional Programs**—Animal/Livestock Husbandry and Production; Aquaculture; Greenhouse Operations and Management; Ornamental Horticulture; Plant Nursery Operations and Management.

Related SOC Job—45-2093 Farmworkers, Farm and Ranch Animals. **Related OOH Job**—Agricultural Workers. **Related DOT Jobs**—410.364-010 Lamber; 410.664-010 Farmworker, Livestock; 410.674-014 Cowpuncher; 410.674-018 Livestock-Yard Attendant; 410.684-010 Farmworker, Dairy; 410.684-014 Sheep Shearer; 410.685-010 Milker, Machine; 410.687-010 Fleece Tier; 410.687-014 Goat Herder; 410.687-022 Sheep Herder; 411.161-018 Poultry Farmer; 411.364-014 Poultry Tender; 411.584-010 Farmworker, Poultry; 411.684-010 Caponizer; 411.684-014 Poultry Vaccinator; 411.687-018 Laborer, Poultry Farm; 411.687-022 Laborer, Poultry Hatchery; others.

45-2099.99 Agricultural Workers, All Other

- **Education/Training Required: No data available**
- **Employed: 8,970**
- **Annual Earnings: $22,060**
- **Growth: 4.3%**
- **Annual Job Openings: 3,000**

All agricultural workers not listed separately.

No task data available.

Note: The Department of Labor has not collected some data for this job, so it has fewer details than the other descriptions.

Related SOC Job—45-2099 Agricultural Workers, All Other. **Related OOH Job**—Agricultural Workers. **Related DOT Jobs**—408.381-010 Scout; 408.687-010 Field Inspector, Disease And Insect Control; 413.687-010 Worm Picker.

45-3000 Fishing and Hunting Workers

45-3011.00 Fishers and Related Fishing Workers

- **Education/Training Required: Moderate-term on-the-job training**
- **Employed: 770**
- **Annual Earnings: $25,130**
- **Growth: −17.2%**
- **Annual Job Openings: 6,000**

Use nets, fishing rods, traps, or other equipment to catch and gather fish or other aquatic animals from rivers, lakes, or oceans for human consumption or other uses. May haul game onto ship.

Locate fish, using fish-finding equipment. Plan fishing operations, establishing the fish to be sought, the fishing location, the method of capture, and the duration of the trip. Wash decks, conveyors, knives, and other equipment, using brushes, detergents, and water. Compute positions and plot courses on charts to navigate vessels, using instruments such as compasses, sextants, and charts. Steer vessels and operate navigational instruments. Stand lookout for schools of fish and for steering and engine-room watches. Sort, pack, and store catch in holds with salt and ice. Signal other workers to move, hoist, and position loads. Pull and guide nets, traps, and lines onto vessels by hand or using hoisting equipment. Put fishing equipment into the water and anchor or tow equipment according to the fishing method used. Remove catches from fishing equipment and measure them to ensure compliance with legal size. Load and unload vessel equipment and supplies by hand or using hoisting equipment. Attach nets, slings, hooks, blades, or lifting devices to cables, booms, hoists, or dredges. Return undesirable or illegal catches to the water. Interpret weather and vessel conditions to determine appropriate responses. Club or gaff large fish to enable hauling them into fishing vessel. Harvest marine life for human or animal consumption, using diving or dredging equipment, traps, barges, rods, reels, or tackle. Connect accessories such as floats, weights, flags, lights, or markers to nets, lines, or traps. Transport fish to processing plants or to buyers. Direct fishing operations and supervise fishing crew members. Estimate costs of operations and plan fishing season budgets accordingly. Hire qualified crew members and assign their duties. Participate in wildlife management, disease control, and research activities. Sell catches by contacting and negotiating with buyers or by sending catches to fish auctions. Operate rowboats, dinghies, or skiffs to transport fishers, divers, or sponge hookers or to tow and position fishing equipment. Maintain engines, fishing gear, and other on-board equipment and perform minor repairs. Monitor distribution of proceeds from sales of catches to ensure that crew members receive their prearranged portions. Oversee the purchase of supplies, gear, and equipment such as fuel, netting, and cables.

Record in logbooks specifics of fishing activities such as dates, harvest areas, yields, and weather and sea conditions.

GOE Information—Interest Area: 01. Agriculture and Natural Resources. **Work Group:** 01.07. Hunting and Fishing. **Personality Type—**Realistic. Realistic occupations frequently involve work activities that include practical, hands-on problems and solutions. They often deal with plants; animals; and real-world materials like wood, tools, and machinery. Many of the occupations require working outside and do not involve a lot of paperwork or working closely with others. **Work Values—**None met the criteria. **Skills—**Repairing; Equipment Maintenance. **Abilities—***Cognitive:* Spatial Orientation. *Psychomotor:* Wrist-Finger Speed; Speed of Limb Movement; Multilimb Coordination; Manual Dexterity; Rate Control; Response Orientation. *Physical:* Static Strength; Dynamic Strength; Extent Flexibility; Trunk Strength; Stamina. *Sensory:* Far Vision; Depth Perception. **General Work Activities—***Information Input:* Identifying Objects, Actions, and Events; Monitoring Processes, Materials, or Surroundings; Inspecting Equipment, Structures, or Materials. *Mental Process:* Organizing, Planning, and Prioritizing; Judging the Qualities of Things, Services, or Other People's Work. *Work Output:* Performing General Physical Activities; Handling and Moving Objects; Operating Vehicles or Equipment. *Interacting with Others:* Resolving Conflicts and Negotiating with Others; Influencing Others or Selling; Communicating with Persons Outside Organization. **Physical Work Conditions—**Outdoors; Contaminants; Minor Burns, Cuts, Bites, or Stings; Standing; Using Hands on Objects, Tools, or Controls. **Other Job Characteristics—**None met the criteria.

Experience—Job Zone 1. No previous work-related skill, knowledge, or experience is needed. **Job Preparation—**SVP below 4.0—less than six months. **Knowledges—**Food Production; Transportation; Biology. **Instructional Program—**Fishing and Fisheries Sciences and Management.

Related SOC Job—45-3011 Fishers and Related Fishing Workers. **Related OOH Job—**Fishers and Fishing Vessel Operators. **Related DOT Jobs—**441.132-010 Boatswain, Otter Trawler; 441.683-010 Skiff Operator; 441.684-010 Fisher, Net; 441.684-014 Fisher, Pot; 441.684-018 Fisher, Terrapin; 441.684-022 Fisher, Weir; 442.684-010 Fisher, Line; 443.664-010 Fisher, Diving; 443.684-010 Fisher, Spear; 446.161-014 Shellfish Grower; 446.663-010 Shellfish Dredge Operator; 446.684-014 Shellfish-Bed Worker; 447.684-010 Sponge Hooker; 447.687-010 Dulser; 447.687-014 Irish-Moss Bleacher; 447.687-018 Irish-Moss Gatherer; 447.687-022 Kelp Cutter; others.

45-3021.00 Hunters and Trappers

- **Education/Training Required: Moderate-term on-the-job training**
- **Employed: 1,115**
- **Annual Earnings: No data available**
- **Growth: 5.2%**
- **Annual Job Openings: Fewer than 500**

Hunt and trap wild animals for human consumption, fur, feed, bait, or other purposes.

Kill or stun trapped quarry, using clubs, poisons, guns, or drowning methods. Secure identification tags to quarry to track migratory movements of released quarry. Remove designated parts such as ears or tails from slain quarry as evidence for killing bounty, using knives. Teach or guide individuals or groups unfamiliar with specific hunting methods or types of prey. Restrain quarry with arms or nets and rig nets or slings under catch to permit hoisting without bodily injury. Scrape fat, blubber, or flesh from skin sides of pelts with knives or hand scrapers. Cure pelts with salt and boric acid. Skin quarry, using knives, and stretch pelts on frames to be cured. Train dogs for hunting. Wash and sort pelts according to species, color, and quality. Publicize hunting activities by writing for outdoor magazines or by making videos of their hunts. Trap and capture quarry dead or alive for identification, relocation, or sale, using baited, scented, or camouflaged traps, snares, cages, or nets. Cut walk tracks for better access to traps and bait stations. Release quarry from traps or nets and transfer to cages. Participate in animal damage control, wildlife management, disease control, and research activities. Mix baits for attracting animals. Pack pelts in containers, load containers onto trucks, and transport pelts to processing plants or to public auctions. Select, bait, and set traps and lay poison along trails, according to species, size, habits, and environs of birds or animals and reasons for trapping them. Maintain and repair trapping equipment. Travel on foot or by using vehicles or equipment such as boats, snowmobiles, helicopters, snowshoes, or skis to reach hunting areas. Drive quarry into traps, nets, or killing areas, using dogs or prods. Track animals by checking for signs such as droppings or destruction of vegetation. Decide where to set traps, using grid maps and aerial maps of hunting areas. Patrol trap lines or nets to inspect settings, remove catch, and reset or relocate traps. Obtain required approvals for using poisons or traps and notify persons in areas where traps and poison are set.

GOE Information—Interest Area: 01. Agriculture and Natural Resources. **Work Group:** 01.07. Hunting and Fishing. **Personality Type—**Realistic. Realistic occupations frequently involve work activities that include practical, hands-on problems and solutions. They often deal with plants; animals; and real-world materials like wood, tools, and machinery. Many of the occupations require working outside and do not involve a lot of paperwork or working closely with others. **Work Values—**Independence; Autonomy; Variety. **Skills—**None met the criteria. **Abilities—***Cognitive:* Spatial Orientation; Flexibility of Closure. *Psychomotor:* Speed of Limb Movement; Wrist-Finger Speed; Reaction Time; Manual Dexterity; Arm-Hand Steadiness; Multilimb Coordination. *Physical:* Explosive Strength; Static Strength; Dynamic Strength; Gross Body Equilibrium; Gross Body Coordination; Stamina. *Sensory:* Night Vision; Peripheral Vision; Depth Perception; Sound Localization; Visual Color Discrimination; Far Vision. **General Work Activities—***Information Input:* Getting Information; Monitoring Processes, Materials, or Surroundings; Identifying Objects, Actions, and Events. *Mental Process:* Judging the Qualities of Things, Services, or Other People's Work; Organizing, Planning, and Prioritizing; Making Decisions and Solving Problems. *Work Output:* Handling and Moving Objects; Performing General Physical Activities; Controlling Machines and Processes. *Interacting with Others:* None met the criteria. **Physical Work Conditions—**Outdoors; Minor Burns, Cuts, Bites, or Stings; Standing; Kneeling, Crouching, Stooping, or Crawling; Using Hands on Objects, Tools, or Controls. **Other Job Characteristics—**None met the criteria.

Experience—Job Zone 2. Some previous work-related skill, knowledge, or experience may be helpful in these occupations, but usually is not needed. **Job Preparation—**SVP 4.0 to less than 6.0—six months to less than two years. **Knowledges—**Food Production; Sales and Security. **Instructional Program—**No related CIP programs.

Related SOC Job—45-3021 Hunters and Trappers. **Related OOH Job—**Hunters and Trappers. **Related DOT Jobs—**461.134-010 Expedition Supervisor; 461.661-010 Predatory-Animal Hunter; 461.664-010 Underwater Hunter-Trapper; 461.684-010 Sealer; 461.684-014 Trapper, Animal; 461.684-018 Trapper, Bird.

45-4000 Forest, Conservation, and Logging Workers

45-4011.00 Forest and Conservation Workers

- **Education/Training Required: Moderate-term on-the-job training**
- **Employed: 8,700**
- **Annual Earnings: $19,680**
- **Growth: 6.0%**
- **Annual Job Openings: 2,000**

Under supervision, perform manual labor necessary to develop, maintain, or protect forest, forested areas, and woodlands through such activities as raising and transporting tree seedlings; combating insects, pests, and diseases harmful to trees; and building erosion and water control structures and leaching of forest soil. Includes forester aides, seedling pullers, and tree planters.

Check equipment to ensure that it is operating properly. Confer with other workers to discuss issues such as safety, cutting heights, and work needs. Fight forest fires or perform prescribed burning tasks under the direction of fire suppression officers or forestry technicians. Perform fire protection and suppression duties such as constructing fire breaks and disposing of brush. Select and cut trees according to markings or sizes, types, and grades. Identify diseased or undesirable trees and remove them, using power saws or handsaws. Spray or inject vegetation with insecticides to kill insects and to protect against disease and with herbicides to reduce competing vegetation. Drag cut trees from cutting areas and load trees onto trucks. Thin and space trees, using power thinning saws. Maintain tallies of trees examined and counted during tree marking and measuring efforts. Gather, package, and deliver forest products to buyers. Erect signs and fences, using posthole diggers, shovels, or other hand tools. Prune or shear tree tops and limbs to control growth, increase density, and improve shape. Select tree seedlings, prepare the ground, and plant the trees in reforestation areas, using manual planting tools. Provide assistance to forest survey crews by clearing site-lines, holding measuring tools, and setting stakes. Explain and enforce regulations regarding camping, vehicle use, fires, use of building, and sanitation. Operate a skidder, bulldozer, or other prime mover to pull a variety of scarification or site preparation equipment over areas to be regenerated. Examine and grade trees according to standard charts and staple color-coded grade tags to limbs. Sort and separate tree seedlings, discarding substandard seedlings, according to standard charts and verbal instructions. Maintain campsites and recreational areas, replenishing firewood and other supplies and cleaning kitchens and restrooms. Sow and harvest cover crops such as alfalfa.

GOE Information—**Interest Area:** 01. Agriculture and Natural Resources. **Work Group:** 01.06. Forestry and Logging. **Personality Type**—Realistic. Realistic occupations frequently involve work activities that include practical, hands-on problems and solutions. They often deal with plants; animals; and real-world materials like wood, tools, and machinery. Many of the occupations require working outside and do not involve a lot of paperwork or working closely with others. **Work Values**—Independence; Achievement; Moral Values; Variety. **Skills**—Science; Management of Financial Resources; Management of Personnel Resources; Equipment Maintenance; Systems Analysis; Equipment Selection. **Abilities**—*Cognitive:* Spatial Orientation; Perceptual Speed; Number Facility; Time Sharing.

Psychomotor: Multilimb Coordination; Control Precision; Speed of Limb Movement; Rate Control; Response Orientation; Manual Dexterity. *Physical:* Static Strength; Dynamic Strength; Stamina; Trunk Strength; Gross Body Coordination; Extent Flexibility. *Sensory:* Depth Perception; Hearing Sensitivity; Visual Color Discrimination; Far Vision; Auditory Attention. **General Work Activities**—*Information Input:* Identifying Objects, Actions, and Events; Estimating the Needed Characteristics of Products, Events, or Information; Monitoring Processes, Materials, or Surroundings. *Mental Process:* Organizing, Planning, and Prioritizing; Making Decisions and Solving Problems; Evaluating Information Against Standards. *Work Output:* Handling and Moving Objects; Performing General Physical Activities; Controlling Machines and Processes. *Interacting with Others:* Coordinating the Work and Activities of Others; Communicating with Other Workers; Establishing and Maintaining Interpersonal Relationships. **Physical Work Conditions**—Outdoors; Noisy; Very Hot or Cold; Minor Burns, Cuts, Bites, or Stings; Using Hands on Objects, Tools, or Controls; Repetitive Motions. **Other Job Characteristics**—Need to Be Exact or Accurate; Errors Have Important Consequences; Pace Determined by Speed of Equipment; Repeat Same Tasks.

Experience—Job Zone 3. Previous work-related skill, knowledge, or experience is required. **Job Preparation**—SVP 6.0 to less than 7.0—more than one year and less than four years. **Knowledges**—Biology; Geography; Transportation; Production and Processing; Mechanical Devices; Personnel and Human Resources. **Instructional Programs**—Forest Management/Forest Resources Management; Forest Resources Production and Management; Forest Sciences; Forestry, General; Forestry, Other; Natural Resources and Conservation, Other; Natural Resources Management and Policy, Other; Natural Resources/Conservation, General; Urban Forestry; Wood Science and Wood Products/Pulp and Paper Technology.

Related SOC Job—45-4011 Forest and Conservation Workers. **Related OOH Job**—Forest, Conservation, and Logging Workers. **Related DOT Jobs**—451.687-010 Christmas-Tree Farm Worker; 451.687-014 Christmas-Tree Grader; 451.687-018 Seedling Puller; 451.687-022 Seedling Sorter; 452.687-010 Forest Worker; 452.687-018 Tree Planter; 453.687-010 Forest-Products Gatherer; 453.687-014 Laborer, Tree Tapping.

45-4021.00 Fallers

- **Education/Training Required: Moderate-term on-the-job training**
- **Employed: 9,780**
- **Annual Earnings: $28,360**
- **Growth: –5.7%**
- **Annual Job Openings: 3,000**

Use axes or chain saws to fell trees, using knowledge of tree characteristics and cutting techniques to control direction of fall and minimize tree damage.

Control the direction of a tree's fall by scoring cutting lines with axes, sawing undercuts along scored lines with chain saws, knocking slabs from cuts with single-bit axes, and driving wedges. Tag unsafe trees with high-visibility ribbons. Mark logs for identification. Work as a member of a team, rotating between chain saw operation and skidder operation. Maintain and repair chain saws and other equipment, cleaning, oiling, and greasing equipment and sharpening equipment properly. Appraise trees for certain characteristics, such as twist, rot, and heavy limb growth, and gauge amount and direction of lean in order to determine how to control the direction of a tree's fall with the least damage. Secure steel cables or chains to logs for dragging by tractors or for pulling by cable yarding systems. Measure felled trees and cut them into specified log lengths, using chain saws and axes. Clear brush from work areas and escape routes and cut saplings and other trees from direction of falls, using axes, chain saws, or bulldozers. Insert jacks or drive wedges behind saws to prevent binding of saws and to start trees falling. Load logs or wood onto trucks, trailers, or railroad cars by hand or using loaders or winches. Assess logs after cutting to ensure that the quality and length are correct. Assemble floating logs into rafts for towing to mills. Trim off the tops and limbs of trees, using chain saws, delimbers, or axes. Stop saw engines, pull cutting bars from cuts, and run to safety as tree falls. Place supporting limbs or poles under felled trees to avoid splitting undersides and to prevent logs from rolling. Saw back-cuts, leaving sufficient sound wood to control direction of fall. Select trees to be cut down, assessing factors such as site, terrain, and weather conditions before beginning work. Split logs, using axes, wedges, and mauls, and stack wood in ricks or cord lots. Determine position, direction, and depth of cuts to be made and placement of wedges or jacks.

GOE Information—Interest Area: 01. Agriculture and Natural Resources. **Work Group:** 01.06. Forestry and Logging. **Personality Type**—Realistic. Realistic occupations frequently involve work activities that include practical, hands-on problems and solutions. They often deal with plants; animals; and real-world materials like wood, tools, and machinery. Many of the occupations require working outside and do not involve a lot of paperwork or working closely with others. **Work Values**—Moral Values; Supervision, Technical; Activity. **Skills**—None met the criteria. **Abilities**—*Cognitive:* Spatial Orientation; Visualization; Time Sharing. *Psychomotor:* Speed of Limb Movement; Wrist-Finger Speed; Reaction Time; Control Precision; Multilimb Coordination; Manual Dexterity. *Physical:* Explosive Strength; Static Strength; Dynamic Strength; Dynamic Flexibility; Stamina; Extent Flexibility. *Sensory:* Peripheral Vision; Depth Perception; Sound Localization; Far Vision. **General Work Activities**—*Information Input:* Identifying Objects, Actions, and Events; Estimating the Needed Characteristics of Products, Events, or Information; Getting Information. *Mental Process:* Judging the Qualities of Things, Services, or Other People's Work; Making Decisions and Solving Problems. *Work Output:* Performing General Physical Activities; Handling and Moving Objects; Operating Vehicles or Equipment. *Interacting with Others:* None met the criteria. **Physical Work Conditions**—Outdoors; Whole-Body Vibration; Hazardous Equipment; Minor Burns, Cuts, Bites, or Stings; Standing; Using Hands on Objects, Tools, or Controls. **Other Job Characteristics**—None met the criteria.

Experience—Job Zone 1. No previous work-related skill, knowledge, or experience is needed. **Job Preparation**—SVP below 4.0—less than six months. **Knowledges**—Mechanical Devices; Public Safety and Security. **Instructional Program**—Forest Resources Production and Management.

Related SOC Job—45-4021 Fallers. **Related OOH Job**—Forest, Conservation, and Logging Workers. **Related DOT Jobs**—454.384-010 Faller I; 454.684-010 Bucker; 454.684-014 Faller II; 454.684-018 Logger, All-Round; 454.684-026 Tree Cutter; 454.687-010 Chain Saw Operator.

45-4022.00 Logging Equipment Operators

- **Education/Training Required: Moderate-term on-the-job training**
- **Employed: 26,880**
- **Annual Earnings: $28,920**
- **Growth: 3.4%**
- **Annual Job Openings: 9,000**

Drive logging tractor or wheeled vehicle equipped with one or more accessories, such as bulldozer blade, frontal shear, grapple, logging arch, cable winches, hoisting rack, or crane boom, to fell tree; to skid, load, unload, or stack logs; or to pull stumps or clear brush.

Inspect equipment for safety prior to use and perform necessary basic maintenance tasks. Drive straight or articulated tractors equipped with accessories such as bulldozer blades, grapples, logging arches, cable winches, and crane booms to skid, load, unload, or stack logs; pull stumps; or clear brush. Drive crawler or wheeled tractors to drag or transport logs from felling sites to log landing areas for processing and loading. Drive tractors for the purpose of building or repairing logging and skid roads. Grade logs according to characteristics such as knot size and straightness and according to established industry or company standards. Control hydraulic tractors equipped with tree clamps and booms to lift, swing, and bunch sheared trees. Drive and maneuver tractors and tree harvesters to shear the tops off of trees, cut and limb the trees, and then cut the logs into desired lengths. Fill out required job or shift report forms. Calculate total board feet, cordage, or other wood measurement units, using conversion tables.

GOE Information—Interest Area: 01. Agriculture and Natural Resources. **Work Group:** 01.06. Forestry and Logging. **Personality Type**—Realistic. Realistic occupations frequently involve work activities that include practical, hands-on problems and solutions. They often deal with plants; animals; and real-world materials like wood, tools, and machinery. Many of the occupations require working outside and do not involve a lot of paperwork or working closely with others. **Work Values**—Moral Values; Supervision, Technical; Co-workers. **Skills**—Repairing; Equipment Maintenance; Operation Monitoring; Troubleshooting; Operation and Control; Installation. **Abilities**—*Cognitive:* Spatial Orientation. *Psychomotor:* Control Precision; Wrist-Finger Speed; Multilimb Coordination; Manual Dexterity. *Physical:* Extent Flexibility; Trunk Strength; Gross Body Coordination; Static Strength. *Sensory:* Depth Perception. **General Work Activities**—*Information Input:* Monitoring Processes, Materials, or Surroundings; Identifying Objects, Actions, and Events; Inspecting Equipment, Structures, or Materials. *Mental Process:* Organizing, Planning, and Prioritizing; Judging the Qualities of Things, Services, or Other People's Work; Making Decisions and Solving Problems. *Work Output:* Controlling Machines and Processes; Operating Vehicles or Equipment; Repairing and Maintaining Mechanical Equipment. *Interacting with Others:* Communicating with Other Workers; Assisting and Caring for Others; Establishing and Maintaining Interpersonal Relationships. **Physical Work Conditions**—Outdoors; Noisy; Contaminants; Hazardous Equipment; Sitting; Using Hands on Objects, Tools, or Controls. **Other Job Characteristics**—Errors Have Important Consequences; Pace Determined by Speed of Equipment; Need to Be Exact or Accurate.

Experience—Job Zone 1. No previous work-related skill, knowledge, or experience is needed. **Job Preparation**—SVP below 4.0—less than six months. **Knowledges**—Mechanical Devices; Transportation; Production and Processing; Public Safety and Security; Administration and Management. **Instructional Program**—Forest Resources Production and Management.

Related SOC Job—45-4022 Logging Equipment Operators. **Related OOH Job**—Forest, Conservation, and Logging Workers. **Related DOT Jobs**—454.683-010 Tree-Shear Operator; 929.663-010 Logging-Tractor Operator.

45-4023.00 Log Graders and Scalers

- **Education/Training Required: Moderate-term on-the-job training**
- **Employed: 4,520**
- **Annual Earnings: $27,680**
- **Growth: 1.7%**
- **Annual Job Openings: 2,000**

Grade logs or estimate the marketable content or value of logs or pulpwood in sorting yards, millpond, log deck, or similar locations. Inspect logs for defects or measure logs to determine volume.

Evaluate log characteristics and determine grades, using established criteria. Record data about individual trees or load volumes into tally books or hand-held collection terminals. Paint identification marks of specified colors on logs to identify grades or species, using spray cans, or call out grades to log markers. Measure felled logs or loads of pulpwood to calculate volume, weight, dimensions, and marketable value, using measuring devices and conversion tables. Measure log lengths and mark boles for bucking into logs according to specifications. Identify logs of substandard or special grade so that they can be returned to shippers, regraded, recut, or transferred for other processing. Jab logs with metal ends of scale sticks and inspect logs to ascertain characteristics or defects such as water damage, splits, knots, broken ends, rotten areas, twists, and curves. Drive to sawmills, wharfs, or skids to inspect logs or pulpwood. Communicate with co-workers by using signals to direct log movement. Weigh log trucks before and after unloading and record load weights and supplier identities. Saw felled trees into lengths. Tend conveyor chains that move logs to and from scaling stations.

GOE Information—**Interest Area:** 01. Agriculture and Natural Resources. **Work Group:** 01.06. Forestry and Logging. **Personality Type**—Realistic. Realistic occupations frequently involve work activities that include practical, hands-on problems and solutions. They often deal with plants; animals; and real-world materials like wood, tools, and machinery. Many of the occupations require working outside and do not involve a lot of paperwork or working closely with others. **Work Values**—Independence; Moral Values; Supervision, Technical; Responsibility. **Skills**—Management of Material Resources; Management of Financial Resources; Negotiation; Equipment Maintenance; Operations Analysis; Repairing. **Abilities**—*Cognitive:* Spatial Orientation; Flexibility of Closure; Category Flexibility; Perceptual Speed; Number Facility; Time Sharing. *Psychomotor:* Control Precision; Multilimb Coordination; Reaction Time;

Arm-Hand Steadiness; Manual Dexterity; Finger Dexterity. *Physical:* Static Strength. *Sensory:* Visual Color Discrimination; Auditory Attention; Depth Perception; Far Vision; Near Vision. **General Work Activities**—*Information Input:* Monitoring Processes, Materials, or Surroundings; Estimating the Needed Characteristics of Products, Events, or Information; Getting Information. *Mental Process:* Organizing, Planning, and Prioritizing; Making Decisions and Solving Problems; Processing Information. *Work Output:* Handling and Moving Objects; Performing General Physical Activities; Operating Vehicles or Equipment. *Interacting with Others:* Communicating with Other Workers; Performing for or Working with the Public; Establishing and Maintaining Interpersonal Relationships. **Physical Work Conditions**—Outdoors; Noisy; Very Hot or Cold; Hazardous Equipment; Standing; Walking and Running. **Other Job Characteristics**—Need to Be Exact or Accurate; Repeat Same Tasks.

Experience—Job Zone 3. Previous work-related skill, knowledge, or experience is required. **Job Preparation**—SVP 6.0 to less than 7.0—more than one year and less than four years. **Knowledges**—Production and Processing; Mathematics; Sales and Marketing; Administration and Management; Transportation; Clerical Practices. **Instructional Program**—Forest Resources Production and Management.

Related SOC Job—45-4023 Log Graders and Scalers. **Related OOH Job**—Forest, Conservation, and Logging Workers. **Related DOT Jobs**—455.367-010 Log Grader; 455.487-010 Log Scaler.

45-4029.99 Logging Workers, All Other

- **Education/Training Required: Moderate-term on-the-job training**
- **Employed: 7,146**
- **Annual Earnings: $31,690**
- **Growth: –4.2%**
- **Annual Job Openings: 1,000**

All logging workers not listed separately.

No task data available.

Note: The Department of Labor has not collected some data for this job, so it has fewer details than the other descriptions.

Related SOC Job—45-4029 Logging Workers, All Other. **Related OOH Job**—Forest, Conservation, and Logging Workers. **Related DOT Jobs**—168.267-070 Logging-Operations Inspector; 454.687-018 Log Marker; 455.664-010 Rafter; 455.684-010 Log Sorter; 455.687-010 Log Marker; 459.387-010 Cruiser; 669.485-010 Power-Barker Operator; 669.687-022 Picker; 921.364-010 Rigging Slinger; 921.667-014 Chaser; 921.686-018 Log-Haul Chain Feeder; 921.686-022 Pond Worker; 921.687-014 Choke Setter; 921.687-022 Log Loader Helper; 921.687-030 Rigger, Third; 922.687-082 Pulp Piler.

47-0000
Construction and Extraction Occupations

47-1000 Supervisors, Construction and Extraction Workers

47-1011.00 First-Line Supervisors/ Managers of Construction Trades and Extraction Workers

- Education/Training Required: Work experience in a related occupation
- Employed: 555,380
- Annual Earnings: $51,970
- Growth: 10.9%
- Annual Job Openings: 57,000

Directly supervise and coordinate activities of construction or extraction workers.

Examine and inspect work progress, equipment, and construction sites to verify safety and to ensure that specifications are met. Read specifications such as blueprints to determine construction requirements and to plan procedures. Estimate material and worker requirements to complete jobs. Supervise, coordinate, and schedule the activities of construction or extractive workers. Confer with managerial and technical personnel, other departments, and contractors to resolve problems and to coordinate activities. Coordinate work activities with other construction project activities. Locate, measure, and mark site locations and placement of structures and equipment, using measuring and marking equipment. Order or requisition materials and supplies. Record information such as personnel, production, and operational data on specified forms and reports. Assign work to employees based on material and worker requirements of specific jobs. Provide assistance to workers engaged in construction or extraction activities, using hand tools and equipment. Train workers in construction methods, operation of equipment, safety procedures, and company policies. Analyze worker and production problems and recommend solutions, such as improving production methods or implementing motivational plans. Arrange for repairs of equipment and machinery. Suggest or initiate personnel actions such as promotions, transfers, and hires.

GOE Information—Interest Area: 01. Agriculture and Natural Resources. **Work Group:** 01.01. Managerial Work in Agriculture and Natural Resources. **Personality Type**—Enterprising. Enterprising occupations frequently involve starting up and carrying out projects. These occupations can involve leading people and making many decisions. They sometimes require risk taking and often deal with business. **Work Values**—Authority; Responsibility; Autonomy; Variety; Co-workers; Social Status. **Skills**—Management of Material Resources; Installation; Equipment Maintenance; Coordination; Repairing; Management of Personnel Resources. **Abilities**—*Cognitive:* Visualization; Number Facility; Perceptual Speed; Time Sharing; Originality; Fluency of Ideas. *Psychomotor:* Multilimb Coordination; Control Precision; Manual Dexterity; Finger Dexterity; Arm-Hand Steadiness. *Physical:* None met the criteria. *Sensory:* Depth Perception; Hearing Sensitivity; Visual Color Discrimination; Far Vision; Auditory Attention. **General Work Activities**—*Information Input:* Monitoring Processes, Materials, or Surroundings; Inspecting Equipment, Structures, or Materials; Identifying Objects, Actions, and Events. *Mental Process:* Organizing, Planning, and Prioritizing; Scheduling Work and Activities; Making Decisions and Solving

Problems. *Work Output:* Handling and Moving Objects; Performing General Physical Activities; Documenting or Recording Information. *Interacting with Others:* Guiding, Directing, and Motivating Subordinates; Coordinating the Work and Activities of Others; Establishing and Maintaining Interpersonal Relationships. **Physical Work Conditions**—Outdoors; Noisy; Very Hot or Cold; Contaminants; Hazardous Equipment; Standing. **Other Job Characteristics**—Need to Be Exact or Accurate; Errors Have Important Consequences; Repeat Same Tasks.

Experience—Job Zone 3. Previous work-related skill, knowledge, or experience is required. **Job Preparation**—SVP 6.0 to less than 7.0—more than one year and less than four years. **Knowledges**—Building and Construction; Mechanical Devices; Design; Engineering and Technology; Administration and Management; Production and Processing. **Instructional Programs**—Blasting/Blaster; Building/Construction Finishing, Management, and Inspection, Other; Building/Construction Site Management/Manager; Building/Construction Trades, Other; Building/Home/Construction Inspection/Inspector; Building/Property Maintenance and Management; Carpentry/Carpenter; Concrete Finishing/Concrete Finisher; Drywall Installation/Drywaller; Electrical and Power Transmission Installation/Installer, General; Electrical and Power Transmission Installer, Other; Electrician; Glazier; Lineworker; Masonry/Mason; Painting/Painter and Wall Coverer; Plumbing Technology/Plumber; Roofer; Well Drilling/Driller.

Related SOC Job—47-1011 First-Line Supervisors/Managers of Construction Trades and Extraction Workers. **Related OOH Job**—First-Line Supervisors/Managers of Construction Trades and Extraction Workers. **Related DOT Jobs**—184.167-234 Supervisor of Way; 801.131-010 Supervisor, Chimney Construction; 801.134-010 Supervisor, Reinforced-Steel-Placing; 809.131-014 Supervisor, Ornamental Ironworking; 809.131-018 Supervisor, Structural-Steel Erection; 821.131-022 Steel-Post-Installer Supervisor; 824.137-010 Electrician, Chief; 825.131-010 Electrician Supervisor; 829.131-014 Electrician Supervisor; 840.131-010 Supervisor, Painting; 840.131-014 Supervisor, Painting, Shipyard; 841.137-010 Supervisor, Billposting; others.

47-2000 Construction Trades Workers

47-2011.00 Boilermakers

- Education/Training Required: Long-term on-the-job training
- Employed: 17,760
- Annual Earnings: $48,050
- Growth: 8.7%
- Annual Job Openings: 2,000

Construct, assemble, maintain, and repair stationary steam boilers and boiler house auxiliaries. Align structures or plate sections to assemble boiler frame tanks or vats, following blueprints. Work involves use of hand and power tools, plumb bobs, levels, wedges, dogs, or turnbuckles. Assist in testing assembled vessels. Direct cleaning of boilers and boiler furnaces. Inspect and repair boiler fittings, such as safety valves, regulators, automatic-control mechanisms, water columns, and auxiliary machines.

Bolt or arc-weld pressure vessel structures and parts together, using wrenches and welding equipment. Examine boilers, pressure vessels, tanks, and vats to locate defects such as leaks, weak spots, and defective sections so that they can be repaired. Repair or replace defective pressure vessel parts, such as safety valves and regulators, using torches, jacks, caulking hammers, power saws, threading dies, welding equipment, and metalworking machinery. Inspect assembled vessels and individual components, such as tubes, fittings, valves, controls, and auxiliary mechanisms, to locate any defects. Attach rigging and signal crane or hoist operators to lift heavy frame and plate sections and other parts into place. Bell, bead with power hammers, or weld pressure vessel tube ends to ensure leakproof joints. Lay out plate, sheet steel, or other heavy metal and locate and mark bending and cutting lines, using protractors, compasses, and drawing instruments or templates. Install manholes, handholes, taps, tubes, valves, gauges, and feedwater connections in drums of water tube boilers, using hand tools. Study blueprints to determine locations, relationships, and dimensions of parts. Straighten or reshape bent pressure vessel plates and structure parts, using hammers, jacks, and torches. Shape seams, joints, and irregular edges of pressure vessel sections and structural parts to attain specified fit of parts, using cutting torches, hammers, files, and metalworking machines. Position, align, and secure structural parts and related assemblies to boiler frames, tanks, or vats of pressure vessels, following blueprints. Locate and mark reference points for columns or plates on boiler foundations, following blueprints and using straightedges, squares, transits, and measuring instruments. Shape and fabricate parts, such as stacks, uptakes, and chutes, to adapt pressure vessels, heat exchangers, and piping to premises, using heavy-metalworking machines such as brakes, rolls, and drill presses. Clean pressure vessel equipment, using scrapers, wire brushes, and cleaning solvents.

GOE Information—Interest Area: 02. Architecture and Construction. **Work Group:** 02.04. Construction Crafts. **Personality Type**—Realistic. Realistic occupations frequently involve work activities that include practical, hands-on problems and solutions. They often deal with plants; animals; and real-world materials like wood, tools, and machinery. Many of the occupations require working outside and do not involve a lot of paperwork or working closely with others. **Work Values**—Supervision, Technical; Moral Values; Supervision, Human Relations; Compensation; Creativity; Company Policies and Practices. **Skills**—Repairing; Installation; Equipment Maintenance; Operation Monitoring; Troubleshooting; Mathematics. **Abilities**—*Cognitive:* Perceptual Speed; Visualization; Time Sharing; Speed of Closure; Flexibility of Closure. *Psychomotor:* Reaction Time; Rate Control; Response Orientation; Control Precision; Multilimb Coordination; Arm-Hand Steadiness. *Physical:* Extent Flexibility; Gross Body Equilibrium; Gross Body Coordination; Stamina; Static Strength; Trunk Strength. *Sensory:* Depth Perception; Hearing Sensitivity; Auditory Attention; Visual Color Discrimination; Far Vision. **General Work Activities**—*Information Input:* Monitoring Processes, Materials, or Surroundings; Identifying Objects, Actions, and Events; Inspecting Equipment, Structures, or Materials. *Mental Process:* Organizing, Planning, and Prioritizing; Scheduling Work and Activities; Updating and Using Relevant Knowledge. *Work Output:* Handling and Moving Objects; Performing General Physical Activities; Repairing and Maintaining Mechanical Equipment. *Interacting with Others:* Communicating with Other Workers; Coordinating the Work and Activities of Others; Establishing and Maintaining Interpersonal Relationships. **Physical Work Conditions**—Noisy; Very Hot or Cold; Contaminants; Minor Burns, Cuts, Bites, or Stings; Using Hands on Objects, Tools, or Controls. **Other Job Characteristics**—Need to Be Exact or Accurate; Errors Have Important Consequences.

Experience—Job Zone 2. Some previous work-related skill, knowledge, or experience may be helpful in these occupations, but usually

is not needed. **Job Preparation**—SVP 4.0 to less than 6.0—six months to less than two years. **Knowledges**—Building and Construction; Mechanical Devices; Engineering and Technology; Design; Physics; Transportation. **Instructional Program**—Boilermaking/Boilermaker.

Related SOC Job—47-2011 Boilermakers. **Related OOH Job**—Boilermakers. **Related DOT Jobs**—805.261-010 Boilermaker Apprentice; 805.261-014 Boilermaker I; 805.361-010 Boilerhouse Mechanic; 805.361-014 Boilermaker Fitter; 805.381-010 Boilermaker II.

47-2021.00 Brickmasons and Blockmasons

- **Education/Training Required: Long-term on-the-job training**
- **Employed: 115,950**
- **Annual Earnings: $41,860**
- **Growth: 12.0%**
- **Annual Job Openings: 17,000**

Lay and bind building materials, such as brick, structural tile, concrete block, cinderblock, glass block, and terra-cotta block, with mortar and other substances to construct or repair walls, partitions, arches, sewers, and other structures.

Construct corners by fastening in plumb position a corner pole or building a corner pyramid of bricks and filling in between the corners, using a line from corner to corner to guide each course, or layer, of brick. Measure distance from reference points and mark guidelines to lay out work, using plumb bobs and levels. Fasten or fuse brick or other building material to structure with wire clamps, anchor holes, torch, or cement. Calculate angles and courses and determine vertical and horizontal alignment of courses. Break or cut bricks, tiles, or blocks to size, using trowel edge, hammer, or power saw. Remove excess mortar with trowels and hand tools and finish mortar joints with jointing tools for a sealed, uniform appearance. Interpret blueprints and drawings to determine specifications and to calculate the materials required. Apply and smooth mortar or other mixture over work surface. Mix specified amounts of sand, clay, dirt, or mortar powder with water to form refractory mixtures. Examine brickwork or structure to determine need for repair. Clean working surface to remove scale, dust, soot, or chips of brick and mortar, using broom, wire brush, or scraper. Lay and align bricks, blocks, or tiles to build or repair structures or high-temperature equipment, such as cupola, kilns, ovens, or furnaces. Remove burned or damaged brick or mortar, using sledgehammer, crowbar, chipping gun, or chisel. Spray or spread refractory material over brickwork to protect against deterioration.

GOE Information—Interest Area: 02. Architecture and Construction. **Work Group:** 02.04. Construction Crafts. **Personality Type**—Realistic. Realistic occupations frequently involve work activities that include practical, hands-on problems and solutions. They often deal with plants; animals; and real-world materials like wood, tools, and machinery. Many of the occupations require working outside and do not involve a lot of paperwork or working closely with others. **Work Values**—Moral Values; Compensation; Independence; Variety. **Skills**—Equipment Maintenance; Mathematics; Installation; Management of Financial Resources; Repairing; Technology Design. **Abilities**—*Cognitive:* Visualization. *Psychomotor:* Reaction Time; Manual Dexterity; Multilimb Coordination; Arm-Hand Steadiness. *Physical:* Extent Flexibility; Trunk Strength; Gross Body Equilibrium; Dynamic Strength; Gross Body Coordination; Stamina. *Sensory:* None met the criteria. **General Work Activities**—*Information Input:* Identifying Objects, Actions, and Events; Inspecting Equipment, Structures, or Materials; Getting Information. *Mental Process:*

Organizing, Planning, and Prioritizing; Making Decisions and Solving Problems; Scheduling Work and Activities. *Work Output:* Handling and Moving Objects; Performing General Physical Activities; Drafting and Specifying Technical Devices. *Interacting with Others:* Coordinating the Work and Activities of Others; Establishing and Maintaining Interpersonal Relationships; Coaching and Developing Others. **Physical Work Conditions**—Outdoors; Very Hot or Cold; Hazardous Equipment; Standing; Using Hands on Objects, Tools, or Controls; Bending or Twisting the Body. **Other Job Characteristics**—Need to Be Exact or Accurate.

Experience—Job Zone 2. Some previous work-related skill, knowledge, or experience may be helpful in these occupations, but usually is not needed. **Job Preparation**—SVP 4.0 to less than 6.0—six months to less than two years. **Knowledges**—Building and Construction; Design; Production and Processing; Mechanical Devices; Public Safety and Security; Mathematics. **Instructional Program**—Masonry/Mason.

Related SOC Job—47-2021 Brickmasons and Blockmasons. **Related OOH Job**—Brickmasons, Blockmasons, and Stonemasons. **Related DOT Jobs**—573.684-010 Kiln-Door Builder; 709.684-046 Hot-Top Liner; 861.381-010 Acid-Tank Liner; 861.381-014 Bricklayer; 861.381-018 Bricklayer; 861.381-022 Bricklayer Apprentice; 861.381-026 Bricklayer, Firebrick and Refractory Tile; 861.684-010 Cupola Patcher; 861.684-014 Patcher; 861.684-022 Repairer, Kiln Car; 899.364-010 Chimney Repairer.

47-2022.00 Stonemasons

- **Education/Training Required: Long-term on-the-job training**
- **Employed: 17,030**
- **Annual Earnings: $34,640**
- **Growth: 13.0%**
- **Annual Job Openings: 2,000**

Build stone structures, such as piers, walls, and abutments. Lay walks; curbstones; or special types of masonry for vats, tanks, and floors.

Lay out wall patterns or foundations, using straight edge, rule, or staked lines. Shape, trim, face, and cut marble or stone preparatory to setting, using power saws, cutting equipment, and hand tools. Set vertical and horizontal alignment of structures, using plumb bob, gauge line, and level. Mix mortar or grout and pour or spread mortar or grout on marble slabs, stone, or foundation. Remove wedges; fill joints between stones; finish joints between stones, using a trowel; and smooth the mortar to an attractive finish, using a tuck-pointer. Clean excess mortar or grout from surface of marble, stone, or monument, using sponge, brush, water, or acid. Set stone or marble in place according to layout or pattern. Lay brick to build shells of chimneys and smokestacks or to line or reline industrial furnaces, kilns, boilers, and similar installations. Replace broken or missing masonry units in walls or floors. Smooth, polish, and bevel surfaces, using hand tools and power tools. Drill holes in marble or ornamental stone and anchor brackets in holes. Repair cracked or chipped areas of stone or marble, using blowtorch and mastic, and remove rough or defective spots from concrete, using power grinder or chisel and hammer. Remove sections of monument from truck bed and guide stone onto foundation, using skids, hoist, or truck crane. Construct and install prefabricated masonry units. Dig trench for foundation of monument, using pick and shovel. Position mold along guidelines of wall, press mold in place, and remove mold and paper from wall. Line interiors of molds with treated paper and fill molds with composition-stone mixture.

GOE Information—Interest Area: 02. Architecture and Construction. **Work Group:** 02.04. Construction Crafts. **Personality Type**—Realistic. Realistic occupations frequently involve work activities that include practical, hands-on problems and solutions. They often deal with plants; animals; and real-world materials like wood, tools, and machinery. Many of the occupations require working outside and do not involve a lot of paperwork or working closely with others. **Work Values**—Moral Values; Compensation; Independence. **Skills**—Installation; Management of Personnel Resources; Repairing; Equipment Maintenance; Equipment Selection; Mathematics. **Abilities**—*Cognitive:* Visualization; Originality. *Psychomotor:* Manual Dexterity; Reaction Time; Multilimb Coordination; Speed of Limb Movement; Arm-Hand Steadiness; Response Orientation. *Physical:* Static Strength; Dynamic Strength; Stamina; Trunk Strength; Extent Flexibility; Gross Body Coordination. *Sensory:* Depth Perception; Hearing Sensitivity; Visual Color Discrimination; Far Vision. **General Work Activities**—*Information Input:* Inspecting Equipment, Structures, or Materials; Estimating the Needed Characteristics of Products, Events, or Information; Identifying Objects, Actions, and Events. *Mental Process:* Making Decisions and Solving Problems; Organizing, Planning, and Prioritizing; Scheduling Work and Activities. *Work Output:* Handling and Moving Objects; Performing General Physical Activities; Drafting and Specifying Technical Devices. *Interacting with Others:* Communicating with Other Workers; Establishing and Maintaining Interpersonal Relationships; Coordinating the Work and Activities of Others. **Physical Work Conditions**—Outdoors; Standing; Walking and Running; Kneeling, Crouching, Stooping, or Crawling; Using Hands on Objects, Tools, or Controls; Bending or Twisting the Body. **Other Job Characteristics**—Need to Be Exact or Accurate.

Experience—Job Zone 3. Previous work-related skill, knowledge, or experience is required. **Job Preparation**—SVP 6.0 to less than 7.0—more than one year and less than four years. **Knowledges**—Building and Construction; Design; Mechanical Devices; Mathematics; Education and Training; Public Safety and Security. **Instructional Program**—Masonry/Mason.

Related SOC Job—47-2022 Stonemasons. **Related OOH Job**—Brickmasons, Blockmasons, and Stonemasons. **Related DOT Jobs**—861.361-010 Composition-Stone Applicator; 861.361-014 Monument Setter; 861.381-030 Marble Setter; 861.381-038 Stonemason; 861.381-042 Stonemason Apprentice.

47-2031.00 Carpenters

- **Education/Training Required: Long-term on-the-job training**
- **Employed: 935,920**
- **Annual Earnings: $35,580**
- **Growth: 13.8%**
- **Annual Job Openings: 210,000**

The job openings listed here are shared with 47-2031.01 Construction Carpenters and 47-2031.02 Rough Carpenters.

Construct, erect, install, or repair structures and fixtures made of wood, such as concrete forms; building frameworks, including partitions, joists, studding, and rafters; wood stairways; window and door frames; and hardwood floors. May also install cabinets, siding, drywall, and batt or roll insulation. Includes brattice builders who build doors or brattices (ventilation walls or partitions) in underground passageways to control the proper circulation of air through the passageways and to the working places.

No task data available.

Note: The Department of Labor has not collected some data for this job, so it has fewer details than the other descriptions.

Instructional Program—Carpentry/Carpenter.

Related SOC Job—47-2031 Carpenters. **Related OOH Job**—Carpenters. **Related DOT Job**—No data available.

47-2031.01 Construction Carpenters

- **Education/Training Required: Long-term on-the-job training**
- **Employed: 935,920**
- **Annual Earnings: $35,580**
- **Growth: 13.8%**
- **Annual Job Openings: 210,000**

The job openings listed here are shared with 47-2031.00 Carpenters and 47-2031.02 Rough Carpenters.

Construct, erect, install, and repair structures and fixtures of wood, plywood, and wallboard, using carpenter's hand tools and power tools.

Measure and mark cutting lines on materials, using ruler, pencil, chalk, and marking gauge. Follow established safety rules and regulations and maintain a safe and clean environment. Verify trueness of structure, using plumb bob and level. Shape or cut materials to specified measurements, using hand tools, machines, or power saw. Study specifications in blueprints, sketches, or building plans to prepare project layout and determine dimensions and materials required. Assemble and fasten materials to make framework or props, using hand tools and wood screws, nails, dowel pins, or glue. Build or repair cabinets, doors, frameworks, floors, and other wooden fixtures used in buildings, using woodworking machines, carpenter's hand tools, and power tools. Erect scaffolding and ladders for assembling structures above ground level. Remove damaged or defective parts or sections of structures and repair or replace, using hand tools. Install structures and fixtures, such as windows, frames, floorings, and trim, or hardware, using carpenter's hand and power tools. Select and order lumber and other required materials. Maintain records, document actions, and present written progress reports. Finish surfaces of woodwork or wallboard in houses and buildings, using paint, hand tools, and paneling. Prepare cost estimates for clients or employers. Arrange for subcontractors to deal with special areas such as heating and electrical wiring work. Inspect ceiling or floor tile, wall coverings, siding, glass, or woodwork to detect broken or damaged structures. Work with or remove hazardous material. Construct forms and chutes for pouring concrete. Cover subfloors with building paper to keep out moisture and lay hardwood, parquet, and wood-strip-block floors by nailing floors to subfloor or cementing them to mastic or asphalt base. Fill cracks and other defects in plaster or plasterboard and sand patch, using patching plaster, trowel, and sanding tool. Perform minor plumbing, welding, or concrete mixing work. Apply shock-absorbing, sound-deadening, and decorative paneling to ceilings and walls.

GOE Information—**Interest Area:** 02. Architecture and Construction. **Work Group:** 02.04. Construction Crafts. **Personality Type**—Realistic. Realistic occupations frequently involve work activities that include practical, hands-on problems and solutions. They often deal with plants; animals; and real-world materials like wood, tools, and machinery. Many of the occupations require working outside and do not involve a lot of paperwork or working closely with others. **Work Values**—Moral Values; Compensation; Creativity; Variety; Ability Utilization. **Skills**—Management of Personnel Resources; Management of Material Resources; Management of Financial Resources; Repairing; Equipment Maintenance; Quality

Control Analysis. **Abilities**—*Cognitive:* Visualization; Information Ordering; Originality; Flexibility of Closure; Perceptual Speed; Fluency of Ideas. *Psychomotor:* Manual Dexterity; Reaction Time; Multilimb Coordination; Arm-Hand Steadiness; Control Precision; Speed of Limb Movement. *Physical:* Extent Flexibility; Gross Body Equilibrium; Static Strength; Dynamic Strength; Gross Body Coordination; Stamina. *Sensory:* Depth Perception; Auditory Attention; Far Vision; Visual Color Discrimination. **General Work Activities**—*Information Input:* Monitoring Processes, Materials, or Surroundings; Identifying Objects, Actions, and Events; Inspecting Equipment, Structures, or Materials. *Mental Process:* Organizing, Planning, and Prioritizing; Updating and Using Relevant Knowledge; Judging the Qualities of Things, Services, or Other People's Work. *Work Output:* Handling and Moving Objects; Performing General Physical Activities; Controlling Machines and Processes. *Interacting with Others:* Coordinating the Work and Activities of Others; Teaching Others; Communicating with Other Workers. **Physical Work Conditions**—Outdoors; Noisy; Hazardous Equipment; Standing; Walking and Running; Using Hands on Objects, Tools, or Controls. **Other Job Characteristics**—Need to Be Exact or Accurate.

Experience—Job Zone 3. Previous work-related skill, knowledge, or experience is required. **Job Preparation**—SVP 6.0 to less than 7.0—more than one year and less than four years. **Knowledges**—Building and Construction; Design; Mechanical Devices; Production and Processing; Engineering and Technology; Public Safety and Security. **Instructional Program**—Carpentry/Carpenter.

Related SOC Job—47-2031 Carpenters. **Related OOH Job**—Carpenters. **Related DOT Jobs**—739.684-190 Casket Assembler; 764.684-022 Cooper; 764.684-026 Hogshead Cooper I; 769.684-038 Repairer, Assembled Wood Products; 806.281-058 Carpenter, Prototype; 807.361-014 Boat Repairer; 842.361-010 Lather; 842.361-014 Lather Apprentice; 860.281-010 Carpenter, Maintenance; 860.281-014 Carpenter, Ship; 860.361-010 Boatbuilder, Wood; 860.361-014 Boatbuilder Apprentice, Wood; 860.381-022 Carpenter; 860.381-026 Carpenter Apprentice; 860.381-034 Carpenter, Mold; 860.381-038 Carpenter, Railcar; others.

47-2031.02 Rough Carpenters

- **Education/Training Required: Long-term on-the-job training**
- **Employed: 935,920**
- **Annual Earnings: $35,580**
- **Growth: 13.8%**
- **Annual Job Openings: 210,000**

The job openings listed here are shared with 47-2031.00 Carpenters and 47-2031.01 Construction Carpenters.

Build rough wooden structures, such as concrete forms, scaffolds, tunnel, bridge, or sewer supports, billboard signs, and temporary frame shelters, according to sketches, blueprints, or oral instructions.

Study blueprints and diagrams to determine dimensions of structure or form to be constructed. Measure materials or distances, using square, measuring tape, or rule to lay out work. Cut or saw boards, timbers, or plywood to required size, using handsaw, power saw, or woodworking machine. Assemble and fasten material together to construct wood or metal framework of structure, using bolts, nails, or screws. Anchor and brace forms and other structures in place, using nails, bolts, anchor rods, steel cables, planks, wedges, and timbers. Mark cutting lines on materials, using pencil and scriber. Erect forms, framework, scaffolds, hoists, roof supports, or chutes, using hand tools, plumb rule, and level. Install rough door and window frames, subflooring, fixtures, or temporary supports in structures undergoing construction or repair. Examine structural timbers and supports to detect decay and replace timbers as required, using hand tools, nuts, and bolts. Bore boltholes in timber, masonry, or concrete walls, using power drill. Fabricate parts, using woodworking and metalworking machines. Dig or direct digging of post holes and set poles to support structures. Build sleds from logs and timbers for use in hauling camp buildings and machinery through wooded areas. Build chutes for pouring concrete.

GOE Information—Interest Area: 02. Architecture and Construction. **Work Group:** 02.04. Construction Crafts. **Personality Type**—Realistic. Realistic occupations frequently involve work activities that include practical, hands-on problems and solutions. They often deal with plants; animals; and real-world materials like wood, tools, and machinery. Many of the occupations require working outside and do not involve a lot of paperwork or working closely with others. **Work Values**—Moral Values; Variety; Compensation; Creativity; Recognition; Activity. **Skills**—Repairing; Installation; Management of Personnel Resources; Equipment Selection; Mathematics; Technology Design. **Abilities**—*Cognitive:* Visualization; Perceptual Speed; Number Facility; Speed of Closure. *Psychomotor:* Reaction Time; Multilimb Coordination; Arm-Hand Steadiness; Response Orientation; Speed of Limb Movement; Wrist-Finger Speed. *Physical:* Gross Body Equilibrium; Dynamic Strength; Static Strength; Extent Flexibility; Trunk Strength; Stamina. *Sensory:* Glare Sensitivity; Depth Perception; Hearing Sensitivity; Far Vision; Auditory Attention; Visual Color Discrimination. **General Work Activities**—*Information Input:* Monitoring Processes, Materials, or Surroundings; Identifying Objects, Actions, and Events; Inspecting Equipment, Structures, or Materials. *Mental Process:* Organizing, Planning, and Prioritizing; Making Decisions and Solving Problems; Judging the Qualities of Things, Services, or Other People's Work. *Work Output:* Handling and Moving Objects; Performing General Physical Activities; Controlling Machines and Processes. *Interacting with Others:* Coordinating the Work and Activities of Others; Communicating with Other Workers; Establishing and Maintaining Interpersonal Relationships. **Physical Work Conditions**—Outdoors; Noisy; Very Hot or Cold; Contaminants; Standing; Using Hands on Objects, Tools, or Controls. **Other Job Characteristics**—Need to Be Exact or Accurate.

Experience—Job Zone 2. Some previous work-related skill, knowledge, or experience may be helpful in these occupations, but usually is not needed. **Job Preparation**—SVP 4.0 to less than 6.0—six months to less than two years. **Knowledges**—Building and Construction; Design; Engineering and Technology; Mechanical Devices; Production and Processing; Physics. **Instructional Program**—Carpentry/Carpenter.

Related SOC Job—47-2031 Carpenters. **Related OOH Job**—Carpenters. **Related DOT Jobs**—860.381-030 Carpenter, Bridge; 860.381-042 Carpenter, Rough; 860.381-046 Form Builder; 860.381-581 Carpenter, Piledriver; 869.361-018 Sign Erector-and-Repairer; 869.381-034 Timber Framer; 869.684-058 Stopping Builder.

47-2041.00 Carpet Installers

- **Education/Training Required: Moderate-term on-the-job training**
- **Employed: 37,050**
- **Annual Earnings: $33,550**
- **Growth: 8.4%**
- **Annual Job Openings: 11,000**

Lay and install carpet from rolls or blocks on floors. Install padding and trim flooring materials.

Join edges of carpet and seam edges where necessary by sewing or by using tape with glue and heated carpet iron. Cut and trim carpet to fit along wall edges, openings, and projections, finishing the edges with a wall trimmer. Roll out, measure, mark, and cut carpeting to size with a carpet knife, following floor sketches and allowing extra carpet for final fitting. Inspect the surface to be covered to determine its condition and correct any imperfections that might show through carpet or cause carpet to wear unevenly. Plan the layout of the carpet, allowing for expected traffic patterns and placing seams for best appearance and longest wear. Stretch carpet to align with walls and ensure a smooth surface and press carpet in place over tack strips or use staples, tape, tacks, or glue to hold carpet in place. Take measurements and study floor sketches to calculate the area to be carpeted and the amount of material needed. Cut carpet padding to size and install padding, following prescribed method. Install carpet on some floors by using adhesive, following prescribed method. Nail tack strips around area to be carpeted or use old strips to attach edges of new carpet. Fasten metal treads across door openings or where carpet meets flooring to hold carpet in place. Measure, cut, and install tackless strips along the baseboard or wall. Draw building diagrams and record dimensions. Move furniture from area to be carpeted and remove old carpet and padding. Cut and bind material.

GOE Information—Interest Area: 02. Architecture and Construction. **Work Group:** 02.04. Construction Crafts. **Personality Type**—Realistic. Realistic occupations frequently involve work activities that include practical, hands-on problems and solutions. They often deal with plants; animals; and real-world materials like wood, tools, and machinery. Many of the occupations require working outside and do not involve a lot of paperwork or working closely with others. **Work Values**—Moral Values. **Skills**—Installation; Equipment Selection; Repairing; Management of Personnel Resources; Mathematics; Equipment Maintenance. **Abilities**—*Cognitive:* Spatial Orientation; Visualization; Flexibility of Closure; Mathematical Reasoning; Category Flexibility; Memorization. *Psychomotor:* Arm-Hand Steadiness; Multilimb Coordination; Reaction Time; Control Precision. *Physical:* Static Strength; Extent Flexibility; Dynamic Strength; Stamina; Trunk Strength; Gross Body Equilibrium. *Sensory:* Depth Perception; Visual Color Discrimination; Far Vision; Speech Recognition. **General Work Activities**—*Information Input:* Inspecting Equipment, Structures, or Materials; Estimating the Needed Characteristics of Products, Events, or Information; Monitoring Processes, Materials, or Surroundings. *Mental Process:* Judging the Qualities of Things, Services, or Other People's Work; Making Decisions and Solving Problems; Organizing, Planning, and Prioritizing. *Work Output:* Performing General Physical Activities; Handling and Moving Objects; Controlling Machines and Processes. *Interacting with Others:* Communicating with Other Workers; Coaching and Developing Others; Establishing and Maintaining Interpersonal Relationships. **Physical Work Conditions**—Minor Burns, Cuts, Bites, or Stings; Standing; Walking and Running; Kneeling, Crouching, Stooping, or Crawling; Using Hands on Objects, Tools, or Controls; Bending or Twisting the Body. **Other Job Characteristics**—Need to Be Exact or Accurate.

Experience—Job Zone 1. No previous work-related skill, knowledge, or experience is needed. **Job Preparation**—SVP below 4.0—less than six months. **Knowledges**—Building and Construction; Public Safety and Security; Sales and Marketing; Transportation; Mechanical Devices; Design. **Instructional Program**—Building/Construction Trades, Other.

Related SOC Job—47-2041 Carpet Installers. **Related OOH Job**—Carpet, Floor, and Tile Installers and Finishers. **Related DOT Job**—864.381-010 Carpet Layer.

47-2042.00 Floor Layers, Except Carpet, Wood, and Hard Tiles

- **Education/Training Required: Moderate-term on-the-job training**
- **Employed: 14,520**
- **Annual Earnings: $33,010**
- **Growth: 10.2%**
- **Annual Job Openings: 4,000**

Apply blocks, strips, or sheets of shock-absorbing, sound-deadening, or decorative coverings to floors.

Sweep, scrape, sand, or chip dirt and irregularities to clean base surfaces, correcting imperfections that may show through the covering. Cut flooring material to fit around obstructions. Inspect surface to be covered to ensure that it is firm and dry. Trim excess covering materials, tack edges, and join sections of covering material to form tight joint. Form a smooth foundation by stapling plywood or Masonite over the floor or by brushing waterproof compound onto surface and filling cracks with plaster, putty, or grout to seal pores. Measure and mark guidelines on surfaces or foundations, using chalk lines and dividers. Cut covering and foundation materials according to blueprints and sketches. Roll and press sheet wall and floor covering into cement base to smooth and finish surface, using hand roller. Apply adhesive cement to floor or wall material to join and adhere foundation material. Determine traffic areas and decide location of seams. Lay out, position, and apply shock-absorbing, sound-deadening, or decorative coverings to floors, walls, and cabinets, following guidelines to keep courses straight and create designs. Remove excess cement to clean finished surface. Disconnect and remove appliances, light fixtures, and worn floor and wall covering from floors, walls, and cabinets. Heat and soften floor covering materials to patch cracks or fit floor coverings around irregular surfaces, using blowtorch.

GOE Information—Interest Area: 02. Architecture and Construction. **Work Group:** 02.04. Construction Crafts. **Personality Type**—Realistic. Realistic occupations frequently involve work activities that include practical, hands-on problems and solutions. They often deal with plants; animals; and real-world materials like wood, tools, and machinery. Many of the occupations require working outside and do not involve a lot of paperwork or working closely with others. **Work Values**—Moral Values. **Skills**—Installation; Repairing; Equipment Maintenance; Equipment Selection; Mathematics; Operations Analysis. **Abilities**—*Cognitive:* Visualization; Selective Attention. *Psychomotor:* Manual Dexterity; Multilimb Coordination; Arm-Hand Steadiness; Control Precision; Finger Dexterity. *Physical:* Extent Flexibility; Trunk Strength; Dynamic Strength; Static Strength; Stamina. *Sensory:* None met the criteria. **General Work Activities**—*Information Input:* Inspecting Equipment, Structures, or Materials; Monitoring Processes, Materials, or Surroundings; Getting Information. *Mental Process:* Making Decisions and Solving Problems; Scheduling Work and Activities; Organizing, Planning, and Prioritizing. *Work Output:* Handling and Moving Objects; Performing General Physical Activities; Controlling Machines and Processes. *Interacting with Others:* Communicating with Other Workers; Performing for or Working with the Public; Establishing and Maintaining Interpersonal Relationships. **Physical Work Conditions**—Indoors; Contaminants; Cramped Work Space, Awkward Positions; Kneeling, Crouching, Stooping, or Crawling; Using Hands on Objects, Tools, or Controls; Bending or Twisting the Body. **Other Job Characteristics**—Need to Be Exact or Accurate.

Experience—Job Zone 2. Some previous work-related skill, knowledge, or experience may be helpful in these occupations, but usually is not needed. **Job Preparation**—SVP 4.0 to less than 6.0—six months to less than two years. **Knowledges**—Building and Construction; Design; Mechanical Devices; Production and Processing; Mathematics; Transportation. **Instructional Program**—Building/Construction Trades, Other.

Related SOC Job—47-2042 Floor Layers, Except Carpet, Wood, and Hard Tiles. **Related OOH Job**—Carpet, Floor, and Tile Installers and Finishers. **Related DOT Jobs**—622.381-026 Floor-Covering Layer; 861.381-034 Soft-Tile Setter; 864.481-010 Floor Layer; 864.481-014 Floor-Layer Apprentice.

47-2043.00 Floor Sanders and Finishers

- **Education/Training Required: Moderate-term on-the-job training**
- **Employed: 5,950**
- **Annual Earnings: $27,340**
- **Growth: 8.2%**
- **Annual Job Openings: 2,000**

Scrape and sand wooden floors to smooth surfaces, using floor scraper and floor sanding machine, and apply coats of finish.

Scrape and sand floor edges and areas inaccessible to floor sanders, using scrapers, disk-type sanders, and sandpaper. Remove excess glue from joints, using knives, scrapers, or wood chisels. Apply filler compound and coats of finish to floors to seal wood. Attach sandpaper to rollers of sanding machines. Guide sanding machines over surfaces of floors until surfaces are smooth. Inspect floors for smoothness.

GOE Information—Interest Area: 02. Architecture and Construction. **Work Group:** 02.04. Construction Crafts. **Personality Type**—Realistic. Realistic occupations frequently involve work activities that include practical, hands-on problems and solutions. They often deal with plants; animals; and real-world materials like wood, tools, and machinery. Many of the occupations require working outside and do not involve a lot of paperwork or working closely with others. **Work Values**—Moral Values. **Skills**—None met the criteria. **Abilities**—*Cognitive:* Spatial Orientation. *Psychomotor:* Speed of Limb Movement; Wrist-Finger Speed; Multilimb Coordination; Manual Dexterity; Control Precision; Arm-Hand Steadiness. *Physical:* Dynamic Flexibility; Explosive Strength; Dynamic Strength; Stamina; Static Strength; Gross Body Coordination. *Sensory:* None met the criteria. **General Work Activities**—*Information Input:* None met the criteria. *Mental Process:* None met the criteria. *Work Output:* Performing General Physical Activities; Handling and Moving Objects; Controlling Machines and Processes. *Interacting with Others:* None met the criteria. **Physical Work Conditions**—Indoors; Contaminants; Standing; Walking and Running; Using Hands on Objects, Tools, or Controls; Repetitive Motions. **Other Job Characteristics**—Automation; Repeat Same Tasks.

Experience—Job Zone 2. Some previous work-related skill, knowledge, or experience may be helpful in these occupations, but usually is not needed. **Job Preparation**—SVP 4.0 to less than 6.0—six months to less than two years. **Knowledges**—Mechanical Devices. **Instructional Program**—Building/Construction Trades, Other.

Related SOC Job—47-2043 Floor Sanders and Finishers. **Related OOH Job**—Carpet, Floor, and Tile Installers and Finishers. **Related DOT Job**—869.664-014 Construction Worker I.

47-2044.00 Tile and Marble Setters

- **Education/Training Required: Long-term on-the-job training**
- **Employed: 47,410**
- **Annual Earnings: $36,530**
- **Growth: 22.9%**
- **Annual Job Openings: 9,000**

Apply hard tile, marble, and wood tile to walls, floors, ceilings, and roof decks.

Align and straighten tile, using levels, squares, and straightedges. Determine and implement the best layout to achieve a desired pattern. Cut and shape tile to fit around obstacles and into odd spaces and corners, using hand- and power-cutting tools. Finish and dress the joints and wipe excess grout from between tiles, using damp sponge. Apply mortar to tile back, position the tile, and press or tap with trowel handle to affix tile to base. Mix, apply, and spread plaster, concrete, mortar, cement, mastic, glue, or other adhesives to form a bed for the tiles, using brush, trowel, and screed. Prepare cost and labor estimates based on calculations of time and materials needed for project. Measure and mark surfaces to be tiled, following blueprints. Level concrete and allow to dry. Build underbeds and install anchor bolts, wires, and brackets. Prepare surfaces for tiling by attaching lath or waterproof paper or by applying a cement mortar coat onto a metal screen. Study blueprints and examine surface to be covered to determine amount of material needed. Cut, surface, polish, and install marble and granite or install pre-cast terrazzo, granite, or marble units. Install and anchor fixtures in designated positions, using hand tools. Cut tile backing to required size, using shears. Remove any old tile, grout, and adhesive, using chisels and scrapers, and clean the surface carefully. Lay and set mosaic tiles to create decorative wall, mural, and floor designs. Assist customers in selection of tile and grout. Remove and replace cracked or damaged tile. Measure and cut metal lath to size for walls and ceilings, using tin snips. Select and order tile and other items to be installed, such as bathroom accessories, walls, panels, and cabinets, according to specifications. Mix and apply mortar or cement to edges and ends of drain tiles to seal halves and joints. Spread mastic or other adhesive base on roof deck to form base for promenade tile, using serrated spreader. Apply a sealer to make grout stain- and water-resistant. Brush glue onto manila paper on which design has been drawn and position tiles, finished side down, onto paper.

GOE Information—Interest Area: 02. Architecture and Construction. **Work Group:** 02.04. Construction Crafts. **Personality Type**—Realistic. Realistic occupations frequently involve work activities that include practical, hands-on problems and solutions. They often deal with plants; animals; and real-world materials like wood, tools, and machinery. Many of the occupations require working outside and do not involve a lot of paperwork or working closely with others. **Work Values**—Moral Values; Independence; Compensation; Supervision, Technical. **Skills**—Installation; Management of Financial Resources; Mathematics; Management of Material Resources; Social Perceptiveness; Equipment Selection. **Abilities**—*Cognitive:* Visualization; Spatial Orientation; Mathematical Reasoning; Originality; Number Facility; Memorization. *Psychomotor:* Arm-Hand Steadiness; Manual Dexterity; Multilimb Coordination; Control Precision; Wrist-Finger Speed. *Physical:* Extent Flexibility; Dynamic Strength; Static Strength; Dynamic Flexibility; Gross Body Coordination; Trunk Strength. *Sensory:* Depth Perception; Visual Color Discrimination. **General Work Activities**—*Information Input:* Identifying Objects, Actions, and Events; Monitoring Processes, Materials, or Surroundings; Getting Information. *Mental Process:* Thinking Creatively; Organizing, Planning, and Prioritizing; Making

Decisions and Solving Problems. *Work Output:* Handling and Moving Objects; Performing General Physical Activities; Controlling Machines and Processes. *Interacting with Others:* Establishing and Maintaining Interpersonal Relationships; Coordinating the Work and Activities of Others; Teaching Others. **Physical Work Conditions**—Noisy; Contaminants; Cramped Work Space, Awkward Positions; Standing; Using Hands on Objects, Tools, or Controls; Bending or Twisting the Body. **Other Job Characteristics**—Need to Be Exact or Accurate.

Experience—Job Zone 2. Some previous work-related skill, knowledge, or experience may be helpful in these occupations, but usually is not needed. **Job Preparation**—SVP 4.0 to less than 6.0—six months to less than two years. **Knowledges**—Building and Construction; Design; Production and Processing; Economics and Accounting; Administration and Management; Transportation. **Instructional Program**—Masonry/Mason.

Related SOC Job—47-2044 Tile and Marble Setters. **Related OOH Job**—Carpet, Floor, and Tile Installers and Finishers. **Related DOT Jobs**—779.381-014 Mosaic Worker; 861.381-054 Tile Setter; 861.381-058 Tile Setter Apprentice; 861.381-062 Tile-Conduit Layer; 861.684-018 Tile Setter.

47-2051.00 Cement Masons and Concrete Finishers

- **Education/Training Required: Moderate-term on-the-job training**
- **Employed: 204,720**
- **Annual Earnings: $32,030**
- **Growth: 15.9%**
- **Annual Job Openings: 32,000**

Smooth and finish surfaces of poured concrete, such as floors, walks, sidewalks, roads, or curbs, using a variety of hand and power tools. Align forms for sidewalks, curbs, or gutters; patch voids; and use saws to cut expansion joints.

Check the forms that hold the concrete to see that they are properly constructed. Set the forms that hold concrete to the desired pitch and depth and align them. Spread, level, and smooth concrete, using rake, shovel, hand or power trowel, hand or power screed, and float. Mold expansion joints and edges, using edging tools, jointers, and straightedge. Monitor how the wind, heat, or cold affect the curing of the concrete throughout the entire process. Signal truck driver to position truck to facilitate pouring concrete and move chute to direct concrete on forms. Produce rough concrete surface, using broom. Operate power vibrator to compact concrete. Direct the casting of the concrete and supervise laborers who use shovels or special tools to spread it. Mix cement, sand, and water to produce concrete, grout, or slurry, using hoe, trowel, tamper, scraper, or concrete-mixing machine. Cut out damaged areas, drill holes for reinforcing rods, and position reinforcing rods to repair concrete, using power saw and drill. Wet surface to prepare for bonding, fill holes and cracks with grout or slurry, and smooth, using trowel. Wet concrete surface and rub with stone to smooth surface and obtain specified finish. Clean chipped area, using wire brush, and feel and observe surface to determine if it is rough or uneven. Apply hardening and sealing compounds to cure surface of concrete and waterproof or restore surface. Chip, scrape, and grind high spots, ridges, and rough projections to finish concrete, using pneumatic chisels, power grinders, or hand tools. Spread roofing paper on surface of foundation and spread concrete onto roofing paper with trowel to form terrazzo base. Build wooden molds and clamp molds around area to be repaired, using hand tools. Sprinkle colored marble or stone chips, powdered steel, or coloring powder over surface to produce prescribed finish. Cut metal division strips and press them into terrazzo base so that top edges form desired design or pattern. Fabricate concrete beams, columns, and panels. Waterproof or restore concrete surfaces, using appropriate compounds.

GOE Information—Interest Area: 02. Architecture and Construction. **Work Group:** 02.04. Construction Crafts. **Personality Type**—Realistic. Realistic occupations frequently involve work activities that include practical, hands-on problems and solutions. They often deal with plants; animals; and real-world materials like wood, tools, and machinery. Many of the occupations require working outside and do not involve a lot of paperwork or working closely with others. **Work Values**—Moral Values; Compensation; Supervision, Technical. **Skills**—Mathematics; Installation; Repairing; Equipment Maintenance; Coordination; Equipment Selection. **Abilities**—*Cognitive:* Perceptual Speed; Visualization. *Psychomotor:* Control Precision; Multilimb Coordination; Reaction Time; Rate Control; Speed of Limb Movement; Manual Dexterity. *Physical:* Gross Body Equilibrium; Extent Flexibility; Trunk Strength; Dynamic Strength; Stamina; Static Strength. *Sensory:* Depth Perception; Hearing Sensitivity; Visual Color Discrimination. **General Work Activities**—*Information Input:* Monitoring Processes, Materials, or Surroundings; Inspecting Equipment, Structures, or Materials; Getting Information. *Mental Process:* Making Decisions and Solving Problems; Updating and Using Relevant Knowledge; Thinking Creatively. *Work Output:* Performing General Physical Activities; Handling and Moving Objects; Operating Vehicles or Equipment. *Interacting with Others:* Communicating with Other Workers; Establishing and Maintaining Interpersonal Relationships; Teaching Others. **Physical Work Conditions**—Outdoors; Noisy; Hazardous Equipment; Standing; Using Hands on Objects, Tools, or Controls; Bending or Twisting the Body. **Other Job Characteristics**—Need to Be Exact or Accurate; Errors Have Important Consequences; Pace Determined by Speed of Equipment.

Experience—Job Zone 3. Previous work-related skill, knowledge, or experience is required. **Job Preparation**—SVP 6.0 to less than 7.0—more than one year and less than four years. **Knowledges**—Building and Construction; Public Safety and Security; Mechanical Devices; Design; Engineering and Technology; Administration and Management. **Instructional Program**—Concrete Finishing/Concrete Finisher.

Related SOC Job—47-2051 Cement Masons and Concrete Finishers. **Related OOH Job**—Cement Masons, Concrete Finishers, Segmental Pavers, and Terrazzo Workers. **Related DOT Jobs**—844.364-010 Cement Mason; 844.364-014 Cement-Mason Apprentice; 844.461-010 Concrete-Stone Finisher; 844.684-010 Concrete Rubber.

47-2053.00 Terrazzo Workers and Finishers

- **Education/Training Required: Long-term on-the-job training**
- **Employed: 5,440**
- **Annual Earnings: $32,030**
- **Growth: 15.2%**
- **Annual Job Openings: 1,000**

Apply a mixture of cement, sand, pigment, or marble chips to floors, stairways, and cabinet fixtures to fashion durable and decorative surfaces.

Blend marble chip mixtures and place into panels; then push a roller over the surface to embed the chips. Cut metal division strips and press them into the terrazzo base wherever there is to be a joint or change of color, to form desired designs or patterns, and to help prevent cracks. Measure designated amounts of ingredients for terrazzo or grout according to standard formulas and specifications, using graduated containers and scale, and load ingredients into portable mixer. Mold expansion joints and edges, using edging tools, jointers, and straightedges. Spread, level, and smooth concrete and terrazzo mixtures to form bases and finished surfaces, using rakes, shovels, hand or power trowels, hand or power screeds, and floats. Grind curved surfaces and areas inaccessible to surfacing machine, such as stairways and cabinet tops, with portable hand grinder. Grind surfaces with a power grinder and polish surfaces with polishing or surfacing machines. Position and secure moisture membrane and wire mesh prior to pouring base materials for terrazzo installation. Modify mixing, grouting, grinding, and cleaning procedures according to type of installation or material used. Wash polished terrazzo surface, using cleaner and water, and apply sealer and curing agent according to manufacturer's specifications, using brush or sprayer. Mix cement, sand, and water to produce concrete, grout, or slurry, using hoe, trowel, tamper, scraper, or concrete-mixing machine. Sprinkle colored marble or stone chips, powdered steel, or coloring powder over surface to produce prescribed finish. Wet surface to prepare for bonding, fill holes and cracks with grout or slurry, and smooth, using trowel. Cut out damaged areas, drill holes for reinforcing rods, and position reinforcing rods to repair concrete, using power saw and drill. Clean installation site, mixing and storage areas, tools, machines, and equipment and store materials and equipment. Fill slight depressions left by grinding with a matching grout material and then hand-trowel for a smooth, uniform surface. Chip, scrape, and grind high spots, ridges, and rough projections to finish concrete, using pneumatic chisel, hand chisel, or other hand tools.

GOE Information—Interest Area: 02. Architecture and Construction. **Work Group:** 02.04. Construction Crafts. **Personality Type**—Realistic. Realistic occupations frequently involve work activities that include practical, hands-on problems and solutions. They often deal with plants; animals; and real-world materials like wood, tools, and machinery. Many of the occupations require working outside and do not involve a lot of paperwork or working closely with others. **Work Values**—Moral Values; Compensation; Supervision, Technical. **Skills**—Installation; Repairing; Equipment Maintenance; Coordination; Equipment Selection; Management of Material Resources. **Abilities**—*Cognitive:* Visualization; Selective Attention. *Psychomotor:* Multilimb Coordination; Speed of Limb Movement; Reaction Time; Manual Dexterity; Rate Control; Control Precision. *Physical:* Extent Flexibility; Static Strength; Trunk Strength; Stamina; Gross Body Coordination. *Sensory:* Depth Perception; Visual Color Discrimination; Auditory Attention; Far Vision. **General Work Activities**—*Information Input:* Inspecting Equipment, Structures, or Materials; Monitoring Processes, Materials, or Surroundings; Estimating the Needed Characteristics of Products, Events, or Information. *Mental Process:* Organizing, Planning, and Prioritizing; Making Decisions and Solving Problems; Updating and Using Relevant Knowledge. *Work Output:* Handling and Moving Objects; Performing General Physical Activities; Controlling Machines and Processes. *Interacting with Others:* Communicating with Other Workers; Establishing and Maintaining Interpersonal Relationships; Interpreting the Meaning of Information for Others. **Physical Work Conditions**—Noisy; Contaminants; Standing; Walking and Running; Using Hands on Objects, Tools, or Controls; Repetitive Motions. **Other Job Characteristics**—Need to Be Exact or Accurate.

Experience—Job Zone 2. Some previous work-related skill, knowledge, or experience may be helpful in these occupations, but usually is not needed. **Job Preparation**—SVP 4.0 to less than 6.0—six months to less than two years. **Knowledges**—Building and Construction; Production and Processing; Mechanical Devices; Administration and Management; Sales and Marketing; Design. **Instructional Programs**—Building/Construction Finishing, Management, and Inspection, Other; Building/Property Maintenance and Management.

Related SOC Job—47-2053 Terrazzo Workers and Finishers. **Related OOH Job**—Cement Masons, Concrete Finishers, Segmental Pavers, and Terrazzo Workers. **Related DOT Jobs**—861.381-046 Terrazzo Worker; 861.381-050 Terrazzo-Worker Apprentice; 861.664-014 Terrazzo Finisher.

47-2061.00 Construction Laborers

- **Education/Training Required: Moderate-term on-the-job training**
- **Employed: 934,000**
- **Annual Earnings: $25,410**
- **Growth: 5.9%**
- **Annual Job Openings: 245,000**

Perform tasks involving physical labor at building, highway, and heavy construction projects; tunnel and shaft excavations; and demolition sites. May operate hand and power tools of all types: air hammers, earth tampers, cement mixers, small mechanical hoists, surveying and measuring equipment, and a variety of other equipment and instruments. May clean and prepare sites; dig trenches; set braces to support the sides of excavations; erect scaffolding; clean up rubble and debris; and remove asbestos, lead, and other hazardous waste materials. May assist other craft workers.

Clean and prepare construction sites to eliminate possible hazards. Read and interpret plans, instructions, and specifications to determine work activities. Control traffic passing near, in, and around work zones. Signal equipment operators to facilitate alignment, movement, and adjustment of machinery, equipment, and materials. Dig ditches or trenches, backfill excavations, and compact and level earth to grade specifications, using picks, shovels, pneumatic tampers, and rakes. Measure, mark, and record openings and distances to lay out areas where construction work will be performed. Position, join, align, and seal structural components, such as concrete wall sections and pipes. Load, unload, and identify building materials, machinery, and tools and distribute them to the appropriate locations according to project plans and specifications. Erect and disassemble scaffolding, shoring, braces, traffic barricades, ramps, and other temporary structures. Build and position forms for pouring concrete and dismantle forms after use, using saws, hammers, nails, or bolts. Lubricate, clean, and repair machinery, equipment, and tools. Operate jackhammers and drills to break up concrete or pavement. Smooth and finish freshly poured cement or concrete, using floats, trowels, screeds, or powered cement-finishing tools. Operate, read, and maintain air monitoring and other sampling devices in confined or hazardous environments. Install sewer, water, and storm drain pipes, using pipe-laying machinery and laser guidance equipment. Transport and set explosives for tunnel, shaft, and road construction. Provide assistance to craft workers, such as carpenters, plasterers, and masons. Tend pumps, compressors, and generators to provide power for tools, machinery, and equipment or to heat and move materials such as asphalt. Mop, brush, or spread paints, cleaning solutions, or other compounds over surfaces to clean them or to provide protection. Place, consolidate, and protect case-in-place concrete or masonry structures. Identify, pack, and transport hazardous or radioactive materials. Use computers and other input devices to control robotic pipe cutters and cleaners.

GOE Information—Interest Area: 02. Architecture and Construction. **Work Group:** 02.06. Construction Support/Labor. **Personality Type**—Realistic. Realistic occupations frequently involve work activities that include practical, hands-on problems and solutions. They often deal with plants; animals; and real-world materials like wood, tools, and machinery. Many of the occupations require working outside and do not involve a lot of paperwork or working closely with others. **Work Values**—Supervision, Technical; Co-workers. **Skills**—Equipment Maintenance; Repairing; Equipment Selection; Installation; Operation Monitoring. **Abilities**—*Cognitive:* None met the criteria. *Psychomotor:* Multilimb Coordination; Manual Dexterity; Rate Control; Response Orientation; Reaction Time; Control Precision. *Physical:* Static Strength; Stamina; Trunk Strength; Dynamic Strength; Extent Flexibility; Gross Body Coordination. *Sensory:* Auditory Attention; Depth Perception; Hearing Sensitivity; Visual Color Discrimination; Far Vision. **General Work Activities**—*Information Input:* Getting Information; Monitoring Processes, Materials, or Surroundings; Identifying Objects, Actions, and Events. *Mental Process:* Updating and Using Relevant Knowledge; Organizing, Planning, and Prioritizing; Making Decisions and Solving Problems. *Work Output:* Performing General Physical Activities; Handling and Moving Objects; Controlling Machines and Processes. *Interacting with Others:* Establishing and Maintaining Interpersonal Relationships; Communicating with Other Workers; Coordinating the Work and Activities of Others. **Physical Work Conditions**—Outdoors; Noisy; Very Hot or Cold; Contaminants; Standing; Using Hands on Objects, Tools, or Controls. **Other Job Characteristics**—Need to Be Exact or Accurate; Pace Determined by Speed of Equipment.

Experience—Job Zone 1. No previous work-related skill, knowledge, or experience is needed. **Job Preparation**—SVP below 4.0—less than six months. **Knowledges**—Building and Construction; Design; Mechanical Devices; Transportation; Public Safety and Security; Engineering and Technology. **Instructional Program**—Building/Construction Trades, Other.

Related SOC Job—47-2061 Construction Laborers. **Related OOH Job**—Construction Laborers. **Related DOT Jobs**—800.684-010 Riveter; 800.684-014 Riveter, Pneumatic; 801.684-018 Playground-Equipment Erector; 809.664-010 Aluminum-Pool Installer; 842.665-010 Plaster-Machine Tender; 849.665-010 Pump Tender, Cement Based Materials; 850.467-010 Grade Checker; 853.665-010 Asphalt-Distributor Tender; 853.685-010 Asphalt-Heater Tender; 862.682-010 Pipe Cutter; 864.684-010 Floor and Wall Applier, Liquid; 869.381-018 Pipe Installer; 869.463-010 Swimming Pool Installer-And-Servicer; others.

47-2071.00 Paving, Surfacing, and Tamping Equipment Operators

- **Education/Training Required: Moderate-term on-the-job training**
- **Employed: 63,220**
- **Annual Earnings: $30,320**
- **Growth: 15.6%**
- **Annual Job Openings: 7,000**

Operate equipment used for applying concrete, asphalt, or other materials to road beds, parking lots, or airport runways and taxiways or equipment used for tamping gravel, dirt, or other materials. Includes concrete and asphalt paving machine operators, form tampers, tamping machine operators, and stone spreader operators.

Start machine, engage clutch, and push and move levers to guide machine along forms or guidelines and to control the operation of machine attachments. Operate machines to spread, smooth, level, or steel-reinforce stone, concrete, or asphalt on road beds. Inspect, clean, maintain, and repair equipment, using mechanics' hand tools, or report malfunctions to supervisors. Operate oil distributors, loaders, chip spreaders, dump trucks, and snowplows. Coordinate truck dumping. Set up and tear down equipment. Operate tamping machines or manually roll surfaces to compact earth fills, foundation forms, and finished road materials according to grade specifications. Shovel blacktop. Drive machines onto truck trailers and drive trucks to transport machines and material to and from job sites. Observe distribution of paving material to adjust machine settings or material flow and indicate low spots for workers to add material. Light burners or start heating units of machines and regulate screed temperatures and asphalt flow rates. Control paving machines to push dump trucks and to maintain a constant flow of asphalt or other material into hoppers or screeds. Set up forms and lay out guidelines for curbs according to written specifications, using string, spray paint, and concrete/water mixes. Fill tanks, hoppers, or machines with paving materials. Drive and operate curbing machines to extrude concrete or asphalt curbing. Cut or break up pavement and drive guardrail posts, using machines equipped with interchangeable hammers. Install dies, cutters, and extensions to screeds onto machines, using hand tools. Operate machines that clean or cut expansion joints in concrete or asphalt and that rout out cracks in pavement. Place strips of material such as cork, asphalt, or steel into joints or place rolls of expansion-joint material on machines that automatically insert material.

GOE Information—Interest Area: 02. Architecture and Construction. **Work Group:** 02.04. Construction Crafts. **Personality Type**—Realistic. Realistic occupations frequently involve work activities that include practical, hands-on problems and solutions. They often deal with plants; animals; and real-world materials like wood, tools, and machinery. Many of the occupations require working outside and do not involve a lot of paperwork or working closely with others. **Work Values**—Moral Values; Supervision, Technical; Independence. **Skills**—Operation Monitoring; Equipment Maintenance; Operation and Control; Repairing; Installation; Equipment Selection. **Abilities**—*Cognitive:* Spatial Orientation; Visualization; Time Sharing; Selective Attention; Perceptual Speed. *Psychomotor:* Multilimb Coordination; Reaction Time; Response Orientation; Control Precision; Rate Control; Speed of Limb Movement. *Physical:* Static Strength; Extent Flexibility; Trunk Strength; Dynamic Strength; Stamina; Gross Body Coordination. *Sensory:* Glare Sensitivity; Depth Perception; Hearing Sensitivity; Auditory Attention; Visual Color Discrimination. **General Work Activities**—*Information Input:* Monitoring Processes, Materials, or Surroundings; Identifying Objects, Actions, and Events; Inspecting Equipment, Structures, or Materials. *Mental Process:* Organizing, Planning, and Prioritizing; Making Decisions and Solving Problems; Thinking Creatively. *Work Output:* Handling and Moving Objects; Controlling Machines and Processes; Performing General Physical Activities. *Interacting with Others:* Communicating with Persons Outside Organization; Establishing and Maintaining Interpersonal Relationships; Coordinating the Work and Activities of Others. **Physical Work Conditions**—Outdoors; Noisy; Very Hot or Cold; Contaminants; Hazardous Equipment; Using Hands on Objects, Tools, or Controls. **Other Job Characteristics**—Pace Determined by Speed of Equipment; Need to Be Exact or Accurate.

Experience—Job Zone 2. Some previous work-related skill, knowledge, or experience may be helpful in these occupations, but usually

is not needed. **Job Preparation**—SVP 4.0 to less than 6.0—six months to less than two years. **Knowledges**—Building and Construction; Mechanical Devices; Transportation; Public Safety and Security; Engineering and Technology; Production and Processing. **Instructional Program**—Construction/Heavy Equipment/Earthmoving Equipment Operation.

Related SOC Job—47-2071 Paving, Surfacing, and Tamping Equipment Operators. **Related OOH Job**—Construction Equipment Operators. **Related DOT Jobs**—853.663-010 Asphalt-Paving-Machine Operator; 853.663-014 Concrete-Paving-Machine Operator; 853.663-018 Road-Oiling-Truck Driver; 853.663-022 Stone-Spreader Operator; 853.683-010 Curb-Machine Operator; 853.683-014 Heater-Planer Operator; 853.683-018 Joint-Cleaning-and-Grooving-Machine Operator; 859.683-022 Reinforcing-Steel-Machine Operator; 859.683-026 Road-Mixer Operator; 859.683-030 Road-Roller Operator; 869.683-010 Form-Tamper Operator; 869.683-018 Tamping-Machine Operator.

47-2072.00 Pile-Driver Operators

- **Education/Training Required: Moderate-term on-the-job training**
- **Employed: 4,410**
- **Annual Earnings: $48,900**
- **Growth: 11.9%**
- **Annual Job Openings: Fewer than 500**

Operate pile drivers mounted on skids, barges, crawler treads, or locomotive cranes to drive pilings for retaining walls, bulkheads, and foundations of structures such as buildings, bridges, and piers.

Move levers and turn valves to activate power hammers or to raise and lower drophammers that drive piles to required depths. Clean, lubricate, and refill equipment. Conduct pre-operational checks on equipment to ensure proper functioning. Drive pilings to provide support for buildings or other structures, using heavy equipment with a pile-driver head. Move hand and foot levers of hoisting equipment to position piling leads, hoist piling into leads, and position hammers over pilings.

GOE Information—Interest Area: 02. Architecture and Construction. **Work Group:** 02.04. Construction Crafts. **Personality Type**—Realistic. Realistic occupations frequently involve work activities that include practical, hands-on problems and solutions. They often deal with plants; animals; and real-world materials like wood, tools, and machinery. Many of the occupations require working outside and do not involve a lot of paperwork or working closely with others. **Work Values**—Moral Values; Independence. **Skills**—Operation and Control; Operation Monitoring. **Abilities**—*Cognitive:* None met the criteria. *Psychomotor:* Multilimb Coordination; Control Precision. *Physical:* Extent Flexibility. *Sensory:* Depth Perception; Far Vision. **General Work Activities**—*Information Input:* None met the criteria. *Mental Process:* None met the criteria. *Work Output:* Controlling Machines and Processes; Operating Vehicles or Equipment; Handling and Moving Objects. *Interacting with Others:* None met the criteria. **Physical Work Conditions**—Outdoors; Noisy; Whole-Body Vibration; Hazardous Equipment; Sitting; Using Hands on Objects, Tools, or Controls. **Other Job Characteristics**—Automation.

Experience—Job Zone 2. Some previous work-related skill, knowledge, or experience may be helpful in these occupations, but usually is not needed. **Job Preparation**—SVP 4.0 to less than 6.0—six months to less than two years. **Knowledges**—Building and Construction; Engineering and Technology; Mechanical Devices. **Instructional**

Program—Construction/Heavy Equipment/Earthmoving Equipment Operation.

Related SOC Job—47-2072 Pile-Driver Operators. **Related OOH Job**—Construction Equipment Operators. **Related DOT Job**—859.682-018 Pile-Driver Operator.

47-2073.00 Operating Engineers and Other Construction Equipment Operators

- **Education/Training Required: Moderate-term on-the-job training**
- **Employed: 378,720**
- **Annual Earnings: $35,830**
- **Growth: 11.6%**
- **Annual Job Openings: 37,000**

Operate one or several types of power construction equipment, such as motor graders, bulldozers, scrapers, compressors, pumps, derricks, shovels, tractors, or front-end loaders, to excavate, move, and grade earth; erect structures; or pour concrete or other hard-surface pavement. May repair and maintain equipment in addition to other duties.

Learn and follow safety regulations. Take actions to avoid potential hazards and obstructions such as utility lines, other equipment, other workers, and falling objects. Adjust handwheels and depress pedals to control attachments such as blades, buckets, scrapers, and swing booms. Start engines; move throttles, switches, and levers; and depress pedals to operate machines such as bulldozers, trench excavators, road graders, and backhoes. Locate underground services, such as pipes and wires, prior to beginning work. Monitor operations to ensure that health and safety standards are met. Align machines, cutterheads, or depth gauge makers with reference stakes and guidelines or ground or position equipment by following hand signals of other workers. Load and move dirt, rocks, equipment, and materials, using trucks, crawler tractors, power cranes, shovels, graders, and related equipment. Drive and maneuver equipment equipped with blades in successive passes over working areas to remove topsoil, vegetation, and rocks and to distribute and level earth or terrain. Coordinate machine actions with other activities, positioning or moving loads in response to hand or audio signals from crew members. Operate tractors and bulldozers to perform such tasks as clearing land, mixing sludge, trimming backfills, and building roadways and parking lots. Repair and maintain equipment, making emergency adjustments or assisting with major repairs as necessary. Check fuel supplies at sites to ensure adequate availability. Connect hydraulic hoses, belts, mechanical linkages, or power takeoff shafts to tractors. Operate loaders to pull out stumps, rip asphalt or concrete, rough-grade properties, bury refuse, or perform general cleanup. Select and fasten bulldozer blades or other attachments to tractors, using hitches. Test atmosphere for adequate oxygen and explosive conditions when working in confined spaces. Operate compactors, scrapers, and rollers to level, compact, and cover refuse at disposal grounds. Talk to clients and study instructions, plans, and diagrams to establish work requirements.

GOE Information—**Interest Area:** 02. Architecture and Construction. **Work Group:** 02.04. Construction Crafts. **Personality Type**—Realistic. Realistic occupations frequently involve work activities that include practical, hands-on problems and solutions. They often deal with plants; animals; and real-world materials like wood, tools, and machinery. Many of the occupations require working outside and do not involve a lot of paperwork or working closely with others. **Work Values**—Supervision, Technical; Moral Values; Independence. **Skills**—Equipment Maintenance; Installation; Operation Monitoring; Operation and Control; Repairing; Management of Financial Resources. **Abilities**—_Cognitive:_ None met the criteria. _Psychomotor:_ Control Precision; Reaction Time; Response Orientation; Rate Control; Multilimb Coordination; Wrist-Finger Speed. _Physical:_ Explosive Strength; Static Strength; Trunk Strength; Extent Flexibility. _Sensory:_ Depth Perception. **General Work Activities**—_Information Input:_ Monitoring Processes, Materials, or Surroundings; Identifying Objects, Actions, and Events; Inspecting Equipment, Structures, or Materials. _Mental Process:_ Organizing, Planning, and Prioritizing; Updating and Using Relevant Knowledge; Judging the Qualities of Things, Services, or Other People's Work. _Work Output:_ Operating Vehicles or Equipment; Handling and Moving Objects; Performing General Physical Activities. _Interacting with Others:_ Establishing and Maintaining Interpersonal Relationships; Coordinating the Work and Activities of Others; Communicating with Other Workers. **Physical Work Conditions**—Outdoors; Noisy; Very Hot or Cold; Contaminants; Whole-Body Vibration; Using Hands on Objects, Tools, or Controls. **Other Job Characteristics**—Pace Determined by Speed of Equipment; Need to Be Exact or Accurate; Errors Have Important Consequences; Repeat Same Tasks.

Experience—Job Zone 3. Previous work-related skill, knowledge, or experience is required. **Job Preparation**—SVP 6.0 to less than 7.0—more than one year and less than four years. **Knowledges**—Building and Construction; Mechanical Devices; Engineering and Technology; Design; Production and Processing; Public Safety and Security. **Instructional Programs**—Construction/Heavy Equipment/Earthmoving Equipment Operation; Mobil Crane Operation/Operator.

Related SOC Job—47-2073 Operating Engineers and Other Construction Equipment Operators. **Related OOH Job**—Construction Equipment Operators. **Related DOT Jobs**—850.663-014 Elevating-Grader Operator; 850.663-022 Motor-Grader Operator; 850.683-010 Bulldozer Operator I; 850.683-014 Ditcher Operator; 850.683-022 Form-Grader Operator; 850.683-038 Scraper Operator; 850.683-046 Utility-Tractor Operator; 859.683-010 Operating Engineer; 859.683-014 Operating-Engineer Apprentice; 955.463-010 Sanitary Landfill Operator.

47-2081.00 Drywall and Ceiling Tile Installers

- **Education/Training Required: Moderate-term on-the-job training**
- **Employed: 126,810**
- **Annual Earnings: $34,740**
- **Growth: 9.0%**
- **Annual Job Openings: 17,000**

Apply plasterboard or other wallboard to ceilings or interior walls of buildings. Apply or mount acoustical tiles or blocks, strips, or sheets of shock-absorbing materials to ceilings and walls of buildings to reduce or reflect sound. Materials may be of decorative quality. Includes lathers who fasten wooden, metal, or rockboard lath to walls, ceilings, or partitions of buildings to provide support base for plaster, fireproofing, or acoustical material.

Fasten metal or rockboard lath to the structural framework of walls, ceilings, and partitions of buildings, using nails, screws, staples, or wire-ties. Apply cement to backs of tiles and press tiles into place, aligning them with layout marks or joints of previously laid tile. Apply or mount acoustical tile or blocks, strips, or sheets of shock-absorbing materials to ceilings and walls of buildings to reduce reflection of sound or to decorate rooms. Assemble and install metal framing and decorative trim for windows, doorways, and vents. Cut and screw together metal channels to make floor and ceiling frames according to plans for the location of rooms and hallways. Cut metal or wood framing and trim to size, using cutting tools. Measure and cut openings in panels or tiles for electrical outlets, windows, vents, and plumbing and other fixtures, using keyhole saws or other cutting tools. Fit and fasten wallboard or drywall into position on wood or metal frameworks, using glue, nails, or screws. Hang dry lines (stretched string) to wall moldings in order to guide positioning of main runners. Hang drywall panels on metal frameworks of walls and ceilings in offices, schools, and other large buildings, using lifts or hoists to adjust panel heights when necessary. Inspect furrings, mechanical mountings, and masonry surface for plumbness and level, using spirit or water levels. Install horizontal and vertical metal or wooden studs to frames so that wallboard can be attached to interior walls. Measure and mark surfaces to lay out work according to blueprints and drawings, using tape measures, straightedges or squares, and marking devices. Nail channels or wood furring strips to surfaces to provide mounting for tile. Read blueprints and other specifications to determine methods of installation, work procedures, and material and tool requirements. Scribe and cut edges of tile to fit walls where wall molding is not specified. Seal joints between ceiling tiles and walls. Cut fixture and border tiles to size, using keyhole saws, and insert them into surrounding frameworks. Suspend angle iron grids and channel irons from ceilings, using wire.

GOE Information—Interest Area: 02. Architecture and Construction. **Work Group:** 02.04. Construction Crafts. **Personality Type—**Realistic. Realistic occupations frequently involve work activities that include practical, hands-on problems and solutions. They often deal with plants; animals; and real-world materials like wood, tools, and machinery. Many of the occupations require working outside and do not involve a lot of paperwork or working closely with others. **Work Values—**Independence; Moral Values; Supervision, Technical; Supervision, Human Relations. **Skills—**Installation. **Abilities—***Cognitive:* None met the criteria. *Psychomotor:* Wrist-Finger Speed; Multilimb Coordination; Manual Dexterity; Arm-Hand Steadiness. *Physical:* Explosive Strength; Extent Flexibility; Static Strength; Trunk Strength. *Sensory:* None met the criteria. **General Work Activities—***Information Input:* Getting Information; Inspecting Equipment, Structures, or Materials. *Mental Process:* None met the criteria. *Work Output:* Performing General Physical Activities; Handling and Moving Objects. *Interacting with Others:* None met the criteria. **Physical Work Conditions—**Indoors; Contaminants; Hazardous Equipment; Minor Burns, Cuts, Bites, or Stings; Standing; Using Hands on Objects, Tools, or Controls. **Other Job Characteristics—**None met the criteria.

Experience—Job Zone 3. Previous work-related skill, knowledge, or experience is required. **Job Preparation—**SVP 6.0 to less than 7.0—more than one year and less than four years. **Knowledges—**Building and Construction; Design. **Instructional Program—**Drywall Installation/Drywaller.

Related SOC Job—47-2081 Drywall and Ceiling Tile Installers. **Related OOH Job—**Drywall Installers, Ceiling Tile Installers, and Tapers. **Related DOT Jobs—**842.361-030 Dry-Wall Applicator; 842.684-014 Dry-Wall Applicator; 860.381-010 Acoustical Carpenter; 869.684-050 Sheetrock Applicator.

47-2082.00 Tapers

- **Education/Training Required: Moderate-term on-the-job training**
- **Employed: 38,570**
- **Annual Earnings: $39,870**
- **Growth: 5.9%**
- **Annual Job Openings: 5,000**

Seal joints between plasterboard or other wallboard to prepare wall surface for painting or papering.

Mix sealing compounds by hand or with portable electric mixers. Sand rough spots of dried cement between applications of compounds. Select the correct sealing compound or tape. Apply additional coats to fill in holes and make surfaces smooth. Sand or patch nicks or cracks in plasterboard or wallboard. Spread sealing compound between boards or panels and over cracks, holes, and nail and screw heads, using trowels, broadknives, or spatulas. Spread and smooth cementing material over tape, using trowels or floating machines to blend joints with wall surfaces. Use mechanical applicators that spread compounds and embed tape in one operation. Press paper tape over joints to embed tape into sealing compound and to seal joints. Install metal molding at wall corners to secure wallboard. Countersink nails or screws below surfaces of walls before applying sealing compounds, using hammers or screwdrivers. Check adhesives to ensure that they will work and will remain durable. Apply texturizing compounds and primers to walls and ceilings before final finishing, using trowels, brushes, rollers, or spray guns. Remove extra compound after surfaces have been covered sufficiently.

GOE Information—Interest Area: 02. Architecture and Construction. **Work Group:** 02.04. Construction Crafts. **Personality Type—**Realistic. Realistic occupations frequently involve work activities that include practical, hands-on problems and solutions. They often deal with plants; animals; and real-world materials like wood, tools, and machinery. Many of the occupations require working outside and do not involve a lot of paperwork or working closely with others. **Work Values—**Moral Values; Independence; Supervision, Technical. **Skills—**None met the criteria. **Abilities—***Cognitive:* None met the criteria. *Psychomotor:* Wrist-Finger Speed; Manual Dexterity; Arm-Hand Steadiness. *Physical:* Explosive Strength; Extent Flexibility. *Sensory:* None met the criteria. **General Work Activities—***Information Input:* None met the criteria. *Mental Process:* None met the criteria. *Work Output:* Performing General Physical Activities; Handling and Moving Objects. *Interacting with Others:* None met the criteria. **Physical Work Conditions—**Indoors; Contaminants; Minor Burns, Cuts, Bites, or Stings; Standing; Using Hands on Objects, Tools, or Controls; Bending or Twisting the Body. **Other Job Characteristics—**None met the criteria.

Experience—Job Zone 2. Some previous work-related skill, knowledge, or experience may be helpful in these occupations, but usually is not needed. **Job Preparation—**SVP 4.0 to less than 6.0—six months to less than two years. **Knowledges—**Building and Construction. **Instructional Program—**Building/Construction Trades, Other.

Related SOC Job—47-2082 Tapers. **Related OOH Job—**Drywall Installers, Ceiling Tile Installers, and Tapers. **Related DOT Job—**842.664-010 Taper.

47-2111.00 Electricians

- Education/Training Required: **Long-term on-the-job training**
- Employed: **606,500**
- Annual Earnings: **$42,790**
- Growth: **11.8%**
- Annual Job Openings: **68,000**

Install, maintain, and repair electrical wiring, equipment, and fixtures. Ensure that work is in accordance with relevant codes. May install or service street lights, intercom systems, or electrical control systems.

Assemble, install, test, and maintain electrical or electronic wiring, equipment, appliances, apparatus, and fixtures, using hand tools and power tools. Diagnose malfunctioning systems, apparatus, and components, using test equipment and hand tools, to locate the cause of a breakdown and correct the problem. Connect wires to circuit breakers, transformers, or other components. Inspect electrical systems, equipment, and components to identify hazards, defects, and the need for adjustment or repair and to ensure compliance with codes. Advise management on whether continued operation of equipment could be hazardous. Test electrical systems and continuity of circuits in electrical wiring, equipment, and fixtures, using testing devices such as ohmmeters, voltmeters, and oscilloscopes, to ensure compatibility and safety of system. Maintain current electrician's license or identification card to meet governmental regulations. Plan layout and installation of electrical wiring, equipment, and fixtures based on job specifications and local codes. Direct and train workers to install, maintain, or repair electrical wiring, equipment, and fixtures. Prepare sketches or follow blueprints to determine the location of wiring and equipment and to ensure conformance to building and safety codes. Use a variety of tools and equipment, such as power construction equipment; measuring devices; power tools; and testing equipment, including oscilloscopes, ammeters, and test lamps. Install ground leads and connect power cables to equipment such as motors. Perform business management duties such as maintaining records and files, preparing reports, and ordering supplies and equipment. Repair or replace wiring, equipment, and fixtures, using hand tools and power tools. Work from ladders, scaffolds, and roofs to install, maintain, or repair electrical wiring, equipment, and fixtures. Place conduit, pipes, or tubing inside designated partitions, walls, or other concealed areas and pull insulated wires or cables through the conduit to complete circuits between boxes. Construct and fabricate parts, using hand tools and specifications.

GOE Information—Interest Area: 02. Architecture and Construction. **Work Group:** 02.04. Construction Crafts. **Personality Type—**Realistic. Realistic occupations frequently involve work activities that include practical, hands-on problems and solutions. They often deal with plants; animals; and real-world materials like wood, tools, and machinery. Many of the occupations require working outside and do not involve a lot of paperwork or working closely with others. **Work Values—**Authority; Ability Utilization; Creativity; Compensation; Variety; Responsibility. **Skills—**Installation; Repairing; Equipment Maintenance; Troubleshooting; Technology Design; Operation and Control. **Abilities—***Cognitive:* Spatial Orientation; Visualization; Speed of Closure; Problem Sensitivity; Flexibility of Closure; Information Ordering. *Psychomotor:* Arm-Hand Steadiness; Reaction Time; Finger Dexterity; Wrist-Finger Speed; Speed of Limb Movement; Manual Dexterity. *Physical:* Extent Flexibility; Gross Body Equilibrium; Dynamic Strength; Static Strength; Stamina; Trunk Strength. *Sensory:* Visual Color Discrimination; Depth Perception; Auditory Attention; Hearing Sensitivity; Near Vision; Far Vision. **General Work Activities—**

Information Input: Monitoring Processes, Materials, or Surroundings; Inspecting Equipment, Structures, or Materials; Identifying Objects, Actions, and Events. *Mental Process:* Updating and Using Relevant Knowledge; Organizing, Planning, and Prioritizing; Making Decisions and Solving Problems. *Work Output:* Performing General Physical Activities; Handling and Moving Objects; Repairing and Maintaining Electronic Equipment. *Interacting with Others:* Establishing and Maintaining Interpersonal Relationships; Coordinating the Work and Activities of Others; Communicating with Other Workers. **Physical Work Conditions—**Outdoors; Noisy; Minor Burns, Cuts, Bites, or Stings; Standing; Walking and Running; Using Hands on Objects, Tools, or Controls. **Other Job Characteristics—**Need to Be Exact or Accurate; Repeat Same Tasks; Errors Have Important Consequences.

Experience—Job Zone 3. Previous work-related skill, knowledge, or experience is required. **Job Preparation—**SVP 6.0 to less than 7.0—more than one year and less than four years. **Knowledges—**Building and Construction; Mechanical Devices; Design; Production and Processing; Physics; Mathematics. **Instructional Program—**Electrician.

Related SOC Job—47-2111 Electricians. **Related OOH Job—**Electricians. **Related DOT Jobs—**729.381-018 Street-Light Repairer; 821.684-018 Wirer, Street Light; 824.261-010 Electrician; 824.261-014 Electrician Apprentice; 824.281-010 Airport Electrician; 824.281-018 Neon-Sign Servicer; 824.381-010 Street-Light Servicer; 824.681-010 Electrician; 825.281-014 Electrician; 825.381-030 Electrician; 825.381-034 Electrician Apprentice; 829.261-018 Electrician, Maintenance; 952.364-010 Trouble Shooter I; 952.381-010 Switch Inspector.

47-2121.00 Glaziers

- Education/Training Required: **Long-term on-the-job training**
- Employed: **49,310**
- Annual Earnings: **$33,530**
- Growth: **14.2%**
- Annual Job Openings: **9,000**

Install glass in windows, skylights, storefronts, and display cases or on surfaces such as building fronts, interior walls, ceilings, and tabletops.

Read and interpret blueprints and specifications to determine size, shape, color, type, and thickness of glass; location of framing; installation procedures; and staging and scaffolding materials required. Determine plumb of walls or ceilings, using plumb-lines and levels. Fabricate and install metal sashes and moldings for glass installation, using aluminum or steel framing. Measure mirrors and dimensions of areas to be covered to determine work procedures. Fasten glass panes into wood sashes or frames with clips, points, or moldings, adding weather seals or putty around pane edges to seal joints. Secure mirrors in position, using mastic cement, putty, bolts, or screws. Cut, fit, install, repair, and replace glass and glass substitutes, such as plastic and aluminum, in building interiors or exteriors and in furniture or other products. Cut and remove broken glass prior to installing replacement glass. Set glass doors into frames and bolt metal hinges, handles, locks, and other hardware to attach doors to frames and walls. Score glass with cutters' wheels, breaking off excess glass by hand or with notched tools. Cut, assemble, fit, and attach metal-framed glass enclosures for showers, bathtubs, display cases, skylights, solariums, and other structures. Drive trucks to installation sites and unload mirrors, glass equipment, and tools. Install pre-assembled metal or wood frameworks for windows or doors to be fitted with glass panels, using hand tools. Cut and attach mounting strips, metal or wood moldings, rubber gaskets, or metal clips to surfaces in preparation for mirror installation. Assemble, erect, and dismantle scaffolds, rigging, and hoisting equipment. Load and arrange glass and mirrors onto delivery trucks, using suction cups or cranes to lift glass. Grind and polish glass and smooth edges when necessary. Measure and mark outlines or patterns on glass to indicate cutting lines. Prepare glass for cutting by resting it on rack edges or against cutting tables and brushing thin layer of oil along cutting lines or dipping cutting tools in oil. Pack spaces between moldings and glass with glazing compounds and trim excess material with glazing knives.

GOE Information—Interest Area: 02. Architecture and Construction. **Work Group:** 02.04. Construction Crafts. **Personality Type**—Realistic. Realistic occupations frequently involve work activities that include practical, hands-on problems and solutions. They often deal with plants; animals; and real-world materials like wood, tools, and machinery. Many of the occupations require working outside and do not involve a lot of paperwork or working closely with others. **Work Values**—Moral Values. **Skills**—Installation; Mathematics; Repairing. **Abilities**—*Cognitive:* Visualization. *Psychomotor:* Multilimb Coordination; Arm-Hand Steadiness; Control Precision; Finger Dexterity; Manual Dexterity. *Physical:* Gross Body Equilibrium; Stamina; Extent Flexibility; Gross Body Coordination; Trunk Strength; Static Strength. *Sensory:* Visual Color Discrimination; Depth Perception. **General Work Activities**—*Information Input:* Inspecting Equipment, Structures, or Materials; Estimating the Needed Characteristics of Products, Events, or Information; Identifying Objects, Actions, and Events. *Mental Process:* Organizing, Planning, and Prioritizing; Evaluating Information Against Standards; Scheduling Work and Activities. *Work Output:* Handling and Moving Objects; Performing General Physical Activities; Operating Vehicles or Equipment. *Interacting with Others:* Communicating with Persons Outside Organization; Communicating with Other Workers; Establishing and Maintaining Interpersonal Relationships. **Physical Work Conditions**—Outdoors; Noisy; Very Hot or Cold; Contaminants; Standing; Using Hands on Objects, Tools, or Controls. **Other Job Characteristics**—Need to Be Exact or Accurate; Errors Have Important Consequences; Repeat Same Tasks.

Experience—Job Zone 2. Some previous work-related skill, knowledge, or experience may be helpful in these occupations, but usually is not needed. **Job Preparation**—SVP 4.0 to less than 6.0—six months to less than two years. **Knowledges**—Building and Construction; Mechanical Devices; Design; Engineering and Technology; Mathematics; Public Safety and Security. **Instructional Program**—Glazier.

Related SOC Job—47-2121 Glaziers. **Related OOH Job**—Glaziers. **Related DOT Jobs**—779.381-010 Glazier, Stained Glass; 865.361-010 Mirror Installer; 865.381-010 Glazier; 865.381-014 Glazier Apprentice.

47-2131.00 Insulation Workers, Floor, Ceiling, and Wall

- ● Education/Training Required: Moderate-term on-the-job training
- ● Employed: 34,250
- ● Annual Earnings: $31,360
- ● Growth: 3.0%
- ● Annual Job Openings: 4,000

Line and cover structures with insulating materials. May work with batt, roll, or blown insulation materials.

Distribute insulating materials evenly into small spaces within floors, ceilings, or walls, using blowers and hose attachments or cement mortars. Cover and line structures with blown or rolled forms of materials to insulate against cold, heat, or moisture, using saws, knives, rasps, trowels, blowers, and other tools and implements. Move controls, buttons, or levers to start blowers and regulate flow of materials through nozzles. Remove old insulation such as asbestos, following safety procedures. Read blueprints and select appropriate insulation, based on space characteristics and the heat-retaining or -excluding characteristics of the material. Prepare surfaces for insulation application by brushing or spreading on adhesives, cement, or asphalt or by attaching metal pins to surfaces. Measure and cut insulation for covering surfaces, using tape measures, hand saws, power saws, knives, or scissors. Fit, wrap, staple, or glue insulating materials to structures or surfaces, using hand tools or wires. Fill blower hoppers with insulating materials. Cover, seal, or finish insulated surfaces or access holes with plastic covers, canvas strips, sealants, tape, cement, or asphalt mastic.

GOE Information—Interest Area: 02. Architecture and Construction. **Work Group:** 02.04. Construction Crafts. **Personality Type**—Realistic. Realistic occupations frequently involve work activities that include practical, hands-on problems and solutions. They often deal with plants; animals; and real-world materials like wood, tools, and machinery. Many of the occupations require working outside and do not involve a lot of paperwork or working closely with others. **Work Values**—Moral Values; Independence. **Skills**—None met the criteria. **Abilities**—*Cognitive:* None met the criteria. *Psychomotor:* Wrist-Finger Speed. *Physical:* Static Strength; Trunk Strength. *Sensory:* None met the criteria. **General Work Activities**—*Information Input:* Getting Information. *Mental Process:* None met the criteria. *Work Output:* Handling and Moving Objects; Performing General Physical Activities. *Interacting with Others:* None met the criteria. **Physical Work Conditions**—Indoors; Contaminants; Standing; Using Hands on Objects, Tools, or Controls. **Other Job Characteristics**—Need to Be Exact or Accurate.

Experience—Job Zone 3. Previous work-related skill, knowledge, or experience is required. **Job Preparation**—SVP 6.0 to less than 7.0—more than one year and less than four years. **Knowledges**—Building and Construction; Mechanical Devices. **Instructional Program**—Building/Construction Trades, Other.

Related SOC Job—47-2131 Insulation Workers, Floor, Ceiling, and Wall. **Related OOH Job**—Insulation Workers. **Related DOT Jobs**—863.364-010 Insulation-Worker Apprentice; 863.364-014 Insulation Worker; 863.381-010 Cork Insulator, Refrigeration Plant; 863.664-010 Blower Insulator; 863.685-010 Insulation-Power-Unit Tender.

47-2132.00 Insulation Workers, Mechanical

- ● Education/Training Required: Moderate-term on-the-job training
- ● Employed: 22,100
- ● Annual Earnings: $35,510
- ● Growth: 1.0%
- ● Annual Job Openings: 2,000

Apply insulating materials to pipes or ductwork or other mechanical systems to help control and maintain temperature.

Read blueprints and specifications to determine job requirements. Remove or seal off old asbestos insulation, following safety procedures. Fill blower hoppers with insulating materials. Distribute insulating materials evenly into small spaces within floors, ceilings, or walls, using blowers and hose attachments or cement mortar. Select appropriate insulation such as fiberglass, Styrofoam, or cork, based on the heat-retaining or -excluding characteristics of the material. Move controls, buttons, or levers to start blowers and to regulate flow of materials through nozzles. Apply, remove, and repair insulation on industrial equipment; pipes; ductwork; or other mechanical systems such as heat exchangers, tanks, and vessels to help control noise and maintain temperatures. Measure and cut insulation for covering surfaces, using tape measures, handsaws, knives, and scissors. Install sheet metal around insulated pipes with screws to protect the insulation from weather conditions or physical damage. Fit insulation around obstructions and shape insulating materials and protective coverings as required. Determine the amounts and types of insulation needed and methods of installation based on factors such as location, surface shape, and equipment use. Prepare surfaces for insulation application by brushing or spreading on adhesives, cement, or asphalt or by attaching metal pins to surfaces. Cover, seal, or finish insulated surfaces or access holes with plastic covers, canvas strips, sealants, tape, cement, or asphalt mastic.

GOE Information—Interest Area: 02. Architecture and Construction. **Work Group:** 02.04. Construction Crafts. **Personality Type**—Realistic. Realistic occupations frequently involve work activities that include practical, hands-on problems and solutions. They often deal with plants; animals; and real-world materials like wood, tools, and machinery. Many of the occupations require working outside and do not involve a lot of paperwork or working closely with others. **Work Values**—Moral Values; Independence. **Skills**—None met the criteria. **Abilities**—*Cognitive:* None met the criteria. *Psychomotor:* Wrist-Finger Speed; Control Precision. *Physical:* Static Strength; Trunk Strength. *Sensory:* None met the criteria. **General Work Activities**—*Information Input:* Getting Information. *Mental Process:* None met the criteria. *Work Output:* Handling and Moving Objects; Performing General Physical Activities. *Interacting with Others:* None met the criteria. **Physical Work Conditions**—Indoors; Contaminants; Standing; Using Hands on Objects, Tools, or Controls. **Other Job Characteristics**—Need to Be Exact or Accurate.

Experience—Job Zone 3. Previous work-related skill, knowledge, or experience is required. **Job Preparation**—SVP 6.0 to less than 7.0—more than one year and less than four years. **Knowledges**—Building and Construction; Mechanical Devices. **Instructional Program**—Building/Construction Trades, Other.

Related SOC Job—47-2132 Insulation Workers, Mechanical. **Related OOH Job**—Insulation Workers. **Related DOT Jobs**—863.364-010 Insulation-Worker Apprentice; 863.364-014 Insulation Worker; 863.381-014 Pipe Coverer and Insulator.

47-2141.00 Painters, Construction and Maintenance

- **Education/Training Required: Moderate-term on-the-job training**
- **Employed: 249,850**
- **Annual Earnings: $30,800**
- **Growth: 12.6%**
- **Annual Job Openings: 102,000**

Paint walls, equipment, buildings, bridges, and other structural surfaces, using brushes, rollers, and spray guns. May remove old paint to prepare surface prior to painting. May mix colors or oils to obtain desired color or consistency.

Cover surfaces with dropcloths or masking tape and paper to protect surfaces during painting. Fill cracks, holes, and joints with caulk, putty, plaster, or other fillers, using caulking guns or putty knives. Apply primers or sealers to prepare new surfaces, such as bare wood or metal, for finish coats. Apply paint, stain, varnish, enamel, and other finishes to equipment, buildings, bridges, and other structures, using brushes, spray guns, or rollers. Calculate amounts of required materials and estimate costs, based on surface measurements and work orders. Read work orders or receive instructions from supervisors or homeowners to determine work requirements. Erect scaffolding and swing gates or set up ladders to work above ground level. Remove fixtures such as pictures, door knobs, lamps, and electric switch covers prior to painting. Wash and treat surfaces with oil, turpentine, mildew remover, or other preparations and sand rough spots to ensure that finishes will adhere properly. Mix and match colors of paint, stain, or varnish with oil and thinning and drying additives to obtain desired colors and consistencies. Remove old finishes by stripping, sanding, wire-brushing, burning, or using water or abrasive blasting. Select and purchase tools and finishes for surfaces to be covered, considering durability, ease of handling, methods of application, and customers' wishes. Smooth surfaces, using sandpaper, scrapers, brushes, steel wool, or sanding machines. Polish final coats to specified finishes. Use special finishing techniques such as sponging, ragging, layering, or faux finishing. Waterproof buildings, using waterproofers and caulking. Spray or brush hot plastics or pitch onto surfaces. Cut stencils and brush and spray lettering and decorations on surfaces. Bake finishes on painted and enameled articles, using baking ovens.

GOE Information—Interest Area: 02. Architecture and Construction. **Work Group:** 02.04. Construction Crafts. **Personality Type**—Realistic. Realistic occupations frequently involve work activities that include practical, hands-on problems and solutions. They often deal with plants; animals; and real-world materials like wood, tools, and machinery. Many of the occupations require working outside and do not involve a lot of paperwork or working closely with others. **Work Values**—Moral Values; Independence; Supervision, Technical. **Skills**—Equipment Maintenance; Management of Material Resources; Management of Personnel Resources; Repairing; Equipment Selection; Monitoring. **Abilities**—*Cognitive:* Visualization. *Psychomotor:* Multilimb Coordination; Arm-Hand Steadiness; Manual Dexterity; Control Precision; Finger Dexterity. *Physical:* Gross Body Equilibrium; Stamina; Extent Flexibility; Gross Body Coordination; Trunk Strength; Dynamic Strength. *Sensory:* Visual Color Discrimination; Depth Perception; Far Vision. **General Work Activities**—*Information Input:* Monitoring Processes, Materials, or Surroundings; Getting Information; Inspecting Equipment, Structures, or Materials. *Mental Process:* Organizing, Planning, and Prioritizing; Making Decisions and Solving Problems; Updating and Using Relevant Knowledge. *Work Output:* Handling and Moving Objects; Performing General Physical Activities; Controlling Machines and Processes. *Interacting with Others:* Coordinating the Work and Activities of Others; Establishing and Maintaining Interpersonal Relationships; Communicating with Other Workers. **Physical Work Conditions**—Contaminants; Standing; Climbing Ladders, Scaffolds, or Poles; Using Hands on Objects, Tools, or Controls; Repetitive Motions; Bending or Twisting the Body; Repetitive Motions. **Other Job Characteristics**—Need to Be Exact or Accurate.

Experience—Job Zone 2. Some previous work-related skill, knowledge, or experience may be helpful in these occupations, but usually is not needed. **Job Preparation**—SVP 4.0 to less than 6.0—six months to less than two years. **Knowledges**—Design; Transportation; Building and Construction; Customer and Personal Service;

Production and Processing; Administration and Management. **Instructional Program**—Painting/Painter and Wall Coverer.

Related SOC Job—47-2141 Painters, Construction and Maintenance. **Related OOH Job**—Painters and Paperhangers. **Related DOT Jobs**—840.381-010 Painter; 840.381-014 Painter Apprentice, Shipyard; 840.381-018 Painter, Shipyard; 840.381-640 Coating Finisher, Architectural; 840.681-010 Painter, Stage Settings.

47-2142.00 Paperhangers

- **Education/Training Required: Moderate-term on-the-job training**
- **Employed: 7,710**
- **Annual Earnings: $33,450**
- **Growth: 3.2%**
- **Annual Job Openings: 3,000**

Cover interior walls and ceilings of rooms with decorative wallpaper or fabric or attach advertising posters on surfaces such as walls and billboards. Duties include removing old materials from surface to be papered.

Smooth rough spots on walls and ceilings, using sandpaper. Place strips or sections of paper on surfaces, aligning section edges and patterns. Staple or tack advertising posters onto fences, walls, billboards, or poles. Apply acetic acid to damp plaster to prevent lime from bleeding through paper. Trim excess material at ceilings or baseboards, using knives. Smooth strips or sections of paper with brushes or rollers to remove wrinkles and bubbles and to smooth joints. Set up equipment such as pasteboards and scaffolds. Remove paint, varnish, dirt, and grease from surfaces, using paint remover and water-soda solutions. Remove old paper, using water, steam machines, or solvents and scrapers. Trim rough edges from strips, using straightedges and trimming knives. Mix paste, using paste powder and water, and brush paste onto surfaces. Apply thinned glue to waterproof porous surfaces, using brushes, rollers, or pasting machines. Check finished wallcoverings for proper alignment, pattern matching, and neatness of seams. Apply adhesives to the backs of paper strips, using brushes, or dunk strips of prepasted wallcovering in water, wiping off any excess adhesive. Cover interior walls and ceilings of rooms with decorative wallpaper or fabric, using hand tools. Fill holes, cracks, and other surface imperfections preparatory to covering surfaces. Mark vertical guidelines on walls to align strips, using plumb bobs and chalk lines. Measure and cut strips from rolls of wallpaper or fabric, using shears or razors. Measure surfaces and review work orders to estimate the quantities of materials needed. Apply sizing to seal surfaces and maximize adhesion of coverings to surfaces.

GOE Information—**Interest Area:** 02. Architecture and Construction. **Work Group:** 02.04. Construction Crafts. **Personality Type**—Realistic. Realistic occupations frequently involve work activities that include practical, hands-on problems and solutions. They often deal with plants; animals; and real-world materials like wood, tools, and machinery. Many of the occupations require working outside and do not involve a lot of paperwork or working closely with others. **Work Values**—Moral Values; Supervision, Technical. **Skills**—None met the criteria. **Abilities**—*Cognitive:* None met the criteria. *Psychomotor:* Wrist-Finger Speed; Multilimb Coordination; Manual Dexterity; Arm-Hand Steadiness. *Physical:* Extent Flexibility; Stamina; Static Strength. *Sensory:* None met the criteria. **General Work Activities**—*Information Input:* Getting Information; Monitoring Processes, Materials, or Surroundings. *Mental Process:* None met the criteria. *Work Output:* Handling and Moving Objects; Performing General Physical Activities. *Interacting with Others:* None

met the criteria. **Physical Work Conditions**—Indoors; Standing; Climbing Ladders, Scaffolds, or Poles; Using Hands on Objects, Tools, or Controls; Repetitive Motions. **Other Job Characteristics**—Need to Be Exact or Accurate.

Experience—Job Zone 2. Some previous work-related skill, knowledge, or experience may be helpful in these occupations, but usually is not needed. **Job Preparation**—SVP 4.0 to less than 6.0—six months to less than two years. **Knowledges**—Building and Construction; Design. **Instructional Program**—Painting/Painter and Wall Coverer.

Related SOC Job—47-2142 Paperhangers. **Related OOH Job**—Painters and Paperhangers. **Related DOT Jobs**—841.381-010 Paperhanger; 841.684-010 Billposter.

47-2151.00 Pipelayers

- **Education/Training Required: Moderate-term on-the-job training**
- **Employed: 56,280**
- **Annual Earnings: $28,760**
- **Growth: 9.9%**
- **Annual Job Openings: 7,000**

Lay pipe for storm or sanitation sewers, drains, and water mains. Perform any combination of the following tasks: grade trenches or culverts, position pipe, or seal joints.

Check slopes for conformance to requirements, using levels or lasers. Cover pipes with earth or other materials. Cut pipes to required lengths. Connect pipe pieces and seal joints, using welding equipment, cement, or glue. Install and repair sanitary and stormwater sewer structures and pipe systems. Install and use instruments such as lasers, grade rods, and transit levels. Grade and level trench bases, using tamping machines and hand tools. Lay out pipe routes, following written instructions or blueprints and coordinating layouts with supervisors. Align and position pipes to prepare them for welding or sealing. Dig trenches to desired or required depths by hand or using trenching tools. Operate mechanized equipment such as pickup trucks, rollers, tandem dump trucks, front-end loaders, and backhoes. Train others in pipe-laying and provide supervision. Tap and drill holes into pipes to introduce auxiliary lines or devices. Locate existing pipes needing repair or replacement, using magnetic or radio indicators.

GOE Information—**Interest Area:** 02. Architecture and Construction. **Work Group:** 02.04. Construction Crafts. **Personality Type**—Realistic. Realistic occupations frequently involve work activities that include practical, hands-on problems and solutions. They often deal with plants; animals; and real-world materials like wood, tools, and machinery. Many of the occupations require working outside and do not involve a lot of paperwork or working closely with others. **Work Values**—Moral Values; Supervision, Technical. **Skills**—Installation; Quality Control Analysis; Operation Monitoring; Operation and Control; Equipment Maintenance; Monitoring. **Abilities**—*Cognitive:* Perceptual Speed; Visualization; Selective Attention. *Psychomotor:* Rate Control; Reaction Time; Control Precision; Manual Dexterity; Arm-Hand Steadiness; Response Orientation. *Physical:* Extent Flexibility; Stamina; Static Strength; Trunk Strength. *Sensory:* Depth Perception; Visual Color Discrimination. **General Work Activities**—*Information Input:* Inspecting Equipment, Structures, or Materials; Monitoring Processes, Materials, or Surroundings; Getting Information. *Mental Process:* Making Decisions and Solving Problems; Updating and Using Relevant Knowledge; Organizing, Planning, and Prioritizing. *Work*

Output: Handling and Moving Objects; Performing General Physical Activities; Controlling Machines and Processes. *Interacting with Others:* Establishing and Maintaining Interpersonal Relationships; Coordinating the Work and Activities of Others; Assisting and Caring for Others. **Physical Work Conditions**—Outdoors; Noisy; Hazardous Equipment; Standing; Using Hands on Objects, Tools, or Controls; Repetitive Motions. **Other Job Characteristics**—Need to Be Exact or Accurate; Pace Determined by Speed of Equipment; Errors Have Important Consequences.

Experience—Job Zone 2. Some previous work-related skill, knowledge, or experience may be helpful in these occupations, but usually is not needed. **Job Preparation**—SVP 4.0 to less than 6.0—six months to less than two years. **Knowledges**—Building and Construction; Mechanical Devices. **Instructional Programs**—Pipefitting/Pipefitter and Sprinkler Fitter; Plumbing Technology/Plumber.

Related SOC Job—47-2151 Pipelayers. **Related OOH Job**—Pipelayers, Plumbers, Pipefitters, and Steamfitters. **Related DOT Jobs**—851.383-010 Irrigation System Installer; 869.664-014 Construction Worker I.

47-2152.00 Plumbers, Pipefitters, and Steamfitters

- **Education/Training Required: Long-term on-the-job training**
- **Employed: 420,770**
- **Annual Earnings: $42,160**
- **Growth: 15.7%**
- **Annual Job Openings: 61,000**

The job openings listed here are shared with 47-2152.01 Pipe Fitters and Steamfitters and 47-2152.02 Plumbers.

Assemble, install, alter, and repair pipelines or pipe systems that carry water, steam, air, or other liquids or gases. May install heating and cooling equipment and mechanical control systems.

No task data available.

GOE Information—**Interest Area:** 02. Architecture and Construction. **Work Group:** 02.04. Construction Crafts. **Note:** The Department of Labor has not collected some data for this job, so it has fewer details than the other descriptions.

Instructional Programs—Pipefitting/Pipefitter and Sprinkler Fitter; Plumbing Technology/Plumber.

Related SOC Job—47-2152 Plumbers, Pipefitters, and Steamfitters. **Related OOH Job**—Pipelayers, Plumbers, Pipefitters, and Steamfitters. **Related DOT Job**—No data available.

47-2152.01 Pipe Fitters and Steamfitters

- **Education/Training Required: Long-term on-the-job training**
- **Employed: 420,770**
- **Annual Earnings: $42,160**
- **Growth: 15.7%**
- **Annual Job Openings: 61,000**

The job openings listed here are shared with 47-2152.00 Plumbers, Pipefitters, and Steamfitters and 47-2152.02 Plumbers.

Lay out, assemble, install, and maintain pipe systems, pipe supports, and related hydraulic and pneumatic equipment for steam, hot water, heating, cooling, lubricating, sprinkling, and industrial production and processing systems.

Cut, thread, and hammer pipe to specifications, using tools such as saws, cutting torches, and pipe threaders and benders. Assemble and secure pipes, tubes, fittings, and related equipment according to specifications by welding, brazing, cementing, soldering, and threading joints. Attach pipes to walls, structures, and fixtures, such as radiators or tanks, using brackets, clamps, tools, or welding equipment. Inspect, examine, and test installed systems and pipelines, using pressure gauge, hydrostatic testing, observation, or other methods. Measure and mark pipes for cutting and threading. Lay out full scale drawings of pipe systems, supports, and related equipment, following blueprints. Plan pipe system layout, installation, or repair according to specifications. Select pipe sizes and types and related materials, such as supports, hangers, and hydraulic cylinders, according to specifications. Cut and bore holes in structures such as bulkheads, decks, walls, and mains prior to pipe installation, using hand and power tools. Modify, clean, and maintain pipe systems, units, fittings, and related machines and equipment, following specifications and using hand and power tools. Install automatic controls used to regulate pipe systems. Turn valves to shut off steam, water, or other gases or liquids from pipe sections, using valve keys or wrenches. Remove and replace worn components. Prepare cost estimates for clients. Inspect work sites for obstructions and to ensure that holes will not cause structural weakness. Operate motorized pumps to remove water from flooded manholes, basements, or facility floors. Dip nonferrous piping materials in a mixture of molten tin and lead to obtain a coating that prevents erosion or galvanic and electrolytic action.

GOE Information—**Interest Area:** 02. Architecture and Construction. **Work Group:** 02.04. Construction Crafts. **Personality Type**—Realistic. Realistic occupations frequently involve work activities that include practical, hands-on problems and solutions. They often deal with plants; animals; and real-world materials like wood, tools, and machinery. Many of the occupations require working outside and do not involve a lot of paperwork or working closely with others. **Work Values**—Moral Values; Independence; Supervision, Technical. **Skills**—Installation; Repairing; Management of Personnel Resources; Systems Analysis; Equipment Maintenance; Operation Monitoring. **Abilities**—*Cognitive:* Visualization; Information Ordering; Mathematical Reasoning. *Psychomotor:* Control Precision; Multilimb Coordination; Arm-Hand Steadiness; Finger Dexterity; Manual Dexterity. *Physical:* Extent Flexibility; Gross Body Equilibrium; Gross Body Coordination; Dynamic Strength; Stamina; Trunk Strength. *Sensory:* Depth Perception. **General Work Activities**—*Information Input:* Monitoring Processes, Materials, or Surroundings; Identifying Objects, Actions, and Events; Getting Information. *Mental Process:* Updating and Using Relevant Knowledge; Making Decisions and Solving Problems; Organizing, Planning, and Prioritizing. *Work Output:* Handling and Moving Objects; Documenting or Recording Information; Repairing and Maintaining Electronic Equipment. *Interacting with Others:* Coordinating the Work and Activities of Others; Performing for or Working with the Public; Communicating with Other Workers. **Physical Work Conditions**—Outdoors; Hazardous Equipment; Minor Burns, Cuts, Bites, or Stings; Standing; Using Hands on Objects, Tools, or Controls; Repetitive Motions. **Other Job Characteristics**—Need to Be Exact or Accurate.

Experience—Job Zone 3. Previous work-related skill, knowledge, or experience is required. **Job Preparation**—SVP 6.0 to less than 7.0—more than one year and less than four years. **Knowledges**—Building and Construction; Design; Mechanical Devices; Engineering and Technology; Economics and Accounting; Transportation. **Instructional Program**—Pipefitting/Pipefitter and Sprinkler Fitter.

Related SOC Job—47-2152 Plumbers, Pipefitters, and Steamfitters. Related OOH Job—Pipelayers, Plumbers, Pipefitters, and Steamfitters. Related DOT Jobs—862.261-010 Pipe Fitter; 862.281-010 Coppersmith; 862.281-014 Coppersmith Apprentice; 862.281-022 Pipe Fitter; 862.281-026 Pipe-Fitter Apprentice; 862.361-014 Gas-Main Fitter; 862.361-018 Pipe Fitter, Diesel Engine I; 862.361-022 Steam Service Inspector; 862.381-014 Industrial-Gas Fitter; 862.381-022 Pipe Fitter, Diesel Engine II.

47-2152.02 Plumbers

- **Education/Training Required: Long-term on-the-job training**
- **Employed: 420,770**
- **Annual Earnings: $42,160**
- **Growth: 15.7%**
- **Annual Job Openings: 61,000**

The job openings listed here are shared with 47-2152.00 Plumbers, Pipefitters, and Steamfitters and 47-2152.01 Pipe Fitters and Steamfitters.

Assemble, install, and repair pipes, fittings, and fixtures of heating, water, and drainage systems according to specifications and plumbing codes.

Assemble pipe sections, tubing, and fittings, using couplings; clamps; screws; bolts; cement; plastic solvent; caulking; or soldering, brazing, and welding equipment. Fill pipes or plumbing fixtures with water or air and observe pressure gauges to detect and locate leaks. Review blueprints and building codes and specifications to determine work details and procedures. Prepare written work cost estimates and negotiate contracts. Study building plans and inspect structures to assess material and equipment needs, to establish the sequence of pipe installations, and to plan installation around obstructions such as electrical wiring. Keep records of assignments and produce detailed work reports. Perform complex calculations and planning for special or very large jobs. Locate and mark the position of pipe installations, connections, passage holes, and fixtures in structures, using measuring instruments such as rulers and levels. Measure, cut, thread, and bend pipe to required angle, using hand and power tools or machines such as pipe cutters, pipe-threading machines, and pipe-bending machines. Cut openings in structures to accommodate pipes and pipe fittings, using hand and power tools. Install pipe assemblies, fittings, valves, appliances such as dishwashers and water heaters, and fixtures such as sinks and toilets, using hand and power tools. Hang steel supports from ceiling joists to hold pipes in place. Repair and maintain plumbing, replacing defective washers, replacing or mending broken pipes, and opening clogged drains. Direct workers engaged in pipe cutting and preassembly and installation of plumbing systems and components. Install underground storm, sanitary, and water piping systems and extend piping to connect fixtures and plumbing to these systems. Clear away debris in a renovation. Install oxygen and medical gas in hospitals. Use specialized techniques, equipment, or materials, such as performing computer-assisted welding of small pipes or working with the special piping used in microchip fabrication.

GOE Information—Interest Area: 02. Architecture and Construction. **Work Group:** 02.04. Construction Crafts. **Personality Type**—Realistic. Realistic occupations frequently involve work activities that include practical, hands-on problems and solutions. They often deal with plants; animals; and real-world materials like wood, tools, and machinery. Many of the occupations require working outside and do not involve a lot of paperwork or working closely with others. **Work Values**—Compensation; Authority; Responsibility; Moral Values; Social Service. **Skills**—Installation; Repairing; Systems

Evaluation; Management of Material Resources; Science; Management of Financial Resources. **Abilities**—*Cognitive:* Spatial Orientation; Mathematical Reasoning; Visualization; Speed of Closure; Deductive Reasoning; Flexibility of Closure. *Psychomotor:* Reaction Time; Arm-Hand Steadiness; Wrist-Finger Speed; Control Precision; Speed of Limb Movement; Multilimb Coordination. *Physical:* Extent Flexibility; Static Strength; Dynamic Strength; Gross Body Equilibrium; Trunk Strength; Gross Body Coordination. *Sensory:* Glare Sensitivity; Hearing Sensitivity; Visual Color Discrimination; Depth Perception; Far Vision; Auditory Attention. **General Work Activities**—*Information Input:* Monitoring Processes, Materials, or Surroundings; Identifying Objects, Actions, and Events; Getting Information. *Mental Process:* Updating and Using Relevant Knowledge; Organizing, Planning, and Prioritizing; Making Decisions and Solving Problems. *Work Output:* Performing General Physical Activities; Handling and Moving Objects; Repairing and Maintaining Mechanical Equipment. *Interacting with Others:* Performing for or Working with the Public; Establishing and Maintaining Interpersonal Relationships; Communicating with Other Workers. **Physical Work Conditions**—Outdoors; Contaminants; Cramped Work Space, Awkward Positions; Hazardous Equipment; Minor Burns, Cuts, Bites, or Stings; Using Hands on Objects, Tools, or Controls. **Other Job Characteristics**—Need to Be Exact or Accurate.

Experience—Job Zone 3. Previous work-related skill, knowledge, or experience is required. **Job Preparation**—SVP 6.0 to less than 7.0—more than one year and less than four years. **Knowledges**—Building and Construction; Physics; Mechanical Devices; Chemistry; Design; Sales and Marketing. **Instructional Programs**—Pipefitting/Pipefitter and Sprinkler Fitter; Plumbing and Related Water Supply Services, Other; Plumbing Technology/Plumber.

Related SOC Job—47-2152 Plumbers, Pipefitters, and Steamfitters. Related OOH Job—Pipelayers, Plumbers, Pipefitters, and Steamfitters. Related DOT Jobs—862.381-030 Plumber; 862.381-034 Plumber Apprentice; 862.681-010 Plumber; 862.684-034 Water-Softener Servicer-And-Installer.

47-2161.00 Plasterers and Stucco Masons

- **Education/Training Required: Long-term on-the-job training**
- **Employed: 47,760**
- **Annual Earnings: $33,440**
- **Growth: 8.2%**
- **Annual Job Openings: 6,000**

Apply interior or exterior plaster, cement, stucco, or similar materials. May also set ornamental plaster.

Apply coats of plaster or stucco to walls, ceilings, or partitions of buildings, using trowels, brushes, or spray guns. Mix mortar and plaster to desired consistency or direct workers who perform mixing. Create decorative textures in finish coat, using brushes or trowels, sand, pebbles, or stones. Apply insulation to building exteriors by installing prefabricated insulation systems over existing walls or by covering the outer wall with insulation board, reinforcing mesh, and a base coat. Cure freshly plastered surfaces. Clean and prepare surfaces for applications of plaster, cement, stucco, or similar materials, such as by drywall taping. Rough the undercoat surface with a scratcher so the finish coat will adhere. Apply weatherproof decorative coverings to exterior surfaces of buildings, such as troweling or spraying on coats of stucco. Install guide wires on exterior surfaces of buildings to indicate thickness of plaster or stucco and nail wire mesh, lath, or similar materials to the outside surface to hold stucco in place. Spray acoustic materials or texture finish over walls and ceilings. Mold and install ornamental plaster pieces, panels, and trim.

GOE Information—Interest Area: 02. Architecture and Construction. **Work Group:** 02.04. Construction Crafts. **Personality Type**—Realistic. Realistic occupations frequently involve work activities that include practical, hands-on problems and solutions. They often deal with plants; animals; and real-world materials like wood, tools, and machinery. Many of the occupations require working outside and do not involve a lot of paperwork or working closely with others. **Work Values**—Moral Values; Co-workers; Supervision, Technical. **Skills**—Management of Material Resources; Repairing; Installation; Technology Design; Management of Financial Resources; Equipment Maintenance. **Abilities**—*Cognitive:* Visualization; Selective Attention; Perceptual Speed. *Psychomotor:* Rate Control; Speed of Limb Movement; Manual Dexterity; Wrist-Finger Speed; Reaction Time; Multilimb Coordination. *Physical:* Extent Flexibility; Stamina; Static Strength; Dynamic Strength; Gross Body Equilibrium; Gross Body Coordination. *Sensory:* Glare Sensitivity; Far Vision; Depth Perception; Visual Color Discrimination; Auditory Attention. **General Work Activities**—*Information Input:* Monitoring Processes, Materials, or Surroundings; Identifying Objects, Actions, and Events; Inspecting Equipment, Structures, or Materials. *Mental Process:* Making Decisions and Solving Problems; Organizing, Planning, and Prioritizing; Thinking Creatively. *Work Output:* Handling and Moving Objects; Performing General Physical Activities; Controlling Machines and Processes. *Interacting with Others:* Establishing and Maintaining Interpersonal Relationships; Communicating with Other Workers; Coordinating the Work and Activities of Others. **Physical Work Conditions**—High Places; Standing; Walking and Running; Using Hands on Objects, Tools, or Controls; Bending or Twisting the Body; Repetitive Motions. **Other Job Characteristics**—Need to Be Exact or Accurate; Repeat Same Tasks; Pace Determined by Speed of Equipment; Errors Have Important Consequences.

Experience—Job Zone 2. Some previous work-related skill, knowledge, or experience may be helpful in these occupations, but usually is not needed. **Job Preparation**—SVP 4.0 to less than 6.0—six months to less than two years. **Knowledges**—Building and Construction; Public Safety and Security. **Instructional Program**—Building/Construction Trades, Other.

Related SOC Job—47-2161 Plasterers and Stucco Masons. **Related OOH Job**—Plasterers and Stucco Masons. **Related DOT Jobs**—842.361-018 Plasterer; 842.361-022 Plasterer Apprentice; 842.361-026 Plasterer, Molding; 842.381-014 Stucco Mason.

47-2171.00 Reinforcing Iron and Rebar Workers

- **Education/Training Required: Long-term on-the-job training**
- **Employed:** 30,270
- **Annual Earnings:** $34,910
- **Growth:** 14.1%
- **Annual Job Openings:** 6,000

Position and secure steel bars or mesh in concrete forms to reinforce concrete. Use a variety of fasteners, rod-bending machines, blowtorches, and hand tools.

Space and fasten together rods in forms according to blueprints, using wire and pliers. Cut and fit wire mesh or fabric, using hooked rods, and position fabric or mesh in concrete to reinforce concrete. Cut rods to required lengths, using metal shears, hacksaws, bar cut-

ters, or acetylene torches. Bend steel rods with hand tools and rod-bending machines and weld them with arc-welding equipment. Position and secure steel bars, rods, cables, or mesh in concrete forms, using fasteners, rod-bending machines, blowtorches, and hand tools. Place blocks under rebar to hold the bars off the deck when reinforcing floors. Determine quantities, sizes, shapes, and locations of reinforcing rods from blueprints, sketches, or oral instructions.

GOE Information—Interest Area: 02. Architecture and Construction. **Work Group:** 02.04. Construction Crafts. **Personality Type**—Realistic. Realistic occupations frequently involve work activities that include practical, hands-on problems and solutions. They often deal with plants; animals; and real-world materials like wood, tools, and machinery. Many of the occupations require working outside and do not involve a lot of paperwork or working closely with others. **Work Values**—Moral Values; Independence; Supervision, Technical. **Skills**—None met the criteria. **Abilities**—*Cognitive:* Spatial Orientation; Visualization. *Psychomotor:* Wrist-Finger Speed; Speed of Limb Movement; Multilimb Coordination; Manual Dexterity. *Physical:* Explosive Strength; Static Strength; Extent Flexibility; Dynamic Strength; Trunk Strength. *Sensory:* None met the criteria. **General Work Activities**—*Information Input:* Getting Information. *Mental Process:* None met the criteria. *Work Output:* Handling and Moving Objects; Performing General Physical Activities; Controlling Machines and Processes. *Interacting with Others:* None met the criteria. **Physical Work Conditions**—Outdoors; Noisy; Contaminants; Minor Burns, Cuts, Bites, or Stings; Standing; Using Hands on Objects, Tools, or Controls. **Other Job Characteristics**—None met the criteria.

Experience—Job Zone 3. Previous work-related skill, knowledge, or experience is required. **Job Preparation**—SVP 6.0 to less than 7.0—more than one year and less than four years. **Knowledges**—Building and Construction; Physics; Design; Engineering and Technology. **Instructional Program**—Building/Construction Trades, Other.

Related SOC Job—47-2171 Reinforcing Iron and Rebar Workers. **Related OOH Job**—Structural and Reinforcing Iron and Metal Workers. **Related DOT Job**—801.684-026 Reinforcing-Metal Worker.

47-2181.00 Roofers

- **Education/Training Required: Moderate-term on-the-job training**
- **Employed:** 120,070
- **Annual Earnings:** $31,230
- **Growth:** 16.8%
- **Annual Job Openings:** 38,000

Cover roofs of structures with shingles, slate, asphalt, aluminum, wood, and related materials. May spray roofs, sidings, and walls with material to bind, seal, insulate, or soundproof sections of structures.

Install, repair, or replace single-ply roofing systems, using waterproof sheet materials such as modified plastics, elastomeric, or other asphaltic compositions. Apply alternate layers of hot asphalt or tar and roofing paper to roofs according to specification. Apply gravel or pebbles over top layers of roofs, using rakes or stiff-bristled brooms. Cement or nail flashing-strips of metal or shingle over joints to make them watertight. Cut roofing paper to size, using knives, and nail or staple roofing paper to roofs in overlapping strips to form bases for other materials. Punch holes in slate, tile, terra cotta, or wooden shingles, using punches and hammers. Hammer and chisel away rough spots or remove them with rubbing bricks to prepare surfaces for waterproofing. Spray roofs, sidings, and walls with material to bind, seal, insulate, or soundproof sections of structures, using spray guns, air compressors, and heaters. Cover exposed nailheads with roofing cement or caulking to prevent water leakage and rust. Clean and maintain equipment. Cut felt, shingles, and strips of flashing and fit them into angles formed by walls, vents, and intersecting roof surfaces. Glaze top layers to make a smooth finish or embed gravel in the bitumen for rough surfaces. Inspect problem roofs to determine the best procedures for repairing them. Align roofing materials with edges of roofs. Mop or pour hot asphalt or tar onto roof bases. Apply plastic coatings and membranes, fiberglass, or felt over sloped roofs before applying shingles. Install vapor barriers or layers of insulation on the roof decks of flat roofs and seal the seams. Install partially overlapping layers of material over roof insulation surfaces, determining distance of roofing material overlap by using chalk lines, gauges on shingling hatchets, or lines on shingles. Cover roofs and exterior walls of structures with slate, asphalt, aluminum, wood, gravel, gypsum, and/or related materials, using brushes, knives, punches, hammers, and other tools. Waterproof and damp-proof walls, floors, roofs, foundations, and basements by painting or spraying surfaces with waterproof coatings, or by attaching waterproofing membranes to surfaces. Estimate roofing materials and labor required to complete jobs and provide price quotes.

GOE Information—Interest Area: 02. Architecture and Construction. **Work Group:** 02.04. Construction Crafts. **Personality Type**—Realistic. Realistic occupations frequently involve work activities that include practical, hands-on problems and solutions. They often deal with plants; animals; and real-world materials like wood, tools, and machinery. Many of the occupations require working outside and do not involve a lot of paperwork or working closely with others. **Work Values**—None met the criteria. **Skills**—Repairing; Installation. **Abilities**—*Cognitive:* None met the criteria. *Psychomotor:* Wrist-Finger Speed; Speed of Limb Movement; Manual Dexterity; Multilimb Coordination. *Physical:* Gross Body Equilibrium; Explosive Strength; Extent Flexibility; Static Strength; Dynamic Strength; Stamina. *Sensory:* None met the criteria. **General Work Activities**—*Information Input:* Identifying Objects, Actions, and Events. *Mental Process:* None met the criteria. *Work Output:* Performing General Physical Activities; Handling and Moving Objects; Controlling Machines and Processes. *Interacting with Others:* None met the criteria. **Physical Work Conditions**—Outdoors; High Places; Kneeling, Crouching, Stooping, or Crawling; Keeping or Regaining Balance; Using Hands on Objects, Tools, or Controls; Bending or Twisting the Body. **Other Job Characteristics**—Need to Be Exact or Accurate.

Experience—Job Zone 3. Previous work-related skill, knowledge, or experience is required. **Job Preparation**—SVP 6.0 to less than 7.0— more than one year and less than four years. **Knowledges**—Building and Construction; Mechanical Devices. **Instructional Program**—Roofer.

Related SOC Job—47-2181 Roofers. **Related OOH Job**—Roofers. **Related DOT Jobs**—866.381-010 Roofer; 866.381-014 Roofer Apprentice; 866.684-010 Roofer Applicator.

47-2211.00 Sheet Metal Workers

- **Education/Training Required: Moderate-term on-the-job training**
- **Employed: 174,550**
- **Annual Earnings: $36,390**
- **Growth: 12.2%**
- **Annual Job Openings: 50,000**

Fabricate, assemble, install, and repair sheet metal products and equipment, such as ducts, control boxes, drainpipes, and furnace casings. Work may involve any of the following: setting up and operating fabricating machines to cut, bend, and straighten sheet metal; shaping metal over anvils, blocks, or forms, using hammer; operating soldering and welding equipment to join sheet metal parts; and inspecting, assembling, and smoothing seams and joints of burred surfaces.

Determine project requirements, including scope, assembly sequences, and required methods and materials, according to blueprints, drawings, and written or verbal instructions. Lay out, measure, and mark dimensions and reference lines on material such as roofing panels according to drawings or templates, using calculators, scribes, dividers, squares, and rulers. Maneuver completed units into position for installation and anchor the units. Convert blueprints into shop drawings to be followed in the construction and assembly of sheet metal products. Install assemblies such as flashing, pipes, tubes, heating and air conditioning ducts, furnace casings, rain gutters, and downspouts in supportive frameworks. Select gauges and types of sheet metal or non-metallic material according to product specifications. Drill and punch holes in metal for screws, bolts, and rivets. Fasten seams and joints together with welds, bolts, cement, rivets, solder, caulks, metal drive clips, and bonds to assemble components into products or to repair sheet metal items. Fabricate or alter parts at construction sites, using shears, hammers, punches, and drills. Finish parts, using hacksaws and hand, rotary, or squaring shears. Trim, file, grind, deburr, buff, and smooth surfaces, seams, and joints of assembled parts, using hand tools and portable power tools. Maintain equipment, making repairs and modifications when necessary. Shape metal material over anvils, blocks, or other forms, using hand tools. Transport prefabricated parts to construction sites for assembly and installation. Develop and lay out patterns that use materials most efficiently, using computerized metalworking equipment to experiment with different layouts. Inspect individual parts, assemblies, and installations for conformance to specifications and building codes, using measuring instruments such as calipers, scales, and micrometers. Secure metal roof panels in place and interlock and fasten grooved panel edges. Fasten roof panel edges and machine-made molding to structures, nailing or welding pieces into place.

GOE Information—Interest Area: 02. Architecture and Construction. **Work Group:** 02.04. Construction Crafts. **Personality Type**—Realistic. Realistic occupations frequently involve work activities that include practical, hands-on problems and solutions. They often deal with plants; animals; and real-world materials like wood, tools, and machinery. Many of the occupations require working outside and do not involve a lot of paperwork or working closely with others. **Work Values**—Moral Values; Supervision, Technical; Advancement; Supervision, Human Relations; Independence; Compensation. **Skills**—Installation; Repairing; Equipment Maintenance; Mathematics; Technology Design; Troubleshooting. **Abilities**—*Cognitive:* Visualization; Information Ordering; Perceptual Speed; Selective Attention; Originality. *Psychomotor:* Manual Dexterity; Control Precision; Multilimb Coordination; Arm-Hand Steadiness; Finger Dexterity. *Physical:* Gross Body Equilibrium; Static Strength; Dynamic Strength; Extent Flexibility; Gross Body Coordination; Stamina. *Sensory:* Auditory Attention; Depth Perception. **General Work Activities**—*Information Input:* Monitoring Processes, Materials, or Surroundings; Inspecting Equipment, Structures, or Materials; Identifying Objects, Actions, and Events. *Mental Process:* Organizing, Planning, and Prioritizing; Updating and Using Relevant Knowledge; Thinking Creatively. *Work Output:* Handling and Moving Objects; Performing General Physical Activities; Controlling Machines and Processes. *Interacting with*

Others: Communicating with Other Workers; Establishing and Maintaining Interpersonal Relationships; Coordinating the Work and Activities of Others. **Physical Work Conditions**—Noisy; Contaminants; Hazardous Equipment; Minor Burns, Cuts, Bites, or Stings; Standing; Using Hands on Objects, Tools, or Controls. **Other Job Characteristics**—Need to Be Exact or Accurate; Errors Have Important Consequences.

Experience—Job Zone 2. Some previous work-related skill, knowledge, or experience may be helpful in these occupations, but usually is not needed. **Job Preparation**—SVP 4.0 to less than 6.0—six months to less than two years. **Knowledges**—Building and Construction; Mechanical Devices; Design; Physics; Production and Processing; Mathematics. **Instructional Program**—Sheet Metal Technology/Sheetworking.

Related SOC Job—47-2211 Sheet Metal Workers. **Related OOH Job**—Sheet Metal Workers. **Related DOT Jobs**—804.281-010 Sheet-Metal Worker; 804.281-014 Sheet-Metal-Worker Apprentice; 804.481-010 Hood Maker.

47-2221.00 Structural Iron and Steel Workers

- **Education/Training Required: Long-term on-the-job training**
- **Employed: 68,900**
- **Annual Earnings: $40,580**
- **Growth: 15.0%**
- **Annual Job Openings: 13,000**

Raise, place, and unite iron or steel girders, columns, and other structural members to form completed structures or structural frameworks. May erect metal storage tanks and assemble prefabricated metal buildings.

Read specifications and blueprints to determine the locations, quantities, and sizes of materials required. Verify vertical and horizontal alignment of structural-steel members, using plumb bobs, laser equipment, transits, and/or levels. Connect columns, beams, and girders with bolts, following blueprints and instructions from supervisors. Hoist steel beams, girders, and columns into place, using cranes, or signal hoisting equipment operators to lift and position structural-steel members. Bolt aligned structural-steel members in position for permanent riveting, bolting, or welding into place. Ride on girders or other structural-steel members to position them or use rope to guide them into position. Fabricate metal parts such as steel frames, columns, beams, and girders according to blueprints or instructions from supervisors. Pull, push, or pry structural-steel members into approximate positions for bolting into place. Cut, bend, and weld steel pieces, using metal shears, torches, and welding equipment. Fasten structural-steel members to hoist cables, using chains, cables, or rope. Assemble hoisting equipment and rigging, such as cables, pulleys, and hooks, to move heavy equipment and materials. Force structural-steel members into final positions, using turnbuckles, crowbars, jacks, and hand tools. Erect metal and precast concrete components for structures such as buildings, bridges, dams, towers, storage tanks, fences, and highway guardrails. Unload and position prefabricated steel units for hoisting as needed. Drive drift pins through rivet holes to align rivet holes in structural-steel members with corresponding holes in previously placed members. Dismantle structures and equipment. Insert sealing strips, wiring, insulating material, ladders, flanges, gauges, and valves, depending on types of structures being assembled. Catch hot rivets in buckets and insert rivets in holes, using tongs. Place blocks under reinforcing bars used to reinforce floors. Hold rivets while riveters use air-hammers to form heads on rivets.

GOE Information—**Interest Area:** 02. Architecture and Construction. **Work Group:** 02.04. Construction Crafts. **Personality Type**—Realistic. Realistic occupations frequently involve work activities that include practical, hands-on problems and solutions. They often deal with plants; animals; and real-world materials like wood, tools, and machinery. Many of the occupations require working outside and do not involve a lot of paperwork or working closely with others. **Work Values**—Moral Values; Supervision, Technical; Co-workers. **Skills**—Equipment Maintenance; Installation; Troubleshooting; Coordination; Operation Monitoring; Equipment Selection. **Abilities**—*Cognitive:* Visualization; Spatial Orientation; Perceptual Speed; Time Sharing; Selective Attention; Flexibility of Closure. *Psychomotor:* Reaction Time; Rate Control; Response Orientation; Multilimb Coordination; Speed of Limb Movement; Wrist-Finger Speed. *Physical:* Gross Body Equilibrium; Static Strength; Dynamic Strength; Extent Flexibility; Stamina; Gross Body Coordination. *Sensory:* Depth Perception; Glare Sensitivity; Peripheral Vision; Auditory Attention; Sound Localization; Hearing Sensitivity. **General Work Activities**—*Information Input:* Inspecting Equipment, Structures, or Materials; Monitoring Processes, Materials, or Surroundings; Identifying Objects, Actions, and Events. *Mental Process:* Organizing, Planning, and Prioritizing; Updating and Using Relevant Knowledge; Making Decisions and Solving Problems. *Work Output:* Handling and Moving Objects; Performing General Physical Activities; Controlling Machines and Processes. *Interacting with Others:* Coordinating the Work and Activities of Others; Guiding, Directing, and Motivating Subordinates; Teaching Others. **Physical Work Conditions**—Outdoors; Noisy; Very Hot or Cold; High Places; Hazardous Equipment; Using Hands on Objects, Tools, or Controls. **Other Job Characteristics**—Need to Be Exact or Accurate; Errors Have Important Consequences.

Experience—Job Zone 2. Some previous work-related skill, knowledge, or experience may be helpful in these occupations, but usually is not needed. **Job Preparation**—SVP 4.0 to less than 6.0—six months to less than two years. **Knowledges**—Building and Construction; Engineering and Technology; Production and Processing; Mechanical Devices; Design; Physics. **Instructional Programs**—Building/Construction Trades, Other; Metal Building Assembly/Assembler.

Related SOC Job—47-2221 Structural Iron and Steel Workers. **Related OOH Job**—Structural and Reinforcing Iron and Metal Workers. **Related DOT Jobs**—801.361-014 Structural-Steel Worker; 801.361-018 Structural-Steel-Worker Apprentice; 801.361-022 Tank Setter; 801.381-010 Assembler, Metal Building.

47-3000 Helpers, Construction Trades

47-3011.00 Helpers—Brickmasons, Blockmasons, Stonemasons, and Tile and Marble Setters

- **Education/Training Required: Short-term on-the-job training**
- **Employed: 58,690**
- **Annual Earnings: $24,600**
- **Growth: 14.9%**
- **Annual Job Openings: 14,000**

Help brickmasons, blockmasons, stonemasons, or tile and marble setters by performing duties of lesser skill. Duties include using, supplying, or holding materials or tools and cleaning work area and equipment.

Transport materials, tools, and machines to installation sites manually or by using conveyance equipment. Mix mortar, plaster, and grout manually or by using machines according to standard formulas. Erect scaffolding or other installation structures. Cut materials to specified sizes for installation, using power saws or tile cutters. Clean installation surfaces, equipment, tools, worksites, and storage areas, using water, chemical solutions, oxygen lances, or polishing machines. Move or position materials such as marble slabs, using cranes, hoists, or dollies. Modify material moving, mixing, grouting, grinding, polishing, or cleaning procedures according to installation or material requirements. Correct surface imperfections or fill chipped, cracked, or broken bricks or tiles, using fillers, adhesives, and grouting materials. Arrange and store materials, machines, tools, and equipment. Apply grout between joints of bricks or tiles, using grouting trowels. Apply caulk, sealants, or other agents to installed surfaces. Select or locate and supply materials to masons for installation, following drawings or numbered sequences. Remove excess grout and residue from tile or brick joints, using sponges or trowels. Remove damaged tile, brick, or mortar and clean and prepare surfaces, using pliers, hammers, chisels, drills, wire brushes, and metal wire anchors. Provide assistance in the preparation, installation, repair, or rebuilding of tile, brick, or stone surfaces. Mix mortar, plaster, and grout manually or by using machines according to standard formulas.

GOE Information—Interest Area: 02. Architecture and Construction. **Work Group:** 02.06. Construction Support/Labor. **Personality Type—**Realistic. Realistic occupations frequently involve work activities that include practical, hands-on problems and solutions. They often deal with plants; animals; and real-world materials like wood, tools, and machinery. Many of the occupations require working outside and do not involve a lot of paperwork or working closely with others. **Work Values—**Supervision, Technical; Moral Values; Advancement; Co-workers. **Skills—**Installation. **Abilities—***Cognitive:* None met the criteria. *Psychomotor:* Wrist-Finger Speed; Speed of Limb Movement; Multilimb Coordination. *Physical:* Static Strength; Dynamic Strength; Explosive Strength; Stamina; Extent Flexibility; Gross Body Coordination. *Sensory:* None met the criteria. **General Work Activities—***Information Input:* None met the criteria. *Mental Process:* None met the criteria. *Work Output:* Handling and Moving Objects; Performing General Physical Activities; Controlling Machines and Processes. *Interacting with Others:* Communicating with Other Workers; Assisting and Caring for Others. **Physical Work Conditions—**Outdoors; Standing; Walking and Running; Kneeling, Crouching, Stooping, or Crawling; Using Hands on Objects, Tools, or Controls; Repetitive Motions. **Other Job Characteristics—**None met the criteria.

Experience—Job Zone 1. No previous work-related skill, knowledge, or experience is needed. **Job Preparation—**SVP below 4.0—less than six months. **Knowledges—**Building and Construction; Mechanical Devices. **Instructional Program—**Masonry/Mason.

Related SOC Job—47-3011 Helpers—Brickmasons, Blockmasons, Stonemasons, and Tile and Marble Setters. **Related OOH Job—**Helpers—Brickmasons, Blockmasons, Stonemasons, and Tile and Marble Setters. **Related DOT Jobs—**709.687-018 Hot-Top-Liner Helper; 861.664-010 Marble Finisher; 861.664-018 Tile Finisher; 861.687-010 Bricklayer Helper, Firebrick and Refractory Tile; 861.687-014 Patcher Helper.

47-3012.00 Helpers—Carpenters

- **Education/Training Required: Short-term on-the-job training**
- **Employed: 101,870**
- **Annual Earnings: $21,990**
- **Growth: 14.5%**
- **Annual Job Openings: 24,000**

Help carpenters by performing duties of lesser skill. Duties include using, supplying, or holding materials or tools and cleaning work area and equipment.

Position and hold timbers, lumber, and paneling in place for fastening or cutting. Erect scaffolding, shoring, and braces. Select tools, equipment, and materials from storage and transport items to worksite. Fasten timbers or lumber with glue, screws, pegs, or nails and install hardware. Clean work areas, machines, and equipment to maintain a clean and safe jobsite. Align, straighten, plumb, and square forms for installation. Hold plumb bobs, sighting rods, and other equipment to aid in establishing reference points and lines. Cut timbers, lumber, or paneling to specified dimensions and drill holes in timbers or lumber. Smooth and sand surfaces to remove ridges, tool marks, glue, or caulking. Perform tie spacing layout; then measure, mark, drill, and cut. Secure stakes to grids for constructions of footings, nail scabs to footing forms, and vibrate and float concrete. Construct forms; then assist in raising them to the required elevation. Install handrails under the direction of a carpenter. Glue and clamp edges or joints of assembled parts. Cut and install insulating or sound-absorbing material. Cut tile or linoleum to fit and spread adhesives on flooring to install tile or linoleum. Cover surfaces with laminated-plastic covering material.

GOE Information—Interest Area: 02. Architecture and Construction. **Work Group:** 02.06. Construction Support/Labor. **Personality Type—**Realistic. Realistic occupations frequently involve work activities that include practical, hands-on problems and solutions. They often deal with plants; animals; and real-world materials like wood, tools, and machinery. Many of the occupations require working outside and do not involve a lot of paperwork or working closely with others. **Work Values—**Advancement; Supervision, Technical; Moral Values; Co-workers. **Skills—**Installation; Repairing; Equipment Maintenance; Management of Material Resources; Troubleshooting; Mathematics. **Abilities—***Cognitive:* Visualization. *Psychomotor:* Rate Control; Reaction Time; Speed of Limb Movement; Response Orientation; Multilimb Coordination; Manual Dexterity. *Physical:* Static Strength; Extent Flexibility; Dynamic Strength; Gross Body Equilibrium; Stamina; Gross Body Coordination. *Sensory:* Depth Perception; Hearing Sensitivity; Far Vision; Auditory Attention. **General Work Activities—***Information Input:* Monitoring Processes, Materials, or Surroundings; Inspecting Equipment, Structures, or Materials; Identifying Objects, Actions, and Events. *Mental Process:* Organizing, Planning, and Prioritizing; Updating and Using Relevant Knowledge; Making Decisions and Solving Problems. *Work Output:* Handling and Moving Objects; Performing General Physical Activities; Controlling Machines and Processes. *Interacting with Others:* Communicating with Other Workers; Establishing and Maintaining Interpersonal Relationships; Coordinating the Work and Activities of Others. **Physical Work Conditions—**Noisy; Very Hot or Cold; Hazardous Equipment; Standing; Walking and Running; Using Hands on Objects, Tools, or Controls. **Other Job Characteristics—**Errors Have Important Consequences; Need to Be Exact or Accurate.

Experience—Job Zone 2. Some previous work-related skill, knowledge, or experience may be helpful in these occupations, but usually is not needed. **Job Preparation**—SVP 4.0 to less than 6.0—six months to less than two years. **Knowledges**—Building and Construction; Design; Engineering and Technology; Mechanical Devices. **Instructional Program**—Carpentry/Carpenter.

Related SOC Job—47-3012 Helpers—Carpenters. **Related OOH Job**—Helpers—Carpenters. **Related DOT Jobs**—764.687-050 Cooper Helper; 860.664-014 Joiner Helper; 860.664-018 Shipwright Helper; 869.664-014 Construction Worker I; 869.687-026 Construction Worker II; 869.687-042 Timber-Framer Helper.

47-3013.00 Helpers—Electricians

- **Education/Training Required: Short-term on-the-job training**
- **Employed: 90,370**
- **Annual Earnings: $23,240**
- **Growth: 4.0%**
- **Annual Job Openings: 19,000**

Help electricians by performing duties of lesser skill. Duties include using, supplying, or holding materials or tools and cleaning work area and equipment.

Trace out short circuits in wiring, using test meter. Measure, cut, and bend wire and conduit, using measuring instruments and hand tools. Maintain tools, vehicles, and equipment and keep parts and supplies in order. Drill holes and pull or push wiring through openings, using hand and power tools. Perform semi-skilled and unskilled laboring duties related to the installation, maintenance, and repair of a wide variety of electrical systems and equipment. Disassemble defective electrical equipment, replace defective or worn parts, and reassemble equipment, using hand tools. Transport tools, materials, equipment, and supplies to worksite by hand; handtruck; or heavy, motorized truck. Examine electrical units for loose connections and broken insulation and tighten connections, using hand tools. Strip insulation from wire ends, using wire-stripping pliers, and attach wires to terminals for subsequent soldering. Construct controllers and panels, using power drills, drill presses, taps, saws, and punches. Thread conduit ends, connect couplings, and fabricate and secure conduit support brackets, using hand tools. String transmission lines or cables through ducts or conduits, under the ground, through equipment, or to towers. Clean work area and wash parts. Erect electrical system components and barricades and rig scaffolds, hoists, and shoring. Install copper-clad ground rods, using a manual post driver. Raise, lower, or position equipment, tools, and materials, using hoist, hand line, or block and tackle. Dig trenches or holes for installation of conduit or supports. Requisition materials, using warehouse requisition or release forms. Bolt component parts together to form tower assemblies, using hand tools. Paint a variety of objects related to electrical functions. Operate cutting torches and welding equipment while working with conduit and metal components to construct devices associated with electrical functions. Break up concrete, using air hammer, to facilitate installation, construction, or repair of equipment. Solder electrical connections, using soldering iron. Trim trees and clear undergrowth along right-of-way.

GOE Information—**Interest Area:** 02. Architecture and Construction. **Work Group:** 02.06. Construction Support/Labor. **Personality Type**—Realistic. Realistic occupations frequently involve work activities that include practical, hands-on problems and solutions. They often deal with plants; animals; and real-world materials like wood, tools, and machinery. Many of the occupations require working outside and do not involve a lot of paperwork or working closely with others. **Work Values**—Supervision, Technical; Advancement; Moral Values; Co-workers. **Skills**—Installation;

Troubleshooting; Repairing; Mathematics; Complex Problem Solving; Equipment Selection. **Abilities**—*Cognitive:* Visualization; Information Ordering; Selective Attention. *Psychomotor:* Manual Dexterity; Arm-Hand Steadiness; Control Precision; Multilimb Coordination; Reaction Time; Finger Dexterity. *Physical:* Extent Flexibility; Gross Body Equilibrium; Dynamic Strength; Gross Body Coordination; Static Strength; Trunk Strength. *Sensory:* Visual Color Discrimination; Depth Perception; Near Vision. **General Work Activities**—*Information Input:* Inspecting Equipment, Structures, or Materials; Monitoring Processes, Materials, or Surroundings; Identifying Objects, Actions, and Events. *Mental Process:* Updating and Using Relevant Knowledge; Making Decisions and Solving Problems; Organizing, Planning, and Prioritizing. *Work Output:* Performing General Physical Activities; Handling and Moving Objects; Controlling Machines and Processes. *Interacting with Others:* Establishing and Maintaining Interpersonal Relationships; Communicating with Other Workers; Coordinating the Work and Activities of Others. **Physical Work Conditions**—Outdoors; Very Hot or Cold; Contaminants; High Places; Standing; Using Hands on Objects, Tools, or Controls. **Other Job Characteristics**—Need to Be Exact or Accurate; Errors Have Important Consequences.

Experience—Job Zone 2. Some previous work-related skill, knowledge, or experience may be helpful in these occupations, but usually is not needed. **Job Preparation**—SVP 4.0 to less than 6.0—six months to less than two years. **Knowledges**—Building and Construction; Mechanical Devices; Design; Engineering and Technology; Mathematics; Public Safety and Security. **Instructional Program**—Electrician.

Related SOC Job—47-3013 Helpers—Electricians. **Related OOH Job**—Helpers—Electricians. **Related DOT Jobs**—821.667-010 Helper, Electrical; 821.684-014 Tower Erector Helper; 822.664-010 Protective-Signal-Installer Helper; 822.684-014 Protective-Signal-Repairer Helper; 825.684-010 Electrician Helper, Automotive; 829.684-022 Electrician Helper; 829.684-026 Electrician Helper.

47-3014.00 Helpers—Painters, Paperhangers, Plasterers, and Stucco Masons

- **Education/Training Required: Short-term on-the-job training**
- **Employed: 21,820**
- **Annual Earnings: $20,560**
- **Growth: 11.5%**
- **Annual Job Openings: 6,000**

Help painters, paperhangers, plasterers, or stucco masons by performing duties of lesser skill. Duties include using, supplying, or holding materials or tools and cleaning work area and equipment.

Fill cracks or breaks in surfaces of plaster articles or areas with putty or epoxy compounds. Clean work areas and equipment. Apply protective coverings such as masking tape to articles or areas that could be damaged or stained by work processes. Supply or hold tools and materials. Place articles to be stripped into stripping tanks. Pour specified amounts of chemical solutions into stripping tanks. Smooth surfaces of articles to be painted, using sanding and buffing tools and equipment. Mix plaster and carry plaster to plasterers. Perform support duties to assist painters, paperhangers, plasterers, or masons. Remove articles such as cabinets, metal furniture, and paint containers from stripping tanks after prescribed periods of time. Erect scaffolding.

GOE Information—Interest Area: 02. Architecture and Construction. **Work Group:** 02.06. Construction Support/Labor. **Personality Type**—Realistic. Realistic occupations frequently involve work activities that include practical, hands-on problems and solutions. They often deal with plants; animals; and real-world materials like wood, tools, and machinery. Many of the occupations require working outside and do not involve a lot of paperwork or working closely with others. **Work Values**—Supervision, Technical; Moral Values; Advancement. **Skills**—None met the criteria. **Abilities**—*Cognitive:* None met the criteria. *Psychomotor:* Manual Dexterity. *Physical:* Static Strength; Dynamic Strength; Extent Flexibility. *Sensory:* Visual Color Discrimination. **General Work Activities**—*Information Input:* None met the criteria. *Mental Process:* None met the criteria. *Work Output:* Handling and Moving Objects; Performing General Physical Activities. *Interacting with Others:* None met the criteria. **Physical Work Conditions**—Indoors; Contaminants; Standing; Climbing Ladders, Scaffolds, or Poles; Using Hands on Objects, Tools, or Controls; Repetitive Motions. **Other Job Characteristics**—None met the criteria.

Experience—Job Zone 1. No previous work-related skill, knowledge, or experience is needed. **Job Preparation**—SVP below 4.0—less than six months. **Knowledges**—Building and Construction. **Instructional Program**—Painting/Painter and Wall Coverer.

Related SOC Job—47-3014 Helpers—Painters, Paperhangers, Plasterers, and Stucco Masons. **Related OOH Job**—Helpers—Painters, Paperhangers, Plasterers, and Stucco Masons. **Related DOT Job**—840.687-010 Painter Helper, Shipyard.

47-3015.00 Helpers—Pipelayers, Plumbers, Pipefitters, and Steamfitters

- **Education/Training Required: Short-term on-the-job training**
- **Employed: 77,630**
- **Annual Earnings: $22,820**
- **Growth: 16.6%**
- **Annual Job Openings: 17,000**

Help plumbers, pipefitters, steamfitters, or pipelayers by performing duties of lesser skill. Duties include using, supplying, or holding materials or tools and cleaning work area and equipment.

Assist plumbers by performing rough-ins, repairing and replacing fixtures, and locating and repairing leaking or broken pipes. Cut or drill holes in walls or floors to accommodate the passage of pipes. Measure, cut, thread, and assemble new pipe, placing the assembled pipe in hangers or other supports. Mount brackets and hangers on walls and ceilings to hold pipes and set sleeves or inserts to provide support for pipes. Requisition tools and equipment, select type and size of pipe, and collect and transport materials and equipment to worksite. Fit or assist in fitting valves, couplings, or assemblies to tanks, pumps, or systems, using hand tools. Assist pipe fitters in the layout, assembly, and installation of piping for air, ammonia, gas, and water systems. Excavate and grade ditches and lay and join pipe for water and sewer service. Cut pipe and lift up to fitters. Disassemble and remove damaged or worn pipe. Clean shop, work area, and machines, using solvent and rags. Install gas burners to convert furnaces from wood, coal, or oil. Immerse pipe in chemical solution to remove dirt, oil, and scale. Clean and renew steam traps. Fill pipes with sand or resin to prevent distortion and hold pipes during bending and installation.

GOE Information—Interest Area: 02. Architecture and Construction. **Work Group:** 02.06. Construction Support/Labor.

Personality Type—Realistic. Realistic occupations frequently involve work activities that include practical, hands-on problems and solutions. They often deal with plants; animals; and real-world materials like wood, tools, and machinery. Many of the occupations require working outside and do not involve a lot of paperwork or working closely with others. **Work Values**—Supervision, Technical; Advancement; Moral Values. **Skills**—Installation; Repairing; Equipment Maintenance; Troubleshooting; Mathematics; Quality Control Analysis. **Abilities**—*Cognitive:* Visualization. *Psychomotor:* Control Precision; Manual Dexterity; Arm-Hand Steadiness; Multilimb Coordination; Finger Dexterity. *Physical:* Extent Flexibility; Gross Body Equilibrium; Static Strength; Trunk Strength; Dynamic Strength; Gross Body Coordination. *Sensory:* Depth Perception. **General Work Activities**—*Information Input:* Inspecting Equipment, Structures, or Materials; Monitoring Processes, Materials, or Surroundings; Identifying Objects, Actions, and Events. *Mental Process:* Updating and Using Relevant Knowledge; Organizing, Planning, and Prioritizing; Judging the Qualities of Things, Services, or Other People's Work. *Work Output:* Handling and Moving Objects; Performing General Physical Activities; Controlling Machines and Processes. *Interacting with Others:* Establishing and Maintaining Interpersonal Relationships; Communicating with Other Workers; Coordinating the Work and Activities of Others. **Physical Work Conditions**—Outdoors; Noisy; Contaminants; Hazardous Equipment; Standing; Using Hands on Objects, Tools, or Controls. **Other Job Characteristics**—Need to Be Exact or Accurate.

Experience—Job Zone 2. Some previous work-related skill, knowledge, or experience may be helpful in these occupations, but usually is not needed. **Job Preparation**—SVP 4.0 to less than 6.0—six months to less than two years. **Knowledges**—Building and Construction; Mechanical Devices; Design; Public Safety and Security; Engineering and Technology; Law and Government. **Instructional Program**—Plumbing Technology/Plumber.

Related SOC Job—47-3015 Helpers—Pipelayers, Plumbers, and Steamfitters. **Related OOH Job**—Helpers—Pipelayers, Plumbers, Pipefitters, and Steamfitters. **Related DOT Jobs**—862.684-018 Pipe-Fitter Helper; 862.684-022 Pipe-Fitter Helper; 862.684-026 Plumbing Assembler-Installer.

47-3016.00 Helpers—Roofers

- **Education/Training Required: Short-term on-the-job training**
- **Employed: 20,510**
- **Annual Earnings: $20,740**
- **Growth: 16.5%**
- **Annual Job Openings: 5,000**

Help roofers by performing duties of lesser skill. Duties include using, supplying, or holding materials or tools and cleaning work area and equipment.

Unload materials and tools from work trucks, and unroll roofing as directed. Cover roofs with layers of roofing felt or asphalt strips before installing tile, slate, or composition materials. Place tiles, nail them to roof boards, and cover nailheads with roofing cement. Apply shingles, gravel, or asphalt over the top layer of tar to protect the roofing material. Attach roofing paper and composition shingles, using nails. Clear drains and downspouts and clean gutters. Locate worn or torn areas in roofs. Perform emergency leak repairs and general maintenance for a variety of roof types. Attach sheets of metal to roof boards or building frameworks when installing metal roofs. Check to ensure that completed roofs are watertight. Remove old roofing materials. Provide assistance to skilled roofers installing and repairing roofs, flashings, and surfaces. Maintain tools and equipment. Hoist tar and roofing materials to roofs, using ropes and pulleys, or carry materials up ladders. Clean work areas and equipment. Set ladders, scaffolds, and hoists in place for taking supplies to roofs. Sweep and clean roofs to prepare them for the application of new roofing materials. Chop tar into small pieces and heat chopped tar in kettles.

GOE Information—Interest Area: 02. Architecture and Construction. **Work Group:** 02.06. Construction Support/Labor. **Note:** The Department of Labor has not collected some data for this job, so it has fewer details than the other descriptions.

Instructional Program—Roofer.

Related SOC Job—47-3016 Helpers—Roofers. **Related OOH Job**—Helpers—Roofers. **Related DOT Job**—869.687-026 Construction Worker II.

47-3019.99 Helpers, Construction Trades, All Other

- **Education/Training Required: Short-term on-the-job training**
- **Employed: 37,590**
- **Annual Earnings: $21,630**
- **Growth: 1.8%**
- **Annual Job Openings: 8,000**

All construction trades helpers not listed separately.

No task data available.

Note: The Department of Labor has not collected some data for this job, so it has fewer details than the other descriptions.

Related SOC Job—47-3019 Helpers, Construction Trades, All Other. **Related OOH Job**—None. **Related DOT Jobs**—844.687-010 Cement Sprayer Helper, Nozzle; 850.684-014 Horizontal-Earth-Boring-Machine-Operator Helper; 864.687-010 Carpet-Layer Helper; 869.567-010 Surveyor Helper; 869.687-010 Awning-Hanger Helper; 869.687-034 House-Mover Helper; 899.664-010 Diver Helper; 911.667-018 Sounder; 930.687-014 Core-Drill-Operator Helper.

47-4000 Other Construction and Related Workers

47-4011.00 Construction and Building Inspectors

- **Education/Training Required: Work experience in a related occupation**
- **Employed: 87,820**
- **Annual Earnings: $44,720**
- **Growth: 22.3%**
- **Annual Job Openings: 6,000**

Inspect structures, using engineering skills to determine structural soundness and compliance with specifications, building codes, and other regulations. Inspections may be general in nature or may be limited to a specific area, such as electrical systems or plumbing.

Use survey instruments; metering devices; tape measures; and test equipment, such as concrete strength measurers, to perform inspections. Inspect bridges, dams, highways, buildings, wiring, plumbing, electrical circuits, sewers, heating systems, and foundations during and after construction for structural quality, general safety, and conformance to specifications and codes. Maintain daily logs and supplement inspection records with photographs. Review and interpret plans, blueprints, site layouts, specifications, and construction methods to ensure compliance to legal requirements and safety regulations. Inspect and monitor construction sites to ensure adherence to safety standards, building codes, and specifications. Measure dimensions and verify level, alignment, and elevation of structures and fixtures to ensure compliance to building plans and codes. Issue violation notices and stop-work orders, conferring with owners, violators, and authorities to explain regulations and recommend rectifications. Issue permits for construction, relocation, demolition, and occupancy. Approve and sign plans that meet required specifications. Compute estimates of work completed or of needed renovations or upgrades and approve payment for contractors. Monitor installation of plumbing, wiring, equipment, and appliances to ensure that installation is performed properly and is in compliance with applicable regulations. Examine lifting and conveying devices, such as elevators, escalators, moving sidewalks, lifts and hoists, inclined railways, ski lifts, and amusement rides, to ensure safety and proper functioning. Train, direct, and supervise other construction inspectors. Evaluate premises for cleanliness, including proper garbage disposal and lack of vermin infestation.

GOE Information—Interest Area: 07. Government and Public Administration. **Work Group:** 07.03. Regulations Enforcement. **Personality Type**—Conventional. Conventional occupations frequently involve following set procedures and routines. These occupations can include working with data and details more than with ideas. Usually there is a clear line of authority to follow. **Work Values**—Responsibility; Autonomy; Independence; Supervision; Technical; Advancement; Security. **Skills**—Mathematics; Persuasion; Quality Control Analysis; Reading Comprehension; Science; Time Management. **Abilities**—*Cognitive:* Problem Sensitivity; Speed of Closure; Spatial Orientation; Deductive Reasoning; Visualization; Perceptual Speed. *Psychomotor:* Control Precision; Multilimb Coordination; Arm-Hand Steadiness. *Physical:* Extent Flexibility; Gross Body Coordination; Trunk Strength. *Sensory:* Auditory Attention; Visual Color Discrimination; Depth Perception; Near Vision; Far Vision; Speech Recognition. **General Work Activities**—*Information Input:* Monitoring Processes, Materials, or Surroundings; Identifying Objects, Actions, and Events; Inspecting Equipment, Structures, or Materials. *Mental Process:* Updating and Using Relevant Knowledge; Evaluating Information Against Standards; Organizing, Planning, and Prioritizing. *Work Output:* Documenting or Recording Information; Handling and Moving Objects; Performing General Physical Activities. *Interacting with Others:* Communicating with Other Workers; Resolving Conflicts and Negotiating with Others; Establishing and Maintaining Interpersonal Relationships. **Physical Work Conditions**—More Often Outdoors Than Indoors; Noisy; Contaminants; Hazardous Equipment; Standing. **Other Job Characteristics**—Need to Be Exact or Accurate; Repeat Same Tasks.

Experience—Job Zone 3. Previous work-related skill, knowledge, or experience is required. **Job Preparation**—SVP 6.0 to less than 7.0—more than one year and less than four years. **Knowledges**—Building and Construction; Design; Engineering and Technology; Public Safety and Security; Mechanical Devices; Customer and Personal Service. **Instructional Programs**—Building/Home/Construction Inspection/Inspector.

Related SOC Job—47-4011 Construction and Building Inspectors. **Related OOH Job**—Construction and Building Inspectors. **Related**

DOT Jobs—168.167-026 Inspector, Boiler; 168.167-030 Inspector, Building; 168.167-034 Inspector, Electrical; 168.167-038 Inspector, Elevators; 168.167-046 Inspector, Heating and Refrigeration; 168.167-050 Inspector, Plumbing; 168.264-018 Gas Inspector; 168.267-102 Plan Checker; 168.367-018 Code Inspector; 182.267-010 Construction Inspector; 821.367-010 Construction Checker; 821.367-014 Safety Inspector; 822.267-010 Line Inspector; 859.267-010 Street-Openings Inspector; 869.287-010 Bridge Inspector; others.

47-4021.00 Elevator Installers and Repairers

- **Education/Training Required: Long-term on-the-job training**
- **Employed: 21,000**
- **Annual Earnings: $59,190**
- **Growth: 14.8%**
- **Annual Job Openings: 3,000**

Assemble, install, repair, or maintain electric or hydraulic freight or passenger elevators, escalators, or dumbwaiters.

Assemble, install, repair, and maintain elevators, escalators, moving sidewalks, and dumbwaiters, using hand and power tools and testing devices such as test lamps, ammeters, and voltmeters. Test newly installed equipment to ensure that it meets specifications, such as stopping at floors for set amounts of time. Locate malfunctions in brakes, motors, switches, and signal and control systems, using test equipment. Check that safety regulations and building codes are met and complete service reports verifying conformance to standards. Connect electrical wiring to control panels and electric motors. Read and interpret blueprints to determine the layout of system components, frameworks, and foundations and to select installation equipment. Adjust safety controls; counterweights; door mechanisms; and components such as valves, ratchets, seals, and brake linings. Inspect wiring connections, control panel hookups, door installations, and alignments and clearances of cars and hoistways to ensure that equipment will operate properly. Disassemble defective units and repair or replace parts such as locks, gears, cables, and electric wiring. Maintain logbooks that detail all repairs and checks performed. Participate in additional training to keep skills up to date. Attach guide shoes and rollers to minimize the lateral motion of cars as they travel through shafts. Connect car frames to counterweights, using steel cables. Bolt or weld steel rails to the walls of shafts to guide elevators, working from scaffolding or platforms. Assemble elevator cars, installing each car's platform, walls, and doors. Install outer doors and door frames at elevator entrances on each floor of a structure. Install electrical wires and controls by attaching conduit along shaft walls from floor to floor and then pulling plastic-covered wires through the conduit. Cut prefabricated sections of framework, rails, and other components to specified dimensions. Operate elevators to determine power demands and test power consumption to detect overload factors. Assemble electrically powered stairs, steel frameworks, and tracks and install associated motors and electrical wiring.

GOE Information—Interest Area: 02. Architecture and Construction. **Work Group:** 02.05. Systems and Equipment Installation, Maintenance, and Repair. **Personality Type**—Realistic. Realistic occupations frequently involve work activities that include practical, hands-on problems and solutions. They often deal with plants; animals; and real-world materials like wood, tools, and machinery. Many of the occupations require working outside and do not involve a lot of paperwork or working closely with others. **Work Values**—Independence; Moral Values; Supervision, Technical; Compensation; Company Policies and Practices; Creativity. **Skills**—

Installation; Repairing; Troubleshooting; Equipment Maintenance; Quality Control Analysis; Technology Design. **Abilities**—*Cognitive:* Perceptual Speed; Visualization; Selective Attention; Flexibility of Closure; Originality; Fluency of Ideas. *Psychomotor:* Reaction Time; Arm-Hand Steadiness; Response Orientation; Manual Dexterity; Multilimb Coordination; Rate Control. *Physical:* Extent Flexibility; Gross Body Equilibrium; Gross Body Coordination; Stamina; Trunk Strength; Static Strength. *Sensory:* Visual Color Discrimination; Depth Perception; Hearing Sensitivity; Far Vision. **General Work Activities**—*Information Input:* Monitoring Processes, Materials, or Surroundings; Inspecting Equipment, Structures, or Materials; Identifying Objects, Actions, and Events. *Mental Process:* Updating and Using Relevant Knowledge; Making Decisions and Solving Problems; Thinking Creatively. *Work Output:* Handling and Moving Objects; Performing General Physical Activities; Repairing and Maintaining Mechanical Equipment. *Interacting with Others:* Establishing and Maintaining Interpersonal Relationships; Communicating with Other Workers; Coaching and Developing Others. **Physical Work Conditions**—Contaminants; High Places; Hazardous Conditions; Hazardous Equipment; Standing; Using Hands on Objects, Tools, or Controls. **Other Job Characteristics**—Need to Be Exact or Accurate; Errors Have Important Consequences; Repeat Same Tasks.

Experience—Job Zone 3. Previous work-related skill, knowledge, or experience is required. **Job Preparation**—SVP 6.0 to less than 7.0—more than one year and less than four years. **Knowledges**—Building and Construction; Mechanical Devices; Design; Physics; Engineering and Technology; Customer and Personal Service. **Instructional Program**—Industrial Mechanics and Maintenance Technology.

Related SOC Job—47-4021 Elevator Installers and Repairers. **Related OOH Job**—Elevator Installers and Repairers. **Related DOT Jobs**—825.261-014 Elevator Examiner-and-Adjuster; 825.281-030 Elevator Repairer; 825.281-034 Elevator-Repairer Apprentice; 825.361-010 Elevator Constructor.

47-4031.00 Fence Erectors

- **Education/Training Required: Moderate-term on-the-job training**
- **Employed: 22,600**
- **Annual Earnings: $24,930**
- **Growth: 9.9%**
- **Annual Job Openings: 5,000**

Erect and repair metal and wooden fences and fence gates around highways, industrial establishments, residences, or farms, using hand and power tools.

Insert metal tubing through rail supports. Discuss fencing needs with customers and estimate and quote prices. Weld metal parts together, using portable gas welding equipment. Stretch wire, wire mesh, or chain link fencing between posts and attach fencing to frames. Set metal or wooden posts in upright positions in postholes. Nail top and bottom rails to fence posts or insert them in slots on posts. Nail pointed slats to rails to construct picket fences. Mix and pour concrete around bases of posts or tamp soil into postholes to embed posts. Blast rock formations and rocky areas with dynamite to facilitate posthole digging. Make rails for fences by sawing lumber or by cutting metal tubing to required lengths. Establish the location for a fence and gather information needed to ensure that there are no electric cables or water lines in the area. Erect alternate panel, basket weave, and louvered fences. Construct and repair barriers, retaining walls, trellises, and other types of fences, walls, and gates. Align posts, using lines or by sighting, and verify vertical alignment of posts, using plumb bobs or spirit levels. Assemble gates and fasten gates into position, using hand tools. Attach fence rail supports to posts, using hammers and pliers. Complete top fence rails of metal fences by connecting tube sections, using metal sleeves. Attach rails or tension wire along bottoms of posts to form fencing frames. Measure and lay out fence lines and mark posthole positions, following instructions, drawings, or specifications. Dig postholes, using spades, posthole diggers, or power-driven augers.

GOE Information—Interest Area: 02. Architecture and Construction. **Work Group:** 02.04. Construction Crafts. **Personality Type**—Realistic. Realistic occupations frequently involve work activities that include practical, hands-on problems and solutions. They often deal with plants; animals; and real-world materials like wood, tools, and machinery. Many of the occupations require working outside and do not involve a lot of paperwork or working closely with others. **Work Values**—Moral Values. **Skills**—Repairing. **Abilities**—*Cognitive:* None met the criteria. *Psychomotor:* Wrist-Finger Speed; Speed of Limb Movement; Manual Dexterity; Multilimb Coordination; Arm-Hand Steadiness. *Physical:* Static Strength; Explosive Strength; Extent Flexibility; Dynamic Strength; Trunk Strength. *Sensory:* None met the criteria. **General Work Activities**—*Information Input:* Estimating the Needed Characteristics of Products, Events, or Information; Getting Information. *Mental Process:* Organizing, Planning, and Prioritizing. *Work Output:* Performing General Physical Activities; Handling and Moving Objects. *Interacting with Others:* None met the criteria. **Physical Work Conditions**—Outdoors; Noisy; Minor Burns, Cuts, Bites, or Stings; Standing; Kneeling, Crouching, Stooping, or Crawling; Using Hands on Objects, Tools, or Controls. **Other Job Characteristics**—None met the criteria.

Experience—Job Zone 2. Some previous work-related skill, knowledge, or experience may be helpful in these occupations, but usually is not needed. **Job Preparation**—SVP 4.0 to less than 6.0—six months to less than two years. **Knowledges**—Building and Construction. **Instructional Program**—Building/Construction Trades, Other.

Related SOC Job—47-4031 Fence Erectors. **Related OOH Job**—Fence Erectors. **Related DOT Job**—869.684-022 Fence Erector.

47-4041.00 Hazardous Materials Removal Workers

- **Education/Training Required: Moderate-term on-the-job training**
- **Employed: 38,260**
- **Annual Earnings: $33,690**
- **Growth: 31.2%**
- **Annual Job Openings: 11,000**

Identify, remove, pack, transport, or dispose of hazardous materials, including asbestos, lead-based paint, waste oil, fuel, transmission fluid, radioactive materials, contaminated soil, and so on. Specialized training and certification in hazardous materials handling or a confined entry permit are generally required. May operate earth-moving equipment or trucks.

Follow prescribed safety procedures and comply with federal laws regulating waste disposal methods. Record numbers of containers stored at disposal sites and specify amounts and types of equipment and waste disposed. Drive trucks or other heavy equipment to convey contaminated waste to designated sea or ground locations. Operate machines and equipment to remove, package, store, or transport loads of waste materials. Load and unload materials into containers and onto trucks, using hoists or forklifts. Clean contaminated equipment or areas for re-use, using detergents and solvents, sandblasters, filter pumps, and steam cleaners. Construct scaffolding or build containment areas prior to beginning abatement or decontamination work. Remove asbestos or lead from surfaces, using hand and power tools such as scrapers, vacuums, and high-pressure sprayers. Unload baskets of irradiated elements onto packaging machines that automatically insert fuel elements into canisters and secure lids. Apply chemical compounds to lead-based paint, allow compounds to dry; then scrape the hazardous material into containers for removal or storage. Identify asbestos, lead, or other hazardous materials that need to be removed, using monitoring devices. Pull tram cars along underwater tracks and position cars to receive irradiated fuel elements; then pull loaded cars to mechanisms that automatically unload elements onto underwater tables. Package, store, and move irradiated fuel elements in the underwater storage basin of a nuclear reactor plant, using machines and equipment. Organize and track the locations of hazardous items in landfills. Operate cranes to move and load baskets, casks, and canisters. Manipulate handgrips of mechanical arms to place irradiated fuel elements into baskets. Mix and pour concrete into forms to encase waste material for disposal.

GOE Information—Interest Area: 02. Architecture and Construction. **Work Group:** 02.04. Construction Crafts. **Personality Type**—Realistic. Realistic occupations frequently involve work activities that include practical, hands-on problems and solutions. They often deal with plants; animals; and real-world materials like wood, tools, and machinery. Many of the occupations require working outside and do not involve a lot of paperwork or working closely with others. **Work Values**—Supervision, Technical; Independence; Supervision, Human Relations. **Skills**—Operation Monitoring; Equipment Maintenance; Repairing; Operation and Control; Troubleshooting; Science. **Abilities**—*Cognitive:* Spatial Orientation; Perceptual Speed; Visualization; Time Sharing; Category Flexibility; Flexibility of Closure. *Psychomotor:* Multilimb Coordination; Rate Control; Response Orientation; Control Precision; Reaction Time; Manual Dexterity. *Physical:* Extent Flexibility; Dynamic Strength; Static Strength; Gross Body Coordination; Trunk Strength. *Sensory:* Depth Perception; Night Vision; Visual Color Discrimination; Hearing Sensitivity; Far Vision; Auditory Attention. **General Work Activities**—*Information Input:* Identifying Objects, Actions, and Events; Monitoring Processes, Materials, or Surroundings; Inspecting Equipment, Structures, or Materials. *Mental Process:* Analyzing Data or Information; Processing Information; Making Decisions and Solving Problems. *Work Output:* Handling and Moving Objects; Controlling Machines and Processes; Performing General Physical Activities. *Interacting with Others:* Communicating with Other Workers; Establishing and Maintaining Interpersonal Relationships; Teaching Others. **Physical Work Conditions**—Outdoors; Very Hot or Cold; Contaminants; Hazardous Conditions; Using Hands on Objects, Tools, or Controls; Repetitive Motions. **Other Job Characteristics**—Repeat Same Tasks; Need to Be Exact or Accurate; Pace Determined by Speed of Equipment.

Experience—Job Zone 2. Some previous work-related skill, knowledge, or experience may be helpful in these occupations, but usually is not needed. **Job Preparation**—SVP 4.0 to less than 6.0—six months to less than two years. **Knowledges**—Chemistry; Building and Construction; Mechanical Devices; Transportation; Physics; Education and Training. **Instructional Programs**—Building/Construction Trades, Other; Hazardous Materials Management and Waste Technology/Technician; Mechanic and Repair Technology, Other.

Related SOC Job—47-4041 Hazardous Materials Removal Workers. **Related OOH Job**—Hazardous Materials Removal Workers. **Related DOT Jobs**—921.663-034 Irradiated-Fuel Handler; 955.383-010 Waste-Disposal Attendant.

47-4051.00 Highway Maintenance Workers

- **Education/Training Required: Moderate-term on-the-job training**
- **Employed: 140,600**
- **Annual Earnings: $30,250**
- **Growth: 23.3%**
- **Annual Job Openings: 27,000**

Maintain highways, municipal and rural roads, airport runways, and rights-of-way. Duties include patching broken or eroded pavement and repairing guardrails, highway markers, and snow fences. May also mow or clear brush from along road or plow snow from roadway.

Flag motorists to warn them of obstacles or repair work ahead. Set out signs and cones around work areas to divert traffic. Drive trucks or tractors with adjustable attachments to sweep debris from paved surfaces, mow grass and weeds, and remove snow and ice. Dump, spread, and tamp asphalt, using pneumatic tampers, to repair joints and patch broken pavement. Drive trucks to transport crews and equipment to worksites. Inspect, clean, and repair drainage systems, bridges, tunnels, and other structures. Haul and spread sand, gravel, and clay to fill washouts and repair road shoulders. Erect, install, or repair guardrails, road shoulders, berms, highway markers, warning signals, and highway lighting, using hand tools and power tools. Remove litter and debris from roadways, including debris from rock slides and mudslides. Clean and clear debris from culverts, catch basins, drop inlets, ditches, and other drain structures. Perform roadside landscaping work, such as clearing weeds and brush and planting and trimming trees. Paint traffic control lines and place pavement traffic messages by hand or using machines. Inspect markers to verify accurate installation. Apply poisons along roadsides and in animal burrows to eliminate unwanted roadside vegetation and rodents. Measure and mark locations for installation of markers, using tape, string, or chalk. Apply oil to road surfaces, using sprayers. Blend compounds to form adhesive mixtures used for marker installation. Place and remove snow fences used to prevent the accumulation of drifting snow on highways.

GOE Information—Interest Area: 02. Architecture and Construction. **Work Group:** 02.06. Construction Support/Labor. **Personality Type**—Realistic. Realistic occupations frequently involve work activities that include practical, hands-on problems and solutions. They often deal with plants; animals; and real-world materials like wood, tools, and machinery. Many of the occupations require working outside and do not involve a lot of paperwork or working closely with others. **Work Values**—Moral Values; Supervision, Human Relations. **Skills**—Equipment Maintenance; Repairing; Installation; Operation and Control; Management of Material Resources; Troubleshooting. **Abilities**—*Cognitive:* Time Sharing. *Psychomotor:* Rate Control; Reaction Time; Multilimb Coordination; Response Orientation; Control Precision; Speed of Limb Movement. *Physical:* Static Strength; Trunk Strength; Dynamic Strength; Gross Body Equilibrium; Stamina; Gross Body Coordination. *Sensory:* Sound Localization; Glare Sensitivity; Depth Perception; Auditory Attention; Hearing Sensitivity. **General Work Activities**—*Information Input:* Inspecting Equipment, Structures, or Materials; Estimating the Needed Characteristics of Products, Events, or Information; Getting Information. *Mental Process:* Making Decisions

and Solving Problems; Updating and Using Relevant Knowledge; Organizing, Planning, and Prioritizing. *Work Output:* Handling and Moving Objects; Operating Vehicles or Equipment; Performing General Physical Activities. *Interacting with Others:* Establishing and Maintaining Interpersonal Relationships; Coordinating the Work and Activities of Others; Communicating with Other Workers. **Physical Work Conditions**—Outdoors; Noisy; Very Hot or Cold; Contaminants; Hazardous Equipment; Using Hands on Objects, Tools, or Controls. **Other Job Characteristics**—Need to Be Exact or Accurate.

Experience—Job Zone 2. Some previous work-related skill, knowledge, or experience may be helpful in these occupations, but usually is not needed. **Job Preparation**—SVP 4.0 to less than 6.0—six months to less than two years. **Knowledges**—Building and Construction; Transportation; Mechanical Devices; Public Safety and Security; Customer and Personal Service; Geography. **Instructional Program**—Construction/Heavy Equipment/Earthmoving Equipment Operation.

Related SOC Job—47-4051 Highway Maintenance Workers. **Related OOH Job**—Highway Maintenance Workers. **Related DOT Jobs**—859.684-010 Lane-Marker Installer; 899.684-014 Highway-Maintenance Worker.

47-4061.00 Rail-Track Laying and Maintenance Equipment Operators

- **Education/Training Required: Moderate-term on-the-job training**
- **Employed: 13,510**
- **Annual Earnings: $39,990**
- **Growth: –10.9%**
- **Annual Job Openings: 1,000**

Lay, repair, and maintain track for standard or narrow-gauge railroad equipment used in regular railroad service or in plant yards, quarries, sand and gravel pits, and mines. Includes ballast-cleaning-machine operators and roadbed-tamping-machine operators.

Drive vehicles that automatically move and lay tracks or rails over sections of track to be constructed, repaired, or maintained. Operate track-wrench machines to tighten or loosen bolts at joints that hold ends of rails together. Clean, grade, and level ballast on railroad tracks. Dress and reshape worn or damaged railroad switch points and frogs, using portable power grinders. Push controls to close grasping devices on track or rail sections so that they can be raised or moved. Drive graders, tamping machines, brooms, and ballast cleaning/spreading machines to redistribute gravel and ballast between rails. Adjust controls of machines that spread, shape, raise, level, and align track according to specifications. Engage mechanisms that lay tracks or rails to specified gauges. Grind ends of new or worn rails to attain smooth joints, using portable grinders. Observe leveling indicator arms to verify levelness and alignment of tracks. Operate single- or multiple-head spike-driving machines to drive spikes into ties and secure rails. Operate single- or multiple-head spike pullers to pull old spikes from ties. Operate tie-adzing machines to cut ties and permit insertion of fishplates that hold rails. Drill holes through rails, tie plates, and fishplates for insertion of bolts and spikes, using power drills. Repair and adjust track switches, using wrenches and replacement parts. Spray ties, fishplates, and joints with oil to protect them from weathering. String and attach wire-guidelines machine to rails so that tracks or rails can be aligned or leveled. Cut rails to specified lengths, using rail saws. Patrol assigned track sections so that damaged or broken track can be located and reported. Paint railroad signs, such as speed limits and gate-crossing warnings. Lubricate machines, change oil, and fill hydraulic reservoirs to specified levels. Clean tracks and clear ice and snow from tracks and switch boxes. Clean and make minor repairs to machines and equipment. Turn wheels of machines, using lever controls, to adjust guidelines for track alignments and grades, following specifications.

GOE Information—Interest Area: 02. Architecture and Construction. **Work Group:** 02.04. Construction Crafts. **Personality Type—**Realistic. Realistic occupations frequently involve work activities that include practical, hands-on problems and solutions. They often deal with plants; animals; and real-world materials like wood, tools, and machinery. Many of the occupations require working outside and do not involve a lot of paperwork or working closely with others. **Work Values—**Moral Values; Supervision, Technical; Supervision, Human Relations. **Skills—**Operation and Control; Operation Monitoring; Equipment Maintenance. **Abilities—***Cognitive:* None met the criteria. *Psychomotor:* Control Precision; Multilimb Coordination. *Physical:* None met the criteria. *Sensory:* Depth Perception. **General Work Activities—***Information Input:* None met the criteria. *Mental Process:* Evaluating Information Against Standards. *Work Output:* Handling and Moving Objects; Controlling Machines and Processes; Operating Vehicles or Equipment. *Interacting with Others:* None met the criteria. **Physical Work Conditions—**Outdoors; Noisy; Contaminants; Hazardous Equipment; Sitting; Using Hands on Objects, Tools, or Controls. **Other Job Characteristics—**Errors Have Important Consequences; Need to Be Exact or Accurate; Automation.

Experience—Job Zone 1. No previous work-related skill, knowledge, or experience is needed. **Job Preparation—**SVP below 4.0—less than six months. **Knowledges—**Building and Construction; Mechanical Devices; Transportation; Engineering and Technology. **Instructional Program—**Construction/Heavy Equipment/Earthmoving Equipment Operation.

Related SOC Job—47-4061 Rail-Track Laying and Maintenance Equipment Operators. **Related OOH Job—**Rail-Track Laying and Maintenance Equipment Operators. **Related DOT Jobs—**859.683-018 Railway-Equipment Operator; 910.663-010 Track-Moving-Machine Operator; 910.683-018 Track-Surfacing-Machine Operator; 910.684-010 Grinding-Machine Operator, Portable; 910.684-014 Track Repairer.

47-4071.00 Septic Tank Servicers and Sewer Pipe Cleaners

- **Education/Training Required: Moderate-term on-the-job training**
- **Employed: 17,940**
- **Annual Earnings: $30,440**
- **Growth: 21.8%**
- **Annual Job Openings: 3,000**

Clean and repair septic tanks, sewer lines, or drains. May patch walls and partitions of tank, replace damaged drain tile, or repair breaks in underground piping.

Drive trucks to transport crews, materials, and equipment. Communicate with supervisors and other workers, using equipment such as wireless phones, pagers, or radio telephones. Prepare and keep records of actions taken, including maintenance and repair work. Operate sewer cleaning equipment, including power rodders, high-velocity water jets, sewer flushers, bucket machines, wayne balls, and vac-alls. Ensure that repaired sewer line joints are tightly sealed before backfilling begins. Withdraw cables from pipes and examine them for evidence of mud, roots, grease, and other deposits indicating broken or clogged sewer lines. Install rotary knives on flexible cables mounted on machine reels according to the diameters of pipes to be cleaned. Measure excavation sites, using plumbers' snakes, tapelines, or lengths of cutting heads within sewers, and mark areas for digging. Locate problems, using specially designed equipment, and mark where digging must occur to reach damaged tanks or pipes. Start machines to feed revolving cables or rods into openings, stopping machines and changing knives to conform to pipe sizes. Clean and repair septic tanks; sewer lines; or related structures such as manholes, culverts, and catch basins. Service, adjust, and make minor repairs to equipment, machines, and attachments. Inspect manholes to locate sewer line stoppages. Cut damaged sections of pipe with cutters, remove broken sections from ditches, and replace pipe sections, using pipe sleeves. Dig out sewer lines manually, using shovels. Break asphalt and other pavement so that pipes can be accessed, using airhammers, picks, and shovels. Cover repaired pipes with dirt and pack backfilled excavations, using air and gasoline tampers. Requisition or order tools and equipment. Rotate cleaning rods manually, using turning pins. Clean and disinfect domestic basements and other areas flooded by sewer stoppages. Tap mainline sewers to install sewer saddles. Update sewer maps and manhole charts.

GOE Information—Interest Area: 02. Architecture and Construction. **Work Group:** 02.06. Construction Support/Labor. **Personality Type—**Realistic. Realistic occupations frequently involve work activities that include practical, hands-on problems and solutions. They often deal with plants; animals; and real-world materials like wood, tools, and machinery. Many of the occupations require working outside and do not involve a lot of paperwork or working closely with others. **Work Values—**Independence; Supervision, Technical. **Skills—**Equipment Maintenance; Repairing; Operation Monitoring; Installation; Operation and Control; Troubleshooting. **Abilities—***Cognitive:* Spatial Orientation; Flexibility of Closure; Visualization; Time Sharing; Speed of Closure; Number Facility. *Psychomotor:* Response Orientation; Reaction Time; Rate Control; Speed of Limb Movement; Control Precision; Multilimb Coordination. *Physical:* Dynamic Strength; Stamina; Trunk Strength; Gross Body Equilibrium; Extent Flexibility; Static Strength. *Sensory:* Glare Sensitivity; Depth Perception; Hearing Sensitivity; Peripheral Vision; Auditory Attention; Far Vision. **General Work Activities—***Information Input:* Monitoring Processes, Materials, or Surroundings; Getting Information; Estimating the Needed Characteristics of Products, Events, or Information. *Mental Process:* Making Decisions and Solving Problems; Organizing, Planning, and Prioritizing; Updating and Using Relevant Knowledge. *Work Output:* Handling and Moving Objects; Performing General Physical Activities; Controlling Machines and Processes. *Interacting with Others:* Performing for or Working with the Public; Establishing and Maintaining Interpersonal Relationships; Influencing Others or Selling. **Physical Work Conditions—**Outdoors; Noisy; Very Hot or Cold; Contaminants; Hazardous Equipment; Using Hands on Objects, Tools, or Controls. **Other Job Characteristics—**Need to Be Exact or Accurate; Errors Have Important Consequences.

Experience—Job Zone 1. No previous work-related skill, knowledge, or experience is needed. **Job Preparation—**SVP below 4.0—less than six months. **Knowledges—**Building and Construction; Mechanical Devices; Sales and Marketing; Transportation; Production and Processing; Customer and Personal Service. **Instructional Program—**Plumbing Technology/Plumber.

Related SOC Job—47-4071 Septic Tank Servicers and Sewer Pipe Cleaners. **Related OOH Job**—Septic Tank Servicers and Sewer Pipe Cleaners. **Related DOT Jobs**—869.664-018 Sewer-Line Repairer; 899.664-014 Sewer-Pipe Cleaner.

47-4091.00 Segmental Pavers

- **Education/Training Required: Moderate-term on-the-job training**
- **Employed: 330**
- **Annual Earnings: $25,000**
- **Growth: 12.5%**
- **Annual Job Openings: Fewer than 500**

Lay out, cut, and paste segmental paving units. Includes installers of bedding and restraining materials for the paving units.

Supply and place base materials, edge restraints, bedding sand, and jointing sand. Prepare base for installation by removing unstable or unsuitable materials, compacting and grading the soil, draining or stabilizing weak or saturated soils, and taking measures to prevent water penetration and migration of bedding sand. Sweep sand from the surface prior to opening to traffic. Set pavers, aligning and spacing them correctly. Sweep sand into the joints and compact pavement until the joints are full. Compact bedding sand and pavers to finish the paved area, using a plate compactor. Design paver installation layout pattern and create markings for directional references of joints and stringlines. Resurface an outside area with cobblestones, terracotta tiles, concrete, or other materials. Discuss the design with the client. Cut paving stones to size and for edges, using a splitter and a masonry saw. Screed sand level to an even thickness and recheck sand exposed to elements, raking and rescreeding if necessary. Cement the edges of the paved area.

GOE Information—Interest Area: 02. Architecture and Construction. **Work Group:** 02.04. Construction Crafts. **Personality Type**—No data available. **Work Values**—No data available. **Skills**—Negotiation; Equipment Maintenance; Management of Material Resources; Management of Personnel Resources; Judgment and Decision Making; Service Orientation. **Abilities**—*Cognitive:* Time Sharing; Visualization; Selective Attention. *Psychomotor:* Multilimb Coordination; Response Orientation; Control Precision; Speed of Limb Movement; Rate Control; Manual Dexterity. *Physical:* Gross Body Coordination; Static Strength; Dynamic Strength; Stamina. *Sensory:* Depth Perception; Auditory Attention. **General Work Activities**—*Information Input:* Monitoring Processes, Materials, or Surroundings; Inspecting Equipment, Structures, or Materials; Estimating the Needed Characteristics of Products, Events, or Information. *Mental Process:* Making Decisions and Solving Problems; Organizing, Planning, and Prioritizing; Thinking Creatively. *Work Output:* Handling and Moving Objects; Performing General Physical Activities; Controlling Machines and Processes. *Interacting with Others:* Establishing and Maintaining Interpersonal Relationships; Coordinating the Work and Activities of Others; Communicating with Other Workers. **Physical Work Conditions**—More Often Outdoors Than Indoors; Noisy; Very Hot or Cold; Walking and Running; Repetitive Motions. **Other Job Characteristics**—Need to Be Exact or Accurate; Repeat Same Tasks.

Experience—Job Zone 2. Some previous work-related skill, knowledge, or experience may be helpful in these occupations, but usually is not needed. **Job Preparation**—SVP 4.0 to less than 6.0—six months to less than two years. **Knowledges**—Building and Construction; Mechanical Devices; Transportation; Engineering and Technology; Customer and Personal Service; Administration and Management. **Instructional Program**—Concrete Finishing/Concrete Finisher.

Related SOC Job—47-4091 Segmental Pavers. **Related OOH Job**—Cement Masons, Concrete Finishers, Segmental Pavers, and Terrazzo Workers. **Related DOT Job**—No data available.

47-4099.99 Construction and Related Workers, All Other

- **Education/Training Required: Moderate-term on-the-job training**
- **Employed: 63,340**
- **Annual Earnings: $29,860**
- **Growth: 27.5%**
- **Annual Job Openings: 9,000**

All construction and related workers not listed separately.

No task data available.

Note: The Department of Labor has not collected some data for this job, so it has fewer details than the other descriptions.

Related SOC Job—47-4099 Construction and Related Workers, All Other. **Related OOH Job**—None. **Related DOT Jobs**—168.364-640 Hazardous-Waste Material Technician; 779.684-058 Stone Repairer; 809.381-022 Ornamental-Iron Worker; 809.381-026 Ornamental-Iron-Worker Apprentice; 821.687-010 Steel-Post Installer; 851.262-010 Sewer-Line Repairer, Tele-Grout; 862.662-010 Pipe-Cleaning-And-Priming-Machine Operator; 862.682-014 Pipe-Wrapping-Machine Operator; 869.261-010 House Mover; 869.261-018 Poured-Concrete-Wall Technician; 869.281-014 House Builder; 869.361-010 Conduit Mechanic; others.

47-5000 Extraction Workers

47-5011.00 Derrick Operators, Oil and Gas

- **Education/Training Required: Moderate-term on-the-job training**
- **Employed: 13,270**
- **Annual Earnings: $33,880**
- **Growth: −0.5%**
- **Annual Job Openings: 1,000**

Rig derrick equipment and operate pumps to circulate mud through drill hole.

Inspect derricks or order their inspection prior to being raised or lowered. Inspect derricks for flaws and clean and oil derricks to maintain proper working conditions. Control the viscosity and weight of the drilling fluid. Repair pumps, mud tanks, and related equipment. Set and bolt crown blocks to posts at tops of derricks. Listen to mud pumps and check regularly for vibration and other problems to ensure that rig pumps and drilling mud systems are working properly. Start pumps that circulate mud through drill pipes and boreholes to cool drill bits and flush out drill cuttings. Position and align derrick elements, using harnesses and platform climbing devices. Supervise crew members and provide assistance in training them. Guide lengths of pipe into and out of elevators. Prepare mud reports and instruct crews about the handling of any chemical additives. Clamp holding fixtures on ends of hoisting cables. Weigh clay and mix with water and chemicals to make drilling mud, using portable mixers. String cables through pulleys and blocks. Steady pipes during connection to or disconnection from drill or casing strings.

GOE Information—Interest Area: 01. Agriculture and Natural Resources. Work Group: 01.08. Mining and Drilling. Personality Type—Realistic. Realistic occupations frequently involve work activities that include practical, hands-on problems and solutions. They often deal with plants; animals; and real-world materials like wood, tools, and machinery. Many of the occupations require working outside and do not involve a lot of paperwork or working closely with others. Work Values—Moral Values; Supervision, Technical; Supervision, Human Relations. Skills—Operation Monitoring; Repairing; Equipment Maintenance; Operation and Control; Installation; Management of Personnel Resources. Abilities—Cognitive: Spatial Orientation; Perceptual Speed; Flexibility of Closure; Time Sharing; Visualization; Selective Attention. Psychomotor: Reaction Time; Rate Control; Speed of Limb Movement; Response Orientation; Multilimb Coordination; Control Precision. Physical: Gross Body Equilibrium; Extent Flexibility; Static Strength; Stamina; Gross Body Coordination; Trunk Strength. Sensory: Depth Perception; Auditory Attention; Glare Sensitivity; Hearing Sensitivity; Sound Localization; Peripheral Vision. General Work Activities—Information Input: Inspecting Equipment, Structures, or Materials; Monitoring Processes, Materials, or Surroundings; Identifying Objects, Actions, and Events. Mental Process: Making Decisions and Solving Problems; Judging the Qualities of Things, Services, or Other People's Work; Updating and Using Relevant Knowledge. Work Output: Handling and Moving Objects; Performing General Physical Activities; Repairing and Maintaining Mechanical Equipment. Interacting with Others: Communicating with Other Workers; Teaching Others; Developing and Building Teams. Physical Work Conditions—Outdoors; Noisy; Very Hot or Cold; Contaminants; Hazardous Equipment; Minor Burns, Cuts, Bites, or Stings. Other Job Characteristics—Repeat Same Tasks; Need to Be Exact or Accurate; Pace Determined by Speed of Equipment.

Experience—Job Zone 1. No previous work-related skill, knowledge, or experience is needed. Job Preparation—SVP below 4.0—less than six months. Knowledges—Mechanical Devices; Building and Construction; Physics; Transportation; Chemistry; Public Safety and Security. Instructional Program—Well Drilling/Driller.

Related SOC Job—47-5011 Derrick Operators, Oil and Gas. Related OOH Job—Derrick Operators, Oil and Gas. Related DOT Job—930.382-022 Rotary Derrick Operator.

47-5012.00 Rotary Drill Operators, Oil and Gas

- Education/Training Required: Moderate-term on-the-job training
- Employed: 15,500
- Annual Earnings: $37,490
- Growth: 0.1%
- Annual Job Openings: 1,000

Set up or operate a variety of drills to remove petroleum products from the earth and to find and remove core samples for testing during oil and gas exploration.

Train crews and introduce procedures to make drill work more safe and effective. Observe pressure gauge and move throttles and levers to control the speed of rotary tables and to regulate pressure of tools at bottoms of boreholes. Count sections of drill rod to determine depths of boreholes. Push levers and brake pedals to control gasoline, diesel, electric, or steam draw works that lower and raise drill pipes and casings in and out of wells. Connect sections of drill pipe, using hand tools and powered wrenches and tongs. Maintain records of footage drilled, location and nature of strata penetrated, materials and tools used, services rendered, and time required. Maintain and adjust machinery to ensure proper performance. Start and examine operation of slush pumps to ensure circulation and consistency of drilling fluid or mud in well. Locate and recover lost or broken bits, casings, and drill pipes from wells, using special tools. Weigh clay and mix with water and chemicals to make drilling mud. Direct rig crews in drilling and other activities, such as setting up rigs and completing or servicing wells. Monitor progress of drilling operations and select and change drill bits according to the nature of strata, using hand tools. Repair or replace defective parts of machinery, such as rotary drill rigs, water trucks, air compressors, and pumps, using hand tools. Clean and oil pulleys, blocks, and cables. Bolt together pump and engine parts and connect tanks and flow lines. Remove core samples during drilling to determine the nature of the strata being drilled. Cap wells with packers or turn valves to regulate outflow of oil from wells. Line drilled holes with pipes and install all necessary hardware to prepare new wells. Position and prepare truck-mounted derricks at drilling areas that are specified on field maps. Plug observation wells and restore sites. Lower and explode charges in boreholes to start flow of oil from wells. Dig holes, set forms, and mix and pour concrete for foundations of steel or wooden derricks.

GOE Information—Interest Area: 01. Agriculture and Natural Resources. Work Group: 01.08. Mining and Drilling. Personality Type—Realistic. Realistic occupations frequently involve work activities that include practical, hands-on problems and solutions. They often deal with plants; animals; and real-world materials like wood, tools, and machinery. Many of the occupations require working outside and do not involve a lot of paperwork or working closely with others. Work Values—Compensation; Supervision, Technical; Supervision, Human Relations; Company Policies and Practices. Skills—Repairing; Equipment Maintenance; Operation Monitoring; Operation and Control; Installation; Troubleshooting. Abilities—Cognitive: Selective Attention; Perceptual Speed; Time Sharing; Visualization; Information Ordering; Flexibility of Closure. Psychomotor: Rate Control; Multilimb Coordination; Response Orientation; Reaction Time; Control Precision; Manual Dexterity. Physical: Static Strength; Gross Body Equilibrium; Dynamic Strength; Gross Body Coordination; Extent Flexibility; Trunk Strength. Sensory: Auditory Attention; Depth Perception; Hearing Sensitivity; Visual Color Discrimination; Far Vision. General Work Activities—Information Input: Inspecting Equipment, Structures, or Materials; Monitoring Processes, Materials, or Surroundings; Identifying Objects, Actions, and Events. Mental Process: Making Decisions and Solving Problems; Thinking Creatively; Updating and Using Relevant Knowledge. Work Output: Handling and Moving Objects; Performing General Physical Activities; Controlling Machines and Processes. Interacting with Others: Communicating with Other Workers; Coordinating the Work and Activities of Others; Guiding, Directing, and Motivating Subordinates. Physical Work Conditions—Outdoors; Noisy; Very Hot or Cold; Contaminants; Hazardous Equipment; Using Hands on Objects, Tools, or Controls. Other Job Characteristics—Need to Be Exact or Accurate; Errors Have Important Consequences; Repeat Same Tasks; Pace Determined by Speed of Equipment.

Experience—Job Zone 2. Some previous work-related skill, knowledge, or experience may be helpful in these occupations, but usually is not needed. Job Preparation—SVP 4.0 to less than 6.0—six months to less than two years. Knowledges—Mechanical Devices; Chemistry; Personnel and Human Resources; Transportation; Education and Training; Mathematics. Instructional Program—Well Drilling/Driller.

Related SOC Job—47-5012 Rotary Drill Operators, Oil and Gas. Related OOH Job—Rotary Drill Operators, Oil and Gas. Related DOT Jobs—930.382-018 Prospecting Driller; 930.382-026 Rotary Driller; 950.382-022 Rotary-Rig Engine Operator.

47-5013.00 Service Unit Operators, Oil, Gas, and Mining

- Education/Training Required: Moderate-term on-the-job training
- Employed: 19,530
- Annual Earnings: $30,670
- Growth: –0.6%
- Annual Job Openings: 1,000

Operate equipment to increase oil flow from producing wells or to remove stuck pipe, casing, tools, or other obstructions from drilling wells. May also perform similar services in mining exploration operations.

Observe load variations on strain gauges, mud pumps, and motor pressure indicators and listen to engines, rotary chains, and other equipment to detect faulty operations or unusual well conditions. Confer with other personnel to gather information regarding pipe and tool sizes and borehole conditions in wells. Drive truck-mounted units to well sites. Install pressure-control devices onto well heads. Thread cables through pulleys in derricks and connect hydraulic lines, using hand tools. Start pumps that circulate water, oil, or other fluids through wells to remove sand and other materials obstructing the free flow of oil. Close and seal wells no longer in use. Operate controls that raise derricks and level rigs. Direct drilling crews performing such activities as assembling and connecting pipe, applying weights to drill pipes, and drilling around lodged obstacles. Perforate well casings or sidewalls of boreholes with explosive charges. Quote prices to customers and prepare reports of services rendered, tools used, and time required so that bills can be produced. Direct lowering of specialized equipment to point of obstruction and push switches or pull levers to back off or sever pipes by chemical or explosive action. Plan fishing methods and select tools for removing obstacles, such as liners, broken casing, screens, and drill pipe, from wells. Analyze conditions of unserviceable wells to determine actions to be taken to improve well conditions. Assemble and lower detection instruments into wells with obstructions. Interpret instrument readings to ascertain the depth of obstruction. Assemble and operate sound-wave generating and detecting mechanisms to determine well fluid levels.

GOE Information—Interest Area: 01. Agriculture and Natural Resources. Work Group: 01.08. Mining and Drilling. Personality Type—Realistic. Realistic occupations frequently involve work activities that include practical, hands-on problems and solutions. They often deal with plants; animals; and real-world materials like wood, tools, and machinery. Many of the occupations require working outside and do not involve a lot of paperwork or working closely with others. Work Values—Supervision, Technical; Authority; Supervision, Human Relations; Compensation; Moral Values; Co-workers. Skills—Repairing; Operation Monitoring; Equipment Maintenance; Installation; Operation and Control; Troubleshooting. Abilities—*Cognitive:* Spatial Orientation; Perceptual Speed; Selective Attention; Time Sharing; Visualization; Speed of Closure. *Psychomotor:* Multilimb Coordination; Control Precision; Response Orientation; Reaction Time; Rate Control; Speed of Limb Movement. *Physical:* Gross Body Equilibrium; Stamina; Static Strength; Extent Flexibility; Dynamic Strength; Gross Body Coordination. *Sensory:* Depth Perception; Sound Localization; Night Vision; Glare

Sensitivity; Auditory Attention; Hearing Sensitivity. General Work Activities—*Information Input:* Monitoring Processes, Materials, or Surroundings; Inspecting Equipment, Structures, or Materials; Identifying Objects, Actions, and Events. *Mental Process:* Updating and Using Relevant Knowledge; Making Decisions and Solving Problems; Organizing, Planning, and Prioritizing. *Work Output:* Performing General Physical Activities; Handling and Moving Objects; Repairing and Maintaining Mechanical Equipment. *Interacting with Others:* Establishing and Maintaining Interpersonal Relationships; Communicating with Other Workers; Coordinating the Work and Activities of Others. Physical Work Conditions—Outdoors; Noisy; Very Hot or Cold; Contaminants; Hazardous Conditions; Using Hands on Objects, Tools, or Controls. Other Job Characteristics—Need to Be Exact or Accurate; Errors Have Important Consequences; Repeat Same Tasks; Pace Determined by Speed of Equipment.

Experience—Job Zone 2. Some previous work-related skill, knowledge, or experience may be helpful in these occupations, but usually is not needed. Job Preparation—SVP 4.0 to less than 6.0—six months to less than two years. Knowledges—Mechanical Devices; Transportation; Customer and Personal Service; Physics; Engineering and Technology; Public Safety and Security. Instructional Program—Mining Technology/Technician.

Related SOC Job—47-5013 Service Unit Operators, Oil, Gas, and Mining. Related OOH Job—Service Unit Operators, Oil, Gas, and Mining. Related DOT Jobs—930.261-010 Fishing-Tool Technician, Oil Well; 930.361-010 Service-Unit Operator, Oil Well; 939.462-010 Oil-Well-Service Operator.

47-5021.00 Earth Drillers, Except Oil and Gas

- Education/Training Required: Moderate-term on-the-job training
- Employed: 18,800
- Annual Earnings: $33,770
- Growth: 7.9%
- Annual Job Openings: 4,000

Operate a variety of drills—such as rotary, churn, and pneumatic—to tap sub-surface water and salt deposits, to remove core samples during mineral exploration or soil testing, and to facilitate the use of explosives in mining or construction. May use explosives. Includes horizontal and earth-boring machine operators.

Drive or guide truck-mounted equipment into position, level and stabilize rigs, and extend telescoping derricks. Operate hoists to lift power line poles into position. Fabricate well casings. Disinfect, reconstruct, and redevelop contaminated wells and water pumping systems and clean and disinfect new wells in preparation for use. Design well pumping systems. Assemble and position machines, augers, casing pipes, and other equipment, using hand and power tools. Signal crane operators to move equipment. Record drilling progress and geological data. Retrieve lost equipment from bore holes, using retrieval tools and equipment. Review client requirements and proposed locations for drilling operations to determine feasibility and cost estimates. Perform routine maintenance and upgrade work on machines and equipment, such as replacing parts, building up drill bits, and lubricating machinery. Perform pumping tests to assess well performance. Drive trucks, tractors, or truck-mounted drills to and from worksites. Verify depths and alignments of boring positions. Withdraw drill rods from holes and extract core samples. Operate water-well drilling rigs and other equipment to drill, bore, and dig for water wells or for environmental assessment purposes. Drill or bore holes in rock for blasting, grouting, anchoring, or building foundations. Inspect core samples to determine nature of strata or take samples to laboratories for analysis. Monitor drilling operations, checking gauges and listening to equipment to assess drilling conditions and to determine the need to adjust drilling or alter equipment. Observe electronic graph recorders and flow meters that monitor the water used to flush debris from holes. Document geological formations encountered during work. Operate machines to flush earth cuttings or to blow dust from holes. Start, stop, and control drilling speed of machines and insertion of casings into holes. Select the appropriate drill for the job, using knowledge of rock or soil conditions. Operate controls to stabilize machines and to position and align drills. Place and install screens, casings, pumps, and other well fixtures to develop wells. Pour water into wells or pump water or slush into wells to cool drill bits and to remove drillings.

GOE Information—Interest Area: 01. Agriculture and Natural Resources. **Work Group:** 01.08. Mining and Drilling. **Personality Type—**Realistic. Realistic occupations frequently involve work activities that include practical, hands-on problems and solutions. They often deal with plants; animals; and real-world materials like wood, tools, and machinery. Many of the occupations require working outside and do not involve a lot of paperwork or working closely with others. **Work Values—**Moral Values; Supervision, Technical. **Skills—**Operation Monitoring; Operation and Control; Equipment Maintenance. **Abilities—***Cognitive:* Spatial Orientation; Visualization; Information Ordering; Perceptual Speed; Number Facility; Memorization. *Psychomotor:* Response Orientation; Reaction Time; Control Precision; Speed of Limb Movement; Multilimb Coordination; Rate Control. *Physical:* Static Strength; Explosive Strength; Dynamic Strength; Extent Flexibility; Trunk Strength; Stamina. *Sensory:* Peripheral Vision; Depth Perception; Sound Localization; Auditory Attention; Hearing Sensitivity; Glare Sensitivity. **General Work Activities—***Information Input:* Monitoring Processes, Materials, or Surroundings; Identifying Objects, Actions, and Events; Inspecting Equipment, Structures, or Materials. *Mental Process:* Judging the Qualities of Things, Services, or Other People's Work; Updating and Using Relevant Knowledge; Making Decisions and Solving Problems. *Work Output:* Controlling Machines and Processes; Handling and Moving Objects; Performing General Physical Activities. *Interacting with Others:* Communicating with Other Workers. **Physical Work Conditions—**Outdoors; Noisy; Contaminants; Hazardous Equipment; Standing; Using Hands on Objects, Tools, or Controls. **Other Job Characteristics—**Need to Be Exact or Accurate; Pace Determined by Speed of Equipment.

Experience—Job Zone 3. Previous work-related skill, knowledge, or experience is required. **Job Preparation—**SVP 6.0 to less than 7.0—more than one year and less than four years. **Knowledges—**Mechanical Devices; Transportation; Physics; Engineering and Technology. **Instructional Programs—**Construction/Heavy Equipment/Earthmoving Equipment Operation; Well Drilling/Driller.

Related SOC Job—47-5021 Earth Drillers, Except Oil and Gas. **Related OOH Job—**Earth Drillers, Except Oil and Gas. **Related DOT Jobs—**850.662-010 Horizontal-Earth-Boring-Machine Operator; 850.662-014 Rock-Drill Operator II; 850.683-034 Rock-Drill Operator I; 859.362-010 Well-Drill Operator; 859.682-010 Earth-Boring-Machine Operator; 859.682-014 Foundation-Drill Operator; 930.662-014 Core-Drill Operator; 930.682-010 Core-Drill Operator.

47-5031.00 Explosives Workers, Ordnance Handling Experts, and Blasters

- **Education/Training Required: Moderate-term on-the-job training**
- **Employed: 4,800**
- **Annual Earnings: $38,780**
- **Growth: 2.2%**
- **Annual Job Openings: 1,000**

Place and detonate explosives to demolish structures or to loosen, remove, or displace earth, rock, or other materials. May perform specialized handling, storage, and accounting procedures. Includes seismograph shooters.

Examine blast areas to determine amounts and kinds of explosive charges needed and to ensure that safety laws are observed. Tie specified lengths of delaying fuses into patterns to time sequences of explosions. Place safety cones around blast areas to alert other workers of danger zones and signal workers as necessary to ensure that they clear blast sites prior to explosions. Place explosive charges in holes or other spots; then detonate explosives to demolish structures or to loosen, remove, or displace earth, rock, or other materials. Insert, pack, and pour explosives, such as dynamite, ammonium nitrate, black powder, or slurries, into blast holes; then shovel drill cuttings, admit water into boreholes, and tamp material to compact charges. Mark patterns, locations, and depths of charge holes for drilling and issue drilling instructions. Compile and keep gun and explosives records in compliance with local and federal laws. Measure depths of drilled blast holes, using weighted tape measures. Connect electrical wire to primers and cover charges or fill blast holes with clay, drill chips, sand, or other material. Lay primacord between rows of charged blast holes and tie cord into main lines to form blast patterns. Assemble and position equipment, explosives, and blasting caps in holes at specified depths or load perforating guns or torpedoes with explosives. Verify detonation of charges by observing control panels or by listening for the sounds of blasts. Move and store inventories of explosives, loaded perforating guns, and other materials according to established safety procedures. Light fuses; drop detonating devices into wells or boreholes; or activate firing devices with plungers, dials, or buttons to set off single or multiple blasts. Drive trucks to transport explosives and blasting equipment to blasting sites. Cut specified lengths of primacord and attach primers to cord ends. Maintain inventory levels, ordering new supplies as necessary. Set up and operate equipment such as hoists, jackhammers, or drills to bore charge holes. Repair and service blasting, shooting, and automotive equipment and electrical wiring and instruments, using hand tools.

GOE Information—Interest Area: 01. Agriculture and Natural Resources. **Work Group:** 01.08. Mining and Drilling. **Personality Type—**Realistic. Realistic occupations frequently involve work activities that include practical, hands-on problems and solutions. They often deal with plants; animals; and real-world materials like wood, tools, and machinery. Many of the occupations require working outside and do not involve a lot of paperwork or working closely with others. **Work Values—**Supervision, Technical; Moral Values. **Skills—**Equipment Maintenance; Operation and Control; Operation Monitoring; Repairing; Troubleshooting; Management of Material Resources. **Abilities—***Cognitive:* Perceptual Speed; Flexibility of Closure; Visualization; Selective Attention; Information Ordering; Time Sharing. *Psychomotor:* Reaction Time; Manual Dexterity; Rate Control; Multilimb Coordination; Response Orientation; Control Precision. *Physical:* Gross Body Equilibrium; Extent Flexibility;

Stamina; Static Strength; Dynamic Strength; Gross Body Coordination. *Sensory:* Visual Color Discrimination; Glare Sensitivity; Depth Perception; Hearing Sensitivity; Far Vision; Auditory Attention. **General Work Activities—***Information Input:* Monitoring Processes, Materials, or Surroundings; Identifying Objects, Actions, and Events; Inspecting Equipment, Structures, or Materials. *Mental Process:* Making Decisions and Solving Problems; Updating and Using Relevant Knowledge; Evaluating Information Against Standards. *Work Output:* Handling and Moving Objects; Performing General Physical Activities; Controlling Machines and Processes. *Interacting with Others:* Communicating with Other Workers; Teaching Others; Coordinating the Work and Activities of Others. **Physical Work Conditions—**Outdoors; Very Hot or Cold; Contaminants; Hazardous Conditions; Standing; Using Hands on Objects, Tools, or Controls. **Other Job Characteristics—**Need to Be Exact or Accurate; Errors Have Important Consequences; Repeat Same Tasks; Pace Determined by Speed of Equipment.

Experience—Job Zone 2. Some previous work-related skill, knowledge, or experience may be helpful in these occupations, but usually is not needed. **Job Preparation—**SVP 4.0 to less than 6.0—six months to less than two years. **Knowledges—**Public Safety and Security; Law and Government; Engineering and Technology; Transportation; Mechanical Devices; Production and Processing. **Instructional Program—**Blasting/Blaster.

Related SOC Job—47-5031 Explosives Workers, Ordnance Handling Experts, and Blasters. **Related OOH Job—**Explosives Workers, Ordnance Handling Experts, and Blasters. **Related DOT Jobs—**850.381-010 Miner; 859.261-010 Blaster; 931.261-010 Blaster; 931.361-010 Sample-Taker Operator; 931.361-014 Shooter; 931.361-018 Shooter, Seismograph; 931.382-010 Perforator Operator, Oil Well; 931.664-010 Tier-and-Detonator; 931.667-010 Powder Loader.

47-5041.00 Continuous Mining Machine Operators

- **Education/Training Required: Moderate-term on-the-job training**
- **Employed: 9,000**
- **Annual Earnings: $39,100**
- **Growth: −12.4%**
- **Annual Job Openings: 1,000**

Operate self-propelled mining machines that rip coal, metal and non-metal ores, rock, stone, or sand from the face and load it onto conveyors or into shuttle cars in a continuous operation.

Drive machines into position at working faces. Move controls to start and regulate movement of conveyors and to start and position drill cutters or torches. Determine locations, boundaries, and depths of holes or channels to be cut. Move levers to raise and lower hydraulic safety bars that support roofs above machines until other workers complete their framing. Install casings to prevent cave-ins. Guide and assist crews laying track and resetting supports and blocking. Start machines to gather coal and convey it to floors or shuttle cars. Reposition machines to make additional holes or cuts. Observe and listen to equipment operation to detect binding or stoppage of tools and other equipment malfunctions. Repair, oil, and adjust machines and change cutting teeth, using wrenches.

GOE Information—Interest Area: 01. Agriculture and Natural Resources. **Work Group:** 01.08. Mining and Drilling. **Personality Type—**Realistic. Realistic occupations frequently involve work activities that include practical, hands-on problems and solutions. They

often deal with plants; animals; and real-world materials like wood, tools, and machinery. Many of the occupations require working outside and do not involve a lot of paperwork or working closely with others. **Work Values—**Supervision, Technical; Moral Values; Supervision, Human Relations. **Skills—**Repairing; Operation and Control; Equipment Maintenance; Operation Monitoring. **Abilities—***Cognitive:* None met the criteria. *Psychomotor:* Multilimb Coordination; Control Precision. *Physical:* Static Strength. *Sensory:* Depth Perception; Night Vision. **General Work Activities—***Information Input:* Monitoring Processes, Materials, or Surroundings. *Mental Process:* None met the criteria. *Work Output:* Controlling Machines and Processes; Operating Vehicles or Equipment; Handling and Moving Objects. *Interacting with Others:* None met the criteria. **Physical Work Conditions—**Outdoors; Noisy; Contaminants; Hazardous Conditions; Hazardous Equipment; Using Hands on Objects, Tools, or Controls. **Other Job Characteristics—**Errors Have Important Consequences; Need to Be Exact or Accurate; Automation; Pace Determined by Speed of Equipment.

Experience—Job Zone 2. Some previous work-related skill, knowledge, or experience may be helpful in these occupations, but usually is not needed. **Job Preparation—**SVP 4.0 to less than 6.0—six months to less than two years. **Knowledges—**Mechanical Devices; Engineering and Technology. **Instructional Program—**Construction/Heavy Equipment/Earthmoving Equipment Operation.

Related SOC Job—47-5041 Continuous Mining Machine Operators. **Related OOH Job—**Continuous Mining Machine Operators. **Related DOT Job—**930.683-010 Continuous-Mining-Machine Operator.

47-5042.00 Mine Cutting and Channeling Machine Operators

- **Education/Training Required: Moderate-term on-the-job training**
- **Employed: 6,080**
- **Annual Earnings: $38,770**
- **Growth: −11.1%**
- **Annual Job Openings: Fewer than 500**

Operate machinery—such as longwall shears, plows, and cutting machines—to cut or channel along the face or seams of coal mines, stone quarries, or other mining surfaces to facilitate blasting, separating, or removing minerals or materials from mines or from the earth's surface.

Position jacks, timbers, or roof supports and install casings to prevent cave-ins. Reposition machines and move controls to make additional holes or cuts. Cut entries between rooms and haulage-ways. Observe indicator lights and gauges and listen to machine operation to detect binding or stoppage of tools or other equipment problems. Replace worn or broken tools and machine bits and parts, using wrenches, pry bars, and other hand tools, and lubricate machines, using grease guns. Press buttons to activate conveyor belts and push or pull chain handles to regulate conveyor movement so that material can be moved or loaded into dinkey cars or dump trucks. Move planer levers to control and adjust the movement of equipment and the speed, height, and depth of cuts and to rotate swivel cutting booms. Cut slots along working faces of coal, salt, or other non-metal deposits to facilitate blasting by moving levers to start the machine and to control the vertical reciprocating drills. Cut and move shale from open pits. Signal that machine plow blades are properly positioned, using electronic buzzers or two-way radios. Drive mobile, truck-mounted, or track-mounted drilling or cutting machine in mines and quarries or on construction sites. Move controls to start and position drill cutters or torches and to advance tools into mines or quarry faces to complete horizontal or vertical cuts. Advance plow blades through coal strata by remote control according to electronic or radio signals from the tailer. Determine locations, boundaries, and depths of holes or channels to be cut. Signal crew members to adjust the speed of equipment to the rate of installation of roof supports and to adjust the speed of conveyors to the volume of coal. Remove debris such as loose shale from channels and planer travel areas. Charge and set off explosives in blasting holes. Signal truck drivers to position their vehicles for receiving shale from planer hoppers. Monitor movement of shale along conveyors from hoppers to trucks or railcars. Guide and assist crews in laying track for machines and resetting planer rails, supports, and blocking, using jacks, shovels, sledges, picks, and pinch bars.

GOE Information—Interest Area: 01. Agriculture and Natural Resources. **Work Group:** 01.08. Mining and Drilling. **Personality Type**—Realistic. Realistic occupations frequently involve work activities that include practical, hands-on problems and solutions. They often deal with plants; animals; and real-world materials like wood, tools, and machinery. Many of the occupations require working outside and do not involve a lot of paperwork or working closely with others. **Work Values**—Supervision, Technical; Moral Values; Supervision, Human Relations. **Skills**—Repairing; Equipment Maintenance; Operation and Control; Operation Monitoring; Coordination; Troubleshooting. **Abilities**—*Cognitive:* Spatial Orientation; Perceptual Speed; Time Sharing; Selective Attention; Flexibility of Closure; Visualization. *Psychomotor:* Reaction Time; Control Precision; Response Orientation; Multilimb Coordination; Rate Control; Speed of Limb Movement. *Physical:* Static Strength; Extent Flexibility; Dynamic Strength; Stamina; Trunk Strength; Gross Body Coordination. *Sensory:* Depth Perception; Glare Sensitivity; Sound Localization; Hearing Sensitivity; Auditory Attention; Far Vision. **General Work Activities**—*Information Input:* Identifying Objects, Actions, and Events; Monitoring Processes, Materials, or Surroundings; Inspecting Equipment, Structures, or Materials. *Mental Process:* Making Decisions and Solving Problems; Evaluating Information Against Standards; Updating and Using Relevant Knowledge. *Work Output:* Controlling Machines and Processes; Handling and Moving Objects; Operating Vehicles or Equipment. *Interacting with Others:* Communicating with Other Workers; Assisting and Caring for Others; Providing Consultation and Advice to Others. **Physical Work Conditions**—Noisy; Contaminants; Hazardous Conditions; Hazardous Equipment; Using Hands on Objects, Tools, or Controls; Repetitive Motions. **Other Job Characteristics**—Pace Determined by Speed of Equipment; Need to Be Exact or Accurate; Errors Have Important Consequences.

Experience—Job Zone 2. Some previous work-related skill, knowledge, or experience may be helpful in these occupations, but usually is not needed. **Job Preparation**—SVP 4.0 to less than 6.0—six months to less than two years. **Knowledges**—Mechanical Devices; Physics; Law and Government. **Instructional Program**—Construction/Heavy Equipment/Earthmoving Equipment Operation.

Related SOC Job—47-5042 Mine Cutting and Channeling Machine Operators. **Related OOH Job**—Mine Cutting and Channeling Machine Operators. **Related DOT Jobs**—930.382-010 Driller, Machine; 930.383-010 Channeling-Machine Runner; 930.482-010 Drilling-Machine Operator; 930.662-010 Long-Wall Shear Operator; 930.663-010 Shale Planer Operator; 930.665-010 Long-Wall-Mining-Machine Tender; 930.683-014 Cutter Operator; 930.684-010 Flame Channeler.

47-5049.99 Mining Machine Operators, All Other

- **Education/Training Required: Moderate-term on-the-job training**
- **Employed: 2,450**
- **Annual Earnings: $36,120**
- **Growth: 0.9%**
- **Annual Job Openings: Fewer than 500**

All mining machine operators not listed separately.

No task data available.

Note: The Department of Labor has not collected some data for this job, so it has fewer details than the other descriptions.

Related SOC Job—47-5049 Mining Machine Operators, All Other. **Related OOH Job**—None. **Related DOT Job**—No data available.

47-5051.00 Rock Splitters, Quarry

- **Education/Training Required: Moderate-term on-the-job training**
- **Employed: 3,600**
- **Annual Earnings: $27,260**
- **Growth: 4.1%**
- **Annual Job Openings: 1,000**

Separate blocks of rough-dimension stone from quarry mass, using jackhammer and wedges.

Insert wedges and feathers into holes and drive wedges with sledgehammers to split stone sections from masses. Set charges of explosives to split rock. Cut slabs of stone into sheets that will be used for floors or counters. Remove pieces of stone from larger masses, using jackhammers, wedges, and other tools. Cut grooves along outlines, using chisels. Locate grain line patterns to determine how rocks will split when cut. Drill holes into sides of stones broken from masses, insert dogs or attach slings, and direct removal of stones. Drill holes along outlines, using jackhammers. Mark dimensions or outlines on stone prior to cutting, using rules and chalk lines.

GOE Information—Interest Area: 01. Agriculture and Natural Resources. **Work Group:** 01.08. Mining and Drilling. **Personality Type**—Realistic. Realistic occupations frequently involve work activities that include practical, hands-on problems and solutions. They often deal with plants; animals; and real-world materials like wood, tools, and machinery. Many of the occupations require working outside and do not involve a lot of paperwork or working closely with others. **Work Values**—Moral Values; Independence. **Skills**—None met the criteria. **Abilities**—*Cognitive:* None met the criteria. *Psychomotor:* Wrist-Finger Speed. *Physical:* Explosive Strength; Static Strength; Dynamic Strength; Trunk Strength; Stamina; Extent Flexibility. *Sensory:* None met the criteria. **General Work Activities**—*Information Input:* None met the criteria. *Mental Process:* None met the criteria. *Work Output:* Performing General Physical Activities; Handling and Moving Objects; Controlling Machines and Processes. *Interacting with Others:* None met the criteria. **Physical Work Conditions**—Outdoors; Noisy; Hazardous Equipment; Standing; Kneeling, Crouching, Stooping, or Crawling; Using Hands on Objects, Tools, or Controls. **Other Job Characteristics**—Errors Have Important Consequences; Need to Be Exact or Accurate.

Experience—Job Zone 2. Some previous work-related skill, knowledge, or experience may be helpful in these occupations, but usually is not needed. **Job Preparation**—SVP 4.0 to less than 6.0—six months to less than two years. **Knowledges**—Mechanical Devices; Physics; Public Safety and Security. **Instructional Program**—No related CIP programs.

Related SOC Job—47-5051 Rock Splitters, Quarry. **Related OOH Job**—Rock Splitters, Quarry. **Related DOT Job**—930.684-022 Quarry Plug-and-Feather Driller.

47-5061.00 Roof Bolters, Mining

- **Education/Training Required: Moderate-term on-the-job training**
- **Employed: 4,140**
- **Annual Earnings: $39,340**
- **Growth: –29.5%**
- **Annual Job Openings: 1,000**

Operate machinery to install roof support bolts in underground mine.

Drill bolt holes into roofs at specified distances from ribs or adjacent bolts. Force bolts into holes, using hydraulic mechanisms of self-propelled bolting machines. Remove drill bits from chucks after drilling holes; then insert bolts into chucks. Test bolts for specified tension, using torque wrenches. Position safety jacks to support underground mine roofs until bolts can be installed. Position bolting machines and insert drill bits into chucks. Rotate chucks to turn bolts and open expansion heads against rock formations. Install truss bolts traversing entire ceiling spans. Tighten ends of anchored truss bolts, using turnbuckles.

GOE Information—Interest Area: 01. Agriculture and Natural Resources. **Work Group:** 01.08. Mining and Drilling. **Personality Type**—Realistic. Realistic occupations frequently involve work activities that include practical, hands-on problems and solutions. They often deal with plants; animals; and real-world materials like wood, tools, and machinery. Many of the occupations require working outside and do not involve a lot of paperwork or working closely with others. **Work Values**—Supervision, Technical; Moral Values. **Skills**—Operation and Control; Installation; Equipment Maintenance; Repairing; Equipment Selection; Operation Monitoring. **Abilities**—*Cognitive:* Spatial Orientation; Time Sharing; Selective Attention; Visualization. *Psychomotor:* Response Orientation; Reaction Time; Control Precision; Speed of Limb Movement; Rate Control; Multilimb Coordination. *Physical:* Extent Flexibility; Dynamic Strength; Static Strength; Stamina; Gross Body Equilibrium; Trunk Strength. *Sensory:* Glare Sensitivity; Night Vision; Depth Perception; Peripheral Vision; Sound Localization; Auditory Attention. **General Work Activities**—*Information Input:* Inspecting Equipment, Structures, or Materials; Monitoring Processes, Materials, or Surroundings; Identifying Objects, Actions, and Events. *Mental Process:* Evaluating Information Against Standards; Making Decisions and Solving Problems; Updating and Using Relevant Knowledge. *Work Output:* Handling and Moving Objects; Performing General Physical Activities; Controlling Machines and Processes. *Interacting with Others:* Communicating with Other Workers; Assisting and Caring for Others; Establishing and Maintaining Interpersonal Relationships. **Physical Work Conditions**—Noisy; Contaminants; Hazardous Equipment; Using Hands on Objects, Tools, or Controls; Bending or Twisting the Body; Repetitive Motions. **Other Job Characteristics**—Pace Determined by Speed of Equipment; Need to Be Exact or Accurate; Errors Have Important Consequences; Repeat Same Tasks.

Experience—Job Zone 2. Some previous work-related skill, knowledge, or experience may be helpful in these occupations, but usually is not needed. **Job Preparation**—SVP 4.0 to less than 6.0—six months to less than two years. **Knowledges**—Mechanical Devices; Medicine and Dentistry; Transportation; Engineering and Technology; Production and Processing; Public Safety and Security. **Instructional Program**—No related CIP programs.

Related SOC Job—47-5061 Roof Bolters, Mining. **Related OOH Job**—Roof Bolters, Mining. **Related DOT Job**—930.683-026 Roof Bolter.

47-5071.00 Roustabouts, Oil and Gas

- **Education/Training Required: Moderate-term on-the-job training**
- **Employed: 33,570**
- **Annual Earnings: $24,880**
- **Growth: 1.0%**
- **Annual Job Openings: 6,000**

Assemble or repair oilfield equipment, using hand and power tools. Perform other tasks as needed.

Clean up spilled oil by bailing it into barrels. Unscrew or tighten pipes, casing, tubing, and pump rods, using hand and power wrenches and tongs. Bolt together pump and engine parts. Walk flow lines to locate leaks, using electronic detectors and making visual inspections. Move pipes to and from trucks by hand or by using truck winches and motorized lifts. Dismantle and repair oilfield machinery, boilers, and steam engine parts, using hand tools and power tools. Dig drainage ditches around wells and storage tanks. Keep pipe deck and main deck areas clean and tidy. Guide cranes to move loads about decks. Supply equipment to rig floors as requested and provide assistance to roughnecks. Dig holes, set forms, and mix and pour concrete into forms to make foundations for wood or steel derricks. Cut down and remove trees and brush to clear drill sites, to reduce fire hazards, and to make way for roads to sites. Bolt or nail together wood or steel framework to erect derricks.

GOE Information—Interest Area: 01. Agriculture and Natural Resources. **Work Group:** 01.08. Mining and Drilling. **Personality Type**—Realistic. Realistic occupations frequently involve work activities that include practical, hands-on problems and solutions. They often deal with plants; animals; and real-world materials like wood, tools, and machinery. Many of the occupations require working outside and do not involve a lot of paperwork or working closely with others. **Work Values**—Moral Values; Supervision, Technical; Supervision, Human Relations. **Skills**—Equipment Maintenance; Installation; Operation Monitoring; Repairing; Operation and Control; Troubleshooting. **Abilities**—*Cognitive:* Visualization; Time Sharing; Perceptual Speed. *Psychomotor:* Control Precision; Response Orientation; Reaction Time; Multilimb Coordination; Speed of Limb Movement; Manual Dexterity. *Physical:* Static Strength; Stamina; Extent Flexibility; Gross Body Equilibrium; Trunk Strength; Dynamic Strength. *Sensory:* Depth Perception; Peripheral Vision; Glare Sensitivity; Sound Localization; Hearing Sensitivity; Auditory Attention. **General Work Activities**—*Information Input:* Inspecting Equipment, Structures, or Materials; Monitoring Processes, Materials, or Surroundings; Identifying Objects, Actions, and Events. *Mental Process:* Processing Information; Organizing, Planning, and Prioritizing; Judging the Qualities of Things, Services, or Other People's Work. *Work Output:* Handling and Moving Objects; Performing General Physical Activities; Repairing and Maintaining Mechanical Equipment. *Interacting with Others:* Establishing and Maintaining Interpersonal Relationships; Communicating with

Other Workers; Coaching and Developing Others. **Physical Work Conditions**—Outdoors; Very Hot or Cold; Contaminants; Hazardous Conditions; Standing; Using Hands on Objects, Tools, or Controls. **Other Job Characteristics**—Need to Be Exact or Accurate; Errors Have Important Consequences.

Experience—Job Zone 2. Some previous work-related skill, knowledge, or experience may be helpful in these occupations, but usually is not needed. **Job Preparation**—SVP 4.0 to less than 6.0–six months to less than two years. **Knowledges**—Mechanical Devices; Physics; Public Safety and Security; Chemistry; Production and Processing; Engineering and Technology. **Instructional Program**—Heavy/Industrial Equipment Maintenance Technologies.

Related SOC Job—47-5071 Roustabouts, Oil and Gas. **Related OOH Job**—Roustabouts, Oil and Gas. **Related DOT Jobs**—869.684-046 Roustabout; 930.684-014 Floor Worker, Well Service; 931.384-010 Gun-Perforator Loader; 931.684-010 Dumper-Bailer Operator.

47-5081.00 Helpers—Extraction Workers

- Education/Training Required: **Short-term on-the-job training**
- Employed: **25,550**
- Annual Earnings: **$27,430**
- Growth: **–0.1%**
- Annual Job Openings: **4,000**

Help extraction craft workers, such as earth drillers, blasters and explosives workers, derrick operators, and mining machine operators, by performing duties of lesser skill. Duties include supplying equipment or cleaning work area.

Set up and adjust equipment used to excavate geological materials. Load materials into well holes or into equipment, using hand tools. Repair and maintain automotive and drilling equipment, using hand tools. Dig trenches. Collect and examine geological matter, using hand tools and testing devices. Unload materials, devices, and machine parts, using hand tools. Signal workers to start geological material extraction or boring. Clean and prepare sites for excavation or boring. Observe and monitor equipment operation during the extraction process to detect any problems. Drive moving equipment to transport materials and parts to excavation sites. Dismantle extracting and boring equipment used for excavation, using hand tools. Clean up work areas and remove debris after extraction activities are complete. Organize materials to prepare for use. Provide assistance to extraction craft workers such as earth drillers and derrick operators.

GOE Information—Interest Area: 01. Agriculture and Natural Resources. **Work Group**: 01.08. Mining and Drilling. **Personality Type**—Realistic. Realistic occupations frequently involve work activities that include practical, hands-on problems and solutions. They often deal with plants; animals; and real-world materials like wood, tools, and machinery. Many of the occupations require working outside and do not involve a lot of paperwork or working closely with others. **Work Values**—Supervision, Technical; Advancement; Moral Values. **Skills**—Repairing; Equipment Maintenance; Operation Monitoring. **Abilities**—*Cognitive:* None met the criteria. *Psychomotor:* Wrist-Finger Speed; Speed of Limb Movement; Reaction Time; Multilimb Coordination; Manual Dexterity. *Physical:* Explosive Strength; Static Strength; Dynamic Flexibility; Dynamic Strength; Stamina; Extent Flexibility. *Sensory:* None met the criteria. **General Work Activities**—*Information Input:* Monitoring Processes, Materials, or Surroundings; Inspecting Equipment, Structures, or Materials. *Mental Process:* None met the criteria. *Work Output:* Performing General Physical Activities; Handling and Moving Objects; Repairing and Maintaining Mechanical Equipment. *Interacting with Others:* Communicating with Other Workers. **Physical Work Conditions**—Outdoors; Noisy; Contaminants; Whole-Body Vibration; Standing; Using Hands on Objects, Tools, or Controls. **Other Job Characteristics**—Errors Have Important Consequences.

Experience—Job Zone 1. No previous work-related skill, knowledge, or experience is needed. **Job Preparation**—SVP below 4.0–less than six months. **Knowledges**—Physics; Mechanical Devices; Transportation; Production and Processing. **Instructional Program**—No related CIP programs.

Related SOC Job—47-5081 Helpers—Extraction Workers. **Related OOH Job**—Helpers—Extraction Workers. **Related DOT Jobs**—859.687-010 Blaster Helper; 899.684-034 Shaft Mechanic; 930.664-014 Clean-Out-Driller Helper; 930.666-010 Driller Helper; 930.666-014 Tailer; 930.667-010 Shale Planer Operator Helper; 930.684-026 Rotary-Driller Helper; 930.687-010 Bottom-Hole-Pressure-Recording-Operator Helper; 939.281-010 Miner I; 939.364-010 Observer Helper, Seismic Prospecting; 939.382-010 Dry-Placer-Machine Operator; 939.485-010 Sandfill Operator; 939.663-010 Observer Helper, Gravity Prospecting; others.

47-5099.99 Extraction Workers, All Other

- Education/Training Required: **Moderate-term on-the-job training**
- Employed: **9,060**
- Annual Earnings: **$34,010**
- Growth: **–0.7%**
- Annual Job Openings: **3,000**

All extraction workers not listed separately.

No task data available.

Note: The Department of Labor has not collected some data for this job, so it has fewer details than the other descriptions.

Related SOC Job—47-5099 Extraction Workers, All Other. **Related OOH Job**—None. **Related DOT Jobs**—850.682-010 Shield Runner; 930.664-010 Caser; 933.664-010 Crusher Setter; 939.667-014 Quarry Worker; 939.687-026 Rock-Dust Sprayer.

49-0000

Installation, Maintenance, and Repair Occupations

49-1000 Supervisors of Installation, Maintenance, and Repair Workers

49-1011.00 First-Line Supervisors/ Managers of Mechanics, Installers, and Repairers

- **Education/Training Required: Work experience in a related occupation**
- **Employed: 455,690**
- **Annual Earnings: $51,980**
- **Growth: 12.4%**
- **Annual Job Openings: 33,000**

Supervise and coordinate the activities of mechanics, installers, and repairers.

Determine schedules, sequences, and assignments for work activities based on work priority, quantity of equipment, and skill of personnel. Patrol and monitor work areas and examine tools and equipment to detect unsafe conditions or violations of procedures or safety rules. Monitor employees' work levels and review work performance. Examine objects, systems, or facilities and analyze information to determine needed installations, services, or repairs. Participate in budget preparation and administration, coordinating purchasing and documentation and monitoring departmental expenditures. Counsel employees about work-related issues and assist employees in correcting job-skill deficiencies. Requisition materials and supplies, such as tools, equipment, and replacement parts. Compute estimates and actual costs of factors such as materials, labor, and outside contractors. Conduct or arrange for worker training in safety, repair, and maintenance techniques; operational procedures; or equipment use. Interpret specifications, blueprints, and job orders to construct templates and lay out reference points for workers. Investigate accidents and injuries and prepare reports of findings. Confer with personnel, such as management, engineering, quality control, customer, and union workers' representatives, to coordinate work activities, resolve employee grievances, and identify and review resource needs. Recommend or initiate personnel actions, such as hires, promotions, transfers, discharges, and disciplinary measures. Perform skilled repair and maintenance operations, using equipment such as hand and power tools, hydraulic presses and shears, and welding equipment. Compile operational and personnel records, such as time and production records, inventory data, repair and maintenance statistics, and test results. Develop, implement, and evaluate maintenance policies and procedures. Monitor tool inventories and the condition and maintenance of shops to ensure adequate working conditions. Inspect, test, and measure completed work, using devices such as hand tools and gauges to verify conformance to standards and repair requirements.

GOE Information—Interest Area: 13. Manufacturing. **Work Group:** 13.01. Managerial Work in Manufacturing. **Personality Type—** Enterprising. Enterprising occupations frequently involve starting up and carrying out projects. These occupations can involve leading people and making many decisions. They sometimes require risk taking and often deal with business. **Work Values—**Authority; Responsibility; Autonomy; Variety; Co-workers; Recognition. **Skills—** Installation; Repairing; Management of Personnel Resources; Management of Material Resources; Management of Financial Resources; Equipment Maintenance. **Abilities—**Cognitive: Visualization; Originality; Mathematical Reasoning; Flexibility of Closure; Perceptual Speed; Oral Expression. *Psychomotor:* Reaction Time; Multilimb Coordination; Control Precision; Finger Dexterity; Arm-Hand Steadiness; Manual Dexterity. *Physical:* Extent Flexibility; Static Strength; Trunk Strength. *Sensory:* Hearing Sensitivity; Auditory Attention; Visual Color Discrimination; Depth Perception; Far Vision; Speech Recognition. **General Work Activities—** *Information Input:* Monitoring Processes, Materials, or Surroundings; Identifying Objects, Actions, and Events; Inspecting Equipment, Structures, or Materials. *Mental Process:* Updating and Using Relevant Knowledge; Organizing, Planning, and Prioritizing; Making Decisions and Solving Problems. *Work Output:* Repairing and Maintaining Mechanical Equipment; Repairing and Maintaining Electronic Equipment; Controlling Machines and Processes. *Interacting with Others:* Coordinating the Work and Activities of Others; Communicating with Other Workers; Establishing and Maintaining Interpersonal Relationships. **Physical Work Conditions—**More Often Indoors Than Outdoors; Noisy; Very Hot or Cold; Contaminants; Standing. **Other Job Characteristics—**Need to Be Exact or Accurate; Repeat Same Tasks.

Experience—Job Zone 4. A minimum of two to four years of work-related skill, knowledge, or experience is needed. **Job Preparation—** SVP 7.0 to less than 8.0–two years to less than 10 years. **Knowledges—**Mechanical Devices; Building and Construction; Design; Personnel and Human Resources; Engineering and Technology; Physics. **Instructional Program—**Operations Management and Supervision.

Related SOC Job—49-1011 First-Line Supervisors/Managers of Mechanics, Installers, and Repairers. **Related OOH Job—**First-Line Supervisors/Managers of Mechanics, Installers, and Repairers. **Related DOT Jobs—**169.167-074 Preventive Maintenance Coordinator; 184.167-050 Maintenance Supervisor; 184.167-194 Superintendent, Meters; 185.164-010 Service Manager; 185.167-058 Service Manager; 185.167-074 Manager, Auto Specialty Services; 187.167-010 Appliance-Service Supervisor; 187.167-130 Manager, Marine Service; 187.167-142 Manager, Service Department; 189.167-046 Superintendent, Maintenance; 375.167-018 Commanding Officer, Motor Equipment; 620.131-010 Supervisor, Endless Track Vehicle; others.

49-2000 Electrical and Electronic Equipment Mechanics, Installers, and Repairers

49-2011.00 Computer, Automated Teller, and Office Machine Repairers

- **Education/Training Required: Postsecondary vocational training**
- **Employed: 138,210**
- **Annual Earnings: $36,060**
- **Growth: 3.8%**
- **Annual Job Openings: 31,000**

Repair, maintain, or install computers; word-processing systems; automated teller machines; and electronic office machines, such as duplicating and fax machines.

Converse with customers to determine details of equipment problems. Reassemble machines after making repairs or replacing parts. Travel to customers' stores or offices to service machines or to provide emergency repair service. Reinstall software programs or adjust settings on existing software to fix machine malfunctions. Advise customers concerning equipment operation, maintenance, and programming. Assemble machines according to specifications, using hand tools, power tools, and measuring devices. Test new systems to ensure that they are in working order. Operate machines to test functioning of parts and mechanisms. Maintain records of equipment maintenance work and repairs. Install and configure new equipment, including operating software and peripheral equipment. Maintain parts inventories and order any additional parts needed for repairs. Update existing equipment, performing tasks such as installing updated circuit boards or additional memory. Test components and circuits of faulty equipment to locate defects, using oscilloscopes, signal generators, ammeters, voltmeters, or special diagnostic software programs. Align, adjust, and calibrate equipment according to specifications. Repair, adjust, or replace electrical and mechanical components and parts, using hand tools, power tools, and soldering or welding equipment. Complete repair bills, shop records, time cards, and expense reports. Disassemble machine to examine parts such as wires, gears, and bearings for wear and defects, using hand tools, power tools, and measuring devices. Clean, oil, and adjust mechanical parts to maintain machines' operating efficiency and to prevent breakdowns. Enter information into computers to copy programs from one electronic component to another or to draw, modify, or store schematics. Read specifications such as blueprints, charts, and schematics to determine machine settings and adjustments. Lay cable and hook up electrical connections between machines, power sources, and phone lines. Analyze equipment performance records to assess equipment functioning.

GOE Information—Interest Area: 11. Information Technology. **Work Group:** 11.03. Digital Equipment Repair. **Personality Type—** Realistic. Realistic occupations frequently involve work activities that include practical, hands-on problems and solutions. They often deal with plants; animals; and real-world materials like wood, tools, and machinery. Many of the occupations require working outside and do not involve a lot of paperwork or working closely with others. **Work Values—**Supervision, Technical; Moral Values; Independence; Variety; Working Conditions; Supervision, Human Relations. **Skills—**Installation; Repairing; Troubleshooting; Equipment Maintenance; Management of Material Resources; Programming. **Abilities—***Cognitive:* Visualization; Perceptual Speed; Flexibility of Closure; Written Expression; Originality; Fluency of Ideas. *Psychomotor:* Arm-Hand Steadiness; Control Precision; Finger Dexterity; Manual Dexterity; Multilimb Coordination. *Physical:* None met the criteria. *Sensory:* Visual Color Discrimination; Hearing Sensitivity; Depth Perception. **General Work Activities—***Information Input:* Identifying Objects, Actions, and Events; Monitoring Processes, Materials, or Surroundings; Getting Information. *Mental Process:* Updating and Using Relevant Knowledge; Thinking Creatively; Making Decisions and Solving Problems. *Work Output:* Interacting With Computers; Repairing and Maintaining Electronic Equipment; Repairing and Maintaining Mechanical Equipment. *Interacting with Others:* Establishing and Maintaining Interpersonal Relationships; Communicating with Other Workers; Communicating with Persons Outside Organization. **Physical Work Conditions—**Indoors; Sitting; Using Hands on Objects, Tools, or Controls; Repetitive Motions. **Other Job Characteristics—**Need to Be Exact or Accurate; Repeat Same Tasks.

Experience—Job Zone 3. Previous work-related skill, knowledge, or experience is required. **Job Preparation—**SVP 6.0 to less than 7.0— more than one year and less than four years. **Knowledges—** Computers and Electronics; Telecommunications; Customer and Personal Service; Mechanical Devices; Engineering and Technology;

Sales and Marketing. **Instructional Programs—**Business Machine Repair; Computer Installation and Repair Technology/Technician.

Related SOC Job—49-2011 Computer, Automated Teller, and Office Machine Repairers. **Related OOH Job—**Computer, Automated Teller, and Office Machine Repairers. **Related DOT Jobs—**633.261-010 Assembly Technician; 633.261-014 Mail-Processing-Equipment Mechanic; 633.281-010 Cash-Register Servicer; 633.281-014 Dictating-Transcribing-Machine Servicer; 633.281-018 Office-Machine Servicer; 633.281-022 Office-Machine-Servicer Apprentice; 633.281-030 Statistical-Machine Servicer; 706.381-010 Aligner, Typewriter; 706.381-030 Repairer, Typewriter; 828.261-022 Electronics Mechanic; 828.261-026 Electronics-Mechanic Apprentice.

49-2021.00 Radio Mechanics

- **Education/Training Required: Postsecondary vocational training**
- **Employed: 6,170**
- **Annual Earnings: $37,960**
- **Growth: –1.1%**
- **Annual Job Openings: 1,000**

Test or repair mobile or stationary radio transmitting and receiving equipment and two-way radio communications systems used in ship-to-shore communications and found in service and emergency vehicles.

Repair circuits, wiring, and soldering, using soldering irons and hand tools to install parts and adjust connections. Turn setscrews to adjust receivers for maximum sensitivity and transmitters for maximum output. Mount equipment on transmission towers and in vehicles such as ships or ambulances. Test equipment functions such as signal strength and quality, transmission capacity, interference, and signal delay, using equipment such as oscilloscopes, circuit analyzers, frequency meters, and wattmeters. Test emergency transmitters to ensure their readiness for immediate use. Test batteries, using hydrometers and ammeters, and charge batteries as necessary. Monitor radio range stations to detect transmission flaws and adjust controls to eliminate flaws. Install, adjust, and repair stationary and mobile radio transmitting and receiving equipment and two-way radio communication systems. Insert plugs into receptacles and bolt or screw leads to terminals to connect equipment to power sources, using hand tools. Examine malfunctioning radio equipment to locate defects such as loose connections, broken wires, or burned-out components, using schematic diagrams and test equipment. Calibrate and align components, using scales, gauges, and other measuring instruments. Remove and replace defective components and parts such as conductors, resistors, semiconductors, and integrated circuits, using soldering irons, wire cutters, and hand tools. Clean and lubricate motor generators.

GOE Information—Interest Area: 13. Manufacturing. **Work Group:** 13.12. Electrical and Electronic Repair. **Personality Type—**Realistic. Realistic occupations frequently involve work activities that include practical, hands-on problems and solutions. They often deal with plants; animals; and real-world materials like wood, tools, and machinery. Many of the occupations require working outside and do not involve a lot of paperwork or working closely with others. **Work Values—**Independence; Moral Values; Supervision, Technical; Variety; Security; Compensation. **Skills—**Installation; Repairing; Troubleshooting; Quality Control Analysis; Equipment Maintenance; Operation Monitoring. **Abilities—***Cognitive:* Speed of Closure; Flexibility of Closure; Visualization. *Psychomotor:* Finger Dexterity; Wrist-Finger Speed; Manual Dexterity; Arm-Hand Steadiness; Control Precision. *Physical:* None met the criteria. *Sensory:* Visual Color

Discrimination; Hearing Sensitivity; Auditory Attention. **General Work Activities**—*Information Input:* Monitoring Processes, Materials, or Surroundings; Getting Information; Inspecting Equipment, Structures, or Materials. *Mental Process:* Updating and Using Relevant Knowledge; Evaluating Information Against Standards; Analyzing Data or Information. *Work Output:* Repairing and Maintaining Electronic Equipment; Handling and Moving Objects; Performing General Physical Activities. *Interacting with Others:* None met the criteria. **Physical Work Conditions**—Indoors; Minor Burns, Cuts, Bites, or Stings; Sitting; Using Hands on Objects, Tools, or Controls. **Other Job Characteristics**—Need to Be Exact or Accurate.

Experience—Job Zone 3. Previous work-related skill, knowledge, or experience is required. **Job Preparation**—SVP 6.0 to less than 7.0—more than one year and less than four years. **Knowledges**—Telecommunications; Engineering and Technology; Computers and Electronics; Physics; Mechanical Devices; Design. **Instructional Program**—Communications Systems Installation and Repair Technology.

Related SOC Job—49-2021 Radio Mechanics. **Related OOH Job**—Radio and Telecommunications Equipment Installers and Repairers. **Related DOT Jobs**—726.381-014 Electronic Equipment Repairer; 823.261-018 Radio Mechanic; 823.281-014 Electrician, Radio.

49-2022.00 Telecommunications Equipment Installers and Repairers, Except Line Installers

- **Education/Training Required: Long-term on-the-job training**
- **Employed: 198,350**
- **Annual Earnings: $50,620**
- **Growth: −4.9%**
- **Annual Job Openings: 21,000**

Set up, rearrange, or remove switching and dialing equipment used in central offices. Service or repair telephones and other communication equipment on customers' property. May install equipment in new locations or install wiring and telephone jacks in buildings under construction.

Note differences in wire and cable colors so that work can be performed correctly. Test circuits and components of malfunctioning telecommunications equipment to isolate sources of malfunctions, using test meters, circuit diagrams, polarity probes, and other hand tools. Test repaired, newly installed, or updated equipment to ensure that it functions properly and conforms to specifications, using test equipment and observation. Drive crew trucks to and from work areas. Inspect equipment on a regular basis to ensure proper functioning. Repair or replace faulty equipment such as defective and damaged telephones, wires, switching system components, and associated equipment. Remove and remake connections to change circuit layouts, following work orders or diagrams. Demonstrate equipment to customers, explain how it is to be used, and respond to any inquiries or complaints. Analyze test readings, computer printouts, and trouble reports to determine equipment repair needs and required repair methods. Adjust or modify equipment to enhance equipment performance or to respond to customer requests. Remove loose wires and other debris after work is completed. Request support from technical service centers when on-site procedures fail to solve installation or maintenance problems. Assemble and install communication equipment such as data and telephone communication lines, wiring, switching equipment, wiring frames, power apparatus, computer systems, and networks. Communicate with bases, using telephones or two-way radios to receive instructions or technical advice or to report equipment status. Collaborate with other workers to locate and correct malfunctions. Review manufacturer's instructions, manuals, technical specifications, building permits, and ordinances to determine communication equipment requirements and procedures. Test connections to ensure that power supplies are adequate and that communications links function. Refer to manufacturers' manuals to obtain maintenance instructions pertaining to specific malfunctions. Climb poles and ladders, use truck-mounted booms, and enter areas such as manholes and cable vaults to install, maintain, or inspect equipment.

GOE Information—**Interest Area:** 02. Architecture and Construction. **Work Group:** 02.05. Systems and Equipment Installation, Maintenance, and Repair. **Personality Type**—Realistic. Realistic occupations frequently involve work activities that include practical, hands-on problems and solutions. They often deal with plants; animals; and real-world materials like wood, tools, and machinery. Many of the occupations require working outside and do not involve a lot of paperwork or working closely with others. **Work Values**—Supervision, Technical; Moral Values; Security; Supervision, Human Relations; Independence; Variety. **Skills**—Installation; Repairing; Troubleshooting; Technology Design; Systems Analysis; Equipment Selection. **Abilities**—*Cognitive:* Spatial Orientation; Visualization; Perceptual Speed; Time Sharing; Memorization; Flexibility of Closure. *Psychomotor:* Response Orientation; Reaction Time; Speed of Limb Movement; Multilimb Coordination; Manual Dexterity; Rate Control. *Physical:* Gross Body Equilibrium; Extent Flexibility; Gross Body Coordination; Dynamic Strength; Stamina; Static Strength. *Sensory:* Visual Color Discrimination; Night Vision; Glare Sensitivity; Hearing Sensitivity; Auditory Attention; Depth Perception. **General Work Activities**—*Information Input:* Monitoring Processes, Materials, or Surroundings; Identifying Objects, Actions, and Events; Getting Information. *Mental Process:* Updating and Using Relevant Knowledge; Organizing, Planning, and Prioritizing; Thinking Creatively. *Work Output:* Performing General Physical Activities; Handling and Moving Objects; Repairing and Maintaining Electronic Equipment. *Interacting with Others:* Establishing and Maintaining Interpersonal Relationships; Performing for or Working with the Public; Communicating with Persons Outside Organization. **Physical Work Conditions**—Outdoors; Noisy; Very Hot or Cold; Contaminants; Cramped Work Space, Awkward Positions; Using Hands on Objects, Tools, or Controls. **Other Job Characteristics**—Need to Be Exact or Accurate.

Experience—Job Zone 3. Previous work-related skill, knowledge, or experience is required. **Job Preparation**—SVP 6.0 to less than 7.0—more than one year and less than four years. **Knowledges**—Telecommunications; Mechanical Devices; Computers and Electronics; Engineering and Technology; Design; Customer and Personal Service. **Instructional Program**—Communications Systems Installation and Repair Technology.

Related SOC Job—49-2022 Telecommunications Equipment Installers and Repairers, Except Line Installers. **Related OOH Job**—Radio and Telecommunications Equipment Installers and Repairers. **Related DOT Jobs**—722.281-010 Instrument Repairer; 821.261-010 Cable Television Line Technician; 822.261-010 Electrician, Office; 822.261-022 Station Installer-and-Repairer; 822.281-010 Automatic-Equipment Technician; 822.281-014 Central-Office Repairer; 822.281-018 Maintenance Mechanic, Telephone; 822.281-022 Private-Branch-Exchange Repairer; 822.281-030 Technician, Plant and Maintenance; 822.281-034 Technician, Submarine Cable Equipment; 822.361-014 Central-Office Installer; 822.381-010 Equipment Installer; others.

49-2091.00 Avionics Technicians

- **Education/Training Required: Postsecondary vocational training**
- **Employed: 22,490**
- **Annual Earnings: $46,630**
- **Growth: 9.1%**
- **Annual Job Openings: 2,000**

Install, inspect, test, adjust, or repair avionics equipment, such as radar, radio, navigation, and missile control systems in aircraft or space vehicles.

Set up and operate ground support and test equipment to perform functional flight tests of electrical and electronic systems. Test and troubleshoot instruments, components, and assemblies, using circuit testers, oscilloscopes, and voltmeters. Keep records of maintenance and repair work. Coordinate work with that of engineers, technicians, and other aircraft maintenance personnel. Interpret flight test data to diagnose malfunctions and systemic performance problems. Install electrical and electronic components, assemblies, and systems in aircraft, using hand tools, power tools, and soldering irons. Adjust, repair, or replace malfunctioning components or assemblies, using hand tools and soldering irons. Connect components to assemblies such as radio systems, instruments, magnetos, inverters, and in-flight refueling systems, using hand tools and soldering irons. Assemble components such as switches, electrical controls, and junction boxes, using hand tools and soldering irons. Fabricate parts and test aids as required. Lay out installation of aircraft assemblies and systems, following documentation such as blueprints, manuals, and wiring diagrams. Assemble prototypes or models of circuits, instruments, and systems so that they can be used for testing. Operate computer-aided drafting and design applications to design avionics system modifications.

GOE Information—Interest Area: 13. Manufacturing. **Work Group:** 13.12. Electrical and Electronic Repair. **Personality Type—**Realistic. Realistic occupations frequently involve work activities that include practical, hands-on problems and solutions. They often deal with plants; animals; and real-world materials like wood, tools, and machinery. Many of the occupations require working outside and do not involve a lot of paperwork or working closely with others. **Work Values—**Supervision, Technical; Moral Values; Supervision, Human Relations; Compensation; Independence; Variety. **Skills—**Installation; Repairing; Equipment Maintenance; Troubleshooting; Operation Monitoring; Operation and Control. **Abilities—***Cognitive:* Visualization; Flexibility of Closure; Selective Attention; Information Ordering; Perceptual Speed; Problem Sensitivity. *Psychomotor:* Manual Dexterity; Control Precision; Finger Dexterity; Multilimb Coordination; Arm-Hand Steadiness. *Physical:* None met the criteria. *Sensory:* Visual Color Discrimination; Hearing Sensitivity; Far Vision; Near Vision. **General Work Activities—***Information Input:* Monitoring Processes, Materials, or Surroundings; Inspecting Equipment, Structures, or Materials; Getting Information. *Mental Process:* Making Decisions and Solving Problems; Updating and Using Relevant Knowledge; Organizing, Planning, and Prioritizing. *Work Output:* Repairing and Maintaining Electronic Equipment; Handling and Moving Objects; Repairing and Maintaining Mechanical Equipment. *Interacting with Others:* Establishing and Maintaining Interpersonal Relationships; Communicating with Other Workers; Teaching Others. **Physical Work Conditions—**Indoors; Noisy; Contaminants; Hazardous Conditions; Sitting; Using Hands on Objects, Tools, or Controls. **Other Job Characteristics—**Need to Be Exact or Accurate; Repeat Same Tasks.

Experience—Job Zone 3. Previous work-related skill, knowledge, or experience is required. **Job Preparation—**SVP 6.0 to less than 7.0—more than one year and less than four years. **Knowledges—**Engineering and Technology; Mechanical Devices; Computers and Electronics; Telecommunications; Production and Processing; Design. **Instructional Programs—**Airframe Mechanics and Aircraft Maintenance Technology/Technician; Avionics Maintenance and Technology/Technician.

Related SOC Job—49-2091 Avionics Technicians. **Related OOH Job—**Aircraft and Avionics Equipment Mechanics and Service Technicians. **Related DOT Jobs—**825.261-018 Electrician, Aircraft; 825.381-010 Aircraft Mechanic, Electrical and Radio; 829.281-018 In-Flight Refueling System Repairer.

49-2092.00 Electric Motor, Power Tool, and Related Repairers

- **Education/Training Required: Postsecondary vocational training**
- **Employed: 20,070**
- **Annual Earnings: $33,460**
- **Growth: 4.1%**
- **Annual Job Openings: 3,000**

Repair, maintain, or install electric motors, wiring, or switches.

Measure velocity, horsepower, revolutions per minute (rpm), amperage, circuitry, and voltage of units or parts to diagnose problems, using ammeters, voltmeters, wattmeters, and other testing devices. Record repairs required, parts used, and labor time. Reassemble repaired electric motors to specified requirements and ratings, using hand tools and electrical meters. Maintain stocks of parts. Repair and rebuild defective mechanical parts in electric motors, generators, and related equipment, using hand tools and power tools. Rewire electrical systems and repair or replace electrical accessories. Inspect electrical connections, wiring, relays, charging resistance boxes, and storage batteries, following wiring diagrams. Read service guides to find information needed to perform repairs. Inspect and test equipment to locate damage or worn parts and diagnose malfunctions or read work orders or schematic drawings to determine required repairs. Solder, wrap, and coat wires to ensure proper insulation. Assemble electrical parts such as alternators, generators, starting devices, and switches, following schematic drawings and using hand, machine, and power tools. Lubricate moving parts. Remove and replace defective parts such as coil leads, carbon brushes, and wires, using soldering equipment. Disassemble defective equipment so that repairs can be made, using hand tools. Lift units or parts such as motors or generators, using cranes or chain hoists, or signal crane operators to lift heavy parts or subassemblies. Weld, braze, or solder electrical connections. Reface, ream, and polish commutators and machine parts to specified tolerances, using machine tools. Adjust working parts, such as fan belts, contacts, and springs, using hand tools and gauges. Clean cells, cell assemblies, glassware, leads, electrical connections, and battery poles, using scrapers, steam, water, emery cloths, power grinders, or acid. Scrape and clean units or parts, using cleaning solvents and equipment such as buffing wheels. Rewind coils on cores in slots or make replacement coils, using coil-winding machines.

GOE Information—Interest Area: 13. Manufacturing. **Work Group:** 13.12. Electrical and Electronic Repair. **Personality Type—**Realistic. Realistic occupations frequently involve work activities that include practical, hands-on problems and solutions. They often deal with plants; animals; and real-world materials like wood, tools, and machinery. Many of the occupations require working outside and do not involve a lot of paperwork or working closely with others. **Work Values**—Supervision, Technical; Moral Values; Independence; Security; Supervision, Human Relations. **Skills**—Installation; Repairing; Troubleshooting; Equipment Maintenance; Technology Design; Operation Monitoring. **Abilities**—*Cognitive:* Visualization; Selective Attention; Speed of Closure; Time Sharing; Category Flexibility; Flexibility of Closure. *Psychomotor:* Reaction Time; Manual Dexterity; Control Precision; Finger Dexterity; Rate Control; Arm-Hand Steadiness. *Physical:* Extent Flexibility; Static Strength; Gross Body Equilibrium; Gross Body Coordination; Trunk Strength. *Sensory:* Depth Perception; Auditory Attention; Hearing Sensitivity; Visual Color Discrimination; Far Vision. **General Work Activities**—*Information Input:* Getting Information; Monitoring Processes, Materials, or Surroundings; Identifying Objects, Actions, and Events. *Mental Process:* Organizing, Planning, and Prioritizing; Making Decisions and Solving Problems; Updating and Using Relevant Knowledge. *Work Output:* Handling and Moving Objects; Performing General Physical Activities; Controlling Machines and Processes. *Interacting with Others:* Establishing and Maintaining Interpersonal Relationships; Communicating with Other Workers; Coaching and Developing Others. **Physical Work Conditions**—Noisy; Contaminants; Hazardous Conditions; Hazardous Equipment; Standing; Using Hands on Objects, Tools, or Controls. **Other Job Characteristics**—Need to Be Exact or Accurate; Errors Have Important Consequences.

Experience—Job Zone 3. Previous work-related skill, knowledge, or experience is required. **Job Preparation**—SVP 6.0 to less than 7.0—more than one year and less than four years. **Knowledges**—Mechanical Devices; Engineering and Technology; Design; Production and Processing. **Instructional Program**—Electrical/Electronics Equipment Installation and Repair, General.

Related SOC Job—49-2092 Electric Motor, Power Tool, and Related Repairers. **Related OOH Job**—Electrical and Electronics Installers and Repairers. **Related DOT Jobs**—519.684-026 Tool Repairer; 620.261-026 Electric-Golf-Cart Repairer; 701.381-010 Repairer, Handtools; 701.384-010 Tool-Maintenance Worker; 701.684-010 Calibrator; 721.261-010 Electric-Motor Analyst; 721.281-010 Automotive-Generator-and-Starter Repairer; 721.281-014 Electric-Motor Assembler and Tester; 721.281-018 Electric-Motor Repairer; 721.281-026 Propulsion-Motor-and-Generator Repairer; 721.381-010 Electric-Motor Fitter; 724.381-010 Adjuster, Electrical Contacts; others.

49-2093.00 Electrical and Electronics Installers and Repairers, Transportation Equipment

- **Education/Training Required: Postsecondary vocational training**
- **Employed: 20,560**
- **Annual Earnings: $41,490**
- **Growth: 6.6%**
- **Annual Job Openings: 2,000**

Install, adjust, or maintain mobile electronics communication equipment, including sound, sonar, security, navigation, and surveillance systems on trains, watercraft, or other mobile equipment.

Inspect and test electrical systems and equipment to locate and diagnose malfunctions, using visual inspections, testing devices, and computer software. Reassemble and test equipment after repairs.

Splice wires with knives or cutting pliers and solder connections to fixtures, outlets, and equipment. Install new fuses, electrical cables, or power sources as required. Locate and remove or repair circuit defects such as blown fuses or malfunctioning transistors. Adjust, repair, or replace defective wiring and relays in ignition, lighting, air-conditioning, and safety control systems, using electrician's tools. Refer to schematics and manufacturers' specifications that show connections and provide instructions on how to locate problems. Maintain equipment service records. Cut openings and drill holes for fixtures, outlet boxes, and fuse holders, using electric drills and routers. Measure, cut, and install frameworks and conduit to support and connect wiring, control panels, and junction boxes, using hand tools. Install electrical equipment such as air-conditioning, heating, or ignition systems and components such as generator brushes and commutators, using hand tools. Install fixtures, outlets, terminal boards, switches, and wall boxes, using hand tools. Repair or rebuild equipment such as starters, generators, distributors, or door controls, using electrician's tools. Confer with customers to determine the nature of malfunctions. Estimate costs of repairs based on parts and labor requirements.

GOE Information—**Interest Area:** 13. Manufacturing. **Work Group:** 13.12. Electrical and Electronic Repair. **Personality Type**—Realistic. Realistic occupations frequently involve work activities that include practical, hands-on problems and solutions. They often deal with plants; animals; and real-world materials like wood, tools, and machinery. Many of the occupations require working outside and do not involve a lot of paperwork or working closely with others. **Work Values**—Supervision, Technical; Moral Values; Supervision, Human Relations; Variety; Advancement; Security. **Skills**—Installation; Repairing; Troubleshooting; Complex Problem Solving; Operation Monitoring; Equipment Selection. **Abilities**—*Cognitive:* Visualization; Category Flexibility; Flexibility of Closure; Selective Attention. *Psychomotor:* Arm-Hand Steadiness; Manual Dexterity; Multilimb Coordination; Control Precision; Finger Dexterity. *Physical:* Extent Flexibility; Trunk Strength. *Sensory:* Visual Color Discrimination; Depth Perception; Hearing Sensitivity. **General Work Activities**—*Information Input:* Monitoring Processes, Materials, or Surroundings; Getting Information; Inspecting Equipment, Structures, or Materials. *Mental Process:* Updating and Using Relevant Knowledge; Processing Information; Thinking Creatively. *Work Output:* Handling and Moving Objects; Repairing and Maintaining Electronic Equipment; Repairing and Maintaining Mechanical Equipment. *Interacting with Others:* Communicating with Other Workers; Establishing and Maintaining Interpersonal Relationships; Interpreting the Meaning of Information to Others. **Physical Work Conditions**—Outdoors; Contaminants; Hazardous Conditions; Standing; Using Hands on Objects, Tools, or Controls; Repetitive Motions. **Other Job Characteristics**—Need to Be Exact or Accurate; Repeat Same Tasks; Errors Have Important Consequences.

Experience—Job Zone 3. Previous work-related skill, knowledge, or experience is required. **Job Preparation**—SVP 6.0 to less than 7.0—more than one year and less than four years. **Knowledges**—Mechanical Devices; Engineering and Technology; Building and Construction; Physics; Design; Production and Processing. **Instructional Program**—Automobile/Automotive Mechanics/Technology/Technician.

Related SOC Job—49-2093 Electrical and Electronics Installers and Repairers, Transportation Equipment. **Related OOH Job**—Electrical and Electronics Installers and Repairers. **Related DOT Jobs**—825.281-026 Electrician, Locomotive; 825.381-018 Controller Repairer-and-Tester; 829.684-014 Body Wirer.

✳ ✳ ✳ ✳ ✳ ✳ ✳ ✳ ✳ ✳ ✳ *O*NET Dictionary of Occupational Titles, Fourth Edition* **499**

49-2094.00 Electrical and Electronics Repairers, Commercial and Industrial Equipment

- Education/Training Required: Postsecondary vocational training
- Employed: 69,620
- Annual Earnings: $44,120
- Growth: 9.7%
- Annual Job Openings: 8,000

Repair, test, adjust, or install electronic equipment, such as industrial controls, transmitters, and antennas.

Perform scheduled preventive maintenance tasks, such as checking, cleaning, and repairing equipment, to detect and prevent problems. Examine work orders and converse with equipment operators to detect equipment problems and to ascertain whether mechanical or human errors contributed to the problems. Operate equipment to demonstrate proper use and to analyze malfunctions. Set up and test industrial equipment to ensure that it functions properly. Test faulty equipment to diagnose malfunctions, using test equipment and software and applying knowledge of the functional operation of electronic units and systems. Repair and adjust equipment, machines, and defective components, replacing worn parts such as gaskets and seals in watertight electrical equipment. Calibrate testing instruments and installed or repaired equipment to prescribed specifications. Advise management regarding customer satisfaction, product performance, and suggestions for product improvements. Study blueprints, schematics, manuals, and other specifications to determine installation procedures. Inspect components of industrial equipment for accurate assembly and installation and for defects such as loose connections and frayed wires. Maintain equipment logs that record performance problems, repairs, calibrations, and tests. Coordinate efforts with other workers involved in installing and maintaining equipment or components. Maintain inventory of spare parts. Consult with customers, supervisors, and engineers to plan layout of equipment and to resolve problems in system operation and maintenance. Install repaired equipment in various settings, such as industrial or military establishments. Send defective units to the manufacturer or to a specialized repair shop for repair. Determine feasibility of using standardized equipment and develop specifications for equipment required to perform additional functions. Enter information into computer to copy program or to draw, modify, or store schematics, applying knowledge of software package used. Sign overhaul documents for equipment replaced or repaired. Develop or modify industrial electronic devices, circuits, and equipment according to available specifications.

GOE Information—Interest Area: 13. Manufacturing. **Work Group:** 13.12. Electrical and Electronic Repair. **Personality Type—**Realistic. Realistic occupations frequently involve work activities that include practical, hands-on problems and solutions. They often deal with plants; animals; and real-world materials like wood, tools, and machinery. Many of the occupations require working outside and do not involve a lot of paperwork or working closely with others. **Work Values—**Authority; Variety; Creativity; Compensation; Advancement; Co-workers. **Skills—**Installation; Repairing; Operation Monitoring; Troubleshooting; Equipment Maintenance; Operation and Control. **Abilities—***Cognitive:* Visualization; Perceptual Speed; Memorization; Selective Attention; Information Ordering; Flexibility of Closure. *Psychomotor:* Control Precision; Arm-Hand Steadiness; Finger Dexterity; Multilimb Coordination; Manual Dexterity. *Physical:*

Extent Flexibility; Static Strength; Gross Body Coordination; Trunk Strength. *Sensory:* Visual Color Discrimination; Auditory Attention; Hearing Sensitivity; Depth Perception; Far Vision. **General Work Activities—***Information Input:* Monitoring Processes, Materials, or Surroundings; Getting Information; Identifying Objects, Actions, and Events. *Mental Process:* Updating and Using Relevant Knowledge; Organizing, Planning, and Prioritizing; Making Decisions and Solving Problems. *Work Output:* Repairing and Maintaining Electronic Equipment; Interacting With Computers; Handling and Moving Objects. *Interacting with Others:* Communicating with Other Workers; Establishing and Maintaining Interpersonal Relationships; Communicating with Persons Outside Organization. **Physical Work Conditions—**Indoors; Noisy; Cramped Work Space, Awkward Positions; Hazardous Conditions; Standing; Using Hands on Objects, Tools, or Controls. **Other Job Characteristics—**Need to Be Exact or Accurate; Errors Have Important Consequences.

Experience—Job Zone 3. Previous work-related skill, knowledge, or experience is required. **Job Preparation—**SVP 6.0 to less than 7.0—more than one year and less than four years. **Knowledges—**Mechanical Devices; Computers and Electronics; Telecommunications; Engineering and Technology. **Instructional Programs—**Computer Installation and Repair Technology/Technician; Industrial Electronics Technology/Technician.

Related SOC Job—49-2094 Electrical and Electronics Repairers, Commercial and Industrial Equipment. **Related OOH Job—**Electrical and Electronics Installers and Repairers. **Related DOT Jobs—**726.361-022 Repairer, Probe Test Card, Semiconductor Wafers; 726.684-090 Reworker, Printed Circuit Board; 823.261-026 Avionics Technician; 823.281-018 Meteorological-Equipment Repairer; 828.251-010 Electronic-Sales-and-Service Technician; 828.261-014 Field Service Engineer; 828.261-022 Electronics Mechanic; 828.261-026 Electronics-Mechanic Apprentice; 828.281-022 Radioactivity-Instrument Maintenance Technician; 828.281-026 Computerized Environmental Control Installer; others.

49-2095.00 Electrical and Electronics Repairers, Powerhouse, Substation, and Relay

- Education/Training Required: Postsecondary vocational training
- Employed: 21,250
- Annual Earnings: $54,970
- Growth: –0.4%
- Annual Job Openings: 2,000

Inspect, test, repair, or maintain electrical equipment in generating stations, substations, and in-service relays.

Construct, test, maintain, and repair substation relay and control systems. Inspect and test equipment and circuits to identify malfunctions or defects, using wiring diagrams and testing devices such as ohmmeters, voltmeters, or ammeters. Consult manuals, schematics, wiring diagrams, and engineering personnel to troubleshoot and solve equipment problems and to determine optimum equipment functioning. Notify facility personnel of equipment shutdowns. Open and close switches to isolate defective relays; then perform adjustments or repairs. Prepare and maintain records detailing tests, repairs, and maintenance. Analyze test data to diagnose malfunctions, to determine performance characteristics of systems, and to evaluate effects of system modifications. Test insulators and bushings of equipment by inducing voltage across insulation, testing current, and calculating insulation loss. Repair, replace, and clean equipment and components such as circuit breakers, brushes, and commutators. Disconnect voltage regulators, bolts, and screws and connect replacement regulators to high-voltage lines. Schedule and supervise the construction and testing of special devices and the implementation of unique monitoring or control systems. Run signal quality and connectivity tests for individual cables and record results. Schedule and supervise splicing or termination of cables in color-code order. Test oil in circuit breakers and transformers for dielectric strength, refilling oil periodically. Maintain inventories of spare parts for all equipment, requisitioning parts as necessary. Set forms and pour concrete footings for installation of heavy equipment.

GOE Information—Interest Area: 02. Architecture and Construction. **Work Group:** 02.05. Systems and Equipment Installation, Maintenance, and Repair. **Personality Type—**Realistic. Realistic occupations frequently involve work activities that include practical, hands-on problems and solutions. They often deal with plants; animals; and real-world materials like wood, tools, and machinery. Many of the occupations require working outside and do not involve a lot of paperwork or working closely with others. **Work Values—**Moral Values; Variety; Supervision, Technical; Responsibility; Compensation; Independence. **Skills—**Installation; Repairing; Equipment Maintenance; Troubleshooting; Operation Monitoring; Operation and Control. **Abilities—**Cognitive: Visualization; Perceptual Speed; Mathematical Reasoning; Selective Attention; Flexibility of Closure; Memorization. Psychomotor: Arm-Hand Steadiness; Control Precision; Manual Dexterity; Finger Dexterity; Multilimb Coordination. Physical: Extent Flexibility; Trunk Strength. Sensory: Visual Color Discrimination; Depth Perception; Hearing Sensitivity; Auditory Attention; Near Vision. **General Work Activities—**Information Input: Monitoring Processes, Materials, or Surroundings; Inspecting Equipment, Structures, or Materials; Identifying Objects, Actions, and Events. Mental Process: Organizing, Planning, and Prioritizing; Updating and Using Relevant Knowledge; Processing Information.. Work Output: Repairing and Maintaining Electronic Equipment; Handling and Moving Objects; Controlling Machines and Processes. Interacting with Others: Communicating with Other Workers; Establishing and Maintaining Interpersonal Relationships; Coaching and Developing Others. **Physical Work Conditions—**Outdoors; Noisy; Very Bright or Dim Lighting; Hazardous Conditions; Standing; Using Hands on Objects, Tools, or Controls. **Other Job Characteristics—**Need to Be Exact or Accurate; Errors Have Important Consequences; Repeat Same Tasks.

Experience—Job Zone 3. Previous work-related skill, knowledge, or experience is required. **Job Preparation—**SVP 6.0 to less than 7.0— more than one year and less than four years. **Knowledges—**Mechanical Devices; Design; Telecommunications; Building and Construction; Physics; Public Safety and Security. **Instructional Program—**No related CIP programs.

Related SOC Job—49-2095 Electrical and Electronics Repairers, Powerhouse, Substation, and Relay. **Related OOH Job—**Electrical and Electronics Installers and Repairers. **Related DOT Jobs—**820.261-010 Electrician Apprentice, Powerhouse; 820.261-014 Electrician, Powerhouse; 820.261-018 Electrician, Substation; 820.361-010 Corrosion-Control Fitter; 821.261-018 Relay Technician.

49-2096.00 Electronic Equipment Installers and Repairers, Motor Vehicles

- **Education/Training Required: Postsecondary vocational training**
- **Employed: 17,650**
- **Annual Earnings: $27,440**
- **Growth: 13.6%**
- **Annual Job Openings: 1,000**

Install, diagnose, or repair communications, sound, security, or navigation equipment in motor vehicles.

Build fiberglass or wooden enclosures for sound components and fit them to automobile dimensions. Confer with customers to determine the nature of malfunctions. Remove seats, carpeting, and interiors of doors; add sound-absorbing material in empty spaces; and reinstall interior parts. Estimate costs of repairs based on parts and labor charges. Splice wires with knives or cutting pliers and solder connections to fixtures and equipment. Run new speaker and electrical cables. Replace and clean electrical or electronic components. Diagnose or repair problems with electronic equipment, such as sound, navigation, communication, and security equipment, in motor vehicles. Install equipment and accessories such as stereos, navigation equipment, communication equipment, and security systems. Inspect and test electrical or electronic systems to locate and diagnose malfunctions, using visual inspections and testing instruments such as oscilloscopes and voltmeters. Cut openings and drill holes for fixtures and equipment, using electric drills and routers. Record results of diagnostic tests.

GOE Information—Interest Area: 13. Manufacturing. **Work Group:** 13.12. Electrical and Electronic Repair. **Personality Type—**Realistic. Realistic occupations frequently involve work activities that include practical, hands-on problems and solutions. They often deal with plants; animals; and real-world materials like wood, tools, and machinery. Many of the occupations require working outside and do not involve a lot of paperwork or working closely with others. **Work Values—**Supervision, Technical; Moral Values; Supervision, Human Relations; Variety; Advancement; Security. **Skills—**Repairing; Installation; Equipment Maintenance. **Abilities—**Cognitive: Memorization; Visualization; Number Facility. Psychomotor: Wrist-Finger Speed; Manual Dexterity; Arm-Hand Steadiness; Control Precision; Finger Dexterity; Multilimb Coordination. Physical: Extent Flexibility; Explosive Strength; Dynamic Flexibility; Static Strength; Trunk Strength; Dynamic Strength. Sensory: Visual Color Discrimination; Near Vision. **General Work Activities—**Information Input: Inspecting Equipment, Structures, or Materials; Monitoring Processes, Materials, or Surroundings; Getting Information. Mental Process: Updating and Using Relevant Knowledge; Judging the Qualities of Things, Services, or Other People's Work; Making Decisions and Solving Problems. Work Output: Repairing and Maintaining Electronic Equipment; Handling and Moving Objects; Repairing and Maintaining Mechanical Equipment. Interacting with Others: Communicating with Persons Outside Organization. **Physical Work Conditions—**Indoors; Hazardous Conditions; Hazardous Equipment; Standing; Kneeling, Crouching, Stooping, or Crawling; Using Hands on Objects, Tools, or Controls. **Other Job Characteristics—**Need to Be Exact or Accurate.

Experience—Job Zone 3. Previous work-related skill, knowledge, or experience is required. **Job Preparation—**SVP 6.0 to less than 7.0—

more than one year and less than four years. **Knowledges—** Mechanical Devices; Building and Construction; Computers and Electronics; Engineering and Technology. **Instructional Program—** Automobile/Automotive Mechanics/Technology/Technician.

Related SOC Job—49-2096 Electronic Equipment Installers and Repairers, Motor Vehicles. **Related OOH Job—**Electrical and Electronics Installers and Repairers. **Related DOT Jobs—**825.281-022 Electrician, Automotive; 828.381-010 Equipment Installer.

49-2097.00 Electronic Home Entertainment Equipment Installers and Repairers

- **Education/Training Required: Postsecondary vocational training**
- **Employed: 35,360**
- **Annual Earnings: $28,940**
- **Growth: 4.7%**
- **Annual Job Openings: 6,000**

Repair, adjust, or install audio or television receivers, stereo systems, camcorders, video systems, or other electronic home entertainment equipment.

Read and interpret electronic circuit diagrams, function block diagrams, specifications, engineering drawings, and service manuals. Install, service, and repair electronic equipment or instruments such as televisions, radios, and videocassette recorders. Position or mount speakers and wire speakers to consoles. Calibrate and test equipment and locate circuit and component faults, using hand and power tools and measuring and testing instruments such as resistance meters and oscilloscopes. Compute cost estimates for labor and materials. Disassemble entertainment equipment and repair or replace loose, worn, or defective components and wiring, using hand tools and soldering irons. Make service calls to repair units in customers' homes or return units to shops for major repairs. Tune or adjust equipment and instruments to obtain optimum visual or auditory reception according to specifications, manuals, and drawings. Instruct customers on the safe and proper use of equipment. Keep records of work orders and test and maintenance reports. Confer with customers to determine the nature of problems or to explain repairs.

GOE Information—Interest Area: 13. Manufacturing. **Work Group:** 13.12. Electrical and Electronic Repair. **Personality Type—**Realistic. Realistic occupations frequently involve work activities that include practical, hands-on problems and solutions. They often deal with plants; animals; and real-world materials like wood, tools, and machinery. Many of the occupations require working outside and do not involve a lot of paperwork or working closely with others. **Work Values—**Variety; Independence; Supervision, Technical; Moral Values; Social Service; Compensation. **Skills—**Installation; Science; Repairing; Equipment Maintenance; Troubleshooting; Technology Design. **Abilities—***Cognitive:* Visualization; Speed of Closure; Number Facility; Mathematical Reasoning; Information Ordering. *Psychomotor:* Finger Dexterity; Wrist-Finger Speed; Arm-Hand Steadiness; Control Precision; Manual Dexterity; Multilimb Coordination. *Physical:* Static Strength; Extent Flexibility; Trunk Strength. *Sensory:* Sound Localization; Visual Color Discrimination; Hearing Sensitivity; Near Vision; Auditory Attention. **General Work Activities—***Information Input:* Monitoring Processes, Materials, or Surroundings; Inspecting Equipment, Structures, or Materials; Getting Information. *Mental Process:* Updating and Using Relevant

Knowledge; Analyzing Data or Information; Organizing, Planning, and Prioritizing. *Work Output:* Repairing and Maintaining Electronic Equipment; Handling and Moving Objects; Controlling Machines and Processes. *Interacting with Others:* Communicating with Persons Outside Organization; Establishing and Maintaining Interpersonal Relationships; Performing for or Working with the Public. **Physical Work Conditions—**Indoors; Sitting; Using Hands on Objects, Tools, or Controls; Bending or Twisting the Body. **Other Job Characteristics—**Need to Be Exact or Accurate.

Experience—Job Zone 3. Previous work-related skill, knowledge, or experience is required. **Job Preparation—**SVP 6.0 to less than 7.0— more than one year and less than four years. **Knowledges—** Computers and Electronics; Telecommunications; Design; Mechanical Devices; Engineering and Technology. **Instructional Program—**Communications Systems Installation and Repair Technology.

Related SOC Job—49-2097 Electronic Home Entertainment Equipment Installers and Repairers. **Related OOH Job—**Electronic Home Entertainment Equipment Installers and Repairers. **Related DOT Jobs—**720.281-010 Radio Repairer; 720.281-014 Tape-Recorder Repairer; 720.281-018 Television-and-Radio Repairer; 729.281-010 Audio-Video Repairer; 730.281-018 Electric-Organ Inspector and Repairer; 823.361-010 Television Installer; 828.261-010 Electronic-Organ Technician.

49-2098.00 Security and Fire Alarm Systems Installers

- **Education/Training Required: Postsecondary vocational training**
- **Employed: 49,470**
- **Annual Earnings: $33,720**
- **Growth: 21.7%**
- **Annual Job Openings: 15,000**

Install, program, maintain, and repair security and fire alarm wiring and equipment. Ensure that work is in accordance with relevant codes.

Examine systems to locate problems such as loose connections or broken insulation. Test backup batteries, keypad programming, sirens, and all security features to ensure proper functioning and to diagnose malfunctions. Mount and fasten control panels, door and window contacts, sensors, and video cameras and attach electrical and telephone wiring to connect components. Install, maintain, or repair security systems, alarm devices, and related equipment, following blueprints of electrical layouts and building plans. Inspect installation sites and study work orders, building plans, and installation manuals to determine materials requirements and installation procedures. Feed cables through access holes, roof spaces, and cavity walls to reach fixture outlets; then position and terminate cables, wires, and strapping. Adjust sensitivity of units based on room structures and manufacturers' recommendations, using programming keypads. Test and repair circuits and sensors, following wiring and system specifications. Drill holes for wiring in wall studs, joists, ceilings, and floors. Demonstrate systems for customers and explain details such as the causes and consequences of false alarms. Consult with clients to assess risks and to determine security requirements. Keep informed of new products and developments. Mount raceways and conduits and fasten wires to wood framing, using staplers. Provide customers with cost estimates for equipment installation. Prepare documents such as invoices and warranties. Order replacement parts.

GOE Information—Interest Area: 02. Architecture and Construction. Work Group: 02.04. Construction Crafts. Personality Type—No data available. Work Values—No data available. Skills—Installation; Repairing; Troubleshooting; Equipment Maintenance; Systems Evaluation; Programming. Abilities—*Cognitive:* Visualization; Perceptual Speed; Time Sharing; Flexibility of Closure; Originality; Selective Attention. *Psychomotor:* Multilimb Coordination; Manual Dexterity; Arm-Hand Steadiness; Control Precision; Finger Dexterity. *Physical:* Extent Flexibility; Gross Body Equilibrium; Gross Body Coordination; Trunk Strength; Static Strength. *Sensory:* Visual Color Discrimination; Depth Perception; Auditory Attention. General Work Activities—*Information Input:* Monitoring Processes, Materials, or Surroundings; Identifying Objects, Actions, and Events; Getting Information. *Mental Process:* Updating and Using Relevant Knowledge; Organizing, Planning, and Prioritizing; Thinking Creatively. *Work Output:* Handling and Moving Objects; Repairing and Maintaining Electronic Equipment; Performing General Physical Activities. *Interacting with Others:* Establishing and Maintaining Interpersonal Relationships; Performing for or Working with the Public; Communicating with Other Workers. Physical Work Conditions—More Often Indoors Than Outdoors; Noisy; Very Hot or Cold; Standing; Using Hands on Objects, Tools, or Controls. Other Job Characteristics—Need to Be Exact or Accurate; Errors Have Important Consequences.

Experience—Job Zone 3. Previous work-related skill, knowledge, or experience is required. Job Preparation—SVP 6.0 to less than 7.0—more than one year and less than four years. Knowledges—Telecommunications; Building and Construction; Mechanical Devices; Computers and Electronics; Public Safety and Security; Design. Instructional Programs—Electrician; Security System Installation, Repair, and Inspection Technology/Technician.

Related SOC Job—49-2098 Security and Fire Alarm Systems Installers. Related OOH Job—Security and Fire Alarm Systems Installers. Related DOT Jobs—822.361-018 Protective-Signal Installer; 822.361-022 Protective-Signal Repairer.

49-3000 Vehicle and Mobile Equipment Mechanics, Installers, and Repairers

49-3011.00 Aircraft Mechanics and Service Technicians

- **Education/Training Required: Postsecondary vocational training**
- **Employed: 115,120**
- **Annual Earnings: $47,310**
- **Growth: 13.4%**
- **Annual Job Openings: 11,000**

Diagnose, adjust, repair, or overhaul aircraft engines and assemblies, such as hydraulic and pneumatic systems.

Read and interpret maintenance manuals, service bulletins, and other specifications to determine the feasibility and method of repairing or replacing malfunctioning or damaged components. Inspect completed work to certify that maintenance meets standards and that aircraft are ready for operation. Maintain repair logs, documenting all preventive and corrective aircraft maintenance. Conduct routine and special inspections as required by regulations. Examine and inspect aircraft components, including landing gear, hydraulic systems, and de-icers, to locate cracks, breaks, leaks, or other problem. Inspect airframes for wear or other defects. Maintain, repair, and rebuild aircraft structures; functional components; and parts such as wings and fuselage, rigging, hydraulic units, oxygen systems, fuel systems, electrical systems, gaskets, and seals. Measure the tension of control cables. Replace or repair worn, defective, or damaged components, using hand tools, gauges, and testing equipment. Measure parts for wear, using precision instruments. Assemble and install electrical, plumbing, mechanical, hydraulic, and structural components and accessories, using hand tools and power tools. Test operation of engines and other systems, using test equipment such as ignition analyzers, compression checkers, distributor timers, and ammeters. Obtain fuel and oil samples and check them for contamination. Reassemble engines following repair or inspection and re-install engines in aircraft. Read and interpret pilots' descriptions of problems to diagnose causes. Modify aircraft structures, space vehicles, systems, or components, following drawings, schematics, charts, engineering orders, and technical publications. Install and align repaired or replacement parts for subsequent riveting or welding, using clamps and wrenches. Locate and mark dimensions and reference lines on defective or replacement parts, using templates, scribes, compasses, and steel rules. Clean, strip, prime, and sand structural surfaces and materials to prepare them for bonding. Service and maintain aircraft and related apparatus by performing activities such as flushing crankcases, cleaning screens, and lubricating moving parts.

GOE Information—Interest Area: 13. Manufacturing. Work Group: 13.14. Vehicle and Facility Mechanical Work. Personality Type—Realistic. Realistic occupations frequently involve work activities that include practical, hands-on problems and solutions. They often deal with plants; animals; and real-world materials like wood, tools, and machinery. Many of the occupations require working outside and do not involve a lot of paperwork or working closely with others. Work Values—Moral Values; Compensation; Security; Supervision, Technical; Company Policies and Practices; Variety. Skills—Repairing; Equipment Maintenance; Operation Monitoring; Installation; Troubleshooting; Operation and Control. Abilities—*Cognitive:* Memorization; Visualization; Speed of Closure; Information Ordering; Number Facility; Inductive Reasoning. *Psychomotor:* Wrist-Finger Speed; Manual Dexterity; Control Precision; Speed of Limb Movement; Multilimb Coordination; Reaction Time. *Physical:* Explosive Strength; Extent Flexibility; Dynamic Flexibility; Static Strength; Dynamic Strength; Trunk Strength. *Sensory:* Hearing Sensitivity; Depth Perception; Visual Color Discrimination. General Work Activities—*Information Input:* Inspecting Equipment, Structures, or Materials; Monitoring Processes, Materials, or Surroundings; Getting Information. *Mental Process:* Updating and Using Relevant Knowledge; Making Decisions and Solving Problems; Organizing, Planning, and Prioritizing. *Work Output:* Repairing and Maintaining Mechanical Equipment; Handling and Moving Objects; Controlling Machines and Processes. *Interacting with Others:* Establishing and Maintaining Interpersonal Relationships; Communicating with Other Workers; Teaching Others. Physical Work Conditions—Noisy; Contaminants; Cramped Work Space, Awkward Positions; Standing; Using Hands on Objects, Tools, or Controls; Bending or Twisting the Body. Other Job Characteristics—Need to Be Exact or Accurate; Repeat Same Tasks.

Experience—Job Zone 3. Previous work-related skill, knowledge, or experience is required. Job Preparation—SVP 6.0 to less than 7.0—more than one year and less than four years. Knowledges—Mechanical Devices; Design; Physics; Chemistry; Engineering and Technology; Transportation. Instructional Programs—Agricultural

Mechanics and Equipment/Machine Technology; Aircraft Powerplant Technology/Technician; Airframe Mechanics and Aircraft Maintenance Technology/Technician.

Related SOC Job—49-3011 Aircraft Mechanics and Service Technicians. **Related OOH Job**—Aircraft and Avionics Equipment Mechanics and Service Technicians. **Related DOT Jobs**—621.261-022 Experimental Aircraft Mechanic; 621.281-014 Airframe-and-Power-Plant Mechanic; 621.281-018 Airframe-and-Power-Plant-Mechanic Apprentice; 621.281-030 Rocket-Engine-Component Mechanic; 807.261-010 Aircraft Body Repairer; 807.381-014 Bonded Structures Repairer; 825.281-038 Experimental-Rocket-Sled Mechanic.

49-3021.00 Automotive Body and Related Repairers

- **Education/Training Required: Long-term on-the-job training**
- **Employed: 158,160**
- **Annual Earnings: $34,810**
- **Growth: 10.3%**
- **Annual Job Openings: 18,000**

Repair and refinish automotive vehicle bodies and straighten vehicle frames.

File, grind, sand, and smooth filled or repaired surfaces, using power tools and hand tools. Sand body areas to be painted and cover bumpers, windows, and trim with masking tape or paper to protect them from the paint. Follow supervisors' instructions as to which parts to restore or replace and how much time the job should take. Remove damaged sections of vehicles, using metal-cutting guns, air grinders, and wrenches, and install replacement parts, using wrenches or welding equipment. Cut and tape plastic separating film to outside repair areas to avoid damaging surrounding surfaces during repair procedure and remove tape and wash surfaces after repairs are complete. Prime and paint repaired surfaces, using paint spray guns and motorized sanders. Inspect repaired vehicles for dimensional accuracy and test drive them to ensure proper alignment and handling. Mix polyester resins and hardeners to be used in restoring damaged areas. Chain or clamp frames and sections to alignment machines that use hydraulic pressure to align damaged components. Fill small dents that cannot be worked out with plastic or solder. Fit and weld replacement parts into place, using wrenches and welding equipment, and grind down welds to smooth them, using power grinders and other tools. Position dolly blocks against surfaces of dented areas and beat opposite surfaces to remove dents, using hammers. Remove damaged panels and identify the family and properties of the plastic used on a vehicle. Review damage reports, prepare or review repair cost estimates, and plan work to be performed. Remove small pits and dimples in body metal, using pick hammers and punches. Remove upholstery, accessories, electrical window-and-seat-operating equipment, and trim to gain access to vehicle bodies and fenders. Clean work areas, using air hoses, to remove damaged material and discarded fiberglass strips used in repair procedures. Adjust or align headlights, wheels, and brake systems. Apply heat to plastic panels, using hot-air welding guns or immersion in hot water, and press the softened panels back into shape by hand. Soak fiberglass matting in resin mixtures and apply layers of matting over repair areas to specified thicknesses.

GOE Information—Interest Area: 13. Manufacturing. **Work Group:** 13.14. Vehicle and Facility Mechanical Work. **Personality Type—** Realistic. Realistic occupations frequently involve work activities that include practical, hands-on problems and solutions. They often

deal with plants; animals; and real-world materials like wood, tools, and machinery. Many of the occupations require working outside and do not involve a lot of paperwork or working closely with others. **Work Values**—Independence; Moral Values; Compensation; Variety. **Skills**—Repairing; Installation; Equipment Maintenance; Troubleshooting; Equipment Selection; Management of Financial Resources. **Abilities**—*Cognitive:* Visualization; Perceptual Speed; Time Sharing; Category Flexibility; Flexibility of Closure; Selective Attention. *Psychomotor:* Reaction Time; Wrist-Finger Speed; Control Precision; Response Orientation; Speed of Limb Movement; Rate Control. *Physical:* Extent Flexibility; Static Strength; Dynamic Strength; Trunk Strength; Stamina; Gross Body Coordination. *Sensory:* Hearing Sensitivity; Sound Localization; Depth Perception; Visual Color Discrimination; Far Vision; Auditory Attention. **General Work Activities**—*Information Input:* Identifying Objects, Actions, and Events; Monitoring Processes, Materials, or Surroundings; Inspecting Equipment, Structures, or Materials. *Mental Process:* Organizing, Planning, and Prioritizing; Updating and Using Relevant Knowledge; Processing Information. *Work Output:* Handling and Moving Objects; Operating Vehicles or Equipment; Performing General Physical Activities. *Interacting with Others:* Establishing and Maintaining Interpersonal Relationships; Communicating with Persons Outside Organization; Communicating with Other Workers. **Physical Work Conditions**—Noisy; Contaminants; Hazardous Equipment; Standing; Using Hands on Objects, Tools, or Controls; Repetitive Motions. **Other Job Characteristics**—Need to Be Exact or Accurate; Repeat Same Tasks; Errors Have Important Consequences.

Experience—Job Zone 2. Some previous work-related skill, knowledge, or experience may be helpful in these occupations, but usually is not needed. **Job Preparation**—SVP 4.0 to less than 6.0—six months to less than two years. **Knowledges**—Mechanical Devices; Building and Construction; Chemistry; Administration and Management; Production and Processing; Transportation. **Instructional Program**—Autobody/Collision and Repair Technology and Technician.

Related SOC Job—49-3021 Automotive Body and Related Repairers. **Related OOH Job**—Automotive Body and Related Repairers. **Related DOT Jobs**—807.281-010 Truck-Body Builder; 807.361-010 Automobile-Body Customizer; 807.381-010 Automobile-Body Repairer; 807.381-022 Service Mechanic; 807.381-030 Auto-Body Repairer, Fiberglass.

49-3022.00 Automotive Glass Installers and Repairers

- **Education/Training Required: Long-term on-the-job training**
- **Employed: 17,760**
- **Annual Earnings: $29,500**
- **Growth: 15.1%**
- **Annual Job Openings: 2,000**

Replace or repair broken windshields and window glass in motor vehicles.

Remove all dirt, foreign matter, and loose glass from damaged areas; then apply primer along windshield or window edges and allow it to dry. Install replacement glass in vehicles after old glass has been removed and all necessary preparations have been made. Allow all glass parts installed with urethane ample time to cure, taking temperature and humidity into account. Prime all scratches on pinch welds with primer and allow primed scratches to dry. Obtain windshields or windows for specific automobile makes and models from stock and examine them for defects prior to installation. Apply a bead of urethane around the perimeter of each pinch weld and dress the remaining urethane on the pinch welds so that it is of uniform level and thickness all the way around. Check for moisture or contamination in damaged areas, dry out any moisture prior to making repairs, and keep damaged areas dry until repairs are complete. Select appropriate tools, safety equipment, and parts according to job requirements. Remove broken or damaged glass windshields or window glass from motor vehicles, using hand tools to remove screws from frames holding glass. Remove all moldings, clips, windshield wipers, screws, bolts, and inside A-pillar moldings; then lower headliners prior to beginning installation or repair work. Install, repair, and replace safety glass and related materials, such as back glass heating elements, on vehicles and equipment. Install rubber channeling strips around edges of glass or frames to weatherproof windows or to prevent rattling. Hold cut or uneven edges of glass against automated abrasive belts to shape or smooth edges. Cut flat safety glass according to specified patterns or perform precision pattern-making and glass-cutting to custom-fit replacement windows. Replace or adjust motorized or manual window-raising mechanisms. Install new foam dams on pinch welds if required. Cool or warm glass in the event of temperature extremes. Replace all moldings, clips, windshield wipers, and other parts that were removed prior to glass replacement or repair.

GOE Information—Interest Area: 13. Manufacturing. **Work Group:** 13.14. Vehicle and Facility Mechanical Work. **Personality Type—** Realistic. Realistic occupations frequently involve work activities that include practical, hands-on problems and solutions. They often deal with plants; animals; and real-world materials like wood, tools, and machinery. Many of the occupations require working outside and do not involve a lot of paperwork or working closely with others. **Work Values—**Independence; Moral Values; Supervision, Technical; Security. **Skills—**Installation; Equipment Maintenance; Repairing; Management of Material Resources; Equipment Selection; Instructing. **Abilities—***Cognitive:* Visualization; Memorization; Time Sharing. *Psychomotor:* Rate Control; Arm-Hand Steadiness; Manual Dexterity; Reaction Time; Control Precision; Multilimb Coordination. *Physical:* Extent Flexibility; Gross Body Coordination; Static Strength; Trunk Strength; Stamina. *Sensory:* Glare Sensitivity; Depth Perception; Visual Color Discrimination; Hearing Sensitivity; Far Vision. **General Work Activities—***Information Input:* Inspecting Equipment, Structures, or Materials; Monitoring Processes, Materials, or Surroundings; Estimating the Needed Characteristics of Products, Events, or Information. *Mental Process:* Scheduling Work and Activities; Organizing, Planning, and Prioritizing; Judging the Qualities of Things, Services, or Other People's Work. *Work Output:* Handling and Moving Objects; Performing General Physical Activities; Operating Vehicles or Equipment. *Interacting with Others:* Performing for or Working with the Public; Communicating with Persons Outside Organization; Coordinating the Work and Activities of Others. **Physical Work Conditions—**Outdoors; Very Hot or Cold; Contaminants; Cramped Work Space, Awkward Positions; Standing; Using Hands on Objects, Tools, or Controls. **Other Job Characteristics—**Need to Be Exact or Accurate.

Experience—Job Zone 2. Some previous work-related skill, knowledge, or experience may be helpful in these occupations, but usually is not needed. **Job Preparation—**SVP 4.0 to less than 6.0—six months to less than two years. **Knowledges—**Mechanical Devices; Production and Processing; Customer and Personal Service; Administration and Management; Sales and Marketing; Transportation. **Instructional Program—**Autobody/Collision and Repair Technology and Technician.

Related SOC Job—49-3022 Automotive Glass Installers and Repairers. **Related OOH Job—**Automotive Body and Related Repairers. **Related DOT Job—**865.684-010 Glass Installer.

49-3023.00 Automotive Service Technicians and Mechanics

- **Education/Training Required: Postsecondary vocational training**
- **Employed: 654,800**
- **Annual Earnings: $33,050**
- **Growth: 15.7%**
- **Annual Job Openings: 93,000**

The job openings listed here are shared with 49-3023.01 Automotive Master Mechanics and 49-3023.02 Automotive Specialty Technicians.

Diagnose, adjust, repair, or overhaul automotive vehicles.

No task data available.

GOE Information—Interest Area: 13. Manufacturing. **Work Group:** 13.14. Vehicle and Facility Mechanical Work. **Note:** The Department of Labor has not collected some data for this job, so it has fewer details than the other descriptions.

Instructional Programs—Alternative Fuel Vehicle Technology/ Technician; Autobody/Collision and Repair Technology and Technician; Automobile/Automotive Mechanics/Technology/Technician; Automotive Engineering Technology/Technician; Medium/ Heavy Vehicle and Truck Technology/Technician; Vehicle Emissions Inspection and Maintenance Technology/Technician.

Related SOC Job—49-3023 Automotive Service Technicians and Mechanics. **Related OOH Job—**Automotive Service Technicians and Mechanics. **Related DOT Job—**No data available.

49-3023.01 Automotive Master Mechanics

- **Education/Training Required: Postsecondary vocational training**
- **Employed: 654,800**
- **Annual Earnings: $33,050**
- **Growth: 15.7%**
- **Annual Job Openings: 93,000**

The job openings listed here are shared with 49-3023.00 Automotive Service Technicians and Mechanics and 49-3023.02 Automotive Specialty Technicians.

Repair automobiles, trucks, buses, and other vehicles. Master mechanics repair virtually any part on the vehicle or specialize in the transmission system.

Examine vehicles to determine extent of damage or malfunctions. Test drive vehicles and test components and systems, using equipment such as infrared engine analyzers, compression gauges, and computerized diagnostic devices. Repair, reline, replace, and adjust brakes. Review work orders and discuss work with supervisors. Follow checklists to ensure all important parts are examined, including belts, hoses, steering systems, spark plugs, brake and fuel systems, wheel bearings, and other potentially troublesome areas. Plan work procedures, using charts, technical manuals, and experience. Test and adjust repaired systems to meet manufacturers' performance specifications. Confer with customers to obtain descriptions of vehicle problems and to discuss work to be performed and future repair requirements. Perform routine and scheduled maintenance services such as oil changes, lubrications, and tune-ups. Disassemble units and inspect parts for wear, using micrometers, calipers, and gauges. Overhaul or replace carburetors, blowers, generators, distributors, starters, and pumps. Repair and service air conditioning, heating, engine-cooling, and electrical systems. Repair or replace parts such as pistons, rods, gears, valves, and bearings. Tear down, repair, and rebuild faulty assemblies such as power systems, steering systems, and linkages. Rewire ignition systems, lights, and instrument panels. Repair radiator leaks. Install and repair accessories such as radios, heaters, mirrors, and windshield wipers. Repair manual and automatic transmissions. Repair or replace shock absorbers. Align vehicles' front ends. Rebuild parts such as crankshafts and cylinder blocks. Repair damaged automobile bodies. Replace and adjust headlights.

GOE Information—Interest Area: 13. Manufacturing. **Work Group:** 13.14. Vehicle and Facility Mechanical Work. **Personality Type—** Realistic. Realistic occupations frequently involve work activities that include practical, hands-on problems and solutions. They often deal with plants; animals; and real-world materials like wood, tools, and machinery. Many of the occupations require working outside and do not involve a lot of paperwork or working closely with others. **Work Values—**Compensation; Independence; Ability Utilization; Responsibility; Variety; Security. **Skills—**Repairing; Troubleshooting; Installation; Equipment Maintenance; Operation Monitoring; Complex Problem Solving. **Abilities—***Cognitive:* Speed of Closure; Spatial Orientation; Visualization; Perceptual Speed; Flexibility of Closure; Information Ordering. *Psychomotor:* Reaction Time; Response Orientation; Control Precision; Finger Dexterity; Rate Control; Arm-Hand Steadiness. *Physical:* Extent Flexibility; Static Strength; Trunk Strength; Dynamic Strength; Stamina; Gross Body Coordination. *Sensory:* Sound Localization; Hearing Sensitivity; Night Vision; Glare Sensitivity; Visual Color Discrimination; Auditory Attention. **General Work Activities—***Information Input:* Inspecting Equipment, Structures, or Materials; Monitoring Processes, Materials, or Surroundings; Getting Information. *Mental Process:* Making Decisions and Solving Problems; Updating and Using Relevant Knowledge; Processing Information. *Work Output:* Repairing and Maintaining Mechanical Equipment; Controlling Machines and Processes; Handling and Moving Objects. *Interacting with Others:* Communicating with Other Workers; Interpreting the Meaning of Information for Others; Establishing and Maintaining Interpersonal Relationships. **Physical Work Conditions—**Noisy; Contaminants; Hazardous Equipment; Minor Burns, Cuts, Bites, or Stings; Standing; Using Hands on Objects, Tools, or Controls. **Other Job Characteristics—**Need to Be Exact or Accurate.

Experience—Job Zone 3. Previous work-related skill, knowledge, or experience is required. **Job Preparation—**SVP 6.0 to less than 7.0— more than one year and less than four years. **Knowledges—** Mechanical Devices; Physics; Computers and Electronics; Engineering and Technology; Chemistry; Public Safety and Security. **Instructional Programs—**Autobody/Collision and Repair Technology and Technician; Automobile/Automotive Mechanics/ Technology/Technician; Automotive Engineering Technology/Technician; Medium/Heavy Vehicle and Truck Technology/ Technician.

Related SOC Job—49-3023 Automotive Service Technicians and Mechanics. **Related OOH Job—**Automotive Service Technicians and Mechanics. **Related DOT Jobs—**620.261-010 Automobile Mechanic; 620.261-012 Automobile-Mechanic Apprentice; 620.281-062 Transmission Mechanic; 620.364-010 Squeak, Rattle, and Leak Repairer; 620.381-022 Repairer, Heavy.

49-3023.02 Automotive Specialty Technicians

- **Education/Training Required:** Postsecondary vocational training
- **Employed:** 654,800
- **Annual Earnings:** $33,050
- **Growth:** 15.7%
- **Annual Job Openings:** 93,000

The job openings listed here are shared with 49-3023.00 Automotive Service Technicians and Mechanics and 49-3023.01 Automotive Master Mechanics.

Repair only one system or component on a vehicle, such as brakes, suspension, or radiator.

Examine vehicles, compile estimates of repair costs, and secure customers' approval to perform repairs. Repair, overhaul, and adjust automobile brake systems. Use electronic test equipment to locate and correct malfunctions in fuel, ignition, and emissions control systems. Repair and replace defective ball joint suspensions, brake shoes, and wheel bearings. Inspect and test new vehicles for damage; then record findings so that necessary repairs can be made. Test electronic computer components in automobiles to ensure that they are working properly. Tune automobile engines to ensure proper and efficient functioning. Install and repair air conditioners and service components such as compressors, condensers, and controls. Repair, replace, and adjust defective carburetor parts and gasoline filters. Remove and replace defective mufflers and tailpipes. Repair and replace automobile leaf springs. Rebuild, repair, and test automotive fuel injection units. Align and repair wheels, axles, frames, torsion bars, and steering mechanisms of automobiles, using special alignment equipment and wheel-balancing machines. Repair, install, and adjust hydraulic and electromagnetic automatic lift mechanisms used to raise and lower automobile windows, seats, and tops. Repair and rebuild clutch systems. Convert vehicle fuel systems from gasoline to butane gas operations and repair and service operating butane fuel units.

GOE Information—Interest Area: 13. Manufacturing. **Work Group:** 13.14. Vehicle and Facility Mechanical Work. **Personality Type—** Realistic. Realistic occupations frequently involve work activities that include practical, hands-on problems and solutions. They often deal with plants; animals; and real-world materials like wood, tools, and machinery. Many of the occupations require working outside and do not involve a lot of paperwork or working closely with others. **Work Values—**Independence; Responsibility. **Skills—**Repairing; Troubleshooting; Operation Monitoring; Equipment Maintenance; Installation; Equipment Selection. **Abilities—***Cognitive:* Visualization; Speed of Closure; Selective Attention; Deductive Reasoning; Time Sharing; Flexibility of Closure. *Psychomotor:* Multilimb Coordination; Control Precision; Reaction Time; Response Orientation; Manual Dexterity; Finger Dexterity. *Physical:* Extent Flexibility; Static Strength; Gross Body Coordination; Trunk Strength. *Sensory:* Hearing Sensitivity; Auditory Attention; Glare Sensitivity; Depth Perception; Visual Color Discrimination. **General Work Activities—***Information Input:* Monitoring Processes, Materials, or Surroundings; Inspecting Equipment, Structures, or Materials; Getting Information. *Mental Process:* Updating and Using Relevant Knowledge; Making Decisions and Solving Problems; Evaluating Information Against Standards. *Work Output:* Handling and Moving Objects; Repairing and Maintaining Mechanical Equipment; Performing General Physical Activities. *Interacting with Others:*

Establishing and Maintaining Interpersonal Relationships; Communicating with Other Workers; Performing for or Working with the Public. **Physical Work Conditions**—Contaminants; Cramped Work Space, Awkward Positions; Minor Burns, Cuts, Bites, or Stings; Standing; Using Hands on Objects, Tools, or Controls; Bending or Twisting the Body. **Other Job Characteristics**—Need to Be Exact or Accurate; Errors Have Important Consequences.

Experience—Job Zone 3. Previous work-related skill, knowledge, or experience is required. **Job Preparation**—SVP 6.0 to less than 7.0— more than one year and less than four years. **Knowledges**— Mechanical Devices; Physics; Engineering and Technology; Customer and Personal Service; Sales and Marketing; Administration and Management. **Instructional Programs**—Alternative Fuel Vehicle Technology/Technician; Automotive Engineering Technology/ Technician; Vehicle Emissions Inspection and Maintenance Technology/Technician.

Related SOC Job—49-3023 Automotive Service Technicians and Mechanics. **Related OOH Job**—Automotive Service Technicians and Mechanics. **Related DOT Jobs**—619.380-018 Spring Repairer, Hand; 620.261-030 Automobile-Service-Station Mechanic; 620.261-034 Automotive-Cooling-System Diagnostic Technician; 620.281-010 Air-Conditioning Mechanic; 620.281-026 Brake Repairer; 620.281-034 Carburetor Mechanic; 620.281-038 Front-End Mechanic; 620.281-066 Tune-Up Mechanic; 620.281-070 Vehicle-Fuel-Systems Converter; 620.381-010 Automobile-Radiator Mechanic; 620.682-010 Brake-Drum-Lathe Operator; 620.684-018 Brake Adjuster; 620.684-022 Clutch Rebuilder; others.

49-3031.00 Bus and Truck Mechanics and Diesel Engine Specialists

- **Education/Training Required:** Postsecondary vocational training
- **Employed:** 248,280
- **Annual Earnings:** $36,620
- **Growth:** 14.4%
- **Annual Job Openings:** 32,000

Diagnose, adjust, repair, or overhaul trucks, buses, and all types of diesel engines. Includes mechanics working primarily with automobile diesel engines.

Use hand tools such as screwdrivers, pliers, wrenches, pressure gauges, and precision instruments, as well as power tools such as pneumatic wrenches, lathes, welding equipment, and jacks and hoists. Inspect brake systems, steering mechanisms, wheel bearings, and other important parts to ensure that they are in proper operating condition. Perform routine maintenance such as changing oil, checking batteries, and lubricating equipment and machinery. Adjust and reline brakes, align wheels, tighten bolts and screws, and reassemble equipment. Raise trucks, buses, and heavy parts or equipment, using hydraulic jacks or hoists. Test drive trucks and buses to diagnose malfunctions or to ensure that they are working properly. Inspect, test, and listen to defective equipment to diagnose malfunctions, using test instruments such as handheld computers, motor analyzers, chassis charts, and pressure gauges. Examine and adjust protective guards, loose bolts, and specified safety devices. Inspect and verify dimensions and clearances of parts to ensure conformance to factory specifications. Specialize in repairing and maintaining parts of the engine, such as fuel injection systems. Attach test instruments to equipment and read dials and gauges to diagnose malfunctions. Rewire ignition systems, lights, and instrument panels. Recondition and replace parts, pistons, bearings, gears, and valves. Repair and adjust seats, doors, and windows and install and repair accessories. Inspect, repair, and maintain automotive and mechanical equipment and machinery such as pumps and compressors. Disassemble and overhaul internal combustion engines, pumps, generators, transmissions, clutches, and differential units. Rebuild gas or diesel engines. Align front ends and suspension systems. Operate valve-grinding machines to grind and reset valves.

GOE Information—**Interest Area:** 13. Manufacturing. **Work Group:** 13.14. Vehicle and Facility Mechanical Work. **Personality Type**— Realistic. Realistic occupations frequently involve work activities that include practical, hands-on problems and solutions. They often deal with plants; animals; and real-world materials like wood, tools, and machinery. Many of the occupations require working outside and do not involve a lot of paperwork or working closely with others. **Work Values**—Independence; Compensation; Variety; Responsibility. **Skills**—Repairing; Equipment Maintenance; Troubleshooting; Installation; Science; Technology Design. **Abilities**—*Cognitive:* Visualization; Problem Sensitivity; Flexibility of Closure; Information Ordering; Inductive Reasoning; Speed of Closure. *Psychomotor:* Multilimb Coordination; Control Precision; Manual Dexterity; Finger Dexterity; Arm-Hand Steadiness; Reaction Time. *Physical:* Extent Flexibility; Static Strength; Gross Body Equilibrium; Gross Body Coordination; Dynamic Strength; Trunk Strength. *Sensory:* Hearing Sensitivity; Glare Sensitivity; Auditory Attention; Depth Perception; Visual Color Discrimination. **General Work Activities**—*Information Input:* Inspecting Equipment, Structures, or Materials; Monitoring Processes, Materials, or Surroundings; Getting Information. *Mental Process:* Updating and Using Relevant Knowledge; Making Decisions and Solving Problems; Judging the Qualities of Things, Services, or Other People's Work. *Work Output:* Handling and Moving Objects; Repairing and Maintaining Mechanical Equipment; Performing General Physical Activities. *Interacting with Others:* Establishing and Maintaining Interpersonal Relationships; Communicating with Other Workers; Interpreting the Meaning of Information for Others. **Physical Work Conditions**—Noisy; Very Bright or Dim Lighting; Contaminants; Hazardous Equipment; Minor Burns, Cuts, Bites, or Stings; Using Hands on Objects, Tools, or Controls. **Other Job Characteristics**— Need to Be Exact or Accurate; Repeat Same Tasks; Errors Have Important Consequences.

Experience—Job Zone 3. Previous work-related skill, knowledge, or experience is required. **Job Preparation**—SVP 6.0 to less than 7.0— more than one year and less than four years. **Knowledges**— Mechanical Devices; Transportation; Public Safety and Security; Physics; Engineering and Technology; Law and Government. **Instructional Programs**—Diesel Mechanics Technology/Technician; Medium/Heavy Vehicle and Truck Technology/Technician.

Related SOC Job—49-3031 Bus and Truck Mechanics and Diesel Engine Specialists. **Related OOH Job**—Diesel Service Technicians and Mechanics. **Related DOT Jobs**—620.281-046 Maintenance Mechanic; 620.281-050 Mechanic, Industrial Truck; 620.281-058 Tractor Mechanic; 623.281-014 Deep Submergence Vehicle Crewmember; 623.281-018 Machinist Apprentice, Marine Engine; 623.281-026 Machinist, Marine Engine; 623.281-034 Maintenance Mechanic, Engine; 625.281-010 Diesel Mechanic; 625.281-014 Diesel-Mechanic Apprentice; 629.381-014 Oil-Field Equipment Mechanic.

49-3041.00 Farm Equipment Mechanics

- **Education/Training Required: Postsecondary vocational training**
- **Employed: 30,800**
- **Annual Earnings: $28,730**
- **Growth: 3.3%**
- **Annual Job Openings: 3,000**

Diagnose, adjust, repair, or overhaul farm machinery and vehicles, such as tractors, harvesters, dairy equipment, and irrigation systems.

Maintain, repair, and overhaul farm machinery and vehicles, such as tractors, harvesters, and irrigation systems. Test and replace electrical components and wiring, using test meters, soldering equipment, and hand tools. Repair bent or torn sheet metal. Calculate bills according to record of repairs made, labor time, and parts used. Record details of repairs made and parts used. Fabricate new metal parts, using drill presses, engine lathes, and other machine tools. Drive trucks to haul tools and equipment for on-site repair of large machinery. Reassemble machines and equipment following repair; test operation; and make adjustments as necessary. Install and repair agricultural irrigation, plumbing, and sprinkler systems. Examine and listen to equipment, read inspection reports, and confer with customers to locate and diagnose malfunctions. Dismantle defective machines for repair, using hand tools. Tune or overhaul engines. Clean and lubricate parts. Repair or replace defective parts, using hand tools, milling and woodworking machines, lathes, welding equipment, grinders, or saws.

GOE Information—Interest Area: 13. Manufacturing. **Work Group:** 13.14. Vehicle and Facility Mechanical Work. **Personality Type—**Realistic. Realistic occupations frequently involve work activities that include practical, hands-on problems and solutions. They often deal with plants; animals; and real-world materials like wood, tools, and machinery. Many of the occupations require working outside and do not involve a lot of paperwork or working closely with others. **Work Values—**Moral Values; Independence; Variety; Responsibility. **Skills—**Installation; Repairing; Equipment Maintenance; Technology Design; Operation Monitoring; Troubleshooting. **Abilities—***Cognitive:* Visualization; Speed of Closure. *Psychomotor:* Control Precision; Wrist-Finger Speed; Multilimb Coordination; Arm-Hand Steadiness; Manual Dexterity; Reaction Time. *Physical:* Extent Flexibility; Explosive Strength; Static Strength; Stamina; Dynamic Strength; Trunk Strength. *Sensory:* Hearing Sensitivity; Sound Localization; Visual Color Discrimination; Auditory Attention. **General Work Activities—***Information Input:* Monitoring Processes, Materials, or Surroundings; Inspecting Equipment, Structures, or Materials; Getting Information. *Mental Process:* Updating and Using Relevant Knowledge; Evaluating Information Against Standards; Making Decisions and Solving Problems. *Work Output:* Repairing and Maintaining Mechanical Equipment; Handling and Moving Objects; Performing General Physical Activities. *Interacting with Others:* None met the criteria. **Physical Work Conditions—**Outdoors; Hazardous Equipment; Standing; Kneeling, Crouching, Stooping, or Crawling; Using Hands on Objects, Tools, or Controls; Bending or Twisting the Body. **Other Job Characteristics—**None met the criteria.

Experience—Job Zone 3. Previous work-related skill, knowledge, or experience is required. **Job Preparation—**SVP 6.0 to less than 7.0—more than one year and less than four years. **Knowledges—**Mechanical Devices; Engineering and Technology. **Instructional Programs—**Agricultural Mechanics and Equipment/Machine Technology; Agricultural Mechanization, General; Agricultural Mechanization, Other; Agricultural Power Machinery Operation.

Related SOC Job—49-3041 Farm Equipment Mechanics. **Related OOH Job—**Heavy Vehicle and Mobile Equipment Service Technicians and Mechanics. **Related DOT Jobs—**624.281-010 Farm-Equipment Mechanic I; 624.281-014 Farm-Equipment-Mechanic Apprentice; 624.361-014 Sprinkler-Irrigation-Equipment Mechanic; 624.381-010 Assembly Repairer; 624.381-014 Farm-Equipment Mechanic II; 629.281-018 Dairy-Equipment Repairer; 809.381-018 Milking-System Installer.

49-3042.00 Mobile Heavy Equipment Mechanics, Except Engines

- **Education/Training Required: Postsecondary vocational training**
- **Employed: 117,500**
- **Annual Earnings: $39,410**
- **Growth: 8.8%**
- **Annual Job Openings: 14,000**

Diagnose, adjust, repair, or overhaul mobile mechanical, hydraulic, and pneumatic equipment, such as cranes, bulldozers, graders, and conveyors, used in construction, logging, and surface mining.

Test mechanical products and equipment after repair or assembly to ensure proper performance and compliance with manufacturers' specifications. Repair and replace damaged or worn parts. Diagnose faults or malfunctions to determine required repairs, using engine diagnostic equipment such as computerized test equipment and calibration devices. Operate and inspect machines or heavy equipment to diagnose defects. Dismantle and reassemble heavy equipment, using hoists and hand tools. Clean, lubricate, and perform other routine maintenance work on equipment and vehicles. Examine parts for damage or excessive wear, using micrometers and gauges. Read and understand operating manuals, blueprints, and technical drawings. Schedule maintenance for industrial machines and equipment and keep equipment service records. Overhaul and test machines or equipment to ensure operating efficiency. Assemble gear systems and align frames and gears. Fit bearings to adjust, repair, or overhaul mobile mechanical, hydraulic, and pneumatic equipment. Weld or solder broken parts and structural members, using electric or gas welders and soldering tools. Clean parts by spraying them with grease solvent or immersing them in tanks of solvent. Adjust, maintain, and repair or replace subassemblies, such as transmissions and crawler heads, using hand tools, jacks, and cranes. Adjust and maintain industrial machinery, using control and regulating devices. Fabricate needed parts or items from sheet metal. Direct workers who are assembling or disassembling equipment or cleaning parts.

GOE Information—Interest Area: 13. Manufacturing. **Work Group:** 13.14. Vehicle and Facility Mechanical Work. **Personality Type—**Realistic. Realistic occupations frequently involve work activities that include practical, hands-on problems and solutions. They often deal with plants; animals; and real-world materials like wood, tools, and machinery. Many of the occupations require working outside and do not involve a lot of paperwork or working closely with others. **Work Values—**Moral Values; Compensation; Authority; Variety; Ability Utilization; Responsibility. **Skills—**Installation; Repairing; Equipment Maintenance; Operation Monitoring; Troubleshooting; Operation and Control. **Abilities—***Cognitive:* Visualization; Selective Attention; Spatial Orientation; Information Ordering; Flexibility of Closure; Perceptual Speed. *Psychomotor:* Multilimb Coordination;

Reaction Time; Control Precision; Manual Dexterity; Arm-Hand Steadiness; Finger Dexterity. *Physical:* Extent Flexibility; Static Strength; Gross Body Coordination; Trunk Strength. *Sensory:* Auditory Attention; Hearing Sensitivity; Depth Perception; Glare Sensitivity. **General Work Activities**—*Information Input:* Monitoring Processes, Materials, or Surroundings; Getting Information; Inspecting Equipment, Structures, or Materials. *Mental Process:* Updating and Using Relevant Knowledge; Making Decisions and Solving Problems; Judging the Qualities of Things, Services, or Other People's Work. *Work Output:* Handling and Moving Objects; Repairing and Maintaining Mechanical Equipment; Controlling Machines and Processes. *Interacting with Others:* Communicating with Other Workers; Guiding, Directing, and Motivating Subordinates; Resolving Conflicts and Negotiating with Others. **Physical Work Conditions**—Noisy; Contaminants; Hazardous Equipment; Minor Burns, Cuts, Bites, or Stings; Standing; Using Hands on Objects, Tools, or Controls. **Other Job Characteristics**—Need to Be Exact or Accurate; Errors Have Important Consequences.

Experience—Job Zone 4. A minimum of two to four years of work-related skill, knowledge, or experience is needed. **Job Preparation**—SVP 7.0 to less than 8.0—two years to less than 10 years. **Knowledges**—Mechanical Devices; Engineering and Technology; Physics; Production and Processing. **Instructional Programs**—Agricultural Mechanics and Equipment/Machine Technology; Heavy Equipment Maintenance/Technology/Technician.

Related SOC Job—49-3042 Mobile Heavy Equipment Mechanics, Except Engines. **Related OOH Job**—Heavy Vehicle and Mobile Equipment Service Technicians and Mechanics. **Related DOT Jobs**—620.261-022 Construction-Equipment Mechanic; 620.281-042 Logging-Equipment Mechanic; 620.381-014 Mechanic, Endless Track Vehicle.

49-3043.00 Rail Car Repairers

- **Education/Training Required: Long-term on-the-job training**
- **Employed: 24,270**
- **Annual Earnings: $42,530**
- **Growth: −1.2%**
- **Annual Job Openings: 2,000**

Diagnose, adjust, repair, or overhaul railroad rolling stock, mine cars, or mass-transit rail cars.

Repair or replace defective or worn parts such as bearings, pistons, and gears, using hand tools, torque wrenches, power tools, and welding equipment. Test units for operability before and after repairs. Remove locomotives, car mechanical units, or other components, using pneumatic hoists and jacks, pinch bars, hand tools, and cutting torches. Record conditions of cars and repair and maintenance work performed or to be performed. Inspect components such as bearings, seals, gaskets, wheels, and coupler assemblies to determine if repairs are needed. Inspect the interior and exterior of rail cars coming into rail yards to identify defects and to determine the extent of wear and damage. Adjust repaired or replaced units as needed to ensure proper operation. Perform scheduled maintenance and clean units and components. Repair and maintain electrical and electronic controls for propulsion and braking systems. Repair, fabricate, and install steel or wood fittings, using blueprints, shop sketches, and instruction manuals. Disassemble units such as water pumps, control valves, and compressors so that repairs can be made. Align car sides for installation of car ends and crossties, using width gauges, turnbuckles, and wrenches. Measure diameters of axle wheel seats, using micrometers, and mark dimensions on axles so that wheels can be bored to specified dimensions. Replace defective wiring and insulation and

tighten electrical connections, using hand tools. Test electrical systems of cars by operating systems and using testing equipment such as ammeters. Install and repair interior flooring, fixtures, walls, plumbing, steps, and platforms. Examine car roofs for wear and damage and repair defective sections, using roofing material, cement, nails, and waterproof paint. Paint car exteriors, interiors, and fixtures. Repair car upholstery. Repair window sash frames, attach weather stripping and channels to frames, and replace window glass, using hand tools.

GOE Information—**Interest Area:** 13. Manufacturing. **Work Group:** 13.14. Vehicle and Facility Mechanical Work. **Personality Type**—Realistic. Realistic occupations frequently involve work activities that include practical, hands-on problems and solutions. They often deal with plants; animals; and real-world materials like wood, tools, and machinery. Many of the occupations require working outside and do not involve a lot of paperwork or working closely with others. **Work Values**—Variety; Moral Values; Independence; Supervision, Human Relations; Compensation; Supervision, Technical. **Skills**—Repairing; Installation; Equipment Maintenance; Troubleshooting; Operation Monitoring; Technology Design. **Abilities**—*Cognitive:* Visualization; Selective Attention; Flexibility of Closure; Perceptual Speed; Speed of Closure; Time Sharing. *Psychomotor:* Reaction Time; Multilimb Coordination; Speed of Limb Movement; Response Orientation; Arm-Hand Steadiness; Control Precision. *Physical:* Extent Flexibility; Stamina; Static Strength; Dynamic Strength; Gross Body Equilibrium; Trunk Strength. *Sensory:* Glare Sensitivity; Visual Color Discrimination; Depth Perception; Auditory Attention; Sound Localization; Hearing Sensitivity. **General Work Activities**—*Information Input:* Identifying Objects, Actions, and Events; Monitoring Processes, Materials, or Surroundings; Inspecting Equipment, Structures, or Materials. *Mental Process:* Updating and Using Relevant Knowledge; Evaluating Information Against Standards; Thinking Creatively. *Work Output:* Handling and Moving Objects; Performing General Physical Activities; Controlling Machines and Processes. *Interacting with Others:* Communicating with Other Workers; Establishing and Maintaining Interpersonal Relationships; Coordinating the Work and Activities of Others. **Physical Work Conditions**—Outdoors; Noisy; Very Hot or Cold; Contaminants; Standing; Using Hands on Objects, Tools, or Controls. **Other Job Characteristics**—Need to Be Exact or Accurate; Errors Have Important Consequences.

Experience—Job Zone 2. Some previous work-related skill, knowledge, or experience may be helpful in these occupations, but usually is not needed. **Job Preparation**—SVP 4.0 to less than 6.0—six months to less than two years. **Knowledges**—Mechanical Devices; Public Safety and Security; Production and Processing. **Instructional Program**—Heavy Equipment Maintenance/Technology/Technician.

Related SOC Job—49-3043 Rail Car Repairers. **Related OOH Job**—Heavy Vehicle and Mobile Equipment Service Technicians and Mechanics. **Related DOT Jobs**—620.381-018 Mechanical-Unit Repairer; 622.261-010 Brake Repairer, Railroad; 622.381-014 Car Repairer; 622.381-018 Car Repairer, Pullman; 622.381-022 Car-Repairer Apprentice; 622.381-030 Mine-Car Repairer; 622.684-010 Air-Compressor Mechanic; 807.381-026 Streetcar Repairer.

49-3051.00 Motorboat Mechanics

- **Education/Training Required: Long-term on-the-job training**
- **Employed: 18,190**
- **Annual Earnings: $32,780**
- **Growth: 15.1%**
- **Annual Job Openings: 7,000**

Repairs and adjusts electrical and mechanical equipment of gasoline or diesel-powered inboard or inboard-outboard boat engines.

Replace parts such as gears, magneto points, piston rings, and spark plugs and reassemble engines. Adjust generators and replace faulty wiring, using hand tools and soldering irons. Mount motors to boats and operate boats at various speeds on waterways to conduct operational tests. Document inspection and test results and work performed or to be performed. Start motors and monitor performance for signs of malfunctioning such as smoke, excessive vibration, and misfiring. Set starter locks and align and repair steering or throttle controls, using gauges, screwdrivers, and wrenches. Repair engine mechanical equipment such as power tilts, bilge pumps, or power take-offs. Inspect and repair or adjust propellers and propeller shafts. Disassemble and inspect motors to locate defective parts, using mechanic's hand tools and gauges. Adjust carburetor mixtures, electrical point settings, and timing while motors are running in water-filled test tanks. Repair or rework parts, using machine tools such as lathes, mills, drills, and grinders. Idle motors and observe thermometers to determine the effectiveness of cooling systems.

GOE Information—Interest Area: 13. Manufacturing. **Work Group:** 13.14. Vehicle and Facility Mechanical Work. **Personality Type—** Realistic. Realistic occupations frequently involve work activities that include practical, hands-on problems and solutions. They often deal with plants; animals; and real-world materials like wood, tools, and machinery. Many of the occupations require working outside and do not involve a lot of paperwork or working closely with others. **Work Values—**Moral Values; Variety; Compensation; Security; Independence; Company Policies and Practices. **Skills—**Repairing; Quality Control Analysis; Installation; Equipment Maintenance; Troubleshooting; Operation Monitoring. **Abilities—***Cognitive:* None met the criteria. *Psychomotor:* Wrist-Finger Speed; Control Precision; Multilimb Coordination; Manual Dexterity; Arm-Hand Steadiness. *Physical:* Static Strength; Extent Flexibility; Trunk Strength. *Sensory:* Hearing Sensitivity. **General Work Activities—***Information Input:* Inspecting Equipment, Structures, or Materials; Monitoring Processes, Materials, or Surroundings; Getting Information. *Mental Process:* Updating and Using Relevant Knowledge; Making Decisions and Solving Problems; Judging the Qualities of Things, Services, or Other People's Work. *Work Output:* Repairing and Maintaining Mechanical Equipment; Performing General Physical Activities; Handling and Moving Objects. *Interacting with Others:* None met the criteria. **Physical Work Conditions—**More Often Indoors Than Outdoors; Standing; Using Hands on Objects, Tools, or Controls. **Other Job Characteristics—**Need to Be Exact or Accurate.

Experience—Job Zone 3. Previous work-related skill, knowledge, or experience is required. **Job Preparation—**SVP 6.0 to less than 7.0— more than one year and less than four years. **Knowledges—** Mechanical Devices; Engineering and Technology. **Instructional Programs—**Marine Maintenance/Fitter and Ship Repair Technology; Small Engine Mechanics and Repair Technology.

Related SOC Job—49-3051 Motorboat Mechanics. **Related OOH Job—** Small Engine Mechanics. **Related DOT Jobs—**623.261-010 Experimental Mechanic, Outboard Motors; 623.261-014 Outboard-Motor Tester; 623.281-038 Motorboat Mechanic; 623.281-042 Outboard-Motor Mechanic.

49-3052.00 Motorcycle Mechanics

- **Education/Training Required: Long-term on-the-job training**
- **Employed: 16,140**
- **Annual Earnings: $29,450**
- **Growth: 13.7%**
- **Annual Job Openings: 6,000**

Diagnose, adjust, repair, or overhaul motorcycles, scooters, mopeds, dirt bikes, or similar motorized vehicles.

Repair and adjust motorcycle subassemblies such as forks, transmissions, brakes, and drive chains according to specifications. Replace defective parts, using hand tools, arbor presses, flexible power presses, or power tools. Connect test panels to engines and measure generator output, ignition timing, and other engine performance indicators. Listen to engines, examine vehicle frames, and confer with customers to determine nature and extent of malfunction or damage. Reassemble and test subassembly units. Dismantle engines and repair or replace defective parts, such as magnetos, carburetors, and generators. Remove cylinder heads; grind valves; scrape off carbon; and replace defective valves, pistons, cylinders, and rings, using hand tools and power tools. Repair or replace other parts, such as headlights, horns, handlebar controls, gasoline and oil tanks, starters, and mufflers. Disassemble subassembly units and examine condition, movement, or alignment of parts visually or by using gauges. Hammer out dents and bends in frames, weld tears and breaks, and reassemble frames and reinstall engines.

GOE Information—Interest Area: 13. Manufacturing. **Work Group:** 13.14. Vehicle and Facility Mechanical Work. **Personality Type—** Realistic. Realistic occupations frequently involve work activities that include practical, hands-on problems and solutions. They often deal with plants; animals; and real-world materials like wood, tools, and machinery. Many of the occupations require working outside and do not involve a lot of paperwork or working closely with others. **Work Values—**Independence; Variety; Compensation; Responsibility. **Skills—**Repairing; Installation; Troubleshooting; Equipment Maintenance; Technology Design; Science. **Abilities—** *Cognitive:* Visualization; Selective Attention; Time Sharing; Deductive Reasoning; Fluency of Ideas. *Psychomotor:* Manual Dexterity; Response Orientation; Multilimb Coordination; Arm-Hand Steadiness; Control Precision; Finger Dexterity. *Physical:* Extent Flexibility; Static Strength; Trunk Strength. *Sensory:* Hearing Sensitivity; Auditory Attention; Depth Perception. **General Work Activities—***Information Input:* Monitoring Processes, Materials, or Surroundings; Inspecting Equipment, Structures, or Materials; Identifying Objects, Actions, and Events. *Mental Process:* Updating and Using Relevant Knowledge; Judging the Qualities of Things, Services, or Other People's Work; Making Decisions and Solving Problems. *Work Output:* Handling and Moving Objects; Controlling Machines and Processes; Repairing and Maintaining Mechanical Equipment. *Interacting with Others:* Establishing and Maintaining Interpersonal Relationships; Performing for or Working with the Public; Communicating with Persons Outside Organization. **Physical Work Conditions—**Indoors; Noisy; Contaminants; Standing; Using Hands on Objects, Tools, or Controls; Bending or Twisting the Body. **Other Job Characteristics—**Errors Have Important Consequences; Need to Be Exact or Accurate.

Experience—Job Zone 3. Previous work-related skill, knowledge, or experience is required. **Job Preparation—**SVP 6.0 to less than 7.0— more than one year and less than four years. **Knowledges—** Mechanical Devices; Design; Engineering and Technology; Physics;

Transportation; Sales and Marketing. **Instructional Program—** Motorcycle Maintenance and Repair Technology/Technician.

Related SOC Job—49-3052 Motorcycle Mechanics. **Related OOH Job—**Small Engine Mechanics. **Related DOT Jobs—**620.281-054 Motorcycle Repairer; 620.684-026 Motorcycle Subassembly Repairer; 807.381-018 Frame Repairer; 807.484-010 Frame Straightener.

49-3053.00 Outdoor Power Equipment and Other Small Engine Mechanics

- **Education/Training Required: Moderate-term on-the-job training**
- **Employed: 24,680**
- **Annual Earnings: $25,810**
- **Growth: 14.0%**
- **Annual Job Openings: 10,000**

Diagnose, adjust, repair, or overhaul small engines used to power lawn mowers, chain saws, and related equipment.

Sell parts and equipment. Show customers how to maintain equipment. Record repairs made, time spent, and parts used. Grind, ream, rebore, and retap parts to obtain specified clearances, using grinders, lathes, taps, reamers, boring machines, and micrometers. Test and inspect engines to determine malfunctions, to locate missing and broken parts, and to verify repairs, using diagnostic instruments. Replace motors. Repair or replace defective parts such as magnetos, water pumps, gears, pistons, and carburetors, using hand tools. Remove engines from equipment and position and bolt engines to repair stands. Perform routine maintenance such as cleaning and oiling parts, honing cylinders, and tuning ignition systems. Obtain problem descriptions from customers and prepare cost estimates for repairs. Dismantle engines, using hand tools, and examine parts for defects. Adjust points, valves, carburetors, distributors, and spark plug gaps, using feeler gauges. Repair and maintain gasoline engines used to power equipment such as portable saws, lawn mowers, generators, and compressors. Reassemble engines after repair or maintenance work is complete.

GOE Information—Interest Area: 13. Manufacturing. **Work Group:** 13.14. Vehicle and Facility Mechanical Work. **Personality Type—** Realistic. Realistic occupations frequently involve work activities that include practical, hands-on problems and solutions. They often deal with plants; animals; and real-world materials like wood, tools, and machinery. Many of the occupations require working outside and do not involve a lot of paperwork or working closely with others. **Work Values—**Moral Values; Company Policies and Practices; Compensation; Independence; Variety; Security. **Skills—**Repairing; Equipment Maintenance; Troubleshooting; Installation; Quality Control Analysis; Operation and Control. **Abilities—***Cognitive:* Visualization. *Psychomotor:* Wrist-Finger Speed; Control Precision; Multilimb Coordination; Finger Dexterity; Manual Dexterity; Arm-Hand Steadiness. *Physical:* Extent Flexibility; Explosive Strength; Static Strength; Trunk Strength. *Sensory:* Hearing Sensitivity. **General Work Activities—***Information Input:* Getting Information; Monitoring Processes, Materials, or Surroundings; Inspecting Equipment, Structures, or Materials. *Mental Process:* Updating and Using Relevant Knowledge; Evaluating Information Against Standards; Analyzing Data or Information. *Work Output:* Repairing and Maintaining Mechanical Equipment; Handling and Moving Objects; Performing General Physical Activities. *Interacting with Others:* None met the criteria. **Physical Work Conditions—**Indoors; Contaminants; Hazardous Equipment; Standing; Kneeling,

Crouching, Stooping, or Crawling; Using Hands on Objects, Tools, or Controls. **Other Job Characteristics—**None met the criteria.

Experience—Job Zone 3. Previous work-related skill, knowledge, or experience is required. **Job Preparation—**SVP 6.0 to less than 7.0— more than one year and less than four years. **Knowledges—** Mechanical Devices; Engineering and Technology. **Instructional Program—**Small Engine Mechanics and Repair Technology.

Related SOC Job—49-3053 Outdoor Power Equipment and Other Small Engine Mechanics. **Related OOH Job—**Small Engine Mechanics. **Related DOT Jobs—**625.281-018 Engine Repairer, Service; 625.281-026 Gas-Engine Repairer; 625.281-030 Power-Saw Mechanic; 625.281-034 Small-Engine Mechanic; 625.381-010 Engine Repairer, Production; 721.281-022 Magneto Repairer.

49-3091.00 Bicycle Repairers

- **Education/Training Required: Moderate-term on-the-job training**
- **Employed: 7,980**
- **Annual Earnings: $20,910**
- **Growth: 14.3%**
- **Annual Job Openings: 2,000**

Repair and service bicycles.

Install and adjust speed and gear mechanisms. Assemble new bicycles. Install, repair, and replace equipment or accessories, such as handlebars, stands, lights, and seats. Align wheels. Disassemble axles to repair, adjust, and replace defective parts, using hand tools. Shape replacement parts, using bench grinders. Repair holes in tire tubes, using scrapers and patches. Weld broken or cracked frames together, using oxyacetylene torches and welding rods. Paint bicycle frames, using spray guns or brushes.

GOE Information—Interest Area: 13. Manufacturing. **Work Group:** 13.13. Machinery Repair. **Personality Type—**Realistic. Realistic occupations frequently involve work activities that include practical, hands-on problems and solutions. They often deal with plants; animals; and real-world materials like wood, tools, and machinery. Many of the occupations require working outside and do not involve a lot of paperwork or working closely with others. **Work Values—** Independence; Moral Values; Social Service; Responsibility; Creativity. **Skills—**Repairing; Installation; Equipment Maintenance; Operations Analysis; Troubleshooting; Management of Material Resources. **Abilities—***Cognitive:* Visualization. *Psychomotor:* Manual Dexterity; Arm-Hand Steadiness; Finger Dexterity; Control Precision; Wrist-Finger Speed; Multilimb Coordination. *Physical:* Extent Flexibility; Static Strength; Trunk Strength. *Sensory:* Depth Perception; Auditory Attention; Speech Recognition. **General Work Activities—***Information Input:* Getting Information; Inspecting Equipment, Structures, or Materials; Monitoring Processes, Materials, or Surroundings. *Mental Process:* Thinking Creatively; Updating and Using Relevant Knowledge; Organizing, Planning, and Prioritizing. *Work Output:* Repairing and Maintaining Mechanical Equipment; Handling and Moving Objects; Controlling Machines and Processes. *Interacting with Others:* Performing for or Working with the Public; Influencing Others or Selling; Establishing and Maintaining Interpersonal Relationships. **Physical Work Conditions—**Indoors; Noisy; Contaminants; Minor Burns, Cuts, Bites, or Stings; Standing; Using Hands on Objects, Tools, or Controls. **Other Job Characteristics—**Need to Be Exact or Accurate; Repeat Same Tasks; Errors Have Important Consequences.

Experience—Job Zone 2. Some previous work-related skill, knowledge, or experience may be helpful in these occupations, but usually is not needed. **Job Preparation**—SVP 4.0 to less than 6.0—six months to less than two years. **Knowledges**—Mechanical Devices; Design; Building and Construction; Sales and Marketing; Engineering and Technology; Customer and Personal Service. **Instructional Program**—Bicycle Mechanics and Repair.

Related SOC Job—49-3091 Bicycle Repairers. **Related OOH Job**—Bicycle Repairers. **Related DOT Job**—639.681-010 Bicycle Repairer.

49-3092.00 Recreational Vehicle Service Technicians

- **Education/Training Required: Long-term on-the-job training**
- **Employed: 13,540**
- **Annual Earnings: $30,480**
- **Growth: 19.5%**
- **Annual Job Openings: 3,000**

Diagnose, inspect, adjust, repair, or overhaul recreational vehicles, including travel trailers. May specialize in maintaining gas, electrical, hydraulic, plumbing, or chassis/towing systems as well as repairing generators, appliances, and interior components.

Examine or test operation of parts or systems that have been repaired to ensure completeness of repairs. Repair plumbing and propane gas lines, using caulking compounds and plastic or copper pipe. Inspect recreational vehicles to diagnose problems; then perform necessary adjustment, repair, or overhaul. Locate and repair frayed wiring, broken connections, or incorrect wiring, using ohmmeters, soldering irons, tape, and hand tools. Confer with customers, read work orders, and examine vehicles needing repair to determine the nature and extent of damage. List parts needed, estimate costs, and plan work procedures, using parts lists, technical manuals, and diagrams. Connect electrical systems to outside power sources and activate switches to test the operation of appliances and light fixtures. Connect water hoses to inlet pipes of plumbing systems and test operation of toilets and sinks. Remove damaged exterior panels and repair and replace structural frame members. Open and close doors, windows, and drawers to test their operation, trimming edges to fit as necessary. Repair leaks with caulking compound or replace pipes, using pipe wrenches. Refinish wood surfaces on cabinets, doors, moldings, and floors, using power sanders, putty, spray equipment, brushes, paints, or varnishes. Reset hardware, using chisels, mallets, and screwdrivers. Seal open sides of modular units to prepare them for shipment, using polyethylene sheets, nails, and hammers.

GOE Information—Interest Area: 13. Manufacturing. **Work Group:** 13.14. Vehicle and Facility Mechanical Work. **Personality Type**—Realistic. Realistic occupations frequently involve work activities that include practical, hands-on problems and solutions. They often deal with plants; animals; and real-world materials like wood, tools, and machinery. Many of the occupations require working outside and do not involve a lot of paperwork or working closely with others. **Work Values**—Supervision, Technical; Moral Values; Variety. **Skills**—Repairing; Installation; Troubleshooting; Equipment Maintenance; Operation Monitoring; Technology Design. **Abilities**—*Cognitive:* Visualization; Perceptual Speed; Flexibility of Closure; Speed of Closure; Selective Attention; Time Sharing. *Psychomotor:* Manual Dexterity; Control Precision; Response Orientation; Multilimb Coordination; Rate Control; Finger Dexterity. *Physical:* Extent Flexibility; Gross Body Equilibrium; Static Strength; Stamina; Trunk Strength. *Sensory:* Hearing Sensitivity; Visual Color Discrimination; Depth Perception; Auditory Attention; Far Vision;

Near Vision. **General Work Activities**—*Information Input:* Monitoring Processes, Materials, or Surroundings; Getting Information; Inspecting Equipment, Structures, or Materials. *Mental Process:* Updating and Using Relevant Knowledge; Organizing, Planning, and Prioritizing; Making Decisions and Solving Problems. *Work Output:* Handling and Moving Objects; Performing General Physical Activities; Repairing and Maintaining Electronic Equipment. *Interacting with Others:* Establishing and Maintaining Interpersonal Relationships; Performing for or Working with the Public; Communicating with Other Workers. **Physical Work Conditions**—Noisy; Contaminants; Cramped Work Space, Awkward Positions; Hazardous Equipment; Standing; Using Hands on Objects, Tools, or Controls. **Other Job Characteristics**—Need to Be Exact or Accurate; Errors Have Important Consequences.

Experience—Job Zone 2. Some previous work-related skill, knowledge, or experience may be helpful in these occupations, but usually is not needed. **Job Preparation**—SVP 4.0 to less than 6.0—six months to less than two years. **Knowledges**—Mechanical Devices; Building and Construction; Chemistry; Physics; Design; Engineering and Technology. **Instructional Program**—Vehicle Maintenance and Repair Technologies, Other.

Related SOC Job—49-3092 Recreational Vehicle Service Technicians. **Related OOH Job**—Recreational Vehicle Service Technicians. **Related DOT Jobs**—806.381-070 Custom Van Converter; 869.261-022 Repairer, Recreational Vehicle.

49-3093.00 Tire Repairers and Changers

- **Education/Training Required: Short-term on-the-job training**
- **Employed: 100,860**
- **Annual Earnings: $20,960**
- **Growth: 4.5%**
- **Annual Job Openings: 17,000**

Repair and replace tires.

Identify and inflate tires correctly for the size and ply. Place wheels on balancing machines to determine counterweights required to balance wheels. Raise vehicles, using hydraulic jacks. Remount wheels onto vehicles. Locate punctures in tubeless tires by visual inspection or by immersing inflated tires in water baths and observing air bubbles. Unbolt wheels from vehicles and remove them, using lug wrenches and other hand and power tools. Reassemble tires onto wheels. Replace valve stems and remove puncturing objects. Hammer required counterweights onto rims of wheels. Rotate tires to different positions on vehicles, using hand tools. Inspect tire casings for defects, such as holes and tears. Seal punctures in tubeless tires by inserting adhesive material and expanding rubber plugs into punctures, using hand tools. Glue boots (tire patches) over ruptures in tire casings, using rubber cement. Assist mechanics and perform other duties as directed. Separate tubed tires from wheels, using rubber mallets and metal bars or mechanical tire changers. Patch tubes with adhesive rubber patches or seal rubber patches to tubes by using hot vulcanizing plates. Inflate innertubes and immerse them in water to locate leaks. Clean sides of whitewall tires. Apply rubber cement to buffed tire casings prior to vulcanization process. Drive automobile or service trucks to industrial sites to provide services and respond to emergency calls. Prepare rims and wheel drums for reassembly by scraping, grinding, or sandblasting. Order replacements for tires and tubes. Roll new rubber treads, known as camelbacks, over tire casings and mold the semi-raw rubber treads onto the buffed casings. Buff defective areas of innertubes, using scrapers. Place casing-camelback assemblies in tire molds for the vulcanization process and exert pressure on the camelbacks to ensure good adhesion.

GOE Information—Interest Area: 13. Manufacturing. Work Group: 13.14. Vehicle and Facility Mechanical Work. Personality Type—Realistic. Realistic occupations frequently involve work activities that include practical, hands-on problems and solutions. They often deal with plants; animals; and real-world materials like wood, tools, and machinery. Many of the occupations require working outside and do not involve a lot of paperwork or working closely with others. Work Values—Moral Values; Independence; Supervision, Technical; Security. Skills—Repairing; Installation; Equipment Maintenance; Troubleshooting; Management of Material Resources; Management of Personnel Resources. Abilities—*Cognitive:* None met the criteria. *Psychomotor:* Reaction Time; Rate Control; Response Orientation; Multilimb Coordination; Speed of Limb Movement; Manual Dexterity. *Physical:* Static Strength; Extent Flexibility; Trunk Strength; Dynamic Strength; Stamina; Gross Body Coordination. *Sensory:* Hearing Sensitivity; Depth Perception; Auditory Attention. General Work Activities—*Information Input:* Getting Information; Monitoring Processes, Materials, or Surroundings; Inspecting Equipment, Structures, or Materials. *Mental Process:* Making Decisions and Solving Problems; Updating and Using Relevant Knowledge; Judging the Qualities of Things, Services, or Other People's Work. *Work Output:* Handling and Moving Objects; Performing General Physical Activities; Controlling Machines and Processes. *Interacting with Others:* Communicating with Other Workers; Establishing and Maintaining Interpersonal Relationships; Performing for or Working with the Public. Physical Work Conditions—Noisy; Contaminants; Standing; Walking and Running; Using Hands on Objects, Tools, or Controls; Repetitive Motions. Other Job Characteristics—Need to Be Exact or Accurate; Repeat Same Tasks; Pace Determined by Speed of Equipment; Errors Have Important Consequences.

Experience—Job Zone 1. No previous work-related skill, knowledge, or experience is needed. Job Preparation—SVP below 4.0—less than six months. Knowledges—Mechanical Devices; Transportation; Sales and Marketing; Engineering and Technology. Instructional Program—No related CIP programs.

Related SOC Job—49-3093 Tire Repairers and Changers. Related OOH Job—Tire Repairers and Changers. Related DOT Jobs—750.681-010 Tire Repairer; 915.684-010 Tire Repairer.

49-9000 Other Installation, Maintenance, and Repair Occupations

49-9011.00 Mechanical Door Repairers

- Education/Training Required: Moderate-term on-the-job training
- Employed: 14,400
- Annual Earnings: $30,310
- Growth: 15.8%
- Annual Job Openings: 1,000

Install, service, or repair opening and closing mechanisms of automatic doors and hydraulic door closers. Includes garage door mechanics.

Adjust doors to open or close with the correct amount of effort and make simple adjustments to electric openers. Wind large springs with upward motion of arm. Inspect job sites, assessing headroom, side room, and other conditions to determine appropriateness of door for

a given location. Collect payment upon job completion. Complete required paperwork, such as work orders, according to services performed or required. Fasten angle iron back-hangers to ceilings and tracks, using fasteners or welding equipment. Repair or replace worn or broken door parts, using hand tools. Carry springs to tops of doors, using ladders or scaffolding, and attach springs to tracks in order to install spring systems. Set doors into place or stack hardware sections into openings after rail or track installation. Remove or disassemble defective automatic mechanical door closers, using hand tools. Install door frames, rails, steel rolling curtains, electronic-eye mechanisms, and electric door openers and closers, using power tools, hand tools, and electronic test equipment. Apply hardware to door sections, such as drilling holes to install locks. Assemble and fasten tracks to structures or bucks, using impact wrenches or welding equipment. Run low-voltage wiring on ceiling surfaces, using insulated staples. Cut door stops and angle irons to fit openings. Study blueprints and schematic diagrams to determine appropriate methods of installing and repairing automated door openers. Operate lifts, winches, or chain falls to move heavy curtain doors. Order replacement springs, sections, and slats. Bore and cut holes in flooring as required for installation, using hand tools and power tools. Set in and secure floor treadles for door-activating mechanisms; then connect power packs and electrical panelboards to treadles. Lubricate door closer oil chambers and pack spindles with leather washers. Install dock seals, bumpers, and shelters. Fabricate replacements for worn or broken parts, using welders, lathes, drill presses, and shaping and milling machines. Clean door closer parts, using caustic soda, rotary brushes, and grinding wheels.

GOE Information—Interest Area: 13. Manufacturing. Work Group: 13.13. Machinery Repair. Personality Type—Realistic. Realistic occupations frequently involve work activities that include practical, hands-on problems and solutions. They often deal with plants; animals; and real-world materials like wood, tools, and machinery. Many of the occupations require working outside and do not involve a lot of paperwork or working closely with others. Work Values—Independence; Moral Values; Supervision, Technical. Skills—Installation; Repairing; Troubleshooting; Equipment Maintenance; Equipment Selection; Time Management. Abilities—*Cognitive:* Spatial Orientation; Visualization; Speed of Closure; Perceptual Speed; Number Facility. *Psychomotor:* Reaction Time; Speed of Limb Movement; Manual Dexterity; Multilimb Coordination; Arm-Hand Steadiness; Control Precision. *Physical:* Extent Flexibility; Gross Body Equilibrium; Static Strength; Dynamic Strength; Gross Body Coordination; Trunk Strength. *Sensory:* Depth Perception; Visual Color Discrimination; Hearing Sensitivity; Far Vision. General Work Activities—*Information Input:* Monitoring Processes, Materials, or Surroundings; Inspecting Equipment, Structures, or Materials; Getting Information. *Mental Process:* Making Decisions and Solving Problems; Updating and Using Relevant Knowledge; Judging the Qualities of Things, Services, or Other People's Work. *Work Output:* Handling and Moving Objects; Performing General Physical Activities; Repairing and Maintaining Electronic Equipment. *Interacting with Others:* Performing for or Working with the Public; Establishing and Maintaining Interpersonal Relationships; Communicating with Other Workers. Physical Work Conditions—Outdoors; Very Hot or Cold; Hazardous Equipment; Standing; Climbing Ladders, Scaffolds, or Poles; Using Hands on Objects, Tools, or Controls. Other Job Characteristics—Need to Be Exact or Accurate; Repeat Same Tasks.

Experience—Job Zone 2. Some previous work-related skill, knowledge, or experience may be helpful in these occupations, but usually is not needed. Job Preparation—SVP 4.0 to less than 6.0—six months to less than two years. Knowledges—Building and Construction;

Mechanical Devices; Engineering and Technology; Sales and Marketing; Design. **Instructional Program**—No related CIP programs.

Related SOC Job—49-9011 Mechanical Door Repairers. **Related OOH Job**—Mechanical Door Repairers. **Related DOT Jobs**—630.381-014 Door-Closer Mechanic; 829.281-010 Automatic-Door Mechanic; 869.381-038 Overhead Door Installer.

49-9012.00 Control and Valve Installers and Repairers, Except Mechanical Door

- **Education/Training Required: Moderate-term on-the-job training**
- **Employed: 38,640**
- **Annual Earnings: $44,120**
- **Growth: 4.9%**
- **Annual Job Openings: 4,000**

Install, repair, and maintain mechanical regulating and controlling devices, such as electric meters, gas regulators, thermostats, safety and flow valves, and other mechanical governors.

Turn meters on or off to establish or close service. Turn valves to allow measured amounts of air or gas to pass through meters at specified flow rates. Report hazardous field situations and damaged or missing meters. Record meter readings and installation data on meter cards, work orders, or field service orders or enter data into handheld computers. Connect regulators to test stands and turn screw adjustments until gauges indicate that inlet and outlet pressures meet specifications. Disassemble and repair mechanical control devices or valves, such as regulators, thermostats, or hydrants, using power tools, hand tools, and cutting torches. Record maintenance information, including test results, material usage, and repairs made. Disconnect and/or remove defective or unauthorized meters, using hand tools. Lubricate wearing surfaces of mechanical parts, using oils or other lubricants. Test valves and regulators for leaks and accurate temperature and pressure settings, using precision testing equipment. Install regulators and related equipment such as gas meters, odorization units, and gas pressure telemetering equipment. Shut off service and notify repair crews when major repairs are required, such as the replacement of underground pipes or wiring. Examine valves or mechanical control device parts for defects, dents, or loose attachments and mark malfunctioning areas of defective units. Attach air hoses to meter inlets; then plug outlets and observe gauges for pressure losses to test internal seams for leaks. Dismantle meters and replace or adjust defective parts such as cases, shafts, gears, disks, and recording mechanisms, using soldering irons and hand tools. Advise customers on proper installation of valves or regulators and related equipment. Connect hoses from provers to meter inlets and outlets and raise prover bells until prover gauges register zero. Make adjustments to meter components, such as setscrews or timing mechanisms, so that they conform to specifications. Replace defective parts, such as bellows, range springs, and toggle switches, and reassemble units according to blueprints, using cam presses and hand tools.

GOE Information—**Interest Area:** 13. Manufacturing. **Work Group:** 13.13. Machinery Repair. **Personality Type**—Realistic. Realistic occupations frequently involve work activities that include practical, hands-on problems and solutions. They often deal with plants; animals; and real-world materials like wood, tools, and machinery. Many of the occupations require working outside and do not involve a lot of paperwork or working closely with others. **Work Values**—Independence; Moral Values; Supervision, Technical; Security;

Supervision, Human Relations. **Skills**—Installation; Repairing; Equipment Maintenance; Operation Monitoring; Troubleshooting; Quality Control Analysis. **Abilities**—*Cognitive:* Perceptual Speed; Visualization; Time Sharing; Selective Attention. *Psychomotor:* Multilimb Coordination; Manual Dexterity; Arm-Hand Steadiness; Reaction Time; Control Precision; Finger Dexterity. *Physical:* Extent Flexibility; Gross Body Equilibrium; Stamina; Trunk Strength. *Sensory:* Glare Sensitivity; Depth Perception; Visual Color Discrimination; Hearing Sensitivity; Auditory Attention; Far Vision. **General Work Activities**—*Information Input:* Inspecting Equipment, Structures, or Materials; Monitoring Processes, Materials, or Surroundings; Identifying Objects, Actions, and Events. *Mental Process:* Updating and Using Relevant Knowledge; Making Decisions and Solving Problems; Scheduling Work and Activities. *Work Output:* Handling and Moving Objects; Performing General Physical Activities; Repairing and Maintaining Mechanical Equipment. *Interacting with Others:* Communicating with Other Workers; Performing for or Working with the Public; Communicating with Persons Outside Organization. **Physical Work Conditions**—Outdoors; Very Hot or Cold; Very Bright or Dim Lighting; Contaminants; Cramped Work Space, Awkward Positions; Hazardous Conditions. **Other Job Characteristics**—Need to Be Exact or Accurate; Repeat Same Tasks; Errors Have Important Consequences.

Experience—Job Zone 3. Previous work-related skill, knowledge, or experience is required. **Job Preparation**—SVP 6.0 to less than 7.0—more than one year and less than four years. **Knowledges**—Mechanical Devices; Transportation; Public Safety and Security; Physics; Design; Chemistry. **Instructional Program**—No related CIP programs.

Related SOC Job—49-9012 Control and Valve Installers and Repairers, Except Mechanical Door. **Related OOH Job**—Control and Valve Installers and Repairers, Except Mechanical Door. **Related DOT Jobs**—622.381-010 Air-Valve Repairer; 630.381-030 Valve Repairer; 637.261-022 Industrial-Gas Servicer; 709.684-070 Salvager; 710.281-022 Gas-Meter Prover; 710.281-034 Meter Repairer; 710.381-022 Gas-Meter Mechanic I; 710.381-026 Gas-Regulator Repairer; 710.381-050 Thermostat Repairer; 710.684-026 Gas-Meter Mechanic II; 729.281-014 Electric-Meter Repairer; 729.281-018 Electric-Meter-Repairer Apprentice; 729.281-034 Inside-Meter Tester; 821.361-014 Electric-Meter Installer I; others.

49-9021.00 Heating, Air Conditioning, and Refrigeration Mechanics and Installers

- **Education/Training Required: Long-term on-the-job training**
- **Employed: 241,380**
- **Annual Earnings: $37,040**
- **Growth: 19.0%**
- **Annual Job Openings: 33,000**

The job openings listed here are shared with 49-9021.01 Heating and Air Conditioning Mechanics and Installers and 49-9021.02 Refrigeration Mechanics and Installers.

Install or repair heating, central air conditioning, or refrigeration systems, including oil burners, hot-air furnaces, and heating stoves.

No task data available.

Note: The Department of Labor has not collected some data for this job, so it has fewer details than the other descriptions.

Instructional Programs—Heating, Air Conditioning and Refrigeration Technology/Technician (ACH/ACR/ACHR/HRAC/HVAC/AC Technology; Heating, Air Conditioning, Ventilation, and Refrigeration Maintenance Technology/Technician (HAC); Solar Energy Technology/Technician.

Related SOC Job—49-9021 Heating, Air Conditioning, and Refrigeration Mechanics and Installers. **Related OOH Job**—Heating, Air-Conditioning, and Refrigeration Mechanics and Installers. **Related DOT Job**—No data available.

49-9021.01 Heating and Air Conditioning Mechanics and Installers

- **Education/Training Required: Long-term on-the-job training**
- **Employed: 241,380**
- **Annual Earnings: $37,040**
- **Growth: 19.0%**
- **Annual Job Openings: 33,000**

The job openings listed here are shared with 49-9021.00 Heating, Air Conditioning, and Refrigeration Mechanics and Installers and 49-9021.02 Refrigeration Mechanics and Installers.

Install, service, and repair heating and air conditioning systems in residences and commercial establishments.

Obtain and maintain required certifications. Comply with all applicable standards, policies, and procedures, including safety procedures and the maintenance of a clean work area. Repair or replace defective equipment, components, or wiring. Test electrical circuits and components for continuity, using electrical test equipment. Reassemble and test equipment following repairs. Inspect and test system to verify system compliance with plans and specifications and to detect and locate malfunctions. Discuss heating-cooling system malfunctions with users to isolate problems or to verify that malfunctions have been corrected. Test pipe or tubing joints and connections for leaks, using pressure gauge or soap-and-water solution. Record and report all faults, deficiencies, and other unusual occurrences, as well as the time and materials expended on work orders. Adjust system controls to setting recommended by manufacturer to balance system, using hand tools. Recommend, develop, and perform preventive and general maintenance procedures such as cleaning, power-washing, and vacuuming equipment; oiling parts; and changing filters. Lay out and connect electrical wiring between controls and equipment according to wiring diagram, using electrician's hand tools. Install auxiliary components to heating-cooling equipment, such as expansion and discharge valves, air ducts, pipes, blowers, dampers, flues, and stokers, following blueprints. Assist with other work in coordination with repair and maintenance teams. Install, connect, and adjust thermostats, humidistats, and timers, using hand tools. Generate work orders that address deficiencies in need of correction. Join pipes or tubing to equipment and to fuel, water, or refrigerant source to form complete circuit. Assemble, position, and mount heating or cooling equipment, following blueprints. Study blueprints, design specifications, and manufacturers' recommendations to ascertain the configuration of heating or cooling equipment components and to ensure the proper installation of components. Cut and drill holes in floors, walls, and roof to install equipment, using power saws and drills.

GOE Information—**Interest Area:** 02. Architecture and Construction. **Work Group:** 02.05. Systems and Equipment Installation, Maintenance, and Repair. **Personality Type**—Realistic. Realistic occupations frequently involve work activities that include practical, hands-on problems and solutions. They often deal with plants; animals; and real-world materials like wood, tools, and machinery. Many of the occupations require working outside and do not involve a lot of paperwork or working closely with others. **Work Values**—Independence; Moral Values; Supervision, Technical; Variety; Responsibility; Compensation. **Skills**—Repairing; Installation; Equipment Maintenance; Troubleshooting; Systems Evaluation; Systems Analysis. **Abilities**—*Cognitive:* Visualization; Speed of Closure; Spatial Orientation; Time Sharing; Flexibility of Closure; Perceptual Speed. *Psychomotor:* Manual Dexterity; Reaction Time; Wrist-Finger Speed; Finger Dexterity; Control Precision; Speed of Limb Movement. *Physical:* Extent Flexibility; Gross Body Equilibrium; Stamina; Static Strength; Gross Body Coordination; Trunk Strength. *Sensory:* Hearing Sensitivity; Glare Sensitivity; Sound Localization; Visual Color Discrimination; Depth Perception; Auditory Attention. **General Work Activities**—*Information Input:* Getting Information; Inspecting Equipment, Structures, or Materials; Monitoring Processes, Materials, or Surroundings. *Mental Process:* Making Decisions and Solving Problems; Organizing, Planning, and Prioritizing; Thinking Creatively. *Work Output:* Handling and Moving Objects; Performing General Physical Activities; Repairing and Maintaining Mechanical Equipment. *Interacting with Others:* Establishing and Maintaining Interpersonal Relationships; Performing for or Working with the Public; Communicating with Persons Outside Organization. **Physical Work Conditions**—Outdoors; Very Hot or Cold; Contaminants; Hazardous Conditions; Minor Burns, Cuts, Bites, or Stings; Using Hands on Objects, Tools, or Controls. **Other Job Characteristics**—Errors Have Important Consequences; Need to Be Exact or Accurate.

Experience—Job Zone 3. Previous work-related skill, knowledge, or experience is required. **Job Preparation**—SVP 6.0 to less than 7.0—more than one year and less than four years. **Knowledges**—Mechanical Devices; Building and Construction; Design; Physics; Engineering and Technology; Sales and Marketing. **Instructional Programs**—Heating, Air Conditioning, and Refrigeration Technology/Technician; Heating, Air Conditioning, Ventilation, and Refrigeration Maintenance Technology/Technician; Solar Energy Technology/Technician.

Related SOC Job—49-9021 Heating, Air Conditioning, and Refrigeration Mechanics and Installers. **Related OOH Job**—Heating, Air-Conditioning, and Refrigeration Mechanics and Installers. **Related DOT Jobs**—637.261-014 Heating-and-Air-Conditioning Installer-Servicer; 637.261-030 Solar-Energy-System Installer; 637.261-034 Air and Hydronic Balancing Technician; 637.381-010 Evaporative-Cooler Installer; 862.281-018 Oil-Burner-Servicer-and-Installer; 862.361-010 Furnace Installer; 869.281-010 Furnace Installer-and-Repairer, Hot Air.

49-9021.02 Refrigeration Mechanics and Installers

- **Education/Training Required: Long-term on-the-job training**
- **Employed: 241,380**
- **Annual Earnings: $37,040**
- **Growth: 19.0%**
- **Annual Job Openings: 33,000**

The job openings listed here are shared with 49-9021.00 Heating, Air Conditioning, and Refrigeration Mechanics and Installers and 49-9021.01 Heating and Air Conditioning Mechanics and Installers.

Install and repair industrial and commercial refrigerating systems.

Braze or solder parts to repair defective joints and leaks. Observe and test system operation, using gauges and instruments. Test lines, components, and connections for leaks. Dismantle malfunctioning systems and test components, using electrical, mechanical, and pneumatic testing equipment. Adjust or replace worn or defective mechanisms and parts and reassemble repaired systems. Read blueprints to determine location, size, capacity, and type of components needed to build refrigeration system. Supervise and instruct assistants. Perform mechanical overhauls and refrigerant reclaiming. Install wiring to connect components to an electric power source. Cut, bend, thread, and connect pipe to functional components and water, power, or refrigeration system. Adjust valves according to specifications and charge system with proper type of refrigerant by pumping the specified gas or fluid into the system. Estimate, order, pick up, deliver, and install materials and supplies needed to maintain equipment in good working condition. Install expansion and control valves, using acetylene torches and wrenches. Mount compressor, condenser, and other components in specified locations on frames, using hand tools and acetylene welding equipment. Keep records of repairs and replacements made and causes of malfunctions. Schedule work with customers and initiate work orders, house requisitions, and orders from stock. Lay out reference points for installation of structural and functional components, using measuring instruments. Fabricate and assemble structural and functional components of refrigeration system, using hand tools, power tools, and welding equipment. Lift and align components into position, using hoist or block and tackle. Drill holes and install mounting brackets and hangers into floor and walls of building. Insulate shells and cabinets of systems.

GOE Information—Interest Area: 02. Architecture and Construction. **Work Group:** 02.05. Systems and Equipment Installation, Maintenance, and Repair. **Personality Type—**Realistic. Realistic occupations frequently involve work activities that include practical, hands-on problems and solutions. They often deal with plants; animals; and real-world materials like wood, tools, and machinery. Many of the occupations require working outside and do not involve a lot of paperwork or working closely with others. **Work Values—**Moral Values; Independence; Supervision, Technical; Variety; Compensation; Responsibility. **Skills—**Installation; Repairing; Equipment Maintenance; Operation Monitoring; Systems Evaluation; Systems Analysis. **Abilities—***Cognitive:* Visualization; Flexibility of Closure; Perceptual Speed; Information Ordering; Inductive Reasoning. *Psychomotor:* Manual Dexterity; Multilimb Coordination; Control Precision; Arm-Hand Steadiness; Finger Dexterity. *Physical:* Extent Flexibility; Gross Body Coordination; Static Strength; Trunk Strength. *Sensory:* Depth Perception; Visual Color Discrimination; Near Vision. **General Work Activities—***Information Input:* Monitoring Processes, Materials, or Surroundings; Identifying Objects, Actions, and Events; Inspecting Equipment, Structures, or Materials. *Mental Process:* Updating and Using Relevant Knowledge; Organizing, Planning, and Prioritizing; Making Decisions and Solving Problems. *Work Output:* Handling and Moving Objects; Repairing and Maintaining Mechanical Equipment; Performing General Physical Activities. *Interacting with Others:* Establishing and Maintaining Interpersonal Relationships; Coordinating the Work and Activities of Others; Communicating with Other Workers. **Physical Work Conditions—**Outdoors; Very Hot or Cold; Cramped Work Space, Awkward Positions; Minor Burns, Cuts, Bites, or Stings; Standing; Using Hands on Objects, Tools, or Controls. **Other Job Characteristics—**Need to Be Exact or Accurate; Errors Have Important Consequences; Repeat Same Tasks.

Experience—Job Zone 3. Previous work-related skill, knowledge, or experience is required. **Job Preparation—**SVP 6.0 to less than 7.0—more than one year and less than four years. **Knowledges—**Building

and Construction; Mechanical Devices; Engineering and Technology; Physics; Design; Chemistry. **Instructional Programs—**Heating, Air Conditioning, and Refrigeration Technology/Technician; Heating, Air Conditioning, Ventilation, and Refrigeration Maintenance Technology/Technician; Solar Energy Technology/Technician.

Related SOC Job—49-9021 Heating, Air Conditioning, and Refrigeration Mechanics and Installers. **Related OOH Job—**Heating, Air-Conditioning, and Refrigeration Mechanics and Installers. **Related DOT Jobs—**637.261-026 Refrigeration Mechanic; 637.381-014 Refrigeration Unit Repairer; 827.361-014 Refrigeration Mechanic.

49-9031.00 Home Appliance Repairers

- **Education/Training Required: Long-term on-the-job training**
- **Employed: 43,110**
- **Annual Earnings: $32,980**
- **Growth: 2.6%**
- **Annual Job Openings: 3,000**

Repair, adjust, or install all types of electric or gas household appliances, such as refrigerators, washers, dryers, and ovens.

Clean, lubricate, and touch up minor defects on newly installed or repaired appliances. Observe and test operation of appliances following installation and make any initial installation adjustments that are necessary. Level refrigerators, adjust doors, and connect water lines to water pipes for ice makers and water dispensers, using hand tools. Level washing machines and connect hoses to water pipes, using hand tools. Maintain stocks of parts used in on-site installation, maintenance, and repair of appliances. Instruct customers regarding operation and care of appliances and provide information such as emergency service numbers. Provide repair cost estimates and recommend whether appliance repair or replacement is a better choice. Conserve, recover, and recycle refrigerants used in cooling systems. Contact supervisors or offices to receive repair assignments. Install gas pipes and water lines to connect appliances to existing gas lines or plumbing. Record maintenance and repair work performed on appliances. Respond to emergency calls for problems such as gas leaks. Assemble new or reconditioned appliances. Disassemble and reinstall existing kitchen cabinets or assemble and install prefabricated kitchen cabinets and trim in conjunction with appliance installation. Hang steel supports from beams or joists to hold hoses, vents, and gas pipes in place. Install appliances such as refrigerators, washing machines, and stoves. Set appliance thermostats and check to ensure that they are functioning properly. Disassemble and reinstall existing kitchen cabinets or assemble and install prefabricated kitchen cabinets and trim in conjunction with appliance installation. Refer to schematic drawings, product manuals, and troubleshooting guides to diagnose and repair problems. Clean and reinstall parts. Disassemble appliances so that problems can be diagnosed and repairs can be made. Light and adjust pilot lights on gas stoves and examine valves and burners for gas leakage and specified flame. Test and examine gas pipelines and equipment to locate leaks and faulty connections and to determine the pressure and flow of gas. Take measurements to determine if appliances will fit in installation locations; perform minor carpentry work when necessary to ensure proper installation. Measure, cut, and thread pipe and connect it to feeder lines and equipment or appliances, using rules and hand tools. Reassemble units after repairs are made, making adjustments and cleaning and lubricating parts as needed.

GOE Information—Interest Area: 13. Manufacturing. **Work Group:** 13.13. Machinery Repair. **Personality Type—**Realistic. Realistic occupations frequently involve work activities that include practical, hands-on problems and solutions. They often deal with plants; animals; and real-world materials like wood, tools, and machinery. Many of the occupations require working outside and do not involve a lot of paperwork or working closely with others. **Work Values**—Moral Values; Independence; Supervision, Technical; Social Service; Variety. **Skills**—Installation; Repairing; Troubleshooting; Operation Monitoring; Equipment Maintenance. **Abilities**—*Cognitive:* Visualization. *Psychomotor:* Wrist-Finger Speed; Manual Dexterity. *Physical:* Static Strength; Extent Flexibility. *Sensory:* None met the criteria. **General Work Activities**—*Information Input:* Inspecting Equipment, Structures, or Materials; Monitoring Processes, Materials, or Surroundings; Getting Information. *Mental Process:* Updating and Using Relevant Knowledge; Evaluating Information Against Standards; Organizing, Planning, and Prioritizing. *Work Output:* Handling and Moving Objects; Performing General Physical Activities; Repairing and Maintaining Mechanical Equipment. *Interacting with Others:* Communicating with Persons Outside Organization; Performing for or Working with the Public. **Physical Work Conditions**—Indoors; Standing; Kneeling, Crouching, Stooping, or Crawling; Using Hands on Objects, Tools, or Controls. **Other Job Characteristics**—Need to Be Exact or Accurate.

Experience—Job Zone 3. Previous work-related skill, knowledge, or experience is required. **Job Preparation**—SVP 6.0 to less than 7.0—more than one year and less than four years. **Knowledges**—Mechanical Devices; Building and Construction; Engineering and Technology. **Instructional Programs**—Appliance Installation and Repair Technology/Technician; Electrical/Electronics Equipment Installation and Repair, General; Home Furnishings and Equipment Installers.

Related SOC Job—49-9031 Home Appliance Repairers. **Related OOH Job**—Home Appliance Repairers. **Related DOT Jobs**—637.261-010 Air-Conditioning Installer-Servicer, Window Unit; 637.261-018 Gas-Appliance Servicer; 723.381-010 Electrical-Appliance Repairer; 723.381-014 Vacuum Cleaner Repairer; 723.584-010 Appliance Repairer; 729.281-022 Electric-Tool Repairer; 827.261-010 Electrical-Appliance Servicer; 827.261-014 Electrical-Appliance-Servicer Apprentice; 827.661-010 Household-Appliance Installer; 959.361-010 Customer Service Representative.

49-9041.00 Industrial Machinery Mechanics

- **Education/Training Required: Long-term on-the-job training**
- **Employed: 234,650**
- **Annual Earnings: $39,740**
- **Growth: –0.2%**
- **Annual Job Openings: 13,000**

Repair, install, adjust, or maintain industrial production and processing machinery or refinery and pipeline distribution systems.

Disassemble machinery and equipment to remove parts and make repairs. Repair and replace broken or malfunctioning components of machinery and equipment. Examine parts for defects such as breakage and excessive wear. Repair and maintain the operating condition of industrial production and processing machinery and equipment. Reassemble equipment after completion of inspections, testing, or repairs. Observe and test the operation of machinery and equipment to diagnose malfunctions, using voltmeters and other testing devices. Operate newly repaired machinery and equipment to verify the adequacy of repairs. Clean, lubricate, and adjust parts, equip-

ment, and machinery. Analyze test results, machine error messages, and information obtained from operators to diagnose equipment problems. Record repairs and maintenance performed. Study blueprints and manufacturers' manuals to determine correct installation and operation of machinery. Record parts and materials used and order or requisition new parts and materials as necessary. Cut and weld metal to repair broken metal parts, fabricate new parts, and assemble new equipment. Demonstrate equipment functions and features to machine operators. Enter codes and instructions to program computer-controlled machinery.

GOE Information—**Interest Area:** 13. Manufacturing. **Work Group:** 13.13. Machinery Repair. **Personality Type**—Realistic. Realistic occupations frequently involve work activities that include practical, hands-on problems and solutions. They often deal with plants; animals; and real-world materials like wood, tools, and machinery. Many of the occupations require working outside and do not involve a lot of paperwork or working closely with others. **Work Values**—Moral Values; Independence; Variety; Supervision, Technical; Advancement; Activity. **Skills**—Repairing; Installation; Equipment Maintenance; Operation Monitoring; Troubleshooting; Technology Design. **Abilities**—*Cognitive:* Spatial Orientation; Visualization; Selective Attention; Perceptual Speed; Speed of Closure; Information Ordering. *Psychomotor:* Reaction Time; Rate Control; Response Orientation; Multilimb Coordination; Control Precision; Manual Dexterity. *Physical:* Extent Flexibility; Static Strength; Gross Body Equilibrium; Dynamic Strength; Gross Body Coordination; Trunk Strength. *Sensory:* Hearing Sensitivity; Auditory Attention; Glare Sensitivity; Visual Color Discrimination; Sound Localization; Depth Perception. **General Work Activities**—*Information Input:* Monitoring Processes, Materials, or Surroundings; Inspecting Equipment, Structures, or Materials; Getting Information. *Mental Process:* Updating and Using Relevant Knowledge; Organizing, Planning, and Prioritizing; Thinking Creatively. *Work Output:* Handling and Moving Objects; Performing General Physical Activities; Repairing and Maintaining Mechanical Equipment. *Interacting with Others:* Establishing and Maintaining Interpersonal Relationships; Communicating with Other Workers; Coordinating the Work and Activities of Others. **Physical Work Conditions**—Noisy; Contaminants; Hazardous Conditions; Hazardous Equipment; Standing; Using Hands on Objects, Tools, or Controls. **Other Job Characteristics**—Need to Be Exact or Accurate; Pace Determined by Speed of Equipment.

Experience—Job Zone 3. Previous work-related skill, knowledge, or experience is required. **Job Preparation**—SVP 6.0 to less than 7.0—more than one year and less than four years. **Knowledges**—Mechanical Devices; Engineering and Technology; Building and Construction; Design; Chemistry; Physics. **Instructional Programs**—Heavy/Industrial Equipment Maintenance Technologies; Industrial Mechanics and Maintenance Technology.

Related SOC Job—49-9041 Industrial Machinery Mechanics. **Related OOH Job**—Industrial Machinery Mechanics and Maintenance Workers. **Related DOT Jobs**—549.381-640 Cooling Tower Technician; 601.281-030 Tool and Fixture Repairer; 620.281-018 Automotive-Maintenance-Equipment Servicer; 626.261-010 Forge-Shop-Machine Repairer; 626.261-014 Repairer, Welding Systems and Equipment; 626.361-010 Repairer, Welding, Brazing, and Burning Machines; 626.381-010 Case-Finishing-Machine Adjuster; 626.381-014 Gas-Welding-Equipment Mechanic; 626.381-018 Hydraulic-Press Servicer; 626.384-010 Repairer, Welding Equipment; 627.261-010 Composing-Room Machinist; others.

49-9042.00 Maintenance and Repair Workers, General

- **Education/Training Required: Moderate-term on-the-job training**
- **Employed: 1,307,820**
- **Annual Earnings: $31,210**
- **Growth: 15.2%**
- **Annual Job Openings: 154,000**

Perform work involving the skills of two or more maintenance or craft occupations to keep machines, mechanical equipment, or the structure of an establishment in repair. Duties may involve pipe fitting; boiler making; insulating; welding; machining; carpentry; repairing electrical or mechanical equipment; installing, aligning, and balancing new equipment; and repairing buildings, floors, or stairs.

Repair or replace defective equipment parts, using hand tools and power tools, and reassemble equipment. Perform routine preventive maintenance to ensure that machines continue to run smoothly, building systems operate efficiently, and the physical condition of buildings does not deteriorate. Inspect drives, motors, and belts; check fluid levels; replace filters; and perform other maintenance actions, following checklists. Use tools ranging from common hand and power tools, such as hammers, hoists, saws, drills, and wrenches, to precision measuring instruments and electrical and electronic testing devices. Assemble, install, or repair wiring, electrical and electronic components, pipe systems and plumbing, machinery, and equipment. Diagnose mechanical problems and determine how to correct them, checking blueprints, repair manuals, and parts catalogs as necessary. Inspect, operate, and test machinery and equipment to diagnose machine malfunctions. Record maintenance and repair work performed and the costs of the work. Clean and lubricate shafts, bearings, gears, and other parts of machinery. Dismantle devices to gain access to and remove defective parts, using hoists, cranes, hand tools, and power tools. Plan and lay out repair work, using diagrams, drawings, blueprints, maintenance manuals, and schematic diagrams. Adjust functional parts of devices and control instruments, using hand tools, levels, plumb bobs, and straightedges. Order parts, supplies, and equipment from catalogs and suppliers or obtain them from storerooms. Paint and repair roofs, windows, doors, floors, woodwork, plaster, drywall, and other parts of building structures. Operate cutting torches or welding equipment to cut or join metal parts. Align and balance new equipment after installation. Inspect used parts to determine changes in dimensional requirements, using rules, calipers, micrometers, and other measuring instruments. Set up and operate machine tools to repair or fabricate machine parts, jigs and fixtures, and tools. Maintain and repair specialized equipment and machinery found in cafeterias, laundries, hospitals, stores, offices, and factories.

GOE Information—Interest Area: 02. Architecture and Construction. **Work Group:** 02.05. Systems and Equipment Installation, Maintenance, and Repair. **Personality Type**—Realistic. Realistic occupations frequently involve work activities that include practical, hands-on problems and solutions. They often deal with plants; animals; and real-world materials like wood, tools, and machinery. Many of the occupations require working outside and do not involve a lot of paperwork or working closely with others. **Work Values**—Moral Values; Variety; Independence; Supervision, Technical; Supervision, Human Relations; Company Policies and Practices. **Skills**—Equipment Maintenance; Installation; Repairing; Troubleshooting; Operation Monitoring; Operation and Control. **Abilities**—*Cognitive:* Visualization; Information Ordering; Flexibility of Closure; Inductive Reasoning; Speed of Closure; Selective Attention. *Psychomotor:* Multilimb Coordination; Manual Dexterity; Control Precision; Arm-Hand Steadiness; Reaction Time; Speed of Limb Movement. *Physical:* Extent Flexibility; Static Strength; Gross Body Equilibrium; Trunk Strength; Gross Body Coordination. *Sensory:* Visual Color Discrimination; Hearing Sensitivity; Depth Perception; Auditory Attention. **General Work Activities**—*Information Input:* Monitoring Processes, Materials, or Surroundings; Inspecting Equipment, Structures, or Materials; Identifying Objects, Actions, and Events. *Mental Process:* Updating and Using Relevant Knowledge; Organizing, Planning, and Prioritizing; Making Decisions and Solving Problems. *Work Output:* Handling and Moving Objects; Performing General Physical Activities; Repairing and Maintaining Mechanical Equipment. *Interacting with Others:* Establishing and Maintaining Interpersonal Relationships; Communicating with Other Workers; Coordinating the Work and Activities of Others. **Physical Work Conditions**—Indoors; Noisy; Minor Burns, Cuts, Bites, or Stings; Standing; Walking and Running; Using Hands on Objects, Tools, or Controls. **Other Job Characteristics**—Need to Be Exact or Accurate; Errors Have Important Consequences.

Experience—Job Zone 3. Previous work-related skill, knowledge, or experience is required. **Job Preparation**—SVP 6.0 to less than 7.0—more than one year and less than four years. **Knowledges**—Building and Construction; Mechanical Devices; Design; Physics; Engineering and Technology; Public Safety and Security. **Instructional Program**—Building/Construction Site Management/Manager.

Related SOC Job—49-9042 Maintenance and Repair Workers, General. **Related OOH Job**—Maintenance and Repair Workers, General. **Related DOT Jobs**—638.281-010 Fire-Fighting-Equipment Specialist; 806.261-026 Marine-Services Technician; 806.381-062 Installer, Electrical, Plumbing, Mechanical; 869.261-014 Mechanical-Test Technician; 899.261-014 Maintenance Repairer, Industrial; 899.381-010 Maintenance Repairer, Building; 899.484-010 Mobile-Home-Lot Utility Worker; 912.364-010 Airport Attendant.

49-9043.00 Maintenance Workers, Machinery

- **Education/Training Required: Short-term on-the-job training**
- **Employed: 83,220**
- **Annual Earnings: $33,650**
- **Growth: 2.8%**
- **Annual Job Openings: 6,000**

Lubricate machinery, change parts, or perform other routine machinery maintenance.

Reassemble machines after the completion of repair or maintenance work. Start machines and observe mechanical operation to determine efficiency and to detect problems. Inspect or test damaged machine parts and mark defective areas or advise supervisors of repair needs. Lubricate or apply adhesives or other materials to machines, machine parts, or other equipment according to specified procedures. Install, replace, or change machine parts and attachments according to production specifications. Dismantle machines and remove parts for repair, using hand tools, chain falls, jacks, cranes, or hoists. Record production, repair, and machine maintenance information. Read work orders and specifications to determine machines and equipment requiring repair or maintenance. Set up and operate machines and adjust controls to regulate operations. Collaborate with other workers to repair or move machines, machine parts, or equipment. Inventory and requisition machine parts, equipment, and other supplies so that stock can be maintained and replenished. Transport machine parts, tools, equipment, and other material between work areas and storage, using cranes, hoists, or dollies. Collect and discard worn machine parts and other refuse to maintain machinery and work areas. Clean machines and machine parts, using cleaning solvents, cloths, air guns, hoses, vacuums, or other equipment. Replace or repair metal, wood, leather, glass, or other lining in machines or in equipment compartments or containers. Remove hardened material from machines or machine parts, using abrasives, power and hand tools, jackhammers, sledgehammers, or other equipment. Measure, mix, prepare, and test chemical solutions used to clean or repair machinery and equipment. Replace, empty, or replenish machine and equipment containers such as gas tanks or boxes.

GOE Information—Interest Area: 13. Manufacturing. **Work Group:** 13.13. Machinery Repair. **Personality Type—Realistic.** Realistic occupations frequently involve work activities that include practical, hands-on problems and solutions. They often deal with plants; animals; and real-world materials like wood, tools, and machinery. Many of the occupations require working outside and do not involve a lot of paperwork or working closely with others. **Work Values—Variety;** Moral Values; Supervision, Human Relations; Supervision, Technical; Co-workers; Independence. **Skills—Installation;** Repairing; Equipment Maintenance; Troubleshooting; Operation Monitoring; Operation and Control. **Abilities—***Cognitive:* Perceptual Speed; Visualization; Flexibility of Closure; Selective Attention. *Psychomotor:* Rate Control; Reaction Time; Control Precision; Arm-Hand Steadiness; Response Orientation; Manual Dexterity. *Physical:* Extent Flexibility; Static Strength; Trunk Strength. *Sensory:* Depth Perception; Auditory Attention; Hearing Sensitivity; Visual Color Discrimination. **General Work Activities—***Information Input:* Monitoring Processes, Materials, or Surroundings; Inspecting Equipment, Structures, or Materials; Identifying Objects, Actions, and Events. *Mental Process:* Updating and Using Relevant Knowledge; Thinking Creatively; Organizing, Planning, and Prioritizing. *Work Output:* Handling and Moving Objects; Repairing and Maintaining Mechanical Equipment; Controlling Machines and Processes. *Interacting with Others:* Establishing and Maintaining Interpersonal Relationships; Communicating with Other Workers; Teaching Others. **Physical Work Conditions—**Noisy; Very Hot or Cold; Contaminants; Hazardous Equipment; Standing; Using Hands on Objects, Tools, or Controls. **Other Job Characteristics—**Need to Be Exact or Accurate; Pace Determined by Speed of Equipment; Errors Have Important Consequences.

Experience—Job Zone 2. Some previous work-related skill, knowledge, or experience may be helpful in these occupations, but usually is not needed. **Job Preparation—**SVP 4.0 to less than 6.0—six months to less than two years. **Knowledges—**Mechanical Devices; Building and Construction; Engineering and Technology; Physics; Chemistry; Design. **Instructional Programs—**Heavy/Industrial Equipment Maintenance Technologies; Industrial Mechanics and Maintenance Technology.

Related SOC Job—49-9043 Maintenance Workers, Machinery. **Related OOH Job—**Industrial Machinery Mechanics and Maintenance Workers. **Related DOT Jobs—**514.684-018 Nozzle-and-Sleeve Worker; 519.664-014 Pot Liner; 519.667-010 Carbon Setter; 519.684-014 Leaf Coverer; 529.667-014 Mash-Filter-Cloth Changer; 564.684-010 Knife Setter, Grinder Machine; 590.384-014 Production Technician, Semiconductor Processing Equipment; 622.684-018 Switch Repairer; 624.684-010 Greaser; 628.684-010 Binder and Box Builder; 628.684-014 Frame Bander; 628.684-022 Overhead Cleaner Maintainer; 628.684-042 Spindle Repairer; 628.684-046 Texturing-Machine Fixer; others.

49-9044.00 Millwrights

- **Education/Training Required: Long-term on-the-job training**
- **Employed: 53,080**
- **Annual Earnings: $44,780**
- **Growth: 5.9%**
- **Annual Job Openings: 5,000**

Install, dismantle, or move machinery and heavy equipment according to layout plans, blueprints, or other drawings.

Replace defective parts of machine or adjust clearances and alignment of moving parts. Align machines and equipment, using hoists, jacks, hand tools, squares, rules, micrometers, and plumb bobs. Connect power unit to machines or steam piping to equipment and test unit to evaluate its mechanical operation. Repair and lubricate machines and equipment. Assemble and install equipment, using hand tools and power tools. Position steel beams to support bedplates of machines and equipment, using blueprints and schematic drawings to determine work procedures. Signal crane operator to lower basic assembly units to bedplate and align unit to centerline. Insert shims, adjust tension on nuts and bolts, or position parts, using hand tools and measuring instruments to set specified clearances between moving and stationary parts. Move machinery and equipment, using hoists, dollies, rollers, and trucks. Attach moving parts and subassemblies to basic assembly unit, using hand tools and power tools. Assemble machines and bolt, weld, rivet, or otherwise fasten them to foundation or other structures, using hand tools and power tools. Lay out mounting holes, using measuring instruments, and drill holes with power drill. Bolt parts, such as side and deck plates, jaw plates, and journals, to basic assembly unit. Dismantle machines, using hammers, wrenches, crowbars, and other hand tools. Level bedplate and establish centerline, using straightedge, levels, and transit. Shrink-fit bushings, sleeves, rings, liners, gears, and wheels to specified items, using portable gas heating equipment. Dismantle machinery and equipment for shipment to installation site, usually performing installation and maintenance work as part of team. Construct foundation for machines, using hand tools and building materials such as wood, cement, and steel. Install robot and modify its program, using teach pendant. Operate engine lathe to grind, file, and turn machine parts to dimensional specifications.

GOE Information—Interest Area: 13. Manufacturing. **Work Group:** 13.13. Machinery Repair. **Personality Type—Realistic.** Realistic occupations frequently involve work activities that include practical, hands-on problems and solutions. They often deal with plants; animals; and real-world materials like wood, tools, and machinery. Many of the occupations require working outside and do not involve a lot of paperwork or working closely with others. **Work Values—Moral** Values; Variety; Supervision, Human Relations; Compensation; Supervision, Technical; Independence. **Skills—Installation;** Repairing; Troubleshooting; Equipment Maintenance; Mathematics; Equipment Selection. **Abilities—***Cognitive:* Visualization; Spatial Orientation; Information Ordering; Selective Attention; Perceptual Speed; Time Sharing. *Psychomotor:* Rate Control; Multilimb Coordination; Reaction Time; Control Precision; Manual Dexterity; Arm-Hand Steadiness. *Physical:* Extent Flexibility; Static Strength; Dynamic Strength; Gross Body Equilibrium; Trunk Strength; Gross Body Coordination. *Sensory:* Auditory Attention; Depth Perception; Glare Sensitivity; Hearing Sensitivity; Near Vision; Visual Color Discrimination. **General Work Activities—***Information Input:* Monitoring Processes, Materials, or Surroundings; Inspecting Equipment, Structures, or Materials; Identifying Objects, Actions, and Events. *Mental Process:* Updating and Using Relevant Knowledge; Making Decisions and Solving Problems; Thinking Creatively. *Work*

Output: Handling and Moving Objects; Repairing and Maintaining Mechanical Equipment; Performing General Physical Activities. *Interacting with Others:* Establishing and Maintaining Interpersonal Relationships; Communicating with Other Workers; Coordinating the Work and Activities of Others. **Physical Work Conditions**—Noisy; Very Hot or Cold; Very Bright or Dim Lighting; Contaminants; Hazardous Equipment; Using Hands on Objects, Tools, or Controls. **Other Job Characteristics**—Need to Be Exact or Accurate; Errors Have Important Consequences.

Experience—Job Zone 3. Previous work-related skill, knowledge, or experience is required. **Job Preparation**—SVP 6.0 to less than 7.0—more than one year and less than four years. **Knowledges**—Mechanical Devices; Building and Construction; Engineering and Technology; Physics; Design; Public Safety and Security. **Instructional Programs**—Heavy/Industrial Equipment Maintenance Technologies; Industrial Mechanics and Maintenance Technology.

Related SOC Job—49-9044 Millwrights. **Related OOH Job**—Millwrights. **Related DOT Jobs**—638.261-010 Automated Equipment Engineer-Technician; 638.261-014 Machinery Erector; 638.261-018 Manufacturer's Service Representative; 638.261-026 Field Service Technician; 638.281-018 Millwright; 638.281-022 Millwright Apprentice.

49-9045.00 Refractory Materials Repairers, Except Brickmasons

- Education/Training Required: Moderate-term on-the-job training
- Employed: 3,250
- Annual Earnings: $40,240
- Growth: –5.2%
- Annual Job Openings: Fewer than 500

Build or repair furnaces, kilns, cupolas, boilers, converters, ladles, soaking pits, ovens, etc., using refractory materials.

Bolt sections of wooden molds together, using wrenches, and line molds with paper to prevent clay from sticking to molds. Mix specified amounts of sand, clay, mortar powder, and water to form refractory clay or mortar, using shovels or mixing machines. Measure furnace walls to determine dimensions; then cut required number of sheets from plastic block, using saws. Install clay structures in melting tanks and drawing kilns to control the flow and temperature of molten glass, using hoists and hand tools. Fasten stopper heads to rods with metal pins to assemble refractory stoppers used to plug pouring nozzles of steel ladles. Dump and tamp clay in molds, using tamping tools. Dry and bake new linings by placing inverted linings over burners, building fires in ladles, or using blowtorches. Drill holes in furnace walls, bolt overlapping layers of plastic to walls, and hammer surfaces to compress layers into solid sheets. Reline or repair ladles and pouring spouts with refractory clay, using trowels. Chip slag from linings of ladles or remove linings when beyond repair, using hammers and chisels. Climb scaffolding, carrying hoses, and spray surfaces of cupolas with refractory mixtures, using spray equipment. Disassemble molds and cut, chip, and smooth clay structures such as floaters, drawbars, and L-blocks. Remove worn or damaged plastic block refractory linings of furnaces, using hand tools. Spread mortar on stopper heads and rods, using trowels, and slide brick sleeves over rods to form refractory jackets. Tighten locknuts holding refractory stopper assemblies together, spread mortar on jackets to seal sleeve joints, and dry mortar in ovens. Install preformed metal scaffolding in interiors of cupolas, using hand tools.

Transfer clay structures to curing ovens, melting tanks, and drawing kilns, using forklifts.

GOE Information—Interest Area: 02. Architecture and Construction. **Work Group:** 02.04. Construction Crafts. **Personality Type**—Realistic. Realistic occupations frequently involve work activities that include practical, hands-on problems and solutions. They often deal with plants; animals; and real-world materials like wood, tools, and machinery. Many of the occupations require working outside and do not involve a lot of paperwork or working closely with others. **Work Values**—Independence; Moral Values; Variety; Company Policies and Practices; Supervision, Technical. **Skills**—Repairing; Installation; Operation and Control. **Abilities**—*Cognitive:* Spatial Orientation; Visualization. *Psychomotor:* Wrist-Finger Speed; Speed of Limb Movement; Multilimb Coordination; Control Precision; Manual Dexterity; Arm-Hand Steadiness. *Physical:* Explosive Strength; Dynamic Strength; Extent Flexibility; Static Strength; Dynamic Flexibility; Stamina. *Sensory:* Depth Perception. **General Work Activities**—*Information Input:* Monitoring Processes, Materials, or Surroundings. *Mental Process:* None met the criteria. *Work Output:* Performing General Physical Activities; Handling and Moving Objects; Repairing and Maintaining Mechanical Equipment. *Interacting with Others:* None met the criteria. **Physical Work Conditions**—Indoors; Very Hot or Cold; Contaminants; Hazardous Equipment; Standing; Using Hands on Objects, Tools, or Controls. **Other Job Characteristics**—None met the criteria.

Experience—Job Zone 1. No previous work-related skill, knowledge, or experience is needed. **Job Preparation**—SVP below 4.0—less than six months. **Knowledges**—Building and Construction; Mechanical Devices. **Instructional Program**—Industrial Mechanics and Maintenance Technology.

Related SOC Job—49-9045 Refractory Materials Repairers, Except Brickmasons. **Related OOH Job**—Refractory Materials Repairers, Except Brickmasons. **Related DOT Jobs**—519.684-010 Ladle Liner; 519.684-022 Stopper Maker; 579.664-010 Clay-Structure Builder and Servicer; 849.484-010 Boiler Reliner, Plastic Block; 899.684-010 Bondactor-Machine Operator.

49-9051.00 Electrical Power-Line Installers and Repairers

- Education/Training Required: Long-term on-the-job training
- Employed: 106,060
- Annual Earnings: $50,150
- Growth: 2.5%
- Annual Job Openings: 11,000

Install or repair cables or wires used in electrical power or distribution systems. May erect poles and light- or heavy-duty transmission towers.

Adhere to safety practices and procedures, such as checking equipment regularly and erecting barriers around work areas. Open switches or attach grounding devices to remove electrical hazards from disturbed or fallen lines or to facilitate repairs. Climb poles or use truck-mounted buckets to access equipment. Place insulating or fireproofing materials over conductors and joints. Install, maintain, and repair electrical distribution and transmission systems, including conduits; cables; wires; and related equipment such as transformers, circuit breakers, and switches. Identify defective sectionalizing devices, circuit breakers, fuses, voltage regulators, transformers, switches, relays, or wiring, using wiring diagrams and electrical-testing instruments. Drive vehicles equipped with tools and materials to job sites. Coordinate work assignment preparation and completion with other workers. String wire conductors and cables between poles, towers, trenches, pylons, and buildings, setting lines in place and using winches to adjust tension. Inspect and test power lines and auxiliary equipment to locate and identify problems, using reading and testing instruments. Test conductors according to electrical diagrams and specifications to identify corresponding conductors and to prevent incorrect connections. Replace damaged poles with new poles and straighten the poles. Install watt-hour meters and connect service drops between power lines and consumers' facilities. Attach crossarms, insulators, and auxiliary equipment to poles prior to installing them. Travel in trucks, helicopters, and airplanes to inspect lines for freedom from obstruction and adequacy of insulation. Dig holes, using augers, and set poles, using cranes and power equipment. Trim trees that could be hazardous to the functioning of cables or wires. Splice or solder cables together or to overhead transmission lines, customer service lines, or street light lines, using hand tools, epoxies, or specialized equipment. Cut and peel lead sheathing and insulation from defective or newly installed cables and conduits prior to splicing.

GOE Information—**Interest Area:** 02. Architecture and Construction. **Work Group:** 02.05. Systems and Equipment Installation, Maintenance, and Repair. **Personality Type**—Realistic. Realistic occupations frequently involve work activities that include practical, hands-on problems and solutions. They often deal with plants; animals; and real-world materials like wood, tools, and machinery. Many of the occupations require working outside and do not involve a lot of paperwork or working closely with others. **Work Values**—Supervision, Technical; Moral Values; Security; Advancement; Supervision, Human Relations; Independence. **Skills**—Repairing; Installation; Equipment Maintenance; Operation Monitoring; Troubleshooting; Operation and Control. **Abilities**—*Cognitive:* Visualization; Selective Attention; Time Sharing; Information Ordering; Flexibility of Closure; Category Flexibility. *Psychomotor:* Reaction Time; Multilimb Coordination; Rate Control; Response Orientation; Manual Dexterity; Control Precision. *Physical:* Gross Body Equilibrium; Static Strength; Extent Flexibility; Dynamic Strength; Gross Body Coordination; Stamina. *Sensory:* Depth Perception; Glare Sensitivity; Visual Color Discrimination; Far Vision; Auditory Attention; Hearing Sensitivity. **General Work Activities**—*Information Input:* Identifying Objects, Actions, and Events; Inspecting Equipment, Structures, or Materials; Monitoring Processes, Materials, or Surroundings. *Mental Process:* Making Decisions and Solving Problems; Updating and Using Relevant Knowledge; Organizing, Planning, and Prioritizing. *Work Output:* Handling and Moving Objects; Performing General Physical Activities; Controlling Machines and Processes. *Interacting with Others:* Communicating with Other Workers; Coordinating the Work and Activities of Others; Performing for or Working with the Public. **Physical Work Conditions**—Outdoors; Very Hot or Cold; High Places; Hazardous Conditions; Hazardous Equipment; Using Hands on Objects, Tools, or Controls. **Other Job Characteristics**—Need to Be Exact or Accurate; Errors Have Important Consequences; Repeat Same Tasks; Pace Determined by Speed of Equipment.

Experience—Job Zone 3. Previous work-related skill, knowledge, or experience is required. **Job Preparation**—SVP 6.0 to less than 7.0—more than one year and less than four years. **Knowledges**—Building and Construction; Mechanical Devices; Customer and Personal Service; Engineering and Technology; Transportation; Design. **Instructional Programs**—Electrical and Power Transmission Installation/Installer, General; Electrical and Power Transmission Installers, Other; Lineworker.

Related SOC Job—49-9051 Electrical Power-Line Installers and Repairers. **Related OOH Job**—Line Installers and Repairers. **Related DOT Jobs**—821.261-014 Line Maintainer; 821.261-022 Service Restorer, Emergency; 821.261-026 Trouble Shooter II; 821.361-010 Cable Installer-Repairer; 821.361-018 Line Erector; 821.361-022 Line Installer, Street Railway; 821.361-026 Line Repairer; 821.361-030 Line-Erector Apprentice; 821.361-038 Tower Erector; 821.684-022 Trolley-Wire Installer; 825.381-038 Third-Rail Installer; 829.361-010 Cable Splicer; 829.361-014 Cable-Splicer Apprentice.

49-9052.00 Telecommunications Line Installers and Repairers

- **Education/Training Required: Long-term on-the-job training**
- **Employed: 142,560**
- **Annual Earnings: $42,410**
- **Growth: 10.8%**
- **Annual Job Openings: 23,000**

String and repair telephone and television cable, including fiber optics and other equipment for transmitting messages or television programming.

Travel to customers' premises to install, maintain, and repair audio and visual electronic reception equipment and accessories. Inspect and test lines and cables, recording and analyzing test results, to assess transmission characteristics and locate faults and malfunctions. Splice cables, using hand tools, epoxy, or mechanical equipment. Measure signal strength at utility poles, using electronic test equipment. Set up service for customers, installing, connecting, testing, and adjusting equipment. Place insulation over conductors and seal splices with moisture-proof covering. Access specific areas to string lines and install terminal boxes, auxiliary equipment, and appliances, using bucket trucks or by climbing poles and ladders or entering tunnels, trenches, or crawl spaces. String cables between structures and lines from poles, towers, or trenches and pull lines to proper tension. Install equipment such as amplifiers and repeaters to maintain the strength of communications transmissions. Lay underground cable directly in trenches or string it through conduits running through trenches. Pull up cable by hand from large reels mounted on trucks; then pull lines through ducts by hand or with winches. Clean and maintain tools and test equipment. Explain cable service to subscribers after installation and collect any installation fees that are due. Compute impedance of wires from poles to houses to determine additional resistance needed for reducing signals to desired levels. Use a variety of construction equipment to complete installations, including digger derricks, trenchers, and cable plows. Dig trenches for underground wires and cables. Dig holes for power poles, using power augers or shovels; set poles in place with cranes; and hoist poles upright, using winches. Fill and tamp holes, using cement, earth, and tamping devices. Participate in the construction and removal of telecommunication towers and associated support structures.

GOE Information—**Interest Area:** 02. Architecture and Construction. **Work Group:** 02.05. Systems and Equipment Installation, Maintenance, and Repair. **Personality Type**—Realistic. Realistic occupations frequently involve work activities that include practical, hands-on problems and solutions. They often deal with plants; animals; and real-world materials like wood, tools, and machinery. Many of the occupations require working outside and do not involve a lot of paperwork or working closely with others. **Work Values**—Supervision, Technical; Independence; Security; Supervision, Human Relations; Advancement; Variety. **Skills**—Installation;

Troubleshooting; Repairing; Programming; Equipment Maintenance; Technology Design. **Abilities**—*Cognitive:* Perceptual Speed; Time Sharing; Visualization; Mathematical Reasoning; Flexibility of Closure. *Psychomotor:* Response Orientation; Multilimb Coordination; Control Precision; Arm-Hand Steadiness; Manual Dexterity; Reaction Time. *Physical:* Extent Flexibility; Gross Body Equilibrium; Static Strength; Gross Body Coordination; Stamina; Trunk Strength. *Sensory:* Visual Color Discrimination; Depth Perception; Auditory Attention; Hearing Sensitivity. **General Work Activities**—*Information Input:* Monitoring Processes, Materials, or Surroundings; Inspecting Equipment, Structures, or Materials; Identifying Objects, Actions, and Events. *Mental Process:* Updating and Using Relevant Knowledge; Organizing, Planning, and Prioritizing; Making Decisions and Solving Problems. *Work Output:* Handling and Moving Objects; Performing General Physical Activities; Operating Vehicles or Equipment. *Interacting with Others:* Establishing and Maintaining Interpersonal Relationships; Performing for or Working with the Public; Communicating with Persons Outside Organization. **Physical Work Conditions**—Outdoors; Very Hot or Cold; Contaminants; Cramped Work Space, Awkward Positions; Hazardous Equipment; Using Hands on Objects, Tools, or Controls. **Other Job Characteristics**—Need to Be Exact or Accurate; Repeat Same Tasks.

Experience—Job Zone 2. Some previous work-related skill, knowledge, or experience may be helpful in these occupations, but usually is not needed. **Job Preparation**—SVP 4.0 to less than 6.0—six months to less than two years. **Knowledges**—Telecommunications; Customer and Personal Service; Engineering and Technology; Building and Construction; Design; Transportation. **Instructional Program**—Communications Systems Installation and Repair Technology.

Related SOC Job—49-9052 Telecommunications Line Installers and Repairers. **Related OOH Job**—Line Installers and Repairers. **Related DOT Jobs**—821.281-010 Cable Television Installer; 822.381-014 Line Installer-Repairer.

49-9061.00 Camera and Photographic Equipment Repairers

- **Education/Training Required: Moderate-term on-the-job training**
- **Employed: 3,160**
- **Annual Earnings: $34,900**
- **Growth: –9.1%**
- **Annual Job Openings: Fewer than 500**

Repair and adjust cameras and photographic equipment, including commercial video and motion picture camera equipment.

Calibrate and verify accuracy of light meters, shutter diaphragm operation, and lens carriers, using timing instruments. Disassemble equipment to gain access to defect, using hand tools. Adjust cameras; photographic mechanisms; and equipment such as range and view finders, shutters, light meters, and lens systems, using hand tools. Clean and lubricate cameras and polish camera lenses, using cleaning materials and work aids. Measure parts to verify specified dimensions/settings, such as camera shutter speed and light meter reading accuracy, using measuring instruments. Test equipment performance, focus of lens system, alignment of diaphragm, lens mounts, and film transport, using precision gauges. Examine cameras, equipment, processed film, and laboratory reports to diagnose malfunction, using work aids and specifications. Requisition parts and

materials. Read and interpret engineering drawings, diagrams, instructions, and specifications to determine needed repairs, fabrication method, and operation sequence. Fabricate or modify defective electronic, electrical, and mechanical components, using bench lathe, milling machine, shaper, grinder, and precision hand tools, according to specifications. Assemble aircraft cameras, still and motion picture cameras, photographic equipment, and frames, using diagrams, blueprints, bench machines, hand tools, and power tools. Install film in aircraft camera and electrical assemblies and wiring in camera housing, following blueprints and using hand tools and soldering equipment. Record test data and document fabrication techniques on reports. Lay out reference points and dimensions on parts and metal stock to be machined, using precision measuring instruments. Recommend design changes or upgrades of microfilming, film developing, and photographic equipment.

GOE Information—**Interest Area:** 13. Manufacturing. **Work Group:** 13.15. Medical and Technical Equipment Repair. **Personality Type**—Realistic. Realistic occupations frequently involve work activities that include practical, hands-on problems and solutions. They often deal with plants; animals; and real-world materials like wood, tools, and machinery. Many of the occupations require working outside and do not involve a lot of paperwork or working closely with others. **Work Values**—Working Conditions; Independence; Autonomy; Moral Values; Compensation; Variety. **Skills**—Repairing; Installation; Troubleshooting; Quality Control Analysis; Equipment Maintenance; Technology Design. **Abilities**—*Cognitive:* Visualization; Number Facility; Memorization; Perceptual Speed; Speed of Closure; Written Comprehension. *Psychomotor:* Arm-Hand Steadiness; Finger Dexterity; Control Precision; Manual Dexterity; Multilimb Coordination. *Physical:* None met the criteria. *Sensory:* Visual Color Discrimination; Depth Perception; Far Vision; Near Vision; Hearing Sensitivity. **General Work Activities**—*Information Input:* Inspecting Equipment, Structures, or Materials; Identifying Objects, Actions, and Events; Monitoring Processes, Materials, or Surroundings. *Mental Process:* Updating and Using Relevant Knowledge; Making Decisions and Solving Problems; Organizing, Planning, and Prioritizing. *Work Output:* Repairing and Maintaining Electronic Equipment; Repairing and Maintaining Mechanical Equipment; Handling and Moving Objects. *Interacting with Others:* Establishing and Maintaining Interpersonal Relationships; Performing for or Working with the Public; Monitoring and Controlling Resources. **Physical Work Conditions**—Indoors; Sitting; Using Hands on Objects, Tools, or Controls. **Other Job Characteristics**—Need to Be Exact or Accurate.

Experience—Job Zone 3. Previous work-related skill, knowledge, or experience is required. **Job Preparation**—SVP 6.0 to less than 7.0—more than one year and less than four years. **Knowledges**—Mechanical Devices; Computers and Electronics; Engineering and Technology; Design; Customer and Personal Service; Clerical Practices. **Instructional Program**—Communications Systems Installation and Repair Technology.

Related SOC Job—49-9061 Camera and Photographic Equipment Repairers. **Related OOH Job**—Precision Instrument and Equipment Repairers. **Related DOT Jobs**—714.281-010 Aircraft-Photographic-Equipment Mechanic; 714.281-014 Camera Repairer; 714.281-018 Machinist, Motion-Picture Equipment; 714.281-022 Photographic Equipment Technician; 714.281-026 Photographic-Equipment-Maintenance Technician; 714.281-030 Service Technician, Computerized-Photofinishing Equipment; 826.261-010 Field-Service Engineer.

49-9062.00 Medical Equipment Repairers

- **Education/Training Required: Associate degree**
- **Employed: 27,940**
- **Annual Earnings: $39,570**
- **Growth: 14.8%**
- **Annual Job Openings: 4,000**

Test, adjust, or repair biomedical or electromedical equipment.

Inspect and test malfunctioning medical and related equipment following manufacturers' specifications, using test and analysis instruments. Examine medical equipment and facility's structural environment and check for proper use of equipment to protect patients and staff from electrical or mechanical hazards and to ensure compliance with safety regulations. Disassemble malfunctioning equipment and remove, repair, and replace defective parts such as motors, clutches, or transformers. Keep records of maintenance, repair, and required updates of equipment. Perform preventive maintenance or service such as cleaning, lubricating, and adjusting equipment. Test and calibrate components and equipment, following manufacturers' manuals and troubleshooting techniques and using hand tools, power tools, and measuring devices. Explain and demonstrate correct operation and preventive maintenance of medical equipment to personnel. Study technical manuals and attend training sessions provided by equipment manufacturers to maintain current knowledge. Plan and carry out work assignments, using blueprints, schematic drawings, technical manuals, wiring diagrams, and liquid and air flow sheets, following prescribed regulations, directives, and other instructions as required. Solder loose connections, using soldering iron. Test, evaluate, and classify excess or in-use medical equipment and determine serviceability, condition, and disposition in accordance with regulations. Research catalogs and repair part lists to locate sources for repair parts, requisitioning parts and recording their receipt. Evaluate technical specifications to identify equipment and systems best suited for intended use and possible purchase based on specifications, user needs, and technical requirements. Contribute expertise to develop medical maintenance standard operating procedures. Compute power and space requirements for installing medical, dental, or related equipment and install units to manufacturers' specifications. Supervise and advise subordinate personnel. Repair shop equipment, metal furniture, and hospital equipment, including welding broken parts and replacing missing parts, or bring item into local shop for major repairs.

GOE Information—Interest Area: 13. Manufacturing. **Work Group:** 13.15. Medical and Technical Equipment Repair. **Personality Type—** Realistic. Realistic occupations frequently involve work activities that include practical, hands-on problems and solutions. They often deal with plants; animals; and real-world materials like wood, tools, and machinery. Many of the occupations require working outside and do not involve a lot of paperwork or working closely with others. **Work Values—**Moral Values; Compensation; Supervision, Technical; Variety; Security; Co-workers. **Skills—**Repairing; Installation; Equipment Maintenance; Troubleshooting; Systems Analysis; Operation Monitoring. **Abilities—***Cognitive:* Visualization; Written Comprehension; Mathematical Reasoning; Flexibility of Closure; Memorization; Perceptual Speed. *Psychomotor:* Control Precision; Finger Dexterity; Manual Dexterity; Arm-Hand Steadiness; Multilimb Coordination; Speed of Limb Movement. *Physical:* Extent Flexibility; Static Strength; Dynamic Strength; Trunk Strength. *Sensory:* Hearing Sensitivity; Visual Color Discrimination; Near

Vision; Depth Perception; Far Vision; Auditory Attention. **General Work Activities—***Information Input:* Inspecting Equipment, Structures, or Materials; Identifying Objects, Actions, and Events; Monitoring Processes, Materials, or Surroundings. *Mental Process:* Updating and Using Relevant Knowledge; Organizing, Planning, and Prioritizing; Making Decisions and Solving Problems. *Work Output:* Repairing and Maintaining Electronic Equipment; Repairing and Maintaining Mechanical Equipment; Handling and Moving Objects. *Interacting with Others:* Establishing and Maintaining Interpersonal Relationships; Communicating with Other Workers; Communicating with Persons Outside Organization. **Physical Work Conditions—** Indoors; Contaminants; Disease or Infections; Standing; Using Hands on Objects, Tools, or Controls. **Other Job Characteristics—**Need to Be Exact or Accurate; Errors Have Important Consequences.

Experience—Job Zone 3. Previous work-related skill, knowledge, or experience is required. **Job Preparation—**SVP 6.0 to less than 7.0— more than one year and less than four years. **Knowledges—** Mechanical Devices; Computers and Electronics; Engineering and Technology; Physics; Telecommunications; Medicine and Dentistry. **Instructional Program—**Biomedical Technology/Technician.

Related SOC Job—49-9062 Medical Equipment Repairers. **Related OOH Job—**Precision Instrument and Equipment Repairers. **Related DOT Jobs—**019.261-010 Biomedical Equipment Technician; 639.281-022 Medical-Equipment Repairer; 719.261-014 Radiological-Equipment Specialist; 729.281-030 Electromedical-Equipment Repairer; 829.261-014 Dental-Equipment Installer and Servicer.

49-9063.00 Musical Instrument Repairers and Tuners

- **Education/Training Required: Long-term on-the-job training**
- **Employed: 4,830**
- **Annual Earnings: $28,560**
- **Growth: 2.8%**
- **Annual Job Openings: 1,000**

Repair percussion, stringed, reed, or wind instruments. May specialize in one area, such as piano tuning.

Play instruments to evaluate their sound quality and to locate any defects. Adjust string tensions to tune instruments, using hand tools and electronic tuning devices. Inspect instruments to locate defects and to determine their value or the level of restoration required. Disassemble instruments and parts for repair and adjustment. Repair cracks in wood or metal instruments, using pinning wire, lathes, fillers, clamps, or soldering irons. Reassemble instruments following repair, using hand tools and power tools and glue, hair, yarn, resin, or clamps, and lubricate instruments as necessary. Compare instrument pitches with tuning tool pitches to tune instruments. String instruments and adjust trusses and bridges of instruments to obtain specified string tensions and heights. Repair or replace musical instrument parts and components, such as strings, bridges, felts, and keys, using hand and power tools. Polish instruments, using rags and polishing compounds, buffing wheels, or burnishing tools. Shape old parts and replacement parts to improve tone or intonation, using hand tools, lathes, or soldering irons. Make wood replacement parts, using woodworking machines and hand tools. Mix and measure glue that will be used for instrument repair. Align pads and keys on reed or wind instruments. Adjust felt hammers on pianos to increase tonal mellowness or brilliance, using sanding paddles, lacquer, or needles.

Solder posts and parts to hold them in their proper places. Remove dents and burrs from metal instruments, using mallets and burnishing tools. Wash metal instruments in lacquer-stripping and cyanide solutions to remove lacquer and tarnish. Test tubes and pickups in electronic amplifier units and solder parts and connections as necessary. Refinish instruments to protect and decorate them, using hand tools, buffing tools, and varnish. Deliver pianos to purchasers or to locations where they are to be used. Cut out sections around cracks on percussion instruments to prevent cracks from advancing, using shears or grinding wheels. Refinish and polish piano cabinets or cases to prepare them for sale.

GOE Information—Interest Area: 03. Arts and Communication. **Work Group:** 03.11. Musical Instrument Repair. **Personality Type—** Realistic. Realistic occupations frequently involve work activities that include practical, hands-on problems and solutions. They often deal with plants; animals; and real-world materials like wood, tools, and machinery. Many of the occupations require working outside and do not involve a lot of paperwork or working closely with others. **Work Values—**Independence; Moral Values; Working Conditions; Autonomy; Supervision, Technical; Responsibility. **Skills—**Repairing; Management of Financial Resources; Troubleshooting; Installation; Equipment Maintenance; Technology Design. **Abilities—***Cognitive:* Visualization; Speed of Closure; Memorization; Selective Attention; Fluency of Ideas; Time Sharing. *Psychomotor:* Finger Dexterity; Manual Dexterity; Arm-Hand Steadiness; Control Precision; Multilimb Coordination; Wrist-Finger Speed. *Physical:* Static Strength; Trunk Strength. *Sensory:* Hearing Sensitivity; Auditory Attention; Visual Color Discrimination; Depth Perception; Far Vision. **General Work Activities—***Information Input:* Getting Information; Identifying Objects, Actions, and Events; Inspecting Equipment, Structures, or Materials. *Mental Process:* Organizing, Planning, and Prioritizing; Updating and Using Relevant Knowledge; Making Decisions and Solving Problems. *Work Output:* Handling and Moving Objects; Repairing and Maintaining Mechanical Equipment; Controlling Machines and Processes. *Interacting with Others:* Performing for or Working with the Public; Establishing and Maintaining Interpersonal Relationships; Communicating with Persons Outside Organization. **Physical Work Conditions—**Indoors; Noisy; Contaminants; Hazardous Equipment; Using Hands on Objects, Tools, or Controls; Repetitive Motions. **Other Job Characteristics—**Need to Be Exact or Accurate; Repeat Same Tasks; Errors Have Important Consequences.

Experience—Job Zone 3. Previous work-related skill, knowledge, or experience is required. **Job Preparation—**SVP 6.0 to less than 7.0—more than one year and less than four years. **Knowledges—**Mechanical Devices; Fine Arts; Sales and Marketing; Engineering and Technology; Design; Customer and Personal Service. **Instructional Program—**Musical Instrument Fabrication and Repair.

Related SOC Job—49-9063 Musical Instrument Repairers and Tuners. **Related OOH Job—**Precision Instrument and Equipment Repairers. **Related DOT Jobs—**730.281-014 Accordion Repairer; 730.281-026 Fretted-Instrument Repairer; 730.281-038 Piano Technician; 730.281-050 Violin Repairer; 730.281-054 Wind-Instrument Repairer; 730.361-010 Piano Tuner; 730.361-014 Pipe-Organ Tuner and Repairer; 730.381-010 Accordion Tuner; 730.381-026 Harp Regulator; 730.381-034 Metal-Reed Tuner; 730.381-038 Organ-Pipe Voicer; 730.381-042 Percussion-Instrument Repairer; 730.381-058 Tuner, Percussion; 730.681-010 Piano Regulator-Inspector; 730.684-022 Bow Rehairer; others.

49-9064.00 Watch Repairers

- **Education/Training Required: Long-term on-the-job training**
- **Employed: 3,080**
- **Annual Earnings: $31,640**
- **Growth: 0.6%**
- **Annual Job Openings: Fewer than 500**

Repair, clean, and adjust mechanisms of timing instruments, such as watches and clocks.

Gather information from customers about a timepiece's problems and its service history. Perform regular adjustment and maintenance on timepieces, watch cases, and watch bands. Reassemble timepieces, replacing glass faces and batteries, before returning them to customers. Disassemble timepieces and inspect them for defective, worn, misaligned, or rusty parts, using loupes. Clean, rinse, and dry timepiece parts, using solutions and ultrasonic or mechanical watch-cleaning machines. Repair or replace broken, damaged, or worn parts on timepieces, using lathes, drill presses, and hand tools. Adjust timing regulators, using truing calipers, watch-rate recorders, and tweezers. Test and replace batteries and other electronic components. Fabricate parts for watches and clocks, using small lathes and other machines. Estimate repair costs and timepiece values. Demagnetize mechanisms, using demagnetizing machines. Test timepiece accuracy and performance, using meters and other electronic instruments. Record quantities and types of timepieces repaired, serial and model numbers of items, work performed, and charges for repairs. Oil moving parts of timepieces.

GOE Information—Interest Area: 13. Manufacturing. **Work Group:** 13.15. Medical and Technical Equipment Repair. **Personality Type—** Realistic. Realistic occupations frequently involve work activities that include practical, hands-on problems and solutions. They often deal with plants; animals; and real-world materials like wood, tools, and machinery. Many of the occupations require working outside and do not involve a lot of paperwork or working closely with others. **Work Values—**Independence; Working Conditions; Moral Values; Ability Utilization; Compensation; Security. **Skills—**Repairing; Equipment Maintenance; Troubleshooting; Quality Control Analysis. **Abilities—***Cognitive:* Number Facility. *Psychomotor:* Finger Dexterity; Arm-Hand Steadiness; Wrist-Finger Speed; Manual Dexterity; Control Precision. *Physical:* None met the criteria. *Sensory:* Near Vision. **General Work Activities—***Information Input:* Inspecting Equipment, Structures, or Materials; Monitoring Processes, Materials, or Surroundings; Identifying Objects, Actions, and Events. *Mental Process:* Evaluating Information Against Standards; Analyzing Data or Information; Updating and Using Relevant Knowledge. *Work Output:* Repairing and Maintaining Mechanical Equipment; Handling and Moving Objects; Controlling Machines and Processes. *Interacting with Others:* Communicating with Persons Outside Organization. **Physical Work Conditions—**Indoors; Sitting; Using Hands on Objects, Tools, or Controls; Repetitive Motions. **Other Job Characteristics—**Need to Be Exact or Accurate.

Experience—Job Zone 3. Previous work-related skill, knowledge, or experience is required. **Job Preparation—**SVP 6.0 to less than 7.0—more than one year and less than four years. **Knowledges—**Mechanical Devices; Engineering and Technology. **Instructional Program—**Watchmaking and Jewelrymaking.

Related SOC Job—49-9064 Watch Repairers. **Related OOH Job—**Precision Instrument and Equipment Repairers. **Related DOT Jobs—**715.281-010 Watch Repairer; 715.281-014 Watch Repairer Apprentice; 715.584-014 Repairer, Auto Clocks.

49-9069.99 Precision Instrument and Equipment Repairers, All Other

- Education/Training Required: Long-term on-the-job training
- Employed: 12,870
- Annual Earnings: $44,460
- Growth: 7.7%
- Annual Job Openings: 2,000

All precision instrument and equipment repairers not listed separately.

No task data available.

Note: The Department of Labor has not collected some data for this job, so it has fewer details than the other descriptions.

Related SOC Job—49-9069 Precision Instrument and Equipment Repairers, All Other. **Related OOH Job**—Precision Instrument and Equipment Repairers. **Related DOT Jobs**—710.281-038 Taximeter Repairer; 710.381-054 Repairer, Gyroscope.

49-9091.00 Coin, Vending, and Amusement Machine Servicers and Repairers

- Education/Training Required: Moderate-term on-the-job training
- Employed: 39,570
- Annual Earnings: $28,200
- Growth: 2.4%
- Annual Job Openings: 7,000

Install, service, adjust, or repair coin, vending, or amusement machines, including video games, jukeboxes, pinball machines, or slot machines.

Clean and oil machine parts. Replace malfunctioning parts, such as worn magnetic heads on automatic teller machine (ATM) card readers. Adjust and repair coin, vending, or amusement machines and meters and replace defective mechanical and electrical parts, using hand tools, soldering irons, and diagrams. Collect coins and bills from machines, prepare invoices, and settle accounts with concessionaires. Disassemble and assemble machines according to specifications, using hand and power tools. Fill machines with products, ingredients, money, and other supplies. Inspect machines and meters to determine causes of malfunctions and fix minor problems such as jammed bills or stuck products. Install machines, making the necessary water and electrical connections in compliance with codes. Make service calls to maintain and repair machines. Adjust machine pressure gauges and thermostats. Test machines to determine proper functioning. Refer to manuals and wiring diagrams to gather information needed to repair machines. Contact other repair personnel or make arrangements for the removal of machines in cases where major repairs are required. Count cash and items deposited at automatic teller machines (ATMs) by customers and compare numbers to transactions indicated on transaction tapes. Install automatic teller machine (ATM) hardware, software, and peripheral equipment and check that all components are configured correctly and connected to power sources and communications lines. Keep records of merchandise distributed and money collected. Maintain records of machine maintenance and repair. Order parts needed for machine repairs. Prepare repair cost estimates. Record transaction information on forms or logs and notify designated personnel of discrepancies. Transport machines to installation sites. Shellac or paint dial markings or mechanism exteriors, using brushes or spray guns.

GOE Information—**Interest Area:** 11. Information Technology. **Work Group:** 11.03. Digital Equipment Repair. **Personality Type**—Realistic. Realistic occupations frequently involve work activities that include practical, hands-on problems and solutions. They often deal with plants; animals; and real-world materials like wood, tools, and machinery. Many of the occupations require working outside and do not involve a lot of paperwork or working closely with others. **Work Values**—Independence; Supervision, Technical; Moral Values; Responsibility; Security. **Skills**—Repairing; Installation; Equipment Maintenance. **Abilities**—*Cognitive:* Spatial Orientation; Number Facility. *Psychomotor:* Wrist-Finger Speed; Control Precision; Manual Dexterity; Finger Dexterity; Arm-Hand Steadiness. *Physical:* Static Strength; Extent Flexibility; Trunk Strength. *Sensory:* None met the criteria. **General Work Activities**—*Information Input:* Getting Information; Inspecting Equipment, Structures, or Materials; Monitoring Processes, Materials, or Surroundings. *Mental Process:* Evaluating Information Against Standards; Making Decisions and Solving Problems; Updating and Using Relevant Knowledge. *Work Output:* Handling and Moving Objects; Repairing and Maintaining Mechanical Equipment; Performing General Physical Activities. *Interacting with Others:* None met the criteria. **Physical Work Conditions**—Indoors; Standing; Kneeling, Crouching, Stooping, or Crawling; Using Hands on Objects, Tools, or Controls; Bending or Twisting the Body; Repetitive Motions. **Other Job Characteristics**—None met the criteria.

Experience—Job Zone 2. Some previous work-related skill, knowledge, or experience may be helpful in these occupations, but usually is not needed. **Job Preparation**—SVP 4.0 to less than 6.0—six months to less than two years. **Knowledges**—Mechanical Devices. **Instructional Programs**—Business Machine Repair; Computer Installation and Repair Technology/Technician; Electrical/Electronics Maintenance and Repair Technology, Other.

Related SOC Job—49-9091 Coin, Vending, and Amusement Machine Servicers and Repairers. **Related OOH Job**—Coin, Vending, and Amusement Machine Servicers and Repairers. **Related DOT Jobs**—211.367-014 Automatic Teller Machine (ATM) Servicer; 349.680-010 Ticket-Dispenser Changer; 639.281-014 Coin-Machine-Service Repairer; 710.384-026 Parking-Meter Servicer; 710.681-018 Register Repairer; 729.381-014 Pin-Game-Machine Inspector; 729.384-014 Fare-Register Repairer.

49-9092.00 Commercial Divers

- Education/Training Required: Moderate-term on-the-job training
- Employed: 2,310
- Annual Earnings: $37,960
- Growth: 9.5%
- Annual Job Openings: Fewer than 500

Work below surface of water, using scuba gear to inspect, repair, remove, or install equipment and structures. May use a variety of power and hand tools, such as drills, sledgehammers, torches, and welding equipment. May conduct tests or experiments, rig explosives, or photograph structures or marine life.

Perform activities related to underwater search and rescue, salvage, recovery, and cleanup operations. Take appropriate safety precautions, such as monitoring dive lengths and depths and registering with authorities before diving expeditions begin. Set or guide placement of pilings and sandbags to provide support for structures such as docks, bridges, cofferdams, and platforms. Salvage wrecked ships or their cargo, using pneumatic power velocity and hydraulic tools and explosive charges when necessary. Repair ships, bridge foundations, and other structures below the water line, using caulk, bolts, and hand tools. Remove obstructions from strainers and marine railway or launching ways, using pneumatic and power hand tools. Inspect and test docks; ships; buoyage systems; plant intakes and outflows; and underwater pipelines, cables, and sewers, using closed-circuit television, still photography, and testing equipment. Perform offshore oil and gas exploration and extraction duties such as conducting underwater surveys and repairing and maintaining drilling rigs and platforms. Install, inspect, clean, and repair piping and valves. Carry out non-destructive testing such as tests for cracks on the legs of oil rigs at sea. Check and maintain diving equipment such as helmets, masks, air tanks, harnesses, and gauges. Communicate with workers on the surface while underwater, using signal lines or telephones. Cut and weld steel, using underwater welding equipment, jigs, and supports. Descend into water with the aid of diver helpers, using scuba gear or diving suits. Recover objects by placing rigging around sunken objects; hooking rigging to crane lines; and operating winches, derricks, or cranes to raise objects. Install pilings or footings for piers and bridges. Supervise and train other divers, including hobby divers. Obtain information about diving tasks and environmental conditions. Remove rubbish and pollution from the sea. Cultivate and harvest marine species and perform routine work on fish farms. Set up dive sites for recreational instruction. Drill holes in rock and rig explosives for underwater demolitions.

GOE Information—Interest Area: 02. Architecture and Construction. **Work Group:** 02.04. Construction Crafts. **Personality Type**—Realistic. Realistic occupations frequently involve work activities that include practical, hands-on problems and solutions. They often deal with plants; animals; and real-world materials like wood, tools, and machinery. Many of the occupations require working outside and do not involve a lot of paperwork or working closely with others. **Work Values**—Variety; Ability Utilization; Responsibility; Moral Values; Achievement; Social Status. **Skills**—Repairing; Installation. **Abilities**—*Cognitive:* Spatial Orientation; Flexibility of Closure; Perceptual Speed; Speed of Closure; Time Sharing; Memorization. *Psychomotor:* Speed of Limb Movement; Wrist-Finger Speed; Manual Dexterity; Reaction Time; Rate Control; Multilimb Coordination. *Physical:* Gross Body Coordination; Dynamic Strength; Dynamic Flexibility; Stamina; Explosive Strength; Extent Flexibility. *Sensory:* Night Vision; Peripheral Vision; Depth Perception; Far Vision; Visual Color Discrimination. **General Work Activities**—*Information Input:* Identifying Objects, Actions, and Events; Inspecting Equipment, Structures, or Materials; Getting Information. *Mental Process:* Making Decisions and Solving Problems. *Work Output:* Performing General Physical Activities; Repairing and Maintaining Mechanical Equipment; Handling and Moving Objects. *Interacting with Others:* Communicating with Other Workers. **Physical Work Conditions**—Outdoors; Very Hot or Cold; Very Bright or Dim Lighting; Minor Burns, Cuts, Bites, or Stings; Kneeling, Crouching, Stooping, or Crawling; Using Hands on Objects, Tools, or Controls. **Other Job Characteristics**—Need to Be Exact or Accurate; Errors Have Important Consequences.

Experience—Job Zone 2. Some previous work-related skill, knowledge, or experience may be helpful in these occupations, but usually is not needed. **Job Preparation**—SVP 4.0 to less than 6.0—six months to less than two years. **Knowledges**—Building and Construction; Mechanical Devices; Physics; Engineering and Technology. **Instructional Program**—Diver, Professional and Instructor.

Related SOC Job—49-9092 Commercial Divers. **Related OOH Job**—Commercial Divers. **Related DOT Jobs**—379.384-010 Scuba Diver; 899.261-010 Diver.

49-9093.00 Fabric Menders, Except Garment

- **Education/Training Required: Moderate-term on-the-job training**
- **Employed: 2,140**
- **Annual Earnings: $34,880**
- **Growth: –0.6%**
- **Annual Job Openings: Fewer than 500**

Repair tears, holes, and other defects in fabrics, such as draperies, linens, parachutes, and tents.

Sew labels and emblems onto articles for identification. Pull knots to the wrong sides of garments, using hooks. Stamp grommets into canvas, using mallets and punches or eyelet machines. Check repaired and repacked survival equipment to ensure that it meets specifications. Sew fringe, tassels, and ruffles onto drapes and curtains and buttons and trimming onto garments. Replace defective shrouds and splice connections between shrouds and harnesses, using hand tools. Measure and hem curtains, garments, and canvas coverings to size, using tape measures. Clean stains from fabric or garments, using spray guns and cleaning fluid. Trim edges of cut or torn fabric, using scissors or knives, and stitch trimmed edges together. Spread out articles or materials and examine them for holes, tears, worn areas, and other defects. Re-knit runs and replace broken threads, using latch needles. Patch holes, sew tears and ripped seams, or darn defects in items, using needles and thread or sewing machines. Operate sewing machines to restitch defective seams, sew up holes, or replace components of fabric articles. Repair holes by weaving thread over them, using needles.

GOE Information—Interest Area: 13. Manufacturing. **Work Group:** 13.11. Apparel, Shoes, Leather, and Fabric Care. **Personality Type**—Realistic. Realistic occupations frequently involve work activities that include practical, hands-on problems and solutions. They often deal with plants; animals; and real-world materials like wood, tools, and machinery. Many of the occupations require working outside and do not involve a lot of paperwork or working closely with others. **Work Values**—Moral Values; Independence; Supervision, Technical; Activity. **Skills**—None met the criteria. **Abilities**—*Cognitive:* None met the criteria. *Psychomotor:* Wrist-Finger Speed; Arm-Hand Steadiness; Finger Dexterity; Manual Dexterity; Control Precision. *Physical:* None met the criteria. *Sensory:* Visual Color Discrimination; Near Vision. **General Work Activities**—*Information Input:* None met the criteria. *Mental Process:* None met the criteria. *Work Output:* Handling and Moving Objects; Controlling Machines and Processes. *Interacting with Others:* None met the criteria. **Physical Work Conditions**—Indoors; Sitting; Using Hands on Objects, Tools, or Controls; Repetitive Motions. **Other Job Characteristics**—Repeat Same Tasks; Need to Be Exact or Accurate.

Experience—Job Zone 1. No previous work-related skill, knowledge, or experience is needed. **Job Preparation**—SVP below 4.0—less than six months. **Knowledges**—Fine Arts; Food Production. **Instructional Program**—No related CIP programs.

Related SOC Job—49-9093 Fabric Menders, Except Garment. **Related OOH Job**—Fabric Menders, Except Garment. **Related DOT Jobs**—782.381-022 Weaver, Hand; 782.684-010 Canvas Repairer; 782.684-046 Mender, Knit Goods; 784.684-046 Mender; 787.682-030 Mender; 789.684-038 Parachute Mender.

49-9094.00 Locksmiths and Safe Repairers

- Education/Training Required: Moderate-term on-the-job training
- Employed: 16,080
- Annual Earnings: $30,880
- Growth: 16.1%
- Annual Job Openings: 5,000

Repair and open locks, make keys, change locks and safe combinations, and install and repair safes.

Cut new or duplicate keys, using keycutting machines. Keep records of company locks and keys. Insert new or repaired tumblers into locks to change combinations. Move picklocks in cylinders to open door locks without keys. Disassemble mechanical or electrical locking devices and repair or replace worn tumblers, springs, and other parts, using hand tools. Repair and adjust safes, vault doors, and vault components, using hand tools, lathes, drill presses, and welding and acetylene cutting apparatus. Install safes, vault doors, and deposit boxes according to blueprints, using equipment such as powered drills, taps, dies, truck cranes, and dollies. Open safe locks by drilling. Remove interior and exterior finishes on safes and vaults and spray on new finishes.

GOE Information—Interest Area: 13. Manufacturing. **Work Group:** 13.13. Machinery Repair. **Personality Type**—Realistic. Realistic occupations frequently involve work activities that include practical, hands-on problems and solutions. They often deal with plants; animals; and real-world materials like wood, tools, and machinery. Many of the occupations require working outside and do not involve a lot of paperwork or working closely with others. **Work Values**—Independence; Supervision, Technical; Responsibility; Moral Values; Security; Compensation. **Skills**—Installation; Repairing; Equipment Maintenance; Troubleshooting; Equipment Selection; Service Orientation. **Abilities**—*Cognitive:* Visualization; Flexibility of Closure; Speed of Closure; Time Sharing. *Psychomotor:* Arm-Hand Steadiness; Reaction Time; Control Precision; Finger Dexterity; Manual Dexterity; Wrist-Finger Speed. *Physical:* Extent Flexibility; Trunk Strength; Static Strength. *Sensory:* Glare Sensitivity; Depth Perception; Hearing Sensitivity; Auditory Attention; Visual Color Discrimination. **General Work Activities**—*Information Input:* Getting Information; Identifying Objects, Actions, and Events; Inspecting Equipment, Structures, or Materials. *Mental Process:* Updating and Using Relevant Knowledge; Making Decisions and Solving Problems; Organizing, Planning, and Prioritizing. *Work Output:* Controlling Machines and Processes; Handling and Moving Objects; Performing General Physical Activities. *Interacting with Others:* Performing for or Working with the Public; Establishing and Maintaining Interpersonal Relationships; Communicating with Persons Outside Organization. **Physical Work Conditions**—More Often Outdoors Than Indoors; Noisy; Very Bright or Dim Lighting; Standing; Using Hands on Objects, Tools, or Controls. **Other Job Characteristics**—Need to Be Exact or Accurate; Repeat Same Tasks.

Experience—Job Zone 2. Some previous work-related skill, knowledge, or experience may be helpful in these occupations, but usually is not needed. **Job Preparation**—SVP 4.0 to less than 6.0—six months to less than two years. **Knowledges**—Customer and Personal Service; Sales and Marketing; Clerical Practices; Administration and Management; Mechanical Devices; Public Safety and Security. **Instructional Program**—Locksmithing and Safe Repair.

Related SOC Job—49-9094 Locksmiths and Safe Repairers. **Related OOH Job**—Locksmiths and Safe Repairers. **Related DOT Jobs—** 709.281-010 Locksmith; 709.281-014 Locksmith Apprentice; 869.381-022 Safe-and-Vault Service Mechanic.

49-9095.00 Manufactured Building and Mobile Home Installers

- Education/Training Required: Moderate-term on-the-job training
- Employed: 10,120
- Annual Earnings: $23,070
- Growth: 7.9%
- Annual Job Openings: 2,000

Move or install mobile homes or prefabricated buildings.

Reset hardware, using chisels, mallets, and screwdrivers. Remove damaged exterior panels, repair and replace structural frame members, and seal leaks, using hand tools. Repair leaks in plumbing or gas lines, using caulking compounds and plastic or copper pipe. Locate and repair frayed wiring, broken connections, or incorrect wiring, using ohmmeters, soldering irons, tape, and hand tools. List parts needed, estimate costs, and plan work procedures, using parts lists, technical manuals, and diagrams. Inspect, examine, and test the operation of parts or systems to evaluate operating condition and to determine if repairs are needed. Confer with customers or read work orders to determine the nature and extent of damage to units. Connect electrical systems to outside power sources and activate switches to test the operation of appliances and light fixtures. Refinish wood surfaces on cabinets, doors, moldings, and floors, using power sanders, putty, spray equipment, brushes, paints, or varnishes. Seal open sides of modular units to prepare them for shipment, using polyethylene sheets, nails, and hammers. Open and close doors, windows, and drawers to test their operation and trim edges to fit, using jackplanes or drawknives. Move and set up mobile homes or prefabricated buildings on owners' lots or at mobile home parks. Install, repair, and replace units, fixtures, appliances, and other items and systems in mobile and modular homes, prefabricated buildings, or travel trailers, using hand tools or power tools. Connect water hoses to inlet pipes of plumbing systems and test operation of plumbing fixtures.

GOE Information—Interest Area: 02. Architecture and Construction. **Work Group:** 02.04. Construction Crafts. **Personality Type**—Realistic. Realistic occupations frequently involve work activities that include practical, hands-on problems and solutions. They often deal with plants; animals; and real-world materials like wood, tools, and machinery. Many of the occupations require working outside and do not involve a lot of paperwork or working closely with others. **Work Values**—Supervision, Technical; Moral Values; Variety. **Skills**—Installation; Repairing; Troubleshooting; Equipment Maintenance. **Abilities**—*Cognitive:* Visualization; Number Facility. *Psychomotor:* Wrist-Finger Speed; Control Precision; Manual Dexterity; Multilimb Coordination; Arm-Hand Steadiness. *Physical:* Extent Flexibility; Explosive Strength; Static Strength; Trunk Strength. *Sensory:* None met the criteria. **General Work Activities**—*Information Input:* Getting Information; Monitoring Processes, Materials, or Surroundings; Inspecting Equipment, Structures, or Materials. *Mental Process:* Judging the Qualities of Things, Services, or Other People's Work; Evaluating Information Against Standards; Organizing, Planning, and Prioritizing. *Work Output:* Performing General Physical Activities; Handling and Moving Objects; Repairing and Maintaining Mechanical Equipment. *Interacting with Others:* None met the criteria. **Physical Work Conditions**—More Often Indoors Than Outdoors; Standing; Using Hands on Objects, Tools, or Controls. **Other Job Characteristics**—None met the criteria.

Experience—Job Zone 2. Some previous work-related skill, knowledge, or experience may be helpful in these occupations, but usually is not needed. **Job Preparation**—SVP 4.0 to less than 6.0—six months to less than two years. **Knowledges**—Building and Construction; Mechanical Devices; Design; Engineering and Technology. **Instructional Program**—Building/Construction Site Management/ Manager.

Related SOC Job—49-9095 Manufactured Building and Mobile Home Installers. **Related OOH Job**—Manufactured Building and Mobile Home Installers. **Related DOT Jobs**—869.384-010 Repairer, Manufactured Buildings; 869.684-074 Utility Worker.

49-9096.00 Riggers

- **Education/Training Required: Short-term on-the-job training**
- **Employed: 11,840**
- **Annual Earnings: $37,010**
- **Growth: 13.9%**
- **Annual Job Openings: 2,000**

Set up or repair rigging for construction projects, manufacturing plants, logging yards, ships and shipyards, or for the entertainment industry.

Manipulate rigging lines, hoists, and pulling gear to move or support materials such as heavy equipment, ships, or theatrical sets. Signal or verbally direct workers engaged in hoisting and moving loads to ensure safety of workers and materials. Dismantle and store rigging equipment after use. Control movement of heavy equipment through narrow openings or confined spaces, using chainfalls, gin poles, gallows frames, and other equipment. Attach pulleys and blocks to fixed overhead structures such as beams, ceilings, and gin pole booms, using bolts and clamps. Attach loads to rigging to provide support or prepare them for moving, using hand and power tools. Align, level, and anchor machinery. Select gear such as cables, pulleys, and winches according to load weights and sizes, facilities, and work schedules. Tilt, dip, and turn suspended loads to maneuver over, under, or around obstacles, using multi-point suspension techniques. Test rigging to ensure safety and reliability. Fabricate, set up, and repair rigging, supporting structures, hoists, and pulling gear, using hand and power tools. Install ground rigging for yarding lines, attaching chokers to logs and then to the lines. Clean and dress machine surfaces and component parts.

GOE Information—**Interest Area:** 02. Architecture and Construction. **Work Group:** 02.04. Construction Crafts. **Personality Type**—Realistic. Realistic occupations frequently involve work activities that include practical, hands-on problems and solutions. They often deal with plants; animals; and real-world materials like wood, tools, and machinery. Many of the occupations require working outside and do not involve a lot of paperwork or working closely with others. **Work Values**—Moral Values; Authority; Supervision, Technical; Co-workers; Responsibility; Supervision, Human Relations. **Skills**—Repairing; Technology Design; Operation and Control; Science; Operation Monitoring; Installation. **Abilities**—*Cognitive:* Spatial Orientation; Visualization; Information Ordering. *Psychomotor:* Wrist-Finger Speed; Reaction Time; Multilimb Coordination; Response Orientation; Speed of Limb Movement; Manual Dexterity. *Physical:* Gross Body Equilibrium; Extent Flexibility; Explosive Strength; Dynamic Strength; Static Strength; Stamina. *Sensory:* Depth Perception; Peripheral Vision; Far Vision. **General Work Activities**—*Information Input:* Identifying Objects, Actions, and Events; Inspecting Equipment, Structures, or Materials; Monitoring Processes, Materials, or Surroundings. *Mental Process:* Organizing, Planning, and Prioritizing. *Work Output:* Handling and

Moving Objects; Performing General Physical Activities; Controlling Machines and Processes. *Interacting with Others:* Coordinating the Work and Activities of Others; Communicating with Other Workers. **Physical Work Conditions**—Outdoors; High Places; Standing; Climbing Ladders, Scaffolds, or Poles; Using Hands on Objects, Tools, or Controls; Bending or Twisting the Body. **Other Job Characteristics**—Need to Be Exact or Accurate; Errors Have Important Consequences.

Experience—Job Zone 3. Previous work-related skill, knowledge, or experience is required. **Job Preparation**—SVP 6.0 to less than 7.0— more than one year and less than four years. **Knowledges**— Mechanical Devices; Public Safety and Security; Engineering and Technology; Building and Construction. **Instructional Program**— Construction/Heavy Equipment/Earthmoving Equipment Operation.

Related SOC Job—49-9096 Riggers. **Related OOH Job**—Riggers. **Related DOT Jobs**—623.381-010 Gear Repairer; 806.261-014 Rigger; 806.261-018 Rigger Apprentice; 921.260-010 Rigger; 921.664-014 Rigger; 962.664-010 High Rigger; 962.684-010 Acrobatic Rigger; 962.684-014 Grip.

49-9097.00 Signal and Track Switch Repairers

- **Education/Training Required: Moderate-term on-the-job training**
- **Employed: 6,100**
- **Annual Earnings: $49,200**
- **Growth: 2.3%**
- **Annual Job Openings: 1,000**

Install, inspect, test, maintain, or repair electric gate crossings, signals, signal equipment, track switches, section lines, or intercommunications systems within a railroad system.

Inspect, maintain, and replace batteries as needed. Tighten loose bolts, using wrenches, and test circuits and connections by opening and closing gates. Inspect switch-controlling mechanisms on trolley wires and in track beds, using hand tools and test equipment. Inspect and test operation, mechanical parts, and circuitry of gate crossings, signals, and signal equipment such as interlocks and hotbox detectors. Lubricate moving parts on gate-crossing mechanisms and swinging signals. Test air lines and air cylinders on pneumatically operated gates. Maintain high tension lines, de-energizing lines for power companies when repairs are requested. Clean lenses of lamps with cloths and solvents. Inspect electrical units of railroad grade crossing gates and repair loose bolts and defective electrical connections and parts. Drive motor vehicles to job sites. Install, inspect, maintain, and repair various railroad service equipment on the road or in the shop, including railroad signal systems. Record and report information about mileage or track inspected, repairs performed, and equipment requiring replacement. Replace defective wiring, broken lenses, or burned-out light bulbs.

GOE Information—**Interest Area:** 13. Manufacturing. **Work Group:** 13.13. Machinery Repair. **Personality Type**—Realistic. Realistic occupations frequently involve work activities that include practical, hands-on problems and solutions. They often deal with plants; animals; and real-world materials like wood, tools, and machinery. Many of the occupations require working outside and do not involve a lot of paperwork or working closely with others. **Work Values**— Supervision, Technical; Moral Values; Supervision, Human Relations; Security; Company Policies and Practices; Variety. **Skills**—

Installation; Repairing; Equipment Maintenance; Troubleshooting; Operation Monitoring; Quality Control Analysis. **Abilities**—*Cognitive:* Visualization. *Psychomotor:* Wrist-Finger Speed; Control Precision; Finger Dexterity; Manual Dexterity. *Physical:* Extent Flexibility. *Sensory:* Visual Color Discrimination. **General Work Activities**—*Information Input:* Getting Information; Inspecting Equipment, Structures, or Materials; Monitoring Processes, Materials, or Surroundings. *Mental Process:* Updating and Using Relevant Knowledge; Making Decisions and Solving Problems; Analyzing Data or Information. *Work Output:* Performing General Physical Activities; Repairing and Maintaining Mechanical Equipment; Handling and Moving Objects. *Interacting with Others:* Communicating with Other Workers. **Physical Work Conditions**—Outdoors; Hazardous Conditions; Hazardous Equipment; Minor Burns, Cuts, Bites, or Stings; Standing; Using Hands on Objects, Tools, or Controls. **Other Job Characteristics**—Errors Have Important Consequences; Need to Be Exact or Accurate.

Experience—Job Zone 4. A minimum of two to four years of work-related skill, knowledge, or experience is needed. **Job Preparation**—SVP 7.0 to less than 8.0—two years to less than 10 years. **Knowledges**—Mechanical Devices; Transportation; Telecommunications; Engineering and Technology; Physics; Public Safety and Security. **Instructional Program**—Electrician.

Related SOC Job—49-9097 Signal and Track Switch Repairers. **Related OOH Job**—Signal and Track Switch Repairers. **Related DOT Jobs**—822.281-026 Signal Maintainer; 825.261-010 Electric-Track-Switch Maintainer.

49-9098.00 Helpers—Installation, Maintenance, and Repair Workers

- **Education/Training Required: Short-term on-the-job training**
- **Employed: 158,520**
- **Annual Earnings: $21,230**
- **Growth: 16.4%**
- **Annual Job Openings: 41,000**

Help installation, maintenance, and repair workers in maintenance, parts replacement, and repair of vehicles, industrial machinery, and electrical and electronic equipment. Perform duties such as furnishing tools, materials, and supplies to other workers; cleaning work area, machines, and tools; and holding materials or tools for other workers.

Tend and observe equipment and machinery to verify efficient and safe operation. Examine and test machinery, equipment, components, and parts for defects and to ensure proper functioning. Adjust, connect, or disconnect wiring, piping, tubing, and other parts, using hand tools or power tools. Install or replace machinery, equipment, and new or replacement parts and instruments, using hand tools or power tools. Clean or lubricate vehicles, machinery, equipment, instruments, tools, work areas, and other objects, using hand tools, power tools, and cleaning equipment. Apply protective materials to equipment, components, and parts to prevent defects and corrosion. Transfer tools, parts, equipment, and supplies to and from workstations and other areas. Disassemble broken or defective equipment in order to facilitate repair; reassemble equipment when repairs are complete. Assemble and maintain physical structures, using hand tools or power tools. Provide assistance to more skilled workers involved in the adjustment, maintenance, part replacement, and repair of tools, equipment, and machines. Position vehicles, machinery, equipment, physical structures, and other objects for assembly or installation, using hand tools, power tools, and moving equipment. Hold or supply tools, parts, equipment, and supplies for other workers. Prepare work stations so mechanics and repairers can conduct work.

GOE Information—Interest Area: 02. Architecture and Construction. **Work Group:** 02.06. Construction Support/Labor. **Personality Type**—Realistic. Realistic occupations frequently involve work activities that include practical, hands-on problems and solutions. They often deal with plants; animals; and real-world materials like wood, tools, and machinery. Many of the occupations require working outside and do not involve a lot of paperwork or working closely with others. **Work Values**—Supervision, Technical; Advancement; Moral Values; Co-workers. **Skills**—Installation; Operation Monitoring; Repairing; Equipment Maintenance; Troubleshooting; Operations Analysis. **Abilities**—*Cognitive:* Flexibility of Closure; Visualization; Perceptual Speed; Category Flexibility; Oral Comprehension; Selective Attention. *Psychomotor:* Reaction Time; Speed of Limb Movement; Rate Control; Arm-Hand Steadiness; Wrist-Finger Speed; Control Precision. *Physical:* Extent Flexibility; Static Strength; Stamina; Dynamic Strength; Gross Body Coordination; Trunk Strength. *Sensory:* Glare Sensitivity; Hearing Sensitivity; Visual Color Discrimination; Depth Perception; Sound Localization; Auditory Attention. **General Work Activities**—*Information Input:* Monitoring Processes, Materials, or Surroundings; Estimating the Needed Characteristics of Products, Events, or Information; Identifying Objects, Actions, and Events. *Mental Process:* Updating and Using Relevant Knowledge; Evaluating Information Against Standards; Organizing, Planning, and Prioritizing. *Work Output:* Handling and Moving Objects; Performing General Physical Activities; Repairing and Maintaining Mechanical Equipment. *Interacting with Others:* Establishing and Maintaining Interpersonal Relationships; Communicating with Other Workers; Communicating with Persons Outside Organization. **Physical Work Conditions**—Noisy; Hazardous Conditions; Hazardous Equipment; Standing; Using Hands on Objects, Tools, or Controls; Bending or Twisting the Body. **Other Job Characteristics**—Errors Have Important Consequences; Need to Be Exact or Accurate.

Experience—Job Zone 2. Some previous work-related skill, knowledge, or experience may be helpful in these occupations, but usually is not needed. **Job Preparation**—SVP 4.0 to less than 6.0—six months to less than two years. **Knowledges**—Mechanical Devices; Engineering and Technology; Building and Construction; Design; Chemistry; Public Safety and Security. **Instructional Program**—Industrial Mechanics and Maintenance Technology.

Related SOC Job—49-9098 Helpers—Installation, Maintenance, and Repair Workers. **Related OOH Job**—Helpers—Installation, Maintenance, and Repair Workers. **Related DOT Jobs**—620.664-010 Construction-Equipment-Mechanic Helper; 620.664-014 Maintenance Mechanic Helper; 620.684-014 Automobile-Mechanic Helper; 620.684-030 Tractor-Mechanic Helper; 621.684-010 Airframe-and-Power-Plant-Mechanic Helper; 622.684-014 Car-Repairer Helper; 623.684-010 Motorboat-Mechanic Helper; 623.687-010 Machinist Helper, Outside; 625.684-010 Diesel-Mechanic Helper; 628.664-010 Overhauler Helper; 630.664-010 Repairer Helper; 630.664-018 Service-Mechanic Helper, Compressed-Gas Equipment; others.

49-9099.99 Installation, Maintenance, and Repair Workers, All Other

- **Education/Training Required: Moderate-term on-the-job training**
- **Employed: 135,560**
- **Annual Earnings: $34,090**
- **Growth: 11.0%**
- **Annual Job Openings: 22,000**

All mechanical, installation, and repair workers and helpers not listed separately.

No task data available.

Note: The Department of Labor has not collected some data for this job, so it has fewer details than the other descriptions.

Related SOC Job—49-9099 Installation, Maintenance, and Repair Workers, All Other. **Related OOH Job**—None. **Related DOT Jobs**—369.684-018 Umbrella Repairer; 616.662-010 Hydraulic Press Operator; 619.281-010 Casting Repairer; 620.684-010 Automobile Wrecker; 621.261-520 Aviation Safety Equipment Technician; 621.684-014 Reclamation Worker; 630.684-018 Pump Installer; 632.381-010 Gun Synchronizer; 705.684-042 Mother Repairer; 709.364-014 Towel-Cabinet Repairer; 709.384-010 Fire-Extinguisher Repairer; 709.684-034 Cigarette-Lighter Repairer; 709.684-062 Repairer; 719.381-014 Hearing-Aid Repairer; others.

51-0000
Production Occupations

51-1000 Supervisors, Production Workers

51-1011.00 First-Line Supervisors/ Managers of Production and Operating Workers

- Education/Training Required: Work experience in a related occupation
- Employed: 679,930
- Annual Earnings: $46,140
- Growth: 2.7%
- Annual Job Openings: 89,000

Supervise and coordinate the activities of production and operating workers, such as inspectors, precision workers, machine setters and operators, assemblers, fabricators, and plant and system operators.

Enforce safety and sanitation regulations. Direct and coordinate the activities of employees engaged in the production or processing of goods, such as inspectors, machine setters, and fabricators. Read and analyze charts, work orders, production schedules, and other records and reports to determine production requirements and to evaluate current production estimates and outputs. Confer with other supervisors to coordinate operations and activities within or between departments. Plan and establish work schedules, assignments, and production sequences to meet production goals. Inspect materials, products, or equipment to detect defects or malfunctions. Demonstrate equipment operations and work and safety procedures to new employees or assign employees to experienced workers for training. Observe work and monitor gauges, dials, and other indicators to ensure that operators conform to production or processing standards. Interpret specifications, blueprints, job orders, and company policies and procedures for workers. Confer with management or subordinates to resolve worker problems, complaints, or grievances. Maintain operations data such as time, production, and cost records and prepare management reports of production results. Recommend or implement measures to motivate employees and to improve production methods, equipment performance, product quality, or efficiency. Determine standards, budgets, production goals, and rates based on company policies, equipment and labor availability, and workloads. Requisition materials, supplies, equipment parts, or repair services. Recommend personnel actions such as hirings and promotions. Set up and adjust machines and equipment. Calculate labor and equipment requirements and production specifications, using standard formulas. Plan and develop new products and production processes.

GOE Information—Interest Area: 13. Manufacturing. **Work Group:** 13.01. Managerial Work in Manufacturing. **Personality Type—** Enterprising. Enterprising occupations frequently involve starting up and carrying out projects. These occupations can involve leading people and making many decisions. They sometimes require risk taking and often deal with business. **Work Values—**Authority; Responsibility; Variety; Co-workers; Autonomy; Social Status. **Skills—** Management of Personnel Resources; Operation Monitoring; Operation and Control; Quality Control Analysis; Systems Analysis; Operations Analysis. **Abilities—***Cognitive:* Originality; Fluency of Ideas; Selective Attention; Perceptual Speed; Written Expression; Visualization. *Psychomotor:* Reaction Time; Multilimb Coordination; Control Precision; Arm-Hand Steadiness; Manual Dexterity; Finger Dexterity. *Physical:* None met the criteria. *Sensory:* Auditory Attention;

Speech Clarity; Far Vision; Speech Recognition. **General Work Activities—***Information Input:* Monitoring Processes, Materials, or Surroundings; Identifying Objects, Actions, and Events; Getting Information. *Mental Process:* Organizing, Planning, and Prioritizing; Making Decisions and Solving Problems; Scheduling Work and Activities. *Work Output:* Controlling Machines and Processes; Documenting or Recording Information; Handling and Moving Objects. *Interacting with Others:* Guiding, Directing, and Motivating Subordinates; Coordinating the Work and Activities of Others; Resolving Conflicts and Negotiating with Others. **Physical Work Conditions—**Indoors; Noisy; Contaminants; Hazardous Equipment; Standing; Walking and Running. **Other Job Characteristics—**Need to Be Exact or Accurate; Pace Determined by Speed of Equipment; Repeat Same Tasks; Errors Have Important Consequences.

Experience—Job Zone 3. Previous work-related skill, knowledge, or experience is required. **Job Preparation—**SVP 6.0 to less than 7.0— more than one year and less than four years. **Knowledges—** Production and Processing; Mechanical Devices; Personnel and Human Resources; Administration and Management; Engineering and Technology; Education and Training. **Instructional Program—** Operations Management and Supervision.

Related SOC Job—51-1011 First-Line Supervisors/Managers of Production and Operating Workers. **Related OOH Job—**First-Line Supervisors/Managers of Production and Operating Workers. **Related DOT Jobs—**184.167-046 Incinerator-Plant-General Supervisor; 184.167-142 Superintendent, Cold Storage; 299.137-018 Sample-Room Supervisor; 361.137-010 Supervisor, Laundry; 365.131-010 Shoe-Repair Supervisor; 369.137-010 Supervisor, Dry Cleaning; 369.137-014 Supervisor, Rug Cleaning; 369.167-010 Manager, Laundromat; 500.131-010 Supervisor; 500.132-010 Supervisor, Sheet Manufacturing; 500.134-010 Supervisor, Matrix; 501.130-010 Supervisor, Hot-Dip-Tinning; 501.137-010 Supervisor, Hot-Dip Plating; others.

51-2000 Assemblers and Fabricators

51-2011.00 Aircraft Structure, Surfaces, Rigging, and Systems Assemblers

- Education/Training Required: Long-term on-the-job training
- Employed: 22,820
- Annual Earnings: $43,990
- Growth: 7.8%
- Annual Job Openings: 4,000

Assemble, fit, fasten, and install parts of airplanes, space vehicles, or missiles, such as tails, wings, fuselage, bulkheads, stabilizers, landing gear, rigging and control equipment, or heating and ventilating systems.

Form loops or splices in cables, using clamps and fittings, or reweave cable strands. Align and fit structural assemblies manually or signal crane operators to position assemblies for joining. Align, fit, assemble, connect, and install system components, using jigs, fixtures, measuring instruments, hand tools, and power tools. Assemble and fit prefabricated parts to form subassemblies. Assemble, install, and connect parts, fittings, and assemblies on aircraft, using layout tools; hand tools; power tools; and fasteners such as bolts, screws, rivets, and clamps. Attach brackets, hinges, or clips to secure or support components and subassemblies, using bolts, screws, rivets, chemical bonding, or welding. Select and install accessories in swaging machines, using hand tools. Fit and fasten sheet metal coverings to surface areas and other sections of aircraft prior to welding or riveting. Lay out and mark reference points and locations for installation of parts and components, using jigs, templates, and measuring and marking instruments. Inspect and test installed units, parts, systems, and assemblies for fit, alignment, performance, defects, and compliance with standards, using measuring instruments and test equipment. Install mechanical linkages and actuators and verify tension of cables, using tensiometers. Join structural assemblies such as wings, tails, and fuselage. Measure and cut cables and tubing, using master templates, measuring instruments, and cable cutters or saws. Read and interpret blueprints, illustrations, and specifications to determine layouts, sequences of operations, or identities and relationships of parts. Prepare and load live ammunition, missiles, and bombs onto aircraft according to established procedures. Adjust, repair, rework, or replace parts and assemblies to eliminate malfunctions and to ensure proper operation. Cut, trim, file, bend, and smooth parts and verify sizes and fitting tolerances to ensure proper fit and clearance of parts. Install and connect control cables to electronically controlled units, using hand tools, ring locks, cotter keys, threaded connectors, turnbuckles, and related devices.

GOE Information—Interest Area: 13. Manufacturing. **Work Group:** 13.14. Vehicle and Facility Mechanical Work. **Personality Type—** Realistic. Realistic occupations frequently involve work activities that include practical, hands-on problems and solutions. They often deal with plants; animals; and real-world materials like wood, tools, and machinery. Many of the occupations require working outside and do not involve a lot of paperwork or working closely with others. **Work Values—**Moral Values; Independence; Supervision, Technical; Advancement; Supervision, Human Relations; Company Policies and Practices. **Skills—**Installation; Repairing; Quality Control Analysis; Equipment Maintenance; Operation and Control; Troubleshooting. **Abilities—***Cognitive:* Spatial Orientation; Visualization; Number Facility. *Psychomotor:* Wrist-Finger Speed; Manual Dexterity; Speed of Limb Movement; Arm-Hand Steadiness; Reaction Time; Multilimb Coordination. *Physical:* Explosive Strength; Dynamic Flexibility; Extent Flexibility; Static Strength; Dynamic Strength; Gross Body Coordination. *Sensory:* Depth Perception. **General Work Activities—***Information Input:* Inspecting Equipment, Structures, or Materials; Monitoring Processes, Materials, or Surroundings; Getting Information. *Mental Process:* Updating and Using Relevant Knowledge; Evaluating Information Against Standards; Judging the Qualities of Things, Services, or Other People's Work. *Work Output:* Handling and Moving Objects; Repairing and Maintaining Mechanical Equipment; Controlling Machines and Processes. *Interacting with Others:* None met the criteria. **Physical Work Conditions—**More Often Indoors Than Outdoors; Hazardous Equipment; Standing; Kneeling, Crouching, Stooping, or Crawling; Using Hands on Objects, Tools, or Controls. **Other Job Characteristics—**Need to Be Exact or Accurate.

Experience—Job Zone 3. Previous work-related skill, knowledge, or experience is required. **Job Preparation—**SVP 6.0 to less than 7.0— more than one year and less than four years. **Knowledges—** Mechanical Devices; Production and Processing; Design; Building and Construction; Engineering and Technology; Physics. **Instructional Programs—**Aircraft Powerplant Technology/Technician; Airframe Mechanics and Aircraft Maintenance Technology/Technician; Avionics Maintenance and Technology/Technician.

Related SOC Job—51-2011 Aircraft Structure, Surfaces, Rigging, and Systems Assemblers. **Related OOH Job—**Assemblers and Fabricators. **Related DOT Jobs—**806.361-014 Assembler-Installer, General;

806.361-030 Aircraft Mechanic, Armament; 806.380-010 Riveting Machine Operator, Automatic; 806.381-014 Aircraft Mechanic, Environmental Control System; 806.381-018 Aircraft Mechanic, Rigging and Controls; 806.381-026 Assembler, Aircraft, Structures and Surfaces; 806.381-034 Assembler, Tubing; 806.381-042 Cable Assembler and Swager; 806.381-066 Aircraft Mechanic, Plumbing and Hydraulics; 806.381-082 Precision Assembler.

51-2021.00 Coil Winders, Tapers, and Finishers

- **Education/Training Required: Short-term on-the-job training**
- **Employed: 23,190**
- **Annual Earnings: $25,630**
- **Growth: –28.5%**
- **Annual Job Openings: 4,000**

Wind wire coils used in electrical components such as resistors and transformers and in electrical equipment and instruments such as field cores, bobbins, armature cores, electrical motors, generators, and control equipment.

Operate or tend wire-coiling machines to wind wire coils used in electrical components such as resistors and transformers and in electrical equipment and instruments such as bobbins and generators. Review work orders and specifications to determine materials needed and types of parts to be processed. Cut, strip, and bend wire leads at ends of coils, using pliers and wire scrapers. Select and load materials such as workpieces, objects, and machine parts onto equipment used in coiling processes. Record production and operational data on specified forms. Attach, alter, and trim materials such as wire, insulation, and coils, using hand tools. Stop machines to remove completed components, using hand tools. Examine and test wired electrical components such as motors, armatures, and stators, using measuring devices, and record test results. Apply solutions or paints to wired electrical components, using hand tools, and bake components. Disassemble and assemble motors and repair and maintain electrical components and machinery parts, using hand tools. Line slots with sheet insulation and insert coils into slots.

GOE Information—Interest Area: 13. Manufacturing. **Work Group:** 13.09. Hands-On Work, Assorted Materials. **Personality Type—** Realistic. Realistic occupations frequently involve work activities that include practical, hands-on problems and solutions. They often deal with plants; animals; and real-world materials like wood, tools, and machinery. Many of the occupations require working outside and do not involve a lot of paperwork or working closely with others. **Work Values—**Supervision, Technical; Moral Values; Independence; Company Policies and Practices; Activity; Supervision, Human Relations. **Skills—**Technology Design; Installation; Operation and Control; Operation Monitoring; Equipment Selection; Equipment Maintenance. **Abilities—***Cognitive:* Perceptual Speed. *Psychomotor:* Reaction Time; Arm-Hand Steadiness; Control Precision; Response Orientation; Manual Dexterity; Multilimb Coordination. *Physical:* Static Strength; Trunk Strength. *Sensory:* Depth Perception; Hearing Sensitivity; Visual Color Discrimination. **General Work Activities—***Information Input:* Getting Information; Monitoring Processes, Materials, or Surroundings; Inspecting Equipment, Structures, or Materials. *Mental Process:* Updating and Using Relevant Knowledge; Making Decisions and Solving Problems; Processing Information. *Work Output:* Handling and Moving Objects; Controlling Machines and Processes; Performing General Physical Activities. *Interacting with Others:* Establishing and Maintaining Interpersonal Relationships;

Communicating with Other Workers; Teaching Others. **Physical Work Conditions**—Indoors; Contaminants; Minor Burns, Cuts, Bites, or Stings; Standing; Using Hands on Objects, Tools, or Controls; Repetitive Motions. **Other Job Characteristics**—Need to Be Exact or Accurate; Repeat Same Tasks; Pace Determined by Speed of Equipment; Errors Have Important Consequences.

Experience—Job Zone 2. Some previous work-related skill, knowledge, or experience may be helpful in these occupations, but usually is not needed. **Job Preparation**—SVP 4.0 to less than 6.0—six months to less than two years. **Knowledges**—Production and Processing; Mechanical Devices; Education and Training. **Instructional Program**—Industrial Electronics Technology/Technician.

Related SOC Job—51-2021 Coil Winders, Tapers, and Finishers. **Related OOH Job**—Assemblers and Fabricators. **Related DOT Jobs**—721.684-018 Coil Connector; 724.362-010 Wire Coiler; 724.381-014 Coil Winder, Repair; 724.684-010 Armature Bander; 724.684-014 Armature Connector II; 724.684-026 Coil Winder; 724.685-010 Element Winding Machine Tender; 726.682-014 Wire-Wrapping-Machine Operator.

51-2022.00 Electrical and Electronic Equipment Assemblers

- **Education/Training Required: Short-term on-the-job training**
- **Employed: 207,270**
- **Annual Earnings: $25,130**
- **Growth: –6.4%**
- **Annual Job Openings: 33,000**

Assemble or modify electrical or electronic equipment, such as computers, test equipment telemetering systems, electric motors, and batteries.

Inspect and test wiring installations, assemblies, and circuits for resistance factors and for operation and record results. Assemble electrical or electronic systems and support structures and install components, units, subassemblies, wiring, and assembly casings, using rivets, bolts, and soldering and micro-welding equipment. Adjust, repair, or replace electrical or electronic component parts to correct defects and to ensure conformance to specifications. Clean parts, using cleaning solutions, air hoses, and cloths. Read and interpret schematic drawings, diagrams, blueprints, specifications, work orders, and reports to determine materials requirements and assembly instructions. Mark and tag components so that stock inventory can be tracked and identified. Position, align, and adjust workpieces and electrical parts to facilitate wiring and assembly. Pack finished assemblies for shipment and transport them to storage areas, using hoists or handtrucks. Confer with supervisors or engineers to plan and review work activities and to resolve production problems. Explain assembly procedures or techniques to other workers. Measure and adjust voltages to specified values to determine operational accuracy of instruments. Fabricate and form parts, coils, and structures according to specifications, using drills, calipers, cutters, and saws. Drill and tap holes in specified equipment locations to mount control units and to provide openings for elements, wiring, and instruments. Complete, review, and maintain production, time, and component waste reports. Paint structures as specified, using paint sprayers. Instruct customers in the installation, repair, and maintenance of products. Distribute materials, supplies, and subassemblies to work areas.

GOE Information—**Interest Area:** 13. Manufacturing. **Work Group:** 13.06. Production Precision Work. **Personality Type**—Realistic. Realistic occupations frequently involve work activities that include

practical, hands-on problems and solutions. They often deal with plants; animals; and real-world materials like wood, tools, and machinery. Many of the occupations require working outside and do not involve a lot of paperwork or working closely with others. **Work Values**—Moral Values; Company Policies and Practices; Advancement; Supervision, Technical; Authority; Supervision, Human Relations. **Skills**—Quality Control Analysis; Installation; Equipment Selection; Repairing; Systems Evaluation; Troubleshooting. **Abilities**—*Cognitive:* Visualization; Perceptual Speed; Selective Attention; Flexibility of Closure; Information Ordering; Oral Comprehension. *Psychomotor:* Arm-Hand Steadiness; Manual Dexterity; Finger Dexterity; Control Precision; Multilimb Coordination; Reaction Time. *Physical:* Static Strength; Extent Flexibility; Trunk Strength. *Sensory:* Visual Color Discrimination; Hearing Sensitivity. **General Work Activities**—*Information Input:* Monitoring Processes, Materials, or Surroundings; Inspecting Equipment, Structures, or Materials; Getting Information. *Mental Process:* Making Decisions and Solving Problems; Updating and Using Relevant Knowledge; Judging the Qualities of Things, Services, or Other People's Work. *Work Output:* Handling and Moving Objects; Controlling Machines and Processes; Performing General Physical Activities. *Interacting with Others:* Establishing and Maintaining Interpersonal Relationships; Resolving Conflicts and Negotiating with Others; Communicating with Other Workers. **Physical Work Conditions**—Indoors; Contaminants; Hazardous Equipment; Sitting; Using Hands on Objects, Tools, or Controls; Repetitive Motions. **Other Job Characteristics**—Need to Be Exact or Accurate; Repeat Same Tasks.

Experience—Job Zone 2. Some previous work-related skill, knowledge, or experience may be helpful in these occupations, but usually is not needed. **Job Preparation**—SVP 4.0 to less than 6.0—six months to less than two years. **Knowledges**—Production and Processing. **Instructional Programs**—Communications Systems Installation and Repair Technology; Industrial Electronics Technology/Technician.

Related SOC Job—51-2022 Electrical and Electronic Equipment Assemblers. **Related OOH Job**—Assemblers and Fabricators. **Related DOT Jobs**—693.381-026 Electrical and Radio Mock-Up Mechanic; 710.281-010 Assembler and Tester, Electronics; 720.684-014 Phonograph-Cartridge Assembler; 720.687-010 Record-Changer Assembler; 721.381-014 Electric-Motor-Control Assembler; 721.484-010 Electric-Motor Winder; 721.484-014 Field-Ring Assembler; 721.484-022 Skein Winder; 721.684-014 Assembler, Carbon Brushes; 721.684-022 Electric-Motor Assembler; 721.684-026 Spider Assembler; 722.381-010 Assembler; 723.684-010 Assembler; 723.684-014 Assembler I; others.

51-2023.00 Electromechanical Equipment Assemblers

- **Education/Training Required: Short-term on-the-job training**
- **Employed: 57,200**
- **Annual Earnings: $26,980**
- **Growth: –13.9%**
- **Annual Job Openings: 8,000**

Assemble or modify electromechanical equipment or devices, such as servomechanisms, gyros, dynamometers, magnetic drums, tape drives, brakes, control linkage, actuators, and appliances.

Clean and lubricate parts and subassemblies, using grease paddles or oilcans. Operate small cranes to transport or position large parts. Disassemble units to replace parts or to crate them for shipping.

Assemble parts or units and position, align, and fasten units to assemblies, subassemblies, or frames, using hand tools and power tools. Connect cables, tubes, and wiring according to specifications. Drill, tap, ream, countersink, and spot-face bolt holes in parts, using drill presses and portable power drills. File, lap, and buff parts to fit, using hand and power tools. Inspect, test, and adjust completed units to ensure that units meet specifications, tolerances, and customer order requirements. Measure parts to determine tolerances, using precision measuring instruments such as micrometers, calipers, and verniers. Position, align, and adjust parts for proper fit and assembly. Read blueprints and specifications to determine component parts and assembly sequences of electromechanical units. Attach name plates and mark identifying information on parts. Operate or tend automated assembling equipment, such as robotics and fixed automation equipment. Pack or fold insulation between panels.

GOE Information—Interest Area: 13. Manufacturing. **Work Group:** 13.06. Production Precision Work. **Personality Type—**Realistic. Realistic occupations frequently involve work activities that include practical, hands-on problems and solutions. They often deal with plants; animals; and real-world materials like wood, tools, and machinery. Many of the occupations require working outside and do not involve a lot of paperwork or working closely with others. **Work Values—**Independence; Supervision, Technical; Advancement; Moral Values; Company Policies and Practices; Supervision, Human Relations. **Skills—**Installation; Quality Control Analysis; Operation Monitoring; Operation and Control; Equipment Maintenance; Technology Design. **Abilities—***Cognitive:* Visualization; Number Facility; Memorization. *Psychomotor:* Wrist-Finger Speed; Manual Dexterity; Arm-Hand Steadiness; Speed of Limb Movement; Multilimb Coordination; Reaction Time. *Physical:* Explosive Strength; Dynamic Strength; Extent Flexibility; Static Strength; Trunk Strength. *Sensory:* Visual Color Discrimination; Depth Perception. **General Work Activities—***Information Input:* Getting Information; Monitoring Processes, Materials, or Surroundings; Inspecting Equipment, Structures, or Materials. *Mental Process:* Updating and Using Relevant Knowledge; Evaluating Information Against Standards. *Work Output:* Handling and Moving Objects; Repairing and Maintaining Electronic Equipment; Controlling Machines and Processes. *Interacting with Others:* None met the criteria. **Physical Work Conditions—**Indoors; Noisy; Hazardous Equipment; Standing; Using Hands on Objects, Tools, or Controls; Repetitive Motions. **Other Job Characteristics—**Need to Be Exact or Accurate.

Experience—Job Zone 3. Previous work-related skill, knowledge, or experience is required. **Job Preparation—**SVP 6.0 to less than 7.0—more than one year and less than four years. **Knowledges—**Mechanical Devices; Computers and Electronics; Production and Processing; Design; Physics; Engineering and Technology. **Instructional Programs—**Electromechanical and Instrumentation and Maintenance Technologies/Technicians, Other; Electromechanical Technology/Electromechanical Engineering Technology; Robotics Technology/Technician.

Related SOC Job—51-2023 Electromechanical Equipment Assemblers. **Related OOH Job—**Assemblers and Fabricators. **Related DOT Jobs—**706.381-018 Final Assembler; 706.381-050 Precision Assembler, Bench; 706.684-010 Air-Conditioning-Coil Assembler; 706.684-014 Assembler I; 706.684-026 Assembler, Type-Bar-And-Segment; 706.684-038 Bearing-Ring Assembler; 706.684-094 Subassembler; 714.381-010 Assembler, Photographic Equipment; 721.381-018 Governor Assembler, Hydraulic; 737.684-010 Assembler, Mechanical Ordnance.

51-2031.00 Engine and Other Machine Assemblers

- **Education/Training Required:** Short-term on-the-job training
- **Employed:** 49,430
- **Annual Earnings:** $34,770
- **Growth:** 0.2%
- **Annual Job Openings:** 2,000

Construct, assemble, or rebuild machines such as engines, turbines, and similar equipment used in such industries as construction, extraction, textiles, and paper manufacturing.

Assemble systems of gears by aligning and meshing gears in gearboxes. Verify conformance of parts to stock lists and blueprints, using measuring instruments such as calipers, gauges, and micrometers. Set and verify parts clearances. Rework, repair, and replace damaged parts or assemblies. Remove rough spots and smooth surfaces to fit, trim, or clean parts, using hand tools and power tools. Read and interpret assembly blueprints and specifications manuals and plan assembly or building operations. Position and align components for assembly manually or by using hoists. Lay out and drill, ream, tap, and cut parts for assembly. Inspect, operate, and test completed products to verify functioning, machine capabilities, and conformance to customer specifications. Fasten and install piping, fixtures, or wiring and electrical components to form assemblies or subassemblies, using hand tools, rivet guns, and welding equipment. Maintain and lubricate parts and components. Set up and operate metalworking machines, such as milling and grinding machines, to shape or fabricate parts.

GOE Information—Interest Area: 13. Manufacturing. **Work Group:** 13.06. Production Precision Work. **Personality Type—**Realistic. Realistic occupations frequently involve work activities that include practical, hands-on problems and solutions. They often deal with plants; animals; and real-world materials like wood, tools, and machinery. Many of the occupations require working outside and do not involve a lot of paperwork or working closely with others. **Work Values—**Moral Values; Independence; Supervision, Technical; Advancement; Supervision, Human Relations; Company Policies and Practices. **Skills—**Installation; Repairing; Quality Control Analysis; Operation and Control; Equipment Maintenance; Operation Monitoring. **Abilities—***Cognitive:* Visualization; Information Ordering. *Psychomotor:* Wrist-Finger Speed; Control Precision; Multilimb Coordination; Speed of Limb Movement; Arm-Hand Steadiness; Finger Dexterity. *Physical:* Extent Flexibility; Explosive Strength; Static Strength; Dynamic Strength; Stamina; Gross Body Coordination. *Sensory:* Visual Color Discrimination; Hearing Sensitivity. **General Work Activities—***Information Input:* Monitoring Processes, Materials, or Surroundings; Inspecting Equipment, Structures, or Materials; Getting Information. *Mental Process:* Evaluating Information Against Standards; Judging the Qualities of Things, Services, or Other People's Work; Analyzing Data or Information. *Work Output:* Repairing and Maintaining Mechanical Equipment; Handling and Moving Objects; Performing General Physical Activities. *Interacting with Others:* None met the criteria. **Physical Work Conditions—**Indoors; Hazardous Equipment; Minor Burns, Cuts, Bites, or Stings; Standing; Kneeling, Crouching, Stooping, or Crawling; Using Hands on Objects, Tools, or Controls. **Other Job Characteristics—**Need to Be Exact or Accurate; Errors Have Important Consequences.

Experience—Job Zone 3. Previous work-related skill, knowledge, or experience is required. **Job Preparation—**SVP 6.0 to less than 7.0—

more than one year and less than four years. **Knowledges—**Mechanical Devices; Design; Building and Construction; Engineering and Technology. **Instructional Programs—**Engine Machinist; Heavy Equipment Maintenance/Technology/Technician; Industrial Mechanics and Maintenance Technology.

Related SOC Job—51-2031 Engine and Other Machine Assemblers. **Related OOH Job—**Assemblers and Fabricators. **Related DOT Jobs—**600.261-010 Assembler, Steam-and-Gas Turbine; 600.281-022 Machine Builder; 600.380-026 Turbine-Blade Assembler; 624.381-018 Farm-Machinery Set-Up Mechanic; 625.361-010 Diesel-Engine Erector; 638.361-010 Machine Assembler; 706.361-010 Assembler; 706.381-034 Sewing-Machine Assembler; 706.381-038 Subassembler; 706.381-042 Turbine Subassembler; 706.481-010 Internal-Combustion-Engine Subassembler; 706.684-062 Injector Assembler; 801.261-010 Assembler, Mining Machinery; others.

51-2041.00 Structural Metal Fabricators and Fitters

- **Education/Training Required: Moderate-term on-the-job training**
- **Employed: 93,490**
- **Annual Earnings: $30,290**
- **Growth: 2.9%**
- **Annual Job Openings: 18,000**

Fabricate, lay out, position, align, and fit parts of structural metal products.

Position, align, fit, and weld parts to form complete units or subunits, following blueprints and layout specifications and using jigs, welding torches, and hand tools. Verify conformance of workpieces to specifications, using squares, rulers, and measuring tapes. Tackweld fitted parts together. Lay out and examine metal stock or workpieces to be processed to ensure that specifications are met. Align and fit parts according to specifications, using jacks, turnbuckles, wedges, drift pins, pry bars, and hammers. Locate and mark workpiece bending and cutting lines, allowing for stock thickness, machine and welding shrinkage, and other component specifications. Position or tighten braces, jacks, clamps, ropes, or bolt straps or bolt parts in position for welding or riveting. Study engineering drawings and blueprints to determine materials requirements and task sequences. Move parts into position manually or by using hoists or cranes. Set up and operate fabricating machines such as brakes, rolls, shears, flame cutters, grinders, and drill presses to bend, cut, form, punch, drill, or otherwise form and assemble metal components. Hammer, chip, and grind workpieces to cut, bend, and straighten metal. Smooth workpiece edges and fix taps, tubes, and valves. Design and construct templates and fixtures, using hand tools. Straighten warped or bent parts, using sledges, hand torches, straightening presses, or bulldozers. Mark reference points onto floors or face blocks and transpose them to workpieces, using measuring devices, squares, chalk, and soapstone. Set up face blocks, jigs, and fixtures. Remove high spots and cut bevels, using hand files, portable grinders, and cutting torches. Direct welders to build up low spots or short pieces with weld. Lift or move materials and finished products, using large cranes. Heat-treat parts, using acetylene torches. Preheat workpieces to make them malleable, using hand torches or furnaces. Install boilers, containers, and other structures. Erect ladders and scaffolding to fit together large assemblies.

GOE Information—Interest Area: 13. Manufacturing. **Work Group:** 13.04. Welding, Brazing, and Soldering. **Personality Type—**Realistic.

Realistic occupations frequently involve work activities that include practical, hands-on problems and solutions. They often deal with plants; animals; and real-world materials like wood, tools, and machinery. Many of the occupations require working outside and do not involve a lot of paperwork or working closely with others. **Work Values—**Moral Values; Independence; Supervision, Technical; Supervision, Human Relations; Company Policies and Practices; Activity. **Skills—**Quality Control Analysis; Operation Monitoring; Equipment Maintenance; Installation; Repairing; Operation and Control. **Abilities—***Cognitive:* Number Facility; Mathematical Reasoning; Visualization. *Psychomotor:* Control Precision; Wrist-Finger Speed; Multilimb Coordination; Manual Dexterity; Arm-Hand Steadiness. *Physical:* Explosive Strength; Static Strength; Extent Flexibility; Dynamic Strength; Trunk Strength. *Sensory:* Depth Perception. **General Work Activities—***Information Input:* Monitoring Processes, Materials, or Surroundings; Getting Information; Identifying Objects, Actions, and Events. *Mental Process:* Judging the Qualities of Things, Services, or Other People's Work; Evaluating Information Against Standards; Organizing, Planning, and Prioritizing. *Work Output:* Handling and Moving Objects; Performing General Physical Activities; Controlling Machines and Processes. *Interacting with Others:* Establishing and Maintaining Interpersonal Relationships; Communicating with Other Workers. **Physical Work Conditions—**Noisy; Contaminants; Hazardous Equipment; Minor Burns, Cuts, Bites, or Stings; Standing; Using Hands on Objects, Tools, or Controls. **Other Job Characteristics—**Need to Be Exact or Accurate; Errors Have Important Consequences.

Experience—Job Zone 3. Previous work-related skill, knowledge, or experience is required. **Job Preparation—**SVP 6.0 to less than 7.0—more than one year and less than four years. **Knowledges—**Design; Building and Construction; Mechanical Devices; Production and Processing. **Instructional Program—**Machine Shop Technology/Assistant.

Related SOC Job—51-2041 Structural Metal Fabricators and Fitters. **Related OOH Job—**Assemblers and Fabricators. **Related DOT Jobs—**619.361-010 Former, Hand; 619.361-014 Metal Fabricator; 619.361-018 Metal-Fabricator Apprentice; 623.281-720 Ship Propeller Finisher; 801.261-014 Fitter I; 801.381-014 Fitter; 809.261-010 Assembler, Ground Support Equipment; 809.381-010 Fabricator-Assembler Metal Products.

51-2091.00 Fiberglass Laminators and Fabricators

- **Education/Training Required: Moderate-term on-the-job training**
- **Employed: 30,560**
- **Annual Earnings: $25,230**
- **Growth: 4.0%**
- **Annual Job Openings: 6,000**

Laminate layers of fiberglass on molds to form boat decks and hulls, bodies for golf carts or automobiles, or other products.

Apply lacquers and waxes to mold surfaces to facilitate assembly and removal of laminated parts. Check all dies, templates, and cutout patterns to be used in the manufacturing process to ensure that they conform to dimensional data, photographs, blueprints, samples, and customer specifications. Check completed products for conformance to specifications and for defects by measuring with rulers or micrometers, by checking them visually, or by tapping them to detect bubbles or dead spots. Cure materials by letting them set at room temperature, placing them under heat lamps, or baking them in ovens. Inspect, clean, and assemble molds before beginning work. Mask off mold areas that are not to be laminated, using cellophane, wax paper, masking tape, or special sprays containing mold-release substances. Mix catalysts into resins and saturate cloth and mats with mixtures, using brushes. Pat or press layers of saturated mat or cloth into place on molds, using brushes or hands, and smooth out wrinkles and air bubbles with hands or squeegees. Release air bubbles and smooth seams, using rollers. Repair or modify damaged or defective glass-fiber parts, checking thicknesses, densities, and contours to ensure a close fit after repair. Select precut fiberglass mats, cloth, and woodbracing materials as required by projects being assembled. Spray chopped fiberglass, resins, and catalysts onto prepared molds or dies using pneumatic spray guns with chopper attachments. Trim cured materials by sawing them with diamond-impregnated cutoff wheels. Trim excess materials from molds, using hand shears or trimming knives. Bond wood reinforcing strips to decks and cabin structures of watercraft, using resin-saturated fiberglass. Apply layers of plastic resin to mold surfaces prior to placement of fiberglass mats, repeating layers until products have the desired thicknesses and plastics have jelled.

GOE Information—Interest Area: 13. Manufacturing. **Work Group:** 13.14. Vehicle and Facility Mechanical Work. **Note:** The Department of Labor has not collected some data for this job, so it has fewer details than the other descriptions.

Instructional Program—Marine Maintenance/Fitter and Ship Repair Technology.

Related SOC Job—51-2091 Fiberglass Laminators and Fabricators. **Related OOH Job—**Assemblers and Fabricators. **Related DOT Job—**806.684-054 Fiberglass Laminator.

51-2092.00 Team Assemblers

- **Education/Training Required: Moderate-term on-the-job training**
- **Employed: 1,242,370**
- **Annual Earnings: $24,120**
- **Growth: 7.3%**
- **Annual Job Openings: 262,000**

Work as part of a team having responsibility for assembling an entire product or component of a product. Team assemblers can perform all tasks conducted by the team in the assembly process and rotate through all or most of them rather than being assigned to a specific task on a permanent basis. May participate in making management decisions affecting the work. Team leaders who work as part of the team should be included.

Rotate through all the tasks required in a particular production process. Determine work assignments and procedures. Shovel and sweep work areas. Operate heavy equipment such as forklifts. Provide assistance in the production of wiring assemblies.

GOE Information—Interest Area: 13. Manufacturing. **Work Group:** 13.03. Production Work, Assorted Materials Processing. **Personality Type—**No data available. **Work Values—**No data available. **Skills—**Operation Monitoring; Installation; Quality Control Analysis; Equipment Maintenance; Technology Design; Repairing. **Abilities—***Cognitive:* Selective Attention; Time Sharing; Visualization. *Psychomotor:* Rate Control; Multilimb Coordination; Reaction Time; Control Precision; Manual Dexterity; Arm-Hand Steadiness. *Physical:* Static Strength; Trunk Strength. *Sensory:* Depth Perception; Auditory

Attention. **General Work Activities—***Information Input:* Identifying Objects, Actions, and Events; Monitoring Processes, Materials, or Surroundings; Inspecting Equipment, Structures, or Materials. *Mental Process:* Making Decisions and Solving Problems; Judging the Qualities of Things, Services, or Other People's Work; Updating and Using Relevant Knowledge. *Work Output:* Handling and Moving Objects; Controlling Machines and Processes; Performing General Physical Activities. *Interacting with Others:* Establishing and Maintaining Interpersonal Relationships; Communicating with Other Workers; Teaching Others. **Physical Work Conditions—**Indoors; Noisy; Contaminants; Standing; Using Hands on Objects, Tools, or Controls; Repetitive Motions. **Other Job Characteristics—**Need to Be Exact or Accurate; Pace Determined by Speed of Equipment; Repeat Same Tasks.

Experience—Job Zone 2. Some previous work-related skill, knowledge, or experience may be helpful in these occupations, but usually is not needed. **Job Preparation—**SVP 4.0 to less than 6.0–six months to less than two years. **Knowledges—**Production and Processing; Mechanical Devices. **Instructional Program—**No related CIP programs.

Related SOC Job—51-2092 Team Assemblers. **Related OOH Job—**Assemblers and Fabricators. **Related DOT Jobs—**726.261-560 Production Technologist; 806.684-010 Assembler, Motor Vehicle.

51-2093.00 Timing Device Assemblers, Adjusters, and Calibrators

- **Education/Training Required: Moderate-term on-the-job training**
- **Employed: 2,460**
- **Annual Earnings: $28,160**
- **Growth: −1.5%**
- **Annual Job Openings: 1,000**

Perform precision assembling or adjusting, within narrow tolerances, of timing devices, such as watches, clocks, or chronometers.

Change timing weights on balance wheels to correct deficient timing. Replace specified parts to repair malfunctioning timepieces, using watchmakers' tools, loupes, and holding fixtures. Observe operation of timepiece parts and subassemblies to determine accuracy of movement and to diagnose causes of defects. Mount mainsprings and balance wheel assemblies between jaws of truing calipers. Examine components of timepieces such as watches, clocks, or chronometers for defects, using loupes or microscopes. Disassemble timepieces such as watches, clocks, and chronometers so that repairs can be made. Clean and lubricate timepiece parts and assemblies, using solvents, buff sticks, and oil. Bend parts, such as hairsprings, pallets, barrel covers, and bridges, to correct deficiencies in truing or endshake, using tweezers. Assemble and install components of timepieces to complete mechanisms, using watchmakers' tools and loupes. Adjust sizes or positioning of timepiece parts to achieve specified fit or function, using calipers, fixtures, and loupes. Bend inner coils of springs away from or toward collets, using tweezers, to locate centers of collets in centers of springs and to correct errors resulting from faulty colleting of coils. Review blueprints, sketches, or work orders to gather information about tasks to be completed. Examine and adjust hairspring assemblies to ensure horizontal and circular alignment of hairsprings, using calipers, loupes, and watchmakers' tools. Tighten or replace loose jewels, using watchmakers' tools. Turn wheels of calipers and examine springs, using loupes, to determine if center coils appear as perfect circles. Estimate spaces between collets and first inner coils to determine if spaces are within acceptable limits. Test operation and fit of timepiece parts and subassemblies, using electronic testing equipment, tweezers, watchmakers' tools, and loupes.

GOE Information—Interest Area: 13. Manufacturing. **Work Group:** 13.06. Production Precision Work. **Personality Type**—Realistic. Realistic occupations frequently involve work activities that include practical, hands-on problems and solutions. They often deal with plants; animals; and real-world materials like wood, tools, and machinery. Many of the occupations require working outside and do not involve a lot of paperwork or working closely with others. **Work Values**—Independence; Moral Values; Working Conditions; Ability Utilization. **Skills**—Repairing; Installation; Science; Technology Design. **Abilities**—*Cognitive:* Visualization. *Psychomotor:* Finger Dexterity; Manual Dexterity; Wrist-Finger Speed; Arm-Hand Steadiness. *Physical:* None met the criteria. *Sensory:* Near Vision. **General Work Activities**—*Information Input:* Inspecting Equipment, Structures, or Materials; Monitoring Processes, Materials, or Surroundings; Getting Information. *Mental Process:* Updating and Using Relevant Knowledge; Evaluating Information Against Standards; Judging the Qualities of Things, Services, or Other People's Work. *Work Output:* Repairing and Maintaining Mechanical Equipment; Repairing and Maintaining Electronic Equipment; Handling and Moving Objects. *Interacting with Others:* None met the criteria. **Physical Work Conditions**—Indoors; Sitting; Using Hands on Objects, Tools, or Controls. **Other Job Characteristics**—Need to Be Exact or Accurate.

Experience—Job Zone 2. Some previous work-related skill, knowledge, or experience may be helpful in these occupations, but usually is not needed. **Job Preparation**—SVP 4.0 to less than 6.0—six months to less than two years. **Knowledges**—Mechanical Devices; Design; Engineering and Technology. **Instructional Program**—Watchmaking and Jewelrymaking.

Related SOC Job—51-2093 Timing Device Assemblers, Adjusters, and Calibrators. **Related OOH Job**—Assemblers and Fabricators. **Related DOT Jobs**—715.381-010 Assembler; 715.381-014 Assembler, Watch Train; 715.381-018 Banking Pin Adjuster; 715.381-022 Barrel Assembler; 715.381-026 Barrel-Bridge Assembler; 715.381-030 Barrel-Endshake Adjuster; 715.381-038 Chronometer Assembler and Adjuster; 715.381-042 Chronometer-Balance-and-Hairspring Assembler; 715.381-054 Hairspring Assembler; 715.381-062 Hairspring Vibrator; 715.381-082 Pallet-Stone Inserter; 715.381-086 Pallet-Stone Positioner; 715.381-094 Watch Assembler; 715.681-010 Timing Adjuster.

51-2099.99 Assemblers and Fabricators, All Other

- **Education/Training Required: Moderate-term on-the-job training**
- **Employed: 258,240**
- **Annual Earnings: $26,250**
- **Growth: 4.5%**
- **Annual Job Openings: 55,000**

All assemblers and fabricators not listed separately.

No task data available.

Note: The Department of Labor has not collected some data for this job, so it has fewer details than the other descriptions.

Related SOC Job—51-2099 Assemblers and Fabricators, All Other. **Related OOH Job**—Assemblers and Fabricators. **Related DOT Jobs**—692.685-230 Trim Attacher; 699.685-026 Power-Screwdriver Operator; 706.381-014 Bench Hand; 706.381-026 Operating-Table Assembler; 706.684-046 Bench Hand; 709.381-010 Atomic-Fuel Assembler; 709.381-030 Organ-Pipe Maker, Metal; 709.381-038 Reed Maker; 709.381-046 Wire-Mesh-Filter Fabricator; 709.684-098 Wire-Frame-Lamp-Shade Maker; 710.381-010 Assembler II; 710.681-026 Thermometer Maker; 730.381-014 Bell Maker; 730.381-018 Brass-Wind-Instrument Maker; 730.381-030 Harp-Action Assembler; others.

51-3000 Food Processing Workers

51-3011.00 Bakers

- **Education/Training Required: Long-term on-the-job training**
- **Employed: 144,110**
- **Annual Earnings: $21,520**
- **Growth: 15.2%**
- **Annual Job Openings: 37,000**

Mix and bake ingredients according to recipes to produce breads, rolls, cookies, cakes, pies, pastries, or other baked goods.

Observe color of products being baked and adjust oven temperatures, humidity, and conveyor speeds accordingly. Set oven temperatures and place items into hot ovens for baking. Combine measured ingredients in bowls of mixing, blending, or cooking machinery. Measure and weigh flour and other ingredients to prepare batters, doughs, fillings, and icings, using scales and graduated containers. Roll, knead, cut, and shape dough to form sweet rolls, pie crusts, tarts, cookies, and other products. Place dough in pans, in molds, or on sheets and bake in production ovens or on grills. Check the quality of raw materials to ensure that standards and specifications are met. Adapt the quantity of ingredients to match the amount of items to be baked. Apply glazes, icings, or other toppings to baked goods, using spatulas or brushes. Check equipment to ensure that it meets health and safety regulations and perform maintenance or cleaning as necessary. Decorate baked goods such as cakes and pastries. Set time and speed controls for mixing machines, blending machines, or steam kettles so that ingredients will be mixed or cooked according to instructions. Prepare and maintain inventory and production records. Direct and coordinate bakery deliveries. Order and receive supplies and equipment. Operate slicing and wrapping machines. Develop new recipes for baked goods.

GOE Information—Interest Area: 13. Manufacturing. **Work Group:** 13.03. Production Work, Assorted Materials Processing. **Personality Type**—Realistic. Realistic occupations frequently involve work activities that include practical, hands-on problems and solutions. They often deal with plants; animals; and real-world materials like wood, tools, and machinery. Many of the occupations require working outside and do not involve a lot of paperwork or working closely with others. **Work Values**—Supervision, Technical; Moral Values; Independence; Company Policies and Practices. **Skills**—Systems Evaluation; Quality Control Analysis; Equipment Maintenance; Operation and Control; Management of Personnel Resources; Systems Analysis. **Abilities**—*Cognitive:* Perceptual Speed; Visualization. *Psychomotor:* Arm-Hand Steadiness; Manual Dexterity; Control Precision; Finger Dexterity; Multilimb Coordination. *Physical:* Trunk Strength. *Sensory:* Visual Color Discrimination;

Hearing Sensitivity. **General Work Activities**—*Information Input:* Identifying Objects, Actions, and Events; Inspecting Equipment, Structures, or Materials; Monitoring Processes, Materials, or Surroundings. *Mental Process:* Organizing, Planning, and Prioritizing; Processing Information; Analyzing Data or Information. *Work Output:* Handling and Moving Objects; Controlling Machines and Processes; Performing General Physical Activities. *Interacting with Others:* Establishing and Maintaining Interpersonal Relationships; Communicating with Other Workers; Performing for or Working with the Public. **Physical Work Conditions**—Indoors; Very Hot or Cold; Minor Burns, Cuts, Bites, or Stings; Standing; Walking and Running; Using Hands on Objects, Tools, or Controls. **Other Job Characteristics**—Need to Be Exact or Accurate.

Experience—Job Zone 2. Some previous work-related skill, knowledge, or experience may be helpful in these occupations, but usually is not needed. **Job Preparation**—SVP 4.0 to less than 6.0—six months to less than two years. **Knowledges**—Food Production; Production and Processing; Personnel and Human Resources; Mathematics; Administration and Management; Sales and Marketing. **Instructional Program**—Baking and Pastry Arts/Baker/Pastry Chef.

Related SOC Job—51-3011 Bakers. **Related OOH Job**—Food Processing Occupations. **Related DOT Jobs**—520.384-010 Bench Hand; 526.381-010 Baker; 526.381-014 Baker Apprentice.

51-3021.00 Butchers and Meat Cutters

- **Education/Training Required: Long-term on-the-job training**
- **Employed: 128,660**
- **Annual Earnings: $26,590**
- **Growth: 7.9%**
- **Annual Job Openings: 20,000**

Cut, trim, or prepare consumer-sized portions of meat for use or sale in retail establishments.

Wrap, weigh, label, and price cuts of meat. Prepare and place meat cuts and products in display counter so they will appear attractive and catch the shopper's eye. Prepare special cuts of meat ordered by customers. Cut, trim, bone, tie, and grind meats, such as beef, pork, poultry, and fish, to prepare meat in cooking form. Receive, inspect, and store meat upon delivery to ensure meat quality. Shape, lace, and tie roasts, using boning knife, skewer, and twine. Estimate requirements and order or requisition meat supplies to maintain inventories. Supervise other butchers or meat cutters. Record quantity of meat received and issued to cooks and keep records of meat sales. Negotiate with representatives from supply companies to determine order details. Cure, smoke, tenderize, and preserve meat. Total sales and collect money from customers.

GOE Information—**Interest Area:** 09. Hospitality, Tourism, and Recreation. **Work Group:** 09.04. Food and Beverage Preparation. **Personality Type**—Realistic. Realistic occupations frequently involve work activities that include practical, hands-on problems and solutions. They often deal with plants; animals; and real-world materials like wood, tools, and machinery. Many of the occupations require working outside and do not involve a lot of paperwork or working closely with others. **Work Values**—Independence; Moral Values; Social Service. **Skills**—Equipment Maintenance. **Abilities**—*Cognitive:* Number Facility. *Psychomotor:* Wrist-Finger Speed; Manual Dexterity; Reaction Time; Arm-Hand Steadiness; Multilimb Coordination; Control Precision. *Physical:* Static Strength; Trunk Strength; Extent Flexibility. *Sensory:* Hearing Sensitivity; Depth Perception; Visual Color Discrimination; Speech Recognition; Auditory Attention.

General Work Activities—*Information Input:* Identifying Objects, Actions, and Events; Monitoring Processes, Materials, or Surroundings; Inspecting Equipment, Structures, or Materials. *Mental Process:* Organizing, Planning, and Prioritizing; Judging the Qualities of Things, Services, or Other People's Work; Scheduling Work and Activities. *Work Output:* Handling and Moving Objects; Performing General Physical Activities. *Interacting with Others:* Communicating with Other Workers; Establishing and Maintaining Interpersonal Relationships; Performing for or Working with the Public. **Physical Work Conditions**—Indoors; Very Hot or Cold; Hazardous Equipment; Standing; Using Hands on Objects, Tools, or Controls; Repetitive Motions. **Other Job Characteristics**—Need to Be Exact or Accurate; Errors Have Important Consequences; Repeat Same Tasks.

Experience—Job Zone 2. Some previous work-related skill, knowledge, or experience may be helpful in these occupations, but usually is not needed. **Job Preparation**—SVP 4.0 to less than 6.0—six months to less than two years. **Knowledges**—Food Production; Production and Processing; Mechanical Devices; Sales and Marketing; Customer and Personal Service. **Instructional Program**—Meat Cutting/Meat Cutter.

Related SOC Job—51-3021 Butchers and Meat Cutters. **Related OOH Job**—Food Processing Occupations. **Related DOT Jobs**—316.681-010 Butcher, Meat; 316.684-018 Meat Cutter; 316.684-022 Meat-Cutter Apprentice.

51-3022.00 Meat, Poultry, and Fish Cutters and Trimmers

- **Education/Training Required: Short-term on-the-job training**
- **Employed: 136,690**
- **Annual Earnings: $19,830**
- **Growth: 15.8%**
- **Annual Job Openings: 23,000**

Use hand tools to perform routine cutting and trimming of meat, poultry, and fish.

Use knives, cleavers, meat saws, band saws, or other equipment to perform meat cutting and trimming. Clean, trim, slice, and section carcasses for future processing. Cut and trim meat to prepare for packing. Remove parts, such as skin, feathers, scales, or bones, from carcass. Inspect meat products for defects, bruises, or blemishes and remove them along with any excess fat. Produce hamburger meat and meat trimmings. Process primal parts into cuts that are ready for retail use. Obtain and distribute specified meat or carcass. Separate meats and byproducts into specified containers and seal containers. Weigh meats and tag containers for weight and contents. Clean and salt hides. Prepare sausages, luncheon meats, hot dogs, and other fabricated meat products, using meat trimmings and hamburger meat. Prepare ready-to-heat foods by filleting meat or fish or cutting it into bite-sized pieces, preparing and adding vegetables or applying sauces or breading.

GOE Information—**Interest Area:** 13. Manufacturing. **Work Group:** 13.03. Production Work, Assorted Materials Processing. **Personality Type**—Realistic. Realistic occupations frequently involve work activities that include practical, hands-on problems and solutions. They often deal with plants; animals; and real-world materials like wood, tools, and machinery. Many of the occupations require working outside and do not involve a lot of paperwork or working closely with others. **Work Values**—Supervision, Technical; Independence. **Skills**—None met the criteria. **Abilities**—*Cognitive:* None met the criteria.

Psychomotor: Wrist-Finger Speed; Reaction Time; Arm-Hand Steadiness; Control Precision; Manual Dexterity. *Physical:* Trunk Strength; Static Strength; Extent Flexibility. *Sensory:* None met the criteria. **General Work Activities**—*Information Input:* Monitoring Processes, Materials, or Surroundings; Identifying Objects, Actions, and Events; Inspecting Equipment, Structures, or Materials. *Mental Process:* Making Decisions and Solving Problems; Judging the Qualities of Things, Services, or Other People's Work. *Work Output:* Handling and Moving Objects; Performing General Physical Activities; Controlling Machines and Processes. *Interacting with Others:* Teaching Others; Coaching and Developing Others; Communicating with Other Workers. **Physical Work Conditions**—Indoors; Very Hot or Cold; Hazardous Equipment; Standing; Using Hands on Objects, Tools, or Controls; Repetitive Motions. **Other Job Characteristics**—Need to Be Exact or Accurate; Pace Determined by Speed of Equipment; Repeat Same Tasks.

Experience—Job Zone 1. No previous work-related skill, knowledge, or experience is needed. **Job Preparation**—SVP below 4.0—less than six months. **Knowledges**—Food Production; Production and Processing; Mechanical Devices; Customer and Personal Service. **Instructional Program**—Meat Cutting/Meat Cutter.

Related SOC Job—51-3022 Meat, Poultry, and Fish Cutters and Trimmers. **Related OOH Job**—Food Processing Occupations. **Related DOT Jobs**—521.687-058 Fish Chopper, Gang Knife; 521.687-106 Sausage-Meat Trimmer; 521.687-126 Skin Lifter, Bacon; 522.687-046 Fish Roe Processor; 525.684-010 Boner, Meat; 525.684-014 Butcher, Fish; 525.684-018 Carcass Splitter; 525.684-022 Crab Butcher; 525.684-026 Final-Dressing Cutter; 525.684-030 Fish Cleaner; 525.684-034 Head Trimmer; 525.684-038 Offal Separator; 525.684-042 Poultry Killer; 525.684-046 Skinner; 525.684-050 Sticker, Animal; 525.684-054 Trimmer, Meat; 525.684-058 Turkey-Roll Maker; others.

51-3023.00 Slaughterers and Meat Packers

- Education/Training Required: Moderate-term on-the-job training
- Employed: 132,000
- Annual Earnings: $21,220
- Growth: 13.8%
- Annual Job Openings: 22,000

Work in slaughtering, meat packing, or wholesale establishments performing precision functions involving the preparation of meat. Work may include specialized slaughtering tasks, cutting standard or premium cuts of meat for marketing, making sausage, or wrapping meats.

Remove bones and cut meat into standard cuts in preparation for marketing. Slaughter animals in accordance with religious law and determine that carcasses meet specified religious standards. Tend assembly lines, performing a few of the many cuts needed to process a carcass. Saw, split, or scribe carcasses into smaller portions to facilitate handling. Grind meat into hamburger and into trimmings used to prepare sausages, luncheon meats, and other meat products. Cut, trim, skin, sort, and wash viscera of slaughtered animals to separate edible portions from offal. Shave or singe and defeather carcasses and wash them in preparation for further processing or packaging. Slit open, eviscerate, and trim carcasses of slaughtered animals. Stun animals prior to slaughtering. Trim head meat and sever or remove parts of animals' heads or skulls. Trim, clean, and cure animal hides. Wrap dressed carcasses and meat cuts. Skin sections of animals or whole animals. Sever jugular veins to drain blood and facilitate

slaughtering. Shackle hind legs of animals to raise them for slaughtering or skinning.

GOE Information—**Interest Area:** 13. Manufacturing. **Work Group:** 13.03. Production Work, Assorted Materials Processing. **Personality Type**—Realistic. Realistic occupations frequently involve work activities that include practical, hands-on problems and solutions. They often deal with plants; animals; and real-world materials like wood, tools, and machinery. Many of the occupations require working outside and do not involve a lot of paperwork or working closely with others. **Work Values**—Independence; Security. **Skills**—None met the criteria. **Abilities**—*Cognitive:* None met the criteria. *Psychomotor:* Wrist-Finger Speed; Manual Dexterity; Arm-Hand Steadiness; Reaction Time; Control Precision; Multilimb Coordination. *Physical:* Static Strength; Explosive Strength; Dynamic Flexibility; Extent Flexibility; Dynamic Strength; Trunk Strength. *Sensory:* Visual Color Discrimination. **General Work Activities**—*Information Input:* Monitoring Processes, Materials, or Surroundings; Identifying Objects, Actions, and Events. *Mental Process:* Evaluating Information Against Standards. *Work Output:* Handling and Moving Objects; Performing General Physical Activities; Controlling Machines and Processes. *Interacting with Others:* None met the criteria. **Physical Work Conditions**—Indoors; Contaminants; Minor Burns, Cuts, Bites, or Stings; Standing; Using Hands on Objects, Tools, or Controls; Repetitive Motions. **Other Job Characteristics**—None met the criteria.

Experience—Job Zone 2. Some previous work-related skill, knowledge, or experience may be helpful in these occupations, but usually is not needed. **Job Preparation**—SVP 4.0 to less than 6.0—six months to less than two years. **Knowledges**—Food Production; Biology; Production and Processing; Public Safety and Security. **Instructional Program**—Meat Cutting/Meat Cutter.

Related SOC Job—51-3023 Slaughterers and Meat Packers. **Related OOH Job**—Food Processing Occupations. **Related DOT Jobs**—525.361-010 Slaughterer, Religious Ritual; 525.381-010 Butcher Apprentice; 525.381-014 Butcher, All-Round; 525.664-010 Meat Dresser.

51-3091.00 Food and Tobacco Roasting, Baking, and Drying Machine Operators and Tenders

- Education/Training Required: Short-term on-the-job training
- Employed: 18,160
- Annual Earnings: $23,230
- Growth: 4.7%
- Annual Job Openings: 2,000

Operate or tend food or tobacco roasting, baking, or drying equipment, including hearth ovens, kiln driers, roasters, char kilns, and vacuum-drying equipment.

Observe, feel, taste, or otherwise examine products during and after processing to ensure conformance to standards. Observe temperature, humidity, pressure gauges, and product samples and adjust controls, such as thermostats and valves, to maintain prescribed operating conditions for specific stages. Operate or tend equipment that roasts, bakes, dries, or cures food items such as cocoa and coffee beans, grains, nuts, and bakery products. Set temperature and time controls; light ovens, burners, driers, or roasters; and start equipment, such as conveyors, cylinders, blowers, driers, or pumps. Observe flow of materials and listen for machine malfunctions, such as jamming or spillage, and notify supervisors if corrective actions fail. Record production data, such as weight and amount of product processed, type of product, and time and temperature of processing. Weigh or measure products, using scale hoppers or scale conveyors. Read work orders to determine quantities and types of products to be baked, dried, or roasted. Take product samples during and after processing for laboratory analyses. Fill or remove product from trays, carts, hoppers, or equipment, using scoops, peels, or shovels or by hand. Open valves, gates, or chutes or use shovels to load or remove products from ovens or other equipment. Clean equipment with steam, hot water, and hoses. Clear or dislodge blockages in bins, screens, or other equipment, using poles, brushes, or mallets. Push racks or carts to transfer products to storage, cooling stations, or the next stage of processing. Start conveyors to move roasted grain to cooling pans and agitate grain with rakes as blowers force air through perforated bottoms of pans. Smooth out products in bins, pans, trays, or conveyors, using rakes or shovels. Install equipment, such as spray units, cutting blades, or screens, using hand tools. Test products for moisture content, using moisture meters. Signal co-workers to synchronize flow of materials. Dump sugar dust from collectors into melting tanks and add water to reclaim sugar lost during processing.

GOE Information—Interest Area: 13. Manufacturing. **Work Group:** 13.03. Production Work, Assorted Materials Processing. **Personality Type—**Realistic. Realistic occupations frequently involve work activities that include practical, hands-on problems and solutions. They often deal with plants; animals; and real-world materials like wood, tools, and machinery. Many of the occupations require working outside and do not involve a lot of paperwork or working closely with others. **Work Values—**Moral Values; Supervision, Technical; Independence; Company Policies and Practices. **Skills—**Operation Monitoring; Operation and Control; Systems Evaluation; Equipment Maintenance; Quality Control Analysis; Management of Material Resources. **Abilities—***Cognitive:* Perceptual Speed; Selective Attention; Visualization. *Psychomotor:* Rate Control; Control Precision; Manual Dexterity; Multilimb Coordination; Reaction Time; Arm-Hand Steadiness. *Physical:* Extent Flexibility; Trunk Strength; Stamina; Static Strength. *Sensory:* Auditory Attention; Hearing Sensitivity; Visual Color Discrimination. **General Work Activities—***Information Input:* Identifying Objects, Actions, and Events; Inspecting Equipment, Structures, or Materials; Getting Information. *Mental Process:* Updating and Using Relevant Knowledge; Organizing, Planning, and Prioritizing; Evaluating Information Against Standards. *Work Output:* Handling and Moving Objects; Controlling Machines and Processes; Performing General Physical Activities. *Interacting with Others:* Establishing and Maintaining Interpersonal Relationships; Communicating with Other Workers; Teaching Others. **Physical Work Conditions—**Noisy; Very Hot or Cold; Contaminants; Standing; Walking and Running; Using Hands on Objects, Tools, or Controls. **Other Job Characteristics—**Pace Determined by Speed of Equipment; Errors Have Important Consequences; Need to Be Exact or Accurate; Repeat Same Tasks; Automation.

Experience—Job Zone 2. Some previous work-related skill, knowledge, or experience may be helpful in these occupations, but usually is not needed. **Job Preparation—**SVP 4.0 to less than 6.0—six months to less than two years. **Knowledges—**Food Production; Production and Processing; Mechanical Devices. **Instructional Program—**Agricultural and Food Products Processing, General.

Related SOC Job—51-3091 Food and Tobacco Roasting, Baking, and Drying Machine Operators and Tenders. **Related OOH Job—**Food Processing Occupations. **Related DOT Jobs—**522.662-014 Redrying-

Machine Operator; 522.685-038 Curing-Bin Operator; 522.685-066 Fish Smoker; 523.362-010 Cocoa-Bean Roaster I; 523.362-014 Drier Operator; 523.382-010 Gunner; 523.585-022 Drier, Long Goods; 523.585-030 Pulp-Drier Firer; 523.585-034 Roaster, Grain; 523.662-010 Bone-Char Kiln Operator; 523.665-010 Sugar Drier; 523.682-014 Coffee Roaster; 523.682-022 Drier Operator; 523.682-026 Drum Drier; 523.682-030 Kiln Operator, Malt House; 523.682-038 Tobacco Curer; others.

51-3092.00 Food Batchmakers

- **Education/Training Required: Short-term on-the-job training**
- **Employed: 89,400**
- **Annual Earnings: $22,510**
- **Growth: 7.9%**
- **Annual Job Openings: 16,000**

Set up and operate equipment that mixes or blends ingredients used in the manufacturing of food products. Includes candy makers and cheese makers.

Record production and test data for each food product batch, such as the ingredients used, temperature, test results, and time cycle. Observe gauges and thermometers to determine if the mixing chamber temperature is within specified limits and turn valves to control the temperature. Clean and sterilize vats and factory processing areas. Press switches and turn knobs to start, adjust, and regulate equipment such as beaters, extruders, discharge pipes, and salt pumps. Observe and listen to equipment to detect possible malfunctions, such as leaks or plugging, and report malfunctions or undesirable tastes to supervisors. Set up, operate, and tend equipment that cooks, mixes, blends, or processes ingredients in the manufacturing of food products according to formulas or recipes. Mix or blend ingredients according to recipes by using a paddle or an agitator or by controlling vats that heat and mix ingredients. Select and measure or weigh ingredients, using English or metric measures and balance scales. Follow recipes to produce food products of specified flavor, texture, clarity, bouquet, or color. Turn valve controls to start equipment and to adjust operation to maintain product quality. Determine mixing sequences, based on knowledge of temperature effects and of the solubility of specific ingredients. Fill processing or cooking containers, such as kettles, rotating cookers, pressure cookers, or vats, with ingredients by opening valves, by starting pumps or injectors, or by hand. Give directions to other workers who are assisting in the batchmaking process. Homogenize or pasteurize material to prevent separation or to obtain prescribed butterfat content, using a homogenizing device. Inspect vats after cleaning to ensure that fermentable residue has been removed. Examine, feel, and taste product samples during production to evaluate quality, color, texture, flavor, and bouquet and document the results. Test food product samples for moisture content, acidity level, specific gravity, or butterfat content and continue processing until desired levels are reached. Formulate or modify recipes for specific kinds of food products.

GOE Information—Interest Area: 13. Manufacturing. **Work Group:** 13.03. Production Work, Assorted Materials Processing. **Personality Type—**Realistic. Realistic occupations frequently involve work activities that include practical, hands-on problems and solutions. They often deal with plants; animals; and real-world materials like wood, tools, and machinery. Many of the occupations require working outside and do not involve a lot of paperwork or working closely with others. **Work Values—**Supervision, Technical; Authority; Moral Values; Supervision, Human Relations; Company Policies and Practices; Variety. **Skills—**Operation Monitoring; Operation and

Control; Equipment Maintenance; Troubleshooting; Repairing; Quality Control Analysis. **Abilities**—*Cognitive:* Perceptual Speed; Selective Attention. *Psychomotor:* Reaction Time; Rate Control; Control Precision; Manual Dexterity; Multilimb Coordination. *Physical:* Extent Flexibility; Trunk Strength. *Sensory:* Hearing Sensitivity; Auditory Attention. **General Work Activities**—*Information Input:* Monitoring Processes, Materials, or Surroundings; Identifying Objects, Actions, and Events; Getting Information. *Mental Process:* Processing Information; Updating and Using Relevant Knowledge; Making Decisions and Solving Problems. *Work Output:* Handling and Moving Objects; Performing General Physical Activities; Controlling Machines and Processes. *Interacting with Others:* Establishing and Maintaining Interpersonal Relationships; Communicating with Other Workers; Teaching Others. **Physical Work Conditions**—Noisy; Contaminants; Standing; Using Hands on Objects, Tools, or Controls; Bending or Twisting the Body; Repetitive Motions. **Other Job Characteristics**—Pace Determined by Speed of Equipment; Repeat Same Tasks; Need to Be Exact or Accurate; Errors Have Important Consequences; Automation.

Experience—Job Zone 2. Some previous work-related skill, knowledge, or experience may be helpful in these occupations, but usually is not needed. **Job Preparation**—SVP 4.0 to less than 6.0—six months to less than two years. **Knowledges**—Production and Processing; Public Safety and Security; Chemistry; Mathematics. **Instructional Programs**—Agricultural and Food Products Processing, General; Foodservice Systems Administration/Management.

Related SOC Job—51-3092 Food Batchmakers. **Related OOH Job**—Food Processing Occupations. **Related DOT Jobs**—520.361-010 Honey Grader-and-Blender; 529.361-010 Almond-Paste Mixer; 529.361-014 Candy Maker; 529.361-018 Cheesemaker; 529.381-010 Compounder, Flavorings.

51-3093.00 Food Cooking Machine Operators and Tenders

- **Education/Training Required: Short-term on-the-job training**
- **Employed: 43,100**
- **Annual Earnings: $21,390**
- **Growth: 2.9%**
- **Annual Job Openings: 3,000**

Operate or tend cooking equipment, such as steam cooking vats, deep-fry cookers, pressure cookers, kettles, and boilers, to prepare food products.

Record production and test data, such as processing steps, temperature and steam readings, cooking time, batches processed, and test results. Listen for malfunction alarms and shut down equipment and notify supervisors when necessary. Collect and examine product samples during production to test them for quality, color, content, consistency, viscosity, acidity, or specific gravity. Observe gauges, dials, and product characteristics and adjust controls to maintain appropriate temperature, pressure, and flow of ingredients. Read work orders, recipes, or formulas to determine cooking times and temperatures and ingredient specifications. Clean, wash, and sterilize equipment and cooking area, using water hoses, cleaning or sterilizing solutions, or rinses. Set temperature, pressure, and time controls and start conveyers, machines, or pumps. Tend or operate and control equipment such as kettles, cookers, vats and tanks, and boilers to cook ingredients or prepare products for further processing. Measure or weigh ingredients, using scales or measuring containers. Admit required amounts of water, steam, cooking oils, or compressed air

into equipment, such as by opening water valves to cool mixtures to the desired consistency. Remove cooked material or products from equipment. Notify or signal other workers to operate equipment or when processing is complete. Turn valves or start pumps to add ingredients or drain products from equipment and to transfer products for storage, cooling, or further processing. Place products on conveyors or carts and monitor product flow. Pour, dump, or load prescribed quantities of ingredients or products into cooking equipment manually or by using a hoist. Activate agitators and paddles to mix or stir ingredients, stopping machines when ingredients are thoroughly mixed. Operate auxiliary machines and equipment such as grinders, canners, and molding presses to prepare or further process products.

GOE Information—**Interest Area:** 13. Manufacturing. **Work Group:** 13.03. Production Work, Assorted Materials Processing. **Personality Type**—Realistic. Realistic occupations frequently involve work activities that include practical, hands-on problems and solutions. They often deal with plants; animals; and real-world materials like wood, tools, and machinery. Many of the occupations require working outside and do not involve a lot of paperwork or working closely with others. **Work Values**—Moral Values; Supervision, Technical; Supervision, Human Relations; Independence; Company Policies and Practices. **Skills**—Operation Monitoring; Quality Control Analysis; Operation and Control; Operations Analysis; Management of Personnel Resources; Systems Evaluation. **Abilities**—*Cognitive:* Perceptual Speed; Selective Attention; Category Flexibility. *Psychomotor:* Reaction Time; Rate Control; Control Precision; Manual Dexterity; Multilimb Coordination; Arm-Hand Steadiness. *Physical:* Static Strength; Trunk Strength. *Sensory:* Auditory Attention; Hearing Sensitivity. **General Work Activities**—*Information Input:* Identifying Objects, Actions, and Events; Getting Information; Inspecting Equipment, Structures, or Materials. *Mental Process:* Making Decisions and Solving Problems; Evaluating Information Against Standards; Updating and Using Relevant Knowledge. *Work Output:* Handling and Moving Objects; Controlling Machines and Processes; Repairing and Maintaining Mechanical Equipment. *Interacting with Others:* Communicating with Other Workers; Establishing and Maintaining Interpersonal Relationships; Coaching and Developing Others. **Physical Work Conditions**—Noisy; Very Hot or Cold; Minor Burns, Cuts, Bites, or Stings; Standing; Walking and Running; Using Hands on Objects, Tools, or Controls. **Other Job Characteristics**—Need to Be Exact or Accurate; Pace Determined by Speed of Equipment; Repeat Same Tasks; Errors Have Important Consequences; Automation.

Experience—Job Zone 2. Some previous work-related skill, knowledge, or experience may be helpful in these occupations, but usually is not needed. **Job Preparation**—SVP 4.0 to less than 6.0—six months to less than two years. **Knowledges**—Food Production; Production and Processing; Chemistry. **Instructional Program**—Agricultural and Food Products Processing, General.

Related SOC Job—51-3093 Food Cooking Machine Operators and Tenders. **Related OOH Job**—Food Processing Occupations. **Related DOT Jobs**—520.685-082 Cooker, Casing; 521.687-090 Nut Steamer; 522.362-010 Yeast Distiller; 522.382-010 Cottage-Cheese Maker; 522.382-022 Mash-Tub-Cooker Operator; 522.382-034 Sugar Boiler; 522.482-010 Masher; 522.682-010 Kettle Operator; 522.682-014 Ordering-Machine Operator; 522.685-018 Brine Maker I; 522.685-034 Corn Cooker; 522.685-094 Steam-Conditioner Operator; 522.685-102 Vacuum-Conditioner Operator; 523.382-022 Processor, Instant Potato; 523.682-010 Chocolate Temperer; 523.682-018 Dextrine Mixer; others.

51-4000 Metal Workers and Plastic Workers

51-4011.00 Computer-Controlled Machine Tool Operators, Metal and Plastic

- **Education/Training Required:** Moderate-term on-the-job training
- **Employed:** 136,490
- **Annual Earnings:** $31,010
- **Growth:** –1.2%
- **Annual Job Openings:** 13,000

Operate computer-controlled machines or robots to perform one or more machine functions on metal or plastic workpieces.

Measure dimensions of finished workpieces to ensure conformance to specifications, using precision measuring instruments, templates, and fixtures. Remove and replace dull cutting tools. Mount, install, align, and secure tools, attachments, fixtures, and workpieces on machines, using hand tools and precision measuring instruments. Listen to machines during operation to detect sounds such as those made by dull cutting tools or excessive vibration and adjust machines to compensate for problems. Adjust machine feed and speed, change cutting tools, or adjust machine controls when automatic programming is faulty or if machines malfunction. Stop machines to remove finished workpieces or to change tooling, setup, or workpiece placement according to required machining sequences. Lift workpieces to machines manually or with hoists or cranes. Modify cutting programs to account for problems encountered during operation and save modified programs. Calculate machine speed and feed ratios and the size and position of cuts. Insert control instructions into machine control units to start operation. Check to ensure that workpieces are properly lubricated and cooled during machine operation. Input initial part dimensions into machine control panels. Set up and operate computer-controlled machines or robots to perform one or more machine functions on metal or plastic workpieces. Confer with supervisors or programmers to resolve machine malfunctions and production errors and to obtain approval to continue production. Review program specifications or blueprints to determine and set machine operations and sequencing, finished workpiece dimensions, or numerical control sequences. Monitor machine operation and control panel displays and compare readings to specifications to detect malfunctions. Control coolant systems. Maintain machines and remove and replace broken or worn machine tools, using hand tools. Stack or load finished items or place items on conveyor systems. Clean machines, tooling, and parts, using solvents or solutions and rags. Enter commands or load control media such as tapes, cards, or disks into machine controllers to retrieve programmed instructions.

GOE Information—Interest Area: 13. Manufacturing. **Work Group:** 13.05. Production Machining Technology. **Personality Type—**Realistic. Realistic occupations frequently involve work activities that include practical, hands-on problems and solutions. They often deal with plants; animals; and real-world materials like wood, tools, and machinery. Many of the occupations require working outside and do not involve a lot of paperwork or working closely with others. **Work Values—**Moral Values; Supervision, Technical; Activity; Independence; Supervision, Human Relations; Company Policies and Practices. **Skills—**Operation Monitoring; Operation and Control; Equipment Maintenance; Quality Control Analysis; Programming; Troubleshooting. **Abilities—***Cognitive:* Selective Attention; Perceptual Speed; Visualization; Flexibility of Closure; Number Facility; Speed of Closure. *Psychomotor:* Reaction Time; Rate Control; Control Precision; Response Orientation; Multilimb Coordination; Speed of Limb Movement. *Physical:* Static Strength; Extent Flexibility; Dynamic Strength; Gross Body Coordination; Stamina; Trunk Strength. *Sensory:* Auditory Attention; Hearing Sensitivity; Depth Perception; Glare Sensitivity; Sound Localization; Visual Color Discrimination. **General Work Activities—***Information Input:* Inspecting Equipment, Structures, or Materials; Monitoring Processes, Materials, or Surroundings; Identifying Objects, Actions, and Events. *Mental Process:* Making Decisions and Solving Problems; Updating and Using Relevant Knowledge; Processing Information. *Work Output:* Controlling Machines and Processes; Handling and Moving Objects; Repairing and Maintaining Mechanical Equipment. *Interacting with Others:* Communicating with Other Workers; Establishing and Maintaining Interpersonal Relationships; Teaching Others. **Physical Work Conditions—**Noisy; Contaminants; Hazardous Equipment; Standing; Using Hands on Objects, Tools, or Controls; Repetitive Motions. **Other Job Characteristics—**Need to Be Exact or Accurate; Repeat Same Tasks; Pace Determined by Speed of Equipment; Errors Have Important Consequences; Automation.

Experience—Job Zone 2. Some previous work-related skill, knowledge, or experience may be helpful in these occupations, but usually is not needed. **Job Preparation—**SVP 4.0 to less than 6.0—six months to less than two years. **Knowledges—**Mechanical Devices; Production and Processing; Engineering and Technology; Design; Mathematics; Computers and Electronics. **Instructional Program—**Machine Shop Technology/Assistant.

Related SOC Job—51-4011 Computer-Controlled Machine Tool Operators, Metal and Plastic. **Related OOH Job—**Computer Control Programmers and Operators. **Related DOT Jobs—**604.362-010 Lathe Operator, Numerical Control; 605.360-010 Router Set-Up Operator, Numerical Control; 605.380-010 Milling-Machine Set-Up Operator, Numerical Control; 605.382-046 Numerical-Control Router Operator; 606.362-010 Drill-Press Operator, Numerical Control; 606.382-014 Jig-Boring Machine Operator, Numerical Control; 606.382-018 Numerical-Control Drill Operator, Printed Circuit Boards; 606.382-026 Robotic Machine Operator; 609.360-010 Numerical Control Machine Set-Up Operator; others.

51-4012.00 Numerical Tool and Process Control Programmers

- **Education/Training Required:** Long-term on-the-job training
- **Employed:** 17,860
- **Annual Earnings:** $41,830
- **Growth:** –1.1%
- **Annual Job Openings:** 2,000

Develop programs to control machining or processing of parts by automatic machine tools, equipment, or systems.

Determine the sequence of machine operations and select the proper cutting tools needed to machine workpieces into the desired shapes. Revise programs or tapes to eliminate errors and retest programs to check that problems have been solved. Analyze job orders, drawings, blueprints, specifications, printed circuit board pattern films, and design data to calculate dimensions, tool selection, machine speeds, and feed rates. Determine reference points, machine cutting paths, or hole locations and compute angular and linear dimensions, radii, and curvatures. Observe machines on trial runs or conduct computer simulations to ensure that programs and machinery will function properly and produce items that meet specifications. Compare encoded tapes or computer printouts with original part specifications and blueprints to verify accuracy of instructions. Enter coordinates of hole locations into program memories by depressing pedals or buttons of programmers. Write programs in the language of a machine's controller and store programs on media such as punch tapes, magnetic tapes, or disks. Modify existing programs to enhance efficiency. Enter computer commands to store or retrieve parts patterns, graphic displays, or programs that transfer data to other media. Prepare geometric layouts from graphic displays, using computer-assisted drafting software or drafting instruments and graph paper. Write instruction sheets and cutter lists for a machine's controller to guide setup and encode numerical control tapes. Sort shop orders into groups to maximize materials utilization and minimize machine setup time. Draw machine tool paths on pattern film, using colored markers and following guidelines for tool speed and efficiency. Align and secure pattern film on reference tables of optical programmers and observe enlarger scope views of printed circuit boards.

GOE Information—Interest Area: 13. Manufacturing. **Work Group:** 13.05. Production Machining Technology. **Personality Type—** Realistic. Realistic occupations frequently involve work activities that include practical, hands-on problems and solutions. They often deal with plants; animals; and real-world materials like wood, tools, and machinery. Many of the occupations require working outside and do not involve a lot of paperwork or working closely with others. **Work Values—**Compensation; Independence; Creativity; Advancement; Autonomy; Supervision, Human Relations. **Skills—** Programming; Installation; Mathematics; Operation Monitoring; Repairing; Equipment Selection. **Abilities—***Cognitive:* Mathematical Reasoning; Visualization; Perceptual Speed; Number Facility; Flexibility of Closure; Speed of Closure. *Psychomotor:* Reaction Time; Rate Control; Response Orientation; Wrist-Finger Speed; Control Precision; Multilimb Coordination. *Physical:* Trunk Strength; Static Strength; Gross Body Coordination. *Sensory:* Auditory Attention; Hearing Sensitivity; Depth Perception; Far Vision; Visual Color Discrimination. **General Work Activities—***Information Input:* Monitoring Processes, Materials, or Surroundings; Getting Information; Inspecting Equipment, Structures, or Materials. *Mental Process:* Updating and Using Relevant Knowledge; Making Decisions and Solving Problems; Processing Information. *Work Output:* Controlling Machines and Processes; Drafting and Specifying Technical Devices; Interacting With Computers. *Interacting with Others:* Establishing and Maintaining Interpersonal Relationships; Communicating with Other Workers; Coaching and Developing Others. **Physical Work Conditions—**Indoors; Noisy; Contaminants; Hazardous Equipment; Standing; Using Hands on Objects, Tools, or Controls. **Other Job Characteristics—**Need to Be Exact or Accurate; Repeat Same Tasks; Errors Have Important Consequences; Pace Determined by Speed of Equipment.

Experience—Job Zone 3. Previous work-related skill, knowledge, or experience is required. **Job Preparation—**SVP 6.0 to less than 7.0— more than one year and less than four years. **Knowledges—**Design; Mechanical Devices; Engineering and Technology; Mathematics; Physics; Production and Processing. **Instructional Programs—** Computer Programming/Programmer, General; Data Processing and Data Processing Technology/Technician.

Related SOC Job—51-4012 Numerical Tool and Process Control Programmers. **Related OOH Job—**Computer Control Programmers and Operators. **Related DOT Jobs—**007.167-018 Tool Programmer, Numerical Control; 007.362-010 Nesting Operator, Numerical Control; 609.262-010 Tool Programmer, Numerical Control.

51-4021.00 Extruding and Drawing Machine Setters, Operators, and Tenders, Metal and Plastic

- **Education/Training Required: Moderate-term on-the-job training**
- **Employed: 87,290**
- **Annual Earnings: $28,000**
- **Growth: –21.3%**
- **Annual Job Openings: 9,000**

Set up, operate, or tend machines to extrude or draw thermoplastic or metal materials into tubes, rods, hoses, wire, bars, or structural shapes.

Measure and examine extruded products to locate defects and to check for conformance to specifications; adjust controls as necessary to alter products. Determine setup procedures and select machine dies and parts according to specifications. Install dies, machine screws, and sizing rings on machines that extrude thermoplastic or metal materials. Change dies on extruding machines according to production line changes. Start machines and set controls to regulate vacuum, air pressure, sizing rings, and temperature and to synchronize speed of extrusion. Replace worn dies when products vary from specifications. Reel extruded products into rolls of specified lengths and weights. Troubleshoot, maintain, and make minor repairs to equipment. Clean work areas. Adjust controls to draw or press metal into specified shapes and diameters. Operate shearing mechanisms to cut rods to specified lengths. Select nozzles, spacers, and wire guides according to diameters and lengths of rods. Weigh and mix pelletized, granular, or powdered thermoplastic materials and coloring pigments. Load machine hoppers with mixed materials, using augers, or stuff rolls of plastic dough into machine cylinders. Test physical properties of products with testing devices such as acid-bath testers, burst testers, and impact testers. Maintain an inventory of materials.

GOE Information—Interest Area: 13. Manufacturing. **Work Group:** 13.02. Machine Setup and Operation. **Personality Type—**Realistic. Realistic occupations frequently involve work activities that include practical, hands-on problems and solutions. They often deal with plants; animals; and real-world materials like wood, tools, and machinery. Many of the occupations require working outside and do not involve a lot of paperwork or working closely with others. **Work Values—**Moral Values; Independence; Supervision, Technical; Activity; Supervision, Human Relations; Company Policies and Practices. **Skills—**Operation Monitoring; Operation and Control; Quality Control Analysis; Installation; Repairing; Science. **Abilities—** *Cognitive:* Perceptual Speed; Selective Attention; Visualization. *Psychomotor:* Reaction Time; Rate Control; Response Orientation; Control Precision; Multilimb Coordination; Speed of Limb Movement. *Physical:* Static Strength; Extent Flexibility; Dynamic Strength; Gross Body Coordination; Trunk Strength; Stamina. *Sensory:* Auditory Attention; Visual Color Discrimination; Depth Perception; Hearing Sensitivity; Far Vision. **General Work Activities—***Information Input:* Monitoring Processes, Materials, or Surroundings; Inspecting Equipment, Structures, or Materials; Identifying Objects, Actions, and Events. *Mental Process:* Evaluating Information Against Standards; Updating and Using Relevant Knowledge; Judging the Qualities of Things, Services, or Other People's Work. *Work Output:* Handling and Moving Objects; Controlling Machines and Processes; Performing General Physical Activities. *Interacting with Others:* Coordinating the Work and Activities of Others; Establishing and Maintaining Interpersonal Relationships; Assisting and Caring for Others. **Physical Work**

Conditions—Noisy; Very Hot or Cold; Contaminants; Minor Burns, Cuts, Bites, or Stings; Standing; Using Hands on Objects, Tools, or Controls. **Other Job Characteristics**—Errors Have Important Consequences; Pace Determined by Speed of Equipment; Need to Be Exact or Accurate; Repeat Same Tasks.

Experience—Job Zone 2. Some previous work-related skill, knowledge, or experience may be helpful in these occupations, but usually is not needed. **Job Preparation**—SVP 4.0 to less than 6.0—six months to less than two years. **Knowledges**—Mechanical Devices; Medicine and Dentistry; Chemistry; Education and Training; Sociology and Anthropology; Engineering and Technology. **Instructional Program**—Machine Tool Technology/Machinist.

Related SOC Job—51-4021 Extruding and Drawing Machine Setters, Operators, and Tenders, Metal and Plastic. **Related OOH Job**—Machine Setters, Operators, and Tenders—Metal and Plastic. **Related DOT Jobs**—557.382-010 Extruder Operator; 557.685-030 Spinning-Bath Patroller; 614.380-010 Extrusion-Press Adjuster; 614.382-010 Wire Drawer; 614.382-014 Wire Drawer; 614.382-018 Wire Drawing Machine Operator; 614.482-010 Draw-Bench Operator; 614.482-014 Extruder Operator; 614.482-018 Extrusion-Press Operator I; 614.682-010 Draw-Bench Operator; 614.685-010 Extruding-Press Operator; 614.685-014 Extrusion-Press Operator II; 614.685-022 Tube Drawer; 614.685-026 Wire-Drawing-Machine Tender.

51-4022.00 Forging Machine Setters, Operators, and Tenders, Metal and Plastic

- **Education/Training Required: Moderate-term on-the-job training**
- **Employed: 33,850**
- **Annual Earnings: $28,970**
- **Growth: −4.6%**
- **Annual Job Openings: 4,000**

Set up, operate, or tend forging machines to taper, shape, or form metal or plastic parts.

Measure and inspect machined parts to ensure conformance to product specifications. Read work orders or blueprints to determine specified tolerances and sequences of operations for machine setup. Start machines to produce sample workpieces and observe operations to detect machine malfunctions and to verify that machine setups conform to specifications. Remove dies from machines when production runs are finished. Turn handles or knobs to set pressures and depths of ram strokes and to synchronize machine operations. Confer with other workers about machine setups and operational specifications. Repair, maintain, and replace parts on dies. Set up, operate, or tend presses and forging machines to perform hot or cold forging by flattening, straightening, bending, cutting, piercing, or other operations to taper, shape, or form metal. Position and move metal wires or workpieces through a series of dies that compress and shape stock to form die impressions. Install, adjust, and remove dies, synchronizing cams, forging hammers, and stop guides, by using overhead cranes or other hoisting devices and hand tools. Select, align, and bolt positioning fixtures, stops, and specified dies to rams and anvils, forging rolls, or presses and hammers. Trim and compress finished forgings to specified tolerances. Sharpen cutting tools and drill bits, using bench grinders.

GOE Information—**Interest Area:** 13. Manufacturing. **Work Group:** 13.02. Machine Setup and Operation. **Personality Type**—Realistic. Realistic occupations frequently involve work activities that include practical, hands-on problems and solutions. They often deal with

plants; animals; and real-world materials like wood, tools, and machinery. Many of the occupations require working outside and do not involve a lot of paperwork or working closely with others. **Work Values**—Moral Values; Independence; Supervision, Technical; Supervision, Human Relations; Company Policies and Practices; Activity. **Skills**—Operation Monitoring; Quality Control Analysis; Programming; Technology Design; Repairing; Operation and Control. **Abilities**—*Cognitive:* Perceptual Speed; Visualization; Selective Attention; Flexibility of Closure. *Psychomotor:* Rate Control; Reaction Time; Control Precision; Multilimb Coordination; Manual Dexterity; Arm-Hand Steadiness. *Physical:* Trunk Strength; Static Strength. *Sensory:* Auditory Attention; Depth Perception; Hearing Sensitivity. **General Work Activities**—*Information Input:* Identifying Objects, Actions, and Events; Monitoring Processes, Materials, or Surroundings; Inspecting Equipment, Structures, or Materials. *Mental Process:* Updating and Using Relevant Knowledge; Making Decisions and Solving Problems; Organizing, Planning, and Prioritizing. *Work Output:* Handling and Moving Objects; Controlling Machines and Processes; Performing General Physical Activities. *Interacting with Others:* Communicating with Other Workers; Establishing and Maintaining Interpersonal Relationships; Teaching Others. **Physical Work Conditions**—Noisy; Contaminants; Standing; Using Hands on Objects, Tools, or Controls. **Other Job Characteristics**—Pace Determined by Speed of Equipment; Need to Be Exact or Accurate; Errors Have Important Consequences.

Experience—Job Zone 2. Some previous work-related skill, knowledge, or experience may be helpful in these occupations, but usually is not needed. **Job Preparation**—SVP 4.0 to less than 6.0—six months to less than two years. **Knowledges**—Mechanical Devices; Production and Processing; Design; Mathematics. **Instructional Program**—Machine Tool Technology/Machinist.

Related SOC Job—51-4022 Forging Machine Setters, Operators, and Tenders, Metal and Plastic. **Related OOH Job**—Machine Setters, Operators, and Tenders—Metal and Plastic. **Related DOT Jobs**—610.362-010 Drophammer Operator; 610.684-014 Spring Salvage Worker; 611.482-010 Forging-Press Operator I; 611.482-014 Roller-Machine Operator; 611.662-010 Upsetter; 611.682-010 Steel-Shot-Header Operator; 611.682-014 Automatic Casting-Forging Machine Operator; 611.685-010 Forging-Press Operator II; 611.685-014 Hydraulic Operator; 612.260-010 Fastener Technologist; 612.360-010 Die Setter; 612.361-010 Heavy Forger; 612.462-010 Multi-Operation-Machine Operator; 612.462-014 Nut Former; others.

51-4023.00 Rolling Machine Setters, Operators, and Tenders, Metal and Plastic

- **Education/Training Required: Moderate-term on-the-job training**
- **Employed: 37,500**
- **Annual Earnings: $30,480**
- **Growth: −3.9%**
- **Annual Job Openings: 4,000**

Set up, operate, or tend machines to roll steel or plastic, forming bends, beads, knurls, rolls, or plate, or to flatten, temper, or reduce gauge of material.

Adjust and correct machine setups to reduce thicknesses, reshape products, and eliminate product defects. Monitor machine cycles and mill operation to detect jamming and to ensure that products conform to specifications. Examine, inspect, and measure raw materials and finished products to verify conformance to specifications. Read rolling orders, blueprints, and mill schedules to determine setup specifications, work sequences, product dimensions, and installation procedures. Manipulate controls and observe dial indicators to monitor, adjust, and regulate speeds of machine mechanisms. Start operation of rolling and milling machines to flatten, temper, form, and reduce sheet metal sections and to produce steel strips. Thread or feed sheets or rods through rolling mechanisms or start and control mechanisms that automatically feed steel into rollers. Set distance points between rolls, guides, meters, and stops according to specifications. Position, align, and secure arbors, spindles, coils, mandrels, dies, and slitting knives. Direct and train other workers to change rolls, operate mill equipment, remove coils and cobbles, and band and load material. Fill oil cups, adjust valves, and observe gauges to control flow of metal coolants and lubricants onto workpieces. Record mill production on schedule sheets. Install equipment such as guides, guards, gears, cooling equipment, and rolls, using hand tools. Signal and assist other workers to remove and position equipment, fill hoppers, and feed materials into machines. Calculate draft space and roll speed for each mill stand to plan rolling sequences and specified dimensions and tempers. Select rolls, dies, roll stands, and chucks from data charts to form specified contours and to fabricate products. Activate shears and grinders to trim workpieces. Remove scratches and polish roll surfaces, using polishing stones and electric buffers. Disassemble sizing mills removed from rolling lines and sort and store parts.

GOE Information—Interest Area: 13. Manufacturing. **Work Group:** 13.02. Machine Setup and Operation. **Personality Type—**Realistic. Realistic occupations frequently involve work activities that include practical, hands-on problems and solutions. They often deal with plants; animals; and real-world materials like wood, tools, and machinery. Many of the occupations require working outside and do not involve a lot of paperwork or working closely with others. **Work Values—**Supervision, Technical; Moral Values; Supervision, Human Relations; Independence; Activity; Company Policies and Practices. **Skills—**Operation Monitoring; Operation and Control; Equipment Maintenance; Repairing; Quality Control Analysis; Troubleshooting. **Abilities—***Cognitive:* Perceptual Speed; Selective Attention; Visualization; Flexibility of Closure; Speed of Closure; Memorization. *Psychomotor:* Reaction Time; Rate Control; Multilimb Coordination; Response Orientation; Speed of Limb Movement; Control Precision. *Physical:* Static Strength; Dynamic Strength; Gross Body Coordination; Stamina; Trunk Strength; Extent Flexibility. *Sensory:* Glare Sensitivity; Auditory Attention; Depth Perception; Hearing Sensitivity; Far Vision; Visual Color Discrimination. **General Work Activities—***Information Input:* Monitoring Processes, Materials, or Surroundings; Inspecting Equipment, Structures, or Materials; Identifying Objects, Actions, and Events. *Mental Process:* Updating and Using Relevant Knowledge; Organizing, Planning, and Prioritizing; Making Decisions and Solving Problems. *Work Output:* Handling and Moving Objects; Controlling Machines and Processes; Performing General Physical Activities. *Interacting with Others:* Communicating with Other Workers; Establishing and Maintaining Interpersonal Relationships; Coordinating the Work and Activities of Others. **Physical Work Conditions—**Noisy; Contaminants; Hazardous Equipment; Minor Burns, Cuts, Bites, or Stings; Standing; Using Hands on Objects, Tools, or Controls. **Other Job Characteristics—**Need to Be Exact or Accurate; Pace Determined by Speed of Equipment; Repeat Same Tasks; Automation; Errors Have Important Consequences.

Experience—Job Zone 2. Some previous work-related skill, knowledge, or experience may be helpful in these occupations, but usually is not needed. **Job Preparation—**SVP 4.0 to less than 6.0—six months to less than two years. **Knowledges—**Mechanical Devices; Production

and Processing; Education and Training. **Instructional Programs—**Machine Tool Technology/Machinist; Sheet Metal Technology/Sheetworking.

Related SOC Job—51-4023 Rolling Machine Setters, Operators, and Tenders, Metal and Plastic. **Related OOH Job—**Machine Setters, Operators, and Tenders—Metal and Plastic. **Related DOT Jobs—**554.682-018 Roll Operator; 613.360-010 Roll-Forming-Machine Set-Up Mechanic; 613.360-014 Roll-Tube Setter; 613.360-018 Tin Roller, Hot Mill; 613.361-010 Guide Setter; 613.362-014 Roller, Primary Mill; 613.362-018 Rougher; 613.362-022 Speed Operator; 613.382-014 Finisher; 613.382-018 Screwdown Operator; 613.462-018 Rolling-Mill Operator; 613.482-014 Piercing-Machine Operator; 613.662-010 Rolling Attendant; 613.662-014 Rougher Operator; 613.662-018 Cold-Mill Operator; others.

51-4031.00 Cutting, Punching, and Press Machine Setters, Operators, and Tenders, Metal and Plastic

- **Education/Training Required: Moderate-term on-the-job training**
- **Employed: 265,480**
- **Annual Earnings: $25,980**
- **Growth: −17.2%**
- **Annual Job Openings: 13,000**

Set up, operate, or tend machines to saw, cut, shear, slit, punch, crimp, notch, bend, or straighten metal or plastic material.

Measure completed workpieces to verify conformance to specifications, using micrometers, gauges, calipers, templates, or rulers. Examine completed workpieces for defects such as chipped edges and marred surfaces and sort defective pieces according to types of flaws. Read work orders and production schedules to determine specifications such as materials to be used, locations of cutting lines, and dimensions and tolerances. Load workpieces, plastic material, or chemical solutions into machines. Start machines, monitor their operations, and record operational data. Test and adjust machine speeds and actions according to product specifications and using gauges and hand tools. Install, align, and lock specified punches, dies, cutting blades, or other fixtures in rams or beds of machines, using gauges, templates, feelers, shims, and hand tools. Clean and lubricate machines. Position, align, and secure workpieces against fixtures or stops on machine beds or on dies. Scribe reference lines on workpieces as guides for cutting operations according to blueprints, templates, sample parts, or specifications. Set blade tensions, heights, and angles to perform prescribed cuts, using wrenches. Adjust ram strokes of presses to specified lengths, using hand tools. Place workpieces on cutting tables manually or using hoists, cranes, or sledges. Position guides, stops, holding blocks, or other fixtures to secure and direct workpieces, using hand tools and measuring devices. Thread ends of metal coils from reels through slitters and secure ends on recoilers. Turn valves to start flow of coolant against cutting areas and to start airflow that blows cuttings away from kerfs. Set stops on machine beds; change dies; and adjust components, such as rams or power presses, when making multiple or successive passes. Lubricate workpieces with oil. Replace defective blades or wheels, using hand tools. Mark identifying data on workpieces. Turn controls to set cutting speeds, feed rates, and table angles for specified operations.

GOE Information—Interest Area: 13. Manufacturing. **Work Group:** 13.02. Machine Setup and Operation. **Personality Type—**Realistic.

Realistic occupations frequently involve work activities that include practical, hands-on problems and solutions. They often deal with plants; animals; and real-world materials like wood, tools, and machinery. Many of the occupations require working outside and do not involve a lot of paperwork or working closely with others. **Work Values**—Independence; Moral Values; Supervision, Technical; Activity; Supervision, Human Relations; Company Policies and Practices. **Skills**—Quality Control Analysis; Operation Monitoring; Operation and Control; Repairing; Troubleshooting; Equipment Maintenance. **Abilities**—*Cognitive:* Visualization. *Psychomotor:* Wrist-Finger Speed; Control Precision; Manual Dexterity; Reaction Time; Arm-Hand Steadiness; Multilimb Coordination. *Physical:* Extent Flexibility; Static Strength; Dynamic Strength; Trunk Strength. *Sensory:* Depth Perception. **General Work Activities**—*Information Input:* Monitoring Processes, Materials, or Surroundings; Inspecting Equipment, Structures, or Materials; Identifying Objects, Actions, and Events. *Mental Process:* Making Decisions and Solving Problems; Processing Information; Updating and Using Relevant Knowledge. *Work Output:* Handling and Moving Objects; Controlling Machines and Processes; Performing General Physical Activities. *Interacting with Others:* Communicating with Other Workers; Establishing and Maintaining Interpersonal Relationships; Teaching Others. **Physical Work Conditions**—Noisy; Contaminants; Minor Burns, Cuts, Bites, or Stings; Standing; Using Hands on Objects, Tools, or Controls; Repetitive Motions. **Other Job Characteristics**—Need to Be Exact or Accurate; Pace Determined by Speed of Equipment; Repeat Same Tasks.

Experience—Job Zone 2. Some previous work-related skill, knowledge, or experience may be helpful in these occupations, but usually is not needed. **Job Preparation**—SVP 4.0 to less than 6.0—six months to less than two years. **Knowledges**—Production and Processing; Mechanical Devices; Administration and Management; Education and Training. **Instructional Programs**—Machine Tool Technology/Machinist; Sheet Metal Technology/Sheetworking.

Related SOC Job—51-4031 Cutting, Punching, and Press Machine Setters, Operators, and Tenders, Metal and Plastic. **Related OOH Job**—Machine Setters, Operators, and Tenders—Metal and Plastic. **Related DOT Jobs**—607.382-010 Contour-Band-Saw Operator, Vertical; 607.382-014 Saw Operator; 607.682-010 Cut-Off-Saw Operator, Metal; 607.682-014 Profile Trimmer; 607.685-010 Cut-Off Saw Tender, Metal; 607.685-014 Debridging-Machine Operator; 609.280-010 Trim-Machine Adjuster; 609.682-030 Screwmaker, Automatic; 612.685-014 Spring Tester I; 615.280-010 Slitter Service and Setter; 615.380-010 Shear Setter; 615.382-010 Punch-Press Operator I; 615.482-010 Angle Shear Operator; 615.482-014 Duplicator-Punch Operator; others.

51-4032.00 Drilling and Boring Machine Tool Setters, Operators, and Tenders, Metal and Plastic

- **Education/Training Required:** Moderate-term on-the-job training
- **Employed:** 43,180
- **Annual Earnings:** $28,800
- **Growth:** −8.4%
- **Annual Job Openings:** 2,000

Set up, operate, or tend drilling machines to drill, bore, ream, mill, or countersink metal or plastic workpieces.

Verify conformance of machined work to specifications, using measuring instruments such as calipers, micrometers, and fixed and telescoping gauges. Study machining instructions, job orders, and blueprints to determine dimensional and finish specifications, sequences of operations, setups, and tooling requirements. Select and set cutting speeds, feed rates, depths of cuts, and cutting tools according to machining instructions or knowledge of metal properties. Install tools in spindles. Change worn cutting tools, using wrenches. Position and secure workpieces on tables, using bolts, jigs, clamps, shims, or other holding devices. Move machine controls to lower tools to workpieces and to engage automatic feeds. Turn valves and direct flow of coolants or cutting oil over cutting areas. Establish zero reference points on workpieces, such as at the intersections of two edges or over hole locations. Operate single- or multiple-spindle drill presses to bore holes so that machining operations can be performed on metal or plastic workpieces. Observe drilling or boring machine operations to detect any problems. Lift workpieces onto work tables, either manually or with hoists, or direct crane operators to lift and position workpieces. Lay out reference lines and machining locations on work, using layout tools and applying knowledge of shop math and layout techniques. Perform minor assembly, such as fastening parts with nuts, bolts, and screws, using power tools and hand tools. Verify that workpiece reference lines are parallel to the axis of table rotation, using dial indicators mounted in spindles. Operate tracing attachments to duplicate contours from templates or models. Sharpen cutting tools, using bench grinders.

GOE Information—**Interest Area:** 13. Manufacturing. **Work Group:** 13.02. Machine Setup and Operation. **Personality Type**—Realistic. Realistic occupations frequently involve work activities that include practical, hands-on problems and solutions. They often deal with plants; animals; and real-world materials like wood, tools, and machinery. Many of the occupations require working outside and do not involve a lot of paperwork or working closely with others. **Work Values**—Independence; Supervision, Technical; Moral Values; Supervision, Human Relations; Activity; Company Policies and Practices. **Skills**—Operation Monitoring; Programming; Equipment Maintenance; Quality Control Analysis; Installation; Equipment Selection. **Abilities**—*Cognitive:* Perceptual Speed; Visualization; Selective Attention; Mathematical Reasoning; Time Sharing. *Psychomotor:* Rate Control; Reaction Time; Control Precision; Response Orientation; Multilimb Coordination; Finger Dexterity. *Physical:* Static Strength; Trunk Strength. *Sensory:* Depth Perception; Hearing Sensitivity; Auditory Attention; Visual Color Discrimination. **General Work Activities**—*Information Input:* Monitoring Processes, Materials, or Surroundings; Inspecting Equipment, Structures, or Materials; Getting Information. *Mental Process:* Making Decisions and Solving Problems; Updating and Using Relevant Knowledge; Organizing, Planning, and Prioritizing. *Work Output:* Handling and Moving Objects; Controlling Machines and Processes; Performing General Physical Activities. *Interacting with Others:* Establishing and Maintaining Interpersonal Relationships; Communicating with Other Workers; Developing and Building Teams. **Physical Work Conditions**—Noisy; Contaminants; Hazardous Equipment; Minor Burns, Cuts, Bites, or Stings; Standing; Using Hands on Objects, Tools, or Controls. **Other Job Characteristics**—Need to Be Exact or Accurate; Pace Determined by Speed of Equipment; Errors Have Important Consequences; Repeat Same Tasks.

Experience—Job Zone 3. Previous work-related skill, knowledge, or experience is required. **Job Preparation**—SVP 6.0 to less than 7.0—more than one year and less than four years. **Knowledges**—Mechanical Devices; Production and Processing; Design; Engineering and Technology; Mathematics; Public Safety and

Security. **Instructional Program**—Machine Tool Technology/ Machinist.

Related SOC Job—51-4032 Drilling and Boring Machine Tool Setters, Operators, and Tenders, Metal and Plastic. **Related OOH Job**— Machine Setters, Operators, and Tenders—Metal and Plastic. **Related DOT Jobs**—606.280-010 Boring-Machine Set-Up Operator, Jig; 606.280-014 Boring-Mill Set-Up Operator, Horizontal; 606.380-010 Drill-Press Set-Up Operator, Multiple Spindle; 606.380-014 Drill-Press Set-Up Operator, Radial; 606.380-018 Drill-Press Set-Up Operator, Radial, Tool; 606.382-010 Driller-And-Reamer, Automatic; 606.382-022 Boring-Machine Operator; 606.682-014 Drill-Press Operator; 606.682-018 Drill-Press Set-Up Operator, Single Spindle; 606.682-022 Tapper Operator; others.

51-4033.00 Grinding, Lapping, Polishing, and Buffing Machine Tool Setters, Operators, and Tenders, Metal and Plastic

- **Education/Training Required: Moderate-term on-the-job training**
- **Employed: 101,530**
- **Annual Earnings: $27,740**
- **Growth: –10.0%**
- **Annual Job Openings: 5,000**

Set up, operate, or tend grinding and related tools that remove excess material or burrs from surfaces; sharpen edges or corners; or buff, hone, or polish metal or plastic workpieces.

Inspect or measure finished workpieces to determine conformance to specifications, using measuring instruments such as gauges or micrometers. Lift and position workpieces, manually or with hoists, and secure them in hoppers or on machine tables, faceplates, or chucks, using clamps. Observe machine operations to detect any problems; make necessary adjustments to correct problems. Set and adjust machine controls according to product specifications, utilizing knowledge of machine operation. Measure workpieces and lay out work, using precision measuring devices. Select machine tooling to be used, utilizing knowledge of machine and production requirements. Study blueprints, work orders, or machining instructions to determine product specifications, tool requirements, and operational sequences. Mount and position tools in machine chucks, spindles, or other tool holding devices, using hand tools. Activate machine start-up switches to grind, lap, hone, debar, shear, or cut workpieces, according to specifications. Move machine controls to index work-pieces and to adjust machines for pre-selected operational settings. Brush or spray lubricating compounds on workpieces or turn valve handles and direct flow of coolant against tools and workpieces. Compute machine indexings and settings for specified dimensions and base reference points. Slide spacers between buffs on spindles to set spacing. Thread and hand-feed materials through machine cutters or abraders. Adjust air cylinders and setting stops to set traverse lengths and feed arm strokes. Repair or replace machine parts, using hand tools, or notify engineering personnel when corrective action is required. Maintain stocks of machine parts and machining tools.

GOE Information—**Interest Area:** 13. Manufacturing. **Work Group:** 13.02. Machine Setup and Operation. **Personality Type**—Realistic. Realistic occupations frequently involve work activities that include practical, hands-on problems and solutions. They often deal with plants; animals; and real-world materials like wood, tools, and machinery. Many of the occupations require working outside and do not involve a lot of paperwork or working closely with others. **Work**

Values—Independence; Moral Values; Supervision, Technical; Activity; Supervision, Human Relations; Company Policies and Practices. **Skills**—Quality Control Analysis; Operation Monitoring; Equipment Maintenance; Installation; Operation and Control; Repairing. **Abilities**—*Cognitive:* Visualization; Number Facility. *Psychomotor:* Control Precision; Wrist-Finger Speed; Manual Dexterity; Speed of Limb Movement; Arm-Hand Steadiness; Multilimb Coordination. *Physical:* Static Strength; Extent Flexibility; Trunk Strength. *Sensory:* None met the criteria. **General Work Activities**—*Information Input:* Inspecting Equipment, Structures, or Materials; Monitoring Processes, Materials, or Surroundings; Identifying Objects, Actions, and Events. *Mental Process:* Making Decisions and Solving Problems; Updating and Using Relevant Knowledge; Thinking Creatively. *Work Output:* Handling and Moving Objects; Controlling Machines and Processes; Performing General Physical Activities. *Interacting with Others:* Establishing and Maintaining Interpersonal Relationships; Communicating with Other Workers; Teaching Others. **Physical Work Conditions**— Indoors; Noisy; Contaminants; Hazardous Equipment; Standing; Using Hands on Objects, Tools, or Controls. **Other Job Characteristics**—Need to Be Exact or Accurate; Pace Determined by Speed of Equipment; Repeat Same Tasks; Errors Have Important Consequences; Automation.

Experience—Job Zone 2. Some previous work-related skill, knowledge, or experience may be helpful in these occupations, but usually is not needed. **Job Preparation**—SVP 4.0 to less than 6.0—six months to less than two years. **Knowledges**—Mechanical Devices; Production and Processing; Design; Engineering and Technology. **Instructional Programs**—Machine Shop Technology/Assistant; Machine Tool Technology/Machinist.

Related SOC Job—51-4033 Grinding, Lapping, Polishing, and Buffing Machine Tool Setters, Operators, and Tenders, Metal and Plastic. **Related OOH Job**—Machine Setters, Operators, and Tenders—Metal and Plastic. **Related DOT Jobs**—601.482-010 Profile-Grinder Technician; 602.360-010 Grinder Set-Up Operator, Gear, Tool; 602.382-034 Grinder, Gear; 602.482-010 Gear-Lapping-Machine Operator; 603.260-010 Grinder Set-Up Operator, Thread Tool; 603.280-026 Grinder Set-Up Operator, Jig; 603.280-034 Job Setter, Honing; 603.360-010 Buffing-Line Set-Up Worker; 603.380-010 Grinder Machine Setter; 603.382-010 Buffing-Machine Operator; 603.382-014 Grinder Set-Up Operator, Centerless; 603.382-018 Honing-Machine Set-Up Operator; others.

51-4034.00 Lathe and Turning Machine Tool Setters, Operators, and Tenders, Metal and Plastic

- **Education/Training Required: Moderate-term on-the-job training**
- **Employed: 71,410**
- **Annual Earnings: $31,750**
- **Growth: –9.0%**
- **Annual Job Openings: 7,000**

Set up, operate, or tend lathe and turning machines to turn, bore, thread, form, or face metal or plastic materials, such as wire, rod, or bar stock.

Inspect sample workpieces to verify conformance with specifications, using instruments such as gauges, micrometers, and dial indicators. Study blueprints, layouts or charts, and job orders for information on specifications and tooling instructions and to determine material requirements and operational sequences. Adjust machine controls and change tool settings to keep dimensions within specified tolerances. Start lath or turning machines and observe operations to ensure that specifications are met. Move controls to set cutting speeds and depths and feed rates and to position tools in relation to workpieces. Select cutting tools and tooling instructions according to written specifications or knowledge of metal properties and shop mathematics. Crank machines through cycles, stopping to adjust tool positions and machine controls to ensure specified timing, clearances, and tolerances. Lift metal stock or workpieces manually or by using hoists and position and secure them in machines, using fasteners and hand tools. Replace worn tools and sharpen dull cutting tools and dies, using bench grinders or cutter-grinding machines. Position, secure, and align cutting tools in toolholders on machines, using hand tools, and verify their positions with measuring instruments. Compute unspecified dimensions and machine settings, using knowledge of metal properties and shop mathematics. Install holding fixtures, cams, gears, and stops to control stock and tool movement, using hand tools, power tools, and measuring instruments. Move toolholders manually or by turning handwheels or engage automatic feeding mechanisms to feed tools to and along workpieces. Turn valve handles to direct the flow of coolant onto work areas or to coat disks with spinning compounds. Mount attachments, such as relieving or tracing attachments, to perform operations such as duplicating contours of templates or trimming workpieces.

GOE Information—Interest Area: 13. Manufacturing. **Work Group:** 13.02. Machine Setup and Operation. **Personality Type—**Realistic. Realistic occupations frequently involve work activities that include practical, hands-on problems and solutions. They often deal with plants; animals; and real-world materials like wood, tools, and machinery. Many of the occupations require working outside and do not involve a lot of paperwork or working closely with others. **Work Values—**Moral Values; Independence; Supervision, Technical; Supervision, Human Relations; Company Policies and Practices; Advancement. **Skills—**Operation Monitoring; Equipment Maintenance; Repairing; Quality Control Analysis; Operation and Control; Programming. **Abilities—***Cognitive:* Visualization; Perceptual Speed; Selective Attention. *Psychomotor:* Reaction Time; Control Precision; Multilimb Coordination; Rate Control; Response Orientation; Arm-Hand Steadiness. *Physical:* Static Strength; Trunk Strength; Extent Flexibility. *Sensory:* Depth Perception; Hearing Sensitivity; Auditory Attention. **General Work Activities—***Information Input:* Monitoring Processes, Materials, or Surroundings; Inspecting Equipment, Structures, or Materials; Identifying Objects, Actions, and Events. *Mental Process:* Making Decisions and Solving Problems; Updating and Using Relevant Knowledge; Evaluating Information Against Standards. *Work Output:* Controlling Machines and Processes; Handling and Moving Objects; Repairing and Maintaining Mechanical Equipment. *Interacting with Others:* Communicating with Other Workers; Establishing and Maintaining Interpersonal Relationships; Teaching Others. **Physical Work Conditions—**Noisy; Contaminants; Hazardous Equipment; Minor Burns, Cuts, Bites, or Stings; Standing; Using Hands on Objects, Tools, or Controls. **Other Job Characteristics—**Need to Be Exact or Accurate; Pace Determined by Speed of Equipment; Repeat Same Tasks.

Experience—Job Zone 2. Some previous work-related skill, knowledge, or experience may be helpful in these occupations, but usually is not needed. **Job Preparation—**SVP 4.0 to less than 6.0—six months to less than two years. **Knowledges—**Mechanical Devices; Design; Engineering and Technology; Mathematics; Production and Processing; Computers and Electronics. **Instructional Program—**Machine Tool Technology/Machinist.

Related SOC Job—51-4034 Lathe and Turning Machine Tool Setters, Operators, and Tenders, Metal and Plastic. **Related OOH Job—**Machine Setters, Operators, and Tenders—Metal and Plastic. **Related DOT Jobs—**604.260-010 Screw-Machine Set-Up Operator, Swiss-Type; 604.280-010 Engine-Lathe Set-Up Operator, Tool; 604.280-014 Screw-Machine Set-Up Operator, Multiple Spindle; 604.280-018 Screw-Machine Set-Up Operator, Single Spindle; 604.280-022 Turret-Lathe Set-Up Operator, Tool; 604.360-010 Setter, Automatic-Spinning Lathe; 604.380-010 Chucking-Machine Set-Up Operator; 604.380-014 Chucking-Machine Set-Up Operator, Multiple Spindle, Vertical; 604.380-018 Engine-Lathe Set-Up Operator; others.

51-4035.00 Milling and Planing Machine Setters, Operators, and Tenders, Metal and Plastic

- **Education/Training Required: Moderate-term on-the-job training**
- **Employed: 29,140**
- **Annual Earnings: $31,460**
- **Growth: –5.3%**
- **Annual Job Openings: 2,000**

Set up, operate, or tend milling or planing machines to mill, plane, shape, groove, or profile metal or plastic workpieces.

Verify alignment of workpieces on machines, using measuring instruments such as rules, gauges, or calipers. Move controls to set cutting specifications, to position cutting tools and workpieces in relation to each other, and to start machines. Position and secure workpieces on machines, using holding devices, measuring instruments, hand tools, and hoists. Remove workpieces from machines and check to ensure that they conform to specifications, using measuring instruments such as microscopes, gauges, calipers, and micrometers. Move cutters or material manually or by turning handwheels or engage automatic feeding mechanisms to mill workpieces to specifications. Turn valves or pull levers to start and regulate the flow of coolant or lubricant to work areas. Select and install cutting tools and other accessories according to specifications, using hand tools or power tools. Compute dimensions, tolerances, and angles of workpieces or machines according to specifications and knowledge of metal properties and shop mathematics. Make templates or cutting tools. Mount attachments and tools such as pantographs, engravers, or routers to perform other operations such as drilling or boring. Record production output. Replace worn tools, using hand tools, and sharpen dull tools, using bench grinders. Select cutting speeds, feed rates, and depths of cuts, applying knowledge of metal properties and shop mathematics. Study blueprints, layouts, sketches, or work orders to assess workpiece specifications and to determine tooling instructions, tools and materials needed, and sequences of operations. Observe milling or planing machine operation and adjust controls to ensure conformance with specified tolerances.

GOE Information—Interest Area: 13. Manufacturing. **Work Group:** 13.02. Machine Setup and Operation. **Personality Type—**Realistic. Realistic occupations frequently involve work activities that include practical, hands-on problems and solutions. They often deal with plants; animals; and real-world materials like wood, tools, and machinery. Many of the occupations require working outside and do not involve a lot of paperwork or working closely with others. **Work Values—**Independence; Moral Values; Supervision, Technical; Supervision, Human Relations; Company Policies and Practices;

Advancement. **Skills**—Equipment Maintenance; Operation and Control; Operation Monitoring; Repairing; Installation; Technology Design. **Abilities**—*Cognitive:* None met the criteria. *Psychomotor:* Wrist-Finger Speed; Control Precision; Reaction Time; Manual Dexterity. *Physical:* Static Strength. *Sensory:* None met the criteria. **General Work Activities**—*Information Input:* Monitoring Processes, Materials, or Surroundings; Inspecting Equipment, Structures, or Materials; Identifying Objects, Actions, and Events. *Mental Process:* Evaluating Information Against Standards. *Work Output:* Controlling Machines and Processes; Handling and Moving Objects; Performing General Physical Activities. *Interacting with Others:* None met the criteria. **Physical Work Conditions**—Indoors; Noisy; Hazardous Equipment; Standing; Using Hands on Objects, Tools, or Controls; Repetitive Motions. **Other Job Characteristics**—Automation; Need to Be Exact or Accurate.

Experience—Job Zone 3. Previous work-related skill, knowledge, or experience is required. **Job Preparation**—SVP 6.0 to less than 7.0—more than one year and less than four years. **Knowledges**—Production and Processing; Mechanical Devices; Physics; Design; Engineering and Technology. **Instructional Program**—Machine Tool Technology/Machinist.

Related SOC Job—51-4035 Milling and Planing Machine Setters, Operators, and Tenders, Metal and Plastic. **Related OOH Job**—Machine Setters, Operators, and Tenders—Metal and Plastic. **Related DOT Jobs**—605.280-010 Milling-Machine Set-Up Operator I; 605.280-014 Profiling-Machine Set-Up Operator I; 605.280-018 Profiling-Machine Set-Up Operator, Tool; 605.282-010 Milling-Machine Set-Up Operator II; 605.282-014 Planer Set-Up Operator, Tool; 605.282-018 Planer-Type-Milling-Machine Set-Up Operator; 605.382-010 Broaching-Machine Set-Up Operator; 605.382-014 Engraver, Tire Mold; 605.382-018 Keyseating-Machine Set-Up Operator; 605.382-022 Pantograph-Machine Set-Up Operator; others.

51-4041.00 Machinists

- **Education/Training Required: Long-term on-the-job training**
- **Employed: 368,380**
- **Annual Earnings: $34,350**
- **Growth: 4.3%**
- **Annual Job Openings: 33,000**

Set up and operate a variety of machine tools to produce precision parts and instruments. Includes precision instrument makers who fabricate, modify, or repair mechanical instruments. May also fabricate and modify parts to make or repair machine tools or maintain industrial machines, applying knowledge of mechanics, shop mathematics, metal properties, layout, and machining procedures.

Calculate dimensions and tolerances, using knowledge of mathematics and instruments such as micrometers and vernier calipers. Machine parts to specifications, using machine tools such as lathes, milling machines, shapers, or grinders. Measure, examine, and test completed units to detect defects and ensure conformance to specifications, using precision instruments such as micrometers. Set up, adjust, and operate all of the basic machine tools and many specialized or advanced variation tools to perform precision machining operations. Align and secure holding fixtures, cutting tools, attachments, accessories, and materials onto machines. Monitor the feed and speed of machines during the machining process. Study sample parts, blueprints, drawings, and engineering information to determine methods and sequences of operations needed to fabricate products and determine product dimensions and tolerances. Select the appropriate tools, machines, and materials to be used in preparation of machinery work. Lay out, measure, and mark metal stock to display placement of cuts. Observe and listen to operating machines or equipment to diagnose machine malfunctions and to determine need for adjustments or repairs. Check workpieces to ensure that they are properly lubricated and cooled. Maintain industrial machines, applying knowledge of mechanics, shop mathematics, metal properties, layout, and machining procedures. Position and fasten workpieces. Operate equipment to verify operational efficiency. Install repaired parts into equipment or install new equipment. Clean and lubricate machines, tools, and equipment to remove grease, rust, stains, and foreign matter. Advise clients about the materials being used for finished products. Program computers and electronic instruments such as numerically controlled machine tools. Set controls to regulate machining or enter commands to retrieve, input, or edit computerized machine control media. Confer with engineering, supervisory, and manufacturing personnel to exchange technical information. Dismantle machines or equipment, using hand tools and power tools, to examine parts for defects and replace defective parts where needed.

GOE Information—**Interest Area:** 13. Manufacturing. **Work Group:** 13.05. Production Machining Technology. **Personality Type**—Realistic. Realistic occupations frequently involve work activities that include practical, hands-on problems and solutions. They often deal with plants; animals; and real-world materials like wood, tools, and machinery. Many of the occupations require working outside and do not involve a lot of paperwork or working closely with others. **Work Values**—Moral Values; Supervision, Technical; Company Policies and Practices; Supervision, Human Relations; Compensation; Creativity. **Skills**—Operation Monitoring; Operation and Control; Equipment Maintenance; Quality Control Analysis; Installation; Equipment Selection. **Abilities**—*Cognitive:* Visualization; Mathematical Reasoning; Information Ordering; Flexibility of Closure; Deductive Reasoning; Selective Attention. *Psychomotor:* Rate Control; Control Precision; Manual Dexterity; Multilimb Coordination; Arm-Hand Steadiness; Wrist-Finger Speed. *Physical:* Static Strength; Extent Flexibility; Trunk Strength. *Sensory:* Hearing Sensitivity; Auditory Attention; Depth Perception; Near Vision. **General Work Activities**—*Information Input:* Monitoring Processes, Materials, or Surroundings; Inspecting Equipment, Structures, or Materials; Getting Information. *Mental Process:* Updating and Using Relevant Knowledge; Making Decisions and Solving Problems; Processing Information. *Work Output:* Controlling Machines and Processes; Handling and Moving Objects; Performing General Physical Activities. *Interacting with Others:* Communicating with Other Workers; Establishing and Maintaining Interpersonal Relationships; Teaching Others. **Physical Work Conditions**—Indoors; Noisy; Hazardous Equipment; Standing; Using Hands on Objects, Tools, or Controls; Repetitive Motions. **Other Job Characteristics**—Need to Be Exact or Accurate; Pace Determined by Speed of Equipment; Errors Have Important Consequences.

Experience—Job Zone 3. Previous work-related skill, knowledge, or experience is required. **Job Preparation**—SVP 6.0 to less than 7.0—more than one year and less than four years. **Knowledges**—Mechanical Devices; Engineering and Technology; Mathematics; Design; Production and Processing; Computers and Electronics. **Instructional Programs**—Machine Shop Technology/Assistant; Machine Tool Technology/Machinist.

Related SOC Job—51-4041 Machinists. **Related OOH Job**—Machinists. **Related DOT Jobs**—019.161-014 Test Technician; 600.260-022 Machinist, Experimental; 600.280-010 Instrument Maker; 600.280-014 Instrument-Maker And Repairer; 600.280-018 Instrument-Maker Apprentice; 600.280-022 Machinist; 600.280-026

Machinist Apprentice; 600.280-030 Machinist Apprentice, Automotive; 600.280-034 Machinist, Automotive; 600.280-042 Maintenance Machinist; 600.281-010 Fluid-Power Mechanic; 600.380-010 Fixture Maker; 623.281-010 Deck Engineer; 623.281-022 Machinist Apprentice, Outside; others.

51-4051.00 Metal-Refining Furnace Operators and Tenders

- **Education/Training Required: Moderate-term on-the-job training**
- **Employed: 17,960**
- **Annual Earnings: $32,920**
- **Growth: –13.5%**
- **Annual Job Openings: 2,000**

Operate or tend furnaces, such as gas, oil, coal, electric-arc or electric induction, open-hearth, or oxygen furnaces, to melt and refine metal before casting or to produce specified types of steel.

Draw smelted metal samples from furnaces or kettles for analysis and calculate types and amounts of materials needed to ensure that materials meet specifications. Drain, transfer, or remove molten metal from furnaces and place it into molds, using hoists, pumps, or ladles. Record production data and maintain production logs. Operate controls to move or discharge metal workpieces from furnaces. Weigh materials to be charged into furnaces, using scales. Regulate supplies of fuel and air or control flow of electric current and water coolant to heat furnaces and adjust temperatures. Inspect furnaces and equipment to locate defects and wear. Observe air and temperature gauges or metal color and fluidity and turn fuel valves or adjust controls to maintain required temperatures. Observe operations inside furnaces, using television screens, to ensure that problems do not occur. Remove impurities from the surface of molten metal, using strainers. Kindle fires and shovel fuel and other materials into furnaces or onto conveyors by hand, with hoists, or by directing crane operators. Sprinkle chemicals over molten metal to bring impurities to the surface. Direct work crews in the cleaning and repair of furnace walls and flooring. Prepare material to load into furnaces, including cleaning, crushing, or applying chemicals, by using crushing machines, shovels, rakes, or sprayers. Scrape accumulations of metal oxides from floors, molds, and crucibles and sift and store them for reclamation.

GOE Information—Interest Area: 13. Manufacturing. **Work Group:** 13.03. Production Work, Assorted Materials Processing. **Personality Type**—Realistic. Realistic occupations frequently involve work activities that include practical, hands-on problems and solutions. They often deal with plants; animals; and real-world materials like wood, tools, and machinery. Many of the occupations require working outside and do not involve a lot of paperwork or working closely with others. **Work Values**—Independence; Moral Values; Supervision, Human Relations; Company Policies and Practices; Supervision, Technical; Activity. **Skills**—Operation Monitoring; Equipment Maintenance; Quality Control Analysis; Operation and Control; Troubleshooting; Repairing. **Abilities**—*Cognitive:* Perceptual Speed; Flexibility of Closure; Number Facility; Visualization; Selective Attention; Time Sharing. *Psychomotor:* Reaction Time; Rate Control; Multilimb Coordination; Control Precision; Response Orientation; Speed of Limb Movement. *Physical:* Extent Flexibility; Stamina; Dynamic Strength; Gross Body Coordination; Trunk Strength; Static Strength. *Sensory:* Glare Sensitivity; Auditory Attention; Depth Perception; Visual Color Discrimination; Far Vision; Hearing Sensitivity. **General Work Activities**—*Information Input:* Monitoring

Processes, Materials, or Surroundings; Inspecting Equipment, Structures, or Materials; Identifying Objects, Actions, and Events. *Mental Process:* Making Decisions and Solving Problems; Processing Information; Judging the Qualities of Things, Services, or Other People's Work. *Work Output:* Handling and Moving Objects; Controlling Machines and Processes; Performing General Physical Activities. *Interacting with Others:* Communicating with Other Workers; Establishing and Maintaining Interpersonal Relationships; Teaching Others. **Physical Work Conditions**—Noisy; Very Hot or Cold; Very Bright or Dim Lighting; Contaminants; Hazardous Conditions; Minor Burns, Cuts, Bites, or Stings. **Other Job Characteristics**—Need to Be Exact or Accurate; Errors Have Important Consequences; Repeat Same Tasks; Pace Determined by Speed of Equipment.

Experience—Job Zone 2. Some previous work-related skill, knowledge, or experience may be helpful in these occupations, but usually is not needed. **Job Preparation**—SVP 4.0 to less than 6.0—six months to less than two years. **Knowledges**—Production and Processing; Chemistry; Mechanical Devices; Engineering and Technology; Mathematics. **Instructional Program**—No related CIP programs.

Related SOC Job—51-4051 Metal-Refining Furnace Operators and Tenders. **Related OOH Job**—Machine Setters, Operators, and Tenders—Metal and Plastic. **Related DOT Jobs**—504.665-014 Charger Operator; 512.362-010 First Helper; 512.362-014 Furnace Operator; 512.362-018 Furnace Operator; 512.382-010 Oxygen-Furnace Operator; 512.382-014 Stove Tender; 512.382-018 Tin Recovery Worker; 512.662-010 Cupola Tender; 512.684-014 Furnace Charger; 512.685-010 Furnace Tender; 512.685-022 Reclamation Kettle Tender, Metal; 553.685-114 Cadmium Burner.

51-4052.00 Pourers and Casters, Metal

- **Education/Training Required: Moderate-term on-the-job training**
- **Employed: 14,340**
- **Annual Earnings: $29,160**
- **Growth: –16.1%**
- **Annual Job Openings: 1,000**

Operate hand-controlled mechanisms to pour and regulate the flow of molten metal into molds to produce castings or ingots.

Collect samples or signal workers to sample metal for analysis. Pour and regulate the flow of molten metal into molds and forms to produce ingots or other castings, using ladles or hand-controlled mechanisms. Read temperature gauges and observe color changes; then adjust furnace flames, torches, or electrical heating units as necessary to melt metal to specifications. Examine molds to ensure they are clean, smooth, and properly coated. Position equipment such as ladles, grinding wheels, pouring nozzles, or crucibles or signal other workers to position equipment. Skim slag or remove excess metal from ingots or equipment, using hand tools, strainers, rakes, or burners; collect scrap for recycling. Turn valves to circulate water through cores or spray water on filled molds to cool and solidify metal. Add metal to molds to compensate for shrinkage. Pull levers to lift ladle stoppers and to allow molten steel to flow into ingot molds to specified heights. Load specified amounts of metal and flux into furnaces or clay crucibles. Remove solidified steel or slag from pouring nozzles, using long bars or oxygen burners. Assemble and embed cores in casting frames, using hand tools and equipment. Remove metal ingots or cores from molds, using hand tools, cranes, and chain hoists. Transport metal ingots to storage areas, using forklifts. Stencil identifying information on ingots and pigs, using special hand tools.

Repair and maintain metal forms and equipment, using hand tools, sledges, and bars.

GOE Information—Interest Area: 13. Manufacturing. **Work Group:** 13.03. Production Work, Assorted Materials Processing. **Personality Type—Realistic.** Realistic occupations frequently involve work activities that include practical, hands-on problems and solutions. They often deal with plants; animals; and real-world materials like wood, tools, and machinery. Many of the occupations require working outside and do not involve a lot of paperwork or working closely with others. **Work Values—**Moral Values; Supervision, Technical; Independence. **Skills—**Repairing; Equipment Maintenance; Operation Monitoring; Operation and Control; Troubleshooting; Management of Material Resources. **Abilities—***Cognitive:* Perceptual Speed; Time Sharing; Selective Attention; Visualization. *Psychomotor:* Reaction Time; Rate Control; Multilimb Coordination; Arm-Hand Steadiness; Control Precision; Manual Dexterity. *Physical:* Static Strength; Trunk Strength; Stamina; Extent Flexibility. *Sensory:* Visual Color Discrimination; Depth Perception; Hearing Sensitivity; Auditory Attention. **General Work Activities—***Information Input:* Inspecting Equipment, Structures, or Materials; Monitoring Processes, Materials, or Surroundings; Identifying Objects, Actions, and Events. *Mental Process:* Evaluating Information Against Standards; Organizing, Planning, and Prioritizing; Making Decisions and Solving Problems. *Work Output:* Handling and Moving Objects; Controlling Machines and Processes; Performing General Physical Activities. *Interacting with Others:* Communicating with Other Workers; Teaching Others; Assisting and Caring for Others. **Physical Work Conditions—**Noisy; Very Hot or Cold; Contaminants; Hazardous Equipment; Minor Burns, Cuts, Bites, or Stings; Using Hands on Objects, Tools, or Controls. **Other Job Characteristics—**Need to Be Exact or Accurate; Pace Determined by Speed of Equipment; Errors Have Important Consequences; Repeat Same Tasks.

Experience—Job Zone 2. Some previous work-related skill, knowledge, or experience may be helpful in these occupations, but usually is not needed. **Job Preparation—**SVP 4.0 to less than 6.0—six months to less than two years. **Knowledges—**Production and Processing. **Instructional Program—**No related CIP programs.

Related SOC Job—51-4052 Pourers and Casters, Metal. **Related OOH Job—**Machine Setters, Operators, and Tenders—Metal and Plastic. **Related DOT Jobs—**502.664-014 Steel Pourer; 502.687-014 Busher; 514.584-010 Ingot Header; 514.684-010 Caster; 514.684-014 Ladle Pourer; 514.684-022 Pourer, Metal; 518.664-010 Mold Maker; 700.687-042 Melter.

51-4061.00 Model Makers, Metal and Plastic

- **Education/Training Required: Moderate-term on-the-job training**
- **Employed: 8,120**
- **Annual Earnings: $44,970**
- **Growth: –4.0%**
- **Annual Job Openings: 1,000**

Set up and operate machines, such as lathes, milling and engraving machines, and jig borers, to make working models of metal or plastic objects.

Study blueprints, drawings, and sketches to determine material dimensions, required equipment, and operations sequences. Set up and operate machines such as lathes, drill presses, punch presses, or band saws to fabricate prototypes or models. Inspect and test products to verify conformance to specifications, using precision measuring instruments or circuit testers. Cut, shape, and form metal parts, using lathes, power saws, snips, power brakes and shears, files, and mallets. Lay out and mark reference points and dimensions on materials, using measuring instruments and drawing or scribing tools. Drill, countersink, and ream holes in parts and assemblies for bolts, screws, and other fasteners, using power tools. Grind, file, and sand parts to finished dimensions. Record specifications, production operations, and final dimensions of models for use in establishing operating standards and procedures. Rework or alter component model or parts as required to ensure that products meet standards. Align, fit, and join parts by using bolts and screws or by welding or gluing. Consult and confer with engineering personnel to discuss developmental problems and to recommend product modifications. Assemble mechanical, electrical, and electronic components into models or prototypes, using hand tools, power tools, and fabricating machines. Devise and construct tools, dies, molds, jigs, and fixtures or modify existing tools and equipment. Wire and solder electrical and electronic connections and components.

GOE Information—Interest Area: 13. Manufacturing. **Work Group:** 13.05. Production Machining Technology. **Personality Type—Realistic.** Realistic occupations frequently involve work activities that include practical, hands-on problems and solutions. They often deal with plants; animals; and real-world materials like wood, tools, and machinery. Many of the occupations require working outside and do not involve a lot of paperwork or working closely with others. **Work Values—**Moral Values; Creativity; Ability Utilization; Supervision, Human Relations; Compensation; Company Policies and Practices. **Skills—**Operation Monitoring; Repairing; Quality Control Analysis; Equipment Maintenance; Operation and Control; Mathematics. **Abilities—***Cognitive:* Visualization; Selective Attention; Number Facility; Flexibility of Closure; Perceptual Speed. *Psychomotor:* Reaction Time; Rate Control; Response Orientation; Multilimb Coordination; Control Precision; Manual Dexterity. *Physical:* Dynamic Strength; Static Strength; Stamina; Extent Flexibility; Trunk Strength. *Sensory:* Auditory Attention; Depth Perception; Hearing Sensitivity; Far Vision; Visual Color Discrimination; Speech Recognition. **General Work Activities—***Information Input:* Inspecting Equipment, Structures, or Materials; Monitoring Processes, Materials, or Surroundings; Getting Information. *Mental Process:* Thinking Creatively; Making Decisions and Solving Problems; Updating and Using Relevant Knowledge. *Work Output:* Controlling Machines and Processes; Handling and Moving Objects; Repairing and Maintaining Mechanical Equipment. *Interacting with Others:* Communicating with Other Workers; Establishing and Maintaining Interpersonal Relationships; Assisting and Caring for Others. **Physical Work Conditions—**Indoors; Noisy; Contaminants; Hazardous Equipment; Standing; Using Hands on Objects, Tools, or Controls. **Other Job Characteristics—**Need to Be Exact or Accurate.

Experience—Job Zone 3. Previous work-related skill, knowledge, or experience is required. **Job Preparation—**SVP 6.0 to less than 7.0—more than one year and less than four years. **Knowledges—**Mechanical Devices; Design; Production and Processing; Engineering and Technology; Computers and Electronics; Mathematics. **Instructional Program—**Sheet Metal Technology/Sheetworking.

Related SOC Job—51-4061 Model Makers, Metal and Plastic. **Related OOH Job—**Machine Setters, Operators, and Tenders—Metal and

Plastic. **Related DOT Jobs**—600.260-014 Experimental Mechanic; 600.260-018 Model Maker, Firearms; 600.280-054 Sample Maker, Appliances; 693.260-018 Engineering Model Maker; 693.280-540 Prototype Model Maker; 693.281-030 Tool Builder; 693.361-014 Mock-Up Builder; 693.380-010 Model Maker; 693.380-014 Model Maker; 709.381-014 Model Builder; 710.361-010 Model Maker, Scale; 723.361-010 Model Maker, Fluorescent Lighting.

51-4062.00 Patternmakers, Metal and Plastic

- **Education/Training Required: Moderate-term on-the-job training**
- **Employed: 6,850**
- **Annual Earnings: $34,460**
- **Growth: –7.5%**
- **Annual Job Openings: 1,000**

Lay out, machine, fit, and assemble castings and parts to metal or plastic foundry patterns, core boxes, or match plates.

Set up and operate machine tools, such as milling machines, lathes, drill presses, and grinders, to machine castings or patterns. Read and interpret blueprints or drawings of parts to be cast or patterns to be made; then compute dimensions and plan operational sequences. Verify conformance of patterns or template dimensions to specifications, using measuring instruments such as calipers, scales, and micrometers. Program computerized numerical control machine tools. Design and create templates, patterns, or coreboxes according to work orders, sample parts, or mockups. Assemble pattern sections, using hand tools, bolts, screws, rivets, glue, or welding equipment. Repair and rework templates and patterns. Lay out and draw or scribe patterns onto material, using compasses, protractors, rulers, scribes, or other instruments. Clean and finish patterns or templates, using emery cloths, files, scrapers, and power grinders. Construct platforms, fixtures, and jigs for holding and placing patterns. Mark identification numbers or symbols onto patterns or templates. Select pattern materials such as wood, resin, and fiberglass. Apply plastic-impregnated fabrics or coats of sealing wax or lacquer to patterns that will be used to produce plastic. Paint or lacquer patterns.

GOE Information—**Interest Area:** 13. Manufacturing. **Work Group:** 13.05. Production Machining Technology. **Personality Type**—Realistic. Realistic occupations frequently involve work activities that include practical, hands-on problems and solutions. They often deal with plants; animals; and real-world materials like wood, tools, and machinery. Many of the occupations require working outside and do not involve a lot of paperwork or working closely with others. **Work Values**—Moral Values; Independence; Supervision, Technical; Company Policies and Practices. **Skills**—Equipment Maintenance; Technology Design; Repairing; Installation; Mathematics; Operation and Control. **Abilities**—*Cognitive:* Visualization; Perceptual Speed; Selective Attention; Time Sharing. *Psychomotor:* Rate Control; Reaction Time; Arm-Hand Steadiness; Control Precision; Multilimb Coordination; Finger Dexterity. *Physical:* Trunk Strength. *Sensory:* Hearing Sensitivity; Depth Perception; Visual Color Discrimination; Auditory Attention; Far Vision. **General Work Activities**—*Information Input:* Monitoring Processes, Materials, or Surroundings; Getting Information; Inspecting Equipment, Structures, or Materials. *Mental Process:* Updating and Using Relevant Knowledge; Making Decisions and Solving Problems; Thinking Creatively. *Work Output:* Controlling Machines and Processes; Handling and Moving Objects; Drafting and Specifying Technical Devices. *Interacting with Others:* Establishing

and Maintaining Interpersonal Relationships; Communicating with Other Workers; Teaching Others. **Physical Work Conditions**—Noisy; Contaminants; Hazardous Equipment; Minor Burns, Cuts, Bites, or Stings; Standing; Using Hands on Objects, Tools, or Controls. **Other Job Characteristics**—Need to Be Exact or Accurate; Errors Have Important Consequences.

Experience—Job Zone 3. Previous work-related skill, knowledge, or experience is required. **Job Preparation**—SVP 6.0 to less than 7.0— more than one year and less than four years. **Knowledges**—Design; Mechanical Devices; Engineering and Technology; Production and Processing; Physics; Mathematics. **Instructional Program**—Sheet Metal Technology/Sheetworking.

Related SOC Job—51-4062 Patternmakers, Metal and Plastic. **Related OOH Job**—Machine Setters, Operators, and Tenders—Metal and Plastic. **Related DOT Jobs**—600.280-046 Patternmaker Apprentice, Metal; 600.280-050 Patternmaker, Metal; 601.280-038 Template Maker, Extrusion Die; 601.381-038 Template Maker; 693.280-014 Patternmaker, All-Around; 693.281-014 Patternmaker; 693.281-018 Patternmaker, Metal, Bench; 693.281-022 Patternmaker, Sample; 703.381-010 Patternmaker; 709.381-034 Patternmaker; 751.381-010 Patternmaker; 754.381-014 Patternmaker, Plastics.

51-4071.00 Foundry Mold and Coremakers

- **Education/Training Required: Moderate-term on-the-job training**
- **Employed: 15,890**
- **Annual Earnings: $29,010**
- **Growth: –13.3%**
- **Annual Job Openings: 2,000**

Make or form wax or sand cores or molds used in the production of metal castings in foundries.

Clean and smooth molds, cores, and core boxes and repair surface imperfections. Move and position workpieces such as mold sections, patterns, and bottom boards, using cranes, or signal others to move workpieces. Sprinkle or spray parting agents onto patterns and mold sections to facilitate removal of patterns from molds. Position patterns inside mold sections and clamp sections together. Position cores into lower sections of molds and reassemble molds for pouring. Sift and pack sand into mold sections, core boxes, and pattern contours, using hand or pneumatic ramming tools. Tend machines that bond cope and drag together to form completed shell molds. Cut spouts, runner holes, and sprue holes into molds. Lift upper mold sections from lower sections and remove molded patterns. Form and assemble slab cores around patterns and position wire in mold sections to reinforce molds, using hand tools and glue. Pour molten metal into molds manually or by using crane ladles. Rotate sweep boards around spindles to make symmetrical molds for convex impressions. Operate ovens or furnaces to bake cores or to melt, skim, and flux metal.

GOE Information—**Interest Area:** 13. Manufacturing. **Work Group:** 13.05. Production Machining Technology. **Personality Type**—Realistic. Realistic occupations frequently involve work activities that include practical, hands-on problems and solutions. They often deal with plants; animals; and real-world materials like wood, tools, and machinery. Many of the occupations require working outside and do not involve a lot of paperwork or working closely with others. **Work Values**—Moral Values; Supervision, Technical; Supervision, Human Relations; Advancement; Independence; Company Policies and Practices. **Skills**—Equipment Maintenance;

Operation Monitoring; Repairing; Operation and Control; Installation; Troubleshooting. **Abilities**—*Cognitive:* Time Sharing. *Psychomotor:* Reaction Time; Multilimb Coordination; Rate Control; Manual Dexterity; Arm-Hand Steadiness; Finger Dexterity. *Physical:* Static Strength; Extent Flexibility; Dynamic Strength; Gross Body Coordination; Stamina; Trunk Strength. *Sensory:* Depth Perception; Auditory Attention; Visual Color Discrimination. **General Work Activities**—*Information Input:* Monitoring Processes, Materials, or Surroundings; Inspecting Equipment, Structures, or Materials; Identifying Objects, Actions, and Events. *Mental Process:* Making Decisions and Solving Problems; Judging the Qualities of Things, Services, or Other People's Work. *Work Output:* Handling and Moving Objects; Performing General Physical Activities; Controlling Machines and Processes. *Interacting with Others:* Establishing and Maintaining Interpersonal Relationships; Communicating with Other Workers. **Physical Work Conditions**—Noisy; Contaminants; Hazardous Equipment; Standing; Using Hands on Objects, Tools, or Controls; Repetitive Motions. **Other Job Characteristics**—Need to Be Exact or Accurate; Pace Determined by Speed of Equipment; Repeat Same Tasks.

Experience—Job Zone 2. Some previous work-related skill, knowledge, or experience may be helpful in these occupations, but usually is not needed. **Job Preparation**—SVP 4.0 to less than 6.0—six months to less than two years. **Knowledges**—Production and Processing; Engineering and Technology; Mechanical Devices; Design; Chemistry. **Instructional Program**—Ironworking/Ironworker.

Related SOC Job—51-4071 Foundry Mold and Coremakers. **Related OOH Job**—Machine Setters, Operators, and Tenders—Metal and Plastic. **Related DOT Jobs**—518.361-010 Molder; 518.361-014 Molder Apprentice; 518.361-018 Molder, Sweep; 518.381-014 Coremaker; 518.381-018 Coremaker Apprentice.

51-4072.00 Molding, Coremaking, and Casting Machine Setters, Operators, and Tenders, Metal and Plastic

- **Education/Training Required: Moderate-term on-the-job training**
- **Employed: 157,080**
- **Annual Earnings: $25,060**
- **Growth: –9.5%**
- **Annual Job Openings: 17,000**

Set up, operate, or tend metal or plastic molding, casting, or coremaking machines to mold or cast metal or thermoplastic parts or products.

Observe continuous operation of automatic machines to ensure that products meet specifications and to detect jams or malfunctions, making adjustments as necessary. Measure and visually inspect products for surface and dimension defects to ensure conformance to specifications, using precision measuring instruments. Position and secure workpieces on machines and start feeding mechanisms. Turn valves and dials of machines to regulate pressure, temperature, and speed and feed rates and to set cycle times. Remove finished or cured products from dies or molds, using hand tools, air hoses, and other equipment; stamp identifying information on products when necessary. Skim or pour dross, slag, or impurities from molten metal, using ladles, rakes, hoes, spatulas, or spoons. Trim excess material from parts, using knives, and grind scrap plastic into powder for reuse. Install dies onto machines or presses; then coat dies with parting agents according to work order specifications. Cool products after processing to prevent distortion. Mix and measure compounds or weigh premixed compounds; then dump them into machine tubs, cavities, or molds. Observe meters and gauges to verify and record temperatures, pressures, and press-cycle times. Spray, smoke, or coat molds with compounds to lubricate or insulate molds, using acetylene torches or sprayers. Read specifications, blueprints, and work orders to determine setups, temperatures, and time settings required to mold, form, or cast plastic materials, as well as to plan production sequences. Adjust equipment and workpiece-holding fixtures, such as mold frames, tubs, and cutting tables, to ensure proper functioning. Remove parts such as dies from machines after production runs are finished. Inventory and record quantities of materials and finished products; requisition additional supplies as necessary. Pour or load metal or sand into melting pots, furnaces, molds, or hoppers, using shovels, ladles, or machines.

GOE Information—**Interest Area:** 13. Manufacturing. **Work Group:** 13.06. Production Precision Work. **Personality Type**—Realistic. Realistic occupations frequently involve work activities that include practical, hands-on problems and solutions. They often deal with plants; animals; and real-world materials like wood, tools, and machinery. Many of the occupations require working outside and do not involve a lot of paperwork or working closely with others. **Work Values**—Moral Values; Independence; Supervision, Human Relations; Supervision, Technical; Company Policies and Practices; Activity. **Skills**—Operation Monitoring; Operation and Control; Quality Control Analysis; Installation; Repairing; Troubleshooting. **Abilities**—*Cognitive:* None met the criteria. *Psychomotor:* Reaction Time; Wrist-Finger Speed; Manual Dexterity; Control Precision; Speed of Limb Movement; Response Orientation. *Physical:* Explosive Strength; Static Strength; Dynamic Strength; Extent Flexibility; Trunk Strength. *Sensory:* None met the criteria. **General Work Activities**—*Information Input:* Inspecting Equipment, Structures, or Materials; Monitoring Processes, Materials, or Surroundings; Getting Information. *Mental Process:* Making Decisions and Solving Problems; Evaluating Information Against Standards; Updating and Using Relevant Knowledge. *Work Output:* Handling and Moving Objects; Controlling Machines and Processes; Performing General Physical Activities. *Interacting with Others:* Establishing and Maintaining Interpersonal Relationships; Communicating with Other Workers; Interpreting the Meaning of Information for Others. **Physical Work Conditions**—Noisy; Very Hot or Cold; Contaminants; Standing; Using Hands on Objects, Tools, or Controls; Repetitive Motions. **Other Job Characteristics**—Pace Determined by Speed of Equipment; Repeat Same Tasks; Need to Be Exact or Accurate.

Experience—Job Zone 2. Some previous work-related skill, knowledge, or experience may be helpful in these occupations, but usually is not needed. **Job Preparation**—SVP 4.0 to less than 6.0—six months to less than two years. **Knowledges**—Production and Processing; Mechanical Devices. **Instructional Program**—No related CIP programs.

Related SOC Job—51-4072 Molding, Coremaking, and Casting Machine Setters, Operators, and Tenders, Metal and Plastic. **Related OOH Job**—Machine Setters, Operators, and Tenders—Metal and Plastic. **Related DOT Jobs**—502.362-010 Shot Dropper; 502.381-014 Molder, Punch; 502.382-010 Bullet-Slug-Casting-Machine Operator; 502.482-010 Caster; 502.482-014 Casting-Machine Operator, Automatic; 502.482-018 Rotor Casting-Machine Operator; 502.682-010 Bullet-Casting Operator; 502.682-014 Casting-Machine Operator; 502.685-010 Molder, Lead Ingot; 502.685-014 Remelter; 514.360-010 Die-Casting-Machine Setter; 514.362-010 Pig-Machine Operator; 514.382-010 Die-Casting-Machine Operator I; others.

51-4081.00 Multiple Machine Tool Setters, Operators, and Tenders, Metal and Plastic

- **Education/Training Required: Moderate-term on-the-job training**
- **Employed: 98,120**
- **Annual Earnings: $29,780**
- **Growth: 0.3%**
- **Annual Job Openings: 6,000**

Set up, operate, or tend more than one type of cutting or forming machine tool or robot.

Inspect workpieces for defects and measure workpieces to determine accuracy of machine operation, using rules, templates, or other measuring instruments. Observe machine operation to detect workpiece defects or machine malfunctions; adjust machines as necessary. Read blueprints or job orders to determine product specifications and tooling instructions and to plan operational sequences. Set up and operate machines such as lathes, cutters, shears, borers, millers, grinders, presses, drills, and auxiliary machines to make metallic and plastic workpieces. Position, adjust, and secure stock material or workpieces against stops; on arbors; or in chucks, fixtures, or automatic feeding mechanisms manually or by using hoists. Select, install, and adjust alignment of drills, cutters, dies, guides, and holding devices, using templates, measuring instruments, and hand tools. Change worn machine accessories such as cutting tools and brushes, using hand tools. Make minor electrical and mechanical repairs and adjustments to machines and notify supervisors when major service is required. Start machines and turn handwheels or valves to engage feeding, cooling, and lubricating mechanisms. Perform minor machine maintenance, such as oiling or cleaning machines, dies, or workpieces or adding coolant to machine reservoirs. Select the proper coolants and lubricants and start their flow. Remove burrs, sharp edges, rust, or scale from workpieces, using files, hand grinders, wire brushes, or power tools. Instruct other workers in machine setup and operation. Record operational data such as pressure readings, lengths of strokes, feed rates, and speeds. Extract or lift jammed pieces from machines, using fingers, wire hooks, or lift bars. Set machine stops or guides to specified lengths as indicated by scales, rules, or templates. Move controls or mount gears, cams, or templates in machines to set feed rates and cutting speeds, depths, and angles. Compute data such as gear dimensions and machine settings, applying knowledge of shop mathematics. Align layout marks with dies or blades. Measure and mark reference points and cutting lines on workpieces, using traced templates, compasses, and rules.

GOE Information—Interest Area: 13. Manufacturing. **Work Group:** 13.02. Machine Setup and Operation. **Personality Type—**Realistic. Realistic occupations frequently involve work activities that include practical, hands-on problems and solutions. They often deal with plants; animals; and real-world materials like wood, tools, and machinery. Many of the occupations require working outside and do not involve a lot of paperwork or working closely with others. **Work Values—**Moral Values; Independence; Company Policies and Practices; Supervision, Technical; Activity; Supervision, Human Relations. **Skills—**Operation Monitoring; Repairing; Equipment Maintenance; Quality Control Analysis; Troubleshooting; Operation and Control. **Abilities—***Cognitive:* Spatial Orientation; Perceptual Speed; Time Sharing; Visualization. *Psychomotor:* Reaction Time; Control Precision; Wrist-Finger Speed; Speed of Limb Movement; Manual Dexterity; Rate Control. *Physical:* Explosive Strength; Static Strength; Extent Flexibility; Trunk Strength. *Sensory:* Visual Color

Discrimination. **General Work Activities—***Information Input:* Monitoring Processes, Materials, or Surroundings; Inspecting Equipment, Structures, or Materials; Identifying Objects, Actions, and Events. *Mental Process:* Updating and Using Relevant Knowledge; Organizing, Planning, and Prioritizing; Thinking Creatively. *Work Output:* Controlling Machines and Processes; Handling and Moving Objects; Repairing and Maintaining Mechanical Equipment. *Interacting with Others:* Establishing and Maintaining Interpersonal Relationships; Communicating with Other Workers; Coordinating the Work and Activities of Others. **Physical Work Conditions—**Noisy; Contaminants; Hazardous Equipment; Minor Burns, Cuts, Bites, or Stings; Standing; Using Hands on Objects, Tools, or Controls. **Other Job Characteristics—**Pace Determined by Speed of Equipment; Need to Be Exact or Accurate; Errors Have Important Consequences; Automation; Repeat Same Tasks.

Experience—Job Zone 2. Some previous work-related skill, knowledge, or experience may be helpful in these occupations, but usually is not needed. **Job Preparation—**SVP 4.0 to less than 6.0—six months to less than two years. **Knowledges—**Mechanical Devices; Production and Processing; Design; Engineering and Technology; Mathematics. **Instructional Programs—**Machine Shop Technology/Assistant; Machine Tool Technology/Machinist.

Related SOC Job—51-4081 Multiple Machine Tool Setters, Operators, and Tenders, Metal and Plastic. **Related OOH Job—**Machine Setters, Operators, and Tenders—Metal and Plastic. **Related DOT Jobs—**600.360-010 Machine Try-Out Setter; 600.360-014 Machine Setter; 600.380-018 Machine Set-Up Operator; 600.380-022 Machine Setter; 601.280-054 Tool-Machine Set-Up Operator; 602.280-010 Gear-Cutting-Machine Set-Up Operator, Tool; 602.380-010 Gear-Cutting-Machine Set-Up Operator; 602.382-010 Gear Hobber Set-Up Operator; 602.382-014 Gear-Generator Set-Up Operator, Spiral Bevel; 602.382-018 Gear-Generator Set-Up Operator, Straight Bevel; 602.382-022 Gear-Milling-Machine Set-Up Operator; others.

51-4111.00 Tool and Die Makers

- **Education/Training Required: Long-term on-the-job training**
- **Employed: 99,680**
- **Annual Earnings: $43,580**
- **Growth: –2.6%**
- **Annual Job Openings: 7,000**

Analyze specifications, lay out metal stock, set up and operate machine tools, and fit and assemble parts to make and repair dies, cutting tools, jigs, fixtures, gauges, and machinists' hand tools.

Study blueprints, sketches, models, or specifications to plan sequences of operations for fabricating tools, dies, or assemblies. Verify dimensions, alignments, and clearances of finished parts for conformance to specifications, using measuring instruments such as calipers, gauge blocks, micrometers, and dial indicators. Visualize and compute dimensions, sizes, shapes, and tolerances of assemblies, based on specifications. Set up and operate conventional or computer numerically controlled machine tools such as lathes, milling machines, and grinders to cut, bore, grind, or otherwise shape parts to prescribed dimensions and finishes. File, grind, shim, and adjust different parts to properly fit them together. Fit and assemble parts to make, repair, or modify dies, jigs, gauges, and tools, using machine tools and hand tools. Conduct test runs with completed tools or dies to ensure that parts meet specifications; make adjustments as necessary. Inspect finished dies for smoothness, contour conformity, and defects. Smooth and polish flat and contoured surfaces of parts or tools, using scrapers, abrasive stones, files, emery cloths, or power grinders. Lift, position, and secure machined parts on surface plates or worktables, using hoists, vises, v-blocks, or angle plates. Measure, mark, and scribe metal or plastic stock to lay out machining, using instruments such as protractors, micrometers, scribes, and rulers. Cut, shape, and trim blanks or blocks to specified lengths or shapes, using power saws, power shears, rules, and hand tools. Select metals to be used from a range of metals and alloys, based on properties such as hardness and heat tolerance. Design jigs, fixtures, and templates for use as work aids in the fabrication of parts or products. Set up and operate drill presses to drill and tap holes in parts for assembly. Develop and design new tools and dies, using computer-aided design software. Set pyrometer controls of heat-treating furnaces and feed or place parts, tools, or assemblies into furnaces to harden.

GOE Information—Interest Area: 13. Manufacturing. **Work Group:** 13.05. Production Machining Technology. **Personality Type—**Realistic. Realistic occupations frequently involve work activities that include practical, hands-on problems and solutions. They often deal with plants; animals; and real-world materials like wood, tools, and machinery. Many of the occupations require working outside and do not involve a lot of paperwork or working closely with others. **Work Values—**Moral Values; Supervision, Technical; Independence; Company Policies and Practices; Advancement. **Skills—**Repairing; Mathematics; Troubleshooting; Technology Design; Equipment Selection; Installation. **Abilities—***Cognitive:* Visualization; Category Flexibility; Selective Attention; Originality; Information Ordering; Inductive Reasoning. *Psychomotor:* Control Precision; Reaction Time; Multilimb Coordination; Response Orientation; Arm-Hand Steadiness; Manual Dexterity. *Physical:* Static Strength; Trunk Strength. *Sensory:* Depth Perception. **General Work Activities—***Information Input:* Getting Information; Monitoring Processes, Materials, or Surroundings; Inspecting Equipment, Structures, or Materials. *Mental Process:* Updating and Using Relevant Knowledge; Thinking Creatively; Making Decisions and Solving Problems. *Work Output:* Controlling Machines and Processes; Handling and Moving Objects; Performing General Physical Activities. *Interacting with Others:* Communicating with Other Workers; Establishing and Maintaining Interpersonal Relationships; Coaching and Developing Others. **Physical Work Conditions—**Noisy; Contaminants; Hazardous Equipment; Minor Burns, Cuts, Bites, or Stings; Standing; Using Hands on Objects, Tools, or Controls. **Other Job Characteristics—**Need to Be Exact or Accurate; Repeat Same Tasks; Errors Have Important Consequences.

Experience—Job Zone 3. Previous work-related skill, knowledge, or experience is required. **Job Preparation—**SVP 6.0 to less than 7.0—more than one year and less than four years. **Knowledges—**Design; Mechanical Devices; Engineering and Technology; Production and Processing; Mathematics; Public Safety and Security. **Instructional Program—**Tool and Die Technology/Technician.

Related SOC Job—51-4111 Tool and Die Makers. **Related OOH Job—**Tool and Die Makers. **Related DOT Jobs—**601.260-010 Tool-and-Die Maker; 601.260-014 Tool-and-Die-Maker Apprentice; 601.280-010 Die Maker, Stamping; 601.280-014 Die Maker, Trim; 601.280-018 Die Maker, Wire Drawing; 601.280-022 Die Sinker; 601.280-030 Mold Maker, Die-Casting and Plastic Molding; 601.280-034 Tap-and-Die-Maker Technician; 601.280-042 Tool Maker; 601.280-058 Tool-Maker Apprentice; 601.281-010 Die Maker, Bench, Stamping; 601.281-014 Die-Try-Out Worker, Stamping; 601.281-026 Tool Maker, Bench; 601.380-010 Carbide Operator; others.

51-4121.00 Welders, Cutters, Solderers, and Brazers

- **Education/Training Required: Long-term on-the-job training**
- **Employed: 358,050**
- **Annual Earnings: $30,990**
- **Growth: 5.0%**
- **Annual Job Openings: 52,000**

The job openings listed here are shared with 51-4121.06 Welders, Cutters, and Welder Fitters and 51-4121.07 Solderers and Brazers.

Use hand-welding, flame-cutting, hand soldering, or brazing equipment to weld or join metal components or to fill holes, indentations, or seams of fabricated metal products.

No task data available.

GOE Information—Interest Area: 13. Manufacturing. **Work Group:** 13.04. Welding, Brazing, and Soldering. **Note:** The Department of Labor has not collected some data for this job, so it has fewer details than the other descriptions.

Instructional Program—Welding Technology/Welder.

Related SOC Job—51-4121 Welders, Cutters, Solderers, and Brazers. **Related OOH Job—**Welding, Soldering, and Brazing Workers. **Related DOT Job—**No data available.

51-4121.06 Welders, Cutters, and Welder Fitters

- **Education/Training Required: Long-term on-the-job training**
- **Employed: 358,050**
- **Annual Earnings: $30,990**
- **Growth: 5.0%**
- **Annual Job Openings: 52,000**

The job openings listed here are shared with 51-4121.00 Welders, Cutters, Solderers, and Brazers and 51-4121.07 Solderers and Brazers.

Use hand-welding or flame-cutting equipment to weld or join metal components or to fill holes, indentations, or seams of fabricated metal products.

Operate safety equipment and use safe work habits. Weld components in flat, vertical, or overhead positions. Ignite torches or start power supplies and strike arcs by touching electrodes to metals being welded, completing electrical circuits. Clamp, hold, tack-weld, heat-bend, grind, or bolt component parts to obtain required configurations and positions for welding. Detect faulty operation of equipment or defective materials and notify supervisors. Operate manual or semi-automatic welding equipment to fuse metal segments, using processes such as gas tungsten arc, gas metal arc, flux-cored arc, plasma arc, shielded metal arc, resistance welding, and submerged arc welding. Monitor the fitting, burning, and welding processes to avoid overheating of parts or warping, shrinking, distortion, or expansion of material. Examine workpieces for defects and measure workpieces with straightedges or templates to ensure conformance with specifications. Recognize, set up, and operate hand and power tools common to the welding trade, such as shielded metal arc and gas metal arc welding equipment. Lay out, position, align, and secure parts and assemblies prior to assembly, using straightedges, combination squares, calipers, and rulers. Chip or grind off excess weld, slag, or spatter, using hand scrapers or power chippers, portable grinders, or arc-cutting equipment. Analyze engineering drawings, blueprints, specifications, sketches, work orders, and material safety data sheets to plan layout, assembly, and welding operations. Connect and turn regulator valves to activate and adjust gas flow and pressure so that desired flames are obtained. Weld separately or in combination, using aluminum, stainless steel, cast iron, and other alloys. Determine required equipment and welding methods, applying knowledge of metallurgy, geometry, and welding techniques. Mark or tag material with proper job number, piece marks, and other identifying marks as required. Prepare all material surfaces to be welded, ensuring that there is no loose or thick scale, slag, rust, moisture, grease, or other foreign matter.

GOE Information—Interest Area: 13. Manufacturing. **Work Group:** 13.04. Welding, Brazing, and Soldering. **Personality Type—**Realistic. Realistic occupations frequently involve work activities that include practical, hands-on problems and solutions. They often deal with plants; animals; and real-world materials like wood, tools, and machinery. Many of the occupations require working outside and do not involve a lot of paperwork or working closely with others. **Work Values—**Moral Values; Activity; Company Policies and Practices; Supervision, Technical; Independence; Advancement. **Skills—**Repairing; Equipment Maintenance; Installation; Quality Control Analysis; Operation and Control; Equipment Selection. **Abilities—***Cognitive:* Visualization; Selective Attention; Category Flexibility; Flexibility of Closure; Perceptual Speed. *Psychomotor:* Reaction Time; Arm-Hand Steadiness; Multilimb Coordination; Manual Dexterity; Rate Control; Control Precision. *Physical:* Extent Flexibility; Static Strength; Trunk Strength; Dynamic Strength; Stamina. *Sensory:* Depth Perception; Visual Color Discrimination. **General Work Activities—***Information Input:* Monitoring Processes, Materials, or Surroundings; Getting Information; Inspecting Equipment, Structures, or Materials. *Mental Process:* Organizing, Planning, and Prioritizing; Making Decisions and Solving Problems; Updating and Using Relevant Knowledge. *Work Output:* Handling and Moving Objects; Controlling Machines and Processes; Performing General Physical Activities. *Interacting with Others:* Establishing and Maintaining Interpersonal Relationships; Communicating with Other Workers; Interpreting the Meaning of Information for Others. **Physical Work Conditions—**Noisy; Contaminants; Minor Burns, Cuts, Bites, or Stings; Standing; Using Hands on Objects, Tools, or Controls; Repetitive Motions. **Other Job Characteristics—**Need to Be Exact or Accurate; Repeat Same Tasks.

Experience—Job Zone 2. Some previous work-related skill, knowledge, or experience may be helpful in these occupations, but usually is not needed. **Job Preparation—**SVP 4.0 to less than 6.0—six months to less than two years. **Knowledges—**Building and Construction; Mechanical Devices; Design; Engineering and Technology. **Instructional Program—**Welding Technology/Welder.

Related SOC Job—51-4121 Welders, Cutters, Solderers, and Brazers. **Related OOH Job—**Welding, Soldering, and Brazing Workers. **Related DOT Jobs—**613.667-010 Liner Assembler; 709.684-086 Torch-Straightener-and Heater; 727.684-022 Lead Burner; 810.384-010 Welder Apprentice, Arc; 810.384-014 Welder, Arc; 810.664-010 Welder, Gun; 810.684-010 Welder, Tack; 811.684-010 Welder Apprentice, Gas; 811.684-014 Welder, Gas; 816.364-010 Arc Cutter; 816.464-010 Thermal Cutter, Hand I; 816.684-010 Thermal Cutter, Hand II; 819.281-010 Lead Burner; 819.281-014 Lead-Burner Apprentice; 819.281-022 Welder, Experimental; 819.361-010 Welder-Fitter; others.

51-4121.07 Solderers and Brazers

- **Education/Training Required: Long-term on-the-job training**
- **Employed: 358,050**
- **Annual Earnings: $30,990**
- **Growth: 5.0%**
- **Annual Job Openings: 52,000**

The job openings listed here are shared with 51-4121.00 Welders, Cutters, Solderers, and Brazers and 51-4121.06 Welders, Cutters, and Welder Fitters.

Braze or solder together components to assemble fabricated metal parts, using soldering iron, torch, or welding machine and flux.

Melt and apply solder along adjoining edges of workpieces to solder joints, using soldering irons, gas torches, or electric-ultrasonic equipment. Heat soldering irons or workpieces to specified temperatures for soldering, using gas flames or electric current. Examine seams for defects and rework defective joints or broken parts. Melt and separate brazed or soldered joints to remove and straighten damaged or misaligned components, using hand torches, irons, or furnaces. Melt and apply solder to fill holes, indentations, and seams of fabricated metal products, using soldering equipment. Clean workpieces to remove dirt and excess acid, using chemical solutions, files, wire brushes, or grinders. Guide torches and rods along joints of workpieces to heat them to brazing temperature, melt braze alloys, and bond workpieces together. Adjust electric current and timing cycles of resistance welding machines to heat metals to bonding temperature. Turn valves to start flow of gases and light flames and adjust valves to obtain desired colors and sizes of flames. Clean equipment parts, such as tips of soldering irons, using chemical solutions or cleaning compounds. Brush flux onto joints of workpieces or dip braze rods into flux to prevent oxidation of metal. Remove workpieces from fixtures, using tongs, and cool workpieces, using air or water. Align and clamp workpieces together, using rules, squares, or hand tools, or position items in fixtures, jigs, or vises. Sweat together workpieces coated with solder. Smooth soldered areas with alternate strokes of paddles and torches, leaving soldered sections slightly higher than surrounding areas for later filing. Remove workpieces from molten solder and hold parts together until color indicates that solder has set. Select torch tips, flux, and brazing alloys from data charts or work orders. Turn dials to set intensity and duration of ultrasonic impulses according to work order specifications. Dip workpieces into molten solder or place solder strips between seams and heat seams with irons to bond items together. Clean joints of workpieces with wire brushes or by dipping them into cleaning solutions.

GOE Information—Interest Area: 13. Manufacturing. **Work Group:** 13.04. Welding, Brazing, and Soldering. **Personality Type—**Realistic. Realistic occupations frequently involve work activities that include practical, hands-on problems and solutions. They often deal with plants; animals; and real-world materials like wood, tools, and machinery. Many of the occupations require working outside and do not involve a lot of paperwork or working closely with others. **Work Values—**Moral Values; Activity; Independence; Company Policies and Practices; Supervision, Technical. **Skills—**Quality Control Analysis; Installation; Operation and Control; Troubleshooting; Equipment Selection; Repairing. **Abilities—***Cognitive:* Visualization; Flexibility of Closure; Perceptual Speed. *Psychomotor:* Arm-Hand Steadiness; Manual Dexterity; Control Precision; Reaction Time; Finger Dexterity; Multilimb Coordination. *Physical:* Static Strength; Trunk Strength. *Sensory:* Auditory Attention; Visual Color Discrimination; Hearing Sensitivity; Depth Perception. **General Work Activities—**

Information Input: Monitoring Processes, Materials, or Surroundings; Identifying Objects, Actions, and Events; Inspecting Equipment, Structures, or Materials. *Mental Process:* Updating and Using Relevant Knowledge; Judging the Qualities of Things, Services, or Other People's Work; Evaluating Information Against Standards. *Work Output:* Handling and Moving Objects; Repairing and Maintaining Electronic Equipment; Performing General Physical Activities. *Interacting with Others:* Communicating with Other Workers; Establishing and Maintaining Interpersonal Relationships; Interpreting the Meaning of Information to Others. **Physical Work Conditions**—Indoors; Noisy; Contaminants; Minor Burns, Cuts, Bites, or Stings; Using Hands on Objects, Tools, or Controls; Repetitive Motions. **Other Job Characteristics**—Need to Be Exact or Accurate; Repeat Same Tasks.

Experience—Job Zone 2. Some previous work-related skill, knowledge, or experience may be helpful in these occupations, but usually is not needed. **Job Preparation**—SVP 4.0 to less than 6.0—six months to less than two years. **Knowledges**—Production and Processing; Mechanical Devices; Engineering and Technology. **Instructional Program**—Welding Technology/Welder.

Related SOC Job—51-4121 Welders, Cutters, Solderers, and Brazers. **Related OOH Job**—Welding, Soldering, and Brazing Workers. **Related DOT Jobs**—736.684-038 Solderer, Barrel Ribs; 739.684-054 Deicer Finisher; 813.682-010 Brazer, Resistance; 813.684-010 Brazer, Assembler; 813.684-014 Solderer-Assembler; 813.684-018 Solderer-Dipper; 813.684-022 Solderer, Production Line; 813.684-026 Solderer, Torch I; 813.684-030 Solderer, Ultrasonic, Hand.

51-4122.00 Welding, Soldering, and Brazing Machine Setters, Operators, and Tenders

- **Education/Training Required: Moderate-term on-the-job training**
- **Employed: 45,220**
- **Annual Earnings: $30,430**
- **Growth: 0.4%**
- **Annual Job Openings: 7,000**

Set up, operate, or tend welding, soldering, or brazing machines or robots that weld, braze, solder, or heat-treat metal products, components, or assemblies.

Turn and press knobs and buttons or enter operating instructions into computers to adjust and start welding machines. Set up, operate, and tend welding machines that join or bond components to fabricate metal products or assemblies. Load or feed workpieces into welding machines to join or bond components. Correct problems by adjusting controls or by stopping machines and opening holding devices. Give directions to other workers regarding machine setup and use. Inspect, measure, or test completed metal workpieces to ensure conformance to specifications, using measuring and testing devices. Record operational information on specified production reports. Start, monitor, and adjust robotic welding production lines. Read blueprints, work orders, and production schedules to determine product or job instructions and specifications. Assemble, align, and clamp workpieces into holding fixtures to bond, heat-treat, or solder fabricated metal components. Lay out, fit, or connect parts to be bonded, calculating production measurements as necessary. Conduct trial runs before welding, soldering or brazing; make necessary adjustments to equipment. Dress electrodes, using tip dressers, files, emery cloths, or dressing wheels. Remove workpieces and parts from machinery after work is complete, using hand tools. Observe meters, gauges, and machine operations to ensure that soldering or brazing processes meet specifications. Select, position, align, and bolt jigs, holding fixtures, guides, and stops onto machines, using measuring instruments and hand tools. Compute and record settings for new work, applying knowledge of metal properties, principles of welding, and shop mathematics. Select torch tips, alloys, flux, coil, tubing, and wire according to metal types and thicknesses, data charts, and records. Clean, lubricate, maintain, and adjust equipment to maintain efficient operation, using air hoses, cleaning fluids, and hand tools. Prepare metal surfaces and workpieces, using hand-operated equipment such as grinders, cutters, or drills. Set dials and timing controls to regulate electrical current, gas flow pressure, heating and cooling cycles, and shutoff.

GOE Information—Interest Area: 13. Manufacturing. **Work Group:** 13.04. Welding, Brazing, and Soldering. **Personality Type**—Realistic. Realistic occupations frequently involve work activities that include practical, hands-on problems and solutions. They often deal with plants; animals; and real-world materials like wood, tools, and machinery. Many of the occupations require working outside and do not involve a lot of paperwork or working closely with others. **Work Values**—Moral Values; Independence; Company Policies and Practices; Supervision, Technical; Supervision, Human Relations; Activity. **Skills**—Equipment Maintenance; Operation Monitoring; Operation and Control; Repairing; Installation; Troubleshooting. **Abilities**—*Cognitive:* None met the criteria. *Psychomotor:* Wrist-Finger Speed; Control Precision; Manual Dexterity; Reaction Time; Arm-Hand Steadiness; Multilimb Coordination. *Physical:* Static Strength; Extent Flexibility. *Sensory:* None met the criteria. **General Work Activities**—*Information Input:* Monitoring Processes, Materials, or Surroundings; Inspecting Equipment, Structures, or Materials; Identifying Objects, Actions, and Events. *Mental Process:* Updating and Using Relevant Knowledge; Making Decisions and Solving Problems; Processing Information. *Work Output:* Handling and Moving Objects; Controlling Machines and Processes; Repairing and Maintaining Mechanical Equipment. *Interacting with Others:* Establishing and Maintaining Interpersonal Relationships; Communicating with Other Workers. **Physical Work Conditions**—Noisy; Contaminants; Standing; Using Hands on Objects, Tools, or Controls; Bending or Twisting the Body; Repetitive Motions. **Other Job Characteristics**—Need to Be Exact or Accurate; Pace Determined by Speed of Equipment; Repeat Same Tasks; Errors Have Important Consequences.

Experience—Job Zone 2. Some previous work-related skill, knowledge, or experience may be helpful in these occupations, but usually is not needed. **Job Preparation**—SVP 4.0 to less than 6.0—six months to less than two years. **Knowledges**—Production and Processing; Mechanical Devices; Engineering and Technology; Design; Personnel and Human Resources; Public Safety and Security. **Instructional Program**—Welding Technology/Welder.

Related SOC Job—51-4122 Welding, Soldering, and Brazing Machine Setters, Operators, and Tenders. **Related OOH Job**—Welding, Soldering, and Brazing Workers. **Related DOT Jobs**—614.684-010 Billet Assembler; 706.685-010 Type-Soldering-Machine Tender; 715.685-058 Solderer; 726.362-014 Wave-Soldering Machine Operator; 726.684-094 Solder Deposit Operator; 726.685-038 Reflow Operator; 727.662-010 Lead Burner, Machine; 810.382-010 Welding-Machine Operator, Arc; 811.482-010 Welding-Machine Operator, Gas; 812.360-010 Welder Setter, Resistance Machine; 812.682-010 Welding-Machine Operator, Resistance; 813.360-010 Brazing-Machine Setter; others.

51-4191.00 Heat Treating Equipment Setters, Operators, and Tenders, Metal and Plastic

- **Education/Training Required:** Moderate-term on-the-job training
- **Employed:** 26,310
- **Annual Earnings:** $30,300
- **Growth:** −0.4%
- **Annual Job Openings:** 3,000

Set up, operate, or tend heating equipment, such as heat-treating furnaces, flame-hardening machines, induction machines, soaking pits, or vacuum equipment to temper, harden, anneal, or heat-treat metal or plastic objects.

Read production schedules and work orders to determine processing sequences, furnace temperatures, and heat cycle requirements for objects to be heat-treated. Record times that parts are removed from furnaces to document that objects have attained specified temperatures for specified times. Set up and operate or tend machines, such as furnaces, baths, flame-hardening machines, and electronic induction machines, that harden, anneal, and heat-treat metal. Determine types and temperatures of baths and quenching media needed to attain specified part hardness, toughness, and ductility, using heat-treating charts and knowledge of methods, equipment, and metals. Remove parts from furnaces after specified times and air dry parts or cool them in water, oil brine, or other baths. Position stock in furnaces, using tongs, chain hoists, or pry bars. Instruct new workers in machine operation. Adjust controls to maintain temperatures and heating times, using thermal instruments and charts, dials and gauges of furnaces, and color of stock in furnaces to make setting determinations. Determine flame temperatures, current frequencies, heating cycles, and induction heating coils needed, based on degree of hardness required and properties of stock to be treated. Load parts into containers and place containers on conveyors to be inserted into furnaces or insert parts into furnaces. Mount workpieces in fixtures, on arbors, or between centers of machines. Set up and operate die-quenching machines to prevent parts from warping. Move controls to light gas burners and to adjust gas and water flow and flame temperature. Reduce heat when processing is complete to allow parts to cool in furnaces or machinery. Signal forklift operators to deposit or extract containers of parts into and from furnaces and quenching rinse tanks. Test parts for hardness by using hardness-testing equipment or by examining and feeling samples. Position plastic sheets and molds in plastic bags, heat material under lamps, and force confrontation of sheets to molds by vacuum pressure. Examine parts to ensure metal shades and colors conform to specifications, utilizing knowledge of metal heat-treating.

GOE Information—Interest Area: 13. Manufacturing. **Work Group:** 13.03. Production Work, Assorted Materials Processing. **Personality Type**—Realistic. Realistic occupations frequently involve work activities that include practical, hands-on problems and solutions. They often deal with plants; animals; and real-world materials like wood, tools, and machinery. Many of the occupations require working outside and do not involve a lot of paperwork or working closely with others. **Work Values**—Moral Values; Supervision, Technical; Supervision, Human Relations; Independence; Company Policies and Practices; Activity. **Skills**—Operation Monitoring; Equipment Maintenance; Quality Control Analysis; Operation and Control; Troubleshooting; Systems Analysis. **Abilities**—*Cognitive:* Selective

Attention; Perceptual Speed; Category Flexibility; Time Sharing; Visualization; Flexibility of Closure. *Psychomotor:* Reaction Time; Rate Control; Response Orientation; Control Precision; Speed of Limb Movement; Multilimb Coordination. *Physical:* Static Strength; Stamina; Extent Flexibility; Trunk Strength; Gross Body Coordination; Dynamic Strength. *Sensory:* Glare Sensitivity; Depth Perception; Hearing Sensitivity; Auditory Attention; Visual Color Discrimination; Far Vision. **General Work Activities**—*Information Input:* Monitoring Processes, Materials, or Surroundings; Inspecting Equipment, Structures, or Materials; Identifying Objects, Actions, and Events. *Mental Process:* Processing Information; Evaluating Information Against Standards; Judging the Qualities of Things, Services, or Other People's Work. *Work Output:* Handling and Moving Objects; Controlling Machines and Processes; Performing General Physical Activities. *Interacting with Others:* Establishing and Maintaining Interpersonal Relationships; Communicating with Other Workers; Coordinating the Work and Activities of Others. **Physical Work Conditions**—Noisy; Very Hot or Cold; Contaminants; Minor Burns, Cuts, Bites, or Stings; Standing; Using Hands on Objects, Tools, or Controls. **Other Job Characteristics**—Need to Be Exact or Accurate; Pace Determined by Speed of Equipment; Repeat Same Tasks; Errors Have Important Consequences.

Experience—Job Zone 2. Some previous work-related skill, knowledge, or experience may be helpful in these occupations, but usually is not needed. **Job Preparation**—SVP 4.0 to less than 6.0—six months to less than two years. **Knowledges**—Production and Processing; Chemistry; Engineering and Technology; Mechanical Devices; Public Safety and Security. **Instructional Programs**—Machine Shop Technology/Assistant; Machine Tool Technology/Machinist.

Related SOC Job—51-4191 Heat Treating Equipment Setters, Operators, and Tenders, Metal and Plastic. **Related OOH Job**—Machine Setters, Operators, and Tenders—Metal and Plastic. **Related DOT Jobs**—504.360-010 Flame-Annealing-Machine Setter; 504.380-010 Flame-Hardening-Machine Setter; 504.380-014 Induction-Machine Setter; 504.382-010 Hardener; 504.382-014 Heat Treater I; 504.382-018 Heat-Treater Apprentice; 504.682-010 Annealer; 504.682-014 Case Hardener; 504.682-018 Heat Treater II; 504.682-022 Heat-Treating Bluer; 504.682-026 Temperer; 504.685-010 Base-Draw Operator; 504.685-014 Flame-Hardening-Machine Operator; 504.685-022 Induction-Machine Operator; 504.685-026 Production Hardener; others.

51-4192.00 Lay-Out Workers, Metal and Plastic

- **Education/Training Required:** Moderate-term on-the-job training
- **Employed:** 10,970
- **Annual Earnings:** $33,350
- **Growth:** −4.6%
- **Annual Job Openings:** 1,000

Lay out reference points and dimensions on metal or plastic stock or workpieces, such as sheets, plates, tubes, structural shapes, castings, or machine parts, for further processing. Includes shipfitters.

Fit and align fabricated parts to be welded or assembled. Plan and develop layouts from blueprints and templates, applying knowledge of trigonometry, design, effects of heat, and properties of metals. Lay out and fabricate metal structural parts such as plates, bulkheads, and frames. Mark curves, lines, holes, dimensions, and welding symbols onto workpieces, using scribes, soapstones, punches, and hand drills. Compute layout dimensions and determine and mark reference points on metal stock or workpieces for further processing, such as welding and assembly. Locate center lines and verify template positions, using measuring instruments such as gauge blocks, height gauges, and dial indicators. Lift and position workpieces in relation to surface plates manually or with hoists and using parallel blocks and angle plates. Plan locations and sequences of cutting, drilling, bending, rolling, punching, and welding operations, using compasses, protractors, dividers, and rules. Inspect machined parts to verify conformance to specifications. Design and prepare templates of wood, paper, or metal. Brace parts in position within hulls or ships for riveting or welding. Add dimensional details to blueprints or drawings made by other workers. Install doors, hatches, brackets, and clips. Apply pigment to layout surfaces, using paintbrushes.

GOE Information—Interest Area: 13. Manufacturing. **Work Group:** 13.05. Production Machining Technology. **Personality Type—** Realistic. Realistic occupations frequently involve work activities that include practical, hands-on problems and solutions. They often deal with plants; animals; and real-world materials like wood, tools, and machinery. Many of the occupations require working outside and do not involve a lot of paperwork or working closely with others. **Work Values—**Moral Values; Independence; Supervision, Technical; Company Policies and Practices; Advancement. **Skills—** Operation and Control; Equipment Maintenance; Installation; Mathematics; Repairing; Coordination. **Abilities—***Cognitive:* Visualization; Perceptual Speed; Selective Attention; Mathematical Reasoning; Category Flexibility; Flexibility of Closure. *Psychomotor:* Multilimb Coordination; Reaction Time; Manual Dexterity; Arm-Hand Steadiness; Control Precision; Finger Dexterity. *Physical:* Extent Flexibility; Static Strength; Trunk Strength. *Sensory:* Depth Perception; Auditory Attention; Far Vision; Visual Color Discrimination; Near Vision. **General Work Activities—***Information Input:* Monitoring Processes, Materials, or Surroundings; Identifying Objects, Actions, and Events; Inspecting Equipment, Structures, or Materials. *Mental Process:* Updating and Using Relevant Knowledge; Making Decisions and Solving Problems; Organizing, Planning, and Prioritizing. *Work Output:* Handling and Moving Objects; Performing General Physical Activities; Controlling Machines and Processes. *Interacting with Others:* Communicating with Other Workers; Teaching Others; Coordinating the Work and Activities of Others. **Physical Work Conditions—**Noisy; Contaminants; Hazardous Equipment; Minor Burns, Cuts, Bites, or Stings; Standing; Using Hands on Objects, Tools, or Controls. **Other Job Characteristics—** Need to Be Exact or Accurate.

Experience—Job Zone 2. Some previous work-related skill, knowledge, or experience may be helpful in these occupations, but usually is not needed. **Job Preparation—**SVP 4.0 to less than 6.0—six months to less than two years. **Knowledges—**Building and Construction; Mechanical Devices; Design; Production and Processing; Mathematics; Engineering and Technology. **Instructional Programs—**Machine Shop Technology/Assistant; Machine Tool Technology/Machinist.

Related SOC Job—51-4192 Lay-Out Workers, Metal and Plastic. **Related OOH Job—**Machine Setters, Operators, and Tenders—Metal and Plastic. **Related DOT Jobs—**600.281-018 Lay-Out Worker; 806.381-046 Shipfitter; 806.381-050 Shipfitter Apprentice; 809.281-010 Lay-Out Worker I; 809.381-014 Lay-Out Worker II.

51-4193.00 Plating and Coating Machine Setters, Operators, and Tenders, Metal and Plastic

- **Education/Training Required: Moderate-term on-the-job training**
- **Employed: 40,550**
- **Annual Earnings: $26,740**
- **Growth: −4.0%**
- **Annual Job Openings: 9,000**

Set up, operate, or tend plating or coating machines to coat metal or plastic products with chromium, zinc, copper, cadmium, nickel, or other metal to protect or decorate surfaces. Includes electrolytic processes.

Inspect coated or plated areas for defects such as air bubbles or uneven coverage. Immerse objects to be coated or plated into cleaning solutions or spray objects with conductive solutions to prepare them for plating. Immerse workpieces in coating solutions or liquid metal or plastic for specified times. Test machinery to ensure that it is operating properly. Position and feed materials into processing machines by hand or by using automated equipment. Operate hoists to place workpieces onto machine feed carriages or spindles. Maintain production records. Adjust controls to set temperatures of coating substances and speeds of machines and equipment. Remove objects from solutions at periodic intervals and observe objects to verify conformance to specifications. Observe gauges to ensure that machines are operating properly; make adjustments or stop machines when problems occur. Position containers to receive parts and load or unload materials in containers, using dollies or handtrucks. Perform equipment maintenance such as cleaning tanks and lubricating moving parts of conveyors. Clean and maintain equipment, using water hoses and scrapers. Determine sizes and compositions of objects to be plated and amounts of electrical current and time required. Suspend sticks or pieces of plating metal from anodes (positive terminals) and immerse metal in plating solutions. Monitor and measure thicknesses of electroplating on component parts to verify conformance to specifications, using micrometers. Adjust dials to regulate flow of current and voltage supplied to terminals to control plating processes. Rinse coated objects in cleansing liquids; then dry them with cloths, with centrifugal driers, or by tumbling in sawdust-filled barrels. Measure or weigh materials, using rulers, calculators, and scales. Examine completed objects to determine thicknesses of metal deposits or measure thicknesses by using instruments such as micrometers.

GOE Information—Interest Area: 13. Manufacturing. **Work Group:** 13.03. Production Work, Assorted Materials Processing. **Personality Type—**Realistic. Realistic occupations frequently involve work activities that include practical, hands-on problems and solutions. They often deal with plants; animals; and real-world materials like wood, tools, and machinery. Many of the occupations require working outside and do not involve a lot of paperwork or working closely with others. **Work Values—**Moral Values; Independence; Supervision, Human Relations; Supervision, Technical; Activity; Company Policies and Practices. **Skills—**Operation Monitoring; Quality Control Analysis; Operation and Control; Equipment Maintenance; Repairing. **Abilities—***Cognitive:* None met the criteria. *Psychomotor:* Control Precision; Wrist-Finger Speed; Manual Dexterity; Multilimb Coordination; Arm-Hand Steadiness. *Physical:* Extent Flexibility; Static Strength. *Sensory:* None met the criteria. **General Work Activities—***Information Input:* Monitoring Processes, Materials, or Surroundings; Inspecting Equipment, Structures, or Materials;

Identifying Objects, Actions, and Events. *Mental Process:* Processing Information; Organizing, Planning, and Prioritizing; Making Decisions and Solving Problems. *Work Output:* Handling and Moving Objects; Performing General Physical Activities; Documenting or Recording Information. *Interacting with Others:* Communicating with Other Workers; Establishing and Maintaining Interpersonal Relationships; Coaching and Developing Others. **Physical Work Conditions**—Noisy; Contaminants; Hazardous Conditions; Standing; Walking and Running; Using Hands on Objects, Tools, or Controls. **Other Job Characteristics**—Need to Be Exact or Accurate; Pace Determined by Speed of Equipment.

Experience—Job Zone 2. Some previous work-related skill, knowledge, or experience may be helpful in these occupations, but usually is not needed. **Job Preparation**—SVP 4.0 to less than 6.0—six months to less than two years. **Knowledges**—Chemistry; Production and Processing; Public Safety and Security; Education and Training; Engineering and Technology; Mechanical Devices. **Instructional Program**—No related CIP programs.

Related SOC Job—51-4193 Plating and Coating Machine Setters, Operators, and Tenders, Metal and Plastic. **Related OOH Job**—Machine Setters, Operators, and Tenders—Metal and Plastic. **Related DOT Jobs**—500.362-010 Electrogalvanizing-Machine Operator; 500.362-014 Plater, Barrel; 500.380-010 Plater; 500.380-014 Plater Apprentice; 500.384-010 Matrix Plater; 500.384-014 Matrix-Bath Attendant; 500.485-010 Zinc-Plating-Machine Operator; 500.682-010 Anodizer; 500.684-010 Electroformer; 500.684-018 Plate Former; 500.684-026 Plater, Printed Circuit Board Panels; 500.684-030 Plater, Semiconductor Wafers and Components; 500.684-034 Plater; 500.685-014 Plating Equipment Tender; others.

51-4194.00 Tool Grinders, Filers, and Sharpeners

- **Education/Training Required: Moderate-term on-the-job training**
- **Employed: 18,180**
- **Annual Earnings: $31,310**
- **Growth: –7.7%**
- **Annual Job Openings: 2,000**

Perform precision smoothing, sharpening, polishing, or grinding of metal objects.

Dress grinding wheels according to specifications. Monitor machine operations to determine whether adjustments are necessary; stop machines when problems occur. Inspect, feel, and measure workpieces to ensure that surfaces and dimensions meet specifications. Set up and operate grinding or polishing machines to grind metal workpieces such as dies, parts, and tools. Remove finished workpieces from machines and place them in boxes or on racks; set aside pieces that are defective. File or finish surfaces of workpieces, using prescribed hand tools. Select and mount grinding wheels on machines according to specifications, using hand tools and applying knowledge of abrasives and grinding procedures. Perform basic maintenance, such as cleaning and lubricating machine parts. Remove and replace worn or broken machine parts, using hand tools. Compute numbers, widths, and angles of cutting tools, micrometers, scales, and gauges and adjust tools to produce specified cuts. Study blueprints or layouts of metal workpieces to determine grinding procedures and to plan machine setups and operational sequences. Turn valves to direct flow of coolant against cutting wheels and work-

pieces during grinding. Fit parts together in preassembly to ensure that dimensions are accurate. Inspect dies to detect defects, assess wear, and verify specifications, using micrometers, steel gauge pins, and loupes. Duplicate workpiece contours, using tracer attachments. Straighten workpieces and remove dents, using straightening presses and hammers. Attach workpieces to grinding machines; then form specified sections and repair cracks, using welding or brazing equipment. Place workpieces in electroplating solutions or apply pigments to surfaces of workpieces to highlight ridges and grooves.

GOE Information—Interest Area: 13. Manufacturing. **Work Group:** 13.05. Production Machining Technology. **Personality Type**—Realistic. Realistic occupations frequently involve work activities that include practical, hands-on problems and solutions. They often deal with plants; animals; and real-world materials like wood, tools, and machinery. Many of the occupations require working outside and do not involve a lot of paperwork or working closely with others. **Work Values**—Moral Values; Supervision, Technical; Supervision, Human Relations; Independence; Company Policies and Practices. **Skills**—Programming; Repairing; Operation Monitoring; Installation; Equipment Maintenance; Quality Control Analysis. **Abilities**—*Cognitive:* Perceptual Speed; Visualization; Number Facility; Flexibility of Closure; Mathematical Reasoning; Selective Attention. *Psychomotor:* Reaction Time; Rate Control; Control Precision; Manual Dexterity; Response Orientation; Arm-Hand Steadiness. *Physical:* Static Strength; Dynamic Strength; Extent Flexibility; Trunk Strength. *Sensory:* Hearing Sensitivity; Auditory Attention; Depth Perception; Far Vision; Visual Color Discrimination; Near Vision. **General Work Activities**—*Information Input:* Identifying Objects, Actions, and Events; Inspecting Equipment, Structures, or Materials; Estimating the Needed Characteristics of Products, Events, or Information. *Mental Process:* Making Decisions and Solving Problems; Judging the Qualities of Things, Services, or Other People's Work; Updating and Using Relevant Knowledge. *Work Output:* Controlling Machines and Processes; Handling and Moving Objects; Repairing and Maintaining Mechanical Equipment. *Interacting with Others:* Establishing and Maintaining Interpersonal Relationships; Communicating with Other Workers; Teaching Others. **Physical Work Conditions**—Noisy; Contaminants; Hazardous Equipment; Standing; Using Hands on Objects, Tools, or Controls; Repetitive Motions. **Other Job Characteristics**—Need to Be Exact or Accurate; Pace Determined by Speed of Equipment.

Experience—Job Zone 2. Some previous work-related skill, knowledge, or experience may be helpful in these occupations, but usually is not needed. **Job Preparation**—SVP 4.0 to less than 6.0—six months to less than two years. **Knowledges**—Mechanical Devices; Production and Processing; Engineering and Technology; Design. **Instructional Program**—Machine Shop Technology/Assistant.

Related SOC Job—51-4194 Tool Grinders, Filers, and Sharpeners. **Related OOH Job**—Machine Setters, Operators, and Tenders—Metal and Plastic. **Related DOT Jobs**—500.381-010 Cylinder Grinder; 601.381-018 Die Polisher; 603.280-010 Grinder Operator, External, Tool; 603.280-014 Grinder Operator, Surface, Tool; 603.280-018 Grinder Operator, Tool; 603.280-022 Grinder Set-Up Operator, Internal; 603.280-030 Grinder Set-Up Operator, Universal; 603.280-038 Tool-Grinder Operator; 680.380-010 Card Grinder; 701.381-014 Saw Filer; 701.381-018 Tool Grinder I; 701.684-030 Tool Filer; 705.381-010 Die Barber; 705.481-010 Filer, Finish; 705.481-014 Lapper, Hand, Tool.

51-4199.99 Metal Workers and Plastic Workers, All Other

- Education/Training Required: Moderate-term on-the-job training
- Employed: 49,650
- Annual Earnings: $35,480
- Growth: –13.6%
- Annual Job Openings: 5,000

All metalworkers and plastic workers not listed separately.

No task data available.

Note: The Department of Labor has not collected some data for this job, so it has fewer details than the other descriptions.

Related SOC Job—51-4199 Metal Workers and Plastic Workers, All Other. **Related OOH Job**—Machine Setters, Operators, and Tenders—Metal and Plastic. **Related DOT Jobs**—500.685-010 Etcher, Electrolytic; 503.362-014 Shotblast-Equipment Operator; 503.685-018 Drifter; 503.685-038 Sandblast Operator; 503.685-042 Sandblast-Or-Shotblast-Equipment Tender; 503.685-046 Strip-Tank Tender; 505.380-010 Metal Sprayer, Machined Parts; 509.362-010 Mixer Operator, Hot Metal; 509.384-010 Case Preparer-And-Liner; 509.485-014 Shot Polisher And Inspector; 509.685-042 Lubricator-Granulator; 509.685-054 Tank Tender; 511.682-010 Dust Collector, Ore Crushing; others.

51-5000 Printing Workers

51-5011.00 Bindery Workers

- Education/Training Required: Short-term on-the-job training
- Employed: 64,330
- Annual Earnings: $25,050
- Growth: –10.4%
- Annual Job Openings: 8,000

Set up or operate binding machines that produce books and other printed materials.

Read work orders to determine setup specifications and instructions. Examine stitched, collated, bound, and unbound product samples for defects such as imperfect bindings, ink spots, torn or loose pages, and loose and uncut threads. Start machines and make trial runs to verify accuracy of machine setups. Set up, or set up and operate, machines that perform binding operations such as pressing, folding, and trimming on books and related articles. Move controls to adjust and activate bindery machines. Observe and monitor machine operations to detect malfunctions and to determine whether adjustments are needed. Install and adjust bindery machine devices, such as knives, guides, rollers, rounding forms, creasing rams, and clamps, to accommodate sheets, signatures, or books of specified sizes, using hand tools. Maintain records of daily production, using specified forms. Fill machine paper feeds. Lubricate and clean machine parts and make minor repairs to keep machines in working condition. Feed books and related articles such as periodicals and pamphlets into binding machines, following specifications. Remove printed material or finished products from machines or conveyors, wrap products in plastic, and stack them on pallets or skids or pack them in boxes. Clean work areas and maintain equipment and workstations, using

hand tools. Stock supplies such as signatures, books, or paper. Punch holes in paper sheets and fasten sheets, signatures, or other material, using hand or machine punches or staplers. Set machine controls to adjust lengths and thicknesses of folds, stitches, or cuts, to synchronize speed of feeding devices and stitching, and to adjust tension on creasing blades and folding rollers. Record production sheet information such as the amount of time spent on specific tasks. Fill glue reservoirs, turn switches to activate heating elements, and adjust flow of glue and speed of conveyors. Secure reels of stitching wire on spindles and thread wire through feeding, cutting, stitch-forming, and driving mechanisms to load stitcher heads for stapling. Open machines and remove and replace damaged covers and books, using hand tools.

GOE Information—**Interest Area:** 13. Manufacturing. **Work Group:** 13.08. Graphic Arts Production. **Personality Type**—Realistic. Realistic occupations frequently involve work activities that include practical, hands-on problems and solutions. They often deal with plants; animals; and real-world materials like wood, tools, and machinery. Many of the occupations require working outside and do not involve a lot of paperwork or working closely with others. **Work Values**—Moral Values; Independence; Supervision, Technical; Activity; Supervision, Human Relations; Company Policies and Practices. **Skills**—Operation and Control; Quality Control Analysis; Equipment Maintenance; Operation Monitoring; Repairing; Systems Analysis. **Abilities**—*Cognitive:* Perceptual Speed. *Psychomotor:* Control Precision; Arm-Hand Steadiness; Wrist-Finger Speed; Speed of Limb Movement; Manual Dexterity; Reaction Time. *Physical:* Static Strength; Extent Flexibility; Trunk Strength. *Sensory:* None met the criteria. **General Work Activities**—*Information Input:* Monitoring Processes, Materials, or Surroundings; Getting Information; Estimating the Needed Characteristics of Products, Events, or Information. *Mental Process:* Judging the Qualities of Things, Services, or Other People's Work; Making Decisions and Solving Problems; Organizing, Planning, and Prioritizing. *Work Output:* Handling and Moving Objects; Performing General Physical Activities; Controlling Machines and Processes. *Interacting with Others:* Communicating with Other Workers; Establishing and Maintaining Interpersonal Relationships; Interpreting the Meaning of Information for Others. **Physical Work Conditions**—Noisy; Contaminants; Standing; Using Hands on Objects, Tools, or Controls; Bending or Twisting the Body; Repetitive Motions. **Other Job Characteristics**—Pace Determined by Speed of Equipment; Need to Be Exact or Accurate; Repeat Same Tasks.

Experience—Job Zone 2. Some previous work-related skill, knowledge, or experience may be helpful in these occupations, but usually is not needed. **Job Preparation**—SVP 4.0 to less than 6.0—six months to less than two years. **Knowledges**—Production and Processing; Mechanical Devices. **Instructional Program**—Graphic Communications, Other.

Related SOC Job—51-5011 Bindery Workers. **Related OOH Job**—Bookbinders and Bindery Workers. **Related DOT Jobs**—653.360-010 Casing-in-Line Setter; 653.360-018 Bindery-Machine Setter; 653.382-010 Folding-Machine Operator; 653.382-014 Collating-Machine Operator; 653.662-010 Stitching-Machine Operator; 653.682-010 Book-Sewing-Machine Operator II; 653.682-014 Covering-Machine Operator; 653.682-018 Head-Bander-and-Liner Operator; 653.682-022 Tinning-Machine Set-Up Operator; 653.685-010 Bindery Worker; 653.685-014 Book-Sewing-Machine Operator I; 653.685-022 Magazine Repairer; others.

51-5012.00 Bookbinders

- **Education/Training Required: Moderate-term on-the-job training**
- **Employed: 7,660**
- **Annual Earnings: $29,200**
- **Growth: −4.5%**
- **Annual Job Openings: 1,000**

Perform highly skilled hand-finishing operations, such as grooving and lettering, to bind books.

Meet with clients, printers, and designers to discuss job requirements and binding plans. Make boxes or specialty items such as binders and photograph albums. Repair, restore, and rebind old or damaged books, including rare books. Fold and sew printed sheets to form signatures and assemble signatures in numerical order to form book bodies. Apply color to edges of signatures, using brushes, pads, or atomizers. Apply glue to backs of books, using brushes or glue machines, and attach cloth backing and headbands. Attach endpapers to tops and bottoms of book bodies, using sewing machines, or glue endpapers and signatures together along spines, using brushes or glue machines. Compress sewed or glued signatures to reduce books to required thicknesses, using hand presses or smashing machines. Imprint and emboss lettering, designs, or numbers on covers, using gold, silver, or colored foil and stamping machines. Cut cover material to specified dimensions and fit and glue material to binder boards manually or by machine. Glue outside endpapers to covers. Establish production procedures based on job orders. Design original or special bindings for limited editions. Trim edges of books to size, using cutting or book-trimming machines or hand cutters. Place bound books in presses that exert pressure on covers until glue dries. Insert book bodies in devices that form back edges of books into convex shapes and produce grooves that facilitate attachment of covers. Pack and weigh books and stack them on pallets to prepare them for shipment. Cut binder boards to specified dimensions, using board shears, hand cutters, or cutting machines.

GOE Information—**Interest Area:** 13. Manufacturing. **Work Group:** 13.06. Production Precision Work. **Personality Type**—Realistic. Realistic occupations frequently involve work activities that include practical, hands-on problems and solutions. They often deal with plants; animals; and real-world materials like wood, tools, and machinery. Many of the occupations require working outside and do not involve a lot of paperwork or working closely with others. **Work Values**—Supervision, Technical; Moral Values; Independence; Working Conditions; Supervision, Human Relations; Company Policies and Practices. **Skills**—None met the criteria. **Abilities**—*Cognitive:* None met the criteria. *Psychomotor:* Wrist-Finger Speed; Manual Dexterity; Arm-Hand Steadiness. *Physical:* Extent Flexibility. *Sensory:* Visual Color Discrimination. **General Work Activities**—*Information Input:* Getting Information; Identifying Objects, Actions, and Events. *Mental Process:* None met the criteria. *Work Output:* Handling and Moving Objects; Performing General Physical Activities; Controlling Machines and Processes. *Interacting with Others:* None met the criteria. **Physical Work Conditions**—Indoors; Contaminants; Minor Burns, Cuts, Bites, or Stings; More Often Sitting Than Standing; Using Hands on Objects, Tools, or Controls. **Other Job Characteristics**—Automation.

Experience—Job Zone 4. A minimum of two to four years of work-related skill, knowledge, or experience is needed. **Job Preparation**—SVP 7.0 to less than 8.0—two years to less than 10 years. **Knowledges**—Production and Processing; Mechanical Devices. **Instructional Program**—Precision Production Trades, Other.

Related SOC Job—51-5012 Bookbinders. **Related OOH Job**—Bookbinders and Bindery Workers. **Related DOT Jobs**—977.381-010 Bookbinder; 977.381-014 Bookbinder Apprentice.

51-5021.00 Job Printers

- **Education/Training Required: Long-term on-the-job training**
- **Employed: 50,580**
- **Annual Earnings: $31,920**
- **Growth: 1.8%**
- **Annual Job Openings: 8,000**

Set type according to copy, operate press to print job order, read proof for errors and clarity of impression, and correct imperfections. Job printers are often found in small establishments where work combines several job skills.

Examine proofs or printed sheets to detect errors and to evaluate the adequacy of impression clarity. Fill ink fountains and move levers to adjust the flow of ink. Set feed guides according to sizes and thicknesses of paper. Operate cylinder or automatic platen presses to print job orders. Clean ink rollers after runs are completed. Position forms (type in locked chases) on beds of presses; then tighten clamps, using wrenches. Lay forms on proof presses; then ink type, fasten paper to press rollers, and pull rollers over forms to make proof copies. Design and set up product compositions and page layouts. Reset type to correct typographical errors.

GOE Information—**Interest Area:** 13. Manufacturing. **Work Group:** 13.08. Graphic Arts Production. **Personality Type**—Realistic. Realistic occupations frequently involve work activities that include practical, hands-on problems and solutions. They often deal with plants; animals; and real-world materials like wood, tools, and machinery. Many of the occupations require working outside and do not involve a lot of paperwork or working closely with others. **Work Values**—Independence; Moral Values; Supervision, Technical; Variety; Activity. **Skills**—Operation Monitoring; Equipment Maintenance; Operation and Control; Repairing; Quality Control Analysis; Troubleshooting. **Abilities**—*Cognitive:* Selective Attention; Perceptual Speed; Visualization; Flexibility of Closure. *Psychomotor:* Reaction Time; Rate Control; Multilimb Coordination; Arm-Hand Steadiness; Control Precision; Manual Dexterity. *Physical:* Trunk Strength; Extent Flexibility; Gross Body Coordination; Stamina; Static Strength. *Sensory:* Visual Color Discrimination; Auditory Attention; Hearing Sensitivity; Depth Perception; Far Vision; Near Vision. **General Work Activities**—*Information Input:* Monitoring Processes, Materials, or Surroundings; Identifying Objects, Actions, and Events; Getting Information. *Mental Process:* Organizing, Planning, and Prioritizing; Updating and Using Relevant Knowledge; Making Decisions and Solving Problems. *Work Output:* Controlling Machines and Processes; Handling and Moving Objects; Performing General Physical Activities. *Interacting with Others:* Establishing and Maintaining Interpersonal Relationships; Communicating with Other Workers; Coordinating the Work and Activities of Others. **Physical Work Conditions**—Indoors; Contaminants; Hazardous Conditions; Standing; Using Hands on Objects, Tools, or Controls; Repetitive Motions. **Other Job Characteristics**—Need to Be Exact or Accurate; Pace Determined by Speed of Equipment; Repeat Same Tasks; Errors Have Important Consequences.

Experience—Job Zone 3. Previous work-related skill, knowledge, or experience is required. **Job Preparation**—SVP 6.0 to less than 7.0—more than one year and less than four years. **Knowledges**—

Production and Processing; Mechanical Devices; Chemistry; Design; Education and Training; Engineering and Technology. **Instructional Programs**—Graphic and Printing Equipment Operator, General Production; Printing Management.

Related **SOC Job**—51-5021 Job Printers. Related **OOH Job**—Prepress Technicians and Workers. **Related DOT Jobs**—973.381-018 Job Printer; 973.381-022 Job-Printer Apprentice.

51-5022.00 Prepress Technicians and Workers

- **Education/Training Required: Long-term on-the-job training**
- **Employed: 72,050**
- **Annual Earnings: $32,840**
- **Growth: −8.4%**
- **Annual Job Openings: 10,000**

Set up and prepare material for printing presses.

Enter, store, and retrieve information on computer-aided equipment. Enter, position, and alter text size, using computers, to make up and arrange pages so that printed materials can be produced. Maintain, adjust, and clean equipment and perform minor repairs. Operate and maintain laser plate-making equipment that converts electronic data to plates without the use of film. Examine photographic images for obvious imperfections prior to platemaking. Operate presses to print proofs of plates, monitoring printing quality to ensure that it is adequate. Monitor contact between cover glass and masks inside vacuum frames to prevent flaws resulting from overexposure or light reflection. Transfer images from master plates to unexposed plates and immerse plates in developing solutions to develop images. Examine unexposed photographic plates to detect flaws or foreign particles prior to printing. Lower vacuum frames onto plate-film assemblies, activate vacuums to establish contact between film and plates, and set timers to activate ultraviolet lights that expose plates. Examine finished plates to detect flaws, verify conformity with master plates, and measure dot sizes and centers, using light-boxes and microscopes. Perform close alignment or registration of double and single flats to sensitized plates prior to exposure to produce composite images. Remove plate-film assemblies from vacuum frames and place exposed plates in automatic processors to develop images and dry plates. Position and angle screens for proper exposure. Inspect developed film for specified results and quality, using magnifying glasses and scopes; forward acceptable negatives or positives to other workers or to customers. Punch holes in light-sensitive plates and insert pins in holes to prepare plates for contact with positive or negative film. Unload exposed film from scanners and place film in automatic processors to develop images. Place masking paper on areas of plates not covered by positives or negatives to prevent exposure. Mount negatives and plates in cameras, set exposure controls, and expose plates to light through negatives to transfer images onto plates.

GOE Information—**Interest Area:** 13. Manufacturing. **Work Group:** 13.08. Graphic Arts Production. **Personality Type**—Realistic. Realistic occupations frequently involve work activities that include practical, hands-on problems and solutions. They often deal with plants; animals; and real-world materials like wood, tools, and machinery. Many of the occupations require working outside and do not involve a lot of paperwork or working closely with others. **Work Values**—Independence; Moral Values; Supervision, Technical. **Skills**—Troubleshooting; Equipment Selection; Installation; Equipment Maintenance; Operation and Control; Operations Analysis. **Abilities**—*Cognitive:* Visualization. *Psychomotor:* Wrist-Finger Speed; Arm-Hand Steadiness; Control Precision; Manual Dexterity. *Physical:*

None met the criteria. *Sensory:* Visual Color Discrimination. **General Work Activities**—*Information Input:* Monitoring Processes, Materials, or Surroundings; Getting Information; Identifying Objects, Actions, and Events. *Mental Process:* Organizing, Planning, and Prioritizing; Updating and Using Relevant Knowledge; Making Decisions and Solving Problems. *Work Output:* Handling and Moving Objects; Controlling Machines and Processes; Interacting With Computers. *Interacting with Others:* Communicating with Other Workers; Establishing and Maintaining Interpersonal Relationships; Coordinating the Work and Activities of Others. **Physical Work Conditions**—Indoors; Noisy; Contaminants; Sitting; Using Hands on Objects, Tools, or Controls; Repetitive Motions. **Other Job Characteristics**—Need to Be Exact or Accurate; Repeat Same Tasks.

Experience—Job Zone 3. Previous work-related skill, knowledge, or experience is required. **Job Preparation**—SVP 6.0 to less than 7.0—more than one year and less than four years. **Knowledges**—Computers and Electronics; Communications and Media; English Language; Design; Production and Processing; Clerical Practices. **Instructional Programs**—Graphic and Printing Equipment Operator, General Production; Graphic Communications, General; Graphic Communications, Other; Graphic Design; Platemaker/Imager; Precision Production Trades, Other; Prepress/Desktop Publishing and Digital Imaging Design; Printing Management.

Related **SOC Job**—51-5022 Prepress Technicians and Workers. Related **OOH Job**—Prepress Technicians and Workers. **Related DOT Jobs**—208.382-010 Terminal-Makeup Operator; 650.582-010 Linotype Operator; 650.582-014 Monotype-Keyboard Operator; 650.582-018 Photocomposing-Machine Operator; 650.582-022 Phototypesetter Operator; 650.682-010 Equipment Monitor, Phototypesetting; 650.685-010 Typesetting-Machine Tender; 652.585-010 Photolettering-Machine Operator; 652.685-106 Type-Proof Reproducer; 659.360-010 Plate Finisher; 714.381-018 Photographic-Plate Maker; 970.361-014 Repeat Chief; 970.381-018 Lay-Out Former; others.

51-5023.00 Printing Machine Operators

- **Education/Training Required: Moderate-term on-the-job training**
- **Employed: 192,520**
- **Annual Earnings: $30,730**
- **Growth: 2.9%**
- **Annual Job Openings: 26,000**

Set up or operate various types of printing machines, such as offset, letterset, intaglio, or gravure presses or screen printers, to produce print on paper or other materials.

Inspect and examine printed products for print clarity, color accuracy, conformance to specifications, and external defects. Push buttons, turn handles, or move controls and levers to start and control printing machines. Reposition printing plates, adjust pressure rolls, or otherwise adjust machines to improve print quality, using knobs, handwheels, or hand tools. Set and adjust speed, temperature, ink flow, and positions and pressure tolerances of equipment. Examine job orders to determine details such as quantities to be printed, production times, stock specifications, colors, and color sequences. Select and install printing plates, rollers, feed guides, gauges, screens, stencils, type, dies, and cylinders in machines according to specifications, using hand tools. Monitor feeding, printing, and racking processes of presses to maintain specified operating levels and to detect malfunctions; make any necessary adjustments. Operate equipment at slow speed to ensure proper ink coverage, alignment, and registration. Load, position, and adjust unprinted materials on holding fixtures or in equipment loading and feeding mechanisms. Pour or spread paint, ink, color compounds, and other materials into reservoirs, troughs, hoppers, or color holders of printing units, making measurements and adjustments to control color and viscosity. Repair, maintain, or adjust equipment. Blend and test paint, inks, stains, and solvents according to types of material being printed and work order specifications. Clean and lubricate printing machines and components, using oil, solvents, brushes, rags, and hoses. Remove printed materials from presses, using handtrucks, electric lifts, or hoists, and transport them to drying, storage, or finishing areas. Input instructions to program automated machinery, using a computer keyboard. Place printed items in ovens to dry or set ink. Squeeze or spread ink on plates, pads, or rollers, using putty knives, brushes, or sponges. Measure screens and use measurements to center and align screens in proper positions and sequences on machines, using gauges and hand tools.

GOE Information—Interest Area: 13. Manufacturing. **Work Group:** 13.08. Graphic Arts Production. **Personality Type—**Realistic. Realistic occupations frequently involve work activities that include practical, hands-on problems and solutions. They often deal with plants; animals; and real-world materials like wood, tools, and machinery. Many of the occupations require working outside and do not involve a lot of paperwork or working closely with others. **Work Values—**Independence; Moral Values; Supervision, Technical; Company Policies and Practices; Activity; Supervision, Human Relations. **Skills—**Operation Monitoring; Operation and Control; Equipment Maintenance; Repairing; Quality Control Analysis; Troubleshooting. **Abilities—***Cognitive:* None met the criteria. *Psychomotor:* Wrist-Finger Speed; Control Precision; Manual Dexterity; Arm-Hand Steadiness. *Physical:* None met the criteria. *Sensory:* Visual Color Discrimination. **General Work Activities—***Information Input:* Inspecting Equipment, Structures, or Materials; Monitoring Processes, Materials, or Surroundings; Identifying Objects, Actions, and Events. *Mental Process:* Updating and Using Relevant Knowledge; Making Decisions and Solving Problems; Organizing, Planning, and Prioritizing. *Work Output:* Controlling Machines and Processes; Handling and Moving Objects; Performing General Physical Activities. *Interacting with Others:* Communicating with Other Workers; Establishing and Maintaining Interpersonal Relationships; Coaching and Developing Others. **Physical Work Conditions—**Noisy; Contaminants; Hazardous Conditions; Hazardous Equipment; Standing; Using Hands on Objects, Tools, or Controls. **Other Job Characteristics—**Pace Determined by Speed of Equipment; Need to Be Exact or Accurate; Errors Have Important Consequences; Repeat Same Tasks.

Experience—Job Zone 2. Some previous work-related skill, knowledge, or experience may be helpful in these occupations, but usually is not needed. **Job Preparation—**SVP 4.0 to less than 6.0—six months to less than two years. **Knowledges—**Mechanical Devices; Production and Processing; Chemistry. **Instructional Programs—**Graphic and Printing Equipment Operator, General Production; Graphic Communications, Other; Printing Management; Printing Press Operator.

Related SOC Job—51-5023 Printing Machine Operators. **Related OOH Job—**Printing Machine Operators. **Related DOT Jobs—**209.582-010 Music Copyist; 209.584-010 Braille Transcriber, Hand; 617.685-018 Embossing-Machine Operator; 651.362-010 Cylinder-Press Operator; 651.362-014 Cylinder-Press-Operator Apprentice; 651.362-018 Platen-Press Operator; 651.362-022 Platen-Press-Operator Apprentice; 651.362-026 Rotogravure-Press Operator; 651.362-030 Web-Press Operator; 651.362-034 Web-Press-Operator Apprentice;

651.382-010 Engraving Press Operator; 651.382-014 Lithograph-Press Operator, Tinware; others.

51-6000 Textile, Apparel, and Furnishings Workers

51-6011.00 Laundry and Dry-Cleaning Workers

- **Education/Training Required: Moderate-term on-the-job training**
- **Employed: 218,360**
- **Annual Earnings: $17,440**
- **Growth: 12.7%**
- **Annual Job Openings: 44,000**

Operate or tend washing or dry-cleaning machines to wash or dry clean industrial or household articles, such as cloth garments, suede, leather, furs, blankets, draperies, fine linens, rugs, and carpets.

Receive and mark articles for laundry or dry cleaning with identifying code numbers or names, using hand or machine markers. Start washers, dry cleaners, driers, or extractors and turn valves or levers to regulate machine processes and the volume of soap, detergent, water, bleach, starch, and other additives. Sort and count articles removed from dryers and fold, wrap, or hang them. Examine articles to be cleaned and sort them into lots according to color, fabric, dirt content, and cleaning technique required. Load articles into washers or dry-cleaning machines or direct other workers to perform loading. Mix and add detergents, dyes, bleaches, starches, and other solutions and chemicals to clean, color, dry, or stiffen articles. Remove items from washers or dry-cleaning machines or direct other workers to do so. Clean machine filters and lubricate equipment. Operate extractors and driers or direct their operation. Inspect soiled articles to determine sources of stains, to locate color imperfections, and to identify items requiring special treatment. Determine spotting procedures and proper solvents based on fabric and stain types. Spray steam, water, or air over spots to flush out chemicals, dry material, raise naps, or brighten colors. Operate dry-cleaning machines to clean soiled articles. Test fabrics in inconspicuous places to determine whether solvents will damage dyes or fabrics. Pre-soak, sterilize, scrub, spot-clean, and dry contaminated or stained articles, using neutralizer solutions and portable machines. Start pumps to operate distilling systems that drain and reclaim dry-cleaning solvents. Operate machines that comb, dry, and polish furs; clean, sterilize, and fluff feathers and blankets; or roll and package towels. Spread soiled articles on work tables and position stained portions over vacuum heads or on marble slabs. Sprinkle chemical solvents over stains and pat areas with brushes or sponges to remove stains. Apply bleaching powders to spots and spray them with steam to remove stains from fabrics that do not respond to other cleaning solvents. Match sample colors, applying knowledge of bleaching agent and dye properties and types, construction, conditions, and colors of articles.

GOE Information—Interest Area: 13. Manufacturing. **Work Group:** 13.11. Apparel, Shoes, Leather, and Fabric Care. **Personality Type—** Realistic. Realistic occupations frequently involve work activities that include practical, hands-on problems and solutions. They often deal with plants; animals; and real-world materials like wood, tools, and machinery. Many of the occupations require working outside and do not involve a lot of paperwork or working closely with others. **Work Values**—Supervision, Technical; Moral Values; Independence. **Skills**—Equipment Maintenance; Management of Financial Resources. **Abilities**—*Cognitive:* None met the criteria. *Psychomotor:* Rate Control; Arm-Hand Steadiness; Control Precision; Manual Dexterity; Finger Dexterity. *Physical:* Trunk Strength. *Sensory:* Visual Color Discrimination. **General Work Activities**—*Information Input:* Monitoring Processes, Materials, or Surroundings; Getting Information; Estimating the Needed Characteristics of Products, Events, or Information. *Mental Process:* Organizing, Planning, and Prioritizing; Making Decisions and Solving Problems; Updating and Using Relevant Knowledge. *Work Output:* Handling and Moving Objects; Controlling Machines and Processes; Performing General Physical Activities. *Interacting with Others:* Establishing and Maintaining Interpersonal Relationships; Resolving Conflicts and Negotiating with Others; Communicating with Other Workers. **Physical Work Conditions**—Indoors; Contaminants; Standing; Walking and Running; Using Hands on Objects, Tools, or Controls; Repetitive Motions. **Other Job Characteristics**—Need to Be Exact or Accurate; Pace Determined by Speed of Equipment; Repeat Same Tasks.

Experience—Job Zone 2. Some previous work-related skill, knowledge, or experience may be helpful in these occupations, but usually is not needed. **Job Preparation**—SVP 4.0 to less than 6.0—six months to less than two years. **Knowledges**—Chemistry; Production and Processing. **Instructional Program**—No related CIP programs.

Related SOC Job—51-6011 Laundry and Dry-Cleaning Workers. **Related OOH Job**—Textile, Apparel, and Furnishings Occupations. **Related DOT Jobs**—361.665-010 Washer, Machine; 361.682-010 Rug Cleaner, Machine; 361.684-010 Launderer, Hand; 361.684-014 Laundry Worker I; 361.684-018 Spotter I; 361.685-014 Continuous-Towel Roller; 361.685-018 Laundry Worker II; 362.381-010 Spotter II; 362.382-010 Dry-Cleaner Apprentice; 362.382-014 Dry Cleaner; 362.684-014 Fur Cleaner; 362.684-026 Leather Cleaner; 362.685-010 Feather Renovator; 364.361-010 Dyer; 364.361-014 Rug Dyer I; 364.684-010 Rug Dyer II; 369.684-014 Laundry Operator; others.

51-6021.00 Pressers, Textile, Garment, and Related Materials

- **Education/Training Required: Short-term on-the-job training**
- **Employed: 78,620**
- **Annual Earnings: $17,570**
- **Growth: 2.9%**
- **Annual Job Openings: 14,000**

Press or shape articles by hand or machine.

Push and pull irons over surfaces of articles to smooth or shape them. Sew ends of new material to leaders or to ends of material in pressing machines, using sewing machines. Select, install, and adjust machine components, including pressing forms, rollers, and guides, using hoists and hand tools. Activate and adjust machine controls to regulate temperature and pressure of rollers, ironing shoes, or plates according to specifications. Block or shape knitted garments after cleaning. Hang, fold, package, and tag finished articles for delivery to customers. Lower irons, rams, or pressing heads of machines into position over material to be pressed. Moisten materials to soften and smooth them. Press ties on small pressing machines. Position materials such as cloth garments, felt, or straw on tables, dies, or feeding mechanisms of pressing machines or on ironing boards or work tables. Finish velvet garments by steaming them on bucks of hot-head presses or steam tables and brushing pile (nap) with handbrushes.

Remove finished pieces from pressing machines and hang or stack them for cooling or forward them for additional processing. Operate steam, hydraulic, or other pressing machines to remove wrinkles from garments and flatwork items or to shape, form, or patch articles. Finish pants, jackets, shirts, skirts, and other dry-cleaned and laundered articles, using hand irons. Shrink, stretch, or block articles by hand to conform to original measurements, using forms, blocks, and steam. Slide material back and forth over heated, metal, ball-shaped forms to smooth and press portions of garments that cannot be satisfactorily pressed with flat pressers or hand irons. Spray water over fabric to soften fibers when not using steam irons. Straighten, smooth, or shape materials to prepare them for pressing. Use covering cloths to prevent equipment from damaging delicate fabrics. Brush materials made of suede, leather, or felt to remove spots or to raise and smooth naps. Clean and maintain pressing machines, using cleaning solutions and lubricants. Examine and measure finished articles to verify conformance to standards, using measuring devices such as tape measures and micrometers.

GOE Information—**Interest Area:** 13. Manufacturing. **Work Group:** 13.11. Apparel, Shoes, Leather, and Fabric Care. **Personality Type**—Realistic. Realistic occupations frequently involve work activities that include practical, hands-on problems and solutions. They often deal with plants; animals; and real-world materials like wood, tools, and machinery. Many of the occupations require working outside and do not involve a lot of paperwork or working closely with others. **Work Values**—Moral Values; Independence; Supervision; Technical. **Skills**—None met the criteria. **Abilities**—*Cognitive:* None met the criteria. *Psychomotor:* Wrist-Finger Speed; Manual Dexterity; Arm-Hand Steadiness; Control Precision; Multilimb Coordination. *Physical:* Extent Flexibility. *Sensory:* None met the criteria. **General Work Activities**—*Information Input:* None met the criteria. *Mental Process:* None met the criteria. *Work Output:* Handling and Moving Objects; Performing General Physical Activities. *Interacting with Others:* None met the criteria. **Physical Work Conditions**—Indoors; Very Hot or Cold; Minor Burns, Cuts, Bites, or Stings; Standing; Using Hands on Objects, Tools, or Controls; Repetitive Motions. **Other Job Characteristics**—None met the criteria.

Experience—Job Zone 1. No previous work-related skill, knowledge, or experience is needed. **Job Preparation**—SVP below 4.0—less than six months. **Knowledges**—Fine Arts; Food Production. **Instructional Program**—No related CIP programs.

Related SOC Job—51-6021 Pressers, Textile, Garment, and Related Materials. **Related OOH Job**—Textile, Apparel, and Furnishings Occupations. **Related DOT Jobs**—361.685-022 Patching-Machine Operator; 363.681-010 Silk Finisher; 363.682-010 Leather Finisher; 363.682-014 Presser, All-Around; 363.682-018 Presser, Machine; 363.684-010 Blocker; 363.684-014 Hat Blocker; 363.684-018 Presser, Hand; 363.685-010 Press Operator; 363.685-014 Presser, Automatic; 363.685-018 Presser, Form; 363.685-022 Presser, Handkerchief; 363.685-026 Shirt Presser; 369.685-018 Fur Ironer; 580.685-042 Molder; 583.585-010 Calender-Machine Operator; 583.685-018 Brim Presser I; others.

51-6031.00 Sewing Machine Operators

- **Education/Training Required: Moderate-term on-the-job training**
- **Employed: 233,130**
- **Annual Earnings: $18,340**
- **Growth: –36.5%**
- **Annual Job Openings: 20,000**

Operate or tend sewing machines to join, reinforce, decorate, or perform related sewing operations in the manufacture of garment or nongarment products.

Monitor machine operation to detect problems such as defective stitching, breaks in thread, or machine malfunctions. Position items under needles, using marks on machines, clamps, templates, or cloth as guides. Place spools of thread, cord, or other materials on spindles; insert bobbins; and thread ends through machine guides and components. Match cloth pieces in correct sequences prior to sewing them and verify that dye lots and patterns match. Guide garments or garment parts under machine needles and presser feet to sew parts together. Start and operate or tend machines, such as single- or double-needle serging and flat-bed felling machines, to automatically join, reinforce, or decorate material or articles. Record quantities of materials processed. Inspect garments, examine repair tags and markings on garments to locate defects or damage, and mark errors as necessary. Mount attachments, such as needles, cutting blades, or pattern plates, and adjust machine guides according to specifications. Select supplies such as fasteners and thread according to job requirements. Cut excess material or thread from finished products. Fold or stretch edges or lengths of items while sewing to facilitate forming specified sections. Perform equipment maintenance tasks such as replacing needles, sanding rough areas of needles, or cleaning and oiling sewing machines. Turn knobs, screws, and dials to adjust settings of machines according to garment styles and equipment performance. Examine and measure finished articles to verify conformance to standards, using rulers. Repair or alter items by adding replacement parts or missing stitches. Cut materials according to specifications, using blades, scissors, or electric knives. Remove holding devices and finished items from machines. Position and mark patterns on materials to prepare for sewing. Position material or articles in clamps, templates, or hoop frames prior to automatic operation of machines. Attach tape, trim, appliques, or elastic to specified garments or garment parts according to item specifications. Perform specialized or automatic sewing machine functions, such as buttonhole making or tacking.

GOE Information—Interest Area: 13. Manufacturing. **Work Group:** 13.03. Production Work, Assorted Materials Processing. **Personality Type—**Realistic. Realistic occupations frequently involve work activities that include practical, hands-on problems and solutions. They often deal with plants; animals; and real-world materials like wood, tools, and machinery. Many of the occupations require working outside and do not involve a lot of paperwork or working closely with others. **Work Values—**Moral Values; Independence; Activity; Supervision, Human Relations; Company Policies and Practices; Supervision, Technical. **Skills—**None met the criteria. **Abilities—***Cognitive:* Perceptual Speed; Visualization. *Psychomotor:* Rate Control; Arm-Hand Steadiness; Reaction Time; Wrist-Finger Speed; Response Orientation; Manual Dexterity. *Physical:* Extent Flexibility; Static Strength. *Sensory:* Visual Color Discrimination; Depth Perception; Hearing Sensitivity; Far Vision. **General Work Activities—***Information Input:* Getting Information; Identifying Objects, Actions, and Events; Inspecting Equipment, Structures, or Materials. *Mental Process:* Organizing, Planning, and Prioritizing; Making Decisions and Solving Problems; Updating and Using Relevant Knowledge. *Work Output:* Handling and Moving Objects; Controlling Machines and Processes; Performing General Physical Activities. *Interacting with Others:* Communicating with Other Workers; Establishing and Maintaining Interpersonal Relationships. **Physical Work Conditions—**Indoors; Sitting; Using Hands on Objects, Tools, or Controls; Bending or Twisting the Body; Repetitive Motions. **Other Job Characteristics—**Need to Be Exact or Accurate; Pace Determined by Speed of Equipment.

Experience—Job Zone 1. No previous work-related skill, knowledge, or experience is needed. **Job Preparation—**SVP below 4.0—less than six months. **Knowledges—**Production and Processing; Food Production. **Instructional Program—**No related CIP programs.

Related SOC Job—51-6031 Sewing Machine Operators. **Related OOH Job—**Textile, Apparel, and Furnishings Occupations. **Related DOT Jobs—**684.682-014 Sewer and Inspector; 689.662-014 Stripe Matcher; 689.682-018 Splicing-Machine Operator; 689.682-022 Stitcher; 689.685-026 Bouffant-Curtain-Machine Tender; 689.685-106 Quilting-Machine Operator; 689.685-118 Sewing-Machine Operator, Special Equipment; 689.685-126 Stitch-Bonding-Machine Tender; 689.685-150 Watcher, Automat; 689.685-154 Watcher, Pantograph; 692.685-254 Window-Shade-Ring Sewer; 731.685-010 Rooter Operator; 780.682-010 Sewing-Machine Operator; 780.682-014 Slip-Cover Sewer; others.

51-6041.00 Shoe and Leather Workers and Repairers

- **Education/Training Required: Long-term on-the-job training**
- **Employed: 7,680**
- **Annual Earnings: $20,010**
- **Growth: −16.0%**
- **Annual Job Openings: 2,000**

Construct, decorate, or repair leather and leather-like products, such as luggage, shoes, and saddles.

Prepare inserts, heel pads, and lifts from casts of customers' feet. Check the texture, color, and strength of leather to ensure that it is adequate for a particular purpose. Clean and polish shoes. Cut, insert, position, and secure paddings, cushioning, and linings, using stitches or glue. Draw patterns, using measurements, designs, plaster casts, or customer specifications, and position or outline patterns on workpieces. Dress and otherwise finish boots or shoes, as by trimming the edges of new soles and heels to the shoe shape. Estimate the costs of requested products or services such as custom footwear or footwear repair and receive payment from customers. Inspect articles for defects and remove damaged or worn parts, using hand tools. Shape shoe heels with a knife and sand them on a buffing wheel for smoothness. Read prescriptions or specifications and take measurements to establish the type of product to be made, using calipers, tape measures, or rules. Nail heel and toe cleats onto shoes. Measure customers for fit and discuss with them the type of footwear to be made, recommending details such as leather quality. Stretch shoes, first dampening parts and then inserting and twisting parts, using an adjustable stretcher. Drill or punch holes; then insert or attach metal rings, handles, and fastening hardware such as buckles. Align and stitch or glue materials such as fabric, fleece, leather, or wood, in order to join parts. Attach accessories or ornamentation to decorate or protect products. Select materials and patterns and trace patterns onto materials to be cut out. Attach insoles to shoe lasts, affix shoe uppers, and apply heels and outsoles. Cement, nail, or sew soles and heels to shoes. Repair or replace soles, heels, and other parts of footwear, using sewing, buffing, and other shoe repair machines, materials, and equipment. Cut out parts, following patterns or outlines and using knives, shears, scissors, or machine presses. Re-sew seams and replace handles and linings of suitcases or handbags. Dye, soak, polish, paint, stamp, stitch, stain, buff, or engrave leather or other materials to obtain desired effects, decorations, or shapes.

GOE Information—Interest Area: 13. Manufacturing. **Work Group:** 13.11. Apparel, Shoes, Leather, and Fabric Care. **Personality Type—**

Realistic. Realistic occupations frequently involve work activities that include practical, hands-on problems and solutions. They often deal with plants; animals; and real-world materials like wood, tools, and machinery. Many of the occupations require working outside and do not involve a lot of paperwork or working closely with others. **Work Values**—Independence; Moral Values; Creativity; Ability Utilization. **Skills**—Repairing. **Abilities**—*Cognitive:* Visualization. *Psychomotor:* Wrist-Finger Speed; Arm-Hand Steadiness; Manual Dexterity; Finger Dexterity; Control Precision; Multilimb Coordination. *Physical:* Extent Flexibility; Static Strength. *Sensory:* Visual Color Discrimination. **General Work Activities**—*Information Input:* Getting Information. *Mental Process:* Evaluating Information Against Standards. *Work Output:* Handling and Moving Objects; Controlling Machines and Processes; Performing General Physical Activities. *Interacting with Others:* None met the criteria. **Physical Work Conditions**—Indoors; Sitting; Using Hands on Objects, Tools, or Controls; Repetitive Motions. **Other Job Characteristics**—None met the criteria.

Experience—Job Zone 2. Some previous work-related skill, knowledge, or experience may be helpful in these occupations, but usually is not needed. **Job Preparation**—SVP 4.0 to less than 6.0—six months to less than two years. **Knowledges**—Production and Processing; Design. **Instructional Programs**—Leatherworking and Upholstery, Other; Shoe, Boot, and Leather Repair.

Related SOC Job—51-6041 Shoe and Leather Workers and Repairers. **Related OOH Job**—Textile, Apparel, and Furnishings Occupations. **Related DOT Jobs**—365.361-010 Luggage Repairer; 365.361-014 Shoe Repairer; 739.684-114 Last-Repairer Helper; 753.381-010 Bootmaker, Hand; 753.684-026 Repairer; 780.381-030 Pad Hand; 781.381-018 Leather Stamper; 783.361-010 Custom-Leather-Products Maker; 783.381-018 Harness Maker; 783.381-022 Luggage Maker; 783.381-026 Saddle Maker; 788.261-010 Orthopedic-Boot-and-Shoe Designer and Maker; 788.381-010 Cobbler; 788.381-014 Shoemaker, Custom; 788.684-046 Finger Cobbler; 788.684-098 Sample Shoe Inspector and Reworker.

51-6042.00 Shoe Machine Operators and Tenders

- **Education/Training Required: Moderate-term on-the-job training**
- **Employed: 3,850**
- **Annual Earnings: $20,600**
- **Growth: –27.3%**
- **Annual Job Openings: Fewer than 500**

Operate or tend a variety of machines to join, decorate, reinforce, or finish shoes and shoe parts.

Switch on machines; then lower pressure feet or rollers to secure parts and start machine stitching, using hand, foot, or knee controls. Turn knobs to adjust stitch length and thread tension. Align parts to be stitched, following seams, edges, or markings, before positioning them under needles. Cut excess thread or material from shoe parts, using scissors or knives. Draw thread through machine guide slots, needles, and presser feet in preparation for stitching or load rolls of wire through machine axles. Fill shuttle spools with thread from a machine's bobbin winder by pressing a foot treadle. Lower levers to open guides for passing wire along and through machine feeders; then raise levers to close guides and turn knobs to adjust wire tension. Operate or tend machines to join, decorate, reinforce, or finish shoes and shoe parts. Remove and examine shoes, shoe parts, and designs to verify conformance to specifications such as proper embedding of stitches in channels. Study work orders or shoe part tags to obtain information about workloads, specifications, and the types of materials to be used. Select and place spools of thread or pre-wound bobbins into shuttles or onto spindles or loupers of stitching machines. Staple sides of shoes, pressing a foot treadle to position and hold each shoe under the feeder of the machine. Turn screws to regulate size of staples. Collect shoe parts from conveyer belts or racks and place them in machinery such as ovens or on molds for dressing, returning them to conveyers or racks to send them to the next workstation. Hammer loose staples for proper attachment. Load hot-melt plastic rod glue through reactivator axles, using wrenches; then switch on reactivators, setting temperature and timers to heat glue to specifications. Perform routine equipment maintenance such as cleaning and lubricating machines or replacing broken needles. Turn setscrews on needle bars and position required numbers of needles in stitching machines. Select and insert cassettes into consoles of stitching machines to stitch decorative designs onto shoe parts.

GOE Information—**Interest Area:** 13. Manufacturing. **Work Group:** 13.03. Production Work, Assorted Materials Processing. **Personality Type**—Realistic. Realistic occupations frequently involve work activities that include practical, hands-on problems and solutions. They often deal with plants; animals; and real-world materials like wood, tools, and machinery. Many of the occupations require working outside and do not involve a lot of paperwork or working closely with others. **Work Values**—Moral Values; Independence; Activity; Supervision, Human Relations; Company Policies and Practices; Supervision, Technical. **Skills**—Operation and Control. **Abilities**—*Cognitive:* None met the criteria. *Psychomotor:* Wrist-Finger Speed; Manual Dexterity; Arm-Hand Steadiness; Finger Dexterity; Multilimb Coordination; Control Precision. *Physical:* None met the criteria. *Sensory:* Visual Color Discrimination. **General Work Activities**—*Information Input:* Monitoring Processes, Materials, or Surroundings. *Mental Process:* None met the criteria. *Work Output:* Handling and Moving Objects; Performing General Physical Activities; Controlling Machines and Processes. *Interacting with Others:* None met the criteria. **Physical Work Conditions**—Indoors; Minor Burns, Cuts, Bites, or Stings; Sitting; Using Hands on Objects, Tools, or Controls; Repetitive Motions. **Other Job Characteristics**—Repeat Same Tasks; Need to Be Exact or Accurate.

Experience—Job Zone 1. No previous work-related skill, knowledge, or experience is needed. **Job Preparation**—SVP below 4.0—less than six months. **Knowledges**—Production and Processing; Fine Arts. **Instructional Program**—Shoe, Boot, and Leather Repair.

Related SOC Job—51-6042 Shoe Machine Operators and Tenders. **Related OOH Job**—Textile, Apparel, and Furnishings Occupations. **Related DOT Jobs**—690.682-078 Stitcher, Special Machine; 690.682-082 Stitcher, Standard Machine; 690.685-494 Stitcher, Tape-Controlled Machine; 788.684-114 Thread Laster.

51-6051.00 Sewers, Hand

- **Education/Training Required: Short-term on-the-job training**
- **Employed: 11,090**
- **Annual Earnings: $19,770**
- **Growth: –19.7%**
- **Annual Job Openings: 2,000**

Sew, join, reinforce, or finish, usually with needle and thread, a variety of manufactured items. Includes weavers and stitchers.

Wax thread by drawing it through a ball of wax. Select thread, twine, cord, or yarn to be used and thread needles. Measure and align parts, fasteners, or trimmings, following seams, edges, or markings on parts. Smooth seams with heated irons, flat bones, or rubbing sticks. Trim excess threads or edges of parts, using scissors or knives. Sew, join, reinforce, or finish parts of articles, such as garments, books, mattresses, toys, and wigs, using needles and thread or other materials. Use different sewing techniques such as felling, tacking, basting, embroidery, and fagoting. Fold, twist, stretch, or drape material and secure articles in preparation for sewing. Tie, knit, weave, or knot ribbon, yarn, or decorative materials. Soften leather or shoe material with water to prepare it for sewing. Sew buttonholes or add lace or other trimming. Draw and cut patterns according to specifications. Attach trimmings and labels to articles with cement, using brushes or cement guns.

GOE Information—Interest Area: 13. Manufacturing. **Work Group:** 13.09. Hands-On Work, Assorted Materials. **Personality Type—** Realistic. Realistic occupations frequently involve work activities that include practical, hands-on problems and solutions. They often deal with plants; animals; and real-world materials like wood, tools, and machinery. Many of the occupations require working outside and do not involve a lot of paperwork or working closely with others. **Work Values—**Independence; Moral Values; Activity. **Skills—** None met the criteria. **Abilities—***Cognitive:* Visualization. *Psychomotor:* Wrist-Finger Speed; Arm-Hand Steadiness; Finger Dexterity; Manual Dexterity. *Physical:* None met the criteria. *Sensory:* Visual Color Discrimination; Near Vision. **General Work Activities—** *Information Input:* None met the criteria. *Mental Process:* None met the criteria. *Work Output:* Handling and Moving Objects. *Interacting with Others:* None met the criteria. **Physical Work Conditions—** Indoors; Sitting; Using Hands on Objects, Tools, or Controls; Repetitive Motions. **Other Job Characteristics—**Need to Be Exact or Accurate; Repeat Same Tasks.

Experience—Job Zone 1. No previous work-related skill, knowledge, or experience is needed. **Job Preparation—**SVP below 4.0—less than six months. **Knowledges—**Production and Processing; Design. **Instructional Program—**No related CIP programs.

Related SOC Job—51-6051 Sewers, Hand. **Related OOH Job—**Textile, Apparel, and Furnishings Occupations. **Related DOT Jobs—**529.687-030 Casing Sewer; 732.684-034 Baseball Sewer, Hand; 732.684-050 Feather Stitcher; 732.684-090 Pelota Maker; 739.384-014 Foundation Maker; 739.684-162 Umbrella Tipper, Hand; 780.684-070 Mattress Finisher; 782.684-030 Hosiery Mender; 782.684-050 Passementerie Worker; 782.684-058 Sewer, Hand; 782.687-018 Cloth-Bale Header; 782.687-058 Thread Marker; 784.684-022 Decorator; 784.684-042 Hat Maker; 787.381-010 Lamp-Shade Sewer; 788.684-054 Hand Sewer, Shoes; 788.684-110 Sole Sewer, Hand; others.

51-6052.00 Tailors, Dressmakers, and Custom Sewers

- **Education/Training Required: Long-term on-the-job training**
- **Employed: 30,150**
- **Annual Earnings: $22,770**
- **Growth: 0.3%**
- **Annual Job Openings: 4,000**

Design, make, alter, repair, or fit garments.

Fit and study garments on customers to determine required alterations. Sew garments, using needles and thread or sewing machines. Measure parts such as sleeves or pant legs and mark or pin-fold alteration lines. Let out or take in seams in suits and other garments to improve fit. Take up or let down hems to shorten or lengthen garment parts such as sleeves. Assemble garment parts and join parts with basting stitches, using needles and thread or sewing machines. Remove stitches from garments to be altered, using rippers or razor blades. Record required alterations and instructions on tags and attach them to garments. Examine tags on garments to determine alterations that are needed. Fit, alter, repair, and make made-to-measure clothing according to customers' and clothing manufacturers' specifications and fit, and apply principles of garment design, construction, and styling. Maintain garment drape and proportions as alterations are performed. Press garments, using hand irons or pressing machines. Trim excess material, using scissors. Develop, copy, or adapt designs for garments and design patterns to fit measurements, applying knowledge of garment design, construction, styling, and fabric. Measure customers, using tape measures, and record measurements. Make garment style changes, such as tapering pant legs, narrowing lapels, and adding or removing padding. Estimate how much a garment will cost to make, based on factors such as time and material requirements. Repair or replace defective garment parts such as pockets, zippers, snaps, buttons, and linings. Confer with customers to determine types of material and garment styles desired. Position patterns of garment parts on fabric and cut fabric along outlines, using scissors. Sew buttonholes and attach buttons to finish garments. Put in padding and shaping materials.

GOE Information—Interest Area: 13. Manufacturing. **Work Group:** 13.11. Apparel, Shoes, Leather, and Fabric Care. **Personality Type—** Realistic. Realistic occupations frequently involve work activities that include practical, hands-on problems and solutions. They often deal with plants; animals; and real-world materials like wood, tools, and machinery. Many of the occupations require working outside and do not involve a lot of paperwork or working closely with others. **Work Values—**Working Conditions; Independence; Autonomy; Social Service; Creativity; Variety. **Skills—**Time Management; Equipment Maintenance; Repairing; Service Orientation; Operations Analysis; Quality Control Analysis. **Abilities—***Cognitive:* Visualization. *Psychomotor:* Arm-Hand Steadiness; Finger Dexterity; Control Precision; Wrist-Finger Speed; Manual Dexterity; Multilimb Coordination. *Physical:* None met the criteria. *Sensory:* Visual Color Discrimination. **General Work Activities—***Information Input:* Getting Information; Identifying Objects, Actions, and Events; Monitoring Processes, Materials, or Surroundings. *Mental Process:* Organizing, Planning, and Prioritizing; Making Decisions and Solving Problems; Thinking Creatively. *Work Output:* Controlling Machines and Processes; Repairing and Maintaining Mechanical Equipment; Handling and Moving Objects. *Interacting with Others:* Establishing and Maintaining Interpersonal Relationships; Performing for or Working with the Public; Interpreting the Meaning of Information to Others. **Physical Work Conditions—**Indoors; Sitting; Using Hands on Objects, Tools, or Controls; Repetitive Motions. **Other Job Characteristics—**Need to Be Exact or Accurate; Repeat Same Tasks.

Experience—Job Zone 2. Some previous work-related skill, knowledge, or experience may be helpful in these occupations, but usually is not needed. **Job Preparation—**SVP 4.0 to less than 6.0—six months to less than two years. **Knowledges—**Design; Customer and Personal Service; Psychology; Sales and Marketing; Clerical Practices; Production and Processing. **Instructional Program—**No related CIP programs.

Related SOC Job—51-6052 Tailors, Dressmakers, and Custom Sewers. **Related OOH Job—**Textile, Apparel, and Furnishings Occupations. **Related DOT Jobs—**782.361-010 Corset Fitter; 782.381-010 Hat Trimmer; 783.261-010 Furrier; 785.261-010 Alteration Tailor; 785.261-014 Custom Tailor; 785.261-018 Tailor Apprentice, Alteration; 785.261-022 Tailor Apprentice, Custom; 785.361-010 Dressmaker;

785.361-014 Garment Fitter; 785.361-018 Sample Stitcher; 785.361-022 Shop Tailor; 785.361-026 Shop Tailor Apprentice; 969.381-010 Wardrobe-Specialty Worker.

51-6061.00 Textile Bleaching and Dyeing Machine Operators and Tenders

- **Education/Training Required: Moderate-term on-the-job training**
- **Employed: 21,660**
- **Annual Earnings: $22,460**
- **Growth: –45.3%**
- **Annual Job Openings: 4,000**

Operate or tend machines to bleach, shrink, wash, dye, or finish textiles or synthetic or glass fibers.

Install, level, and align components such as gears, chains, dies, cutters, and needles. Record production information such as fabric yardage processed, temperature readings, fabric tensions, and machine speeds. Perform machine maintenance, such as cleaning and oiling equipment, and repair or replace worn or defective parts. Notify supervisors or mechanics of equipment malfunctions. Key in processing instructions to program electronic equipment. Inspect machinery to determine necessary adjustments and repairs. Confer with co-workers to get information about order details, processing plans, or problems that occur. Thread ends of cloth or twine through specified sections of equipment prior to processing. Test solutions used to process textile goods to detect variations from standards. Start and control machines and equipment to wash, bleach, dye, or otherwise process and finish fabric, yarn, thread, or other textile goods. Prepare dyeing machines for production runs and conduct test runs of machines to ensure their proper operation. Study guides, charts, and specification sheets and confer with supervisors to determine machine setup requirements. Add dyes, water, detergents, or chemicals to tanks to dilute or strengthen solutions according to established formulas and solution test results. Adjust equipment controls to maintain specified heat, tension, and speed. Mount rolls of cloth on machines, using hoists, or place textile goods in machines or pieces of equipment. Creel machines with bobbins or twine. Weigh ingredients to be mixed together for use in textile processing. Examine and feel products to identify defects and variations from coloring and other processing standards. Soak specified textile products for designated times. Remove dyed articles from tanks and machines for drying and further processing. Ravel seams that connect cloth ends when processing is completed. Observe display screens, control panels, equipment, and cloth entering or exiting processes to determine if equipment is operating correctly. Sew ends of cloth together, by hand or using machines, to form endless lengths of cloth to facilitate processing.

GOE Information—Interest Area: 13. Manufacturing. **Work Group:** 13.03. Production Work, Assorted Materials Processing. **Personality Type**—Realistic. Realistic occupations frequently involve work activities that include practical, hands-on problems and solutions. They often deal with plants; animals; and real-world materials like wood, tools, and machinery. Many of the occupations require working outside and do not involve a lot of paperwork or working closely with others. **Work Values**—Moral Values; Supervision, Technical; Supervision, Human Relations; Company Policies and Practices; Advancement; Activity. **Skills**—Operation and Control; Operation Monitoring. **Abilities**—*Cognitive:* Memorization; Perceptual Speed; Time Sharing; Number Facility; Information Ordering. *Psychomotor:* Wrist-Finger Speed; Rate Control; Arm-Hand Steadiness; Control

Precision; Manual Dexterity; Reaction Time. *Physical:* Dynamic Flexibility; Explosive Strength; Static Strength; Dynamic Strength; Extent Flexibility; Trunk Strength. *Sensory:* Visual Color Discrimination. **General Work Activities**—*Information Input:* Monitoring Processes, Materials, or Surroundings; Identifying Objects, Actions, and Events; Inspecting Equipment, Structures, or Materials. *Mental Process:* Evaluating Information Against Standards; Processing Information; Judging the Qualities of Things, Services, or Other People's Work. *Work Output:* Controlling Machines and Processes; Handling and Moving Objects; Performing General Physical Activities. *Interacting with Others:* Communicating with Other Workers. **Physical Work Conditions**—Indoors; Contaminants; Hazardous Equipment; Standing; Using Hands on Objects, Tools, or Controls; Repetitive Motions. **Other Job Characteristics**—Automation; Pace Determined by Speed of Equipment; Need to Be Exact or Accurate.

Experience—Job Zone 1. No previous work-related skill, knowledge, or experience is needed. **Job Preparation**—SVP below 4.0—less than six months. **Knowledges**—Production and Processing; Chemistry. **Instructional Program**—No related CIP programs.

Related SOC Job—51-6061 Textile Bleaching and Dyeing Machine Operators and Tenders. **Related OOH Job**—Textile, Apparel, and Furnishings Occupations. **Related DOT Jobs**—582.362-010 Panelboard Operator; 582.362-014 Dye Automation Operator; 582.582-010 Dye-Range Operator, Cloth; 582.665-014 Dye-Reel Operator; 582.665-018 Jigger; 582.685-014 Beam-Dyer Operator; 582.685-018 Bleach-Range Operator; 582.685-022 Boil-Off-Machine Operator, Cloth; 582.685-030 Cloth-Washer Operator; 582.685-034 Coloring-Machine Operator; 582.685-054 Dye-Tank Tender; 582.685-058 Dyed-Yarn Operator; 582.685-070 Felt-Washing-Machine Tender; 582.685-090 Jet-Dyeing-Machine Tender; others.

51-6062.00 Textile Cutting Machine Setters, Operators, and Tenders

- **Education/Training Required: Moderate-term on-the-job training**
- **Employed: 21,420**
- **Annual Earnings: $21,430**
- **Growth: –25.0%**
- **Annual Job Openings: 1,000**

Set up, operate, or tend machines that cut textiles.

Record information about work completed and machine settings. Install, level, and align components such as gears, chains, guides, dies, cutters, or needles to set up machinery for operation. Study guides, samples, charts, and specification sheets or confer with supervisors or engineering staff to determine setup requirements. Notify supervisors of mechanical malfunctions. Inspect machinery to determine whether repairs are needed. Confer with co-workers to obtain information about orders, processes, or problems. Clean, oil, and lubricate machines, using air hoses, cleaning solutions, rags, oilcans, and grease guns. Thread yarn, thread, or fabric through guides, needles, and rollers of machines. Repair or replace worn or defective parts or components, using hand tools. Program electronic equipment. Stop machines when specified amounts of product have been produced. Start machines, monitor operations, and make adjustments as needed. Place patterns on top of layers of fabric and cut fabric, following patterns, by using electric or manual knives, cutters, or computer numerically controlled cutting devices. Operate machines for test runs to verify adjustments and to obtain product samples.

Inspect products to ensure that specifications are met and to determine whether machines require adjustment. Adjust machine controls such as heating mechanisms, tensions, and speeds to produce specified products. Adjust cutting techniques to types of fabrics and styles of garments. Operate machines to cut multiple layers of fabric into parts for articles such as canvas goods, house furnishings, garments, hats, or stuffed toys.

GOE Information—Interest Area: 13. Manufacturing. **Work Group:** 13.02. Machine Setup and Operation. **Personality Type**—Realistic. Realistic occupations frequently involve work activities that include practical, hands-on problems and solutions. They often deal with plants; animals; and real-world materials like wood, tools, and machinery. Many of the occupations require working outside and do not involve a lot of paperwork or working closely with others. **Work Values**—Moral Values; Supervision, Technical; Supervision, Human Relations; Independence; Company Policies and Practices; Activity. **Skills**—Operation Monitoring; Installation; Operation and Control; Equipment Maintenance; Repairing; Quality Control Analysis. **Abilities**—*Cognitive:* Visualization; Information Ordering. *Psychomotor:* Control Precision; Arm-Hand Steadiness; Reaction Time; Wrist-Finger Speed; Manual Dexterity; Finger Dexterity. *Physical:* Extent Flexibility; Static Strength; Trunk Strength. *Sensory:* Visual Color Discrimination. **General Work Activities**—*Information Input:* Inspecting Equipment, Structures, or Materials; Monitoring Processes, Materials, or Surroundings; Identifying Objects, Actions, and Events. *Mental Process:* Updating and Using Relevant Knowledge; Evaluating Information Against Standards. *Work Output:* Repairing and Maintaining Mechanical Equipment; Handling and Moving Objects; Controlling Machines and Processes. *Interacting with Others:* Communicating with Other Workers. **Physical Work Conditions**—Indoors; Hazardous Equipment; Minor Burns, Cuts, Bites, or Stings; Standing; Using Hands on Objects, Tools, or Controls; Repetitive Motions. **Other Job Characteristics**—Need to Be Exact or Accurate; Automation.

Experience—Job Zone 3. Previous work-related skill, knowledge, or experience is required. **Job Preparation**—SVP 6.0 to less than 7.0—more than one year and less than four years. **Knowledges**—Mechanical Devices; Design. **Instructional Program**—Industrial Mechanics and Maintenance Technology.

Related SOC Job—51-6062 Textile Cutting Machine Setters, Operators, and Tenders. **Related OOH Job**—Textile, Apparel, and Furnishings Occupations. **Related DOT Jobs**—585.380-010 Cutting-Machine Fixer; 585.565-010 Corduroy-Cutter Operator; 585.685-026 Cloth Trimmer, Machine; 585.685-046 Fur-Cutting-Machine Operator; 585.685-062 Label Pinker; 585.685-086 Rounding-Machine Operator; 585.685-102 Shearing-Machine Operator; 585.685-118 Stripping Cutter And Winder; 585.685-122 Sweatband Separator; 680.685-022 Chopped-Strand Operator; 680.685-102 Staple Cutter; 686.462-010 Die-Cutting-Machine Operator, Automatic; 686.585-010 Cutting-Machine Operator; others.

51-6063.00 Textile Knitting and Weaving Machine Setters, Operators, and Tenders

- **Education/Training Required: Long-term on-the-job training**
- **Employed: 42,760**
- **Annual Earnings: $23,710**
- **Growth: −56.2%**
- **Annual Job Openings: 6,000**

Set up, operate, or tend machines that knit, loop, weave, or draw in textiles.

Wash and blend wool, yarn, or cloth. Repair or replace worn or defective needles and other components, using hand tools. Remove defects in cloth by cutting and pulling out filling. Confer with co-workers to obtain information about orders, processes, or problems. Adjust machine heating mechanisms, tensions, and speeds to produce specified products. Thread yarn, thread, and fabric through guides, needles, and rollers of machines for weaving, knitting, or other processing. Inspect products to ensure that specifications are met and to determine if machines need adjustment. Install, level, and align machine components such as gears, chains, guides, dies, cutters, and needles to set up machinery for operation. Observe woven cloth to detect weaving defects. Operate machines for test runs to verify adjustments and to obtain product samples. Set up or set up and operate textile machines that perform textile processing and manufacturing operations such as winding, twisting, knitting, weaving, bonding, and stretching. Start machines, monitor operations, and make adjustments as needed. Study guides, loom patterns, samples, charts, or specification sheets or confer with supervisors or engineering staff to determine setup requirements. Clean, oil, and lubricate machines, using air hoses, cleaning solutions, rags, oilcans, or grease guns. Examine looms to determine causes of loom stoppage, such as warp filling, harness breaks, or mechanical defects. Program electronic equipment. Record information about work completed and machine settings. Notify supervisors or repair staff of mechanical malfunctions. Stop machines when specified amounts of product have been produced. Inspect machinery to determine whether repairs are needed.

GOE Information—Interest Area: 13. Manufacturing. **Work Group:** 13.02. Machine Setup and Operation. **Personality Type**—Realistic. Realistic occupations frequently involve work activities that include practical, hands-on problems and solutions. They often deal with plants; animals; and real-world materials like wood, tools, and machinery. Many of the occupations require working outside and do not involve a lot of paperwork or working closely with others. **Work Values**—Moral Values; Supervision, Technical; Supervision, Human Relations; Independence; Company Policies and Practices; Activity. **Skills**—Operation Monitoring; Installation; Operation and Control; Equipment Maintenance; Repairing; Quality Control Analysis. **Abilities**—*Cognitive:* Visualization; Information Ordering. *Psychomotor:* Control Precision; Arm-Hand Steadiness; Reaction Time; Wrist-Finger Speed; Manual Dexterity; Finger Dexterity. *Physical:* Extent Flexibility; Static Strength; Trunk Strength. *Sensory:* Visual Color Discrimination. **General Work Activities**—*Information Input:* Inspecting Equipment, Structures, or Materials; Monitoring Processes, Materials, or Surroundings; Identifying Objects, Actions, and Events. *Mental Process:* Updating and Using Relevant Knowledge; Evaluating Information Against Standards. *Work Output:* Repairing and Maintaining Mechanical Equipment; Handling and Moving Objects; Controlling Machines and Processes. *Interacting with Others:* Communicating with Other Workers. **Physical Work Conditions**—Indoors; Hazardous Equipment; Minor Burns, Cuts, Bites, or Stings; Standing; Using Hands on Objects, Tools, or Controls; Repetitive Motions. **Other Job Characteristics**—Need to Be Exact or Accurate; Automation.

Experience—Job Zone 3. Previous work-related skill, knowledge, or experience is required. **Job Preparation**—SVP 6.0 to less than 7.0—more than one year and less than four years. **Knowledges**—Mechanical Devices; Design. **Instructional Program**—Industrial Mechanics and Maintenance Technology.

Related SOC Job—51-6063 Textile Knitting and Weaving Machine Setters, Operators, and Tenders. **Related OOH Job**—Textile, Apparel, and Furnishings Occupations. **Related DOT Jobs**—616.382-014 Wire

Weaver, Cloth; 683.260-014 Carpet-Loom Fixer; 683.260-018 Loom Fixer; 683.360-010 Loom Changer; 683.381-010 Chain Builder, Loom Control; 683.662-010 Jacquard-Loom Weaver; 683.665-010 Weaver, Needle Loom; 683.680-010 Harness Placer; 683.680-014 Heddles Tier, Jacquard Loom; 683.682-010 Carpet Weaver; 683.682-014 Carpet Weaver, Jacquard Loom; 683.682-018 Drawing-in-Machine Tender; 683.682-022 Jacquard-Loom Weaver; 683.682-026 Levers-Lace Machine Operator; 683.682-030 Plush Weaver; others.

51-6064.00 Textile Winding, Twisting, and Drawing Out Machine Setters, Operators, and Tenders

- **Education/Training Required: Moderate-term on-the-job training**
- **Employed: 47,670**
- **Annual Earnings: $22,960**
- **Growth: −45.5%**
- **Annual Job Openings: 9,000**

Set up, operate, or tend machines that wind or twist textiles or draw out and combine sliver, such as wool, hemp, or synthetic fibers.

Thread yarn, thread, or fabric through guides, needles, and rollers of machines. Remove spindles from machines and bobbins from spindles. Replace depleted supply packages with full packages. Start machines, monitor operation, and make adjustments as needed. Stop machines when specified amount of products has been produced. Study guides, samples, charts, and specification sheets or confer with supervisors or engineering staff to determine setup requirements. Tend machines that wind wire onto bobbins preparatory to formation of wire netting used in reinforcing sheet glass. Unwind lengths of yarn, thread, or twine from spools and wind onto bobbins. Tend spinning frames that draw out and twist roving or sliver into yarn. Tend machines with multiple winding units that wind thread onto shuttle bobbins for use on sewing machines or other kinds of bobbins for sole-stitching, knitting, or weaving machinery. Place bobbins on spindles and insert spindles into bobbin-winding machines. Tend machines that twist together two or more strands of yarn or insert additional twists into single strands of yarn to increase strength, smoothness, or uniformity of yarn. Clean, oil, and lubricate machines, using air hoses, cleaning solutions, rags, oilcans, and grease guns. Inspect machinery to determine whether repairs are needed. Record production data such as numbers and types of bobbins wound. Operate machines for test runs to verify adjustments and to obtain product samples. Repair or replace worn or defective parts or components, using hand tools. Notify supervisors or mechanics of equipment malfunctions. Adjust machine settings such as speed or tension to produce products that meet specifications. Inspect products to verify that they meet specifications and to determine whether machine adjustment is needed. Install, level, and align machine components such as gears, chains, guides, dies, cutters, or needles to set up machinery for operation. Measure bobbins periodically, using gauges, and turn screws to adjust tension if bobbins are not of specified size. Observe bobbins as they are winding and cut threads to remove loaded bobbins, using knives.

GOE Information—Interest Area: 13. Manufacturing. **Work Group:** 13.02. Machine Setup and Operation. **Personality Type—**Realistic. Realistic occupations frequently involve work activities that include practical, hands-on problems and solutions. They often deal with plants; animals; and real-world materials like wood, tools, and machinery. Many of the occupations require working outside and do

not involve a lot of paperwork or working closely with others. **Work Values—**Moral Values; Supervision, Technical; Supervision, Human Relations; Independence; Company Policies and Practices; Activity. **Skills—**Operation Monitoring; Installation; Operation and Control; Equipment Maintenance; Repairing; Quality Control Analysis. **Abilities—***Cognitive:* Visualization; Information Ordering. *Psychomotor:* Control Precision; Arm-Hand Steadiness; Reaction Time; Wrist-Finger Speed; Manual Dexterity; Finger Dexterity. *Physical:* Extent Flexibility; Static Strength; Trunk Strength. *Sensory:* Visual Color Discrimination. **General Work Activities—***Information Input:* Inspecting Equipment, Structures, or Materials; Monitoring Processes, Materials, or Surroundings; Identifying Objects, Actions, and Events. *Mental Process:* Updating and Using Relevant Knowledge; Evaluating Information Against Standards. *Work Output:* Repairing and Maintaining Mechanical Equipment; Handling and Moving Objects; Controlling Machines and Processes. *Interacting with Others:* Communicating with Other Workers. **Physical Work Conditions—**Indoors; Hazardous Equipment; Minor Burns, Cuts, Bites, or Stings; Standing; Using Hands on Objects, Tools, or Controls; Repetitive Motions. **Other Job Characteristics—**Need to Be Exact or Accurate; Automation.

Experience—Job Zone 3. Previous work-related skill, knowledge, or experience is required. **Job Preparation—**SVP 6.0 to less than 7.0—more than one year and less than four years. **Knowledges—**Mechanical Devices; Design. **Instructional Program—**Industrial Mechanics and Maintenance Technology.

Related SOC Job—51-6064 Textile Winding, Twisting, and Drawing Out Machine Setters, Operators, and Tenders. **Related OOH Job—**Textile, Apparel, and Furnishings Occupations. **Related DOT Jobs—**554.665-010 Calender-Wind-Up Tender; 557.685-034 Take-Up Operator; 580.685-034 Hooking-Machine Operator; 581.685-074 Winding-Rack Operator; 583.685-122 Trimming-Machine Operator; 589.360-010 Bonding-Machine Setter; 680.585-010 Batting-Machine Operator; 680.585-014 Staple-Processing-Machine Operator; 680.665-014 Draw-Machine Operator; 680.685-034 Draw-Frame Tender; 680.685-038 Drawing-Frame Tender; 680.685-042 Finisher-Card Tender; 680.685-058 Gill-Box Tender; others.

51-6091.00 Extruding and Forming Machine Setters, Operators, and Tenders, Synthetic and Glass Fibers

- **Education/Training Required: Moderate-term on-the-job training**
- **Employed: 23,040**
- **Annual Earnings: $28,750**
- **Growth: −25.3%**
- **Annual Job Openings: 2,000**

Set up, operate, or tend machines that extrude and form continuous filaments from synthetic materials, such as liquid polymer, rayon, and fiberglass.

Wipe finish rollers with cloths and wash finish trays with water when necessary. Set up, operate, or tend machines that extrude and form filaments from synthetic materials such as rayon, fiberglass, or liquid polymers. Remove excess, entangled, or completed filaments from machines, using hand tools. Open cabinet doors to cut multifilament threadlines away from guides, using scissors. Record operational data on tags and attach tags to machines. Record details of machine malfunctions. Notify other workers of defects and direct them to adjust extruding and forming machines. Clean and maintain extruding and forming machines, using hand tools. Start metering pumps and observe operation of machines and equipment to ensure continuous flow of filaments extruded through spinnerettes and to detect processing defects. Remove polymer deposits from spinnerettes and equipment, using silicone spray, brass chisels, and bronze-wool pads. Move controls to activate and adjust extruding and forming machines. Turn rheostats to obtain specified temperatures in electric furnaces where glass is melted. Pull extruded fiberglass filaments over sleeves where binding solution is applied and then into grooves of graphite shoes that bind filaments into single strands of sliver. Load materials into extruding and forming machines, using hand tools, and adjust feed mechanisms to set feed rates. Observe machine operations, control boards, and gauges to detect malfunctions such as clogged bushings and defective binder applicators. Turn petcocks to adjust the flow of binding fluid to sleeves. Observe flow of finish across finish rollers and turn valves to adjust flow to specifications. Pass sliver strands through openings in floors to workers on floors below who wind slivers onto tubes. Press buttons to stop machines when processes are complete or when malfunctions are detected. Press metering-pump buttons and turn valves to stop flow of polymers. Lower pans inside cabinets to catch molten filaments until flow of polymer through packs has stopped.

GOE Information—Interest Area: 13. Manufacturing. **Work Group:** 13.03. Production Work, Assorted Materials Processing. **Personality Type**—Realistic. Realistic occupations frequently involve work activities that include practical, hands-on problems and solutions. They often deal with plants; animals; and real-world materials like wood, tools, and machinery. Many of the occupations require working outside and do not involve a lot of paperwork or working closely with others. **Work Values**—Moral Values; Supervision, Technical; Independence; Supervision, Human Relations; Company Policies and Practices; Activity. **Skills**—Operation Monitoring; Equipment Maintenance; Operation and Control. **Abilities**—*Cognitive:* Perceptual Speed. *Psychomotor:* Wrist-Finger Speed; Control Precision; Manual Dexterity. *Physical:* Static Strength; Extent Flexibility; Trunk Strength. *Sensory:* None met the criteria. **General Work Activities**—*Information Input:* Monitoring Processes, Materials, or Surroundings; Inspecting Equipment, Structures, or Materials; Getting Information. *Mental Process:* None met the criteria. *Work Output:* Handling and Moving Objects; Controlling Machines and Processes; Repairing and Maintaining Mechanical Equipment. *Interacting with Others:* Communicating with Other Workers. **Physical Work Conditions**—Indoors; Standing; Using Hands on Objects, Tools, or Controls; Repetitive Motions. **Other Job Characteristics**—Need to Be Exact or Accurate; Automation.

Experience—Job Zone 1. No previous work-related skill, knowledge, or experience is needed. **Job Preparation**—SVP below 4.0—less than six months. **Knowledges**—Mechanical Devices; Production and Processing. **Instructional Program**—No related CIP programs.

Related SOC Job—51-6091 Extruding and Forming Machine Setters, Operators, and Tenders, Synthetic and Glass Fibers. **Related OOH Job**—Textile, Apparel, and Furnishings Occupations. **Related DOT Jobs**—557.565-014 Synthetic-Filament Extruder; 557.665-010 Synthetic-Staple Extruder; 557.685-018 Processor; 557.685-022 Second-Floor Operator; 557.685-026 Spinner; 575.685-030 Fiber-Machine Tender; 575.685-082 Test-Skein Winder.

51-6092.00 Fabric and Apparel Patternmakers

- **Education/Training Required: Long-term on-the-job training**
- Employed: 9,650
- Annual Earnings: $31,340
- Growth: –30.5%
- Annual Job Openings: 1,000

Draw and construct sets of precision master fabric patterns or layouts. May also mark and cut fabrics and apparel.

Test patterns by making and fitting sample garments. Draw details on outlined parts to indicate where parts are to be joined, as well as the positions of pleats, pockets, buttonholes, and other features, using computers or drafting instruments. Determine the best layout of pattern pieces to minimize waste of material and mark fabric accordingly. Draw outlines of pattern parts by adapting or copying existing patterns or by drafting new patterns. Create a master pattern for each size within a range of garment sizes, using charts, drafting instruments, computers, or grading devices. Position and cut out master or sample patterns, using scissors and knives, or print out copies of patterns, using computers. Create a paper pattern from which to mass-produce a design concept. Discuss design specifications with designers and convert their original models of garments into patterns of separate parts that can be laid out on a length of fabric. Mark samples and finished patterns with information such as garment size, section, style, identification, and sewing instructions. Compute dimensions of patterns according to sizes, considering stretching of material. Examine sketches, sample articles, and design specifications to determine quantities, shapes, and sizes of pattern parts and to determine the amount of material or fabric required to make a product. Trace outlines of paper onto cardboard patterns and cut patterns into parts to make templates. Trace outlines of specified patterns onto material and cut fabric, using scissors.

GOE Information—Interest Area: 13. Manufacturing. **Work Group:** 13.09. Hands-On Work, Assorted Materials. **Personality Type**—Realistic. Realistic occupations frequently involve work activities that include practical, hands-on problems and solutions. They often deal with plants; animals; and real-world materials like wood, tools, and machinery. Many of the occupations require working outside and do not involve a lot of paperwork or working closely with others. **Work Values**—Independence; Moral Values; Working Conditions. **Skills**—Technology Design; Operations Analysis. **Abilities**—*Cognitive:* Visualization; Originality; Number Facility; Fluency of Ideas; Mathematical Reasoning; Category Flexibility. *Psychomotor:* Arm-Hand Steadiness; Finger Dexterity; Manual Dexterity; Control Precision; Multilimb Coordination. *Physical:* Trunk Strength. *Sensory:* Visual Color Discrimination; Depth Perception; Far Vision; Near Vision. **General Work Activities**—*Information Input:* Monitoring Processes, Materials, or Surroundings; Getting Information; Identifying Objects, Actions, and Events. *Mental Process:* Organizing, Planning, and Prioritizing; Thinking Creatively; Scheduling Work and Activities. *Work Output:* Interacting With Computers; Drafting and Specifying Technical Devices; Documenting or Recording Information. *Interacting with Others:* Communicating with Other Workers; Establishing and Maintaining Interpersonal Relationships; Interpreting the Meaning of Information to Others. **Physical Work Conditions**—Indoors; Sitting; Using Hands on Objects, Tools, or Controls; Repetitive Motions. **Other Job Characteristics**—Need to Be Exact or Accurate; Repeat Same Tasks.

Experience—Job Zone 3. Previous work-related skill, knowledge, or experience is required. **Job Preparation**—SVP 6.0 to less than 7.0—more than one year and less than four years. **Knowledges**—Design; Production and Processing; Clerical Practices; Administration and Management. **Instructional Program**—Apparel and Textile Manufacture.

Related SOC Job—51-6092 Fabric and Apparel Patternmakers. **Related OOH Job**—Textile, Apparel, and Furnishings Occupations. **Related DOT Jobs**—781.361-010 Assistant Designer; 781.361-014 Patternmaker; 781.381-010 Cartoon Designer; 781.381-022 Pattern Grader-Cutter; 781.381-030 Sail-Lay-Out Worker; 781.381-034 Grader Marker; 781.484-010 Pleat Patternmaker; 782.361-014 Embroidery Patternmaker; 784.361-010 Patternmaker; 788.281-010 Designer and Patternmaker; 789.381-014 Pattern Chart-Writer; 962.381-010 Draper.

51-6093.00 Upholsterers

- **Education/Training Required: Long-term on-the-job training**
- **Employed: 41,040**
- **Annual Earnings: $26,710**
- **Growth: –16.5%**
- **Annual Job Openings: 4,000**

Make, repair, or replace upholstery for household furniture or transportation vehicles.

Repair furniture frames and refinish exposed wood. Adjust or replace webbing, padding, or springs and secure them in place. Attach bindings or apply solutions to edges of cut material to prevent raveling. Attach fasteners, grommets, buttons, buckles, ornamental trim, and other accessories to covers or frames, using hand tools. Build furniture up with loose fiber stuffing, cotton, felt, or foam padding to form smooth rounded surfaces. Design upholstery cover patterns and cutting plans based on sketches, customer descriptions, or blueprints. Discuss upholstery fabrics, colors, and styles with customers and provide cost estimates. Examine furniture frames, upholstery, springs, and webbing to locate defects. Interweave and fasten strips of webbing to the backs and undersides of furniture, using small hand tools and fasteners. Fit, install, and secure material on frames, using hand tools, power tools, glue, cement, or staples. Maintain records of time required to perform each job. Pick up and deliver furniture. Draw cutting lines on material, following patterns, templates, sketches, or blueprints and using chalk, pencils, paint, or other methods. Stretch webbing and fabric, using webbing stretchers. Sew rips or tears in material or create tufting, using needles and thread. Remove covering, webbing, padding, and defective springs from workpieces, using hand tools such as hammers and tack pullers. Read work orders and apply knowledge and experience with materials to determine types and amounts of materials required to cover workpieces. Operate sewing machines or sew upholstery by hand to seam cushions and join various sections of covering material. Make, repair, or replace automobile upholstery and convertible and vinyl tops, using knowledge of fabric and upholstery methods. Measure and cut new covering materials, using patterns and measuring and cutting instruments and following sketches and design specifications. Make, restore, or create custom upholstered furniture, using hand tools and knowledge of fabrics and upholstery methods. Collaborate with interior designers to decorate rooms and coordinate furnishing fabrics.

GOE Information—**Interest Area:** 13. Manufacturing. **Work Group:** 13.11. Apparel, Shoes, Leather, and Fabric Care. **Personality Type**—Realistic. Realistic occupations frequently involve work activities that include practical, hands-on problems and solutions. They often deal with plants; animals; and real-world materials like wood, tools, and machinery. Many of the occupations require working outside and do not involve a lot of paperwork or working closely with others. **Work Values**—Autonomy; Independence; Creativity; Moral Values; Working Conditions. **Skills**—Repairing. **Abilities**—*Cognitive:* Visualization. *Psychomotor:* Wrist-Finger Speed; Manual Dexterity; Finger Dexterity; Arm-Hand Steadiness. *Physical:* Static Strength; Extent Flexibility; Dynamic Strength; Trunk Strength. *Sensory:* None met the criteria. **General Work Activities**—*Information Input:* Getting Information; Estimating the Needed Characteristics of Products, Events, or Information. *Mental Process:* Thinking Creatively; Organizing, Planning, and Prioritizing. *Work Output:* Handling and Moving Objects; Performing General Physical Activities; Drafting and Specifying Technical Devices. *Interacting with Others:* None met the criteria. **Physical Work Conditions**—Indoors; Standing; Kneeling, Crouching, Stooping, or Crawling; Using Hands on Objects, Tools, or Controls; Bending or Twisting the Body; Repetitive Motions. **Other Job Characteristics**—Need to Be Exact or Accurate.

Experience—Job Zone 3. Previous work-related skill, knowledge, or experience is required. **Job Preparation**—SVP 6.0 to less than 7.0—more than one year and less than four years. **Knowledges**—Building and Construction; Production and Processing. **Instructional Program**—Upholstery/Upholsterer.

Related SOC Job—51-6093 Upholsterers. **Related OOH Job**—Textile, Apparel, and Furnishings Occupations. **Related DOT Jobs**—780.381-010 Automobile Upholsterer; 780.381-014 Automobile-Upholsterer Apprentice; 780.381-018 Furniture Upholsterer; 780.381-022 Furniture-Upholsterer Apprentice; 780.381-026 Upholsterer, Limousine and Hearse; 780.381-034 Slipcover Cutter; 780.381-038 Upholsterer, Inside; 780.384-014 Upholsterer; 780.684-122 Upholstery Repairer.

51-6099.99 Textile, Apparel, and Furnishings Workers, All Other

- **Education/Training Required: Short-term on-the-job training**
- **Employed: 24,740**
- **Annual Earnings: $22,900**
- **Growth: –29.8%**
- **Annual Job Openings: 3,000**

All textile, apparel, and furnishings workers not listed separately.

No task data available.

Note: The Department of Labor has not collected some data for this job, so it has fewer details than the other descriptions.

Related SOC Job—51-6099 Textile, Apparel, and Furnishings Workers, All Other. **Related OOH Job**—Textile, Apparel, and Furnishings Occupations. **Related DOT Jobs**—580.380-010 Fixer, Boarding Room; 585.681-010 Flesher; 585.681-014 Fur Plucker; 589.361-010 Fur Dresser; 589.685-086 Rolling-Down-Machine Operator; 683.582-010 Card Cutter, Jacquard; 712.281-014 Designer; 782.381-014 Oriental-Rug Repairer; 782.381-018 Rug Repairer; 782.684-042 Mender; 784.261-010 Milliner; 789.261-010 Boat-Canvas Maker-Installer; 789.381-018 Trawl Net Maker.

51-7000 Woodworkers

51-7011.00 Cabinetmakers and Bench Carpenters

- **Education/Training Required: Long-term on-the-job training**
- **Employed: 121,660**
- **Annual Earnings: $26,020**
- **Growth: 4.1%**
- **Annual Job Openings: 12,000**

Cut, shape, and assemble wooden articles or set up and operate a variety of woodworking machines such as power saws, jointers, and mortisers to surface, cut, or shape lumber or to fabricate parts for wood products.

Produce and assemble components of articles such as store fixtures, office equipment, cabinets, and high-grade furniture. Verify dimensions and check the quality and fit of pieces to ensure adherence to specifications. Set up and operate machines, including power saws, jointers, mortisers, tenoners, molders, and shapers, to cut, mold, and shape woodstock and wood substitutes. Measure and mark dimensions of parts on paper or lumber stock prior to cutting, following blueprints, to ensure a tight fit and quality product. Reinforce joints with nails or other fasteners to prepare articles for finishing. Attach parts and subassemblies together to form completed units, using glue, dowels, nails, screws, or clamps. Establish the specifications of articles to be constructed or repaired and plan the methods and operations for shaping and assembling parts, based on blueprints, drawings, diagrams, or oral or written instructions. Cut timber to the right size and shape and trim parts of joints to ensure a snug fit, using hand tools such as planes, chisels, or wood files. Trim, sand, and scrape surfaces and joints to prepare articles for finishing. Match materials for color, grain, and texture, giving attention to knots and other features of the wood. Bore holes for insertion of screws or dowels by hand or using boring machines. Program computers to operate machinery. Estimate the amounts, types, and costs of needed materials. Perform final touch-ups with sandpaper and steel wool. Install hardware such as hinges, handles, catches, and drawer pulls, using hand tools. Discuss projects with customers and draw up detailed specifications. Repair or alter wooden furniture, cabinetry, fixtures, paneling, and other pieces. Apply Masonite, formica, and vinyl surfacing materials. Design furniture, using computer-aided drawing programs. Dip, brush, or spray assembled articles with protective or decorative finishes such as stain, varnish, paint, or lacquer.

GOE Information—Interest Area: 13. Manufacturing. **Work Group:** 13.10. Woodworking Technology. **Personality Type**—Realistic. Realistic occupations frequently involve work activities that include practical, hands-on problems and solutions. They often deal with plants; animals; and real-world materials like wood, tools, and machinery. Many of the occupations require working outside and do not involve a lot of paperwork or working closely with others. **Work Values**—Independence; Moral Values; Recognition; Social Status; Supervision, Technical. **Skills**—Installation; Quality Control Analysis; Instructing; Mathematics; Equipment Maintenance. **Abilities**—*Cognitive:* Visualization; Selective Attention; Flexibility of Closure; Time Sharing; Speed of Closure; Information Ordering. *Psychomotor:* Reaction Time; Rate Control; Manual Dexterity; Response Orientation; Control Precision; Speed of Limb Movement. *Physical:* Static Strength; Dynamic Strength; Stamina; Extent Flexibility; Gross Body Coordination; Trunk Strength. *Sensory:* Visual Color Discrimination; Auditory Attention; Depth Perception; Hearing Sensitivity; Far Vision. **General Work Activities**—*Information Input:*

Monitoring Processes, Materials, or Surroundings; Identifying Objects, Actions, and Events; Inspecting Equipment, Structures, or Materials. *Mental Process:* Judging the Qualities of Things, Services, or Other People's Work; Organizing, Planning, and Prioritizing; Making Decisions and Solving Problems. *Work Output:* Handling and Moving Objects; Controlling Machines and Processes; Performing General Physical Activities. *Interacting with Others:* Coordinating the Work and Activities of Others; Establishing and Maintaining Interpersonal Relationships; Guiding, Directing, and Motivating Subordinates. **Physical Work Conditions**—Noisy; Contaminants; Hazardous Equipment; Standing; Walking and Running; Using Hands on Objects, Tools, or Controls. **Other Job Characteristics**—Need to Be Exact or Accurate; Pace Determined by Speed of Equipment; Repeat Same Tasks.

Experience—Job Zone 3. Previous work-related skill, knowledge, or experience is required. **Job Preparation**—SVP 6.0 to less than 7.0—more than one year and less than four years. **Knowledges**—Design; Production and Processing; Mechanical Devices; Building and Construction; Engineering and Technology; Mathematics. **Instructional Program**—Cabinetmaking and Millwork/Millwright.

Related SOC Job—51-7011 Cabinetmakers and Bench Carpenters. **Related OOH Job**—Woodworkers. **Related DOT Jobs**—660.280-010 Cabinetmaker; 660.280-014 Cabinetmaker Apprentice; 661.381-010 Hat-Block Maker; 669.380-010 Machinist Apprentice, Wood; 669.380-014 Machinist, Wood; 730.281-010 Accordion Maker; 730.281-022 Fretted-Instrument Maker, Hand; 730.281-030 Harp Maker; 730.281-034 Harpsichord Maker; 730.281-042 Pipe-Organ Builder; 730.281-046 Violin Maker, Hand; 730.281-058 Bow Maker; 761.281-010 Carver, Hand; 761.281-014 Experimental-Box Tester; 761.281-018 Marquetry Worker; 761.381-010 Boat-Oar Maker; others.

51-7021.00 Furniture Finishers

- **Education/Training Required: Long-term on-the-job training**
- **Employed: 24,610**
- **Annual Earnings: $24,600**
- **Growth: −13.3%**
- **Annual Job Openings: 2,000**

Shape, finish, and refinish damaged, worn, or used furniture or new high-grade furniture to specified color or finish.

Remove accessories prior to finishing and mask areas that should not be exposed to finishing processes or substances. Stencil, gild, emboss, mark, or paint designs or borders to reproduce the original appearance of restored pieces or to decorate new pieces. Spread graining ink over metal portions of furniture to simulate wood-grain finish. Replace or refurbish upholstery of items, using tacks, adhesives, softeners, solvents, stains, or polish. Disassemble items to prepare them for finishing, using hand tools. Examine furniture to determine the extent of damage or deterioration and to decide on the best method for repair or restoration. Fill and smooth cracks or depressions, remove marks and imperfections, and repair broken parts, using plastic or wood putty, glue, nails, and screws. Mix finish ingredients to obtain desired colors or shades. Remove excess solvent, using cloths soaked in paint thinner. Remove old finishes and damaged or deteriorated parts, using hand tools, stripping tools, sandpaper, steel wool, abrasives, solvents, and dip baths. Design, create, and decorate entire pieces or specific parts of furniture, such as draws for cabinets. Brush, spray, or hand-rub finishing ingredients, such as paint, oil, stain, or wax, onto and into wood grain; then apply lacquer or other sealers. Paint metal surfaces electrostatically or by using a spray gun or other painting equipment. Follow blueprints to produce specific designs. Distress surfaces with woodworking tools or abrasives before staining to create an antique appearance or rub surfaces to bring out highlights and shadings. Select appropriate finishing ingredients, such as paint, stain, lacquer, shellac, or varnish, depending on factors such as wood hardness and surface type. Confer with customers to determine furniture colors and finishes. Brush bleaching agents on wood surfaces to restore natural color. Wash surfaces to prepare them for finish application. Treat warped or stained surfaces to restore original contours and colors. Smooth, shape, and touch up surfaces to prepare them for finishing, using sandpaper, pumice stones, steel wool, chisels, sanders, or grinders.

GOE Information—Interest Area: 13. Manufacturing. **Work Group:** 13.10. Woodworking Technology. **Personality Type—**Realistic. Realistic occupations frequently involve work activities that include practical, hands-on problems and solutions. They often deal with plants; animals; and real-world materials like wood, tools, and machinery. Many of the occupations require working outside and do not involve a lot of paperwork or working closely with others. **Work Values—**Independence; Moral Values; Recognition; Creativity. **Skills—**Repairing; Equipment Selection. **Abilities—***Cognitive:* Visualization. *Psychomotor:* Wrist-Finger Speed; Manual Dexterity; Arm-Hand Steadiness; Finger Dexterity. *Physical:* Extent Flexibility. *Sensory:* Visual Color Discrimination. **General Work Activities—***Information Input:* Getting Information; Identifying Objects, Actions, and Events; Inspecting Equipment, Structures, or Materials. *Mental Process:* Judging the Qualities of Things, Services, or Other People's Work. *Work Output:* Handling and Moving Objects; Performing General Physical Activities. *Interacting with Others:* None met the criteria. **Physical Work Conditions—**Indoors; Contaminants; Hazardous Conditions; Standing; Kneeling, Crouching, Stooping, or Crawling; Using Hands on Objects, Tools, or Controls. **Other Job Characteristics—**None met the criteria.

Experience—Job Zone 2. Some previous work-related skill, knowledge, or experience may be helpful in these occupations, but usually is not needed. **Job Preparation—**SVP 4.0 to less than 6.0—six months to less than two years. **Knowledges—**Building and Construction; Chemistry. **Instructional Program—**Furniture Design and Manufacturing.

Related SOC Job—51-7021 Furniture Finishers. **Related OOH Job—**Woodworkers. **Related DOT Jobs—**763.380-010 Furniture Restorer; 763.381-010 Furniture Finisher; 763.381-014 Furniture-Finisher Apprentice; 763.681-010 Frame Repairer; 763.684-022 Caner II; 763.684-034 Finish Patcher.

51-7031.00 Model Makers, Wood

- **Education/Training Required: Long-term on-the-job training**
- **Employed: 2,280**
- **Annual Earnings: $27,990**
- **Growth: 9.0%**
- **Annual Job Openings: 1,000**

Construct full-size and scale wooden precision models of products. Includes wood jig builders and loft workers.

Select wooden stock, determine layouts, and mark layouts of parts on stock, using precision equipment such as scribers, squares, and protractors. Mark identifying information on patterns, parts, and templates to indicate assembly methods and details. Construct wooden models, patterns, templates, full scale mock-ups, and molds for parts of products and production tools. Finish patterns or models with protective or decorative coatings such as shellac, lacquer, or wax. Fit, fasten, and assemble wood parts together to form patterns, models,

or sections, using glue, nails, dowels, bolts, screws, and other fasteners. Plan, lay out, and draw outlines of units, sectional patterns, or full-scale mock-ups of products. Read blueprints, drawings, or written specifications and consult with designers to determine sizes and shapes of patterns and required machine setups. Set up, operate, and adjust a variety of woodworking machines such as band saws and planers to cut and shape sections, parts, and patterns according to specifications. Trim, smooth, and shape surfaces and plane, shave, file, scrape, and sand models to attain specified shapes, using hand tools. Verify dimensions and contours of models during hand-forming processes, using templates and measuring devices. Build jigs that can be used as guides for assembling oversized or special types of box shooks. Fabricate work aids such as scrapers or templates. Issue patterns to designated machine operators. Maintain pattern records for reference.

GOE Information—Interest Area: 13. Manufacturing. **Work Group:** 13.10. Woodworking Technology. **Personality Type—**Realistic. Realistic occupations frequently involve work activities that include practical, hands-on problems and solutions. They often deal with plants; animals; and real-world materials like wood, tools, and machinery. Many of the occupations require working outside and do not involve a lot of paperwork or working closely with others. **Work Values—**Moral Values; Independence; Supervision, Technical. **Skills—**Operation and Control. **Abilities—***Cognitive:* Visualization. *Psychomotor:* Wrist-Finger Speed; Multilimb Coordination; Control Precision; Arm-Hand Steadiness. *Physical:* Extent Flexibility; Trunk Strength; Static Strength. *Sensory:* None met the criteria. **General Work Activities—***Information Input:* Getting Information; Estimating the Needed Characteristics of Products, Events, or Information; Identifying Objects, Actions, and Events. *Mental Process:* Making Decisions and Solving Problems; Evaluating Information Against Standards; Processing Information. *Work Output:* Handling and Moving Objects; Performing General Physical Activities; Drafting and Specifying Technical Devices. *Interacting with Others:* Communicating with Other Workers. **Physical Work Conditions—**Indoors; Minor Burns, Cuts, Bites, or Stings; Standing; Using Hands on Objects, Tools, or Controls. **Other Job Characteristics—**Need to Be Exact or Accurate.

Experience—Job Zone 4. A minimum of two to four years of work-related skill, knowledge, or experience is needed. **Job Preparation—**SVP 7.0 to less than 8.0—two years to less than 10 years. **Knowledges—**Building and Construction; Design; Mechanical Devices; Engineering and Technology. **Instructional Program—**Cabinetmaking and Millwork/Millwright.

Related SOC Job—51-7031 Model Makers, Wood. **Related OOH Job—**Woodworkers. **Related DOT Jobs—**661.281-010 Loft Worker; 661.380-010 Model Maker, Wood; 693.261-018 Model Maker; 761.381-014 Jig Builder.

51-7032.00 Patternmakers, Wood

- **Education/Training Required: Long-term on-the-job training**
- **Employed: 2,000**
- **Annual Earnings: $28,660**
- **Growth: 3.3%**
- **Annual Job Openings: Fewer than 500**

Plan, lay out, and construct wooden unit or sectional patterns used in forming sand molds for castings.

Read blueprints, drawings, or written specifications to determine sizes and shapes of patterns and required machine setups. Lay out patterns on wood stock and draw outlines of units, sectional patterns, or full-scale mock-ups of products based on blueprint specifications and sketches, using marking and measuring devices. Verify dimensions of completed patterns, using templates, straightedges, calipers, or protractors. Set up, operate, and adjust a variety of woodworking machines such as band saws and lathes to cut and shape sections, parts, and patterns according to specifications. Trim, smooth, and shape surfaces and plane, shave, file, scrape, and sand models to attain specified shapes, using hand tools. Fit, fasten, and assemble wood parts together to form patterns, models, or sections, using glue, nails, dowels, bolts, and screws. Correct patterns to compensate for defects in castings. Construct wooden models, templates, full-scale mock-ups, jigs, or molds for shaping parts of products. Compute dimensions, areas, volumes, and weights. Mark identifying information such as colors or codes on patterns, parts, and templates to indicate assembly methods. Finish completed products or models with shellac, lacquer, wax, or paint. Glue fillets along interior angles of patterns. Select lumber to be used for patterns. Repair broken or damaged patterns. Maintain pattern records for reference. Inventory equipment and supplies, ordering parts and tools as necessary. Estimate costs for patternmaking jobs. Divide patterns into sections according to shapes of castings to facilitate removal of patterns from molds. Issue patterns to designated machine operators. Collect and store patterns and lumber.

GOE Information—Interest Area: 13. Manufacturing. **Work Group:** 13.10. Woodworking Technology. **Personality Type—**Realistic. Realistic occupations frequently involve work activities that include practical, hands-on problems and solutions. They often deal with plants; animals; and real-world materials like wood, tools, and machinery. Many of the occupations require working outside and do not involve a lot of paperwork or working closely with others. **Work Values—**Moral Values; Independence; Supervision, Technical. **Skills—**Mathematics; Repairing; Equipment Maintenance; Quality Control Analysis; Management of Material Resources; Troubleshooting. **Abilities—***Cognitive:* Visualization; Perceptual Speed; Number Facility; Time Sharing; Selective Attention. *Psychomotor:* Reaction Time; Control Precision; Response Orientation; Speed of Limb Movement; Manual Dexterity; Arm-Hand Steadiness. *Physical:* Static Strength; Extent Flexibility; Trunk Strength. *Sensory:* Auditory Attention; Depth Perception; Visual Color Discrimination; Hearing Sensitivity; Far Vision; Near Vision. **General Work Activities—***Information Input:* Inspecting Equipment, Structures, or Materials; Getting Information; Monitoring Processes, Materials, or Surroundings. *Mental Process:* Thinking Creatively; Updating and Using Relevant Knowledge; Organizing, Planning, and Prioritizing. *Work Output:* Handling and Moving Objects; Controlling Machines and Processes; Drafting and Specifying Technical Devices. *Interacting with Others:* Establishing and Maintaining Interpersonal Relationships; Communicating with Other Workers; Coaching and Developing Others. **Physical Work Conditions—**Noisy; Contaminants; Hazardous Equipment; Minor Burns, Cuts, Bites, or Stings; Standing; Using Hands on Objects, Tools, or Controls. **Other Job Characteristics—**Need to Be Exact or Accurate.

Experience—Job Zone 3. Previous work-related skill, knowledge, or experience is required. **Job Preparation—**SVP 6.0 to less than 7.0—more than one year and less than four years. **Knowledges—**Mechanical Devices; Design; Engineering and Technology; Building and Construction; Production and Processing; Mathematics. **Instructional Program—**Cabinetmaking and Millwork/Millwright.

Related SOC Job—51-7032 Patternmakers, Wood. **Related OOH Job—**Woodworkers. **Related DOT Jobs—**661.281-018 Patternmaker Apprentice, Wood; 661.281-022 Patternmaker, Wood.

51-7041.00 Sawing Machine Setters, Operators, and Tenders, Wood

- **Education/Training Required: Moderate-term on-the-job training**
- **Employed: 60,280**
- **Annual Earnings: $23,200**
- **Growth: −11.3%**
- **Annual Job Openings: 11,000**

Set up, operate, or tend wood sawing machines. Includes head sawyers.

Adjust saw blades by using wrenches and rulers or by turning handwheels or pressing pedals, levers, or panel buttons. Inspect and measure workpieces to mark for cuts and to verify the accuracy of cuts, using rulers, squares, or caliper rules. Examine logs or lumber to plan the best cuts. Set up, operate, or tend saws and machines that cut or trim wood to specified dimensions, such as circular saws, band saws, multiple-blade sawing machines, scroll saws, ripsaws, and crozer machines. Inspect stock for imperfections and to estimate grades or qualities of stock or workpieces. Operate panelboards of saw and conveyor systems to move stock through processes and to cut stock to specified dimensions. Mount and bolt sawing blades or attachments to machine shafts. Monitor sawing machines, adjusting speed and tension and clearing jams to ensure proper operation. Select saw blades, types and grades of stock, and cutting procedures to be used according to work orders or supervisors' instructions. Guide workpieces against saws, guide saw over workpieces by hand, or operate automatic feeding devices to guide cuts. Adjust bolts, clamps, stops, guides, and table angles and heights, using hand tools. Sharpen blades or replace defective or worn blades and bands, using hand tools. Count, sort, and stack finished workpieces. Lubricate and clean machines, using wrenches, grease guns, and solvents. Clear machine jams, using hand tools. Dispose of waste material after completing work assignments. Measure and mark stock for cuts. Examine blueprints, drawings, work orders, or patterns to determine equipment setup and selection details, procedures to be used, and dimensions of final products. Pull tables back against stops and depress pedals to advance cutterheads that shape stock ends. Trim lumber to straighten rough edges and remove defects, using circular saws. Position and clamp stock on tables, conveyors, or carriages, using hoists, guides, stops, dogs, wedges, and wrenches. Cut grooves, bevels, and miters; saw curved or irregular designs; and sever or shape metals, according to specifications or work orders.

GOE Information—Interest Area: 13. Manufacturing. **Work Group:** 13.03. Production Work, Assorted Materials Processing. **Personality Type—**Realistic. Realistic occupations frequently involve work activities that include practical, hands-on problems and solutions. They often deal with plants; animals; and real-world materials like wood, tools, and machinery. Many of the occupations require working outside and do not involve a lot of paperwork or working closely with others. **Work Values—**Independence; Moral Values; Supervision, Technical; Company Policies and Practices; Activity; Supervision, Human Relations. **Skills—**Equipment Maintenance; Repairing; Operation Monitoring; Operation and Control; Systems Analysis; Installation. **Abilities—***Cognitive:* Perceptual Speed; Visualization; Flexibility of Closure; Selective Attention. *Psychomotor:* Reaction Time; Multilimb Coordination; Rate Control; Control Precision; Arm-Hand Steadiness; Response Orientation. *Physical:* Stamina; Static Strength; Trunk Strength. *Sensory:* Depth Perception; Hearing Sensitivity; Visual Color Discrimination; Auditory Attention. **General Work Activities—***Information Input:* Monitoring Processes,

Materials, or Surroundings; Inspecting Equipment, Structures, or Materials; Identifying Objects, Actions, and Events. *Mental Process:* Judging the Qualities of Things, Services, or Other People's Work; Organizing, Planning, and Prioritizing; Making Decisions and Solving Problems. *Work Output:* Handling and Moving Objects; Controlling Machines and Processes; Performing General Physical Activities. *Interacting with Others:* Establishing and Maintaining Interpersonal Relationships; Communicating with Other Workers; Assisting and Caring for Others. **Physical Work Conditions**—Noisy; Contaminants; Hazardous Equipment; Using Hands on Objects, Tools, or Controls; Repetitive Motions. **Other Job Characteristics**—Need to Be Exact or Accurate; Pace Determined by Speed of Equipment; Repeat Same Tasks; Errors Have Important Consequences.

Experience—Job Zone 2. Some previous work-related skill, knowledge, or experience may be helpful in these occupations, but usually is not needed. **Job Preparation**—SVP 4.0 to less than 6.0—six months to less than two years. **Knowledges**—Mechanical Devices; Production and Processing; Design; Engineering and Technology. **Instructional Program**—Cabinetmaking and Millwork/Millwright.

Related SOC Job—51-7041 Sawing Machine Setters, Operators, and Tenders, Wood. **Related OOH Job**—Woodworkers. **Related DOT Jobs**—665.685-046 Shaping Machine Tender; 667.382-010 Stock Grader; 667.482-014 Pocket Cutter; 667.482-018 Stock Cutter; 667.485-010 Shingle Sawyer; 667.662-010 Head Sawyer; 667.662-014 Machine-Tank Operator; 667.682-010 Band-Scroll-Saw Operator; 667.682-014 Bottom-Saw Operator; 667.682-018 Corner-Trimmer Operator; 667.682-022 Cut-Off-Saw Operator I; 667.682-026 Edger, Automatic; 667.682-030 Gang Sawyer; 667.682-034 Head Sawyer, Automatic; 667.682-038 Heading-Saw Operator; 667.682-042 Jigsaw Operator; others.

51-7042.00 Woodworking Machine Setters, Operators, and Tenders, Except Sawing

- **Education/Training Required: Moderate-term on-the-job training**
- **Employed: 94,690**
- **Annual Earnings: $23,400**
- **Growth: –11.0%**
- **Annual Job Openings: 13,000**

Set up, operate, or tend woodworking machines, such as drill presses, lathes, shapers, routers, sanders, planers, and wood-nailing machines.

Start machines, adjust controls, and make trial cuts to ensure that machinery is operating properly. Determine product specifications and materials, work methods, and machine setup requirements according to blueprints, oral or written instructions, drawings, or work orders. Feed stock through feed mechanisms or conveyors into planing, shaping, boring, mortising, or sanding machines to produce desired components. Adjust machine tables or cutting devices and set controls on machines to produce specified cuts or operations. Set up, program, operate, or tend computerized or manual woodworking machines, such as drill presses, lathes, shapers, routers, sanders, planers, and wood-nailing machines. Monitor operation of machines and make adjustments to correct problems and ensure conformance to specifications. Select knives, saws, blades, cutter heads, cams, bits, or belts according to workpiece, machine functions, and product specifications. Examine finished workpieces for smoothness, shape, angle, depth of cut, and conformity to specifications and verify dimensions visually and by using hands, rules, calipers, templates, or gauges.

Install and adjust blades, cutterheads, boring bits, or sanding belts, using hand tools and rules. Inspect and mark completed workpieces and stack them on pallets, in boxes, or on conveyors so that they can be moved to the next workstation. Push or hold workpieces against, under, or through cutting, boring, or shaping mechanisms. Change alignment and adjustment of sanding, cutting, or boring machine guides to prevent defects in finished products, using hand tools. Inspect pulleys, drive belts, guards, and fences on machines to ensure that machines will operate safely. Remove and replace worn parts, bits, belts, sandpaper, and shaping tools. Secure woodstock against a guide or in a holding device, place woodstock on a conveyor, or dump woodstock in a hopper to feed woodstock into machines. Clean and maintain products, machines, and work areas. Attach and adjust guides, stops, clamps, chucks, and feed mechanisms, using hand tools. Examine raw woodstock for defects and to ensure conformity to size and other specification standards.

GOE Information—**Interest Area:** 13. Manufacturing. **Work Group:** 13.03. Production Work, Assorted Materials Processing. **Personality Type**—Realistic. Realistic occupations frequently involve work activities that include practical, hands-on problems and solutions. They often deal with plants; animals; and real-world materials like wood, tools, and machinery. Many of the occupations require working outside and do not involve a lot of paperwork or working closely with others. **Work Values**—Independence; Moral Values; Supervision, Technical; Activity; Company Policies and Practices; Supervision, Human Relations. **Skills**—Equipment Maintenance; Operation Monitoring; Repairing; Operation and Control; Troubleshooting; Quality Control Analysis. **Abilities**—*Cognitive:* Visualization; Selective Attention; Perceptual Speed; Time Sharing; Speed of Closure; Number Facility. *Psychomotor:* Reaction Time; Rate Control; Response Orientation; Control Precision; Wrist-Finger Speed; Manual Dexterity. *Physical:* Dynamic Strength; Static Strength; Extent Flexibility; Trunk Strength; Gross Body Coordination. *Sensory:* Auditory Attention; Depth Perception; Hearing Sensitivity; Visual Color Discrimination; Far Vision. **General Work Activities**—*Information Input:* Monitoring Processes, Materials, or Surroundings; Inspecting Equipment, Structures, or Materials; Getting Information. *Mental Process:* Making Decisions and Solving Problems; Judging the Qualities of Things, Services, or Other People's Work; Processing Information. *Work Output:* Handling and Moving Objects; Controlling Machines and Processes; Repairing and Maintaining Mechanical Equipment. *Interacting with Others:* Communicating with Other Workers; Establishing and Maintaining Interpersonal Relationships; Assisting and Caring for Others. **Physical Work Conditions**—Noisy; Contaminants; Hazardous Equipment; Standing; Using Hands on Objects, Tools, or Controls; Repetitive Motions. **Other Job Characteristics**—Need to Be Exact or Accurate; Pace Determined by Speed of Equipment; Repeat Same Tasks.

Experience—Job Zone 2. Some previous work-related skill, knowledge, or experience may be helpful in these occupations, but usually is not needed. **Job Preparation**—SVP 4.0 to less than 6.0—six months to less than two years. **Knowledges**—Production and Processing; Mechanical Devices; Design; Mathematics. **Instructional Programs**—Cabinetmaking and Millwork/Millwright; Woodworking, General.

Related SOC Job—51-7042 Woodworking Machine Setters, Operators, and Tenders, Except Sawing. **Related OOH Job**—Woodworkers. **Related DOT Jobs**—564.682-010 Chipping-Machine Operator; 569.662-010 Incising-Machine Operator; 569.685-014 Bender, Machine; 662.682-010 Molding Sander; 662.682-014 Multiple-Drum Sander; 662.682-018 Stroke-Belt-Sander Operator; 662.685-010 Cork Grinder; 662.685-014 Cylinder-Sander Operator; 662.685-018 Last Scourer; 662.685-022 Sanding-Machine Buffer; 662.685-026

Sanding-Machine Tender; 662.685-030 Sizing-Machine Tender; 662.685-034 Speed-Belt-Sander Tender; 662.685-038 Turning-Sander Tender; others.

51-7099.99 Woodworkers, All Other

- **Education/Training Required: Moderate-term on-the-job training**
- **Employed: 10,550**
- **Annual Earnings: $21,210**
- **Growth: –13.9%**
- **Annual Job Openings: 5,000**

All woodworkers not listed separately.

No task data available.

Note: The Department of Labor has not collected some data for this job, so it has fewer details than the other descriptions.

Related SOC Job—51-7099 Woodworkers, All Other. **Related OOH Job**—Woodworkers. **Related DOT Jobs**—149.281-010 Furniture Reproducer; 661.280-010 Patternmaker; 661.281-014 Loft Worker Apprentice; 761.381-022 Pattern Marker I.

51-8000 Plant and System Operators

51-8011.00 Nuclear Power Reactor Operators

- **Education/Training Required: Long-term on-the-job training**
- **Employed: 3,730**
- **Annual Earnings: $66,230**
- **Growth: –0.5%**
- **Annual Job Openings: 1,000**

Control nuclear reactors.

Adjust controls to position rod and to regulate flux level, reactor period, coolant temperature, and rate of power flow, following standard procedures. Respond to system or unit abnormalities, diagnosing the cause and recommending or taking corrective action. Monitor all systems for normal running conditions, performing activities such as checking gauges to assess output or assess the effects of generator loading on other equipment. Implement operational procedures such as those controlling startup and shutdown activities. Note malfunctions of equipment, instruments, or controls and report these conditions to supervisors. Monitor and operate boilers, turbines, wells, and auxiliary power plant equipment. Dispatch orders and instructions to personnel through radiotelephone or intercommunication systems to coordinate auxiliary equipment operation. Record operating data such as the results of surveillance tests. Participate in nuclear fuel element handling activities such as preparation, transfer, loading, and unloading. Conduct inspections and operations outside of control rooms as necessary. Direct reactor operators in emergency situations in accordance with emergency operating procedures. Authorize maintenance activities on units and changes in equipment and system operational status.

GOE Information—Interest Area: 13. Manufacturing. **Work Group:** 13.16. Utility Operation and Energy Distribution. **Personality Type—**

Realistic. Realistic occupations frequently involve work activities that include practical, hands-on problems and solutions. They often deal with plants; animals; and real-world materials like wood, tools, and machinery. Many of the occupations require working outside and do not involve a lot of paperwork or working closely with others. **Work Values**—Supervision, Technical; Supervision, Human Relations; Authority; Advancement; Co-workers; Compensation. **Skills**—Operation Monitoring; Operation and Control; Science; Systems Analysis; Troubleshooting; Equipment Maintenance. **Abilities**—*Cognitive:* Perceptual Speed; Time Sharing; Selective Attention; Problem Sensitivity; Speed of Closure; Flexibility of Closure. *Psychomotor:* Response Orientation; Reaction Time; Control Precision; Arm-Hand Steadiness. *Physical:* None met the criteria. *Sensory:* Auditory Attention; Hearing Sensitivity; Speech Clarity; Far Vision; Near Vision. **General Work Activities**—*Information Input:* Monitoring Processes, Materials, or Surroundings; Inspecting Equipment, Structures, or Materials; Identifying Objects, Actions, and Events. *Mental Process:* Evaluating Information Against Standards; Processing Information; Updating and Using Relevant Knowledge. *Work Output:* Controlling Machines and Processes; Documenting or Recording Information; Interacting With Computers. *Interacting with Others:* Communicating with Other Workers; Establishing and Maintaining Interpersonal Relationships; Coaching and Developing Others. **Physical Work Conditions**—Indoors; Noisy; Radiation; Hazardous Conditions; Hazardous Equipment; Using Hands on Objects, Tools, or Controls. **Other Job Characteristics**—Need to Be Exact or Accurate; Errors Have Important Consequences; Repeat Same Tasks; Automation.

Experience—Job Zone 3. Previous work-related skill, knowledge, or experience is required. **Job Preparation**—SVP 6.0 to less than 7.0—more than one year and less than four years. **Knowledges**—Physics; Engineering and Technology; Chemistry; Mechanical Devices; Public Safety and Security; Design. **Instructional Program**—Nuclear/Nuclear Power Technology/Technician.

Related SOC Job—51-8011 Nuclear Power Reactor Operators. **Related OOH Job**—Power Plant Operators, Distributors, and Dispatchers. **Related DOT Job**—952.362-022 Power-Reactor Operator.

51-8012.00 Power Distributors and Dispatchers

- **Education/Training Required: Long-term on-the-job training**
- **Employed: 7,520**
- **Annual Earnings: $59,160**
- **Growth: 0.0%**
- **Annual Job Openings: 1,000**

Coordinate, regulate, or distribute electricity or steam.

Respond to emergencies, such as transformer or transmission line failures, and route current around affected areas. Prepare switching orders that will isolate work areas without causing power outages, referring to drawings of power systems. Control, monitor, or operate equipment that regulates or distributes electricity or steam, using data obtained from instruments or computers. Coordinate with engineers, planners, field personnel, and other utility workers to provide information such as clearances, switching orders, and distribution process changes. Direct personnel engaged in controlling and operating distribution equipment and machinery, for example, instructing control room operators to start boilers and generators. Distribute and regulate the flow of power between entities such as generating stations, substations, distribution lines, and users, keeping track of the status of circuits and connections. Monitor and record switch-board and control board readings to ensure that electrical or steam distribution equipment is operating properly. Track conditions that could affect power needs, such as changes in the weather, and adjust equipment to meet any anticipated changes. Manipulate controls to adjust and activate power distribution equipment and machines. Calculate and determine load estimates or equipment requirements to determine required control settings. Record and compile operational data, such as chart and meter readings, power demands, and usage and operating times, using transmission system maps. Inspect equipment to ensure that specifications are met and to detect any defects. Tend auxiliary equipment used in the power distribution process. Accept and implement energy schedules, including real-time transmission reservations and schedules. Repair, maintain, and clean equipment and machinery, using hand tools.

GOE Information—Interest Area: 13. Manufacturing. **Work Group:** 13.16. Utility Operation and Energy Distribution. **Personality Type—** Realistic. Realistic occupations frequently involve work activities that include practical, hands-on problems and solutions. They often deal with plants; animals; and real-world materials like wood, tools, and machinery. Many of the occupations require working outside and do not involve a lot of paperwork or working closely with others. **Work Values—**Authority; Supervision, Technical; Security; Supervision, Human Relations; Compensation; Company Policies and Practices. **Skills—**Operation Monitoring; Operation and Control; Troubleshooting; Systems Analysis; Repairing; Technology Design. **Abilities—***Cognitive:* Perceptual Speed; Mathematical Reasoning; Flexibility of Closure; Number Facility; Category Flexibility; Written Expression. *Psychomotor:* Finger Dexterity. *Physical:* None met the criteria. *Sensory:* Far Vision; Visual Color Discrimination; Speech Clarity; Near Vision; Speech Recognition. **General Work Activities—** *Information Input:* Monitoring Processes, Materials, or Surroundings; Identifying Objects, Actions, and Events; Estimating the Needed Characteristics of Products, Events, or Information. *Mental Process:* Making Decisions and Solving Problems; Analyzing Data or Information; Evaluating Information Against Standards. *Work Output:* Documenting or Recording Information; Interacting With Computers; Controlling Machines and Processes. *Interacting with Others:* Communicating with Other Workers; Coordinating the Work and Activities of Others; Establishing and Maintaining Interpersonal Relationships. **Physical Work Conditions—**Indoors; Sitting; Using Hands on Objects, Tools, or Controls. **Other Job Characteristics—** Errors Have Important Consequences; Need to Be Exact or Accurate; Repeat Same Tasks.

Experience—Job Zone 3. Previous work-related skill, knowledge, or experience is required. **Job Preparation—**SVP 6.0 to less than 7.0— more than one year and less than four years. **Knowledges—**Public Safety and Security; Customer and Personal Service; Mechanical Devices; Telecommunications; Physics; Engineering and Technology. **Instructional Program—**No related CIP programs.

Related SOC Job—51-8012 Power Distributors and Dispatchers. **Related OOH Job—**Power Plant Operators, Distributors, and Dispatchers. **Related DOT Jobs—**820.662-010 Motor-Room Controller; 952.167-014 Load Dispatcher; 952.362-014 Feeder-Switchboard Operator; 952.362-026 Substation Operator; 952.362-030 Substation Operator Apprentice; 952.362-034 Switchboard Operator; 952.362-038 Switchboard Operator; 952.367-014 Switchboard Operator Assistant.

51-8013.00 Power Plant Operators

- **Education/Training Required: Long-term on-the-job training**
- **Employed: 33,650**
- **Annual Earnings: $53,170**
- **Growth: –0.4%**
- **Annual Job Openings: 5,000**

Control, operate, or maintain machinery to generate electric power. Includes auxiliary equipment operators.

Monitor and inspect power plant equipment and indicators to detect evidence of operating problems. Adjust controls to generate specified electrical power or to regulate the flow of power between generating stations and substations. Operate or control power-generating equipment, including boilers, turbines, generators, and reactors, using control boards or semi-automatic equipment. Regulate equipment operations and conditions such as water levels based on data from recording and indicating instruments or from computers. Take readings from charts, meters, and gauges at established intervals and take corrective steps as necessary. Inspect records and logbook entries and communicate with other plant personnel to assess equipment operating status. Start or stop generators, auxiliary pumping equipment, turbines, and other power plant equipment and connect or disconnect equipment from circuits. Control and maintain auxiliary equipment, such as pumps, fans, compressors, condensers, feedwater heaters, filters, and chlorinators, to supply water, fuel, lubricants, air, and auxiliary power. Clean, lubricate, and maintain equipment such as generators, turbines, pumps, and compressors to prevent equipment failure or deterioration. Communicate with systems operators to regulate and coordinate transmission loads and frequencies and line voltages. Record and compile operational data, completing and maintaining forms, logs, and reports. Open and close valves and switches in sequence upon signals from other workers to start or shut down auxiliary units. Collect oil, water, and electrolyte samples for laboratory analysis. Make adjustments or minor repairs, such as tightening leaking gland and pipe joints; report any needs for major repairs. Control generator output to match the phase, frequency, and voltage of electricity supplied to panels. Place standby emergency electrical generators on line in emergencies and monitor the temperature, output, and lubrication of the system. Receive outage calls and call in necessary personnel during power outages and emergencies.

GOE Information—Interest Area: 13. Manufacturing. **Work Group:** 13.16. Utility Operation and Energy Distribution. **Personality Type—** Realistic. Realistic occupations frequently involve work activities that include practical, hands-on problems and solutions. They often deal with plants; animals; and real-world materials like wood, tools, and machinery. Many of the occupations require working outside and do not involve a lot of paperwork or working closely with others. **Work Values—**Supervision, Technical; Moral Values; Supervision, Human Relations; Security. **Skills—**Operation Monitoring; Equipment Maintenance; Operation and Control; Technology Design; Systems Evaluation; Coordination. **Abilities—** *Cognitive:* Perceptual Speed; Time Sharing; Selective Attention; Flexibility of Closure; Visualization; Oral Expression. *Psychomotor:* Rate Control; Response Orientation; Reaction Time; Control Precision; Arm-Hand Steadiness; Manual Dexterity. *Physical:* Extent Flexibility; Stamina; Trunk Strength. *Sensory:* Auditory Attention; Depth Perception; Hearing Sensitivity; Visual Color Discrimination. **General Work Activities—***Information Input:* Monitoring Processes, Materials, or Surroundings; Identifying Objects, Actions, and Events; Inspecting Equipment, Structures, or Materials. *Mental Process:* Making Decisions and Solving Problems; Updating and Using

Relevant Knowledge; Evaluating Information Against Standards. *Work Output:* Controlling Machines and Processes; Handling and Moving Objects; Performing General Physical Activities. *Interacting with Others:* Establishing and Maintaining Interpersonal Relationships; Communicating with Other Workers; Teaching Others. **Physical Work Conditions**—Indoors; Noisy; Very Hot or Cold; Contaminants; High Places; Hazardous Conditions. **Other Job Characteristics**—Errors Have Important Consequences; Need to Be Exact or Accurate; Automation; Repeat Same Tasks.

Experience—Job Zone 3. Previous work-related skill, knowledge, or experience is required. **Job Preparation**—SVP 6.0 to less than 7.0—more than one year and less than four years. **Knowledges**—Physics; Mechanical Devices; Chemistry; Engineering and Technology; Public Safety and Security; Computers and Electronics. **Instructional Program**—No related CIP programs.

Related SOC Job—51-8013 Power Plant Operators. **Related OOH Job**—Power Plant Operators, Distributors, and Dispatchers. **Related DOT Jobs**—951.685-010 Firer, High Pressure; 952.362-010 Auxiliary-Equipment Operator; 952.362-018 Hydroelectric-Station Operator; 952.362-042 Turbine Operator; 952.382-010 Diesel-Plant Operator; 952.382-014 Power Operator; 952.382-018 Power-Plant Operator.

51-8021.00 Stationary Engineers and Boiler Operators

- **Education/Training Required: Long-term on-the-job training**
- **Employed: 43,110**
- **Annual Earnings: $44,600**
- **Growth: 3.4%**
- **Annual Job Openings: 5,000**

Operate or maintain stationary engines, boilers, or other mechanical equipment to provide utilities for buildings or industrial processes. Operate equipment such as steam engines, generators, motors, turbines, and steam boilers.

Operate or tend stationary engines; boilers; and auxiliary equipment such as pumps, compressors and air-conditioning equipment to supply and maintain steam or heat for buildings, marine vessels, or pneumatic tools. Observe and interpret readings on gauges, meters, and charts registering various aspects of boiler operation to ensure that boilers are operating properly. Test boiler water quality or arrange for testing and take any necessary corrective action, such as adding chemicals to prevent corrosion and harmful deposits. Activate valves to maintain required amounts of water in boilers, to adjust supplies of combustion air, and to control the flow of fuel into burners. Monitor boiler water, chemical, and fuel levels and make adjustments to maintain required levels. Fire coal furnaces by hand or with stokers and gas- or oil-fed boilers, using automatic gas feeds or oil pumps. Monitor and inspect equipment, computer terminals, switches, valves, gauges, alarms, safety devices, and meters to detect leaks or malfunctions and to ensure that equipment is operating efficiently and safely. Analyze problems and take appropriate action to ensure continuous and reliable operation of equipment and systems. Maintain daily logs of operation, maintenance, and safety activities, including test results, instrument readings, and details of equipment malfunctions and maintenance work. Adjust controls or valves on equipment to provide power and to regulate and set operations of system or industrial processes. Switch from automatic controls to manual controls and isolate equipment mechanically and electrically to allow for safe inspection and repair work. Clean and lubricate boilers and auxiliary equipment and make minor adjustments as needed,

using hand tools. Check the air quality of ventilation systems and make adjustments to ensure compliance with mandated safety codes. Perform or arrange for repairs, such as complete overhauls; replacement of defective valves, gaskets, or bearings; or fabrication of new parts. Weigh, measure, and record fuel used.

GOE Information—**Interest Area:** 13. Manufacturing. **Work Group:** 13.16. Utility Operation and Energy Distribution. **Personality Type**—Realistic. Realistic occupations frequently involve work activities that include practical, hands-on problems and solutions. They often deal with plants; animals; and real-world materials like wood, tools, and machinery. Many of the occupations require working outside and do not involve a lot of paperwork or working closely with others. **Work Values**—Supervision, Technical; Moral Values; Independence; Supervision, Human Relations. **Skills**—Repairing; Operation Monitoring; Equipment Maintenance; Installation; Systems Analysis; Operation and Control. **Abilities**—*Cognitive:* None met the criteria. *Psychomotor:* Control Precision; Manual Dexterity; Arm-Hand Steadiness; Multilimb Coordination; Finger Dexterity. *Physical:* Explosive Strength; Static Strength; Extent Flexibility; Trunk Strength. *Sensory:* None met the criteria. **General Work Activities**—*Information Input:* Monitoring Processes, Materials, or Surroundings; Inspecting Equipment, Structures, or Materials; Identifying Objects, Actions, and Events. *Mental Process:* Making Decisions and Solving Problems; Organizing, Planning, and Prioritizing; Updating and Using Relevant Knowledge. *Work Output:* Repairing and Maintaining Mechanical Equipment; Handling and Moving Objects; Performing General Physical Activities. *Interacting with Others:* Communicating with Other Workers; Coordinating the Work and Activities of Others; Establishing and Maintaining Interpersonal Relationships. **Physical Work Conditions**—Noisy; Very Hot or Cold; Very Bright or Dim Lighting; Contaminants; Hazardous Conditions; Hazardous Equipment. **Other Job Characteristics**—Need to Be Exact or Accurate; Errors Have Important Consequences; Automation.

Experience—Job Zone 3. Previous work-related skill, knowledge, or experience is required. **Job Preparation**—SVP 6.0 to less than 7.0—more than one year and less than four years. **Knowledges**—Mechanical Devices; Building and Construction; Chemistry; Physics; Design; Engineering and Technology. **Instructional Program**—No related CIP programs.

Related SOC Job—51-8021 Stationary Engineers and Boiler Operators. **Related OOH Job**—Stationary Engineers and Boiler Operators. **Related DOT Jobs**—553.685-066 Firer, Retort; 950.362-014 Refrigerating Engineer; 950.382-010 Boiler Operator; 950.382-018 Gas-Engine Operator; 950.382-026 Stationary Engineer; 950.382-030 Stationary-Engineer Apprentice; 950.485-010 Humidifier Attendant; 950.585-014 Boiler-Operator Helper; 950.685-010 Air-Compressor Operator; 950.685-014 Boiler-Room Helper; 951.685-014 Firer, Low Pressure; 951.685-018 Firer, Marine.

51-8031.00 Water and Liquid Waste Treatment Plant and System Operators

- **Education/Training Required: Long-term on-the-job training**
- **Employed: 102,940**
- **Annual Earnings: $34,930**
- **Growth: 16.2%**
- **Annual Job Openings: 6,000**

Operate or control an entire process or system of machines, often through the use of control boards, to transfer or treat water or liquid waste.

Add chemicals such as ammonia, chlorine, or lime to disinfect and deodorize water and other liquids. Operate and adjust controls on equipment to purify and clarify water, process or dispose of sewage, and generate power. Inspect equipment or monitor operating conditions, meters, and gauges to determine load requirements and detect malfunctions. Collect and test water and sewage samples, using test equipment and color analysis standards. Record operational data, personnel attendance, or meter and gauge readings on specified forms. Maintain, repair, and lubricate equipment, using hand tools and power tools. Clean and maintain tanks and filter beds, using hand tools and power tools. Direct and coordinate plant workers engaged in routine operations and maintenance activities.

GOE Information—Interest Area: 13. Manufacturing. **Work Group:** 13.16. Utility Operation and Energy Distribution. **Personality Type—**Realistic. Realistic occupations frequently involve work activities that include practical, hands-on problems and solutions. They often deal with plants; animals; and real-world materials like wood, tools, and machinery. Many of the occupations require working outside and do not involve a lot of paperwork or working closely with others. **Work Values—**Supervision, Technical; Security; Company Policies and Practices; Authority; Co-workers; Supervision, Human Relations. **Skills—**Operation Monitoring; Installation; Operation and Control; Troubleshooting; Management of Material Resources; Operations Analysis. **Abilities—***Cognitive:* Spatial Orientation; Flexibility of Closure; Selective Attention; Perceptual Speed; Time Sharing; Visualization. *Psychomotor:* Control Precision; Reaction Time; Multilimb Coordination; Response Orientation; Manual Dexterity; Rate Control. *Physical:* Extent Flexibility; Gross Body Coordination; Trunk Strength; Static Strength. *Sensory:* Glare Sensitivity; Depth Perception; Auditory Attention; Visual Color Discrimination; Hearing Sensitivity; Far Vision. **General Work Activities—***Information Input:* Monitoring Processes, Materials, or Surroundings; Identifying Objects, Actions, and Events; Inspecting Equipment, Structures, or Materials. *Mental Process:* Updating and Using Relevant Knowledge; Making Decisions and Solving Problems; Organizing, Planning, and Prioritizing. *Work Output:* Handling and Moving Objects; Performing General Physical Activities; Documenting or Recording Information. *Interacting with Others:* Communicating with Other Workers; Establishing and Maintaining Interpersonal Relationships; Monitoring and Controlling Resources. **Physical Work Conditions—**More Often Outdoors Than Indoors; Noisy; Very Hot or Cold; Contaminants; Minor Burns, Cuts, Bites, or Stings. **Other Job Characteristics—**Need to Be Exact or Accurate; Errors Have Important Consequences; Repeat Same Tasks; Automation.

Experience—Job Zone 3. Previous work-related skill, knowledge, or experience is required. **Job Preparation—**SVP 6.0 to less than 7.0—more than one year and less than four years. **Knowledges—**Biology; Chemistry; Physics; Public Safety and Security; Mechanical Devices; Law and Government. **Instructional Program—**Water Quality and Wastewater Treatment Management and Recycling Technology/Technician.

Related SOC Job—51-8031 Water and Liquid Waste Treatment Plant and System Operators. **Related OOH Job—**Water and Liquid Waste Treatment Plant and System Operators. **Related DOT Jobs—**954.382-010 Pump-Station Operator, Waterworks; 954.382-014 Water-Treatment-Plant Operator; 955.362-010 Wastewater-Treatment-Plant Operator; 955.382-010 Clarifying-Plant Operator; 955.382-014 Waste-Treatment Operator.

51-8091.00 Chemical Plant and System Operators

- **Education/Training Required: Long-term on-the-job training**
- **Employed: 58,640**
- **Annual Earnings: $46,710**
- **Growth: –17.7%**
- **Annual Job Openings: 8,000**

Control or operate an entire chemical process or system of machines.

Move control settings to make necessary adjustments on equipment units affecting speeds of chemical reactions, quality, and yields. Monitor recording instruments, flowmeters, panel lights, and other indicators and listen for warning signals to verify conformity of process conditions. Control or operate chemical processes or systems of machines, using panelboards, control boards, or semi-automatic equipment. Record operating data such as process conditions, test results, and instrument readings. Confer with technical and supervisory personnel to report or resolve conditions affecting safety, efficiency, and product quality. Draw samples of products and conduct quality control tests to monitor processing and to ensure that standards are met. Regulate or shut down equipment during emergency situations as directed by supervisory personnel. Start pumps to wash and rinse reactor vessels; to exhaust gases and vapors; to regulate the flow of oil, steam, air, and perfume to towers; and to add products to converter or blending vessels. Interpret chemical reactions visible through sight glasses or on television monitors and review laboratory test reports for process adjustments. Patrol work areas to ensure that solutions in tanks and troughs are not in danger of overflowing. Notify maintenance, stationary-engineering, and other auxiliary personnel to correct equipment malfunctions and to adjust power, steam, water, or air supplies. Direct workers engaged in operating machinery that regulates the flow of materials and products. Inspect operating units such as towers, soap-spray storage tanks, scrubbers, collectors, and driers to ensure that all are functioning and to maintain maximum efficiency. Turn valves to regulate flow of products or byproducts through agitator tanks, storage drums, or neutralizer tanks. Calculate material requirements or yields according to formulas. Gauge tank levels, using calibrated rods. Repair and replace damaged equipment. Defrost frozen valves, using steam hoses. Supervise the cleaning of towers, strainers, and spray tips.

GOE Information—Interest Area: 13. Manufacturing. **Work Group:** 13.16. Utility Operation and Energy Distribution. **Personality Type—**Realistic. Realistic occupations frequently involve work activities that include practical, hands-on problems and solutions. They often deal with plants; animals; and real-world materials like wood, tools, and machinery. Many of the occupations require working outside and do not involve a lot of paperwork or working closely with others. **Work Values—**Supervision, Technical; Compensation; Security; Supervision, Human Relations; Company Policies and Practices; Advancement. **Skills—**Operation Monitoring; Operation and Control; Troubleshooting; Equipment Maintenance; Systems Analysis; Science. **Abilities—***Cognitive:* Perceptual Speed; Selective Attention; Speed of Closure; Number Facility; Mathematical Reasoning; Problem Sensitivity. *Psychomotor:* Response Orientation; Reaction Time; Rate Control; Control Precision; Multilimb Coordination; Wrist-Finger Speed. *Physical:* Gross Body Equilibrium; Extent Flexibility; Gross Body Coordination; Stamina; Static Strength; Trunk Strength. *Sensory:* Auditory Attention; Hearing Sensitivity; Far Vision; Visual Color Discrimination; Depth Perception; Speech Clarity. **General Work Activities—***Information Input:* Monitoring

Processes, Materials, or Surroundings; Inspecting Equipment, Structures, or Materials; Identifying Objects, Actions, and Events. *Mental Process:* Updating and Using Relevant Knowledge; Making Decisions and Solving Problems; Processing Information. *Work Output:* Performing General Physical Activities; Controlling Machines and Processes; Handling and Moving Objects. *Interacting with Others:* Establishing and Maintaining Interpersonal Relationships; Communicating with Other Workers; Teaching Others. **Physical Work Conditions**—More Often Indoors Than Outdoors; Noisy; Very Hot or Cold; Contaminants; Hazardous Conditions. **Other Job Characteristics**—Need to Be Exact or Accurate; Errors Have Important Consequences; Pace Determined by Speed of Equipment; Repeat Same Tasks; Automation.

Experience—Job Zone 2. Some previous work-related skill, knowledge, or experience may be helpful in these occupations, but usually is not needed. **Job Preparation**—SVP 4.0 to less than 6.0—six months to less than two years. **Knowledges**—Production and Processing; Chemistry; Mechanical Devices; Physics; Engineering and Technology; Public Safety and Security. **Instructional Program**—Chemical Technology/Technician.

Related SOC Job—51-8091 Chemical Plant and System Operators. **Related OOH Job**—Chemical Plant and System Operators. **Related DOT Jobs**—558.260-010 Chief Operator; 559.165-010 Checker; 559.362-026 Plant Operator, Furnace Process; 559.382-010 Ammonia-Still Operator; 559.382-038 Naphtha-Washing-System Operator; 559.662-014 Wash Operator.

51-8092.00 Gas Plant Operators

- **Education/Training Required: Long-term on-the-job training**
- **Employed: 10,530**
- **Annual Earnings: $51,920**
- **Growth: 7.7%**
- **Annual Job Openings: 2,000**

Distribute or process gas for utility companies and others by controlling compressors to maintain specified pressures on main pipelines.

Determine causes of abnormal pressure variances and make corrective recommendations such as installation of pipes to relieve overloading. Distribute or process gas for utility companies or industrial plants, using panel boards, control boards, and semi-automatic equipment. Start and shut down plant equipment. Test gas, chemicals, and air during processing to assess factors such as purity and moisture content and to detect quality problems or gas or chemical leaks. Adjust temperature, pressure, vacuum, level, flow rate, and transfer of gas to maintain processes at required levels or to correct problems. Change charts in recording meters. Calculate gas ratios to detect deviations from specifications, using testing apparatus. Clean, maintain, and repair equipment, using hand tools, or request that repair and maintenance work be performed. Collaborate with other operators to solve unit problems. Monitor equipment functioning; observe temperature, level, and flow gauges; and perform regular unit checks to ensure that all equipment is operating as it should. Control fractioning columns, compressors, purifying towers, heat exchangers, and related equipment to extract nitrogen and oxygen from air. Control equipment to regulate flow and pressure of gas to feedlines of boilers, furnaces, and related steam-generating or heating equipment. Operate construction equipment to install and maintain gas distribution systems. Signal or direct workers who tend auxiliary equipment. Record, review, and compile operations records; test results; and gauge readings such as temperatures, pressures, concentrations, and flows. Read logsheets to determine prod-

uct demand and disposition or to detect malfunctions. Monitor transportation and storage of flammable and other potentially dangerous products to ensure that safety guidelines are followed. Contact maintenance crews when necessary. Control operation of compressors, scrubbers, evaporators, and refrigeration equipment to liquefy, compress, or regasify natural gas.

GOE Information—Interest Area: 13. Manufacturing. **Work Group:** 13.16. Utility Operation and Energy Distribution. **Personality Type**—Realistic. Realistic occupations frequently involve work activities that include practical, hands-on problems and solutions. They often deal with plants; animals; and real-world materials like wood, tools, and machinery. Many of the occupations require working outside and do not involve a lot of paperwork or working closely with others. **Work Values**—Security; Supervision, Technical; Supervision, Human Relations; Advancement; Company Policies and Practices; Moral Values. **Skills**—Operation Monitoring; Operation and Control; Repairing; Equipment Maintenance; Troubleshooting. **Abilities**—*Cognitive:* None met the criteria. *Psychomotor:* Control Precision. *Physical:* None met the criteria. *Sensory:* None met the criteria. **General Work Activities**—*Information Input:* Inspecting Equipment, Structures, or Materials; Monitoring Processes, Materials, or Surroundings; Getting Information. *Mental Process:* Evaluating Information Against Standards; Making Decisions and Solving Problems; Judging the Qualities of Things, Services, or Other People's Work. *Work Output:* Repairing and Maintaining Mechanical Equipment; Performing General Physical Activities; Handling and Moving Objects. *Interacting with Others:* Communicating with Other Workers. **Physical Work Conditions**—Indoors; Contaminants; Hazardous Conditions; Standing; Using Hands on Objects, Tools, or Controls. **Other Job Characteristics**—Need to Be Exact or Accurate; Errors Have Important Consequences; Automation.

Experience—Job Zone 3. Previous work-related skill, knowledge, or experience is required. **Job Preparation**—SVP 6.0 to less than 7.0—more than one year and less than four years. **Knowledges**—Mechanical Devices; Physics; Engineering and Technology; Production and Processing; Chemistry. **Instructional Program**—No related CIP programs.

Related SOC Job—51-8092 Gas Plant Operators. **Related OOH Job**—Gas Plant Operators. **Related DOT Jobs**—552.362-014 Oxygen-Plant Operator; 559.362-018 Liquefaction-Plant Operator; 953.362-010 Fuel Attendant; 953.362-014 Liquefaction-and-Regasification-Plant Operator; 953.362-018 Pressure Controller.

51-8093.00 Petroleum Pump System Operators, Refinery Operators, and Gaugers

- **Education/Training Required: Long-term on-the-job training**
- **Employed: 40,470**
- **Annual Earnings: $51,060**
- **Growth: –8.6%**
- **Annual Job Openings: 6,000**

Control the operation of petroleum-refining or -processing units. May specialize in controlling manifold and pumping systems, gauging or testing oil in storage tanks, or regulating the flow of oil into pipelines.

Calculate test result values, using standard formulas. Clamp seals around valves to secure tanks. Signal other workers by telephone or radio to operate pumps, open and close valves, and check temperatures. Start pumps and open valves or use automated equipment to regulate the flow of oil in pipelines and into and out of tanks. Synchronize activities with other pumphouses to ensure a continuous flow of products and a minimum of contamination between products. Verify that incoming and outgoing products are moving through the correct meters and that meters are working properly. Prepare calculations for receipts and deliveries of oil and oil products. Read automatic gauges at specified intervals to determine the flow rate of oil into or from tanks and the amount of oil in tanks. Record and compile operating data, instrument readings, documentation, and results of laboratory analyses. Control or operate manifold and pumping systems to circulate liquids through a petroleum refinery. Monitor process indicators, instruments, gauges, and meters to detect and report any possible problems. Clean interiors of processing units by circulating chemicals and solvents within units. Operate control panels to coordinate and regulate process variables such as temperature and pressure and to direct product flow rate according to process schedules. Read and analyze specifications, schedules, logs, test results, and laboratory recommendations to determine how to set equipment controls to produce the required qualities and quantities of products. Perform tests to check the qualities and grades of products, such as assessing levels of bottom sediment, water, and foreign materials in oil samples, using centrifugal testers. Collect product samples by turning bleeder valves or by lowering containers into tanks to obtain oil samples. Patrol units to monitor the amount of oil in storage tanks and to verify that activities and operations are safe, efficient, and in compliance with regulations. Operate auxiliary equipment and control multiple processing units during distilling or treating operations, moving controls that regulate valves, pumps, compressors, and auxiliary equipment.

GOE Information—Interest Area: 13. Manufacturing. **Work Group:** 13.16. Utility Operation and Energy Distribution. **Personality Type**—Realistic. Realistic occupations frequently involve work activities that include practical, hands-on problems and solutions. They often deal with plants; animals; and real-world materials like wood, tools, and machinery. Many of the occupations require working outside and do not involve a lot of paperwork or working closely with others. **Work Values**—Supervision, Technical; Supervision, Human Relations; Moral Values; Independence; Company Policies and Practices; Security. **Skills**—Operation Monitoring; Operation and Control; Repairing; Equipment Maintenance; Troubleshooting; Science. **Abilities**—*Cognitive:* None met the criteria. *Psychomotor:* Rate Control; Wrist-Finger Speed; Control Precision; Reaction Time; Manual Dexterity; Arm-Hand Steadiness. *Physical:* Extent Flexibility. *Sensory:* None met the criteria. **General Work Activities**—*Information Input:* Inspecting Equipment, Structures, or Materials; Getting Information; Monitoring Processes, Materials, or Surroundings. *Mental Process:* Evaluating Information Against Standards; Processing Information; Analyzing Data or Information. *Work Output:* Controlling Machines and Processes; Handling and Moving Objects; Repairing and Maintaining Mechanical Equipment. *Interacting with Others:* Communicating with Other Workers. **Physical Work Conditions**—Indoors; Contaminants; Hazardous Conditions; Standing; Using Hands on Objects, Tools, or Controls. **Other Job Characteristics**—Need to Be Exact or Accurate; Automation.

Experience—Job Zone 3. Previous work-related skill, knowledge, or experience is required. **Job Preparation**—SVP 6.0 to less than 7.0—more than one year and less than four years. **Knowledges**—Mechanical Devices; Chemistry; Physics; Production and Processing; Engineering and Technology. **Instructional Program**—No related CIP programs.

Related SOC Job—51-8093 Petroleum Pump System Operators, Refinery Operators, and Gaugers. **Related OOH Job**—Petroleum Pump System Operators, Refinery Operators, and Gaugers. **Related DOT Jobs**—546.382-010 Control-Panel Operator; 549.260-010 Refinery Operator; 549.360-010 Pumper; 914.384-010 Gauger.

51-8099.99 Plant and System Operators, All Other

- **Education/Training Required: Long-term on-the-job training**
- **Employed: 13,920**
- **Annual Earnings: $44,850**
- **Growth: 7.1%**
- **Annual Job Openings: 2,000**

All plant and system operators not listed separately.

No task data available.

Note: The Department of Labor has not collected some data for this job, so it has fewer details than the other descriptions.

Related SOC Job—51-8099 Plant and System Operators, All Other. **Related OOH Job**—None. **Related DOT Jobs**—590.362-010 Forming-Process Worker; 850.663-018 Lock Tender II; 914.362-010 Coal Pipeline Operator; 921.662-014 Charge-Machine Operator; 921.665-010 Cement-Boat-And-Barge Loader; 939.362-014 Panelboard Operator; 950.562-010 Panelboard Operator; 950.585-010 Ventilation Equipment Tender; 954.382-018 Watershed Tender; 955.362-014 Incinerator Operator II; 955.585-010 Wastewater-Treatment-Plant Attendant.

51-9000 Other Production Occupations

51-9011.00 Chemical Equipment Operators and Tenders

- **Education/Training Required: Moderate-term on-the-job training**
- **Employed: 50,610**
- **Annual Earnings: $39,030**
- **Growth: –4.5%**
- **Annual Job Openings: 6,000**

Operate or tend equipment to control chemical changes or reactions in the processing of industrial or consumer products. Equipment used includes devulcanizers, steam-jacketed kettles, and reactor vessels.

Adjust controls to regulate temperature, pressure, feed, and flow of liquids and gases and times of prescribed reactions according to knowledge of equipment and processes. Observe safety precautions to prevent fires and explosions. Monitor gauges, recording instruments, flowmeters, or products to ensure that specified conditions are maintained. Control and operate equipment in which chemical changes or reactions take place during the processing of industrial or consumer products. Measure, weigh, and mix chemical ingredients according to specifications. Inspect equipment or units to detect leaks and malfunctions, shutting equipment down if necessary. Patrol work areas to detect leaks and equipment malfunctions and to monitor operating conditions. Test product samples for specific gravity, chemical characteristics, pH levels, and concentrations or viscosities or send them to laboratories for testing. Draw samples of products at specified stages so that analyses can be performed. Record operational data such as temperatures, pressures, ingredients used, processing times, or test results. Notify maintenance engineers of equipment malfunctions. Add treating or neutralizing agents to products and pump products through filters or centrifuges to remove impurities or to precipitate products. Open valves or start pumps, agitators, reactors, blowers, or automatic feed of materials. Read plant specifications to determine products, ingredients, and prescribed modifications of plant procedures. Drain equipment and pump water or other solutions through to flush and clean tanks and equipment. Make minor repairs and lubricate and maintain equipment, using hand tools. Flush or clean equipment, using steam hoses or mechanical reamers. Observe colors and consistencies of products and compare them to instrument readings and to laboratory and standard test results. Implement appropriate industrial emergency response procedures. Dump or scoop prescribed solid, granular, or powdered materials into equipment. Estimate materials required for production and manufacturing of products.

GOE Information—Interest Area: 13. Manufacturing. **Work Group:** 13.03. Production Work, Assorted Materials Processing. **Personality Type**—Realistic. Realistic occupations frequently involve work activities that include practical, hands-on problems and solutions. They often deal with plants; animals; and real-world materials like wood, tools, and machinery. Many of the occupations require working outside and do not involve a lot of paperwork or working closely with others. **Work Values**—Moral Values; Supervision, Technical; Company Policies and Practices; Advancement; Supervision, Human Relations; Independence. **Skills**—Operation Monitoring; Operation and Control; Troubleshooting; Equipment Maintenance; Repairing; Science. **Abilities**—*Cognitive:* Perceptual Speed; Selective Attention; Category Flexibility; Flexibility of Closure; Number Facility; Speed of Closure. *Psychomotor:* Rate Control; Reaction Time; Response Orientation; Multilimb Coordination; Control Precision; Speed of Limb Movement. *Physical:* Gross Body Equilibrium; Static Strength; Trunk Strength. *Sensory:* Auditory Attention; Depth Perception; Visual Color Discrimination; Hearing Sensitivity; Far Vision; Near Vision. **General Work Activities**—*Information Input:* Monitoring Processes, Materials, or Surroundings; Inspecting Equipment, Structures, or Materials; Identifying Objects, Actions, and Events. *Mental Process:* Evaluating Information Against Standards; Processing Information; Updating and Using Relevant Knowledge. *Work Output:* Controlling Machines and Processes; Performing General Physical Activities; Handling and Moving Objects. *Interacting with Others:* Communicating with Other Workers; Teaching Others; Establishing and Maintaining Interpersonal Relationships. **Physical Work Conditions**—More Often Outdoors Than Indoors; Noisy; Very Hot or Cold; Contaminants; Hazardous Conditions. **Other Job Characteristics**—Need to Be Exact or Accurate; Errors Have Important Consequences; Pace Determined by Speed of Equipment; Automation; Repeat Same Tasks.

Experience—Job Zone 2. Some previous work-related skill, knowledge, or experience may be helpful in these occupations, but usually is not needed. **Job Preparation**—SVP 4.0 to less than 6.0—six months to less than two years. **Knowledges**—Chemistry; Mechanical Devices; Production and Processing; Public Safety and Security; English Language; Computers and Electronics. **Instructional Program**—Chemical Technology/Technician.

Related SOC Job—51-9011 Chemical Equipment Operators and Tenders. **Related OOH Job**—Chemical Equipment Operators and Tenders. **Related DOT Jobs**—521.685-190 Ion Exchange Operator; 546.385-010 Gas Treater; 551.465-010 Purification-Operator Helper; 551.585-018 Pan Helper; 551.685-094 Lye Treater; 553.685-026

Cadmium-Liquor Maker; 558.385-010 Cd-Reactor Operator; 558.385-014 Tower Helper; 558.485-010 Caustic Operator; 558.565-010 Acid-Plant Helper; 558.585-010 Catalytic-Converter-Operator Helper; 558.585-018 Contact-Acid-Plant Operator; 558.585-022 Cuprous-Chloride Helper; 558.585-026 Devulcanizer Tender; 558.585-034 Neutralizer; others.

51-9012.00 Separating, Filtering, Clarifying, Precipitating, and Still Machine Setters, Operators, and Tenders

- **Education/Training Required: Moderate-term on-the-job training**
- **Employed: 41,250**
- **Annual Earnings: $34,650**
- **Growth: 1.6%**
- **Annual Job Openings: 5,000**

Set up, operate, or tend continuous flow or vat-type equipment; filter presses; shaker screens; centrifuges; condenser tubes; precipitating, fermenting, or evaporating tanks; scrubbing towers; or batch stills. These machines extract, sort, or separate liquids, gases, or solids from other materials to recover a refined product. Includes dairy processing equipment operators.

Set or adjust machine controls to regulate conditions such as material flow, temperature, and pressure. Monitor material flow and instruments such as temperature and pressure gauges, indicators, and meters to ensure optimal processing conditions. Start agitators, shakers, conveyors, pumps, or centrifuge machines; then turn valves or move controls to admit, drain, separate, filter, clarify, mix, or transfer materials. Examine samples visually or by hand to verify qualities such as clarity, cleanliness, consistency, dryness, and texture. Collect samples of materials or products for laboratory analysis. Maintain logs of instrument readings, test results, and shift production and send production information to computer databases. Test samples to determine viscosity, acidity, specific gravity, or degree of concentration, using test equipment such as viscometers, pH meters, and hydrometers. Measure or weigh materials to be refined, mixed, transferred, stored, or otherwise processed. Clean and sterilize tanks, screens, inflow pipes, production areas, and equipment, using hoses, brushes, scrapers, or chemical solutions. Inspect machines and equipment for hazards, operating efficiency, malfunctions, wear, and leaks. Dump, pour, or load specified amounts of refined or unrefined materials into equipment or containers for further processing or storage. Connect pipes between vats and processing equipment. Communicate processing instructions to other workers. Remove clogs, defects, and impurities from machines, tanks, conveyors, screens, or other processing equipment. Assemble fittings, valves, bowls, plates, disks, impeller shafts, and other parts to equipment to prepare equipment for operation. Install and maintain or repair hoses, pumps, filters, or screens to maintain processing equipment, using hand tools. Turn valves to pump sterilizing solutions and rinsewater through pipes and equipment and to spray vats with atomizers. Remove full bags or containers from discharge outlets and replace them with empty ones. Pack bottles into cartons or crates, using machines.

GOE Information—Interest Area: 13. Manufacturing. **Work Group:** 13.03. Production Work, Assorted Materials Processing. **Personality Type**—Realistic. Realistic occupations frequently involve work activities that include practical, hands-on problems and solutions. They often deal with plants; animals; and real-world materials like wood, tools, and machinery. Many of the occupations require working outside and do not involve a lot of paperwork or working closely with others. **Work Values**—Moral Values; Supervision, Technical; Supervision, Human Relations; Company Policies and Practices; Advancement; Independence. **Skills**—Operation Monitoring; Repairing; Equipment Maintenance; Operation and Control; Troubleshooting; Quality Control Analysis. **Abilities**—*Cognitive:* Perceptual Speed; Visualization; Flexibility of Closure; Time Sharing; Memorization; Speed of Closure. *Psychomotor:* Reaction Time; Rate Control; Response Orientation; Speed of Limb Movement; Multilimb Coordination; Wrist-Finger Speed. *Physical:* Gross Body Equilibrium; Static Strength; Stamina; Extent Flexibility; Gross Body Coordination; Trunk Strength. *Sensory:* Glare Sensitivity; Auditory Attention; Hearing Sensitivity; Depth Perception; Visual Color Discrimination; Far Vision. **General Work Activities**—*Information Input:* Monitoring Processes, Materials, or Surroundings; Identifying Objects, Actions, and Events; Inspecting Equipment, Structures, or Materials. *Mental Process:* Making Decisions and Solving Problems; Updating and Using Relevant Knowledge; Organizing, Planning, and Prioritizing. *Work Output:* Handling and Moving Objects; Controlling Machines and Processes; Performing General Physical Activities. *Interacting with Others:* Establishing and Maintaining Interpersonal Relationships; Communicating with Other Workers; Coaching and Developing Others. **Physical Work Conditions**—Noisy; Very Hot or Cold; Contaminants; High Places; Hazardous Conditions; Hazardous Equipment. **Other Job Characteristics**—Need to Be Exact or Accurate; Pace Determined by Speed of Equipment; Repeat Same Tasks; Errors Have Important Consequences; Automation.

Experience—Job Zone 2. Some previous work-related skill, knowledge, or experience may be helpful in these occupations, but usually is not needed. **Job Preparation**—SVP 4.0 to less than 6.0—six months to less than two years. **Knowledges**—Production and Processing; Chemistry; Food Production; Mechanical Devices; Public Safety and Security; Education and Training. **Instructional Program**—No related CIP programs.

Related SOC Job—51-9012 Separating, Filtering, Clarifying, Precipitating, and Still Machine Setters, Operators, and Tenders. **Related OOH Job**—Separating, Filtering, Clarifying, Precipitating, and Still Machine Setters, Operators and Tenders. **Related DOT Jobs**—509.685-050 Scrap Handler; 511.385-010 Zinc-Chloride Operator; 511.462-010 Concentrator Operator; 511.465-010 Top-Precipitator Operator; 511.482-014 Cryolite-Recovery Operator; 511.485-010 Molybdenum-Steamer Operator; 511.485-014 Thickener Operator; 511.562-010 Classifier Operator; 511.565-010 Dewaterer Operator; 511.565-018 Iron-Launder Operator; 511.582-010 Leacher; 511.585-010 Hydrate-Control Tender; 511.662-010 Clarifier Operator; 511.664-010 Bottom-Precipitator Operator; others.

51-9021.00 Crushing, Grinding, and Polishing Machine Setters, Operators, and Tenders

- Education/Training Required: Moderate-term on-the-job training
- Employed: 41,480
- Annual Earnings: $27,470
- Growth: 0.8%
- Annual Job Openings: 6,000

Set up, operate, or tend machines to crush, grind, or polish materials such as coal, glass, grain, stone, food, or rubber.

Read work orders to determine production specifications and information. Observe operation of equipment to ensure continuity of flow, safety, and efficient operation and to detect malfunctions. Move controls to start, stop, or adjust machinery and equipment that crushes, grinds, polishes, or blends materials. Record data from operations, testing, and production on specified forms. Examine materials, ingredients, or products visually or with hands to ensure conformance to established standards. Weigh or measure materials, ingredients, or products at specified intervals to ensure conformance to requirements. Clean, adjust, and maintain equipment, using hand tools. Notify supervisors of needed repairs. Set mill gauges to specified fineness of grind. Reject defective products and readjust equipment to eliminate problems. Clean work areas. Transfer materials, supplies, and products between work areas, using moving equipment and hand tools. Dislodge and clear jammed materials or other items from machinery and equipment, using hand tools. Inspect chains, belts, and scrolls for signs of wear. Tend accessory equipment such as pumps and conveyors to move materials or ingredients through production processes. Test samples of materials or products to ensure compliance with specifications, using test equipment. Collect samples of materials or products for laboratory testing. Mark bins as to types of mixtures stored. Turn valves to regulate the moisture contents of materials. Load materials into machinery and equipment, using hand tools. Add or mix chemicals and ingredients for processing, using hand tools or other devices. Break mixtures to size, using picks.

GOE Information—**Interest Area:** 13. Manufacturing. **Work Group:** 13.02. Machine Setup and Operation. **Personality Type**—Realistic. Realistic occupations frequently involve work activities that include practical, hands-on problems and solutions. They often deal with plants; animals; and real-world materials like wood, tools, and machinery. Many of the occupations require working outside and do not involve a lot of paperwork or working closely with others. **Work Values**—Moral Values; Independence; Supervision, Technical; Supervision, Human Relations; Company Policies and Practices; Advancement. **Skills**—Operation Monitoring; Equipment Maintenance; Installation; Operation and Control; Repairing; Quality Control Analysis. **Abilities**—*Cognitive:* Perceptual Speed; Selective Attention; Visualization; Flexibility of Closure; Time Sharing; Memorization. *Psychomotor:* Reaction Time; Rate Control; Response Orientation; Multilimb Coordination; Control Precision; Arm-Hand Steadiness. *Physical:* Static Strength; Dynamic Strength; Stamina; Extent Flexibility; Trunk Strength; Gross Body Coordination. *Sensory:* Hearing Sensitivity; Auditory Attention; Depth Perception; Visual Color Discrimination; Far Vision. **General Work Activities**—*Information Input:* Monitoring Processes, Materials, or Surroundings; Inspecting Equipment, Structures, or Materials; Identifying Objects, Actions, and Events. *Mental Process:* Organizing, Planning, and Prioritizing; Updating and Using Relevant Knowledge; Processing Information. *Work Output:* Controlling Machines and Processes; Handling and Moving Objects; Performing General Physical Activities. *Interacting with Others:* Communicating with Other Workers; Teaching Others; Establishing and Maintaining Interpersonal Relationships. **Physical Work Conditions**—Noisy; Very Hot or Cold; Contaminants; Hazardous Equipment; Standing; Using Hands on Objects, Tools, or Controls. **Other Job Characteristics**—Need to Be Exact or Accurate; Pace Determined by Speed of Equipment.

Experience—Job Zone 2. Some previous work-related skill, knowledge, or experience may be helpful in these occupations, but usually is not needed. **Job Preparation**—SVP 4.0 to less than 6.0—six months to less than two years. **Knowledges**—Mechanical Devices; Production and Processing; Chemistry; Engineering and Technology; Design; Physics. **Instructional Program**—No related CIP programs.

Related SOC Job—51-9021 Crushing, Grinding, and Polishing Machine Setters, Operators, and Tenders. **Related OOH Job**—Crushing, Grinding, and Polishing Machine Setters, Operators, and Tenders. **Related DOT Jobs**—515.382-010 Grinding-Mill Operator; 515.585-010 Scale-Reclamation Tender; 515.685-010 Batch Maker; 515.685-014 Crusher Tender; 515.685-018 Stamping-Mill Tender; 515.687-010 Hammer-Mill Operator; 519.485-010 Grinder-Mill Operator; 519.685-030 Rod-Mill Tender; 521.362-014 Miller, Distillery; 521.585-014 Miller; 521.585-018 Powder-Mill Operator; 521.662-010 Miller, Wet Process; 521.682-022 Flake Miller, Wheat and Oats; 521.682-026 Grinder Operator; 521.682-034 Refining-Machine Operator; others.

51-9022.00 Grinding and Polishing Workers, Hand

- **Education/Training Required: Moderate-term on-the-job training**
- **Employed: 44,890**
- **Annual Earnings: $23,450**
- **Growth: –8.7%**
- **Annual Job Openings: 6,000**

Grind, sand, or polish, using hand tools or hand-held power tools, a variety of metal, wood, stone, clay, plastic, or glass objects.

Clean brass particles from files by drawing file cards through file grooves. Wash grit from stone, using hoses. Verify quality of finished workpieces by inspecting them, comparing them to templates, measuring their dimensions, or testing them in working machinery. Transfer equipment, objects, or parts to specified work areas, using moving devices. Spread emery powder or other polishing compounds on stone or wet stone surfaces, using hoses; then guide buffing wheels over stone to polish surfaces. Sharpen abrasive grinding tools, using machines and hand tools. Repair and maintain equipment, objects, or parts, using hand tools. Record product and processing data on specified forms. Fill cracks or imperfections in marble with wax that matches the stone color. Apply solutions and chemicals to equipment, objects, or parts, using hand tools. Study blueprints or layouts to determine how to lay out workpieces or saw out templates. Select files or other abrasives according to materials, sizes and shapes of workpieces, amount of stock to be removed, finishes specified, and steps in finishing processes. Mark defects such as knotholes, cracks, and splits for repair. Grind, sand, clean, or polish objects or parts to correct defects or to prepare surfaces for further finishing, using hand tools and power tools. Move controls to adjust, start, or stop equipment during grinding and polishing processes. Measure and mark equipment, objects, or parts to ensure grinding and polishing standards are met. Load and adjust workpieces onto equipment or work tables, using hand tools. Remove completed workpieces from equipment or work tables, using hand tools, and place workpieces in containers. File grooved, contoured, and irregular surfaces of metal objects, such as metalworking dies and machine parts, to conform to templates, other parts, layouts, or blueprint specifications. Trim, scrape, or deburr objects or parts, using chisels, scrapers, and other hand tools and equipment.

GOE Information—**Interest Area:** 13. Manufacturing. **Work Group:** 13.09. Hands-On Work, Assorted Materials. **Personality Type**—Realistic. Realistic occupations frequently involve work activities that include practical, hands-on problems and solutions. They often deal with plants; animals; and real-world materials like wood, tools,

and machinery. Many of the occupations require working outside and do not involve a lot of paperwork or working closely with others. **Work Values**—Moral Values; Independence; Supervision, Technical. **Skills**—Operation Monitoring; Operation and Control; Repairing. **Abilities**—*Cognitive:* None met the criteria. *Psychomotor:* Wrist-Finger Speed; Control Precision; Manual Dexterity; Multilimb Coordination. *Physical:* Extent Flexibility; Trunk Strength; Static Strength. *Sensory:* None met the criteria. **General Work Activities**—*Information Input:* Inspecting Equipment, Structures, or Materials; Monitoring Processes, Materials, or Surroundings. *Mental Process:* Evaluating Information Against Standards. *Work Output:* Handling and Moving Objects; Performing General Physical Activities; Controlling Machines and Processes. *Interacting with Others:* None met the criteria. **Physical Work Conditions**—Indoors; Noisy; Hazardous Equipment; Standing; Using Hands on Objects, Tools, or Controls; Repetitive Motions. **Other Job Characteristics**—None met the criteria.

Experience—Job Zone 1. No previous work-related skill, knowledge, or experience is needed. **Job Preparation**—SVP below 4.0—less than six months. **Knowledges**—Mechanical Devices; Production and Processing; Chemistry. **Instructional Program**—No related CIP programs.

Related SOC Job—51-9022 Grinding and Polishing Workers, Hand. **Related OOH Job**—Grinding and Polishing Workers, Hand. **Related DOT Jobs**—519.684-018 Mold Dresser; 700.684-034 Filer; 700.687-058 Polisher; 703.687-022 Steel-Barrel Reamer; 705.384-010 Scraper, Hand; 705.484-010 Filer, Hand, Tool; 705.484-014 Final Finisher, Forging Dies; 705.684-022 Grease Buffer; 705.684-026 Grinder I; 705.684-030 Grinder-Chipper I; 705.684-034 Metal Finisher; 705.684-038 Mold Finisher; 705.684-046 Needle Polisher; 705.684-050 Nib Finisher; 705.684-054 Pipe Buffer; 705.684-062 Polisher and Buffer II; 705.687-014 Laborer, Grinding and Polishing; others.

51-9023.00 Mixing and Blending Machine Setters, Operators, and Tenders

- **Education/Training Required: Moderate-term on-the-job training**
- **Employed: 129,440**
- **Annual Earnings: $28,890**
- **Growth: 2.0%**
- **Annual Job Openings: 16,000**

Set up, operate, or tend machines to mix or blend materials such as chemicals, tobacco, liquids, color pigments, or explosive ingredients.

Weigh or measure materials, ingredients, and products to ensure conformance to requirements. Test samples of materials or products to ensure compliance with specifications, using test equipment. Start machines to mix or blend ingredients; then allow them to mix for specified times. Dump or pour specified amounts of materials into machinery and equipment. Operate or tend machines to mix or blend any of a wide variety of materials such as spices, dough batter, tobacco, fruit juices, chemicals, livestock feed, food products, color pigments, or explosive ingredients. Observe production and monitor equipment to ensure safe and efficient operation. Stop mixing or blending machines when specified product qualities are obtained and open valves and start pumps to transfer mixtures. Collect samples of materials or products for laboratory testing. Add or mix chemicals and ingredients for processing, using hand tools or other devices. Examine materials, ingredients, or products visually or with hands to ensure conformance to established standards. Record operational and production data on specified forms. Transfer materials, supplies, and products between work areas, using moving equipment and hand tools. Tend accessory equipment such as pumps and conveyors to move materials or ingredients through production processes. Read work orders to determine production specifications and information. Compound and process ingredients or dyes according to formulas. Unload mixtures into containers or onto conveyors for further processing. Clean and maintain equipment, using hand tools. Dislodge and clear jammed materials or other items from machinery and equipment, using hand tools. Open valves to drain slurry from mixers into storage tanks.

GOE Information—Interest Area: 13. Manufacturing. **Work Group:** 13.03. Production Work, Assorted Materials Processing. **Personality Type**—Realistic. Realistic occupations frequently involve work activities that include practical, hands-on problems and solutions. They often deal with plants; animals; and real-world materials like wood, tools, and machinery. Many of the occupations require working outside and do not involve a lot of paperwork or working closely with others. **Work Values**—Moral Values; Independence; Supervision, Technical; Supervision, Human Relations; Company Policies and Practices; Advancement. **Skills**—Operation Monitoring; Operation and Control; Equipment Maintenance; Repairing; Troubleshooting; Technology Design. **Abilities**—*Cognitive:* Perceptual Speed; Selective Attention; Category Flexibility; Flexibility of Closure; Time Sharing. *Psychomotor:* Rate Control; Reaction Time; Response Orientation; Manual Dexterity; Control Precision; Multilimb Coordination. *Physical:* Gross Body Equilibrium; Static Strength; Extent Flexibility; Gross Body Coordination; Stamina; Trunk Strength. *Sensory:* Depth Perception; Visual Color Discrimination; Auditory Attention; Hearing Sensitivity; Far Vision. **General Work Activities**—*Information Input:* Inspecting Equipment, Structures, or Materials; Monitoring Processes, Materials, or Surroundings; Identifying Objects, Actions, and Events. *Mental Process:* Making Decisions and Solving Problems; Evaluating Information Against Standards; Updating and Using Relevant Knowledge. *Work Output:* Handling and Moving Objects; Controlling Machines and Processes; Performing General Physical Activities; . *Interacting with Others:* Communicating with Other Workers; Establishing and Maintaining Interpersonal Relationships; Teaching Others. **Physical Work Conditions**—Noisy; Contaminants; Hazardous conditions; Standing; Walking and Running; Using Hands on Objects, Tools, or Controls. **Other Job Characteristics**—Need to Be Exact or Accurate; Errors Have Important Consequences; Pace Determined by Speed of Equipment; Repeat Same Tasks.

Experience—Job Zone 2. Some previous work-related skill, knowledge, or experience may be helpful in these occupations, but usually is not needed. **Job Preparation**—SVP 4.0 to less than 6.0—six months to less than two years. **Knowledges**—Production and Processing; Chemistry; Mechanical Devices; Physics; Education and Training; Mathematics. **Instructional Program**—Agricultural and Food Products Processing, General.

Related SOC Job—51-9023 Mixing and Blending Machine Setters, Operators, and Tenders. **Related OOH Job**—Mixing and Blending Machine Setters, Operators, and Tenders. **Related DOT Jobs**—509.485-010 Compound Mixer; 510.465-010 Carbide-Powder Processor; 510.465-014 Slurry-Control Tender; 510.685-010 Dust Mixer; 510.685-014 Mix-House Tender; 510.685-018 Mixer; 510.685-022 Pug-Mill Operator; 510.685-026 Sinter-Machine Operator; 510.685-030 Slime-Plant Operator I; 511.685-046 Reagent Tender; 514.685-022 Lime Mixer Tender; 519.685-026 Mud-Mill Tender; 520.362-010 Bulk-Plant Operator; 520.362-014 Dry-Starch Operator; 520.382-010 Cistern-Room Operator; 520.382-014 Liquid-Sugar Melter; others.

51-9031.00 Cutters and Trimmers, Hand

- **Education/Training Required: Short-term on-the-job training**
- **Employed: 28,360**
- **Annual Earnings: $21,840**
- **Growth: 2.4%**
- **Annual Job Openings: 3,000**

Use hand tools or hand-held power tools to cut and trim a variety of manufactured items, such as carpet, fabric, stone, glass, or rubber.

Mark identification numbers, trademarks, grades, marketing data, sizes, or model numbers on products. Mark or discard items with defects such as spots, stains, scars, snags, chips, scratches, or unacceptable shapes or finishes. Trim excess material or cut threads off finished products, such as cutting loose ends of plastic off a manufactured toy for a smoother finish. Transport items to work or storage areas, using carts. Stack cut items and load them on racks or conveyors or onto trucks. Mark cutting lines around patterns or templates or follow layout points, using squares, rules, and straightedges and chalk, pencils, or scribes. Cut, shape, and trim materials, such as textiles, food, glass, stone, and metal, using knives, scissors, and other hand tools; portable power tools; or bench-mounted tools. Position templates or measure materials to locate specified points of cuts or to obtain maximum yields, using rules, scales, or patterns. Read work orders to determine dimensions, cutting locations, and quantities to cut. Unroll, lay out, attach, or mount materials or items on cutting tables or machines. Clean, treat, buff, or polish finished items, using grinders, brushes, chisels, and cleaning solutions and polishing materials. Fold or shape materials before or after cutting them. Replace or sharpen dulled cutting tools such as saws. Route items to provide cutouts for parts, using portable routers, grinders, and hand tools. Count or weigh and bundle items. Adjust guides and stops to control depths and widths of cuts. Lower table-mounted cutters such as knife blades, cutting wheels, or saws to cut items to specified sizes. Separate materials or products according to size, weight, type, condition, color, or shade.

GOE Information—Interest Area: 13. Manufacturing. **Work Group:** 13.09. Hands-On Work, Assorted Materials. **Personality Type**—Realistic. Realistic occupations frequently involve work activities that include practical, hands-on problems and solutions. They often deal with plants; animals; and real-world materials like wood, tools, and machinery. Many of the occupations require working outside and do not involve a lot of paperwork or working closely with others. **Work Values**—Independence; Moral Values; Supervision, Technical. **Skills**—None met the criteria. **Abilities**—*Cognitive:* Visualization; Number Facility. *Psychomotor:* Wrist-Finger Speed; Manual Dexterity; Speed of Limb Movement; Arm-Hand Steadiness; Control Precision; Multilimb Coordination. *Physical:* Static Strength; Trunk Strength; Extent Flexibility. *Sensory:* Visual Color Discrimination. **General Work Activities**—*Information Input:* None met the criteria. *Mental Process:* None met the criteria. *Work Output:* Handling and Moving Objects; Performing General Physical Activities; Controlling Machines and Processes. *Interacting with Others:* None met the criteria. **Physical Work Conditions**—Indoors; Hazardous Equipment; Minor Burns, Cuts, Bites, or Stings; Standing; Using Hands on Objects, Tools, or Controls; Repetitive Motions. **Other Job Characteristics**—Need to Be Exact or Accurate.

Experience—Job Zone 1. No previous work-related skill, knowledge, or experience is needed. **Job Preparation**—SVP below 4.0—less than six months. **Knowledges**—Production and Processing. **Instructional Program**—No related CIP programs.

Related SOC Job—51-9031 Cutters and Trimmers, Hand. **Related OOH Job**—Cutters and Trimmers, Hand. **Related DOT Jobs**—521.687-014 Binder Cutter, Hand; 521.687-026 Bunch Trimmer, Mold; 521.687-066 Fruit Cutter; 524.687-010 Cherry Cutter; 525.687-046 Hide Trimmer; 539.686-010 Cutter, Wet Machine; 569.684-010 Log Peeler; 569.687-026 Wood Hacker; 575.684-022 Crosscutter, Rolled Glass; 579.684-030 Cutter; 585.684-010 Trimmer, Hand; 585.687-014 Carpet Cutter II; 590.687-022 Rug Cutter; 673.666-014 Stripper; 689.687-090 Lapper; 700.684-018 Bright Cutter; 700.684-038 Gold Cutter; 700.684-050 Mesh Cutter; others.

51-9032.00 Cutting and Slicing Machine Setters, Operators, and Tenders

- **Education/Training Required: Moderate-term on-the-job training**
- **Employed: 78,030**
- **Annual Earnings: $27,570**
- **Growth: –2.7%**
- **Annual Job Openings: 6,000**

Set up, operate, or tend machines that cut or slice materials, such as glass, stone, cork, rubber, tobacco, food, paper, or insulating material.

Type instructions on computer keyboards; push buttons to activate computer programs; or manually set cutting guides, clamps, and knives. Remove completed materials or products from cutting or slicing machines and stack or store them for additional processing. Press buttons, pull levers, or depress pedals to start and operate cutting and slicing machines. Position width gauge blocks between blades, level blades, and insert wedges into frames to secure blades to frames. Position stock along cutting lines or against stops on beds of scoring or cutting machines. Monitor operation of cutting or slicing machines to detect malfunctions or to determine whether supplies need replenishment. Mark cutting lines or identifying information on stock, using marking pencils, rulers, or scribes. Feed stock into cutting machines, onto conveyors, or under cutting blades by threading, guiding, pushing, or turning handwheels. Examine, measure, and weigh materials or products to verify conformance to specifications, using measuring devices such as rulers, micrometers, or scales. Change or replace saw blades, cables, cutter heads, and grinding wheels, using hand tools. Turn cranks or press buttons to activate winches that move cars under sawing cables or saw frames. Adjust timing mechanisms to synchronize breaker bars to snap glass at scores. Build beds of timbers on cars and align and level stone on beds, using crowbars, sledgehammers, wedges, blocks, rules, and spirit levels. Tighten pulleys or add abrasives to maintain cutting speeds. Start pumps to circulate water and abrasives onto blades or cables during cutting. Start machines to verify setups and make any necessary adjustments. Select and install machine components such as cutting blades, rollers, and templates according to specifications, using hand tools. Review work orders, blueprints, specifications, or job samples to determine components, settings, and adjustments for cutting and slicing machines.

GOE Information—Interest Area: 13. Manufacturing. **Work Group:** 13.03. Production Work, Assorted Materials Processing. **Personality Type**—Realistic. Realistic occupations frequently involve work activities that include practical, hands-on problems and solutions. They often deal with plants; animals; and real-world materials like wood, tools, and machinery. Many of the occupations require working outside and do not involve a lot of paperwork or working closely with others. **Work Values**—Moral Values; Supervision, Technical; Independence; Activity; Company Policies and Practices;

Supervision, Human Relations. **Skills**—Equipment Maintenance; Operation Monitoring; Operation and Control; Repairing; Quality Control Analysis; Troubleshooting. **Abilities**—*Cognitive:* Perceptual Speed; Visualization; Selective Attention; Category Flexibility; Flexibility of Closure; Time Sharing. *Psychomotor:* Rate Control; Reaction Time; Multilimb Coordination; Wrist-Finger Speed; Response Orientation; Speed of Limb Movement. *Physical:* Stamina; Extent Flexibility; Trunk Strength; Static Strength. *Sensory:* Depth Perception; Auditory Attention; Hearing Sensitivity; Far Vision; Visual Color Discrimination. **General Work Activities**—*Information Input:* Monitoring Processes, Materials, or Surroundings; Identifying Objects, Actions, and Events; Getting Information. *Mental Process:* Processing Information; Judging the Qualities of Things, Services, or Other People's Work; Organizing, Planning, and Prioritizing. *Work Output:* Controlling Machines and Processes; Handling and Moving Objects; Performing General Physical Activities. *Interacting with Others:* Establishing and Maintaining Interpersonal Relationships; Communicating with Other Workers; Coaching and Developing Others. **Physical Work Conditions**—Noisy; Contaminants; Minor Burns, Cuts, Bites, or Stings; Standing; Using Hands on Objects, Tools, or Controls; Repetitive Motions. **Other Job Characteristics**—Automation; Need to Be Exact or Accurate; Pace Determined by Speed of Equipment; Repeat Same Tasks; Errors Have Important Consequences.

Experience—Job Zone 2. Some previous work-related skill, knowledge, or experience may be helpful in these occupations, but usually is not needed. **Job Preparation**—SVP 4.0 to less than 6.0—six months to less than two years. **Knowledges**—Production and Processing. **Instructional Program**—No related CIP programs.

Related SOC Job—51-9032 Cutting and Slicing Machine Setters, Operators, and Tenders. **Related OOH Job**—Cutting and Slicing Machine Setters, Operators, and Tenders. **Related DOT Jobs**—520.682-022 Gum-Scoring-Machine Operator; 521.685-018 Almond-Cutting-Machine Tender; 521.685-098 Cutter, Frozen Meat; 521.685-102 Cutting-Machine Operator; 521.685-158 Granulating-Machine Operator; 521.685-170 Hasher Operator; 521.685-298 Slice-Plug-Cutter Operator; 521.685-302 Slicing-Machine Operator; 521.685-306 Slicing-Machine Operator; 521.685-310 Smoking-Tobacco-Cutter Operator; 521.685-338 Strip-Cutting-Machine Operator; 521.685-342 Stripper-Cutter, Machine; others.

51-9041.00 Extruding, Forming, Pressing, and Compacting Machine Setters, Operators, and Tenders

- **Education/Training Required: Moderate-term on-the-job training**
- **Employed: 80,420**
- **Annual Earnings: $27,790**
- **Growth: –2.2%**
- **Annual Job Openings: 8,000**

Set up, operate, or tend machines, such as glass-forming machines, plodder machines, and tuber machines, to shape and form products such as glassware, food, rubber, soap, brick, tile, clay, wax, tobacco, or cosmetics.

Adjust machine components to regulate speeds, pressures, and temperatures and amounts, dimensions, and flow of materials or ingredients. Examine, measure, and weigh materials or products to verify conformance to standards, using measuring devices such as templates, micrometers, or scales. Monitor machine operations and observe lights and gauges to detect malfunctions. Press control buttons to activate machinery and equipment. Turn controls to adjust machine functions, such as regulating air pressure, creating vacuums, and adjusting coolant flow. Review work orders, specifications, or instructions to determine materials, ingredients, procedures, components, settings, and adjustments for extruding, forming, pressing, or compacting machines. Select and install machine components such as dies, molds, and cutters according to specifications, using hand tools and measuring devices. Record and maintain production data such as meter readings and quantities, types, and dimensions of materials produced. Notify supervisors when extruded filaments fail to meet standards. Synchronize speeds of sections of machines when producing products involving several steps or processes. Feed products into machines by hand or conveyor. Clear jams and remove defective or substandard materials or products. Move materials, supplies, components, and finished products between storage and work areas, using work aids such as racks, hoists, and handtrucks. Swab molds with solutions to prevent products from sticking. Complete work tickets and place them with products. Activate machines to shape or form products such as candy bars, light bulbs, balloons, or insulation panels. Remove molds, mold components, and feeder tubes from machinery after production is complete. Remove materials or products from molds or from extruding, forming, pressing, or compacting machines and stack or store them for additional processing. Measure, mix, cut, shape, soften, and join materials and ingredients such as powder, cornmeal, or rubber to prepare them for machine processing. Send product samples to laboratories for analysis.

GOE Information—Interest Area: 13. Manufacturing. **Work Group:** 13.03. Production Work, Assorted Materials Processing. **Personality Type**—Realistic. Realistic occupations frequently involve work activities that involve practical, hands-on problems and solutions. They often deal with plants; animals; and real-world materials like wood, tools, and machinery. Many of the occupations require working outside and do not involve a lot of paperwork or working closely with others. **Work Values**—Moral Values; Independence; Supervision, Technical; Supervision, Human Relations; Company Policies and Practices; Activity. **Skills**—Operation Monitoring; Equipment Maintenance; Operation and Control; Repairing; Troubleshooting; Installation. **Abilities**—*Cognitive:* Perceptual Speed; Visualization; Selective Attention; Time Sharing. *Psychomotor:* Rate Control; Reaction Time; Response Orientation; Multilimb Coordination; Speed of Limb Movement; Manual Dexterity. *Physical:* Static Strength; Dynamic Strength; Gross Body Coordination; Extent Flexibility; Stamina; Trunk Strength. *Sensory:* Auditory Attention; Depth Perception; Hearing Sensitivity; Far Vision; Visual Color Discrimination. **General Work Activities**—*Information Input:* Identifying Objects, Actions, and Events; Getting Information; Monitoring Processes, Materials, or Surroundings. *Mental Process:* Organizing, Planning, and Prioritizing; Updating and Using Relevant Knowledge; Thinking Creatively. *Work Output:* Handling and Moving Objects; Controlling Machines and Processes; Performing General Physical Activities. *Interacting with Others:* Communicating with Other Workers; Teaching Others; Interpreting the Meaning of Information to Others. **Physical Work Conditions**—Contaminants; Minor Burns, Cuts, Bites, or Stings; Standing; Walking and Running; Using Hands on Objects, Tools, or Controls; Repetitive Motions. **Other Job Characteristics**—Pace Determined by Speed of Equipment; Need to Be Exact or Accurate; Repeat Same Tasks; Errors Have Important Consequences.

Experience—Job Zone 2. Some previous work-related skill, knowledge, or experience may be helpful in these occupations, but usually is not needed. **Job Preparation**—SVP 4.0 to less than 6.0—six months to less than two years. **Knowledges**—Production and Processing;

Mechanical Devices; Administration and Management. **Instructional Program**—No related CIP programs.

Related SOC Job—51-9041 Extruding, Forming, Pressing, and Compacting Machine Setters, Operators, and Tenders. **Related OOH Job**—Extruding, Forming, Pressing, and Compacting Machine Setters, Operators, and Tenders. **Related DOT Jobs**—520.682-014 Center-Machine Operator; 520.682-030 Spinner; 520.682-034 Cracker-and-Cookie-Machine Operator; 520.685-038 Cake Former; 520.685-058 Casting-Machine Operator; 520.685-062 Casting-Machine Operator; 520.685-078 Confectionery-Drops-Machine Operator; 520.685-086 Dividing-Machine Operator; 520.685-102 Flaking-Roll Operator; 520.685-178 Pellet-Mill Operator; 520.685-182 Press Operator, Meat; 520.685-186 Press Tender; 520.685-190 Pretzel-Twisting-Machine Operator; others.

51-9051.00 Furnace, Kiln, Oven, Drier, and Kettle Operators and Tenders

- **Education/Training Required: Moderate-term on-the-job training**
- **Employed: 28,140**
- **Annual Earnings: $30,400**
- **Growth: –4.2%**
- **Annual Job Openings: 3,000**

Operate or tend heating equipment other than basic metal, plastic, or food-processing equipment. Includes activities such as annealing glass, drying lumber, curing rubber, removing moisture from materials, or boiling soap.

Weigh or measure specified amounts of ingredients or materials for processing, using devices such as scales and calipers. Press and adjust controls to activate, set, and regulate equipment according to specifications. Monitor equipment operation, gauges, and panel lights to detect deviations from standards. Read and interpret work orders and instructions to determine work assignments, process specifications, and production schedules. Record gauge readings, test results, and shift production in logbooks. Confer with supervisors or other equipment operators to report equipment malfunctions or to resolve production problems. Examine or test samples of processed substances or collect samples for laboratory testing to ensure conformance to specifications. Clean, lubricate, and adjust equipment, using scrapers, solvents, air hoses, oil, and hand tools. Transport materials and products to and from work areas manually or by using carts, handtrucks, or hoists. Stop equipment and clear blockages or jams, using fingers, wire, or hand tools. Remove products from equipment manually or by using hoists and prepare them for storage, shipment, or additional processing. Calculate amounts of materials to be loaded into furnaces, adjusting amounts as necessary for specific conditions. Feed fuel, such as coal and coke, into fireboxes or onto conveyors and remove ashes from furnaces, using shovels and buckets. Melt or refine metal before casting, calculating required temperatures, and observe metal color and adjust controls as necessary to maintain required temperatures. Replace worn or defective equipment parts, using hand tools. Load equipment receptacles or conveyors with material to be processed by hand or using hoists. Sprinkle chemicals on the surface of molten metal to bring impurities to surface and remove impurities, using strainers. Direct crane operators and crew members to load vessels with materials to be processed.

GOE Information—Interest Area: 13. Manufacturing. **Work Group:** 13.03. Production Work, Assorted Materials Processing. **Personality**

Type—Realistic. Realistic occupations frequently involve work activities that include practical, hands-on problems and solutions. They often deal with plants; animals; and real-world materials like wood, tools, and machinery. Many of the occupations require working outside and do not involve a lot of paperwork or working closely with others. **Work Values**—Moral Values; Supervision, Technical; Supervision, Human Relations; Independence; Company Policies and Practices. **Skills**—Operation Monitoring; Operation and Control; Repairing; Equipment Maintenance; Troubleshooting. **Abilities**—*Cognitive:* Perceptual Speed; Selective Attention. *Psychomotor:* Reaction Time; Rate Control; Control Precision; Multilimb Coordination; Manual Dexterity; Arm-Hand Steadiness. *Physical:* Extent Flexibility; Gross Body Equilibrium; Static Strength; Gross Body Coordination; Stamina; Trunk Strength. *Sensory:* Depth Perception; Auditory Attention; Near Vision. **General Work Activities**—*Information Input:* Inspecting Equipment, Structures, or Materials; Monitoring Processes, Materials, or Surroundings; Identifying Objects, Actions, and Events. *Mental Process:* Organizing, Planning, and Prioritizing; Making Decisions and Solving Problems; Processing Information. *Work Output:* Handling and Moving Objects; Performing General Physical Activities; Controlling Machines and Processes. *Interacting with Others:* Communicating with Other Workers; Establishing and Maintaining Interpersonal Relationships; Teaching Others. **Physical Work Conditions**—Noisy; Contaminants; High Places; Hazardous Conditions; Hazardous Equipment; Minor Burns, Cuts, Bites, or Stings. **Other Job Characteristics**—Need to Be Exact or Accurate; Pace Determined by Speed of Equipment; Errors Have Important Consequences; Repeat Same Tasks.

Experience—Job Zone 2. Some previous work-related skill, knowledge, or experience may be helpful in these occupations, but usually is not needed. **Job Preparation**—SVP 4.0 to less than 6.0—six months to less than two years. **Knowledges**—Production and Processing; Mechanical Devices; Engineering and Technology; Public Safety and Security; Education and Training; Physics. **Instructional Program**—No related CIP programs.

Related SOC Job—51-9051 Furnace, Kiln, Oven, Drier, and Kettle Operators and Tenders. **Related OOH Job**—Furnace, Kiln, Oven, Drier, and Kettle Operators and Tenders. **Related DOT Jobs**—361.685-010 Conditioner-Tumbler Operator; 369.685-026 Rug-Dry-Room Attendant; 369.685-034 Tumbler Operator; 503.685-022 Flame Degreaser; 504.485-010 Rivet Heater; 504.685-030 Reel-Blade-Bender Furnace Tender; 509.565-010 Kiln Operator; 509.685-018 Burning-Plant Operator; 511.482-010 Control Operator; 511.565-014 Drier Tender; 512.685-018 Pot Tender; 513.362-010 Calciner Operator; 513.462-010 Furnace Operator; 513.565-010 Kiln Operator; 513.682-010 Rotary-Kiln Operator; others.

51-9061.00 Inspectors, Testers, Sorters, Samplers, and Weighers

- **Education/Training Required: Moderate-term on-the-job training**
- **Employed: 506,160**
- **Annual Earnings: $29,200**
- **Growth: −2.6%**
- **Annual Job Openings: 85,000**

Inspect, test, sort, sample, or weigh nonagricultural raw materials or processed, machined, fabricated, or assembled parts or products for defects, wear, and deviations from specifications. May use precision measuring instruments and complex test equipment.

Discard or reject products, materials, and equipment not meeting specifications. Analyze and interpret blueprints, data, manuals, and other materials to determine specifications, inspection and testing procedures, adjustment and certification methods, formulas, and measuring instruments required. Inspect, test, or measure materials, products, installations, and work for conformance to specifications. Notify supervisors and other personnel of production problems and assist in identifying and correcting these problems. Discuss inspection results with those responsible for products and recommend necessary corrective actions. Record inspection or test data, such as weights, temperatures, grades, or moisture content and quantities inspected or graded. Mark items with details such as grade and acceptance or rejection status. Observe and monitor production operations and equipment to ensure conformance to specifications and make or order necessary process or assembly adjustments. Measure dimensions of products to verify conformance to specifications, using measuring instruments such as rulers, calipers, gauges, or micrometers. Analyze test data and make computations as necessary to determine test results. Collect or select samples for testing or for use as models. Check arriving materials to ensure that they match purchase orders and submit discrepancy reports when problems are found. Compare colors, shapes, textures, or grades of products or materials with color charts, templates, or samples to verify conformance to standards. Write test and inspection reports describing results, recommendations, and needed repairs. Read dials and meters to verify that equipment is functioning at specified levels. Remove defects, such as chips and burrs, and lap corroded or pitted surfaces. Clean, maintain, repair, and calibrate measuring instruments and test equipment such as dial indicators, fixed gauges, and height gauges. Adjust, clean, or repair products or processing equipment to correct defects found during inspections. Stack and arrange tested products for further processing, shipping, or packaging and transport products to other workstations as necessary.

GOE Information—**Interest Area:** 13. Manufacturing. **Work Group:** 13.07. Production Quality Control. **Personality Type**—Realistic. Realistic occupations frequently involve work activities that include practical, hands-on problems and solutions. They often deal with plants; animals; and real-world materials like wood, tools, and machinery. Many of the occupations require working outside and do not involve a lot of paperwork or working closely with others. **Work Values**—Responsibility; Supervision, Technical; Independence; Activity; Supervision, Human Relations; Autonomy. **Skills**—Quality Control Analysis; Operation Monitoring; Operation and Control; Repairing; Instructing; Systems Evaluation. **Abilities**—*Cognitive:* Category Flexibility; Flexibility of Closure; Perceptual Speed; Selective Attention; Visualization. *Psychomotor:* Manual Dexterity; Arm-Hand Steadiness; Finger Dexterity; Control Precision; Multilimb Coordination. *Physical:* Trunk Strength. *Sensory:* Auditory Attention; Visual Color Discrimination. **General Work Activities**—*Information Input:* Monitoring Processes, Materials, or Surroundings; Identifying Objects, Actions, and Events; Inspecting Equipment, Structures, or Materials. *Mental Process:* Updating and Using Relevant Knowledge; Judging the Qualities of Things, Services, or Other People's Work; Processing Information. *Work Output:* Handling and Moving Objects; Documenting or Recording Information; Controlling Machines and Processes. *Interacting with Others:* Establishing and Maintaining Interpersonal Relationships; Communicating with Other Workers; Interpreting the Meaning of Information to Others. **Physical Work Conditions**—Noisy; Standing; Using Hands on Objects, Tools, or Controls; Repetitive Motions. **Other Job Characteristics**—Need to Be Exact or Accurate; Errors Have Important Consequences.

Experience—Job Zone 2. Some previous work-related skill, knowledge, or experience may be helpful in these occupations, but usually is not needed. **Job Preparation**—SVP 4.0 to less than 6.0—six months to less than two years. **Knowledges**—Production and Processing. **Instructional Program**—Quality Control Technology/Technician.

Related SOC Job—51-9061 Inspectors, Testers, Sorters, Samplers, and Weighers. **Related OOH Job**—Inspectors, Testers, Sorters, Samplers, and Weighers. **Related DOT Jobs**—194.387-010 Quality-Control Inspector; 194.387-014 Record Tester; 199.171-010 Proof Technician; 199.361-010 Radiographer; 222.367-046 Petroleum Inspector; 222.384-010 Inspector, Receiving; 222.687-042 Inspector, Handbag Frames; 343.687-010 Plastic-Card Grader, Cardroom; 361.587-010 Flatwork Tier; 361.687-010 Assembler, Wet Wash; 361.687-014 Classifier; 361.687-022 Linen Grader; 369.687-010 Assembler; 369.687-014 Checker; 369.687-022 Inspector; 369.687-026 Marker; 369.687-030 Rug Inspector; others.

51-9071.00 Jewelers and Precious Stone and Metal Workers

- **Education/Training Required: Postsecondary vocational training**
- **Employed: 28,100**
- **Annual Earnings: $29,430**
- **Growth: 0.0%**
- **Annual Job Openings: 6,000**

The job openings listed here are shared with 51-9071.01 Jewelers, 51-9071.06 Gem and Diamond Workers, and 51-9071.07 Precious Metal Workers.

Design, fabricate, adjust, repair, or appraise jewelry, gold, silver, other precious metals, or gems. Includes diamond polishers and gem cutters and persons who perform precision casting and modeling of molds, casting metal in molds, or setting precious and semi-precious stones for jewelry and related products.

No task data available.

GOE Information—Interest Area: 13. Manufacturing. **Work Group:** 13.06. Production Precision Work. **Note:** The Department of Labor has not collected some data for this job, so it has fewer details than the other descriptions.

Instructional Program—Watchmaking and Jewelrymaking.

Related SOC Job—51-9071 Jewelers and Precious Stone and Metal Workers. **Related OOH Job**—Jewelers and Precious Stone and Metal Workers. **Related DOT Job**—No data available.

51-9071.01 Jewelers

- **Education/Training Required: Postsecondary vocational training**
- **Employed: 28,100**
- **Annual Earnings: $29,430**
- **Growth: 0.0%**
- **Annual Job Openings: 6,000**

The job openings listed here are shared with 51-9071.00 Jewelers and Precious Stone and Metal Workers, 51-9071.06 Gem and Diamond Workers, and 51-9071.07 Precious Metal Workers.

Fabricate and repair jewelry articles. Make models or molds to create jewelry items.

Plate articles such as jewelry pieces and watch dials, using silver, gold, nickel, or other metals. Burn grooves or crevices in molds to correct defects, using soldering guns. Immerse gemstones in chemical

solutions to determine specific gravity and other key properties necessary for identification and appraisal. Position stones and metal pieces and set, mount, and secure items in place, using setting and hand tools. Pour molten metal alloys or other materials into molds to cast models of jewelry. Remove mold castings from metal or jewelry workpieces and place workpieces in water or on trays to cool. Melt and roll out metal into sheets or bars and stamp out jewelry such as gold and silver chains, using presses or dies. Select and acquire metals and gems for designs. Record the weights and processing times of finished pieces. Press models into clay and build up clay around exposed parts of models to retain plaster. Mark and drill holes in jewelry mountings to center stones according to design specifications. Grade stones based on their color, perfection, and quality of cut. Examine gemstone surfaces and internal structures to evaluate genuineness, quality, and value, using polariscopes, refractometers, and other optical instruments. Determine appraised values of diamonds and other gemstones based on price guides, market fluctuations, and stone grades and rarity. Design and fabricate molds, models, and machine accessories and modify hand tools used to cast metal and jewelry pieces. Smooth soldered joints and rough spots, using hand files and emery paper, and polish smoothed areas with polishing wheels or buffing wire. Compute costs of labor and materials to determine production costs of products and articles. Build sand molds in flasks, following patterns, and heat flasks to dry and harden molds, using furnaces or torches. Alter existing jewelry mountings to reposition jewels or to adjust mountings. Soften metal to be used in designs by heating it with a gas torch and shape it, using hammers and dies. Buy and sell jewelry or serve as agents between buyers and sellers.

GOE Information—Interest Area: 13. Manufacturing. **Work Group:** 13.06. Production Precision Work. **Personality Type**—Realistic. Realistic occupations frequently involve work activities that include practical, hands-on problems and solutions. They often deal with plants; animals; and real-world materials like wood, tools, and machinery. Many of the occupations require working outside and do not involve a lot of paperwork or working closely with others. **Work Values**—Working Conditions; Independence; Ability Utilization; Autonomy; Creativity; Variety. **Skills**—Repairing; Quality Control Analysis; Science; Installation. **Abilities**—*Cognitive:* Visualization; Category Flexibility; Memorization; Originality. *Psychomotor:* Finger Dexterity; Arm-Hand Steadiness; Manual Dexterity; Wrist-Finger Speed; Control Precision; Multilimb Coordination. *Physical:* None met the criteria. *Sensory:* Visual Color Discrimination; Near Vision. **General Work Activities**—*Information Input:* Identifying Objects, Actions, and Events; Getting Information; Monitoring Processes, Materials, or Surroundings. *Mental Process:* Judging the Qualities of Things, Services, or Other People's Work; Thinking Creatively; Updating and Using Relevant Knowledge. *Work Output:* Handling and Moving Objects; Controlling Machines and Processes. *Interacting with Others:* None met the criteria. **Physical Work Conditions**—Indoors; Sitting; Using Hands on Objects, Tools, or Controls; Repetitive Motions. **Other Job Characteristics**—Need to Be Exact or Accurate.

Experience—Job Zone 4. A minimum of two to four years of work-related skill, knowledge, or experience is needed. **Job Preparation**—SVP 7.0 to less than 8.0—two years to less than 10 years. **Knowledges**—Fine Arts; Production and Processing; Design; Chemistry; Mechanical Devices. **Instructional Program**—Watchmaking and Jewelrymaking.

Related SOC Job—51-9071 Jewelers and Precious Stone and Metal Workers. **Related OOH Job**—Jewelers and Precious Stone and Metal Workers. **Related DOT Jobs**—199.281-010 Gemologist; 502.381-010

Caster; 502.682-018 Centrifugal-Casting-Machine Operator; 518.381-010 Bench-Molder Apprentice; 518.381-022 Molder, Bench; 700.281-010 Jeweler; 700.281-014 Jeweler Apprentice; 700.281-018 Model Maker I; 700.381-010 Chain Maker, Hand; 700.381-014 Fancy-Wire Drawer; 700.381-018 Goldbeater; 700.381-026 Lay-Out Worker; 700.381-030 Locket Maker; 700.381-034 Mold Maker I; 700.381-038 Mold-Maker Apprentice; 700.381-042 Ring Maker; 700.381-046 Sample Maker I; others.

51-9071.06 Gem and Diamond Workers

- **Education/Training Required: Postsecondary vocational training**
- **Employed: 28,100**
- **Annual Earnings: $29,430**
- **Growth: 0.0%**
- **Annual Job Openings: 6,000**

The job openings listed here are shared with 51-9071.00 Jewelers and Precious Stone and Metal Workers, 51-9071.01 Jewelers, and 51-9071.07 Precious Metal Workers.

Fabricate, finish, or evaluate the quality of gems and diamonds used in jewelry or industrial tools.

Regulate the speed of revolutions and reciprocating actions of drilling mechanisms. Regrind drill points and advance drill cutting points according to specifications for channel depths and shapes. Measure sizes of stones' bore holes and cuts to ensure adherence to specifications, using precision measuring instruments. Assign polish, symmetry, and clarity grades to stones according to established grading systems. Replace, true, and sharpen blades, drills, and plates. Lap girdles on rough diamonds, using diamond-girdling lathes. Locate and mark drilling or cutting positions on stones or dies, using diamond chips and power hand tools. Lap inner walls of channels, using machines that revolve stones and rotate wires or needles in channels. Secure gems or diamonds in holders, chucks, dops, lapidary sticks, or blocks for cutting, polishing, grinding, drilling, or shaping. Select shaping wheels for tasks and mix and apply abrasives, bort, or polishing compounds. Sort rough diamonds into categories based on shape, size, color, and quality. Test accuracy of die holes by pulling specified lengths of wire through dies and measuring their resistance or by taking a series of readings along the lengths of wires, using electronic micrometers. Secure stones in metal mountings, using solder. Immerse stones in prescribed chemical solutions to determine specific gravities and key properties of gemstones or substitutes. Examine gem surfaces and internal structures, using polariscopes, refractometers, microscopes, and other optical instruments to differentiate between stones; to identify rare specimens; or to detect flaws, defects, or peculiarities affecting gem values. Split gems along pre-marked lines to remove imperfections, using blades and jewelers' hammers. Estimate wholesale and retail value of gems, following pricing guides, market fluctuations, and other relevant economic factors. Grind, drill, and finish jewel bearings for use in precision instruments such as compasses and chronometers. Dismantle lapping, boring, cutting, polishing, and shaping equipment and machinery to clean and lubricate it.

GOE Information—Interest Area: 13. Manufacturing. **Work Group:** 13.06. Production Precision Work. **Personality Type—**Realistic. Realistic occupations frequently involve work activities that include practical, hands-on problems and solutions. They often deal with plants; animals; and real-world materials like wood, tools, and machinery. Many of the occupations require working outside and do not involve a lot of paperwork or working closely with others. **Work Values—**Independence; Supervision, Technical; Compensation;

Ability Utilization; Working Conditions; Recognition. **Skills—**Equipment Maintenance. **Abilities—***Cognitive:* Visualization; Selective Attention. *Psychomotor:* Arm-Hand Steadiness; Control Precision; Finger Dexterity; Wrist-Finger Speed; Manual Dexterity. *Physical:* None met the criteria. *Sensory:* Near Vision; Visual Color Discrimination. **General Work Activities—***Information Input:* Getting Information; Identifying Objects, Actions, and Events; Monitoring Processes, Materials, or Surroundings. *Mental Process:* Judging the Qualities of Things, Services, or Other People's Work; Evaluating Information Against Standards. *Work Output:* Handling and Moving Objects; Controlling Machines and Processes; Performing General Physical Activities. *Interacting with Others:* None met the criteria. **Physical Work Conditions—**Indoors; Hazardous Equipment; Minor Burns, Cuts, Bites, or Stings; Sitting; Using Hands on Objects, Tools, or Controls. **Other Job Characteristics—**Need to Be Exact or Accurate; Errors Have Important Consequences.

Experience—Job Zone 2. Some previous work-related skill, knowledge, or experience may be helpful in these occupations, but usually is not needed. **Job Preparation—**SVP 4.0 to less than 6.0—six months to less than two years. **Knowledges—**Mechanical Devices; Engineering and Technology; Production and Processing. **Instructional Program—**Watchmaking and Jewelrymaking.

Related SOC Job—51-9071 Jewelers and Precious Stone and Metal Workers. **Related OOH Job—**Jewelers and Precious Stone and Metal Workers. **Related DOT Jobs—**770.261-010 Brilliandeer-Lopper; 770.261-014 Girdler; 770.281-010 Diamond Selector; 770.281-014 Gem Cutter; 770.381-014 Diamond Cleaver; 770.381-018 Diamond Driller; 770.381-022 Diamond-Die Polisher; 770.381-026 Jewel Blocker and Sawyer; 770.381-030 Jewel-Bearing Maker; 770.381-034 Oliving-Machine Operator; 770.381-038 Sapphire-Stylus Grinder; 770.381-042 Spotter; 770.382-010 Lathe Operator; 770.382-014 Phonograph-Needle-Tip Maker.

51-9071.07 Precious Metal Workers

- **Education/Training Required: Postsecondary vocational training**
- **Employed: 28,100**
- **Annual Earnings: $29,430**
- **Growth: 0.0%**
- **Annual Job Openings: 6,000**

The job openings listed here are shared with 51-9071.00 Jewelers and Precious Stone and Metal Workers, 51-9071.01 Jewelers, and 51-9071.06 Gem and Diamond Workers.

Cast, anneal, solder, hammer, or shape gold, silver, pewter, or other metals to form jewelry or other metal items such as goblets or candlesticks.

Weigh completed items to determine weights and record any deviations. Shape and straighten damaged or twisted articles by hand or using pliers. Solder parts together or fill holes and cracks with metal solder, using gas torches. Strike articles with small tools or punch them with hammers to indent them or restore embossing. Trim gates and sharp points from cast parts, using band saws. Verify that bottom edges of articles are level by using straightedges or by rocking them back and forth on flat surfaces. Weigh and mix alloy ingredients, using formulas and knowledge of ingredients' chemical properties. Wire parts such as legs, spouts, and handles to article bodies in preparation for soldering. Strike molds to separate dried castings from molds. Carry castings or finished items to storage areas or to different workstations. Route out locations where parts are to be joined to items, using routing machines. Secure molded items in chucks of lathes and activate lathes to finish inner and outer surfaces of items. Sand interior mold parts to remove glaze residue, apply new glaze to molds, and allow it to dry for mold assembly. Design silver articles such as jewelry and serving pieces. Design and fabricate models of new casting molds and chipping and turning tools used to finish product surfaces. Research reference materials, analyze production data, and consult with interested parties to develop ideas for new products. Assemble molds, wrap molds in heat-resistant cloth, and ladle molten alloy into mold openings, repeating casting processes as necessary to produce specified numbers of parts. Glue plastic separators to handles of coffeepots and teapots. Rotate molds to distribute alloys and to prevent formation of air pockets. Anneal precious metal objects such as coffeepots, tea sets, and trays in gas ovens for prescribed times to soften metal for reworking. Cut and file pieces of jewelry such as rings, brooches, bracelets, and lockets. Determine placement of auxiliary parts, such as handles and spouts, and mark locations of parts. Engrave decorative lines on items, using engraving tools.

GOE Information—Interest Area: 13. Manufacturing. **Work Group:** 13.06. Production Precision Work. **Personality Type—**Realistic. Realistic occupations frequently involve work activities that include practical, hands-on problems and solutions. They often deal with plants; animals; and real-world materials like wood, tools, and machinery. Many of the occupations require working outside and do not involve a lot of paperwork or working closely with others. **Work Values—**Independence; Creativity; Variety; Autonomy; Ability Utilization; Working Conditions. **Skills—**None met the criteria. **Abilities—***Cognitive:* Visualization; Originality. *Psychomotor:* Arm-Hand Steadiness; Wrist-Finger Speed; Manual Dexterity; Speed of Limb Movement; Control Precision; Finger Dexterity. *Physical:* Explosive Strength; Extent Flexibility; Static Strength. *Sensory:* None met the criteria. **General Work Activities—***Information Input:* Getting Information; Identifying Objects, Actions, and Events; Monitoring Processes, Materials, or Surroundings. *Mental Process:* Thinking Creatively; Judging the Qualities of Things, Services, or Other People's Work. *Work Output:* Handling and Moving Objects; Performing General Physical Activities; Controlling Machines and Processes. *Interacting with Others:* None met the criteria. **Physical Work Conditions—**Indoors; Very Hot or Cold; Hazardous Equipment; More Often Sitting Than Standing; Using Hands on Objects, Tools, or Controls. **Other Job Characteristics—**None met the criteria.

Experience—Job Zone 3. Previous work-related skill, knowledge, or experience is required. **Job Preparation—**SVP 6.0 to less than 7.0—more than one year and less than four years. **Knowledges—**Fine Arts; Production and Processing; Mechanical Devices; Design. **Instructional Program—**Watchmaking and Jewelrymaking.

Related SOC Job—51-9071 Jewelers and Precious Stone and Metal Workers. **Related OOH Job—**Jewelers and Precious Stone and Metal Workers. **Related DOT Jobs—**502.384-010 Pewter Caster; 700.261-010 Pewterer; 700.281-022 Silversmith II; 700.281-026 Pewter Finisher; 700.381-022 Hammersmith; 700.381-581 Pewter Fabricator; 704.381-010 Chaser.

51-9081.00 Dental Laboratory Technicians

- **Education/Training Required: Long-term on-the-job training**
- **Employed: 45,600**
- **Annual Earnings: $32,240**
- **Growth: 7.6%**
- **Annual Job Openings: 3,000**

Construct and repair full or partial dentures or dental appliances.

Read prescriptions or specifications and examine models and impressions to determine the design of dental products to be constructed. Fabricate, alter, and repair dental devices such as dentures, crowns, bridges, inlays, and appliances for straightening teeth. Place tooth models on apparatus that mimics bite and movement of patient's jaw to evaluate functionality of model. Test appliances for conformance to specifications and accuracy of occlusion, using articulators and micrometers. Melt metals or mix plaster, porcelain, or acrylic pastes and pour materials into molds or over frameworks to form dental prostheses or apparatus. Prepare metal surfaces for bonding with porcelain to create artificial teeth, using small hand tools. Remove excess metal or porcelain and polish surfaces of prostheses or frameworks, using polishing machines. Create a model of patient's mouth by pouring plaster into a dental impression and allowing plaster to set. Load newly constructed teeth into porcelain furnaces to bake the porcelain onto the metal framework. Build and shape wax teeth, using small hand instruments and information from observations or dentists' specifications. Apply porcelain paste or wax over prosthesis frameworks or setups, using brushes and spatulas. Fill chipped or low spots in surfaces of devices, using acrylic resins. Prepare wax bite-blocks and impression trays for use. Mold wax over denture setups to form the full contours of artificial gums. Train and supervise other dental technicians or dental laboratory bench workers. Rebuild or replace linings, wire sections, and missing teeth to repair dentures. Shape and solder wire and metal frames or bands for dental products, using soldering irons and hand tools.

GOE Information—Interest Area: 13. Manufacturing. **Work Group:** 13.06. Production Precision Work. **Personality Type—**Realistic. Realistic occupations frequently involve work activities that include practical, hands-on problems and solutions. They often deal with plants; animals; and real-world materials like wood, tools, and machinery. Many of the occupations require working outside and do not involve a lot of paperwork or working closely with others. **Work Values—**Independence; Supervision, Technical; Working Conditions; Moral Values; Recognition; Supervision, Human Relations. **Skills—**Equipment Maintenance; Equipment Selection; Management of Material Resources; Repairing; Quality Control Analysis; Operation Monitoring. **Abilities—***Cognitive:* Perceptual Speed; Visualization; Flexibility of Closure. *Psychomotor:* Control Precision; Arm-Hand Steadiness; Wrist-Finger Speed; Finger Dexterity; Manual Dexterity; Reaction Time. *Physical:* None met the criteria. *Sensory:* Hearing Sensitivity; Depth Perception; Auditory Attention; Visual Color Discrimination; Far Vision. **General Work Activities—***Information Input:* Monitoring Processes, Materials, or Surroundings; Identifying Objects, Actions, and Events; Inspecting Equipment, Structures, or Materials. *Mental Process:* Organizing, Planning, and Prioritizing; Updating and Using Relevant Knowledge; Thinking Creatively. *Work Output:* Controlling Machines and Processes; Handling and Moving Objects. *Interacting with Others:* Establishing and Maintaining Interpersonal Relationships; Communicating with Other Workers; Teaching Others. **Physical Work Conditions—**Indoors; Noisy; Contaminants; Sitting; Using Hands on Objects, Tools, or Controls; Repetitive Motions. **Other Job Characteristics—**Need to Be Exact or Accurate; Repeat Same Tasks.

Experience—Job Zone 2. Some previous work-related skill, knowledge, or experience may be helpful in these occupations, but usually is not needed. **Job Preparation—**SVP 4.0 to less than 6.0—six months to less than two years. **Knowledges—**Medicine and Dentistry; Design; Production and Processing; Engineering and Technology; Mechanical Devices; Chemistry. **Instructional Program—**Dental Laboratory Technology/Technician.

Related SOC Job—51-9081 Dental Laboratory Technicians. **Related OOH Job**—Medical, Dental, and Ophthalmic Laboratory Technicians. **Related DOT Jobs**—712.381-014 Contour Wire Specialist, Denture; 712.381-018 Dental-Laboratory Technician; 712.381-022 Dental-Laboratory-Technician Apprentice; 712.381-026 Orthodontic Band Maker; 712.381-030 Orthodontic Technician; 712.381-042 Dental Ceramist; 712.381-046 Denture Waxer; 712.381-050 Finisher, Denture; 712.664-010 Dental Ceramist Assistant.

51-9082.00 Medical Appliance Technicians

- **Education/Training Required: Long-term on-the-job training**
- **Employed: 10,810**
- **Annual Earnings: $29,080**
- **Growth: 13.2%**
- **Annual Job Openings: 1,000**

Construct, fit, maintain, or repair medical supportive devices, such as braces, artificial limbs, joints, arch supports, and other surgical and medical appliances.

Fit appliances onto patients and make any necessary adjustments. Make orthotic/prosthetic devices using materials such as thermoplastic and thermosetting materials, metal alloys and leather, and hand and power tools. Read prescriptions or specifications to determine the type of product or device to be fabricated and the materials and tools that will be required. Repair, modify, and maintain medical supportive devices, such as artificial limbs, braces, and surgical supports, according to specifications. Instruct patients in use of prosthetic or orthotic devices. Take patients' body or limb measurements for use in device construction. Construct or receive casts or impressions of patients' torsos or limbs for use as cutting and fabrication patterns. Bend, form, and shape fabric or material so that it conforms to prescribed contours needed to fabricate structural components. Drill and tap holes for rivets and glue, weld, bolt, and rivet parts together to form prosthetic or orthotic devices. Lay out and mark dimensions of parts, using templates and precision measuring instruments. Test medical supportive devices for proper alignment, movement, and biomechanical stability, using meters and alignment fixtures. Cover or pad metal or plastic structures and devices, using coverings such as rubber, leather, felt, plastic, or fiberglass. Polish artificial limbs, braces, and supports, using grinding and buffing wheels. Service and repair machinery used in the fabrication of appliances. Mix pigments to match patients' skin coloring, according to formulas, and apply mixtures to orthotic or prosthetic devices.

GOE Information—Interest Area: 13. Manufacturing. **Work Group:** 13.06. Production Precision Work. **Personality Type**—Realistic. Realistic occupations frequently involve work activities that include practical, hands-on problems and solutions. They often deal with plants; animals; and real-world materials like wood, tools, and machinery. Many of the occupations require working outside and do not involve a lot of paperwork or working closely with others. **Work Values**—Independence; Social Service; Achievement; Recognition; Supervision, Technical; Social Status. **Skills**—Technology Design; Repairing; Installation; Quality Control Analysis; Active Learning; Science. **Abilities**—*Cognitive:* Visualization; Mathematical Reasoning; Number Facility; Perceptual Speed; Problem Sensitivity; Deductive Reasoning. *Psychomotor:* Control Precision; Arm-Hand Steadiness; Wrist-Finger Speed; Finger Dexterity; Multilimb Coordination; Reaction Time. *Physical:* Dynamic Strength; Static Strength; Trunk Strength. *Sensory:* Visual Color Discrimination; Hearing Sensitivity; Depth Perception; Far Vision; Auditory Attention; Speech Recognition. **General Work Activities**—*Information Input:* Monitoring Processes, Materials, or Surroundings; Getting Information; Identifying Objects, Actions, and Events. *Mental Process:* Updating and Using Relevant Knowledge; Thinking Creatively; Scheduling Work and Activities. *Work Output:* Handling and Moving Objects; Controlling Machines and Processes; Performing General Physical Activities. *Interacting with Others:* Establishing and Maintaining Interpersonal Relationships; Assisting and Caring for Others; Resolving Conflicts and Negotiating with Others. **Physical Work Conditions**—Indoors; Noisy; Contaminants; Disease or Infections; Hazardous Equipment; Using Hands on Objects, Tools, or Controls. **Other Job Characteristics**—Need to Be Exact or Accurate.

Experience—Job Zone 3. Previous work-related skill, knowledge, or experience is required. **Job Preparation**—SVP 6.0 to less than 7.0—more than one year and less than four years. **Knowledges**—Production and Processing; Design; Mechanical Devices; Medicine and Dentistry; Customer and Personal Service; Engineering and Technology. **Instructional Programs**—Assistive/Augmentative Technology and Rehabiliation Engineering; Orthotist/Prosthetist.

Related SOC Job—51-9082 Medical Appliance Technicians. **Related OOH Job**—Medical, Dental, and Ophthalmic Laboratory Technicians. **Related DOT Jobs**—712.381-010 Arch-Support Technician; 712.381-034 Orthotics Technician; 712.381-038 Prosthetics Technician; 713.261-014 Artificial-Plastic-Eye Maker.

51-9083.00 Ophthalmic Laboratory Technicians

- **Education/Training Required: Moderate-term on-the-job training**
- **Employed: 26,740**
- **Annual Earnings: $24,740**
- **Growth: 7.8%**
- **Annual Job Openings: 2,000**

Cut, grind, and polish eyeglasses, contact lenses, or other precision optical elements. Assemble and mount lenses into frames or process other optical elements.

Adjust lenses and frames to correct alignment. Mount, secure, and align finished lenses in frames or optical assemblies, using precision hand tools. Mount and secure lens blanks or optical lenses in holding tools or chucks of cutting, polishing, grinding, or coating machines. Shape lenses appropriately so that they can be inserted into frames. Assemble eyeglass frames and attach shields, nose pads, and temple pieces, using pliers, screwdrivers, and drills. Inspect lens blanks to detect flaws, verify smoothness of surface, and ensure thickness of coating on lenses. Clean finished lenses and eyeglasses, using cloths and solvents. Select lens blanks, molds, tools, and polishing or grinding wheels according to production specifications. Examine prescriptions, work orders, or broken or used eyeglasses to determine specifications for lenses, contact lenses, and other optical elements. Set dials and start machines to polish lenses or hold lenses against rotating wheels to polish them manually. Set up machines to polish, bevel, edge, and grind lenses, flats, blanks, and other precision optical elements. Repair broken parts, using precision hand tools and soldering irons. Position and adjust cutting tools to specified curvature, dimensions, and depth of cut. Inspect, weigh, and measure mounted or unmounted lenses after completion to verify alignment and conformance to specifications, using precision instruments. Remove lenses from molds and separate lenses in containers for further processing or storage. Lay out lenses and trace lens outlines on glass, using templates. Immerse eyeglass frames in solutions to harden, soften, or dye frames. Control equipment that coats lenses to alter their reflective qualities.

GOE Information—Interest Area: 13. Manufacturing. **Work Group:** 13.06. Production Precision Work. **Personality Type—**Realistic. Realistic occupations frequently involve work activities that include practical, hands-on problems and solutions. They often deal with plants; animals; and real-world materials like wood, tools, and machinery. Many of the occupations require working outside and do not involve a lot of paperwork or working closely with others. **Work Values—**Independence; Moral Values; Supervision, Technical; Working Conditions; Supervision, Human Relations; Advancement. **Skills—**Repairing; Service Orientation; Operation Monitoring; Quality Control Analysis; Instructing; Management of Material Resources. **Abilities—***Cognitive:* Number Facility; Mathematical Reasoning; Memorization. *Psychomotor:* Arm-Hand Steadiness; Manual Dexterity; Finger Dexterity; Wrist-Finger Speed; Control Precision; Multilimb Coordination. *Physical:* Extent Flexibility; Trunk Strength. *Sensory:* Near Vision; Visual Color Discrimination; Depth Perception. **General Work Activities—***Information Input:* Monitoring Processes, Materials, or Surroundings; Inspecting Equipment, Structures, or Materials; Identifying Objects, Actions, and Events. *Mental Process:* Updating and Using Relevant Knowledge; Making Decisions and Solving Problems; Organizing, Planning, and Prioritizing. *Work Output:* Controlling Machines and Processes; Handling and Moving Objects; Repairing and Maintaining Mechanical Equipment. *Interacting with Others:* Establishing and Maintaining Interpersonal Relationships; Providing Consultation and Advice to Others; Communicating with Other Workers. **Physical Work Conditions—**Indoors; Noisy; Standing; Walking and Running; Using Hands on Objects, Tools, or Controls; Repetitive Motions. **Other Job Characteristics—**Need to Be Exact or Accurate; Pace Determined by Speed of Equipment; Repeat Same Tasks.

Experience—Job Zone 2. Some previous work-related skill, knowledge, or experience may be helpful in these occupations, but usually is not needed. **Job Preparation—**SVP 4.0 to less than 6.0—six months to less than two years. **Knowledges—**Computers and Electronics; Administration and Management; Mathematics. **Instructional Program—**Ophthalmic Laboratory Technology/Technician.

Related SOC Job—51-9083 Ophthalmic Laboratory Technicians. **Related OOH Job—**Medical, Dental, and Ophthalmic Laboratory Technicians. **Related DOT Jobs—**711.381-010 Optical-Instrument Assembler; 713.381-010 Lens-Mold Setter; 713.681-010 Lens Mounter II; 716.280-010 Optician Apprentice; 716.280-014 Optician; 716.280-018 Optician; 716.280-540 Shop Optician, Surface Room; 716.280-541 Shop Optician, Benchroom; 716.381-014 Lay-Out Technician; 716.382-010 Lathe Operator, Contact Lens; 716.382-014 Optical-Element Coater; 716.382-018 Precision-Lens Grinder; 716.382-022 Precision-Lens-Grinder Apprentice; 716.462-010 Precision-Lens Centerer and Edger; others.

51-9111.00 Packaging and Filling Machine Operators and Tenders

- **Education/Training Required: Short-term on-the-job training**
- **Employed: 396,270**
- **Annual Earnings: $22,930**
- **Growth: 2.3%**
- **Annual Job Openings: 80,000**

Operate or tend machines to prepare industrial or consumer products for storage or shipment. Includes cannery workers who pack food products.

Observe machine operations to ensure quality and conformity of filled or packaged products to standards. Adjust machine components and machine tension and pressure according to size or processing angle of product. Tend or operate machine that packages product. Remove finished packaged items from machine and separate rejected items. Regulate machine flow, speed, or temperature. Stop or reset machines when malfunctions occur, clear machine jams, and report malfunctions to a supervisor. Secure finished packaged items by hand-tying, sewing, gluing, stapling, or attaching fastener. Stock and sort product for packaging or filling machine operation and replenish packaging supplies, such as wrapping paper, plastic sheet, boxes, cartons, glue, ink, or labels. Inspect and remove defective products and packaging material. Clean and remove damaged or otherwise inferior materials to prepare raw products for processing. Sort, grade, weigh, and inspect products, verifying and adjusting product weight or measurement to meet specifications. Clean, oil, and make minor adjustments or repairs to machinery and equipment, such as opening valves or setting guides. Monitor the production line, watching for problems such as pile-ups, jams, or glue that isn't sticking properly. Stack finished packaged items or wrap protective material around each item and pack the items in cartons or containers. Start machine by engaging controls. Count and record finished and rejected packaged items. Package the product in the form in which it will be sent out, for example, filling bags with flour from a chute or spout. Supply materials to spindles, conveyors, hoppers, or other feeding devices and unload packaged product. Attach identification labels to finished packaged items or cut stencils and stencil information on containers, such as lot numbers or shipping destinations. Clean packaging containers, line and pad crates, or assemble cartons to prepare for product packing.

GOE Information—Interest Area: 13. Manufacturing. **Work Group:** 13.03. Production Work, Assorted Materials Processing. **Personality Type—**Realistic. Realistic occupations frequently involve work activities that include practical, hands-on problems and solutions. They often deal with plants; animals; and real-world materials like wood, tools, and machinery. Many of the occupations require working outside and do not involve a lot of paperwork or working closely with others. **Work Values—**Moral Values; Independence; Supervision, Technical; Supervision, Human Relations; Activity; Company Policies and Practices. **Skills—**Equipment Maintenance; Operation and Control; Operation Monitoring; Quality Control Analysis; Repairing; Troubleshooting. **Abilities—***Cognitive:* Perceptual Speed; Selective Attention; Flexibility of Closure; Speed of Closure; Spatial Orientation; Visualization. *Psychomotor:* Reaction Time; Response Orientation; Wrist-Finger Speed; Control Precision; Rate Control; Manual Dexterity. *Physical:* Static Strength; Extent Flexibility; Dynamic Strength; Trunk Strength; Stamina; Gross Body Coordination. *Sensory:* Auditory Attention; Peripheral Vision; Hearing Sensitivity; Depth Perception; Far Vision; Visual Color Discrimination. **General Work Activities—***Information Input:* Identifying Objects, Actions, and Events; Monitoring Processes, Materials, or Surroundings; Inspecting Equipment, Structures, or Materials. *Mental Process:* Updating and Using Relevant Knowledge; Thinking Creatively; Making Decisions and Solving Problems. *Work Output:* Performing General Physical Activities; Handling and Moving Objects; Controlling Machines and Processes. *Interacting with Others:* Communicating with Other Workers; Establishing and Maintaining Interpersonal Relationships; Teaching Others. **Physical Work Conditions—**Noisy; Contaminants; Hazardous Equipment; Standing; Using Hands on Objects, Tools, or Controls; Repetitive Motions. **Other Job Characteristics—**Need to Be Exact or Accurate; Repeat Same Tasks; Pace Determined by Speed of Equipment; Automation.

Experience—Job Zone 2. Some previous work-related skill, knowledge, or experience may be helpful in these occupations, but usually is not needed. **Job Preparation**—SVP 4.0 to less than 6.0—six months to less than two years. **Knowledges**—Production and Processing; Mechanical Devices; Sociology and Anthropology; Psychology; Public Safety and Security; Education and Training. **Instructional Program**—No related CIP programs.

Related SOC Job—51-9111 Packaging and Filling Machine Operators and Tenders. **Related OOH Job**—Packaging and Filling Machine Operators and Tenders. **Related DOT Jobs**—509.685-046 Scrap Baller; 518.683-010 Sand-Slinger Operator; 520.685-174 Molder, Meat; 520.685-210 Stuffer; 520.685-218 Tray-Casting-Machine Operator; 524.685-030 Filling Machine Tender; 525.685-014 Casing-Running-Machine Tender; 529.665-010 Fruit-Grader Operator; 529.665-022 Yeast-Cutting-and-Wrapping-Machine Operator; 529.685-010 Auto Roller; 529.685-038 Bunch Maker, Machine; 529.685-138 Ham-Rolling-Machine Operator; 529.685-162 Linking-Machine Operator; others.

51-9121.00 Coating, Painting, and Spraying Machine Setters, Operators, and Tenders

- **Education/Training Required: Moderate-term on-the-job training**
- **Employed: 100,830**
- **Annual Earnings: $26,670**
- **Growth: –3.4%**
- **Annual Job Openings: 16,000**

Set up, operate, or tend machines to coat or paint any of a wide variety of products, including food, glassware, cloth, ceramics, metal, plastic, paper, or wood, with lacquer, silver, copper, rubber, varnish, glaze, enamel, oil, or rustproofing materials.

Observe machine gauges and equipment operation to detect defects or deviations from standards and make adjustments as necessary. Determine paint flow, viscosity, and coating quality by performing visual inspections or by using viscometers. Weigh or measure chemicals, coatings, or paints before adding them to machines. Select appropriate coatings, paints, or sprays or prepare them by mixing substances according to formulas, using automated paint mixing equipment. Set up and operate machines to paint or coat products with such materials as silver and copper solution, rubber, paint, glaze, oil, or rustproofing materials. Turn dials, handwheels, valves, or switches to regulate conveyor speeds, machine temperature, air pressure and circulation, and the flow or spray of coatings or paints. Start and stop operation of machines, using levers or buttons. Record operational data on specified forms. Start pumps to mix solutions and fill tanks. Fill hoppers, reservoirs, troughs, or pans with material used to coat, paint, or spray, using conveyors or pails. Operate auxiliary machines or equipment used in coating or painting processes. Perform test runs to ensure that equipment is set up properly. Clean machines, related equipment, and work areas, using water, solvents, and other cleaning aids. Thread or feed items or products through or around machine rollers and dryers. Attach hoses or nozzles to machines, using wrenches and pliers, and make adjustments to obtain the proper dispersion of spray. Remove materials, parts, or workpieces from painting or coating machines, using hand tools. Transfer completed items or products from machines to drying or

storage areas, using handcarts, handtrucks, or cranes. Attach and align machine parts such as rollers, guides, brushes, and blades, using hand tools. Examine, measure, weigh, or test sample products to ensure conformance to specifications. Hold or position spray guns to direct spray onto articles. Place items or products on feedracks, spindles, or reel strands to coat, paint, or spray them, using hands, hoists, or trucklifts. Prepare and apply stencils, computer-generated decals, or other decorative items to finished products.

GOE Information—**Interest Area:** 13. Manufacturing. **Work Group:** 13.03. Production Work, Assorted Materials Processing. **Personality Type**—Realistic. Realistic occupations frequently involve work activities that include practical, hands-on problems and solutions. They often deal with plants; animals; and real-world materials like wood, tools, and machinery. Many of the occupations require working outside and do not involve a lot of paperwork or working closely with others. **Work Values**—Moral Values; Independence; Supervision, Technical; Activity; Supervision, Human Relations; Company Policies and Practices. **Skills**—Operation Monitoring; Equipment Maintenance; Operation and Control; Quality Control Analysis; Installation; Repairing. **Abilities**—*Cognitive:* Perceptual Speed; Visualization; Memorization; Speed of Closure; Flexibility of Closure; Time Sharing. *Psychomotor:* Rate Control; Reaction Time; Response Orientation; Multilimb Coordination; Control Precision; Manual Dexterity. *Physical:* Extent Flexibility; Static Strength; Trunk Strength; Dynamic Strength; Gross Body Coordination; Stamina. *Sensory:* Visual Color Discrimination; Depth Perception; Glare Sensitivity; Hearing Sensitivity; Far Vision; Auditory Attention. **General Work Activities**—*Information Input:* Monitoring Processes, Materials, or Surroundings; Inspecting Equipment, Structures, or Materials; Identifying Objects, Actions, and Events. *Mental Process:* Judging the Qualities of Things, Services, or Other People's Work; Updating and Using Relevant Knowledge; Making Decisions and Solving Problems. *Work Output:* Controlling Machines and Processes; Handling and Moving Objects; Performing General Physical Activities. *Interacting with Others:* Communicating with Other Workers; Establishing and Maintaining Interpersonal Relationships; Interpreting the Meaning of Information to Others. **Physical Work Conditions**—Noisy; Contaminants; Hazardous Conditions; Standing; Using Hands on Objects, Tools, or Controls; Repetitive Motions. **Other Job Characteristics**—Need to Be Exact or Accurate; Pace Determined by Speed of Equipment; Repeat Same Tasks.

Experience—Job Zone 2. Some previous work-related skill, knowledge, or experience may be helpful in these occupations, but usually is not needed. **Job Preparation**—SVP 4.0 to less than 6.0—six months to less than two years. **Knowledges**—Production and Processing; Mechanical Devices. **Instructional Program**—No related CIP programs.

Related SOC Job—51-9121 Coating, Painting, and Spraying Machine Setters, Operators, and Tenders. **Related OOH Job**—Painting and Coating Workers, Except Construction and Maintenance. **Related DOT Jobs**—524.382-010 Coating-Machine Operator; 524.382-014 Enrobing-Machine Operator; 524.665-010 Sanding-Machine Operator; 524.682-010 Depositing-Machine Operator; 524.685-014 Cheese Sprayer; 524.685-018 Coating Operator; 524.685-022 Cracker Sprayer; 524.685-026 Enrobing-Machine Operator; 524.685-034 Icer, Machine; 534.380-010 Carbon-Paper-Coating-Machine Setter; 534.482-010 Waxing-Machine Operator; 534.582-010 Paper-Coating-Machine Operator; 534.682-010 Air-Drier-Machine Operator; others.

51-9122.00 Painters, Transportation Equipment

- **Education/Training Required: Moderate-term on-the-job training**
- **Employed: 52,650**
- **Annual Earnings: $34,840**
- **Growth: 14.1%**
- **Annual Job Openings: 10,000**

Operate or tend painting machines to paint surfaces of transportation equipment, such as automobiles, buses, trucks, trains, boats, and airplanes.

Dispose of hazardous waste in an appropriate manner. Select paint according to company requirements and match colors of paint following specified color charts. Mix paints to match color specifications or vehicles' original colors; then stir and thin the paints, using spatulas or power mixing equipment. Remove grease, dirt, paint, and rust from vehicle surfaces in preparation for paint application, using abrasives, solvents, brushes, blowtorches, washing tanks, or sandblasters. Pour paint into spray guns and adjust nozzles and paint mixes to get the proper paint flow and coating thickness. Monitor painting operations to identify flaws such as blisters and streaks so that their causes can be corrected. Sand vehicle surfaces between coats of paint or primer to remove flaws and enhance adhesion for subsequent coats. Disassemble, clean, and reassemble sprayers and power equipment, using solvents, wire brushes, and cloths for cleaning duties. Remove accessories from vehicles, such as chrome or mirrors, and mask other surfaces with tape or paper to protect them from paint. Spray prepared surfaces with specified amounts of primers and decorative or finish coatings. Allow the sprayed product to dry and then touch up any spots that may have been missed. Apply rust-resistant undercoats and caulk and seal seams. Select the correct spray gun system for the material being applied. Apply primer over any repairs made to vehicle surfaces. Adjust controls on infrared ovens, heat lamps, portable ventilators, and exhaust units to speed the drying of vehicles between coats. Fill small dents and scratches with body fillers and smooth surfaces to prepare vehicles for painting. Apply designs, lettering, or other identifying or decorative items to finished products, using paint brushes or paint sprayers. Paint by hand areas that cannot be reached with a spray gun or those that need retouching, using brushes. Sand the final finish and apply sealer once a vehicle has dried properly. Buff and wax the finished paintwork. Lay out logos, symbols, or designs on painted surfaces according to blueprint specifications, using measuring instruments, stencils, and patterns.

GOE Information—Interest Area: 13. Manufacturing. **Work Group:** 13.09. Hands-On Work, Assorted Materials. **Personality Type—** Realistic. Realistic occupations frequently involve work activities that include practical, hands-on problems and solutions. They often deal with plants; animals; and real-world materials like wood, tools, and machinery. Many of the occupations require working outside and do not involve a lot of paperwork or working closely with others. **Work Values—**Moral Values; Independence; Supervision, Technical; Supervision, Human Relations; Company Policies and Practices. **Skills—**Repairing; Equipment Maintenance; Monitoring; Technology Design; Operation and Control; Coordination. **Abilities—***Cognitive:* Visualization; Selective Attention. *Psychomotor:* Reaction Time; Manual Dexterity; Multilimb Coordination; Rate Control; Arm-Hand Steadiness; Control Precision. *Physical:* Extent Flexibility; Static Strength; Gross Body Equilibrium; Trunk Strength; Dynamic Strength; Gross Body Coordination. *Sensory:* Visual Color Discrimination; Glare Sensitivity; Depth Perception. **General Work Activities—***Information Input:* Inspecting Equipment, Structures, or Materials; Getting Information; Monitoring Processes, Materials, or Surroundings. *Mental Process:* Updating and Using Relevant Knowledge; Evaluating Information Against Standards; Organizing, Planning, and Prioritizing. *Work Output:* Handling and Moving Objects; Performing General Physical Activities; Repairing and Maintaining Mechanical Equipment. *Interacting with Others:* Establishing and Maintaining Interpersonal Relationships; Communicating with Other Workers; Coordinating the Work and Activities of Others. **Physical Work Conditions—**Noisy; Contaminants; Hazardous Conditions; Standing; Using Hands on Objects, Tools, or Controls; Repetitive Motions. **Other Job Characteristics—**Need to Be Exact or Accurate; Repeat Same Tasks.

Experience—Job Zone 2. Some previous work-related skill, knowledge, or experience may be helpful in these occupations, but usually is not needed. **Job Preparation—**SVP 4.0 to less than 6.0—six months to less than two years. **Knowledges—**Chemistry; Production and Processing; Mechanical Devices. **Instructional Program—** Autobody/Collision and Repair Technology and Technician.

Related SOC Job—51-9122 Painters, Transportation Equipment. **Related OOH Job—**Painting and Coating Workers, Except Construction and Maintenance. **Related DOT Jobs—**845.381-010 Painter Apprentice, Transportation Equipment; 845.381-014 Painter, Transportation Equipment; 845.381-018 Paint Sprayer, Sandblaster; 845.681-010 Railroad-Car Letterer.

51-9123.00 Painting, Coating, and Decorating Workers

- **Education/Training Required: Short-term on-the-job training**
- **Employed: 27,830**
- **Annual Earnings: $22,640**
- **Growth: 7.9%**
- **Annual Job Openings: 5,000**

Paint, coat, or decorate articles such as furniture, glass, plateware, pottery, jewelry, cakes, toys, books, or leather.

Apply coatings, such as paint, ink, or lacquer, to protect or decorate workpiece surfaces, using spray guns, pens, or brushes. Examine finished surfaces of workpieces to verify conformance to specifications; then retouch any defective areas. Clean and maintain tools and equipment, using solvents, brushes, and rags. Read job orders and inspect workpieces to determine work procedures and materials required. Clean surfaces of workpieces in preparation for coating, using cleaning fluids, solvents, brushes, scrapers, steam, sandpaper, or cloth. Rinse, drain, or wipe coated workpieces to remove excess coating material or to facilitate setting of finish coats on workpieces. Place coated workpieces in ovens or dryers for specified times to dry or harden finishes. Select and mix ingredients to prepare coating substances according to specifications, using paddles or mechanical mixers. Melt or heat coating materials to specified temperatures. Conceal blemishes in workpieces, such as nicks and dents, using fillers such as putty. Immerse workpieces into coating materials for specified times. Cut out sections in surfaces of materials to be inlaid with decorative pieces, using patterns and knives or scissors. Position and glue decorative pieces in cutout sections of workpieces, following patterns.

GOE Information—Interest Area: 13. Manufacturing. **Work Group:** 13.09. Hands-On Work, Assorted Materials. **Personality Type—** Realistic. Realistic occupations frequently involve work activities that include practical, hands-on problems and solutions. They often deal with plants; animals; and real-world materials like wood, tools, and machinery. Many of the occupations require working outside and do not involve a lot of paperwork or working closely with others. **Work Values**—Moral Values; Independence; Supervision, Technical. **Skills**—Repairing; Equipment Maintenance; Equipment Selection; Monitoring; Learning Strategies; Quality Control Analysis. **Abilities**—*Cognitive:* None met the criteria. *Psychomotor:* Arm-Hand Steadiness; Control Precision; Wrist-Finger Speed; Multilimb Coordination; Manual Dexterity; Finger Dexterity. *Physical:* Trunk Strength; Extent Flexibility. *Sensory:* Visual Color Discrimination; Depth Perception. **General Work Activities**—*Information Input:* Inspecting Equipment, Structures, or Materials; Monitoring Processes, Materials, or Surroundings; Getting Information. *Mental Process:* Organizing, Planning, and Prioritizing; Making Decisions and Solving Problems; Thinking Creatively. *Work Output:* Handling and Moving Objects; Controlling Machines and Processes; Performing General Physical Activities. *Interacting with Others:* Establishing and Maintaining Interpersonal Relationships; Teaching Others; Communicating with Other Workers. **Physical Work Conditions**—Noisy; Contaminants; Standing; Using Hands on Objects, Tools, or Controls; Bending or Twisting the Body; Repetitive Motions. **Other Job Characteristics**—Need to Be Exact or Accurate; Repeat Same Tasks; Pace Determined by Speed of Equipment.

Experience—Job Zone 2. Some previous work-related skill, knowledge, or experience may be helpful in these occupations, but usually is not needed. **Job Preparation**—SVP 4.0 to less than 6.0–six months to less than two years. **Knowledges**—Fine Arts; Production and Processing; Design; Sales and Marketing; Transportation. **Instructional Program**—Graphic Design.

Related SOC Job—51-9123 Painting, Coating, and Decorating Workers. **Related OOH Job**—Painting and Coating Workers, Except Construction and Maintenance. **Related DOT Jobs**—364.381-010 Painter, Rug Touch-Up; 500.684-022 Silver Spray Worker; 505.684-010 Electroless Plater; 505.684-014 Metal Sprayer, Production; 509.684-010 Enameler; 524.381-010 Cake Decorator; 524.381-014 Decorator; 524.684-010 Candy Dipper, Hand; 524.684-014 Decorator; 524.684-018 Enrobing-Machine Corder; 524.684-022 Icer, Hand; 554.384-010 Dyer; 554.684-010 Caustic Operator; 562.687-010 Dyer; 562.687-014 Resin Coater; 574.484-010 Optical-Glass Silverer; 574.684-010 Ground Layer; others.

51-9131.00 Photographic Process Workers

- **Education/Training Required: Moderate-term on-the-job training**
- **Employed: 28,000**
- **Annual Earnings: $21,870**
- **Growth: –11.4%**
- **Annual Job Openings: 7,000**

Perform precision work involved in photographic processing, such as editing photographic negatives and prints, using photo-mechanical, chemical, or computerized methods.

Read work orders to determine required processes, techniques, materials, and equipment. Produce color or black-and-white photographs, negatives, and slides, applying standard photographic reproduction techniques and procedures. Examine drawings, negatives, or photographic prints to determine coloring, shading, accenting, and other changes required for retouching or restoration. Mix developing and fixing solutions according to established formulas. Create work prints according to customer specifications and lab protocols. Cut

negatives and put them in order. Place identification on film as necessary. Examine developed prints for defects such as broken lines, spots, and blurs. Reprint originals to enlarge them, or reprint them in sections to be pieced together. Trim edges of prints to enhance appearance, using scissors or paper cutters. Produce timed prints with separate densities and color settings for each scene of a production. Immerse film, negatives, paper, or prints in developing solutions, fixing solutions, and water to complete photographic development processes. Place sensitized paper in frames of projection printers, photostats, or other reproduction machines. Correct color work prints to adjust for outdoor filming. Thread film strips through densitometers and expose film to light to determine density of film and necessary color corrections. Mount original photographs, negatives, or other printed material in holders or vacuum frames beneath lights. Select lens assemblies according to sizes and types of negatives or photographs to be printed. Record test data from film that has been examined and route film to film developers and film printers for further processing. Set automatic timers, lens openings, and printer carriages to specified focus and exposure times and start exposure to duplicate originals, photographs, or negatives. Evaluate film and negatives to determine characteristics such as sensitivity to light, density, and exposure time required for printing. Dry prints or negatives, using sponges or squeegees, mechanical air dryers, or drying cabinets.

GOE Information—**Interest Area:** 13. Manufacturing. **Work Group:** 13.08. Graphic Arts Production. **Personality Type**—Realistic. Realistic occupations frequently involve work activities that include practical, hands-on problems and solutions. They often deal with plants; animals; and real-world materials like wood, tools, and machinery. Many of the occupations require working outside and do not involve a lot of paperwork or working closely with others. **Work Values**—Independence; Moral Values; Supervision, Technical; Working Conditions. **Skills**—Equipment Maintenance; Operation and Control; Operation Monitoring; Quality Control Analysis; Troubleshooting; Time Management. **Abilities**—*Cognitive:* Flexibility of Closure; Visualization; Time Sharing; Memorization; Perceptual Speed; Selective Attention. *Psychomotor:* Rate Control; Reaction Time; Arm-Hand Steadiness; Manual Dexterity; Control Precision; Wrist-Finger Speed. *Physical:* Trunk Strength. *Sensory:* Visual Color Discrimination; Far Vision; Depth Perception; Hearing Sensitivity; Near Vision. **General Work Activities**—*Information Input:* Monitoring Processes, Materials, or Surroundings; Inspecting Equipment, Structures, or Materials; Getting Information. *Mental Process:* Updating and Using Relevant Knowledge; Thinking Creatively; Organizing, Planning, and Prioritizing. *Work Output:* Handling and Moving Objects; Controlling Machines and Processes; Interacting With Computers. *Interacting with Others:* Establishing and Maintaining Interpersonal Relationships; Communicating with Other Workers; Performing for or Working with the Public. **Physical Work Conditions**—Indoors; Contaminants; Hazardous Conditions; Standing; Using Hands on Objects, Tools, or Controls; Repetitive Motions. **Other Job Characteristics**—Need to Be Exact or Accurate; Repeat Same Tasks; Pace Determined by Speed of Equipment.

Experience—Job Zone 2. Some previous work-related skill, knowledge, or experience may be helpful in these occupations, but usually is not needed. **Job Preparation**—SVP 4.0 to less than 6.0–six months to less than two years. **Knowledges**—Fine Arts; Chemistry; Sales and Marketing; Production and Processing; Mechanical Devices; Computers and Electronics. **Instructional Program**—Photographic and Film/Video Technology/Technician and Assistant.

Related SOC Job—51-9131 Photographic Process Workers. **Related OOH Job**—Photographic Process Workers and Processing Machine

Operators. **Related DOT Jobs**—970.281-010 Airbrush Artist; 970.281-018 Photograph Retoucher; 970.381-010 Colorist, Photography; 970.381-034 Spotter, Photographic; 976.361-010 Reproduction Technician; 976.381-010 Film Laboratory Technician I; 976.381-018 Projection Printer; 976.381-022 Template Reproduction Technician; 976.382-022 Photostat Operator; 976.681-010 Developer.

51-9132.00 Photographic Processing Machine Operators

- **Education/Training Required: Short-term on-the-job training**
- **Employed: 53,970**
- **Annual Earnings: $19,250**
- **Growth: –30.7%**
- **Annual Job Openings: 10,000**

Operate photographic processing machines, such as photographic printing machines, film-developing machines, and mounting presses.

Remove completed work from equipment. Place film in labeled containers or number film for identification by hand or by using numbering machines. Read work orders and examine negatives and film to determine machine settings and processing requirements. Load circuit boards, racks or rolls of film, negatives, and printing paper into processing or printing machines. Insert processed negatives and prints into envelopes so that they can be returned to customers. Fill tanks of processing machines with solutions such as developer, dyes, stop-baths, fixers, bleaches, and washes. Sort film to be developed according to criteria such as film type or completion date. Measure and mix chemicals to prepare solutions for processing according to formulas. Monitor equipment operation to detect malfunctions. Clean and maintain photoprocessing equipment, using cleaning and rinsing solutions and ultrasonic equipment. Operate special equipment to perform tasks such as transferring film to videotape or producing photographic enlargements. Set and adjust machine controls, according to specifications, type of operation, and material requirements. Maintain records such as quantities and types of processing completed, rate of materials usage, and customer charges. Start and operate machines to prepare circuit boards and to expose, develop, etch, fix, wash, dry, and print film or plates. Inspect film or circuit patterns on photographic plates to locate any defects; discard defective products or repair them, using cleaning solutions and hand tools. Splice broken or separated film and mount film on reels. Retouch photographic negatives or original prints to correct defects.

GOE Information—Interest Area: 13. Manufacturing. **Work Group:** 13.08. Graphic Arts Production. **Personality Type**—Realistic. Realistic occupations frequently involve work activities that include practical, hands-on problems and solutions. They often deal with plants; animals; and real-world materials like wood, tools, and machinery. Many of the occupations require working outside and do not involve a lot of paperwork or working closely with others. **Work Values**—Independence; Moral Values; Working Conditions; Supervision, Technical; Supervision, Human Relations; Company Policies and Practices. **Skills**—Operation Monitoring; Operation and Control; Equipment Maintenance; Repairing; Science; Technology Design. **Abilities**—*Cognitive:* Flexibility of Closure; Perceptual Speed. *Psychomotor:* Control Precision; Arm-Hand Steadiness; Manual Dexterity; Multilimb Coordination; Finger Dexterity. *Physical:* None met the criteria. *Sensory:* Visual Color Discrimination; Hearing Sensitivity. **General Work Activities**—*Information Input:* Inspecting Equipment, Structures, or Materials; Monitoring Processes, Materials, or Surroundings; Identifying Objects, Actions, and Events. *Mental Process:* Updating and Using Relevant Knowledge; Organizing,

Planning, and Prioritizing; Making Decisions and Solving Problems. *Work Output:* Handling and Moving Objects; Controlling Machines and Processes; Repairing and Maintaining Electronic Equipment. *Interacting with Others:* Establishing and Maintaining Interpersonal Relationships; Communicating with Other Workers; Coordinating the Work and Activities of Others. **Physical Work Conditions**—Indoors; Hazardous Conditions; Standing; Using Hands on Objects, Tools, or Controls; Repetitive Motions. **Other Job Characteristics**—Need to Be Exact or Accurate; Pace Determined by Speed of Equipment; Repeat Same Tasks.

Experience—Job Zone 2. Some previous work-related skill, knowledge, or experience may be helpful in these occupations, but usually is not needed. **Job Preparation**—SVP 4.0 to less than 6.0—six months to less than two years. **Knowledges**—Production and Processing; Chemistry; Sales and Marketing; Administration and Management; Customer and Personal Service; Education and Training. **Instructional Program**—Photographic and Film/Video Technology/Technician and Assistant.

Related SOC Job—51-9132 Photographic Processing Machine Operators. **Related OOH Job**—Photographic Process Workers and Processing Machine Operators. **Related DOT Jobs**—976.380-010 Computer-Controlled-Color-Photograph-Printer Operator; 976.382-014 Color-Printer Operator; 976.382-018 Film Developer; 976.382-030 Photographic Aligner, Semiconductor Wafers; 976.382-034 Step-and-Repeat Reduction Camera Operator; 976.382-038 Photo Mask Pattern Generator; 976.384-010 Photo Technician; 976.384-014 Photo Mask Processor; 976.385-010 Microfilm Processor; 976.665-010 Take-Down Sorter; 976.682-010 Film Printer; 976.682-014 Printer Operator, Black-and-White; others.

51-9141.00 Semiconductor Processors

- **Education/Training Required: Associate degree**
- **Employed: 44,720**
- **Annual Earnings: $31,030**
- **Growth: –7.5%**
- **Annual Job Openings: 7,000**

Perform any or all of the following functions in the manufacture of electronic semiconductors: Load semiconductor material into furnace; saw formed ingots into segments; load individual segment into crystal-growing chamber and monitor controls; locate crystal axis in ingot, using X-ray equipment, and saw ingots into wafers; and clean, polish, and load wafers into series of special-purpose furnaces, chemical baths, and equipment used to form circuitry and change conductive properties.

Manipulate valves, switches, and buttons or key commands into control panels to start semiconductor processing cycles. Inspect materials, components, or products for surface defects and measure circuitry, using electronic test equipment, precision measuring instruments, microscope, and standard procedures. Maintain processing, production, and inspection information and reports. Clean semiconductor wafers, using cleaning equipment, such as chemical baths, automatic wafer cleaners, or blow-off wands. Study work orders, instructions, formulas, and processing charts to determine specifications and sequence of operations. Load and unload equipment chambers and transport finished product to storage or to area for further processing. Clean and maintain equipment, including replacing etching and rinsing solutions and cleaning bath containers and work area. Place semiconductor wafers in processing containers or equipment holders, using vacuum wand or tweezers. Set, adjust, and readjust computerized or mechanical equipment controls to regulate power level, temperature, vacuum, and rotation speed of furnace, according to crystal-growing specifications. Etch, lap, polish, or grind wafers or ingots to form circuitry and change conductive properties, using etching, lapping, polishing, or grinding equipment. Load semiconductor material into furnace. Monitor operation and adjust controls of processing machines and equipment to produce compositions with specific electronic properties, using computer terminals. Count, sort, and weigh processed items. Calculate etching time based on thickness of material to be removed from wafers or crystals. Inspect equipment for leaks, diagnose malfunctions, and request repairs. Align photo mask pattern on photoresist layer, expose pattern to ultraviolet light, and develop pattern, using specialized equipment. Stamp, etch, or scribe identifying information on finished component according to specifications. Operate saw to cut remelt into sections of specified size or to cut ingots into wafers. Scribe or separate wafers into dice. Connect reactor to computer, using hand tools and power tools.

GOE Information—Interest Area: 13. Manufacturing. Work Group: 13.06. Production Precision Work. Personality Type—Realistic. Realistic occupations frequently involve work activities that include practical, hands-on problems and solutions. They often deal with plants; animals; and real-world materials like wood, tools, and machinery. Many of the occupations require working outside and do not involve a lot of paperwork or working closely with others. Work Values—Independence; Moral Values; Company Policies and Practices; Supervision, Human Relations; Supervision, Technical; Advancement. Skills—Operation Monitoring; Repairing; Equipment Maintenance; Installation; Troubleshooting; Operation and Control. Abilities—Cognitive: Perceptual Speed; Visualization; Written Expression; Selective Attention. Psychomotor: Rate Control; Response Orientation; Arm-Hand Steadiness; Finger Dexterity; Reaction Time; Control Precision. Physical: Static Strength; Trunk Strength. Sensory: Visual Color Discrimination; Depth Perception. General Work Activities—Information Input: Monitoring Processes, Materials, or Surroundings; Identifying Objects, Actions, and Events; Inspecting Equipment, Structures, or Materials. Mental Process: Organizing, Planning, and Prioritizing; Updating and Using Relevant Knowledge; Evaluating Information Against Standards. Work Output: Handling and Moving Objects; Controlling Machines and Processes; Performing General Physical Activities. Interacting with Others: Communicating with Other Workers; Establishing and Maintaining Interpersonal Relationships; Coordinating the Work and Activities of Others. Physical Work Conditions—Indoors; Noisy; Contaminants; Hazardous Conditions; Standing; Using Hands on Objects, Tools, or Controls. Other Job Characteristics—Need to Be Exact or Accurate; Errors Have Important Consequences; Repeat Same Tasks; Pace Determined by Speed of Equipment.

Experience—Job Zone 2. Some previous work-related skill, knowledge, or experience may be helpful in these occupations, but usually is not needed. Job Preparation—SVP 4.0 to less than 6.0—six months to less than two years. Knowledges—Production and Processing; Chemistry; Computers and Electronics; English Language; Education and Training; Engineering and Technology. Instructional Program—Industrial Electronics Technology/Technician.

Related SOC Job—51-9141 Semiconductor Processors. Related OOH Job—Semiconductor Processors. Related DOT Jobs—590.262-010 Crystal Growing Technician; 590.262-014 Test Technician, Semiconductor Processing Equipment; 590.282-010 Epitaxial Reactor Technician; 590.362-018 Group Leader, Semiconductor Processing; 590.362-022 Microelectronics Technician; 590.364-010 Lead Worker, Wafer Production; 590.382-014 Crystal Grower; 590.382-018 Epitaxial Reactor Operator; 590.382-022 Ion Implant Machine Operator; 590.384-010 Charge Preparation Technician; 590.684-014 Electronic-Component Processor; others.

51-9191.00 Cementing and Gluing Machine Operators and Tenders

- Education/Training Required: Moderate-term on-the-job training
- Employed: 25,650
- Annual Earnings: $24,490
- Growth: 1.9%
- Annual Job Openings: 4,000

Operate or tend cementing and gluing machines to join items for further processing or to form a completed product. Processes include joining veneer sheets into plywood; gluing paper; and joining rubber and rubberized fabric parts, plastic, simulated leather, or other materials.

Examine and measure completed materials or products to verify conformance to specifications, using measuring devices such as tape measures, gauges, or calipers. Monitor machine operations to detect malfunctions; report or resolve problems. Adjust machine components according to specifications such as widths, lengths, and thickness of materials and amounts of glue, cement, or adhesive required. Read work orders and communicate with co-workers to determine machine and equipment settings and adjustments and supply and product specifications. Fill machines with glue, cement, or adhesives. Mount or load material such as paper, plastic, wood, or rubber in feeding mechanisms of cementing or gluing machines. Maintain production records such as quantities, dimensions, and thicknesses of materials processed. Start machines and turn valves or move controls to feed, admit, apply, or transfer materials and adhesives and to adjust temperature, pressure, and time settings. Perform test production runs and make adjustments as necessary to ensure that completed products meet standards and specifications. Remove jammed materials from machines and readjust components as necessary to resume normal operations. Align and position materials being joined to ensure accurate application of adhesive or heat sealing. Observe gauges, meters, and control panels to obtain information about equipment temperatures and pressures or the speed of feeders or conveyors. Remove and stack completed materials or products and restock materials to be joined. Clean and maintain gluing and cementing machines, using solutions, lubricants, brushes, and scrapers. Transport materials, supplies, and finished products between storage and work areas, using forklifts. Measure and mix ingredients to prepare glue. Depress pedals to lower electrodes that heat and seal edges of material.

GOE Information—Interest Area: 13. Manufacturing. Work Group: 13.03. Production Work, Assorted Materials Processing. Personality Type—Realistic. Realistic occupations frequently involve work activities that include practical, hands-on problems and solutions. They often deal with plants; animals; and real-world materials like wood, tools, and machinery. Many of the occupations require working outside and do not involve a lot of paperwork or working closely with others. Work Values—Moral Values; Supervision, Technical; Supervision, Human Relations; Independence; Company Policies and Practices. Skills—Operation Monitoring; Equipment Maintenance; Operation and Control; Installation; Repairing; Troubleshooting. Abilities—Cognitive: Perceptual Speed; Visualization; Selective Attention; Flexibility of Closure. Psychomotor: Reaction Time; Rate Control; Response Orientation; Multilimb Coordination; Speed of Limb Movement; Control Precision. Physical: Extent Flexibility; Static Strength; Dynamic Strength; Gross Body Coordination; Stamina; Gross Body Equilibrium. Sensory: Depth Perception; Auditory Attention; Hearing Sensitivity; Visual Color Discrimination; Far Vision. General Work Activities—Information Input: Monitoring

Processes, Materials, or Surroundings; Getting Information; Identifying Objects, Actions, and Events. *Mental Process:* Making Decisions and Solving Problems; Organizing, Planning, and Prioritizing; Processing Information. *Work Output:* Handling and Moving Objects; Performing General Physical Activities; Controlling Machines and Processes. *Interacting with Others:* Communicating with Other Workers; Establishing and Maintaining Interpersonal Relationships; Teaching Others. **Physical Work Conditions**—Noisy; Contaminants; Standing; Using Hands on Objects, Tools, or Controls; Bending or Twisting the Body; Repetitive Motions. **Other Job Characteristics**—Pace Determined by Speed of Equipment; Need to Be Exact or Accurate; Errors Have Important Consequences; Repeat Same Tasks.

Experience—Job Zone 2. Some previous work-related skill, knowledge, or experience may be helpful in these occupations, but usually is not needed. **Job Preparation**—SVP 4.0 to less than 6.0—six months to less than two years. **Knowledges**—Production and Processing; Mechanical Devices. **Instructional Program**—No related CIP programs.

Related SOC Job—51-9191 Cementing and Gluing Machine Operators and Tenders. **Related OOH Job**—Cementing and Gluing Machine Operators and Tenders. **Related DOT Jobs**—554.682-014 Masking-Machine Operator; 554.685-030 Laminator; 569.565-010 Crew Leader, Gluing; 569.685-018 Core Feeder, Plywood Layup Line; 569.685-022 Core-Composer-Machine Tender; 569.685-026 Core-Laying-Machine Operator; 569.685-034 Edge-Glue-Machine Tender; 569.685-042 Glue Spreader, Veneer; 569.685-054 Hot-Plate-Plywood-Press Operator; 569.685-062 Splicer Operator; 579.685-022 Glass-Wool-Blanket-Machine Feeder; 584.665-014 Glue-Spreading-Machine Operator; others.

51-9192.00 Cleaning, Washing, and Metal Pickling Equipment Operators and Tenders

- Education/Training Required: Moderate-term on-the-job training
- Employed: 15,250
- Annual Earnings: $22,770
- Growth: 1.0%
- Annual Job Openings: 3,000

Operate or tend machines to wash or clean products such as barrels or kegs, glass items, tin plate, food, pulp, coal, plastic, or rubber to remove impurities.

Add specified amounts of chemicals to equipment at required times to maintain solution levels and concentrations. Drain, clean, and refill machines or tanks at designated intervals, using cleaning solutions or water. Load machines with objects to be processed; then unload objects after cleaning and place them on conveyors or racks. Measure, weigh, or mix cleaning solutions, using measuring tanks, calibrated rods, or suction tubes. Examine and inspect machines to detect malfunctions. Operate or tend machines to wash and remove impurities from items such as barrels or kegs, glass products, tin plate surfaces, dried fruit, pulp, animal stock, coal, manufactured articles, plastic, or rubber. Set controls to regulate temperature and length of cycles and start conveyors, pumps, agitators, and machines. Draw samples for laboratory analysis or test solutions for conformance to specifications, such as acidity or specific gravity. Record gauge readings, materials used, processing times, and test results in production logs. Adjust, clean, and lubricate mechanical parts of machines, using hand tools and grease guns. Observe machine operations, gauges, or thermometers and adjust controls to maintain specified conditions.

GOE Information—Interest Area: 13. Manufacturing. **Work Group:** 13.03. Production Work, Assorted Materials Processing. **Personality Type**—Realistic. Realistic occupations frequently involve work activities that include practical, hands-on problems and solutions. They often deal with plants; animals; and real-world materials like wood, tools, and machinery. Many of the occupations require working outside and do not involve a lot of paperwork or working closely with others. **Work Values**—Moral Values; Independence; Supervision, Technical; Supervision, Human Relations; Company Policies and Practices; Activity. **Skills**—Operation Monitoring; Operation and Control; Equipment Maintenance; Quality Control Analysis. **Abilities**—*Cognitive:* Number Facility. *Psychomotor:* Rate Control; Control Precision; Manual Dexterity. *Physical:* None met the criteria. *Sensory:* None met the criteria. **General Work Activities**—*Information Input:* Inspecting Equipment, Structures, or Materials; Identifying Objects, Actions, and Events; Monitoring Processes, Materials, or Surroundings. *Mental Process:* Evaluating Information Against Standards. *Work Output:* Handling and Moving Objects; Controlling Machines and Processes; Performing General Physical Activities. *Interacting with Others:* Performing Administrative Activities. **Physical Work Conditions**—Indoors; Noisy; Hazardous Equipment; Standing; Using Hands on Objects, Tools, or Controls; Repetitive Motions. **Other Job Characteristics**—Pace Determined by Speed of Equipment; Automation.

Experience—Job Zone 1. No previous work-related skill, knowledge, or experience is needed. **Job Preparation**—SVP below 4.0—less than six months. **Knowledges**—Production and Processing; Mechanical Devices. **Instructional Program**—No related CIP programs.

Related SOC Job—51-9192 Cleaning, Washing, and Metal Pickling Equipment Operators and Tenders. **Related OOH Job**—Cleaning, Washing, and Metal Pickling Equipment Operators and Tenders. **Related DOT Jobs**—503.685-026 Furnace-and-Wash-Equipment Operator; 503.685-030 Metal-Cleaner, Immersion; 503.685-034 Metal-Washing-Machine Operator; 509.685-014 Branner-Machine Tender; 511.685-022 Dust-Collector Attendant; 511.685-066 Trommel Tender; 521.685-110 Dried Fruit Washer; 529.665-014 Washroom Operator; 529.685-074 Container Washer, Machine; 529.685-226 Steamer; 529.685-254 Wash-House Worker; 529.685-258 Washer, Agricultural Produce; 529.685-262 Wheat Cleaner; 529.685-278 Yeast Washer; others.

51-9193.00 Cooling and Freezing Equipment Operators and Tenders

- Education/Training Required: Moderate-term on-the-job training
- Employed: 9,640
- Annual Earnings: $23,150
- Growth: 0.8%
- Annual Job Openings: 1,000

Operate or tend equipment, such as cooling and freezing units, refrigerators, batch freezers, and freezing tunnels, to cool or freeze products, food, blood plasma, and chemicals.

Adjust machine or freezer speed and air intake to obtain desired consistency and amount of product. Monitor pressure gauges, ammeters, flowmeters, thermometers, or products and adjust controls to maintain specified conditions, such as feed rate, product consistency, temperature, air pressure, and machine speed. Record temperatures, amounts of materials processed, and test results on report forms. Read dials and gauges on panel control boards to ascertain temperatures, alkalinities, and densities of mixtures and turn valves to obtain specified mixtures. Correct machinery malfunctions by performing actions such as removing jams and inform supervisors of malfunctions as necessary. Start machinery such as pumps, feeders, or conveyors and turn valves to heat, admit, or transfer products, refrigerants, or mixes. Assemble equipment and attach pipes, fittings, or valves, using hand tools. Scrape, dislodge, or break excess frost, ice, or frozen product from equipment to prevent accumulation, using hands and hand tools. Weigh packages and adjust freezer air valves or switches on filler heads to obtain specified amounts of product in each container. Stir material with spoons or paddles to mix ingredients or allow even cooling and prevent coagulation. Start agitators to blend contents or start beater, scraper, and expeller blades to mix contents with air and prevent sticking. Measure or weigh specified amounts of ingredients or materials and load them into tanks, vats, hoppers, or other equipment. Load and position wrapping paper, sticks, bags, or cartons into dispensing machines. Insert forming fixtures and start machines that cut frozen products into measured portions or specified shapes. Inspect and flush lines with solutions or steam and spray equipment with sterilizing solutions. Place or position containers into equipment and remove containers after completion of cooling or freezing processes. Position molds on conveyors and measure and adjust level of fill, using depth gauges. Sample and test product characteristics such as specific gravity, acidity, and sugar content, using hydrometers, pH meters, or refractometers.

GOE Information—Interest Area: 13. Manufacturing. Work Group: 13.03. Production Work, Assorted Materials Processing. Personality Type—Realistic. Realistic occupations frequently involve work activities that include practical, hands-on problems and solutions. They often deal with plants; animals; and real-world materials like wood, tools, and machinery. Many of the occupations require working outside and do not involve a lot of paperwork or working closely with others. Work Values—Moral Values; Independence; Supervision, Technical; Supervision, Human Relations; Company Policies and Practices. Skills—Repairing; Installation; Operation Monitoring; Equipment Maintenance; Operation and Control; Systems Analysis. Abilities—*Cognitive:* Perceptual Speed; Visualization; Selective Attention; Number Facility. *Psychomotor:* Reaction Time; Rate Control; Wrist-Finger Speed; Response Orientation; Control Precision; Speed of Limb Movement. *Physical:* Static Strength; Extent Flexibility; Trunk Strength; Dynamic Strength; Gross Body Coordination; Stamina. *Sensory:* Auditory Attention; Depth Perception; Visual Color Discrimination; Hearing Sensitivity; Far Vision. General Work Activities—*Information Input:* Monitoring Processes, Materials, or Surroundings; Identifying Objects, Actions, and Events; Inspecting Equipment, Structures, or Materials. *Mental Process:* Making Decisions and Solving Problems; Updating and Using Relevant Knowledge; Organizing, Planning, and Prioritizing. *Work Output:* Controlling Machines and Processes; Handling and Moving Objects; Performing General Physical Activities. *Interacting with Others:* Communicating with Other Workers; Establishing and Maintaining Interpersonal Relationships; Monitoring and Controlling Resources. Physical Work Conditions—Indoors; Noisy; Very Hot or Cold; Contaminants; Hazardous Equipment; Using Hands on Objects, Tools, or Controls. Other Job Characteristics—Need to Be Exact or Accurate; Pace Determined by Speed of Equipment; Errors Have Important Consequences; Repeat Same Tasks; Automation.

Experience—Job Zone 2. Some previous work-related skill, knowledge, or experience may be helpful in these occupations, but usually is not needed. Job Preparation—SVP 4.0 to less than 6.0—six months to less than two years. Knowledges—Mechanical Devices; Food

Production; Chemistry; Building and Construction; Physics; Design. Instructional Program—No related CIP programs.

Related SOC Job—51-9193 Cooling and Freezing Equipment Operators and Tenders. Related OOH Job—Cooling and Freezing Equipment Operators and Tenders. Related DOT Jobs—522.685-014 Brewery Cellar Worker; 523.585-014 Chiller Tender; 523.585-018 Crystallizer Operator; 523.685-010 Batch Freezer; 523.685-018 Chilling-Hood Operator; 523.685-038 Cooler Tender; 523.685-042 Cooling-Machine Operator; 523.685-046 Cooling-Pan Tender; 523.685-050 Crystallizer Operator; 523.685-082 Freezer Tunnel Operator; 523.685-102 Ice Maker; 529.482-010 Freezer Operator; 529.482-014 Novelty Maker I; 529.482-018 Novelty Maker II; 529.485-010 Barrel Filler; others.

51-9194.00 Etchers and Engravers

- Education/Training Required: Long-term on-the-job training
- Employed: 10,050
- Annual Earnings: $25,050
- Growth: 2.1%
- Annual Job Openings: 2,000

Engrave or etch metal, wood, rubber, or other materials for identification or decorative purposes. Includes such workers as etcher-circuit processors, pantograph engravers, and silk screen etchers.

Measure and compute dimensions of lettering, designs, or patterns to be engraved. Prepare etching chemicals according to formulas, diluting acid with water to obtain solutions of specified concentration. Position and clamp workpieces, plates, or rollers in holding fixtures. Guide stylus over template, causing cutting tool to duplicate design or letters on workpiece. Clean rollers prior to etching, using sponges, cleaning chemicals, and water. Prepare workpieces for etching or engraving by cutting, sanding, cleaning, polishing, or treating them with wax, acid resist, lime, etching powder, or light-sensitive enamel. Neutralize workpieces to remove acid, wax, or enamel, using water, solvents, brushes, or specialized machines. Select and mount wheels and miters on lathes and equip lathes with water to cool wheels and prevent dust when grinding glass. Inspect etched work for depth of etching, uniformity, and defects, using calibrated microscopes, gauges, fingers, or magnifying lenses. Insert cutting tools or bits into machines and secure them with wrenches. Observe actions of cutting tools through microscopes and adjust stylus movement to ensure accurate reproduction. Print proofs or examine designs to verify accuracy of engraving and rework engraving as required. Select and insert required templates into pattern frames beneath the stylus of a machine cutting tool or router. Set reduction scales to attain specified sizes of reproduction on workpieces and set pantograph controls for required heights, depths, and widths of cuts. Sketch, trace, or scribe layout lines and designs on workpieces, plates, dies, or rollers, using compasses, scribers, gravers, or pencils. Start machines and lower cutting tools to beginning points on patterns. Brush or smear abrasives on cutting wheels. Brush or wipe acid over engraving to darken or highlight inscriptions. Carve designs and letters onto metal for transfer to other surfaces. Clean and polish engraved areas. Cut outlines of impressions with gravers and remove excess material with knives. Remove completed workpieces and place them in trays.

GOE Information—Interest Area: 13. Manufacturing. Work Group: 13.08. Graphic Arts Production. Personality Type—Realistic. Realistic occupations frequently involve work activities that include practical, hands-on problems and solutions. They often deal with plants; animals; and real-world materials like wood, tools, and machinery. Many of the occupations require working outside and do not involve a lot of paperwork or working closely with others. **Work Values**—Independence; Moral Values; Supervision, Technical. **Skills**—None met the criteria. **Abilities**—*Cognitive:* Visualization. *Psychomotor:* Arm-Hand Steadiness; Wrist-Finger Speed; Manual Dexterity; Control Precision; Finger Dexterity; Multilimb Coordination. *Physical:* None met the criteria. *Sensory:* Depth Perception. **General Work Activities**—*Information Input:* Monitoring Processes, Materials, or Surroundings; Inspecting Equipment, Structures, or Materials; Getting Information. *Mental Process:* Judging the Qualities of Things, Services, or Other People's Work; Thinking Creatively. *Work Output:* Handling and Moving Objects; Controlling Machines and Processes. *Interacting with Others:* None met the criteria. **Physical Work Conditions**—Indoors; Hazardous Equipment; More Often Sitting Than Standing; Using Hands on Objects, Tools, or Controls; Repetitive Motions. **Other Job Characteristics**—Need to Be Exact or Accurate.

Experience—Job Zone 3. Previous work-related skill, knowledge, or experience is required. **Job Preparation**—SVP 6.0 to less than 7.0—more than one year and less than four years. **Knowledges**—Fine Arts; Design; Production and Processing. **Instructional Program**—Graphic Communications, Other.

Related SOC Job—51-9194 Etchers and Engravers. **Related OOH Job**—Etchers and Engravers. **Related DOT Jobs**—590.684-018 Etched-Circuit Processor; 704.381-022 Engraver Apprentice, Decorative; 704.381-026 Engraver, Hand, Hard Metals; 704.381-030 Engraver, Hand, Soft Metals; 704.381-034 Engraver, Seals; 704.382-010 Engraver, Pantograph I; 704.582-010 Engraver, Machine II; 704.682-010 Engraver, Machine I; 704.682-014 Engraver, Pantograph II; 704.684-010 Etcher; 704.684-014 Silk-Screen Etcher; 704.687-014 Etcher, Hand; 716.681-022 Optical-Glass Etcher; 732.584-010 Bowling-Ball Engraver; others.

51-9195.00 Molders, Shapers, and Casters, Except Metal and Plastic

- **Education/Training Required: Moderate-term on-the-job training**
- **Employed: 41,250**
- **Annual Earnings: $23,700**
- **Growth: –7.0%**
- **Annual Job Openings: 7,000**

The job openings listed here are shared with 51-9195.03 Stone Cutters and Carvers, Manufacturing, 51-9195.04 Glass Blowers, Molders, Benders, and Finishers, 51-9195.05 Potters, Manufacturing, and 51-9195.07 Molding and Casting Workers.

Mold, shape, form, cast, or carve products, such as food products, figurines, tile, pipes, and candles, consisting of clay, glass, plaster, concrete, stone, or combinations of materials.

No task data available.

Note: The Department of Labor has not collected some data for this job, so it has fewer details than the other descriptions.

Instructional Program—No related CIP programs.

Related SOC Job—51-9195 Molders, Shapers, and Casters, Except Metal and Plastic. **Related OOH Job**—Molders, Shapers, and Casters, Except Metal and Plastic. **Related DOT Job**—No data available.

51-9195.03 Stone Cutters and Carvers, Manufacturing

- **Education/Training Required: Moderate-term on-the-job training**
- **Employed: 41,250**
- **Annual Earnings: $23,700**
- **Growth: –7.0%**
- **Annual Job Openings: 7,000**

The job openings listed here are shared with 51-9195.00 Molders, Shapers, and Casters, Except Metal and Plastic, 51-9195.04 Glass Blowers, Molders, Benders, and Finishers, 51-9195.05 Potters, Manufacturing, and 51-9195.07 Molding and Casting Workers.

Cut or carve stone according to diagrams and patterns.

Carve designs and figures in full and bas relief on stone, employing knowledge of stone-carving techniques and sense of artistry to produce carvings consistent with designers' plans. Verify depths and dimensions of cuts or carvings to ensure adherence to specifications, blueprints, or models, using measuring instruments. Lay out designs or dimensions from sketches or blueprints on stone surfaces, by freehand, or by transferring them from tracing paper, using scribes or chalk and measuring instruments. Study artistic objects or graphic materials such as models, sketches, or blueprints to plan carving or cutting techniques. Drill holes and cut or carve moldings and grooves in stone according to diagrams and patterns. Shape, trim, or touch up roughed-out designs with appropriate tools to finish carvings. Select chisels, pneumatic or surfacing tools, or sandblasting nozzles and determine sequence of use. Move fingers over surfaces of carvings to ensure smoothness of finish. Carve rough designs freehand or by chipping along marks on stone, using mallets and chisels or pneumatic tools. Guide nozzles over stone, following stencil outlines, or chip along marks to create designs or to work surfaces down to specified finishes. Cut, shape, and finish rough blocks of building or monumental stone according to diagrams or patterns. Smooth surfaces of carvings, using rubbing stones. Remove or add stencils during blasting to create differing cut depths; intricate designs; or rough, pitted finishes. Copy drawings on rough clay or plaster models. Load sandblasting equipment with abrasives, attach nozzles to hoses, and turn valves to admit compressed air and activate jets. Dress stone surfaces, using bushhammers.

GOE Information—Interest Area: 02. Architecture and Construction. **Work Group:** 02.04. Construction Crafts. **Personality Type**—Realistic. Realistic occupations frequently involve work activities that include practical, hands-on problems and solutions. They often deal with plants; animals; and real-world materials like wood, tools, and machinery. Many of the occupations require working outside and do not involve a lot of paperwork or working closely with others. **Work Values**—Independence; Moral Values; Recognition; Achievement; Autonomy; Creativity. **Skills**—Equipment Selection; Mathematics; Repairing; Equipment Maintenance; Quality Control Analysis; Instructing. **Abilities**—*Cognitive:* Visualization. *Psychomotor:* Arm-Hand Steadiness; Manual Dexterity; Multilimb Coordination; Control Precision; Finger Dexterity. *Physical:* Static Strength; Extent Flexibility; Trunk Strength; Stamina. *Sensory:* Depth Perception. **General Work Activities**—*Information Input:* Getting Information; Monitoring Processes, Materials, or Surroundings; Inspecting Equipment, Structures, or Materials. *Mental Process:* Thinking Creatively; Making Decisions and Solving Problems; Organizing, Planning, and Prioritizing. *Work Output:* Handling and Moving Objects; Performing General Physical Activities; Controlling Machines and Processes. *Interacting with Others:* Communicating with Other Workers; Establishing and Maintaining Interpersonal Relationships; Teaching Others. **Physical Work Conditions**—Noisy; Contaminants; Hazardous Equipment; Standing; Using Hands on Objects, Tools, or Controls; Repetitive Motions. **Other Job Characteristics**—Need to Be Exact or Accurate; Errors Have Important Consequences; Repeat Same Tasks.

Experience—Job Zone 2. Some previous work-related skill, knowledge, or experience may be helpful in these occupations, but usually is not needed. **Job Preparation**—SVP 4.0 to less than 6.0—six months to less than two years. **Knowledges**—Design; Fine Arts; Production and Processing; Building and Construction; Mechanical Devices; Mathematics. **Instructional Program**—No related CIP programs.

Related SOC Job—51-9195 Molders, Shapers, and Casters, Except Metal and Plastic. **Related OOH Job**—Molders, Shapers, and Casters, Except Metal and Plastic. **Related DOT Jobs**—673.382-010 Sandblaster, Stone; 673.382-014 Sandblaster, Stone Apprentice; 771.281-014 Stone Carver; 771.381-010 Stonecutter Apprentice, Hand; 771.381-014 Stonecutter, Hand.

51-9195.04 Glass Blowers, Molders, Benders, and Finishers

- **Education/Training Required: Moderate-term on-the-job training**
- **Employed: 41,250**
- **Annual Earnings: $23,700**
- **Growth: −7.0%**
- **Annual Job Openings: 7,000**

The job openings listed here are shared with 51-9195.00 Molders, Shapers, and Casters, Except Metal and Plastic, 51-9195.03 Stone Cutters and Carvers, Manufacturing, 51-9195.05 Potters, Manufacturing, and 51-9195.07 Molding and Casting Workers.

Shape molten glass according to patterns.

Place electrodes in tube ends and heat them with glass burners to fuse them into place. Inspect, weigh, and measure products to verify conformance to specifications, using instruments such as micrometers, calipers, magnifiers, and rulers. Heat glass to pliable stage, using gas flames or ovens and rotating glass to heat it uniformly. Place rubber hoses on ends of tubing and charge tubing with gas. Design and create glass objects, using blowpipes and artisans' hand tools and equipment. Repair broken scrolls by replacing them with new sections of tubing. Set up and adjust machine press stroke lengths and pressures and regulate oven temperatures according to glass types to be processed. Shape, bend, or join sections of glass, using paddles, pressing and flattening hand tools, or cork. Spray or swab molds with oil solutions to prevent adhesion of glass. Strike necks of finished articles to separate articles from blowpipes. Superimpose bent tubing on asbestos patterns to ensure accuracy. Place glass into dies or molds of presses and control presses to form products such as glassware components or optical blanks. Operate electric kilns that heat glass sheets and molds to the shape and curve of metal jigs. Determine types and quantities of glass required to fabricate products. Dip ends of blowpipes into molten glass to collect gobs on pipe heads or cut gobs from molten glass, using shears. Record manufacturing information such as quantities, sizes, and types of goods produced. Operate and maintain finishing machines to grind, drill, sand, bevel, decorate, wash, or polish glass or glass products. Develop sketches of glass products into blueprint specifications, applying knowledge of glass technology and glass blowing. Blow tubing into specified shapes to prevent glass from collapsing, using compressed air or own breath, or blow and rotate gathers in molds or on boards

to obtain final shapes. Cut lengths of tubing to specified sizes, using files or cutting wheels.

GOE Information—**Interest Area:** 13. Manufacturing. **Work Group:** 13.09. Hands-On Work, Assorted Materials. **Personality Type**—Realistic. Realistic occupations frequently involve work activities that include practical, hands-on problems and solutions. They often deal with plants; animals; and real-world materials like wood, tools, and machinery. Many of the occupations require working outside and do not involve a lot of paperwork or working closely with others. **Work Values**—Independence; Moral Values; Ability Utilization; Achievement; Supervision, Technical; Recognition. **Skills**—Operation Monitoring; Equipment Maintenance; Repairing; Installation; Quality Control Analysis; Troubleshooting. **Abilities**—*Cognitive:* Visualization; Perceptual Speed; Selective Attention; Flexibility of Closure; Category Flexibility; Memorization. *Psychomotor:* Reaction Time; Rate Control; Manual Dexterity; Arm-Hand Steadiness; Wrist-Finger Speed; Control Precision. *Physical:* Static Strength; Dynamic Strength; Gross Body Coordination; Stamina; Trunk Strength. *Sensory:* Visual Color Discrimination; Auditory Attention; Hearing Sensitivity; Depth Perception; Far Vision; Near Vision. **General Work Activities**—*Information Input:* Monitoring Processes, Materials, or Surroundings; Identifying Objects, Actions, and Events; Inspecting Equipment, Structures, or Materials. *Mental Process:* Updating and Using Relevant Knowledge; Judging the Qualities of Things, Services, or Other People's Work; Thinking Creatively. *Work Output:* Handling and Moving Objects; Controlling Machines and Processes; Performing General Physical Activities. *Interacting with Others:* Communicating with Other Workers; Coordinating the Work and Activities of Others; Coaching and Developing Others. **Physical Work Conditions**—Noisy; Very Hot or Cold; Contaminants; Minor Burns, Cuts, Bites, or Stings; Standing; Using Hands on Objects, Tools, or Controls. **Other Job Characteristics**—Need to Be Exact or Accurate; Repeat Same Tasks; Pace Determined by Speed of Equipment.

Experience—Job Zone 3. Previous work-related skill, knowledge, or experience is required. **Job Preparation**—SVP 6.0 to less than 7.0—more than one year and less than four years. **Knowledges**—Production and Processing; Mechanical Devices; Design; Chemistry; Physics; Engineering and Technology. **Instructional Program**—No related CIP programs.

Related SOC Job—51-9195 Molders, Shapers, and Casters, Except Metal and Plastic. **Related OOH Job**—Molders, Shapers, and Casters, Except Metal and Plastic. **Related DOT Jobs**—006.261-010 Scientific Glass Blower; 575.381-010 Molder; 713.261-010 Artificial-Glass-Eye Maker; 772.281-010 Glass Blower, Laboratory Apparatus; 772.381-010 Glass Bender; 772.381-018 Ware Finisher; 772.381-022 Glass Blower; 772.482-010 Glass-Blowing-Lathe Operator.

51-9195.05 Potters, Manufacturing

- **Education/Training Required: Moderate-term on-the-job training**
- **Employed: 41,250**
- **Annual Earnings: $23,700**
- **Growth: −7.0%**
- **Annual Job Openings: 7,000**

The job openings listed here are shared with 51-9195.00 Molders, Shapers, and Casters, Except Metal and Plastic, 51-9195.03 Stone Cutters and Carvers, Manufacturing, 51-9195.04 Glass Blowers, Molders, Benders, and Finishers, and 51-9195.07 Molding and Casting Workers.

Operate production machines such as pug mill, jigger machine, or potter's wheel to process clay in manufacture of ceramic, pottery, and stoneware products.

Adjust pressures, temperatures, and trimming tool settings as required. Move pieces from wheels so that they can dry. Teach pottery classes. Maintain supplies of tools, equipment, and materials and order additional supplies as needed. Start machine units and conveyors and observe lights and gauges on panel board to verify operational efficiency. Operate drying chambers to dry or finish molded ceramic ware. Operate jigger machines to form ceramic ware, such as bowls, cups, plates, and saucers. Prepare work for sale or exhibition and maintain relationships with retail, pottery, art, and resource networks that can facilitate sale or exhibition of work. Perform test-fires of pottery to determine how to achieve specific colors and textures. Examine finished ware for defects and measure dimensions, using rule and thickness gauge. Mix and apply glazes and load glazed pieces into kilns for firing. Operate pug mills to blend and extrude clay. Design clay forms and molds and decorations for forms. Adjust wheel speeds according to the feel of the clay as pieces enlarge and walls become thinner. Position balls of clay in centers of potters' wheels and start motors or pump treadles with feet to revolve wheels. Press thumbs into centers of revolving clay to form hollows and press on the inside and outside of emerging clay cylinders with hands and fingers, gradually raising and shaping clay to desired forms and sizes. Pull wires through bases of articles and wheels to separate finished pieces. Raise and shape clay into wares such as vases and pitchers on revolving wheels, using hands, fingers, and thumbs. Smooth surfaces of finished pieces, using rubber scrapers and wet sponges. Verify accuracy of shapes and sizes of objects, using calipers and templates.

GOE Information—Interest Area: 03. Arts and Communication. **Work Group:** 03.04. Studio Art. **Personality Type—**Realistic. Realistic occupations frequently involve work activities that include practical, hands-on problems and solutions. They often deal with plants; animals; and real-world materials like wood, tools, and machinery. Many of the occupations require working outside and do not involve a lot of paperwork or working closely with others. **Work Values—**Moral Values; Independence; Creativity; Autonomy; Recognition; Variety. **Skills—**None met the criteria. **Abilities—***Cognitive:* Visualization. *Psychomotor:* Arm-Hand Steadiness; Manual Dexterity; Wrist-Finger Speed; Multilimb Coordination; Reaction Time; Finger Dexterity. *Physical:* Extent Flexibility. *Sensory:* None met the criteria. **General Work Activities—***Information Input:* Monitoring Processes, Materials, or Surroundings. *Mental Process:* Thinking Creatively. *Work Output:* Handling and Moving Objects; Controlling Machines and Processes; Performing General Physical Activities. *Interacting with Others:* None met the criteria. **Physical Work Conditions—**Indoors; Sitting; Using Hands on Objects, Tools, or Controls; Bending or Twisting the Body; Repetitive Motions. **Other Job Characteristics—**Repeat Same Tasks.

Experience—Job Zone 4. A minimum of two to four years of work-related skill, knowledge, or experience is needed. **Job Preparation—**SVP 7.0 to less than 8.0—two years to less than 10 years. **Knowledges—**Fine Arts; Production and Processing. **Instructional Program—**No related CIP programs.

Related SOC Job—51-9195 Molders, Shapers, and Casters, Except Metal and Plastic. **Related OOH Job—**Molders, Shapers, and Casters, Except Metal and Plastic. **Related DOT Jobs—**774.381-010 Thrower; 774.382-010 Pottery-Machine Operator; 777.281-014 Model Maker.

51-9195.07 Molding and Casting Workers

- **Education/Training Required: Moderate-term on-the-job training**
- **Employed: 41,250**
- **Annual Earnings: $23,700**
- **Growth: –7.0%**
- **Annual Job Openings: 7,000**

The job openings listed here are shared with 51-9195.00 Molders, Shapers, and Casters, Except Metal and Plastic, 51-9195.03 Stone Cutters and Carvers, Manufacturing, 51-9195.04 Glass Blowers, Molders, Benders, and Finishers, and 51-9195.05 Potters, Manufacturing.

Perform a variety of duties such as mixing materials, assembling mold parts, filling molds, and stacking molds to mold and cast a wide range of products.

Brush or spray mold surfaces with parting agents or insert paper into molds to ensure smoothness and prevent sticking or seepage. Clean, finish, and lubricate molds and mold parts. Separate models or patterns from molds and examine products for accuracy. Pour, pack, spread, or press plaster, concrete, liquid plastic, or other materials into or around models or molds. Operate and adjust controls of heating equipment to melt material or to cure, dry, or bake filled molds. Read work orders or examine parts to determine parts or sections of products to be produced. Load or stack filled molds in ovens, dryers, or curing boxes or on storage racks or carts. Set the proper operating temperature for each casting. Measure and cut products to specified dimensions, using measuring and cutting instruments. Remove excess materials and level and smooth wet mold mixtures. Melt metal pieces, using torches, and cast products such as inlays and crowns, using centrifugal casting machines. Select sizes and types of molds according to instructions. Align and assemble parts to produce completed products, using gauges and hand tools. Trim or remove excess material, using scrapers, knives, or band saws. Bore holes or cut grates, risers, and pouring spouts in molds, using power tools. Withdraw cores and other loose mold members after castings solidify. Construct or form molds for use in casting metal, clay, or plaster objects, using plaster, fiberglass, rubber, casting machines, patterns, or flasks. Verify dimensions of products, using measuring instruments such as calipers, vernier gauges, and protractors. Tap or tilt molds to ensure uniform distribution of materials. Locate and scribe parting lines on patterns, using measuring instruments such as calipers, squares, and depth gauges. Patch broken edges or fractures, using clay or plaster. Smooth surfaces of molds, using scraping tools and sandpaper. Measure ingredients and mix molding, casting material, or sealing compounds to prescribed consistencies according to formulas. Repair mold defects such as cracks and broken edges, using patterns, mold boxes, or hand tools.

GOE Information—Interest Area: 13. Manufacturing. **Work Group:** 13.09. Hands-On Work, Assorted Materials. **Personality Type—**Realistic. Realistic occupations frequently involve work activities that include practical, hands-on problems and solutions. They often deal with plants; animals; and real-world materials like wood, tools, and machinery. Many of the occupations require working outside and do not involve a lot of paperwork or working closely with others. **Work Values—**Moral Values; Independence; Supervision, Technical; Supervision, Human Relations. **Skills—**Quality Control Analysis; Installation; Repairing; Equipment Selection; Operation Monitoring; Equipment Maintenance. **Abilities—***Cognitive:* Perceptual Speed; Visualization; Flexibility of Closure. *Psychomotor:* Rate Control; Reaction Time; Manual Dexterity; Arm-Hand

Steadiness; Response Orientation; Multilimb Coordination. *Physical:* Static Strength; Dynamic Strength; Extent Flexibility; Trunk Strength; Stamina; Gross Body Coordination. *Sensory:* Depth Perception; Auditory Attention; Visual Color Discrimination; Hearing Sensitivity; Far Vision. **General Work Activities**—*Information Input:* Monitoring Processes, Materials, or Surroundings; Inspecting Equipment, Structures, or Materials; Identifying Objects, Actions, and Events. *Mental Process:* Making Decisions and Solving Problems; Judging the Qualities of Things, Services, or Other People's Work; Updating and Using Relevant Knowledge. *Work Output:* Handling and Moving Objects; Performing General Physical Activities; Controlling Machines and Processes. *Interacting with Others:* Coordinating the Work and Activities of Others; Establishing and Maintaining Interpersonal Relationships; Communicating with Other Workers. **Physical Work Conditions**—Noisy; Very Hot or Cold; Contaminants; Standing; Using Hands on Objects, Tools, or Controls; Repetitive Motions. **Other Job Characteristics**—Need to Be Exact or Accurate; Errors Have Important Consequences; Pace Determined by Speed of Equipment; Repeat Same Tasks.

Experience—Job Zone 2. Some previous work-related skill, knowledge, or experience may be helpful in these occupations, but usually is not needed. **Job Preparation**—SVP 4.0 to less than 6.0—six months to less than two years. **Knowledges**—Production and Processing; Mechanical Devices. **Instructional Program**—No related CIP programs.

Related SOC Job—51-9195 Molders, Shapers, and Casters, Except Metal and Plastic. **Related OOH Job**—Molders, Shapers, and Casters, Except Metal and Plastic. **Related DOT Jobs**—502.684-010 Lead Caster; 502.684-014 Mill Helper; 502.684-022 Needle Leader; 518.484-010 Plaster Molder II; 518.684-014 Coremaker, Pipe; 556.484-010 Scagliola Mechanic; 556.684-014 Encapsulator; 556.684-018 Mold-Filling Operator; 556.684-026 Rubber Molder; 556.684-030 Loader-Demolder; 556.687-022 Molder, Toilet Products; 556.687-030 Mold Filler; 575.461-010 Concrete-Stone Fabricator; 575.684-014 Caster; 575.684-018 Caster; 575.684-030 Handle Maker; 575.684-034 Laundry-Tub Maker; others.

51-9196.00 Paper Goods Machine Setters, Operators, and Tenders

- **Education/Training Required: Moderate-term on-the-job training**
- **Employed: 107,560**
- **Annual Earnings: $31,160**
- **Growth: 2.4%**
- **Annual Job Openings: 15,000**

Set up, operate, or tend paper goods machines that perform a variety of functions, such as converting, sawing, corrugating, banding, wrapping, boxing, stitching, forming, or sealing paper or paperboard sheets into products.

Examine completed work to detect defects and verify conformance to work orders and adjust machinery as necessary to correct production problems. Start machines and move controls to regulate tension on pressure rolls, to synchronize speed of machine components, and to adjust temperatures of glue or paraffin. Adjust guide assemblies, forming bars, and folding mechanisms according to specifications, using hand tools. Install attachments to machines for gluing, folding, printing, or cutting. Measure, space, and set saw blades, cutters, and

perforators according to product specifications. Observe operation of various machines to detect and correct machine malfunctions such as improper forming, glue flow, or pasteboard tension. Place rolls of paper or cardboard on machine feedtracks and thread paper through gluing, coating, and slitting rollers. Stamp products with information such as dates, using hand stamps or automatic stamping devices. Fill glue and paraffin reservoirs and position rollers to dispense glue onto paperboard. Cut products to specified dimensions, using hand or power cutters. Monitor finished cartons as they drop from forming machines into rotating hoppers and then into gravity feed chutes to prevent jamming. Disassemble machines to maintain, repair, or replace broken or worn parts, using hand or power tools. Remove finished cores and stack or place them on conveyors for transfer to other work areas. Lift tote boxes of finished cartons and dump cartons into feed hoppers. Load automatic stapling mechanisms.

GOE Information—**Interest Area:** 13. Manufacturing. **Work Group:** 13.02. Machine Setup and Operation. **Personality Type**—Realistic. Realistic occupations frequently involve work activities that include practical, hands-on problems and solutions. They often deal with plants; animals; and real-world materials like wood, tools, and machinery. Many of the occupations require working outside and do not involve a lot of paperwork or working closely with others. **Work Values**—Moral Values; Independence; Supervision, Human Relations; Supervision, Technical; Company Policies and Practices. **Skills**—Operation Monitoring; Operation and Control; Equipment Maintenance; Repairing; Troubleshooting; Quality Control Analysis. **Abilities**—*Cognitive:* Perceptual Speed; Selective Attention; Time Sharing. *Psychomotor:* Reaction Time; Rate Control; Control Precision; Multilimb Coordination; Arm-Hand Steadiness; Manual Dexterity. *Physical:* Stamina; Extent Flexibility; Trunk Strength. *Sensory:* Auditory Attention; Depth Perception; Hearing Sensitivity; Visual Color Discrimination. **General Work Activities**—*Information Input:* Inspecting Equipment, Structures, or Materials; Identifying Objects, Actions, and Events; Monitoring Processes, Materials, or Surroundings. *Mental Process:* Organizing, Planning, and Prioritizing; Scheduling Work and Activities; Processing Information. *Work Output:* Handling and Moving Objects; Controlling Machines and Processes; Repairing and Maintaining Mechanical Equipment. *Interacting with Others:* Communicating with Other Workers; Establishing and Maintaining Interpersonal Relationships; Developing and Building Teams. **Physical Work Conditions**—Noisy; Contaminants; Standing; Walking and Running; Using Hands on Objects, Tools, or Controls; Repetitive Motions. **Other Job Characteristics**—Pace Determined by Speed of Equipment; Need to Be Exact or Accurate; Repeat Same Tasks.

Experience—Job Zone 2. Some previous work-related skill, knowledge, or experience may be helpful in these occupations, but usually is not needed. **Job Preparation**—SVP 4.0 to less than 6.0—six months to less than two years. **Knowledges**—Production and Processing; Mechanical Devices; Engineering and Technology. **Instructional Program**—No related CIP programs.

Related SOC Job—51-9196 Paper Goods Machine Setters, Operators, and Tenders. **Related OOH Job**—Paper Goods Machine Setters, Operators, and Tenders. **Related DOT Jobs**—640.682-010 Convolute-Tube Winder; 640.682-022 Spiral-Tube Winder; 641.380-010 Envelope-Folding-Machine Adjuster; 649.380-010 Machine Set-Up Operator, Paper Goods; 649.682-010 Box-Folding-Machine Operator.

51-9197.00 Tire Builders

- **Education/Training Required:** Moderate-term on-the-job training
- **Employed:** 19,860
- **Annual Earnings:** $36,770
- **Growth:** −16.6%
- **Annual Job Openings:** 4,000

Operate machines to build tires from rubber components.

Cut plies at splice points and press ends together to form continuous bands. Position rollers that turn ply edges under and over beads or use steel rods to turn ply edges. Activate bead setters that press prefabricated beads onto plies. Align treads with guides, start drums to wind treads onto plies, and slice ends. Brush or spray solvents onto plies to ensure adhesion and repeat process as specified, alternating direction of each ply to strengthen tires. Trim excess rubber and imperfections during retreading processes. Start rollers that bond tread and plies as drums revolve. Wind chafers and breakers onto plies. Build semi-raw rubber treads onto buffed tire casings to prepare tires for vulcanization in recapping or retreading processes. Clean and paint completed tires. Inspect worn tires for faults, cracks, cuts, and nail holes and to determine if tires are suitable for retreading. Place rebuilt casings in molds for vulcanization processes. Place tires into molds for new tread. Roll camelbacks onto casings by hand and cut camelbacks, using knives. Roll hand rollers over rebuilt casings, exerting pressure to ensure adhesion between camelbacks and casings. Measure tires to determine mold size requirements. Spray tires with vulcanizing cement. Depress pedals to collapse drums after processing is complete. Rub cement sticks on drum edges to provide adhesive surfaces for plies. Pull plies from supply racks and align plies with edges of drums. Position ply stitcher rollers and drums according to width of stock, using hand tools and gauges. Fit inner tubes and final layers of rubber onto tires. Fill cuts and holes in tires, using hot rubber. Depress pedals to rotate drums and wind specified numbers of plies around drums to form tire bodies. Select camelbacks according to specified tire widths and tread thicknesses and whether tires are to be retreaded or recapped.

GOE Information—Interest Area: 13. Manufacturing. **Work Group:** 13.03. Production Work, Assorted Materials Processing. **Personality Type**—Realistic. Realistic occupations frequently involve work activities that include practical, hands-on problems and solutions. They often deal with plants; animals; and real-world materials like wood, tools, and machinery. Many of the occupations require working outside and do not involve a lot of paperwork or working closely with others. **Work Values**—Moral Values; Independence; Supervision, Technical; Supervision, Human Relations; Company Policies and Practices; Activity. **Skills**—Operation and Control. **Abilities**—*Cognitive:* None met the criteria. *Psychomotor:* Wrist-Finger Speed; Manual Dexterity; Multilimb Coordination; Control Precision. *Physical:* Static Strength; Extent Flexibility. *Sensory:* None met the criteria. **General Work Activities**—*Information Input:* Monitoring Processes, Materials, or Surroundings. *Mental Process:* None met the criteria. *Work Output:* Handling and Moving Objects; Performing General Physical Activities; Controlling Machines and Processes. *Interacting with Others:* None met the criteria. **Physical Work Conditions**—Indoors; Contaminants; Hazardous Equipment; Minor Burns, Cuts, Bites, or Stings; Standing; Using Hands on Objects, Tools, or Controls. **Other Job Characteristics**—Automation; Pace Determined by Speed of Equipment.

Experience—Job Zone 1. No previous work-related skill, knowledge, or experience is needed. **Job Preparation**—SVP below 4.0—less than six months. **Knowledges**—Production and Processing; Mechanical Devices. **Instructional Program**—No related CIP programs.

Related SOC Job—51-9197 Tire Builders. **Related OOH Job**—Tire Builders. **Related DOT Jobs**—750.384-010 Tire Builder, Automobile; 750.684-014 Bead Builder.

51-9198.00 Helpers—Production Workers

- **Education/Training Required:** Short-term on-the-job training
- **Employed:** 528,610
- **Annual Earnings:** $20,390
- **Growth:** 7.9%
- **Annual Job Openings:** 107,000

Help production workers by performing duties of lesser skill. Duties include supplying or holding materials or tools and cleaning work area and equipment.

Operate machinery used in the production process or assist machine operators. Examine products to verify conformance to quality standards. Observe equipment operations so that malfunctions can be detected and notify operators of any malfunctions. Lift raw materials, finished products, and packed items manually or using hoists. Count finished products to determine if product orders are complete. Mark or tag identification on parts. Load and unload items from machines, conveyors, and conveyances. Help production workers by performing duties of lesser skill, such as supplying or holding materials or tools and cleaning work areas and equipment. Clean and lubricate equipment. Record information such as the number of products tested, meter readings, and dates and times of product production. Start machines or equipment to begin production processes. Separate products according to weight, grade, size, and composition of materials used to produce them. Turn valves to regulate flow of liquids or air, to reverse machines, to start pumps, or to regulate equipment. Place products in equipment or on work surfaces for further processing, inspecting, or wrapping. Pack and store materials and products. Remove products, machine attachments, and waste material from machines. Tie products in bundles for further processing or shipment, following prescribed procedures. Transfer finished products, raw materials, tools, or equipment between storage and work areas of plants and warehouses by hand or using hand trucks or powered lift trucks. Signal co-workers to direct them to move products during the production process. Prepare raw materials for processing. Measure amounts of products, lengths of extruded articles, or weights of filled containers to ensure conformance to specifications. Thread ends of items such as thread, cloth, and lace through needles and rollers and around take-up tubes. Read gauges and charts and record data obtained. Mix ingredients according to specified procedures and formulas. Position spouts or chutes of storage bins so that containers can be filled. Fold products and product parts during processing.

GOE Information—Interest Area: 13. Manufacturing. **Work Group:** 13.03. Production Work, Assorted Materials Processing. **Personality Type**—Realistic. Realistic occupations frequently involve work activities that include practical, hands-on problems and solutions. They often deal with plants; animals; and real-world materials like wood, tools, and machinery. Many of the occupations require working outside and do not involve a lot of paperwork or working closely with others. **Work Values**—Moral Values; Supervision, Technical; Activity.

Skills—Equipment Selection; Equipment Maintenance; Installation; Troubleshooting; Management of Material Resources; Quality Control Analysis. **Abilities**—*Cognitive:* Perceptual Speed. *Psychomotor:* Control Precision; Multilimb Coordination; Arm-Hand Steadiness; Reaction Time; Manual Dexterity; Finger Dexterity. *Physical:* Extent Flexibility; Stamina; Trunk Strength; Static Strength; Gross Body Coordination. *Sensory:* Depth Perception; Auditory Attention; Hearing Sensitivity; Visual Color Discrimination. **General Work Activities**—*Information Input:* Monitoring Processes, Materials, or Surroundings; Inspecting Equipment, Structures, or Materials; Identifying Objects, Actions, and Events. *Mental Process:* Organizing, Planning, and Prioritizing; Making Decisions and Solving Problems; Processing Information. *Work Output:* Handling and Moving Objects; Performing General Physical Activities; Controlling Machines and Processes. *Interacting with Others:* Establishing and Maintaining Interpersonal Relationships; Teaching Others; Communicating with Other Workers. **Physical Work Conditions**—Noisy; Contaminants; Minor Burns, Cuts, Bites, or Stings; Standing; Using Hands on Objects, Tools, or Controls; Bending or Twisting the Body. **Other Job Characteristics**—Need to Be Exact or Accurate; Pace Determined by Speed of Equipment.

Experience—Job Zone 1. No previous work-related skill, knowledge, or experience is needed. **Job Preparation**—SVP below 4.0—less than six months. **Knowledges**—Food Production; Production and Processing. **Instructional Program**—No related CIP programs.

Related SOC Job—51-9198 Helpers—Production Workers. **Related OOH Job**—Helpers—Production Workers. **Related DOT Jobs**—230.667-014 Telephone-Directory Deliverer; 230.687-010 Advertising-Material Distributor; 299.667-010 Billposter; 299.687-010 Porter, Sample Case; 361.687-018 Laundry Laborer; 361.687-026 Shaker, Wearing Apparel; 361.687-030 Washer, Hand; 362.686-010 Dry-Cleaner Helper; 362.686-014 Rug-Cleaner Helper; 362.687-010 Glove Cleaner, Hand; 362.687-014 Lining Scrubber; 362.687-018 Shaver; 363.687-010 Glove Former; 363.687-014 Ironer, Sock; 363.687-018 Puff Ironer; 363.687-022 Stretcher-Drier Operator; others.

51-9199.99 Production Workers, All Other

- **Education/Training Required: Moderate-term on-the-job training**
- **Employed: 296,340**
- **Annual Earnings: $23,630**
- **Growth: –1.3%**
- **Annual Job Openings: 45,000**

All production workers not listed separately.

No task data available.

Note: The Department of Labor has not collected some data for this job, so it has fewer details than the other descriptions.

Related SOC Job—51-9199 Production Workers, All Other. **Related OOH Job**—None. **Related DOT Jobs**—017.684-010 Taper, Printed Circuit Layout; 222.687-014 Garment Sorter; 362.684-010 Dry Cleaner, Hand; 362.684-018 Fur Cleaner, Hand; 362.684-022 Furniture Cleaner; 364.684-014 Shoe Dyer; 364.684-018 Sprayer, Leather; 369.384-010 Hatter; 369.684-010 Fur Glazer; 369.685-030 Shirt-Folding-Machine Operator; 410.687-018 Pelter; 500.684-014 Matrix Worker; 502.664-010 Blast-Furnace Keeper; 502.684-018 Mold Setter; 503.362-010 Pickler, Continuous Pickling Line; 503.684-010 Cleaner; others.

53-0000
Transportation and Material Moving Occupations

53-1000 Supervisors, Transportation and Material Moving Workers

53-1011.00 Aircraft Cargo Handling Supervisors

- Education/Training Required: Work experience in a related occupation
- Employed: 6,210
- Annual Earnings: $34,900
- Growth: 17.3%
- Annual Job Openings: 1,000

Direct ground crew in the loading, unloading, securing, and staging of aircraft cargo or baggage. Determine the quantity and orientation of cargo and compute aircraft center of gravity. May accompany aircraft as member of flight crew, monitor and handle cargo in flight, and assist and brief passengers on safety and emergency procedures.

Brief aircraft passengers on safety and emergency procedures. Calculate load weights for different aircraft compartments, using charts and computers. Determine the quantity and orientation of cargo and compute an aircraft's center of gravity. Direct ground crews in the loading, unloading, securing, and staging of aircraft cargo or baggage. Distribute cargo in such a manner that space use is maximized. Accompany aircraft as a member of the flight crew to monitor and handle cargo in flight.

GOE Information—Interest Area: 16. Transportation, Distribution, and Logistics. Work Group: 16.01. Managerial Work in Transportation. Note: The Department of Labor has not collected some data for this job, so it has fewer details than the other descriptions.

Instructional Program—No related CIP programs.

Related SOC Job—53-1011 Aircraft Cargo Handling Supervisors. Related OOH Job—Aircraft Cargo Handling Supervisors. Related DOT Job—912.367-014 Transportation Agent.

53-1021.00 First-Line Supervisors/ Managers of Helpers, Laborers, and Material Movers, Hand

- Education/Training Required: Work experience in a related occupation
- Employed: 176,030
- Annual Earnings: $39,000
- Growth: 8.1%
- Annual Job Openings: 15,000

Supervise and coordinate the activities of helpers, laborers, or material movers.

Plan work schedules and assign duties to maintain adequate staffing levels, to ensure that activities are performed effectively, and to respond to fluctuating workloads. Collaborate with workers and managers to solve work-related problems. Review work throughout the work process and at completion to ensure that it has been performed properly. Transmit and explain work orders to laborers. Check specifications of materials loaded or unloaded against information contained in work orders. Inform designated employees or departments of items loaded and problems encountered. Examine freight to determine loading sequences. Evaluate employee performance and prepare performance appraisals. Perform the same work duties as those whom they supervise or perform more difficult or skilled tasks or assist in their performance. Prepare and maintain work records and reports that include information such as employee time and wages, daily receipts, and inspection results. Counsel employees in work-related activities, personal growth, and career development. Conduct staff meetings to relay general information or to address specific topics such as safety. Inspect equipment for wear and for conformance to specifications. Resolve personnel problems, complaints, and formal grievances when possible or refer them to higher-level supervisors for resolution. Recommend or initiate personnel actions such as promotions, transfers, and disciplinary measures. Assess training needs of staff; then arrange for or provide appropriate instruction. Schedule times of shipment and modes of transportation for materials. Quote prices to customers. Estimate material, time, and staffing requirements for a given project based on work orders, job specifications, and experience. Provide assistance in balancing books; tracking, monitoring, and projecting a unit's budget needs; and developing unit policies and procedures. Inspect job sites to determine the extent of maintenance or repairs needed. Participate in the hiring process by reviewing credentials, conducting interviews, and making hiring decisions or recommendations.

GOE Information—Interest Area: 13. Manufacturing. Work Group: 13.01. Managerial Work in Manufacturing. Personality Type—Enterprising. Enterprising occupations frequently involve starting up and carrying out projects. These occupations can involve leading people and making many decisions. They sometimes require risk taking and often deal with business. Work Values—Authority; Responsibility; Co-workers; Autonomy; Variety; Activity. Skills—Management of Personnel Resources; Monitoring; Persuasion; Time Management; Social Perceptiveness; Systems Evaluation. Abilities—Cognitive: Written Expression; Number Facility; Originality; Fluency of Ideas; Time Sharing; Visualization. Psychomotor: Manual Dexterity; Arm-Hand Steadiness. Physical: Trunk Strength. Sensory: Auditory Attention; Hearing Sensitivity; Speech Clarity; Speech Recognition. General Work Activities—Information Input: Identifying Objects, Actions, and Events; Monitoring Processes, Materials, or Surroundings; Getting Information. Mental Process: Organizing, Planning, and Prioritizing; Scheduling Work and Activities; Making Decisions and Solving Problems. Work Output: Handling and Moving Objects; Performing General Physical Activities; Interacting With Computers. Interacting with Others: Establishing and Maintaining Interpersonal Relationships; Resolving Conflicts and Negotiating with Others; Guiding, Directing, and Motivating Subordinates. Physical Work Conditions—Indoors; Noisy; Very Hot or Cold; Contaminants; Standing; Walking and Running. Other Job Characteristics—Need to Be Exact or Accurate; Errors Have Important Consequences.

Experience—Job Zone 3. Previous work-related skill, knowledge, or experience is required. Job Preparation—SVP 6.0 to less than 7.0—more than one year and less than four years. Knowledges—Production and Processing; Transportation; Administration and Management; Personnel and Human Resources; Public Safety and Security; Customer and Personal Service. Instructional Program—No related CIP programs.

Related SOC Job—53-1021 First-Line Supervisors/Managers of Helpers, Laborers, and Material Movers, Hand. Related OOH Job—Material Moving Occupations. Related DOT Jobs—189.167-042 Superintendent, Labor Utilization; 519.137-014 Supervisor, Scrap

Preparation; 559.137-050 Supervisor, Tank Cleaning; 570.132-022 Supervisor; 699.137-010 Supervisor, Cleaning; 860.137-010 Carpenter-Labor Supervisor; 891.137-014 Supervisor, Aircraft Cleaning; 891.137-018 Supervisor, Tank Cleaning; 899.131-022 Utility Supervisor, Boat and Plant; 910.137-014 Car-Cleaning Supervisor; 910.137-018 Circus-Train Supervisor; 910.137-026 Freight-Loading Supervisor; others.

53-1031.00 First-Line Supervisors/ Managers of Transportation and Material-Moving Machine and Vehicle Operators

- Education/Training Required: Work experience in a related occupation
- Employed: 221,520
- Annual Earnings: $47,530
- Growth: 15.3%
- Annual Job Openings: 22,000

Directly supervise and coordinate activities of transportation and material-moving machine and vehicle operators and helpers.

Enforce safety rules and regulations. Plan work assignments and equipment allocations to meet transportation, operations, or production goals. Confer with customers, supervisors, contractors, and other personnel to exchange information and to resolve problems. Direct workers in transportation or related services, such as pumping, moving, storing, and loading and unloading of materials or people. Resolve worker problems or collaborate with employees to assist in problem resolution. Review orders, production schedules, blueprints, and shipping and receiving notices to determine work sequences and material shipping dates, types, volumes, and destinations. Monitor fieldwork to ensure that it is being performed properly and that materials are being used as they should be. Recommend and implement measures to improve worker motivation, equipment performance, work methods, and customer services. Maintain or verify records of time, materials, expenditures, and crew activities. Interpret transportation and tariff regulations, shipping orders, safety regulations, and company policies and procedures for workers. Explain and demonstrate work tasks to new workers or assign workers to more experienced workers for further training. Prepare, compile, and submit reports on work activities, operations, production, and work-related accidents. Recommend or implement personnel actions such as employee selection, evaluation, and rewards or disciplinary actions. Requisition needed personnel, supplies, equipment, parts, or repair services. Inspect or test materials, stock, vehicles, equipment, and facilities to ensure that they are safe, are free of defects, and meet specifications. Plan and establish transportation routes. Compute and estimate cash, payroll, transportation, personnel, and storage requirements. Dispatch personnel and vehicles in response to telephone or radio reports of emergencies. Perform or schedule repairs and preventive maintenance of vehicles and other equipment. Examine, measure, and weigh cargo or materials to determine specific handling requirements. Provide workers with assistance in performing tasks such as coupling railroad cars or loading vehicles.

GOE Information—Interest Area: 16. Transportation, Distribution, and Logistics. **Work Group:** 16.01. Managerial Work in Transportation. **Personality Type—**Enterprising. Enterprising occupations frequently involve starting up and carrying out projects. These occupations can involve leading people and making many decisions. They sometimes require risk taking and often deal with business. **Work Values—**Authority; Responsibility; Variety;

Autonomy; Co-workers; Recognition. **Skills—**Management of Personnel Resources; Management of Financial Resources; Management of Material Resources; Social Perceptiveness; Systems Evaluation; Monitoring. **Abilities—***Cognitive:* Originality; Written Expression; Number Facility; Time Sharing; Mathematical Reasoning; Speed of Closure. *Psychomotor:* Arm-Hand Steadiness. *Physical:* None met the criteria. *Sensory:* Depth Perception; Auditory Attention; Far Vision; Speech Recognition. **General Work Activities—***Information Input:* Getting Information; Monitoring Processes, Materials, or Surroundings; Identifying Objects, Actions, and Events. *Mental Process:* Organizing, Planning, and Prioritizing; Updating and Using Relevant Knowledge; Scheduling Work and Activities. *Work Output:* Handling and Moving Objects; Interacting With Computers; Documenting or Recording Information. *Interacting with Others:* Establishing and Maintaining Interpersonal Relationships; Resolving Conflicts and Negotiating with Others; Guiding, Directing, and Motivating Subordinates. **Physical Work Conditions—**Indoors; Noisy; Contaminants; Sitting. **Other Job Characteristics—**Need to Be Exact or Accurate; Repeat Same Tasks.

Experience—Job Zone 3. Previous work-related skill, knowledge, or experience is required. **Job Preparation—**SVP 6.0 to less than 7.0—more than one year and less than four years. **Knowledges—**Transportation; Production and Processing; Personnel and Human Resources; Customer and Personal Service; Public Safety and Security; Administration and Management. **Instructional Program—**No related CIP programs.

Related SOC Job—53-1031 First-Line Supervisors/Managers of Transportation and Material-Moving Machine and Vehicle Operators. **Related OOH Job—**First-Line Supervisors/Managers of Transportation and Material Moving Machine and Vehicle Operators. **Related DOT Jobs—**185.167-018 Manager, Distribution Warehouse; 187.167-150 Manager, Storage Garage; 292.137-014 Supervisor, Route Sales-Delivery Drivers; 579.137-030 Dispatcher, Concrete Products; 859.137-010 Supervisor, Grading; 909.137-010 Driver Supervisor; 909.137-014 Garbage-Collection Supervisor; 909.137-018 Truck Supervisor; 910.137-022 Conductor, Yard; 910.137-034 Road Supervisor of Engines; 910.137-046 Yard Manager; 911.131-010 Boatswain; 911.137-018 Header; 911.137-022 Superintendent, Stevedoring; others.

53-2000 Air Transportation Workers

53-2011.00 Airline Pilots, Copilots, and Flight Engineers

- Education/Training Required: Bachelor's degree
- Employed: 76,240
- Annual Earnings: $138,170
- Growth: 17.2%
- Annual Job Openings: 7,000

Pilot and navigate the flight of multi-engine aircraft in regularly scheduled service for the transport of passengers and cargo. Requires Federal Air Transport rating and certification in specific aircraft type used.

Use instrumentation to guide flights when visibility is poor. Respond to and report in-flight emergencies and malfunctions. Work as part of a flight team with other crew members, especially during takeoffs and landings. Contact control towers for takeoff clearances, arrival instructions, and other information, using radio equipment. Steer aircraft along planned routes with the assistance of autopilot and flight management computers. Monitor gauges, warning devices, and control panels to verify aircraft performance and to regulate engine speed. Start engines, operate controls, and pilot airplanes to transport passengers, mail, or freight while adhering to flight plans, regulations, and procedures. Inspect aircraft for defects and malfunctions according to pre-flight checklists. Check passenger and cargo distributions and fuel amounts to ensure that weight and balance specifications are met. Monitor engine operation, fuel consumption, and functioning of aircraft systems during flights. Confer with flight dispatchers and weather forecasters to keep abreast of flight conditions. Coordinate flight activities with ground crews and air-traffic control and inform crew members of flight and test procedures. Order changes in fuel supplies, loads, routes, or schedules to ensure safety of flights. Choose routes, altitudes, and speeds that will provide the fastest, safest, and smoothest flights. Direct activities of aircraft crews during flights. Brief crews about flight details such as destinations, duties, and responsibilities. Record in logbooks information such as flight times, distances flown, and fuel consumption. Make announcements regarding flights, using public address systems. File instrument flight plans with air traffic control to ensure that flights are coordinated with other air traffic. Perform minor maintenance work or arrange for major maintenance. Instruct other pilots and student pilots in aircraft operations and the principles of flight. Conduct in-flight tests and evaluations at specified altitudes and in all types of weather to determine the receptivity and other characteristics of equipment and systems.

GOE Information—Interest Area: 16. Transportation, Distribution, and Logistics. **Work Group:** 16.02. Air Vehicle Operation. **Personality Type—**Realistic. Realistic occupations frequently involve work activities that include practical, hands-on problems and solutions. They often deal with plants; animals; and real-world materials like wood, tools, and machinery. Many of the occupations require working outside and do not involve a lot of paperwork or working closely with others. **Work Values—**Recognition; Compensation; Authority; Ability Utilization; Social Status; Company Policies and Practices. **Skills—**Operation Monitoring; Operation and Control; Systems Analysis; Judgment and Decision Making; Troubleshooting; Systems Evaluation. **Abilities—***Cognitive:* Spatial Orientation; Time Sharing; Flexibility of Closure; Speed of Closure; Perceptual Speed; Selective Attention. *Psychomotor:* Response Orientation; Rate Control; Reaction Time; Multilimb Coordination; Control Precision; Speed of Limb Movement. *Physical:* Extent Flexibility; Static Strength. *Sensory:* Night Vision; Glare Sensitivity; Peripheral Vision; Far Vision; Depth Perception; Hearing Sensitivity. **General Work Activities—***Information Input:* Identifying Objects, Actions, and Events; Monitoring Processes, Materials, or Surroundings; Getting Information. *Mental Process:* Making Decisions and Solving Problems; Updating and Using Relevant Knowledge; Analyzing Data or Information. *Work Output:* Operating Vehicles or Equipment; Controlling Machines and Processes; Interacting With Computers. *Interacting with Others:* Communicating with Other Workers; Coordinating the Work and Activities of Others; Performing for or Working with the Public. **Physical Work Conditions—**Indoors; Noisy; Contaminants; Radiation; Sitting; Using Hands on Objects, Tools, or Controls. **Other Job Characteristics—**Need to Be Exact or Accurate; Errors Have Important Consequences; Repeat Same Tasks; Automation; Pace Determined by Speed of Equipment.

Experience—Job Zone 4. A minimum of two to four years of work-related skill, knowledge, or experience is needed. **Job Preparation—**SVP 7.0 to less than 8.0—two years to less than 10 years. **Knowledges—**Transportation; Geography; Physics; Public Safety and Security; Psychology; Law and Government. **Instructional Programs—**Airline/Commercial/Professional Pilot and Flight Crew; Flight Instructor.

Related SOC Job—53-2011 Airline Pilots, Copilots, and Flight Engineers. **Related OOH Job—**Aircraft Pilots and Flight Engineers. **Related DOT Jobs—**196.167-014 Navigator; 196.263-030 Executive Pilot; 196.263-034 Facilities-Flight-Check Pilot; 621.261-018 Flight Engineer.

53-2012.00 Commercial Pilots

- **Education/Training Required: Postsecondary vocational training**
- **Employed: 24,860**
- **Annual Earnings: $55,810**
- **Growth: 16.8%**
- **Annual Job Openings: 2,000**

Pilot and navigate the flight of small fixed or rotary winged aircraft primarily for the transport of cargo and passengers. Requires Commercial Rating.

Check aircraft prior to flights to ensure that the engines, controls, instruments, and other systems are functioning properly. Start engines, operate controls, and pilot airplanes to transport passengers, mail, or freight while adhering to flight plans, regulations, and procedures. Contact control towers for takeoff clearances, arrival instructions, and other information, using radio equipment. Monitor engine operation, fuel consumption, and functioning of aircraft systems during flights. Consider airport altitudes, outside temperatures, plane weights, and wind speeds and directions to calculate the speed needed to become airborne. Order changes in fuel supplies, loads, routes, or schedules to ensure safety of flights. Obtain and review data such as load weights, fuel supplies, weather conditions, and flight schedules to determine flight plans and to see if changes might be necessary. Plan flights, following government and company regulations, using aeronautical charts and navigation instruments. Use instrumentation to pilot aircraft when visibility is poor. Check baggage or cargo to ensure that it has been loaded correctly. Request changes in altitudes or routes as circumstances dictate. Choose routes, altitudes, and speeds that will provide the fastest, safest, and smoothest flights. Coordinate flight activities with ground crews and air-traffic control and inform crew members of flight and test procedures. Write specified information in flight records, such as flight times, altitudes flown, and fuel consumption. Teach company regulations and procedures to other pilots. Instruct other pilots and student pilots in aircraft operations. Co-pilot aircraft or perform captain's duties if required. File instrument flight plans with air traffic control so that flights can be coordinated with other air traffic. Conduct in-flight tests and evaluations at specified altitudes and in all types of weather to determine the receptivity and other characteristics of equipment and systems. Rescue and evacuate injured persons. Supervise other crew members. Perform minor aircraft maintenance and repair work or arrange for major maintenance.

GOE Information—Interest Area: 16. Transportation, Distribution, and Logistics. **Work Group:** 16.02. Air Vehicle Operation. **Personality Type—**Realistic. Realistic occupations frequently involve work activities that include practical, hands-on problems and solutions. They often deal with plants; animals; and real-world materials like wood, tools, and machinery. Many of the occupations require working outside and do not involve a lot of paperwork or working closely with others. **Work Values**—Recognition; Compensation; Authority; Ability Utilization; Social Status; Company Policies and Practices. **Skills**—Operation Monitoring; Operation and Control; Troubleshooting; Judgment and Decision Making; Systems Evaluation; Critical Thinking. **Abilities**—*Cognitive:* Spatial Orientation; Perceptual Speed; Time Sharing; Selective Attention; Problem Sensitivity; Speed of Closure. *Psychomotor:* Response Orientation; Rate Control; Reaction Time; Control Precision; Multilimb Coordination; Speed of Limb Movement. *Physical:* Static Strength. *Sensory:* Night Vision; Glare Sensitivity; Peripheral Vision; Depth Perception; Far Vision; Sound Localization. **General Work Activities**—*Information Input:* Monitoring Processes, Materials, or Surroundings; Identifying Objects, Actions, and Events; Getting Information. *Mental Process:* Making Decisions and Solving Problems; Updating and Using Relevant Knowledge; Processing Information. *Work Output:* Operating Vehicles or Equipment; Controlling Machines and Processes; Handling and Moving Objects. *Interacting with Others:* Establishing and Maintaining Interpersonal Relationships; Communicating with Other Workers; Communicating with Persons Outside Organization. **Physical Work Conditions**—Outdoors; Noisy; Very Hot or Cold; Contaminants; Sitting; Using Hands on Objects, Tools, or Controls. **Other Job Characteristics**—Need to Be Exact or Accurate; Errors Have Important Consequences; Pace Determined by Speed of Equipment.

Experience—Job Zone 3. Previous work-related skill, knowledge, or experience is required. **Job Preparation**—SVP 6.0 to less than 7.0—more than one year and less than four years. **Knowledges**—Transportation; Geography; Mechanical Devices; Physics; Customer and Personal Service; Psychology. **Instructional Programs**—Airline/Commercial/Professional Pilot and Flight Crew; Flight Instructor.

Related SOC Job—53-2012 Commercial Pilots. **Related OOH Job**—Aircraft Pilots and Flight Engineers. **Related DOT Jobs**—196.263-010 Airplane Pilot; 196.263-014 Airplane Pilot, Commercial; 196.263-018 Airplane Pilot, Photogrammetry; 196.263-038 Helicopter Pilot.

53-2021.00 Air Traffic Controllers

- **Education/Training Required: Long-term on-the-job training**
- **Employed: 21,590**
- **Annual Earnings: $107,590**
- **Growth: 14.3%**
- **Annual Job Openings: 2,000**

Control air traffic on and within vicinity of airport and movement of air traffic between altitude sectors and control centers according to established procedures and policies. Authorize, regulate, and control commercial airline flights according to government or company regulations to expedite and ensure flight safety.

Issue landing and take-off authorizations and instructions. Monitor and direct the movement of aircraft within an assigned air space and on the ground at airports to minimize delays and maximize safety. Monitor aircraft within a specific airspace, using radar, computer equipment, and visual references. Inform pilots about nearby planes as well as potentially hazardous conditions such as weather, speed and direction of wind, and visibility problems. Provide flight path changes or directions to emergency landing fields for pilots traveling in bad weather or in emergency situations. Alert airport emergency

services in cases of emergency and when aircraft are experiencing difficulties. Direct pilots to runways when space is available or direct them to maintain a traffic pattern until there is space for them to land. Transfer control of departing flights to traffic control centers and accept control of arriving flights. Direct ground traffic, including taxiing aircraft, maintenance and baggage vehicles, and airport workers. Determine the timing and procedures for flight vector changes. Maintain radio and telephone contact with adjacent control towers, terminal control units, and other area control centers to coordinate aircraft movement. Contact pilots by radio to provide meteorological, navigational, and other information. Initiate and coordinate searches for missing aircraft. Check conditions and traffic at different altitudes in response to pilots' requests for altitude changes. Relay to control centers such air traffic information as courses, altitudes, and expected arrival times. Compile information about flights from flight plans, pilot reports, radar, and observations. Inspect, adjust, and control radio equipment and airport lights. Conduct pre-flight briefings on weather conditions, suggested routes, altitudes, indications of turbulence, and other flight safety information. Analyze factors such as weather reports, fuel requirements, and maps to determine air routes. Organize flight plans and traffic management plans to prepare for planes about to enter assigned airspace.

GOE Information—**Interest Area:** 03. Arts and Communication. **Work Group:** 03.10. Communications Technology. **Personality Type**—Conventional. Conventional occupations frequently involve following set procedures and routines. These occupations can include working with data and details more than with ideas. Usually there is a clear line of authority to follow. **Work Values**—Authority; Supervision, Technical; Responsibility; Ability Utilization; Security; Achievement. **Skills**—Operation Monitoring; Operation and Control; Coordination; Complex Problem Solving; Instructing; Active Listening. **Abilities**—*Cognitive:* Time Sharing; Speed of Closure; Flexibility of Closure; Perceptual Speed; Visualization; Selective Attention. *Psychomotor:* Finger Dexterity; Control Precision; Manual Dexterity; Arm-Hand Steadiness. *Physical:* None met the criteria. *Sensory:* Auditory Attention; Far Vision; Speech Recognition; Speech Clarity; Hearing Sensitivity; Visual Color Discrimination. **General Work Activities**—*Information Input:* Identifying Objects, Actions, and Events; Monitoring Processes, Materials, or Surroundings; Getting Information. *Mental Process:* Making Decisions and Solving Problems; Processing Information; Evaluating Information Against Standards. *Work Output:* Documenting or Recording Information; Interacting With Computers. *Interacting with Others:* Communicating with Persons Outside Organization; Performing for or Working with the Public; Communicating with Other Workers. **Physical Work Conditions**—Indoors; Noisy; Sitting; Using Hands on Objects, Tools, or Controls; Repetitive Motions. **Other Job Characteristics**—Need to Be Exact or Accurate; Repeat Same Tasks; Errors Have Important Consequences; Automation.

Experience—Job Zone 3. Previous work-related skill, knowledge, or experience is required. **Job Preparation**—SVP 6.0 to less than 7.0—more than one year and less than four years. **Knowledges**—Transportation; Geography; Telecommunications; Public Safety and Security; Education and Training; Physics. **Instructional Program**—Air Traffic Controller.

Related SOC Job—53-2021 Air Traffic Controllers. **Related OOH Job**—Air Traffic Controllers. **Related DOT Jobs**—193.162-010 Air-Traffic Coordinator; 193.162-014 Air-Traffic-Control Specialist, Station; 193.162-018 Air-Traffic-Control Specialist, Tower; 193.167-010 Chief Controller; 912.167-010 Dispatcher.

53-2022.00 Airfield Operations Specialists

- **Education/Training Required: Long-term on-the-job training**
- **Employed: 4,510**
- **Annual Earnings: $37,330**
- **Growth: 15.0%**
- **Annual Job Openings: Fewer than 500**

Ensure the safe takeoff and landing of commercial and military aircraft. Duties include coordination between air traffic control and maintenance personnel; dispatching; using airfield landing and navigational aids; implementing airfield safety procedures; monitoring and maintaining flight records; and applying knowledge of weather information.

Implement airfield safety procedures to ensure a safe operating environment for personnel and aircraft operation. Plan and coordinate airfield construction. Coordinate with agencies such as air traffic control, civil engineers, and command posts to ensure support of airfield management activities. Monitor the arrival, parking, refueling, loading, and departure of all aircraft. Maintain air-to-ground and point-to-point radio contact with aircraft commanders. Train operations staff. Relay departure, arrival, delay, aircraft and airfield status, and other pertinent information to upline controlling agencies. Procure, produce, and provide information on the safe operation of aircraft, such as flight-planning publications, operations publications, charts and maps, and weather information. Coordinate communications between air traffic control and maintenance personnel. Perform and supervise airfield management activities, which may include mobile airfield management functions. Receive, transmit, and control message traffic. Receive and post weather information and flight plan data such as air routes and arrival and departure times. Maintain flight and events logs, air crew flying records, and flight operations records of incoming and outgoing flights. Coordinate with agencies to meet aircrew requirements for billeting, messing, refueling, ground transportation, and transient aircraft maintenance. Collaborate with others to plan flight schedules and air crew assignments. Coordinate changes to flight itineraries with appropriate Air Traffic Control (ATC) agencies. Anticipate aircraft equipment needs for air evacuation and cargo flights. Provide air crews with information and services needed for airfield management and flight planning. Conduct departure and arrival briefings. Use airfield landing and navigational aids and digital data terminal communications equipment to perform duties. Post visual display boards and status boards. Check military flight plans with civilian agencies.

GOE Information—**Interest Area:** 03. Arts and Communication. **Work Group:** 03.10. Communications Technology. **Personality Type**—No data available. **Work Values**—No data available. **Skills**—Operation Monitoring; Instructing; Operations Analysis; Management of Personnel Resources; Active Learning; Writing. **Abilities**—*Cognitive:* Perceptual Speed; Speed of Closure; Problem Sensitivity; Deductive Reasoning; Selective Attention; Inductive Reasoning. *Psychomotor:* Control Precision; Manual Dexterity. *Physical:* None met the criteria. *Sensory:* Far Vision; Auditory Attention; Depth Perception; Hearing Sensitivity; Visual Color Discrimination; Near Vision. **General Work Activities**—*Information Input:* Identifying Objects, Actions, and Events; Monitoring Processes, Materials, or Surroundings; Inspecting Equipment, Structures, or Materials. *Mental Process:* Updating and Using Relevant Knowledge; Evaluating Information Against Standards; Organizing, Planning, and Prioritizing. *Work Output:* Documenting or Recording Information; Handling and Moving Objects; Operating Vehicles or Equipment. *Interacting with Others:* Establishing and Maintaining Interpersonal Relationships; Communicating with Persons Outside

Organization; Performing for or Working with the Public. **Physical Work Conditions**—More Often Indoors Than Outdoors; Noisy; Very Hot or Cold; Contaminants; Sitting. **Other Job Characteristics**—Need to Be Exact or Accurate; Repeat Same Tasks; Errors Have Important Consequences.

Experience—Job Zone 3. Previous work-related skill, knowledge, or experience is required. **Job Preparation**—SVP 6.0 to less than 7.0—more than one year and less than four years. **Knowledges**—Transportation; Geography; Customer and Personal Service; Telecommunications; Computers and Electronics; Physics. **Instructional Program**—Air Traffic Controller.

Related SOC Job—53-2022 Airfield Operations Specialists. **Related OOH Job**—Airfield Operations Specialists. **Related DOT Job**—912.367-010 Flight-Information Expediter.

53-3000 Motor Vehicle Operators

53-3011.00 Ambulance Drivers and Attendants, Except Emergency Medical Technicians

- **Education/Training Required: Moderate-term on-the-job training**
- **Employed: 18,320**
- **Annual Earnings: $18,790**
- **Growth: 28.0%**
- **Annual Job Openings: 5,000**

Drive ambulance or assist ambulance driver in transporting sick, injured, or convalescent persons. Assist in lifting patients.

Drive ambulances or assist ambulance drivers in transporting sick, injured, or convalescent persons. Remove and replace soiled linens and equipment to maintain sanitary conditions. Accompany and assist emergency medical technicians on calls. Place patients on stretchers and load stretchers into ambulances, usually with assistance from other attendants. Earn and maintain appropriate certifications. Replace supplies and disposable items on ambulances. Report facts concerning accidents or emergencies to hospital personnel or law enforcement officials. Administer first aid such as bandaging, splinting, and administering oxygen. Restrain or shackle violent patients.

GOE Information—**Interest Area:** 16. Transportation, Distribution, and Logistics. **Work Group:** 16.06. Other Services Requiring Driving. **Personality Type**—Social. Social occupations frequently involve working with, communicating with, and teaching people. These occupations often involve helping or providing service to others. **Work Values**—Social Service; Variety; Supervision, Technical; Security; Co-workers; Achievement. **Skills**—Equipment Maintenance; Operation Monitoring; Operation and Control; Repairing; Technology Design; Service Orientation. **Abilities**—*Cognitive:* Spatial Orientation; Time Sharing; Perceptual Speed; Selective Attention; Speed of Closure; Flexibility of Closure. *Psychomotor:* Reaction Time; Response Orientation; Speed of Limb Movement; Rate Control; Control Precision; Manual Dexterity. *Physical:* Static Strength; Dynamic Strength; Gross Body Coordination; Stamina; Extent Flexibility; Trunk Strength. *Sensory:* Depth Perception; Far Vision;

Auditory Attention; Hearing Sensitivity; Visual Color Discrimination. **General Work Activities**—*Information Input:* Monitoring Processes, Materials, or Surroundings; Identifying Objects, Actions, and Events; Inspecting Equipment, Structures, or Materials. *Mental Process:* Making Decisions and Solving Problems; Organizing, Planning, and Prioritizing; Judging the Qualities of Things, Services, or Other People's Work. *Work Output:* Handling and Moving Objects; Operating Vehicles or Equipment; Documenting or Recording Information. *Interacting with Others:* Assisting and Caring for Others; Performing for or Working with the Public; Establishing and Maintaining Interpersonal Relationships. **Physical Work Conditions**—Outdoors; Noisy; Very Hot or Cold; Disease or Infections; Sitting; Using Hands on Objects, Tools, or Controls. **Other Job Characteristics**—Need to Be Exact or Accurate; Errors Have Important Consequences.

Experience—Job Zone 2. Some previous work-related skill, knowledge, or experience may be helpful in these occupations, but usually is not needed. **Job Preparation**—SVP 4.0 to less than 6.0—six months to less than two years. **Knowledges**—Transportation; Psychology; Medicine and Dentistry; Customer and Personal Service; Telecommunications; Public Safety and Security. **Instructional Program**—Emergency Medical Technology/Technician (Paramedic).

Related SOC Job—53-3011 Ambulance Drivers and Attendants, Except Emergency Medical Technicians. **Related OOH Job**—Ambulance Drivers and Attendants, Except Emergency Medical Technicians. **Related DOT Jobs**—355.374-010 Ambulance Attendant; 913.683-010 Ambulance Driver.

53-3021.00 Bus Drivers, Transit and Intercity

- **Education/Training Required:** Moderate-term on-the-job training
- **Employed:** 183,450
- **Annual Earnings:** $31,010
- **Growth:** 21.7%
- **Annual Job Openings:** 34,000

Drive bus or motor coach, including regular route operations, charters, and private carriage. May assist passengers with baggage. May collect fares or tickets.

Inspect vehicles and check gas, oil, and water levels prior to departure. Drive vehicles over specified routes or to specified destinations according to time schedules to transport passengers, complying with traffic regulations. Park vehicles at loading areas so that passengers can board. Assist passengers with baggage and collect tickets or cash fares. Report delays or accidents. Advise passengers to be seated and orderly while on vehicles. Regulate heating, lighting, and ventilating systems for passenger comfort. Load and unload baggage in baggage compartments. Record cash receipts and ticket fares. Make minor repairs to vehicle and change tires.

GOE Information—**Interest Area:** 16. Transportation, Distribution, and Logistics. **Work Group:** 16.06. Other Services Requiring Driving. **Personality Type**—Realistic. Realistic occupations frequently involve work activities that include practical, hands-on problems and solutions. They often deal with plants; animals; and real-world materials like wood, tools, and machinery. Many of the occupations require working outside and do not involve a lot of paperwork or working closely with others. **Work Values**—Supervision, Technical; Supervision, Human Relations; Company Policies and Practices;

Independence; Social Service; Security. **Skills**—Equipment Maintenance; Operation and Control; Social Perceptiveness; Operation Monitoring; Troubleshooting; Repairing. **Abilities**—*Cognitive:* Spatial Orientation; Time Sharing; Perceptual Speed; Selective Attention; Flexibility of Closure; Speed of Closure. *Psychomotor:* Response Orientation; Reaction Time; Rate Control; Control Precision; Multilimb Coordination; Speed of Limb Movement. *Physical:* Static Strength; Extent Flexibility; Trunk Strength. *Sensory:* Peripheral Vision; Sound Localization; Night Vision; Glare Sensitivity; Hearing Sensitivity; Far Vision. **General Work Activities**—*Information Input:* Getting Information; Monitoring Processes, Materials, or Surroundings; Identifying Objects, Actions, and Events. *Mental Process:* Making Decisions and Solving Problems; Evaluating Information Against Standards; Updating and Using Relevant Knowledge. *Work Output:* Operating Vehicles or Equipment; Handling and Moving Objects; Performing General Physical Activities. *Interacting with Others:* Establishing and Maintaining Interpersonal Relationships; Performing for or Working with the Public; Communicating with Persons Outside Organization. **Physical Work Conditions**—Outdoors; Noisy; Contaminants; Sitting; Using Hands on Objects, Tools, or Controls; Repetitive Motions. **Other Job Characteristics**—Need to Be Exact or Accurate; Repeat Same Tasks; Errors Have Important Consequences; Pace Determined by Speed of Equipment.

Experience—Job Zone 2. Some previous work-related skill, knowledge, or experience may be helpful in these occupations, but usually is not needed. **Job Preparation**—SVP 4.0 to less than 6.0—six months to less than two years. **Knowledges**—Transportation; Geography; Public Safety and Security; Customer and Personal Service; Psychology; Law and Government. **Instructional Program**—Truck and Bus Driver/Commercial Vehicle Operation.

Related SOC Job—53-3021 Bus Drivers, Transit and Intercity. **Related OOH Job**—Bus Drivers. **Related DOT Jobs**—913.363-010 Bus Driver, Day-Haul or Farm Charter; 913.463-010 Bus Driver; 913.663-014 Mobile-Lounge Driver.

53-3022.00 Bus Drivers, School

- **Education/Training Required:** Short-term on-the-job training
- **Employed:** 465,880
- **Annual Earnings:** $24,070
- **Growth:** 13.6%
- **Annual Job Openings:** 76,000

Transport students or special clients, such as the elderly or persons with disabilities. Ensure adherence to safety rules. May assist passengers in boarding or exiting.

Follow safety rules as students are boarding and exiting buses and as they cross streets near bus stops. Comply with traffic regulations to operate vehicles in a safe and courteous manner. Check the condition of a vehicle's tires, brakes, windshield wipers, lights, oil, fuel, water, and safety equipment to ensure that everything is in working order. Maintain order among pupils during trips to ensure safety. Pick up and drop off students at regularly scheduled neighborhood locations, following strict time schedules. Report any bus malfunctions or needed repairs. Drive gasoline, diesel, or electrically powered multi-passenger vehicles to transport students between neighborhoods, schools, and school activities. Prepare and submit reports that may include the number of passengers or trips, hours worked, mileage, fuel consumption, and fares received. Maintain knowledge of first-aid procedures. Keep bus interiors clean for passengers. Read maps and follow written and verbal geographic directions. Report delays, accidents, or other traffic and transportation situations, using telephones or mobile two-way radios. Regulate heating, lighting, and ventilation systems for passenger comfort. Escort small children across roads and highways. Make minor repairs to vehicles.

GOE Information—Interest Area: 16. Transportation, Distribution, and Logistics. **Work Group:** 16.06. Other Services Requiring Driving. **Personality Type**—Realistic. Realistic occupations frequently involve work activities that include practical, hands-on problems and solutions. They often deal with plants; animals; and real-world materials like wood, tools, and machinery. Many of the occupations require working outside and do not involve a lot of paperwork or working closely with others. **Work Values**—Supervision, Technical; Supervision, Human Relations; Independence; Company Policies and Practices; Social Service. **Skills**—Operation Monitoring; Equipment Maintenance; Operation and Control; Social Perceptiveness; Persuasion; Negotiation. **Abilities**—*Cognitive:* Spatial Orientation; Time Sharing; Selective Attention; Perceptual Speed; Speed of Closure. *Psychomotor:* Reaction Time; Response Orientation; Rate Control; Multilimb Coordination; Speed of Limb Movement; Control Precision. *Physical:* None met the criteria. *Sensory:* Sound Localization; Glare Sensitivity; Peripheral Vision; Hearing Sensitivity; Depth Perception; Auditory Attention. **General Work Activities**—*Information Input:* Inspecting Equipment, Structures, or Materials; Monitoring Processes, Materials, or Surroundings; Identifying Objects, Actions, and Events. *Mental Process:* Making Decisions and Solving Problems; Evaluating Information Against Standards; Judging the Qualities of Things, Services, or Other People's Work. *Work Output:* Operating Vehicles or Equipment; Handling and Moving Objects; Repairing and Maintaining Mechanical Equipment. *Interacting with Others:* Resolving Conflicts and Negotiating with Others; Performing for or Working with the Public; Assisting and Caring for Others. **Physical Work Conditions**—Noisy; Contaminants; Disease or Infections; Sitting; Using Hands on Objects, Tools, or Controls; Repetitive Motions. **Other Job Characteristics**—Need to Be Exact or Accurate; Repeat Same Tasks; Errors Have Important Consequences.

Experience—Job Zone 2. Some previous work-related skill, knowledge, or experience may be helpful in these occupations, but usually is not needed. **Job Preparation**—SVP 4.0 to less than 6.0—six months to less than two years. **Knowledges**—Transportation; Psychology; Public Safety and Security; Law and Government. **Instructional Program**—Truck and Bus Driver/Commercial Vehicle Operation.

Related SOC Job—53-3022 Bus Drivers, School. **Related OOH Job**—Bus Drivers. **Related DOT Job**—913.463-010 Bus Driver.

53-3031.00 Driver/Sales Workers

- **Education/Training Required: Short-term on-the-job training**
- **Employed: 400,530**
- **Annual Earnings: $20,120**
- **Growth: 13.8%**
- **Annual Job Openings: 72,000**

Drive truck or other vehicle over established routes or within an established territory and sell goods, such as food products, including restaurant take-out items, or pick up and deliver items such as laundry. May also take orders and collect payments. Includes newspaper delivery drivers.

Collect money from customers, make change, and record transactions on customer receipts. Listen to and resolve customers' complaints regarding products or services. Inform regular customers of new products or services and price changes. Write customer orders and sales contracts according to company guidelines. Drive trucks to deliver such items as food, medical supplies, or newspapers. Collect coins from vending machines, refill machines, and remove aged merchandise. Call on prospective customers to explain company services and to solicit new business. Record sales or delivery information on daily sales or delivery record. Review lists of dealers, customers, or station drops and load trucks. Arrange merchandise and sales promotion displays or issue sales promotion materials to customers. Maintain trucks and food-dispensing equipment and clean inside of machines that dispense food or beverages. Sell food specialties, such as sandwiches and beverages, to office workers and patrons of sports events.

GOE Information—Interest Area: 16. Transportation, Distribution, and Logistics. **Work Group:** 16.06. Other Services Requiring Driving. **Personality Type**—Enterprising. Enterprising occupations frequently involve starting up and carrying out projects. These occupations can involve leading people and making many decisions. They sometimes require risk taking and often deal with business. **Work Values**—Independence; Supervision, Technical. **Skills**—None met the criteria. **Abilities**—*Cognitive:* Spatial Orientation; Time Sharing; Fluency of Ideas; Memorization; Perceptual Speed; Visualization. *Psychomotor:* Response Orientation; Reaction Time; Rate Control; Multilimb Coordination; Manual Dexterity; Control Precision. *Physical:* Static Strength; Trunk Strength. *Sensory:* Peripheral Vision; Night Vision; Glare Sensitivity; Depth Perception; Hearing Sensitivity; Speech Recognition. **General Work Activities**—*Information Input:* Identifying Objects, Actions, and Events; Getting Information; Monitoring Processes, Materials, or Surroundings. *Mental Process:* Judging the Qualities of Things, Services, or Other People's Work; Making Decisions and Solving Problems; Scheduling Work and Activities. *Work Output:* Handling and Moving Objects; Controlling Machines and Processes; Performing General Physical Activities. *Interacting with Others:* Communicating with Persons Outside Organization; Establishing and Maintaining Interpersonal Relationships; Influencing Others or Selling. **Physical Work Conditions**—More Often Outdoors Than Indoors; Very Hot or Cold; Sitting; Using Hands on Objects, Tools, or Controls; Repetitive Motions. **Other Job Characteristics**—Need to Be Exact or Accurate; Errors Have Important Consequences.

Experience—Job Zone 1. No previous work-related skill, knowledge, or experience is needed. **Job Preparation**—SVP below 4.0—less than six months. **Knowledges**—Transportation; Sales and Marketing; Public Safety and Security. **Instructional Program**—Retailing and Retail Operations.

Related SOC Job—53-3031 Driver/Sales Workers. **Related OOH Job**—Truck Drivers and Driver/Sales Workers. **Related DOT Jobs**—292.353-010 Driver, Sales Route; 292.363-010 Newspaper-Delivery Driver; 292.463-010 Lunch-Truck Driver; 292.483-010 Coin Collector; 292.667-010 Driver Helper, Sales Route; 292.687-010 Coin-Machine Collector.

53-3032.00 Truck Drivers, Heavy and Tractor-Trailer

- **Education/Training Required: Moderate-term on-the-job training**
- **Employed: 1,624,740**
- **Annual Earnings: $34,280**
- **Growth: 12.9%**
- **Annual Job Openings: 274,000**

Drive a tractor-trailer combination or a truck with a capacity of at least 26,000 GVW to transport and deliver goods, livestock, or materials in liquid, loose, or packaged form. May be required to unload truck. May require use of automated routing equipment. Requires commercial driver's license.

Follow appropriate safety procedures when transporting dangerous goods. Check vehicles before driving them to ensure that mechanical, safety, and emergency equipment is in good working order. Maintain logs of working hours and of vehicle service and repair status, following applicable state and federal regulations. Obtain receipts or signatures when loads are delivered and collect payment for services when required. Check all load-related documentation to ensure that it is complete and accurate. Maneuver trucks into loading or unloading positions, following signals from loading crew as needed; check that vehicle position is correct and any special loading equipment is properly positioned. Drive trucks with capacities greater than 3 tons, including tractor-trailer combinations, to transport and deliver products, livestock, or other materials. Secure cargo for transport, using ropes, blocks, chain, binders, or covers. Read bills of lading to determine assignment details. Report vehicle defects, accidents, traffic violations, or damage to the vehicles. Read and interpret maps to determine vehicle routes. Couple and uncouple trailers by changing trailer jack positions, connecting or disconnecting air and electrical lines, and manipulating fifth-wheel locks. Collect delivery instructions from appropriate sources, verifying instructions and routes. Drive trucks to weigh stations before and after loading and along routes to document weights and to comply with state regulations. Operate equipment such as truck cab computers, CB radios, and telephones to exchange necessary information with bases, supervisors, or other drivers. Check conditions of trailers after contents have been unloaded to ensure that there has been no damage. Crank trailer landing gear up and down to safely secure vehicles. Wrap goods, using pads, packing paper, and containers, and secure loads to trailer walls, using straps. Perform basic vehicle maintenance tasks such as adding oil, fuel, and radiator fluid or performing minor repairs. Load and unload trucks or help others with loading and unloading, operating any special loading-related equipment on vehicles and using other equipment as necessary.

GOE Information—Interest Area: 16. Transportation, Distribution, and Logistics. **Work Group:** 16.03. Truck Driving. **Personality Type—**Realistic. Realistic occupations frequently involve work activities that include practical, hands-on problems and solutions. They often deal with plants; animals; and real-world materials like wood, tools, and machinery. Many of the occupations require working outside and do not involve a lot of paperwork or working closely with others. **Work Values—**Compensation; Independence; Company Policies and Practices; Supervision, Technical; Supervision, Human Relations. **Skills—**Equipment Maintenance; Repairing; Operation Monitoring; Troubleshooting; Operation and Control. **Abilities—** *Cognitive:* Spatial Orientation; Time Sharing; Visualization; Memorization; Perceptual Speed. *Psychomotor:* Reaction Time; Response Orientation; Rate Control; Wrist-Finger Speed; Speed of Limb Movement; Multilimb Coordination. *Physical:* Static Strength; Explosive Strength; Extent Flexibility; Dynamic Flexibility; Dynamic Strength; Trunk Strength. *Sensory:* Night Vision; Peripheral Vision; Depth Perception; Glare Sensitivity; Hearing Sensitivity; Far Vision. **General Work Activities—***Information Input:* Inspecting Equipment, Structures, or Materials; Monitoring Processes, Materials, or Surroundings; Identifying Objects, Actions, and Events. *Mental Process:* Making Decisions and Solving Problems; Organizing, Planning, and Prioritizing; Evaluating Information Against Standards. *Work Output:* Handling and Moving Objects; Operating Vehicles or Equipment; Performing General Physical Activities.

Interacting with Others: Communicating with Persons Outside Organization; Establishing and Maintaining Interpersonal Relationships; Communicating with Other Workers. **Physical Work Conditions—**Outdoors; Very Hot or Cold; Contaminants; Sitting; Using Hands on Objects, Tools, or Controls; Repetitive Motions. **Other Job Characteristics—**Need to Be Exact or Accurate; Errors Have Important Consequences; Pace Determined by Speed of Equipment; Repeat Same Tasks.

Experience—Job Zone 2. Some previous work-related skill, knowledge, or experience may be helpful in these occupations, but usually is not needed. **Job Preparation—**SVP 4.0 to less than 6.0—six months to less than two years. **Knowledges—**Transportation; Geography; Public Safety and Security; Law and Government; Mechanical Devices. **Instructional Program—**Truck and Bus Driver/Commercial Vehicle Operation.

Related SOC Job—53-3032 Truck Drivers, Heavy and Tractor-Trailer. **Related OOH Job—**Truck Drivers and Driver/Sales Workers. **Related DOT Jobs—**900.683-010 Concrete-Mixing-Truck Driver; 902.683-010 Dump-Truck Driver; 903.683-010 Explosives-Truck Driver; 903.683-014 Powder-Truck Driver; 903.683-018 Tank-Truck Driver; 904.363-010 Tractor-Trailer Moving Van Driver; 904.383-010 Tractor-Trailer-Truck Driver; 904.683-010 Log-Truck Driver; 905.363-900 Construction Driver; 905.483-010 Milk Driver; 905.663-010 Garbage Collector Driver; 905.663-014 Truck Driver, Heavy; 905.663-018 Van Driver; 905.683-010 Water-Truck Driver II; others.

53-3033.00 Truck Drivers, Light or Delivery Services

- **Education/Training Required: Short-term on-the-job training**
- **Employed: 938,280**
- **Annual Earnings: $24,790**
- **Growth: 15.7%**
- **Annual Job Openings: 169,000**

Drive a truck or van with a capacity of under 26,000 GVW primarily to deliver or pick up merchandise or to deliver packages within a specified area. May require use of automatic routing or location software. May load and unload truck.

Obey traffic laws and follow established traffic and transportation procedures. Inspect and maintain vehicle supplies and equipment such as gas, oil, water, tires, lights, and brakes to ensure that vehicles are in proper working condition. Report any mechanical problems encountered with vehicles. Present bills and receipts and collect payments for goods delivered or loaded. Load and unload trucks, vans, or automobiles. Turn in receipts and money received from deliveries. Verify the contents of inventory loads against shipping papers. Maintain records such as vehicle logs, records of cargo, or billing statements in accordance with regulations. Read maps and follow written and verbal geographic directions. Report delays, accidents, or other traffic and transportation situations to bases or other vehicles, using telephones or mobile two-way radios. Sell and keep records of sales for products from truck inventory. Drive vehicles with capacities under three tons to transport materials to and from specified destinations such as railroad stations, plants, residences, and offices or within industrial yards. Drive trucks equipped with public address systems through city streets to broadcast announcements for advertising or publicity purposes. Use and maintain the tools and equipment found on commercial vehicles, such as weighing and measuring devices. Perform emergency repairs such as changing tires or installing light bulbs, fuses, tire chains, and spark plugs.

GOE Information—Interest Area: 16. Transportation, Distribution, and Logistics. Work Group: 16.03. Truck Driving. Personality Type—Realistic. Realistic occupations frequently involve work activities that include practical, hands-on problems and solutions. They often deal with plants; animals; and real-world materials like wood, tools, and machinery. Many of the occupations require working outside and do not involve a lot of paperwork or working closely with others. Work Values—Independence; Compensation; Supervision, Technical; Company Policies and Practices. Skills—Equipment Maintenance; Operation Monitoring; Operation and Control; Social Perceptiveness; Service Orientation. Abilities—*Cognitive:* Spatial Orientation; Time Sharing; Oral Expression; Perceptual Speed; Number Facility; Speed of Closure. *Psychomotor:* Response Orientation; Reaction Time; Rate Control; Multilimb Coordination; Speed of Limb Movement; Manual Dexterity. *Physical:* Static Strength; Extent Flexibility; Dynamic Strength; Trunk Strength; Gross Body Coordination; Stamina. *Sensory:* Night Vision; Glare Sensitivity; Peripheral Vision; Depth Perception; Far Vision; Hearing Sensitivity. General Work Activities—*Information Input:* Identifying Objects, Actions, and Events; Getting Information; Monitoring Processes, Materials, or Surroundings. *Mental Process:* Updating and Using Relevant Knowledge; Organizing, Planning, and Prioritizing; Processing Information. *Work Output:* Handling and Moving Objects; Performing General Physical Activities; Operating Vehicles or Equipment. *Interacting with Others:* Performing for or Working with the Public; Establishing and Maintaining Interpersonal Relationships; Communicating with Other Workers. Physical Work Conditions—Outdoors; Very Hot or Cold; Contaminants; Cramped Work Space, Awkward Positions; Minor Burns, Cuts, Bites, or Stings; Using Hands on Objects, Tools, or Controls. Other Job Characteristics—Need to Be Exact or Accurate; Repeat Same Tasks.

Experience—Job Zone 2. Some previous work-related skill, knowledge, or experience may be helpful in these occupations, but usually is not needed. Job Preparation—SVP 4.0 to less than 6.0—six months to less than two years. Knowledges—Transportation; Production and Processing. Instructional Program—Truck and Bus Driver/Commercial Vehicle Operation.

Related SOC Job—53-3033 Truck Drivers, Light or Delivery Services. Related OOH Job—Truck Drivers and Driver/Sales Workers. Related DOT Jobs—906.683-010 Food-Service Driver; 906.683-014 Liquid-Fertilizer Servicer; 906.683-018 Telephone-Directory-Distributor Driver; 906.683-022 Truck Driver, Light; 913.663-018 Driver; 919.663-022 Escort-Vehicle Driver.

53-3041.00 Taxi Drivers and Chauffeurs

- **Education/Training Required: Short-term on-the-job training**
- **Employed: 144,280**
- **Annual Earnings: $19,980**
- **Growth: 24.8%**
- **Annual Job Openings: 43,000**

Drive automobiles, vans, or limousines to transport passengers. May occasionally carry cargo.

Test vehicle equipment such as lights, brakes, horns, or windshield wipers to ensure proper operation. Notify dispatchers or company mechanics of vehicle problems. Drive taxicabs, limousines, company cars, or privately owned vehicles to transport passengers. Follow regulations governing taxi operation and ensure that passengers follow safety regulations. Pick up passengers at prearranged locations, at taxi stands, or by cruising streets in high-traffic areas. Perform routine vehicle maintenance such as regulating tire pressure and adding gasoline, oil, and water. Communicate with dispatchers by radio, telephone, or computer to exchange information and receive requests for passenger service. Record name, date, and taxi identification information on trip sheets, along with trip information such as time and place of pickup and dropoff and total fee. Complete accident reports when necessary. Provide passengers with assistance entering and exiting vehicles and help them with any luggage. Arrange to pick up particular customers or groups on a regular schedule. Vacuum and clean interiors and wash and polish exteriors of automobiles. Pick up or meet employers according to requests, appointments, or schedules. Operate vans with special equipment such as wheelchair lifts to transport people with special needs. Collect fares or vouchers from passengers and make change or issue receipts as necessary. Determine fares based on trip distances and times, using taximeters and fee schedules, and announce fares to passengers. Perform minor vehicle repairs such as cleaning spark plugs or take vehicles to mechanics for servicing. Turn the taximeter on when passengers enter the cab and turn it off when they reach the final destination. Report to taxicab services or garages to receive vehicle assignments. Perform errands for customers or employers, such as delivering or picking up mail and packages. Provide passengers with information about the local area and points of interest or give advice on hotels and restaurants.

GOE Information—Interest Area: 16. Transportation, Distribution, and Logistics. Work Group: 16.06. Other Services Requiring Driving. Personality Type—Realistic. Realistic occupations frequently involve work activities that include practical, hands-on problems and solutions. They often deal with plants; animals; and real-world materials like wood, tools, and machinery. Many of the occupations require working outside and do not involve a lot of paperwork or working closely with others. Work Values—Social Service; Independence. Skills—Operation and Control; Installation; Equipment Maintenance. Abilities—*Cognitive:* Spatial Orientation; Time Sharing; Perceptual Speed; Flexibility of Closure; Selective Attention; Speed of Closure. *Psychomotor:* Reaction Time; Response Orientation; Rate Control; Control Precision; Multilimb Coordination; Manual Dexterity. *Physical:* Static Strength; Gross Body Coordination; Trunk Strength. *Sensory:* Sound Localization; Peripheral Vision; Night Vision; Glare Sensitivity; Hearing Sensitivity; Far Vision. General Work Activities—*Information Input:* Monitoring Processes, Materials, or Surroundings; Inspecting Equipment, Structures, or Materials; Getting Information. *Mental Process:* Judging the Qualities of Things, Services, or Other People's Work; Evaluating Information Against Standards; Updating and Using Relevant Knowledge. *Work Output:* Handling and Moving Objects; Operating Vehicles or Equipment; Performing General Physical Activities. *Interacting with Others:* Performing for or Working with the Public; Assisting and Caring for Others; Establishing and Maintaining Interpersonal Relationships. Physical Work Conditions—Outdoors; Contaminants; Sitting; Using Hands on Objects, Tools, or Controls. Other Job Characteristics—Need to Be Exact or Accurate; Errors Have Important Consequences.

Experience—Job Zone 1. No previous work-related skill, knowledge, or experience is needed. Job Preparation—SVP below 4.0—less than six months. Knowledges—Transportation; English Language. Instructional Program—Truck and Bus Driver/Commercial Vehicle Operation.

Related SOC Job—53-3041 Taxi Drivers and Chauffeurs. Related OOH Job—Taxi Drivers and Chauffeurs. Related DOT Jobs—359.673-010 Chauffeur; 359.673-014 Chauffeur, Funeral Car; 913.463-018 Taxi Driver; 913.663-010 Chauffeur; 919.663-010 Deliverer, Car Rental; 919.683-014 Driver.

53-3099.99 Motor Vehicle Operators, All Other

- **Education/Training Required: Short-term on-the-job training**
- **Employed: 76,500**
- **Annual Earnings: $22,280**
- **Growth: 25.7%**
- **Annual Job Openings: 23,000**

All motor vehicle operators not listed separately.

No task data available.

Note: The Department of Labor has not collected some data for this job, so it has fewer details than the other descriptions.

Related SOC Job—53-3099 Motor Vehicle Operators, All Other. **Related OOH Job**—None. **Related DOT Jobs**—919.683-022 Street-Sweeper Operator; 919.683-030 Driver, Starting Gate.

53-4000 Rail Transportation Workers

53-4011.00 Locomotive Engineers

- **Education/Training Required: Work experience in a related occupation**
- **Employed: 37,390**
- **Annual Earnings: $55,520**
- **Growth: –2.5%**
- **Annual Job Openings: 2,000**

Drive electric, diesel-electric, steam, or gas-turbine-electric locomotives to transport passengers or freight. Interpret train orders, electronic or manual signals, and railroad rules and regulations.

Monitor gauges and meters that measure speed, amperage, battery charge, and air pressure in brake lines and in main reservoirs. Observe tracks to detect obstructions. Interpret train orders, signals, and railroad rules and regulations that govern the operation of locomotives. Receive starting signals from conductors; then move controls such as throttles and air brakes to drive electric, diesel-electric, steam, or gas-turbine-electric locomotives. Confer with conductors or traffic control center personnel via radiophones to issue or receive information concerning stops, delays, or oncoming trains. Operate locomotives to transport freight or passengers between stations and to assemble and disassemble trains within rail yards. Respond to emergency conditions or breakdowns, following applicable safety procedures and rules. Check to ensure that brake examination tests are conducted at shunting stations. Call out train signals to assistants to verify meanings. Inspect locomotives to verify adequate fuel, sand, water, and other supplies before each run and to check for mechanical problems. Prepare reports regarding any problems encountered, such as accidents, signaling problems, unscheduled stops, or delays. Check to ensure that documentation, including procedure manuals and logbooks, is in the driver's cab and available for staff use. Inspect locomotives after runs to detect damaged or defective equipment. Drive diesel-electric rail-detector cars to transport rail-flaw-detecting machines over tracks. Monitor train-loading procedures to ensure that freight and rolling stock are loaded or unloaded without damage.

GOE Information—**Interest Area:** 16. Transportation, Distribution, and Logistics. **Work Group:** 16.04. Rail Vehicle Operation. **Personality Type**—Realistic. Realistic occupations frequently involve work activities that include practical, hands-on problems and solutions. They often deal with plants; animals; and real-world materials like wood, tools, and machinery. Many of the occupations require working outside and do not involve a lot of paperwork or working closely with others. **Work Values**—Supervision, Technical; Supervision, Human Relations; Compensation; Company Policies and Practices; Security; Social Status. **Skills**—Operation Monitoring; Operation and Control; Troubleshooting; Instructing; Active Listening; Service Orientation. **Abilities**—*Cognitive:* Spatial Orientation; Perceptual Speed; Flexibility of Closure; Time Sharing; Selective Attention; Visualization. *Psychomotor:* Reaction Time; Response Orientation; Rate Control; Multilimb Coordination; Control Precision; Speed of Limb Movement. *Physical:* Static Strength; Trunk Strength. *Sensory:* Auditory Attention; Peripheral Vision; Glare Sensitivity; Far Vision; Night Vision; Depth Perception. **General Work Activities**—*Information Input:* Identifying Objects, Actions, and Events; Inspecting Equipment, Structures, or Materials; Getting Information. *Mental Process:* Evaluating Information Against Standards; Updating and Using Relevant Knowledge; Processing Information. *Work Output:* Controlling Machines and Processes; Handling and Moving Objects; Operating Vehicles or Equipment. *Interacting with Others:* Communicating with Other Workers; Establishing and Maintaining Interpersonal Relationships; Resolving Conflicts and Negotiating with Others. **Physical Work Conditions**—Outdoors; Noisy; Contaminants; Hazardous Equipment; Using Hands on Objects, Tools, or Controls; Repetitive Motions. **Other Job Characteristics**—Need to Be Exact or Accurate; Repeat Same Tasks; Errors Have Important Consequences.

Experience—Job Zone 2. Some previous work-related skill, knowledge, or experience may be helpful in these occupations, but usually is not needed. **Job Preparation**—SVP 4.0 to less than 6.0—six months to less than two years. **Knowledges**—Transportation; Mechanical Devices; Public Safety and Security. **Instructional Program**—Transportation and Material-Moving Services, Other.

Related SOC Job—53-4011 Locomotive Engineers. **Related OOH Job**—Rail Transportation Occupations. **Related DOT Job**—910.363-014 Locomotive Engineer.

53-4012.00 Locomotive Firers

- **Education/Training Required: Postsecondary vocational training**
- **Employed: 540**
- **Annual Earnings: $38,790**
- **Growth: –2.5%**
- **Annual Job Openings: 2,000**

Monitor locomotive instruments and watch for dragging equipment, obstacles on rights-of-way, and train signals during run. Watch for and relay traffic signals from yard workers to yard engineer in railroad yard.

Signal other workers to set brakes and to throw track switches when switching cars from trains to way stations. Monitor oil, temperature, and pressure gauges on dashboards to determine if engines are operating safely and efficiently. Check to see that trains are equipped with supplies such as fuel, water, and sand. Inspect locomotives to detect damaged or worn parts. Operate locomotives in emergency situations. Receive signals from workers in rear of train and relay that information to engineers. Start diesel engines to warm engines before runs. Observe train signals along routes and verify their meanings for engineers. Observe tracks from left sides of locomotives to detect obstructions on tracks. Monitor trains as they go around curves to detect dragging equipment and smoking journal boxes.

GOE Information—Interest Area: 16. Transportation, Distribution, and Logistics. **Work Group:** 16.04. Rail Vehicle Operation. **Personality Type—**Realistic. Realistic occupations frequently involve work activities that include practical, hands-on problems and solutions. They often deal with plants; animals; and real-world materials like wood, tools, and machinery. Many of the occupations require working outside and do not involve a lot of paperwork or working closely with others. **Work Values—**Supervision, Technical; Supervision, Human Relations; Company Policies and Practices; Moral Values; Advancement; Security. **Skills—**Operation Monitoring; Operation and Control; Systems Analysis. **Abilities—***Cognitive:* Perceptual Speed; Time Sharing. *Psychomotor:* Reaction Time; Response Orientation; Rate Control; Manual Dexterity; Control Precision. *Physical:* Extent Flexibility. *Sensory:* Night Vision; Peripheral Vision; Far Vision; Glare Sensitivity; Depth Perception. **General Work Activities—***Information Input:* Monitoring Processes, Materials, or Surroundings; Getting Information; Inspecting Equipment, Structures, or Materials. *Mental Process:* Evaluating Information Against Standards. *Work Output:* Operating Vehicles or Equipment; Handling and Moving Objects; Performing General Physical Activities. *Interacting with Others:* Establishing and Maintaining Interpersonal Relationships; Communicating with Other Workers. **Physical Work Conditions—**Outdoors; Noisy; Very Hot or Cold; Contaminants; Whole-Body Vibration; Hazardous Equipment. **Other Job Characteristics—**Errors Have Important Consequences; Need to Be Exact or Accurate; Automation.

Experience—Job Zone 3. Previous work-related skill, knowledge, or experience is required. **Job Preparation—**SVP 6.0 to less than 7.0—more than one year and less than four years. **Knowledges—**Transportation; Geography; Mechanical Devices; Engineering and Technology. **Instructional Program—**Transportation and Materials Moving Services, Other.

Related SOC Job—53-4012 Locomotive Firers. **Related OOH Job—**Rail Transportation Occupations. **Related DOT Job—**910.363-010 Firer, Locomotive.

53-4013.00 Rail Yard Engineers, Dinkey Operators, and Hostlers

- **Education/Training Required: Work experience in a related occupation**
- **Employed: 6,970**
- **Annual Earnings: $38,020**
- **Growth: –2.5%**
- **Annual Job Openings: 2,000**

Drive switching or other locomotive or dinkey engines within railroad yard, industrial plant, quarry, construction project, or similar location.

Confer with conductors and other workers via radio-telephones or computers to exchange switching information. Signal crew members for movement of engines or trains, using lanterns, hand signals, radios, or telephones. Observe and respond to wayside and cab signals, including colored light signals, position signals, torpedoes, flags, and hot box detectors. Drive engines within railroad yards or other establishments to couple, uncouple, or switch railroad cars. Inspect engines before and after use to ensure proper operation. Apply and release hand brakes. Read switching instructions and daily car schedules to determine work to be performed or receive orders from yard conductors. Inspect the condition of stationary trains, rolling stock, and equipment. Observe water levels and oil, air, and steam pressure gauges to ensure proper operation of equipment. Spot cars for loading and unloading at customer locations. Inspect track for defects such as broken rails and switch malfunctions. Ride on moving cars by holding onto grab irons and standing on ladder steps. Operate track switches, derails, automatic switches, and retarders to change routing of train or cars. Receive, relay, and act upon instructions and inquiries from train operations and customer service center personnel. Couple and uncouple air hoses and electrical connections between cars. Report arrival and departure times, train delays, work order completion, and time on duty. Pull knuckles to open them for coupling. Provide assistance in aligning drawbars, using available equipment to lift, pull, or push on the drawbars. Drive locomotives to and from various stations in roundhouses to have locomotives cleaned, serviced, repaired, or supplied. Record numbers of cars available, numbers of cars sent to repair stations, and types of service needed. Perform routine repair and maintenance duties. Operate and control dinkey engines to transport and shunt cars at industrial or mine sites. Operate flatcars equipped with derricks or railcars to transport personnel or equipment. Provide assistance in the installation or repair of rails and ties.

GOE Information—Interest Area: 16. Transportation, Distribution, and Logistics. **Work Group:** 16.04. Rail Vehicle Operation. **Personality Type—**Realistic. Realistic occupations frequently involve work activities that include practical, hands-on problems and solutions. They often deal with plants; animals; and real-world materials like wood, tools, and machinery. Many of the occupations require working outside and do not involve a lot of paperwork or working closely with others. **Work Values—**Supervision, Technical; Supervision, Human Relations; Company Policies and Practices; Security; Advancement. **Skills—**Operation and Control; Operation Monitoring; Equipment Maintenance; Troubleshooting; Instructing; Repairing. **Abilities—***Cognitive:* Spatial Orientation; Perceptual Speed; Time Sharing; Selective Attention; Flexibility of Closure; Visualization. *Psychomotor:* Response Orientation; Reaction Time; Rate Control; Multilimb Coordination; Control Precision; Speed of Limb Movement. *Physical:* Gross Body Equilibrium; Extent Flexibility; Gross Body Coordination; Static Strength; Trunk Strength; Stamina. *Sensory:* Glare Sensitivity; Sound Localization; Auditory Attention; Peripheral Vision; Far Vision; Depth Perception. **General Work Activities—***Information Input:* Inspecting Equipment, Structures, or Materials; Monitoring Processes, Materials, or Surroundings; Getting Information. *Mental Process:* Evaluating Information Against Standards; Organizing, Planning, and Prioritizing; Making Decisions and Solving Problems. *Work Output:* Operating Vehicles or Equipment; Controlling Machines and Processes; Handling and Moving Objects. *Interacting with Others:* Establishing and Maintaining Interpersonal Relationships; Communicating with Other Workers; Coaching and Developing Others. **Physical Work Conditions—**Outdoors; Noisy; Very Hot or Cold; Contaminants; Sitting; Using Hands on Objects, Tools, or Controls. **Other Job Characteristics—**Need to Be Exact or Accurate; Errors Have Important Consequences; Repeat Same Tasks.

Experience—Job Zone 2. Some previous work-related skill, knowledge, or experience may be helpful in these occupations, but usually is not needed. **Job Preparation—**SVP 4.0 to less than 6.0—six months to less than two years. **Knowledges—**Transportation; Telecommunications; Public Safety and Security; Personnel and Human Resources; Law and Government; Education and Training. **Instructional Program—**Truck and Bus Driver/Commercial Vehicle Operation.

✳ ✳ ✳ ✳ ✳ ✳ ✳ ✳ ✳ ✳ ✳ ✳ ✳

Related SOC Job—53-4013 Rail Yard Engineers, Dinkey Operators, and Hostlers. Related OOH Job—Rail Transportation Occupations. Related DOT Jobs—910.363-018 Yard Engineer; 910.583-010 Laborer, Car Barn; 910.683-010 Hostler; 919.663-014 Dinkey Operator.

53-4021.00 Railroad Brake, Signal, and Switch Operators

- Education/Training Required: Work experience in a related occupation
- Employed: 20,700
- Annual Earnings: $49,700
- Growth: –38.5%
- Annual Job Openings: 1,000

Operate railroad track switches. Couple or uncouple rolling stock to make up or break up trains. Signal engineers by hand or by flagging. May inspect couplings, air hoses, journal boxes, and hand brakes.

Answer questions from passengers concerning train rules, stations, and timetable information. Monitor oil, air, and steam pressure gauges and make sure water levels are adequate. Open and close chute gates to load and unload cars. Repair and install rails and ties. Provide passengers with assistance entering and exiting trains. Place passengers' baggage in racks above seats on trains. Collect tickets, fares, and passes from passengers. Attach cables to cars being hoisted by cables or chains in mines, quarries, or industrial plants. Set flares, flags, lanterns, or torpedoes in front and at rear of trains during emergency stops to warn oncoming trains. Refuel and lubricate engines. Record numbers of cars available, numbers of cars sent to repair stations, and types of service needed. Operate and drive locomotives, diesel switch engines, dinkey engines, flatcars, and railcars in train yards and at industrial sites. Adjust controls to regulate air conditioning, heating, and lighting on trains for comfort of passengers. Watch for and relay traffic signals to start and stop cars during shunting. Observe signals from other crewmembers so that work activities can be coordinated. Pull or push track switches to reroute cars. Inspect tracks, cars, and engines for defects and to determine service needs, sending engines and cars for repairs as necessary. Signal locomotive engineers to start or stop trains when coupling or uncoupling cars, using hand signals, lanterns, or radio communication. Open and close ventilation doors. Ride atop cars that have been shunted and turn handwheels to control speeds or stop cars at specified positions. Receive oral or written instructions from yardmasters or yard conductors indicating track assignments and cars to be switched. Climb ladders to tops of cars to set brakes. Connect air hoses to cars, using wrenches. Inspect couplings, air hoses, journal boxes, and handbrakes to ensure that they are securely fastened and functioning properly. Make minor repairs to couplings, air hoses, and journal boxes, using hand tools. Raise levers to couple and uncouple cars for makeup and breakup of trains.

GOE Information—Interest Area: 16. Transportation, Distribution, and Logistics. Work Group: 16.07. Transportation Support Work. Personality Type—Realistic. Realistic occupations frequently involve work activities that include practical, hands-on problems and solutions. They often deal with plants; animals; and real-world materials like wood, tools, and machinery. Many of the occupations require working outside and do not involve a lot of paperwork or working closely with others. Work Values—Supervision, Technical; Supervision, Human Relations; Company Policies and Practices; Moral Values; Advancement. Skills—Operation and Control; Repairing. Abilities—*Cognitive:* Spatial Orientation. *Psychomotor:* Reaction Time; Response Orientation; Rate Control; Speed of Limb

Movement; Control Precision; Wrist-Finger Speed. *Physical:* Explosive Strength; Gross Body Equilibrium; Dynamic Strength; Static Strength; Gross Body Coordination; Stamina. *Sensory:* Night Vision; Auditory Attention; Far Vision; Depth Perception; Visual Color Discrimination. General Work Activities—*Information Input:* Getting Information. *Mental Process:* None met the criteria. *Work Output:* Performing General Physical Activities; Handling and Moving Objects; Controlling Machines and Processes. *Interacting with Others:* Communicating with Other Workers. Physical Work Conditions—Outdoors; Noisy; Hazardous Equipment; Standing; Walking and Running; Using Hands on Objects, Tools, or Controls. Other Job Characteristics—Need to Be Exact or Accurate; Errors Have Important Consequences.

Experience—Job Zone 2. Some previous work-related skill, knowledge, or experience may be helpful in these occupations, but usually is not needed. Job Preparation—SVP 4.0 to less than 6.0—six months to less than two years. Knowledges—Transportation; Mechanical Devices. Instructional Program—Truck and Bus Driver/Commercial Vehicle Operation.

Related SOC Job—53-4021 Railroad Brake, Signal, and Switch Operators. Related OOH Job—Rail Transportation Occupations. Related DOT Jobs—910.364-010 Braker, Passenger Train; 910.367-010 Brake Coupler, Road Freight; 910.367-022 Locomotive Operator Helper; 910.664-010 Yard Coupler; 910.667-026 Switch Tender; 932.664-010 Brake Holder.

53-4031.00 Railroad Conductors and Yardmasters

- Education/Training Required: Work experience in a related occupation
- Employed: 38,330
- Annual Earnings: $54,040
- Growth: 20.3%
- Annual Job Openings: 3,000

Conductors coordinate activities of train crew on passenger or freight train. Coordinate activities of switch-engine crew within yard of railroad, industrial plant, or similar location. Yardmasters coordinate activities of workers engaged in railroad traffic operations, such as the makeup or breakup of trains; yard switching; and review train schedules and switching orders.

Signal engineers to begin train runs, stop trains, or change speed, using telecommunications equipment or hand signals. Receive information regarding train or rail problems from dispatchers or from electronic monitoring devices. Direct and instruct workers engaged in yard activities, such as switching tracks, coupling and uncoupling cars, and routing inbound and outbound traffic. Keep records of the contents and destination of each train car and make sure that cars are added or removed at proper points on routes. Operate controls to activate track switches and traffic signals. Instruct workers to set warning signals in front and at rear of trains during emergency stops. Direct engineers to move cars to fit planned train configurations, combining or separating cars to make up or break up trains. Receive instructions from dispatchers regarding trains' routes, timetables, and cargoes. Review schedules, switching orders, way bills, and shipping records to obtain cargo loading and unloading information and to plan work. Confer with engineers regarding train routes, timetables, and cargoes and to discuss alternative routes when there are rail defects or obstructions. Arrange for the removal of defective cars from trains at stations or stops. Inspect each car periodically during runs. Observe yard traffic to determine tracks available to accommodate inbound and outbound traffic. Document and prepare reports of accidents, unscheduled stops, or delays. Confirm routes and destination information for freight cars. Supervise and coordinate crew activities to transport freight and passengers and to provide boarding, porter, maid, and meal services to passengers. Supervise workers in the inspection and maintenance of mechanical equipment to ensure efficient and safe train operation. Record departure and arrival times, messages, tickets and revenue collected, and passenger accommodations and destinations. Inspect freight cars for compliance with sealing procedures and record car numbers and seal numbers. Collect tickets, fares, or passes from passengers. Verify accuracy of timekeeping instruments with engineers to ensure that trains depart on time.

GOE Information—Interest Area: 16. Transportation, Distribution, and Logistics. **Work Group:** 16.01. Managerial Work in Transportation. **Personality Type—**Realistic. Realistic occupations frequently involve work activities that include practical, hands-on problems and solutions. They often deal with plants; animals; and real-world materials like wood, tools, and machinery. Many of the occupations require working outside and do not involve a lot of paperwork or working closely with others. **Work Values—**Authority; Supervision, Technical; Company Policies and Practices; Security; Autonomy; Supervision, Human Relations. **Skills—**Operation and Control; Operation Monitoring; Coordination; Equipment Maintenance; Troubleshooting; Instructing. **Abilities—**Cognitive: Spatial Orientation; Perceptual Speed; Selective Attention; Oral Expression; Visualization; Time Sharing. Psychomotor: Reaction Time; Response Orientation; Rate Control; Speed of Limb Movement; Control Precision; Multilimb Coordination. Physical: Gross Body Equilibrium; Gross Body Coordination; Stamina; Extent Flexibility; Trunk Strength; Static Strength. Sensory: Auditory Attention; Glare Sensitivity; Peripheral Vision; Far Vision; Depth Perception; Hearing Sensitivity. **General Work Activities—**Information Input: Getting Information; Monitoring Processes, Materials, or Surroundings; Identifying Objects, Actions, and Events. Mental Process: Evaluating Information Against Standards; Organizing, Planning, and Prioritizing; Updating and Using Relevant Knowledge. Work Output: Handling and Moving Objects; Performing General Physical Activities; Controlling Machines and Processes. Interacting with Others: Communicating with Other Workers; Establishing and Maintaining Interpersonal Relationships; Coordinating the Work and Activities of Others. **Physical Work Conditions—**Outdoors; Noisy; Very Hot or Cold; Very Bright or Dim Lighting; Contaminants; Hazardous Equipment. **Other Job Characteristics—**Errors Have Important Consequences; Need to Be Exact or Accurate; Repeat Same Tasks.

Experience—Job Zone 2. Some previous work-related skill, knowledge, or experience may be helpful in these occupations, but usually is not needed. **Job Preparation—**SVP 4.0 to less than 6.0—six months to less than two years. **Knowledges—**Transportation; Public Safety and Security; Mechanical Devices. **Instructional Program—**Truck and Bus Driver/Commercial Vehicle Operation.

Related SOC Job—53-4031 Railroad Conductors and Yardmasters. **Related OOH Job—**Rail Transportation Occupations. **Related DOT Jobs—**184.167-262 Train Dispatcher; 184.167-278 Yard Manager; 198.167-010 Conductor, Passenger Car; 198.167-014 Conductor, Pullman; 198.167-018 Conductor, Road Freight; 910.167-010 Car Chaser.

53-4041.00 Subway and Streetcar Operators

- **Education/Training Required: Moderate-term on-the-job training**
- **Employed: 7,430**
- **Annual Earnings: $47,500**
- **Growth: 13.7%**
- **Annual Job Openings: 1,000**

Operate subway or elevated suburban train with no separate locomotive or electric-powered streetcar to transport passengers. May handle fares.

Operate controls to open and close transit vehicle doors. Drive and control rail-guided public transportation, such as subways; elevated trains; and electric-powered streetcars, trams, or trolleys, to transport passengers. Monitor lights indicating obstructions or other trains ahead and watch for car and truck traffic at crossings to stay alert to potential hazards. Direct emergency evacuation procedures. Regulate vehicle speed and the time spent at each stop to maintain schedules. Report delays, mechanical problems, and emergencies to supervisors or dispatchers, using radios. Make announcements to passengers, such as notifications of upcoming stops or schedule delays. Complete reports, including shift summaries and incident or accident reports. Greet passengers; provide information; and answer questions concerning fares, schedules, transfers, and routings. Attend meetings on driver and passenger safety to learn ways in which job performance might be affected. Collect fares from passengers and issue change and transfers. Record transactions and coin receptor readings to verify the amount of money collected.

GOE Information—Interest Area: 16. Transportation, Distribution, and Logistics. **Work Group:** 16.04. Rail Vehicle Operation. **Personality Type—**Realistic. Realistic occupations frequently involve work activities that include practical, hands-on problems and solutions. They often deal with plants; animals; and real-world materials like wood, tools, and machinery. Many of the occupations require working outside and do not involve a lot of paperwork or working closely with others. **Work Values—**Supervision, Technical; Supervision, Human Relations; Independence; Company Policies and Practices; Security; Moral Values. **Skills—**Operation and Control; Operation Monitoring; Troubleshooting; Service Orientation; Active Listening. **Abilities—**Cognitive: Spatial Orientation; Perceptual Speed; Time Sharing; Selective Attention; Flexibility of Closure; Memorization. Psychomotor: Reaction Time; Response Orientation; Rate Control; Multilimb Coordination; Control Precision; Speed of Limb Movement. Physical: Gross Body Coordination; Static Strength. Sensory: Sound Localization; Glare Sensitivity; Peripheral Vision; Night Vision; Auditory Attention; Depth Perception. **General Work Activities—**Information Input: Identifying Objects, Actions, and Events; Monitoring Processes, Materials, or Surroundings; Inspecting Equipment, Structures, or Materials. Mental Process: Updating and Using Relevant Knowledge; Making Decisions and Solving Problems; Processing Information. Work Output: Operating Vehicles or Equipment; Controlling Machines and Processes; Handling and Moving Objects. Interacting with Others: Performing for or Working with the Public; Communicating with Other Workers; Establishing and Maintaining Interpersonal Relationships. **Physical Work Conditions—**Outdoors; Noisy; Contaminants; Sitting; Using Hands on Objects, Tools, or Controls; Repetitive Motions. **Other Job Characteristics—**Need to Be Exact or Accurate; Errors Have Important Consequences; Repeat Same Tasks; Pace Determined by Speed of Equipment.

Experience—Job Zone 2. Some previous work-related skill, knowledge, or experience may be helpful in these occupations, but usually is not needed. **Job Preparation**—SVP 4.0 to less than 6.0—six months to less than two years. **Knowledges**—Transportation; Public Safety and Security; Customer and Personal Service; Telecommunications; Mechanical Devices; Psychology. **Instructional Program**—Truck and Bus Driver/Commercial Vehicle Operation.

Related SOC Job—53-4041 Subway and Streetcar Operators. **Related OOH Job**—Rail Transportation Occupations. **Related DOT Jobs**—910.683-014 Motor Operator; 913.463-014 Streetcar Operator.

53-4099.99 Rail Transportation Workers, All Other

- **Education/Training Required: No data available**
- **Employed: 7,500**
- **Annual Earnings: $38,990**
- **Growth: –30.8%**
- **Annual Job Openings: Fewer than 500**

All rail transportation workers not listed separately.

No task data available.

Note: The Department of Labor has not collected some data for this job, so it has fewer details than the other descriptions.

Related SOC Job—53-4099 Rail Transportation Workers, All Other. **Related OOH Job**—Rail Transportation Occupations. **Related DOT Jobs**—910.362-010 Tower Operator; 910.382-010 Car-Retarder Operator; 910.683-022 Transfer-Table Operator; 919.683-026 Trackmobile Operator.

53-5000 Water Transportation Workers

53-5011.00 Sailors and Marine Oilers

- **Education/Training Required: Short-term on-the-job training**
- **Employed: 31,090**
- **Annual Earnings: $29,360**
- **Growth: 5.2%**
- **Annual Job Openings: 4,000**

Stand watch to look for obstructions in path of vessel; measure water depth; turn wheel on bridge; or use emergency equipment as directed by captain, mate, or pilot. Break out, rig, overhaul, and store cargo-handling gear, stationary rigging, and running gear. Perform a variety of maintenance tasks to preserve the painted surface of the ship and to maintain line and ship equipment. Must hold government-issued certification and tankerman certification when working aboard liquid-carrying vessels.

Steer ships under the direction of commanders or navigating officers or direct helmsmen to steer, following designated courses. Break out, rig, and stow cargo-handling gear, stationary rigging, and running gear. Chip and clean rust spots on decks, superstructures, and sides of ships, using wire brushes and hand or air chipping machines. Overhaul lifeboats and lifeboat gear and lower or raise lifeboats with winches or falls. Tie barges together into tow units for tugboats to handle, inspecting barges periodically during voyages and disconnecting them when destinations are reached. Paint or varnish decks, superstructures, lifeboats, or sides of ships. Stand gangway watches to prevent unauthorized persons from boarding ships while they are in port. Measure depth of water in shallow or unfamiliar waters, using leadlines, and telephone or shout depth information to vessel bridges. Maintain a ship's engines under the direction of the ship's engineering officers. Lubricate machinery, equipment, and engine parts such as gears, shafts, and bearings. Handle lines to moor vessels to wharfs, to tie up vessels to other vessels, or to rig towing lines. Examine machinery to verify specified pressures and lubricant flows. Maintain government-issued certifications as required. Give directions to crew members engaged in cleaning wheelhouses and quarterdecks. Record in ships' logs data such as weather conditions and distances traveled. Read pressure and temperature gauges or displays and record data in engineering logs. Participate in shore patrols. Lower and man lifeboats when emergencies occur. Operate, maintain, and repair ship equipment such as winches, cranes, derricks, and weapons system. Load or unload materials from vessels. Stand by wheels when ships are on automatic pilot and verify accuracy of courses, using magnetic compasses. Attach hoses and operate pumps to transfer substances to and from liquid cargo tanks. Sweep, mop, and wash down decks to remove oil, dirt, and debris, using brooms, mops, brushes, and hoses. Stand watch in ships' bows or bridge wings to look for obstructions in a ship's path or to locate navigational aids such as buoys and lighthouses.

GOE Information—**Interest Area:** 16. Transportation, Distribution, and Logistics. **Work Group:** 16.05. Water Vehicle Operation. **Personality Type**—Realistic. Realistic occupations frequently involve work activities that include practical, hands-on problems and solutions. They often deal with plants; animals; and real-world materials like wood, tools, and machinery. Many of the occupations require working outside and do not involve a lot of paperwork or working closely with others. **Work Values**—Supervision, Technical; Advancement; Co-workers. **Skills**—Equipment Maintenance; Repairing; Operation and Control; Operation Monitoring. **Abilities**—*Cognitive:* Spatial Orientation; Time Sharing. *Psychomotor:* Control Precision; Speed of Limb Movement; Wrist-Finger Speed; Reaction Time; Rate Control; Response Orientation. *Physical:* Dynamic Flexibility; Gross Body Equilibrium; Static Strength; Extent Flexibility; Stamina; Trunk Strength. *Sensory:* Night Vision; Peripheral Vision; Glare Sensitivity; Depth Perception; Far Vision; Auditory Attention. **General Work Activities**—*Information Input:* Getting Information; Monitoring Processes, Materials, or Surroundings; Inspecting Equipment, Structures, or Materials. *Mental Process:* None met the criteria. *Work Output:* Performing General Physical Activities; Handling and Moving Objects; Operating Vehicles or Equipment. *Interacting with Others:* Establishing and Maintaining Interpersonal Relationships; Communicating with Other Workers. **Physical Work Conditions**—Outdoors; Hazardous Equipment; Minor Burns, Cuts, Bites, or Stings; Standing; Using Hands on Objects, Tools, or Controls; Bending or Twisting the Body. **Other Job Characteristics**—Errors Have Important Consequences; Need to Be Exact or Accurate.

Experience—Job Zone 2. Some previous work-related skill, knowledge, or experience may be helpful in these occupations, but usually is not needed. **Job Preparation**—SVP 4.0 to less than 6.0—six months to less than two years. **Knowledges**—Transportation; Geography; Mechanical Devices; Engineering and Technology. **Instructional Program**—Marine Transportation Services, Other.

Related SOC Job—53-5011 Sailors and Marine Oilers. **Related OOH Job**—Water Transportation Occupations. **Related DOT Jobs**—911.363-014 Quartermaster; 911.364-010 Able Seaman; 911.584-010 Marine Oiler; 911.664-014 Sailor, Pleasure Craft; 911.687-022 Deckhand; 911.687-030 Ordinary Seaman.

53-5021.00 Captains, Mates, and Pilots of Water Vessels

- Education/Training Required: Work experience in a related occupation
- Employed: 28,570
- Annual Earnings: $50,940
- Growth: 4.8%
- Annual Job Openings: 2,000

The job openings listed here are shared with 53-5021.01 Ship and Boat Captains, 53-5021.02 Mates—Ship, Boat, and Barge, and 53-5021.03 Pilots, Ship.

Command or supervise operations of ships and water vessels, such as tugboats and ferryboats, that travel into and out of harbors, estuaries, straits, and sounds and on rivers, lakes, bays, and oceans. Required to hold license issued by U.S. Coast Guard.

No task data available.

GOE Information—Interest Area: 16. Transportation, Distribution, and Logistics. **Work Group:** 16.05. Water Vehicle Operation. **Note:** The Department of Labor has not collected some data for this job, so it has fewer details than the other descriptions.

Instructional Programs—Commercial Fishing; Marine Science/ Merchant Marine Officer; Marine Transportation Services, Other.

Related SOC Job—53-5021 Captains, Mates, and Pilots of Water Vessels. **Related OOH Job**—Water Transportation Occupations. **Related DOT Job**—No data available.

53-5021.01 Ship and Boat Captains

- Education/Training Required: Work experience in a related occupation
- Employed: 28,570
- Annual Earnings: $50,940
- Growth: 4.8%
- Annual Job Openings: 2,000

The job openings listed here are shared with 53-5021.00 Captains, Mates, and Pilots of Water Vessels, 53-5021.02 Mates—Ship, Boat, and Barge, and 53-5021.03 Pilots, Ship.

Command vessels in oceans, bays, lakes, rivers, and coastal waters.

Steer and operate vessels, using radios, depth finders, radars, lights, buoys, and lighthouses. Interview and hire crew members. Sort logs, form log booms, and salvage lost logs. Perform various marine duties such as checking for oil spills or other pollutants around ports and harbors and patrolling beaches. Contact buyers to sell cargo such as fish. Tow and maneuver barges or signal tugboats to tow barges to destinations. Signal passing vessels, using whistles, flashing lights, flags, and radios. Resolve questions or problems with customs officials. Read gauges to verify sufficient levels of hydraulic fluid, air pressure, and oxygen. Monitor the loading and discharging of cargo or passengers. Measure depths of water, using depth-measuring equipment. Calculate sightings of land, using electronic sounding devices and following contour lines on charts. Assign watches and living quarters to crew members. Arrange for ships to be fueled, restocked with supplies, or repaired. Collect fares from customers or signal ferryboat helpers to collect fares. Signal crew members or deckhands to rig tow lines, open or close gates and ramps, and pull

guard chains across entries. Maintain records of daily activities, personnel reports, ship positions and movements, ports of call, weather and sea conditions, pollution control efforts, and cargo and passenger status. Inspect vessels to ensure efficient and safe operation of vessels and equipment and conformance to regulations. Direct and coordinate crew members or workers performing activities such as loading and unloading cargo; steering vessels; operating engines; and operating, maintaining, and repairing ship equipment. Compute positions, set courses, and determine speeds by using charts, area plotting sheets, compasses, sextants, and knowledge of local conditions. Purchase supplies and equipment. Maintain boats and equipment on board, such as engines, winches, navigational systems, fire extinguishers, and life preservers.

GOE Information—Interest Area: 16. Transportation, Distribution, and Logistics. **Work Group:** 16.05. Water Vehicle Operation. **Personality Type**—Enterprising. Enterprising occupations frequently involve starting up and carrying out projects. These occupations can involve leading people and making many decisions. They sometimes require risk taking and often deal with business. **Work Values**—Authority; Responsibility; Autonomy; Recognition; Social Status; Compensation. **Skills**—Management of Personnel Resources; Operation Monitoring; Operation and Control; Management of Material Resources; Systems Evaluation; Systems Analysis. **Abilities**—*Cognitive:* Spatial Orientation; Time Sharing; Number Facility; Mathematical Reasoning; Speed of Closure; Oral Expression. *Psychomotor:* Response Orientation; Reaction Time; Control Precision; Rate Control; Wrist-Finger Speed; Multilimb Coordination. *Physical:* None met the criteria. *Sensory:* Night Vision; Glare Sensitivity; Far Vision; Peripheral Vision; Sound Localization; Depth Perception. **General Work Activities**—*Information Input:* Getting Information; Monitoring Processes, Materials, or Surroundings; Identifying Objects, Actions, and Events. *Mental Process:* Making Decisions and Solving Problems; Updating and Using Relevant Knowledge; Analyzing Data or Information. *Work Output:* Operating Vehicles or Equipment; Documenting or Recording Information; Handling and Moving Objects. *Interacting with Others:* Communicating with Other Workers; Coordinating the Work and Activities of Others; Staffing Organizational Units. **Physical Work Conditions**—Outdoors; Standing; Using Hands on Objects, Tools, or Controls; Repetitive Motions. **Other Job Characteristics**—Need to Be Exact or Accurate; Errors Have Important Consequences.

Experience—Job Zone 4. A minimum of two to four years of work-related skill, knowledge, or experience is needed. **Job Preparation**—SVP 7.0 to less than 8.0—two years to less than 10 years. **Knowledges**—Transportation; Geography; Physics; Administration and Management; Personnel and Human Resources; Telecommunications. **Instructional Programs**—Commercial Fishing; Marine Science/Merchant Marine Officer; Marine Transportation Services, Other.

Related SOC Job—53-5021 Captains, Mates, and Pilots of Water Vessels. **Related OOH Job**—Water Transportation Occupations. **Related DOT Jobs**—197.133-010 Captain, Fishing Vessel; 197.133-014 Master, Yacht; 197.133-030 Tugboat Captain; 197.161-010 Dredge Captain; 197.163-010 Ferryboat Captain; 197.163-014 Master, Passenger Barge; 197.163-018 Master, Riverboat; 197.167-010 Master, Ship; 911.137-010 Barge Captain; 911.137-014 Derrick-Boat Captain; 911.263-010 Deep Submergence Vehicle Operator; 911.363-010 Ferryboat Operator.

53-5021.02 Mates—Ship, Boat, and Barge

- Education/Training Required: Work experience in a related occupation
- Employed: 28,570
- Annual Earnings: $50,940
- Growth: 4.8%
- Annual Job Openings: 2,000

The job openings listed here are shared with 53-5021.00 Captains, Mates, and Pilots of Water Vessels, 53-5021.01 Ship and Boat Captains, and 53-5021.03 Pilots, Ship.

Supervise and coordinate activities of crew aboard ships, boats, barges, or dredges.

Participate in activities related to maintenance of vessel security. Assume command of vessels in the event that ships' masters become incapacitated. Arrange for ships to be stocked, fueled, and repaired. Supervise crews in cleaning and maintaining decks, superstructures, and bridges. Determine geographical positions of ships, using lorans, azimuths of celestial bodies, or computers, and use this information to determine the course and speed of a ship. Inspect equipment such as cargo-handling gear; lifesaving equipment; visual-signaling equipment; and fishing, towing, or dredging gear to detect problems. Observe loading and unloading of cargo and equipment to ensure that handling and storage are performed according to specifications. Observe water from ships' mastheads to advise on navigational direction. Steer vessels, utilizing navigational devices such as compasses and sextons and navigational aids such as lighthouses and buoys. Supervise crew members in the repair or replacement of defective gear and equipment. Stand watches on vessels during specified periods while vessels are under way.

GOE Information—Interest Area: 16. Transportation, Distribution, and Logistics. **Work Group:** 16.05. Water Vehicle Operation. **Personality Type—Realistic.** Realistic occupations frequently involve work activities that include practical, hands-on problems and solutions. They often deal with plants; animals; and real-world materials like wood, tools, and machinery. Many of the occupations require working outside and do not involve a lot of paperwork or working closely with others. **Work Values—Authority; Advancement; Co-workers; Supervision, Technical; Autonomy; Company Policies and Practices. Skills—Operation and Control; Repairing; Management of Personnel Resources; Operation Monitoring; Systems Analysis; Systems Evaluation. Abilities—Cognitive:** Spatial Orientation; Mathematical Reasoning; Number Facility. *Psychomotor:* Control Precision; Reaction Time; Multilimb Coordination. *Physical:* None met the criteria. *Sensory:* Glare Sensitivity; Far Vision; Night Vision; Depth Perception. **General Work Activities—Information Input:** Getting Information; Inspecting Equipment, Structures, or Materials; Monitoring Processes, Materials, or Surroundings. *Mental Process:* Making Decisions and Solving Problems; Judging the Qualities of Things, Services, or Other People's Work; Organizing, Planning, and Prioritizing. *Work Output:* Operating Vehicles or Equipment; Performing General Physical Activities; Handling and Moving Objects. *Interacting with Others:* Guiding, Directing, and Motivating Subordinates; Coordinating the Work and Activities of Others; Establishing and Maintaining Interpersonal Relationships. **Physical Work Conditions—More Often Outdoors Than Indoors; Very Hot or Cold; Standing; Using Hands on Objects, Tools, or Controls. Other Job Characteristics—None met the criteria.

Experience—Job Zone 3. Previous work-related skill, knowledge, or experience is required. Job Preparation—SVP 6.0 to less than 7.0—more than one year and less than four years. Knowledges—

Transportation; Geography; Mechanical Devices; Physics; Public Safety and Security; Administration and Management. **Instructional Programs—**Commercial Fishing; Marine Science/Merchant Marine Officer; Marine Transportation Services, Other.

Related SOC Job—53-5021 Captains, Mates, and Pilots of Water Vessels. **Related OOH Job—**Water Transportation Occupations. **Related DOT Jobs—**197.133-018 Mate, Fishing Vessel; 197.133-022 Mate, Ship; 197.133-034 Tugboat Mate; 197.137-010 Dredge Mate; 911.133-010 Cadet, Deck.

53-5021.03 Pilots, Ship

- Education/Training Required: Work experience in a related occupation
- Employed: 28,570
- Annual Earnings: $50,940
- Growth: 4.8%
- Annual Job Openings: 2,000

The job openings listed here are shared with 53-5021.00 Captains, Mates, and Pilots of Water Vessels, 53-5021.01 Ship and Boat Captains, and 53-5021.02 Mates—Ship, Boat, and Barge.

Command ships to steer them into and out of harbors, estuaries, straits, and sounds and on rivers, lakes, and bays. Must be licensed by U.S. Coast Guard with limitations indicating class and tonnage of vessels for which license is valid and route and waters that may be piloted.

Serve as a vessel's docking master upon arrival at a port and when at a berth. Prevent ships under their navigational control from engaging in unsafe operations. Provide assistance to vessels approaching or leaving seacoasts, navigating harbors, and docking and undocking. Steer ships into and out of berths or signal tugboat captains to berth and unberth ships. Advise ships' masters on harbor rules and customs procedures. Learn to operate new technology systems and procedures through the use of instruction, simulators, and models. Maintain and repair boats and equipment. Maintain ship logs. Oversee cargo storage on or below decks. Provide assistance in maritime rescue operations. Relieve crew members on tugs and launches. Report to appropriate authorities any violations of federal or state pilotage laws. Make nautical maps. Operate amphibious craft during troop landings. Operate ship-to-shore radios to exchange information needed for ship operations. Direct courses and speeds of ships based on specialized knowledge of local winds, weather, water depths, tides, currents, and hazards. Give directions to crew members who are steering ships. Set ships' courses that avoid reefs, outlying shoals, and other hazards, utilizing navigational aids such as lighthouses and buoys. Consult maps, charts, weather reports, and navigation equipment to determine and direct ship movements.

GOE Information—Interest Area: 16. Transportation, Distribution, and Logistics. **Work Group:** 16.05. Water Vehicle Operation. **Personality Type—Realistic.** Realistic occupations frequently involve work activities that include practical, hands-on problems and solutions. They often deal with plants; animals; and real-world materials like wood, tools, and machinery. Many of the occupations require working outside and do not involve a lot of paperwork or working closely with others. **Work Values—Authority; Responsibility; Autonomy; Social Status; Recognition; Compensation. Skills—Operation and Control; Systems Analysis; Operation Monitoring; Systems Evaluation; Judgment and Decision Making; Management of Personnel Resources. Abilities—Cognitive:** Spatial Orientation; Time Sharing; Memorization; Flexibility of Closure; Selective Attention. *Psychomotor:* Rate Control; Response Orientation; Reaction Time;

Control Precision. *Physical:* Gross Body Equilibrium. *Sensory:* Night Vision; Far Vision; Glare Sensitivity; Peripheral Vision; Depth Perception; Speech Clarity. **General Work Activities—***Information Input:* Monitoring Processes, Materials, or Surroundings; Getting Information; Identifying Objects, Actions, and Events. *Mental Process:* Analyzing Data or Information; Making Decisions and Solving Problems; Updating and Using Relevant Knowledge. *Work Output:* Operating Vehicles or Equipment; Performing General Physical Activities. *Interacting with Others:* Communicating with Other Workers; Communicating with Persons Outside Organization; Establishing and Maintaining Interpersonal Relationships. **Physical Work Conditions—**More Often Indoors Than Outdoors; More Often Standing Than Sitting; Keeping or Regaining Balance; Using Hands on Objects, Tools, or Controls. **Other Job Characteristics—**Errors Have Important Consequences; Need to Be Exact or Accurate; Automation.

Experience—Job Zone 5. Extensive skill, knowledge, and experience are needed. **Job Preparation—**SVP 8.0 and above—four years to more than 10 years. **Knowledges—**Transportation; Geography; Physics; Law and Government; Engineering and Technology; Public Safety and Security. **Instructional Programs—**Commercial Fishing; Marine Science/Merchant Marine Officer; Marine Transportation Services, Other.

Related SOC Job—53-5021 Captains, Mates, and Pilots of Water Vessels. **Related OOH Job—**Water Transportation Occupations. **Related DOT Job—**197.133-026 Pilot, Ship.

53-5022.00 Motorboat Operators

- **Education/Training Required: Moderate-term on-the-job training**
- **Employed: 2,700**
- **Annual Earnings: $34,280**
- **Growth: 4.4%**
- **Annual Job Openings: Fewer than 500**

Operate small motor-driven boats to carry passengers and freight between ships or between ship and shore. May patrol harbors and beach areas. May assist in navigational activities.

Organize and direct the activities of crew members. Issue directions for loading, unloading, and seating in boats. Operate engine throttles and steering mechanisms to guide boats on desired courses. Oversee operation of vessels used for carrying passengers, motor vehicles, or goods across rivers, harbors, lakes, and coastal waters. Secure boats to docks with mooring lines and cast off lines to enable departure. Arrange repairs, fuel, and supplies for vessels. Clean boats and repair hulls and superstructures, using hand tools, paint, and brushes. Maintain equipment such as range markers, fire extinguishers, boat fenders, lines, pumps, and fittings. Follow safety procedures to ensure the protection of passengers, cargo, and vessels. Report any observed navigational hazards to authorities. Service motors by performing tasks such as changing oil and lubricating parts. Tow, push, or guide other boats, barges, logs, or rafts. Perform general labor duties such as repairing booms. Position booms around docked ships. Direct safety operations in emergency situations. Take depth soundings in turning basins. Maintain desired courses, using compasses or electronic navigational aids.

GOE Information—Interest Area: 16. Transportation, Distribution, and Logistics. **Work Group:** 16.05. Water Vehicle Operation. **Personality Type—**Realistic. Realistic occupations frequently involve work activities that include practical, hands-on problems and solutions. They often deal with plants; animals; and real-world materials like wood, tools, and machinery. Many of the occupations require working outside and do not involve a lot of paperwork or working closely with others. **Work Values—**Autonomy; Independence; Recognition; Authority; Responsibility. **Skills—**Repairing; Equipment Maintenance; Operation and Control; Operation Monitoring; Troubleshooting. **Abilities—***Cognitive:* Spatial Orientation; Visualization. *Psychomotor:* Reaction Time; Rate Control; Wrist-Finger Speed; Control Precision; Speed of Limb Movement; Manual Dexterity. *Physical:* Extent Flexibility; Static Strength; Gross Body Equilibrium. *Sensory:* Peripheral Vision; Glare Sensitivity; Depth Perception; Far Vision. **General Work Activities—***Information Input:* Monitoring Processes, Materials, or Surroundings; Inspecting Equipment, Structures, or Materials; Getting Information. *Mental Process:* Updating and Using Relevant Knowledge. *Work Output:* Repairing and Maintaining Mechanical Equipment; Operating Vehicles or Equipment; Performing General Physical Activities. *Interacting with Others:* Performing for or Working with the Public; Communicating with Persons Outside Organization. **Physical Work Conditions—**Outdoors; Hazardous Equipment; More Often Standing Than Sitting; Keeping or Regaining Balance; Using Hands on Objects, Tools, or Controls. **Other Job Characteristics—**Errors Have Important Consequences.

Experience—Job Zone 2. Some previous work-related skill, knowledge, or experience may be helpful in these occupations, but usually is not needed. **Job Preparation—**SVP 4.0 to less than 6.0—six months to less than two years. **Knowledges—**Mechanical Devices; Transportation; Geography. **Instructional Program—**Marine Transportation Services, Other.

Related SOC Job—53-5022 Motorboat Operators. **Related OOH Job—**Water Transportation Occupations. **Related DOT Jobs—**911.663-010 Motorboat Operator; 919.683-010 Dock Hand.

53-5031.00 Ship Engineers

- **Education/Training Required: Postsecondary vocational training**
- **Employed: 13,240**
- **Annual Earnings: $52,780**
- **Growth: 12.7%**
- **Annual Job Openings: 1,000**

Supervise and coordinate activities of crew engaged in operating and maintaining engines; boilers; deck machinery; and electrical, sanitary, and refrigeration equipment aboard ship.

Monitor engine, machinery, and equipment indicators when vessels are under way and report abnormalities to appropriate shipboard staff. Record orders for changes in ship speed and direction and note gauge readings and test data, such as revolutions per minute and voltage output, in engineering logs and bellbooks. Perform and participate in emergency drills as required. Fabricate engine replacement parts such as valves, stay rods, and bolts, using metalworking machinery. Install engine controls, propeller shafts, and propellers. Maintain and repair engines, electric motors, pumps, winches, and other mechanical and electrical equipment or assist other crew members with maintenance and repair duties. Monitor and test operations of engines and other equipment so that malfunctions and their causes can be identified. Operate and maintain off-loading liquid pumps and valves. Perform general marine vessel maintenance and repair work such as repairing leaks, finishing interiors, refueling, and maintaining decks. Start engines to propel ships and regulate engines and power transmissions to control speeds of ships according to directions from captains or bridge computers. Supervise the activities of marine engine technicians engaged in the maintenance and repair of mechanical and electrical marine vessels and inspect their work to ensure that it is performed properly. Act as a liaison between a ship's captain and shore personnel to ensure that schedules and budgets are maintained and that the ship is operated safely and efficiently. Order and receive engine room's stores such as oil and spare parts; maintain inventories and record usage of supplies. Maintain complete records of engineering department activities, including machine operations. Monitor the availability, use, and condition of lifesaving equipment and pollution preventatives to ensure that international regulations are followed. Maintain electrical power, heating, ventilation, refrigeration, water, and sewerage systems. Clean engine parts and keep engine rooms clean.

GOE Information—Interest Area: 13. Manufacturing. **Work Group:** 13.16. Utility Operation and Energy Distribution. **Personality Type—** Realistic. Realistic occupations frequently involve work activities that include practical, hands-on problems and solutions. They often deal with plants; animals; and real-world materials like wood, tools, and machinery. Many of the occupations require working outside and do not involve a lot of paperwork or working closely with others. **Work Values—**Authority; Responsibility; Compensation; Autonomy; Social Status; Recognition. **Skills—**Operation and Control; Operation Monitoring; Repairing; Equipment Maintenance; Management of Personnel Resources; Systems Evaluation. **Abilities—** *Cognitive:* Spatial Orientation; Oral Expression; Number Facility. *Psychomotor:* Control Precision; Reaction Time. *Physical:* Extent Flexibility. *Sensory:* None met the criteria. **General Work Activities—** *Information Input:* Inspecting Equipment, Structures, or Materials; Monitoring Processes, Materials, or Surroundings; Identifying Objects, Actions, and Events. *Mental Process:* Analyzing Data or Information; Updating and Using Relevant Knowledge; Making Decisions and Solving Problems. *Work Output:* Repairing and Maintaining Mechanical Equipment; Controlling Machines and Processes; Performing General Physical Activities. *Interacting with Others:* Coordinating the Work and Activities of Others; Communicating with Other Workers; Guiding, Directing, and Motivating Subordinates; Establishing and Maintaining Interpersonal Relationships. **Physical Work Conditions—**Indoors; Standing; Using Hands on Objects, Tools, or Controls. **Other Job Characteristics—** Errors Have Important Consequences; Need to Be Exact or Accurate.

Experience—Job Zone 5. Extensive skill, knowledge, and experience are needed. **Job Preparation—**SVP 8.0 and above—four years to more than 10 years. **Knowledges—**Mechanical Devices; Transportation; Engineering and Technology; Physics. **Instructional Program—**No related CIP programs.

Related SOC Job—53-5031 Ship Engineers. **Related OOH Job—**Water Transportation Occupations. **Related DOT Job—**197.130-010 Engineer.

53-6000 Other Transportation Workers

53-6011.00 Bridge and Lock Tenders

- **Education/Training Required: Short-term on-the-job training**
- **Employed: 3,620**
- **Annual Earnings: $37,980**
- **Growth: 7.2%**
- **Annual Job Openings: Fewer than 500**

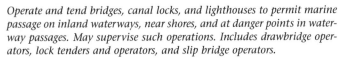

Operate and tend bridges, canal locks, and lighthouses to permit marine passage on inland waterways, near shores, and at danger points in waterway passages. May supervise such operations. Includes drawbridge operators, lock tenders and operators, and slip bridge operators.

Move levers to activate traffic signals, navigation lights, and alarms. Record names, types, and destinations of vessels passing through bridge openings or locks and numbers of trains or vehicles crossing bridges. Control machinery to open and close canal locks and dams, railroad or highway drawbridges, or horizontally or vertically adjustable bridges. Direct movements of vessels in locks or bridge areas, using signals, telecommunication equipment, or loudspeakers. Prepare accident reports. Observe approaching vessels to determine size and speed and listen for whistle signals indicating desire to pass. Observe position and progress of vessels to ensure best utilization of lock spaces or bridge opening spaces. Maintain and guard stations in bridges to check waterways for boat traffic. Inspect canal and bridge equipment and areas such as roadbeds for damage or defects, reporting problems to supervisors as necessary. Clean and lubricate equipment and make minor repairs and adjustments. Log data such as water levels and weather conditions. Write and submit maintenance work requisitions. Perform maintenance duties such as sweeping, painting, and yard work to keep facilities clean and in order. Check that bridges are clear of vehicles and pedestrians prior to opening. Turn valves to increase or decrease water levels in locks. Stop automobile and pedestrian traffic on bridges and lower automobile gates prior to moving bridges. Raise drawbridges and observe passage of water traffic; then lower drawbridges and raise automobile gates. Operate lighthouses to assist marine passage near shores and dangerous waters. Add and remove balance weights to bridge mechanisms as necessary. Attach ropes or cable lines to bits on lock decks or wharfs to secure vessels.

GOE Information—Interest Area: 16. Transportation, Distribution, and Logistics. **Work Group:** 16.07. Transportation Support Work. **Personality Type—**Realistic. Realistic occupations frequently involve work activities that include practical, hands-on problems and solutions. They often deal with plants; animals; and real-world materials like wood, tools, and machinery. Many of the occupations require working outside and do not involve a lot of paperwork or working closely with others. **Work Values—**Independence; Moral Values; Supervision, Human Relations; Security. **Skills—**Operation and Control; Operation Monitoring; Equipment Maintenance; Troubleshooting. **Abilities—***Cognitive:* Time Sharing; Selective Attention; Perceptual Speed; Speed of Closure. *Psychomotor:* Reaction Time; Rate Control; Response Orientation; Control Precision; Multilimb Coordination; Manual Dexterity. *Physical:* Gross Body Equilibrium; Trunk Strength. *Sensory:* Glare Sensitivity; Sound Localization; Depth Perception; Far Vision; Hearing Sensitivity; Auditory Attention. **General Work Activities—***Information Input:* Inspecting Equipment, Structures, or Materials; Monitoring Processes, Materials, or Surroundings; Getting Information. *Mental Process:* Making Decisions and Solving Problems; Processing Information; Judging the Qualities of Things, Services, or Other People's Work. *Work Output:* Controlling Machines and Processes; Performing General Physical Activities; Documenting or Recording Information. *Interacting with Others:* Establishing and Maintaining Interpersonal Relationships; Performing for or Working with the Public; Communicating with Other Workers. **Physical Work Conditions—**More Often Indoors Than Outdoors; Noisy; Standing; Using Hands on Objects, Tools, or Controls. **Other Job Characteristics—**Need to Be Exact or Accurate; Errors Have Important Consequences; Repeat Same Tasks; Automation.

Experience—Job Zone 1. No previous work-related skill, knowledge, or experience is needed. **Job Preparation**—SVP below 4.0—less than six months. **Knowledges**—Public Safety and Security; Transportation; Personnel and Human Resources; Psychology; Education and Training; Communications and Media. **Instructional Program**—No related CIP programs.

Related SOC Job—53-6011 Bridge and Lock Tenders. **Related OOH Job**—Bridge and Lock Tenders. **Related DOT Jobs**—371.362-010 Drawbridge Operator; 911.131-014 Lock Tender, Chief Operator; 911.362-010 Lock Operator; 919.682-010 Bridge Operator, Slip.

53-6021.00 Parking Lot Attendants

- **Education/Training Required: Short-term on-the-job training**
- **Employed: 124,250**
- **Annual Earnings: $16,930**
- **Growth: –8.7%**
- **Annual Job Openings: 28,000**

Park automobiles or issue tickets for customers in a parking lot or garage. May collect fee.

Take numbered tags from customers, locate vehicles, and deliver vehicles or provide customers with instructions for locating vehicles. Keep parking areas clean and orderly to ensure that space usage is maximized. Direct motorists to parking areas or parking spaces, using hand signals or flashlights as necessary. Patrol parking areas to prevent vehicle damage and vehicle or property thefts. Park and retrieve automobiles for customers in parking lots, storage garages, or new car lots. Greet customers and open their car doors. Calculate parking charges and collect fees from customers. Issue ticket stubs or place numbered tags on windshields and give customers matching tags for locating parked vehicles. Lift, position, and remove barricades to open or close parking areas. Inspect vehicles to detect any damage. Review motorists' identification before allowing them to enter parking facilities. Escort customers to their vehicles to ensure their safety. Service vehicles with gas, oil, and water. Perform maintenance on cars in storage to protect tires, batteries, and exteriors from deterioration.

GOE Information—**Interest Area:** 16. Transportation, Distribution, and Logistics. **Work Group:** 16.06. Other Services Requiring Driving. **Personality Type**—Realistic. Realistic occupations frequently involve work activities that include practical, hands-on problems and solutions. They often deal with plants; animals; and real-world materials like wood, tools, and machinery. Many of the occupations require working outside and do not involve a lot of paperwork or working closely with others. **Work Values**—Social Service; Independence. **Skills**—Service Orientation. **Abilities**—*Cognitive:* Spatial Orientation; Selective Attention; Flexibility of Closure; Perceptual Speed; Time Sharing; Visualization. *Psychomotor:* Response Orientation; Reaction Time; Speed of Limb Movement; Rate Control; Multilimb Coordination; Manual Dexterity. *Physical:* Stamina; Gross Body Coordination; Extent Flexibility; Static Strength; Trunk Strength. *Sensory:* Night Vision; Peripheral Vision; Glare Sensitivity; Sound Localization; Depth Perception; Far Vision. **General Work Activities**—*Information Input:* Monitoring Processes, Materials, or Surroundings; Identifying Objects, Actions, and Events; Inspecting Equipment, Structures, or Materials. *Mental Process:* Organizing, Planning, and Prioritizing; Making Decisions and Solving Problems; Processing Information. *Work Output:* Handling and Moving Objects; Performing General Physical Activities; Operating Vehicles or Equipment. *Interacting with Others:* Establishing and Maintaining Interpersonal Relationships; Performing for or Working with the

Public; Assisting and Caring for Others. **Physical Work Conditions**—Outdoors; Very Hot or Cold; Contaminants; Standing; Walking and Running; Repetitive Motions. **Other Job Characteristics**—Need to Be Exact or Accurate; Repeat Same Tasks.

Experience—Job Zone 1. No previous work-related skill, knowledge, or experience is needed. **Job Preparation**—SVP below 4.0—less than six months. **Knowledges**—Public Safety and Security; Customer and Personal Service; Public Safety and Security; Transportation. **Instructional Program**—No related CIP programs.

Related SOC Job—53-6021 Parking Lot Attendants. **Related OOH Job**—Parking Lot Attendants. **Related DOT Jobs**—915.473-010 Parking-Lot Attendant; 915.583-010 Lot Attendant; 915.667-014 Parking Lot Signaler.

53-6031.00 Service Station Attendants

- **Education/Training Required: Short-term on-the-job training**
- **Employed: 96,340**
- **Annual Earnings: $17,300**
- **Growth: 7.5%**
- **Annual Job Openings: 26,000**

Service automobiles, buses, trucks, boats, and other automotive or marine vehicles with fuel, lubricants, and accessories. Collect payment for services and supplies. May lubricate vehicle; change motor oil; install antifreeze; or replace lights or other accessories, such as windshield wiper blades or fan belts. May repair or replace tires.

Collect cash payments from customers and make change or charge purchases to customers' credit cards and provide customers with receipts. Activate fuel pumps and fill fuel tanks of vehicles with gasoline or diesel fuel to specified levels. Prepare daily reports of fuel, oil, and accessory sales. Clean parking areas, offices, restrooms, and equipment and remove trash. Check air pressure in vehicle tires; check levels of fuel, motor oil, transmission, radiator, battery, and other fluids; and add air, oil, water, or other fluids as required. Clean windshields or wash and wax vehicles. Provide customers with information about local roads and highways. Perform minor repairs such as adjusting brakes, replacing spark plugs, and changing engine oil and filters. Order stock and price and shelve incoming goods. Rotate, test, and repair or replace tires. Sell prepared food, groceries, and related items. Maintain customer records and follow up periodically with telephone, mail, or personal reminders of service due. Grease and lubricate vehicles or specified units, such as springs, universal joints, and steering knuckles, using grease guns or spray lubricants. Sell and install accessories, such as batteries, windshield wiper blades, fan belts, bulbs, and headlamps. Test and charge batteries. Operate car washes.

GOE Information—**Interest Area:** 14. Retail and Wholesale Sales and Service. **Work Group:** 14.03. General Sales. **Personality Type**—Realistic. Realistic occupations frequently involve work activities that include practical, hands-on problems and solutions. They often deal with plants; animals; and real-world materials like wood, tools, and machinery. Many of the occupations require working outside and do not involve a lot of paperwork or working closely with others. **Work Values**—Social Service. **Skills**—Repairing; Troubleshooting; Operation Monitoring; Equipment Maintenance; Operation and Control; Management of Financial Resources. **Abilities**—*Cognitive:* Oral Expression. *Psychomotor:* Response Orientation; Reaction Time; Speed of Limb Movement; Multilimb Coordination; Wrist-Finger Speed; Manual Dexterity. *Physical:* Extent Flexibility; Stamina; Gross Body Coordination; Trunk Strength;

Static Strength. *Sensory:* Visual Color Discrimination; Hearing Sensitivity; Auditory Attention; Depth Perception; Far Vision. **General Work Activities**—*Information Input:* Monitoring Processes, Materials, or Surroundings; Inspecting Equipment, Structures, or Materials; Identifying Objects, Actions, and Events. *Mental Process:* Updating and Using Relevant Knowledge; Making Decisions and Solving Problems; Organizing, Planning, and Prioritizing. *Work Output:* Performing General Physical Activities; Handling and Moving Objects; Controlling Machines and Processes. *Interacting with Others:* Establishing and Maintaining Interpersonal Relationships; Performing for or Working with the Public; Communicating with Other Workers. **Physical Work Conditions**—Outdoors; Contaminants; Hazardous Conditions; Standing; Walking and Running; Using Hands on Objects, Tools, or Controls. **Other Job Characteristics**—Need to Be Exact or Accurate; Repeat Same Tasks; Errors Have Important Consequences.

Experience—Job Zone 1. No previous work-related skill, knowledge, or experience is needed. **Job Preparation**—SVP below 4.0—less than six months. **Knowledges**—Customer and Personal Service; Mechanical Devices; Sales and Marketing. **Instructional Program**—No related CIP programs.

Related SOC Job—53-6031 Service Station Attendants. **Related OOH Job**—Service Station Attendants. **Related DOT Jobs**—915.467-010 Automobile-Service-Station Attendant; 915.477-010 Automobile-Self-Serve-Service-Station Attendant; 915.587-010 Gas-and-Oil Servicer; 915.687-014 Garage Servicer, Industrial; 915.687-018 Lubrication Servicer; 915.687-030 Taxi Servicer.

53-6041.00 Traffic Technicians

- **Education/Training Required: Short-term on-the-job training**
- **Employed: 6,990**
- **Annual Earnings: $37,070**
- **Growth: 14.1%**
- **Annual Job Openings: 1,000**

Conduct field studies to determine traffic volume, speed, effectiveness of signals, adequacy of lighting, and other factors influencing traffic conditions under direction of traffic engineer.

Interact with the public to answer traffic-related questions; respond to complaints and requests; or discuss traffic control ordinances, plans, policies, and procedures. Prepare drawings of proposed signal installations or other control devices, using drafting instruments or computer automated drafting equipment. Plan, design, and improve components of traffic control systems to accommodate current and projected traffic and to increase usability and efficiency. Analyze data related to traffic flow, accident rate data, and proposed development to determine the most efficient methods to expedite traffic flow. Prepare work orders for repair, maintenance, and changes in traffic systems. Study factors affecting traffic conditions, such as lighting and sign and marking visibility, to assess their effectiveness. Visit development and worksites to determine projects' effect on traffic and the adequacy of plans to control traffic and maintain safety and to suggest traffic control measures. Lay out pavement markings for striping crews. Operate counters and record data to assess the volume, type, and movement of vehicular and pedestrian traffic at specified times. Provide technical supervision regarding traffic control devices to other traffic technicians and laborers. Gather and compile data from hand-count sheets, machine-count tapes, and radar speed checks and code data for computer input. Place and secure automatic counters, using power tools, and retrieve counters after counting periods end. Measure and record the speed of vehicular traffic, using

electrical timing devices or radar equipment. Study traffic delays by noting times of delays, the numbers of vehicles affected, and vehicle speed through the delay area. Review traffic control/barricade plans to issue permits for parades and other special events and for construction work that affects rights-of-way, providing assistance with plan preparation or revision as necessary. Prepare graphs, charts, diagrams, and other aids to illustrate observations and conclusions.

GOE Information—**Interest Area:** 16. Transportation, Distribution, and Logistics. **Work Group:** 16.07. Transportation Support Work. **Personality Type**—Realistic. Realistic occupations frequently involve work activities that include practical, hands-on problems and solutions. They often deal with plants; animals; and real-world materials like wood, tools, and machinery. Many of the occupations require working outside and do not involve a lot of paperwork or working closely with others. **Work Values**—Independence; Variety; Supervision, Human Relations; Supervision, Technical; Company Policies and Practices; Advancement. **Skills**—Operation Monitoring; Coordination; Technology Design; Systems Evaluation; Systems Analysis; Writing. **Abilities**—*Cognitive:* Visualization; Mathematical Reasoning; Selective Attention; Number Facility; Fluency of Ideas; Originality. *Psychomotor:* Control Precision; Reaction Time; Multilimb Coordination; Finger Dexterity. *Physical:* None met the criteria. *Sensory:* Far Vision; Speech Recognition; Depth Perception; Visual Color Discrimination; Speech Clarity; Auditory Attention. **General Work Activities**—*Information Input:* Inspecting Equipment, Structures, or Materials; Getting Information; Estimating the Needed Characteristics of Products, Events, or Information. *Mental Process:* Updating and Using Relevant Knowledge; Organizing, Planning, and Prioritizing; Thinking Creatively. *Work Output:* Interacting With Computers; Documenting or Recording Information; Drafting and Specifying Technical Devices. *Interacting with Others:* Coordinating the Work and Activities of Others; Communicating with Other Workers; Establishing and Maintaining Interpersonal Relationships. **Physical Work Conditions**—More Often Indoors Than Outdoors; Noisy; Very Hot or Cold; Hazardous Equipment; Sitting. **Other Job Characteristics**—Need to Be Exact or Accurate; Errors Have Important Consequences; Repeat Same Tasks.

Experience—Job Zone 4. A minimum of two to four years of work-related skill, knowledge, or experience is needed. **Job Preparation**—SVP 7.0 to less than 8.0—two years to less than 10 years. **Knowledges**—Design; Building and Construction; Engineering and Technology; Customer and Personal Service; Law and Government; Public Safety and Security. **Instructional Program**—Traffic, Customs, and Transportation Clerk/Technician.

Related SOC Job—53-6041 Traffic Technicians. **Related OOH Job**—Traffic Technicians. **Related DOT Job**—199.267-030 Traffic Technician.

53-6051.00 Transportation Inspectors

- **Education/Training Required: Work experience in a related occupation**
- **Employed: 25,570**
- **Annual Earnings: $49,490**
- **Growth: 11.4%**
- **Annual Job Openings: 2,000**

The job openings listed here are shared with 53-6051.01 Aviation Inspectors, 53-6051.07 Transportation Vehicle, Equipment, and Systems Inspectors, Except Aviation, and 53-6051.08 Freight and Cargo Inspectors.

Inspect equipment or goods in connection with the safe transport of cargo or people. Includes rail transport inspectors, such as freight inspectors, car inspectors, rail inspectors, and other nonprecision inspectors of other types of transportation vehicles.

No task data available.

Note: The Department of Labor has not collected some data for this job, so it has fewer details than the other descriptions.

Instructional Program—No related CIP programs.

Related SOC Job—53-6051 Transportation Inspectors. **Related OOH Job**—Transportation Inspectors. **Related DOT Job**—No data available.

53-6051.01 Aviation Inspectors

- **Education/Training Required: Work experience in a related occupation**
- **Employed: 25,570**
- **Annual Earnings: $49,490**
- **Growth: 11.4%**
- **Annual Job Openings: 2,000**

The job openings listed here are shared with 53-6051.00 Transportation Inspectors, 53-6051.07 Transportation Vehicle, Equipment, and Systems Inspectors, Except Aviation, and 53-6051.08 Freight and Cargo Inspectors.

Inspect aircraft, maintenance procedures, air navigational aids, air traffic controls, and communications equipment to ensure conformance with federal safety regulations.

Inspect work of aircraft mechanics performing maintenance, modification, or repair and overhaul of aircraft and aircraft mechanical systems to ensure adherence to standards and procedures. Start aircraft and observe gauges, meters, and other instruments to detect evidence of malfunctions. Examine aircraft access plates and doors for security. Examine landing gear, tires, and exteriors of fuselage, wings, and engines for evidence of damage or corrosion and to determine whether repairs are needed. Prepare and maintain detailed repair, inspection, investigation, and certification records and reports. Inspect new, repaired, or modified aircraft to identify damage or defects and to assess airworthiness and conformance to standards, using checklists, hand tools, and test instruments. Examine maintenance records and flight logs to determine if service and maintenance checks and overhauls were performed at prescribed intervals. Recommend replacement, repair, or modification of aircraft equipment. Recommend changes in rules, policies, standards, and regulations based on knowledge of operating conditions, aircraft improvements, and other factors. Issue pilots' licenses to individuals meeting standards. Investigate air accidents and complaints to determine causes. Observe flight activities of pilots to assess flying skills and to ensure conformance to flight and safety regulations. Conduct flight test programs to test equipment, instruments, and systems under a variety of conditions, using both manual and automatic controls. Approve or deny issuance of certificates of airworthiness. Analyze training programs and conduct oral and written examinations to ensure the competency of persons operating, installing, and repairing aircraft equipment. Schedule and coordinate in-flight testing programs with ground crews and air traffic control to ensure availability of ground tracking, equipment monitoring, and related services.

GOE Information—**Interest Area:** 07. Government and Public Administration. **Work Group:** 07.03. Regulations Enforcement. **Personality Type**—Realistic. Realistic occupations frequently involve work activities that include practical, hands-on problems and solutions. They often deal with plants; animals; and real-world materials like wood, tools, and machinery. Many of the occupations require

working outside and do not involve a lot of paperwork or working closely with others. **Work Values**—Supervision, Technical; Responsibility; Supervision, Human Relations; Compensation; Authority; Autonomy. **Skills**—Systems Analysis; Systems Evaluation; Quality Control Analysis; Operation Monitoring; Troubleshooting; Reading Comprehension. **Abilities**—*Cognitive:* Perceptual Speed; Flexibility of Closure; Written Expression; Speed of Closure; Visualization; Problem Sensitivity. *Psychomotor:* Response Orientation; Multilimb Coordination; Reaction Time; Control Precision; Manual Dexterity; Arm-Hand Steadiness. *Physical:* Stamina; Static Strength. *Sensory:* Depth Perception; Hearing Sensitivity; Auditory Attention; Visual Color Discrimination; Far Vision. **General Work Activities**—*Information Input:* Inspecting Equipment, Structures, or Materials; Monitoring Processes, Materials, or Surroundings; Getting Information. *Mental Process:* Updating and Using Relevant Knowledge; Evaluating Information Against Standards; Analyzing Data or Information. *Work Output:* Controlling Machines and Processes; Repairing and Maintaining Mechanical Equipment; Documenting or Recording Information. *Interacting with Others:* Communicating with Other Workers; Interpreting the Meaning of Information for Others; Establishing and Maintaining Interpersonal Relationships. **Physical Work Conditions**—More Often Indoors Than Outdoors; Noisy; Sitting. **Other Job Characteristics**—Need to Be Exact or Accurate; Repeat Same Tasks; Automation.

Experience—Job Zone 3. Previous work-related skill, knowledge, or experience is required. **Job Preparation**—SVP 6.0 to less than 7.0—more than one year and less than four years. **Knowledges**—Mechanical Devices; Physics; Transportation; Design; Chemistry; Law and Government. **Instructional Program**—No related CIP programs.

Related SOC Job—53-6051 Transportation Inspectors. **Related OOH Job**—Transportation Inspectors. **Related DOT Jobs**—168.264-010 Inspector, Air-Carrier; 196.163-014 Supervising Airplane Pilot.

53-6051.07 Transportation Vehicle, Equipment, and Systems Inspectors, Except Aviation

- **Education/Training Required: Work experience in a related occupation**
- **Employed: 25,570**
- **Annual Earnings: $49,490**
- **Growth: 11.4%**
- **Annual Job Openings: 2,000**

The job openings listed here are shared with 53-6051.00 Transportation Inspectors, 53-6051.01 Aviation Inspectors, and 53-6051.08 Freight and Cargo Inspectors.

Inspect and monitor transportation equipment, vehicles, or systems to ensure compliance with regulations and safety standards.

Investigate and make recommendations on carrier requests for waiver of federal standards. Prepare reports on investigations or inspections and actions taken. Examine carrier operating rules, employee qualification guidelines, and carrier training and testing programs for compliance with regulations or safety standards. Examine transportation vehicles, equipment, or systems to detect damage, wear, or malfunction. Inspect repairs to transportation vehicles and equipment to ensure that repair work was performed properly. Inspect vehicles or equipment to ensure compliance with rules, standards, or regulations. Investigate complaints regarding safety violations. Investigate incidents or violations, such as delays, accidents, and equipment failures. Issue notices and recommend corrective actions when infractions or problems are found. Inspect vehicles and other equipment for evidence of abuse, damage, or mechanical malfunction. Conduct vehicle or transportation equipment tests, using diagnostic equipment.

GOE Information—Interest Area: 07. Government and Public Administration. **Work Group:** 07.03. Regulations Enforcement. **Personality Type—Realistic.** Realistic occupations frequently involve work activities that include practical, hands-on problems and solutions. They often deal with plants; animals; and real-world materials like wood, tools, and machinery. Many of the occupations require working outside and do not involve a lot of paperwork or working closely with others. **Work Values—Supervision, Technical; Responsibility; Supervision, Human Relations; Autonomy; Authority; Security. Skills—Operation Monitoring; Quality Control Analysis; Systems Evaluation; Troubleshooting. Abilities—***Cognitive:* Time Sharing; Written Expression. *Psychomotor:* Wrist-Finger Speed; Control Precision; Reaction Time; Multilimb Coordination; Manual Dexterity. *Physical:* Extent Flexibility. *Sensory:* Hearing Sensitivity. **General Work Activities—***Information Input:* Inspecting Equipment, Structures, or Materials; Monitoring Processes, Materials, or Surroundings; Identifying Objects, Actions, and Events. *Mental Process:* Evaluating Information Against Standards; Making Decisions and Solving Problems; Updating and Using Relevant Knowledge. *Work Output:* Repairing and Maintaining Mechanical Equipment; Performing General Physical Activities; Handling and Moving Objects. *Interacting with Others:* Communicating with Other Workers. **Physical Work Conditions—**Outdoors; Standing; Using Hands on Objects, Tools, or Controls. **Other Job Characteristics—**Need to Be Exact or Accurate; Errors Have Important Consequences.

Experience—Job Zone 3. Previous work-related skill, knowledge, or experience is required. **Job Preparation—**SVP 6.0 to less than 7.0—more than one year and less than four years. **Knowledges—**Transportation; Public Safety and Security; Mechanical Devices. **Instructional Program—**No related CIP programs.

Related SOC Job—53-6051 Transportation Inspectors. **Related OOH Job—**Transportation Inspectors. **Related DOT Jobs—**168.167-082 Transportation Inspector; 168.267-058 Inspector, Motor Vehicles; 168.287-018 Inspector, Railroad; 184.163-010 Traffic Inspector; 379.364-010 Automobile Tester; 910.263-010 Rail-Flaw-Detector Operator; 910.367-030 Way Inspector; 910.384-010 Tank-Car Inspector; 910.387-014 Railroad-Car Inspector; 910.667-010 Car Inspector; 919.363-010 New-Car Inspector; 919.687-018 Safety Inspector, Truck.

53-6051.08 *Freight and Cargo Inspectors*

- **Education/Training Required: Work experience in a related occupation**
- **Employed: 25,570**
- **Annual Earnings: $49,490**
- **Growth: 11.4%**
- **Annual Job Openings: 2,000**

The job openings listed here are shared with 53-6051.00 Transportation Inspectors, 53-6051.01 Aviation Inspectors, and 53-6051.07 Transportation Vehicle, Equipment, and Systems Inspectors, Except Aviation.

Inspect the handling, storage, and stowing of freight and cargoes.

Review commercial vehicle logs, shipping papers, and driver and equipment records to detect any problems and to ensure compliance with regulations. Prepare and submit reports after completion of freight shipments. Recommend remedial procedures to correct any violations found during inspections. Record details about freight conditions, handling of freight, and any problems encountered. Calculate gross and net tonnage, hold capacities, volumes of stored fuel and water, cargo weights, and ship stability factors, using mathematical formulas. Evaluate new methods of packaging, testing, shipping, and transporting hazardous materials to ensure adequate public safety protection. Measure ships' holds and depths of fuel and water in tanks, using sounding lines and tape measures. Write certificates of admeasurement that list details such as designs, lengths, depths, and breadths of vessels and methods of propulsion. Read draft markings to determine depths of vessels in water. Post warning signs on vehicles containing explosives or flammable or radioactive materials. Negotiate with authorities, such as local government officials, to eliminate hazards along transportation routes. Observe loading of freight to ensure that crews comply with procedures. Notify workers of any special treatment required for shipments. Measure heights and widths of loads to ensure they will pass over bridges or through tunnels on scheduled routes. Issue certificates of compliance for vessels without violations. Inspect shipments to ensure that freight is securely braced and blocked. Inspect loaded cargo, cargo lashed to decks or in storage facilities, and cargo-handling devices to determine compliance with health and safety regulations and need for maintenance. Direct crews to reload freight or to insert additional bracing or packing as necessary. Determine types of licenses and safety equipment required and compute applicable fees such as tolls and wharfage fees. Determine cargo transportation capabilities by reading documents that set forth cargo loading and securing procedures, capacities, and stability factors.

GOE Information—Interest Area: 07. Government and Public Administration. **Work Group:** 07.03. Regulations Enforcement. **Personality Type—Conventional.** Conventional occupations frequently involve following set procedures and routines. These occupations can include working with data and details more than with ideas. Usually there is a clear line of authority to follow. **Work Values—**Supervision, Technical; Responsibility; Independence; Autonomy; Security; Supervision, Human Relations. **Skills—**Mathematics. **Abilities—***Cognitive:* Spatial Orientation; Number Facility; Mathematical Reasoning; Memorization; Perceptual Speed; Written Comprehension. *Psychomotor:* None met the criteria. *Physical:* Extent Flexibility. *Sensory:* None met the criteria. **General Work Activities—***Information Input:* Inspecting Equipment, Structures, or Materials; Identifying Objects, Actions, and Events; Getting Information. *Mental Process:* Evaluating Information Against Standards; Processing Information; Making Decisions and Solving Problems. *Work Output:* Documenting or Recording Information; Handling and Moving Objects; Performing General Physical Activities. *Interacting with Others:* Communicating with Other Workers; Performing Administrative Activities. **Physical Work Conditions—**Outdoors; Standing; Walking and Running; Using Hands on Objects, Tools, or Controls. **Other Job Characteristics—**Need to Be Exact or Accurate; Errors Have Important Consequences.

Experience—Job Zone 3. Previous work-related skill, knowledge, or experience is required. **Job Preparation—**SVP 6.0 to less than 7.0—more than one year and less than four years. **Knowledges—**Transportation; Public Safety and Security; Mathematics. **Instructional Program—**No related CIP programs.

Related SOC Job—53-6051 Transportation Inspectors. **Related OOH Job—**Transportation Inspectors. **Related DOT Jobs—**168.267-094 Marine-Cargo Surveyor; 169.284-010 Admeasurer; 910.387-010 Perishable-Fruit Inspector; 910.667-018 Loading Inspector; 910.667-022 Perishable-Freight Inspector.

53-6099.99 Transportation Workers, All Other

- **Education/Training Required: Short-term on-the-job training**
- **Employed: 54,010**
- **Annual Earnings: $32,610**
- **Growth: 13.9%**
- **Annual Job Openings: 4,000**

All transportation workers not listed separately.

No task data available.

Note: The Department of Labor has not collected some data for this job, so it has fewer details than the other descriptions.

Related SOC Job—53-6099 Transportation Workers, All Other. **Related OOH Job**—None. **Related DOT Jobs**—196.223-010 Instructor, Flying I; 196.223-014 Instructor, Pilot; 196.263-022 Check Pilot; 388.663-010 Elevator Operator; 911.664-010 Ferryboat Operator, Cable; 912.663-010 Airport Utility Worker.

53-7000 Material Moving Workers

53-7011.00 Conveyor Operators and Tenders

- **Education/Training Required: Short-term on-the-job training**
- **Employed: 49,220**
- **Annual Earnings: $26,640**
- **Growth: 7.7%**
- **Annual Job Openings: 3,000**

Control or tend conveyors or conveyor systems that move materials or products to and from stockpiles, processing stations, departments, or vehicles. May control speed and routing of materials or products.

Position deflector bars, gates, chutes, or spouts to divert flow of materials from one conveyor onto another conveyor. Weigh or measure materials and products, using scales or other measuring instruments, or read scales on conveyors that continually weigh products to verify specified tonnages and prevent overloads. Manipulate controls, levers, and valves to start pumps, auxiliary equipment, or conveyors and to adjust equipment positions, speeds, timing, and material flows. Record production data such as weights, types, quantities, and storage locations of materials, as well as equipment performance problems and downtime. Inform supervisors of equipment malfunctions that need to be addressed. Clean, sterilize, and maintain equipment, machinery, and workstations, using hand tools, shovels, brooms, chemicals, hoses, and lubricants. Observe conveyor operations and monitor lights, dials, and gauges to maintain specified operating levels and to detect equipment malfunctions. Operate elevator systems in conjunction with conveyor systems. Read production and delivery schedules and confer with supervisors to determine sorting and transfer procedures, arrangement of packages on pallets, and destinations of loaded pallets. Repair or replace equipment components or parts such as blades, rolls, and pumps. Contact workers in workstations or other departments to request movement of materials, products, or machinery or to notify them of incoming shipments and their estimated delivery times. Stop equipment or machinery and clear jams, using poles, bars, and hand tools, or remove damaged materials from conveyors. Collect samples of materials or products, checking them to ensure conformance to specifications or sending them to laboratories for analysis. Load, unload, or adjust materials or products on conveyors by hand; by using lifts, hoists, and scoops; or by opening gates, chutes, or hoppers. Operate consoles to control automatic palletizing equipment. Affix identifying information to materials or products, using hand tools. Distribute materials, supplies, and equipment to workstations, using lifts and trucks.

GOE Information—**Interest Area:** 13. Manufacturing. **Work Group:** 13.17. Loading, Moving, Hoisting, and Conveying. **Personality Type**—Realistic. Realistic occupations frequently involve work activities that include practical, hands-on problems and solutions. They often deal with plants; animals; and real-world materials like wood, tools, and machinery. Many of the occupations require working outside and do not involve a lot of paperwork or working closely with others. **Work Values**—Supervision, Technical; Supervision, Human Relations; Moral Values; Activity; Independence; Company Policies and Practices. **Skills**—Operation Monitoring; Operation and Control; Quality Control Analysis; Equipment Maintenance; Repairing; Systems Analysis. **Abilities**—*Cognitive:* Perceptual Speed; Selective Attention; Visualization; Category Flexibility; Speed of Closure; Information Ordering. *Psychomotor:* Multilimb Coordination; Rate Control; Response Orientation; Control Precision; Reaction Time; Manual Dexterity. *Physical:* Static Strength; Trunk Strength. *Sensory:* Glare Sensitivity; Depth Perception; Auditory Attention; Hearing Sensitivity; Visual Color Discrimination; Far Vision. **General Work Activities**—*Information Input:* Monitoring Processes, Materials, or Surroundings; Identifying Objects, Actions, and Events; Getting Information. *Mental Process:* Organizing, Planning, and Prioritizing; Making Decisions and Solving Problems; Judging the Qualities of Things, Services, or Other People's Work. *Work Output:* Handling and Moving Objects; Controlling Machines and Processes; Performing General Physical Activities. *Interacting with Others:* Establishing and Maintaining Interpersonal Relationships; Providing Consultation and Advice to Others; Communicating with Other Workers. **Physical Work Conditions**—Outdoors; Noisy; Contaminants; High Places; Hazardous Conditions; Minor Burns, Cuts, Bites, or Stings. **Other Job Characteristics**—Need to Be Exact or Accurate; Pace Determined by Speed of Equipment.

Experience—Job Zone 2. Some previous work-related skill, knowledge, or experience may be helpful in these occupations, but usually is not needed. **Job Preparation**—SVP 4.0 to less than 6.0—six months to less than two years. **Knowledges**—Mechanical Devices; Chemistry; Engineering and Technology; Physics; Education and Training; Production and Processing. **Instructional Program**—Vehicle and Equipment Operators, Other.

Related SOC Job—53-7011 Conveyor Operators and Tenders. **Related OOH Job**—Material Moving Occupations. **Related DOT Jobs**—513.685-010 Sinter Feeder; 524.565-010 Trolley Operator; 529.682-030 Silo Operator; 529.685-050 Char-Conveyor Tender; 553.685-078 Milled-Rubber Tender; 575.687-038 Tip-Out Worker; 579.685-050 Silo Tender; 579.685-062 Brick Unloader Tender; 613.685-034 Bed Operator; 669.685-090 Tipple Tender; 921.382-010 Conveyor Operator, Pneumatic System; 921.563-010 Coke Loader; 921.565-010 Cement Loader; 921.662-018 Conveyor-System Operator; 921.662-026 Tipple Operator; 921.682-014 Palletizer Operator I; others.

53-7021.00 Crane and Tower Operators

- **Education/Training Required: Moderate-term on-the-job training**
- **Employed: 43,690**
- **Annual Earnings: $38,870**
- **Growth: 8.2%**
- **Annual Job Openings: 4,000**

Operate mechanical boom and cable or tower and cable equipment to lift and move materials, machines, or products in many directions.

Determine load weights and check them against lifting capacities to prevent overload. Move levers, depress foot pedals, and turn dials to operate cranes, cherry pickers, electromagnets, or other moving equipment for lifting, moving, and placing loads. Inspect cables and grappling devices for wear and install or replace cables as needed. Clean, lubricate, and maintain mechanisms such as cables, pulleys, and grappling devices, making repairs as necessary. Inspect and adjust crane mechanisms and lifting accessories to prevent malfunctions and damage. Direct helpers engaged in placing blocking and outrigging under cranes. Load and unload bundles from trucks and move containers to storage bins, using moving equipment. Weigh bundles, using floor scales, and record weights for company records. Review daily work and delivery schedules to determine orders, sequences of deliveries, and special loading instructions. Direct truck drivers backing vehicles into loading bays and cover, uncover, and secure loads for delivery. Inspect bundle packaging for conformance to regulations and customer requirements and remove and batch packaging tickets.

GOE Information—Interest Area: 02. Architecture and Construction. **Work Group:** 02.04. Construction Crafts. **Personality Type—**Realistic. Realistic occupations frequently involve work activities that include practical, hands-on problems and solutions. They often deal with plants; animals; and real-world materials like wood, tools, and machinery. Many of the occupations require working outside and do not involve a lot of paperwork or working closely with others. **Work Values—**Supervision, Technical; Moral Values; Supervision, Human Relations. **Skills—**Equipment Maintenance; Operation Monitoring; Operation and Control; Repairing; Equipment Selection; Installation. **Abilities—***Cognitive:* Spatial Orientation; Perceptual Speed; Selective Attention; Visualization; Flexibility of Closure. *Psychomotor:* Rate Control; Response Orientation; Reaction Time; Multilimb Coordination; Control Precision; Speed of Limb Movement. *Physical:* Gross Body Equilibrium; Static Strength; Extent Flexibility; Trunk Strength. *Sensory:* Glare Sensitivity; Depth Perception; Peripheral Vision; Sound Localization; Far Vision; Auditory Attention. **General Work Activities—***Information Input:* Inspecting Equipment, Structures, or Materials; Monitoring Processes, Materials, or Surroundings; Identifying Objects, Actions, and Events. *Mental Process:* Updating and Using Relevant Knowledge; Making Decisions and Solving Problems; Judging the Qualities of Things, Services, or Other People's Work. *Work Output:* Handling and Moving Objects; Controlling Machines and Processes; Operating Vehicles or Equipment. *Interacting with Others:* Communicating with Other Workers; Establishing and Maintaining Interpersonal Relationships; Teaching Others. **Physical Work Conditions—**Noisy; Very Bright or Dim Lighting; Contaminants; High Places; Using Hands on Objects, Tools, or Controls; Repetitive Motions. **Other Job Characteristics—**Errors Have Important Consequences; Need to Be Exact or Accurate; Repeat Same Tasks; Pace Determined by Speed of Equipment.

Experience—Job Zone 3. Previous work-related skill, knowledge, or experience is required. **Job Preparation—**SVP 6.0 to less than 7.0—more than one year and less than four years. **Knowledges—**Building and Construction; Mechanical Devices; Transportation; Engineering and Technology; Public Safety and Security; Administration and Management. **Instructional Programs—**Construction/Heavy Equipment/Earthmoving Equipment Operation; Mobil Crane Operation/Operator.

Related SOC Job—53-7021 Crane and Tower Operators. **Related OOH Job—**Material Moving Occupations. **Related DOT Jobs—**519.683-010 Dross Skimmer; 921.663-010 Overhead Crane Operator; 921.663-014 Cherry-Picker Operator; 921.663-022 Derrick Operator; 921.663-038 Locomotive-Crane Operator; 921.663-042 Monorail Crane Operator; 921.663-054 Tower-Crane Operator; 921.663-058 Tractor-Crane Operator; 921.663-062 Truck-Crane Operator; 921.663-070 Truck Loader, Overhead Crane; 921.683-018 Cantilever-Crane Operator; 921.683-034 Derrick-Boat Operator; 921.683-066 Sorting-Grapple Operator; 921.683-074 Tower-Loader Operator.

53-7031.00 Dredge Operators

- **Education/Training Required: Moderate-term on-the-job training**
- **Employed: 1,720**
- **Annual Earnings: $31,030**
- **Growth: 3.7%**
- **Annual Job Openings: Fewer than 500**

Operate dredge to remove sand, gravel, or other materials from lakes, rivers, or streams and to excavate and maintain navigable channels in waterways.

Start power winches that draw in or let out cables to change positions of dredges or pull in and let out cables manually. Start and stop engines to operate equipment. Pump water to clear machinery pipelines. Move levers to position dredges for excavation, to engage hydraulic pumps, to raise and lower suction booms, and to control rotation of cutterheads. Direct or assist workers placing shore anchors and cables, laying additional pipes from dredges to shore, and pumping water from pontoons. Lower anchor poles to verify depths of excavations, using winches, or scan depth gauges to determine depths of excavations.

GOE Information—Interest Area: 16. Transportation, Distribution, and Logistics. **Work Group:** 16.05. Water Vehicle Operation. **Personality Type—**Realistic. Realistic occupations frequently involve work activities that include practical, hands-on problems and solutions. They often deal with plants; animals; and real-world materials like wood, tools, and machinery. Many of the occupations require working outside and do not involve a lot of paperwork or working closely with others. **Work Values—**Authority; Supervision, Technical; Moral Values. **Skills—**Operation and Control; Operation Monitoring; Management of Personnel Resources. **Abilities—***Cognitive:* None met the criteria. *Psychomotor:* Control Precision; Multilimb Coordination. *Physical:* Static Strength; Extent Flexibility. *Sensory:* Depth Perception; Far Vision; Speech Clarity. **General Work Activities—***Information Input:* Monitoring Processes, Materials, or Surroundings. *Mental Process:* None met the criteria. *Work Output:* Controlling Machines and Processes; Handling and Moving Objects; Performing General Physical Activities. *Interacting with Others:* Communicating with Other Workers; Coordinating the Work and Activities of Others; Guiding, Directing, and Motivating Subordinates. **Physical Work Conditions—**Outdoors; Noisy; Hazardous Equipment; Minor Burns,

Cuts, Bites, or Stings; Sitting; Using Hands on Objects, Tools, or Controls. **Other Job Characteristics**—Automation; Errors Have Important Consequences.

Experience—Job Zone 2. Some previous work-related skill, knowledge, or experience may be helpful in these occupations, but usually is not needed. **Job Preparation**—SVP 4.0 to less than 6.0—six months to less than two years. **Knowledges**—Engineering and Technology; Mechanical Devices. **Instructional Program**—Construction/Heavy Equipment/Earthmoving Equipment Operation.

Related SOC Job—53-7031 Dredge Operators. **Related OOH Job**—Material Moving Occupations. **Related DOT Job**—850.663-010 Dredge Operator.

53-7032.00 Excavating and Loading Machine and Dragline Operators

- **Education/Training Required: Moderate-term on-the-job training**
- **Employed: 66,030**
- **Annual Earnings: $32,380**
- **Growth: 8.0%**
- **Annual Job Openings: 11,000**

Operate or tend machinery equipped with scoops, shovels, or buckets to excavate and load loose materials.

Move levers, depress foot pedals, and turn dials to operate power machinery such as power shovels, stripping shovels, scraper loaders, or backhoes. Set up and inspect equipment prior to operation. Observe hand signals, grade stakes, and other markings when operating machines so that work can be performed to specifications. Become familiar with digging plans, machine capabilities and limitations, and efficient and safe digging procedures in a given application. Operate machinery to perform activities such as backfilling excavations, vibrating or breaking rock or concrete, and making winter roads. Create and maintain inclines and ramps and handle slides, mud, and pit cleanings and maintenance. Lubricate, adjust, and repair machinery and replace parts such as gears, bearings, and bucket teeth. Move materials over short distances, such as around a construction site, factory, or warehouse. Measure and verify levels of rock or gravel, bases, and other excavated material. Receive written or oral instructions regarding material movement or excavation. Adjust dig face angles for varying overburden depths and set lengths. Drive machines to worksites. Perform manual labor to prepare or finish sites, such as shoveling materials by hand. Direct ground workers engaged in activities such as moving stakes or markers or changing positions of towers. Direct workers engaged in placing blocks and outriggers to prevent capsizing of machines when lifting heavy loads.

GOE Information—Interest Area: 01. Agriculture and Natural Resources. **Work Group:** 01.08. Mining and Drilling. **Personality Type**—Realistic. Realistic occupations frequently involve work activities that include practical, hands-on problems and solutions. They often deal with plants; animals; and real-world materials like wood, tools, and machinery. Many of the occupations require working outside and do not involve a lot of paperwork or working closely with others. **Work Values**—Supervision, Technical; Moral Values; Authority. **Skills**—Repairing; Operation Monitoring; Equipment Maintenance; Operation and Control; Installation; Systems Analysis. **Abilities**—*Cognitive:* Spatial Orientation; Time Sharing; Visualization; Perceptual Speed; Selective Attention; Flexibility of Closure. *Psychomotor:* Reaction Time; Response Orientation; Rate Control;

Multilimb Coordination; Speed of Limb Movement; Control Precision. *Physical:* Static Strength; Dynamic Strength; Trunk Strength; Stamina; Gross Body Coordination; Extent Flexibility. *Sensory:* Peripheral Vision; Depth Perception; Sound Localization; Auditory Attention; Glare Sensitivity; Night Vision. **General Work Activities**—*Information Input:* Monitoring Processes, Materials, or Surroundings; Identifying Objects, Actions, and Events; Inspecting Equipment, Structures, or Materials. *Mental Process:* Making Decisions and Solving Problems; Organizing, Planning, and Prioritizing; Updating and Using Relevant Knowledge. *Work Output:* Handling and Moving Objects; Controlling Machines and Processes; Operating Vehicles or Equipment. *Interacting with Others:* Establishing and Maintaining Interpersonal Relationships; Communicating with Other Workers; Coordinating the Work and Activities of Others. **Physical Work Conditions**—Outdoors; Noisy; Contaminants; Whole-Body Vibration; Sitting; Using Hands on Objects, Tools, or Controls. **Other Job Characteristics**—Pace Determined by Speed of Equipment; Need to Be Exact or Accurate; Errors Have Important Consequences.

Experience—Job Zone 2. Some previous work-related skill, knowledge, or experience may be helpful in these occupations, but usually is not needed. **Job Preparation**—SVP 4.0 to less than 6.0—six months to less than two years. **Knowledges**—Building and Construction; Mechanical Devices; Transportation; Production and Processing; Public Safety and Security; Engineering and Technology. **Instructional Program**—Construction/Heavy Equipment/Earthmoving Equipment Operation.

Related SOC Job—53-7032 Excavating and Loading Machine and Dragline Operators. **Related OOH Job**—Material Moving Occupations. **Related DOT Jobs**—850.663-026 Stripping-Shovel Operator; 850.683-018 Dragline Operator; 850.683-026 Mucking-Machine Operator; 850.683-030 Power-Shovel Operator; 850.683-042 Tower-Excavator Operator; 851.663-010 Septic-Tank Installer; 921.683-022 Coal-Equipment Operator; 930.683-022 Harvester Operator.

53-7033.00 Loading Machine Operators, Underground Mining

- **Education/Training Required: Moderate-term on-the-job training**
- **Employed: 2,390**
- **Annual Earnings: $35,660**
- **Growth: –8.3%**
- **Annual Job Openings: Fewer than 500**

Operate underground loading machine to load coal, ore, or rock into shuttle or mine car or onto conveyors. Loading equipment may include power shovels, hoisting engines equipped with cable-drawn scraper or scoop, or machines equipped with gathering arms and conveyor.

Clean hoppers and clean spillage from tracks, walks, driveways, and conveyor decking. Replace hydraulic hoses, headlight bulbs, and gathering-arm teeth. Pry off loose material from roofs and move it into the paths of machines, using crowbars. Oil, lubricate, and adjust conveyors, crushers, and other equipment, using hand tools and lubricating equipment. Observe and record car numbers, carriers, customers, tonnages, and grades and conditions of material. Notify switching departments to deliver specific types of cars. Move trailing electrical cables clear of obstructions, using rubber safety gloves. Estimate and record amounts of material in bins. Stop gathering arms when cars are full. Start conveyor booms and gathering-arm motors and operate winches to position cars under boom conveyors for loading. Signal workers to move loaded cars. Operate levers to move conveyor booms or shovels so that mine contents such as coal, rock, and ore can be placed into cars or onto conveyors. Drive machines into piles of material blasted from working faces. Advance machines to gather material and convey it into cars. Inspect boarding and locking of open-top boxcars and wedging of side-drop and hopper cars to prevent loss of material in transit.

GOE Information—Interest Area: 01. Agriculture and Natural Resources. **Work Group:** 01.08. Mining and Drilling. **Personality Type**—Realistic. Realistic occupations frequently involve work activities that include practical, hands-on problems and solutions. They often deal with plants; animals; and real-world materials like wood, tools, and machinery. Many of the occupations require working outside and do not involve a lot of paperwork or working closely with others. **Work Values**—Supervision, Technical; Independence; Supervision, Human Relations; Moral Values; Advancement. **Skills**—Repairing; Operation and Control; Equipment Maintenance; Operation Monitoring. **Abilities**—*Cognitive:* Spatial Orientation. *Psychomotor:* Wrist-Finger Speed; Multilimb Coordination; Control Precision; Manual Dexterity. *Physical:* Static Strength; Extent Flexibility; Trunk Strength. *Sensory:* Night Vision; Depth Perception. **General Work Activities**—*Information Input:* Inspecting Equipment, Structures, or Materials. *Mental Process:* None met the criteria. *Work Output:* Handling and Moving Objects; Operating Vehicles or Equipment; Performing General Physical Activities. *Interacting with Others:* None met the criteria. **Physical Work Conditions**—Outdoors; Noisy; Contaminants; Hazardous Equipment; Minor Burns, Cuts, Bites, or Stings; Using Hands on Objects, Tools, or Controls. **Other Job Characteristics**—Automation.

Experience—Job Zone 2. Some previous work-related skill, knowledge, or experience may be helpful in these occupations, but usually is not needed. **Job Preparation**—SVP 4.0 to less than 6.0—six months to less than two years. **Knowledges**—Mechanical Devices; Engineering and Technology. **Instructional Program**—Vehicle and Equipment Operators, Other.

Related SOC Job—53-7033 Loading Machine Operators, Underground Mining. **Related OOH Job**—Material Moving Occupations. **Related DOT Jobs**—932.683-014 Loading-Machine Operator; 932.683-018 Mechanical-Shovel Operator.

53-7041.00 Hoist and Winch Operators

- **Education/Training Required: Moderate-term on-the-job training**
- **Employed: 3,110**
- **Annual Earnings: $32,570**
- **Growth: 7.0%**
- **Annual Job Openings: 1,000**

Operate or tend hoists or winches to lift and pull loads, using power-operated cable equipment.

Move levers, pedals, and throttles to stop, start, and regulate speeds of hoist or winch drums in response to hand, bell, buzzer, telephone, loudspeaker, or whistle signals or by observing dial indicators or cable marks. Start engines of hoists or winches and use levers and pedals to wind or unwind cable on drums. Observe equipment gauges and indicators and hand signals of other workers to verify load positions or depths. Operate compressed air, diesel, electric, gasoline, or steam-driven hoists or winches to control movement of cableways, cages, derricks, draglines, loaders, railcars, or skips. Move

or reposition hoists, winches, loads, and materials manually or by using equipment and machines such as trucks, cars, and handtrucks. Select loads or materials according to weight and size specifications. Signal and assist other workers loading or unloading materials. Attach, fasten, and disconnect cables or lines to loads, materials, and equipment, using hand tools. Apply hand or foot brakes and move levers to lock hoists or winches. Oil winch drums so that cables will wind smoothly. Climb ladders to position and set up vehicle-mounted derricks. Repair, maintain, and adjust equipment, using hand tools. Tend auxiliary equipment such as jacks, slings, cables, or stop blocks to facilitate moving items or materials for further processing.

GOE Information—Interest Area: 13. Manufacturing. **Work Group:** 13.17. Loading, Moving, Hoisting, and Conveying. **Personality Type**—Realistic. Realistic occupations frequently involve work activities that include practical, hands-on problems and solutions. They often deal with plants; animals; and real-world materials like wood, tools, and machinery. Many of the occupations require working outside and do not involve a lot of paperwork or working closely with others. **Work Values**—Independence; Moral Values; Supervision, Technical. **Skills**—Operation and Control; Equipment Maintenance; Repairing; Operation Monitoring; Equipment Selection; Coordination. **Abilities**—*Cognitive:* Perceptual Speed; Time Sharing; Visualization. *Psychomotor:* Response Orientation; Reaction Time; Multilimb Coordination; Control Precision; Rate Control; Speed of Limb Movement. *Physical:* Extent Flexibility; Gross Body Equilibrium; Static Strength; Gross Body Coordination; Trunk Strength. *Sensory:* Depth Perception; Glare Sensitivity; Sound Localization; Peripheral Vision; Hearing Sensitivity; Auditory Attention. **General Work Activities**—*Information Input:* Monitoring Processes, Materials, or Surroundings; Inspecting Equipment, Structures, or Materials; Identifying Objects, Actions, and Events. *Mental Process:* Organizing, Planning, and Prioritizing; Making Decisions and Solving Problems; Processing Information. *Work Output:* Handling and Moving Objects; Controlling Machines and Processes; Repairing and Maintaining Mechanical Equipment. *Interacting with Others:* Communicating with Other Workers; Teaching Others; Monitoring and Controlling Resources. **Physical Work Conditions**—Noisy; Contaminants; High Places; Hazardous Equipment; Using Hands on Objects, Tools, or Controls; Repetitive Motions. **Other Job Characteristics**—Need to Be Exact or Accurate; Errors Have Important Consequences; Pace Determined by Speed of Equipment; Repeat Same Tasks.

Experience—Job Zone 2. Some previous work-related skill, knowledge, or experience may be helpful in these occupations, but usually is not needed. **Job Preparation**—SVP 4.0 to less than 6.0—six months to less than two years. **Knowledges**—Mechanical Devices; Transportation; Public Safety and Security; Engineering and Technology. **Instructional Program**—Construction/Heavy Equipment/Earthmoving Equipment Operation.

Related SOC Job—53-7041 Hoist and Winch Operators. **Related OOH Job**—Material Moving Occupations. **Related DOT Jobs**—663.686-022 Lathe Spotter; 869.683-014 Rigger; 911.663-014 Stevedore I; 911.687-018 Coal Trimmer; 921.662-022 Marine Railway Operator; 921.663-026 Hoist Operator; 921.663-030 Hoisting Engineer; 921.663-046 Pneumatic-Hoist Operator; 921.663-050 Scraper-Loader Operator; 921.663-066 Yarding Engineer; 921.682-022 Transfer Controller; 921.683-010 Boat-Hoist Operator; 921.683-030 Cupola Hoist Operator; 921.683-046 Hydraulic-Boom Operator; 921.683-054 Jammer Operator; 921.683-058 Log Loader; others.

53-7051.00 Industrial Truck and Tractor Operators

- **Education/Training Required: Short-term on-the-job training**
- **Employed: 627,060**
- **Annual Earnings: $27,080**
- **Growth: 7.9%**
- **Annual Job Openings: 114,000**

Operate industrial trucks or tractors equipped to move materials around a warehouse, storage yard, factory, construction site, or similar location.

Move controls to drive gasoline- or electric-powered trucks, cars, or tractors and transport materials between loading, processing, and storage areas. Move levers and controls that operate lifting devices, such as forklifts, lift beams and swivel hooks, hoists, and elevating platforms, to load, unload, transport, and stack material. Position lifting devices under, over, or around loaded pallets, skids, and boxes and secure material or products for transport to designated areas. Manually load or unload materials onto or off pallets, skids, platforms, cars, or lifting devices. Perform routine maintenance on vehicles and auxiliary equipment, such as cleaning, lubricating, recharging batteries, fueling, or replacing liquefied-gas tank. Weigh materials or products and record weight and other production data on tags or labels. Operate or tend automatic stacking, loading, packaging, or cutting machines. Signal workers to discharge, dump, or level materials. Hook tow trucks to trailer hitches and fasten attachments, such as graders, plows, rollers, and winch cables, to tractors, using hitchpins. Turn valves and open chutes to dump, spray, or release materials from dump cars or storage bins into hoppers.

GOE Information—Interest Area: 13. Manufacturing. **Work Group:** 13.17. Loading, Moving, Hoisting, and Conveying. **Personality Type**—Realistic. Realistic occupations frequently involve work activities that include practical, hands-on problems and solutions. They often deal with plants; animals; and real-world materials like wood, tools, and machinery. Many of the occupations require working outside and do not involve a lot of paperwork or working closely with others. **Work Values**—Supervision, Technical; Moral Values; Supervision, Human Relations. **Skills**—Operation Monitoring; Equipment Maintenance; Operation and Control; Repairing; Systems Analysis; Troubleshooting. **Abilities**—*Cognitive:* Spatial Orientation; Visualization; Perceptual Speed; Selective Attention; Flexibility of Closure; Time Sharing. *Psychomotor:* Response Orientation; Reaction Time; Multilimb Coordination; Rate Control; Control Precision; Speed of Limb Movement. *Physical:* Static Strength; Extent Flexibility; Stamina; Dynamic Strength; Trunk Strength; Gross Body Equilibrium. *Sensory:* Depth Perception; Peripheral Vision; Sound Localization; Night Vision; Glare Sensitivity; Hearing Sensitivity. **General Work Activities**—*Information Input:* Getting Information; Identifying Objects, Actions, and Events; Inspecting Equipment, Structures, or Materials. *Mental Process:* Organizing, Planning, and Prioritizing; Making Decisions and Solving Problems; Thinking Creatively. *Work Output:* Handling and Moving Objects; Performing General Physical Activities; Controlling Machines and Processes. *Interacting with Others:* Establishing and Maintaining Interpersonal Relationships; Communicating with Other Workers; Resolving Conflicts and Negotiating with Others. **Physical Work Conditions**—Noisy; Very Hot or Cold; Contaminants; Standing; Using Hands on Objects, Tools, or Controls; Bending or Twisting the Body. **Other Job Characteristics**—Need to Be Exact or Accurate; Repeat Same Tasks; Errors Have Important Consequences.

Experience—Job Zone 2. Some previous work-related skill, knowledge, or experience may be helpful in these occupations, but usually is not needed. **Job Preparation**—SVP 4.0 to less than 6.0—six months to less than two years. **Knowledges**—Transportation; Mechanical Devices; Production and Processing. **Instructional Program**—Vehicle and Equipment Operators, Other.

Related SOC Job—53-7051 Industrial Truck and Tractor Operators. **Related OOH Job**—Material Moving Occupations. **Related DOT Jobs**—519.663-014 Hot-Car Operator; 519.683-014 Larry Operator; 569.683-010 Kiln-Transfer Operator; 921.583-010 Transfer-Car Operator, Drier; 921.683-042 Front-End Loader Operator; 921.683-050 Industrial-Truck Operator; 921.683-070 Straddle-Truck Operator; 921.683-078 Transfer-Car Operator; 929.583-010 Yard Worker; 929.683-014 Tractor Operator.

53-7061.00 Cleaners of Vehicles and Equipment

- **Education/Training Required: Short-term on-the-job training**
- **Employed: 333,350**
- **Annual Earnings: $17,620**
- **Growth: 8.3%**
- **Annual Job Openings: 111,000**

Wash or otherwise clean vehicles, machinery, and other equipment. Use such materials as water, cleaning agents, brushes, cloths, and hoses.

Inspect parts, equipment, and vehicles for cleanliness, damage, and compliance with standards or regulations. Scrub, scrape, or spray machine parts, equipment, or vehicles, using scrapers, brushes, clothes, cleaners, disinfectants, insecticides, acid, abrasives, vacuums, and hoses. Mix cleaning solutions, abrasive compositions, and other compounds according to formulas. Press buttons to activate cleaning equipment or machines. Clean and polish vehicle windows. Rinse objects and place them on drying racks or use cloth, squeegees, or air compressors to dry surfaces. Drive vehicles to and from workshops or customers' workplaces or homes. Turn valves or handles on equipment to regulate pressure and flow of water, air, steam, or abrasives from sprayer nozzles. Pre-soak or rinse machine parts, equipment, or vehicles by immersing objects in cleaning solutions or water manually or by using hoists. Lubricate machinery, vehicles, and equipment and perform minor repairs and adjustments, using hand tools. Monitor operation of cleaning machines and stop machines or notify supervisors when malfunctions occur. Disassemble and reassemble machines or equipment or remove and reattach vehicle parts and trim, using hand tools. Connect hoses and lines to pumps and other equipment. Maintain inventories of supplies. Apply paints, dyes, polishes, reconditioners, waxes, and masking materials to vehicles to preserve, protect, or restore color and condition. Turn valves or disconnect hoses to eliminate water, cleaning solutions, or vapors from machinery or tanks. Sweep, shovel, or vacuum loose debris and salvageable scrap into containers and remove containers from work areas. Transport materials, equipment, or supplies to and from work areas, using carts or hoists. Collect and test samples of cleaning solutions and vapors. Clean the plastic work inside cars, using paintbrushes. Fit boot spoilers, side skirts, and mud flaps to cars.

GOE Information—Interest Area: 16. Transportation, Distribution, and Logistics. **Work Group:** 16.07. Transportation Support Work. **Personality Type**—Realistic. Realistic occupations frequently involve work activities that include practical, hands-on problems and solutions. They often deal with plants; animals; and real-world materials like wood, tools, and machinery. Many of the occupations require working outside and do not involve a lot of paperwork or working closely with others. **Work Values**—Independence; Moral Values; Supervision, Technical. **Skills**—Equipment Maintenance; Repairing. **Abilities**—*Cognitive:* None met the criteria. *Psychomotor:* Multilimb Coordination; Control Precision; Manual Dexterity. *Physical:* Extent Flexibility; Gross Body Coordination; Stamina; Trunk Strength. *Sensory:* Depth Perception. **General Work Activities**—*Information Input:* Inspecting Equipment, Structures, or Materials; Monitoring Processes, Materials, or Surroundings; Getting Information. *Mental Process:* Updating and Using Relevant Knowledge; Making Decisions and Solving Problems; Developing Objectives and Strategies. *Work Output:* Handling and Moving Objects; Performing General Physical Activities; Repairing and Maintaining Mechanical Equipment. *Interacting with Others:* Establishing and Maintaining Interpersonal Relationships; Performing for or Working with the Public; Communicating with Other Workers. **Physical Work Conditions**—Outdoors; Noisy; Contaminants; Standing; Walking and Running; Repetitive Motions. **Other Job Characteristics**—Need to Be Exact or Accurate.

Experience—Job Zone 1. No previous work-related skill, knowledge, or experience is needed. **Job Preparation**—SVP below 4.0—less than six months. **Knowledges**—Chemistry; Mechanical Devices; Public Safety and Security; Transportation; Economics and Accounting; Physics. **Instructional Program**—No related CIP programs.

Related SOC Job—53-7061 Cleaners of Vehicles and Equipment. **Related OOH Job**—Material Moving Occupations. **Related DOT Jobs**—503.687-010 Sandblaster; 511.687-010 Blanket Washer; 519.664-010 Assembly Cleaner; 521.687-030 Char Puller; 521.687-054 Filter-Screen Cleaner; 521.687-114 Shaker Washer; 529.685-230 Stem-Dryer Maintainer; 529.687-014 Bin Cleaner; 529.687-018 Box-Truck Washer; 529.687-054 Cooker Cleaner; 529.687-062 Die Cleaner; 529.687-190 Stone Cleaner; 529.687-194 Suction-Plate-Carrier Cleaner; 529.687-206 Trolley Cleaner; 529.687-210 Washer; 529.687-214 Washroom Cleaner; 557.684-010 Jet Handler; others.

53-7062.00 Laborers and Freight, Stock, and Material Movers, Hand

- **Education/Training Required: Short-term on-the-job training**
- **Employed: 2,363,960**
- **Annual Earnings: $20,610**
- **Growth: 10.2%**
- **Annual Job Openings: 671,000**

Manually move freight, stock, or other materials or perform other unskilled general labor. Includes all unskilled manual laborers not elsewhere classified.

Attach identifying tags to containers or mark them with identifying information. Read work orders or receive oral instructions to determine work assignments and material and equipment needs. Record numbers of units handled and moved, using daily production sheets or work tickets. Move freight, stock, and other materials to and from storage and production areas, loading docks, delivery vehicles, ships, and containers by hand or using trucks, tractors, and other equipment. Sort cargo before loading and unloading. Assemble product containers and crates, using hand tools and precut lumber. Load and unload ship cargo, using winches and other hoisting devices. Connect hoses and operate equipment to move liquid materials into and out of storage tanks on vessels. Pack containers and re-pack damaged containers. Carry needed tools and supplies from storage or

trucks and return them after use. Install protective devices, such as bracing, padding, or strapping, to prevent shifting or damage to items being transported. Maintain equipment storage areas to ensure that inventory is protected. Attach slings, hooks, and other devices to lift cargo and guide loads. Carry out general yard duties such as performing shunting on railway lines. Adjust controls to guide, position, and move equipment such as cranes, booms, and cameras. Guide loads being lifted to prevent swinging. Adjust or replace equipment parts such as rollers, belts, plugs, and caps, using hand tools. Stack cargo in locations such as transit sheds or in holds of ships as directed, using pallets or cargo boards. Connect electrical equipment to power sources so that it can be tested before use. Set up the equipment needed to produce special lighting and sound effects during performances. Bundle and band material such as fodder and tobacco leaves, using banding machines. Rig and dismantle props and equipment such as frames, scaffolding, platforms, or backdrops, using hand tools. Check out, rent, or requisition all equipment needed for productions or for set construction. Direct spouts and position receptacles such as bins, carts, and containers so they can be loaded.

GOE Information—**Interest Area:** 16. Transportation, Distribution, and Logistics. **Work Group:** 16.07. Transportation Support Work. **Personality Type**—Realistic. Realistic occupations frequently involve work activities that include practical, hands-on problems and solutions. They often deal with plants; animals; and real-world materials like wood, tools, and machinery. Many of the occupations require working outside and do not involve a lot of paperwork or working closely with others. **Work Values**—Supervision, Technical; Moral Values. **Skills**—None met the criteria. **Abilities**—*Cognitive:* Spatial Orientation. *Psychomotor:* Multilimb Coordination; Manual Dexterity. *Physical:* Static Strength; Explosive Strength; Extent Flexibility; Dynamic Strength; Trunk Strength; Stamina. *Sensory:* Depth Perception. **General Work Activities**—*Information Input:* Inspecting Equipment, Structures, or Materials; Getting Information; Monitoring Processes, Materials, or Surroundings. *Mental Process:* Judging the Qualities of Things, Services, or Other People's Work; Processing Information; Organizing, Planning, and Prioritizing. *Work Output:* Handling and Moving Objects; Performing General Physical Activities; Controlling Machines and Processes. *Interacting with Others:* Coordinating the Work and Activities of Others; Performing for or Working with the Public; Providing Consultation and Advice to Others. **Physical Work Conditions**—Outdoors; Noisy; Very Hot or Cold; Contaminants; Standing; Using Hands on Objects, Tools, or Controls. **Other Job Characteristics**—Need to Be Exact or Accurate; Repeat Same Tasks.

Experience—Job Zone 2. Some previous work-related skill, knowledge, or experience may be helpful in these occupations, but usually is not needed. **Job Preparation**—SVP 4.0 to less than 6.0—six months to less than two years. **Knowledges**—Transportation; Public Safety and Security; Production and Processing. **Instructional Program**—No related CIP programs.

Related SOC Job—53-7062 Laborers and Freight, Stock, and Material Movers, Hand. **Related OOH Job**—Material Moving Occupations. **Related DOT Jobs**—412.687-010 Commissary Assistant; 520.687-010 Blender Laborer; 520.687-038 Gum Puller; 523.687-022 Freezing-Room Worker; 525.687-054 Offal Icer, Poultry; 525.687-086 Shackler; 529.687-138 Leaf Tier; 542.667-010 Wharf Tender; 573.687-030 Setter Helper; 575.687-026 Pipe Stripper; 579.665-014 Laborer, Concrete-Mixing Plant; 579.687-018 Floor Attendant; 669.687-018 Lumber Straightener; 677.687-010 Log Roller; 684.687-022 Collector; 727.687-030 Battery Stacker; 860.684-018 Car Blocker; others.

53-7063.00 Machine Feeders and Offbearers

- **Education/Training Required:** Short-term on-the-job training
- **Employed:** 145,740
- **Annual Earnings:** $22,330
- **Growth:** –18.0%
- **Annual Job Openings:** 20,000

Feed materials into or remove materials from machines or equipment that is automatic or tended by other workers.

Shovel or scoop materials into containers, machines, or equipment for processing, storage, or transport. Record production and operational data, such as amount of materials processed. Open and close gates of belt and pneumatic conveyors on machines that are fed directly from preceding machines. Inspect materials and products for defects and to ensure conformance to specifications. Identify and mark materials, products, and samples, following instructions. Weigh or measure materials or products to ensure conformance to specifications. Fasten, package, or stack materials and products, using hand tools and fastening equipment. Remove materials and products from machines and equipment and place them in boxes, trucks, or conveyors, using hand tools and moving devices. Push dual control buttons and move controls to start, stop, or adjust machinery and equipment. Load materials and products into machines and equipment or onto conveyors, using hand tools and moving devices. Add chemicals, solutions, or ingredients to machines or equipment as required by the manufacturing process. Clean and maintain machinery, equipment, and work areas to ensure proper functioning and safe working conditions. Transfer materials and products to and from machinery and equipment, using industrial trucks or hand trucks.

GOE Information—Interest Area: 13. Manufacturing. **Work Group:** 13.17. Loading, Moving, Hoisting, and Conveying. **Personality Type**—Realistic. Realistic occupations frequently involve work activities that include practical, hands-on problems and solutions. They often deal with plants; animals; and real-world materials like wood, tools, and machinery. Many of the occupations require working outside and do not involve a lot of paperwork or working closely with others. **Work Values**—Moral Values; Supervision, Technical; Activity. **Skills**—Equipment Maintenance; Operation and Control. **Abilities**—*Cognitive:* Spatial Orientation; Perceptual Speed. *Psychomotor:* Manual Dexterity; Multilimb Coordination; Speed of Limb Movement; Reaction Time; Wrist-Finger Speed; Control Precision. *Physical:* Explosive Strength; Static Strength; Dynamic Flexibility; Dynamic Strength; Extent Flexibility; Stamina. *Sensory:* Depth Perception. **General Work Activities**—*Information Input:* Inspecting Equipment, Structures, or Materials. *Mental Process:* None met the criteria. *Work Output:* Handling and Moving Objects; Performing General Physical Activities; Controlling Machines and Processes. *Interacting with Others:* None met the criteria. **Physical Work Conditions**—Indoors; Noisy; Hazardous Equipment; Standing; Using Hands on Objects, Tools, or Controls; Repetitive Motions. **Other Job Characteristics**—Pace Determined by Speed of Equipment; Automation; Repeat Same Tasks.

Experience—Job Zone 1. No previous work-related skill, knowledge, or experience is needed. **Job Preparation**—SVP below 4.0—less than six months. **Knowledges**—Production and Processing; Mechanical Devices. **Instructional Program**—No related CIP programs.

Related SOC Job—53-7063 Machine Feeders and Offbearers. **Related OOH Job**—Material Moving Occupations. **Related DOT Jobs**—361.686-010 Washing-Machine Loader-and-Puller; 363.686-010 Flatwork Finisher; 369.686-010 Folding-Machine Operator; 429.686-010 Press Feeder, Broomcorn; 504.686-014 Furnace Helper; 504.686-022 Heat Treater; 509.666-010 Compound-Coating-Machine Offbearer; 509.686-014 Pasting-Machine Offbearer; 509.687-026 Laborer, General; 512.686-010 Cupola Charger; 515.686-010 Battery-Wrecker Operator; 519.686-010 Laborer, General; 520.686-010 Ball-Machine Operator; 520.686-014 Dessert-Cup-Machine Feeder; others.

53-7064.00 Packers and Packagers, Hand

- **Education/Training Required:** Short-term on-the-job training
- **Employed:** 840,410
- **Annual Earnings:** $17,390
- **Growth:** 10.1%
- **Annual Job Openings:** 194,000

Pack or package by hand a wide variety of products and materials.

Mark and label containers, container tags, or products, using marking tools. Measure, weigh, and count products and materials. Examine and inspect containers, materials, and products to ensure that packing specifications are met. Record product, packaging, and order information on specified forms and records. Remove completed or defective products or materials, placing them on moving equipment such as conveyors or in specified areas such as loading docks. Seal containers or materials, using glues, fasteners, nails, and hand tools. Load materials and products into package-processing equipment. Assemble, line, and pad cartons, crates, and containers, using hand tools. Clean containers, materials, supplies, or work areas, using cleaning solutions and hand tools. Transport packages to customers' vehicles. Place or pour products or materials into containers, using hand tools and equipment, or fill containers from spouts or chutes. Obtain, move, and sort products, materials, containers, and orders, using hand tools.

GOE Information—Interest Area: 13. Manufacturing. **Work Group:** 13.17. Loading, Moving, Hoisting, and Conveying. **Personality Type**—Realistic. Realistic occupations frequently involve work activities that include practical, hands-on problems and solutions. They often deal with plants; animals; and real-world materials like wood, tools, and machinery. Many of the occupations require working outside and do not involve a lot of paperwork or working closely with others. **Work Values**—Supervision, Technical; Moral Values; Activity. **Skills**—None met the criteria. **Abilities**—*Cognitive:* None met the criteria. *Psychomotor:* Manual Dexterity; Multilimb Coordination. *Physical:* Extent Flexibility; Static Strength; Stamina; Trunk Strength. *Sensory:* None met the criteria. **General Work Activities**—*Information Input:* Identifying Objects, Actions, and Events; Inspecting Equipment, Structures, or Materials; Getting Information. *Mental Process:* Making Decisions and Solving Problems; Judging the Qualities of Things, Services, or Other People's Work. *Work Output:* Handling and Moving Objects; Performing General Physical Activities; Controlling Machines and Processes. *Interacting with Others:* Establishing and Maintaining Interpersonal Relationships; Communicating with Other Workers; Assisting and Caring for Others. **Physical Work Conditions**—Indoors; Noisy; Standing; Walking and Running; Using Hands on Objects, Tools, or Controls; Repetitive Motions. **Other Job Characteristics**—None met the criteria.

Experience—Job Zone 1. No previous work-related skill, knowledge, or experience is needed. **Job Preparation**—SVP below 4.0—less than six months. **Knowledges**—Production and Processing; Public Safety and Security. **Instructional Program**—No related CIP programs.

Related SOC Job—53-7064 Packers and Packagers, Hand. **Related OOH Job**—Material Moving Occupations. **Related DOT Jobs**—522.687-010 Barrel Filler I; 522.687-018 Bulker; 525.687-082 Poultry-Dressing Worker; 525.687-118 Tier; 529.687-022 Bulk Filler; 529.687-086 Fish-Egg Packer; 529.687-150 Linker; 559.687-014 Ampoule Sealer; 585.687-030 Singer; 700.687-038 Laborer, Gold Leaf; 710.687-034 Tie-Up Worker; 737.587-018 Primer Boxer; 737.687-014 Bag Loader; 737.687-030 Core Loader; 737.687-094 Packer-Fuser; 753.687-038 Packing-Line Worker; 784.687-042 Inspector-Packer; 789.687-106 Mophead Trimmer-and-Wrapper; others.

53-7071.00 Gas Compressor and Gas Pumping Station Operators

- **Education/Training Required: Moderate-term on-the-job training**
- **Employed: 3,950**
- **Annual Earnings: $43,830**
- **Growth: −21.3%**
- **Annual Job Openings: 1,000**

Operate steam, gas, electric motor, or internal combustion engine-driven compressors. Transmit, compress, or recover gases such as butane, nitrogen, hydrogen, and natural gas.

Turn knobs or switches to regulate pressures. Take samples of gases and conduct chemical tests to determine gas quality and sulfur or moisture content or send samples to laboratories for analysis. Submit daily reports on facility operations. Record instrument readings and operational changes in operating logs. Maintain each station by performing general housekeeping duties such as painting, washing, and cleaning. Clean, lubricate, and adjust equipment and replace filters and gaskets, using hand tools. Respond to problems by adjusting control room equipment or instructing other personnel to adjust equipment at problem locations or in other control areas. Read gas meters and maintain records of the amounts of gas received and dispensed from holders. Operate power-driven pumps that transfer liquids, semi-liquids, gases, or powdered materials. Move controls and turn valves to start compressor engines, pumps, and auxiliary equipment. Monitor meters and pressure gauges to determine consumption rate variations, temperatures, and pressures. Adjust valves and equipment to obtain specified performance. Connect pipelines between pumps and containers that are being filled or emptied.

GOE Information—Interest Area: 13. Manufacturing. **Work Group:** 13.16. Utility Operation and Energy Distribution. **Personality Type**—Realistic. Realistic occupations frequently involve work activities that include practical, hands-on problems and solutions. They often deal with plants; animals; and real-world materials like wood, tools, and machinery. Many of the occupations require working outside and do not involve a lot of paperwork or working closely with others. **Work Values**—Independence; Supervision, Technical; Supervision, Human Relations; Moral Values. **Skills**—Operation Monitoring; Operation and Control; Repairing. **Abilities**—*Cognitive:* None met the criteria. *Psychomotor:* Control Precision. *Physical:* Extent Flexibility. *Sensory:* None met the criteria. **General Work Activities**—*Information Input:* Monitoring Processes, Materials, or Surroundings; Inspecting Equipment, Structures, or Materials; Getting Information. *Mental Process:* Processing Information. *Work Output:* Handling and Moving Objects; Controlling Machines and Processes; Repairing and Maintaining Mechanical Equipment. *Interacting with Others:* None met the criteria. **Physical Work Conditions**—Indoors; Contaminants; Standing; Using Hands on Objects, Tools, or Controls. **Other Job Characteristics**—Need to Be Exact or Accurate; Automation.

Experience—Job Zone 2. Some previous work-related skill, knowledge, or experience may be helpful in these occupations, but usually is not needed. **Job Preparation**—SVP 4.0 to less than 6.0—six months to less than two years. **Knowledges**—Mechanical Devices; Engineering and Technology. **Instructional Program**—No related CIP programs.

Related SOC Job—53-7071 Gas Compressor and Gas Pumping Station Operators. **Related OOH Job**—Material Moving Occupations. **Related DOT Jobs**—950.382-014 Gas-Compressor Operator; 953.382-010 Gas-Pumping-Station Operator.

53-7072.00 Pump Operators, Except Wellhead Pumpers

- **Education/Training Required: Moderate-term on-the-job training**
- **Employed: 9,970**
- **Annual Earnings: $36,150**
- **Growth: −22.2%**
- **Annual Job Openings: 2,000**

Tend, control, or operate power-driven, stationary, or portable pumps and manifold systems to transfer gases, oil, other liquids, slurries, or powdered materials to and from various vessels and processes.

Add chemicals and solutions to tanks to ensure that specifications are met. Tend vessels that store substances such as gases, liquids, slurries, or powdered materials, checking levels of substances by using calibrated rods or by reading mercury gauges and tank charts. Tend auxiliary equipment such as water treatment and refrigeration units and heat exchangers. Record operating data such as products and quantities pumped, stocks used, gauging results, and operating times. Communicate with other workers, using signals, radios, or telephones, to start and stop flows of materials or substances. Test materials and solutions, using testing equipment. Clean, lubricate, and repair pumps and vessels, using hand tools and equipment. Read operating schedules or instructions or receive verbal orders to determine amounts to be pumped. Pump two or more materials into one tank to blend mixtures. Plan movement of products through lines to processing, storage, and shipping units, utilizing knowledge of interconnections and capacities of pipelines, valve manifolds, pumps, and tankage. Monitor gauges and flowmeters and inspect equipment to ensure that tank levels, temperatures, chemical amounts, and pressures are at specified levels, reporting abnormalities as necessary. Connect hoses and pipelines to pumps and vessels prior to material transfer, using hand tools. Collect and deliver sample solutions for laboratory analysis. Turn valves and start pumps to start or regulate flows of substances such as gases, liquids, slurries, or powdered materials.

GOE Information—Interest Area: 13. Manufacturing. **Work Group:** 13.17. Loading, Moving, Hoisting, and Conveying. **Personality Type**—Realistic. Realistic occupations frequently involve work activities that include practical, hands-on problems and solutions. They often deal with plants; animals; and real-world materials like wood, tools, and machinery. Many of the occupations require working outside and do not involve a lot of paperwork or working closely with others. **Work Values**—Supervision, Technical; Supervision, Human Relations; Moral Values; Independence; Advancement. **Skills**—Operation Monitoring; Operation and Control; Equipment Maintenance. **Abilities**—*Cognitive:* Memorization; Time Sharing; Number Facility. *Psychomotor:* Control Precision; Rate Control; Wrist-Finger Speed; Response Orientation; Manual Dexterity; Reaction Time. *Physical:* Extent Flexibility; Stamina; Static Strength; Trunk

Strength. *Sensory:* None met the criteria. **General Work Activities—** *Information Input:* Inspecting Equipment, Structures, or Materials; Monitoring Processes, Materials, or Surroundings; Identifying Objects, Actions, and Events. *Mental Process:* Judging the Qualities of Things, Services, or Other People's Work; Evaluating Information Against Standards. *Work Output:* Controlling Machines and Processes; Handling and Moving Objects; Performing General Physical Activities. *Interacting with Others:* Communicating with Other Workers. **Physical Work Conditions—**Indoors; Hazardous Conditions; Hazardous Equipment; Standing; Using Hands on Objects, Tools, or Controls; Repetitive Motions. **Other Job Characteristics—**Automation; Need to Be Exact or Accurate; Pace Determined by Speed of Equipment.

Experience—Job Zone 2. Some previous work-related skill, knowledge, or experience may be helpful in these occupations, but usually is not needed. **Job Preparation—**SVP 4.0 to less than 6.0—six months to less than two years. **Knowledges—**Mechanical Devices; Physics; Chemistry; Production and Processing. **Instructional Program—**No related CIP programs.

Related SOC Job—53-7072 Pump Operators, Except Wellhead Pumpers. **Related OOH Job—**Material Moving Occupations. **Related DOT Jobs—**521.565-010 Liquor-Bridge Operator; 522.662-010 Receiver, Fermenting Cellars; 529.585-014 Tank Tender; 529.685-242 Tank Pumper, Panelboard; 529.685-246 Tapper; 549.362-010 Still-Pump Operator; 549.382-018 Wash-Oil-Pump Operator; 549.685-042 Utility Operator III; 559.585-014 Grease-and-Tallow Pumper; 559.665-038 Tank-Farm Attendant; 559.684-034 Utility Worker, Production; 559.685-026 Brine-Well Operator; 914.362-018 Station Engineer, Main Line; 914.585-010 Gas-Transfer Operator; others.

53-7073.00 Wellhead Pumpers

- **Education/Training Required: Moderate-term on-the-job training**
- **Employed: 10,190**
- **Annual Earnings: $37,690**
- **Growth: –23.6%**
- **Annual Job Openings: 2,000**

Operate power pumps and auxiliary equipment to produce flow of oil or gas from wells in oil field.

Monitor control panels during pumping operations to ensure that materials are being pumped at the correct pressure, density, rate, and concentration. Operate engines and pumps to shut off wells according to production schedules and to switch flow of oil into storage tanks. Perform routine maintenance on vehicles and equipment. Repair gas and oil meters and gauges. Unload and assemble pipes and pumping equipment, using hand tools. Attach pumps and hoses to wellheads. Start compressor engines and divert oil from storage tanks into compressor units and auxiliary equipment to recover natural gas from oil. Open valves to return compressed gas to bottoms of specified wells to repressurize them and force oil to surface. Supervise oil pumpers and other workers engaged in producing oil from wells. Drive trucks to transport high-pressure pumping equipment and chemicals, fluids, or gases to be pumped into wells. Prepare trucks and equipment necessary for the type of pumping service required. Control pumping and blending equipment to acidize, cement, or fracture gas or oil wells and permeable rock formations. Mix acids, chemicals, or dry cement as required for a specific job.

GOE Information—Interest Area: 01. Agriculture and Natural Resources. **Work Group:** 01.08. Mining and Drilling. **Personality Type—**Realistic. Realistic occupations frequently involve work activities that include practical, hands-on problems and solutions. They often deal with plants; animals; and real-world materials like wood, tools, and machinery. Many of the occupations require working outside and do not involve a lot of paperwork or working closely with others. **Work Values—**Independence; Supervision, Technical; Moral Values; Supervision, Human Relations. **Skills—**Repairing; Operation Monitoring; Equipment Maintenance; Installation; Operation and Control; Systems Analysis. **Abilities—***Cognitive:* Perceptual Speed; Selective Attention; Visualization; Category Flexibility. *Psychomotor:* Reaction Time; Control Precision; Multilimb Coordination; Response Orientation; Manual Dexterity; Finger Dexterity. *Physical:* Gross Body Equilibrium; Extent Flexibility; Dynamic Strength; Gross Body Coordination; Static Strength; Trunk Strength. *Sensory:* Auditory Attention; Depth Perception. **General Work Activities—***Information Input:* Monitoring Processes, Materials, or Surroundings; Inspecting Equipment, Structures, or Materials; Identifying Objects, Actions, and Events. *Mental Process:* Updating and Using Relevant Knowledge; Organizing, Planning, and Prioritizing; Making Decisions and Solving Problems. *Work Output:* Handling and Moving Objects; Performing General Physical Activities; Repairing and Maintaining Mechanical Equipment. *Interacting with Others:* Communicating with Other Workers; Establishing and Maintaining Interpersonal Relationships; Communicating with Persons Outside Organization. **Physical Work Conditions—**Outdoors; Very Hot or Cold; Contaminants; High Places; Hazardous Conditions; Hazardous Equipment. **Other Job Characteristics—**Errors Have Important Consequences; Need to Be Exact or Accurate; Repeat Same Tasks; Pace Determined by Speed of Equipment.

Experience—Job Zone 2. Some previous work-related skill, knowledge, or experience may be helpful in these occupations, but usually is not needed. **Job Preparation—**SVP 4.0 to less than 6.0—six months to less than two years. **Knowledges—**Mechanical Devices; Physics; Production and Processing; Chemistry; Engineering and Technology; Design. **Instructional Program—**No related CIP programs.

Related SOC Job—53-7073 Wellhead Pumpers. **Related OOH Job—**Material Moving Occupations. **Related DOT Jobs—**914.382-010 Oil Pumper; 914.382-022 Pumper, Head.

53-7081.00 Refuse and Recyclable Material Collectors

- **Education/Training Required: Short-term on-the-job training**
- **Employed: 133,930**
- **Annual Earnings: $28,460**
- **Growth: 8.9%**
- **Annual Job Openings: 31,000**

Collect and dump refuse or recyclable materials from containers into truck. May drive truck.

Inspect trucks prior to beginning routes to ensure safe operating condition. Refuel trucks and add other necessary fluids, such as oil. Fill out any needed reports for defective equipment. Drive to disposal sites to empty trucks that have been filled. Drive trucks along established routes through residential streets and alleys or through business and industrial areas. Operate equipment that compresses the collected refuse. Operate automated or semi-automated hoisting devices that raise refuse bins and dump contents into openings in truck bodies. Dismount garbage trucks to collect garbage and remount trucks to ride to the next collection point. Communicate with dispatchers concerning delays, unsafe sites, accidents, equipment breakdowns, and other maintenance problems. Keep informed of road and weather conditions to determine how routes will be affected. Tag garbage or recycling containers to inform customers of problems such as excess garbage or inclusion of items that are not permitted. Clean trucks and compactor bodies after routes have been completed. Sort items set out for recycling and throw materials into designated truck compartments. Organize schedules for refuse collection. Provide quotes for refuse collection contracts.

GOE Information—Interest Area: 13. Manufacturing. **Work Group:** 13.17. Loading, Moving, Hoisting, and Conveying. **Personality Type**—Realistic. Realistic occupations frequently involve work activities that include practical, hands-on problems and solutions. They often deal with plants; animals; and real-world materials like wood, tools, and machinery. Many of the occupations require working outside and do not involve a lot of paperwork or working closely with others. **Work Values**—Supervision, Technical; Supervision, Human Relations; Company Policies and Practices; Security. **Skills**—Equipment Maintenance; Operation Monitoring; Operation and Control; Repairing. **Abilities**—*Cognitive:* Spatial Orientation. *Psychomotor:* Rate Control; Response Orientation; Control Precision; Multilimb Coordination; Speed of Limb Movement; Reaction Time. *Physical:* Static Strength; Dynamic Strength; Stamina; Extent Flexibility; Gross Body Coordination; Trunk Strength. *Sensory:* Glare Sensitivity; Depth Perception; Hearing Sensitivity; Visual Color Discrimination; Auditory Attention. **General Work Activities**—*Information Input:* Inspecting Equipment, Structures, or Materials; Identifying Objects, Actions, and Events; Monitoring Processes, Materials, or Surroundings. *Mental Process:* Making Decisions and Solving Problems; Evaluating Information Against Standards; Judging the Qualities of Things, Services, or Other People's Work. *Work Output:* Handling and Moving Objects; Performing General Physical Activities; Controlling Machines and Processes. *Interacting with Others:* Establishing and Maintaining Interpersonal Relationships; Communicating with Other Workers; Performing for or Working with the Public. **Physical Work Conditions**—Outdoors; Noisy; Contaminants; Using Hands on Objects, Tools, or Controls; Bending or Twisting the Body; Repetitive Motions. **Other Job Characteristics**—Need to Be Exact or Accurate; Errors Have Important Consequences; Repeat Same Tasks.

Experience—Job Zone 2. Some previous work-related skill, knowledge, or experience may be helpful in these occupations, but usually is not needed. **Job Preparation**—SVP 4.0 to less than 6.0—six months to less than two years. **Knowledges**—Transportation; Customer and Personal Service; Public Safety and Security; Education and Training; Mechanical Devices. **Instructional Program**—No related CIP programs.

Related SOC Job—53-7081 Refuse and Recyclable Material Collectors. **Related OOH Job**—Material Moving Occupations. **Related DOT Job**—955.687-022 Garbage Collector.

53-7111.00 Shuttle Car Operators

- **Education/Training Required:** Short-term on-the-job training
- **Employed:** 3,100
- **Annual Earnings:** $38,310
- **Growth:** −42.4%
- **Annual Job Openings:** Fewer than 500

Operate diesel or electric-powered shuttle car in underground mine to transport materials from working face to mine cars or conveyor.

Control conveyors that run the entire length of shuttle cars to distribute loads as loading progresses. Drive loaded shuttle cars to ramps and move controls to discharge loads into mine cars or onto conveyors. Clean, fuel, and service equipment and repair and replace parts as necessary. Move mine cars into position for loading and unloading, using pinchbars inserted under car wheels to position cars under loading spouts. Guide and stop cars by switching, applying brakes, or placing scotches (wooden wedges) between wheels and rails. Push or ride cars down slopes or hook cars to cables and control cable drum brakes to ease cars down inclines. Observe hand signals, grade stakes, or other markings when operating machines. Open and close bottom doors of cars to dump contents. Direct other workers to move stakes, place blocks, position anchors or cables, or move materials. Monitor loading processes to ensure that materials are loaded according to specifications. Measure, weigh, or verify levels of rock, gravel, or other excavated material to prevent equipment overloads. Read written instructions or confer with supervisors about schedules and materials to be moved. Maintain records of materials moved.

GOE Information—Interest Area: 01. Agriculture and Natural Resources. **Work Group:** 01.08. Mining and Drilling. **Personality Type**—Realistic. Realistic occupations frequently involve work activities that include practical, hands-on problems and solutions. They often deal with plants; animals; and real-world materials like wood, tools, and machinery. Many of the occupations require working outside and do not involve a lot of paperwork or working closely with others. **Work Values**—Independence; Supervision, Technical; Supervision, Human Relations; Moral Values; Advancement. **Skills**—Operation and Control; Equipment Maintenance; Repairing; Operation Monitoring; Troubleshooting; Installation. **Abilities**—*Cognitive:* Spatial Orientation; Time Sharing. *Psychomotor:* Reaction Time; Rate Control; Response Orientation; Control Precision; Multilimb Coordination; Manual Dexterity. *Physical:* Static Strength; Extent Flexibility. *Sensory:* Depth Perception. **General Work Activities**—*Information Input:* Inspecting Equipment, Structures, or Materials; Monitoring Processes, Materials, or Surroundings; Identifying Objects, Actions, and Events. *Mental Process:* Making Decisions and Solving Problems; Evaluating Information Against Standards; Thinking Creatively. *Work Output:* Controlling Machines and Processes; Handling and Moving Objects; Operating Vehicles or Equipment. *Interacting with Others:* Establishing and Maintaining Interpersonal Relationships; Communicating with Other Workers; Assisting and Caring for Others. **Physical Work Conditions**—Noisy; Contaminants; Cramped Work Space, Awkward Positions; Hazardous Equipment; Using Hands on Objects, Tools, or Controls; Repetitive Motions. **Other Job Characteristics**—Errors Have Important Consequences; Pace Determined by Speed of Equipment; Need to Be Exact or Accurate.

Experience—Job Zone 2. Some previous work-related skill, knowledge, or experience may be helpful in these occupations, but usually is not needed. **Job Preparation**—SVP 4.0 to less than 6.0—six months to less than two years. **Knowledges**—Mechanical Devices; Transportation; Law and Government. **Instructional Program**—No related CIP programs.

Related SOC Job—53-7111 Shuttle Car Operators. **Related OOH Job**—Material Moving Occupations. **Related DOT Job**—932.683-022 Shuttle-Car Operator.

53-7121.00 Tank Car, Truck, and Ship Loaders

- **Education/Training Required: Moderate-term on-the-job training**
- **Employed: 15,950**
- **Annual Earnings: $31,310**
- **Growth: –11.0%**
- **Annual Job Openings: 2,000**

Load and unload chemicals and bulk solids such as coal, sand, and grain into or from tank cars, trucks, or ships, using material moving equipment. May perform a variety of other tasks relating to shipment of products. May gauge or sample shipping tanks and test them for leaks.

Verify tank car, barge, or truck load numbers to ensure car placement accuracy based on written or verbal instructions. Observe positions of cars passing loading spouts and swing spouts into the correct positions at the appropriate times. Operate ship loading and unloading equipment, conveyors, hoists, and other specialized material handling equipment such as railroad tank car unloading equipment. Monitor product movement to and from storage tanks, coordinating activities with other workers to ensure constant product flow. Record operating data such as products and quantities pumped, gauge readings, and operating times manually or by using computers. Check conditions and weights of vessels to ensure cleanliness and compliance with loading procedures. Operate industrial trucks, tractors, loaders, and other equipment to transport materials to and from transportation vehicles and loading docks and to store and retrieve materials in warehouses. Connect ground cables to carry off static electricity when unloading tanker cars. Seal outlet valves on tank cars, barges, and trucks. Test samples for specific gravity, using hydrometers, or send samples to laboratories for testing. Remove and replace tank car dome caps or direct other workers in their removal and replacement. Lower gauge rods into tanks or read meters to verify contents, temperatures, and volumes of liquid loads. Clean interiors of tank cars or tank trucks, using mechanical spray nozzles. Operate conveyors and equipment to transfer grain or other materials from transportation vehicles. Test vessels for leaks, damage, and defects and repair or replace defective parts as necessary. Unload cars containing liquids by connecting hoses to outlet plugs and pumping compressed air into cars to force liquids into storage tanks. Copy and attach load specifications to loaded tanks. Start pumps and adjust valves or cables to regulate the flow of products to vessels, utilizing knowledge of loading procedures.

GOE Information—Interest Area: 13. Manufacturing. **Work Group:** 13.17. Loading, Moving, Hoisting, and Conveying. **Personality Type**—Realistic. Realistic occupations frequently involve work activities that include practical, hands-on problems and solutions. They often deal with plants; animals; and real-world materials like wood, tools, and machinery. Many of the occupations require working outside and do not involve a lot of paperwork or working closely with others. **Work Values**—Independence; Supervision, Technical; Moral Values. **Skills**—Operation Monitoring; Operation and Control; Troubleshooting; Repairing; Equipment Maintenance. **Abilities**—*Cognitive:* Spatial Orientation; Perceptual Speed; Time Sharing; Selective Attention; Flexibility of Closure; Number Facility. *Psychomotor:* Reaction Time; Rate Control; Multilimb Coordination;

Response Orientation; Control Precision; Speed of Limb Movement. *Physical:* Static Strength; Gross Body Equilibrium; Extent Flexibility; Stamina; Dynamic Strength; Trunk Strength. *Sensory:* Depth Perception; Glare Sensitivity; Peripheral Vision; Auditory Attention; Hearing Sensitivity; Far Vision. **General Work Activities**—*Information Input:* Monitoring Processes, Materials, or Surroundings; Inspecting Equipment, Structures, or Materials; Identifying Objects, Actions, and Events. *Mental Process:* Updating and Using Relevant Knowledge; Scheduling Work and Activities; Making Decisions and Solving Problems. *Work Output:* Handling and Moving Objects; Performing General Physical Activities; Controlling Machines and Processes. *Interacting with Others:* Communicating with Other Workers; Establishing and Maintaining Interpersonal Relationships; Providing Consultation and Advice to Others. **Physical Work Conditions**—Outdoors; Noisy; Very Hot or Cold; Contaminants; High Places; Hazardous Equipment. **Other Job Characteristics**—Need to Be Exact or Accurate; Pace Determined by Speed of Equipment; Errors Have Important Consequences; Repeat Same Tasks.

Experience—Job Zone 2. Some previous work-related skill, knowledge, or experience may be helpful in these occupations, but usually is not needed. **Job Preparation**—SVP 4.0 to less than 6.0—six months to less than two years. **Knowledges**—Production and Processing; Transportation; Mechanical Devices; Public Safety and Security; Building and Construction; Chemistry. **Instructional Program**—No related CIP programs.

Related SOC Job—53-7121 Tank Car, Truck, and Ship Loaders. **Related OOH Job**—Material Moving Occupations. **Related DOT Jobs**—914.382-014 Pumper-Gauger; 914.382-018 Pumper-Gauger Apprentice; 914.667-010 Loader I.

53-7199.99 Material Moving Workers, All Other

- **Education/Training Required: Moderate-term on-the-job training**
- **Employed: 52,970**
- **Annual Earnings: $30,220**
- **Growth: –5.3%**
- **Annual Job Openings: 8,000**

All material moving workers not listed separately.

No task data available.

Note: The Department of Labor has not collected some data for this job, so it has fewer details than the other descriptions.

Related SOC Job—53-7199 Material Moving Workers, All Other. **Related OOH Job**—Material Moving Occupations. **Related DOT Jobs**—504.665-010 Slab-Depiler Operator; 521.685-278 Routing-Equipment Tender; 521.685-366 Tipple Tender; 529.685-102 Dumping-Machine Operator; 569.685-066 Stacker, Machine; 575.683-010 Bucket Operator; 612.683-010 Manipulator Operator; 850.387-010 Inspector Of Dredging; 911.364-014 Boat Loader I; 914.685-010 Fish Bailer; 919.664-010 Teamster; 919.683-018 Rail-Tractor Operator; 921.662-010 Car-Dumper Operator; 921.663-018 Chip Unloader; 921.667-018 Dumper; 921.682-010 Loader, Malt House; others.

Military Specific Occupations

55-1000 Military Officer Special and Tactical Operations Leaders/Managers

55-1011.00 Air Crew Officers

- Education/Training Required: Long-term on-the-job training
- Employed: No data available
- Annual Earnings: No data available
- Growth: No data available
- Annual Job Openings: No data available

Perform and direct in-flight duties to ensure the successful completion of combat, reconnaissance, transport, and search and rescue missions. Duties include operating aircraft communications and radar equipment, such as establishing satellite linkages and jamming enemy communications capabilities; operating aircraft weapons and defensive systems; conducting pre-flight, in-flight, and post-flight inspections of onboard equipment; and directing cargo and personnel drops.

No task data available.

GOE Information—Interest Area: 12. Law and Public Safety. **Work Group:** 12.07. Military. **Note:** The Department of Labor has not collected some data for this job, so it has fewer details than the other descriptions.

Instructional Program—No related CIP programs.

Related SOC Job—55-1011 Air Crew Officers. **Related OOH Job—**Job Opportunities in the Armed Forces. **Related DOT Job—**No data available.

55-1012.00 Aircraft Launch and Recovery Officers

- Education/Training Required: Long-term on-the-job training
- Employed: No data available
- Annual Earnings: No data available
- Growth: No data available
- Annual Job Openings: No data available

Plan and direct the operation and maintenance of catapults; arresting gear; and associated mechanical, hydraulic, and control systems involved primarily in aircraft carrier takeoff and landing operations. Duties include supervision of readiness and safety of arresting gear; launching equipment, barricades, and visual landing aid systems; planning and coordinating the design, development, and testing of launch and recovery systems; preparing specifications for catapult and arresting gear installations; evaluating design proposals; determining handling equipment needed for new aircraft; preparing technical data and instructions for operation of landing aids; and training personnel in carrier takeoff and landing procedures.

No task data available.

GOE Information—Interest Area: 12. Law and Public Safety. **Work Group:** 12.07. Military. **Note:** The Department of Labor has not collected some data for this job, so it has fewer details than the other descriptions.

Instructional Program—No related CIP programs.

Related SOC Job—55-1012 Aircraft Launch and Recovery Officers. **Related OOH Job—**Job Opportunities in the Armed Forces. **Related DOT Job—**No data available.

55-1013.00 Armored Assault Vehicle Officers

- Education/Training Required: Long-term on-the-job training
- Employed: No data available
- Annual Earnings: No data available
- Growth: No data available
- Annual Job Openings: No data available

Direct the operation of tanks, light armor, and amphibious assault vehicle units during combat situations on land or in aquatic environments. Duties include directing crew members in the operation of targeting and firing systems; coordinating the operation of advanced onboard communications and navigation equipment; directing the transport of personnel and equipment during combat; formulating and implementing battle plans, including the tactical employment of armored vehicle units; and coordinating with infantry, artillery, and air support units.

No task data available.

GOE Information—Interest Area: 12. Law and Public Safety. **Work Group:** 12.07. Military. **Note:** The Department of Labor has not collected some data for this job, so it has fewer details than the other descriptions.

Instructional Program—No related CIP programs.

Related SOC Job—55-1013 Armored Assault Vehicle Officers. **Related OOH Job—**Job Opportunities in the Armed Forces. **Related DOT Job—**No data available.

55-1014.00 Artillery and Missile Officers

- Education/Training Required: Long-term on-the-job training
- Employed: No data available
- Annual Earnings: No data available
- Growth: No data available
- Annual Job Openings: No data available

Manage personnel and weapons operations to destroy enemy positions, aircraft, and vessels. Duties include planning, targeting, and coordinating the tactical deployment of field artillery and air defense artillery missile systems units; directing the establishment and operation of fire control communications systems; targeting and launching intercontinental ballistic missiles; directing the storage and handling of nuclear munitions and components; overseeing security of weapons storage and launch facilities; and managing maintenance of weapons systems.

No task data available.

GOE Information—Interest Area: 12. Law and Public Safety. **Work Group:** 12.07. Military. **Note:** The Department of Labor has not collected some data for this job, so it has fewer details than the other descriptions.

Instructional Program—No related CIP programs.

Related SOC Job—55-1014 Artillery and Missile Officers. **Related OOH Job—**Job Opportunities in the Armed Forces. **Related DOT Job—**378.132-010 Field Artillery Senior Sergeant.

55-1015.00 Command and Control Center Officers

- **Education/Training Required:** Long-term on-the-job training
- **Employed:** No data available
- **Annual Earnings:** No data available
- **Growth:** No data available
- **Annual Job Openings:** No data available

Manage the operation of communications, detection, and weapons systems essential for controlling air, ground, and naval operations. Duties include managing critical communication links between air, naval, and ground forces; formulating and implementing emergency plans for natural and wartime disasters; coordinating emergency response teams and agencies; evaluating command center information and need for high-level military and government reporting; managing the operation of surveillance and detection systems; providing technical information and advice on capabilities and operational readiness; and directing operation of weapons-targeting, -firing, and -launch computer systems.

No task data available.

GOE Information—Interest Area: 12. Law and Public Safety. **Work Group:** 12.07. Military. **Note:** The Department of Labor has not collected some data for this job, so it has fewer details than the other descriptions.

Instructional Program—No related CIP programs.

Related SOC Job—55-1015 Command and Control Center Officers. **Related OOH Job—**Job Opportunities in the Armed Forces. **Related DOT Job—**No data available.

55-1016.00 Infantry Officers

- **Education/Training Required:** Long-term on-the-job training
- **Employed:** No data available
- **Annual Earnings:** No data available
- **Growth:** No data available
- **Annual Job Openings:** No data available

Direct, train, and lead infantry units in ground combat operations. Duties include directing deployment of infantry weapons, vehicles, and equipment; directing location, construction, and camouflage of infantry positions and equipment; managing field communications operations; coordinating with armor, artillery, and air support units; performing strategic and tactical planning, including battle plan development; and leading basic reconnaissance operations.

No task data available.

GOE Information—Interest Area: 12. Law and Public Safety. **Work Group:** 12.07. Military. **Note:** The Department of Labor has not collected some data for this job, so it has fewer details than the other descriptions.

Instructional Program—No related CIP programs.

Related SOC Job—55-1016 Infantry Officers. **Related OOH Job—**Job Opportunities in the Armed Forces. **Related DOT Job—**378.137-010 Infantry Unit Leader.

55-1017.00 Special Forces Officers

- **Education/Training Required:** Long-term on-the-job training
- **Employed:** No data available
- **Annual Earnings:** No data available
- **Growth:** No data available
- **Annual Job Openings:** No data available

Lead elite teams that implement unconventional operations by air, land, or sea during combat or peacetime. These activities include offensive raids, demolitions, reconnaissance, search and rescue, and counterterrorism. In addition to their combat training, special forces officers often have specialized training in swimming, diving, parachuting, survival, emergency medicine, and foreign languages. Duties include directing advanced reconnaissance operations and evaluating intelligence information; recruiting, training, and equipping friendly forces; leading raids and invasions on enemy territories; training personnel to implement individual missions and contingency plans; performing strategic and tactical planning for politically sensitive missions; and operating sophisticated communications equipment.

No task data available.

GOE Information—Interest Area: 12. Law and Public Safety. **Work Group:** 12.07. Military. **Note:** The Department of Labor has not collected some data for this job, so it has fewer details than the other descriptions.

Instructional Program—No related CIP programs.

Related SOC Job—55-1017 Special Forces Officers. **Related OOH Job—**Job Opportunities in the Armed Forces. **Related DOT Job—**No data available.

55-1019.99 Military Officer Special and Tactical Operations Leaders/Managers, All Other

- **Education/Training Required:** Long-term on-the-job training
- **Employed:** No data available
- **Annual Earnings:** No data available
- **Growth:** No data available
- **Annual Job Openings:** No data available

All military officer special and tactical operations leaders/managers not listed separately.

No task data available.

Note: The Department of Labor has not collected some data for this job, so it has fewer details than the other descriptions.

Related SOC Job—55-1019 Military Officer Special and Tactical Operations Leaders/Managers, All Other. **Related OOH Job—**Job Opportunities in the Armed Forces. **Related DOT Job—**No data available.

55-2000 First-Line Enlisted Military Supervisor/Managers

55-2011.00 First-Line Supervisors/ Managers of Air Crew Members

- Education/Training Required: Work experience in a related occupation
- Employed: No data available
- Annual Earnings: No data available
- Growth: No data available
- Annual Job Openings: No data available

Supervise and coordinate the activities of air crew members. Supervisors may also perform the same activities as the workers they supervise.

No task data available.

GOE Information—Interest Area: 12. Law and Public Safety. **Work Group:** 12.07. Military. **Note:** The Department of Labor has not collected some data for this job, so it has fewer details than the other descriptions.

Instructional Program—No related CIP programs.

Related SOC Job—55-2011 First-Line Supervisors/Managers of Air Crew Members. **Related OOH Job**—Job Opportunities in the Armed Forces. **Related DOT Job**—No data available.

55-2012.00 First-Line Supervisors/ Managers of Weapons Specialists/ Crew Members

- Education/Training Required: Work experience in a related occupation
- Employed: No data available
- Annual Earnings: No data available
- Growth: No data available
- Annual Job Openings: No data available

Supervise and coordinate the activities of weapons specialists/crew members. Supervisors may also perform the same activities as the workers they supervise.

No task data available.

GOE Information—Interest Area: 12. Law and Public Safety. **Work Group:** 12.07. Military. **Note:** The Department of Labor has not collected some data for this job, so it has fewer details than the other descriptions.

Instructional Program—No related CIP programs.

Related SOC Job—55-2012 First-Line Supervisors/Managers of Weapons Specialists/Crew Members. **Related OOH Job**—Job Opportunities in the Armed Forces. **Related DOT Job**—No data available.

55-2013.00 First-Line Supervisors/ Managers of All Other Tactical Operations Specialists

- Education/Training Required: Work experience in a related occupation
- Employed: No data available
- Annual Earnings: No data available
- Growth: No data available
- Annual Job Openings: No data available

Supervise and coordinate the activities of all other tactical operations specialists not classified separately. Supervisors may also perform the same activities as the workers they supervise.

No task data available.

GOE Information—Interest Area: 12. Law and Public Safety. **Work Group:** 12.07. Military. **Note:** The Department of Labor has not collected some data for this job, so it has fewer details than the other descriptions.

Instructional Program—No related CIP programs.

Related SOC Job—55-2013 First-Line Supervisors/Managers of All Other Tactical Operations Specialists. **Related OOH Job**—Job Opportunities in the Armed Forces. **Related DOT Job**—No data available.

55-3000 Military Enlisted Tactical Operations and Air/Weapons Specialists and Crew Members

55-3011.00 Air Crew Members

- Education/Training Required: Moderate-term on-the-job training
- Employed: No data available
- Annual Earnings: No data available
- Growth: No data available
- Annual Job Openings: No data available

Perform in-flight duties to ensure the successful completion of combat, reconnaissance, transport, and search and rescue missions. Duties include operating aircraft communications and detection equipment, including establishing satellite linkages and jamming enemy communications capabilities; conducting pre-flight, in-flight, and post-flight inspections of onboard equipment; operating and maintaining aircraft weapons and defensive systems; operating and maintaining aircraft in-flight refueling systems; executing aircraft safety and emergency procedures; computing and verifying passenger, cargo, fuel, and emergency and special equipment weight and balance data; and conducting cargo and personnel drops.

No task data available.

GOE Information—Interest Area: 12. Law and Public Safety. **Work Group:** 12.07. Military. **Note:** The Department of Labor has not collected some data for this job, so it has fewer details than the other descriptions.

Instructional Program—No related CIP programs.

Related SOC Job—55-3011 Air Crew Members. Related OOH Job—Job Opportunities in the Armed Forces. Related DOT Job—No data available.

55-3012.00 Aircraft Launch and Recovery Specialists

- Education/Training Required: Moderate-term on-the-job training
- Employed: No data available
- Annual Earnings: No data available
- Growth: No data available
- Annual Job Openings: No data available

Operate and maintain catapults; arresting gear; and associated mechanical, hydraulic, and control systems involved primarily in aircraft carrier takeoff and landing operations. Duties include installing and maintaining visual landing aids; testing and maintaining launch and recovery equipment, using electric and mechanical test equipment and hand tools; activating airfield arresting systems, such as crash barriers and cables, during emergency landing situations; directing aircraft launch and recovery operations, using hand or light signals; and maintaining logs of airplane launches, recoveries, and equipment maintenance.

No task data available.

GOE Information—Interest Area: 12. Law and Public Safety. Work Group: 12.07. Military. Note: The Department of Labor has not collected some data for this job, so it has fewer details than the other descriptions.

Instructional Program—No related CIP programs.

Related SOC Job—55-3012 Aircraft Launch and Recovery Specialists. Related OOH Job—Job Opportunities in the Armed Forces. Related DOT Job—912.682-010 Aircraft Launch And Recovery Technician.

55-3013.00 Armored Assault Vehicle Crew Members

- Education/Training Required: Moderate-term on-the-job training
- Employed: No data available
- Annual Earnings: No data available
- Growth: No data available
- Annual Job Openings: No data available

Operate tanks, light armor, and amphibious assault vehicles during combat situations on land or in aquatic environments. Duties include driving armored vehicles that require specialized training; operating and maintaining targeting and firing systems; operating and maintaining advanced onboard communications and navigation equipment; transporting personnel and equipment in a combat environment; and operating and maintaining auxiliary weapons, including machine guns and grenade launchers.

No task data available.

GOE Information—Interest Area: 12. Law and Public Safety. Work Group: 12.07. Military. Note: The Department of Labor has not collected some data for this job, so it has fewer details than the other descriptions.

Instructional Program—No related CIP programs.

Related SOC Job—55-3013 Armored Assault Vehicle Crew Members. Related OOH Job—Job Opportunities in the Armed Forces. Related DOT Job—378.683-018 Tank Crewmember.

55-3014.00 Artillery and Missile Crew Members

- Education/Training Required: Moderate-term on-the-job training
- Employed: No data available
- Annual Earnings: No data available
- Growth: No data available
- Annual Job Openings: No data available

Target, fire, and maintain weapons used to destroy enemy positions, aircraft, and vessels. Field artillery crew members predominantly use guns, cannons, and howitzers in ground combat operations, whereas air defense artillery crew members predominantly use missiles and rockets. Naval artillery crew members predominantly use torpedoes and missiles launched from a ship or submarine. Duties include testing, inspecting, and storing ammunition, missiles, and torpedoes; conducting preventive and routine maintenance on weapons and related equipment; establishing and maintaining radio and wire communications; and operating weapons-targeting, -firing, and -launch computer systems.

No task data available.

GOE Information—Interest Area: 12. Law and Public Safety. Work Group: 12.07. Military. Note: The Department of Labor has not collected some data for this job, so it has fewer details than the other descriptions.

Instructional Program—No related CIP programs.

Related SOC Job—55-3014 Artillery and Missile Crew Members. Related OOH Job—Job Opportunities in the Armed Forces. Related DOT Jobs—378.663-010 Vulcan Crewmember; 378.682-010 Redeye Gunner; 378.684-018 Field Artillery Crewmember; 632.261-010 Aircraft-Armament Mechanic; 632.261-014 Fire-Control Mechanic; 632.261-018 Ordnance Artificer.

55-3015.00 Command and Control Center Specialists

- Education/Training Required: Moderate-term on-the-job training
- Employed: No data available
- Annual Earnings: No data available
- Growth: No data available
- Annual Job Openings: No data available

Operate and monitor communications, detection, and weapons systems essential for controlling air, ground, and naval operations. Duties include maintaining and relaying critical communications between air, naval, and ground forces; implementing emergency plans for natural and wartime disasters; relaying command center information to high-level military and government decision makers; monitoring surveillance and detection systems, such as air defense; interpreting and evaluating tactical situations and making recommendations to superiors; and operating weapons-targeting, -firing, and -launch computer systems.

No task data available.

GOE Information—Interest Area: 12. Law and Public Safety. Work Group: 12.07. Military. Note: The Department of Labor has not collected some data for this job, so it has fewer details than the other descriptions.

Instructional Program—No related CIP programs.

Related SOC Job—55-3015 Command and Control Center Specialists. **Related OOH Job**—Job Opportunities in the Armed Forces. **Related DOT Jobs**—235.662-010 Command And Control Specialist; 378.367-026 Operations And Intelligence Assistant.

55-3016.00 Infantry

- **Education/Training Required: Moderate-term on-the-job training**
- **Employed: No data available**
- **Annual Earnings: No data available**
- **Growth: No data available**
- **Annual Job Openings: No data available**

Operate weapons and equipment in ground combat operations. Duties include operating and maintaining weapons, such as rifles, machine guns, mortars, and hand grenades; locating, constructing, and camouflaging infantry positions and equipment; evaluating terrain and recording topographical information; operating and maintaining field communications equipment; assessing need for and directing supporting fire; placing explosives and performing minesweeping activities on land; and participating in basic reconnaissance operations.

No task data available.

GOE Information—**Interest Area:** 12. Law and Public Safety. **Work Group:** 12.07. Military. **Note:** The Department of Labor has not collected some data for this job, so it has fewer details than the other descriptions.

Instructional Program—No related CIP programs.

Related SOC Job—55-3016 Infantry. **Related OOH Job**—Job Opportunities in the Armed Forces. **Related DOT Job**—378.684-014 Combat Rifle Crewmember.

55-3017.00 Radar and Sonar Technicians

- **Education/Training Required: Moderate-term on-the-job training**
- **Employed: No data available**
- **Annual Earnings: No data available**
- **Growth: No data available**
- **Annual Job Openings: No data available**

Operate equipment using radio or sound wave technology to identify, track, and analyze objects or natural phenomena of military interest. Includes airborne, shipboard, and terrestrial positions. May perform minor maintenance.

No task data available.

GOE Information—**Interest Area:** 12. Law and Public Safety. **Work Group:** 12.07. Military. **Note:** The Department of Labor has not collected some data for this job, so it has fewer details than the other descriptions.

Instructional Program—No related CIP programs.

Related SOC Job—55-3017 Radar and Sonar Technicians. **Related OOH Job**—Job Opportunities in the Armed Forces. **Related DOT Job**—No data available.

55-3018.00 Special Forces

- **Education/Training Required: Long-term on-the-job training**
- **Employed: No data available**
- **Annual Earnings: No data available**
- **Growth: No data available**
- **Annual Job Openings: No data available**

Implement unconventional operations by air, land, or sea during combat or peacetime as members of elite teams. These activities include offensive raids, demolitions, reconnaissance, search and rescue, and counterterrorism. In addition to their combat training, Special Forces members often have specialized training in swimming, diving, parachuting, survival, emergency medicine, and foreign languages. Duties include conducting advanced reconnaissance operations and collecting intelligence information; recruiting, training, and equipping friendly forces; conducting raids and invasions on enemy territories; laying and detonating explosives for demolition targets; locating, identifying, defusing, and disposing of ordnance; and operating and maintaining sophisticated communications equipment.

No task data available.

GOE Information—**Interest Area:** 12. Law and Public Safety. **Work Group:** 12.07. Military. **Note:** The Department of Labor has not collected some data for this job, so it has fewer details than the other descriptions.

Instructional Program—No related CIP programs.

Related SOC Job—55-3018 Special Forces. **Related OOH Job**—Job Opportunities in the Armed Forces. **Related DOT Jobs**—378.227-018 Survival Specialist; 378.367-030 Reconnaissance Crewmember; 378.683-010 Amphibian Crewmember.

55-3019.99 Military Enlisted Tactical Operations and Air/Weapons Specialists and Crew Members, All Other

- **Education/Training Required: No data available**
- **Employed: No data available**
- **Annual Earnings: No data available**
- **Growth: No data available**
- **Annual Job Openings: No data available**

All military enlisted tactical operations and air/weapons specialists and crewmembers not listed separately.

No task data available.

Note: The Department of Labor has not collected some data for this job, so it has fewer details than the other descriptions.

Related SOC Job—55-3019 Military Enlisted Tactical Operations and Air/Weapons Specialists and Crew Members, All Other. **Related OOH Job**—Job Opportunities in the Armed Forces. **Related DOT Jobs**—199.682-010 Aerospace Physiological Technician; 248.387-010 Flight Operations Specialist; 249.387-014 Intelligence Clerk; 378.161-010 Combat Surveillance And Target Acquisition Noncommissioned Officer; 378.227-014 Recruit Instructor; 378.267-010 Counterintelligence Agent; 378.281-010 Target Aircraft Technician; 378.362-010 Sound Ranging Crewmember; 378.363-010 Armor Reconnaissance Specialist; 378.367-010 Artillery Or Naval Gunfire Observer; 378.367-014 Field Artillery Operations Specialist; others.

APPENDIX

O*NET Jobs by Personality Type

The following table will help you to identify occupations that may be a good match for your personality type. Occupations are listed by their two-letter Holland code—the abbreviation for their two principal personality types. The six Holland personality types are defined in the introduction.

The abbreviations used here are as follows: R=Realistic, I=Investigative, A=Artistic, S=Social, E=Enterprising, and C=Conventional. The codes are arranged alphabetically, and occupations that share the same code are arranged numerically by O*NET code.

Note that you may find it useful to consider both combinations of your primary and secondary personality types. For example, if your primary type is Artistic and your secondary type is Social, you may want to look at occupations coded AS and SA.

Two-Letter RIASEC Codes for Occupations

RIASEC Code	O*NET Number	Job Title
A	27-2041.04	Music Composers and Arrangers
A	27-2042.02	Musicians, Instrumental
A	27-4032.00	Film and Video Editors
AC	25-4021.00	Librarians
AE	11-2011.00	Advertising and Promotions Managers
AE	27-1011.00	Art Directors
AE	27-1022.00	Fashion Designers
AE	27-1024.00	Graphic Designers
AE	27-1025.00	Interior Designers
AE	27-2011.00	Actors
AE	27-2012.01	Producers
AE	27-2012.02	Directors—Stage, Motion Pictures, Television, and Radio
AE	27-2012.04	Talent Directors
AE	27-2042.01	Singers
AE	27-3043.04	Copy Writers
AE	41-9012.00	Models
AI	25-4012.00	Curators
AI	27-3022.00	Reporters and Correspondents
AI	27-3042.00	Technical Writers
AI	27-3043.05	Poets, Lyricists, and Creative Writers
AR	17-1011.00	Architects, Except Landscape and Naval
AR	17-1012.00	Landscape Architects
AR	25-4013.00	Museum Technicians and Conservators
AR	27-1013.00	Fine Artists, Including Painters, Sculptors, and Illustrators
AR	27-1021.00	Commercial and Industrial Designers
AR	27-1023.00	Floral Designers
AR	27-1026.00	Merchandise Displayers and Window Trimmers
AR	27-1027.00	Set and Exhibit Designers
AR	27-4021.00	Photographers
AR	27-4031.00	Camera Operators, Television, Video, and Motion Picture
AR	39-3092.00	Costume Attendants
AR	39-5091.00	Makeup Artists, Theatrical and Performance
AS	23-2091.00	Court Reporters
AS	25-1121.00	Art, Drama, and Music Teachers, Postsecondary
AS	25-1123.00	English Language and Literature Teachers, Postsecondary
AS	25-1124.00	Foreign Language and Literature Teachers, Postsecondary
AS	27-2031.00	Dancers
AS	27-2032.00	Choreographers
AS	27-2041.01	Music Directors
AS	27-3011.00	Radio and Television Announcers
AS	27-3021.00	Broadcast News Analysts
AS	27-3041.00	Editors
AS	27-3091.00	Interpreters and Translators
C	29-2071.00	Medical Records and Health Information Technicians
C	43-9061.00	Office Clerks, General
C	43-9081.00	Proofreaders and Copy Markers
C	43-9111.00	Statistical Assistants
CE	13-1031.01	Claims Examiners, Property and Casualty Insurance
CE	13-1041.02	Licensing Examiners and Inspectors
CE	13-1051.00	Cost Estimators
CE	13-2011.01	Accountants
CE	13-2011.02	Auditors
CE	13-2021.01	Assessors
CE	13-2031.00	Budget Analysts
CE	13-2041.00	Credit Analysts
CE	13-2053.00	Insurance Underwriters
CE	13-2081.00	Tax Examiners, Collectors, and Revenue Agents
CE	13-2082.00	Tax Preparers
CE	23-2093.00	Title Examiners, Abstractors, and Searchers
CE	33-3021.05	Immigration and Customs Inspectors
CE	41-2011.00	Cashiers
CE	41-2021.00	Counter and Rental Clerks
CE	43-3011.00	Bill and Account Collectors
CE	43-3021.01	Statement Clerks
CE	43-3021.02	Billing, Cost, and Rate Clerks
CE	43-3031.00	Bookkeeping, Accounting, and Auditing Clerks
CE	43-3051.00	Payroll and Timekeeping Clerks
CE	43-3061.00	Procurement Clerks
CE	43-3071.00	Tellers
CE	43-4011.00	Brokerage Clerks
CE	43-4021.00	Correspondence Clerks
CE	43-4031.01	Court Clerks
CE	43-4031.02	Municipal Clerks
CE	43-4031.03	License Clerks
CE	43-4041.01	Credit Authorizers

CE	43-4041.02	Credit Checkers
CE	43-4051.00	Customer Service Representatives
CE	43-4071.00	File Clerks
CE	43-4081.00	Hotel, Motel, and Resort Desk Clerks
CE	43-4131.00	Loan Interviewers and Clerks
CE	43-4141.00	New Accounts Clerks
CE	43-4151.00	Order Clerks
CE	43-4161.00	Human Resources Assistants, Except Payroll and Timekeeping
CE	43-4171.00	Receptionists and Information Clerks
CE	43-4181.00	Reservation and Transportation Ticket Agents and Travel Clerks
CE	43-5061.00	Production, Planning, and Expediting Clerks
CE	43-5081.04	Order Fillers, Wholesale and Retail Sales
CE	43-6011.00	Executive Secretaries and Administrative Assistants
CE	43-6012.00	Legal Secretaries
CE	43-6013.00	Medical Secretaries
CE	43-6014.00	Secretaries, Except Legal, Medical, and Executive
CE	43-9041.01	Insurance Claims Clerks
CE	43-9041.02	Insurance Policy Processing Clerks
CI	15-2011.00	Actuaries
CI	19-4061.01	City and Regional Planning Aides
CR	13-1032.00	Insurance Appraisers, Auto Damage
CR	17-1021.00	Cartographers and Photogrammetrists
CR	17-3012.02	Electrical Drafters
CR	17-3031.02	Mapping Technicians
CR	29-2052.00	Pharmacy Technicians
CR	33-2021.01	Fire Inspectors
CR	33-3021.02	Police Identification and Records Officers
CR	33-3041.00	Parking Enforcement Workers
CR	43-2011.00	Switchboard Operators, Including Answering Service
CR	43-2021.00	Telephone Operators
CR	43-3021.03	Billing, Posting, and Calculating Machine Operators
CR	43-4121.00	Library Assistants, Clerical
CR	43-5011.00	Cargo and Freight Agents
CR	43-5032.00	Dispatchers, Except Police, Fire, and Ambulance
CR	43-5041.00	Meter Readers, Utilities
CR	43-5051.00	Postal Service Clerks
CR	43-5052.00	Postal Service Mail Carriers
CR	43-5071.00	Shipping, Receiving, and Traffic Clerks
CR	43-5081.02	Marking Clerks
CR	43-5081.03	Stock Clerks—Stockroom, Warehouse, or Storage Yard
CR	43-5111.00	Weighers, Measurers, Checkers, and Samplers, Recordkeeping

CR	43-9011.00	Computer Operators
CR	43-9021.00	Data Entry Keyers
CR	43-9022.00	Word Processors and Typists
CR	43-9051.00	Mail Clerks and Mail Machine Operators, Except Postal Service
CR	43-9071.00	Office Machine Operators, Except Computer
CR	47-4011.00	Construction and Building Inspectors
CR	53-2021.00	Air Traffic Controllers
CR	53-6051.08	Freight and Cargo Inspectors
CS	25-4031.00	Library Technicians
CS	25-9011.00	Audio-Visual Collections Specialists
CS	27-4011.00	Audio and Video Equipment Technicians
CS	43-4061.00	Eligibility Interviewers, Government Programs
CS	43-4111.00	Interviewers, Except Eligibility and Loan
EA	27-2012.03	Program Directors
EA	27-3031.00	Public Relations Specialists
EC	11-1011.00	Chief Executives
EC	11-2021.00	Marketing Managers
EC	11-2022.00	Sales Managers
EC	11-3011.00	Administrative Services Managers
EC	11-3021.00	Computer and Information Systems Managers
EC	11-3031.01	Treasurers and Controllers
EC	11-3031.02	Financial Managers, Branch or Department
EC	11-3051.00	Industrial Production Managers
EC	11-3061.00	Purchasing Managers
EC	11-3071.01	Transportation Managers
EC	11-3071.02	Storage and Distribution Managers
EC	11-9051.00	Food Service Managers
EC	11-9071.00	Gaming Managers
EC	11-9081.00	Lodging Managers
EC	11-9131.00	Postmasters and Mail Superintendents
EC	11-9141.00	Property, Real Estate, and Community Association Managers
EC	13-1021.00	Purchasing Agents and Buyers, Farm Products
EC	13-1022.00	Wholesale and Retail Buyers, Except Farm Products
EC	13-1023.00	Purchasing Agents, Except Wholesale, Retail, and Farm Products
EC	13-1041.04	Government Property Inspectors and Investigators
EC	13-1111.00	Management Analysts
EC	13-1121.00	Meeting and Convention Planners
EC	13-2021.02	Appraisers, Real Estate
EC	13-2061.00	Financial Examiners
EC	23-1011.00	Lawyers
EC	23-2011.00	Paralegals and Legal Assistants
EC	23-2092.00	Law Clerks

(continued)

(continued)

Two-Letter RIASEC Codes for Occupations

RIASEC Code	O*NET Number	Job Title
EC	29-2081.00	Opticians, Dispensing
EC	39-1011.00	Gaming Supervisors
EC	39-1021.00	First-Line Supervisors/Managers of Personal Service Workers
EC	39-3011.00	Gaming Dealers
EC	39-3012.00	Gaming and Sports Book Writers and Runners
EC	41-1011.00	First-Line Supervisors/Managers of Retail Sales Workers
EC	41-1012.00	First-Line Supervisors/Managers of Non-Retail Sales Workers
EC	41-3031.01	Sales Agents, Securities and Commodities
EC	41-3031.02	Sales Agents, Financial Services
EC	41-9041.00	Telemarketers
EC	41-9091.00	Door-To-Door Sales Workers, News and Street Vendors, and Related Workers
EC	43-1011.00	First-Line Supervisors/Managers of Office and Administrative Support Workers
EC	53-1021.00	First-Line Supervisors/Managers of Helpers, Laborers, and Material Movers, Hand
EI	13-1031.02	Insurance Adjusters, Examiners, and Investigators
EI	17-2112.00	Industrial Engineers
EI	33-3021.03	Criminal Investigators and Special Agents
ER	11-9011.01	Nursery and Greenhouse Managers
ER	11-9011.02	Crop and Livestock Managers
ER	11-9011.03	Aquacultural Managers
ER	11-9021.00	Construction Managers
ER	11-9041.00	Engineering Managers
ER	27-2021.00	Athletes and Sports Competitors
ER	27-2022.00	Coaches and Scouts
ER	35-1011.00	Chefs and Head Cooks
ER	35-1012.00	First-Line Supervisors/Managers of Food Preparation and Serving Workers
ER	37-1011.00	First-Line Supervisors/Managers of Housekeeping and Janitorial Workers
ER	39-6011.00	Baggage Porters and Bellhops
ER	41-2022.00	Parts Salespersons
ER	41-4011.00	Sales Representatives, Wholesale and Manufacturing, Technical and Scientific Products
ER	41-9031.00	Sales Engineers
ER	47-1011.00	First-Line Supervisors/Managers of Construction Trades and Extraction Workers
ER	49-1011.00	First-Line Supervisors/Managers of Mechanics, Installers, and Repairers
ER	51-1011.00	First-Line Supervisors/Managers of Production and Operating Workers
ER	53-1031.00	First-Line Supervisors/Managers of Transportation and Material-Moving Machine and Vehicle Operators
ER	53-3031.00	Driver/Sales Workers
ER	53-5021.01	Ship and Boat Captains
ES	11-3040.00	Human Resources Managers
ES	11-3041.00	Compensation and Benefits Managers
ES	11-3042.00	Training and Development Managers
ES	11-9033.00	Education Administrators, Postsecondary
ES	11-9061.00	Funeral Directors
ES	11-9111.00	Medical and Health Services Managers
ES	13-1011.00	Agents and Business Managers of Artists, Performers, and Athletes
ES	13-1071.02	Personnel Recruiters
ES	13-2071.00	Loan Counselors
ES	13-2072.00	Loan Officers
ES	23-1021.00	Administrative Law Judges, Adjudicators, and Hearing Officers
ES	23-1022.00	Arbitrators, Mediators, and Conciliators
ES	23-1023.00	Judges, Magistrate Judges, and Magistrates
ES	27-2023.00	Umpires, Referees, and Other Sports Officials
ES	33-1012.00	First-Line Supervisors/Managers of Police and Detectives
ES	33-3021.01	Police Detectives
ES	33-3052.00	Transit and Railroad Police
ES	33-9021.00	Private Detectives and Investigators
ES	35-3011.00	Bartenders
ES	35-9031.00	Hosts and Hostesses, Restaurant, Lounge, and Coffee Shop
ES	39-5012.00	Hairdressers, Hairstylists, and Cosmetologists
ES	39-5092.00	Manicurists and Pedicurists
ES	39-6022.00	Travel Guides
ES	39-6031.00	Flight Attendants
ES	39-6032.00	Transportation Attendants, Except Flight Attendants and Baggage Porters
ES	41-2031.00	Retail Salespersons
ES	41-3011.00	Advertising Sales Agents
ES	41-3021.00	Insurance Sales Agents
ES	41-3041.00	Travel Agents
ES	41-4012.00	Sales Representatives, Wholesale and Manufacturing, Except Technical and Scientific Products
ES	41-9011.00	Demonstrators and Product Promoters
ES	41-9022.00	Real Estate Sales Agents
I	29-1062.00	Family and General Practitioners

I	29-1063.00	Internists, General
I	29-1064.00	Obstetricians and Gynecologists
I	29-1065.00	Pediatricians, General
IA	19-3031.02	Clinical Psychologists
IA	19-3041.00	Sociologists
IA	19-3093.00	Historians
IA	19-3094.00	Political Scientists
IA	29-1066.00	Psychiatrists
IC	13-1041.01	Environmental Compliance Inspectors
IC	13-1041.06	Coroners
IC	13-1072.00	Compensation, Benefits, and Job Analysis Specialists
IC	13-2051.00	Financial Analysts
IC	15-1041.00	Computer Support Specialists
IC	15-1051.00	Computer Systems Analysts
IC	15-1061.00	Database Administrators
IC	15-2021.00	Mathematicians
IC	15-2031.00	Operations Research Analysts
IC	15-2041.00	Statisticians
IC	17-3026.00	Industrial Engineering Technicians
IC	19-4092.00	Forensic Science Technicians
IC	25-1021.00	Computer Science Teachers, Postsecondary
IC	25-4011.00	Archivists
IC	29-1051.00	Pharmacists
IE	11-9121.00	Natural Sciences Managers
IE	17-1022.00	Surveyors
IE	17-2111.01	Industrial Safety and Health Engineers
IE	17-2111.02	Fire-Prevention and Protection Engineers
IE	19-3011.00	Economists
IE	19-3021.00	Market Research Analysts
IE	19-3032.00	Industrial-Organizational Psychologists
IE	19-3051.00	Urban and Regional Planners
IE	29-1031.00	Dietitians and Nutritionists
IR	15-1021.00	Computer Programmers
IR	15-1031.00	Computer Software Engineers, Applications
IR	15-1032.00	Computer Software Engineers, Systems Software
IR	15-1071.01	Computer Security Specialists
IR	15-1081.00	Network Systems and Data Communications Analysts
IR	15-2091.00	Mathematical Technicians
IR	17-2011.00	Aerospace Engineers
IR	17-2021.00	Agricultural Engineers
IR	17-2041.00	Chemical Engineers
IR	17-2061.00	Computer Hardware Engineers
IR	17-2071.00	Electrical Engineers
IR	17-2072.00	Electronics Engineers, Except Computer
IR	17-2111.03	Product Safety Engineers
IR	17-2131.00	Materials Engineers
IR	17-2151.00	Mining and Geological Engineers, Including Mining Safety Engineers
IR	17-2161.00	Nuclear Engineers
IR	17-3021.00	Aerospace Engineering and Operations Technicians
IR	19-1011.00	Animal Scientists
IR	19-1012.00	Food Scientists and Technologists
IR	19-1013.00	Soil and Plant Scientists
IR	19-1020.01	Biologists
IR	19-1021.00	Biochemists and Biophysicists
IR	19-1022.00	Microbiologists
IR	19-1023.00	Zoologists and Wildlife Biologists
IR	19-1031.01	Soil and Water Conservationists
IR	19-1031.02	Range Managers
IR	19-1041.00	Epidemiologists
IR	19-1042.00	Medical Scientists, Except Epidemiologists
IR	19-2011.00	Astronomers
IR	19-2012.00	Physicists
IR	19-2021.00	Atmospheric and Space Scientists
IR	19-2031.00	Chemists
IR	19-2032.00	Materials Scientists
IR	19-2041.00	Environmental Scientists and Specialists, Including Health
IR	19-2042.00	Geoscientists, Except Hydrologists and Geographers
IR	19-2043.00	Hydrologists
IR	19-3091.02	Archeologists
IR	19-3092.00	Geographers
IR	19-4091.00	Environmental Science and Protection Technicians, Including Health
IR	25-1032.00	Engineering Teachers, Postsecondary
IR	29-1011.00	Chiropractors
IR	29-1021.00	Dentists, General
IR	29-1022.00	Oral and Maxillofacial Surgeons
IR	29-1023.00	Orthodontists
IR	29-1024.00	Prosthodontists
IR	29-1041.00	Optometrists
IR	29-1061.00	Anesthesiologists
IR	29-1067.00	Surgeons
IR	29-1126.00	Respiratory Therapists
IR	29-1131.00	Veterinarians
IR	29-2011.00	Medical and Clinical Laboratory Technologists
IR	29-2031.00	Cardiovascular Technologists and Technicians
IR	29-2033.00	Nuclear Medicine Technologists
IR	33-2021.02	Fire Investigators
IS	19-3031.01	School Psychologists
IS	19-3091.01	Anthropologists
IS	25-1022.00	Mathematical Science Teachers, Postsecondary

(continued)

(continued)

Two-Letter RIASEC Codes for Occupations

RIASEC Code	O*NET Number	Job Title
IS	25-1041.00	Agricultural Sciences Teachers, Postsecondary
IS	25-1042.00	Biological Science Teachers, Postsecondary
IS	25-1043.00	Forestry and Conservation Science Teachers, Postsecondary
IS	25-1052.00	Chemistry Teachers, Postsecondary
IS	25-1054.00	Physics Teachers, Postsecondary
IS	25-1071.00	Health Specialties Teachers, Postsecondary
IS	29-1071.00	Physician Assistants
R	35-3021.00	Combined Food Preparation and Serving Workers, Including Fast Food
R	37-2011.00	Janitors and Cleaners, Except Maids and Housekeeping Cleaners
R	37-3011.00	Landscaping and Groundskeeping Workers
R	37-3012.00	Pesticide Handlers, Sprayers, and Applicators, Vegetation
R	39-2021.00	Nonfarm Animal Caretakers
R	45-2091.00	Agricultural Equipment Operators
R	45-2092.01	Nursery Workers
R	45-3021.00	Hunters and Trappers
R	45-4022.00	Logging Equipment Operators
R	47-2011.00	Boilermakers
R	47-2021.00	Brickmasons and Blockmasons
R	47-2022.00	Stonemasons
R	47-2031.01	Construction Carpenters
R	47-2041.00	Carpet Installers
R	47-2042.00	Floor Layers, Except Carpet, Wood, and Hard Tiles
R	47-2043.00	Floor Sanders and Finishers
R	47-2051.00	Cement Masons and Concrete Finishers
R	47-2053.00	Terrazzo Workers and Finishers
R	47-2071.00	Paving, Surfacing, and Tamping Equipment Operators
R	47-2072.00	Pile-Driver Operators
R	47-2081.00	Drywall and Ceiling Tile Installers
R	47-2082.00	Tapers
R	47-2121.00	Glaziers
R	47-2131.00	Insulation Workers, Floor, Ceiling, and Wall
R	47-2132.00	Insulation Workers, Mechanical
R	47-2141.00	Painters, Construction and Maintenance
R	47-2142.00	Paperhangers
R	47-2152.01	Pipe Fitters and Steamfitters
R	47-2152.02	Plumbers
R	47-2181.00	Roofers
R	47-2211.00	Sheet Metal Workers
R	47-2221.00	Structural Iron and Steel Workers
R	47-4021.00	Elevator Installers and Repairers
R	47-4031.00	Fence Erectors
R	47-4051.00	Highway Maintenance Workers
R	47-4061.00	Rail-Track Laying and Maintenance Equipment Operators
R	47-4071.00	Septic Tank Servicers and Sewer Pipe Cleaners
R	47-5011.00	Derrick Operators, Oil and Gas
R	47-5013.00	Service Unit Operators, Oil, Gas, and Mining
R	47-5021.00	Earth Drillers, Except Oil and Gas
R	47-5051.00	Rock Splitters, Quarry
R	47-5071.00	Roustabouts, Oil and Gas
R	49-2092.00	Electric Motor, Power Tool, and Related Repairers
R	49-3041.00	Farm Equipment Mechanics
R	49-3042.00	Mobile Heavy Equipment Mechanics, Except Engines
R	49-3052.00	Motorcycle Mechanics
R	49-3092.00	Recreational Vehicle Service Technicians
R	49-3093.00	Tire Repairers and Changers
R	49-9011.00	Mechanical Door Repairers
R	49-9031.00	Home Appliance Repairers
R	49-9041.00	Industrial Machinery Mechanics
R	49-9045.00	Refractory Materials Repairers, Except Brickmasons
R	49-9052.00	Telecommunications Line Installers and Repairers
R	49-9061.00	Camera and Photographic Equipment Repairers
R	49-9091.00	Coin, Vending, and Amusement Machine Servicers and Repairers
R	49-9092.00	Commercial Divers
R	49-9095.00	Manufactured Building and Mobile Home Installers
R	51-2011.00	Aircraft Structure, Surfaces, Rigging, and Systems Assemblers
R	51-2021.00	Coil Winders, Tapers, and Finishers
R	51-2023.00	Electromechanical Equipment Assemblers
R	51-3011.00	Bakers
R	51-3023.00	Slaughterers and Meat Packers
R	51-3092.00	Food Batchmakers
R	51-6093.00	Upholsterers
R	51-7011.00	Cabinetmakers and Bench Carpenters
R	51-7021.00	Furniture Finishers
R	51-9022.00	Grinding and Polishing Workers, Hand
R	51-9031.00	Cutters and Trimmers, Hand
R	51-9071.06	Gem and Diamond Workers

R	51-9071.07	Precious Metal Workers
R	51-9123.00	Painting, Coating, and Decorating Workers
R	51-9195.07	Molding and Casting Workers
R	51-9198.00	Helpers—Production Workers
R	53-7121.00	Tank Car, Truck, and Ship Loaders
RA	17-3011.01	Architectural Drafters
RA	27-2012.05	Technical Directors/Managers
RA	27-4012.00	Broadcast Technicians
RA	27-4014.00	Sound Engineering Technicians
RA	37-3013.00	Tree Trimmers and Pruners
RA	43-9031.00	Desktop Publishers
RA	49-9063.00	Musical Instrument Repairers and Tuners
RA	51-5012.00	Bookbinders
RA	51-6041.00	Shoe and Leather Workers and Repairers
RA	51-6052.00	Tailors, Dressmakers, and Custom Sewers
RA	51-9131.00	Photographic Process Workers
RA	51-9194.00	Etchers and Engravers
RA	51-9195.03	Stone Cutters and Carvers, Manufacturing
RA	51-9195.05	Potters, Manufacturing
RC	17-3011.02	Civil Drafters
RC	17-3012.01	Electronic Drafters
RC	17-3013.00	Mechanical Drafters
RC	17-3031.01	Surveying Technicians
RC	19-4041.01	Geophysical Data Technicians
RC	27-4013.00	Radio Operators
RC	29-2034.02	Radiologic Technicians
RC	31-9093.00	Medical Equipment Preparers
RC	33-2022.00	Forest Fire Inspectors and Prevention Specialists
RC	35-2011.00	Cooks, Fast Food
RC	35-2012.00	Cooks, Institution and Cafeteria
RC	35-2021.00	Food Preparation Workers
RC	35-9021.00	Dishwashers
RC	37-2012.00	Maids and Housekeeping Cleaners
RC	37-2021.00	Pest Control Workers
RC	39-3021.00	Motion Picture Projectionists
RC	39-3091.00	Amusement and Recreation Attendants
RC	39-4011.00	Embalmers
RC	43-5021.00	Couriers and Messengers
RC	43-5081.01	Stock Clerks, Sales Floor
RC	45-2041.00	Graders and Sorters, Agricultural Products
RC	45-2093.00	Farmworkers, Farm and Ranch Animals
RC	45-4021.00	Fallers
RC	45-4023.00	Log Graders and Scalers
RC	47-2031.02	Rough Carpenters
RC	47-2044.00	Tile and Marble Setters
RC	47-2061.00	Construction Laborers
RC	47-2073.00	Operating Engineers and Other Construction Equipment Operators
RC	47-2151.00	Pipelayers
RC	47-2161.00	Plasterers and Stucco Masons
RC	47-2171.00	Reinforcing Iron and Rebar Workers
RC	47-3011.00	Helpers—Brickmasons, Blockmasons, Stonemasons, and Tile and Marble Setters
RC	47-3012.00	Helpers—Carpenters
RC	47-3013.00	Helpers—Electricians
RC	47-3014.00	Helpers—Painters, Paperhangers, Plasterers, and Stucco Masons
RC	47-3015.00	Helpers—Pipelayers, Plumbers, Pipefitters, and Steamfitters
RC	47-4041.00	Hazardous Materials Removal Workers
RC	47-5012.00	Rotary Drill Operators, Oil and Gas
RC	47-5031.00	Explosives Workers, Ordnance Handling Experts, and Blasters
RC	47-5041.00	Continuous Mining Machine Operators
RC	47-5042.00	Mine Cutting and Channeling Machine Operators
RC	47-5061.00	Roof Bolters, Mining
RC	47-5081.00	Helpers—Extraction Workers
RC	49-2011.00	Computer, Automated Teller, and Office Machine Repairers
RC	49-2021.00	Radio Mechanics
RC	49-2022.00	Telecommunications Equipment Installers and Repairers, Except Line Installers
RC	49-2093.00	Electrical and Electronics Installers and Repairers, Transportation Equipment
RC	49-2096.00	Electronic Equipment Installers and Repairers, Motor Vehicles
RC	49-2097.00	Electronic Home Entertainment Equipment Installers and Repairers
RC	49-3021.00	Automotive Body and Related Repairers
RC	49-3022.00	Automotive Glass Installers and Repairers
RC	49-3023.01	Automotive Master Mechanics
RC	49-3023.02	Automotive Specialty Technicians
RC	49-3031.00	Bus and Truck Mechanics and Diesel Engine Specialists
RC	49-3043.00	Rail Car Repairers
RC	49-3053.00	Outdoor Power Equipment and Other Small Engine Mechanics
RC	49-3091.00	Bicycle Repairers
RC	49-9012.00	Control and Valve Installers and Repairers, Except Mechanical Door
RC	49-9021.01	Heating and Air Conditioning Mechanics and Installers
RC	49-9021.02	Refrigeration Mechanics and Installers

(continued)

(continued)

Two-Letter RIASEC Codes for Occupations

RIASEC Code	O*NET Number	Job Title
RC	49-9042.00	Maintenance and Repair Workers, General
RC	49-9043.00	Maintenance Workers, Machinery
RC	49-9051.00	Electrical Power-Line Installers and Repairers
RC	49-9064.00	Watch Repairers
RC	49-9093.00	Fabric Menders, Except Garment
RC	49-9094.00	Locksmiths and Safe Repairers
RC	49-9097.00	Signal and Track Switch Repairers
RC	49-9098.00	Helpers—Installation, Maintenance, and Repair Workers
RC	51-2022.00	Electrical and Electronic Equipment Assemblers
RC	51-2031.00	Engine and Other Machine Assemblers
RC	51-2041.00	Structural Metal Fabricators and Fitters
RC	51-2093.00	Timing Device Assemblers, Adjusters, and Calibrators
RC	51-3022.00	Meat, Poultry, and Fish Cutters and Trimmers
RC	51-3091.00	Food and Tobacco Roasting, Baking, and Drying Machine Operators and Tenders
RC	51-3093.00	Food Cooking Machine Operators and Tenders
RC	51-4011.00	Computer-Controlled Machine Tool Operators, Metal and Plastic
RC	51-4012.00	Numerical Tool and Process Control Programmers
RC	51-4021.00	Extruding and Drawing Machine Setters, Operators, and Tenders, Metal and Plastic
RC	51-4022.00	Forging Machine Setters, Operators, and Tenders, Metal and Plastic
RC	51-4023.00	Rolling Machine Setters, Operators, and Tenders, Metal and Plastic
RC	51-4031.00	Cutting, Punching, and Press Machine Setters, Operators, and Tenders, Metal and Plastic
RC	51-4032.00	Drilling and Boring Machine Tool Setters, Operators, and Tenders, Metal and Plastic
RC	51-4033.00	Grinding, Lapping, Polishing, and Buffing Machine Tool Setters, Operators, and Tenders, Metal and Plastic
RC	51-4034.00	Lathe and Turning Machine Tool Setters, Operators, and Tenders, Metal and Plastic
RC	51-4035.00	Milling and Planing Machine Setters, Operators, and Tenders, Metal and Plastic
RC	51-4051.00	Metal-Refining Furnace Operators and Tenders
RC	51-4052.00	Pourers and Casters, Metal
RC	51-4061.00	Model Makers, Metal and Plastic
RC	51-4062.00	Patternmakers, Metal and Plastic
RC	51-4071.00	Foundry Mold and Coremakers
RC	51-4072.00	Molding, Coremaking, and Casting Machine Setters, Operators, and Tenders, Metal and Plastic
RC	51-4081.00	Multiple Machine Tool Setters, Operators, and Tenders, Metal and Plastic
RC	51-4111.00	Tool and Die Makers
RC	51-4121.06	Welders, Cutters, and Welder Fitters
RC	51-4121.07	Solderers and Brazers
RC	51-4122.00	Welding, Soldering, and Brazing Machine Setters, Operators, and Tenders
RC	51-4191.00	Heat Treating Equipment Setters, Operators, and Tenders, Metal and Plastic
RC	51-4192.00	Lay-Out Workers, Metal and Plastic
RC	51-4193.00	Plating and Coating Machine Setters, Operators, and Tenders, Metal and Plastic
RC	51-4194.00	Tool Grinders, Filers, and Sharpeners
RC	51-5011.00	Bindery Workers
RC	51-5021.00	Job Printers
RC	51-5022.00	Prepress Technicians and Workers
RC	51-5023.00	Printing Machine Operators
RC	51-6011.00	Laundry and Dry-Cleaning Workers
RC	51-6021.00	Pressers, Textile, Garment, and Related Materials
RC	51-6031.00	Sewing Machine Operators
RC	51-6042.00	Shoe Machine Operators and Tenders
RC	51-6051.00	Sewers, Hand
RC	51-6061.00	Textile Bleaching and Dyeing Machine Operators and Tenders
RC	51-6062.00	Textile Cutting Machine Setters, Operators, and Tenders
RC	51-6063.00	Textile Knitting and Weaving Machine Setters, Operators, and Tenders
RC	51-6064.00	Textile Winding, Twisting, and Drawing Out Machine Setters, Operators, and Tenders
RC	51-6091.00	Extruding and Forming Machine Setters, Operators, and Tenders, Synthetic and Glass Fibers
RC	51-6092.00	Fabric and Apparel Patternmakers
RC	51-7031.00	Model Makers, Wood
RC	51-7032.00	Patternmakers, Wood

RC	51-7041.00	Sawing Machine Setters, Operators, and Tenders, Wood
RC	51-7042.00	Woodworking Machine Setters, Operators, and Tenders, Except Sawing
RC	51-8011.00	Nuclear Power Reactor Operators
RC	51-8012.00	Power Distributors and Dispatchers
RC	51-8013.00	Power Plant Operators
RC	51-8021.00	Stationary Engineers and Boiler Operators
RC	51-8031.00	Water and Liquid Waste Treatment Plant and System Operators
RC	51-8091.00	Chemical Plant and System Operators
RC	51-8092.00	Gas Plant Operators
RC	51-8093.00	Petroleum Pump System Operators, Refinery Operators, and Gaugers
RC	51-9011.00	Chemical Equipment Operators and Tenders
RC	51-9012.00	Separating, Filtering, Clarifying, Precipitating, and Still Machine Setters, Operators, and Tenders
RC	51-9021.00	Crushing, Grinding, and Polishing Machine Setters, Operators, and Tenders
RC	51-9023.00	Mixing and Blending Machine Setters, Operators, and Tenders
RC	51-9032.00	Cutting and Slicing Machine Setters, Operators, and Tenders
RC	51-9041.00	Extruding, Forming, Pressing, and Compacting Machine Setters, Operators, and Tenders
RC	51-9051.00	Furnace, Kiln, Oven, Drier, and Kettle Operators and Tenders
RC	51-9061.00	Inspectors, Testers, Sorters, Samplers, and Weighers
RC	51-9083.00	Ophthalmic Laboratory Technicians
RC	51-9111.00	Packaging and Filling Machine Operators and Tenders
RC	51-9121.00	Coating, Painting, and Spraying Machine Setters, Operators, and Tenders
RC	51-9122.00	Painters, Transportation Equipment
RC	51-9132.00	Photographic Processing Machine Operators
RC	51-9141.00	Semiconductor Processors
RC	51-9191.00	Cementing and Gluing Machine Operators and Tenders
RC	51-9192.00	Cleaning, Washing, and Metal Pickling Equipment Operators and Tenders
RC	51-9193.00	Cooling and Freezing Equipment Operators and Tenders
RC	51-9195.04	Glass Blowers, Molders, Benders, and Finishers
RC	51-9196.00	Paper Goods Machine Setters, Operators, and Tenders
RC	51-9197.00	Tire Builders
RC	53-3032.00	Truck Drivers, Heavy and Tractor-Trailer
RC	53-3033.00	Truck Drivers, Light or Delivery Services
RC	53-4011.00	Locomotive Engineers
RC	53-4012.00	Locomotive Firers
RC	53-4013.00	Rail Yard Engineers, Dinkey Operators, and Hostlers
RC	53-4021.00	Railroad Brake, Signal, and Switch Operators
RC	53-4041.00	Subway and Streetcar Operators
RC	53-5011.00	Sailors and Marine Oilers
RC	53-6011.00	Bridge and Lock Tenders
RC	53-6051.07	Transportation Vehicle, Equipment, and Systems Inspectors, Except Aviation
RC	53-7011.00	Conveyor Operators and Tenders
RC	53-7021.00	Crane and Tower Operators
RC	53-7031.00	Dredge Operators
RC	53-7032.00	Excavating and Loading Machine and Dragline Operators
RC	53-7033.00	Loading Machine Operators, Underground Mining
RC	53-7041.00	Hoist and Winch Operators
RC	53-7051.00	Industrial Truck and Tractor Operators
RC	53-7061.00	Cleaners of Vehicles and Equipment
RC	53-7062.00	Laborers and Freight, Stock, and Material Movers, Hand
RC	53-7063.00	Machine Feeders and Offbearers
RC	53-7064.00	Packers and Packagers, Hand
RC	53-7071.00	Gas Compressor and Gas Pumping Station Operators
RC	53-7072.00	Pump Operators, Except Wellhead Pumpers
RC	53-7073.00	Wellhead Pumpers
RC	53-7081.00	Refuse and Recyclable Material Collectors
RC	53-7111.00	Shuttle Car Operators
RE	11-9012.00	Farmers and Ranchers
RE	33-1021.01	Municipal Fire Fighting and Prevention Supervisors
RE	33-1021.02	Forest Fire Fighting and Prevention Supervisors
RE	35-2014.00	Cooks, Restaurant
RE	35-2015.00	Cooks, Short Order
RE	35-9011.00	Dining Room and Cafeteria Attendants and Bartender Helpers
RE	37-1012.00	First-Line Supervisors/Managers of Landscaping, Lawn Service, and Groundskeeping Workers
RE	45-1011.05	First-Line Supervisors/Managers of Logging Workers
RE	45-1011.06	First-Line Supervisors/Managers of Aquacultural Workers

(continued)

(continued)

Two-Letter RIASEC Codes for Occupations

RIASEC Code	O*NET Number	Job Title
RE	45-1011.07	First-Line Supervisors/Managers of Agricultural Crop and Horticultural Workers
RE	45-1011.08	First-Line Supervisors/Managers of Animal Husbandry and Animal Care Workers
RE	45-2092.02	Farmworkers and Laborers, Crop
RE	45-3011.00	Fishers and Related Fishing Workers
RE	49-9096.00	Riggers
RE	51-3021.00	Butchers and Meat Cutters
RE	51-9071.01	Jewelers
RE	53-2011.00	Airline Pilots, Copilots, and Flight Engineers
RE	53-2012.00	Commercial Pilots
RE	53-3041.00	Taxi Drivers and Chauffeurs
RE	53-4031.00	Railroad Conductors and Yardmasters
RE	53-5021.02	Mates—Ship, Boat, and Barge
RE	53-5021.03	Pilots, Ship
RE	53-5022.00	Motorboat Operators
RE	53-5031.00	Ship Engineers
RE	53-6021.00	Parking Lot Attendants
RE	53-6031.00	Service Station Attendants
RI	17-2051.00	Civil Engineers
RI	17-2121.01	Marine Engineers
RI	17-2121.02	Marine Architects
RI	17-2141.00	Mechanical Engineers
RI	17-2171.00	Petroleum Engineers
RI	17-3022.00	Civil Engineering Technicians
RI	17-3023.01	Electronics Engineering Technicians
RI	17-3023.03	Electrical Engineering Technicians
RI	17-3024.00	Electro-Mechanical Technicians
RI	17-3027.00	Mechanical Engineering Technicians
RI	19-1032.00	Foresters
RI	19-4011.01	Agricultural Technicians
RI	19-4011.02	Food Science Technicians
RI	19-4021.00	Biological Technicians
RI	19-4031.00	Chemical Technicians
RI	19-4041.02	Geological Sample Test Technicians
RI	19-4051.01	Nuclear Equipment Operation Technicians
RI	19-4051.02	Nuclear Monitoring Technicians
RI	29-2012.00	Medical and Clinical Laboratory Technicians
RI	29-2034.01	Radiologic Technologists
RI	31-9096.00	Veterinary Assistants and Laboratory Animal Caretakers
RI	33-3031.00	Fish and Game Wardens
RI	45-2011.00	Agricultural Inspectors
RI	45-2021.00	Animal Breeders
RI	45-4011.00	Forest and Conservation Workers
RI	47-2111.00	Electricians
RI	49-2091.00	Avionics Technicians
RI	49-2094.00	Electrical and Electronics Repairers, Commercial and Industrial Equipment
RI	49-2095.00	Electrical and Electronics Repairers, Powerhouse, Substation, and Relay
RI	49-3011.00	Aircraft Mechanics and Service Technicians
RI	49-3051.00	Motorboat Mechanics
RI	49-9044.00	Millwrights
RI	49-9062.00	Medical Equipment Repairers
RI	51-4041.00	Machinists
RI	51-9081.00	Dental Laboratory Technicians
RI	51-9082.00	Medical Appliance Technicians
RI	53-6041.00	Traffic Technicians
RI	53-6051.01	Aviation Inspectors
RS	29-2055.00	Surgical Technologists
RS	33-2011.01	Municipal Fire Fighters
RS	33-2011.02	Forest Fire Fighters
RS	33-3012.00	Correctional Officers and Jailers
RS	33-9092.00	Lifeguards, Ski Patrol, and Other Recreational Protective Service Workers
RS	39-5011.00	Barbers
RS	53-3021.00	Bus Drivers, Transit and Intercity
RS	53-3022.00	Bus Drivers, School
S	21-1021.00	Child, Family, and School Social Workers
SA	21-1012.00	Educational, Vocational, and School Counselors
SA	21-2011.00	Clergy
SA	25-2011.00	Preschool Teachers, Except Special Education
SA	25-2012.00	Kindergarten Teachers, Except Special Education
SA	25-2021.00	Elementary School Teachers, Except Special Education
SA	25-2022.00	Middle School Teachers, Except Special and Vocational Education
SA	25-2023.00	Vocational Education Teachers, Middle School
SA	25-2031.00	Secondary School Teachers, Except Special and Vocational Education
SA	25-2032.00	Vocational Education Teachers, Secondary School
SA	25-2041.00	Special Education Teachers, Preschool, Kindergarten, and Elementary School
SA	25-2042.00	Special Education Teachers, Middle School
SA	25-2043.00	Special Education Teachers, Secondary School
SA	25-3011.00	Adult Literacy, Remedial Education, and GED Teachers and Instructors

SA	25-3021.00	Self-Enrichment Education Teachers
SA	27-3012.00	Public Address System and Other Announcers
SA	29-1125.00	Recreational Therapists
SA	39-9011.00	Child Care Workers
SA	39-9011.01	Nannies
SA	39-9032.00	Recreation Workers
SC	21-1092.00	Probation Officers and Correctional Treatment Specialists
SC	21-1093.00	Social and Human Service Assistants
SC	25-9041.00	Teacher Assistants
SC	29-2021.00	Dental Hygienists
SC	31-9092.00	Medical Assistants
SC	39-3031.00	Ushers, Lobby Attendants, and Ticket Takers
SC	39-9041.00	Residential Advisors
SC	43-5031.00	Police, Fire, and Ambulance Dispatchers
SE	11-9031.00	Education Administrators, Preschool and Child Care Center/Program
SE	11-9032.00	Education Administrators, Elementary and Secondary School
SE	11-9151.00	Social and Community Service Managers
SE	13-1041.03	Equal Opportunity Representatives and Officers
SE	13-1071.01	Employment Interviewers
SE	13-1073.00	Training and Development Specialists
SE	13-2052.00	Personal Financial Advisors
SE	21-1091.00	Health Educators
SE	21-2021.00	Directors, Religious Activities and Education
SE	29-9011.00	Occupational Health and Safety Specialists
SE	33-3011.00	Bailiffs
SE	33-3051.03	Sheriffs and Deputy Sheriffs
SE	33-9032.00	Security Guards
SE	35-3031.00	Waiters and Waitresses
SE	39-3093.00	Locker Room, Coatroom, and Dressing Room Attendants
SE	39-4021.00	Funeral Attendants
SE	39-6021.00	Tour Guides and Escorts
SI	19-3031.03	Counseling Psychologists
SI	21-1011.00	Substance Abuse and Behavioral Disorder Counselors
SI	21-1014.00	Mental Health Counselors
SI	21-1022.00	Medical and Public Health Social Workers
SI	21-1023.00	Mental Health and Substance Abuse Social Workers
SI	25-1061.00	Anthropology and Archeology Teachers, Postsecondary
SI	25-1062.00	Area, Ethnic, and Cultural Studies Teachers, Postsecondary
SI	25-1063.00	Economics Teachers, Postsecondary
SI	25-1065.00	Political Science Teachers, Postsecondary
SI	25-1066.00	Psychology Teachers, Postsecondary
SI	25-1067.00	Sociology Teachers, Postsecondary
SI	25-1072.00	Nursing Instructors and Teachers, Postsecondary
SI	25-1125.00	History Teachers, Postsecondary
SI	25-1191.00	Graduate Teaching Assistants
SI	25-9031.00	Instructional Coordinators
SI	29-1081.00	Podiatrists
SI	29-1111.00	Registered Nurses
SI	29-1121.00	Audiologists
SI	29-1127.00	Speech-Language Pathologists
SI	29-2091.00	Orthotists and Prosthetists
SR	19-1031.03	Park Naturalists
SR	25-1194.00	Vocational Education Teachers, Postsecondary
SR	25-9021.00	Farm and Home Management Advisors
SR	29-1122.00	Occupational Therapists
SR	29-1123.00	Physical Therapists
SR	29-1124.00	Radiation Therapists
SR	29-2041.00	Emergency Medical Technicians and Paramedics
SR	29-2051.00	Dietetic Technicians
SR	29-2053.00	Psychiatric Technicians
SR	29-2061.00	Licensed Practical and Licensed Vocational Nurses
SR	29-9091.00	Athletic Trainers
SR	31-1011.00	Home Health Aides
SR	31-1012.00	Nursing Aides, Orderlies, and Attendants
SR	31-1013.00	Psychiatric Aides
SR	31-2011.00	Occupational Therapist Assistants
SR	31-2012.00	Occupational Therapist Aides
SR	31-2021.00	Physical Therapist Assistants
SR	31-2022.00	Physical Therapist Aides
SR	31-9091.00	Dental Assistants
SR	33-3051.01	Police Patrol Officers
SR	33-9011.00	Animal Control Workers
SR	33-9091.00	Crossing Guards
SR	35-3022.00	Counter Attendants, Cafeteria, Food Concession, and Coffee Shop
SR	35-3041.00	Food Servers, Nonrestaurant
SR	39-2011.00	Animal Trainers
SR	39-9021.00	Personal and Home Care Aides
SR	39-9031.00	Fitness Trainers and Aerobics Instructors
SR	53-3011.00	Ambulance Drivers and Attendants, Except Emergency Medical Technicians

Index of O*NET Job Titles

F

✳ ✳ ✳ ✳ ✳ ✳ ✳ ✳ ✳ ✳ ✳ © JIST Works

R

U

V

W

X–Z